리얼 오리지널

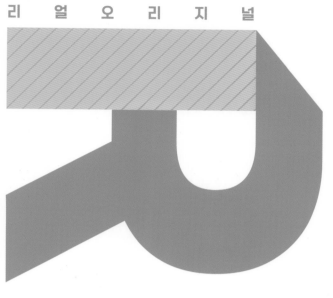
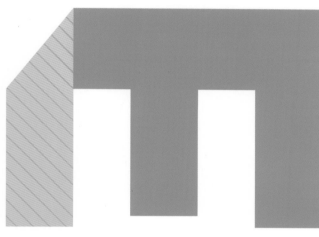
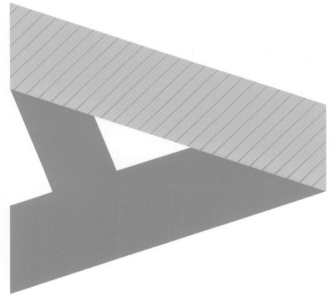

The Real series ipsifly provide questions in previous real test and you can practice as real college scholastic ability test.

2025 학력평가 + 내신대비

전국연합
학력평가
5 개 년
기출문제집

20회 [3월·6월·9월·11월 학력평가 기출 20회]

- **2020~2024 최신 5개년 [고2] 전국연합 학력평가 20회**
- 영어 **[독해 28문항]**을 회차별로 구성한 **[유형별]** 모의고사
- 학교시험 **[중간·기말고사]**를 대비한 내신 필수 문제집
- 매회 어휘를 복습할 수 있는 **[어휘 리뷰 TEST]** 20회
- 친절한 입체적 해설 **[직독직해·구문 풀이·고난도 꿀팁]**
- 회차별 **[SPEED 정답 체크표·STUDY 플래너·정답률]**
- **[특별 부록]** 회차별 **영단어**

고2 영어 독해

모바일로 학습하는
회차별 영단어 **QR 코드 제공**

● 문 제 편 ●

수능 모의고사 전문 출판
ipy 입시플라이

REAL

REAL ORIGINAL

입시플라이

전국연합학력평가
5개년 기출 문제집

고2 영어 독해

Contents

독해는 18번부터 45번까지 일정한 흐름과 출제 패턴이 고정 되어 있기 때문에 「유형별로 푸는 것도 중요」하지만 독해 28문항을 「한 세트로 풀어보는 훈련」이 매우 중요합니다.

수능 모의고사 전문 출판
입시플라이

실전은 연습처럼! 연습은 실전처럼! 「리얼 오리지널」

수능 시험장에 가면 낯선 환경과 긴장감 때문에 실력을 제대로 발휘 못하는 경우가 많습니다. 실전 연습은 여러분의 실력이 됩니다.

01

실제 시험지와 똑같은 문제지

고2 영어 독해는 전국연합 학력평가 영어 [독해 28문항]을 회차별로 20회를 구성한 모의고사입니다.

❶ 실제 시험지의 크기와 느낌을 그대로 살려 실전과 동일한 조건 속에서 영어 독해 문제만 풀어 볼 수 있습니다.

❷ 문제를 풀기 전에 먼저 학습 체크 표에 학습 날짜와 시간을 기록 하고, [45분] 타이머를 작동해 실전처럼 풀어 보십시오.

02

하루 28문항 · 20일 완성

영어 영역에서 듣기 문항을 제외한 영어 [독해 문항]만 집중 학습할 수 있도록 만든 [20일 완성] 교재입니다.

❶ 독해 [18번~45번] 문제만 수록했으며, 영어 독해는 전체 유형의 문제를 [통으로 푸는 훈련]을 해야 점수가 올라갑니다.

❷ 독해 문제만 하루 [28문항 · 20일] 완성 교재이며, 독해 파트만 집중해 학습할 수 있는 효율적인 교재입니다.

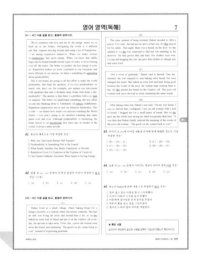

03

회차별 [VOCA LIST]

회차별로 쉬운 단어부터 어려운 단어까지 모든 단어를 정리한 [VOCA LIST]를 제공합니다.

❶ 회차별, 문항별로 단어를 정리하여 매회 문제편 뒤에 제공되며 출제된 모든 핵심 단어를 수록했습니다.

❷ 빠른 독해와 영어의 생명은 어휘입니다. 회차별 단어를 문항별로 정리한 VOCA LIST로 어휘를 복습해 보세요.

※ 모바일로 영단어를 학습할 수 있도록 VOCA 상단에 QR 코드를 제공합니다.

★ 해설편 앞 부분에 「SPEED 정답 체크 표」가 있습니다.
오려서 정답을 확인하거나 책갈피로 사용하시면 됩니다.

04

회차별 [어휘 리뷰 TEST]

어휘와 독해력까지 동시에 잡을 수 있도록 [어휘 리뷰 TEST]를
총 20회 부록으로 제공합니다.

❶ VOCA LIST와 함께 매회 문제편 뒤에 제공되며 단어를 복습할
수 있도록 [어휘 리뷰 TEST]를 수록했습니다.
❷ 먼저 VOCA LIST로 학습하고 [어휘 리뷰 TEST]로 복습을
하시면 어휘력도, 독해력도 쑥~쑥 올라갑니다.

05

입체적 해설 & 문제 해결 꿀 팁

혼자서도 학습이 충분하도록 자세한 [입체적 해설]과 함께
고난도 문제는 문제 해결 꿀~팁까지 수록을 했습니다.

❶ 입체적 해설로 직독직해, 구문 풀이가 수록되어 있으며 혼자서도
학습이 충분하도록 자세한 해설을 수록했습니다.
❷ 등급을 가르는 고난도 문제는 많이 틀린 이유와 함께 문제 해결
꿀 팁까지 명쾌한 해설을 수록했습니다.

06

정답률 & SPEED 정답 체크 표

문제를 푼 후 빠르게 정답을 확인할 수 있는 SPEED 정답
체크 표와, 문항별 정답률까지 제공합니다.

❶ 문제를 푼 후 빠르게 정답을 확인할 수 있는 SPEED 정답 체크
표를 제공하며, 오려서 책갈피로도 사용할 수 있습니다.
❷ 문항별로 정답률을 제공하므로 문제의 난이도를 파악할 수 있어
문제 풀이에 답답함이 없습니다.

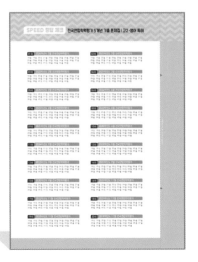

STUDY 플래너

① 문제를 풀기 전 먼저 〈학습 체크표〉에 학습 날짜와 시간을 기록하세요.
② 회분별 기출 문제는 영역별로 정해진 시간 안에 푸는 습관을 기르세요.
③ 정답 확인 후 점수를 적고 성적 변화를 체크하면서 학습 계획을 세우세요.
④ **리얼 오리지널**은 실제 수능 시험과 똑같이 학습하는 교재이므로 실전을 연습하는 것처럼 문제를 풀어 보세요.

● 영어 [독해] | 시험 개요

문항 수	문항당 배점	문항별 점수 표기	원점수 만점	학습 시간	문항 형태
28문항	2점, 3점	•3점 문항에 점수 표시 •점수 표시 없는 문항 모두 2점	63점	45분	5지 선다형

● 영어 [독해] | 학습 체크

회분	학습 날짜	학습 시간	채점 결과	틀린 문제	시간 부족 문제
01회 2024학년도 3월	월 일	시 분 ~ 시 분			
02회 2023학년도 3월	월 일	시 분 ~ 시 분			
03회 2022학년도 3월	월 일	시 분 ~ 시 분			
04회 2021학년도 3월	월 일	시 분 ~ 시 분			
05회 2020학년도 3월	월 일	시 분 ~ 시 분			
06회 2024학년도 6월	월 일	시 분 ~ 시 분			
07회 2023학년도 6월	월 일	시 분 ~ 시 분			
08회 2022학년도 6월	월 일	시 분 ~ 시 분			
09회 2021학년도 6월	월 일	시 분 ~ 시 분			
10회 2020학년도 6월	월 일	시 분 ~ 시 분			
11회 2024학년도 9월	월 일	시 분 ~ 시 분			
12회 2023학년도 9월	월 일	시 분 ~ 시 분			
13회 2022학년도 9월	월 일	시 분 ~ 시 분			
14회 2021학년도 9월	월 일	시 분 ~ 시 분			
15회 2020학년도 9월	월 일	시 분 ~ 시 분			
16회 2023학년도 11월	월 일	시 분 ~ 시 분			
17회 2022학년도 11월	월 일	시 분 ~ 시 분			
18회 2021학년도 11월	월 일	시 분 ~ 시 분			
19회 2020학년도 11월	월 일	시 분 ~ 시 분			
20회 2019학년도 11월	월 일	시 분 ~ 시 분			

※ 영어 [독해] 파트만 수록한 문제지이므로 18번부터 시작합니다.

● 점수 표시가 없는 문항은 모두 **2점** ● 문항수 **28개** | 배점 **63점** | 제한 시간 **45분**

18. 다음 글의 목적으로 가장 적절한 것은?

Dear Art Crafts People of Greenville,
For the annual Crafts Fair on May 25 from 1 p.m. to 6 p.m., the Greenville Community Center is providing booth spaces to rent as in previous years. To reserve your space, please visit our website and complete a registration form by April 20. The rental fee is $50. All the money we receive from rental fees goes to support upcoming activities throughout the year. We expect all available spaces to be fully booked soon, so don't get left out. We hope to see you at the fair.

① 지역 예술가를 위한 정기 후원을 요청하려고
② 공예품 박람회의 부스 예약을 안내하려고
③ 대여 물품의 반환 방법을 설명하려고
④ 지역 예술가가 만든 물품을 홍보하려고
⑤ 지역 행사 일정의 변경 사항을 공지하려고

19. 다음 글에 드러난 Sarah의 심경 변화로 가장 적절한 것은?

Sarah, a young artist with a love for painting, entered a local art contest. As she looked at the amazing artworks made by others, her confidence dropped. She quietly thought, 'I might not win an award.' The moment of judgment arrived, and the judges began announcing winners one by one. It wasn't until the end that she heard her name. The head of the judges said, "Congratulations, Sarah Parker! You won first prize. We loved the uniqueness of your work." Sarah was overcome with joy, and she couldn't stop smiling. This experience meant more than just winning; it confirmed her identity as an artist.

① hopeful → regretful
② relieved → grateful
③ excited → disappointed
④ depressed → frightened
⑤ discouraged → delighted

20. 다음 글에서 필자가 주장하는 바로 가장 적절한 것은?

Too many times people, especially in today's generation, expect things to just happen overnight. When we have these false expectations, it tends to discourage us from continuing to move forward. Because this is a high tech society, everything we want has to be within the parameters of our comfort and convenience. If it doesn't happen fast enough, we're tempted to lose interest. So many people don't want to take the time it requires to be successful. Success is not a matter of mere desire; you should develop patience in order to achieve it. Have you fallen prey to impatience? Great things take time to build.

* parameter: 매개 변수, 제한

① 성공하기 위해서는 인내심을 길러야 한다.
② 안락함을 추구하기보다 한계에 도전해야 한다.
③ 사회 변화의 속도에 맞춰 빠르게 대응해야 한다.
④ 기회를 기다리기보다 능동적으로 행동해야 한다.
⑤ 흥미를 잃지 않으려면 자신이 좋아하는 일을 해야 한다.

21. 밑줄 친 we were still taping bricks to accelerators가 다음 글에서 의미하는 바로 가장 적절한 것은? [3점]

If you had wanted to create a "self-driving" car in the 1950s, your best option might have been to strap a brick to the accelerator. Yes, the vehicle would have been able to move forward on its own, but it could not slow down, stop, or turn to avoid barriers. Obviously not ideal. But does that mean the entire concept of the self-driving car is not worth pursuing? No, it only means that at the time we did not yet have the tools we now possess to help enable vehicles to operate both autonomously and safely. This once-distant dream now seems within our reach. It is much the same story in medicine. Two decades ago, we were still taping bricks to accelerators. Today, we are approaching the point where we can begin to bring some appropriate technology to bear in ways that advance our understanding of patients as unique individuals. In fact, many patients are already wearing devices that monitor their conditions in real time, which allows doctors to talk to their patients in a specific, refined, and feedback-driven way that was not even possible a decade ago.

* strap: 끈으로 묶다 ** autonomously: 자율적으로

① the importance of medical education was overlooked
② self-driving cars enabled patients to move around freely
③ the devices for safe driving were unavailable at that time
④ lack of advanced tools posed a challenge in understanding patients
⑤ appropriate technologies led to success in developing a new medicine

22. 다음 글의 요지로 가장 적절한 것은?

We tend to overrate the impact of new technologies in part because older technologies have become absorbed into the furniture of our lives, so as to be almost invisible. Take the baby bottle. Here is a simple implement that has transformed a fundamental human experience for vast numbers of infants and mothers, yet it finds no place in our histories of technology. This technology might be thought of as a classic time-shifting device, as it enables mothers to exercise more control over the timing of feeding. It can also function to save time, as bottle feeding allows for someone else to substitute for the mother's time. Potentially, therefore, it has huge implications for the management of time in everyday life, yet it is entirely overlooked in discussions of high-speed society.

① 새로운 기술은 효율적인 시간 관리에 도움이 된다.
② 새로운 기술에 비해 기존 기술의 영향력이 간과되고 있다.
③ 현대 사회의 새로운 기술이 양육자의 역할을 대체하고 있다.
④ 새로운 기술의 사용을 장려하는 사회적 인식이 요구된다.
⑤ 기존 기술의 활용은 새로운 기술의 개발에 도움이 된다.

23. 다음 글의 주제로 가장 적절한 것은?

Empathy is frequently listed as one of the most desired skills in an employer or employee, although without specifying exactly what is meant by *empathy*. Some businesses stress cognitive empathy, emphasizing the need for leaders to understand the perspective of employees and customers when negotiating deals and making decisions. Others stress affective empathy and empathic concern, emphasizing the ability of leaders to gain trust from employees and customers by treating them with real concern and compassion. When some consultants argue that successful companies foster empathy, what that translates to is that companies should conduct good market research. In other words, an "empathic" company understands the needs and wants of its customers and seeks to fulfill those needs and wants. When some people speak of design with empathy, what that translates to is that companies should take into account the specific needs of different populations — the blind, the deaf, the elderly, non-English speakers, the color-blind, and so on — when designing products.

* empathy: 공감, 공감 능력 ** compassion: 동정심

① diverse benefits of good market research
② negative factors in making business decisions
③ difficulties in designing products with empathic concern
④ efforts to build cognitive empathy among employees
⑤ different interpretations of empathy in business

24. 다음 글의 제목으로 가장 적절한 것은?

The most prevalent problem kids report is that they feel like they need to be accessible at all times. Because technology allows for it, they feel an obligation. It's easy for most of us to relate — you probably feel the same pressure in your own life! It is really challenging to deal with the fact that we're human and can't always respond instantly. For a teen or tween who's still learning the ins and outs of social interactions, it's even worse. Here's how this behavior plays out sometimes: Your child texts one of his friends, and the friend doesn't text back right away. Now it's easy for your child to think, "This person doesn't want to be my friend anymore!" So he texts again, and again, and again — "blowing up their phone." This can be stress-inducing and even read as aggressive. But you can see how easily this could happen.

* tween: (10 ~ 12세 사이의) 십대 초반의 아동

① From Symbols to Bytes: History of Communication
② Parents' Desire to Keep Their Children Within Reach
③ Building Trust: The Key to Ideal Human Relationships
④ The Positive Role of Digital Technology in Teen Friendships
⑤ Connected but Stressed: Challenges for Kids in the Digital Era

25. 다음 도표의 내용과 일치하지 <u>않는</u> 것은?

Animal Protein Consumption, 2020
measured as the average daily supply per person (unit: g)

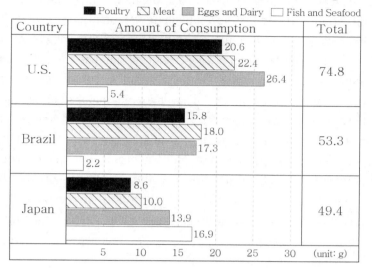

Country	Amount of Consumption	Total
U.S.	Poultry 20.6 / Meat 22.4 / Eggs and Dairy 26.4 / Fish and Seafood 5.4	74.8
Brazil	Poultry 15.8 / Meat 18.0 / Eggs and Dairy 17.3 / Fish and Seafood 2.2	53.3
Japan	Poultry 8.6 / Meat 10.0 / Eggs and Dairy 13.9 / Fish and Seafood 16.9	49.4

The graph above shows the animal protein consumption measured as the average daily supply per person in three different countries in 2020. ① The U.S. showed the largest amount of total animal protein consumption per person among the three countries. ② Eggs and Dairy was the top animal protein consumption source among four categories in the U.S., followed by Meat and Poultry at 22.4g and 20.6g, respectively. ③ Unlike the U.S., Brazil consumed the most animal protein from Meat, with Eggs and Dairy being the second most. ④ Japan had less than 50g of the total animal protein consumption per person, which was the smallest among the three countries. ⑤ Fish and Seafood, which was the least consumed animal protein consumption source in the U.S. and Brazil, ranked the second highest in Japan.

26. Theodore von Kármán에 관한 다음 글의 내용과 일치하지 <u>않는</u> 것은?

Theodore von Kármán, a Hungarian-American engineer, was one of the greatest minds of the twentieth century. He was born in Hungary and at an early age, he showed a talent for math and science. In 1908, he received a doctoral degree in engineering at the University of Göttingen in Germany. In the 1920s, he began traveling as a lecturer and consultant to industry. He was invited to the United States to advise engineers on the design of a wind tunnel at California Institute of Technology (Caltech). He became the director of the Guggenheim Aeronautical Laboratory at Caltech in 1930. Later, he was awarded the National Medal of Science for his leadership in science and engineering.

① 어린 시절 수학과 과학에 재능을 보였다.
② University of Göttingen에서 공학 박사 학위를 받았다.
③ 1920년대에 강연자 겸 자문 위원으로 다니기 시작했다.
④ Caltech의 공학자를 초청하여 조언을 구했다.
⑤ National Medal of Science를 받았다.

27. Basic Latte Art Class에 관한 다음 안내문의 내용과 일치하지 <u>않는</u> 것은?

Basic Latte Art Class

Make perfect lattes and present them in the most beautiful way! In this class, you will learn how to steam and pour milk. You will make three latte art designs on your own: heart, tulip, and leaf.

Date: April 27, 2024
Time: 9 a.m. — 1 p.m.
Place: Camefort Community Center
Registration & Fee
• Register online at www.camefortcc.com, from April 22 to April 24.
• $60 per person (cost of ingredients included)
Notes
• Dairy alternatives will be available for non-milk drinkers.
• Students can get a 10% discount.

① 세 가지 라떼 아트 디자인을 직접 만들 것이다.
② 수업은 4시간 동안 진행된다.
③ 등록은 4월 24일부터 시작된다.
④ 비용에 재료비가 포함되어 있다.
⑤ 우유를 마시지 않는 사람은 대체 유제품을 사용할 수 있다.

28. Family Night-hiking Event에 관한 다음 안내문의 내용과 일치하는 것은?

Family Night-hiking Event

Join us for a fun-filled night of hiking and family bonding!

Date: Saturday, May 4
Time: 6 p.m. — 9 p.m.
Location: Skyline Preserve
Cost
• Adults: $20
• Children under 19: $10
Guidelines
• Children must be accompanied by legal guardians.
• Bring a flashlight and a bottle of water.
• Follow the instructions of the guides at all times.
Registration
• Visit www.familyhiking.com and register by April 26.
• A free first aid kit is provided for all who register by April 12.

① 토요일과 일요일 이틀간 진행된다.
② 오후 5시에 시작된다.
③ 어른과 어린이의 참가비는 같다.
④ 어린이는 법적 보호자를 동반해야 한다.
⑤ 추첨을 통해 구급상자가 무료로 제공된다.

29. 다음 글의 밑줄 친 부분 중, 어법상 틀린 것은?

For years, many psychologists have held strongly to the belief ① that the key to addressing negative health habits is to change behavior. This, more than values and attitudes, ② is the part of personality that is easiest to change. Ingestive habits such as smoking, drinking and various eating behaviors are the most common health concerns targeted for behavioral changes. Process-addiction behaviors (workaholism, shopaholism, and the like) fall into this category as well. Mental imagery combined with power of suggestion was taken up as the premise of behavioral medicine to help people change negative health behaviors into positive ③ ones. Although this technique alone will not produce changes, when ④ using alongside other behavior modification tactics and coping strategies, behavioral changes have proved effective for some people. ⑤ What mental imagery does is reinforce a new desired behavior. Repeated use of images reinforces the desired behavior more strongly over time.

* ingestive: (음식) 섭취의 ** premise: 전제

30. 다음 글의 밑줄 친 부분 중, 문맥상 낱말의 쓰임이 적절하지 않은 것은? [3점]

Emotion socialization — learning from other people about emotions and how to deal with them — starts early in life and plays a foundational role for emotion regulation development. Although extra-familial influences, such as peers or media, gain in importance during adolescence, parents remain the ① primary socialization agents. For example, their own responses to emotional situations serve as a role model for emotion regulation, increasing the likelihood that their children will show ② similar reactions in comparable situations. Parental practices at times when their children are faced with emotional challenges also impact emotion regulation development. Whereas direct soothing and directive guidance of what to do are beneficial for younger children, they may ③ cultivate adolescents' autonomy striving. In consequence, adolescents might pull away from, rather than turn toward, their parents in times of emotional crisis, unless parental practices are ④ adjusted. More suitable in adolescence is ⑤ indirect support of autonomous emotion regulation, such as through interest in, as well as awareness and nonjudgmental acceptance of, adolescents' emotional experiences, and being available when the adolescent wants to talk.

[31 ~ 34] 다음 빈칸에 들어갈 말로 가장 적절한 것을 고르시오.

31. Dancers often push themselves to the limits of their physical capabilities. But that push is misguided if it is directed toward accomplishing something physically impossible. For instance, a tall dancer with long feet may wish to perform repetitive vertical jumps to fast music, pointing his feet while in the air and lowering his heels to the floor between jumps. That may be impossible no matter how strong the dancer is. But a short-footed dancer may have no trouble! Another dancer may be struggling to complete a half-turn in the air. Understanding the connection between a rapid turn rate and the alignment of the body close to the rotation axis tells her how to accomplish her turn successfully. In both of these cases, understanding and working within the _____ imposed by nature and described by physical laws allows dancers to work efficiently, minimizing potential risk of injury.

* alignment: 정렬 ** rotation axis: 회전축

① habits ② cultures ③ constraints
④ hostilities ⑤ moralities

32. We must explore the relationship between children's film production and consumption habits. The term "children's film" implies ownership by children — *their* cinema — but films supposedly made for children have always been _____, particularly in commercial cinemas. The considerable crossover in audience composition for children's films can be shown by the fact that, in 2007, eleven Danish children's and youth films attracted 59 per cent of theatrical admissions, and in 2014, German children's films comprised seven out of the top twenty films at the national box office. This phenomenon corresponds with a broader, international embrace of what is seemingly children's culture among audiences of diverse ages. The old prejudice that children's film is some other realm, separate from (and forever subordinate to) a more legitimate cinema for adults is not supported by the realities of consumption: children's film is at the heart of contemporary popular culture.

* subordinate: 하위의

① centered on giving moral lessons
② consumed by audiences of all ages
③ appreciated through an artistic view
④ produced by inexperienced directors
⑤ separated from the cinema for adults

33. Beethoven's drive to create something novel is a reflection of his state of curiosity. Our brains experience a sense of reward when we create something new in the process of exploring something uncertain, such as a musical phrase that we've never played or heard before. When our curiosity leads to something novel, the resulting reward brings us a sense of pleasure. A number of investigators have modeled how curiosity influences musical composition. In the case of Beethoven, computer modeling focused on the thirty-two piano sonatas written after age thirteen revealed that the musical patterns found in all of Beethoven's music decreased in later sonatas, while novel patterns, including patterns that were unique to a particular sonata, increased. In other words, Beethoven's music _____ as his curiosity drove the exploration of new musical ideas. Curiosity is a powerful driver of human creativity. [3점]

* sonata: 악곡의 한 형식

① had more standardized patterns
② obtained more public popularity
③ became less predictable over time
④ reflected his unstable mental state
⑤ attracted less attention from the critics

34. Technologists are always on the lookout for quantifiable metrics. Measurable inputs to a model are their lifeblood, and like a social scientist, a technologist needs to identify concrete measures, or "proxies," for assessing progress. This need for quantifiable proxies produces a bias toward measuring things that are easy to quantify. But simple metrics can take us further away from the important goals we really care about, which may require complicated metrics or be extremely difficult, or perhaps impossible, to reduce to any measure. And when we have imperfect or bad proxies, we can easily fall under the illusion that we are solving for a good end without actually making genuine progress toward a worthy solution. The problem of proxies results in technologists frequently _____. As the saying goes, "Not everything that counts can be counted, and not everything that can be counted counts." [3점]

* metric: 측정 기준

① regarding continuous progress as a valid solution
② prioritizing short-term goals over long-term visions
③ mistaking a personal bias for an established theory
④ substituting what is measurable for what is meaningful
⑤ focusing more on possible risks than concrete measures

35. 다음 글에서 전체 흐름과 관계 <u>없는</u> 문장은?

We are the only species that seasons its food, deliberately altering it with the highly flavored plant parts we call herbs and spices. It's quite possible that our taste for spices has an evolutionary root. ① Many spices have antibacterial properties—in fact, common seasonings such as garlic, onion, and oregano inhibit the growth of almost every bacterium tested. ② And the cultures that make the heaviest use of spices—think of the garlic and black pepper of Thai food, the ginger and coriander of India, the chili peppers of Mexico—come from warmer climates, where bacterial spoilage is a bigger issue. ③ The changing climate can have a significant impact on the production and availability of spices, influencing their growth patterns and ultimately affecting global spice markets. ④ In contrast, the most lightly spiced cuisines—those of Scandinavia and northern Europe—are from cooler climates. ⑤ Our uniquely human attention to flavor, in this case the flavor of spices, turns out to have arisen as a matter of life and death.

* cuisine: 요리(법)

[36 ~ 37] 주어진 글 다음에 이어질 글의 순서로 가장 적절한 것을 고르시오.

36.

> Development of the human body from a single cell provides many examples of the structural richness that is possible when the repeated production of random variation is combined with nonrandom selection.

(A) Those in the right place that make the right connections are stimulated, and those that don't are eliminated. This process is much like sculpting. A natural consequence of the strategy is great variability from individual to individual at the cell and molecular levels, even though large-scale structures are quite similar.

(B) The survivors serve to produce new cells that undergo further rounds of selection. Except in the immune system, cells and extensions of cells are not genetically selected during development, but rather, are positionally selected.

(C) All phases of body development from embryo to adult exhibit random activities at the cellular level, and body formation depends on the new possibilities generated by these activities coupled with selection of those outcomes that satisfy previously built-in criteria. Always new structure is based on old structure, and at every stage selection favors some cells and eliminates others. [3점]

* molecular: 분자의 ** embryo: 배아

① (A) − (C) − (B)　　　② (B) − (A) − (C)
③ (B) − (C) − (A)　　　④ (C) − (A) − (B)
⑤ (C) − (B) − (A)

37.

In order to bring the ever-increasing costs of home care for elderly and needy persons under control, managers of home care providers have introduced management systems.

(A) This, in the view of managers, has contributed to the resolution of the problem. The home care workers, on the other hand, may perceive their work not as a set of separate tasks to be performed as efficiently as possible, but as a service to be provided to a client with whom they may have developed a relationship.

(B) These systems specify tasks of home care workers and the time and budget available to perform these tasks. Electronic reporting systems require home care workers to report on their activities and the time spent, thus making the distribution of time and money visible and, in the perception of managers, controllable.

(C) This includes having conversations with clients and enquiring about the person's well-being. Restricted time and the requirement to report may be perceived as obstacles that make it impossible to deliver the service that is needed. If the management systems are too rigid, this may result in home care workers becoming overloaded and demotivated. [3점]

① (A) − (C) − (B)   ② (B) − (A) − (C)
③ (B) − (C) − (A)   ④ (C) − (A) − (B)
⑤ (C) − (B) − (A)

[38 ~ 39] 글의 흐름으로 보아, 주어진 문장이 들어가기에 가장 적절한 곳을 고르시오.

38.

However, there are many lines of evidence to suggest that vagrancy can, on rare occasions, dramatically alter the fate of populations, species or even whole ecosystems.

It is a common assumption that most vagrant birds are ultimately doomed, aside from the rare cases where individuals are able to reorientate and return to their normal ranges. (①) In turn, it is also commonly assumed that vagrancy itself is a relatively unimportant biological phenomenon. (②) This is undoubtedly true for the majority of cases, as the most likely outcome of any given vagrancy event is that the individual will fail to find enough resources, and/or be exposed to inhospitable environmental conditions, and perish. (③) Despite being infrequent, these events can be extremely important when viewed at the timescales over which ecological and evolutionary processes unfold. (④) The most profound consequences of vagrancy relate to the establishment of new breeding sites, new migration routes and wintering locations. (⑤) Each of these can occur through different mechanisms, and at different frequencies, and they each have their own unique importance. [3점]

* vagrancy: 무리에서 떨어져 헤맴 ** doomed: 죽을 운명의
*** inhospitable: 살기 힘든

39.

Only then are they able to act quickly in accordance with their internalized expertise and evidence-based experience.

Intuition can be great, but it ought to be hard-earned. (①) Experts, for example, are able to think on their feet because they've invested thousands of hours in learning and practice: their intuition has become data-driven. (②) Yet most people are not experts, though they often think they are. (③) Most of us, especially when we interact with others on social media, act with expert-like speed and conviction, offering a wide range of opinions on global crises, without the substance of knowledge that supports it. (④) And thanks to AI, which ensures that our messages are delivered to an audience more inclined to believing it, our delusions of expertise can be reinforced by our personal filter bubble. (⑤) We have an interesting tendency to find people more open-minded, rational, and sensible when they think just like us.

* intuition: 직관 ** delusion: 착각

40. 다음 글의 내용을 한 문장으로 요약하고자 한다. 빈칸 (A), (B)에 들어갈 말로 가장 적절한 것은?

The fast-growing, tremendous amount of data, collected and stored in large and numerous data repositories, has far exceeded our human ability for understanding without powerful tools. As a result, data collected in large data repositories become "data tombs"—data archives that are hardly visited. Important decisions are often made based not on the information-rich data stored in data repositories but rather on a decision maker's instinct, simply because the decision maker does not have the tools to extract the valuable knowledge hidden in the vast amounts of data. Efforts have been made to develop expert system and knowledge-based technologies, which typically rely on users or domain experts to *manually* input knowledge into knowledge bases. However, this procedure is likely to cause biases and errors and is extremely costly and time consuming. The widening gap between data and information calls for the systematic development of tools that can turn data tombs into "golden nuggets" of knowledge.

* repository: 저장소 ** golden nugget: 금괴

↓

As the vast amounts of data stored in repositories ___(A)___ human understanding, effective tools to ___(B)___ valuable knowledge are required for better decision-making.

	(A)		(B)
①	overwhelm	┈┈┈	obtain
②	overwhelm	┈┈┈	exchange
③	enhance	┈┈┈	apply
④	enhance	┈┈┈	discover
⑤	fulfill	┈┈┈	access

[41 ~ 42] 다음 글을 읽고, 물음에 답하시오.

It's untrue that teens can focus on two things at once—what they're doing is shifting their attention from one task to another. In this digital age, teens wire their brains to make these shifts very quickly, but they are still, like everyone else, paying attention to one thing at a time, sequentially. Common sense tells us multitasking should (a) increase brain activity, but Carnegie Mellon University scientists using the latest brain imaging technology find it doesn't. As a matter of fact, they discovered that multitasking actually decreases brain activity. Neither task is done as well as if each were performed (b) individually. Fractions of a second are lost every time we make a switch, and a person's interrupted task can take 50 percent (c) longer to finish, with 50 percent more errors. Turns out the latest brain research (d) contradicts the old advice "one thing at a time."

It's not that kids can't do some tasks simultaneously. But if two tasks are performed at once, one of them has to be familiar. Our brains perform a familiar task on "automatic pilot" while really paying attention to the other one. That's why insurance companies consider talking on a cell phone and driving to be as (e) dangerous as driving while drunk—it's the driving that goes on "automatic pilot" while the conversation really holds our attention. Our kids may be living in the Information Age but our brains have not been redesigned yet.

41. 윗글의 제목으로 가장 적절한 것은?

① Multitasking Unveiled: What Really Happens in Teens' Brains
② Optimal Ways to Expand the Attention Span of Teens
③ Unknown Approaches to Enhance Brain Development
④ Multitasking for a Balanced Life in a Busy World
⑤ How to Build Automaticity in Performing Tasks

42. 밑줄 친 (a)~(e) 중에서 문맥상 낱말의 쓰임이 적절하지 <u>않은</u> 것은?

① (a)　　② (b)　　③ (c)　　④ (d)　　⑤ (e)

[43 ~ 45] 다음 글을 읽고, 물음에 답하시오.

(A)

Christine was a cat owner who loved her furry companion, Leo. One morning, she noticed that Leo was not feeling well. Concerned for her beloved cat, Christine decided to take him to the animal hospital. As she always brought Leo to this hospital, she was certain that the vet knew well about Leo. (a) She desperately hoped Leo got the necessary care as soon as possible.

(B)

"I'll call (b) you with updates as soon as we know anything," said the vet. Throughout the day, Christine anxiously awaited news about Leo. Later that day, the phone rang and it was the vet. "The tests revealed a minor infection. Leo needs some medication and rest, but he'll be back to his playful self soon." Relieved to hear the news, Christine rushed back to the animal hospital to pick up Leo.

(C)

The vet provided detailed instructions on how to administer the medication and shared tips for a speedy recovery. Back at home, Christine created a comfortable space for Leo to rest and heal. (c) She patted him with love and attention, ensuring that he would recover in no time. As the days passed, Leo gradually regained his strength and playful spirit.

(D)

The waiting room was filled with other pet owners. Finally, it was Leo's turn to see the vet. Christine watched as the vet gently examined him. The vet said, "(d) I think Leo has a minor infection." "Infection? Will he be okay?" asked Christine. "We need to do some tests to see if he is infected. But for the tests, it's best for Leo to stay here," replied the vet. It was heartbreaking for Christine to leave Leo at the animal hospital, but (e) she had to accept it was for the best.

43. 주어진 글 (A)에 이어질 내용을 순서에 맞게 배열한 것으로 가장 적절한 것은?

① (B) - (D) - (C)　　② (C) - (B) - (D)
③ (C) - (D) - (B)　　④ (D) - (B) - (C)
⑤ (D) - (C) - (B)

44. 밑줄 친 (a)~(e) 중에서 가리키는 대상이 나머지 넷과 <u>다른</u> 것은?

① (a)　　② (b)　　③ (c)　　④ (d)　　⑤ (e)

45. 윗글에 관한 내용으로 적절하지 <u>않은</u> 것은?

① Christine은 수의사가 Leo에 대해 잘 알고 있을 거라고 확신했다.
② Christine은 병원을 방문한 다음 날 수의사의 전화를 받았다.
③ 수의사는 Leo의 빠른 회복을 위한 조언을 했다.
④ 대기실은 다른 반려동물의 주인들로 꽉 차 있었다.
⑤ Leo의 감염 여부를 알기 위해 검사를 할 필요가 있었다.

＊ 확인 사항
○ 답안지의 해당란에 필요한 내용을 정확히 기입(표기)했는지 확인하시오.

회차별 영단어 **QR 코드** ※ QR 코드를 스캔 후 모바일로 단어장처럼 학습할 수 있습니다.

● 고2 2024학년도 3월

18
001 annual ⓐ 매년의, 연례의
002 craft ⓝ 수공예품
003 fair ⓝ 전시회
004 provide ⓥ 제공하다
005 previous ⓐ (시간·순서적으로) 앞의, 이전의
006 reserve ⓥ 예약하다
007 complete ⓥ 기입하다, 작성하다
008 registration form 신청서
009 rental fee 대여료, 사용료
010 support ⓥ 지원하다
011 upcoming ⓐ 다가오는, 곧 있을
012 expect ⓥ 예상하다
013 available ⓐ 이용할 수 있는
014 book ⓥ 예약하다

19
015 painting ⓝ 그림 그리기
016 enter ⓥ 출전하다, 참가하다
017 local ⓐ 지역의
018 artwork ⓝ 작품
019 confidence ⓝ 자신감
020 drop ⓥ 떨어지다
021 quietly ad 조용히
022 judgment ⓝ 심사, 심판
023 announce ⓥ 발표하다
024 prize ⓝ 상
025 overcome ⓥ 극복하다
026 confirm ⓥ 확인하다
027 identity ⓝ 정체성

20
028 especially ad 특히
029 generation ⓝ 세대
030 happen ⓥ 일어나다
031 overnight ad 밤사이에, 하룻밤 동안
032 expectation ⓝ 기대
033 tend ⓥ 경향이 있다
034 discourage ⓥ 방해하다
035 forward ad ~향해
036 parameter ⓝ 매개 변수, 제한
037 comfort ⓝ 편안
038 convenience ⓝ 편리
039 tempt ⓥ 유혹하다
040 require ⓥ 필요하다
041 successful ⓐ 성공한
042 matter ⓝ (고려하거나 처리해야 할) 문제
043 mere ⓐ 단순한
044 desire ⓝ 욕망
045 patience ⓝ 인내력, 인내심
046 achieve ⓥ 이루다
047 prey ⓝ 먹이
048 impatience ⓝ 조바심

21
049 self-driving 자율 주행의
050 option ⓝ 선택
051 strap ⓝ 끈
052 brick ⓝ 벽돌
053 accelerator ⓝ 가속 페달
054 vehicle ⓝ 탈것
055 avoid ⓥ 피하다

056 barrier ⓝ 장애물
057 obviously ad 명백히
058 entire ⓐ 전체의
059 concept ⓝ 개념
060 worth ⓐ ~할 가치가 있는
061 pursue ⓥ 추구하다
062 tool ⓝ 도구
063 possess ⓥ 소유하다
064 operate ⓥ 작동하다
065 autonomously ad 자율의
066 safely ad 안전하게
067 reach ⓥ 도달하다
068 medicine ⓝ 의학
069 approach ⓥ 접근하다
070 appropriate ⓐ 적절한
071 technology ⓝ (과학) 기술
072 patient ⓝ 환자
073 unique ⓐ 고유의
074 wear ⓥ 착용하고 있다, 입고 있다
075 device ⓝ 장치
076 monitor ⓥ 감시하다
077 condition ⓝ 상태
078 specific ⓐ 구체적인
079 refined ⓐ 제한된

22
080 overrate ⓥ 과대평가하다
081 impact ⓝ 영향
082 absorb ⓥ 흡수하다
083 furniture ⓝ 가구
084 invisible ⓐ 눈에 보이지 않는
085 baby bottle 젖병
086 implement ⓝ 도구
087 transform ⓥ 바꾸다
088 fundamental ⓐ 기초의
089 infant ⓝ 유아
090 classic ⓐ 전형적인, 대표적인
091 function ⓝ 기능
092 substitute for ~을 대신하다
093 huge ⓐ 거대한, 막대
094 implication ⓝ 영향
095 management ⓝ 관리
096 overlook ⓥ 간과하다
097 discussion ⓝ 논의
098 society ⓝ 사회

23
099 empathy ⓝ 공감
100 frequently ad 종종
101 employer ⓝ 고용주
102 employee ⓝ 종업원
103 specify ⓥ 구체화하다
104 exactly ad 정확히
105 stress ⓥ 강조하다
106 cognitive ⓐ 인지적인
107 emphasize ⓥ 강조하다
108 perspective ⓝ 관점
109 customer ⓝ 손님, 고객
110 negotiate ⓥ 협상하다
111 deal ⓥ 거래하다
112 decision ⓝ 결정
113 affective ⓐ 정서적인

114 concern ⓝ 관심
115 gain ⓥ 얻다
116 trust ⓝ 신뢰, 신임
117 treat ⓥ 대하다
118 compassion ⓝ 열정
119 company ⓝ 회사
120 foster ⓥ 기르다
121 conduct ⓥ 수행하다, 처리하다
122 seek ⓥ 추구하다
123 diverse ⓐ 다양한
124 interpretation ⓝ 이해

24
125 prevalent ⓐ 일반적인
126 accessible ⓐ 연락될 수 있는
127 allow ⓥ 허용하다, 인정하다
128 obligation ⓝ 의무
129 probably ad 아마
130 pressure ⓝ 압박
131 respond ⓥ 응답하다
132 instantly ad 즉각, 즉시
133 social interaction 사회적 상호 작용
134 blow up 폭파하다, 터뜨리다
135 induce ⓥ 유발하다
136 aggressive ⓐ 공격적인

25
137 protein ⓝ 단백질
138 consumption ⓝ 섭취, 소비
139 measure ⓥ 측정하다
140 supply ⓝ 공급량
141 dairy ⓝ 유제품
142 follow ⓥ 뒤를 잇다
143 poultry ⓝ 가금류
144 respectively ad 각각
145 consume ⓥ 소비하다
146 rank ⓥ 차지하다

26
147 mind ⓝ 지성인
148 talent ⓝ 재능
149 receive ⓥ 받다
150 doctoral degree 박사 학위
151 engineering ⓝ 공학
152 lecturer ⓝ 강사, 강연자
153 consultant ⓝ 자문 위원
154 advise ⓥ 조언하다
155 award ⓥ 수상하다

27
156 present ⓥ 표현하다
157 pour ⓥ 따르다
158 on your own 혼자
159 ingredient ⓝ 재료
160 alternative ⓝ 대체품

28
161 preserve 보호 구역
162 adult ⓝ 성인
163 be accompanied by ~을 동반하다
164 legal ⓐ 법률상의
165 guardian ⓝ 보호자, 수호자

166 instruction ⓝ 지시

29
167 psychologist ⓝ 심리학자
168 belief ⓝ 믿음
169 negative ⓐ 부정적인
170 habit ⓝ 습관, 버릇
171 attitude ⓝ 태도
172 personality ⓝ 성격
173 ingestive ⓐ 섭취의
174 smoking ⓝ 흡연
175 drinking ⓝ 음주
176 workaholism ⓝ 일중독
177 shopaholism ⓝ 쇼핑 중독
178 imagery ⓝ 사진
179 suggestion ⓝ 암시, 제안
180 premise ⓝ 전제
181 behavioral ⓐ 행동의
182 alongside ~와 함께
183 modification ⓝ 수정
184 tactics ⓝ 기법
185 cope ⓥ 대응하다
186 strategy ⓝ 전략
187 effective ⓐ 효과적인
188 reinforce ⓥ 강화하다

30
189 emotion ⓝ 감정
190 socialization ⓝ 사회화
191 foundational ⓐ 기초적인
192 role ⓝ 역할
193 regulation ⓝ 규제
194 peer ⓝ 또래
195 adolescence ⓝ 청소년기
196 remain ⓥ 여전히 ~이다
197 primary ⓐ 주된, 주요한
198 agent ⓝ 주체
199 response ⓝ 반응
200 emotional ⓐ 감정의
201 likelihood ⓝ 가능성
202 reaction ⓝ 반응
203 comparable ⓐ 비슷한
204 parental ⓐ 부모의
205 soothing ⓐ 위로
206 directive ⓐ 지시적인
207 guidance ⓝ 안내, 지도
208 beneficial ⓐ 도움이 되는
209 cultivate ⓥ 구축하다
210 autonomy ⓝ 자율성, 자주성
211 crisis ⓝ 위기
212 adjust ⓥ 조정하다
213 suitable ⓐ 적합한, 적절한
214 autonomous ⓐ 자율적인, 자주적인
215 awareness ⓝ 인식, 자각
216 nonjudgmental ⓐ (도덕 문제에서) 개인적 판단을 피하는
217 acceptance ⓝ 받아들임, 수용

31
218 limit ⓝ 한계
219 capability ⓝ 능력
220 misguided ⓐ 잘못 이해한

221 ☐ accomplish ⓥ 달성하다
222 ☐ physically ad 물리적으로
223 ☐ impossible ⓐ 불가능한
224 ☐ perform ⓥ 수행하다, 실행하다
225 ☐ repetitive ⓐ 반복적인
226 ☐ vertical ⓐ 수직의
227 ☐ lower ⓥ 내리다
228 ☐ trouble ⓝ 문제, 곤란
229 ☐ complete ⓥ 완성하다, 완료하다
230 ☐ rapid ⓐ 빠른
231 ☐ rotation ⓝ 회전
232 ☐ axis ⓝ 축
233 ☐ impose ⓥ 주다
234 ☐ by nature 선천적으로
235 ☐ constraint ⓝ 제약, 제한
236 ☐ potential ⓐ 잠재적인
237 ☐ injury ⓝ 부상

32
238 ☐ relationship ⓝ 관계
239 ☐ production ⓝ 생산, 제조
240 ☐ imply ⓥ 암시하다
241 ☐ ownership ⓝ 소유권
242 ☐ cinema ⓝ 영화
243 ☐ supposedly ad 소위
244 ☐ particularly ad 특히
245 ☐ commercial ⓐ 상업의
246 ☐ considerable ⓐ 상당한
247 ☐ crossover ⓝ 넘나듦
248 ☐ composition ⓝ 구성
249 ☐ attract ⓥ 끌어들이다
250 ☐ theatrical ⓐ 극장의
251 ☐ admission ⓝ 입장료
252 ☐ comprise ⓥ 차지하다
253 ☐ phenomenon ⓝ 현상
254 ☐ correspond with ~와 일치하다
255 ☐ embrace ⓥ 수용
256 ☐ seemingly ad 외견상으로, 겉보기에는
257 ☐ prejudice ⓝ 편견
258 ☐ realm ⓝ 영역
259 ☐ separate ⓐ 분리된, 독립된
260 ☐ subordinate ⓐ 부차적인
261 ☐ legitimate ⓐ 제대로 된

33
262 ☐ drive ⓝ 욕구
263 ☐ novel ⓐ 새로운
264 ☐ reflection ⓝ 반영
265 ☐ state ⓝ 상태
266 ☐ curiosity ⓝ 호기심
267 ☐ reward ⓝ 보상
268 ☐ uncertain ⓐ 불확실한
269 ☐ pleasure ⓝ 쾌감, 만족
270 ☐ investigator ⓝ 연구자
271 ☐ composition ⓝ 작곡
272 ☐ reveal ⓥ 보여주다
273 ☐ predictable ⓐ 예측할 수 있는
274 ☐ exploration ⓝ 탐구
275 ☐ obtain ⓥ 얻다

34
276 ☐ technologist ⓝ 과학 기술자

277 ☐ on the lookout for ~를 찾고 있는
278 ☐ quantifiable ⓐ 정량화할 수 있는
279 ☐ measurable ⓐ 측정할 수 있는
280 ☐ input ⓥ 입력하다
281 ☐ lifeblood ⓝ 생명선
282 ☐ social scientist 사회 과학자
283 ☐ identify ⓥ 식별하다
284 ☐ concrete ⓐ 구체적인
285 ☐ assess ⓥ 평가하다
286 ☐ bias ⓝ 편향
287 ☐ quantify ⓥ 양을 나타내다, 양을 정하다
288 ☐ further ad 더 멀리
289 ☐ complicated ⓐ 복잡한
290 ☐ extremely ad 매우
291 ☐ imperfect ⓐ 불완전한, 결함이 있는
292 ☐ illusion ⓝ 환영
293 ☐ genuine ⓐ 진정한
294 ☐ worthy ⓐ 가치 있는, 훌륭한
295 ☐ meaningful ⓐ 의미 있는, 중요한
296 ☐ count ⓥ 중요하다

35
297 ☐ season ⓥ 양념을 하다
298 ☐ deliberately ad 의도적으로
299 ☐ alter ⓥ 바꾸다
300 ☐ flavored ⓐ 맛이 나는
301 ☐ plant ⓝ 식물
302 ☐ quite ad 꽤
303 ☐ taste ⓝ 미각, 입맛
304 ☐ evolutionary ⓐ 진화적인
305 ☐ antibacterial ⓐ 항균의
306 ☐ property ⓝ 특성
307 ☐ seasoning ⓝ 양념
308 ☐ garlic ⓝ 마늘
309 ☐ onion ⓝ 양파
310 ☐ inhibit ⓥ 억제하다
311 ☐ ginger ⓝ 생강
312 ☐ coriander ⓝ 고수
313 ☐ spoilage ⓝ 부패
314 ☐ issue ⓝ 문제
315 ☐ significant ⓐ 많은
316 ☐ availability ⓝ 이용 가능성
317 ☐ ultimately ad 궁극적으로, 결국
318 ☐ affect ⓥ 영향을 미치다
319 ☐ cuisine ⓝ 요리, 요리법
320 ☐ arise ⓥ 생겨나다

36
321 ☐ structural ⓐ 구조상의, 구조적인
322 ☐ variation ⓝ 변이
323 ☐ selection ⓝ 선택
324 ☐ connection ⓝ 연결
325 ☐ stimulate ⓥ 활성화시키다
326 ☐ eliminate ⓥ 제거하다
327 ☐ sculpt ⓥ 조각하다
328 ☐ consequence ⓝ 결과
329 ☐ molecular ⓐ 분자의
330 ☐ undergo ⓥ 겪다
331 ☐ immune system 면역 체계
332 ☐ extension ⓝ 확장
333 ☐ genetically ad 유전적으로
334 ☐ positionally ad 위치적으로

335 ☐ embryo ⓝ 배아
336 ☐ cellular ⓐ 세포의
337 ☐ formation ⓝ 형성
338 ☐ criteria ⓝ 기준

37
339 ☐ ever-increasing 계속 증가하는
340 ☐ cost ⓝ 비용
341 ☐ elderly ⓐ 노인의
342 ☐ needy ⓐ 빈곤한
343 ☐ contribute ⓥ 기여하다
344 ☐ resolution ⓝ 해결
345 ☐ perceive ⓥ 인지하다
346 ☐ a set of 일련의
347 ☐ task ⓝ 일, 직무
348 ☐ efficiently ad 효율적으로
349 ☐ client ⓝ 고객, 의뢰인
350 ☐ budget ⓝ 예산
351 ☐ distribution ⓝ 분배
352 ☐ controllable ⓐ 통제 가능한
353 ☐ conversation ⓝ 대화
354 ☐ enquire ⓥ 묻다
355 ☐ restrict ⓥ 제한하다
356 ☐ requirement ⓝ 필요조건, 요건
357 ☐ obstacle ⓝ 장애물
358 ☐ rigid ⓐ 엄격한
359 ☐ demotivated ⓐ 의욕을 잃은

38
360 ☐ evidence ⓝ 증거, 흔적
361 ☐ suggest ⓥ 시사하다
362 ☐ vagrancy ⓝ 부랑자
363 ☐ rare ⓐ 드문
364 ☐ occasion ⓝ 경우
365 ☐ assumption ⓝ 가정
366 ☐ vagrant ⓐ 방랑하는, 정처 없이 떠돌아다니는
367 ☐ doom ⓥ (불행한)운명을 맞다
368 ☐ reorientate ⓥ 방향을 다시 잡다
369 ☐ range ⓝ 범위
370 ☐ commonly ad 일반적으로, 흔히, 보통
371 ☐ undoubtedly ad 의심할 여지없이
372 ☐ majority ⓝ 대부분, 대다수
373 ☐ inhospitable ⓐ 힘든
374 ☐ environmental ⓐ 환경의
375 ☐ perish ⓥ 죽다, 소멸되다
376 ☐ infrequent ⓐ 드문
377 ☐ timescale ⓝ 시간
378 ☐ profound ⓐ 중대한
379 ☐ breeding ⓝ 번식
380 ☐ migration ⓝ 이동

39
381 ☐ in accordance with ~에 따라
382 ☐ expertise ⓝ 전문 지식
383 ☐ intuition ⓝ 직관
384 ☐ on one's feet 즉각적으로
385 ☐ conviction ⓝ 확신
386 ☐ opinion ⓝ 의견
387 ☐ substance ⓝ 실체
388 ☐ delusions ⓝ 망상
389 ☐ tendency ⓝ 경향

390 ☐ rational ⓐ 합리적인

40
391 ☐ tremendous ⓐ 엄청난
392 ☐ repository ⓝ 저장소
393 ☐ exceed ⓥ 뛰어넘다
394 ☐ tomb ⓝ 무덤
395 ☐ instinct ⓝ 직관
396 ☐ vast ⓐ 방대한
397 ☐ manually ad 수동으로
398 ☐ procedure ⓝ 방법
399 ☐ overwhelm ⓥ 압도하다
400 ☐ enhance ⓥ 강화하다
401 ☐ fulfill ⓥ 수행하다

41~42
402 ☐ shift ⓥ 전환하다
403 ☐ age ⓝ 시대
404 ☐ sequentially ad 순차적으로
405 ☐ fraction ⓝ 아주 조금
406 ☐ switch ⓥ 전환
407 ☐ interrupt ⓥ 중단시키다
408 ☐ contradict ⓥ 반박하다
409 ☐ simultaneously ad 동시에
410 ☐ familiar ⓐ 친숙한
411 ☐ redesign ⓥ 재설계하다

43~45
412 ☐ furry ⓐ 털북숭이의
413 ☐ notice ⓥ 알리다
414 ☐ beloved ⓐ 사랑스러운
415 ☐ hospital ⓝ 병원
416 ☐ certain ⓥ 확신하다
417 ☐ desperately ad 절망적으로
418 ☐ vet ⓝ 수의사
419 ☐ anxiously ad 초조하게
420 ☐ await ⓥ 기다리다
421 ☐ medication ⓝ 약물
422 ☐ rush ⓥ 서두르다
423 ☐ pick up 데리고 오다
424 ☐ administer ⓥ 투여하다
425 ☐ ensure ⓥ 보장하다
426 ☐ pass ⓥ 지나다
427 ☐ spirit ⓝ 활기
428 ☐ be filled with ~로 채우다
429 ☐ examine ⓥ 진찰하다
430 ☐ infection ⓝ 감염
431 ☐ heartbreaking ⓐ 가슴 아픈
432 ☐ accept ⓥ 받아들이다

● 채점 : 맞은 개수 _____ / 80

TEST A-B 각 단어의 뜻을 [A] 영어는 우리말로, [B] 우리말은 영어로 쓰시오.

A	English	Korean
01	impatience	
02	fulfill	
03	inhibit	
04	deal	
05	vertical	
06	tempt	
07	restrict	
08	needy	
09	repetitive	
10	tomb	
11	injury	
12	absorb	
13	fundamental	
14	empathy	
15	arise	
16	fraction	
17	substance	
18	rush	
19	exceed	
20	prejudice	

B	Korean	English
01	관심	
02	수용	
03	단순한	
04	압도하다	
05	암시하다	
06	환영	
07	중단시키다	
08	규제	
09	작동하다	
10	간과하다	
11	기대	
12	가정	
13	작품	
14	방대한	
15	눈에 보이지 않는	
16	전체의	
17	수동으로	
18	협상하다	
19	정서적인	
20	인지적인	

▶ A-D 정답 : 해설편 012쪽

TEST C-D 각 단어의 뜻을 골라 기호를 쓰시오.

C	English			Korean
01	quietly	(	)	ⓐ ~와 함께
02	criteria	(	)	ⓑ 중대한
03	investigator	(	)	ⓒ 투여하다
04	premise	(	)	ⓓ 연구자
05	realm	(	)	ⓔ 망상
06	on one's feet	(	)	ⓕ 대응하다
07	breeding	(	)	ⓖ 중요하다
08	cultivate	(	)	ⓗ 영역
09	count	(	)	ⓘ 매개 변수, 제한
10	foster	(	)	ⓙ 기르다
11	cope	(	)	ⓚ 구축하다
12	constraint	(	)	ⓛ 약물
13	medication	(	)	ⓜ 제약, 강제, 압박
14	delusions	(	)	ⓝ 번식
15	parameter	(	)	ⓞ 전제
16	concrete	(	)	ⓟ 기준
17	profound	(	)	ⓠ 새로운
18	novel	(	)	ⓡ 즉각적으로
19	alongside	(	)	ⓢ 구체적인
20	administer	(	)	ⓣ 꽤

D	Korean			English
01	힘든	(	)	ⓐ consumption
02	차지하다	(	)	ⓑ inhospitable
03	절망적으로	(	)	ⓒ contradict
04	수정	(	)	ⓓ overrate
05	기법	(	)	ⓔ examine
06	진정한	(	)	ⓕ desperately
07	재료	(	)	ⓖ furniture
08	반박하다	(	)	ⓗ infection
09	저장소	(	)	ⓘ pour
10	엄청난	(	)	ⓙ modification
11	감염	(	)	ⓚ tactics
12	가구	(	)	ⓛ repository
13	따르다	(	)	ⓜ comprise
14	겪다	(	)	ⓝ undergo
15	섭취	(	)	ⓞ sequentially
16	과대평가하다	(	)	ⓟ doom
17	운명을 맞다	(	)	ⓠ tremendous
18	순차적으로	(	)	ⓡ ingredient
19	진찰하다	(	)	ⓢ genuine
20	의무	(	)	ⓣ obligation

※ 영어 [독해] 파트만 수록한 문제지이므로 18번부터 시작합니다. ● 점수 표시가 없는 문항은 모두 2점 ● 문항수 28개 | 배점 63점 | 제한 시간 45분

18. 다음 글의 목적으로 가장 적절한 것은?

It was a pleasure meeting you at your gallery last week. I appreciate your effort to select and exhibit diverse artwork. As I mentioned, I greatly admire Robert D. Parker's paintings, which emphasize the beauty of nature. Over the past few days, I have been researching and learning about Robert D. Parker's online viewing room through your gallery's website. I'm especially interested in purchasing the painting that depicts the horizon, titled *Sunrise*. I would like to know if the piece is still available for purchase. It would be a great pleasure to house this wonderful piece of art. I look forward to your reply to this inquiry.

① 좋아하는 화가와의 만남을 요청하려고
② 미술 작품의 구매 가능 여부를 문의하려고
③ 소장 중인 미술 작품의 감정을 의뢰하려고
④ 미술 작품의 소유자 변경 내역을 확인하려고
⑤ 기획 중인 전시회에 참여하는 화가를 홍보하려고

19. 다음 글에 드러난 Isabel의 심경 변화로 가장 적절한 것은?

On opening day, Isabel arrives at the cafe very early with nervous anticipation. She looks around the cafe, but she can't shake off the feeling that something is missing. As she sets out cups, spoons, and plates, Isabel's doubts grow. She looks around, trying to imagine what else she could do to make the cafe perfect, but nothing comes to mind. Then, in a sudden burst of inspiration, Isabel grabs her paintbrush and transforms the blank walls into landscapes, adding flowers and trees. As she paints, her doubts begin to fade. Looking at her handiwork, which is beautifully done, she is certain that the cafe will be a success. 'Now, success is not exactly guaranteed,' she thinks to herself, 'but I'll definitely get there.'

① calm → surprised
② doubtful → confident
③ envious → delighted
④ grateful → frightened
⑤ indifferent → uneasy

20. 다음 글에서 필자가 주장하는 바로 가장 적절한 것은?

The more people have to do unwanted things the more chances are that they create unpleasant environment for themselves and others. If you hate the thing you do but have to do it nonetheless, you have choice between hating the thing and accepting that it needs to be done. Either way you will do it. Doing it from place of hatred will develop hatred towards the self and others around you; doing it from the place of acceptance will create compassion towards the self and allow for opportunities to find a more suitable way of accomplishing the task. If you decide to accept the fact that your task has to be done, start from recognising that your situation is a gift from life; this will help you to see it as a lesson in acceptance.

① 창의력을 기르려면 익숙한 환경에서 벗어나야 한다.
② 상대방의 무리한 요구는 최대한 분명하게 거절해야 한다.
③ 주어진 과업을 정확하게 파악한 후에 일을 시작해야 한다.
④ 효율적으로 일을 처리하기 위해 좋아하는 일부터 해야 한다.
⑤ 원치 않는 일을 해야만 할 때 수용적인 태도를 갖춰야 한다.

21. 밑줄 친 helping move the needle forward가 다음 글에서 의미하는 바로 가장 적절한 것은? [3점]

Everyone's heard the expression *don't let the perfect become the enemy of the good*. If you want to get over an obstacle so that your idea can become the solution-based policy you've long dreamed of, you can't have an all-or-nothing mentality. You have to be willing to alter your idea and let others influence its outcome. You have to be okay with the outcome being a little different, even a little *less*, than you wanted. Say you're pushing for a clean water act. Even if what emerges isn't as well-funded as you wished, or doesn't match how you originally conceived the bill, you'll have still succeeded in ensuring that kids in troubled areas have access to clean water. That's what counts, that *they* will be safer because of your idea and your effort. Is it perfect? No. Is there more work to be done? Absolutely. But in almost every case, helping move the needle forward is vastly better than not helping at all.

① spending time and money on celebrating perfection
② suggesting cost-saving strategies for a good cause
③ making a difference as best as the situation allows
④ checking your resources before altering the original goal
⑤ collecting donations to help the education of poor children

22. 다음 글의 요지로 가장 적절한 것은?

Brands that fail to grow and develop lose their relevance. Think about the person you knew who was once on the fast track at your company, who is either no longer with the firm or, worse yet, appears to have hit a plateau in his or her career. Assuming he or she did not make an ambitious move, more often than not, this individual is a victim of having failed to stay relevant and embrace the advances in his or her industry. Think about the impact personal computing technology had on the first wave of executive leadership exposed to the technology. Those who embraced the technology were able to integrate it into their work styles and excel. Those who were resistant many times found few opportunities to advance their careers and in many cases were ultimately let go through early retirement for failure to stay relevant and update their skills.

* hit a plateau: 정체기에 들다

① 다양한 업종의 경력이 있으면 구직 활동에 유리하다.
② 직원의 다양한 능력을 활용하면 업계를 주도할 수 있다.
③ 기술이 발전함에 따라 단순 반복 업무가 사라지고 있다.
④ 자신의 약점을 인정하면 동료들로부터 도움을 얻기 쉽다.
⑤ 변화를 받아들이지 못하면 업계에서의 적합성을 잃게 된다.

23. 다음 글의 주제로 가장 적절한 것은?

What consequences of eating too many grapes and other sweet fruit could there possibly be for our brains? A few large studies have helped to shed some light. In one, higher fruit intake in older, cognitively healthy adults was linked with less volume in the hippocampus. This finding was unusual, since people who eat more fruit usually display the benefits associated with a healthy diet. In this study, however, the researchers isolated various components of the subjects' diets and found that fruit didn't seem to be doing their memory centers any favors. Another study from the Mayo Clinic saw a similar inverse relationship between fruit intake and volume of the cortex, the large outer layer of the brain. Researchers in the latter study noted that excessive consumption of high-sugar fruit (such as mangoes, bananas, and pineapples) may cause metabolic and cognitive problems as much as processed carbs do.

* hippocampus: (대뇌 측두엽의) 해마 ** carb: 탄수화물 식품

① benefits of eating whole fruit on the brain health
② universal preference for sweet fruit among children
③ types of brain exercises enhancing long-term memory
④ nutritional differences between fruit and processed carbs
⑤ negative effect of fruit overconsumption on the cognitive brain

24. 다음 글의 제목으로 가장 적절한 것은?

Winning turns on a self-conscious awareness that others are watching. It's a lot easier to move under the radar when no one knows you and no one is paying attention. You can mess up and be rough and get dirty because no one even knows you're there. But as soon as you start to win, and others start to notice, you're suddenly aware that you're being observed. You're being judged. You worry that others will discover your flaws and weaknesses, and you start hiding your true personality, so you can be a good role model and good citizen and a leader that others can respect. There is nothing wrong with that. But if you do it at the expense of being who you really are, making decisions that please others instead of pleasing yourself, you're not going to be in that position very long. When you start apologizing for who you are, you stop growing and you stop winning. Permanently.

① Stop Judging Others to Win the Race of Life
② Why Disappointment Hurts More than Criticism
③ Winning vs. Losing: A Dangerously Misleading Mindset
④ Winners in a Trap: Too Self-Conscious to Be Themselves
⑤ Is Honesty the Best Policy to Turn Enemies into Friends?

25. 다음 도표의 내용과 일치하지 <u>않는</u> 것은?

How Often Do You Read a Book? (Germany 2022)

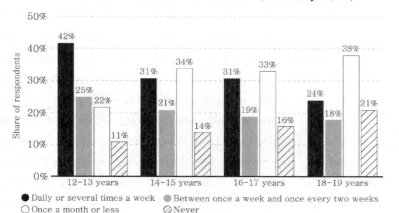

● Daily or several times a week　● Between once a week and once every two weeks
○ Once a month or less　⊘ Never

Note: All percentages may not total 100% due to rounding.

　The above graph shows how often German children and young adults read books in 2022 according to age groups. ① In each age group except 12 to 13-year-olds, those who said they read books once a month or less accounted for the largest proportion. ② Of the 12 to 13-year-old group, 42% stated they read daily or several times a week, which was the highest share within that group. ③ In the 14 to 15-year-old group, the percentage of teenagers who read daily or several times a week was three times higher than that of those who never read a book in the same age group. ④ In the 16 to 17-year-old group, those who read between once a week and once every two weeks were less than 20%. ⑤ More than one fifth of the age group of 18 to 19 years responded that they never read any book.

26. Julia Margaret Cameron에 관한 다음 글의 내용과 일치하지 <u>않는</u> 것은?

　British photographer Julia Margaret Cameron is considered one of the greatest portrait photographers of the 19th century. Born in Calcutta, India, into a British family, Cameron was educated in France. Given a camera as a gift by her daughter in December 1863, she quickly and energetically devoted herself to the art of photography. She cleared out a chicken coop and converted it into studio space where she began to work as a photographer. Cameron made illustrative studio photographs, convincing friends and family members to pose for photographs, fitting them in theatrical costumes and carefully composing them into scenes. Criticized for her so-called bad technique by art critics in her own time, she ignored convention and experimented with composition and focus. Later critics appreciated her valuing of spiritual depth over technical perfection and now consider her portraits to be among the finest expressions of the artistic possibilities of the medium.

* chicken coop: 닭장

① 인도에서 태어나고 프랑스에서 교육받았다.
② 딸로부터 카메라를 선물로 받았다.
③ 친구들과 가족 구성원에게 연극 의상을 입히고 촬영했다.
④ 능숙한 사진 기술로 자기 시대 예술 비평가에게 인정받았다.
⑤ 정신적 깊이에 가치를 둔 점을 훗날 높이 평가받았다.

27. Have a Good Night App에 관한 다음 안내문의 내용과 일치하지 <u>않는</u> 것은?

Have a Good Night App
This smart app helps you have a refreshing sleep!

FEATURES

■ **Sounds for Sleep**
－ Providing relaxing sounds for sleep

■ **Sleep Recorder**
－ Recording sounds such as coughing or snoring while sleeping

■ **Sleep Pattern Tracker**
－ Checking and analyzing the user's sleep pattern

■ **Stress-Free Alarm Tones**
－ Adjusting alarm tones to the user's sleep pattern

PRICE

■ **Basic version**: Free
■ **Premium version (extra soundtracks)**: $30 per year

<u>Click HERE to Download the App!</u>

① 수면을 위한 편안한 소리를 제공한다.
② 자는 동안 기침이나 코를 고는 소리를 녹음한다.
③ 이용자의 수면 패턴을 확인하고 분석한다.
④ 수면 패턴에 따라 알람음을 조정한다.
⑤ 기본 버전은 1년에 30달러이다.

28. 2023 Online Talent Show에 관한 다음 안내문의 내용과 일치하는 것은?

2023 Online Talent Show
Show off your amazing talents!

■ **Categories**: singing, dancing, playing instruments

■ **How to Enter**
－ Record a 3-minute video of your talent and send it to talent@westhigh.edu.
－ Submit the entry between March 27 and March 31.

■ **How We Select a Winner**
1. All the videos will be uploaded on the school website on April 5.
2. Students and teachers will vote for their favorite video.
3. The video that receives the most votes will win.

＊ The winning video will be played at the school festival.

For more information, please visit www.westhigh.edu.

① 참가 부문은 노래와 춤을 포함한 네 가지이다.
② 비디오의 길이에는 제한이 없다.
③ 제출 기간은 3월 27일부터 7일 동안이다.
④ 학생들만 우승작 선정 투표에 참여할 수 있다.
⑤ 우승한 비디오는 학교 축제에서 상영될 것이다.

29. 다음 글의 밑줄 친 부분 중, 어법상 틀린 것은? [3점]

Human beings like certainty. This liking stems from our ancient ancestors ① <u>who</u> needed to survive alongside saber-toothed tigers and poisonous berries. Our brains evolved to help us attend to threats, keep away from ② <u>them</u>, and remain alive afterward. In fact, we learned that the more ③ <u>certain</u> we were about something, the better chance we had of making the right choice. Is this berry the same shape as last time? The same size? If I know for certain it ④ <u>is</u>, my brain will direct me to eat it because I know it's safe. And if I'm uncertain, my brain will send out a danger alert to protect me. The dependence on certainty all those millennia ago ensured our survival to the present day, and the danger-alert system continues to protect us. This is achieved by our brains labeling new, vague, or unpredictable everyday events and experiences as uncertain. Our brains then ⑤ <u>generating</u> sensations, thoughts, and action plans to keep us safe from the uncertain element, and we live to see another day.

* saber-toothed tiger: 검치호(검 모양의 송곳니를 가진 호랑이)

30. 다음 글의 밑줄 친 부분 중, 문맥상 낱말의 쓰임이 적절하지 <u>않은</u> 것은? [3점]

Robert Blattberg and Steven Hoch noted that, in a changing environment, it is not clear that consistency is always a virtue and that one of the advantages of human judgment is the ability to detect change. Thus, in changing environments, it might be ① <u>advantageous</u> to combine human judgment and statistical models. Blattberg and Hoch examined this possibility by having supermarket managers forecast demand for certain products and then creating a composite forecast by averaging these judgments with the forecasts of statistical models based on ② <u>past</u> data. The logic was that statistical models ③ <u>deny</u> stable conditions and therefore cannot account for the effects on demand of novel events such as actions taken by competitors or the introduction of new products. Humans, however, can ④ <u>incorporate</u> these novel factors in their judgments. The composite — or average of human judgments and statistical models — proved to be more ⑤ <u>accurate</u> than either the statistical models or the managers working alone.

* composite: 종합적인; 종합된 것

[31 ~ 34] 다음 빈칸에 들어갈 말로 가장 적절한 것을 고르시오.

31. Free play is nature's means of teaching children that they are not _____. In play, away from adults, children really do have control and can practice asserting it. In free play, children learn to make their own decisions, solve their own problems, create and follow rules, and get along with others as equals rather than as obedient or rebellious subordinates. In active outdoor play, children deliberately dose themselves with moderate amounts of fear and they thereby learn how to control not only their bodies, but also their fear. In social play children learn how to negotiate with others, how to please others, and how to manage and overcome the anger that can arise from conflicts. None of these lessons can be taught through verbal means; they can be learned only through experience, which free play provides.

* rebellious: 반항적인

① noisy　　　　② sociable　　　　③ complicated
④ helpless　　　⑤ selective

32. Many early dot-com investors focused almost entirely on revenue growth instead of net income. Many early dot-com companies earned most of their revenue from selling advertising space on their Web sites. To boost reported revenue, some sites began exchanging ad space. Company A would put an ad for its Web site on company B's Web site, and company B would put an ad for its Web site on company A's Web site. No money ever changed hands, but each company recorded revenue (for the value of the space that it gave up on its site) and expense (for the value of its ad that it placed on the other company's site). This practice did little to boost net income and _____ — but it did boost *reported* revenue. This practice was quickly put to an end because accountants felt that it did not meet the criteria of the revenue recognition principle.

* revenue: 수익　** net income: 순이익

① simplified the Web design process
② resulted in no additional cash inflow
③ decreased the salaries of the employees
④ intensified competition among companies
⑤ triggered conflicts on the content of Web ads

33. Scholars of myth have long argued that myth gives structure and meaning to human life; that meaning is amplified when a myth evolves into a world. A virtual world's ability to fulfill needs grows when lots and lots of people believe in the world. Conversely, a virtual world cannot be long sustained by a mere handful of adherents. Consider the difference between a global sport and a game I invent with my nine friends and play regularly. My game might be a great game, one that is completely immersive, one that consumes all of my group's time and attention. If its reach is limited to the ten of us, though, then it's ultimately just a weird hobby, and it has limited social function. For a virtual world to provide lasting, wide-ranging value, its participants must _____.
When that threshold is reached, psychological value can turn into wide-ranging social value. [3점]

* adherent: 추종자 ** threshold: 기준점

① be a large enough group to be considered a society
② have historical evidence to make it worth believing
③ apply their individual values to all of their affairs
④ follow a strict order to enhance their self-esteem
⑤ get approval in light of the religious value system

34. It seems natural to describe certain environmental conditions as 'extreme', 'harsh', 'benign' or 'stressful'. It may seem obvious when conditions are 'extreme': the midday heat of a desert, the cold of an Antarctic winter, the salinity of the Great Salt Lake. But this only means that these conditions are extreme *for us*, given our particular physiological characteristics and tolerances. To a cactus there is nothing extreme about the desert conditions in which cacti have evolved; nor are the icy lands of Antarctica an extreme environment for penguins. It is lazy and dangerous for the ecologist to assume that _____.
Rather, the ecologist should try to gain a worm's-eye or plant's-eye view of the environment: to see the world as others see it. Emotive words like harsh and benign, even relativities such as hot and cold, should be used by ecologists only with care. [3점]

* benign: 온화한 ** salinity: 염도

① complex organisms are superior to simple ones
② technologies help us survive extreme environments
③ ecological diversity is supported by extreme environments
④ all other organisms sense the environment in the way we do
⑤ species adapt to environmental changes in predictable ways

35. 다음 글에서 전체 흐름과 관계 없는 문장은?
Human processes differ from rational processes in their outcome. A process is *rational* if it always does the right thing based on the current information, given an ideal performance measure. In short, rational processes go by the book and assume that the book is actually correct. ① Human processes involve instinct, intuition, and other variables that don't necessarily reflect the book and may not even consider the existing data. ② As an example, the rational way to drive a car is to always follow the laws. ③ Likewise, pedestrian crossing signs vary depending on the country with differing appearances of a person crossing the street. ④ However, traffic isn't rational; if you follow the laws precisely, you end up stuck somewhere because other drivers aren't following the laws precisely. ⑤ To be successful, a self-driving car must therefore act humanly, rather than rationally.

[36~37] 주어진 글 다음에 이어질 글의 순서로 가장 적절한 것을 고르시오.
36.
Like positive habits, bad habits exist on a continuum of easy-to-change and hard-to-change.

(A) But this kind of language (and the approaches it spawns) frames these challenges in a way that isn't helpful or effective. I specifically hope we will stop using this phrase: "break a habit." This language misguides people. The word "break" sets the wrong expectation for how you get rid of a bad habit.

(B) This word implies that if you input a lot of force in one moment, the habit will be gone. However, that rarely works, because you usually cannot get rid of an unwanted habit by applying force one time.

(C) When you get toward the "hard" end of the spectrum, note the language you hear—*breaking* bad habits and *battling* addiction. It's as if an unwanted behavior is a nefarious villain to be aggressively defeated.

* spawn: 낳다 ** nefarious: 사악한

① (A) − (C) − (B)   ② (B) − (A) − (C)
③ (B) − (C) − (A)   ④ (C) − (A) − (B)
⑤ (C) − (B) − (A)

37.

A common but incorrect assumption is that we are creatures of reason when, in fact, we are creatures of both reason and emotion. We cannot get by on reason alone since any reason always eventually leads to a feeling. Should I get a wholegrain cereal or a chocolate cereal?

(A) These deep-seated values, feelings, and emotions we have are rarely a result of reasoning, but can certainly be influenced by reasoning. We have values, feelings, and emotions before we begin to reason and long before we begin to reason effectively.

(B) I can list all the reasons I want, but the reasons have to be based on something. For example, if my goal is to eat healthy, I can choose the wholegrain cereal, but what is my reason for wanting to be healthy?

(C) I can list more and more reasons such as wanting to live longer, spending more quality time with loved ones, etc., but what are the reasons for those reasons? You should be able to see by now that reasons are ultimately based on non-reason such as values, feelings, or emotions. [3점]

① (A) − (C) − (B) ② (B) − (A) − (C)
③ (B) − (C) − (A) ④ (C) − (A) − (B)
⑤ (C) − (B) − (A)

[38 ~ 39] 글의 흐름으로 보아, 주어진 문장이 들어가기에 가장 적절한 곳을 고르시오.

38.

In the electric organ the muscle cells are connected in larger chunks, which makes the total current intensity larger than in ordinary muscles.

Electric communication is mainly known in fish. The electric signals are produced in special electric organs. When the signal is discharged the electric organ will be negatively loaded compared to the head and an electric field is created around the fish. (①) A weak electric current is created also in ordinary muscle cells when they contract. (②) The fish varies the signals by changing the form of the electric field or the frequency of discharging. (③) The system is only working over small distances, about one to two meters. (④) This is an advantage since the species using the signal system often live in large groups with several other species. (⑤) If many fish send out signals at the same time, the short range decreases the risk of interference.

39.

For others, whose creativity is more focused on methods and technique, creativity may lead to solutions that drastically reduce the work necessary to solve a problem.

Creativity can have an effect on productivity. Creativity leads some individuals to recognize problems that others do not see, but which may be very difficult. (①) Charles Darwin's approach to the speciation problem is a good example of this; he chose a very difficult and tangled problem, speciation, which led him into a long period of data collection and deliberation. (②) This choice of problem did not allow for a quick attack or a simple experiment. (③) In such cases creativity may actually decrease productivity (as measured by publication counts) because effort is focused on difficult problems. (④) We can see an example in the development of the polymerase chain reaction (PCR) which enables us to amplify small pieces of DNA in a short time. (⑤) This type of creativity might reduce the number of steps or substitute steps that are less likely to fail, thus increasing productivity. [3점]

* speciation: 종(種) 분화 ** polymerase chain reaction: 중합 효소 연쇄 반응

40. 다음 글의 내용을 한 문장으로 요약하고자 한다. 빈칸 (A), (B)에 들어갈 말로 가장 적절한 것은?

A young child may be puzzled when asked to distinguish between the directions of right and left. But that same child may have no difficulty in determining the directions of up and down or back and front. Scientists propose that this occurs because, although we experience three dimensions, only two had a strong influence on our evolution: the vertical dimension as defined by gravity and, in mobile species, the front/back dimension as defined by the positioning of sensory and feeding mechanisms. These influence our perception of vertical versus horizontal, far versus close, and the search for dangers from above (such as an eagle) or below (such as a snake). However, the left-right axis is not as relevant in nature. A bear is equally dangerous from its left or the right side, but not if it is upside down. In fact, when observing a scene containing plants, animals, and man-made objects such as cars or street signs, we can only tell when left and right have been inverted if we observe those artificial items.

* axis: 축

⬇

Having affected the evolution of our __(A)__ perception, vertical and front/back dimensions are easily perceived, but the left-right axis, which is not __(B)__ in nature, doesn't come instantly to us.

    (A)   (B)   (A)   (B)
① spatial …… significant ② spatial …… scarce
③ auditory …… different ④ cultural …… accessible
⑤ cultural …… desirable

[41~42] 다음 글을 읽고, 물음에 답하시오.

Creative people aren't all cut from the same cloth. They have (a) varying levels of maturity and sensitivity. They have different approaches to work. And they're each motivated by different things. Managing people is about being aware of their unique personalities. It's also about empathy and adaptability, and knowing how the things you do and say will be interpreted and adapting accordingly. Who you are and what you say may not be the (b) same from one person to the next. For instance, if you're asking someone to work a second weekend in a row, or telling them they aren't getting that deserved promotion just yet, you need to bear in mind the (c) group. Vincent will have a very different reaction to the news than Emily, and they will each be more receptive to the news if it's bundled with different things. Perhaps that promotion news will land (d) easier if Vincent is given a few extra vacation days for the holidays, while you can promise Emily a bigger promotion a year from now. Consider each person's complex positive and negative personality traits, their life circumstances, and their mindset in the moment when deciding what to say and how to say it. Personal connection, compassion, and an individualized management style are (e) key to drawing consistent, rock star-level work out of everyone.

41. 윗글의 제목으로 가장 적절한 것은?

① Know Each Person to Guarantee Best Performance
② Flexible Hours: An Appealing Working Condition
③ Talk to Employees More Often in Hard Times
④ How Empathy and Recognition Are Different
⑤ Why Creativity Suffers in Competition

42. 밑줄 친 (a)~(e) 중에서 문맥상 낱말의 쓰임이 적절하지 않은 것은?

① (a)   ② (b)   ③ (c)   ④ (d)   ⑤ (e)

[43~45] 다음 글을 읽고, 물음에 답하시오.

(A)

It was a hot day in early fall. Wylder was heading to the school field for his first training. He had just joined the team with five other students after a successful tryout. Approaching the field, (a) he saw players getting ready, pulling up their socks and strapping on shin guards. But they weren't together. New players were sitting in the shade by the garage, while the others were standing in the sun by the right pole. Then Coach McGraw came and watched the players.

* shin: 정강이

(B)

'Wow,' thought Wylder. From his new location on the grass, he stretched out his legs. He liked what he was hearing. A new sense of team spirit came across (b) him, a deeper sense of connection. It was encouraging to hear Coach talk about this, to see him face the challenge head-on. Now his speech was over. The players got up and started walking on the field to warm up. "Good job, Coach. That was good," Wylder said to McGraw in a low voice as he walked past him, keeping (c) his eyes down out of respect.

(C)

McGraw continued to point, calling each player out, until he was satisfied with the rearrangement. "Okay, this is how it's going to be," he began. "We need to learn how to trust and work with each other. This is how a team plays. This is how I want you to be on and off the field: together." The players looked at each other. Almost immediately, McGraw noticed a change in their postures and faces. (d) He saw some of them starting to smile.

(D)

Coach McGraw, too, saw the pattern—new kids and others grouping separately. 'This has to change,' he thought. He wanted a winning team. To do that, he needed to build relationships. "I want you guys to come over here in the middle and sit," he called the players as he walked over. "You!" McGraw roared, pointing at Wylder. "Come here onto the field and sit. And Jonny! You sit over there!" He started pointing, making sure they mixed together. Wylder realized what Coach was trying to do, so (e) he hopped onto the field.

43. 주어진 글 (A)에 이어질 내용을 순서에 맞게 배열한 것으로 가장 적절한 것은?

① (B) - (D) - (C)   ② (C) - (B) - (D)
③ (C) - (D) - (B)   ④ (D) - (B) - (C)
⑤ (D) - (C) - (B)

44. 밑줄 친 (a)~(e) 중에서 가리키는 대상이 나머지 넷과 다른 것은?

① (a)   ② (b)   ③ (c)   ④ (d)   ⑤ (e)

45. 윗글에 관한 내용으로 적절하지 않은 것은?

① Wylder는 다섯 명의 다른 학생과 팀에 합류했다.
② Wylder는 잔디 위의 새로운 자리에서 다리를 쭉 폈다.
③ McGraw는 재배열이 마음에 들 때까지 선수들을 불러냈다.
④ McGraw는 선수들의 자세와 얼굴의 변화를 알아차렸다.
⑤ McGraw는 선수들에게 운동장 밖으로 나가라고 말했다.

* 확인 사항
○ 답안지의 해당란에 필요한 내용을 정확히 기입(표기) 했는지 확인하시오.

18

001 □ appreciate ⓥ 고마워하다
002 □ effort ⓝ 노력
003 □ select ⓥ 고르다
004 □ exhibit ⓥ 전시하다
005 □ artwork ⓝ 예술작품
006 □ mention ⓥ 언급하다
007 □ greatly [ad] 대단히
008 □ admire ⓥ 존경하다, 찬탄하다
009 □ emphasize ⓥ 강조하다
010 □ beauty ⓝ 아름다움
011 □ over the past few days 지난 며칠 동안
012 □ viewing ⓝ 전시, 조망, 감상
013 □ especially [ad] 특히
014 □ purchase ⓥ 구매하다 ⓝ 구매
015 □ depict ⓥ 그리다, 묘사하다
016 □ horizon ⓝ 수평선
017 □ sunrise ⓝ 일출, 해돋이
018 □ available ⓐ 이용 가능한
019 □ house ⓥ 소장하다, 보관하다
020 □ inquiry ⓝ 문의

19

021 □ opening day 개업일
022 □ anticipation ⓝ 기대
023 □ look around ～을 둘러보다
024 □ shake off 떨쳐내다
025 □ missing ⓐ 빠진, 실종된
026 □ set out 차려내다, 착수하다, 시작하다
027 □ plate ⓝ 접시
028 □ doubt ⓝ 의심
029 □ imagine ⓥ 상상하다
030 □ come to mind ～이 떠오르다
031 □ sudden ⓐ 갑작스러운
032 □ burst ⓝ 폭발
033 □ inspiration ⓝ 영감
034 □ grab ⓥ 집어들다
035 □ paintbrush ⓝ (그림) 붓
036 □ transform ⓥ 변모시키다
037 □ blank ⓐ 텅 빈
038 □ landscape ⓝ 풍경(화)
039 □ add ⓥ 더하다
040 □ fade ⓥ 옅어지다
041 □ handiwork ⓝ (솜씨를 발휘한) 작품, 피조물
042 □ certain ⓐ 확신하는
043 □ guarantee ⓥ 보장하다, 보증하다
044 □ envious ⓐ 부러워하는
045 □ grateful ⓐ 고마워하는
046 □ frightened ⓐ 겁에 질린
047 □ uneasy ⓐ 불안한

20

048 □ unwanted ⓐ 원치 않는
049 □ unpleasant ⓐ 불쾌한
050 □ environment ⓝ 환경
051 □ hate ⓥ 싫어하다
052 □ nonetheless [ad] 그럼에도 불구하고
053 □ have choice 선택권이 있다
054 □ accept ⓥ 수용하다, 받아들이다
055 □ either ⓐ 둘 중 하나의
056 □ hatred ⓝ 증오
057 □ develop ⓥ 키우다, 발전시키다

058 □ self ⓝ 자아
059 □ acceptance ⓝ 수용
060 □ compassion ⓝ 연민, 동정
061 □ allow for ～을 허용하다, 고려하다
062 □ accomplish ⓥ 달성하다, 이루다
063 □ task ⓝ 과제
064 □ situation ⓝ 상황
065 □ see A as B A를 B로 여기다
066 □ lesson ⓝ 교훈

21

067 □ get over ～을 극복하다
068 □ obstacle ⓝ 장애물
069 □ policy ⓝ 정책, 방책
070 □ all-or-nothing ⓐ 전부 아니면 전무의, 양자택일의
071 □ mentality ⓝ 사고방식
072 □ be willing to 기꺼이 ～하다
073 □ alter ⓥ 바꾸다, 수정하다
074 □ influence ⓥ 영향을 미치다 ⓝ 영향
075 □ outcome ⓝ 결과
076 □ push for ～을 추진하다
077 □ act ⓝ 법안
078 □ emerge ⓥ 나타나다, 출현하다
079 □ well-funded ⓐ 자금을 잘 지원받는
080 □ conceive ⓥ 고안하다, 떠올리다
081 □ succeed in ～하는 데 성공하다
082 □ ensure ⓥ 보장하다
083 □ troubled ⓐ 힘든, 곤란한
084 □ have access to ～을 이용하다
085 □ needle ⓝ 바늘
086 □ vastly [ad] 대단히, 엄청나게
087 □ celebrate ⓥ 칭송하다, 축하하다
088 □ perfection ⓝ 완벽함
089 □ cost-saving ⓐ 비용을 절감하는
090 □ make difference 변화를 일으키다, 달라지게 하다

22

091 □ fail to ～하지 못하다
092 □ relevance ⓝ 적합성, 적절성
093 □ on the fast track 성공 가도를 달리는
094 □ hit a plateau 정체기에 들다
095 □ assume ⓥ 가정하다
096 □ make a move 행동하다
097 □ ambitious ⓐ 야망 있는
098 □ more often than not 대개
099 □ victim ⓝ 희생자
100 □ embrace ⓥ 포용하다
101 □ advance ⓝ 발전, 진보
102 □ industry ⓝ 업계, 산업
103 □ executive ⓐ 경영의, 간부의
104 □ exposed to ～을 접한, ～에 노출된
105 □ integrate ⓥ 통합하다
106 □ excel ⓥ 탁월하다, 능가하다
107 □ resistant ⓐ 저항하는, 내성 있는
108 □ ultimately [ad] 궁극적으로
109 □ let go ～을 해고하다
110 □ retirement ⓝ 은퇴

23

111 □ consequence ⓝ 결과, 영향

112 □ shed light (on) (～을) 밝히다
113 □ intake ⓝ 섭취(량) ⓥ 섭취하다
114 □ cognitively [ad] 인지적으로
115 □ be linked with ～와 연관되다
116 □ volume ⓝ 부피
117 □ hippocampus ⓝ (대뇌 측두엽의) 해마
118 □ unusual ⓐ 특이한
119 □ isolate ⓥ 분리하다
120 □ component ⓝ 구성요소
121 □ subject ⓝ 실험 대상자
122 □ do A a favor A의 부탁을 들어주다, A를 이롭게 하다
123 □ inverse ⓐ 역의, 반대의
124 □ cortex ⓝ (대뇌) 피질
125 □ outer ⓐ 외부의
126 □ layer ⓝ 층
127 □ the latter 후자(의)
128 □ excessive ⓐ 과도한
129 □ consumption ⓝ 소비, 섭취
130 □ metabolic ⓐ 신진대사의
131 □ processed ⓐ 가공된
132 □ carb ⓝ 탄수화물 식품
133 □ universal ⓐ 보편적인
134 □ long-term ⓐ 장기의
135 □ nutritional ⓐ 영양의

24

136 □ turn on ～을 켜다, 작동시키다
137 □ self-conscious ⓐ 남을 의식하는
138 □ awareness ⓝ 의식, 인식
139 □ under the radar 눈에 띄지 않게, 몰래
140 □ mess up 엉망으로 하다, 망치다
141 □ rough ⓐ 거친
142 □ flaw ⓝ 결점
143 □ weakness ⓝ 약점
144 □ personality ⓝ 성격
145 □ role model 역할 모델
146 □ citizen ⓝ 시민
147 □ respect ⓥ 존경하다
148 □ at the expense of ～을 희생하며
149 □ please ⓥ 기쁘게 하다
150 □ apologize ⓥ 사과하다
151 □ permanently [ad] 영구적으로
152 □ disappointment ⓝ 실망
153 □ criticism ⓝ 비판
154 □ misleading ⓐ 오해의 소지가 있는, 오도하는

25

155 □ German ⓐ 독일의
156 □ according to ～에 따라
157 □ age group 연령 집단
158 □ account for ～을 차지하다
159 □ proportion ⓝ 비율
160 □ daily [ad] 매일
161 □ share ⓝ 몫, 점유율
162 □ one fifth 5분의 1
163 □ respond ⓥ 대답하다

26

164 □ portrait ⓝ 인물 사진, 초상화
165 □ energetically [ad] 활기차게

166 □ devote oneself to ～에 전념하다
167 □ clear out ～을 치우다
168 □ chicken coop 닭장
169 □ convert ⓥ 바꾸다, 전환하다
170 □ convince ⓥ 설득하다
171 □ pose for ～을 위해 포즈를 취하다
172 □ fit ⓥ (의복을) 입히다, ～에 꼭 맞추다
173 □ theatrical ⓐ 연극적인
174 □ costume ⓝ 의상
175 □ so-called ⓐ 소위 말하는
176 □ critic ⓝ 비평가
177 □ in one's own time 동시대의, 당대의
178 □ ignore ⓥ 무시하다
179 □ convention ⓝ 관습
180 □ composition ⓝ 구성
181 □ spiritual ⓐ 영적인
182 □ depth ⓝ 깊이
183 □ technical ⓐ 기술적인
184 □ artistic ⓐ 예술적인
185 □ medium ⓝ 매체, 수단

27

186 □ have a good night 숙면을 취하다
187 □ refreshing ⓐ 상쾌한
188 □ relaxing ⓐ 편안해지는, 여유로운
189 □ cough ⓥ 기침하다
190 □ snore ⓥ 코 골다
191 □ analyze ⓥ 분석하다
192 □ adjust ⓥ 조절하다

28

193 □ talent show 장기자랑
194 □ show off ～을 뽐내다
195 □ entry ⓝ 출품작
196 □ vote for ～에 투표하다

29

197 □ certainty ⓝ 확실성
198 □ liking ⓝ 선호
199 □ stem from ～에서 기원하다
200 □ saber-toothed tiger 검치호(검 모양의 송곳니를 가진 호랑이)
201 □ poisonous ⓐ 독이 든
202 □ attend to ～에 주의를 기울이다
203 □ threat ⓝ 위협
204 □ keep away from ～에서 벗어나다
205 □ have chance of ～할 가능성을 갖다
206 □ uncertain ⓐ 확신이 없는
207 □ send out 내보내다
208 □ alert ⓝ 경고, 경계 태세 ⓐ 경계하는, 기민한
209 □ dependence ⓝ 의존
210 □ millennium (pl. millennia) ⓝ 천년
211 □ to the present day 오늘날까지
212 □ vague ⓐ 희미한
213 □ unpredictable ⓐ 예측 불가한
214 □ generate ⓥ 만들어내다

30

215 □ consistency ⓝ 일관성
216 □ virtue ⓝ 미덕
217 □ judgment ⓝ 판단(력)
218 □ detect ⓥ 감지하다

219 □ advantageous ⓐ 유리한
220 □ statistical ⓐ 통계적인
221 □ forecast ⓥ 예측하다
222 □ composite ⓐ 종합적인 ⓝ 종합된 것
223 □ deny ⓥ 부인하다
224 □ stable ⓐ 안정된
225 □ novel ⓐ 새로운, 신기한
226 □ take action 행동을 취하다, 조치를 취하다
227 □ accurate ⓐ 정확한

31
228 □ free play 자유 놀이
229 □ means ⓝ 수단
230 □ assert ⓥ (권리 등을) 행사하다, 주장하다
231 □ follow a rule 규칙을 따르다
232 □ equal ⓝ 동등한 사람 ⓐ 동등한
233 □ obedient ⓐ 복종하는
234 □ rebellious ⓐ 반항적인
235 □ subordinate ⓝ 하급자, 부하
236 □ deliberately ⓐⓓ 의도적으로
237 □ dose ⓥ (약을) 투여하다, 먹이다
238 □ moderate ⓐ 적당한
239 □ thereby ⓐⓓ 그렇게 함으로써
240 □ negotiate ⓥ 협상하다
241 □ overcome ⓥ 극복하다
242 □ anger ⓝ 화, 분노
243 □ arise from ~에서 발생하다
244 □ conflict ⓝ 갈등
245 □ verbal ⓐ 언어적인
246 □ sociable ⓐ 사교적인
247 □ helpless ⓐ 무력한
248 □ selective ⓐ 선택적인

32
249 □ investor ⓝ 투자자
250 □ entirely ⓐⓓ 전적으로
251 □ revenue ⓝ 수익
252 □ net income 순이익
253 □ earn ⓥ 벌다
254 □ boost ⓥ 신장시키다, 높이다
255 □ put an ad for ~을 위한 광고를 싣다
256 □ give up on ~을 포기하다, 단념하다
257 □ do little to ~하는 데 거의 효과가 없다
258 □ put to an end ~을 끝내다
259 □ accountant ⓝ 회계사
260 □ criterion (pl. criteria) ⓝ 기준
261 □ principle ⓝ 원리
262 □ inflow ⓝ 유입
263 □ intensify ⓥ 강화하다
264 □ trigger ⓥ 촉발하다

33
265 □ scholar ⓝ 학자
266 □ myth ⓝ 신화
267 □ amplify ⓥ 증폭하다
268 □ fulfill ⓥ 충족하다, 이루다
269 □ conversely ⓐⓓ 반대로
270 □ sustain ⓥ 지탱하다
271 □ a handful of 소수의, 얼마 안 되는
272 □ mere ⓐ 단지 ~인
273 □ adherent ⓝ 추종자
274 □ immersive ⓐ 몰입시키는

275 □ attention ⓝ 주의, 관심
276 □ reach ⓝ 범위 ⓥ 도달하다
277 □ weird ⓐ 이상한
278 □ lasting ⓐ 지속적인, 오래 가는
279 □ wide-ranging ⓐ 광범위한
280 □ threshold ⓝ 기준점
281 □ turn into ~로 변하다
282 □ affair ⓝ 일, 사건
283 □ strict ⓐ 엄격한
284 □ enhance ⓥ 향상시키다
285 □ self-esteem ⓝ 자존감
286 □ in light of ~의 관점에서, ~을 고려하여

34
287 □ extreme ⓐ 극심한, 극도의
288 □ harsh ⓐ 혹독한
289 □ benign ⓐ 온화한
290 □ obvious ⓐ 명백한
291 □ midday ⓝ 한낮
292 □ desert ⓝ 사막
293 □ Antarctic ⓐ 남극의
294 □ salinity ⓝ 염도
295 □ given prep ~을 고려하면
296 □ physiological ⓐ 생리적인
297 □ characteristic ⓝ 특성
298 □ tolerance ⓝ 내성, 저항력, 인내
299 □ cactus (pl. cacti) ⓝ 선인장
300 □ lazy ⓐ 나태한, 게으른
301 □ ecologist ⓝ 생태학자
302 □ emotive ⓐ 감정적인, 감정을 나타내는
303 □ relativity ⓝ 상대성
304 □ with care 조심해서, 주의 깊게, 신중하게
305 □ complex organism 다세포 생물
306 □ superior to ~보다 우월한
307 □ sense ⓥ 감지하다

35
308 □ rational ⓐ 이성적인, 합리적인
309 □ ideal ⓐ 이상적인
310 □ go by ~에 따르다
311 □ instinct ⓝ 본능
312 □ intuition ⓝ 직관
313 □ variable ⓝ 변수
314 □ not necessarily 반드시 ~하지는 않은
315 □ existing ⓐ 기존의
316 □ likewise ⓐⓓ 마찬가지로
317 □ pedestrian ⓝ 보행자
318 □ vary ⓥ 다르다, 달리하다
319 □ differing ⓐ 다른
320 □ precisely ⓐⓓ 정확하게
321 □ end up 결국 ~하다
322 □ stuck ⓐ (어딘가에) 갇힌
323 □ self-driving car 자율 주행 자동차

36
324 □ positive ⓐ 긍정적인
325 □ continuum ⓝ 연속체
326 □ spawn ⓥ 낳다
327 □ frame ⓥ (특정한 방식으로) 표현하다
328 □ phrase ⓝ 어구
329 □ break a habit (흔히 나쁜) 습관을 고치다
330 □ expectation ⓝ 기대

331 □ get rid of ~을 제거하다
332 □ imply ⓥ 암시하다
333 □ input ⓥ 투입하다
334 □ addiction ⓝ 중독
335 □ nefarious ⓐ 사악한
336 □ villain ⓝ 악당
337 □ aggressively ⓐⓓ 맹렬하게, 격렬하게
338 □ defeat ⓥ 이기다, 패배시키다

37
339 □ incorrect ⓐ 부정확한
340 □ assumption ⓝ 가정
341 □ creature ⓝ 피조물, 창조물
342 □ reason ⓝ 이성, 근거 ⓥ 추론하다
343 □ emotion ⓝ 감정, 정서
344 □ get by on ~로 그럭저럭 살아가다
345 □ wholegrain ⓝ 통곡물
346 □ deep-seated ⓐ 뿌리 깊은
347 □ long before ~하기 훨씬 이전에
348 □ effectively ⓐⓓ 효과적으로
349 □ list ⓥ 열거하다
350 □ eat healthy 건강한 음식을 먹다
351 □ live long 장수하다
352 □ loved one 사랑하는 사람

38
353 □ electric ⓐ 전기의
354 □ organ ⓝ (신체) 기관
355 □ muscle ⓝ 근육
356 □ chunk ⓝ 덩어리
357 □ intensity ⓝ 강도
358 □ ordinary ⓐ 일반적인, 보통의
359 □ produce ⓥ 생산하다
360 □ discharge ⓥ 방출하다, 내보내다
361 □ negatively ⓐⓓ (전기) 음전하로, 부정적으로
362 □ load ⓥ (짐, 부담을) 실어주다
363 □ compared to ~에 비해
364 □ contract ⓥ 수축하다
365 □ frequency ⓝ 주파수
366 □ interference ⓝ 전파 방해, 간섭

39
367 □ technique ⓝ 기술
368 □ lead to ~로 이어지다
369 □ drastically ⓐⓓ 극적으로
370 □ have an effect on ~에 영향을 끼치다
371 □ productivity ⓝ 생산성
372 □ speciation ⓝ 종(種) 분화
373 □ tangled ⓐ 복잡한, 뒤엉킨
374 □ deliberation ⓝ 숙고
375 □ as measured 측정된 대로
376 □ publication ⓝ 출판(물)
377 □ development ⓝ 개발, 발전, 전개
378 □ polymerase chain reaction 중합 효소 연쇄 반응
379 □ amplify ⓥ 증폭하다
380 □ substitute ⓥ 대체하다

40
381 □ puzzled ⓐ 혼란스러워하는
382 □ distinguish ⓥ 구별하다
383 □ direction ⓝ 방향

384 □ have difficulty (in) ~ing ~하는 데 어려움이 있다
385 □ propose ⓥ 제시하다, 주장하다
386 □ dimension ⓝ 차원
387 □ have an influence on ~에 영향을 미치다
388 □ evolution ⓝ 진화
389 □ vertical ⓐ 수직인
390 □ gravity ⓝ 중력
391 □ mobile ⓐ 이동하는
392 □ positioning ⓝ 배치
393 □ perception ⓝ 지각, 인식
394 □ horizontal ⓐ 수평인
395 □ axis ⓝ 축
396 □ upside down 거꾸로
397 □ man-made ⓐ 인간이 만든, 인공의
398 □ invert ⓥ 뒤집다, 도치시키다
399 □ artificial ⓐ 인공적인
400 □ instantly ⓐⓓ 즉각
401 □ spatial ⓐ 공간적인
402 □ significant ⓐ 유의미한, 중요한
403 □ scarce ⓐ 드문
404 □ auditory ⓐ 청각적인
405 □ accessible ⓐ 이해하기 쉬운, 접근 가능한
406 □ desirable ⓐ 바람직한

41~42
407 □ cut from the same cloth 비슷한, 같은 부류인
408 □ maturity ⓝ 성숙
409 □ sensitivity ⓝ 민감성
410 □ personality ⓝ 개성, 성격
411 □ empathy ⓝ 공감, 감정 이입
412 □ adaptability ⓝ 적응력
413 □ accordingly ⓐⓓ 그에 따라
414 □ promotion ⓝ 승진
415 □ bear in mind ~을 유념하다
416 □ receptive to ~에 수용적인, ~을 잘 받아들이는
417 □ bundle ⓥ 다발로 하다, 묶다
418 □ trait ⓝ 특성
419 □ circumstance ⓝ 상황
420 □ individualize ⓥ 개인의 요구에 맞추다, 개별화하다
421 □ flexible hours 탄력 근로제, 유연 근무제 (근무시간을 자유롭게 조정하여 일하는 것)
422 □ appealing ⓐ 매력적인

43~45
423 □ tryout ⓝ 실력 테스트, 적격 시험
424 □ pull up 끌어올리다
425 □ strap on (시계, 배낭 등을) 차다
426 □ shin ⓝ 정강이
427 □ pole ⓝ 기둥
428 □ location ⓝ 위치, 장소
429 □ stretch out ~을 펴다
430 □ encouraging ⓐ 고무적인
431 □ head-on ⓐⓓ 정면으로 ⓐ 정면으로 맞서는
432 □ warm up 몸을 풀다
433 □ rearrangement ⓝ 재배치
434 □ separately ⓐⓓ 따로
435 □ hop ⓥ (깡충깡충) 뛰다

TEST A-B 각 단어의 뜻을 [A] 영어는 우리말로, [B] 우리말은 영어로 쓰시오.

A	English	Korean	B	Korean	English
01	appreciate		01	강조하다	
02	nonetheless		02	달성하다, 이루다	
03	be willing to		03	정책, 방책	
04	assume		04	칭송하다, 축하하다	
05	embrace		05	희생자	
06	processed		06	과도한	
07	subject		07	5분의 1	
08	flaw		08	위협	
09	convert		09	의존	
10	stem from		10	행동을 취하다, 조치를 취하다	
11	verbal		11	갈등	
12	variable		12	(약을) 투여하다, 먹이다	
13	get by on		13	신화	
14	distinguish		14	이상적인	
15	head-on		15	생산성	
16	complex organism		16	중력	
17	virtue		17	받을 자격이 있다	
18	consistency		18	고무적인	
19	conceive		19	특성	
20	grateful		20	수축하다	

▶ A-D 정답 : 해설편 022쪽

TEST C-D 각 단어의 뜻을 골라 기호를 쓰시오.

C	English			Korean	D	Korean			English
01	anticipation	(	)	ⓐ 신진대사의	01	연민, 동정	(	)	ⓐ retirement
02	resistant	(	)	ⓑ ~을 뽐내다	02	풍경(화)	(	)	ⓑ account for
03	alert	(	)	ⓒ 기대	03	은퇴	(	)	ⓒ unpredictable
04	metabolic	(	)	ⓓ 기준	04	분리하다	(	)	ⓓ accountant
05	self-conscious	(	)	ⓔ 기존의	05	오해의 소지가 있는, 오도하는	(	)	ⓔ subordinate
06	snore	(	)	ⓕ 온화한	06	~을 차지하다	(	)	ⓕ statistical
07	show off	(	)	ⓖ 몰입시키는	07	~에 전념하다	(	)	ⓖ proportion
08	attend to	(	)	ⓗ ~을 제거하다	08	예측 불가한	(	)	ⓗ substitute
09	obedient	(	)	ⓘ 증폭하다	09	통계적인	(	)	ⓘ composite
10	criterion	(	)	ⓙ ~을 희생하며	10	하급자, 부하	(	)	ⓙ isolate
11	immersive	(	)	ⓚ 저항하는, 내성 있는	11	회계사	(	)	ⓚ consequence
12	benign	(	)	ⓛ 경고, 경계하는	12	남극의	(	)	ⓛ compassion
13	existing	(	)	ⓜ 복종하는	13	본능	(	)	ⓜ devote oneself to
14	get rid of	(	)	ⓝ (짐, 부담을) 실어주다	14	비율	(	)	ⓝ significant
15	amplify	(	)	ⓞ 악당	15	대체하다	(	)	ⓞ accordingly
16	frequency	(	)	ⓟ 의도적으로	16	유의미한, 중요한	(	)	ⓟ pedestrian
17	villain	(	)	ⓠ ~에 주의를 기울이다	17	보행자	(	)	ⓠ Antarctic
18	load	(	)	ⓡ 코골다	18	그에 따라	(	)	ⓡ instinct
19	deliberately	(	)	ⓢ 남을 의식하는	19	종합적인, 종합된 것	(	)	ⓢ misleading
20	at the expense of	(	)	ⓣ 주파수	20	결과, 영향	(	)	ⓣ landscape

03회 ● 2022학년도 3월 학력평가 고2 영어 독해

※ 영어 [독해] 파트만 수록한 문제지이므로 18번부터 시작합니다.　　● 점수 표시가 없는 문항은 모두 2점　● 문항수 28개 | 배점 63점 | 제한 시간 45분

18. 다음 글의 목적으로 가장 적절한 것은?

As I explained on the telephone, I don't want to take my two children by myself on a train trip to visit my parents in Springfield this Saturday since it is the same day the Riverside Warriors will play the Greenville Trojans in the National Soccer Championship. I would really appreciate it, therefore, if you could change my tickets to the following weekend (April 23). I fully appreciate that the original, special-offer ticket was non-exchangeable, but I did not know about the soccer match when I booked the tickets and I would be really grateful if you could do this for me. Thank you in advance.

① 특가로 제공되는 기차표를 구매하려고
② 축구 경기 입장권의 환불을 요구하려고
③ 다른 날짜로 기차표 변경을 요청하려고
④ 기차표 예약이 가능한 날짜를 알아보려고
⑤ 축구 경기 날짜가 연기되었는지를 확인하려고

19. 다음 글에 드러난 'I'의 심경으로 가장 적절한 것은?

Hours later — when my back aches from sitting, my hair is styled and dry, and my almost invisible makeup has been applied — Ash tells me it's time to change into my dress. We've been waiting until the last minute, afraid any refreshments I eat might accidentally fall onto it and stain it. There's only thirty minutes left until the show starts, and the nerves that have been torturing Ash seem to have escaped her, choosing a new victim in me. My palms are sweating, and I have butterflies in my stomach. Nearly all the models are ready, some of them already dressed in their nineteenth-century costumes. Ash tightens my corset.

① tense and nervous
② proud and confident
③ relieved and pleased
④ indifferent and bored
⑤ irritated and disappointed

20. 다음 글에서 필자가 주장하는 바로 가장 적절한 것은?

Though we are marching toward a more global society, various ethnic groups traditionally do things quite differently, and a fresh perspective is valuable in creating an open-minded child. Extensive multicultural experience makes kids more creative (measured by how many ideas they can come up with and by association skills) and allows them to capture unconventional ideas from other cultures to expand on their own ideas. As a parent, you should expose your children to other cultures as often as possible. If you can, travel with your child to other countries; live there if possible. If neither is possible, there are lots of things you can do at home, such as exploring local festivals, borrowing library books about other cultures, and cooking foods from different cultures at your house.

① 자녀가 전통문화를 자랑스럽게 여기게 해야 한다.
② 자녀가 주어진 문제를 깊이 있게 탐구하도록 이끌어야 한다.
③ 자녀가 다른 문화를 가능한 한 자주 접할 수 있게 해야 한다.
④ 창의성 발달을 위해 자녀의 실수에 대해 너그러워야 한다.
⑤ 경험한 것을 돌이켜 볼 시간을 자녀에게 주어야 한다.

21. 밑줄 친 _Fish is Fish-style assimilation_이 다음 글에서 의미하는 바로 가장 적절한 것은? [3점]

Studies by Vosniado and Brewer illustrate _Fish is Fish-style assimilation_ in the context of young children's thinking about the earth. They worked with children who believed that the earth is flat (because this fit their experiences) and attempted to help them understand that, in fact, it is spherical. When told it is round, children often pictured the earth as a pancake rather than as a sphere. If they were then told that it is round like a sphere, they interpreted the new information about a spherical earth within their flat-earth view by picturing a pancake-like flat surface inside or on top of a sphere, with humans standing on top of the pancake. The model of the earth that they had developed — and that helped them explain how they could stand or walk upon its surface — did not fit the model of a spherical earth. Like the story _Fish is Fish_, where a fish imagines everything on land to be fish-like, everything the children heard was incorporated into their preexisting views.

① established knowledge is questioned and criticized
② novel views are always favored over existing ones
③ all one's claims are evaluated based on others' opinions
④ new information is interpreted within one's own views
⑤ new theories are established through experiments

22. 다음 글의 요지로 가장 적절한 것은?

Advice from a friend or family member is the most well-meaning of all, but it's not the best way to match yourself with a new habit. While hot yoga may have changed your friend's life, does that mean it's the right practice for you? We all have friends who _swear_ their new habit of getting up at 4:30 a.m. changed their lives and that we have to do it. I don't doubt that getting up super early changes people's lives, sometimes in good ways and sometimes not. But be cautious: You don't know if this habit will actually make your life better, especially if it means you get less sleep. So yes, you can try what worked for your friend, but don't beat yourself up if your friend's answer doesn't change you in the same way. All of these approaches involve guessing and chance. And that's not a good way to strive for change in your life.

① 한번 잘못 들인 습관은 바로잡기가 어렵다.
② 꾸준한 반복을 통해 올바른 습관을 들일 수 있다.
③ 친구나 가족의 조언은 항상 귀담아들을 필요가 있다.
④ 사소하더라도 좋은 습관을 들이면 인생이 바뀔 수 있다.
⑤ 타인에게 유익했던 습관이 자신에게는 효과가 없을 수 있다.

23. 다음 글의 주제로 가장 적절한 것은?

Individual human beings differ from one another physically in a multitude of visible and invisible ways. If races — as most people define them — are real biological entities, then people of African ancestry would share a wide variety of traits while people of European ancestry would share a wide variety of _different_ traits. But once we add traits that are less visible than skin coloration, hair texture, and the like, we find that the people we identify as "the same race" are less and less like one another and more and more like people we identify as "different races." Add to this point that the physical features used to identify a person as a representative of some race (e.g. skin coloration) are continuously variable, so that one cannot say where "brown skin" becomes "white skin." Although the physical differences themselves are real, the way we use physical differences to classify people into discrete races is a cultural construction.

* entity: 실체 ** discrete: 별개의

① causes of physical variations among different races
② cultural differences between various races
③ social policies to overcome racism
④ importance of environmental factors in evolution
⑤ misconception about race as a biological construct

24. 다음 글의 제목으로 가장 적절한 것은?

The realization of human domination over the environment began in the late 1700s with the industrial revolution. Advances in manufacturing transformed societies and economies while producing significant impacts on the environment. American society became structured on multiple industries' capitalistic goals as the development of the steam engine led to the mechanized production of goods in mass quantities. Rural agricultural communities with economies based on handmade goods and agriculture were abandoned for life in urban cities with large factories based on an economy of industrialized manufacturing. Innovations in the production of textiles, iron, and steel provided increased profits to private companies. Simultaneously, those industries exerted authority over the environment and began dumping hazardous by-products in public lands and waterways.

① Strategies for Industrial Innovations
② Urbanization: A Road to a Better Life
③ Industrial Development Hurt the Environment
④ Technology: A Key to Sustainable Development
⑤ The Driving Force of Capitalism Was Not Greed

25. 다음 도표의 내용과 일치하지 <u>않는</u> 것은?

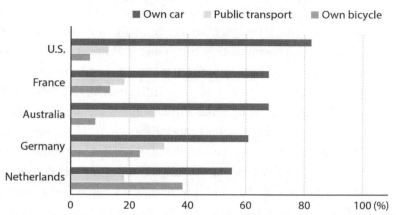

How People Commute in Five Countries

The above graph shows which modes of transportation people use for their daily commute to work, school, or university in five selected countries. ① In each of the five countries, the percentage of commuters using their own car is the highest among all three modes of transportation. ② The U.S. has the highest percentage of commuters using their own car among the five countries, but it has the lowest percentages for the other two modes of transportation. ③ Public transport is the second most popular mode of transportation in all the countries except for the Netherlands. ④ Among the five countries, France has the biggest gap between the percentage of commuters using their own car and that of commuters using public transport. ⑤ In terms of commuters using public transport, Germany leads all of the countries, immediately followed by Australia.

26. 2022 Bluehill Virtual Gala에 관한 다음 안내문의 내용과 일치하지 <u>않는</u> 것은?

2022 Bluehill Virtual Gala

You're invited to the 2022 Bluehill Virtual Gala hosted by the Bluehill Community Center. We'll have an online party to raise funds for our charity programs! Because we can't gather together in person this year, we are joining together virtually.

- Our Virtual Gala is on April 2 from 6 p.m. to 8 p.m.
- It will include musical performances, special lectures, and live auctions!
- Our MC will be Edward Jones, the famous actor from *A Good Neighbor*.

Everyone is welcome. This event will stream for free!
To join the party, simply visit www.bluehillgala.org.
---

① 자선 프로그램 기금 마련을 위한 온라인 파티이다.
② 4월 2일 오후 6시부터 8시까지 진행된다.
③ 음악 공연과 특별 강연, 라이브 경매가 있을 것이다.
④ 배우 Edward Jones가 사회를 볼 것이다.
⑤ 유료로 스트리밍될 것이다.

27. Woodside Clay Workshop에 관한 다음 안내문의 내용과 일치하는 것은?

Woodside Clay Workshop

7 p.m. Thursday March 31, 2022
7 p.m. Thursday April 7, 2022

This is a two-session workshop for adults. In the first session, you will learn the basics of clay and create unique ceramic pendants. In the second session, you will decorate the pieces before we glaze and fire them. Your pendants will be ready to be picked up from April 14.

- This workshop is suitable for beginners, so no experience is necessary.
- Fee: £25 (including all materials, instruction and a glass of wine)
- There are limited spaces, so book early. Advance bookings only.

For more information, visit our website at www.woodsideclay.co.uk.
---

* glaze: 유약을 바르다

① 목요일 오전에 진행된다.
② 어린이를 대상으로 한다.
③ 두 번째 시간에 펜던트를 찾아갈 수 있다.
④ 모든 재료가 참가비에 포함된다.
⑤ 사전 예약을 받지 않는다.

28. Gordon Parks에 관한 다음 글의 내용과 일치하지 <u>않는</u> 것은?

Gordon Parks was a photographer, author, film director, and musician. He documented the everyday lives of African Americans at a time when few people outside the black community were familiar with their lives. Parks was born the youngest of 15 children and grew up on his family's farm. After the death of his mother, he went to live with a sister in Minnesota. Parks eventually dropped out of school and worked at various jobs. His interest in photography was inspired by a photo-essay he read about migrant farm workers. After he moved to Chicago, Parks began taking photos of poor African Americans. In 1949, he became the first African American to be a staff photographer for *Life* magazine. He also wrote music pieces in his life and in 1956 the Vienna Orchestra performed a piano concerto he wrote. Parks was an inspiring artist until he died in 2006.

① 15명의 자녀 중 막내로 태어났다.
② 어머니가 돌아가신 후 Minnesota에 있는 누나와 살러 갔다.
③ 학교를 중퇴하지 않고 다양한 일자리에서 일했다.
④ *Life* 지의 사진 기자가 된 최초의 아프리카계 미국인이었다.
⑤ 그가 작곡한 피아노 협주곡을 1956년에 Vienna Orchestra가 연주했다.

29. 다음 글의 밑줄 친 부분 중, 어법상 틀린 것은? [3점]

Despite abundant warnings that we shouldn't measure ourselves against others, most of us still do. We're not only meaning-seeking creatures but social ① ones as well, constantly making interpersonal comparisons to evaluate ourselves, improve our standing, and enhance our self-esteem. But the problem with social comparison is that it often backfires. When comparing ourselves to someone who's doing better than we are, we often feel ② inadequate for not doing as well. This sometimes leads to what psychologists call *malignant envy*, the desire for someone ③ to meet with misfortune ("I wish she didn't have what she has"). Also, comparing ourselves with someone who's doing worse than we are ④ risk scorn, the feeling that others are something undeserving of our beneficence ("She's beneath my notice"). Then again, comparing ourselves to others can also lead to *benign envy*, the longing to reproduce someone else's accomplishments without wishing them ill ("I wish I had what she has"), ⑤ which has been shown in some circumstances to inspire and motivate us to increase our efforts in spite of a recent failure.

* backfire: 역효과를 내다 ** scorn: 경멸

30. 다음 글의 밑줄 친 부분 중, 문맥상 낱말의 쓰임이 적절하지 않은 것은? [3점]

What exactly does normal science involve? According to Thomas Kuhn it is primarily a matter of *puzzle-solving*. However successful a paradigm is, it will always ① encounter certain problems — phenomena which it cannot easily accommodate, or mismatches between the theory's predictions and the experimental facts. The job of the normal scientist is to try to ② eliminate these minor puzzles while making as few changes as possible to the paradigm. So normal science is a ③ conservative activity — its practitioners are not trying to make any earth-shattering discoveries, but rather just to develop and extend the existing paradigm. In Kuhn's words, 'normal science does not aim at novelties of fact or theory, and when successful finds none'. Above all, Kuhn stressed that normal scientists are not trying to *test* the paradigm. On the contrary, they accept the paradigm ④ unquestioningly, and conduct their research within the limits it sets. If a normal scientist gets an experimental result which ⑤ corresponds with the paradigm, they will usually assume that their experimental technique is faulty, not that the paradigm is wrong.

* practitioner: (어떤 일을) 실행하는 사람

[31 ~ 34] 다음 빈칸에 들어갈 말로 가장 적절한 것을 고르시오.

31. Around the boss, you will always find people coming across as friends, good subordinates, or even great sympathizers. But some do not truly belong. One day, an incident will blow their cover, and then you will know where they truly belong. When it is all cosy and safe, they will be there, loitering the corridors and fawning at the slightest opportunity. But as soon as difficulties arrive, they are the first to be found missing. And difficult times are the true test of _____. Dr. Martin Luther King said, "The ultimate test of a man is not where he stands in moments of comfort and convenience, but where he stands at times of challenge and controversy." And so be careful of friends who are always eager to take from you but reluctant to give back even in their little ways. If they lack the commitment to sail with you through difficult weather, then they are more likely to abandon your ship when it stops.

* loiter: 서성거리다 ** fawn: 알랑거리다

① leadership   ② loyalty   ③ creativity
④ intelligence   ⑤ independence

32. When you're driving a car, your memory of how to operate the vehicle comes from one set of brain cells; the memory of how to navigate the streets to get to your destination springs from another set of neurons; the memory of driving rules and following street signs originates from another family of brain cells; and the thoughts and feelings you have about the driving experience itself, including any close calls with other cars, come from yet another group of cells. You do not have conscious awareness of all these separate mental plays and cognitive neural firings, yet they somehow work together in beautiful harmony to synthesize your overall experience. In fact, we don't even know the real difference between how we remember and how we think. But, we do know they are strongly intertwined. That is why truly improving memory can never simply be about using memory tricks, although they can be helpful in strengthening certain components of memory. Here's the bottom line: To improve and preserve memory at the cognitive level, you have to _____.

* close call: 위기일발 ** intertwine: 뒤얽히게 하다

① keep your body and mind healthy
② calm your mind in stressful times
③ concentrate on one thing at a time
④ work on all functions of your brain
⑤ share what you learn with other people

33. According to many philosophers, there is a purely logical reason why science will never be able to explain everything. For in order to explain something, whatever it is, we need to invoke something else. But what explains the second thing? To illustrate, recall that Newton explained a diverse range of phenomena using his law of gravity. But what explains the law of gravity itself? If someone asks *why* all bodies exert a gravitational attraction on each other, what should we tell them? Newton had no answer to this question. In Newtonian science the law of gravity was a fundamental principle: it explained other things, but could not itself be explained. The moral generalizes. However much the science of the future can explain, the explanations it gives will have to make use of certain fundamental laws and principles. Since nothing can explain itself, it follows that at least some of these laws and principles _____. [3점]

* invoke: 언급하다

① govern human's relationship with nature
② are based on objective observations
③ will themselves remain unexplained
④ will be compared with other theories
⑤ are difficult to use to explain phenomena

34. In one example of the important role of laughter in social contexts, Devereux and Ginsburg examined frequency of laughter in matched pairs of strangers or friends who watched a humorous video together compared to those who watched it alone. The time individuals spent laughing was nearly twice as frequent in pairs as when alone. Frequency of laughing was only slightly shorter for friends than strangers. According to Devereux and Ginsburg, laughing with strangers served to create a social bond that made each person in the pair feel comfortable. This explanation is supported by the fact that in their stranger condition, when one person laughed, the other was likely to laugh as well. Interestingly, the three social conditions (alone, paired with a stranger, or paired with a friend) did not differ in their ratings of funniness of the video or of feelings of happiness or anxiousness. This finding implies that their frequency of laughter was not because we find things funnier when we are with others but instead we _____. [3점]

① have similar tastes in comedy and humor
② are using laughter to connect with others
③ are reluctant to reveal our innermost feelings
④ focus on the content rather than the situation
⑤ feel more comfortable around others than alone

35. 다음 글에서 전체 흐름과 관계 <u>없는</u> 문장은?

Today's "digital natives" have grown up immersed in digital technologies and possess the technical aptitude to utilize the powers of their devices fully. ① But although they know which apps to use or which websites to visit, they do not necessarily understand the workings behind the touch screen. ② People need technological literacy if they are to understand machines' mechanics and uses. ③ In much the same way as factory workers a hundred years ago needed to understand the basic structures of engines, we need to understand the elemental principles behind our devices. ④ The lifespan of devices depends on the quality of software operating them as well as the structure of hardware. ⑤ This empowers us to deploy software and hardware to their fullest utility, maximizing our powers to achieve and create.

* deploy: 사용하다

[36 ~ 37] 주어진 글 다음에 이어질 글의 순서로 가장 적절한 것을 고르시오.

36.

> The ancient Greeks used to describe two very different ways of thinking—*logos* and *mythos*. *Logos* roughly referred to the world of the logical, the empirical, the scientific.

(A) But lots of scholars then and now—including many anthropologists, sociologists and philosophers today—see a more complicated picture, where *mythos* and *logos* are intertwined and interdependent. Science itself, according to this view, relies on stories.

(B) *Mythos* referred to the world of dreams, storytelling and symbols. Like many rationalists today, some philosophers of Greece prized *logos* and looked down at *mythos*. Logic and reason, they concluded, make us modern; storytelling and mythmaking are primitive.

(C) The frames and metaphors we use to understand the world shape the scientific discoveries we make; they even shape what we see. When our frames and metaphors change, the world itself is transformed. The Copernican Revolution involved more than just scientific calculation; it involved a new story about the place of Earth in the universe.

* empirical: 경험적인

① (A) − (C) − (B) ② (B) − (A) − (C)
③ (B) − (C) − (A) ④ (C) − (A) − (B)
⑤ (C) − (B) − (A)

37.

> There is no doubt that the length of some literary works is overwhelming. Reading or translating a work in class, hour after hour, week after week, can be such a boring experience that many students never want to open a foreign language book again.

(A) Moreover, there are some literary features that cannot be adequately illustrated by a short excerpt: the development of plot or character, for instance, with the gradual involvement of the reader that this implies; or the unfolding of a complex theme through the juxtaposition of contrasting views.

(B) Extracts provide one type of solution. The advantages are obvious: reading a series of passages from different works produces more variety in the classroom, so that the teacher has a greater chance of avoiding monotony, while still giving learners a taste at least of an author's special flavour.

(C) On the other hand, a student who is only exposed to 'bite-sized chunks' will never have the satisfaction of knowing the overall pattern of a book, which is after all the satisfaction most of us seek when we read something in our own language.

* excerpt: 발췌 ** juxtaposition: 병치

① (A) − (C) − (B)
② (B) − (A) − (C)
③ (B) − (C) − (A)
④ (C) − (A) − (B)
⑤ (C) − (B) − (A)

[38 ~ 39] 글의 흐름으로 보아, 주어진 문장이 들어가기에 가장 적절한 곳을 고르시오.

38.

> For instance, the revolutionary ideas that earned Einstein his Nobel Prize — concerning the special theory of relativity and the photoelectric effect — appeared as papers in the *Annalen der Physik.*

In the early stages of modern science, scientists communicated their creative ideas largely by publishing books. (①) This modus operandi is illustrated not only by Newton's *Principia*, but also by Copernicus' *On the Revolutions of the Heavenly Spheres,* Kepler's *The Harmonies of the World*, and Galileo's *Dialogues Concerning the Two New Sciences.* (②) With the advent of scientific periodicals, such as the *Transactions of the Royal Society of London*, books gradually yielded ground to the technical journal article as the chief form of scientific communication. (③) Of course, books were not abandoned altogether, as Darwin's *Origin of Species* shows. (④) Even so, it eventually became possible for scientists to establish a reputation for their creative contributions without publishing a single book-length treatment of their ideas. (⑤) His status as one of the greatest scientists of all time does not depend on the publication of a single book.

* photoelectric effect: 광전 효과 ** modus operandi: 작업 방식[절차]

39.

> Although sport clubs and leagues may have a fixed supply schedule, it is possible to increase the number of consumers who watch.

A supply schedule refers to the ability of a business to change their production rates to meet the demand of consumers. Some businesses are able to increase their production level quickly in order to meet increased demand. However, sporting clubs have a fixed, or inflexible(inelastic) production capacity. (①) They have what is known as a fixed supply schedule. (②) It is worth noting that this is not the case for sales of clothing, equipment, memberships and memorabilia. (③) But clubs and teams can only play a certain number of times during their season. (④) If fans and members are unable to get into a venue, that revenue is lost forever. (⑤) For example, the supply of a sport product can be increased by providing more seats, changing the venue, extending the playing season or even through new television, radio or Internet distribution. [3점]

* memorabilia: 기념품 ** venue: 경기장

40. 다음 글의 내용을 한 문장으로 요약하고자 한다. 빈칸 (A), (B)에 들어갈 말로 가장 적절한 것은?

> Distance is a reliable indicator of the relationship between two people. Strangers stand further apart than do acquaintances, acquaintances stand further apart than friends, and friends stand further apart than romantic partners. Sometimes, of course, these rules are violated. Recall the last time you rode 20 stories in an elevator packed with total strangers. The sardine-like experience no doubt made the situation a bit uncomfortable. With your physical space violated, you may have tried to create "psychological" space by avoiding eye contact, focusing instead on the elevator buttons. By reducing closeness in one nonverbal channel (eye contact), one can compensate for unwanted closeness in another channel (proximity). Similarly, if you are talking with someone who is seated several feet away at a large table, you are likely to maintain constant eye contact — something you might feel uncomfortable doing if you were standing next to each other.

* sardine-like: 승객이 빽빽이 들어찬 ** proximity: 근접성

↓

> Physical distance between people is __(A)__ by relationship status, but when the distance is not appropriate, people __(B)__ their nonverbal communication to establish a comfortable psychological distance.

	(A)	(B)		(A)	(B)
①	determined	adjust	②	concealed	interpret
③	influenced	ignore	④	predicted	stop
⑤	measured	decrease			

[41 ~ 42] 다음 글을 읽고, 물음에 답하시오.

Being able to have a good fight doesn't just make us more civil; it also develops our creative muscles. In a classic study, highly creative architects were more likely than their technically competent but less original peers to come from homes with (a) plenty of friction. They often grew up in households that were "tense but secure," as psychologist Robert Albert notes: "The creative person-to-be comes from a family that is anything but (b) harmonious." The parents weren't physically or verbally abusive, but they didn't shy away from conflict, either. Instead of telling their children to be seen but not heard, they (c) encouraged them to stand up for themselves. The kids learned to dish it out—and take it. That's exactly what happened to Wilbur and Orville Wright, who invented the airplane.

When the Wright brothers said they thought together, what they really meant is that they fought together. When they were solving problems, they had arguments that lasted not just for hours but for weeks and months at a time. They didn't have such (d) ceaseless fights because they were angry. They kept quarreling because they enjoyed it and learned from the experience. "I like scrapping with Orv," Wilbur reflected. As you'll see, it was one of their most passionate and prolonged arguments that led them to (e) support a critical assumption that had prevented humans from soaring through the skies.

*dish it out: 남을 비판하다 **scrap with: ~과 다투다

41. 윗글의 제목으로 가장 적절한 것은?

① The Power of Constructive Conflict
② Lighten Tense Moments with Humor
③ Strategies to Cope with Family Stress
④ Compromise: A Key to Resolving Conflict
⑤ Rivalry Between Brothers: A Serious Crisis

42. 밑줄 친 (a)~(e) 중에서 문맥상 낱말의 쓰임이 적절하지 <u>않은</u> 것은? [3점]

① (a) ② (b) ③ (c) ④ (d) ⑤ (e)

[43 ~ 45] 다음 글을 읽고, 물음에 답하시오.

(A)

John was a sensitive boy. Even his hair was ticklish. When breeze touched his hair he would burst out laughing. And when this ticklish laughter started, no one could make him stop. John's laughter was so contagious that when John started feeling ticklish, everyone ended up in endless laughter. He tried everything to control his ticklishness: wearing a thousand different hats, using ultra strong hairsprays, and shaving his head. But nothing worked. One day he met a clown in the street. The clown was very old and could hardly walk, but when he saw John in tears, he went to cheer (a) him up.

*ticklish: 간지럼을 타는

(B)

All were full of children who were sick, or orphaned, children with very serious problems. But as soon as they saw the clown, their faces changed completely and lit up with a smile. That day was even more special, because in every show John's contagious laughter would end up making the kids laugh a lot. The old clown winked at (b) him and said "Now do you see what a serious job it is? That's why I can't retire, even at my age."

(C)

It didn't take long to make John laugh, and they started to talk. John told (c) him about his ticklish problem. Then he asked the clown how such an old man could carry on being a clown. "I have no one to replace me," said the clown, "and I have a very serious job to do." And then he took John to many hospitals, shelters, and schools.

(D)

And he added, "Not everyone could do it. He or she has to have a special gift for laughter." This said, the wind again set off John's ticklishness and (d) his laughter. After a while, John decided to replace the old clown. From that day onward, the fact that John was different actually made (e) him happy, thanks to his special gift.

43. 주어진 글 (A)에 이어질 내용을 순서에 맞게 배열한 것으로 가장 적절한 것은?

① (B) − (D) − (C)   ② (C) − (B) − (D)
③ (C) − (D) − (B)   ④ (D) − (B) − (C)
⑤ (D) − (C) − (B)

44. 밑줄 친 (a)~(e) 중에서 가리키는 대상이 나머지 넷과 <u>다른</u> 것은?

① (a) ② (b) ③ (c) ④ (d) ⑤ (e)

45. 윗글의 John에 관한 내용으로 적절하지 <u>않은</u> 것은?

① 간지럼을 타지 않으려고 온갖 시도를 했다.
② 전염성 있는 웃음으로 아이들을 많이 웃게 했다.
③ 광대에게 그렇게 늙어서도 어떻게 계속 일할 수 있는지 물었다.
④ 광대와 함께 여러 병원과 보호 시설, 학교에 갔다.
⑤ 광대의 뒤를 잇지 않기로 했다.

★ 확인 사항
○ 답안지의 해당란에 필요한 내용을 정확히 기입(표기)했는지 확인하시오.

회차별 영단어 **QR 코드** ※ QR 코드를 스캔 후 모바일로 단어장처럼 학습할 수 있습니다.

● 고2 2022학년도 3월

18
001 ☐ by oneself 혼자
002 ☐ appreciate ⓥ 감사하다, (제대로) 이해하다
003 ☐ fully ᵃᵈ 충분히
004 ☐ special-offer 특가로 제공되는
005 ☐ non-exchangeable ⓐ 교환 불가한
006 ☐ match ⓝ 경기
007 ☐ book ⓥ 예약하다
008 ☐ grateful ⓐ 고마워하는

19
009 ☐ ache ⓥ 아프다
010 ☐ invisible ⓐ 보이지 않는
011 ☐ makeup ⓝ 화장
012 ☐ apply ⓥ (연고, 화장품 등을) 바르다
013 ☐ refreshment ⓝ 다과
014 ☐ accidentally ᵃᵈ 우연히, 실수로
015 ☐ stain ⓥ 얼룩지게 하다
016 ☐ nerve ⓝ 신경, 긴장, 불안
017 ☐ torture ⓥ 괴롭히다, 고문하다
018 ☐ victim ⓝ 희생자
019 ☐ palm ⓝ 손바닥
020 ☐ sweat ⓥ 땀이 나다
021 ☐ have butterflies in one's stomach
안절부절 못하다, 긴장하다
022 ☐ tighten ⓥ 조이다
023 ☐ tense ⓐ 긴장된
024 ☐ confident ⓐ 자신감 있는
025 ☐ indifferent ⓐ 무관심한
026 ☐ irritated ⓐ 짜증난

20
027 ☐ march ⓥ 나아가다
028 ☐ ethnic ⓐ 민족의
029 ☐ traditionally ᵃᵈ 전통적으로
030 ☐ perspective ⓝ 관점, 시각
031 ☐ valuable ⓐ 가치가 있는
032 ☐ open-minded ⓐ (사고가) 개방적인
033 ☐ extensive ⓐ 광범위한
034 ☐ multicultural ⓐ 다문화적인
035 ☐ come up with ~을 떠올리다
036 ☐ association ⓝ 연상, 연관
037 ☐ allow ⓥ 허락하다, 가능하게 하다
038 ☐ capture ⓥ 포착하다, 붙잡다
039 ☐ unconventional ⓐ 색다른, 관습에 얽매
이지 않는
040 ☐ expand ⓥ 확장하다
041 ☐ expose ⓥ 접하게 하다
042 ☐ at home 국내에서
043 ☐ explore ⓥ 탐방하다, 탐험하다

21
044 ☐ illustrate ⓥ (예를 들어) 보여주다
045 ☐ assimilation ⓝ 동화, 흡수
046 ☐ flat ⓐ 평평한
047 ☐ fit ⓥ ~에 맞다, 적합하다
048 ☐ attempt ⓥ 시도하다
049 ☐ spherical ⓐ (도형) 구의
050 ☐ sphere ⓝ 구, 구체
051 ☐ interpret ⓥ 해석하다, 이해하다
052 ☐ on top of ~ 위에
053 ☐ incorporate ⓥ 통합하다

054 ☐ preexisting ⓐ 기존의
055 ☐ evaluate ⓥ 평가하다

22
056 ☐ well-meaning ⓐ 선의로 하는
057 ☐ habit ⓝ 버릇, 습관
058 ☐ practice ⓝ 연습
059 ☐ swear ⓥ 장담하다, 맹세하다
060 ☐ doubt ⓥ 의심하다
061 ☐ cautious ⓐ 조심하는, 신중한
062 ☐ especially ᵃᵈ 특히
063 ☐ beat oneself up 자책하다
064 ☐ approach ⓝ 접근법
065 ☐ involve ⓥ 포함하다, 수반하다
066 ☐ strive for ~을 위해 노력하다

23
067 ☐ differ ⓥ 다르다
068 ☐ physically ᵃᵈ 신체적으로
069 ☐ a multitude of 많은, 다수의
070 ☐ visible ⓐ 눈에 보이는
071 ☐ race ⓝ 인종
072 ☐ define ⓥ 정의하다
073 ☐ biological ⓐ 생물학적
074 ☐ ancestry ⓝ 혈통, 가계
075 ☐ trait ⓝ 특성
076 ☐ coloration ⓝ (생물의) 천연색
077 ☐ texture ⓝ 결
078 ☐ less and less 점점 적게
079 ☐ more and more 더욱더
080 ☐ identify ⓥ 확인하다, (…임을) 알다
081 ☐ and the like 기타 등등
082 ☐ feature ⓝ 특징
083 ☐ representative ⓝ 전형, 대표
084 ☐ continuously ᵃᵈ 계속해서, 연속적으로
085 ☐ variable ⓐ 가변적인
086 ☐ classify ⓥ 분류하다
087 ☐ overcome ⓥ 극복하다
088 ☐ racism ⓝ 인종 차별(주의)
089 ☐ misconception ⓝ 오해

24
090 ☐ realization ⓝ 실현
091 ☐ domination ⓝ 지배
092 ☐ industrial revolution 산업 혁명
093 ☐ manufacturing ⓝ 제조(업)
094 ☐ transform ⓥ 변모시키다
095 ☐ significant ⓐ 중대한
096 ☐ structure ⓥ 구조화하다, 구축하다
097 ☐ capitalistic ⓐ 자본주의적인
098 ☐ steam engine 증기 기관(차)
099 ☐ mechanize ⓥ 기계화하다
100 ☐ in mass quantities 대량으로
101 ☐ rural ⓐ 시골의
102 ☐ agriculture ⓝ 농업
103 ☐ urban ⓐ 도시의
104 ☐ innovation ⓝ 혁신, 쇄신
105 ☐ textile ⓝ 직물, 섬유
106 ☐ private company 개인 회사, 사기업
107 ☐ simultaneously ᵃᵈ 동시에
108 ☐ exert ⓥ (힘, 영향 등을) 행사하다, 가하다
109 ☐ authority ⓝ 권위

110 ☐ dump ⓥ (쓰레기 따위를) 내버리다
111 ☐ hazardous ⓐ 유해한
112 ☐ by-product ⓝ 부산물
113 ☐ waterway ⓝ 수로
114 ☐ sustainable ⓐ 지속 가능한
115 ☐ driving force 추진력, 원동력
116 ☐ greed ⓝ 탐욕

25
117 ☐ mode of transportation 교통수단
118 ☐ commute ⓝ 통근(길) ⓥ 통근하다
119 ☐ public transport 대중교통
120 ☐ in terms of ~의 관점에서
121 ☐ lead ⓥ 앞서다
122 ☐ immediately ᵃᵈ 즉시, 바로

26
123 ☐ virtual ⓐ 가상의
124 ☐ gala ⓝ 경축 행사
125 ☐ host ⓥ 주최하다
126 ☐ raise a fund 기금을 마련하다
127 ☐ charity ⓝ 자선
128 ☐ gather ⓥ 모이다
129 ☐ virtually ᵃᵈ 가상으로
130 ☐ auction ⓝ 경매

27
131 ☐ adult ⓝ 성인
132 ☐ clay ⓝ 점토
133 ☐ ceramic ⓝ 도자기
134 ☐ decorate ⓥ 장식하다, 꾸미다
135 ☐ piece ⓝ 조각
136 ☐ glaze ⓝ 유약
137 ☐ fire ⓥ (도자기 등을) 굽다
138 ☐ suitable ⓐ 적합한
139 ☐ necessary ⓐ 필요한
140 ☐ instruction ⓝ 강습

28
141 ☐ author ⓝ 작가, 저자
142 ☐ film director 영화감독
143 ☐ musician ⓝ 음악가
144 ☐ document ⓥ 기록하다
145 ☐ familiar with ~에 친숙한
146 ☐ drop out of ~을 그만두다
147 ☐ various ⓐ 다양한
148 ☐ inspire ⓥ 영감을 주다
149 ☐ migrant ⓝ 떠돌이, 이주자
150 ☐ staff ⓝ 직원
151 ☐ perform ⓥ 공연하다, 연주하다
152 ☐ concerto ⓝ 협주곡

29
153 ☐ abundant ⓐ 많은, 풍부한
154 ☐ measure A against B B에 견주어 A를
평가하다, 측정하다
155 ☐ meaning-seeking 의미를 추구하는
156 ☐ creature ⓝ 생명이 있는 존재, 생물
157 ☐ interpersonal ⓐ 사람들끼리의
158 ☐ comparison ⓝ 비교
159 ☐ standing ⓝ 지위
160 ☐ self-esteem ⓝ 자존감

161 ☐ backfire ⓥ 역효과를 낳다
162 ☐ inadequate ⓐ (상황을 처리하기에) 부족한,
무능한
163 ☐ malignant ⓐ 악의 있는
164 ☐ envy ⓝ 질투, 선망
165 ☐ misfortune ⓝ 불행
166 ☐ risk ⓥ (~의 위험을) 감수하다
167 ☐ scorn ⓝ 경멸, 멸시
168 ☐ undeserving ⓐ (~을 가질) 자격이 없는
169 ☐ beneath one's notice 주목할 가치가 없는
170 ☐ benign ⓐ 양성의, 상냥한
171 ☐ longing ⓝ 열망, 동경
172 ☐ reproduce ⓥ 재생산하다
173 ☐ accomplishment ⓝ 업적, 성취
174 ☐ circumstance ⓝ 상황
175 ☐ motivate ⓥ 동기를 부여하다
176 ☐ effort ⓝ 노력, 수고
177 ☐ in spite of ~에도 불구하고

30
178 ☐ normal ⓐ 정상
179 ☐ primarily ᵃᵈ 주로
180 ☐ matter ⓝ 문제, 일, 사건
181 ☐ puzzle ⓝ (어려운) 문제
182 ☐ encounter ⓥ 마주하다
183 ☐ phenomenon ⓝ 현상
184 ☐ accommodate ⓥ 수용하다
185 ☐ mismatch ⓝ 부조화
186 ☐ prediction ⓝ 예측, 예견
187 ☐ experimental ⓐ 실험에 근거한
188 ☐ eliminate ⓥ 제거하다
189 ☐ minor ⓐ 사소한
190 ☐ conservative ⓐ 보수적인
191 ☐ earth-shattering ⓐ 세상이 깜짝 놀랄,
경천동지할
192 ☐ extend ⓥ 확장하다
193 ☐ novelty ⓝ 참신함, 새로움
194 ☐ stress ⓥ 강조하다
195 ☐ unquestioningly ᵃᵈ 의심 없이
196 ☐ correspond with ~와 부합하다, 일치하다
197 ☐ assume ⓥ 추정하다
198 ☐ faulty ⓐ 결함이 있는

31
199 ☐ boss ⓝ 상관, 상사
200 ☐ come across as ~이라는 인상을 주다
201 ☐ subordinate ⓝ 부하
202 ☐ sympathizer ⓝ 동조자
203 ☐ belong ⓥ 속하다
204 ☐ incident ⓝ 사건, 일
205 ☐ blow ⓥ 날리다, 불다
206 ☐ cover ⓝ 위장
207 ☐ truly ᵃᵈ 진정으로
208 ☐ cosy ⓐ 편안한
209 ☐ safe ⓐ 안전한
210 ☐ loiter ⓥ 어슬렁어슬렁 걷다
211 ☐ corridor ⓝ 복도
212 ☐ fawn ⓥ 알랑거리다, 아양을 떨다
213 ☐ slightest ⓐ 최소의
214 ☐ arrive ⓥ (어떤 순간이) 도래하다, 찾아오다
215 ☐ ultimate ⓐ 궁극적인
216 ☐ controversy ⓝ 논란

03회

217 □ be eager to ~하려고 열망하는
218 □ reluctant ⓐ (~하기를) 꺼리는, 마지못해 하는
219 □ give back 돌려주다
220 □ lack ⓥ 부족하다
221 □ commitment ⓝ 헌신
222 □ sail ⓥ 항해하다
223 □ abandon ⓥ 버리다

32
224 □ operate ⓥ 조작하다, 운전하다, 작동하다
225 □ vehicle ⓝ 탈것
226 □ cell ⓝ 세포
227 □ navigate ⓥ 주행하다
228 □ destination ⓝ 목적지, 도착지
229 □ spring from ~로부터 일어나다, 비롯되다
230 □ neuron ⓝ 신경 세포
231 □ street sign ⓝ 도로 표지
232 □ conscious ⓐ 의식적인
233 □ awareness ⓝ 인식, 앎
234 □ separate ⓐ 별개의
235 □ cognitive ⓐ 인지의
236 □ neural ⓐ 신경(계)의
237 □ firing ⓝ 활성화
238 □ harmony ⓝ 조화, 화합
239 □ synthesize ⓥ 종합하다, 합성하다
240 □ intertwine ⓥ 뒤얽히다
241 □ trick ⓝ 기술, 속임수
242 □ strengthen ⓥ 강화하다
243 □ certain ⓐ 특정한, 어떤 정해진
244 □ component ⓝ 구성요소
245 □ the bottom line 가장 중요한 점, 핵심
246 □ preserve ⓥ 보존하다, 유지하다
247 □ calm ⓥ 진정시키다, 가라앉히다
248 □ stressful ⓐ 스트레스가 많은
249 □ concentrate on ~에 집중하다

33
250 □ philosopher ⓝ 철학자
251 □ logical ⓐ 논리적인
252 □ reason ⓝ 이유, 까닭, 동기
253 □ invoke ⓥ 들다[언급하다]
254 □ recall ⓥ 떠올리다, 상기하다
255 □ diverse ⓐ 다양한
256 □ gravity ⓝ 중력
257 □ body ⓝ 물체
258 □ gravitational attraction 중력
259 □ fundamental ⓐ 기본적인, 근본적인
260 □ principle ⓝ 원리
261 □ moral ⓝ 교훈
262 □ generalize ⓥ 일반화하다
263 □ make use of ~을 이용하다, 활용하다
264 □ govern ⓥ 지배하다
265 □ objective ⓐ 객관적인

34
266 □ laughter ⓝ 웃음
267 □ examine ⓥ 조사하다
268 □ frequency ⓝ 빈도
269 □ match ⓥ 짝을 이루다
270 □ pair ⓝ (짝진 것의) 한 쌍
271 □ stranger ⓝ 모르는 사람

272 □ humorous ⓐ 익살스러운
273 □ compare ⓥ (A와 B를) 비교하다
274 □ slightly ⓐⓓ 약간
275 □ serve ⓥ ~에 이바지하다
276 □ bond ⓝ 유대감
277 □ rating ⓝ 평가
278 □ anxiousness ⓝ 불안감
279 □ imply ⓥ 의미하다
280 □ connect with ~와 관계를 맺다, 연결하다
281 □ reveal ⓥ 드러내다
282 □ innermost ⓐ 가장 사적인[내밀한]

35
283 □ digital native 디지털 원주민
284 □ immersed in ~에 몰입한
285 □ possess ⓥ 가지다
286 □ aptitude ⓝ 소질, 적성
287 □ utilize ⓥ 이용하다, 활용하다
288 □ device ⓝ 기기
289 □ necessarily ⓐⓓ 반드시
290 □ behind prep (위치가) 뒤에
291 □ technological literacy 기술 활용 능력
292 □ mechanics ⓝ 역학, 기계학
293 □ elemental ⓐ 기본적인
294 □ lifespan ⓝ 수명
295 □ empower ⓥ 권한을 주다
296 □ utility ⓝ 유용, 쓸모가 있음
297 □ maximize ⓥ 극대화하다

36
298 □ ancient ⓐ 고대의
299 □ describe ⓥ 말로 설명하다, 묘사하다
300 □ roughly ⓐⓓ 대략
301 □ refer to ~을 지칭하다
302 □ scholar ⓝ 학자
303 □ anthropologist ⓝ 인류학자
304 □ sociologist ⓝ 사회학자
305 □ complicated ⓐ 복잡한
306 □ picture ⓝ 상황 (파악)
307 □ intertwined ⓐ 뒤얽힌
308 □ interdependent ⓐ 상호 의존적인
309 □ rationalist ⓝ 합리주의자
310 □ prize ⓥ 높이 평가하다, 존중하다
311 □ look down at ~을 경시하다
312 □ conclude ⓥ 결론을 내리다
313 □ primitive ⓐ 원시적인
314 □ frame ⓝ (생각의) 틀
315 □ metaphor ⓝ 은유
316 □ shape ⓥ 형성하다
317 □ calculation ⓝ 계산

37
318 □ doubt ⓝ 의심, 의혹
319 □ literary ⓐ 문학의
320 □ overwhelming ⓐ 압도적인
321 □ translate ⓥ 번역하다
322 □ week after week 여러 주 동안
323 □ moreover ⓐⓓ 게다가, 더욱이
324 □ adequately ⓐⓓ 충분히
325 □ illustrate ⓥ 설명하다, 예증하다
326 □ excerpt ⓝ 발췌
327 □ plot ⓝ 줄거리

328 □ for instance 예를 들어
329 □ gradual ⓐ 점진적인
330 □ involvement ⓝ 몰입, 몰두
331 □ imply ⓥ 내포하다
332 □ unfolding ⓝ 전개, 펼침
333 □ juxtaposition ⓝ 병치
334 □ contrasting ⓐ 대조되는, 상충하는
335 □ extract ⓝ 발췌(본) ⓥ 발췌하다, 뽑아내다
336 □ passage ⓝ 단락
337 □ have a greater chance of ~할 가능성이 더 크다
338 □ monotony ⓝ 단조로움
339 □ flavour ⓝ 묘미, 맛
340 □ chunk ⓝ 토막, 덩어리
341 □ satisfaction ⓝ 만족감
342 □ pattern ⓝ 구성, 양식

38
343 □ revolutionary ⓐ 혁명적인
344 □ concerning prep ~에 관하여
345 □ special theory of relativity 특수 상대성 이론
346 □ photoelectric effect 광전 효과
347 □ paper ⓝ 논문
348 □ communicate ⓥ 전달하다
349 □ largely ⓐⓓ 주로, 대개
350 □ publish ⓥ 출판하다
351 □ advent ⓝ 출현
352 □ periodical ⓝ 정기 간행물
353 □ gradually ⓐⓓ 점차로
354 □ yield ground to ~에 자리를 내주다, ~로 대체되다
355 □ journal ⓝ 학술지
356 □ altogether ⓐⓓ 완전히, 전적으로
357 □ establish ⓥ 세우다, 확립하다
358 □ reputation ⓝ 명성
359 □ contribution ⓝ 기여, 공헌
360 □ treatment ⓝ 취급, 대우
361 □ status ⓝ 지위, 상태
362 □ depend on ~에 달려 있다

39
363 □ fixed ⓐ 고정된
364 □ supply ⓝ 공급
365 □ production rate 생산율
366 □ demand ⓝ 수요
367 □ production level 조업도
368 □ inflexible ⓐ 유연하지 못한, 융통성 없는
369 □ inelastic ⓐ 비탄력적인, 적응력이 없는
370 □ it is worth -ing ~할 가치가 있다
371 □ note ⓥ 알아차리다
372 □ equipment ⓝ 장비
373 □ revenue ⓝ 수입, 수익
374 □ distribution ⓝ 배급, 분배

40
375 □ distance ⓝ 거리
376 □ reliable ⓐ 믿을 만한
377 □ indicator ⓝ 지표
378 □ acquaintance ⓝ 아는 사람, 약간의 친분
379 □ violate ⓥ 위반하다
380 □ packed ⓐ 가득 찬

381 □ sardine-like 승객이 빽빽이 들어찬
382 □ closeness ⓝ 가까움, 근접함
383 □ nonverbal ⓐ 비언어적인
384 □ compensate for ~을 보상하다, 상쇄하다
385 □ proximity ⓝ 근접성, 가까움
386 □ maintain ⓥ 지속하다, 유지하다
387 □ constant ⓐ 계속적인
388 □ uncomfortable ⓐ 불편한
389 □ appropriate ⓐ 적절한
390 □ adjust ⓥ 조절하다

41~42
391 □ civil ⓐ 정중한, 예의 바른
392 □ architect ⓝ 건축가
393 □ competent ⓐ 유능한
394 □ original ⓐ 독창적인
395 □ peer ⓝ 동료
396 □ friction ⓝ 마찰, 저항, 갈등
397 □ household ⓝ 가정
398 □ secure ⓐ 안전한
399 □ anything but ~이 결코 아닌
400 □ harmonious ⓐ 조화로운
401 □ verbally ⓐⓓ 언어적으로
402 □ abusive ⓐ 학대하는
403 □ shy away from ~을 피하다
404 □ stand up for ~을 대변하다, 옹호하다
405 □ solve ⓥ (문제 등을) 풀다, 해결하다
406 □ argument ⓝ 논쟁
407 □ last ⓥ 지속되다
408 □ ceaseless ⓐ 끊임없는
409 □ quarrel ⓥ 싸우다, 말다툼하다
410 □ reflect ⓥ 회고하다
411 □ passionate ⓐ 열정적인
412 □ prolonged ⓐ 장기간의
413 □ critical ⓐ 결정적인, 중대한
414 □ assumption ⓝ 가정
415 □ prevent ⓥ (~를/~가 ~하는 것을) 막다
416 □ soar ⓥ 솟구치다
417 □ cope with ~에 대처하다
418 □ compromise ⓝ 타협, 절충 ⓥ 타협하다

43~45
419 □ sensitive ⓐ 민감한
420 □ ticklish ⓐ 간지럼을 잘 타는
421 □ breeze ⓝ 산들바람
422 □ touch ⓥ 닿다
423 □ burst out laughing 웃음을 터뜨리다
424 □ contagious ⓐ 전염되는
425 □ endless ⓐ 끝없는
426 □ control ⓥ 억제하다, 조절하다
427 □ shave ⓥ 면도하다, 깎다
428 □ clown ⓝ 광대
429 □ cheer up ~을 격려하다
430 □ orphaned ⓐ 고아가 된
431 □ completely ⓐⓓ 완전히
432 □ light up with ~로 빛나다
433 □ wink ⓥ 윙크하다
434 □ retire ⓥ 은퇴하다
435 □ carry on 계속해서 ~하다
436 □ replace ⓥ 대체하다
437 □ add ⓥ 덧붙여 말하다
438 □ set off 유발하다, 일으키다

TEST A-B 각 단어의 뜻을 [A] 영어는 우리말로, [B] 우리말은 영어로 쓰시오.

A	English	Korean
01	mismatch	
02	sweat	
03	ancient	
04	perspective	
05	interpret	
06	commitment	
07	phenomenon	
08	cautious	
09	aptitude	
10	indicator	
11	authority	
12	control	
13	conscious	
14	bond	
15	slightly	
16	significant	
17	self-esteem	
18	recall	
19	traditionally	
20	approach	

B	Korean	English
01	궁극적인	
02	~에 맞다, 적합하다	
03	적합한	
04	극복하다	
05	지속 가능한	
06	수입, 수익	
07	기록하다	
08	공연하다, 연주하다	
09	출판하다	
10	사건, 일	
11	민감한	
12	실현	
13	조작하다, 운전하다, 작동하다	
14	주로	
15	대략	
16	광범위한	
17	객관적인	
18	대체하다	
19	특징	
20	확장하다	

▶ A-D 정답 : 해설편 033쪽

TEST C-D 각 단어의 뜻을 골라 기호를 쓰시오.

C	English	( )	Korean
01	non-exchangeable	( )	ⓐ 신경, 긴장, 불안
02	novelty	( )	ⓑ 지속하다, 유지하다
03	ancestry	( )	ⓒ 가변적인
04	preexisting	( )	ⓓ 배급, 분배
05	primitive	( )	ⓔ 기계화하다
06	variable	( )	ⓕ 위장
07	conservative	( )	ⓖ 설명하다, 예증하다
08	abundant	( )	ⓗ 위반하다
09	distribution	( )	ⓘ 오해
10	mechanize	( )	ⓙ 많은, 풍부한
11	maintain	( )	ⓚ 구성, 양식
12	gala	( )	ⓛ 원시적인
13	pattern	( )	ⓜ 혈통, 가계
14	misconception	( )	ⓝ 참신함, 새로움
15	packed	( )	ⓞ 교환 불가한
16	violate	( )	ⓟ 기존의
17	incorporate	( )	ⓠ 가득 찬
18	illustrate	( )	ⓡ 보수적인
19	nerve	( )	ⓢ 경축 행사
20	cover	( )	ⓣ 통합하다

D	Korean	( )	English
01	장담하다, 맹세하다	( )	ⓐ victim
02	동조자	( )	ⓑ grateful
03	이유, 까닭, 동기	( )	ⓒ ethnic
04	열망, 동경	( )	ⓓ undeserving
05	기본적인	( )	ⓔ concerning
06	수명	( )	ⓕ ache
07	(~을 가질) 자격이 없는	( )	ⓖ swear
08	의심, 의혹	( )	ⓗ elemental
09	도로 표지	( )	ⓘ reason
10	계속적인	( )	ⓙ longing
11	민족의	( )	ⓚ virtual
12	논문	( )	ⓛ doubt
13	~에 관하여	( )	ⓜ commute
14	평가	( )	ⓝ constant
15	희생자	( )	ⓞ street sign
16	고마워하는	( )	ⓟ unfolding
17	아프다	( )	ⓠ sympathizer
18	통근하다	( )	ⓡ lifespan
19	가상의	( )	ⓢ paper
20	전개, 펼침	( )	ⓣ rating

※ 영어 [독해] 파트만 수록한 문제지이므로 **18번**부터 시작합니다.　　　　● 점수 표시가 없는 문항은 모두 **2점**　　● 문항수 **28개** | 배점 **63점** | 제한 시간 **45분**

18. 다음 글의 목적으로 가장 적절한 것은?

My name is Anthony Thompson and I am writing on behalf of the residents' association. Our recycling program has been working well thanks to your participation. However, a problem has recently occurred that needs your attention. Because there is no given day for recycling, residents are putting their recycling out at any time. This makes the recycling area messy, which requires extra labor and cost. To deal with this problem, the residents' association has decided on a day to recycle. I would like to let you know that you can put out your recycling on Wednesdays only. I am sure it will make our apartment complex look much more pleasant. Thank you in advance for your cooperation.

① 재활용품 배출 허용 요일을 알리려고
② 쓰레기 분리배출의 필요성을 설명하려고
③ 쓰레기 분리배출 후 주변 정리를 부탁하려고
④ 입주민 대표 선출 결과를 공지하려고
⑤ 쓰레기장 재정비 비용을 청구하려고

19. 다음 글에 드러난 'I'의 심경으로 가장 적절한 것은?

It was a day I was due to give a presentation at work, not something I'd do often. As I stood up to begin, I froze. A chilly 'pins-and-needles' feeling crept over me, starting in my hands. Time seemed to stand still as I struggled to start speaking, and I felt a pressure around my throat, as though my voice was trapped and couldn't come out. Gazing around at the blur of faces, I realized they were all waiting for me to begin, but by now I knew I couldn't continue.

① panicked　　② angry　　③ relieved
④ grateful　　⑤ bored

20. 다음 글에서 필자가 주장하는 바로 가장 적절한 것은?

No matter what your situation, whether you are an insider or an outsider, you need to become the voice that challenges yesterday's answers. Think about the characteristics that make outsiders valuable to an organization. They are the people who have the perspective to see problems that the insiders are too close to really notice. They are the ones who have the freedom to point out these problems and criticize them without risking their job or their career. Part of adopting an outsider mentality is forcing yourself to look around your organization with this disassociated, less emotional perspective. If you didn't know your coworkers and feel bonded to them by your shared experiences, what would you think of them? You may not have the job security or confidence to speak your mind to management, but you can make these "outsider" assessments of your organization on your own and use what you determine to advance your career.

① 조직 내의 의사소통이 원활한지 수시로 살피라.
② 외부자의 관점으로 자기 조직을 비판적으로 바라보라.
③ 관심사의 공유를 통해 직장 동료와의 관계를 개선하라.
④ 과거의 성공에 도취되어 자기 계발을 소홀히 하지 말라.
⑤ 동료의 실수를 비판하기보다는 먼저 이해하려고 노력하라.

21. 밑줄 친 training for a marathon이 다음 글에서 의미하는 바로 가장 적절한 것은? [3점]

The known fact of contingencies, without knowing precisely what those contingencies will be, shows that disaster preparation is not the same thing as disaster rehearsal. No matter how many mock disasters are staged according to prior plans, the real disaster will never mirror any one of them. Disaster-preparation planning is more like training for a marathon than training for a high-jump competition or a sprinting event. Marathon runners do not practice by running the full course of twenty-six miles; rather, they get into shape by running shorter distances and building up their endurance with cross-training. If they have prepared successfully, then they are in optimal condition to run the marathon over its predetermined course and length, assuming a range of weather conditions, predicted or not. This is normal marathon preparation.

* contingency: 비상사태 ** mock: 모의의
*** cross-training: 여러 가지 운동을 조합하여 행하는 훈련법

① developing the potential to respond to a real disaster
② making a long-term recovery plan for a disaster
③ seeking cooperation among related organizations
④ saving basic disaster supplies for an emergency
⑤ testing a runner's speed as often as possible

22. 다음 글의 요지로 가장 적절한 것은?

Fears of damaging ecosystems are based on the sound conservationist principle that we should aim to minimize the disruption we cause, but there is a risk that this principle may be confused with the old idea of a 'balance of nature.' This supposes a perfect order of nature that will seek to maintain itself and that we should not change. It is a romantic, not to say idyllic, notion, but deeply misleading because it supposes a static condition. Ecosystems are dynamic, and although some may endure, apparently unchanged, for periods that are long in comparison with the human lifespan, they must and do change eventually. Species come and go, climates change, plant and animal communities adapt to altered circumstances, and when examined in fine detail such adaptation and consequent change can be seen to be taking place constantly. The 'balance of nature' is a myth. Our planet is dynamic, and so are the arrangements by which its inhabitants live together.

* idyllic: 목가적인

① 생물 다양성이 높은 생태계가 기후 변화에 더 잘 적응한다.
② 인간의 부적절한 개입은 자연의 균형을 깨뜨린다.
③ 자연은 정적이지 않고 역동적으로 계속 변한다.
④ 모든 생물은 적자생존의 원칙에 순응하기 마련이다.
⑤ 동식물은 상호 경쟁을 통해 생태계의 균형을 이룬다.

23. 다음 글의 주제로 가장 적절한 것은?

Before the modern scientific era, creativity was attributed to a superhuman force; all novel ideas originated with the gods. After all, how could a person create something that did not exist before the divine act of creation? In fact, the Latin meaning of the verb "inspire" is "to breathe into," reflecting the belief that creative inspiration was similar to the moment in creation when God first breathed life into man. Plato argued that the poet was possessed by divine inspiration, and Plotin wrote that art could only be beautiful if it descended from God. The artist's job was not to imitate nature but rather to reveal the sacred and transcendent qualities of nature. Art could only be a pale imitation of the perfection of the world of ideas. Greek artists did not blindly imitate what they saw in reality; instead they tried to represent the pure, true forms underlying reality, resulting in a sort of compromise between abstraction and accuracy.

* transcendent: 초월적인

① conflicting views on the role of artists
② positive effects of imitation on creativity
③ contribution of art to sharing religious beliefs
④ gods as a source of creativity in the pre-modern era
⑤ collaboration between philosophy and art in ancient times

24. 다음 글의 제목으로 가장 적절한 것은?

Some beginning researchers mistakenly believe that a good hypothesis is one that is guaranteed to be right (e.g., *alcohol will slow down reaction time*). However, if we already know your hypothesis is true before you test it, testing your hypothesis won't tell us anything new. Remember, research is supposed to produce *new* knowledge. To get new knowledge, you, as a researcher-explorer, need to leave the safety of the shore (established facts) and venture into uncharted waters (as Einstein said, "If we knew what we were doing, it would not be called research, would it?"). If your predictions about what will happen in these uncharted waters are wrong, that's okay: Scientists are allowed to make mistakes (as Bates said, "Research is the process of going up alleys to see if they are blind"). Indeed, scientists often learn more from predictions that do not turn out than from those that do.

* uncharted waters: 미개척 영역

① Researchers, Don't Be Afraid to Be Wrong
② Hypotheses Are Different from Wild Guesses
③ Why Researchers Are Reluctant to Share Their Data
④ One Small Mistake Can Ruin Your Whole Research
⑤ Why Hard Facts Don't Change Our Minds

25. 다음 도표의 내용과 일치하지 <u>않는</u> 것은?

Average Class Size in Primary Education

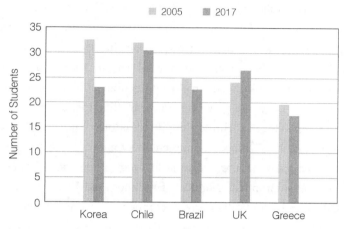

The above graph shows the average class size in primary education of five countries in 2005 and 2017. ① In every country except the UK, the average class size in 2017 decreased compared to that in 2005. ② In 2005, Korea's average class size was the largest of all the countries, with more than 30 students in a class. ③ In 2017, however, Chile's average class size was the largest of all the countries, with fewer than 30 students in a class. ④ In 2005, the average class size in Brazil was larger than that in the UK, whereas the reverse was true in 2017. ⑤ In Greece, the average class size was fewer than 20 students in a class in both 2005 and 2017.

26. Grey County 2021 Job Fair에 관한 다음 안내문의 내용과 일치하는 것은?

Grey County 2021 Job Fair

April 28, 2:00 p.m. − 6:00 p.m.
Bayshore Community Center

Businesses across Grey County can now register for a booth at the 2021 Job Fair. Last year's was the largest ever held in this area with more than 80 employers and over 1,000 job seekers. This year, we're moving to an even larger location with plenty of space for all attendees.

− Registration Fee: $80
− Registration Deadline: April 14, 6:00 p.m.

Enhanced Services to Employers
• 5 m × 5 m booth
• Free wifi
• Employer-only lounge and refreshments

For more information, visit www.greycountyjobfair.org.

---

① 행사 진행 시간은 6시간이다.
② 작년보다 더 좁은 장소에서 열린다.
③ 등록 마감일은 4월 28일이다.
④ 가로세로 각각 10m인 부스가 제공된다.
⑤ 고용주 전용 라운지와 다과가 제공된다.

27. The Riverside Escape에 관한 다음 안내문의 내용과 일치하지 <u>않는</u> 것은?

The Riverside Escape

The Riverside Escape is a city-wide escape game played on your smartphone. We turn the city of Riverside into a giant escape game wherein teams must race around the city completing challenges without getting caught.

How to Play
• Get your ticket ─ one ticket per team of up to 6 players.
• Choose the start date for the game. We will send you detailed information via email before your date of choice.
• Arrive at the start location and start anytime you want on the day.
• Score as many points as possible by answering the puzzles while moving around the city.

Opening Times
March 1, 2021 − May 31, 2021
Monday − Sunday, 10:00 − 20:00

Ticket Price
$50 per ticket (This price may change on a daily basis.)

Come join us for an escape adventure!

---

① 도시 전역에서 벌어지는 탈출 게임이다.
② 최대 여섯 명으로 구성된 팀당 티켓 한 장을 사야 한다.
③ 선택한 게임 시작일 이전에 전화로 상세한 정보를 알려 준다.
④ 2021년 3월 1일부터 세 달간 열린다.
⑤ 티켓 가격은 매일 달라질 수 있다.

28. Ingrid Bergman에 관한 다음 글의 내용과 일치하지 <u>않는</u> 것은?

Ingrid Bergman was born in Stockholm, Sweden on August 29, 1915. Her mother was German and her father Swedish. Her mother died when she was three, and her father passed away when she was 12. Eventually she was brought up by her Uncle Otto and Aunt Hulda. She was interested in acting from an early age. When she was 17, she attended the Royal Dramatic Theater School in Stockholm. She made her debut on the stage but was more interested in working in films. In the early 1940s, she gained star status in Hollywood, playing many roles as the heroine of the film. Bergman was considered to have tremendous acting talent, an angelic natural beauty and the willingness to work hard to get the best out of films. She was fluent in five languages and appeared in a range of films, plays and TV productions.

① 어머니는 독일인이었고 아버지는 스웨덴인이었다.
② 17세에 Royal Dramatic Theater School에 다녔다.
③ 영화를 통해 데뷔했으나 연극에 더 관심이 있었다.
④ 1940년대 초에 할리우드에서 스타의 지위를 얻었다.
⑤ 다섯 개의 언어에 유창했다.

29. 다음 글의 밑줄 친 부분 중, 어법상 틀린 것은?

While reflecting on the needs of organizations, leaders, and families today, we realize that one of the unique characteristics ① is inclusivity. Why? Because inclusivity supports ② what everyone ultimately wants from their relationships: collaboration. Yet the majority of leaders, organizations, and families are still using the language of the old paradigm in which one person — typically the oldest, most educated, and/or wealthiest — makes all the decisions, and their decisions rule with little discussion or inclusion of others, ③ resulting in exclusivity. Today, this person could be a director, CEO, or other senior leader of an organization. There is no need for others to present their ideas because they are considered ④ inadequate. Yet research shows that exclusivity in problem solving, even with a genius, is not as effective as inclusivity, ⑤ which everyone's ideas are heard and a solution is developed through collaboration.

30. 다음 글의 밑줄 친 부분 중, 문맥상 낱말의 쓰임이 적절하지 않은 것은? [3점]

The objective point of view is illustrated by John Ford's "philosophy of camera." Ford considered the camera to be a window and the audience to be ① outside the window viewing the people and events within. We are asked to watch the actions as if they were taking place at a distance, and we are not asked to participate. The objective point of view employs a static camera as much as possible in order to ② avoid this window effect, and it concentrates on the actors and the action without drawing attention to the camera. The objective camera suggests an emotional distance between camera and subject; the camera seems simply to be recording, as ③ straightforwardly as possible, the characters and actions of the story. For the most part, the director uses natural, normal types of camera positioning and camera angles. The objective camera does not comment on or ④ interpret the action but merely records it, letting it unfold. We see the action from the viewpoint of an impersonal observer. If the camera moves, it does so unnoticeably, calling as ⑤ little attention to itself as possible.

[31 ~ 34] 다음 빈칸에 들어갈 말로 가장 적절한 것을 고르시오.

31. Even the most respectable of all musical institutions, the symphony orchestra, carries inside its DNA the legacy of the _____. The various instruments in the orchestra can be traced back to these primitive origins — their earliest forms were made either from the animal (horn, hide, gut, bone) or the weapons employed in bringing the animal under control (stick, bow). Are we wrong to hear this history in the music itself, in the formidable aggression and awe-inspiring assertiveness of those monumental symphonies that remain the core repertoire of the world's leading orchestras? Listening to Beethoven, Brahms, Mahler, Bruckner, Berlioz, Tchaikovsky, Shostakovich, and other great composers, I can easily summon up images of bands of men starting to chase animals, using sound as a source and symbol of dominance, an expression of the will to predatory power. [3점]

* legacy: 유산 ** formidable: 강력한

① hunt   ② law   ③ charity
④ remedy   ⑤ dance

32. Our brains have evolved to remember unexpected events because basic survival depends on the ability to perceive causes and predict effects. If the brain predicts one event and experiences another, the unusualness will be especially interesting and will be encoded accordingly. Neurologist and classroom teacher Judith Willis has claimed that surprise in the classroom is one of the most effective ways of teaching with brain stimulation in mind. If students are exposed to new experiences via demonstrations or through the unexpected enthusiasm of their teachers or peers, they will be much more likely to connect with the information that follows. Willis has written that encouraging active discovery in the classroom allows students to interact with new information, moving it beyond working memory to be processed in the frontal lobe, which is devoted to advanced cognitive functioning. _____ sets us up for learning by directing attention, providing stimulation to developing perceptual systems, and feeding curious and exploratory behavior.

* frontal lobe: (대뇌의) 전두엽

① Awareness of social responsibility
② Memorization of historical facts
③ Competition with rivals
④ Preference for novelty
⑤ Fear of failure

33. Psychological research has shown that people naturally _____, often without thinking about it. Imagine you're cooking up a special dinner with a friend. You're a great cook, but your friend is the wine expert, an amateur sommelier. A neighbor drops by and starts telling you both about the terrific new wines being sold at the liquor store just down the street. There are many new wines, so there's a lot to remember. How hard are you going to try to remember what the neighbor has to say about which wines to buy? Why bother when the information would be better retained by the wine expert sitting next to you? If your friend wasn't around, you might try harder. After all, it would be good to know what a good wine would be for the evening's festivities. But your friend, the wine expert, is likely to remember the information without even trying. [3점]

① divide up cognitive labor
② try to avoid disagreements
③ seek people with similar tastes
④ like to share old wisdom
⑤ balance work and leisure

34. Even companies that sell physical products to make profit are forced by their boards and investors to reconsider their underlying motives and to collect as much data as possible from consumers. Supermarkets no longer make all their money selling their produce and manufactured goods. They give you loyalty cards with which they track your purchasing behaviors precisely. Then supermarkets sell this purchasing behavior to marketing analytics companies. The marketing analytics companies perform machine learning procedures, slicing the data in new ways, and resell behavioral data back to product manufacturers as marketing insights. When data and machine learning become currencies of value in a capitalist system, then every company's natural tendency is to maximize its ability to conduct surveillance on its own customers because _____. [3점]

* surveillance: 관찰, 감시

① its success relies on the number of its innovative products
② more customers come through word-of-mouth marketing
③ it has come to realize the importance of offline stores
④ the customers are themselves the new value-creation devices
⑤ questions are raised on the effectiveness of the capitalist system

35. 다음 글에서 전체 흐름과 관계 없는 문장은?

Academics, politicians, marketers and others have in the past debated whether or not it is ethically correct to market products and services directly to young consumers. ① This is also a dilemma for psychologists who have questioned whether they ought to help advertisers manipulate children into purchasing more products they have seen advertised. ② Advertisers have admitted to taking advantage of the fact that it is easy to make children feel that they are losers if they do not own the 'right' products. ③ When products become more popular, more competitors enter the marketplace and marketers lower their marketing costs to remain competitive. ④ Clever advertising informs children that they will be viewed by their peers in an unfavorable way if they do not have the products that are advertised, thereby playing on their emotional vulnerabilities. ⑤ The constant feelings of inadequateness created by advertising have been suggested to contribute to children becoming fixated with instant gratification and beliefs that material possessions are important.

* fixated: 집착하는   ** gratification: 만족(감)

[36~37] 주어진 글 다음에 이어질 글의 순서로 가장 적절한 것을 고르시오.

36.

> Once we recognize the false-cause issue, we see it everywhere. For example, a recent long-term study of University of Toronto medical students concluded that medical school class presidents lived an average of 2.4 years less than other medical school graduates.

(A) Perhaps this extra stress, and the corresponding lack of social and relaxation time — rather than being class president per se — contributes to lower life expectancy. If so, the real lesson of the study is that we should all relax a little and not let our work take over our lives.

(B) Probably not. Just because being class president is correlated with shorter life expectancy does not mean that it *causes* shorter life expectancy. In fact, it seems likely that the sort of person who becomes medical school class president is, on average, extremely hard-working, serious, and ambitious.

(C) At first glance, this seemed to imply that being a medical school class president is bad for you. Does this mean that you should avoid being medical school class president at all costs? [3점]

* per se: 그 자체로

① (A) − (C) − (B)   ② (B) − (A) − (C)
③ (B) − (C) − (A)   ④ (C) − (A) − (B)
⑤ (C) − (B) − (A)

37.

> We commonly argue about the fairness of taxation — whether this or that tax will fall more heavily on the rich or the poor.

(A) Taxes on tobacco, alcohol, and casinos are called "sin taxes" because they seek to discourage activities considered harmful or undesirable. Such taxes express society's disapproval of these activities by raising the cost of engaging in them. Proposals to tax sugary sodas (to combat obesity) or carbon emissions (to address climate change) likewise seek to change norms and shape behavior.

(B) But the expressive dimension of taxation goes beyond debates about fairness, to the moral judgements societies make about which activities are worthy of honor and recognition, and which ones should be discouraged. Sometimes, these judgements are explicit.

(C) Not all taxes have this aim. We do not tax income to express disapproval of paid employment or to discourage people from engaging in it. Nor is a general sales tax intended as a deterrent to buying things. These are simply ways of raising revenue.

* deterrent: 억제책

① (A) − (C) − (B)
② (B) − (A) − (C)
③ (B) − (C) − (A)
④ (C) − (A) − (B)
⑤ (C) − (B) − (A)

[38 ~ 39] 글의 흐름으로 보아, 주어진 문장이 들어가기에 가장 적절한 곳을 고르시오.

38.

> However, some types of beliefs cannot be tested for truth because we cannot get external evidence in our lifetimes (such as a belief that the Earth will stop spinning on its axis by the year 9999 or that there is life on a planet 100-million light-years away).

Most beliefs — but not all — are open to tests of verification. This means that beliefs can be tested to see if they are correct or false. (①) Beliefs can be verified or falsified with objective criteria external to the person. (②) There are people who believe the Earth is flat and not a sphere. (③) Because we have objective evidence that the Earth is in fact a sphere, the flat Earth belief can be shown to be false. (④) Also, the belief that it will rain tomorrow can be tested for truth by waiting until tomorrow and seeing whether it rains or not. (⑤) Also, meta-physical beliefs (such as the existence and nature of a god) present considerable challenges in generating evidence that everyone is willing to use as a truth criterion. [3점]

* verification: 검증, 확인 ** falsify: 거짓임을 입증하다

39.

> But the necessary and useful instinct to generalize can distort our world view.

Everyone automatically categorizes and generalizes all the time. Unconsciously. It is not a question of being prejudiced or enlightened. Categories are absolutely necessary for us to function. (①) They give structure to our thoughts. (②) Imagine if we saw every item and every scenario as truly unique — we would not even have a language to describe the world around us. (③) It can make us mistakenly group together things, or people, or countries that are actually very different. (④) It can make us assume everything or everyone in one category is similar. (⑤) And, maybe, most unfortunate of all, it can make us jump to conclusions about a whole category based on a few, or even just one, unusual example.

40. 다음 글의 내용을 한 문장으로 요약하고자 한다. 빈칸 (A), (B)에 들어갈 말로 가장 적절한 것은?

> At the University of Iowa, students were briefly shown numbers that they had to memorize. Then they were offered the choice of either a fruit salad or a chocolate cake. When the number the students memorized was seven digits long, 63% of them chose the cake. When the number they were asked to remember had just two digits, however, 59% opted for the fruit salad. Our reflective brains know that the fruit salad is better for our health, but our reflexive brains desire that soft, fattening chocolate cake. If the reflective brain is busy figuring something else out — like trying to remember a seven-digit number — then impulse can easily win. On the other hand, if we're not thinking too hard about something else (with only a minor distraction like memorizing two digits), then the reflective system can deny the emotional impulse of the reflexive side.
>
> * reflective: 숙고하는 ** reflexive: 반사적인

↓

> According to the above experiment, the ___(A)___ intellective load on the brain leads the reflexive side of the brain to become ___(B)___.

	(A)		(B)
①	limited	……	powerful
②	limited	……	divided
③	varied	……	passive
④	increased	……	dominant
⑤	increased	……	weakened

[41 ~ 42] 다음 글을 읽고, 물음에 답하시오.

Test scores are not a measure of self-worth; however, we often associate our sense of worthiness with our performance on an exam. Thoughts such as "If I don't pass this test, I'm a failure" are mental traps not rooted in truth. Failing a test is failing a test, nothing more. It is in no way (a) descriptive of your value as a person. Believing that test performance is a reflection of your virtue places (b) unreasonable pressure on your performance. Not passing the certification test only means that your certification status has been delayed. (c) Maintaining a positive attitude is therefore important. If you have studied hard, reaffirm this mentally and believe that you will do well. If, on the other hand, you did not study as hard as you should have or wanted to, (d) accept that as beyond your control for now and attend to the task of doing the best you can. If things do not go well this time, you know what needs to be done in preparation for the next exam. Talk to yourself in positive terms. Avoid rationalizing past or future test performance by placing the blame on secondary variables. Thoughts such as, "I didn't have enough time," or "I should have ...," (e) relieve the stress of test-taking. Take control by affirming your value, self-worth, and dedication to meeting the test challenge head on. Repeat to yourself "I can and I will pass this exam."

41. 윗글의 제목으로 가장 적절한 것은?

① Attitude Toward a Test: It's Just a Test
② Some Stress Is Good for Performance
③ Studying Together Works for a Test
④ Repetition: The Road to Perfection
⑤ Sound Body: The Key to Success

42. 밑줄 친 (a)~(e) 중에서 문맥상 낱말의 쓰임이 적절하지 <u>않은</u> 것은?

① (a) ② (b) ③ (c) ④ (d) ⑤ (e)

[43 ~ 45] 다음 글을 읽고, 물음에 답하시오.

(A)

Once upon a time there lived a poor but cheerful shoemaker. He was so happy, he sang all day long. The children loved to stand around his window to listen to (a) him. Next door to the shoemaker lived a rich man. He used to sit up all night to count his gold. In the morning, he went to bed, but he could not sleep because of the sound of the shoemaker's singing.

(B)

He could not sleep, or work, or sing—and, worst of all, the children no longer came to see (b) him. At last, the shoemaker felt so unhappy that he seized his bag of gold and ran next door to the rich man. "Please take back your gold," he said. "The worry of it is making me ill, and I have lost all of my friends. I would rather be a poor shoemaker, as I was before." And so the shoemaker was happy again and sang all day at his work.

(C)

There was so much there that the shoemaker was afraid to let it out of his sight. So he took it to bed with him. But he could not sleep for worrying about it. Very early in the morning, he got up and brought his gold down from the bedroom. He had decided to hide it up the chimney instead. But he was still uneasy, and in a little while he dug a hole in the garden and buried his bag of gold in it. It was no use trying to work. (c) He was too worried about the safety of his gold. And as for singing, he was too miserable to utter a note.

(D)

One day, (d) he thought of a way of stopping the singing. He wrote a letter to the shoemaker asking him to visit. The shoemaker came at once, and to his surprise the rich man gave him a bag of gold. When he got home again, the shoemaker opened the bag. (e) He had never seen so much gold before! When he sat down at his bench and began, carefully, to count it, the children watched through the window.

43. 주어진 글 (A)에 이어질 내용을 순서에 맞게 배열한 것으로 가장 적절한 것은?

① (B) − (D) − (C)   ② (C) − (B) − (D)
③ (C) − (D) − (B)   ④ (D) − (B) − (C)
⑤ (D) − (C) − (B)

44. 다음 밑줄 친 (a)~(e) 중에서 가리키는 대상이 나머지 넷과 <u>다른</u> 것은?

① (a) ② (b) ③ (c) ④ (d) ⑤ (e)

45. 윗글의 shoemaker에 관한 내용으로 적절하지 <u>않은</u> 것은?

① 그의 노래로 인해 옆집 사람이 잠을 잘 수 없었다.
② 예전처럼 가난하게 살고 싶지 않다고 말했다.
③ 정원에 구멍을 파고 금화가 든 가방을 묻었다.
④ 부자가 보낸 편지에 즉시 그를 만나러 갔다.
⑤ 금화를 셀 때 아이들이 그 모습을 봤다.

★ 확인 사항
○ 답안지의 해당란에 필요한 내용을 정확히 기입(표기)했는지 확인하시오.

18

001 ☐ on behalf of ~을 대표하여
002 ☐ association ⓝ 조합, 협회
003 ☐ participation ⓝ 참여
004 ☐ occur ⓥ 발생하다
005 ☐ attention ⓝ 관심
006 ☐ given ⓐ 정해진
007 ☐ messy ⓐ 엉망인, 지저분한
008 ☐ labor ⓝ 노동
009 ☐ apartment complex 아파트 단지
010 ☐ pleasant ⓐ 쾌적한
011 ☐ in advance 미리

19

012 ☐ due to ~하기로 한[예정된]
013 ☐ give a presentation 발표하다
014 ☐ chilly ⓐ 차가운
015 ☐ pins-and-needles ⓐ 저릿저릿한, 조마조마한
016 ☐ creep over ~을 엄습하다
017 ☐ still ⓐ 정지한
018 ☐ struggle ⓥ (~하려고) 애쓰다, 고생하다
019 ☐ throat ⓝ 목구멍
020 ☐ trap ⓥ 가두다
021 ☐ gaze at ~을 응시하다
022 ☐ blur ⓝ 흐릿한 형체 ⓥ 흐릿해지다
023 ☐ panicked ⓐ 어쩔 줄 모르는

20

024 ☐ insider ⓝ 내부자
025 ☐ outsider ⓝ 외부자
026 ☐ challenge ⓥ 이의를 제기하다, 반박하다
027 ☐ characteristic ⓝ 특성
028 ☐ perspective ⓝ 관점, 시각
029 ☐ point out ~을 지적하다
030 ☐ criticize ⓥ 비판하다
031 ☐ risk ⓥ 위태롭게 하다
032 ☐ career ⓝ 경력
033 ☐ adopt ⓥ 채택하다
034 ☐ mentality ⓝ 사고방식
035 ☐ disassociated ⓐ 고립된, 결속되지 않은
036 ☐ bonded ⓐ 결속되어 있는
037 ☐ job security 직업 안정성
038 ☐ management ⓝ 경영진
039 ☐ assessment ⓝ 평가
040 ☐ on one's own 독자적으로
041 ☐ determine ⓥ 판정하다, 결정하다
042 ☐ advance ⓥ 발전시키다

21

043 ☐ precisely ⓐ 정확히
044 ☐ disaster ⓝ 재난, 재해
045 ☐ preparation ⓝ 대비, 준비
046 ☐ rehearsal ⓝ 예행연습
047 ☐ stage ⓥ 기획하다, 조직하다
048 ☐ prior ⓐ 사전의
049 ☐ mirror ⓥ (그대로) 반영하다[나타내다]
050 ☐ sprint ⓥ (짧은 거리를) 전력 질주하다
051 ☐ get into shape 건강을 유지하다
052 ☐ build up ~을 단련하다
053 ☐ endurance ⓝ 지구력, 인내
054 ☐ optimal ⓐ 최적의

055 ☐ predetermined ⓐ 미리 설정된
056 ☐ assume ⓥ 가정하다
057 ☐ a range of 다양한
058 ☐ long-term ⓐ 장기적인
059 ☐ recovery ⓝ 복구
060 ☐ seek ⓥ 구하다

22

061 ☐ fear ⓝ 두려움
062 ☐ damage ⓥ 해치다, 피해를 입히다
063 ☐ sound ⓐ 건전한
064 ☐ conservationist ⓝ 환경 보호 활동가
065 ☐ principle ⓝ 원칙, 원리
066 ☐ minimize ⓥ 최소화하다
067 ☐ disruption ⓝ 파괴, 붕괴
068 ☐ not to say ~라고까지는 할 수 없어도
069 ☐ misleading ⓐ 오도하는, 잘못된
070 ☐ static ⓐ 정적인
071 ☐ dynamic ⓐ 역동적인
072 ☐ endure ⓥ 지속되다
073 ☐ apparently ⓐ 겉보기에
074 ☐ in comparison with ~에 비해서
075 ☐ lifespan ⓝ 수명
076 ☐ community ⓝ (동식물의) 군집
077 ☐ adapt to ~에 적응하다
078 ☐ alter ⓥ 변화시키다, 바꾸다
079 ☐ circumstances ⓝ 환경, 상황
080 ☐ examine ⓥ 검토하다
081 ☐ fine ⓐ 미세한
082 ☐ consequent ⓐ 결과적인
083 ☐ constantly ⓐ 항상
084 ☐ myth ⓝ 잘못된 통념
085 ☐ arrangement ⓝ (사는) 모습, (생활) 방식
086 ☐ inhabitant ⓝ 정착 주민, 서식자, 원주민

23

087 ☐ creativity ⓝ 창의성
088 ☐ attribute A to B A를 B의 탓으로 돌리다
089 ☐ superhuman ⓐ 초인적인
090 ☐ originate with ~에서 유래하다
091 ☐ divine ⓐ 성스러운
092 ☐ creation ⓝ 창조
093 ☐ verb ⓝ 동사
094 ☐ inspire ⓥ 영감을 주다
095 ☐ breathe ⓥ 호흡하다
096 ☐ inspiration ⓝ 영감
097 ☐ possess ⓥ 사로잡다, 지니다
098 ☐ descend ⓥ 내려오다
099 ☐ imitate ⓥ 모방하다
100 ☐ reveal ⓥ 드러내다
101 ☐ sacred ⓐ 신성한
102 ☐ quality ⓝ 특성
103 ☐ pale imitation 어설프게 흉내 낸 것
104 ☐ perfection ⓝ 완벽함
105 ☐ blindly ⓐ 맹목적으로
106 ☐ represent ⓥ 나타내다, 표현하다
107 ☐ pure ⓐ 순수한
108 ☐ underlying ⓐ 근저에 있는
109 ☐ compromise ⓝ 타협
110 ☐ abstraction ⓝ 추상
111 ☐ accuracy ⓝ 정확성
112 ☐ conflicting ⓐ 상충하는

113 ☐ contribution ⓝ 기여, 이바지
114 ☐ religious ⓐ 종교의
115 ☐ collaboration ⓝ 협력
116 ☐ philosophy ⓝ 철학

24

117 ☐ mistakenly ⓐ 잘못, 실수하여
118 ☐ hypothesis ⓝ 가설
119 ☐ guarantee ⓥ 보장하다
120 ☐ slow down ~을 둔화시키다
121 ☐ be supposed to ~하기로 되어 있다
122 ☐ shore ⓝ 해변
123 ☐ established ⓐ 확립된, 공고한
124 ☐ venture into ~에 발을 들여놓다, ~을 탐험하다
125 ☐ uncharted ⓐ 미지의, 잘 알지 못하는
126 ☐ waters 미지의[위험한] 영역
127 ☐ prediction ⓝ 예측
128 ☐ go up 올라가다
129 ☐ alley ⓝ 골목길
130 ☐ blind ⓐ 막다른
131 ☐ turn out 모습을 드러내다
132 ☐ reluctant ⓐ 마지못해 하는, 꺼리는
133 ☐ ruin ⓥ 망치다
134 ☐ hard facts 확실한 정보, 엄격한 사실

25

135 ☐ except ⓟ (누구·무엇을) 제외하고는
136 ☐ average ⓐ 평균의
137 ☐ primary education 초등 교육
138 ☐ decrease ⓥ 줄다, 감소하다
139 ☐ compared to ~와 비교해서
140 ☐ reverse ⓝ 반대

26

141 ☐ county ⓝ (영국 등에서) 자치주[군(郡)]
142 ☐ job fair 채용 박람회
143 ☐ business ⓝ 사업체
144 ☐ register for ~에 등록하다
145 ☐ employer ⓝ 고용주
146 ☐ job seeker 구직자
147 ☐ location ⓝ 장소
148 ☐ plenty of 충분히 큰, 많은
149 ☐ attendee ⓝ 참가자
150 ☐ deadline ⓝ 마감 일자
151 ☐ enhance ⓥ 향상하다
152 ☐ refreshment ⓝ 다과

27

153 ☐ escape ⓝ 탈출
154 ☐ complete ⓥ 완수하다
155 ☐ challenge ⓝ 도전 과제
156 ☐ up to ~까지
157 ☐ via ⓟ ~을 통하여
158 ☐ on a daily basis 매일

28

159 ☐ pass away 사망하다, 돌아가시다
160 ☐ bring up ~을 기르다, 양육하다
161 ☐ acting ⓝ 연기
162 ☐ make one's debut 데뷔하다
163 ☐ status ⓝ 지위

164 ☐ heroine ⓝ 여주인공
165 ☐ tremendous ⓐ 엄청난, 굉장한
166 ☐ angelic ⓐ 천사 같은
167 ☐ willingness ⓝ 기꺼이 ~하려는 마음
168 ☐ get the best out of ~을 최대한 활용하다, ~에게 최선을 다하게 하다
169 ☐ fluent ⓐ 유창한
170 ☐ production ⓝ 작품

29

171 ☐ reflect on ~에 대해 곰곰이 생각하다
172 ☐ organization ⓝ 조직
173 ☐ inclusivity ⓝ 포용성
174 ☐ support ⓥ 뒷받침하다
175 ☐ ultimately ⓐ 궁극적으로
176 ☐ majority ⓝ 대다수
177 ☐ paradigm ⓝ 패러다임
178 ☐ typically ⓐ 보통, 대개
179 ☐ educated ⓐ 교육을 받은, 교양 있는
180 ☐ rule ⓥ 지배하다
181 ☐ discussion ⓝ 토론
182 ☐ inclusion ⓝ 포함
183 ☐ exclusivity ⓝ 배타성
184 ☐ senior ⓐ 상급의
185 ☐ inadequate ⓐ 부적절한

30

186 ☐ objective ⓐ 객관적인
187 ☐ point of view 관점
188 ☐ illustrate ⓥ (예를 들어) 보여주다, 자세히 설명하다
189 ☐ audience ⓝ 관객
190 ☐ at a distance 멀리 떨어져서
191 ☐ employ ⓥ (기술, 방법 등을) 쓰다[이용하다]
192 ☐ as...as possible 될 수 있는 대로, 가급적
193 ☐ concentrate on ~에 집중하다
194 ☐ draw attention to ~에 관심을 끌다
195 ☐ subject ⓝ 대상
196 ☐ record ⓥ 기록하다
197 ☐ straightforwardly ⓐ 단도직입적으로, 있는 그대로
198 ☐ positioning ⓝ 위치 선정
199 ☐ comment on ~에 대해 논평하다
200 ☐ interpret ⓥ 해석하다
201 ☐ merely ⓐ 그저
202 ☐ unfold ⓥ 펼쳐지다, 펴다
203 ☐ viewpoint ⓝ 관점
204 ☐ impersonal ⓐ 냉담한
205 ☐ observer ⓝ 관찰자
206 ☐ unnoticeably ⓐ 눈에 띄지 않게

31

207 ☐ respectable ⓐ 훌륭한, 존경할 만한
208 ☐ institution ⓝ 기관, 제도
209 ☐ instrument ⓝ 악기
210 ☐ trace back to ~으로 거슬러 올라가다
211 ☐ primitive ⓐ 원시적인
212 ☐ origin ⓝ 기원
213 ☐ horn ⓝ 뿔
214 ☐ hide ⓝ (동물의) 가죽
215 ☐ gut ⓝ 내장
216 ☐ aggression ⓝ 공격성

217 ☐ **awe-inspiring** ⓐ 경외감을 불러일으키는
218 ☐ **assertiveness** ⓝ 적극성, 자기 주장
219 ☐ **monumental** ⓐ 기념비적인, 엄청난
220 ☐ **remain** ⓥ 남아 있다
221 ☐ **repertoire** ⓝ 연주 목록, 레퍼토리
222 ☐ **core** ⓐ 핵심의
223 ☐ **leading** ⓐ 주요한, 일류의
224 ☐ **composer** ⓝ 작곡가
225 ☐ **summon up** (생각, 기억 등을) 불러 일으키다
226 ☐ **band** ⓝ 무리
227 ☐ **chase** ⓥ 쫓다
228 ☐ **source** ⓝ 원천
229 ☐ **dominance** ⓝ 지배, 우월함
230 ☐ **expression** ⓝ 표현
231 ☐ **predatory** ⓐ 포식하는, 생물을 잡아먹는
232 ☐ **remedy** ⓝ 치료법

32
233 ☐ **evolve** ⓥ 진화하다
234 ☐ **unexpected** ⓐ 예상치 못한
235 ☐ **perceive** ⓥ 인지하다
236 ☐ **predict** ⓥ 예측하다
237 ☐ **unusualness** ⓝ 특이함
238 ☐ **encode** ⓥ (정보를 특정한 형식으로) 입력하다
239 ☐ **accordingly** ⓐⓓ 그에 따라
240 ☐ **neurologist** ⓝ 신경학자
241 ☐ **claim** ⓥ 주장하다
242 ☐ **stimulation** ⓝ 자극
243 ☐ **expose** ⓥ 노출하다
244 ☐ **demonstration** ⓝ (작동 과정 또는 사용법에 대한) 실연
245 ☐ **enthusiasm** ⓝ 열정
246 ☐ **working memory** 작동 기억
247 ☐ **be devoted to** ~에 전념하다
248 ☐ **cognitive functioning** 인지 기능
249 ☐ **set up** ~을 마련하다
250 ☐ **direct** ⓥ 인도하다
251 ☐ **perceptual** ⓐ 지각의
252 ☐ **feed** ⓥ 충족하다
253 ☐ **exploratory** ⓐ 탐구적인
254 ☐ **awareness** ⓝ 인식
255 ☐ **memorization** ⓝ 암기
256 ☐ **historical** ⓐ 역사적
257 ☐ **novelty** ⓝ 새로움

33
258 ☐ **psychological** ⓐ 심리적인
259 ☐ **expert** ⓝ 전문가
260 ☐ **amateur** ⓐ 아마추어의
261 ☐ **sommelier** ⓝ 소믈리에(식당에서 요리와 어울리는 와인을 추천해 주는 직원)
262 ☐ **drop by** 잠깐 들르다
263 ☐ **terrific** ⓐ 아주 멋진
264 ☐ **liquor** ⓝ 독한 술, 독주
265 ☐ **bother** ⓥ 애를 쓰다, 신경 쓰다
266 ☐ **retain** ⓥ 보유하다
267 ☐ **festivity** ⓝ 만찬, 축제 행사
268 ☐ **divide up** ~을 나누다
269 ☐ **cognitive** ⓐ 인지적인
270 ☐ **disagreement** ⓝ 의견 충돌

271 ☐ **wisdom** ⓝ 지혜
272 ☐ **leisure** ⓝ 여가

34
273 ☐ **make profit** 수익을 내다
274 ☐ **board** ⓝ 이사회
275 ☐ **investor** ⓝ 투자자
276 ☐ **reconsider** ⓥ 재고하다
277 ☐ **motive** ⓝ 동기, 동인
278 ☐ **produce** ⓝ 농산물
279 ☐ **manufacture** ⓥ 제조하다, 생산하다
280 ☐ **loyalty card** 고객 우대 카드
281 ☐ **track** ⓥ 추적하다
282 ☐ **analytics** ⓝ 분석 (정보)
283 ☐ **machine learning** 기계 학습(과거의 작동 축적을 통해 자기 동작을 개선하는 슈퍼컴퓨터의 능력)
284 ☐ **slice** ⓥ 쪼개다, 자르다
285 ☐ **behavioral** ⓐ 행동의
286 ☐ **insight** ⓝ 통찰(력)
287 ☐ **currency** ⓝ 통화, 화폐
288 ☐ **capitalist** ⓝ 자본주의(자)
289 ☐ **maximize** ⓥ 최대화하다
290 ☐ **conduct** ⓥ 수행하다
291 ☐ **innovative** ⓐ 혁신적인
292 ☐ **word-of-mouth** ⓐ 구두의, 구전의
293 ☐ **value-creation** 가치 창출
294 ☐ **effectiveness** ⓝ 효과성

35
295 ☐ **academic** ⓝ (대학) 교수
296 ☐ **politician** ⓝ 정치인
297 ☐ **in the past** (완료형과 함께) 지금까지
298 ☐ **ethically** ⓐⓓ 윤리적으로
299 ☐ **dilemma** ⓝ 딜레마
300 ☐ **psychologist** ⓝ 심리학자
301 ☐ **manipulate A into B** A를 조종해 B하게 하다
302 ☐ **admit to** ~한 것을 인정하다
303 ☐ **take advantage of** ~을 이용하다
304 ☐ **competitor** ⓝ 경쟁자
305 ☐ **marketplace** ⓝ 시장
306 ☐ **unfavorable** ⓐ 비판적인, 호의적이 아닌
307 ☐ **thereby** ⓐⓓ 그로 인해
308 ☐ **play on** (감정 등을) 이용하다
309 ☐ **emotional** ⓐ 정서적인
310 ☐ **vulnerability** ⓝ 취약성, 연약함
311 ☐ **constant** ⓐ 끊임없는
312 ☐ **inadequateness** ⓝ 부적절성
313 ☐ **contribute to** ~에 기여하다, ~의 원인이 되다
314 ☐ **instant** ⓐ 즉각적인
315 ☐ **material** ⓐ 물질적인
316 ☐ **possession** ⓝ 소유물

36
317 ☐ **conclude** ⓥ 결론을 내리다
318 ☐ **graduate** ⓥ 졸업생
319 ☐ **corresponding** ⓐ 상응하는, 해당하는
320 ☐ **lack** ⓝ 부족
321 ☐ **relaxation** ⓝ 휴식
322 ☐ **life expectancy** 기대 수명, 평균 수명

323 ☐ **take over** ~을 장악하다
324 ☐ **be correlated with** ~와 서로 관련되다
325 ☐ **extremely** ⓐⓓ 극도로, 몹시
326 ☐ **hard-working** ⓐ 근면한
327 ☐ **ambitious** ⓐ 야망 있는
328 ☐ **at first glance** 처음 언뜻 보면
329 ☐ **imply** ⓥ 의미하다
330 ☐ **at all costs** 무슨 수를 써서라도, 기어코

37
331 ☐ **fairness** ⓝ 공정성
332 ☐ **taxation** ⓝ 과세, 조세
333 ☐ **fall on** (부담이) ~에게 떨어지다, ~의 책임이다
334 ☐ **tobacco** ⓝ 담배
335 ☐ **sin tax** 죄악세(술·담배·도박 등에 부과되는 세금)
336 ☐ **discourage** ⓥ 낙담시키다
337 ☐ **undesirable** ⓐ 바람직하지 않은
338 ☐ **disapproval** ⓝ 반대, 못마땅함
339 ☐ **proposal** ⓝ 제안
340 ☐ **sugary** ⓐ 설탕이 든
341 ☐ **combat** ⓥ 방지하다, 퇴치하다, 싸우다
342 ☐ **obesity** ⓝ 비만
343 ☐ **emission** ⓝ 배출(량)
344 ☐ **address** ⓥ 해결하다, 대처하다, 다루다
345 ☐ **likewise** ⓐⓓ 마찬가지로
346 ☐ **norm** ⓝ 규범
347 ☐ **expressive** ⓐ 표현적인
348 ☐ **dimension** ⓝ 차원
349 ☐ **worthy** ⓐ 가치가 있는
350 ☐ **recognition** ⓝ 인정
351 ☐ **explicit** ⓐ 명백한
352 ☐ **income** ⓝ 소득
353 ☐ **intend** ⓥ 의도하다
354 ☐ **revenue** ⓝ 수입

38
355 ☐ **external** ⓐ 외부의, 외적인
356 ☐ **lifetime** ⓝ 일생
357 ☐ **axis** ⓝ 축
358 ☐ **verify** ⓥ 검증하다, 확인하다
359 ☐ **criterion** ⓝ 기준
360 ☐ **sphere** ⓝ 구(球)
361 ☐ **meta-physical** ⓐ 형이상학의
362 ☐ **existence** ⓝ 존재, 실재
363 ☐ **nature** ⓝ 본질
364 ☐ **present a challenge** 난제가 되다
365 ☐ **considerable** ⓐ 상당한
366 ☐ **generate** ⓥ 만들어 내다
367 ☐ **willing** ⓐ 기꺼이 ~하려는

39
368 ☐ **generalize** ⓥ 일반화하다
369 ☐ **distort** ⓥ 왜곡하다
370 ☐ **automatically** ⓐⓓ 자동적으로, 저절로
371 ☐ **categorize** ⓥ (개개의 범주로) 분류하다
372 ☐ **unconsciously** ⓐⓓ 무의식적으로
373 ☐ **prejudice** ⓝ 편견을 갖게 하다
374 ☐ **enlighten** ⓥ 계몽하다
375 ☐ **function** ⓥ (정상적으로) 활동하다
376 ☐ **structure** ⓝ 체계

377 ☐ **group together** ~을 하나로 묶다
378 ☐ **jump to a conclusion** 성급한 결론을 내리다

40
379 ☐ **briefly** ⓐⓓ 잠시, 짧게
380 ☐ **memorize** ⓥ 암기하다
381 ☐ **digit** ⓝ 숫자
382 ☐ **opt for** ~을 선택하다
383 ☐ **fatten** ⓥ 살찌게 하다
384 ☐ **be busy ~ing** ~하느라 바쁘다
385 ☐ **impulse** ⓝ 충동
386 ☐ **distraction** ⓝ 주의를 산만하게 하는 것
387 ☐ **deny** ⓥ 부인하다
388 ☐ **intellective** ⓐ 인지적인, 지적인
389 ☐ **load** ⓝ 부담, 무거운 짐
390 ☐ **limited** ⓐ 제한된, 한정된
391 ☐ **passive** ⓐ 수동적인
392 ☐ **dominant** ⓐ 지배적인

41~42
393 ☐ **self-worth** ⓝ 자아 존중감, 자부심
394 ☐ **associate A with B** A를 B와 연관시키다
395 ☐ **trap** ⓝ 함정
396 ☐ **rooted in** ~에 뿌리를 둔
397 ☐ **descriptive** ⓐ 설명하는
398 ☐ **reflection** ⓝ 반영, 반사
399 ☐ **virtue** ⓝ 미덕
400 ☐ **place pressure on** ~에 압력을 가하다
401 ☐ **unreasonable** ⓐ 부당한
402 ☐ **certification** ⓝ 자격, 증명
403 ☐ **reaffirm** ⓥ 재확인하다
404 ☐ **attend to** ~에 주의를 기울이다
405 ☐ **in preparation for** ~의 준비로
406 ☐ **term** ⓝ 말
407 ☐ **rationalize** ⓥ 합리화하다
408 ☐ **blame** ⓝ 책임
409 ☐ **secondary** ⓐ 부차적인
410 ☐ **variable** ⓝ 변수
411 ☐ **relieve** ⓥ 완화하다
412 ☐ **affirm** ⓥ 확인하다
413 ☐ **dedication** ⓝ 헌신
414 ☐ **meet ~ head on** ~에 정면으로 맞서다

43~45
415 ☐ **cheerful** ⓐ 쾌활한
416 ☐ **shoemaker** ⓝ 제화공, 구두장이
417 ☐ **sit up all night** 밤을 꼴딱 새우다
418 ☐ **worst of all** 무엇보다도 나쁜 것은
419 ☐ **seize** ⓥ 붙잡다
420 ☐ **ill** ⓐ 아픈
421 ☐ **out of one's sight** 보이지 않는 곳에
422 ☐ **chimney** ⓝ 굴뚝
423 ☐ **uneasy** ⓐ 불안한
424 ☐ **in a little while** 잠시 후에
425 ☐ **bury** ⓥ 묻다
426 ☐ **it is no use -ing** ~해도 소용없다
427 ☐ **as for** ~에 관해 말하자면
428 ☐ **miserable** ⓐ 몹시 불행한, 비참한
429 ☐ **utter** ⓥ (입으로) 소리를 내다, 말하다
430 ☐ **note** ⓝ 음, 음표
431 ☐ **at once** 즉시, 당장

04회

TEST A-B 각 단어의 뜻을 [A] 영어는 우리말로, [B] 우리말은 영어로 쓰시오.

A	English	Korean
01	revenue	
02	hypothesis	
03	mentality	
04	majority	
05	chilly	
06	static	
07	virtue	
08	bury	
09	novelty	
10	criterion	
11	discourage	
12	fatten	
13	conduct	
14	leisure	
15	optimal	
16	accuracy	
17	examine	
18	up to	
19	labor	
20	compared to	

B	Korean	English
01	보장하다	
02	배출(량)	
03	열정	
04	유창한	
05	무의식적으로	
06	충동	
07	수명	
08	끊임없는	
09	성스러운	
10	극도로, 몹시	
11	해석하다	
12	수동적인	
13	배타성	
14	관점, 시각	
15	참가자	
16	부인하다	
17	내려오다	
18	재고하다	
19	예측하다	
20	공격성	

▶ A-D 정답 : 해설편 044쪽

TEST C-D 각 단어의 뜻을 골라 기호를 쓰시오.

C	English			Korean
01	assertiveness	(	)	ⓐ 경쟁자
02	tremendous	(	)	ⓑ 행동의
03	enlighten	(	)	ⓒ 포용성
04	manufacture	(	)	ⓓ 지배적인
05	objective	(	)	ⓔ 제조하다, 생산하다
06	conflicting	(	)	ⓕ ~을 기르다, 양육하다
07	certification	(	)	ⓖ 잠시, 짧게
08	ethically	(	)	ⓗ 계몽하다
09	behavioral	(	)	ⓘ 윤리적으로
10	institution	(	)	ⓙ 엄청난, 굉장한
11	bring up	(	)	ⓚ 상충하는
12	accordingly	(	)	ⓛ 적극성, 자기 주장
13	in advance	(	)	ⓜ 미리
14	established	(	)	ⓝ 기꺼이 ~하려는
15	obesity	(	)	ⓞ 기관, 제도
16	willing	(	)	ⓟ 그에 따라
17	briefly	(	)	ⓠ 비만
18	inclusivity	(	)	ⓡ 확립된, 공고한
19	dominant	(	)	ⓢ 객관적인
20	competitor	(	)	ⓣ 자격, 증명

D	Korean			English
01	환경, 상황	(	)	ⓐ verify
02	~을 엄습하다	(	)	ⓑ unexpected
03	정확히	(	)	ⓒ stage
04	기획하다, 조직하다	(	)	ⓓ seize
05	겉보기에	(	)	ⓔ rooted in
06	원칙, 원리	(	)	ⓕ retain
07	나타내다, 표현하다	(	)	ⓖ represent
08	붙잡다	(	)	ⓗ principle
09	반대, 못마땅함	(	)	ⓘ precisely
10	충분히 큰, 많은	(	)	ⓙ plenty of
11	검증하다, 확인하다	(	)	ⓚ impersonal
12	예상치 못한	(	)	ⓛ gaze at
13	조합, 협회	(	)	ⓜ external
14	~에 집중하다	(	)	ⓝ disapproval
15	냉담한	(	)	ⓞ creep over
16	~에 뿌리를 둔	(	)	ⓟ concentrate on
17	보유하다	(	)	ⓠ circumstances
18	외부의, 외적인	(	)	ⓡ association
19	~을 응시하다	(	)	ⓢ apparently
20	야망 있는	(	)	ⓣ ambitious

※ 영어 [독해] 파트만 수록한 문제지이므로 18번부터 시작합니다.

● 점수 표시가 없는 문항은 모두 2점 ● 문항수 28개 | 배점 63점 | 제한 시간 45분

18. 다음 글의 목적으로 가장 적절한 것은?

> Dear Tony,
>
> I'm writing to ask if you could possibly do me a favour. For this year's workshop, we would really like to take all our staff on a trip to Bridgend to learn more about new leadership skills in the industry. I remember that your company took a similar course last year, which included a lecture by an Australian lady whom you all found inspiring. Are you still in contact with her? If so, do you think that you could possibly let me have a number for her, or an email address? I would really appreciate your assistance.
>
> Kind regards,
> Luke Schreider

① 직원 연수 진행을 부탁하려고
② 연수 강사의 연락처를 문의하려고
③ 연수에서 강연할 원고를 의뢰하려고
④ 리더십 개발 연수 참석을 권유하려고
⑤ 연수자 명단을 보내 줄 것을 요청하려고

19. 다음 글에 드러난 Alice의 심경 변화로 가장 적절한 것은?

Alice looked up from her speech for the first time since she began talking. She hadn't dared to break eye contact with the words on the pages until she finished, for fear of losing her place. Actually, she'd just hoped for two simple things — not to lose the ability to read during the talk and to get through it without making a fool of herself. Now the entire ballroom was standing, clapping. It was more than she had hoped for. Smiling brightly, she looked at the familiar faces in the front row. Tom clapped and cheered and looked like he could barely keep himself from running up to hug and congratulate her. She couldn't wait to hug him, too.

① nervous → delighted
② embarrassed → scared
③ amazed → annoyed
④ hopeful → disappointed
⑤ angry → grateful

20. 다음 글에서 필자가 주장하는 바로 가장 적절한 것은?

When I started my career, I looked forward to the annual report from the organization showing statistics for each of its leaders. As soon as I received them in the mail, I'd look for my standing and compare my progress with the progress of all the other leaders. After about five years of doing that, I realized how harmful it was. Comparing yourself to others is really just a needless distraction. The only one you should compare yourself to is you. Your mission is to become better today than you were yesterday. You do that by focusing on what you can do today to improve and grow. Do that enough, and if you look back and compare the you of weeks, months, or years ago to the you of today, you should be greatly encouraged by your progress.

① 남과 비교하기보다는 자신의 성장에 주목해야 한다.
② 진로를 결정할 때는 다양한 의견을 경청해야 한다.
③ 발전을 위해서는 선의의 경쟁 상대가 있어야 한다.
④ 타인의 성공 사례를 자신의 본보기로 삼아야 한다.
⑤ 객관적 자료에 근거하여 직원을 평가해야 한다.

21. 밑줄 친 creating a buffer가 다음 글에서 의미하는 바로 가장 적절한 것은?

On one occasion I was trying to explain the concept of buffers to my children. We were in the car together at the time and I tried to explain the idea using a game. Imagine, I said, that we had to get to our destination three miles away without stopping. We couldn't predict what was going to happen in front of us and around us. We didn't know how long the light would stay on green or if the car in front would suddenly put on its brakes. The only way to keep from crashing was to put extra space between our car and the car in front of us. This space acts as a buffer. It gives us time to respond and adapt to any sudden moves by other cars. Similarly, we can reduce the friction of doing the essential in our work and lives simply by creating a buffer.

* friction: 마찰

① knowing that learning is more important than winning
② always being prepared for unexpected events
③ never stopping what we have already started
④ having a definite destination when we drive
⑤ keeping peaceful relationships with others

22. 다음 글의 요지로 가장 적절한 것은?

Many of the leaders I know in the media industry are intelligent, capable, and honest. But they are leaders of companies that appear to have only one purpose: the single-minded pursuit of short-term profit and "shareholder value." I believe, however, that the media industry, by its very nature and role in our society and global culture, must act differently than other industries — especially because they have the free use of our public airwaves and our digital spectrum, and have almost unlimited access to our children's hearts and minds. These are priceless assets, and the right to use them should necessarily carry serious and long-lasting responsibilities to promote the public good.

* shareholder: 주주(株主)

① 방송 통신과 관련된 법 개정이 시급하다.
② 공익 방송 시청률이 점점 하락하고 있다.
③ 미디어 산업은 공익을 증진할 책임이 있다.
④ 미디어 산업은 시설의 현대화를 꾀하고 있다.
⑤ 미디어에 대한 비판적 시각을 기를 필요가 있다.

23. 다음 글의 주제로 가장 적절한 것은?

In addition to the varied forms that recreation may take, it also meets a wide range of individual needs and interests. Many participants take part in recreation as a form of relaxation and release from work pressures or other tensions. Often they may be passive spectators of entertainment provided by television, movies, or other forms of electronic amusement. However, other significant play motivations are based on the need to express creativity, discover hidden talents, or pursue excellence in varied forms of personal expression. For some participants, active, competitive recreation may offer a channel for releasing hostility and aggression or for struggling against others or the environment in adventurous, high-risk activities. Others enjoy recreation that is highly social and provides the opportunity for making new friends or cooperating with others in group settings.

① effects of recreational participation on memory
② various motivations for recreational participation
③ importance of balance between work and leisure
④ social factors promoting the recreation movement
⑤ economic trends affecting recreational participation

24. 다음 글의 제목으로 가장 적절한 것은?

If a food contains more sugar than any other ingredient, government regulations require that sugar be listed first on the label. But if a food contains several different kinds of sweeteners, they can be listed separately, which pushes each one farther down the list. This requirement has led the food industry to put in three different sources of sugar so that they don't have to say the food has that much sugar. So sugar doesn't appear first. Whatever the true motive, ingredient labeling still does not fully convey the amount of sugar being added to food, certainly not in a language that's easy for consumers to understand. A world-famous cereal brand's label, for example, indicates that the cereal has 11 grams of sugar per serving. But nowhere does it tell consumers that more than one-third of the box contains added sugar.

① Artificial Sweeteners: Good or Bad?
② Consumer Benefits of Ingredient Labeling
③ Sugar: An Energy Booster for Your Brain
④ Truth About Sugar Hidden in Food Labels
⑤ What Should We Do to Reduce Sugar Intake?

25. 다음 도표의 내용과 일치하지 <u>않는</u> 것은?

Injury Rate by Day of Game in NFL (2014-2017)

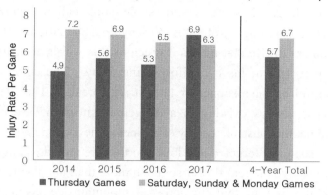

The above graph shows the injury rate by day of game in the National Football League (NFL) from 2014 to 2017. ① The injury rate of Thursday games was the lowest in 2014 and the highest in 2017. ② The injury rate of Saturday, Sunday and Monday games decreased steadily from 2014 to 2017. ③ In all the years except 2017, the injury rate of Thursday games was lower than that of Saturday, Sunday and Monday games. ④ The gap between the injury rate of Thursday games and that of Saturday, Sunday and Monday games was the largest in 2014 and the smallest in 2017. ⑤ In two years out of the four, the injury rate of Thursday games was higher than that of the 4-year total.

26. Christiaan Huygens에 관한 다음 글의 내용과 일치하지 <u>않는</u> 것은?

Dutch mathematician and astronomer Christiaan Huygens was born in The Hague in 1629. He studied law and mathematics at his university, and then devoted some time to his own research, initially in mathematics but then also in optics, working on telescopes and grinding his own lenses. Huygens visited England several times, and met Isaac Newton in 1689. In addition to his work on light, Huygens had studied forces and motion, but he did not accept Newton's law of universal gravitation. Huygens' wide-ranging achievements included some of the most accurate clocks of his time, the result of his work on pendulums. His astronomical work, carried out using his own telescopes, included the discovery of Titan, the largest of Saturn's moons, and the first correct description of Saturn's rings.

* pendulum: 시계추

① 대학에서 법과 수학을 공부했다.
② 1689년에 뉴턴을 만났다.
③ 뉴턴의 만유인력 법칙을 받아들였다.
④ 당대의 가장 정확한 시계 중 몇몇이 업적에 포함되었다.
⑤ 자신의 망원경을 사용하여 천문학 연구를 수행했다.

27. Flower Arranging Contest에 관한 다음 안내문의 내용과 일치하지 <u>않는</u> 것은?

Flower Arranging Contest
Join our annual Flower Arranging Contest!

When: May 7, 2020 at 4:00 p.m.
Where: Jade High School Educational Exhibit Building

Who Can Enter?
- Category I - Students enrolled in Home Economics
- Category II - Parents (not open to professionals)

Rules
- Each contestant must bring their own materials.
- 30 minutes will be allowed for finishing arrangements.

Prizes for Each Category
1st Place: $80.00 2nd Place: $60.00 3rd Place: $40.00

* Arrangements will be on display until May 9, 2020.

---

① 학부모 중에서 전문가는 참여할 수 없다.
② 참가자에게 재료를 제공한다.
③ 꽃꽂이를 끝내는 데 30분이 주어진다.
④ 부문별 1등, 2등, 3등에게 상금을 준다.
⑤ 2020년 5월 9일까지 꽃꽂이 작품이 전시된다.

28. Bright Cat Toy에 관한 다음 안내문의 내용과 일치하는 것은?

Bright Cat Toy

Attract your cat's attention and satisfy their hunting instincts with a unique electronic cat toy.

Key Benefits
- The feather appears randomly in the 6 holes.
- Feathers can be exchanged easily.
- It automatically stops running after 8 minutes.
- It is fully charged in 30 minutes via USB-cable, and it runs for 5 hours.

How to Use
- Short press the button to power on / off the device.
- Long press the button to change feathers.

What's in the Box
- Bright Cat Toy: 1 piece
- Feather: 2 pieces (1 installed, 1 extra)

---

① 구멍에서 정해진 순서대로 깃털이 나온다.
② 8분 후에 자동으로 작동을 멈춘다.
③ 완전히 충전하는 데 5시간이 걸린다.
④ 켜거나 끄려면 버튼을 길게 눌러야 한다.
⑤ 총 세 개의 깃털이 제공된다.

29. 다음 글의 밑줄 친 부분 중, 어법상 틀린 것은?

Commercial airplanes generally travel airways similar to roads, although they are not physical structures. Airways have fixed widths and defined altitudes, ① which separate traffic moving in opposite directions. Vertical separation of aircraft allows some flights ② to pass over airports while other processes occur below. Air travel usually covers long distances, with short periods of intense pilot activity at takeoff and landing and long periods of lower pilot activity while in the air, the portion of the flight ③ known as the "long haul." During the long-haul portion of a flight, pilots spend more time assessing aircraft status than ④ searching out nearby planes. This is because collisions between aircraft usually occur in the surrounding area of airports, while crashes due to aircraft malfunction ⑤ tends to occur during long-haul flight.

* altitude: 고도   ** long haul: 장거리 비행

30. 다음 글의 밑줄 친 부분 중, 문맥상 낱말의 쓰임이 적절하지 않은 것은? [3점]

I was sitting outside a restaurant in Spain one summer evening, waiting for dinner. The aroma of the kitchens excited my taste buds. My future meal was coming to me in the form of molecules drifting through the air, too small for my eyes to see but ① detected by my nose. The ancient Greeks first came upon the idea of atoms this way; the smell of baking bread suggested to them that small particles of bread ② existed beyond vision. The cycle of weather ③ disproved this idea: a puddle of water on the ground gradually dries out, disappears, and then falls later as rain. They reasoned that there must be particles of water that turn into steam, form clouds, and fall to earth, so that the water is ④ conserved even though the little particles are too small to see. My paella in Spain had inspired me, four thousand years too ⑤ late, to take the credit for atomic theory.

* taste bud: 미뢰(혀의 미각 기관)   ** molecule: 분자
*** paella: 파에야(스페인 요리의 하나)

[31~34] 다음 빈칸에 들어갈 말로 가장 적절한 것을 고르시오.

31. When he was dying, the contemporary Buddhist teacher Dainin Katagiri wrote a remarkable book called *Returning to Silence*. Life, he wrote, "is a dangerous situation." It is the weakness of life that makes it precious; his words are filled with the very fact of his own life passing away. "The china bowl is beautiful because sooner or later it will break.... The life of the bowl is always existing in a dangerous situation." Such is our struggle: this unstable beauty. This inevitable wound. We forget — how easily we forget — that love and loss are intimate companions, that we love the real flower so much more than the plastic one and love the cast of twilight across a mountainside lasting only a moment. It is this very _____ that opens our hearts. [3점]

① fragility   ② stability   ③ harmony
④ satisfaction   ⑤ diversity

32. Nothing happens immediately, so in the beginning we can't see any results from our practice. This is like the example of the man who tries to make fire by rubbing two sticks of wood together. He says to himself, "They say there's fire here," and he begins rubbing energetically. He rubs on and on, but he's very impatient. He wants to have that fire, but the fire doesn't come. So he gets discouraged and stops to rest for a while. Then he starts again, but the going is slow, so he rests again. By then the heat has disappeared; he didn't keep at it long enough. He rubs and rubs until he gets tired and then he stops altogether. Not only is he tired, but he becomes more and more discouraged until he gives up completely, "There's no fire here." Actually, he was doing the work, but there wasn't enough heat to start a fire. The fire was there all the time, but _____.

① he didn't carry on to the end
② someone told him not to give up
③ the sticks were not strong enough
④ he started without planning in advance
⑤ the weather was not suitable to start a fire

[해설편 p.048]

33. Translating academic language into everyday language can be an essential tool for you as a writer to _____. For, as writing theorists often note, writing is generally not a process in which we start with a fully formed idea in our heads that we then simply transcribe in an unchanged state onto the page. On the contrary, writing is more often a means of discovery in which we use the writing process to figure out what our idea is. This is why writers are often surprised to find that what they end up with on the page is quite different from what they thought it would be when they started. What we are trying to say here is that everyday language is often crucial for this discovery process. Translating your ideas into more common, simpler terms can help you figure out what your ideas really are, as opposed to what you initially imagined they were. [3점]

* transcribe: 옮겨 쓰다

① finish writing quickly
② reduce sentence errors
③ appeal to various readers
④ come up with creative ideas
⑤ clarify your ideas to yourself

34. The growing field of genetics is showing us what many scientists have suspected for years — _____. This information helps us better understand that genes are under our control and not something we must obey. Consider identical twins; both individuals are given the same genes. In mid-life, one twin develops cancer, and the other lives a long healthy life without cancer. A specific gene instructed one twin to develop cancer, but in the other the same gene did not initiate the disease. One possibility is that the healthy twin had a diet that turned off the cancer gene — the same gene that instructed the other person to get sick. For many years, scientists have recognized other environmental factors, such as chemical toxins (tobacco for example), can contribute to cancer through their actions on genes. The notion that food has a specific influence on gene expression is relatively new. [3점]

① identical twins have the same genetic makeup
② our preference for food is influenced by genes
③ balanced diet is essential for our mental health
④ genetic engineering can cure some fatal diseases
⑤ foods can immediately influence the genetic blueprint

35. 다음 글에서 전체 흐름과 관계 <u>없는</u> 문장은?

There are many superstitions surrounding the world of the theater. ① Superstitions can be anything from not wanting to say the last line of a play before the first audience comes, to not wanting to rehearse the curtain call before the final rehearsal. ② Shakespeare's famous tragedy *Macbeth* is said to be cursed, and to avoid problems actors never say the title of the play out loud when inside a theater or a theatrical space (like a rehearsal room or costume shop). ③ The interaction between the audience and the actors in the play influences the actors' performance. ④ Since the play is set in Scotland, the secret code you say when you need to say the title of the play is "the Scottish play." ⑤ If you do say the title by accident, legend has it that you have to go outside, turn around three times, and come back into the theater.

[36 ~ 37] 주어진 글 다음에 이어질 글의 순서로 가장 적절한 것을 고르시오.

36.

Habits create the foundation for mastery. In chess, it is only after the basic movements of the pieces have become automatic that a player can focus on the next level of the game. Each chunk of information that is memorized opens up the mental space for more effortful thinking.

(A) You fall into mindless repetition. It becomes easier to let mistakes slide. When you can do it "good enough" automatically, you stop thinking about how to do it better.

(B) However, the benefits of habits come at a cost. At first, each repetition develops fluency, speed, and skill. But then, as a habit becomes automatic, you become less sensitive to feedback.

(C) This is true for anything you attempt. When you know the simple movements so well that you can perform them without thinking, you are free to pay attention to more advanced details. In this way, habits are the backbone of any pursuit of excellence. [3점]

① (A) − (C) − (B)   ② (B) − (A) − (C)
③ (B) − (C) − (A)   ④ (C) − (A) − (B)
⑤ (C) − (B) − (A)

37.

> Regardless of whether the people existing after agriculture were happier, healthier, or neither, it is undeniable that there were more of them. Agriculture both supports and requires more people to grow the crops that sustain them.

(A) And a larger population doesn't just mean increasing the size of everything, like buying a bigger box of cereal for a larger family. It brings qualitative changes in the way people live.

(B) Estimates vary, of course, but evidence points to an increase in the human population from 1-5 million people worldwide to a few hundred million once agriculture had become established.

(C) For example, more people means more kinds of diseases, particularly when those people are sedentary. Those groups of people can also store food for long periods, which creates a society with haves and have-nots. [3점]

*sedentary: 한 곳에 정착해 있는

① (A) − (C) − (B) ② (B) − (A) − (C)
③ (B) − (C) − (A) ④ (C) − (A) − (B)
⑤ (C) − (B) − (A)

[38~39] 글의 흐름으로 보아, 주어진 문장이 들어가기에 가장 적절한 곳을 고르시오.

38.

> Yet today if you program that same position into an ordinary chess program, it will immediately suggest the exact moves that Fischer made.

The boundary between uniquely human creativity and machine capabilities continues to change. (①) Returning to the game of chess, back in 1956, thirteen-year-old child prodigy Bobby Fischer made a pair of remarkably creative moves against grandmaster Donald Byrne. (②) First he sacrificed his knight, seemingly for no gain, and then exposed his queen to capture. (③) On the surface, these moves seemed insane, but several moves later, Fischer used these moves to win the game. (④) His creativity was praised at the time as the mark of genius. (⑤) It's not because the computer has memorized the Fischer-Byrne game, but rather because it searches far enough ahead to see that these moves really do pay off.

*prodigy: 신동, 영재

39.

> In some cases, their brains had ceased to function altogether.

Of all the medical achievements of the 1960s, the most widely known was the first heart transplant, performed by the South African surgeon Christiaan Barnard in 1967. (①) The patient's death 18 days later did not weaken the spirits of those who welcomed a new era of medicine. (②) The ability to perform heart transplants was linked to the development of respirators, which had been introduced to hospitals in the 1950s. (③) Respirators could save many lives, but not all those whose hearts kept beating ever recovered any other significant functions. (④) The realization that such patients could be a source of organs for transplantation led to the setting up of the Harvard Brain Death Committee, and to its recommendation that the absence of all "discernible central nervous system activity" should be "a new criterion for death". (⑤) The recommendation has since been adopted, with some modifications, almost everywhere. [3점]

*respirator: 인공호흡기 **discernible: 식별 가능한
***criterion: 기준

40. 다음 글의 내용을 한 문장으로 요약하고자 한다. 빈칸 (A), (B)에 들어갈 말로 가장 적절한 것은?

> Some natural resource-rich developing countries tend to create an excessive dependence on their natural resources, which generates a lower productive diversification and a lower rate of growth. Resource abundance in itself need not do any harm: many countries have abundant natural resources and have managed to outgrow their dependence on them by diversifying their economic activity. That is the case of Canada, Australia, or the US, to name the most important ones. But some developing countries are trapped in their dependence on their large natural resources. They suffer from a series of problems since a heavy dependence on natural capital tends to exclude other types of capital and thereby interfere with economic growth.

↓

> Relying on rich natural resources without __(A)__ economic activities can be a __(B)__ to economic growth.

	(A)		(B)
①	varying	.....	barrier
②	varying	.....	shortcut
③	limiting	.....	challenge
④	limiting	.....	barrier
⑤	connecting	.....	shortcut

05회

[41 ~ 42] 다음 글을 읽고, 물음에 답하시오.

Animal studies have dealt with the distances creatures may keep between themselves and members of other species. These distances determine the functioning of the so-called 'flight or fight' mechanism. As an animal senses what it considers to be a predator approaching within its 'flight' distance, it will quite simply run away. The distance at which this happens is amazingly (a) underline consistent, and Hediger, a Swiss biologist, claimed to have measured it remarkably precisely for some of the species that he studied. Naturally, it varies from species to species, and usually the larger the animal the (b) shorter its flight distance. I have had to use a long focus lens to take photographs of giraffes, which have very large flight distances. By contrast, I have several times nearly stepped on a squirrel in my garden before it drew attention to itself by suddenly escaping! We can only assume that this (c) variation in distance matches the animal's own assessment of its ability to accelerate and run.

The 'fight' distance is always (d) smaller than the flight distance. If a perceived predator approaches within the flight distance but the animal is trapped by obstacles or other predators and cannot (e) flee, it must stand its ground. Eventually, however, attack becomes the best form of defence, and so the trapped animal will turn and fight.

41. 윗글의 제목으로 가장 적절한 것은?

① How Animals Migrate Without Getting Lost
② Flight or Fight Mechanism: Still in Our Brain
③ Why the Size Matters in the Survival of Animals
④ Distances: A Determining Factor for Flight or Attack
⑤ Competition for Food Between Large and Small Animals

42. 밑줄 친 (a) ~ (e) 중에서 문맥상 낱말의 쓰임이 적절하지 <u>않은</u> 것은?

① (a)　② (b)　③ (c)　④ (d)　⑤ (e)

[43 ~ 45] 다음 글을 읽고, 물음에 답하시오.

(A)

Eight-year-old Yolanda went to her grandmother's and proudly announced that she was going to be very successful when she grew up and asked her grandmother if she could give her any tips on how to achieve this. The grandmother nodded, took the girl by the hand, and walked (a) her to a nearby plant nursery. There, the two of them chose and purchased two small trees.

(B)

The grandmother smiled and said, "Remember this, and you will be successful in whatever you do: If you choose the safe option all of your life, you will never grow. But if you are willing to face the world with all of its challenges, you will learn from those challenges and grow to achieve great heights." Yolanda looked up at the tall tree, took a deep breath, and nodded (b) her head, realizing that her wise grandmother was right.

(C)

They returned home and planted one of them in the back yard and planted the other tree in a pot and kept it indoors. Then her grandmother asked her which of the trees (c) she thought would be more successful in the future. Yolanda thought for a moment and said the indoor tree would be more successful because it was protected and safe, while the outdoor tree had to cope with the elements. Her grandmother shrugged and said, "We'll see." Her grandmother took good care of both trees.

* elements: 악천후

(D)

In a few years, Yolanda, now a teenager, came to visit her grandmother again. Yolanda reminded her that (d) she had never really answered her question from when she was a little girl about how she could become successful when she grew up. The grandmother showed Yolanda the indoor tree and then took (e) her outside to have a look at the towering tree outside. "Which one is greater?" the grandmother asked. Yolanda replied, "The outside one. But that doesn't make sense; it had to cope with many more challenges than the one inside."

43. 주어진 글 (A)에 이어질 내용을 순서에 맞게 배열한 것으로 가장 적절한 것은?

① (B) − (D) − (C)　② (C) − (B) − (D)
③ (C) − (D) − (B)　④ (D) − (B) − (C)
⑤ (D) − (C) − (B)

44. 밑줄 친 (a) ~ (e) 중에서 가리키는 대상이 나머지 넷과 <u>다른</u> 것은?

① (a)　② (b)　③ (c)　④ (d)　⑤ (e)

45. 윗글에 관한 내용으로 적절하지 <u>않은</u> 것은?

① Yolanda는 자신이 크게 성공할 것이라고 자랑스럽게 말했다.
② 할머니는 역경으로부터 배울 수 있다고 말했다.
③ Yolanda는 집 밖에 심은 나무가 더 잘 자랄 거라고 말했다.
④ 할머니는 두 나무를 정성스럽게 돌보았다.
⑤ Yolanda는 십 대가 되어 할머니를 다시 방문했다.

★ 확인 사항
○ 답안지의 해당란에 필요한 내용을 정확히 기입(표기) 했는지 확인하시오.

18
001 ☐ favour ⓝ 부탁
002 ☐ industry ⓝ (특정 분야의) 업계
003 ☐ take a course 수업을 받다, 강좌를 듣다
004 ☐ lecture ⓝ 강연
005 ☐ inspiring ⓐ 고무적인, 영감을 주는
006 ☐ address ⓝ 주소
007 ☐ appreciate ⓥ 감사하다
008 ☐ assistance ⓝ 도움

19
009 ☐ dare ⓥ 감히 ~하다
010 ☐ break eye contact with ~에서 눈을 떼다, 시선을 피하다
011 ☐ for fear of ~할까봐 두려워서
012 ☐ get through ~을 마치다
013 ☐ make a fool of oneself 웃음거리가 되다
014 ☐ entire ⓐ 전체의, 온
015 ☐ ballroom ⓝ 강연장, 연회장
016 ☐ clap ⓥ 박수 치다
017 ☐ brightly ⓐⓓ 밝게, 환히
018 ☐ row ⓝ 줄, 열
019 ☐ cheer ⓥ 환호성을 지르다
020 ☐ barely ⓐⓓ 간신히
021 ☐ congratulate ⓥ 축하하다
022 ☐ hug ⓥ 껴안다, 포옹하다
023 ☐ nervous ⓐ 긴장한
024 ☐ embarrassed ⓐ 당황한

20
025 ☐ career ⓝ 일, 경력
026 ☐ look forward to ~을 고대하다
027 ☐ organization ⓝ 조직
028 ☐ statistics ⓝ 통계
029 ☐ standing ⓝ 순위, 지위
030 ☐ compare ⓥ 비교하다
031 ☐ progress ⓝ 발전, 진전
032 ☐ needless ⓐ 불필요한
033 ☐ distraction ⓝ 정신을 흩뜨리는 것
034 ☐ focus on ~에 집중하다
035 ☐ improve ⓥ 나아지다, 향상되다
036 ☐ look back 되돌아보다
037 ☐ encourage ⓥ 고무시키다, 용기를 북돋우다

21
038 ☐ occasion ⓝ (어떤 일이 일어나는) 때, 경우
039 ☐ concept ⓝ 개념
040 ☐ buffer ⓝ 완충 지대
041 ☐ destination ⓝ 목적지
042 ☐ away ⓐⓓ 떨어져
043 ☐ predict ⓥ 예측하다
044 ☐ in front of ~ 앞에
045 ☐ put on a brake 브레이크를 밟다
046 ☐ crash ⓥ 추돌[충돌]하다
047 ☐ act as ~으로 작용하다
048 ☐ respond ⓥ 반응하다
049 ☐ adapt to ~에 적응하다
050 ☐ similarly ⓐⓓ 마찬가지로
051 ☐ reduce ⓥ 줄이다, 축소하다
052 ☐ unexpected ⓐ 예상치 못한
053 ☐ definite ⓐ 확실한
054 ☐ relationship ⓝ 관계

22
055 ☐ media industry 미디어 업계[산업]
056 ☐ intelligent ⓐ 지적인
057 ☐ capable ⓐ 유능한
058 ☐ single-minded (한 가지 목적에만) 전념하는
059 ☐ pursuit ⓝ 추구
060 ☐ profit ⓝ 이익
061 ☐ nature ⓝ 본질
062 ☐ role ⓝ 역할
063 ☐ airwaves ⓝ 방송 전파, 채널
064 ☐ have access to ~에 접근하다
065 ☐ unlimited ⓐ 제한 없는, 무한한
066 ☐ priceless ⓐ 귀중한
067 ☐ asset ⓝ 자산
068 ☐ necessarily ⓐⓓ 반드시
069 ☐ long-lasting ⓐ 장기적인
070 ☐ responsibility ⓝ 책임
071 ☐ promote ⓥ 증진하다
072 ☐ public good ⓝ 공익

23
073 ☐ in addition to ~뿐만 아니라
074 ☐ a wide range of 광범위한
075 ☐ participant ⓝ 참여자
076 ☐ take part in ~에 참여하다
077 ☐ relaxation ⓝ 휴식
078 ☐ release ⓝ 분출구 ⓥ 분출하다
079 ☐ pressure ⓝ 압박
080 ☐ tension ⓝ 긴장
081 ☐ passive ⓐ 수동적인
082 ☐ spectator ⓝ 구경꾼, 관중
083 ☐ electronic ⓐ 전자적인, 전자의
084 ☐ amusement ⓝ 오락
085 ☐ significant ⓐ 중요한
086 ☐ pursue ⓥ 추구하다
087 ☐ competitive ⓐ 경쟁적인
088 ☐ hostility ⓝ 적의, 반감
089 ☐ aggression ⓝ 공격성
090 ☐ struggle against ~와 맞서 싸우다
091 ☐ adventurous ⓐ 모험적인
092 ☐ high-risk 위험성이 높은
093 ☐ opportunity ⓝ 기회
094 ☐ cooperate ⓥ 협력하다, 협조하다
095 ☐ promote ⓥ 촉진하다
096 ☐ economic ⓐ 경제의
097 ☐ trend ⓝ 동향, 경향

24
098 ☐ contain ⓥ ~이 들어[함유되어]있다
099 ☐ ingredient ⓝ 성분, 재료
100 ☐ regulation ⓝ 규제
101 ☐ sweetener ⓝ 감미료
102 ☐ separately ⓐⓓ 각각, 개별적으로
103 ☐ requirement ⓝ 요구
104 ☐ convey ⓥ 전달하다
105 ☐ indicate ⓥ 나타내다, 보여 주다
106 ☐ serving ⓝ 1인분, 1회 제공량
107 ☐ nowhere ⓐⓓ 어디에도
108 ☐ booster ⓝ 촉진제
109 ☐ hidden ⓐ 숨겨진
110 ☐ intake ⓝ 섭취량

25
111 ☐ injury ⓝ 부상
112 ☐ rate ⓝ 비율
113 ☐ decrease ⓥ 줄다, 감소하다
114 ☐ steadily ⓐⓓ 꾸준히
115 ☐ gap ⓝ 격차, 차이
116 ☐ out of ~ 중에서, ~로부터

26
117 ☐ mathematician ⓝ 수학자
118 ☐ astronomer ⓝ 천문학자
119 ☐ devote A to B A를 B에 바치다
120 ☐ initially ⓐⓓ 처음에는
121 ☐ optics ⓝ 광학
122 ☐ telescope ⓝ 망원경
123 ☐ grind ⓥ (칼 등을) 갈다
124 ☐ motion ⓝ 운동
125 ☐ universal gravitation 만유인력
126 ☐ wide-ranging ⓐ 광범위한
127 ☐ achievement ⓝ 업적, 성취
128 ☐ accurate ⓐ 정확한
129 ☐ astronomical ⓐ 천문학의
130 ☐ carry out ~을 수행하다
131 ☐ moon ⓝ 위성
132 ☐ description ⓝ 기술, 설명, 묘사

27
133 ☐ flower arranging 꽃꽂이
134 ☐ contest ⓝ 대회
135 ☐ exhibit ⓥ 전시
136 ☐ category ⓝ 부문, 범주
137 ☐ enroll in ~에 등록하다
138 ☐ home economics (학과) 가정
139 ☐ professional ⓝ 전문가 ⓐ 전문적인
140 ☐ contestant ⓝ 참가자
141 ☐ material ⓝ 재료
142 ☐ arrangement ⓝ 배치, 배열, 배열 방법
143 ☐ on display 전시 중인

28
144 ☐ attract one's attention ~의 관심을 끌다
145 ☐ satisfy ⓥ 충족시키다
146 ☐ instinct ⓝ 본능
147 ☐ feather ⓝ 깃털
148 ☐ randomly ⓐⓓ 무작위로
149 ☐ hole ⓝ 구멍
150 ☐ exchange ⓥ 교체하다
151 ☐ easily ⓐⓓ 쉽게
152 ☐ automatically ⓐⓓ 자동으로, 저절로
153 ☐ fully ⓐⓓ 완전히, 충분히
154 ☐ charge ⓥ 충전하다
155 ☐ run ⓥ 작동하다
156 ☐ press ⓥ 누르다
157 ☐ device ⓝ 기기, 장치
158 ☐ install ⓥ 장착하다, 설치하다

29
159 ☐ commercial ⓐ 민간의, 상업적인
160 ☐ airway ⓝ 항로
161 ☐ physical ⓐ 물리적인
162 ☐ structure ⓝ 구조(물)
163 ☐ fixed ⓐ 고정된

30
164 ☐ width ⓝ 폭
165 ☐ defined ⓐ 정해진
166 ☐ separate ⓥ 분리시키다
167 ☐ opposite ⓐ 반대의
168 ☐ direction ⓝ 방향
169 ☐ vertical ⓐ 상하의, 수직의
170 ☐ aircraft ⓝ 항공기
171 ☐ flight ⓝ 비행(기), 항공편
172 ☐ cover ⓥ (거리를) 이동하다
173 ☐ intense ⓐ 강도 높은
174 ☐ takeoff ⓝ 이륙
175 ☐ landing ⓝ 착륙
176 ☐ portion ⓝ 부분
177 ☐ assess ⓥ 평가하다
178 ☐ collision ⓝ 충돌
179 ☐ surrounding ⓐ 주위의, 주변의
180 ☐ crash ⓝ (비행기의) 추락
181 ☐ malfunction ⓝ 오작동, 기능 불량
182 ☐ tend ⓥ ~하는 경향이 있다

30
183 ☐ aroma ⓝ 향기
184 ☐ excite ⓥ 자극하다, 흥분시키다
185 ☐ drift ⓥ 떠다니다
186 ☐ detect ⓥ 감지하다
187 ☐ ancient ⓐ 고대의
188 ☐ come upon an idea 생각이 떠오르다
189 ☐ atom ⓝ 원자
190 ☐ suggest ⓥ 생각나게 하다, 암시하다
191 ☐ particle ⓝ 알갱이, 입자
192 ☐ vision ⓝ 시야
193 ☐ disprove ⓥ 틀렸음을 입증하다
194 ☐ puddle ⓝ 물웅덩이
195 ☐ gradually ⓐⓓ 점차
196 ☐ dry out 메마르다, 고갈되다
197 ☐ disappear ⓥ 사라지다
198 ☐ reason ⓥ 추론하다
199 ☐ steam ⓝ 수증기
200 ☐ conserve ⓥ 보존하다
201 ☐ inspire ⓥ 영감을 주다
202 ☐ take the credit for ~의 공적을 인정받다
203 ☐ theory ⓝ 이론

31
204 ☐ contemporary ⓐ 현대의
205 ☐ buddhist ⓐ 불교의
206 ☐ remarkable ⓐ 경이로운, 주목할 만한
207 ☐ silence ⓝ 침묵, 정적
208 ☐ dangerous ⓐ 위험한
209 ☐ situation ⓝ 상황
210 ☐ weakness ⓝ 약함
211 ☐ precious ⓐ 소중한
212 ☐ very ⓐ 바로 그
213 ☐ pass away (존재하던 것이) 없어지다
214 ☐ china ⓝ 자기, 도자기 ⓐ 자기의, 도자기의
215 ☐ bowl ⓝ 그릇
216 ☐ sooner or later 언젠가, 곧, 조만간
217 ☐ struggle ⓝ 고행, 고투, 분투
218 ☐ unstable ⓐ 불안정한
219 ☐ inevitable ⓐ 피할 수 없는
220 ☐ wound ⓝ 상처 ⓥ 상처 입히다
221 ☐ loss ⓝ 상실, 손실

05회

222 intimate ⓐ 친밀한
223 companion ⓝ 동반자
224 cast ⓝ 색조, 빛깔
225 twilight ⓝ 황혼
226 mountainside ⓝ 산 중턱, 산허리
227 lasting ⓐ 지속되는
228 fragility ⓝ 연약함
229 stability ⓝ 안정성
230 harmony ⓝ 조화
231 diversity ⓝ 다양성

32
232 immediately ⓐⓓ 즉시
233 practice ⓥ 실행
234 rub ⓥ 문지르다
235 energetically ⓐⓓ 힘차게, 열심히
236 on and on 계속해서
237 impatient ⓐ 참을성이 없는
238 discouraged ⓐ 풀이 죽은, 낙담한
239 rest 쉬다, 휴식을 취하다
240 altogether ⓐⓓ 완전히
241 completely ⓐⓓ 완전히
242 actually ⓐⓓ 사실은
243 carry on ~을 계속하다
244 in advance 미리
245 suitable ⓐ 적합한

33
246 translate A into B A를 B로 번역하다
247 academic ⓐ 학문적인, 이론적인
248 tool ⓝ 도구
249 theorist ⓝ 이론가
250 note ⓥ 지적하다
251 unchanged ⓐ 원래대로의
252 state ⓝ 상태
253 on the contrary 도리어, 반대로
254 means ⓝ 수단
255 figure out ~을 알아내다[이해하다]
256 end up with 결국 ~하게 되다
257 crucial ⓐ 중요한
258 discovery ⓝ 발견
259 common ⓐ 흔한, 일반적인
260 term ⓝ 용어, 말
261 as opposed to ~와 대조적으로
262 come up with ~을 떠올리다
263 clarify ⓥ 명확하게 하다

34
264 genetics ⓝ 유전학
265 suspect ⓥ 의심하다
266 gene ⓝ 유전자
267 under control 통제 하에 있는, 통제되는
268 obey ⓥ 복종하다
269 identical twin 일란성 쌍둥이
270 mid-life 중년
271 specific ⓐ 특정한
272 instruct ⓥ 명령하다, 지시하다
273 initiate ⓥ 시작되게 하다
274 possibility ⓝ 가능성
275 turn off ~을 차단하다[끄다]
276 recognize ⓥ 인정하다, 인지하다
277 environmental ⓐ 환경적인

278 factor ⓝ 요인
279 toxin ⓝ 독소
280 contribute to ~의 원인이 되다
281 notion ⓝ 생각, 개념
282 relatively ⓐⓓ 비교적
283 makeup ⓝ 구성
284 preference ⓝ 선호
285 cure ⓥ 치료하다
286 fatal ⓐ 치명적인
287 immediately ⓐⓓ 직접적으로, 즉각
288 influence ⓥ 영향을 주다
289 blueprint ⓝ 청사진, 설계도

35
290 superstition ⓝ 미신
291 surround ⓥ 둘러싸다, 에워싸다
292 theater ⓝ 극장
293 play ⓝ 연극
294 audience ⓝ 관객
295 rehearse ⓥ 예행연습하다
296 rehearsal ⓝ 예행연습
297 famous ⓐ 유명한
298 tragedy ⓝ 비극
299 curse ⓥ 저주하다
300 avoid ⓥ 피하다
301 say out loud 소리 내어 말하다
302 theatrical ⓐ 극장의, 연극의
303 interaction ⓝ 상호 작용
304 performance ⓝ 연기
305 be set in ~을 배경으로 하다
306 by accident 우연히
307 legend has it that 전설에 따르면 ~이다

36
308 habit ⓝ 습관
309 create ⓥ 만들다
310 foundation ⓝ 토대, 기초
311 mastery ⓝ 숙달, 통달
312 basic ⓐ 기본적인
313 movement ⓝ 움직임
314 automatic ⓐ 자동의, 자동적인
315 focus on ~에 집중하다
316 chunk ⓝ (큰) 덩어리, 상당히 많은 양
317 memorize ⓥ 암기하다
318 mental ⓐ 정신의, 마음의
319 effortful ⓐ 노력이 필요한
320 fall into ... ...에 빠져들다
321 mindless ⓐ 아무 생각 없이 하는
322 repetition ⓝ 반복
323 let ~ slide ~을 되어가는 대로 내버려 두다
324 come at a cost 대가가 따르다
325 develop ⓥ 발달하다
326 fluency ⓝ 유창함
327 sensitive ⓐ 민감한
328 attempt ⓥ 시도하다
329 detail ⓝ 세부 사항
330 backbone ⓝ 중추, 근간

37
331 regardless of ~에 관계없이
332 agriculture ⓝ 농경
333 undeniable ⓐ 부인할 수 없는

334 support ⓥ 부양하다, 지지하다
335 require ⓥ 필요로 하다, 요구하다
336 crop ⓝ 농작물
337 sustain ⓥ 지탱하다, 부양하다
338 population ⓝ 인구
339 increase ⓥ 증가하다
340 qualitative ⓐ 질적인
341 estimate ⓝ 추정치 ⓥ 추정하다
342 vary ⓥ 다양하다, 다르다
343 evidence ⓝ 증거
344 point to ~을 보여주다, 시사하다
345 established ⓐ 확립된
346 store ⓥ 저장하다

38
347 yet ⓐⓓ 하지만
348 program ⓥ 프로그램을 설정하다
349 position ⓝ 위치, 배치
350 ordinary ⓐ 보통의
351 suggest ⓥ 제안[제의]하다
352 move ⓝ (체스의) 수
353 boundary ⓝ 경계(선)
354 capability ⓝ 능력
355 remarkably ⓐⓓ 대단히, 두드러지게
356 grandmaster ⓝ 거장
357 sacrifice ⓥ 희생시키다
358 seemingly ⓐⓓ 겉보기에
359 capture ⓝ 잡힘, 포획, 생포
360 insane ⓐ 비상식적인
361 praise ⓥ 칭송하다
362 pay off 성과를 거두다

39
363 case ⓝ 경우
364 cease ⓥ 멈추다
365 function ⓝ 기능 ⓥ 기능하다
366 widely ⓐⓓ 널리
367 transplant ⓝ 이식
368 perform ⓥ 행하다
369 surgeon ⓝ 외과 의사, 외과 전문의
370 era ⓝ 시대
371 realization ⓝ 인식, 깨달음
372 organ ⓝ 장기
373 brain death 뇌사
374 recommendation ⓝ 권고, 추천
375 absence ⓝ 부재
376 central nervous system 중추 신경계
377 adopt ⓥ 받아들이다, 채택하다
378 modification ⓝ 수정

40
379 tend to do ~하는 경향이 있다
380 excessive ⓐ 지나친, 과도한
381 dependence ⓝ 의존
382 generate ⓥ 만들어 내다
383 productive ⓐ 생산적인
384 diversification ⓝ 다양화
385 growth ⓝ 성장
386 abundance ⓝ 풍요, 풍부함
387 in oneself 그 자체로는
388 do harm 해를 끼치다
389 abundant ⓐ 풍부한

390 outgrow ⓥ ~에서 벗어나다
391 diversify ⓥ 다양화하다
392 economic activity 경제 활동
393 trap ⓥ 가두다
394 capital ⓝ 자본(금), 자원
395 exclude ⓥ 배제하다
396 thereby ⓐⓓ 그로 인해
397 interfere with ~을 방해하다
398 rely on ~에 의존하다
399 varying ⓐ 다양화하는 것
400 barrier ⓝ 장벽
401 shortcut ⓝ 지름길
402 limiting ⓐ 제한[한정]하는
403 connecting ⓐ 연결하는

41~42
404 deal with ~을 다루다
405 determine ⓥ 결정짓다, 결정하다
406 functioning ⓝ 기능
407 flight or fight 도주 또는 공격
408 predator ⓝ 포식자
409 consistent ⓐ 일관적인
410 measure ⓥ 측정하다
411 remarkably ⓐⓓ 놀라울 만큼
412 precisely ⓐⓓ 정확하게
413 assume ⓥ 추정하다, 가정하다
414 variation ⓝ 차이, 변화
415 assessment ⓝ 평가
416 accelerate ⓥ 가속화하다
417 perceive ⓥ 인식하다
418 obstacle ⓝ 장애물
419 flee ⓥ 달아나다, 도망가다
420 stand one's ground 버티다, 공격에 견디다
421 migrate ⓥ 이주하다
422 survival ⓝ 생존
423 determining ⓐ 결정적인
424 competition ⓝ 경쟁

43~45
425 announce ⓥ 선언하다, 알리다
426 achieve ⓥ 성취하다
427 nod ⓥ (머리를) 끄덕이다
428 plant nursery 식물 묘목장
429 purchase ⓥ 사다, 구매하다
430 option ⓝ 선택
431 all of one's life 평생
432 be willing to 기꺼이 ~하려고 하다
433 face ⓥ (대담하게) 맞서다
434 challenge ⓝ 역경, 도전
435 height ⓝ (성공, 성취에서 높은) 단계, 최고조
436 take a deep breath 심호흡을 하다
437 back yard 뒷마당
438 indoors ⓐⓓ 실내에
439 outdoor ⓐ 집 밖의
440 cope with ~에 대처하다
441 shrug ⓥ 어깨를 으쓱하다
442 take care of ~을 돌보다
443 remind ⓥ 일깨워주다
444 towering ⓐ 높이 솟은, 우뚝 솟은
445 reply ⓥ 대답하다
446 make sense 이해가 되다, 일리가 있다

TEST A-B 각 단어의 뜻을 [A] 영어는 우리말로, [B] 우리말은 영어로 쓰시오.

A	English	Korean
01	contribute to	
02	estimate	
03	end up with	
04	sacrifice	
05	carry on	
06	cease	
07	satisfy	
08	insane	
09	assess	
10	diversification	
11	collision	
12	as opposed to	
13	dry out	
14	fragility	
15	take the credit for	
16	for fear of	
17	progress	
18	needless	
19	devote A to B	
20	gradually	

B	Korean	English
01	농경	
02	복종하다	
03	이식(하다)	
04	미신	
05	비극	
06	저주하다	
07	피할 수 없는	
08	민감한	
09	감지하다	
10	친밀한	
11	오작동, 기능 불량	
12	상하의, 수직의	
13	통계	
14	자산	
15	공격성	
16	~에 접근하다	
17	규제	
18	부상	
19	업적, 성취	
20	달아나다, 도망가다	

▶ A-D 정답 : 해설편 054쪽

TEST C-D 각 단어의 뜻을 골라 기호를 쓰시오.

C	English		Korean
01	stability	( )	ⓐ 추구하다
02	crucial	( )	ⓑ 중추, 근간
03	drift	( )	ⓒ 풍요, 풍부함
04	excessive	( )	ⓓ 지나친, 과도한
05	adapt to	( )	ⓔ ~에 적응하다
06	initiate	( )	ⓕ 능력
07	public good	( )	ⓖ 전달하다
08	abundance	( )	ⓗ 중요한
09	convey	( )	ⓘ 명확하게 하다
10	clarify	( )	ⓙ 증진하다
11	promote	( )	ⓚ 안정성
12	backbone	( )	ⓛ 시작되게 하다
13	assistance	( )	ⓜ 도움
14	pursue	( )	ⓝ 떠다니다
15	capability	( )	ⓞ 공익
16	measure	( )	ⓟ 부재
17	absence	( )	ⓠ 겉보기에
18	seemingly	( )	ⓡ 이주하다
19	in oneself	( )	ⓢ 그 자체로는
20	migrate	( )	ⓣ 측정하다

D	Korean		English
01	천문학자	( )	ⓐ come up with
02	~에 대처하다	( )	ⓑ come at a cost
03	~에 등록하다	( )	ⓒ hostility
04	유전학	( )	ⓓ modification
05	주의를 분산시키는 것	( )	ⓔ genetics
06	수정	( )	ⓕ legend has it that
07	적의, 반감	( )	ⓖ enroll in
08	전설에 따르면 ~이다	( )	ⓗ barely
09	미리	( )	ⓘ astronomer
10	간신히	( )	ⓙ let ~ slide
11	~을 떠올리다	( )	ⓚ established
12	확립된	( )	ⓛ distraction
13	대가가 따르다	( )	ⓜ pay off
14	성과를 거두다	( )	ⓝ cope with
15	~을 내버려 두다	( )	ⓞ in advance
16	기꺼이 ~하려고 하다	( )	ⓟ be willing to
17	예측하다	( )	ⓠ interfere with
18	그로 인해	( )	ⓡ predict
19	~을 방해하다	( )	ⓢ thereby
20	노력이 필요한	( )	ⓣ effortful

※ 영어 [독해] 파트만 수록한 문제지이므로 18번부터 시작합니다.

● 점수 표시가 없는 문항은 모두 2점   ● 문항수 28개 | 배점 63점 | 제한 시간 45분

18. 다음 글의 목적으로 가장 적절한 것은?

Dear Residents,

My name is Kari Patterson, and I'm the manager of the River View Apartments. It's time to take advantage of the sunny weather to make our community more beautiful. On Saturday, July 13 at 9 a.m., residents will meet in the north parking lot. We will divide into teams to plant flowers and small trees, pull weeds, and put colorful decorations on the lawn. Please join us for this year's Gardening Day, and remember no special skills or tools are required. Last year, we had a great time working together, so come out and make this year's event even better!

Warm regards,
Kari Patterson

① 아파트 내 정원 조성에 대한 의견을 수렴하려고
② 정원가꾸기 날 행사에 참여할 것을 독려하려고
③ 쓰레기를 지정된 장소에 버릴 것을 당부하려고
④ 지하 주차장 공사 일정에 대해 공지하려고
⑤ 정원박람회 개최 날짜 변경을 안내하려고

19. 다음 글에 드러난 Emma의 심경 변화로 가장 적절한 것은?

It was the championship race. Emma was the final runner on her relay team. She anxiously waited in her spot for her teammate to pass her the baton. Emma wasn't sure she could perform her role without making a mistake. Her hands shook as she thought, "What if I drop the baton?" She felt her heart rate increasing as her teammate approached. But as she started running, she received the baton smoothly. In the final 10 meters, she passed two other runners and crossed the finish line in first place! She raised her hands in the air, and a huge smile came across her face. As her teammates hugged her, she shouted, "We did it!" All of her hard training had been worth it.

① nervous   → excited   ② doubtful → regretful
③ confident   → upset   ④ hopeful   → disappointed
⑤ indifferent → amused

20. 다음 글에서 필자가 주장하는 바로 가장 적절한 것은?

Most people resist the idea of a true self-estimate, probably because they fear it might mean downgrading some of their beliefs about who they are and what they're capable of. As Goethe's maxim goes, it is a great failing "to see yourself as more than you are." How could you really be considered self-aware if you refuse to consider your weaknesses? Don't fear self-assessment because you're worried you might have to admit some things about yourself. The second half of Goethe's maxim is important too. He states that it is equally damaging to "value yourself at less than your true worth." We underestimate our capabilities just as much and just as dangerously as we overestimate other abilities. Cultivate the ability to judge yourself accurately and honestly. Look inward to discern what you're capable of and what it will take to unlock that potential.

* maxim: 격언

① 주관적 기준으로 타인을 평가하는 것을 피해야 한다.
② 정확하고 정직하게 자신을 평가하는 능력을 길러야 한다.
③ 자신이 가진 잠재력을 믿고 다양한 분야에 도전해야 한다.
④ 다른 사람과 비교하기보다는 자신의 성장에 주목해야 한다.
⑤ 문제를 해결하기 위해 근본 원인을 정확하게 분석해야 한다.

21. 밑줄 친 "Slavery resides under marble and gold."가 다음 글에서 의미하는 바로 가장 적절한 것은? [3점]

Take a look at some of the most powerful, rich, and famous people in the world. Ignore the trappings of their success and what they're able to buy. Look instead at what they're forced to trade in return—look at what success has cost them. Mostly? Freedom. Their work demands they wear a suit. Their success depends on attending certain parties, kissing up to people they don't like. It will require—inevitably—realizing they are unable to say what they actually think. Worse, it demands that they become a different type of person or do bad things. Sure, it might pay well—but they haven't truly examined the transaction. As Seneca put it, "Slavery resides under marble and gold." Too many successful people are prisoners in jails of their own making. Is that what you want? Is that what you're working hard toward? Let's hope not.

* trappings: 장식

① Your success requires you to act in ways you don't want to.
② Fame cannot be achieved without the help of others.
③ Comparing yourself to others makes you miserable.
④ Hard labor guarantees glory and happiness in the future.
⑤ There exists freedom in the appearance of your success.

22. 다음 글의 요지로 가장 적절한 것은?

If a firm is going to be saved by the government, it might be easier to concentrate on lobbying the government for more money rather than taking the harder decision of restructuring the company to be able to be profitable and viable in the long term. This is an example of something known as moral hazard—when government support alters the decisions firms take. For example, if governments rescue banks who get into difficulty, as they did during the credit crisis of 2007—08, this could encourage banks to take greater risks in the future because they know there is a possibility that governments will intervene if they lose money. Although the government rescue may be well intended, it can negatively affect the behavior of banks, encouraging risky and poor decision making.

* viable: 성장할 수 있는

① 기업에 대한 정부의 지원이 새로운 기술의 도입을 촉진한다.
② 현명한 소비자들은 윤리적 기업의 제품을 선택하는 경향이 있다.
③ 정부와 기업은 협력으로 사회적 문제의 해결책을 모색할 수 있다.
④ 정부의 구제는 기업의 의사 결정에 부정적인 영향을 미칠 수 있다.
⑤ 합리적 의사 결정은 다양한 대안에 대한 평가를 통해 이루어진다.

23. 다음 글의 주제로 가장 적절한 것은?

If there is little or no diversity of views, and all scientists see, think, and question the world in a similar way, then they will not, as a community, be as objective as they maintain they are, or at least aspire to be. The solution is that there should be far greater diversity in the practice of science: in gender, ethnicity, and social and cultural backgrounds. Science works because it is carried out by people who pursue their curiosity about the natural world and test their and each other's ideas from as many varied perspectives and angles as possible. When science is done by a diverse group of people, and if consensus builds up about a particular area of scientific knowledge, then we can have more confidence in its objectivity and truth.

* consensus: 일치

① value of acquiring scientific knowledge through trial and error
② necessity of various perspectives in practicing science
③ benefits of building good relationships among scientists
④ curiosity as a key factor in designing experiments
⑤ importance of specialization in scientific research

24. 다음 글의 제목으로 가장 적절한 것은?

We tend to break up time into units, such as weeks, months, and seasons; in a series of studies among farmers in India and students in North America, psychologists found that if a deadline is on the other side of a "break"—such as in the New Year—we're more likely to see it as remote, and, as a result, be less ready to jump into action. What you need to do in that situation is find another way to think about the timeframe. For example, if it's November and the deadline is in January, it's better to tell yourself you have to get it done "this winter" rather than "next year." The best approach is to view deadlines as a challenge that you have to meet within a period that's imminent. That way the stress is more manageable, and you have a better chance of starting—and therefore finishing—in good time.

* imminent: 임박한

① Delayed Deadlines: No Hurries, No Worries
② How Stress Affects Your Perception of Time
③ Why Do We Manage Our Tasks Worse in Winter?
④ Trick Your Mind to Get Your Work Done in Time
⑤ The Sooner You Start, The More Errors You Make

25. 다음 도표의 내용과 일치하지 <u>않는</u> 것은?

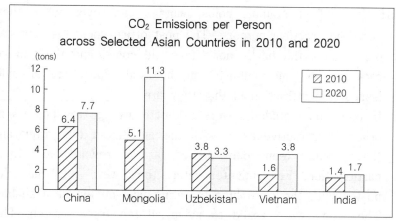

CO₂ Emissions per Person
across Selected Asian Countries in 2010 and 2020

The graph above shows the amount of CO₂ emissions per person across selected Asian countries in 2010 and 2020. ① All the countries except Uzbekistan had a greater amount of CO₂ emissions per person in 2020 than that in 2010. ② In 2010, the amount of CO₂ emissions per person of China was the largest among the five countries, followed by that of Mongolia. ③ However, in 2020, Mongolia surpassed China in terms of the amount of CO₂ emissions per person, with the amount of Mongolia more than twice that of China. ④ In 2010, Uzbekistan produced a larger amount of CO₂ emissions per person than Vietnam, while the opposite was true in 2020. ⑤ Among the five countries, India was the only one where the amount of CO₂ emissions per person was less than 2 tons in 2020.

26. Henry David Thoreau에 관한 다음 글의 내용과 일치하지 <u>않는</u> 것은?

Henry David Thoreau was born in Concord, Massachusetts in 1817. When he was 16, he entered Harvard College. After graduating, Thoreau worked as a schoolteacher but he quit after two weeks. In June of 1838 he set up a school with his brother John. However, he had hopes of becoming a nature poet. In 1845, he moved into a small self-built house near Walden Pond. At Walden, Thoreau did an incredible amount of reading. The journal he wrote there became the source of his most famous book, *Walden*. In his later life, Thoreau traveled to the Maine woods, to Cape Cod, and to Canada. At the age of 43, he ended his travels and returned to Concord. Although his works were not widely read during his lifetime, he never stopped writing, and his works fill 20 volumes.

① 졸업한 후에 교사로 일했다.
② 자연 시인이 되기를 희망했다.
③ Walden에서 엄청난 양의 독서를 했다.
④ 43세에 여행을 마치고 Concord로 돌아왔다.
⑤ 그의 작품은 그의 일생 동안 널리 읽혔다.

27. 2024 Future Engineers Camp에 관한 다음 안내문의 내용과 일치하지 <u>않는</u> 것은?

2024 Future Engineers Camp

Calling all young creators! Join us at Southside Maker Space to explore the wonders of engineering with exciting activities.

Date: Saturday, July 20 & Sunday, July 21
Time: 10 a.m. − 4 p.m.
Ages: 14 to 16
Participation Fee: $100

Day 1 − Robotics Workshop
• Learn basic coding skills.
• Work in teams to build mini-robots.

Day 2 − Flying Challenge
• Make and test toy airplanes.
• Participate in an airplane flying race.

Notes
• Lunch is included in the participation fee.
• All tools and materials for the projects are provided.

For more information, please visit www.southsidemaker.com.

① 오전 10시부터 오후 4시까지 진행된다.
② 참가비는 100달러이다.
③ 기본적인 코딩 기술을 배운다.
④ 장난감 비행기를 만들고 테스트한다.
⑤ 점심 식사는 참가비에 포함되지 않는다.

28. Taste the City에 관한 다음 안내문의 내용과 일치하는 것은?

Taste the City

Experience Jamestown's diverse and delicious food culture all in one place. Enjoy tasty treats, and discover new restaurants!

When & Where
• September 6th − 8th (10 a.m. − 9 p.m.)
• Grand Park

Highlights
• 30 kinds of food samples provided by local restaurants
• Live music performances each evening
• Cooking classes with experienced chefs

Entry Tickets
• Adult: $15
• Child: $10

※ No pre-reservations necessary, just show up and enjoy.

① 9월 6일부터 일주일 동안 열린다.
② 라이브 음악 공연이 하루 종일 진행된다.
③ 숙련된 요리사들과의 요리 수업이 있다.
④ 어른과 아이의 입장권 가격은 동일하다.
⑤ 사전 예약이 필요하다.

29. 다음 글의 밑줄 친 부분 중, 어법상 틀린 것은? [3점]

The built-in capacity for smiling is proven by the remarkable observation ① that babies who are congenitally both deaf and blind, who have never seen a human face, also start to smile at around 2 months. However, smiling in blind babies eventually ② disappears if nothing is done to reinforce it. Without the right feedback, smiling dies out. But here's a fascinating fact: blind babies will continue to smile if they are cuddled, bounced, nudged, and tickled by an adult — anything to let ③ them know that they are not alone and that someone cares about them. This social feedback encourages the baby to continue smiling. In this way, early experience operates with our biology ④ to establish social behaviors. In fact, you don't need the cases of blind babies to make the point. Babies with sight smile more at you when you look at them or, better still, ⑤ smiling back at them.

* congenitally: 선천적으로 ** cuddle: 껴안다
*** nudge: 팔꿈치로 쿡쿡 찌르다

30. 다음 글의 밑줄 친 부분 중, 문맥상 낱말의 쓰임이 적절하지 않은 것은? [3점]

Because people tend to adapt, interrupting positive things with negative ones can actually increase enjoyment. Take commercials. Most people hate them, so ① removing them should make shows or other entertainment more enjoyable. But the opposite is true. Shows are actually ② more enjoyable when they're broken up by annoying commercials. Because these less enjoyable moments break up adaptation to the ③ positive experience of the show. Think about eating chocolate chips. The first chip is delicious: sweet, melt-in-your-mouth goodness. The second chip is also pretty good. But by the fourth, fifth, or tenth chip in a row, the goodness is no longer as pleasurable. We adapt. Interspersing positive experiences with less positive ones, however, can ④ accelerate adaptation. Eating a Brussels sprout between chocolate chips or viewing commercials between parts of TV shows disrupts the process. The less positive moment makes the ⑤ following positive one new again and thus more enjoyable.

* intersperse: 흩뿌리다 ** Brussels sprout: 방울양배추

[31~34] 다음 빈칸에 들어갈 말로 가장 적절한 것을 고르시오.

31. We collect stamps, coins, vintage cars even when they serve no practical purpose. The post office doesn't accept the old stamps, the banks don't take old coins, and the vintage cars are no longer allowed on the road. These are all side issues; the attraction is that they are in _____. In one study, students were asked to arrange ten posters in order of attractiveness — with the agreement that afterward they could keep one poster as a reward for their participation. Five minutes later, they were told that the poster with the third highest rating was no longer available. Then they were asked to judge all ten from scratch. The poster that was no longer available was suddenly classified as the most beautiful. In psychology, this phenomenon is called *reactance*: when we are deprived of an option, we suddenly deem it more attractive.

① short supply   ② good shape
③ current use   ④ great excess
⑤ constant production

32. If we've invested in something that hasn't repaid us — be it money in a failing venture, or time in an unhappy relationship — we find it very difficult to walk away. This is the sunk cost fallacy. Our instinct is to continue investing money or time as we hope that our investment will prove to be worthwhile in the end. Giving up would mean acknowledging that we've wasted something we can't get back, and that thought is so painful that we prefer to avoid it if we can. The problem, of course, is that if something really is a bad bet, then staying with it simply increases the amount we lose. Rather than walk away from a bad five-year relationship, for example, we turn it into a bad 10-year relationship; rather than accept that we've lost a thousand dollars, we lay down another thousand and lose that too. In the end, by delaying the pain of admitting our problem, we only add to it. Sometimes we just have to _____.

① reduce profit
② offer rewards
③ cut our losses
④ stick to the plan
⑤ pay off our debt

33. On our little world, light travels, for all practical purposes, instantaneously. If a lightbulb is glowing, then of course it's physically where we see it, shining away. We reach out our hand and touch it: It's there all right, and unpleasantly hot. If the filament fails, then the light goes out. We don't see it in the same place, glowing, illuminating the room years after the bulb breaks and it's removed from its socket. The very notion seems nonsensical. But if we're far enough away, an entire sun can go out and we'll continue to see it shining brightly; we won't learn of its death, it may be, for ages to come — in fact, for how long it takes light, which travels fast but not infinitely fast, to cross the intervening vastness. The immense distances to the stars and the galaxies mean that we _____. [3점]

* instantaneously: 순간적으로 ** intervene: 사이에 들다

① see everything in space in the past
② can predict when our sun will go out
③ lack evidence of life on other planets
④ rely on the sun as a measure of time
⑤ can witness the death of a star as it dies

34. Financial markets do more than take capital from the rich and lend it to everyone else. They enable each of us to smooth consumption over our lifetimes, which is a fancy way of saying that we don't have to spend income at the same time we earn it. Shakespeare may have admonished us to be neither borrowers nor lenders; the fact is that most of us will be both at some point. If we lived in an agrarian society, we would have to eat our crops reasonably soon after the harvest or find some way to store them. Financial markets are a more sophisticated way of managing the harvest. We can spend income now that we have not yet earned — as by borrowing for college or a home — or we can earn income now and spend it later, as by saving for retirement. The important point is that _____, allowing us much more flexibility in life. [3점]

* admonish: 권고하다 ** agrarian: 농업(농민)의

① we can ignore the complexity of financial markets
② earning income has been divorced from spending it
③ financial markets can regulate our impulses
④ we sell our crops as soon as we harvest them
⑤ managing working hours has become easier than ever

35. 다음 글에서 전체 흐름과 관계 <u>없는</u> 문장은?

As the old joke goes: "Software, free. User manual, $10,000." But it's no joke. A couple of high-profile companies make their living selling instruction and paid support for free software. The copy of code, being mere bits, is free. The lines of free code become valuable to you only through support and guidance. ① A lot of medical and genetic information will go this route in the coming decades. ② Right now getting a full copy of all your DNA is very expensive ($10,000), but soon it won't be. ③ The public exposure of people's personal genetic information will undoubtedly cause serious legal and ethical problems. ④ The price is dropping so fast, it will be $100 soon, and then the next year insurance companies will offer to sequence you for free. ⑤ When a copy of your sequence costs nothing, the interpretation of what it means, what you can do about it, and how to use it — the manual for your genes — will be expensive.

* sequence: (유전자) 배열 순서를 밝히다

[36~37] 주어진 글 다음에 이어질 글의 순서로 가장 적절한 것을 고르시오.

36.

Brains are expensive in terms of energy. Twenty percent of the calories we consume are used to power the brain.

(A) By directing your attention, they perform tricks with their hands in full view. Their actions should give away the game, but they can rest assured that your brain processes only small bits of the visual scene.

(B) So brains try to operate in the most energy-efficient way possible, and that means processing only the minimum amount of information from our senses that we need to navigate the world. Neuroscientists weren't the first to discover that fixing your gaze on something is no guarantee of seeing it. Magicians figured this out long ago.

(C) This all helps to explain the prevalence of traffic accidents in which drivers hit pedestrians in plain view, or collide with cars directly in front of them. In many of these cases, the eyes are pointed in the right direction, but the brain isn't seeing what's really out there.

* prevalence: 널리 행하여짐 ** pedestrian: 보행자 *** collide: 충돌하다

① (A) — (C) — (B)   ② (B) — (A) — (C)
③ (B) — (C) — (A)   ④ (C) — (A) — (B)
⑤ (C) — (B) — (A)

37.

Buying a television is current consumption. It makes us happy today but does nothing to make us richer tomorrow. Yes, money spent on a television keeps workers employed at the television factory.

(A) The crucial difference between these scenarios is that a college education makes a young person more productive for the rest of his or her life; a sports car does not. Thus, college tuition is an investment; buying a sports car is consumption.

(B) But if the same money were invested, it would create jobs somewhere else, say for scientists in a laboratory or workers on a construction site, while also making us richer in the long run.

(C) Think about college as an example. Sending students to college creates jobs for professors. Using the same money to buy fancy sports cars for high school graduates would create jobs for auto workers. [3점]

① (A) − (C) − (B)   ② (B) − (A) − (C)
③ (B) − (C) − (A)   ④ (C) − (A) − (B)
⑤ (C) − (B) − (A)

[38~39] 글의 흐름으로 보아, 주어진 문장이 들어가기에 가장 적절한 곳을 고르시오.

38.

But the Net doesn't just connect us with businesses; it connects us with one another.

The Net differs from most of the mass media it replaces in an obvious and very important way: it's bidirectional. (①) We can send messages through the network as well as receive them, which has made the system all the more useful. (②) The ability to exchange information online, to upload as well as download, has turned the Net into a thoroughfare for business and commerce. (③) With a few clicks, people can search virtual catalogues, place orders, track shipments, and update information in corporate databases. (④) It's a personal broadcasting medium as well as a commercial one. (⑤) Millions of people use it to distribute their own digital creations, in the form of blogs, videos, photos, songs, and podcasts, as well as to critique, edit, or otherwise modify the creations of others.

* bidirectional: 두 방향으로 작용하는 ** thoroughfare: 통로

39.

Instead, automation created hundreds of millions of jobs in entirely new fields.

Imagine that seven out of ten working Americans got fired tomorrow. What would they all do? It's hard to believe you'd have an economy at all if you gave pink slips to more than half the labor force. But that is what the industrial revolution did to the workforce of the early 19th century. Two hundred years ago, 70 percent of American workers lived on the farm. (①) Today automation has eliminated all but 1 percent of their jobs, replacing them with machines. (②) But the displaced workers did not sit idle. (③) Those who once farmed were now manning the factories that manufactured farm equipment, cars, and other industrial products. (④) Since then, wave upon wave of new occupations have arrived— appliance repair person, food chemist, photographer, web designer—each building on previous automation. (⑤) Today, the vast majority of us are doing jobs that no farmer from the 1800s could have imagined.

* pink slip: 해고 통지서

40. 다음 글의 내용을 한 문장으로 요약하고자 한다. 빈칸 (A), (B)에 들어갈 말로 가장 적절한 것은?

Many things spark *envy*: ownership, status, health, youth, talent, popularity, beauty. It is often confused with jealousy because the physical reactions are identical. The difference: the subject of *envy* is a thing (status, money, health etc.). The subject of jealousy is the behaviour of a third person. *Envy* needs two people. Jealousy, on the other hand, requires three: Peter is jealous of Sam because the beautiful girl next door rings him instead. Paradoxically, with envy we direct resentments toward those who are most similar to us in age, career and residence. We don't envy businesspeople from the century before last. We don't envy millionaires on the other side of the globe. As a writer, I don't envy musicians, managers or dentists, but other writers. As a CEO you envy other, bigger CEOs. As a supermodel you envy more successful supermodels. Aristotle knew this: 'Potters envy potters.'

↓

Jealousy involves three parties, focusing on the ___(A)___ of a third person, whereas envy involves two individuals whose personal circumstances are most ___(B)___, with one person resenting the other.

	(A)		(B)
①	actions	......	different
②	possessions	......	unique
③	goals	......	ordinary
④	possessions	......	favorable
⑤	actions	......	alike

영어 영역(독해)

[41~42] 다음 글을 읽고, 물음에 답하시오.

We have biases that support our biases! If we're partial to one option—perhaps because it's more memorable, or framed to minimize loss, or seemingly consistent with a promising pattern—we tend to search for information that will (a) justify choosing that option. On the one hand, it's sensible to make choices that we can defend with data and a list of reasons. On the other hand, if we're not careful, we're (b) likely to conduct an imbalanced analysis, falling prey to a cluster of errors collectively known as "confirmation biases."

For example, nearly all companies include classic "tell me about yourself" job interviews as part of the hiring process, and many rely on these interviews alone to evaluate applicants. But it turns out that traditional interviews are actually one of the (c) least useful tools for predicting an employee's future success. This is because interviewers often subconsciously make up their minds about interviewees based on their first few moments of interaction and spend the rest of the interview cherry-picking evidence and phrasing their questions to (d) confirm that initial impression: "I see here you left a good position at your previous job. You must be pretty ambitious, right?" versus "You must not have been very committed, huh?" This means that interviewers can be prone to (e) noticing significant information that would clearly indicate whether this candidate was actually the best person to hire. More structured approaches, like obtaining samples of a candidate's work or asking how he would respond to difficult hypothetical situations, are dramatically better at assessing future success, with a nearly threefold advantage over traditional interviews.

41. 윗글의 제목으로 가장 적절한 것은?

① Bias Trap: How Our Preconceptions Mislead Us
② Utilize the Power of Similar Personality Types!
③ More Information Adds Up to Worse Choices
④ Why Are You Persuaded by Others' Perspectives?
⑤ Interviews: The Fairest Judgment for All Applicants

42. 밑줄 친 (a)~(e) 중에서 문맥상 낱말의 쓰임이 적절하지 <u>않은</u> 것은? [3점]

① (a)　② (b)　③ (c)　④ (d)　⑤ (e)

[43~45] 다음 글을 읽고, 물음에 답하시오.

(A)

On Saturday morning, Todd and his 5-year-old daughter Ava walked out of the store with the groceries they had just purchased. As they pushed their grocery cart through the parking lot, they saw a red car pulling into the space next to their pick-up truck. A young man named Greg was driving. "That's a cool car," Ava said to her dad. (a) He agreed and looked at Greg, who finished parking and opened his door.

(B)

By this time, Greg had already pulled one thin wheel out of his car and attached it to the frame. He was now pulling a second wheel out when he looked up and saw Todd standing near him. Todd said, "Hi there! Have a great weekend!" Greg seemed a bit surprised, but replied by wishing (b) him a great weekend too. Then Greg added, "Thanks for letting me have my independence." "Of course," Todd said.

(C)

As Todd finished loading his groceries, Greg's door remained open. Todd noticed Greg didn't get out of his car. But he was pulling something from his car. He put a metal frame on the ground beside his door. Remaining in the driver's seat, he then reached back into (c) his car to grab something else. Todd realized what he was doing and considered whether (d) he should try to help him. After a moment, he decided to approach Greg.

(D)

After Todd and Ava climbed into their truck, Ava became curious. So she asked why (e) he didn't offer to help the man with his wheelchair. Todd said, "Why do you insist on brushing your teeth without my help?" She answered, "Because I know how to!" He said, "And the man knows how to put together his wheelchair." Ava understood that sometimes the best way to help someone is to not help at all.

43. 주어진 글 (A)에 이어질 내용을 순서에 맞게 배열한 것으로 가장 적절한 것은?

① (B) − (D) − (C)　② (C) − (B) − (D)
③ (C) − (D) − (B)　④ (D) − (B) − (C)
⑤ (D) − (C) − (B)

44. 밑줄 친 (a)~(e) 중에서 가리키는 대상이 나머지 넷과 <u>다른</u> 것은?

① (a)　② (b)　③ (c)　④ (d)　⑤ (e)

45. 윗글에 관한 내용으로 적절하지 <u>않은</u> 것은?

① Ava는 차가 멋지다고 말했다.
② Greg는 얇은 바퀴를 프레임에 끼웠다.
③ Greg는 휠체어를 꺼내준 것에 감사하다고 말했다.
④ Todd는 Greg가 차에서 내리지 않은 것을 알아차렸다.
⑤ Ava는 트럭에 오른 후 호기심이 생겼다.

---

* 확인 사항

○ 답안지의 해당란에 필요한 내용을 정확히 기입(표기)했는지 확인 하시오.

[해설편 p.063]

[06회] 2024학년도 6월 **057**

18
001 manager ⓝ 관리인, 지배인
002 advantage ⓝ 이점, 혜택
003 sunny ⓐ 화창한
004 weather ⓝ 날씨, 기상
005 community ⓝ 공동체, 지역사회
006 resident ⓝ 주민
007 north ⓝ 북쪽
008 divide ⓥ 나누다
009 plant ⓥ 심다
010 weed ⓝ 잡초
011 colorful ⓐ 다채로운
012 decoration ⓝ 장식
013 lawn ⓝ 잔디밭
014 skill ⓝ 기술, 능력
015 tool ⓝ 도구
016 require ⓥ 필요로 하다
017 event ⓝ 행사, 이벤트

19
018 championship ⓝ 챔피언십, 선수권 대회
019 race ⓝ 경주, 달리기(시합)
020 runner ⓝ 경주자, 달리는 사람
021 relay ⓝ 계주, 릴레이
022 anxiously ⓐⓓ 걱정스럽게, 불안하게
023 spot ⓝ 지점, 장소, 곳, 현장
024 teammate ⓝ 팀 동료
025 perform ⓥ 수행하다, 공연하다
026 role ⓝ 역할
027 mistake ⓝ 실수
028 shake ⓥ 떨다, 떨리다
029 drop ⓥ 떨어뜨리다, 떨어지다
030 heart rate 심장박동수
031 increase ⓥ 증가하다, 늘다
032 receive ⓥ 받다
033 smoothly ⓐⓓ 원활하게
034 pass ⓥ 지나가다, 통과하다
035 finish line 결승선
036 raise ⓥ 올리다, 들어 올리다
037 air ⓝ 공중, 허공
038 huge ⓐ (모양·크기 등이) 거대한
039 shout ⓥ 외치다
040 training ⓝ 훈련, 연습
041 worth ⓐ ~할 가치가 있는

20
042 resist ⓥ 저항하다, 반대하다
043 true ⓐ 진정한, 참된
044 estimate ⓝ 평가, 추정
045 probably ⓐⓓ 아마도
046 fear ⓥ 두려워하다
047 downgrade ⓥ 격하시키다, 떨어뜨리다
048 belief ⓝ 생각, 믿음
049 capable ⓐ 능력이 있는
050 maxim ⓝ 격언, 금언
051 self-aware ⓐ 자기 인식이 있는
052 refuse ⓥ 거절하다, 거부하다
053 weakness ⓝ 약점
054 assessment ⓝ 평가
055 worry ⓥ 걱정하다
056 admit ⓥ 인정하다
057 second half 후반전

058 important ⓐ 중요한
059 state ⓥ 말하다, 진술하다
060 equally ⓐⓓ 똑같이
061 damaging ⓐ 해로운
062 value ⓥ 평가하다
063 underestimate ⓥ 과소평가하다
064 dangerously ⓐⓓ 위험하게, 위태롭게
065 overestimate ⓥ 과대평가하다
066 ability ⓝ 능력
067 cultivate ⓥ 기르다
068 accurately ⓐⓓ 정확하게, 정밀하게
069 honestly ⓐⓓ 정직하게, 솔직하게
070 inward ⓐ 마음속의, 내심의
071 discern ⓥ 분별하다, 식별하다
072 unlock ⓥ 드러내다
073 potential ⓝ 잠재력

21
074 powerful ⓐ 강력한, 강한
075 rich ⓐ 부유한
076 famous ⓐ 유명한
077 ignore ⓥ 무시하다
078 trappings ⓝ 장식물, 외양
079 success ⓝ 성공
080 instead ⓐⓓ 대신에
081 cost ⓝ 대가
082 mostly ⓐⓓ 대부분
083 freedom ⓝ 자유
084 demand ⓝ 요구 사항
085 wear ⓥ 입고 있다
086 suit ⓝ 정장
087 depend ⓥ ~에 달려 있다, 좌우되다
088 attend ⓥ 참석하다
089 certain ⓐ 특정한, 확실한
090 inevitably ⓐⓓ 필연적이다시피
091 realize ⓥ 깨닫다, 실현하다
092 are unable to ~할 수 없다
093 actually ⓐⓓ 실제로, 정말로
094 worse ⓐ 더 나쁜
095 type ⓝ 유형, 종류
096 truly ⓐⓓ 엄밀히, 정확히
097 examine ⓥ 검토하다, 조사하다
098 transaction ⓝ 거래
099 slavery ⓝ 노예제도
100 reside ⓥ 존재하다
101 marble ⓝ 대리석
102 prisoner ⓝ 죄수, 포로
103 jail ⓝ 감옥, 교도소
104 hard ⓐⓓ 열심히
105 hope ⓥ 바라다
106 achieve ⓥ 이루다, 성취하다
107 compare ⓥ 비교하다
108 miserable ⓐ 비참한, 불행한
109 labor ⓝ 노동
110 glory ⓝ 영광
111 future ⓝ 미래
112 appearance ⓝ (겉)모습, 외모

22
113 firm ⓝ 회사
114 save ⓥ 구하다
115 government ⓝ 정부

116 concentrate ⓥ 집중하다
117 lobby ⓥ 로비하다, 압력을 가하다
118 decision ⓝ 결정, 판단
119 restructure ⓥ 재구조화하다
120 profitable ⓐ 수익성이 있는
121 viable ⓐ 실행 가능한
122 long term 장기적인
123 moral hazard 도덕적 해이
124 alter ⓥ 바꾸다, 고치다
125 get into ~을 하게 되다
126 crisis ⓝ 위기
127 encourage ⓥ 장려하다
128 possibility ⓝ 가능성
129 although conj. 비록 ~이긴 하지만
130 rescue ⓝ 구조, 구제
131 intend ⓥ 의도하다
132 negatively ⓐⓓ 부정적으로
133 affect 영향을 미치다
134 risky ⓐ 위험한
135 poor ⓐ 좋지 못한

23
136 diversity ⓝ 다양성
137 view ⓝ 관점
138 scientists ⓝ 과학자
139 question ⓥ 질문하다
140 similar ⓐ 비슷한, 유사한
141 way ⓝ 방법, 방식
142 objective ⓐ 객관적인
143 maintain ⓥ 주장하다
144 at least 최소한
145 aspire ⓥ 열망하다
146 solution ⓝ 해결책
147 practice ⓝ 실행, 실천
148 ethnicity ⓝ 민족성
149 cultural ⓐ 문화의
150 background ⓝ 배경
151 carry out 수행하다
152 pursue ⓥ 추구하다
153 curiosity ⓝ 호기심
154 natural ⓐ 자연의
155 varied ⓐ 다양한
156 perspective ⓝ 관점, 시각
157 consensus ⓝ 합의, 의견 일치
158 particular ⓐ 특정한
159 area ⓝ 분야, 부문
160 knowledge ⓝ 지식
161 confidence ⓝ 신뢰, 자신감
162 truth ⓝ 진리, 진실

24
163 tend ⓥ (~하는) 경향이 있다
164 break up ~을 나누다(분해하다)
165 unit ⓝ 단위
166 season ⓝ 계절
167 farmer ⓝ 농부
168 psychologist ⓝ 심리학자
169 deadline ⓝ 마감일
170 remote ⓐ 멀리 떨어진, 원격의
171 situation ⓝ 상황
172 timeframe ⓝ 시간(기간)
173 rather than ~보다는

116 concentrate... (col 4)
174 approach ⓝ 접근법 ⓥ 접근하다
175 challenge ⓝ 도전
176 within prep 이내에
177 period ⓝ 기간
178 imminent ⓐ 임박한
179 manageable ⓐ 관리 가능한
180 chance ⓝ (특히 원하는 일이 일어날) 가능성
181 in good time 적시에, 제때에

25
182 show ⓥ 보여 주다
183 amount ⓝ 양
184 CO₂ 이산화탄소
185 emission ⓝ 배출, 방출
186 selected ⓐ 선택된
187 country ⓝ 국가
188 except prep 제외하고는
189 follow ⓥ (···의 뒤를) 따라가다
190 surpass ⓥ 능가하다, 넘어서다
191 twice ⓐⓓ 두 배로
192 produce ⓥ 생산하다
193 opposite ⓐ 반대
194 ton ⓝ 톤

26
195 schoolteacher ⓝ 교사
196 nature ⓝ 자연
197 journal ⓝ 일기, 기록
198 volume ⓝ 책, 권

27
199 Engineer ⓝ 공학자
200 participation ⓝ 참가
201 Robotics ⓝ 로봇 공학
202 Workshop ⓝ 워크숍
203 airplane ⓝ 비행기

28
204 taste ⓝ 맛
205 delicious ⓐ 아주 맛있는
206 food ⓝ 음식
207 culture ⓝ 문화
208 treat ⓝ 간식
209 discover ⓥ 발견하다
210 sample ⓝ 샘플
211 local ⓐ 지역의
212 performances ⓝ 공연
213 chef ⓝ 요리사
214 ticket ⓝ 티켓
215 prereservation 사전 예약
216 necessary ⓐ 필요한

29
217 capacity ⓝ 능력, 용량
218 smile ⓥ 미소 짓다
219 proven ⓥ 입증하다
220 remarkable ⓐ 놀라운
221 observation ⓝ 관찰
222 congenitally ⓐⓓ 선천적으로
223 deaf ⓐ 청각 장애가 있는
224 blind ⓐ 눈이 먼
225 eventually ⓐⓓ 결국

226 ☐ disappear ⓥ 사라지다
227 ☐ reinforce ⓥ 강화하다
228 ☐ feedback ⓝ 피드백
229 ☐ die out 사라지다, 자취를 감추다
230 ☐ fascinating ⓐ 대단히 흥미로운
231 ☐ cuddle ⓥ 껴안다
232 ☐ bounce ⓥ 튀다, 튀기다
233 ☐ nudge ⓥ 쿡 찌르다
234 ☐ tickle ⓥ 간지럽히다
235 ☐ social ⓐ 사회적인
236 ☐ early ⓐ 초(창)기의
237 ☐ operate ⓥ 작용하다
238 ☐ biology ⓝ 생물학
239 ☐ establish ⓥ 확립하다
240 ☐ behavior ⓝ 행동
241 ☐ sight ⓝ 시력

30
242 ☐ adapt ⓥ 적응하다
243 ☐ interrupt ⓥ 방해하다
244 ☐ positive ⓐ 긍정적인
245 ☐ negative ⓐ 부정적인
246 ☐ enjoyment ⓝ 즐거움
247 ☐ commercial ⓝ 광고
248 ☐ remove ⓥ 없애다
249 ☐ entertainment ⓝ 오락(물)
250 ☐ enjoyable ⓐ 즐거운
251 ☐ annoying ⓐ 짜증스러운
252 ☐ experience ⓝ 경험
253 ☐ melt ⓥ 녹다, 녹이다
254 ☐ no longer 더이상 ~아닌
255 ☐ pleasurable ⓐ 즐거운
256 ☐ intersperse ⓥ (…속에·사이에) 들어가다, 배치하다
257 ☐ Brussels sprout 방울양배추
258 ☐ between ⓟⓡⓔⓟ 사이[중간]에
259 ☐ disrupt ⓥ 방해하다
260 ☐ process ⓝ 과정, 절차

31
261 ☐ stamp ⓝ 우표
262 ☐ coin ⓝ 동전
263 ☐ vintage ⓐ 고전적인, 오래된
264 ☐ practical ⓐ 실용적인
265 ☐ purpose ⓝ 목적
266 ☐ attraction ⓝ 매력
267 ☐ arrange ⓥ 배열하다
268 ☐ poster ⓝ 포스터
269 ☐ agreement ⓝ 동의, 합의
270 ☐ afterward ⓐⓓ 그 후에
271 ☐ reward ⓝ 보상
272 ☐ rate ⓥ 평가하다
273 ☐ classify ⓥ 분류하다
274 ☐ psychology ⓝ 심리학
275 ☐ phenomenon ⓝ 현상
276 ☐ reactance ⓝ 반발
277 ☐ deprive ⓥ 빼앗다, 박탈하다

32
278 ☐ invest ⓥ 투자하다
279 ☐ repay ⓥ 갚다, 보답하다
280 ☐ venture ⓝ (벤처) 사업

281 ☐ relationship ⓝ 관계
282 ☐ fallacy ⓝ 오류
283 ☐ instinct ⓝ 본능
284 ☐ worthwhile ⓐ 가치 있는
285 ☐ in the end 결국에
286 ☐ acknowledge ⓥ 인정하다
287 ☐ waste ⓥ 낭비하다
288 ☐ prefer ⓥ 선호하다
289 ☐ stay with ~를 계속하다
290 ☐ simply ⓐⓓ 단순히
291 ☐ turn into ~으로 변하다
292 ☐ delay ⓥ 지연하다
293 ☐ losses ⓝ 손실, 손해

33
294 ☐ instantaneously ⓐⓓ 즉시, 순간적으로
295 ☐ lightbulb ⓝ 백열 전구
296 ☐ glow ⓥ 빛나다
297 ☐ reach out (손 등을) 뻗다
298 ☐ filament ⓝ 필라멘트
299 ☐ notion ⓝ 개념
300 ☐ nonsensical ⓐ 무의미한, 터무니없는
301 ☐ entire ⓐ 전체의
302 ☐ infinitely ⓐⓓ 무한히, 한없이
303 ☐ intervening ⓐ 사이에 있는
304 ☐ vastness ⓝ 광대함
305 ☐ immense ⓐ 엄청난
306 ☐ distance ⓝ 거리
307 ☐ past ⓝ 과거
308 ☐ predict ⓥ 예측하다
309 ☐ evidence ⓝ 증거
310 ☐ planet ⓝ 행성
311 ☐ rely on 기대다, 의존하다
312 ☐ measure ⓥ 측정하다
313 ☐ witness ⓥ 목격하다

34
314 ☐ financial ⓐ 재정의
315 ☐ market ⓝ 시장
316 ☐ capital ⓝ 자본
317 ☐ income ⓝ 수입
318 ☐ admonish ⓥ 훈계하다
319 ☐ neither A nor B A도 B도 아닌
320 ☐ agrarian ⓐ 농업의
321 ☐ crop ⓝ (농)작물
322 ☐ reasonably ⓐⓓ 상당히, 꽤
323 ☐ harvest ⓥ 수확하다
324 ☐ store ⓥ 저장하다
325 ☐ sophisticated ⓐ 정교한, 복잡한
326 ☐ manage ⓥ 관리하다
327 ☐ earn ⓥ 벌다
328 ☐ retirement ⓝ 은퇴
329 ☐ flexibility ⓝ 유연성, 탄력성

35
330 ☐ software ⓝ 소프트웨어
331 ☐ a couple of 몇 개의
332 ☐ highprofile 세간의 이목을 끄는
333 ☐ instruction ⓝ 지시, 설명서
334 ☐ guidance ⓝ 지도, 안내
335 ☐ genetic ⓐ 유전의
336 ☐ route ⓝ 길, 경로

337 ☐ decade ⓝ 10년
338 ☐ expensive ⓐ 비싼
339 ☐ exposure ⓝ 노출
340 ☐ undoubtedly ⓐⓓ 분명히, 확실히
341 ☐ serious ⓐ 심각한
342 ☐ legal ⓐ 법률과 관련된
343 ☐ ethical ⓐ 윤리적인
344 ☐ insurance ⓝ 보험
345 ☐ sequence ⓝ 서열, 순서
346 ☐ interpretation ⓝ 해석

36
347 ☐ brain ⓝ 뇌
348 ☐ energy ⓝ 에너지
349 ☐ calory ⓝ 칼로리
350 ☐ direct ⓥ ~로 향하다
351 ☐ trick ⓝ 묘기, 요령
352 ☐ minimum ⓐ 최소한의
353 ☐ sense ⓝ 감각
354 ☐ neuroscientist ⓝ 신경과학자
355 ☐ gaze ⓝ 시선, 응시
356 ☐ guarantee ⓝ 보장(하는 것)
357 ☐ explain ⓥ 설명하다
358 ☐ prevalence ⓝ 널리 퍼짐, 유행
359 ☐ accident ⓝ 사고
360 ☐ pedestrian ⓝ 보행자
361 ☐ collide ⓥ 충돌하다
362 ☐ in front of ~의 앞쪽에

37
363 ☐ television ⓝ 텔레비전
364 ☐ consumption ⓝ 소비
365 ☐ productive ⓐ 생산적인
366 ☐ sports car 스포츠카
367 ☐ tuition ⓝ 학비
368 ☐ investment ⓝ 투자
369 ☐ fancy ⓐ 화려한, 값비싼

38
370 ☐ bidirectional ⓐ 양방향의
371 ☐ commerce ⓝ 상업
372 ☐ virtual ⓐ 가상의
373 ☐ catalogue ⓝ 카탈로그
374 ☐ corporate ⓐ 기업의
375 ☐ medium ⓝ 매체
376 ☐ distribute ⓥ 배포하다

39
377 ☐ automation ⓝ 자동화
378 ☐ revolution ⓝ 혁명
379 ☐ displaced ⓐ 대체된, 쫓겨난
380 ☐ wave ⓝ 물결, 파도
381 ☐ occupation ⓝ 직업
382 ☐ appliance ⓝ 기구, 장치
383 ☐ vast ⓐ 광대한

40
384 ☐ envy ⓝ 부러움
385 ☐ ownership ⓝ 소유(권)
386 ☐ status ⓝ 지위
387 ☐ often ⓐⓓ 자주, 종종
388 ☐ jealousy ⓝ 질투

389 ☐ paradoxically ⓐⓓ 역설적으로
390 ☐ resentment ⓝ 원한, 분노
391 ☐ residence ⓝ 주택, 거주지
392 ☐ aristotle ⓝ 아리스토텔레스
393 ☐ potter ⓝ 도예가
394 ☐ circumstance ⓝ 상황

41~42
395 ☐ bias ⓝ 편견
396 ☐ support ⓥ 지원하다
397 ☐ partial ⓐ 부분의
398 ☐ seemingly ⓐⓓ 겉보기에는, 보아하니
399 ☐ information ⓝ 정보
400 ☐ imbalanced ⓐ 불균형의
401 ☐ confirmation ⓝ 확신
402 ☐ nearly ⓐⓓ 거의
403 ☐ include ⓥ 포함하다
404 ☐ subconsciously ⓐⓓ 잠재의식적으로
405 ☐ spend ⓥ 소비하다
406 ☐ cherry-picking 원하는 것만 선택하는 것
407 ☐ impression ⓝ 인상
408 ☐ ambitious ⓐ 야심 있는
409 ☐ candidate ⓝ 지원자, 응시자

43~45
410 ☐ walk out 걸어 나가다
411 ☐ grocery ⓝ 식료품점
412 ☐ attach ⓥ 붙이다
413 ☐ reply ⓥ 대답하다
414 ☐ independence ⓝ 독립
415 ☐ load ⓥ 짐을 싣다
416 ☐ beside ⓟⓡⓔⓟ 옆에
417 ☐ moment ⓝ 순간
418 ☐ climb ⓥ 오르다
419 ☐ curious ⓐ 궁금한, 호기심이 많은
420 ☐ insist ⓥ 고집하다
421 ☐ without ~없이

● 채점 : 맞은 개수 _____ / 80

TEST A-B 각 단어의 뜻을 [A] 영어는 우리말로, [B] 우리말은 영어로 쓰시오.

A	English	Korean
01	prisoner	
02	demand	
03	freedom	
04	miserable	
05	anxiously	
06	smoothly	
07	weakness	
08	diversity	
09	estimate	
10	resist	
11	perform	
12	transaction	
13	aspire	
14	decoration	
15	remote	
16	ethnicity	
17	intervene	
18	advantage	
19	consensus	
20	divide	

B	Korean	English
01	오류	
02	임박한	
03	강화하다	
04	포함하다	
05	고전적인, 오래된	
06	능력, 용량	
07	행동	
08	투자하다	
09	인정하다	
10	부러움	
11	매력	
12	지연하다	
13	일기, 기록	
14	참가	
15	가치 있는	
16	적응하다	
17	반발	
18	방해하다	
19	능가하다, 넘어서다	
20	화려한, 값비싼	

▶ A-D 정답 : 해설편 064쪽

TEST C-D 각 단어의 뜻을 골라 기호를 쓰시오.

C	English	( )	Korean
01	automation	( )	ⓐ 광고
02	nonsensical	( )	ⓑ 서열, 순서
03	accident	( )	ⓒ 다르다
04	vastness	( )	ⓓ 상황
05	sequence	( )	ⓔ 목격하다
06	differ	( )	ⓕ 소유
07	virtual	( )	ⓖ 사고들
08	ownership	( )	ⓗ 부분의
09	paid	( )	ⓘ 오르다
10	admonish	( )	ⓙ 가상의
11	capital	( )	ⓚ 자본
12	volume	( )	ⓛ 훈계하다
13	climb	( )	ⓜ 자동화
14	commercial	( )	ⓝ 독립
15	partial	( )	ⓞ 광대함
16	witness	( )	ⓟ 무의미한, 터무니없는
17	circumstance	( )	ⓠ 대신하다, 대체하다
18	replace	( )	ⓡ 짐을 싣다
19	independence	( )	ⓢ 유급의
20	load	( )	ⓣ 책, 권

D	Korean	( )	English
01	원한, 분노	( )	ⓐ prevalence
02	학비	( )	ⓑ resentment
03	상당히, 꽤	( )	ⓒ receive
04	소비하다	( )	ⓓ instruction
05	선천적으로	( )	ⓔ reasonably
06	수신하다	( )	ⓕ agrarian
07	배포하다	( )	ⓖ appliance
08	널리 퍼짐, 유행	( )	ⓗ instantaneously
09	인상	( )	ⓘ support
10	대체된, 쫓겨난	( )	ⓙ distribute
11	지원하다	( )	ⓚ displaced
12	지시, 설명서	( )	ⓛ grocery
13	식료품점	( )	ⓜ gaze
14	은퇴	( )	ⓝ retirement
15	농업의	( )	ⓞ congenitally
16	시선, 응시	( )	ⓟ tuition
17	기구, 장치	( )	ⓠ occupation
18	포함하다	( )	ⓡ impression
19	즉시, 순간적으로	( )	ⓢ include
20	직업	( )	ⓣ spend

※ 영어 [독해] 파트만 수록한 문제지이므로 18번부터 시작합니다. ● 점수 표시가 없는 문항은 모두 2점 ● 문항수 28개 | 배점 63점 | 제한 시간 45분

18. 다음 글의 목적으로 가장 적절한 것은?

Dear parents,

Regular attendance at school is essential in maximizing student potential. Recently, we've become concerned about the number of unapproved absences across all grades. I would like to further clarify that your role as a parent is to approve any school absence. Parents must provide an explanation for absences to the school within 7 days from the first day of any period of absence. Where an explanation has not been received within the 7-day time frame, the school will record the absence as unjustified on the student's record. Please ensure that you go to the parent portal site and register the reason any time your child is absent. Please approve all absences, so that your child will not be at a disadvantage. Many thanks for your cooperation.

Sincerely,
Natalie Brown, Vice Principal

① 자녀의 결석 사유를 등록해 줄 것을 요청하려고
② 학교 홈페이지의 일시적 운영 중단을 공지하려고
③ 자녀가 지각하지 않도록 부모의 지도를 당부하려고
④ 방과 후 프로그램에 대한 부모의 관심을 독려하려고
⑤ 인정 결석은 최대 7일까지 허용된다는 것을 안내하려고

19. 다음 글에 드러난 Ester의 심경 변화로 가장 적절한 것은?

Ester stood up as soon as she heard the hum of a hover engine outside. "Mail," she shouted and ran down the third set of stairs and swung open the door. It was pouring now, but she ran out into the rain. She was facing the mailbox. There was a single, unopened letter inside. She was sure this must be what she was eagerly waiting for. Without hesitation, she tore open the envelope. She pulled out the paper and unfolded it. The letter said, 'Thank you for applying to our company. We would like to invite you to our internship program. We look forward to seeing you soon.' She jumped up and down and looked down at the letter again. She couldn't wait to tell this news to her family.

① anticipating → excited
② confident → ashamed
③ curious → embarrassed
④ surprised → confused
⑤ indifferent → grateful

20. 다음 글에서 필자가 주장하는 바로 가장 적절한 것은?

The introduction of new technologies clearly has both positive and negative impacts for sustainable development. Good management of technological resources needs to take them fully into account. Technological developments in sectors such as nuclear energy and agriculture provide examples of how not only environmental benefits but also risks to the environment or human health can accompany technological advances. New technologies have profound social impacts as well. Since the industrial revolution, technological advances have changed the nature of skills needed in workplaces, creating certain types of jobs and destroying others, with impacts on employment patterns. New technologies need to be assessed for their full potential impacts, both positive and negative.

① 기술 혁신을 저해하는 과도한 법률적 규제를 완화해야 한다.
② 기술의 도입으로 인한 잠재적인 영향들을 충분히 고려해야 한다.
③ 혁신적 농업 기술을 적용할 때는 환경적인 측면을 검토해야 한다.
④ 기술 진보가 가져온 일자리 위협에 대한 대비책을 마련해야 한다.
⑤ 기술 발전을 위해서는 혁신적 사고와 창의성이 뒷받침되어야 한다.

21. 밑줄 친 have entirely lost our marbles가 다음 글에서 의미하는 바로 가장 적절한 것은? [3점]

North America's native cuisine met the same unfortunate fate as its native people, save for a few relics like the Thanksgiving turkey. Certainly, we still have regional specialties, but the Carolina barbecue will almost certainly have California tomatoes in its sauce, and the Louisiana gumbo is just as likely to contain Indonesian farmed shrimp. If either of these shows up on a fast-food menu with lots of added fats or HFCS, we seem unable either to discern or resist the corruption. We have yet to come up with a strong set of generalized norms, passed down through families, for savoring and sensibly consuming what our land and climate give us. We have, instead, a string of fad diets convulsing our bookstores and bellies, one after another, at the scale of the national best seller. Nine out of ten nutritionists view this as evidence that we have entirely lost our marbles.

*relic: 전해 내려오는 풍속 **HFCS: 액상 과당
***convulse: 큰 소동을 일으키다

① have utterly disrupted our complex food supply chain
② have vividly witnessed the rebirth of our classic recipes
③ have completely denied ourselves access to healthy food
④ have become totally confused about our distinctive food identity
⑤ have fully recognized the cultural significance of our local foods

22. 다음 글의 요지로 가장 적절한 것은?

Perhaps, the advent of Artificial Intelligence (AI) in the workplace may bode well for Emotional Intelligence (EI). As AI gains momentum and replaces people in jobs at every level, predictions are, there will be a premium placed on people who have high ability in EI. The emotional messages people send and respond to while interacting are, at this point, far beyond the ability of AI programs to mimic. As we get further into the age of the smart machine, it is likely that sensing and managing emotions will remain one type of intelligence that puzzles AI. This means people and jobs involving EI are safe from being taken over by machines. In a survey, almost three out of four executives see EI as a "must-have" skill for the workplace in the future as the automatizing of routine tasks bumps up against the impossibility of creating effective AI for activities that require emotional skill.

*bode: ~의 징조가 되다 **momentum: 추진력

① 감성 지능의 결여는 직장 내 대인 관계 갈등을 심화시킨다.
② 미래의 직장에서는 감성 지능의 가치가 더욱 높아질 것이다.
③ 미래 사회에서는 감성 지능을 갖춘 기계가 보편화될 것이다.
④ 미래에는 대부분의 직장 업무를 인공 지능이 대신할 것이다.
⑤ 인간과 인공 지능 간의 상호 작용은 감성 지능의 발달을 저해한다.

23. 다음 글의 주제로 가장 적절한 것은? [3점]

Education must focus on the trunk of the tree of knowledge, revealing the ways in which the branches, twigs, and leaves all emerge from a common core. Tools for thinking stem from this core, providing a common language with which practitioners in different fields may share their experience of the process of innovation and discover links between their creative activities. When the same terms are employed across the curriculum, students begin to link different subjects and classes. If they practice abstracting in writing class, if they work on abstracting in painting or drawing class, and if, in all cases, they call it abstracting, they begin to understand how to think beyond disciplinary boundaries. They see how to transform their thoughts from one mode of conception and expression to another. Linking the disciplines comes naturally when the terms and tools are presented as part of a universal imagination.

① difficulties in finding meaningful links between disciplines
② drawbacks of applying a common language to various fields
③ effects of diversifying the curriculum on students' creativity
④ necessity of using a common language to integrate the curriculum
⑤ usefulness of turning abstract thoughts into concrete expressions

24. 다음 글의 제목으로 가장 적절한 것은?

New words and expressions emerge continually in response to new situations, ideas and feelings. *The Oxford English Dictionary* publishes supplements of new words and expressions that have entered the language. Some people deplore this kind of thing and see it as a drift from correct English. But it was only in the eighteenth century that any attempt was made to formalize spelling and punctuation of English at all. The language we speak in the twenty-first century would be virtually unintelligible to Shakespeare, and so would his way of speaking to us. Alvin Toffler estimated that Shakespeare would probably only understand about 250,000 of the 450,000 words in general use in the English language now. In other words, so to speak, if Shakespeare were to materialize in London today he would understand, on average, only five out of every nine words in our vocabulary.

*deplore: 한탄하다

① Original Meanings of Words Fade with Time
② Dictionary: A Gradual Continuation of the Past
③ Literature: The Driving Force Behind New Words
④ How Can We Bridge the Ever-Widening Language Gap?
⑤ Language Evolution Makes Even Shakespeare Semi-literate!

25. 다음 도표의 내용과 일치하지 <u>않는</u> 것은?

Average Number of Students per Teacher in Public Elementary and Secondary Schools across Selected Countries in 2019

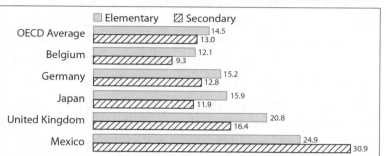

	Elementary	Secondary
OECD Average	14.5	13.0
Belgium	12.1	9.3
Germany	15.2	12.8
Japan	15.9	11.9
United Kingdom	20.8	16.4
Mexico	24.9	30.9

The graph above shows the average number of students per teacher in public elementary and secondary schools across selected countries in 2019. ① Belgium was the only country with a smaller number of students per teacher than the OECD average in both public elementary and secondary schools. ② In both public elementary and secondary schools, the average number of students per teacher was the largest in Mexico. ③ In public elementary schools, there was a smaller number of students per teacher on average in Germany than in Japan, whereas the reverse was true in public secondary schools. ④ The average number of students per teacher in public secondary schools in Germany was less than half that in the United Kingdom. ⑤ Of the five countries, Mexico was the only country with more students per teacher in public secondary schools than in public elementary schools.

26. John Ray에 관한 다음 글의 내용과 일치하지 <u>않는</u> 것은?

Born in 1627 in Black Notley, Essex, England, John Ray was the son of the village blacksmith. At 16, he went to Cambridge University, where he studied widely and lectured on topics from Greek to mathematics, before joining the priesthood in 1660. To recover from an illness in 1650, he had taken to nature walks and developed an interest in botany. Accompanied by his wealthy student and supporter Francis Willughby, Ray toured Britain and Europe in the 1660s, studying and collecting plants and animals. He married Margaret Oakley in 1673 and, after leaving Willughby's household, lived quietly in Black Notley to the age of 77. He spent his later years studying samples in order to assemble plant and animal catalogues. He wrote more than twenty works on theology and his travels, as well as on plants and their form and function.

* theology: 신학

① 마을 대장장이의 아들이었다.
② 성직자의 길로 들어서기 전 Cambridge 대학에 다녔다.
③ 병에서 회복하기 위해 자연을 산책하기 시작했다.
④ Francis Willughby에게 후원받아 홀로 유럽을 여행하였다.
⑤ 동식물의 목록을 만들기 위해 표본을 연구하며 말년을 보냈다.

27. Peace Marathon Festival에 관한 다음 안내문의 내용과 일치하지 <u>않는</u> 것은?

Peace Marathon Festival

The Peace Marathon Festival will be held to promote world peace and share compassion for people in need. Join us to enjoy running and make a better world.

When & Where
• Sunday, September 3, 2023 (Start time: 10 a.m.)
• Civic Stadium

Participation Fee & Qualification
• Full & Half: $30 (20 years or older)
• 10 km & 5 km: $15 (No age limit)

Registration
• The number of participants is limited to 1,000. (First come, first served.)
• Online only at ipmarathon.com

Notes
• Souvenirs and medals will be given to all participants.
• Changing rooms will be available at no charge.
• Water will be provided every 2.5 km and at the finish line.

① 출발 시각은 오전 10시이다.
② 5킬로미터 코스는 참가에 나이 제한이 없다.
③ 참가자는 선착순 1,000명으로 제한된다.
④ 모든 참가자들에게 기념품과 메달이 주어진다.
⑤ 물은 결승선에서만 제공된다.

28. Out to Lunch에 관한 다음 안내문의 내용과 일치하는 것은?

Out to Lunch

Do you want to enjoy an afternoon with tasty food and great music? 'Out to Lunch' is the perfect event to meet your needs! Come and enjoy this event held in Caras Park in downtown Missoula!

Dates & Times
• Every Wednesday in June, 12 p.m. – 3 p.m.

Highlights
• 10% discount at all food trucks including Diamond Ice Cream
• Live music performance of the new group Cello Brigade
• Face-painting and water balloon fight for kids

Notices
• Bring your own lawn chairs and blankets.
• Dispose of your waste properly.
• Drinking alcoholic beverages is strictly banned.

① 일 년 내내 수요일마다 열리는 행사이다.
② 푸드 트럭에서는 가격을 20% 할인해 준다.
③ 라이브 음악 공연이 마련되어 있다.
④ 개인 의자와 담요를 가지고 올 수 없다.
⑤ 주류를 포함한 음료를 마실 수 있다.

29. 다음 글의 밑줄 친 부분 중, 어법상 틀린 것은? [3점]

Research psychologists often work with *self-report data*, made up of participants' verbal accounts of their behavior. This is the case ① whenever questionnaires, interviews, or personality inventories are used to measure variables. Self-report methods can be quite useful. They take advantage of the fact that people have a unique opportunity to observe ② themselves full-time. However, self-reports can be plagued by several kinds of distortion. One of the most problematic of these distortions is the social desirability bias, which is a tendency to give ③ socially approved answers to questions about oneself. Subjects who are influenced by this bias work overtime trying to create a favorable impression, especially when subjects ④ ask about sensitive issues. For example, many survey respondents will report that they voted in an election or ⑤ gave to a charity when in fact it is possible to determine that they did not.

30. 다음 글의 밑줄 친 부분 중, 문맥상 낱말의 쓰임이 적절하지 않은 것은? [3점]

Over the past several decades, there have been some agreements to reduce the debt of poor nations, but other economic challenges (like trade barriers) ① remain. Nontariff trade measures, such as quotas, subsidies, and restrictions on exports, are increasingly prevalent and may be enacted for policy reasons having nothing to do with trade. However, they have a ② discriminatory effect on exports from countries that lack the resources to comply with requirements of nontariff measures imposed by rich nations. For example, the huge subsidies that ③ poor nations give to their farmers make it very difficult for farmers in the rest of the world to compete with them. Another example would be domestic health or safety regulations, which, though not specifically targeting imports, could ④ impose significant costs on foreign manufacturers seeking to conform to the importer's market. Industries in developing markets may have more ⑤ difficulty absorbing these additional costs.

* nontariff: 비관세의 ** subsidy: 보조금

[31~34] 다음 빈칸에 들어갈 말로 가장 적절한 것을 고르시오.

31. In the course of his research on business strategy and the environment, Michael Porter noticed a peculiar pattern: Businesses seemed to be profiting from regulation. He also discovered that the stricter regulations were prompting more _____ than the weaker ones. The Dutch flower industry provides an illustration. For many years, the companies producing Holland's world-renowned tulips and other cut flowers were also contaminating the country's water and soil with fertilizers and pesticides. In 1991, the Dutch government adopted a policy designed to cut pesticide use in half by 2000 — a goal they ultimately achieved. Facing increasingly strict regulation, greenhouse growers realized they had to develop new methods if they were going to maintain product quality with fewer pesticides. In response, they shifted to a cultivation method that circulates water in closed-loop systems and grows flowers in a rock wool substrate. The new system not only reduced the pollution released into the environment; it also increased profits by giving companies greater control over growing conditions.

* substrate: 배양판

① innovation　　　　② resistance
③ fairness　　　　④ neglect
⑤ unity

32. It's hard to pay more for the speedy but highly skilled person, simply because there's less effort being observed. Two researchers once did a study in which they asked people how much they would pay for data recovery. They found that people would pay a little more for a greater quantity of rescued data, but what they were most sensitive to was the number of hours the technician worked. When the data recovery took only a few minutes, willingness to pay was low, but when it took more than a week to recover the same amount of data, people were willing to pay much more. Think about it: They were willing to pay more for the slower service with the same outcome. Fundamentally, when we _____, we're paying for incompetence. Although it is actually irrational, we *feel* more rational, and more comfortable, paying for incompetence. [3점]

① prefer money to time
② ignore the hours put in
③ value effort over outcome
④ can't stand any malfunction
⑤ are biased toward the quality

33. In adolescence many of us had the experience of falling under the sway of a great book or writer. We became entranced by the novel ideas in the book, and because we were so open to influence, these early encounters with exciting ideas sank deeply into our minds and became part of our own thought processes, affecting us decades after we absorbed them. Such influences enriched our mental landscape, and in fact our intelligence depends on the ability to absorb the lessons and ideas of those who are older and wiser. Just as the body tightens with age, however, so does the mind. And just as our sense of weakness and vulnerability motivated the desire to learn, so does our creeping sense of superiority slowly close us off to new ideas and influences. Some may advocate that we all become more skeptical in the modern world, but in fact a far greater danger comes from _____ that burdens us as individuals as we get older, and seems to be burdening our culture in general. [3점]

* entrance: 매료시키다

① the high dependence on others
② the obsession with our inferiority
③ the increasing closing of the mind
④ the misconception about our psychology
⑤ the self-destructive pattern of behavior

34. Many people look for safety and security in popular thinking. They figure that if a lot of people are doing something, then it must be right. It must be a good idea. If most people accept it, then it probably represents fairness, equality, compassion, and sensitivity, right? Not necessarily. Popular thinking said the earth was the center of the universe, yet Copernicus studied the stars and planets and proved mathematically that the earth and the other planets in our solar system revolved around the sun. Popular thinking said surgery didn't require clean instruments, yet Joseph Lister studied the high death rates in hospitals and introduced antiseptic practices that immediately saved lives. Popular thinking said that women shouldn't have the right to vote, yet people like Emmeline Pankhurst and Susan B. Anthony fought for and won that right. We must always remember _____.
People may say that there's safety in numbers, but that's not always true. [3점]

* antiseptic: 멸균의

① majority rule should be founded on fairness
② the crowd is generally going in the right direction
③ the roles of leaders and followers can change at any time
④ people behave in a different fashion to others around them
⑤ there is a huge difference between acceptance and intelligence

35. 다음 글에서 전체 흐름과 관계 <u>없는</u> 문장은?

Before getting licensed to drive a cab in London, a person has to pass an incredibly difficult test with an intimidating name—"The Knowledge." ① The test involves memorizing the layout of more than 20,000 streets in the Greater London area—a feat that involves an incredible amount of memory resources. ② In fact, fewer than 50 percent of the people who sign up for taxi driver training pass the test, even after spending two or three years studying for it! ③ And as it turns out, the brains of London cabbies are different from non-cab-driving humans in ways that reflect their herculean memory efforts. ④ In other words, they must hold a full driving license, issued by the Driver and Vehicle Licensing Authority, for at least a year. ⑤ In fact, the part of the brain that has been most frequently associated with spatial memory, the tail of the sea horse-shaped brain region called the hippocampus, is *bigger* than average in these taxi drivers.

* herculean: 초인적인 ** hippocampus: 해마

[36~37] 주어진 글 다음에 이어질 글의 순서로 가장 적절한 것을 고르시오.

36.

> When evaluating a policy, people tend to concentrate on how the policy will fix some particular problem while ignoring or downplaying other effects it may have. Economists often refer to this situation as *The Law of Unintended Consequences*.

(A) But an unintended consequence is that the jobs of some autoworkers will be lost to foreign competition. Why? The tariff that protects steelworkers raises the price of the steel that domestic automobile makers need to build their cars.

(B) For instance, suppose that you impose a tariff on imported steel in order to protect the jobs of domestic steelworkers. If you impose a high enough tariff, their jobs will indeed be protected from competition by foreign steel companies.

(C) As a result, domestic automobile manufacturers have to raise the prices of their cars, making them relatively less attractive than foreign cars. Raising prices tends to reduce domestic car sales, so some domestic autoworkers lose their jobs.

① (A) - (C) - (B)   ② (B) - (A) - (C)
③ (B) - (C) - (A)   ④ (C) - (A) - (B)
⑤ (C) - (B) - (A)

37.

> Species that are found in only one area are called endemic species and are especially vulnerable to extinction.

(A) But warmer air from global climate change caused these clouds to rise, depriving the forests of moisture, and the habitat for the golden toad and many other species dried up. The golden toad appears to be one of the first victims of climate change caused largely by global warming.

(B) They exist on islands and in other unique small areas, especially in tropical rain forests where most species are highly specialized. One example is the brilliantly colored golden toad once found only in a small area of lush rain forests in Costa Rica's mountainous region.

(C) Despite living in the country's well-protected Monteverde Cloud Forest Reserve, by 1989, the golden toad had apparently become extinct. Much of the moisture that supported its rain forest habitat came in the form of moisture-laden clouds blowing in from the Caribbean Sea.

*lush: 무성한, 우거진

① (A) − (C) − (B) ② (B) − (A) − (C)
③ (B) − (C) − (A) ④ (C) − (A) − (B)
⑤ (C) − (B) − (A)

[38~39] 글의 흐름으로 보아, 주어진 문장이 들어가기에 가장 적절한 곳을 고르시오.

38.

> Rather, we have to create a situation that doesn't actually occur in the real world.

The fundamental nature of the experimental method is manipulation and control. Scientists manipulate a variable of interest, and see if there's a difference. At the same time, they attempt to control for the potential effects of all other variables. The importance of controlled experiments in identifying the underlying causes of events cannot be overstated. (①) In the real-uncontrolled-world, variables are often correlated. (②) For example, people who take vitamin supplements may have different eating and exercise habits than people who don't take vitamins. (③) As a result, if we want to study the health effects of vitamins, we can't merely observe the real world, since any of these factors (the vitamins, diet, or exercise) may affect health. (④) That's just what scientific experiments do. (⑤) They try to separate the naturally occurring relationship in the world by manipulating one specific variable at a time, while holding everything else constant.

39.

> These healthful, non-nutritive compounds in plants provide color and function to the plant and add to the health of the human body.

Why do people in the Mediterranean live longer and have a lower incidence of disease? Some people say it's because of what they eat. Their diet is full of fresh fruits, fish, vegetables, whole grains, and nuts. Individuals in these cultures drink red wine and use great amounts of olive oil. Why is that food pattern healthy? (①) One reason is that they are eating a palette of colors. (②) More and more research is surfacing that shows us the benefits of the thousands of colorful "phytochemicals" (*phyto*=plant) that exist in foods. (③) Each color connects to a particular compound that serves a specific function in the body. (④) For example, if you don't eat purple foods, you are probably missing out on anthocyanins, important brain protection compounds. (⑤) Similarly, if you avoid green-colored foods, you may be lacking chlorophyll, a plant antioxidant that guards your cells from damage.

*antioxidant: 산화 방지제

40. 다음 글의 내용을 한 문장으로 요약하고자 한다. 빈칸 (A), (B)에 들어갈 말로 가장 적절한 것은?

> People behave in highly predictable ways when they experience certain thoughts. When they agree, they nod their heads. So far, no surprise, but according to an area of research known as "proprioceptive psychology," the process also works in reverse. Get people to behave in a certain way and you cause them to have certain thoughts. The idea was initially controversial, but fortunately it was supported by a compelling experiment. Participants in a study were asked to fixate on various products moving across a large computer screen and then indicate whether the items appealed to them. Some of the items moved vertically (causing the participants to nod their heads while watching), and others moved horizontally (resulting in a side-to-side head movement). Participants preferred vertically moving products without being aware that their "yes" and "no" head movements had played a key role in their decisions.

↓

> In one study, participants responded ___(A)___ to products on a computer screen when they moved their heads up and down, which showed that their decisions were unconsciously influenced by their ___(B)___.

　　　　(A)　　　　　　　　　　(B)
① favorably　　……　　behavior
② favorably　　……　　instinct
③ unfavorably　……　　feeling
④ unfavorably　……　　gesture
⑤ irrationally　……　　prejudice

[41~42] 다음 글을 읽고, 물음에 답하시오.

Events or experiences that are out of ordinary tend to be remembered better because there is nothing competing with them when your brain tries to access them from its storehouse of remembered events. In other words, the reason it can be (a) difficult to remember what you ate for breakfast two Thursdays ago is that there was probably nothing special about that Thursday or that particular breakfast — consequently, all your breakfast memories combine together into a sort of generic impression of a breakfast. Your memory (b) merges similar events not only because it's more efficient to do so, but also because this is fundamental to how we learn things — our brains extract abstract rules that tie experiences together.

This is especially true for things that are (c) routine. If your breakfast is always the same — cereal with milk, a glass of orange juice, and a cup of coffee for instance — there is no easy way for your brain to extract the details from one particular breakfast. Ironically, then, for behaviors that are routinized, you can remember the generic content of the behavior (such as the things you ate, since you always eat the same thing), but (d) particulars to that one instance can be very difficult to call up (such as the sound of a garbage truck going by or a bird that passed by your window) *unless* they were especially distinctive. On the other hand, if you did something unique that broke your routine — perhaps you had leftover pizza for breakfast and spilled tomato sauce on your dress shirt — you are (e) less likely to remember it.

41. 윗글의 제목으로 가장 적절한 것은?

① Repetition Makes Your Memory Sharp!
② How Does Your Memory Get Distorted?
③ What to Consider in Routinizing Your Work
④ Merging Experiences: Key to Remembering Details
⑤ The More Unique Events, the More Vivid Recollection

42. 밑줄 친 (a)~(e) 중에서 문맥상 낱말의 쓰임이 적절하지 않은 것은?

① (a) ② (b) ③ (c) ④ (d) ⑤ (e)

[43~45] 다음 글을 읽고, 물음에 답하시오.

(A)

Henrietta is one of the greatest "queens of song." She had to go through a severe struggle before (a) she attained the enviable position as the greatest singer Germany had produced. At the beginning of her career she was hissed off a Vienna stage by the friends of her rival, Amelia. But in spite of this defeat, Henrietta endured until all Europe was at her feet.

*hiss off: 야유하여 쫓아내다

(B)

The answer was, "That's my mother, Amelia Steininger. She used to be a great singer, but she lost her voice, and she cried so much about it that now (b) she can't see anymore." Henrietta inquired their address and then told the child, "Tell your mother an old acquaintance will call on her this afternoon." She searched out their place and undertook the care of both mother and daughter. At her request, a skilled doctor tried to restore Amelia's sight, but it was in vain.

(C)

But Henrietta's kindness to (c) her former rival did not stop here. The next week she gave a benefit concert for the poor woman, and it was said that on that occasion Henrietta sang as (d) she had never sung before. And who can doubt that with the applause of that vast audience there was mingled the applause of the angels in heaven who rejoice over the good deeds of those below?

(D)

Many years later, when Henrietta was at the height of her fame, one day she was riding through the streets of Berlin. Soon she came across a little girl leading a blind woman. She was touched by the woman's helplessness, and she impulsively beckoned the child to (e) her, saying "Come here, my child. Who is that you are leading by the hand?"

43. 주어진 글 (A)에 이어질 내용을 순서에 맞게 배열한 것으로 가장 적절한 것은?

① (B) – (D) – (C)　　② (C) – (B) – (D)
③ (C) – (D) – (B)　　④ (D) – (B) – (C)
⑤ (D) – (C) – (B)

44. 밑줄 친 (a)~(e) 중에서 가리키는 대상이 나머지 넷과 다른 것은?

① (a)　② (b)　③ (c)　④ (d)　⑤ (e)

45. 윗글에 관한 내용으로 적절하지 않은 것은?

① Amelia와 Henrietta는 라이벌 관계였다.
② Henrietta는 모녀의 거처를 찾아내서 그들을 돌보았다.
③ 숙련된 의사가 Amelia의 시력을 회복시켰다.
④ 불쌍한 여성을 위해 Henrietta는 자선 콘서트를 열었다.
⑤ Henrietta는 눈먼 여성을 데리고 가는 여자 아이와 마주쳤다.

* 확인 사항

○ 답안지의 해당란에 필요한 내용을 정확히 기입(표기)했는지 확인하시오.

18

001 □ attendance ⓝ 출석, 참석
002 □ essential ⓐ 필수적인
003 □ maximize ⓥ 극대화하다
004 □ potential ⓝ 잠재력
005 □ concerned about ~에 대해 걱정하는
006 □ the number of ~의 수
007 □ unapproved ⓐ 승인되지 않은
008 □ absence ⓝ 결석
009 □ grade ⓝ 학년
010 □ clarify ⓥ 밝히다
011 □ role ⓝ 역할
012 □ explanation ⓝ 해명, 설명
013 □ within prep ~ 이내에
014 □ unjustified ⓐ 정당하지 않은
015 □ student's record 학생부
016 □ disadvantage ⓝ 불리(한 점)
017 □ many thanks for ~에 대해 대단히 고맙습니다

19

018 □ hum ⓝ 웅웅거리는 소리
019 □ stairs ⓝ 계단
020 □ swing open 활짝 열다
021 □ pour ⓥ (비가) 퍼붓다
022 □ face ⓥ 마주보다, 직면하다
023 □ mailbox ⓝ 우편함
024 □ unopened ⓐ 개봉되지 않은
025 □ eagerly ⓐⓓ 간절히
026 □ pull out 꺼내다
027 □ unfold ⓥ 펼치다
028 □ apply to ~에 지원하다
029 □ look forward to ~을 기대하다
030 □ look down at ~을 내려다보다
031 □ can't wait to ~하기를 몹시 기대하다
032 □ anticipating ⓥ 기대하는
033 □ embarrassed ⓐ 당황한

20

034 □ introduction ⓝ 소개, 도입
035 □ positive ⓐ 긍정적인
036 □ negative ⓐ 부정적인
037 □ impact ⓝ 영향
038 □ sustainable development (환경적으로) 지속 가능한 개발
039 □ resource ⓝ 자원
040 □ take into account ~을 고려하다
041 □ sector ⓝ 부문
042 □ nuclear ⓐ 핵의
043 □ agriculture ⓝ 농업
044 □ benefit ⓝ 이점
045 □ risk ⓝ 위험 ⓥ 위험을 감수하다
046 □ profound ⓐ 심오한, 깊은
047 □ as well (문장 끝에서) 또한
048 □ assess ⓥ 평가하다

21

049 □ native ⓐ 토착의
050 □ cuisine ⓝ 요리
051 □ unfortunate ⓐ 불행한
052 □ fate ⓝ 운명
053 □ save for ~을 빼고는

054 □ relic ⓝ 전해 내려오는 풍속
055 □ turkey ⓝ 칠면조
056 □ regional ⓐ 지역적인
057 □ specialty ⓝ 특산품, 특색 요리
058 □ contain ⓥ 포함하다
059 □ show up 나타나다
060 □ fat ⓝ 지방
061 □ HFCS ⓝ 액상과당
062 □ discern ⓥ 분간하다
063 □ corruption ⓝ 붕괴
064 □ have yet to 아직 ~해야 하다
065 □ generalize ⓥ 일반화하다
066 □ norm ⓝ 규범
067 □ savor ⓥ 음미하다
068 □ sensibly ⓐⓓ 분별력 있게, 현명하게
069 □ fad ⓝ (일시적) 유행
070 □ convulse ⓥ 큰 소동을 일으키다
071 □ entirely ⓐⓓ 전적으로
072 □ lose one's marble 분별력을 잃다
073 □ disrupt ⓥ 파괴하다, 방해하다
074 □ witness ⓥ 목격하다
075 □ significance ⓝ 의미, 중요성

22

076 □ advent ⓝ 출현
077 □ bode ⓥ ~의 징조가 되다
078 □ gain ⓥ 얻다
079 □ momentum ⓝ 추진력, 기세
080 □ replace ⓥ 대체하다
081 □ prediction ⓝ 예측
082 □ emotional ⓐ 정서적인
083 □ respond to ~에 응답하다
084 □ interact ⓥ 상호 작용하다
085 □ far beyond ~을 훨씬 넘어서는
086 □ mimic ⓥ 모방하다
087 □ puzzle ⓥ 당황하게 하다
088 □ take over 장악하다, 탈취하다, 인수하다
089 □ executive ⓝ 임원
090 □ automatize ⓥ 자동화하다
091 □ bump up against ~에 부딪치다, ~와 우연히 만나다
092 □ impossibility ⓝ 불가능함

23

093 □ education ⓝ 교육
094 □ trunk ⓝ (나무) 줄기
095 □ reveal ⓥ 드러내다
096 □ branch ⓝ (나무) 가지
097 □ twig ⓝ 잔가지
098 □ emerge from ~에서 생겨나다
099 □ core ⓝ 핵심
100 □ stem from ~에서 유래하다
101 □ language ⓝ 언어
102 □ practitioner ⓝ 실무자
103 □ process ⓝ 과정 ⓥ 가공하다
104 □ innovation ⓝ 혁신
105 □ link ⓝ 연결고리
106 □ term ⓝ 용어
107 □ employ ⓥ 사용하다
108 □ abstract ⓥ 추상하다, (글쓰기) 요약하다
109 □ disciplinary ⓐ (학문) 분야의
110 □ conception ⓝ 개념

111 □ naturally ⓐⓓ 자연적으로
112 □ as part of ~의 일환으로
113 □ universal ⓐ 보편적인
114 □ drawback ⓝ 문제
115 □ diversify ⓥ 다양화하다
116 □ necessity ⓝ 필요성
117 □ concrete ⓐ 구체적인

24

118 □ continually ⓐⓓ 지속적으로
119 □ in response to ~에 반응하여
120 □ publish ⓥ 출판하다
121 □ supplement ⓝ 보충
122 □ deplore ⓥ 한탄하다
123 □ see A as B A를 B라고 여기다
124 □ drift ⓝ 표류, 부유
125 □ attempt ⓝ 시도, 노력
126 □ formalize ⓥ 공식화하다
127 □ punctuation ⓝ 구두법
128 □ virtually ⓐⓓ 거의, 사실상
129 □ unintelligible to ~가 이해할 수 없는
130 □ estimate ⓥ 추정하다
131 □ in use 사용 중인
132 □ so to speak 가령, 말하자면
133 □ materialize ⓥ (갑자기) 나타나다
134 □ vocabulary ⓝ 어휘
135 □ fade ⓥ 바래다, 옅어지다
136 □ literature ⓝ 문학
137 □ driving force 원동력
138 □ bridge ⓥ 격차를 줄이다, 다리를 놓다
139 □ ever-widening ⓐ 점점 커지는, 계속 벌어지는

25

140 □ public ⓐ 공립의 ⓝ 대중
141 □ elementary ⓐ 초등의
142 □ secondary ⓐ 중등의
143 □ select ⓥ 선정하다
144 □ reverse ⓝ 역, 반대
145 □ half ⓝ 절반
146 □ United Kingdom 영국

26

147 □ blacksmith ⓝ 대장장이
148 □ widely ⓐⓓ 널리
149 □ lecture on ~에 관해 강의하다
150 □ Greek ⓝ 그리스어 ⓐ 그리스의
151 □ mathematics ⓝ 수학
152 □ priesthood ⓝ 성직, 사제직
153 □ recover from ~에서 회복하다
154 □ illness ⓝ 질병
155 □ botany ⓝ 식물학
156 □ accompany ⓥ ~을 동반하다
157 □ wealthy ⓐ 부유한
158 □ supporter ⓝ 후원자, 지지자
159 □ household ⓝ 집, 가정
160 □ quietly ⓐⓓ 조용히
161 □ spend A ~ing A를 ~하는 데 쓰다, 들이다, 보내다
162 □ assemble ⓥ 모으다, 조립하다
163 □ theology ⓝ 신학
164 □ function ⓝ 기능

27

165 □ promote ⓥ 촉진하다, 장려하다
166 □ compassion ⓝ 연민, 동정
167 □ in need 도움이 필요한
168 □ civic ⓐ 시민의
169 □ stadium ⓝ 경기장
170 □ qualification ⓝ 자격 (사항)
171 □ age limit 나이 제한
172 □ registration ⓝ 등록
173 □ first come, first served 선착순
174 □ souvenir ⓝ 기념품
175 □ at no charge 무료로

28

176 □ tasty ⓐ 맛있는
177 □ perfect ⓐ 완벽한
178 □ meet one's needs ~의 필요를 충족시키다
179 □ downtown ⓝ 시내 ⓐ 시내의
180 □ live performance 라이브 공연
181 □ lawn chair 접이식 의자
182 □ dispose of ~을 처리하다, ~을 버리다
183 □ properly ⓐⓓ 적절하게
184 □ beverage ⓝ 음료
185 □ strictly ⓐⓓ 엄히
186 □ ban ⓥ 금지하다

29

187 □ self-report ⓝ 자기 보고
188 □ made up of ~로 이뤄진
189 □ verbal ⓐ 구두의
190 □ account ⓝ 설명
191 □ this is the case 이것은 사실이다[그러하다]
192 □ questionnaire ⓝ 설문지
193 □ personality inventory (연구를 위한) 성격 특성 목록
194 □ variable ⓝ 변수, 변인
195 □ take advantage of ~을 이용하다
196 □ unique ⓐ 고유한, 독특한, 특유의
197 □ opportunity ⓝ 기회
198 □ plague ⓥ 괴롭히다, 감염시키다
199 □ problematic ⓐ 문제가 되는
200 □ distortion ⓝ 왜곡
201 □ desirability ⓝ 바람직함
202 □ socially approved 사회적으로 받아들여지는
203 □ subject ⓝ 실험 대상자
204 □ bias ⓝ 편향
205 □ impression ⓝ 인상
206 □ sensitive ⓐ 민감한
207 □ respondent ⓝ 응답자
208 □ vote ⓥ 투표하다
209 □ election ⓝ 선거
210 □ give to (a) charity 자선 단체에 기부하다

30

211 □ debt ⓝ 부채, 빚
212 □ trade barrier 무역 장벽
213 □ nontariff ⓐ 비관세의
214 □ quota ⓝ 할당(제)
215 □ subsidy ⓝ 보조금
216 □ restriction ⓝ 제한, 규제

217 □ export ⓝ 수출
218 □ prevalent ⓐ 만연한, 널리 퍼진
219 □ enact ⓥ 제정하다
220 □ have nothing to do with ～와 관련이 없다
221 □ discriminatory ⓐ 차별적인
222 □ comply with ～을 준수하다
223 □ impose ⓥ 부과하다
224 □ huge ⓐ 막대한
225 □ domestic ⓐ 국내의, 가정의
226 □ safety regulation 안전 규제
227 □ specifically ⓐ 구체적으로, 특정하게
228 □ significant ⓐ 상당한
229 □ conform to ～에 맞추다, 순응하다
230 □ absorb ⓥ (비용을) 감당하다, 빨아들이다, 흡수하다

31
231 □ peculiar ⓐ 특이한
232 □ profit from ～로부터 이득을 보다
233 □ prompt ⓥ 유발하다
234 □ illustration ⓝ (잘 보여주는) 예
235 □ world-renowned ⓐ 세계적으로 유명한
236 □ contaminate ⓥ 오염시키다
237 □ fertilizer ⓝ 비료
238 □ pesticide ⓝ 살충제
239 □ adopt ⓥ 채택하다
240 □ cut in half 반으로 줄이다
241 □ increasingly ⓐ 점점 더
242 □ greenhouse ⓝ 온실
243 □ shift to ～로 이동하다, 변하다
244 □ cultivation ⓝ 경작, 재배
245 □ substrate ⓝ 배양판
246 □ release ⓥ 배출하다, 내보내다, 풀어주다
247 □ resistance ⓝ 저항
248 □ neglect ⓥ 방치, 태만, 소홀
249 □ unity ⓝ 통합

32
250 □ skilled ⓐ 숙련된
251 □ simply because 단지 ～하므로
252 □ researcher ⓝ 연구자
253 □ recovery ⓝ 회복, 복구
254 □ quantity ⓝ 양
255 □ rescue ⓥ 복구하다, 구조하다
256 □ technician ⓝ 기술자
257 □ willingness ⓝ 기꺼이 ～함, 의향
258 □ amount ⓝ 양
259 □ outcome ⓝ 결과
260 □ fundamentally ⓐ 근본적으로
261 □ irrational ⓐ 불합리한
262 □ incompetence ⓝ 무능
263 □ put in (시간이나 돈을) 들이다, 투입하다
264 □ value A over B A를 B보다 중시하다
265 □ malfunction ⓝ 불량

33
266 □ adolescence ⓝ 청소년기, 사춘기
267 □ sway ⓝ 영향, 지배, 장악
268 □ entrance ⓥ 매료시키다
269 □ novel ⓐ 새로운, 신기한
270 □ encounter ⓝ 만남, 조우

271 □ sink into ～로 가라앉다
272 □ deeply ⓐ 깊이
273 □ thought process 사고 과정
274 □ enrich ⓥ 풍부하게 하다
275 □ landscape ⓝ 정경, 풍경
276 □ tighten ⓥ 조여들다, 경직되다
277 □ vulnerability ⓝ 취약함, 상처받기 쉬움
278 □ creeping ⓐ 서서히 진행되는
279 □ superiority ⓝ 우월함
280 □ close off ～을 닫다
281 □ advocate ⓥ 주장하다, 변호하다, 옹호하다
282 □ skeptical ⓐ 회의적인
283 □ burden ⓥ 부담을 주다 ⓝ 짐, 부담
284 □ obsession ⓝ 강박, 집착
285 □ inferiority ⓝ 열등함
286 □ self-destructive ⓐ 자기 파괴적인

34
287 □ security ⓝ 안정
288 □ figure ⓥ 생각하다, 판단하다
289 □ represent ⓥ 나타내다, 표현하다
290 □ fairness ⓝ 공정
291 □ equality ⓝ 평등
292 □ earth ⓝ 지구, 흙
293 □ planet ⓝ 행성
294 □ solar system 태양계
295 □ revolve around ～ 주위를 돌다
296 □ surgery ⓝ 수술
297 □ instrument ⓝ 도구
298 □ death rate 사망률
299 □ antiseptic ⓐ 멸균의
300 □ majority rule 다수결의 원칙
301 □ be founded on ～에 근거를 두다

35
302 □ license ⓥ 면허를 주다 ⓝ 면허
303 □ cab ⓝ 택시
304 □ intimidating ⓐ 위협적인
305 □ memorize ⓥ 암기하다
306 □ layout ⓝ 배치
307 □ feat ⓝ 능력, 기술
308 □ even after 심지어 ～한 뒤에도
309 □ study for ～을 위해 공부하다
310 □ as it turns out 밝혀진 바에 따르면
311 □ cabbie(cabby) ⓝ 택시 기사
312 □ herculean ⓐ 초인적인
313 □ issue ⓥ 발행하다
314 □ sea horse ⓝ (동물) 해마
315 □ hippocampus ⓝ (대뇌의) 해마

36
316 □ evaluate ⓥ 평가하다
317 □ concentrate on ～에 집중하다
318 □ downplay ⓥ 경시하다
319 □ economist ⓝ 경제학자
320 □ refer to A as B A를 B라고 부르다
321 □ unintended ⓐ 의도되지 않은
322 □ consequence ⓝ 결과
323 □ autoworker ⓝ 자동차 업체 근로자
324 □ tariff ⓝ 관세
325 □ steelworker ⓝ 철강 노동자
326 □ raise ⓥ 올리다

327 □ import ⓥ 수입하다
328 □ attractive ⓐ 매력적인

37
329 □ endemic ⓐ 토착의, 풍토의, 고유의
330 □ vulnerable to ～에 취약한
331 □ extinction ⓝ 멸종
332 □ deprive A of B A에게서 B를 빼앗다
333 □ habitat ⓝ 서식지
334 □ dry up 말라버리다
335 □ victim ⓝ 희생자
336 □ largely ⓐ 대체로
337 □ tropical rain forest 열대 우림
338 □ brilliantly ⓐ 눈부시게
339 □ lush ⓐ 무성한, 우거진
340 □ mountainous ⓐ 산악의
341 □ reserve ⓝ 보호 구역
342 □ apparently ⓐ 겉보기에, 분명히
343 □ moisture-laden ⓐ 습기 찬

38
344 □ fundamental ⓐ 근본적인
345 □ experimental ⓐ 실험의
346 □ manipulation ⓝ 조작
347 □ identify ⓥ 식별하다
348 □ underlying ⓐ 근본적인, 기저에 있는
349 □ cannot be overstated 아무리 과장해도 지나치지 않다
350 □ correlate ⓥ 상호 관련시키다
351 □ merely ⓐ 단지
352 □ since ⓒⓞⓝⓙ ～ 때문에
353 □ affect ⓥ 영향을 끼치다
354 □ separate ⓥ 분리하다 ⓐ 개별의
355 □ at a time 한 번에
356 □ constant ⓐ 일정한

39
357 □ healthful ⓐ 건강에 좋은
358 □ non-nutritive ⓐ 비영양성의
359 □ compound ⓝ 화합물
360 □ Mediterranean ⓝ 지중해 (지역) ⓐ 지중해의
361 □ incidence ⓝ (사건의) 발생
362 □ whole grain 통곡물
363 □ palette ⓝ 팔레트, 색깔들
364 □ colorful ⓐ 다채로운, 색색의
365 □ connect to ～에 연결되다
366 □ serve ⓥ 제공하다, 수행하다
367 □ miss out on ～을 놓치다
368 □ antioxidant ⓝ 산화 방지제
369 □ guard ⓥ 지키다
370 □ damage ⓝ 손상

40
371 □ nod ⓥ 끄덕이다
372 □ so far 여기까지는, 지금까지는
373 □ known as ～라고 알려진
374 □ initially ⓐ 처음에는
375 □ controversial ⓐ 논쟁의 여지가 있는
376 □ fortunately ⓐ 다행히도
377 □ compelling ⓐ 설득력 있는
378 □ fixate on ～에 고정시키다

379 □ across ⓟⓡⓔⓟ ～을 가로질러
380 □ indicate ⓥ 가리키다, 나타내다
381 □ appeal to ～에게 매력적으로 보이다, 호소하다
382 □ vertically ⓐ 수직으로, 세로로
383 □ horizontally ⓐ 수평으로, 가로로
384 □ side-to-side ⓐ 좌우의
385 □ play a role in ～에 (…한) 역할을 하다
386 □ unconsciously ⓐ 무의식적으로
387 □ favorably ⓐ 호의적으로
388 □ instinct ⓝ 본능
389 □ prejudice ⓝ 편견

41~42
390 □ out of (the) ordinary 평범하지 않은
391 □ compete with ～와 경쟁하다
392 □ storehouse ⓝ 창고
393 □ combine into ～로 합쳐지다
394 □ generic ⓐ 일반적인
395 □ merge ⓥ 병합하다
396 □ extract ⓥ 추출하다
397 □ abstract ⓐ 추상적인
398 □ tie ⓥ 결합하다
399 □ true for ～에 해당한다, 적용되다
400 □ ironically ⓐ 역설적으로
401 □ routinize ⓥ 일상화하다, 습관화하다
402 □ garbage ⓝ 쓰레기
403 □ pass by ～을 지나치다
404 □ distinctive ⓐ 독특한
405 □ leftover ⓐ 남긴 ⓝ 남은 음식
406 □ spill ⓥ 쏟다
407 □ dress shirt 와이셔츠
408 □ sharp ⓐ 예리한
409 □ distort ⓥ 왜곡하다
410 □ recollection ⓝ 회상, 기억

43~45
411 □ severe ⓐ 혹독한
412 □ attain ⓥ 얻다, 달성하다
413 □ enviable ⓐ 부러운, 선망의 대상인
414 □ hiss off 야유하여 쫓아내다
415 □ in spite of ～에도 불구하고
416 □ endure ⓥ 견디다
417 □ at one's feet 발밑에
418 □ inquire ⓥ 묻다
419 □ acquaintance ⓝ 아는 사람, 지인
420 □ call on 방문하다
421 □ search out 뒤지다, 수색하다
422 □ undertake ⓥ 맡다, 착수하다, 약속하다
423 □ restore ⓥ 복구하다
424 □ in vain 허사가 되어
425 □ benefit concert 자선 콘서트
426 □ occasion ⓝ 행사
427 □ doubt ⓥ 의심하다
428 □ applause ⓝ 박수갈채
429 □ mingle ⓥ 섞이다
430 □ rejoice over ～에 기뻐하다
431 □ at the height of ～의 정점에
432 □ come across 우연히 마주치다
433 □ helplessness ⓝ 무력함
434 □ impulsively ⓐ 충동적으로
435 □ beckon ⓥ 손짓하다

07회

● 채점 : 맞은 개수 _____ / 80

TEST A-B 각 단어의 뜻을 [A] 영어는 우리말로, [B] 우리말은 영어로 쓰시오.

A	English	Korean
01	attendance	
02	profound	
03	fad	
04	stem from	
05	abstract	
06	accompany	
07	quota	
08	questionnaire	
09	discriminatory	
10	contaminate	
11	rescue	
12	novel	
13	intimidating	
14	be founded on	
15	underlying	
16	vertically	
17	distinctive	
18	beckon	
19	extract	
20	sustainable development	

B	Korean	English
01	승인되지 않은	
02	분간하다	
03	출현	
04	역, 반대	
05	금지하다	
06	엄히	
07	실험대상자	
08	국내의, 가정의	
09	살충제	
10	불량	
11	주장하다, 변호하다, 옹호하다	
12	능력, 기술	
13	수입하다	
14	조작	
15	편견	
16	일상화하다, 습관화하다	
17	아무리 과장해도 지나치지 않다	
18	자격 (사항)	
19	당황한	
20	~을 고려하다	

▶ A-D 정답 : 해설편 074쪽

TEST C-D 각 단어의 뜻을 골라 기호를 쓰시오.

C	English			Korean
01	unfold	(	)	ⓐ 충동적으로
02	save for	(	)	ⓑ 괴롭히다, 감염시키다
03	momentum	(	)	ⓒ 핵의
04	dispose of	(	)	ⓓ ~에 맞추다, 순응하다
05	compassion	(	)	ⓔ 열등함
06	plague	(	)	ⓕ 지중해(지역)
07	nuclear	(	)	ⓖ 일반적인
08	distortion	(	)	ⓗ 논란의 여지가 있는
09	prevalent	(	)	ⓘ 본능
10	conform to	(	)	ⓙ 멸균의
11	neglect	(	)	ⓚ 펼치다
12	incompetence	(	)	ⓛ 혹독한
13	inferiority	(	)	ⓜ 추진력, 기세
14	antiseptic	(	)	ⓝ ~를 처리하다, 버리다
15	controversial	(	)	ⓞ 왜곡
16	Mediterranean	(	)	ⓟ 만연한, 널리 퍼진
17	instinct	(	)	ⓠ 태만, 방치, 소홀
18	generic	(	)	ⓡ ~를 빼고는
19	impulsively	(	)	ⓢ 무능
20	severe	(	)	ⓣ 연민, 동정

D	Korean			English
01	평가하다	(	)	ⓐ punctuation
02	전해 내려오는 풍속	(	)	ⓑ account
03	~에서 생겨나다	(	)	ⓒ assess
04	구두법	(	)	ⓓ illustration
05	준수하다	(	)	ⓔ obsession
06	설명	(	)	ⓕ antioxidant
07	편향	(	)	ⓖ spill
08	(잘 보여주는) 예	(	)	ⓗ downplay
09	청소년기, 사춘기	(	)	ⓘ in vain
10	강박, 집착	(	)	ⓙ comply with
11	경시하다	(	)	ⓚ agriculture
12	산화 방지제	(	)	ⓛ endure
13	병합하다	(	)	ⓜ lose one's marble
14	쏟다	(	)	ⓝ emerge from
15	농업	(	)	ⓞ bias
16	견디다	(	)	ⓟ merge
17	분별력을 잃다	(	)	ⓠ prompt
18	구두의	(	)	ⓡ relic
19	허사가 되어	(	)	ⓢ adolescence
20	유발하다	(	)	ⓣ verbal

※ 영어 [독해] 파트만 수록한 문제지이므로 18번부터 시작합니다.

● 점수 표시가 없는 문항은 모두 2점 ● 문항수 28개 | 배점 63점 | 제한 시간 45분

18. 다음 글의 목적으로 가장 적절한 것은?

Dear Ms. Stevens,

My name is Peter Watson, and I'm the manager of the Springton Library. Our storytelling program has been so well-attended that we are planning to expand the program to 6 days each week. This means that we need to recruit more volunteers to read to the children. People still talk about the week you filled in for us when one of our volunteers couldn't come. You really brought those stories to life! So, would you be willing to read to the preschoolers for an hour, from 10 to 11 a.m. every Friday? I hope you will take this opportunity to let more children hear your voice. We are looking forward to your positive reply.

Best regards,
Peter Watson

① 도서관의 운영 시간 연장을 제안하려고
② 봉사 활동 시간이 변경된 것을 안내하려고
③ 독서 토론 수업에 참여할 아동을 모집하려고
④ 봉사 활동에 참여하지 못하게 된 것을 사과하려고
⑤ 책 읽어 주기 자원봉사에 참여해 줄 것을 요청하려고

19. 다음 글에 드러난 'I'의 심경 변화로 가장 적절한 것은?

I walked up to the little dark brown door and knocked. Nobody answered. I pushed on the door carefully. When the door swung open with a rusty creak, a man was standing in a back corner of the room. My hands flew over my mouth as I started to scream. He was just standing there, watching me! As my heart continued to race, I saw that he had also put his hands over his mouth. Wait a minute... It was a mirror! I took a deep breath and walked past a table to the old mirror that stood in the back of the room. I felt my heartbeat returning to normal, and calmly looked at my reflection in the mirror.

① terrified → relieved
② hopeful → nervous
③ confident → anxious
④ annoyed → grateful
⑤ disappointed → thrilled

20. 다음 글에서 필자가 주장하는 바로 가장 적절한 것은?

In the rush towards individual achievement and recognition, the majority of those who make it forget their humble beginnings. They often forget those who helped them on their way up. If you forget where you came from, if you neglect those who were there for you when things were tough and slow, then your success is valueless. No one can make it up there without the help of others. There are parents, friends, advisers, and coaches that help. You need to be grateful to all of those who helped you. Gratitude is the glue that keeps you connected to others. It is the bridge that keeps you connected with those who were there for you in the past and who are likely to be there in the end. Relationships and the way you treat others determine your real success.

① 원만한 인간관계를 위하여 사고의 유연성을 길러야 한다.
② 성공에 도움을 준 사람들에게 감사하는 마음을 가져야 한다.
③ 자신의 분야에서 성공하기 위해서는 경험의 폭을 넓혀야 한다.
④ 원하는 직업을 갖기 위해서는 다른 사람의 조언을 경청해야 한다.
⑤ 타인의 시선을 의식하지 않고 부단히 새로운 일에 도전해야 한다.

21. 밑줄 친 'give away the house'가 다음 글에서 의미하는 바로 가장 적절한 것은? [3점]

For companies interested in delighting customers, exceptional value and service become part of the overall company culture. For example, year after year, Pazano ranks at or near the top of the hospitality industry in terms of customer satisfaction. The company's passion for satisfying customers is summed up in its credo, which promises that its luxury hotels will deliver a truly memorable experience. Although a customer-centered firm seeks to deliver high customer satisfaction relative to competitors, it does not attempt to *maximize* customer satisfaction. A company can always increase customer satisfaction by lowering its price or increasing its services. But this may result in lower profits. Thus, the purpose of marketing is to generate customer value profitably. This requires a very delicate balance: the marketer must continue to generate more customer value and satisfaction but not 'give away the house'.

* credo: 신조

① risk the company's profitability
② overlook a competitor's strengths
③ hurt the reputation of the company
④ generate more customer complaints
⑤ abandon customer-oriented marketing

22. 다음 글의 요지로 가장 적절한 것은?

The problem with simply adopting any popular method of parenting is that it ignores the most important variable in the equation: the uniqueness of your child. So, rather than insist that one style of parenting will work with every child, we might take a page from the gardener's handbook. Just as the gardener accepts, without question or resistance, the plant's requirements and provides the right conditions each plant needs to grow and flourish, so, too, do we parents need to custom-design our parenting to fit the natural needs of each individual child. Although that may seem difficult, it is possible. Once we understand who our children really are, we can begin to figure out how to make changes in our parenting style to be more positive and accepting of each child we've been blessed to parent.

* equation: 방정식

① 자녀의 특성에 맞는 개별화된 양육이 필요하다.
② 식물을 키우는 것이 자녀의 창의성 발달에 도움이 된다.
③ 정서적 교감은 자녀의 바람직한 인격 형성에 필수적이다.
④ 자녀에게 타인을 존중하는 태도를 가르치는 것이 중요하다.
⑤ 전문가에 의해 검증된 양육 방식을 따르는 것이 바람직하다.

23. 다음 글의 주제로 가장 적절한 것은?

In the movie *Groundhog Day*, a weatherman played by Bill Murray is forced to re-live a single day over and over again. Confronted with this seemingly endless loop, he eventually rebels against living through the same day the same way twice. He learns French, becomes a great pianist, befriends his neighbors, helps the poor. Why do we cheer him on? Because we don't want perfect predictability, even if what's on repeat is appealing. Surprise engages us. It allows us to escape autopilot. It keeps us awake to our experience. In fact, the neurotransmitter systems involved in reward are tied to the level of surprise: rewards delivered at regular, predictable times yield a lot less activity in the brain than the same rewards delivered at random unpredictable times. Surprise gratifies.

* loop: 고리   ** neurotransmitter: 신경전달물질

① considerations in learning foreign languages
② people's inclination towards unpredictability
③ hidden devices to make a movie plot unexpected
④ positive effects of routine on human brain function
⑤ danger of predicting the future based on the present

24. 다음 글의 제목으로 가장 적절한 것은?

A building is an inanimate object, but it is not an inarticulate one. Even the simplest house always makes a statement, one expressed in brick and stone, in wood and glass, rather than in words — but no less loud and obvious. When we see a rusting trailer surrounded by weeds and abandoned cars, or a brand-new mini-mansion with a high wall, we instantly get a message. In both of these cases, though in different accents, it is "Stay Out of Here." It is not only houses, of course, that communicate with us. All kinds of buildings — churches, museums, schools, hospitals, restaurants, and offices — speak to us silently. Sometimes the statement is deliberate. A store or restaurant can be designed so that it welcomes mostly low-income or high-income customers. Buildings tell us what to think and how to act, though we may not register their messages consciously.

* inarticulate: 표현을 제대로 하지 못하는

① Buildings Do Talk in Their Own Ways!
② Design of Buildings Starts from Nature
③ Language of Buildings: Too Vague to Grasp
④ Which Is More Important, Safety or Beauty?
⑤ How Do Architects Attach Emotions to Buildings?

25. 다음 도표의 내용과 일치하지 <u>않는</u> 것은?

Travel and Tourism's Contribution to GDP

(unit: billions of US dollars)

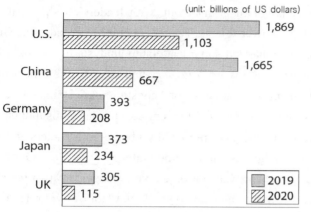

	2019	2020
U.S.	1,869	1,103
China	1,665	667
Germany	393	208
Japan	373	234
UK	305	115

The above graph shows travel and tourism's contribution to GDP for each of the five countries in 2019 and in 2020. ① In all five countries, travel and tourism's contribution to GDP in 2020 decreased compared to the previous year. ② Both in 2019 and in 2020, the U.S. showed the largest contribution of travel and tourism to GDP among the five countries, followed by China. ③ In China, travel and tourism's contribution to GDP in 2020 was less than a third that in 2019. ④ In 2019, Germany showed a larger contribution of travel and tourism to GDP than Japan, whereas the reverse was true in 2020. ⑤ In 2020, the UK was the only country where the contribution of travel and tourism to GDP was less than $200 billion.

26. monarch butterfly에 관한 다음 글의 내용과 일치하지 <u>않는</u> 것은?

The monarch butterfly has lovely bright colors splashed on its wings. The wings have white spots on the outer margins. The hind wings are rounded, and they are lighter in color than the front wings. The body is black with white spots. The mother butterfly lays only one egg on the underside of milkweed leaves, which hatches about three to five days later. The monarch loves to fly around in the warm sunshine, from March through October, all across the United States. The monarch cannot survive the cold winter temperatures of the northern states. So, it very wisely migrates from the northern states to the south, and hibernates. The monarch is the only insect that can fly more than four thousand kilometers to a warmer climate.

* hibernate: 동면하다

① 날개의 바깥 가장자리에 흰 점이 있다.
② 뒷날개는 앞날개보다 색이 더 밝다.
③ 알은 약 3일에서 5일 후에 부화한다.
④ 북부 주의 추운 겨울 기온에 잘 버틴다.
⑤ 4천 킬로미터 넘게 날 수 있다.

27. 2022 Korean Speech Contest에 관한 다음 안내문의 내용과 일치하지 <u>않는</u> 것은?

2022 Korean Speech Contest

Are you a foreign student who wants to show off your Korean? Make your own video sharing your experiences in Korea.

- **Theme:** "My Experiences While Staying in Korea"
- **Video Submission Deadline:** September 5th
- **Prizes**
  - 1st place: $100 and traditional Korean tea
  - 2nd place: $50 and a traditional Korean doll
- **Details**
  - Your name must be mentioned at the beginning of the video.
  - Your video must be between 3 to 5 minutes.
  - Please email your video file to k-speech@kcontest.com.

① 한국에서 지내는 동안의 경험을 주제로 한다.
② 영상 제출 마감일은 9월 5일이다.
③ 1등에게는 상금과 한국 전통 인형이 주어진다.
④ 영상 도입부에 이름이 언급되어야 한다.
⑤ 이메일로 영상 파일을 보내야 한다.

28. EZ Portable Photo Printer 사용에 관한 다음 안내문의 내용과 일치하는 것은?

EZ Portable Photo Printer User Manual

Note on LED Indicator
- White: Power on
- Red: Battery charging

Top Cover
Power Button
USB Port
LED Indicator

How to Operate
- Press the power button to turn the printer on.
- Press the power button twice to turn the printer off.
- To charge the battery, connect the cable to the USB port. It takes 60 – 90 minutes for a full charge.
- To connect to the printer wirelessly, download the 'EZ Printer App' on your mobile device.

How to Load Photo Paper
- Lift the printer's top cover.
- Insert the photo paper with any logos facing downward.

① LED 표시기의 흰색은 충전 중임을 나타낸다.
② 전원 버튼을 한 번 누르면 전원이 꺼진다.
③ 배터리가 완전히 충전되는 데 2시간 이상 걸린다.
④ 무선 연결을 위해 앱을 다운로드해야 한다.
⑤ 인화지를 로고가 위로 향하도록 넣어야 한다.

29. 다음 글의 밑줄 친 부분 중, 어법상 틀린 것은? [3점]

Even though institutions like the World Bank use wealth ① to differentiate between "developed" and "developing" countries, they also agree that development is more than economic growth. "Development" can also include the social and environmental changes that are caused by or accompany economic growth, some of ② which are positive and thus may be negative. Awareness has grown — and continues to grow — that the question of how economic growth is affecting people and the planet ③ needs to be addressed. Countries are slowly learning that it is cheaper and causes ④ much less suffering to try to reduce the harmful effects of an economic activity or project at the beginning, when it is planned, than after the damage appears. To do this is not easy and is always imperfect. But an awareness of the need for such an effort indicates a greater understanding and moral concern than ⑤ was the previous widespread attitude that focused only on creating new products and services.

30. 다음 글의 밑줄 친 부분 중, 문맥상 낱말의 쓰임이 적절하지 않은 것은?

The most advanced military jets are fly-by-wire: They are so unstable that they require an automated system that can sense and act more quickly than a human operator to maintain control. Our dependence on smart technology has led to a ① paradox. As technology improves, it becomes more reliable and more efficient, and human operators depend on it even more. Eventually they lose focus, become ② distracted, and check out, leaving the system to run on its own. In the most extreme case, piloting a massive airliner could become a ③ passive occupation, like watching TV. This is fine until something unexpected happens. The unexpected reveals the value of humans; what we bring to the table is the ④ flexibility to handle new situations. Machines aren't collaborating in pursuit of a joint goal; they are merely serving as tools. So when the human operator gives up oversight, the system is ⑤ less likely to have a serious accident.

* fly-by-wire: 전자식 비행 조종 장치

[31~34] 다음 빈칸에 들어갈 말로 가장 적절한 것을 고르시오.

31. Followers can be defined by their position as subordinates or by their behavior of going along with leaders' wishes. But followers also have power to lead. Followers empower leaders as well as vice versa. This has led some leadership analysts like Ronald Heifetz to avoid using the word *followers* and refer to the others in a power relationship as "citizens" or "constituents." Heifetz is correct that too simple a view of followers can produce misunderstanding. In modern life, most people wind up being both leaders and followers, and the categories can become quite _____. Our behavior as followers changes as our objectives change. If I trust your judgment in music more than my own, I may follow your lead on which concert we attend (even though you may be formally my subordinate in position). But if I am an expert on fishing, you may follow my lead on where we fish, regardless of our formal positions or the fact that I followed your lead on concerts yesterday.

* vice versa: 반대로, 거꾸로

① rigid
② unfair
③ fluid
④ stable
⑤ apparent

32. Color is an interpretation of wavelengths, one that only exists internally. And it gets stranger, because the wavelengths we're talking about involve only what we call "visible light", a spectrum of wavelengths that runs from red to violet. But visible light constitutes only a tiny fraction of the electromagnetic spectrum — less than one ten-trillionth of it. All the rest of the spectrum — including radio waves, microwaves, X-rays, gamma rays, cell phone conversations, wi-fi, and so on — all of this is flowing through us right now, and we're completely unaware of it. This is because we don't have any specialized biological receptors to pick up on these signals from other parts of the spectrum. The slice of reality that we can see is _____.

* electromagnetic: 전자기의 ** receptor: 수용체

① hindered by other wavelengths
② derived from our imagination
③ perceived through all senses
④ filtered by our stereotypes
⑤ limited by our biology

33. What is unusual about journalism as a profession is _____. In theory, practitioners in the classic professions, like medicine or the clergy, contain the means of production in their heads and hands, and therefore do not have to work for a company or an employer. They can draw their income directly from their clients or patients. Because the professionals hold knowledge, moreover, their clients are dependent on them. Journalists hold knowledge, but it is not theoretical in nature; one might argue that the public depends on journalists in the same way that patients depend on doctors, but in practice a journalist can serve the public usually only by working for a news organization, which can fire her or him at will. Journalists' income depends not on the public, but on the employing news organization, which often derives the large majority of its revenue from advertisers. [3점]

① its lack of independence
② the constant search for truth
③ the disregard of public opinion
④ its balance of income and faith
⑤ its overconfidence in its social influence

34. In most of the world, capitalism and free markets are accepted today as constituting the best system for allocating economic resources and encouraging economic output. Nations have tried other systems, such as socialism and communism, but in many cases they have either switched wholesale to or adopted aspects of free markets. Despite the widespread acceptance of the free-market system, _____ . Government involvement takes many forms, ranging from the enactment and enforcement of laws and regulations to direct participation in the economy through entities like the U.S.'s mortgage agencies. Perhaps the most important form of government involvement, however, comes in the attempts of central banks and national treasuries to control and affect the ups and downs of economic cycles. [3점]

* enactment: (법률의) 제정 ** entity: 실체

① markets are rarely left entirely free
② governments are reluctant to intervene
③ supply and demand are not always balanced
④ economic inequality continues to get worse
⑤ competition does not guarantee the maximum profit

35. 다음 글에서 전체 흐름과 관계 없는 문장은?

Inflationary risk refers to uncertainty regarding the future real value of one's investments. Say, for instance, that you hold $100 in a bank account that has no fees and accrues no interest. If left untouched there will always be $100 in that bank account. ① If you keep that money in the bank for a year, during which inflation is 100 percent, you've still got $100. ② Only now, if you take it out and put it in your wallet, you'll only be able to purchase half the goods you could have bought a year ago. ③ In other words, if inflation increases faster than the amount of interest you are earning, this will decrease the purchasing power of your investments over time. ④ It would be very useful to know in advance what would happen to your firm's total revenue if you increased your product's price. ⑤ That's why we differentiate between nominal value and real value.

* accrue: 생기다 ** nominal: 명목의, 액면(상)의

[36~37] 주어진 글 다음에 이어질 글의 순서로 가장 적절한 것을 고르시오.

36.

> Touch receptors are spread over all parts of the body, but they are not spread evenly. Most of the touch receptors are found in your fingertips, tongue, and lips.

(A) But if the fingers are spread far apart, you can feel them individually. Yet if the person does the same thing on the back of your hand (with your eyes closed, so that you don't see how many fingers are being used), you probably will be able to tell easily, even when the fingers are close together.

(B) You can test this for yourself. Have someone poke you in the back with one, two, or three fingers and try to guess how many fingers the person used. If the fingers are close together, you will probably think it was only one.

(C) On the tip of each of your fingers, for example, there are about five thousand separate touch receptors. In other parts of the body there are far fewer. In the skin of your back, the touch receptors may be as much as 2 inches apart.

① (A) - (C) - (B)   ② (B) - (A) - (C)
③ (B) - (C) - (A)   ④ (C) - (A) - (B)
⑤ (C) - (B) - (A)

37.

One interesting feature of network markets is that "history matters." A famous example is the QWERTY keyboard used with your computer.

(A) Replacing the QWERTY keyboard with a more efficient design would have been both expensive and difficult to coordinate. Thus, the placement of the letters stays with the obsolete QWERTY on today's English-language keyboards.

(B) You might wonder why this particular configuration of keys, with its awkward placement of the letters, became the standard. The QWERTY keyboard in the 19th century was developed in the era of manual typewriters with physical keys.

(C) The keyboard was designed to keep frequently used keys (like E and O) physically separated in order to prevent them from jamming. By the time the technology for electronic typing evolved, millions of people had already learned to type on millions of QWERTY typewriters. [3점]

* obsolete: 구식의 ** configuration: 배열

① (A) − (C) − (B)
② (B) − (A) − (C)
③ (B) − (C) − (A)
④ (C) − (A) − (B)
⑤ (C) − (B) − (A)

[38~39] 글의 흐름으로 보아, 주어진 문장이 들어가기에 가장 적절한 곳을 고르시오.

38.

This temperature is of the surface of the star, the part of the star which is emitting the light that can be seen.

One way of measuring temperature occurs if an object is hot enough to visibly glow, such as a metal poker that has been left in a fire. (①) The color of a glowing object is related to its temperature: as the temperature rises, the object is first red and then orange, and finally it gets white, the "hottest" color. (②) The relation between temperature and the color of a glowing object is useful to astronomers. (③) The color of stars is related to their temperature, and since people cannot as yet travel the great distances to the stars and measure their temperature in a more precise way, astronomers rely on their color. (④) The interior of the star is at a much higher temperature, though it is concealed. (⑤) But the information obtained from the color of the star is still useful. [3점]

39.

But by the 1970s, psychologists realized there was no such thing as a general "creativity quotient."

The holy grail of the first wave of creativity research was a personality test to measure general creativity ability, in the same way that IQ measured general intelligence. (①) A person's creativity score should tell us his or her creative potential in any field of endeavor, just like an IQ score is not limited to physics, math, or literature. (②) Creative people aren't creative in a general, universal way; they're creative in a specific sphere of activity, a particular domain. (③) We don't expect a creative scientist to also be a gifted painter. (④) A creative violinist may not be a creative conductor, and a creative conductor may not be very good at composing new works. (⑤) Psychologists now know that creativity is domain specific.

* quotient: 지수 ** holy grail: 궁극적 목표

40. 다음 글의 내용을 한 문장으로 요약하고자 한다. 빈칸 (A), (B)에 들어갈 말로 가장 적절한 것은?

The great irony of performance psychology is that it teaches each sportsman to believe, as far as he is able, that he will win. No man doubts. No man indulges his inner skepticism. That is the logic of sports psychology. But only one man *can* win. That is the logic of sport. Note the difference between a scientist and an athlete. Doubt is a scientist's stock in trade. Progress is made by focusing on the evidence that refutes a theory and by improving the theory accordingly. Skepticism is the rocket fuel of scientific advance. But doubt, to an athlete, is poison. Progress is made by ignoring the evidence; it is about creating a mindset that is immune to doubt and uncertainty. Just to reiterate: From a rational perspective, this is nothing less than crazy. Why should an athlete convince himself he will win when he knows that there is every possibility he will lose? Because, to win, one must proportion one's belief, not to the evidence, but to whatever the mind can usefully get away with.

* reiterate: 되풀이하다

↓

Unlike scientists whose ___(A)___ attitude is needed to make scientific progress, sports psychology says that to succeed, athletes must ___(B)___ feelings of uncertainty about whether they can win.

　　　(A)　　　　　　　(B)
① confident　······　keep
② skeptical　······　eliminate
③ arrogant　······　express
④ critical　······　keep
⑤ stubborn　······　eliminate

08회

[41~42] 다음 글을 읽고, 물음에 답하시오.

Common sense suggests that discussion with others who express different opinions should produce more moderate attitudes for everyone in the group. Surprisingly, this is not always the case. In group polarization, a period of discussion pushes group members to take more extreme positions in the direction that they were already inclined to prefer. Group polarization does not (a) reverse the direction of attitudes, but rather accentuates the attitudes held at the beginning. Two pressures appear to push individuals to take more extreme positions following a group discussion. First, conformity and desire for affiliation contribute to group polarization. If the majority of a group is leaning in a particular direction, what could be a better way of fitting in than (b) agreeing with that majority, and maybe even taking its argument one step farther? There is also a tendency for like-minded people to affiliate with one another, which can provide (c) reinforcement for existing opinions, increase people's confidence in those opinions, lead to the discovery of new reasons for those opinions and counterarguments to opposing views, and reduce exposure to conflicting ideas. Second, exposure to discussion on a topic introduces new reasons for (d) changing an attitude. If you are already opposed to gun control and you listen to additional arguments supporting your position, you might end up more (e) opposed than you were originally.

* accentuate: 강화하다 ** affiliation: 소속

41. 윗글의 제목으로 가장 적절한 것은?

① Have More Companions and Perform Better!
② Group Competition: Not Necessarily Harmful
③ Exposure to New Ideas Weakens Group Identity
④ Sharing Ideas: The Surest Way to Foster Creativity
⑤ Black Gets Darker, White Gets Brighter in Group Discussion

42. 밑줄 친 (a)~(e) 중에서 문맥상 낱말의 쓰임이 적절하지 <u>않은</u> 것은? [3점]

① (a) ② (b) ③ (c) ④ (d) ⑤ (e)

[43~45] 다음 글을 읽고, 물음에 답하시오.

(A)

A businessman boarded a flight. Arriving at his seat, he greeted his travel companions: a middle-aged woman sitting at the window, and a little boy sitting in the aisle seat. After putting his bag in the overhead bin, he took his place between them. After the flight took off, he began a conversation with the little boy. He appeared to be about the same age as (a) his son and was busy with a coloring book.

(B)

As the plane rose and fell several times, people got nervous and sat up in their seats. The man was also nervous and grabbing (b) his seat as tightly as he could. Meanwhile, the little boy was sitting quietly beside (c) him. His coloring book and crayons were put away neatly in the seat pocket in front of him, and his hands were calmly resting on his legs. Incredibly, he didn't seem worried at all.

(C)

Then, suddenly, the turbulence ended. The pilot apologized for the bumpy ride and announced that they would be landing soon. As the plane began its descent, the man said to the little boy, "You are just a little boy, but (d) I have never met a braver person in all my life! Tell me, how is it that you remained so calm while all of us adults were so afraid?" Looking him in the eyes, he said, "My father is the pilot, and he's taking me home."

* turbulence: 난기류

(D)

He asked the boy a few usual questions, such as his age, his hobbies, as well as his favorite animal. He found it strange that such a young boy would be traveling alone, so he decided to keep an eye on (e) him to make sure he was okay. About an hour into the flight, the plane suddenly began experiencing turbulence. The pilot told everyone to fasten their seat belts and remain calm, as they had encountered rough weather.

43. 주어진 글 (A)에 이어질 내용을 순서에 맞게 배열한 것으로 가장 적절한 것은?

① (B) - (D) - (C)   ② (C) - (B) - (D)
③ (C) - (D) - (B)   ④ (D) - (B) - (C)
⑤ (D) - (C) - (B)

44. 밑줄 친 (a)~(e) 중에서 가리키는 대상이 나머지 넷과 <u>다른</u> 것은?

① (a) ② (b) ③ (c) ④ (d) ⑤ (e)

45. 윗글에 관한 내용으로 적절하지 <u>않은</u> 것은?

① 사업가는 중년 여성과 소년 사이에 앉았다.
② 비행기가 오르락내리락하자 사람들은 긴장했다.
③ 소년은 색칠 공부 책과 크레용을 가방에 넣었다.
④ 소년은 자신의 아버지가 조종사라고 말했다.
⑤ 조종사는 사람들에게 안전벨트를 매고 침착하라고 말했다.

* 확인 사항
○ 답안지의 해당란에 필요한 내용을 정확히 기입(표기)했는지 확인하시오.

18

001 ☐ manager ⓝ 관리자
002 ☐ well-attended ⓐ 많은 사람들이 참석하는
003 ☐ expand ⓥ 확대하다
004 ☐ recruit ⓥ 모집하다
005 ☐ volunteer ⓝ 자원봉사자
006 ☐ fill in ~을 대신하다, 채워넣다
007 ☐ bring to life (이야기를) 활기 넘치게 하다, 생동감 있게 하다
008 ☐ preschooler ⓝ 미취학 아동
009 ☐ opportunity ⓝ 기회
010 ☐ positive ⓐ 긍정적인

19

011 ☐ carefully ⓐⓓ 조심스럽게
012 ☐ swing open (문이 좌우로) 활짝 열리다
013 ☐ rusty ⓐ 녹슨
014 ☐ creak ⓝ 삐걱거리는 소리
015 ☐ scream ⓥ 비명지르다
016 ☐ breath ⓝ 호흡
017 ☐ heartbeat ⓝ 심장 박동
018 ☐ reflection ⓝ (거울이나 물에 비친) 그림자
019 ☐ relieved ⓐ 안도한
020 ☐ confident ⓐ 자신감 있는
021 ☐ anxious ⓐ 불안한
022 ☐ annoyed ⓐ 짜증이 난
023 ☐ disappointed ⓐ 실망한

20

024 ☐ individual ⓐ 개인의
025 ☐ achievement ⓝ 성취
026 ☐ recognition ⓝ 인정, 표창
027 ☐ majority ⓝ 대다수
028 ☐ make it 성공하다
029 ☐ humble ⓐ 작은, 변변찮은, 겸손한
030 ☐ beginning ⓝ 시작
031 ☐ often ⓐⓓ 종종
032 ☐ neglect ⓥ 소홀히 하다
033 ☐ valueless ⓐ 가치 없는
034 ☐ grateful ⓐ 감사하는, 고마워하는
035 ☐ gratitude ⓝ 감사
036 ☐ treat ⓥ 대하다
037 ☐ determine ⓥ 결정하다

21

038 ☐ delight ⓥ (~을) 즐겁게 하다, 기쁘게 하다
039 ☐ customer ⓝ 고객
040 ☐ exceptional ⓐ 뛰어난, 예외적인
041 ☐ company culture 기업 문화
042 ☐ hospitality industry 서비스업(호텔 산업, 식당업 등)
043 ☐ customer satisfaction 고객 만족
044 ☐ passion ⓝ 열정
045 ☐ sum up 요약하다, 압축해서 보여주다
046 ☐ memorable ⓐ 기억할 만한
047 ☐ firm ⓝ 회사
048 ☐ relative to ~에 비해
049 ☐ attempt ⓥ 시도하다
050 ☐ result in ~로 이어지다, ~을 낳다
051 ☐ generate ⓥ 발생시키다, 만들어 내다
052 ☐ profitably ⓐⓓ 수익을 내며, 수익성 있게
053 ☐ delicate ⓐ 섬세한, 미묘한

054 ☐ balance ⓝ 균형
055 ☐ give away 거저 주다
056 ☐ profitability ⓝ 수익성
057 ☐ overlook ⓥ 간과하다

22

058 ☐ adopt ⓥ 채택하다
059 ☐ method ⓝ 방법
060 ☐ ignore ⓥ 무시하다
061 ☐ variable ⓝ 변수 ⓐ 가변적인
062 ☐ uniqueness ⓝ 독특함, 고유함
063 ☐ gardner ⓝ 정원사, 원예사
064 ☐ insist ⓥ 주장하다
065 ☐ handbook ⓝ 안내서
066 ☐ resistance ⓝ 저항
067 ☐ requirement ⓝ 필요조건
068 ☐ provide ⓥ 제공하다
069 ☐ flourish ⓥ 번성하다
070 ☐ possible ⓐ 가능한
071 ☐ blessed ⓐ 축복 받은

23

072 ☐ play ⓥ 연기하다
073 ☐ over and over 반복해서
074 ☐ confront ⓥ 직면하다
075 ☐ loop ⓝ 고리
076 ☐ rebel against ~에 저항하다
077 ☐ befriend ⓥ ~의 친구가 되다
078 ☐ cheer on ~을 응원하다
079 ☐ predictability ⓝ 예측 가능성
080 ☐ repeat ⓥ 반복하다
081 ☐ appealing ⓐ 매력적인
082 ☐ engage ⓥ 사로잡다
083 ☐ autopilot ⓝ 자동 조종 장치
084 ☐ neurotransmitter ⓝ 신경 전달 물질
085 ☐ reward ⓝ 보상
086 ☐ predictable ⓐ 예측할 수 있는
087 ☐ yield ⓥ 산출하다
088 ☐ random ⓐ 임의의
089 ☐ unpredictable ⓐ 예측이 불가능한
090 ☐ gratify ⓥ 기쁘게 하다, 충족시키다
091 ☐ consideration ⓝ 고려 사항
092 ☐ inclination ⓝ 성향, 경향
093 ☐ plot ⓝ 줄거리
094 ☐ routine ⓝ 일상
095 ☐ function ⓝ 기능

24

096 ☐ inanimate ⓐ 무생물의
097 ☐ make a statement 말하다, 진술하다
098 ☐ express ⓥ 표현하다
099 ☐ brick ⓝ 벽돌
100 ☐ rust ⓥ 녹슬다
101 ☐ weed ⓝ 잡초
102 ☐ brand-new ⓐ 아주 새로운
103 ☐ instantly ⓐⓓ 즉시
104 ☐ accent ⓝ 억양
105 ☐ church ⓝ 교회
106 ☐ museum ⓝ 박물관
107 ☐ statement ⓝ 진술
108 ☐ deliberate ⓐ 의도적인, 고의의
109 ☐ low-income ⓐ 저소득의

110 ☐ register ⓥ 알아채다, 기억하다
111 ☐ consciously ⓐⓓ 의식적으로
112 ☐ grasp ⓥ 이해하다
113 ☐ attach ⓥ 부여하다

25

114 ☐ contribution ⓝ 기여
115 ☐ billion ⓝ 10억
116 ☐ previous ⓐ 이전의
117 ☐ reverse ⓝ 반대, 역

26

118 ☐ monarch ⓝ 제왕, 군주
119 ☐ splash ⓥ (선명한 색으로) 알록달록하게 장식하다
120 ☐ wing ⓝ 날개
121 ☐ spot ⓝ 점, 반점
122 ☐ outer ⓐ (안·중심에서 가장) 바깥쪽의
123 ☐ margin ⓝ 가장자리
124 ☐ hind wing (곤충의) 뒷날개
125 ☐ rounded ⓐ 둥근
126 ☐ lay ⓥ (알을) 낳다
127 ☐ underside ⓝ 아랫면, 밑면
128 ☐ hatch ⓥ 부화하다
129 ☐ survive ⓥ 살아남다
130 ☐ migrate ⓥ 이주하다
131 ☐ insect ⓝ 곤충
132 ☐ climate ⓝ (기후상으로 본) 지방, 지대, 지역

27

133 ☐ traditional ⓐ 전통의
134 ☐ show off ~을 과시하다
135 ☐ mention ⓥ 언급하다

28

136 ☐ portable ⓐ 휴대 가능한
137 ☐ indicator ⓝ 표시(기), 장치, 지표
138 ☐ twice ⓐⓓ 두 번
139 ☐ wirelessly ⓐⓓ 무선으로
140 ☐ load ⓥ 장착하다, 싣다
141 ☐ cover ⓥ 덮개
142 ☐ insert ⓥ 끼워 넣다

29

143 ☐ institution ⓝ 기관
144 ☐ wealth ⓝ 부, 재산
145 ☐ differentiate ⓥ 구별하다
146 ☐ economic growth 경제 성장
147 ☐ include ⓥ 포함하다
148 ☐ environmental ⓐ 환경적인
149 ☐ accompany ⓥ 동반하다
150 ☐ affect ⓥ 영향을 미치다
151 ☐ address ⓥ 다루다, 처리하다
152 ☐ cheap ⓐ 돈이 적게 드는
153 ☐ suffering ⓝ 고통
154 ☐ harmful ⓐ 해로운
155 ☐ damage ⓝ 피해
156 ☐ imperfect ⓐ 불완전한
157 ☐ indicate ⓥ 나타내다
158 ☐ concern ⓝ 우려
159 ☐ widespread ⓐ 광범위한, 널리 퍼진
160 ☐ attitude ⓝ 태도

30

161 ☐ advanced ⓐ 진보된, 고급의
162 ☐ military ⓐ 군사의
163 ☐ jet ⓝ 제트기
164 ☐ unstable ⓐ 불안정한
165 ☐ automate ⓥ 자동화하다
166 ☐ operator ⓝ 조작자
167 ☐ dependence ⓝ 의존
168 ☐ paradox ⓝ 역설
169 ☐ reliable ⓐ 믿을 만한
170 ☐ lose focus 집중력을 잃다
171 ☐ distracted ⓐ 산만한, 주의가 분산된
172 ☐ pilot ⓥ 조종하다
173 ☐ massive ⓐ 거대한
174 ☐ airliner ⓝ 여객기
175 ☐ passive ⓐ 수동적인
176 ☐ occupation ⓝ 직업, 일
177 ☐ unexpected ⓐ 예상치 못한
178 ☐ bring to the table 제시하다, 화두를 꺼내다
179 ☐ collaborate ⓥ 협력하다
180 ☐ in pursuit of ~을 추구하여
181 ☐ merely ⓐⓓ 단지
182 ☐ oversight ⓝ 관리, 감독
183 ☐ serious ⓐ 심각한
184 ☐ accident ⓝ 사고

31

185 ☐ follower ⓝ 추종자
186 ☐ define ⓥ 정의하다
187 ☐ subordinate ⓝ 부하, 추종자
188 ☐ empower ⓥ 권한을 주다
189 ☐ analyst ⓝ 분석가
190 ☐ constituent ⓝ 구성원, 구성 요소
191 ☐ correct ⓐ 옳은
192 ☐ view ⓝ 관점
193 ☐ misunderstanding ⓝ 오해
194 ☐ objective ⓝ 목표
195 ☐ trust ⓥ 신뢰하다
196 ☐ judgment ⓝ 판단
197 ☐ attend ⓥ 참석하다
198 ☐ formally ⓐⓓ 공식적으로
199 ☐ regardless of ~에 관계없이
200 ☐ formal ⓐ 공식적인, ⓝ 지위
201 ☐ rigid ⓐ 엄격한
202 ☐ fluid ⓐ 유동적인

32

203 ☐ interpretation ⓝ 해석
204 ☐ wavelength ⓝ 파장, 주파수
205 ☐ internally ⓐⓓ 내부적으로
206 ☐ visible light 가시광선
207 ☐ constitute ⓥ 구성하다
208 ☐ fraction ⓝ 부분, 파편
209 ☐ rest ⓝ 나머지
210 ☐ radio waves 무선 전파
211 ☐ conversation ⓝ 대화
212 ☐ completely ⓐⓓ 완전히
213 ☐ unaware ⓐ 알지 못하는
214 ☐ specialized ⓐ 전문화된, 분화된
215 ☐ pick up on ~을 알아차리다
216 ☐ signal ⓝ 신호

217 □ hinder ⓥ 방해하다		328 □ quotient ⓝ 지수	386 □ conformity ⓝ 순응
218 □ derive ⓥ ~에서 나오다	**35**	329 □ holy grail 궁극적 목표	387 □ desire ⓝ 욕구
219 □ perceive ⓥ 인식하다	275 □ inflationary ⓐ 인플레이션의	330 □ wave ⓝ 급증	388 □ affiliation ⓝ 소속
220 □ filter ⓥ 거르다	276 □ uncertainty ⓝ 불확실성	331 □ personality test 성격 검사	389 □ contribute ⓥ 기여하다
221 □ stereotype ⓝ 고정관념	277 □ investment ⓝ 투자	332 □ intelligence ⓝ 지능	390 □ lean ⓥ 기울다, 기대다
	278 □ account ⓝ 계좌, 계정	333 □ potential ⓝ 잠재력	391 □ farther ad 더 멀리
33	279 □ accrue ⓥ 생기다	334 □ endeavor ⓝ 노력	392 □ tendency ⓝ 경향
222 □ unusual ⓐ 특이한	280 □ interest ⓝ 이자	335 □ literature ⓝ 문학	393 □ like-minded ⓐ 생각이 비슷한
223 □ profession ⓝ 직업	281 □ wallet ⓝ 지갑	336 □ universal ⓐ 보편적인	394 □ reinforcement ⓝ 강화
224 □ practitioner ⓝ 전문직 종사자, 현역	282 □ purchase ⓥ 구입하다	337 □ specific ⓐ 특정한	395 □ discovery ⓝ 발견
225 □ medicine ⓝ 의학	283 □ in other words 다시 말해서	338 □ sphere ⓝ 범위, 영역	396 □ reason ⓝ 이유
226 □ clergy ⓝ 성직자	284 □ purchasing power 구매력	339 □ domain ⓝ 영역	397 □ counterargument ⓝ 반론
227 □ the means of production 생산 수단	285 □ useful ⓐ 유용한	340 □ expect ⓥ 기대하다	398 □ opposing ⓐ 상반되는, 대립되는
228 □ employer ⓝ 고용주	286 □ total revenue 총수입	341 □ gifted ⓐ 재능이 있는	399 □ exposure ⓝ 노출
229 □ directly ad 직접(으로)		342 □ conductor ⓝ 지휘자	400 □ conflicting ⓐ 상충되는
230 □ draw A from B A를 B로부터 끌어내다	**36**	343 □ compose ⓥ 작곡하다	401 □ topic ⓝ 주제
231 □ client ⓝ 의뢰인, 고객	287 □ touch ⓝ 촉각		402 □ introduce ⓥ 도입하다
232 □ patient ⓝ 환자	288 □ evenly ad 고르게	**40**	403 □ oppose ⓥ 반대하다
233 □ professional ⓝ 전문직 종사자	289 □ fingertip ⓝ 손가락 끝	344 □ irony ⓝ 아이러니, 반어	404 □ gun control 총기 규제
234 □ moreover ad 게다가, 더욱이	290 □ tongue ⓝ 혀	345 □ indulge ⓥ (~에) 빠지다, 탐닉하다	405 □ additional ⓐ 추가의
235 □ dependent ⓐ 의존하는	291 □ individually ad 개별적으로	346 □ skepticism ⓝ 회의론	406 □ argument ⓝ 주장
236 □ theoretical ⓐ 이론적인	292 □ probably ad 아마	347 □ logic ⓝ 논리	407 □ end up 결국 ~이 되다
237 □ in nature 본질적으로	293 □ for oneself 스스로, 혼자 힘으로	348 □ athlete ⓝ 운동선수	408 □ companion ⓝ 동반자
238 □ argue ⓥ 주장하다	294 □ poke ⓥ 쿡 찌르다	349 □ stock in trade 상투적 요소, 장사 도구	409 □ foster ⓥ 기르다, 육성하다
239 □ public ⓝ 대중	295 □ guess ⓥ 추측하다	350 □ evidence ⓝ 증거	
240 □ in practice 실제로	296 □ tip ⓝ 끝	351 □ refute ⓥ 반박하다	**43~45**
241 □ serve ⓥ 봉사하다	297 □ separate ⓐ 각각의, 별개의 ⓥ 분리하다	352 □ improve ⓥ 개선하다	410 □ businessman ⓝ 사업가
242 □ organization ⓝ 단체, 협회	298 □ back ⓝ 등, 허리	353 □ accordingly ad 그에 따라	411 □ board ⓥ 탑승하다
243 □ fire ⓥ 해고하다		354 □ scientific ⓐ 과학적인	412 □ arrive ⓥ 도착하다
244 □ at will 마음대로	**37**	355 □ advance ⓝ 진보	413 □ greet ⓥ 인사하다
245 □ income ⓝ 수입	299 □ matter ⓥ 중요하다	356 □ progress ⓝ 진보	414 □ middle-aged ⓐ 중년의
246 □ employ ⓥ 고용하다	300 □ famous ⓐ 유명한	357 □ mindset ⓝ 사고방식	415 □ aisle ⓝ 통로
247 □ disregard ⓝ 무시	301 □ expensive ⓐ 비용이 많이 드는	358 □ immune ⓐ ~의 영향을 받지 않는	416 □ overhead bin (여객기 객석 위에 있는) 짐
248 □ faith ⓝ 신념	302 □ coordinate ⓥ 조정하다	359 □ rational ⓐ 이성적인	넣는 곳
249 □ overconfidence ⓝ 과신	303 □ placement ⓝ 배열	360 □ perspective ⓝ 관점, 시각	417 □ take off 이륙하다
	304 □ letter ⓝ 문자	361 □ nothing less than 다름 아닌	418 □ nervous ⓐ 긴장한
34	305 □ particular ⓐ 독특한	362 □ convince ⓥ 확신시키다	419 □ grab ⓥ 쥐다, 잡다
250 □ capitalism ⓝ 자본주의	306 □ awkward ⓐ 어색한	363 □ proportion ⓥ 적절한 비율로 조화시키다	420 □ sit up 자세를 바로 하다[바로 앉다]
251 □ free market 자유 시장	307 □ standard ⓝ 표준	364 □ belief ⓝ 신념	421 □ meanwhile ad 그러는 동안
252 □ allocate ⓥ 배분하다, 할당하다	308 □ manual ⓐ 수동의	365 □ get away with ~을 잘 해내다	422 □ beside prep 옆에
253 □ resource ⓝ 자원	309 □ typewriter ⓝ 타자기	366 □ skeptical ⓐ 회의적인	423 □ neatly ad 가지런히, 깔끔하게
254 □ output ⓝ 생산	310 □ physical ⓐ 물리적인	367 □ eliminate ⓥ 없애다, 제거하다	424 □ rest on ~ 위에 놓여 있다
255 □ socialism ⓝ 사회주의	311 □ prevent A from B A가 B하지 못하게 하다	368 □ arrogant ⓐ 거만한	425 □ at all 전혀
256 □ communism ⓝ 공산주의	312 □ jam ⓥ 걸리다, 움직이지 않게 하다	369 □ stubborn ⓐ 고집 센, 완고한	426 □ turbulence ⓝ 난기류
257 □ wholesale ad 완전히, 모조리			427 □ apologize ⓥ 사과하다
258 □ despite prep ~에도 불구하고	**38**	**41~42**	428 □ bumpy ride 험난한 주행, 곤란, 우여곡절
259 □ acceptance ⓝ 수용	313 □ surface ⓝ 표면	370 □ common sense 상식	(이 많은 상황)
260 □ involvement ⓝ 개입	314 □ emit ⓥ (빛이나 열을) 뿜다	371 □ discussion ⓝ 토론	429 □ announce ⓥ 발표하다, 알리다
261 □ enforcement ⓝ 시행, 집행	315 □ measure ⓥ 측정하다	372 □ opinion ⓝ 의견	430 □ descent ⓝ 하강
262 □ regulation ⓝ 규정, 규제	316 □ occur ⓥ 일어나다, 생기다	373 □ moderate ⓐ 온건한, 중간의	431 □ brave ⓐ 용감한
263 □ mortgage ⓝ (담보) 대출	317 □ visibly ad 눈에 보이게	374 □ be not the case 사실이 아니다	432 □ calm ⓐ 침착한
264 □ perhaps ad 아마도	318 □ glow ⓥ 빛나다	375 □ polarization ⓝ 양극화	433 □ afraid ⓐ 두려워하는
265 □ central bank 중앙은행	319 □ poker ⓝ 부지깽이	376 □ period ⓝ 기간	434 □ hobby ⓝ 취미
266 □ treasury ⓝ 재무부, 금고	320 □ relate ⓥ 관련이 있다	377 □ extreme ⓐ 극단적인	435 □ favorite ⓐ 좋아하는
267 □ ups and downs 흥망성쇠	321 □ astronomer ⓝ 천문학자	378 □ position ⓝ 입장	436 □ strange ⓐ 이상한
268 □ entirely ad 완전히	322 □ precise ⓐ 정확한	379 □ direction ⓝ 경향	437 □ travel ⓥ 여행하다
269 □ reluctant ⓐ 꺼리는, 마지못해 하는	323 □ interior ⓝ 내부 ⓐ 내부의	380 □ inclined to ~하는 경향이 있는	438 □ alone ad 혼자
270 □ intervene ⓥ 개입하다	324 □ conceal ⓥ 숨기다	381 □ prefer ⓥ 선호하다	439 □ keep an eye on ~을 주시하다
271 □ supply and demand 수요와 공급	325 □ obtain ⓥ 얻다	382 □ reverse ⓥ 뒤집다	440 □ suddenly ad 갑자기
272 □ inequality ⓝ 불평등		383 □ accentuate ⓥ 강화하다	441 □ seat belt 안전벨트
273 □ competition ⓝ 경쟁	**39**	384 □ at the beginning 처음에	442 □ encounter ⓥ 만나다
274 □ guarantee ⓥ 보장하다	326 □ realize ⓥ 깨닫다	385 □ pressure ⓝ 압력	443 □ rough weather 악천후
	327 □ general ⓐ 전반적인		

08회

● 채점 : 맞은 개수 _____ / 80

TEST A-B 각 단어의 뜻을 [A] 영어는 우리말로, [B] 우리말은 영어로 쓰시오.

A	English	Korean
01	reflection	
02	theoretical	
03	achievement	
04	accident	
05	counterargument	
06	overlook	
07	contribution	
08	imperfect	
09	hinder	
10	occupation	
11	monarch	
12	address	
13	oversight	
14	flourish	
15	overconfidence	
16	analyst	
17	valueless	
18	grasp	
19	domain	
20	aisle	

B	Korean	English
01	채택하다	
02	양육	
03	알아채다, 기억하다	
04	언급하다	
05	반대, 역	
06	양극화	
07	예상치 못한	
08	동반하다	
09	부하, 추종자	
10	부분, 파편	
11	투자	
12	어색한	
13	각각의, 별개의	
14	반박하다	
15	뛰어난, 예외적인	
16	배열	
17	내부의	
18	조정하다	
19	계좌, 계정	
20	축복 받은	

▶ A-D 정답 : 해설편 084쪽

TEST C-D 각 단어의 뜻을 골라 기호를 쓰시오.

C	English		Korean
01	load	( )	ⓐ 이주하다
02	determine	( )	ⓑ 벽돌
03	survive	( )	ⓒ 의도적인, 고의의
04	automate	( )	ⓓ 조작자
05	universal	( )	ⓔ ~에 빠지다, 탐닉하다
06	reliable	( )	ⓕ 유동적인
07	portable	( )	ⓖ 산출하다
08	hatch	( )	ⓗ 살아남다
09	consciously	( )	ⓘ 믿을 만한
10	fluid	( )	ⓙ 부화하다
11	yield	( )	ⓚ 자동화하다
12	operator	( )	ⓛ 환경적인
13	brick	( )	ⓜ 규정, 규제
14	environmental	( )	ⓝ 결정하다
15	glow	( )	ⓞ 보편적인
16	splash	( )	ⓟ 장착하다, 싣다
17	migrate	( )	ⓠ 의식적으로
18	regulation	( )	ⓡ 알록달록하게 장식하다
19	indulge	( )	ⓢ 휴대 가능한
20	deliberate	( )	ⓣ 빛나다

D	Korean		English
01	목표	( )	ⓐ descent
02	소홀히 하다	( )	ⓑ mortgage
03	파장, 주파수	( )	ⓒ margin
04	순응	( )	ⓓ resistance
05	(담보) 대출	( )	ⓔ appealing
06	공식적으로	( )	ⓕ unstable
07	회의론	( )	ⓖ conformity
08	불안정한	( )	ⓗ emit
09	기관	( )	ⓘ neglect
10	가장자리	( )	ⓙ rigid
11	저항	( )	ⓚ evenly
12	하강	( )	ⓛ differentiate
13	불확실성	( )	ⓜ formally
14	구분하다, 구별하다	( )	ⓝ objective
15	매력적인	( )	ⓞ skepticism
16	방출하다, (빛이나 열을) 뿜다	( )	ⓟ companion
17	엄격한	( )	ⓠ reluctant
18	골고루, 고르게	( )	ⓡ wavelength
19	꺼리는, 마지못해 하는	( )	ⓢ uncertainty
20	동반자	( )	ⓣ institution

※ 영어 [독해] 파트만 수록한 문제지이므로 18번부터 시작합니다. ● 점수 표시가 없는 문항은 모두 2점 ● 문항수 28개 | 배점 63점 | 제한 시간 45분

18. 다음 글의 목적으로 가장 적절한 것은?

Dear animal lovers,

I am writing on behalf of the Protect Animal Organization. Our organization was founded on the belief that all animals should be respected and treated with kindness, and must be protected by law. Over the past 20 years, we have provided lost animals with protection, new homes, and sometimes health care. Currently, our animal shelter is full, and we need your help to build a new shelter. We are seeking donations in any amount. Every dollar raised goes to building homes for animals in need. You can donate to us online at www.protectanimal.org. Thank you for considering supporting us.

Sincerely,
Stella Anderson

① 사무실을 빌려준 것에 대해 감사하려고
② 동물 병원 설립의 필요성을 주장하려고
③ 새롭게 시행되는 동물 보호법에 대해 설명하려고
④ 동물 보호 단체의 봉사 활동 프로그램을 안내하려고
⑤ 새로운 동물 보호소를 짓기 위한 기부를 요청하려고

19. 다음 글에 드러난 Dave의 심경 변화로 가장 적절한 것은?

Dave sat up on his surfboard and looked around. He was the last person in the water that afternoon. Suddenly something out toward the horizon caught his eye and his heart froze. It was every surfer's worst nightmare — the fin of a shark. And it was no more than 20 meters away! He turned his board toward the beach and started kicking his way to the shore. Shivering, he gripped his board tighter and kicked harder. 'I'm going to be okay,' he thought to himself. 'I need to let go of the fear.' Five minutes of terror that felt like a lifetime passed before he was on dry land again. Dave sat on the beach and caught his breath. His mind was at ease. He was safe. He let out a contented sigh as the sun started setting behind the waves.

* fin: 지느러미

① scared → relieved
② indifferent → proud
③ amazed → horrified
④ hopeful → worried
⑤ ashamed → grateful

20. 다음 글에서 필자가 주장하는 바로 가장 적절한 것은?

Sibling rivalry is natural, especially between strong-willed kids. As parents, one of the dangers is comparing children unfavorably with each other, since they are always looking for a competitive advantage. The issue is not how fast a child can run, but who crosses the finish line first. A boy does not care how tall he is; he is vitally interested in who is tallest. Children systematically measure themselves against their peers on everything from skateboarding ability to who has the most friends. They are especially sensitive to any failure that is talked about openly within their own family. Accordingly, parents who want a little peace at home should guard against comparative comments that routinely favor one child over another. To violate this principle is to set up even greater rivalry between them.

* sibling: 형제, 자매

① 아이를 칭찬할 때는 일관성 있게 하라.
② 자녀를 서로 비교하는 발언을 자제하라.
③ 아이의 발전을 위하여 경쟁을 활용하라.
④ 아이에게 실패를 두려워하지 말라고 가르쳐라.
⑤ 자녀가 구체적인 목표를 설정하도록 조언하라.

21. 밑줄 친 the silent killers가 다음 글에서 의미하는 바로 가장 적절한 것은?

Author Elizabeth Gilbert tells the fable of a great saint who would lead his followers in meditation. Just as the followers were dropping into their zen moment, they would be disrupted by a cat that would walk through the temple meowing and bothering everyone. The saint came up with a simple solution: He began to tie the cat to a pole during meditation sessions. This solution quickly developed into a ritual: Tie the cat to the pole first, meditate second. When the cat eventually died of natural causes, a religious crisis followed. What were the followers supposed to do? How could they possibly meditate without tying the cat to the pole? This story illustrates what I call invisible rules. These are habits and behaviors that have unnecessarily rigidified into rules. Although written rules can be resistant to change, invisible ones are more stubborn. They're the silent killers.

* zen: (불교) 선(禪) ** rigidify: 굳게 하다

① hidden rules that govern our actions unconsciously
② noises that restrict one's level of concentration
③ surroundings that lead to the death of a cat
④ internal forces that slowly lower our self-esteem
⑤ experiences that discourage us from following rules

22. 다음 글의 요지로 가장 적절한 것은?

When it comes to the decision to get more exercise, you are setting goals that are similar to running a half marathon with very little training! You make a decision to buy a gym membership and decide to spend an hour at the gym every day. Well, you might stick to that for a day or two, but chances are you won't be able to continue to meet that commitment in the long term. If, however, you make a commitment to go jogging for a few minutes a day or add a few sit-ups to your daily routine before bed, then you are far more likely to stick to your decision and to create a habit that offers you long-term results. The key is to start small. Small habits lead to long-term success.

① 상황에 따른 유연한 태도가 목표 달성에 효과적이다.
② 올바른 식습관과 규칙적인 운동이 건강 유지에 도움이 된다.
③ 나쁜 습관을 고치기 위해서는 장기적인 계획이 필수적이다.
④ 꿈을 이루기 위해서는 원대한 목표를 세우는 것이 중요하다.
⑤ 장기적인 성공을 위해 작은 습관부터 시작하는 것이 필요하다.

23. 다음 글의 주제로 가장 적절한 것은?

Creativity is a step further on from imagination. Imagination can be an entirely private process of internal consciousness. You might be lying motionless on your bed in a fever of imagination and no one would ever know. Private imaginings may have no outcomes in the world at all. Creativity does. Being creative involves doing something. It would be odd to describe as creative someone who never did anything. To call somebody creative suggests they are actively producing something in a deliberate way. People are not creative in the abstract; they are creative in something: in mathematics, in engineering, in writing, in music, in business, in whatever. Creativity involves putting your imagination to work. In a sense, creativity is applied imagination.

① the various meanings of imagination
② creativity as the realization of imagination
③ factors which make imaginative people attractive
④ the necessity of art education to enhance creativity
⑤ effects of a creative attitude on academic achievement

24. 다음 글의 제목으로 가장 적절한 것은?

News reporters are taught to start their stories with the most important information. The first sentence, called the lead, contains the most essential elements of the story. A good lead can convey a lot of information. After the lead, information is presented in decreasing order of importance. Journalists call this the "inverted pyramid" structure — the most important information (the widest part of the pyramid) is at the top. The inverted pyramid is great for readers. No matter what the reader's attention span — whether she reads only the lead or the entire story — the inverted pyramid maximizes the information she gets. Think of the alternative: If news stories were written like mysteries with a dramatic payoff at the end, then readers who broke off in mid-story would miss the point. Imagine waiting until the last sentence of a story to find out who won the presidential election or the Super Bowl.

* inverted: 거꾸로 된

① Inverted Pyramid: Logically Impossible Structure
② Curiosity Is What Makes Readers Keep Reading
③ Where to Put Key Points in News Writing
④ The More Information, the Less Attention
⑤ Readers, Tell the Facts from the Fakes!

25. 다음 표의 내용과 일치하지 <u>않는</u> 것은?

Top Seven Natural Gas Producing Countries Worldwide

(unit: billion cubic meters)

2014			2018		
Rank	Country	Amount	Rank	Country	Amount
1	The United States	729	1	The United States	863
2	Russia	610	2	Russia	725
3	Iran	172	3	Iran	248
4	Canada	161	4	Qatar	181
5	Qatar	160	5	China	176
6	China	132	6	Canada	172
7	Norway	108	7	Australia	131

The table above shows the top seven natural gas producing countries worldwide in 2014 and 2018. ① The United States, Russia, and Iran were the top three natural gas producing countries in both 2014 and 2018. ② In 2014 and 2018 respectively, the gap of the amount of natural gas production between Russia and Iran was larger than 400 billion cubic meters. ③ Canada ranked lower in 2018 than in 2014 even though the amount of natural gas produced in Canada increased. ④ Between 2014 and 2018, the increase in natural gas production in China was more than three times that in Qatar. ⑤ Australia, which was not included among the top seven natural gas producing countries in 2014, ranked seventh in 2018.

26. Carol Ryrie Brink에 관한 다음 글의 내용과 일치하지 <u>않는</u> 것은?

Born in 1895, Carol Ryrie Brink was orphaned by age 8 and raised by her grandmother. Her grandmother's life and storytelling abilities inspired her writing. She married Raymond Woodard Brink, a young mathematics professor she had met in Moscow, Idaho many years before. After their son and daughter were born, early in her career, she started to write children's stories and edited a yearly collection of short stories. She and her husband spent several years living in France, and her first novel *Anything Can Happen on the River* was published in 1934. After that, she wrote more than thirty fiction and nonfiction books for children and adults. She received the Newbery Award in 1936 for *Caddie Woodlawn*.

① 할머니에 의해 길러졌다.
② Moscow에서 만났던 수학 교수와 결혼했다.
③ 자녀가 태어나기 전에 어린이 이야기를 쓰기 시작했다.
④ 1934년에 그녀의 첫 번째 소설이 출간되었다.
⑤ *Caddie Woodlawn*으로 Newbery 상을 받았다.

27. One Day Camp at Seattle Children's Museum에 관한 다음 안내문의 내용과 일치하지 <u>않는</u> 것은?

> **One Day Camp at Seattle Children's Museum**
>
> One Day Camp at Seattle Children's Museum is an experience that promises to inspire creativity in children. Join us on an amazing journey of discovery!
>
> • **Date:** Thursday, July 8, 2021
> • **Ages:** 5－10
> • **Schedule**
>
> | Time | Activity |
> |---|---|
> | 10:30 － 12:30 | Arts &Crafts |
> | 12:30 － 13:30 | Lunch |
> | 13:30 － 15:30 | Music & Dance |
>
> • **Participation Fees**
> － Child: $30
> － Adult: $10
>
> • **Notes**
> － All children must be accompanied by an adult.
> － The participation fee includes lunch and materials for the program.

① 7월 8일 목요일에 진행된다.
② 음악과 춤 활동이 있다.
③ 아이의 참가비는 30달러이다.
④ 모든 아이들은 어른과 동행해야 한다.
⑤ 점심 식사는 참가비에 포함되지 않는다.

28. Summer Rock Concert에 관한 다음 안내문의 내용과 일치하는 것은?

> **Summer Rock Concert**
>
> Five rock bands will provide great entertainment, joy, and music to all visitors.
>
> • **Date:** Saturday, August 14, 2021
> • **Time:** 7 p.m.
> • **Place:** Citizens Hall in the Blue Creek Building
> • **Details**
> － All seats are $30.
> － Tickets must be purchased online by Saturday, August 7.
> － Only 13-year-olds and older can attend the concert.
> • **Notice**
> － Food is not allowed in the concert hall.
> － All forms of photography and video recording are prohibited during the performance.
> － If you have any questions, please visit www.rock5.info.

① 이틀간 진행된다.
② 티켓은 현장에서만 구매할 수 있다.
③ 콘서트 관람에 나이 제한은 없다.
④ 음식은 콘서트 홀에서 허용되지 않는다.
⑤ 공연 중 사진 촬영이 가능하다.

29. 다음 글의 밑줄 친 부분 중, 어법상 틀린 것은? [3점]

While working as a research fellow at Harvard, B. F. Skinner carried out a series of experiments on rats, using an invention that later became known as a "Skinner box." A rat was placed in one of these boxes, ① which had a special bar fitted on the inside. Every time the rat pressed this bar, it was presented with food. The rate of bar-pressing was ② automatically recorded. Initially, the rat might press the bar accidentally, or simply out of curiosity, and as a consequence ③ receive some food. Over time, the rat learned that food appeared whenever the bar was pressed, and began to press ④ it purposefully in order to be fed. Comparing results from rats ⑤ gives the "positive reinforcement" of food for their bar-pressing behavior with those that were not, or were presented with food at different rates, it became clear that when food appeared as a consequence of the rat's actions, this influenced its future behavior.

30. 다음 글의 밑줄 친 부분 중, 문맥상 낱말의 쓰임이 적절하지 않은 것은? [3점]

Let's return to a time in which photographs were not in living color. During that period, people referred to pictures as "photographs" rather than "black-and-white photographs" as we do today. The possibility of color did not exist, so it was ① unnecessary to insert the adjective "black-and-white." However, suppose we did include the phrase "black-and-white" before the existence of color photography. By ② highlighting that reality, we become conscious of current limitations and thus open our minds to new possibilities and potential opportunities. World War I was given that name only ③ after we were deeply embattled in World War II. Before that horrific period of the 1940s, World War I was simply called "The Great War" or, even worse, "The War to End All Wars." What if we had called it "World War I" back in 1918? Such a label might have made the possibility of a second worldwide conflict an ④ unpredictable reality for governments and individuals. We become conscious of issues when we explicitly ⑤ identify them.

[31~34] 다음 빈칸에 들어갈 말로 가장 적절한 것을 고르시오.

31. The tendency for one purchase to lead to another one has a name: the Diderot Effect. The Diderot Effect states that obtaining a new possession often creates a spiral of consumption that leads to additional purchases. You can spot this pattern everywhere. You buy a dress and have to get new shoes and earrings to match. You buy a toy for your child and soon find yourself purchasing all of the accessories that go with it. It's a chain reaction of purchases. Many human behaviors follow this cycle. You often decide what to do next based on what you have just finished doing. Going to the bathroom leads to washing and drying your hands, which reminds you that you need to put the dirty towels in the laundry, so you add laundry detergent to the shopping list, and so on. No behavior happens in _____. Each action becomes a cue that triggers the next behavior.

① isolation   ② comfort   ③ observation
④ fairness   ⑤ harmony

32. While leaders often face enormous pressures to make decisions quickly, premature decisions are the leading cause of decision failure. This is primarily because leaders respond to the superficial issue of a decision rather than taking the time to explore the underlying issues. Bob Carlson is a good example of a leader _____ in the face of diverse issues. In the economic downturn of early 2001, Reell Precision Manufacturing faced a 30 percent drop in revenues. Some members of the senior leadership team favored layoffs and some favored salary reductions. While it would have been easy to push for a decision or call for a vote in order to ease the tension of the economic pressures, as co-CEO, Bob Carlson helped the team work together and examine all of the issues. The team finally agreed on salary reductions, knowing that, to the best of their ability, they had thoroughly examined the implications of both possible decisions. [3점]

        * revenue: 총수입   ** implication: 영향

① justifying layoffs
② exercising patience
③ increasing employment
④ sticking to his opinions
⑤ training unskilled members

33. When self-handicapping, you're engaging in behaviour that you know will harm your chances of succeeding: you know that you won't do as well on the test if you go out the night before, but you do it anyway. Why would anyone intentionally harm their chances of success? Well, here's a possible answer. Say that you do study hard. You go to bed at a decent time and get eight hours of sleep. Then you take the maths test, but don't do well: you only get a C. What can you conclude about yourself? Probably that you're just not good at maths, which is a pretty hard blow to your self-esteem. But if you self-handicap, you'll never be in this position because _____. You were bound to get a C, you can tell yourself, because you went out till 1 a.m. That C doesn't mean that you're bad at maths; it just means that you like to party. Self-handicapping seems like a paradox, because people are deliberately harming their chances of success. [3점]

① getting some rest from studying is necessary
② failure serves as the foundation for success
③ you're creating a reason for your failure
④ studying is not about winning or losing
⑤ you have already achieved a lot

34. Early in the term, our art professor projected an image of a monk, his back to the viewer, standing on the shore, looking off into a blue sea and an enormous sky. The professor asked the class, "What do you see?" The darkened auditorium was silent. We looked and looked and thought and thought as hard as possible to unearth the hidden meaning, but came up with nothing — we must have missed it. With dramatic exasperation she answered her own question, "It's a painting of a monk! His back is to us! He is standing near the shore! There's a blue sea and enormous sky!" Hmm... why didn't we see it? So as not to bias us, she'd posed the question without revealing the artist or title of the work. In fact, it was Caspar David Friedrich's *The Monk by the Sea*. To better understand your world, _____ rather than guess at what you think you are supposed to see. [3점]

* exasperation: 격분

① consciously acknowledge what you actually see
② accept different opinions with a broad mind
③ reflect on what you've already learned
④ personally experience even a small thing
⑤ analyze the answers from various perspectives

35. 다음 글에서 전체 흐름과 관계 <u>없는</u> 문장은?

An interesting phenomenon that arose from social media is the concept of *social proof*. It's easier for a person to accept new values or ideas when they see that others have already done so. ① If the person they see accepting the new idea happens to be a friend, then social proof has even more power by exerting peer pressure as well as relying on the trust that people put in the judgments of their close friends. ② For example, a video about some issue may be controversial on its own but more credible if it got thousands of *likes*. ③ When expressing feelings of liking to friends, you can express them using nonverbal cues such as facial expressions. ④ If a friend recommends the video to you, in many cases, the credibility of the idea it presents will rise in direct proportion to the trust you place in the friend recommending the video. ⑤ This is the power of social media and part of the reason why videos or "posts" can become "viral."

* exert: 발휘하다 ** viral: 바이러스성의, 입소문이 나는

[36~37] 주어진 글 다음에 이어질 글의 순서로 가장 적절한 것을 고르시오.

36.

Consider the story of two men quarreling in a library. One wants the window open and the other wants it closed. They argue back and forth about how much to leave it open: a crack, halfway, or three-quarters of the way.

(A) The librarian could not have invented the solution she did if she had focused only on the two men's stated positions of wanting the window open or closed. Instead, she looked to their underlying interests of fresh air and no draft.

(B) After thinking a minute, she opens wide a window in the next room, bringing in fresh air without a draft. This story is typical of many negotiations. Since the parties' problem appears to be a conflict of positions, they naturally tend to talk about positions — and often reach an impasse.

(C) No solution satisfies them both. Enter the librarian. She asks one why he wants the window open: "To get some fresh air." She asks the other why he wants it closed: "To avoid a draft."

* draft: 외풍 ** impasse: 막다름

① (A) - (C) - (B) ② (B) - (A) - (C)
③ (B) - (C) - (A) ④ (C) - (A) - (B)
⑤ (C) - (B) - (A)

37.

> In one survey, 61 percent of Americans said that they supported the government spending more on 'assistance to the poor'.

(A) Therefore, the framing of a question can heavily influence the answer in many ways, which matters if your aim is to obtain a 'true measure' of what people think. And next time you hear a politician say 'surveys prove that the majority of the people agree with me', be very wary.

(B) But when the same population was asked whether they supported spending more government money on 'welfare', only 21 percent were in favour. In other words, if you ask people about individual welfare programmes — such as giving financial help to people who have long-term illnesses and paying for school meals for families with low income — people are broadly in favour of them.

(C) But if you ask about 'welfare' — which refers to those exact same programmes that you've just listed — they're against it. The word 'welfare' has negative connotations, perhaps because of the way many politicians and newspapers portray it.

* wary: 조심성 있는 ** connotation: 함축

① (A) − (C) − (B)　　　② (B) − (A) − (C)
③ (B) − (C) − (A)　　　④ (C) − (A) − (B)
⑤ (C) − (B) − (A)

[38~39] 글의 흐름으로 보아, 주어진 문장이 들어가기에 가장 적절한 곳을 고르시오.

38.

> However, transfer of one kind of risk often means inheriting another kind.

Risk often arises from uncertainty about how to approach a problem or situation. (①) One way to avoid such risk is to contract with a party who is experienced and knows how to do it. (②) For example, to minimize the financial risk associated with the capital cost of tooling and equipment for production of a large, complex system, a manufacturer might subcontract the production of the system's major components to suppliers familiar with those components. (③) This relieves the manufacturer of the financial risk associated with the tooling and equipment to produce these components. (④) For example, subcontracting work for the components puts the manufacturer in the position of relying on outsiders, which increases the risks associated with quality control, scheduling, and the performance of the end-item system. (⑤) But these risks often can be reduced through careful management of the suppliers. [3점]

* subcontract: 하청을 주다(일감을 다른 사람에게 맡기다)

39.

> While other competitors were in awe of this incredible volume, Henry Ford dared to ask, "Can we do even better?"

Ransom Olds, the father of the Oldsmobile, could not produce his "horseless carriages" fast enough. In 1901 he had an idea to speed up the manufacturing process — instead of building one car at a time, he created the assembly line. (①) The acceleration in production was unheard-of — from an output of 425 automobiles in 1901 to an impressive 2,500 cars the following year. (②) He was, in fact, able to improve upon Olds's clever idea by introducing conveyor belts to the assembly line. (③) As a result, Ford's production went through the roof. (④) Instead of taking a day and a half to manufacture a Model T, as in the past, he was now able to spit them out at a rate of one car every ninety minutes. (⑤) The moral of the story is that good progress is often the herald of great progress.

* in awe of: ~에 깊은 감명을 받은 ** herald: 선구자

40. 다음 글의 내용을 한 문장으로 요약하고자 한다. 빈칸 (A), (B)에 들어갈 말로 가장 적절한 것은?

> Anne Thorndike, a primary care physician in Boston, had a crazy idea. She believed she could improve the eating habits of thousands of hospital staff and visitors without changing their willpower or motivation in the slightest way. In fact, she didn't plan on talking to them at all. Thorndike designed a study to alter the "choice architecture" of the hospital cafeteria. She started by changing how drinks were arranged in the room. Originally, the refrigerators located next to the cash registers in the cafeteria were filled with only soda. She added water as an option to each one. Additionally, she placed baskets of bottled water next to the food stations throughout the room. Soda was still in the primary refrigerators, but water was now available at all drink locations. Over the next three months, the number of soda sales at the hospital dropped by 11.4 percent. Meanwhile, sales of bottled water increased by 25.8 percent.

↓

> The study performed by Thorndike showed that the ___(A)___ of drinks at the hospital cafeteria influenced the choices people made, which ___(B)___ the consumption of soda.

	(A)		(B)
①	placement	......	lowered
②	placement	......	boosted
③	price	......	lowered
④	price	......	boosted
⑤	flavor	......	maintained

[41~42] 다음 글을 읽고, 물음에 답하시오.

Paralysis by analysis is a state of overthinking and analyzing a particular problem, but you still end up not making a decision. One famous ancient fable of the fox and the cat explains this situation of paralysis by analysis in the simplest way. In the story, the fox and the cat discuss how many ways they have to escape their hunters. Cat quickly climbs a tree. Fox, on the other hand, begins to analyze all the ways to escape that he knows. But unable to decide which one would be the best, he (a) fails to act and gets caught by the dogs. This story perfectly illustrates the analysis paralysis phenomenon: the (b) inability to act or decide due to overthinking about available alternatives. People experience that although they start with a good intention to find a solution to a problem, they often analyze indefinitely about various factors that might lead to wrong decisions. They don't feel satisfied with the available information and think they still need (c) more data to perfect their decision. Most often this situation of paralysis by analysis (d) arises when somebody is afraid of making an erroneous decision that can lead to potential catastrophic consequences: it might impact their careers or their organizations' productivity. So that's why people are generally (e) confident in making decisions that involve huge stakes.

*paralysis: 마비 **stakes: (계획·행동 등의 성공 여부에) 걸려 있는 것

41. 윗글의 제목으로 가장 적절한 것은?

① Best Ways to Keep You from Overthinking
② Overthinking or Overdoing: Which Is Worse?
③ Costs and Benefits of Having Various Alternatives
④ Overthinking: A Barrier to Effective Decision-making
⑤ Trapped in Moral Dilemma: Harmful for Your Survival

42. 밑줄 친 (a)~(e) 중에서 문맥상 낱말의 쓰임이 적절하지 않은 것은? [3점]

① (a)　　② (b)　　③ (c)　　④ (d)　　⑤ (e)

[43~45] 다음 글을 읽고, 물음에 답하시오.

(A)

Victor applied for the position of office cleaner at a very big company. The manager interviewed him, then gave him a test: cleaning, stocking, and supplying designated facility areas. After observing what (a) he was doing, the manager said, "You are hired. Give me your email address, and I'll send you some documents to fill out."

(B)

(b) He then sold the tomatoes in a door to door round. In two hours, he succeeded to double his capital. He repeated the operation three times and returned home with 60 dollars. Victor realized that he could survive by this way, and started to go every day earlier, and returned late. Thus, (c) his money doubled or tripled each day. Shortly later, he bought a cart, then a truck, and then he had his own fleet of delivery vehicles.

(C)

Victor replied, "I don't have a computer, nor an email." "I'm sorry," said the manager. And he added, "If you don't have an email, how do you intend to do this job? This job requires you to have an email address. I can't hire you." Victor left with no hope at all. (d) He didn't know what to do, with only 10 dollars in his pocket. He then decided to go to the supermarket and bought a 10kg box of tomatoes.

(D)

Several years later, Victor's company became the biggest food company in his city. He started to plan his family's future, and decided to get a life insurance. He called an insurance broker. When the conversation was concluded, (e) he asked him his email. Victor replied: "I don't have an email." The broker replied curiously, "You don't have an email, and yet have succeeded to build an empire. Do you imagine what you could have been if you had an email?" He thought for a while, and replied, "An office cleaner!"

43. 주어진 글 (A)에 이어질 내용을 순서에 맞게 배열한 것으로 가장 적절한 것은?

① (B) － (D) － (C)　　② (C) － (B) － (D)
③ (C) － (D) － (B)　　④ (D) － (B) － (C)
⑤ (D) － (C) － (B)

44. 밑줄 친 (a) ~ (e) 중에서 가리키는 대상이 나머지 넷과 다른 것은?

① (a)　　② (b)　　③ (c)　　④ (d)　　⑤ (e)

45. 윗글의 Victor에 관한 내용으로 적절하지 않은 것은?

① 사무실 청소부 자리에 지원하였다.
② 2시간 만에 자본금을 두 배로 만들었다.
③ 슈퍼마켓에 가서 토마토를 샀다.
④ 그의 회사는 도시에서 가장 큰 식품 회사가 되었다.
⑤ 이메일이 있다고 보험 중개인에게 답했다.

* 확인 사항
∘ 답안지의 해당란에 필요한 내용을 정확히 기입(표기)했는지 확인하시오.

18
001 ☐ on behalf of ~을 대표하여
002 ☐ organization ⓝ 조직, 단체, 기구
003 ☐ found(-founded-founded) ⓥ 설립하다
004 ☐ belief ⓝ 신념, 믿음
005 ☐ respect ⓥ 존경하다, 존중하다
006 ☐ treat with ~로 대하다
007 ☐ protect ⓥ 보호하다
008 ☐ provide ⓥ 제공[공급]하다, 주다
009 ☐ protection ⓝ 보호
010 ☐ shelter ⓝ 주거지
011 ☐ seek ⓥ 찾다, 구하다
012 ☐ donation ⓝ 기부(금)
013 ☐ amount ⓝ 양, 액수
014 ☐ in need 도움이 필요한
015 ☐ donate ⓥ 기부하다, 기증하다
016 ☐ support ⓥ 지지하다, 지원하다
017 ☐ sincerely ad 진심으로
018 ☐ considering prep …을 고려[감안]하면

19
019 ☐ sit up (앉아 있는 상태에서) 자세를 바로 하다 [바로 앉다]
020 ☐ surfboard ⓝ 서핑보드
021 ☐ toward prep ~쪽으로, ~을 향하여
022 ☐ horizon ⓝ 수평선, 지평선
023 ☐ worst ⓐ 최악의, 가장 나쁜
024 ☐ nightmare ⓝ 악몽
025 ☐ no more than 단지 ~일 뿐인
026 ☐ shore ⓝ 해변, 해안가
027 ☐ shiver ⓥ (몸을) 떨다
028 ☐ grip ⓥ 잡다
029 ☐ let go of ~을 놓다
030 ☐ lifetime ⓝ 일생, 평생
031 ☐ dry land ⓝ 육지
032 ☐ catch one's breath 한숨 돌리다, 숨을 고르다
033 ☐ at ease 편안한
034 ☐ contented ⓐ 만족한
035 ☐ sigh ⓝ 한숨, 한숨 소리
036 ☐ indifferent ⓐ 무관심한
037 ☐ horrified ⓐ 겁에 질린

20
038 ☐ rivalry ⓝ 경쟁
039 ☐ strong-willed ⓐ 의지가 강한
040 ☐ compare ⓥ (A와 B를) 비교하다
041 ☐ unfavorably ad 비판적으로, 호의적이지 않게
042 ☐ competitive advantage 경쟁 우위
043 ☐ vitally ad 극도로, 지극히
044 ☐ systematically ad 체계적으로
045 ☐ measure ⓥ 측정하다, 재다
046 ☐ sensitive ⓐ 민감한, 예민한
047 ☐ failure ⓝ 실패
048 ☐ openly ad 공개적으로
049 ☐ accordingly ad 따라서
050 ☐ guard against 경계하다, 조심하다
051 ☐ comparative ⓐ 비교의
052 ☐ comment ⓝ 언급, 지적
053 ☐ routinely ad 일상적으로
054 ☐ violate ⓥ 위반하다

21
055 ☐ fable ⓝ 우화
056 ☐ saint ⓝ 성인(聖人), 성-
057 ☐ follower ⓝ 신도, 신봉자
058 ☐ meditation ⓝ 명상
059 ☐ disrupt ⓥ 방해하다, 지장을 주다
060 ☐ temple ⓝ 신전, 사원
061 ☐ meow ⓥ (고양이가) 야옹하고 울다
062 ☐ bother ⓥ 신경 쓰이게 하다, 괴롭히다
063 ☐ come up with ~을 떠올리다
064 ☐ pole ⓝ 기둥, 장대
065 ☐ session ⓝ (특정한 활동을 위한) 시간[기간]
066 ☐ ritual ⓝ 의식
067 ☐ meditate ⓥ 명상[묵상]하다
068 ☐ religious ⓐ 종교적인
069 ☐ crisis ⓝ 위기
070 ☐ illustrate ⓥ (예를 들어 분명히) 보여주다
071 ☐ invisible ⓐ 보이지 않는
072 ☐ unnecessarily ad 불필요하게
073 ☐ resistant ⓐ (~에) 저항하는, 내성이 있는
074 ☐ stubborn ⓐ 완고한
075 ☐ govern ⓥ 지배하다, 통치하다
076 ☐ unconsciously ad 무의식적으로
077 ☐ restrict ⓥ 제한하다
078 ☐ concentration ⓝ 집중
079 ☐ surroundings ⓝ 환경
080 ☐ internal ⓐ 내부의
081 ☐ self-esteem 자부심

22
082 ☐ when it comes to ~에 관하여
083 ☐ decision ⓝ 결정
084 ☐ exercise ⓝ 운동
085 ☐ decide ⓥ 결정하다
086 ☐ stick to ~을 지키다, 고수하다
087 ☐ commitment ⓝ 약속, 다짐, 헌신
088 ☐ sit-up ⓝ 윗몸 일으키기 (운동)
089 ☐ routine ⓝ 일상
090 ☐ create ⓥ 만들다
091 ☐ offer ⓥ 제공하다
092 ☐ long-term 장기적인

23
093 ☐ creativity ⓝ 창의성, 독창성
094 ☐ imagination ⓝ 상상, 상상력
095 ☐ entirely ad 전적으로
096 ☐ consciousness ⓝ 의식, 자각
097 ☐ motionless ⓐ 움직이지 않는, 가만히 있는
098 ☐ fever ⓝ 흥분
099 ☐ outcome ⓝ 결과
100 ☐ odd ⓐ 이상한
101 ☐ describe ⓥ 묘사하다
102 ☐ deliberate ⓐ 의도적인
103 ☐ abstract ⓝ 추상적인 것 ⓐ 추상적인
104 ☐ mathematics ⓝ 수학
105 ☐ in a sense 어느 정도(까지는)
106 ☐ realization ⓝ 실현
107 ☐ imaginative ⓐ 상상력이 풍부한
108 ☐ attractive ⓐ 멋진, 매력적인
109 ☐ necessity ⓝ 필요성
110 ☐ enhance ⓥ 향상시키다
111 ☐ achievement ⓝ 업적, 성취

24
112 ☐ reporter ⓝ 기자, 리포터
113 ☐ sentence ⓝ 문장
114 ☐ essential ⓐ 필수적인, 본질적인
115 ☐ element ⓝ 요소
116 ☐ lead ⓝ (신문 기사의) 머리글, 첫머리
117 ☐ convey ⓥ 전달하다
118 ☐ present ⓥ 제시하다
119 ☐ decrease ⓥ 줄다, 감소하다
120 ☐ journalist ⓝ 언론인, (신문·방송·잡지사의) 기자
121 ☐ structure ⓝ 구조
122 ☐ attention span 주의 지속 시간
123 ☐ entire ⓐ 전체의
124 ☐ maximize ⓥ 극대화하다
125 ☐ alternative ⓝ 대안
126 ☐ dramatic ⓐ 극적인
127 ☐ payoff ⓝ (뜻밖의) 결말
128 ☐ break off (갑자기) 중단하다
129 ☐ presidential ⓐ 대통령 (선거)의
130 ☐ logically ad 논리적으로
131 ☐ curiosity ⓝ 호기심
132 ☐ tell A from B A와 B를 구별하다

25
133 ☐ natural gas ⓝ 천연 가스
134 ☐ cubic ⓐ 세제곱의, 입체의
135 ☐ above prep …보다 위에[위로]
136 ☐ worldwide ad 전 세계적으로
137 ☐ respectively ad 각각
138 ☐ gap ⓝ 차이, 격차
139 ☐ production ⓝ 생산
140 ☐ increase ⓥ 증가하다, 인상되다

26
141 ☐ orphan ⓥ 고아로 만들다 ⓝ 고아
142 ☐ storytelling ⓝ 이야기를 하는
143 ☐ inspire ⓥ 영감을 주다
144 ☐ professor ⓝ 교수
145 ☐ edit ⓥ (글 등을 발간할 수 있게) 수정하다
146 ☐ early ad 초기
147 ☐ career ⓝ 경력
148 ☐ yearly ⓐ 연간의
149 ☐ spend A ~ing ~하는 데 A를 쓰다
150 ☐ publish ⓥ 출판하다
151 ☐ fiction ⓝ 허구, 소설
152 ☐ nonfiction ⓝ 논픽션(소설이나 허구의 이야기가 아닌 전기·역사·사건 기록 따위)
153 ☐ award ⓝ 상

27
154 ☐ experience ⓝ 체험
155 ☐ promise ⓥ 약속하다
156 ☐ journey ⓝ 여행, 여정
157 ☐ discovery ⓝ 발견
158 ☐ accompany ⓥ 동반하다, 동행하다
159 ☐ material ⓝ (특정 활동에 필요한) 재료

28
160 ☐ entertainment ⓝ 오락
161 ☐ visitor ⓝ 방문객
162 ☐ citizen ⓝ 시민

29
163 ☐ purchase ⓥ 구매하다
164 ☐ attend ⓥ 참석하다
165 ☐ photography ⓝ 사진 촬영
166 ☐ prohibit ⓥ 금지시키다

29
167 ☐ fellow ⓝ (일부 대학의) 선임 연구원
168 ☐ carry out ~을 수행하다
169 ☐ a series of 일련의
170 ☐ experiment ⓝ 실험
171 ☐ rat ⓝ 쥐(생쥐보다 몸집이 크고 꼬리가 긴)
172 ☐ invention ⓝ 발명품
173 ☐ known as ~으로 알려진
174 ☐ present A with B A에게 B를 주다, 제시하다
175 ☐ automatically ad 자동적으로
176 ☐ record ⓥ 기록하다
177 ☐ initially ad 처음에
178 ☐ accidentally ad 우연히
179 ☐ as a consequence 그 결과
180 ☐ purposefully ad 일부러, 목적을 갖고
181 ☐ feed ⓥ 먹이를 주다
182 ☐ reinforcement ⓝ 강화
183 ☐ influence ⓥ 영향을 미치다

30
184 ☐ return ⓥ 돌아가다
185 ☐ photograph ⓝ 사진
186 ☐ living ⓐ 자연 그대로의, 생생한
187 ☐ refer to ~에 대해 언급하다
188 ☐ black-and-white 흑백의
189 ☐ unnecessary ⓐ 불필요한
190 ☐ insert ⓥ 삽입하다
191 ☐ adjective ⓝ 형용사
192 ☐ phrase ⓝ 구(句)
193 ☐ existence ⓝ 존재
194 ☐ highlight ⓥ 강조하다
195 ☐ be conscious of ~을 자각하다[의식하다]
196 ☐ current ⓐ 현재의, 지금의
197 ☐ limitation ⓝ 한계
198 ☐ potential ⓐ 잠재적인
199 ☐ embattle ⓥ 전쟁 준비를 갖추다
200 ☐ horrific ⓐ 끔찍한, 무시무시한
201 ☐ conflict ⓝ 충돌, 갈등
202 ☐ unpredictable ⓐ 예측 불가능한
203 ☐ government ⓝ 정부, 통치 체제
204 ☐ individual ⓝ 개인
205 ☐ explicitly ad 명시적으로
206 ☐ identify ⓥ 확인하다, 알아보다

31
207 ☐ state ⓥ 진술하다
208 ☐ obtain ⓥ 얻다, 입수하다
209 ☐ possession ⓝ 소유물
210 ☐ spiral ⓝ 소용돌이
211 ☐ consumption ⓝ 소비
212 ☐ additional ⓐ 추가의
213 ☐ spot ⓥ 발견하다
214 ☐ pattern ⓝ (정형화된) 양식, 패턴, 경향
215 ☐ go with ~와 어울리다
216 ☐ chain reaction 연쇄 반응
217 ☐ remind ⓥ 상기시키다

218 ☐ laundry ⓝ 세탁실
219 ☐ detergent ⓝ 세제
220 ☐ cue ⓝ 신호
221 ☐ trigger ⓥ 유발하다
222 ☐ isolation ⓝ 고립
223 ☐ fairness ⓝ 공정함, 공평함

32
224 ☐ enormous ⓐ 거대한
225 ☐ pressure ⓝ 압박, 압력
226 ☐ premature ⓐ 너무 이른, 시기상조의
227 ☐ leading ⓐ 주된
228 ☐ primarily ⓐⓓ 주로
229 ☐ superficial ⓐ 피상적인
230 ☐ explore ⓥ 탐구하다, 분석하다
231 ☐ underlying ⓐ 근본적인
232 ☐ in the face of ~에 직면하여, ~에도 불구하고
233 ☐ diverse ⓐ 다양한
234 ☐ downturn ⓝ 하강, 침체
235 ☐ manufacturing ⓝ 제조업
236 ☐ favor ⓥ 찬성하다, 선호하다
237 ☐ layoff ⓝ 해고
238 ☐ salary ⓝ 급여, 봉급
239 ☐ reduction ⓝ 삭감, 감소
240 ☐ call for ~을 요구하다[청하다]
241 ☐ in order to (목적) 위하여
242 ☐ ease ⓥ (고통·불편 등을) 덜어주다
243 ☐ tension ⓝ 긴장 상태, 긴장
244 ☐ examine ⓥ 검토하다
245 ☐ thoroughly ⓐⓓ 철저하게
246 ☐ justify ⓥ 정당화하다

33
247 ☐ self-handicap 자기 불구화하다, 실패의 구실을 만들기 위해 최대한의 노력을 다하지 않는다
248 ☐ engage in ~에 관여하다
249 ☐ harm ⓥ 해를 입히다
250 ☐ intentionally ⓐⓓ 의도적으로
251 ☐ decent ⓐ 적절한, 온당한
252 ☐ conclude ⓥ 결론을 내리다
253 ☐ probably ⓐⓓ 아마도
254 ☐ pretty ⓐⓓ 꽤
255 ☐ blow ⓝ (정신적) 충격[타격]
256 ☐ be bound to ~하기 마련이다
257 ☐ paradox ⓝ 역설
258 ☐ deliberately ⓐⓓ 의도적으로, 고의로
259 ☐ necessary ⓐ 필수적인
260 ☐ serve as ~의 역할을 하다
261 ☐ foundation ⓝ 기반, 기초
262 ☐ achieve ⓥ 성취하다

34
263 ☐ term ⓝ 기간, 학기
264 ☐ project ⓥ 제시하다, 투사하다
265 ☐ monk ⓝ 수도자, 수도승
266 ☐ darken ⓥ 캄캄하게 만들다
267 ☐ auditorium ⓝ 강당
268 ☐ hard ⓐⓓ 열심히
269 ☐ unearth ⓥ 파헤치다, 밝혀내다
270 ☐ (so as) not to ~하지 않기 위해

271 ☐ bias ⓥ 편견을 갖게 하다 ⓝ 편견
272 ☐ reveal ⓥ 드러내다
273 ☐ consciously ⓐⓓ 의식적으로
274 ☐ acknowledge ⓥ 인정하다
275 ☐ accept ⓥ (기꺼이) 받아들이다
276 ☐ opinion ⓝ (개인의) 의견[견해]
277 ☐ broad ⓐ 넓은
278 ☐ reflect on ~을 반추하다, 되돌아 보다
279 ☐ analyze ⓥ 분석하다
280 ☐ perspective ⓝ 시각, 관점

35
281 ☐ phenomenon ⓝ 현상
282 ☐ arise from ~에서 발생하다
283 ☐ concept ⓝ 개념
284 ☐ proof ⓝ 증거, 증명
285 ☐ value ⓝ 가치
286 ☐ rely on ~에 의존하다
287 ☐ judgment ⓝ 판단, 심사
288 ☐ controversial ⓐ 논란의 여지가 있는
289 ☐ credible ⓐ 신뢰할 만한
290 ☐ nonverbal ⓐ 비언어적인
291 ☐ facial expression 표정
292 ☐ credibility ⓝ 신뢰성
293 ☐ in proportion to ~에 비례하여

36
294 ☐ quarrel ⓥ 싸우다
295 ☐ argue back and forth 옥신각신하다, 설왕설래하다
296 ☐ crack ⓝ (좁은) 틈, (갈라진) 금
297 ☐ librarian ⓝ (도서관의) 사서
298 ☐ invent ⓥ 발명하다, ~을 지어내다
299 ☐ state ⓥ 언급하다, 말하다
300 ☐ instead ⓐⓓ 대신에
301 ☐ typical ⓝ 전형 ⓐ 전형적인
302 ☐ negotiation ⓝ 협상
303 ☐ party ⓝ (소송·계약 등의) 당사자
304 ☐ satisfy ⓥ 만족시키다
305 ☐ avoid ⓥ 피하다

37
306 ☐ survey ⓝ (설문) 조사
307 ☐ assistance ⓝ 도움, 원조
308 ☐ framing ⓝ 프레이밍, (특정한 방식의) 표현
309 ☐ aim ⓝ 목적, 목표
310 ☐ politician ⓝ 정치인
311 ☐ prove ⓥ 입증하다, 증명하다
312 ☐ majority ⓝ (특정 집단 내에서) 가장 많은 수[다수]
313 ☐ welfare ⓝ 복지
314 ☐ in favour 찬성하는
315 ☐ individual ⓐ 각각의, 개인의
316 ☐ financial ⓐ 재정의
317 ☐ illness ⓝ 병, 질환
318 ☐ income ⓝ 소득, 수입
319 ☐ broadly ⓐⓓ 대략
320 ☐ refer to ~을 나타내다
321 ☐ exact ⓐ 정확한
322 ☐ negative ⓐ 부정적인
323 ☐ newspaper ⓝ 신문
324 ☐ portray ⓥ 묘사하다

38
325 ☐ transfer ⓝ 이전, 이동
326 ☐ inherit ⓥ 물려받다
327 ☐ arise ⓥ 발생하다
328 ☐ uncertainty ⓝ 불확실성
329 ☐ approach ⓥ 접근하다
330 ☐ contract with ~와 계약하다
331 ☐ experienced ⓐ 경험이 풍부한
332 ☐ minimize ⓥ 최소화하다
333 ☐ associate ⓥ 관련시키다, 연관짓다
334 ☐ capital cost 자본 비용
335 ☐ tooling ⓝ 연장을 쓰는 일, 도구
336 ☐ equipment ⓝ 장비, 용품
337 ☐ complex ⓐ 복잡한
338 ☐ manufacturer ⓝ 제조업체
339 ☐ component ⓝ 부품
340 ☐ supplier ⓝ 공급업자
341 ☐ familiar with ~에 익숙한, 정통한
342 ☐ relieve ⓥ (문제의 심각성을) 완화하다 [줄이다]
343 ☐ end-item 완제품

39
344 ☐ competitor ⓝ 경쟁자
345 ☐ incredible ⓐ 놀라운, 믿기지 않는
346 ☐ volume ⓝ 양
347 ☐ dare ⓥ 감히 ~하다
348 ☐ horseless ⓐ 말(馬))이 없는
349 ☐ carriage ⓝ 마차
350 ☐ manufacturing process 제조 과정
351 ☐ assembly ⓝ 조립
352 ☐ acceleration ⓝ 가속화
353 ☐ unheard-of ⓐ 전례 없는
354 ☐ impressive ⓐ 인상적인
355 ☐ following ⓐ (시간상으로) 그 다음의
356 ☐ improve ⓥ 향상하다
357 ☐ introduce ⓥ 도입하다
358 ☐ conveyor belt 컨베이어 벨트
359 ☐ go through the roof 치솟다, 급등하다
360 ☐ spit out 내뱉다
361 ☐ moral ⓝ (이야기나 경험의) 교훈, 도덕률
362 ☐ progress ⓝ 진보, 진척

40
363 ☐ primary ⓐ (순서·단계상으로) 최초의
364 ☐ physician ⓝ (내과) 의사
365 ☐ improve ⓥ 향상시키다
366 ☐ willpower ⓝ 의지력
367 ☐ motivation ⓝ 동기
368 ☐ slight ⓐ 약간의, 조금의, 경미한
369 ☐ design ⓥ 설계하다
370 ☐ study ⓝ 연구
371 ☐ alter ⓥ 바꾸다
372 ☐ architecture ⓝ 구성, 건축
373 ☐ arrange ⓥ 배열하다
374 ☐ originally ⓐⓓ 본래, 원래
375 ☐ refrigerator ⓝ 냉장고
376 ☐ locate ⓥ 위치하고 있다
377 ☐ cash register 금전 등록기
378 ☐ be filled with ~로 채워지다
379 ☐ additionally ⓐⓓ 추가적으로, 게다가
380 ☐ available ⓐ 구할[이용할] 수 있는

381 ☐ drop ⓥ 떨어지다
382 ☐ meanwhile ⓐⓓ 한편, 반면에
383 ☐ perform ⓥ (일·과제·의무 등을) 행하다
384 ☐ placement ⓝ 배치
385 ☐ lowered ⓐ 낮아진
386 ☐ boosted ⓐ 증가된
387 ☐ flavor ⓝ 맛
388 ☐ maintain ⓥ 유지하다

41~42
389 ☐ paralysis ⓝ 마비, (기능의) 마비
390 ☐ analysis ⓝ 분석
391 ☐ state ⓝ 상태
392 ☐ overthink ⓥ 지나치게 생각하다
393 ☐ end up ~ing 결국 ~하게 되다
394 ☐ escape ⓥ 달아나다, 탈출하다
395 ☐ climb ⓥ 오르다
396 ☐ unable ⓐ 할 수 없는, 하지 못하는
397 ☐ inability ⓝ ~할 수 없음, 무능력
398 ☐ due to ~ 때문에
399 ☐ intention ⓝ 의도
400 ☐ indefinitely ⓐⓓ 무한히
401 ☐ satisfied with ~에 만족하는
402 ☐ erroneous ⓐ 잘못된
403 ☐ catastrophic ⓐ 처참한, 재앙 같은
404 ☐ consequence ⓝ 결과, 영향
405 ☐ impact ⓥ 영향을 미치다
406 ☐ productivity ⓝ 생산성
407 ☐ huge ⓐ 거대한
408 ☐ keep A from B A가 B하지 못하게 하다
409 ☐ overdo ⓥ 지나치게 하다, 과장하다
410 ☐ barrier ⓝ 장벽, 장애물
411 ☐ trap ⓥ 가두다, 빠뜨리다
412 ☐ moral ⓐ 도덕과 관련된, 도덕상의
413 ☐ dilemma ⓝ 딜레마, 궁지

43~45
414 ☐ apply for ~에 지원하다[신청하다]
415 ☐ cleaner ⓝ 청소부
416 ☐ stock ⓥ (식품·책 등으로) 채우다[갖추다]
417 ☐ supply ⓥ 보급하다, 제공하다
418 ☐ designate ⓥ 지정하다
419 ☐ facility ⓝ 시설
420 ☐ observe ⓥ 관찰하다
421 ☐ fill out (서류 등을) 작성하다
422 ☐ double ⓥ 두 배로 만들다, 두 배가 되다
423 ☐ capital ⓝ 자본
424 ☐ repeated ⓐ 반복[되풀이]되는
425 ☐ operation ⓝ (조직적인) 작업 [활동]
426 ☐ triple ⓥ 3배가 되다
427 ☐ fleet ⓝ (한 기관이 소유한 전체 비행기·버스·택시 등의) 무리
428 ☐ vehicle ⓝ 차량
429 ☐ reply ⓥ 대답하다
430 ☐ intend ⓥ 의도하다, 작정하다
431 ☐ require ⓥ 필요[요구]하다, 필요로 하다
432 ☐ several ⓟⓡⓞⓝ (몇)몇의
433 ☐ life insurance 생명 보험
434 ☐ broker ⓝ 중개인
435 ☐ conclude ⓥ 끝내다, 마치다
436 ☐ curiously ⓐⓓ 의아해하며, 신기한 듯이
437 ☐ empire ⓝ 거대 기업, 제국

09회

● 채점 : 맞은 개수 _____ / 80

TEST A-B 각 단어의 뜻을 [A] 영어는 우리말로, [B] 우리말은 영어로 쓰시오.

A	English	Korean
01	alternative	
02	shiver	
03	analysis	
04	curiosity	
05	restrict	
06	improve	
07	foundation	
08	erroneous	
09	conflict	
10	portray	
11	perspective	
12	entirely	
13	trigger	
14	come up with	
15	violate	
16	acknowledge	
17	discovery	
18	respectively	
19	examine	
20	on behalf of	

B	Korean	English
01	~에 의존하다	
02	근본적인	
03	영감을 주다	
04	의도적으로	
05	감히 ~하다	
06	논리적으로	
07	기부하다, 기증하다	
08	체계적으로	
09	~을 수행하다	
10	금지하다	
11	신뢰성, 신뢰도	
12	싸우다	
13	종교적인	
14	보이지 않는	
15	의도적인	
16	지정하다	
17	자본	
18	도움, 원조	
19	비언어적인	
20	존재	

▶ A-D 정답 : 해설편 095쪽

TEST C-D 각 단어의 뜻을 골라 기호를 쓰시오.

C	English			Korean
01	several	(	)	ⓐ 확인하다, 알아보다
02	influence	(	)	ⓑ 제공[공급]하다, 주다
03	opinion	(	)	ⓒ 증가하다, 인상되다
04	realization	(	)	ⓓ ~에 익숙한, 정통한
05	necessity	(	)	ⓔ 필요성
06	possession	(	)	ⓕ 가속화
07	identify	(	)	ⓖ 구성, 건축
08	negotiation	(	)	ⓗ 무관심한
09	consumption	(	)	ⓘ (대명사) (몇)몇의
10	architecture	(	)	ⓙ 소유물
11	be filled with	(	)	ⓚ 실현
12	let go of	(	)	ⓛ 영향을 미치다; 영향
13	provide	(	)	ⓜ 전달하다
14	improve	(	)	ⓝ ~을 놓다
15	acceleration	(	)	ⓞ (개인의) 의견[견해]
16	familiar with	(	)	ⓟ 철저하게
17	indifferent	(	)	ⓠ ~로 채워지다
18	increase	(	)	ⓡ 향상시키다
19	thoroughly	(	)	ⓢ 협상
20	convey	(	)	ⓣ 소비

D	Korean			English
01	불확실성	(	)	ⓐ fairness
02	거대한	(	)	ⓑ accompany
03	고립	(	)	ⓒ primarily
04	공정함, 공평함	(	)	ⓓ break off
05	불필요하게	(	)	ⓔ consequence
06	결국 ~하게 되다	(	)	ⓕ consumption
07	동반하다, 동행하다	(	)	ⓖ credible
08	~을 지키다, 고수하다	(	)	ⓗ end up ~ing
09	소비	(	)	ⓘ uncertainty
10	명시적으로	(	)	ⓙ enormous
11	특정한	(	)	ⓚ explicitly
12	의도	(	)	ⓛ enormous
13	결과, 영향	(	)	ⓜ intention
14	우연히	(	)	ⓝ automatically
15	내적인	(	)	ⓞ isolation
16	주로	(	)	ⓟ particular
17	거대한	(	)	ⓠ accidentally
18	신뢰할 만한	(	)	ⓡ stick to
19	자동적으로	(	)	ⓢ internal
20	(갑자기) 중단하다	(	)	ⓣ unnecessarily

※ 영어 [독해] 파트만 수록한 문제지이므로 18번부터 시작합니다.

● 점수 표시가 없는 문항은 모두 2점　● 문항수 28개 | 배점 63점 | 제한 시간 45분

18. 다음 글의 목적으로 가장 적절한 것은?

Dear Mr. Stanton:

We at the Future Music School have been providing music education to talented children for 10 years. We hold an annual festival to give our students a chance to share their music with the community and we always invite a famous musician to perform in the opening event. Your reputation as a world-class violinist precedes you and the students consider you the musician who has influenced them the most. That's why we want to ask you to perform at the opening event of the festival. It would be an honor for them to watch one of the most famous violinists of all time play at the show. It would make the festival more colorful and splendid. We look forward to receiving a positive reply.

Sincerely,
Steven Forman

① 개막 행사에서 연주를 요청하려고
② 공연 스케줄 변경을 공지하려고
③ 학교 행사 취소를 통보하려고
④ 모금 행사 참여를 독려하려고
⑤ 올해의 음악가 상 수상을 축하하려고

19. 다음 글에 드러난 'I'의 심경 변화로 가장 적절한 것은?

It was time for the results of the speech contest. I was still skeptical whether I would win a prize or not. My hands were trembling due to the anxiety. I thought to myself, 'Did I work hard enough to outperform the other participants?' After a long wait, an envelope was handed to the announcer. She tore open the envelope to pull out the winner's name. My hands were now sweating and my heart started pounding really hard and fast. "The winner of the speech contest is Josh Brown!" the announcer declared. As I realized my name had been called, I jumped with joy. "I can't believe it. I did it!" I exclaimed. I felt like I was in heaven. Almost everybody gathered around me and started congratulating me for my victory.

① nervous → excited
② delighted → jealous
③ indifferent → thrilled
④ confident → disappointed
⑤ furious → relieved

20. 다음 글에서 필자가 주장하는 바로 가장 적절한 것은?

We all have set patterns in life. We like to label ourselves as this or that and are quite proud of our opinions and beliefs. We all like to read a particular newspaper, watch the same sorts of TV programs or movies, go to the same sort of shops every time, eat the sort of food that suits us, and wear the same type of clothes. And all this is fine. But if we cut ourselves off from all other possibilities, we become boring, rigid, hardened — and thus likely to get knocked about a bit. You have to see life as a series of adventures. Each adventure is a chance to have fun, learn something, explore the world, expand your circle of friends and experience, and broaden your horizons. Shutting down to adventure means exactly that — you are shut down.

① 반복되는 경험 속에서 인생의 의미를 발견하라.
② 도전하기 전에 실패의 가능성을 신중하게 생각하라.
③ 정해진 일상에 안주하기보다 삶에서 모험을 시도하라.
④ 타인의 삶의 방식을 수용하고 인정하는 자세를 지녀라.
⑤ 결단을 실천으로 옮기는 삶 속에서 즐거움을 발견하라.

21. 밑줄 친 constantly wearing masks가 다음 글에서 의미하는 바로 가장 적절한 것은? [3점]

Over the centuries various writers and thinkers, looking at humans from an outside perspective, have been struck by the theatrical quality of social life. The most famous quote expressing this comes from Shakespeare: "All the world's a stage, / And all the men and women merely players; / They have their exits and their entrances, / And one man in his time plays many parts." If the theater and actors were traditionally represented by the image of masks, writers such as Shakespeare are implying that all of us are constantly wearing masks. Some people are better actors than others. Evil types such as Iago in the play *Othello* are able to conceal their hostile intentions behind a friendly smile. Others are able to act with more confidence and bravado — they often become leaders. People with excellent acting skills can better navigate our complex social environments and get ahead.

* bravado: 허세

① protecting our faces from harmful external forces
② performing on stage to show off our acting skills
③ feeling confident by beating others in competition
④ doing completely the opposite of what others expect
⑤ adjusting our behavior based on the social context given

22. 다음 글의 요지로 가장 적절한 것은?

Personal blind spots are areas that are visible to others but not to you. The developmental challenge of blind spots is that you don't know what you don't know. Like that area in the side mirror of your car where you can't see that truck in the lane next to you, personal blind spots can easily be overlooked because you are completely unaware of their presence. They can be equally dangerous as well. That truck you don't see? It's really there! So are your blind spots. Just because you don't see them, doesn't mean they can't run you over. This is where you need to enlist the help of others. You have to develop a crew of special people, people who are willing to hold up that mirror, who not only know you well enough to see that truck, but who also care enough about you to let you know that it's there.

① 모르는 부분을 인정하고 질문하는 것이 중요하다.
② 폭넓은 인간관계는 성공에 결정적인 영향을 미친다.
③ 자기발전은 실수를 기회로 만드는 능력에서 비롯된다.
④ 주변에 관심을 가지고 타인을 도와주는 것이 바람직하다.
⑤ 자신의 맹점을 인지하도록 도와줄 수 있는 사람이 필요하다.

23. 다음 글의 주제로 가장 적절한 것은?

A child whose behavior is out of control improves when clear limits on their behavior are set and enforced. However, parents must agree on where a limit will be set and how it will be enforced. The limit and the consequence of breaking the limit must be clearly presented to the child. Enforcement of the limit should be consistent and firm. Too many limits are difficult to learn and may spoil the normal development of autonomy. The limit must be reasonable in terms of the child's age, temperament, and developmental level. To be effective, both parents (and other adults in the home) must enforce limits. Otherwise, children may effectively split the parents and seek to test the limits with the more indulgent parent. In all situations, to be effective, punishment must be brief and linked directly to a behavior.

* indulgent: 멋대로 하게 하는

① ways of giving reward and punishment fairly
② considerations when placing limits on children's behavior
③ increasing necessity of parents' participation in discipline
④ impact of caregivers' personality on children's development
⑤ reasons for encouraging children to do socially right things

24. 다음 글의 제목으로 가장 적절한 것은?

Many inventions were invented thousands of years ago so it can be difficult to know their exact origins. Sometimes scientists discover a model of an early invention and from this model they can accurately tell us how old it is and where it came from. However, there is always the possibility that in the future other scientists will discover an even older model of the same invention in a different part of the world. In fact, we are forever discovering the history of ancient inventions. An example of this is the invention of pottery. For many years archaeologists believed that pottery was first invented in the Near East (around modern Iran) where they had found pots dating back to 9,000 B.C. In the 1960s, however, older pots from 10,000 B.C. were found on Honshu Island, Japan. There is always a possibility that in the future archaeologists will find even older pots somewhere else.

① How Can You Tell Original from Fake?
② Exploring the Materials of Ancient Pottery
③ Origin of Inventions: Never-Ending Journey
④ Learn from the Past, Change for the Better
⑤ Science as a Driving Force for Human Civilization

25. 다음 도표의 내용과 일치하지 <u>않는</u> 것은?

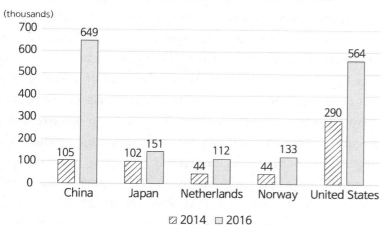

Electric Car Stock in Five Countries in 2014 and 2016

☑ 2014 ☐ 2016

The graph above shows the amount of the electric car stock in five countries in 2014 and 2016. ① All five countries had more electric car stock in 2016 than in 2014. ② In 2014, the electric car stock of the United States ranked first among the five countries, followed by that of China. ③ However, China showed the biggest increase of electric car stock from 2014 to 2016, surpassing the United States in electric car stock in 2016. ④ Between 2014 and 2016, the increase in electric car stock in Japan was less than that in Norway. ⑤ In the Netherlands, the electric car stock was more than three times larger in 2016 than in 2014.

26. impala에 관한 다음 글의 내용과 일치하지 <u>않는</u> 것은?

The impala is one of the most graceful four-legged animals. Impalas have the ability to adapt to different environments of the savannas. Both male and female impalas are similar in color, with white bellies and black-tipped ears. Male impalas have long and pointed horns which can measure 90 centimeters in length. Female impalas have no horns. Impalas feed upon grass, fruits, and leaves from trees. When conditions are harsh in the dry season, they come together to search for food in mixed herds which can number as many as 100-200 individuals. The breeding season occurs at the end of the wet season around May. Females give birth in an isolated spot away from the herd. The average life span of an impala is between 13 and 15 years in the wild.

① 암컷과 수컷 모두 배가 하얗다.
② 수컷은 길고 뾰족한 뿔이 있다.
③ 풀, 과일, 나뭇잎을 먹고 산다.
④ 우기가 시작될 무렵 번식기를 가진다.
⑤ 평균 수명은 야생에서 13년에서 15년이다.

27. Silver Aqua Classes에 관한 다음 안내문의 내용과 일치하지 <u>않는</u> 것은?

Silver Aqua Classes

Are you bored with your current exercise routine? Parkside Pool will host special one-day water exercise classes for senior customers. Please come and enjoy our senior-friendly pool.

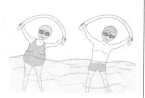

Program
- Date: Tuesday, June 9
- Special Classes
  9:00 a.m. – 10:00 a.m.: water walking
  10:30 a.m. – 11:30 a.m.: recreational swimming
  2:00 p.m. – 3:00 p.m.: water aerobics

Admission Fee
  – $5 per person (This includes all classes.)

Notes
  – No pre-registration necessary, just show up and have fun!
  – For more information, please visit our website at www.parksidepool.org.

① 노인 고객들을 위한 일일 강좌이다.
② 6월 9일 화요일에 진행된다.
③ 오후에 수중 에어로빅 수업이 있다.
④ 1인당 입장료는 5달러이다.
⑤ 사전 참가 등록이 필요하다.

28. Fanstaville Magic Festival에 관한 다음 안내문의 내용과 일치하는 것은?

Fanstaville Magic Festival

Welcome to the Fanstaville Magic Festival! Enjoy a magical experience with your family and make special memories!

- When: July 4th (Saturday), 12:00 – 18:00
- Where: Fanstaville Center playground
  (If it rains, the event will be held in the gym.)
- What:
  – Learn simple magic tricks.
  – Take pictures at the trick art photo zone.
  – Watch a magic stage show.
- Tickets:
  – $20 per person
  – All participants will receive a free T-shirt as a gift.
  – Purchase tickets online at www.fanstaville.com or at the entrance on the day of the festival.

① 8시간 동안 진행된다.
② 우천 시 취소된다.
③ 간단한 마술을 배울 수 있다.
④ 참가자에게 기념품은 제공되지 않는다.
⑤ 입장권은 온라인으로만 구매할 수 있다.

29. 다음 글의 밑줄 친 부분 중, 어법상 <u>틀린</u> 것은?

Every farmer knows that the hard part is getting the field ① <u>prepared</u>. Inserting seeds and watching ② <u>them</u> grow is easy. In the case of science and industry, the community prepares the field, yet society tends to give all the credit to the individual who happens to plant a successful seed. Planting a seed does not necessarily require overwhelming intelligence; creating an environment that allows seeds to prosper ③ <u>does</u>. We need to give more credit to the community in science, politics, business, and daily life. Martin Luther King Jr. was a great man. Perhaps his greatest strength was his ability ④ <u>to inspire</u> people to work together to achieve, against all odds, revolutionary changes in society's perception of race and in the fairness of the law. But to really understand ⑤ <u>that</u> he accomplished requires looking beyond the man. Instead of treating him as the manifestation of everything great, we should appreciate his role in allowing America to show that it can be great.

* manifestation: 표명

30. 다음 글의 밑줄 친 부분 중, 문맥상 낱말의 쓰임이 적절하지 <u>않은</u> 것은? [3점]

Sudden success or winnings can be very dangerous. Neurologically, chemicals are released in the brain that give a powerful burst of excitement and energy, leading to the desire to ① <u>repeat</u> this experience. It can be the start of any kind of addiction or manic behavior. Also, when gains come quickly we tend to ② <u>lose</u> sight of the basic wisdom that true success, to really last, must come through hard work. We do not take into account the role that luck plays in such ③ <u>hard-earned</u> gains. We try again and again to recapture that high from winning so much money or attention. We acquire feelings of superiority. We become especially ④ <u>resistant</u> to anyone who tries to warn us — they don't understand, we tell ourselves. Because this cannot be sustained, we experience an inevitable ⑤ <u>fall</u>, which is all the more painful, leading to the depression part of the cycle. Although gamblers are the most prone to this, it equally applies to businesspeople during bubbles and to people who gain sudden attention from the public.

[31~34] 다음 빈칸에 들어갈 말로 가장 적절한 것을 고르시오.

31. When is the right time for the predator to consume the fruit? The plant uses the color of the fruit to signal to predators that it is ripe, which means that the seed's hull has hardened — and therefore the sugar content is at its height. Incredibly, the plant has chosen to manufacture fructose, instead of glucose, as the sugar in the fruit. Glucose raises insulin levels in primates and humans, which initially raises levels of leptin, a hunger-blocking hormone — but fructose does not. As a result, the predator never receives the normal message that it is _____. That makes for a win-win for predator and prey. The animal obtains more calories, and because it keeps eating more and more fruit and therefore more seeds, the plant has a better chance of distributing more of its babies. [3점]

* hull: 겉껍질 ** primate: 영장류

① full   ② strong   ③ tired
④ dangerous   ⑤ hungry

32. We are often faced with high-level decisions, where we are unable to predict the results of those decisions. In such situations, most people end up quitting the option altogether, because the stakes are high and results are very unpredictable. But there is a solution for this. You should use the process of _____. In many situations, it's wise to dip your toe in the water rather than dive in headfirst. Recently, I was about to enroll in an expensive coaching program. But I was not fully convinced of how the outcome would be. Therefore, I used this process by enrolling in a low-cost mini course with the same instructor. This helped me understand his methodology, style, and content; and I was able to test it with a lower investment, and less time and effort before committing fully to the expensive program.

* stakes: (계획·행동 등의 성공 여부에) 걸려 있는 것

① trying out what other people do
② erasing the least preferred options
③ testing the option on a smaller scale
④ sharing your plans with professionals
⑤ collecting as many examples as possible

33. Sociologists have proven that people bring their own views and values to the culture they encounter; books, TV programs, movies, and music may affect everyone, but they affect different people in different ways. In a study, Neil Vidmar and Milton Rokeach showed episodes of the sitcom *All in the Family* to viewers with a range of different views on race. The show centers on a character named Archie Bunker, an intolerant bigot who often gets into fights with his more progressive family members. Vidmar and Rokeach found that viewers who didn't share Archie Bunker's views thought the show was very funny in the way it made fun of Archie's absurd racism — in fact, this was the producers' intention. On the other hand, though, viewers who were themselves bigots thought Archie Bunker was the hero of the show and that the producers meant to make fun of his foolish family! This demonstrates why it's a mistake to assume that a certain cultural product _____. [3점]

* bigot: 고집쟁이

① can provide many valuable views
② reflects the idea of the sociologists
③ forms prejudices to certain characters
④ will have the same effect on everyone
⑤ might resolve social conflicts among people

34. The availability heuristic refers to a common mistake that our brains make by assuming that the instances or examples that come to mind easily are also the most important or prevalent. It shows that we make our decisions based on the recency of events. We often misjudge the frequency and magnitude of the events that have happened recently because of the limitations of our memories. According to Harvard professor, Max Bazerman, managers conducting performance appraisals often fall victim to the availability heuristic. The recency of events highly influences a supervisor's opinion during performance appraisals. Managers give more weight to performance during the three months prior to the evaluation than to the previous nine months of the evaluation period because _____.
The availability heuristic is influenced by the ease of recall or retrievability of information of some event. Ease of recall suggests that if something is more easily recalled in your memory, you think that it will occur with a high probability. [3점]

* appraisal: 평가 ** retrievability: 회복력

① there is little reliable data about workers
② the frequent contacts help the relationship
③ they want to evaluate employees objectively
④ the recent instances dominate their memories
⑤ distorted data have no impact on the evaluation

35. 다음 글에서 전체 흐름과 관계 없는 문장은?

Marketing management is concerned not only with finding and increasing demand but also with changing or even reducing it. For example, Uluru (Ayers Rock) might have too many tourists wanting to climb it, and Daintree National Park in North Queensland can become overcrowded in the tourist season. ① Power companies sometimes have trouble meeting demand during peak usage periods. ② In these and other cases of excess demand, the needed marketing task, called demarketing, is to reduce demand temporarily or permanently. ③ Efforts should be made to compensate for the losses caused by the increase in supply. ④ The aim of demarketing is not to completely destroy demand, but only to reduce or shift it to another time, or even another product. ⑤ Thus, marketing management seeks to affect the level, timing, and nature of demand in a way that helps the organisation achieve its objectives.

[36~37] 주어진 글 다음에 이어질 글의 순서로 가장 적절한 것을 고르시오.

36.

The invention of the mechanical clock was influenced by monks who lived in monasteries that were the examples of order and routine.

(A) Time was determined by watching the length of the weighted rope. The discovery of the pendulum in the seventeenth century led to the widespread use of clocks and enormous public clocks. Eventually, keeping time turned into serving time.

(B) They had to keep accurate time so that monastery bells could be rung at regular intervals to announce the seven hours of the day reserved for prayer. Early clocks were nothing more than a weight tied to a rope wrapped around a revolving drum.

(C) People started to follow the mechanical time of clocks rather than their natural body time. They ate at meal time, rather than when they were hungry, and went to bed when it was time, rather than when they were sleepy. Even periodicals and fashions became "yearly." The world had become orderly.

* monastery: 수도원 ** pendulum: 흔들리는 추

① (A) − (C) − (B)   ② (B) − (A) − (C)
③ (B) − (C) − (A)   ④ (C) − (A) − (B)
⑤ (C) − (B) − (A)

37.

Since we know we can't completely eliminate our biases, we need to try to limit the harmful impacts they can have on the objectivity and rationality of our decisions and judgments.

(A) If it did, we can move on and make an objective and informed decision. If it didn't, we can try the same strategy again or implement a new one until we are ready to make a rational judgment.

(B) Then we can choose an appropriate de-biasing strategy to combat it. After we have implemented a strategy, we should check in again to see if it worked in the way we had hoped.

(C) It is important that we are aware when one of our cognitive biases is activated and make a conscious choice to overcome that bias. We need to be aware of the impact the bias has on our decision making process and our life. [3점]

① (A) - (C) - (B) ② (B) - (A) - (C)
③ (B) - (C) - (A) ④ (C) - (A) - (B)
⑤ (C) - (B) - (A)

[38~39] 글의 흐름으로 보아, 주어진 문장이 들어가기에 가장 적절한 곳을 고르시오.

38.

A computer cannot make independent decisions, however, or formulate steps for solving problems, unless programmed to do so by humans.

It is important to remember that computers can only carry out instructions that humans give them. Computers can process data accurately at far greater speeds than people can, yet they are limited in many respects — most importantly, they lack common sense. (①) However, combining the strengths of these machines with human strengths creates synergy. (②) Synergy occurs when combined resources produce output that exceeds the sum of the outputs of the same resources employed separately. (③) A computer works quickly and accurately; humans work relatively slowly and make mistakes. (④) Even with sophisticated artificial intelligence, which enables the computer to learn and then implement what it learns, the initial programming must be done by humans. (⑤) Thus, a human-computer combination allows the results of human thought to be translated into efficient processing of large amounts of data.

39.

We have a continual desire to communicate our feelings and yet at the same time the need to conceal them for proper social functioning.

For hundreds of thousands of years our hunter-gatherer ancestors could survive only by constantly communicating with one another through nonverbal cues. Developed over so much time, before the invention of language, that is how the human face became so expressive, and gestures so elaborate. (①) With these counterforces battling inside us, we cannot completely control what we communicate. (②) Our real feelings continually leak out in the form of gestures, tones of voice, facial expressions, and posture. (③) We are not trained, however, to pay attention to people's nonverbal cues. (④) By sheer habit, we fixate on the words people say, while also thinking about what we'll say next. (⑤) What this means is that we are using only a small percentage of the potential social skills we all possess. [3점]

* counterforce: 반대 세력 ** sheer: 순전한

40. 다음 글의 내용을 한 문장으로 요약하고자 한다. 빈칸 (A), (B)에 들어갈 말로 가장 적절한 것은?

Why do we help? One widely held view is that self-interest underlies all human interactions, that our constant goal is to maximize rewards and minimize costs. Accountants call it *cost-benefit analysis*. Philosophers call it *utilitarianism*. Social psychologists call it social exchange theory. If you are considering whether to donate blood, you may weigh the costs of doing so (time, discomfort, and anxiety) against the benefits (reduced guilt, social approval, and good feelings). If the rewards exceed the costs, you will help. Others believe that we help because we have been socialized to do so, through norms that prescribe how we ought to behave. Through socialization, we learn the reciprocity norm: the expectation that we should return help, not harm, to those who have helped us. In our relations with others of similar status, the reciprocity norm compels us to give (in favors, gifts, or social invitations) about as much as we receive.

↓

People help because helping gives them ___(A)___, but also because they are socially learned to ___(B)___ what others have done for them.

	(A)	(B)
①	advantages	repay
②	patience	evaluate
③	wisdom	forget
④	advantages	accept
⑤	patience	appreciate

[41~42] 다음 글을 읽고, 물음에 답하시오.

An organization imported new machinery with the capacity to produce quality products at a lesser price. A manager was responsible for large quantities in a relatively short span of time. He started with the (a) full utilization of the new machinery. He operated it 24/7 at maximum capacity. He paid the least attention to downtime, recovery breaks or the general maintenance of the machinery. As the machinery was new, it continued to produce results and, therefore, the organization's profitability (b) soared and the manager was appreciated for his performance. Now after some time, this manager was promoted and transferred to a different location. A new manager came in his place to be in charge of running the manufacturing location. But this manager realized that with heavy utilization and without any downtime for maintenance, a lot of the parts of the machinery were significantly (c) worn and needed to be replaced or repaired. The new manager had to put significant time and effort into repair and maintenance of the machines, which resulted in lower production and thus a loss of profits. The earlier manager had only taken care of the goal of production and (d) ignored the machinery although he had short-term good results. But ultimately not giving attention to recovery and maintenance resulted in long-term (e) positive consequences.

41. 윗글의 제목으로 가장 적절한 것은?

① Why Are Quality Products Important?
② Give Machines a Break to Avoid Overuse
③ Providing Incentives to Maximize Workers' Abilities
④ Tip for Managers: The Right Man in the Right Place
⑤ Wars for High Productivity in a World of Competition

42. 밑줄 친 (a)~(e) 중에서 문맥상 낱말의 쓰임이 적절하지 않은 것은?

① (a)   ② (b)   ③ (c)   ④ (d)   ⑤ (e)

[43~45] 다음 글을 읽고, 물음에 답하시오.

(A)

Maria Sutton was a social worker in a place where the average income was very low. Many of Maria's clients had lost their jobs when the coal industry in a nearby town collapsed. Every Christmas season, knowing how much children loved presents at Christmas, Maria tried to arrange a special visit from Santa Claus for one family. Alice, the seven-year-old daughter of Maria, was very enthusiastic about helping with (a) her mother's Christmas event.

(B)

On Christmas Eve, Maria and Alice visited Karen's house with Christmas gifts. When Karen opened the door, Maria and Alice wished the astonished woman a merry Christmas. Then Alice began to unload the gifts from the car, handing them to Karen one by one. Karen laughed in disbelief, and said she hoped she would one day be able to do something similar for someone else in need. On her way home, Maria said to Alice, "God multiplied (b) your gift."

(C)

This year's lucky family was a 25-year-old mother named Karen and her 3-year-old son, who she was raising by herself. However, things went wrong. Two weeks before Christmas Day, a representative from a local organization called Maria to say that the aid she had requested for Karen had fallen through. No Santa Claus. No presents. Maria saw the cheer disappear from Alice's face at the news. After hearing this, (c) she ran to her room.

(D)

When Alice returned, her face was set with determination. She counted out the coins from her piggy bank: $4.30. "Mom," she told Maria, "(d) I know it's not much. But maybe this will buy a present for the kid." Maria gave her daughter a lovely hug. The next day, Maria told her coworkers about her daughter's latest project. To (e) her surprise, staff members began to open their purses. The story of Alice's gift had spread beyond Maria's office, and Maria was able to raise $300 — plenty for a Christmas gift for Karen and her son.

43. 주어진 글 (A)에 이어질 내용을 순서에 맞게 배열한 것으로 가장 적절한 것은?

① (B) - (D) - (C)   ② (C) - (B) - (D)
③ (C) - (D) - (B)   ④ (D) - (B) - (C)
⑤ (D) - (C) - (B)

44. 밑줄 친 (a)~(e) 중에서 가리키는 대상이 나머지 넷과 다른 것은?

① (a)   ② (b)   ③ (c)   ④ (d)   ⑤ (e)

45. 윗글에 관한 내용으로 적절하지 않은 것은?

① Maria는 평균 소득이 매우 낮은 지역의 사회복지사였다.
② 크리스마스 전날 Karen은 선물을 받았다.
③ Karen은 세 살 된 아들을 키우고 있었다.
④ Maria는 지역 단체 대표의 연락을 받지 못했다.
⑤ Maria는 300달러를 모금할 수 있었다.

* 확인 사항
○ 답안지의 해당란에 필요한 내용을 정확히 기입(표기)했는지 확인하시오.

18

001 □ provide ⓥ 제공하다
002 □ education ⓝ 교육
003 □ talented ⓐ 재능 있는
004 □ annual ⓐ 매년의
005 □ perform ⓥ 공연[연주]하다
006 □ reputation ⓝ 명성
007 □ precede ⓥ 앞서다, 선행하다
008 □ influence ⓥ 영향을 끼치다
009 □ honor ⓝ 영광
010 □ of all time 역대, 지금껏
011 □ splendid ⓐ 훌륭한
012 □ look forward to ~을 고대하다
013 □ receive ⓥ 받다
014 □ positive ⓐ 긍정적인
015 □ reply ⓝ 대답, 답장

19

016 □ result ⓝ 결과
017 □ skeptical ⓐ 회의적인
018 □ win a prize 상을 타다
019 □ tremble ⓥ 떨다
020 □ anxiety ⓝ 불안
021 □ outperform ⓥ ~을 능가하다, ~보다 더 나은 결과를 내다
022 □ participant ⓝ 참가자
023 □ envelope ⓝ 봉투
024 □ hand ⓥ 건네주다, 넘겨주다
025 □ tear open ~을 찢어서 열다
026 □ sweat ⓥ 땀을 흘리다
027 □ pound ⓥ (심장이) 세차게 뛰다
028 □ declare ⓥ 선언하다, 분명히 말하다
029 □ realize ⓥ 깨닫다
030 □ exclaim ⓥ 소리치다, 외치다
031 □ gather ⓥ 모이다
032 □ delighted ⓐ 기쁜
033 □ indifferent ⓐ 무관심한
034 □ furious ⓐ 분노한

20

035 □ set ⓐ 정해진
036 □ label A as B A를 B라고 이름 짓다
037 □ opinion ⓝ 견해
038 □ particular ⓐ 특정한
039 □ same ⓐ 같은
040 □ sort ⓝ 종류
041 □ suit ⓥ (~에게) 맞다
042 □ cut off from ~에서 단절시키다
043 □ possibility ⓝ 가능성
044 □ rigid ⓐ 완고한, 엄격한
045 □ hardened ⓐ 굳어진
046 □ knock about ~을 혹사시키다
047 □ a series of 일련의
048 □ explore ⓥ 탐험하다
049 □ expand ⓥ 확장시키다
050 □ broaden ⓥ 확장하다
051 □ horizon ⓝ 지평선, (사고, 지식 등의 범위를 나타내는), 시야

21

052 □ perspective ⓝ 관점
053 □ strike ⓥ ~와 만나다
054 □ theatrical ⓐ 연극적인
055 □ quality ⓝ 속성, 본질
056 □ quote ⓝ 인용문
057 □ express ⓥ 표현하다
058 □ stage ⓝ 무대
059 □ merely ⓐⓓ 단지
060 □ exit ⓝ 퇴장
061 □ entrance ⓝ 입장
062 □ represent ⓥ 표현하다, 나타내다
063 □ imply ⓥ 암시하다
064 □ constantly ⓐⓓ 끊임없이
065 □ hostile ⓐ 적대적인
066 □ intention ⓝ 의도
067 □ confidence ⓝ 자신감
068 □ navigate ⓥ (상황을) 다루다, (길을 가며) 방향을 찾다
069 □ complex ⓐ 복잡한
070 □ environment ⓝ 환경
071 □ get ahead 앞서다
072 □ harmful ⓐ 해로운, 위험한
073 □ external ⓐ 외부적인
074 □ show off 뽐내다
075 □ adjusting ⓝ 조절

22

076 □ blind spot 맹점
077 □ visible ⓐ (눈에) 보이는
078 □ developmental ⓐ 발달상의
079 □ lane ⓝ 길, 도로
080 □ overlook ⓥ 간과하다
081 □ unaware ⓐ 인지하지 못하는
082 □ presence ⓝ 존재
083 □ equally ⓐⓓ 똑같이
084 □ run over (차 등이) ~을 치다
085 □ enlist ⓥ (협조나 도움을) 구하다, 요청하다
086 □ be willing to ⓥ 기꺼이 ~하다

23

087 □ behavior ⓝ 행동
088 □ be out of control 통제력을 벗어나다
089 □ improve ⓥ 개선되다
090 □ clear ⓐ 분명한
091 □ enforce ⓥ 시행하다
092 □ consequence ⓝ 결과
093 □ present ⓥ 제시하다
094 □ enforcement ⓝ 시행
095 □ consistent ⓐ 일관성 있는
096 □ firm ⓐ 단호한
097 □ spoil ⓥ 망치다
098 □ autonomy ⓝ 자율성
099 □ reasonable ⓐ 합당한
100 □ in terms of ~ 면에서
101 □ temperament ⓝ 기질
102 □ effectively ⓐⓓ 효과적으로
103 □ split ⓥ 갈라놓다, 분리시키다
104 □ punishment ⓝ 처벌
105 □ be linked to ~와 연관되다
106 □ reward ⓝ 보상
107 □ fairly ⓐⓓ 공정하게, 꽤
108 □ consideration ⓝ 고려 사항
109 □ necessity ⓝ 필요성
110 □ discipline ⓝ 훈육, 규율

111 □ impact ⓝ 영향
112 □ caregiver ⓝ (병자·아이들을) 돌보는 사람

24

113 □ invention ⓝ 발명품
114 □ invent ⓥ 발명하다
115 □ exact ⓐ 정확한
116 □ origin ⓝ 기원
117 □ discover ⓥ 발견하다
118 □ accurately ⓐⓓ 정확하게
119 □ ancient ⓐ 고대의
120 □ pottery ⓝ 도자기
121 □ archaeologist ⓝ 고고학자
122 □ date back to ~로 거슬러 올라가다
123 □ tell A from B A와 B를 구별하다
124 □ fake ⓝ 모조품
125 □ driving force 동인(動因), 추동하는 힘
126 □ civilization ⓝ 문명

25

127 □ amount ⓝ 양, 액수
128 □ electric car 전기 차
129 □ stock ⓝ 재고품
130 □ rank ⓥ (등급, 순위 등을) 차지하다
131 □ surpass ⓥ 넘어서다, 능가하다

26

132 □ graceful ⓐ 우아한
133 □ adapt ⓥ 적응하다
134 □ belly ⓝ 배
135 □ pointed ⓐ 뾰족한
136 □ horn ⓝ 뿔
137 □ measure ⓥ (길이, 양 등이) ~이다
138 □ feed upon ~을 먹고 살다
139 □ grass ⓝ 풀
140 □ condition ⓝ 상황
141 □ harsh ⓐ 혹독한, 가혹한
142 □ dry ⓐ 건조한
143 □ herd ⓝ 무리, 떼
144 □ breeding season 번식기
145 □ wet ⓐ 젖은
146 □ give birth 출산하다
147 □ isolated ⓐ 고립된
148 □ life span 수명

27

149 □ be bored with ~에 싫증이 나다
150 □ current ⓐ 지금의
151 □ routine ⓝ 일과
152 □ senior-friendly 노인 친화적인
153 □ recreational ⓐ 오락의
154 □ admission fee 입장료, 참가비
155 □ include ⓥ 포함하다
156 □ pre-registration 사전 등록
157 □ necessary ⓐ 필요한

28

158 □ magical ⓐ 마술적인, 신기한
159 □ simple ⓐ 간단한, 단순한
160 □ magic trick 마술 묘기
161 □ purchase ⓥ 구매하다
162 □ entrance ⓝ 입구

29

163 □ insert ⓥ 끼우다, 넣다
164 □ seed ⓝ 씨앗
165 □ industry ⓝ 산업
166 □ prepare ⓥ 준비하다
167 □ give credit to ~에게 공로를 주다
168 □ individual ⓝ 개인
169 □ plant ⓥ 심다
170 □ successful ⓐ 성공적인
171 □ necessarily ⓐⓓ 반드시
172 □ overwhelming ⓐ 엄청난, 압도적인
173 □ intelligence ⓝ 지능
174 □ prosper ⓥ 번성하다
175 □ community ⓝ 공동체, 지역사회
176 □ strength ⓝ 강점, 장점
177 □ inspire ⓥ 고무하다, 격려하다
178 □ against all odds 모든 역경을 딛고
179 □ revolutionary ⓐ 혁명적인
180 □ perception ⓝ 인식
181 □ race ⓝ 인종
182 □ fairness ⓝ 공정함
183 □ accomplish ⓥ 성취하다, 달성하다
184 □ treat ⓥ 대하다, 여기다
185 □ appreciate ⓥ (진가를) 인정하다

30

186 □ sudden ⓐ 갑작스러운
187 □ neurologically ⓐⓓ 신경학적으로
188 □ chemical ⓝ 화학물질
189 □ release ⓥ 분비하다
190 □ burst ⓝ 분출
191 □ addiction ⓝ 중독
192 □ manic ⓐ 광적인
193 □ gain ⓝ 이득, 이익
194 □ wisdom ⓝ 지혜
195 □ last ⓥ 지속되다
196 □ take into account ~을 고려하다
197 □ hard-earned 어렵게 얻은
198 □ recapture ⓥ 되찾다
199 □ high ⓝ 황홀감, 도취감
200 □ attention ⓝ 관심
201 □ acquire ⓥ 얻다
202 □ superiority ⓝ 우월함
203 □ resistant ⓐ 저항하는
204 □ warn ⓥ 경고하다
205 □ sustain ⓥ 지속시키다, 지탱하다
206 □ inevitable ⓐ 필연적인, 불가피한
207 □ painful ⓐ 고통스러운
208 □ depression ⓝ 우울, 낮게 패인 곳
209 □ prone to ~하기 쉬운

31

210 □ predator ⓝ 포식자
211 □ consume ⓥ 먹다, 마시다
212 □ signal ⓥ 신호를 보내다
213 □ ripe ⓐ (과일 등이) 다 익은
214 □ harden ⓥ 딱딱해지다
215 □ content ⓝ 함량
216 □ at one's height 최고조에 이른
217 □ incredibly ⓐⓓ 놀랍게도, 믿기 힘들게도
218 □ manufacture ⓥ 생산하다
219 □ fructose ⓝ 과당

220 □ glucose ⓝ 포도당
221 □ prey ⓝ 먹이
222 □ obtain ⓥ 얻다
223 □ distribute ⓥ 퍼뜨리다, 분포시키다

32
224 □ be faced with ～에 직면하다
225 □ predict ⓥ 예측하다
226 □ decision ⓝ 결정
227 □ situation ⓝ 상황, 경우
228 □ end up 결국 ～하게 되다
229 □ altogether ⓐⓓ 전적으로, 완전히
230 □ unpredictable ⓐ 예측할 수 없는
231 □ dip ⓥ 담그다, 적시다
232 □ dive ⓥ 뛰어들다
233 □ be about to 막 ～하려고 하다
234 □ enroll in ～에 등록하다
235 □ fully ⓐⓓ 완전히
236 □ convinced ⓐ 확신하는
237 □ outcome ⓝ 결과
238 □ instructor ⓝ 강사
239 □ methodology ⓝ 방법론
240 □ investment ⓝ 투자
241 □ commit ⓥ 전념하다

33
242 □ sociologist ⓝ 사회학자
243 □ prove ⓥ 입증하다
244 □ view ⓝ 관점
245 □ value ⓝ 가치
246 □ encounter ⓥ 직면하다, 마주치다
247 □ affect ⓥ 영향을 주다
248 □ intolerant ⓐ 편협한
249 □ get into (특정한 상태에) 처하다
250 □ progressive ⓐ 진보적인
251 □ share ⓥ 공유하다
252 □ absurd ⓐ 어처구니없는, 불합리한
253 □ racism ⓝ 인종 차별주의
254 □ make fun of ～을 놀리다, 비웃다
255 □ foolish ⓐ 어리석은
256 □ demonstrate ⓥ 분명히 보여주다
257 □ assume ⓥ 가정하다
258 □ prejudice ⓝ 편견
259 □ have an effect on ～에게 영향을 주다
260 □ resolve ⓥ 해결하다

34
261 □ availability ⓝ 가용성, 이용 가능성
262 □ common ⓐ 일반적인
263 □ come to mind 떠오르다
264 □ prevalent ⓐ 널리 퍼진, 만연한
265 □ recency ⓝ 최신성
266 □ misjudge ⓥ 잘못 판단하다
267 □ frequency ⓝ 빈도
268 □ magnitude ⓝ 규모
269 □ fall victim to ～의 희생양이 되다
270 □ heuristic ⓐ (교수법·교육이) 체험적인, 스스로 발견하게 하는
271 □ supervisor ⓝ 관리자, 상사
272 □ prior to ～에 앞서, 먼저
273 □ evaluation ⓝ 평가
274 □ previous ⓐ 바로 앞의, 이전의

275 □ dominate ⓥ 지배하다
276 □ ease ⓝ 쉬움, 용이함
277 □ recall ⓥ 회상
278 □ probability ⓝ 가능성
279 □ reliable ⓐ 신뢰할 만한
280 □ frequent ⓐ 잦은
281 □ contact ⓝ 접촉
282 □ evaluate ⓥ 평가하다
283 □ objectively ⓐⓓ 객관적으로
284 □ distorted ⓐ 왜곡된

35
285 □ management ⓝ 경영
286 □ climb ⓥ 등반하다
287 □ overcrowded ⓐ 과하게 붐비는
288 □ demand ⓝ 수요
289 □ usage ⓝ 사용, 사용량
290 □ excess ⓐ 초과한
291 □ task ⓝ 일, 과업, 과제
292 □ demarketing ⓝ 역 마케팅(수요 억제를 위한 선전 활동)
293 □ temporarily ⓐⓓ 일시적으로
294 □ permanently ⓐⓓ 영구적으로
295 □ compensate for ～을 보상하다, 상쇄하다
296 □ loss ⓝ 손실
297 □ supply ⓝ 공급
298 □ aim ⓝ 목적, 목표
299 □ shift ⓥ 이동시키다
300 □ seek ⓥ 추구하다
301 □ objective ⓝ 목표

36
302 □ invention ⓝ 발명
303 □ mechanical ⓐ 기계의
304 □ monk ⓝ 수도사, 승려
305 □ determine ⓥ 결정하다, 확정하다
306 □ widespread ⓐ 널리 퍼진
307 □ enormous ⓐ 거대한, 엄청난
308 □ serve ⓥ ～을 섬기다, ～을 위해 일하다
309 □ accurate ⓐ 정확한
310 □ ring ⓥ (종이) 울리다
311 □ interval ⓝ 간격
312 □ announce ⓥ 알리다
313 □ reserved ⓐ 지정된, 예약한
314 □ tie ⓥ 묶다
315 □ revolve ⓥ 회전하다, 돌다
316 □ periodical ⓝ 정기 간행물
317 □ yearly ⓐ 연간의, 해마다 있는
318 □ orderly ⓐ 질서 정연한

37
319 □ eliminate ⓥ 없애다, 제거하다
320 □ bias ⓝ 편향, 편견
321 □ limit ⓥ 제한하다
322 □ objectivity ⓝ 객관성
323 □ rationality ⓝ 합리성
324 □ judgment ⓝ 판단
325 □ move on (새로운 일·주제로) 넘어가다
326 □ informed ⓐ 정보에 근거한
327 □ strategy ⓝ 전략
328 □ implement ⓥ 실행하다
329 □ rational ⓐ 이성적인

330 □ appropriate ⓐ 적절한
331 □ combat ⓥ 싸우다
332 □ cognitive ⓐ 인지적인
333 □ activate ⓥ 활성화시키다
334 □ conscious ⓐ 의식적인
335 □ overcome ⓥ 극복하다

38
336 □ independent ⓐ 독립적인
337 □ formulate ⓥ 만들어 내다, 공식화하다
338 □ carry out 수행하다
339 □ instruction ⓝ 지시
340 □ process ⓥ 처리하다
341 □ respect ⓝ 측면, 사항
342 □ lack ⓥ ～이 부족하다
343 □ common sense 상식
344 □ combine ⓥ 결합하다
345 □ synergy ⓝ 시너지, 상승효과
346 □ occur ⓥ 일어나다, 발생하다
347 □ output ⓝ 산출
348 □ exceed ⓥ 초과하다
349 □ sum ⓝ 합
350 □ employ ⓥ 사용하다
351 □ separately ⓐⓓ 각각, 별개로
352 □ relatively ⓐⓓ 상대적으로, 비교적
353 □ sophisticated ⓐ 정교한, 세련된
354 □ enable ⓥ ～을 가능하게 하다
355 □ initial ⓐ 초기의
356 □ combination ⓝ 결합
357 □ translate ⓥ (다른 형태로) 바꾸다, 고치다
358 □ efficient ⓐ 효율적인

39
359 □ continual ⓐ 끊임없는
360 □ desire ⓝ 욕망, 욕구
361 □ communicate ⓥ 전달하다
362 □ feeling ⓝ 감정
363 □ proper ⓐ 적절한
364 □ functioning ⓝ 기능
365 □ nonverbal ⓐ 비언어적인
366 □ cue ⓝ 신호
367 □ expressive ⓐ (감정을) 나타내는
368 □ elaborate ⓐ 정교한
369 □ battle ⓥ 다투다
370 □ continually ⓐⓓ 끊임없이
371 □ leak out 새어 나오다
372 □ in the form of ～의 형태로
373 □ posture ⓝ 자세
374 □ fixate on ～에 집착하다, ～을 고수하다
375 □ potential ⓐ 잠재적인
376 □ possess ⓥ 소유하다

40
377 □ widely ⓐⓓ 널리
378 □ underlie ⓥ ～의 기초를 이루다
379 □ interaction ⓝ 상호작용
380 □ maximize ⓥ 극대화하다
381 □ minimize ⓥ 최소화하다
382 □ accountant ⓝ 회계사
383 □ benefit ⓝ 수익, 이익
384 □ analysis ⓝ 분석
385 □ philosopher ⓝ 철학자

386 □ utilitarianism ⓝ 공리주의
387 □ weigh ⓥ 따져 보다
388 □ discomfort ⓝ 불편함
389 □ guilt ⓝ 죄책감
390 □ approval ⓝ 인정, 승인
391 □ prescribe ⓥ 규정하다, 처방하다
392 □ socialization ⓝ 사회화
393 □ reciprocity ⓝ 상호성
394 □ expectation ⓝ 기대
395 □ relation ⓝ 관계
396 □ status ⓝ 지위
397 □ compel ⓥ 강요하다

41~42
398 □ organization ⓝ 조직
399 □ import ⓥ 수입하다
400 □ machinery ⓝ 기계(류)
401 □ capacity ⓝ 능력
402 □ produce ⓥ 생산하다
403 □ be responsible for ～에 책임이 있다
404 □ quantity ⓝ 양
405 □ span ⓝ 기간, 시간
406 □ utilization ⓝ 사용
407 □ operate ⓥ 작동시키다
408 □ maximum ⓐ 최대의
409 □ downtime ⓝ (기계 등의) 비가동 시간
410 □ recovery ⓝ 회복
411 □ general ⓐ 일반적인
412 □ maintenance ⓝ 유지 보수
413 □ profitability ⓝ 수익성
414 □ soar ⓥ 치솟다
415 □ promote ⓥ 승진하다
416 □ location ⓝ 장소, 위치
417 □ in charge of ～을 맡아서, 담당해서
418 □ significantly ⓐⓓ 상당히
419 □ worn ⓐ 닳은, 해진
420 □ production ⓝ 생산
421 □ ignore ⓥ 무시하다
422 □ ultimately ⓐⓓ 궁극적으로
423 □ overuse ⓝ 과도한 사용, 남용

43~45
424 □ social worker 사회 복지사
425 □ income ⓝ 소득
426 □ client ⓝ 고객
427 □ coal ⓝ 석탄
428 □ collapse ⓥ 붕괴하다
429 □ arrange ⓥ 마련하다
430 □ enthusiastic ⓐ 열성적인
431 □ astonished ⓐ 깜짝 놀란
432 □ unload ⓥ (짐을) 내리다
433 □ laugh ⓥ 웃다
434 □ disbelief ⓝ 믿기지 않음, 불신
435 □ in need 어려운, 도움이 필요한
436 □ multiply ⓥ 배가시키다
437 □ representative ⓝ 대표 ⓐ 대표하는
438 □ aid ⓝ 도움, 지원
439 □ fall through 성사되지 않다, 실현되지 못하다
440 □ cheer ⓝ 쾌활함, 생기
441 □ disappear ⓥ 사라지다
442 □ determination ⓝ 결의
443 □ purse ⓝ 지갑

10회

어휘 Review test 10

TEST A-B 각 단어의 뜻을 [A] 영어는 우리말로, [B] 우리말은 영어로 쓰시오.

A	English	Korean
01	prosper	
02	discipline	
03	astonished	
04	spoil	
05	manic	
06	enforce	
07	reciprocity	
08	declare	
09	fall victim to	
10	splendid	
11	intolerant	
12	collapse	
13	tear open	
14	leak out	
15	knock about	
16	tell A from B	
17	harmful	
18	compel	
19	approval	
20	broaden	

B	Korean	English
01	왜곡된	
02	진보적인	
03	중독	
04	합리성	
05	자율성	
06	영구적으로	
07	뽐내다	
08	인종 차별주의	
09	무관심한	
10	분노한	
11	불안	
12	넘어서다, 능가하다	
13	명성	
14	(차 등이) ~을 치다	
15	간격	
16	비언어적인	
17	A를 B라고 이름 짓다	
18	우아한	
19	편견	
20	투자	

▶ A-D 정답 : 해설편 105쪽

TEST C-D 각 단어의 뜻을 골라 기호를 쓰시오.

C	English		Korean
01	absurd	( )	ⓐ 방법론
02	neurologically	( )	ⓑ 신경학적으로
03	bias	( )	ⓒ ~로 거슬러 올라가다
04	against all odds	( )	ⓓ 모든 역경을 딛고
05	take into account	( )	ⓔ 널리 퍼진, 만연한
06	possess	( )	ⓕ 일시적으로
07	prevalent	( )	ⓖ 인지하지 못하는
08	methodology	( )	ⓗ ~을 고려하다
09	temporarily	( )	ⓘ 처벌
10	unaware	( )	ⓙ 편향, 편견
11	compensate for	( )	ⓚ 맹점
12	punishment	( )	ⓛ 어처구니없는, 불합리한
13	combat	( )	ⓜ 싸우다
14	blind spot	( )	ⓝ ~을 보상[상쇄]하다
15	date back to	( )	ⓞ 소유하다
16	hard-earned	( )	ⓟ 최신성
17	elaborate	( )	ⓠ 공리주의
18	utilitarianism	( )	ⓡ 정교한
19	recency	( )	ⓢ 어렵게 얻은
20	at one's height	( )	ⓣ 최고조에 이른

D	Korean		English
01	떠오르다	( )	ⓐ skeptical
02	혁명적인	( )	ⓑ driving force
03	규모	( )	ⓒ import
04	~하기 쉬운	( )	ⓓ come to mind
05	~에 집착하다	( )	ⓔ split
06	회의적인	( )	ⓕ magnitude
07	성사되지 않다	( )	ⓖ periodical
08	정기 간행물	( )	ⓗ fixate on
09	~을 고대하다	( )	ⓘ breeding season
10	갈라놓다, 분리시키다	( )	ⓙ fall through
11	구하다, 요청하다	( )	ⓚ look forward to
12	동인(動因), 추동하는 힘	( )	ⓛ prone to
13	번식기	( )	ⓜ enlist
14	~을 먹고 살다	( )	ⓝ revolutionary
15	수입하다	( )	ⓞ feed upon
16	질서 정연한	( )	ⓟ orderly
17	널리 퍼진	( )	ⓠ underlie
18	~의 기초를 이루다	( )	ⓡ widespread
19	~에 등록하다	( )	ⓢ pottery
20	도자기	( )	ⓣ enroll in

※ 영어 [독해] 파트만 수록한 문제지이므로 **18번**부터 시작합니다. ● 점수 표시가 없는 문항은 모두 **2점** ● 문항수 **28개** | 배점 **63점** | 제한 시간 **45분**

18. 다음 글의 목적으로 가장 적절한 것은?

> To whom it may concern,
>
> My name is Peter Jackson and I am thinking of applying for the Advanced Licensed Counselor Program that the university provides. I found that the certification for 100 hours of counseling experience is required for the application. However, I do not think I could possibly complete the required counseling experience by the current deadline. So, if possible, I kindly request an extension of the deadline until the end of this summer vacation. I am actively working on obtaining the certification, and I am sure I will be able to submit it by then. I understand the importance of following the application process, and would greatly appreciate your consideration of this request. I look forward to your response.
>
> Sincerely,
> Peter Jackson

① 상담 경력 증명서의 제출 기한 연장을 요청하려고
② 서류 심사 결과 발표의 지연에 대해 항의하려고
③ 전문 상담 강좌의 추가 개설을 제안하려고
④ 대학의 편의 시설 확충을 건의하려고
⑤ 대학 진학 상담 예약을 취소하려고

19. 다음 글에 드러난 'I'의 심경 변화로 가장 적절한 것은?

The passport control line was short and the inspectors looked relaxed; except the inspector at my window. He seemed to want to model the seriousness of the task at hand for the other inspectors. Maybe that's why I felt uneasy when he studied my passport more carefully than I expected. "You were here in September," he said. "Why are you back so soon?" "I came in September to prepare to return this month," I replied with a trembling voice, considering if I missed any Italian regulations. "For how long?" he asked. "One month, this time," I answered truthfully. I knew it was not against the rules to stay in Italy for three months. "Enjoy your stay," he finally said, as he stamped my passport. Whew! As I walked away, the burden I had carried, even though I did nothing wrong, vanished into the air. My shoulders, once weighed down, now stretched out with comfort.

① angry → ashamed
② nervous → relieved
③ bored → grateful
④ curious → frightened
⑤ hopeful → disappointed

20. 다음 글에서 필자가 주장하는 바로 가장 적절한 것은?

Merely convincing your children that worry is senseless and that they would be more content if they didn't worry isn't going to stop them from worrying. For some reason, young people seem to believe that worry is a fact of life over which they have little or no control. Consequently, they don't even try to stop. Therefore, you need to convince them that worry, like guilt and fear, is nothing more than an emotion, and like all emotions, is subject to the power of the will. Tell them that they can eliminate worry from their lives by simply refusing to attend to it. Explain to them that if they refuse to act worried regardless of how they feel, they will eventually stop feeling worried and will begin to experience the contentment that accompanies a worry-free life.

① 아이가 죄책감과 책임감을 구분하도록 가르쳐야 한다.
② 아이가 스스로 불안의 원인을 찾도록 도와주어야 한다.
③ 아이의 감정에 공감하고 있음을 구체적으로 표현해야 한다.
④ 부모로서 느끼는 감정에 관해 아이와 솔직하게 대화해야 한다.
⑤ 아이에게 자기 의지로 걱정을 멈출 수 있음을 알려주어야 한다.

21. 밑줄 친 Build a jazz band가 다음 글에서 의미하는 바로 가장 적절한 것은?

In today's information age, in many companies and on many teams, the objective is no longer error prevention and replicability. On the contrary, it's creativity, speed, and keenness. In the industrial era, the goal was to minimize variation. But in creative companies today, maximizing variation is more essential. In these situations, the biggest risk isn't making a mistake or losing consistency; it's failing to attract top talent, to invent new products, or to change direction quickly when the environment shifts. Consistency and repeatability are more likely to suppress fresh thinking than to bring your company profit. A lot of little mistakes, while sometimes painful, help the organization learn quickly and are a critical part of the innovation cycle. In these situations, rules and process are no longer the best answer. A symphony isn't what you're going for. Leave the conductor and the sheet music behind. Build a jazz band instead.

① Foster variation within an organization.
② Limit the scope of variability in businesses.
③ Invent a new way of minimizing risk-taking.
④ Promote teamwork to forecast upcoming changes.
⑤ Share innovations over a sufficient period of time.

22. 다음 글의 요지로 가장 적절한 것은?

Any new or threatening situation may require us to make decisions and this requires information. So important is communication during a disaster that normal social barriers are often lowered. We will talk to strangers in a way we would never consider normally. Even relatively low grade disruption of our life such as a fire drill or a very late train seems to give us the permission to break normal etiquette and talk to strangers. The more important an event to a particular public, the more detailed and urgent the requirement for news becomes. Without an authoritative source of facts, whether that is a newspaper or trusted broadcast station, rumours often run riot. Rumours start because people believe their group to be in danger and so, although the rumour is unproven, feel they should pass it on. For example, if a worker heard that their employer's business was doing badly and people were going to be made redundant, they would pass that information on to colleagues.

* redundant: (일시) 해고된

① 소수에 의한 정보 독점은 합리적 의사 결정을 방해한다.
② 대중의 지속적 관심이 뉴스의 공정성을 향상시킬 수 있다.
③ 위기에 처한 사람은 권위 있는 전문가의 의견을 구하려고 한다.
④ 소문은 유사한 성향을 지닌 사람들 사이에서 더 빠르게 퍼진다.
⑤ 위기 상황에서는 확인되지 않은 정보라도 전달하려는 경향이 크다.

23. 다음 글의 주제로 가장 적절한 것은?

People seem to recognize that the arts are cultural activities that draw on (or react against) certain cultural traditions, certain shared understanding, and certain values and ideas that are characteristic of the time and place in which the art is created. In the case of science, however, opinions differ. Some scientists, like the great biologist J. B. S. Haldane, see science in a similar light — as a historical activity that occurs in a particular time and place, and that needs to be understood within that context. Others, however, see science as a purely "objective" pursuit, uninfluenced by the cultural viewpoint and values of those who create it. In describing this view of science, philosopher Hugh Lacey speaks of the belief that there is an underlying order of the world which is simply there to be discovered — the world of pure "fact" stripped of any link with value. The aim of science according to this view is to represent this world of pure "fact", independently of any relationship it might bear contingently to human practices and experiences.

* contingently: 혹여라도

① misconceptions on how experimental data should be measured
② views on whether science is free from cultural context or not
③ ways for minimizing cultural bias in scientific pursuits
④ challenges in achieving objectivity in scientific studies
⑤ functions of science in analyzing cultural phenomena

24. 다음 글의 제목으로 가장 적절한 것은?

Mental development consists of individuals increasingly mastering social codes and signals themselves, which they can master only in social situations with the support of more competent individuals, typically adults. In this sense, mental development consists of internalizing social patterns and gradually becoming a responsible actor among other responsible actors. In Denmark, the age of criminal responsibility is 15 years, which means that we then say that people have developed sufficient mental maturity to be accountable for their actions at this point. And at the age of 18 people are given the right to vote and are thereby formally included in the basic democratic process. I do not know whether these age boundaries are optimal, but it is clear that mental development takes place at different rates for different individuals, and depends especially on the social and family environment they have been given. Therefore, having formal limits for responsibility from a specific age that apply to everyone is a somewhat questionable practice. But the question, of course, is whether it can be done any differently.

① Adult Influence Is Key to Child Development
② How Can Social Codes Limit People's Cognition?
③ Democracy Grows Only with Responsible Youth
④ Setting Responsibilities Based on Age: Is It Appropriate?
⑤ Aging: A Possible Obstacle to Consistent Personal Growth

25. 다음 도표의 내용과 일치하지 <u>않는</u> 것은?

Proportion of People Who Provide Unpaid Care to Children and Adults in Canada in 2022

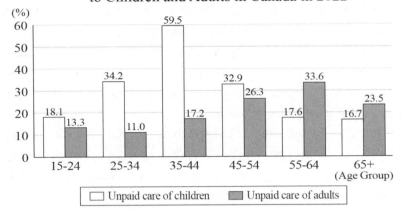

Legend: □ Unpaid care of children ■ Unpaid care of adults

The graph above shows the percentage of people who provided unpaid care to children and adults by age group in Canada in 2022. ① Notably, the 35-44 group had the highest percentage of individuals providing unpaid care to children, reaching 59.5%. ② However, the highest percentage of individuals providing unpaid care to adults was found in the 55-64 group. ③ Compared to the 25-34 group, the 15-24 group had a lower percentage of individuals providing unpaid care to children and a higher percentage of individuals providing unpaid care to adults. ④ The percentage of people providing unpaid care to adults in the 45-54 group was more than twice as high as that in the 35-44 group. ⑤ The 55-64 group and the 65 and older group showed a similar percentage of individuals providing unpaid care to children, with a difference of less than 1 percentage point.

26. Charles Elton에 관한 다음 글의 내용과 일치하지 <u>않는</u> 것은?

Born in the English city of Liverpool, Charles Elton studied zoology under Julian Huxley at Oxford University from 1918 to 1922. After graduating, he began teaching as a part-time instructor and had a long and distinguished teaching career at Oxford from 1922 to 1967. After a series of arctic expeditions with Huxley, he worked with a fur-collecting and trading company as a biological consultant, and examined the company's records to study animal populations. In 1927, he wrote his first and most important book, *Animal Ecology*, in which he demonstrated the nature of food chains and cycles. In 1932, he helped establish the Bureau of Animal Population at Oxford. In the same year he became the editor of the new *Journal of Animal Ecology*. Throughout his career, Elton wrote six books and played a major role in shaping the modern science of ecology.

① 대학에서 동물학을 공부했다.
② 대학 졸업 후 가르치는 일을 시작했다.
③ 생물학 컨설턴트로서 한 회사와 함께 일했다.
④ 마지막으로 쓴 저서는 *Animal Ecology*였다.
⑤ 1932년에 *Journal of Animal Ecology*의 편집자가 되었다.

27. Clifton Fall Clean-up Day 2024에 관한 다음 안내문의 내용과 일치하지 <u>않는</u> 것은?

Clifton Fall Clean-up Day 2024

Join us for this annual event to clean up the fallen leaves in Central Park, and enjoy meeting your neighbors!

When: Sunday, October 20th, 1 p.m. – 3 p.m.

Details
• Clean-up will be done in groups of 10 people based on age.
• After the clean-up, you can enjoy a casual gathering with neighbors.
• Food trucks will be set up for your gathering.

Notes
• A T-shirt with the event's logo will be provided as a gift.
• You'll be supplied with cleaning materials, such as bags and gloves, so you don't have to bring them.

We're looking forward to seeing you there!

① 매년 열리는 행사이다.
② 10명씩 조를 이루어 청소할 것이다.
③ 푸드 트럭이 설치될 것이다.
④ 행사 로고가 있는 티셔츠가 제공될 것이다.
⑤ 청소 도구를 가져와야 한다.

28. Sustainable Fashion Festival 2024에 관한 다음 안내문의 내용과 일치하는 것은?

Sustainable Fashion Festival 2024

Sustainable Fashion Festival 2024 is coming! Be inspired and learn how to live sustainably while looking fabulous.

When & Where
• Friday, September 13th, 5 p.m. – 9 p.m.
• Aimes Community Center

Tickets: $20 for early birds / $25 at the door
(Early purchase discount ends two days before the event.)

Programs
• Marketplace for sustainable products: You can sell or buy new, vintage, or upcycled clothing.
• Talks from eco-fashion experts on fashion's sustainable future
• Clothing exchange: You can exchange 5 or fewer items.
• Runway showcase of sustainable designs

※ To sell your sustainable products at our marketplace, registration is required in advance.

Contact us on social media for more information.

① 금요일 오전에 진행된다.
② 티켓 조기 구매 할인은 행사 사흘 전 종료된다.
③ 장터에서 새 의류를 구입할 수 없다.
④ 5개 이하의 의류 물품을 교환할 수 있다.
⑤ 사전 등록 없이도 지속 가능 제품을 판매할 수 있다.

29. 다음 글의 밑줄 친 부분 중, 어법상 틀린 것은? [3점]

One well-known shift took place when the accepted view —that the Earth was the center of the universe—changed to one where we understood that we are only inhabitants on one planet ① orbiting the Sun. With each person who grasped the solar system view, ② it became easier for the next person to do so. So it is with the notion that the world revolves around the human economy. This is slowly being replaced by the view that the economy is a part of the larger system of material flows that connect all living things. When this perspective shifts into place, it will be obvious that our economic well-being requires that we account for, and ③ respond to, factors of ecological health. Unfortunately we do not have a century or two ④ make the change. By clarifying the nature of the old and new perspectives, and by identifying actions ⑤ on which we might cooperate to move the process along, we can help accelerate the shift.

30. 다음 글의 밑줄 친 부분 중, 문맥상 낱말의 쓰임이 적절하지 않은 것은?

The first human beings probably evolved in tropical regions where survival was possible without clothing. It is likely that they had very dark skin because light skin would have given ① little protection against the burning rays of the sun. There is a debate about whether these people spread into other parts of the world or, instead, whether people developed independently in various parts of the world. Whichever the case, it is believed that in time they became ② capable of spreading out from Africa, eventually to most of the world. This was probably because their ③ physical characteristics changed. For instance, early hominids probably did not walk upright, but when they developed that ability, they could travel more efficiently. More important, perhaps, was their ④ development of tool making. With tools, they could hunt other animals, so they could consume more protein and fat than their low-energy vegetarian diet would have provided. Not only their bodies but also their brains would have been changed with more energy. The brain needs lots of energy to grow. As their diet ⑤ reduced, hominids could physically and intellectually expand their territory.

*hominid: 인류

[31~34] 다음 빈칸에 들어갈 말로 가장 적절한 것을 고르시오.

31. When we get an unfavorable outcome, in some ways the *last* thing we want to hear is that the process was fair. As outraging as the combination of an unfavorable outcome and an unfair process is, this combination also brings with it a consolation prize: the possibility of attributing the bad outcome to something other than ourselves. We may reassure ourselves by believing that our bad outcome had little to do with us and everything to do with the unfair process. If the process is fair, however, we cannot nearly as easily _____ the outcome; we got what we got "fair and square." When the process is fair we believe that our outcome is deserved, which is another way of saying that there must have been something about ourselves (what we did or who we are) that caused the outcome. [3점]

*consolation: 위로

① expect   ② diversify   ③ externalize
④ generate   ⑤ overestimate

32. The well-known American ethnologist Alfred Louis Kroeber made a rich and in-depth study of women's evening dress in the West, stretching back about three centuries and using reproductions of engravings. Having adjusted the dimensions of these plates due to their diverse origins, he was able to analyse the constant elements in fashion features and to come up with a study that was neither intuitive nor approximate, but precise, mathematical and statistical. He reduced women's clothing to a certain number of features: length and size of the skirt, size and depth of the neckline, height of the waistline. He demonstrated unambiguously that fashion is _____ which is not located at the level of annual variations but on the scale of history. For practically 300 years, women's dress was subject to a very precise periodic cycle: forms reach the furthest point in their variations every fifty years. If, at any one moment, skirts are at their longest, fifty years later they will be at their shortest; thus skirts become long again fifty years after being short and a hundred years after being long. [3점]

*engraving: 판화 **dimension: 크기

① a profoundly regular phenomenon
② a practical and progressive trend
③ an intentionally created art form
④ a socially influenced tradition
⑤ a swiftly occurring event

33. Over the last few centuries, humanity's collective prosperity has skyrocketed, as technological progress has made us far wealthier than ever before. To share out those riches, almost all societies have settled upon the market mechanism, rewarding people in various ways for the work that they do and the things that they own. But rising inequality, itself often driven by technology, has started to put that mechanism under strain. Today, markets already provide immense rewards to some people but leave many others with very little. And now, technological unemployment threatens to become a more radical version of the same story, taking place in the particular market we rely upon the most: the labor market. As that market begins to break down, more and more people will be in danger of _____. [3점]

① not receiving a share of society's prosperity at all
② making too large of an investment in new areas
③ not fully comprehending technological terms
④ unconsciously wasting the rewards from their work
⑤ not realizing the reason to raise their cost of living

34. It's often said that those who can't do, teach. It would be more accurate to say that those who can do, can't teach the basics. A great deal of expert knowledge is implicit, not explicit. The further you progress toward mastery, _____. Experiments show that skilled golfers and wine aficionados have a hard time describing their putting and tasting techniques—even asking them to explain their approaches is enough to interfere with their performance, so they often stay on autopilot. When I first saw an elite diver do four and a half somersaults, I asked how he managed to spin so fast. His answer: "Just go up in a ball." Experts often have an intuitive understanding of a route, but they struggle to clearly express all the steps to take. Their brain dump is partially filled with garbage. [3점]

* aficionado: 애호가   ** somersault: 공중제비

① the greater efforts you have to put into your work
② the smaller number of strategies you use to solve problems
③ the less you tend to show off your excellent skills to others
④ the more detail-oriented you are likely to be for task completion
⑤ the less conscious awareness you often have of the fundamentals

35. 다음 글에서 전체 흐름과 관계 <u>없는</u> 문장은?

Minimal processing can be one of the best ways to keep original flavors and taste, without any need to add artificial flavoring or additives, or too much salt. This would also be the efficient way to keep most nutrients, especially the most sensitive ones such as many vitamins and anti-oxidants. ① Milling of cereals is one of the most harsh processes which dramatically affect nutrient content. ② While grains are naturally very rich in micronutrients, anti-oxidants and fiber (i.e. in wholemeal flour or flakes), milling usually removes the vast majority of minerals, vitamins and fibers to raise white flour. ③ To increase grain production, the use of chemical fertilizers should be minimized, and insect-resistant grain varieties should be developed. ④ Such a spoilage of key nutrients and fiber is no longer acceptable in the context of a sustainable diet aiming at an optimal nutrient density and health protection. ⑤ In contrast, fermentation of various foodstuffs or germination of grains are traditional, locally accessible, low-energy and highly nutritious processes of sounded interest.

* fermentation: 발효   ** germination: 발아

[36~37] 주어진 글 다음에 이어질 글의 순서로 가장 적절한 것을 고르시오.

36.

> It would seem obvious that the more competent someone is, the more we will like that person. By "competence," I mean a cluster of qualities: smartness, the ability to get things done, wise decisions, etc.

(A) If this were true, we might like people more if they reveal some evidence of fallibility. For example, if your friend is a brilliant mathematician, superb athlete, and gourmet cook, you might like him or her better if, every once in a while, they screwed up.

(B) One possibility is that, although we like to be around competent people, those who are *too* competent make us uncomfortable. They may seem unapproachable, distant, superhuman—and make us look bad (and feel worse) by comparison.

(C) We stand a better chance of doing well at our life tasks if we surround ourselves with people who know what they're doing and have a lot to teach us. But the research evidence is paradoxical: In problem-solving groups, the participants who are considered the most competent and have the best ideas tend not to be the ones who are best liked. Why?

* fallibility: 실수를 저지르기 쉬움

① (A) - (C) - (B)   ② (B) - (A) - (C)
③ (B) - (C) - (A)   ④ (C) - (A) - (B)
⑤ (C) - (B) - (A)

37.

> A computational algorithm that takes input data and generates some output from it doesn't really embody any notion of meaning. Certainly, such a computation does not generally have as its purpose its own survival and well-being.

(A) Some bees might not bother to make the journey, considering it not worthwhile. The input, such as it is, is processed in the light of the organism's own internal states and history; there is nothing prescriptive about its effects.

(B) It does not, in general, assign value to the inputs. Compare, for example, a computer algorithm with the waggle dance of the honeybee, by which means a foraging bee conveys to others in the hive information about the source of food (such as nectar) it has located.

(C) The "dance"—a series of stylized movements on the comb—shows the bees how far away the food is and in which direction. But this input does not simply program other bees to go out and look for it. Rather, they evaluate this information, comparing it with their own knowledge of the surroundings. [3점]

* forage: 먹이를 찾아다니다 ** comb: 벌집

① (A) − (C) − (B)   ② (B) − (A) − (C)
③ (B) − (C) − (A)   ④ (C) − (A) − (B)
⑤ (C) − (B) − (A)

[38~39] 글의 흐름으로 보아, 주어진 문장이 들어가기에 가장 적절한 곳을 고르시오.

38.

> But there are also important differences between the two types of contagion.

There are deep similarities between viral contagion and behavioral contagion. (①) For example, people in close or extended proximity to others infected by a virus are themselves more likely to become infected, just as people are more likely to drink excessively when they spend more time in the company of heavy drinkers. (②) One is that visibility promotes behavioral contagion but inhibits the spread of infectious diseases. (③) Solar panels that are visible from the street, for instance, are more likely to stimulate neighboring installations. (④) In contrast, we try to avoid others who are visibly ill. (⑤) Another important difference is that whereas viral contagion is almost always a bad thing, behavioral contagion is sometimes negative—as in the case of smoking—but sometimes positive, as in the case of solar installations.

* contagion: 전염

39.

> Real hibernation involves profound unconsciousness and a dramatic fall in body temperature—often to around 32 degrees Fahrenheit.

Sleep is clearly about more than just resting. One curious fact is that animals that are hibernating also have periods of sleep. It comes as a surprise to most of us, but hibernation and sleep are not the same thing at all, at least not from a neurological and metabolic perspective. (①) Hibernating is more like being anesthetized: the subject is unconscious but not actually asleep. (②) So a hibernating animal needs to get a few hours of conventional sleep each day within the larger unconsciousness. (③) A further surprise to most of us is that bears, the most famous of wintry sleepers, don't actually hibernate. (④) By this definition, bears don't hibernate, because their body temperature stays near normal and they are easily awakened. (⑤) Their winter sleeps are more accurately called a state of torpor. [3점]

* hibernation: 동면 ** anesthetize: 마취시키다 *** torpor: 휴면

40. 다음 글의 내용을 한 문장으로 요약하고자 한다. 빈칸 (A), (B)에 들어갈 말로 가장 적절한 것은?

> The concern about how we appear to others can be seen in children, though work by the psychologist Ervin Staub suggests that the effect may vary with age. In a study where children heard another child in distress, young children (kindergarten through second grade) were more likely to help the child in distress when with another child than when alone. But for older children—in fourth and sixth grade—the effect reversed: they were less likely to help a child in distress when they were with a peer than when they were alone. Staub suggested that younger children might feel more comfortable acting when they have the company of a peer, whereas older children might feel more concern about being judged by their peers and fear feeling embarrassed by overreacting. Staub noted that "older children seemed to discuss the distress sounds less and to react to them less openly than younger children." In other words, the older children were deliberately putting on a poker face in front of their peers.

↓

> The study suggests that, contrary to younger children, older children are less likely to help those in distress in the ___(A)___ of others because they care more about how they are ___(B)___.

	(A)		(B)
①	presence	······	evaluated
②	presence	······	motivated
③	absence	······	viewed
④	absence	······	assisted
⑤	audience	······	trained

[41~42] 다음 글을 읽고, 물음에 답하시오.

What makes questioning authority so hard? The (a) difficulties start in childhood, when parents — the first and most powerful authority figures — show children "the way things are." This is a necessary element of learning language and socialization, and certainly most things learned in early childhood are (b) noncontroversial: the English alphabet starts with A and ends with Z, the numbers 1 through 10 come before the numbers 11 through 20, and so on. Children, however, will spontaneously question things that are quite obvious to adults and even to older kids. The word "why?" becomes a challenge, as in, "Why is the sky blue?" Answers such as "because it just is" or "because I say so" tell children that they must unquestioningly (c) accept what authorities say "just because," and children who persist in their questioning are likely to find themselves dismissed or yelled at for "bothering" adults with "meaningless" or "unimportant" questions. But these questions are in fact perfectly (d) unreasonable. Why is the sky blue? Many adults do not themselves know the answer. And who says the sky's color needs to be called "blue," anyway? How do we know that what one person calls "blue" is the same color that another calls "blue"? The scientific answers come from physics, but those are not the answers that children are seeking. They are trying to understand the world, and no matter how (e) irritating the repeated questions may become to stressed and time-pressed parents, it is important to take them seriously to encourage kids to question authority to think for themselves.

41. 윗글의 제목으로 가장 적절한 것은?

① Things Plain to You Aren't to Children: Let Them Question
② Children's Complaints: Should Parents Accept All of Them?
③ Want More Challenges? They'll Make Your Energy Dry Up!
④ Authority Has Hidden Power to Nurture Children's Morality
⑤ Answering Is More Crucial than Questioning for Quick Learning

42. 밑줄 친 (a)~(e) 중에서 문맥상 낱말의 쓰임이 적절하지 <u>않은</u> 것은?

① (a)　② (b)　③ (c)　④ (d)　⑤ (e)

[43~45] 다음 글을 읽고, 물음에 답하시오.

(A)

My two girls grew up without challenges with respect to development and social interaction. My son Benjamin, however, was quite delayed. He struggled through his childhood, not fitting in with the other children and wondering what he was doing wrong at every turn. He was teased by the other children and frowned upon by a number of unsympathetic adults. But his Grade 1 teacher was a wonderful, caring person who took the time to ask why Benjamin behaved the way (a) he did.

(B)

I suspected the teacher had paid for it out of his own pocket. It was a story-board book with a place for a photo. On each page there was an outline of an animal and a hole so that the face in the photo appeared to be the face of the animal. Wondering if Benjamin would really be interested in the book, I brought it home. He loved it! Through that book, he saw that (b) he could be anything he wanted to be: a cat, an octopus, a dinosaur — even a frog!

(C)

The teacher was determined to understand Benjamin and to accept him as he was. One day he came home with a note from his teacher. He suggested I go to the school library. They were having a sale, and (c) he thought my son would like one of the books. I couldn't go for a couple of days and was concerned I'd missed the opportunity. When I finally went to the school, his teacher told me that the sale had ended but that the library had saved the book for my little boy.

(D)

Benjamin joyfully embarked on an imaginative journey through the book, and little did we know, it laid the groundwork for his future successes. And thankfully, his teacher had taken the time to observe and understand (d) him and had discovered a way to help him reach out of his own world and join ours through a story-board book. My son later became a child actor and performed for seven years with a Toronto casting agency. (e) He is now a published author who writes fantasy and science-fiction! Who would have guessed?

43. 주어진 글 (A)에 이어질 내용을 순서에 맞게 배열한 것으로 가장 적절한 것은?

① (B) − (D) − (C)　② (C) − (B) − (D)
③ (C) − (D) − (B)　④ (D) − (B) − (C)
⑤ (D) − (C) − (B)

44. 밑줄 친 (a)~(e) 중에서 가리키는 대상이 나머지 넷과 <u>다른</u> 것은?

① (a)　② (b)　③ (c)　④ (d)　⑤ (e)

45. 윗글에 관한 내용으로 적절하지 <u>않은</u> 것은?

① Benjamin은 어린 시절 다른 아이들과 잘 어울리지 않았다.
② 'I'는 선생님이 책값을 지불했다고 짐작했다.
③ Benjamin은 'I'가 가져온 책을 좋아하지 않았다.
④ 선생님은 'I'에게 학교 도서관에 방문할 것을 제안했다.
⑤ Benjamin은 아역 배우가 되었다.

★ 확인 사항

○ 답안지의 해당란에 필요한 내용을 정확히 기입(표기)했는지 확인하시오.

회차별 영단어 QR 코드 ※ QR 코드를 스캔 후 모바일로 단어장처럼 학습할 수 있습니다. ● 고2 2024학년도 9월

18

001 applying ⓥ 신청하다, 지원하다
002 provide ⓥ 제공하다, 주다
003 certification ⓝ 증명서
004 counseling ⓝ 상담
005 require ⓥ 필요하다, 필요로 하다
006 application ⓝ 지원
007 possibly ⓐⓓ 아마도
008 complete ⓥ 완료하다
009 current ⓐ 현재의, 지금의
010 deadline ⓝ 기한, 마감 시간
011 kindly ⓐⓓ 정중하게, 친절하게
012 request ⓝ 요청, 신청 ⓥ 요청하다, 신청하다
013 extension ⓝ 연장
014 until ⓒⓞⓝⓙ …(때)까지
015 actively ⓐⓓ 적극적으로, 열심히
016 obtaining ⓝ 취득, 획득
017 sure ⓐ 확신하는, 확실히 아는
018 submit ⓥ 제출하다
019 consideration ⓝ 고려
020 response ⓝ 대답, 응답, 회신, 답장

19

021 passport control 입국 심사, 출국 수속
022 relaxed ⓐ 편안한
023 inspector ⓝ 심사관
024 window ⓝ 창구, 창문
025 model ⓝ 모범, 견본
026 seriousness ⓝ 심각성, 진지함
027 task at hand 당면한 과제
028 uneasy ⓐ 불안한, 우려되는
029 studied ⓐ 살펴보다
030 carefully ⓐⓓ 신중하게, 꼼꼼히
031 expected ⓐ 예상되는
032 prepare ⓥ 준비하다
033 trembling ⓐ 떨리는
034 regulation ⓝ 규정, 규제
035 truthfully ⓐⓓ 진실하게, 솔직하게
036 against ⓟⓡⓔⓟ ~에 반하여
037 stay ⓥ 체류하다, 머무르다
038 vanish ⓥ 사라지다
039 weigh down ~을 짓누르다
040 comfort ⓝ 안락, 편안

20

041 merely ⓐⓓ 그저, 단지
042 convince ⓥ 설득하다
043 senseless ⓐ 무의미한
044 content ⓝ 내용 ⓥ 걱정하다
045 worry ⓝ 걱정, 우려
046 reason ⓝ 이유, 까닭, 사유
047 guilt ⓝ 죄책감
048 eliminate ⓥ 없애다
049 regardless of ~와 상관없이
050 worry-free 걱정 없음

21

051 information age 정보화 시대
052 objective ⓝ 목적, 목표
053 error ⓝ 실수, 오류
054 prevention ⓝ 예방, 방지
055 replicability ⓝ 반복 가능성

056 On the contrary 반대로, 그와는 달리
057 creativity ⓝ 창의성
058 keenness ⓝ 명민함
059 industrial era 산업화 시대
060 variation ⓝ 변화
061 consistency ⓝ 일관성
062 talent ⓝ 재능, 재능 있는 사람
063 invent ⓥ 만들다, 발명하다
064 repeatability ⓝ 반복성
065 suppress ⓥ 짓누르다
066 profit ⓝ 이익, 수익
067 painful ⓐ 고통스러운
068 critical ⓐ 대단히 중요한
069 innovation ⓝ 혁신
070 cycle ⓝ 순환, 주기
071 conductor ⓝ 지휘자
072 foster ⓥ 기르다

22

073 threatening ⓐ 긴박한, 위협적인
074 decision ⓝ 결정, 판단
075 during ⓟⓡⓔⓟ … 동안, ~ 중에
076 disaster ⓝ 참사, 재난, 재해
077 barrier ⓝ 장벽
078 lower ⓥ 낮추다, 완화하다
079 normally ⓐⓓ 평상시에는, 보통 때는
080 even ⓐⓓ 심지어, ~조차도
081 fire drill 소방 훈련
082 etiquette ⓝ 예의, 에티켓
083 permission ⓝ 허용
084 urgent ⓐ 긴급한
085 authoritative ⓐ 권위 있는
086 run riot 제멋대로 뻗어나가다
087 although ⓒⓞⓝⓙ ~임에도 불구하고
088 unproven ⓐ 입증되지 않은
089 badly ⓐⓓ 안 좋은
090 redundant ⓐ (일시)해고된

23

091 recognize ⓥ 인식하다, 알아보다
092 cultural ⓐ 문화의
093 certain ⓐ 특정한
094 shared ⓐ 공유된, 공통의
095 value ⓝ 가치
096 In the case of ~의 경우에
097 differ ⓥ 다르다
098 biologist ⓝ 생물학자
099 similar ⓐ 비슷한, 유사한
100 historical ⓐ 역사적, 역사상의
101 purely ⓐⓓ 순전히
102 pursuit ⓥ 추구하다
103 uninfluenced ⓐ 영향을 받지 않은
104 viewpoint ⓝ 관점, 시각
105 describing ⓐ 묘사하는, 설명하는
106 underlying ⓐ 근본적인
107 strip of ~을 빼앗다
108 contingently ⓐⓓ 혹여라도
109 misconception ⓝ 오해

24

110 consist of ~로 구성되다
111 increasingly ⓐⓓ 점점 더, 갈수록 더

112 support ⓝ 도움, 지지
113 competent ⓐ 유능한
114 In this sense 이러한 의미에서
115 internalize ⓥ 내면화하는
116 pattern ⓝ 양식, 패턴
117 gradually ⓐⓓ 점차
118 among ⓟⓡⓔⓟ ~사이에서, ~중에서
119 sufficient ⓐ 충분한
120 maturity ⓝ 성숙함
121 be accountable for ~에 대해 책임이 있다
122 right to vote 투표권, 선거권
123 thereby ⓐⓓ 그렇게 함으로써
124 democratic ⓐ 민주주의의, 민주적인
125 whether ⓒⓞⓝⓙ ~인지
126 boundary ⓝ 경계
127 take place 발생하다, 일어나다
128 somewhat ⓐⓓ 다소
129 apply ⓥ 적용하다, 지원하다

25

130 above ⓟⓡⓔⓟ ~위에
131 unpaid ⓐ 무급의
132 care ⓝ 돌봄, 치료
133 notably ⓐⓓ 두드러지게, 특히
134 highest ⓐ 가장 높은
135 reach ⓥ 도달하다

26

136 born ⓥ 태어나다
137 zoology ⓝ 동물학
138 after ⓟⓡⓔⓟ ~후에
139 instructor ⓝ 강사
140 distinguished ⓐ 유명한
141 career ⓝ 직업, 경력
142 arctic ⓐ 북극
143 expedition ⓝ 탐험
144 fur ⓝ 모피, 털
145 biological ⓐ 생물학의
146 examine ⓥ 조사하다, 검토하다
147 population ⓝ 개체
148 demonstrate ⓥ 입증하다
149 food chain ⓝ 먹이사슬
150 establish ⓥ 설립하다
151 editor ⓝ 편집자
152 throughout ⓟⓡⓔⓟ ~내내, ~동안 쭉
153 shape ⓥ 형성하다
154 ecology ⓝ 생태학

27

155 fall ⓥ 떨어지다, 넘어지다
156 leaf ⓝ 잎사귀 (복수형: leaves)
157 meet ⓥ 만나다
158 neighbor ⓝ 이웃
159 based on ⓟⓡⓔⓟ ~에 기초하여
160 casual ⓐ 가벼운
161 gathering ⓝ 모임, 수집
162 material ⓝ 도구, 재료
163 bring ⓥ 가져오다, 데려오다

28

164 sustainable ⓐ 지속 가능한

165 inspire ⓥ 영감을 주다
166 fabulous ⓐ 굉장한
167 sell ⓥ 팔다
168 clothing ⓝ 의류, 옷
169 expert ⓝ 전문가
170 few ⓐ 적은
171 in advance 사전에

29

172 center ⓝ 중심, 중앙
173 inhabitant ⓝ 주민
174 planet ⓝ 행성
175 orbit ⓥ 궤도를 돌다
176 grasp ⓥ 잡다, 이해하다
177 solar system ⓝ 태양계
178 notion ⓝ 개념, 생각
179 economy ⓝ 경제학
180 flow ⓝ 흐름
181 perspective ⓝ 관점
182 shift ⓝ 변화
183 account for 설명하다
184 identify ⓥ 식별하다, 확인하다
185 cooperate ⓥ 협력하다
186 accelerate ⓥ 가속화하다

30

187 tropical ⓐ 열대의
188 region ⓝ 지역, 구역
189 survival ⓝ 생존
190 without ⓟⓡⓔⓟ ~없이
191 protection ⓝ 보호
192 burn ⓥ 태우다, 불타다
193 ray ⓝ 광선, 빛줄기
194 debate ⓝ 논쟁
195 spread ⓥ 퍼지다, 펼치다
196 instead ⓐⓓ 대신에
197 independently ⓐⓓ 독립적으로
198 case ⓝ 사례, 경우, 사건
199 became capable of ~할 수 있다
200 spread out 펴다, 확장하다
201 eventually ⓐⓓ 결국, 최종적으로
202 hominid ⓝ 인류
203 upright ⓐ 똑바른, 직립한
204 ability ⓝ 능력
205 travel ⓥ 여행하다, 이동하다
206 efficiently ⓐⓓ 효율적으로
207 important ⓐ 중요한
208 perhaps ⓐⓓ 아마도
209 hunt ⓥ 사냥하다
210 consume ⓥ 소비하다, 먹다
211 protein ⓝ 단백질
212 fat ⓝ 지방
213 diet ⓝ 식단
214 body ⓝ 몸, 신체
215 also ⓐⓓ 또한, 역시
216 brain ⓝ 뇌
217 intellectually ⓐⓓ 지적으로
218 expand ⓥ 확장하다
219 territory ⓝ 지역

31

220 unfavorable ⓐ 불리한

221 □ outcome ⓝ 결과, 성과
222 □ fair ⓐ 공정한, 공평한
223 □ outrage ⓝ 분노
224 □ combination ⓝ 결합
225 □ consolation ⓝ 위로
226 □ attribute ⓥ ~의 탓으로 돌리다
227 □ ourselves pron 우리 자신
228 □ reassure ⓥ 안심시키다
229 □ nearly ⓐd 거의
230 □ fair and square 정정당당하게, 공명정대하게
231 □ unfair ⓐ 불공정한
232 □ deserved ⓐ 마땅한
233 □ cause ⓥ 초래하다, 야기하다, 원인이 되다

32
234 □ ethnologist ⓝ 민족학자
235 □ in-depth ⓐ 깊이 있는, 심층적인
236 □ stretching back to ~이래로, ~까지 거슬러 올라가서
237 □ reproduction ⓝ 복제품
238 □ engraving ⓝ 판화
239 □ dimension ⓝ 크기
240 □ plate ⓝ 접시, 판
241 □ due to ~때문에, ~로 인해
242 □ diverse ⓐ 다양한, 여러 가지의
243 □ origin ⓝ 기원
244 □ analyze ⓥ 분석하다
245 □ constant ⓐ 끊임없는
246 □ feature ⓝ 특징
247 □ come up with ⓥ 생각해내다, 제안하다
248 □ neither conj ~도 아닌, ~도 아니다
249 □ intuitive ⓐ 직관적인
250 □ approximate ⓐ 대략적이지 않은
251 □ precise ⓐ 정확한
252 □ mathematical ⓐ 수학의, 수리적인
253 □ statistical ⓐ 통계의, 통계적인
254 □ length ⓝ 길이, 기간
255 □ neckline ⓝ 목선
256 □ height ⓝ 높이, 키
257 □ waistline ⓝ 허리선
258 □ unambiguously ⓐd 분명하게
259 □ locate ⓥ 위치하다, 위치를 찾다
260 □ practically ⓐd 사실상
261 □ periodic ⓐ 주기적인
262 □ profoundly ⓐd 매우, 대단히
263 □ regular ⓐ 규칙적인, 정기적인, 보통의

33
264 □ collective ⓐ 집합적인, 공동의
265 □ prosperity ⓝ 번영
266 □ skyrocket ⓥ 급증하다
267 □ wealthy ⓐ 부유한
268 □ share ⓥ 공유하다, 나누다
269 □ settle ⓥ 정착하다, 해결하다
270 □ rise ⓥ 증가하다, 오르다, 상승하다
271 □ inequality ⓝ 불평등
272 □ itself pron 그 자체
273 □ strain ⓝ 부담, 압박
274 □ already ⓐd 이미, 벌써
275 □ immense ⓐ 엄청난
276 □ leave ⓥ 떠나다, 남기다

277 □ unemployment ⓝ 실업
278 □ threaten ⓥ 위협하다
279 □ radical ⓐ 급진적인
280 □ rely ⓥ 의지하다, 믿다
281 □ labor ⓝ 노동, 노동력
282 □ break down ⓥ 무너지다
283 □ comprehend ⓥ 이해하다

34
284 □ accurate ⓐ 정확한
285 □ a great deal of 많은 양의
286 □ implicit ⓐ 암시적
287 □ further ⓐd 더 멀리, 더 나아가서
288 □ progress ⓝ 진전, 발전 ⓥ 진행하다, 나아가다
289 □ toward prep ~쪽으로, ~을 향하여
290 □ explicit ⓐ 명시적
291 □ mastery ⓝ 숙달
292 □ experiment ⓝ 실험 ⓥ 실험하다
293 □ aficionado ⓝ 애호가
294 □ describe ⓥ 묘사하다, 설명하다
295 □ explain ⓥ 설명하다, 해명하다
296 □ approach ⓝ 접근법, 접근 방식
297 □ interfere with ~을 방해하다
298 □ autopilot ⓝ 자동 조종 장치
299 □ somersault ⓝ 공중제비
300 □ spin ⓥ 돌다, 회전하다
301 □ route ⓝ 경로, 길, 방법
302 □ partially ⓐd 부분적으로
303 □ fill with ~으로 가득 차다
304 □ detail-oriented 자세한 것을 지향하는
305 □ completion ⓝ 완료
306 □ conscious ⓐ 의식하는, 자각하는
307 □ awareness ⓝ 의식, 자각, 인식

35
308 □ way ⓝ 방법, 방식, 길
309 □ flavor ⓝ 맛
310 □ artificial ⓐ 인공적인
311 □ additive ⓝ 첨가물
312 □ nutrient ⓝ 영양소
313 □ especially ⓐd 특히, 특별히
314 □ sensitive ⓐ 민감한
315 □ anti-oxidants 항산화물질
316 □ mill ⓥ 제분하다
317 □ cereal ⓝ 곡물, 시리얼
318 □ harsh ⓐ 가혹한
319 □ process ⓝ 과정, 절차
320 □ dramatically ⓐd 극적으로, 급격히
321 □ affect ⓥ 영향을 미치다
322 □ naturally ⓐd 자연스럽게, 당연히
323 □ micronutrient ⓝ 미량영양소
324 □ fiber ⓝ 섬유질
325 □ wholemeal ⓐ 통밀의, 전분 가루의
326 □ flour ⓝ 밀가루, 가루
327 □ flake ⓝ 조각, (특히) 곡물 플레이크
328 □ usually ⓐd 보통, 일반적으로
329 □ remove ⓥ 제거하다, 없애다
330 □ vast majority 최대의, 대부분의
331 □ fertilizer ⓝ 비료
332 □ insect-resistant 곤충에 저항력이 있는
333 □ develop ⓥ 발전하다, 개발하다

334 □ spoilage ⓝ 부패
335 □ aim ⓥ 목표로 하다, 겨냥하다
336 □ density ⓝ 밀도
337 □ fermentation ⓝ 발효
338 □ germination ⓝ 발아
339 □ accessible ⓐ 접근 가능한

36
340 □ obvious ⓐ 분명한
341 □ cluster ⓝ 집단
342 □ quality ⓝ 특성, 특징
343 □ wise ⓐ 현명한, 지혜로운
344 □ stand ⓥ 서다, 위치하다
345 □ chance ⓝ 기회, 가능성
346 □ task ⓝ 과제, 일
347 □ surround ⓥ 둘러싸다, 에워싸다
348 □ fallibility ⓝ 실수
349 □ brilliant ⓐ 훌륭한
350 □ superb ⓐ 뛰어난
351 □ athlete ⓝ 운동선수
352 □ gourmet ⓝ 미식가
353 □ screw up ⓥ 망치다
354 □ possibility ⓝ 가능성
355 □ unapproachable ⓐ 접근할 수 없는
356 □ distant ⓐ 먼, 떨어져 있는
357 □ worse ⓐ 더 나쁘게, 악화된
358 □ comparison ⓝ 비교
359 □ paradoxical ⓐ 역설적인
360 □ participant ⓝ 참가자

37
361 □ computational ⓐ 컴퓨터의
362 □ algorithm ⓝ 알고리즘
363 □ input ⓝ 입력
364 □ generate ⓥ 발생하다
365 □ embody ⓥ 구현하다
366 □ meaning ⓝ 의미, 뜻
367 □ certainly ⓐd 확실히, 분명히
368 □ computation ⓝ 계산, 연산
369 □ purpose ⓝ 목적
370 □ internal ⓐ 내부의, 내적인
371 □ state ⓝ 상태, 상황
372 □ worthwhile ⓐ 가치 있는
373 □ organism ⓝ 유기체, 생물
374 □ prescriptive ⓐ 규정하는
375 □ effect ⓝ 효과, 영향
376 □ assign ⓥ 부여하다
377 □ compare ⓥ 비교하다, 견주다
378 □ honeybee ⓝ 꿀벌
379 □ foraging ⓝ 수렵 채집
380 □ convey ⓥ 전달하다
381 □ nectar ⓝ 꿀, 꽃의 꿀
382 □ a series of 일련의, 연속적인
383 □ stylize ⓥ 양식화하다
384 □ movement ⓝ 움직임, 동작
385 □ comb ⓝ 벌집
386 □ simply ⓐd 단순히, 그냥
387 □ evaluate ⓥ 평가하다

38
388 □ contagion ⓝ 전염
389 □ viral ⓐ 바이러스의

390 □ proximity ⓝ 가까움
391 □ excessively ⓐd 과도하게
392 □ visibility ⓝ 가시성
393 □ inhibit ⓥ 억제하다
394 □ infectious ⓐ 전염되는
395 □ stimulate ⓥ 촉진하다

39
396 □ hibernation ⓝ 동면
397 □ profound ⓐ 깊은
398 □ unconsciousness ⓝ 무의식
399 □ Fahrenheit ⓐ 화씨의
400 □ neurological ⓐ 신경의
401 □ metabolic ⓐ 신진대사적인
402 □ anesthetize ⓥ 마취시키다
403 □ wintry ⓐ 겨울의
404 □ awakened ⓥ 깨다
405 □ torpor ⓝ 휴면

40
406 □ psychologist ⓝ 심리학자
407 □ vary ⓥ 다르다
408 □ reverse ⓥ 뒤집다
409 □ peer ⓝ 또래
410 □ overreact ⓥ 과잉 반응을 보이다
411 □ note ⓥ 주목하다
412 □ deliberately ⓐd 의도적으로
413 □ contrary to ~와 반대로
414 □ distress ⓝ 곤경

41~42
415 □ figure ⓝ 인물
416 □ necessary ⓐ 필요한
417 □ socialization ⓝ 사회화
418 □ noncontroversial ⓐ 논란의 여지가 없는
419 □ spontaneously ⓐd 자발적으로
420 □ unquestioningly ⓐd 의문을 품지 않고
421 □ persist ⓥ 계속하다
422 □ dismiss ⓥ 묵살하다
423 □ yell ⓥ 소리치다
424 □ bother ⓥ 성가시게 하다
425 □ unreasonable ⓐ 비합리적인
426 □ irritate ⓥ 짜증나게 하다
427 □ encourage ⓥ 독려하다

43~45
428 □ interaction ⓝ 상호 작용
429 □ struggle ⓥ 고군분투하다
430 □ unsympathetic ⓐ 인정 없는
431 □ behave ⓥ 행동하다
432 □ suspect ⓥ 의심하다
433 □ determine ⓥ 결심하다
434 □ accept ⓥ 받아들이다
435 □ concern ⓝ 걱정
436 □ embark ⓥ 시작하다
437 □ imaginative ⓐ 상상력이 풍부한
438 □ journey ⓝ 여정
439 □ groundwork ⓝ 준비작업
440 □ observe ⓥ 관찰하다
441 □ publish ⓥ 출판하다
442 □ author ⓝ 작가
443 □ guess ⓥ 짐작하다

11회

어휘 Review test 11

TEST A-B 각 단어의 뜻을 [A] 영어는 우리말로, [B] 우리말은 영어로 쓰시오.

A	English	Korean
01	counseling	
02	certification	
03	consideration	
04	prepare	
05	seriousness	
06	truthfully	
07	variation	
08	suppress	
09	innovation	
10	authoritative	
11	unproven	
12	urgent	
13	purely	
14	misconception	
15	gradually	
16	somewhat	
17	thereby	
18	reach	
19	care	
20	distinguished	

B	Korean	English
01	강사	
02	입증하다	
03	탐험	
04	가벼운	
05	도구, 재료	
06	지속 가능한	
07	굉장한	
08	전문가	
09	주민	
10	가속화하다	
11	흐름	
12	논쟁	
13	아마도	
14	지적으로	
15	지역	
16	불리한	
17	위로	
18	안심시키다	
19	불공정한	
20	복제품	

▶ A-D 정답 : 해설편 116쪽

TEST C-D 각 단어의 뜻을 골라 기호를 쓰시오.

C	English		Korean
01	brilliant	( )	ⓐ 기원
02	radical	( )	ⓑ 특징
03	density	( )	ⓒ 분명하게
04	visibility	( )	ⓓ 번영
05	origin	( )	ⓔ 급진적인
06	sensitive	( )	ⓕ 위협하다
07	worthwhile	( )	ⓖ 암시적
08	feature	( )	ⓗ 쓰레기
09	evaluate	( )	ⓘ 부분적으로
10	obvious	( )	ⓙ 민감한
11	garbage	( )	ⓚ 섬유질
12	convey	( )	ⓛ 밀도
13	implicit	( )	ⓜ 분명한
14	input	( )	ⓝ 비교
15	partially	( )	ⓞ 훌륭한
16	unambiguously	( )	ⓟ 입력
17	fiber	( )	ⓠ 전달하다
18	prosperity	( )	ⓡ 가치 있는
19	threaten	( )	ⓢ 평가하다
20	comparison	( )	ⓣ 가시성

D	Korean		English
01	상호 작용	( )	ⓐ stimulate
02	자발적으로	( )	ⓑ excessively
03	깊은	( )	ⓒ awakened
04	곤경	( )	ⓓ profound
05	필요한	( )	ⓔ neurological
06	성가시게 하다	( )	ⓕ peer
07	인물	( )	ⓖ vary
08	소리치다	( )	ⓗ distress
09	또래	( )	ⓘ deliberately
10	계속하다	( )	ⓙ figure
11	깨다	( )	ⓚ necessary
12	신경의	( )	ⓛ spontaneously
13	결심하다	( )	ⓜ persist
14	시작하다	( )	ⓝ yell
15	짜증나게 하다	( )	ⓞ bother
16	촉진하다	( )	ⓟ irritate
17	다르다	( )	ⓠ interaction
18	과도하게	( )	ⓡ struggle
19	고군분투하다	( )	ⓢ determine
20	의도적으로	( )	ⓣ embark

※ 영어 [독해] 파트만 수록한 문제지이므로 18번부터 시작합니다.

● 점수 표시가 없는 문항은 모두 2점 ● 문항수 28개 | 배점 63점 | 제한 시간 45분

18. 다음 글의 목적으로 가장 적절한 것은?

To whom it may concern,

I would like to draw your attention to a problem that frequently occurs with the No. 35 buses. There is a bus stop about halfway along Fenny Road, at which the No. 35 buses are supposed to stop. It would appear, however, that some of your drivers are either unaware of this bus stop or for some reason choose to ignore it, driving past even though the buses are not full. I would be grateful if you could remind your drivers that this bus stop exists and that they should be prepared to stop at it. I look forward to seeing an improvement in this service soon.

Yours faithfully,

John Williams

① 버스 운전기사 채용 계획을 문의하려고
② 버스 정류장의 위치 변경을 요청하려고
③ 도로 공사로 인한 소음에 대해 항의하려고
④ 출퇴근 시간의 버스 배차 간격 단축을 제안하려고
⑤ 버스 정류장 무정차 통과에 대한 시정을 요구하려고

19. 다음 글에 드러난 'I'의 심경 변화로 가장 적절한 것은?

My 10-year-old appeared, in desperate need of a quarter. "A quarter? What on earth do you need a quarter for?" My tone bordered on irritation. I didn't want to be bothered with such a trivial demand. "There's a garage sale up the street, and there's something I just gotta have! It only costs a quarter. Please?" I placed a quarter in my son's hand. Moments later, a little voice said, "Here, Mommy, this is for you." I glanced down at the hands of my little son and saw a four-inch cream-colored statue of two small children hugging one another. Inscribed at their feet were words that read *It starts with 'L' ends with 'E' and in between are 'O' and 'V.'* As I watched him race back to the garage sale, I smiled with a heart full of happiness. That 25-cent garage sale purchase brought me a lot of joy.

* quarter: 25센트 동전   ** inscribe: 새기다

① annoyed → delighted
② ashamed → relieved
③ excited → confused
④ scared → confident
⑤ indifferent → jealous

20. 다음 글에서 필자가 주장하는 바로 가장 적절한 것은?

Managers frequently try to play psychologist, to "figure out" why an employee has acted in a certain way. Empathizing with employees in order to understand their point of view can be very helpful. However, when dealing with a problem area, in particular, remember that it is not the person who is bad, but the actions exhibited on the job. Avoid making suggestions to employees about personal traits they should change; instead suggest more acceptable ways of performing. For example, instead of focusing on a person's "unreliability," a manager might focus on the fact that the employee "has been late to work seven times this month." It is difficult for employees to change who they are; it is usually much easier for them to change how they act.

① 직원의 개인적 성향을 고려하여 업무를 배정하라.
② 업무 효율성 향상을 위해 직원의 자율성을 존중하라.
③ 조직의 안정을 위해 직원의 심리 상태를 수시로 확인하라.
④ 직원의 업무상 고충을 이해하기 위해 직원과 적극적으로 소통하라.
⑤ 문제를 보이는 직원에게 인격적 특성보다는 행동 방식에 대해 제안하라.

21. 밑줄 친 forward "thinking"이 다음 글에서 의미하는 바로 가장 적절한 것은?

I suspect fungi are a little more forward "thinking" than their larger partners. Among trees, each species fights other species. Let's assume the beeches native to Central Europe could emerge victorious in most forests there. Would this really be an advantage? What would happen if a new pathogen came along that infected most of the beeches and killed them? In that case, wouldn't it be more advantageous if there were a certain number of other species around — oaks, maples, or firs — that would continue to grow and provide the shade needed for a new generation of young beeches to sprout and grow up? Diversity provides security for ancient forests. Because fungi are also very dependent on stable conditions, they support other species underground and protect them from complete collapse to ensure that one species of tree doesn't manage to dominate.

* fungus: 균류, 곰팡이류 (*pl.* fungi) ** beech: 너도밤나무
*** pathogen: 병원균

① responsible for the invasion of foreign species
② eager to support the dominance of one species
③ aware that diversity leads to the stability of forests
④ indifferent to helping forests regenerate after collapse
⑤ careful that their territories are not occupied by other species

22. 다음 글의 요지로 가장 적절한 것은?

It's remarkable that positive fantasies help us relax to such an extent that it shows up in physiological tests. If you want to unwind, you can take some deep breaths, get a massage, or go for a walk — but you can also try simply closing your eyes and fantasizing about some future outcome that you might enjoy. But what about when your objective is to make your wish a reality? The *last* thing you want to be is relaxed. You want to be energized enough to get off the couch and lose those pounds or find that job or study for that test, and you want to be motivated enough to stay engaged even when the inevitable obstacles or challenges arise. The principle of "Dream it. Wish it. Do it." does not hold true, and now we know why: in dreaming it, you undercut the energy you need to do it. You put yourself in a temporary state of complete happiness, calmness — and inactivity.

* physiological: 생리학적인

① 과도한 목표 지향적 태도는 삶의 만족감을 떨어뜨린다.
② 긍정적 자세로 역경을 극복할 때 잠재 능력이 발휘된다.
③ 편안함을 느끼는 상황에서 자기 개선에 대한 동기가 생긴다.
④ 낙관적인 상상은 소망을 실현하는 데 필요한 동력을 약화시킨다.
⑤ 막연한 목표보다는 명확하고 구체적인 목표가 실현 가능성이 크다.

23. 다음 글의 주제로 가장 적절한 것은?

If cooking is as central to human identity, biology, and culture as the biological anthropologist Richard Wrangham suggests, it stands to reason that the decline of cooking in our time would have serious consequences for modern life, and so it has. Are they all bad? Not at all. The outsourcing of much of the work of cooking to corporations has relieved women of what has traditionally been their exclusive responsibility for feeding the family, making it easier for them to work outside the home and have careers. It has headed off many of the domestic conflicts that such a large shift in gender roles and family dynamics was bound to spark. It has relieved other pressures in the household, including longer workdays and overscheduled children, and saved us time that we can now invest in other pursuits. It has also allowed us to diversify our diets substantially, making it possible even for people with no cooking skills and little money to enjoy a whole different cuisine. All that's required is a microwave.

① current trends in commercial cooking equipment
② environmental impacts of shifts in dietary patterns
③ cost-effective ways to cook healthy meals at home
④ reasons behind the decline of the food service industry
⑤ benefits of reduced domestic cooking duties through outsourcing

24. 다음 글의 제목으로 가장 적절한 것은?

As you may already know, what and how you buy can be political. To whom do you want to give your money? Which companies and corporations do you value and respect? Be mindful about every purchase by carefully researching the corporations that are taking our money to decide if they deserve our support. Do they have a record of polluting the environment, or do they have fair-trade practices and an end-of-life plan for the products they make? Are they committed to bringing about good in the world? For instance, my family has found a company producing recycled, plastic-packaging-free toilet paper with a social conscience. They contribute 50 percent of their profits to the construction of toilets around the world, and we're genuinely happy to spend our money on this special toilet paper each month. Remember that the corporate world is built on consumers, so as a consumer you have the power to vote with your wallet and encourage companies to embrace healthier and more sustainable practices with every purchase you choose to make.

① Green Businesses: Are They Really Green?
② Fair Trade Does Not Always Appeal to Consumers
③ Buy Consciously, Make Companies Do the Right Things
④ Do Voters Have a Powerful Impact on Economic Policy?
⑤ The Secret to Saving Your Money: Record Your Spending

25. 다음 도표의 내용과 일치하지 <u>않는</u> 것은?

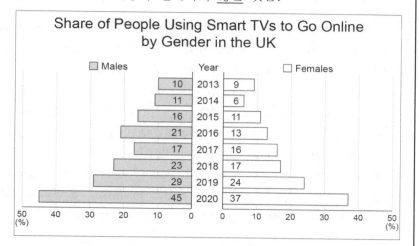

Share of People Using Smart TVs to Go Online by Gender in the UK

Males	Year	Females
10	2013	9
11	2014	6
16	2015	11
21	2016	13
17	2017	16
23	2018	17
29	2019	24
45	2020	37

The graph above shows the findings of a survey on the use of smart TVs to go online in the UK from 2013 to 2020, by gender. ① In each year from 2013 to 2020, the percentage of male respondents who used smart TVs to access the Internet was higher than that of female respondents. ② The percentage gap between the two genders was the largest in 2016 and in 2020, which both had an 8 percentage point difference. ③ In 2020, the percentage of respondents who reported using smart TVs to go online was higher than 30% for both males and females. ④ For male respondents, 2017 was the only year that saw a decrease in the percentage of those accessing the Internet via smart TVs compared to the previous year, during the given period. ⑤ In 2014, the percentage of females using smart TVs to access the Internet was the lowest during the given period at 6%, and it was still below 10% in 2015.

26. Camille Flammarion에 관한 다음 글의 내용과 일치하지 <u>않는</u> 것은?

Camille Flammarion was born at Montigny-le-Roi, France. He became interested in astronomy at an early age, and when he was only sixteen he wrote a book on the origin of the world. The manuscript was not published at the time, but it came to the attention of Urbain Le Verrier, the director of the Paris Observatory. He became an assistant to Le Verrier in 1858 and worked as a calculator. At nineteen, he wrote another book called *The Plurality of Inhabited Worlds*, in which he passionately claimed that life exists outside the planet Earth. His most successful work, *Popular Astronomy*, was published in 1880, and eventually sold 130,000 copies. With his own funds, he built an observatory at Juvisy and spent May to November of each year there. In 1887, he founded the French Astronomical Society and served as editor of its monthly publication.

* observatory: 천문대

① 어린 나이에 천문학에 흥미가 생겼다.
② 1858년에 Le Verrier의 조수가 되었다.
③ 19세에 쓴 책에서 외계 생명체의 존재를 부인했다.
④ 자신의 자금으로 Juvisy에 천문대를 세웠다.
⑤ French Astronomical Society를 설립했다.

27. Roselands Virtual Sports Day에 관한 다음 안내문의 내용과 일치하지 <u>않는</u> 것은?

Roselands Virtual Sports Day

Roselands Virtual Sports Day is an athletic competition that you can participate in from anywhere.

When: October 16th – 22nd, 2023

How the event works
• There are 10 challenges in total.
• You can see videos explaining each challenge on our school website.
• The more challenges you complete, the more points you will gain for your class.
• The class with the most points will get a prize.
• Parents and teachers can also participate.

How to submit your entry
• Email us videos of you completing the challenges at virtualsportsday@roselands.com.
• The size of the video file must not exceed 500MB.

① 10월 16일부터 22일까지 열린다.
② 총 10개의 도전 과제가 있다.
③ 학교 웹사이트에서 도전 과제를 설명하는 영상을 볼 수 있다.
④ 학부모와 교사는 참여할 수 없다.
⑤ 제출할 영상파일 용량이 500MB를 초과하면 안 된다.

28. Back-to-school Giveaway Event에 관한 다음 안내문의 내용과 일치하는 것은?

Back-to-school Giveaway Event

The City of Easton will host a free back-to-school giveaway event. Join us for this fun event to help children of all ages prepare to go back to school after summer vacation.

When: Saturday, September 2nd, 9 a.m. – 11 a.m.

Location: City of Easton Central Park
(This event will be held rain or shine.)

Participation requirements
• Open to City of Easton residents only
• Must bring a valid ID

Note
• 500 backpacks will be given out on a first-come, first-served basis.
• A parent or a guardian must come with their child to receive the backpack.

For more information, call the City Council at 612-248-6633.

① 토요일 오후에 진행된다.
② 우천 시에는 취소된다.
③ Easton시 주민이 아니어도 참여할 수 있다.
④ 가방 500개가 선착순으로 배부될 것이다.
⑤ 부모 또는 보호자만 와도 가방을 받을 수 있다.

29. 다음 글의 밑줄 친 부분 중, 어법상 <u>틀린</u> 것은?

There is little doubt that we are driven by the sell-by date. Once an item is past that date it goes into the waste stream, further ① <u>increasing</u> its carbon footprint. Remember those items have already travelled hundreds of miles ② <u>reach</u> the shelves and once they go into waste they start a new carbon mile journey. But we all make our own judgement about sell-by dates; those brought up during the Second World War ③ <u>are</u> often scornful of the terrible waste they believe such caution encourages. The manufacturer of the food has a view when making or growing something ④ <u>that</u> by the time the product reaches the shelves it has already been travelling for so many days and possibly many miles. The manufacturer then decides that a product can reasonably be consumed within say 90 days and 90 days minus so many days for travelling gives the sell-by date. But ⑤ <u>whether</u> it becomes toxic is something each individual can decide. It would seem to make sense not to buy large packs of perishable goods but non-perishable items may become cost-effective.

* sell-by date: 판매 유효 기한 ** scornful: 경멸하는

30. 다음 글의 밑줄 친 부분 중, 문맥상 낱말의 쓰임이 적절하지 <u>않은</u> 것은?

The "jolt" of caffeine does wear off. Caffeine is ① <u>removed</u> from your system by an enzyme within your liver, which gradually degrades it over time. Based in large part on genetics, some people have a more efficient version of the enzyme that degrades caffeine, ② <u>allowing</u> the liver to rapidly clear it from the bloodstream. These rare individuals can drink an espresso with dinner and fall fast asleep at midnight without a problem. Others, however, have a slower-acting version of the enzyme. It takes far ③ <u>longer</u> for their system to eliminate the same amount of caffeine. As a result, they are very ④ <u>insensitive</u> to caffeine's effects. One cup of tea or coffee in the morning will last much of the day, and should they have a second cup, even early in the afternoon, they will find it difficult to fall asleep in the evening. Aging also ⑤ <u>alters</u> the speed of caffeine clearance: the older we are, the longer it takes our brain and body to remove caffeine, and thus the more sensitive we become in later life to caffeine's sleep-disrupting influence.

* jolt: 충격 ** enzyme: 효소

[31~34] 다음 빈칸에 들어갈 말로 가장 적절한 것을 고르시오.

31. Rebels may think they're rebels, but clever marketers influence them just like the rest of us. Saying, "Everyone is doing it" may turn some people off from an idea. These people will look for alternatives, which (if cleverly planned) can be exactly what a marketer or persuader wants you to believe. If I want you to consider an idea, and know you strongly reject popular opinion in favor of maintaining your independence and uniqueness, I would present the majority option first, which you would reject in favor of my actual preference. We are often tricked when we try to maintain a position of defiance. People use this _____ to make us "independently" choose an option which suits their purposes. Some brands have taken full effect of our defiance towards the mainstream and positioned themselves as rebels; which has created even stronger brand loyalty. [3점]

* defiance: 반항

① reversal   ② imitation   ③ repetition
④ conformity   ⑤ collaboration

32. A typical soap opera creates an abstract world, in which a highly complex web of relationships connects fictional characters that exist first only in the minds of the program's creators and are then recreated in the minds of the viewer. If you were to think about how much human psychology, law, and even everyday physics the viewer must know in order to follow and speculate about the plot, you would discover it is considerable — at least as much as the knowledge required to follow and speculate about a piece of modern mathematics, and in most cases, much more. Yet viewers follow soap operas with ease. How are they able to cope with such abstraction? Because, of course, the abstraction _____.
The characters in a soap opera and the relationships between them are very much like the real people and relationships we experience every day. The abstraction of a soap opera is only a step removed from the real world. The mental "training" required to follow a soap opera is provided by our everyday lives. [3점]

* soap opera: 드라마, 연속극

① is separated from the dramatic contents
② is a reflection of our unrealistic desires
③ demonstrates our poor taste in TV shows
④ is built on an extremely familiar framework
⑤ indicates that unnecessary details are hidden

33. As always happens with natural selection, bats and their prey have _____ for millions of years. It's believed that hearing in moths arose specifically in response to the threat of being eaten by bats. (Not all insects can hear.) Over millions of years, moths have evolved the ability to detect sounds at ever higher frequencies, and, as they have, the frequencies of bats' vocalizations have risen, too. Some moth species have also evolved scales on their wings and a fur-like coat on their bodies; both act as "acoustic camouflage," by absorbing sound waves in the frequencies emitted by bats, thereby preventing those sound waves from bouncing back. The B-2 bomber and other "stealth" aircraft have fuselages made of materials that do something similar with radar beams. [3점]

* frequency: 주파수 ** camouflage: 위장 *** fuselage: (비행기의) 기체

① been in a fierce war over scarce food sources
② been engaged in a life-or-death sensory arms race
③ invented weapons that are not part of their bodies
④ evolved to cope with other noise-producing wildlife
⑤ adapted to flying in night skies absent of any lights

34. Much of human thought is designed to screen out information and to sort the rest into a manageable condition. The inflow of data from our senses could create an overwhelming chaos, especially given the enormous amount of information available in culture and society. Out of all the sensory impressions and possible information, it is vital to find a small amount that is most relevant to our individual needs and to organize that into a usable stock of knowledge. Expectancies accomplish some of this work, helping to screen out information that is irrelevant to what is expected, and focusing our attention on clear contradictions. The processes of learning and memory _____. People notice only a part of the world around them. Then, only a fraction of what they notice gets processed and stored into memory. And only part of what gets committed to memory can be retrieved. [3점]

* retrieve: 생각해 내다

① tend to favor learners with great social skills
② are marked by a steady elimination of information
③ require an external aid to support our memory capacity
④ are determined by the accuracy of incoming information
⑤ are facilitated by embracing chaotic situations as they are

35. 다음 글에서 전체 흐름과 관계 없는 문장은?

The irony of early democracy in Europe is that it thrived and prospered precisely because European rulers for a very long time were remarkably weak. ① For more than a millennium after the fall of Rome, European rulers lacked the ability to assess what their people were producing and to levy substantial taxes based on this. ② The most striking way to illustrate European weakness is to show how little revenue they collected. ③ For this reason, tax collectors in Europe were able to collect a huge amount of revenue and therefore had a great influence on how society should function. ④ Europeans would eventually develop strong systems of revenue collection, but it took them an awfully long time to do so. ⑤ In medieval times, and for part of the early modern era, Chinese emperors and Muslim caliphs were able to extract much more of economic production than any European ruler with the exception of small city-states.

* levy: 부과하다 ** caliph: 칼리프(과거 이슬람 국가의 통치자)

[36~37] 주어진 글 다음에 이어질 글의 순서로 가장 적절한 것을 고르시오.

36.

If you drive down a busy street, you will find many competing businesses, often right next to one another. For example, in most places a consumer in search of a quick meal has many choices, and more fast-food restaurants appear all the time.

(A) Yes, costs rise, but consumers also gain information to help make purchasing decisions. Consumers also benefit from added variety, and we all get a product that's pretty close to our vision of a perfect good — and no other market structure delivers that outcome.

(B) However, this misconception doesn't account for why firms advertise. In markets where competitors sell slightly differentiated products, advertising enables firms to inform their customers about new products and services.

(C) These competing firms advertise heavily. The temptation is to see advertising as driving up the price of a product without any benefit to the consumer.

① (A) - (C) - (B)   ② (B) - (A) - (C)
③ (B) - (C) - (A)   ④ (C) - (A) - (B)
⑤ (C) - (B) - (A)

37.

Architects might say a machine can never design an innovative or impressive building because a computer cannot be "creative." Yet consider the Elbphilharmonie, a new concert hall in Hamburg, which contains a remarkably beautiful auditorium composed of ten thousand interlocking acoustic panels.

(A) Are these systems behaving "creatively"? No, they are using lots of processing power to blindly generate varied possible designs, working in a very different way from a human being.

(B) It is the sort of space that makes one instinctively think that only a human being—and a human with a remarkably refined creative sensibility, at that—could design something so aesthetically impressive. Yet the auditorium was, in fact, designed algorithmically, using a technique known as "parametric design."

(C) The architects gave the system a set of criteria, and it generated a set of possible designs for the architects to choose from. Similar software has been used to design lightweight bicycle frames and sturdier chairs, among much else. [3점]

* aesthetically: 미적으로 ** sturdy: 튼튼한, 견고한

① (A) − (C) − (B)　　② (B) − (A) − (C)
③ (B) − (C) − (A)　　④ (C) − (A) − (B)
⑤ (C) − (B) − (A)

[38~39] 글의 흐름으로 보아, 주어진 문장이 들어가기에 가장 적절한 곳을 고르시오.

38.

You don't sit back and speculate about the meaning of life when you are stressed.

The brain is a high-energy consumer of glucose, which is its fuel. Although the brain accounts for merely 3 percent of a person's body weight, it consumes 20 percent of the available fuel. (①) Your brain can't store fuel, however, so it has to "pay as it goes." (②) Since your brain is incredibly adaptive, it economizes its fuel resources. (③) Thus, during a period of high stress, it shifts away from the analysis of the nuances of a situation to a singular and fixed focus on the stressful situation at hand. (④) Instead, you devote all your energy to trying to figure out what action to take. (⑤) Sometimes, however, this shift from the higher-thinking parts of the brain to the automatic and reflexive parts of the brain can lead you to do something too quickly, without thinking.

* glucose: 포도당

39.

It is, however, noteworthy that although engagement drives job performance, job performance also drives engagement.

Much research has been carried out on the causes of engagement, an issue that is important from both a theoretical and practical standpoint: identifying the drivers of work engagement may enable us to manipulate or influence it. (①) The causes of engagement fall into two major camps: situational and personal. (②) The most influential situational causes are job resources, feedback and leadership, the latter, of course, being responsible for job resources and feedback. (③) Indeed, leaders influence engagement by giving their employees honest and constructive feedback on their performance, and by providing them with the necessary resources that enable them to perform their job well. (④) In other words, when employees are able to do their jobs well—to the point that they match or exceed their own expectations and ambitions—they will engage more, be proud of their achievements, and find work more meaningful. (⑤) This is especially evident when people are employed in jobs that align with their values. [3점]

* align with: ~과 일치하다

40. 다음 글의 내용을 한 문장으로 요약하고자 한다. 빈칸 (A), (B)에 들어갈 말로 가장 적절한 것은?

In 2006, researchers conducted a study on the motivations for helping after the September 11th terrorist attacks against the United States. In the study, they found that individuals who gave money, blood, goods, or other forms of assistance because of other-focused motives (giving to reduce another's discomfort) were almost four times more likely to still be giving support one year later than those whose original motivation was to reduce personal distress. This effect likely stems from differences in emotional arousal. The events of September 11th emotionally affected people throughout the United States. Those who gave to reduce their own distress reduced their emotional arousal with their initial gift, discharging that emotional distress. However, those who gave to reduce others' distress did not stop empathizing with victims who continued to struggle long after the attacks.

* distress: (정신적) 고통 ** arousal: 자극

↓

A study found that the act of giving was less likely to be ___(A)___ when driven by self-centered motives rather than by other-focused motives, possibly because of the ___(B)___ in emotional arousal.

　　(A)　　　　　(B)
① sustained ······ decline
② sustained ······ maximization
③ indirect ······ variation
④ discouraged ······ reduction
⑤ discouraged ······ increase

[41~42] 다음 글을 읽고, 물음에 답하시오.

In England in the 1680s, it was unusual to live to the age of fifty. This was a period when knowledge was not spread (a) widely, there were few books and most people could not read. As a consequence, knowledge passed down through the oral traditions of stories and shared experiences. And since older people had accumulated more knowledge, the social norm was that to be over fifty was to be wise. This social perception of age began to shift with the advent of new technologies such as the printing press. Over time, as more books were printed, literacy (b) increased, and the oral traditions of knowledge transfer began to fade. With the fading of oral traditions, the wisdom of the old became less important and as a consequence being over fifty was no longer seen as (c) signifying wisdom.

We are living in a period when the gap between chronological and biological age is changing fast and where social norms are struggling to (d) adapt. In a video produced by the AARP (formerly the American Association of Retired Persons), young people were asked to do various activities 'just like an old person'. When older people joined them in the video, the gap between the stereotype and the older people's actual behaviour was (e) unnoticeable. It is clear that in today's world our social norms need to be updated quickly.

41. 윗글의 제목으로 가장 적절한 것은?

① Our Social Norms on Aging: An Ongoing Evolution
② The Power of Oral Tradition in the Modern World
③ Generational Differences: Not As Big As You Think
④ There's More to Aging than What the Media Shows
⑤ How Well You Age Depends on Your Views of Aging

42. 밑줄 친 (a)~(e) 중에서 문맥상 낱말의 쓰임이 적절하지 않은 것은? [3점]

① (a)　② (b)　③ (c)　④ (d)　⑤ (e)

[43~45] 다음 글을 읽고, 물음에 답하시오.

(A)

When Jack was a young man in his early twenties during the 1960s, he had tried to work in his father's insurance business, as was expected of him. His two older brothers fit in easily and seemed to enjoy their work. But Jack was bored with the insurance industry. "It was worse than being bored," he said. "I felt like I was dying inside." Jack felt drawn to hair styling and dreamed of owning a hair shop with a lively environment. He was sure that (a) he would enjoy the creative and social aspects of it and that he'd be successful.

(B)

Jack understood that his father feared adoption, in this case especially because the child was of a different racial background than their family. Jack and Michele risked rejection and went ahead with the adoption. It took years but eventually Jack's father loved the little girl and accepted (b) his son's independent choices. Jack realized that, although he often felt fear and still does, he has always had courage. In fact, courage was the scaffolding around which (c) he had built richness into his life.

* scaffolding: 발판

(C)

When he was twenty-six, Jack approached his father and expressed his intentions of leaving the business to become a hairstylist. As Jack anticipated, his father raged and accused Jack of being selfish, ungrateful, and unmanly. In the face of his father's fury, Jack felt confusion and fear. His resolve became weak. But then a force filled (d) his chest and he stood firm in his decision. In following his path, Jack not only ran three flourishing hair shops, but also helped his clients experience their inner beauty by listening and encouraging them when they faced dark times.

(D)

His love for his work led to donating time and talent at nursing homes, which in turn led to becoming a hospice volunteer, and eventually to starting fundraising efforts for the hospice program in his community. And all this laid a strong stepping stone for another courageous move in his life. When, after having two healthy children of their own, Jack and his wife, Michele, decided to bring an orphaned child into their family, (e) his father threatened to disown them.

43. 주어진 글 (A)에 이어질 내용을 순서에 맞게 배열한 것으로 가장 적절한 것은?

① (B) - (D) - (C)　② (C) - (B) - (D)
③ (C) - (D) - (B)　④ (D) - (B) - (C)
⑤ (D) - (C) - (B)

44. 밑줄 친 (a)~(e) 중에서 가리키는 대상이 나머지 넷과 다른 것은?

① (a)　② (b)　③ (c)　④ (d)　⑤ (e)

45. 윗글의 Jack에 관한 내용으로 적절하지 않은 것은?

① 두 형은 자신들의 일을 즐기는 것으로 보였다.
② 아버지의 반대로 입양을 포기했다.
③ 아버지에게 회사를 떠나겠다는 의사를 밝혔다.
④ 세 개의 번창하는 미용실을 운영했다.
⑤ 지역사회에서 모금 운동을 시작했다.

★ 확인 사항

○ 답안지의 해당란에 필요한 내용을 정확히 기입(표기)했는지 확인하시오.

18
001 □ to whom it may concern 담당자 귀하
002 □ draw ⓥ 끌다
003 □ frequently ⓐ 자주
004 □ attention ⓝ 주의
005 □ be supposed to ~하기로 되어 있다
006 □ appear ⓥ ~처럼 보이다
007 □ unaware ⓐ 모르는
008 □ for some reason 모종의 이유로
009 □ grateful ⓐ 고마워하는
010 □ be prepared to ~할 대비를 하다

19
011 □ in need of ~이 필요한, ~이 없는
012 □ desperate ⓐ 간절한
013 □ quarter ⓝ 25센트 동전
014 □ on earth (의문사 뒤에서) 도대체
015 □ tone ⓝ 어조
016 □ border on 거의 ~에 달하다
017 □ irritation ⓝ 짜증
018 □ be bothered with ~로 귀찮다
019 □ trivial ⓐ 사소한
020 □ demand ⓝ 요구
021 □ cost ⓥ ~의 비용이 들다
022 □ glance ⓥ 흘깃 보다
023 □ one another 서로
024 □ inscribe ⓥ 새기다
025 □ annoyed ⓐ 짜증 난
026 □ delighted ⓐ 기쁜
027 □ confused ⓐ 혼란스러운
028 □ jealous ⓐ 질투하는

20
029 □ figure out 알아내다, 파악하다
030 □ employee ⓝ 직원
031 □ certain ⓐ 특정한, 어떤
032 □ empathize with ~에 공감하다
033 □ point of view 관점, 견해
034 □ deal with ~을 다루다, ~에 대처하다
035 □ exhibit ⓥ 보여주다
036 □ avoid ⓥ 피하다
037 □ make a suggestion 제안하다
038 □ personal ⓐ 개인적인, 인격적인
039 □ trait ⓝ 특성
040 □ acceptable ⓐ 수용 가능한
041 □ unreliability ⓝ 미덥지 못함

21
042 □ fungus (*pl*. fungi) ⓝ 균류
043 □ beech ⓝ 너도밤나무
044 □ native to ~이 원산지인
045 □ emerge ⓥ 부상하다, 출현하다
046 □ victorious ⓐ 승리한, 우세한
047 □ pathogen ⓝ 병원균
048 □ infect ⓥ 감염시키다
049 □ oak ⓝ 떡갈나무, 오크
050 □ maple ⓝ 단풍나무
051 □ fir ⓝ 전나무
052 □ sprout ⓥ 싹을 틔우다
053 □ diversity ⓝ 다양성
054 □ security ⓝ 안정(성)
055 □ stable ⓐ 안정된

056 □ protect A from B A를 B로부터 보호하다
057 □ collapse ⓝ 붕괴 ⓥ 붕괴하다, 무너지다, 쓰러지다
058 □ ensure ⓥ 확실히 하다
059 □ dominate ⓥ 우세하다, 지배하다
060 □ responsible for ~의 원인이 되는, ~에 책임이 있는
061 □ invasion ⓝ 침입
062 □ foreign species 외래종
063 □ stability ⓝ 안정성
064 □ regenerate ⓥ 재생되다
065 □ territory ⓝ 영역, 영토
066 □ occupy ⓥ 점유하다, 차지하다

22
067 □ remarkable ⓐ 두드러지는
068 □ extent ⓝ 정도
069 □ physiological ⓐ 생리학적인
070 □ unwind ⓥ 긴장을 풀다, (감긴 것을) 풀다
071 □ outcome ⓝ 결과
072 □ objective ⓝ 목표
073 □ be motivated to ~하도록 동기 부여받다
074 □ inevitable ⓐ 피할 수 없는, 필연적인
075 □ obstacle ⓝ 장애물
076 □ arise ⓥ 발생하다
077 □ hold true 사실이다
078 □ undercut ⓥ 약화하다
079 □ temporary ⓐ 일시적인
080 □ inactivity ⓝ 무활동

23
081 □ anthropologist ⓝ 인류학자
082 □ stand to reason 당연하다, 이치에 맞다
083 □ decline ⓝ 감소, 쇠퇴 ⓥ 줄어들다
084 □ consequence ⓝ 결과, 영향
085 □ outsource ⓥ (외부에) 위탁하다
086 □ corporation ⓝ 회사, 기업
087 □ exclusive ⓐ 전적인, 배타적인
088 □ head off ~을 막다, 차단하다
089 □ domestic ⓐ 가정의
090 □ gender role 성 역할
091 □ be bound to ~하게 마련이다
092 □ spark ⓥ 촉발하다
093 □ household ⓝ 가정, 가구
094 □ save A B A에게 B를 아껴주다
095 □ pursuit ⓝ (시간과 에너지를 들여 하는) 활동, 취미
096 □ diversify ⓥ 다양화하다
097 □ substantially ⓐ 상당히
098 □ cuisine ⓝ 요리
099 □ microwave ⓝ 전자레인지
100 □ dietary ⓐ 식단의
101 □ cost-effective ⓐ 가성비 좋은

24
102 □ mindful ⓐ 의식하는, 염두에 두는
103 □ deserve ⓥ ~을 받을 만하다
104 □ pollute ⓥ 오염시키다
105 □ fair-trade ⓐ 공정 무역의
106 □ practice ⓝ 관행
107 □ end-of-life plan 수명 종료 계획(제품, 폐기, 교체, 중단 등에 관한 계획)

108 □ be committed to ~에 헌신하다, 전념하다
109 □ bring about ~을 초래하다
110 □ conscience ⓝ 양심
111 □ contribute ⓥ 기부하다
112 □ genuinely ⓐ 진짜로
113 □ vote ⓥ 투표하다
114 □ embrace ⓥ 받아들이다, 수용하다
115 □ sustainable ⓐ 지속 가능한
116 □ green ⓐ 친환경의

25
117 □ survey ⓝ 설문 조사
118 □ go online 온라인에 접속하다
119 □ respondent ⓝ 응답자
120 □ access ⓥ 접속하다
121 □ compared to ~에 비해
122 □ previous year 작년, 전년도
123 □ below [prep] ~ 아래에

26
124 □ astronomy ⓝ 천문학
125 □ origin ⓝ 기원
126 □ manuscript ⓝ 원고
127 □ publish ⓥ 출판하다, 게재하다
128 □ observatory ⓝ 천문대
129 □ assistant ⓝ 조수
130 □ calculator ⓝ 계산원, 계산기
131 □ plurality ⓝ 다원성, 많은 수
132 □ inhabit ⓥ 거주하다
133 □ passionately ⓐ 열정적으로
134 □ eventually ⓐ 결국
135 □ serve as ~로 일하다, ~의 역할을 하다
136 □ editor ⓝ 편집자
137 □ monthly ⓐ 월간의
138 □ publication ⓝ 간행물, 발행

27
139 □ virtual ⓐ 가상의
140 □ athletic ⓐ 운동의, 육상의
141 □ participate in ~에 참여하다
142 □ complete ⓥ 완수하다 ⓐ 완수된
143 □ gain ⓥ 얻다, 따다
144 □ entry ⓝ 출품, 입장
145 □ exceed ⓥ 초과하다, 능가하다

28
146 □ giveaway ⓝ 무료 나눔, 증정
147 □ host ⓥ 주최하다
148 □ location ⓝ 위치
149 □ requirement ⓝ 요구 사항, 필수 요건
150 □ resident ⓝ 주민
151 □ valid ⓐ 유효한, 타당한
152 □ backpack ⓝ 배낭
153 □ give out 나눠주다
154 □ on a first-come, first-served basis 선착순으로
155 □ guardian ⓝ 보호자

29
156 □ sell-by date 판매 유효 기한
157 □ stream ⓝ 흐름
158 □ further ⓐ 더욱

159 □ carbon footprint 탄소 발자국
160 □ bring up 양육하다
161 □ scornful ⓐ 경멸하는
162 □ terrible ⓐ 끔찍한
163 □ caution ⓝ 경고
164 □ manufacturer ⓝ 제조업체
165 □ by the time ~할 무렵에
166 □ possibly ⓐ 아마도
167 □ reasonably ⓐ 적당하게, 타당하게
168 □ consume ⓥ 소비하다
169 □ toxic ⓐ 유독한
170 □ make sense 이치에 맞다
171 □ perishable ⓐ 상하기 쉬운

30
172 □ jolt ⓝ 충격
173 □ wear off 차츰 사라지다, 없어지다
174 □ enzyme ⓝ 효소
175 □ liver ⓝ 간
176 □ gradually ⓐ 점점
177 □ degrade ⓥ 분해하다, 저하시키다
178 □ over time 시간이 흐르며
179 □ in part 대부분, 상당히, 아주 많이
180 □ genetics ⓝ 유전적 특징
181 □ efficient ⓐ 효율적인
182 □ bloodstream ⓝ 혈류
183 □ rare ⓐ 몇 안 되는, 드문
184 □ fast asleep 깊이 잠든
185 □ eliminate ⓥ 제거하다
186 □ insensitive ⓐ 둔감한
187 □ last ⓥ 지속되다
188 □ aging ⓝ 노화
189 □ alter ⓥ 변화시키다
190 □ clearance ⓝ 없애기, 정리
191 □ sensitive ⓐ 민감한
192 □ in later life 노후에, 만년에
193 □ disrupt ⓥ 지장을 주다

31
194 □ rebel ⓝ 반항아
195 □ clever ⓐ 영리한
196 □ influence ⓥ 영향을 미치다
197 □ turn off ~을 지루하게 만들다
198 □ alternative ⓝ 대안
199 □ reject ⓥ 거부하다
200 □ in favor of ~을 위해
201 □ independence ⓝ 독립
202 □ uniqueness ⓝ 고유성
203 □ majority ⓝ 대다수
204 □ trick ⓥ 속이다
205 □ defiance ⓝ 반항
206 □ suit ⓥ ~에 맞추다
207 □ mainstream ⓝ 주류
208 □ loyalty ⓝ 충성도
209 □ reversal ⓝ 반전
210 □ repetition ⓝ 반복
211 □ conformity ⓝ 순응

32
212 □ soap opera 드라마, 연속극
213 □ abstract ⓐ 추상적인
214 □ complex ⓐ 복잡한

215 ☐ web ⓝ 망	269 ☐ accomplish ⓥ 해내다, 성취하다	325 ☐ varied ⓐ 다양한
216 ☐ fictional ⓐ 허구의	270 ☐ irrelevant ⓐ 무관한	326 ☐ instinctively ⓐⓓ 본능적으로
217 ☐ recreate ⓥ 되살리다	271 ☐ contradiction ⓝ 모순	327 ☐ refine ⓥ 개선하다
218 ☐ psychology ⓝ 심리	272 ☐ fraction ⓝ 부분	328 ☐ sensibility ⓝ 감수성
219 ☐ physics ⓝ 물리학	273 ☐ commit A to memory A를 기억하다	329 ☐ aesthetically ⓐⓓ 미적으로
220 ☐ speculate ⓥ 추측하다	274 ☐ retrieve ⓥ 생각해 내다	330 ☐ algorithmically ⓐⓓ 알고리즘에 의해
221 ☐ plot ⓝ 플롯, 줄거리	275 ☐ steady ⓐ 꾸준한	331 ☐ architect ⓝ 건축가
222 ☐ considerable ⓐ 상당한	276 ☐ accuracy ⓝ 정확성	332 ☐ criterion (*pl.* criteria) ⓝ 기준
223 ☐ mathematics ⓝ 수학	277 ☐ facilitate ⓥ 촉진하다	333 ☐ sturdy ⓐ 튼튼한, 견고한
224 ☐ with ease 쉽게, 용이하게		
225 ☐ cope with ~에 대처하다	**35**	**38**
226 ☐ abstraction ⓝ 추상	278 ☐ irony ⓝ 아이러니, 반의	334 ☐ glucose ⓝ 포도당
227 ☐ reflection ⓝ 반영	279 ☐ democracy ⓝ 민주주의	335 ☐ fuel ⓝ 연료 ⓥ 부추기다
228 ☐ unrealistic ⓐ 비현실적인	280 ☐ thrive ⓥ 번성하다	336 ☐ merely ⓐⓓ 단지, 그저
229 ☐ demonstrate ⓥ 입증하다, 보여주다	281 ☐ prosper ⓥ 번영하다	337 ☐ body weight 체중
230 ☐ taste ⓝ 취향	282 ☐ ruler ⓝ 통치자	338 ☐ incredibly ⓐⓓ 놀라울 정도로
231 ☐ extremely ⓐⓓ 극도로, 몹시	283 ☐ remarkably ⓐⓓ 현저하게	339 ☐ adaptive ⓐ 적응하는
232 ☐ framework ⓝ 틀, 뼈대	284 ☐ millennium ⓝ 천년	340 ☐ economize ⓥ 절약하다, 아끼다
	285 ☐ fall ⓥ 몰락	341 ☐ shift ⓥ 옮기다, 바뀌다 ⓝ 전환, 이동
33	286 ☐ assess ⓥ 평가하다	342 ☐ analysis ⓝ 분석
233 ☐ natural selection 자연 선택	287 ☐ levy ⓥ 부과하다	343 ☐ nuance ⓝ 미묘한 차이
234 ☐ prey ⓝ 먹이 동물	288 ☐ substantial ⓐ 상당한	344 ☐ singular ⓐ 단일한
235 ☐ moth ⓝ 나방	289 ☐ tax ⓝ 세금	345 ☐ fixed ⓐ 고정된
236 ☐ in response to ~에 대응해	290 ☐ striking ⓐ 눈에 띄는	346 ☐ at hand 당면한, 눈앞에 있는
237 ☐ threat ⓝ 위협	291 ☐ illustrate ⓥ 분명히 보여주다	347 ☐ devote A to B A를 B에 바치다
238 ☐ detect ⓥ 감지하다	292 ☐ revenue ⓝ 세입, 수입	348 ☐ automatic ⓐ 자동적인
239 ☐ frequency ⓝ 주파수	293 ☐ for this reason 이런 이유로	349 ☐ reflexive ⓐ 반사적인
240 ☐ vocalization ⓝ 발성	294 ☐ huge ⓐ 거대한, 막대한	
241 ☐ rise ⓥ 오르다	295 ☐ function ⓥ 기능하다	**39**
242 ☐ scale ⓝ 비늘	296 ☐ awfully ⓐⓓ 몹시, 지독히	350 ☐ noteworthy ⓐ 주목할 만한
243 ☐ acoustic ⓐ 청각적인	297 ☐ medieval ⓐ 중세의	351 ☐ drive ⓥ 유도하다
244 ☐ camouflage ⓝ 위장	298 ☐ modern ⓐ 현대의	352 ☐ engagement ⓝ 몰입, 참여
245 ☐ absorb ⓥ 흡수하다	299 ☐ era ⓝ 시대	353 ☐ performance ⓝ 수행, 성과
246 ☐ emit ⓥ 방출하다	300 ☐ emperor ⓝ 황제	354 ☐ carry out 수행하다
247 ☐ bounce back 반향하다, (튕겨서) 되돌아가다	301 ☐ caliph ⓝ 칼리프(과거 이슬람 국가의 통치자)	355 ☐ theoretical ⓐ 이론적인
248 ☐ bomber ⓝ 폭격기	302 ☐ extract ⓥ 뽑아내다, 얻어내다	356 ☐ practical ⓐ 실제적인
249 ☐ stealth ⓐ (레이더가 탐지하기 힘든) 스텔스 기의, 숨어서 하는	303 ☐ with the exception of ~을 제외하고	357 ☐ standpoint ⓝ 관점, 견지
250 ☐ fuselage ⓝ (비행기의) 기체		358 ☐ identify ⓥ 식별하다, 알아내다
251 ☐ made of ~로 만들어진	**36**	359 ☐ manipulate ⓥ 조작하다
252 ☐ fierce ⓐ 맹렬한	304 ☐ in search of ~을 찾아서	360 ☐ fall into ~로 나뉘다, ~에 빠지다
253 ☐ arms race 군비 경쟁(군사적 우위를 차지하기 위한 소모적 경쟁)	305 ☐ quick meal 간단한 식사	361 ☐ major ⓐ 주요한
254 ☐ wildlife ⓝ 야생 생물	306 ☐ benefit from ~에서 이득을 보다	362 ☐ situational ⓐ 상황적인
255 ☐ absent of ~이 없는	307 ☐ variety ⓝ 다양성, 품종	363 ☐ influential ⓐ 영향력 있는
	308 ☐ vision ⓝ 상상	364 ☐ the latter (주로 둘 중) 후자
34	309 ☐ deliver ⓥ (결과를) 내놓다, 산출하다	365 ☐ honest ⓐ 정직한
256 ☐ screen out 차단하다	310 ☐ misconception ⓝ 오해	366 ☐ constructive ⓐ 건설적인
257 ☐ sort ⓥ 분류하다	311 ☐ account for ~을 설명하다	367 ☐ provide A with B A에게 B를 제공하다
258 ☐ manageable ⓐ 처리하기 쉬운, 감당할 만한	312 ☐ advertise ⓥ 광고하다	368 ☐ evident ⓐ 분명한
259 ☐ inflow ⓝ 유입	313 ☐ slightly ⓐⓓ 약간	369 ☐ be employed in ~에 종사하다
260 ☐ overwhelming ⓐ 압도적인	314 ☐ differentiate ⓥ 차별(화)하다, 구별하다	370 ☐ align with ~과 일치하다
261 ☐ chaos ⓝ 혼돈	315 ☐ heavily ⓐⓓ 많이, 심하게	
262 ☐ enormous ⓐ 막대한	316 ☐ temptation ⓝ 유혹	**40**
263 ☐ impression ⓝ 인상	317 ☐ drive up (값 등을) 끌어올리다	371 ☐ motivation ⓝ 동기
264 ☐ vital ⓐ 매우 중요한		372 ☐ terrorist attack 테러 사건
265 ☐ amount ⓝ 양	**37**	373 ☐ against ⓟ️ⓡⓔⓟ ~에 반대하여
266 ☐ relevant ⓐ 적절한, 관련된	318 ☐ innovative ⓐ 혁신적인	374 ☐ assistance ⓝ 도움, 원조
267 ☐ usable ⓐ 사용 가능한	319 ☐ impressive ⓐ 인상적인	375 ☐ discomfort ⓝ 불편
268 ☐ stock ⓝ 저장, 축적 ⓥ 저장하다, 보관하다	320 ☐ auditorium ⓝ 강당	376 ☐ distress ⓝ (정신적) 고통
	321 ☐ composed of ~로 구성된	377 ☐ stem from ~에서 기인하다
	322 ☐ interlock ⓥ 서로 맞물리다	378 ☐ emotional ⓐ 감정적인
	323 ☐ blindly ⓐⓓ 무턱대고, 맹목적으로	379 ☐ arousal ⓝ 자극
	324 ☐ generate ⓥ 만들어내다, 생성하다	380 ☐ affect ⓥ 영향을 미치다

381 ☐ throughout ⓟ️ⓡⓔⓟ ~을 통틀어
382 ☐ initial ⓐ 처음의
383 ☐ discharge ⓥ 해소하다, 내보내다
384 ☐ struggle ⓥ 고생하다
385 ☐ sustain ⓥ 지속되다
386 ☐ indirect ⓐ 간접적인
387 ☐ discourage ⓥ 낙담시키다, 좌절시키다

41~42

388 ☐ unusual ⓐ 이례적인
389 ☐ spread ⓥ 퍼뜨리다
390 ☐ as a consequence 결과적으로
391 ☐ pass down 전해지다
392 ☐ oral tradition 구전
393 ☐ accumulate ⓥ 축적하다
394 ☐ norm ⓝ 규범
395 ☐ perception ⓝ 인식
396 ☐ advent ⓝ 출현, 도래
397 ☐ printing press 인쇄기
398 ☐ literacy ⓝ 문해력, 읽고 쓰는 능력
399 ☐ transfer ⓝ 이동, 전파
400 ☐ fade ⓥ 사라지다, 옅어지다
401 ☐ no longer 더 이상 ~않다
402 ☐ signify ⓥ 의미하다
403 ☐ chronological age (신체적·정신적 수준을 비추어볼 때 실제로 산) 생활 연령
404 ☐ biological age 생물학적 연령
405 ☐ adapt ⓥ 적응하다
406 ☐ formerly ⓐⓓ 이전에
407 ☐ stereotype ⓝ 고정관념
408 ☐ unnoticeable ⓐ 눈에 띄지 않는

43~45

409 ☐ insurance ⓝ 보험
410 ☐ dream of ~을 꿈꾸다
411 ☐ lively ⓐ 활기찬
412 ☐ adoption ⓝ 입양
413 ☐ racial ⓐ 인종적인
414 ☐ risk ⓥ (위험을) 감수하다, 무릅쓰다
415 ☐ rejection ⓝ 거부
416 ☐ courage ⓝ 용기
417 ☐ scaffolding ⓝ 발판
418 ☐ richness ⓝ 풍요로움
419 ☐ intention ⓝ 의도
420 ☐ anticipate ⓥ 예상하다
421 ☐ rage ⓥ 분노하다
422 ☐ accuse A of B A를 B에 대해 비난하다
423 ☐ selfish ⓐ 이기적인
424 ☐ ungrateful ⓐ 배은망덕한
425 ☐ unmanly ⓐ 남자답지 못한
426 ☐ in the face of ~에도 불구하고
427 ☐ fury ⓝ 분노
428 ☐ resolve ⓝ 결심 ⓥ 결심하다
429 ☐ firm ⓐ 확고한
430 ☐ path ⓝ 길
431 ☐ flourishing ⓐ 무성한, 번영하는
432 ☐ in turn 결과적으로
433 ☐ hospice ⓝ 호스피스(말기 환자용 병원)
434 ☐ fundraising ⓝ 모금
435 ☐ stepping stone 디딤돌
436 ☐ orphaned ⓐ 고아인
437 ☐ disown ⓥ 의절하다

12회

● 채점 : 맞은 개수 _____ / 80

TEST A-B 각 단어의 뜻을 [A] 영어는 우리말로, [B] 우리말은 영어로 쓰시오.

A	English	Korean
01	in need of	
02	empathize with	
03	sprout	
04	obstacle	
05	respondent	
06	scornful	
07	wear off	
08	defiance	
09	abstract	
10	emit	
11	overwhelming	
12	account for	
13	distress	
14	arousal	
15	stereotype	
16	fade	
17	standpoint	
18	evident	
19	temptation	
20	be motivated to	

B	Korean	English
01	고마워하는	
02	두드러지는	
03	감염시키다	
04	안정성	
05	회사, 기업	
06	거주하다	
07	이치에 맞다	
08	분해하다, 저하시키다	
09	순응	
10	~에 대처하다	
11	상당한	
12	맹렬한	
13	민주주의	
14	건축가	
15	반사적인	
16	문해력, 읽고 쓰는 능력	
17	보험	
18	인식	
19	~와 일치하다	
20	사소한	

▶ A-D 정답 : 해설편 127쪽

TEST C-D 각 단어의 뜻을 골라 기호를 쓰시오.

C	English			Korean
01	irritation	(	)	ⓐ 유효한, 타당한
02	border on	(	)	ⓑ 눈에 띄는
03	collapse	(	)	ⓒ 튼튼한, 견고한
04	outsource	(	)	ⓓ 해소하다, 내보내다
05	valid	(	)	ⓔ 이전에
06	fast asleep	(	)	ⓕ 결심, 결심하다
07	fictional	(	)	ⓖ 출현, 도래
08	physics	(	)	ⓗ 판매 유효 기간
09	retrieve	(	)	ⓘ ~에도 불구하고
10	formerly	(	)	ⓙ 발판
11	bring about	(	)	ⓚ 붕괴, 붕괴하다
12	sturdy	(	)	ⓛ 물리학
13	sell-by date	(	)	ⓜ 거의 ~에 달하다
14	striking	(	)	ⓝ ~을 초래하다
15	at hand	(	)	ⓞ (외부에) 위탁하다
16	discharge	(	)	ⓟ 깊이 잠든
17	advent	(	)	ⓠ 짜증
18	resolve	(	)	ⓡ 허구의
19	scaffolding	(	)	ⓢ 당면한, 눈앞에 있는
20	in the face of	(	)	ⓣ 생각해 내다

D	Korean			English
01	~하기로 되어 있다	(	)	ⓐ pathogen
02	간절한	(	)	ⓑ conscience
03	우세하다, 지배하다	(	)	ⓒ rebel
04	병원균	(	)	ⓓ economize
05	전적인, 배타적인	(	)	ⓔ giveaway
06	오염시키다	(	)	ⓕ manipulate
07	양심	(	)	ⓖ noteworthy
08	무료 나눔, 증정	(	)	ⓗ bring up
09	양육하다	(	)	ⓘ signify
10	반항아	(	)	ⓙ dominate
11	추측하다	(	)	ⓚ natural selection
12	자연 선택	(	)	ⓛ accuse A of B
13	촉진하다	(	)	ⓜ identify
14	절약하다	(	)	ⓝ pollute
15	조작하다	(	)	ⓞ exclusive
16	의미하다	(	)	ⓟ be supposed to
17	A를 B에 대해 비난하다	(	)	ⓠ glucose
18	주목할 만한	(	)	ⓡ speculate
19	알아내다, 식별하다	(	)	ⓢ facilitate
20	포도당	(	)	ⓣ desperate

※ 영어 [독해] 파트만 수록한 문제지이므로 **18**번부터 시작합니다.

● 점수 표시가 없는 문항은 모두 **2점** ● 문항수 **28개** | 배점 **63점** | 제한 시간 **45분**

18. 다음 글의 목적으로 가장 적절한 것은?

Dear Customer Service,
    I am writing in regard to my magazine subscription. Currently, I have just over a year to go on my subscription to *Economy Tomorrow* and would like to continue my subscription as I have enjoyed the magazine for many years. Unfortunately, due to my bad eyesight, I have trouble reading your magazine. My doctor has told me that I need to look for large print magazines and books. I'd like to know whether there's a large print version of your magazine. Please contact me if this is something you offer. Thank you for your time. I look forward to hearing from you soon.
Sincerely,
Martin Gray

① 잡지 기삿거리를 제보하려고
② 구독 기간 변경을 신청하려고
③ 구독료 인상에 대해 항의하려고
④ 잡지의 큰 글자판이 있는지 문의하려고
⑤ 잡지 기사 내용에 대한 정정을 요구하려고

19. 다음 글에 나타난 'I'의 심경 변화로 가장 적절한 것은?

    There was no choice next morning but to turn in my private reminiscence of Belleville. Two days passed before Mr. Fleagle returned the graded papers, and he returned everyone's but mine. I was anxiously expecting for a command to report to Mr. Fleagle immediately after school for discipline when I saw him lift my paper from his desk and rap for the class's attention. "Now, boys," he said, "I want to read you an essay. This is titled 'The Art of Eating Spaghetti.'" And he started to read. My words! He was reading *my words* out loud to the entire class. What's more, the entire class was listening attentively. Then somebody laughed, then the entire class was laughing, and not in contempt and ridicule, but with openhearted enjoyment. I did my best to avoid showing pleasure, but what I was feeling was pure ecstasy at this startling demonstration that my words had the power to make people laugh.

*reminiscence: 회상

① relieved → scared
② nervous → delighted
③ bored → confident
④ satisfied → depressed
⑤ confused → ashamed

20. 다음 글에서 필자가 주장하는 바로 가장 적절한 것은?

    We usually take time out only when we really need to switch off, and when this happens we are often overtired, sick, and in need of recuperation. Me time is complicated by negative associations with escapism, guilt, and regret as well as overwhelm, stress, and fatigue. All these negative connotations mean we tend to steer clear of it. Well, I am about to change your perception of the importance of me time, to persuade you that you should view it as vital for your health and wellbeing. Take this as permission to set aside some time for yourself! Our need for time in which to do what we choose is increasingly urgent in an overconnected, overwhelmed, and overstimulated world.

*recuperation: 회복

① 나를 위한 시간의 중요성을 인식해야 한다.
② 자신의 잘못을 성찰하는 자세를 가져야 한다.
③ 어려운 일이라고 해서 처음부터 회피해서는 안 된다.
④ 사회의 건강과 행복을 위하여 타인과 연대해야 한다.
⑤ 급변하는 사회에서 가치 판단을 신속하게 할 수 있어야 한다.

21. 밑줄 친 the innocent messenger who falls before a firing line이 다음 글에서 의미하는 바로 가장 적절한 것은? [3점]

Perhaps worse than attempting to get the bad news out of the way is attempting to soften it or simply not address it at all. This "Mum Effect" — a term coined by psychologists Sidney Rosen and Abraham Tesser in the early 1970s — happens because people want to avoid becoming the target of others' negative emotions. We all have the opportunity to lead change, yet it often requires of us the courage to deliver bad news to our superiors. We don't want to be the innocent messenger who falls before a firing line. When our survival instincts kick in, they can override our courage until the truth of a situation gets watered down. "The Mum Effect and the resulting filtering can have devastating effects in a steep hierarchy," writes Robert Sutton, an organizational psychologist. "What starts out as bad news becomes happier and happier as it travels up the ranks — because after each boss hears the news from his or her subordinates, he or she makes it sound a bit less bad before passing it up the chain."

① the employee being criticized for being silent
② the peacemaker who pursues non-violent solutions
③ the negotiator who looks for a mutual understanding
④ the subordinate who wants to get attention from the boss
⑤ the person who gets the blame for reporting unpleasant news

22. 다음 글의 요지로 가장 적절한 것은?

Most parents think that if our child would just "behave," we could stay calm as parents. The truth is that managing our own emotions and actions is what allows us to feel peaceful as parents. Ultimately we can't control our children or the obstacles they will face — but we can always control our own actions. Parenting isn't about what our child does, but about how we respond. In fact, most of what we call parenting doesn't take place between a parent and child but within the parent. When a storm brews, a parent's response will either calm it or trigger a full-scale tsunami. Staying calm enough to respond constructively to all that childish behavior — and the stormy emotions behind it — requires that we grow, too. If we can use those times when our buttons get pushed to reflect, not just react, we can notice when we lose equilibrium and steer ourselves back on track. This inner growth is the hardest work there is, but it's what enables you to become a more peaceful parent, one day at a time.

① 자녀의 행동 변화를 위해 부모의 즉각적인 반응이 필요하다.
② 부모의 내적 성장을 통한 평정심 유지가 양육에 중요하다.
③ 부모는 자녀가 감정을 다스릴 수 있게 도와주어야 한다.
④ 부모와 자녀는 건설적인 의견을 나눌 수 있어야 한다.
⑤ 바람직한 양육은 자녀에게 모범을 보이는 것이다.

23. 다음 글의 주제로 가장 적절한 것은?

We have already seen that learning is much more efficient when done at regular intervals: rather than cramming an entire lesson into one day, we are better off spreading out the learning. The reason is simple: every night, our brain consolidates what it has learned during the day. This is one of the most important neuroscience discoveries of the last thirty years: sleep is not just a period of inactivity or a garbage collection of the waste products that the brain accumulated while we were awake. Quite the contrary: while we sleep, our brain remains active; it runs a specific algorithm that replays the important events it recorded during the previous day and gradually transfers them into a more efficient compartment of our memory.

* consolidate: 통합 정리하다

① how to get an adequate amount of sleep
② the role that sleep plays in the learning process
③ a new method of stimulating engagement in learning
④ an effective way to keep your mind alert and active
⑤ the side effects of certain medications on brain function

24. 다음 글의 제목으로 가장 적절한 것은? [3점]

From the earliest times, healthcare services have been recognized to have two equal aspects, namely clinical care and public healthcare. In classical Greek mythology, the god of medicine, Asklepios, had two daughters, Hygiea and Panacea. The former was the goddess of preventive health and wellness, or hygiene, and the latter the goddess of treatment and curing. In modern times, the societal ascendancy of medical professionalism has caused treatment of sick patients to overshadow those preventive healthcare services provided by the less heroic figures of sanitary engineers, biologists, and governmental public health officers. Nevertheless, the quality of health that human populations enjoy is attributable less to surgical dexterity, innovative pharmaceutical products, and bioengineered devices than to the availability of public sanitation, sewage management, and services which control the pollution of the air, drinking water, urban noise, and food for human consumption. The human right to the highest attainable standard of health depends on public healthcare services no less than on the skills and equipment of doctors and hospitals.

* ascendancy: 우세 ** dexterity: 기민함

① Public Healthcare: A Co-Star, Not a Supporting Actor
② The Historical Development of Medicine and Surgery
③ Clinical Care Controversies: What You Don't Know
④ The Massive Similarities Between Different Mythologies
⑤ Initiatives Opening up Health Innovation Around the World

25. 다음 도표의 내용과 일치하지 <u>않는</u> 것은?

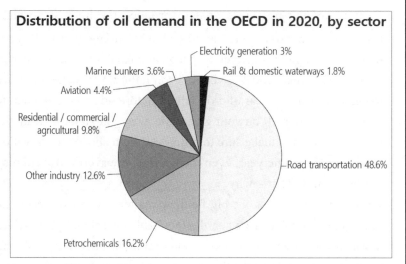

Distribution of oil demand in the OECD in 2020, by sector

- Electricity generation 3%
- Rail & domestic waterways 1.8%
- Marine bunkers 3.6%
- Aviation 4.4%
- Residential / commercial / agricultural 9.8%
- Other industry 12.6%
- Road transportation 48.6%
- Petrochemicals 16.2%

The above graph shows the distribution of oil demand by sector in the OECD in 2020. ① The Road transportation sector, which took up 48.6%, was the greatest oil demanding sector in the OECD member states. ② The percentage of oil demand in the Petrochemicals sector was one-third that of the Road transportation sector. ③ The difference in oil demand between the Other industry sector and the Petrochemicals sector was smaller than the difference in oil demand between the Aviation sector and the Electricity generation sector. ④ The oil demand in the Residential, commercial and agricultural sector took up 9.8% of all oil demand in the OECD, which was the fourth largest among all the sectors. ⑤ The percentage of oil demand in the Marine bunkers sector was twice that of the oil demand in the Rail & domestic waterways sector.

26. Carl-Gustaf Rossby에 관한 다음 글의 내용과 일치하지 <u>않는</u> 것은?

Carl-Gustaf Rossby was one of a group of notable Scandinavian researchers who worked with the Norwegian meteorologist Vilhelm Bjerknes at the University of Bergen. While growing up in Stockholm, Rossby received a traditional education. He earned a degree in mathematical physics at the University of Stockholm in 1918, but after hearing a lecture by Bjerknes, and apparently bored with Stockholm, he moved to the newly established Geophysical Institute in Bergen. In 1925, Rossby received a scholarship from the Sweden-America Foundation to go to the United States, where he joined the United States Weather Bureau. Based in part on his practical experience in weather forecasting, Rossby had become a supporter of the "polar front theory," which explains the cyclonic circulation that develops at the boundary between warm and cold air masses. In 1947, Rossby accepted the chair of the Institute of Meteorology, which had been set up for him at the University of Stockholm, where he remained until his death ten years later.

① Stockholm에서 성장하면서 전통적인 교육을 받았다.
② University of Stockholm에서 수리 물리학 학위를 받았다.
③ 1925년에 장학금을 받았다.
④ polar front theory를 지지했다.
⑤ University of Stockholm에 마련된 직책을 거절했다.

27. The Colchester Zoo Charity Race에 관한 다음 안내문의 내용과 일치하지 <u>않는</u> 것은?

The Colchester Zoo Charity Race

Join us for a charity event to help endangered species.
You will be running through Colchester Zoo,
home to over 260 species!

Date: Sunday, Sep. 25th, 2022

Time: 9:00 a.m. − 11:00 a.m.

Registration Fee: $50
- Registration fee includes a free pass to the zoo, food and drinks, and official photos.
- Register at www.info.colchesters.com.

Course Length: 10km
- Every runner will run 1km of the race through the zoo before going out to the main road.

Other Information
- Only the runners who complete the race will receive a medal at the finish line.
- Event T-shirts can be purchased at the zoo.
---

① 2시간 동안 진행된다.
② 등록비에는 음식과 음료가 포함된다.
③ 코스 길이는 10km이다.
④ 모든 참가자는 메달을 받는다.
⑤ 행사 티셔츠는 동물원에서 구입할 수 있다.

28. 7-Day Story Writing Competition에 관한 다음 안내문의 내용과 일치하는 것은?

7-Day Story Writing Competition

Is writing your talent? This is the stage for you.

When: From Monday, Dec. 5th to Sunday, Dec. 11th, 2022

Age: 17 and over

Content
- All participants will write about the same topic.
- You will be randomly assigned one of 12 literary genres for your story.
- You'll have exactly 7 days to write and submit your story.

Submission
- Only one entry per person
- You can revise and resubmit your entry until the deadline.

Prize
- We will choose 12 finalists, one from each genre, and the 12 entries will be published online and shared via social media.
- From the 12 finalists, one overall winner will be chosen and awarded $500.

※ To register and for more information, visit our website at www.7challenge_globestory.com.
---

① 17세 미만 누구나 참여할 수 있다.
② 참가자들은 동일한 주제에 대하여 글을 쓴다.
③ 참가자들은 12가지 문학 장르 중 하나를 선택할 수 있다.
④ 1인당 출품작을 최대 3편까지 제출할 수 있다.
⑤ 결승 진출자 전원에게 상금이 수여된다.

29. 다음 글의 밑줄 친 부분 중, 어법상 <u>틀린</u> 것은? [3점]

By noticing the relation between their own actions and resultant external changes, infants develop self-efficacy, a sense ① <u>that</u> they are agents of the perceived changes. Although infants can notice the effect of their behavior on the physical environment, it is in early social interactions that infants most ② <u>readily</u> perceive the consequence of their actions. People have perceptual characteristics that virtually ③ <u>assure</u> that infants will orient toward them. They have visually contrasting and moving faces. They produce sound, provide touch, and have interesting smells. In addition, people engage with infants by exaggerating their facial expressions and inflecting their voices in ways that infants find ④ <u>fascinated</u>. But most importantly, these antics are responsive to infants' vocalizations, facial expressions, and gestures; people vary the pace and level of their behavior in response to infant actions. Consequentially, early social interactions provide a context ⑤ <u>where</u> infants can easily notice the effect of their behavior.

* inflect: (음성을) 조절하다 ** antics: 익살스러운 행동

30. 다음 글의 밑줄 친 부분 중, 문맥상 낱말의 쓰임이 적절하지 <u>않은</u> 것은?

Adam Smith pointed out that specialization, where each of us focuses on one specific skill, leads to a general improvement of everybody's well-being. The idea is simple and powerful. By specializing in just one activity — such as food raising, clothing production, or home construction — each worker gains ① <u>mastery</u> over the particular activity. Specialization makes sense, however, only if the specialist can subsequently ② <u>trade</u> his or her output with the output of specialists in other lines of activity. It would make no sense to produce more food than a household needs unless there is a market outlet to exchange that ③ <u>scarce</u> food for clothing, shelter, and so forth. At the same time, without the ability to buy food on the market, it would not be possible to be a specialist home builder or clothing maker, since it would be ④ <u>necessary</u> to farm for one's own survival. Thus Smith realized that the division of labor is ⑤ <u>limited</u> by the extent of the market, whereas the extent of the market is determined by the degree of specialization.

[31 ~ 34] 다음 빈칸에 들어갈 말로 가장 적절한 것을 고르시오.

31. It is not the peasant's goal to produce the highest possible time-averaged crop yield, averaged over many years. If your time-averaged yield is marvelously high as a result of the combination of nine great years and one year of crop failure, you will still starve to death in that one year of crop failure before you can look back to congratulate yourself on your great time-averaged yield. Instead, the peasant's aim is to make sure to produce a yield above the starvation level in every single year, even though the time-averaged yield may not be highest. That's why _____ may make sense. If you have just one big field, no matter how good it is on the average, you will starve when the inevitable occasional year arrives in which your one field has a low yield. But if you have many different fields, varying independently of each other, then in any given year some of your fields will produce well even when your other fields are producing poorly. [3점]

① land leveling
② weed trimming
③ field scattering
④ organic farming
⑤ soil fertilization

32. There are several reasons why support may not be effective. One possible reason is that receiving help could be a blow to self-esteem. A recent study by Christopher Burke and Jessica Goren at Lehigh University examined this possibility. According to the threat to self-esteem model, help can be perceived as supportive and loving, or it can be seen as threatening if that help is interpreted as implying incompetence. According to Burke and Goren, support is especially likely to be seen as threatening if it is in an area that is self-relevant or self-defining — that is, in an area where your own success and achievement are especially important. Receiving help with a self-relevant task can _____, and this can undermine the potential positive effects of the help. For example, if your self-concept rests, in part, on your great cooking ability, it may be a blow to your ego when a friend helps you prepare a meal for guests because it suggests that you're not the master chef you thought you were.

① make you feel bad about yourself
② improve your ability to deal with challenges
③ be seen as a way of asking for another favor
④ trick you into thinking that you were successful
⑤ discourage the person trying to model your behavior

33. As well as making sense of events through narratives, historians in the ancient world established the tradition of history as a(n) _____ . The history writing of Livy or Tacitus, for instance, was in part designed to examine the behavior of heroes and villains, meditating on the strengths and weaknesses in the characters of emperors and generals, providing exemplars for the virtuous to imitate or avoid. This continues to be one of the functions of history. French chronicler Jean Froissart said he had written his accounts of chivalrous knights fighting in the Hundred Years' War "so that brave men should be inspired thereby to follow such examples." Today, historical studies of Lincoln, Churchill, Gandhi, or Martin Luther King, Jr. perform the same function.

* chivalrous: 기사도적인

① source of moral lessons and reflections
② record of the rise and fall of empires
③ war against violence and oppression
④ means of mediating conflict
⑤ integral part of innovation

34. Psychologist Christopher Bryan finds that when we _____, people evaluate choices differently. His team was able to cut cheating in half: instead of "Please don't cheat," they changed the appeal to "Please don't be a cheater." When you're urged not to cheat, you can do it and still see an ethical person in the mirror. But when you're told not to be a cheater, the act casts a shadow; immorality is tied to your identity, making the behavior much less attractive. Cheating is an isolated action that gets evaluated with the logic of consequence: Can I get away with it? Being a cheater evokes a sense of self, triggering the logic of appropriateness: What kind of person am I, and who do I want to be? In light of this evidence, Bryan suggests that we should embrace nouns more thoughtfully. "Don't Drink and Drive" could be rephrased as: "Don't Be a Drunk Driver." The same thinking can be applied to originality. When a child draws a picture, instead of calling the artwork creative, we can say "You are creative."

① ignore what experts say
② keep a close eye on the situation
③ shift our emphasis from behavior to character
④ focus on appealing to emotion rather than reason
⑤ place more importance on the individual instead of the group

35. 다음 글에서 전체 흐름과 관계 없는 문장은?

Taking a stand is important because you become a beacon for those individuals who are your people, your tribe, and your audience. ① When you raise your viewpoint up like a flag, people know where to find you; it becomes a rallying point. ② Displaying your perspective lets prospective (and current) customers know that you don't just sell your products or services. ③ The best marketing is never just about selling a product or service, but about taking a stand — showing an audience why they should believe in what you're marketing enough to want it at any cost, simply because they agree with what you're doing. ④ If you want to retain your existing customers, you need to create ways that a customer can feel like another member of the team, participating in the process of product development. ⑤ Products can be changed or adjusted if they aren't functioning, but rallying points align with the values and meaning behind what you do.

* beacon: 횃불 ** rallying point: 집합 지점

[36 ~ 37] 주어진 글 다음에 이어질 글의 순서로 가장 적절한 것을 고르시오.

36.

If DNA were the only thing that mattered, there would be no particular reason to build meaningful social programs to pour good experiences into children and protect them from bad experiences.

(A) This number came as a surprise to biologists: given the complexity of the brain and the body, it had been assumed that hundreds of thousands of genes would be required.

(B) So how does the massively complicated brain, with its eighty-six billion neurons, get built from such a small recipe book? The answer relies on a clever strategy implemented by the genome: build incompletely and let world experience refine.

(C) But brains require the right kind of environment if they are to correctly develop. When the first draft of the Human Genome Project came to completion at the turn of the millennium, one of the great surprises was that humans have only about twenty thousand genes.

① (A) − (C) − (B)   ② (B) − (A) − (C)
③ (B) − (C) − (A)   ④ (C) − (A) − (B)
⑤ (C) − (B) − (A)

37.

One benefit of reasons and arguments is that they can foster humility. If two people disagree without arguing, all they do is yell at each other. No progress is made.

(A) That is one way to achieve humility — on one side at least. Another possibility is that neither argument is refuted. Both have a degree of reason on their side. Even if neither person involved is convinced by the other's argument, both can still come to appreciate the opposing view.

(B) Both still think that they are right. In contrast, if both sides give arguments that articulate reasons for their positions, then new possibilities open up. One of the arguments gets refuted — that is, it is shown to fail. In that case, the person who depended on the refuted argument learns that he needs to change his view.

(C) They also realize that, even if they have some truth, they do not have the whole truth. They can gain humility when they recognize and appreciate the reasons against their own view. [3점]

* humility: 겸손 ** articulate: 분명히 말하다

① (A) − (C) − (B) ② (B) − (A) − (C)
③ (B) − (C) − (A) ④ (C) − (A) − (B)
⑤ (C) − (B) − (A)

[38 ~ 39] 글의 흐름으로 보아, 주어진 문장이 들어가기에 가장 적절한 곳을 고르시오.

38.

However, the capacity to produce skin pigments is inherited.

Adaptation involves changes in a population, with characteristics that are passed from one generation to the next. This is different from acclimation — an individual organism's changes in response to an altered environment. (①) For example, if you spend the summer outside, you may acclimate to the sunlight: your skin will increase its concentration of dark pigments that protect you from the sun. (②) This is a temporary change, and you won't pass the temporary change on to future generations. (③) For populations living in intensely sunny environments, individuals with a good ability to produce skin pigments are more likely to thrive, or to survive, than people with a poor ability to produce pigments, and that trait becomes increasingly common in subsequent generations. (④) If you look around, you can find countless examples of adaptation. (⑤) The distinctive long neck of a giraffe, for example, developed as individuals that happened to have longer necks had an advantage in feeding on the leaves of tall trees. [3점]

* pigment: 색소

39.

This inequality produces the necessary conditions for the operation of a huge, global-scale engine that takes on heat in the tropics and gives it off in the polar regions.

On any day of the year, the tropics and the hemisphere that is experiencing its warm season receive much more solar radiation than do the polar regions and the colder hemisphere. (①) Averaged over the course of the year, the tropics and latitudes up to about 40° receive more total heat than they lose by radiation. (②) Latitudes above 40° receive less total heat than they lose by radiation. (③) Its working fluid is the atmosphere, especially the moisture it contains. (④) Air is heated over the warm earth of the tropics, expands, rises, and flows away both northward and southward at high altitudes, cooling as it goes. (⑤) It descends and flows toward the equator again from more northerly and southerly latitudes.

* latitude: 위도

40. 다음 글의 내용을 한 문장으로 요약하고자 한다. 빈칸 (A), (B)에 들어갈 말로 가장 적절한 것은? [3점]

Greenwashing involves misleading a consumer into thinking a good or service is more environmentally friendly than it really is. Greenwashing ranges from making environmental claims required by law, and therefore irrelevant (CFC-free for example), to puffery (exaggerating environmental claims) to fraud. Researchers have shown that claims on products are often too vague or misleading. Some products are labeled "chemical-free," when the fact is everything contains chemicals, including plants and animals. Products with the highest number of misleading or unverifiable claims were laundry detergents, household cleaners, and paints. Environmental advocates agree there is still a long way to go to ensure shoppers are adequately informed about the environmental impact of the products they buy. The most common reason for greenwashing is to attract environmentally conscious consumers. Many consumers do not find out about the false claims until after the purchase. Therefore, greenwashing may increase sales in the short term. However, this strategy can seriously backfire when consumers find out they are being deceived.

* CFC: 염화불화탄소 ** fraud: 사기

↓

While greenwashing might bring a company profits ___(A)___ by deceiving environmentally conscious consumers, the company will face serious trouble when the consumers figure out they were ___(B)___.

	(A)		(B)
①	permanently	……	manipulated
②	temporarily	……	misinformed
③	momentarily	……	advocated
④	ultimately	……	underestimated
⑤	consistently	……	analyzed

[41~42] 다음 글을 읽고, 물음에 답하시오.

The driver of FOMO (the fear of missing out) is the social pressure to be at the right place with the right people, whether it's from a sense of duty or just trying to get ahead, we feel (a) obligated to attend certain events for work, for family and for friends. This pressure from society combined with FOMO can wear us down. According to a recent survey, 70 percent of employees admit that when they take a vacation, they still don't (b) disconnect from work. Our digital habits, which include constantly checking emails, and social media timelines, have become so firmly established, it is nearly impossible to simply enjoy the moment, along with the people with whom we are sharing these moments.

JOMO (the joy of missing out) is the emotionally intelligent antidote to FOMO and is essentially about being present and being (c) content with where you are at in life. You do not need to compare your life to others but instead, practice tuning out the background noise of the "shoulds" and "wants" and learn to let go of worrying whether you are doing something wrong. JOMO allows us to live life in the slow lane, to appreciate human connections, to be (d) intentional with our time, to practice saying "no," to give ourselves "tech-free breaks," and to give ourselves permission to acknowledge where we are and to feel emotions. Instead of constantly trying to keep up with the rest of society, JOMO allows us to be who we are in the present moment. When you (e) activate that competitive and anxious space in your brain, you have so much more time, energy, and emotion to conquer your true priorities.

* antidote: 해독제

41. 윗글의 제목으로 가장 적절한 것은?

① Missing Out Has Its Benefits
② JOMO: Another Form of Self-Deception
③ How to Catch up with Digital Technology
④ Being Isolated from Others Makes You Lonely
⑤ Using Social Media Wisely: The Dos and Don'ts

42. 밑줄 친 (a)~(e) 중에서 문맥상 낱말의 쓰임이 적절하지 <u>않은</u> 것은?

① (a) ② (b) ③ (c) ④ (d) ⑤ (e)

[43~45] 다음 글을 읽고, 물음에 답하시오.

(A)

There was a very wealthy man who was bothered by severe eye pain. He consulted many doctors and was treated by several of them. He did not stop consulting a galaxy of medical experts; he was heavily medicated and underwent hundreds of injections. However, the pain persisted and was worse than before. At last, (a) he heard about a monk who was famous for treating patients with his condition. Within a few days, the monk was called for by the suffering man.

* monk: 수도사

(B)

In a few days everything around (b) <u>that man</u> was green. The wealthy man made sure that nothing around him could be any other colour. When the monk came to visit him after a few days, the wealthy man's servants ran with buckets of green paint and poured them all over him because he was wearing red clothes. (c) <u>He</u> asked the servants why they did that.

(C)

They replied, "We can't let our master see any other colour." Hearing this, the monk laughed and said "If only you had purchased a pair of green glasses for just a few dollars, you could have saved these walls, trees, pots, and everything else and you could have saved a large share of (d) <u>his</u> fortune. You cannot paint the whole world green."

(D)

The monk understood the wealthy man's problem and said that for some time (e) <u>he</u> should concentrate only on green colours and not let his eyes see any other colours. The wealthy man thought it was a strange prescription, but he was desperate and decided to try it. He got together a group of painters and purchased barrels of green paint and ordered that every object he was likely to see be painted green just as the monk had suggested.

43. 주어진 글 (A)에 이어질 내용을 순서에 맞게 배열한 것으로 가장 적절한 것은?

① (B) − (D) − (C)　　　② (C) − (B) − (D)
③ (C) − (D) − (B)　　　④ (D) − (B) − (C)
⑤ (D) − (C) − (B)

44. 밑줄 친 (a)~(e) 중에서 가리키는 대상이 나머지 넷과 <u>다른</u> 것은?

① (a) ② (b) ③ (c) ④ (d) ⑤ (e)

45. 윗글에 관한 내용으로 적절하지 <u>않은</u> 것은?

① 부자는 눈 통증으로 여러 명의 의사에게 치료받았다.
② 수도사는 붉은 옷을 입고 부자를 다시 찾아갔다.
③ 하인들은 녹색 안경을 구입했다.
④ 부자는 수도사의 처방이 이상하다고 생각했다.
⑤ 부자는 주변을 모두 녹색으로 칠하게 했다.

---

* 확인 사항

○ 답안지의 해당란에 필요한 내용을 정확히 기입(표기)
했는지 확인하시오.

18
001 ☐ **in regard to** ~에 관해서
002 ☐ **currently** ⓐⓓ 현재
003 ☐ **subscription** ⓝ 구독
004 ☐ **unfortunately** ⓐⓓ 안타깝게도
005 ☐ **due to** ~ 때문에
006 ☐ **eyesight** ⓝ 시력
007 ☐ **have trouble ~ing** ~하는 데 어려움이 있다
008 ☐ **print** ⓝ 활자
009 ☐ **offer** ⓥ 제공하다

19
010 ☐ **there is no choice but** ~할 수밖에 없다
011 ☐ **private** ⓐ 개인적인, 사적인
012 ☐ **anxiously** ⓐⓓ 걱정스럽게, 불안하게
013 ☐ **command** ⓝ 지시, 명령
014 ☐ **report to** ~에게 출두하다, 보고하다
015 ☐ **discipline** ⓝ 훈육, 징계
016 ☐ **lift** ⓥ 들어올리다
017 ☐ **rap** ⓥ (빠르게) 톡톡 두드리다
018 ☐ **read out loud** 소리 내어 읽다
019 ☐ **what's more** 더구나, 게다가
020 ☐ **attentively** ⓐⓓ 주의 깊게
021 ☐ **contempt** ⓝ 경멸
022 ☐ **ridicule** ⓝ 조롱, 조소
023 ☐ **openhearted** ⓐ 솔직한, 숨김없는
024 ☐ **ecstasy** ⓝ 황홀감
025 ☐ **startling** ⓐ 놀라운
026 ☐ **demonstration** ⓝ 시연, 증명
027 ☐ **nervous** ⓐ 긴장한
028 ☐ **delighted** ⓐ 기쁜
029 ☐ **depressed** ⓐ 우울한

20
030 ☐ **switch off** (신경을) 끄다
031 ☐ **overtired** ⓐ 지나치게 피곤한
032 ☐ **in need of** ~이 필요한
033 ☐ **complicated** ⓐ 복잡한
034 ☐ **escapism** ⓝ 현실 도피
035 ☐ **guilt** ⓝ 죄책감
036 ☐ **regret** ⓝ 후회, 유감
037 ☐ **fatigue** ⓝ 피로
038 ☐ **steer clear of** ~을 피하다, 가까이 가지 않다
039 ☐ **vital** ⓐ 매우 필요한
040 ☐ **set aside** ~을 따로 두다, 마련하다
041 ☐ **increasingly** ⓐⓓ 점점 더
042 ☐ **urgent** ⓐ 긴급한
043 ☐ **overconnected** ⓐ 과도하게 연결된
044 ☐ **overstimulate** ⓥ 과도하게 자극하다

21
045 ☐ **out of the way** 처리된, 끝난
046 ☐ **address** ⓥ 다루다, 대처하다
047 ☐ **mum** ⓐ 침묵, 잠자코 있는
048 ☐ **require A of B** B에게 A를 요구하다
049 ☐ **courage** ⓝ 용기
050 ☐ **superior** ⓝ 상사, 윗사람 ⓐ 상위의, 우등한
051 ☐ **innocent** ⓐ 무고한
052 ☐ **firing line** (화기가 발사되는) 사선, 방화선
053 ☐ **kick in** 효과가 나타나다

054 ☐ **override** ⓥ 중단시키다
055 ☐ **water down** (물로) 희석하다
056 ☐ **devastating** ⓐ 파괴적인
057 ☐ **hierarchy** ⓝ 위계질서
058 ☐ **subordinate** ⓝ 부하직원
059 ☐ **peacemaker** ⓝ 중재자
060 ☐ **non-violent** ⓐ 비폭력적인
061 ☐ **negotiator** ⓝ 협상가
062 ☐ **mutual** ⓐ 서로의, 상호의
063 ☐ **get the blame for** ~에 대한 비난을 받다

22
064 ☐ **behave** ⓥ (잘) 처신하다, 행동하다
065 ☐ **obstacle** ⓝ 장애물
066 ☐ **parenting** ⓝ 양육
067 ☐ **take place** 일어나다, 발생하다
068 ☐ **brew** ⓥ (불쾌한 일이 일어나려고) 태동하다, (차가) 끓다
069 ☐ **trigger** ⓥ 유발하다
070 ☐ **constructively** ⓐⓓ 건설적으로
071 ☐ **childish** ⓐ 유치한
072 ☐ **equilibrium** ⓝ 평정, 균형
073 ☐ **steer** ⓥ 조종하다
074 ☐ **back on track** 정상 궤도로 돌아온
075 ☐ **enable** ⓥ 가능하게 하다
076 ☐ **peaceful** ⓐ 평화로운

23
077 ☐ **interval** ⓝ 간격
078 ☐ **cram** ⓥ 밀어 넣다, 벼락치기하다
079 ☐ **well off** 잘 사는, 사정이 좋은
080 ☐ **spread out** 펼쳐놓다
081 ☐ **neuroscience** ⓝ 신경과학
082 ☐ **inactivity** ⓝ 비활동
083 ☐ **collection** ⓝ 수집, 모음
084 ☐ **accumulate** ⓥ 축적하다, 모으다
085 ☐ **quite the contrary** 그와는 정반대이다
086 ☐ **replay** ⓥ 재생하다
087 ☐ **previous** ⓐ 이전의
088 ☐ **gradually** ⓐⓓ 점진적으로, 점차
089 ☐ **compartment** ⓝ 구획
090 ☐ **adequate** ⓐ 적절한
091 ☐ **engagement** ⓝ 참여, 몰입
092 ☐ **alert** ⓐ 기민한, 정신이 초롱초롱한
093 ☐ **side effect** 부작용
094 ☐ **medication** ⓝ 약물

24
095 ☐ **healthcare service** 공공 보건 서비스
096 ☐ **namely** ⓐⓓ 즉
097 ☐ **clinical care** 임상 진료
098 ☐ **mythology** ⓝ 신화
099 ☐ **the former** (둘 중) 전자
100 ☐ **preventive** ⓐ 예방적인
101 ☐ **wellness** ⓝ 건강
102 ☐ **hygiene** ⓝ 위생
103 ☐ **the latter** (둘 중) 후자
104 ☐ **treatment** ⓝ 치료
105 ☐ **professionalism** ⓝ 전문성
106 ☐ **overshadow** ⓥ 빛을 잃게 하다, 가리다
107 ☐ **heroic** ⓐ 영웅적인
108 ☐ **sanitary** ⓐ 위생의

109 ☐ **be attributable to** ~에 기인하다
110 ☐ **surgical** ⓐ 수술적인
111 ☐ **pharmaceutical** ⓐ 약학의
112 ☐ **sewage** ⓝ 오물
113 ☐ **attainable** ⓐ 달성 가능한
114 ☐ **no less than** ~에 못지 않게
115 ☐ **equipment** ⓝ 장비
116 ☐ **co-star** ⓝ 공동 주연 ⓥ 공동 주연을 맡다
117 ☐ **supporting actor** 조연
118 ☐ **controversy** ⓝ 논란, 논쟁의 여지
119 ☐ **massive** ⓐ 엄청나게 큰, 거대한
120 ☐ **initiative** ⓝ 계획

25
121 ☐ **distribution** ⓝ 분배, 분포
122 ☐ **sector** ⓝ 부문, 분야
123 ☐ **transportation** ⓝ 교통
124 ☐ **take up** ~을 차지하다
125 ☐ **state** ⓝ 국가
126 ☐ **petrochemical** ⓝ 석유화학의
127 ☐ **generation** ⓝ (동력) 발생, 생성
128 ☐ **aviation** ⓝ 항공
129 ☐ **residential** ⓐ 거주의, 주거의
130 ☐ **commercial** ⓐ 상업적인
131 ☐ **agricultural** ⓐ 농업의
132 ☐ **domestic** ⓐ 국내의, 가정의

26
133 ☐ **notable** ⓐ 저명한
134 ☐ **meteorologist** ⓝ 기상학자
135 ☐ **earn a degree** 학위를 받다
136 ☐ **receive a scholarship** 장학금을 받다
137 ☐ **in part** 부분적으로
138 ☐ **practical** ⓐ 실질적인, 현실적인
139 ☐ **weather forecasting** 기상 예보
140 ☐ **cyclonic** ⓐ 사이클론의, 격렬한
141 ☐ **circulation** ⓝ 순환
142 ☐ **chair** ⓝ 의장, (기관)장

27
143 ☐ **charity event** 자선 행사
144 ☐ **race** ⓝ 경주 ⓥ 뛰다
145 ☐ **endangered** ⓐ 멸종 위기에 처한
146 ☐ **species** ⓝ (생물) 종
147 ☐ **fee** ⓝ 요금
148 ☐ **official** ⓐ 공식적인
149 ☐ **length** ⓝ 길이
150 ☐ **complete** ⓥ 끝내다, 완수하다
151 ☐ **finish line** 결승선
152 ☐ **purchase** ⓥ 구매하다

28
153 ☐ **writing competition** 글쓰기 대회
154 ☐ **randomly** ⓐⓓ 무작위로
155 ☐ **literary** ⓐ 문학의
156 ☐ **genre** ⓝ 장르
157 ☐ **submit** ⓥ 제출하다
158 ☐ **entry** ⓝ 출품작
159 ☐ **revise** ⓥ 수정하다
160 ☐ **finalist** ⓝ 결승 진출자
161 ☐ **overall** ⓐ 전체의, 종합의
162 ☐ **award** ⓥ 수여하다 ⓝ 상

29
163 ☐ **notice** ⓥ 알아차리다
164 ☐ **resultant** ⓐ 그로 인한
165 ☐ **external** ⓐ 외부적인
166 ☐ **self-efficacy** ⓝ 자기 효능감
167 ☐ **agent** ⓝ 주체, 행위자
168 ☐ **readily** ⓐⓓ 쉽게, 순조롭게
169 ☐ **perceptual** ⓐ 지각과 관련된
170 ☐ **characteristic** ⓝ 특성
171 ☐ **virtually** ⓐⓓ 실제로
172 ☐ **assure** ⓥ 확실히 하다
173 ☐ **engage with** ~와 관계를 맺다, ~을 상대하다
174 ☐ **exaggerate** ⓥ 과장하다
175 ☐ **fascinated** ⓐ 매혹된
176 ☐ **most importantly** 가장 중요한 것은
177 ☐ **responsive to** ~에 잘 호응하는
178 ☐ **consequentially** ⓐⓓ 결과적으로

30
179 ☐ **specialization** ⓝ 전문화
180 ☐ **lead to** ~을 낳다
181 ☐ **general** ⓐ 전반적인
182 ☐ **improvement** ⓝ 향상, 개선
183 ☐ **raise** ⓥ 기르다, 키우다
184 ☐ **production** ⓝ 생산
185 ☐ **construction** ⓝ 건설
186 ☐ **subsequently** ⓐⓓ 차후에
187 ☐ **trade** ⓥ 교역하다, 거래하다
188 ☐ **household** ⓝ 가정, 가구
189 ☐ **outlet** ⓝ 직판점
190 ☐ **scarce** ⓐ 부족한
191 ☐ **and so forth** 기타 등등
192 ☐ **division of labor** 분업
193 ☐ **extent** ⓝ 규모, 정도

31
194 ☐ **peasant** ⓝ 농부, 소작농
195 ☐ **yield** ⓝ 수확량, 산출량
196 ☐ **marvelously** ⓐⓓ 놀랍도록
197 ☐ **combination** ⓝ 결합
198 ☐ **failure** ⓝ 실패
199 ☐ **starve to death** 굶어 죽다
200 ☐ **congratulate** ⓥ 기념하다
201 ☐ **make sure to** 확실히 ~하다
202 ☐ **no matter how** 아무리 ~하더라도
203 ☐ **inevitable** ⓐ 불가피한
204 ☐ **occasional** ⓐ 이따금의
205 ☐ **vary** ⓥ 다르다, 달라지다
206 ☐ **independently of** ~와 상관없이
207 ☐ **poorly** ⓐⓓ 형편없이
208 ☐ **leveling** (땅을) 고름, 평평하게 함
209 ☐ **trim** ⓥ 다듬다, 손질하다
210 ☐ **scatter** ⓥ 흩어놓다
211 ☐ **organic farming** 유기농법
212 ☐ **fertilization** ⓝ (땅을) 비옥하게 하기

32
213 ☐ **blow** ⓝ 타격, 충격
214 ☐ **self-esteem** ⓝ 자아 존중감
215 ☐ **examine** ⓥ 조사하다, 연구하다
216 ☐ **threat** ⓝ 위협

217 be perceived as ~로 여겨지다	271 at any cost 반드시, 기필코	325 organism ⓝ 유기체	380 impact ⓝ 영향, 충격
218 incompetence ⓝ 무능	272 simply 〔ad〕 단지, 그저	326 in response to ~에 반응해	381 attract ⓥ 유인하다, 끌다
219 self-relevant ⓐ 자아 관련의	273 agree with ~에 동의하다	327 alter ⓥ 바꾸다, 변경하다	382 in the short term 단기적으로
220 undermine ⓥ 손상시키다	274 retain ⓥ 보유하다, 유지하다	328 concentration ⓝ 농도	383 backfire ⓥ 역효과를 낳다
221 self-concept ⓝ 자아 개념	275 existing ⓐ 기존의	329 temporary ⓐ 일시적인	384 deceive ⓥ 속이다
222 rest on ~에 놓여 있다	276 participate in ~에 참가하다	330 intensely 〔ad〕 강렬하게	385 permanently 〔ad〕 영구적으로
223 suggest ⓥ 암시하다, 시사하다	277 product development 상품 개발	331 thrive ⓥ 번성하다	386 manipulate ⓥ 조종하다
224 feel bad about ~에 대해 안 좋게 느끼다, ~에 대해 나쁘게 느끼다	278 align with ~와 나란히 있다	332 trait ⓝ 특성	387 temporarily 〔ad〕 일시적으로
225 challenge ⓝ 도전, 과제	**36**	333 subsequent ⓐ 차후의	388 momentarily 〔ad〕 잠시
226 trick A into B A를 속여 B하게 하다	279 matter ⓥ 중요하다	334 look around 둘러보다	389 underestimate ⓥ 과소평가하다
227 discourage ⓥ 낙담시키다	280 particular ⓐ 특정한, 특별한	335 countless ⓐ 수없이 많은	**41~42**
33	281 meaningful ⓐ 의미 있는	336 distinctive ⓐ 독특한	390 driver ⓝ 원동력
228 make sense of ~을 이해하다	282 pour ⓥ 쏟아 붓다	337 giraffe ⓝ 기린	391 miss out 놓치다, 소외되다
229 narrative ⓝ 이야기	283 protect A from B A를 B로부터 보호하다	338 happen to 우연히 ~하다	392 sense of duty 의무감
230 villain ⓝ 악당	284 come as a surprise 놀라움으로 다가 오다	339 advantage ⓝ 이점	393 get ahead 앞서 나가다
231 meditate on ~에 관해 곰곰이 생각해보다	285 given 〔prep〕 ~을 고려할 때	340 feed on ~을 먹고 살다	394 feel obligated to ~해야 한다는 의무감이 들다
232 strength ⓝ 장점	286 gene ⓝ 유전자	**39**	395 combined with ~와 결합된
233 emperor ⓝ 황제	287 hundreds of thousands of 수십만의, 다수의	341 inequality ⓝ 불균형	396 wear down ~을 지치게 하다
234 general ⓝ 장군, 제독	288 massively 〔ad〕 엄청나게	342 necessary condition 필요조건	397 admit ⓥ 인정하다
235 exemplar ⓝ 본보기	289 billion ⓝ 10억	343 operation ⓝ 작동, 가동	398 disconnect from ~로부터 단절되다
236 virtuous ⓐ 도덕적인	290 neuron ⓝ 뉴런, 신경 세포	344 take on ~을 떠맡다	399 firmly 〔ad〕 확고히, 단단히
237 chronicler ⓝ 연대기 작가, 기록가	291 recipe book 요리책	345 tropics ⓝ 열대	400 established ⓐ 확립된, 자리 잡은
238 account ⓝ 설명	292 clever ⓐ 영리한	346 give off 방출하다, 내뿜다	401 nearly 〔ad〕 거의
239 thereby 〔ad〕 그렇게 함으로써	293 implement ⓥ 실행하다	347 polar ⓐ 극지방의	402 along with ~와 함께
240 reflection ⓝ 성찰	294 incompletely 〔ad〕 불완전하게	348 hemisphere ⓝ 반구	403 emotionally 〔ad〕 정서적으로
241 rise and fall 흥망성쇠	295 refine ⓥ 다듬다, 정제하다	349 solar ⓐ 태양의	404 intelligent ⓐ 현명한, 똑똑한
242 empire ⓝ 제국	296 first draft 초안	350 radiation ⓝ (열, 에너지 등의) 복사	405 essentially 〔ad〕 본질적으로
243 oppression ⓝ 억압	297 come to completion 완수되다	351 over the course of the year 연중, 한 해 동안	406 present ⓐ 존재하는, 현재의
244 mediate ⓥ 중재하다	298 at the turn of ~의 전환기에	352 up to ~까지	407 content ⓐ 만족하는
245 integral part 필수 요소	299 millennium ⓝ 새천년	353 above 〔prep〕 ~을 넘는, 위에	408 tune out ~을 듣지 않다, 무시하다
34	**37**	354 working fluid 작동유(동력을 전달해주는 매체)	409 let go of ~을 버리다, 놓아주다
246 evaluate ⓥ 평가하다	300 reason ⓝ 근거, 이유	355 atmosphere ⓝ 대기	410 intentional ⓐ 의도하는
247 cut in half 절반으로 줄이다	301 argument ⓝ 주장, 논쟁	356 moisture ⓝ 수분, 습기	411 give permission to ~하도록 허락하다
248 cheat ⓥ 속이다	302 foster ⓥ 기르다, 키우다, 양성하다	357 rise ⓥ 상승하다	412 acknowledge ⓥ 인식하다, 인정하다
249 urge ⓥ 촉구하다	303 yell at ~에게 소리 지르다	358 flow away 흘러가다	413 keep up with ~을 따라잡다
250 ethical ⓐ 도덕적인, 윤리적인	304 progress ⓝ 진전, 진행	359 northward 〔ad〕 북쪽으로	414 conquer ⓥ 정복하다, 이기다
251 cast a shadow 그림자를 드리우다	305 neither 둘 중 어느 것도 ~않은	360 southward 〔ad〕 남쪽으로	415 priority ⓝ 우선순위
252 immorality ⓝ 부도덕함	306 refute ⓥ 반박하다	361 altitude ⓝ 고도	416 self-deception ⓝ 자기 기만
253 be tied to ~와 결부되다	307 a degree of 어느 정도의	362 descend ⓥ 하강하다	417 catch up with ~을 따라잡다, ~에 발맞 추다
254 isolated ⓐ 고립된, 동떨어진	308 involved ⓐ 연루된, 연관된	363 equator ⓝ 적도	**43~45**
255 get away with ~에서 벗어나다	309 convince ⓥ 설득하다, 납득시키다	**40**	418 bother ⓥ 괴롭게 하다
256 evoke ⓥ (감정 등을) 불러일으키다	310 appreciate ⓥ 제대로 이해하다	364 greenwashing ⓝ 그린워싱, 위장 환경주의	419 severe ⓐ 심각한
257 appropriateness ⓝ 적절성	311 opposing ⓐ 반대되는, 상충하는	365 mislead ⓥ 현혹하다, 오도하다	420 heavily 〔ad〕 아주 많이, 심하게
258 in light of ~에 비추어볼 때	312 right ⓐ 옳은	366 environmentally friendly 환경 친화 적인	421 medicate ⓥ 약을 투여하다
259 embrace ⓥ 받아들이다	313 in contrast 대조적으로	367 range from A to B A부터 B에 이르다	422 undergo ⓥ 겪다, 경험하다
260 thoughtfully 〔ad〕 사려 깊게	314 fail ⓥ 무너지다	368 make a claim 주장하다	423 injection ⓝ 주사
261 originality ⓝ 독창성, 창의성	315 whole ⓐ 온전한, 전체의	369 irrelevant ⓐ 부적절한, 관련이 없는	424 persist ⓥ 지속되다
262 keep a close eye on ~을 면밀히 관찰 하다	316 gain ⓥ 얻다	370 puffery ⓝ 과대 선전	425 call for ~을 필요로 하다, 데리러 가다, 부르다
263 emphasis ⓝ 강조, 역점	**38**	371 vague ⓐ 애매모호한	426 bucket ⓝ 양동이
264 place importance on ~에 중점을 두다	317 capacity ⓝ 능력	372 label ⓥ 이름을 붙이다, 명명하다	427 share ⓝ 부분, 몫
35	318 produce ⓥ 만들어내다	373 chemical ⓝ 화학물질 ⓐ 화학의	428 fortune ⓝ 재산
265 take a stand 입장을 취하다	319 inherit ⓥ 물려주다, 상속하다	374 unverifiable ⓐ 증명할 수 없는	429 for some time 얼마 동안, 일정 기간
266 tribe ⓝ 부족	320 adaptation ⓝ 적응	375 detergent ⓝ 세제	430 concentrate on ~에 집중하다
267 viewpoint ⓝ 견해, 시각	321 population ⓝ 개체군, 인구	376 advocate ⓝ 옹호자, 지지자	431 prescription ⓝ 처방
268 flag ⓝ 깃발	322 pass from A to B A에서 B로 전하다	377 ensure ⓥ 확실히 하다, 보장하다	432 desperate ⓐ 절박한
269 prospective ⓐ 장래의	323 generation ⓝ 세대	378 adequately 〔ad〕 적절하게	433 get together 모으다
270 believe in ~을 믿다	324 acclimation ⓝ (새 환경에 대한) 순응	379 informed ⓐ 정보를 제공받은	434 barrel ⓝ (목재나 금속으로 된) 통

TEST A-B 각 단어의 뜻을 [A] 영어는 우리말로, [B] 우리말은 영어로 쓰시오.

A	English	Korean		B	Korean	English
01	sewage			01	조종하다	
02	interval			02	시력	
03	preventive			03	번성하다	
04	subscription			04	쉽게, 순조롭게	
05	mythology			05	지시, 명령	
06	devastating			06	손상시키다	
07	villain			07	도덕적인, 윤리적인	
08	accumulate			08	쏟아 붓다	
09	distribution			09	건강	
10	hierarchy			10	중단시키다	
11	aviation			11	진전, 진행	
12	exemplar			12	걱정스럽게, 불안하게	
13	practical			13	순환	
14	mutual			14	흩어놓다	
15	regret			15	거주의, 주거의	
16	characteristic			16	전문화	
17	randomly			17	공식적인	
18	appreciate			18	수정하다	
19	marvelously			19	절박한	
20	blow			20	설명	

▶ A-D 정답 : 해설편 138쪽

TEST C-D 각 단어의 뜻을 골라 기호를 쓰시오.

C	English			Korean	D	Korean			English
01	viewpoint	( )	ⓐ 경멸		01	확립된, 자리 잡은	( )	ⓐ self-concept
02	refute	( )	ⓑ 지나치게 피곤한		02	과장하다	( )	ⓑ inherit
03	undergo	( )	ⓒ 지속되다		03	(감정 등을) 불러일으키다	( )	ⓒ hygiene
04	tropics	( )	ⓓ 도덕적인		04	다듬다, 정제하다	( )	ⓓ self-esteem
05	persist	( )	ⓔ 부도덕함		05	기존의	( )	ⓔ childish
06	virtuous	( )	ⓕ 반박하다		06	~을 떠맡다	( )	ⓕ medicate
07	overtired	( )	ⓖ 겪다, 경험하다		07	강조, 역점	( )	ⓖ exaggerate
08	contempt	( )	ⓗ 역효과를 낳다		08	빛을 잃게 하다, 가리다	( )	ⓗ obstacle
09	sector	( )	ⓘ 적도		09	물려주다, 상속하다	( )	ⓘ refine
10	immorality	( )	ⓙ 고립된, 동떨어진		10	유치한	( )	ⓙ emphasis
11	compartment	( )	ⓚ 억압		11	자아 개념	( )	ⓚ established
12	openhearted	( )	ⓛ 견해, 시각		12	극지방의	( )	ⓛ prospective
13	trait	( )	ⓜ 열대		13	정복하다, 이기다	( )	ⓜ overshadow
14	equator	( )	ⓝ 부하직원		14	장래의	( )	ⓝ existing
15	isolated	( )	ⓞ 평정, 균형		15	자아 존중감	( )	ⓞ conquer
16	equilibrium	( )	ⓟ 특성		16	조롱, 조소	( )	ⓟ take on
17	subordinate	( )	ⓠ 저명한		17	위생	( )	ⓠ ridicule
18	notable	( )	ⓡ 솔직한, 숨김없는		18	장애물	( )	ⓡ evoke
19	oppression	( )	ⓢ 부문, 분야		19	약을 투여하다	( )	ⓢ subsequently
20	backfire	( )	ⓣ 구획		20	차후에	( )	ⓣ polar

※ 영어 [독해] 파트만 수록한 문제지이므로 18번부터 시작합니다.

● 점수 표시가 없는 문항은 모두 2점 ● 문항수 28개 | 배점 63점 | 제한 시간 45분

18. 다음 글의 목적으로 가장 적절한 것은?

Dear parents and students of Douglas School,

As you know, our school was built over 150 years ago. While we are proud of our school's history, the facilities are not exactly what they should be for modern schooling. Thanks to a generous donation to the school foundation, we will be able to start renovating those parts of our campus that have become outdated. We hope this will help provide our students with the best education possible. I'm writing to inform you that the auditorium will be the first building closed for repairs. Students will not be able to use the auditorium for about one month while the repairs are taking place. We hope that you will understand how this brief inconvenience will encourage community-wide benefits for years to come.

Sincerely,
Vice Principal Kyla Andrews

① 수리로 인한 강당 폐쇄를 안내하려고
② 캠퍼스 투어 프로그램 일정을 조정하려고
③ 강당 사용을 위한 신청 방법을 공지하려고
④ 강당 신축을 위한 기금 모금 행사를 홍보하려고
⑤ 집짓기 행사에 참여할 자원 봉사자를 모집하려고

19. 다음 글에 드러난 Evan의 심경으로 가장 적절한 것은?

Evan's eyes opened wide and his mouth made the shape of an O, which happened whenever something surprised him. "You don't mean we're leaving Sydney?" he asked. His mother had just told him they were leaving Sydney for his father's work. "But what about school?" said Evan, interrupting her, a thing he knew he was not supposed to do but which he felt he would be forgiven for on this occasion. "And what about Carl and Daniel and Martin? How will they know where I am when we want to do things together?" His mother told him that he would have to say goodbye to his friends for the time being but that she was sure Evan would see them again. "Say goodbye to them? Say goodbye to them?" He kept repeating himself, sounding more and more anxious with every repetition.

① shocked and worried
② excited and pleased
③ grateful and relieved
④ bored and indifferent
⑤ jealous and envious

20. 다음 글에서 필자가 주장하는 바로 가장 적절한 것은?

Without guidance from their teacher, students will not embark on a journey of personal development that recognizes the value of cooperation. Left to their own devices, they will instinctively become increasingly competitive with each other. They will compare scores, reports, and feedback within the classroom environment—just as they do in the sporting arena. We don't need to teach our students about winners and losers. The playground and the media do that for them. However, we do need to teach them that there is more to life than winning and about the skills they need for successful cooperation. A group working together successfully requires individuals with a multitude of social skills, as well as a high level of interpersonal awareness. While some students inherently bring a natural understanding of these skills with them, they are always in the minority. To bring cooperation between peers into your classroom, you need to teach these skills consciously and carefully, and nurture them continuously throughout the school years.

① 학생의 참여가 활발한 수업 방법을 개발해야 한다.
② 학생에게 성공적인 협동을 위한 기술을 가르쳐야 한다.
③ 학생의 의견을 존중하는 학교 분위기를 조성해야 한다.
④ 학생의 전인적 발달을 위해 체육활동을 강화해야 한다.
⑤ 정보를 올바르게 선별하도록 미디어 교육을 실시해야 한다.

21. 밑줄 친 bringing together contradictory characteristics가 다음 글에서 의미하는 바로 가장 적절한 것은?

The creative team exhibits paradoxical characteristics. It shows tendencies of thought and action that we'd assume to be mutually exclusive or contradictory. For example, to do its best work, a team needs deep knowledge of subjects relevant to the problem it's trying to solve, and a mastery of the processes involved. But at the same time, the team needs fresh perspectives that are unencumbered by the prevailing wisdom or established ways of doing things. Often called a "beginner's mind," this is the newcomers' perspective: people who are curious, even playful, and willing to ask anything — no matter how naive the question may seem — because they don't know what they don't know. Thus, bringing together contradictory characteristics can accelerate the process of new ideas.

* unencumbered: 방해 없는

① establishing short-term and long-term goals
② performing both challenging and easy tasks
③ adopting temporary and permanent solutions
④ utilizing aspects of both experts and rookies
⑤ considering processes and results simultaneously

22. 다음 글의 요지로 가장 적절한 것은?

Too many officials in troubled cities wrongly imagine that they can lead their city back to its former glories with some massive construction project — a new stadium or light rail system, a convention center, or a housing project. With very few exceptions, no public policy can slow the tidal forces of urban change. We mustn't ignore the needs of the poor people who live in the Rust Belt, but public policy should help poor *people*, not poor places. Shiny new real estate may dress up a declining city, but it doesn't solve its underlying problems. The hallmark of declining cities is that they have *too much* housing and infrastructure relative to the strength of their economies. With all that supply of structure and so little demand, it makes no sense to use public money to build more supply. The folly of building-centric urban renewal reminds us that cities aren't structures; cities are people.

① 도시 재생을 위한 공공정책은 건설보다 사람에 중점을 두어야 한다.
② 대중 교통 이용이 편리하도록 도시 교통 체계를 구축해야 한다.
③ 사회기반시설 확충을 통해 지역 경제를 활성화해야 한다.
④ 에너지를 절감할 수 있는 친환경 건물을 설계해야 한다.
⑤ 문화유산 보존을 우선하는 도시 계획을 수립해야 한다.

23. 다음 글의 주제로 가장 적절한 것은?

Many marine species including oysters, marsh grasses, and fish were deliberately introduced for food or for erosion control, with little knowledge of the impacts they could have. Fish and shellfish have been intentionally introduced all over the world for aquaculture, providing food and jobs, but they can escape and become a threat to native species, ecosystem function, or livelihoods. Atlantic salmon are reared in ocean net-pens in Washington State and British Columbia. Many escape each year, and they have been recovered in both saltwater and freshwater in Washington State, British Columbia, and Alaska. Recreational fishing can also spread invasive species. Bait worms from Maine are popular throughout the country. They are commonly packed in seaweed which contains many other organisms. If the seaweed is discarded, it or the organisms on it can colonize new areas. Fishing boots, recreational boats, and trailers can pick up organisms at one location and move them elsewhere.

* aquaculture: 양식(업)

① benefits of recreational ocean fishing
② ways to maintain marine biodiversity
③ potential value of the ocean for ecotourism
④ contribution of ocean farming to food supply
⑤ human influence on the spread of invasive species

24. 다음 글의 제목으로 가장 적절한 것은?

Before the fancy high-rises, financial headquarters, tourist centers, and souvenir peddlers made their way to Battery Park City, the area behind the World Trade Center was a giant, gross landfill. In 1982, artist Agnes Denes decided to return that landfill back to its roots, although temporarily. Denes was commissioned by the Public Art Fund to create one of the most significant and fantastical pieces of public work Manhattan has ever seen. Her concept was not a traditional sculpture, but a living installation that changed the way the public looked at art. In the name of art, Denes put a beautiful golden wheat field right in the shadow of the gleaming Twin Towers. For *Wheatfield — A Confrontation*, Denes and volunteers removed trash from four acres of land, then planted amber waves of grain atop the area. After months of farming and irrigation, the wheat field was thriving and ready. The artist and her volunteers harvested thousands of pounds of wheat to give to food banks in the city, nourishing both the minds and bodies of New Yorkers.

① Living Public Art Grows from a Landfill
② Why Does Art Fade Away in Urban Areas?
③ New York: Skyscraper Capital of the World
④ Art Narrows the Gap Between the Old and Young
⑤ How City Expansion Could Affect Food Production

25. 다음 도표의 내용과 일치하지 <u>않는</u> 것은?

The Number of Korean and Foreign Visitors to Korean Palaces

Changgyeonggung Palace   Deoksugung Palace

(in thousands)   (in thousands)

	Korean	Foreign	Total
2018	1,716	345	2,061
2019	874	94	968
Overall Total			3,029

	Korean	Foreign	Total
2018	767	77	844
2019	2,414	369	2,783
Overall Total			3,627

※ Note: Details may not add to totals due to rounding.

The tables above show the number of Korean and foreign visitors to Korean palaces in 2018 and 2019. ① For the two-year period of 2018 to 2019, the overall total number of visitors to Deoksugung Palace was larger than that to Changgyeonggung Palace. ② While the total number of visitors to Changgyeonggung Palace decreased from 2018 to 2019, the total number of visitors to Deoksugung Palace increased during the same period. ③ During both 2018 and 2019, the two palaces had more Korean visitors than foreign visitors. ④ In 2018, the number of Korean visitors to Deoksugung Palace was less than half the number of Korean visitors to Changgyeonggung Palace. ⑤ In 2019, the number of Korean visitors to Changgyeonggung Palace was more than 10 times the number of foreign visitors.

26. Patricia Bath에 관한 다음 글의 내용과 일치하지 <u>않는</u> 것은?

Patricia Bath spent her life advocating for eye health. Born in 1942, she was raised in the Harlem area of New York City. She graduated from Howard University's College of Medicine in 1968. It was during her time as a medical intern that she saw that many poor people and Black people were becoming blind because of the lack of eye care. She decided to concentrate on ophthalmology, which is the branch of medicine that works with eye diseases and disorders. As her career progressed, Bath taught students in medical schools and trained other doctors. In 1976, she co-founded the American Institute for the Prevention of Blindness (AiPB) with the basic principle that "eyesight is a basic human right." In the 1980s, Bath began researching the use of lasers in eye treatments. Her research led to her becoming the first African-American female doctor to receive a patent for a medical device.

① 뉴욕 시의 Harlem 지역에서 성장했다.
② 1968년에 의과 대학을 졸업했다.
③ 의과 대학에서 학생을 가르쳤다.
④ 1976년에 AiPB를 단독으로 설립했다.
⑤ 의료 장비 특허를 받았다.

27. Bright Future Walkathon에 관한 다음 안내문의 내용과 일치하지 <u>않는</u> 것은?

Bright Future Walkathon

Sunny Side Foundation is hosting the annual Bright Future Walkathon in support of people in need.

Date & Place
· Date: Saturday, September 25th (Start Time: 9:00 a.m.)
· Place: Green Brook Park

Registration
· Fee: $10
· All registration fees will be donated to local charities.
· Register online at www.ssfwalkathon.com.

Course (Choose one)
· Course A: 3km (all ages welcome)
· Course B: 5km (for ages 15 and older)

Details
· Each participant who completes the course will receive a T-shirt.
· No refund will be made for cancellations.

① 오전 9시에 시작한다.
② 모든 등록비는 기부될 것이다.
③ B 코스는 15세 이상 참가자가 선택할 수 있다.
④ 코스를 완주한 참가자는 티셔츠를 받는다.
⑤ 취소 시 환불이 가능하다.

28. South High School Reunion에 관한 다음 안내문의 내용과 일치하는 것은?

South High School Reunion
Class of 2011

Don't you miss your old friends from high school? Come meet them and remember your high school days!

◎ **When & Where**
  − Saturday, November 6th, 2021 7:00 p.m. − 10:00 p.m.
  − Bay Street Park

◎ **Ticket Reservation (per person)**
  − Ticket price: $40
  − If you reserve by October 15th, the price will be $30.
  − Refunds will only be available until October 31st.

◎ **Main Events**
  − Quiz Show: Answer 50 questions about our old buddies, teachers, and memories. The champion will receive two movie tickets.
  − The barbecue party will start at 8:00 p.m.

◎ **Notes**
  − Dress Code: Wear a red jacket to show your South High School spirit.
  − Feel free to invite up to three friends.

① 오후 7시부터 오후 11시까지 진행된다.
② 11월 1일 이후에 티켓 환불이 가능하다.
③ 퀴즈 쇼 챔피언은 영화 티켓 두 장을 받는다.
④ 정해진 복장 규정은 없다.
⑤ 친구는 네 명까지 초대할 수 있다.

29. 다음 글의 밑줄 친 부분 중, 어법상 틀린 것은? [3점]

Organisms living in the deep sea have adapted to the high pressure by storing water in their bodies, some ① consisting almost entirely of water. Most deep-sea organisms lack gas bladders. They are cold-blooded organisms that adjust their body temperature to their environment, allowing them ② to survive in the cold water while maintaining a low metabolism. Many species lower their metabolism so much that they are able to survive without food for long periods of time, as finding the sparse food ③ that is available expends a lot of energy. Many predatory fish of the deep sea are equipped with enormous mouths and sharp teeth, enabling them to hold on to prey and overpower ④ it. Some predators hunting in the residual light zone of the ocean ⑤ has excellent visual capabilities, while others are able to create their own light to attract prey or a mating partner.

* bladder: (물고기의) 부레

30. 다음 글의 밑줄 친 부분 중, 문맥상 낱말의 쓰임이 적절하지 않은 것은? [3점]

Human innovation in agriculture has unlocked modifications in apples, tulips, and potatoes that never would have been realized through a plant's natural reproductive cycles. This cultivation process has created some of the recognizable vegetables and fruits consumers look for in their grocery stores. However, relying on only a few varieties of cultivated crops can leave humankind ① vulnerable to starvation and agricultural loss if a harvest is destroyed. For example, a million people died over the course of three years during the Irish potato famine because the Irish relied ② primarily on potatoes and milk to create a nutritionally balanced meal. In order to continue its symbiotic relationship with cultivated plants, humanity must allow for biodiversity and recognize the potential ③ benefits that monocultures of plants can introduce. Planting seeds of all kinds, even if they don't seem immediately useful or profitable, can ④ ensure the longevity of those plants for generations to come. A ⑤ balance must be struck between nature's capacity for wildness and humanity's desire for control.

* symbiotic: 공생의

[31~34] 다음 빈칸에 들어갈 말로 가장 적절한 것을 고르시오.

31. _____ works as a general mechanism for the mind, in many ways and across many different areas of life. For example, Brian Wansink, author of *Mindless Eating*, showed that it can also affect our waistlines. We decide how much to eat not simply as a function of how much food we actually consume, but by a comparison to its alternatives. Say we have to choose between three burgers on a menu, at 8, 10, and 12 ounces. We are likely to pick the 10-ounce burger and be perfectly satisfied at the end of the meal. But if our options are instead 10, 12, and 14 ounces, we are likely again to choose the middle one, and again feel equally happy and satisfied with the 12-ounce burger at the end of the meal, even though we ate more, which we did not need in order to get our daily nourishment or in order to feel full.

① Originality
② Relativity
③ Visualization
④ Imitation
⑤ Forgetfulness

32. Philosophical activity is based on the _____. The philosopher's thirst for knowledge is shown through attempts to find better answers to questions even if those answers are never found. At the same time, a philosopher also knows that being too sure can hinder the discovery of other and better possibilities. In a philosophical dialogue, the participants are aware that there are things they do not know or understand. The goal of the dialogue is to arrive at a conception that one did not know or understand beforehand. In traditional schools, where philosophy is not present, students often work with factual questions, they learn specific content listed in the curriculum, and they are not required to solve philosophical problems. However, we know that awareness of what one does not know can be a good way to acquire knowledge. Knowledge and understanding are developed through thinking and talking. Putting things into words makes things clearer. Therefore, students must not be afraid of saying something wrong or talking without first being sure that they are right.

① recognition of ignorance
② emphasis on self-assurance
③ conformity to established values
④ achievements of ancient thinkers
⑤ comprehension of natural phenomena

33. The most powerful emotional experiences are those that bring joy, inspiration, and the kind of love that makes suffering bearable. These emotional experiences are the result of choices and behaviors that result in our feeling happy. When we look at happiness through a spiritual filter, we realize that it does not mean the absence of pain or heartache. Sitting with a sick or injured child, every parent gets to know the profound joy that bubbles over when a son or daughter begins to heal. This is a simple example of how we can be flooded with happiness that becomes more intense as we contrast it with previous suffering. Experiences such as this go into the chemical archives of the limbic system. Each time you experience true happiness, the stored emotions are activated as you are flooded with even deeper joy than you remembered. Your spiritual genes are, in a sense, _____. [3점]

* limbic system: 변연계(인체의 기본적인 감정·욕구 등을 관장하는 신경계)

① your biological treasure map to joy
② your hidden key to lasting friendships
③ a mirror showing your unique personality
④ a facilitator for communication with others
⑤ a barrier to looking back to your joyful childhood

34. Deep-fried foods are tastier than bland foods, and children and adults develop a taste for such foods. Fatty foods cause the brain to release oxytocin, a powerful hormone with a calming, antistress, and relaxing influence, said to be the opposite of adrenaline, into the blood stream; hence the term "comfort foods." We may even be genetically programmed to eat too much. For thousands of years, food was very scarce. Food, along with salt, carbs, and fat, was hard to get, and the more you got, the better. All of these things are necessary nutrients in the human diet, and when their availability was limited, you could never get too much. People also had to hunt down animals or gather plants for their food, and that took a lot of calories. It's different these days. We have food at every turn—lots of those fast-food places and grocery stores with carry-out food. But that ingrained "caveman mentality" says that we can't ever get too much to eat. So craving for "unhealthy" food may _____. [3점]

① actually be our body's attempt to stay healthy
② ultimately lead to harm to the ecosystem
③ dramatically reduce our overall appetite
④ simply be the result of a modern lifestyle
⑤ partly strengthen our preference for fresh food

35. 다음 글에서 전체 흐름과 관계 <u>없는</u> 문장은?

Nurses hold a pivotal position in the mental health care structure and are placed at the centre of the communication network, partly because of their high degree of contact with patients, but also because they have well-developed relationships with other professionals. ① Because of this, nurses play a crucial role in interdisciplinary communication. ② They have a mediating role between the various groups of professionals and the patient and carer. ③ Mental healthcare professionals are legally bound to protect the privacy of their patients, so they may be, rather than unwilling, unable to talk about care needs. ④ This involves translating communication between groups into language that is acceptable and comprehensible to people who have different ways of understanding mental health problems. ⑤ This is a highly sensitive and skilled task, requiring a high level of attention to alternative views and a high level of understanding of communication.

[36~37] 주어진 글 다음에 이어질 글의 순서로 가장 적절한 것을 고르시오.

36.

> When trying to sustain an independent ethos, cultures face a problem of critical mass. No single individual, acting on his or her own, can produce an ethos.

(A) They manage this feat through a combination of trade, to support their way of life, and geographic isolation. The Inuit occupy remote territory, removed from major population centers of Canada. If cross-cultural contact were to become sufficiently close, the Inuit ethos would disappear.

(B) Rather, an ethos results from the interdependent acts of many individuals. This cluster of produced meaning may require some degree of insulation from larger and wealthier outside forces. The Canadian Inuit maintain their own ethos, even though they number no more than twenty-four thousand.

(C) Distinct cultural groups of similar size do not, in the long run, persist in downtown Toronto, Canada, where they come in contact with many outside influences and pursue essentially Western paths for their lives. [3점]

* ethos: 민족(사회) 정신 ** insulation: 단절

① (A) − (C) − (B)
② (B) − (A) − (C)
③ (B) − (C) − (A)
④ (C) − (A) − (B)
⑤ (C) − (B) − (A)

37.

> Heat is lost at the surface, so the more surface area you have relative to volume, the harder you must work to stay warm. That means that little creatures have to produce heat more rapidly than large creatures.

(A) Despite the vast differences in heart rates, nearly all mammals have about 800 million heartbeats in them if they live an average life. The exception is humans. We pass 800 million heartbeats after twenty-five years, and just keep on going for another fifty years and 1.6 billion heartbeats or so.

(B) They must therefore lead completely different lifestyles. An elephant's heart beats just thirty times a minute, a human's sixty, a cow's between fifty and eighty, but a mouse's beats six hundred times a minute — ten times a second. Every day, just to survive, the mouse must eat about 50 percent of its own body weight.

(C) We humans, by contrast, need to consume only about 2 percent of our body weight to supply our energy requirements. One area where animals are curiously uniform is with the number of heartbeats they have in a lifetime. [3점]

① (A) − (C) − (B)　　　② (B) − (A) − (C)
③ (B) − (C) − (A)　　　④ (C) − (A) − (B)
⑤ (C) − (B) − (A)

[38~39] 글의 흐름으로 보아, 주어진 문장이 들어가기에 가장 적절한 곳을 고르시오.

38.

> It is possible to argue, for example, that, today, the influence of books is vastly overshadowed by that of television.

Interest in ideology in children's literature arises from a belief that children's literary texts are culturally formative, and of massive importance educationally, intellectually, and socially. (①) Perhaps more than any other texts, they reflect society as it wishes to be, as it wishes to be seen, and as it unconsciously reveals itself to be, at least to writers. (②) Clearly, literature is not the only socialising agent in the life of children, even among the media. (③) There is, however, a considerable degree of interaction between the two media. (④) Many so-called children's literary classics are televised, and the resultant new book editions strongly suggest that viewing can encourage subsequent reading. (⑤) Similarly, some television series for children are published in book form.

* resultant: 그 결과로 생긴

39.

> There isn't really a way for us to pick up smaller pieces of debris such as bits of paint and metal.

The United Nations asks that all companies remove their satellites from orbit within 25 years after the end of their mission. This is tricky to enforce, though, because satellites can (and often do) fail. (①) To tackle this problem, several companies around the world have come up with novel solutions. (②) These include removing dead satellites from orbit and dragging them back into the atmosphere, where they will burn up. (③) Ways we could do this include using a harpoon to grab a satellite, catching it in a huge net, using magnets to grab it, or even firing lasers to heat up the satellite, increasing its atmospheric drag so that it falls out of orbit. (④) However, these methods are only useful for large satellites orbiting Earth. (⑤) We just have to wait for them to naturally re-enter Earth's atmosphere. [3점]

* harpoon: 작살

40. 다음 글의 내용을 한 문장으로 요약하고자 한다. 빈칸 (A), (B)에 들어갈 말로 가장 적절한 것은?

> Music is used to mold customer experience and behavior. A study was conducted that explored what impact it has on employees. Results from the study indicate that participants who listen to rhythmic music were inclined to cooperate more irrespective of factors like age, gender, and academic background, compared to those who listened to less rhythmic music. This positive boost in the participants' willingness to cooperate was induced regardless of whether they liked the music or not. When people are in a more positive state of mind, they tend to become more agreeable and creative, while those on the opposite spectrum tend to focus on their individual problems rather than giving attention to solving group problems. The rhythm of music has a strong pull on people's behavior. This is because when people listen to music with a steady pulse, they tend to match their actions to the beat. This translates to better teamwork when making decisions because everyone is following one tempo.

↓

> According to the study, the music played in workplaces can lead employees to be _____(A)_____ because the beat of the music creates a _____(B)_____ for working.

　　　(A)　　　　　　　　(B)
① uncomfortable　⋯⋯　competitive mood
② cooperative　⋯⋯　shared rhythm
③ distracted　⋯⋯　shared rhythm
④ attentive　⋯⋯　competitive mood
⑤ indifferent　⋯⋯　disturbing pattern

[41~42] 다음 글을 읽고, 물음에 답하시오.

In this day and age, it is difficult to imagine our lives without email. But how often do we consider the environmental impact of these virtual messages? At first glance, digital messages appear to (a) save resources. Unlike traditional letters, no paper or stamps are needed; nothing has to be packaged or transported. Many of us tend to assume that using email requires little more than the electricity used to power our computers. It's easy to (b) overlook the invisible energy usage involved in running the network — particularly when it comes to sending and storing data.

Every single email in every single inbox in the world is stored on a server. The incredible quantity of data requires huge server farms — gigantic centres with millions of computers which store and transmit information. These servers consume (c) minimum amounts of energy, 24 hours a day, and require countless litres of water, or air conditioning systems, for cooling. The more messages we send, receive and store, the (d) more servers are needed — which means more energy consumed, and more carbon emissions. Clearly, sending and receiving electronic messages in an environmentally conscious manner is by no means enough to stop climate change. But with a few careful, mindful changes, (e) unnecessary CO_2 emissions can easily be avoided.

41. 윗글의 제목으로 가장 적절한 것은?

① Recycling Makes Your Life Even Better
② Eco-friendly Use of Email Saves the Earth
③ Traditional Letters: The Bridge Between Us
④ Email Servers: Records of Past and Present
⑤ Technicians Looking for Alternative Energy

42. 밑줄 친 (a)~(e) 중에서 문맥상 낱말의 쓰임이 적절하지 <u>않은</u> 것은?

① (a)　　② (b)　　③ (c)　　④ (d)　　⑤ (e)

[43~45] 다음 글을 읽고, 물음에 답하시오.

(A)

There once lived a girl named Melanie. She wanted to be a ballet dancer. One day, Melanie's mother saw her dancing with the flawless steps and enthusiasm of a ballerina. "Isn't it strange? Melanie is dancing so well without any formal training!" her mother said. "I must get (a) her professional lessons to help her polish her skill."

(B)

Disappointed, they returned home, tears rolling down Melanie's cheeks. With her confidence and ego hurt, Melanie never danced again. (b) She completed her studies and became a schoolteacher. One day, the ballet instructor at her school was running late, and Melanie was asked to keep an eye on the class so that they wouldn't roam around the school. Once inside the ballet room, she couldn't control herself. She taught the students some steps and kept on dancing for some time. Unaware of time or the people around her, (c) she was lost in her own little world of dancing.

(C)

Just then, the ballet instructor entered the classroom and was surprised to see Melanie's incredible skill. "What a performance!" the instructor said with a sparkle in her eyes. Melanie was embarrassed to see the instructor in front of her. "Sorry, Ma'am!" she said. "For what?" the instructor asked. "You are a true ballerina!" The instructor invited Melanie to accompany (d) her to a ballet training center, and Melanie has never stopped dancing since. Today, she is a world-renowned ballet dancer.

(D)

The following day, Melanie accompanied her mother to a local dance institute. Upon meeting the dance teacher, Mr. Edler, her mother requested to admit Melanie to his institute. The teacher asked Melanie to audition. (e) She was happy and showed him some of her favorite dance steps. However, he wasn't interested in her dance. He was busy with other tasks in the dance room. "You can leave now! The girl is just average. Don't let her waste her time aspiring to be a dancer," he said. Melanie and her mother were shocked to hear this.

43. 주어진 글 (A)에 이어질 내용을 순서에 맞게 배열한 것으로 가장 적절한 것은?

① (B) - (D) - (C)　　　　② (C) - (B) - (D)
③ (C) - (D) - (B)　　　　④ (D) - (B) - (C)
⑤ (D) - (C) - (B)

44. 밑줄 친 (a)~(e) 중에서 가리키는 대상이 나머지 넷과 <u>다른</u> 것은?

① (a)　　② (b)　　③ (c)　　④ (d)　　⑤ (e)

45. 윗글에 관한 내용으로 적절하지 <u>않은</u> 것은?

① 엄마는 Melanie가 발레리나의 열정을 가지고 춤추는 것을 보았다.
② Melanie는 학생들에게 스텝을 가르쳤다.
③ Melanie는 세계적으로 유명한 발레 댄서이다.
④ Melanie는 지역 댄스 학원에 엄마와 동행했다.
⑤ Mr. Edler는 Melanie의 춤에 관심을 보였다.

---

* 확인 사항
ㅇ 답안지의 해당란에 필요한 내용을 정확히 기입(표기)했는지 확인하시오.

18

001 ☐ facility ⓝ 시설
002 ☐ generous ⓐ (무엇을 주는 데 있어서) 후한 [너그러운]
003 ☐ donation ⓝ 기부, 기증
004 ☐ foundation ⓝ 재단
005 ☐ renovate ⓥ 수리하다, 보수하다
006 ☐ outdated ⓐ 구식인, 시대에 뒤처진
007 ☐ auditorium ⓝ 강당
008 ☐ inform (~에게 …을) 알리다
009 ☐ repair ⓝ 수리, 보수
010 ☐ brief ⓐ 짧은, 잠시 동안의
011 ☐ inconvenience ⓝ 불편, 폐

19

012 ☐ interrupt ⓥ 끼어들다, 간섭하다
013 ☐ be supposed to ⓥ ~해야 한다, ~하기로 되어 있다
014 ☐ forgive ⓥ 용서하다
015 ☐ occasion ⓝ 경우, 때
016 ☐ for the time being 당분간은, 지금 당장은
017 ☐ anxious ⓐ 걱정하는
018 ☐ shocked ⓐ 충격을 받은
019 ☐ grateful ⓐ 고마워하는
020 ☐ indifferent ⓐ 무관심한
021 ☐ envious ⓐ 부러워하는

20

022 ☐ guidance ⓝ (특히 연장자에 의한) 지도 [안내]
023 ☐ embark on ~에 착수하다
024 ☐ journey ⓝ 여정, 여행
025 ☐ leave ~ to one's devices ~을 자기 뜻대로 하게 내버려두다
026 ☐ instinctively ⓐⓓ 본능적으로
027 ☐ report ⓝ 성적표
028 ☐ arena ⓝ 경기장, 무대
029 ☐ a multitude of 다수의, 아주 많은
030 ☐ interpersonal ⓐ 대인 관계에 관련된
031 ☐ inherently ⓐⓓ 본래, 선천적으로
032 ☐ minority ⓝ (한 사회·국가 내의) 소수집단
033 ☐ nurture ⓥ 육성하다
034 ☐ consciously ⓐⓓ 의식적으로
035 ☐ continuously ⓐⓓ 계속해서
036 ☐ throughout ⓟⓡⓔⓟ ~동안 쭉, 내내

21

037 ☐ exhibit ⓥ (감정 등을) 보이다[드러내다]
038 ☐ paradoxical ⓐ 역설적인
039 ☐ mutually exclusive 상호 배타적인
040 ☐ contradictory ⓐ 모순적인
041 ☐ relevant to ~에 관련 있는
042 ☐ mastery ⓝ 숙달, 통달
043 ☐ prevailing ⓐ 만연한, 널리 퍼진
044 ☐ established ⓐ 확립된, 자리를 잡은
045 ☐ newcomer ⓝ 신입자, 신참
046 ☐ naive ⓐ 모자란, 순진한
047 ☐ accelerate ⓥ 가속화하다
048 ☐ short-term 단기의, 단기적인
049 ☐ long-term 장기의, 장기적인
050 ☐ challenging ⓐ 힘드는, 까다로운
051 ☐ temporary ⓐ 일시적인, 임시의

052 ☐ permanent ⓐ 영구적인
053 ☐ utilize ⓥ 활용하다
054 ☐ rookie ⓝ 초보자
055 ☐ simultaneously ⓐⓓ 동시에

22

056 ☐ official ⓝ 공무원
057 ☐ wrongly ⓐⓓ 잘못되게, 그릇되게
058 ☐ lead back to ~로 되돌리다
059 ☐ glory ⓝ 영광, 영예
060 ☐ massive ⓐ 거대한, 큰
061 ☐ construction ⓝ 건설
062 ☐ light rail 경(輕)철도
063 ☐ convention center 전시 장소나 숙박 시설이 집중된 지역 또는 종합 빌딩
064 ☐ housing ⓝ 주택 (공급)
065 ☐ exception ⓝ 예외
066 ☐ tidal ⓐ (바다) 조수의
067 ☐ ignore ⓥ 무시하다
068 ☐ real estate 부동산 (중개업)
069 ☐ dress up (보기 좋게 또는 달라 보이게) ~을 꾸미다
070 ☐ decline ⓥ 쇠퇴하다
071 ☐ underlying ⓐ 기저에 있는, 근본적인
072 ☐ hallmark ⓝ 특징
073 ☐ infrastructure ⓝ 기반 시설
074 ☐ folly ⓝ 어리석음, 판단력 부족
075 ☐ renewal ⓝ 재생, 부활

23

076 ☐ marine ⓐ 바다의, 해양의
077 ☐ oyster ⓝ (바다) 굴
078 ☐ marsh ⓝ 습지
079 ☐ deliberately ⓐⓓ 의도적으로
080 ☐ erosion ⓝ 침식
081 ☐ fish and shellfish 어패류
082 ☐ intentionally ⓐⓓ 의도적으로
083 ☐ threat ⓝ 위협
084 ☐ ecosystem ⓝ 생태계
085 ☐ livelihood ⓝ 생계 (수단)
086 ☐ salmon ⓝ 연어
087 ☐ rear ⓥ 기르다, 재배하다
088 ☐ recover ⓥ (분실물·도난물 등을) 되찾다 [찾아내다]
089 ☐ saltwater ⓝ 해수, 바닷물
090 ☐ freshwater ⓝ 담수, 민물
091 ☐ recreational ⓐ 오락의, 여가의
092 ☐ spread ⓥ 퍼뜨리다
093 ☐ invasive ⓐ 침입의
094 ☐ seaweed ⓝ 해초
095 ☐ discard ⓥ 버리다
096 ☐ colonize ⓥ 식민지로 만들다
097 ☐ biodiversity ⓝ 생물의 다양성
098 ☐ potential ⓐ 잠재적인
099 ☐ ecotourism ⓝ 생태 관광

24

100 ☐ fancy ⓐ 화려한, 고급의
101 ☐ high-rise ⓝ 고층 건물
102 ☐ headquarter ⓝ 본부
103 ☐ souvenir ⓝ 기념품
104 ☐ peddler ⓝ 행상인, 판매원

105 ☐ gross ⓐ 혐오스러운, 징그러운
106 ☐ landfill ⓝ 쓰레기 매립지
107 ☐ temporarily ⓐⓓ 일시적으로
108 ☐ commission ⓥ 의뢰하다
109 ☐ significant ⓐ 중대한
110 ☐ public work 공공사업
111 ☐ installation ⓝ 설치 미술품
112 ☐ wheat field 밀밭
113 ☐ gleaming ⓐ 반짝이는, 빛나는
114 ☐ confrontation ⓝ 대립
115 ☐ acre ⓝ 에이커(약 4,050평방미터에 해당하는 크기의 땅)
116 ☐ amber ⓐ 호박색의, 황색의
117 ☐ grain ⓝ 곡물
118 ☐ atop ⓟⓡⓔⓟ 꼭대기, 맨 위
119 ☐ irrigation ⓝ 관개, 물 대기
120 ☐ thriving ⓐ 무성한, 잘 자라는
121 ☐ nourish ⓥ 풍요롭게 하다, 영양분을 공급하다
122 ☐ fade away 사라지다, 꺼지다
123 ☐ skyscraper ⓝ (초)고층 건물
124 ☐ narrow the gap 격차를 좁히다
125 ☐ expansion ⓝ 확장, 팽창

25

126 ☐ palace ⓝ 궁, 궁전
127 ☐ overall ⓐ 전반적인
128 ☐ detail ⓝ 세부 사항
129 ☐ round ⓥ 반올림[반내림]하다
130 ☐ larger (large의 비교급) 더 큰
131 ☐ decrease ⓥ 줄다, 감소하다
132 ☐ increase ⓥ 늘다, 증가하다
133 ☐ period ⓝ 기간

26

134 ☐ advocate for ~을 옹호하다
135 ☐ graduate ⓥ 졸업하다, (학사) 학위를 받다
136 ☐ intern ⓝ 인턴, 수련의
137 ☐ lack ⓝ 부족, 결여
138 ☐ concentrate on ~에 집중하다
139 ☐ ophthalmology ⓝ 안과학
140 ☐ branch ⓝ (지식의) 분야
141 ☐ disease ⓝ 질병, 질환
142 ☐ disorder ⓝ 장애, 이상
143 ☐ progress ⓥ 진척하다, 진행되다
144 ☐ prevention ⓝ 예방
145 ☐ blindness ⓝ 시각 장애
146 ☐ principle ⓝ 원칙, 주의, 신조
147 ☐ treatment ⓝ 치료
148 ☐ patent ⓝ 특허
149 ☐ medical device 의료 기기

27

150 ☐ walkathon ⓝ 걷기 대회, 장거리 경보
151 ☐ annual ⓐ 매년의, 연례의
152 ☐ in support of ~을 후원하여
153 ☐ in need 도움이 필요한, 불우한
154 ☐ registration ⓝ 등록
155 ☐ donate ⓥ 기부하다
156 ☐ charity ⓝ 자선 단체
157 ☐ complete ⓥ 완료하다, 끝마치다
158 ☐ cancellation ⓝ 취소

28

159 ☐ reunion ⓝ 모임, 재결합
160 ☐ reserve ⓥ 예약하다
161 ☐ refund ⓝ 환불
162 ☐ buddy ⓝ 친구
163 ☐ dress code 복장 규정
164 ☐ wear ⓥ (옷 등을) 입고있다
165 ☐ spirit ⓝ 정신
166 ☐ feel free to 자유롭게 ~하다
167 ☐ invite ⓥ 초대하다
168 ☐ up to ~까지

29

169 ☐ store ⓥ 저장하다, 보관하다
170 ☐ entirely ⓐⓓ 전적으로
171 ☐ body temperature 체온
172 ☐ metabolism ⓝ 신진대사
173 ☐ sparse ⓐ 드문, (밀도가) 희박한
174 ☐ expend ⓥ (돈·시간·에너지를) 쏟다[들이다]
175 ☐ predatory ⓐ 포식성의
176 ☐ be equipped with ~을 갖추다
177 ☐ enormous ⓐ 거대한
178 ☐ enable ⓥ ~을 할 수 있게 하다
179 ☐ hold on to ~을 계속 보유하다
180 ☐ overpower ⓥ 제압하다, 압도하다
181 ☐ predator ⓝ 포식자, 포식 동물
182 ☐ residual ⓐ 잔여의
183 ☐ attract ⓥ 끌어들이다

30

184 ☐ unlock ⓥ ~을 열다
185 ☐ modification ⓝ 개량, 수정
186 ☐ reproductive ⓐ 번식의, 재생의
187 ☐ cultivation ⓝ 재배, 경작
188 ☐ recognizable ⓐ 알아보기 쉬운
189 ☐ variety ⓝ 품종, 종류
190 ☐ cultivate ⓥ (식물·작물을) 재배하다
191 ☐ crop ⓝ 작물
192 ☐ humankind ⓝ 인류, 인간
193 ☐ vulnerable ⓐ 취약한
194 ☐ starvation ⓝ 기아, 굶주림
195 ☐ loss ⓝ 손실, 손해
196 ☐ harvest ⓝ 추수, 수확
197 ☐ destroy ⓥ 망치다, 파괴하다
198 ☐ famine ⓝ 기근
199 ☐ nutritionally ⓐⓓ 영양학적으로
200 ☐ humanity ⓝ 인류, 인간
201 ☐ monoculture ⓝ 단일 경작
202 ☐ profitable ⓐ 수익성 있는
203 ☐ longevity ⓝ 오래 감, 장수
204 ☐ generations to come 후대, 후세
205 ☐ strike a balance 균형을 유지하다
206 ☐ wildness ⓝ 야생

31

207 ☐ mechanism ⓝ (목적을 달성하기 위한) 방법, 메커니즘
208 ☐ waistline ⓝ 허리둘레
209 ☐ function ⓝ (수학) 함수
210 ☐ consume ⓥ 먹다, 마시다
211 ☐ comparison ⓝ 비교
212 ☐ alternative ⓝ 대안

213 □ satisfied ⓐ 만족하는
214 □ equally ⓐ𝖽 똑같이, 동일하게
215 □ nourishment ⓝ 영양분
216 □ originality ⓝ 독창성
217 □ relativity ⓝ 상대성
218 □ forgetfulness ⓝ 건망증, 잘 잊어버림

32
219 □ philosophical ⓐ 철학적인
220 □ philosopher ⓝ 철학자
221 □ thirst ⓝ 갈망
222 □ hinder ⓥ 방해하다
223 □ conception ⓝ 생각
224 □ beforehand ⓐ𝖽 미리, 사전에
225 □ factual ⓐ 사실적인
226 □ specific ⓐ 특정한
227 □ acquire ⓥ 습득하다
228 □ put into words 말로 옮기다
229 □ recognition ⓝ 인식
230 □ ignorance ⓝ 무지
231 □ emphasis ⓝ 강조
232 □ self-assurance ⓝ 자기 확신
233 □ conformity ⓝ 순응
234 □ thinker ⓝ 철학자, 사상가
235 □ comprehension ⓝ 이해
236 □ phenomenon ⓝ 현상

33
237 □ emotional ⓐ 감정의, 정서의
238 □ inspiration ⓝ 영감
239 □ suffering ⓝ (마음의) 고통, 괴로움
240 □ bearable ⓐ 견딜 수 있는
241 □ spiritual ⓐ 정신적인
242 □ absence ⓝ 부재
243 □ heartache ⓝ 심적 고통
244 □ injured ⓐ 다친, 부상을 입은
245 □ profound ⓐ 깊은
246 □ bubble over 벅차오르다
247 □ be flooded with ~로 넘쳐나다
248 □ intense ⓐ 강렬한
249 □ contrast A with B A와 B를 대조하다
250 □ archive ⓝ 기록 보관소
251 □ biological ⓐ 생물학의
252 □ treasure ⓝ 보물
253 □ lasting ⓐ 지속되는
254 □ personality ⓝ 성격
255 □ facilitator ⓝ 촉진제
256 □ barrier ⓝ (어떤 일에 대한) 장애물[장벽]
257 □ look back to ~을 돌아보다
258 □ joyful ⓐ 기쁨을 주는

34
259 □ deep-fried 튀긴
260 □ tasty ⓐ (풍미가 강하고) 맛있는
261 □ bland ⓐ 싱거운, 담백한, 특징 없는
262 □ fatty ⓐ 지방이 많은
263 □ release ⓥ 분비하다
264 □ calming ⓐ 진정시키는
265 □ antistress ⓐ 스트레스 예방의, 항 스트레스의
266 □ influence ⓝ 효과, 영향
267 □ opposite ⓝ 반대되는 것

268 □ adrenaline ⓝ 아드레날린, 흥분시키는 것
269 □ comfort food 위안을 주는 음식, 기분 좋게 해주는 음식
270 □ genetically ⓐ𝖽 유전적으로
271 □ scarce ⓐ 드문
272 □ nutrient ⓝ 영양소[분]
273 □ availability ⓝ 이용 가능성
274 □ gather ⓥ 모으다
275 □ grocery store 식료품점, 슈퍼마켓
276 □ carry-out food 포장음식
277 □ ingrained ⓐ 뿌리 깊은
278 □ caveman ⓝ 원시인
279 □ mentality ⓝ 사고방식
280 □ craving ⓝ 갈망, 열망
281 □ ultimately ⓐ𝖽 궁극적으로
282 □ lead to ~로 이어지다
283 □ dramatically ⓐ𝖽 극적으로
284 □ appetite ⓝ 식욕
285 □ strengthen ⓥ 강화하다
286 □ preference ⓝ 선호

35
287 □ pivotal ⓐ 핵심적인
288 □ care ⓝ 돌봄, 관리
289 □ structure ⓝ 구조, 체계
290 □ centre ⓝ 중심, 가운데
291 □ well-developed 잘 발달된 [다듬어진]
292 □ crucial ⓐ 중요한
293 □ interdisciplinary ⓐ 여러 학문 분야가 관련된, 학제적인
294 □ mediate ⓥ 중재하다
295 □ legally ⓐ𝖽 법적으로
296 □ be bound to ~하게 되어 있다
297 □ unwilling ⓐ ~하려 하지 않는, 내키지 않는
298 □ translate ⓥ 번역하다
299 □ acceptable ⓐ 용인되는
300 □ comprehensible ⓐ 이해 가능한
301 □ sensitive ⓐ 민감한, 예민한
302 □ skilled ⓐ 숙련된, 노련한
303 □ alternative ⓐ 대안이 되는

36
304 □ sustain ⓥ 지속하다
305 □ independent ⓐ 독립된
306 □ critical mass 임계 질량
307 □ feat ⓝ 위업, 공적
308 □ combination ⓝ 조합
309 □ trade ⓝ 거래, 무역
310 □ geographic ⓐ 지리적인
311 □ isolation ⓝ 고립
312 □ occupy ⓥ 차지하다, 점유하다
313 □ remote ⓐ 외진, 외딴
314 □ territory ⓝ 지역, 영토
315 □ cross-cultural 여러 문화가 섞인
316 □ sufficiently ⓐ𝖽 충분히
317 □ cluster ⓝ 군집, 무리
318 □ insulation ⓝ 단절, 절연
319 □ distinct ⓐ 구별되는, 다른
320 □ persist ⓥ 지속하다
321 □ come in contact with ~와 접촉하다
322 □ pursue ⓥ 추구하다
323 □ path ⓝ (행동) 계획[방식]

37
324 □ relative to ~에 비해
325 □ volume ⓝ 부피, 체적
326 □ creature ⓝ 생명이 있는 존재, 생물
327 □ vast ⓐ 큰, 방대한
328 □ nearly ⓐ𝖽 거의
329 □ heartbeat ⓝ 심장 박동
330 □ completely ⓐ𝖽 완전히
331 □ requirement ⓝ 필요, 요구
332 □ supply ⓥ 공급[제공]하다
333 □ curiously ⓐ𝖽 기묘하게도
334 □ uniform ⓐ 동일한

38
335 □ vastly ⓐ𝖽 크게
336 □ overshadow ⓥ 그늘을 드리우다, 가리다, 빛을 잃게 하다
337 □ ideology ⓝ 이데올로기, 이념
338 □ literature ⓝ 문학
339 □ arise from ~에서 발생하다
340 □ literary ⓐ 문학의
341 □ formative ⓐ 모양을 만드는, 형성하는
342 □ intellectually ⓐ𝖽 지적으로
343 □ reflect ⓥ 반영하다
344 □ unconsciously ⓐ𝖽 무의식적으로
345 □ reveal ⓥ 드러내다
346 □ socialise ⓥ 사회화시키다
347 □ considerable ⓐ 상당한
348 □ so-called ⓐ 소위 말하는
349 □ televise ⓥ 텔레비전으로 방송하다
350 □ resultant ⓐ 그 결과로 생긴, 그에 따른
351 □ subsequent ⓐ 뒤이은

39
352 □ debris ⓝ 잔해
353 □ satellite ⓝ 인공위성
354 □ orbit ⓝ 궤도
355 □ mission ⓝ 임무
356 □ tricky ⓐ 까다로운
357 □ enforce ⓥ 시행하다
358 □ tackle ⓥ 다루다, 해결하다
359 □ come up with ~을 떠올리다
360 □ novel ⓐ 새로운, 신기한
361 □ drag ⓝ 항력, 끌림
362 □ atmosphere ⓝ (지구의) 대기
363 □ burn up 타 버리다
364 □ magnet ⓝ 자석, 자철
365 □ heat up 데우다, 열을 가하다
366 □ fall out of ~을 빠져나오다, 떨어져 나오다
367 □ method ⓝ 방법

40
368 □ mold ⓥ 형성하다, 빚다
369 □ employee ⓝ 직원
370 □ indicate ⓥ 보여주다
371 □ rhythmic ⓐ 리드미컬한, 리듬감이 있는
372 □ be inclined to ~하는 경향이 있다
373 □ irrespective of ~와 관계없이
374 □ academic background 학력
375 □ boost ⓝ 증진
376 □ willingness ⓝ (기꺼이) ~하려는 마음
377 □ induce ⓥ 유발하다

378 □ regardless of ~와 상관없이
379 □ agreeable ⓐ 기분 좋은, 선뜻 동의하는
380 □ spectrum ⓝ 스펙트럼, 빛 띠
381 □ rhythm ⓝ 리듬
382 □ steady ⓐ 고정적인, 한결같은
383 □ pulse ⓝ 리듬, 맥박
384 □ beat ⓝ 박자, 운율
385 □ translate to ~로 이해되다, 해석되다
386 □ tempo ⓝ 박자, 속도
387 □ workplace ⓝ 직장, 업무 현장
388 □ distracted ⓐ 산만해진
389 □ disturbing ⓐ 골치 아픈, 불안감을 주는

41~42
390 □ impact ⓝ 영향
391 □ virtual ⓐ 가상의
392 □ at first glance 언뜻 보기에는
393 □ package ⓥ 포장하다
394 □ transport ⓥ 운송하다, 수송하다
395 □ overlook ⓥ 간과하다
396 □ invisible ⓐ 눈에 보이지 않는
397 □ particularly ⓐ𝖽 특히
398 □ when it comes to ~에 관해서
399 □ incredible ⓐ (너무 좋거나 커서) 믿어지지 않을 정도인
400 □ quantity ⓝ 양
401 □ huge ⓐ 거대한
402 □ gigantic ⓐ 거대한
403 □ transmit ⓥ 전송하다
404 □ consume ⓥ 소비하다, 소모하다
405 □ minimum ⓐ 최소한의, 최저의
406 □ countless ⓐ 무수히 많은
407 □ air conditioning 에어컨
408 □ cooling ⓝ 냉각
409 □ emission ⓝ (빛·열·가스 등의) 배출
410 □ environmentally conscious 환경 의식이 있는
411 □ mindful ⓐ 의식하는, 유념하는
412 □ record ⓝ 기록

43~45
413 □ flawless ⓐ 흠 없는
414 □ enthusiasm ⓝ 열정
415 □ formal ⓐ 공식적인, 형식적인
416 □ polish ⓥ 연마하다, 다듬다
417 □ cheek ⓝ 볼, 뺨
418 □ confidence ⓝ 자신감
419 □ ego ⓝ 자아, 에고
420 □ instructor ⓝ 강사
421 □ run late 늦다
422 □ roam ⓥ 이리저리 돌아다니다, 배회하다
423 □ control oneself 자제하다, 통제하다
424 □ unaware ⓐ 알지 못하는
425 □ sparkle ⓝ 반짝거림
426 □ embarrassed ⓐ 당황한
427 □ accompany ⓥ 동반하다, 데리고 가다
428 □ world-renowned ⓐ 세계적으로 유명한
429 □ request ⓥ 요청하다
430 □ admit ⓥ (입학 등을) 받아주다
431 □ average ⓐ 평균의
432 □ waste ⓥ 낭비하다
433 □ aspire ⓥ 열망하다, 바라다

14회

● 채점 : 맞은 개수 _____ / 80

TEST A-B 각 단어의 뜻을 [A] 영어는 우리말로, [B] 우리말은 영어로 쓰시오.

A	English	Korean
01	interrupt	
02	reflect	
03	release	
04	strengthen	
05	sustain	
06	intentionally	
07	induce	
08	residual	
09	challenging	
10	famine	
11	alternative	
12	relativity	
13	curiously	
14	embarrassed	
15	orbit	
16	intense	
17	prevention	
18	conformity	
19	confrontation	
20	vastly	

B	Korean	English
01	취소	
02	항력, 끌림	
03	계속해서	
04	~와 상관없이	
05	무수히 많은	
06	오래 감, 장수	
07	차지하다, 점유하다	
08	핵심적인	
09	위협	
10	특징	
11	무지	
12	공식적인, 형식적인	
13	~에 비해	
14	열망하다, 바라다	
15	기념품	
16	거대한	
17	전적으로	
18	의뢰하다	
19	시행하다	
20	부재	

▶ A-D 정답 : 해설편 149쪽

TEST C-D 각 단어의 뜻을 골라 기호를 쓰시오.

C	English		Korean
01	unconsciously	( )	ⓐ 진정시키는
02	concentrate on	( )	ⓑ 가속화하다
03	decline	( )	ⓒ 증진
04	virtual	( )	ⓓ 중요한
05	crucial	( )	ⓔ ~을 돌아보다
06	mentality	( )	ⓕ 완전히
07	scarce	( )	ⓖ 예외
08	calming	( )	ⓗ 습득하다
09	simultaneously	( )	ⓘ 지속하다
10	accelerate	( )	ⓙ 사고방식
11	contradictory	( )	ⓚ 방해하다
12	look back to	( )	ⓛ 무의식적으로
13	overlook	( )	ⓜ 모순적인
14	persist	( )	ⓝ 드문
15	boost	( )	ⓞ 동시에
16	spiritual	( )	ⓟ 간과하다
17	acquire	( )	ⓠ 쇠퇴하다
18	hinder	( )	ⓡ 가상의
19	exception	( )	ⓢ 정신적인
20	completely	( )	ⓣ ~에 집중하다

D	Korean		English
01	취약한	( )	ⓐ sufficiently
02	이해 가능한	( )	ⓑ bearable
03	환불	( )	ⓒ comprehensible
04	유전적으로	( )	ⓓ requirement
05	~와 관계없이	( )	ⓔ exception
06	본능적으로	( )	ⓕ indifferent
07	불편, 폐	( )	ⓖ geographic
08	~에서 발생하다	( )	ⓗ inconvenience
09	새로운, 신기한	( )	ⓘ predatory
10	거대한	( )	ⓙ instinctively
11	예외	( )	ⓚ invasive
12	충분히	( )	ⓛ enormous
13	침입의	( )	ⓜ irrigation
14	지리적인	( )	ⓝ novel
15	포식성의	( )	ⓞ irrespective of
16	무관심한	( )	ⓟ prevailing
17	관개, 물 대기	( )	ⓠ refund
18	만연한, 널리 퍼진	( )	ⓡ genetically
19	견딜 수 있는	( )	ⓢ arise from
20	필요, 요구	( )	ⓣ vulnerable

18. 다음 글의 목적으로 가장 적절한 것은?

Dear Residents,

We truly value and appreciate all of our residents, including those with pets. We believe that allowing people to live with their pets enriches their lives. While we encourage you to enjoy your pets, we also want to ensure that you do not do so at the expense of your neighbors or your community. We have received reports that some residents have been disturbed by noise from dogs barking. Excessive barking by dogs disrupts everyone within hearing, particularly those who are elderly or sick or who have small children. We kindly ask that you keep your dogs' noise levels to a minimum. Thank you for your assistance with this.

Regards,

Conway Forest Apartments Management Office

① 반려견이 짖는 소리를 최소화 해줄 것을 요청하려고
② 아파트 내 반려동물 출입 가능 구역을 안내하려고
③ 아파트 공사로 인한 소음 발생에 대해 사과하려고
④ 반려견 대소변 관련 민원처리 결과를 공지하려고
⑤ 반려동물과 외출 시 목줄 사용을 당부하려고

19. 다음 글의 상황에 나타난 분위기로 가장 적절한 것은?

Meghan looked up and saw angry gray clouds rolling across the water. The storm had turned and was coming her way. She stood up and reached for her sandals. That's when she spotted the dog splashing around in the middle of the lake. At first she thought he was playing. She watched for a second or two, then realized the dog wasn't playing. He was trying to keep from going under. With her heart pounding like a trip-hammer, she ran into the water and started swimming toward the dog. Before she got to the dog, the rain started. She saw the dog, and seconds later he was gone. She pushed forward frantically, her arms reaching out in long strokes, her legs kicking harder and faster.

① grave and solemn
② tense and urgent
③ calm and peaceful
④ festive and lively
⑤ monotonous and boring

20. 다음 글에서 필자가 주장하는 바로 가장 적절한 것은?

Children may develop imaginary friends around three or four years of age. Imaginary friends are only a concern if children replace all social interactions with pretend friends. As long as children are developing socially with other children, then imaginary friends are beneficial. Parents often will need reassurance about imaginary friends; they should be respectful of the pretend friends, as well as of their child. Children who create imaginary friends should never be teased, humiliated, or ridiculed in any way. Parents may tire of including the friends in daily activities, such as setting an extra plate at dinner, but they should be reassured that the imaginary friends stage will pass. Until then, imaginary friends should be respected and welcomed by parents because they signify a child's developing imagination.

① 아이들의 상상력을 자극하는 질문을 해야 한다.
② 식사 시간을 자녀와 대화하는 기회로 삼아야 한다.
③ 사회성 발달을 위해 단체 활동에 적극 참여해야 한다.
④ 자녀의 노력을 구체적으로 칭찬하는 부모가 되어야 한다.
⑤ 부모는 자녀의 가상의 친구를 존중하고 받아들여야 한다.

21. 밑줄 친 got "colder"가 다음 글에서 의미하는 바로 가장 적절한 것은? [3점]

If creators knew when they were on their way to fashioning a masterpiece, their work would progress only forward: they would halt their idea-generation efforts as they struck gold. But in fact, they backtrack, returning to versions that they had earlier discarded as inadequate. In Beethoven's most celebrated work, the Fifth Symphony, he scrapped the conclusion of the first movement because it felt too short, only to come back to it later. Had Beethoven been able to distinguish an extraordinary from an ordinary work, he would have accepted his composition immediately as a hit. When Picasso was painting his famous *Guernica* in protest of fascism, he produced 79 different drawings. Many of the images in the painting were based on his early sketches, not the later variations. If Picasso could judge his creations as he produced them, he would get consistently "warmer" and use the later drawings. But in reality, it was just as common that he got "colder."

① moved away from the desired outcome
② lost his reputation due to public criticism
③ became unwilling to follow new art trends
④ appreciated others' artwork with less enthusiasm
⑤ imitated masters' styles rather than creating his own

22. 다음 글의 요지로 가장 적절한 것은?

The psychology professor Dr. Kelly Lambert's research explains that keeping what she calls the "effort-driven rewards circuit" well engaged helps you deal with challenges in the environment around you or in your emotional life more effectively and efficiently. Doing hands-on activities that produce results you can see and touch — such as knitting a scarf, cooking from scratch, or tending a garden — fuels the reward circuit so that it functions optimally. She argues that the documented increase in depression among Americans may be directly correlated with the decline of purposeful physical activity. When we work with our hands, it increases the release of the neurochemicals dopamine and serotonin, both responsible for generating positive emotions. She also explains that working with our hands gives us a greater sense of control over our environment and more connection to the world around us. All of which contributes to a reduction in stress and anxiety and builds resilience against the onset of depression.

① 긍정적인 감정은 타인에게 쉽게 전이된다.
② 감정 조절은 대인 관계 능력의 핵심 요소이다.
③ 수작업 활동은 정신 건강에 도움을 줄 수 있다.
④ 과도한 신체활동은 호르몬 분비의 불균형을 초래한다.
⑤ 취미 활동을 통해 여러 분야의 사람들을 만날 수 있다.

23. 다음 글의 주제로 가장 적절한 것은?

It has long been held that the capacity for laughter is a peculiarly human characteristic. The witty Lucian of Samosata (2nd century A.D.) noted that the way to distinguish a man from a donkey is that one laughs and the other does not. In all societies humor is important not only in individual communication but also as a molding force of social groups, reinforcing their norms and regulating behavior. "Each particular time, each era, in fact each moment, has its own condition and themes for laughter . . . because of the major preoccupations, concerns, interests, activities, relations, and mode prevailing at the time." The ultimate goal of anyone who studies another culture, such as ancient Greece, is to understand the people themselves who were more than the sum total of monuments, historical incidents, or social groupings. One way to approach this goal directly is to study the culture's humor. As Goethe aptly observed: "Men show their characters in nothing more clearly than in what they think laughable."

① typical process of cultural assimilation
② function of laughter in building friendship
③ educational need for intercultural competence
④ roles of humor in criticizing social problems
⑤ humor as a tool for understanding a culture

24. 다음 글의 제목으로 가장 적절한 것은?

Since the early 1980s, Black Friday has been a kind of unofficial U.S. holiday marking the beginning of the holiday season and, consequently, the most profitable time for retailers in the year. But in recent years, a new movement has come to light, adding a more ecological philosophy. The movement is called Green Friday, and it seeks to raise awareness about the damage that Black Friday brings to the environment. Think of the carbon emissions caused by driving to the mall, the shipping of millions of items around the world, the plastic waste produced by packaging, and even the long-term waste produced by mindlessly buying things we don't need. Green Friday is about changing the way we see this day and switching our mindset from "buy, buy, buy" to finding alternative ways to give gifts during the holiday season so we don't cause further damage to the Earth. Even if only a small percentage of the population makes the switch, it'll mean great things for the environment.

① Compare Deals, Save Money
② Turning Black Friday Green
③ Online Shops for Green Consumers
④ Marketing Tricks Used on Black Friday
⑤ What Makes You Spend Beyond Your Budget?

25. 다음 도표의 내용과 일치하지 <u>않는</u> 것은?

Materials Landfilled as Municipal Waste in the U.S.

(unit: thousand of tons)

2000

Material	Amount
Paper	40,450
Plastics	19,950
Metals	10,290
Wood	9,910
Glass	8,100
Textiles	6,280
Other Materials	6,360
Total	101,340

2017

Material	Amount
Plastics	26,820
Paper	18,350
Metals	13,800
Wood	12,140
Textiles	11,150
Glass	6,870
Other Materials	7,930
Total	97,060

※ Note: Details may not add to totals due to rounding.

The tables above show the materials landfilled as municipal waste in the U.S. in 2000 and 2017. ① The total amount of materials landfilled in 2017 was smaller than in 2000. ② While paper was the material most landfilled as municipal waste in 2000, plastics were the most landfilled material in 2017. ③ In 2000, metals and wood were the third and fourth most landfilled materials, respectively, and this remained the same in 2017. ④ More glass was landfilled than textiles in 2000, but more textiles were landfilled than glass in 2017. ⑤ The amount of textiles landfilled in 2017 was more than twice that in 2000.

26. Vera Rubin에 관한 다음 글의 내용과 일치하지 <u>않는</u> 것은?

Vera Rubin was born in 1928 in Philadelphia and grew up in Washington, D.C. It was in Washington, D.C. that she started to develop an interest in astronomy. She earned a master's degree from Cornell University in 1951 and a doctor's degree from Georgetown University in 1954. At the age of 22, she made headlines and shocked scientists with her theory about the motion of galaxies. In 1965, Rubin started as a researcher at the Carnegie Institution and became the first woman permitted to use the Hale Telescope. She made groundbreaking observations that provided evidence for the existence of a vast amount of dark matter in the universe. She won many prizes for her work, but never the Nobel Prize. She died in 2016 and is celebrated as someone who worked to lead the way for women in astronomy and physics.

① Washington, D.C.에서 천문학에 대한 관심을 키우기 시작했다.
② 1954년에 Georgetown 대학교에서 박사 학위를 받았다.
③ 은하의 움직임에 관한 이론으로 과학자들을 놀라게 했다.
④ Hale 망원경을 사용하도록 허가받은 최초의 여성이었다.
⑤ 노벨상을 포함하여 많은 상을 받았다.

27. 2020 Game-Coding Workshop에 관한 다음 안내문의 내용과 일치하지 <u>않는</u> 것은?

2020 Game-Coding Workshop

Turn your children's love for computer games into a skill. This game-coding workshop will teach them to use block-based coding software to create their own games!

□ **Date & Time**
· Saturday, December 12th, 1:00 pm to 3:00 pm

□ **Registration**
· Closes Friday, November 27th
· Participation fee is $30 (free for Lansing Kids Club members).
· Sign up in person at Kid's Coding Center or online at www.lanskidscoding.com.

□ **Requirements**
· Open only to children 9 to 12 years old
· Laptops will not be provided. Participants must bring their own.
· No prior coding knowledge is required.

Please visit our website for more information.

① 토요일 오후에 진행된다.
② Lansing 키즈 클럽 회원은 참가비가 무료이다.
③ 온라인 등록이 가능하다.
④ 참가자들에게 노트북 컴퓨터가 제공된다.
⑤ 코딩에 대한 사전 지식이 필요 없다.

28. Young Filmmakers Contest에 관한 다음 안내문의 내용과 일치하는 것은?

Young Filmmakers Contest

Join our annual Young Filmmakers Contest, and demonstrate your filmmaking skills!

◇ **Contest Rules**
· Contest is open only to high school students.
· Total running time of each entry must be less than fifteen minutes.
· Participants must choose one of the following two topics: Family | Friendship

◇ **Submission**
· Submit by Wednesday, September 16th.
· Do not mail entries to our offices. Only submissions uploaded to our official Young Filmmakers Contest website will be accepted.

◇ **Prizes**
· 1st place: $300 | 2nd place: $200 | 3rd place: $100
· All winning entries will be posted on the official website.

If you have any questions, please visit www.2020yfc.org.

① 중학생을 대상으로 한다.
② 각 출품작의 전체 길이는 15분 이상이어야 한다.
③ 참가자는 세 개의 주제 중 하나를 선택해야 한다.
④ 출품작은 우편으로 제출할 수 있다.
⑤ 모든 수상작은 공식 웹사이트에 게시될 것이다.

29. 다음 글의 밑줄 친 부분 중, 어법상 틀린 것은? [3점]

All social interactions require some common ground upon which the involved parties can coordinate their behavior. In the interdependent groups ① in which humans and other primates live, individuals must have even greater common ground to establish and maintain social relationships. This common ground is morality. This is why morality often is defined as a shared set of standards for ② judging right and wrong in the conduct of social relationships. No matter how it is conceptualized — whether as trustworthiness, cooperation, justice, or caring — morality ③ to be always about the treatment of people in social relationships. This is likely why there is surprising agreement across a wide range of perspectives ④ that a shared sense of morality is necessary to social relations. Evolutionary biologists, sociologists, and philosophers all seem to agree with social psychologists that the interdependent relationships within groups that humans depend on ⑤ are not possible without a shared morality.

30. 다음 글의 밑줄 친 부분 중, 문맥상 낱말의 쓰임이 적절하지 않은 것은?

Spine-tingling ghost stories are fun to tell if they are really scary, and even more so if you claim that they are true. People get a ① thrill from passing on those stories. The same applies to miracle stories. If a rumor of a miracle gets written down in a book, the rumor becomes hard to ② believe, especially if the book is ancient. If a rumor is ③ old enough, it starts to be called a "tradition" instead, and then people believe it all the more. This is rather odd because you might think they would realize that older rumors have had more time to get ④ distorted than younger rumors that are close in time to the alleged events themselves. Elvis Presley and Michael Jackson lived too ⑤ recently for traditions to have grown up, so not many people believe stories like "Elvis seen on Mars."

[31~34] 다음 빈칸에 들어갈 말로 가장 적절한 것을 고르시오.

31. Firms in almost every industry tend to be clustered. Suppose you threw darts at random on a map of the United States. You'd find the holes left by the darts to be more or less evenly distributed across the map. But the real map of any given industry looks nothing like that; it looks more as if someone had thrown all the darts in the same place. This is probably in part because of reputation; buyers may be suspicious of a software firm in the middle of the cornfields. It would also be hard to recruit workers if every time you needed a new employee you had to persuade someone to move across the country, rather than just poach one from your neighbor. There are also regulatory reasons: zoning laws often try to concentrate dirty industries in one place and restaurants and bars in another. Finally, people in the same industry often have similar preferences (computer engineers like coffee, financiers show off with expensive bottles of wine). _____ makes it easier to provide the amenities they like.

* poach: (인력을) 빼내다

① Automation   ② Concentration   ③ Transportation
④ Globalization   ⑤ Liberalization

32. When we are emotionally charged, we often use anger to hide our more primary and deeper emotions, such as sadness and fear, which doesn't allow for true resolution to occur. Separating yourself from an emotionally upsetting situation gives you the space you need to better understand what you are truly feeling so you can more clearly articulate your emotions in a logical and less emotional way. A time-out also helps _____. When confronted with situations that don't allow us to deal with our emotions or that cause us to suppress them, we may transfer those feelings to other people or situations at a later point. For instance, if you had a bad day at work, you may suppress your feelings at the office, only to find that you release them by getting into a fight with your kids or spouse when you get home later that evening. Clearly, your anger didn't originate at home, but you released it there. When you take the appropriate time to digest and analyze your feelings, you can mitigate hurting or upsetting other people who have nothing to do with the situation. [3점]

* mitigate: 완화하다

① restrain your curiosity
② mask your true emotions
③ spare innocent bystanders
④ provoke emotional behavior
⑤ establish unhealthy relationships

33. A recent study shows that dogs appear to _____.
Scientists placed 28 dogs in front of a computer monitor blocked by an opaque screen, then played a recording of the dog's human guardian or a stranger saying the dog's name five times through speakers in the monitor. Finally, the screen was removed to reveal either the face of the dog's human companion or a stranger's face. The dogs' reactions were videotaped. Naturally, the dogs were attentive to the sound of their name, and they typically stared about six seconds at the face after the screen was removed. But they spent significantly more time gazing at a strange face after they had heard the familiar voice of their guardian. That they paused for an extra second or two suggests that they realized something was wrong. The conclusion drawn is that dogs form a picture in their mind, and that they can think about it and make predictions based on that picture. And, like us, they are puzzled when what they see or hear doesn't match what they were expecting.

* opaque: 불투명한

① form mental images of people's faces
② sense people's moods from their voices
③ detect possible danger and prepare for it
④ imitate their guardians' habitual behaviors
⑤ selectively obey commands from strangers

34. In the current landscape, social enterprises tend to rely either on grant capital (e.g., grants, donations, or project funding) or commercial financing products (e.g., bank loans). Ironically, many social enterprises at the same time report of significant drawbacks related to each of these two forms of financing. Many social enterprises are for instance reluctant to make use of traditional commercial finance products, fearing that they might not be able to pay back the loans. In addition, a significant number of social enterprise leaders report that relying too much on grant funding can be a risky strategy since individual grants are time limited and are not reliable in the long term. Grant funding can also lower the incentive for leaders and employees to professionalize the business aspects, thus leading to unhealthy business behavior. In other words, there seems to be a substantial need among social enterprises for _____. [3점]

* grant: (정부나 단체에서 주는) 보조금

① alternatives to the traditional forms of financing
② guidelines for promoting employee welfare
③ measures to protect employees' privacy
④ departments for better customer service
⑤ incentives to significantly increase productivity

35. 다음 글에서 전체 흐름과 관계 없는 문장은?

The major oceans are all interconnected, so that their geographical boundaries are less clear than those of the continents. As a result, their biotas show fewer clear differences than those on land. ① The oceans themselves are continually moving because the water within each ocean basin slowly rotates. ② These moving waters carry marine organisms from place to place, and also help the dispersal of their young or larvae. ③ In other words, coastal ocean currents not only move animals much less often than expected, but they also trap animals within near-shore regions. ④ Furthermore, the gradients between the environments of different areas of ocean water mass are very gradual and often extend over wide areas that are inhabited by a great variety of organisms of differing ecological tolerances. ⑤ There are no firm boundaries within the open oceans although there may be barriers to the movement of organisms.

* biota: 생물 군집 ** gradient: 변화도

[36~37] 주어진 글 다음에 이어질 글의 순서로 가장 적절한 것을 고르시오.

36.

When a change in the environment occurs, there is a relative increase or decrease in the rate at which the neurons fire, which is how intensity is coded. Furthermore, relativity operates to calibrate our sensations.

(A) Although both hands are now in the same water, one feels that it is colder and the other feels warmer because of the relative change from prior experience. This process, called *adaptation*, is one of the organizing principles operating throughout the central nervous system.

(B) For example, if you place one hand in hot water and the other in iced water for some time before immersing them both into lukewarm water, you will experience conflicting sensations of temperature because of the relative change in the receptors registering hot and cold.

(C) It explains why you can't see well inside a dark room if you have come in from a sunny day. Your eyes have to become accustomed to the new level of luminance. Adaptation explains why apples taste sour after eating sweet chocolate and why traffic seems louder in the city if you normally live in the country.

* calibrate: 조정하다 ** luminance: (빛의) 밝기

① (A) − (C) − (B) ② (B) − (A) − (C)
③ (B) − (C) − (A) ④ (C) − (A) − (B)
⑤ (C) − (B) − (A)

37.

> When an important change takes place in your life, observe your response. If you resist accepting the change it is because you are afraid; afraid of losing something.

(A) To learn to let go, to not cling and allow the flow of the river, is to live without resistances; being the creators of constructive changes that bring about improvements and widen our horizons.

(B) In life, all these things come and go and then others appear, which will also go. It is like a river in constant movement. If we try to stop the flow, we create a dam; the water stagnates and causes a pressure which accumulates inside us.

(C) Perhaps you might lose your position, property, possession, or money. The change might mean that you lose privileges or prestige. Perhaps with the change you lose the closeness of a person or a place.

* stagnate: (물이) 고이다

① (A) − (C) − (B)
② (B) − (A) − (C)
③ (B) − (C) − (A)
④ (C) − (A) − (B)
⑤ (C) − (B) − (A)

[38~39] 글의 흐름으로 보아, 주어진 문장이 들어가기에 가장 적절한 곳을 고르시오.

38.

> In terms of the overall value of an automobile, you can't drive without tires, but you can drive without cup holders and a portable technology dock.

Some resources, decisions, or activities are *important* (highly valuable on average) while others are *pivotal* (small changes make a big difference). Consider how two components of a car relate to a consumer's purchase decision: tires and interior design. Which adds more value on average? The tires. (①) They are essential to the car's ability to move, and they impact both safety and performance. (②) Yet tires generally do not influence purchase decisions because safety standards guarantee that all tires will be very safe and reliable. (③) Differences in interior features — optimal sound system, portable technology docks, number and location of cup holders — likely have far more effect on the consumer's buying decision. (④) Interior features, however, clearly have a greater impact on the purchase decision. (⑤) In our language, the tires are important, but the interior design is pivotal. [3점]

39.

> When an overall silence appears on beats 4 and 13, it is not because each musician is thinking, "On beats 4 and 13, I will rest."

In the West, an individual composer writes the music long before it is performed. The patterns and melodies we hear are pre-planned and intended. (①) Some African tribal music, however, results from collaboration by the players on the spur of the moment. (②) The patterns heard, whether they are the silences when all players rest on a beat or the accented beats when all play together, are not planned but serendipitous. (③) Rather, it occurs randomly as the patterns of all the players converge upon a simultaneous rest. (④) The musicians are probably as surprised as their listeners to hear the silences at beats 4 and 13. (⑤) Surely that surprise is one of the joys tribal musicians experience in making their music. [3점]

* serendipitous: 우연히 얻은 ** converge: 한데 모아지다

40. 다음 글의 내용을 한 문장으로 요약하고자 한다. 빈칸 (A), (B)에 들어갈 말로 가장 적절한 것은?

> Some researchers at Sheffield University recruited 129 hobbyists to look at how the time spent on their hobbies shaped their work life. To begin with, the team measured the seriousness of each participant's hobby, asking them to rate their agreement with statements like "I regularly train for this activity," and also assessed how similar the demands of their job and hobby were. Then, each month for seven months, participants recorded how many hours they had dedicated to their activity, and completed a scale measuring their belief in their ability to effectively do their job, or their "self-efficacy." The researchers found that when participants spent longer than normal doing their leisure activity, their belief in their ability to perform their job increased. But this was only the case when they had a serious hobby that was dissimilar to their job. When their hobby was both serious and similar to their job, then spending more time on it actually decreased their self-efficacy.

↓

> Research suggests that spending more time on serious hobbies can boost ___(A)___ at work if the hobbies and the job are sufficiently ___(B)___.

	(A)		(B)
①	confidence	......	different
②	productivity	......	connected
③	relationships	......	balanced
④	creativity	......	separate
⑤	dedication	......	similar

[41~42] 다음 글을 읽고, 물음에 답하시오.

U.S. commercial aviation has long had an extremely effective system for encouraging pilots to submit reports of errors. The program has resulted in numerous improvements to aviation safety. It wasn't easy to establish: pilots had severe self-induced social pressures against (a) admitting to errors. Moreover, to whom would they report them? Certainly not to their employers. Not even to the Federal Aviation Authority (FAA), for then they would probably be punished. The solution was to let the National Aeronautics and Space Administration (NASA) set up a (b) voluntary accident reporting system whereby pilots could submit semi-anonymous reports of errors they had made or observed in others.

Once NASA personnel had acquired the necessary information, they would (c) detach the contact information from the report and mail it back to the pilot. This meant that NASA no longer knew who had reported the error, which made it impossible for the airline companies or the FAA (which enforced penalties against errors) to find out who had (d) rejected the report. If the FAA had independently noticed the error and tried to invoke a civil penalty or certificate suspension, the receipt of self-report automatically exempted the pilot from punishment. When a sufficient number of similar errors had been collected, NASA would analyze them and issue reports and recommendations to the airlines and to the FAA. These reports also helped the pilots realize that their error reports were (e) valuable tools for increasing safety.

41. 윗글의 제목으로 가장 적절한 것은?

① Aviation Safety Built on Anonymous Reports
② More Flexible Manuals Mean Ignored Safety
③ Great Inventions from Unexpected Mistakes
④ Controversies over New Safety Regulations
⑤ Who Is Innovating Technology in the Air?

42. 밑줄 친 (a)~(e) 중에서 문맥상 낱말의 쓰임이 적절하지 <u>않은</u> 것은? [3점]

① (a)   ② (b)   ③ (c)   ④ (d)   ⑤ (e)

[43~45] 다음 글을 읽고, 물음에 답하시오.

(A)

I was on a train in Switzerland. The train came to a stop, and the conductor's voice over the loudspeaker delivered a message in German, then Italian, then French. I had made the mistake of not learning any of those languages before my vacation. After the announcement, everyone started getting off the train, and an old woman saw I was confused and stressed. (a) She came up to me.

(B)

So we went from one train station to the next, getting to know each other along the way. It was a 2.5-hour journey in total, and when we finally made it to the destination, we got off and said our good-byes. I had made it just in time to catch my train to Rome, and she told me she had a train to catch too. I asked (b) her how much farther she had to go, and it turned out her home was two hours back the other way.

(C)

She spoke some English, and she told me that an accident had happened on the tracks. She asked me where I was trying to get to, then she got off the train and went to a woman in the ticket booth. The old woman got a rail map and timetable from (c) her and came back to tell me that we'd have to hop trains three or four times to get there. I was really glad (d) she was headed the same way because it would have been hopeless for me to figure it out on my own.

(D)

She had jumped from train to train and traveled the whole way just to make sure I made it. "You are the nicest person I've ever met," I said. She smiled gently and hugged me and told me I'd better hurry off so I wouldn't miss my train. This woman spent her entire day sitting on trains taking (e) her hours away from her home just to help out a confused tourist visiting her country. No matter how many countries I visit or sites I see, I always say the most beautiful country in the world is Switzerland.

43. 주어진 글 (A)에 이어질 내용을 순서에 맞게 배열한 것으로 가장 적절한 것은?

① (B) − (D) − (C)   ② (C) − (B) − (D)
③ (C) − (D) − (B)   ④ (D) − (B) − (C)
⑤ (D) − (C) − (B)

44. 밑줄 친 (a)~(e) 중에서 가리키는 대상이 나머지 넷과 <u>다른</u> 것은?

① (a)   ② (b)   ③ (c)   ④ (d)   ⑤ (e)

45. 윗글에 관한 내용으로 적절하지 <u>않은</u> 것은?

① 안내 방송 후 모두가 기차에서 내리기 시작했다.
② 'I'는 로마로 가는 기차 시간에 맞춰 도착하지 못했다.
③ 노부인은 선로에서 사고가 발생했다고 말했다.
④ 노부인은 기차에서 내려 티켓 부스로 갔다.
⑤ 'I'는 세계에서 가장 아름다운 나라가 스위스라고 항상 말한다.

* 확인 사항
◦ 답안지의 해당란에 필요한 내용을 정확히 기입(표기)했는지 확인하시오.

15회

18
001 resident ⓝ 거주자, 주민
002 truly ⓐⓓ 정말로, 진심으로
003 value ⓥ 소중히 하다, 귀중히 여기다
004 appreciate ⓥ 고마워하다
005 enrich ⓥ 풍요롭게 하다
006 ensure ⓥ 확실히 하다
007 at the expense of ~을 희생하여
008 neighbor ⓝ 이웃
009 disturb ⓥ 방해하다, 어지럽히다
010 bark ⓥ 짖다
011 excessive ⓐ 과도한
012 disrupt ⓥ 방해하다, 지장을 주다
013 elderly ⓝ 연세 드신 분들, 어르신들
014 assistance ⓝ 도움, 원조, 지원

19
015 reach ⓥ 뻗다, 내밀다
016 spot ⓥ 발견하다
017 splash ⓥ 첨벙거리다
018 lake ⓝ 호수
019 pound ⓥ (심장이) 쿵쾅거리다
020 trip-hammer 스프링 해머, 기계 해머
021 frantically ⓐⓓ 미친 듯이
022 stroke ⓝ (수영에서 팔을) 젓기
023 grave ⓐ (문제 등이) 심각한
024 solemn ⓐ 엄숙한
025 festive ⓐ 축제의, 기념일의
026 monotonous ⓐ 단조로운

20
027 imaginary ⓐ 가상의
028 concern ⓝ 걱정거리
029 replace A with B A를 B로 대체하다
030 interaction ⓝ 상호 작용
031 pretend ⓐ 가상의 ⓥ ~인 체하다
032 socially ⓐⓓ 사회적으로
033 beneficial ⓐ 유익한, 이로운
034 reassurance ⓝ 안심
035 respectful ⓐ 존중하는
036 tease ⓥ 놀리다
037 humiliate ⓥ 창피를 주다
038 ridicule ⓥ 조롱하다
039 tire of ~에 지치다, 싫증 내다
040 plate ⓝ 접시, 그릇
041 signify ⓥ 의미하다, 나타내다
042 imagination ⓝ 상상력

21
043 fashion ⓥ (특히 손으로) 만들다, 빚다
044 masterpiece ⓝ 걸작
045 progress ⓥ 나아가다
046 halt ⓥ 멈추다
047 generation ⓝ 발생, 유발, 생성
048 strike gold 노다지를 캐다, 큰 성공을 거두다
049 backtrack ⓥ (왔던 길을) 되짚어가다
050 version ⓝ 판, 형태, 버전
051 discard A as B A를 B로 간주해서 폐기하다
052 inadequate ⓐ 부적당한, 불충분한
053 scrap ⓥ 폐기하다, 버리다
054 conclusion ⓝ 결말

055 distinguish A from B A와 B를 구별하다
056 extraordinary ⓐ 비범한
057 ordinary ⓐ 평범한
058 composition ⓝ 작곡
059 immediately ⓐⓓ 즉시
060 in protest of ~에 저항하는
061 variation ⓝ 변형, 변주
062 consistently ⓐⓓ 일관되게
063 move away from ~에서 멀어지다, 벗어나다
064 outcome ⓝ 결과
065 criticism ⓝ 비판
066 unwilling ⓐ 꺼리는, 싫어하는
067 enthusiasm ⓝ 열정, 열광
068 imitate ⓥ 모방하다

22
069 reward ⓝ 보상
070 circuit ⓝ 회로
071 engaged ⓐ 사용 중인, 쓰고 있는
072 deal with ~을 처리하다
073 efficiently ⓐⓓ 효율적으로
074 hands-on 손으로 하는, 직접 해보는
075 knit ⓥ (실로 옷 등을) 뜨다, 짜다
076 from scratch 처음부터
077 tend ⓥ 돌보다, 보살피다
078 function ⓥ 기능하다, 작동하다
079 optimally ⓐⓓ 최적으로
080 documented ⓐ 문서로 기록된
081 depression ⓝ 우울(증), 침체
082 correlate ⓥ 연관성이 있다
083 decline ⓝ 감소
084 purposeful ⓐ 목적이 있는
085 release ⓝ 분비, 배출
086 neurochemical ⓝ 신경 화학 물질
087 generate ⓥ 발생시키다, 만들어 내다
088 sense of control 통제감, 통제력
089 contribute to ~에 기여하다
090 reduction ⓝ 감소, 축소
091 anxiety ⓝ 불안
092 resilience ⓝ 회복력, 탄력성
093 onset ⓝ (특히 불쾌한 일의) 시작

23
094 capacity ⓝ 능력
095 laughter ⓝ 웃음
096 peculiarly ⓐⓓ 독특하게
097 characteristic ⓝ 특징, 특질
098 witty ⓐ 재치 있는
099 note ⓥ 주목하다, 언급하다
100 distinguish ⓥ 구별하다
101 donkey ⓝ 당나귀
102 mold ⓥ 만들다, 주조하다
103 reinforce ⓥ 강화하다
104 norm ⓝ 규범, 규준
105 regulate ⓥ 규제하다
106 era ⓝ 시대, 연대
107 preoccupation ⓝ (뇌리를 사로잡고 있는) 생각, 집착
108 prevail ⓥ 만연하다, 팽배하다
109 ultimate ⓐ 궁극적인
110 sum total 총계, 합계

111 monument ⓝ 기념물
112 incident ⓝ 일, 사건
113 approach ⓥ 접근하다
114 aptly ⓐⓓ 적절하게
115 observe ⓥ (의견을) 말하다
116 assimilation ⓝ 동화
117 intercultural ⓐ 문화 간의
118 competence ⓝ 역량, 능숙함, 권한
119 criticize ⓥ 비판하다

24
120 unofficial ⓐ 비공식적인
121 mark ⓥ 나타내다
122 consequently ⓐⓓ 결과적으로
123 profitable ⓐ 이득이 되는, 수익성이 있는
124 retailer ⓝ 소매상
125 come to light 나타나다, 드러나다, 밝혀지다
126 ecological ⓐ 생태학적인
127 philosophy ⓝ 철학
128 seek ⓥ 추구하다
129 raise ⓥ 불러일으키다, 자아내다
130 awareness ⓝ 의식[관심]
131 emission ⓝ 배출
132 cause ⓥ ~을 야기하다, 초래하다
133 waste ⓥ 낭비하다
134 mindlessly ⓐⓓ 생각 없이, 무분별하게, 어리석게
135 switch ⓥ 바꾸다, 전환하다 ⓝ 전환, 바꾸기
136 mindset ⓝ 사고방식[태도]
137 alternative ⓐ 대안적인, 대체의
138 population ⓝ 인구
139 beyond 〔prep〕 ~ 이상으로, ~을 넘어서
140 budget ⓝ 예산, 비용

25
141 material ⓝ 물질, 재료, 소재
142 landfill ⓥ 매립하다 ⓝ 매립 쓰레기
143 municipal ⓐ 도시의
144 respectively ⓐⓓ 각각
145 remain ⓥ 계속[여전히] ~이다
146 textile ⓝ 직물

26
147 interest ⓝ 관심
148 astronomy ⓝ 천문학
149 earn ⓥ 얻다, 받다
150 master's degree 석사 학위
151 make headlines 대서특필되다, 화제가 되다
152 shock ⓥ 충격을 주다, 깜짝 놀라게 하다
153 theory ⓝ 이론
154 motion ⓝ 운동, 움직임
155 galaxy ⓝ 은하계, 은하수
156 telescope ⓝ 망원경
157 groundbreaking ⓐ 혁신적인, 획기적인
158 observation ⓝ 관측, 관찰
159 evidence ⓝ 증거, 흔적
160 existence ⓝ 존재
161 vast ⓐ 막대한, 광대한
162 matter ⓝ 물질
163 universe ⓝ 우주
164 celebrate ⓥ 칭송하다, 기념하다

27
165 turn A into B A를 B로 바꾸다
166 registration ⓝ 등록
167 participation fee 참가비
168 sign up 등록하다
169 in person 직접
170 requirement ⓝ 필요(한 것), 요건
171 laptop ⓝ 노트북 컴퓨터
172 provide ⓥ 제공하다
173 prior ⓐ 사전의
174 knowledge ⓝ 지식

28
175 demonstrate ⓥ 보여주다, 입증하다
176 filmmaking ⓝ 영화 제작
177 official ⓐ 공식적인, 공식의
178 entry ⓝ 출품(작)
179 topic ⓝ 화제, 주제
180 submission ⓝ 제출
181 post ⓥ 게시하다

29
182 social interaction 사회적 상호 작용
183 coordinate ⓥ 조정하다
184 interdependent ⓐ 상호 의존적인
185 primate ⓝ 영장류
186 establish ⓥ 확립하다
187 morality ⓝ 도덕성
188 define ⓥ 정의하다, 규정하다
189 standard ⓝ 기준, 표준
190 conduct ⓝ 행위, 행동
191 no matter how 어떻게 하더라도, 아무리 ~한들
192 conceptualize ⓥ 개념화하다
193 trustworthiness ⓝ 신뢰성
194 cooperation ⓝ 협력, 협동
195 justice ⓝ 정의
196 caring ⓝ 복지, 돌보기
197 treatment ⓝ 대우, 처리
198 agreement ⓝ 일치, 합의
199 perspective ⓝ 관점
200 evolutionary ⓐ 진화의
201 philosopher ⓝ 철학자

30
202 spine-tingling 등골이 오싹한, 스릴 넘치는
203 scary ⓐ 무서운
204 claim ⓥ 주장하다
205 thrill ⓝ 황홀감, 흥분, 스릴
206 pass on ~을 전해주다
207 apply to ~에 적용되다
208 especially ⓐⓓ 특히
209 instead ⓐⓓ 대신에
210 odd ⓐ 이상한
211 distort ⓥ 왜곡하다
212 alleged ⓐ (증거 없이) 주장된, ~이라고들 말하는
213 recently ⓐⓓ 최근에

31
214 firm ⓝ 회사
215 industry ⓝ (특정 분야의) 산업

VOCA LIST 15

216 cluster	ⓥ 밀집하다, 모이다
217 suppose	ⓥ 가정하다, 추정하다
218 at random	무작위로[임의로]
219 more or less	거의, 약
220 evenly	ⓐⓓ 고르게
221 distribute	ⓥ 분포하다
222 reputation	ⓝ 평판, 명성
223 suspicious	ⓐ 수상쩍어하는, 의심스러운
224 cornfield	ⓝ 옥수수밭
225 recruit	ⓥ 채용하다, 모집하다
226 persuade	ⓥ 설득하다
227 regulatory	ⓐ 규제의, 단속력을 지닌
228 concentrate	ⓥ 집중시키다
229 preference	ⓝ 선호(도)
230 financier	ⓝ 금융업자, 자본가
231 amenity	ⓝ 편의시설
232 automation	ⓝ 자동화
233 liberalization	ⓝ 자유화

32

234 charged	ⓐ (어떤 감정에) 차 있는, 격앙된
235 primary	ⓐ 원초적인, 기본적인
236 resolution	ⓝ 해결책, 결심
237 upsetting	ⓐ 화가 나는, 속상하게 하는
238 articulate	ⓥ 명확하게 표현하다
239 spare	ⓥ (불쾌한 일을) 모면하게[당하지 않게] 하다
240 innocent	ⓐ 무고한, 결백한
241 bystander	ⓝ 구경꾼
242 confront	ⓥ 직면하게 하다
243 suppress	ⓥ 억누르다
244 transfer	ⓥ 전이하다, 옮기다
245 release	ⓥ 표출하다
246 spouse	ⓝ 배우자
247 originate	ⓥ 비롯되다, 기원하다
248 appropriate	ⓐ 적절한
249 digest	ⓥ 소화하다
250 analyze	ⓥ 분석하다
251 have nothing to do with	~와 무관하다
252 restrain	ⓥ 억누르다, 제한하다
253 provoke	ⓥ 촉발시키다, 자극하다

33

254 appear	ⓥ ~인 것 같다
255 block	ⓥ 막다, 차단하다
256 companion	ⓝ 동반자, 동행
257 reaction	ⓝ 반응
258 attentive	ⓐ 주의를 기울이는
259 typically	ⓐⓓ 일반적으로, 전형적으로
260 stare	ⓥ 응시하다
261 gaze at	~을 응시하다
262 familiar	ⓐ 익숙한, 친숙한
263 pause	ⓥ 잠시 멈추다
264 make a prediction	예측하다
265 puzzle	ⓥ 당황하게 하다
266 sense	ⓥ 감지하다, 느끼다
267 detect	ⓥ 감지하다
268 imitate	ⓥ 모방하다, 흉내내다
269 habitual	ⓐ 습관적인
270 selectively	ⓐⓓ 선택적으로
271 obey	ⓥ 복종[순종]하다
272 command	ⓝ 명령

34

273 current	ⓐ 현재의
274 landscape	ⓝ 전망, 조망
275 enterprise	ⓝ 기업
276 rely on	~에 의존하다
277 capital	ⓝ 자본금, 자금
278 donations	ⓝ 기부금
279 commercial	ⓐ 상업의, 상업적인
280 financing	ⓝ 자금 조달, 융자
281 ironically	ⓐⓓ 반어적으로
282 significant	ⓐ 중대한, 중요한, 상당한
283 drawback	ⓝ 결점
284 reluctant	ⓐ 꺼리는, 마지못해 하는
285 make use of	~을 이용하다
286 loan	ⓝ 대출금
287 risky	ⓐ 위험한
288 strategy	ⓝ 계획, 전략
289 reliable	ⓐ 신뢰할 수 있는
290 incentive	ⓝ 장려[우대]책
291 professionalize	ⓥ 전문화하다
292 aspect	ⓝ 양상, 측면
293 substantial	ⓐ 상당한
294 alternative	ⓝ 대안
295 welfare	ⓝ 복지
296 measure	ⓝ 정책, 조치
297 productivity	ⓝ 생산성

35

298 interconnected	ⓐ 상호 연결된
299 geographical	ⓐ 지리적인
300 boundary	ⓝ 경계
301 continent	ⓝ 대륙
302 clear	ⓐ 분명한, 명확한
303 continually	ⓐⓓ 계속해서
304 basin	ⓝ 분지, (큰 강의) 유역
305 rotate	ⓥ 회전하다
306 marine	ⓐ 바다의, 해양의
307 organism	ⓝ 유기체, 생물
308 dispersal	ⓝ 분산
309 larva	ⓝ 유충, 애벌레
310 coastal	ⓐ 해안[연안]의
311 current	ⓝ 해류
312 trap	ⓥ 가두다
313 near-shore	연안의, 해변의
314 gradual	ⓐ 점진적인
315 extend	ⓥ 확장하다
316 inhabit	ⓥ ~에 거주하다
317 differ	ⓥ 다르다
318 tolerance	ⓝ 내성, 관용
319 firm	ⓐ 확고한, 확실한
320 barrier	ⓝ 장애물, 장벽

36

321 neuron	ⓝ 뉴런, 신경 세포
322 intensity	ⓝ 강도
323 code	ⓥ 암호로 처리하다
324 relativity	ⓝ 상대성
325 operate	ⓥ 작용하다, 운용되다
326 sensation	ⓝ (자극을 받아서 느끼는) 감각
327 adaptation	ⓝ 순응, 적응
328 principle	ⓝ 원리, 원칙
329 central nervous system	중추 신경계

37

330 immerse	ⓥ (액체 속에) 담그다, 몰두하게 만들다
331 lukewarm	ⓐ 미지근한
332 conflicting	ⓐ 상충하는, 모순되는
333 receptor	ⓝ 수용체
334 register	ⓥ 인식하다, 알아채다, 등록하다
335 accustomed to	~에 익숙한
336 normally	ⓐⓓ 보통은

37

337 take place	일어나다
338 observe	ⓥ 관찰하다
339 response	ⓝ 반응
340 resist	ⓥ 저항[반대]하다
341 cling	ⓥ 집착하다, 고수하다
342 flow	ⓝ 흐름
343 resistance	ⓝ 저항
344 creator	ⓝ 창조자, 창작자
345 constructive	ⓐ 건설적인
346 bring about	~을 가져오다
347 improvement	ⓝ 개선, 향상
348 widen	ⓥ 넓히다, 키우다
349 horizon	ⓝ 시야, 수평선
350 constant	ⓐ 끊임없는
351 accumulate	ⓥ 축적되다
352 property	ⓝ 재산, 특성
353 possession	ⓝ 소유물
354 privilege	ⓝ 특권
355 prestige	ⓝ 명성, 위신

38

356 in terms of	~의 면에서
357 overall	ⓐ 종합적인, 전반적인
358 automobile	ⓝ 자동차
359 portable	ⓐ 휴대용의
360 dock	ⓝ 거치대
361 valuable	ⓐ 가치가 큰, 소중한
362 pivotal	ⓐ 중추적인
363 component	ⓝ (구성) 요소
364 relate to	~와 관계가 있다[관련되다]
365 essential	ⓐ 필수적인
366 impact	ⓥ 영향을 미치다 ⓝ 영향
367 guarantee	ⓥ 보장[약속]하다
368 feature	ⓝ 기능, 특징
369 optimal	ⓐ 최적의
370 have (an) effect on	~에 영향을 미치다

39

371 silence	ⓝ 휴지(休止), 침묵, 정적
372 beat	ⓝ 박자, 비트
373 rest	ⓥ 쉬다, 휴식을 취하다
374 composer	ⓝ 작곡가
375 intend	ⓥ 의도하다
376 tribal	ⓐ 부족의
377 result from	~로 생겨나다, ~이 원인이다
378 collaboration	ⓝ 합작, 협연
379 on the spur of the moment	즉석에서, 순간적인 충동으로
380 accent	ⓥ 강조하다
381 randomly	ⓐⓓ 무작위로
382 simultaneous	ⓐ 동시의
383 surely	ⓐⓓ 확실히

40

384 hobbyist	ⓝ 취미에 아주 열심인 사람
385 to begin with	먼저, 우선
386 measure	ⓥ 측정하다
387 seriousness	ⓝ 진지함
388 rate	ⓥ 평가하다
389 statement	ⓝ 진술, 서술
390 assess	ⓥ 평가하다
391 dedicate	ⓥ 바치다, 전념하다
392 scale	ⓝ 척도
393 self-efficacy	자기 효능감
394 dissimilar	ⓐ 다른, 같지 않은
395 boost	ⓥ 높이다, 신장시키다
396 sufficiently	ⓐⓓ 충분히

41~42

397 aviation	ⓝ 항공
398 extremely	ⓐⓓ 매우, 극도로
399 numerous	ⓐ 수많은
400 severe	ⓐ 극심한, 심각한
401 self-induced	자기 유도의, 저절로 생긴
402 admit to	~을 인정하다
403 punish	ⓥ 처벌하다
404 semi-anonymous	반익명의
405 personnel	ⓝ (회사의) 인사과
406 acquire	ⓥ 얻다, 습득하다
407 detach	ⓥ 떼어내다, 분리시키다
408 contact information	연락처
409 enforce	ⓥ 집행하다, 실시하다
410 penalty	ⓝ 제재, 처벌
411 independently	ⓐⓓ 독립적으로
412 invoke	ⓥ 적용하다, 들먹이다
413 civil penalty	민사상 처벌(주로 벌금형)
414 certificate	ⓝ 자격(증)
415 suspension	ⓝ 정지, 연기, 보류
416 automatically	ⓐⓓ 자동적으로
417 exempt A from B	A로 하여금 B를 면하게 하다
418 sufficient	ⓐ 충분한
419 issue	ⓥ 발부[지급]하다
420 recommendation	ⓝ 권고, 충고
421 anonymous	ⓐ 익명의
422 unexpected	ⓐ 예상치 못한, 뜻밖의
423 controversy	ⓝ 논란

43~45

424 come to a stop	멈추다, 서다
425 conductor	ⓝ 차장, 안내원, 지휘자
426 loudspeaker	ⓝ 확성기, 스피커
427 deliver	ⓥ 전하다, 말하다
428 confused	ⓐ 혼란스러운
429 in total	전체로서, 통틀어
430 destination	ⓝ 목적지
431 in time	때맞춰, 제시간에
432 catch	ⓥ (기차 등을 시간 맞춰)타다
433 accident	ⓝ 사고, 재해
434 hop	ⓥ (비행기, 버스, 기차 등에)타다
435 head	ⓥ (특정 방향으로) 가다[향하다]
436 hopeless	ⓐ 가망 없는, 절망적인
437 figure out	~을 이해하다[알아내다]
438 gently	ⓐⓓ 부드럽게
439 hurry off	서둘러[급히] 떠나다

15회

어휘 Review test 15

TEST A-B 각 단어의 뜻을 [A] 영어는 우리말로, [B] 우리말은 영어로 쓰시오.

A	English	Korean
01	dissimilar	
02	detach	
03	inhabit	
04	suspension	
05	provoke	
06	controversy	
07	spouse	
08	prestige	
09	concentrate	
10	lukewarm	
11	evenly	
12	tolerance	
13	spine-tingling	
14	welfare	
15	emission	
16	liberalization	
17	from scratch	
18	reinforce	
19	primate	
20	larva	

B	Korean	English
01	동화	
02	집행하다, 실시하다	
03	왜곡하다	
04	처벌하다	
05	만들다, 주조하다	
06	특권	
07	놀리다	
08	소유물	
09	막대한, 광대한	
10	순응, 적응	
11	조롱하다	
12	꺼리는, 마지못해 하는	
13	도시의	
14	불안	
15	소화하다	
16	도덕성	
17	조정하다	
18	폐기하다, 버리다	
19	첨벙거리다	
20	결점	

▶ A-D 정답 : 해설편 159쪽

TEST C-D 각 단어의 뜻을 골라 기호를 쓰시오.

C	English		Korean
01	make headlines	( )	ⓐ 회복력, 탄력성
02	monument	( )	ⓑ 기념물
03	prior	( )	ⓒ 습관적인
04	resilience	( )	ⓓ 명확하게 표현하다
05	articulate	( )	ⓔ 회전하다
06	correlate	( )	ⓕ 방해하다, 어지럽히다
07	habitual	( )	ⓖ 엄숙한
08	strike gold	( )	ⓗ 큰 성공을 거두다
09	rotate	( )	ⓘ 화제가 되다
10	pretend	( )	ⓙ 가상의; ~인 체하다
11	immerse	( )	ⓚ 축적되다
12	solemn	( )	ⓛ 사전의
13	accumulate	( )	ⓜ 중추적인
14	disturb	( )	ⓝ 연관성이 있다
15	pivotal	( )	ⓞ 몰두하게 만들다
16	in terms of	( )	ⓟ 신뢰성
17	conceptualize	( )	ⓠ ~의 면에서
18	on the spur of the moment	( )	ⓡ 즉석에서, 순간적인 충동으로
19	trustworthiness	( )	ⓢ 믿을 만한
20	reliable	( )	ⓣ 개념화하다

D	Korean		English
01	익명의	( )	ⓐ anonymous
02	~에 익숙한	( )	ⓑ gaze at
03	항공	( )	ⓒ come to light
04	A를 B로 보고 폐기하다	( )	ⓓ cling
05	집착하다, 고수하다	( )	ⓔ exempt A from B
06	차장, 안내원, 지휘자	( )	ⓕ discard A as B
07	~을 응시하다	( )	ⓖ civil penalty
08	때맞춰, 제시간에	( )	ⓗ conductor
09	편의시설	( )	ⓘ dispersal
10	민사상 처벌	( )	ⓙ amenity
11	드러나다, 밝혀지다	( )	ⓚ accustomed to
12	자기 효능감	( )	ⓛ in person
13	A에게 B를 면하게 하다	( )	ⓜ self-efficacy
14	직접	( )	ⓝ in time
15	분산	( )	ⓞ aviation
16	~에 의존하다	( )	ⓟ suppress
17	주장된, ~이라고들 말하는	( )	ⓠ rely on
18	각각	( )	ⓡ numerous
19	수많은	( )	ⓢ alleged
20	억누르다	( )	ⓣ respectively

18. 다음 글의 목적으로 가장 적절한 것은?

> To whom it may concern,
>
> I am writing to inform you of an ongoing noise issue that I am experiencing. My apartment faces the basketball courts of the community center. While I fully support the community center's services, I am constantly being disrupted by individuals playing basketball late at night. Many nights, I struggle to fall asleep because I can hear people bouncing balls and shouting on the basketball courts well after 11 p.m.. Could you restrict the time the basketball court is open to before 9 p.m.? I'm sure I'm not the only person in the neighborhood that is affected by this noise issue. I appreciate your assistance.
>
> Sincerely,
> Ian Baldwin

① 체육관의 바닥 교체 공사를 요구하려고
② 농구 코트의 운영 시간 제한을 요청하려고
③ 문화 센터 시설의 대관 날짜를 변경하려고
④ 건강 증진 프로그램 신청 방법을 문의하려고
⑤ 지역 내 체육 시설의 증설 가능 여부를 확인하려고

19. 다음 글에 드러난 Chaske의 심경 변화로 가장 적절한 것은?

Chaske, a Cherokee boy, was sitting on a tree stump. As a rite of passage for youths in his tribe, Chaske had to survive one night in the forest wearing a blindfold, not knowing he was observed by his father. After the sunset, Chaske could hear all kinds of noises. The wind blew the grass and shook his stump. A sense of dread swept through his body. *What if wild beasts are looking at me? I can't stand this!* Just as he was about to take off the blindfold to run away, a voice came in from somewhere. "I'm here around you. Don't give up, and complete your mission." It was his father's voice. *He has been watching me from nearby!* With just the presence of his father, the boy regained stability. What panicked him awfully a moment ago vanished into thin air.

① nervous → doubtful
② horrified → relieved
③ disappointed → curious
④ ashamed → frightened
⑤ bored → delighted

20. 다음 글에서 필자가 주장하는 바로 가장 적절한 것은?

Agriculture includes a range of activities such as planting, harvesting, fertilizing, pest management, raising animals, and distributing food and agricultural products. It is one of the oldest and most essential human activities, dating back thousands of years, and has played a critical role in the development of human civilizations, allowing people to create stable food supplies and settle in one place. Today, agriculture remains a vital industry that feeds the world's population, supports rural communities, and provides raw materials for other industries. However, agriculture faces numerous challenges such as climate change, water scarcity, soil degradation, and biodiversity loss. As the world's population continues to grow, it is essential to find sustainable solutions to address the challenges facing agriculture and ensure the continued production of food and other agricultural products.

① 토양의 질을 개선하기 위해 친환경 농법의 연구와 개발이 필요하다.
② 세계 인구의 증가에 대응하기 위해 농산물 품종의 다양화가 필요하다.
③ 기후 변화에 대한 지속 가능한 대책은 경제적 관점에서 고려되어야 한다.
④ 다른 산업 분야와의 공동 연구를 통해 상품성을 가진 농작물을 개발해야 한다.
⑤ 농업이 직면한 문제 해결 및 식량과 농산물의 지속적 생산을 위한 방안이 필요하다.

21. 밑줄 친 be more than just sugar on the tongue이 다음 글에서 의미하는 바로 가장 적절한 것은? [3점]

The arts and aesthetics offer emotional connection to the full range of human experience. "The arts can be more than just sugar on the tongue," Anjan Chatterjee, a professor at the University of Pennsylvania, says. "In art, when there's something challenging, which can also be uncomfortable, this discomfort, if we're willing to engage with it, offers the possibility of some change, some transformation. That can also be a powerful aesthetic experience." The arts, in this way, become vehicles to contend with ideas and concepts that are difficult and uncomfortable otherwise. When Picasso painted his masterpiece *Guernica* in 1937, he captured the heartbreaking and cruel nature of war, and offered the world a way to consider the universal suffering caused by the Spanish Civil War. When Lorraine Hansberry wrote her play *A Raisin in the Sun*, she gave us a powerful story of people struggling with racism, discrimination, and the pursuit of the American dream while also offering a touching portrait of family life.

① play a role in relieving psychological anxiety
② enlighten us about the absoluteness of beauty
③ conceal the artist's cultural and ethnic traditions
④ embrace a variety of experiences beyond pleasure
⑤ distort the viewers' accurate understanding of history

22. 다음 글의 요지로 가장 적절한 것은?

Many historians have pointed to the significance of accurate time measurement to Western economic progress. The French historian Jacques Le Goff called the birth of the public mechanical clock a turning point in Western society. Until the late Middle Ages, people had sun or water clocks, which did not play any meaningful role in business activities. Market openings and activities started with the sunrise and typically ended at noon when the sun was at its peak. But when the first public mechanical clocks were introduced and spread across European cities, market times were set by the stroke of the hour. Public clocks thus greatly contributed to public life and work by providing a new concept of time that was easy for everyone to understand. This, in turn, helped facilitate trade and commerce. Interactions and transactions between consumers, retailers, and wholesalers became less irregular. Important town meetings began to follow the pace of the clock, allowing people to better plan their time and allocate resources in a more efficient manner.

① 공공 시계는 서양 사회의 경제적 진보에 영향을 미쳤다.
② 서양에서 생산된 시계는 세계적으로 정교함을 인정받았다.
③ 서양의 시계는 교역을 통해 전파되어 세계적으로 대중화되었다.
④ 기계 시계의 발명은 다른 측량 장비들의 개발에 도움을 주었다.
⑤ 중세 시대의 시계 발명은 자연법칙을 이해하는 데 큰 전환점이 되었다.

23. 다음 글의 주제로 가장 적절한 것은?

Sylvan Goldman invented the shopping cart and introduced it in his stores in 1937. It was an excellent device that would make it easy for shoppers to buy as much as they wanted without getting tired or seeking others' help. But Goldman discovered that in spite of his repeated advertisements and explanations, he could not persuade his shoppers to use the wheeled carts. Men were reluctant because they thought they would appear weak if they pushed such carts instead of carrying their shopping. Women wouldn't touch them because the carts reminded them of baby carriages. It was only a few elderly shoppers who used them. That made the carts even less attractive to the majority of the shoppers. Then Goldman hit upon an idea. He hired several models, men and women, of different ages and asked them to wheel the carts in the store and shop. A young woman employee standing near the entrance told the regular shoppers, 'Look, everyone is using the carts. Why don't you?' That was the turning point. A few shills disguised as regular shoppers easily accomplished what logic, explanations, and advertisements failed to do. Within a few weeks shoppers readily accepted those carts.

*shill: 바람잡이

① persuasive power of peer behavior
② methods to help consumers shop less
③ innovative ways to reduce waste in retail
④ hidden nature of human beings to support materialism
⑤ importance of a store layout based on customer needs

24. 다음 글의 제목으로 가장 적절한 것은?

In response to human-like care robots, critics might charge that human-robot interactions create moral hazards for dementia patients. Even if deception is sometimes allowed when it serves worthy goals, should it be allowed for vulnerable users? Just as children on the autism spectrum with robot companions might be easily fooled into thinking of robots as friends, older adults with cognitive deficits might be. According to Alexis Elder, a professor at UMD, robots are *false* friends, inferior to true friendship. Reasoning along similar lines, John Sullins, a professor at Sonoma State University, holds that robots should "remain iconic or cartoonish so that they are easily distinguished as synthetic even by unsophisticated users." At least then no one is fooled. Making robots clearly fake also avoids the so-called "uncanny valley," where robots are perceived as scary because they so closely resemble us, but not quite. Other critics of robot deception argue that when care recipients are deceived into thinking that robots care, this crosses a line and violates human *dignity*.

*dementia: 치매 **autism: 자폐성

① The Importance of Protecting Human Dignity
② Robots Can't Surpass Human Beings in Nursing Jobs
③ Why Robots for Vulnerable People Should Look Like Robots
④ Can Robots Learn Ethical Behavior Through Human Interaction?
⑤ Healthcare Robots: Opening the Era of Online Medical Checkups

25. 다음 도표의 내용과 일치하지 <u>않는</u> 것은?

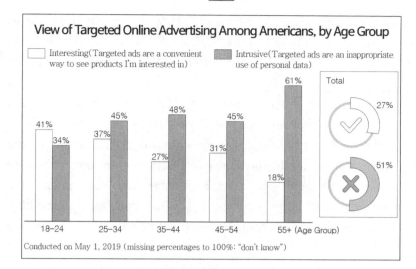

View of Targeted Online Advertising Among Americans, by Age Group

□ Interesting(Targeted ads are a convenient way to see products I'm interested in)
■ Intrusive(Targeted ads are an inappropriate use of personal data)

18–24: 41% / 34%
25–34: 37% / 45%
35–44: 27% / 48%
45–54: 31% / 45%
55+ (Age Group): 18% / 61%

Total: 27% ✓, 51% ✗

Conducted on May 1, 2019 (missing percentages to 100%: "don't know")

The graph above shows the results of a 2019 survey on the views of American age groups on targeted online advertising. ① In total, while 51% of the respondents said targeted ads were intrusive, 27% said they were interesting. ② The percentage of respondents who believed that targeted ads were interesting was the highest in the age group of 18 to 24. ③ The percentage of respondents aged 25 to 34 who said that targeted ads were intrusive was the same as that of respondents aged 45 to 54 who said the same. ④ Among all age groups, the gap between respondents who said targeted ads were interesting and those who believed them to be intrusive was the largest in the 35-to-44 age group. ⑤ The age group of 55 and above was the only group where the percentage of respondents who believed targeted ads were intrusive was more than 50%.

26. Maggie L. Walker에 관한 다음 글의 내용과 일치하지 <u>않는</u> 것은?

Maggie L. Walker achieved national prominence as a businesswoman and community leader. She was among the earliest Black students to attend newly-established public schools for African Americans. After graduating, she worked as a teacher for three years at the Valley School, where she had studied. In the early 1900s, Virginia banks owned by white bankers were unwilling to do business with African American organizations or individuals. The racial discrimination by white bankers drove her to study banking and financial laws. She established a newspaper to promote closer communication between the charitable organization she belonged to and the public. Soon after, she founded the St. Luke Penny Savings Bank, which survived the Great Depression and merged with two other banks. It thrived as the oldest continually African American-operated bank until 2009. Walker achieved successes with the vision to make improvements in the way of life for African Americans.

① 아프리카계 미국인을 위해 설립된 학교에 다녔다.
② 졸업 후 자신이 공부했던 학교에서 교사로 일했다.
③ 인종 차별로 인해 은행 금융법 공부를 시작할 수 없었다.
④ 자선 단체와 대중 간의 소통을 장려하고자 신문사를 설립했다.
⑤ 그녀가 설립한 은행은 대공황에서 살아남아 다른 은행들과 합병했다.

27. 2024 Youth Tennis Camp에 관한 다음 안내문의 내용과 일치하지 <u>않는</u> 것은?

2024 Youth Tennis Camp

2024 Youth Tennis Camp is where your child can get instruction from qualified tennis players at indoor tennis courts. It will provide fundamental tennis skills to your children!

Who: Ages 13 to 18
When: January 15 − 18, 2024
Monday to Thursday, 9:00 a.m. − 12:00 p.m.
Registration Fee: $100(lunch included)

Cancellation Policy
• 5 days before the class: 100% refund
• 1−4 days before the class: 50% refund
• On the day of the class and afterwards: No refund

Notes
• No outside food is allowed.
• Participants must bring their own tennis equipment.

Registration is ONLY available online and will start on December 16. Visit our website at www.ytc2024.com to register.

① 자격을 가진 테니스 선수가 지도한다.
② 금요일에는 강습이 없다.
③ 등록비에는 점심 식사가 포함된다.
④ 강습 당일 취소 시 환불받을 수 있다.
⑤ 참가자들은 테니스 장비를 가져와야 한다.

28. Cherrywood High School's T-shirt Design Contest에 관한 다음 안내문의 내용과 일치하는 것은?

Cherrywood High School's T-shirt Design Contest

Help us to design our new school shirts! A panel of student council members will select the winning design. Take this chance at being the designer for the new school T-shirt. This contest is open to all students!

Submission Deadline: 16:00 on December 22, 2023
Winner Announcement Date: December 29, 2023
Location for Submissions: Art Teacher's Office

Contest Rules
• Sketch your design on a piece of plain paper.
• Write your student number and name on your paper.
• Include the school name and logo in your design.
• Max of 4 colors can be used.

Good luck and thanks for your participation!

① 교사들이 수상 디자인을 선정할 예정이다.
② 수상자 발표일은 제출 마감일 다음 날이다.
③ 출품작은 학생회실에 제출해야 한다.
④ 종이에 자신의 학번과 이름을 써야 한다.
⑤ 사용 가능한 색상 수에 제한이 없다.

16회

29. 다음 글의 밑줄 친 부분 중, 어법상 틀린 것은?

Lectins are large proteins that serve as a crucial weapon that plants use to defend ① themselves. The lectins in most plants bind to carbohydrates as we consume the plant. They also bind to sugar molecules ② found in the gut, in the brain, between nerve endings, in joints and in all bodily fluids. According to Dr. Steven Gundry, these sticky proteins can interrupt messaging between cells and ③ cause toxic and inflammatory reactions. Brain fog is just one result of lectins interrupting communication between nerves. An upset stomach is another common symptom of lectin overload. Dr. Gundry lists a wide range of other health problems including aching joints, dementia, headaches and infertility ④ that have been resolved in his patients once they eliminated lectins from their diets. Dr. Paul Saladino writes that the hypothesis that lectins are involved in Parkinson's disease is also gaining support, with animal studies ⑤ showed that 'lectins, once eaten, may be damaging the gut and travelling to the brain, where they appear to be toxic to dopaminergic neurons'.

* inflammatory: 염증성의

30. 다음 글의 밑줄 친 부분 중, 문맥상 낱말의 쓰임이 적절하지 <u>않은</u> 것은? [3점]

Technology changes how individuals and societies understand the concept of privacy. The fact that someone has a new ability to access information or watch the actions of another does not ① justify doing so. Rather, advances in technology require citizens and policy makers to consider how privacy protections should be expanded. For example, when cameras first became available for commercial and private use, nations and citizens struggled over whether new laws should be enacted to ② protect individuals from being photographed without their permission. The ③ reconsideration of privacy brought about by this new technology re-affirmed a distinction between private and public spaces. It was determined by most cultures that people automatically gave ④ consent to being seen — and thus recorded — once they voluntarily stepped into a public space. Although some people might be uncomfortable with the spread of surveillance cameras, citizens in most cultures have adjusted to the fact that giving up the right not to be observed in these circumstances causes ⑤ more harm to the community than failing to have surveillance.

* surveillance: 감시

[31 ~ 34] 다음 빈칸에 들어갈 말로 가장 적절한 것을 고르시오.

31. Coincidence that is statistically impossible seems to us like an irrational event, and some define it as a miracle. But, as Montaigne has said, "the origin of a miracle is in our _____, at the level of our knowledge of nature, and not in nature itself." Glorious miracles have been later on discovered to be obedience to the laws of nature or a technological development that was not widely known at the time. As the German poet, Goethe, phrased it: "Things that are *mysterious* are *not* yet *miracles*." The miracle assumes the intervention of a "higher power" in its occurrence that is beyond human capability to grasp. Yet there are methodical and simple ways to "cause a miracle" without divine revelation and inspiration. Instead of checking it out, investigating and finding the source of the event, we define it as a miracle. The miracle, then, is the excuse of those who are too lazy to think. [3점]

* revelation: 계시

① ignorance
② flexibility
③ excellence
④ satisfaction
⑤ exaggeration

32. Information encountered after an event can influence subsequent remembering. External information can easily integrate into a witness's memory, especially if the event was poorly encoded or the memory is from a distant event, in which case time and forgetting have degraded the original memory. With reduced information available in memory with which to confirm the validity of post-event misinformation, it is less likely that

_____.

Instead, especially when it fits the witness's current thinking and can be used to create a story that makes sense to him or her, it may be integrated as part of the original experience. This process can be explicit (i.e., the witness knows it is happening), but it is often unconscious. That is, the witness might find himself or herself thinking about the event differently without awareness. Over time, the witness may not even know the source of information that led to the (new) memory. Sources of misinformation in forensic contexts can be encountered anywhere, from discussions with other witnesses to social media searches to multiple interviews with investigators or other legal professionals, and even in court. [3점]

* forensic: 법정의

① this new information will be rejected
② people will deny the experience of forgetting
③ interference between conflicting data will occur
④ the unconscious will be involved in the recall process
⑤ a recent event will last longer in memory than a distant one

[해설편 p.164]

33. Correlations are powerful because the insights they offer are relatively clear. These insights are often covered up when we bring causality back into the picture. For instance, a used−car dealer supplied data to statisticians to predict which of the vehicles available for purchase at an auction were likely to have problems. A correlation analysis showed that orange−colored cars were far less likely to have defects. Even as we read this, we already think about why it might be so: Are orange−colored car owners likely to be car enthusiasts and take better care of their vehicles? Or, is it because orange−colored cars are more noticeable on the road and therefore less likely to be in accidents, so they're in better condition when resold? Quickly we are caught in a web of competing causal hypotheses. But our attempts to illuminate things this way only make them cloudier. Correlations exist; we can show them mathematically. We can't easily do the same for causal links. So we would do well to _____.

[3점]

① stay away from simply accepting the data as they are
② point out every phenomenon in light of cause and effect
③ apply a psychological approach to color preferences
④ admit that correlations are within the framework of causality
⑤ hold off from trying to explain the reason behind the correlations

34. Most mice in the wild are eaten or die before their life span of two years is over. They die from *external causes*, such as disease, starvation, or predators, not due to *internal causes*, such as aging. That is why nature has made mice to live, on average, for no longer than two years. Now we have arrived at an important point: The average life span of an animal species, or the rate at which it ages, is determined by _____.

That explains why a bat can live to be 30 years old. In contrast to mice, bats can fly, which is why they can escape from danger much faster. Thanks to their wings, bats can also cover longer distances and are better able to find food. Every genetic change in the past that made it possible for a bat to live longer was useful, because bats are much better able than mice to flee from danger, find food, and survive.

① the distance that migrating species can travel for their survival
② the average time that this animal species can survive in the wild
③ the amount of energy that members of the species expend in a day
④ the extent to which this species is able to protect its source of food
⑤ the maximum size of the habitat in which it and its neighbors coexist

35. 다음 글에서 전체 흐름과 관계 <u>없는</u> 문장은? [3점]

Moral excellence, according to Aristotle, is the result of habit and repetition, though modern science would also suggest that it may have an innate, genetic component. ① This means that moral excellence will be broadly set early in our lives, which is why the question of how early to teach it is so important. ② Freud suggested that we don't change our personality much after age five or thereabouts, but as in many other things, Freud was wrong. ③ A person of moral excellence cannot help doing good — it is as natural as the change of seasons or the rotation of the planets. ④ Recent psychological research shows that personality traits stabilize around age thirty in both men and women and regardless of ethnicity as the human brain continues to develop, both neuroanatomically and in terms of cognitive skills, until the mid−twenties. ⑤ The advantage of this new understanding is that we can be a bit more optimistic than Aristotle and Freud about being able to teach moral excellence.

* neuroanatomically: 신경 해부학적으로

16회

[36 ~ 37] 주어진 글 다음에 이어질 글의 순서로 가장 적절한 것을 고르시오.

36.

> The size of a species is not accidental. It's a fine−tuned interaction between a species and the world it inhabits. Over large periods of time, size fluctuations have often signalled significant changes in the environment.

(A) But we are beginning to see changes in this trend. Scientists have discovered that many animals are shrinking. Around the world, species in every category have been found to be getting smaller, and one major cause appears to be the heat.

(B) Generally speaking, over the last five hundred million years, the trend has been towards animals getting larger. It's particularly notable in marine animals, whose average body size has increased 150−fold in this time.

(C) Animals living in the Italian Alps, for example, have seen temperatures rise by three to four degrees Celsius since the 1980s. To avoid overheating, chamois goats now spend more of their days resting rather than searching for food, and as a result, in just a few decades, the new generations of chamois are 25 percent smaller.

① (A) − (C) − (B)　　　② (B) − (A) − (C)
③ (B) − (C) − (A)　　　④ (C) − (A) − (B)
⑤ (C) − (B) − (A)

37.

For a long time, random sampling was a good shortcut. It made analysis of large data problems possible in the pre-digital era.

(A) There is no need to focus at the beginning, since collecting all the information makes it possible to do that afterwards. Because rays from the entire light field are included, it is closer to all the data. As a result, the information is more "reuseable" than ordinary pictures, where the photographer has to decide what to focus on before she presses the shutter.

(B) But much as converting a digital image or song into a smaller file results in loss of data, information is lost when sampling. Having the full (or close to the full) dataset provides a lot more freedom to explore, to look at the data from different angles or to look closer at certain aspects of it.

(C) A fitting example may be the light-field camera, which captures not just a single plane of light, as with conventional cameras, but rays from the entire light field, some 11 million of them. The photographers can decide later which element of an image to focus on in the digital file. [3점]

① (A) - (C) - (B)
② (B) - (A) - (C)
③ (B) - (C) - (A)
④ (C) - (A) - (B)
⑤ (C) - (B) - (A)

[38 ~ 39] 글의 흐름으로 보아, 주어진 문장이 들어가기에 가장 적절한 곳을 고르시오.

38.

We must reexamine this stereotype, however, as it doesn't always hold true.

Introverted leaders do have to overcome the strong cultural presumption that extroverts are more effective leaders. (①) Although the population splits into almost equal parts between introverts and extroverts, more than 96 percent of managers and executives are extroverted. (②) In a study done in 2006, 65 percent of senior corporate executives viewed introversion as a barrier to leadership. (③) Regent University found that a desire to be of service to others and to empower them to grow, which is more common among introverts than extroverts, is a key factor in becoming a leader and retaining leadership. (④) So-called servant leadership, dating back to ancient philosophical literature, adheres to the belief that a company's goals are best achieved by helping workers or customers achieve their goals. (⑤) Such leaders do not seek attention but rather want to shine a light on others' wins and achievements; servant leadership requires humility, but that humility ultimately pays off.

* humility: 겸손

39.

However, contrary to the trend of the past several decades, in many new situations that are occurring today, allowing for imprecision—for messiness—may be a positive feature, not a shortcoming.

By the nineteenth century, France had developed a system of precisely defined units of measurement to capture space, time, and more, and had begun to get other nations to adopt the same standards. (①) Just half a century later, in the 1920s, the discoveries of quantum mechanics forever destroyed the dream of comprehensive and perfect measurement. (②) And yet, outside a relatively small circle of physicists, the mindset of humankind's drive to flawlessly measure continued among engineers and scientists. (③) In the world of business it even expanded, as the precision-oriented sciences of mathematics and statistics began to influence all areas of commerce. (④) As a tradeoff for relaxing the standards of allowable errors, one can get a hold of much more data. (⑤) It isn't just that "more is better than some," but that, in fact, sometimes "more is greater than better."

40. 다음 글의 내용을 한 문장으로 요약하고자 한다. 빈칸 (A), (B)에 들어갈 말로 가장 적절한 것은?

Multiple laboratory studies show that cooperative people tend to receive social advantages from others. One way to demonstrate this is to give people the opportunity to act positively or negatively toward contributors. For example, Pat Barclay, a professor at the University of Guelph, had participants play a cooperative game where people could contribute money toward a group fund which helped all group members, and then allowed participants to give money to other participants based on their reputations. People who contributed more to the group fund were given responsibility for more money than people who contributed less. Similar results have been found by other researchers. People who contribute toward their groups are also chosen more often as interaction partners, preferred as leaders, rated as more desirable partners for long-term relationships, and are perceived to be trustworthy and have high social status. Uncooperative people tend to receive verbal criticism or even more severe punishment.

↓

Studies suggest that individuals who act with ___(A)___ toward their communities are more likely to be viewed as deserving of ___(B)___ by members of that community than those who don't.

	(A)	(B)		(A)	(B)
①	generosity	benefit	②	hostility	support
③	generosity	humiliation	④	hostility	hospitality
⑤	tolerance	dishonor			

[41 ~ 42] 다음 글을 읽고, 물음에 답하시오.

In Western society, many music performance settings make a clear distinction between performers and audience members: the performers are the "doers" and those in the audience take a decidedly passive role. The performance space itself may further (a) <u>reinforce</u> the distinction with a physical separation between the stage and audience seating. Perhaps because this distinction is so common, audiences seem to greatly value opportunities to have special "access" to performers that affords understanding about performers' style of music. Some performing musicians have won great approval by regularly (b) <u>incorporating</u> "audience participation" into their concerts. Whether by leading a sing—along activity or teaching a rhythm to be clapped at certain points, including audience members in the music making can (c) <u>boost</u> the level of engagement and enjoyment for all involved. Performers who are uncomfortable leading audience participation can still connect with the audience simply by giving a special glimpse of the performer (d) <u>perspective</u>. It is quite common in classical music to provide audiences with program notes. Typically, this text in a program gives background information about pieces of music being performed and perhaps biographical information about historically significant composers. What may be of more interest to audience members is background information about the very performers who are onstage, including an explanation of why they have chosen the music they are presenting. Such insight can make audience members feel (e) <u>distant</u> to the musicians onstage, both metaphorically and emotionally. This connection will likely enhance the expressive and communicative experience.

41. 윗글의 제목으로 가장 적절한 것은?

① Bridge the Divide and Get the Audience Involved
② Musical Composition Reflects the Musician's Experience
③ Why a Performer's Style Changes with Each Performance
④ Understanding Performers on Stage: An Audience's Responsibility
⑤ The Effect of Theater Facilities on the Success of a Performance

42. 밑줄 친 (a)~(e) 중에서 문맥상 낱말의 쓰임이 적절하지 <u>않은</u> 것은?

① (a)　　② (b)　　③ (c)　　④ (d)　　⑤ (e)

[43 ~ 45] 다음 글을 읽고, 물음에 답하시오.

(A)

Once upon a time, two brothers, Robert and James, who lived on neighboring farms fell into conflict. It was the first serious fight in 40 years of farming side by side. It began with a small misunderstanding and it grew into a major argument, and finally it exploded into an exchange of bitter words followed by weeks of silence. One morning there was a knock on Robert's door. (a) <u>He</u> opened it to find a carpenter with a toolbox.

(B)

The two brothers stood awkwardly for a moment, but soon met on the bridge and shook hands. They saw the carpenter leaving with his toolbox. "No, wait! Stay a few more days." Robert told him. "Thank you for (b) <u>your</u> invitation. But I need to go build more bridges. Don't forget. The fence leads to isolation and the bridge to openness," said carpenter. The two brothers nodded at the carpenter's words.

(C)

Looking at Robert, the carpenter said, "I'm looking for a few days' work. Do (c) <u>you</u> have anything to repair?" "I have nothing to be repaired, but I have a job for you. Look across the creek at that farm. Last week, my younger brother James took his bulldozer and put that creek in the meadow between us. Well, (d) <u>I</u> will do even worse. I want you to build me an 8—foot tall fence which will block him from seeing my place," said Robert. The carpenter seemed to understand the situation.

(D)

Robert prepared all the materials the carpenter needed. The next day, Robert left to work on another farm, so he couldn't watch the carpenter for some days. When Robert returned and saw the carpenter's work, his jaw dropped. Instead of a fence, the carpenter had built a bridge that stretched from one side of the creek to the other. His brother was walking over, waving (e) <u>his</u> hand in the air. Robert laughed and said to the carpenter, "You really can fix anything."

43. 주어진 글 (A)에 이어질 내용을 순서에 맞게 배열한 것으로 가장 적절한 것은?

① (B) − (C) − (D)　　　② (C) − (B) − (D)
③ (C) − (D) − (B)　　　④ (D) − (B) − (C)
⑤ (D) − (C) − (B)

44. 밑줄 친 (a)~(e) 중에서 가리키는 대상이 나머지 넷과 <u>다른</u> 것은?

① (a)　　② (b)　　③ (c)　　④ (d)　　⑤ (e)

45. 윗글에 관한 내용으로 적절하지 <u>않은</u> 것은?

① Robert와 James는 40년간 나란히 농사를 지었다.
② Robert는 떠나려는 목수에게 더 머무르라고 말했다.
③ James는 불도저로 초원에 샛강을 만들었다.
④ Robert는 목수가 필요로 하는 재료들을 준비해 주었다.
⑤ 목수는 샛강에 다리 대신 울타리를 설치했다.

※ 확인 사항

○ 답안지의 해당란에 필요한 내용을 정확히 기입(표기)했는지 확인하시오.

18

001 inform ⓥ 알리다
002 ongoing ⓐ 진행 중인
003 experience ⓥ 경험하다
004 fully ⓐⓓ 완전히, 충분히
005 support ⓥ 지지하다, 지원하다
006 constantly ⓐⓓ 끊임없이, 계속해서
007 disrupt ⓥ 방해하다, 중단시키다
008 bounce ⓥ 튀기다
009 struggle ⓥ 투쟁하다, 애쓰다
010 restrict ⓥ 제한하다, 한정하다
011 neighborhood ⓝ 이웃

19

012 stump ⓝ 그루터기
013 rite ⓝ 의례
014 youth ⓝ 청년
015 tribe ⓝ 부족, 종족
016 survive ⓥ 살아남다
017 blindfold ⓝ 눈가리개 ⓥ 눈을 가리다
018 observe ⓥ 관찰하다
019 blow ⓥ 불다, 날리다
020 dread ⓝ 두려움, 공포
021 sweep ⓥ 쓸다, 청소하다
022 stability ⓝ 안정, 안정성
023 panic ⓥ 당황하다, 공포에 질리다
024 awfully ⓐⓓ 아주, 몹시
025 a moment ago 방금 전에, 잠시 전에
026 vanish ⓥ 사라지다, 없어지다
027 into thin air 온데간데없이, 흔적도 없이

20

028 agriculture ⓝ 농업
029 a range of 다양한, 범위의
030 planting ⓝ 파종
031 fertilize ⓥ 비료를 주다
032 pest ⓝ 해충, 성가신 사람이나 것
033 distribute ⓥ 배포하다, 분배하다
034 essential ⓐ 필수적인, 본질적인
035 critical ⓐ 중요한, 비판적인
036 development ⓝ 개발, 발전
037 allow ⓥ 허락하다, 가능하게 하다
038 remain ⓥ 남다, 머무르다
039 vital ⓐ 중요한, 필수적인
040 industry ⓝ 산업, 공업
041 feed ⓥ 먹이다, 공급하다 ⓝ 먹이, 공급
042 provide ⓥ 제공하다, 공급하다
043 material ⓝ 재료, 물질
044 numerous ⓐ 다수의, 수많은
045 challenge ⓝ 도전
046 scarcity ⓝ 부족, 희소성
047 degradation ⓝ 저하
048 biodiversity ⓝ 생물다양성

21

049 aesthetics ⓝ 미학
050 offer ⓥ 제공하다, 제안하다
051 emotional ⓐ 감정적인
052 connection ⓝ 연결
053 range ⓝ 범위, 영역
054 discomfort ⓝ 불편, 불쾌
055 engage ⓥ 참여하다, 끌어들이다

22

056 possibility ⓝ 가능성, 잠재력
057 vehicle ⓝ 차량, 탈것
058 otherwise ⓐⓓ 그렇지 않으면, 달리
059 masterpiece ⓝ 걸작, 명작
060 cruel ⓐ 잔인한, 무자비한
061 cause ⓥ 일으키다, 야기하다
062 Civil War 내전, 시민 전쟁
063 discrimination ⓝ 차별
064 portrait ⓝ 초상화

22

065 historian ⓝ 역사학자
066 significance ⓝ 중요성, 의의
067 accurate ⓐ 정확한
068 measurement ⓝ 측정, 치수
069 mechanical ⓐ 기계의
070 turning point 전환점, 분기점
071 stroke ⓝ 뇌졸중, 타격
072 contribute ⓥ 기여하다
073 concept ⓝ 개념, 구상
074 commerce ⓝ 상업
075 transaction ⓝ 거래, 처리
076 irregular ⓐ 불규칙한, 고르지 않은
077 allocate ⓥ 할당하다, 분배하다
078 efficient ⓐ 효율적인, 능률적인
079 manner ⓝ 방식, 태도

23

080 device ⓝ 장치, 기기
081 spite ⓝ 악의, 앙심
082 repeat ⓥ 반복하다, 되풀이하다
083 advertisement ⓝ 광고
084 persuade ⓥ 설득하다, 납득시키다
085 reluctant ⓐ 꺼리는, 주저하는
086 remind ⓥ 상기시키다, 연상시키다
087 attractive ⓐ 매력적인, 마음을 끄는
088 hit upon …을 (우연히) 생각해내다
089 hire ⓥ 고용하다, 채용하다
090 regular ⓐ 보통의
091 shill ⓝ 바람잡이
092 disguise ⓥ 변장하다
093 accomplish ⓥ 달성하다
094 logic ⓝ 논리, 이치

24

095 response ⓝ 답변
096 critic ⓝ 비평가
097 charge ⓥ 고소하다
098 moral ⓐ 도덕적인, 윤리적인
099 hazard ⓝ 위험, 위험 요소
100 dementia ⓝ 치매
101 vulnerable ⓐ 취약한, 연약한
102 autism ⓝ 자폐성
103 cognitive ⓐ 인지의, 인식의
104 deficit ⓝ 결함, 부족
105 according ⓟ ~에 따르면, ~에 의하면
106 inferior ⓐ 열등한, 하위의
107 reasoning ⓝ 추리, 추론, 논리적 사고
108 State University 주립 대학
109 synthetic ⓐ 합성의, 인조의
110 unsophisticated ⓐ 순수한, 단순한, 소박한
111 uncanny valley 불쾌한 골짜기

25

112 resemble ⓥ 닮다, 비슷하다
113 violate ⓥ 위반하다, 침해하다
114 dignity ⓝ 존엄성, 위엄, 품위

25

115 above ⓟ ~위에, ~보다 높이
116 result ⓝ 결과, 성과
117 survey ⓝ 조사
118 targeted ⓐ 표적이 된
119 advertising ⓝ 광고, 홍보
120 respondent ⓝ 응답자
121 intrusive ⓐ 침해적

26

122 prominence ⓝ 명성
123 unwilling ⓐ 꺼리는, 마지못한
124 organization ⓝ 조직
125 individual ⓝ 개인
126 financial ⓐ 금융의, 재정의
127 promote ⓥ 홍보하다
128 charitable ⓐ 자비로운, 자선의
129 belong ⓥ 속하다, 소속되다
130 the Great Depression 대공황
131 merge ⓥ 합병하다
132 thrive ⓥ 번창하다, 성공하다

27

133 instruction ⓝ 지도
134 qualified ⓐ 자격이 있는
135 indoor ⓐ 실내의
136 fundamental ⓐ 기초의
137 refund ⓝ 환불
138 outside ⓐ 외부의, 밖의
139 equipment ⓝ 장비, 설비
140 available ⓐ 이용 가능한

28

141 contest ⓝ 대회
142 design ⓥ 디자인하다
143 council ⓝ 의회
144 submission ⓝ 제출
145 announcement ⓝ 발표

29

146 protein ⓝ 단백질
147 serve as ~로서 역할을 하다
148 crucial ⓐ 중요한
149 weapon ⓝ 무기
150 plant ⓝ 식물 ⓥ 심다
151 defend ⓥ 방어하다, 변호하다
152 carbohydrates ⓝ 탄수화물
153 consume ⓥ 소비하다, 섭취하다
154 bind to ~에 결합하다, ~에 붙다
155 molecules ⓝ 분자
156 joint ⓝ 관절, 이음새
157 bodily fluids 체액
158 sticky ⓐ 끈적거리는, 찐득찐득한
159 cell ⓝ 세포, 작은 방
160 inflammatory ⓐ 염증성의
161 reaction ⓝ 반응, 반작용
162 common ⓐ 흔한, 공통의
163 symptom ⓝ 증상

30

164 overload ⓝ 과부하, 과잉
165 a wide range of 광범위한, 다양한
166 ache ⓝ 통증, 아픔 ⓥ 아프다, 통증이 있다
167 infertility ⓝ 불임
168 eliminate ⓥ 제거하다
169 hypothesis ⓝ 가설
170 Parkinson's disease ⓝ 파킨슨병

30

171 technology ⓝ 기술
172 privacy ⓝ 사생활, 프라이버시
173 ability ⓝ 능력, 재능
174 justify ⓥ 정당화하다, 해명하다
175 rather ⓐⓓ 오히려, 차라리, 다소
176 advance ⓝ 발전, 진보
177 require ⓥ 필요로 하다, 요구하다
178 citizen ⓝ 시민
179 policy maker 정책 결정자, 정책 입안자
180 enact ⓥ (법을) 제정하다, 시행하다
181 permission ⓝ 허가, 승인
182 reconsideration ⓝ 재고, 재검토
183 distinction ⓝ 구별, 차이, 우수성
184 determine ⓥ 결정하다, 결심하다, 측정하다
185 consent ⓝ 동의하다
186 surveillance ⓝ 감시
187 circumstance ⓝ 상황, 환경, 사정

31

188 coincidence ⓝ 우연의 일치, 동시 발생
189 statistically ⓐⓓ 통계적으로
190 irrational ⓐ 비합리적인
191 define ⓥ 정의하다, 규정하다
192 miracle ⓝ 기적
193 ignorance ⓝ 무지, 무식
194 glorious ⓐ 영광스러운, 멋진, 훌륭한
195 obedience ⓝ 순응, 복종, 순종
196 phrase ⓥ 표현하다, 말로 나타내다
197 assume ⓥ 가정하다, 추정하다
198 intervention ⓝ 개입, 중재
199 occurrence ⓝ 발생, 사건
200 beyond ⓐⓓ 그 너머에
201 methodical ⓐ 체계적인
202 capability ⓝ 능력, 역량, 가능성
203 grasp ⓥ 이해하다, 잡다
204 divine ⓐ 신성한, 신의
205 revelation ⓝ 계시
206 inspiration ⓝ 영감, 감화
207 instead of ~대신에, ~하지 않고
208 investigate ⓥ 조사하다
209 excuse ⓝ 변명
210 lazy ⓐ 게으른, 나태한

32

211 encounter ⓥ 마주치다
212 influence ⓝ 영향
213 subsequent ⓐ 그[이] 다음의
214 integrate ⓥ 통합되다
215 poorly ⓐⓓ 형편없이, 저조하게
216 encode ⓥ 부호화하다
217 distant ⓐ 먼, (멀리) 떨어져 있는
218 forgetting ⓝ 망각
219 degrade ⓥ 저하시키다

220 ☐ **reduced** ⓐ 줄인, 축소한	278 ☐ **distance** ⓝ 거리	333 ☐ **decide** ⓥ 결정하다	389 ☐ **reputation** ⓝ 명성
221 ☐ **confirm** ⓥ 확인하다	279 ☐ **useful** ⓐ 유용한	334 ☐ **press** ⓥ 누르다	390 ☐ **prefer** ⓥ 선호하다, 더 좋아하다
222 ☐ **validity** ⓝ 유효함		335 ☐ **shutter** ⓝ (카메라의) 셔터	391 ☐ **desirable** ⓐ 바람직한, 원하는
223 ☐ **post-event** 사건 후	**35**	336 ☐ **convert** ⓥ 변환하다	392 ☐ **long-term** 장기적인
224 ☐ **misinformation** ⓝ 잘못된 정보	280 ☐ **excellence** ⓝ 우수성	337 ☐ **freedom** ⓝ 자유	393 ☐ **relationship** ⓝ 관계, 연관성
225 ☐ **reject** ⓥ 거부하다	281 ☐ **habit** ⓝ 습관	338 ☐ **aspect** ⓝ 양상, 측면	394 ☐ **trustworthy** ⓐ 신뢰할 수 있는, 믿을 만한
226 ☐ **current** ⓐ 현재의	282 ☐ **repetition** ⓝ 반복	339 ☐ **fitting** ⓐ 적합한	395 ☐ **status** ⓝ 상태, 지위, 신분
227 ☐ **makes sense** 이해가 되다	283 ☐ **modern** ⓐ 현대의	340 ☐ **plane** ⓝ (평평한) 면	396 ☐ **uncooperative** ⓐ 협조적이지 않은, 비협조적인
228 ☐ **integrate** ⓥ 통합되다	284 ☐ **suggest** ⓥ 제안하다	341 ☐ **conventional** ⓐ 극히 평범한	397 ☐ **verbal** ⓐ 언어의, 말로 된, 구두의
229 ☐ **explicit** ⓐ 분명한, 명쾌한	285 ☐ **innate** ⓐ 타고난	342 ☐ **element** ⓝ 요소	398 ☐ **generosity** ⓝ 관대함, 너그러움
230 ☐ **unconscious** ⓐ 무의식적인	286 ☐ **component** ⓝ 요소		399 ☐ **view** ⓥ 보다, 간주하다
231 ☐ **awareness** ⓝ 의식[관심]	287 ☐ **broadly** ⓐ𝑑 대략적으로	**38**	400 ☐ **deserving** ⓐ 자격이 있는, 받을 만한
232 ☐ **forensic** ⓐ 법정의	288 ☐ **personality** ⓝ 성격	343 ☐ **reexamine** ⓥ 재검토하다	401 ☐ **benefit** ⓝ 혜택, 이익
233 ☐ **context** ⓝ 맥락, 상황	289 ☐ **thereabouts** ⓐ𝑑 대략, 그쯤	344 ☐ **stereotype** ⓝ 고정관념	402 ☐ **humiliation** ⓝ 굴욕, 창피
234 ☐ **discussion** ⓝ 논의	290 ☐ **rotation** ⓝ 회전	345 ☐ **introverted** ⓐ 내성적인	403 ☐ **hostility** ⓝ 적대감, 적대 행위
235 ☐ **investigator** ⓝ 조사관	291 ☐ **trait** ⓝ (성격상의) 특성	346 ☐ **overcome** ⓥ 극복하다	404 ☐ **hospitality** ⓝ 환대, 접대
236 ☐ **legal** ⓐ 법적의	292 ☐ **stabilize** ⓥ 안정되다	347 ☐ **presumption** ⓝ 추정(되는 것)	405 ☐ **tolerance** ⓝ 관용, 인내
237 ☐ **professional** ⓝ 전문직 종사자	293 ☐ **regardless of** 𝑝𝑟𝑒𝑝 ~에 상관없이	348 ☐ **extrovert** 외향적인 사람	406 ☐ **dishonor** ⓝ 불명예, 치욕
238 ☐ **court** ⓝ 법정, 법원	294 ☐ **ethnicity** ⓝ 민족성	349 ☐ **population** ⓝ 인구	
	295 ☐ **develop** ⓥ 발달하다	350 ☐ **split** ⓥ 나뉘다	**41~42**
33	296 ☐ **neuroanatomically** ⓐ𝑑 신경 해부학적으로	351 ☐ **equal** ⓐ 동일한, 같은	407 ☐ **performance** ⓝ 수행
239 ☐ **correlation** ⓝ 상관관계	297 ☐ **in terms of** ~면에서	352 ☐ **executive** ⓝ 임원	408 ☐ **audience** ⓝ 청중
240 ☐ **insight** ⓝ 통찰력	298 ☐ **optimistic** ⓐ 낙관적인	353 ☐ **corporate** ⓐ 기업의	409 ☐ **decidedly** ⓐ𝑑 단호히
241 ☐ **relatively** ⓐ𝑑 비교적		354 ☐ **barrier** ⓝ 장벽	410 ☐ **passive** ⓐ 수동적인
242 ☐ **cover up** 숨기다, 가리다	**36**	355 ☐ **retain** ⓥ 얻다	411 ☐ **reinforce** ⓥ 강화하다
243 ☐ **causality** ⓝ 인과 관계	299 ☐ **species** ⓝ 종	356 ☐ **so-called** ⓐ 소위, 이른바	412 ☐ **separation** ⓝ 분리, 구분
244 ☐ **used-car** 중고차	300 ☐ **accidental** ⓐ 우연한	357 ☐ **ancient** ⓐ 고대의	413 ☐ **access** ⓝ 접근 ⓥ 접근하다
245 ☐ **statistician** ⓝ 통계학자	301 ☐ **fine-tune** 미세 조정을 하다	358 ☐ **philosophical** ⓐ 철학적인	414 ☐ **afford** ⓥ 제공하다
246 ☐ **predict** ⓥ 예측하다	302 ☐ **interaction** ⓝ 상호 작용	359 ☐ **literature** ⓝ 문헌	415 ☐ **regularly** ⓐ𝑑 규칙적으로
247 ☐ **purchase** ⓝ 구입, 구매	303 ☐ **inhabit** ⓥ 살다, 서식하다	360 ☐ **attention** ⓝ 주의, 주목	416 ☐ **clap** ⓥ 박수를 치다
248 ☐ **auction** ⓝ 경매	304 ☐ **fluctuation** ⓝ 변동	361 ☐ **achievement** ⓝ 성취, 성과	417 ☐ **perspective** ⓝ 관점
249 ☐ **defect** ⓝ 결함	305 ☐ **signal** ⓥ 신호를 보내다	362 ☐ **ultimately** ⓐ𝑑 결국	418 ☐ **biographical** ⓐ 전기체의
250 ☐ **enthusiast** ⓝ 열광적인 팬	306 ☐ **significant** ⓐ 중요한		
251 ☐ **accident** ⓝ 사고	307 ☐ **environment** ⓝ 환경	**39**	**43~45**
252 ☐ **resell** ⓥ 되팔다	308 ☐ **shrink** ⓥ 줄어들다	363 ☐ **contrary** ⓐ 반대의, 상반되는	419 ☐ **farm** ⓝ 농장
253 ☐ **web** ⓝ 망(거미줄)	309 ☐ **major** ⓐ 주요한	364 ☐ **situation** ⓝ 상황, 상태	420 ☐ **conflict** ⓝ 갈등
254 ☐ **compete** ⓥ 경쟁하다	310 ☐ **appear** ⓥ ~인 것 같다	365 ☐ **occur** ⓥ 발생하다	421 ☐ **argument** ⓝ 논쟁
255 ☐ **hypotheses** ⓝ 가설	311 ☐ **heat** ⓝ 열	366 ☐ **imprecision** ⓝ 부정확, 불명확	422 ☐ **exchange** ⓝ 말싸움, 언쟁
256 ☐ **attempt** ⓝ 시도	312 ☐ **trend** ⓝ 동향, 추세	367 ☐ **messiness** ⓝ 어지러움, 지저분함	423 ☐ **bitter** ⓐ 격렬한
257 ☐ **illuminate** ⓥ 밝히다, 분명히 하다	313 ☐ **particularly** ⓐ𝑑 특히	368 ☐ **positive** ⓐ 긍정적인, 확신하는, 양성의	424 ☐ **silence** ⓝ 침묵
258 ☐ **cloudy** ⓐ 흐린	314 ☐ **notable** ⓐ 주목할 만한, 눈에 띄는	369 ☐ **feature** ⓝ 특징, 특성	425 ☐ **carpenter** ⓝ 목수
259 ☐ **exist** ⓥ 존재하다	315 ☐ **marine** ⓐ 해양의	370 ☐ **shortcoming** ⓝ 결점, 단점	426 ☐ **toolbox** ⓝ 공구함, 연장통
260 ☐ **mathematically** ⓐ𝑑 수학적으로	316 ☐ **increase** ⓥ 증가하다	371 ☐ **precisely** ⓐ𝑑 정확하게, 정밀하게	427 ☐ **awkwardly** ⓐ𝑑 어색하게
261 ☐ **casual** ⓐ 원인의	317 ☐ **temperature** ⓝ 온도	372 ☐ **standard** ⓝ 기준, 표준	428 ☐ **bridge** ⓝ 다리
262 ☐ **hold off** 시작하지 않다	318 ☐ **rise** ⓝ 증가, 상승	373 ☐ **quantum mechanics** 양자 역학	429 ☐ **repair** ⓥ 수리하다
	319 ☐ **degree** ⓝ (온도 단위인) 도	374 ☐ **destroy** ⓥ 파괴하다	430 ☐ **creek** ⓝ 개울
34	320 ☐ **avoid** ⓥ 피하다	375 ☐ **comprehensive** ⓐ 포괄적인, 종합적인	431 ☐ **meadow** ⓝ 초원, 목초지
263 ☐ **mouse** 쥐(𝑝𝑙. mice)	321 ☐ **overheating** ⓝ 과열	376 ☐ **physicist** ⓝ 물리학자	432 ☐ **worse** ⓐ 더 심한
264 ☐ **wild** ⓐ 야생의	322 ☐ **decade** ⓝ 10년	377 ☐ **mindset** ⓝ 사고방식, 태도	433 ☐ **fence** ⓝ 울타리
265 ☐ **span** ⓝ 기간	323 ☐ **generation** ⓝ 세대	378 ☐ **flawlessly** ⓐ𝑑 완벽하게, 흠없이	434 ☐ **jaw** ⓝ 턱
266 ☐ **external** ⓐ 외부의		379 ☐ **continue** ⓥ 계속하다	435 ☐ **stretch** ⓥ 뻗어 있다
267 ☐ **disease** ⓝ 질병	**37**	380 ☐ **oriented** ⓐ 유래된	
268 ☐ **starvation** ⓝ 기아	324 ☐ **sampling** ⓝ 표본 추출	381 ☐ **tradeoff** ⓝ 균형, 절충, 맞바꿈	
269 ☐ **predator** ⓝ 포식자	325 ☐ **shortcut** ⓝ 지름길	382 ☐ **allowable** ⓐ 허용 가능한, 허용되는	
270 ☐ **internal** ⓐ 내부의	326 ☐ **analysis** ⓝ 분석		
271 ☐ **aging** ⓝ 노화	327 ☐ **era** ⓝ 시대	**40**	
272 ☐ **arrive** ⓥ 도착하다	328 ☐ **collect** ⓥ 수집하다	383 ☐ **laboratory** ⓝ 연구실	
273 ☐ **lifespan** ⓝ 수명	329 ☐ **afterwards** ⓐ𝑑 나중에	384 ☐ **cooperative** ⓐ 협력적인	
274 ☐ **rate** ⓝ 속도	330 ☐ **ray** ⓝ 광선	385 ☐ **receive** ⓥ 받다	
275 ☐ **bat** ⓝ 박쥐	331 ☐ **reusable** ⓐ 재사용이 가능한	386 ☐ **advantage** ⓝ 이점, 유리한 점	
276 ☐ **in contrast** ~와 대조적으로	332 ☐ **ordinary** ⓐ 보통의	387 ☐ **fund** ⓝ 기금, 자금	
277 ☐ **escape** ⓥ 탈출하다		388 ☐ **based on** ~에 기초하여, ~을 바탕으로	

16회

● 채점 : 맞은 개수 _____ / 80

TEST A-B 각 단어의 뜻을 [A] 영어는 우리말로, [B] 우리말은 영어로 쓰시오.

A	English	Korean
01	inform	
02	ongoing	
03	neighborhood	
04	youth	
05	observe	
06	agriculture	
07	degradation	
08	critical	
09	challenge	
10	possibility	
11	portrait	
12	vehicle	
13	historian	
14	typically	
15	contribute	
16	commerce	
17	mechanical	
18	introduce	
19	device	
20	reluctant	

B	Korean	English
01	달성하다	
02	설득하다	
03	답변	
04	열등한	
05	인지의, 인식의	
06	조사	
07	침해적	
08	개인	
09	지도	
10	기초의	
11	제출	
12	발표	
13	무기	
14	중요한	
15	제거하다	
16	사생활	
17	자발적으로, 자진해서	
18	감시	
19	통계적으로	
20	체계적인	

▶ A-D 정답 : 해설편 170쪽

TEST C-D 각 단어의 뜻을 골라 기호를 쓰시오.

C	English		Korean
01	escape	( )	ⓐ 개입
02	intervention	( )	ⓑ 확인하다
03	accidental	( )	ⓒ 조사관
04	develop	( )	ⓓ 경쟁하다
05	laboratory	( )	ⓔ 기간
06	oriented	( )	ⓕ 탈출하다
07	confirm	( )	ⓖ 성격
08	cooperative	( )	ⓗ 발달하다
09	personality	( )	ⓘ 제안하다
10	reputation	( )	ⓙ 우연한
11	suggest	( )	ⓚ 종
12	destroy	( )	ⓛ 요소
13	compete	( )	ⓜ 고정관념
14	element	( )	ⓝ 철학적인
15	investigator	( )	ⓞ 유지하다
16	species	( )	ⓟ 파괴하다
17	stereotype	( )	ⓠ 유래된
18	philosophical	( )	ⓡ 협력적인
19	retain	( )	ⓢ 연구실
20	span	( )	ⓣ 명성

D	Korean		English
01	의회	( )	ⓐ reinforce
02	온도	( )	ⓑ awkwardly
03	목수	( )	ⓒ carpenter
04	법적의	( )	ⓓ isolation
05	포함하다	( )	ⓔ openness
06	조직	( )	ⓕ repair
07	살아남다	( )	ⓖ refund
08	강화하다	( )	ⓗ critic
09	개방	( )	ⓘ uncomfortable
10	수리하다	( )	ⓙ meaningful
11	가설	( )	ⓚ significance
12	비평가	( )	ⓛ include
13	의미 있는	( )	ⓜ survive
14	어색하게	( )	ⓝ organization
15	비합리적인	( )	ⓞ council
16	접근하다	( )	ⓟ access
17	고립	( )	ⓠ legal
18	환불	( )	ⓡ irrational
19	불편한	( )	ⓢ hypothesis
20	중요성, 중대성	( )	ⓣ temperature

※ 영어 [독해] 파트만 수록한 문제지이므로 **18번**부터 시작합니다.
● 점수 표시가 없는 문항은 모두 2점 ● 문항수 **28개** | 배점 **63점** | 제한 시간 **45분**

18. 다음 글의 목적으로 가장 적절한 것은?

Dear local business owners,

My name is Carol Williams, president of the student council at Yellowstone High School. We are hosting our annual quiz night on March 30 and plan to give prizes to the winning team. However, this event won't be possible without the support of local businesses who provide valuable products and services. Would you be willing to donate a gift certificate that we can use as a prize? We would be grateful for any amount on the certificate. In exchange for your generosity, we would place an advertisement for your business on our answer sheets. Thank you for taking time to read this letter and consider our request. If you'd like to donate or need more information, please call or email me. I look forward to hearing from you soon.

Carol Williams

① 행사 홍보물 게시가 가능한지를 문의하려고
② 학교 퀴즈 행사에 사용할 물품 제작을 의뢰하려고
③ 우승 상품으로 사용할 상품권을 기부해 줄 것을 요청하려고
④ 학교 행사로 예상되는 소음 발생에 대해 양해를 구하려고
⑤ 퀴즈 행사 개최를 위한 장소 사용 허가를 받으려고

19. 다음 글에 드러난 'I'의 심경 변화로 가장 적절한 것은?

Dan and I were supposed to make a presentation that day. Right after the class started, my phone buzzed. It was a text from Dan saying, "I can't make it on time. There's been a car accident on the road!" I almost fainted. 'What should I do?' Dan didn't show up before our turn, and soon I was standing in front of the whole class. I managed to finish my portion, and my mind went blank for a few seconds, wondering what to do. 'Hold yourself together!' I quickly came to my senses and worked through Dan's part of the presentation as best as I could. After a few moments, I finished the entire presentation on my own. Only then did the tension vanish. I could see our professor's beaming face.

① panicked → relieved
② sorrowful → indifferent
③ sympathetic → content
④ jealous → delighted
⑤ confused → humiliated

20. 다음 글에서 필자가 주장하는 바로 가장 적절한 것은?

Clarity in an organization keeps everyone working in one accord and energizes key leadership components like trust and transparency. No matter who or what is being assessed in your organization, what they are being assessed on must be clear and the people must be aware of it. If individuals in your organization are assessed without knowing what they are being assessed on, it can cause mistrust and move your organization away from clarity. For your organization to be productive, cohesive, and successful, trust is essential. Failure to have trust in your organization will have a negative effect on the results of any assessment. It will also significantly hinder the growth of your organization. To conduct accurate assessments, trust is a must — which comes through clarity. In turn, assessments help you see clearer, which then empowers your organization to reach optimal success.

① 조직이 구성원에게 제공하는 보상은 즉각적이어야 한다.
② 조직의 발전을 위해 구성원은 동료의 능력을 신뢰해야 한다.
③ 조직 내 구성원의 능력에 맞는 명확한 목표를 설정해야 한다.
④ 조직의 신뢰 형성을 위해 구성원에 대한 평가 요소가 명확해야 한다.
⑤ 구성원의 의견 수용을 위해 신뢰에 기반한 조직 문화가 구축되어야 한다.

21. 밑줄 친 "eating my problems for breakfast"가 다음 글에서 의미하는 바로 가장 적절한 것은?

Research in the science of peak performance and motivation points to the fact that different tasks should ideally be matched to our energy level. For example, analytical tasks are best accomplished when our energy is high and we are free from distractions and able to focus. I generally wake up energized. Over the years, I have consistently stuck to the habit of "eating my problems for breakfast." I'm someone who tends to overthink different scenarios and conversations that haven't happened yet. When I procrastinate on talking with an unhappy client or dealing with an unpleasant email, I find I waste too much emotional energy during the day. It's as if the task hangs over my head, and I'll spend more time worrying about it, talking about it, and avoiding it, than it would actually take to just take care of it. So for me, it'll always be the first thing I get done. If you know you are not a morning person, be strategic about scheduling your difficult work later in the day.

* procrastinate: 미루다

① thinking of breakfast as fuel for the day
② trying to reflect on pleasant events from yesterday
③ handling the most demanding tasks while full of energy
④ spending the morning time improving my physical health
⑤ preparing at night to avoid decision making in the morning

22. 다음 글의 요지로 가장 적절한 것은?

In one study, when researchers suggested that a date was associated with a new beginning (such as "the first day of spring"), students viewed it as a more attractive time to kick-start goal pursuit than when researchers presented it as an unremarkable day (such as "the third Thursday in March"). Whether it was starting a new gym habit or spending less time on social media, when the date that researchers suggested was associated with a new beginning, more students wanted to begin changes right then. And more recent research by a different team found that similar benefits were achieved by showing goal seekers modified weekly calendars. When calendars depicted the current day (either Monday or Sunday) as the first day of the week, people reported feeling more motivated to make immediate progress on their goals.

① 새로운 시작을 하기 전에 장기적인 계획을 세우는 것이 바람직하다.
② 자신이 해야 할 일을 일정표에 표시하는 것이 목표 달성에 효과적이다.
③ 문제 행동을 개선하기 위해 원인이 되는 요소를 파악할 필요가 있다.
④ 날짜가 시작이라는 의미와 관련지어질 때 목표 추구에 강한 동기가 부여된다.
⑤ 상세한 일정표를 작성하는 것은 여러 목표를 동시에 달성하는 데 도움이 된다.

23. 다음 글의 주제로 가장 적절한 것은?

Native Americans often sang and danced in preparation for launching an attack. The emotional and neurochemical excitement that resulted from this preparatory singing gave them stamina to carry out their attacks. What may have begun as an unconscious, uncontrolled act — rushing their victims with singing and beating drums in a frenzy — could have become a strategy as the victors saw firsthand the effect their actions had on those they were attacking. Although war dances risk warning an enemy of an upcoming attack, the arousal and synchronizing benefits for the attackers may compensate for the loss of surprise. Humans who sang, danced, and marched may have enjoyed a strong advantage on the battlefield as well as intimidated enemies who witnessed such a spectacle. Nineteenth-and twentieth-century Germans feared no one more than the Scots — the bagpipes and drums were disturbing in their sheer loudness and visual spectacle.

* frenzy: 격분   ** synchronize: 동시에 움직이게 하다

① cultural differences in honoring war victims
② benefits of utilizing sound and motion in warfare
③ functions of music in preventing or resolving conflicts
④ strategies of analyzing an enemy's vulnerable points in war
⑤ effects of religious dances on lowering anxiety on the battlefield

24. 다음 글의 제목으로 가장 적절한 것은?

The recent "cycling as a lifestyle" craze has expressed itself in an increase in the number of active cyclists and in growth of cycling club membership in several European, American, Australian and Asian urban areas. It has also been accompanied by a symbolic reinterpretation of the bicycle. After the bicycle had been associated with poverty for many years, expensive recreational bicycles or recreationally-inspired commuting bicycles have suddenly become aspirational products in urban environments. In present times, cycling has become an activity which is also performed for its demonstrative value, its role in identity construction and its effectiveness in impressing others and signaling social status. To a certain extent, cycling has turned into a symbolic marker of the well-off. Obviously, value-laden consumption behavior is by no means limited to cycling. However, the link with identity construction and conspicuous consumption has become particularly manifest in the case of cycling.

* conspicuous: 눈에 잘 띄는

① Cycling Contributes to a City's Atmosphere and Identity
② The Rise of Cycling: A New Status Symbol of City Dwellers
③ Cycling Is Wealth-Building but Worsens Social Inequality
④ How to Encourage and Sustain the Bicycle Craze in Urban Areas
⑤ Expanding Bike Lane Networks Can Lead to More Inclusive Cities

25. 다음 도표의 내용과 일치하지 <u>않는</u> 것은?

Second-Dose Measles Vaccinations among Children by Region in 2000 and in 2020

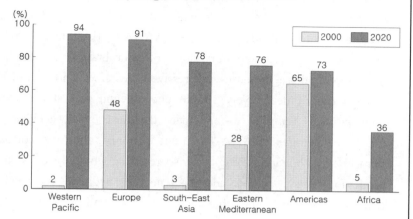

* measles: 홍역

The graph above shows the percentage of children who received second-dose measles vaccinations in six regions in 2000 and in 2020. ① The percentage of vaccinated children in the Western Pacific was lower than that of Europe in 2000, but the vaccination percentage in 2020 of the Western Pacific exceeded that of Europe by 3 percentage points. ② Among all regions, South-East Asia achieved the second biggest increase in its percentage of vaccinated children over the two decades, and it ranked third in the percentage of vaccinated children among the six regions in 2020. ③ In the Eastern Mediterranean, the percentage of vaccinated children more than doubled from 2000 to 2020, but did not exceed that of the Americas in either year. ④ The percentage of vaccinated children in the Americas was the highest among the six regions in 2000, but it increased the least of all regions over the two decades. ⑤ In Africa, the percentage of children who received the vaccine in 2020 was more than seven times higher than in 2000, but was still the lowest among the six regions in 2020.

26. Janaki Ammal에 관한 다음 글의 내용과 일치하지 <u>않는</u> 것은?

Janaki Ammal, one of India's most notable scientists, was born in 1897, and was expected to wed through an arranged marriage. Despite living at a time when literacy among women in India was less than one percent, she decided to reject tradition and attend college. In 1924, she went to the U.S. and eventually received a doctorate in botany from the University of Michigan. Ammal contributed to the development of the sweetest sugarcane variety in the world. She moved to England where she co-authored the *Chromosome Atlas of Cultivated Plants*. Following a series of famines, she returned to India to help increase food production at the request of the Prime Minister. However, Ammal disagreed with the deforestation taking place in an effort to grow more food. She became an advocate for the preservation of native plants and successfully saved the Silent Valley from the construction of a hydroelectric dam.

① 관습을 따르지 않고 대학에 입학하기로 결심했다.
② 세계에서 가장 단 사탕수수 품종 개발에 기여했다.
③ *Chromosome Atlas of Cultivated Plants*를 공동 집필했다.
④ 식량 생산을 증가시키는 데 도움을 주기 위해 인도로 돌아갔다.
⑤ 수력 발전 댐의 건설로부터 Silent Valley를 지키는 데 실패했다.

27. 2022 Strawberry Festival에 관한 다음 안내문의 내용과 일치하지 <u>않는</u> 것은?

2022 Strawberry Festival

Join us for a fun family festival. This year, we are back to hosting an in-person event in Berry Square!

□ **Date**: November 26, 2022 (11:00 a.m. — 5:00 p.m.)
□ **Tickets**: $20 per person
(Children 6 and under are FREE.)

□ **Special Events**
· 11:00 a.m. : Baking Class for Kids
· 1:00 p.m. : Strawberry Pie-Eating Contest
· 3:00 p.m. : Strawberry Costume Contest

□ **Note**
· The parking fee is $5 and includes tram service to the ticket booth.
· If you are interested in volunteering, complete an application form and email it to manager@strawberryfestival.org.

① 올해는 대면 행사로 개최된다.
② 6세 이하의 어린이에게는 입장료를 받지 않는다.
③ 딸기파이 먹기 대회가 오후에 열린다.
④ 매표소로 가는 트램 서비스는 주차비에 포함되지 않는다.
⑤ 자원봉사에 관심이 있다면 신청서를 이메일로 보내야 한다.

28. Maple Spring Light Art Exhibition에 관한 다음 안내문의 내용과 일치하는 것은?

Maple Spring Light Art Exhibition

The Maple Spring Light Art Exhibition will illuminate you, with a route surrounded by light artwork. Admire the beautiful light artwork as you walk through Maple Spring.

□ **Date**: December 1 — 31, 2022
(closed on the 2nd and 4th Monday of the month)
□ **Time**: 7 p.m. — 11 p.m.
□ **Entrance Fee**: $5 per person
□ **Exhibition Route**: alongside the Bow River in central Maple Spring (Only digital maps of the route are available.)
· Souvenirs will be available on site and online.
· Local residents can get a 10% discount off the entrance fee.

Please visit www.maplespringlight.com for more information.

① 매주 월요일은 운영하지 않는다.
② 밤 11시 이후에도 입장이 가능하다.
③ 관람 경로가 담긴 지도는 종이로만 제공한다.
④ 기념품은 현장에서만 구매 가능하다.
⑤ 지역 주민은 입장료의 10% 할인을 받을 수 있다.

29. 다음 글의 밑줄 친 부분 중, 어법상 틀린 것은? [3점]

Pre-emption means that a strategy is designed to prevent a rival from starting some particular activity. In some case a pre-emptive move may simply be an announcement of some intent ① that might discourage rivals from doing the same. The idea of pre-emption implies that timing is sometimes very important — a decision or an action at one point in time might be much more rewarding than ② doing it at a different time point. Pre-emption may involve up-weighting advertising for a period before and during ③ when a new entrant launches into a market. The intent is to make it more difficult for the new entrant's advertising to make an impression on potential buyers. Product proliferation is another potential pre-emption strategy. The general idea is to launch a large variety of product variants so that there is very little in the way of market demand that ④ are not accommodated. Arguably, if a market is already filled with product variants it is more difficult for competitors to find ⑤ untapped pockets of market demand.

* pre-emption: 선매 행위 ** proliferation: 확산

30. 다음 글의 밑줄 친 부분 중, 문맥상 낱말의 쓰임이 적절하지 않은 것은? [3점]

Countershading is the process of optical flattening that provides camouflage to animals. When sunlight illuminates an object from above, the object will be brightest on top. The color of the object will gradually shade darker toward the ① bottom. This shading gives the object ② depth and allows the viewer to distinguish its shape. Thus even if an animal is exactly, but uniformly, the same color as the substrate, it will be easily ③ visible when illuminated. Most animals, however, are darker above than they are below. When they are illuminated from above, the darker back is lightened and the lighter belly is shaded. The animal thus appears to be a ④ single color and easily blends in with the substrate. This pattern of coloration, or countershading, ⑤ reinforces the visual impression of shape in the organism. It allows the animal to blend in with its background.

* camouflage: 위장 ** substrate: 밑바탕, 기질(基質)

[31~34] 다음 빈칸에 들어갈 말로 가장 적절한 것을 고르시오.

31. No learning is possible without an error signal. Organisms only learn when events violate their expectations. In other words, surprise is one of the fundamental drivers of learning. Imagine hearing a series of identical notes, AAAAA. Each note draws out a response in the auditory areas of your brain — but as the notes repeat, those responses progressively decrease. This is called "adaptation," a deceptively simple phenomenon that shows that your brain is learning to anticipate the next event. Suddenly, the note changes: AAAAA#. Your primary auditory cortex immediately shows a strong surprise reaction: not only does the adaptation fade away, but additional neurons begin to vigorously fire in response to the unexpected sound. And it is not just repetition that leads to adaptation: what matters is whether the notes are _____. For instance, if you hear an alternating set of notes, such as ABABA, your brain gets used to this alternation, and the activity in your auditory areas again decreases. This time, however, it is an unexpected repetition, such as ABABB, that triggers a surprise response.

① audible
② predictable
③ objective
④ countable
⑤ recorded

32. The connectedness of the global economic market makes it vulnerable to potential "infection." A financial failure can make its way from borrowers to banks to insurers, spreading like a flu. However, there are unexpected characteristics when it comes to such infection in the market. Infection can occur even without any contact. A bank might become insolvent even without having any of its investments fail. _____ to financial markets, just as cascading failures due to bad investments. If we all woke up tomorrow and believed that Bank X would be insolvent, then it would become insolvent. In fact, it would be enough for us to fear that others believed that Bank X was going to fail, or just to fear our collective fear! We might all even know that Bank X was well-managed with healthy investments, but if we expected others to pull their money out, then we would fear being the last to pull our money out. Financial distress can be self-fulfilling and is a particularly troublesome aspect of financial markets.

* insolvent: 지급 불능의, 파산한 ** cascading: 연속된

① Fear and uncertainty can be damaging
② Unaffordable personal loans may pose a risk
③ Ignorance about legal restrictions may matter
④ Accurate knowledge of investors can be poisonous
⑤ Strong connections between banks can create a scare

33. Negative numbers are a lot more abstract than positive numbers — you can't see negative 4 cookies and you certainly can't eat them — but you can think about them, and you *have to*, in all aspects of daily life, from debts to contending with freezing temperatures and parking garages. Still, many of us haven't quite made peace with negative numbers. People have invented all sorts of funny little mental strategies to _____. On mutual fund statements, losses (negative numbers) are printed in red or stuck in parentheses with no negative sign to be found. The history books tell us that Julius Caesar was born in 100 B.C., not −100. The underground levels in a parking garage often have designations like B1 and B2. Temperatures are one of the few exceptions: folks do say, especially here in Ithaca, New York, that it's −5 degrees outside, though even then, many prefer to say 5 below zero. There's something about that negative sign that just looks so unpleasant.

* parentheses: 괄호

① sidestep the dreaded negative sign
② resolve stock market uncertainties
③ compensate for complicated calculating processes
④ unify the systems of expressing numbers below zero
⑤ face the truth that subtraction can create negative numbers

34. Observational studies of humans cannot be properly controlled. Humans live different lifestyles and in different environments. Thus, they are insufficiently homogeneous to be suitable experimental subjects. These *confounding factors* undermine our ability to draw sound causal conclusions from human epidemiological surveys. Confounding factors are variables (known or unknown) that make it difficult for epidemiologists to _____. For example, Taubes argued that since many people who drink also smoke, researchers have difficulty determining the link between alcohol consumption and cancer. Similarly, researchers in the famous Framingham study identified a significant correlation between coffee drinking and coronary heart disease. However, most of this correlation disappeared once researchers corrected for the fact that many coffee drinkers also smoke. If the confounding factors are known, it is often possible to correct for them. However, if they are unknown, they will undermine the reliability of the causal conclusions we draw from epidemiological surveys. [3점]

* homogeneous: 동질적인 ** epidemiological: 역학의

① distort the interpretation of the medical research results
② isolate the effects of the specific variable being studied
③ conceal the purpose of their research from subjects
④ conduct observational studies in an ethical way
⑤ refrain from intervening in their experiments

35. 다음 글에서 전체 흐름과 관계 <u>없는</u> 문장은?

Of all the human emotions, none is trickier or more elusive than envy. It is very difficult to actually discern the envy that motivates people's actions. ① The reason for this elusiveness is simple: we almost never directly express the envy we are feeling. ② Envy entails the admission to ourselves that we are inferior to another person in something we value. ③ Not only is it painful to admit this inferiority, but it is even worse for others to see that we are feeling this. ④ Envy can cause illness because people with envy can cast the "evil eye" on someone they envy, even unwittingly, or the envious person can become ill from the emotion. ⑤ And so almost as soon as we experience the initial feelings of envy, we are motivated to disguise it to ourselves — it is not envy we feel but unfairness at the distribution of goods or attention, resentment at this unfairness, even anger.

* elusive: 이해하기 어려운

[36~37] 주어진 글 다음에 이어질 글의 순서로 가장 적절한 것을 고르시오.

36.

The right to be forgotten is a right distinct from but related to a right to privacy. The right to privacy is, among other things, the right for information traditionally regarded as protected or personal not to be revealed.

(A) One motivation for such a right is to allow individuals to move on with their lives and not be defined by a specific event or period in their lives. For example, it has long been recognized in some countries, such as the UK and France, that even past criminal convictions should eventually be "spent" and not continue to affect a person's life.

(B) The right to be forgotten, in contrast, can be applied to information that has been in the public domain. The right to be forgotten broadly includes the right of an individual not to be forever defined by information from a specific point in time.

(C) Despite the reason for supporting the right to be forgotten, the right to be forgotten can sometimes come into conflict with other rights. For example, formal exceptions are sometimes made for security or public health reasons.

① (A) − (C) − (B)   ② (B) − (A) − (C)
③ (B) − (C) − (A)   ④ (C) − (A) − (B)
⑤ (C) − (B) − (A)

37.

To an economist who succeeds in figuring out a person's preference structure — understanding whether the satisfaction gained from consuming one good is greater than that of another — explaining behavior in terms of changes in underlying likes and dislikes is usually highly problematic.

(A) When income rises, for example, people want more children (or, as you will see later, more satisfaction derived from children), even if their inherent desire for children stays the same.

(B) To argue, for instance, that the baby boom and then the baby bust resulted from an increase and then a decrease in the public's inherent taste for children, rather than a change in relative prices against a background of stable preferences, places a social scientist in an unsound position.

(C) In economics, such an argument about birth rates would be equivalent to saying that a rise and fall in mortality could be attributed to an increase in the inherent desire change for death. For an economist, changes in income and prices, rather than changes in tastes, affect birth rates. [3점]

① (A) − (C) − (B)　　② (B) − (A) − (C)
③ (B) − (C) − (A)　　④ (C) − (A) − (B)
⑤ (C) − (B) − (A)

[38~39] 글의 흐름으로 보아, 주어진 문장이 들어가기에 가장 적절한 곳을 고르시오.

38.

It does this by making your taste buds perceive these flavors as bad and even disgusting.

In the natural world, if an animal consumes a plant with enough antinutrients to make it feel unwell, it won't eat that plant again. Intuitively, animals also know to stay away from these plants. Years of evolution and information being passed down created this innate intelligence. (①) This "intuition," though, is not just seen in animals. (②) Have you ever wondered why most children hate vegetables? (③) Dr. Steven Gundry justifies this as part of our genetic programming, our inner intelligence. (④) Since many vegetables are full of antinutrients, your body tries to keep you away from them while you are still fragile and in development. (⑤) As you grow and your body becomes stronger enough to tolerate these antinutrients, suddenly they no longer taste as bad as before.

* taste bud: 미뢰(味蕾)

39.

However, the rigidity of rock means that land rises and falls with the tides by a much smaller amount than water, which is why we notice only the ocean tides.

The difference in the Moon's gravitational pull on different parts of our planet effectively creates a "stretching force." (①) It makes our planet slightly stretched out along the line of sight to the Moon and slightly compressed along a line perpendicular to that. (②) The tidal stretching caused by the Moon's gravity affects our entire planet, including both land and water, inside and out. (③) The stretching also explains why there are generally *two* high tides (and two low tides) in the ocean each day. (④) Because Earth is stretched much like a rubber band, the oceans bulge out both on the side facing toward the Moon and on the side facing away from the Moon. (⑤) As Earth rotates, we are carried through both of these tidal bulges each day, so we have high tide when we are in each of the two bulges and low tide at the midpoints in between. [3점]

* rigidity: 단단함　** perpendicular: 직각을 이루는
*** bulge: 팽창하다

40. 다음 글의 내용을 한 문장으로 요약하고자 한다. 빈칸 (A), (B)에 들어갈 말로 가장 적절한 것은? [3점]

A study investigated the economic cost of prejudice based on blind assumptions. Researchers gave a group of Danish teenagers the choice of working with one of two people. The teenager had never met either of them. One of the people had a name that suggested they were from a similar ethnic or religious background to the teenager. The other had a name that suggested they were from a different ethnic or religious background. The study showed that the teenagers were prepared to earn an average of 8% less if they could work with someone they thought came from the same ethnic or religious background. And this prejudice was evident among teenagers with ethnic majority names as well as those with ethnic minority names. The teenagers were blindly making assumptions about the race of their potential colleagues. They then applied prejudice to those assumptions, to the point where they actually allowed that prejudice to reduce *their own* potential income. The job required the two teenagers to work together for just *90 minutes*.

↓

A study in which teenagers expressed a(n) ___(A)___ to work with someone of a similar background, even at a financial cost to themselves, suggests that an assumption-based prejudice can ___(B)___ rational economic behavior.

　　(A)　　　　　　(B)　　　　　　(A)　　　　　　(B)
① preference ‥‥‥ outweigh　② hesitation ‥‥‥ reinforce
③ preference ‥‥‥ strengthen　④ hesitation ‥‥‥ overwhelm
⑤ inability ‥‥‥ underlie

[41~42] 다음 글을 읽고, 물음에 답하시오.

A neuropsychologist, Michael Gazzaniga conducted a study that shows that our brains (a) <u>excel</u> at creating coherent (but not necessarily true) stories that deceive us. In the study, split-brain patients were shown an image such that it was visible to only their left eye and asked to select a related card with their left hand. Left-eye vision and left-side body movement are controlled by the right hemisphere. In a split-brain patient, the connection between the right and left hemispheres has been broken, meaning no information can cross from one hemisphere to the other. Therefore, in this experiment, the right hemisphere was doing all of the work, and the left hemisphere was (b) <u>aware</u> of what was happening.

Gazzaniga then asked participants why they chose the card that they did. Because language is processed and generated in the left hemisphere, the left hemisphere is required to respond. However, because of the experiment's design, only the right hemisphere knew why the participant selected the card. As a result, Gazzaniga expected the participants to be (c) <u>silent</u> when asked to answer the question. But instead, every subject fabricated a response. The left hemisphere was being asked to provide a (d) <u>rationalization</u> for a behavior done by the right hemisphere. The left hemisphere didn't know the answer. But that didn't keep it from fabricating an answer. That answer, however, had no basis in reality. Now if this study had been limited to split-brain patients, it would be interesting but not very (e) <u>relevant</u> to us. It turns out split-brain patients aren't the only ones who fabricate reasons. We all do it. We all need a coherent story about ourselves, and when information in that story is missing, our brains simply fill in the details.

* coherent: 일관성 있는

41. 윗글의 제목으로 가장 적절한 것은?

① Which Side of the Brain Do We Tend to Use More?
② How Our Brain's Hemispheres Interact in Storytelling
③ The Deceptive Brain: Insights from a Split-Brain Patient Study
④ To Be Creative, Activate Both Hemispheres of Your Brain!
⑤ The Dominance of the Left Brain in Image Processing

42. 밑줄 친 (a)~(e) 중에서 문맥상 낱말의 쓰임이 적절하지 <u>않은</u> 것은? [3점]

① (a)　　② (b)　　③ (c)　　④ (d)　　⑤ (e)

[43~45] 다음 글을 읽고, 물음에 답하시오.

(A)

The basketball felt like it belonged in Chanel's hands even though it was only a practice game. She decided not to pass the ball to her twin sister, Vasha. Instead, (a) <u>she</u> stopped, jumped, and shot the ball toward the basket, but it bounced off the backboard. Chanel could see that her teammates were disappointed. The other team got the ball and soon scored, ending the game.

(B)

The next day, Chanel played in the championship game against a rival school. It was an intense game and the score was tied when Chanel was passed the ball by Vasha, with ten seconds left in the game. (b) <u>She</u> leaped into the air and shot the ball. It went straight into the basket! Chanel's last shot had made her team the champions. Vasha and all her other teammates cheered for her.

(C)

At first, Chanel did not like practicing with Vasha because every time Vasha shot the ball, it went in. But whenever it was Chanel's turn, she missed. (c) <u>She</u> got frustrated at not making a shot. "Don't give up!" Vasha shouted after each missed shot. After twelve misses in a row, her thirteenth shot went in and she screamed, "I finally did it!" Her twin said, "I knew (d) <u>you</u> could! Now let's keep practicing!"

(D)

When the practice game ended, Chanel felt her eyes sting with tears. "It's okay," Vasha said in a comforting voice. Chanel appreciated her, but Vasha wasn't making her feel any better. Vasha wanted to help her twin improve. She invited her twin to practice with (e) <u>her</u>. After school, they got their basketball and started practicing their basketball shots.

43. 주어진 글 (A)에 이어질 내용을 순서에 맞게 배열한 것으로 가장 적절한 것은?

① (B) − (D) − (C)　　② (C) − (B) − (D)
③ (C) − (D) − (B)　　④ (D) − (B) − (C)
⑤ (D) − (C) − (B)

44. 밑줄 친 (a)~(e) 중에서 가리키는 대상이 나머지 넷과 <u>다른</u> 것은?

① (a)　　② (b)　　③ (c)　　④ (d)　　⑤ (e)

45. 윗글의 Chanel에 관한 내용으로 적절하지 <u>않은</u> 것은?

① 연습 경기 중에 팀원들의 실망한 모습을 보았다.
② 라이벌 학교와의 챔피언십 경기에 출전했다.
③ 팀을 우승시키는 마지막 슛을 성공했다.
④ 슛 연습에서 연이은 실패 후에 12번째 슛이 들어갔다.
⑤ 방과 후에 농구 슛을 연습하기 시작했다.

* 확인 사항
◦ 답안지의 해당란에 필요한 내용을 정확히 기입(표기)했는지 확인하시오.

18

001 local ⓐ 지역의
002 president ⓝ 회장
003 student council 학생회
004 host ⓥ 주최하다
005 annual ⓐ 연마다 하는
006 prize ⓝ 상, 상품
007 winning team 우승팀
008 support ⓝ 후원, 지지
009 valuable ⓐ 가치 있는
010 be willing to 기꺼이 ~하다
011 gift certificate 상품권
012 grateful for ~에 감사하는
013 amount ⓝ 양, 액수
014 in exchange for ~에 대한 대가로
015 generosity ⓝ 관대함
016 place ⓥ 싣다, 두다
017 answer sheet 답안지

19

018 be supposed to ~하기로 되어 있다
019 buzz ⓥ (윙윙) 울리다
020 make it 도착하다
021 on time 제 시간에
022 faint ⓥ 기절하다
023 show up 나타나다
024 whole ⓐ 전체의
025 manage to 가까스로 ~하다
026 portion ⓝ 부분
027 go blank (마음 따위가) 텅 비다
028 hold oneself together 정신을 차리다
029 come to one's senses 의식을 되찾다, 정신을 차리다
030 work through 해치우다
031 tension ⓝ 긴장
032 vanish ⓥ 사라지다
033 beaming ⓐ 미소 띤, 기쁨에 넘치는
034 panicked ⓐ 당황한, 공포에 질린
035 sympathetic ⓐ 연민 어린
036 content ⓐ 만족한
037 humiliated ⓐ 굴욕을 느끼는, 수치스러운

20

038 clarity ⓝ 명확성
039 organization ⓝ 조직
040 in one accord 합심하여, 이구동성으로
041 component ⓝ 구성 요소
042 transparency ⓝ 투명성
043 assess ⓥ 평가하다
044 be aware of ~을 알다
045 individual ⓝ 개인
046 mistrust ⓝ 불신
047 productive ⓐ 생산적인
048 cohesive ⓐ 응집력 있는
049 essential ⓐ 필수적인
050 failure to ~하지 못하는 것, ~에 있어서의 실패
051 negative ⓐ 부정적인
052 significantly ⓐⓓ 현저히, 상당히
053 hinder ⓥ 막다, 방해하다
054 growth ⓝ 성장
055 accurate ⓐ 정확한

056 in turn 결국
057 empower ⓥ 권한을 부여하다
058 optimal ⓐ 최적의

21

059 peak ⓝ 최상, 정점
060 performance ⓝ 수행, 성과
061 point to ~을 지적하다
062 ideally ⓐⓓ 이상적으로
063 match A to B A를 B에 맞추다
064 accomplish ⓥ 성취하다
065 free from ~로부터 자유로운, 해방된
066 distraction ⓝ 방해물, 정신을 산만하게 하는 것
067 generally ⓐⓓ 대체로
068 over the years 몇 년에 걸쳐
069 consistently ⓐⓓ 꾸준하게, 일관성 있게
070 stick to ~을 고수하다
071 overthink ⓥ 과도하게 생각하다
072 procrastinate ⓥ 미루다
073 unpleasant ⓐ 불쾌한
074 as if 마치 ~한 것처럼
075 take care of 처리하다, 다루다
076 get done 끝내다
077 strategic ⓐ 전략적인
078 fuel ⓝ 연료
079 demanding ⓐ 까다로운
080 decision-making ⓝ 의사 결정

22

081 beginning ⓝ 시작
082 spring ⓝ 봄
083 view A as B A를 B로 여기다
084 attractive ⓐ 매력적인
085 kick-start ⓥ 시동을 걸다
086 pursuit ⓝ 추구
087 present A as B A를 B라고 제시하다
088 unremarkable ⓐ 특별할 것 없는, 평범한
089 right then 바로 그때
090 achieve ⓥ 얻다, 성취하다
091 goal seeker 목표를 추구하는 사람
092 modify ⓥ 수정하다
093 depict ⓥ 묘사하다, 설명하다
094 immediate ⓐ 즉각적인
095 progress ⓝ 진전

23

096 Native American 북미 원주민(의)
097 in preparation for ~을 준비하며
098 launch ⓥ 개시하다, 시작하다
099 emotional ⓐ 정서적인
100 neurochemical ⓐ 신경 화학적인
101 excitement ⓝ 흥분
102 result from ~에서 기인하다
103 carry out ~을 수행하다
104 unconscious ⓐ 무의식적인
105 uncontrolled ⓐ 통제되지 않은
106 frenzy ⓝ 격분
107 firsthand ⓐⓓ 직접
108 enemy ⓝ 적
109 arousal ⓝ 자극, 흥분
110 synchronize ⓥ 동시에 움직이게 하다

111 compensate for ~을 보충하다, 보상하다
112 march ⓥ 행진하다
113 advantage ⓝ 이점
114 intimidate ⓥ 위협하다
115 witness ⓥ 목격하다
116 spectacle ⓝ 장관
117 disturb ⓥ 교란시키다
118 sheer ⓐ 순전한, 큰
119 utilize ⓥ 이용하다
120 warfare ⓝ 전쟁, 싸움
121 vulnerable ⓐ 취약한
122 religious ⓐ 종교적인
123 anxiety ⓝ 불안, 걱정

24

124 express ⓥ 표현하다
125 membership ⓝ 회원 수, 회원 자격
126 accompany ⓥ 동반하다, 수반하다
127 symbolic ⓐ 상징적인
128 reinterpretation ⓝ 재해석
129 poverty ⓝ 가난
130 recreational ⓐ 오락의
131 inspire ⓥ 영감을 주다
132 aspirational ⓐ 열망의, 출세지향적인
133 present ⓐ 현재의
134 demonstrative ⓐ 표현적인, 분명히 나타내는
135 construction ⓝ 구축, 건설
136 effectiveness ⓝ 유효성
137 signal ⓥ 알리다
138 social status 사회적 지위
139 to a certain extent 어느 정도는
140 well-off ⓐ 부유한
141 value-laden ⓐ 가치 판단적인, 개인의 의견에 영향을 받는
142 by no means 결코 ~않다
143 conspicuous ⓐ 눈에 잘 띄는
144 manifest ⓐ 나타나는, 분명한
145 dweller ⓝ 거주자
146 worsen ⓥ 악화시키다
147 inequality ⓝ 불평등

25

148 dose ⓝ (약의) 투여량, 복용량
149 measles ⓝ 홍역
150 vaccination ⓝ 백신 접종
151 region ⓝ 지역
152 exceed ⓥ 능가하다, 넘어서다
153 among prep ~ 중에서
154 decade ⓝ 10년
155 rank ⓥ ~의 순위를 차지하다
156 Mediterranean ⓐ 지중해의
157 double ⓥ 2배가 되다

26

158 notable ⓐ 유명한, 저명한
159 be expected to ~할 것으로 예상되다
160 wed ⓥ 결혼하다
161 arranged marriage 중매결혼
162 literacy ⓝ 문해력, 식자율
163 attend college 대학에 다니다
164 doctorate ⓝ 박사 학위

165 botany ⓝ 식물학
166 sugarcane ⓝ 사탕수수
167 co-author ⓥ 공동 저술하다
168 famine ⓝ 기근
169 deforestation ⓝ 삼림벌채
170 advocate ⓝ 지지자, 옹호자
171 preservation ⓝ 보존
172 hydroelectric ⓐ 수력 전기의

27

173 be back to 다시 ~하게 되다
174 in-person ⓐ 직접 하는, 대면의
175 square ⓝ 광장
176 ticket booth 매표소
177 volunteer ⓥ 자원봉사하다
178 application ⓝ 신청, 지원

28

179 exhibition ⓝ 전시
180 illuminate ⓥ 비추다
181 route ⓝ 경로
182 surround ⓥ 둘러싸다
183 artwork ⓝ 예술 작품
184 entrance ⓝ 입장, 입구
185 alongside prep ~을 따라, ~와 나란히
186 souvenir ⓝ 기념품
187 on site 현장에서

29

188 pre-emption ⓝ 선매 행위
189 rival ⓐ 적수, 경쟁 상대
190 announcement ⓝ 공표, 안내
191 intent ⓝ 의도, 취지
192 discourage A from B A가 B하지 못하게 단념시키다
193 rewarding ⓐ 보람된
194 weight ⓥ 가중치를 두다 ⓝ 가중치, 무게
195 entrant ⓝ 갓 들어온 사람, 진입자, 출전자
196 proliferation ⓝ 확산
197 variant ⓝ 변형
198 accommodate ⓥ (수요나 필요를) 맞추다, 수용하다
199 arguably ⓐⓓ 거의 틀림없이
200 untapped ⓐ 아직 손대지 않은

30

201 optical ⓐ 시각적인
202 flatten ⓥ 평평하게 하다
203 camouflage ⓝ 위장
204 on top 맨 위에
205 gradually ⓐⓓ 점점
206 distinguish ⓥ 구별하다
207 uniformly ⓐⓓ 균일하게
208 substrate ⓝ 밑바탕, 기질(基質)
209 visible ⓐ 눈에 띄는
210 lighten ⓥ 밝게 하다, 밝아지다
211 blend in with ~에 섞여들다
212 reinforce ⓥ 강화하다
213 organism ⓝ 유기체

31

214 violate ⓥ 위반하다

215 ☐ expectation ⓝ 기대, 예상
216 ☐ fundamental ⓐ 근본적인
217 ☐ identical ⓐ 동일한
218 ☐ note ⓝ 음
219 ☐ draw out ~을 끌어내다
220 ☐ auditory ⓐ 청각의
221 ☐ progressively ⓐⓓ 점진적으로
222 ☐ adaptation ⓝ 적응
223 ☐ deceptively ⓐⓓ 현혹될 정도로
224 ☐ phenomenon ⓝ 현상
225 ☐ anticipate ⓥ 기대하다, 예상하다
226 ☐ primary ⓐ 1차의, 주요한, 기본적인
227 ☐ cortex ⓝ (대뇌의) 피질
228 ☐ fade away 흐려지다, 옅어지다
229 ☐ vigorously ⓐⓓ 힘차게
230 ☐ alternate ⓥ 번갈아 나오다, 교대로 나오다
231 ☐ trigger ⓥ 유발하다, 촉발하다
232 ☐ audible ⓐ 잘 들리는, 들을 수 있는
233 ☐ predictable ⓐ 예측 가능한
234 ☐ countable ⓐ 셀 수 있는

32
235 ☐ connectedness ⓝ 연결성
236 ☐ infection ⓝ 감염
237 ☐ insurer ⓝ 보증인, 보험업자
238 ☐ when it comes to ~에 관해서
239 ☐ insolvent ⓐ 지급 불능의, 파산한
240 ☐ investment ⓝ 투자
241 ☐ cascading ⓐ 연속된
242 ☐ collective ⓐ 집단적인
243 ☐ well-managed ⓐ 잘 경영되는
244 ☐ healthy ⓐ 건전한
245 ☐ pull out 꺼내다, 인출하다
246 ☐ distress ⓝ 고통
247 ☐ self-fulfilling ⓐ 자기 충족적인, 예고대로 성취되는
248 ☐ troublesome ⓐ 골치 아픈
249 ☐ uncertainty ⓝ 불확실성
250 ☐ unaffordable ⓐ 감당할 수 없는
251 ☐ restriction ⓝ 제재, 제한
252 ☐ poisonous ⓐ 유독한, 유해한
253 ☐ scare ⓝ 놀람, 공포 ⓥ 겁먹게 하다

33
254 ☐ negative ⓐ (수가) 음수인
255 ☐ abstract ⓐ 추상적인
256 ☐ positive ⓐ (수가) 양수인
257 ☐ contend with ~와 씨름하다
258 ☐ freezing ⓐ 몹시 추운
259 ☐ make peace with ~와 잘 지내다
260 ☐ all sorts of 온갖
261 ☐ statement ⓝ 설명(서)
262 ☐ parentheses ⓝ 괄호
263 ☐ underground ⓐ 지하의
264 ☐ designation ⓝ 명칭, 직함
265 ☐ folks ⓝ 사람들
266 ☐ unpleasant ⓐ 불쾌한
267 ☐ sidestep ⓥ 회피하다
268 ☐ dread ⓥ 두려워하다, 겁내다
269 ☐ resolve ⓥ 해결하다
270 ☐ face the truth 진실을 직시하다
271 ☐ subtraction ⓝ 빼기, 뺄셈

34
272 ☐ observational ⓐ 관찰의
273 ☐ insufficiently ⓐⓓ 불충분하게
274 ☐ homogeneous ⓐ 동질적인
275 ☐ suitable ⓐ 적절한
276 ☐ confounding factor (결과에 간섭하는) 교란 변수
277 ☐ undermine ⓥ 약화시키다
278 ☐ draw a conclusion 결론을 내리다
279 ☐ epidemiological ⓐ 역학의
280 ☐ variable ⓝ 변수
281 ☐ unknown ⓐ 미지의
282 ☐ epidemiologist ⓝ 전염병학자, 역학자
283 ☐ consumption ⓝ 복용, 소비
284 ☐ identify ⓥ 찾아내다, 알아보다
285 ☐ correlation ⓝ 상관관계
286 ☐ coronary ⓐ 관상 동맥의
287 ☐ heart disease 심장병
288 ☐ reliability ⓝ 신뢰도
289 ☐ distort ⓥ 왜곡하다
290 ☐ isolate ⓥ 분리하다
291 ☐ interpretation ⓝ 해석, 이해
292 ☐ conceal ⓥ 숨기다, 가리다
293 ☐ refrain from ~을 자제하다, 삼가다
294 ☐ intervene ⓥ 간섭하다

35
295 ☐ tricky ⓐ 까다로운
296 ☐ elusive ⓐ 이해하기 어려운
297 ☐ envy ⓝ 부러움, 질투
298 ☐ discern ⓥ 분간하다, 알아차리다
299 ☐ motivate ⓥ 동기 부여하다, 자극하다
300 ☐ elusiveness ⓝ 모호함, 이해하기 어려움
301 ☐ entail ⓥ 수반하다
302 ☐ admission ⓝ 인정
303 ☐ inferior to ~보다 열등한
304 ☐ painful ⓐ 고통스러운
305 ☐ inferiority ⓝ 열등함
306 ☐ illness ⓝ 질병
307 ☐ cast ⓥ 던지다
308 ☐ unwittingly ⓐⓓ 자기도 모르게
309 ☐ disguise ⓥ 속이다
310 ☐ unfairness ⓝ 불공평함
311 ☐ resentment ⓝ 분개

36
312 ☐ right to be forgotten 잊힐 권리
313 ☐ distinct from ~와 구별되는
314 ☐ right to privacy 사생활 권리
315 ☐ traditionally ⓐⓓ 전통적으로
316 ☐ regard ⓥ 여기다, 간주하다
317 ☐ reveal ⓥ 드러내다, 폭로하다
318 ☐ move on with 나아가다, 정진하다
319 ☐ define ⓥ 규정하다, 한정짓다
320 ☐ criminal ⓐ 형사상의, 범죄의
321 ☐ conviction ⓝ 유죄 판결
322 ☐ spent ⓐ 소모된, 영향력이 없어진
323 ☐ domain ⓝ 영역
324 ☐ broadly ⓐⓓ 넓게
325 ☐ formal ⓐ 공식적인
326 ☐ security ⓝ 안보
327 ☐ public health 공중 보건

37
328 ☐ economist ⓝ 경제학자
329 ☐ underlying ⓐ 기저에 있는
330 ☐ like and dislikes 호불호
331 ☐ problematic ⓐ 문제가 있는
332 ☐ income ⓝ 소득, 수입
333 ☐ derive from ~로부터 얻다, ~에서 비롯되다
334 ☐ inherent ⓐ 내재된
335 ☐ baby boom 베이비 붐(일시적으로 출생률이 증가하는 시기)
336 ☐ baby bust 출생률 급감
337 ☐ taste ⓝ 취향
338 ☐ stable ⓐ 안정된
339 ☐ unsound ⓐ 불안정한, 불건전한
340 ☐ be equivalent to ~와 같다
341 ☐ rise and fall 증감, 흥망성쇠
342 ☐ mortality ⓝ 사망률
343 ☐ be attributed to ~에서 비롯되다, 기인하다

38
344 ☐ taste bud 맛봉오리, 미뢰(味蕾)
345 ☐ flavor ⓝ 맛, 풍미
346 ☐ disgusting ⓐ 역겨운
347 ☐ antinutrient ⓝ 항영양소
348 ☐ unwell ⓐ 몸이 편치 않은
349 ☐ intuitively ⓐⓓ 직관적으로
350 ☐ stay away from ~을 멀리하다
351 ☐ pass down 전해주다
352 ☐ innate ⓐ 타고난
353 ☐ intuition ⓝ 직관
354 ☐ though ⓐⓓ 하지만
355 ☐ justify ⓥ 정당화하다, 옳음을 보여주다
356 ☐ as part of ~의 일환으로, 일부로
357 ☐ genetic ⓐ 유전적인
358 ☐ fragile ⓐ 연약한
359 ☐ tolerate ⓥ 견디다

39
360 ☐ rigidity ⓝ 단단함
361 ☐ tide ⓝ 조수, 밀물과 썰물
362 ☐ gravitational ⓐ 중력의
363 ☐ slightly ⓐⓓ 약간
364 ☐ along ⓟⓡⓔⓟ ~을 따라
365 ☐ compress ⓥ 압축하다, 수축하다
366 ☐ perpendicular ⓐ 직각을 이루는
367 ☐ entire ⓐ 온, 전체의
368 ☐ inside and out 안팎으로
369 ☐ rubber band 고무줄
370 ☐ bulge ⓥ 팽창하다 ⓝ 튀어나온 것
371 ☐ carry through 헤쳐나가다, 달성하다
372 ☐ midpoint ⓝ 중간 지점
373 ☐ in between 사이에

40
374 ☐ investigate ⓥ 조사하다, 연구하다
375 ☐ prejudice ⓝ 편견
376 ☐ blind ⓐ 맹목적인
377 ☐ assumption ⓝ 가정, 추정
378 ☐ teenager ⓝ 십 대
379 ☐ ethnic ⓐ 민족적인

380 ☐ earn ⓥ 얻다, 벌다
381 ☐ evident ⓐ 명백한
382 ☐ race ⓝ 인종
383 ☐ reduce ⓥ 줄이다, 감소시키다
384 ☐ financial ⓐ 재정적인
385 ☐ outweigh ⓥ ~보다 중요하다
386 ☐ hesitation ⓝ 망설임
387 ☐ strengthen ⓥ 강화하다
388 ☐ overwhelm ⓥ 압도하다
389 ☐ inability ⓝ ~하지 못함, 무능
390 ☐ underlie ⓥ ~의 근간이 되다

41~42
391 ☐ neuropsychologist ⓝ 신경 심리학자
392 ☐ excel at ~에 능하다
393 ☐ coherent ⓐ 일관성 있는
394 ☐ necessarily ⓐⓓ 반드시, 꼭
395 ☐ deceive ⓥ 속이다
396 ☐ split ⓐ 분리된, 쪼개진
397 ☐ such that ~할 정도로
398 ☐ vision ⓝ 시야, 시력
399 ☐ movement ⓝ 움직임, 운동
400 ☐ hemisphere ⓝ 반구, (뇌의 한쪽) 뇌
401 ☐ cross ⓥ 건너가다
402 ☐ the other (둘 중) 나머지 하나, 상대방
403 ☐ process ⓥ 처리하다
404 ☐ generate ⓥ 만들어내다, 생성하다
405 ☐ respond ⓥ 반응하다, 응수하다
406 ☐ design ⓝ 설계
407 ☐ fabricate ⓥ 꾸며내다, 날조하다
408 ☐ rationalization ⓝ 합리적 설명, 합리화
409 ☐ behavior ⓝ 행동
410 ☐ keep A from B A가 B하지 못하게 하다
411 ☐ basis ⓝ 근거, 기반
412 ☐ relevant ⓐ 관련 있는, 적절한
413 ☐ interact ⓥ 상호작용하다
414 ☐ deceptive ⓐ 속이는, 교묘한
415 ☐ insight ⓝ 통찰력
416 ☐ activate ⓥ 활성화하다
417 ☐ dominance ⓝ 우세

43~45
418 ☐ belong in ~에 속하다, ~에 알맞다, ~의 자격이 있다
419 ☐ practice game 연습 게임
420 ☐ shoot a ball 공을 던지다, 슈팅하다
421 ☐ bounce off 튕겨 나오다
422 ☐ backboard ⓝ (농구 골대의) 백보드
423 ☐ disappointed ⓐ 실망한
424 ☐ championship ⓝ 챔피언십, 선수권 대회
425 ☐ intense ⓐ 격렬한
426 ☐ tie ⓥ 동점을 이루다
427 ☐ leap ⓥ 뛰어오르다
428 ☐ cheer for ~을 응원하다
429 ☐ frustrated ⓐ 좌절한
430 ☐ give up 포기하다
431 ☐ in a row 연속으로
432 ☐ scream ⓥ (무서움이나 흥분으로) 비명을 지르다
433 ☐ sting ⓥ 따끔거리다, 쓰라리다
434 ☐ comfort ⓥ 위로하다
435 ☐ appreciate ⓥ 고마워하다

● 채점 : 맞은 개수 _____ / 80

TEST A-B 각 단어의 뜻을 [A] 영어는 우리말로, [B] 우리말은 영어로 쓰시오.

A	English	Korean
01	generosity	
02	assess	
03	stick to	
04	demanding	
05	launch	
06	religious	
07	anxiety	
08	accompany	
09	notable	
10	in-person	
11	accommodate	
12	violate	
13	distress	
14	designation	
15	conviction	
16	intuitively	
17	ethnic	
18	intense	
19	weight	
20	humiliated	

B	Korean	English
01	생산적인	
02	후원, 지지	
03	정확한	
04	이상적으로	
05	진전	
06	영감을 주다	
07	백신 접종	
08	전시	
09	A가 B하지 못하게 단념시키다	
10	시각적인	
11	근본적인	
12	기대하다, 예상하다	
13	동일한	
14	해결하다	
15	부러움, 질투	
16	맛, 풍미	
17	처리하다	
18	기근	
19	가난	
20	가치 있는	

▶ A-D 정답 : 해설편 181쪽

TEST C-D 각 단어의 뜻을 골라 기호를 쓰시오.

C	English		Korean
01	hinder	( )	ⓐ 주최하다
02	host	( )	ⓑ 지중해
03	come to one's senses	( )	ⓒ 위협하다
04	accomplish	( )	ⓓ 확산
05	modify	( )	ⓔ 따끔거리다, 쓰라리다
06	intimidate	( )	ⓕ 1차의, 주요한, 기본적인
07	Mediterranean	( )	ⓖ 동질적인
08	proliferation	( )	ⓗ 기저에 있는
09	sting	( )	ⓘ 사망률
10	reinforce	( )	ⓙ 역겨운
11	primary	( )	ⓚ 열등함
12	investment	( )	ⓛ 성취하다
13	contend with	( )	ⓜ 막다, 방해하다
14	homogeneous	( )	ⓝ 수정하다
15	inferiority	( )	ⓞ 조수, 밀물과 썰물
16	mortality	( )	ⓟ 망설임
17	underlying	( )	ⓠ 투자
18	disgusting	( )	ⓡ 강화하다
19	tide	( )	ⓢ ~와 씨름하다
20	hesitation	( )	ⓣ 의식을 되찾다, 정신을 차리다

D	Korean		English
01	구성요소	( )	ⓐ procrastinate
02	연민 어린	( )	ⓑ vulnerable
03	미루다	( )	ⓒ dose
04	묘사하다, 설명하다	( )	ⓓ literacy
05	장관	( )	ⓔ deceptively
06	교란시키다	( )	ⓕ cohesive
07	(약의) 투여량, 복용량	( )	ⓖ undermine
08	문해율, 식자율	( )	ⓗ inherent
09	균일하게	( )	ⓘ unsound
10	구별하다	( )	ⓙ prejudice
11	현혹될 정도로	( )	ⓚ audible
12	잘 들리는, 들을 수 있는	( )	ⓛ spectacle
13	추상적인	( )	ⓜ depict
14	약화시키다	( )	ⓝ sympathetic
15	내재된	( )	ⓞ component
16	불안정한, 불건전한	( )	ⓟ disturb
17	편견	( )	ⓠ comfort
18	위로하다	( )	ⓡ abstract
19	취약한	( )	ⓢ distinguish
20	응집력 있는	( )	ⓣ uniformly

※ 영어 [독해] 파트만 수록한 문제지이므로 18번부터 시작합니다.

● 점수 표시가 없는 문항은 모두 2점 ● 문항수 28개 | 배점 63점 | 제한 시간 45분

18. 다음 글의 목적으로 가장 적절한 것은?

To whom it may concern,

I am a parent of a high school student who takes the 145 bus to commute to Clarkson High School. This is the only public transport available from our area and is used by many students. Recently, I heard that the city council is planning to discontinue this service. My husband and I start work early in the morning and this makes it impossible for us to drop our son off at school. It would take him nearly an hour to walk to school and there is a lot of traffic in the morning, so I do not consider it safe to bike. This matter will place many families, including ours, under a lot of stress. As a resident of Sunnyville, I think such a plan is unacceptable. I urge the council to listen to the concerns of the community.

Sincerely,

Lucy Jackson

① 버스 노선 변경에 항의하려고
② 버스 운행 중단 계획에 반대하려고
③ 버스 배차 간격 조정을 요청하려고
④ 자전거 전용 도로 설치를 건의하려고
⑤ 통학로 안전 관리 강화를 촉구하려고

19. 다음 글에 드러난 Ted의 심경 변화로 가장 적절한 것은?

One Friday afternoon, Ted was called to the vice president of human resources. Ted sat down, beaming in anticipation. Today was the big day and this meeting would mark a turning point in his career! Ted felt sure that it was for his promotion and that the vice president would make him the marketing manager. "Ted, there is no easy way to say this." Ted suddenly realized this meeting wasn't going to be as he expected. Ted's mind went blank. The vice president continued, "Ted, I know you've desperately wanted this promotion, but we decided Mike is more suitable." Ted just sat there, frozen. He felt as if he had been hit by a truck. *Don't panic.* All he was able to do was repeat that sentence over and over to himself.

① hopeful → shocked
② relaxed → lonely
③ ashamed → relieved
④ indifferent → upset
⑤ embarrassed → pleased

20. 다음 글에서 필자가 주장하는 바로 가장 적절한 것은?

In 2003, British Airways made an announcement that they would no longer be able to operate the London to New York Concorde flight twice a day because it was starting to prove uneconomical. Well, the sales for the flight on this route increased the very next day. There was nothing that changed about the route or the service offered by the airlines. Merely because it became a scarce resource, the demand for it increased. If you are interested in persuading people, then the principle of scarcity can be effectively used. If you are a salesperson trying to increase the sales of a certain product, then you must not merely point out the benefits the customer can derive from the said product, but also point out its uniqueness and what they will miss out on if they don't purchase the product soon. In selling, you should keep in mind that the more limited something is, the more desirable it becomes.

① 상품 판매 시 실현 가능한 판매 목표를 설정해야 한다.
② 판매를 촉진하기 위해서는 가격 경쟁력을 갖추어야 한다.
③ 효과적인 판매를 위해서는 상품의 희소성을 강조해야 한다.
④ 고객의 신뢰를 얻기 위해서는 일관된 태도를 유지해야 한다.
⑤ 고객의 특성에 맞춰 다양한 판매 전략을 수립하고 적용해야 한다.

21. 밑줄 친 a "media diet"가 다음 글에서 의미하는 바로 가장 적절한 것은?

The most dangerous threat to our ability to concentrate is not that we use our smartphone during working hours, but that we use it too irregularly. By checking our emails every now and then on the computer and our text messages here and there on our phone with no particular schedule or rhythm in mind, our brain loses its ability to effectively filter. The solution is to regulate your devices as if you were on a strict diet. When it comes to nutrition, sticking to a fixed time plan for breakfast, lunch, and dinner allows your metabolism to adjust, thereby causing less hunger during the in-between phases. Your belly will start to rumble around 12:30 p.m. each day, but that's okay because that's a good time to eat lunch. If something unexpected happens, you can add a snack every now and then to get fresh energy, but your metabolism will remain under control. It's the same with our brain when you put it on a "media diet."

* rumble: 우르르 울리다

① balancing the consumption of traditional and online media
② regulating the use of media devices with a set schedule
③ avoiding false nutritional information from the media
④ stimulating your brain with various media sources
⑤ separating yourself from toxic media contents

22. 다음 글의 요지로 가장 적절한 것은?

Who is this person? This is the question all stories ask. It emerges first at the ignition point. When the initial change strikes, the protagonist overreacts or behaves in an otherwise unexpected way. We sit up, suddenly attentive. *Who is this person who behaves like this?* The question then re-emerges every time the protagonist is challenged by the plot and compelled to make a choice. Everywhere in the narrative that the question is present, the reader or viewer will likely be engaged. Where the question is absent, and the events of drama move out of its narrative beam, they are at risk of becoming detached — perhaps even bored. If there's a single secret to storytelling then I believe it's this. *Who is this person?* Or, from the perspective of the character, *Who am I?* It's the definition of drama. It is its electricity, its heartbeat, its fire.

* ignition: 발화 ** protagonist: 주인공

① 독자의 공감을 얻기 위해 구체적인 인물 묘사가 중요하다.
② 이야기의 줄거리를 단순화시키는 것이 독자의 이해를 높인다.
③ 거리를 두고 주인공의 상황을 객관적으로 바라볼 필요가 있다.
④ 주인공의 역경과 행복이 적절히 섞여야 이야기가 흥미로워진다.
⑤ 주인공에 대한 지속적인 궁금증 유발이 독자의 몰입을 도와준다.

23. 다음 글의 주제로 가장 적절한 것은?

Shutter speed refers to the speed of a camera shutter. In behavior profiling, it refers to the speed of the eyelid. When we blink, we reveal more than just blink rate. Changes in the speed of the eyelid can indicate important information; shutter speed is a measurement of fear. Think of an animal that has a reputation for being fearful. A Chihuahua might come to mind. In mammals, because of evolution, our eyelids will speed up to minimize the amount of time that we can't see an approaching predator. The greater the degree of fear an animal is experiencing, the more the animal is concerned with an approaching predator. In an attempt to keep the eyes open as much as possible, the eyelids involuntarily speed up. Speed, when it comes to behavior, almost always equals fear. In humans, if we experience fear about something, our eyelids will do the same thing as the Chihuahua; they will close and open more quickly.

* eyelid: 눈꺼풀

① eye contact as a way to frighten others
② fast blinking as a symptom of eye fatigue
③ blink speed as a significant indicator of fear
④ fast eye movement as proof of predatory instinct
⑤ blink rate as a difference between humans and animals

24. 다음 글의 제목으로 가장 적절한 것은?

The free market has liberated people in a way that Marxism never could. What is more, as A. O. Hirschman, the Harvard economic historian, showed in his classic study *The Passions and the Interests*, the market was seen by Enlightenment thinkers Adam Smith, David Hume, and Montesquieu as a powerful solution to one of humanity's greatest traditional weaknesses: violence. When two nations meet, said Montesquieu, they can do one of two things: they can wage war or they can trade. If they wage war, both are likely to lose in the long run. If they trade, both will gain. That, of course, was the logic behind the establishment of the European Union: to lock together the destinies of its nations, especially France and Germany, in such a way that they would have an overwhelming interest not to wage war again as they had done to such devastating cost in the first half of the twentieth century.

* Marxism: 마르크스주의

① Trade War: A Reflection of Human's Innate Violence
② Free Market: Winning Together over Losing Together
③ New Economic Framework Stabilizes the Free Market
④ Violence Is the Invisible Hand That Disrupts Capitalism!
⑤ How Are Governments Involved in Controlling the Market?

25. 다음 표의 내용과 일치하지 <u>않는</u> 것은?

Share of Respondents Familiar with/Engaged in E-Sports in 2020

Country	Familiarity (%)	Engagement (%)
China	72	47
Denmark	67	10
Indonesia	57	40
U.S.	34	8
Spain	33	17
UAE	26	19
Iraq	26	16

The above table shows the share of respondents familiar with or engaged in e-sports in selected countries in 2020. ① Among the countries in the table, China was the country with the highest percentage both in e-sports familiarity and in e-sports engagement. ② When it comes to e-sports familiarity, Denmark showed a higher percentage than Indonesia, but the percentage of e-sports engagement in Denmark was lower than Indonesia's. ③ The percentage of U.S. respondents familiar with e-sports was higher than that of Spanish respondents, and with e-sports engagement, the percentage in the U.S. was more than twice that of Spain. ④ While the percentage of e-sports familiarity in Spain was higher than that in the UAE, the percentage of e-sports engagement in Spain was two percentage points lower than that in the UAE. ⑤ As for e-sports familiarity, among the selected countries, the UAE and Iraq showed the lowest percentage, where fewer than a third of respondents in each country were familiar with e-sports.

26. John Bowlby에 관한 다음 글의 내용과 일치하지 <u>않는</u> 것은?

John Bowlby, British developmental psychologist and psychiatrist, was born in 1907, to an upper-middle-class family. His father, who was a member of the King's medical staff, was often absent. Bowlby was cared for primarily by a nanny and did not spend much time with his mother, as was customary at that time for his class. Bowlby was sent to a boarding school at the age of seven. He later recalled this as being traumatic to his development. This experience, however, proved to have a large impact on Bowlby, whose work focused on children's development. Following his father's suggestion, Bowlby enrolled at Trinity College, Cambridge to study medicine, but by his third year, he changed his focus to psychology. During the 1950s, Bowlby briefly worked as a mental health consultant for the World Health Organization. His attachment theory has been described as the dominant approach to understanding early social development.

① 아버지는 왕의 의료진의 일원이었다.
② 어머니와 많은 시간을 보내지 못했다.
③ 기숙 학교로 보내진 것이 성장에 있어 충격적인 일이었다.
④ Trinity 대학에 심리학을 공부하기 위해 입학했다.
⑤ 세계 보건 기구에서 정신 건강 자문 위원으로 일했다.

27. The Great Pumpkin Roll에 관한 다음 안내문의 내용과 일치하지 <u>않는</u> 것은?

The Great Pumpkin Roll

Let's race pumpkins by rolling them down a hill! How far will they go across the road?

□ **Date**: The last Sunday of May, 2021
□ **Location**: Branford Hill in the town of Goomeri
□ **Registration Fee**: $10 for adults, $2 for teens
□ **Rules**
 • The participant who rolls their pumpkin farthest wins.
 • Pumpkins must be at least 15 cm in width.
 • Participants must roll pumpkins only using an underarm action.
 • Each participant has only one opportunity to roll a pumpkin.
□ **Prizes**
 • $1,000 for the person whose pumpkin lands in the Lucky Spot (If more than one participant lands their pumpkin in the Lucky Spot, the money will be divided equally.)
 • $500 for the adult champion and $200 for the teen champion
  Please visit www.goomeripumpkinfestival.com.

① 2021년 5월의 마지막 일요일에 열린다.
② 경기에 사용하는 호박의 최소 너비에 제한이 있다.
③ 참가자는 팔을 아래로 내려 호박을 굴려야 한다.
④ 참가자에게 호박을 굴릴 수 있는 기회를 여러 번 준다.
⑤ Lucky Spot에 호박을 넣은 모두가 상금을 균등하게 나눠 갖는다.

28. Plogging Event에 관한 다음 안내문의 내용과 일치하는 것은?

Plogging Event

Have you heard of Plogging? It comes from the Swedish word for pick up, "plocka upp" and is a combination of jogging and picking up litter. In 2016, it started in Sweden and has recently come to the UK, becoming a new movement for saving nature.

When & Where
• 9 a.m. on the first Monday of each month
• Outside the ETNA Centre, East Twickenham

What to Prepare
• Just bring your running shoes, and we will provide all the other equipment.
• There is no fee to participate, but you are welcome to donate toward our conservation work.

※ No reservations are necessary to participate.
 For more information, visit www.environmenttrust.org.

① 2016년에 영국에서 시작되었다.
② 매달 첫 번째 일요일 오전 9시에 열린다.
③ 운동화를 포함한 장비들이 지급된다.
④ 참가비는 무료이다.
⑤ 참가하려면 예약이 필요하다.

29. 다음 글의 밑줄 친 부분 중, 어법상 틀린 것은? [3점]

Anchoring bias describes the cognitive error you make when you tend to give more weight to information arriving early in a situation ① compared to information arriving later — regardless of the relative quality or relevance of that initial information. Whatever data is presented to you first when you start to look at a situation can form an "anchor" and it becomes significantly more challenging ② to alter your mental course away from this anchor than it logically should be. A classic example of anchoring bias in emergency medicine is "triage bias," ③ where whatever the first impression you develop, or are given, about a patient tends to influence all subsequent providers seeing that patient. For example, imagine two patients presenting for emergency care with aching jaw pain that occasionally ④ extends down to their chest. Differences in how the intake providers label the chart — "jaw pain" vs. "chest pain," for example — ⑤ creating anchors that might result in significant differences in how the patients are treated.

* triage: 부상자 분류 ** intake provider: 환자를 예진하는 의료 종사자

30. 다음 글의 밑줄 친 부분 중, 문맥상 낱말의 쓰임이 적절하지 않은 것은?

In order for us to be able to retain valuable pieces of information, our brain has to ① forget in a manner that is both targeted and controlled. Can you recall, for example, your very first day of school? You most likely have one or two noteworthy images in your head, such as putting your crayons and pencils into your pencil case. But that's probably the extent of the ② specifics. Those additional details that are apparently unimportant are actively deleted from your brain the more you go about remembering the situation. The reason for this is that the brain does not consider it ③ valuable to remember all of the details as long as it is able to convey the main message (i.e., your first day of school was great). In fact, studies have shown that the brain actively ④ strengthens regions responsible for insignificant or minor memory content that tends to disturb the main memory. Over time, the minor details vanish more and more, though this in turn serves to ⑤ sharpen the most important messages of the past.

[31~34] 다음 빈칸에 들어갈 말로 가장 적절한 것을 고르시오.

31. The elements any particular animal needs are relatively predictable. They are predictable based on the past: what an animal's ancestors needed is likely to be what that animal also needs. _____, therefore, can be hardwired. Consider sodium (Na). The bodies of terrestrial vertebrates, including those of mammals, tend to have a concentration of sodium nearly fifty times that of the primary producers on land, plants. This is, in part, because vertebrates evolved in the sea and so evolved cells dependent upon the ingredients that were common in the sea, including sodium. To remedy the difference between their needs for sodium and that available in plants, herbivores can eat fifty times more plant material than they otherwise need (and eliminate the excess). Or they can seek out other sources of sodium. The salt taste receptor rewards animals for doing the latter, seeking out salt in order to satisfy their great need.

* terrestrial: 육생의 ** vertebrate: 척추동물 *** herbivore: 초식 동물

① Taste preferences
② Hunting strategies
③ Migration patterns
④ Protective instincts
⑤ Periodic starvations

32. We might think that our gut instinct is just an inner feeling — a secret interior voice — but in fact it is shaped by a perception of something visible around us, such as a facial expression or a visual inconsistency so fleeting that often we're not even aware we've noticed it. Psychologists now think of this moment as a 'visual matching game'. So a stressed, rushed or tired person is more likely to resort to this visual matching. When they see a situation in front of them, they quickly match it to a sea of past experiences stored in a mental knowledge bank and then, based on a match, they assign meaning to the information in front of them. The brain then sends a signal to the gut, which has many hundreds of nerve cells. So the visceral feeling we get in the pit of our stomach and the butterflies we feel are a(n) _____.

[3점]

* gut: 직감, 창자 ** visceral: 본능적인

① result of our cognitive processing system
② instance of discarding negative memories
③ mechanism of overcoming our internal conflicts
④ visual representation of our emotional vulnerability
⑤ concrete signal of miscommunication within the brain

33. When it comes to climates in the interior areas of continents, mountains _____. A great example of this can be seen along the West Coast of the United States. Air moving from the Pacific Ocean toward the land usually has a great deal of moisture in it. When this humid air moves across the land, it encounters the Coast Range Mountains. As the air moves up and over the mountains, it begins to cool, which causes precipitation on the windward side of the mountains. Once the air moves down the opposite side of the mountains (called the leeward side) it has lost a great deal of moisture. The air continues to move and then hits the even higher Sierra Nevada mountain range. This second uplift causes most of the remaining moisture to fall out of the air, so by the time it reaches the leeward side of the Sierras, the air is extremely dry. The result is that much of the state of Nevada is a desert. [3점]

① increase annual rainfall in dry regions
② prevent drastic changes in air temperature
③ play a huge role in stopping the flow of moisture
④ change wind speed as air ascends and descends them
⑤ equalize the amount of moisture of surrounding land areas

34. One vivid example of how _____ is given by Dan Ariely in his book *Predictably Irrational*. He tells the story of a day care center in Israel that decided to fine parents who arrived late to pick up their children, in the hope that this would discourage them from doing so. In fact, the exact opposite happened. Before the imposition of fines, parents felt guilty about arriving late, and guilt was effective in ensuring that only a few did so. Once a fine was introduced, it seems that in the minds of the parents the entire scenario was changed from a social contract to a market one. Essentially, they were paying for the center to look after their children after hours. Some parents thought it worth the price, and the rate of late arrivals increased. Significantly, once the center abandoned the fines and went back to the previous arrangement, late arrivals remained at the high level they had reached during the period of the fines.

[3점]

① people can put aside their interests for the common good
② changing an existing agreement can cause a sense of guilt
③ imposing a fine can compensate for broken social contracts
④ social bonds can be insufficient to change people's behavior
⑤ a market mindset can transform and undermine an institution

35. 다음 글에서 전체 흐름과 관계 <u>없는</u> 문장은?

There is a pervasive idea in Western culture that humans are essentially rational, skillfully sorting fact from fiction, and, ultimately, arriving at timeless truths about the world. ① This line of thinking holds that humans follow the rules of logic, calculate probabilities accurately, and make decisions about the world that are perfectly informed by all available information. ② Conversely, failures to make effective and well-informed decisions are often attributed to failures of human reasoning — resulting, say, from psychological disorders or cognitive biases. ③ In this picture, whether we succeed or fail turns out to be a matter of whether individual humans are rational and intelligent. ④ Our ability to make a reasonable decision has more to do with our social interactions than our individual psychology. ⑤ And so, if we want to achieve better outcomes — truer beliefs, better decisions — we need to focus on improving individual human reasoning.

* pervasive: 널리 스며 있는

[36~37] 주어진 글 다음에 이어질 글의 순서로 가장 적절한 것을 고르시오.

36.

Regarding food production, under the British government, there was a different conception of responsibility from that of French government. In France, the responsibility for producing good food lay with the producers.

(A) It would be unfair to interfere with the shopkeeper's right to make money. In the 1840s, a patent was granted for a machine designed for making fake coffee beans out of chicory, using the same technology that went into manufacturing bullets.

(B) The state would police their activities and, if they should fail, would punish them for neglecting the interests of its citizens. By contrast, the British government — except in extreme cases — placed most of the responsibility with the individual consumers.

(C) This machine was clearly designed for the purposes of swindling, and yet the government allowed it. A machine for forging money would never have been licensed, so why this? As one consumer complained, the British system of government was weighted against the consumer in favour of the swindler.

* swindle: 사기 치다 ** forge: 위조하다

① (A) − (C) − (B)   ② (B) − (A) − (C)
③ (B) − (C) − (A)   ④ (C) − (A) − (B)
⑤ (C) − (B) − (A)

37.

Because we are told that the planet is doomed, we do not register the growing number of scientific studies demonstrating the resilience of other species. For instance, climate-driven disturbances are affecting the world's coastal marine ecosystems more frequently and with greater intensity.

(A) Similarly, kelp forests hammered by intense El Niño water-temperature increases recovered within five years. By studying these "bright spots," situations where ecosystems persist even in the face of major climatic impacts, we can learn what management strategies help to minimize destructive forces and nurture resilience.

(B) In a region in Western Australia, for instance, up to 90 percent of live coral was lost when ocean water temperatures rose, causing what scientists call coral bleaching. Yet in some sections of the reef surface, 44 percent of the corals recovered within twelve years.

(C) This is a global problem that demands urgent action. Yet, as detailed in a 2017 paper in *BioScience*, there are also instances where marine ecosystems show remarkable resilience to acute climatic events. [3점]

* doomed: 운이 다한 ** resilience: 회복력 *** kelp: 켈프(해초의 일종)

① (A) − (C) − (B) 　② (B) − (A) − (C)
③ (B) − (C) − (A) 　④ (C) − (A) − (B)
⑤ (C) − (B) − (A)

[38~39] 글의 흐름으로 보아, 주어진 문장이 들어가기에 가장 적절한 곳을 고르시오.

38.

But this is a short-lived effect, and in the long run, people find such sounds too bright.

Brightness of sounds means much energy in higher frequencies, which can be calculated from the sounds easily. A violin has many more overtones compared to a flute and sounds brighter. (①) An oboe is brighter than a classical guitar, and a crash cymbal brighter than a double bass. (②) This is obvious, and indeed people like brightness. (③) One reason is that it makes sound subjectively louder, which is part of the loudness war in modern electronic music, and in the classical music of the 19th century. (④) All sound engineers know that if they play back a track to a musician that just has recorded this track and add some higher frequencies, the musician will immediately like the track much better. (⑤) So it is wise not to play back such a track with too much brightness, as it normally takes quite some time to convince the musician that less brightness serves his music better in the end. [3점]

39.

In full light, seedlings reduce the amount of energy they allocate to stem elongation.

Scientists who have observed plants growing in the dark have found that they are vastly different in appearance, form, and function from those grown in the light. (①) This is true even when the plants in the different light conditions are genetically identical and are grown under identical conditions of temperature, water, and nutrient level. (②) Seedlings grown in the dark limit the amount of energy going to organs that do not function at full capacity in the dark, like cotyledons and roots, and instead initiate elongation of the seedling stem to propel the plant out of darkness. (③) The energy is directed to expanding their leaves and developing extensive root systems. (④) This is a good example of phenotypic plasticity. (⑤) The seedling adapts to distinct environmental conditions by modifying its form and the underlying metabolic and biochemical processes. [3점]

* elongation: 연장 ** cotyledon: 떡잎
*** phenotypic plasticity: 표현형 적응성

40. 다음 글의 내용을 한 문장으로 요약하고자 한다. 빈칸 (A), (B)에 들어갈 말로 가장 적절한 것은?

In a study, Guy Mayraz, a behavioral economist, showed his experimental subjects graphs of a price rising and falling over time. The graphs were actually of past changes in the stock market, but Mayraz told people that the graphs showed recent changes in the price of wheat. He asked each person to predict where the price would move next — and offered them a reward if their forecasts came true. But Mayraz had also divided his participants into two categories, "farmers" and "bakers". Farmers would be paid extra if wheat prices were high. Bakers would earn a bonus if wheat was cheap. So the subjects might earn two separate payments: one for an accurate forecast, and a bonus if the price of wheat moved in their direction. Mayraz found that the prospect of the bonus influenced the forecast itself. The farmers hoped and *predicted* that the price of wheat would rise. The bakers hoped for — and predicted — the opposite. They let their hopes influence their reasoning.

↓

When participants were asked to predict the price change of wheat, their _____(A)_____ for where the price would go, which was determined by the group they belonged to, _____(B)_____ their predictions.

	(A)	(B)		(A)	(B)
①	wish	affected	②	wish	contradicted
③	disregard	restricted	④	disregard	changed
⑤	assurance	realized			

[41~42] 다음 글을 읽고, 물음에 답하시오.

Stories populate our lives. If you are not a fan of stories, you might imagine that the best world is a world without them, where we can only see the facts in front of us. But to do this is to (a) deny how our brains work, how they are *designed* to work. Evolution has given us minds that are alert to stories and suggestion because, through many hundreds of thousands of years of natural selection, minds that can attend to stories have been more (b) successful at passing on their owners' genes.

Think about what happens, for example, when animals face one another in conflict. They rarely plunge into battle right away. No, they first try to (c) signal in all kinds of ways what the *outcome* of the battle is going to be. They puff up their chests, they roar, and they bare their fangs. Animals evolved to attend to stories and signals because these turn out to be an efficient way to navigate the world. If you and I were a pair of lions on the Serengeti, and we were trying to decide the strongest lion, it would be most (d) sensible — for both of us — to plunge straight into a conflict. It is far better for each of us to make a show of strength, to tell *the story* of how our victory is inevitable. If one of those stories is much more (e) convincing than the other, we might be able to agree on the outcome without actually having the fight.

* fang: 송곳니

41. 윗글의 제목으로 가장 적절한 것은?

① The Light and Dark Sides of Storytelling
② How to Interpret Various Signals of Animals
③ Why Are We Built to Pay Attention to Stories?
④ Story: A Game Changer for Overturning a Losing Battle
⑤ Evolution: A History of Human's Coexistence with Animals

42. 밑줄 친 (a)~(e) 중에서 문맥상 낱말의 쓰임이 적절하지 <u>않은</u> 것은?

① (a)   ② (b)   ③ (c)   ④ (d)   ⑤ (e)

[43~45] 다음 글을 읽고, 물음에 답하시오.

(A)

Jennifer was on her way home. She decided to stop at a gas station to get coffee. After she paid for her coffee, she got back into her car, but before she started it, she noticed a woman standing outside in front of the building. (a) She could tell that the woman was homeless by her appearance. Her clothes were worn and she was nothing but skin and bones. *She must have not had enough money to get something to eat.* Jennifer thought to herself, feeling pity for her.

(B)

Watching the scene changed Jennifer's life entirely. You see, that day was Mother's Day. It took a homeless woman to show (b) her what selfless giving and love is. From that day on, Jennifer has helped people in trouble, especially mothers struggling to raise children. The homeless woman made Jennifer a better person.

(C)

Jennifer sat in her car, looking at the dog. She noticed that people were walking by without paying attention to the dog. But (c) she still did not do anything. However, someone did. The homeless woman, who Jennifer thought did not have money to buy herself anything to eat, went into the store. And what she did brought tears to Jennifer's eyes. She had gone into the store, bought a can of dog food, and fed that dog. (d) She looked so happy to do it as well.

(D)

Suddenly, a dog walked up to the front of the building. Being a dog lover, Jennifer noticed that the dog was a German Shepherd. She could also tell that the dog was a mother, because anyone could notice that she had been feeding puppies. The dog was terribly in need of something to eat and (e) she felt so bad for her. She knew if the dog didn't eat soon, she and her puppies would not make it.

43. 주어진 글 (A)에 이어질 내용을 순서에 맞게 배열한 것으로 가장 적절한 것은?

① (B) − (D) − (C)   ② (C) − (B) − (D)
③ (C) − (D) − (B)   ④ (D) − (B) − (C)
⑤ (D) − (C) − (B)

44. 밑줄 친 (a)~(e) 중에서 가리키는 대상이 나머지 넷과 <u>다른</u> 것은?

① (a)   ② (b)   ③ (c)   ④ (d)   ⑤ (e)

45. 윗글에 관한 내용으로 적절하지 <u>않은</u> 것은?

① Jennifer는 커피를 사기 위해 주유소에 들렀다.
② 사건이 일어난 날은 어머니날이었다.
③ 지나가던 사람들은 개에게 관심을 보이지 않았다.
④ Jennifer는 가게에 들어가서 개의 먹이를 샀다.
⑤ Jennifer는 개가 어미 개라는 것을 알았다.

* 확인 사항
○ 답안지의 해당란에 필요한 내용을 정확히 기입(표기)했는지 확인하시오.

18

001 whom it may concern [불특정 상대에 대한 편지·증명서 따위의 첫머리에 써서] 관계자 제위, 관계자 분께
002 commute ⓥ 통근하다, 통학하다
003 public transport 대중교통
004 city council 시 의회
005 discontinue ⓥ 중단하다
006 drop off (차로) 내려주다
007 traffic ⓝ 교통량
008 bike ⓝ 자전거
009 resident ⓝ 주민
010 unacceptable ⓐ 받아들일 수 없는
011 urge ⓥ 촉구하다, 권고하다

19

012 vice president 부사장
013 human resources (회사) 인사과
014 beam ⓥ 활짝 웃다
015 anticipation ⓝ 기대
016 turning point 전환점
017 career ⓝ 경력
018 promotion ⓝ 승진
019 realize ⓥ 깨닫다
020 expect ⓥ 예상하다
021 desperately ⓐⓓ 간절히
022 suitable ⓐ 적합한
023 frozen ⓐ 얼어붙은
024 panic ⓥ 당황하다
025 repeat ⓥ 되풀이하다, 반복하다
026 sentence ⓝ 문장
027 relaxed ⓐ 여유 있는
028 relieved ⓐ 안도하는
029 embarrassed ⓐ 당황한
030 pleased ⓐ 기쁜

20

031 make an announcement 발표하다
032 prove ⓥ 판명되다
033 uneconomical ⓐ 비경제적인, 수익이 안 나는
034 route ⓝ 노선
035 merely ⓐⓓ 단지
036 scarce ⓐ 부족한, 희소한
037 persuade ⓥ 설득하다
038 principle ⓝ 원리
039 scarcity ⓝ 부족, 희귀
040 effectively ⓐⓓ 효과적으로
041 salesperson ⓝ 판매원
042 derive A from B B로부터 A를 얻어내다
043 uniqueness ⓝ 유일함, 고유함
044 miss out on ~을 놓치다
045 desirable ⓐ 바람직한, 가치 있는

21

046 concentrate ⓥ 집중하다
047 irregularly ⓐⓓ 불규칙적으로
048 every now and then 이따금, 가끔
049 filter ⓥ 여과하다
050 regulate ⓥ 조절하다, 통제하다
051 strict ⓐ 엄격한
052 nutrition ⓝ 영양

053 stick to ~을 고수하다
054 fixed ⓐ 고정된
055 metabolism ⓝ 신진대사
056 adjust ⓥ 적응하다
057 thereby ⓐⓓ 그렇게 함으로써
058 hunger ⓝ 배고픔, 허기
059 in-between ⓐ 중간의
060 phase ⓝ 단계
061 belly ⓝ 배
062 rumble ⓥ 우르르 울리다
063 unexpected ⓐ 예기치 않은
064 happen ⓥ 일어나다
065 snack ⓝ 간식
066 energy ⓝ 활기
067 under control 통제되는
068 balance ⓥ 균형을 유지하다
069 consumption ⓝ 소비
070 false ⓐ 잘못된
071 stimulate ⓥ 자극하다
072 toxic ⓐ 유독한

22

073 emerge ⓥ 나타나다, 출현하다
074 ignition ⓝ 발화
075 protagonist ⓝ 주인공
076 overreact ⓥ 과민 반응하다
077 behave ⓥ 행동하다
078 otherwise ⓐ 다른
079 attentive ⓐ 주의를 기울이는
080 compel ⓥ 강요하다
081 narrative ⓝ 이야기
082 reader ⓝ 독자
083 viewer ⓝ 시청자
084 engaged ⓐ 몰입한
085 absent ⓐ 부재한
086 at risk of ~할 위험에 처한
087 perhaps ⓐⓓ 어쩌면
088 single ⓐ 단 하나의
089 definition ⓝ 정의
090 electricity ⓝ 전기
091 heartbeat ⓝ 심장박동

23

092 refer ⓥ 가리켜 말하다
093 profiling ⓝ 프로파일링, (개요 작성을 위한) 자료 수집
094 eyelid ⓝ 눈꺼풀
095 blink ⓝ 눈을 깜박거림 ⓥ 눈을 깜박이다
096 reveal ⓥ 드러내다
097 rate ⓝ 속도, 비율
098 indicate ⓥ 나타내다
099 measurement ⓝ 척도
100 fear ⓝ 두려움
101 reputation ⓝ 평판, 명성
102 fearful ⓐ 겁이 많은
103 minimize ⓥ 최소화하다
104 predator ⓝ 포식자
105 degree ⓝ 정도
106 attempt ⓝ 시도
107 involuntarily ⓐⓓ 모르는 사이에, 본의 아니게
108 equal ⓐ 같다

109 frighten ⓥ 겁을 주다
110 fatigue ⓝ 피로
111 significant ⓐ 중요한, 유의미한
112 indicator ⓝ 지표, 표시
113 proof ⓝ 증거
114 instinct ⓝ 본능

24

115 free market 자유시장
116 liberate ⓥ 자유롭게 해주다
117 classic ⓐ 전형적인, 고전적인
118 passion ⓝ 열정
119 Enlightenment ⓝ (18세기) 계몽주의
120 weakness ⓝ 약점
121 violence ⓝ 폭력
122 wage war 전쟁을 벌이다
123 long run 장기간
124 establishment ⓝ 설립
125 destiny ⓝ 운명
126 overwhelming ⓐ 저항할 수 없는, 압도적인
127 devastating ⓐ 참담한
128 cost ⓝ 대가
129 first half 전반기
130 reflection ⓝ 반영, 성찰
131 innate ⓐ 타고난, 선천적인
132 framework ⓝ 체제
133 stabilize ⓥ 안정시키다
134 disrupt ⓥ 교란시키다

25

135 respondent ⓝ 응답자
136 selected ⓐ 선택된, 선정된
137 familiar with ~에 친숙한
138 engagement ⓝ 참여, 몰입

26

139 upper-middle-class 상위 중산 계급
140 medical staff 의료진
141 often ⓐⓓ 자주
142 psychiatrist ⓝ 정신과 의사
143 primarily ⓐⓓ 주로
144 nanny ⓝ 유모
145 customary ⓐ 관습적인
146 class ⓝ 계급
147 boarding school 기숙 학교
148 recall ⓥ 회상하다, 기억해 내다
149 traumatic ⓐ 대단히 충격적인
150 have an impact on ~에 영향을 미치다
151 enroll at ~에 등록하다
152 mental health 정신 건강
153 consultant ⓝ 자문위원
154 World Health Organization 세계보건 기구(WHO)
155 attachment ⓝ (유아와 부모의) 애착
156 describe ⓥ 평하다, 말하다
157 dominant ⓐ 지배적인

27

158 roll ⓥ 굴리다
159 hill ⓝ 언덕
160 registration fee 등록비

161 farthest ⓐⓓ 가장 멀리
162 width ⓝ 너비
163 underarm ⓐ (투구 시) 팔을 내려서 하는
164 land ⓥ 착륙하다
165 equally ⓐⓓ 균등하게

28

166 combination ⓝ 조합
167 litter ⓝ 쓰레기
168 movement ⓝ (사람들이 조직적으로 벌이는) 운동
169 running shoes 운동화
170 equipment ⓝ 장비
171 donate ⓥ 기부하다
172 toward prep ~을 위하여
173 conservation ⓝ (환경) 보호
174 necessary ⓐ 필요한

29

175 anchor ⓥ 닻을 내리다, 정박하다, 기준점을 잡다 ⓝ 기준점
176 cognitive ⓐ 인지적인
177 give weight to ~을 중요시하다
178 regardless of ~와 관계없이
179 relevance ⓝ 적절성
180 significantly ⓐⓓ 상당히
181 bias ⓝ 편향
182 triage bias 부상자 분류
183 impression ⓝ 인상
184 influence ⓥ 영향을 미치다
185 subsequent ⓐ 다음의, 이후의
186 imagine ⓥ 상상하다
187 present ⓥ (환자가) 진찰을 받으러 가다, (증상이) 나타나다
188 emergency care 응급 치료
189 aching ⓐ 쑤시는
190 jaw ⓝ 턱
191 occasionally ⓐⓓ 때때로
192 chest ⓝ 가슴, 흉부
193 intake providers 환자를 예진하는 의료 종사자
194 treat ⓥ 치료하다

30

195 retain ⓥ 지니다, 보유하다
196 valuable ⓐ 가치가 있는
197 piece ⓝ 조각
198 manner ⓝ 방식
199 noteworthy ⓐ 주목할 만한
200 extent ⓝ 정도, 범위
201 specific ⓝ 세부 사항, 구체적인 것
202 detail ⓝ 세부 사항
203 apparently ⓐⓓ 명백히
204 delete ⓥ 삭제하다
205 convey ⓥ 전달하다
206 region ⓝ 영역
207 responsible for ~을 담당하는, 책임지는
208 insignificant ⓐ 중요하지 않은
209 minor ⓐ 대수롭지 않은, 사소한
210 disturb ⓥ 저해하다, 방해하다
211 vanish ⓥ 사라지다
212 sharpen ⓥ 선명하게 하다, 연마하다

31

213 □ element ⓝ 요소
214 □ predictable ⓐ 예측 가능한
215 □ ancestor ⓝ 조상
216 □ hardwired ⓐ 타고난, 내장된
217 □ terrestrial ⓐ 육생의
218 □ vertebrate ⓝ 척추동물
219 □ concentration ⓝ 농도
220 □ sodium ⓝ 나트륨
221 □ in part 부분적으로는, 어느 정도는
222 □ evolve ⓥ 진화하다
223 □ cell ⓝ 세포
224 □ dependent upon ~에 의존하는
225 □ ingredient ⓝ 성분
226 □ remedy ⓥ 해결하다, 바로잡다
227 □ herbivore ⓝ 초식동물
228 □ eliminate ⓥ 배설하다, 제거하다
229 □ taste ⓝ 맛
230 □ receptor ⓝ (신체의) 수용기, 감각기
231 □ reward ⓥ 보상하다
232 □ latter ⓐ (둘 중의) 후자의
233 □ satisfy ⓥ 충족시키다
234 □ preference ⓝ 선호도
235 □ periodic ⓐ 주기적인
236 □ starvation ⓝ 기아, 굶주림

32

237 □ interior ⓐ 내부의
238 □ perception ⓝ 인식
239 □ visible ⓐ 가시적인
240 □ facial expression 얼굴 표정
241 □ visual ⓐ 시각의
242 □ inconsistency ⓝ 불일치, 모순
243 □ fleeting ⓐ 순식간의, 잠깐 동안의
244 □ aware ⓐ 알아차린
245 □ rush ⓥ 서두르다
246 □ resort ⓥ 의지하다
247 □ assign A to B A를 B에 부여하다, 할당하다
248 □ gut ⓝ 직감, 창자
249 □ nerve cell 신경세포
250 □ visceral ⓐ 본능적인
251 □ stomach ⓝ 배, 복부
252 □ instance ⓝ 예시
253 □ discard ⓥ 버리다
254 □ overcome ⓥ 극복하다
255 □ conflict ⓝ 갈등
256 □ representation ⓝ 표현
257 □ miscommunication ⓝ 의사소통의 오류
258 □ vulnerability ⓝ 취약성, 연약함
259 □ concrete ⓐ 구체적인

33

260 □ climate ⓝ 기후
261 □ humid ⓐ 습한
262 □ continent ⓝ 대륙
263 □ encounter ⓥ 마주치다, 접하다
264 □ precipitation ⓝ 강수
265 □ windward ⓐ 바람이 불어오는 쪽의
266 □ leeward ⓐ 바람이 가려지는 쪽의
267 □ a great deal of 많은 양의
268 □ uplift ⓝ 상승
269 □ fall out of ~에서 빠져나오다

270 □ reach ⓥ 도달하다
271 □ extremely ⓐⓓ 매우, 극도로
272 □ desert ⓝ 사막
273 □ rainfall ⓝ 강우량
274 □ drastic ⓐ 급격한, 과감한
275 □ wind speed 풍속(風速)
276 □ ascend ⓥ 올라가다
277 □ equalize ⓥ 균등하게 하다

34

278 □ vivid ⓐ 생생한
279 □ irrational ⓐ 불합리한
280 □ discourage A from B A를 B하지 못하게 하다
281 □ opposite ⓐ 반대의
282 □ imposition ⓝ 부과
283 □ guilty ⓐ 죄책감이 드는
284 □ introduce ⓥ 도입하다
285 □ contract ⓝ 계약
286 □ pay for 대금을 지불하다, 비용을 지불하다
287 □ look after ~을 맡다[돌보다/건사하다]
288 □ worth ⓐ ~의 가치가 있는
289 □ abandon ⓥ (하다가) 포기하다, 그만두다
290 □ previous ⓐ 이전의
291 □ arrangement ⓝ 방식
292 □ put aside ~을 무시하다, 제쳐두다, 따로 떼어놓다
293 □ compensate for ~을 보상하다
294 □ insufficient ⓐ 불충분한
295 □ mindset ⓝ 사고방식
296 □ undermine ⓥ 훼손하다, (기반을) 약화시키다
297 □ institution ⓝ 제도, 관습

35

298 □ pervasive ⓐ 스며드는
299 □ idea ⓝ 관념
300 □ rational ⓐ 이성적인
301 □ skillfully ⓐⓓ 능숙하게
302 □ sort A from B A와 B를 가려내다
303 □ fiction ⓝ 허구
304 □ ultimately ⓐⓓ 궁극적으로
305 □ timeless ⓐ 영원한
306 □ calculate ⓥ 계산하다
307 □ probability ⓝ 확률, 가능성
308 □ accurately ⓐⓓ 정확하게
309 □ failure ⓝ 실패
310 □ be attributed to ~의 탓이다
311 □ disorder ⓝ 장애
312 □ intelligent ⓐ 지적인
313 □ have to do with ~와 관련이 있다
314 □ social interaction 사회적 상호작용
315 □ outcome ⓝ 결과

36

316 □ conception ⓝ 개념
317 □ unfair ⓐ 부당한
318 □ shopkeeper ⓝ 가게주인
319 □ right ⓝ 권리
320 □ patent ⓝ 특허
321 □ grant ⓥ (공식적으로) 주다
322 □ manufacture ⓥ 생산하다, 제조하다

323 □ bullet ⓝ 총알
324 □ police ⓥ 감시하다
325 □ punish ⓥ 처벌하다
326 □ neglect ⓥ 등한시하다
327 □ by contrast 그와 대조적으로, 그에 반해서
328 □ except ⓟⓡ➋ⓟ 제외하고는
329 □ clearly ⓐⓓ 분명히
330 □ swindle ⓥ 사기 치다
331 □ forge ⓥ 위조하다
332 □ license ⓥ 허가하다
333 □ complain ⓥ 불평하다
334 □ weigh against ~에 불리하다

37

335 □ doomed ⓐ 운이 다한
336 □ register ⓥ (흔히 부정문에서) 알아채다, 기억하다
337 □ demonstrate ⓥ 입증하다
338 □ resilience ⓝ 회복력
339 □ disturbance ⓝ 교란
340 □ coastal ⓐ 해안의
341 □ marine ecosystem 해양생태계
342 □ intensity ⓝ 강도
343 □ water-temperature 수온
344 □ recover ⓥ 복구되다
345 □ persist ⓥ 지속되다
346 □ in the face of ~에 직면하여, ~에도 불구하고
347 □ destructive ⓐ 파괴적인
348 □ nurture ⓥ 양성하다, 키우다
349 □ coral ⓝ 산호
350 □ bleaching ⓝ 표백
351 □ section ⓝ 부분
352 □ reef ⓝ 암초
353 □ urgent ⓐ 긴급한
354 □ remarkable ⓐ 놀라운, 주목할 만한
355 □ acute ⓐ 극심한

38

356 □ short-lived ⓐ 단기적인
357 □ brightness ⓝ 밝기
358 □ frequency ⓝ 주파수
359 □ overtone ⓝ 상음(上音)
360 □ subjectively ⓐⓓ 주관적으로
361 □ loudness ⓝ 소리의 세기
362 □ sound engineer ⓝ 음향기사
363 □ track ⓝ (테이프로 녹음한) 곡
364 □ musician ⓝ 음악가
365 □ record ⓥ 녹음하다
366 □ immediately ⓐⓓ 즉시, 곧바로
367 □ normally ⓐⓓ 보통
368 □ convince ⓥ 납득시키다
369 □ serve ⓥ 도움이 되다

39

370 □ seedling ⓝ 묘목
371 □ allocate ⓥ 할당하다
372 □ stem ⓝ 줄기
373 □ elongation ⓝ 연장
374 □ vastly ⓐⓓ 상당히, 대단히, 엄청나게
375 □ genetically ⓐⓓ 유전적으로
376 □ identical ⓐ 동일한

377 □ nutrient ⓝ 영양소
378 □ organ ⓝ 기관(器官)
379 □ cotyledon ⓝ 떡잎
380 □ initiate ⓥ 시작하다
381 □ propel ⓥ 나아가게 하다, 추진시키다
382 □ extensive ⓐ 광범위한
383 □ distinct ⓐ 별개의, 다른
384 □ underlying ⓐ 기저의, 근본적인

40

385 □ economist ⓝ 경제학자
386 □ experimental ⓐ 실험의
387 □ actually ⓐⓓ 사실
388 □ stock market 주식 시장
389 □ wheat ⓝ 밀
390 □ predict ⓥ 예측하다
391 □ forecast ⓝ 예측, 예보
392 □ come true 실현되다
393 □ divide ⓥ 나누다
394 □ separate ⓐ 별개의
395 □ accurate ⓐ 정확한
396 □ prospect ⓝ 예상, 전망
397 □ reasoning ⓝ 추론
398 □ contradict ⓥ ~와 모순되다
399 □ disregard ⓝ 무시 ⓥ 무시하다
400 □ assurance ⓝ 확언, 장담, 자신감

41~42

401 □ populate ⓥ 거주하다
402 □ deny ⓥ 부인하다
403 □ natural selection 자연 선택
404 □ pass on ~을 전해주다
405 □ alert ⓝ 유전자
406 □ plunge into ~에 뛰어들다
407 □ battle ⓝ 전투
408 □ puff up 부풀리다
409 □ roar ⓥ 으르렁거리다
410 □ bare ⓥ (신체의 일부를) 드러내다
411 □ fang ⓝ 송곳니
412 □ sensible ⓐ 분별 있는
413 □ make a show of ~을 과시하다, 자랑하다
414 □ inevitable ⓐ 불가피한
415 □ convincing ⓐ 설득력 있는

43~45

416 □ gas station 주유소
417 □ notice ⓥ 주목하다
418 □ in front of ~의 앞에
419 □ homeless ⓐ 노숙자의
420 □ appearance ⓝ 겉모습
421 □ nothing but skin and bones 피골이 상접한, 매우 마른
422 □ scene ⓝ 장면
423 □ pity ⓝ 유감, 연민
424 □ entirely ⓐⓓ 완전히
425 □ selfless ⓐ 이타적인
426 □ from that day on 그날부터
427 □ struggling ⓐ 애쓰는, 고군분투하는
428 □ raise children 아이들을 키우다
429 □ bring tears to one's eyes ~의 눈물을 짓게 하다
430 □ in need of ~이 필요한

● 채점 : 맞은 개수 _____ / 80

TEST A-B 각 단어의 뜻을 [A] 영어는 우리말로, [B] 우리말은 영어로 쓰시오.

A	English	Korean
01	unacceptable	
02	anticipation	
03	equally	
04	attentive	
05	identical	
06	significant	
07	probability	
08	manufacture	
09	rate	
10	insignificant	
11	regulate	
12	predator	
13	overwhelming	
14	stock market	
15	entirely	
16	demonstrate	
17	guilty	
18	recall	
19	appearance	
20	equipment	

B	Korean	English
01	중단하다	
02	바람직한, 가치 있는	
03	세부 사항, 구체적인 것	
04	포기하다, 그만두다	
05	부당한	
06	보상하다	
07	이타적인	
08	지니다, 보유하다	
09	평판, 명성	
10	불합리한	
11	결과	
12	주로	
13	예상, 전망	
14	나타나다, 출현하다	
15	때때로	
16	반영, 성찰	
17	집중하다	
18	관습적인	
19	대륙	
20	보통	

▶ A-D 정답 : 해설편 192쪽

TEST C-D 각 단어의 뜻을 골라 기호를 쓰시오.

C	English		Korean
01	institution	( )	ⓐ 정도, 범위
02	persist	( )	ⓑ 갈등
03	extent	( )	ⓒ 주기적인
04	adjust	( )	ⓓ 과민 반응하다
05	predictable	( )	ⓔ 예측, 예보
06	dominant	( )	ⓕ 적응하다
07	conflict	( )	ⓖ 간절히
08	commute	( )	ⓗ 지속되다
09	overreact	( )	ⓘ 제도, 관습
10	desperately	( )	ⓙ 착륙하다
11	definition	( )	ⓚ 주관적으로
12	instinct	( )	ⓛ 놀라운, 주목할 만한
13	periodic	( )	ⓜ 양성하다, 키우다
14	forecast	( )	ⓝ 예측 가능한
15	land	( )	ⓞ 척도
16	measurement	( )	ⓟ 선명하게 하다, 연마하다
17	nurture	( )	ⓠ 통근하다, 통학하다
18	subjectively	( )	ⓡ 본능, 직감
19	sharpen	( )	ⓢ 정의
20	remarkable	( )	ⓣ 지배적인

D	Korean		English
01	등한시하다	( )	ⓐ discard
02	납득시키다	( )	ⓑ width
03	광범위한	( )	ⓒ scarce
04	적절성	( )	ⓓ sensible
05	모르는 사이에, 본의 아니게	( )	ⓔ inconsistency
06	단기적인	( )	ⓕ disrupt
07	불일치, 모순	( )	ⓖ neglect
08	너비	( )	ⓗ windward
09	올라가다	( )	ⓘ relevance
10	쓰레기	( )	ⓙ involuntarily
11	교란시키다	( )	ⓚ eliminate
12	별개의	( )	ⓛ ascend
13	버리다	( )	ⓜ fixed
14	설립	( )	ⓝ genetically
15	고정된	( )	ⓞ separate
16	유전적으로	( )	ⓟ extensive
17	배설하다, 제거하다	( )	ⓠ short-lived
18	바람이 불어오는 쪽의	( )	ⓡ establishment
19	부족한, 희소한	( )	ⓢ litter
20	분별 있는	( )	ⓣ convince

※ 영어 [독해] 파트만 수록한 문제지이므로 18번부터 시작합니다.

● 점수 표시가 없는 문항은 모두 2점   ● 문항수 28개 | 배점 63점 | 제한 시간 45분

18. 다음 글의 목적으로 가장 적절한 것은?

To the Principal of Gullard High School,

My name is Nancy Watson, and I am the captain of the student dance club at Gullard High School. We are one of the biggest faces of the school, winning a lot of awards and trophies. However, the school isn't allowing our club to practice on the school field because a lot of teachers worry that we are going to mess up the field. This is causing us to lose practice time and ultimately results in creating a bad high school experience for us. We promise to use the space respectfully. Therefore, I'm asking you to allow us to use the school field for our dance practice. I would be grateful if you reconsider your decision. Thank you very much.

Sincerely,
Nancy Watson

① 학생 동아리 운영 성과를 보고하려고
② 댄스 동아리 특별 공연을 홍보하려고
③ 댄스 동아리실 시설 보수를 건의하려고
④ 댄스 동아리의 운동장 사용 허락을 요청하려고
⑤ 학생 동아리 부원 모집 기간의 연장을 부탁하려고

19. 다음 글에 드러난 Ryan의 심경 변화로 가장 적절한 것은?

Ryan, an eleven-year-old boy, ran home as fast as he could. Finally, summer break had started! When he entered the house, his mom was standing in front of the refrigerator, waiting for him. She told him to pack his bags. Ryan's heart soared like a balloon. *Pack for what? Are we going to Disneyland?* He couldn't remember the last time his parents had taken him on a vacation. His eyes beamed. "You're spending the summer with uncle Tim and aunt Gina." Ryan groaned. "The whole summer?" "Yes, t he who l e s ummer." The anticipation he had felt disappeared in a flash. For three whole miserable weeks, he would be on his aunt and uncle's farm. He sighed.

① excited → disappointed
② furious → regretful
③ irritated → satisfied
④ nervous → relaxed
⑤ pleased → jealous

20. 다음 글에서 필자가 주장하는 바로 가장 적절한 것은?

When trying to convince someone to change their mind, most people try to lay out a logical argument, or make a passionate plea as to why their view is right and the other person's opinion is wrong. But when you think about it, you'll realize that this doesn't often work. As soon as someone figures out that you are on a mission to change their mind, the metaphorical shutters go down. You'll have better luck if you ask well-chosen, open-ended questions that let someone challenge their own assumptions. We tend to approve of an idea if we thought of it first — or at least, if we *think* we thought of it first. Therefore, encouraging someone to question their own worldview will often yield better results than trying to force them into accepting your opinion as fact. Ask someone well-chosen questions to look at their own views from another angle, and this might trigger fresh insights.

① 타인의 신뢰를 얻기 위해서는 일관된 행동을 보여 주어라.
② 협상을 잘하기 위해 질문에 담긴 상대방의 의도를 파악하라.
③ 논쟁을 잘하려면 자신의 가치관에서 벗어나려는 시도를 하라.
④ 원만한 대인 관계를 유지하려면 상대를 배려하는 태도를 갖춰라.
⑤ 설득하고자 할 때 상대방이 스스로 관점을 돌아보게 하는 질문을 하라.

21. 밑줄 친 turns the life stories of these scientists from lead to gold가 다음 글에서 의미하는 바로 가장 적절한 것은? [3점]

In school, there's one curriculum, one right way to study science, and one right formula that spits out the correct answer on a standardized test. Textbooks with grand titles like *The Principles of Physics* magically reveal "the principles" in three hundred pages. An authority figure then steps up to the lectern to feed us "the truth." As theoretical physicist David Gross explained in his Nobel lecture, textbooks often ignore the many alternate paths that people wandered down, the many false clues they followed, the many misconceptions they had. We learn about Newton's "laws" — as if they arrived by a grand divine visitation or a stroke of genius — but not the years he spent exploring, revising, and changing them. The laws that Newton failed to establish — most notably his experiments in alchemy, which attempted, and spectacularly failed, to turn lead into gold — don't make the cut as part of the one-dimensional story told in physics classrooms. Instead, our education system turns the life stories of these scientists from lead to gold.

* lectern: 강의대 ** alchemy: 연금술

① discovers the valuable relationships between scientists
② emphasizes difficulties in establishing new scientific theories
③ mixes the various stories of great scientists across the world
④ focuses more on the scientists' work than their personal lives
⑤ reveals only the scientists' success ignoring their processes and errors

22. 다음 글의 요지로 가장 적절한 것은?

The vast majority of companies, schools, and organizations measure and reward "high performance" in terms of individual metrics such as sales numbers, résumé accolades, and test scores. The problem with this approach is that it is based on a belief we thought science had fully confirmed: that we live in a world of "survival of the fittest." It teaches us that those with the best grades, or the *most* impressive résumé, or the *highest* point score, will be the ONLY ones to succeed. The formula is simple: be better and smarter and more creative than everyone else, and you will be successful. But this formula is inaccurate. Thanks to new research, we now know that achieving our highest potential is not about survival of the fittest but survival of the best fit. In other words, success is not just about how creative or smart or driven you are, but how well you are able to connect with, contribute to, and benefit from the ecosystem of people around you.

* accolade: 수상, 표창

① 효율적인 업무 배분은 조직의 생산성을 향상시킨다.
② 유연한 사고방식은 원활한 의사소통에 도움이 된다.
③ 사람들과 잘 어울려 일하는 능력이 성공을 가능하게 한다.
④ 비판적 사고 능력은 정확성을 추구하는 태도에서 출발한다.
⑤ 치열한 경쟁 사회에서 최고의 실력을 갖추는 것이 필수적이다.

23. 다음 글의 주제로 가장 적절한 것은?

I was brought up to believe that if I get lost in a large forest, I will sooner or later end up where I started. Without knowing it, people who are lost will always walk in a circle. In the book *Finding Your Way Without Map or Compass*, author Harold Gatty confirms that this is true. We tend to walk in circles for several reasons. The most important is that virtually no human has two legs of the exact same length. One leg is always slightly longer than the other, and this causes us to turn without even noticing it. In addition, if you are hiking with a backpack on, the weight of that backpack will inevitably throw you off balance. Our dominant hand factors into the mix too. If you are right-handed, you will have a tendency to turn toward the right. And when you meet an obstacle, you will subconsciously decide to pass it on the right side.

① abilities to construct a mental map for walking
② factors that result in people walking in a circle
③ reasons why dominance exists in nature
④ instincts that help people return home
⑤ solutions to finding the right direction

24. 다음 글의 제목으로 가장 적절한 것은?

In government, in law, in culture, and in routine everyday interaction beyond family and immediate neighbours, a widely understood and clearly formulated language is a great aid to mutual confidence. When dealing with property, with contracts, or even just with the routine exchange of goods and services, concepts and descriptions need to be as precise and unambiguous as possible, otherwise misunderstandings will arise. If full communication with a potential counterparty in a deal is not possible, then uncertainty and probably a measure of distrust will remain. As economic life became more complex in the later Middle Ages, the need for fuller and more precise communication was accentuated. A shared language facilitated clarification and possibly settlement of any disputes. In international trade also the use of a precise and well-formulated language aided the process of translation. The Silk Road could only function at all because translators were always available at interchange points.

* accentuate: 강조하다

① Earn Trust with Reliable Goods Rather Than with Words!
② Linguistic Precision: A Key to Successful Economic Transactions
③ Difficulties in Overcoming Language Barriers and Distrust in Trade
④ The More the Economy Grows, the More Complex the World Gets
⑤ Excessive Confidence: The Biggest Reason for Miscommunication

25. 다음 도표의 내용과 일치하지 <u>않는</u> 것은?

Percentage of Commuters Using Eco-friendly Transportation in Canada by City, 2016

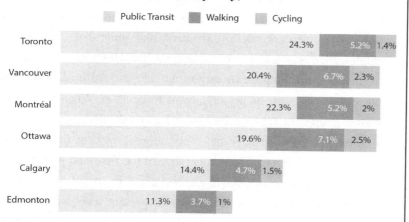

	Public Transit	Walking	Cycling
Toronto	24.3%	5.2%	1.4%
Vancouver	20.4%	6.7%	2.3%
Montréal	22.3%	5.2%	2%
Ottawa	19.6%	7.1%	2.5%
Calgary	14.4%	4.7%	1.5%
Edmonton	11.3%	3.7%	1%

The above graph shows the percentage of commuters using eco-friendly transportation to get to work in six large cities in Canada in 2016. ① For all six given cities, the percentage of people who commuted by public transit was the highest, while the percentage of people who commuted by cycling was the lowest. ② The percentages of people who commuted by walking were the same in both Toronto and Montréal even though the percentages of people who commuted by public transit in those two cities were different. ③ In Vancouver, the percentage of people who commuted by public transit was over ten times higher than that of people who commuted by cycling. ④ Even though Ottawa ranked fourth in the percentage of people who commuted by public transit, this city was in first place in the percentage of people who commuted by walking or cycling. ⑤ Compared with Calgary, Edmonton recorded lower percentages for all three given types of eco-friendly transportation.

26. Alice Coachman에 관한 다음 글의 내용과 일치하지 <u>않는</u> 것은?

Alice Coachman was born in 1923, in Albany, Georgia, U.S.A. Since she was unable to access athletic training facilities because of the racism of the time, she trained using what was available to her, running barefoot along the dirt roads near her home and using homemade equipment to practice her jumping. Her talent in track and field was noticeable as early as elementary school. Coachman kept practicing hard and gained attention with her achievements in several competitions during her time in high school and college. In the 1948 London Olympics, Coachman competed in the high jump, reaching 5 feet, 6.5 inches, setting both an Olympic and an American record. This accomplishment made her the first black woman to win an Olympic gold medal. She is in nine different Halls of Fame, including the U.S. Olympic Hall of Fame. Coachman died in 2014, at the age of 90 in Georgia after she had dedicated her life to education.

① 집 근처에서 맨발로 달리며 훈련했다.
② 육상 경기에서의 재능을 고등학교 때부터 보였다.
③ 런던 올림픽에서 높이뛰기 올림픽 기록과 미국 기록을 세웠다.
④ 흑인 여성 최초로 올림픽 금메달리스트가 되었다.
⑤ 9개의 명예의 전당에 올랐다.

27. Zero Waste Day 2020에 관한 다음 안내문의 내용과 일치하지 <u>않는</u> 것은?

Zero Waste Day 2020

Zero Waste Day (ZWD) 2020 is an opportunity for you to clean out your attic and donate items for reuse.

When & Where:
First Saturday in November (November 7, 2020),
9:00 a.m. − 12:00 p.m. (rain or shine)
At 400 Union Square

Accepted Items:
- **Wearable clothes / shoes**
  All sizes of clothes and shoes MUST BE DRY.
- **Bedding (pillows, blankets, or mattress covers)**
  Worn or torn is fine, but no oil stains are allowed.
- **Electronics (computers, laptops, or cell phones)**
  All data on the device must be deleted.

Note: If an item isn't accepted, please be prepared to take it home. There is no place for you to drop off garbage.

ZWD is open to ALL!
For more information, please visit www.zwd.org.

---

① 우천 시에도 행사가 예정대로 진행된다.
② 의류와 신발은 건조된 상태의 것만 받는다.
③ 헤지거나 찢어진 침구류도 기부가 가능하다.
④ 전자 기기에 저장된 모든 정보는 삭제되어야 한다.
⑤ 기부 물품 접수가 거절되면 현장에서 버릴 수 있다.

28. Sign Language Class에 관한 다음 안내문의 내용과 일치하는 것은?

Sign Language Class

If you've ever considered studying sign language, our class is one of the best ways to do it! The class is open to people of all ages, but all children must be accompanied by an adult.

Class Schedule
- Where: Coorparoo Community Center
- When: September − October, 2020
  (7:00 p.m. − 9:00 p.m.)

Levels
- Class #1 (Monday and Tuesday)
  − No previous sign language experience is required.
- Class #2 (Wednesday and Thursday)
  − Knowledge of at least 1,000 signs is required.

Note
- Tuition is $100.
- We do not provide refunds unless class is cancelled due to low registration.
- Registration is available only online and before August 31.
  Visit our website at www.CRsignlgs.com.

---

① 어린이들도 어른 동반 없이 참여할 수 있다.
② 수업은 주 3일 진행된다.
③ 수화 경험이 없어도 참여할 수 있는 수업이 있다.
④ 환불은 예외 없이 불가능하다.
⑤ 현장 등록이 가능하다.

영어 영역(독해)

29. 다음 글의 밑줄 친 부분 중, 어법상 틀린 것은? [3점]

One of the keys to insects' successful survival in the open air ① lies in their outer covering — a hard waxy layer that helps prevent their tiny bodies from dehydrating. To take oxygen from the air, they use narrow breathing holes in the body-segments, which take in air ② passively and can be opened and closed as needed. Instead of blood ③ containing in vessels, they have free-flowing hemolymph, which helps keep their bodies rigid, aids movement, and assists the transportation of nutrients and waste materials to the appropriate parts of the body. The nervous system is modular — in a sense, each of the body segments has ④ its own individual and autonomous brain — and some other body systems show a similar modularization. These are just a few of the many ways ⑤ in which insect bodies are structured and function completely differently from our own.

* hemolymph: 혈림프
** modular: 모듈식의(여러 개의 개별 단위로 되어 있는)

30. (A), (B), (C)의 각 네모 안에서 문맥에 맞는 낱말로 가장 적절한 것은?

On projects in the built environment, people consider safety and functionality nonnegotiable. But the aesthetics of a new project — how it is *designed* — is too often considered (A) relevant / irrelevant. The question of how its design *affects* human beings is rarely asked. People think that design makes something highfalutin, called architecture, and that architecture differs from building, just as surely as the Washington National Cathedral differs from the local community church. This (B) connection / distinction between architecture and building — or more generally, between design and utility — couldn't be more wrong. More and more we are learning that the design of all our built environments matters so profoundly that safety and functionality must not be our only urgent priorities. All kinds of design elements influence people's experiences, not only of the environment but also of themselves. They (C) overlook / shape our cognitions, emotions, and actions, and even our well-being. They actually help constitute our very sense of identity.

* highfalutin: 허세를 부리는

	(A)		(B)		(C)
①	relevant	⋯⋯	distinction	⋯⋯	shape
②	relevant	⋯⋯	connection	⋯⋯	overlook
③	irrelevant	⋯⋯	distinction	⋯⋯	overlook
④	irrelevant	⋯⋯	connection	⋯⋯	overlook
⑤	irrelevant	⋯⋯	distinction	⋯⋯	shape

[31~34] 다음 빈칸에 들어갈 말로 가장 적절한 것을 고르시오.

31. Over 4.5 billion years ago, the Earth's primordial atmosphere was probably largely water vapour, carbon dioxide, sulfur dioxide and nitrogen. The appearance and subsequent evolution of exceedingly primitive living organisms (bacteria-like microbes and simple single-celled plants) began to change the atmosphere, liberating oxygen and breaking down carbon dioxide and sulfur dioxide. This made it possible for higher organisms to develop. When the earliest known plant cells with nuclei evolved about 2 billion years ago, the atmosphere seems to have had only about 1 percent of its present content of oxygen. With the emergence of the first land plants, about 500 million years ago, oxygen reached about one-third of its present concentration. It had risen to almost its present level by about 370 million years ago, when animals first spread on to land. Today's atmosphere is thus not just a requirement to sustain life as we know it — it is also _____.

* primordial: 원시의 ** sulfur dioxide: 이산화황

① a barrier to evolution
② a consequence of life
③ a record of primitive culture
④ a sign of the constancy of nature
⑤ a reason for cooperation among species

32. One of the primary ways by which music is able to take on significance in our inner world is by the way it interacts with memory. Memories associated with important emotions tend to be more deeply embedded in our memory than other events. Emotional memories are more likely to be vividly remembered and are more likely to be recalled with the passing of time than neutral memories. Since music can be extremely emotionally evocative, key life events can be emotionally heightened by the presence of music, ensuring that memories of the event become deeply encoded. Retrieval of those memories is then enhanced by contextual effects, in which a recreation of a similar context to that in which the memories were encoded can facilitate their retrieval. Thus, _____ can activate intensely vivid memories of the event.

* evocative: 불러일으키는 ** retrieval: 회복

① analyzing memories of the event thoroughly
② increasing storage space for recalling the event
③ re-hearing the same music associated with the event
④ reconstructing the event in the absence of background music
⑤ enhancing musical competence to deliver emotional messages

[해설편 p.196]

33. We are now _____, instead of the other way around. Perhaps the clearest way to see this is to look at changes in the biomass — the total worldwide weight — of mammals. A long time ago, all of us humans together probably weighed only about two-thirds as much as all the bison in North America, and less than one-eighth as much as all the elephants in Africa. But in the Industrial Era our population exploded and we killed bison and elephants at industrial scale and in terrible numbers. The balance shifted greatly as a result. At present, we humans weigh more than 350 times as much as all bison and elephants put together. We weigh over ten times more than all the earth's wild mammals combined. And if we add in all the mammals we've domesticated — cattle, sheep, pigs, horses, and so on — the comparison becomes truly ridiculous: we and our tamed animals now represent 97 percent of the earth's mammalian biomass. This comparison illustrates a fundamental point: instead of being limited by the environment, we learned to shape it to our own ends. [3점]

* bison: 들소

① imposing ourselves on nature
② limiting our ecological impact
③ yielding our land to mammals
④ encouraging biological diversity
⑤ doing useful work for the environment

34. In the modern world, we look for certainty in uncertain places. We search for order in chaos, the right answer in ambiguity, and conviction in complexity. "We spend far more time and effort on trying to control the world," best-selling writer Yuval Noah Harari says, "than on trying to understand it." We look for the easy-to-follow formula. Over time, we _____.
Our approach reminds me of the classic story of the drunk man searching for his keys under a street lamp at night. He knows he lost his keys somewhere on the dark side of the street but looks for them underneath the lamp, because that's where the light is. Our yearning for certainty leads us to pursue seemingly safe solutions — by looking for our keys under street lamps. Instead of taking the risky walk into the dark, we stay within our current state, however inferior it may be. [3점]

① weigh the pros and cons of our actions
② develop the patience to bear ambiguity
③ enjoy adventure rather than settle down
④ gain insight from solving complex problems
⑤ lose our ability to interact with the unknown

35. 다음 글에서 전체 흐름과 관계 <u>없는</u> 문장은?

As far back as the seventeenth century, hair had a special spiritual significance in Africa. Many African cultures saw the head as the center of control, communication, and identity in the body. ① Hair was regarded as a source of power that personified the individual and could be used for spiritual purposes or even to cast a spell. ② Since it rests on the highest point on the body, hair itself was a means to communicate with divine spirits and it was treated in ways that were thought to bring good luck or protect against evil. ③ People had the opportunity to socialize while styling each other's hair, and the shared tradition of hair was passed down. ④ According to authors Ayana Byrd and Lori Tharps, "communication from the gods and spirits was thought to pass through the hair to get to the soul." ⑤ In Cameroon, for example, medicine men attached hair to containers that held their healing potions in order to protect the potions and enhance their effectiveness.

* potion: (마법의) 물약

[36~37] 주어진 글 다음에 이어질 글의 순서로 가장 적절한 것을 고르시오.

36.

> Mark Granovetter examined the extent to which information about jobs flowed through weak versus strong ties among a group of people.

(A) This means that they might have information that is most relevant to us, but it also means that it is information to which we may already be exposed. In contrast, our weaker relationships are often with people who are more distant both geographically and demographically.

(B) Their information is more novel. Even though we talk to these people less frequently, we have so many weak ties that they end up being a sizable source of information, especially of information to which we don't otherwise have access.

(C) He found that only a sixth of jobs that came via the network were from strong ties, with the rest coming via medium or weak ties; and with more than a quarter coming via weak ties. Strong ties can be more homophilistic. Our closest friends are often those who are most like us.

* demographically: 인구통계학적으로 ** homophilistic: 동족친화적인

① (A) − (C) − (B)　　　② (B) − (A) − (C)
③ (B) − (C) − (A)　　　④ (C) − (A) − (B)
⑤ (C) − (B) − (A)

37.

When we think of culture, we first think of human cultures, of *our* culture. We think of computers, airplanes, fashions, teams, and pop stars. For most of human cultural history, none of those things existed.

(A) Sadly, this remains true as the final tribal peoples get overwhelmed by those who value money above humanity. We are living in their end times and, to varying extents, we're all contributing to those endings. Ultimately our values may even prove self-defeating.

(B) They held extensive knowledge, knew deep secrets of their lands and creatures. And they experienced rich and rewarding lives; we know so because when their ways were threatened, they fought to hold on to them, to the death.

(C) For hundreds of thousands of years, no human culture had a tool with moving parts. Well into the twentieth century, various human foraging cultures retained tools of stone, wood, and bone. We might pity human hunter-gatherers for their stuck simplicity, but we would be making a mistake. [3점]

* forage: 수렵 채집하다

① (A) − (C) − (B)　　　② (B) − (A) − (C)
③ (B) − (C) − (A)　　　④ (C) − (A) − (B)
⑤ (C) − (B) − (A)

[38~39] 글의 흐름으로 보아, 주어진 문장이 들어가기에 가장 적절한 곳을 고르시오.

38.

But the flowing takes time, and if your speed of impact is too great, the water won't be able to flow away fast enough, and so it pushes back at you.

Liquids are destructive. Foams feel soft because they are easily compressed; if you jump on to a foam mattress, you'll feel it give beneath you. (①) Liquids don't do this; instead they flow. (②) You see this in a river, or when you turn on a tap, or if you use a spoon to stir your coffee. (③) When you jump off a diving board and hit a body of water, the water has to flow away from you. (④) It's that force that stings your skin as you belly-flop into a pool, and makes falling into water from a great height like landing on concrete. (⑤) The incompressibility of water is also why waves can have such deadly power, and in the case of tsunamis, why they can destroy buildings and cities, tossing cars around easily.

* compress: 압축하다 ** give: (힘을 받아) 휘다

39.

However, according to Christakis and Fowler, we cannot transmit ideas and behaviours much beyond our friends' friends' friends (in other words, across just three degrees of separation).

In the late twentieth century, researchers sought to measure how fast and how far news, rumours or innovations moved. (①) More recent research has shown that ideas — even emotional states and conditions — can be transmitted through a social network. (②) The evidence of this kind of contagion is clear: 'Students with studious roommates become more studious. Diners sitting next to heavy eaters eat more food.' (③) This is because the transmission and reception of an idea or behaviour requires a stronger connection than the relaying of a letter or the communication that a certain employment opportunity exists. (④) Merely knowing people is not the same as being able to influence them to study more or over-eat. (⑤) Imitation is indeed the sincerest form of flattery, even when it is unconscious. [3점]

* flattery: 아첨

40. 다음 글의 내용을 한 문장으로 요약하고자 한다. 빈칸 (A), (B)에 들어갈 말로 가장 적절한 것은?

In 2011, Micah Edelson and his colleagues conducted an interesting experiment about external factors of memory manipulation. In their experiment, participants were shown a two minute documentary film and then asked a series of questions about the video. Directly after viewing the videos, participants made few errors in their responses and were correctly able to recall the details. Four days later, they could still remember the details and didn't allow their memories to be swayed when they were presented with any false information about the film. This changed, however, when participants were shown fake responses about the film made by other participants. Upon seeing the incorrect answers of others, participants were also drawn toward the wrong answers themselves. Even after they found out that the other answers had been fabricated and didn't have anything to do with the documentary, it was too late. The participants were no longer able to distinguish between truth and fiction. They had already modified their memories to fit the group.

↓

According to the experiment, when participants were given false information itself, their memories remained ____(A)____, but their memories were ____(B)____ when they were exposed to other participants' fake responses.

　　　(A)　　　　　(B)　　　　　　(A)　　　　　(B)
① stable ······ falsified　　② fragile ······ modified
③ stable ······ intensified　　④ fragile ······ solidified
⑤ concrete ······ maintained

[41~42] 다음 글을 읽고, 물음에 답하시오.

Evolutionary biologists believe sociability drove the evolution of our complex brains. Fossil evidence shows that as far back as 130,000 years ago, it was not (a) unusual for *Homo sapiens* to travel more than a hundred and fifty miles to trade, share food and, no doubt, gossip. Unlike the Neanderthals, their social groups extended far beyond their own families. Remembering all those (b) connections, who was related to whom, and where they lived required considerable processing power.

It also required wayfinding savvy. Imagine trying to (c) maintain a social network across tens or hundreds of square miles of Palaeolithic wilderness. You couldn't send a text message to your friends to find out where they were — you had to go out and visit them, remember where you last saw them or imagine where they might have gone. To do this, you needed navigation skills, spatial awareness, a sense of direction, the ability to store maps of the landscape in your mind and the motivation to travel around. Canadian anthropologist Ariane Burke believes that our ancestors (d) developed all these attributes while trying to keep in touch with their neighbours. Eventually, our brains became primed for wayfinding. Meanwhile the Neanderthals, who didn't travel as far, never fostered a spatial skill set; despite being sophisticated hunters, well adapted to the cold and able to see in the dark, they went extinct. In the prehistoric badlands, nothing was more (e) useless than a circle of friends.

* savvy: 요령, 지식 ** Palaeolithic: 구석기 시대의

41. 윗글의 제목으로 가장 적절한 것은?

① Social Networks: An Evolutionary Advantage
② Our Brain Forced Us to Stay Close to Our Family!
③ How We Split from Our Way and Kept Going on My Way
④ Why Do Some People Have Difficulty in Social Relationships?
⑤ Being Connected to Each Other Leads to Communicative Skills

42. 밑줄 친 (a)~(e) 중에서 문맥상 낱말의 쓰임이 적절하지 않은 것은? [3점]

① (a)   ② (b)   ③ (c)   ④ (d)   ⑤ (e)

[43~45] 다음 글을 읽고, 물음에 답하시오.

(A)

"You've been a very good girl this year, Emma. Tonight, Santa will drop by our house to leave you some presents." Martha told (a) her little girl, smiling. "And for you too, Fred," she added. She wanted to give her two children so much more, but this year had been especially hard for Martha. She had worked day and night to buy some Christmas gifts for her children.

(B)

Emma came running up to her mother the next morning. "Mommy, Santa really did come last night!" Martha smiled, thinking of the candies and cookies (b) she must have found in her socks. "Did you like his gifts?" "Yes, they are wonderful. Fred loves his toys, too." Martha was confused. She wondered how the candies and cookies had become toys overnight. Martha ran into Emma's room and saw a small red box that was half open. She knelt down and glanced inside to see its contents.

(C)

That night, after everyone had gone to bed, Emma slowly climbed out of bed. She took out a page from a notebook to write a letter to Santa. She whispered to herself as she wrote. "Dear Santa, will you send a few smiles and laughs for my mother? (c) She doesn't laugh much. And will you send a few toys for Fred as well? Thank you." Emma folded the letter twice and sealed it within an envelope. She left the envelope outside the front door and went back to sleep.

(D)

The box contained some toys, countless little candies and cookies. "Mommy, this is for you from Santa." Emma said holding out a card towards Martha. Puzzled, (d) she opened it. It said, "Dear Emma's mother. A very merry Christmas! Hi, I am Amelia. I found your child's letter blowing across the street last night. I was touched and couldn't help but respond. Please accept the gift as a Christmas greeting." Martha felt tears falling down (e) her cheeks. She slowly wiped them off and hugged her daughter. "Merry Christmas, Emma. Didn't I tell you Santa would come?"

43. 주어진 글 (A)에 이어질 내용을 순서에 맞게 배열한 것으로 가장 적절한 것은?

① (B) − (D) − (C)   ② (C) − (B) − (D)
③ (C) − (D) − (B)   ④ (D) − (B) − (C)
⑤ (D) − (C) − (B)

44. 밑줄 친 (a)~(e) 중에서 가리키는 대상이 나머지 넷과 다른 것은?

① (a)   ② (b)   ③ (c)   ④ (d)   ⑤ (e)

45. 윗글에 관한 내용으로 적절하지 않은 것은?

① 올해는 Martha에게 힘든 한 해였다.
② Fred가 선물받은 장난감을 마음에 들어 했다.
③ Martha가 자신의 방에서 작은 빨간 상자를 보았다.
④ Emma가 산타에게 편지를 썼다.
⑤ Emma가 Martha에게 산타가 보냈다고 말하며 카드를 내밀었다.

* 확인 사항
○ 답안지의 해당란에 필요한 내용을 정확히 기입(표기)했는지 확인하시오.

18

001 principal ⓝ 교장 선생님
002 captain ⓝ 회장
003 win ⓥ (경기에서 이겨 무엇을) 타다, 차지하다
004 award ⓝ 상
005 trophy ⓝ 트로피
006 allow ⓥ 허락하다, 용납하다
007 mess up ~을 엉망으로 만들다
008 ultimately ⓐⓓ 결국, 궁극적으로
009 respectfully ⓐⓓ 공손히, 정중하게
010 grateful ⓐ 감사하는, 고마워하는
011 reconsider ⓥ 재고하다

19

012 break ⓝ 휴식, 방학
013 refrigerator ⓝ 냉장고
014 pack ⓥ (짐 등을) 싸다
015 soar ⓥ 날아오르다, 치솟다
016 balloon ⓝ 풍선
017 beam ⓥ 빛나다, 활짝 웃다
018 groan ⓥ 신음소리를 내다
019 anticipation ⓝ 기대감
020 disappear ⓥ 사라지다
021 in a flash 순식간에
022 miserable ⓐ 끔찍한, 비참한
023 sigh ⓥ 한숨을 쉬다
024 regretful ⓐ 후회하는, 유감스러운
025 irritated ⓐ 짜증 난

20

026 convince ⓥ 설득하다
027 lay out 펼치다
028 argument ⓝ 주장, 논거
029 make a plea 항변하다, 간청하다
030 passionate ⓐ 열정적인
031 as to ~에 관해
032 work ⓥ 효과가 있다, 작용하다
033 metaphorical ⓐ 비유의, 은유의
034 shutter ⓝ 셔터, 덧문
035 open-ended ⓐ 정해진 답이 없는, 주관식의
036 challenge ⓥ 이의를 제기하다
037 assumption ⓝ 가정
038 approve of ~을 인정하다
039 question ⓥ 의문을 제기하다
040 worldview ⓝ 세계관
041 yield ⓥ (결과를) 내다, 산출하다
042 trigger ⓥ 유발하다
043 insight ⓝ 통찰(력)

21

044 curriculum ⓝ 교육과정, 커리큘럼
045 formula ⓝ 공식, 제조법
046 spit out ~을 뱉어내다
047 standardize ⓥ 표준화하다, 규격화하다
048 grand ⓐ 대단한, 웅장한
049 authority figure 권위자
050 theoretical ⓐ 이론적인
051 alternate ⓐ 대안의
052 path ⓝ 경로, 길
053 wander ⓥ 헤매다, 돌아다니다
054 clue ⓝ 단서, 실마리
055 misconception ⓝ 오해

056 arrive ⓥ 도래하다, 찾아오다
057 divine ⓐ 신의, 신성한
058 visitation ⓝ (격식) 방문, 사찰
059 stroke of genius 천재성, 신의 한 수
060 revise ⓥ 수정하다, 변경하다
061 establish ⓥ 확립하다
062 notably ⓐⓓ 특히, 현저히
063 spectacularly ⓐⓓ 구경거리로, 볼 만하게
064 lead ⓝ 납
065 make the cut 목표를 달성하다, 최종 명단에 들다, 성공하다
066 one-dimensional 일차원적인
067 emphasize ⓥ 강조하다

22

068 vast ⓐ 거대한, 막대한
069 performance ⓝ 실적, 성과
070 in terms of ~의 관점에서
071 individual ⓐ 개인의, 개별적인
072 metrics ⓝ 수량적 분석
073 résumé ⓝ 이력서, 경력
074 accolade ⓝ 수상, 표창
075 approach ⓝ 접근(법)
076 confirm ⓥ (맞다고) 확인하다
077 survival of the fittest 적자생존
078 impressive ⓐ 인상적인
079 formula ⓝ 공식
080 inaccurate ⓐ 부정확한
081 potential ⓝ 가능성, 잠재력
082 driven ⓐ 투지가 넘치는, 주도적인
083 ecosystem ⓝ 생태계

23

084 bring up ~을 기르다[양육하다]
085 get lost 길을 잃다, 헤매다
086 sooner or later 머지않아
087 end up 결국 ~이다
088 compass ⓝ 나침반
089 virtually ⓐⓓ 거의, 사실상
090 slightly ⓐⓓ 약간
091 hike ⓥ 하이킹하다, 걷다
092 backpack ⓝ 배낭
093 inevitably ⓐⓓ 불가피하게
094 off balance 균형을 잃고
095 dominant ⓐ 우성의, 지배적인
096 factor into ~을 요인으로 포함하다
097 right-handed 오른손잡이의
098 obstacle ⓝ 장애물
099 subconsciously ⓐⓓ 무의식적으로
100 dominance ⓝ (유전적) 우성, 우세함, 지배

24

101 interaction ⓝ 상호 작용
102 immediate ⓐ 가까운, 당면한, 즉각적인
103 formulate ⓥ 만들어내다, 표현하다
104 aid ⓝ 도움, 원조
105 mutual ⓐ 상호의
106 property ⓝ 재산, 소유물
107 contract ⓝ 계약서
108 exchange ⓝ 교환, 주고받음
109 description ⓝ 설명, 묘사
110 precise ⓐ 정확한, 정교한

111 unambiguous ⓐ 모호하지 않은
112 misunderstanding ⓝ 오해, 착오
113 arise ⓥ 발생하다
114 counterparty ⓝ 한쪽 당사자
115 uncertainty ⓝ 불확실성
116 a measure of 어느 정도의, 꽤 많은 양의
117 distrust ⓝ 불신
118 facilitate ⓥ 용이하게 하다
119 clarification ⓝ 해명, 설명
120 settlement ⓝ 해결, 합의
121 dispute ⓝ 논쟁
122 translation ⓝ 통역
123 interchange ⓝ (특히 생각·정보의) 교환
124 earn ⓥ 얻다, 받다
125 transaction ⓝ 거래, 매매

25

126 commuter ⓝ 통근자
127 eco-friendly 친환경적인
128 transportation ⓝ 교통수단
129 given ⓐ 주어진
130 public transit 대중교통
131 record ⓥ 기록하다

26

132 access ⓥ 접근하다, 이용하다
133 athletic ⓐ 운동의, 육상의
134 racism ⓝ 인종 차별주의
135 of the time 그 당시의, 당대의
136 barefoot ⓐⓓ 맨발로
137 dirt road 비포장도로, 흙길
138 homemade ⓐ 집에서 만든
139 equipment ⓝ 장비
140 track and field 육상 경기
141 noticeable ⓐ 눈에 띄는, 두드러지는
142 competition ⓝ 대회
143 compete ⓥ 겨루다, (시합 등에) 참가하다
144 accomplishment ⓝ 성취
145 dedicate A to B A를 B에 바치다

27

146 clean out ~을 깨끗이 치우다
147 attic ⓝ 다락방
148 donate ⓥ 기부하다
149 reuse ⓝ 재사용
150 rain or shine 날씨에 상관없이
151 wearable ⓐ 착용할 수 있는
152 pillow ⓝ 베개
153 blanket ⓝ 담요
154 wear(-wore-worn) ⓥ 닳다, 마모되다
155 stain ⓝ 얼룩, 오점
156 electronics ⓝ 전자 기기
157 device ⓝ 기기, 장치
158 delete ⓥ 삭제하다
159 drop off ~을 버리다
160 garbage ⓝ 쓰레기

28

161 sign language 수화, 수어
162 accompany ⓥ 동반하다
163 previous ⓐ 이전의
164 require ⓥ 요구하다, 필요로 하다

165 tuition ⓝ 수업료
166 refund ⓝ 환불
167 cancel ⓥ 취소하다
168 registration ⓝ 등록

29

169 open air 야외, 옥외
170 outer ⓐ 외부의, 바깥 표면의
171 covering ⓝ 외피, 피복
172 waxy ⓐ 왁스[밀랍] 같은
173 layer ⓝ 층, 막
174 tiny ⓐ 아주 작은
175 dehydrate ⓥ 탈수 상태가 되다, 건조시키다
176 narrow ⓐ 좁은
177 segment ⓝ (동물의) 몸의 마디
178 take in (몸속으로) ~을 섭취[흡수]하다
179 passively ⓐⓓ 수동적으로
180 as needed 필요에 따라
181 vessel ⓝ 혈관
182 free-flowing ⓐ 자유롭게 흐르는
183 rigid ⓐ 단단한, 엄격한
184 assist ⓥ 돕다, 도움이 되다
185 nutrient ⓝ 영양분
186 waste material 쓰레기, 폐기물
187 appropriate ⓐ 적절한
188 nervous ⓐ 신경의
189 in a sense 어떤 의미에서
190 autonomous ⓐ 자율적인

30

191 project ⓝ 설계, 계획
192 built ⓐ 구조의, 조립된
193 environment ⓝ 환경
194 functionality ⓝ 기능성
195 nonnegotiable ⓐ 협상의 여지가 없는
196 aesthetics ⓝ 미학
197 irrelevant ⓐ 무관한
198 rarely ⓐⓓ 드물게, 좀처럼 ~하지 않는
199 highfalutin ⓐ 허세를 부리는
200 architecture ⓝ 건축
201 differ from ~와 다르다
202 surely ⓐⓓ 분명히, 확실히
203 cathedral ⓝ 대성당
204 distinction ⓝ 구분
205 utility ⓝ 실용성
206 matter ⓥ 중요하다, 의미가 있다
207 profoundly ⓐⓓ 완전히, 깊이
208 urgent ⓐ 긴박한, 시급한
209 priority ⓝ 우선 사항
210 element ⓝ 요소, 성분
211 overlook ⓥ 간과하다
212 cognition ⓝ 인지, 인식
213 emotion ⓝ 감정
214 well-being (건강과) 행복, 웰빙
215 constitute ⓥ 구성하다
216 identity ⓝ 정체성

31

217 billion ⓝ 10억
218 primordial ⓐ 원시의, 태고의
219 atmosphere ⓝ 대기(권)
220 largely ⓐⓓ 대부분, 거의

221 □ vapour ⓝ 증기
222 □ carbon dioxide 이산화탄소
223 □ nitrogen ⓝ 질소
224 □ appearance ⓝ 출현, 등장
225 □ subsequent ⓐ 연이은, 그다음의
226 □ exceedingly ad 극히, 대단히
227 □ primitive ⓐ 원시적인
228 □ organism ⓝ 유기체
229 □ bacteria ⓝ 박테리아
230 □ microbe ⓝ 미생물
231 □ liberate ⓥ (화학) 유리시키다
232 □ break down ~을 분해하다
233 □ nucleus ⓝ (원자)핵, 세포핵 (*pl.* nuclei)
234 □ emergence ⓝ 출현
235 □ concentration ⓝ 농도
236 □ requirement ⓝ 필요조건
237 □ sustain ⓥ 유지하다, 지탱하다
238 □ consequence ⓝ 결과
239 □ constancy ⓝ 불변성
240 □ cooperation ⓝ 협력, 합동

32

241 □ primary ⓐ 주요한
242 □ take on (특징 등을) 띠다, (일을) 맡다
243 □ significance ⓝ 중요성
244 □ inner ⓐ 내면의
245 □ associated ⓐ 관련된
246 □ be embedded in ~에 박혀있다
247 □ vividly ad 생생하게
248 □ with the passing of time 시간이 지남에 따라
249 □ neutral ⓐ 중립적인
250 □ extremely ad 극도로
251 □ evocative ⓐ ~을 환기시키는
252 □ heighten ⓥ 고조시키다
253 □ presence ⓝ 존재
254 □ retrieval ⓝ 회복, 회수
255 □ enhance ⓥ 강화하다
256 □ contextual ⓐ 맥락과 관련된, 맥락의
257 □ recreation ⓝ 재창조
258 □ activate ⓥ 활성화하다
259 □ intensely ad 강렬하게, 매우
260 □ thoroughly ad 면밀하게, 철저하게
261 □ storage ⓝ 저장, 보관
262 □ reconstruct ⓥ 재구성하다
263 □ in the absence of ~이 없을 때, ~의 부재 시에
264 □ competence ⓝ 능력, 능숙함

33

265 □ the other way around 반대로, 거꾸로
266 □ biomass ⓝ (특정 지역 내의) 생물량
267 □ mammal ⓝ 포유류
268 □ weigh ⓥ 무게가 나가다
269 □ Industrial Era 산업시대
270 □ explode ⓥ 폭발하다, 폭발적으로 증가하다
271 □ at industrial scale 대규모로
272 □ shift ⓥ 변화하다, 바뀌다
273 □ add in ~을 포함하다
274 □ domesticate ⓥ 가축화하다, 길들이다
275 □ cattle ⓝ (집합적으로) 소
276 □ comparison ⓝ 비교
277 □ ridiculous ⓐ 터무니없는, 우스꽝스러운
278 □ tame ⓥ 길들이다
279 □ represent ⓥ 나타내다
280 □ mammalian ⓐ 포유류의
281 □ illustrate ⓥ 보여주다
282 □ fundamental ⓐ 기본적인
283 □ to one's end ~의 목적을 위해서
284 □ impose ⓥ 강요하다, (의무나 책임을) 부과하다
285 □ ecological ⓐ 생태학의
286 □ yield ⓥ (~에게) 양도하다
287 □ diversity ⓝ 다양성

34

288 □ certainty ⓝ 확실성
289 □ uncertain ⓐ 불확실한
290 □ chaos ⓝ 혼란
291 □ ambiguity ⓝ 애매모호함
292 □ conviction ⓝ 확신
293 □ complexity ⓝ 복잡성
294 □ easy-to-follow ⓐ 따르기 쉬운
295 □ classic ⓐ 전형적인, 고전의
296 □ drunk ⓐ 술에 취한
297 □ street lamp 가로등
298 □ underneath prep ~ 밑에서
299 □ yearning ⓝ 갈망, 열망
300 □ pursue ⓥ 추구하다
301 □ seemingly ad 겉으로 보기에
302 □ risky ⓐ 위험한
303 □ inferior ⓐ 열등한
304 □ pros and cons 장단점
305 □ bear ⓥ 참다, (아이를) 낳다

35

306 □ spiritual ⓐ 영적인
307 □ personify ⓥ 인격화하다
308 □ cast a spell 주문을 걸다
309 □ rest ⓥ 놓여 있다
310 □ means ⓝ 수단
311 □ socialize ⓥ (사람을) 사귀다, 어울리다
312 □ pass down 전해주다
313 □ effectiveness ⓝ 효과성

36

314 □ examine ⓥ 조사하다
315 □ versus prep ~ 대(對), ~에 비해
316 □ tie ⓝ 유대관계
317 □ relevant ⓐ 관련 있는
318 □ expose ⓥ 노출시키다
319 □ geographically ad 지리적으로
320 □ novel ⓐ 새로운, 참신한
321 □ frequently ad 자주
322 □ sizable ⓐ (크기 등이) 상당한
323 □ have access to ~을 이용하다, ~에 접근하다
324 □ via prep ~을 통해
325 □ medium ⓝ 중간, 보통

37

326 □ tribal ⓐ 부족의
327 □ people ⓝ (단수 명사) 민족
328 □ overwhelm ⓥ 압도하다, 제압하다
329 □ value ⓥ 가치 있게 여기다
330 □ humanity ⓝ 인간성
331 □ varying ⓐ 다양한, 바뀌는
332 □ contribute to ~에 기여하다, ~의 원인이 되다
333 □ self-defeating ⓐ 스스로를 파괴하는, 자멸적인
334 □ extensive ⓐ 광범위한
335 □ rewarding ⓐ 가치 있는, 보람 있는
336 □ hold on to ~을 고수하다
337 □ retain ⓥ 보유하다
338 □ pity ⓥ 동정하다
339 □ hunter-gatherer 수렵채집인
340 □ stuck ⓐ 꽉 막힌
341 □ simplicity ⓝ 단순함

38

342 □ impact ⓝ 충격, 충돌
343 □ flow away 흘러가다
344 □ push back 밀어내다
345 □ liquid ⓝ 액체
346 □ destructive ⓐ 파괴적인
347 □ foam ⓝ (매트리스에 주로 쓰이는) 발포 고무
348 □ beneath prep ~ 밑에서
349 □ stir ⓥ 젓다, 섞다
350 □ a body of (양이) 많은
351 □ sting ⓥ 쓰리게 하다, 쏘다, 찌르다
352 □ belly-flop 배로 수면을 치며 뛰어들다
353 □ height ⓝ 높이
354 □ land on ~에 착륙하다
355 □ incompressibility ⓝ 비압축성
356 □ deadly ⓐ 치명적인
357 □ in the case of ~의 경우에
358 □ tsunami ⓝ (일본어에서) 쓰나미, 해일
359 □ destroy ⓥ 파괴하다, 부수다
360 □ toss ⓥ 던지다

39

361 □ transmit ⓥ 전파하다
362 □ beyond prep ~을 넘어서
363 □ separation ⓝ 떨어짐, 분리
364 □ innovation ⓝ 혁신
365 □ contagion ⓝ 전염
366 □ studious ⓐ 학구적인
367 □ diner ⓝ 식사하는 사람 (dine ⓥ 식사하다)
368 □ heavy eater 과식하는 사람
369 □ transmission ⓝ 전파, 전염
370 □ reception ⓝ 받아들임, 수용
371 □ relaying ⓝ (정보나 뉴스 등의) 전달
372 □ merely ad 단지, 그저
373 □ over-eat 과식하다
374 □ imitation ⓝ 모방
375 □ sincere ⓐ 순수한
376 □ unconscious ⓐ 무의식적인

40

377 □ colleague ⓝ 동료
378 □ conduct ⓥ 수행하다
379 □ experiment ⓝ 실험
380 □ external ⓐ 외부의
381 □ factor ⓝ 요소, 요인
382 □ manipulation ⓝ 조작
383 □ a series of 일련의
384 □ sway ⓥ 흔들다, 동요시키다
385 □ false ⓐ 잘못된
386 □ present A with B A에게 B를 제시하다
387 □ fake ⓐ 거짓의
388 □ draw ⓥ 끌다, 끌어당기다
389 □ fabricate ⓥ (거짓 정보를) 날조하다, 조작하다
390 □ distinguish between A and B A와 B를 구별하다
391 □ modify ⓥ 수정하다
392 □ fit ⓥ 꼭 맞추다
393 □ intensify ⓥ 강화하다
394 □ solidify ⓥ 공고히 하다

41~42

395 □ evolutionary ⓐ 진화의, 진화론적인
396 □ biologist ⓝ 생물학자
397 □ sociability ⓝ 사교성, 사회성
398 □ fossil ⓝ 화석
399 □ gossip ⓥ 잡담하다
400 □ extend ⓥ 뻗다, 확장하다
401 □ considerable ⓐ 상당한
402 □ wayfinding ⓝ 길 찾기
403 □ square ⓐ 제곱의
404 □ wilderness ⓝ 황무지
405 □ navigation ⓝ 길 찾기
406 □ spatial ⓐ 공간의
407 □ awareness ⓝ 인지, 인식
408 □ landscape ⓝ 풍경
409 □ motivation ⓝ 동기
410 □ anthropologist ⓝ 인류학자
411 □ ancestor ⓝ 조상
412 □ attribute ⓝ 특성
413 □ keep in touch with ~와 연락하다
414 □ primed for ~의 준비가 된
415 □ foster ⓥ 기르다, 발전시키다
416 □ sophisticated ⓐ 수준 높은, 정교한
417 □ extinct ⓐ 멸종된
418 □ prehistoric ⓐ 선사 시대의
419 □ badland ⓝ 악지, 불모지

43~45

420 □ drop by ~에 들르다
421 □ day and night 밤낮으로
422 □ run up to ~에 뛰어오다
423 □ overnight ad 하룻밤 사이에
424 □ kneel down 꿇어 앉다
425 □ glance ⓥ 흘긋 보다
426 □ whisper ⓥ 속삭이다
427 □ as well ~도, 또한
428 □ fold ⓥ 접다
429 □ seal ⓥ 봉인하다
430 □ envelope ⓝ 봉투
431 □ contain ⓥ 담다, 포함하다
432 □ countless ⓐ 무수히 많은
433 □ towards ad (어떤 방향을) 향하여
434 □ puzzled ⓐ 당황한
435 □ respond ⓥ 응답하다
436 □ greeting ⓝ 인사
437 □ cheek ⓝ 볼, 뺨
438 □ wipe off ~을 닦다

● 채점 : 맞은 개수 _____ / 80

TEST A-B 각 단어의 뜻을 [A] 영어는 우리말로, [B] 우리말은 영어로 쓰시오.

A	English	Korean
01	irritated	
02	facilitate	
03	formula	
04	inferior	
05	formulate	
06	spiritual	
07	sway	
08	represent	
09	competence	
10	extensive	
11	uncertainty	
12	assumption	
13	modify	
14	constitute	
15	extinct	
16	relevant	
17	emergence	
18	aesthetics	
19	uncertain	
20	as needed	

B	Korean	English
01	인상적인	
02	확립하다	
03	해명, 설명	
04	보유하다	
05	치명적인	
06	적절한	
07	상당한	
08	압도하다, 제압하다	
09	불변성	
10	기능성	
11	특성	
12	이전의	
13	설득하다	
14	재고하다	
15	운동의, 육상의	
16	성취	
17	극도로	
18	파괴적인	
19	면밀하게, 철저하게	
20	대안의	

▶ A-D 정답 : 해설편 203쪽

TEST C-D 각 단어의 뜻을 골라 기호를 쓰시오.

C	English		Korean
01	lay out	( )	ⓐ 약간
02	covering	( )	ⓑ 확실성
03	certainty	( )	ⓒ 동반하다
04	intensify	( )	ⓓ 펼치다
05	a body of	( )	ⓔ 자주
06	unambiguous	( )	ⓕ 흘긋 보다
07	respectfully	( )	ⓖ 유지하다, 지탱하다
08	merely	( )	ⓗ 인격화하다
09	unconscious	( )	ⓘ 확신
10	conviction	( )	ⓙ 사교성, 사회성
11	inaccurate	( )	ⓚ 부정확한
12	sustain	( )	ⓛ 무의식적인
13	exceedingly	( )	ⓜ 외피, 피복
14	sociability	( )	ⓝ 모호하지 않은
15	personify	( )	ⓞ (양이) 많은
16	frequently	( )	ⓟ 단지, 그저
17	slightly	( )	ⓠ 극히, 대단히
18	countless	( )	ⓡ 공손히, 정중하게
19	glance	( )	ⓢ 강화하다
20	accompany	( )	ⓣ 무수히 많은

D	Korean		English
01	눈에 띄는, 두드러지는	( )	ⓐ varying
02	중립적인	( )	ⓑ trigger
03	기대감	( )	ⓒ ridiculous
04	오해	( )	ⓓ subconsciously
05	~을 인정하다	( )	ⓔ sophisticated
06	완전히, 깊이	( )	ⓕ significance
07	중요성	( )	ⓖ misconception
08	수준 높은, 정교한	( )	ⓗ requirement
09	조사하다	( )	ⓘ profoundly
10	특히, 현저히	( )	ⓙ noticeable
11	조작	( )	ⓚ insight
12	터무니없는	( )	ⓛ neutral
13	무의식적으로	( )	ⓜ transportation
14	(맞다고) 확인하다	( )	ⓝ manipulation
15	필요조건	( )	ⓞ land on
16	교통수단	( )	ⓟ approve of
17	~에 착륙하다	( )	ⓠ examine
18	유발하다	( )	ⓡ confirm
19	통찰력	( )	ⓢ notably
20	다양한, 바뀌는	( )	ⓣ anticipation

18. 다음 글의 목적으로 가장 적절한 것은?

Dear Mr. Coleman,

I'm Aaron Brown, the director of TAC company. To celebrate our company's 10th anniversary and to boost further growth, we have arranged a small event. It will be an informative afternoon with enlightening discussions on business trends. I recently attended your lecture about recent issues in business and it was really impressive. I am writing this letter to request that you be our guest speaker for the afternoon. Your experience and knowledge will benefit our businesses in many ways. It would be a pleasure to have you with us. The planned schedule includes a guest speaker's speech and a question and answer session on Thursday, the 21st of November, 2019 at 3:00 p.m. We would sincerely appreciate it if you could make some time for us. We will be looking forward to hearing from you soon.

Yours Sincerely,
Aaron Brown

① 회사 행사에 초청 연사로 와 줄 것을 요청하려고
② 회사의 행사 일정이 변경된 이유를 설명하려고
③ 체계적인 시간 관리 방법을 제안하려고
④ 기업의 효율적 경영에 대한 조언을 부탁하려고
⑤ 의사 결정 과정에서 토의의 중요성을 강조하려고

19. 다음 글에 드러난 'I'의 심경 변화로 가장 적절한 것은?

One night, my family was having a party with a couple from another city who had two daughters. The girls were just a few years older than I, and I played lots of fun games together with them. The father of the family had an amusing, jolly, witty character, and I had a memorable night full of laughter and joy. While we laughed, joked, and had our dinner, the TV suddenly broadcast an air attack, and a screeching siren started to scream, announcing the "red" situation. We all stopped dinner, and we squeezed into the basement. The siren kept screaming and the roar of planes was heard in the sky. The terror of war was overwhelming. Shivering with fear, I murmured a panicked prayer that this desperate situation would end quickly.

① indifferent → satisfied
② relaxed → envious
③ frustrated → relieved
④ excited → bored
⑤ pleased → terrified

20. 다음 글에서 필자가 주장하는 바로 가장 적절한 것은?

Over the years, memory has been given a bad name. It has been associated with rote learning and cramming information into your brain. Educators have said that understanding is the key to learning, but how can you understand something if you can't remember it? We have all had this experience: we recognize and understand information but can't recall it when we need it. For example, how many jokes do you know? You've probably heard thousands, but you can only recall about four or five right now. There is a big difference between remembering your four jokes and recognizing or understanding thousands. Understanding doesn't create use: only when you can instantly recall what you understand, and practice using your remembered understanding, do you achieve mastery. Memory means storing what you have learned; otherwise, why would we bother learning in the first place?

① 창의력 신장을 학습 활동의 목표로 삼아야 한다.
② 배운 것을 활용하기 위해서는 내용을 기억해야 한다.
③ 기억력 저하를 예방하기 위해 자신의 일상을 기록해야 한다.
④ 자연스러운 분위기를 만들 수 있는 농담을 알고 있어야 한다.
⑤ 학습 의욕을 유지하기 위해서는 실천 가능한 계획을 세워야 한다.

21. 밑줄 친 the democratization of business financing이 다음 글에서 의미하는 바로 가장 적절한 것은?

Crowdfunding is a new and more collaborative way to secure funding for projects. It can be used in different ways such as requesting donations for a worthy cause anywhere in the world and generating funding for a project with the contributors then becoming partners in the project. In essence, crowdfunding is the fusion of social networking and venture capitalism. In just the same way as social networks have rewritten the conventional rules about how people communicate and interact with each other, crowdfunding in all its variations has the potential to rewrite the rules on how businesses and other projects get funded in the future. Crowdfunding can be viewed as the democratization of business financing. Instead of restricting capital sourcing and allocation to a relatively small and fixed minority, crowdfunding empowers everyone connected to the Internet to access both the collective wisdom and the pocket money of everyone else who connects to the Internet.

① More people can be involved in funding a business.
② More people will participate in developing new products.
③ Crowdfunding can reinforce the conventional way of financing.
④ Crowdfunding keeps social networking from facilitating funding.
⑤ The Internet helps employees of a company interact with each other.

22. 다음 글의 요지로 가장 적절한 것은?

You meet many different kinds of people in your life. Sometimes you run into those who are full of energy, and you wonder if they are from the same planet as you. After a closer look, you realize that they too face challenges and problems. They are under the same amount of pressure and stress as you. One word makes a world of difference: attitude! Attitude is your psychological disposition, a proactive way to approach life. It is a personal predetermination not to let anything or anyone take control of your life or manipulate your mood. Attitude allows you to anticipate, excuse, forgive and forget, without being naive or stupid. It is a personal decision to stay in control and not to lose your temper. Attitude provides safe conduct through all kinds of storms. It helps you to get up every morning happy and determined to get the most out of a brand new day. Whatever happens — good or bad — the proper attitude makes the difference. It may not always be easy to have a positive attitude; nevertheless, you need to remember you can face a kind or cruel world based on your perception and your actions.

* safe conduct: 안전 통행권

① 근거 없는 낙관주의는 문제 해결을 어렵게 한다.
② 차이에 대한 관용은 조화로운 공동체 생활에 필요하다.
③ 인식과 행동의 일관성은 정신적 스트레스를 감소시킨다.
④ 적극적인 의사 표현이 효율적 의사소통에 도움이 된다.
⑤ 긍정적인 태도를 갖는 것이 삶의 변화를 가져온다.

23. 다음 글의 주제로 가장 적절한 것은?

Our world today is comparatively harmless. We don't have to be careful every moment that a tiger is behind us. We do not have to worry about starving. Our dangers today are, for example, high blood pressure or diabetes. To be clear, we have a Stone Age brain that lives in a modern world. Because of this, many situations are considered a threat by our brains, although they are harmless to our survival. In the past, danger meant we either had to flee or fight. If we have an appointment but are stuck in a traffic jam, that does not really threaten our lives. However, our brain considers this a danger. That is the point. There is no danger, but our brain rates it as such. If we have an unpleasant conversation with our partner, it does not threaten our lives, and we do not have to flee or fight. The danger is an illusion. Our Stone Age brain sees a mortal danger that is not there.

① the role of instinct in deciding to flee or fight
② benefits of danger perception for humans' survival
③ our perception of harmless situations as threatening
④ the human brain's evolution for telling friend from foe
⑤ primitive people's ways of quickly dealing with dangers

24. 다음 글의 제목으로 가장 적절한 것은?

There has been a general belief that sport is a way of reducing violence. Anthropologist Richard Sipes tests this notion in a classic study of the relationship between sport and violence. Focusing on what he calls "combative sports," those sports including actual body contact between opponents or simulated warfare, he hypothesizes that if sport is an alternative to violence, then one would expect to find an inverse correlation between the popularity of combative sports and the frequency and intensity of warfare. In other words, the more combative sports (e.g., football, boxing) the less likely warfare. Using the Human Relations Area Files and a sample of 20 societies, Sipes tests the hypothesis and discovers a significant relationship between combative sports and violence, but a direct one, not the inverse correlation of his hypothesis. According to Sipes' analysis, the more pervasive and popular combative sports are in a society, the more likely that society is to engage in war. So, Sipes draws the obvious conclusion that combative sports are not alternatives to war but rather are reflections of the same aggressive impulses in human society.

① Is There a Distinction among Combative Sports?
② Combative Sports Mirror Human Aggressiveness
③ Never Let Your Aggressive Impulses Consume You!
④ International Conflicts: Creating New Military Alliances
⑤ Combative Sports Are More Common among the Oppressed

25. 다음 표의 내용과 일치하지 <u>않는</u> 것은?

Jobs in Renewable Energy Technology in 2014 and 2015

Year of 2014		Year of 2015	
Renewable Energy Technology	Jobs (thousands)	Renewable Energy Technology	Jobs (thousands)
Solar Photovoltaic	2,495	Solar Photovoltaic	2,772
Liquid Biofuels	1,788	Liquid Biofuels	1,678
Wind Power	1,027	Wind Power	1,081
Biomass	822	Solar Heating/Cooling	939
Solar Heating/Cooling	764	Biomass	822
Biogas	381	Biogas	382
Small Hydropower	209	Small Hydropower	204
Geothermal Energy	154	Geothermal Energy	160
Total	**7,600**	**Total**	**8,000**

• Note: Figures may not add to total shown because of rounding.

The tables above show the number of jobs in renewable energy technology around the world in 2014 and 2015. ① The total number of jobs was larger in 2015 than in 2014. ② In both years, solar photovoltaic had the largest number of jobs, and the number of jobs increased in 2015. ③ The rank of liquid biofuels remained the same in both years though the number of jobs decreased in 2015. ④ Solar heating/cooling ranked higher in 2015 than in 2014, but still had fewer than 900 thousand jobs. ⑤ Among the lowest three ranks in 2014, only small hydropower showed a decrease in the number of jobs in 2015.

26. Lotte Laserstein에 관한 다음 글의 내용과 일치하지 <u>않는</u> 것은?

Lotte Laserstein was born into a Jewish family in East Prussia. One of her relatives ran a private painting school, which allowed Lotte to learn painting and drawing at a young age. Later, she earned admission to the Berlin Academy of Arts and completed her master studies as one of the first women in the school. In 1928 her career skyrocketed as she gained widespread recognition, but after the seizure of power by the Nazi Party, she was forbidden to exhibit her artwork in Germany. In 1937 she emigrated to Sweden. She continued to work in Sweden but never recaptured the fame she had enjoyed before. In her work, Lotte repeatedly portrayed Gertrud Rose, her closest friend. To Lotte, she embodied the type of the "New Woman" and was so represented.

① 어린 나이에 회화와 소묘를 배웠다.
② Berlin Academy of Arts에 입학 허가를 받았다.
③ 나치당의 권력 장악 이후 독일에서 작품 전시를 금지 당했다.
④ 이전에 누렸던 명성을 스웨덴에서 되찾았다.
⑤ 가장 가까운 친구인 Gertrud Rose를 그렸다.

27. Springfield Photo Contest에 관한 다음 안내문의 내용과 일치하지 <u>않는</u> 것은?

Springfield Photo Contest

Show off your pictures taken in this beautiful town. All the winning entries will be included in the official Springfield tour guide book!

Prizes
• 1st Place: $500
• 2nd Place: $250
• 3rd Place: $150

Contest Rules
• Limit of 5 photos per entrant
• Photos must be taken in Springfield.
• Photos must be submitted digitally as JPEG files.
• Photos should be in color (black-and-white photos are not accepted).

The submission must be completed on our website (www.visitspringfield.org) by December 27, 2019.

Please email us at info@visitspringfield.org for further information.

① 모든 수상작은 공식 여행 안내 책자에 수록될 것이다.
② 1등 상금은 2등 상금의 두 배이다.
③ Springfield에서 촬영한 사진이어야 한다.
④ 컬러 사진 및 흑백 사진이 허용된다.
⑤ 12월 27일까지 웹 사이트로 제출이 완료되어야 한다.

28. 2019 Upcycling Festival에 관한 다음 안내문의 내용과 일치하는 것은?

2019 Upcycling Festival

The Riverside Art Center is proud to announce the 2019 Upcycling Festival, a festival for the whole family to create, see and learn about the art of upcycling. There is no admission fee and booking is not needed.

Date & Time
Saturday, November 23, 2:00 pm − 5:00 pm

Location
The Riverside Art Center

Programs
• Hands-on activities for children: making art pieces utilizing used or waste materials at the center's garden
• Exhibition: famous upcycled artwork in the lobby
• Movie: documentaries on environmental topics in the meeting room

Parking
• The parking lot is open from 1:00 pm to 6:00 pm.
• The parking fee is $5.

For more information, please call 123-456-0987.

① 입장료가 있고 예약이 필요하다.
② 토요일 오전부터 시작된다.
③ 어린이를 위한 체험 활동이 있다.
④ 예술 작품이 회의실에 전시된다.
⑤ 주차 요금은 무료이다.

29. 다음 글의 밑줄 친 부분 중, 어법상 <u>틀린</u> 것은? [3점]

There is a reason why so many of us are attracted to recorded music these days, especially considering personal music players are common and people are listening to music through headphones a lot. Recording engineers and musicians have learned to create special effects that tickle our brains by exploiting neural circuits that evolved ① <u>to discern</u> important features of our auditory environment. These special effects are similar in principle to 3-D art, motion pictures, or visual illusions, none of ② <u>which</u> have been around long enough for our brains to have evolved special mechanisms to perceive them. Rather, 3-D art, motion pictures, and visual illusions leverage perceptual systems that ③ <u>are</u> in place to accomplish other things. Because they use these neural circuits in novel ways, we find them especially ④ <u>interested</u>. The same is true of the way ⑤ <u>that</u> modern recordings are made.

* auditory: 청각의 ** leverage: 이용하다

30. (A), (B), (C)의 각 네모 안에서 문맥에 맞는 낱말로 가장 적절한 것은? [3점]

A story is only as believable as the storyteller. For story to be effective, trust must be established. Yes, trust. Whenever someone stops to listen to you, an element of unspoken trust (A) exists / vanishes . Your listener unconsciously trusts you to say something worthwhile to him, something that will not waste his time. The few minutes of attention he is giving you is (B) deceptive / sacrificial . He could choose to spend his time elsewhere, yet he has stopped to respect your part in a conversation. This is where story comes in. Because a story illustrates points clearly and often bridges topics easily, trust can be established *quickly*, and recognizing this time element to story is essential to trust. (C) Respecting / Wasting your listener's time is the capital letter at the beginning of your sentence — it leads the conversation into a sentence worth listening to *if* trust is earned and not taken for granted.

	(A)		(B)		(C)
①	exists	......	deceptive	......	Respecting
②	exists	......	sacrificial	......	Respecting
③	exists	......	sacrificial	......	Wasting
④	vanishes	......	sacrificial	......	Respecting
⑤	vanishes	......	deceptive	......	Wasting

[31 ~ 34] 다음 빈칸에 들어갈 말로 가장 적절한 것을 고르시오.

31. Once we own something, we're far more likely to _____ it. In a study conducted at Duke University, students who won basketball tickets in an extremely onerous lottery (one that they had to wait in line to enter for more than a day) said they wouldn't sell their tickets for less than, on average, $2,400. But students who had waited and hadn't won said they would only pay, on average, $170 per ticket. Once a student owned the tickets, he or she saw them as being worth much more in the market than they were. In another example, during the housing market crash of 2008, a real estate website conducted a survey to see how homeowners felt the crash affected the price of their homes. 92% of respondents, aware of nearby foreclosures, asserted these had hurt the price of homes in their neighborhood. However, when asked about the price of their *own* home, 62% believed it had increased.

* onerous: 성가신 ** foreclosure: 압류

① overvalue   ② exchange   ③ disregard
④ conceal   ⑤ share

32. Are the different types of mobile device, smartphones and tablets, substitutes or complements? Let's explore this question by considering the case of Madeleine and Alexandra, two users of these devices. Madeleine uses her tablet to take notes in class. These notes are synced to her smartphone wirelessly, via a cloud computing service, allowing Madeleine to review her notes on her phone during the bus trip home. Alexandra uses both her phone and tablet to surf the Internet, write emails and check social media. Both of these devices allow Alexandra to access online services when she is away from her desktop computer. For Madeleine, smartphones and tablets are *complements*. She gets greater functionality out of her two devices when they are used together. For Alexandra, they are *substitutes*. Both smartphones and tablets fulfil more or less the same function in Alexandra's life. This case illustrates the role that an _____ plays in determining the nature of the relationship between two goods or services.

① interaction with other people
② individual consumer's behavior
③ obvious change in social status
④ innovative technological advancement
⑤ objective assessment of current conditions

33. Thomas Edison was indeed a creative genius, but it was not until he discovered some of the principles of marketing that he found increased success. One of his first inventions was, although much needed, a failure. In 1869, he created and patented an electronic vote recorder, which recorded and totalled the votes in the Massachusetts state legislature faster than the chamber's old manual system. To Edison's astonishment, it failed. Edison had not taken into account legislators' habits. They didn't like to vote quickly and efficiently. They liked to lobby their fellow legislators as voting took place. Edison had a great idea, but he completely misunderstood the needs of his customers. He learned from his failure the relationship between invention and marketing. Edison learned that marketing and invention must be integrated. "Anything that won't sell, I don't want to invent," he said. "Its sale is proof of utility, and utility is success." He realized he needed to _____ and tailor his thinking accordingly. [3점]

① consider the likelihood of mass production
② simplify the design of his inventions
③ work with other inventors regularly
④ have knowledge of law in advance
⑤ put the customers' needs first

34. Attitude has been conceptualized into four main components: affective (feelings of liking or disliking), cognitive (beliefs and evaluation of those beliefs), behavioral intention (a statement of how one would behave in a certain situation), and behavior. Public attitudes toward a wildlife species and its management are generated based on the interaction of those components. In forming our attitudes toward wolves, people strive to keep their affective components of attitude consistent with their cognitive component. For example, I could dislike wolves; I believe they have killed people (cognitive belief), and having people killed is of course bad (evaluation of belief). The behavioral intention that could result from this is to support a wolf control program and actual behavior may be a history of shooting wolves. In this example, _____, producing a negative overall attitude toward wolves. [3점]

① attitude drives the various forms of belief
② all aspects of attitude are consistent with each other
③ cognitive components of attitude outweigh affective ones
④ the components of attitude are not simultaneously evaluated
⑤ our biased attitudes get in the way of preserving biodiversity

35. 다음 글에서 전체 흐름과 관계 <u>없는</u> 문장은?

Cultural globalization has multiple centers in Asia like Bollywood movies made in India and Kung Fu movies made in Hong Kong. ① They are subtitled in as many as 17 languages and distributed to specific diasporas. ② These cultural spaces, which are dominated by languages like Hindi and Mandarin, ignore and challenge the spread of English. ③ Professor Vaish has shown how Chinese and Indian children in Singapore are networked into the pan-Chinese and pan-Indian culture through their engagement with Chinese pop music and Indian movies respectively. ④ As the world's two most populous nations, China is India's largest trading partner, with the size of trade between them valuing $71.5 billion. ⑤ She thus empirically challenges the idea that Asian youth are passive victims of cultural globalization, or "world culture" that comes out of the West.

* diaspora: 디아스포라(이주하여 해외에 사는 사람들 또는 그 집단)

[36 ~ 37] 주어진 글 다음에 이어질 글의 순서로 가장 적절한 것을 고르시오.

36.

> The lotus plant (a white water lily) grows in the dirty, muddy bottom of lakes and ponds, yet despite this, its leaves are always clean.

(A) As a result of this investigation, a German company produced a house paint. On the market in Europe and Asia, the product even came with a guarantee that it would stay clean for five years without detergents or sandblasting.

(B) That is because whenever the smallest particle of dust lands on the plant, it immediately waves the leaf, directing the dust particles to one particular spot. Raindrops falling on the leaves are sent to that same place, to thus wash the dirt away.

(C) This property of the lotus led researchers to design a new house paint. Researchers began working on how to develop paints that wash clean in the rain, in much the same way as lotus leaves do.

① (A) − (C) − (B)   ② (B) − (A) − (C)
③ (B) − (C) − (A)   ④ (C) − (A) − (B)
⑤ (C) − (B) − (A)

37.

Like the physiological discoveries of the late nineteenth century, today's biological breakthrough has fundamentally altered our understanding of how the human organism works and will change medical practice fundamentally and thoroughly.

(A) Remember the scientific method, which you probably first learned about back in elementary school? It has a long and difficult process of observation, hypothesis, experiment, testing, modifying, retesting, and retesting again and again and again.

(B) That's how science works, and the breakthrough understanding of the relationship between our genes and chronic disease happened in just that way, building on the work of scientists from decades — even centuries — ago. In fact, it is still happening; the story continues to unfold as the research presses on.

(C) The word "breakthrough," however, seems to imply in many people's minds an amazing, unprecedented revelation that, in an instant, makes everything clear. Science doesn't actually work that way. [3점]

① (A) − (C) − (B)　　　② (B) − (A) − (C)
③ (B) − (C) − (A)　　　④ (C) − (A) − (B)
⑤ (C) − (B) − (A)

[38 ~ 39] 글의 흐름으로 보아, 주어진 문장이 들어가기에 가장 적절한 곳을 고르시오.

38.

In describing the service, a recent newspaper article warned consumers that sharing the yacht means "there is no guarantee you will always be able to use it when you want."

Car-sharing is now a familiar concept, but creative companies are making it possible for their clients to share ownership and access to just about everything, such as villas, handbags and even diamond necklaces. (①) According to a Portuguese saying, "You should never have a yacht; you should have a friend with a yacht." (②) By joining a yacht sharing service, members can live the Portuguese dream by sharing a yacht with up to seven other people. (③) This apparent limitation is precisely what helps consumers make it a treat. (④) Limiting your access to everything from sandwiches to luxury cars helps to reset your cheerometer. (⑤) That is, knowing you can't have access to something all the time may help you appreciate it more when you do.

39.

Houses in the historic district of Key West, Florida, for example, whether new or remodeled, must be built of wood in a traditional style, and there are only a few permissible colors of paint, white being preferred.

In the US, regional styles of speech have always been associated with regional styles of building: the Midwestern farmhouse, the Southern plantation mansion, and the Cape Cod cottage all have their equivalent in spoken dialect. (①) These buildings may be old and genuine, or they may be recent reproductions, the equivalent of an assumed rather than a native accent. (②) As James Kunstler says, "half-baked versions of Scarlett O'Hara's Tara now stand replicated in countless suburban subdivisions around the United States." (③) In some cities and towns, especially where tourism is an important part of the economy, zoning codes may make a sort of artificial authenticity compulsory. (④) From the street these houses may look like the simple sea captains' mansions they imitate. (⑤) Inside, however, where zoning does not reach, they often contain modern lighting and state-of-the-art kitchens and bathrooms. [3점]

40. 다음 글의 내용을 한 문장으로 요약하고자 한다. 빈칸 (A), (B)에 들어갈 말로 가장 적절한 것은?

Psychologist John Bargh did an experiment showing human perception and behavior can be influenced by external factors. He told a bunch of healthy undergraduates that he was testing their language abilities. He presented them with a list of words and asked them to create a coherent sentence from it. One of the lists was "DOWN SAT LONELY THE MAN WRINKLED BITTERLY THE WITH FACE OLD". "Bitterly, the lonely old man with the wrinkled face sat down" is one possible solution. But this was no linguistics test. Bargh was interested in how long it took the students to leave the lab and walk down the hall after they were exposed to the words. What he found was extraordinary. Those students who had been exposed to an "elderly" mix of words took almost 40 percent longer to walk down the hall than those who had been exposed to "random" words. Some students even walked with their shoulders bent forwards, dragging their feet as they left, as if they were 50 years older than they actually were.

↓

In an experiment about human perception and behavior, participants who experienced _____(A)_____ to words related to "elderly" showed　pace, and some of them even showed posture, _____(B)_____ to what the words suggested.

	(A)	(B)		(A)	(B)
①	exposure	corresponding	②	resistance	irrelevant
③	exposure	contrary	④	resistance	similar
⑤	preference	comparable			

[41 ~ 42] 다음 글을 읽고, 물음에 답하시오.

We're creatures who live and die by the energy stores we've built up in our bodies. Navigating the world is a difficult job that requires moving around and using a lot of brainpower — an energy-expensive endeavor. When we make correct (a) predictions, that saves energy. When you know that edible bugs can be found beneath certain types of rocks, it saves turning over *all* the rocks. The better we predict, the less energy it costs us. Repetition makes us more confident in our forecasts and more efficient in our actions. So there's something (b) appealing about predictability.

But if our brains are going to all this effort to make the world predictable, that begs the question: if we love predictability so much, why don't we, for example, just replace our televisions with machines that emit a rhythmic beep twenty-four hours a day, predictably? The answer is that there's a problem with a (c) lack of surprise. The better we understand something, the less effort we put into thinking about it. Familiarity (d) reduces indifference. Repetition suppression sets in and our attention diminishes. This is why — no matter how much you enjoyed watching the World Series — you aren't going to be satisfied watching that same game over and over. Although predictability is reassuring, the brain strives to (e) incorporate new facts into its model of the world. It always seeks novelty.

41. 윗글의 제목으로 가장 적절한 것은?

① Why Are Television Reruns Still Popular?
② Predictability Is Something Not to Be Feared!
③ What Really Satisfies Our Brain: Familiarity or Novelty
④ Repetition Gives Us Expertise at the Expense of Creativity
⑤ Our Hunter-Gatherer Ancestors Were Smart in Saving Energy

42. 밑줄 친 (a) ~ (e) 중에서 문맥상 낱말의 쓰임이 적절하지 않은 것은? [3점]

① (a) ② (b) ③ (c) ④ (d) ⑤ (e)

[43 ~ 45] 다음 글을 읽고, 물음에 답하시오.

(A)

Bahati lived in a small village, where baking bread for a hungry passerby is a custom when one misses someone. She had an only son living far away and missed him a lot, so (a) she baked an extra loaf of bread and put it on the window sill every day, for anyone to take away. Every day, a poor old woman took away the bread, just muttering "The good you do, comes back to you!" instead of expressing gratitude.

(B)

This time, instead of being irritated, Bahati decided to offer a prayer. For years, she had got no news of her son. (b) She prayed for his safety. That night, there was a knock on the door. As she opened it, (c) she was surprised to find her son standing in the doorway. He had grown thin and lean. His clothes were torn. Crying and hugging her son, she gave him clothes to change into and some food.

(C)

"Not a word of gratitude," Bahati said to herself. One day, irritated, she was tempted to stop baking extra bread, but soon changed her mind. She baked an extra loaf and kept doing good because the words of the poor old woman kept coming back to her. (d) She placed the bread on the window sill. The poor old woman took away the loaf as usual, muttering the same words.

(D)

After taking some rest, Bahati's son said, "On my way home, I was so starved that I collapsed. I saw an old woman with a loaf of bread. I begged her for a small piece of bread. But (e) she gave me the whole loaf saying my need was greater than hers." It was then that Bahati finally realized the meaning of the words of the poor old woman: "The good you do, comes back to you!"

43. 주어진 글 (A)에 이어질 내용을 순서에 맞게 배열한 것으로 가장 적절한 것은?

① (B) − (D) − (C) ② (C) − (B) − (D)
③ (C) − (D) − (B) ④ (D) − (B) − (C)
⑤ (D) − (C) − (B)

44. 밑줄 친 (a) ~ (e) 중에서 가리키는 대상이 나머지 넷과 다른 것은?

① (a) ② (b) ③ (c) ④ (d) ⑤ (e)

45. 윗글의 Bahati에 관한 내용으로 적절하지 않은 것은?

① 멀리 살고 있는 아들을 몹시 그리워했다.
② 수년간 아들의 소식을 듣지 못했다.
③ 아들에게 갈아입을 옷과 음식을 주었다.
④ 여분의 빵을 굽는 일을 그만두었다.
⑤ 결국은 노파의 말의 의미를 깨달았다.

※ 확인 사항
답안지의 해당란에 필요한 내용을 정확히 기입(표기)했는지 확인하시오.

18

001 ☐ celebrate ⓥ 기념하다, 축하하다
002 ☐ anniversary ⓝ 기념일
003 ☐ boost ⓥ 돋우다, 촉진하다
004 ☐ arrange ⓥ 마련하다
005 ☐ informative ⓐ 유익한
006 ☐ enlightening ⓐ 깨우침을 주는
007 ☐ recently ⓐⓓ 최근에
008 ☐ attend ⓥ 참석하다
009 ☐ impressive ⓐ 인상적인
010 ☐ request ⓥ 요청하다
011 ☐ guest speaker 초청 연사
012 ☐ session ⓝ 시간, 기간
013 ☐ sincerely ⓐⓓ 진심으로

19

014 ☐ amusing ⓐ 재미있는
015 ☐ jolly ⓐ 쾌활한
016 ☐ witty ⓐ 재치 있는
017 ☐ laughter ⓝ 웃음
018 ☐ broadcast ⓥ 퍼뜨리다, 방송하다
019 ☐ air attack 공습
020 ☐ screeching ⓐ 날카로운 소리를 내는
021 ☐ squeeze into ~로 비집고 들어가다
022 ☐ basement ⓝ 지하
023 ☐ roar ⓝ 굉음, 함성
024 ☐ overwhelming ⓐ 압도적인
025 ☐ shiver ⓥ 떨다
026 ☐ murmur ⓥ 중얼거리다
027 ☐ prayer ⓝ 기도
028 ☐ desperate ⓐ 절망적인
029 ☐ frustrated ⓐ 좌절한
030 ☐ terrified ⓐ 공포에 질린

20

031 ☐ bad name 오명
032 ☐ be associated with ~와 연관되다
033 ☐ rote learning (기계적인) 암기 학습
034 ☐ cram into ~에 쑤셔 넣다
035 ☐ information ⓝ 정보
036 ☐ educator ⓝ 교육자
037 ☐ recall ⓥ 기억해 내다
038 ☐ joke ⓝ 농담
039 ☐ instantly ⓐⓓ 즉각적으로
040 ☐ mastery ⓝ 숙달
041 ☐ store ⓥ 저장하다
042 ☐ bother ⓥ 굳이 ~하다
043 ☐ in the first place 애초에

21

044 ☐ collaborative ⓐ 협력적인
045 ☐ secure ⓥ 확보하다
046 ☐ donation ⓝ 기부, 기증
047 ☐ worthy ⓐ 가치 있는
048 ☐ cause 대의명분
049 ☐ contributor ⓝ 기부자
050 ☐ in essence 본질적으로
051 ☐ fusion ⓝ 융합, 혼합
052 ☐ venture ⓝ 벤처 (사업)
053 ☐ capitalism ⓝ 자본주의
054 ☐ conventional ⓐ 전통적인
055 ☐ variation ⓝ 변주, 변형

056 ☐ view ⓥ (…라고) 여기다, 보다
057 ☐ democratization ⓝ 민주화
058 ☐ restrict ⓥ 한정하다, 제한하다
059 ☐ capital ⓝ 자본
060 ☐ allocation ⓝ 할당
061 ☐ minority ⓝ 소수
062 ☐ empower ⓥ 권한을 주다, ~할 수 있게 하다
063 ☐ collective wisdom 집단 지혜
064 ☐ pocket money 쌈짓돈, 용돈
065 ☐ reinforce ⓥ 강화하다
066 ☐ keep A from B A가 B하지 못하게 하다
067 ☐ facilitate ⓥ 용이하게 하다

22

068 ☐ run into ~을 마주치다
069 ☐ face ⓥ 직면하다, 닥쳐오다
070 ☐ disposition ⓝ 기질
071 ☐ proactive ⓐ 상황을 앞서서 주도하는, 사전 대책을 강구하는
072 ☐ predetermination ⓝ 사전 결정, 선결
073 ☐ manipulate ⓥ 조종하다, 조작하다
074 ☐ mood ⓝ 기분, 분위기
075 ☐ anticipate ⓥ 기대하다
076 ☐ excuse ⓥ 용서하다, 봐주다
077 ☐ naive ⓐ 고지식한, 순진한
078 ☐ lose temper 화가 나 이성을 잃다
079 ☐ safe conduct ⓝ 안전 통행권
080 ☐ storm ⓝ 폭풍, 폭풍우
081 ☐ determined ⓐ 단단히 결심한
082 ☐ get the most out of ~을 최대한 활용하다
083 ☐ proper ⓐ 적절한, 제대로 된
084 ☐ positive ⓐ 긍정적인
085 ☐ nevertheless ⓐⓓ 그럼에도 불구하고
086 ☐ cruel ⓐ 잔인한, 잔혹한

23

087 ☐ comparatively ⓐⓓ 비교적
088 ☐ harmless ⓐ 무해한
089 ☐ starve ⓥ 굶어죽다
090 ☐ high blood pressure 고혈압
091 ☐ diabetes ⓝ 당뇨병
092 ☐ stone age ⓝ 석기 시대
093 ☐ threat ⓝ 위협
094 ☐ flee ⓥ 도피하다, 도망하다
095 ☐ appointment ⓝ 약속
096 ☐ stuck ⓐ (~에) 갇힌, 꼼짝 못하는
097 ☐ traffic jam 교통 체증
098 ☐ rate A as B A를 B로 여기다, 평가하다
099 ☐ unpleasant ⓐ 불쾌한
100 ☐ conversation ⓝ 대화
101 ☐ illusion ⓝ 환상
102 ☐ mortal ⓐ 치명적인
103 ☐ instinct ⓝ 본능
104 ☐ tell A from B A와 B를 구별하다
105 ☐ foe ⓝ 적, 원수
106 ☐ primitive ⓐ 원시 사회의

24

107 ☐ violence ⓝ 폭력
108 ☐ anthropologist ⓝ 인류학자
109 ☐ notion ⓝ 개념, 관념
110 ☐ combative ⓐ 전투적인

111 ☐ actual ⓐ 실제의
112 ☐ opponent ⓝ 상대방
113 ☐ simulated ⓐ 모의의, 모조의
114 ☐ warfare ⓝ 전투, 전쟁
115 ☐ hypothesize ⓥ 가설을 세우다
116 ☐ alternative ⓝ 대안, 선택 가능한 것
117 ☐ inverse ⓝ 역의, 정반대의
118 ☐ correlation ⓝ 상관관계
119 ☐ frequency ⓝ 빈도
120 ☐ intensity ⓝ 강도
121 ☐ discover ⓥ 발견하다
122 ☐ significant ⓐ 중요한
123 ☐ hypothesis ⓝ 가설
124 ☐ pervasive ⓐ 만연한
125 ☐ reflection ⓝ 반영(물)
126 ☐ aggressive ⓐ 공격적인
127 ☐ impulse ⓝ 충동
128 ☐ distinction ⓝ 차이, 구별
129 ☐ consume ⓥ 사로잡다
130 ☐ military ⓐ 군사의
131 ☐ alliance ⓝ 동맹
132 ☐ the oppressed 억압받는 사람들

25

133 ☐ renewable ⓐ 재생 가능한
134 ☐ photovoltaic ⓐ 광발전의
135 ☐ biofuel ⓝ 바이오 연료
136 ☐ hydropower ⓝ 수력 발전
137 ☐ geothermal ⓐ 지열의

26

138 ☐ Jewish ⓐ 유대인의 ⓝ 유대인
139 ☐ private ⓐ 사립의, 사적인
140 ☐ complete ⓥ 완료하다, 끝마치다
141 ☐ master ⓝ 석사 학위
142 ☐ skyrocket ⓥ 급부상하다, 급증하다
143 ☐ widespread ⓐ 폭넓은, 널리 퍼진
144 ☐ recognition ⓝ 인정
145 ☐ seizure ⓝ 장악, 점령
146 ☐ forbid ⓥ 금지하다
147 ☐ artwork ⓝ (특히 박물관의) 미술품
148 ☐ emigrate to ⓥ ~로 이주하다
149 ☐ recapture ⓥ 되찾다, 다시 붙잡다
150 ☐ repeatedly ⓐⓓ 반복해서
151 ☐ portray ⓥ 그리다
152 ☐ embody ⓥ 구현하다, 구체화하다
153 ☐ represent ⓥ 표현하다, 대표하다

27

154 ☐ show off ~을 뽐내다
155 ☐ entry ⓝ 출품작
156 ☐ official ⓐ 공식적인
157 ☐ entrant ⓝ 참가자, 출전자
158 ☐ submission ⓝ 제출

28

159 ☐ upcycling ⓝ 업사이클링(재활용품으로 더 품질이 좋거나 가치가 높은 새 제품을 만드는 과정)
160 ☐ learn ⓥ 배우다, 학습하다
161 ☐ admission ⓝ 입장
162 ☐ booking ⓝ 예약

163 ☐ hands-on 직접 해 보는
164 ☐ activity ⓝ 활동
165 ☐ utilize ⓥ 이용하다
166 ☐ waste ⓐ 쓸모없어진
167 ☐ exhibition ⓝ 전시, 전시회
168 ☐ environmental ⓐ 환경과 관련된
169 ☐ topic ⓝ 화제, 주제

29

170 ☐ attracted to ~에 끌리는, 매혹되는
171 ☐ considering ⓟⓡⓔⓟ ~을 고려할 때
172 ☐ tickle ⓥ 자극하다, 간질이다
173 ☐ exploit ⓥ 이용하다
174 ☐ neural ⓐ 신경의
175 ☐ circuit ⓝ 회로
176 ☐ evolve ⓥ 진화하다
177 ☐ discern ⓥ 분간하다, 식별하다
178 ☐ feature ⓝ 특징
179 ☐ auditory ⓐ 청각의
180 ☐ in principle 원리적으로
181 ☐ visual illusion 착시
182 ☐ mechanism ⓝ 기제
183 ☐ perceive ⓥ 인식하다
184 ☐ leverage ⓥ 이용하다
185 ☐ perceptual ⓐ 지각의
186 ☐ accomplish ⓥ 성취하다
187 ☐ novel ⓐ 새로운
188 ☐ true of ~에 해당되는, 적용되는

30

189 ☐ establish ⓥ 확립하다
190 ☐ element ⓝ 요소, 성분
191 ☐ unspoken ⓐ 무언의
192 ☐ vanish ⓥ 사라지다
193 ☐ unconsciously ⓐⓓ 무의식적으로
194 ☐ worthwhile ⓐ 가치 있는
195 ☐ deceptive ⓐ 기만적인
196 ☐ sacrificial ⓐ 희생적인
197 ☐ spend ⓥ (시간을) 보내다, 들이다
198 ☐ elsewhere ⓐⓓ (어딘가) 다른 곳에서
199 ☐ part ⓝ (배역의) 말, 대사
200 ☐ illustrate ⓥ 분명하게 보였다
201 ☐ bridge ⓥ 연결하다
202 ☐ essential ⓐ 필수적인, 본질적인
203 ☐ respect ⓥ 존중하다
204 ☐ sentence ⓝ 문장
205 ☐ take for granted 당연하게 여기다, 대수롭지 않게 여기다

31

206 ☐ conduct ⓥ (특정한 활동을) 하다
207 ☐ extremely ⓐⓓ 극도로
208 ☐ onerous ⓐ 성가신, 아주 힘든
209 ☐ lottery ⓝ 추첨, 복권
210 ☐ wait in line 줄을 서서 기다리다
211 ☐ on average 평균적으로
212 ☐ per ⓐⓓ 각 …당
213 ☐ worth ⓐ ~의 가치가 있는
214 ☐ housing ⓝ 주택
215 ☐ crash ⓝ 붕괴, 도산
216 ☐ real estate 부동산
217 ☐ homeowner ⓝ 주택 소유자

218 □ respondent ⓝ 응답자
219 □ aware of ~을 깨달은
220 □ nearby ⓐ 인근의, 가까운 곳의
221 □ foreclosure ⓝ 압류
222 □ assert ⓥ 단언하다, 확고히 하다
223 □ hurt ⓥ 해를 끼치다
224 □ neighborhood ⓝ 근처, 인근, 이웃
225 □ overvalue ⓥ 과대평가하다
226 □ disregard ⓥ 무시하다

32

227 □ device ⓝ 장치
228 □ substitute ⓝ 대체재, 대체물
229 □ complement ⓝ 보완재, 보충물
230 □ explore ⓥ 탐구하다, 분석하다
231 □ case ⓝ 사례, 경우
232 □ take notes 필기하다
233 □ be synced to ~에 동기화되다
234 □ wirelessly ad 무선으로
235 □ via prep ~을 통해
236 □ be away from ~로부터 떨어져 있다
237 □ functionality ⓝ 기능성
238 □ fulfill ⓥ 수행하다, 달성하다
239 □ more or less 거의, 대략
240 □ status ⓝ (사회적) 지위, 신분
241 □ advancement ⓝ 발전, 진보
242 □ assessment ⓝ 평가
243 □ current ⓐ 현재의, 지금의
244 □ condition ⓝ 상태, 상황

33

245 □ indeed ad 정말, 확실히
246 □ genius ⓝ 천재
247 □ patent ⓥ 특허를 받다
248 □ electronic ⓐ 전자의
249 □ total ⓥ 합계를 내다
250 □ vote ⓝ 투표
251 □ legislature ⓝ 의회
252 □ chamber ⓝ 의회
253 □ manual ⓐ 손으로 하는, 수기의
254 □ astonishment ⓝ 놀람
255 □ take into account ~을 고려하다
256 □ legislator ⓝ 국회의원, 입법자
257 □ efficiently ad 효율적으로, 유효하게
258 □ fellow ⓐ 동료의
259 □ misunderstand ⓥ 오해하다, 잘못 해석하다
260 □ integrate ⓥ 통합시키다
261 □ proof ⓝ 증거, 증명
262 □ utility ⓝ 유용성
263 □ tailor ⓥ ~에 맞추다
264 □ accordingly ad 그에 따라
265 □ likelihood ⓝ (어떤 일이 있을) 가능성
266 □ mass production 대량 생산
267 □ regularly ad 정기적으로

34

268 □ conceptualize ⓥ 개념화하다
269 □ component ⓝ 구성 요소
270 □ affective ⓐ 감정적인
271 □ dislike ⓥ 싫어하다
272 □ cognitive ⓐ 인지의, 인식의
273 □ evaluation ⓝ 평가
274 □ behavioral ⓐ 행동의
275 □ intention ⓝ 의사, 의도
276 □ statement ⓝ 진술, 서술
277 □ management ⓝ 관리
278 □ generate ⓥ 생성하다, 만들어 내다
279 □ form ⓥ 형성하다
280 □ strive ⓥ 노력하다, 분투하다
281 □ consistent with ~와 일관되는, 일치하는
282 □ overall ⓐ 종합적인, 전체의
283 □ outweigh ⓥ ~보다 중요하다
284 □ simultaneously ad 동시에
285 □ get in the way of ~을 방해하다
286 □ preserve ⓥ 보존하다
287 □ biodiversity ⓝ 생물 다양성

35

288 □ globalization ⓝ 세계화
289 □ multiple ⓐ 다수의, 많은
290 □ subtitle ⓥ 자막 처리를 하다, 자막을 달다
291 □ distribute ⓥ 배급하다, 배포하다
292 □ specific ⓐ 특정한
293 □ dominate ⓥ 지배하다
294 □ challenge ⓥ 저항하다, 반박하다
295 □ spread ⓝ 확산 ⓥ 퍼뜨리다
296 □ engagement ⓝ 참여, 관여
297 □ respectively ad 각각
298 □ populous ⓐ 인구가 많은
299 □ value ⓥ 값을 매기다
300 □ empirically ad 실증적으로
301 □ passive ⓐ 수동적인, 소극적인
302 □ victim ⓝ 희생자

36

303 □ lotus ⓝ 연꽃, 수련
304 □ muddy ⓐ 진흙투성이인
305 □ pond ⓝ 연못
306 □ investigation ⓝ 연구, 조사
307 □ guarantee ⓝ 보증 ⓥ 보장하다
308 □ detergent ⓝ 세제
309 □ sandblasting ⓝ 모래 분사
310 □ particle ⓝ 입자
311 □ dust ⓝ 먼지
312 □ immediately ad 즉시
313 □ wave ⓥ 흔들다
314 □ direct ⓥ ~로 향하다
315 □ particular ⓐ 특정한
316 □ raindrop ⓝ 빗방울
317 □ fall on ~에 떨어지다
318 □ property ⓝ 특성

37

319 □ breakthrough ⓝ 획기적 발견
320 □ fundamentally ad 근본적으로
321 □ alter ⓥ 바꾸다
322 □ organism ⓝ 유기체
323 □ medical ⓐ 의료의, 의학의
324 □ practice ⓝ 행위, 업무
325 □ thoroughly ad 철저히
326 □ observation ⓝ 관찰
327 □ modify ⓥ 수정하다
328 □ gene ⓝ 유전자
329 □ chronic ⓐ 만성의
330 □ disease ⓝ 질병, 병
331 □ unfold ⓥ 펼쳐지다, 펴다
332 □ press on 밀고 나가다
333 □ imply ⓥ 의미하다, 암시하다
334 □ unprecedented ⓐ 전례 없는
335 □ revelation ⓝ 발견
336 □ in an instant 즉시, 순식간에

38

337 □ warn ⓥ 경고하다, 주의를 주다
338 □ familiar ⓐ 친숙한, 익숙한
339 □ ownership ⓝ 소유권
340 □ necklace ⓝ 목걸이
341 □ apparent ⓐ 외관상의, 겉보기의
342 □ limitation ⓝ 제한
343 □ precisely ad 정확히, 꼭
344 □ reset ⓥ 다시 맞추다
345 □ cheerometer ⓝ 활기 온도계(사람의 활기를 측정하는 장치라는 뜻의 비유적 표현)
346 □ appreciate ⓥ 감사하다, 고마워하다

39

347 □ historic ⓐ 역사적으로 중요한
348 □ district ⓝ 지역
349 □ permissible ⓐ 허용 가능한
350 □ regional ⓐ 지방의, 지역의
351 □ plantation ⓝ 대농장
352 □ mansion ⓝ 저택
353 □ cottage ⓝ 오두막
354 □ equivalent ⓝ 상응하는 것, 등가물
355 □ dialect ⓝ 방언
356 □ genuine ⓐ 진품의, 진짜인
357 □ reproduction ⓝ 복제, 복사
358 □ replicate ⓥ 복제하다
359 □ countless ⓐ 무수한, 셀 수 없이 많은
360 □ suburban ⓐ 교외의
361 □ subdivision ⓝ 구획
362 □ artificial ⓐ 인위적인
363 □ authenticity ⓝ 진정성
364 □ compulsory ⓐ 의무적인, 필수의
365 □ imitate ⓥ 모방하다, 본뜨다
366 □ contain ⓥ 포함하다
367 □ state-of-the-art 최신식의

40

368 □ perception ⓝ 인식
369 □ external ⓐ 외부의
370 □ factor ⓝ 요인, 요소
371 □ undergraduate ⓝ 대학생, 학부
372 □ present A with B ⓥ A에게 B를 제시하다
373 □ coherent ⓐ 일관되는, 조리 있는
374 □ wrinkled ⓐ 주름이 진
375 □ bitterly ad 씁쓸하게도
376 □ linguistics ⓝ 언어학
377 □ extraordinary ⓐ 놀라운, 대단한
378 □ forward ad 앞으로
379 □ drag ⓥ 끌다, 끌고 가다
380 □ posture ⓝ 자세, 태도
381 □ suggest ⓥ 시사하다
382 □ corresponding ⓐ (~와) 일치하는
383 □ comparable ⓐ 맞먹는, 필적할 만한

41~42

384 □ creature ⓝ 생명이 있는 존재, 생물
385 □ build up 쌓아 올리다
386 □ navigate ⓥ 항해하다
387 □ endeavor ⓝ 수고, 노력
388 □ make a prediction 예측하다
389 □ correct ⓐ 정확한
390 □ save ⓥ 아끼다, 절약하다
391 □ edible ⓐ 먹을 수 있는
392 □ beneath prep 아래에, 밑에
393 □ certain ⓐ 특정한
394 □ turn over 뒤집다
395 □ forecast ⓝ 예측
396 □ appealing ⓐ 매력적인
397 □ predictability ⓝ 예측 가능성
398 □ beg the question 질문을 하게 만들다
399 □ replace ⓥ 대체하다
400 □ emit ⓥ 내보내다, 방출하다
401 □ beep ⓝ 삑 하는 소리
402 □ put effort into ~에 노력을 들이다
403 □ familiarity ⓝ 익숙함
404 □ indifference ⓝ 무관심
405 □ suppression ⓝ 억제
406 □ set in 시작되다
407 □ diminish ⓥ 줄어들다, 감소하다
408 □ satisfy ⓥ 만족시키다
409 □ over and over 반복해서
410 □ reassuring ⓐ 안심시키는
411 □ strive ⓥ 노력하다, 힘쓰다
412 □ incorporate ⓥ 포함시키다, 통합시키다
413 □ seek ⓥ 추구하다
414 □ novelty ⓝ 새로움
415 □ rerun ⓝ 재방송
416 □ expertise ⓝ 전문성, 전문기술
417 □ at the expense of ~을 희생하여

43~45

418 □ village ⓝ 마을
419 □ bake ⓥ 굽다
420 □ passerby ⓝ 행인
421 □ custom ⓝ 관습
422 □ miss ⓥ 그리워하다
423 □ far away 멀리
424 □ extra ⓐ 여분의
425 □ loaf ⓝ (빵) 덩어리
426 □ sill ⓝ (문이나 창문의) 틀
427 □ take away 가져가다
428 □ mutter ⓥ 중얼거리다
429 □ good ⓝ 선(善)
430 □ express ⓥ 표현하다
431 □ gratitude ⓝ 감사
432 □ irritated ⓐ 짜증 난
433 □ pray ⓥ 기도하다
434 □ doorway ⓝ 대문간, 출입구
435 □ lean ⓐ 야윈
436 □ tear ⓥ 찢다
437 □ be tempted to ~하고 싶다
438 □ place ⓥ 두다
439 □ collapse ⓥ 쓰러지다, 붕괴하다
440 □ whole ⓐ 전부의, 모든
441 □ realize ⓥ 깨닫다
442 □ meaning ⓝ 의미

TEST A-B 각 단어의 뜻을 [A] 영어는 우리말로, [B] 우리말은 영어로 쓰시오.

A	English	Korean
01	astonishment	
02	dominate	
03	true of	
04	property	
05	considering	
06	empirically	
07	alliance	
08	authenticity	
09	combative	
10	emit	
11	lose temper	
12	lean	
13	disposition	
14	outweigh	
15	starve	
16	familiarity	
17	linguistics	
18	tailor	
19	vanish	
20	pocket money	

B	Korean	English
01	새로움	
02	전문성, 전문기술	
03	일관되는, 조리 있는	
04	수정하다	
05	만성의	
06	부동산	
07	행동의	
08	인식	
09	통합시키다	
10	분간하다, 식별하다	
11	고지식한, 순진한	
12	~을 뽐내다	
13	융합, 혼합	
14	상대방	
15	중얼거리다	
16	쓰러지다, 붕괴하다	
17	중얼거리다	
18	기만적인	
19	위협	
20	공격적인	

▶ A-D 정답 : 해설편 214쪽

TEST C-D 각 단어의 뜻을 골라 기호를 쓰시오.

C	English			Korean
01	beg the question	(	)	ⓐ 연결하다
02	more or less	(	)	ⓑ ~에 동기화되다
03	cottage	(	)	ⓒ 저택
04	inverse	(	)	ⓓ 거의, 대략
05	revelation	(	)	ⓔ 억제
06	illustrate	(	)	ⓕ 역의, 정반대의
07	bridge	(	)	ⓖ 분명히 보여주다
08	lotus	(	)	ⓗ 질문을 하게 만들다
09	be synced to	(	)	ⓘ 오두막
10	mortal	(	)	ⓙ 연꽃, 수련
11	suppression	(	)	ⓚ ~에 노력을 들이다
12	visual illusion	(	)	ⓛ 발견
13	put effort into	(	)	ⓜ 치명적인
14	mansion	(	)	ⓝ 착시
15	take into account	(	)	ⓞ ~을 고려하다
16	emigrate to	(	)	ⓟ A와 B를 구별하다
17	tell A from B	(	)	ⓠ ~와 연관되다
18	present A with B	(	)	ⓡ A에게 B를 제시하다
19	bitterly	(	)	ⓢ ~로 이주하다
20	be associated with	(	)	ⓣ 씁쓸하게도

D	Korean			English
01	깨우침을 주는	(	)	ⓐ enlightening
02	개념화하다	(	)	ⓑ get the most out of
03	가설을 세우다	(	)	ⓒ entrant
04	대의명분	(	)	ⓓ cause
05	~을 마주치다	(	)	ⓔ run into
06	참가자, 출전자	(	)	ⓕ secure
07	~로 비집고 들어가다	(	)	ⓖ proactive
08	자막 처리를 하다	(	)	ⓗ subtitle
09	본질적으로	(	)	ⓘ conceptualize
10	~을 최대한 활용하다	(	)	ⓙ shiver
11	상황을 앞서서 주도하는	(	)	ⓚ complement
12	보완재, 보충물	(	)	ⓛ in essence
13	확보하다	(	)	ⓜ cram into
14	~에 쑤셔 넣다	(	)	ⓝ hypothesize
15	떨다	(	)	ⓞ squeeze into
16	~을 방해하다	(	)	ⓟ fulfill
17	수력 발전	(	)	ⓠ hydropower
18	좌절한	(	)	ⓡ get in the way of
19	수행하다, 달성하다	(	)	ⓢ frustrated
20	외관상의, 겉보기의	(	)	ⓣ apparent

575만권
베스트셀러
리얼 오리지널 시리즈 누적 판매
2006~2024

리얼 오리지널

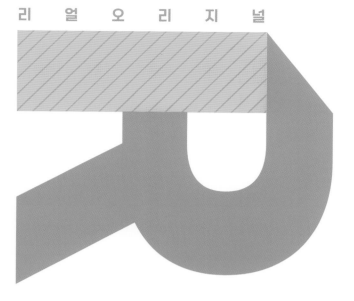
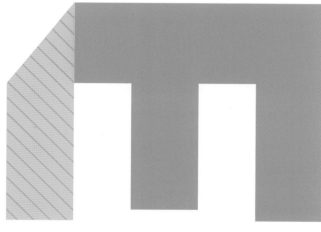
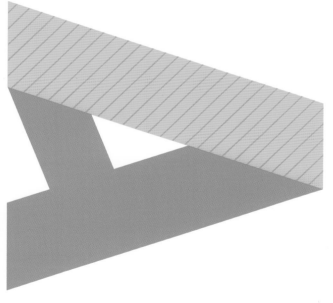

The Real series ipsifly
provide questions in previous
real test and you can practice
as real college scholastic
ability test.

2025 학력평가 + 내신대비

전국연합
학력평가
5개년
기출문제집

20회 [3월·6월·9월·11월
학력평가 기출 20회]

- 2020~2024 최신 5개년 [고2] 전국연합 학력평가 20회
- 영어 [독해 28문항]을 회차별로 구성한 [유형별] 모의고사
- 학교시험 [중간·기말고사]를 대비한 내신 필수 문제집
- 매회 어휘를 복습할 수 있는 [어휘 리뷰 TEST] 20회
- 친절한 입체적 해설 [직독직해·구문 풀이·고난도 꿀팁]
- 회차별 [SPEED 정답 체크표·STUDY 플래너·정답률]
- [특별 부록] 회차별 영단어

고2 영어 독해

모바일로 학습하는
회차별 영단어 QR 코드 제공

● 해 설 편 ●

수능 모의고사 전문 출판
 입시플라이

01회 2024학년도 3월 전국연합학력평가

18② 19⑤ 20① 21④ 22② 23⑤ 24⑤ 25⑤ 26④ 27③
28④ 29④ 30③ 31③ 32② 33③ 34④ 35③ 36⑤ 37②
38③ 39② 40① 41① 42④ 43④ 44④ 45②

02회 2023학년도 3월 전국연합학력평가

18② 19② 20⑤ 21③ 22⑤ 23⑤ 24④ 25③ 26④ 27⑤
28⑤ 29⑤ 30③ 31④ 32② 33① 34④ 35③ 36④ 37③
38② 39④ 40① 41① 42③ 43⑤ 44④ 45⑤

03회 2022학년도 3월 전국연합학력평가

18③ 19① 20④ 21④ 22⑤ 23⑤ 24③ 25④ 26⑤ 27④
28③ 29④ 30⑤ 31② 32④ 33③ 34④ 35④ 36② 37③
38⑤ 39⑤ 40① 41① 42⑤ 43② 44③ 45⑤

04회 2021학년도 3월 전국연합학력평가

18① 19① 20④ 21③ 22③ 23④ 24① 25③ 26⑤ 27③
28③ 29⑤ 30② 31① 32④ 33① 34④ 35③ 36⑤ 37②
38⑤ 39③ 40④ 41① 42⑤ 43⑤ 44④ 45②

05회 2020학년도 3월 전국연합학력평가

18② 19① 20④ 21② 22③ 23② 24④ 25⑤ 26③ 27②
28② 29⑤ 30③ 31① 32① 33⑤ 34⑤ 35③ 36⑤ 37②
38⑤ 39④ 40① 41④ 42② 43③ 44④ 45③

06회 2024학년도 6월 전국연합학력평가

18② 19① 20④ 21① 22④ 23② 24④ 25③ 26⑤ 27⑤
28③ 29⑤ 30④ 31① 32③ 33① 34② 35③ 36② 37③
38④ 39③ 40⑤ 41① 42⑤ 43② 44③ 45③

07회 2023학년도 6월 전국연합학력평가

18① 19① 20② 21④ 22② 23④ 24⑤ 25④ 26④ 27⑤
28③ 29④ 30③ 31① 32③ 33③ 34⑤ 35④ 36③ 37③
38④ 39③ 40① 41⑤ 42⑤ 43④ 44② 45③

08회 2022학년도 6월 전국연합학력평가

18⑤ 19① 20② 21① 22③ 23② 24① 25③ 26④ 27③
28④ 29⑤ 30⑤ 31③ 32⑤ 33① 34① 35④ 36⑤ 37③
38④ 39② 40② 41⑤ 42④ 43④ 44⑤ 45③

09회 2021학년도 6월 전국연합학력평가

18⑤ 19① 20② 21① 22⑤ 23② 24③ 25④ 26③ 27⑤
28④ 29⑤ 30④ 31① 32② 33③ 34① 35③ 36⑤ 37③
38④ 39② 40① 41④ 42⑤ 43② 44⑤ 45⑤

10회 2020학년도 6월 전국연합학력평가

18① 19① 20③ 21⑤ 22⑤ 23② 24⑤ 25⑤ 26④ 27⑤
28③ 29⑤ 30③ 31① 32③ 33④ 34④ 35③ 36② 37⑤
38④ 39① 40① 41② 42⑤ 43③ 44⑤ 45④

11회 2024학년도 9월 전국연합학력평가

18① 19② 20⑤ 21① 22⑤ 23② 24④ 25④ 26④ 27⑤
28④ 29④ 30⑤ 31③ 32② 33① 34⑤ 35③ 36⑤ 37③
38② 39④ 40① 41① 42④ 43② 44③ 45③

12회 2023학년도 9월 전국연합학력평가

18⑤ 19① 20⑤ 21③ 22④ 23⑤ 24③ 25⑤ 26③ 27④
28④ 29② 30④ 31③ 32③ 33② 34② 35③ 36⑤ 37②
38④ 39④ 40① 41① 42⑤ 43③ 44② 45②

13회 2022학년도 9월 전국연합학력평가

18④ 19② 20① 21⑤ 22② 23② 24① 25③ 26⑤ 27④
28② 29④ 30③ 31③ 32① 33① 34④ 35④ 36④ 37②
38③ 39③ 40② 41① 42⑤ 43④ 44③ 45③

14회 2021학년도 9월 전국연합학력평가

18① 19① 20② 21④ 22① 23⑤ 24① 25⑤ 26④ 27⑤
28③ 29⑤ 30③ 31② 32① 33① 34① 35③ 36② 37③
38③ 39⑤ 40① 41② 42③ 43④ 44④ 45⑤

15회 2020학년도 9월 전국연합학력평가

18① 19② 20⑤ 21① 22③ 23⑤ 24② 25⑤ 26⑤ 27④
28⑤ 29③ 30② 31② 32③ 33① 34① 35③ 36② 37⑤
38④ 39④ 40① 41① 42④ 43② 44③ 45②

16회 2023학년도 11월 전국연합학력평가

18② 19② 20⑤ 21④ 22① 23① 24⑤ 25④ 26③ 27④
28④ 29⑤ 30⑤ 31① 32① 33⑤ 34② 35③ 36② 37③
38③ 39④ 40① 41① 42⑤ 43③ 44⑤ 45⑤

17회 2022학년도 11월 전국연합학력평가

18③ 19① 20④ 21③ 22④ 23② 24② 25③ 26⑤ 27④
28⑤ 29④ 30⑤ 31② 32① 33① 34② 35④ 36② 37③
38⑤ 39③ 40① 41③ 42② 43⑤ 44⑤ 45④

18회 2021학년도 11월 전국연합학력평가

18② 19① 20③ 21② 22⑤ 23③ 24② 25③ 26④ 27④
28④ 29⑤ 30④ 31① 32① 33③ 34⑤ 35④ 36② 37⑤
38⑤ 39③ 40① 41③ 42④ 43⑤ 44④ 45④

19회 2020학년도 11월 전국연합학력평가

18④ 19① 20⑤ 21⑤ 22③ 23② 24② 25③ 26② 27⑤
28③ 29③ 30⑤ 31② 32③ 33① 34⑤ 35③ 36④ 37⑤
38④ 39④ 40① 41① 42④ 43③ 44② 45③

20회 2019학년도 11월 전국연합학력평가

18① 19⑤ 20② 21① 22⑤ 23③ 24② 25④ 26④ 27④
28③ 29④ 30② 31① 32② 33⑤ 34② 35④ 36③ 37④
38⑤ 39④ 40① 41② 42④ 43② 44④ 45④

REAL
ORIGINAL

전국연합학력평가
5개년 기출 문제집

고2 영어 독해 해설편

Contents

REAL ORIGINAL

※ 수록된 정답률은 실제와 차이가 있을 수 있습니다.
문제 난도를 파악하는데 참고용으로 활용하시기
바랍니다.

수능 모의고사 전문 출판
입시플라이

---

18 마을 공예가들에게 부스 대여 안내   정답률 85% | 정답 ②

다음 글의 목적으로 가장 적절한 것은?

① 지역 예술가를 위한 정기 후원을 요청하려고
✓ 공예품 박람회의 부스 예약을 안내하려고
③ 대여 물품의 반환 방법을 설명하려고
④ 지역 예술가가 만든 물품을 홍보하려고
⑤ 지역 행사 일정의 변경 사항을 공지하려고

Dear Art Crafts People of Greenville,
친애하는 Greenville의 공예가들에게,
For the annual Crafts Fair on May 25 from 1 p.m. to 6 p.m., / the Greenville Community
Center is providing booth spaces to rent / as in previous years.
5월 25일 오후 1시부터 6시까지 열리는 연례 공예품 박람회를 위해서 / Greenville 커뮤니티 센터에서는 대여 부스 공간을 제공합니다. / 지난 몇 간년처럼
To reserve your space, please visit our website / and complete a registration form /
by April 20.
공간을 예약하기 위해서는 / 저희 웹사이트를 방문해주세요. / 그리고 신청서를 작성해주세요. / 4월 20일까지
The rental fee is $50.
대여 요금은 50달러입니다.
All the money / we receive from rental fees / goes to support upcoming activities
throughout the year.
모든 돈은 / 대여료로 받은 / 연중 예정된 활동을 지원하는데 사용됩니다.
We expect / all available spaces / to be fully booked soon, / so don't get left out.
우리는 예상합니다. / 모든 이용할 수 있는 공간이 / 곧 모두 예약될 것으로 / 그러니 놓치지 마세요.
We hope to see you at the fair.
박람회에서 뵙기를 희망합니다.

친애하는 Greenville의 공예가들에게,
5월 25일 오후 1시부터 6시까지 열리는 연례 공예품 박람회를 위해서, Greenville 커뮤니티 센터에서는 지난 몇 간년처럼 대여 부스 공간을 제공합니다. 공간을 예약하기 위해서는 저희 웹사이트를 방문하여 4월 20일까지 신청서를 작성해 주세요. 대여 요금은 50달러입니다. 대여료로 받은 모든 돈은 연중 예정된 활동을 지원하는데 사용됩니다. 우리는 모든 이용할 수 있는 공간이 곧 모두 예약될 것으로 예상되니 놓치지 마세요. 박람회에서 뵙기를 희망합니다.

Why? 왜 정답일까?

마을 공예가에게 부스 대여와 함께 박람회를 홍보하는 내용(For the annual Crafts Fair on May 25 from 1 p.m. to 6 p.m., the Greenville Community Center is providing booth spaces to rent as in previous years.)이므로, 글의 목적으로 가장 적절한 것은 ② '공예품 박람회의 부스 예약을 안내하려고'이다.

● craft ⓝ 수공예품
● book ⓥ 예약하다
● reserve ⓥ 예약하다
● fair ⓝ 전시회

구문 풀이

[4행] To reserve your space, please visit our website and complete a registration
  to부정사(부사적)   동사(병렬1)   동사(병렬2)
form by April 20.

---

19 미술 대회 수상 발표   정답률 83% | 정답 ⑤

다음 글에 드러난 Sarah의 심경 변화로 가장 적절한 것은?

① hopeful → regretful
  희망찬   후회하는
② relieved → grateful
  안도하는   감사한
③ excited → disappointed
  흥분한   실망한
④ depressed → frightened
  우울한   놀란
✓ discouraged → delighted
  낙담한   기쁜

Sarah, a young artist with a love for painting, / entered local art contest.
그림 그리기를 좋아하는 젊은 예술가 Sarah는 / 지역 미술 대회에 참가했다.
As she looked at the amazing artworks / made by others, / her confidence dropped.
그녀는 놀라운 예술 작품을 보면서 / 다른 사람들이 만든 / 자신감이 떨어졌다.
She quietly thought, / 'I might not win an award.'
그녀는 조용히 생각했다. / '내가 상을 받지 못할 수도 있겠네.'라고
The moment of judgment arrived, / and the judges began announcing winners / one by one.
심사의 순간이 다가왔다. / 그리고 심사위원들은 수상자를 발표하기 시작했다. / 한 명씩
It wasn't until the end / that she heard her name.
마지막까지 아니었다. / 그녀는 그녀의 이름을 들었다.
The head of the judges said, / "Congratulations, Sarah Parker! // You won first prize.
심사위원장이 말했다. / "축하해요 Sarah Parker! // 당신이 1등을 했습니다.
We loved the uniqueness / of your work."
우리는 독창성이 좋았어요. / 당신 작품의
Sarah was overcome with joy, / and she couldn't stop smiling.
Sarah는 기쁨에 휩싸였다. / 그리고 웃는 것을 멈출 수 없었다.
This experience meant / more than just winning; / it confirmed her identity / as an artist.
이 경험은 의미했다. / 단순한 우승 이상을 / 그리고 그녀의 정체성을 확인해 주었다. / 예술가로서의

그림 그리기를 좋아하는 젊은 예술가 Sarah는 지역 미술 대회에 참가했다. 다른 사람들이 만든 놀라운 예술 작품들을 보면서 그녀의 자신감은 떨어졌다. 그녀는 '내가 상을 받지 못할 수

(우측 단)

도 있겠네.'라고 조용히 생각했다. 심사의 순간이 다가왔고, 심사위원들은 수상자를 한 명씩 발표하기 시작했다. 그녀는 마지막에야 자신의 이름을 들었다. 심사위원장이 "축하해요, Sarah Parker! 당신이 1등을 했습니다. 당신 작품의 독창성이 좋았습니다."라고 말했다. Sarah는 기쁨에 휩싸였고 웃는 것을 멈출 수 없었다. 이 경험은 단순한 우승 이상을 의미했고, 그녀에게 예술가로서의 정체성을 확인해 주었다.

Why? 왜 정답일까?

수상자 발표 때 이름이 불리지 않다가 가장 마지막에 이름이 불리는 것을 들었다(It wasn't until the end that she heard her name.)는 글이다. 따라서 'I'의 심경 변화로 가장 적절한 것은 ⑤ '낙담한 → 기쁜'이다.

● artwork ⓝ 작품
● quietly ⓐⓓ 꽤
● prize ⓝ 상
● confirm ⓥ 확인하다
● regretful ⓐ 후회하는
● frightened ⓐ 놀란
● confidence ⓝ 자신감
● judgment ⓝ 심판, 심사
● overcome ⓥ 극복하다
● identity ⓝ 정체성
● disappointed ⓐ 실망하는
● discouraged ⓐ 낙담한

구문 풀이

[2행] As she looked at the amazing artworks made by others, her confidence
  접속사(~하면서)   주어   동사   주어
dropped.
동사

---

20 성공을 위한 인내심   정답률 82% | 정답 ①

다음 글에서 필자가 주장하는 바로 가장 적절한 것은?

✓ 성공하기 위해서는 인내심을 길러야 한다.
② 안락함을 추구하기보다 한계에 도전해야 한다.
③ 사회 변화의 속도에 맞춰 빠르게 대응해야 한다.
④ 기회를 기다리기보다 능동적으로 행동해야 한다.
⑤ 흥미를 잃지 않으려면 자신이 좋아하는 일을 해야 한다.

Too many times / people, especially in today's generation, / expect things to just happen
overnight.
너무나 많은 경우에 / 사람들, 특히 오늘날의 세대는 / 일이 하룻밤 사이에 일어나기를 기대한다.
When we have these false expectations, / it tends to discourage / us from continuing to
move forward.
우리가 이러한 잘못된 기대를 가질 때 / 그것은 방해하는 경향이 있다. / 우리가 계속해서 앞으로 나아가는 것을
Because this is a high tech society, / everything we want / has to be within the parameters /
of our comfort and convenience.
지금은 첨단 기술 사회이기 때문에 / 우리가 원하는 모든 것은 / 제한 내에 있어야 한다. / 우리의 편안함과 편리함이라는
If it doesn't happen fast enough, / we're tempted / to lose interest.
그 일이 충분히 빨리 일어나지 않으면 / 우리는 유혹을 받는다. / 흥미를 잃게끔
So many people don't want / to take the time / it requires to be successful.
그래서 많은 사람들은 원하지 않는다. / 시간을 들이는 것을 / 성공하는데 필요한
Success is not a matter / of mere desire; / you should develop patience / in order to achieve
it.
성공은 문제가 아니다. / 단순한 욕망의 / 여러분은 인내심을 길러야 한다. / 성공을 이루기 위해서
Have you fallen prey to impatience? // Great things take time to build.
여러분은 인내심의 먹이가 되어 본 적은 있는가? // 위대한 일이 일어나는 데에는 시간이 걸린다.

너무나 많은 경우에, 사람들, 특히 오늘날의 세대는, 일이 하룻밤 사이에 일어나기를 기대한다. 우리가 이러한 잘못된 기대를 가질 때, 그것은 우리가 계속해서 앞으로 나아가는 것을 방해하는 경향이 있다. 지금은 첨단 기술 사회이기 때문에, 우리가 원하는 모든 것은 편안함과 편리함이라는 제한 내에 있어야 한다. 그 일이 충분히 빨리 일어나지 않으면, 우리는 흥미를 잃게끔 유혹을 받는다. 그래서 많은 사람들은 성공하는 데 필요한 시간을 들이는 것을 원하지 않는다. 성공은 단순한 욕망의 문제가 아니다. 여러분은 그것(성공)을 이루기 위해 인내심을 길러야 한다. 여러분은 조바심의 먹잇감이 되어 본 적이 있는가? 위대한 일이 이루어지는 데에는 시간이 걸린다.

Why? 왜 정답일까?

요즘 사람들은 편안함과 편리함을 느끼며 일이 빨리 해결되기를 바라지만 성공을 위해서는 인내심이 필요하다(Success is not a matter of mere desire; you should develop patience in order to achieve it.)는 내용의 글이므로, 필자가 주장하는 바로 가장 적절한 것은 ① '성공하기 위해서는 인내심을 길러야 한다.'이다.

● expectation ⓝ 기대
● parameter ⓝ 매개 변수, 제한
● convenience ⓝ 편리
● mere ⓐ 단순한
● achieve ⓥ 이루다
● forward ⓐⓓ ~향해
● comfort ⓝ 편안
● tempt ⓥ 유혹하다
● desire ⓝ 욕망
● impatience ⓝ 조바심

구문 풀이

[10행] Have you fallen prey to impatience?
  현재완료(경험)

---

21 자율 주행 자동차에 빗대어 보는 환자   정답률 49% | 정답 ④

밑줄 친 we were still taping bricks to accelerators가 다음 글에서 의미하는 바로 가장 적절한 것은? [3점]

① the importance of medical education was overlooked
의학 교육의 중요성이 간과되었다
② self-driving cars enabled patients to move around freely
자율 자동차는 환자들이 자유롭게 이동할 수 있게 해주었다
③ the devices for safe driving were unavailable at that time
안전 운전을 위한 장치는 그 당시에 사용할 수 없었다
✓ lack of advanced tools posed a challenge in understanding patients
고급 도구의 부족은 환자들을 이해시키기에 어렵다
⑤ appropriate technologies led to success in developing a new medicine
새로운 약 개발을 성공으로 이끈 적절한 기술

If you had wanted / to create a "self-driving" car / in the 1950s, / your best option might have been / to strap a brick to the accelerator.
만약 원했다면 / '자율 주행' 자동차를 만들기를 / 1950년대에 / 가장 좋은 선택은 ~었을 것이다. / 가속 페달에 벽돌을 끈으로 묶는

Yes, / the vehicle would have been able to move forward / on its own, / but it could not slow down, stop, or turn / to avoid barriers.
물론, / 자동차는 앞으로 나아갈 수 있었다. / 스스로 / 하지만 속도를 줄이거나, 멈추거나, 방향을 전환할 수는 없었다. / 장애물을 피하기 위해서

Obviously not ideal.
분명히 이상적이지는 않다.

But / does that mean / the entire concept of the self-driving car / is not worth pursuing?
그러나 / 의미일까? / 자율 주행 자동차라는 전체 개념이 / 추구할 만한 가치가 없다는

No, / it only means / that at the time / we did not yet have the tools / we now possess / to help enable vehicles to operate / both autonomously and safely.
아니다. / 그것은 단지 의미할 뿐이다. / 그 당시에 / 우리가 아직 도구를 갖고 있지 않았다는 것을 / 우리가 지금 갖고 있는 / 자동차를 작동할 수 있도록 도와주는 / 자율적이면서 안전하게

This once-distant dream / now seems within our reach.
이 한때 멀게 느껴진 꿈은 / 이제 우리의 손이 닿는 곳에 있는 것처럼 보인다.

It is much the same story / in medicine.
이는 마찬가지이다. / 의학에서도

Two decades ago, / we were still taping bricks / to accelerators.
20년 전에 / 우리는 여전히 벽돌을 테이프로 묶어두고 있었다. / 가속 페달에

Today, / we are approaching the point / where we can begin to bring some appropriate technology / to bear in ways that advance / our understanding of patients / as unique individuals.
오늘날 / 우리는 지점에 접근하고 있다. / 우리가 적절한 기술을 도입하기 시작하는 지점에 / 증진하는 방식에 맞는 / 환자를 이해하는 것을 / 고유한 개인으로서

In fact, / many patients are already wearing devices / that monitor their conditions / in real time, / which allows doctors to talk to their patients / in a specific, refined, and feedback-driven way / that was not even possible a decade ago.
사실 / 많은 환자들이 이미 장치를 착용하고 있다. / 상태를 관찰하는 / 실시간으로 / 이는 의사가 환자에게 말할 수 있도록 해주었다. / 구체적으로도 정제되었으며 피드백을 기반으로 하는 방식으로 / 십 년 전에는 전혀 가능하지 않았던

만약 '자율 주행' 자동차를 1950년대에 만들기를 원했었다면, 가장 좋은 선택은 가속 페달에 벽돌을 끈으로 묶는 것이었을 것이다. 물론, 자동차가 스스로 앞으로 나아갈 수는 있었겠지만, 속도를 줄이거나 멈추거나 또는 장애물을 피하기 위해 방향을 전환할 수는 없었다. 분명히, 이상적이지는 않다. 그러나 그것이 자율 주행 자동차라는 전체 개념이 추구할 만한 가치가 없다는 의미일까? 아니다. 그것은 단지 우리가 지금은 갖고 있는, 자동차를 자율적이면서 안전하게 작동할 수 있도록 도와 주는 도구를, 그 당시에는 우리가 아직 갖고 있지 않았다는 것을 의미할 뿐이다. 한때 멀게만 느껴졌던 이 꿈이 이제 우리의 손이 닿는 곳에 있는 것처럼 보인다. 이는 의학에서도 마찬가지이다. 20년 전에, 우리는 여전히 가속 페달에 벽돌을 테이프로 묶어 두고 있었다. 오늘날, 우리는 환자를 고유한 개인으로서 이해하는 것을 증진하는 방식에 맞는 적절한 기술을 도입하기 시작하는 지점에 접근하고 있다. 사실, 많은 환자들이 이미 자신의 상태를 실시간으로 관찰하는 장치를 착용하고 있는데, 이는 의사가 구체적이고도 정제되었으며 피드백을 기반으로 하는, 십 년 전에는 전혀 가능하지 않았던 방식으로 환자에게 말할 수 있도록 해 주었다.

Why? 왜 정답일까?

그 당시 안전한 자율 주행이 가능하도록 돕는 도구가 없었다고(No, it only means that at the time we did not yet have the tools we now possess to help enable vehicles to operate both autonomously and safely.) 말하는 것으로 보아, 밑줄 친 부분의 의미로 가장 적절한 것은 ④ '고급 도구의 부족은 환자들을 이해시키기 어렵다'이다.

- **self-driving** 자율 주행의
- **strap** ⓝ 끈
- **accelerator** ⓝ 가속 페달
- **avoid** ⓥ 피하다
- **obviously** ⓐⓓ 명백히
- **concept** ⓝ 개념
- **operate** ⓥ 작동하다
- **reach** ⓥ 도달하다
- **patient** ⓝ 환자
- **monitor** ⓥ 감시하다
- **refined** ⓐ 제한된
- **appropriate** ⓐ 적절한
- **option** ⓝ 선택
- **brick** ⓝ 벽돌
- **vehicle** ⓝ 탈것
- **barrier** ⓝ 장애물
- **entire** ⓐ 전체의
- **possess** ⓥ 소유하다
- **autonomously** ⓐⓓ 자율의
- **medicine** ⓝ 의학
- **unique** ⓐ 고유의
- **specific** ⓐ 구체적인
- **overlook** ⓥ 간과하다

구문 풀이

1행 If you had wanted to create a "self-driving" car in the 1950s,
[가정법 과거 : If + 주어 + had p.p ~.]
your best option might have been to strap a brick to the accelerator.
[주어 + 조동사과거 + have p.p]

---

22 새로운 기술을 과대평가 하는 이유 정답률 47% | 정답 ②

다음 글의 요지로 가장 적절한 것은?

① 새로운 기술은 효율적인 시간 관리에 도움이 된다.
✓② 새로운 기술에 비해 기존 기술의 영향력이 간과되고 있다.
③ 현대 사회의 새로운 기술이 양육자의 역할을 대체하고 있다.
④ 새로운 기술의 사용을 장려하는 사회적 인식이 요구된다.
⑤ 기존 기술의 활용은 새로운 기술의 개발에 도움이 된다.

We tend to overrate the impact / of new technologies / in part / because older technologies have become absorbed / into the furniture of our lives, / so as to be almost invisible.
우리는 영향을 과대평가 하는 경향이 있다. / 새로운 기술의 / 부분적으로 / 그 이유는 기존 기술이 흡수되었기 때문이다. / 우리 삶의 일부로 / 눈에 거의 보이지 않을 만큼

Take the baby bottle.
젖병을 예로 들어 보자.

Here is a simple implement / that has transformed a fundamental human experience / for vast numbers of infants and mothers, / yet it finds no place in our histories of technology.
여기 단순한 도구가 있다. / 인간으로서의 근본적인 경험을 바꾼 / 수많은 영유아와 엄마들을 / 그러나 그것은 기술의 역사에서 그 자리를 찾지 못한다.

This technology might be thought of / as a classic time-shifting device, / as it enables mothers to exercise / more control / over the timing of feeding.
이 기술은 여겨진다. / 전형적으로 시간을 조절하는 장치라고 / 엄마가 발휘할 수 있게 하기 때문에 / 더 많은 통제력을 / 수유 시간에

It can also function to save time, / as bottle feeding allows for someone else to substitute for the mother's time.
또한 시간을 절약하는 기능도 한다. / 젖병 수유는 다른 사람이 엄마의 시간을 대신하도록 허락하기 때문에

Potentially, / therefore, / it has huge implications for the management of time / in everyday life, / yet it is entirely overlooked / in discussions of high-speed society.
잠재적으로 / 그러므로 / 그것은 시간 관리에 큰 영향을 미친다. / 일상생활의 / 그러나 완전히 간과되고 있다. / 빠른 속도의 사회적 논의에서는

우리는 새로운 기술의 영향을 과대평가하는 경향이 있는데, 부분적으로 그 이유는 기존 기술이 눈에 거의 보이지 않을 만큼 우리 삶의 일부로 흡수되었기 때문이다. 젖병을 예로 들어 보자. 여기 수많은 영유아와 엄마들의 인간으로서의 근본적인 경험을 바꿨으나, 기술의 역사에서 그 자리를 찾지 못한 단순한 도구가 있다. 이 기술은 전형적으로 시간을 조절하는 장치라고 여겨지는데 이는 엄마가 수유 시간에 대해 더 많은 통제력을 발휘할 수 있게 하기 때문이다. 또한 젖병 수유는 시간을 절약하는 기능도 하는데, 이는 다른 사람이 엄마의 (수유) 시간을 대신하도록 허락하기 때문이다. 그러므로, 잠재적으로 그것(젖병)은 일상생활의 시간 관리에 큰 영향을 미치지만, 빠른 속도의 사회적 논의에서는 완전히 간과되고 있다.

Why? 왜 정답일까?

새로운 기술을 과대평가하는 이유는 기존의 기술이 인간의 삶의 일부로 흡수되었기 때문이라는(We tend to overrate the impact of new technologies in part because older technologies have become absorbed into the furniture of our lives, so as to be almost invisible.) 내용이다. 따라서 글의 요지로 가장 적절한 것은 ② '새로운 기술에 비해 기존 기술의 영향력이 간과되고 있다.'이다.

- **overrate** ⓥ 과대평가하다
- **absorb** ⓥ 흡수하다
- **invisible** ⓐ 눈에 보이지 않는
- **transform** ⓥ 바꾸다
- **infant** ⓝ 유아
- **implication** ⓝ 영향
- **discussion** ⓝ 논의
- **impact** ⓝ 영향
- **furniture** ⓝ 가구
- **implement** ⓝ 도구
- **fundamental** ⓐ 기초의
- **substitute for** ~을 대신하다
- **overlook** ⓥ 간과하다
- **society** ⓝ 사회

구문 풀이

1행 We tend to overrate the impact of new technologies in part because [to부정사]
older technologies have become absorbed into the furniture of our lives, so as to [현재완료수동태] [「so as to : ~할 만큼」]
be almost invisible.

★★★ 등급을 가르는 문제!

23 사업에서의 공감 정답률 42% | 정답 ⑤

다음 글의 주제로 가장 적절한 것은?

① diverse benefits of good market research
좋은 시장 조사의 다양한 이점들
② negative factors in making business decisions
사업 결정에 있어서 부정적인 요소들
③ difficulties in designing products with empathic concern
공감할 수 있는 제품을 디자인하는 것의 어려움
④ efforts to build cognitive empathy among employees
직원들 간의 인지적 공감을 형성하기 위한 노력
✓⑤ different interpretations of empathy in business
사업상의 공감에 대한 다양한 해석

Empathy is frequently listed / as one of the most desired skills / in an employer or employee, / although without specifying exactly / what is meant by *empathy*.
공감은 목록에 종종 오른다. / 가장 바라는 기술 중 하나로 / 고용주나 직원에게 / 정확히 명시하지는 않지만 / '공감'이 무엇을 의미하는지

Some businesses stress cognitive empathy, / emphasizing the need for leaders to understand / the perspective of employees and customers / when negotiating deals and making decisions.
일부 기업은 인지적 공감을 강조한다. / 리더가 이해할 필요성에 중점을 두면서 / 직원과 고객의 관점을 / 거래를 협상하고 결정을 내릴 때

Others stress affective empathy and empathic concern, / emphasizing the ability of leaders / to gain trust from employees and customers / by treating them with real concern and compassion.
다른 기업은 정서적 공감과 공감적 관심을 강조한다. / 리더의 능력을 강조하면서 / 직원과 고객에게 신뢰를 얻는 / 진정한 관심과 동정심으로 그들을 대함으로써

When some consultants argue / that successful companies foster empathy, / what that translates to is / that companies should conduct good market research.
일부 자문 위원이 주장할 때 / 성공하려는 기업은 공감 능력을 길러야 한다고 / 그것이 의미하는 바는 ~이다. / 기업이 시장 조사를 잘 수행해야 한다는 것

In other words, / an "empathic" company understands the needs and wants of its customers / and seeks to fulfill those needs and wants.
다시 말해 / '공감적인' 기업은 고객의 필요와 요구를 이해한다. / 그리고 그 필요와 요구를 충족시키기 위해 노력한다.

When some people speak of design with empathy, / what that translates to is / that companies should take into account the specific needs / of different populations — the blind, the deaf, the elderly, non-English speakers, the color-blind, and so on / — when designing products.
일부 사람들이 공감을 담은 디자인을 말할 때 / 그것이 의미하는 바는 ~이다. / 기업이 구체적인 필요 사항을 고려해야 한다는 것 / 다양한 사람들의 시각 장애인, 청각 장애인, 노인, 비영어권 화자, 색맹 등 / 제품을 디자인 할 때

'공감'이 무엇을 의미하는지 정확히 명시하지는 않지만, 공감은 고용주나 직원에게 가장 바라는 기술 중 하나로 목록에 종종 오른다. 일부 기업은 인지적 공감을 강조하여 리더가 거래를 협상하고 결정을 내릴 때 직원과 고객의 관점을 이해할 필요성에 중점을 둔다. 다른 기업은 정서적 공감과 공감적 관심을 강조하여 진정한 관심과 동정심으로 직원과 고객을 대함으로써 그들에게 신뢰를 얻는 리더의 능력에 중점을 둔다. 일부 자문 위원이 성공하려는 기업은 공감 능력을 길러야 한다고 주장할 때, 그것이 의미하는 바는 기업이 시장 조사를 잘 수행해야 한다는 것이다. 다시 말해, '공감적인' 기업은 고객의 필요와 요구를 이해하고, 그 필요와 요구를 충족시키기 위해 노력한다. 일부 사람들이 공감을 담은 디자인을 말할 때, 그것이 의미하는

바는 기업이 제품을 디자인할 때 시각 장애인, 청각 장애인, 노인, 비영어권 화자, 색맹 등 다양한 사람들의 구체적인 필요 사항을 고려해야 한다는 것이다.

Why? 왜 정답일까?

기업은 '공감'을 정확하게 밝히고 있지 않지만, 기업별로 다르게 해석하여 직원의 필수 덕목으로 추구하고 있다는 내용이다. (Empathy is frequently listed as one of the most desired skills in an employer or employee, although without specifying exactly what is meant by *empathy*.) 따라서 글의 주제로 가장 적절한 것은 ⑤ '사업상의 공감에 대한 다양한 해석'이다.

- empathy ⓝ 공감
- specify ⓥ 구체화하다
- perspective ⓝ 관점
- deal ⓥ 거래하다
- concern ⓝ 관심
- consultants ⓝ 자문 위원
- seek ⓥ 추구하다
- diverse ⓐ 다양한
- frequently ⓐⓓ 종종
- cognitive ⓐ 인지적인
- negotiate ⓥ 협상하다
- affective ⓐ 정서적인
- compassion ⓝ 열정
- foster ⓥ 기르다
- fulfill ⓥ 이행하다
- interpretation ⓝ 이해

구문 풀이

3행 Some businesses stress cognitive empathy, emphasizing the need for
분사구문(= as they emphasize)
leaders to understand the perspective of employees and customers when
분사구문(병렬1)
negotiating deals and making decisions.
분사구문(병렬2)

★★ 문제 해결 꿀~팁 ★★

▶ 많이 틀린 이유는?
기업은 공감을 정확히 명시하고 있지 않지만 직원에게 바라는 기술로 여기며, 어떤 기업은 인지적 공감에, 어떤 기업은 정서적 공감에, 어떤 기업은 고객의 필요와 요구를 파악하는 공감에 중점을 두고 있다고 얘기하고 있다. ⑤를 제외한 나머지 선택지는 글에 언급된 단어를 이용하여 만들어졌으나 글 전체를 아우르는 얘기와는 거리가 멀다.

▶ 문제 해결 방법은?
글에서 나온 단어가 등장하더라도 주제와 맞는지, 너무 지엽적인 부분을 이야기하고 있거나 성급한 일반화를 하고 있진 않은지 파악해야 한다.

---

24 디지털 시대 아이들의 고충 정답률 70% | 정답 ⑤

다음 글의 제목으로 가장 적절한 것은?

① From Symbols to Bytes: History of Communication
기호에서 바이트까지: 통신의 역사
② Parents' Desire to Keep Their Children Within Reach
아이들을 곁에 두고 싶은 부모님의 바람
③ Building Trust: The Key to Ideal Human Relationships
친숙한 경험을 추구하는 것에 대한 인간의 끝없는 욕망
④ The Positive Role of Digital Technology in Teen Friendships
인간 생존의 대가로의 자연 파괴
✔ Connected but Stressed: Challenges for Kids in the Digital Era
연결되어 있지만 스트레스 받는: 디지털 시대의 아이들을 위한 과제

The most prevalent problem kids report / is that they feel like / they need to be accessible at all times.
아이들이 이야기하는 가장 일반적인 문제는 / 그들이 느낀다는 것이다. / 그들이 항상 연락될 수 있어야 한다고
Because technology allows for it, / they feel an obligation.
기술이 그것을 허용하기 때문에 / 그들은 의무감을 느낀다.
It's easy for most of us to relate / — you probably feel the same pressure / in your own life!
우리 대부분은 공감하기 쉽다 / 아마 여러분은 같은 압박을 느낄 것이다. / 자신의 삶에서
It is really challenging to deal / with the fact / that we're human and can't always respond instantly.
대처하는 것은 매우 힘들다. / 사실에 / 우리가 인간이고 항상 즉각적으로 응답할 수 없다는
For a teen or tween / who's still learning the ins and outs of social interactions, / it's even worse.
십대나 십대 초반의 아동에게 / 아직 사회적 상호 작용의 세부적인 것들을 배우고 있는 / 상황은 훨씬 더 심각하다.
Here's how this behavior plays out sometimes: / Your child texts one of his friends, / and the friend doesn't text back right away.
때때로 이 행동이 나타나는 방식은 다음과 같다: / 예를 들어 여러분의 자녀가 친구 중 한 명에게 문자 메시지를 보낸다. / 그리고 친구가 즉시 답장을 보내지 않는다.
Now it's easy for your child to think, / "This person doesn't want to be my friend anymore!"
이제 여러분의 자녀는 생각하기 쉽다. / "얘는 더 이상 내 친구가 되기를 원하지 않는구나!"라고
So he texts again, and again, and again / — "blowing up their phone."
그래서 그는 다시, 다시, 그리고 또 다시 문자 메시지를 보낸다. / 그리고 '전화기를 폭파하는 것'이다.
This can be stress-inducing / and even read as aggressive.
이것은 스트레스를 유발할 수 있다. / 그리고 공격적인 것으로 읽힐 수도 있다.
But you can see / how easily this could happen.
그러나 여러분은 볼 수 있다. / 이것이 얼마나 쉽게 일어날 수 있는지

아이들이 이야기하는 가장 일반적인 문제는 그들이 항상 연락될 수 있어야 한다고 느낀다는 것이다. 기술이 그것을 허용하기 때문에, 그들은 의무감을 느낀다. 우리 대부분은 공감하기 쉬운데, 아마 여러분도 자신의 삶에서 같은 압박을 느낄 것이다! 우리가 인간이고 항상 즉각적으로 응답할 수 없다는 사실에 대처하는 것은 매우 힘들다. 아직 사회적 상호 작용의 세부적인 것들을 배우고 있는 십대(13~19세)나 십대 초반(10~12세)의 아동에게 상황은 훨씬 더 심각하다. 때때로 이 행동이 나타나는 방식은 다음과 같다. 예를 들어, 여러분의 자녀가 친구 중 한 명에게 문자 메시지를 보내고, 그 친구가 즉시 답장을 보내지 않는다면, 이제 여러분의 자녀는 "얘는 더 이상 내 친구가 되기를 원하지 않는구나!"라고 생각하기 쉽다. 그래서 다시, 다시, 그리고 또 다시 문자 메시지를 보내다가, '전화기를 폭파하는(과부하 상태로 만드는)' 것이다. 이것은 스트레스를 유발하고, 심지어 공격적인 것으로 읽힐 수 있다. 하지만 여러분은 이것이 얼마나 쉽게 일어날 수 있는지 알 수 있다.

Why? 왜 정답일까?

디지털 시대의 아이들은 기술의 발달로 인해 부모님과 항상 연락이 되어야 한다는 의무감을 느끼고 있다는 (The most prevalent problem kids report is that they feel like they need to be accessible at all times. Because technology allows for it, they feel an obligation.)

내용이므로, 글의 제목으로 가장 적절한 것은 ⑤ '연결되어 있지만 스트레스 받는: 디지털 시대의 아이들을 위한 과제'이다.

- prevalent ⓐ 일반적인
- obligation ⓝ 의무
- accessible ⓐ 연락될 수 있는
- induce ⓥ 유발하다

구문 풀이

14행 But you can see how easily this could happen.
「간접의문문: 의문사 + 형용사/부사 + 주어 + 동사」

---

25 동물성 단백질 섭취량 정답률 85% | 정답 ⑤

다음 도표의 내용과 일치하지 <u>않는</u> 것은?

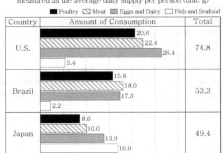

Animal Protein Consumption, 2020
measured as the average daily supply per person (unit: g)

■ Poultry ▧ Meat ▤ Eggs and Dairy □ Fish and Seafood

Country	Amount of Consumption	Total
U.S.	20.6 / 22.4 / 26.4 / 5.4	74.8
Brazil	15.8 / 18.0 / 17.3 / 2.2	53.3
Japan	8.6 / 10.0 / 13.9 / 16.9	49.4

5 10 15 20 25 30 (unit: g)

The graph above shows the animal protein consumption / measured as the average daily supply per person / in three different countries in 2020.
위 그래프는 동물성 단백질 섭취량을 나타낸다. / 1인당 일일 평균 공급량으로 측정한 / 2020년 3개국의
① The U.S. showed / the largest amount of total animal protein consumption / per person among the three countries.
미국은 나타났다. / 총 동물성 단백질 섭취량이 가장 많은 것으로 / 3개국 중 1인당
② Eggs and Dairy was the top animal protein consumption source / among four categories in the U.S., / followed by Meat and Poultry at 22.4g and 20.6g, respectively.
계란과 유제품이 가장 많은 동물성 단백질 공급원이었다. / 미국에서 네 가지 범주 가운데 / 육류와 가금류가 각각 22.4g과 20.6g으로 그 뒤를 이었다.
③ Unlike the U.S., / Brazil consumed / the most animal protein from Meat, / with Eggs and Dairy being the second most.
미국과 달리 / 브라질은 섭취했다. / 가장 많은 동물성 단백질을 / 육류로부터 / 계란과 유제품을 두 번째로 많이 섭취했다.
④ Japan had less than 50g / of the total animal protein consumption / per person, / which was the smallest among the three countries.
일본은 50g 미만을 가지고 있었다. / 총 동물 단백질 섭취량의 / 1인당 / 이는 세 나라 중 가장 적은 양이었다.
✔ Fish and Seafood, / which was the least consumed animal protein consumption source / in the U.S. and Brazil, / ranked the second highest in Japan.
생선과 해산물은 / 가장 적게 섭취한 동물성 단백질 섭취원이었다. / 미국과 브라질에서 / 일본에서는 두 번째로 높은 순위를 차지했다.

위 그래프는 2020년 3개국의 1인당 일일 평균 공급량으로 측정한 동물성 단백질 섭취량을 나타낸다. ① 미국은 3개국 중 1인당 총 동물성 단백질 섭취량이 가장 많은 것으로 나타났다. ② 계란과 유제품이 미국에서 네 가지 범주 가운데 가장 많은 동물성 단백질 공급원이었고, 육류와 가금류가 각각 22.4g과 20.6g으로 그 뒤를 이었다. ③ 미국과 달리, 브라질은 가장 많은 동물성 단백질을 육류로부터 섭취했고, 계란과 유제품을 두 번째로 많이 섭취했다. ④ 일본은 1인당 50g 미만의 총 동물 단백질을 섭취했고, 이는 세 나라 중 가장 적은 양이었다. ⑤ 생선과 해산물은 미국과 브라질에서 가장 적게 섭취한 동물성 단백질 섭취원이었는데, 일본에서는 두 번째로 높은 순위를 차지했다.

Why? 왜 정답일까?

도표에 따르면 생선과 해산물은 일본에서 첫 번째로 높은 순위를 차지하는 동물성 단백질 섭취원이다. 따라서 도표와 일치하지 않는 것은 ⑤이다.

- protein ⓝ 단백질
- dairy ⓝ 유제품
- rank ⓥ 차지하다
- consumption ⓝ 섭취
- poultry ⓝ 가금류

구문 풀이

5행 Eggs and Dairy was the top animal protein consumption source among four categories in the U.S., followed by Meat and Poultry at 22.4g and 20.6g,
「A be followed by B : A에 뒤이어 B가 나타나다」
respectively.

---

26 Theodore von Kármán의 학술적 역사 정답률 85% | 정답 ④

Theodore von Kármán에 관한 다음 글의 내용과 일치하지 <u>않는</u> 것은?

① 어린 시절 수학과 과학에 재능을 보였다.
② University of Göttingen에서 공학 박사 학위를 받았다.
③ 1920년대에 강연자 겸 자문 위원으로 다니기 시작했다.
✔ Caltech의 공학자를 초청하여 조언을 구했다.
⑤ National Medal of Science를 받았다.

Theodore von Kármán, a Hungarian-American engineer, / was one of the greatest minds of the twentieth century.
Theodore von Kármán은 헝가리계 미국인 공학자로 / 20세기의 가장 위대한 지성 중 한 명이었다.
「He was born in Hungary / and at an early age, / he showed a talent for math and science.」
그는 헝가리에서 태어났다. / 그리고 어린 시절에 / 그는 수학과 과학에 재능을 보였다. ①의 근거 일치
「In 1908, / he received a doctoral degree in engineering / at the University of Göttingen in Germany.」 ②의 근거 일치
1908년에 / 그는 공학 박사 학위를 받았다. / 독일의 University of Göttingen에서

『In the 1920s, / he began traveling / as a lecturer and consultant to industry.』 ③의근거 일치
1920년대에, 그는 다니기 시작했다. / 관련 분야의 강연자 겸 자문 위원으로

『He was invited to the United States / to advise engineers on the design of a wind tunnel / at California Institute of Technology (Caltech).』 ④의근거 불일치
그는 미국에 초청되었다. / 공학자들에게 윈드 터널 설계에 관한 조언을 하기 위해서 / 캘리포니아 공과대학(Caltech)에서

He became the director of the Guggenheim Aeronautical Laboratory / at Caltech in 1930.
그는 Guggenheim Aeronautical Laboratory의 소장이 되었다. / 1930년에 Caltech의

『Later, / he was awarded the National Medal of Science / for his leadership in science and engineering.』 ⑤의근거 일치
나중에는 / 그는 National Medal of Science를 받았다. / 과학과 공학 분야에서의 리더십으로

Theodore von Kármán은 헝가리계 미국인 공학자로, 20세기의 가장 위대한 지성인 중 한 명이었다. 그는 헝가리에서 태어나 어린 시절 수학과 과학에 재능을 보였다. 1908년, 독일 University of Göttingen에서 공학 박사 학위를 받았다. 1920년대에, 관련 분야의 강연자 겸 자문 위원으로 다니기 시작했다. 캘리포니아 공과대학(Caltech)에서 공학자들에게 윈드 터널 설계에 관한 조언을 하기 위해 미국에 초청되었다. 1930년에 Caltech의 Guggenheim Aeronautical Laboratory의 소장이 되었다. 나중에는 과학과 공학 분야에서의 리더십으로 National Medal of Science를 받았다.

Why? 왜 정답일까?
'He was invited to the United States to advise engineers on the design of a wind tunnel at California Institute of Technology (Caltech).'에서 Caltech에 초청되어 조언을 했다고 하므로, 내용과 일치하지 않는 것은 ④ 'Claltech의 공학자를 초청하여 조언을 구했다.'이다.

Why? 왜 오답일까?
① 'He was born in Hungary and at an early age, he showed a talent for math and science.'의 내용과 일치한다.
② 'In 1908, he received a doctoral degree in engineering at the University of Göttingen in Germany.'의 내용과 일치한다.
③ 'In the 1920s, he began traveling as a lecturer and consultant to industry.'의 내용과 일치한다.
⑤ 'Later, he was awarded the National Medal of Science for his leadership in science and engineering.'의 내용과 일치한다.

● mind ⓝ 지성인
● lecturer ⓝ 강사, 강연자
● advise ⓥ 조언하다
● doctoral degree 박사 학위
● consultant ⓝ 자문 위원
● award ⓥ 수상하다

구문 풀이

7행 He was invited to the United States to advise engineers on the design of
전치사 to / to부정사(부사적)
a wind tunnel at California Institute of Technology (Caltech).

---

27 라떼 아트 수업 정답률 93% | 정답 ③

Basic Latte Art Class에 관한 다음 안내문의 내용과 일치하지 <u>않는</u> 것은?
① 세 가지 라떼 아트 디자인을 직접 만들 것이다.
② 수업은 4시간 동안 진행된다.
☑ 등록은 4월 24일부터 시작된다.
④ 비용에 재료비가 포함되어 있다.
⑤ 우유를 마시지 않는 사람은 대체 유제품을 사용할 수 있다.

Basic Latte Art Class
기초 라떼 아트 수업

Make perfect lattes / and present them / in the most beautiful way!
완벽한 라떼를 만들어 보세요. / 그리고 표현해 보세요. / 가장 아름다운 방법으로

In this class, / you will learn / how to steam and pour milk.
이 수업에서 / 여러분은 배울 것입니다. / 우유를 데우고 따르는 방법을

『You will make three latte art designs / on your own: / heart, tulip, and leaf.』 ①의근거 일치
여러분은 세 가지 라떼 아트 디자인을 만들 것입니다. / 직접 / 하트, 튤립, 그리고 나뭇잎

Date: April 27, 2024
날짜: 2024년 4월 27일

『Time: 9 a.m. – 1 p.m.』 ②의근거 일치
시간: 오전 9시 ~ 오후 1시

Place: Camefort Community Center
장소: Camefort 커뮤니티 센터

Registration & Fee
등록 & 비용

『Register online at www.camefortcc.com, from April 22 to April 24.』 ③의근거 불일치
온라인으로 등록하세요. / www.camefortcc.com에서 / 4월 22일부터 4월 24일까지

『$60 per person (cost of ingredients included)』 ④의근거 일치
1인당 60달러 (재료비 포함)

Notes
참고

『Dairy alternatives will be available / for non-milk drinkers.』 ⑤의근거 일치
대체 유제품을 사용할 수 있습니다. / 우유를 마시지 않는 사람은

Students can get a 10% discount.
학생은 10$ 할인을 받을 수 있습니다.

기초 라떼 아트 수업

완벽한 라떼를 만들어 가장 아름다운 방법으로 표현해 보세요! 이 수업에서, 여러분은 우유를 데우고 따르는 방법을 배울 것입니다. 여러분은 세 가지 라떼 아트 디자인(하트, 튤립, 그리고 나뭇잎)을 직접 만들 것입니다.

날짜: 2024년 4월 27일
시간: 오전 9시 ~ 오후 1시
장소: Camefort 커뮤니티 센터
등록 & 비용
• 4월 22일부터 4월 24일까지 www.camefortcc.com에서 온라인으로 등록하세요.

• 1인당 60달러 (재료비 포함)
참고
• 우유를 마시지 않는 사람은 대체 유제품을 사용할 수 있습니다.
• 학생은 10% 할인을 받을 수 있습니다.

Why? 왜 정답일까?
'Register online at www.camefortcc.com, from April 22 to April 24.'에서 4월 22일부터 등록이 시작된다고 하므로, 안내문의 내용과 일치하지 않는 것은 ③ '등록은 4월 24일부터 시작된다.'이다.

Why? 왜 오답일까?
① 'You will make three latte art designs on your own: heart, tulip, and leaf.'의 내용과 일치한다.
② 'Time: 9 a.m. – 1 p.m.'의 내용과 일치한다.
④ '$60 per person (cost of ingredients included)'의 내용과 일치한다.
⑤ 'Dairy alternatives will be available for non-milk drinkers'의 내용과 일치한다.

● present ⓥ 표현하다
● ingredient ⓝ 재료
● pour ⓥ 따르다
● alternative ⓝ 대체품

---

28 야간 하이킹 행사 안내 정답률 92% | 정답 ④

Family Night-hiking Event에 관한 다음 안내문의 내용과 일치하는 것은?
① 토요일과 일요일 이틀간 진행된다.
② 오후 5시에 시작된다.
③ 어른과 어린이의 참가비는 같다.
☑ 어린이는 법적 보호자를 동반해야 한다.
⑤ 추첨을 통해 구급상자가 무료로 제공된다.

Family Night-hiking Event
가족 야간 하이킹 이벤트

Join us / for a fun-filled night / of hiking and family bonding!
함께하세요. / 즐거움이 가득한 밤을 / 하이킹과 가족 간의 유대로

『Date: Saturday, May 4』 ①의근거 불일치
날짜: 5월 4일, 토요일

『Time: 6 p.m. – 9 p.m.』 ②의근거 불일치
시간: 오후 6시~9시

Location: Skyline Preserve
장소: Skyline 보호 구역

Cost
비용

『Adults: $20』
성인: 20달러

『Children under 19: $10』 ③의근거 불일치
19세 미만 어린이: 10달러

Guidelines
지침

『Children must be accompanied / by legal guardians.』 ④의근거 일치
어린이는 동반해야만 합니다. / 법적 보호자를

Bring a flashlight and a bottle of water.
손전등과 물 한 병을 가져오세요.

Follow the instructions of the guides / at all times.
안내원의 지시를 따라오세요. / 항상

Registration
등록

Visit www.familyhiking.com / and register by April 26.
www.familyhiking.com에 방문하세요. / 그리고 4월 26일까지 등록하세요.

『A free first aid kit is provided / for all who register by April 12.』 ⑤의근거 불일치
구급상자가 무료로 제공됩니다. / 4월 12일까지 등록하는 모든 분께

가족 야간 하이킹 이벤트

하이킹과 가족 간의 유대로 즐거움이 가득한 밤을 함께하세요!

날짜: 5월 4일, 토요일
시간: 오후 6시 ~ 9시
장소: Skyline 보호 구역
비용
• 성인: 20달러
• 19세 미만 어린이: 10달러
지침
• 어린이는 법적 보호자를 동반해야 합니다.
• 손전등과 물 한 병을 가져오세요.
• 항상 안내원의 지시를 따라 주세요.
등록
• www.familyhiking.com에 방문하여 4월 26일까지 등록하세요.
• 4월 12일까지 등록하시는 모든 분께 구급상자가 무료로 제공됩니다.

Why? 왜 정답일까?
'Children must be accompanied by legal guardians.'에서 어린이는 법적 보호자를 동반해야 한다는 지침을 안내하고 있으므로, 안내문의 내용과 일치하는 것은 ④ '어린이는 법적 보호자를 동반해야 한다.'이다.

Why? 왜 오답일까?
① 'Date: Saturday, May 4'에서 토요일 하루만 진행한다고 하였다.
② 'Time: 6 p.m. – 9 p.m.'에서 오후 여섯시에 시작한다고 하였다.
③ 'Adults: $20, Children under 19: $10'에서 어른은 20달러 어린이는 10달러로 참가비가 다른 것을 알 수 있다.
⑤ 'A free first aid kit is provided for all who register by April 12.'에서 4월 12일까지 등록하는 모든 분께 구급상자를 무료로 제공한다고 하였다.

- preserve 보호 구역
- instruction ⓝ 지시
- be accompanied by ~을 동반하다

29 상상을 통한 행동 교정
정답률 45% | 정답 ④

다음 글의 밑줄 친 부분 중, 어법상 틀린 것은?

For years, / many psychologists have held strongly to the belief / ① that the key to addressing negative health habits / is to change behavior.
수년 동안 / 많은 심리학자들이 믿음을 굳게 갖고 있었다. / 부정적인 건강 습관을 해결하기 위한 열쇠는 / 행동을 바꾸는 것이라는
This, / more than values and attitudes, / ② is the part of personality / that is easiest to change.
이것이 / 가치관이나 태도보다 / 성격의 한 부분이다. / 바꾸기 가장 쉬운
Ingestive habits such as smoking, drinking and various eating behaviors / are the most common health concerns / targeted for behavioral changes.
흡연, 음주, 그리고 다양한 섭식 행동과 같은 섭취 습관은 / 가장 일반적인 건강 문제이다. / 행동 변화의 대상이 되는
Process-addiction behaviors (workaholism, shopaholism, and the like) / fall into this category / as well.
과정 중독 행동(일중독, 쇼핑 중독 등) / 이 범주에 속한다 / 또한
Mental imagery combined with power of suggestion / was taken up as the premise of behavioral medicine / to help people change negative health behaviors / into positive ③ ones.
암시의 힘과 결합된 마음속 이미지는 / 행동 의학의 전제가 되었다. / 사람들이 부정적인 건강 행동을 긍정적인 것으로 바꾸는데 도움을 주는
Although this technique alone will not produce changes, / when ✔ used alongside other behavior modification tactics and coping strategies, / behavioral changes have proved effective / for some people.
이 기술만으로는 변화를 만들어내지 않지만, / 다른 행동 수정 기법 및 대응 전략과 함께 사용되면, / 행동 변화가 효과적인 것으로 입증되었다. / 일부 사람들에게는
⑤ What mental imagery does is reinforce / a new desired behavior.
마음속 이미지가 하는 일은 강화하는 것이다. / 새로운 바람직한 행동을
Repeated use of images / reinforces the desired behavior / more strongly over time.
이미지의 반복적 사용은 / 그 바람직한 행동을 강화한다. / 시간이 지남에 따라 더욱 강력하게

수년 동안 많은 심리학자들이 부정적인 건강 습관을 해결하기 위한 열쇠는 행동을 바꾸는 것이라는 믿음을 굳게 갖고 있었다. 가치관이나 태도보다, 이것이 가장 바꾸기 쉬운 성격의 한 부분이다. 흡연, 음주, 그리고 다양한 섭식 습관과 같은 섭취 습관은 행동 변화의 대상이 되는 가장 일반적인 건강 문제이다. 과정 중독 행동(일중독, 쇼핑 중독 등) 또한 이 범주에 속한다. 암시의 힘과 결합된 마음속 이미지는 사람들이 부정적인 건강 행동을 긍정적인 것으로 바꾸는 데 도움을 주는 행동 의학의 전제가 되었다. 이 기술만으로는 변화를 만들어 내지는 않지만, 다른 행동 수정 기법 및 대응 전략과 함께 사용되면, 행동 변화가 일부 사람들에게는 효과적인 것으로 입증되었다. 마음속 이미지가 하는 일은 새로운 바람직한 행동을 강화하는 것이다. 이미지의 반복적 사용은 시간이 지남에 따라 그 바람직한 행동을 더욱 강력하게 강화한다.

Why? 왜 정답일까?
주어는 주절의 주어 this technique과 같이 생략되었다. 주어와의 관계를 생각해 보면 using이 아니라 수동의 형태인 used로 고쳐야 한다. 따라서 어법상 틀린 것은 ④이다.

Why? 왜 오답일까?
① belief에 대해 구체적으로 설명해주는 동격의 접속사 that이다.
② 주어는 this로 단수 형태이기에 단수 동사 is가 오는 것이 맞다.
③ ones는 앞의 behaviors를 대신하는 대명사로 복수형이 오는 것이 맞다.
⑤ 관계대명사 what으로 선행사를 포함하고 있으며 주어 역할을 하고 있다.

- psychologist ⓝ 심리학자
- personality ⓝ 성격
- imagery ⓝ 사진
- behavioral ⓐ 행동의
- modification ⓝ 수정
- cope ⓥ 대응하다
- reinforce ⓥ 강화하다
- attitude ⓝ 태도
- ingestive ⓐ 섭취의
- premise ⓝ 전제
- alongside ~와 함께
- tactics ⓝ 기법
- strategy ⓝ 전략

구문 풀이
15행 What mental imagery does is reinforce a new desired behavior.
선행사를 포함한 관계대명사 / 단수 동사

★★★ 등급을 가르는 문제!

30 청소년기의 감정 사회화
정답률 28% | 정답 ③

다음 글의 밑줄 친 부분 중, 문맥상 낱말의 쓰임이 적절하지 않은 것은? [3점]

Emotion socialization / — learning from other people about emotions / and how to deal with them / — starts early in life / and plays a foundational role / for emotion regulation development.
감정 사회화는 / 다른 사람들로부터 감정을 배우는 / 그리고 감정을 다루는 방법을 / 어릴 때부터 시작된다. / 그리고 기초적인 역할을 한다 / 감정 조절 발달에
Although / extra-familial influences, such as peers or media, / gain in importance / during adolescence, / parents remain the ① primary socialization agents.
하지만 / 또래나 미디어와 같은 가족 이외의 영향이 / 중요해진다 / 청소년기에는 / 부모는 여전히 주된 사회화 주체이다.
For example, / their own responses to emotional situations / serve as a role model for emotion regulation, / increasing the likelihood / that their children will show ② similar reactions / in comparable situations.
예를 들어 / 감정적 상황에 대한 부모 자신의 반응이 / 감정 조절의 롤 모델이 된다. / 가능성을 높인다. / 자녀가 유사한 반응을 보일 / 비슷한 상황에서
Parental practices at times / when their children are faced with emotional challenges / also impact emotion regulation development.
그때 부모의 (습관적) 행동은 / 자녀가 정서적 어려움에 직면했을 때 / 또한 감정 조절 발달에 영향을 미친다.
Whereas / direct soothing and directive guidance / of what to do / are beneficial for younger children, / they may ✔ intrude on adolescents' autonomy striving.
반면에 / 직접적인 위로와 지시적 안내는 / 어떻게 해야 하는지에 대한 / 어린 자녀에게 도움이 된다. / 그들은 아마도 청소년의 자율성 추구를 방해할 수 있다.
In consequence, / adolescents might pull away from, / rather than turn toward, / their parents / in times of emotional crisis, / unless parental practices are ④ adjusted.
결과적으로 / 청소년은 더 멀어질 수 있다. / 의지하기보다 오히려 / 부모로부터 / 정서적 위기 상황에서 / 부모의 행동이 조정되지 않는다면
More suitable in adolescence / is ⑤ indirect support / of autonomous emotion regulation, / such as through interest in, / as well as awareness and nonjudgmental acceptance of, / adolescents' emotional experiences, / and being available / when the adolescent wants to talk.
청소년기에 더 적합한 것은 / 간접적으로 지원하는 것이다. / 자율적 감정 조절을 / (그에 대한) 관심 같은 방법으로 / 인식과 무비판적 수용뿐만 아니라 / 청소년의 정서적 경험에 대한 / 그리고 곁에 있어 주는 것이다. / 청소년이 대화하고 싶을 때

다른 사람들로부터 감정과 감정을 다루는 방법을 배우는 감정 사회화는 어릴 때부터 시작되며 감정 조절 발달에 기초적인 역할을 한다. 청소년기에는 또래나 미디어와 같은 가족 이외의 영향이 중요해지지만, 부모는 여전히 주된 사회화 주체이다. 예를 들어, 감정적 상황에 대한 부모 자신의 반응이 감정 조절의 롤 모델이 되어 자녀가 비슷한 상황에서 유사한 반응을 보일 가능성을 높인다. 자녀가 정서적 어려움에 직면했을 때 부모의 (습관적) 행동 또한 감정 조절 발달에 영향을 미친다. 직접적인 위로와 어떻게 해야 하는지에 대한 지시적 안내가 어린 자녀에게는 도움이 되는 반면, 청소년의 자율성 추구를 장려할 수(→ 방해할 수) 있다. 결과적으로 부모의 행동이 조정되지 않는다면, 청소년은 정서적 위기 상황에서 부모에게 의지하기보다 오히려 부모로부터 멀어질 수 있다. 청소년기에 더 적합한 것은 청소년의 정서적 경험에 대한 인식과 무비판적 수용뿐만 아니라 (그에 대한) 관심, 그리고 청소년이 대화하고 싶을 때 곁에 있어 주는 것과 같은 방법으로 자율적 감정 조절을 간접적으로 지원하는 것이다.

Why? 왜 정답일까?
자녀가 정서적 어려움에 직면했을 때 부모의 직접적인 개입은 청소년의 자율성 추구를 방해할 수 있다는 말이 논리적으로 옳다. 따라서 cultivate를 intrude on으로 고쳐야 한다.

- regulation ⓝ 규제
- socialization ⓝ 사회화
- comparable ⓐ 비슷한
- directive ⓐ 지시적인
- cultivate ⓥ 구축하다
- adolescence ⓝ 청소년기
- agent ⓝ 주체
- soothing ⓝ 위로
- beneficial ⓐ 도움이 되는
- adjust ⓥ 조정하다

구문 풀이
10행 Parental practices at times when their children are faced with emotional challenges also impact emotion regulation development.
관계부사 / 수동태

★★ 문제 해결 꿀~팁 ★★
▶ 많이 틀린 이유는?
감정 사회화는 어렸을 때부터 시작되며, 부모가 주된 사회화 주체라고 주장하고 있다. 이어서 등장한 예시는 주장을 뒷받침해야 하기 때문에 비슷한 상황에서 유사한 반응을 보이는 것이 논리적으로 맞다. ③의 경우 문장 앞에 등장한 'whereas'를 고려하면 부사절의 내용과 주절의 내용이 대조되어야 하기 때문에 장려하는 것이 아니라 방해하는 것이 맞다.
▶ 문제 해결 방법은?
글에서 주장하는 것이 무엇인지 먼저 파악하고, 글의 주장과 반대되는 문장을 찾으면 쉽다. 다만 문장에서 부정어나 대조를 의미하는 접속사가 쓰였는지 확인하여 꼼꼼하게 문장을 해석하는 것이 좋다.

31 무용수의 물리적 제약에 대한 자세
정답률 57% | 정답 ③

다음 빈칸에 들어갈 말로 가장 적절한 것을 고르시오.

① habits – 습관
② cultures – 문화
✔ constraints – 제약
④ hostilities – 적개심
⑤ moralities – 도덕성

Dancers often push themselves to the limits / of their physical capabilities.
무용수는 종종 자신을 한계까지 밀어붙인다. / 자신의 신체 능력의
But that push is misguided / if it is directed toward accomplishing something physically impossible.
그러나 그렇게 밀어붙이는 것은 잘못 이해된 것이다. / 만약 물리적으로 불가능한 것을 달성하는 쪽으로 향하게 된다면
For instance, / a tall dancer with long feet may wish / to perform repetitive vertical jumps to fast music, / pointing his feet while in the air / and lowering his heels to the floor between jumps.
예를 들어 / 키가 크고 발이 긴 무용수가 소망할 수 있다. / 빠른 음악에 맞춰 반복적인 수직 점프를 수행하기를 / 공중에서 발끝을 뾰족하게 세우면서 / 그리고 점프 사이에 발뒤꿈치를 바닥에 내리면서
That may be impossible / no matter how strong the dancer is.
그것은 불가능할 수 있다. / 무용수가 아무리 힘이 좋을지라도
But a short-footed dancer / may have no trouble!
하지만 발이 짧은 무용수는 / 전혀 문제가 없을 것이다!
Another dancer may be struggling / to complete a half-turn in the air.
또 다른 무용수는 애쓰고 있을 수 있다. / 공중에서 반 회전을 완성하려고
Understanding the connection / between a rapid turn rate and the alignment of the body / close to the rotation axis / tells her / how to accomplish her turn successfully.
연관성을 이해하는 것은 / 빠른 회전속도와 몸을 정렬하는 것의 / 회전축에 가깝게 / 그 무용수에게 알려 준다. / 성공적으로 회전을 해내는 방법을
In both of these cases, / understanding and imposed by nature / and working within the constraints imposed by nature / and described by physical laws / allows dancers to work efficiently, / minimizing potential risk of injury.
이 두 경우 모두에서 / 선천적으로 주어지고 이해하는 것 / 그리고 선천적으로 주어진 제약 안에서 움직이는 것은 / 물리적 법칙에 의해 설명되는 / 무용수가 효율적으로 움직이게 해 준다. / 잠재적 부상 위험을 최소화 하면서

무용수는 종종 자신의 신체 능력의 한계까지 자신을 밀어붙인다. 그러나 그렇게 밀어붙이는 것이 물리적으로 불가능한 것을 달성하는 쪽으로 향하게 된다면, 잘못 이해된 것이다. 예를 들어, 키가 크고 발이 긴 무용수가 공중에서 발끝을 뾰족하게 세우고 점프 사이에 발뒤꿈치를 바닥에 내리면서 빠른 음악에 맞춰 반복적인 수직 점프를 수행하기를 소망할 수 있다. 무용수가 아무리 힘이 좋을지라도 그것은 불가능할 수 있다. 하지만 발이 짧은 무용수는 전혀 문제가 없을 것이다! 또 다른 무용수는 공중에서 반 회전을 완성하려고 애쓰고 있을 수 있다. 빠른 회전 속도와 회전축에 가깝게 몸을 정렬하는 것의 연관성을 이해하는 것은 그 무용수에게 성공적으로 회전을 해내는 방법을 알려 준다. 이 두 경우 모두에서, 선천적으로 주어지고 물리적 법칙에 의해 설명되는 제약을 이해하고 그 안에서 움직이는 것은 잠재적인 부상 위험을 최소화하면서 무용수가 효율적으로 움직이게 해 준다.

Why? 왜 정답일까?

무용수는 종종 신체 능력의 한계까지 밀어붙이는데 물리적으로 불가능한 것을 밀어붙이기 보단 제약 내에서 움직이면 부상 위험을 줄이고 효율적으로 무용을 할 수 있다고 말한다. 따라서 빈칸에 들어갈 말로 가장 적절한 것은 ③ '제약'이다.

- **limit** ⓝ 한계
- **misguided** ⓐ 잘못 이해한
- **accomplish** ⓥ 달성하다
- **impossible** ⓐ 불가능한
- **repetitive** ⓐ 반복적인
- **lower** ⓥ 내리다
- **rapid** ⓐ 빠른
- **axis** ⓝ 축
- **impose** ⓥ 주다
- **constraint** ⓝ 제약, 제한
- **injury** ⓝ 부상
- **capability** ⓝ 능력
- **toward** [prep] 쪽으로
- **physically** [ad] 물리적으로
- **perform** ⓥ 이행하다, 수행하다
- **vertical** ⓐ 수직의
- **complete** ⓥ 완성하다, 완료하다
- **rotation** ⓝ 회전
- **constraint** ⓝ 제약, 강제, 압박
- **by nature** 선천적으로
- **potential** ⓐ 잠재적인

구문 풀이

10행 Understanding the connection between a rapid turn rate and the
주어(동명사)
alignment of the body close to the rotation axis tells her how to accomplish her
동사   간접목적어   직접목적어
turn successfully.

---

32 대중문화의 중심인 어린이 영화   정답률 54% | 정답 ②

다음 빈칸에 들어갈 말로 가장 적절한 것을 고르시오.

① centered on giving moral lessons – 도덕적 교훈을 주는데 중심을 두어왔다
✓ consumed by audiences of all ages – 모든 연령대의 관객들에게 소비되어 왔다
③ appreciated through an artistic view – 예술적 견해를 통해 감상해왔다
④ produced by inexperienced directors – 경험이 부족한 감독에 의해 제작되어 왔다
⑤ separated from the cinema for adults – 어른들을 위한 영화관과 분리되어 왔다

We must explore the relationship / between children's film production and consumption habits.
우리는 관계를 탐구해야 한다. / 어린이 영화 제작과 소비 습관 사이의
The term "children's film" implies ownership by children / — *their* cinema / — but films supposedly made for children / have always been consumed / by audiences of all ages, / particularly in commercial cinemas.
'어린이 영화'라는 용어는 어린이에의 소유권을 암시한다. / 즉 '그들의' 영화 / 그러나 소위 어린이를 위해 만들어진 영화는 / 항상 소비되어왔다. / 모든 연령대의 관객들에게, 특히 상업 영화에서
The considerable crossover / in audience composition for children's films / can be shown by the fact that, / in 2007, eleven Danish children's and youth films attracted / 59 per cent of theatrical admissions, / and in 2014, German children's films comprised seven out of the top twenty films / at the national box office.
상당한 넘나듦은 / 어린이 영화의 관객 구성에서 / 사실에 의해 증명될 수 있다. / 2007년에 11개의 덴마크의 어린이 및 청소년 영화가 끌어모았고 / 극장 입장객의 59퍼센트를 / 2014년에는 독일의 어린이 영화가 상위 20개 중 7개를 차지했다는 / 전국 극장 흥행 수익의
This phenomenon corresponds / with a broader, international embrace / of what is seemingly children's culture / among audiences of diverse ages.
이 현상은 일치한다. / 더 광범위하고 / 국제적으로 수용되는 것 / 어린이 문화처럼 보이는 것이 / 다양한 연령대의 관객들 사이에서
The old prejudice / that children's film is some other realm, / separate from (and forever subordinate to) a more legitimate cinema for adults / is not supported by the realities of consumption: / children's film is / at the heart of contemporary popular culture.
오래된 편견은 / 어린이 영화가 다른 영역이라는 / 성인을 위한 더 제대로 된 영화와는 별개의(그리고 영원히 하위의) / 소비의 실상에 의해 뒷받침되지 않는다. / 즉 어린이 영화가 / 현대 대중문화의 중심에 있다.

우리는 어린이 영화 제작과 소비 습관 사이의 관계를 탐구해야 한다. '어린이 영화'라는 용어는 어린이에 의한 소유권, 즉 '그들의' 영화를 암시하지만, 소위 어린이를 위해 만들어진 영화는 특히 상업 영화에서, 항상 모든 연령대의 관객들에게 소비되어 왔다. 어린이 영화의 관객 구성에서 상당한 (연령 간의) 넘나듦이 있다는 것은, 2007년에 11개의 덴마크의 어린이 및 청소년 영화가 극장 입장객의 59퍼센트를 끌어모았고 2014년에는 독일의 어린이 영화가 전국 극장 흥행 수익 상위 20개 영화 중 7개를 차지했다는 사실에 의해 증명될 수 있다. 이 현상은 다양한 연령대의 관객들 사이에서 겉으로는 어린이 문화처럼 보이는 것이 더 광범위하고 국제적으로 수용되는 것과 일치한다. 어린이 영화가 성인을 위한 더 제대로 된 영화와는 별개의(그리고 영원히 하위의) 다른 영역이라는 오래된 편견은 소비의 실상에 의해 뒷받침되지 않는다. 즉, 어린이 영화가 현대 대중문화의 중심에 있다.

Why? 왜 정답일까?

어린이 영화가 상업영화에서 입장객의 반 이상을 끌어모으고, 독일에서는 흥행 상위 20개 중 7개를 차지하는 등 소비의 실상으로 보아 대중문화에 중심에 있다는 (The old prejudice that children's film is some other realm, separate from (and forever subordinate to) a more legitimate cinema for adults is not supported by the realities of consumption: children's film is at the heart of contemporary popular culture.) 내용이므로, 빈칸에 들어갈 말로 가장 적절한 것은 ② '모든 연령대의 관객들에게 소비되어 왔다'이다.

- **imply** ⓥ 암시하다
- **supposedly** [ad] 소위
- **crossover** ⓝ 넘나듦
- **attract** ⓥ 끌어들이다
- **comprise** ⓥ 차지하다
- **correspond with** ~와 일치하다
- **prejudice** ⓝ 편견
- **subordinate** ⓐ 부차적인
- **commercial** ⓐ 상업의
- **considerable** ⓐ 상당한
- **composition** ⓝ 구성
- **theatrical** ⓐ 극장의
- **phenomenon** ⓝ 현상
- **embrace** ⓝ 수용
- **realm** ⓝ 영역
- **legitimate** ⓐ 제대로 된

구문 풀이

11행 This phenomenon corresponds with a broader, international embrace of what is seemingly children's culture among audiences of diverse ages.
선행사를 포함한 관계대명사(= the thing which)

---

33 베토벤의 호기심에서 비롯된 창의성   정답률 43% | 정답 ③

다음 빈칸에 들어갈 말로 가장 적절한 것을 고르시오. [3점]

① had more standardized patterns – 더 표준화된 패턴을 가지게 되었다
② obtained more public popularity – 더 많은 대중의 인기를 얻게 되었다
✓ became less predictable over time – 시간이 지날수록 덜 예측 가능하게 되었다
④ reflected his unstable mental state – 그의 불안한 정신이 반영되었다
⑤ attracted less attention from the critics – 비평가들의 관심을 덜 끌게 되었다

Beethoven's drive to create something novel / is a reflection of his state of curiosity.
새로운 것을 창작하려는 베토벤의 욕구는 / 그의 호기심 상태의 반영이다.
Our brains experience a sense of reward / when we create something new / in the process of exploring something uncertain, / such as a musical phrase / that we've never played or heard before.
우리의 뇌는 보상감을 경험한다. / 우리가 새로운 것을 창작할 때 / 불확실한 것을 탐구하는 과정에서 / 악절과 같이 / 우리가 이전에 연주하거나 들어본 적이 없는
When our curiosity leads to something novel, / the resulting reward brings us a sense of pleasure.
우리의 호기심이 새로운 것으로 이어지면 / 그 결과로 얻어지는 보상은 우리에게 쾌감을 가져다 준다.
A number of investigators have modeled / how curiosity influences musical composition.
많은 연구자들이 모델링해 왔다. / 음악 작곡에 호기심이 어떻게 영향을 미치는지를
In the case of Beethoven, / computer modeling focused on the thirty-two piano sonatas written / after age thirteen revealed / that the musical patterns found in all of Beethoven's music decreased / in later sonatas, / while novel patterns, / including patterns / that were unique to a particular sonata, / increased.
베토벤의 경우 / 32개의 피아노 소나타에 초점을 맞춘 컴퓨터 모델링에서 / 13세 이후로 작곡된 / 베토벤의 모든 음악에서 발견되는 음악 패턴이 감소했는 / 후기 소나타에서 / 반면 새로운 패턴은 / 패턴을 포함한 / 특정 소나타에만 나타나는 / 증가했다.
In other words, / Beethoven's music became less predictable over time / as his curiosity drove the exploration of new musical ideas.
다시 말해, / 베토벤의 음악은 시간이 지날수록 덜 예측 가능하게 되었다. / 그의 호기심이 새로운 음악적 아이디어의 탐구를 이끌게 됨에 따라
Curiosity is a powerful driver / of human creativity.
호기심은 강력한 원동력이다. / 인간의 창의성의

새로운 것을 창작하려는 베토벤의 욕구는 그의 호기심 상태의 반영이다. 우리의 뇌는 우리가 이전에 연주하거나 들어본 적이 없는 악절과 같이 불확실한 것을 탐구하는 과정에서 새로운 것을 창작할 때 보상감을 경험한다. 우리의 호기심이 새로운 것으로 이어지면, 그 결과로 얻어지는 보상은 우리에게 쾌감을 가져다준다. 많은 연구자들이 음악 작곡에 호기심이 어떻게 영향을 미치는지를 모델링해 왔다. 베토벤의 경우, 13세 이후로 작곡된 32개의 피아노 소나타에 초점을 맞춘 컴퓨터 모델링에서 베토벤의 모든 음악에서 발견되는 음악 패턴이 후기 소나타에서는 감소한 반면, 특정 소나타에만 나타나는 패턴을 포함한 새로운 패턴은 증가한 것을 보여 주었다. 다시 말해, 베토벤의 호기심이 새로운 음악적 아이디어의 탐구를 이끌게 됨에 따라 그의 음악이 시간이 지날수록 덜 예측 가능하게 되었다. 호기심은 인간의 창의성의 강력한 원동력이다.

Why? 왜 정답일까?

베토벤의 공통적인 음악 패턴이 후기 음악 작품에서는 감소한 반면 새로운 패턴이 증가했다는 것을 예로 들어 호기심이 창의성의 강력한 원동력(In the case of Beethoven, computer modeling focused on the thirty-two piano sonatas written after age thirteen revealed that the musical patterns found in all of Beethoven's music decreased in later sonatas, while novel patterns, including patterns that were unique to a particular sonata, increased.)이라고 이야기하고 있으므로, 빈칸에 들어갈 말로 가장 적절한 것은 ③ '시간이 지날수록 덜 예측 가능하게 되었다'이다.

- **drive** ⓝ 욕구
- **uncertain** ⓐ 불확실한
- **investigator** ⓝ 연구자
- **reveal** ⓥ 보여주다
- **obtain** ⓥ 얻다
- **curiosity** ⓝ 호기심
- **novel** ⓐ 새로운
- **composition** ⓝ 작곡
- **exploration** ⓝ 탐구
- **predictable** ⓐ 예측할 수 있는

구문 풀이

7행 A number of investigators have modeled how curiosity influences musical
현재완료
composition.

★★★ 등급을 가르는 문제!

34 기술자들의 딜레마   정답률 30% | 정답 ④

다음 빈칸에 들어갈 말로 가장 적절한 것을 고르시오. [3점]

① regarding continuous progress as a valid solution
유효한 해결책으로 지속적인 진전에 관해
② prioritizing short-term goals over long-term visions
장기적 비전보다 단기적 목표를 우선시하는
③ mistaking a personal bias for an established theory
개인적 편견을 정설로 착각하는
✓ substituting what is measurable for what is meaningful
의미 있는 것을 측정 가능한 것으로 대체하는
⑤ focusing more on possible risks than concrete measures
구체적인 조치보다 가능한 위험에 더 초점을 맞추는

Technologists are always on the lookout / for quantifiable metrics.
기술자들은 항상 찾고 있다. / 정량화할 수 있는 측정 기준을
Measurable inputs to a model / are their lifeblood, / and like a social scientist, / a technologist needs to identify / concrete measures, / or "proxies," / for assessing progress.
모델에 측정 가능한 입력을 하는 것은 / 그들의 생명줄이다. / 그리고 사회 과학자와 마찬가지로 / 기술자는 식별할 필요가 있다. / 구체적인 측정 방법 / 즉 '프록시'를 / 진척 상황을 평가하기 위한
This need for quantifiable proxies / produces a bias / toward measuring / things that are easy to quantify.
이러한 정량화할 수 있는 프록시에 대한 필요성은 / 편향을 만든다. / 측정하는 쪽으로 / 정량화하기 쉬운 것들을
But / simple metrics can take us further away / from the important goals / we really care about, / which may require complicated metrics / or be extremely difficult, / or perhaps impossible, / to reduce to any measure.

하지만 / 단순한 측정 기준은 우리를 더 멀어지게 할 수 있다. / 중요한 목표로부터 / 우리가 정말로 신경 쓰는 / 이는 복잡한 측정 기준을 요구할 수 있다. / 또는 매우 어렵다 / 또는 아마 불가능할 수 있다. / 어떤 하나의 측정 방법만으로 한정하기가

And when we have imperfect or bad proxies, / we can easily fall / under the illusion / that we are solving for a good end / without actually making genuine progress / toward a worthy solution.
그리고 우리가 불완전하거나 잘못된 프록시를 가지고 있을 때 / 우리는 쉽게 빠질 수 있다 / 착각에 / 우리가 좋은 목적을 위해 문제를 해결하고 있다는 / 진정한 진전을 실제로 이루지 못하면서 / 가치 있는 해결책을 향한

The problem of proxies results in / technologists frequently substituting / what is measurable for / what is meaningful.
프록시의 문제는 결과를 낳는다 / 기술자들이 흔히 대체하는 / 측정 가능한 것으로 / 의미 있는 것을

As the saying goes, / "Not everything that counts can be counted, / and not everything that can be counted counts."
흔히 말하듯이 / 중요한 모든 것들이 셀 수 있는 것은 아니다. / 그리고 셀 수 있는 모든 것들이 중요한 것도 아니다.

기술자들은 항상 정량화할 수 있는 측정 기준을 찾고 있다. 모델에 측정 가능한 입력(을 하는 것)은 그들의 생명줄이며, 사회 과학자와 마찬가지로 기술자는 진척 상황을 평가하기 위한 구체적인 측정 방법, 즉 '프록시'를 식별할 필요가 있다. 이러한 정량화할 수 있는 프록시에 대한 필요성은 정량화하기 쉬운 것들을 측정하는 쪽으로 편향을 만든다. 하지만 단순한 측정 기준은 우리가 정말로 신경 쓰는 중요한 목표로부터 우리를 더 멀어지게 할 수 있는데, 이 목표는 복잡한 측정 기준을 요구하거나, 또는 (이 목표를) 어떤 하나의 측정 방법만으로 한정(하여 측정)하기가 매우 어렵거나 아마 불가능할 수도 있다. 그리고 우리가 불완전하거나 잘못된 프록시를 가지고 있을 때, 우리는 가치 있는 해결책을 향한 진정한 진전을 실제로 이루지 못하면서 좋은 목적을 위해 문제를 해결하고 있다는 착각에 쉽게 빠질 수 있다. 프록시의 문제는 기술자들이 흔히 의미 있는 것을 측정 가능한 것으로 대체하는 결과를 낳는다. 흔히 말하듯이, "중요한 모든 것들이 셀 수 있는 것은 아니고, 셀 수 있는 모든 것들이 중요한 것도 아니다."

Why? 왜 정답일까?

기술자들은 항상 정량화할 수 있는 측정 기준을 찾고 있는데 중요한 모든 것들이 셀 수 있는 것은 아니고, 셀 수 있는 모든 것들이 중요한 것도 아니라 (As the saying goes, "Not everything that counts can be counted, and not everything that can be counted counts.") 말하고 있으므로, 빈칸에 들어갈 말로 가장 적절한 것은 ④ '의미 있는 것을 측정 가능한 것으로 대체하는'이다.

- on the lookout for ~를 찾고 있는
- measurable ⓐ 측정할 수 있는
- concrete ⓐ 구체적인
- quantify ⓥ 양을 나타내다, 양을 정하다
- complicated ⓐ 복잡한
- genuine ⓐ 진정한
- quantifiable ⓐ 정량화할 수 있는
- lifeblood ⓝ 생명선
- bias ⓝ 편향
- further ⓐ 더 멀리
- illusion ⓝ 환영
- count ⓥ 중요하다

구문 풀이

13행 The problem of proxies results in technologists frequently substituting
동명사(result in의 목적어)
{what is measurable} for {what is meaningful.} 'substitute A for B : B를 A로 대체하다'
관계대명사(병렬1)   관계대명사(병렬2)

★★ 문제 해결 꿀~팁 ★★

▶ 많이 틀린 이유는?
이 글은 기술자들은 항상 정량화할 수 있는 측정 기준을 찾고 있는데, 이때 구체적인 측정 방법인 프록시를 식별할 필요가 있다고 주장한다. 빈칸이 있는 문장은 프록시의 문제점이 낳을 수 있는 결과를 이야기하고 있다. 여러 문장에 걸쳐 설명한 문제를 한 문장으로 요약해본다면 ④이 오는 것이 가장 적절하다.

▶ 문제 해결 방법은?
글의 주제를 파악하고 자주 언급되는 단어를 확인하며 주제에서 벗어나지 않도록 노력해야 한다. 글은 계속해서 측정방법에 대한 이야기를 하고 있으므로 사람의 편견이나 정설이 등장한 ③은 주제와 무관한 문장이므로 답이 될 수 없다.

35 음식에 양념을 하는 유일한 종 인간   정답률 56% | 정답 ③

다음 글에서 전체 흐름과 관계 없는 문장은?

We are the only species / that seasons its food, / deliberately altering it / with the highly flavored plant parts / we call herbs and spices.
우리는 유일한 종이다. / 음식에 양념을 하는 / 의도적으로 그것을 바꾼다. / 강한 맛을 내는 식물의 부분을 이용하여 / 허브와 향신료라고 부른

It's quite possible / that our taste for spices / has an evolutionary root.
가능성이 높다. / 향신료에 대한 우리의 미각은 / 진화적 뿌리를 가지고 있

① Many spices have antibacterial properties / — in fact, common seasonings such as garlic, onion, and oregano / inhibit the growth of almost every bacterium tested.
많은 향신료가 항균성을 가지고 있다. / 실제로 마늘, 양파, 오레가노와 같은 흔한 조미료들이 / 거의 모든 확인된 박테리아의 성장을 억제한다.

② And the cultures that make the heaviest use of spices / — think of the garlic and black pepper of Thai food, / the ginger and coriander of India, / the chili peppers of Mexico / — come from warmer climates, / where bacterial spoilage is a bigger issue.
그리고 향신료를 가장 많이 사용하는 문화권은 / 태국 음식의 마늘과 후추를 생각해 보면 / 그리고 인도의 생강과 고수, / 그리고 멕시코의 고추를 / 더 따뜻한 기후에서 유래하는데 / 그곳에서는 박테리아에 의한 부패가 큰 문제이다.

✔ The changing climate can have a significant impact on / the production and availability of spices, / influencing their growth patterns / and ultimately affecting global spice markets.
변화하는 기후는 많은 영향을 미칠 수 있다 / 향신료의 생산과 이용 가능성에 / 그들의 성장 방식에 영향을 주면서 / 그리고 궁극적으로 세계 향신료 시장에 영향을 미치면서

④ In contrast, / the most lightly spiced cuisines / — those of Scandinavia and northern Europe / — are from cooler climates.
반대로 / 가장 향신료를 적게 쓰는 요리 / 스칸디나비아와 북유럽의 요리 같이 / 더 서늘한 기후에서 유래한다.

⑤ Our uniquely human attention to flavor, / in this case the flavor of spices, / turns out to have arisen / as a matter of life and death.
맛에 대한 인간의 특유한 관심 / 이 경우 향신료의 맛은 / 생겨난 것으로 드러난다. / 사느냐 죽느냐의 문제로서

우리는 음식에 양념을 하는 유일한 종으로, 허브와 향신료라고 부르는 강한 맛을 내는 식물의 부분을 이용하여 그것(음식)을 의도적으로 바꾼다. 향신료에 대한 우리의 미각은 진화적

뿌리를 가지고 있을 가능성이 높다. ① 많은 향신료가 항균성을 가지고 있는데, 실제로 마늘, 양파, 오레가노와 같은 흔한 조미료들이 거의 모든 확인된 박테리아의 성장을 억제한다. ② 그리고 태국 음식의 마늘과 후추, 인도의 생강과 고수, 멕시코의 고추를 생각해 보면, 향신료를 가장 많이 사용하는 문화권은 더 따뜻한 기후에서 유래하는데, 그곳에서는 박테리아에 의한 (음식의) 부패가 큰 문제이다. ③ 변화하는 기후는 향신료의 생산과 이용 가능성에 많은 영향을 미칠 수 있기 때문에, 그들(향신료)의 성장 방식에 영향을 주고, 궁극적으로 세계 향신료 시장에 영향을 미친다. ④ 반대로, 스칸디나비아와 북유럽의 요리같이 가장 향신료를 적게 쓰는 요리는 더 서늘한 기후에서 유래한다. ⑤ 맛에 대한 인간 특유의 관심, 이 경우 향신료의 맛은 사느냐 죽느냐의 문제로서 생겨난 것으로 드러난다.

Why? 왜 정답일까?

향신료는 항균성을 갖고 있는데 실제로 향신료를 많이 쓰는 나라는 따뜻한 기후를 가진 나라로 박테리아에 의한 부패를 막기 위해 썼을 것이라고 가정하고 있다. ③은 기후의 변화가 세계 향신료 시장에 영향을 미친다고 얘기하고 있으므로 전체 흐름과 관계없는 문장이다.

- season ⓥ 양념을 하다
- alter ⓥ 바꾸다
- evolutionary ⓐ 진화적인
- property ⓝ 특성
- ginger ⓝ 생강
- spoilage ⓝ 부패
- availability ⓝ 이용 가능성
- deliberately ⓐ 의도적으로
- quite ⓐ 꽤
- antibacterial ⓐ 항균의
- inhibit ⓥ 억제하다
- coriander ⓝ 고수
- significant ⓐ 많은
- arise ⓥ 생겨나다

구문 풀이

7행 And the cultures that make the heaviest use of spices — think of the
주어   관계대명사(주격)
garlic and black pepper of Thai food, the ginger and coriander of India, the chili
peppers of Mexico — come from warmer climates, where bacterial spoilage is a
동사   관계부사(계속적용법)
bigger issue.

★★★ 등급을 가르는 문제!

36 무작위적이면서 비작위적인 세포의 발달   정답률 36% | 정답 ⑤

주어진 글 다음에 이어질 글의 순서로 가장 적절한 것을 고르시오. [3점]
① (A) – (C) – (B)   ② (B) – (A) – (C)
③ (B) – (C) – (A)   ④ (C) – (A) – (B)
✔ (C) – (B) – (A)

Development of the human body / from a single cell / provides many examples of the structural richness / that is possible / when the repeated production of random variation / is combined with nonrandom selection.
인체가 발달하는 것은 / 단일 세포로부터 / 구조적 풍부함의 많은 예를 제공한다. / 가능해지는 / 무작위적인 변이의 반복적 생성이 ~할 때 / 비무작위적인 선택과 결합될

(C) All phases of body development / from embryo to adult / exhibit random activities / at the cellular level, / and body formation depends on / the new possibilities / generated by these activities / coupled with selection of those outcomes / that satisfy previously built-in criteria.
신체 발달의 모든 단계는 / 배아에서 성체에 이르기까지 / 무작위 활동을 보인다. / 세포 수준에서 / 그리고 신체 형성은 달려 있다. / 새로운 가능성에 / 이러한 활동에 의해 만들어진 / 결과물의 선택에 더불어 / 이전에 확립된 기준을 만족시키는

Always new structure is based on old structure, / and at every stage / selection favors some cells / and eliminates others.
항상 새로운 구조는 오래된 구조를 기반으로 한다. / 그리고 모든 단계에서 / 선택은 일부 세포들을 선호한다. / 그리고 다른 세포들은 제거한다.

(B) The survivors serve to produce new cells / that undergo further rounds of selection.
생존한 세포들은 새로운 세포를 만들어 내는 역할을 한다. / 추가적인 선택의 과정을 거치는

Except in the immune system, / cells and extensions of cells are not genetically selected / during development, / but rather, are positionally selected.
면역계를 제외하면 / 세포와 세포의 확장은 유전적으로 선택되는 것이 아니다. / 발달 과정에서 / 위치에 의해 선택된다.

(A) Those in the right place / that make the right connections / are stimulated, / and those that don't are eliminated.
제자리에 있는 것들은 / 제대로 된 연결을 만들어 낸 / 활성화된다. / 그리고 그렇지 않은 것들은 제거된다.

This process is much like sculpting.
이 과정은 마치 조각을 하는 것과 같다.

A natural consequence of the strategy / is great variability / from individual to individual / at the cell and molecular levels, / even though large-scale structures are quite similar.
이 전략의 필연적 결과는 / 큰 변이성이 있다는 것이다. / 개인마다 / 세포와 분자 수준에서 / 전체 구조가 상당히 비슷하더라도

단일 세포로부터 인체가 발달하는 것은 무작위적인 변이의 반복적 생성이 비무작위적인 선택과 결합될 때 가능해지는 구조적 풍부함의 많은 예를 제공한다.

(C) 배아에서 성체에 이르기까지 신체 발달의 모든 단계는 세포 수준에서는 무작위 활동을 보이고, 신체 형성은 이러한 활동(무작위 활동)에 의해 만들어진 새로운 가능성과 더불어, 이전에 확립된 기준을 만족시키는 결과물의 선택에 달려 있다. 항상 새로운 구조는 오래된 구조를 기반으로 하며, 모든 단계에서 선택은 일부 세포들을 선호하고 다른 세포들은 제거한다.

(B) 생존한 세포들은 추가적인 선택의 과정을 거치는 새로운 세포들을 만들어 내는 역할을 한다. 면역계를 제외하면 세포와 세포의 확장은 발달 과정에서 유전적으로 선택되는 것이 아니라 위치에 의해 선택된다.

(A) 제 자리에서 제대로 된 연결을 만들어 낸 것(세포)들은 활성화되고, 그렇지 않은 것들은 제거된다. 이 과정은 마치 조각을 하는 것과 같다. 이 전략의 필연적 결과는 전체 구조가 상당히 비슷하더라도 세포와 분자 수준에서 개인마다 큰 변이성이 있다는 것이다.

Why? 왜 정답일까?

주어진 글에서는 단일 세포로부터 인체가 발달하는 것이 구조적 풍부함의 예라고 이야기하고 있다. 이후 (C)에서 배아에서 성체에 이르기까지의 단계가 무작위 활동이라고 주장을 뒷받침하고 있으며, (B)에는 (C)의 마지막에서 이야기했던 일부 생존 세포들을 언급하고 있다. 이후 면역계를 제외하고 세포의 확장은 위치에 의해 선택된다고 이야기하고 있는데 (A)에서 제 자리에 위치한 세포에 대해 이야기하고 있다. 그러므로 글의 순서로 가장 적절한 것은 ⑤ '(C) – (B) – (A)'이다.

- variation ⓝ 변이
- stimulate ⓥ 활성화시키다
- sculpt ⓥ 조각하다
- undergo ⓥ 겪다
- extension ⓝ 확장
- positionally ⓐⓓ 위치적으로
- cellular ⓐ 세포의
- connection ⓝ 연결
- eliminate ⓥ 제거하다
- molecular ⓐ 분자의
- immune system 면역 체계
- genetically ⓐⓓ 유전적으로
- embryo ⓝ 배아
- criteria ⓝ 기준

구문 풀이

12행 Except in the immune system, cells and extensions of cells are not genetically selected during development, but rather, are positionally selected.
└─「not A but B : A가 아니라 B」─┘

★★ 문제 해결 꿀~팁 ★★

▶ 많이 틀린 이유는?
주어진 글에서 단일 세포에서 인간의 신체가 발달한다고 이야기하고 있기 때문에 그 다음에 올 글이 (C)라는 것은 알기 쉽다. 그 다음 (A)가 올지 (B)가 올지 살펴봐야 하는데, (A)에서 첫 문장의 주어 those와 (B)의 the survivor가 의미하는 것이 무엇인지 찾으면 된다. (B)의 the survivor는 (C)에서 선택된 일부의 세포를 의미한다. 이후 생존한 세포들은 발달될 때 유전적이기 보다 위치적으로 선택된다고 말한다. (A)의 Those in the right place는 위치적으로 선택된 세포들을 말하는 것이다. 따라서 (B)뒤에 (A)가 오는 것이 맞다.

▶ 문제 해결 방법은?
글의 내용이 과학과 관련된 지문이라 낯설거나 어려워 논리적으로 풀어가기 힘들 때는, 문장에서 언급된 대명사나 접속사 등을 활용해 글의 순서를 유추해 볼 수 있다.

---

37 재택 간호사 관리 시스템 정답률 49% | 정답 ②

주어진 글 다음에 이어질 글의 순서로 가장 적절한 것을 고르시오. [3점]

① (A) - (C) - (B) ✓② (B) - (A) - (C)
③ (B) - (C) - (A) ④ (C) - (A) - (B)
⑤ (C) - (B) - (A)

In order to bring / the ever-increasing costs / of home care for elderly and needy persons / under control, / managers of home care providers / have introduced management systems.
가져오기 위해서 / 계속적으로 증가하는 비용을 / 노인과 빈곤층을 위한 재택 간호의 / 통제 아래서 / 재택 간호 제공 업체의 관리자는 / 관리 시스템을 도입했다.

(B) These systems specify tasks of home care workers / and the time and budget / available to perform these tasks.
이러한 시스템은 재택 간호 종사자의 업무를 명시한다. / 그리고 시간과 예산을 / 이러한 업무를 수행하는데 사용할 수 있는

Electronic reporting systems require / home care workers to report on their activities and the time spent, / thus making the distribution of time and money visible / and, in the perception of managers, controllable.
전자 보고 시스템은 요구한다. / 재택 간호 종사자가 자신의 활동과 소요 시간을 보고하도록 / 따라서 시간과 비용의 분배를 잘 보이게 만든다. / 그리고 관리자의 입장에서는 통제 가능하게 만든다.

(A) This, / in the view of managers, / has contributed to the resolution of the problem.
이것이 / 관리자의 관점에서는 / 문제 해결에 기여해 왔다.

The home care workers, / on the other hand, / may perceive their work / not as a set of separate tasks / to be performed as efficiently as possible, / but as a service to be provided to a client / with whom they may have developed a relationship.
재택 간호 종사자들은 / 반면에 / 그들의 업무를 인식할 것이다. / 일련의 분리된 업무가 아니라 / 가능한 한 효율적으로 수행되어야 하는 / 고객에게 제공되는 서비스로 인식할 것이다. / 그들이 관계를 맺어 온

(C) This includes having conversations with clients / and enquiring about the person's well-being.
이것은 고객과 대화를 나누는 것을 포함한다. / 그리고 고객의 안부를 묻는 것을

Restricted time and the requirement to report / may be perceived as obstacles / that make it impossible / to deliver the service that is needed.
제한된 시간과 보고를 해야 한다는 요구 사항은 / 장애물로 여겨질 것이다. / 불가능하게 하는 / 필요한 서비스를 제공하는

If the management systems are too rigid, / this may result in / home care workers becoming overloaded and demotivated.
만약 관리 시스템이 너무 엄격하면 / 이것은 결과를 초래할 것이다. / 재택 간호 종사자가 너무 많은 부담을 지게 되고 의욕을 잃는

노인과 빈곤층을 위한 재택 간호의 계속적으로 증가하는 비용을 통제하기 위해 재택 간호 제공 업체의 관리자는 관리 시스템을 도입했다.

(B) 이러한 시스템은 재택 간호 종사자의 업무와 이러한 업무를 수행하는데 사용할 수 있는 시간과 예산을 명시한다. 전자 보고 시스템은 재택 간호 종사자가 자신의 활동과 소요시간을 보고하도록 요구하므로 시간과 비용의 분배를 잘 보이게 만들고, 관리자의 입장에서는 통제 가능하게 만든다.

(A) 관리자의 관점에서는, 이것이 문제 해결에 기여해 왔다. 반면에, 재택 간호 종사자들은 자신의 업무를 가능한 한 효율적으로 수행되어야 하는 일련의 분리된 업무가 아니라, 그들이 관계를 맺어 온 고객에게 제공되는 서비스로 인식할 것이다.

(C) 이것은 고객과 대화를 나누고 고객의 안부를 묻는 것을 포함한다. 제한된 시간과 보고를 해야 한다는 요구 사항은 필요한 서비스를 제공하는 것을 불가능하게 하는 장애물로 여겨질 것이다. 만약 관리 시스템이 너무 엄격하면, 이것은 재택 간호 종사자가 너무 많은 부담을 지게 되고 의욕을 잃는 결과를 초래할 것이다.

Why? 왜 정답일까?

재택 간호에 관리 시스템을 도입했다는 주어진 글 뒤로, 시스템을 통해 시간과 예산을 명시할 수 있게 되었다는 (B), 관리자의 입장과 달리 재택 간호 종사자들에게는 다르게 비춰질 수 있다는 내용의 (A), 이후 시스템이 너무 엄격하면 재택 간호 종사자에게 부담이 커 의욕을 잃게 할 수 있다는 내용인 (C)가 이어져야 자연스럽다. 따라서 글의 순서로 가장 적절한 것은 ② '(B) - (A) - (C)'이다.

- ever-increasing 계속 증가하는
- needy ⓐ 빈곤한
- a set of 일련의
- enquire ⓥ 묻다
- perceive ⓥ 인지하다
- elderly ⓐ 노인의
- contribute ⓥ 기여하다
- efficiently ⓐⓓ 효율적으로
- restrict ⓥ 제한하다
- demotivated ⓐ 의욕을 잃은

구문 풀이

13행 Electronic reporting systems require home care workers to report on their
          동사   목적어(to부정사)
activities and the time spent, thus making the distribution of time and money
분사구문(= and thus they make)   목적어
visible and, in the perception of managers, controllable.
목적보어(병렬1)   목적보어(병렬2)

---

38 무리에서 떨어진 새 정답률 48% | 정답 ③

글의 흐름으로 보아, 주어진 문장이 들어가기에 가장 적절한 곳을 고르시오. [3점]

It is a common assumption / that most vagrant birds are ultimately doomed, / aside from the rare cases / where individuals are able to reorientate / and return to their normal ranges.
일반적인 가정이다. / 무리에서 떨어진 대부분의 새들은 궁극적으로 죽을 운명이라는 것이 / 드문 경우의 개체를 제외하고 / 개체들이 방향을 다시 잡을 수 있는 / 그리고 그들의 일반적인 범위로 돌아갈 수 있는

① In turn, / it is also commonly assumed / that vagrancy itself is a relatively unimportant biological phenomenon.
결국 / 일반적으로 여겨지기도 한다. / 무리에서 떨어져 헤매는 것 자체가 비교적 중요하지 않은 생물학적 현상이라고

② This is undoubtedly true for the majority of cases, / as the most likely outcome of any given vagrancy event / is that the individual will fail to find enough resources, / and / or be exposed to inhospitable environmental conditions, and perish.
이것은 의심할 여지없이 대부분의 경우에 사실인데 / 무리에서 떨어져 헤매는 어떤 경우든 가장 가능성 있는 결과는 ~기 때문이다. / 개체가 충분한 자원을 찾지 못할 것이기 / 그리고 / 또는 살기 힘든 환경 조건에 노출되어 죽기

✓ However, / there are many lines of evidence to suggest / that vagrancy can, / on rare occasions, / dramatically alter the fate / of populations, species or even whole ecosystems.
하지만 / 시사하는 많은 증거가 있다. / 무리에서 떨어져 헤매는 것이 할 수 있다. / 드문 경우에 / 운명을 극적으로 바꿀 수 있다. / 개체 수, 종, 심지어 생태계 전체의

Despite being infrequent, / these events can be extremely important / when viewed at the timescales over which ecological and evolutionary processes unfold.
드물기는 하지만 / 이러한 경우들은 매우 중요할 수 있다. / 생태학적이고 진화적인 과정이 진행되는 관점에서 볼 때

④ The most profound consequences of vagrancy / relate to the establishment of new breeding sites, new migration routes and wintering locations.
무리에서 떨어져 헤매는 것의 가장 중대한 결과는 / 새로운 번식지, 새로운 이동 경로 및 월동 장소의 확보와 관련이 있다.

⑤ Each of these can occur through different mechanisms, / and at different frequencies, / and they each have their own unique importance.
이들 각각은 서로 다른 메커니즘을 통해 발생할 수 있다. / 서로 다른 빈도로 / 그리고 각각 고유한 중요성을 가지고 있다.

무리에서 떨어져 헤매는 대부분의 새들은 방향을 다시 잡고 그들의 일반적인 (서식) 범위로 돌아갈 수 있는 드문 경우의 개체들을 제외하고, 궁극적으로 죽을 운명이라는 것이 일반적인 가정이다. ① 결국, 무리에서 떨어져 헤매는 것 자체가 비교적 중요하지 않은 생물학적 현상이라고 일반적으로 여겨지기도 한다. ② 이것은 의심할 여지없이 대부분의 경우에 사실인데, 무리에서 떨어져 헤매는 어떤 경우든 가장 가능성 있는 결과는 개체가 충분한 자원을 찾지 못하고/못하거나, 살기 힘든 환경 조건에 노출되어 죽기 때문이다. ③ 하지만, 드문 경우에, 무리에서 떨어져 헤매는 것이 개체 수, 종, 심지어 생태계 전체의 운명을 극적으로 바꿀 수 있다는 것을 시사하는 많은 증거가 있다. 드물기는 하지만, 이러한 경우들은 생태학적이고 진화적인 과정이 진행되는 시간의 관점에서 볼 때 매우 중요할 수 있다. ④ 무리에서 떨어져 헤매는 것의 가장 중대한 결과는 새로운 번식지, 새로운 이동 경로 및 월동 장소의 확보와 관련이 있다. ⑤ 이들 각각은 서로 다른 메커니즘을 통해, 서로 다른 빈도로 발생할 수 있으며, 각각 고유한 중요성을 가지고 있다.

Why? 왜 정답일까?

글의 앞부분은 새가 무리에서 떨어지게 되면 궁극적으로 죽을 운명이라고 말하고 있다 하지만 뒷부분은 새가 무리에서 떨어져도 드문 경우 살 수도 있다고 이야기하고 있으므로, 주어진 글의 however를 이용하여 자연스럽게 연결할 수 있다. 따라서 주어진 문장이 들어가기에 가장 적절한 곳은 ③이다.

- evidence ⓝ 증거, 흔적
- vagrancy ⓝ 부랑자
- occasion ⓝ 경우
- doom ⓥ (불행한) 운명을 맞다
- undoubtedly ⓐⓓ 의심할 여지없이
- infrequent ⓐ 드문
- evolutionary ⓐ 진화의
- migration ⓝ 이동
- suggest ⓥ 시사하다
- rare ⓐ 드문
- assumption ⓝ 가정
- reorientate ⓥ 방향을 다시 잡다
- inhospitable ⓐ 힘든
- timescale ⓝ 시간
- profound ⓐ 중대한
- breeding ⓝ 번식

구문 풀이

8행 In turn, it is also commonly assumed that vagrancy itself is a relatively
                  가주어   진주어(접속사 that)
unimportant biological phenomenon.

★★★ 등급을 가르는 문제!

39 직관의 정의 정답률 25% | 정답 ②

글의 흐름으로 보아, 주어진 문장이 들어가기에 가장 적절한 곳을 고르시오.

Intuition can be great, / but it ought to be hard-earned.
직관은 탁월할 수 있다. / 하지만 힘들여 얻은 것이어야 한다.

① Experts, / for example, / are able to think on their feet / because they've invested thousands of hours / in learning and practice: / their intuition has become data-driven.
전문가들은 / 예를 들어 / 즉각적으로 생각할 수 있다. / 왜냐하면 그들은 수천 시간을 투자했다. / 학습과 경험에 / 데이터로부터 직관이 얻어졌기 때문이다.

✓ Only then / are they able to act quickly / in accordance with their internalized expertise and evidence-based experience.
그래야만 / 그들이 빠르게 행동할 수 있다. / 내재화된 전문 지식과 증거에 기반한 경험에 따라

Yet / most people are not experts, / though they often think they are.
그러나 / 대부분의 사람들은 전문가가 아니다. / 그들이 종종 스스로를 전문가로 생각하지만

③ Most of us, / especially when we interact with others on social media, / act with expert-like speed and conviction, / offering a wide range of opinions on global crises, / without the substance of knowledge that supports it.

우리 중 대부분은 / 특히 소셜 미디어에서 다른 사람들과 소통할 때 / 전문가와 같은 속도와 확신을 가지고 행동한다. / 국제적 위기에 대한 다양한 의견을 제시하면서 / 이를 뒷받침하는 지식의 실체 없이

④ And thanks to AI, / which ensures that our messages are delivered / to an audience more inclined to believing it, / our delusions of expertise / can be reinforce / by our personal filter bubble.
그리고 인공 지능 덕분에 / 우리의 메시지가 전달되도록 확실히 하는 / 그것을 더 믿으려는 성향이 있는 독자에게 / 전문 지식에 대한 우리의 착각은 강화될 수 있다. / 개인적 필터 버블에 의해

⑤ We have an interesting tendency / to find people more open-minded, rational, and sensible / when they think just like us.
우리는 흥미로운 경향을 가지고 있다. / 그들을 더 개방적이고 합리적이며 분별 있다고 여기는 / 남들이 우리와 똑같이 생각할 때

직관은 탁월할 수 있지만, 힘들여 얻은 것이어야 한다. ① 예를 들어, 전문가들은 수천 시간을 학습과 경험에 투자하여, 데이터로부터 직관이 얻어졌기 때문에 즉각적으로 생각할 수 있다. ② 그래야만 그들이 내재화된 전문 지식과 증거에 기반한 경험에 따라 빠르게 행동할 수 있다. 그러나 대부분의 사람들은 종종 스스로를 전문가라고 생각하지만 실제로는 전문가가 아니다. ③ 우리 중 대부분은, 특히 소셜 미디어에서 다른 사람들과 소통할 때, 전문가와 같은 속도와 확신을 가지고 행동하며, 이를 뒷받침하는 지식의 실체 없이 국제적 위기에 대한 다양한 의견을 제시한다. ④ 그리고 우리의 메시지가 그것을 더 믿으려는 성향이 있는 독자에게 확실히 전달되도록 하는 인공 지능 덕분에, 전문 지식에 대한 우리의 착각은 개인적 필터 버블(자신의 관심사에 맞게 필터링된 정보만을 접하게 되는 현상)에 의해 강화될 수 있다. ⑤ 우리는 남들이 우리와 똑같이 생각할 때 그들을 더 개방적이고 합리적이며 분별 있다고 여기는 흥미로운 경향을 가지고 있다.

② 앞은 직관은 오랜 학습과 경험에 의해서 얻어져야 한다고 말하고 있다. 반면 이후에는 접속사 'Yet'을 사용하여 오랜 학습과 경험에 의해 얻어지지 않은 직관에 대해 이야기 하고 있다. 그러므로 주어진 문장이 들어가기에 가장 적절한 곳은 ②이다.

- in accordance with ~에 따라
- intuition ⓝ 직관
- conviction ⓝ 확신
- substance ⓝ 실체
- tendency ⓝ 경향
- expertise ⓝ 전문 지식
- on one's feet 즉각적으로
- opinion ⓝ 의견
- delusions ⓝ 망상
- rational ⓐ 합리적인

구문 풀이

1행 Only then are they able to act quickly in accordance with their internalized expertise and evidence-based experience.
(부정어 도치 / 동사 / 주어)

★★ 문제 해결 꿀~팁 ★★

▶ 많이 틀린 이유는?
주어진 문장에서 살펴 볼 단어는 then과 they이다. then이 의미하는 상황과 they가 의미하는 명사가 이전에 언급되었어야 한다. 주어진 문장은 내재화된 전문 지식과 증거에 기반한 경험에 따라 빠르게 행동할 수 있다고 이야기하므로 then이 의미하는 것은 'has become data-driven'이며 they는 'experts'를 의미한다. 그 이후 Yet이라는 접속사로 대부분의 사람들은 전문가와 다르다고 이야기하고 있기 때문에 흐름상 ②에 오는 것이 맞다.

▶ 문제 해결 방법은?
주어진 문장을 완벽하게 해석하는 것이 많은 도움이 된다. 그 다음 글의 흐름을 파악하여 논조가 바뀌는 구간을 확인하고 주어진 문장이 어느 쪽인지 살펴본 후 점차 선택지를 줄여나가는 것이 좋다.

40 데이터 무덤을 금괴로 바꿀 수 있는 도구의 필요성   정답률 46% | 정답 ①

다음 글의 내용을 한 문장으로 요약하고자 한다. 빈칸 (A), (B)에 들어갈 말로 가장 적절한 것은?

(A)	(B)	(A)	(B)
✓ overwhelm 압도하기	obtain 얻기	② overwhelm 압도하기	exchange 교환하기
③ enhance 강화하기	apply 적용하기	④ enhance 강화하기	discover 발견하기
⑤ fulfill 수행하기	access 접근하기		

The fast-growing, / tremendous amount of data, / collected and stored / in large and numerous data repositories, / has far exceeded our human ability for understanding / without powerful tools.
빠르게 증가하는 / 엄청난 양의 데이터는 / 수집되고 저장된다. / 크고 많은 데이터 저장소에 / 우리 인간이 이해할 수 있는 능력을 훨씬 뛰어 넘었다. / 도구 없는

As a result, / data collected in large data repositories / become "data tombs" / — data archives that are hardly visited.
결과적으로 / 대규모 데이터 저장소에서 수집된 데이터는 / '데이터 무덤'이 된다. / 즉 찾는 사람이 거의 없는 데이터 보관소가 된다.

Important decisions are often made / based not on the information-rich data stored in data repositories / but rather on a decision maker's instinct, / simply because the decision maker does not have the tools / to extract the valuable knowledge hidden / in the vast amounts of data.
중요한 의사 결정이 종종 내려지기도 한다. / 데이터 저장소에 저장된 정보가 풍부한 데이터가 아닌 / 의사 결정자의 직관에 기반하여 / 이는 단지 의사 결정자가 도구를 가지고 있지 않기 때문이다. / 숨겨진 가치 있는 지식을 추출할 수 있는 / 방대한 양의 데이터에서

Efforts have been made / to develop expert system and knowledge-based technologies, / which typically rely on / users or domain experts to *manually* input knowledge into knowledge bases.
노력이 있어 왔다 / 전문가 시스템과 지식 기반 기술을 개발하려는 / 이는 일반적으로 의존한다. / 사용자나 분야 전문가가 '수동으로' 지식 기반에 입력하는 것에

However, / this procedure is likely to cause biases and errors / and is extremely costly and time consuming.
그러나 / 이 방법은 편견과 오류를 일으키기 쉽다. / 그리고 비용과 시간이 엄청나게 든다.

The widening gap / between data and information / calls for the systematic development of tools / that can turn data tombs into "golden nuggets" of knowledge.
점점 더 벌어지는 격차는 / 데이터와 정보 간의 / 도구의 체계적인 개발을 요구한다. / 데이터 무덤을 지식의 '금괴'로 바꿀 수 있는

→ As / the vast amounts of data stored in repositories / (A) overwhelm human understanding, / effective tools / to (B) obtain valuable knowledge / are required for better decision-making.
때문에 / 저장소에 저장된 방대한 양의 데이터는 / 인간의 이해를 압도한다. / 효과적인 도구는 / 가치 있는 지식을 얻기 위한 / 요구된다. / 더 나은 의사 결정을 위해

빠르게 증가하는 엄청난 양의 데이터는, 크고 많은 데이터 저장소에 수집되고 저장되어, 우리 인간이 효과적인 도구 없이는 이해할 수 있는 능력을 훨씬 뛰어넘었다. 결과적으로, 대규모 데이터 저장소에서 수집된 데이터는 '데이터 무덤', 즉 찾는 사람이 거의 없는 데이터 보관소가 된다. 중요한 의사 결정이 종종 데이터 저장소에 저장된 정보가 풍부한 데이터가 아닌 의사 결정자의 직관에 기반하여 내려지기도 하는데, 이는 단지 의사 결정자가 방대한 양의 데이터에 숨겨진 가치 있는 지식을 추출할 수 있는 도구를 가지고 있지 않기 때문이다. 전문가 시스템과 지식 기반 기술을 개발하려는 노력이 있어 왔는데, 이는 일반적으로 사용자나 분야(별) 전문가가 지식을 '수동으로' 지식 기반에 입력하는 것에 의존한다. 이 방법은 편견과 오류를 일으키기 쉽고 비용과 시간이 엄청나게 든다. 점점 더 벌어지는 데이터와 정보 간의 격차로 인해 데이터 무덤을 지식의 '금괴'로 바꿀 수 있는 도구의 체계적인 개발이 요구된다.

→ 저장소에 저장된 방대한 양의 데이터는 인간의 이해를 (A) 압도하기 때문에, 더 나은 의사 결정을 위해 가치 있는 지식을 (B) 얻기 위한 효과적인 도구가 요구된다.

빠르게 증가하는 엄청난 양의 데이터는 인간의 이해 능력을 훨씬 뛰어넘었다(The fast-growing, tremendous amount of data, collected and stored in large and numerous data repositories, has far exceeded our human ability for understanding without powerful tools.)는 내용이 서두에 언급되어 있으며, 기술을 추출할 수 있는 도구를 갖고 있지 않기 때문에 데이터 무덤을 금괴로 바꿀 도구의 개발이 필요하다(The widening gap between data and information calls for the systematic development of tools that can turn data tombs into "golden nuggets" of knowledge.)고 이야기하고 있다. 따라서 요약문의 빈칸 (A), (B)에 들어갈 말로 가장 적절한 것은 ① '(A) overwhelm(압도하기), (B) obtain(얻기)'이다.

- tremendous ⓐ 엄청난
- exceed ⓥ 뛰어넘다
- instinct ⓝ 직관
- manually ⓐⓓ 수동으로
- overwhelm ⓥ 압도하다
- fulfill ⓥ 수행하다
- repository ⓝ 저장소
- tomb ⓝ 무덤
- vast ⓐ 방대한
- procedure ⓝ 방법
- enhance ⓥ 강화하다

구문 풀이

11행 Efforts have been made to develop expert system and knowledge-based technologies, which typically rely on users or domain experts to manually input knowledge into knowledge bases.
(to부정사(형용사적) / to부정사(부사적))

41-42 십 대의 멀티태스킹

It's untrue / that teens can focus on two things at once / — what they're doing / is shifting their attention / from one task to another.
사실이 아니다 / 십대들이 동시에 두 가지 일에 집중할 수 있다는 것은 / 그들이 하고 있는 것은 / 주의를 전환하는 것이다. / 한 작업에서 다른 작업으로

「In this digital age, / teens wire their brains / to make these shifts very quickly, / but they are still, like everyone else, paying attention / to one thing at a time, / sequentially.」   【41번의 근거】
디지털 시대에 / 십 대들은 그들의 뇌를 연결한다. / 매우 빠르게 작업을 전환하도록 / 하지만 그들은 여전히 다른 모든 사람들과 마찬가지로 주의를 기울이고 있다. / 한 번에 한 가지씩 / 순차적으로

Common sense tells us / multitasking should (a) increase brain activity, / but Carnegie Mellon University scientists / using the latest brain imaging technology find it doesn't.
상식은 우리에게 말한다 / 멀티태스킹이 뇌 활동을 증가시킬 것이라고 / 하지만 Carnegie Mellon 대학의 과학자들은 / ; 최신 뇌 영상 기술을 사용하는 / 찾는다 그렇지 않다는 것을

「As a matter of fact, / they discovered / that multitasking actually decreases brain activity.」   【42번의 근거】
사실 / 그들은 발견했다. / 멀티태스킹이 실제로는 두뇌 활동을 감소시킨다는 것을

Neither task is done / as well as if each were performed (b) individually.
어느 작업도 잘 되지 못한다. / 각각 개별적으로 수행될 때만큼

Fractions of a second are lost / every time we make a switch, / and a person's interrupted task can take 50 percent (c) longer / to finish, / with 50 percent more errors.
시간이 아주 조금씩 낭비된다. / 우리가 전환할 때마다 / 그리고 사람의 중단된 작업은 50퍼센트 더 오래 걸린다. / 완료하기까지 / 50퍼센트 더 많은 에러와 함께

Turns out / the latest brain research (d) supports the old advice / "one thing at a time."
드러났다. / 최신 뇌 연구가 오래된 조언을 뒷받침하는 것으로 / 한 번에 한 가지 일만 하라는

It's not that kids can't do some tasks simultaneously.
아이들이 동시에 여러 작업을 할 수 없다는 것은 아니다.

But / two tasks are performed at once, / one of them has to be familiar.
그러나 / 동시에 두 가지 작업이 수행된다면 / 그중 하나는 익숙한 작업이어야 한다.

Our brains perform / a familiar task on "automatic pilot" / while really paying attention to the other one.
우리의 뇌는 수행한다. / 익숙한 작업을 '자동 조종' 상태에서 / 반면 실제로는 다른 작업에 주의를 기울인다.

That's why / insurance companies consider / talking on a cell phone and driving / to be as (e) dangerous as driving / while drunk / — it's the driving / that goes on "automatic pilot" / while the conversation really holds our attention.
그것이 이유이다. / 보험 회사가 간주하는 / 휴대 전화로 통화하면서 운전하는 것을 / 운전하는 것만큼 위험한 것으로 / 술 취한 상태에서 / 운전이다. / '자동 조종' 상태에서 수행 되는 것은 / 대화가 실제로 우리의 주의를 끌고 있는 동안

Our kids may be living / in the Information Age / but our brains have not been redesigned yet.
우리 아이들이 살고 있을지 모른다. / 정보화 시대에 / 그러나 우리의 뇌는 아직 재설계되지 않았다.

십 대들이 동시에 두 가지 일에 집중할 수 있다는 것은 사실이 아니며, 그들이 하고 있는 것은 한 작업에서 다른 작업으로 주의를 전환하는 것이다. 디지털 시대에, 십 대의 뇌는 매우 빠르게 작업을 전환하도록 발달하지만, 여전히 다른 모든 사람들과 마찬가지로 십 대들도 한 번에 한 가지씩 순차적으로 주의를 기울이고 있다. 상식적으로 멀티태스킹이 뇌 활동을 (a) 증가시킬 것이라고 생각하지만, Carnegie Mellon 대학의 과학자들은 최신 뇌 영상 기술을 사용하여 그렇지 않다는 것을 발견했다. 사실, 그들은 멀티태스킹이 실제로는 두뇌 활동을 감소시킨다는 것을 발견했다. 어느 작업도 각각 (b) 개별적으로 수행될 때만큼 잘 되지 못한다. 우리가 (작업을) 전환할 때마다 시간이 아주 조금씩 낭비되며, 중단된 작업은 완료하기까지 50퍼센트 (c) 더 오래 걸리고, 50퍼센트 더 많은 오류가 발생할 수 있다. 최신 뇌 연구가 '한 번에 한 가지 일만 하라'는 오래된 조언을 (d) 반박하는(→ 뒷받침하는) 것으로 드러났다. 아이들이 동시에 여러 작업을 할 수 없다는 것은 아니다. 하지만 동시에 두 가지 작업이 수행된다면, 그중 하나는 익숙한 작업이어야 한다. 우리의 뇌는 익숙한 작업을 '자동 조종' 상태에서 수행하고 실제로는 다른 작업에 주의를 기울인다. 그것이 보험 회사가 휴대 전화로 통화하면서

운전하는 것을 술에 취한 상태에서 운전하는 것만큼 (e) 위험한 것으로 간주하는 이유이다. 대화가 실제로 우리의 주의를 끌고 있는 동안 '자동 조종' 상태에서 수행되는 것은 운전이다. 우리 아이들이 정보화 시대에 살고 있을지 모르지만, 우리의 뇌는 아직 (정보화 시대에 맞게) 재설계되지 않았다.

- **shift** ⓥ 전환하다
- **sequentially** ⓐⓓ 순차적으로
- **switch** ⓝ 전환
- **contradict** ⓥ 반박하다
- **familiar** ⓐ 친숙한
- **age** ⓝ 시대
- **fraction** ⓝ 아주 조금
- **interrupt** ⓥ 중단시키다
- **simultaneously** ⓐⓓ 동시에
- **redesign** ⓥ 재설계하다

구문 풀이

10행 Neither task is done as well as if each were performed individually.
가정법과거(마치 ~인 것처럼)

41 제목 파악
정답률 71% | 정답 ①

윗글의 제목으로 가장 적절한 것은?

☑ Multitasking Unveiled: What Really Happens in Teens' Brains
멀티태스킹의 비밀: 십 대의 뇌에서 실제로 일어나는 일
② Optimal Ways to Expand the Attention Span of Teens
청소년의 주의력을 향상시키는 최적의 방법
③ Unknown Approaches to Enhance Brain Development
뇌 발달을 향상시키기 위한 알려지지 않은 접근법
④ Multitasking for a Balanced Life in a Busy World
바쁜 세상에서 균형 잡힌 삶을 위한 멀티태스킹
⑤ How to Build Automaticity in Performing Tasks
작업을 수행할 때 자동성을 구축하는 법

Why? 왜 정답일까?

십 대의 뇌는 매우 빠르게 작업을 전환하도록 발달하지만 멀티태스킹보다는 한 번에 한 가지씩 순차적으로 주의를 기울일 수 있다(In this digital age, teens wire their brains to make these shifts very quickly, but they are still, like everyone else, paying attention to one thing at a time, sequentially.)고 말하고 있으므로, 글의 제목으로 가장 적절한 것은 ① '멀티태스킹의 비밀: 십 대의 뇌에서 실제로 일어나는 일'이다.

42 어휘 추론
정답률 46% | 정답 ④

밑줄 친 (a)~(e) 중에서 문맥상 낱말의 쓰임이 적절하지 않은 것은?

① (a) ② (b) ③ (c) ☑ (d) ⑤ (e)

Why? 왜 정답일까?

멀티태스킹은 두뇌 활동을 감소시켜 작업 속도를 늦추고 더 많은 오류를 만들어 낸다(As a matter of fact, they discovered that multitasking actually decreases brain activity.)고 이야기하고 있으므로 contradicts 대신 supports를 써야 자연스럽다. 낱말의 쓰임이 문맥상 적절하지 않은 것은 ④ '(d)'이다.

43-45 반려동물 Leo

(A)
Christine was a cat owner / who loved her furry companion, Leo.
Christine은 고양이 주인이다. / 그녀의 털북숭이 반려동물인 Leo를 사랑하는
One morning, / she noticed / that Leo was not feeling well.
어느 날 아침 / 그녀는 알게 되었다 / Leo의 몸 상태가 좋지 않다는 것을
Concerned for her beloved cat, / Christine decided / to take him to the animal hospital.
사랑하는 고양이가 걱정되어서 / christine은 결심했다. / 그를 동물 병원에 데려가기로
『As she always brought Leo to this hospital, / she was certain / that the vet knew well about Leo.』 45번 ①의 근거 일치
그녀가 항상 이 병원에 데려왔기 때문에 / 그녀는 확신했다. / 수의사가 Leo에 대해 잘 알고 있을 것이라고
(a) She desperately hoped / Leo got the necessary care / as soon as possible.
그녀는 간절히 희망했다. / Leo가 필요한 보살핌을 받기를 / 가능한 한 빨리

(D)
『The waiting room was filled / with other pet owners.』 45번 ④의 근거 일치
대기실은 꽉 차 있었다. / 다른 반려동물의 주인들로
Finally, / it was Leo's turn to see the vet.
마침내 / Leo가 수의사를 만날 차례가 되었다.
Christine watched / as the vet gently examined him.
Christine은 지켜보았다. / 수의사가 그를 조심스럽게 진찰하는 모습을
The vet said, / "(d) I think Leo has a minor infection."
수의사가 말했다. / "저는 Leo에게 경미한 감염이 있다고 생각합니다."
"Infection? / Will he be okay?" / asked Christine.
감염이요? / 그는 괜찮을까요? / christine이 물었다.
『"We need to do some tests / to see / if he is infected.』 45번 ⑤의 근거 일치
우리는 몇 가지 검사를 할 필요가 있습니다. / 알기 위해서 / 그가 감염되어 있는지
But / for the tests, / it's best for Leo to stay here," / replied the vet.
하지만 / 검사를 위해서 / Leo가 여기 머무는 것이 가장 좋습니다. / 수의사가 대답했다
It was heartbreaking for Christine / to leave Leo / at the animal hospital, / but (e) she had to accept / it was for the best.
Christine에게는 가슴 아팠다. / Leo를 두고 가는 것이 / 동물병원에 / 하지만 그녀는 받아들여야만 했다. / 이것이 최선이라는 것을

(B)
"I'll call (b) you / with updates / as soon as we know anything," / said the vet.
당신에게 전화하겠습니다. / 새로운 소식과 함께 / 저희가 뭔가 알게 되는 즉시 / 수의사가 말했다.
Throughout the day, / Christine anxiously awaited news / about Leo.
그날 내내 / Christine은 초조하게 소식을 기다렸다. / Leo에 대한
『Later that day, / the phone rang / and it was the vet.』 45번 ②의 근거 불일치
그날 늦게 / 전화가 울렸다. / 그리고 그건 수의사였다.
"The tests revealed / a minor infection.
검사 결과 경미한 감염이 발견되었습니다.
Leo needs some medication and rest, / but he'll be back / to his playful self / soon."
Leo는 약간의 약물 치료와 휴식이 필요합니다. / 하지만 그는 돌아올 것입니다. / 장난기 넘치는 모습으로 / 곧

Relieved to hear the news, / Christine rushed back to the animal hospital / to pick up Leo.
그 소식을 듣고 안도하며 / Christine은 동물병원에 서둘러 되돌아갔다. / Leo를 데리러

(C)
『The vet provided detailed instructions / on how to administer the medication / and shared tips for a speedy recovery.』 45번 ③의 근거 일치
수의사는 자세히 설명했다. / 약을 투여하는 방법을 / 그리고 빠른 회복을 위한 조언을 했다.
Back at home, / Christine created a comfortable space / for Leo to rest and heal.
집으로 돌아와서 / Christine은 편안한 공간을 만들었다. / Leo가 쉬고 회복할 수 있는
(c) She patted him / with love and attention, / ensuring that he would recover in no time.
그녀는 그를 쓰다듬었다. / 사랑과 관심으로 / 그가 금방 회복할 수 있도록
As the days passed, / Leo gradually regained / his strength and playful spirit.
며칠이 지나자 / Leo는 점차 되찾았다. / 체력과 장난기 넘치는 활기를

(A)
Christine은 고양이 주인으로 그녀의 털북숭이 반려동물인 Leo를 사랑한다. 어느 날 아침, 그녀는 Leo의 몸 상태가 좋지 않다는 것을 알게 되었다. 사랑하는 고양이가 걱정되어서, Christine은 Leo를 동물병원에 데려가기로 결심했다. 그녀가 항상 Leo를 이 병원에 데려왔기 때문에, 수의사가 Leo에 대해 잘 알고 있을 것이라고 그녀는 확신했다. Leo가 필요한 보살핌을 가능한 한 빨리 받기를 (a) 그녀는 간절히 바랐다.

(D)
대기실은 다른 반려동물의 주인들로 꽉 차 있었다. 마침내, Leo가 수의사를 만날 차례가 되었다. Christine은 수의사가 Leo를 조심스럽게 진찰하는 모습을 지켜보았다. "(d) 저는 Leo에게 경미한 감염이 있다고 생각합니다." 수의사가 말했다. "감염이요? Leo는 괜찮을까요?" Christine이 물었다. "감염 여부를 알기 위해 우리는 몇 가지 검사를 할 필요가 있습니다. 하지만 검사를 위해서 Leo가 여기 머무는 것이 가장 좋습니다." 수의사가 대답했다. Leo를 병원에 두고 가는 것이 Christine에게는 가슴 아팠지만, (e) 그녀는 그것이 최선이라는 것을 받아들여야만 했다.

(B)
"저희가 뭔가 알게 되는 즉시 (b) 당신에게 전화로 새로운 소식을 알려 드리겠습니다."라고 수의사가 말했다. 그날 내내 Christine은 초조하게 Leo에 대한 소식을 기다렸다. 그날 늦게 전화가 울렸고 그것(전화를 건 사람)은 수의사였다. "검사 결과 경미한 감염이 발견되었습니다. Leo는 약간의 약물 치료와 휴식이 필요하긴 하지만 곧 장난기 넘치는 모습으로 돌아올 거예요." 그 소식을 듣고 안도하며, Christine은 Leo를 데리러 동물병원으로 서둘러 되돌아갔다.

(C)
수의사는 약을 투여하는 방법을 자세히 설명해 주고 빠른 회복을 위한 조언을 했다. 집으로 돌아와서, Christine은 Leo가 쉬고 회복할 수 있는 편안한 공간을 만들었다. (c) 그녀는 Leo가 금방 회복할 수 있도록 사랑과 관심으로 Leo를 쓰다듬어 주었다. 며칠이 지나자, Leo는 점차 체력과 장난기 넘치는 활기를 되찾았다.

- **furry** ⓐ 털북숭이의
- **beloved** ⓐ 사랑스러운
- **certain** ⓥ 확신하다
- **be filled with** ~로 채우다
- **infection** ⓝ 감염
- **accept** ⓥ 받아들이다
- **anxiously** ⓐⓓ 초조하게
- **reveal** ⓥ 드러내다
- **rush** ⓥ 서두르다
- **administer** ⓥ 투여하다
- **pass** ⓥ 지나다
- **notice** ⓥ 알리다
- **hospital** ⓝ 병원
- **desperately** ⓐⓓ 절망적으로
- **examine** ⓥ 진찰하다
- **heartbreaking** ⓐ 가슴 아픈
- **vet** ⓝ 수의사
- **await** ⓥ 기다리다
- **medication** ⓝ 약물
- **pick up** 데리고 오다
- **ensure** ⓥ 보장하다
- **spirit** ⓝ 활기

구문 풀이

(D) 7행 It was heartbreaking for Christine to leave Leo at the animal hospital, but
가주어 / 의미상 주어 / 진주어(to부정사)
she had to accept it was for the best.

43 글의 순서 파악
정답률 80% | 정답 ④

주어진 글 (A)에 이어질 내용을 순서에 맞게 배열한 것으로 가장 적절한 것은?

① (B) - (D) - (C) ② (C) - (B) - (D)
③ (C) - (D) - (B) ☑ (D) - (B) - (C)
⑤ (D) - (C) - (B)

Why? 왜 정답일까?

Leo가 아팠다는 내용의 (A)뒤로, 병원에 도착한 내용의 (D), 검사 결과에 대한 내용의 (B), 다시 활기를 되찾은 내용의 (C)가 순서대로 이어져야 자연스럽다. 따라서 글의 순서로 가장 적절한 것은 ④ '(D) – (B) – (C)'이다.

44 지칭 추론
정답률 82% | 정답 ④

밑줄 친 (a)~(e) 중에서 가리키는 대상이 나머지 넷과 다른 것은?

① (a) ② (b) ③ (c) ☑ (d) ⑤ (e)

Why? 왜 정답일까?

(a), (b), (c), (e)는 she(Leo의 주인) (b)는 the vet을 가리키므로, (a)~(e) 중에서 가리키는 대상이 다른 하나는 ④ '(d)'이다.

45 세부 내용 파악
정답률 67% | 정답 ②

윗글에 관한 내용으로 적절하지 않은 것은?

① Christine은 수의사가 Leo에 대해 잘 알고 있을 거라고 확신했다.
☑ Christine은 병원을 방문한 다음 날 수의사의 전화를 받았다.
③ 수의사는 Leo의 빠른 회복을 위한 조언을 했다.

④ 대기실은 다른 반려동물의 주인들로 꽉 차 있었다.
⑤ Leo의 감염 여부를 알기 위해 검사를 할 필요가 있었다.

Why? 왜 정답일까?

(B) 'Later that day, the phone rang and it was the vet.'에서 그날 늦게 전화가 울렸다고 했으므로, 내용과 일치하지 않는 것은 ② 'Christine은 병원을 방문한 다음 날 수의사의 전화를 받았다.'이다.

Why? 왜 오답일까?

① (A) 'As she always brought Leo to this hospital, she was certain that the vet knew well about Leo.'의 내용과 일치한다.
③ (C) 'The vet provided detailed instructions on how to administer the medication and shared tips for a speedy recovery.'의 내용과 일치한다.
④ (D) 'The waiting room was filled with other pet owners.'의 내용과 일치한다.
⑤ (D) 'We need to do some tests to see if he is infected.'의 내용과 일치한다.

어휘 Review Test 01

문제편 010쪽

A	B	C	D
01 조바심	01 concern	01 ⓘ	01 ⓑ
02 이행하다	02 embrace	02 ⓟ	02 ⓜ
03 억제하다	03 mere	03 ⓓ	03 ⓕ
04 거래하다	04 overwhelm	04 ⓞ	04 ⓙ
05 수직의	05 imply	05 ⓗ	05 ⓚ
06 유혹하다	06 illusion	06 ⓡ	06 ⓢ
07 제한하다	07 interrupt	07 ⓝ	07 ⓡ
08 빈곤한	08 regulation	08 ⓚ	08 ⓒ
09 반복적인	09 operate	09 ⓖ	09 ⓓ
10 무덤	10 overlook	10 ⓘ	10 ⓠ
11 부상	11 expectation	11 ⓕ	11 ⓗ
12 흡수하다	12 assumption	12 ⓜ	12 ⓖ
13 기초의	13 artwork	13 ⓙ	13 ⓘ
14 공감	14 vast	14 ⓔ	14 ⓝ
15 생겨나다	15 invisible	15 ⓘ	15 ⓐ
16 아주 조금	16 entire	16 ⓢ	16 ⓞ
17 실체	17 manually	17 ⓑ	17 ⓟ
18 서두르다	18 negotiate	18 ⓠ	18 ⓘ
19 뛰어넘다	19 affective	19 ⓐ	19 ⓔ
20 편견	20 cognitive	20 ⓒ	20 ⓘ

- 정답 -

18 ② 19 ② 20 ⑤ 21 ③ 22 ⑤ 23 ⑤ 24 ④ 25 ③ 26 ④ 27 ⑤ 28 ⑤ 29 ⑤ 30 ③ 31 ④ 32 ②
33 ① 34 ④ 35 ③ 36 ④ 37 ③ 38 ② 39 ④ 40 ① 41 ① 42 ③ 43 ⑤ 44 ④ 45 ⑤

★ 표기된 문항은 [등급을 가르는 문제]에 해당하는 문항입니다.

18 미술 작품 구매 가능 여부 묻기   정답률 88% | 정답 ②

다음 글의 목적으로 가장 적절한 것은?

① 좋아하는 화가와의 만남을 요청하려고
☑ 미술 작품의 구매 가능 여부를 문의하려고
③ 소장 중인 미술 작품의 감정을 의뢰하려고
④ 미술 작품의 소유자 변경 내역을 확인하려고
⑤ 기획 중인 전시회에 참여하는 화가를 홍보하려고

It was a pleasure meeting you / at your gallery last week.
만나서 즐거웠습니다. / 지난주에 귀하의 화랑에서
I appreciate your effort / to select and exhibit diverse artwork.
저는 귀하의 노력에 감사드립니다. / 다양한 미술 작품을 선정하고 전시한
As I mentioned, / I greatly admire Robert D. Parker's paintings, / which emphasize the beauty of nature.
제가 말씀드렸듯이, / 저는 Robert D. Parker의 그림을 대단히 좋아하는데, / 그것은 자연의 아름다움을 강조합니다.
Over the past few days, / I have been researching and learning about Robert D. Parker's online viewing room / through your gallery's website.
지난 며칠 동안, / 저는 Robert D. Parker의 온라인 전시 공간에 관해 조사하고 알아보았습니다. / 귀하의 화랑 웹사이트를 통해
I'm especially interested in purchasing the painting / that depicts the horizon, / titled *Sunrise*.
저는 그림을 구매하는 데 특히 관심이 있습니다. / 수평선을 묘사한 / *Sunrise*라는 제목의
I would like to know / if the piece is still available for purchase.
저는 알고 싶습니다. / 그 작품을 아직 구매할 수 있는지를
It would be a great pleasure / to house this wonderful piece of art.
큰 기쁨이 될 것입니다. / 이 훌륭한 미술 작품을 소장할 수 있는 것은
I look forward to your reply to this inquiry.
저는 이 문의에 대한 귀하의 답변을 손꼽아 기다립니다.

지난주에 귀하의 화랑에서 만나서 즐거웠습니다. 다양한 미술 작품을 선정하고 전시한 귀하의 노력에 감사드립니다. 제가 말씀드렸듯이, 저는 Robert D. Parker의 그림을 대단히 좋아하는데, 그의 그림은 자연의 아름다움을 강조합니다. 지난 며칠 동안, 저는 귀하의 화랑 웹사이트를 통해 Robert D. Parker의 온라인 전시 공간에 관해 조사하고 알아보았습니다. 저는 수평선을 묘사한 *Sunrise*라는 제목의 그림을 구매하는 데 특히 관심이 있습니다. 저는 그 작품을 아직 구매할 수 있는지를 알고 싶습니다. 이 훌륭한 미술 작품을 소장할 수 있다면 큰 기쁨이 될 것입니다. 이 문의에 대한 귀하의 답변을 손꼽아 기다립니다.

Why? 왜 정답일까?

관심 있는 미술 작품을 아직 구매할 수 있는지(I would like to know if the piece is still available for purchase.) 물어보는 글이므로, 글의 목적으로 가장 적절한 것은 ② '미술 작품의 구매 가능 여부를 문의하려고'이다.

- appreciate ⓥ 고마워하다
- mention ⓥ 언급하다
- emphasize ⓥ 강조하다
- depict ⓥ 그리다, 묘사하다
- house ⓥ 소장하다, 보관하다
- exhibit ⓥ 전시하다
- admire ⓥ 존경하다, 찬탄하다
- purchase ⓥ 구매하다 ⓝ 구매
- available ⓐ 이용 가능한
- inquiry ⓝ 문의

구문 풀이

8행   I would like to know **if** the piece is still available for purchase.
명사절 접속사(~인지 아닌지)

19 카페 개업을 앞둔 Isabel   정답률 78% | 정답 ②

다음 글에 드러난 Isabel의 심경 변화로 가장 적절한 것은?

① calm → surprised
  평온한   놀란
☑ doubtful → confident
  의심하는   자신 있는
③ envious → delighted
  부러워하는   기쁜
④ grateful → frightened
  고마워하는   겁에 질린
⑤ indifferent → uneasy
  무관심한   불안한

On opening day, / Isabel arrives at the cafe very early / with nervous anticipation.
개업식날, / Isabel은 카페에 매우 일찍 도착한다. / 초조한 기대감을 품고
She looks around the cafe, / but she can't shake off the feeling / that something is missing.
그녀는 카페를 둘러보지만, / 그녀는 느낌을 떨쳐낼 수 없다. / 뭔가 빠졌다는
As she sets out cups, spoons, and plates, / Isabel's doubts grow.
그녀가 컵과 숟가락, 접시를 차려 놓으며 / Isabel의 의심은 커진다.
She looks around, / trying to imagine what else she could do / to make the cafe perfect, / but nothing comes to mind.
그녀는 주변을 둘러보지만, / 뭘 더 할 수 있을지를 상상하려고 애쓰며 / 카페를 완벽하게 만들기 위해 / 아무것도 머릿속에 떠오르지 않는다.
Then, in a sudden burst of inspiration, / Isabel grabs her paintbrush / and transforms the blank walls into landscapes, / adding flowers and trees.
그때, 갑작스러운 영감의 폭발과 함께, / Isabel은 붓을 쥐고 / 텅 빈 벽을 풍경화로 변화시킨다. / 꽃과 나무를 더해
As she paints, / her doubts begin to fade.
그녀가 그림을 그리면서, / 그녀의 불안도 서서히 사라지기 시작한다.
Looking at her handiwork, / which is beautifully done, / she is certain / that the cafe will be a success.
그녀의 작품을 보며, / 아름답게 완성된 / 그녀는 확신한다. / 카페가 성공할 거라고

'Now, success is not exactly guaranteed,' / she thinks to herself, / 'but I'll definitely get there.'
'자, 성공이 확실히 보장되지는 않았지만,' / 그녀는 혼자 생각한다. / '나는 분명 이르게 될 거야.'라고

개업식날, Isabel은 초조한 기대감을 품고 카페에 매우 일찍 도착한다. 그녀는 카페를 둘러보지만, 뭔가 빠졌다는 느낌을 떨쳐 낼 수 없다. 컵과 숟가락, 접시를 차려 놓으며 Isabel의 의심은 커진다. 그녀는 카페를 완벽하게 만들기 위해 뭘 더 할 수 있을지를 상상하려 애쓰며 주변을 둘러보지만, 아무것도 머릿속에 떠오르지 않는다. 그때, 갑작스러운 영감의 폭발과 함께, Isabel은 붓을 쥐고 꽃과 나무를 더해 텅 빈 벽을 풍경화로 변화시킨다. 그림을 그리면서, 그녀의 불안도 서서히 사라지기 시작한다. 아름답게 완성된 그녀의 작품을 보며, 그녀는 카페가 성공할 거라고 확신한다. '자, 성공이 확실히 보장되지는 않았지만, 나는 분명 이르게 될 거야.'라고 혼자 생각한다.

Why? 왜 정답일까?

카페 개업을 앞두고 뭔가 빠진 느낌에 의심(doubts)을 품었던 Isabel이 벽면에 그림을 그려넣고는 카페가 잘 될거라는 확신을 느꼈다(she is certain that the cafe will be a success)는 내용이다. 따라서 Isabel의 심경 변화로 가장 적절한 것은 ② '의심하는 → 자신 있는'이다.

- **anticipation** ⓝ 기대
- **set out** 차려내다, 착수하다, 시작하다
- **sudden** ⓐ 갑작스러운
- **inspiration** ⓝ 영감
- **transform** ⓥ 변모시키다
- **fade** ⓥ 옅어지다
- **certain** ⓐ 확신하는
- **envious** ⓐ 부러워하는
- **frightened** ⓐ 겁에 질린
- **shake off** 떨쳐내다
- **doubt** ⓝ 의심
- **burst** ⓝ 폭발
- **grab** ⓥ 집어들다
- **landscape** ⓝ 풍경(화)
- **handiwork** ⓝ (솜씨를 발휘한) 작품, 피조물
- **guarantee** ⓥ 보장하다, 보증하다
- **grateful** ⓐ 고마워하는
- **uneasy** ⓐ 불안한

구문 풀이

4행 She looks around the cafe, but she can't shake off the feeling [that something is missing].   [ ]: 동격(= the feeling)

---

20 일과 상황을 수용하고 받아들이기   정답률 73% | 정답 ⑤

다음 글에서 필자가 주장하는 바로 가장 적절한 것은?
① 창의력을 기르려면 익숙한 환경에서 벗어나야 한다.
② 상대방의 무리한 요구는 최대한 분명하게 거절해야 한다.
③ 주어진 과업을 정확하게 파악한 후에 일을 시작해야 한다.
④ 효율적으로 일을 처리하기 위해 좋아하는 일부터 해야 한다.
☑ 원치 않는 일을 해야만 할 때 수용적인 태도를 갖춰야 한다.

The more people have to do unwanted things / the more chances are / that they create unpleasant environment / for themselves and others.
사람들은 원치 않는 일을 더 해야 할수록, / 가능성이 더 커진다. / 그들이 불편한 환경을 만들 / 자신과 다른 사람에게
If you hate the thing you do / but have to do it nonetheless, / you have choice / between hating the thing / and accepting that it needs to be done.
만약 여러분이 하는 일을 싫어하지만 / 그럼에도 불구하고 그것을 해야 한다면, / 여러분은 선택할 수 있다. / 그 일을 싫어하는 것과 / 그 일을 끝내야 한다는 사실을 받아들이는 것 중에
Either way / you will do it.
어느 쪽이든, / 여러분은 그 일을 할 것이다.
Doing it from place of hatred / will develop hatred / towards the self and others around you; / doing it from the place of acceptance / will create compassion towards the self / and allow for opportunities / to find a more suitable way of accomplishing the task.
증오의 영역에서 그 일을 한다면, / 증오를 키우게 된다 / 여러분 자신과 주변 사람들을 향한 / 수용의 영역에서 그 일을 하는 것은 / 자신을 향한 연민을 만들어 내며 / 기회를 갖게 해준다. / 그 과업을 달성할 더 적합한 방법을 찾을
If you decide to accept the fact / that your task has to be done, / start from recognising / that your situation is a gift from life; / this will help you to see it / as a lesson in acceptance.
여러분이 사실을 받아들이기로 한다면, / 과업이 완료되어야 한다는 / 인식하는 것으로부터 시작하라. / 여러분의 상황이 삶이 준 선물임을 / 이는 여러분이 그것을 여기게 도울 것이다. / 수용의 교훈으로

사람들은 원하지 않는 일을 더 해야 할수록, 자신과 다른 사람에게 불편한 환경을 만들 가능성이 더 커진다. 만약 여러분이 하는 일을 싫어하지만 그럼에도 불구하고 해야 한다면, 여러분은 그 일을 싫어하는 것과 그 일을 끝내야 한다는 사실을 받아들이는 것 중 하나를 선택할 수 있다. 어느 쪽이든, 여러분은 그 일을 할 것이다. 증오의 영역에서 그 일을 한다면, 여러분 자신과 주변 사람들을 향한 증오를 키우게 된다. (하지만) 수용의 영역에서 그 일을 한다면 자신을 향한 연민을 갖게 되며 그 과업을 달성할 더 적합한 방법을 찾을 기회를 갖게 된다. 과업이 완료되어야 한다는 사실을 받아들이기로 한다면, 여러분의 상황이 삶이 준 선물임을 인식하는 것으로부터 시작하라. 이는 여러분이 그것을 수용의 교훈으로 여기게 도울 것이다.

Why? 왜 정답일까?

일이 싫더라도 끝내야 한다는 것을 받아들이기로 했다면, 그것을 삶이 준 선물로 받아들이고 수용의 교훈으로 삼으라(If you decide to accept the fact that your task has to be done, start from recognising that your situation is a gift from life; ~ see it as a lesson in acceptance.)는 내용의 글이다. 따라서 필자가 주장하는 바로 가장 적절한 것은 ⑤ '원치 않는 일을 해야만 할 때 수용적인 태도를 갖춰야 한다.'이다.

- **unwanted** ⓐ 원치 않는
- **environment** ⓝ 환경
- **develop** ⓥ 키우다, 발전시키다
- **compassion** ⓝ 연민, 동정
- **accomplish** ⓥ 달성하다, 이루다
- **unpleasant** ⓐ 불쾌한
- **nonetheless** ⓐ 그럼에도 불구하고
- **acceptance** ⓝ 수용
- **allow for** ~을 허용하다, 고려하다
- **task** ⓝ 과제

구문 풀이

1행 The more people have to do unwanted things the more chances are that they create unpleasant environment for themselves and others.
the+비교급 ~, the+비교급 ~: ~할수록 …하다   접속사

---

21 상황이 허락하는 한, 완벽하지 않더라도 실행하기   정답률 55% | 정답 ③

밑줄 친 helping move the needle forward가 다음 글에서 의미하는 바로 가장 적절한 것은?   [3점]
① spending time and money on celebrating perfection
완벽을 칭송하는 데 시간과 돈을 쓰는 것
② suggesting cost-saving strategies for a good cause
좋은 대의명분을 위해 비용 절감 전략을 제안하는 것
☑ making a difference as best as the situation allows
상황이 허락하는 한 최대한 차이를 만드는 것
④ checking your resources before altering the original goal
원래 목표를 바꾸기 앞서 자원을 확인해보는 것
⑤ collecting donations to help the education of poor children
가난한 아이들의 교육을 돕기 위해 기부금을 모으는 것

Everyone's heard the expression / don't let the perfect become the enemy of the good.
표현은 누구나 들어 본 적이 있다. / 완벽하다는 것이 좋다는 것의 적이 되게 두지 말라는
If you want to get over an obstacle / so that your idea can become the solution-based policy / you've long dreamed of, / you can't have an all-or-nothing mentality.
여러분이 장애물을 극복하고 싶다면, / 여러분의 아이디어가 해결책 중심의 방책이 될 수 있도록 / 여러분이 오랫동안 꿈꿔 왔던 / 여러분은 전부 아니면 전무라는 식의 사고방식을 가져서는 안 된다.
You have to be willing to alter your idea / and let others influence its outcome.
여러분은 기꺼이 아이디어를 바꿔야 한다. / 그리고 다른 사람이 그 결과에 영향을 미치게
You have to be okay / with the outcome being a little different, / even a little less, / than you wanted.
여러분은 괜찮다고 여겨야 한다. / 결과가 여러분이 원했던 것과 조금 다르거나, / 심지어 조금 못해도 / 원했던 것보다
Say you're pushing for a clean water act.
여러분이 수질 오염 방지법을 추진하고 있다고 가정해 보자.
Even if what emerges isn't as well-funded / as you wished, / or doesn't match how you originally conceived the bill, / you'll have still succeeded in ensuring / that kids in troubled areas have access to clean water.
비록 나타난 결과가 자금을 충분히 지원받지 못한 것이거나, / 여러분이 원했던 만큼 / 여러분이 처음에 이 법안을 고안한 방식과 일치하지 않더라도, / 여러분은 보장하는 데 여전히 성공할 것이다. / 힘든 지역의 아이들이 깨끗한 물을 이용할 수 있게
That's what counts, / that they will be safer / because of your idea and your effort.
그게 중요한 것이다. / 바로 그들이 더 안전할 거라는 것 / 여러분의 아이디어와 노력 덕분에
Is it perfect? // No.
완벽한가? // 아니다.
Is there more work to be done? // Absolutely.
더 해야 할 일이 있는가? // 당연하다.
But in almost every case, / helping move the needle forward / is vastly better / than not helping at all.
하지만 거의 모든 경우에, / 바늘이 앞으로 가게 돕는 것이 / 훨씬 더 낫다. / 전혀 돕지 않는 것보다

완벽하다는 것이 좋다는 것의 적이 되게 두지 말라는 표현은 누구나 들어 본 적이 있다. 여러분이 장애물을 극복해서 여러분의 아이디어가 오랫동안 꿈꿔 왔던 대로 해결책 중심의 방책이 되게 하고 싶다면, 전부 아니면 전무라는 식의 사고방식을 가져서는 안 된다. 여러분은 기꺼이 아이디어를 바꾸고 다른 사람이 그 결과에 영향을 미치게 해야 한다. 결과가 여러분이 원했던 것과 조금 다르거나, 심지어 원했던 것보다 조금 못해도 괜찮다고 여겨야 한다. 여러분이 수질 오염 방지법을 추진하고 있다고 가정해 보자. 비록 나타난 결과가 여러분이 원했던 만큼 자금을 충분히 지원받지 못한 것이거나, 여러분이 처음에 이 법안을 고안한 방식과 일치하지 않더라도, 여러분은 힘든 지역의 아이들이 깨끗한 물을 이용할 수 있게 하는 데 여전히 성공할 것이다. 중요한 것은 바로 여러분의 아이디어와 노력 덕분에 그들이 더 안전할 거라는 것이다. 완벽한가? 아니다. 더 해야 할 일이 있는가? 당연하다. 하지만 거의 모든 경우에, 바늘이 앞으로 가게 돕는 것이 전혀 돕지 않는 것보다 훨씬 더 낫다.

Why? 왜 정답일까?

완벽하지 않은 아이디어라도 실행해 결과를 만들어내는 것이 중요하다는 내용의 글이다. 결과가 애초 원했던 바와 다르거나, 심지어 약간 못하다고 여겨질지라도 나름의 의미가 있다는 내용을 통해, 상황의 한계 안에서 '일단 조금이라도 해보는 것'이 중요하다는 주제를 파악할 수 있다. 따라서 밑줄 친 부분의 의미로 가장 적절한 것은 ③ '상황이 허락하는 한 최대한 차이를 만드는 것'이다.

- **get over** ~을 극복하다
- **policy** ⓝ 정책, 방책
- **mentality** ⓝ 사고방식
- **alter** ⓥ 바꾸다, 수정하다
- **outcome** ⓝ 결과
- **act** ⓝ 법안
- **well-funded** ⓐ 자금을 잘 지원받는
- **ensure** ⓥ 보장하다
- **vastly** ⓐ 대단히, 엄청나게
- **cost-saving** ⓐ 비용을 절감하는
- **obstacle** ⓝ 장애물
- **all-or-nothing** ⓐ 전부 아니면 전무의, 양자택일의
- **be willing to** 기꺼이 ~하다
- **influence** ⓥ 영향을 미치다 ⓝ 영향
- **push for** ~을 추진하다
- **emerge** ⓥ 나타나다, 출현하다
- **conceive** ⓥ 고안하다, 떠올리다
- **have access to** ~을 이용하다
- **celebrate** ⓥ 칭송하다, 축하하다

구문 풀이

13행 But in almost every case, helping move the needle forward is vastly better than not helping at all.
동명사구 주어   동사(단수)   동명사 부정 표현(not + 동명사)

---

22 변화를 받아들이고 성장하는 것의 중요성   정답률 60% | 정답 ⑤

다음 글의 요지로 가장 적절한 것은?
① 다양한 업종의 경력이 있으면 구직 활동에 유리하다.
② 직원의 다양한 능력을 활용하면 업계를 주도할 수 있다.
③ 기술이 발전함에 따라 단순 반복 업무가 사라지고 있다.
④ 자신의 약점을 인정하면 동료들로부터 도움을 얻기 쉽다.
☑ 변화를 받아들이지 못하면 업계에서의 적합성을 잃게 된다.

Brands that fail to grow and develop / lose their relevance.
성장과 발전에 실패한 브랜드는 / 그 적합성을 잃는다.
Think about the person you knew / who was once on the fast track at your company, / who is either no longer with the firm / or, worse yet, / appears to have hit a plateau in his or her career.

여러분이 알던 사람을 생각해 보라. / 한때 여러분의 회사에서 승진 가도에 있었는데 / 더 이상 회사에 있지 않거나, / 더 나쁜 예로는 / 경력의 정체기에 든 것으로 보이는

Assuming / he or she did not make an ambitious move, / more often than not, / this individual is a victim of having failed / to stay relevant and embrace the advances in his or her industry.
가정하면, / 그 사람이 야심에 찬 행동을 하지 않았다고 / 대개 / 이 사람은 하지 못한 것의 희생자이다. / 자기 업계에서 적합성을 유지하고 발전을 포용하지

Think about the impact / personal computing technology had / on the first wave of executive leadership / exposed to the technology.
영향을 생각해 보라. / 개인용 컴퓨터 사용 기술이 미친 / 첫 물결의 경영 지도자에게 / 이 기술을 접한

Those who embraced the technology / were able to integrate it into their work styles / and excel.
기술을 포용한 이들은 / 그것을 그들의 작업 스타일에 흡수시켜서 / 탁월해질 수 있었다.

Those who were resistant many times / found few opportunities / to advance their careers / and in many cases were ultimately let go / through early retirement / for failure to stay relevant and update their skills.
여러 번 (기술에) 저항한 이들은 / 기회를 거의 찾을 수 없었고, / 자기 경력을 발전시키기 위한 / 많은 경우 이들은 결국 해고되었다. / 이른 은퇴를 통해 / 적합성을 유지하고 기술을 새롭게 하는 데 실패하여

성장과 발전에 실패한 브랜드는 그 적합성을 잃는다. 한때 여러분의 회사에서 승진 가도에 있었는데 더 이상 회사에 있지 않거나, 더 나쁜 예로는 경력의 정체기에 든 것으로 보이는 지인을 생각해 보라. 그 사람이 야심에 찬 행동을 하지 않았다고 가정하면, 대개 이 사람은 자기 업계에서 적합성을 유지하고 발전을 포용하지 못한 것의 희생자이다. 개인용 컴퓨터 사용 기술이 이 기술을 접한 첫 물결의 경영 지도자에게 미친 영향을 생각해 보라. 기술을 포용한 이들은 그것을 그들의 작업 스타일에 흡수시켜서 탁월해질 수 있었다. 여러 번 (기술에) 저항한 이들은 경력을 발전시키기 위한 기회를 거의 찾을 수 없었고, 많은 경우 이들은 결국 적합성을 유지하고 기술을 새롭게 하는 데 실패하여 이른 은퇴를 통해 해고되었다.

Why? 왜 정답일까?
첫 문장에서 성장과 발전에 실패한 브랜드는 그 적합성을 잃게 된다고 한다. 두 번째 문장부터는 이를 직장 상황에 적용하여, 변화에 적응해 자신의 가치를 높이지 못한 직원들은 일찍이 도태되는 결과를 맞는다고 설명하고 있다. 따라서 글의 요지로 가장 적절한 것은 ⑤ '변화를 받아들이지 못하면 업계에서의 적합성을 잃게 된다.'이다.

- relevance ⓝ 적합성, 적절성
- hit a plateau 정체기에 들다
- ambitious ⓐ 야망 있는
- embrace ⓥ 포용하다
- industry ⓝ 업계, 산업
- integrate ⓥ 통합하다
- ultimately ⓐⓓ 궁극적으로
- retirement ⓝ 은퇴
- on the fast track 성공 가도를 달리는
- assume ⓥ 가정하다
- victim ⓝ 희생자
- advance ⓝ 발전, 진보
- executive ⓐ 경영의, 간부의
- resistant ⓐ 저항하는, 내성 있는
- let go ~을 해고하다

구문 풀이
1행 Brands [that fail to grow and develop] lose their relevance.
주어 [ ]: 주어 수식 동사(복수)

---

23 단 과일 섭취가 뇌에 미치는 영향   정답률 69% | 정답 ⑤

다음 글의 주제로 가장 적절한 것은?
① benefits of eating whole fruit on the brain health
통과일을 먹는 것이 뇌 건강에 미치는 이점
② universal preference for sweet fruit among children
아이들 사이에서 보편적으로 단 과일을 선호하는 것
③ types of brain exercises enhancing long-term memory
장기 기억을 향상시키는 여러 뇌 운동 유형
④ nutritional differences between fruit and processed carbs
과일과 가공 탄수화물의 영양적 차이
✓⑤ negative effect of fruit overconsumption on the cognitive brain
과일의 과도한 섭취가 인지적 뇌에 미치는 부정적 영향

What consequences of eating too many grapes and other sweet fruit / could there possibly be / for our brains?
포도와 그 외 달콤한 과일을 너무 많이 먹는 것의 어떤 영향이 / 과연 있을까? / 우리의 뇌에

A few large studies / have helped to shed some light.
몇 가지 대규모 연구가 / 새로운 견해를 밝히는 데 도움이

In one, / higher fruit intake / in older, cognitively healthy adults / was linked with less volume in the hippocampus.
한 연구에서는, / 더 많은 과일 섭취가 / 나이가 더 많고 인지적으로 건강한 성인에서 / 해마의 더 작은 용적과 연관되었다.

This finding was unusual, / since people who eat more fruit / usually display the benefits / associated with a healthy diet.
이 결과는 특이했는데, / 왜냐하면 과일을 더 많이 먹는 사람들은 / 보통 이점을 보여 주기 때문이었다. / 건강한 식단과 관련된

In this study, however, / the researchers isolated various components of the subjects' diets / and found / that fruit didn't seem to be doing their memory centers any favors.
하지만 이 연구에서, / 연구원들은 피실험자 식단의 다양한 요소를 분리했고 / 발견했다. / 과일이 기억 중추에 아무 도움도 주지 않는 것처럼 보인다는 것을

Another study from the Mayo Clinic / saw a similar inverse relationship / between fruit intake and volume of the cortex, / the large outer layer of the brain.
Mayo Clinic의 또 다른 연구에서는 / 유사한 역관계를 확인했다. / 과일 섭취와 피질의 용적 사이의 / 뇌의 커다란 바깥쪽인

Researchers in the latter study noted / that excessive consumption of high-sugar fruit / (such as mangoes, bananas, and pineapples) / may cause metabolic and cognitive problems / as much as processed carbs do.
후자의 연구에서 연구원들은 주목했다. / 고당도 과일의 과도한 섭취가 / (망고, 바나나, 파인애플 같은) / 신진대사 문제와 인지적 문제를 일으킬 수 있다는 점에 / 가공된 탄수화물 식품만큼이나

포도와 그 외 달콤한 과일을 너무 많이 먹는 것이 과연 뇌에 어떤 영향을 미칠 수 있을까? 몇 가지 대규모 연구가 새로운 견해를 밝히는 데 도움이 되었다. 한 연구에서는, 나이가 더 많고 인지적으로 건강한 성인에서 더 많은 과일 섭취가 해마의 더 작은 용적과 연관되었다. 이 결과는 특이했는데, 왜냐하면 과일을 더 많이 먹는 사람들은 보통 건강한 식단과 관련된 이점을 보여 주기 때문이었다. 하지만 이 연구에서, 연구원들은 피실험자 식단의 다양한 요소들을 분리했고 과일이 기억 중추에 아무 도움도 주지 않는 것처럼 보인다는 것을 발견했다. Mayo Clinic의 또 다른 연구에서는 과일 섭취와 뇌의 커다란 바깥쪽인 피질의 용적 사이의 유사한 역관계를 확인했다. 후자의 연구에서 연구원들은 (망고, 바나나, 파인애플 같은) 고당도 과일의 과도한 섭취가 가공된 탄수화물 식품만큼이나 신진대사 문제와 인지적 문제를 일으킬 수 있다는 점에 주목했다.

Why? 왜 정답일까?
두 가지 실험 결과를 모두 아우를 수 있는 내용을 주제로 삼아야 한다. 과일을 많이 먹었을 때 해마 용적이 더 작아지고 기억력에 도움이 되지 않았으며, 가공된 탄수화물과 마찬가지로 신진대사 및 인지 문제를 일으킬 수 있다는 내용으로 보아, 과일 섭취가 뇌에 '안 좋은' 영향을 미칠 수 있다는 것이 핵심 내용이다. 따라서 글의 주제로 가장 적절한 것은 ⑤ '과일의 과도한 섭취가 인지적 뇌에 미치는 부정적 영향'이다.

- consequence ⓝ 결과, 영향
- intake ⓝ 섭취(량) ⓥ 섭취하다
- hippocampus ⓝ (대뇌 측두엽의) 해마
- component ⓝ 구성요소
- inverse ⓐ 역의, 반대의
- the latter 후자(의)
- consumption ⓝ 소비, 섭취
- processed ⓐ 가공된
- universal ⓐ 보편적인
- shed light (on) (~을) 밝히다
- cognitively ⓐⓓ 인지적으로
- isolate ⓥ 분리하다
- subject ⓝ 실험 대상자
- cortex ⓝ (대뇌) 피질
- excessive ⓐ 과도한
- metabolic ⓐ 신진대사의
- carb ⓝ 탄수화물 식품
- nutritional ⓐ 영양의

구문 풀이
1행
의문형용사(어떤)
What consequences (of eating too many grapes and other sweet fruit)
명사 수식
could there possibly be for our brains?
조동사+there+be: 의문문 어순

---

24 승리의 어두운 단면   정답률 62% | 정답 ④

다음 글의 제목으로 가장 적절한 것은?
① Stop Judging Others to Win the Race of Life
인생의 경주에서 이기기 위해 남들을 평가하지 말라
② Why Disappointment Hurts More than Criticism
왜 실망이 비판보다 더 마음 아플까
③ Winning vs. Losing: A Dangerously Misleading Mindset
이기는 것 vs. 지는 것: 위험할 정도로 오해의 소지가 있는 사고방식
✓④ Winners in a Trap: Too Self-Conscious to Be Themselves
덫에 갇힌 승리자들: 너무 남을 의식하여 자기 자신이 되지 못하는
⑤ Is Honesty the Best Policy to Turn Enemies into Friends?
정직은 적을 친구로 돌리기 위한 최선의 방책일까?

Winning turns on a self-conscious awareness / that others are watching.
승리는 자의식적 인식을 촉발한다. / 다른 사람이 바라보고 있다는

It's a lot easier / to move under the radar / when no one knows you / and no one is paying attention.
훨씬 더 쉽다. / 눈에 안 띄게 움직이기가 / 아무도 여러분을 모르고 / 아무도 여러분에게 집중하고 있지 않으면

You can mess up and be rough and get dirty / because no one even knows / you're there.
여러분은 일을 망치고 난폭해지고 비열해져도 되는데, / 왜냐하면 아무도 알지조차 못하기 때문이다. / 여러분이 거기 있다는 것을

But as soon as you start to win, / and others start to notice, / you're suddenly aware / that you're being observed.
하지만 여러분이 승리하기 시작하자마자 / 그리고 다른 사람이 인지하기 시작하자마자 / 여러분은 갑자기 인식한다. / 여러분이 관찰되고 있다는 것을

You're being judged.
여러분은 평가받고 있다.

You worry / that others will discover your flaws and weaknesses, / and you start hiding your true personality, / so you can be a good role model and good citizen / and a leader that others can respect.
여러분은 걱정하고, / 다른 사람이 여러분의 실수와 약점을 발견할까봐 / 여러분은 본래의 성격을 숨기기 시작한다. / 여러분이 좋은 본보기이자 훌륭한 시민이 될 수 있도록 / 그리고 다른 사람이 존경할 수 있는 지도자가

There is nothing wrong with that.
이렇게 하는 데 문제는 없다.

But if you do it / at the expense of being who you really are, / making decisions / that please others instead of pleasing yourself, / you're not going to be in that position very long.
하지만 여러분이 그렇게 해나간다면 / 진정한 자기 모습이 되기를 희생하면서까지 / 결정을 내리며 / 자기 자신보다는 남을 기쁘게 하는 / 여러분은 그 지위에 그리 오래 머물지 못할 것이다.

When you start apologizing for who you are, / you stop growing / and you stop winning. // Permanently.
여러분이 자기 자신의 모습에 대해 사과하기 시작하는 순간, / 여러분은 성장을 멈추고, / 여러분은 승리를 멈추게 된다. // 영원히.

승리는 다른 사람이 바라보고 있다는 자의식적 인식을 촉발한다. 아무도 여러분을 모르고 아무도 여러분에게 집중하고 있지 않으면 눈에 안 띄게 움직이기가 훨씬 더 쉽다. 여러분은 일을 망치고 난폭해지고 비열해져도 되는데, 왜냐하면 여러분이 거기 있다는 것을 아무도 알지조차 못하기 때문이다. 하지만 여러분이 승리하기 시작하거나, 다른 사람이 (여러분을) 인지하기 시작하는 순간부터, 여러분은 관찰되고 있다는 것을 갑자기 인식한다. 여러분은 평가받고 있다. 여러분은 다른 사람이 여러분의 실수와 약점을 발견할까봐 걱정하고, 여러분이 좋은 본보기이자 훌륭한 시민이고 다른 사람이 존경할 수 있는 지도자가 될 수 있도록 본래의 성격을 숨기기 시작한다. 이렇게 하는 데 문제는 없다. 하지만 여러분이 진정한 자기 모습이 되기를 희생하면서까지 자기 자신을 기쁘게 하는 결정보다는 남을 기쁘게 하는 결정을 내리며 그렇게 해나간다면, 여러분은 그 지위에 그리 오래 머물지 못할 것이다. 자기 자신의 모습에 대해 사과하기 시작하는 순간, 여러분은 성장을 멈추고, 승리를 멈추게 된다. 영원히.

Why? 왜 정답일까?
마지막 세 문장을 통해, 자기 자신을 버리면서까지 남들의 시선을 의식하는 지경에 이른다면 성공의 입지를 오래 유지할 수 없다(When you start apologizing for who you are, you stop growing and you stop winning.)는 핵심 내용을 파악할 수 있다. 따라서 글의 제목으로 가장 적절한 것은 ④ '덫에 갇힌 승리자들: 너무 남을 의식하여 자기 자신이 되지 못하는'이다.

- turn on ~을 켜다, 작동시키다
- awareness ⓝ 의식, 인식
- mess up 엉망으로 하다, 망치다
- flaw ⓝ 결점
- apologize ⓥ 사과하다
- disappointment ⓝ 실망
- misleading ⓐ 오해의 소지가 있는, 오도하는
- self-conscious ⓐ 남을 의식하는
- under the radar 눈에 띄지 않게, 몰래
- rough ⓐ 거친
- at the expense of ~을 희생하며
- permanently ⓐⓓ 영구적으로
- criticism ⓝ 비판

구문 풀이

10행 But if you do it at the expense of being who you really are, making decisions [that please others instead of pleasing yourself], you're not going to be in that position very long.

~을 희생하여 / 분사구문 / 주격 관계대명사

---

25 독일의 연령별 독서 빈도 비율   정답률 73% | 정답 ③

다음 도표의 내용과 일치하지 <u>않는</u> 것은?

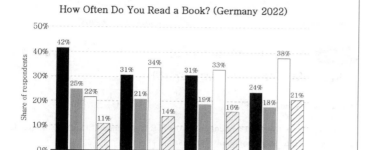

How Often Do You Read a Book? (Germany 2022)

● Daily or several times a week   ○ Once a month or less
◎ Between once a week and once every two weeks   ▨ Never

Note: All percentages may not total 100% due to rounding.

The above graph shows / how often German children and young adults / read books in 2022 / according to age groups.
위 그래프는 보여 준다. / 독일의 어린이와 젊은 성인이 얼마나 자주 / 2022년에 책을 읽었는지를 / 연령 집단에 따라

① In each age group / except 12 to 13-year-olds, / those who said they read books once a month or less / accounted for the largest proportion.
각각의 연령 집단에서 / 12~13세 연령 집단을 제외한 / 월 1회 또는 그 미만으로 책을 읽었다고 말한 이들은 / 가장 높은 비율을 차지했다.

② Of the 12 to 13-year-old group, / 42% stated / they read daily or several times a week, / which was the highest share within that group.
12~13세 연령 집단에서 / 42%가 말했고, / 그들이 매일 또는 일주일에 여러 번 책을 읽었다고 / 이는 그 집단 내에서 가장 높은 비율이었다.

✔③ In the 14 to 15-year-old group, / the percentage of teenagers / who read daily or several times a week / was three times higher / than that of those / who never read a book in the same age group.
14~15세 연령 집단에서 / 십 대의 비율은 / 매일 또는 일주일에 여러 번 책을 읽은 / 3배 높았다. / 이들 비율의 / 같은 연령 집단 내에서 전혀 책을 읽지 않은

④ In the 16 to 17-year-old group, / those who read between once a week and once every two weeks / were less than 20%.
16~17세 연령 집단에서 / 1주에 한 번에서 2주에 한 번 책을 읽은 이들은 / 20% 미만이었다.

⑤ More than one fifth of the age group of 18 to 19 years / responded / that they never read any book.
18~19세 연령 집단의 5분의 1 이상은 / 답했다. / 아무 책도 읽지 않았다고

위 그래프는 2022년 독일의 어린이와 젊은 성인이 책을 얼마나 자주 읽었는지를 연령 집단에 따라 보여 준다. ① 12~13세 연령 집단을 제외한 각각의 연령 집단에서 월 1회 또는 그 미만으로 책을 읽었다고 말한 이들은 가장 높은 비율을 차지했다. ② 12~13세 연령 집단에서 42%가 매일 또는 일주일에 여러 번 책을 읽었다고 말했고, 이는 그 집단 내에서 가장 높은 비율이었다. ③ 14~15세 연령 집단에서 매일 또는 일주일에 여러 번 책을 읽은 십 대의 비율은 같은 연령 집단 내에서 전혀 책을 읽지 않은 이들 비율의 3배였다. ④ 16~17세 연령 집단에서 1주에 한 번에서 2주에 한 번 책을 읽은 이들의 비율은 20% 미만이었다. ⑤ 18~19세 연령 집단의 5분의 1 이상은 아무 책도 읽지 않았다고 답했다.

Why? 왜 정답일까?

도표에 따르면 14~15세 연령 집단에서 책을 매일 혹은 일주일에 여러 번 읽은 이들은 31%, 책을 전혀 읽지 않은 이들은 14%이다. 따라서 도표와 일치하지 않는 것은 이를 3배 차이로 잘못 설명한 ③이다.

● account for ~을 차지하다   ● proportion ⓝ 비율
● one fifth 5분의 1

구문 풀이

11행 More than one fifth of the age group of 18 to 19 years responded that they never read any book.
분수 표현(분자 : 기수/ 분모 : 서수) / 접속사(~것)

---

26 Julia Margaret Cameron의 생애   정답률 89% | 정답 ④

Julia Margaret Cameron에 관한 다음 글의 내용과 일치하지 <u>않는</u> 것은?

① 인도에서 태어나고 프랑스에서 교육받았다.
② 딸로부터 카메라를 선물로 받았다.
③ 친구들과 가족 구성원에게 연극 의상을 입히고 촬영했다.
✔④ 능숙한 사진 기술로 자기 시대 예술 비평가에게 인정받았다.
⑤ 정신적 깊이에 가치를 둔 점을 훗날 높이 평가받았다.

British photographer Julia Margaret Cameron / is considered / one of the greatest portrait photographers of the 19th century.
영국인 사진작가인 Julia Margaret Cameron은 / 여겨진다. / 19세기의 가장 뛰어난 인물 사진작가 중 한 명으로

「Born in Calcutta, India, into a British family, / Cameron was educated in France.」 ①의근거 일치
인도 Calcutta의 영국인 가족에서 태어난 / Cameron은 프랑스에서 교육받았다.

「Given a camera as a gift by her daughter / in December 1863, / she quickly and energetically devoted herself / to the art of photography.」 ②의근거 일치
딸로부터 카메라를 선물로 받고서 / 1863년 12월에 / 그녀는 곧 활기차게 전념했다. / 사진 촬영 기술에

She cleared out a chicken coop / and converted it into studio space / where she began to work as a photographer.

그녀는 닭장을 비우고 / 그곳을 스튜디오 공간으로 바꾸었다. / 그녀가 사진작가로 일하기 시작한

「Cameron made illustrative studio photographs, / convincing friends and family members / to pose for photographs, / fitting them in theatrical costumes / and carefully composing them into scenes.」 ③의근거 일치
Cameron은 화보 같은 스튜디오 사진을 찍었는데 / 친구들과 가족 구성원을 설득하고 / 사진을 위해 포즈를 잡도록 / 그들에게 연극 의상을 입혀 / 신중하게 장면으로 구성했다.

「Criticized for her so-called bad technique / by art critics in her own time, / she ignored convention / and experimented with composition and focus.」 ④의근거 불일치
소위 서툰 기술로 인해 비판받으면서도, / 자기 시대 예술 비평가들로부터 / 그녀는 관습을 무시하고 / 구도와 초점을 실험했다.

「Later critics appreciated her valuing of spiritual depth / over technical perfection / and now consider her portraits / to be among the finest expressions of the artistic possibilities of the medium.」 ⑤의근거 일치
훗날 비평가들은 그녀가 정신적 깊이에 가치를 둔 것을 높이 평가했으며, / 기술적 완벽함보다 / 오늘날 그녀의 인물 사진을 여긴다. / 그 매체의 예술적 가능성을 가장 뛰어나게 표현한 작품 중 하나라고

영국인 사진작가인 Julia Margaret Cameron은 19세기의 가장 뛰어난 인물 사진작가 중 한 명으로 여겨진다. 인도 Calcutta의 영국인 가족에서 태어난 Cameron은 프랑스에서 교육받았다. 1863년 12월에 딸로부터 카메라를 선물로 받고서, 그녀는 곧 활기차게 사진 촬영 기술에 전념했다. 그녀는 닭장을 비우고 그곳을 스튜디오 공간으로 바꾸어 거기서 사진작가로 일하기 시작했다. Cameron은 화보 같은 스튜디오 사진을 찍었는데 친구들과 가족 구성원이 사진을 위해 포즈를 잡도록 설득하고, 그들에게 연극 의상을 입혀 신중하게 장면으로 구성했다. 소위 서툰 기술로 인해 자기 시대 예술 비평가들로부터 비판받으면서도, 그녀는 관습을 무시하고 구도와 초점을 실험했다. 훗날 비평가들은 그녀가 기술적 완벽함보다 정신적 깊이에 가치를 둔 것을 높이 평가했으며, 오늘날 그녀의 인물 사진이 이 매체(사진)의 예술적 가능성을 가장 뛰어나게 표현한 작품 중 하나라고 여긴다.

Why? 왜 정답일까?

'Criticized for her so-called bad technique by art critics in her own time, ~'에서 Julia Margaret Cameron은 서툰 기술 때문에 동시대 비평가들에게 비판을 받았다고 하므로, 내용과 일치하지 않는 것은 ④ '능숙한 사진 기술로 자기 시대 예술 비평가에게 인정받았다.'이다.

Why? 왜 오답일까?

① 'Born in Calcutta, India, into a British family, Cameron was educated in France.'의 내용과 일치한다.
② 'Given a camera as a gift by her daughter in December 1863, ~'의 내용과 일치한다.
③ '~ fitting them in theatrical costumes and carefully composing them into scenes.'의 내용과 일치한다.
⑤ 'Later critics appreciated her valuing of spiritual depth over technical perfection ~'의 내용과 일치한다.

● portrait ⓝ 인물 사진, 초상화   ● devote oneself to ~에 전념하다
● chicken coop 닭장   ● convert ⓥ 바꾸다, 전환하다
● fit ⓥ (의복을) 입히다, ~에 꼭 맞추다   ● theatrical ⓐ 연극적인
● costume ⓝ 의상   ● ignore ⓥ 무시하다
● convention ⓝ 관습   ● composition ⓝ 구성
● spiritual ⓐ 영적인   ● technical ⓐ 기술적인
● artistic ⓐ 예술적인   ● medium ⓝ 매체, 수단

구문 풀이

4행 Given a camera as a gift by her daughter in December 1863, she quickly and energetically devoted herself to the art of photography.
수동 분사구문 / 직접목적어 / ~에 헌신하다

---

27 숙면을 돕는 사운드 앱   정답률 94% | 정답 ⑤

Have a Good Night App에 관한 다음 안내문의 내용과 일치하지 <u>않는</u> 것은?

① 수면을 위한 편안한 소리를 제공한다.
② 자는 동안 기침이나 코를 고는 소리를 녹음한다.
③ 이용자의 수면 패턴을 확인하고 분석한다.
④ 수면 패턴에 따라 알람음을 조정한다.
✔⑤ 기본 버전은 1년에 30달러이다.

Have a Good Night App
Have a Good Night 앱
This smart app helps you have a refreshing sleep!
이 스마트 앱은 상쾌한 잠을 자도록 도와드립니다!
FEATURES
기능
Sounds for Sleep
수면을 위한 소리
「Providing relaxing sounds for sleep」 ①의근거 일치
수면을 위한 편안한 소리를 제공함
Sleep Recorder
수면 녹음기
「Recording sounds / such as coughing or snoring / while sleeping」 ②의근거 일치
소리를 녹음함 / 기침이나 코를 고는 소리와 같은 / 자는 동안
Sleep Pattern Tracker
수면 패턴 추적기
「Checking and analyzing the user's sleep pattern」 ③의근거 일치
이용자의 수면 패턴을 확인하고 분석함
Stress-Free Alarm Tones
스트레스가 없는 알람음
「Adjusting alarm tones to the user's sleep pattern」 ④의근거 일치
이용자의 수면 패턴에 따라 알람음을 조정함
PRICE
가격
「Basic version: Free」 ⑤의근거 불일치
기본 버전: 무료
Premium version (extra soundtracks): $30 per year

프리미엄 버전 (추가 사운드트랙): 1년에 $30
Click HERE to Download the App!
여기를 클릭해서 앱을 다운받으세요!

___

Have a Good Night 앱

이 스마트 앱은 상쾌한 잠을 자도록 도와드립니다!

기능

■ **수면을 위한 소리**
– 수면을 위한 편안한 소리를 제공함

■ **수면 녹음기**
– 자는 동안 기침이나 코를 고는 소리와 같은 소리를 녹음함

■ **수면 패턴 추적기**
– 이용자의 수면 패턴을 확인하고 분석함

■ **스트레스가 없는 알람**
– 이용자의 수면 패턴에 따라 알람음을 조정함

가격

■ **기본 버전:** 무료
■ **프리미엄 버전 (추가 사운드트랙):** 1년에 $30

여기를 클릭해서 앱을 다운받으세요!

Why? 왜 정답일까?

가격(PRICE) 항목의 'Basic version: Free'에서 기본 버전은 무료라고 하였다. 1년에 30달러를 지불해야 하는 것은 프리미엄 버전이다. 따라서 안내문의 내용과 일치하지 않는 것은 ⑤ '기본 버전은 1년에 30달러이다.'이다.

Why? 왜 오답일까?

① 'Providing relaxing sounds for sleep'의 내용과 일치한다.
② 'Recording sounds such as coughing or snoring while sleeping'의 내용과 일치한다.
③ 'Checking and analyzing the user's sleep pattern'의 내용과 일치한다.
④ 'Adjusting alarm tones to the user's sleep pattern'의 내용과 일치한다.

● have a good night 숙면을 취하다 ● cough ⓥ 기침하다
● snore ⓥ 코 골다

28 교내 온라인 장기자랑 대회   정답률 91% | 정답 ⑤

2023 Online Talent Show에 관한 다음 안내문의 내용과 일치하는 것은?
① 참가 부문은 노래와 춤을 포함한 네 가지이다.
② 비디오의 길이에는 제한이 없다.
③ 제출 기간은 3월 27일부터 7일 동안이다.
④ 학생들만 우승작 선정 투표에 참여할 수 있다.
☑ 우승한 비디오는 학교 축제에서 상영될 것이다.

2023 Online Talent Show
2023 온라인 장기자랑 대회
Show off your amazing talents!
여러분의 놀라운 재능을 뽐내세요!
「Categories: singing, dancing, playing instruments」 ①의 근거 불일치
부문: 노래, 춤, 악기 연주
How to Enter
참가 방법
「Record a 3-minute video of your talent / and send it to talent@westhigh.edu.」 ②의 근거 불일치
여러분의 재능을 3분 길이의 영상으로 녹화해 / 그것을 talent@westhigh.edu로 보내세요.
「Submit the entry / between March 27 and March 31.」 ③의 근거 불일치
참가작을 제출하세요. / 3월 27일과 3월 31일 사이에
How We Select a Winner
우승작 선정 방법
1. All the videos will be uploaded on the school website on April 5.
모든 비디오는 4월 5일에 학교 웹사이트에 업로드될 것입니다.
2. 「Students and teachers will vote for their favorite video.」 ④의 근거 불일치
학생과 교사가 가장 좋아하는 비디오에 투표할 것입니다.
3. The video that receives the most votes / will win.
가장 많은 표를 받은 비디오가 / 우승할 것입니다.
「The winning video will be played at the school festival.」 ⑤의 근거 일치
우승한 비디오는 학교 축제에서 상영될 예정입니다.
For more information, / please visit www.westhigh.edu.
더 많은 정보를 위해 / www.westhigh.edu를 방문하세요.

2023 온라인 장기자랑 대회

여러분의 놀라운 재능을 뽐내세요!

■ **부문:** 노래, 춤, 악기 연주

■ **참가 방법**
– 여러분의 재능을 3분 길이의 영상으로 녹화해 talent@westhigh.edu로 보내세요.
– 참가작을 3월 27일과 3월 31일 사이에 제출하세요.

■ **우승작 선정 방법**
1. 모든 비디오는 4월 5일에 학교 웹사이트에 업로드될 것입니다.
2. 학생과 교사가 가장 좋아하는 비디오에 투표할 것입니다.
3. 가장 많은 표를 받은 비디오가 우승할 것입니다.

＊ 우승한 비디오는 학교 축제에서 상영될 예정입니다.

더 많은 정보를 위해 www.westhigh.edu를 방문하세요.

Why? 왜 정답일까?

'The winning video will be played at the school festival.'에서 우승한 비디오는 학교 축제

___

에서 상영될 예정이라고 하므로, 안내문의 내용과 일치하는 것은 ⑤ '우승한 비디오는 학교 축제에서 상영될 것이다.'이다.

Why? 왜 오답일까?

① 'Categories: singing, dancing, playing instruments'에서 참가 부문은 총 3가지라고 하였다.
② 'Record a 3-minute video of your talent ～'에서 영상 길이는 3분으로 제한된다고 하였다.
③ 'Submit the entry between March 27 and March 31.'에서 제출 기간은 3월 27일부터 31일까지 5일이라고 하였다.
④ 'Students and teachers will vote for their favorite video.'에서 학생들뿐 아니라 교사들도 우승자 결정 투표에 참여한다고 하였다.

● talent show 장기자랑   ● show off ～을 뽐내다

29 확실성에 대한 선호로 생존해가는 인간   정답률 58% | 정답 ⑤

다음 글의 밑줄 친 부분 중, 어법상 틀린 것은? [3점]

Human beings like certainty.
인간은 확실성을 좋아한다.
This liking stems from our ancient ancestors / ① who needed to survive alongside saber-toothed tigers and poisonous berries.
이 선호는 우리의 고대 선조들로부터 유래한다. / 검치호와 독이 있는 딸기류 열매 곁에서 살아남아야 했던
Our brains evolved / to help us attend to threats, / keep away from ② them, / and remain alive afterward.
우리의 뇌는 진화했다. / 우리가 위협에 주의하게 돕도록 / 그것에서 벗어나 / 그리고 이후 살아남을 수 있게
In fact, / we learned / that the more ③ certain we were about something, / the better chance we had of making the right choice.
사실, / 우리는 학습했다. / 우리가 무언가에 대해 더 확신할수록 / 우리가 옳은 선택을 할 가능성이 더 크다는 것을
Is this berry the same shape as last time? // The same size?
이 딸기류 열매는 지난번과 모양이 같은가? // 같은 크기인가?
If I know for certain it ④ is, / my brain will direct me to eat it / because I know it's safe.
내가 그게 그렇다는 것을 확실히 안다면, / 내 뇌는 내가 그것을 먹도록 지시할 텐데, / 그것이 안전하다는 것을 내가 알기 때문이다.
And if I'm uncertain, / my brain will send out a danger alert / to protect me.
그리고 만약 내게 확신이 없다면, / 내 뇌는 위험 신호를 보낼 것이다. / 나를 보호하고자
The dependence on certainty / all those millennia ago / ensured our survival to the present day, / and the danger-alert system continues to protect us.
확실성에 대한 의존은 / 그 모든 수천 년 전의 / 현재까지 우리의 생존을 책임졌고, / 그 위험을 알리는 시스템은 계속하여 우리를 지키고 있다.
This is achieved by our brains / labeling new, vague, or unpredictable everyday events and experiences / as uncertain.
이것은 우리의 뇌에 의해 이루어진다. / 새롭거나 모호하거나 예측할 수 없는 매일의 사건과 경험을 명명함으로써 / 불확실한 것으로
Our brains then ☑ generate sensations, thoughts, and action plans / to keep us safe from the uncertain element, / and we live to see another day.
그런 후 우리의 뇌는 감각, 사고, 그리고 행동 계획을 만들어 내고 / 그 불확실한 요소로부터 우리를 안전하게 지키기 위해 / 우리는 살아서 또 다른 날을 보게 된다.

___

인간은 확실성을 좋아한다. 이 선호는 검치호와 독이 있는 딸기류 열매 곁에서 살아남아야 했던 우리의 고대 선조들로부터 유래한다. 우리의 뇌는 우리가 위협에 주의하고 그것에서 벗어나 이후 살아남을 수 있게 진화했다. 사실, 우리는 무언가에 대해 더 확신할수록 옳은 선택을 할 가능성이 더 크다는 것을 학습했다. 이 딸기류 열매는 지난번과 모양이 같은가? 같은 크기인가? 그게 그렇다는 것을 확실히 안다면, 내 뇌는 내가 그것을 먹도록 지시할 텐데, 그것이 안전하다는 것을 내가 알기 때문이다. 그리고 만약 내게 확신이 없다면, 내 뇌는 나를 보호하고자 위험 신호를 보낼 것이다. 그 모든 수천 년 전의 확실성에 대한 의존은 현재까지 우리의 생존을 책임졌고, 그 위험을 알리는 시스템은 계속하여 우리를 지키고 있다. 이것은 우리의 뇌가 새롭거나 모호하거나 예측할 수 없는 매일의 사건과 경험을 불확실한 것으로 명명함으로써 이루어진다. 그런 후 우리의 뇌는 그 불확실한 요소로부터 우리를 안전하게 지키기 위해 감각, 사고, 그리고 행동 계획을 만들어 내고, 우리는 살아서 또 다른 날을 보게 된다.

Why? 왜 정답일까?

주어 Our brains 뒤로 동사가 필요하므로 generating을 generate로 고쳐야 한다. 뒤에 따로 술어가 나오지 않는 것으로 보아 ⑤가 곧 술어 자리이기 때문이다. 따라서 어법상 틀린 것은 ⑤이다.

Why? 왜 오답일까?

① our ancient ancestors가 사람 선행사이므로 이를 수식하는 주격 관계대명사 who를 썼다.
② keep away의 주어는 Our brains인데 목적어는 threats이므로, '자기 자신'을 가리키는 재귀대명사 themselves가 아닌 인칭대명사 them을 썼다.
③ 'the＋비교급 ～, the＋비교급 …(～할수록 더 …하다)' 구문이다. 비교급의 품사가 형용사일지 부사일지 알려면 비교급 뒤를 보면 되는데, 여기서는 we were와 같이 2형식 문장이 나온다. 즉 ③이 were의 보어 자리이므로 형용사인 certain이 적절하게 쓰였다.
④ it is (the same shape and size)의 의미이므로 be동사가 알맞게 쓰였다.

● certainty ⓝ 확실성   ● stem from ～에서 기원하다
● saber-toothed tiger 검치호   ● attend to ～에 주의를 기울이다
● threat ⓝ 위협   ● uncertain ⓐ 확신이 없는
● send out 내보내다   ● alert ⓝ 경고, 경계 태세 ⓐ 경계하는, 기민한
● dependence ⓝ 의존   ● vague ⓐ 희미한
● unpredictable ⓐ 예측 불가한   ● generate ⓥ 만들어내다

구문 풀이

接続사(조건)
7행 If I know for certain it is, my brain will direct me to eat it because I know
현재시제   미래시제
it's safe.

★★★ 등급을 가르는 문제!
30 인간의 판단과 통계 자료의 결합   정답률 43% | 정답 ③

다음 글의 밑줄 친 부분 중, 문맥상 낱말의 쓰임이 적절하지 <u>않은</u> 것은? [3점]

Robert Blattberg and Steven Hoch noted / that, in a changing environment, / it is not clear / that consistency is always a virtue / and that one of the advantages of human judgment / is the ability to detect change.
Robert Blattberg와 Steven Hoch는 주목했다. / 변화하는 환경에서 / 분명하지 않다는 것 / 일관성이 항상 장점인지가 / 그리고 인간이 판단하는 것의 이점 중 하나는 / 변화를 감지하는 능력이라는 것에

Thus, / in changing environments, / it might be ① advantageous / to combine human judgment and statistical models.
따라서 / 변화하는 환경에서는 / ~ 유리할 수 있다 / 인간의 판단과 통계 모델을 결합하는 것이

Blattberg and Hoch examined this possibility / by having supermarket managers forecast demand for certain products / and then creating a composite forecast / by averaging these judgments with the forecasts of statistical models / based on ② past data.
Blattberg와 Hoch는 이러한 가능성을 조사했다. / 슈퍼마켓 관리자들에게 특정한 제품에 대한 수요를 예측하게 해서 / 그런 다음 종합적인 예측을 생성해서 / 이 판단을 통계 모델의 평균을 내어 / 지난 데이터에 근거한

The logic was / that statistical models ✓ assume stable conditions / and therefore cannot account for the effects on demand of novel events / such as actions taken by competitors / or the introduction of new products.
논리는 ~이었다. / 통계 모델들은 변동이 없는 조건을 가정한다 / 그렇기 때문에 새로운 사건이 수요에 미치는 영향을 설명할 수 없다는 것 / 경쟁자들에 의해 취해진 행동이나 / 신제품의 도입과 같은

Humans, however, / can ④ incorporate these novel factors in their judgments.
하지만 인간은 / 이러한 새로운 요인들을 판단에 통합할 수 있다.

The composite / — or average of human judgments and statistical models — / proved to be more ⑤ accurate / than either the statistical models or the managers working alone.
종합된 것 / 즉 인간의 판단과 통계 모델의 평균이 / 더 정확하다는 것이 증명되었다. / 통계 모델이나 관리자들이 각자 처리하는 것보다

Robert Blattberg와 Steven Hoch는 변화하는 환경에서 일관성이 항상 장점인지가 분명하지 않다는 것과, 인간이 판단하는 것의 이점 중 하나는 변화를 감지하는 능력이라는 데 주목했다. 따라서 변화하는 환경에서는 인간의 판단과 통계 모델들을 결합하는 것이 ① 유리할 수 있다. Blattberg와 Hoch는 슈퍼마켓 관리자들에게 특정한 제품에 대한 수요를 예측하게 한 다음, 이 판단을 ② 지난 데이터에 근거한 통계 모델의 예측과 평균을 내어 종합적인 예측을 생성해서 이러한 가능성을 조사했다. (그들의) 논리는 통계 모델들은 변동이 없는 조건을 ③ 부정하기(→ 가정하기) 때문에 경쟁자들에 의해 취해진 행동이나 신제품의 도입과 같은 새로운 사건이 수요에 미치는 영향을 설명할 수 없다는 것이었다. 하지만 인간은 이러한 새로운 요인들을 판단에 ④ 통합할 수 있다. 종합된 것, 즉 인간의 판단과 통계 모델의 평균이 통계 모델이나 관리자들이 각자 처리하는 것보다 더 ⑤ 정확하다는 것이 증명되었다.

Why? 왜 정답일까?

상황이 일관적이지 않고 변화하는 중일 때는 통계 자료에 더해 인간의 판단력을 결합해야 더 정확한 결정을 내릴 수 있다는 내용이다. ④가 포함된 문장에서 역접어(however)와 함께, 인간은 변화하는 상황을 고려해 판단을 내릴 수 있다고 한다. 이러한 문맥으로 보아, ③이 포함된 however 앞 문장은 '인간과는 달리' 통계 자료는 일관된 상황만을 '전제로 한다'는 의미여야 하므로, ③의 deny는 assume으로 바뀌어야 적절하다. 따라서 문맥상 낱말의 쓰임이 적절하지 않은 것은 ③이다.

- consistency ⑩ 일관성
- detect ⓥ 감지하다
- forecast ⓥ 예측하다
- deny ⓥ 부인하다
- take action 행동을 취하다, 조치를 취하다
- virtue ⑩ 미덕
- statistical ⓐ 통계적인
- composite ⓐ 종합적인 ⑩ 종합된 것
- novel ⓐ 새로운, 신기한
- accurate ⓐ 정확한

구문 풀이

1행 ~ it is not clear [that consistency is always a virtue] and [that one of the advantages of human judgment is the ability to detect change].
가주어 / 주어(one of the + 복수 명사) / 동사(단수) / [ ]: 진주어

★★ 문제 해결 꿀~팁 ★★

▶ 많이 틀린 이유는?
첫 문장에서 인간 판단력의 이점은 '변화를 감지하는(detect change)' 능력이라고 했다. 이 말을 ④가 포함된 문장에서는 '새로운 요인을 포함한다(incorporate these novel factors)'는 말로 바꾸었다. 따라서 ④는 문맥상 어색하지 않다.
▶ 문제 해결 방법은?
and 앞뒤는 서로 같은 내용이 연결되어야 하는데, ③의 deny는 같은 문장의 and 뒤에 나오는 'cannot account for ~ novel events'와 정반대된다. 따라서 ③이 어색한 것을 바로 파악할 수 있다.

★★★ 등급을 가르는 문제! ★★★

31 자유 놀이의 기능   정답률 29% | 정답 ④

다음 빈칸에 들어갈 말로 가장 적절한 것을 고르시오.

① noisy – 시끄럽지
② sociable – 사교적이지
③ complicated – 복잡하지
✓ helpless – 무력하지
⑤ selective – 선택적이지

Free play is nature's means of teaching children / that they are not helpless.
자유 놀이는 아이들에게 가르치는 자연적 수단이다. / 자신이 무력하지 않다는 것을

In play, away from adults, / children really do have control / and can practice asserting it.
어른과 떨어져 놀면서, / 아이들은 통제력을 정말로 가지고 / 그것을 발휘하는 것을 연습할 수 있다.

In free play, / children learn / to make their own decisions, / solve their own problems, / create and follow rules, / and get along with others as equals / rather than as obedient or rebellious subordinates.
자유 놀이를 통해, / 아이들은 배운다. / 스스로 결정을 내리고, / 자신들만의 문제를 해결하고, / 규칙을 만들고 지키며, / 동등한 사람 자격으로 다른 사람과 어울리는 것을 / 복종적이거나 반항적인 아랫사람이라기보다는

In active outdoor play, / children deliberately dose themselves with moderate amounts of fear / and they thereby learn / how to control not only their bodies, but also their fear.
활동적인 야외 놀이를 통해, / 아이들은 의도적으로 자기 자신에게 적절한 수준의 두려움을 주고, / 그렇게 하여 그들은 배운다. / 자기 신체뿐만 아니라 두려움 또한 통제하는 법을

In social play / children learn / how to negotiate with others, / how to please others, / and how to manage and overcome the anger / that can arise from conflicts.
사회적인 놀이를 통해, / 아이들은 배운다. / 어떻게 다른 사람과 협상하고, / 다른 사람을 기쁘게 하며, / 분노를 다스리고 극복할 수 있는지를 / 갈등으로부터 생길 수 있는

None of these lessons / can be taught through verbal means; / they can be learned only through experience, / which free play provides.
이러한 교훈 중 어느 것도 / 언어적 수단을 통해서는 배울 수 없다. / 그것들은 오로지 경험을 통해서만 배울 수 있는데, / 그것은 자유 놀이가 제공하는 것이다.

자유 놀이는 아이들에게 자신이 무력하지 않다는 것을 가르치는 자연적 수단이다. 어른과 떨어져 놀면서, 아이들은 통제력을 정말로 가지고 그것을 발휘하는 것을 연습할 수 있다. 자유 놀이를 통해, 아이들은 스스로 결정을 내리고, 자신들만의 문제를 해결하고, 규칙을 만들고 지키며, 복종적이거나 반항적인 아랫사람보다는 동등한 사람 자격으로 다른 사람과 어울리는 것을 배운다. 활동적인 야외 놀이를 통해, 아이들은 의도적으로 자기 자신에게 적절한 수준의 두려움을 주고, 그렇게 하여 자기 신체뿐만 아니라 두려움 또한 통제하는 법을 배운다. 사회적인 놀이를 통해 아이들은 어떻게 다른 사람과 협상하고, 다른 사람을 기쁘게 하며, 갈등으로부터 생길 수 있는 분노를 다스리고 극복할 수 있는지를 배운다. 이러한 교훈 중 어느 것도 언어적 수단을 통해서는 배울 수 없다. 그것들은 오로지 경험을 통해서만 배울 수 있는데, 그것은 자유 놀이가 제공하는 것이다.

Why? 왜 정답일까?

두 번째 문장에서 자유 놀이를 통해 아이들은 통제력을 갖고 발휘하는 연습(~ do have control and can practice asserting it.)을 해볼 수 있다는 핵심 내용이 나온다. 이어서 글 전체에 걸쳐 아이들은 놀이 속에서 스스로 결정하고 문제를 해결하며, 타인과 동등한 인격체로 어울리고 협상하는 법을 익히는 한편, 자신의 감정을 통제하는 법도 익혀나간다는 보충 설명이 제시된다. 이때 빈칸 바로 앞에는 not이 있으므로, 빈칸에는 '통제력이 없는' 상태에 관한 말이 들어가야 'not + 빈칸'이 주제를 나타낼 수 있다. 따라서 빈칸에 들어갈 말로 가장 적절한 것은 ④ '무력하지'이다.

- assert ⓥ (권리 등을) 행사하다, 주장하다
- rebellious ⓐ 반항적인
- deliberately ⓐ 의도적으로
- moderate ⓐ 적당한
- negotiate ⓥ 협상하다
- arise from ~에서 발생하다
- verbal ⓐ 언어적인
- helpless ⓐ 무력한
- obedient ⓐ 복종하는
- subordinate ⑩ 하급자, 부하
- dose ⓥ (약을) 투여하다, 먹이다
- thereby ⓐ 그렇게 함으로써
- overcome ⓥ 극복하다
- conflict ⑩ 갈등
- sociable ⓐ 사교적인
- selective ⓐ 선택적인

구문 풀이

9행 In social play children learn how to negotiate with others, how to please others, and how to manage and overcome the anger [that can arise from conflicts].
명사구1 / 명사구2 / 명사구3(~하는 방법) / [ ]: anger 수식

★★ 문제 해결 꿀~팁 ★★

▶ 많이 틀린 이유는?
글에 get along with others, social play 등의 표현이 나와 ②가 답으로 적절해 보일 수 있다. 하지만 아이들의 놀이의 의미를 설명하는 두 번째 문장을 보면, 놀이를 통해 아이들은 스스로 '통제력'을 지니고 있음을 알고, 그것을 행사하는 방법을 익히게 된다고 한다. 이는 아이들이 '무력한 존재가 아니라' 놀이 속 경험을 통해 행동이나 감정의 조절, 사회적 규칙 등을 배워갈 수 있는 힘을 지닌 존재라는 뜻이다.
▶ 문제 해결 방법은?
빈칸 앞에 not이 있으므로, 'not+빈칸'이 함께 주제를 나타내려면 빈칸에는 주제와 반대되는 말이 들어가야 한다. 즉 do have control과 의미상 반대되는 표현이 빈칸에 적합하다.

32 명목 수익을 중시했던 관행의 종식   정답률 49% | 정답 ②

다음 빈칸에 들어갈 말로 가장 적절한 것을 고르시오.

① simplified the Web design process – 웹 디자인 과정을 단순화했지만
✓ resulted in no additional cash inflow – 부가적인 현금 유입을 초래하지 않았지만
③ decreased the salaries of the employees – 직원들의 임금을 떨어뜨렸지만
④ intensified competition among companies – 회사들 간 경쟁을 심화시켰지만
⑤ triggered conflicts on the content of Web ads – 웹 광고 내용에 관한 갈등을 촉발했지만

Many early dot-com investors focused / almost entirely on revenue growth / instead of net income.
초기의 많은 닷컴 투자자들은 집중했다. / 거의 전적으로 수익 증가에만 / 순이익 대신

Many early dot-com companies / earned most of their revenue / from selling advertising space on their Web sites.
초기의 많은 닷컴 회사들은 / 자신들의 수익 대부분을 벌어들였다. / 웹사이트에 광고를 게재하는 공간을 판매하여

To boost reported revenue, / some sites began exchanging ad space.
보고되는 수익을 끌어올리기 위해, / 몇몇 사이트는 광고 게재 공간을 서로 주고받기 시작했다.

Company A would put an ad for its Web site / on company B's Web site, / and company B would put an ad for its Web site / on company A's Web site.
A 회사는 자기 회사의 웹 사이트 광고를 게시하곤 했고, / B 회사의 웹 사이트에 / B 회사에 자기 회사의 웹 사이트 광고를 게시하곤 했다. / A 회사의 웹 사이트에

No money ever changed hands, / but each company recorded revenue / (for the value of the space / that it gave up on its site) / and expense / (for the value of its ad / that it placed on the other company's site).
돈은 다른 회사에게로 전혀 넘어가지 않았지만, / 각 회사는 수익을 보고했다. / (광고 게재 공간의 가치에 대한 / 그곳이 자기 웹 사이트에서 포기한) / 그리고 비용을 / (광고의 가치에 대한 / 그곳이 타 회사의 사이트에 게재한)

This practice did little to boost net income / and resulted in no additional cash inflow / — but it did boost reported revenue.
이러한 관행은 순이익을 끌어올리는 데 거의 효과가 없었고 / 부가적인 현금 유입을 초래하지 않았다 / 그러나 보고되는 수익은 정말로 끌어올렸다.

This practice was quickly put to an end / because accountants felt / that it did not meet the criteria of the revenue recognition principle.
이 관행은 빠르게 종식되었다. / 회계사들이 생각했기 때문에 / 이러한 관행이 수익 인식 기준을 충족시키지 못한다고

초기의 많은 닷컴 투자자들은 거의 전적으로 순이익 대신 수익 증가에만 집중했다. 초기의 많은 닷컴 회사들은 수익 대부분을 자신들의 웹사이트에 광고를 게재하는 공간을 판매하여 벌어들였다. 보고되는 수익을 끌어올리기 위해, 몇몇 사이트는 광고 게재 공간을 서로 주고받기 시작했다. A 회사는 자기 회사의 웹 사이트 광고를 B 회사의 웹 사이트에 게시하곤 했고,

B 회사는 자기 회사의 웹 사이트 광고를 A 회사의 웹 사이트에 게시하곤 했다. 돈은 다른 회사에게로 전혀 넘어가지 않았지만, 각 회사는 (자기 웹 사이트에서 포기한 광고 게재 공간의 가치에 대한) 수익과 (타 회사의 사이트에 게재한 광고의 가치에 대한) 비용을 보고했다. 이러한 관행은 순이익을 끌어올리는 데 거의 효과가 없었고 부가적인 현금 유입을 초래하지 않았지만, 보고되는 수익은 정말로 끌어올렸다. 회계사들이 이러한 관행은 수익 인식 기준을 충족시키지 못한다고 생각했기 때문에 이 관행은 빠르게 종식되었다.

Why? 왜 정답일까?

과거 웹 사이트 회사들이 광고 공간을 팔아 수익을 내다가, 명목상의 수익을 부풀리기 위해 서로 광고 공간을 주고받았던 관행을 설명하는 글이다. 이렇듯 공간을 주고받는 것은 돈의 실제적 이동을 수반하지 않았으며(No money ever changed hands), 순이익의 증가도 이끌어내지 않았다(did little to boost net income)는 설명으로 보아, 빈칸에 들어갈 말로 가장 적절한 것은 '실제적 이득이 없었다'는 의미를 완성하는 ② '부가적인 현금 유입을 초래하지 않았지만'이다.

- **revenue** ⓝ 수익
- **put to an end** ~을 끝내다
- **criterion** (*pl.* criteria) ⓝ 기준
- **inflow** ⓝ 유입
- **trigger** ⓥ 촉발하다
- **give up on** ~을 포기하다, 단념하다
- **accountant** ⓝ 회계사
- **principle** ⓝ 원리
- **intensify** ⓥ 강화하다

구문 풀이

4행 To boost reported revenue, some sites began exchanging ad space.
목적(~하려면) 목적어(동명사)

---

33 가상 세계를 지탱하는 군중의 힘 | 정답률 46% | 정답 ①

다음 빈칸에 들어갈 말로 가장 적절한 것을 고르시오. [3점]

✓① be a large enough group to be considered a society
사회로 여겨질 정도로 충분히 큰 규모의 집단이어야
② have historical evidence to make it worth believing
그것을 믿을 가치가 있게 만들어주는 역사적 증거가 있어야
③ apply their individual values to all of their affairs
그들의 개인적 가치들을 그들의 모든 일에 적용해야
④ follow a strict order to enhance their self-esteem
그들의 자존감을 높이기 위해 엄격한 질서를 따라야
⑤ get approval in light of the religious value system
종교적 가치 체계의 관점에서 승인을 받아야

Scholars of myth have long argued / that myth gives structure and meaning to human life; / that meaning is amplified / when a myth evolves into a world.
신화 학자들은 오랫동안 주장해 왔다. / 신화가 인간의 삶에 구조와 의미를 부여한다고 / 그 의미는 증폭된다. / 하나의 신화가 하나의 세상으로 진화할 때

A virtual world's ability to fulfill needs / grows / when lots and lots of people believe in the world.
욕구를 충족시킬 수 있는 가상 세계의 능력은 / 커진다. / 수많은 사람이 그 세상의 존재를 믿을 때

Conversely, / a virtual world cannot be long sustained / by a mere handful of adherents.
이와 반대로, / 가상 세계는 오래 지속될 수 없다. / 단지 몇 명뿐인 추종자들에 의해서는

Consider the difference / between a global sport / and a game I invent with my nine friends / and play regularly.
차이를 고려해 보라. / 전 세계적인 스포츠와 / 내가 내 친구 9명과 만들어 정기적으로 하는 게임 사이의

My game might be a great game, / one that is completely immersive, / one that consumes all of my group's time and attention.
나의 게임은 훌륭한 게임이고 / 완전히 몰입하게 하는 게임이며, / 내 집단의 시간과 관심 모두를 소모하는 게임일 수 있다.

If its reach is limited to the ten of us, / though, / then it's ultimately just a weird hobby, / and it has limited social function.
그것이 미치는 범위가 우리 10명으로 제한된다면, / 하지만 / 그것은 최종적으로 그저 이상한 취미일 뿐이고, / 그것은 제한된 사회적 기능을 가진다.

For a virtual world / to provide lasting, wide-ranging value, / its participants must be a large enough group / to be considered a society.
가상 세계가 / 지속적이고 넓은 범위에 퍼지는 가치를 제공하려면 / 그 참여자들이 충분히 큰 규모의 집단이어야 한다. / 사회로 여겨질 정도로

When that threshold is reached, / psychological value can turn into wide-ranging social value.
그 기준점에 도달했을 때, / 심리적 가치가 넓은 범위에 퍼지는 사회적 가치로 변할 수 있다.

신화(를 연구하는) 학자들은 신화가 인간의 삶에 구조와 의미를 부여한다고 오랫동안 주장해 왔다. 그 의미는 하나의 신화가 하나의 세상으로 진화할 때 증폭된다. 욕구를 충족시킬 수 있는 가상 세계의 능력은 수많은 사람이 그 세상의 존재를 믿을 때 커진다. 이와 반대로, 가상 세계는 단지 몇 명뿐인 추종자들에 의해서는 오래 지속될 수 없다. 전 세계적인 스포츠와 내가 내 친구 9명과 만들어 정기적으로 하는 게임의 차이를 고려해 보라. 나의 게임은 훌륭한 게임이고 완전히 몰입하게 하는 게임이며, 내 집단의 시간과 관심 모두를 소모하는 게임일 수 있다. 하지만 그것이 미치는 범위가 우리 10명으로 제한된다면, 그것은 최종적으로 그저 이상한 취미일 뿐이고, 제한된 사회적 기능을 가진다. 가상 세계가 지속적이고 넓은 범위에 퍼지는 가치를 제공하려면 그 참여자들이 사회로 여겨질 정도로 충분히 큰 규모의 집단이어야 한다. 그 기준점에 도달했을 때, 심리적 가치가 넓은 범위에 퍼지는 사회적 가치로 변할 수 있다.

Why? 왜 정답일까?

신화, 게임, 혹은 다른 어떤 가상 세계가 지속적인 영향력을 갖기 위해서는 '많은 사람'이 필요하다(A virtual world's ability to fulfill needs grows when lots and lots of people believe in the world.)는 내용의 글이다. 따라서 빈칸에 들어갈 말로 가장 적절한 것은 ① '사회로 여겨질 정도로 충분히 큰 규모의 집단이어야'이다.

- **scholar** ⓝ 학자
- **amplify** ⓥ 증폭하다
- **conversely** [ad] 반대로
- **adherent** ⓝ 추종자
- **attention** ⓝ 주의, 관심
- **wide-ranging** @ 광범위한
- **affair** ⓝ 일, 사건
- **enhance** ⓥ 향상시키다
- **in light of** ~의 관점에서, ~을 고려하여
- **myth** ⓝ 신화
- **fulfill** ⓥ 충족하다, 이루다
- **sustain** ⓥ 지탱하다
- **immersive** @ 몰입시키는
- **weird** @ 이상한
- **threshold** ⓝ 기준점
- **strict** @ 엄격한
- **self-esteem** ⓝ 자존감

구문 풀이

11행 For a virtual world to provide lasting, wide-ranging value, its participants
의미상 주어 부사적 용법(~하려면)
must be a large enough group to be considered a society.
「형/부+enough ~ to 부정사」: '~할 정도로 충분히 …한 ~」

---

34 생태 환경에 대한 감정적 묘사에 신중하기 | 정답률 44% | 정답 ④

다음 빈칸에 들어갈 말로 가장 적절한 것을 고르시오. [3점]

① complex organisms are superior to simple ones
다세포 생물이 단세포보다 우월하다
② technologies help us survive extreme environments
기술은 우리가 극심한 환경에서 생존하도록 돕는다
③ ecological diversity is supported by extreme environments
생태적 다양성이 극심한 환경에 의해 뒷받침된다
✓④ all other organisms sense the environment in the way we do
모든 다른 유기체가 우리가 느끼는 방식으로 환경을 느낀다
⑤ species adapt to environmental changes in predictable ways
생물 종들은 예측 가능한 방식으로 환경 변화에 적응한다

It seems natural / to describe certain environmental conditions / as 'extreme', 'harsh', 'benign' or 'stressful'.
당연해 보인다. / 특정한 환경 조건을 묘사하는 것은 / '극심한', '혹독한', '온화한' 또는 '스트레스를 주는'이라고

It may seem obvious / when conditions are 'extreme': / the midday heat of a desert, / the cold of an Antarctic winter, / the salinity of the Great Salt Lake.
그것이 명백해 보일지도 모른다. / 상태가 '극심한' 경우는 / 사막 한낮의 열기, / 남극 겨울의 추위, / 그레이트솔트호의 염도와 같이

But this only means / that these conditions are extreme *for us*, / given our particular physiological characteristics and tolerances.
하지만 이것은 의미할 뿐이다. / 이러한 조건이 *우리에게* 극심하다는 것을 / 우리의 특정한 생리적 특징과 내성을 고려할 때

To a cactus / there is nothing extreme about the desert conditions / in which cacti have evolved; / nor are the icy lands of Antarctica / an extreme environment for penguins.
선인장에게 / 사막의 환경 조건은 전혀 극심한 것이 아니며, / 선인장들이 진화해 온 / 남극의 얼음에 뒤덮인 땅도 아니다 / 펭귄에게 극심한 환경

It is lazy and dangerous / for the ecologist to assume / that all other organisms sense the environment / in the way we do.
나태하고 위험하다. / 생태학자가 추정하는 것은 / 모든 다른 유기체가 환경을 느낀다고 / 우리가 느끼는 방식으로

Rather, / the ecologist should try to gain a worm's-eye or plant's-eye view of the environment: / to see the world as others see it.
오히려 / 생태학자는 환경에 대한 벌레의 관점이나 식물의 관점을 취하려고 노력해야 한다. / 다른 유기체가 세계를 보는 방식으로 세계를 바라보기 위해

Emotive words like harsh and benign, / even relativities such as hot and cold, / should be used by ecologists / only with care.
혹독한, 그리고 온화한 같은 감정적 단어들, / 심지어 덥고 추운 것과 같은 상대적인 단어들은 / 생태학자들에 의해 사용되어야 한다. / 오로지 신중하게

특정한 환경 조건을 '극심한', '혹독한', '온화한' 또는 '스트레스를 주는'이라고 묘사하는 것은 당연해 보인다. 사막 한낮의 열기, 남극 겨울의 추위, 그레이트솔트호의 염도와 같이 상태가 '극심한' 경우에는 그것이 명백해 보일지도 모른다. 하지만 이것은 우리의 특정한 생리적 특징과 내성을 고려할 때 이러한 조건이 *우리에게* 극심하다는 것을 의미할 뿐이다. 선인장에게 선인장들이 진화해 온 사막의 환경 조건은 전혀 극심한 것이 아니며, 펭귄에게 남극의 얼음에 뒤덮인 땅은 극심한 환경이 아니다. 생태학자가 모든 다른 유기체가 우리가 느끼는 방식으로 환경을 느낀다고 추정하는 것은 나태하고 위험하다. 오히려 생태학자는 다른 유기체가 세계를 보는 방식으로 세계를 바라보기 위해 환경에 대한 벌레의 관점이나 식물의 관점을 취하려고 노력해야 한다. 혹독한, 그리고 온화한 같은 감정적 단어들, 심지어 덥고 추운 것과 같은 상대적인 단어들은 생태학자들에 의해 오로지 신중하게 사용되어야 한다.

Why? 왜 정답일까?

Rather로 시작하는 문장에서, 생태학자는 우리 자신의 시각으로 어떤 환경을 바라보기보다, 그 환경에 적응해 사는 다른 생물의 관점을 두루 취할 의무가 있다(~ the ecologist should try to gain a worm's-eye or plant's-eye view of the environment: to see the world as others see it.)고 한다. 즉 '모두가 우리와 같게 느낄 것이라고' 나태하게 가정하지 말아야 한다는 것이 글의 주제이다. 따라서 빈칸에 들어갈 말로 가장 적절한 것은 ④ '모든 다른 유기체가 우리가 느끼는 방식으로 환경을 느낀다'이다.

- **extreme** @ 극심한, 극도의
- **benign** @ 온화한
- **Antarctic** @ 남극의
- **physiological** @ 생리적인
- **tolerance** ⓝ 내성, 저항력, 인내
- **lazy** @ 나태한, 게으른
- **emotive** @ 감정적인, 감정을 나타내는
- **complex organism** 다세포 생물
- **harsh** @ 혹독한
- **obvious** @ 명백한
- **salinity** ⓝ 염도
- **characteristic** ⓝ 특성
- **cactus** (*pl.* cacti) ⓝ 선인장
- **ecologist** ⓝ 생태학자
- **relativity** ⓝ 상대성

구문 풀이

9행 It is lazy and dangerous for the ecologist to assume that all other organisms
가주어 의미상 주어 진주어
sense the environment in the way we do.
대동사(= sense)

---

35 인간의 과정의 특성 고려하기 | 정답률 54% | 정답 ③

다음 글에서 전체 흐름과 관계 없는 문장은?

Human processes differ from rational processes / in their outcome.
인간의 과정은 이성적인 과정과 다르다. / 그 결과에 있어서

A process is *rational* / if it always does the right thing / based on the current information, / given an ideal performance measure.
어떤 과정은 *이성적인* / 만일 그것이 맞는 일을 항상 수행한다면 / 현재의 정보를 바탕으로 / 이상적인 수행 척도를 고려할 때

In short, / rational processes go by the book / and assume that the book is actually correct.
요컨대 / 이성적인 과정은 책에 나와 있는 규칙대로 진행하고, / 책은 실제로 옳다고 간주한다.

① Human processes involve instinct, intuition, and other variables / that don't necessarily reflect the book / and may not even consider the existing data.

인간의 과정은 본능, 직관 그리고 다른 변인들을 포함하며, / 책을 반드시 반영하지는 않는 / 심지어 기존의 데이터를 고려하지 않을 수도 있다.

② As an example, / the rational way to drive a car / is to always follow the laws.
예를 들어, / 자동차를 운전하는 이성적인 방식은 / 항상 법규를 따르는 것이다.

✓ Likewise, / pedestrian crossing signs vary / depending on the country / with differing appearances of a person crossing the street.
마찬가지로, / 보행자 횡단 신호는 다르고, / 나라에 따라 / 길을 건너는 사람의 모양이 서로 다르다.

④ However, / traffic isn't rational; / if you follow the laws precisely, / you end up stuck somewhere / because other drivers aren't following the laws precisely.
그러나 / 차량 흐름은 이성적이지 않아서, / 만일 여러분이 법규를 정확히 따른다면 / 여러분은 결국 어딘가에 갇혀 꼼짝 못하는 결과를 맞게 될 것이다. / 다른 운전자는 법규를 정확히 따르지 않기 때문에

⑤ To be successful, / a self-driving car must therefore act humanly, / rather than rationally.
성공을 거두려면, / 따라서 자율 주행 자동차는 인간적으로 행동해야 한다. / 이성적이기보다는

인간의 과정은 그 결과에 있어서 이성적인 과정과 다르다. 이상적인 수행 척도를 고려할 때, 만일 하나의 과정이 현재의 정보를 바탕으로 맞는 일을 항상 수행한다면 그 과정은 이성적이다. 요컨대 이성적인 과정은 책에 나와 있는 규칙대로 진행하고, 책은 실제로 옳다고 간주한다. ① 인간의 과정은 본능, 직관 그리고 책을 반드시 반영하지는 않는 다른 변인들을 포함하며, 심지어 기존의 데이터를 고려하지 않을 수도 있다. ② 예를 들어, 자동차를 운전하는 이성적인 방식은 항상 법규를 따르는 것이다. ③ 마찬가지로, 보행자 횡단 신호는 나라에 따라 다르고, 길을 건너는 사람의 모양이 서로 다르다. ④ 그러나 차량 흐름은 이성적이지 않아서, 만일 여러분이 법규를 정확히 따른다면 다른 운전자는 법규를 정확히 따르지 않기 때문에 여러분은 결국 어딘가에 갇혀 꼼짝 못하는 결과를 맞게 될 것이다. ⑤ 따라서 자율 주행 자동차는 성공을 거두려면 이성적이기보다는 인간적으로 행동해야 한다.

Why? 왜 정답일까?

인간의 과정은 반드시 합리적으로 움직이지는 않는다는 일반적 내용 뒤로, 인간의 과정이 꼭 책에 나오는 것 같지는 않다고 주제를 한 번 더 풀어 설명하는 ①, 예를 제시하는 ②와 ④, 이를 토대로 자율 주행 차가 나아갈 방향을 결론 짓는 ⑤가 자연스럽게 연결된다. 하지만 ③은 교통 법규의 세부적 내용이 나라마다 다르다는 의미여서 앞뒤 내용과 연결되지 않는다. 따라서 전체 흐름과 관계 없는 문장은 ③이다.

- ideal ⓐ 이상적인
- intuition ⓝ 직관
- existing ⓐ 기존의
- pedestrian ⓝ 보행자
- end up 결국 ~하다
- self-driving car 자율 주행 자동차
- instinct ⓝ 본능
- variable ⓝ 변수
- likewise ⓐⓓ 마찬가지로
- precisely ⓐⓓ 정확하게
- stuck (어딘가에) 갇힌

구문 풀이

13행 To be successful, a self-driving car must therefore act **humanly**, rather than **rationally**.
「A + rather than + B : B라기보다는 A인(A, B는 병렬)」

---

36 나쁜 습관을 '깬다'는 언어 표현   정답률 53% | 정답 ④

주어진 글 다음에 이어질 글의 순서로 가장 적절한 것을 고르시오.

① (A) – (C) – (B)   ② (B) – (A) – (C)
③ (B) – (C) – (A)   ✓ (C) – (A) – (B)
⑤ (C) – (B) – (A)

Like positive habits, / bad habits exist / on a continuum of easy-to-change and hard-to-change.
긍정적인 습관과 마찬가지로, / 나쁜 습관은 존재한다. / 바꾸기 쉽다와 바꾸기 어려움의 연속체에

(C) When you get toward the "hard" end of the spectrum, / note the language you hear / — *breaking* bad habits and *battling* addiction.
여러분이 그 연속체의 '어려운 쪽' 끝에 가까워질 때, / 여러분이 듣는 언어에 주목하라. / 즉 나쁜 습관을 *깨*는 것과 중독과 *싸우*는 것

It's as if an unwanted behavior is a nefarious villain / to be aggressively defeated.
바람직하지 못한 행동은 마치 사악한 악당인 것 같다. / 격렬히 패배시켜야 할

(A) But / this kind of language / (and the approaches it spawns) / frames these challenges / in a way that isn't helpful or effective.
그러나 / 이러한 종류의 언어는 / (그리고 그것이 낳는 접근법) / 이러한 도전에 틀을 씌운다. / 도움이 되지 않거나 효과적이지 않은 방식으로

I specifically hope / we will stop using this phrase: "break a habit."
특히 나는 바란다. / 우리가 이 문구를 그만 사용하기를 / '습관을 깨라'는

This language misguides people.
이 언어는 사람들을 잘못된 길로 이끈다.

The word "break" sets the wrong expectation / for how you get rid of a bad habit.
'깨다'라는 단어는 잘못된 기대를 형성한다. / 여러분이 나쁜 습관을 없애는 방법에 대해

(B) This word implies / that if you input a lot of force in one moment, / the habit will be gone.
이 단어는 의미를 담는다. / 여러분이 한순간에 많은 힘을 가하면 / 그 습관이 없어질 거라는

However, that rarely works, / because you usually cannot get rid of an unwanted habit / by applying force one time.
하지만 그것은 거의 효과가 없는데, / 대체로 여러분이 바람직하지 못한 습관을 없앨 수 없기 때문이다. / 한 번 힘을 가하는 것으로

긍정적인 습관과 마찬가지로, 나쁜 습관은 바꾸기 쉽다와 바꾸기 어렵다의 연속체에 존재한다.

(C) 그 연속체의 '어려운 쪽' 끝에 가까워질 때, 여러분이 듣는 언어, 즉 나쁜 습관을 *깨*는 것과 중독과 *싸우*는 것에 주목하라. 바람직하지 못한 행동은 마치 격렬히 패배시켜야 할 사악한 악당인 것 같다.

(A) 그러나 이러한 종류의 언어(와 그것이 낳는 접근법)는 도움이 되지 않거나 효과적이지 않은 방식으로 이러한 도전에 틀을 씌운다. 특히 나는 우리가 '습관을 깨다'라는 문구를 그만 사용하기를 바란다. 이 언어는 사람들을 잘못된 길로 이끈다. '깨다'라는 단어는 나쁜 습관을 없애는 방법에 대해 잘못된 기대를 형성한다.

(B) 이 단어는 여러분이 한순간에 많은 힘을 가하면 그 습관이 없어질 거라는 의미를 담는다. 하지만 그것은 거의 효과가 없는데, 대체로 여러분이 한 번 힘을 가하는 것으로 바람직하지 못한 습관을 없앨 수 없기 때문이다.

Why? 왜 정답일까?

습관이 바꾸기 쉽다와 어렵다라는 연속체 안에 존재한다는 주어진 글 뒤로, '연속체'를 다시 언급하며 사람

들이 흔히 습관을 '깬다'는 표현을 사용한다고 언급하는 (C)가 먼저 연결된다. 이어서 But으로 시작하는 (A)는 이런 식의 언어, 즉 '습관을 깬다'고 말하는 것이 사람들에게 잘못된 기대를 품게 한다는 내용을 전개한다. 마지막으로 (B)는 (A)에서 언급된 The word "break"를 This word라는 지시어로 가리키며 왜 이 표현에 담긴 의미가 현실성이 없는지 설명한다. 따라서 주어진 글의 순서로 가장 적절한 것은 ④ '(C) – (A) – (B)'이다.

- continuum ⓝ 연속체
- frame ⓥ (특정한 방식으로) 표현하다
- get rid of ~을 제거하다
- addiction ⓝ 중독
- villain ⓝ 악당
- spawn ⓥ 낳다
- break a habit (흔히 나쁜) 습관을 고치다
- input ⓥ 투입하다
- nefarious ⓐ 사악한
- aggressively ⓐⓓ 맹렬하게, 격렬하게

구문 풀이

14행 It's as if an unwanted behavior is a nefarious villain to be aggressively defeated.
마치 ~인 것 같다(비유) / 형용사적 용법

---

37 이성적 판단 이면의 감정   정답률 65% | 정답 ③

주어진 글 다음에 이어질 글의 순서로 가장 적절한 것을 고르시오. [3점]

① (A) – (C) – (B)   ② (B) – (A) – (C)
✓ (B) – (C) – (A)   ④ (C) – (A) – (B)
⑤ (C) – (B) – (A)

A common but incorrect assumption / is / that we are creatures of reason / when, in fact, we are creatures of both reason and emotion.
일반적이지만 잘못된 가정은 / ~이다 / 우리가 이성의 피조물이라는 것 / 사실 우리는 이성과 감정 둘 다의 피조물이다.

We cannot get by on reason alone / since any reason always eventually leads to a feeling.
우리는 이성만으로 살아갈 수 없다. / 어떤 이성도 항상 결국 감정으로 이어지기 때문에

Should I get a wholegrain cereal or a chocolate cereal?
내가 통곡물 시리얼을 선택해야 할까, 혹은 초콜릿 시리얼을 선택해야 할까?

(B) I can list all the reasons I want, / but the reasons have to be based on something.
나는 내가 원하는 모든 이유를 열거할 수 있지만, / 그 이유는 뭔가에 근거해야 한다.

For example, / if my goal is to eat healthy, / I can choose the wholegrain cereal, / but what is my reason / for wanting to be healthy?
예를 들어 / 나의 목표가 건강하게 먹는 것이라면 / 나는 통곡물 시리얼을 선택할 수 있지만, / 내 근거는 무엇일까? / 건강해지고 싶다는 것을 뒷받침하는

(C) I can list more and more reasons / such as wanting to live longer, / spending more quality time with loved ones, etc., / but what are the reasons / for those reasons?
나는 더 많은 이유를 열거할 수 있지만, / 더 오래 살고 싶은 것 같은 / 사랑하는 사람들과 양질의 시간을 더 많이 보내고 싶은 것 등 / 이유는 무엇인가? / 그러한 이유를 뒷받침하는

You should be able to see by now / that reasons are ultimately based on non-reason / such as values, feelings, or emotions.
여러분은 이제 알 수 있을 것이다. / 이유가 궁극적으로 비이성에 근거한다는 것을 / 가치, 느낌, 또는 감정과 같은

(A) These deep-seated values, feelings, and emotions we have / are rarely a result of reasoning, / but can certainly be influenced by reasoning.
우리가 가진 이러한 뿌리 깊은 가치, 느낌, 감정은 / 추론의 산물인 경우가 거의 없지만, / 물론 추론의 영향을 받을 수 있다.

We have values, feelings, and emotions / before we begin to reason / and long before we begin to reason effectively.
우리는 가치, 느낌, 감정을 갖는다. / 우리가 추론을 시작하기 전에, / 우리가 추론을 효과적으로 시작하기 훨씬 전에

일반적이지만 잘못된 가정은 우리가 이성의 피조물이라는 것이지만, 사실 우리는 이성과 감정 둘 다의 피조물이다. 어떤 이성도 항상 결국 감정으로 이어지기 때문에 우리는 이성만으로 살아갈 수 없다. 내가 통곡물 시리얼을 선택해야 할까, 혹은 초콜릿 시리얼을 선택해야 할까?

(B) 나는 내가 원하는 모든 이유를 열거할 수 있지만, 그 이유는 뭔가에 근거해야 한다. 예를 들어 건강하게 먹는 것이 나의 목표라면 통곡물 시리얼을 선택할 수 있지만, 건강해지고 싶다는 것을 뒷받침하는 내 근거는 무엇일까?

(C) 나는 더 오래 살고 싶은 것, 사랑하는 사람들과 양질의 시간을 더 많이 보내고 싶은 것 등과 같은 더 많은 이유를 열거할 수 있지만, 그러한 이유를 뒷받침하는 이유는 무엇인가? 여러분은 이유가 궁극적으로 가치, 느낌, 또는 감정과 같은 비이성에 근거한다는 것을 이제 알 수 있을 것이다.

(A) 우리가 가진 이러한 뿌리 깊은 가치, 느낌, 감정은 추론의 산물인 경우가 거의 없지만, 물론 추론의 영향을 받을 수 있다. 우리는 추론을 시작하기 전에, (더 정확히는) 추론을 효과적으로 시작하기 훨씬 전에 가치, 느낌, 감정을 갖는다.

Why? 왜 정답일까?

주어진 글은 우리가 이성과 동시에 감정도 가진 존재임을 언급하며 선택의 상황을 예로 든다. 이어서 (B)는 주어진 글에서 언급된 선택 상황에 대해 근거를 생각해보고 언급하고, (C)는 근거를 열거하다 보면 결국 그 이면에 '비이성'이 있다는 것을 알게 된다고 말한다. (A)는 (C) 후반부에서 언급된 비이성적 요소, 즉 가치관이나 느낌, 감정 등을 다시 언급하며 이런 것들이 우리가 이성적 추론을 시작하기 훨씬 앞서 자리잡고 있던 것임을 설명한다. 따라서 글의 순서로 가장 적절한 것은 ③ '(B) – (C) – (A)'이다.

- incorrect ⓐ 부정확한
- wholegrain ⓝ 통곡물
- effectively ⓐⓓ 효과적으로
- loved one 사랑하는 사람
- get by on ~로 그럭저럭 살아가다
- deep-seated ⓐ 뿌리 깊은
- live long 장수하다

구문 풀이

1행 A common but incorrect assumption is that we are creatures of reason when, (in fact), we are creatures of both reason and emotion.
접속사(~을 때) / 접속사(~것) / ( ) : 삽입구

★★★ 등급을 가르는 문제!
38 물고기의 전기 신호   정답률 30% | 정답 ②

글의 흐름으로 보아, 주어진 문장이 들어가기에 가장 적절한 곳을 고르시오.

Electric communication is mainly known in fish.
전기적 의사소통은 주로 물고기에서 알려져 있다.
The electric signals are produced / in special electric organs.
전기 신호는 생성된다. / 특수 전기 기관에서
When the signal is discharged / the electric organ will be negatively loaded / compared to the head / and an electric field is created around the fish.
신호가 방출되면 / 전기 기관이 음전하를 띠고 / 머리에 대해 / 물고기 주위에 전기장이 생긴다.
① A weak electric current is created / also in ordinary muscle cells / when they contract.
약한 전류가 발생한다. / 일반 근육 세포 안에서도 / 그것이 수축할 때
✔ In the electric organ / the muscle cells are connected in larger chunks, / which makes the total current intensity larger / than in ordinary muscles.
전기 기관 안에서 / 근육 세포는 더 큰 덩어리로 연결되어 있으며, / 이는 총 전류 강도를 더 크게 만든다. / 일반 근육에서보다
The fish varies the signals / by changing the form of the electric field / or the frequency of discharging.
물고기는 신호를 다양하게 한다. / 전기장의 형태를 변화시켜 / 혹은 방출 주파수를
③ The system is only working over small distances, / about one to two meters.
이 체계는 짧은 거리에서만 작동한다. / 약 1∼2미터 정도의
④ This is an advantage / since the species using the signal system / often live in large groups / with several other species.
이것은 이점이 있다. / 신호 체계를 사용하는 종들은 ~때문에 / 흔히 큰 무리를 지어 살기 / 다른 여러 종과 함께
⑤ If many fish send out signals at the same time, / the short range decreases the risk of interference.
많은 물고기가 동시에 신호를 보내면, / 짧은 범위는 전파 방해의 위험을 줄여 준다.

전기적 의사소통은 주로 물고기에서 알려져 있다. 전기 신호는 특수 전기 기관에서 생성된다. 신호가 방출되면 머리에 대해 전기 기관이 음전하를 띠고 물고기 주위에 전기장이 생긴다. ① 일반 근육 세포가 수축할 때 약한 전류가 그 안에서도 발생한다. ② 전기 기관 안에서 근육 세포는 더 큰 덩어리로 연결되어 있으며, 이는 일반 근육에서보다 총 전류 강도를 더 크게 만든다. 물고기는 전기장의 형태나 방출 주파수를 변화시켜 신호를 다양하게 한다. ③ 이 체계는 약 1∼2미터 정도의 짧은 거리에서만 작동한다. ④ 신호 체계를 사용하는 종들은 흔히 큰 무리를 지어 다른 여러 종과 함께 살기 때문에 이것은 이점이다. ⑤ 많은 물고기가 동시에 신호를 보내면, 짧은 (도달 가능) 범위는 전파 방해의 위험을 줄여 준다.

물고기가 사용하는 전기적 의사소통 과정을 소개하는 글이다. ② 앞에서 전기 신호는 특수 전기 기관에서 생성되거나, 일반 근육 세포에서도 미세하게 발생할 수 있다고 언급하는데, 주어진 문장은 전기 기관에서는 근육 세포가 더 큰 덩어리로 연결돼 있어 전류 강도가 더 크다고 설명한다. 이어서 ③ 뒤부터는 물고기가 신호를 다양하게 만들어낼 수 있다는 것과 이 신호가 작동하는 범위에 관해 주로 설명하고 있다. 따라서 근육 세포에서 만들어진 신호에 관한 설명을 마무리하는 주어진 문장이 들어가기에 가장 적절한 곳은 ②이다.

- chunk ⓝ 덩어리
- discharge ⓥ 방출하다, 내보내다
- contract ⓥ 수축하다
- interference ⓝ 전파 방해, 간섭
- intensity ⓝ 강도
- load ⓥ (짐, 부담을) 실어주다
- frequency ⓝ 주파수

구문 풀이

1행 In the electric organ the muscle cells are connected in larger chunks,
선행사(문장)
which makes the total current intensity larger than in ordinary muscles.
계속적 용법

★★ 문제 해결 꿀~팁 ★★
▶ 많이 틀린 이유는?
④가 만일 정답이면, ④ 뒤의 This가 앞 문장과 이어지지 않아 논리적 공백이 생길 것이다. 하지만 여기서는 This 자리에 앞 문장 내용을 넣어서 읽어도 흐름이 어색하지 않다. 즉 '전기 신호 체계가 짧은 거리에 작용한다는 사실'이 물고기에게 이점이 맞고, 그 이유를 설명하는 문장이 'since ~'와 ⑤ 뒤의 문장이므로 흐름상 어색하지 않다.
▶ 문제 해결 방법은?
② 앞과 주어진 문장은 둘 다 전기 강도와 근육 세포를 언급한다. ② 뒤를 보면 근육에 대한 언급은 없고 바로 신호 종류가 다양하다는 새로운 내용으로 넘어간다. 따라서 전류가 '어디서 발생하는지'에 대한 이야기는 ②에서 마무리되어야 한다.

39 창의성과 생산성의 관계   정답률 47% | 정답 ④
글의 흐름으로 보아, 주어진 문장이 들어가기에 가장 적절한 곳을 고르시오. [3점]

Creativity can have an effect on productivity.
창의성은 생산성에 영향을 미칠 수 있다.
Creativity leads some individuals to recognize problems / that others do not see, / but which may be very difficult.
창의성은 어떤 이들이 문제들을 인식하게 하지만, / 남들은 보지 못하는 / 이는 매우 어려울 수도 있다.
① Charles Darwin's approach to the speciation problem / is a good example of this; / he chose a very difficult and tangled problem, speciation, / which led him / into a long period of data collection and deliberation.
종 분화 문제에 대한 찰스 다윈의 접근이 이것의 좋은 예시인데, / 그는 매우 어렵고 복잡한 문제인 종 분화를 선택했고, / 이것은 그를 이끌었다. / 오랜 자료 수집과 심사숙고의 기간으로
② This choice of problem / did not allow for a quick attack or a simple experiment.
이러한 문제 선택은 / 빠른 착수나 간단한 실험을 허용하지 않았다.
③ In such cases / creativity may actually decrease productivity / (as measured by publication counts) / because effort is focused on difficult problems.
이 경우, / 창의성은 사실 생산성을 감소시킬 수 있다. / (출판물의 수로 측정되듯) / 노력은 어려운 문제에 집중되기 때문에
✔ For others, / whose creativity is more focused on methods and technique, / creativity may lead to solutions / that drastically reduce the work / necessary to solve a problem.
다른 이들의 경우, / 창의성이 방법과 기술에 더 집중돼 있는 / 창의성은 해결책으로 이어질 수 있다. / 작업을 극적으로 줄이는 / 문제해결에 필요한
We can see an example / in the development of the polymerase chain reaction (PCR) / which enables us to amplify small pieces of DNA in a short time.
우리는 한 예를 볼 수 있다. / 중합 효소 연쇄 반응(PCR)의 개발에서 / 작은 DNA 조각들을 짧은 시간에 증폭시켜 주는

⑤ This type of creativity / might reduce the number of steps / or substitute steps / that are less likely to fail, / thus increasing productivity.
이러한 유형의 창의성은 / 단계의 수를 줄이거나 / 단계로 대체해주고, / 실패할 가능성이 더 낮은 / 그리하여 생산성을 높일 수도 있다.

창의성은 생산성에 영향을 미칠 수 있다. 창의성은 어떤 이들이 남들은 보지 못하는 문제들을 인식하게 하지만, 이는 매우 어려울 수도 있다. ① 종 분화 문제에 대한 찰스 다윈의 접근이 이것의 좋은 예시인데, 그는 매우 어렵고 복잡한 문제인 종 분화를 선택했고, 이것은 그를 오랜 자료 수집과 심사숙고의 기간으로 이끌었다. ② 이러한 문제 선택은 빠른 착수나 간단한 실험을 허용하지 않았다. ③ 이 경우, 노력은 어려운 문제에 집중되기 때문에 창의성은 (출판물의 수로 측정되듯) 사실 생산성을 감소시킬 수 있다. ④ 창의성이 방법과 기술에 더 집중돼 있는 다른 이들의 경우, 창의성은 문제 해결에 필요한 작업을 극적으로 줄이는 해결책으로 이어질 수 있다. 우리는 작은 DNA 조각들을 짧은 시간에 증폭시켜 주는 중합 효소 연쇄 반응(PCR)의 개발에서 한 예를 볼 수 있다. ⑤ 이러한 유형의 창의성은 단계의 수를 줄이거나 실패할 가능성이 더 낮은 단계로 대체해주고, 그리하여 생산성을 높일 수도 있다.

창의성이 생산성에 부정적 또는 긍정적 영향을 끼친다는 내용으로, ④ 앞에서는 창의성으로 인해 생산성이 떨어지는 예시를, ④ 뒤에서는 생산성이 오르는 사례를 보여주고 있다. 따라서 생산성의 긍정적 영향에 관한 설명으로 넘어가는 주어진 문장이 들어가기에 가장 적절한 곳은 ④이다.

- drastically ⓐⓓ 극적으로
- speciation ⓝ 종(種) 분화
- deliberation ⓝ 숙고
- development ⓝ 개발, 발전, 전개
- amplify ⓥ 증폭하다
- productivity ⓝ 생산성
- tangled ⓐ 복잡한, 뒤엉킨
- publication ⓝ 출판(물)
- polymerase chain reaction 중합 효소 연쇄 반응
- substitute ⓥ 대체하다

구문 풀이

1행 For others, whose creativity is more focused on methods and technique,
선행사 소유격 관계대명사
creativity may lead to solutions [that drastically reduce the work necessary to
형용사구
solve a problem]. [ ] : 형용사절(solutions 수식)

40 좌우보다 위아래나 앞뒤를 구별하기 더 쉬운 이유   정답률 53% | 정답 ①
다음 글의 내용을 한 문장으로 요약하고자 한다. 빈칸 (A), (B)에 들어갈 말로 가장 적절한 것은?

	(A)		(B)
✔①	spatial 공간적	……	significant 유의미한
②	spatial 공간적	……	scarce 드문
③	auditory 청각적	……	different 서로 다른
④	cultural 문화적	……	accessible 이해하기 쉬운
⑤	cultural 문화적	……	desirable 바람직한

A young child may be puzzled / when asked to distinguish / between the directions of right and left.
어린아이는 당황할 수 있다. / 구분하라고 요구받으면 / 오른쪽과 왼쪽의 방향을
But that same child may have no difficulty / in determining the directions of up and down or back and front.
하지만 그 아이는 전혀 어려움이 없을 것이다. / 위아래나 앞뒤의 방향을 알아내는 데에는
Scientists propose / that this occurs / because, although we experience three dimensions, / only two had a strong influence on our evolution: / the vertical dimension as defined by gravity / and, in mobile species, the front/back dimension / as defined by the positioning of sensory and feeding mechanisms.
과학자들은 주장한다 / 이것이 발생한다고 / 왜냐하면 비록 우리가 세 가지 차원을 경험하지만 / 두 가지만이 우리의 진화에 강력한 영향을 미쳤기 때문에 / 중력으로 정의되는 수직적 차원 / 그리고 이동하는 종에서는 앞뒤 차원 / 감각 먹이 섭취 기제의 배치로 정의되는
These influence our perception of vertical versus horizontal, / far versus close, / and the search for dangers from above (such as an eagle) / or below (such as a snake).
이것들은 수직 대 수평에 대한 우리의 지각에 영향을 미친다. / 원거리 대 근거리에 대한 / 그리고 (독수리처럼) 위로부터의 위험 탐색에 / 또는 (뱀처럼) 아래로부터의
However, / the left-right axis is not as relevant in nature.
그러나 / 좌우 축은 자연에서는 그만큼 중요하지 않다.
A bear is equally dangerous / from its left or the right side, / but not if it is upside down.
곰은 똑같이 위험하지만, / 왼쪽에서든 오른쪽에서든 / 그것이 거꾸로 뒤집혀 있다면 그렇지 않다.
In fact, / when observing a scene / containing plants, animals, and man-made objects such as cars or street signs, / we can only tell / when left and right have been inverted / if we observe those artificial items.
사실, / 장면을 관찰할 때, / 식물이나 동물, 자동차, 도로 표지판 같이 인간이 만든 물체가 포함된 / 우리는 겨우 구별할 수 있을 뿐이다. / 좌우가 뒤바뀐 것을 / 만약 우리가 그 인공적인 물체들을 관찰한다면
➡ Having affected the evolution of our (A) spatial perception, / vertical and front/back dimensions are easily perceived, / but the left-right axis, / which is not (B) significant in nature, / doesn't come instantly to us.
우리의 공간적 지각의 진화에 영향을 미쳤기 때문에 / 수직적 차원과 앞뒤 차원은 쉽게 인식되지만 / 좌우 축은 / 자연에서 유의미하지 않은 / 우리에게 즉각 이해되지 않는다.

오른쪽과 왼쪽의 방향을 구분하라고 요구받으면 어린아이는 당황할 수 있다. 하지만 그 아이는 위아래나 앞뒤의 방향을 알아내는 데에는 전혀 어려움이 없을 것이다. 과학자들이 주장하기로 이것이 발생하는 이유는 비록 우리가 세 가지 차원을 경험하지만 두 가지만이 우리의 진화에 강력한 영향을 미쳤기 때문이다. 바로 중력으로 정의되는 수직적 차원과, 이동하는 종의 경우 감각 먹이 섭취 기제의 배치로 정의되는 앞뒤 차원이다. 이것들은 수직 대 수평, 원거리 대 근거리에 대한 우리의 지각과 (독수리처럼) 위 또는 (뱀처럼) 아래로부터의 위험 탐색에 영향을 미친다. 그러나 좌우 축은 자연에서는 그만큼 중요하지 않다. 곰은 왼쪽에서든 오른쪽에서든 똑같이 위험하지만, 거꾸로 뒤집혀 있다면 그렇지 않다. 사실, 우리가 식물이나 동물, 자동차, 도로 표지판 같이 인간이 만든 물체가 포함된 장면을 관찰할 때, 만약 우리가 그 인공적인 물체들을 관찰한다면 좌우가 뒤바뀐 것을 겨우 구별할 수 있을 뿐이다.

➡ 수직적 차원과 앞뒤 차원은 우리의 (A) 공간적 지각의 진화에 영향을 미쳤기 때문에 쉽게 인식되지만, 자연에서 (B) 유의미하지 않은 좌우 축은 우리에게 즉각 이해되지 않는다.

Why? 왜 정답일까?

수직적 차원과 앞뒤 차원은 인간의 공간 지각에 많은 영향을 미쳤지만(~ the vertical dimension ~ and, ~ the front/back dimension ~. These influence our perception, ~) 좌우 축은 그 영향이 덜했다(~ the left-right axis is not as relevant in nature.)는 내용이다. 따라서 요약문의 빈칸 (A), (B)에 들어갈 말로 가장 적절한 것은 ① '(A) spatial(공간적), (B) significant(유의미한)' 이다.

- **puzzled** ⓐ 혼란스러워하는
- **dimension** ⓝ 차원
- **gravity** ⓝ 중력
- **perception** ⓝ 지각, 인식
- **axis** ⓝ 축
- **artificial** ⓐ 인공적인
- **scarce** ⓐ 드문
- **accessible** ⓐ 이해하기 쉬운, 접근 가능한
- **distinguish** ⓥ 구별하다
- **vertical** ⓐ 수직적인
- **mobile** ⓐ 이동하는
- **horizontal** ⓐ 수평적인
- **invert** ⓥ 뒤집다, 도치시키다
- **significant** ⓐ 유의미한, 중요한
- **auditory** ⓐ 청각적인
- **desirable** ⓐ 바람직한

구문 풀이

2행 But that same child may have no difficulty in determining the directions
「have no difficulty in+동명사 : ~하는 데 어려움이 없다」
of up and down or back and front.

41-42 사람 관리에서 중요한 것

Creative people aren't all cut from the same cloth.
창의적인 사람들이 모두 같은 부류인 것은 아니다.

They have (a) varying levels of maturity and sensitivity.
그들은 다양한 수준의 성숙도와 민감성을 지닌다.

They have different approaches to work.
그들은 일에 대한 접근법이 서로 다르다.

And they're each motivated by different things.
그리고 그들은 각자 서로 다른 것에 의해 동기 부여된다.

Managing people / is about being aware of their unique personalities. **41번의 근거**
사람 관리는 / 그들의 고유한 개성을 아는 것에 관한 것이다.

It's also about empathy and adaptability, / and knowing how the things you do and say will be interpreted / and adapting accordingly.
또한 그것은 공감과 적응성에 관한 것이다. / 그리고 여러분이 하는 일과 하는 말이 어떻게 해석될지 알고 / 그에 따라 보조를 맞추는 것

Who you are and what you say / may not be the (b) same / from one person to the next.
여러분이 누구인지와 무슨 말을 하는지는 / 같지 않을 수 있다. / 사람마다

For instance, / if you're asking someone / to work a second weekend in a row, / or telling them / they aren't getting that deserved promotion just yet, / you need to bear in mind the (c) individual.
예를 들어, / 여러분이 누군가에게 요청하고 있다면, / 2주 연속 주말에 일하라고 / 또는 그들에게 말하고 있다면 / 그들이 받아 마땅한 승진을 지금 당장은 받지 못할 것이라고 / 여러분은 개인을 명심해야 한다.

Vincent will have a very different reaction to the news than Emily, / and they will each be more receptive to the news / if it's bundled with different things. **42번의 근거**
Vincent는 그 소식에 Emily와 매우 다른 반응을 보일 것이고, / 그들 각자는 그 소식을 더 잘 받아들일 것이다. / 그것이 서로 다른 것과 묶인다면

Perhaps that promotion news will land (d) easier / if Vincent is given a few extra vacation days for the holidays, / while you can promise Emily a bigger promotion a year from now.
아마 그 승진 소식은 더 쉽게 도달할 것이고, / Vincent에게 명절에 며칠간의 추가적인 휴무일이 주어진다면 / 한편 Emily에게는 지금보다 1년 후에 더 큰 승진을 약속할 수도 있을 것이다.

Consider each person's complex positive and negative personality traits, / their life circumstances, / and their mindset in the moment / when deciding what to say and how to say it.
사람 각각의 복잡한 긍정적 및 부정적인 개성의 특징을 고려하라. / 그들의 인생 상황, / 그리고 그 순간 그들의 사고방식을 / 무슨 말을 할지와 그 말을 어떻게 할지를 정할 때

Personal connection, compassion, and an individualized management style / are (e) key / to drawing consistent, rock star-level work out of everyone.
개인적인 연관, 동감, 그리고 개별화된 관리 방식은 / 핵심이다 / 모든 사람으로부터 일관되고 록 스타 수준의(엄청난) 일을 끌어내는 데 있어

창의적인 사람들이 모두 같은 부류인 것은 아니다. 그들은 (a) 다양한 수준의 성숙도와 민감성을 지닌다. 그들은 일에 대한 접근법이 서로 다르다. 그리고 그들은 각자 서로 다른 것에 의해 동기 부여된다. 사람 관리에서 중요한 것은 그들의 고유한 개성을 아는 것이다. 또한 중요한 것은 공감과 적응성, 그리고 여러분이 하는 일과 하는 말이 어떻게 해석될지 알고 그에 따라 보조를 맞추는 것이다. 여러분이 누구인지와 무슨 말을 하는지는 사람마다 (b) 같지 않을 수 있다. 예를 들어, 여러분이 누군가에게 2주 연속 주말에 일하라고 요청하고 있다면, 또는 그들이 받아 마땅한 승진을 지금 당장은 받지 못할 것이라고 말하고 있다면, 그 (c) 집단(→ 개인)을 명심해야 한다. Vincent는 그 소식에 Emily와 매우 다른 반응을 보일 것이고, 그 소식이 서로 다른 것과 묶인다면 그들 각자는 더 잘 받아들일 것이다. 아마 Vincent에게 명절에 며칠간의 추가적인 휴무일이 주어진다면 그 승진 소식은 (d) 더 쉽게 도달할(받아들여질) 것이고, 한편 Emily에게는 지금보다 1년 후에 더 큰 승진을 약속할 수도 있을 것이다. 무슨 말을 할지와 그 말을 어떻게 할지를 정할 때 사람 각각의 복잡한 긍정적 및 부정적인 개성의 특징, 그들의 인생 상황, 그 순간 그들의 사고방식을 고려하라. 개인적인 연관, 동감, 그리고 개별화된 관리 방식은 모든 사람으로부터 일관되고 록 스타 수준의(엄청난) 일을 끌어내는 데 (e) 핵심이다.

- **cut from the same cloth** 비슷한, 같은 부류인
- **maturity** ⓝ 성숙
- **unique** ⓐ 고유한
- **empathy** ⓝ 공감, 감정 이입
- **accordingly** ⓐⓓ 그에 따라
- **deserve** ⓥ (받을) 자격이 있다
- **bear in mind** ~을 유념하다
- **receptive** ⓐ ~에 수용적인, ~을 잘 받아들이는
- **land** ⓥ 도달하다
- **circumstance** ⓝ 상황
- **flexible hours** 탄력 근로제, 유연 근무제(근무시간을 자유롭게 조정하여 일하는 것)
- **appealing** ⓐ 매력적인
- **varying** ⓐ 다양한
- **sensitivity** ⓝ 민감성
- **personality** ⓝ 개성, 성격
- **adaptability** ⓝ 적응력
- **in a row** 연달아
- **promotion** ⓝ 승진
- **reaction** ⓝ 반응
- **bundle** ⓥ 대발로 하다, 묶다
- **trait** ⓝ 특성
- **individualize** ⓥ 개인의 요구에 맞추다, 개별화하다

구문 풀이

14행 Perhaps that promotion news will land easier if Vincent is given
4형식 수동태
a few extra vacation days for the holidays, while you can promise Emily a bigger
직접목적어   접속사(~한 한편)
promotion a year from now.

★★★ 등급을 가르는 문제!

41 제목 파악 정답률 42% | 정답 ①

윗글의 제목으로 가장 적절한 것은?

✓① Know Each Person to Guarantee Best Performance – 최상의 수행을 보장하려면 사람 각각을 알라
② Flexible Hours: An Appealing Working Condition – 탄력 근무제: 매력적인 근로 조건
③ Talk to Employees More Often in Hard Times – 어려운 시기에는 직원들과 더 자주 이야기하라
④ How Empathy and Recognition Are Different – 공감과 인정은 어떻게 다른가
⑤ Why Creativity Suffers in Competition – 왜 창의성은 경쟁 속에서 약화되는가

Why? 왜 정답일까?

사람마다 개성이 다르기에 이 개성을 활용해야 사람들을 잘 관리할 수 있다(Managing people is about being aware of their unique personalities.)는 내용의 글이다. 따라서 글의 제목으로 가장 적절한 것은 ① '최상의 수행을 보장하려면 사람 각각을 알라'이다.

★★ 문제 해결 꿀~팁 ★★

▶ 많이 틀린 이유는?
사람 관리에 개성이 중요하다는 내용의 글로, empathy가 핵심 소재로 등장하므로 ④가 제목으로 그럴듯해 보일 수 있다. 하지만 '공감과 인정의 차이'를 설명하는 내용은 글에서 다루지 않았다.

▶ 문제 해결 방법은?
분량은 길지만, 명확한 주제문(Managing people is about being aware of their unique personalities.)이 있어 지엽적 소재와 관련된 함정에 주의하면 쉽게 답을 고를 수 있다. For instance 이하는 주제를 뒷받침하는 예시를 주로 다룬다.

★★★ 등급을 가르는 문제!

42 어휘 추론 정답률 34% | 정답 ③

밑줄 친 (a) ~ (e) 중에서 문맥상 낱말의 쓰임이 적절하지 않은 것은?

① (a) ② (b) ✓③ (c) ④ (d) ⑤ (e)

Why? 왜 정답일까?

(c)가 포함된 문장 뒤를 보면, 사람마다 같은 소식에 대해 다른 반응을 보일 수도 있고, 그렇기 때문에 소식을 더 잘 받아들이게 하려면 각자 다른 것을 제시해야 한다는 내용이다. 이 예시에 앞서 일반적 내용을 정리하는 (c)가 포함된 문장은 집단보다 '개인'을 고려하라는 의미여야 하므로, group을 individual로 고쳐야 한다. 따라서 문맥상 낱말의 쓰임이 적절하지 않은 것은 ③ '(c)'이다.

★★ 문제 해결 꿀~팁 ★★

▶ 많이 틀린 이유는?
④가 예시를 다루고 있어 주제를 적용해야 하므로 다소 까다롭다. 내용을 살펴보면, Vincent와 Emily에게 똑같이 '승진 유예'라는 소식을 전하는 상황에서, Vincent에게는 추가 휴가를 주고, Emily에게는 훗날 더 큰 승진을 약속해야 각자 소식을 '더 쉽게' 받아들일 것이라고 한다. 즉 ④가 포함된 문장은 '~ they will each be more receptive to the news if it's bundled with different things.'에 대한 적절한 예를 제시하고 있다.

▶ 문제 해결 방법은?
예시 앞의 unique personalities, empathy and adaptability, not be the same from one person to the next가 모두 한 논지를 가리키고 있다. 즉, '개인의 특징'을 고려해야 한다는 것이다.

43-45 Wylder의 첫 훈련

(A)

It was a hot day in early fall.
초가을의 더운 날이었다.

Wylder was heading to the school field / for his first training.
Wylder는 학교 운동장으로 향하고 있었다. / 첫 훈련을 하러

「He had just joined the team with five other students / after a successful tryout.」
그는 다른 학생 다섯 명과 함께 팀에 막 합류했다. / 성공적인 실력 테스트 후 **45번 ①의 근거** 일치

Approaching the field, / (a) he saw players getting ready, / pulling up their socks / and strapping on shin guards.
운동장에 다가가면서, / 그는 선수들이 준비하는 것을 보았다. / 양말을 당겨 올리고 / 정강이 보호대를 착용하면서

But they weren't together.
그러나 그들은 함께가 아니었다.

New players were sitting in the shade by the garage, / while the others were standing in the sun by the right pole.
새 선수들은 차고 옆 그늘에 앉아 있었다. / 다른 선수들은 오른편 골대 옆의 양지에 서 있었던 반면

Then Coach McGraw came / and watched the players.
그때 McGraw 코치가 도착해서 / 선수들을 보았다.

(D)

Coach McGraw, too, saw the pattern / — new kids and others grouping separately.
McGraw 코치도 패턴을 보았다. / 새로운 아이들과 다른 아이들이 따로 떨어져서 무리를 짓고 있는

'This is to change,' he thought.
그는 '이건 바꿔야겠군.'이라고 생각했다.

He wanted a winning team.
그는 승리하는 팀을 원했다.

To do that, / he needed to build relationships.
그렇게 하려면, / 그는 관계를 구축해야 했다.

그렇게 하려면, / 그는 관계를 형성해야 했다.

『"I want you guys / to come over here in the middle and sit," / he called the players / as he walked over.』 45번 ⑤의 근거 불일치

"나는 너희들이 ~하면 좋겠다. / 여기 중앙에 와서 앉았으면"이라며 / 그는 선수들을 불렀다. / 그가 걸어가면서

"You!" McGraw roared, / pointing at Wylder.

McGraw는 "너!"라고 소리치며 / Wylder를 가리켰다.

"Come here onto the field and sit. / And Jonny! You sit over there!"

"여기 필드 쪽에 와서 앉아라. / 그리고 Jonny! 너 저기 앉아라!"

He started pointing, / making sure they mixed together.

그는 가리키기 시작했고, / 그들이 반드시 서로 섞이도록 했다.

Wylder realized / what Coach was trying to do, / so (e) he hopped onto the field.

Wylder는 알아차렸고, / 코치가 무엇을 하려는지 / 그래서 그는 운동장 안으로 뛰어 들어갔다.

(C)

『McGraw continued to point, / calling each player out, / until he was satisfied with the rearrangement.』 45번 ③의 근거 일치

McGraw는 계속 가리켰다. / 각 선수를 불러내면서 / 그가 재배열이 마음에 들 때까지

"Okay, this is how it's going to be," / he began.

"자, 이렇게 되어갈 거다."라고 / 그는 말하기 시작했다.

"We need to learn / how to trust and work with each other. / This is how a team plays. / This is how I want you to be on and off the field: / together."

"우리는 배워야 해. / 서로 신뢰하고 함께 경기하는 방식을 / 이게 팀이 경기하는 방식이다. / 이게 내가 경기장 안과 밖에서 너희에게 바라는 거야. / 함께하는 것 말이다."라고

The players looked at each other.

선수들은 서로 쳐다보았다.

『Almost immediately, / McGraw noticed a change in their postures and faces.』 45번 ④의 근거 일치

거의 곧바로, / McGraw는 그들의 자세와 얼굴 변화를 알아차렸다.

(d) He saw some of them starting to smile.

그는 그들 중 몇몇이 미소 짓기 시작한 것을 보았다.

(B)

'Wow,' thought Wylder.

'와,' Wylder는 생각했다.

『From his new location on the grass, / he stretched out his legs.』 45번 ②의 근거 일치

잔디 위 새로운 자리에서, / 그는 다리를 쭉 폈다.

He liked what he was hearing.

그는 듣고 있는 말이 마음에 들었다.

A new sense of team spirit came across (b) him, / a deeper sense of connection.

그는 새로운 공동체 정신의 감각을 느꼈다. / 더 깊은 연대감

It was encouraging, / to hear Coach talk about this, / to see him face the challenge head-on.

고무적이었다. / 코치가 이것에 관해 말하는 것을 듣고, / 그가 그 도전에 정면으로 맞서는 것을 보는 것

Now his speech was over.

이제 그의 연설이 끝났다.

The players got up / and started walking on the field / to warm up.

선수들은 일어서서 / 운동장을 걸어 다니기 시작했다. / 몸을 풀려고

"Good job, Coach. That was good," / Wylder said to McGraw in a low voice / as he walked past him, / keeping (c) his eyes down out of respect.

"잘하셨습니다, 코치님. 좋았습니다."/ Wylder는 McGraw에게 낮은 목소리로 말했다. / 코치를 지나쳐 걸어가면서, / 존경의 마음을 담아 그의 눈을 내리깐 채로

(A)

초가을의 더운 날이었다. Wylder는 첫 훈련을 하러 학교 운동장으로 향하고 있었다. 그는 성공적인 실력 테스트 후 다른 학생 다섯 명과 함께 팀에 막 합류했다. 운동장에 다가가면서, (a) 그는 선수들이 양말을 당겨 올리고 정강이 보호대를 착용하면서 준비하는 것을 보았다. 그러나 그들은 함께가 아니었다. 새 선수들은 차고 옆 그늘에 앉아 있던 반면 다른 선수들은 오른편 골대 옆의 양지에 서 있었다. 그런 다음 McGraw 코치가 도착해서 선수들을 보았다.

(D)

McGraw 코치도 새로운 아이들과 다른 아이들이 따로 떨어져서 무리를 짓고 있는 패턴을 보았다. 그는 '이건 바꿔야겠군.'이라고 생각했다. 그는 승리하는 팀을 원했다. 그렇게 하려면, 그는 관계를 형성해야 했다. 그는 걸어가면서 "너희를 여기 중앙에 와서 앉았으면 좋겠다."라며 선수들을 불렀다. McGraw는 "너!"라고 소리치며 Wylder를 가리켰다. "여기 필드 쪽에 필드 쪽에 와서 앉아라. 그리고 Jonny! 너 저기 앉아라!" 그는 (앉을 위치들을) 가리키기 시작했고, 그들이 반드시 서로 섞이도록 했다. Wylder는 코치가 무엇을 하려는지 알아차렸고, 그래서 (e) 그는 운동장 안으로 뛰어 들어갔다.

(C)

재배열이 마음에 들 때까지 McGraw는 각 선수를 불러내면서 계속 가리켰다. 그는 "자, 이렇게 되어갈 거다. 우리는 서로 신뢰하고 함께 경기하는 방식을 배워야 해. 이게 팀이 경기하는 방식이다. 이게 내가 경기장 안과 밖에서 너희들에게 바라는 거야. 함께하는 것 말이다."라고 말했다. 선수들은 서로 쳐다보았다. 거의 곧바로, McGraw는 그들의 자세와 얼굴 변화를 알아차렸다. (d) 그는 그들 중 몇몇이 미소 짓기 시작한 것을 보았다.

(B)

'와,' Wylder는 생각했다. 잔디 위 새로운 자리에서, 그는 다리를 쭉 폈다. 그는 듣고 있는 (코치의) 말이 마음에 들었다. (b) 그는 새로운 공동체 정신의 감각, 더 깊은 연대감을 느꼈다. 코치가 이것에 관해 말하는 것을 듣고, 그가 그 도전에 정면으로 맞서는 것을 보는 것은 고무적이었다. 이제 그의 연설이 끝났다. 선수들은 몸을 풀려고 일어서서 걸어가면서, 존경의 마음을 담아 (e) 그의 눈을 내리깐 채로, Wylder는 McGraw에게 낮은 목소리로 말했다. "잘하셨습니다, 코치님. 좋았습니다."

- tryout ⓝ 실력 테스트, 적격 시험
- shin ⓝ 정강이
- stretch out ~을 펴다
- head-on ⓐⓓ 정면으로 ⓐ 정면으로 맞서는
- rearrangement ⓝ 재배치
- hop ⓥ (깡충깡충) 뛰다
- strap on (시계, 배낭 등을) 차다
- pole ⓝ 기둥
- encouraging ⓐ 고무적인
- warm up 몸을 풀다
- separately ⓐⓓ 따로

구문 풀이

(A) 3행 Approaching the field, he saw players getting ready, pulling up their

분사구문(~하면서) 지각동사 목적격 보어1 목적격 보어2

socks and strapping on shin guards.

목적격 보어3

---

43 글의 순서 파악
정답률 59% | 정답 ⑤

주어진 글 (A)에 이어질 내용을 순서에 맞게 배열한 것으로 가장 적절한 것은?

① (B) – (D) – (C)
② (C) – (B) – (D)
③ (C) – (D) – (B)
④ (D) – (B) – (C)
☑ (D) – (C) – (B)

Why? 왜 정답일까?

Wylder의 첫 훈련 날 운동장에 선수들이 서로 갈라져 있었다는 (A) 뒤로, 코치인 McGraw가 선수들을 서로 섞으려고 자리를 지정해주기 시작했다는 (D), 재배치 이후 선수들의 표정이 달라졌다는 (C), Wylder가 McGraw 코치의 뜻에 공감하며 그에게 존경을 표현한다는 (B)가 차례로 이어지는 것이 자연스럽다. 따라서 글의 순서로 가장 적절한 것은 ⑤ '(D) – (C) – (B)'이다.

44 지칭 추론
정답률 69% | 정답 ④

밑줄 친 (a) ~ (e) 중에서 가리키는 대상이 나머지 넷과 다른 것은?

① (a)   ② (b)   ③ (c)   ☑ (d)   ⑤ (e)

Why? 왜 정답일까?

(a), (b), (c), (e)는 Wylder, (d)는 Coach McGraw를 가리키므로, (a) ~ (e) 중에서 가리키는 대상이 다른 하나는 ④ '(d)'이다.

45 세부 내용 파악
정답률 75% | 정답 ⑤

윗글에 관한 내용으로 적절하지 않은 것은?

① Wylder는 다섯 명의 다른 학생과 팀에 합류했다.
② Wylder는 잔디 위의 새로운 자리에서 다리를 쭉 폈다.
③ McGraw는 재배열이 마음에 들 때까지 선수들을 불러냈다.
④ McGraw는 선수들의 자세와 얼굴의 변화를 알아차렸다.
☑ McGraw는 선수들에게 운동장 밖으로 나가라고 말했다.

Why? 왜 정답일까?

(D) '"I want you guys to come over here in the middle and sit," ~'에 따르면 코치인 McGraw는 선수들을 운동장 중간에 와서 앉으라고 불렀다. 따라서 내용과 일치하지 않는 것은 ⑤ 'McGraw는 선수들에게 운동장 밖으로 나가라고 말했다.'이다.

Why? 왜 오답일까?

① (A) 'He had just joined the team with five other students after a successful tryout.'의 내용과 일치한다.
② (B) 'From his new location on the grass, he stretched out his legs.'의 내용과 일치한다.
③ (C) '~ calling each player out, until he was satisfied with the rearrangement.'의 내용과 일치한다.
④ (C) 'Almost immediately, McGraw noticed a change in their postures and faces.'의 내용과 일치한다.

어휘 Review Test 02
문제편 020쪽

A	B	C	D
01 고마워하다	01 emphasize	01 ⓒ	01 ⓛ
02 그럼에도 불구하고	02 accomplish	02 ⓚ	02 ⓞ
03 기꺼이 ~하다	03 policy	03 ⓛ	03 ⓐ
04 가정하다	04 celebrate	04 ⓐ	04 ⓙ
05 포용하다	05 victim	05 ⓢ	05 ⓢ
06 가공된	06 excessive	06 ⓕ	06 ⓑ
07 실험 대상자	07 one fifth	07 ⓑ	07 ⓜ
08 결점	08 threat	08 ⓠ	08 ⓒ
09 바꾸다, 전환하다	09 dependence	09 ⓜ	09 ⓕ
10 ~에서 기원하다	10 take action	10 ⓓ	10 ⓔ
11 언어적인	11 conflict	11 ⓖ	11 ⓓ
12 변수	12 dose	12 ⓕ	12 ⓖ
13 ~로 그럭저럭 살아가다	13 myth	13 ⓔ	13 ⓕ
14 구별하다	14 ideal	14 ⓗ	14 ⓖ
15 정면으로, 정면으로 맞서는	15 productivity	15 ⓛ	15 ⓗ
16 다세포 생물	16 gravity	16 ⓞ	16 ⓝ
17 미덕	17 deserve	17 ⓞ	17 ⓟ
18 일관성	18 encouraging	18 ⓝ	18 ⓛ
19 고안하다, 떠올리다	19 trait	19 ⓟ	19 ⓘ
20 고마워하는	20 contract	20 ⓙ	20 ⓚ

★ 표기된 문항은 [등급을 가르는 문제]에 해당하는 문항입니다.

---

18 기차표 날짜 변경 요청   정답률 86% | 정답 ③

다음 글의 목적으로 가장 적절한 것은?
① 특가로 제공되는 기차표를 구매하려고
② 축구 경기 입장권의 환불을 요구하려고
☑ 다른 날짜로 기차표 변경을 요청하려고
④ 기차표 예약이 가능한 날짜를 알아보려고
⑤ 축구 경기 날짜가 연기되었는지를 확인하려고

As I explained on the telephone, / I don't want to take my two children by myself on a train trip / to visit my parents in Springfield / this Saturday / since it is the same day / the Riverside Warriors will play the Greenville Trojans / in the National Soccer Championship.
제가 전화로 설명드렸듯이, / 저는 혼자 두 아이를 데리고 기차 여행을 하고 싶지 않습니다. / Springfield에 사시는 저희 부모님을 뵈러 / 이번 주 토요일에 / 그날이 같은 날이어서 / Riverside Warriors가 Greenville Trojans와 시합할 / National Soccer Championship에서

I would really appreciate it, therefore, / if you could change my tickets / to the following weekend (April 23).
그래서 저는 정말 감사하겠습니다. / 당신이 제 기차표를 바꿔 주시면 / 다음 주말(4월 23일)로

I fully appreciate / that the original, special-offer ticket was non-exchangeable, / but I did not know about the soccer match / when I booked the tickets / and I would be really grateful / if you could do this for me.
저는 잘 압니다. / 특가로 제공되는 원래 기차표는 교환할 수 없다는 것을 / 하지만 저는 축구 경기에 관해 알지 못했으니 / 제가 기차표를 예매할 당시에는 / 저는 정말 감사하겠습니다. / 당신이 제게 이렇게 해 주시면

Thank you in advance.
미리 감사드립니다.

전화로 설명드렸듯이, 이번 주 토요일이 National Soccer Championship에서 Riverside Warriors가 Greenville Trojans와 시합할 날과 같은 날이어서 그날 Springfield에 사시는 저희 부모님을 뵈러 혼자 두 아이를 데리고 기차 여행을 하고 싶지 않습니다. 그래서 제 기차표를 다음 주말(4월 23일)로 바꿔 주시면 정말 감사하겠습니다. 특가로 제공되는 원래 기차표는 교환할 수 없다는 것을 잘 알지만, 기차표를 예매할 당시에는 축구 경기에 관해 알지 못했으니 이렇게 해 주시면 정말 감사하겠습니다. 미리 감사드립니다.

Why? 왜 정답일까?

'I would really appreciate it, therefore, if you could change my tickets to the following weekend (April 23).'에서 기차표 날짜를 변경해줬으면 좋겠다는 내용이 나오는 것으로 보아, 글의 목적으로 가장 적절한 것은 ③ '다른 날짜로 기차표 변경을 요청하려고'이다.

● **appreciate** ⓥ 감사하다. (제대로) 이해하다 ● **non-exchangeable** ⓐ 교환 불가한
● **book** ⓥ 예약하다 ● **grateful** ⓐ 고마워하는
● **in advance** 미리, 사전에

구문 풀이

1행 As I explained on the telephone, I don't want to take my two children
접속사(~듯이)
by myself on a train trip to visit my parents in Springfield this Saturday since it is
혼자서   부사적 용법(~하기 위해)   접속사(~ 때문에)
the same day [(that) the Riverside Warriors will play the Greenville Trojans in the
선행사(시간)   생략
National Soccer Championship].

---

19 패션쇼 대기 상황   정답률 86% | 정답 ①

다음 글에 드러난 'I'의 심경으로 가장 적절한 것은?
☑ tense and nervous – 긴장되고 불안한
② proud and confident – 자랑스럽고 자신 있는
③ relieved and pleased – 안도하고 기쁜
④ indifferent and bored – 무관심하고 지루한
⑤ irritated and disappointed – 짜증나고 실망한

Hours later / — when my back aches from sitting, / my hair is styled and dry, / and my almost invisible makeup has been applied — / Ash tells me / it's time to change into my dress.
몇 시간 후에, / 앉아 있어서 허리가 아프고, / 머리는 스타일링된 채 마르고, / 거의 보이지 않는 화장을 했을 때, / Ash는 나에게 말한다. / 드레스로 갈아입을 시간이라고

We've been waiting until the last minute, / afraid / any refreshments I eat / might accidentally fall onto it and stain it.
우리는 마지막 순간까지 기다리고 있었다. / 두려워하며 / 내가 먹는 다과가 / 우연히 드레스에 떨어져 얼룩질까 봐

There's only thirty minutes left / until the show starts, / and the nerves that have been torturing Ash / seem to have escaped her, / choosing a new victim in me.
30분밖에 남지 않았고 / 쇼가 시작될 때까지 / Ash를 괴롭히던 초조함이 / 그녀에게서 빠져나와 / 새로운 희생자로 나를 선택한 것 같다.

My palms are sweating, / and I have butterflies in my stomach.
내 손바닥에서 땀이 나고, / 나는 안절부절못한다.

Nearly all the models are ready, / some of them already dressed in their nineteenth-century costumes.
거의 모든 모델이 준비가 되었고, / 일부 모델은 이미 19세기 복장을 입고 있다.

Ash tightens my corset.
Ash가 내 코르셋을 조인다.

몇 시간 후에, 앉아 있어서 허리가 아프고, 머리는 스타일링된 채로 마르고, 눈에 거의 안 띄는 (열은) 화장을 했을 때, Ash는 나에게 드레스로 갈아입을 시간이라고 말한다. 내가 먹는 다과가 우연히 드레스에 떨어져 얼룩질까 두려워 우리는 마지막 순간까지 기다리고 있었다. 쇼가 시작될 때까지 30분밖에 남지 않았고 Ash를 괴롭히던 초조함이 그녀에게서 빠져나와 새로운 희생자로 나를 선택한 것 같다. 내 손바닥에서 땀이 나고, 나는 안절부절못한다. 거의 모든 모델이 준비가 되었고, 일부 모델은 이미 19세기 복장을 입고 있다. Ash가 내 코르셋을 조인다.

Why? 왜 정답일까?

패션쇼를 기다리며 초조함을 느끼는(My palms are sweating, and I have butterflies in my stomach.) 상황을 묘사한 글이므로, 'I'의 심경으로 가장 적절한 것은 ① '긴장되고 불안한'이다.

● **invisible** ⓐ 보이지 않는 ● **apply** ⓥ (연고, 화장품 등을) 바르다
● **refreshment** ⓝ 다과 ● **accidentally** ⓐ 우연히, 실수로
● **stain** ⓥ 얼룩지게 하다 ● **nerve** ⓝ 신경, 긴장, 불안
● **torture** ⓥ 괴롭히다, 고문하다 ● **victim** ⓝ 희생자
● **have butterflies in one's stomach** 안절부절 못한다. 긴장하다 ● **tense** ⓐ 긴장된
● **tighten** ⓥ 조이다
● **irritated** ⓐ 짜증난

구문 풀이

3행 We've been waiting until the last minute, (being) afraid {any refreshments
동사(현재완료 진행)   생략(분사구문)   주어
[I eat] might accidentally fall onto it and stain it}.
조동사   동사원형1   동사원형2

---

20 풍부한 다문화 경험을 자녀에게 제공하기   정답률 95% | 정답 ③

다음 글에서 필자가 주장하는 바로 가장 적절한 것은?
① 자녀가 전통문화를 자랑스럽게 여기게 해야 한다.
② 자녀가 주어진 문제를 깊이 있게 탐구하도록 이끌어야 한다.
☑ 자녀가 다른 문화를 가능한 한 자주 접할 수 있게 해야 한다.
④ 창의성 발달을 위해 자녀의 실수에 대해 너그러워야 한다.
⑤ 경험한 것을 돌이켜 볼 시간을 자녀에게 주어야 한다.

Though we are marching toward a more global society, / various ethnic groups traditionally do things quite differently, / and a fresh perspective is valuable / in creating an open-minded child.
우리는 더 글로벌한 사회로 나아가고 있지만, / 다양한 민족 집단들은 전통적으로 상당히 다르게 일을 하고 있어, / 새로운 관점이 가치가 있다. / 개방적인 아이를 만드는 데

Extensive multicultural experience / makes kids more creative / (measured by how many ideas they can come up with / and by association skills) / and allows them / to capture unconventional ideas from other cultures / to expand on their own ideas.
광범위한 다문화 경험은 / 아이를 더 창의적으로 만들고 / (그들이 얼마나 많은 생각을 떠올릴 수 있는지로 측정됨 / 그리고 연상 능력으로) / 그들이 ~할 수 있게 한다. / 다른 문화로부터 색다른 생각을 포착할 / 아이 자신의 생각을 확장하기 위해

As a parent, / you should expose your children to other cultures / as often as possible.
부모로서, / 당신은 자녀가 다른 문화를 접하게 해야 한다. / 가능한 한 자주

If you can, / travel with your child to other countries; / live there if possible.
당신이 할 수 있다면 / 자녀와 다른 나라로 여행하고, / 가능하면 거기서 살라.

If neither is possible, / there are lots of things you can do at home, / such as exploring local festivals, / borrowing library books about other cultures, / and cooking foods from different cultures at your house.
둘 다 가능하지 않은 경우에는 / 국내에서 할 수 있는 일이 많다. / 지역 축제 탐방하기와 / 다른 문화에 대한 도서관 책 빌리기, / 집에서 다른 문화의 음식 요리하기와 같이

우리는 더 글로벌한 사회로 나아가고 있지만, 다양한 민족 집단들은 전통적으로 상당히 다르게 일을 하고 있어, 새로운 관점이 개방적인 아이를 만드는 데 가치가 있다. 광범위한 다문화 경험은 아이를 더 창의적으로 (얼마나 많은 생각을 떠올릴 수 있는지와 연상 능력으로 측정됨) 만들고 아이가 자신의 생각을 확장하기 위해 다른 문화로부터 색다른 생각을 포착할 수 있게 한다. 부모로서 가능한 한 자주 자녀가 다른 문화를 접하게 해야 한다. 할 수 있다면 자녀와 다른 나라로 여행하고, 가능하면 거기서 살라. 둘 다 가능하지 않은 경우에는 지역 축제 탐방하기와 다른 문화에 대한 도서관 책 빌리기, 집에서 다른 문화의 음식 요리하기와 같이 국내에서 할 수 있는 일이 많다.

Why? 왜 정답일까?

'As a parent, you should expose your children to other cultures as often as possible.'에서 자녀에게 다른 문화를 가급적 많이 접할 수 있게 해 주어야 한다고 하므로, 필자의 주장으로 가장 적절한 것은 ③ '자녀가 다른 문화를 가능한 한 자주 접할 수 있게 해야 한다.'이다.

● **ethnic** ⓐ 민족의 ● **perspective** ⓝ 관점, 시각
● **open-minded** ⓐ (사고가) 개방적인 ● **extensive** ⓐ 광범위한
● **multicultural** ⓐ 다문화적인 ● **come up with** ~을 떠올리다
● **association** ⓝ 연상, 연관 ● **unconventional** ⓐ 색다른, 관습에 얽매이지 않는
● **expand** ⓥ 확장하다

구문 풀이

3행 Extensive multicultural experience makes kids more creative (measured
동사   목적어1   목적격 보어1(형용사)
{by how many ideas they can come up with} and {by association skills}) and
allows them to capture unconventional ideas from other cultures to expand on
동사2   목적어2   목적격 보어2   부사적 용법(~하기 위해)
their own ideas.

---

21 기존 견해의 틀 안에서 이해되는 새로운 관념   정답률 73% | 정답 ④

밑줄 친 *Fish is Fish–style* assimilation이 다음 글에서 의미하는 바로 가장 적절한 것은?
[3점]

① established knowledge is questioned and criticized
확립된 지식에 의문을 갖고 그것을 비판한다
② novel views are always favored over existing ones
새로운 견해는 항상 기존 견해보다 선호된다
③ all one's claims are evaluated based on others' opinions
자신의 모든 주장은 타인의 의견에 기반하여 평가된다
✔ new information is interpreted within one's own views
자기 자신의 견해 안에서 새로운 정보를 해석한다
⑤ new theories are established through experiments
새로운 이론은 실험을 통해 확립된다

Studies by Vosniado and Brewer / illustrate *Fish is Fish*-style assimilation / in the context of young children's thinking about the earth.
Vosniado와 Brewer의 연구는 / *Fish is Fish*식의 동화를 보여준다. / 지구에 관한 어린아이들의 생각이라는 맥락에서
They worked with children / who believed that the earth is flat / (because this fit their experiences) / and attempted to help them understand / that, in fact, it is spherical.
그들은 아이들을 대상으로 연구했고 / 지구가 평평하다고 믿는 / (이것이 자기 경험과 일치하기 때문에) / 이들이 이해하도록 돕고자 했다. / 사실은 지구가 구형이라는 것을
When told it is round, / children often pictured the earth as a pancake / rather than as a sphere.
지구가 둥글다는 말을 들으면 / 아이들은 흔히 지구를 팬케이크와 같다고 상상했다. / 구의 형태보다는
If they were then told / that it is round like a sphere, / they interpreted the new information about a spherical earth / within their flat-earth view / by picturing a pancake-like flat surface / inside or on top of a sphere, / with humans standing on top of the pancake.
그런 다음 지구가 구처럼 둥글다는 말을 / 그들은 구형의 지구에 관한 새로운 정보를 해석했다. / 자신들의 평평한 지구라는 관점 안에서 / 팬케이크처럼 평평한 표면을 상상함으로써 / 구의 안쪽이나 위쪽에 있는 / 사람들이 그 팬케이크 위에 서 있는
The model of the earth / that they had developed / — and that helped them explain / how they could stand or walk upon its surface — / did not fit the model of a spherical earth.
지구의 모형은 / 그리고 그들이 개발한 / 그들이 설명하는 데 도움이 된 / 자신들이 어떻게 지구의 표면에 서 있거나 걸을 수 있는지를 / 구형의 지구라는 모형과 일치하지 않았다.
Like the story *Fish is Fish*, / where a fish imagines everything on land to be fish-like, / everything the children heard / was incorporated into their preexisting views.
*Fish is Fish*의 이야기처럼, / 물고기가 육지의 모든 것을 물고기와 닮은 것으로 상상한다는 / 아이들이 들은 모든 것은 / 그들의 기존 견해에 통합되었다.

Vosniado와 Brewer의 연구는 어린아이들이 지구에 관해 지닌 생각이라는 맥락에서 *Fish is Fish*식의 동화를 보여준다. 그들은 (자기 경험과 일치하기 때문에) 지구가 평평하다고 믿는 아이들을 대상으로 연구했고 사실은 지구가 구형이라는 것을 이들이 이해하도록 돕고자 했다. 지구가 둥글다는 말을 들으면 아이들은 흔히 지구를 구의 형태보다는 팬케이크와 같다고 상상했다. 그런 다음 지구가 구처럼 둥글다는 말을 들으면 그들은 팬케이크처럼 평평한 표면이 구의 안쪽이나 위쪽에 있으며 사람들이 그 팬케이크 위에 서 있는 것을 상상함으로써, 자신들의 평평한 지구라는 관점 안에서 구형의 지구에 관한 새로운 정보를 해석했다. 자신들이 어떻게 지구의 표면에 서 있거나 걸을 수 있는지를 설명하는 데 도움이 된, 그들이 개발한 지구의 모형은 구형의 지구라는 모형과 일치하지 않았다. 물고기가 육지의 모든 것을 물고기와 닮은 것으로 상상한다는 *Fish is Fish*의 이야기처럼, 아이들이 들은 모든 것은 그들의 기존 견해에 통합되었다.

Why? 왜 정답일까?

예시에 따르면 지구를 평평하다고 믿었던 아이들은 구형의 지구에 관한 설명을 들었을 때 자신이 이미 지구에 대해 갖고 있는 관념을 기준으로 그 정보를 해석해 받아들였다고 한다. 이를 가리켜 마지막 문장에서는 아이들이 들은 모든 것들이 아이들이 기존에 지녔던 견해 안에 통합되었다(~ **everything the children heard was incorporated into their preexisting views.**)고 한다. 따라서 밑줄 친 부분의 의미로 가장 적절한 것은 ④ '자기 자신의 견해 안에서 새로운 정보를 해석한다'이다.

● illustrate ⓥ (예를 들어) 보여주다
● fit ⓥ ~에 맞다, 적합하다
● interpret ⓥ 해석하다, 이해하다
● incorporate ⓥ 통합하다
● assimilation ⓝ 동화, 흡수
● spherical ⓐ (도형) 구의
● on top of ~ 위에
● preexisting ⓐ 기존의

구문 풀이

```
         접속사(만일 ~라면)
7행  If they were then told {that it is round like a sphere}, they interpreted the
          4형식 수동태                          { }: 목적어
     new information about a spherical earth within their flat-earth view by picturing a
                                                                              ~함으로써
     pancake-like flat surface inside or on top of a sphere, with humans standing on
                                                              「with + 명사 + 분사: ~한 채로」
     top of the pancake.
```

22 습관에 관한 타인의 조언   정답률 82% | 정답 ⑤

다음 글의 요지로 가장 적절한 것은?
① 한번 잘못 들인 습관은 바로잡기가 어렵다.
② 꾸준한 반복을 통해 올바른 습관을 들일 수 있다.
③ 친구나 가족의 조언은 항상 귀담아들을 필요가 있다.
④ 사소하더라도 좋은 습관을 들이면 인생이 바뀔 수 있다.
✔ 타인에게 유익했던 습관이 자신에게는 효과가 없을 수 있다.

Advice from a friend or family member / is the most well-meaning of all, / but it's not the best way / to match yourself with a new habit.
친구나 가족의 조언은 / 모든 것 중에서 가장 좋은 뜻으로 하는 말이지만, / 최선의 방법은 아니다. / 새로운 습관에 자신을 맞추는
While hot yoga may have changed your friend's life, / does that mean it's the right practice for you?
핫 요가가 여러분 친구의 삶을 바꿔 놓았을지 모르지만, / 그것이 여러분에게 맞는 운동임을 의미할까?
We all have friends / who *swear* / their new habit of getting up at 4:30 a.m. / changed their lives / and that we have to do it.
우리 모두에게는 친구들이 있다. / *확언하는* / 새벽 4시 30분에 일어나는 새로운 습관이 / 자신의 삶을 바꿨고 / 우리도 그렇게 해야 한다고
I don't doubt / that getting up super early changes people's lives, / sometimes in good ways and sometimes not.
나는 의심하지 않는다. / 엄청 일찍 일어나는 것이 사람들의 삶을 바꾼다는 것을 / 때로는 좋은 방식으로, 때로는 그렇지
But be cautious:
그러나 주의하라.

You don't know / if this habit will actually make your life better, / especially if it means you get less sleep.
여러분은 알 수 없다. / 이 습관이 실제로 여러분의 삶을 더 낫게 만들지 / 특히 그것이 잠을 더 적게 자는 것을 의미한다면
So yes, / you can try what worked for your friend, / but don't beat yourself up / if your friend's answer doesn't change you in the same way.
그러니 맞다, / 여러분은 친구에게 효과가 있었던 것을 시도해 볼 수 있지만, / 자책하지 말라. / 여러분의 친구의 해결책이 여러분을 똑같은 방식으로 바꾸지 않는다고 해서
All of these approaches involve guessing and chance.
이 모든 접근법은 추측과 우연을 포함한다.
And that's not a good way / to strive for change in your life.
그리고 그것은 좋은 방법은 아니다. / 여러분 삶의 변화를 위해 노력하는

친구나 가족의 조언은 모든 것 중에서 가장 좋은 뜻으로 하는 말이지만, 새로운 습관에 자신을 맞추는 최선의 방법은 아니다. 핫 요가가 여러분 친구의 삶을 바꿔 놓았을지 모르지만, 그것이 여러분에게 맞는 운동임을 의미할까? 우리 모두에게는 새벽 4시 30분에 일어나는 새로운 습관이 자신의 삶을 바꿨고 우리도 그렇게 해야 한다고 확신하는 친구들이 있다. 나는 엄청 일찍 일어나는 것이 사람들의 삶을 때로는 좋은 방식으로, 때로는 그렇지 않게 바꾼다는 것을 의심하지 않는다. 그러나 주의하라. 이 습관이 특히 잠을 더 적게 자는 것을 의미한다면, 그것이 실제로 여러분의 삶을 더 낫게 만들지 알 수 없다. 그러니, 친구에게 효과가 있었던 것을 시도해 볼 수 있지만, 친구의 해결책이 여러분을 똑같은 방식으로 바꾸지 않는다고 해서 자책하지 말라. 이 모든 접근법은 추측과 우연을 포함한다. 그리고 그것은 여러분 삶의 변화를 위해 노력하는 좋은 방법은 아니다.

Why? 왜 정답일까?

첫 문장과 마지막 세 문장을 통해, 생활 습관에 관한 친구와 가족의 조언이 우리에게 꼭 맞지는 않을 수도 있으므로 시도해본 뒤 효과가 없다고 해서 자책하지 말라(~ **don't beat yourself up if your friend's answer doesn't change you in the same way.**)는 내용이 주제임을 알 수 있다. 따라서 글의 요지로 가장 적절한 것은 ⑤ '타인에게 유익했던 습관이 자신에게는 효과가 없을 수 있다.'이다.

● well-meaning ⓐ 선의로 하는
● doubt ⓥ 의심하다
● beat oneself up 자책하다
● swear ⓥ 장담하다, 맹세하다
● cautious ⓐ 조심하는, 신중한

구문 풀이

```
                          주격 관·대
4행  We all have friends [who *swear* {(that) their new habit of getting up at 4:30
                           선행사       동사     생략
     a.m. changed their lives} and {that we have to do it}].  [ ]: 목적어
```

★★★ 등급을 가르는 문제!
23 문화적으로 이뤄지는 인종의 구별   정답률 37% | 정답 ⑤

다음 글의 주제로 가장 적절한 것은?
① causes of physical variations among different races – 다른 인종 간 신체적 차이의 원인
② cultural differences between various races – 다양한 인종 간의 문화 차이
③ social policies to overcome racism – 인종 차별주의를 극복하기 위한 사회 정책
④ importance of environmental factors in evolution – 진화에 있어서 환경적 요인의 중요성
✔ misconception about race as a biological construct – 생물학적 구성물로서의 인종에 대한 오해

Individual human beings / differ from one another physically / in a multitude of visible and invisible ways.
인간 개개인은 / 신체적으로 서로 다르다. / 많은 가시적이고 비가시적인 면에서
If races / — as most people define them — / are real biological entities, / then people of African ancestry / would share a wide variety of traits / while people of European ancestry / would share a wide variety of *different* traits.
만일 인종이 / 대부분의 사람이 정의하듯이, / 정말 생물학적 실체라면 / 아프리카계 혈통인 사람들은 / 매우 다양한 특성을 공유할 것이다. / 유럽계 혈통인 사람들은 ~한 한편 / *다른* 매우 다양한 특성을 공유할 것인
But once we add traits / that are less visible than skin coloration, hair texture, and the like, / we find / that the people we identify as "the same race" / are less and less like one another / and more and more like people we identify as "different races."
하지만 우리가 특성들을 추가해 보면, / 피부색, 머릿결 등등보다 덜 가시적인 / 우리는 알게 된다. / 우리가 '같은 인종'이라고 식별하는 사람들이 / 서로 점점 덜 닮았고 / 사람들과 더욱 더 닮았다는 것을 / 우리가 '다른 인종'이라고 식별하는
Add to this point / that the physical features used to identify a person / as a representative of some race / (e.g. skin coloration) / are continuously variable, / so that one cannot say / where "brown skin" becomes "white skin."
이 점에 추가해 보라. / 어떤 사람을 식별하는 데 사용되는 신체적 특성이 / 어떤 인종의 전형이라고 / (예를 들어, 피부색) / 지속적으로 변할 수 있어서 / 사람들이 말할 수 없다는 것을 / 어디서 '갈색 피부'가 '흰 피부'가 되는지를
Although the physical differences themselves are real, / the way we use physical differences / to classify people into discrete races / is a cultural construction.
비록 신체적 차이 그 자체가 실재하더라도, / 우리가 신체적 차이를 사용하는 방식은 / 사람들을 별개의 인종으로 분류하기 위해 / 문화적 구성이다.

인간 개개인은 많은 가시적이고 비가시적인 면에서 신체적으로 서로 다르다. 대부분의 사람이 정의하듯이, 인종이 정말 생물학적 실체라면, 아프리카계 혈통인 사람들은 매우 다양한 특성을 공유하는 한편, 유럽계 혈통인 사람들은 (그것과) 다른 매우 다양한 특성을 공유할 것이다. 하지만 우리가 피부색, 머릿결 등등보다 덜 가시적인 특성들을 추가해 보면, 우리가 '같은 인종'이라고 식별하는 사람들이 서로 점점 덜 닮았고 우리가 '다른 인종'이라고 식별하는 사람들과 더욱 더 닮았다는 것을 알게 된다. 어떤 사람을 어떤 인종의 전형이라고 식별하는 데 사용되는 신체적 특성(예를 들어, 피부색)이 지속적으로 변할 수 있어서 어디서 '갈색 피부'가 '흰 피부'가 되는지를 말할 수 없는 것을 이 점에 추가해 보라. 비록 신체적 차이 그 자체가 실재하더라도, 사람들을 별개의 인종으로 분류하기 위해 우리가 신체적 차이를 사용하는 방식은 문화적 구성이다.

Why? 왜 정답일까?

마지막 문장에서 비록 서로 다른 인종들 간의 생물학적 차이가 실제로 있다고 해도, 인종의 구별은 문화적으로 이루어진다(Although the physical differences themselves are real, the way we use physical differences to classify people into discrete races is a cultural construction.)는 내용이 제시된다. 따라서 글의 주제로 가장 적절한 것은 ⑤ '생물학적 구성물로서의 인종에 대한 오해'이다.

- **physically** [ad] 신체적으로
- **ancestry** [n] 혈통, 가계
- **coloration** [n] (생물의) 천연색
- **identify as** ~라고 식별하다
- **representative** [n] 전형, 대표
- **construction** [n] 구성
- **racism** [n] 인종 차별(주의)
- **multitude** [n] 다수
- **trait** [n] 특성
- **and the like** 기타 등등
- **feature** [n] 특징
- **variable** [a] 가변적인
- **overcome** [v] 극복하다
- **misconception** [n] 오해

구문 풀이

9행 Add to this point that the physical features used to identify a person as a
(동사(명령문)) (주어) (과거분사구)
representative of some race (e.g. skin coloration) are continuously variable, so that
(동사(복수)) (그래서 ~하다)
one cannot say {where "brown skin" becomes "white skin."} [ ] : 간접의문문

★★ 문제 해결 꿀~팁 ★★

▶ 많이 틀린 이유는?
difference, cultural, races 등 키워드만 보고 오답을 고르지 않도록 주의해야 한다. 먼저 ①은 서로 다른 인종 간 '신체적 차이'의 '원인'을 언급하는데, 글에서는 인종 간 '신체적' 차이가 실제로 개념이 아닐 수 있다고 했으며, 그 원인을 밝히지도 않았다. 이어서 ②는 서로 다른 인종 간 '문화적 차이'를 언급하는데, 글에서는 인종적 차이라는 개념이 문화적으로 구성된 개념일 수 있다고만 언급할 뿐, 인종들 간에 어떤 문화적 차이가 있는지는 구체적으로 다루지 않았다.

▶ 문제 해결 방법은?
인종이 생물학적 개념이라는 통념에 대해 사실 이것이 문화적으로 구성된 개념임을 언급하며 반박하는 글이므로, 가리켜 '오해'라고 지적하는 선택지가 정답이다.

24 환경에 대한 인간 지배의 시작 정답률 61% | 정답 ③

다음 글의 제목으로 가장 적절한 것은?
① Strategies for Industrial Innovations – 산업 혁신을 위한 전략
② Urbanization: A Road to a Better Life – 도시화: 더 나은 삶으로 가는 길
✔ Industrial Development Hurt the Environment – 산업 발달이 환경을 해쳤다
④ Technology: A Key to Sustainable Development – 기술: 지속 가능한 발전의 열쇠
⑤ The Driving Force of Capitalism Was Not Greed – 자본주의의 원동력은 탐욕이 아니었다

The realization of human domination over the environment / began in the late 1700s with the industrial revolution.
환경에 대한 인간 지배의 실현은 / 1700년대 후반 산업 혁명과 함께 시작되었다.
Advances in manufacturing / transformed societies and economies / while producing significant impacts on the environment.
제조업의 발달은 / 사회와 경제를 변화시키면서 / 환경에 중대한 영향을 미쳤다.
American society became structured / on multiple industries' capitalistic goals / as the development of the steam engine / led to the mechanized production of goods in mass quantities.
미국 사회는 구축되었다. / 여러 산업의 자본주의적 목표에 따라 / 증기 기관의 발달이 / 기계화를 통한 상품의 대량 생산으로 이어지면서
Rural agricultural communities with economies / based on handmade goods and agriculture / were abandoned for life in urban cities with large factories / based on an economy of industrialized manufacturing.
경제를 가진 시골의 농업 사회는 / 수제 상품과 농업에 기반을 둔 / 대규모 공장이 있는 도시에서의 삶을 위해 버려졌다. / 산업화된 제조업 경제를 기반으로 한
Innovations in the production of textiles, iron, and steel / provided increased profits to private companies.
직물, 철, 철강 생산의 혁신은 / 사기업의 이윤을 증대하였다.
Simultaneously, / those industries exerted authority over the environment / and began dumping hazardous by-products in public lands and waterways.
동시에, / 그런 산업들은 환경에 권력을 행사하였고 / 공공 토지와 수로에 유해한 부산물을 내버리기 시작했다.

환경에 대한 인간 지배의 실현은 1700년대 후반 산업 혁명과 함께 시작되었다. 제조업의 발달은 사회와 경제를 변화시키면서 환경에 중대한 영향을 미쳤다. 증기 기관의 발달이 기계화를 통한 상품의 대량 생산으로 이어지면서 미국 사회는 여러 산업의 자본주의적 목표에 따라 구축되었다. 수제 상품과 농업에 기반을 둔 경제를 가진 시골의 농업 사회는 산업화된 제조업 경제를 기반으로 한 대규모 공장이 있는 도시에서의 삶을 위해 버려졌다. 직물, 철, 철강 생산의 혁신은 사기업의 이윤을 증대하였다. 동시에, 그런 산업들은 환경에 권력을 행사하였고 공공 토지와 수로에 유해한 부산물을 내버리기 시작했다.

Why? 왜 정답일까?

첫 문장에서 환경에 대한 인간의 지배가 산업화와 함께 시작되었다(The realization of human domination over the environment began in the late 1700s with the industrial revolution.)고 언급한 뒤, 산업 발달과 함께 착취되고 오염되기 시작한 환경에 관해 서술하고 있다. 따라서 글의 제목으로 가장 적절한 것은 ③ '산업 발달이 환경을 해쳤다'이다.

- **realization** [n] 실현
- **industrial revolution** 산업 혁명
- **transform** [v] 변모시키다
- **capitalistic** [a] 자본주의적인
- **mass** [a] 대량, 많음
- **exert** [v] (힘, 영향 등을) 행사하다, 가하다
- **hazardous** [a] 유해한
- **sustainable** [a] 지속 가능한
- **greed** [n] 탐욕
- **domination** [n] 지배
- **advance** [n] 진보, 발달
- **significant** [a] 중대한
- **mechanize** [v] 기계화하다
- **abandon** [v] 버리다
- **authority** [n] 권위
- **by-product** [n] 부산물
- **driving force** 추진력, 원동력

구문 풀이

1행 The realization of human domination over the environment began
(주어) (동사(과거))
in the late 1700s with the industrial revolution.
(시간 부사구)

25 통근길 교통수단별 이용자 비율 정답률 83% | 정답 ④

다음 도표의 내용과 일치하지 않는 것은?

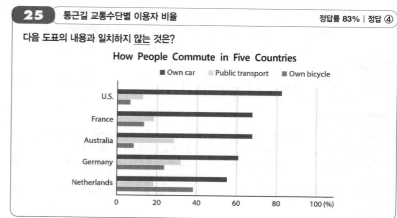

How People Commute in Five Countries
■ Own car ▨ Public transport ■ Own bicycle

(U.S., France, Australia, Germany, Netherlands / 0 20 40 60 80 100 (%))

The above graph shows / which modes of transportation people use / for their daily commute to work, school, or university / in five selected countries.
위 그래프는 보여준다. / 사람들이 어떤 교통수단을 이용하는지 / 직장, 학교, 또는 대학교로 매일 통근을 위해 / 선택된 5개국에서
① In each of the five countries, / the percentage of commuters using their own car / is the highest among all three modes of transportation.
5개국 각각에서 / 자가용을 이용하는 통근자의 비율이 / 세 가지 교통수단 중 가장 높다.
② The U.S. has the highest percentage of commuters / using their own car / among the five countries, / but it has the lowest percentages / for the other two modes of transportation.
미국은 통근자의 비율이 가장 높지만, / 자가용을 이용하는 / 5개국 중에서 / 그것은 가장 낮은 비율을 지닌다. / 다른 두 교통수단에 관해서는
③ Public transport is the second most popular mode of transportation / in all the countries / except for the Netherlands.
대중교통은 두 번째로 인기 있는 교통수단이다. / 모든 국가에서 / 네덜란드를 제외한
✔ Among the five countries, / France has the biggest gap / between the percentage of commuters using their own car / and that of commuters using public transport.
5개국 중 / 프랑스는 차이가 가장 크다. / 자가용을 이용하는 통근자의 비율과 / 대중교통을 이용하는 통근자의 비율 간의
⑤ In terms of commuters using public transport, / Germany leads all of the countries, / immediately followed by Australia.
대중교통을 이용하는 통근자의 경우에는, / 독일이 모든 나라를 앞서고 / 바로 그다음이 오스트레일리아이다.

위 그래프는 선택된 5개국에서 사람들이 직장, 학교, 또는 대학교로 매일 통근을 위해 어떤 교통수단을 이용하는지 보여준다. ① 5개국 각각에서 자가용을 이용하는 통근자의 비율이 세 가지 교통수단 중 가장 높다. ② 미국은 5개국 중에서 자가용을 이용하는 통근자의 비율이 가장 높지만, 다른 두 교통수단의 비율은 가장 낮다. ③ 네덜란드를 제외한 모든 국가에서 대중교통은 두 번째로 인기 있는 교통수단이다. ④ 5개국 중 프랑스는 자가용을 이용하는 통근자의 비율과 대중교통을 이용하는 통근자의 비율 간의 차이가 가장 크다. ⑤ 대중교통을 이용하는 통근자의 경우에는, 독일이 모든 나라를 앞서고 바로 그다음이 오스트레일리아이다.

Why? 왜 정답일까?

도표에 따르면 자가용 이용자와 대중교통 이용자 사이의 비율 격차가 가장 큰 국가는 프랑스가 아닌 미국이므로, 도표와 일치하지 않는 것은 ④이다.

- **mode of transportation** 교통수단
- **public transport** 대중교통
- **commute** [n] 통근(길) [v] 통근하다
- **in terms of** ~의 관점에서

26 가상 자선 행사 안내 정답률 96% | 정답 ⑤

2022 Bluehill Virtual Gala에 관한 다음 안내문의 내용과 일치하지 않는 것은?
① 자선 프로그램 기금 마련을 위한 온라인 파티이다.
② 4월 2일 오후 6시부터 8시까지 진행된다.
③ 음악 공연과 특별 강연, 라이브 경매가 있을 것이다.
④ 배우 Edward Jones가 사회를 볼 것이다.
✔ 유료로 스트리밍될 것이다.

2022 Bluehill Virtual Gala
2022 Bluehill 가상 행사
You're invited to the 2022 Bluehill Virtual Gala / hosted by the Bluehill Community Center.
2022 Bluehill 가상 행사에 여러분을 초대합니다. / Bluehill 커뮤니티 센터가 주최하는
『We'll have an online party / to raise funds for our charity programs!』 ①의 근거 일치
우리는 온라인 파티를 할 것입니다! / 자선 프로그램 기금을 마련하기 위한
Because we can't gather together in person this year, / we are joining together virtually.
올해는 우리가 직접 함께 모일 수 없어서 / 우리는 가상으로 함께 모일 것입니다.
『Our Virtual Gala is on April 2 from 6 p.m. to 8 p.m.』 ②의 근거 일치
가상 행사는 4월 2일 오후 6시부터 8시까지입니다.
『It will have musical performances, special lectures, and live auctions!』 ③의 근거 일치
음악 공연과 특별 강연, 라이브 경매가 포함될 것입니다.
『Our MC will be Edward Jones, / the famous actor from A Good Neighbor.』 ④의 근거 일치
사회자는 Edward Jones일 것입니다. / A Good Neighbor에 나온 유명 배우인
Everyone is welcome.
누구나 참가할 수 있습니다.
『This event will stream for free!』 ⑤의 근거 불일치
이 행사는 무료로 스트리밍될 것입니다!
To join the party, simply visit www.bluehillgala.org.
파티에 참가하려면 그저 www.bluehillgala.org로 오세요.

2022 Bluehill 가상 행사

Bluehill 커뮤니티 센터가 주최하는 2022 Bluehill 가상 행사에 여러분을 초대합니다. 자선 프로그램 기금을 마련하기 위한 온라인 파티를 할 것입니다! 올해는 직접 함께 모일 수 없어서 가상으로 함께 모일 것입니다.

– 가상 행사는 4월 2일 오후 6시부터 8시까지입니다.
– 음악 공연과 특별 강연, 라이브 경매가 포함될 것입니다!

03회

– 사회자는 *A Good Neighbor*에 나온 유명 배우인 Edward Jones일 것입니다.

누구나 참가할 수 있습니다. 이 행사는 무료로 스트리밍될 것입니다!

파티에 참가하려면 그저 www.bluehillgala.org로 오세요.

Why? 왜 정답일까?

'This event will stream for free!'에서 무료로 스트리밍이 이뤄진다고 하므로, 안내문의 내용과 일치하지 않는 것은 ⑤ '유료로 스트리밍될 것이다.'이다.

Why? 왜 오답일까?

① 'We'll have an online party to raise funds for our charity programs!'의 내용과 일치한다.
② 'Our Virtual Gala is on April 2 from 6 p.m. to 8 p.m.'의 내용과 일치한다.
③ 'It will include musical performances, special lectures, and live auctions!'의 내용과 일치한다.
④ 'Our MC will be Edward Jones, the famous actor from *A Good Neighbor*.'의 내용과 일치한다.

- **gala** ⓝ 경축 행사
- **charity** ⓝ 자선
- **virtually** ⓐⓓ 가상으로
- **raise a fund** 기금을 마련하다
- **gather** ⓥ 모이다
- **auction** ⓝ 경매

---

27 점토 공예 워크숍 안내   정답률 92% | 정답 ④

Woodside Clay Workshop에 관한 다음 안내문의 내용과 일치하는 것은?

① 목요일 오전에 진행된다.
② 어린이를 대상으로 한다.
③ 두 번째 시간에 펜던트를 찾아갈 수 있다.
☑ 모든 재료가 참가비에 포함된다.
⑤ 사전 예약을 받지 않는다.

Woodside Clay Workshop
Woodside 점토 공예 워크숍

『7 p.m. Thursday March 31, 2022
2022년 3월 31일 목요일 오후 7시
7 p.m. Thursday April 7, 2022』①의 근거 불일치
2022년 4월 7일 목요일 오후 7시

『This is a two-session workshop for adults.』②의 근거 불일치
성인을 위한 2차시짜리 워크숍입니다.

In the first session, / you will learn the basics of clay / and create unique ceramic pendants.
첫 번째 시간에, / 여러분은 점토의 기본을 배우고 / 독특한 도자기 펜던트를 만들 것입니다.

In the second session, / you will decorate the pieces / before we glaze and fire them.
두 번째 시간에는, / 여러분이 작품을 장식할 것입니다. / 우리가 유약을 바르고 굽기 전에

『Your pendants will be ready to be picked up / from April 14.』③의 근거 불일치
여러분의 펜던트는 찾아가실 수 있도록 준비될 것입니다. / 4월 14일부터

This workshop is suitable for beginners, / so no experience is necessary.
이 워크숍은 초보자에게 적합하므로 / 경험이 필요하지 않습니다.

『Fee: £25 / (including all materials, instruction and a glass of wine)』④의 근거 일치
참가비: 25파운드 / (모든 재료와 강습, 와인 한 잔 포함)

There are limited spaces, so book early.
자리가 한정되어 있으니 일찍 예약하십시오.

『Advance bookings only.』⑤의 근거 불일치
사전 예약만 가능합니다.

For more information, / visit our website at www.woodsideclay.co.uk.
더 많은 정보를 원하시면 / 저희 웹 사이트 www.woodsideclay.co.uk를 방문하십시오.

Woodside 점토 공예 워크숍

2022년 3월 31일 목요일 오후 7시
2022년 4월 7일 목요일 오후 7시

성인을 위한 2차시짜리 워크숍입니다. 첫 번째 시간에 점토의 기본을 배우고 독특한 도자기 펜던트를 만들 것입니다. 두 번째 시간에는 우리가 유약을 바르고 굽기 전에 여러분이 작품을 장식할 것입니다. 여러분의 펜던트는 4월 14일부터 찾아가실 수 있도록 준비될 것입니다.

– 이 워크숍은 초보자에게 적합하므로 경험이 필요하지 않습니다.
– 참가비: 25파운드(모든 재료와 강습, 와인 한 잔 포함)
– 자리가 한정되어 있으니 일찍 예약하십시오. 사전 예약만 가능합니다.

더 많은 정보를 원하시면 저희 웹 사이트 www.woodsideclay.co.uk를 방문하십시오.

Why? 왜 정답일까?

'Fee: £25 (including all materials, instruction and a glass of wine)'에서 모든 재료비가 포함된 참가비가 25파운드라고 하므로, 안내문의 내용과 일치하는 것은 ④ '모든 재료가 참가비에 포함된다.'이다.

Why? 왜 오답일까?

① '7 p.m. Thursday March 31, 2022 / 7 p.m. Thursday April 7, 2022'에서 2차시 수업 모두 목요일 오후 7시에 진행된다고 하였다.
② 'This is a two-session workshop for adults.'에서 수강 대상은 성인이라고 하였다.
③ 'Your pendants will be ready to be picked up from April 14.'에서 두 번째 시간은 4월 7일인데, 펜던트를 찾아갈 수 있는 날짜는 그로부터 일주일 뒤인 4월 14일이라고 하였다.
⑤ 'Advance bookings only.'에서 사전 예약만 가능하다고 하였다.

- **clay** ⓝ 점토
- **suitable** ⓐ 적합한
- **ceramic** ⓝ 도자기

---

28 Gordon Parks의 생애   정답률 94% | 정답 ③

Gordon Parks에 관한 다음 글의 내용과 일치하지 <u>않는</u> 것은?

① 15명의 자녀 중 막내로 태어났다.

---

② 어머니가 돌아가신 후 Minnesota에 있는 누나와 살러 갔다.
☑ 학교를 중퇴하지 않고 다양한 일자리에서 일했다.
④ *Life* 지의 사진 기자가 된 최초의 아프리카계 미국인이었다.
⑤ 그가 작곡한 피아노 협주곡을 1956년에 Vienna Orchestra가 연주했다.

Gordon Parks was a photographer, author, film director, and musician.
Gordon Parks는 사진작가이자 작가, 영화감독, 음악가였다.

He documented the everyday lives of African Americans / at a time / when few people outside the black community / were familiar with their lives.
그는 아프리카계 미국인의 일상생활을 기록했다. / 시절에 / 흑인 사회 밖에서는 사람이 거의 없던 / 그들의 삶에 익숙한

『Parks was born the youngest of 15 children / and grew up on his family's farm.』①의 근거 일치
Parks는 15명의 자녀 중 막내로 태어나 / 가족 농장에서 자랐다.

『After the death of his mother, / he went to live with a sister in Minnesota.』②의 근거 일치
어머니가 돌아가신 후, / 그는 Minnesota에 있는 누나와 살러 갔다.

『Parks eventually dropped out of school / and worked at various jobs.』③의 근거 불일치
Parks는 결국 학교를 중퇴하고 / 다양한 일자리에서 일했다.

His interest in photography / was inspired by a photo-essay / he read about migrant farm workers.
사진에 대한 그의 관심은 / 포토에세이 덕분에 생겼다. / 그가 떠돌이 농장 일꾼에 관해 읽은

After he moved to Chicago, / Parks began taking photos of poor African Americans.
그가 시카고로 옮겨간 후, / Parks는 가난한 아프리카계 미국인들을 사진 찍기 시작했다.

『In 1949, / he became the first African American / to be a staff photographer for *Life* magazine.』④의 근거 일치
1949년에, / 그는 최초의 아프리카계 미국인이 되었다. / *Life* 지의 사진 기자가 된

『He also wrote music pieces in his life / and in 1956 the Vienna Orchestra performed a piano concerto he wrote.』⑤의 근거 일치
그는 또한 살아생전에 음악 작품을 작곡했고 / 1956년에 Vienna Orchestra는 그가 작곡한 피아노 협주곡을 연주했다.

Parks was an inspiring artist / until he died in 2006.
Parks는 영감을 주는 예술가였다. / 그가 2006년에 사망할 때까지

Gordon Parks는 사진작가이자 작가, 영화감독, 음악가였다. 그는 흑인 사회 밖에서는 아프리카계 미국인의 삶에 익숙한 사람이 거의 없던 시절에 그들의 일상생활을 기록했다. Parks는 15명의 자녀 중 막내로 태어나 가족 농장에서 자랐다. 어머니가 돌아가신 후, 그는 Minnesota에 있는 누나와 살러 갔다. Parks는 결국 학교를 중퇴하고 다양한 일자리에서 일했다. 그가 읽은 농장 이주 노동자에 관한 포토에세이 덕분에 그는 사진에 관심이 생겼다. 그가 시카고로 옮겨간 후, Parks는 가난한 아프리카계 미국인들을 사진 찍기 시작했다. 1949년에 그는 *Life* 지의 사진 기자가 된 최초의 아프리카계 미국인이 되었다. 그는 또한 살아생전에 음악 작품을 작곡했고, 1956년에 Vienna Orchestra는 그가 작곡한 피아노 협주곡을 연주했다. Parks는 2006년에 사망할 때까지 영감을 주는 예술가였다.

Why? 왜 정답일까?

'Parks eventually dropped out of school and worked at various jobs.'에서 Parks는 학교를 결국 중퇴하고 다양한 일자리에서 일했다고 하므로, 내용과 일치하지 않는 것은 ③ '학교를 중퇴하지 않고 다양한 일자리에서 일했다.'이다.

Why? 왜 오답일까?

① 'Parks was born the youngest of 15 children ~'의 내용과 일치한다.
② 'After the death of his mother, he went to live with a sister in Minnesota.'의 내용과 일치한다.
④ 'In 1949, he became the first African American to be a staff photographer for *Life* magazine.'의 내용과 일치한다.
⑤ '~ in 1956 the Vienna Orchestra performed a piano concerto he wrote.'의 내용과 일치한다.

- **author** ⓝ 작가, 저자
- **familiar with** ~에 친숙한
- **inspire** ⓥ 영감을 주다
- **document** ⓥ 기록하다
- **drop out of** ~을 그만두다
- **perform** ⓥ 공연하다, 연주하다

구문 풀이

2행 He documented the everyday lives of African Americans at a time [when few people outside the black community were familiar with their lives].
관계부사절 / 시간 선행사

---

29 사회적 비교의 결과   정답률 56% | 정답 ④

다음 글의 밑줄 친 부분 중, 어법상 틀린 것은? [3점]

Despite abundant warnings / that we shouldn't measure ourselves against others, / most of us still do.
많은 경고에도 불구하고, / 우리가 타인과 견주어 우리 자신을 평가해서는 안 된다는 / 우리 대부분은 여전히 그렇게 하고 있다.

We're not only meaning-seeking creatures / but social ① ones as well, / constantly making interpersonal comparisons / to evaluate ourselves, / improve our standing, / and enhance our self-esteem.
우리는 의미를 추구하는 존재일 뿐만 아니라 / 사회적인 존재라서, / 끊임없이 사람들끼리 비교한다. / 우리 자신을 평가하고, / 지위를 개선하고, / 자존감을 높이기 위해

But the problem with social comparison / is that it often backfires.
그러나 / 사회적 비교의 문제는 / 그것이 흔히 역효과를 낸다는 것이다.

When comparing ourselves to someone / who's doing better than we are, / we often feel ② inadequate for not doing as well.
누군가와 우리 자신을 비교할 때, / 우리보다 더 잘하고 있는 / 우리는 흔히 그만큼 잘하지 못하는 것에 대해서 무능하다고 느낀다.

This sometimes leads to / what psychologists call *malignant envy*, / the desire for someone ③ to meet with misfortune / ("I wish she didn't have what she has").
이것은 때로는 ~로 이어진다. / 심리학자들이 악성 질투라고 부르는 것, / 누군가가 불행을 만나기를 바라는 욕망 / ("그녀가 지금 가진 것을 가지고 있지 않으면 좋을 텐데.")

Also, / comparing ourselves with someone / who's doing worse than we are / ☑ risks scorn, / the feeling that others are something undeserving of our beneficence / ("She's beneath my notice").
마찬가지로, / 누군가와 자신을 비교하는 것은 / 우리보다 더 못하고 있는 / 경멸로 이어질 위험이 있다. / 다른 사람이 우리의 호의를 받을 가치가 없다는 느낌 / ("그녀는 내가 주목할 가치가 없어.")

Then again, / comparing ourselves to others / can also lead to *benign envy*, / the longing to

---

reproduce someone else's accomplishments / without wishing them ill / ("I wish I had what she has"), / ⑤ which has been shown in some circumstances / to inspire and motivate us / to increase our efforts in spite of a recent failure.

그렇지 않고, / 우리 자신을 타인과 비교하는 것은 / 또한 *양성* 질투로 이어질 수 있으며, / 다른 사람의 성취를 재생산하려는 열망 / 그들이 불행해지기를 바라지 않으면서 / ("그녀가 가진 것을 나도 가지면 좋을 텐데.") / 이는 몇몇 상황에서 알려져 왔다. / 우리에게 영감을 주고 동기를 부여한다고 / 우리가 최근의 실패에도 불구하고 노력을 더 하도록

타인과 견주어 우리 자신을 평가해서는 안 된다는 많은 경고에도 불구하고, 우리 대부분은 여전히 그렇게 하고 있다. 우리는 의미를 추구하는 존재일 뿐만 아니라 사회적인 존재라서, 우리 자신을 평가하고, 지위를 개선하며, 자존감을 높이기 위해 끊임없이 사람들끼리 비교한다. 그러나 사회적 비교의 문제는 그것이 흔히 역효과를 낸다는 것이다. 우리보다 더 잘하고 있는 사람과 우리 자신을 비교할 때, 우리는 흔히 그만큼 잘하지 못하는 것에 대해서 무능하다고 느낀다. 이것은 때로는 심리학자들이 *악성* 질투라고 부르는 것, 즉 누군가가 불행을 만나기를 바라는 욕망("그녀가 지금 가진 것을 가지고 있지 않으면 좋을 텐데.")으로 이어진다. 마찬가지로, 우리보다 더 못하고 있는 사람과 자신을 비교하는 것은 경멸, 즉 다른 사람이 우리의 호의를 받을 가치가 없다는 느낌("그녀는 내가 주목할 가치가 없어.")으로 이어질 위험이 있다. 그렇지 않고, 우리 자신을 타인과 비교하는 것은 또한 양성 질투, 즉 다른 사람이 불행해지기를 바라지 않고 그들의 성취를 재생산하려는 열망("그녀가 가진 것을 나도 가지면 좋을 텐데.")으로 이어질 수 있으며, 이는 몇몇 상황에서 우리가 최근의 실패에도 불구하고 노력을 더 하도록 우리에게 영감을 주고 동기를 부여한다고 알려져 왔다.

Why? 왜 정답일까?
동명사구 주어인 'comparing ourselves with someone ~'는 단수 동사와 함께 쓰므로, risk를 risks로 고쳐야 한다. 따라서 어법상 틀린 것은 ④이다.

Why? 왜 오답일까?
① creatures를 받는 복수의 부정대명사 ones가 바르게 쓰였다.
② 2형식 동사 feel 뒤에서 주격 보어 역할을 하기 위해 형용사 inadequate가 바르게 쓰였다.
③ the desire는 to부정사구의 꾸밈을 받는 명사이므로, 형용사적 용법의 to meet이 바르게 쓰였다.
⑤ 선행사 the longing을 받으면서 뒤에 주어가 없는 관계절을 이끌기 위해 which가 바르게 쓰였다. 이 which는 콤마 뒤에서 선행사를 보충 설명하는 계속적 용법으로 쓰였다.

- **abundant** ⓐ 많은, 풍부한
- **measure A against B** B에 견주어 A를 평가하다, 측정하다
- **enhance** ⓥ 높이다, 향상시키다
- **inadequate** ⓐ (상황을 처리하기에) 부족한, 무능한
- **risk** ⓥ (~의 위험을) 감수하다
- **beneficence** ⓝ 선행, 자선
- **circumstance** ⓝ 상황
- **self-esteem** ⓝ 자존감
- **malignant** ⓐ 악의 있는
- **undeserving** ⓐ (~을 가질) 자격이 없는
- **benign** ⓐ 양성의, 상냥한
- **in spite of** ~에도 불구하고

구문 풀이
1행 Despite abundant warnings {that we shouldn't measure ourselves against
전치사 ／ 명사구 ／ { }: 동격절(= warnings)
others}, most of us still do.
= measure ~ others

★★★ 등급을 가르는 문제!
30 정상 과학의 특징 정답률 34% | 정답 ⑤
다음 글의 밑줄 친 부분 중, 문맥상 낱말의 쓰임이 적절하지 <u>않은</u> 것은? [3점]

What exactly does normal science involve?
정상 과학은 정확히 무엇을 포함하는가?
According to Thomas Kuhn / it is primarily a matter of *puzzle-solving*.
Thomas Kuhn에 따르면, / 그것은 주로 *문제 해결*의 문제이다.
However successful a paradigm is, / it will always ① encounter certain problems / — phenomena which it cannot easily accommodate, / or mismatches between the theory's predictions and the experimental facts.
패러다임이 아무리 성공적이더라도, / 그것은 항상 특정한 문제를 마주할 것이다. / 그것이 쉽게 수용할 수 없는 현상이나, / 이론의 예측과 실험적 사실 간의 불일치
The job of the normal scientist / is to try to ② eliminate these minor puzzles / while making as few changes as possible to the paradigm.
정상 과학자들의 일은 / 이러한 사소한 문제를 제거하려고 노력하는 것이다. / 패러다임에 가능한 한 변화를 거의 주지 않으면서
So normal science is a ③ conservative activity / — its practitioners are not trying / to make any earth-shattering discoveries, / but rather just to develop and extend the existing paradigm.
그래서 정상 과학은 보수적인 활동으로, / 그것을 실행하는 사람은 노력하고 있지 않고, / 세상이 깜짝 놀랄 어떤 발견이라도 하고자 / 오히려 단지 현존하는 패러다임을 발전시키고 확장하려는 것이다.
In Kuhn's words, / 'normal science does not aim at novelties of fact or theory, / and when successful finds none'.
Kuhn의 말로 하자면, / '정상 과학은 사실이나 이론의 참신함을 목표로 하지 않으며, / 성공적일 때에는 아무것도 못 찾아낸다.'
Above all, / Kuhn stressed / that normal scientists are not trying to *test* the paradigm.
무엇보다도, / Kuhn은 강조했다. / 정상 과학자들이 패러다임을 *시험하려* 노력하지 않는다는 것을
On the contrary, / they accept the paradigm ④ unquestioningly, / and conduct their research within the limits it sets.
오히려 / 그들은 패러다임을 의심하지 않고 받아들이고, / 그것이 설정한 한계 안에서 자신의 연구를 수행한다.
If a normal scientist gets an experimental result / which ✓conflicts with the paradigm, / they will usually assume / that their experimental technique is faulty, / not that the paradigm is wrong.
만약 정상 과학자가 실험 결과를 얻는다면, / 패러다임과 상충하는 / 그들은 보통 여긴다. / 자신의 실험 기술에 결함이 있고, / 패러다임이 틀린 것은 아니라고

정상 과학은 정확히 무엇을 포함하는가? Thomas Kuhn에 따르면, 그것은 주로 *문제 해결*의 문제이다. 패러다임이 아무리 성공적이더라도, 그것은 항상 특정한 문제, 즉 그것이 쉽게 수용할 수 없는 현상이나, 이론의 예측과 실험적 사실 간의 불일치를 ① 마주할 것이다. 정상 과학자들의 일은 패러다임에 가능한 한 변화를 거의 주지 않으면서, 이러한 사소한 문제를 ② 제거하려고 노력하는 것이다. 그래서 정상 과학은 ③ 보수적인 활동으로, 그것을 실행하는 사람은 세상이 깜짝 놀랄 어떤 발견이라도 하고자 노력하고 있지 않고, 오히려 단지 현존하는 패러다임을 발전시키고 확장하려는 것이다. Kuhn의 말로 하자면, '정상 과학은 사실이나

이론의 참신함을 목표로 하지 않으며, 성공적일 때에는 아무것도 못 찾아낸다.' 무엇보다도, Kuhn은 정상 과학자들이 패러다임을 *시험하려* 노력하지 않는다는 것을 강조했다. 오히려 그들은 패러다임을 ④ 의심하지 않고 받아들이고, 그것이 설정한 한계 안에서 자신의 연구를 수행한다. 만약 정상 과학자가 패러다임과 ⑤ 상응하는(→ 상충하는) 실험 결과를 얻는다면, 그들은 보통 자신의 실험 기술에 결함이 있고, 패러다임이 틀린 것은 아니라고 여긴다.

Why? 왜 정답일까?
④가 포함된 문장에서 정상 과학자들은 패러다임을 시험하려 하기보다는 의심 없이 받아들인다고 하므로, 흐름상 마지막 문장은 심지어 패러다임과 '맞지 않는' 실험 결과가 나오더라도 과학자들이 패러다임에 의문을 갖기보다는 실험 기술에 문제가 있다고 본다는 의미여야 한다. 즉 ⑤의 corresponds를 conflicts로 고쳐야 문맥이 자연스럽다. 따라서 문맥상 낱말의 쓰임이 가장 어색한 것은 ⑤이다.

- **primarily** ⓐⓓ 주로
- **phenomenon** ⓝ 현상
- **mismatch** ⓝ 부조화
- **eliminate** ⓥ 제거하다
- **earth-shattering** ⓐ 세상이 깜짝 놀랄
- **novelty** ⓝ 참신함, 새로움
- **correspond with** ~와 부합하다, 일치하다
- **encounter** ⓥ 마주하다
- **accommodate** ⓥ 수용하다
- **experimental** ⓐ 실험에 근거한
- **conservative** ⓐ 보수적인
- **extend** ⓥ 확장하다
- **unquestioningly** ⓐⓓ 의심 없이

구문 풀이
2행 However successful a paradigm is, it will always encounter certain
「however + 형/부 + 주어 + 동사」: 아무리 ~하더라도
problems — phenomena [which it cannot easily accommodate], or mismatches
선행사 ／ 목적격 관·대
(between the theory's predictions and the experimental facts.)
( ): 전치사구(수식)

★★ 문제 해결 꿀~팁 ★★
▶ 많이 틀린 이유는?
정상 과학자들은 기존의 패러다임을 수용하고 이를 유지보수하는 선에서 연구를 진행한다는 내용의 글이므로, 이들이 패러다임을 '의심 없이' 받아들인다는 의미의 ④는 문맥상 적합하다.
▶ 문제 해결 방법은?
정답인 ⑤의 주변 문장을 보면, 정상 과학자들이 패러다임을 의심하는 대신 자기 실험이 잘못됐다고 느끼는 상황을 언급하고 있다. 이는 패러다임과 실험 결과가 '맞지 않아서' 사고 체계에 의문을 제기해 볼 법한데도 그렇게 하지 않는 경우를 설명하는 것이므로, ⑤의 corresponds가 부적절함을 알 수 있다.

★★★ 등급을 가르는 문제!
31 충성심의 시험대가 되는 어려운 시기 정답률 36% | 정답 ②
다음 빈칸에 들어갈 말로 가장 적절한 것을 고르시오.
① leadership – 지도력
✓ loyalty – 충성심
③ creativity – 창의력
④ intelligence – 지성
⑤ independence – 독립성

Around the boss, / you will always find people / coming across as friends, good subordinates, or even great sympathizers.
우두머리 주변에서, / 여러분은 항상 사람들을 발견할 수 있다. / 친구나 좋은 부하, 심지어는 대단한 동조자라는 인상을 주는
But some do not truly belong.
그러나 일부는 진정으로 속해 있는 것은 아니다.
One day, / an incident will blow their cover, / and then you will know where they truly belong.
언젠가는, / 어떤 사건이 그들의 껍데기를 날려 버릴 것이고, / 여러분은 그들이 진정으로 속한 곳을 알게 될 것이다.
When it is all cosy and safe, / they will be there, / loitering the corridors and fawning at the slightest opportunity.
모든 것이 편안하고 안전할 때, / 그들은 그곳에 있을 것이다. / 복도를 서성거리고 아주 작은 기회에도 알랑거리면서
But as soon as difficulties arrive, / they are the first to be found missing.
하지만 어려움이 닥치자마자, / 그들은 가장 먼저 보이지 않을 것이다.
And difficult times are the true test of loyalty.
그래서 어려운 시기는 충성심의 진정한 시험대이다.
Dr. Martin Luther King said, / "The ultimate test of a man / is not where he stands in moments of comfort and convenience, / but where he stands at times of challenge and controversy."
Dr. Martin Luther King은 말했다. / "어떤 사람을 판단하는 궁극적인 시험대는 / 그 사람이 편안함과 안락함의 순간에 있는 곳이 아니라, / 도전과 논쟁의 시기에 있는 곳이다."라고
And so be careful of friends / who are always eager to take from you / but reluctant to give back even in their little ways.
그러므로 친구를 조심하라. / 항상 여러분에게서 뭔가 얻어가려고 열망하면서 / 사소하게라도 돌려주기를 꺼리는
If they lack the commitment / to sail with you through difficult weather, / then they are more likely to abandon your ship / when it stops.
만약 그들에게 헌신이 부족하다면, / 여러분과 함께 악천후를 뚫고 항해하려는 / 그렇다면 그들은 여러분의 배를 버릴 가능성이 더 크다. / 그것이 멈출 때

우두머리 주변에서, 여러분은 항상 친구나 좋은 부하, 심지어는 대단한 동조자라는 인상을 주는 사람들을 발견할 수 있다. 그러나 일부는 진정으로 속해 있는 것은 아니다. 언젠가는, 어떤 사건이 그들의 껍데기를 날려 버릴 것이고, 여러분은 그들이 진정으로 속한 곳을 알게 될 것이다. 모든 것이 편안하고 안전할 때, 그들은 복도를 서성거리고 아주 작은 기회에도 알랑거리면서 그곳에 있을 것이다. 하지만 어려움이 닥치자마자, 그들은 가장 먼저 보이지 않을 것이다. 그래서 어려운 시기는 충성심의 진정한 시험대이다. Dr. Martin Luther King은 "어떤 사람을 판단하는 궁극적인 시험대는 그 사람이 편안함과 안락함의 순간에 있는 곳이 아니라, 도전과 논쟁의 시기에 있는 곳이다."라고 말했다. 그러므로 항상 여러분에게서 뭔가 얻어가려고 열망하면서 사소하게라도 돌려주기를 꺼리는 친구를 조심하라. 만약 그들에게 여러분과 함께 악천후를 뚫고 항해하려는 헌신이 부족하다면, 여러분의 배가 멈출 때 그것을 버릴 가능성이 더 크다.

Why? 왜 정답일까?

마지막 문장에서 어려운 시기를 악천후에 빗대어, '헌신(commitment)'이 부족한 친구라면 이러한 악천후의 시기에 우리 곁을 떠나고 말 것이라는 내용을 제시하고 있다. 따라서 빈칸에 들어갈 말로 가장 적절한 것은 '헌신'과 같은 의미인 ② '충성심'이다.

● subordinate ⓝ 부하
● incident ⓝ 사건, 일
● corridor ⓝ 복도
● controversy ⓝ 논란
● reluctant ⓐ (~하기를) 꺼리는, 마지못해 하는
● abandon ⓥ 버리다
● sympathizer ⓝ 동조자
● blow ⓥ 날리다, 불다
● ultimate ⓐ 궁극적인
● be eager to ~하려고 열망하는
● commitment ⓝ 헌신

구문 풀이

6행 But as soon as difficulties arrive, they are the first to be found missing.
접속사(~하자마자)　　　　「be found + 형용사: ~한 것으로 발견되다」

★★ 문제 해결 꿀~팁 ★★

▶ 많이 틀린 이유는?
첫 문장에 the boss가 언급되므로 얼핏 보면 '리더십'에 관한 글처럼 보여 ①을 고르기 쉽다. 하지만 글에서 팀이나 무리를 이끄는 상황, 리더의 자질 등에 관해서는 전혀 언급되지 않는다.

▶ 문제 해결 방법은?
시기가 좋을 때와 어려울 때를 나눠, 좋을 때 곁에 있고 어려울 때 떠나는 사람을 경계해야 한다고 언급하는 글이다. 즉 '어려운' 시기는 곁에 있는 이들의 '진실성, 충실함'을 시험할 계기 역할을 한다는 것이다.

---

32 기억을 개선하고 보존할 방법　　　　정답률 54% | 정답 ④

다음 빈칸에 들어갈 말로 가장 적절한 것을 고르시오.
① keep your body and mind healthy – 몸과 마음을 건강하게 유지해야
② calm your mind in stressful times – 스트레스를 받을 때 마음을 가라앉혀야
③ concentrate on one thing at a time – 한 번에 한 가지 일에 집중해야
✔ work on all functions of your brain – 뇌의 모든 기능을 작동시켜야
⑤ share what you learn with other people – 배우는 것을 다른 사람과 공유해야

When you're driving a car, / your memory of how to operate the vehicle / comes from one set of brain cells; / the memory of how to navigate the streets / to get to your destination / springs from another set of neurons; / the memory of driving rules and following street signs / originates from another family of brain cells; / and the thoughts and feelings / you have about the driving experience itself, / including any close calls with other cars, / come from yet another group of cells.
여러분이 자동차를 운전할 때, / 차량을 조작하는 방법에 관한 기억은 / 일련의 뇌세포에서 나오고, / 도로를 주행하는 방법에 관한 기억은 / 목적지에 도착하기 위해 / 또 다른 일련의 신경 세포로부터 발생하며, / 운전 규칙에 관한 기억과 도로 표지를 따르는 것에 관한 기억은 / 또 다른 뇌세포 집단으로부터 생기고, / 생각과 느낌은 / 운전 경험 자체에 대해 여러분이 가지고 있는 / 다른 자동차와의 위기일발을 포함하여 / 또 다른 세포 집단에서 나온다.
You do not have conscious awareness / of all these separate mental plays and cognitive neural firings, / yet they somehow work together in beautiful harmony / to synthesize your overall experience.
여러분은 의식적인 인지를 하고 있지는 않지만, / 이 모든 별개의 정신적 활동과 인지적 신경 활성화에 관한 / 그것들은 아름다운 조화를 이루며 어떻게든 함께 작동한다. / 여러분의 전반적인 경험을 종합하기 위해
In fact, / we don't even know the real difference / between how we remember and how we think.
사실, / 우리는 진정한 차이를 알지도 못한다. / 우리가 기억하는 방식과 우리가 생각하는 방식 사이의
But, / we do know they are strongly intertwined.
하지만, / 우리는 그것들이 강력하게 뒤얽혀 있다는 것을 정말로 안다.
That is why / truly improving memory / can never simply be about using memory tricks, / although they can be helpful / in strengthening certain components of memory.
그것이 ~한 이유이다. / 진정으로 기억력을 향상시키는 것은 / 결코 단지 기억력 기술을 사용하는 것에 관한 것일 수 없는 / 그것들이 도움이 될 수 있다 하더라도, / 기억력의 특정 구성 요소를 강화하는 데
Here's the bottom line:
여기 요점이 있다.
To improve and preserve memory at the cognitive level, / you have to work on all functions of your brain.
인지적 수준에서 기억력을 개선하고 보존하기 위해서는 / 여러분은 뇌의 모든 기능을 작동시켜야 한다.

자동차를 운전할 때, 차량을 조작하는 방법에 관한 기억은 일련의 뇌세포에서 나오고, 목적지에 도착하기 위해 도로를 주행하는 방법에 관한 기억은 또 다른 일련의 신경 세포로부터 발생하며, 운전 규칙에 관한 기억과 도로 표지를 따르는 것에 관한 기억은 또 다른 뇌세포 집단으로부터 생기고, 다른 자동차와의 위기일발을 포함하여 운전 경험 자체에 대해 여러분이 가지고 있는 생각과 느낌은 또 다른 세포 집단에서 나온다. 여러분은 이 모든 별개의 정신적 활동과 인지적 신경 활성화에 관한 의식적으로 인지하고 있지는 않지만, 그것들은 여러분의 전반적인 경험을 종합하기 위해 아름다운 조화를 이루며 어떻게든 함께 작동한다. 사실, 우리가 기억하는 방식과 우리가 생각하는 방식 사이의 진정한 차이를 우리는 알지도 못한다. 하지만, 우리는 그것들이 강력하게 뒤얽혀 있다는 것을 정말로 안다. 그런 이유로 기억력 기술이 기억력의 특정 구성 요소를 강화하는 데 도움이 될 수 있다 하더라도, 진정으로 기억력을 향상시키는 것은 결코 단지 기억력 기술의 사용에 관한 것일 수 없다. 요컨대, 인지적 수준에서 기억력을 개선하고 보존하기 위해서는 뇌의 모든 기능을 작동시켜야 한다.

Why? 왜 정답일까?

정신적 활동은 서로 밀접하게 연결된(strongly intertwined) 여러 기능이 함께 작동하여(work together) 이루어진다는 설명으로 보아, 기억력을 높이기 위해서는 단지 기억에 관련된 요소만을 사용하기 보다 뇌를 전방위적으로 사용할 필요가 있다는 결론을 내릴 수 있다. 따라서 빈칸에 들어갈 말로 가장 적절한 것은 ④ '뇌의 모든 기능을 작동시켜야'이다.

● spring from ~로부터 일어나다, 비롯되다
● conscious ⓐ 의식적인
● synthesize ⓥ 종합하다, 합성하다
● originate from ~에서 기원하다
● awareness ⓝ 인식, 앎
● strengthen ⓥ 강화하다

구문 풀이

1행 When you're driving a car, your memory of {how to operate the vehicle}
　　　　주어1　　　　　　 { }: 명사구(how + to부정사: ~하는 방법)
comes from one set of brain cells; the memory of {how to navigate the streets to
동사1　　　　　　　　　주어2
get to your destination} springs from another set of neurons; the memory of
　　　　동사2　　　　　　　　　　　　　주어3
driving rules and following street signs originates from another family of brain
동사3
cells; and the thoughts and feelings [(that) you have about the driving experience
주어4(복수)　　　　 생략(목적격 관계대명사)
itself], (including any close calls with other cars), come from yet another group of
삽입구　　　　　　　　　　　　　　　　동사4
cells.

---

33 과학이 모든 것을 설명하지 못하는 이유　　　　정답률 45% | 정답 ③

다음 빈칸에 들어갈 말로 가장 적절한 것을 고르시오. [3점]
① govern human's relationship with nature – 인간이 자연과 맺는 관계를 지배한다
② are based on objective observations – 객관적인 관찰에 기초한다
✔ will themselves remain unexplained – 그 자체로 설명되지 않은 채 남을 것이다
④ will be compared with other theories – 다른 이론들과 비교될 것이다
⑤ are difficult to use to explain phenomena – 현상을 설명하기 위해 사용하기 어렵다

According to many philosophers, / there is a purely logical reason / why science will never be able to explain everything.
많은 철학자에 따르면, / 순전히 논리적인 이유가 있다. / 과학이 결코 모든 것을 설명하지는 못할 것이라는
For in order to explain something, / whatever it is, / we need to invoke something else.
왜냐하면 무언가를 설명하기 위해서는, / 그것이 무엇이든 / 우리는 다른 어떤 것을 언급해야 한다.
But what explains the second thing?
하지만 두 번째 것은 무엇으로 설명하는가?
To illustrate, / recall that Newton explained a diverse range of phenomena / using his law of gravity.
예를 들어, / 뉴턴이 매우 다양한 범위의 현상을 설명했음을 떠올려 보라. / 자신의 중력 법칙을 사용하여
But what explains the law of gravity itself?
하지만 중력 법칙 자체는 무엇이 설명하는가?
If someone asks / why all bodies exert a gravitational attraction on each other, / what should we tell them?
만약 누군가가 묻는다면, / 왜 모든 물체가 서로에게 중력을 행사하는지 / 우리는 그들에게 뭐라고 말해야 하는가?
Newton had no answer to this question.
뉴턴은 이 질문에 답이 없었다.
In Newtonian science / the law of gravity was a fundamental principle: / it explained other things, / but could not itself be explained.
뉴턴의 과학에서 / 중력 법칙은 기본 원리였다. / 그것은 다른 것들을 설명했지만, / 그 자체는 설명될 수 없었다.
The moral generalizes.
이 교훈이 일반화된다.
However much the science of the future can explain, / the explanations it gives / will have to make use of certain fundamental laws and principles.
미래의 과학이 아무리 많이 설명할 수 있다 하더라도, / 그것이 제공하는 설명은 / 어떤 기본 법칙과 원리를 이용해야만 할 것이다.
Since nothing can explain itself, / it follows that / at least some of these laws and principles / will themselves remain unexplained.
어떤 것도 스스로를 설명할 수 없기 때문에, / 결론적으로 ~이다. / 적어도 이러한 법칙과 원리 중 일부는 / 그 자체로 설명되지 않은 채 남을 것

많은 철학자에 따르면, 과학이 결코 모든 것을 설명하지는 못할 것이라는 순전히 논리적인 이유가 있다. 왜냐하면 무언가를 설명하기 위해서는, 우리는 무엇이든 다른 어떤 것을 언급해야 한다. 하지만 두 번째 것은 무엇으로 설명하는가? 예를 들어, 뉴턴이 자신의 중력 법칙을 사용하여 매우 다양한 범위의 현상을 설명했음을 떠올려 보라. 하지만 중력 법칙 자체는 무엇이 설명하는가? 만약 누군가가 왜 모든 물체가 서로에게 중력을 행사하는지 묻는다면, 우리는 그들에게 뭐라고 말해야 하는가? 뉴턴은 이 질문에 답이 없었다. 뉴턴의 과학에서 중력 법칙은 기본 원리였다. 즉, 그것이 다른 것들을 설명했지만, 그 자체는 설명될 수 없었다. 이 교훈이 일반화된다. 미래의 과학이 아무리 많이 설명할 수 있다 하더라도, 그것이 제공하는 설명은 어떤 기본 법칙과 원리를 이용해야만 할 것이다. 어떤 것도 스스로를 설명할 수 없기 때문에, 결론적으로 적어도 이러한 법칙과 원리 중 일부는 그 자체로 설명되지 않은 채 남을 것이다.

Why? 왜 정답일까?

첫 두 문장에 따르면 과학은 모든 것을 설명하지 못하는데, 왜냐하면 한 가지를 설명하기 위해 무엇이든 다른 개념을 동원해야만 하기 때문이다. 이어서 마지막 문장에서 어떤 것도 자기 자신을 설명할 수는 없다(nothing can explain itself)고 언급하는 것으로 보아, 끝내 설명되지 않고 남는 대상이 존재하기 마련이라는 결론을 내릴 수 있다. 따라서 빈칸에 들어갈 말로 가장 적절한 것은 ③ '그 자체로 설명되지 않은 채 남을 것이다'이다.

● philosopher ⓝ 철학자
● gravity ⓝ 중력
● fundamental ⓐ 기본적인, 근본적인
● make use of ~을 이용하다, 활용하다
● objective ⓐ 객관적인
● illustrate ⓥ (예를 들어) 보여주다
● attraction ⓝ 끌어당김
● generalize ⓥ 일반화하다
● govern ⓥ 지배하다

구문 풀이

3행 For in order to explain something, whatever it is, we need to invoke
　　~ 때문이다(앞과 연결) 부사적 용법(~하기 위해)　 복합관계대명사(어떤 것이 ~하든 간에)
something else.

---

34 사회적 상황에서의 웃음의 역할　　　　정답률 49% | 정답 ②

다음 빈칸에 들어갈 말로 가장 적절한 것을 고르시오. [3점]
① have similar tastes in comedy and humor – 희극과 유머에 대한 비슷한 취향을 갖고 있기

✔ are using laughter to connect with others – 다른 사람과 가까워지기 위해 웃음을 이용하고 있기
③ are reluctant to reveal our innermost feelings – 우리의 가장 내밀한 감정을 드러내기를 꺼리기
④ focus on the content rather than the situation – 상황보다 내용에 집중하기
⑤ feel more comfortable around others than alone – 혼자보다 다른 사람 곁에 있을 때 더 편안함을 느끼기

In one example of the important role of laughter in social contexts, / Devereux and Ginsburg examined frequency of laughter / in matched pairs of strangers or friends / who watched a humorous video together / compared to those who watched it alone.
사회적 상황에서 웃음의 중요한 역할의 한 예로, / Devereux와 Ginsburg는 웃음의 빈도를 조사했다. / 모르는 사람이나 친구끼리 짝지어진 쌍에서 / 익살스러운 동영상을 함께 본, / 그것을 혼자 본 사람들과 비교하여

The time individuals spent laughing / was nearly twice as frequent in pairs / as when alone.
사람들이 웃은 시간은 / 짝을 이루어 있을 때의 거의 두 배로 잦았다. / 혼자 있을 때보다

Frequency of laughing / was only slightly shorter for friends than strangers.
웃음의 빈도는 / 모르는 사람들보다 친구들의 경우가 약간 더 적었을 뿐이다.

According to Devereux and Ginsburg, / laughing with strangers served to create a social bond / that made each person in the pair feel comfortable.
Devereux와 Ginsburg에 따르면, / 모르는 사람과 함께 웃는 것은 사회적 유대를 형성하는 데 이바지했다. / 쌍을 이루는 각각의 사람을 편안하게 만드는

This explanation is supported by the fact / that in their stranger condition, / when one person laughed, / the other was likely to laugh as well.
이 설명은 사실에 의해 뒷받침된다. / 모르는 사람과 함께 있는 조건에서 / 한 사람이 웃을 때 / 상대방도 웃을 가능성이 있었다는

Interestingly, / the three social conditions / (alone, paired with a stranger, or paired with a friend) / did not differ in their ratings of funniness of the video / or of feelings of happiness or anxiousness.
흥미롭게도, / 세 가지 사회적 조건은 / (혼자인 경우, 모르는 사람과 쌍을 이룬 경우, 친구와 쌍을 이룬 경우) / 동영상의 재미에 대한 그들의 평가에서는 다르지 않았다. / 또는 행복감이나 불안감에 대한

This finding implies / that their frequency of laughter / was not because we find things funnier / when we are with others / but instead we are using laughter to connect with others.
이 발견은 의미한다. / 그들의 웃음의 빈도는 / 우리가 어떤 것이 더 재미있다고 생각하기 때문이 아니라 / 우리가 다른 사람들과 함께 있을 때 / 오히려 우리가 다른 사람과 가까워지기 위해 웃음을 이용하고 있기 때문이었음을

사회적 상황에서 웃음의 중요한 역할의 한 예로, Devereux와 Ginsburg는 익살스러운 동영상을 혼자 본 사람들과 비교하여 그것을 함께 본 모르는 사람끼리 짝지어진 쌍에서 웃음의 빈도를 조사했다. 사람들이 웃은 시간은, 혼자 있을 때보다 짝을 이루어 있을 때 거의 두 배 더 잦았다. 웃음의 빈도는 모르는 사람들보다 친구들의 경우가 약간 더 적었을 뿐이다. Devereux와 Ginsburg에 따르면, 모르는 사람과 함께 웃는 것은 쌍을 이루는 각각의 사람을 편안하게 만드는 사회적 유대를 형성하는 데 이바지했다. 이 설명은 모르는 사람과 함께 있는 조건에서 한 사람이 웃을 때 상대방도 웃을 가능성이 있었다는 사실에 의해 뒷받침된다. 흥미롭게도, 세 가지 사회적 조건(혼자인 경우, 모르는 사람과 쌍을 이룬 경우, 친구와 쌍을 이룬 경우)은 동영상의 재미나 행복감 또는 불안감에 대한 그들의 평가에서는 다르지 않았다. 이 발견이 의미하기로, 그들의 웃음 빈도는 우리가 다른 사람들과 함께 있을 때 어떤 것이 더 재미있다고 생각하기 때문이 아니라 오히려 우리가 다른 사람과 가까워지기 위해 웃음을 이용하고 있기 때문이었다.

Why? 왜 정답일까?
글 중반부에서 모르는 사람끼리 함께 웃는 것이 사회적 유대를 형성한다(~ laughing with strangers served to create a social bond that made each person in the pair feel comfortable.)는 내용이 나오는 것으로 보아, 빈칸에 들어갈 말로 가장 적절한 것은 ② '다른 사람과 가까워지기 위해 웃음을 이용하고 있기'이다.

- frequency ⓝ 빈도
- bond ⓝ 유대감
- anxiousness ⓝ 불안감
- reveal ⓥ 드러내다
- slightly ㉮ⓓ 약간
- rating ⓝ 평가
- connect with ~와 관계를 맺다, 연결하다
- content ⓝ 내용

구문 풀이

4행 The time [(that) individuals spent laughing] was nearly twice as frequent in pairs as when (they are) alone.
주어 / 목적격 관·대 / 동사 / 「배수사 + as + 원급 + as : ~배만큼 …한」 / 부사절 축약(대명사+be 생략)

---

35 디지털 기기의 작동 원리에 대한 이해 정답률 55% | 정답 ④

다음 글에서 전체 흐름과 관계 없는 문장은?

Today's "digital natives" have grown up / immersed in digital technologies / and possess the technical aptitude / to utilize the powers of their devices fully.
오늘날의 '디지털 원주민'들은 성장했고, / 디지털 기술에 몰입한 채로 / 기술적 소질을 가지고 있다. / 자기가 가진 기기의 힘을 충분히 활용할 수 있는

① But although they know / which apps to use or which websites to visit, / they do not necessarily understand the workings / behind the touch screen.
하지만 그들이 알고 있을지라도, / 어떤 앱을 사용해야 하는지 혹은 어떤 웹 사이트를 방문해야 하는지 / 그들이 작동 방식을 반드시 이해하는 것은 아니다. / 터치스크린 뒤의

② People need technological literacy / if they are to understand machines' mechanics and uses.
사람들은 기술 활용 능력이 필요하다. / 그들이 기계의 역학과 용도를 이해하려면

③ In much the same way / as factory workers a hundred years ago / needed to understand the basic structures of engines, / we need to understand the elemental principles behind our devices.
~와 마찬가지로, / 100년 전 공장 근로자들이 / 엔진의 기본 구조를 이해할 필요가 있었던 것과 / 우리는 우리의 기기 뒤에 숨겨진 기본 원리를 이해할 필요가 있다.

✔ The lifespan of devices / depends on the quality of software operating them / as well as the structure of hardware.
기기의 수명은 / 기기를 작동하는 소프트웨어의 우수성에 달려 있다. / 하드웨어의 구조뿐만 아니라

⑤ This empowers us / to deploy software and hardware to their fullest utility, / maximizing our powers to achieve and create.
이것은 우리에게 권한을 주고 / 소프트웨어와 하드웨어를 최대한 유용하게 사용할 수 있도록 / 성취하고 만들어 낼 수 있는 우리의 능력을 극대화한다.

오늘날의 '디지털 원주민'들은 디지털 기술에 몰입한 채로 성장했고, 자기가 가진 기기의 힘을 충분히 활용할 수 있는 기술적 소질을 가지고 있다. ① 하지만 그들이 어떤 앱을 사용해야 하는지 혹은 어떤 웹 사이트를 방문해야 하는지 알고 있을지라도, 터치스크린 뒤에 숨겨진 작동 방식을 반드시 이해한다는 것은 아니다. ② 사람들이 기계의 역학과 용도를 이해하려면 기술 활용 능력이 필요하다. ③ 100년 전 공장 근로자들이 엔진의 기본 구조를 이해할 필요가 있었던 것과 마찬가지로, 우리는 우리의 기기 뒤에 숨겨진 기본 원리를 이해할 필요가 있다. ④ 기기의 수명은 하드웨어의 구조뿐만 아니라 기기를 작동하는 소프트웨어의 우수성에 달려 있다. ⑤ 이것은 우리가 소프트웨어와 하드웨어를 최대한 유용하게 사용하여, 성취하고 만들어 낼 수 있는 우리의 능력을 극대화한다.

Why? 왜 정답일까?
디지털 기기의 작동 원리를 이해할 필요가 있다는 내용의 글로, ④의 경우 디지털 기기의 수명을 결정짓는 요소에 관해 이야기하므로 흐름상 무관하다. 따라서 전체 흐름과 관계 없는 문장은 ④이다.

- immersed in ~에 몰입한
- utilize ⓥ 이용하다, 활용하다
- elemental ⓐ 기본적인
- operate ⓥ 작동하다, 조작하다
- maximize ⓥ 극대화하다
- aptitude ⓝ 소질, 적성
- literacy ⓝ (글을) 읽고 쓰는 능력, 문해력
- lifespan ⓝ 수명
- empower ⓥ 권한을 주다

구문 풀이

5행 People need technological literacy if they are to understand machines' mechanics and uses.
be to 용법(의도 : ~하려면)

---

36 logos와 mythos의 관계 정답률 55% | 정답 ②

주어진 글 다음에 이어질 글의 순서로 가장 적절한 것을 고르시오.
① (A) – (C) – (B) ✔ (B) – (A) – (C)
③ (B) – (C) – (A) ④ (C) – (A) – (B)
⑤ (C) – (B) – (A)

The ancient Greeks / used to describe two very different ways of thinking / — *logos* and *mythos*.
고대 그리스인들은 / 두 가지의 매우 다른 사고방식을 설명하곤 했다. / *logos*와 *mythos*라는

Logos roughly referred to / the world of the logical, the empirical, the scientific.
*logos*는 대략 ~을 지칭했다. / 논리적, 경험적, 과학적 세계

(B) *Mythos* referred to / the world of dreams, storytelling and symbols.
*mythos*는 ~을 지칭했다. / 꿈, 스토리텔링, 상징의 세계

Like many rationalists today, / some philosophers of Greece prized *logos* / and looked down at *mythos*.
오늘날의 많은 합리주의자처럼, / 그리스의 일부 철학자들은 *logos*를 높이 평가하고 / *mythos*를 경시했다.

Logic and reason, / they concluded, / make us modern; / storytelling and mythmaking are primitive.
논리와 이성은 / 그들은 결론지었다. / 우리를 현대적으로 만들고, / 스토리텔링과 신화 만들기는 원시적이라고

(A) But lots of scholars then and now / — including many anthropologists, sociologists and philosophers today — / see a more complicated picture, / where *mythos* and *logos* are intertwined and interdependent.
그러나 그때나 지금이나 많은 학자는 / 오늘날의 많은 인류학자, 사회학자, 철학자를 포함하여, / 더 복잡한 상황을 이해하는데, / *mythos*와 *logos*는 뒤얽혀 있고 상호 의존적이라는 것이다.

Science itself, / according to this view, / relies on stories.
과학 자체는 / 이 관점에 따르면 / 이야기에 의존한다.

(C) The frames and metaphors / we use to understand the world / shape the scientific discoveries we make; / they even shape what we see.
생각의 틀과 은유는 / 우리가 세상을 이해하기 위해 사용하는 / 우리가 하는 과학적 발견을 형성하고, / 그것은 심지어 우리가 보는 것을 형성한다.

When our frames and metaphors change, / the world itself is transformed.
우리의 생각의 틀과 은유가 바뀌면 / 세상 자체가 변한다.

The Copernican Revolution / involved more than just scientific calculation; / it involved a new story / about the place of Earth in the universe.
코페르니쿠스 혁명은 / 단순한 과학적 계산보다 더 많은 것을 포함하는데, / 그것은 새로운 이야기를 포함했다. / 우주 속 지구의 위치에 관한

고대 그리스인들은 *logos*와 *mythos*라는 두 가지의 매우 다른 사고방식을 설명하곤 했다. *logos*는 대략 논리적, 경험적, 과학적 세계를 지칭했다.

(B) *mythos*는 꿈, 스토리텔링, 상징의 세계를 지칭했다. 오늘날의 많은 합리주의자처럼, 그리스의 일부 철학자들은 *logos*를 높이 평가하고 *mythos*를 경시했다. 그들은 논리와 이성이 우리를 현대적으로 만들고, 스토리텔링과 신화 만들기를 원시적이라고 결론지었다.

(A) 그러나 오늘날의 많은 인류학자, 사회학자, 철학자를 포함하여, 그때나 지금이나 많은 학자는 더 복잡하게 상황을 이해하는데, *mythos*와 *logos*는 뒤얽혀 있고 상호 의존적이라는 것이다. 이 관점에 따르면 과학 자체가 이야기에 의존한다.

(C) 우리가 세상을 이해하기 위해 사용하는 생각의 틀과 은유는 우리의 과학적 발견을 형성하고, 심지어 우리가 보는 것을 형성한다. 우리 생각의 틀과 은유가 바뀌면 세상 자체가 변한다. 코페르니쿠스 혁명은 단순한 과학적 계산보다 더 많은 것을 포함하는데, 우주 속 지구의 위치에 관한 새로운 이야기를 포함했다.

Why? 왜 정답일까?
주어진 글은 고대 그리스의 logos와 mythos 개념을 언급한 후, 먼저 logos가 무엇을 지칭하는지 설명한다. (B)는 이어서 mythos가 지칭하는 바를 설명한 뒤, 그리스의 철학자들 사이에서는 logos가 중시되고 mythos가 격하되었음을 언급한다. 한편 (A)는 But으로 흐름을 반전시키며, 오늘날 두 개념은 상호 의존적인 관계로 이해됨을 서술한다. 마지막으로 (C)에서는 (A)의 마지막 문장에서 언급된, '과학 자체가 이야기에 의존한다'는 내용을 보충 설명한다. 따라서 글의 순서로 가장 적절한 것은 ② '(B) – (A) – (C)'이다.

- anthropologist ⓝ 인류학자
- intertwined ⓐ 뒤얽힌
- rely on ~에 의존하다
- complicated ⓐ 복잡한
- interdependent ⓐ 상호 의존적인
- rationalist ⓝ 합리주의자

- **look down at** ~을 경시하다
- **metaphor** ⓝ 은유
- **primitive** ⓐ 원시적인
- **calculation** ⓝ 계산

구문 풀이

> **4행** But lots of scholars then and now — (including many anthropologists,
> 삽입구
> sociologists and philosophers today) — see a more complicated picture, where
> 선행사(공간) 계속적 용법
> *mythos* and *logos* are intertwined and inter-dependent.

★★★ 등급을 가르는 문제!

37 발췌본의 유용함과 한계 정답률 29% | 정답 ③

주어진 글 다음에 이어질 글의 순서로 가장 적절한 것을 고르시오.

① (A) - (C) - (B) ② (B) - (A) - (C)
☑ (B) - (C) - (A) ④ (C) - (A) - (B)
⑤ (C) - (B) - (A)

There is no doubt / that the length of some literary works is overwhelming.
의심의 여지가 없다. / 일부 문학 작품의 길이가 압도적이라는 데에는

Reading or translating a work in class, / hour after hour, week after week, / can be such a
boring experience / that many students never want to open a foreign language book again.
수업 시간에 작품을 읽거나 번역하는 것은 / 몇 시간, 몇 주 동안 / 너무나 지루한 경험일 수 있어서 / 많은 학생이 다시는 외국어
서적을 펴고 싶어 하지 않는다.

(B) Extracts provide one type of solution.
발췌본은 한 가지 해결책을 제공한다.

The advantages are obvious: / reading a series of passages from different works / produces
more variety in the classroom, / so that the teacher has a greater chance of avoiding
monotony, / while still giving learners a taste / of at least of an author's special flavour.
장점들은 분명하다. / 다양한 작품에서 가져온 일련의 단락을 읽는 것은 / 교실에서 더 많은 다양성을 만들어 내서 / 교사는 단조로움
을 피할 가능성이 더 크다. / 학습자에게 여전히 맛보기 하는 한편 / 최소한이라도 어떤 작가의 특별한 묘미를

(C) On the other hand, / a student / who is only exposed to 'bite-sized chunks' / will never
have the satisfaction / of knowing the overall pattern of a book, / which is after all the
satisfaction most of us seek / when we read something in our own language.
반면에, / 학생은 / '짧은 토막글'만 접한 / 만족감을 결코 가질 수 없을 것이며, / 책의 전반적인 구성을 안다는 / 결국 그 만족감은 우리
대부분이 찾고자 하는 것이다. / 우리가 모국어로 된 어떤 글을 읽을 때

(A) Moreover, / there are some literary features / that cannot be adequately illustrated by a
short excerpt: / the development of plot or character, / for instance, / with the gradual
involvement of the reader / that this implies; / or the unfolding of a complex theme /
through the juxtaposition of contrasting views.
게다가 / 문학적인 특징이 몇 가지 있다. / 짧은 발췌로는 충분히 설명될 수 없는 / 줄거리나 등장인물의 전개 / 예를 들면 / 독자의
점진적 몰입과 더불어 / 이것이 내포하는 / 또는 복잡한 주제의 전개 / 대조적인 관점의 병치를 통해

일부 문학 작품의 길이가 압도적이라는 데는 의심의 여지가 없다. 수업 시간에 작품을 몇 시간,
몇 주 동안 읽거나 번역하는 것은 너무나 지루한 경험일 수 있어서 많은 학생이 다시는 외국
어 서적을 절대 펴고 싶어 하지 않는다.
(B) 발췌본은 한 가지 해결책을 제공한다. 장점들은 분명하다. 즉, 다양한 작품에서 가져온
  일련의 단락을 읽는 것은 교실에서 더 많은 다양성을 만들어 내서, 교사는 단조로움을
  피할 가능성이 더 큰 한편으로, 여전히 최소한이라도 어떤 작가의 특별한 묘미를 학습자
  에게 맛보게 한다.
(C) 반면에, '짧은 토막글'만 접한 학생은 책의 전반적인 구성을 아는 만족감을 결코 가질 수
  없을 것이며, 결국 그 만족감은 모국어로 된 어떤 글을 읽을 때 우리 대부분이 찾고자 하는
  것이다.
(A) 게다가 짧은 발췌로는 충분히 설명될 수 없는 문학적인 특징이 몇 가지 있는데, 예를 들면
  줄거리나 등장인물의 전개와 더불어 이것이 내포하는 독자의 점진적 몰입, 또는 대조적
  인 관점의 병치를 통한 복잡한 주제 전개 등이 있다.

Why? 왜 정답일까?

긴 문학 작품을 다루는 경우를 언급하는 주어진 글 뒤로, 발췌본을 활용하는 것이 해결책이 될 수 있다는
내용의 **(B)**, On the other hand로 흐름을 반전시키며 발췌본에 한계가 있음을 설명하는 **(C)**,
Moreover와 함께 한계점을 추가로 열거하는 **(A)**가 차례로 연결된다. 따라서 글의 순서로 가장 적절한
것은 ③ '**(B) - (C) - (A)**'이다.

- **literary** ⓐ 문학의
- **translate** ⓥ 번역하다
- **adequately** ⓐ 충분히
- **unfolding** ⓝ 전개, 펼침
- **extract** ⓝ 발췌(본) ⓥ 발췌하다, 뽑아내다
- **flavour** ⓝ 묘미, 맛
- **overwhelming** ⓐ 압도적인
- **feature** ⓝ 특징
- **gradual** ⓐ 점진적인
- **contrasting** ⓐ 대조되는, 상충하는
- **monotony** ⓝ 단조로움
- **overall** ⓐ 전반적인

구문 풀이

> **2행** Reading or translating a work in class, hour after hour, week after week,
> 주어(동명사구)
> can be such a boring experience that many students never want to open a
> 동사 「such ~ that …: 너무 ~해서 …하다」
> foreign language book again.

★★ 문제 해결 꿀~팁 ★★

▶ 많이 틀린 이유는?
발췌본의 한계를 연이어 설명하는 **(C)-(A)**의 연결고리를 파악했다면, **(B)**의 순서를 잡는 것이 관건이다.
주어진 글에서 '발췌본'에 관한 언급이 아예 나오지 않는데, 바로 On the other hand로 시작하는
(C)가 연결되어 발췌본의 한계를 지적하면 글의 흐름이 어색하다. 따라서 **(C)** 앞에 **(B)**가 나와 '발췌본'
이라는 소재를 등장시켜야 흐름이 매끄러워진다.

▶ 문제 해결 방법은?
주어진 글이 아닌 **(B)**에서 중심 소재가 등장하므로, 일단 **(B)**가 전제되어야 나머지 단락을 연결할 수
있다는 점을 파악하도록 한다.

---

38 과학자들이 생각을 전달하는 수단의 변화 정답률 38% | 정답 ⑤

글의 흐름으로 보아, 주어진 문장이 들어가기에 가장 적절한 곳을 고르시오.

In the early stages of modern science, / scientists communicated their creative ideas /
largely by publishing books.
현대 과학의 초기 단계에서 / 과학자들은 자신의 창의적인 생각을 전달했다. / 주로 책을 출판하여

① This modus operandi is illustrated / not only by Newton's *Principia*, / but also by
Copernicus' *On the Revolutions of the Heavenly Spheres*, / Kepler's *The Harmonies of the
World*, / and Galileo's *Dialogues Concerning the Two New Sciences*.
이런 작업 방식은 설명된다. / 뉴턴의 *Principia*로뿐만 아니라 / 코페르니쿠스의 *On the Revolutions of the Heavenly
Spheres*와 / 케플러의 *The Harmonies of the World*, / 갈릴레오의 *Dialogues Concerning the Two New Sciences*로도

② With the advent of scientific periodicals, / such as the *Transactions of the Royal Society
of London*, / books gradually yielded ground / to the technical journal article / as the chief
form of scientific communication.
과학 정기 간행물의 출현과 함께, / *Transactions of the Royal Society of London* 같은 / 책은 점차 자리를 내주었다. / 전문
학술지 논문에 / 과학적 의사소통의 주요한 형식으로

③ Of course, / books were not abandoned altogether, / as Darwin's *Origin of Species* shows.
물론 / 책이 완전히 버려진 것은 아니었다. / 다윈의 *Origin of Species*가 보여주듯이

④ Even so, / it eventually became possible for scientists / to establish a reputation for their
creative contributions / without publishing a single book-length treatment of their ideas.
그랬다고 하더라도, / 결국 과학자들은 가능해졌다. / 자신이 창의적으로 기여한 바에 대한 명성을 세우는 것이 / 자기 생각을
다룬 책 한 권 길이의 출간물을 내지 않고도

☑ For instance, / the revolutionary ideas / that earned Einstein his Nobel Prize /
— concerning the special theory of relativity and the photoelectric effect — / appeared as
papers in the *Annalen der Physik*.
예를 들어, / 혁명적인 생각들은 / 아인슈타인에게 노벨상을 안겨 준, / 특수 상대성 이론과 광전 효과에 관한 / *Annalen der
Physik*에 논문으로 등장했다.

His status as one of the greatest scientists of all time / does not depend on the publication
of a single book.
역사상 가장 위대한 과학자 중 한 명이라는 그의 지위는 / 단 한 권의 책의 출간에 달려 있지는 않다.

현대 과학의 초기 단계에서 과학자들은 주로 책을 출판하여 자신의 창의적인 생각을 전달했
다. ① 이런 작업 방식은 뉴턴의 *Principia*뿐만 아니라 코페르니쿠스의 *On the Revolutions of
the Heavenly Spheres*와 케플러의 *The Harmonies of the World*, 갈릴레오의 *Dialogues
Concerning the Two New Sciences*로도 설명된다. ② *Transactions of the Royal Society of
London* 같은 과학 정기 간행물의 출현과 함께, 책은 과학적 의사소통의 주요한 형식으로 전
문 학술지 논문에 점차 자리를 내주었다. ③ 물론 다윈의 *Origin of Species*가 보여주듯이, 책
이 완전히 버려진 것은 아니었다. ④ 그랬다고 하더라도, 과학자들은 자기 생각을 다룬 책 한
권 길이의 출간물을 내지 않고도 자신이 창의적으로 기여한 바에 대한 명성을 세우는 것이
결국 가능해졌다. ⑤ 예를 들어, 아인슈타인에게 노벨상을 안겨 준, 특수 상대성 이론과 광전
효과에 관한 혁명적인 생각들은 *Annalen der Physik*에 논문으로 등장했다. 역사상 가장 위대
한 과학자 중 한 명이라는 그의 지위는 단 한 권의 책의 출간에 달려 있지는 않다.

Why? 왜 정답일까?

현대 과학 초기에 과학자들은 책을 출판해 자신의 생각을 세상에 알렸지만, 시간이 흐르며 책보다 짧은 학술
논문의 형태로 생각을 발표하게 되었다는 내용의 글이다. ⑤ 앞에서 책 한 권 길이의 출간물 없이도 과학자
들이 자신의 업적을 드러낼 수 있게 되었다고 설명한 데 이어, 주어진 문장에서는 책 대신 '논문'을 활용한
과학자의 예로 아인슈타인을 언급한다. 이어서 ⑤ 뒤에서는 아인슈타인을 His로 지칭하며, '그'의 입지가
책 출간 여부에 좌우되지는 않는다고 부연한다. 따라서 주어진 문장이 들어가기에 가장 적절한 곳은 ⑤이다.

- **revolutionary** ⓐ 혁명적인
- **relativity** ⓝ 상대성
- **largely** ⓐ 주로, 대개
- **advent** ⓝ 출현
- **gradually** ⓐ 점차로
- **abandon** ⓥ 버리다
- **reputation** ⓝ 명성
- **concerning** prep ~에 관하여
- **communicate** ⓥ 전달하다
- **publish** ⓥ 출판하다
- **periodical** ⓝ 정기 간행물
- **yield ground to** ~에 자리를 내주다, ~로 대체되다
- **altogether** ⓐ 완전히, 전적으로

구문 풀이

> **15행** Even so, it eventually became possible for scientists to establish a
> 가주어 2형식 동사 보어 의미상 주어 진주어(~것)
> reputation for their creative contributions without publishing a single book-length
> ~하지 않은 채
> treatment of their ideas.

---

39 고정 공급 일정 정답률 38% | 정답 ⑤

글의 흐름으로 보아, 주어진 문장이 들어가기에 가장 적절한 곳을 고르시오. [3점]

A supply schedule refers to the ability of a business / to change their production rates / to
meet the demand of consumers.
공급 일정은 업체의 능력을 말한다. / 생산율을 바꿀 수 있는 / 소비자의 수요를 충족하기 위해

Some businesses are able to increase their production level quickly / in order to meet
increased demand.
몇몇 업체는 조업도를 빠르게 늘릴 수 있다. / 증가한 수요를 맞추고자

However, / sporting clubs have a fixed, or inflexible (inelastic) production capacity.
그러나, / 스포츠 클럽은 고정된, 혹은 유연하지 못한(비탄력적인) 생산 능력을 가지고 있다.

① They have / what is known as a fixed supply schedule.
그들은 가지고 있다. / 소위 고정 공급 일정이라는 것을

② It is worth noting / that this is not the case / for sales of clothing, equipment,
memberships and memorabilia.
주목할 가치가 있다. / 이것이 해당하지 않는다는 것에 / 의류, 장비, 회원권, 기념품 판매에는

③ But / clubs and teams can only play a certain number of times / during their season.
그러나 / 클럽과 팀은 / 일정 횟수만 경기할 수 있다. / 시즌 동안

④ If fans and members are unable to get into a venue, / that revenue is lost forever.
팬과 회원이 경기장에 들어갈 수 없으면, / 그 수익은 영원히 손실된다.

☑ Although sport clubs and leagues / may have a fixed supply schedule, / it is possible / to
increase the number of consumers who watch.
스포츠 클럽과 리그는 / ~할지라도 / 고정 공급 일정을 가지고 있을 / 가능하다. / (경기를) 보는 소비자의 수를 늘리는 것이

For example, / the supply of a sport product can be increased / by providing more seats, /
예를 들어, / 스포츠 상품의 공급은 늘어날 수 있다. / 더 많은 좌석을 제공함으로써 /

changing the venue, / extending the playing season / or even through new television, radio or Internet distribution.
예를 들어, / 스포츠 제품의 공급은 증가될 수 있다. / 더 많은 좌석을 제공하거나, / 경기장을 바꾸거나, / 경기 시즌을 연장하거나, / 심지어 새로운 텔레비전, 라디오, 혹은 인터넷 배급으로

공급 일정은 소비자의 수요를 충족하기 위해 생산율을 바꿀 수 있는 업체의 능력을 말한다. 몇몇 업체는 증가한 수요를 맞추고자 조업도를 빠르게 늘릴 수 있다. 그러나, 스포츠 클럽은 고정된, 혹은 유연하지 못한(비탄력적인) 생산 능력을 가지고 있다. ① 그들은 소위 고정 공급 일정이라는 것을 가지고 있다. ② 이것이 의류, 장비, 회원권, 기념품 판매에는 해당하지 않는다는 것에 주목할 가치가 있다. ③ 그러나 클럽과 팀은 시즌 동안 일정 횟수만 경기할 수 있다. ④ 팬과 회원이 경기장에 들어갈 수 없으면, 그 수익은 영원히 손실된다. ⑤ 스포츠 클럽과 리그가 고정 공급 일정을 가지고 있을지라도, (경기를) 보는 소비자의 수를 늘리는 것이 가능하다. 예를 들어, 더 많은 좌석을 제공하거나, 경기장을 바꾸거나, 경기 시즌을 연장하거나, 심지어 새로운 텔레비전, 라디오, 혹은 인터넷 배급으로 스포츠 제품의 공급을 늘릴 수 있다.

Why? 왜 정답일까?

⑤ 앞에서는 고정 공급 일정으로 인해 수요에 빠르게 대응하기 어려운 스포츠 클럽의 상황을 설명한다. 한편 주어진 문장은 이렇게 고정 공급 일정일지라도 소비자의 수를 늘릴 수 있다는 내용으로 흐름을 반전시키고, ⑤ 뒤에서는 그 구체적인 방법을 열거한다. 따라서 주어진 문장이 들어가기에 가장 적절한 곳은 ⑤이다.

- **inflexible** ⓐ 유연하지 못한, 융통성 없는
- **note** ⓥ 알아차리다
- **revenue** ⓝ 수입, 수익
- **distribution** ⓝ 배급, 분배
- **inelastic** ⓐ 비탄력적인, 적응력이 없는
- **equipment** ⓝ 장비
- **extend** ⓥ 연장하다

구문 풀이

9행 It is worth noting that this is not the case for sales of clothing, equipment,
「be worth + 동명사 : ~할 가치가 있다」
memberships and memorabilia.

---

40 인간 관계의 지표가 되는 거리   정답률 39% | 정답 ①

다음 글의 내용을 한 문장으로 요약하고자 한다. 빈칸 (A), (B)에 들어갈 말로 가장 적절한 것은?

	(A)		(B)
✓①	determined 결정된	……	adjust 조절하다
②	concealed 숨겨진	……	interpret 해석하다
③	influenced 영향을 받은	……	ignore 무시하다
④	predicted 예견된	……	stop 중단하다
⑤	measured 측정된	……	decrease 줄이다

Distance is a reliable indicator / of the relationship between two people.
거리는 믿을 수 있는 지표이다. / 두 사람 간의 관계에 관한

Strangers stand further apart than do acquaintances, / acquaintances stand further apart than friends, / and friends stand further apart than romantic partners.
모르는 사람들은 지인들보다 더 멀리 떨어져 서 있고, / 지인들은 친구들보다 더 멀리 떨어져 서 있고, / 친구는 연인들보다 더 멀리 떨어져 서 있다.

Sometimes, of course, these rules are violated.
물론 때로는 이들 규칙은 위반된다.

Recall the last time / you rode 20 stories in an elevator / packed with total strangers.
마지막 때를 떠올려 보라. / 여러분이 엘리베이터를 타고 20개 층을 이동했던 / 전혀 모르는 사람들로 가득 찬

The sardine-like experience / no doubt made the situation a bit uncomfortable.
승객이 빽빽이 들어찬 경험은 / 분명히 그 상황을 약간 불편하게 만들었을 것이다.

With your physical space violated, / you may have tried to create "psychological" space / by avoiding eye contact, / focusing instead on the elevator buttons.
물리적 공간이 침범된 상태에서, / 여러분은 '심리적' 공간을 만들어 내려고 했을 수도 있다. / 눈 맞춤을 피하고, / 그 대신 엘리베이터 버튼에 집중해서

By reducing closeness in one nonverbal channel (eye contact), / one can compensate for unwanted closeness in another channel (proximity).
하나의 비언어적 채널(눈맞춤)에서의 가까움을 줄임으로써, / 사람들은 또 다른 채널(근접성)에서의 원치 않는 가까움을 상쇄할 수 있다.

Similarly, / if you are talking with someone / who is seated several feet away at a large table, / you are likely to maintain constant eye contact / — something you might feel uncomfortable doing / if you were standing next to each other.
마찬가지로, / 여러분이 누군가와 이야기를 하고 있다면 / 큰 테이블에서 몇 피트 떨어져 앉아 있는 / 여러분은 아마도 계속 눈을 마주칠 것이다. / 여러분이 하기에 불편해할 수도 있는 것 / 여러분이 서로 옆에 서 있는 경우에

➡ Physical distance between people / is (A) determined by relationship status, / but when the distance is not appropriate, / people (B) adjust their nonverbal communication / to establish a comfortable psychological distance.
사람들 사이의 물리적 거리는 / 관계의 상태에 의해 결정되지만, / 그 거리가 적절하지 않을 때 / 사람들은 비언어적 의사소통을 조절한다. / 편안한 심리적 거리를 설정하기 위해

거리는 두 사람 간의 관계에 관한 믿을 수 있는 지표이다. 모르는 사람들은 지인들보다 더 멀리 떨어져 서 있고, 지인들은 친구들보다 더 멀리 떨어져 서 있고, 친구는 연인들보다 더 멀리 떨어져 서 있다. 물론 때로는 이들 규칙은 위반된다. 마지막으로 전혀 모르는 사람들로 가득 찬 엘리베이터를 타고 20개 층을 이동했던 때를 떠올려 보라. 승객이 빽빽이 들어찬 경험은 분명히 그 상황을 약간 불편하게 만들었을 것이다. 물리적 공간이 침범된 상태에서, 여러분은 눈을 마주치지 않고, 그 대신 엘리베이터 버튼에 집중해서 '심리적' 공간을 만들어 내려고 했을 수도 있다. 하나의 비언어적인 채널(눈맞춤)에서의 가까움을 줄임으로써, 또 다른 채널(근접성)에서의 원치 않는 가까움을 상쇄할 수 있다. 마찬가지로, 여러분이 큰 테이블에서 몇 피트 떨어져 앉아 있는 누군가와 이야기를 하고 있다면, 아마도 계속 눈을 마주칠 것인데, (그것은) 여러분이 서로 옆에 서 있는 경우에 하기에는 불편할할 수도 있는 것이다.

➡ 사람들 사이의 물리적 거리는 관계의 상태에 의해 (A) 결정되지만, 그 거리가 적절하지 않을 때 사람들은 편안한 심리적 거리를 설정하기 위해 비언어적 의사소통을 (B) 조절한다.

Why? 왜 정답일까?

거리는 관계를 보여주는 지표로 작용할 수 있다(Distance is a reliable indicator of the

---

relationship ~)는 내용에 이어, 예시를 통해 물리적인 공간 조절이 어려운 경우에는 비언어적 표현을 활용해 심리적 거리를 조절한다는 내용을 설명하고 있다. 따라서 요약문의 빈칸 (A), (B)에 들어갈 말로 가장 적절한 것은 ① '(A) determined(결정된), (B) adjust(조절하다)'이다.

- **reliable** ⓐ 믿을 만한
- **acquaintance** ⓝ 아는 사람, 약간의 친분
- **recall** ⓥ 회상하다
- **closeness** ⓝ 가까움, 근접함
- **appropriate** ⓐ 적절한
- **adjust** ⓥ 조절하다
- **indicator** ⓝ 지표
- **violate** ⓥ 위반하다
- **psychological** ⓐ 심리적인
- **compensate for** ~을 보상하다, 상쇄하다
- **establish** ⓥ 설정하다, 확립하다

구문 풀이

8행 With your physical space violated, you may have tried to create
「with + 명사 + 분사 : ~이 …한 채로」   「may have + 과거분사 : ~했을지도 모른다」
"psychological" space by avoiding eye contact, focusing instead on the elevator
분사구문(~하면서)
buttons.

41-42 잘 싸우는 것의 이점

『Being able to have a good fight / doesn't just make us more civil; it also develops our creative muscles.』 41번의 근거
잘 싸울 수 있다는 것은 / 우리를 더 정중하게 만들 뿐 아니라 / 그것은 우리의 창의적 근력을 발달시킨다.

In a classic study, / highly creative architects were more likely / than their technically competent but less original peers / to come from homes with (a) plenty of friction.
고전적인 연구에 따르면, / 매우 창의적인 건축가는 가능성이 더 크다. / 기술적으로 유능하지만 덜 독창적인 그들의 동료보다 / 충돌이 많은 가정에서 나올

They often grew up in households / that were "tense but secure," / as psychologist Robert Albert notes: / "The creative person-to-be comes from a family / that is anything but (b) harmonious."
그들은 흔히 집안에서 자랐는데, / '긴장감이 있지만 안전한' / 심리학자 Robert Albert는 언급한다. / "창의적인 사람이 될 사람은 가정에서 나온다. / 전혀 화목하지 않은"

The parents weren't physically or verbally abusive, / but they didn't shy away from conflict, either.
그 부모들이 신체적으로나 언어적으로 학대한 것은 아니었지만 / 그들은 갈등을 피하지도 않았다.

Instead of telling their children to be seen but not heard, / they (c) encouraged them to stand up for themselves.
자녀에게 눈앞에 있되 아무 말도 하지 말라고 말하는 대신 / 그들은 자녀에게 자신의 입장을 내세우라고 권장했다.

『The kids learned to dish it out — and take it.
그 자녀들은 남을 비판하고 비판을 받아들이는 것을 배웠다.

That's exactly what happened to Wilbur and Orville Wright, / who invented the airplane.』
그것이 바로 Wilbur와 Orville Wright 형제에게 일어난 일이었다. / 비행기를 발명한   42번의 근거

When the Wright brothers said they thought together, / what they really meant is that they fought together.
Wright 형제가 자기들은 함께 생각한다고 말했을 때 / 그 말의 진짜 의미는 함께 싸웠다는 것이다.

When they were solving problems, / they had arguments / that lasted not just for hours / but for weeks and months / at a time.
그들이 문제를 풀고 있었을 때 / 그들은 논쟁을 했다. / 몇 시간 동안만 지속된 것이 아닌 / 몇 주, 몇 달 동안 지속된 / 한 번에

They didn't have such (d) ceaseless fights / because they were angry.
그들이 그토록 끊임없는 싸움을 한 것은 아니었다. / 그들이 화가 났기 때문에

They kept quarreling / because they enjoyed it and learned from the experience.
그들은 계속 싸웠다. / 그들이 그것을 즐기고 그 경험으로부터 배웠기 때문에

"I like scrapping with Orv," / Wilbur reflected.
"나는 Orv와 다투는 것을 좋아한다." / Wilbur는 회고했다.

As you'll see, / it was one of their most passionate and prolonged arguments / that led them to (e) rethink a critical assumption / that had prevented humans from soaring through the skies.
여러분이 보다시피, / 바로 그들의 가장 열정적이고 장기적인 논쟁 중 하나였다. / 그들이 결정적 가정을 재고하도록 이끌었던 것은 / 인간이 하늘에 날아오르지 못하게 했던

잘 싸울 수 있다는 것은 우리를 더 정중하게 만들 뿐 아니라 우리의 창의적 근력을 발달시킨다. 고전적인 연구에 따르면, 매우 창의적인 건축가는 기술적으로 유능하지만 덜 독창적인 그들의 동료보다 충돌이 (a) 많은 가정에서 나올 가능성이 더 크다. 그들은 흔히 '긴장감이 있지만 안전한' 집안에서 자랐는데, 심리학자 Robert Albert는 "창의적인 사람이 될 사람은 전혀 (b) 화목하지 않은 가정에서 나온다."라고 언급한다. 그 부모들이 신체적으로나 언어적으로 학대한 것은 아니었지만 갈등을 피하지도 않았다. 그들은 자녀에게 눈앞에 있되 아무 말도 하지 말라고 말하는 대신 자신의 입장을 내세우라고 (c) 권장했다. 그 자녀들은 남을 비판하고 비판을 받아들이는 것을 배웠다. 그것이 바로 비행기를 발명한 Wilbur와 Orville Wright 형제에게 일어난 일이었다.

Wright 형제가 자기들은 함께 생각한다고 말했을 때 그 말의 진짜 의미는 함께 싸웠다는 것이다. 그들이 문제를 풀고 있었을 때 그들은 한 번에 몇 시간 동안뿐만 아니라 몇 주, 몇 달 동안 지속된 논쟁을 했다. 그들이 화가 나서 그토록 (d) 끊임없는 싸움을 한 것은 아니었다. 그들은 그것을 즐기고 그 경험으로부터 배웠기 때문에 계속 싸웠다. "나는 Orv와 다투는 것을 좋아한다."라고 Wilbur는 회고했다. 보다시피, 바로 그들의 가장 열정이고 장기적인 논쟁 중 하나가 인간이 하늘로 날아오르지 못하게 했던 결정적 가정을 그들이 (e) 지지하도록(→ 재고하도록) 이끌었다.

- **civil** ⓐ 정중한, 예의 바른
- **technically** ⓪ 기술적으로
- **friction** ⓝ 마찰, 저항, 갈등
- **anything but** ~이 결코 아닌
- **abusive** ⓐ 학대하는
- **stand up for** ~을 대변하다, 옹호하다
- **prolonged** ⓐ 장기간의
- **cope with** ~에 대처하다
- **architect** ⓝ 건축가
- **competent** ⓐ 유능한
- **secure** ⓐ 안전한
- **harmonious** ⓐ 조화로운
- **shy away from** ~을 피하다
- **ceaseless** ⓐ 끊임없는
- **soar** ⓥ 솟구치다
- **compromise** ⓝ 타협, 절충 ⓥ 타협하다

구문 풀이

20행 As you'll see, it was one of their most passionate and prolonged arguments
「it is[was] ~ that … 강조 구문 : …한 것은 바로 ~이대였다」
that led them to rethink a critical assumption [that had prevented humans from
선행사   「prevent + A + from + B
soaring through the skies].
A가 B하지 못하게 막다」

41 제목 파악 | 정답률 54% | 정답 ①

윗글의 제목으로 가장 적절한 것은?

☑ The Power of Constructive Conflict – 건설적인 갈등의 힘
② Lighten Tense Moments with Humor – 유머로 긴장된 순간을 가볍게 하라
③ Strategies to Cope with Family Stress – 가족 스트레스에 대처하는 전략
④ Compromise: A Key to Resolving Conflict – 타협: 갈등 해결의 열쇠
⑤ Rivalry Between Brothers: A Serious Crisis – 형제 간의 경쟁: 심각한 위기

Why? 왜 정답일까?

주제문인 첫 문장에서 건설적인 갈등은 우리를 정중하게 만들 뿐 아니라 창의력도 길러준다(Being able to have a good fight doesn't just make us more civil; it also develops our creative muscles.)고 하므로, 글의 제목으로 가장 적절한 것은 ① '건설적인 갈등의 힘'이다.

★★★ 등급을 가르는 문제!

42 어휘 추론 | 정답률 17% | 정답 ⑤

밑줄 친 (a)~(e) 중에서 문맥상 낱말의 쓰임이 적절하지 않은 것은? [3점]

① (a)　② (b)　③ (c)　④ (d)　☑ (e)

Why? 왜 정답일까?

첫 단락의 마지막 두 문장에서 Wright 형제는 남을 비판하고 자신에 대한 비판도 받아들이는 법을 배웠으며, 그 결과 비행기의 발명이라는 창의적인 업적까지 이르렀다고 한다. 다시 말해, 이들 형제는 끝없이 서로 논쟁하는 과정에서 사람이 날지 못할 것이라는 믿음을 '지지하는' 대신 '다시 생각하고 비판하여' 사고의 성장을 이루었다는 것이므로, (e)의 support를 rethink로 고쳐야 문맥이 자연스럽다. 따라서 문맥상 낱말의 쓰임이 가장 적절하지 않은 것은 ⑤ '(e)'이다.

★★ 문제 해결 꿀~팁 ★★

▶ 많이 틀린 이유는?
밑줄 주변 문맥에 답의 근거가 있다. ④ 'd' 바로 앞에서 Wright 형제는 문제를 해결하는 도중 몇 시간, 몇 주, 심지어 몇 달간 이어지는 싸움을 했다고 언급하는 것으로 보아, 싸움이 '끊임없었다'는 의미의 ceaseless는 적합하다.

▶ 문제 해결 방법은?
정답인 ⑤ '(e)'가 포함된 문장은 호흡이 길기 때문에 시간을 들여 정확하게 읽어야 한다. Wright 형제가 끊임없는 싸움과 문제 해결 과정을 통해 결국 비행에 '성공한' 인물임을 고려할 때, 기존에 비행을 좌절시켰던 생각을 이들이 '지지했다'는 설명은 적합하지 않다. 이들이 통념을 '깨려' 했기 때문에 남들이 하지 못한 창의적인 생각을 할 수 있었던 것이다.

43-45 잘 웃는 John의 특별한 재능

(A)

John was a sensitive boy.
John은 민감한 소년이었다.
Even his hair was ticklish.
심지어 그의 머리카락도 간지럼을 탔다.
When breeze touched his hair / he would burst out laughing.
산들바람이 그의 머리카락에 닿으면 / 그는 웃음을 터뜨리곤 했다.
And when this ticklish laughter started, / no one could make him stop.
그리고 간지럼으로 인한 웃음이 시작되면, / 아무도 그를 멈추게 할 수 없었다.
John's laughter was so contagious / that when John started feeling ticklish, / everyone ended up in endless laughter.
John의 웃음은 전염성이 매우 강해서 / John이 간지럼을 타기 시작하면 / 모두가 결국 끝없이 웃게 되었다.
「He tried everything to control his ticklishness: / wearing a thousand different hats, / using ultra strong hairsprays, / and shaving his head.」 45번 ①의 근거 일치
그는 간지럼을 잘 타는 것을 억제하기 위해 온갖 노력을 했다. / 수없이 많은 다양한 모자를 써 보기도 했고, / 초강력 헤어스프레이를 사용해 보기도 하며, / 머리를 밀기도 하는 등
But nothing worked.
하지만 아무것도 효과가 없었다.
One day he met a clown in the street.
어느 날 그는 거리에서 어떤 광대를 만났다.
The clown was very old and could hardly walk, / but when he saw John in tears, / he went to cheer (a) him up.
그 광대는 매우 늙어서 걸음을 겨우 걸었지만 / John이 울고 있는 것을 보았을 때 / 그는 그를 격려하러 갔다.

(C)

It didn't take long to make John laugh, / and they started to talk.
John을 웃게 하는 데 오래 걸리지 않았고, / 그들은 이야기를 나누기 시작했다.
John told (c) him about his ticklish problem.
John은 그에게 간지럼을 타는 자신의 문제에 관해 말했다.
「Then he asked the clown / how such an old man could carry on being a clown.」 그러고 나서 늙은 사람이 어떻게 광대 일을 계속할 수 있는지 45번 ③의 근거 일치
"I have no one to replace me," / said the clown, / "and I have a very serious job to do."
"나를 대신할 사람은 없고, / 그 광대는 말했다. / 내게는 해야 할 매우 중요한 일이 있단다."라고
「And then he took John / to many hospitals, shelters, and schools.」 45번 ④의 근거 일치
그러고 나서 그는 John을 데려갔다. / 여러 병원과 보호 시설, 학교로

(B)

All were full of children / who were sick, or orphaned, / children with very serious problems.
모든 곳은 아이들로 가득했다. / 아프거나 고아가 된 / 매우 심각한 문제를 가진 아이들로
But as soon as they saw the clown, / their faces changed completely and lit up with a smile.
하지만 그들은 그 광대를 보자마자, / 그들의 표정은 완전히 바뀌고 미소로 밝아졌다.
That day was even more special, / because 「in every show / John's contagious laughter / would end up making the kids laugh a lot.」 45번 ②의 근거 일치
그날은 훨씬 더 특별했는데, / 모든 쇼에서 / John의 전염성 있는 웃음이 / 결국 아이들을 많이 웃게 만들곤 했기 때문이다.
The old clown winked at (b) him and said, / "Now do you see what a serious job it is? / That's why I can't retire, even at my age."
그 늙은 광대는 그에게 윙크하며 말했다. / "이제 이 일이 얼마나 중요한 일인지 알겠니? / 그래서 내 나이에도 나는 은퇴할 수가 없단다."

(D)

And he added, / "Not everyone could do it. / He or she has to have a special gift for laughter."
그리고 그는 덧붙여 말했다. / "아무나 그 일을 할 수 있는 게 아니란다. / 웃음에 특별한 재능이 있는 사람이어야 한단다."라고
This said, / the wind again set off John's ticklishness and (d) his laughter.
이 말을 했을 때 / 바람이 다시 John의 간지럼과 그의 웃음을 터지게 했다.
「After a while, / John decided to replace the old clown.」 45번 ⑤의 근거 불일치
얼마 후, / John은 그 늙은 광대의 뒤를 잇기로 했다.
From that day onward, / the fact that John was different / actually made (e) him happy, / thanks to his special gift.
그날 이후로 / John이 남다르다는 사실은 / 실제로 그를 행복하게 만들었다. / 그의 특별한 재능 덕분에

(A)

John은 민감한 소년이었다. 심지어 그의 머리카락도 간지럼을 탔다. 산들바람이 그의 머리카락에 닿으면 그는 웃음을 터뜨리곤 했다. 그리고 간지럼으로 인한 웃음이 시작되면, 아무도 그를 멈추게 할 수 없었다. John의 웃음은 전염성이 매우 강해서 John이 간지럼을 타기 시작하면 모두 결국 끝없이 웃게 되었다. 간지럼을 잘 타는 것을 억제하기 위해 수없이 많은 다양한 모자를 써 보기도 했고, 초강력 헤어스프레이를 사용해 보기도 하며, 머리를 밀기도 하는 등 온갖 노력을 했다. 하지만 어떤 것도 효과가 없었다. 어느 날 그는 거리에서 어떤 광대를 만났다. 그 광대는 매우 늙어서 걸음을 겨우 걸었지만 John이 울고 있는 것을 보았을 때 (a) 그를 격려하러 갔다.

(C)

John을 웃게 하는 데 오래 걸리지 않았고, 그들은 이야기를 나누기 시작했다. John은 (c) 그에게 간지럼을 타는 자신의 문제에 관해 말했다. 그러고 나서 그는 광대에게 그렇게 늙어서도 어떻게 광대 일을 계속할 수 있는지 물었다. "나를 대신할 사람은 없고, 내게는 해야 할 매우 중요한 일이 있단다."라고 그 광대는 말했다. 그러고 나서 그는 John을 여러 병원과 보호 시설, 학교로 데려갔다.

(B)

가는 곳마다 아프거나 고아가 된 아이들, 매우 심각한 문제를 가진 아이들로 가득했다. 하지만 그들은 그 광대를 보자마자, 그들의 표정은 완전히 바뀌고 미소로 밝아졌다. 그날은 훨씬 더 특별했는데, 모든 쇼에서 John의 전염성 있는 웃음이 결국 아이들을 많이 웃게 만들곤 했기 때문이다. 그 늙은 광대는 (b) 그에게 윙크하며 말했다. "이제 이 일이 얼마나 중요한 일인지 알겠니? 그래서 내 나이에도 나는 은퇴할 수가 없단다."

(D)

그리고 그는 "아무나 그 일을 할 수 있는 게 아니란다. 웃음에 특별한 재능이 있는 사람이어야 한단다."라고 덧붙여 말했다. 이 말을 했을 때 바람이 다시 John의 간지럼과 (d) 그의 웃음을 터지게 했다. 얼마 후, John은 그 늙은 광대의 뒤를 잇기로 했다. 그날 이후로 특별한 재능 덕분에 남다르다는 사실은 실제로 (e) John을 행복하게 만들었다.

- sensitive ⓐ 민감한
- contagious ⓐ 전염되는
- shave ⓥ 면도하다, 깎다
- light up with ~로 빛나다
- carry on 계속해서 ~하다
- set off 유발하다, 일으키다
- burst out laughing 웃음을 터뜨리다
- end up in 결국 ~로 끝나다
- orphaned ⓐ 고아가 된
- retire ⓥ 은퇴하다
- replace ⓥ 대체하다

구문 풀이

(A) 4행 John's laughter was so contagious that when John started feeling
〔so ~ that … : 너무 ~해서 …하다〕
ticklish, everyone ended up in endless laughter.

(B) 3행 That day was even more special, because in every show John's
contagious laughter would end up making the kids laugh a lot.
〔end up+동명사: 결국 ~하게 되다〕 → 원형부정사

(D) 2행 This said, the wind again set off John's ticklishness and his laughter.
→ 분사구문(수동)　의미상 주어　주어　동사

(D) 4행 From that day onward, the fact {that John was different} actually made
주어　{ }: 동격절　동사
him happy, thanks to his special gift.
목적어 └→ 목적격 보어

43 글의 순서 파악 | 정답률 77% | 정답 ②

주어진 글 (A)에 이어질 내용을 순서에 맞게 배열한 것으로 가장 적절한 것은?

① (B) – (D) – (C)　☑ (C) – (B) – (D)
③ (C) – (D) – (B)　④ (D) – (B) – (C)
⑤ (D) – (C) – (B)

Why? 왜 정답일까?

간지럼을 잘 타고 잘 웃는 John이 어느 날 광대를 만났다는 내용의 (A) 뒤에는, John이 광대에게 자신의 문제를 상담하며 광대 일에 관해 물었다는 내용의 (C)가 연결된다. 이어서 (B)에서는 광대가 John을 데리고 웃음이 필요한 사람들에게로 향했다고 하고, (D)에서는 광대와 함께 다니며 자신의 장점을 깨달은 John이 광대의 뒤를 잇기로 결심했다고 한다. 따라서 글의 순서로 가장 적절한 것은 ② '(C) – (B) – (D)'이다.

44 지칭 추론 | 정답률 71% | 정답 ③

밑줄 친 (a)~(e) 중에서 가리키는 대상이 나머지 넷과 다른 것은?

① (a)　② (b)　☑ (c)　④ (d)　⑤ (e)

Why? 왜 정답일까?

(a), (b), (d), (e)는 John, (c)는 (A)의 The clown을 가리키므로, (a)~(e) 중에서 가리키는 대상이 다른 하나는 ③ '(c)'이다.

45 세부 내용 파악
정답률 85% | 정답 ⑤

윗글의 John에 관한 내용으로 적절하지 <u>않은</u> 것은?
① 간지럼을 타지 않으려고 온갖 시도를 했다.
② 전염성 있는 웃음으로 아이들을 많이 웃게 했다.
③ 광대에게 그렇게 늙어서도 어떻게 계속 일할 수 있는지 물었다.
④ 광대와 함께 여러 병원과 보호 시설, 학교에 갔다.
☑ 광대의 뒤를 잇지 않기로 했다.

Why? 왜 정답일까?

(D) 'After a while, John decided to replace the old clown.'에서 늙은 광대와 하루를 보내고 난 얼마 후 John은 광대의 뒤를 잇기로 결심했다고 하므로, 내용과 일치하지 않는 것은 ⑤ '광대의 뒤를 잇지 않기로 했다.'이다.

Why? 왜 오답일까?

① (A) 'He tried everything to control his ticklishness: ~'의 내용과 일치한다.
② (B) '~ John's contagious laughter would end up making the kids laugh a lot.'의 내용과 일치한다.
③ (C) 'Then he asked the clown how such an old man could carry on being a clown.'의 내용과 일치한다.
④ (C) 'And then he took John to many hospitals, shelters, and schools.'의 내용과 일치한다.

어휘 Review Test 03
문제편 030쪽

A	B	C	D
01 부조화	01 ultimate	01 ⓞ	01 ⑨
02 땀이 나다	02 fit	02 ⓝ	02 ⑨
03 고대의	03 suitable	03 ⓜ	03 ⓘ
04 관점, 시각	04 overcome	04 ⓟ	04 ⓙ
05 해석하다, 이해하다	05 sustainable	05 ⓘ	05 ⓗ
06 헌신	06 revenue	06 ⓒ	06 ⓡ
07 현상	07 document	07 ⓡ	07 ⓓ
08 조심하는, 신중한	08 perform	08 ⓙ	08 ⓘ
09 소질, 적성	09 publish	09 ⓓ	09 ⓞ
10 지표	10 incident	10 ⓔ	10 ⓝ
11 권위	11 sensitive	11 ⓑ	11 ⓒ
12 억제하다, 조절하다	12 realization	12 ⓢ	12 ⓢ
13 의식적인	13 operate	13 ⓚ	13 ⓔ
14 유대감	14 primarily	14 ⓘ	14 ⓕ
15 약간	15 roughly	15 ⓠ	15 ⓐ
16 중대한	16 extensive	16 ⓗ	16 ⓑ
17 자존감	17 objective	17 ⓘ	17 ⓘ
18 떠올리다, 상기하다	18 replace	18 ⓖ	18 ⓜ
19 전통적으로	19 feature	19 ⓐ	19 ⓚ
20 접근법	20 expand	20 ⓕ	20 ⓟ

04회 | 2021학년도 3월 학력평가

• 정답 •

18① 19① 20② 21① 22③ 23④ 24① 25③ 26⑤ 27③ 28★③ 29⑤ 30② 31① 32④ 33① 34④ 35③ 36⑤ 37② 38★⑤ 39③ 40★④ 41① 42⑤ 43⑤ 44④ 45②

★ 표기된 문항은 [등급을 가르는 문제]에 해당하는 문항입니다.

18 재활용품 배출 가능 요일 공지
정답률 93% | 정답 ①

다음 글의 목적으로 가장 적절한 것은?
☑ 재활용품 배출 허용 요일을 알리려고
② 쓰레기 분리배출의 필요성을 설명하려고
③ 쓰레기 분리배출 후 주변 정리를 부탁하려고
④ 입주민 대표 선출 결과를 공지하려고
⑤ 쓰레기장 재정비 비용을 청구하려고

My name is Anthony Thompson / and I am writing on behalf of the residents' association.
제 이름은 Anthony Thompson이고 / 저는 입주민 조합을 대표하여 이 글을 쓰고 있습니다.
Our recycling program has been working well / thanks to your participation.
우리의 재활용 프로그램은 잘 운영되고 있습니다. / 여러분의 참여 덕분에
However, / a problem has recently occurred / that needs your attention.
그런데 / 최근에 문제가 생겼습니다. / 여러분의 관심이 필요한
Because there is no given day for recycling, / residents are putting their recycling out at any time.
재활용을 위해 정해진 날이 없어서 / 입주민들은 아무 때나 자신들의 재활용품을 내놓습니다.
This makes the recycling area messy, / which requires extra labor and cost.
이것이 재활용 구역을 어지럽혀서 / 추가 노동과 비용이 필요하게 합니다.
To deal with this problem, / the residents' association has decided on a day to recycle.
이 문제를 처리하기 위해서 / 입주민 조합은 재활용하는 날을 결정했습니다.
I would like to let you know / that you can put out your recycling on Wednesdays only.
저는 여러분께 알려드리고 싶습니다. / 여러분이 수요일에만 여러분의 재활용품을 내놓을 수 있다는 것을
I am sure / it will make our apartment complex look much more pleasant.
저는 확신합니다. / 그것이 우리 아파트 단지를 훨씬 더 쾌적하게 보이도록 만들 것이라고
Thank you in advance for your cooperation.
여러분의 협조에 미리 감사드립니다.

제 이름은 Anthony Thompson이고 저는 입주민 조합을 대표하여 이 글을 쓰고 있습니다. 우리의 재활용 프로그램은 여러분의 참여 덕분에 잘 운영되고 있습니다. 그런데 최근에 여러분의 관심이 필요한 문제가 생겼습니다. 재활용을 위해 정해진 날이 없어서 입주민들은 아무 때나 자신들의 재활용품을 내놓습니다. 이것이 재활용 구역을 어지럽혀서 추가 노동과 비용이 필요하게 합니다. 이 문제를 처리하기 위해서 입주민 조합은 재활용하는 날을 결정했습니다. 수요일에만 재활용품을 내놓을 수 있다는 것을 알려드리고 싶습니다. 그것이 우리 아파트 단지를 훨씬 더 쾌적하게 보이도록 만들 것이라고 저는 확신합니다. 여러분의 협조에 미리 감사드립니다.

Why? 왜 정답일까?

'I would like to let you know that you can put out your recycling on Wednesdays only.'에서 아파트 입주민들은 앞으로 재활용품을 수요일에만 배출할 수 있다고 공지하고 있으므로, 글의 목적으로 가장 적절한 것은 ① '재활용품 배출 허용 요일을 알리려고'이다.

● on behalf of ~을 대표하여 ● association ⓝ 조합, 협회
● messy ⓐ 엉망인, 지저분한 ● labor ⓝ 노동
● deal with ~을 처리하다, 다루다 ● in advance 미리

구문 풀이

8행 To deal with this problem, the residents' association has decided on
목적(~하기 위해) ~에 대해 결정하다
a day to recycle.
형용사적 용법

19 발표를 앞두고 몹시 긴장한 필자
정답률 87% | 정답 ①

다음 글에 드러난 'I'의 심경으로 가장 적절한 것은?
☑ panicked – 어쩔 줄 모르는 ② angry – 화가 난 ③ relieved – 안도한
④ grateful – 고마워하는 ⑤ bored – 지루한

It was a day / I was due to give a presentation at work, / not something I'd do often.
날이었고 / 내가 직장에서 발표를 하기로 한 / 이는 내가 자주 하던 일이 아니었다.
As I stood up to begin, / I froze.
내가 시작하려고 일어섰을 때 / 나는 얼어붙었다.
A chilly 'pins-and-needles' feeling crept over me, / starting in my hands.
'저릿저릿한' 차가운 느낌이 나를 엄습했다. / 손에서 시작해서
Time seemed to stand still / as I struggled to start speaking, / and I felt a pressure around my throat, / as though my voice was trapped and couldn't come out.
시간이 정지해 있는 것 같았고 / 내가 말하기 시작하려고 애쓸 때 / 나는 목구멍이 조이는 느낌이 들었는데 / 마치 내 목소리가 갇혀서 빠져나올 수 없는 것 같았다.
Gazing around at the blur of faces, / I realized they were all waiting for me to begin, / but by now I knew I couldn't continue.
흐릿한 형체의 얼굴들을 둘러보며 / 나는 그들이 모두 내가 시작하기를 기다리고 있다는 것을 깨달았지만 / 그때쯤 나는 내가 계속할 수 없다는 것을 알았다.

내가 직장에서 발표를 하기로 한 날이었고 이는 내가 자주 하던 일이 아니었다. 시작하려고 일어섰을 때 나는 얼어붙었다. '저릿저릿한' 차가운 느낌이 손에서 시작해서 나를 엄습했다. 내가 말하기 시작하려고 애쓸 때 시간이 정지해 있는 것 같았고 목구멍이 조이는 느낌이 들었는데 마치 내 목소리가 갇혀서 빠져나올 수 없는 것 같았다. 흐릿한 형체의 얼굴들을 둘러

보며 나는 그들이 모두 내가 시작하기를 기다리고 있다는 것을 깨달았지만 그때쯤 내가 계속할 수 없다는 것을 알았다.

Why? 왜 정답일까?

'As I stood up to begin, I froze.' 이후로 필자가 발표를 시작하게 되자 너무 긴장하여 얼어붙었고 압박감에 목소리조차 내지 못하는 상황에 처했음을 알 수 있다. 따라서 'I'의 심경으로 가장 적절한 것은 ① '어쩔 줄 모르는'이다.

- give a presentation 발표하다
- chilly ⓐ 차가운
- pins-and-needles ⓐ 저릿저릿한, 조마조마한
- creep over ~을 엄습하다
- struggle ⓥ (~하려고) 애쓰다, 고생하다
- gaze at ~을 응시하다
- blur ⓝ 흐릿한 형체 ⓥ 흐릿해지다
- panicked ⓐ (당황하거나 겁에 질려서) 어쩔 줄 모르는

구문 풀이

4행 Time seemed to stand still as I struggled to start speaking, and I felt a
　　　　　　　　　　 동사구　　　　　　　　　형용사 보어
pressure around my throat, as though my voice was trapped and couldn't come
　　　　　　　　　　　접속사(마치 ~인 것처럼)　주어　　동사1　　　　　동사2
out.

---

20 외부자의 눈으로 조직을 비판하기　　　　　정답률 74% | 정답 ②

다음 글에서 필자가 주장하는 바로 가장 적절한 것은?
① 조직 내의 의사소통이 원활한지 수시로 살피라.
✔ 외부자의 관점으로 자기 조직을 비판적으로 바라보라.
③ 관심사의 공유를 통해 직장 동료와의 관계를 개선하라.
④ 과거의 성공에 도취되어 자기 계발을 소홀히 하지 말라.
⑤ 동료의 실수를 비판하기보다는 먼저 이해하려고 노력하라.

No matter what your situation, / whether you are an insider or an outsider, / you need to become the voice / that challenges yesterday's answers.
여러분의 상황이 어떠하든, / 여러분이 내부자이건 외부자이건, / 여러분은 목소리가 될 필요가 있다. / 어제의 정답에 이의를 제기하는
Think about the characteristics / that make outsiders valuable to an organization.
특성들에 관해 생각해 보라. / 외부자를 조직에 가치 있게 만드는
They are the people / who have the perspective to see problems / that the insiders are too close to really notice.
그들은 사람들이다. / 문제들을 볼 수 있는 관점을 가진 / 내부자가 너무 가까이 있어서 정말 알아차릴 수 없는
They are the ones / who have the freedom / to point out these problems and criticize them / without risking their job or their career.
그들은 사람들이다. / 자유를 가진 / 이런 문제들을 지적하고 그것들을 비판할 수 있는 / 자신의 일자리나 자신의 경력을 걸지 않고
Part of adopting an outsider mentality / is forcing yourself / to look around your organization / with this disassociated, less emotional perspective.
외부자의 사고방식을 채택하는 것의 일부는 / 여러분 스스로에게 강제하는 것이다. / 여러분의 조직을 둘러보도록 / 이렇게 분리된, 덜 감정적인 관점으로
If you didn't know your coworkers / and feel bonded to them by your shared experiences, / what would you think of them?
여러분이 자신의 동료를 모르고 / 그들과 공유한 경험으로 결속되어 있다고 느끼지 않는다면 / 여러분은 그들에 관해 어떻게 생각하겠는가?
You may not have the job security or confidence / to speak your mind to management, / but you can make these "outsider" assessments of your organization on your own / and use what you determine to advance your career.
여러분이 직업 안정성이나 자신감을 갖고 있지 않을지도 모르지만 / 자신의 생각을 경영진에게 말할 / 여러분은 자신의 조직에 관해 이런 '외부자의' 평가를 독자적으로 할 수 있고 / 경력을 발전시키기 위해 여러분이 판단한 것을 이용할 수 있다.

여러분의 상황이 어떠하든, 여러분이 내부자이건 외부자이건, 여러분은 어제의 정답에 이의를 제기하는 목소리가 될 필요가 있다. 외부자를 조직에 가치 있게 만드는 특성들에 관해 생각해 보라. 그들은 내부자가 너무 가까이 있어서 정말 알아차릴 수 없는 문제들을 볼 수 있는 관점을 가진 사람들이다. 그들은 자신의 일자리나 자신의 경력을 걸지 않고 이런 문제들을 지적하고 그것들을 비판할 수 있는 자유를 가진 사람들이다. 외부자의 사고방식을 채택하는 것의 일부는 이렇게 분리된, 덜 감정적인 관점으로 여러분의 조직을 스스로 둘러보도록 강제하는 것이다. 여러분이 자신의 동료를 모르고 공유한 경험으로 결속되어 있다고 느끼지 않는다면 여러분은 그들에 관해 어떻게 생각하겠는가? 여러분이 자신의 생각을 경영진에게 말할 직업 안정성이나 자신감을 갖고 있지 않을지도 모르지만 여러분은 자신의 조직에 관해 이런 '외부자의' 평가를 독자적으로 할 수 있고 경력을 발전시키기 위해 여러분이 판단한 것을 이용할 수 있다.

Why? 왜 정답일까?

첫 문장에서 상황과 입지가 어떠하든 조직 내에서 기존의 답에 의문을 제기하는 사람이 될 필요가 있다고 언급한 후, 마지막 문장에서 외부자로서의 시각을 갖추고 조직을 비판적으로 바라보며 경력을 발전시킬 것을 조언하고 있다. 따라서 필자가 주장하는 바로 가장 적절한 것은 ② '외부자의 관점으로 자기 조직을 비판적으로 바라보라.'이다.

- challenge ⓥ 이의를 제기하다, 반박하다
- characteristic ⓝ 특성, 특징
- perspective ⓝ 관점, 시각
- criticize ⓥ 비판하다
- risk ⓥ ~을 걸다, 위태롭게 하다
- mentality ⓝ 사고방식
- disassociated ⓐ 고립된, 결속되지 않은
- security ⓝ 안정성
- confidence ⓝ 자신감
- assessment ⓝ 평가

구문 풀이

1행 No matter what your situation (is), whether you are an insider or an outsider,
　　　　= whatever(무엇이 ~이든 간에)　　　　'whether + A + or + B : A이든 B이든」
you need to become the voice [that challenges yesterday's answers].
　　　　　　　　　　　　선행사　　　주격 관계대명사

---

21 비상사태를 대비하는 훈련의 의의　　　　　정답률 57% | 정답 ①

밑줄 친 training for a marathon이 다음 글에서 의미하는 바로 가장 적절한 것은? [3점]
✔ developing the potential to respond to a real disaster – 실제 재난에 대응할 수 있는 잠재력을 기르기

② making a long-term recovery plan for a disaster – 재난에 대한 장기적인 복구 계획을 수립하기
③ seeking cooperation among related organizations – 관련 기관들 간의 협조를 구하기
④ saving basic disaster supplies for an emergency – 비상사태를 위해 기본적인 재난 물자를 비축하기
⑤ testing a runner's speed as often as possible – 가능한 한 자주 달리기 선수의 속도를 검사하기

The known fact of contingencies, / without knowing precisely what those contingencies will be, / shows / that disaster preparation is not the same thing as disaster rehearsal.
비상사태에 관해 이미 알려진 사실은, / 그 비상사태가 어떠할지를 정확히 알지는 못하겠지만, / 보여 준다. / 재난 대비가 재난 예행연습과 똑같지 않다는 것을
No matter how many mock disasters are staged / according to prior plans, / the real disaster will never mirror any one of them.
아무리 많은 모의 재난이 조직되더라도 / 사전 계획에 따라 / 실제 재난은 그런 것들 중 어느 하나라도 그대로 반영하지 않을 것이다.
Disaster-preparation planning is more like training for a marathon / than training for a high-jump competition or a sprinting event.
재난 대비 계획 세우기는 마라톤을 위해 훈련하는 것과 더 비슷하다. / 높이뛰기 시합이나 단거리 달리기 경주를 위해 훈련하는 것보다는
Marathon runners do not practice / by running the full course of twenty-six miles; / rather, they get into shape / by running shorter distances / and building up their endurance with cross-training.
마라톤 선수들은 연습하는 것이 아니라 / 26마일 전체 코스를 달리는 것으로 / 오히려 그들은 몸 상태를 좋게 만든다. / 더 짧은 거리를 달리고 / 여러 가지 운동을 조합하여 행하는 훈련법으로 자신의 지구력을 강화함으로써
If they have prepared successfully, / then they are in optimal condition / to run the marathon over its predetermined course and length, / assuming a range of weather conditions, / predicted or not.
만약 그들이 성공적으로 준비했다면 / 그들은 최적의 상태에 있다. / 마라톤의 미리 정해진 코스와 길이에 걸쳐 마라톤을 달릴 수 있는 / 다양한 기상 조건을 가정하면서 / 예상되었던 아니든
This is normal marathon preparation.
이것이 보통의 마라톤 준비이다.

비상사태에 관해 이미 알려진 사실은, 그 비상사태가 어떠할지를 정확히 알지는 못하겠지만, 재난 대비가 재난 예행연습과 똑같지 않다는 것을 보여 준다. 아무리 많은 모의 재난이 사전 계획에 따라 조직되더라도 실제 재난은 그런 것들 중 어느 하나라도 그대로 반영하지 않을 것이다. 재난 대비 계획 세우기는 높이뛰기 시합이나 단거리 달리기 경주를 위해 훈련하는 것보다는 마라톤을 위해 훈련하는 것과 더 비슷하다. 마라톤 선수들은 26마일 전체 코스를 달리는 것으로 연습하는 것이 아니라 오히려 더 짧은 거리를 달리고 여러 가지 운동을 조합하여 행하는 훈련법으로 자신의 지구력을 강화함으로써 몸 상태를 좋게 만든다. 만약 그들이 성공적으로 준비했다면 그들은 마라톤의 미리 정해진 코스와 길이에 걸쳐 예상되었든 아니든 다양한 기상 조건을 가정하면서 마라톤을 달릴 수 있는 최적의 상태에 있다. 이것이 보통의 마라톤 준비이다.

Why? 왜 정답일까?

'If they have prepared successfully, then they are in optimal condition to run the marathon over its predetermined course and length, assuming a range of weather conditions, predicted or not.'에서 마라톤 선수들은 매번 전체 코스를 달리지는 않지만, 더 짧은 거리를 달리는 훈련 등으로 몸 상태를 좋게 만들어 두어서 결전의 날 다양한 기상 조건 하에서도 무사히 마라톤을 달려낼 컨디션을 갖추게 된다고 언급하고 있다. 이를 근거로 볼 때, 밑줄 친 부분에서 재난 훈련이 '마라톤 준비'와 비슷하다고 언급한 것은 훈련이 재난을 그대로 재현하기보다는 혹시라도 있을 재난에 우리가 대비하도록 잠재력을 키워주는 과정과 같다는 의미로 이해할 수 있다. 따라서 밑줄 친 부분이 의미하는 바로 가장 적절한 것은 ① '실제 재난에 대응할 수 있는 잠재력을 기르기'이다.

- precisely ⓐⓓ 정확히
- disaster ⓝ 재난, 재해
- preparation ⓝ 대비, 준비
- stage ⓥ 기획하다, 조직하다
- get into shape 건강을 유지하다
- endurance ⓝ 지구력, 인내
- optimal ⓐ 최적의
- predetermined ⓐ 미리 설정된

구문 풀이

1행 The known fact of contingencies, without knowing precisely what those
　　　　　　　주어　　　　　　　　　　　　 ~하지 않은 채　　　 의문사(무엇이)
contingencies will be, shows that disaster preparation is not the same thing as
　　　　　　　　　　　 동사(단수) 접속사(~것)
disaster rehearsal.

---

22 지구와 생태계의 역동성　　　　　정답률 69% | 정답 ③

다음 글의 요지로 가장 적절한 것은?
① 생물 다양성이 높은 생태계가 기후 변화에 더 잘 적응한다.
② 인간의 부적절한 개입은 자연의 균형을 깨뜨린다.
✔ 자연은 정적이지 않고 역동적으로 계속 변한다.
④ 모든 생물은 적자생존의 원칙에 순응하기 마련이다.
⑤ 동식물은 상호 경쟁을 통해 생태계의 균형을 이룬다.

Fears of damaging ecosystems / are based on the sound conservationist principle / that we should aim to minimize the disruption we cause, / but there is a risk / that this principle may be confused / with the old idea of a 'balance of nature.'
생태계를 손상시키는 것에 대한 두려움은 / 건전한 환경 보호주의자 원칙을 바탕으로 하지만, / 우리가 초래하는 파괴를 최소화하는 것을 목표로 해야 한다는 / 위험이 있다. / 이 원칙이 혼동될지도 모른다는 / '자연의 균형'이라는 오래된 생각과
This supposes a perfect order of nature / that will seek to maintain itself / and that we should not change.
이것은 완벽한 자연의 질서를 전제로 한다. / 그 자체를 유지하려고 노력하는 / 우리가 바꾸어서는 안 되는
It is a romantic, not to say idyllic, notion, / but deeply misleading / because it supposes a static condition.
그것은 목가적이라고까지는 할 수 없어도 낭만적인 개념이지만 / 매우 잘못된 것이다. / 그것이 정적인 상태를 전제로 하기 때문에
Ecosystems are dynamic, / and although some may endure, apparently unchanged, / for periods that are long in comparison with the human lifespan, / they must and do change eventually.
생태계는 역동적이고, / 일부는 겉보기에는 변하지 않는 채로 지속될지 모르지만, / 인간의 수명과 비교해 보면 오랜 기간에 걸쳐 / 그것은 결국 변할 것임에 틀림없고 정말 변한다.
Species come and go, / climates change, / plant and animal communities adapt to altered circumstances, / and when examined in fine detail / such adaptation and consequent change / can be seen to be taking place constantly.

생물 종(種)들은 생겼다 사라지고 / 기후는 변하며 / 동식물 군집은 달라진 환경에 적응하고 / 아주 자세히 검토하면 / 그런 적응과 결과적인 변화는 / 항상 일어나고 있는 것으로 보일 수 있다.

The 'balance of nature' is a myth.
'자연의 균형'은 잘못된 통념이다.

Our planet is dynamic, / and so are the arrangements / by which its inhabitants live together.
지구는 역동적이고 / 방식도 그러하다. / 지구의 서식자들이 함께 살아가는

생태계를 손상시키는 것에 대한 두려움은 우리가 초래하는 (환경) 파괴를 최소화하는 것을 목표로 해야 한다는 건전한 환경 보호주의자 원칙을 바탕으로 하지만, 이 원칙이 '자연의 균형'이라는 오래된 생각과 혼동될지도 모른다는 위험이 있다. 이것은 그 자체를 유지하려고 노력하고 우리가 바꾸어서는 안 되는 완벽한 자연의 질서를 전제로 한다. 그것은 목가적이라고까지는 할 수 없어도 낭만적인 개념이지만 정적인 상태를 전제로 하기 때문에 매우 잘못된 것이다. 생태계는 역동적이고, 일부는 겉보기에는 변하지 않는 채로 인간의 수명과 비교해 보면 오랜 기간에 걸쳐 지속될지 모르지만, 그것은 결국 변할 것임에 틀림없고 정말 변한다. 생물 종(種)들은 생겼다 사라지고, 기후는 변하며, 동식물 군집은 달라진 환경에 적응하고, 아주 자세히 검토하면 그런 적응과 결과적인 변화는 항상 일어나고 있는 것으로 보일 수 있다. '자연의 균형'은 잘못된 통념이다. 지구는 역동적이고 지구의 서식자들이 함께 살아가는 방식도 그러하다.

Why? **왜 정답일까?**

'Ecosystems are dynamic, and ~, they must and do change eventually.'와 'Our planet is dynamic, and so are the arrangements by which its inhabitants live together.'에서 우리 지구는 역동적이며 지구의 생물이 살아가는 방식 또한 계속 변한다고 언급하는 것으로 보아, 글의 요지로 가장 적절한 것은 ③ '자연은 정적이지 않고 역동적으로 계속 변한다.'이다.

- sound ⓐ 건전한
- principle ⓝ 원칙, 원리
- disruption ⓝ 파괴, 붕괴
- static ⓐ 정적인
- in comparison with ~에 비해서
- alter ⓥ 변화시키다, 바꾸다
- examine ⓥ 검토하다
- inhabitant ⓝ 정착 주민, 서식자, 원주민
- conservationist ⓝ 환경 보호 활동가
- minimize ⓥ 최소화하다
- misleading ⓐ 오도하는, 잘못된
- apparently ⓐⓓ 겉보기에
- lifespan ⓝ 수명
- circumstances ⓝ 환경, 상황
- fine ⓐ 미세한

구문 풀이

1행 Fears of damaging ecosystems are based on the sound conservationist principle {that we should aim to minimize the disruption [we cause]}, but there is a risk {that this principle may be confused with the old idea of a 'balance of nature}.'
동격 유도 추상명사1
~하는 것을 목표로 하다
동격 유도 추상명사2
~와 혼동하다
{ }: 동격절

---

23 근대 이전에 예술가의 창작 행위에 관한 생각 정답률 53% | 정답 ④

다음 글의 주제로 가장 적절한 것은?

① conflicting views on the role of artists – 예술가의 역할에 관한 상충하는 견해들
② positive effects of imitation on creativity – 모방이 창의성에 미치는 긍정적 영향
③ contribution of art to sharing religious beliefs – 종교적 믿음을 공유하는 것에 대한 예술의 기여
✔ gods as a source of creativity in the pre-modern era – 전근대적인 시대에 창의성의 원천이었던 신
⑤ collaboration between philosophy and art in ancient times – 고대 철학과 예술 간의 협력

Before the modern scientific era, / creativity was attributed to a superhuman force; / all novel ideas originated with the gods.
근대의 과학적인 시대 이전에 / 창의성은 초인적인 힘에 기인한 것으로 여겨졌는데 / 모든 새로운 생각은 신에게서 유래했다.

After all, / how could a person create something / that did not exist before the divine act of creation?
결국 / 무언가를 인간이 어떻게 만들 수 있었겠는가? / 신의 창조 행위 이전에 존재하지 않았던

In fact, / the Latin meaning of the verb "inspire" / is "to breathe into," / reflecting the belief / that creative inspiration was similar to the moment in creation / when God first breathed life into man.
사실, / '영감을 주다'라는 동사의 라틴어 의미는 / '숨결을 불어넣다'인데 / 믿음을 반영한다. / 창의적 영감은 창조의 순간과 비슷했다는 / 신이 처음에 인간에게 생명을 불어 넣었을 때

Plato argued / that the poet was possessed by divine inspiration, / and Plotin wrote / that art could only be beautiful / if it descended from God.
플라톤은 주장했고 / 시인은 신이 내린 영감에 사로잡혔다고 / 플로티노스는 썼다. / 예술은 아름다울 수 있다고 / 그것이 신으로부터 내려온 경우에만

The artist's job was not to imitate nature / but rather to reveal the sacred and transcendent qualities of nature.
예술가의 일은 자연을 모방하는 것이라기보다는 / 오히려 자연의 신성함과 초월적인 특성을 드러내는 것이었다.

Art could only be a pale imitation / of the perfection of the world of ideas.
예술은 어설픈 흉내에 불과한 것일 수 있었다. / 관념의 세계의 완벽함

Greek artists did not blindly imitate / what they saw in reality; / instead they tried to represent the pure, true forms underlying reality, / resulting in a sort of compromise / between abstraction and accuracy.
그리스의 예술가들은 맹목적으로 모방하지 않았고 / 그들이 현실에서 본 것을 / 그 대신 현실의 근저에 있는 순수하고 진정한 형태를 나타내려고 애썼는데 / 그 결과 일종의 타협을 발생시켰다 / 추상과 정확성 간의

근대의 과학적인 시대 이전에 창의성은 초인적인 힘에 기인한 것으로 여겨졌는데, 모든 새로운 생각은 신에게서 유래했다. 결국 신의 창조 행위 이전에 존재하지 않았던 무언가를 인간이 어떻게 만들 수 있었겠는가? 사실, '영감을 주다'라는 동사의 라틴어의 의미는 '숨결을 불어넣다'인데, 이것은 창의적 영감은 신이 처음에 인간에게 생명을 불어 넣었을 때 창조의 순간과 비슷했다는 믿음을 반영한다. 플라톤은 시인은 신이 내린 영감에 사로잡혔다고 주장했고 플로티노스는 예술은 신으로부터 내려온 경우에만 아름다울 수 있다고 썼다. 예술가의 일은 자연을 모방하는 것이라기보다는 오히려 자연의 신성하고 초월적인 특성을 드러내는 것이었다. 예술은 관념(이데아)의 세계의 완벽함을 어설프게 흉내 낸 것에 불과한 것일 수 있었다. 그리스의 예술가들은 그들이 현실에서 본 것을 맹목적으로 모방하지 않았고 그 대신 현실의 근저에 있는 순수하고 진정한 형태를 나타내려고 애썼는데 그 결과 추상과 정확성 간의 일종의 타협을 발생시켰다.

Why? **왜 정답일까?**

'Before the modern scientific era, creativity was attributed to a superhuman force; all novel ideas originated with the gods.'에서 근대 과학 이전에 창의성은 초인적인 힘, 즉 신에게서 기원한다고 여겨졌다는 핵심 내용이 제시되는 것으로 보아, 글의 주제로 가장 적절한 것은 ④ '전근대적인 시대에 창의성의 원천이었던 신'이다.

- attribute A to B A를 B의 탓으로 돌리다
- divine ⓐ 성스러운
- descend ⓥ 내려오다
- represent ⓥ 나타내다, 표현하다
- abstraction ⓝ 추상
- conflicting ⓐ 상충하는
- collaboration ⓝ 협력
- novel ⓐ 새로운, 창의적인
- possess ⓥ 사로잡다, 지니다
- imitate ⓥ 모방하다
- compromise ⓝ 타협
- accuracy ⓝ 정확성
- contribution ⓝ 기여, 이바지

구문 풀이

4행 In fact, the Latin meaning of the verb "inspire" is "to breathe into," reflecting the belief {that creative inspiration was similar to the moment in creation [when God first breathed life into man]}.
주어 동사(단수) 주격 보어 분사구문
시간 선행사 관계부사
{ }: 동격절(= the belief)

---

24 미개척 영역에 대한 탐구의 중요성 정답률 71% | 정답 ①

다음 글의 제목으로 가장 적절한 것은?

✔ Researchers, Don't Be Afraid to Be Wrong
연구자여, 틀리는 것을 두려워 말라
② Hypotheses Are Different from Wild Guesses
가설은 터무니없는 추측과 다르다
③ Why Researchers Are Reluctant to Share Their Data
연구자가 데이터를 공유하기 주저하는 이유
④ One Small Mistake Can Ruin Your Whole Research
하나의 작은 실수가 여러분의 연구 전체를 망칠 수 있다
⑤ Why Hard Facts Don't Change Our Minds
확실한 사실이 우리의 생각을 바꾸지 않는 이유

Some beginning researchers mistakenly believe / that a good hypothesis is one / that is guaranteed to be right / (e.g., *alcohol will slow down reaction time*).
일부 처음 시작하는 연구자들은 잘못 믿는다. / 좋은 가설은 가설이라고 / 옳다는 것이 보장된 (예를 들면, 알코올은 반응 시간을 둔화시킬 것이다)

However, / if we already know / your hypothesis is true / before you test it, / testing your hypothesis won't tell us anything new.
하지만 / 이미 우리가 알고 있다면 / 여러분의 가설이 사실이라고 / 여러분이 그것을 검사해 보기 전에 / 여러분의 가설을 검사하는 것은 우리에게 아무런 새로운 것도 말해 주지 않을 것이다.

Remember, research is supposed to produce *new* knowledge.
연구란 새로운 지식을 생산해야 한다는 것을 기억하라.

To get new knowledge, / you, as a researcher-explorer, / need to leave the safety of the shore (established facts) / and venture into uncharted waters / (as Einstein said, / "If we knew what we were doing, / it would not be called research, would it?").
새로운 지식을 얻기 위해서 / 연구자이자 탐험가로서 여러분은 / 해변의 안전함(기정사실)을 떠나 미개척 영역으로 과감히 들어가 볼 필요가 있다 / (아인슈타인이 말했듯이, / "우리가 무엇을 하고 있는지 안다면 / 그것은 연구라고 불리지 않을 것이다, 그렇지 않은가?").

If your predictions about what will happen in these uncharted waters / are wrong, / that's okay:
이런 미개척 영역에서 무엇이 일어날 것인지에 관한 여러분의 예측이 / 틀린다면 / 그것은 괜찮다:

Scientists are allowed to make mistakes / (as Bates said, / "Research is the process of going up alleys / to see if they are blind")
과학자는 실수를 하는 것이 허용되어 있다. / (Bates가 말했듯이, / "연구는 골목길을 올라가 보는 과정이다. / 그 길이 막다른 길인지 보려고")

Indeed, / scientists often learn more from predictions / that do not turn out / than from those that do.
정말로 / 과학자는 흔히 예측들로부터 더 많이 배운다. / 결과를 내지 않는 / 결과를 내는 예측들보다는

일부 처음 시작하는 연구자들은 좋은 가설은 옳다는 것이 보장된 것(예를 들면, 알코올은 반응 시간을 둔화시킬 것이다.)이라고 잘못 믿는다. 하지만 여러분의 가설을 여러분이 검사해 보기 전에 그것이 사실이라고 이미 우리가 알고 있다면 여러분의 가설을 검사하는 것은 우리에게 아무런 새로운 것도 말해 주지 않을 것이다. 연구란 새로운 지식을 생산해야 한다는 것을 기억하라. 새로운 지식을 얻기 위해서 연구자이자 탐험가로서 여러분은 해변의 안전함(기정사실)을 떠나 미개척 영역으로 과감히 들어가 볼 필요가 있다(아인슈타인이 말했듯이, "우리가 무엇을 하고 있는지 안다면 그것은 연구라고 불리지 않을 것이다, 그렇지 않은가?"). 이런 미개척 영역에서 무엇이 일어날 것인지에 관한 여러분의 예측이 틀린다면 그것은 괜찮다. 과학자는 실수를 하는 것이 허용된다(Bates가 말했듯이, "연구는 막다른 길인지 보려고 골목길을 올라가 보는 과정이다."). 정말로 과학자는 흔히 결과를 내는 예측들보다는 결과를 내지 않는 예측들로부터 더 많이 배운다.

Why? **왜 정답일까?**

'To get new knowledge, you, as a researcher-explorer, need to leave the safety of the shore ~'에서 과학자들은 새로운 지식을 얻기 위해서는 기정사실, 즉 이미 사실로 밝혀진 것들의 영역을 넘어 아직 개척되지 않은 영역으로 들어가 볼 필요가 있다고 언급한다. 이어서 마지막 문장에서는 과학자들이 결과를 실제로 내지 못한 예측이나 가정을 통해 도리어 더 많이 배운다는 언급을 통해 '틀리는 것'을 두려워할 필요가 없다는 내용을 시사한다. 따라서 글의 제목으로 가장 적절한 것은 ① '연구자여, 틀리는 것을 두려워 말라'이다.

- mistakenly ⓐⓓ 잘못, 실수하여
- guarantee ⓥ 보장하다
- established ⓐ 확립된, 공고한
- prediction ⓝ 예측
- hard facts 확실한 정보, 엄격한 사실
- hypothesis ⓝ 가설
- be supposed to ~하기로 되어 있다
- venture into ~에 발을 들여놓다, ~을 탐험하다
- reluctant ⓐ 마지못해 하는, 꺼리는

구문 풀이

6행 To get new knowledge, you, (as a researcher-explorer), need to leave the safety of the shore (established facts) and (need to) venture into uncharted waters (as Einstein said, "If we knew what we were doing, it would not be called research, would it?").
목적(~하기 위해) 주어 ( ): 삽입구 동사구1
동사구2
접속사(~듯이/~대로) 'if + 주어 + 과거 동사 ~.
주어 + 조동사 과거형 + 동사원형':
가정법 과거(현재 사실의 반대 가정)

[문제편 p.032]

[04회] 2021학년도 3월 **035**

04회

다음 도표의 내용과 일치하지 <u>않는</u> 것은?

Average Class Size in Primary Education

■ 2005　■ 2017

The above graph shows the average class size / in primary education of five countries / in 2005 and 2017.
위 그래프는 평균 학급 크기를 보여 준다. / 다섯 나라의 초등 교육에서 / 2005년과 2017년에

① In every country except the UK, / the average class size in 2017 / decreased compared to that in 2005.
영국을 제외한 모든 나라에서 / 2017년의 평균 학급 크기는 / 2005년의 그것과 비교하면 줄었다.

② In 2005, / Korea's average class size was the largest of all the countries, / with more than 30 students in a class.
2005년에 / 한국의 평균 학급 크기는 그 모든 나라 중에서 가장 컸는데, / 학급에 서른 명이 넘는 학생이 있었다.

✔ In 2017, however, / Chile's average class size was the largest of all the countries, / with fewer than 30 students in a class.
그런데 2017년에는 / 칠레의 평균 학급 크기가 모든 나라 중에서 가장 컸는데, / 학급에 서른 명이 안 되는 학생이 있었다.

④ In 2005, / the average class size in Brazil was larger than that in the UK, / whereas the reverse was true in 2017.
2005년에 / 브라질의 평균 학급 크기는 영국의 그것보다 더 컸지만, / 2017년에는 그 반대였다.

⑤ In Greece, / the average class size was fewer than 20 students in a class / in both 2005 and 2017.
그리스에서 / 평균 학급 크기는 학급에 스무 명이 안 되는 학생이 있었다. / 2005년과 2017년 두 해 모두

위 그래프는 2005년과 2017년에 다섯 나라의 초등 교육에서 평균 학급 크기를 보여 준다. ① 영국을 제외한 모든 나라에서 2017년의 평균 학급 크기는 2005년과 비교하면 줄었다. ② 2005년에 한국의 평균 학급 크기는 그 모든 나라 중에서 가장 컸는데, 학급에 서른 명이 넘는 학생이 있었다. ③ 그런데 2017년에는 칠레의 평균 학급 크기가 모든 나라 중에서 가장 컸는데, 학급에 서른 명이 안 되는 학생이 있었다. ④ 2005년에 브라질의 평균 학급 크기는 영국보다 더 컸지만, 2017년에는 그 반대였다. ⑤ 그리스에서 평균 학급 크기는 2005년과 2017년 두 해 모두 학급에 스무 명이 안 되는 학생이 있었다.

Why? 왜 정답일까?

도표에 따르면 2017년 칠레의 평균 학급 크기는 30명을 약간 웃돌아 다섯 나라 중 제일 컸다. 따라서 도표와 일치하지 않는 것은 칠레의 평균 학급 크기가 30명을 넘지 못했다고 언급한 ③이다.

- primary education 초등 교육
- reverse ⓝ 역, 반대 @ 거꾸로의
- compared to ~와 비교해서

구문 풀이

8행　In 2005, the average class size in Brazil was larger than that in the UK,
　　　　　　　　　　　　　　　　　[비교급+than : ~보다 더 —한/하게]　　대명사(= class size)
whereas the reverse was true in 2017.
접속사(~한 반면에)

Grey County 2021 Job Fair에 관한 다음 안내문의 내용과 일치하는 것은?

① 행사 진행 시간은 6시간이다.
② 작년보다 더 좁은 장소에서 열린다.
③ 등록 마감일은 4월 28일이다.
④ 가로세로 각각 10m인 부스가 제공된다.
✔ 고용주 전용 라운지와 다과가 제공된다.

Grey County 2021 Job Fair
Grey County 2021 채용 박람회

「April 28, 2:00 p.m. – 6:00 p.m.」 ①의근거 불일치
4월 28일 오후 2시 ~ 오후 6시

Bayshore Community Center
Bayshore 커뮤니티 센터

Businesses across Grey County / can now register for a booth at the 2021 Job Fair.
Grey County 전역의 사업체들은 / 지금 2021 채용 박람회에 부스를 신청 등록할 수 있습니다.

Last year's was the largest ever held in this area / with more than 80 employers and over 1,000 job seekers.
작년의 채용 박람회는 지금껏 이 지역에서 열린 가장 큰 행사였고 / 80명이 넘는 고용주와 1천 명이 넘는 구직자가 참가했습니다.

「This year, / we're moving to an even larger location / with plenty of space for all attendees.」 ②의근거 불일치
올해 / 저희는 훨씬 더 넓은 장소로 옮길 겁니다. / 모든 참가자를 위한 충분한 공간이 있는

Registration Fee: $80
등록비: 80달러

「Registration Deadline: April 14, 6:00 p.m.」 ③의근거 불일치
등록 마감 일시: 4월 14일 오후 6시

Enhanced Services to Employers
고용주들에게 더 나아진 서비스

「5 m × 5 m booth」 ④의근거 불일치
5미터×5미터 부스

Free wifi
무료 와이파이

「Employer-only lounge and refreshments」 ⑤의근거 일치
고용주 전용 라운지와 다과

For more information, visit www.greycountyjobfair.org.
더 많은 정보를 원하시면 www.greycountyjobfair.org를 방문하세요.

Grey County 2021 채용 박람회

4월 28일 오후 2시 ~ 오후 6시
Bayshore 커뮤니티 센터

Grey County 전역의 사업체들은 지금 2021 채용 박람회에 부스를 신청할 수 있습니다. 작년의 채용 박람회는 지금껏 이 지역에서 열린 가장 큰 행사였고 80명이 넘는 고용주와 1천 명이 넘는 구직자가 참가했습니다. 올해 저희는 모든 참가자를 위한 충분한 공간이 있는 훨씬 더 넓은 장소로 옮길 겁니다.

– 등록비: 80달러
– 등록 마감 일시: 4월 14일 오후 6시

고용주들에게 더 나아진 서비스

- 5미터×5미터 부스
- 무료 와이파이
- 고용주 전용 라운지와 다과

더 많은 정보를 원하시면 www.greycountyjobfair.org를 방문하세요.

Why? 왜 정답일까?

'Employer-only lounge and refreshments'에서 고용주 전용 라운지와 다과가 서비스로 제공된다고 하므로, 안내문의 내용과 일치하는 것은 ⑤ '고용주 전용 라운지와 다과가 제공된다.'이다.

Why? 왜 오답일까?

① 'April 28, 2:00 p.m. – 6:00 p.m.'에서 행사 진행 시간은 4시간임을 알 수 있다.
② 'This year, we're moving to an even larger location with plenty of space for all attendees.'에서 올해 행사는 작년보다 더 큰 곳으로 옮겨 진행된다고 하였다.
③ 'Registration Deadline: April 14, 6:00 p.m.'에서 등록 마감일은 4월 14일이라고 하였다. 4월 28일은 행사 개최일이다.
④ '5m×5m booth'에서 부스의 가로세로 크기는 각각 5미터라고 하였다.

- register for ~에 등록하다
- plenty of 충분히 큰, 많은
- enhance ⓥ 향상시키다
- job seeker 구직자
- attendee ⓝ 참가자
- refreshment ⓝ 다과

The Riverside Escape에 관한 다음 안내문의 내용과 일치하지 <u>않는</u> 것은?

① 도시 전역에서 벌어지는 탈출 게임이다.
② 최대 여섯 명으로 구성된 팀당 티켓 한 장을 사야 한다.
✔ 선택한 게임 시작일 이전에 전화로 상세한 정보를 알려 준다.
④ 2021년 3월 1일부터 세 달간 열린다.
⑤ 티켓 가격은 매일 달라질 수 있다.

The Riverside Escape
Riverside 탈출

「The Riverside Escape is a city-wide escape game / played on your smartphone.」 ①의근거 일치
Riverside 탈출은 도시 전역에서 벌어지는 탈출 게임입니다. / 여러분의 스마트폰으로 하는

We turn the city of Riverside into a giant escape game / wherein teams must race around the city / completing challenges without getting caught.
우리는 Riverside 도시를 거대한 탈출 게임의 장소로 바꾸고 / 거기서 팀들은 도시 이곳저곳을 질주해야 합니다. / 붙잡히지 않고 도전 과제를 완수하면서

How to Play
게임 방법

「Get your ticket / — one ticket per team of up to 6 players.」 ②의근거 일치
티켓을 구입하세요 / 최대 여섯 명의 선수로 구성된 팀당 티켓 한 장입니다.

Choose the start date for the game.
게임 시작 날짜를 선택하세요.

「We will send you detailed information via email / before your date of choice.」 ③의근거 불일치
이메일로 상세한 정보를 여러분에게 보내 드릴 겁니다. / 여러분이 고른 날짜 이전에

Arrive at the start location / and start anytime you want on the day.
시작 장소에 도착해서 / 그날 여러분이 원하는 아무때나 시작하세요.

Score as many points as possible / by answering the puzzles / while moving around the city.
가능한 한 많은 점수를 얻으세요. / 수수께끼에 응답하여서 / 도시를 이곳저곳 돌아다니는 동안

Opening Times
운영 시간

「March 1, 2021 – May 31, 2021」 ④의근거 일치
2021년 3월 1일 ~ 2021년 5월 31일

Monday – Sunday, 10:00 – 20:00
월요일 ~ 일요일, 10시~20시

Ticket Price
티켓 가격

「$50 per ticket / (This price may change on a daily basis.)」 ⑤의근거 일치
티켓당 50달러 / (이 가격은 매일 달라질 수 있습니다.)

Come join us for an escape adventure!
탈출 모험에 와서 저희와 함께 하세요!

Riverside 탈출

Riverside 탈출은 여러분의 스마트폰으로 하는 도시 전역에서 벌어지는 탈출 게임입니다. 우리는 Riverside 도시를 거대한 탈출 게임의 장소로 바꾸고 거기서 팀들은 붙잡히지 않고 도전 과제를 완수하면서 도시 이곳저곳을 질주해야 합니다.

게임 방법

- 티켓을 구입하세요 — 최대 여섯 명의 선수로 구성된 팀당 티켓 한 장입니다.
- 게임 시작 날짜를 선택하세요. 여러분이 고른 날짜 이전에 이메일로 상세한 정보를 여러분에게 보내 드릴 겁니다.
- 시작 장소에 도착해서 그날 여러분이 원하는 아무때나 시작하세요.
- 도시를 이곳저곳 돌아다니는 동안 수수께끼에 응답하여서 가능한 한 많은 점수를 얻으세요.

운영 시간
2021년 3월 1일 ~ 2021년 5월 31일
월요일 ~ 일요일, 10시 ~ 20시

티켓 가격
티켓당 50달러(이 가격은 매일 달라질 수 있습니다.)

탈출 모험을 위해 와서 저희와 함께 하세요!

Why? 왜 정답일까?

'We will send you detailed information via email before your date of choice.'에서 플레이어들이 선택한 게임 시작일 이전에 이메일로 상세한 정보를 보내준다고 하였다. 따라서 안내문의 내용과 일치하지 않는 것은 ③ '선택한 게임 시작일 이전에 전화로 상세한 정보를 알려 준다.'이다.

Why? 왜 오답일까?

① 'The Riverside Escape is a city-wide escape game played on your smartphone.'의 내용과 일치한다.
② 'Get your ticket—one ticket per team of up to 6 players.'의 내용과 일치한다.
④ 'March 1, 2021 – May 31, 2021'의 내용과 일치한다.
⑤ '$50 per ticket (This price may change on a daily basis.)'의 내용과 일치한다.

- complete ⓥ 완수하다
- on a daily basis 매일
- up to ~까지

---

28 Ingrid Bergman의 생애 ····· 정답률 93% | 정답 ③

Ingrid Bergman에 관한 다음 글의 내용과 일치하지 않는 것은?
① 어머니는 독일인이었고 아버지는 스웨덴인이었다.
② 17세에 Royal Dramatic Theater School에 다녔다.
☑ ③ 영화를 통해 데뷔했으나 연극에 더 관심이 있었다.
④ 1940년대 초에 할리우드에서 스타의 지위를 얻었다.
⑤ 다섯 개의 언어에 유창했다.

Ingrid Bergman was born in Stockholm, Sweden / on August 29, 1915.
Ingrid Bergman은 스웨덴의 스톡홀름에서 태어났다. / 1915년 8월 29일에
「Her mother was German / and her father Swedish.」 ①의 근거 일치
어머니는 독일인이었고 / 아버지는 스웨덴인이었다.
Her mother died when she was three, / and her father passed away when she was 12.
어머니는 그녀가 세 살 때 돌아가셨고, / 아버지는 그녀가 열두 살 때 돌아가셨다.
Eventually she was brought up / by her Uncle Otto and Aunt Hulda.
결국 그녀는 키워졌다. / Otto 삼촌과 Hulda 이모에 의해
She was interested in acting from an early age.
그녀는 어릴 때부터 연기에 관심이 있었다.
「When she was 17, / she attended the Royal Dramatic Theater School in Stockholm.」 ②의 근거 일치
그녀가 열일곱 살 때 / 그녀는 스톡홀름에 있는 Royal Dramatic Theater School에 다녔다.
「She made her debut on the stage / but was more interested in working in films.」 ③의 근거 불일치
그녀는 연극으로 데뷔했지만 / 영화계에서 일하는 데 더 관심이 있었다.
「In the early 1940s, / she gained star status in Hollywood, / playing many roles as the heroine of the film.」 ④의 근거 일치
1940년대 초에 / 그녀는 할리우드에서 스타의 지위를 얻었고 / 영화의 여주인공으로 많은 역할을 맡았다.
Bergman was considered / to have tremendous acting talent, / an angelic natural beauty / and the willingness to work hard / to get the best out of films.
Bergman은 여겨졌다. / 굉장한 연기 재능을 가진 것으로 / 천사 같은 자연미가 / 그리고 기꺼이 열심히 일하려는 태도를 / 영화에서 최상의 것을 얻으려고
「She was fluent in five languages / and appeared in a range of films, plays and TV productions.」 ⑤의 근거 일치
그녀는 다섯 개의 언어에 유창했고 / 다양한 영화, 연극, 그리고 TV 작품에 출연했다.

Ingrid Bergman은 1915년 8월 29일에 스웨덴의 스톡홀름에서 태어났다. 어머니는 독일인이었고 아버지는 스웨덴인이었다. 어머니는 그녀가 세 살 때 돌아가셨고, 아버지는 그녀가 열두 살 때 돌아가셨다. 결국 그녀는 Otto 삼촌과 Hulda 이모에 의해 키워졌다. 그녀는 어릴 때부터 연기에 관심이 있었다. 그녀가 열일곱 살 때 스톡홀름에 있는 Royal Dramatic Theater School에 다녔다. 그녀는 연극으로 데뷔했지만 영화계 일에 더 관심이 있었다. 1940년대 초에 그녀는 할리우드에서 스타의 지위를 얻었고 영화의 여주인공으로 많은 역할을 맡았다. Bergman은 굉장한 연기 재능과 천사 같은 자연미와 영화에서 최상의 것을 얻으려고 기꺼이 열심히 일하려는 태도를 가진 것으로 여겨졌다. 그녀는 다섯 개의 언어에 유창했고 다양한 영화, 연극, 그리고 TV 작품에 출연했다.

Why? 왜 정답일까?

'She made her debut on the stage but was more interested in working in films.'에서 Ingrid Bergman은 연극으로 데뷔했으나 영화계 일에 더 관심이 있었다고 하므로, 내용과 일치하지 않는 것은 이를 반대로 진술한 ③ '영화를 통해 데뷔했으나 연극에 더 관심이 있었다.'이다.

Why? 왜 오답일까?

① 'Her mother was German and her father Swedish.'의 내용과 일치한다.
② 'When she was 17, she attended the Royal Dramatic Theater School in Stockholm.'의 내용과 일치한다.
④ 'In the early 1940s, she gained star status in Hollywood, ~'의 내용과 일치한다.
⑤ 'She was fluent in five languages ~'의 내용과 일치한다.

- pass away 사망하다, 돌아가시다
- make one's debut 데뷔하다
- tremendous ⓐ 엄청난, 굉장한
- bring up ~을 기르다, 양육하다
- heroine ⓝ 여주인공
- willingness ⓝ 기꺼이 ~하려는 마음

- get the best out of ~을 최대한 활용하다, ~에게 최선을 다하게 하다
- fluent ⓐ 유창한

구문 풀이

2행 Her mother was German and her father (was) Swedish.
주어1 동사1 보어1 주어2 →동사2(중복되어 생략) 보어2

★★★ 등급을 가르는 문제!

29 협력과 문제 해결을 뒷받침하는 포용성 ····· 정답률 30% | 정답 ⑤

다음 글의 밑줄 친 부분 중, 어법상 틀린 것은?

While reflecting on the needs of organizations, leaders, and families today, / we realize / that one of the unique characteristics / ① is inclusivity.
오늘날 조직, 지도자, 그리고 가족의 요구에 관해 곰곰이 생각할 때 / 우리는 깨닫는다. / 독특한 특성 중 하나가 / 포용성이라는 것을
Why? 왜 그런가?
Because inclusivity supports / ② what everyone ultimately wants from their relationships: / collaboration.
포용성은 뒷받침하기 때문이다. / 모든 사람이 자신의 관계에서 궁극적으로 원하는 것인 / 협력을
Yet / the majority of leaders, organizations, and families / are still using the language of the old paradigm / in which one person — typically the oldest, most educated, and/or wealthiest — / makes all the decisions, / and their decisions rule / with little discussion or inclusion of others, / ③ resulting in exclusivity.
그러나 / 대다수의 지도자, 조직, 그리고 가정은 / 낡은 패러다임의 언어를 여전히 사용하고 있다. / 한 사람이 / 보통 가장 연장자, 가장 교육을 많이 받은 사람, 그리고/또는 가장 부유한 사람인 / 모든 결정을 내리고, / 그들의 결정이 지배하고 / 토론이나 다른 사람의 관여가 거의 없이 / 결과적으로 배타성을 초래하는
Today, / this person could be a director, CEO, or other senior leader of an organization.
오늘날 / 이 사람은 어떤 조직의 관리자, 최고 경영자, 또는 다른 상급 지도자일 수 있다.
There is no need / for others to present their ideas / because they are considered ④ inadequate.
필요가 없는데 / 다른 사람들이 자신의 생각을 제시할 / 왜냐하면 그것은 부적절한 것으로 여겨지기 때문이다.
Yet research shows / that exclusivity in problem solving, / even with a genius, / is not as effective as inclusivity, / ☑ ⑤ where everyone's ideas are heard / and a solution is developed / through collaboration.
그러나 연구에 따르면 / 문제 해결에 있어서 배타성은, / 심지어 천재와 함께하는 것이더라도, / 포용성만큼 효과적이지 않은데, / 이 경우에는 모든 사람의 생각을 듣게 되고 / 해결책은 발전된다. / 협력을 통해

오늘날 조직, 지도자, 그리고 가족의 요구에 관해 곰곰이 생각할 때 우리는 독특한 특성 중 하나가 포용성이라는 것을 깨닫는다. 왜 그런가? 포용성은 모든 사람이 자신의 관계에서 궁극적으로 원하는 것인 협력을 뒷받침하기 때문이다. 그러나 대다수의 지도자, 조직, 그리고 가정은 보통 가장 연장자, 가장 교육을 많이 받은 사람, 그리고/또는 가장 부유한 사람인 한 사람이 모든 결정을 내리고, 토론이나 다른 사람의 관여가 거의 없이 그들의 결정이 지배하고 결과적으로 배타성을 초래하는 낡은 패러다임의 언어를 여전히 사용하고 있다. 오늘날 이 사람은 어떤 조직의 관리자, 최고 경영자, 또는 다른 상급 지도자일 수 있다. 다른 사람들이 자신의 생각을 제시할 필요가 없는데 왜냐하면 그것은 부적절한 것으로 여겨지기 때문이다. 그러나 연구에 따르면 문제 해결에 있어서 배타성은, 심지어 천재와 함께하는 것이더라도, 포용성만큼 효과적이지 않은데, 포용성이 있는 경우에는 모든 사람의 생각을 듣게 되고 해결책은 협력을 통해 발전된다.

Why? 왜 정답일까?

'everyone's ideas are heard and a solution is developed ~'는 완전한 수동태 문장이므로, 불완전한 절을 수반하는 관계대명사 which 뒤에 나올 수 없다. 따라서 which를 관계부사로 바꾸어야 하는데, 여기서는 선행사 inclusivity를 공간처럼 취급하여 which 대신 where를 써야 한다. 어법상 틀린 것은 ⑤이다.

Why? 왜 오답일까?

① 'one of the+복수 명사'가 that절의 주어이므로 뒤따르는 동사가 단수형인 is로 바르게 쓰였다.
② 앞에 선행사가 없고, 뒤따르는 'everyone ultimately wants'는 동사의 목적어가 빠진 불완전한 문장이다. 따라서 선행사가 없는 맥락에서 선행사의 역할을 대신하며 불완전한 관계절을 수반하는 what이 바르게 쓰였다.
③ 현재분사 resulting이 전치사 in과 짝을 이루어 '(결과적으로) ~을 초래하는'이라는 의미를 나타내며 뒤에 목적어 exclusivity를 수반한 구조로 바르게 쓰였다.
④ 5형식 동사 consider는 주로 명사 또는 형용사 보어를 수반하는데, 특히 형용사 보어가 쓰인 'consider+명+형'을 수동태로 바꾸면 '명+be considered+형'이 된다. 따라서 are considered라는 수동태 뒤에 형용사 inadequate가 바르게 쓰였다.

- reflect on ~에 대해 곰곰이 생각하다
- inclusivity ⓝ 포용성
- collaboration ⓝ 협력
- typically ⓐⓓ 보통, 대개
- wealthy ⓐ 부유한
- exclusivity ⓝ 배타성
- genius ⓝ 천재
- characteristic ⓝ 특성
- ultimately ⓐⓓ 궁극적으로
- majority ⓝ 대다수
- educated ⓐ 교육을 받은, 교양 있는
- rule ⓥ 지배하다, 통치하다
- inadequate ⓐ 부적절한

구문 풀이

12행 Yet research shows that exclusivity in problem solving, even with a genius,
접속사(~것) 주어
is not as effective as inclusivity, where everyone's ideas are heard and a solution
동사 선행사 관계부사 주어1 동사1
is developed through collaboration.
동사2

★★ 문제 해결 꿀~팁 ★★

▶ 많이 틀린 이유는?
④ '형용사 vs. 부사'는 자주 출제되는 문법 포인트이지만, 이 문제에서는 5형식 동사 consider의 수동태를 결합시켜 난이도를 높였다. consider는 능동태로 쓸 때 뒤에 목적어와 목적격 보어를 수반하지만, 목적어를 주어로 삼아 수동태인 be considered 형태로 쓰이면 뒤에 보어만 수반한다. 이 보어 자리에는 명사 또는 형용사가 들어갈 수 있고, inadequate는 형용사이므로, ④는 어법상

바르게 쓰였다. 해석하면 '부적절하게 여겨진다'이기 때문에 부사처럼 느껴지지만, 보어 자리이기 때문에 부사인 inadequately를 써서는 안 된다는 점에 주의해야 한다.

▶ 문제 해결 방법은?
정답인 ⑤ '관계대명사 vs. 관계부사'는 가장 많이 출제되는 문법 포인트 중 하나로, 앞보다는 뒤를 보아 어법상 적절한지를 판단해야 한다. 뒤에 주어, 목적어, 보어 중 하나가 빠진 불완전한 문장이 나오면 관계대명사를, 수동태나 자동사 등이 쓰인 완전한 문장이 나오면 관계부사를 써야 한다.

---

30 객관적인 카메라 정답률 40% | 정답 ②

다음 글의 밑줄 친 부분 중, 문맥상 낱말의 쓰임이 적절하지 않은 것은? [3점]

The objective point of view / is illustrated by John Ford's "philosophy of camera."
객관적인 관점은 / John Ford의 '카메라의 철학'에 의해 설명된다.
Ford considered the camera to be a window / and the audience to be ① outside the window / viewing the people and events within.
Ford는 카메라를 창문이라고 생각했고 / 관객은 창문 밖에 있다고 생각했다. / 창문 안에 있는 사람과 사건을 바라보면서
We are asked to watch the actions / as if they were taking place at a distance, / and we are not asked to participate.
우리는 사건들을 바라보도록 요청받고, / 그것들이 멀리서 일어나고 있는 것처럼 / 우리는 참여하도록 요청받지 않는다.
The objective point of view / employs a static camera as much as possible / in order to ② produce this window effect, / and it concentrates on the actors and the action / without drawing attention to the camera.
객관적인 관점은 / 정적인 카메라를 가능한 한 많이 이용하고, / 이런 창문 효과를 만들기 위해 / 그것은 배우와 사건에 집중한다. / 카메라에 관심을 끄는 것 없이
The objective camera suggests an emotional distance / between camera and subject; / the camera seems simply to be recording, / as ③ straightforwardly as possible, / the characters and actions of the story.
객관적인 카메라는 감정적인 거리를 보여 주는데, / 카메라와 대상 간의 / 카메라는 그저 기록하고 있는 것으로 보인다. / 가능한 한 있는 그대로 / 이야기의 등장인물과 사건을
For the most part, / the director uses natural, normal types of camera positioning and camera angles.
대부분의 경우, / 감독은 자연스럽고 일반적인 종류의 카메라 위치와 카메라 각도를 사용한다.
The objective camera does not comment on or ④ interpret the action / but merely records it, / letting it unfold.
객관적인 카메라는 사건에 관해 논평하거나 해석하지 않고 / 그저 그것을 기록한다. / 그것이 전개되게 하면서
We see the action / from the viewpoint of an impersonal observer.
우리는 사건을 본다. / 냉담한 관찰자의 관점에서
If the camera moves, / it does so unnoticeably, / calling as ⑤ little attention to itself as possible.
만약 카메라가 움직인다면 / 그것은 눈에 띄지 않게 그렇게 한다. / 가능한 한 카메라 자체에 관심을 불러일으키는 일이 거의 없이

객관적인 관점은 John Ford의 '카메라의 철학'에 의해 설명된다. Ford는 카메라를 창문이라고 생각했고 관객은 창문 안쪽 사람과 사건을 바라보면서 창문 ① 밖에 있다고 생각했다. 우리는 사건들이 멀리서 일어나고 있는 것처럼 그것들을 바라보도록 요청받고, 참여하도록 요청받지 않는다. 객관적인 관점은 이런 창문 효과를 ② 피하기(→ 만들기) 위해 정적인 카메라를 가능한 한 많이 이용하고, 카메라에 관심을 끄는 것 없이 배우와 사건에 집중한다. 객관적인 카메라는 카메라와 대상 간의 감정적인 거리를 보여 주는데, 카메라는 이야기의 등장인물과 사건을 가능한 한 ③ 있는 그대로 그저 기록하고 있는 것으로 보인다. 대부분의 경우, 감독은 자연스럽고 일반적인 종류의 카메라 위치와 카메라 각도를 사용한다. 객관적인 카메라는 사건에 관해 논평하거나 ④ 해석하지 않고 그것이 전개되게 하면서 그저 그것을 기록한다. 우리는 냉담한 관찰자의 관점에서 사건을 본다. 만약 카메라가 움직인다면 그것은 눈에 띄지 않게, 가능한 한 카메라 자체에 관심을 불러일으키는 일이 ⑤ 거의 없이 그렇게 한다.

Why? 왜 정답일까?

'~ it concentrates on the actors and the action without drawing attention to the camera.'와 'We see the action from the viewpoint of an impersonal observer.'에서 객관적인 카메라는 우리가 카메라 자체에 관심을 두지 않은 채 관찰자의 시점에서 사건을 바라보도록 도와준다고 한다. 이를 근거로 볼 때, 객관적 카메라는 첫 두 문장에서 언급한 카메라의 '창문 효과'를 피하지 않고 적절히 이용하여 관객이 인물과 사건으로부터 거리를 두게 해 준다는 것을 알 수 있다. 따라서 ②의 avoid를 produce로 고쳐야 한다. 문맥상 낱말의 쓰임이 적절하지 않은 것은 ②이다.

- objective ⓐ 객관적인
- philosophy ⓝ 철학
- static ⓐ 정적인
- draw attention to ~에 관심을 끌다
- straightforwardly ⓐⓓ 단도직입적으로, 있는 그대로
- comment on ~에 대해 논평하다
- unfold ⓥ 펼쳐지다, 펴다
- unnoticeably ⓐⓓ 눈에 띄지 않게
- illustrate ⓥ (예를 들어) 보여주다, 자세히 설명하다
- at a distance 멀리 떨어져서
- concentrate on ~에 집중하다
- interpret ⓥ 해석하다
- impersonal ⓐ 냉담한

구문 풀이

4행 We are asked to watch the actions as if they were taking place at a distance, and we are not asked to participate.
「be asked +to부정사 : ~하도록 요청받다」 「as if + 주어 + 과거 동사 : 마치 (현재 ~하지 않는데) ~한 것처럼」

---

31 사냥의 역사를 지니고 있는 음악 정답률 57% | 정답 ①

다음 빈칸에 들어갈 말로 가장 적절한 것을 고르시오.
① hunt - 사냥 ② law - 법 ③ charity - 자선 (행위)
④ remedy - 치료법 ⑤ dance - 춤

Even the most respectable of all musical institutions, / the symphony orchestra, / carries inside its DNA the legacy of the hunt.
심지어 모든 음악 단체 중 가장 훌륭한 단체인, / 교향악단도 / 자신의 DNA 안에 사냥의 유산을 지니고 있다.
The various instruments in the orchestra / can be traced back to these primitive origins /

— their earliest forms were made / either from the animal (horn, hide, gut, bone) / or the weapons employed in bringing the animal under control (stick, bow).
교향악단에 있는 다양한 악기들은 / 다음의 원시적인 기원으로 거슬러 올라갈 수 있는데, / 그것들의 초기 형태는 만들어졌다. / 동물(뿔, 가죽, 내장, 뼈) / 또는 동물을 진압하기 위해 사용된 무기(막대, 활)로
Are we wrong to hear this history in the music itself, / in the formidable aggression and awe-inspiring assertiveness of those monumental symphonies / that remain the core repertoire of the world's leading orchestras?
음악 그 자체에서 이러한 역사를 듣는다면 우리가 틀린 것인가? / 기념비적인 교향곡들의 강력한 공격성과 경외감을 자아내는 당당함에서 / 세계의 주요한 교향악단의 핵심 레퍼토리로 남아 있는
Listening to Beethoven, Brahms, Mahler, Bruckner, Berlioz, Tchaikovsky, Shostakovich, and other great composers, / I can easily summon up images of bands of men / starting to chase animals, / using sound as a source and symbol of dominance, / an expression of the will to predatory power.
베토벤, 브람스, 말러, 브루크너, 베를리오즈, 차이코프스키, 쇼스타코비치 및 다른 위대한 작곡가들의 음악을 들으며, / 나는 사람들 무리의 이미지를 쉽게 떠올릴 수 있다. / 동물을 쫓기 시작하는 / 소리를 지배의 원천이자 상징으로 사용하면서 / 공격적인 힘에 대한 의지의 표현으로

심지어 모든 음악 단체 중 가장 훌륭한 단체인 교향악단도 자신의 DNA 안에 사냥의 유산을 지니고 있다. 교향악단에 있는 다양한 악기들은 다음의 원시적인 기원으로 거슬러 올라갈 수 있는데, 그것들의 초기 형태는 동물(뿔, 가죽, 내장, 뼈) 또는 동물을 진압하기 위해 사용된 무기(막대, 활)로 만들어졌다. 음악 그 자체에서, 세계의 주요한 교향악단의 핵심 레퍼토리로 남아 있는 기념비적인 교향곡들의 강력한 공격성과 경외감을 자아내는 당당함에서 이러한 역사를 듣는다면 우리가 틀린 것인가? 베토벤, 브람스, 말러, 브루크너, 베를리오즈, 차이코프스키, 쇼스타코비치 및 다른 위대한 작곡가들의 음악을 들으며, 나는 소리를 지배의 원천이자 상징으로, 공격적인 힘에 대한 의지의 표현으로 사용하면서 동물을 쫓기 시작하는 사람들 무리의 이미지를 쉽게 떠올릴 수 있다.

Why? 왜 정답일까?

두 번째 문장에서 초기 악기는 동물의 신체 부위로 만들어지거나 동물을 진압하기 위한 무기(either from the animal ~ or the weapons employed in bringing the animal under control)에서 기원했다고 설명한다. 마지막 문장에서는 유명한 음악가의 음악을 들으면 과거 조상들이 소리로 공격의 의지를 표현하면서 동물들을 사냥하던 모습을 상상할 수 있다고 언급한다. 따라서 빈칸에 들어갈 말로 가장 적절한 것은 ① '사냥'이다.

- respectable ⓐ 훌륭한, 존경할 만한
- trace back to ~으로 거슬러 올라가다
- hide ⓝ (동물의) 가죽
- awe-inspiring ⓐ 경외감을 불러일으키는, 장엄한
- monumental ⓐ 기념비적인, 엄청난
- predatory ⓐ 포식하는, 생물을 잡아먹는
- institution ⓝ 기관, 제도
- primitive ⓐ 원시적인
- aggression ⓝ 공격성
- assertiveness ⓝ 적극성, 자기 주장
- summon up (생각, 기억 등을) 불러일으키다

구문 풀이

10행 Listening to Beethoven, Brahms, Mahler, Bruckner, Berlioz, Tchaikovsky, Shostakovich, and other great composers, I can easily summon up images of bands of men starting to chase animals, using sound as a source and symbol of dominance, an expression of the will to predatory power.
분사구문(~하면서) / 동사구 / 목적어 / 꾸밈 받는 명사 / 현재분사 / 분사구문(~하면서) / 전치사(~로서)

★★★ 등급을 가르는 문제!

32 새롭고 예기치 못한 사건과 정보를 잘 기억하는 뇌 정답률 32% | 정답 ④

다음 빈칸에 들어갈 말로 가장 적절한 것을 고르시오.
① Awareness of social responsibility - 사회적 책임에 대한 인식
② Memorization of historical facts - 역사적 사실의 암기
③ Competition with rivals - 라이벌과의 경쟁
④ Preference for novelty - 새로움에 대한 선호
⑤ Fear of failure - 실패에 대한 두려움

Our brains have evolved to remember unexpected events / because basic survival depends on the ability / to perceive causes and predict effects.
우리의 뇌는 예상치 못한 사건들을 기억하도록 진화해 왔는데, / 왜냐하면 기본적인 생존이 능력에 달려 있기 때문이다. / 원인을 인식하고 결과를 예측하는
If the brain predicts one event and experiences another, / the unusualness will be especially interesting / and will be encoded accordingly.
만약 뇌가 어떤 사건을 예측하고 다른 사건을 경험한다면, / 그 특이함은 특히 흥미로울 것이고 / 그에 따라 입력될 것이다.
Neurologist and classroom teacher Judith Willis has claimed / that surprise in the classroom / is one of the most effective ways of teaching / with brain stimulation in mind.
신경학자이자 학급 교사인 Judith Willis는 주장했다. / 교실에서의 놀라움은 / 가르치는 가장 효과적인 방법 중 하나라고 / 뇌 자극을 염두에 두고
If students are exposed to new experiences / via demonstrations / or through the unexpected enthusiasm of their teachers or peers, / they will be much more likely to connect with the information that follows.
학생들이 새로운 경험에 노출된다면, / 실연을 통해 / 혹은 교사나 또래 친구의 예상치 못한 열의를 통해 / 그들은 뒤따르는 정보와 연결될 가능성이 훨씬 더 클 것이다.
Willis has written / that encouraging active discovery in the classroom / allows students to interact with new information, / moving it beyond working memory to be processed in the frontal lobe, / which is devoted to advanced cognitive functioning.
Willis는 기술했는데, / 교실에서 능동적인 발견을 장려하는 것이 / 학생들로 하여금 새로운 정보와 상호 작용하게 해 주어서, / 그것이 작업 기억을 넘어 전두엽에서 처리되도록 한다고 / 그 전두엽은 고도의 인지 기능을 전담한다.
Preference for novelty sets us up for learning / by directing attention, / providing stimulation to developing perceptual systems, / and feeding curious and exploratory behavior.
새로움에 대한 선호는 우리를 학습하도록 준비시킨다. / 주의를 이끌고, / 지각 체계를 발전시키는 데 자극을 제공하며, / 호기심 많고 탐구적인 행동을 충족함으로써

우리의 뇌는 예상치 못한 사건들을 기억하도록 진화해 왔는데, 왜냐하면 기본적인 생존이 원인을 인식하고 결과를 예측하는 능력에 달려 있기 때문이다. 만약 뇌가 어떤 사건을 예측하고 (그것과) 다른 사건을 경험한다면, 그 특이함은 특히 흥미로울 것이고 그에 따라 (뇌 속의 정보

로) 입력될 것이다. 신경학자이자 학급 교사인 Judith Willis는 교실에서의 놀라움은 뇌 자극을 염두에 두고 가르치는 가장 효과적인 방법 중 하나라고 주장했다. 학생들이 실연, 혹은 교사나 또래 친구의 예상치 못한 열의를 통해 새로운 경험에 노출되면, 그들은 뒤따르는 정보와 연결될 가능성이 훨씬 더 클 것이다. Willis는 교실에서 능동적인 발견을 장려하는 것이 학생들로 하여금 새로운 정보와 상호 작용하게 해 주어서, 그것(새로운 정보)이 작업 기억을 넘어 전두엽에서 처리되도록 한다고 기술했는데, 이 전두엽은 고도의 인지 기능을 전담한다. 새로움에 대한 선호는 주의를 이끌고, 지각 체계를 발전시키는 데 자극을 제공하며, 호기심 많고 탐구적인 행동을 충족함으로써 우리를 학습하도록 준비시킨다.

'Our brains have evolved to remember unexpected events because basic survival depends on the ability to perceive causes and predict effects.'에서 우리 뇌는 기본적인 생존을 위해 '예기치 못한' 사건을 기억하도록 진화해 왔다고 언급하는 것으로 볼 때, 빈칸에 들어갈 말로 가장 적절한 것은 ④ '새로움에 대한 선호'이다. 본문의 unexpected, unusualness, surprise, new 등이 novelty로 재진술되었다.

- **unexpected** ⓐ 예상치 못한
- **predict** ⓥ 예측하다
- **encode** ⓥ 부호화하다
- **stimulation** ⓝ 자극
- **demonstration** ⓝ (작동 과정 또는 사용법에 대한) 실연
- **enthusiasm** ⓝ 열정
- **exploratory** ⓐ 탐구적인
- **perceive** ⓥ 인지하다
- **unusualness** ⓝ 특이함
- **accordingly** ⓐⓓ 그에 따라
- **be devoted to** ~에 전념하다
- **novelty** ⓝ 새로움

구문 풀이

11행 Willis has written that encouraging active discovery in the classroom
접속사(~것) 동명사구 주어
allows students to interact with new information, moving it beyond working
「allow + 목적어 + to부정사 : ~이 …하게 해주다」 분사구문(그리고 ~하다)
memory to be processed in the frontal lobe, which is devoted to advanced
선행사 관·대 계속적 용법
cognitive functioning.

★★ 문제 해결 꿀~팁 ★★

▶ 많이 틀린 이유는?
뇌는 새롭고 예기치 못한 사건이나 정보를 더 잘 기억한다는 내용의 글이다. 역사적 사실을 단순 암기하는 것에 관해서는 언급되지 않으므로 ②는 답으로 부적절하다.
▶ 문제 해결 방법은?
첫 두 문장에서 주제를 제시한 뒤 연구 내용을 예시로 들고 마지막 문장에서 주제를 한 번 더 정리하고 있으므로, 글 서두의 내용과 상통하는 내용의 선택지를 답으로 골라야 한다.

★★★ 등급을 가르는 문제! ★★★

33 인간의 무의식적인 인지 과업 분담   정답률 37% | 정답 ①

다음 빈칸에 들어갈 말로 가장 적절한 것을 고르시오. [3점]
✓① divide up cognitive labor – 인지 노동을 나누는데
② try to avoid disagreements – 의견 불일치를 피하려고 노력하는데
③ seek people with similar tastes – 비슷한 취향을 가진 사람을 찾는데
④ like to share old wisdom – 옛 지혜를 공유하기 좋아하는데
⑤ balance work and leisure – 일과 여가의 균형을 맞추는데

Psychological research has shown / that people naturally divide up cognitive labor, / often without thinking about it.
심리학 연구는 보여준다. / 사람들은 자연스럽게 인지 노동을 나누는데, / 흔히 그것에 대해서 별 생각 없이 그렇게 한다고

Imagine you're cooking up a special dinner with a friend.
여러분이 친구와 함께 특별한 저녁식사를 요리하고 있다고 상상해 보라.

You're a great cook, / but your friend is the wine expert, an amateur sommelier.
여러분은 요리를 잘하지만, / 친구는 아마추어 소믈리에라고 할 수 있는 와인 전문가이다.

A neighbor drops by / and starts telling you both / about the terrific new wines / being sold at the liquor store just down the street.
이웃이 들르더니 / 여러분 두 사람에게 말하기 시작한다. / 기막히게 좋은 새로운 와인에 대해 / 거리를 따라가면 바로 있는 주류 가게에서 파는

There are many new wines, / so there's a lot to remember.
많은 새로운 와인이 있어서 / 기억해야 할 것이 많다.

How hard are you going to try / to remember what the neighbor has to say about which wines to buy?
여러분은 얼마나 열심히 노력할까? / 어떤 와인을 사야 하는지에 관해 이웃이 할 말을 기억하기 위해

Why bother / when the information would be better retained / by the wine expert sitting next to you?
무엇 하러 그러겠는가? / 그 정보가 더 잘 기억될 텐데 / 여러분 옆에 앉아 있는 와인 전문가에 의해

If your friend wasn't around, / you might try harder.
여러분의 친구가 곁에 없다면 / 여러분은 더 열심히 애쓸지 모른다.

After all, / it would be good to know / what a good wine would be for the evening's festivities.
어쨌든 / 아는 것은 좋은 일일 것이다. / 뭐가 저녁 만찬을 위해 좋은 와인일지

But / your friend, the wine expert, / is likely to remember the information without even trying.
하지만, / 와인 전문가인 여러분의 친구는 / 애쓰지도 않고 그 정보를 기억하기 쉽다.

심리학 연구에 따르면, 사람들은 자연스럽게 인지 노동을 나누는데, 흔히 그것에 대해서 별 생각 없이 그렇게 한다. 여러분이 친구와 함께 특별한 저녁식사를 요리하고 있다고 상상해 보라. 여러분은 요리를 잘하지만, 친구는 아마추어 소믈리에라고 할 수 있는 와인 전문가이다. 이웃이 들르더니 여러분 두 사람에게 거리를 따라가면 바로 있는 주류 가게에서 파는 기막히게 좋은 새로운 와인에 대해 말하기 시작한다. 많은 새로운 와인이 있어서 기억해야 할 것이 많다. 어떤 와인을 사야 하는지에 관해 이웃이 할 말을 기억하기 위해 여러분은 얼마나 열심히 노력할까? 여러분 옆에 앉아 있는 와인 전문가가 그 정보를 더 잘 기억하고 있는데 무엇 하러 그러겠는가? 여러분의 친구가 곁에 없다면 더 열심히 애쓸지도 모른다. 어쨌든 뭐가 저녁 만찬을 위해 좋은 와인일지 아는 것은 좋은 일일 것이다. 하지만, 와인 전문가인 여러분의 친구는 애쓰지도 않고 그 정보를 기억하기 쉽다.

Why? 왜 정답일까?

첫 문장에서 주제를 제시하고 두 번째 문장부터 주제를 뒷받침하는 예를 소개한다. 예시에 따르면 와인 전문가인 친구와 함께 새로 들어온 와인에 관한 이야기를 들을 때, 친구가 그 정보를 큰 노력 없이 더 잘 기억할 것이기 때문에 우리는 무의식적으로 별 노력을 들이지 않게 된다고 한다. 이에 근거할 때, 우리는 무의식적으로 함께 있는 사람과 인지적인 노력을 '분담해서' 효율적으로 정보를 처리하려는 경향이 있다는 내용을 추론할 수 있다. 따라서 빈칸에 들어갈 말로 가장 적절한 것은 ① '인지 노동을 나누는데'이다.

- **expert** ⓝ 전문가
- **terrific** ⓐ 아주 멋진
- **retain** ⓥ 보유하다
- **cognitive** ⓐ 인지적인
- **leisure** ⓝ 여가
- **sommelier** ⓝ 소믈리에(와인 담당 웨이터)
- **liquor** ⓝ (독한) 술
- **festivity** ⓝ 축제 기분
- **disagreement** ⓝ 불일치

구문 풀이

8행 How hard are you going to try to remember what the neighbor has to say about which wines to buy?
관계대명사(~것)
「which + 명 + to부정사 : 어떤 ~을 …할지」

★★ 문제 해결 꿀~팁 ★★

▶ 많이 틀린 이유는?
어떤 정보를 더 잘 기억할 사람이 옆에 있다면 우리는 무의식적으로 그 정보를 기억하려는 노력을 덜 들일 것이라는 내용의 글이다. 의견 불일치를 피하거나 서로 비슷한 취향을 가진 사람을 찾는다는 내용은 언급되지 않으므로 ②, ③은 모두 답으로 부적절하다.
▶ 문제 해결 방법은?
빈칸 뒤의 예시를 읽고 그 전체적인 내용을 근거로 도출할 수 있는 논리적 결론을 추론해내는 문제이다. 와인에 대한 정보를 별로 애쓰지도 않고 쉽게 기억해낼 친구가 있다면, 이웃이 와인에 대한 정보를 이야기해낼 때 그 정보를 처리하기 위한 인지적 노력을 덜 기울일 것이라는 내용을 통해, 인간은 무의식 속에서도 '인지적 부담'을 나눌 수 있는지 살펴보고 행동한다는 내용이 빈칸에 들어가야 한다.

34 고객을 관찰하며 고객 정보를 수집하는 것이 가장 중요해진 오늘날 기업들   정답률 42% | 정답 ④

다음 빈칸에 들어갈 말로 가장 적절한 것을 고르시오. [3점]
① its success relies on the number of its innovative products
기업의 성공은 혁신적인 제품의 수에 달려있기
② more customers come through word-of-mouth marketing
더 많은 고객이 입소문 마케팅을 통해 오기
③ it has come to realize the importance of offline stores
기업은 오프라인 매장의 중요성을 깨닫게 되었기
✓④ the customers are themselves the new value-creation devices
고객 자체가 새로운 가치 창출 장치이기
⑤ questions are raised on the effectiveness of the capitalist system
자본주의 체제의 효율성에 관해 의문이 제기되기

Even companies / that sell physical products to make profit / are forced by their boards and investors / to reconsider their underlying motives / and to collect as much data as possible from consumers.
기업조차 / 수익을 내기 위해 물적 제품을 판매하는 / 이사회와 투자자에 의해 어쩔 수 없이 ~하게 된다. / 자신의 근원적인 동기를 재고하게 되고 / 고객에게서 가능한 한 많은 정보를 수집하게

Supermarkets no longer make all their money / selling their produce and manufactured goods.
슈퍼마켓은 더 이상 자신의 모든 돈을 버는 것이 아니다. / 자신의 농산물과 제조된 물품을 판매해서

They give you loyalty cards / with which they track your purchasing behaviors precisely.
그들은 고객 우대 카드를 여러분에게 준다. / 여러분의 구매 행동을 정밀하게 추적하게 해 주는

Then supermarkets sell this purchasing behavior / to marketing analytics companies.
그러고 나서 슈퍼마켓은 이 구매 행위를 판매한다. / 마케팅 분석 기업에

The marketing analytics companies / perform machine learning procedures, / slicing the data in new ways, / and resell behavioral data back to product manufacturers / as marketing insights.
마케팅 분석 기업은 / 기계 학습 절차를 수행하고 / 그 정보를 새로운 방식으로 쪼개서 / 행동 정보를 제품 제조 기업에 다시 되판다. / 통찰력 있는 마케팅 정보로

When data and machine learning / become currencies of value in a capitalist system, / then every company's natural tendency / is to maximize its ability / to conduct surveillance on its own customers / because the customers are themselves the new value-creation devices.
정보와 기계 학습이 / 자본주의 체제에서 가치 있는 통화가 될 때, / 모든 기업의 자연스러운 경향은 / 그들의 능력을 최대화하는 것이다. / 자신의 고객을 관찰하는 / 고객 자체가 새로운 가치 창출 장치이기 때문에

수익을 내기 위해 물적 제품을 판매하는 기업조차도 이사회와 투자자에 의해 어쩔 수 없이 자신의 근원적인 동기를 재고하게 되고 고객에게서 가능한 한 많은 정보를 수집하게 된다. 슈퍼마켓은 더 이상 자신의 농산물과 제조된 물품을 판매해서 자신의 모든 돈을 버는 것이 아니다. 그들은 여러분의 구매 행동을 정밀하게 추적하게 해 주는 고객 우대 카드를 여러분에게 준다. 그러고 나서 슈퍼마켓은 이 구매 행위를 마케팅 분석 기업에 판매한다. 마케팅 분석 기업은 기계 학습 절차를 수행하고 그 정보를 새로운 방식으로 쪼개서 행동 정보를 제품 제조 기업에 통찰력 있는 마케팅 정보로 다시 되판다. 정보와 기계 학습이 자본주의 체제에서 가치 있는 통화가 될 때, 고객 자체가 새로운 가치 창출 장치이기 때문에 모든 기업의 자연스러운 경향은 자신의 고객을 관찰하는 능력을 최대화하는 것이다.

Why? 왜 정답일까?

첫 두 문장에서 오늘날 기업들은 가급적 고객 정보를 많이 수집할 수밖에 없는 상황에 처해 있는데 더 이상 제품을 팔아 돈을 버는 시대가 아니기 때문이라고 언급하고 있다. 세 번째 문장부터는 고객의 구매 행위 정보를 추적하고 이를 다시 마케팅 분석에 활용하는 과정이 이루어지면서 고객을 관찰하는 행위 자체가 기업의 중대 과업이 되었다는 내용이 이어지고 있다. 이에 근거할 때, 빈칸에 들어갈 말로 가장 적절한 것은 고객 자체가 정보적 가치를 갖게 되었기 때문에 기업들로서는 고객을 관찰하는 능력을 최대화하는 것이 당연하다는 의미를 완성하는 ④ '고객 자체가 새로운 가치 창출 장치이기'이다.

- **make profit** 수익을 내다
- **underlying** ⓐ 근본적인, 기저에 있는
- **precisely** ⓐⓓ 정밀하게, 정확히
- **reconsider** ⓥ 재고하다
- **manufacture** ⓥ 제조하다, 생산하다
- **analytics** ⓝ 분석 (정보)

[문제편 p.035]   [04회] 2021학년도 3월 **039**

- **procedure** ⓝ 절차
- **capitalist** ⓝ 자본주의(자)
- **innovative** ⓐ 혁신적인
- **raise** ⓥ (의문을) 제기하다
- **behavioral** ⓐ 행동의
- **conduct** ⓥ 수행하다
- **word-of-mouth** ⓐ 구두의, 구전의
- **effectiveness** ⓝ 효과성

구문 풀이

1행 Even companies [that sell physical products to make profit] are forced by
주어   ↳주격 관계대명사   「be forced +
their boards and investors to reconsider their underlying motives and to collect
to부정사1 +   to부정사2 : 어쩔 수 없이 ~하고 …하게 되다」
as much data as possible from consumers.

---

35 아이들을 대상으로 한 제품 광고의 윤리적 타당성   정답률 62% | 정답 ③

다음 글에서 전체 흐름과 관계 없는 문장은?

Academics, politicians, marketers and others / have in the past debated / whether or not it is ethically correct / to market products and services directly to young consumers.
대학 교수, 정치인, 마케팅 담당자, 그리고 그 외의 사람들은 / 지금까지 논쟁해 왔다. / 윤리적으로 옳은지 그렇지 않은지를 / 제품과 서비스를 어린 소비자들에게 직접 판촉하는 것이

① This is also a dilemma for psychologists / who have questioned / whether they ought to help advertisers / manipulate children into purchasing more products / they have seen advertised.
이것은 또한, 심리학자들에게도 딜레마이다. / 의문을 제기하는 / 그들이 광고주들을 도와야 하는지 / 아이들이 더 많은 제품을 구매하도록 조종하는 것을 / 광고되는 것을 본

② Advertisers have admitted to taking advantage of the fact / that it is easy to make children feel / that they are losers / if they do not own the 'right' products.
광고주들은 사실을 이용한 것을 인정했다. / 아이들이 느끼게 만드는 것이 쉽다는 / 자신이 패배자라고 / 그들이 그 '적절한' 제품을 소유하고 있지 않으면

☑ When products become more popular, / more competitors enter the marketplace / and marketers lower their marketing costs / to remain competitive.
제품이 더 인기 있어질 때 / 더 많은 경쟁자들이 시장에 진출하고 / 마케팅 담당자들은 그들의 마케팅 비용을 줄인다. / 경쟁력을 유지하기 위해

④ Clever advertising informs children / that they will be viewed by their peers in an unfavorable way / if they do not have the products that are advertised, / thereby playing on their emotional vulnerabilities.
영리한 광고는 아이들에게 알려 주고, / 그들이 자신의 또래 친구들에게 부정적으로 보일 것이라고 / 만약 그들이 광고되는 제품을 가지고 있지 않으면 / 그렇게 해서 아이들의 정서적인 취약성을 이용한다.

⑤ The constant feelings of inadequateness / created by advertising / have been suggested to contribute to / children becoming fixated with instant gratification / and beliefs that material possessions are important.
끊임없는 부적절함의 감정은 / 광고에 의해 만들어지는, / ~에 기여한다고 언급되어 왔다 / 아이들이 즉각적인 만족감에 집착하게 되는 데 / 그리고 물질적 소유물이 중요하다는 믿음에

지금까지 대학 교수, 정치인, 마케팅 담당자, 그리고 그 외의 사람들은 제품과 서비스를 어린 소비자들에게 직접 판촉하는 것이 윤리적으로 옳은지 그렇지 않은지를 논쟁해 왔다. ① 이것은 또한, 광고주들이 아이들을 조종해서 아이들이 광고되는 것을 본 더 많은 제품을 구매하게 만드는 것을 도와야 하는지 의문을 제기하는 심리학자들에게도 딜레마이다. ② 광고주들은 아이들이 그 '적절한' 제품을 소유하고 있지 않으면 자신이 패배자라고 느끼게 만드는 것이 쉽다는 사실을 이용한 것을 인정했다. ③ 제품이 더 인기 있어질 때 많은 경쟁자들이 시장에 진출하고 마케팅 담당자들은 경쟁력을 유지하기 위해 그들의 마케팅 비용을 줄인다. ④ 영리한 광고는 아이들에게 만약 그들이 광고되는 제품을 가지고 있지 않으면 자신의 또래 친구들에게 부정적으로 보일 것이라고 알려 주고, 그렇게 해서 아이들의 정서적인 취약성을 이용한다. ⑤ 광고가 만들어 내는, 끊임없이 부적절하다고 느끼는 감정은 아이들이 즉각적인 만족감과 물질적 소유물이 중요하다는 믿음에 집착하게 되는 데 기여한다고 언급되어 왔다.

Why? 왜 정답일까?

첫 문장에서 어린 소비자를 겨냥해 제품을 직접 판촉하고 광고하는 것이 윤리적으로 옳은가에 관한 논쟁이 있다고 언급한다. 이어서 ①, ②, ④, ⑤에서는 어린 소비자가 광고 속 제품을 자신만 갖고 있지 않을 때 또래들로부터 느낄 소외감을 자극하여, 제품을 갖고 있지 않은 상황을 '부적절하다'고 여기게 만들고, 그리하여 제품 구매를 촉진한다는 내용을 일관되게 보충 설명한다. 하지만 ③은 제품이 인기 있어질 때 마케팅 담당자들은 경쟁력을 유지하고자 마케팅 비용을 줄인다는 내용을 다루어 흐름에서 벗어난다. 따라서 전체 흐름과 관계없는 문장은 ③이다.

- **ethically** ⓐⓓ 윤리적으로
- **take advantage of** ~을 이용하다
- **unfavorable** ⓐ 비판적인, 호의적이 아닌
- **constant** ⓐ 끊임없는
- **instant** ⓐ 즉각적인
- **manipulate A into B** A를 조종하여 B하게 하다
- **competitor** ⓝ 경쟁자
- **vulnerability** ⓝ 취약성, 연약함
- **inadequateness** ⓝ 부적절성
- **possession** ⓝ 소유물

구문 풀이

6행 Advertisers have admitted to taking advantage of the fact {that it is easy
「admit to +동명사 : ~하는 것을 인정하다」   가주어
to make children feel that they are losers if they do not own the 'right' products}.
진주어(사역동사)   원형부정사   접속사(~것)   접속사(~라면)   { } : 동격절(=the fact)

---

36 원인 파악 오류   정답률 73% | 정답 ⑤

주어진 글 다음에 이어질 글의 순서로 가장 적절한 것을 고르시오. [3점]

① (A) – (C) – (B)   ② (B) – (A) – (C)
③ (B) – (C) – (A)   ④ (C) – (A) – (B)
☑ (C) – (B) – (A)

Once we recognize the false-cause issue, / we see it everywhere.
일단 잘못 파악한 원인 문제를 우리가 인식하면, / 우리는 그것을 어디에서나 보게 된다.
For example, / a recent long-term study of University of Toronto medical students / concluded / that medical school class presidents lived an average of 2.4 years less / than other medical school graduates.
예를 들어, / 토론토 대학의 의대생들에 대한 최근의 장기 연구는 / 결론을 내렸다 / 의대 학년 대표들이 평균 2.4년 더 적게 살았다는 / 다른 의대 졸업생들보다

(C) At first glance, / this seemed to imply / that being a medical school class president is bad for you.
처음 언뜻 봐서는, / 이것은 의미하는 것처럼 보였다 / 의대 학년 대표인 것이 여러분에게 해롭다는 것을
Does this mean / that you should avoid being medical school class president at all costs?
이것은 의미하는가? / 여러분이 무슨 수를 써서라도 의대 학년 대표가 되는 것을 피해야 한다는 것을
(B) Probably not.
아마도 그렇지는 않을 것이다.
Just because being class president is correlated with shorter life expectancy / does not mean / that it *causes* shorter life expectancy.
단지 학년 대표인 것이 더 짧은 평균 수명과 서로 관련된다고 해서 / 의미는 아니다 / 그것이 더 짧은 평균 수명을 *유발한다*는
In fact, / it seems likely / that the sort of person / who becomes medical school class president / is, on average, extremely hard-working, serious, and ambitious.
사실, / 아마도 ~한 것 같다. / 그런 부류의 사람은 / 의대 학년 대표가 되는 / 평균적으로 몹시 열심히 공부하고, 진지하며, 야망이 있는
(A) Perhaps this extra stress, / and the corresponding lack of social and relaxation time / — rather than being class president per se — / contributes to lower life expectancy.
아마도 이러한 가중된 스트레스와 / 그에 상응하는 사교와 휴식 시간의 부족이 / 의대 학년 대표인 것 그 자체보다, / 더 짧은 평균 수명의 원인인 것 같다.
If so, / the real lesson of the study is / that we should all relax a little / and not let our work take over our lives.
만약 그렇다면, / 이 연구의 진정한 교훈은 / 우리 모두가 약간의 휴식을 취해야 하고 / 우리의 일이 우리의 삶을 장악하게 해서는 안 된다는 것이다.

일단 잘못 파악한 원인 문제를 우리가 인식하면, 우리는 그것을 어디에서나 보게 된다. 예를 들어, 토론토 대학의 의대생들에 대한 최근의 장기 연구는 의대 학년 대표들이 다른 의대 졸업생들보다 평균 2.4년 더 적게 살았다는 결론을 내렸다.

(C) 처음 언뜻 봐서는, 이것은 의대 학년 대표인 것이 여러분에게 해롭다는 것을 의미하는 것처럼 보였다. 이것은 여러분이 무슨 수를 써서라도 의대 학년 대표가 되는 것을 피해야 한다는 것을 의미하는가?

(B) 아마도 그렇지는 않을 것이다. 단지 학년 대표인 것이 더 짧은 평균 수명과 서로 관련된다고 해서 그것이 더 짧은 평균 수명을 *유발한다*는 의미는 아니다. 사실, 아마도 의대 학년 대표가 되는 그런 부류의 사람은 평균적으로 몹시 열심히 공부하고, 진지하며, 야망이 있는 것 같다.

(A) 의대 학년 대표인 것 그 자체보다, 아마도 이러한 가중된 스트레스와 그에 상응하는 사교와 휴식 시간의 부족이 더 짧은 평균 수명의 원인인 것 같다. 만약 그렇다면, 이 연구의 진정한 교훈은 우리 모두가 약간의 휴식을 취해야 하고 우리의 일이 우리의 삶을 장악하게 해서는 안 된다는 것이다.

Why? 왜 정답일까?

주어진 글에서 원인 파악 오류를 화제로 언급하며, 의대생 학년 대표들이 다른 의대 졸업생보다 평균적으로 2.4년 더 적게 산다는 연구 결과를 예시로 든다. (C)는 이 연구 결과를 '처음 언뜻 보면' 의대 학년 대표를 맡는 것이 수명에 해롭다는 의미로 해석할 수 있는데, 그렇다면 이 결과로부터 의대 학년 대표가 되는 것을 피해야 한다는 의미까지 도출할 수 있는지 자문한다. (B)는 이 질문에 'Probably not'이라는 부정의 답을 제시하며, 의대 학년 대표가 평균 수명이 더 적은 경향이 있다는 연구 결과만으로 의대 학년 대표가 되는 것 자체가 건강에 부정적 영향을 끼치는 원인이라는 결론을 내릴 수는 없다고 설명한다. (A)는 (B)의 후반부에 이어서 의대 학년 대표들의 어떤 다른 특성들이 실제로 수명에 부정적 영향을 끼친 원인으로 분석될 수 있는지를 보충 설명한다. 따라서 글의 순서로 가장 적절한 것은 ⑤ '(C) – (B) – (A)'이다.

- **corresponding** ⓐ 상응하는, 해당하는
- **be correlated with** ~와 서로 관련되다
- **ambitious** ⓐ 야망 있는
- **at all costs** 무슨 수를 써서라도, 기어코
- **life expectancy** 기대 수명, 평균 수명
- **extremely** ⓐⓓ 극도로, 몹시
- **at first glance** 처음 언뜻 보면

구문 풀이

11행 {Just because being class president is correlated with shorter life
동명사구 주어   동사(수동태)
expectancy} does not mean that it *causes* shorter life expectancy.
[ ] : 주어 역할   동사   접속사(~것)

---

37 행동을 억제하거나 형성할 수 있는 과세   정답률 42% | 정답 ②

주어진 글 다음에 이어질 글의 순서로 가장 적절한 것을 고르시오.

① (A) – (C) – (B)   ☑ (B) – (A) – (C)   ③ (B) – (C) – (A)
④ (C) – (A) – (B)   ⑤ (C) – (B) – (A)

We commonly argue about the fairness of taxation / — whether this or that tax / will fall more heavily on the rich or the poor.
우리는 흔히 과세의 공정성에 관해 논한다. / 즉 이런저런 세금이 / 부자들에게 더 과중하게 부과될 것인지 아니면 가난한 사람들에게 그럴 것인지
(B) But the expressive dimension of taxation / goes beyond debates about fairness, / to the moral judgements societies make / about which activities are worthy of honor and recognition, / and which ones should be discouraged.
그러나 과세의 표현적 차원은 / 공정성에 대한 논쟁을 넘어, / 사회가 내리는 도덕적 판단에까지 이른다. / 어떤 활동이 명예와 인정을 받을 가치가 있고 / 어떤 활동이 억제되어야 하는지에 대해
Sometimes, these judgements are explicit.
때때로 이러한 판단은 명백하다.
(A) Taxes on tobacco, alcohol, and casinos / are called "sin taxes" / because they seek to discourage activities / considered harmful or undesirable.
담배, 술, 그리고 카지노에 대한 세금은 / '죄악세'라고 불린다 / 그것들이 활동들을 억제하려고 하기 때문에 / 해롭거나 바람직하지 않은 것으로 간주되는
Such taxes express society's disapproval of these activities / by raising the cost of engaging in them.
그런 세금은 이러한 활동에 대한 사회의 반대를 표현한다. / 그것을 하는 데 드는 비용을 증가시킴으로써
Proposals to tax sugary sodas (to combat obesity) / or carbon emissions (to address climate change) / likewise seek to change norms and shape behavior.
(비만을 퇴치하기 위해) 설탕이 든 탄산음료에 세금을 부과하는 제안은 / 또는 (기후 변화에 대처하기 위해) 탄소 배출에 / 마찬가지로 규범을 바꾸고 행동을 형성하려 한다.
(C) Not all taxes have this aim.
모든 세금이 이런 목적을 가진 것은 아니다.

We do not tax income / to express disapproval of paid employment / or to discourage people from engaging in it.
우리는 소득에 세금을 부과하는 것이 아니다. / 유급 고용에 대한 반대를 표명하거나 / 혹은 사람들이 그것을 하는 것을 막기 위해
Nor is a general sales tax intended / as a deterrent to buying things.
일반 판매세 역시 의도된 것이 아니다. / 물건을 사는 것의 억제책으로서
These are simply ways of raising revenue.
이것들은 단순히 세입을 올리는 방법이다.

우리는 흔히 과세의 공정성, 즉 이런저런 세금이 부자들에게 더 과중하게 부과될 것인지 아니면 가난한 사람들에게 그럴 것인지에 관해 논한다.

(B) 그러나 과세의 표현적 차원은 공정성에 대한 논쟁을 넘어, 어떤 활동이 명예와 인정을 받을 가치가 있고 어떤 활동이 억제되어야 하는지에 대해 사회가 내리는 도덕적 판단에까지 이른다. 때때로 이러한 판단은 명백하다.

(A) 담배, 술, 그리고 카지노에 대한 세금은 해롭거나 바람직하지 않은 것으로 간주되는 활동들을 억제하려고 하기 때문에 '죄악세'라고 불린다. 그런 세금은 이러한 활동을 하는 데 드는 비용을 증가시킴으로써 그것에 대한 사회의 반대를 표현한다. 마찬가지로 (비만을 퇴치하기 위해) 설탕이 든 탄산음료에 세금을 부과하는 제안이나 (기후 변화에 대처하기 위해) 탄소 배출에 세금을 부과하는 제안은 규범을 바꾸고 행동을 형성하려 한다.

(C) 모든 세금이 이런 목적을 가진 것은 아니다. 우리는 유급 고용에 대한 반대를 표명하거나 사람들이 그것을 하는 것을 막기 위해 소득에 세금을 부과하는 것은 아니다. 일반 판매세 역시 물건을 사는 것의 억제책으로서 의도된 것이 아니다. 이것들은 단순히 세입을 올리는 방법이다.

Why? 왜 정답일까?

과세의 공정성에 관한 논의를 화제로 제시한 주어진 글 뒤에는 이러한 논의가 특정 행위에 대한 사회의 도덕적 판단에 이를 수 있다고 언급하는 (B)가 먼저 연결된다. 이어서 (A)는 담배, 술, 카지노 등에 부과되는 세금을 예로 들며, 이러한 행위를 사회에서 '바람직하지 않다'고 보고 억제하려는 시각이 반영된 결과로서 세금이 부과된다는 보충 설명을 제시한다. 마지막으로 (C)는 모든 세금이 '이러한 목적', 즉 (A)에서 언급한 대로 '사람들의 행동을 바꾸려는' 목적으로 매겨지는 것은 아니라고 언급하며 소득세, 일반 판매세 등 다른 세금의 예를 든다. 따라서 글의 순서로 가장 적절한 것은 ② '(B) – (A) – (C)'이다.

- **fairness** ⓝ 공정함
- **fall on** (부담이) ~에게 떨어지다, ~의 책임이다
- **undesirable** ⓐ 바람직하지 않은
- **combat** ⓥ 방지하다, 퇴치하다, 싸우다
- **emission** ⓝ 배출(량)
- **explicit** ⓐ 명백한
- **taxation** ⓝ 과세, 조세
- **discourage** ⓥ 낙담시키다
- **disapproval** ⓝ 반대, 못마땅함
- **obesity** ⓝ 비만
- **address** ⓥ 해결하다, 대처하다, 다루다
- **revenue** ⓝ 수입

구문 풀이

19행 Nor is a general sales tax intended as a deterrent to buying things.
「부정어구 + be + 주어 + p.p.」: 도치 구문(~도 또한 아니다)

---

38 객관적 증거에 의한 믿음의 검증   정답률 41% | 정답 ⑤

글의 흐름으로 보아, 주어진 문장이 들어가기에 가장 적절한 곳을 고르시오. [3점]

Most beliefs — but not all — / are open to tests of verification.
전부는 아니지만 대부분의 믿음은 / 검증 시험을 받을 수 있다.
This means / that beliefs can be tested / to see if they are correct or false.
이것은 의미한다. / 믿음이 시험될 수 있다는 것을 / 그것들이 옳거나 그른지를 확인하기 위해
① Beliefs can be verified or falsified / with objective criteria external to the person.
믿음은 진실임이 입증되거나 거짓임이 입증될 수 있다. / 그 사람의 외부에 있는 객관적인 기준을 통해
② There are people / who believe the Earth is flat and not a sphere.
사람들이 있다. / 지구가 평평하고 구가 아니라고 믿는
③ Because we have objective evidence / that the Earth is in fact a sphere, / the flat Earth belief can be shown to be false.
우리는 객관적인 증거를 가지고 있기 때문에, / 지구가 실제로 구라는 / 지구가 평평하다는 믿음은 거짓임이 증명될 수 있다.
④ Also, / the belief that it will rain tomorrow / can be tested for truth / by waiting until tomorrow / and seeing whether it rains or not.
또한, / 내일 비가 올 것이라는 믿음은 / 진실인지 확인될 수 있다. / 내일까지 기다려 / 비가 오는지 안 오는지 봄으로써
✓ However, / some types of beliefs cannot be tested for truth / because we cannot get external evidence in our lifetimes / (such as a belief / that the Earth will stop spinning on its axis by the year 9999 / or that there is life on a planet 100-million light-years away).
하지만, / 어떤 종류의 믿음은 진실인지 확인될 수 없다. / 우리가 일생 동안 외부 증거를 얻을 수 없기 때문에 / (믿음 같은 / 9999년이 되면 지구가 자전하는 것을 멈출 것이라는 / 혹은 1억 광년 떨어진 행성에 생명체가 있다는 것 같은)
Also, / meta-physical beliefs / (such as the existence and nature of a god) / present considerable challenges / in generating evidence / that everyone is willing to use as a truth criterion.
또한, / 형이상학적 믿음은 / (신의 존재와 본질과 같은) / 상당한 난제가 된다. / 증거를 만드는 데 있어서 / 모든 사람이 진리 기준으로 기꺼이 사용할

전부는 아니지만 대부분의 믿음은 검증 시험을 받을 수 있다. 이것은 믿음이 옳거나 그른지를 확인하기 위해 시험될 수 있다는 것을 의미한다. ① 믿음은 그 사람의 외부에 있는 객관적인 기준을 통해 진실임이 입증되거나 거짓임이 입증될 수 있다. ② 지구가 평평하고 구가 아니라고 믿는 사람들이 있다. ③ 우리는 지구가 실제로 구라는 객관적인 증거를 가지고 있기 때문에, 지구가 평평하다는 믿음은 거짓임이 증명될 수 있다. ④ 또한, 내일 비가 올 것이라는 믿음은 내일까지 기다려 비가 오는지 안 오는지 봄으로써 진실인지 확인될 수 있다. ⑤ 하지만, (9999년이 되면 지구가 자전하는 것을 멈출 것이라는 믿음이나 1억 광년 떨어진 행성에 생명체가 있다는 것 같은) 어떤 종류의 믿음은 우리가 일생 동안 외부 증거를 얻을 수 없기 때문에 진실인지 확인될 수 없다. 또한, (신의 존재와 본질과 같은) 형이상학적 믿음은 모든 사람이 진리 기준으로 기꺼이 사용할 증거를 만드는 데 있어서 상당한 난제가 된다.

Why? 왜 정답일까?

⑤ 앞에서 지구가 둥글다는 믿음과 내일 비가 올 것이라는 믿음을 예로 들어, 믿음을 외부의 객관적 기준으로 검증할 수 있는 경우를 언급하고 있다. 이와는 반대로 주어진 문장은 지구가 미래 어느 시점에는 자전을 멈출 것이라는 믿음, 또는 외계 생명체가 있다는 믿음 등은 이를 뒷받침하는 외부적 증거를 얻을 수 없기 때문에 검증이 이루어지기 어렵다는 내용을 제시하고 있다. 이어서 ⑤ 뒤의 문장은 주어진 문장과

Also로 연결되며, 신의 존재 등에 관한 형이상학적 믿음 또한 객관적 증거로 뒷받침되기 어려울 수 있다는 점을 추가로 제시한다. 따라서 주어진 문장이 들어가기에 가장 적절한 곳은 ⑤이다.

- **external** ⓐ 외부의, 외적인
- **verify** ⓥ 검증하다, 확인하다
- **criterion** ⓝ 기준 (pl. criteria)
- **meta-physical** ⓐ 형이상학의
- **generate** ⓥ 만들어 내다
- **axis** ⓝ 축
- **objective** ⓐ 객관적인
- **sphere** ⓝ 구
- **considerable** ⓐ 상당한
- **willing** ⓐ 기꺼이 ~하려는

구문 풀이

13행 Also, the belief {that it will rain tomorrow} can be tested for truth by
( ): 동격절(= the belief)   조동사 수동태   전치사
waiting until tomorrow and seeing whether it rains or not.
동명사1   동명사2   명사절 접속사(~인지 아닌지)

★★★ 등급을 가르는 문제!
39 일반화하려는 본능의 순기능과 역기능   정답률 38% | 정답 ③

글의 흐름으로 보아, 주어진 문장이 들어가기에 가장 적절한 곳을 고르시오.

Everyone automatically categorizes and generalizes all the time.
모든 사람들은 항상 자동적으로 분류하고 일반화한다.
Unconsciously.
무의식적으로.
It is not a question of being prejudiced or enlightened.
그것은 편견을 갖고 있다거나 계몽되어 있다는 것의 문제가 아니다.
Categories are absolutely necessary for us to function.
범주는 우리가 제 기능을 하는 데 반드시 필요하다.
① They give structure to our thoughts.
그것들은 우리의 사고에 체계를 준다.
② Imagine / if we saw every item and every scenario as truly unique / — we would not even have a language / to describe the world around us.
상상해 보라. / 만일 우리가 모든 품목과 모든 있을 법한 상황을 정말로 유일무이한 것으로 본다고 / 우리는 언어조차 갖지 못할 것이다. / 우리 주변의 세계를 설명할
✓ But the necessary and useful instinct to generalize / can distort our world view.
그러나 필연적이고 유용한 일반화 본능은 / 우리의 세계관을 왜곡할 수 있다.
It can make us / mistakenly group together things, or people, or countries / that are actually very different.
그것은 우리를 만들 수 있다. / 사물들이나, 사람들, 혹은 나라들을 하나로 잘못 묶게 / 실제로는 아주 다른
④ It can make us assume / everything or everyone in one category is similar.
그것은 우리가 가정하게 만들 수 있다. / 하나의 범주 안에 있는 모든 것이나 모든 사람이 비슷하다고
⑤ And, maybe, most unfortunate of all, / it can make us jump to conclusions about a whole category / based on a few, or even just one, unusual example.
그리고 어쩌면 모든 것 중에서 가장 유감스러운 것은, / 그것이 우리로 하여금 전체 범주에 대해 성급하게 결론을 내리게 만들 수 있다는 것이다. / 몇 가지, 또는 심지어 고작 하나의 특이한 사례를 바탕으로

모든 사람들은 항상 자동적으로 분류하고 일반화한다. 무의식적으로 (그렇게 한다). 그것은 편견을 갖고 있다거나 계몽되어 있다는 것의 문제가 아니다. 범주는 우리가 제 기능을 하는 데 반드시 필요하다. ① 그것들은 우리의 사고에 체계를 준다. ② 만일 우리가 모든 품목과 모든 있을 법한 상황을 정말로 유일무이한 것으로 본다고 상상해 보라. 우리는 우리 주변의 세계를 설명할 언어조차 갖지 못할 것이다. ③ 그러나 필연적이고 유용한 일반화 본능은 우리의 세계관을 왜곡할 수 있다. 그것은 우리가 실제로는 아주 다른 사물들이나 사람들, 혹은 나라들을 하나로 잘못 묶게 만들 수 있다. ④ 그것은 우리가 하나의 범주 안에 있는 모든 것이나 모든 사람이 비슷하다고 가정하게 만들 수 있다. ⑤ 그리고 어쩌면 모든 것 중에서 가장 유감스러운 것은, 그것이 우리로 하여금 몇 가지, 또는 심지어 고작 하나의 특이한 사례를 바탕으로 전체 범주에 대해 성급하게 결론을 내리게 만들 수 있다는 것이다.

Why? 왜 정답일까?

③ 앞까지 인간은 대상을 무의식적으로 범주에 따라 분류하고 일반화하려는 경향이 있어, 이를 토대로 체계적인 사고를 해나갈 수 있다는 내용이 언급되고 있다. But으로 시작하는 주어진 문장은 이와 같은 흐름을 반전시키며 이러한 일반화 본능이 역으로 우리 세계관을 '왜곡'할 여지가 있음을 상기시키고 있다. ③ 뒤부터는 주어진 문장의 'the necessary and useful instinct'를 It으로 가리키며, 일반화 본능으로 인해 우리가 실제로 굉장히 다른 대상을 한 범주로 잘못 묶거나 한 범주 안의 개별적인 대상들을 비슷하다고 오해할 여지가 생긴다고 설명한다. 따라서 주어진 문장이 들어가기에 가장 적절한 곳은 ③이다.

- **instinct** ⓝ 본능
- **distort** ⓥ 왜곡하다
- **unconsciously** ⓐⓓ 무의식적으로
- **enlighten** ⓥ 계몽하다
- **jump to a conclusion** 성급한 결론을 내리다
- **generalize** ⓥ 일반화하다
- **automatically** ⓐⓓ 자동적으로, 저절로
- **prejudice** ⓥ 편견을 갖게 하다
- **mistakenly** ⓐⓓ 잘못하여, 실수로

구문 풀이

7행 Imagine (that) if we saw every item and every scenario as truly unique —
생략   「if + 주어 + 과거 동사 ~.
we would not even have a language to describe the world around us.
주어 + 조동사 과거형 +   동사원형 ~ : 가정법 과거」   형용사적 용법

★★ 문제 해결 꿀~팁 ★★

▶ 많이 틀린 이유는?
④ 앞에서, 우리는 일반화 본능 때문에 실제로 서로 다른 대상을 한 가지 범주 안에 묶을지도 모른다고 언급한다. 이어서 ④ 뒤의 문장에서는 '나아가' 우리가 한 범주 안의 대상이 다 비슷할 것이라고 잘못 가정할 수도 있다는 점을 언급한다. 즉 ④ 앞뒤가 흐름 단절 없이 자연스럽게 서로 연결되므로, 주어진 문장이 ④에 들어가는 것은 적합하지 않다.

▶ 문제 해결 방법은?
③ 앞뒤의 논리적 공백을 포착해야 한다. ③ 앞에서는 우리가 일반화 본능 '덕분에' 주변 세계를 설명할 수 있다는 내용인 반면, ③ 뒤에서는 일반화 본능 '때문에' 우리가 서로 다른 대상을 하나로 잘못 묶을 수도 있다는 내용이 이어진다. 즉 '일반화 본능'이라는 한 가지 소재에 대해 ③ 앞은 긍정적 시각, ③ 뒤는 부정적 시각을 비치고 있기 때문에, ③ 앞뒤로 논리적 공백이 발생하고 있다.

40 뇌에 가해지는 인지적 부담에 따른 충동 억제 정도
정답률 31% | 정답 ④

다음 글의 내용을 한 문장으로 요약하고자 한다. 빈칸 (A), (B)에 들어갈 말로 가장 적절한 것은?

(A)		(B)
① limited 제한된	……	powerful 강력한
② limited 제한된	……	divided 분리된
③ varied 달라지는	……	passive 수동적인
✔④ increased 증가된	……	dominant 우세해지게
⑤ increased 증가된	……	weakened 약화된

At the University of Iowa, / students were briefly shown numbers / that they had to memorize.
Iowa 대학교에서, / 학생들에게 숫자를 잠시 보여 주었다. / 그들이 암기해야 하는

Then they were offered the choice / of either a fruit salad or a chocolate cake.
그러고 나서 그들은 선택권을 받았다. / 과일 샐러드나 초콜릿 케이크 중 하나라는

When the number the students memorized / was seven digits long, / 63% of them chose the cake.
학생들이 외운 숫자가 / 일곱 자리일 때, / 그들 중 63%가 케이크를 선택했다.

When the number they were asked to remember / had just two digits, / however, / 59% opted for the fruit salad.
그들이 기억하도록 요청받은 숫자가 / 두 자리밖에 되지 않았을 때, / 그러나, / 59%가 과일 샐러드를 선택했다.

Our reflective brains know / that the fruit salad is better for our health, / but our reflexive brains desire that soft, fattening chocolate cake.
우리의 숙고하는 뇌는 알지만, / 과일 샐러드가 우리의 건강에 더 좋다는 것을 / 우리의 반사적인 뇌는 그 부드럽고 살이 찌는 초콜릿 케이크를 원한다.

If the reflective brain is busy figuring something else out — / like trying to remember a seven-digit number — / then impulse can easily win.
만약 숙고하는 뇌가 다른 어떤 것을 해결하느라 애쓰는 일과 같은, / 일곱 자리 숫자를 기억하려고 애쓰는 일과 같은 / 충동이 쉽게 이길 수 있다.

On the other hand, / if we're not thinking too hard about something else / (with only a minor distraction like memorizing two digits), / then the reflective system / can deny the emotional impulse of the reflexive side.
반면에, / 우리가 다른 것에 관해 너무 열심히 생각하고 있지 않다면 / (두 자리 숫자를 외우는 것처럼 사소한 주의를 산만하게 하는 일만 있을 때), / 숙고하는 (뇌의) 계통은 / 반사적인 쪽의 감정적인 충동을 억제할 수 있다.

➡ According to the above experiment, / the (A) increased intellective load on the brain / leads the reflexive side of the brain / to become (B) dominant.
위 실험에 따르면, / 뇌에 가해지는 증가된 지적 부담은 / 뇌의 반사적인 부분이 / ~하게 한다. / 우세해지게

Iowa 대학교에서, 학생들에게 그들이 암기해야 하는 숫자를 잠시 보여 주었다. 그러고 나서 그들에게 과일 샐러드나 초콜릿 케이크 중 하나를 선택하게 했다. 학생들이 외운 숫자가 일곱 자리일 때, 그들 중 63%가 케이크를 선택했다. 그러나 그들이 기억하도록 요청받은 숫자가 두 자리밖에 되지 않았을 때, 59%가 과일 샐러드를 선택했다. 우리의 숙고하는 뇌는 과일 샐러드가 우리의 건강에 더 좋다는 것을 알지만, 우리의 반사적인 뇌는 그 부드럽고 살이 찌는 초콜릿 케이크를 원한다. 만약 숙고하는 뇌가 일곱 자리 숫자를 기억하려고 애쓰는 일과 같은 다른 어떤 것을 해결하느라 바쁘다면, 충동이 쉽게 이길 수 있다. 반면에, 우리가 다른 것에 관해 너무 열심히 생각하고 있지 않다면(두 자리 숫자를 외우는 것처럼 사소하게 주의를 산만하게 하는 일만 있을 때), 숙고하는 (뇌의) 계통은 반사적인 쪽의 감정적인 충동을 억제할 수 있다.

➡ 위 실험에 따르면, 뇌에 가해지는 (A) 증가된 지적 부담은 뇌의 반사적인 부분이 (B) 우세해지게 한다.

Why? 왜 정답일까?

실험 결과를 제시하는 'If the reflective brain is busy figuring something else out — like trying to remember a seven-digit number — then impulse can easily win.' 이후로 뇌에 부담된 인지 과업이 많다면 충동에 대한 억제가 덜 일어나지만, 인지 과업이 적은 경우에는 억제가 잘 이루어진다고 언급하고 있다. 이에 근거할 때, 요약문은 뇌에 부담된 인지적 부담이 '늘어나면' 반사, 즉 충동을 따르려는 경향이 '우세해진다'는 내용이어야 하므로, 요약문의 빈칸에 들어갈 말로 가장 적절한 것은 ④ '(A) increased(증가된), (B) dominant(우세해지게)'이다.

- briefly [ad] 잠시, 짧게
- fatten [v] 살찌게 하다
- impulse [n] 충동
- deny [v] 부인하다
- limited [a] 제한된, 한정된
- dominant [a] 지배적인
- digit [n] 숫자
- be busy ~ing ~하느라 바쁘다
- distraction [n] 주의를 산만하게 하는 것
- intellective [a] 인지적인, 지적인
- passive [a] 수동적인

구문 풀이

2행 Then they were offered the choice of either a fruit salad or a chocolate cake.
4형식 수동태(~을 제공받다) / 목적어 / 「either + A + or + B : A와 B 중 하나」

★★ 문제 해결 꿀~팁 ★★

▶ 많이 틀린 이유는?
마지막 두 문장에서 뇌에 인지적 부담이 많이 가해지면 충동에 지기 쉽지만, 뇌에 인지적 부담이 적게 가해지면 충동을 억제하기가 쉽다고 했다. ①의 경우, 인지적 부담이 '제한되면' 뇌의 반사적인 부분, 즉 인지적 부담이 '우세해진다'는 의미이므로 주제와 반대되는 선택지이다. 마찬가지로 ⑤ 또한 인지적 부담이 '커지면' 충동에 의해 좌우되는 부분이 '약해진다'는 의미이므로 주제와 반대된다.

▶ 문제 해결 방법은?
마지막 두 문장의 내용을 '인지적 부담↑ 충동↑, 인지적 부담↓ 충동↓'과 같이 간단히 도식화해보면 요약문에 들어갈 단어를 쉽게 찾을 수 있다.

41-42 시험에 대한 긍정적 태도 갖기

Test scores are not a measure of self-worth; / however, / we often associate our sense of worthiness / with our performance on an exam.
시험 점수는 자부심의 척도가 아니다 / 하지만, / 우리는 흔히 우리의 자부심을 연관시킨다. / 우리의 시험 성적과

Thoughts / such as "If I don't pass this test, I'm a failure" / are mental traps / not rooted in truth.
생각은 / "이 시험에 합격하지 못하면 나는 실패자야."와 같은 / 정신적 함정이다. / 사실에 뿌리를 두고 있지 않은

「Failing a test is failing a test, nothing more.
시험에 실패하는 것은 시험에 실패하는 것이지, 그 이상이 아니다.

It is in no way (a) descriptive of your value as a person.」 **41번의 근거**
그것은 결코 사람으로서의 여러분의 가치를 설명하지 않는다.

Believing that test performance is a reflection of your virtue / places (b) unreasonable pressure on your performance.
시험 성적이 여러분의 미덕을 반영하는 것이라고 믿는 것은 / 여러분의 수행에 부당한 압력을 가한다.

Not passing the certification test / only means / that your certification status has been delayed.
자격 시험을 통과하지 못한 것은 / 단지 의미할 따름이다. / 여러분의 자격 지위가 지연되었다는 것을

「(c) Maintaining a positive attitude is therefore important.」 **41번의 근거**
그러므로 긍정적인 태도를 유지하는 것이 중요하다.

If you have studied hard, / reaffirm this mentally / and believe that you will do well.
만약 여러분이 열심히 공부했다면, / 마음속으로 이것을 재확인하고 / 여러분이 잘할 것이라고 믿으라.

If, on the other hand, / you did not study as hard / as you should have or wanted to, / (d) accept that as beyond your control for now / and attend to the task of doing the best you can.
반면에 만일 / 여러분이 열심히 공부하지 않았다면, / 여러분이 했어야 하거나 원했던 만큼 / 지금으로서는 그것을 여러분이 어찌할 수 없는 것으로 받아들이고 / 여러분이 할 수 있는 최선의 것을 하는 과업에 주의를 기울이라.

If things do not go well this time, / you know what needs to be done / in preparation for the next exam.
만약 이번에 잘되지 않는다면, / 여러분은 무엇을 해야 할지 알게 된다. / 다음 시험을 준비하는 데 있어

「Talk to yourself in positive terms.」 **41번의 근거**
긍정적인 말로 자신에게 이야기하라.

「Avoid rationalizing past or future test performance / by placing the blame on secondary variables.」 **42번의 근거**
과거 또는 미래의 시험 성적을 합리화하는 것을 피하라. / 부차적인 변수에 책임을 지움으로써

Thoughts / such as, "I didn't have enough time," or "I should have …," / (e) compound the stress of test-taking.
생각은 / "나는 시간이 충분하지 않았어."라거나 / "내가 그랬어야 했는데…"와 같은 / 시험 보는 것의 스트레스를 가중시킨다.

Take control / by affirming your value, self-worth, and dedication / to meeting the test challenge head on.
통제권을 잡으라. / 자신의 가치, 자부심, 그리고 헌신을 확인함으로써 / 시험 과제에 정면으로 맞서는 것에 대한

Repeat to yourself "I can and I will pass this exam."
"난 할 수 있고 이 시험에 합격할 거야."라고 자신에게 되풀이해 말하라.

시험 점수는 자부심의 척도가 아니지만, 우리는 흔히 우리의 자부심과 우리의 시험 성적을 연관시킨다. "이 시험에 합격하지 못하면 나는 실패자야."와 같은 생각은 사실에 뿌리를 두고 있지 않은 정신적 함정이다. 시험에 실패하는 것은 시험에 실패하는 것이지, 그 이상이 아니다. 시험 성적이 여러분의 미덕을 반영하는 것이라고 믿는 것은 여러분의 수행에 (b) 부당한 압력을 가한다. 자격 시험을 통과하지 못한 것은 단지 여러분의 자격 지위가 지연되었다는 것을 의미할 따름이다. 그러므로 긍정적인 태도를 (c) 유지하는 것이 중요하다. 만약 여러분이 열심히 공부했다면, 마음속으로 이것을 재확인하고 잘할 것이라고 믿으라. 반면에 만일 여러분이 했어야 하거나 했던 만큼 열심히 공부하지 않았다면, 지금으로서는 그것을 여러분이 어찌할 수 없는 것으로 (d) 받아들이고 여러분이 할 수 있는 최선의 것을 하는 과업에 주의를 기울이라. 만약 이번에 잘되지 않는다면, 다음 시험 준비에서는 무엇을 해야 할지 알게 된다. 긍정적인 말로 자신에게 이야기하라. 부차적인 변수에 책임을 지움으로써 과거 또는 미래의 시험 성적을 합리화하는 것을 피하라. "나는 시간이 충분하지 않았어."라거나 "내가 그랬어야 했는데…"와 같은 생각은 시험 보는 것의 스트레스를 (e) 덜어준다(→ 가중시킨다). 자신의 가치, 자부심, 그리고 시험 과제에 정면으로 맞서는 것에 대한 헌신을 확인함으로써 통제권을 잡으라. "난 할 수 있고 이 시험에 합격할 거야."라고 자신에게 되풀이해 말하라.

- self-worth 자아 존중감, 자부심
- rooted in ~에 뿌리를 둔
- reflection [n] 반영, 반사
- place pressure on ~에 압력을 가하다
- certification [n] 자격, 증명
- attend to ~에 주의를 기울이다
- rationalize [v] 합리화하다
- variable [n] 변수
- associate A with B A를 B와 연관시키다
- descriptive [a] 설명하는
- virtue [n] 미덕
- unreasonable [a] 부당한
- reaffirm [v] 재확인하다
- in preparation for ~의 준비로
- secondary [a] 부차적인
- dedication [n] 헌신

구문 풀이

8행 Not passing the certification test only means that your certification status
동명사구 주어(~하지 않는 것) / 동사(단수) / 접속사(~것)
has been delayed.
현재완료 수동태(~되었다)

41 제목 파악
정답률 73% | 정답 ①

윗글의 제목으로 가장 적절한 것은?
✔① Attitude Toward a Test: It's Just a Test – 시험에 대한 태도: 시험은 시험일 뿐이다
② Some Stress Is Good for Performance – 약간의 스트레스는 수행에 유익하다
③ Studying Together Works for a Test – 함께 공부하는 것이 시험에 효과적이다
④ Repetition: The Road to Perfection – 반복: 완벽에 이르는 길
⑤ Sound Body: The Key to Success – 건강한 신체: 성공의 열쇠

Why? 왜 정답일까?

'Failing a test is failing a test, nothing more. It is in no way descriptive of your value as a person.'에서 시험에 통과하지 못한 것은 말 그대로 통과를 못했다는 의미일 뿐, 수험자의 인간으로서의 가치에 대한 평가가 아니라고 언급하고 있다. 이어서 'Maintaining a positive attitude is therefore important.', 'Talk to yourself in positive terms.'에서는 그렇기에 긍정적인 태도를 유지하는 것이 중요하다고 이야기한다. 따라서 글의 제목으로 가장 적절한 것은 ① '시험에 대한 태도: 시험은 시험일 뿐이다'이다.

42 어휘 추론
정답률 46% | 정답 ⑤

밑줄 친 (a)~(e) 중에서 문맥상 낱말의 쓰임이 적절하지 않은 것은?
① (a)　　② (b)　　③ (c)　　④ (d)　　✔(e)

Why? 왜 정답일까?

'Avoid rationalizing past or future test performance by placing the blame on secondary variables.'에서 잘 나오지 않았거나 잘 안 나올 수 있는 성적을 부차적인 변수 탓으로 돌리지 말라고 언급한 데 이어, (e)가 포함된 문장은 '시간이 부족했다'는 등 '부차적인' 변수 탓을 하는 경우를 예로 들고 있다. 이렇듯 소위 핑계를 대는 것은 시험에 대해 긍정적인 태도를 갖는 것과는 거리가 먼 행동으로, 수험자의 스트레스를 도리어 '증가시킬' 수 있다는 맥락이 되어야 한다. 따라서 (e)의 relieve는 compound로 고쳐야 한다. 문맥상 낱말의 쓰임이 적절하지 않은 것은 ⑤ '(e)'이다.

43-45 금화로 인해 불행을 알게 된 구두 만드는 사람

(A)

Once upon a time / there lived a poor but cheerful shoemaker.
옛날 옛적에 / 가난하지만 쾌활한 구두 만드는 사람이 살았다.

He was so happy, / he sang all day long.
그는 너무 행복해서 / 그는 온종일 노래를 불렀다.

The children loved to stand around his window / to listen to (a) him.
아이들은 그의 창문에 둘러서 있기를 좋아했다. / 그의 노래를 듣기 위해서

Next door to the shoemaker / lived a rich man.
구두 만드는 사람 옆집에는 / 부자가 살았다.

He used to sit up all night to count his gold.
그는 자신의 금화를 세기 위해 밤을 새곤 했다.

「In the morning, he went to bed, / but he could not sleep / because of the sound of the shoemaker's singing.」 45번 ①의 근거 일치
아침에 그는 잠자리에 들었지만 / 그는 잠을 잘 수 없었다. / 구두 만드는 사람의 노랫소리 때문에

(D)

One day, / (d) he thought of a way of stopping the singing.
어느 날, / 그는 그 노래를 멈출 방법을 생각해냈다.

He wrote a letter to the shoemaker / asking him to visit.
그는 구두 만드는 사람에게 편지를 써 보냈다. / 그에게 방문해 달라고 요청하는

「The shoemaker came at once, / and to his surprise the rich man gave him a bag of gold.」 45번 ④의 근거 일치
구두 만드는 사람은 즉시 왔고, / 놀랍게도 부자는 그에게 금화가 든 가방을 주었다.

When he got home again, / the shoemaker opened the bag.
그가 집에 다시 돌아왔을 때, / 구두 만드는 사람은 그 가방을 열었다.

(e) He had never seen so much gold before!
그는 그때까지 그렇게 많은 금화를 본 적이 없었다!

「When he sat down at his bench / and began, carefully, to count it, / the children watched through the window.」 45번 ⑤의 근거 일치
그가 의자에 앉았을 때 / 조심스럽게 그것을 세기 시작하면서, / 아이들이 창문을 통해서 지켜보았다.

(C)

There was so much there / that the shoemaker was afraid to let it out of his sight.
거기엔 (금화가) 너무 많아서 / 구두 만드는 사람은 그것을 자신에게 보이지 않는 곳에 두기가 겁났다.

So he took it to bed with him.
그래서 그는 그것을 잠자리에 가져갔다.

But he could not sleep for worrying about it.
그러나 그는 그것에 대한 걱정으로 잠을 잘 수 없었다.

Very early in the morning, / he got up and brought his gold down from the bedroom.
매우 이른 아침에, / 그는 일어나서 금화를 침실에서 가지고 내려왔다.

He had decided to hide it up the chimney instead.
대신에 그는 그것을 굴뚝에 숨기로 결정했다.

「But he was still uneasy, / and in a little while he dug a hole in the garden / and buried his bag of gold in it.」 45번 ③의 근거 일치
그러나 그는 여전히 불안했고, / 잠시 후에 그는 정원에 구멍을 파고 / 그 안에 금화가 든 가방을 묻었다.

It was no use trying to work.
일을 해 보려고 해도 소용없었다.

(c) He was too worried about the safety of his gold.
그는 자신의 금화의 안전이 너무나 걱정되었다.

And as for singing, / he was too miserable to utter a note.
그리고 노래에 관해서라면, / 그는 너무 불행해서 한 음도 낼 수 없었다.

(B)

He could not sleep, or work, or sing / — and, worst of all, / the children no longer came to see (b) him.
그는 잠을 잘 수도, 일을 할 수도, 노래를 부를 수도 없었고, / 최악으로는 / 아이들이 더 이상 그를 보러 오지 않았다.

At last, the shoemaker felt so unhappy / that he seized his bag of gold / and ran next door to the rich man.
마침내, 구두 만드는 사람은 너무 불행해져서 / 그의 금화가 든 가방을 움켜쥐고 / 옆집 부자에게 달려갔다.

"Please take back your gold," he said.
"제발 당신의 금화를 다시 가져가세요."라고 그가 말했다.

"The worry of it is making me ill, / and I have lost all of my friends.
"그것에 대한 걱정이 저를 아프게 하고, / 저는 제 친구들을 모두 잃었어요.

「I would rather be a poor shoemaker, / as I was before.」" 45번 ②의 근거 불일치
저는 차라리 가난한 구두 만드는 사람이 되겠어요. / 제가 예전에 그랬듯이"

And so the shoemaker was happy again / and sang all day at his work.
그래서 구두 만드는 사람은 다시 행복해졌고 / 일을 하면서 온종일 노래를 불렀다.

(A)

옛날 옛적에 가난하지만 쾌활한 구두 만드는 사람이 살았다. 그는 너무 행복해서 온종일 노래를 불렀다. 아이들은 그의 창문에 둘러서서 (a) 그의 노래를 듣기 좋아했다. 구두 만드는 사람 옆집에는 부자가 살았다. 그는 자신의 금화를 세기 위해 밤을 새곤 했다. 아침에 그는 잠자리에 들었지만 구두 만드는 사람의 노랫소리 때문에 잠을 잘 수 없었다.

(D)

어느 날, (d) 그는 그 노래를 멈출 방법을 생각해냈다. 그는 구두 만드는 사람에게 방문해 달라고 요청하는 편지를 써 보냈다. 구두 만드는 사람은 즉시 왔고, 놀랍게도 부자는 그에게 금화가 든 가방을 주었다. 집에 다시 돌아왔을 때, 구두 만드는 사람은 그 가방을 열었다.

(e) 그는 그때까지 그렇게 많은 금화를 본 적이 없었다! 그가 의자에 앉아 조심스럽게 그것을 세기 시작했을 때, 아이들이 창문을 통해서 지켜보았다.

(C)

거기엔 금화가 너무 많아서 구두 만드는 사람은 그것을 자신에게 보이지 않는 곳에 두기가 겁났다. 그래서 그는 그것을 잠자리에 가져갔다. 그러나 그는 그것에 대한 걱정으로 잠을 잘 수 없었다. 매우 이른 아침에, 그는 일어나서 금화를 침실에서 가지고 내려왔다. 대신에 그는 그것을 굴뚝에 숨기로 결정했다. 그러나 그는 여전히 불안했고, 잠시 후에 정원에 구멍을 파고 그 안에 금화가 든 가방을 묻었다. 일을 해 보려고 해도 소용없었다. (c) 그는 자신의 금화의 안전이 너무나 걱정되었다. 그리고 노래에 관해서라면, 그는 너무 불행해서 한 음도 낼 수 없었다.

(B)

그는 잠을 잘 수도, 일을 할 수도, 노래를 부를 수도 없었고, 최악으로는 아이들이 더 이상 (b) 그를 보러 오지 않았다. 마침내, 구두 만드는 사람은 너무 불행해져서 그의 금화가 든 가방을 움켜쥐고 옆집 부자에게 달려갔다. "제발 당신의 금화를 다시 가져가세요."라고 그가 말했다. "그것에 대한 걱정이 저를 아프게 하고, 저는 제 친구들을 모두 잃었어요. 저는 예전처럼 차라리 가난한 구두 만드는 사람이 되겠어요." 그래서 구두 만드는 사람은 다시 행복해졌고 일을 하면서 온종일 노래를 불렀다.

- **sit up all night** 밤을 꼴딱 새우다
- **chimney** ⓝ 굴뚝
- **bury** ⓥ 묻다
- **utter** ⓥ (입으로) 소리를 내다, 말하다
- **seize** ⓥ 붙잡다
- **uneasy** ⓐ 불안한
- **as for** ~에 관해 말하자면
- **note** ⓝ (음악의) 음

구문 풀이

(A) 4행 Next door to the shoemaker lived a rich man.
「부사구 + 동사 + 주어 : 도치 구문」

(B) 2행 At last, the shoemaker felt so unhappy that he seized his bag of gold and ran next door to the rich man.
「so ~that ... : 너무 ~해서 ...하다」

(C) 8행 It was no use trying to work.
「it is no use + 동명사 : ~하는 것도 소용없다」

(D) 6행 When he sat down at his bench and began, (carefully), to count it, the children watched through the window.
접속사(~할 때) / 동사1 / 동사2 / ( ) : 삽입구 / 목적어(begin + to부정사 : ~하기 시작하다)

43 글의 순서 파악
정답률 73% | 정답 ⑤

주어진 글 (A)에 이어질 내용을 순서에 맞게 배열한 것으로 가장 적절한 것은?
① (B) − (D) − (C)　　② (C) − (B) − (D)
③ (C) − (D) − (B)　　④ (D) − (B) − (C)
✔(D) − (C) − (B)

Why? 왜 정답일까?

쾌활한 성격으로 온종일 노래를 부르는 구두 만드는 사람과 금화를 밤새 세느라 아침에서야 잠자리에 들려고 하지만 구두 만드는 사람의 노랫소리 때문에 잠 못드는 옆집 부자의 상황을 제시한 (A) 뒤에는, 부자가 구두 만드는 사람의 노래를 멈추게 하기 위해 집으로 불러 금화를 맡겼다는 내용의 (D)가 먼저 연결된다. 이어 (C)에서는 구두 만드는 사람이 금화가 너무 많은 것을 알고 내내 불안해하며 어쩔 줄 몰라 했다는 내용을 제시한다. 마지막으로 (B)는 잠도 못 이루고 노래도 못 부르고 친구까지 잃게 된 구두 만드는 사람이 다시 부자를 찾아가 금화를 돌려주고 이전의 가난한 생활로 돌아갔다는 결말을 제시한다. 따라서 글의 순서로 가장 적절한 것은 ⑤ '(D) − (C) − (B)'이다.

44 지칭 추론
정답률 73% | 정답 ④

다음 밑줄 친 (a)~(e) 중에서 가리키는 대상이 나머지 넷과 다른 것은?
① (a)　　② (b)　　③ (c)　　✔(d)　　⑤ (e)

Why? 왜 정답일까?

(a), (b), (c), (e)는 the shoemaker를, (d)는 the rich man을 가리키므로, (a)~(e) 중에서 가리키는 대상이 다른 하나는 ④ '(d)'이다.

45 세부 내용 파악
정답률 72% | 정답 ②

윗글의 shoemaker에 관한 내용으로 적절하지 않은 것은?
① 그의 노래로 인해 옆집 사람이 잠을 잘 수 없었다.
✔② 예전처럼 가난하게 살고 싶지 않다고 말했다.
③ 정원에 구멍을 파고 금화가 든 가방을 묻었다.
④ 부자가 보낸 편지에 즉시 그를 만나러 갔다.
⑤ 금화를 셀 때 아이들이 그 모습을 봤다.

Why? 왜 정답일까?

(B) 'I would rather be a poor shoemaker, as I was before.'에서 구두 만드는 사람은 금화로 인해 너무 걱정하게 된 자신의 처지가 싫어 차라리 예전처럼 가난한 삶을 택하겠다고 말했음을 알 수 있다. 따라서 내용과 일치하지 않는 것은 ② '예전처럼 가난하게 살고 싶지 않다고 말했다.'이다.

Why? 왜 오답일까?

① (A) '~ he could not sleep because of the sound of the shoemaker's singing.'의 내용과 일치한다.
③ (C) '~ he dug a hole in the garden and buried his bag of gold in it.'의 내용과 일치한다.
④ (D) 'The shoemaker came at once, ~'의 내용과 일치한다.
⑤ (D) 'When he sat down at his bench and began, carefully, to count it, the children watched through the window.'의 내용과 일치한다.

A	B	C	D
01 수입	01 guarantee	01 ①	01 ⑨
02 가설	02 emission	02 ①	02 ⓞ
03 사고방식	03 enthusiasm	03 ⓗ	03 ①
04 대다수	04 fluent	04 ⓔ	04 ⓒ
05 차가운	05 unconsciously	05 ⓢ	05 ⓢ
06 정적인	06 impulse	06 ⓚ	06 ⓗ
07 미덕	07 lifespan	07 ①	07 ⓖ
08 묻다	08 constant	08 ①	08 ⓓ
09 새로움	09 divine	09 ⓑ	09 ⓝ
10 기준	10 extremely	10 ⓞ	10 ①
11 낙담시키다	11 interpret	11 ①	11 ⓐ
12 살찌게 하다	12 passive	12 ⓟ	12 ⓑ
13 수행하다	13 exclusivity	13 ⓜ	13 ⓡ
14 여가	14 perspective	14 ⓡ	14 ⓟ
15 최적의	15 attendee	15 ⓠ	15 ⓚ
16 정확성	16 deny	16 ⓝ	16 ⓔ
17 검토하다	17 descend	17 ⓖ	17 ①
18 ~까지	18 reconsider	18 ⓒ	18 ⓜ
19 노동	19 predict	19 ⓓ	19 ①
20 ~와 비교해서	20 aggression	20 ⓐ	20 ①

· 정답 ·

18 ② 19 ① 20 ① 21 ② 22 ③ 23 ② 24 ④ 25 ⑤ 26 ③ 27 ② 28 ② 29 ⑤ 30 ③ 31★① 32 ①
33 ⑤ 34★⑤ 35 ③ 36 ⑤ 37★② 38 ⑤ 39 ④ 40 ① 41 ④ 42★② 43 ③ 44 ④ 45 ③

★ 표기된 문항은 [등급을 가르는 문제]에 해당하는 문항입니다.

18　연수 강사 연락처 묻기　　　　정답률 83% | 정답 ②

다음 글의 목적으로 가장 적절한 것은?
① 직원 연수 진행을 부탁하려고
☑ 연수 강사의 연락처를 문의하려고
③ 연수에서 강연할 원고를 의뢰하려고
④ 리더십 개발 연수 참석을 권유하려고
⑤ 연수자 명단을 보내 줄 것을 요청하려고

Dear Tony,
Tony 씨께,
I'm writing to ask / if you could possibly do me a favour.
저는 여쭤보려고 편지를 씁니다. / 당신이 제 부탁을 들어주실 수 있는지
For this year's workshop, / we would really like to take all our staff on a trip to Bridgend / to learn more about new leadership skills in the industry.
올해 연수를 위해 / 저희는 모든 직원을 데리고 Bridgend로 꼭 가고자 합니다. / 업계의 새로운 리더십 기술에 대해 더 많이 배우기 위해
I remember / that your company took a similar course last year, / which included a lecture by an Australian lady / whom you all found inspiring.
저는 기억합니다. / 귀사에서 작년에 비슷한 연수 과정을 하셨고, / 거기에는 호주 출신 여성분의 강연이 포함되었던 것으로 / 여러분 모두가 고무적이라고 생각한
Are you still in contact with her?
아직도 그분과 연락을 하고 계십니까?
If so, / do you think / that you could possibly let me have a number for her, or an email address?
그러시다면, / 생각하십니까? / 당신이 제게 그분의 전화번호 또는 이메일 주소를 알려주실 수 있다고
I would really appreciate your assistance.
귀하께서 도와주신다면 정말 감사하겠습니다.
Kind regards, // Luke Schreider
Luke Schreider 올림

Tony 씨께,

제 부탁을 들어주실 수 있는지 여쭤보려고 편지를 씁니다. 올해 연수로 저희는 업계의 새로운 리더십 기술에 대해 더 많이 배우기 위해 모든 직원을 데리고 Bridgend로 꼭 가고자 합니다. 귀사에서 작년에 비슷한 연수 과정을 하셨고, 거기에는 여러분 모두가 고무적이라고 생각한 호주 출신 여성분의 강연이 포함되었던 것으로 기억합니다. 아직도 그분과 연락을 하고 계십니까? 그러시다면, 그분의 전화번호 또는 이메일 주소를 알려주실 수 있으십니까? 귀하께서 도와주신다면 정말 감사하겠습니다.

Luke Schreider 올림

Why? 왜 정답일까?

리더십 연수를 계획하고 있는 필자는 편지 수신자가 작년에 연수를 받을 때 만났던 호주 출신 여성 강사의 연락처를 알려줄 수 있는지(If so, do you think that you could possibly let me have a number for her, or an email address?) 묻고 있다. 따라서 글의 목적으로 가장 적절한 것은 ② '연수 강사의 연락처를 문의하려고'이다.

● industry ⓝ (특정 분야의) 업계　　● inspiring ⓐ 고무적인, 영감을 주는
● in contact with ~와 연락하는　　● assistance ⓝ 도움

구문 풀이

5행　I remember that your company took a similar course last year, which
　　　　접속사(~것)　　　　　　　　　　　　선행사　　　　　계속적 용법
included a lecture by an Australian lady [whom you all found inspiring].
　　　　　　　　선행사　　목적격 관·대 5형식 동사↩ 목적격 보어

19　몹시 긴장했지만 연설을 무사히 마친 Alice　　　　정답률 85% | 정답 ①

다음 글에 드러난 Alice의 심경 변화로 가장 적절한 것은?
☑ nervous → delighted
　긴장한　　　기쁜
② embarrassed → scared
　당황한　　　　겁이 난
③ amazed → annoyed
　놀란　　　　짜증난
④ hopeful → disappointed
　희망에 찬　　실망한
⑤ angry → grateful
　화난　　　감사한

Alice looked up from her speech / for the first time since she began talking.
Alice는 자신의 연설문으로부터 고개를 들었다. / 연설을 시작한 이후 처음으로
She hadn't dared to break eye contact with the words on the pages / until she finished, / for fear of losing her place.
그녀는 페이지에 있는 단어들로부터 감히 눈을 뗄 수가 없었다. / 그녀가 마칠 때까지 / 연설할 부분을 놓칠까 두려워
Actually, she'd just hoped for two simple things / — not to lose the ability to read during the talk / and to get through it without making a fool of herself.
사실 그녀는 단지 두 가지 간단한 것들을 바랐을 뿐이었는데, / 연설하는 동안 읽는 능력을 잃지 않는 것과 / 웃음거리가 되지 않고 연설을 마치는 것이었다.
Now the entire ballroom was standing, clapping.
이제 강연장에 있는 모두가 일어서서 박수를 치고 있었다.

It was more than she had hoped for.
그것은 그녀가 희망했던 것 이상이었다.
Smiling brightly, / she looked at the familiar faces in the front row.
환하게 웃으며, / 그녀는 앞줄에 있는 낯익은 얼굴들을 바라보았다.
Tom clapped and cheered / and looked like he could barely keep himself / from running up to hug and congratulate her.
Tom이 박수를 치고 환호성을 질렀고, / 그는 간신히 참는 것처럼 보였다. / 달려와 그녀를 껴안고 축하해주고 싶은 것
She couldn't wait to hug him, too.
그녀도 정말로 그를 껴안고 싶었다.

연설을 시작한 이후 처음으로 Alice는 자신의 연설문으로부터 고개를 들었다. 연설할 부분을 놓칠까 두려워 마칠 때까지 그녀는 페이지에 있는 단어들로부터 감히 눈을 뗄 수가 없었다. 사실 그녀는 단지 두 가지 간단한 것들을 바랐을 뿐이었는데, 연설하는 동안 읽는 능력을 잃지 않는 것과 웃음거리가 되지 않고 연설을 마치는 것이었다. 이제 강연장에 있는 모두가 일어서서 박수를 치고 있었다. 그것은 그녀가 희망했던 것 이상이었다. 환하게 웃으며, 그녀는 앞줄에 있는 낯익은 얼굴들을 바라보았다. Tom이 박수를 치고 환호성을 질렀고, 달려와 그녀를 껴안고 축하해주고 싶은 것을 간신히 참는 것처럼 보였다. 그녀도 정말로 그를 껴안고 싶었다.

Why? 왜 정답일까?
'She hadn't dared to break eye contact with the words on the pages until she finished, for fear of losing her place.'에서 Alice가 연설하는 도중 놓치는 부분이 있을까 몹시 긴장하며 연설했음을 알 수 있고, 'Smiling brightly, ~' 이후로는 연설을 잘 마친 Alice가 모두의 박수를 받으며 몹시 기뻐했음을 알 수 있다. 따라서 Alice의 심경 변화로 가장 적절한 것은 ① '긴장한 → 기쁜'이다.

- break eye contact with ~에서 눈을 떼다, 시선을 피하다
- for fear of ~할까봐 두려워서
- make a fool of oneself 웃음거리가 되다
- barely [ad] 간신히
- get through ~을 마치다
- clap [v] 박수를 치다
- congratulate [v] 축하하다

구문 풀이
2행 She hadn't dared to break eye contact with the words on the pages until she finished, for fear of losing her place.
과거완료 「dare + to부정사」 감히 ~하지 못하다 / 시간 접속사(~까지) / ~할까봐 두려워서 동명사

20 남이 아닌 자기 자신을 비교대상으로 삼아 성장하기 | 정답률 88% | 정답 ①
다음 글에서 필자가 주장하는 바로 가장 적절한 것은?
☑ ① 남과 비교하기보다는 자신의 성장에 주목해야 한다.
② 진로를 결정할 때는 다양한 의견을 경청해야 한다.
③ 발전을 위해서는 선의의 경쟁 상대가 있어야 한다.
④ 타인의 성공 사례를 자신의 본보기로 삼아야 한다.
⑤ 객관적 자료에 근거하여 직원을 평가해야 한다.

When I started my career, / I looked forward to the annual report from the organization / showing statistics for each of its leaders.
내가 일을 시작했을 때, / 나는 조직의 연간 보고서를 손꼽아 기다렸다. / 각 지도자에 대한 통계를 보여주는
As soon as I received them in the mail, / I'd look for my standing / and compare my progress with the progress of all the other leaders.
내가 그것을 메일로 받자마자, / 나는 내 순위를 찾아 / 다른 모든 지도자의 발전과 나의 발전을 비교하곤 했다.
After about five years of doing that, / I realized how harmful it was.
그렇게 한 지 5년쯤 지나서, / 나는 그것이 얼마나 해로운지 깨달았다.
Comparing yourself to others / is really just a needless distraction.
여러분 자신과 다른 사람을 비교하는 것은 / 사실 불필요하게 정신을 흩뜨리는 것일 뿐이다.
The only one you should compare yourself to / is you.
여러분 자신과 비교해야 하는 유일한 대상은 / 여러분뿐이다.
Your mission is to become better today / than you were yesterday.
여러분의 임무는 오늘 더 나아지는 것이다. / 어제의 여러분 모습보다
You do that / by focusing on what you can do today to improve and grow.
여러분은 그렇게 한다(나아져 간다). / 나아지고 성장하기 위해 오늘 여러분이 할 수 있는 것에 집중하여
Do that enough, / and if you look back / and compare the you of weeks, months, or years ago / to the you of today, / you should be greatly encouraged by your progress.
충분히 그렇게 하라, / 그리고 여러분이 되돌아보고, / 몇 주, 몇 달, 또는 몇 년 전의 여러분을 비교한다면, / 오늘의 여러분과 / 여러분은 자신의 발전에 대단히 고무될 것이다.

내가 일을 시작했을 때, 나는 각 지도자에 대한 통계를 보여주는 조직의 연간 보고서를 손꼽아 기다렸다. 그것을 메일로 받자마자, 나는 내 순위를 찾아 다른 모든 지도자의 발전과 나의 발전을 비교하곤 했다. 그렇게 한 지 5년쯤 지나서, 나는 그것이 얼마나 해로운지 깨달았다. 여러분 자신과 다른 사람을 비교하는 것은 사실 불필요하게 정신을 흩뜨리는 것일 뿐이다. 여러분 자신과 비교해야 하는 유일한 대상은 여러분뿐이다. 여러분의 임무는 어제보다 오늘 더 나아지는 것이다. 나아지고 성장하기 위해 오늘 여러분이 할 수 있는 것에 집중하여 나아져가는 것이다. 충분히 그렇게 한 다음, 되돌아보고, 몇 주, 몇 달, 또는 몇 년 전의 여러분과 오늘의 여러분을 비교한다면, 여러분은 자신의 발전에 대단히 고무될 것이다.

Why? 왜 정답일까?
'Comparing yourself to others is really just a needless distraction. The only one you should compare yourself to is you.'에서 남과 자신을 비교하는 것은 불필요하며 자기 자신을 유일한 비교 대상으로 삼아야 한다고 하므로, 필자가 주장하는 바로 가장 적절한 것은 ① '남과 비교하기보다는 자신의 성장에 주목해야 한다.'이다.

- look forward to ~을 고대하다
- organization [n] 조직
- progress [n] 발전, 진전
- needless [a] 불필요한
- distraction [n] 정신을 흩뜨리는 것, 주의를 분산시키는 것
- improve [v] 나아지다, 향상되다
- annual [a] 연간의, 1년의
- statistics [n] 통계
- harmful [a] 해로운
- encourage [v] 고무시키다, 용기를 북돋우다

구문 풀이
9행 You do that by focusing on what you can do today to improve and grow.
지시대명사(그것) / ~함으로써 / 관계대명사(~것) / 부사적 용법(~하기 위해)

21 완충 지대 마련의 중요성 | 정답률 60% | 정답 ②
밑줄 친 creating a buffer가 다음 글에서 의미하는 바로 가장 적절한 것은?
① knowing that learning is more important than winning
배우는 것이 이기는 것보다 더 중요함을 아는 것
☑ ② always being prepared for unexpected events
예상치 못한 사건에 항상 대비하는 것
③ never stopping what we have already started
이미 시작한 것을 결코 멈추지 않는 것
④ having a definite destination when we drive
운전할 때 확실한 목적지를 갖는 것
⑤ keeping peaceful relationships with others
다른 사람들과 평화로운 관계를 유지하는 것

On one occasion / I was trying to explain the concept of buffers to my children.
한 번은 / 나는 나의 아이들에게 완충 지대의 개념을 설명하려고 했다.
We were in the car together at the time / and I tried to explain the idea using a game.
우리는 그때 차에 함께 있었고 / 나는 게임을 이용하여 그 개념을 설명하려고 했다.
Imagine, I said, / that we had to get to our destination three miles away / without stopping.
나는 상상해 보자고 말했다. / 우리가 3마일 떨어진 목적지까지 도착해야 했다고 / 멈추지 않고
We couldn't predict / what was going to happen in front of us and around us.
우리는 예측할 수 없었을 것이다. / 우리 앞과 주위에서 무슨 일이 일어날지
We didn't know / how long the light would stay on green / or if the car in front would suddenly put on its brakes.
우리는 몰랐을 것이다. / 신호등이 얼마나 오랫동안 녹색일지, / 아니면 앞차의 운전자가 갑자기 브레이크를 밟을지
The only way to keep from crashing / was to put extra space / between our car and the car in front of us.
충돌을 막는 유일한 방법은 / 여분의 공간을 두는 것이었을 것이다. / 우리 차와 우리 앞에 있는 차 사이에
This space acts as a buffer.
이 공간은 완충 지대로 작용한다.
It gives us time / to respond and adapt to any sudden moves by other cars.
그것은 우리에게 시간을 준다. / 다른 차들의 갑작스러운 움직임에 반응하고 적응할
Similarly, / we can reduce the friction / of doing the essential in our work and lives / simply by creating a buffer.
마찬가지로, / 우리는 마찰을 줄일 수 있다. / 우리의 일과 삶에서 필수적인 일을 할 때의 / 단지 완충 지대를 만듦으로써

한 번은 나는 나의 아이들에게 완충 지대의 개념을 설명하려고 했다. 우리는 그때 차에 함께 있었고 나는 게임을 이용하여 그 개념을 설명하려고 했다. 나는 우리가 멈추지 않고 3마일 떨어진 목적지까지 도착해야 했다고 상상해 보자고 말했다. 우리는 우리 앞과 주위에서 무슨 일이 일어날지 예측할 수 없었을 것이다. 우리는 신호등이 얼마나 오랫동안 녹색일지, 아니면 앞차의 운전자가 갑자기 브레이크를 밟을지 몰랐을 것이다. 충돌을 막는 유일한 방법은 우리 차와 앞 차 사이에 여분의 공간을 두는 것이었을 것이다. 이 공간은 완충 지대로 작용한다. 그것은 우리에게 다른 차들의 갑작스러운 움직임에 반응하고 적응할 시간을 준다. 마찬가지로, 우리는 단지 완충 지대를 만듦으로써 우리의 일과 삶에서 필수적인 일을 할 때의 마찰을 줄일 수 있다.

Why? 왜 정답일까?
'The only way to keep from crashing was to put extra space ~' 이후에서 자동차 충돌을 막는 유일한 방법은 앞차와 일정 거리를 유지하여 다른 차의 움직임에 반응하고 적응할 충분한 시간을 확보하는 것이라고 설명한다. 이 내용에 비추어볼 때, 인생에서도 '완충 지대를 만들어야' 한다는 말은 언제 있을지 모르는 사고에 항상 대비할 필요가 있다는 의미임을 알 수 있다. 따라서 밑줄 친 부분이 의미하는 바로 가장 적절한 것은 ② '예상치 못한 사건에 항상 대비하는 것'이다.

- occasion [n] (어떤 일이 일어나는) 때, 경우
- destination [n] 목적지
- put on a brake 브레이크를 밟다, 제동을 걸다
- adapt to ~에 적응하다
- definite [a] 확실한
- buffer [n] 완충 지대
- predict [v] 예측하다
- act as ~로 작용하다, 기능하다
- essential [a] 필수적인

구문 풀이
3행 Imagine, I said, that we had to get to our destination three miles away without stopping.
명령문 / 삽입절 / 접속사(~것)
「without + 동명사」 ~하지 않은 채

22 미디어 산업의 책임 | 정답률 74% | 정답 ③
다음 글의 요지로 가장 적절한 것은?
① 방송 통신과 관련된 법 개정이 시급하다.
② 공익 방송 시청률이 점점 하락하고 있다.
☑ ③ 미디어 산업은 공익을 증진할 책임이 있다.
④ 미디어 산업은 시설의 현대화를 꾀하고 있다.
⑤ 미디어에 대한 비판적 시각을 기를 필요가 있다.

Many of the leaders I know in the media industry / are intelligent, capable, and honest.
내가 미디어 업계에 알고 있는 지도자 중 다수가 / 지적이고, 유능하고, 정직하다.
But they are leaders of companies / that appear to have only one purpose: / the single-minded pursuit of short-term profit and "shareholder value."
그러나 그들은 회사의 지도자들이다. / 유일한 목표를 가진 것처럼 보이는 / 단기간의 이익과 '주주 가치'의 전념된 추구라는
I believe, however, / that the media industry, / by its very nature and role in our society and global culture, / must act differently than other industries / — especially because they have the free use of our public airwaves and our digital spectrum, / and have almost unlimited access to our children's hearts and minds.
그러나 나는 믿는데, / 미디어 산업이 / 우리 사회와 세계 문화 속에서의 그것의 바로 그 본질과 역할로 인해, / 다른 산업과는 달리 행동해야 한다고 / 특히 미디어 산업이 우리의 공중파와 디지털 스펙트럼을 자유롭게 이용하고, / 우리 아이들의 감정과 생각에 거의 제한 없이 접근하기 때문이다.
These are priceless assets, / and the right to use them / should necessarily carry serious and long-lasting responsibilities / to promote the public good.

내가 미디어 업계에서 알고 있는 지도자 중 다수가 지적이고, 유능하고, 정직하다. 그러나 그들은 오로지 단기간의 이익과 '주주 가치'만을 추구하는 것이 유일한 목표인 것 같아 보이는 회사의 지도자들이다. 그러나 나는 미디어 산업이 우리 사회와 세계 문화 속에서 갖는 그것의 바로 그 본질과 역할로 인해, 다른 산업과는 달리 행동해야 한다고 믿는데, 특히 미디어 산업이 우리의 공중파와 디지털 스펙트럼을 자유롭게 이용하고, 우리 아이들의 감정과 생각에 거의 제한 없이 접근하기 때문이다. 이것들은 매우 귀중한 자산이며, 그것들을 사용할 권리는 공공의 이익을 증진해야 한다는 중대하고 장기간에 걸친 책임을 반드시 수반해야 한다.

Why? 왜 정답일까?

'I believe, however, ~' 문장에서 미디어 산업은 공중파와 디지털 스펙트럼이라는 자산을 자유롭게 이용하며 아이들의 생각과 마음에도 제한 없이 접근할 수 있다고 설명한다. 이를 토대로 마지막 문장인 '~ the right to use them should necessarily carry serious and long-lasting responsibilities to promote the public good.'에서는 이렇듯 특별한 권리를 부여받은 미디어가 공공의 이익을 증진하는 책임을 마땅히 져야 한다고 주장하고 있다. 따라서 글의 요지로 가장 적절한 것은 ③ '미디어 산업은 공익을 증진할 책임이 있다.'이다.

- **intelligent** ⓐ 지적인
- **pursuit** ⓝ 추구
- **airwaves** ⓝ 방송 전파, 채널
- **unlimited** ⓐ 제한 없는, 무한한
- **priceless** ⓐ 귀중한
- **long-lasting** ⓐ 장기적인
- **public good** ⓝ 공익
- **single-minded** (한 가지 목적에만) 전념하는
- **nature** ⓝ 본질
- **have access to** ~에 접근하다
- **necessarily** ⓐⓓ 반드시
- **asset** ⓝ 자산
- **promote** ⓥ 증진하다

구문 풀이

4행 I believe, however, that the media industry, (by its very nature and role in
접속사(~것) · 주어 · ( ) : 삽입구
our society and global culture), must act differently than other industries — especially
자동사 · ~와는 달리
because they have the free use of our public airwaves and our digital spectrum,
이유 접속사 · 주어 · 동사1
and have almost unlimited access to our children's hearts and minds.
동사2

---

23 레크리에이션에 참여하는 다양한 이유
정답률 55% | 정답 ②

다음 글의 주제로 가장 적절한 것은?

① effects of recreational participation on memory – 레크리에이션 참여가 기억력에 미치는 영향
✓ various motivations for recreational participation – 레크리에이션 참여의 다양한 동기
③ importance of balance between work and leisure – 일과 여가 사이 균형의 중요성
④ social factors promoting the recreation movement – 레크리에이션 운동을 촉진하는 사회적 요인
⑤ economic trends affecting recreational participation – 레크리에이션 참여에 영향을 주는 경제 동향

In addition to the varied forms that recreation may take, / it also meets a wide range of individual needs and interests.
레크리에이션이 취할 수 있는 다양한 형태뿐 아니라, / 그것은 또한 광범위한 개인의 욕구와 관심사를 충족시킨다.
Many participants take part in recreation / as a form of relaxation and release / from work pressures or other tensions.
많은 참여자들은 레크리에이션에 참여한다. / 휴식과 분출구의 형태로 / 업무상의 압박이나 다른 긴장으로부터의
Often they may be passive spectators of entertainment / provided by television, movies, or other forms of electronic amusement.
흔히 그들은 오락의 수동적인 구경꾼일 수 있다. / 텔레비전, 영화 또는 다른 형태의 전자 오락에 의해 제공되는
However, other significant play motivations / are based on the need / to express creativity, / discover hidden talents, / or pursue excellence in varied forms of personal expression.
그러나, 다른 중요한 놀이 동기는 / 욕구에 근거한다. / 창의성을 표현하거나, / 숨겨진 재능을 발견하거나, / 다양한 형태의 개인적 표현에서의 탁월함을 추구하려는
For some participants, / active, competitive recreation may offer a channel / for releasing hostility and aggression / or for struggling against others or the environment / in adventurous, high-risk activities.
일부 참여자들에게, / 활동적이고 경쟁적인 레크리에이션은 통로를 제공할 수 있다. / 적의와 공격성을 분출하거나 / 타인이나 환경에 맞서 싸울 수 있는 / 모험적이고 위험성이 높은 활동에서
Others enjoy recreation / that is highly social / and provides the opportunity / for making new friends or cooperating with others in group settings.
다른 사람들은 레크리에이션을 즐긴다. / 매우 사교적이고, / 기회를 제공하는 / 새로운 친구를 사귀거나 집단 환경에서 다른 사람들과 협력할

레크리에이션은 다양한 형태를 취할 수 있을 뿐만 아니라, 광범위한 개인의 욕구와 관심사를 충족시킨다. 많은 참여자들은 업무상의 압박이나 다른 긴장으로부터의 휴식과 분출구의 형태로 레크리에이션에 참여한다. 흔히 그들은 텔레비전, 영화 또는 다른 형태의 전자오락이 제공하는 즐거움의 수동적인 구경꾼일 수 있다. 그러나, 다른 중요한 놀이 동기는 창의성을 표현하거나, 숨겨진 재능을 발견하거나, 다양한 형태의 개인적 표현에서의 탁월함을 추구하려는 욕구에 근거한다. 일부 참여자들에게 활동적이고 경쟁적인 레크리에이션은 적의와 공격성을 분출하거나 모험적이고 위험성이 높은 활동에서 타인이나 환경에 맞서 싸울 수 있는 통로를 제공할 수 있다. 다른 사람들은, 매우 사교적이고, 새로운 친구를 사귀거나 집단 환경에서 다른 사람들과 협력할 기회를 제공하는 레크리에이션을 즐긴다.

Why? 왜 정답일까?

'In addition to the varied forms that recreation may take, it also meets a wide range of individual needs and interests.'에서 레크리에이션은 광범위한 개인의 욕구와 관심사를 충족시킨다는 일반적인 진술을 제시한 후, 다양한 참여 이유를 소개하고 있다. 따라서 글의 주제로 가장 적절한 것은 ② '레크리에이션 참여의 다양한 동기'이다.

- **in addition to** ~뿐만 아니라
- **tension** ⓝ 긴장
- **spectator** ⓝ 구경꾼, 관중
- **significant** ⓐ 중요한
- **excellence** ⓝ 탁월함
- **relaxation** ⓝ 휴식
- **passive** ⓐ 수동적인
- **amusement** ⓝ 오락
- **pursue** ⓥ 추구하다
- **competitive** ⓐ 경쟁적인

- **hostility** ⓝ 적의, 반감
- **adventurous** ⓐ 모험적인
- **promote** ⓥ 촉진하다
- **aggression** ⓝ 공격성
- **high-risk** 위험성이 높은

구문 풀이

1행 In addition to the varied forms [that recreation may take], it also meets a
~뿐만 아니라 · 선행사 · 목적격 관계대명사 · = recreation
wide range of individual needs and interests.

---

24 설탕량 표기의 신뢰성
정답률 76% | 정답 ④

다음 글의 제목으로 가장 적절한 것은?

① Artificial Sweeteners: Good or Bad? – 인공 감미료: 이로울까, 해로울까?
② Consumer Benefits of Ingredient Labeling – 성분 라벨 표기로 얻는 소비자 이익
③ Sugar: An Energy Booster for Your Brain – 설탕: 여러분의 두뇌를 위한 에너지 촉진제
✓ Truth About Sugar Hidden in Food Labels – 식품 라벨에 숨겨진 설탕에 대한 진실
⑤ What Should We Do to Reduce Sugar Intake? – 설탕 섭취를 줄이기 위해 우리는 무엇을 해야 하는가?

If a food contains more sugar than any other ingredient, / government regulations require / that sugar be listed first on the label.
한 식품이 다른 어떤 성분보다 설탕을 더 많이 함유하고 있다면, / 정부 규제에서는 요구한다. / 설탕이 라벨에 첫 번째로 기재될 것을
But if a food contains several different kinds of sweeteners, / they can be listed separately, / which pushes each one farther down the list.
그러나 어떤 식품이 몇 가지 다른 종류의 감미료를 함유하고 있다면, / 그것들은 각각 기재될 수 있는데, / 그것은 각각의 감미료를 목록에서 더 아래로 밀어 내린다.
This requirement has led the food industry / to put in three different sources of sugar / so that they don't have to say the food has that much sugar.
이 요구는 식품업계가 ~하게 했다. / 세 가지 다른 당의 원료를 넣도록 / 그 식품에 설탕이 그렇게 많이 들어 있다고 말할 필요가 없도록
So sugar doesn't appear first.
그래서 설탕이 첫 번째로 나타나지 않는다.
Whatever the true motive, / ingredient labeling / still does not fully convey the amount of sugar / being added to food, / certainly not in a language / that's easy for consumers to understand.
진짜 동기가 무엇이든, / 성분 라벨 표기는 / 설탕의 양을 여전히 충분히 전달하지 못하고 있으며, / 식품에 첨가되고 있는 / 분명히 소비자가 이해하기 쉬운 언어로 되어있지 않다.
A world-famous cereal brand's label, for example, / indicates that the cereal has 11 grams of sugar per serving.
예를 들어, 세계적으로 유명한 어떤 시리얼 브랜드의 라벨은 / 시리얼이 1회분에 11g의 설탕을 함유하고 있음을 보여준다.
But nowhere does it tell consumers / that more than one-third of the box contains added sugar.
그러나 라벨의 어디에서도 소비자들에게 알려주지 않는다. / 상자의 3분의 1 이상 첨가당을 함유하고 있다는 것을

한 식품이 다른 어떤 성분보다 설탕을 더 많이 함유하고 있다면, 정부 규제에서는 설탕이 라벨에 첫 번째로 기재될 것을 요구한다. 그러나 어떤 식품이 몇 가지 다른 종류의 감미료를 함유하고 있다면, 그것들은 각각 기재될 수 있는데, 그것은 각각의 감미료를 목록에서 더 아래로 밀어 내린다. 이 요구는 식품업계가 그 식품에 설탕이 그렇게 많이 들어 있다고 말할 필요가 없도록 세 가지 다른 당의 원료를 넣게 만들었다. 그래서 설탕이 첫 번째로 나타나지 않는다. 진짜 동기가 무엇이든, 성분 라벨 표기는 식품에 첨가되고 있는 설탕의 양을 여전히 충분히 전달하지 못하고 있으며, 분명히 소비자가 이해하기 쉬운 언어로 되어있지 않다. 예를 들어, 세계적으로 유명한 어떤 시리얼 브랜드의 라벨은 시리얼이 1회분에 11g의 설탕을 함유하고 있음을 보여준다. 그러나 라벨의 어디에서도 상자의 3분의 1 이상 첨가당을 함유하고 있다는 것을 소비자들에게 알려주지 않는다.

Why? 왜 정답일까?

'~ ingredient labeling still does not fully convey the amount of sugar being added to food, certainly not in a language that's easy for consumers to understand.'에서 성분 라벨 표기는 식품에 첨가된 설탕량을 제대로 보여주지 못하고 있으며 소비자가 이해하기 쉽게 쓰여있지도 않다는 점을 지적하고 있다. 따라서 글의 제목으로 가장 적절한 것은 ④ '식품 라벨에 숨겨진 설탕에 대한 진실'이다.

- **ingredient** ⓝ 성분, 재료
- **sweetener** ⓝ 감미료
- **requirement** ⓝ 요구
- **serving** ⓝ (음식의) 1인분, 1회 제공량
- **regulation** ⓝ 규제
- **separately** ⓐⓓ 각각, 개별적으로
- **convey** ⓥ 전달하다
- **intake** ⓝ 섭취량

구문 풀이

1행 If a food contains more sugar than any other ingredient, government
「비교급 + than any other + 단수명사 : 다른 어떤 ~보다 더 …하다(최상급 의미)」
regulations require that sugar (should) be listed first on the label.
「require + that + 주어 + (should) 동사원형 : ~이 …할 것을 요구하다」

12행 But nowhere does it tell consumers that more than one-third of the box
「부정어구 + do/does/did + 주어 + 동사원형 : 도치 구문」
contains added sugar.

---

25 요일별 풋볼 리그 경기 부상률
정답률 69% | 정답 ⑤

다음 도표의 내용과 일치하지 않는 것은?

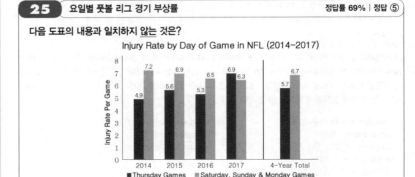

Injury Rate by Day of Game in NFL (2014-2017)

The above graph shows the injury rate by day of game / in the National Football League (NFL) / from 2014 to 2017.
위 그래프는 경기 요일별 부상률을 보여 준다. / 내셔널 풋볼 리그(NFL)의 / 2014년부터 2017년까지
① The injury rate of Thursday games / was the lowest in 2014 and the highest in 2017.
목요일 경기 부상률은 / 2014년에 가장 낮았고 2017년에 가장 높았다.
② The injury rate of Saturday, Sunday and Monday games / decreased steadily from 2014 to 2017.
토요일과 일요일과 월요일 경기 부상률은 / 2014년부터 2017년까지 꾸준히 감소하였다.
③ In all the years except 2017, / the injury rate of Thursday games / was lower than that of Saturday, Sunday and Monday games.
2017년을 제외한 모든 해에 / 목요일 경기 부상률이 / 토요일, 일요일 그리고 월요일 경기 부상률보다 더 낮았다.
④ The gap / between the injury rate of Thursday games / and that of Saturday, Sunday and Monday games / was the largest in 2014 and the smallest in 2017.
차이는 / 목요일 경기 부상률과 / 토요일, 일요일 그리고 월요일 경기 부상률 간의 / 2014년에 가장 컸고 2017년에 가장 작았다.
☑ In two years out of the four, / the injury rate of Thursday games / was higher than that of the 4-year total.
4년 중 두 해에, / 목요일 경기 부상률이 / 4년 전체의 목요일 경기 부상률보다 더 높았다.

위 그래프는 2014년부터 2017년까지 내셔널 풋볼 리그(NFL) 경기의 요일별 부상률을 보여 준다. ① 목요일 경기 부상률은 2014년에 가장 낮았고 2017년에 가장 높았다. ② 토요일과 일요일과 월요일 경기 부상률은 2014년부터 2017년까지 꾸준히 감소하였다. ③ 2017년을 제외한 모든 해에 목요일 경기 부상률이 토요일, 일요일 그리고 월요일 경기 부상률보다 더 낮았다. ④ 목요일 경기 부상률과 토요일, 일요일 그리고 월요일 경기 부상률 간의 차이는 2014년에 가장 컸고 2017년에 가장 작았다. ⑤ 4년 중 두 해에, 목요일 경기 부상률이 4년 전체의 목요일 경기 부상률보다 더 높았다.

Why? 왜 정답일까?
도표에 따르면 한 해의 목요일 경기 부상률이 4년 합계 목요일 경기 부상률보다 높았던 해는 2017년뿐이다. 따라서 도표의 내용과 일치하지 않는 것은 ⑤이다.

- injury ⓝ 부상
- steadily ⓐⓓ 꾸준히
- rate ⓝ 비율
- out of ~ 중에서, ~로부터

---

26 Christiaan Huygens의 생애   정답률 84% | 정답 ③

Christiaan Huygens에 관한 다음 글의 내용과 일치하지 않는 것은?
① 대학에서 법과 수학을 공부했다.
② 1689년에 뉴턴을 만났다.
☑ 뉴턴의 만유인력 법칙을 받아들였다.
④ 당대의 가장 정확한 시계 중 몇몇이 업적에 포함되었다.
⑤ 자신의 망원경을 사용하여 천문학 연구를 수행했다.

Dutch mathematician and astronomer Christiaan Huygens / was born in The Hague in 1629.
네덜란드의 수학자이자 천문학자인 Christiaan Huygens는 / 1629년 헤이그에서 태어났다.
「He studied law and mathematics at his university,」 ①의 근거 일치
/ and then devoted some time to his own research, / initially in mathematics / but then also in optics, / working on telescopes and grinding his own lenses.
그는 대학에서 법과 수학을 공부했고, / 이후 얼마간의 시간을 자기 연구에 바쳤다. / 처음에는 수학에서, / 그다음에는 광학에서도 / 망원경에 대한 작업을 하고 자신의 렌즈를 갈면서
「Huygens visited England several times, / and met Isaac Newton in 1689.」 ②의 근거 일치
Huygens는 영국을 몇 차례 방문했고, / 1689년에 아이작 뉴턴을 만났다.
「In addition to his work on light, / Huygens had studied forces and motion, / but he did not accept Newton's law of universal gravitation.」 ③의 근거 불일치
빛에 관한 연구 외에도 / Huygens는 힘과 운동을 연구했으나, / 뉴턴의 만유인력 법칙을 받아들이지 않았다.
「Huygens' wide-ranging achievements / included some of the most accurate clocks of his time, / the result of his work on pendulums.」 ④의 근거 일치
Huygens의 광범위한 업적에는 / 당대의 가장 정확한 시계 중 몇몇이 포함되었다. / 시계추에 대한 그의 연구의 결과물인
「His astronomical work, / carried out using his own telescopes, / included the discovery of Titan, the largest of Saturn's moons, / and the first correct description of Saturn's rings.」 ⑤의 근거 일치
그의 천문학 연구에는 / 자신의 망원경을 사용하여 수행된 / 토성의 위성 중 가장 큰 타이탄의 발견과 / 토성의 고리에 대한 최초의 정확한 기술이 포함되었다.

네덜란드의 수학자이자 천문학자인 Christiaan Huygens는 1629년 헤이그에서 태어났다. 그는 대학에서 법과 수학을 공부했고, 이후 처음에는 수학에서, 그다음에는 망원경에 대한 작업을 하고 자신의 렌즈를 갈면서 광학에서도 얼마간의 시간을 연구에 바쳤다. Huygens는 영국을 몇 차례 방문했고, 1689년에 아이작 뉴턴을 만났다. 빛에 관한 연구 외에도 Huygens는 힘과 운동을 연구했으나, 뉴턴의 만유인력 법칙을 받아들이지 않았다. Huygens의 광범위한 업적에는 시계추에 대한 그의 연구의 결과물인, 당대의 가장 정확한 시계 중 몇몇이 포함되었다. 자신의 망원경을 사용하여 수행된 그의 천문학 연구에는 토성의 위성 중 가장 큰 타이탄의 발견과 토성의 고리에 대한 최초의 정확한 기술이 포함되었다.

Why? 왜 정답일까?
'~ he did not accept Newton's law of universal gravitation.'에서 Christiaan Huygens는 힘과 운동을 연구하였으나 뉴턴의 만유인력 법칙을 받아들이지는 않았다고 설명하므로, 내용과 일치하지 않는 것은 ③ '뉴턴의 만유인력 법칙을 받아들였다.'이다.

Why? 왜 오답일까?
① 'He studied law and mathematics at his university, ~'의 내용과 일치한다.
② 'Huygens ~ met Isaac Newton in 1689.'의 내용과 일치한다.
④ 'Huygens' wide-ranging achievements included some of the most accurate clocks of his time, ~'의 내용과 일치한다.
⑤ 'His astronomical work, carried out using his own telescopes, ~'의 내용과 일치한다.

- mathematician ⓝ 수학자
- devote A to B A를 B에 바치다
- optics ⓝ 광학
- in addition to ~뿐만 아니라
- wide-ranging 광범위한
- accurate ⓐ 정확한
- astronomer ⓝ 천문학자
- initially ⓐⓓ 처음에는
- grind ⓥ (칼 등을) 갈다
- universal gravitation 만유인력
- achievement ⓝ 업적, 성취
- description ⓝ 기술, 설명

구문 풀이
2행 He studied law and mathematics at his university, and then devoted
　　　　동사1
some time to his own research, initially in mathematics but then also in optics,
　　　　　　　　　　　　　　　　　　　　　　　　　　동사2
「devote+A+to+B : A를 B에 바치다」
working on telescopes and grinding his own lenses.
분사구문1　　　　　　　　　　　분사구문2

---

27 꽃꽂이 대회 안내   정답률 85% | 정답 ②

Flower Arranging Contest에 관한 다음 안내문의 내용과 일치하지 않는 것은?
① 학부모 중에서 전문가는 참여할 수 없다.
☑ 참가자에게 재료를 제공한다.
③ 꽃꽂이를 끝내는 데 30분이 주어진다.
④ 부문별 1등, 2등, 3등에게 상금을 준다.
⑤ 2020년 5월 9일까지 꽃꽂이 작품이 전시된다.

Flower Arranging Contest
Flower Arranging Contest(꽃꽂이 대회)
Join our annual Flower Arranging Contest!
연례 꽃꽂이 대회에 참가하십시오!
When: May 7, 2020 at 4:00 p.m.
언제: 2020년 5월 7일 오후 4시
Where: Jade High School Educational Exhibit Building
어디서: Jade 고등학교 교육 전시관
Who Can Enter?
참가 대상
Category Ⅰ – Students enrolled in Home Economics
부문 Ⅰ / 가정 과목 등록 학생
「Category Ⅱ / – Parents (not open to professionals)」 ①의 근거 일치
부문 Ⅱ / 학부모(전문가는 참여할 수 없음)
Rules
규칙
「Each contestant must bring their own materials.」 ②의 근거 불일치
각 참가자는 자신의 재료를 가져와야 합니다.
「30 minutes will be allowed for finishing arrangements.」 ③의 근거 일치
꽃꽂이를 끝내는 데 30분이 주어집니다.
Prizes for Each Category
부문별 시상
「1st Place: $80.00 / 2nd Place: $60.00 / 3rd Place: $40.00」 ④의 근거 일치
1위: 80달러 / 2위: 60달러 / 3위: 40달러
「Arrangements will be on display until May 9, 2020.」 ⑤의 근거 일치
꽃꽂이 작품은 2020년 5월 9일까지 전시될 것입니다.

Flower Arranging Contest(꽃꽂이 대회)

연례 꽃꽂이 대회에 참가하십시오!

언제: 2020년 5월 7일 오후 4시
어디서: Jade 고등학교 교육 전시관

참가 대상
■ 부문 Ⅰ – 가정 과목 등록 학생
■ 부문 Ⅱ – 학부모(전문가는 참여할 수 없음)

규칙
■ 각 참가자는 자신의 재료를 가져와야 합니다.
■ 꽃꽂이를 끝내는 데 30분이 주어집니다.

부문별 시상
1위: 80달러　2위: 60달러　3위: 40달러

＊ 꽃꽂이 작품은 2020년 5월 9일까지 전시될 것입니다.

Why? 왜 정답일까?
'Each contestant must bring their own materials.'에서 참가자는 각자 재료를 가져와야 한다고 하므로, 안내문의 내용과 일치하지 않는 것은 ② '참가자에게 재료를 제공한다.'이다.

Why? 왜 오답일까?
① 'Parents (not open to professionals)'의 내용과 일치한다.
③ '30 minutes will be allowed for finishing arrangements.'의 내용과 일치한다.
④ '1st Place: $80.00 / 2nd Place: $60.00 / 3rd Place: $40.00'의 내용과 일치한다.
⑤ 'Arrangements will be on display until May 9, 2020.'의 내용과 일치한다.

- flower arranging 꽃꽂이
- home economics (학과) 가정
- contestant ⓝ 참가자
- enroll in ~에 등록하다
- professional ⓝ 전문가 ⓐ 전문적인
- on display 전시 중인

---

28 고양이 장난감 설명서   정답률 83% | 정답 ②

Bright Cat Toy에 관한 다음 안내문의 내용과 일치하는 것은?
① 구멍에서 정해진 순서대로 깃털이 나온다.
☑ 8분 후에 자동으로 작동을 멈춘다.
③ 완전히 충전하는 데 5시간이 걸린다.
④ 켜거나 끄려면 버튼을 길게 눌러야 한다.
⑤ 총 세 개의 깃털이 제공된다.

Bright Cat Toy
Bright Cat Toy(멋진 고양이 장난감)
Attract your cat's attention / and satisfy their hunting instincts / with a unique electronic cat toy.
여러분 고양이의 관심을 끌고 / 그들의 사냥 본능을 충족시키세요. / 독특한 전자 고양이 장난감으로

Key Benefits
주요 이점
「The feather appears randomly in the 6 holes.」 ①의근거 불일치
깃털이 6개의 구멍에서 무작위로 나옵니다.
Feathers can be exchanged easily.
깃털은 쉽게 교체될 수 있습니다.
「It automatically stops running after 8 minutes.」 ②의근거 일치
그것은 8분 후 자동으로 작동을 멈춥니다.
「It is fully charged in 30 minutes via USB-cable, / and it runs for 5 hours.」 ③의근거 불일치
그것은 USB 케이블을 통해 30분 만에 완전히 충전되며, / 5시간 동안 작동합니다.
How to Use
사용법
「Short press the button to power on / off the device.」 ④의근거 불일치
기기의 전원을 켜거나 끄려면 버튼을 짧게 누르세요.
Long press the button to change feathers.
깃털을 바꾸려면 버튼을 길게 누르세요.
What's in the Box
상자 속 내용물
Bright Cat Toy: 1 piece
Bright Cat Toy: 1개
「Feather: 2 pieces (1 installed, 1 extra)」 ⑤의근거 불일치
깃털: 2개(장착된 것 1개, 여분 1개)

Bright Cat Toy(멋진 고양이 장난감)

독특한 전자 고양이 장난감으로 여러분 고양이의 관심을 끌고 사냥 본능을 충족시키세요.

주요 이점
- 깃털이 6개의 구멍에서 무작위로 나옵니다.
- 깃털을 쉽게 교체할 수 있습니다.
- 8분 후 자동으로 작동을 멈춥니다.
- USB 케이블을 통해 30분 만에 완전히 충전되며, 5시간 동안 작동합니다.

사용법
- 기기의 전원을 켜거나 끄려면 버튼을 짧게 누르세요.
- 깃털을 바꾸려면 버튼을 길게 누르세요.

상자 속 내용물
- Bright Cat Toy: 1개
- 깃털: 2개(장착된 것 1개, 여분 1개)

Why? 왜 정답일까?
'It automatically stops running after 8 minutes.'에서 장난감은 8분 후 저절로 작동을 멈춘다고 하므로, 안내문의 내용과 일치하는 것은 ② '8분 후에 자동으로 작동을 멈춘다.'이다.

Why? 왜 오답일까?
① 'The feather appears randomly in the 6 holes.'에서 깃털은 무작위로 나온다고 하였다.
③ 'It is fully charged in 30 minutes via USB-cable, and it runs for 5 hours.'에서 완전 충전하는 데 30분이 걸리고, 완충 이후 작동 가능한 시간이 5시간이라고 하였다.
④ 'Short press the button to power on / off the device.'에서 장난감을 켜거나 끄려면 버튼을 짧게 눌러야 한다고 하였다.
⑤ 'Feather: 2 pieces (1 installed, 1 extra)'에서 깃털은 두 개가 제공된다고 하였다.

- attract one's attention ~의 관심을 끌다
- instinct ⓝ 본능
- automatically ⓐⓓ 자동으로, 저절로
- satisfy ⓥ 충족시키다
- randomly ⓐⓓ 무작위로

29 민간 항공기 운항 정답률 55% | 정답 ⑤

다음 글의 밑줄 친 부분 중, 어법상 틀린 것은?

Commercial airplanes / generally travel airways similar to roads, / although they are not physical structures.
민간 항공기는 / 일반적으로 도로와 유사한 항로로 운항한다. / 그것이 물리적 구조물은 아니지만
Airways have fixed widths and defined altitudes, / ① which separate traffic moving in opposite directions.
항로에는 고정된 폭과 정해진 고도가 있으며, / 이것이 반대 방향으로 움직이는 통행을 분리한다.
Vertical separation of aircraft / allows some flights ② to pass over airports / while other processes occur below.
항공기 간의 상하 분리는 / 일부 비행기가 공항 위를 통과하는 것을 가능하게 한다. / 아래에서 다른 과정이 이루어지는 동안
Air travel usually covers long distances, / with short periods of intense pilot activity at takeoff and landing / and long periods of lower pilot activity while in the air, / the portion of the flight ③ known as the "long haul."
항공 여행은 보통 장거리를 이동하며, / 이륙과 착륙 시 짧은 시간의 고강도 조종사 활동과, / 공중에 있는 동안 긴 시간의 저강도 조종사 활동이 있다. / '장거리 비행'이라고 알려진 비행 부분인
During the long-haul portion of a flight, / pilots spend more time assessing aircraft status / than ④ searching out nearby planes.
비행에서 장거리 비행 부분 동안 / 조종사들은 항공기 상태를 평가하는 데 더 많은 시간을 보낸다. / 근처의 비행기를 탐색하는 것보다
This is because collisions between aircraft / usually occur in the surrounding area of airports, / while crashes due to aircraft malfunction / ⑤ tend to occur during long-haul flight.
이는 항공기 간의 충돌은 / 대개 공항 주변 지역에서 발생하는 반면 / 항공기 오작동으로 인한 추락은 / 장거리 비행 중에 발생하는 경향이 있기 때문이다.

일반적으로 민간 항공기는 물리적 구조물은 아니지만 도로와 유사한 항로로 운항한다. 항로에는 고정된 폭과 정해진 고도가 있으며, 이것이 반대 방향으로 움직이는 통행을 분리한다. 항공기 간에 상하 간격을 둠으로써 아래에서 다른 과정이 이루어지는 동안 일부 비행기가 공항 위를 통과할 수 있게 된다. 항공 여행은 보통 장거리를 이동하며, 이륙과 착륙 시 짧은 시간의 고강도 조종사 활동과, '장거리 비행'이라고 알려진 비행 부분인, 공중에 있는 동안 긴 시간의 저강도 조종사 활동이 있다. 비행에서 장거리 비행 부분 동안 조종사들은 근처의 비행기를 탐색하는 것보다 항공기 상태를 평가하는 데 더 많은 시간을 보낸다. 이는 항공기 간의 충돌은 대개 공항 주변 지역에서 발생하는 반면 항공기 오작동으로 인한 추락은 장거리 비행 중에 발생하는 경향이 있기 때문이다.

Why? 왜 정답일까?
접속사 while 뒤로 복수 명사 crashes가 주어로 나오므로, 동사 tends를 복수형인 tend로 고쳐야 한다. 어법상 틀린 것은 ⑤이다.

Why? 왜 오답일까?
① 콤마 뒤에 쓰인 관계대명사의 계속적 용법으로 which가 바르게 쓰였다.
② 'allow + 목적어 + to부정사(~이 …하게 하다)'의 5형식 구문이므로 to pass가 바르게 쓰였다.
③ the portion of the flight가 '알려진' 대상이므로 과거분사 known이 수식어로 바르게 쓰였다.
④ 'spend + 시간/돈 + 동명사(~하는 데 …을 쓰다)' 구문이므로, 비교의 than 앞뒤로 assessing과 searching이 짝을 이루어 바르게 쓰였다.

- generally ⓐⓓ 일반적으로
- separate ⓥ 분리시키다
- cover ⓥ (거리를) 이동하다, 가다
- portion ⓝ 부분
- collision ⓝ 충돌
- defined ⓐ 정해진
- vertical ⓐ 상하의, 수직의
- intense ⓐ 강도 높은
- assess ⓥ 평가하다
- malfunction ⓝ 오작동, 기능 불량

구문 풀이

> **6행** Air travel usually covers long distances, with short periods of intense pilot activity at takeoff and landing and long periods of lower pilot activity while in the air, the portion of the flight known as the "long haul."
> 전치사 / 목적어1
> 목적어2 / 부사절(주어 + be 동사절 생략)
> 동격(= long periods of lower pilot activity) / 과거분사구(~라고 알려진)

30 음식을 기다리는 중 되짚어본 원자 개념 정답률 57% | 정답 ③

다음 글의 밑줄 친 부분 중, 문맥상 낱말의 쓰임이 적절하지 않은 것은? [3점]

I was sitting outside a restaurant in Spain one summer evening, / waiting for dinner.
나는 어느 여름날 저녁 스페인에 한 식당 밖에 앉아 / 저녁 식사를 기다리고 있었다.
The aroma of the kitchens excited my taste buds.
주방의 향기가 나의 미뢰를 자극했다.
My future meal was coming to me / in the form of molecules drifting through the air, / too small for my eyes to see / but ① detected by my nose.
곧 먹게 될 내 음식은 내게 오고 있었다. / 공중을 떠다니는 분자의 형태로 / 너무 작아 눈으로 볼 수는 없지만 / 코로는 감지되는
The ancient Greeks / first came upon the idea of atoms this way; / the smell of baking bread suggested to them / that small particles of bread ② existed beyond vision.
고대 그리스인들은 / 이런 식으로 원자의 개념을 최초로 생각해 냈는데, / 빵 굽는 냄새는 그들에게 암시했다. / 작은 빵 입자가 눈에 보이지 않게 존재한다는
The cycle of weather ☑ reinforced this idea: / a puddle of water on the ground / gradually dries out, disappears, and then falls later as rain.
날씨의 순환은 이 생각을 강화했다. / 지면 위 물웅덩이는 / 점차 말라 사라지고, 그런 다음 나중에 비가 되어 떨어진다.
They reasoned / that there must be particles of water / that turn into steam, form clouds, and fall to earth, / so that the water is ④ conserved / even though the little particles are too small to see.
그들은 추론했다. / 물 입자가 존재하는 게 틀림없고, / 수증기로 변하여 구름을 형성하고 땅으로 떨어지는 / 그래서 그 물이 보존된다고 / 그 작은 입자들이 너무 작아 눈에 보이지 않더라도
My paella in Spain had inspired me, / four thousand years too ⑤ late, / to take the credit for atomic theory.
스페인에서 먹은 나의 파에야가 내게 영감을 주었다. / 4천 년이나 너무 늦게 / 원자 이론에 대한 공로를 인정받기에는

나는 어느 여름날 저녁 스페인에 한 식당 밖에 앉아 저녁 식사를 기다리고 있었다. 주방의 향기가 나의 미뢰를 자극했다. 곧 먹게 될 내 음식은, 너무 작아 눈으로 볼 수는 없지만 코로는 ① 감지되는, 공중을 떠다니는 분자의 형태로 내게 오고 있었다. 고대 그리스인들은 이런 식으로 원자의 개념을 최초로 생각해 냈는데, 빵 굽는 냄새는 그들에게 작은 빵 입자가 눈에 보이지 않게 ② 존재한다는 생각이 들게 했다. 날씨의 순환은 이 생각을 ③ 뒤집었다(→ 강화했다). 지면 위 물웅덩이는 점차 말라 사라지고, 그런 다음 나중에 비가 되어 떨어진다. 그들은 수증기로 변하여 구름을 형성하고 땅으로 떨어지는 물 입자가 존재하는 게 틀림없고, 그래서 그 작은 입자들이 너무 작아 눈에 보이지 않더라도 그 물이 ④ 보존된다고 추론했다. 스페인에서 먹은 나의 파에야가 원자 이론에 대한 공로를 인정받기에는 4천 년이나 너무 ⑤ 늦게 내게 영감을 주었다.

Why? 왜 정답일까?
'They reasoned that there must be particles of water that turn into steam, form clouds, and fall to earth, so that the water is conserved even though the little particles are too small to see.'에서 물웅덩이가 수증기로 증발하여 구름을 이루고 나중에 비가 되어 떨어지는 것으로 볼 때 너무 작아 눈에 보이지 않더라도 항상 보존되는 물 입자가 있을 것으로 추론되었다는 설명이 나온다. 이에 비추어볼 때, ③이 포함된 문장은 날씨의 순환 과정이 항상 보존되는 입자가 있다는 생각을 '강화해 주었다'는 의미를 나타내야 한다. 따라서 ③의 disproved를 reinforced로 고쳐야 한다. 문맥상 낱말의 쓰임이 적절하지 않은 것은 ③이다.

- drift ⓥ 떠다니다
- atom ⓝ 원자
- gradually ⓐⓓ 점차
- disappear ⓥ 사라지다
- take the credit for ~의 공적을 인정받다
- detect ⓥ 감지하다
- disprove ⓥ 틀렸음을 입증하다
- dry out ⓥ 메마르다, 고갈되다
- conserve ⓥ 보존하다

구문 풀이

> **9행** They reasoned that there must be particles of water [that turn into steam, form clouds, and fall to earth], so that the water is conserved even though the little particles are too small to see.
> 접속사(~것) / 동사 / 주어(선행사) / 주격 관·대 복수 동사1
> 복수 동사2 / 복수 동사3 / (~해서) ~하다 / 비록 ~일지라도
> 「too ~ to : 너무 ~해서 …할 수 없다」

★★★ 등급을 가르는 문제!

31 연약해서 아름다운 삶 정답률 45% | 정답 ①

다음 빈칸에 들어갈 말로 가장 적절한 것을 고르시오. [3점]

① fragility – 연약함　　② stability – 안정성　　③ harmony – 조화
④ satisfaction – 만족감　　⑤ diversity – 다양성

When he was dying, / the contemporary Buddhist teacher Dainin Katagiri / wrote a remarkable book called *Returning to Silence.*
그가 죽어가고 있었을 때, / 현대의 불교 스승인 Dainin Katagiri는 / 침묵으로의 회귀라는 경이로운 책을 집필했다.
Life, he wrote, "is a dangerous situation."
그는 삶이란 "위험한 상황이다."라고 썼다.
It is the weakness of life / that makes it precious; / his words are filled / with the very fact of his own life passing away.
바로 삶의 취약함이, / 삶을 소중하게 만드는 것은 / 그의 글은 채워져 있다. / 자신의 삶이 끝나가고 있다는 바로 그 사실로
"The china bowl is beautiful / because sooner or later it will break.... / The life of the bowl is always existing in a dangerous situation."
"자기 그릇은 아름답다. / 언젠가 깨질 것이기 때문에… / 그 그릇의 생명은 늘 위험한 상황에 놓여 있다."
Such is our struggle: / this unstable beauty.
그런 것이 우리의 고행이다. / 이 불안정한 아름다움.
This inevitable wound.
이 피할 수 없는 상처.
We forget — / how easily we forget — / that love and loss are intimate companions, / that we love the real flower so much more than the plastic one / and love the cast of twilight across a mountainside / lasting only a moment.
우리는 잊는다. / — 그것도 너무나 쉽게 잊는다. / 사랑과 상실이 친밀한 동반자라는 것을, / 우리가 진짜 꽃을 플라스틱 꽃보다 훨씬 더 사랑하고 / 산 중턱을 가로지르는 황혼의 색조를 사랑하는 것을 / 한 순간만 지속하는
It is this very fragility / that opens our hearts.
바로 이 연약함이다. / 우리의 마음을 여는 것은

현대의 불교 스승인 Dainin Katagiri는 죽음을 앞두고 침묵으로의 회귀라는 경이로운 책을 집필했다. 그는 삶이란 "위험한 상황이다."라고 썼다. 삶을 소중하게 만드는 것은 바로 삶의 취약함이며, 그의 글은 자신의 삶이 끝나가고 있다는 바로 그 사실로 채워져 있다. "자기 그릇은 언젠가 깨질 것이기 때문에 아름답다…. 그 그릇의 생명은 늘 위험한 상황에 놓여 있다." 그런 것이 우리의 고행이다. 이 불안정한 아름다움. 이 피할 수 없는 상처. 우리는 사랑과 상실이 친밀한 동반자라는 것을, 우리가 진짜 꽃을 플라스틱 꽃보다 훨씬 더 사랑하고 산 중턱을 가로지르는 한 순간만 지속하는 황혼의 색조를 사랑한다는 것을 잊는다 — 그것도 너무나 쉽게 잊는다. 우리의 마음을 여는 것은 바로 이 연약함이다.

Why? 왜 정답일까?
'It is the weakness of life that makes it precious; ~'에서 Dainin Katagiri는 죽음을 앞두고 쓴 책에서 삶을 소중하게 만드는 것이 삶의 취약함이라고 기술했다는 내용이 나온다. 따라서 빈칸에 들어갈 말로 가장 적절한 것은 weakness의 동의어인 ① '연약함'이다.

- **contemporary** ⓐ 현대의
- **pass away** (존재하던 것이) 없어지다
- **unstable** ⓐ 불안정한
- **wound** ⓝ 상처 ⓥ 상처 입히다
- **companion** ⓝ 동반자
- **stability** ⓝ 안정성
- **remarkable** ⓐ 경이로운, 주목할 만한
- **sooner or later** 언젠가, 곧, 조만간
- **inevitable** ⓐ 피할 수 없는
- **intimate** ⓐ 친밀한
- **fragility** ⓝ 연약함

구문 풀이
8행 We forget — (how easily we forget) — that love and loss are intimate
동사　　( ): 삽입절　　접속사1(~것)
companions, that we love the real flower so much more than the plastic one and
접속사2(~것)　　비교급 강조
love the cast of twilight across a mountainside lasting only a moment.
전명구　　현재분사구(twilight 꾸밈)

★★ 문제 해결 꿀~팁 ★★
▶ 많이 틀린 이유는?
삶은 언젠가 끝나기 마련인 특유의 연약함 때문에 아름답게 여겨진다는 내용의 글로, ②의 '안정성'은 주제와 반대된다. ③의 '조화', ④의 '만족감'은 글에서 언급되지 않았다.
▶ 문제 해결 방법은?
강조구문인 'It is the weakness of life ~'에서 삶의 연약함을, 도치 구문인 'Such is our struggle: this unstable beauty.'에서 삶의 불안정한 아름다움을 강조하고 있는 것으로 볼 때 ①이 답으로 적절하다.

32 인내심의 중요성　　정답률 56% | 정답 ①
다음 빈칸에 들어갈 말로 가장 적절한 것을 고르시오.
① he didn't carry on to the end – 그는 끝까지 계속하지 못했다
② someone told him not to give up – 누군가 그에게 그만두지 말라고 했다
③ the sticks were not strong enough – 막대기가 충분히 튼튼하지 않았다
④ he started without planning in advance – 그는 미리 계획하지 않은 채로 시작했다
⑤ the weather was not suitable to start a fire – 불을 피우기에 날씨가 적당하지 않았다

Nothing happens immediately, / so in the beginning / we can't see any results from our practice.
아무것도 즉시 일어나는 것은 없으므로, / 처음에 / 우리는 우리가 하는 일로부터 어떤 결과도 볼 수 없다.
This is like the example of the man / who tries to make fire / by rubbing two sticks of wood together.
이것은 사람의 예와 같다. / 불을 피우려고 하는 / 두 개의 나무 막대기를 서로 문질러서
He says to himself, "They say there's fire here," / and he begins rubbing energetically.
그는 "여기에 불이 있다고들 하잖아."라고 혼잣말을 하고 / 힘차게 문지르기 시작한다.
He rubs on and on, / but he's very impatient.
그는 계속해서 문지르지만, / 그는 매우 참을성이 없다.
He wants to have that fire, / but the fire doesn't come.
그는 그 불을 갖고 싶어 하지만, / 불은 일어나지 않는다.
So he gets discouraged / and stops to rest for a while.
그래서 그는 풀이 죽어서 / 잠시 쉬러 멈춘다.
Then he starts again, / but the going is slow, / so he rests again.
그러고 나서 그는 다시 시작하지만, / 진행이 더디므로, / 그는 다시 휴식을 취한다.
By then the heat has disappeared; / he didn't keep at it long enough.

그때쯤에는 열이 사라져 버렸는데, / 그가 충분히 오랫동안 그것을 계속하지 않았기 때문이다.
He rubs and rubs until he gets tired / and then he stops altogether.
그는 결국 지치게 되기까지 문지르고 문지르다가, / 그런 다음에 완전히 멈춘다.
Not only is he tired, / but he becomes more and more discouraged / until he gives up completely, "There's no fire here."
그는 지쳤을 뿐만 아니라, / 점점 더 좌절하여 "여기에는 불이 없어."라고 하며 완전히 포기한다.
Actually, he was doing the work, / but there wasn't enough heat to start a fire.
사실 그는 작업을 하고 있었지만, / 불을 피울 수 있을 만큼의 충분한 열이 없었다.
The fire was there all the time, / but he didn't carry on to the end.
불은 줄곧 거기에 있었지만, / 그는 끝까지 계속하지 못했다.

아무것도 즉시 일어나는 것은 없으므로, 처음에 우리는 우리가 하는 일로부터 어떤 결과도 볼 수 없다. 이것은 두 개의 나무 막대기를 서로 문질러서 불을 피우려고 하는 사람의 예와 같다. 그는 "여기에 불이 있다고들 하잖아."라고 혼잣말을 하고 힘차게 문지르기 시작한다. 계속해서 문지르지만, 그는 매우 참을성이 없다. 그는 그 불을 갖고 싶어 하지만, 불은 일어나지 않는다. 그래서 그는 풀이 죽어서 잠시 쉬러 멈춘다. 그러고 나서 다시 시작하지만, 진행이 더디므로, 그는 다시 휴식을 취한다. 그때쯤에는 열이 사라져 버렸는데, 그가 충분히 오랫동안 그것을 계속하지 않았기 때문이다. 그는 문지르고 또 문지르다가 결국 지치게 되고, 그런 다음에 완전히 멈춘다. 그는 지쳤을 뿐만 아니라, 점점 더 좌절하여 "여기에는 불이 없어."라고 하며 완전히 포기한다. 사실 그는 작업을 하고 있었지만, 불을 피울 수 있을 만큼의 충분한 열이 없었다. 불은 줄곧 거기에 있었지만, 그는 끝까지 계속하지 못했다.

Why? 왜 정답일까?
첫 문장에서 어떤 일도 즉시 일어나지 않으므로 일의 시작 단계에서는 아무런 결실도 볼 수 없다는 내용을 제시한 후 나뭇가지를 비벼 불을 켜려고 시도하는 남자의 예를 든다. 예시에 따르면 남자는 참을성이 없어서(he's very impatient), 불을 피울 만큼의 열이 유지되도록 계속해서 비비는 일을 하지 못한다(he didn't keep at it long enough)고 한다. 따라서 빈칸에 들어갈 말로 가장 적절한 것은 남자의 인내심 부족을 지적하는 ① '그는 끝까지 계속하지 못했다'이다.

- **practice** ⓐ 실행
- **impatient** ⓐ 참을성이 없는
- **altogether** [ad] 완전히
- **in advance** 미리
- **energetically** [ad] 힘차게, 열심히
- **discouraged** ⓐ 풀이 죽은, 낙담한
- **carry on** ~을 계속하다
- **suitable** ⓐ 적합한

구문 풀이
10행 「부정어구 + be + 주어 : 도치 구문」 Not only is he tired, but he becomes more and more discouraged until he
「not only + A + but (also) + B : A뿐만 아니라 B도」　시간 접속사(~까지)
gives up completely, "There's no fire here."

33 생각을 일상 언어로 풀어보기　　정답률 47% | 정답 ⑤
다음 빈칸에 들어갈 말로 가장 적절한 것을 고르시오. [3점]
① finish writing quickly – 글쓰기를 빨리 끝낼
② reduce sentence errors – 문장의 오류를 줄일
③ appeal to various readers – 다양한 독자의 흥미를 끌
④ come up with creative ideas – 창의적인 생각을 떠올릴
⑤ clarify your ideas to yourself – 자신의 생각을 스스로에게 명료하게 할

Translating academic language into everyday language / can be an essential tool for you as a writer / to clarify your ideas to yourself.
학문적인 언어를 일상 언어로 바꿔 보는 것은 / 작가인 여러분에게 필수적인 도구가 될 수 있다. / 자신의 생각을 스스로에게 명료하게 할 수 있는
For, as writing theorists often note, / writing is generally not a process / in which we start with a fully formed idea in our heads / that we then simply transcribe / in an unchanged state onto the page.
왜냐하면, 글쓰기 이론가들이 흔히 지적하듯이, / 글쓰기는 일반적으로 과정이 아니기 때문이다. / 머릿속에 완전하게 만들어진 한 가지 생각으로 시작하는 / 우리가 단순히 옮겨 쓰는 / 본래 그대로의 상태로 페이지 위에
On the contrary, / writing is more often a means of discovery / in which we use the writing process / to figure out what our idea is.
도리어 / 글쓰기는 발견의 수단인 경우가 더 흔하다. / 우리가 글쓰기 과정을 사용하는 / 우리의 생각이 무엇인지를 알아내기 위해
This is why writers are often surprised to find / that what they end up with on the page / is quite different / from what they thought it would be when they started.
이것이 글을 쓰는 사람들이 발견하고는 자주 놀라는 이유이다. / 결국 그들이 페이지 위에 적는 내용이 / 상당히 다르다는 것을 / 그들이 처음에 시작할 때 그렇게 되리라고 생각했던 것과
What we are trying to say here is / that everyday language is often crucial for this discovery process.
우리가 여기서 하고자 하는 말은 / 일상 언어가 이런 발견 과정에 흔히 매우 중요하다는 것이다.
Translating your ideas into more common, simpler terms / can help you figure out what your ideas really are, / as opposed to what you initially imagined they were.
여러분의 생각을 더 평범하고 더 간단한 말로 바꿔 보는 것은 / 실제 여러분의 생각이 무엇인지 알아내도록 도와줄 수 있을 것이다. / 여러분이 처음에 그럴 것이라고 상상했던 것이 아니라

학문적인 언어를 일상 언어로 바꿔 보는 것은 여러분이 작가로서 자신의 생각을 스스로에게 명료하게 할 수 있는 필수적인 도구가 될 수 있다. 왜냐하면, 글쓰기 이론가들이 흔히 지적하듯이, 글쓰기는 일반적으로 머릿속에 완전하게 만들어진 한 가지 생각으로 시작하여, 그 생각을 본래 그대로의 상태로 페이지 위에 단순히 옮겨 쓰는 과정이 아니기 때문이다. 도리어 글쓰기는 글쓰기 과정을 사용하여 우리의 생각이 무엇인지를 알아내는 발견의 수단인 경우가 더 흔하다. 이래서 글을 쓰는 사람들은 결국 페이지 위에 적히는 내용이 처음에 시작할 때 그렇게 되리라고 생각했던 것과 상당히 다르다는 것을 발견하고는 자주 놀란다. 우리가 여기서 하고자 하는 말은 일상 언어가 이런 발견 과정에 흔히 매우 중요하다는 것이다. 여러분의 생각을 더 평범하고 더 간단한 말로 바꿔 보는 것은 여러분이 처음에 그럴 것이라고 상상했던 것이 아니라 실제 여러분의 생각이 무엇인지 알아내도록 도와줄 수 있을 것이다.

Why? 왜 정답일까?
'Translating your ideas into more common, simpler terms can help you figure out what your ideas really are, as opposed to what you initially imagined they were.'에서 머릿속 생각을 쉬운 말로 풀어보면 그 생각의 내용이 실제로 어떤지 깨닫는 데 도움이 될 것이라고 하므로, 빈칸에 들어갈 말로 가장 적절한 것은 ⑤ '자신의 생각을 스스로에게 명료하게 할'이다.

- translate A into B A를 B로 번역하다, 옮기다
- theorist ⓝ 이론가
- unchanged ⓐ 변하지 않은
- end up with 결국 ~하게 되다
- as opposed to ~이 아니라, ~와 대조적으로
- come up with ~을 떠올리다
- essential ⓐ 필수적인
- generally ⓐ 일반적으로
- discovery ⓝ 발견
- crucial ⓐ 중요한
- initially ⓐ 처음에
- clarify ⓥ 명확하게 하다

구문 풀이

2행 For, as writing theorists often note, writing is generally not a process [in which we start with a fully formed idea in our heads {that we then simply transcribe in an unchanged state onto the page}]. [ ] : a fully formed idea 수식

7행 This is why writers are often surprised to find {that what they end up with on the page is quite different from what (they thought) it would be when they started}.

★★★ 등급을 가르는 문제!

34 유전자 발현에 영향을 주는 음식 정답률 37% | 정답 ⑤

다음 빈칸에 들어갈 말로 가장 적절한 것을 고르시오. [3점]

① identical twins have the same genetic makeup
일란성 쌍둥이는 똑같은 유전자 구성을 지니고 있다
② our preference for food is influenced by genes
우리의 음식 선호는 유전자에 영향을 받는다
③ balanced diet is essential for our mental health
균형잡힌 식사가 우리의 정신 건강에 필수적이다
④ genetic engineering can cure some fatal diseases
유전공학은 몇몇 치명적인 질병을 고칠 수 있다
✓⑤ foods can immediately influence the genetic blueprint
식품이 유전자 청사진에 직접 영향을 줄 수 있다

The growing field of genetics is showing us / what many scientists have suspected for years / — foods can immediately influence the genetic blueprint.
성장하고 있는 유전학 분야는 우리에게 보여주고 있다. / 많은 과학자가 여러 해 동안 의구심을 가져왔던 것을 / 즉 식품이 유전자 청사진에 직접 영향을 줄 수 있다는 것

This information helps us better understand / that genes are under our control / and not something we must obey.
이 정보는 우리가 더 잘 이해하도록 도와준다. / 유전자가 우리의 통제 하에 있는 것이지 / 우리가 복종해야 하는 것이 아니라는 것을

Consider identical twins; / both individuals are given the same genes.
일란성 쌍둥이를 생각해보자. / 두 사람은 모두 똑같은 유전자를 부여받는다.

In mid-life, one twin develops cancer, / and the other lives a long healthy life without cancer.
중년에, 쌍둥이 중 한 명은 암에 걸리고, / 다른 한 명은 암 없이 건강하게 오래 산다.

A specific gene instructed one twin to develop cancer, / but in the other the same gene did not initiate the disease.
특정 유전자가 쌍둥이 중 한 명에게 암에 걸리도록 명령했지만, / 나머지 한 명에서는 똑같은 유전자가 그 질병을 발생시키지 않았다.

One possibility is / that the healthy twin had a diet / that turned off the cancer gene / — the same gene that instructed the other person to get sick.
한 가지 가능성은 / 쌍둥이 중 건강한 사람이 식사를 했다는 것이다. / 암 유전자를 차단하는 / 즉 나머지 한 명이 병에 걸리도록 명령했던 바로 그 유전자를

For many years, scientists have recognized / other environmental factors, / such as chemical toxins (tobacco for example), / can contribute to cancer through their actions on genes.
여러 해 동안 과학자들은 인정해 왔다. / 다른 환경적 요인들이 / 화학적 독소(예를 들어 담배)와 같은 / 유전자에 작용하여 암의 원인이 될 수 있다는 것을

The notion / that food has a specific influence on gene expression / is relatively new.
생각은 / 음식이 유전자 발현에 특정한 영향을 미친다는 / 비교적 새로운 것이다.

성장하고 있는 유전학 분야는 많은 과학자가 여러 해 동안 의구심을 가져왔던 것, 즉 식품이 유전자 청사진에 직접 영향을 줄 수 있다는 것을 우리에게 보여주고 있다. 이 정보는 유전자가 우리의 통제 하에 있는 것이지 우리가 복종해야 하는 것이 아니라는 것을 더 잘 이해하도록 도와준다. 일란성 쌍둥이를 생각해보자. 두 사람은 모두 똑같은 유전자를 부여받는다. 중년에, 쌍둥이 중 한 명은 암에 걸리고, 다른 한 명은 암 없이 건강하게 오래 산다. 특정 유전자가 쌍둥이 중 한 명에게 암에 걸리도록 명령했지만, 나머지 한 명에서는 똑같은 유전자가 그 질병을 발생시키지 않았다. 한 가지 가능성은 쌍둥이 중 건강한 사람이 암 유전자를 차단하는 식사를 했다는 것이다. 즉 나머지 한 명이 병에 걸리도록 명령했던 바로 그 유전자를 차단하는 식사를 한 것이다. 여러 해 동안 과학자들은 화학적 독소(예를 들어 담배)와 같은 다른 환경적 요인들이 유전자에 작용하여 암의 원인이 될 수 있다는 것을 인정해 왔다. 음식이 유전자 발현에 특정한 영향을 미친다는 생각은 비교적 새로운 것이다.

Why? 왜 정답일까?

유전자가 완전히 서로 같지만 둘 중 한 사람만 암에 걸린 일란성 쌍둥이를 생각해 볼 때, 음식이 유전자 발현에 특정한 영향을 끼친다는 사실(The notion that food has a specific influence on gene expression ~)을 알 수 있음을 소개한 글이다. 따라서 빈칸에 들어갈 말로 가장 적절한 것은 ⑤ '식품이 유전자 청사진에 직접 영향을 줄 수 있다'이다.

- genetics ⓝ 유전학
- under control 통제 하에 있는, 통제되는
- identical twin 일란성 쌍둥이
- initiate ⓥ 시작하게 하다
- contribute to ~의 원인이 되다
- makeup ⓝ 구성
- immediately ⓐ 직접적으로, 즉각
- suspect ⓥ 의심하다
- obey ⓥ 복종하다
- instruct ⓥ 명령하다, 지시하다
- environmental ⓐ 환경적인
- relatively ⓐ 비교적
- preference ⓝ 선호
- blueprint ⓝ 청사진, 설계도

구문 풀이

9행 One possibility is that the healthy twin had a diet [that turned off the cancer gene] — the same gene [that instructed the other person to get sick].

★★ 문제 해결 꿀~팁 ★★

▶ 많이 틀린 이유는?
우리가 먹는 음식이 유전자 발현에 영향을 미칠 수 있다는 내용을 ④에서 언급하는 genetic

---

engineering(유전공학)이나 fatal diseases(치명적인 질병)에 대한 언급은 없다. 또한 ②는 유전자가 음식 선호에 영향을 준다는 내용으로 이 글의 내용과 반대되는 내용이다.

▶ 문제 해결 방법은?
글의 주제가 처음과 마지막에서 두 번 언급되고 있고 이를 예를 들어 설명한 내용이 가운데에 배치된 글이다. 빈칸이 주제를 나타내고 있으므로 예시를 잘 파악하고 주제가 다시 언급되는 부분에 주목하여 읽는다.

35 연극계의 미신 정답률 59% | 정답 ③

다음 글에서 전체 흐름과 관계 없는 문장은?

There are many superstitions / surrounding the world of the theater.
많은 미신이 있다. / 연극계를 둘러싸고 있는

① Superstitions can be anything / from not wanting to say the last line of a play / before the first audience comes, / to not wanting to rehearse the curtain call / before the final rehearsal.
미신은 무엇이든 될 수 있다. / 연극의 마지막 대사를 말하지 말아야 하는 것부터, / 첫 관객이 오기 전에 / 커튼콜을 예행연습하지 말아야 하는 것까지 / 마지막 예행연습 전에

② Shakespeare's famous tragedy *Macbeth* is said to be cursed, / and to avoid problems / actors never say the title of the play out loud / when inside a theater / or a theatrical space (like a rehearsal room or costume shop).
셰익스피어의 유명한 비극 *Macbeth*는 저주받았다는 이야기가 있으며, / 문제를 피하고자 / 배우들은 그 연극의 제목을 절대 소리 내어 말하지 않는다. / 극장 안이나 / (예행연습실이나 의상실 같은) 극장 공간 내에서

✓③ The interaction between the audience and the actors in the play / influences the actors' performance.
연극에서 관객과 배우들 사이의 상호 작용은 / 배우들의 연기에 영향을 미친다.

④ Since the play is set in Scotland, / the secret code you say / when you need to say the title of the play / is "the Scottish play."
그 연극은 스코틀랜드를 배경으로 하고 있기 때문에, / 당신이 말하는 암호는 / 당신이 연극의 제목을 말할 필요가 있을 때 / '그 스코틀랜드 연극'이다.

⑤ If you do say the title by accident, / legend has it / that you have to go outside, / turn around three times, / and come back into the theater.
당신이 우연히 제목을 정말 말하게 된다면, / 전설이 있다. / 당신은 밖으로 나가 / 세 바퀴를 돌고 / 극장으로 다시 돌아와야 한다는

연극계를 둘러싸고 있는 많은 미신이 있다. ① 미신은 첫 관객이 오기 전에 연극의 마지막 대사를 말하지 말아야 한다는 것부터, 마지막 예행연습 전에 커튼콜을 예행연습하지 말아야 한다는 것까지 무엇이든 될 수 있다. ② 셰익스피어의 유명한 비극 *Macbeth*는 저주받았다는 이야기가 있으며, 문제를 피하고자 배우들은 극장이나 (예행연습실이나 의상실 같은) 극장 공간 내에서 그 연극의 제목을 절대 소리 내어 말하지 않는다. ③ 연극에서 관객과 배우들 사이의 상호 작용은 배우들의 연기에 영향을 미친다. ④ 그 연극은 스코틀랜드를 배경으로 하고 있기 때문에, 연극의 제목을 말할 필요가 있을 때 말하는 암호는 '그 스코틀랜드 연극'이다. ⑤ 우연히 제목을 정말 말하게 된다면, 밖으로 나가 세 바퀴를 돌고 극장으로 다시 돌아와야 한다는 전설이 있다.

Why? 왜 정답일까?

연극계의 미신을 소재로 한 글인데, ③은 연극에서 관객과 배우의 상호작용이 배우의 연기에 영향을 준다는 무관한 내용을 다루고 있다. 따라서 전체 흐름과 관계 없는 문장은 ③이다.

- superstition ⓝ 미신
- audience ⓝ 관객
- tragedy ⓝ 비극
- say out loud 소리 내어 말하다
- influence ⓥ 영향을 미치다
- legend has it that 전설에 따르면 ~이다
- surround ⓥ 둘러싸다, 에워싸다
- rehearse ⓥ 예행연습하다
- curse ⓥ 저주하다
- theatrical ⓐ 극장의, 연극의
- by accident 우연히

구문 풀이

11행 If you do say the title by accident, legend has it that you have to go outside, turn around three times, and come back into the theater.

36 습관화의 장단점 정답률 50% | 정답 ⑤

주어진 글 다음에 이어질 글의 순서로 가장 적절한 것을 고르시오. [3점]

① (A) − (C) − (B) ② (B) − (A) − (C)
③ (B) − (C) − (A) ④ (C) − (A) − (B)
✓⑤ (C) − (B) − (A)

Habits create the foundation for mastery.
습관은 숙달의 토대를 만든다.

In chess, / it is only after the basic movements of the pieces / have become automatic / that a player can focus on the next level of the game.
체스에서, / 오직 말의 기본적인 움직임이 / 자동적으로 이루어지고 나서야, / 체스를 두는 사람이 게임의 다음 레벨에 집중할 수 있게 되는 것은

Each chunk of information that is memorized / opens up the mental space for more effortful thinking.
암기된 각각의 정보 덩어리는 / 더 노력이 필요한 사고를 할 수 있도록 정신적 공간을 열어준다.

(C) This is true for anything you attempt.
이것은 여러분이 시도하는 어떤 것에도 적용된다.

When you know the simple movements so well / that you can perform them without thinking, / you are free to pay attention to more advanced details.
여러분이 간단한 동작을 매우 잘 알고 있어서 / 그것을 생각하지 않고도 할 수 있을 때, / 여러분은 더 높은 수준의 세부 사항에 자유롭게 집중하게 된다.

In this way, / habits are the backbone of any pursuit of excellence.
이런 식으로, / 습관은 그 어떤 탁월함을 추구할 때도 중추적인 역할을 한다.

(B) However, the benefits of habits come at a cost.
그러나 습관의 이점에는 대가가 따른다.

At first, each repetition develops fluency, speed, and skill.

처음에, 각각의 반복은 유창함, 속도, 그리고 기술을 발달시킨다.
But then, as a habit becomes automatic, / you become less sensitive to feedback.
그러나 그 다음에 습관이 자동화되면서 / 여러분은 피드백에 덜 민감해지게 된다.
(A) You fall into mindless repetition.
여러분은 아무 생각 없이 하는 반복으로 빠져든다.
It becomes easier to let mistakes slide.
실수를 대수롭지 않게 여기기가 더 쉬워진다.
When you can do it "good enough" automatically, / you stop thinking about how to do it better.
여러분이 저절로 '충분히 잘' 할 수 있을 때, / 여러분은 그것을 더 잘 할 수 있는 방법에 대해 생각하기를 멈춘다.

습관은 숙달의 토대를 만든다. 체스에서 체스를 두는 사람이 게임의 다음 레벨에 집중할 수 있게 되는 것은 오직 말의 기본적인 움직임이 자동적으로 이루어지고 나서이다. 암기된 각각의 정보 덩어리는 더 노력이 필요한 사고를 할 수 있도록 정신적 공간을 열어준다.
(C) 이것은 여러분이 시도하는 어떤 것에도 적용된다. 간단한 동작을 매우 잘 알고 있어서 생각하지 않고도 할 수 있을 때, 더 높은 수준의 세부 사항에 자유롭게 집중하게 된다. 이런 식으로, 습관은 그 어떤 탁월함을 추구할 때도 중추적인 역할을 한다.
(B) 그러나 습관의 이점에는 대가가 따른다. 처음에, 각각의 반복은 유창함, 속도, 그리고 기술을 발달시킨다. 그러나 그 다음에 습관이 자동화되면서 여러분은 피드백에 덜 민감해지게 된다.
(A) 여러분은 아무 생각 없이 하는 반복으로 빠져든다. 실수를 대수롭지 않게 여기기가 더 쉬워진다. 여러분이 저절로 '충분히 잘' 할 수 있을 때, 그것을 더 잘 할 수 있는 방법에 대해 생각하기를 멈춘다.

Why? 왜 정답일까?
습관이 숙달의 토대가 된다며 체스 두는 사람의 예를 드는 주어진 글 뒤에는, 다른 예에도 이 명제가 적용된다는 내용의 (C), 습관의 이점에는 대가가 따른다는 반전된 내용으로 연결되는 (B), 습관이 자동화되면 우리는 무의식적인 반복에 빠져들며 더 잘하려고 고민하지 않게 된다는 내용의 (A)가 차례로 이어져야 한다. 따라서 글의 순서로 가장 적절한 것은 ⑤ '(C) – (B) – (A)'이다.

- foundation ⓝ 토대, 기초
- mindless ⓐ 아무 생각 없이 하는, 머리를 쓸 필요가 없는
- repetition ⓝ 반복
- come at a cost 대가가 따르다
- fluency ⓝ 유창함
- attempt ⓥ 시도하다
- pursuit ⓝ 추구
- effortful ⓐ 노력이 필요한
- let ~ slide ~을 되어가는 대로 내버려 두다
- automatically ⓐⓓ 저절로, 자동적으로
- sensitive ⓐ 민감한
- backbone ⓝ 중추, 근간

구문 풀이
13행 When you know the simple movements so well that you can perform
「so ~ that : 너무 ~해서 …하다」
them without thinking, you are free to pay attention to more advanced details.
자유롭게 ~하다

★★★ 등급을 가르는 문제!
37 농경 이후 사회의 인구 | 정답률 37% | 정답 ②
주어진 글 다음에 이어질 글의 순서로 가장 적절한 것을 고르시오. [3점]
① (A) – (C) – (B) ✔ (B) – (A) – (C)
③ (B) – (C) – (A) ④ (C) – (A) – (B)
⑤ (C) – (B) – (A)

Regardless of whether the people existing after agriculture / were happier, healthier, or neither, / it is undeniable that there were more of them.
농경 이후에 존재했던 사람들이 / 더 행복했든, 더 건강했든, 아니면 둘 다 아니었든 간에 관계없이, / 더 많은 수의 사람들이 있었다는 것은 부인할 수 없다.
Agriculture both supports and requires / more people to grow the crops / that sustain them.
농경은 더 많은 사람을 부양하는 동시에, 필요로 한다. / 농작물을 기를 더 많은 사람을 / 그들을 지탱해 주는
(B) Estimates vary, of course, / but evidence points to an increase in the human population / from 1-5 million people worldwide to a few hundred million / once agriculture had become established.
물론, 추정치는 다양하지만, / 증거는 인구의 증가를 보여준다. / 전 세계적으로 1~5백만 명에서 수억 명으로 / 농경이 확립된 후
(A) And a larger population / doesn't just mean increasing the size of everything, / like buying a bigger box of cereal for a larger family.
그리고 더 많은 인구는 / 단지 모든 것의 규모를 확장하는 것을 의미하지는 않는다. / 더 큰 가족을 위해 더 큰 상자의 시리얼을 사는 것 같이
It brings qualitative changes / in the way people live.
그것은 질적인 변화를 가져온다. / 사람들이 사는 방식에
(C) For example, / more people means more kinds of diseases, / particularly when those people are sedentary.
예를 들어, / 더 많은 사람은 더 많은 종류의 질병을 의미하는데, / 특히 그 사람들이 한 곳에 정착해 있을 때 그렇다.
Those groups of people / can also store food for long periods, / which creates a society with haves and have-nots.
그러한 사람들의 집단은 / 또한 음식을 장기간 보관할 수 있고, / 이것은 가진 자와 가지지 못한 자가 있는 사회를 만들어 낸다.

농경 이후에 존재했던 사람들이 더 행복했든, 더 건강했든, 아니면 둘 다 아니었든 간에 관계없이, 더 많은 수의 사람들이 있었다는 것은 부인할 수 없다. 농경은 더 많은 사람을 부양하는 동시에, 그들을 지탱해 주는 농작물을 기를 더 많은 사람을 필요로 한다.
(B) 물론, 추정치는 다양하지만, 증거에 따르면 농경이 확립된 후 전 세계적으로 인구가 1~5백만 명에서 수억 명으로 증가했다.
(A) 그리고 더 많은 인구는 더 큰 가족을 위해 더 큰 상자의 시리얼을 사는 것 같이 단지 모든 것의 규모를 확장하는 것을 의미하지는 않는다. 그것은 사람들의 생활 방식에 질적인 변화를 가져온다.
(C) 예를 들어 더 많은 사람은 더 많은 종류의 질병을 의미하는데, 특히 그 사람들이 한 곳에 정착해 있을 때 그렇다. 그러한 사람들의 집단은 또한 음식을 장기간 보관할 수 있고, 이것은 가진 자와 가지지 못한 자가 있는 사회를 만들어 낸다.

Why? 왜 정답일까?
농경 이후 사회의 인구는 이전보다 더 많아졌다는 내용을 제시하는 주어진 글 뒤에는, 농경 이후의 인구 증가를 수치로 보여주는 (B), 농경이 사람들의 생활 방식에 질적인 변화를 가져왔다는 내용의 (A), 질적 변화에 대한 예를 드는 (C)가 차례로 이어져야 한다. 따라서 글의 순서로 가장 적절한 것은 ② '(B) – (A) – (C)'이다.

- regardless of ~에 관계없이
- undeniable ⓐ 부인할 수 없는
- qualitative ⓐ 질적인
- vary ⓥ 다양하다, 다르다
- established ⓐ 확립된
- agriculture ⓝ 농경
- population ⓝ 인구
- estimate ⓝ 추정치 ⓥ 추정하다
- point to ~을 보여주다, 시사하다

구문 풀이
8행 Estimates vary, of course, but evidence points to an increase in the human
주어1   └동사1(자동사)   주어2   동사2(~을 시사하다)
population from 1-5 million people worldwide to a few hundred million / once
「from + A + to + B : A에서 B까지」   일단 ~한 후에
agriculture had become established.
과거완료

★★ 문제 해결 꿀~팁 ★★
▶ 많이 틀린 이유는?
(B)는 농경 이후 세계 인구가 1~5백만에서 수억까지 증가했다는 내용으로 끝나는데 (C)는 사람들이 많아지면 질병도 많아진다는 내용으로 이어지고 있어 두 단락 사이에 논리적 연관성이 없다. 따라서 (B) 뒤로 '사람들이 많아지면 단순히 양적인 변화뿐 아니라 질적인 변화도 야기된다'는 내용을 제시하는 (A)가 먼저 나온 후 '질적인 변화'를 부가 설명하는 (C)가 연결되어야 한다.
▶ 문제 해결 방법은?
For example 등 연결어는 순서 문제 풀이에 큰 힌트를 제공한다. 여기서도 (C)의 For example 뒤로 소개되는 예시가 (A)와 (B) 중 어느 단락과 연결되는지를 중점적으로 파악해보면 정답을 찾을 수 있다.

38 기계 능력의 진화 | 정답률 49% | 정답 ⑤
글의 흐름으로 보아, 주어진 문장이 들어가기에 가장 적절한 곳을 고르시오.

The boundary between uniquely human creativity and machine capabilities / continues to change.
인간 고유의 창의력과 기계의 능력 사이 경계가 / 계속 변화하고 있다.
① Returning to the game of chess, back in 1956, / thirteen-year-old child prodigy Bobby Fischer / made a pair of remarkably creative moves / against grandmaster Donald Byrne.
과거 1956년의 체스 게임으로 돌아가 보면, / 13세 신동 Bobby Fischer는 / 대단히 창의적인 두 수를 두었다. / 거장 Donald Byrne을 상대로
② First he sacrificed his knight, seemingly for no gain, / and then exposed his queen to capture.
먼저 그는 겉으로 보기에 아무런 이득도 없이 자신의 나이트를 희생시켰고, / 그런 다음 퀸을 노출시켜 잡히게 했다.
③ On the surface, these moves seemed insane, / but several moves later, / Fischer used these moves to win the game.
겉으로 보기에는 이러한 수들은 비상식적으로 보였지만, / 몇 수를 더 두고 나서, / Fischer는 이 수를 이용하여 그 게임에서 승리했다.
④ His creativity was praised at the time / as the mark of genius.
당시 그의 창의성은 칭송받았다 / 천재성을 나타내는 표시로
✔ Yet today / if you program that same position into an ordinary chess program, / it will immediately suggest the exact moves / that Fischer made.
하지만 오늘날 / 여러분이 보통의 체스 프로그램에 그와 똑같은 배치를 설정하면, / 그것은 즉시 바로 그 수를 제안할 것이다. / Fischer가 두었던
It's not because the computer has memorized the Fischer-Byrne game, / but rather because it searches far enough ahead / to see that these moves really do pay off.
그것은 컴퓨터가 Fischer와 Byrne의 게임을 암기했기 때문이 아니라, / 그것이 충분히 멀리 앞을 탐색하기 때문이다. / 이러한 수가 실제로 성과를 거둔다는 것을 볼 수 있을 만큼

인간 고유의 창의력과 기계의 능력 사이 경계가 계속 변화하고 있다. ① 과거 1956년의 체스 게임으로 돌아가 보면, 13세 신동 Bobby Fischer는 거장 Donald Byrne을 상대로 대단히 창의적인 두 수를 두었다. ② 먼저 그는 겉으로 보기에 아무런 이득도 없이 자신의 나이트를 희생시켰고, 그런 다음 퀸을 노출시켜 잡히게 했다. ③ 겉으로 보기에는 이러한 수들은 비상식적으로 보였지만, 몇 수를 더 두고 나서, Fischer는 이 수를 이용하여 그 게임에서 승리했다. ④ 당시 그의 창의성은 천재성을 나타내는 표시로 칭송받았다. ⑤ 하지만 오늘날 보통의 체스 프로그램에 그와 똑같은 배치를 설정하면, 그것은 즉시 Fischer가 두었던 바로 그 수를 제안할 것이다. 그것은 컴퓨터가 Fischer와 Byrne의 게임을 암기했기 때문이 아니라, 이러한 수가 실제로 성과를 거둔다는 것을 볼 수 있을 만큼 충분히 멀리 앞을 탐색하기 때문이다.

Why? 왜 정답일까?
인간의 창의력과 기계의 능력 사이 경계가 모호해지고 있다는 내용의 글로, 서두부터 체스 게임 신동의 예가 제시되고 있다. 이 신동은 겉으로 이득이 없어 보이는 수를 두었으나 결과적으로는 승리했고, 그의 창의성은 천재성의 표시로 칭송받았다는 내용이 ⑤ 앞까지 이어진다. 한편 주어진 문장은 Yet으로 흐름을 반전시키며, 오늘날 컴퓨터에게 당시의 체스판을 똑같이 재현해주면, 컴퓨터가 바로 그 신동이 두었던 수를 제안할 것이라고 설명한다. ⑤ 뒤에서는 그 이유로 컴퓨터가 그때의 게임을 외우고 있기 때문이 아니라 그 수의 유효성을 실제로 미리 탐색할 수 있기 때문이라는 내용을 제시한다. 따라서 주어진 문장이 들어가기에 가장 적절한 곳은 ⑤이다.

- capability ⓝ 능력
- sacrifice ⓥ 희생시키다
- insane ⓐ 비상식적인, 제정신이 아닌
- pay off 성과를 거두다
- remarkably ⓐⓓ 대단히, 두드러지게
- seemingly ⓐⓓ 겉보기에
- memorize ⓥ 암기하다

구문 풀이
13행 It's not because the computer has memorized the Fischer-Byrne game,
「not + A + but rather + B : A가 아니라 B인(A, B 자리에 because절)」
but rather because it searches far enough to see that these moves really
「형/부 + enough + to부정사 : ~할 만큼 충분히 …한/하게」
do pay off.
동사 강조

글의 흐름으로 보아, 주어진 문장이 들어가기에 가장 적절한 곳을 고르시오. [3점]

Of all the medical achievements of the 1960s, / the most widely known was the first heart transplant, / performed by the South African surgeon Christiaan Barnard in 1967.
1960년대의 모든 의학적 성취 중에서 / 가장 널리 알려진 것은 최초의 심장 이식이었다. / 1967년 남아프리카 공화국의 외과 의사 Christiaan Barnard에 의해서 행해진

① The patient's death 18 days later / did not weaken the spirits of those / who welcomed a new era of medicine.
18일 후 그 환자의 사망이 / 사람들의 사기를 떨어뜨리지 않았다. / 의학의 새로운 시대를 환영하는

② The ability to perform heart transplants / was linked to the development of respirators, / which had been introduced to hospitals in the 1950s.
심장 이식을 할 수 있는 능력이 / 인공호흡기의 개발과 관련이 있었는데, / 이것은 1950년대에 병원에 도입되었다.

③ Respirators could save many lives, / but not all those whose hearts kept beating / ever recovered any other significant functions.
인공호흡기는 많은 생명을 구할 수 있었지만, / 심장이 계속해서 뛰는 사람들 모두가 / 어떤 다른 중요한 기능을 회복한 것은 아니었다.

☑ In some cases, / their brains had ceased to function altogether.
어떤 경우에는 / 그들의 뇌가 완전히 기능을 멈추었다.

The realization / that such patients could be a source of organs for transplantation / led to the setting up of the Harvard Brain Death Committee, / and to its recommendation / that the absence of all "discernible central nervous system activity" / should be "a new criterion for death".
그 인식이 / 그러한 환자들이 이식용 장기 공급자가 될 수 있다는 / 하버드 뇌사 위원회의 설립으로 이어졌고, / 그 위원회의 권고로 이어졌다. / 모든 '식별 가능한 중추 신경계 활동'의 부재가 / '사망의 새로운 기준'이 되어야 한다는

⑤ The recommendation has since been adopted, with some modifications, / almost everywhere.
그 권고는 그 후 일부 수정을 거쳐 받아들여졌다. / 거의 모든 곳에서

1960년대의 모든 의학적 성취 중에서 가장 널리 알려진 것은 1967년 남아프리카 공화국의 외과 의사 Christiaan Barnard에 의해서 행해진 최초의 심장 이식이었다. ① 18일 후에 그 환자가 사망한 것이 의학의 새로운 시대를 환영하는 사람들의 사기를 떨어뜨리지 않았다. ② 심장 이식을 할 수 있는 능력이 인공호흡기의 개발과 관련이 있었는데, 이것은 1950년대에 병원에 도입되었다. ③ 인공호흡기는 많은 생명을 구할 수 있었지만, 심장이 계속해서 뛰는 사람들이 모두 다 어떤 다른 중요한 기능을 회복한 것은 아니었다. ④ 어떤 경우에는 그들의 뇌가 완전히 기능을 멈추었다. 그러한 환자들이 이식용 장기 공급자가 될 수 있다는 인식으로 인해 하버드 뇌사 위원회가 설립되었고, 모든 '식별 가능한 중추 신경계 활동'의 부재가 '사망의 새로운 기준'이 되어야 한다는 그 위원회의 권고로 이어졌다. ⑤ 그 권고는 그 후 일부 수정을 거쳐 거의 모든 곳에서 받아들여졌다.

Why?　왜 정답일까?

심장 이식의 시작을 소재로 다룬 글이다. ④ 앞의 두 문장에서 심장 이식은 인공호흡기의 개발로 가능해졌는데, 이 인공호흡기는 많은 생명을 구할 수 있기는 했지만 모든 이가 온전히 기능을 회복하게 해주는 것은 아니라는 내용을 제시한다. 주어진 문장은 인공호흡기로 인해 심장이 계속 뛰게 된 환자들 중 일부를 their로 받으며 때때로 이들의 뇌 기능이 완전히 정지되기도 했다는 내용을 언급한다. ④ 뒤의 문장은 뇌 기능이 멈춘 환자들을 다시 such patients로 받으며 이들의 장기를 이식하기 위한 뇌사 위원회가 설립되었다고 설명한다. 따라서 주어진 문장이 들어가기에 가장 적절한 곳은 ④이다.

- cease ⓥ 멈추다
- transplant ⓝ 이식
- realization ⓝ 인식, 깨달음
- absence ⓝ 부재
- altogether ⓐⅾ 완전히
- significant ⓐ 중요한
- recommendation ⓝ 권고, 추천
- modification ⓝ 수정

구문 풀이

2행 Of all the medical achievements of the 1960s, the most widely known
　　　　　　　　　모든 ~들 중에서　　　　　　　　「보어 +
was the first heart transplant, (which was) performed by the South African surgeon
동사 + 주어 : 도치 구문」　　　　생략
Christiaan Barnard in 1967.

★★★ 등급을 가르는 문제!

40 풍부한 천연자원에 대한 지나친 의존이 부르는 부작용　정답률 46% | 정답 ①

다음 글의 내용을 한 문장으로 요약하고자 한다. 빈칸 (A), (B)에 들어갈 말로 가장 적절한 것은?

	(A)		(B)		(A)		(B)
☑	varying 다양화하는	·····	barrier 장애	②	varying 다양화하는	·····	shortcut 지름길
③	limiting 제한하는 것	·····	challenge 도전	④	limiting 제한하는 것	·····	barrier 장애
⑤	connecting 연결시키는 것	·····	shortcut 지름길				

Some natural resource-rich developing countries / tend to create an excessive dependence on their natural resources, / which generates a lower productive diversification and a lower rate of growth.
천연자원이 풍부한 일부 개발 도상국들은 / 자국의 천연자원에 대한 지나친 의존을 초래하는 경향이 있으며, / 더 낮은 생산적 다양화와 더 낮은 성장률을 초래한다.

Resource abundance in itself / need not do any harm: / many countries have abundant natural resources / and have managed to outgrow their dependence on them / by diversifying their economic activity.
자원의 풍요가 그 자체로 / 해가 되어야 하는 것은 아닌데, / 많은 나라들은 풍부한 천연자원을 가지고 있고 / 그것에 대한 의존을 그럭저럭 벗어났다. / 자국의 경제 활동을 다양화함으로써

That is the case of Canada, Australia, or the US, / to name the most important ones.
캐나다, 호주, 또는 미국의 경우가 그러하다. / 가장 중요한 나라들을 꼽자면

But some developing countries / are trapped in their dependence on their large natural resources.
하지만 일부 개발 도상국들은 / 자국의 많은 천연자원에 대한 의존에 갇혀 있다.

They suffer from a series of problems / since a heavy dependence on natural capital / tends to exclude other types of capital / and thereby interfere with economic growth.
그들은 일련의 문제를 겪고 있다. / 자연 자본에 대한 과도한 의존은 / 다른 형태의 자본을 배제하고 / 그로 인해 경제 성장을 저해하는 경향이 있기 때문에

➡ Relying on rich natural resources / without (A) varying economic activities / can be a (B) barrier to economic growth.
풍부한 천연자원에 의존하는 것은 / 경제 활동을 다양화하지 않은 채 / 경제 성장에 장애가 될 수 있다.

천연자원이 풍부한 일부 개발 도상국들은 자국의 천연자원에 대한 지나친 의존을 초래하는 경향이 있으며, (이로 인해) 더 낮은 생산적 다양화와 더 낮은 성장률을 초래한다. 자원의 풍요가 그 자체로 해가 되어야 하는 것은 아닌데, 많은 나라들이 풍부한 천연자원을 가지고 있고 자국의 경제 활동을 다양화함으로써 그것(풍부한 천연자원)에 대한 의존에서 그럭저럭 벗어났다. 가장 중요한 나라들을 꼽자면 캐나다, 호주, 또는 미국의 경우가 그러하다. 하지만 일부 개발 도상국들은 자국의 많은 천연자원에 대한 의존에 갇혀 있다. 자연 자본에 대한 과도한 의존은 다른 형태의 자본을 배제하고 그로 인해 경제 성장을 저해하는 경향이 있기 때문에 그들은 일련의 문제를 겪고 있다.

➡ 경제 활동을 (A) 다양화하지 않은 채 풍부한 천연자원에 의존하는 것은 경제 성장에 (B) 장애가 될 수 있다.

Why?　왜 정답일까?

첫 문장과 마지막 문장에서 개발도상국은 천연자원에 지나치게 의존한 나머지(~ developing countries tend to create an excessive dependence on their natural resources ~) 다른 형태의 자본을 배제하고 있고 그로 인해 경제 성장에 방해를 받는다(~ a heavy dependence on natural capital tends to exclude other types of capital and thereby interfere with economic growth.)고 언급하는 것으로 볼 때, 요약문의 빈칸 (A), (B)에 들어갈 말로 가장 적절한 것은 ① '(A) varying(다양화하는 것), (B) barrier(장애)'이다.

- excessive ⓐ 지나친, 과도한
- generate ⓥ 만들어 내다
- diversification ⓝ 다양화
- in oneself 그 자체로는
- outgrow ⓥ ~에서 벗어나다, ~보다 더 커지다
- thereby ⓐⅾ 그로 인해
- dependence ⓝ 의존
- productive ⓐ 생산적인
- abundance ⓝ 풍요, 풍부함
- do harm 해를 끼치다
- exclude ⓥ 배제하다
- interfere with ~을 방해하다

구문 풀이

1행 Some natural resource-rich developing countries tend to create an excessive
　　　　　　　　　　　　　　　　　　　　　　　　　　　　　　　　선행사(단수)
dependence on their natural resources, which generates a lower productive
　　　　　　　　　　　　　　　　계속적 용법　　단수 동사　　　목적어1
diversification and a lower rate of growth.
목적어2

★★ 문제 해결 꿀~팁 ★★

▶ 많이 틀린 이유는?
첫 문장에서 천연자원에만 너무 의존하면 생산적 다양화와 경제 성장이 더뎌진다고 하였다. 즉 생산 수단이나 경제 활동을 '다양화'하지 않고 자원에만 의존하는 경우의 문제점을 지적하는 것이 글의 목적임을 알 수 있다. (A)에 limiting을 넣으면 경제 활동을 '제한하지' 않고 자원에 의존하는 경우를 언급하게 되므로 글의 내용과 맞지 않다.

▶ 문제 해결 방법은?
중간에 흐름이 반전되는 부분 없이 처음부터 끝까지 일관된 흐름으로 주제를 전개하는 글이다. 따라서 첫 문장과 마지막 문장을 주의 깊게 읽어 요약문을 완성토록 한다.

41-42 도주와 공격을 결정짓는 거리

Animal studies have dealt with the distances / creatures may keep / between themselves and members of other species.
동물 연구는 거리를 다루어 왔다. / 동물들이 유지할 수도 있는 / 그들 자신과 다른 종의 구성원들 사이에

These distances / determine the functioning of the so-called 'flight or fight' mechanism. `41번의 근거`
이러한 거리는 / 소위 '도주 또는 공격' 메커니즘의 기능을 결정짓는다.

As an animal senses / what it considers to be a predator / approaching within its 'flight' distance, / it will quite simply run away.
동물이 감지하면, / 자기가 포식자라고 여기는 것이 / 자신의 '도주' 거리 내로 접근하는 것을 / 그것은 정말 그야말로 도망갈 것이다.

The distance at which this happens / is amazingly (a) consistent, / and Hediger, a Swiss biologist, claimed / to have measured it remarkably precisely / for some of the species that he studied.
이러한 현상이 일어나는 거리는 / 놀라울 정도로 일관되며, / 스위스 생물학자 Hediger는 주장했다. / 그것을 놀라울 만큼 정확하게 측정했다고 / 자신이 연구하는 일부 종에 대해

Naturally, it varies from species to species, / and usually the larger the animal / the (b) longer its flight distance.
당연히 그것은 종에 따라 다르며, / 보통 동물이 더 클수록 / 그것의 도주 거리는 더 길다.

I have had to use a long focus lens / to take photographs of giraffes, / which have very large flight distances.
나는 초점 렌즈를 사용해야만 했는데, / 기린의 사진을 찍기 위해서는 / 기린은 도주 거리가 매우 크기 때문이다.

By contrast, / I have several times nearly stepped on a squirrel in my garden / before it drew attention to itself by suddenly escaping! `42번의 근거`
대조적으로, / 나는 내 정원에서 다람쥐를 거의 밟을 뻔한 적이 몇 번 있었는데 / 다람쥐가 갑자기 도망쳐서 자신에게 관심을 갖게 하기 전에

We can only assume / that this (c) variation in distance / matches the animal's own assessment of its ability / to accelerate and run.
우리는 추정할 수 있을 뿐이다. / 거리에서의 이러한 차이가 / 동물 자신의 평가와 일치한다고 / 속력을 내서 달릴 수 있는

The 'fight' distance is always (d) smaller than the flight distance.
'공격' 거리는 항상 도주 거리보다 더 짧다.

If a perceived predator approaches within the flight distance / but the animal is trapped by obstacles or other predators / and cannot (e) flee, / it must stand its ground.
인식된 포식자가 도주 거리 내로 접근하지만, / 그 동물이 장애물이나 다른 포식자들에 의해 갇혀서 / 달아날 수 없다면, / 그 동물은 버텨야 한다.

Eventually, however, / attack becomes the best form of defence, / and so the trapped animal will turn and fight.
하지만, 결국에는 / 공격이 가장 좋은 형태의 방어 수단이 되므로, / 그 갇힌 동물은 돌아서서 싸울 것이다.

동물 연구는 동물들이 그들 자신과 다른 종의 구성원들 사이에 유지할 수도 있는 거리를 다루어 왔다. 이러한 거리는 소위 '도주 또는 공격' 메커니즘의 기능을 결정짓는다. 동물은 자기가 포식자라고 여기는 것이 자신의 '도주' 거리 내로 접근하는 것을 감지하면, 정말 그야말로 도망

갈 것이다. 이러한 현상이 일어나는 거리는 놀라울 정도로 (a) 일관되며, 스위스 생물학자 Hediger는 자신이 연구하는 일부 종에 대해 그것을 놀라울 만큼 정확하게 측정했다고 주장했다. 당연히 그것은 종에 따라 다르며, 보통 동물이 더 클수록 그것의 도주 거리는 (b) 더 짧다(→ 더 길다). 나는 기린의 사진을 찍기 위해서는 원거리 초점 렌즈를 사용해야만 했는데, 기린은 도주 거리가 매우 크기 때문이다. 대조적으로, 정원에서 다람쥐를 거의 밟을 뻔했을 때 다람쥐가 갑자기 도망쳐서 나의 주의를 끈 적이 몇 번 있었다! 우리는 거리에서의 이러한 (c) 차이가 속력을 내서 달릴 수 있는 능력에 대한 동물 자신의 평가와 일치한다고 추정할 수 있을 뿐이다. '공격' 거리는 항상 도주 거리보다 더 (d) 짧다. 인식된 포식자가 도주 거리 내로 접근하지만, 그 동물이 장애물이나 다른 포식자들에 의해 갇혀서 (e) 달아날 수 없다면, 그 동물은 (물러나지 않고) 버텨야 한다. 하지만, 결국에는 공격이 가장 좋은 형태의 방어 수단이 되므로, 그 갇힌 동물은 돌아서서 싸울 것이다.

- **deal with** ~을 다루다
- **flight or fight** 도주 또는 공격
- **consistent** ⓐ 일관적인
- **remarkably** ⓐⓓ 놀라울 만큼
- **variation** ⓝ 차이, 변화
- **accelerate** ⓥ 가속화하다
- **flee** ⓥ 달아나다, 도망가다
- **migrate** ⓥ 이주하다
- **functioning** ⓝ 기능
- **predator** ⓝ 포식자
- **measure** ⓥ 측정하다
- **precisely** ⓐⓓ 정확하게
- **assessment** ⓝ 평가
- **obstacle** ⓝ 장애물
- **stand one's ground** 버티다, 공격에 견디다
- **determining** ⓐ 결정적인

구문 풀이

6행 The distance [at which this happens] is amazingly consistent, and
주어1 〈전치사+관·대〉 동사1
Hediger, a Swiss biologist, claimed to have measured it remarkably precisely for
주어2 동사2 목적어(완료부정사)
some of the species [that he studied].
선행사 목적격 관·대

---

41 제목 파악 정답률 61% | 정답 ④

윗글의 제목으로 가장 적절한 것은?

① How Animals Migrate Without Getting Lost – 동물이 길을 잃지 않고 이동하는 방법
② Flight or Fight Mechanism: Still in Our Brain – 도주 또는 공격 메커니즘: 아직도 우리 뇌 속에
③ Why the Size Matters in the Survival of Animals – 동물의 생존에서 크기가 중요한 이유
✔④ Distances: A Determining Factor for Flight or Attack – 거리: 도주나 공격의 결정 요인
⑤ Competition for Food Between Large and Small Animals – 큰 동물과 작은 동물 간의 먹이 경쟁

Why? 왜 정답일까?

두 번째 문장인 'These distances determine the functioning of the so-called 'flight or fight' mechanism.'에서 도주 또는 공격 중 무엇을 택할지를 결정해주는 요인은 바로 거리라는 주제를 제시하므로, 글의 제목으로 가장 적절한 것은 ④ '거리: 도주나 공격의 결정 요인'이다.

★★★ 등급을 가르는 문제!

42 어휘 추론 정답률 44% | 정답 ②

밑줄 친 (a) ~ (e) 중에서 문맥상 낱말의 쓰임이 적절하지 않은 것은?

① (a) ✔② (b) ③ (c) ④ (d) ⑤ (e)

Why? 왜 정답일까?

'I have had to use a long focus lens to take photographs of giraffes, which have very large flight distances. By contrast, I have several times nearly stepped on a squirrel in my garden before it drew attention to itself by suddenly escaping!' 몸집이 큰 기린과 작은 다람쥐를 예로 들어 큰 동물은 도주 거리가 길다는 내용을 제시하고 있다. 따라서 (b)의 smaller를 반의어인 longer로 고쳐야 한다. 문맥상 낱말의 쓰임이 적절하지 않은 것은 ② '(b)'이다.

★★ 문제 해결 꿀~팁 ★★

▶ 많이 틀린 이유는?
첫 단락에서 '도주' 거리가 동물의 크기에 따라 달라진다는 내용이 나온 뒤, (d)가 포함된 문장은 '공격'의 거리를 언급하고 있다. 'If a perceived predator approaches ~'에서 도주 거리 안에 포식자가 들어왔으나 장애물이나 다른 포식자가 더 있어 '도주하기 어려운' 경우에 먹이 동물은 공격을 선택한다고 하므로, 공격 거리는 도주 거리보다 '더 짧을' 것임을 유추할 수 있다.

▶ 문제 해결 방법은?
밑줄 어휘 문제는 앞뒤 맥락이 주로 답의 근거를 제시한다. 여기서도 (b) 뒤의 두 문장이 기린과 다람쥐의 예를 통해 몸집의 크기에 따른 도주 거리 차이를 설명하고 있으므로 이 내용을 잘 읽어 (b)의 쓰임이 적합한지를 결정해야 한다.

43~45 Yolanda가 나무 두 그루를 통해 배운 삶의 교훈

(A)

『Eight-year-old Yolanda went to her grandmother's / and proudly announced / that she was going to be very successful when she grew up』 / and asked her grandmother / if she could give her any tips on how to achieve this. ◀ 45번 ①의 근거 일치
여덟 살의 Yolanda는 할머니 댁에 가서 / 자랑스럽게 선언하고 / 자기가 커서 크게 성공할 것이라고 / 할머니께 여쭤었다. / 할머니가 이것을 성취할 방법에 대해 조언을 해줄 수 있는지

The grandmother nodded, / took the girl by the hand, / and walked (a) her to a nearby plant nursery.
할머니는 고개를 끄덕이더니, / 소녀의 손을 잡고 / 그녀를 가까운 식물 묘목장으로 데리고 갔다.

There, the two of them chose and purchased two small trees.
그곳에서 두 사람은 두 개의 작은 나무를 골라서 샀다.

(C)

They returned home / and planted one of them in the back yard / and planted the other tree in a pot and kept it indoors.
그들은 집으로 돌아와 그중 하나를 뒷마당에 심고 / 다른 나무는 화분에 심어 실내에 두었다.

Then her grandmother asked her / which of the trees (c) she thought / would be more successful in the future.
그런 다음 그녀의 할머니는 그녀에게 물었다. / 그녀가 생각하기에 그 나무 중 어느 것이 / 미래에 더 성공적일 것인지

『Yolanda thought for a moment / and said / the indoor tree would be more successful / because it was protected and safe, / while the outdoor tree had to cope with the elements.』 ◀ 45번 ③의 근거 불일치
Yolanda는 잠시 생각하더니, / 말했다. / 실내의 나무가 더 성공적일 것이라고 / 그것은 보호를 받아 안전하지만 / 집 밖의 나무는 악천후를 이겨내야 하기 때문에

Her grandmother shrugged and said, "We'll see."
그녀의 할머니는 어깨를 으쓱하더니, / "두고 보자꾸나."라고 말했다.

『Her grandmother took good care of both trees.』 ◀ 45번 ④의 근거 일치
그녀의 할머니는 두 나무를 모두 정성스럽게 돌보았다.

(D)

『In a few years, Yolanda, now a teenager, / came to visit her grandmother again.』 ◀ 45번 ⑤의 근거 일치
몇 년 후, 이제 십 대가 된 Yolanda가 / 할머니를 다시 찾아왔다.

Yolanda reminded her / that (d) she had never really answered her question / from when she was a little girl / about how she could become successful when she grew up.
Yolanda는 할머니께 일깨워주었다. / 할머니가 실제로 질문에 대답한 적이 전혀 없었다는 것을 / 자신이 어렸을 때의 / 자신이 어떻게 하면 커서 성공할 수 있는지에 대한

The grandmother showed Yolanda the indoor tree / and then took (e) her outside / to have a look at the towering tree outside.
할머니는 Yolanda에게 실내의 나무를 보여주고는 / 그녀를 밖으로 데리고 나가 / 밖에 있는 높이 솟은 나무를 보게 했다.

"Which one is greater?" the grandmother asked.
"어느 것이 더 크니?"라고 할머니가 물었다.

Yolanda replied, / "The outside one. / But that doesn't make sense; / it had to cope with many more challenges than the one inside."
Yolanda는 대답했다. / "밖에 있는 거요. / 하지만 이해가 되질 않아요. / 그것은 실내의 것보다 더 많은 역경을 이겨내야만 했잖아요." 라고

(B)

The grandmother smiled and said, / "Remember this, / and you will be successful in whatever you do: / If you choose the safe option all of your life, / you will never grow.
할머니는 미소를 지으며, 말했다. / "이것을 기억해라, / 네가 무엇을 하든 그 일에서 성공할 거야. / 그러면 네가 평생 안전한 선택을 한다면 / 너는 결코 성장하지 못할 테지.

『But if you are willing to face the world with all of its challenges, / you will learn from those challenges / and grow to achieve great heights."』 ◀ 45번 ②의 근거 일치
그러나 네가 모든 역경에도 불구하고 세상에 기꺼이 맞선다면, / 너는 그 역경으로부터 배우게 되고 / 성장하여 대단히 높은 수준까지 성취하게 될 거야."라고

Yolanda looked up at the tall tree, / took a deep breath, / and nodded (b) her head, / realizing that her wise grandmother was right.
Yolanda는 큰 나무를 올려다보고, / 심호흡을 하고, / 자신의 머리를 끄덕였다. / 지혜로운 할머니가 옳다는 것을 깨달으며

(A)

여덟 살의 Yolanda는 할머니 댁에 가서 자기가 커서 크게 성공할 것이라고 자랑스럽게 선언하고 할머니께 이것을 성취할 방법에 대해 조언을 해줄 수 있는지 여쭈었다. 할머니는 고개를 끄덕이더니, 소녀의 손을 잡고 (a) 그녀를 가까운 식물 묘목장으로 데리고 갔다. 그곳에서 두 사람은 두 개의 작은 나무를 골라서 샀다.

(C)

그들은 집으로 돌아와 그중 하나를 뒷마당에 심고 다른 나무는 화분에 심어 실내에 두었다. 그런 다음 그녀의 할머니는 (c) 그녀가 생각하기에 그 나무 중 어느 것이 미래에 더 성공적일 것인지 그녀에게 물었다. Yolanda는 잠시 생각하더니, 실내의 나무는 보호를 받아 안전하지만 집 밖의 나무는 악천후를 이겨내야 하기 때문에, 실내의 나무가 더 성공적일 것이라고 말했다. 그녀의 할머니는 어깨를 으쓱하더니, "두고 보자꾸나."라고 말했다. 그녀의 할머니는 두 나무를 모두 정성스럽게 돌보았다.

(D)

몇 년 후, 이제 십 대가 된 Yolanda가 할머니를 다시 찾아왔다. Yolanda는 어떻게 하면 커서 성공할 수 있는지에 대한 어렸을 때의 질문에 (d) 할머니가 실제로 대답한 적이 전혀 없었다는 것을 일깨워주었다. 할머니는 Yolanda에게 실내의 나무를 보여주고는 (e) 그녀를 밖으로 데리고 나가 밖에 있는 높이 솟은 나무를 보게 했다. "어느 것이 더 크니?"라고 할머니가 물었다. Yolanda는 "밖에 있는 거요. 하지만 이해가 되질 않아요. 그것은 실내의 것보다 더 많은 역경을 이겨내야만 했잖아요."라고 대답했다.

(B)

할머니는 미소를 지으며, "이것을 기억하면, 네가 무엇을 하든 그 일에서 성공할 거야. 평생 안전한 선택을 한다면 너는 결코 성장하지 못할 테지. 그러나 네가 모든 역경에도 불구하고 세상에 기꺼이 맞선다면, 너는 그 역경으로부터 배우게 되고 성장하여 대단히 높은 수준까지 성취하게 될 거야."라고 말했다. Yolanda는 큰 나무를 올려다보고, 심호흡을 하고, 지혜로운 할머니가 옳다는 것을 깨달으며 (b) 자신의 머리를 끄덕였다.

- **plant nursery** 식물 묘목장
- **height** ⓝ (성공, 성취에서 높은) 단계, 최고조
- **shrug** ⓥ 어깨를 으쓱하다
- **make sense** 이해가 되다, 일리가 있다
- **be willing to** 기꺼이 ~하려고 하다
- **cope with** ~에 대처하다
- **towering** ⓐ 높이 솟은, 우뚝 솟은

구문 풀이

(A) 1행 Eight-year-old Yolanda went to her grandmother's and proudly
동사1
announced that she was going to be very successful when she grew up and
동사2 접속사(~것) 시간 접속사(~할 때)
asked her grandmother if she could give her any tips on how to achieve this.
동사3 간접 목적어 직접 목적어(~인지 아닌지) 〈how + to부정사: ~하는 방법〉

(B) 1행 Remember this, and you will be successful in {whatever you do}:
〈명령문 + and : ~하라, 그러면 …〉 복합관계대명사(~하는 것은 무엇이든지)

(C) 4행 Yolanda thought for a moment and said (that) the indoor tree would be
동사1 동사2 접속사(생략)
more successful because it was protected and safe, while the outdoor tree had
= the indoor tree ~하는 반면에
to cope with the elements.
~에 대처하다

(D) 2행 Yolanda reminded her that she had never really answered her question
〈remind + A + that ~ : A에게 ~임을 일깨우다〉 과거완료
from when she was a little girl about how she could become successful when
전치사 간접의문문(의문사 + 주어 + 동사)
she grew up.

| **43** | 글의 순서 파악 | 정답률 67% | 정답 ③ |

주어진 글 (A)에 이어질 내용을 순서에 맞게 배열한 것으로 가장 적절한 것은?

① (B) − (D) − (C)
② (C) − (B) − (D)
✓③ (C) − (D) − (B)
④ (D) − (B) − (C)
⑤ (D) − (C) − (B)

Why? 왜 정답일까?

어린 Yolanda가 할머니를 찾아가 성공에 대한 조언을 해줄 것을 청하자 할머니가 Yolanda를 데리고 가 묘목 두 그루를 샀다고 언급하는 (A) 뒤에는, 할머니가 두 그루를 각각 다른 곳에 심고는 어느 나무가 더 잘 자랄 것인지 Yolanda에게 물었다는 내용을 다룬 (C)가 연결된다. 이어서 (D)는 Yolanda가 십 대가 되어 다시 할머니에게 찾아갔고, 두 나무 중 밖에 심었던 것이 더 우뚝 자랐음을 보게 되었다는 내용을 전개한다. 마지막으로 (B)는 할머니가 두 나무를 통해 얻을 수 있는 교훈을 Yolanda에게 이야기해 주었다는 결말로 마무리된다. 따라서 글의 순서로 가장 적절한 것은 ③ '(C) − (D) − (B)'이다.

| **44** | 지칭 추론 | 정답률 58% | 정답 ④ |

밑줄 친 (a) ~ (e) 중에서 가리키는 대상이 나머지 넷과 다른 것은?

① (a) ② (b) ③ (c) ✓④ (d) ⑤ (e)

Why? 왜 정답일까?

(a), (b), (c), (e)는 Yolanda를, (d)는 앞 문장의 her grandmother를 가리키므로, (a) ~ (e) 중에 가리키는 대상이 다른 하나는 ④ '(d)'이다.

| **45** | 세부 내용 파악 | 정답률 70% | 정답 ③ |

윗글에 관한 내용으로 적절하지 않은 것은?

① Yolanda는 자신이 크게 성공할 것이라고 자랑스럽게 말했다.
② 할머니는 역경으로부터 배울 수 있다고 말했다.
✓③ Yolanda는 집 밖에 심은 나무가 더 잘 자랄 거라고 말했다.
④ 할머니는 두 나무를 정성스럽게 돌보았다.
⑤ Yolanda는 십 대가 되어 할머니를 다시 방문했다.

Why? 왜 정답일까?

(C) 'Yolanda thought for a moment and said the indoor tree would be more successful ~'에 따르면 어린 Yolanda는 안에 심은 나무가 더 안전하고 보호받는 환경에 있어 더 잘 자랄 것이라고 대답했다. 따라서 내용과 일치하지 않는 것은 ③ 'Yolanda는 집 밖에 심은 나무가 더 잘 자랄 거라고 말했다.'이다.

Why? 왜 오답일까?

① (A) 'Eight-year-old Yolanda went to her grandmother's and proudly announced that she was going to be very successful when she grew up ~'의 내용과 일치한다.
② (B) 'But if you are willing to face the world with all of its challenges, you will learn from those challenges and grow to achieve great heights.'의 내용과 일치한다.
④ (C) 'Her grandmother took good care of both trees.'의 내용과 일치한다.
⑤ (D) 'In a few years, Yolanda, now a teenager, came to visit her grandmother again.'의 내용과 일치한다.

어휘 Review Test 05

문제편 050쪽

A		B		C	D
01 ~의 원인이 되다		01 agriculture		01 ⓚ	01 ①
02 추정치; 추정하다		02 obey		02 ⓗ	02 ⓝ
03 결국 ~하게 되다		03 transplant		03 ⓝ	03 ⑨
04 희생시키다		04 superstition		04 ⓓ	04 ⓔ
05 ~을 계속하다		05 tragedy		05 ⓔ	05 ①
06 멈추다		06 curse		06 ①	06 ⓓ
07 충족시키다		07 inevitable		07 ⓞ	07 ⓒ
08 비상식적인, 제정신이 아닌		08 sensitive		08 ⓒ	08 ①
09 평가하다		09 detect		09 ⑨	09 ⓞ
10 다양화		10 intimate		10 ①	10 ⓗ
11 충돌		11 malfunction		11 ①	11 ⓐ
12 ~이 아니라, ~와 대조적으로		12 vertical		12 ⓑ	12 ⓚ
13 메마르다, 고갈되다		13 statistics		13 ⓜ	13 ⓑ
14 연약함		14 asset		14 ⓐ	14 ⓜ
15 ~의 공적을 인정받다		15 aggression		15 ①	15 ①
16 ~할까봐 두려워서		16 have access to		16 ①	16 ⓟ
17 발전, 진전		17 regulation		17 ①	17 ①
18 불필요한		18 injury		18 ⓠ	18 ⓢ
19 A를 B에 바치다		19 achievement		19 ⓢ	19 ⓠ
20 점차		20 flee		20 ①	20 ①

06회 | 2024학년도 6월 학력평가 [고2]

· 정답 ·

18 ② 19 ① 20 ② 21 ① 22 ④ 23 ② 24 ④ 25 ③ 26 ⑤ 27 ⑤ 28 ③ 29 ⑤ 30 ④ 31 ① 32 ③
33 ① 34 ② 35 ③ 36 ② 37 ③ 38 ④ 39 ① 40 ⑤ 41 ① 42 ⑤ 43 ② 44 ④ 45 ③

★ 표기된 문항은 [등급을 가르는 문제]에 해당하는 문항입니다.

| **18** | 정원가꾸기 날 참여 독려 | 정답률 95% | 정답 ② |

다음 글의 목적으로 가장 적절한 것은?

① 아파트 내 정원 조성에 대한 의견을 수렴하려고
✓② 정원가꾸기 날 행사에 참여할 것을 독려하려고
③ 쓰레기를 지정된 장소에 버릴 것을 당부하려고
④ 지하 주차장 공사 일정에 대해 공지하려고
⑤ 정원박람회 개최 날짜 변경을 안내하려고

Dear Residents,
친애하는 주민 여러분.
My name is Kari Patterson, / and I'm the manager of the River View Apartments.
제 이름은 Kari Patterson이고, / 저는 River View 아파트의 관리인입니다.
It's time to take advantage / of the sunny weather / to make our community more beautiful.
이용할 때입니다. / 화창한 날씨를 / 우리의 커뮤니티를 / 더 아름답게 만들기 위해서
On Saturday, July 13 at 9 a.m., residents will meet / in the north parking lot.
7월 13일 토요일 오전 9시에, / 주민들은 만날 것입니다. / 북쪽 주차장에서
We will divide into teams / to plant flowers and small trees, / pull weeds, / and put colorful decorations on the lawn.
우리는 팀으로 나누어서 / 꽃과 작은 나무를 심고, / 잡초를 뽑고, / 잔디밭에 다채로운 장식을 할 것입니다.
Please join us for this year's Gardening Day, / and remember / no special skills or tools are required.
올해의 정원가꾸기 날에 꼭 함께해 주세요, / 그리고 기억하세요. / 특별한 기술이나 도구가 / 필요하지 않다는 것을
Last year, / we had a great time / working together, / so come out and make / this year's event / even better!
작년에, / 우리는 즐거운 시간을 보냈습니다. / 함께 일하며 / 그러니 나와서 만듭시다! / 이번 해의 행사를 / 더욱 멋지게
Warm regards,
따뜻한 마음을 담아,
Kari Patterson
Kari Patterson

주민들께,
제 이름은 Kari Patterson이고, 저는 River View 아파트의 관리인입니다. 우리의 커뮤니티를 더욱 아름답게 만들기 위해 화창한 날씨를 이용할 때입니다. 7월 13일 토요일 오전 9시에, 주민들은 .북쪽 주차장에서 만날 예정입니다. 우리는 팀을 나누어 꽃과 작은 나무를 심고, 잡초를 뽑고, 잔디밭에 다채로운 장식을 할 것입니다. 올해 정원가꾸기 날에 우리와 함께 해 주시고, 특별한 기술이나 도구는 필요하지 않다는 것을 기억하세요. 작년에, 우리는 함께 일하며 즐거운 시간을 보냈으니, 오셔서 올해 행사도 더 멋지게 만들어 주세요!
따뜻한 마음을 담아, Kari Patterson

Why? 왜 정답일까?

아파트 관리인이 작년 정원가꾸기 날이 즐거웠음을 언급하며 올해의 정원가꾸기 날에 참여를 독려하고 있다. 따라서 글의 목적으로 가장 적절한 것은 ② '정원가꾸기 날 행사에 참여할 것을 독려하려고'이다.

- advantage ⓝ 이점, 혜택
- divide ⓥ 나누다
- weed ⓝ 잡초
- require ⓥ 필요로 하다
- event ⓝ 행사, 이벤트
- community ⓝ 공동체, 지역 사회
- plant ⓥ 심다
- decoration ⓝ 장식
- skill ⓝ 기술, 능력

구문 풀이

8행 Please join us for this year's Gardening Day, and remember no special
　　　　　　명령문　　　　　　　　　　　　　　　　　　　부정어
skills or tools are required.
　　　　　수동태

| **19** | 계주 주자 Emma의 심경변화 | 정답률 95% | 정답 ① |

다음 글에 드러난 Emma의 심경 변화로 가장 적절한 것은?

✓① nervous → excited
　긴장한　신난
② doubtful → regretful
　의심스러운　후회스러운
③ confident → upset
　자신감 있는　화난
④ hopeful → disappointed
　희망찬　실망한
⑤ indifferent → amused
　무관심한　즐거운

It was / the championship race.
그것은 / 챔피언십 경주였다.
Emma was / the final runner / on her relay team.
Emma는 / 마지막 주자였다. / 그녀의 릴레이 팀에서
She anxiously waited / in her spot / for her teammate / to pass her the baton.
그녀는 불안하게 기다렸다. / 그녀의 자리에서 / 그녀의 팀원이 / 배턴을 넘겨주기를
Emma wasn't sure / she could perform her role / without making a mistake.
Emma는 확신하지 못했다. / 그녀가 그녀의 역할을 해낼 수 있을지 / 실수 없이
Her hands shook / as she thought, / "What if I drop the baton?"
그녀의 손은 떨렸다. / 그녀가 ~라고 생각하며, / "내가 배턴을 떨어뜨리면 어쩌지?"
She felt / her heart rate increasing / as her teammate approached.
그녀는 느꼈다. / 그녀의 심장 박동이 빨라지는 것을 / 그녀의 팀원이 다가올 때
But / as she started running, / she received the baton / smoothly.
하지만 / 그녀가 달리기 시작했을 때, / 그녀는 배턴을 부드럽게 받았다.

In the final 10 meters, / she passed / two other runners / and crossed the finish line / in first place!
마지막 10미터에서, / 그녀는 제치고 / 두 명의 다른 주자를 / 결승선을 통과했다! / 첫 번째로

She raised her hands in the air, / and a huge smile / came across her face.
그녀는 그녀의 손을 공중에 들었고, / 커다란 미소가 / 그녀의 얼굴에 번졌다.

As her teammates hugged her, / she shouted, / "We did it!"
그녀의 팀원들이 그녀를 껴안았을 때, / 그녀는 외쳤다, / "우리가 해냈어!"

All of her hard training / had been worth it.
그녀의 모든 힘든 훈련이 / 가치 있었다.

결승전 경주였다. Emma는 그녀의 계주 팀의 마지막 주자였다. 그녀는 그녀의 자리에서 팀 동료가 그녀에게 바통을 건네주기를 초조하게 기다렸다. Emma는 그녀가 실수를 하지 않고 자신의 역할을 수행할 수 있을지 확신하지 못했다. "만약 내가 바통을 떨어뜨리면 어떡하지?" 라고 생각하면서 그녀의 손이 떨렸다. 그녀는 그녀의 팀 동료가 다가올수록 심박수가 증가하는 것을 느꼈다. 하지만 그녀가 달리기 시작했을 때, 그녀는 순조롭게 바통을 받았다. 마지막 10미터에서, 그녀는 두 명의 다른 주자를 제치고 나서 1위로 결승선을 통과했다! 그녀는 두 손을 하늘로 치켜들고, 얼굴에 큰 미소를 지었다. 팀 동료들이 그녀를 안아주자, 그녀는 "우리가 해냈어!"라고 소리쳤다. 그녀의 모든 힘든 훈련이 그럴만한 가치가 있었다.

Why? 왜 정답일까?

Emma는 바통을 받기 전에 바통을 떨어뜨릴까봐 걱정했지만, 바통을 순조롭게 받고 1위로 결승선을 통과했기 때문에 글에 드러난 Emma의 심경 변화로 가장 적절한 것은 ① '긴장한 → 신난'이다.

- championship ⓝ 챔피언십, 선수권 대회
- anxiously ⓐⓓ 걱정스럽게, 불안하게
- smoothly ⓐⓓ 원활하게
- training ⓝ 훈련, 연습
- relay ⓝ 계주, 릴레이
- perform ⓥ 수행하다, 공연하다
- finish line 결승선

구문 풀이

6행 But as she started <u>running</u>, she received the baton smoothly.
　　　　전치사　　　　동명사

20 진정한 자기 평가의 중요성　　정답률 74% | 정답 ②

다음 글에서 필자가 주장하는 바로 가장 적절한 것은?

① 주관적 기준으로 타인을 평가하는 것을 피해야 한다.
☑ 정확하고 정직하게 자신을 평가하는 능력을 길러야 한다.
③ 자신이 가진 잠재력을 믿고 다양한 분야에 도전해야 한다.
④ 다른 사람과 비교하기보다는 자신의 성장에 주목해야 한다.
⑤ 문제를 해결하기 위해 근본 원인을 정확하게 분석해야 한다.

Most people / resist the idea of a true self-estimate, / probably because they fear / it might mean downgrading / some of their beliefs / about who they are / and what they're capable of.
대부분의 사람들은 / 진정한 자기 평가의 개념에 저항한다, / 아마도 그들이 두려워하기 때문일 것이다, / 그것이 격하하는 것을 의미할까봐 / 그들의 믿음 중 일부를 / 자신이 누구인지에 대해서 / 그리고 자신이 무엇을 할 수 있는지에

As Goethe's maxim goes, / it is a great failing / "to see yourself / as more than you are."
괴테의 격언에 따르면, / 그것은 큰 실패이다 / "자신을 본다는 것" / 실제 자신보다 더 큰 존재로

How could you really be considered self-aware / if you refuse / to consider your weaknesses?
어떻게 정말로 자각할 수 있겠는가? / 만약 네가 거부한다면 / 너의 약점을 생각하는 것을?

Don't fear self-assessment / because you're worried / you might have to admit / some things about yourself.
자기 평가를 두려워하지 마라. / 네가 걱정한다고 / 네가 인정해야 할 수도 있을까 봐 / 자신에 관한 몇 가지를

The second half of Goethe's maxim / is important too.
괴테 격언의 후반부도 / 중요하다.

He states / that it is equally damaging / to "value yourself / at less than your true worth."
그는 말한다. / 그것이 똑같이 해롭다고 / "자신을 평가하는 것" / 실제 가치보다 낮게

We underestimate our capabilities / just as much / and just as dangerously / as we overestimate / other abilities.
우리는 우리의 능력을 과소평가한다, / 똑같이 많이 / 그리고 똑같이 위험하게 / 우리가 과대평가하는 것처럼 / 다른 능력들을

Cultivate the ability / to judge yourself / accurately and honestly.
능력을 키워라. / 자신을 판단하는 / 정확하게 그리고 정직하게

Look inward / to discern / what you're capable of / and what it will take / to unlock that potential.
내면을 들여다봐라. / 분별하기 위해 / 네가 무엇을 할 수 있는지 / 그리고 무엇이 필요한지 / 그 잠재력을 발휘하기 위해

대부분의 사람들은 그것(진정한 자기 평가)이 그들이 누구인지, 무엇을 할 수 있는지에 대한 믿음을 낮추는 것을 의미할지도 모른다고 두려워하기 때문에, 진정한 자기 평가에 대한 생각을 거부한다. Goethe의 격언처럼, "너 자신을 현재의 너의 모습 이상으로 보는 것"은 큰 실수이다. 네가 너의 단점을 생각해 보기를 거부한다면 어떻게 너 자신을 인식하고 있다고 여겨질 수 있을까? 네가 너 자신에 대해 몇 가지를 인정해야 할지도 모른다는 걱정 때문에 자기를 평가하는 것을 두려워하지 마라. Goethe 격언의 후반부도 역시 중요하다. 그는 "너의 진정한 가치보다 너 자신을 낮게 평가하는 것"도 똑같이 해롭다고 말한다. 우리는 다른 능력들을 과대평가하는 것만큼 많이 그리고 위험하게 우리의 능력을 과소평가한다. 너 자신을 정확하게 그리고 정직하게 판단하는 능력을 길러라. 네가 할 수 있는 것과 너의 잠재력을 열기 위해 필요한 것을 파악하기 위해 내면을 들여다 봐라.

Why? 왜 정답일까?

너무 높거나 너무 낮지 않은, 진정한 자기 평가의 중요성에 대해서 이야기하고 있기 때문에 필자의 주장으로 가장 적절한 것은 ② '정확하고 정직하게 자신을 평가하는 능력을 길러야 한다.'이다.

- estimate ⓝ 평가, 추정
- capable ⓐ 능력이 있는
- weakness ⓝ 약점
- underestimate ⓥ 과소평가하다
- resist ⓥ 저항하다, 반대하다
- self-aware ⓐ 자기 인식이 있는
- assessment ⓝ 평가

구문 풀이

6행 Don't fear self-assessment because you're worried (that) you might have
　　　명령문　　　　　　　　　　　　접속사 that 생략↲　　조동사＋동사원형
to admit some things about yourself.

---

21 성공의 대가　　정답률 63% | 정답 ①

밑줄 친 "Slavery resides under marble and gold."가 다음 글에서 의미하는 바로 가장 적절한 것은? [3점]

☑ Your success requires you to act in ways you don't want to.
　당신의 성공은 당신이 원하지 않는 방식으로 행동하는 것을 요구한다.
② Fame cannot be achieved without the help of others.
　유명세는 타인의 도움 없이 이뤄지지 않는다.
③ Comparing yourself to others makes you miserable.
　스스로를 타인과 비교하는 것은 당신을 비참하게 만든다.
④ Hard labor guarantees glory and happiness in the future.
　고된 노동은 미래의 영광과 행복을 보장한다.
⑤ There exists freedom in the appearance of your success.
　당신의 성공의 모습에는 자유가 존재한다.

Take a look / at some of the most powerful, / rich, / and famous people / in the world.
살펴봐라. / 가장 강력하고, / 부유하고, / 유명한 사람들을 / 세상에서

Ignore / the trappings of their success / and what they're able to buy.
무시해라. / 그들의 성공의 장식과 / 그들이 살 수 있는 것을

Look instead / at what they're forced to trade in return — / look at what success has cost them.
대신 봐라. / 그들이 무엇을 대가로 / 강요받았는지 — / 성공이 그들에게 어떤 대가를 요구했는지

Mostly? / Freedom.
대부분은? / 자유.

Their work demands / they wear a suit.
그들의 일은 요구한다. / 그들이 정장을 입어야 한다고

Their success depends / on attending certain parties, / kissing up to people / they don't like.
그들의 성공은 달려 있다. / 특정 파티에 참석하는 것에, / 아부하는 것에 / 그들이 좋아하지 않는 사람들에게

It will require — / inevitably — / realizing they are unable to say / what they actually think.
그것은 요구할 것이다. — / 필연적으로 — / 그들이 말할 수 없다는 것을 깨닫는 것을 / 그들이 실제로 생각하는 것을

Worse, / it demands / that they become a different type of person / or do bad things.
더 나쁜 것은, / 그것은 요구한다. / 그들이 다른 유형의 사람이 되거나 / 나쁜 일을 해야 한다고

Sure, / it might pay well — / but they haven't truly examined / the transaction.
물론, / 그것이 많은 돈을 줄 수도 있다. — / 하지만 그들은 제대로 검토하지 않았습니다. / 그 거래를

As Seneca put it, / "Slavery resides under marble and gold."
Seneca가 말했듯이, / "노예제는 대리석과 금 아래에 존재한다."

Too many successful people / are prisoners / in jails of their own making.
너무 많은 성공한 사람들이 / 죄수다. / 그들 스스로 만든 감옥 안에서

Is that what you want? / Is that what you're working hard toward?
그것이 당신이 원하는 것인가? / 그것이 당신이 열심히 노력하는 이유인가?

Let's hope not.
그렇지 않기를 바란다.

세계에서 가장 힘있고, 부유하며, 유명한 사람들 중 몇몇을 살펴봐라. 그들의 성공의 장식과 그들이 살 수 있는 것을 무시해라. 대신 그들이 맞바꿔야 하는 것을 봐라 — 성공이 그들에게 치르게 한 것을 봐라. 대부분은? 자유이다. 그들의 업무는 그들이 정장을 입는 것을 요구한다. 그들의 성공은 특정 파티에 참석하여, 그들이 좋아하지 않는 사람들에게 아첨하는 것에 달려 있다. 그것은 요구할 것이다 — 필연적으로 — 그들이 실제로 생각하는 것을 말할 수 없다는 사실을 깨닫는 것을. 더 나쁜 것은, 그것은 그들이 다른 유형의 사람이 되거나 부당한 일을 하도록 요구한다는 것이다. 물론, 그것은 많은 이익이 될지도 모른다 — 그러나 그들은 그 거래를 제대로 고찰한 적이 없다. Seneca가 말했듯이, "대리석과 황금 아래에 노예 상태가 존재한다." 너무 많은 성공한 사람들은 그들이 스스로 만든 감옥의 죄수들이다. 그것이 당신이 원하는 것인가? 그것이 당신이 목표로 하여 열심히 일하고 있는 것인가? 그렇지 않기를 바라자.

Why? 왜 정답일까?

성공한 사람들이 자유롭지 않음을 언급하며 성공하려면 원하지 않는 것도 해야한다(Worse, it demands that they become a different type of person or do bad things.)고 이야기하고 있기 때문에, "Slavery resides under marble and gold.(노예제는 대리석과 금 아래에 산다)"가 의미하는 바로 가장 적절한 것은 ① 'Your success requires you to act in ways you don't want to.'이다.

- trappings ⓝ 장식물, 외양
- cost ⓝ 대가, 값, 가격
- freedom ⓝ 자유
- success ⓝ 성공
- realize ⓥ 깨닫다, 실현하다
- require ⓥ 요구하다
- labor ⓝ 노동
- instead ⓐⓓ 대신에
- mostly ⓐⓓ 대부분
- demand ⓝ 요구 사항
- transaction ⓝ 거래
- prisoner ⓝ 죄수, 포로
- miserable ⓐ 비참한
- appearance ⓝ (겉)모습, 외모

구문 풀이

6행 Their success depends on attending certain parties, kissing up to people
　　　　　　　　　　　　　　　동명사1　　　　　　　　　　　　동명사2
(who/that) they don't like.
목적격 관계대명사 생략

---

22 기업의 도덕적 해이　　정답률 85% | 정답 ④

다음 글의 요지로 가장 적절한 것은?

① 기업에 대한 정부의 지원이 새로운 기술의 도입을 촉진한다.
② 현명한 소비자들은 윤리적 기업의 제품을 선택하는 경향이 있다.
③ 정부와 기업은 협력으로 사회적 문제의 해결책을 모색할 수 있다.
☑ 정부의 구제는 기업의 의사 결정에 부정적인 영향을 미칠 수 있다.
⑤ 합리적 의사 결정은 다양한 대안에 대한 평가를 통해 이루어진다.

If a firm is going to be saved / by the government, / it might be easier / to concentrate on lobbying the government / for more money / rather than taking the harder decision / of restructuring the company / to be able to be profitable and viable / in the long term.
회사가 구제 받게 된다면 / 정부에 의해, / 더 쉬울 수 있다. / 정부를 대상으로 로비에 집중하는 것이 / 더 많은 자금을 위해 / 더 어려운 결정을 내리는 것보다 / 회사를 구조조정하는 / 수익성과 생존 가능성을 갖추기 위해 / 장기적으로

This is an example / of something known as moral hazard — / when government support / alters the decisions firms take.
이것은 예시이다 / 도덕적 해이로 알려진 현상의 — / 정부 지원이 / 기업들이 내리는 결정을 바꿀 때

For example, / if governments rescue banks / who get into difficulty, / as they did during

the credit crisis of 2007 – 08, / this could encourage banks / to take greater risks / in the future / because they know / there is a possibility / that governments will intervene / if they lose money.
예를 들어, / 만약 정부가 은행을 구제하면 / 어려움에 처한, / 2007-08년 금융 위기 동안 그랬던 것처럼, / 이것은 은행에 장려한다. / 더 큰 위험을 감수하도록 / 장래에 / 왜냐하면 그들은 알고 있기 때문입니다. / 가능성이 있다는 것을 / 정부가 개입할 수 있다는 / 돈을 잃을 경우.
Although the government rescue / may be well intended, / it can negatively affect / the behavior of banks, / encouraging risky and poor decision making.
비록 정부의 구제가 / 의도가 좋을지라도, / 그것은 부정적인 영향을 미칠 수 있다. / 은행들의 행동에, / 위험하고 잘못된 결정을 내리도록 장려하며

기업이 정부로부터 구제 받으려면, 장기적으로 수익성이 나고 성장할 수 있도록 회사를 구조 조정 하는 어려운 결정을 내리기보다는 더 많은 돈을 받기 위해 정부에 로비하는 것에 집중하는 것이 더 쉬울지도 모른다. 이것은 도덕적 해이라고 불리는 것이다─정부의 지원이 기업이 내리는 결정을 바꿀 때. 예를 들어, 2007-08년 신용 위기 때 그들이 그랬던 것처럼, 만약 정부가 어려움에 처한 은행을 구제하면, 이것은 은행이 앞으로 더 큰 위험을 감수하도록 조장하는데 그 이유는 그들이 손해를 보는 경우 정부가 개입할 가능성이 있다는 것을 그들이 알기 때문이다. 정부의 구제는 좋은 의도일지라도, 그것은 은행의 행동에 부정적으로 영향을 미쳐, 위험하고 형편없는 의사 결정을 조장할 수 있다.

Why? 왜 정답일까?

정부가 은행에 개입한 예시를 들며, 정부의 기업 구제가 기업의 도덕적 해이를 자극하여 부정적인 영향을 끼칠 수 있음을 언급하고 있기 때문에 글의 요지로 가장 적절한 것은 ④ '정부의 구제는 기업의 의사 결정에 부정적인 영향을 미칠 수 있다.'이다.

- government ⓝ 정부
- lobby ⓥ 로비하다, 압력을 가하다
- viable ⓐ 실행 가능한
- intervene ⓥ 개입하다
- crisis ⓝ 위기
- concentrate ⓥ 집중하다
- restructure ⓥ 재구조화하다
- moral hazard 도덕적 해이
- rescue ⓝ 구조, 구제

구문 풀이

7행 For example, if governments rescue banks who get into difficulty, as they
가정법   선행사 주격 관계대명사   전치사(~처럼)
did during the credit crisis of 2007 – 08, this could encourage bank s to take
대동사(rescue)
greater risks in the future because they know there is a possibility that governments
명사절의 접속사
will intervene if they lose money.

23 다양한 의견의 중요성 정답률 77% | 정답 ②

다음 글의 주제로 가장 적절한 것은?

① value of acquiring scientific knowledge through trial and error
시도와 실패로 과학적 지식을 얻는 것의 가치
✓② necessity of various perspectives in practicing science
과학 실행의 다양한 관점의 필요성
③ benefits of building good relationships among scientists
과학자들 사이에서 좋은 관계를 맺는 것의 혜택
④ curiosity as a key factor in designing experiments
실험 설계의 중요한 요소로서의 호기심
⑤ importance of specialization in scientific research
과학적 연구에서 전문성의 중요성

If there is little or no diversity of views, / and all scientists see, think, and question the world / in a similar way, / then they will not, / as a community, / be as objective as they maintain they are, / or at least aspire to be.
만약 다양한 관점이 거의 없거나 전혀 없다면, / 그리고 모든 과학자들이 보고, 생각하고, 세상에 질문을 한다면, / 비슷한 방식으로, / 그러면 그들은 ~ 않을 것이다. / 공동체로서, / 그들이 주장하는 만큼 객관적이지 / 또는 최소한 그렇게 되기를 열망하지 않을 것이다.
The solution is / that there should be far greater diversity / in the practice of science: / in gender, ethnicity, and social and cultural backgrounds.
해결책은 ~ 이다. / 훨씬 더 큰 다양성이 있어야 한다는 것이다. / 과학의 실행에서: / 성별에서, 인종에서, 그리고 사회적 및 문화적 배경에서
Science works / because it is carried out / by people / who pursue their curiosity / about the natural world / and test their and each other's ideas / from as many varied perspectives and angles as possible.
과학은 작동한다. / 왜냐하면 그것은 수행되기 때문에 / 사람들에 의해 / 그들의 호기심을 추구하는 / 자연 세계에 대한 / 그리고 그들 자신의 아이디어와 서로의 아이디어를 검증하는 / 가능한 한 다양한 관점과 각도에서
When science is done / by a diverse group of people, / and if consensus builds up / about a particular area of scientific knowledge, / then we can have more confidence / in its objectivity and truth.
과학이 이루어질 때 / 다양한 사람들에 의해, / 그리고 만약 합의가 형성된다면 / 특정 과학 지식 분야에 대해, / 그러면 우리는 더 큰 신뢰를 가질 수 있다. / 그것의 객관성과 진리에 대해

만약 견해의 다양성이 거의 없거나 전혀 없고, 모든 과학자들이 비슷한 방식으로 세상을 보고, 생각하고, 의문을 제기한다면, 그러면 그들은, 하나의 공동체로서, 자신들이 주장하는 것만큼, 혹은 적어도 그렇게 되기를 열망하는 것만큼, 객관적이지 않을 것이다. 해결책은 과학의 실행에 있어 훨씬 더 많은 다양성이 있어야 한다는 것이다: 성별, 인종, 그리고 사회적 문화적 배경에서, 과학은 그것이 자연 세계에 대한 호기심을 추구하고 가능한 한 다양한 관점과 각도에서 그들의 그리고 서로의 아이디어를 검증하는 사람들에 의해 수행되기 때문에 작동한다. 과학이 다양한 집단의 사람들에 의해 행해질 때, 그리고 만약 과학 지식의 특정 영역에 대한 의견 일치가 이루어진다면, 그러면 우리는 그것의 객관성과 진실성에 있어서 더 큰 자신감을 가질 수 있다.

Why? 왜 정답일까?

과학에서 한 가지 의견만 있다면 객관적이지 않을 것이라며 다양한 의견의 중요성에 대해 이야기하고 있다. 따라서 글의 주제로 가장 적절한 것은 ② 'necessity of various perspectives in practicing science'이다.

- diversity ⓝ 다양성
- similar ⓐ 비슷한, 유사한
- aspire ⓥ 열망하다
- perspective ⓝ 관점, 시각
- confidence ⓝ 신뢰, 자신감
- view ⓝ 관점
- objective ⓐ 객관적인
- ethnicity ⓝ 민족성
- consensus ⓝ 합의, 의견 일치

구문 풀이

7행 Science works because it is carried out by people who pursue their
수동태   주격 관계대명사   동사1
curiosity about the natural world and test their and each other's ideas from
동사2
as many varied perspectives and angles as possible.
└ as many as possible : 가능한 많이 ┘

24 시간의 단위 정답률 69% | 정답 ④

다음 글의 제목으로 가장 적절한 것은?

① Delayed Deadlines: No Hurries, No Worries - 늦춰진 마감일: 서두를 필요도, 걱정할 필요도 없다
② How Stress Affects Your Perception of Time - 스트레스가 시간의 인식에 어떻게 영향을 끼치는가
③ Why Do We Manage Our Tasks Worse in Winter? - 왜 겨울에 작업을 끝내기 더 못할까?
✓④ Trick Your Mind to Get Your Work Done in Time - 제시간에 작업을 끝내기 위해서 마음을 속이라
⑤ The Sooner You Start, The More Errors You Make - 더 빨리 시작할수록, 더 많은 오류를 만든다

We tend to break up time / into units, / such as weeks, months, and seasons; / in a series of studies / among farmers in India and students in North America, / psychologists found / that if a deadline is on the other side of a "break" — / such as in the New Year — / we're more likely to see it as remote, / and, as a result, / be less ready to jump into action.
우리는 시간을 나누는 경향이 있다. / 단위로, / 예를 들어 주, 달, 그리고 계절처럼; / 일련의 연구에서 / 인도의 농부들과 북미의 학생들을 대상으로, / 심리학자들은 발견했다. / 만약 마감일이 "나눔"의 반대편에 있다면 / 예를 들어 새해에 / 우리는 그것을 더 멀리 있는 것으로 인식할 가능성이 높아지고, / 그리고 그 결과 / 즉각적으로 행동에 나설 준비가 덜 되어 있게 된다.
What you need to do / in that situation / is find another way / to think about the timeframe.
여러분이 해야 할 일은 / 그 상황에서 / 다른 방법을 찾는 것이다. / 시간 프레임을 생각할
For example, / if it's November / and the deadline is in January, / it's better to tell yourself / you have to get it done "this winter" / rather than "next year."
예를 들어, / 지금이 11월이고 / 마감일이 1월이라면, / 스스로에게 말하는 것이 더 좋다. / "올겨울"까지 끝내야 한다고 / "내년"보다는
The best approach / is to view deadlines as a challenge / that you have to meet / within a period that's imminent.
최선의 접근 방법은 / 마감일을 도전으로 보는 것이다. / 당신이 달성해야 하는 / 임박한 기간 내에
That way / the stress is more manageable, / and you have a better chance of starting — / and therefore finishing — / in good time.
그렇게 하면 / 스트레스가 더 관리하기 쉬워지고, / 당신은 시작할 더 큰 가능성이 있다. — / 따라서 마무리하는 — / 제때에

우리는 시간을 주, 월, 계절과 같은 단위로 나누는 경향이 있다; 인도의 농부들과 북미의 학생들을 대상으로 한 일련의 연구에서, 심리학자들은 마감일이 "나눔" — 새해와 같이 — 의 반대편에 있는 경우, 우리는 그것을 멀리 있는 것으로 여기고, 그 결과, 실행에 옮길 준비를 덜 할 가능성이 더 많다는 사실을 발견했다. 그러한 상황에서 당신이 해야 할 일은 그 시간 틀에 대해 생각하는 또 다른 방식을 찾는 것이다. 예를 들어, 지금이 11월이고 마감일이 1월이라면, 네가 "내년"보다는 "이번 겨울"에 일을 끝내야 한다고 너 자신에게 말하는 것이 더 좋다. 최고의 접근법은 마감일을 임박한 기간 내에 맞춰야 하는 도전으로 여기는 것이다. 그런 식으로 스트레스는 더 잘 관리될 수 있고, 적시에 작업을 시작 — 따라서 마무리 — 할 수 있는 가능성이 높아진다.

Why? 왜 정답일까?

시간의 단위가 "나눔"의 반대편에 있을 때 더 멀리 있다고 느낀다는 것을 언급하며 작업을 빨리 끝내고 싶다면 마감일을 "나눔"의 반대편에 두지 말라고 조언한다. 따라서 제목으로 가장 적절한 것은 ④ 'Trick Your Mind to Get Your Work Done in Time'이다.

- tend ⓥ (~하는) 경향이 있다
- unit ⓝ 단위
- farmer ⓝ 농부
- deadline ⓝ 마감일
- rather than ~보다는
- within prep 이내에
- imminent ⓐ 임박한
- challenge ⓝ 도전
- break up ~을 나누다(분해하다)
- season ⓝ 계절
- remote ⓐ 멀리 떨어진, 원격의
- situation ⓝ 상황
- approach ⓝ 접근법, 방법
- period ⓝ 기간
- manageable ⓐ 관리 가능한

구문 풀이

10행 The best approach is to view deadlines as a challenge that you have to
최상급   to 부정사 명사적 용법   목적격 관계대명사(생략가능)
meet within a period that's imminent.

25 2010년과 2020년 1인당 CO₂배출량 정답률 79% | 정답 ③

다음 도표의 내용과 일치하지 <u>않는</u> 것은?

CO₂ Emissions per Person
across Selected Asian Countries in 2010 and 2020

(tons)
☑ 2010 □ 2020
China: 6.4, 7.7
Mongolia: 5.1, 11.3
Uzbekistan: 3.8, 3.3
Vietnam: 1.6, 3.8
India: 1.4, 1.7

The graph above shows / the amount of CO₂ emissions per person / across selected Asian countries / in 2010 and 2020.
위의 그래프는 보여준다. / 1인당 CO₂ 배출량을 / 선택된 아시아 국가들에 / 2010년과 2020년에
① All the countries except Uzbekistan / had a greater amount of CO₂ emissions per person / in 2020 / than that in 2010.
우즈베키스탄을 제외한 모든 국가들이 / 더 많은 1인당 CO₂ 배출량을 보였다. / 2020년에 / 2010년의 배출량보다

② In 2010, / the amount of CO₂ emissions per person of China / was the largest / among the five countries, / followed by that of Mongolia.
2010년에, / 중국의 1인당 CO₂ 배출량이 / 가장 컸다. / 다섯 국가 중에서, / 몽골이 그 뒤를 이으며

⑤ However, / in 2020, / Mongolia surpassed China / in terms of the amount of CO₂ emissions per person, / with the amount of Mongolia / more than twice that of China.
그러나, / 2020년에는, / 몽골이 중국을 앞질렀다. / 1인당 CO₂ 배출량 면에서, / 몽골의 배출량은 / 중국의 두 배가 넘으며

④ In 2010, / Uzbekistan produced a larger amount of CO₂ emissions per person / than Vietnam, / while the opposite was true in 2020.
2010년에, / 우즈키스탄은 더 많은 CO₂ 배출량을 1인당 생산했다. / 베트남보다, / 2020년에는 반대였지만

⑤ Among the five countries, / India was the only one / where the amount of CO₂ emissions per person / was less than 2 tons in 2020.
다섯 국가 중에서, / 인도만이 유일한 / 1인당 CO₂ 배출량이 / 2020년에 2톤 이하였다.

위 그래프는 선택된 아시아 국가들의 2010년과 2020년 1인당 CO₂배출량을 보여준다. ① 우즈베키스탄을 제외한 모든 국가들은 2010년의 배출량보다 2020년의 1인당 CO₂ 배출량이 더 많았다. ② 2010년에는, 중국의 1인당 CO₂ 배출량이 5개국 중 가장 많았고, 몽골의 배출량이 그 뒤를 이었다. ③ 그러나, 2020년에는, 1인당 CO₂ 배출량에 있어서 몽골이 중국을 능가했는데, 몽골의 배출량은 중국의 배출량보다 두 배 이상이었다. ④ 2010년에는, 우즈베키스탄이 베트남보다 더 많은 1인당 CO₂ 배출량을 만들어 냈지만, 2020년에는 그 반대였다. ⑤ 5개국 중, 인도는 2020년에 1인당 CO₂ 배출량이 2톤 미만인 유일한 국가였다.

Why? 왜 정답일까?
2020년에 1인당 CO₂배출량은 몽골이 5.1톤으로 중국의 6.4톤을 능가하지 않았고, 몽골의 배출량은 중국의 배출량보다 두 배 이상이 아니었다. 따라서 도표의 내용과 일치하지 않는 것은 ③이다.

- **emission** ⓝ 배출, 방출
- **amount** ⓝ 양
- **ton** ⓝ 톤
- **CO₂** ⓝ 이산화탄소
- **surpass** ⓥ 능가하다, 넘어서다
- **country** ⓝ 국가

구문 풀이

7행 However, in 2020, Mongolia surpassed China in terms of the amount of CO₂ emissions per person, with the amount of Mongolia more than twice that of China.
~라는 점에서 / 비교급

---

26 Henry David Thoreau의 일생 | 정답률 91% | 정답 ⑤

Henry David Thoreau에 관한 다음 글의 내용과 일치하지 않는 것은?
① 졸업한 후에 교사로 일했다.
② 자연 시인이 되기를 희망했다.
③ Walden에서 엄청난 양의 독서를 했다.
④ 43세에 여행을 마치고 Concord로 돌아왔다.
☑ 그의 작품은 그의 일생 동안 널리 읽혔다.

Henry David Thoreau was born / in Concord, Massachusetts / in 1817.
Henry David Thoreau는 태어났다. / 매사추세츠주 콩코드에서 / 1817년에

When he was 16, / he entered Harvard College.
그가 16살이었을 때, / 그는 하버드 대학에 입학했다.

「After graduating, / Thoreau worked as a schoolteacher / but he quit after two weeks.」 ①의 근거 일치
졸업 후, / Thoreau는 교사로 일했지만 / 그는 2주 후에 그만두었다.

In June of 1838 / he set up a school / with his brother John.
1838년 6월에 / 그는 학교를 설립했다. / 그의 형 John과 함께

「However, / he had hopes of becoming a nature poet.」 ②의 근거 일치
그러나, / 그는 자연 시인이 되기를 희망했다.

In 1845, / he moved into a small self-built house / near Walden Pond.
1845년에, / 그는 스스로 지은 작은 집으로 이사했다. / Walden 연못 근처에

「At Walden, / Thoreau did an incredible amount of reading.」 ③의 근거 일치
Walden에서, / Thoreau는 엄청난 양의 독서를 했다.

The journal he wrote there / became the source of his most famous book, *Walden*.
그가 그곳에서 쓴 일기는 / 그의 가장 유명한 책인 'Walden'의 원천이 되었다.

In his later life, / Thoreau traveled to the Maine woods, / to Cape Cod, / and to Canada.
말년에, / Thoreau는 Maine 숲, Cape Cod, 그리고 캐나다를 여행했다.

「At the age of 43, / he ended his travels / and returned to Concord.」 ④의 근거 일치
43세에, / 그는 여행을 마치고 / 콩코드로 돌아왔다.

「Although his works were not widely read / during his lifetime, / he never stopped writing, / and his works fill 20 volumes.」 ⑤의 근거 불일치
그의 작품들이 널리 읽히지 않았지만 / 그의 생애 동안, / 그는 글쓰기를 멈추지 않았고, / 그의 작품들은 20권이나 된다.

Henry David Thoreau는 1817년 Massachusetts주 Concord에서 태어났다. 그가 16세 때, 그는 Harvard 대학에 입학했다. 졸업 후, Thoreau는 학교 교사로 일했지만 2주 후에 그만두었다. 1838년 6월에 그는 그의 형제인 John과 함께 학교를 세웠다. 그러나, 그는 자연 시인이 되기를 희망했다. 1845년, 그는 Walden 연못 근처에 직접 지은 작은 집으로 이사했다. Walden에서, Thoreau는 엄청난 양의 독서를 했다. 그가 그곳에서 쓴 저널이 그의 가장 유명한 저서인 *Walden*의 원천이 되었다. 그의 인생 후반부에, Thoreau는 Maine 숲으로, Cape Cod로, 그리고 캐나다로 여행을 떠났다. 43세의 나이에, 그는 그의 여행을 마치고 Concord로 돌아왔다. 비록 그의 작품이 그의 일생 동안 널리 읽히지 않았지만, 그는 집필을 멈추지 않았고, 그의 작품은 20권에 달한다.

Why? 왜 정답일까?
Henry David Thoreau는 졸업한 후에 교사로 일했고, 자연 시인이 되기를 희망했으며 Walden에서 엄청난 양을 독서를 했다. 또한 43세에 여행을 마치고 Concord로 돌아왔지만 그의 작품은 그의 일생 동안 널리 읽히지 않았다.(Although his works were not widely read during his lifetime, he never stopped writing, and his works fill 20 volumes.) 따라서 글의 내용과 일치하지 않는 것은 ⑤ '그의 작품은 그의 일생 동안 널리 읽혔다.'이다.

- **schoolteacher** ⓝ 교사
- **incredible** ⓐ 놀라운, 대단한, 굉장한
- **source** ⓝ 원천
- **nature** ⓝ 자연
- **nature** ⓝ 자연
- **journal** ⓝ 일기, 기록
- **volume** ⓝ 책, 권

문제편 p.053

구문 풀이

12행 Although his works were not widely read during his lifetime, he never stopped writing, and his works fill 20 volumes.
수동태 / 부정어 / 동명사

---

27 2024 미래 엔지니어 캠프 | 정답률 95% | 정답 ⑤

2024 Future Engineers Camp에 관한 다음 안내문의 내용과 일치하지 않는 것은?
① 오전 10시부터 오후 4시까지 진행된다.
② 참가비는 100달러이다.
③ 기본적인 코딩 기술을 배운다.
④ 장난감 비행기를 만들고 테스트한다.
☑ 점심 식사는 참가비에 포함되지 않는다.

2024 Future Engineers Camp
2024 미래 공학 캠프
Calling all young creators!
젊은이들을 부릅니다!
Join us at Southside Maker Space / to explore the wonders of engineering / with exciting activities.
South Maker Space에 참여하세요. / 공학의 신비를 탐색하기 위해서 / 신나는 활동들로
Date: Saturday, July 20 & Sunday, July 21
날짜: 6월 20일 토요일 & 7월 21일 일요일
「Time: 10 a.m. − 4 p.m.」 ①의 근거 일치
시간: 오전 10시~오후 4시
Ages: 14 to 16
나이: 14살부터 16살
「Participation Fee: $100」 ②의 근거 일치
참가 비용 : 100 달러
Day 1 − Robotics Workshop
1일차 − 로봇 워크숍
「Learn basic coding skills.」 ③의 근거 일치
기본 코딩 기술을 배우세요.
Work in teams to build mini-robots.
미니 로봇을 만들기 위해서 팀으로 작업하세요.
Day 2 − Flying Challenge
2일차 − 비행 도전
「Make and test toy airplanes.」 ④의 근거 일치
장난감 비행기를 만들고 시험하세요.
Participate in an airplane flying race.
비행기 날리기 경주에 참여하세요.
Notes
주의사항
「Lunch is included in the participation fee.」 ⑤의 근거 불일치
점심은 참가비에 포함되어 있습니다.
All tools and materials for the projects / are provided.
프로젝트를 위한 모든 도구와 재료는 / 제공됩니다.
For more information, / please visit www.southsidemaker.com.
더 많은 정보를 위해서, / www.southsidemaker.com에 방문하세요.

2024 미래 엔지니어 캠프

모든 젊은 크리에이터들을 모집합니다! 흥미진진한 활동과 함께 공학기술의 경이로움을 탐험하기 위해 Southside Maker Space에 와서 함께 해요.

날짜: 7월 20일 토요일 & 7월 21일 일요일
시간: 오전 10시 - 오후 4시
연령: 14세에서 16세
참가비: 100달러

1일 차 - 로봇 공학 워크숍
• 기본적인 코딩 기술을 배웁니다.
• 팀을 이루어 미니 로봇을 만듭니다.

2일 차 - 플라잉 챌린지
• 장난감 비행기를 만들고 테스트합니다.
• 비행기 날리기 경주에 참가합니다.

공지사항
• 점심 식사는 참가비에 포함됩니다.
• 프로젝트를 위한 모든 도구들과 재료들이 제공됩니다.

더 많은 정보를 위해서는, www.southsidemaker.com을 방문하세요.

Why? 왜 정답일까?
점심 식사는 참가비에 포함된다고 하였으므로(Lunch is included in the participation fee), 안내문의 내용과 일치하지 않는 것은 ⑤ '점심 식사는 참가비에 포함되지 않는다.'이다.

- **engineer** ⓝ 공학자
- **workshop** ⓝ 워크숍
- **challenge** ⓝ 도전
- **robotics** ⓝ 로봇 공학
- **participation** ⓝ 참가
- **airplane** ⓝ 비행기

---

28 음식 문화 경험 안내문 | 정답률 94% | 정답 ③

Taste the City에 관한 다음 안내문의 내용과 일치하는 것은?
① 9월 6일부터 일주일 동안 열린다.
② 라이브 음악 공연이 하루 종일 진행된다.
☑ 숙련된 요리사들과의 요리 수업이 있다.
④ 어른과 아이의 입장권 가격이 동일하다.
⑤ 사전 예약이 필요하다.

Taste the City
도시를 맛보세요

Experience Jamestown's diverse and delicious food culture / all in one place.
Jamestown의 다양하고 맛있는 음식 문화를 경험하세요 / 한 장소에서

Enjoy tasty treats, / and discover new restaurants!
맛있는 간식을 즐기고, / 새로운 식당을 발견하세요!

When & Where
장소 & 시간

「September 6th − 8th (10 a.m. − 9 p.m.)」 ①의근거 불일치
9월 6일~8일 (오전 10시~오후 9시)

Grand Park Highlights
Grand Park Highlights에서

30 kinds of food samples provided by local restaurants
지역 식당에서 제공된 30종의 음식 샘플

「Live music performances each evening」 ②의근거 불일치
매일 저녁 라이브 음악 공연

「Cooking classes with experienced chefs」 ③의근거 일치
숙련된 요리사와의 요리 수업

Entry Tickets
입장표

「Adult: $15
성인: 15달러

Child: $10」 ④의근거 불일치
아동: 10달러

「No pre-reservations necessary, / just show up and enjoy.」 ⑤의근거 불일치
사전 예약이 필요하지 않습니다. / 오셔서 즐기세요.

도시를 맛보세요

Jamestown의 다양하고 맛있는 음식 문화를 한자리에서 모두 경험해 보세요. 맛있는 음식들을 즐기고, 새로운 레스토랑들을 발견해 보세요!

언제 & 어디서
• 9월 6일 − 8일 (오전 10시 − 오후 9시)
• Grand Park

주요사항
지역 식당에서 제공되는 30가지 종류의 음식 샘플
• 저녁마다 라이브 음악 공연
• 숙련된 요리사들과의 요리 수업

입장권
• 어른: 15달러
• 어린이: 10달러

※ 사전 예약은 필요하지 않으며, 바로 와서 즐기세요.

Why? 왜 정답일까?

숙련된 요리사들과의 요리 수업이 있다(Cooking classes with experienced chefs)고 하였으므로, 안내문의 내용과 일치하는 것은 ③ '숙련된 요리사들과의 요리 수업이 있다.'이다.

- taste ⓝ 맛
- ticket ⓝ 티켓
- culture ⓝ 문화
- performances ⓝ 공연

---

29 미소 짓기의 선천적인 능력   정답률 53% | 정답 ⑤

다음 글의 밑줄 친 부분 중, 어법상 틀린 것은? [3점]

The built-in capacity for smiling / is proven by the remarkable observation / ① that babies who are congenitally both deaf and blind, / who have never seen a human face, / also start to smile at around 2 months.
타고난 미소 짓는 능력은 / 놀라운 관찰에 의해 입증되었다. / 선천적으로 청각과 시각을 모두 잃은 아기들이, / 사람의 얼굴을 본 적이 없는 / 또한 생후 약 2개월에 미소를 짓기 시작한다는 것이

However, / smiling in blind babies eventually ② disappears / if nothing is done to reinforce it.
그러나, / 시각 장애 아기들의 미소는 결국 사라진다 / 그것을 강화하기 위한 조치가 없다면

Without the right feedback, / smiling dies out.
적절한 피드백이 없으면, / 미소는 사라진다.

But here's a fascinating fact: / blind babies will continue to smile / if they are cuddled, bounced, nudged, and tickled by an adult — / anything to let ③ them know / that they are not alone / and that someone cares about them.
하지만 여기 흥미로운 사실이 있습니다: / 시각 장애 아기들은 계속 미소를 지을 것이다. / 만약 그들이 어른에 의해 껴안기거나, 튕겨지거나, 눌리거나, 간지럼을 타게 되면 — / 그들에게 알릴 어느 것이든 / 그들이 혼자가 아니라는 것과 / 누군가가 그들을 돌보고 있다는

This social feedback / encourages the baby to continue smiling.
이러한 사회적 피드백은 / 아기가 계속 미소를 짓도록 격려한다.

In this way, / early experience operates with our biology / ④ to establish social behaviors.
이런 식으로, / 초기 경험은 생물학과 함께 작용하여 / 사회적 행동을 확립한다.

In fact, / you don't need the cases of blind babies / to make the point.
사실, / 시각 장애 아기의 사례가 필요하지 않다. / 요점을 말하기 위해

Babies with sight smile more at you / when you look at them or, / better still, ✔ smile back at them.
시력이 있는 아기들은 더 많이 당신에게 미소를 짓는다. / 당신이 그들을 볼 때 / 혹은 더 나아가, 그들에게 미소를 지어줄 때

미소 짓기에 대한 선천적인 능력은 선천적으로 청각장애와 시각장애가 있고, 사람 얼굴을 한 번도 본 적이 없는 아기들도, 약 2개월 즈음에 미소를 짓기 시작한다는 놀라운 관찰에 의해 증명된다. 그러나, 시각장애를 가진 아기의 미소 짓기는 그것을 강화하기 위해 아무것도 행해지지 않으면 결국 사라진다. 적절한 피드백이 없으면, 미소 짓기는 사라진다. 하지만 여기에 흥미로운 사실이 있다: 만약 그들이 어른에 의해서 안기고, 흔들리고, 슬쩍 찔리고, 간지럽혀지면 — 그들이 혼자가 아니며 누군가 그들에게 관심을 갖고 있다는 것을 알게 하는 것 — 시각 장애를 가진 아기들은 계속 미소를 지을 것이다. 이러한 사회적 피드백은 그 아기가 계속 미소를 지을 수 있도록 조장한다. 이런 방식으로, 초기 경험은 우리의 생리 작용과 함께 작용하여 사회적 행동을 형성한다. 사실, 당신은 이를 설명하기 위해 시각장애를 가진 아기의 사례를 필요로 하지 않는다. 시력이 있는 아기들은 당신이 그들을 바라볼 때나, 더 나아가, 당신이 그들에게 미소를 지어줄 때, 당신에게 더 많이 미소를 짓는다.

Why? 왜 정답일까?

Babies with sight smile more at you when you look at them or, better still, smiling → smile back at them. 주어가 "Babies with sight"이기 때문에 동사로 "smile"이 와야 적절하다. 따라서 어법상 틀린 것은 ⑤이다.

- capacity ⓝ 능력, 용량
- remarkable ⓐ 놀라운
- congenitally ⓐⓓ 선천적으로
- disappear ⓥ 사라지다
- feedback ⓝ 피드백
- behavior ⓝ 행동
- smile ⓥ 미소 짓다
- observation ⓝ 관찰
- eventually ⓐⓓ 결국
- reinforce ⓥ 강화하다
- social ⓐ 사회적인

구문 풀이

1행 The built-in capacity for smiling is proven by the remarkable observation
수동태 by 행위자
that babies who are congenitally both deaf and blind, who have never seen
명사절의 접속사 주격 관계대명사   주격 관계대명사
a human face, also start to smile at around 2 months.
to 부정사

---

30 적응을 중단하기   정답률 54% | 정답 ④

다음 글의 밑줄 친 부분 중, 문맥상 낱말의 쓰임이 적절하지 않은 것은? [3점]

Because people tend to adapt, / interrupting positive things with negative ones / can actually increase enjoyment.
사람들이 적응하는 경향이 있기 때문에, / 긍정적인 것들 사이에 부정적인 것들을 끼워 넣으며 / 실제로 즐거움을 증가시킬 수 있다.

Take commercials. // Most people hate them, / so ① removing them / should make shows or other entertainment more enjoyable.
광고를 예로 들어보자. // 대부분의 사람들은 광고를 싫어한다. / 그래서 광고를 없애는 것이 / 프로그램이나 다른 오락을 더 즐겁게 만들어 줄 것이라고 생각한다.

But the opposite is true. // Shows are actually ② more enjoyable / when they're broken up by annoying commercials.
하지만 실제로는 반대이다. // 프로그램은 사실 덜 즐거워진다. / 짜증 나는 광고들로 나누어졌을 때

Because these less enjoyable moments / break up adaptation to the ③ positive experience of the show.
왜냐하면 이러한 덜 즐거운 순간들이 / 프로그램의 긍정적인 경험에 대한 적응을 끊기 때문이다.

Think about eating chocolate chips. // The first chip is delicious: / sweet, melt-in-your-mouth goodness.
초콜릿 칩을 먹는 것을 생각해 보라. // 첫 번째 칩은 맛있다: / 달콤하고, 입안에서 녹는 좋은 맛

The second chip is also pretty good. // But by the fourth, fifth, or tenth chip in a row, / the goodness is no longer as pleasurable.
두 번째 칩도 꽤 좋다. // 하지만 네 번째, 다섯 번째, 또는 열 번째 칩이 될 때쯤, / 그 좋은 맛은 더 이상 그렇게 즐겁지 않다.

We adapt. // Interspersing positive experiences with less positive ones, however, / can ✔ slow down adaptation.
우리는 적응한다. // 그러나 긍정적인 경험 사이에 덜 긍정적인 경험을 끼워 넣으면 / 적응을 늦출 수 있다.

Eating a Brussels sprout between chocolate chips / or viewing commercials between parts of TV shows / disrupts the process.
초콜릿 칩 사이에 방울양배추를 먹거나 / TV 프로그램의 일부 사이에 광고를 보는 것이 / 그 과정을 방해한다.

The less positive moment / makes the ⑤ following positive one new again / and thus more enjoyable.
덜 긍정적인 순간이 / 그 다음 긍정적인 순간을 다시 새롭게 만들고, / 결과적으로 더 즐겁게 만든다.

사람들은 적응하는 경향이 있기 때문에, 긍정적인 것을 부정적인 것으로 방해하는 것이 실제로는 즐거움을 향상시킬 수 있다. 광고를 예로 들어 보자. 대부분의 사람들은 그것들을 싫어해서, 그것들을 ① 제거하는 것이 쇼나 다른 오락물을 더 즐겁게 만들 수 있다. 하지만 그 반대가 사실이다. 쇼는 그것들이 성가신 광고들에 의해 중단될 때 실제로 ② 더 즐거워진다. 왜냐하면 이러한 덜 즐거운 순간들이 쇼의 ③ 긍정적인 경험에 대한 적응을 깨뜨리기 때문이다. 초콜릿 칩을 먹는 것을 생각해 보라. 첫 번째 칩은 맛있다: 달콤하고, 입안에서 살살 녹는 좋은 맛. 두 번째 칩도 꽤 맛있다. 하지만 네 번째, 다섯 번째, 혹은 열 번째 칩을 연속으로 먹으면 그 좋은 맛은 더 이상 즐겁지 않다. 우리는 적응한다. 그러나, 긍정적인 경험들에 덜 긍정적인 경험들을 간격을 두고 배치하는 것은 적응을 ④ 빠르게 할(→ 늦출) 수 있다. 초콜릿 칩 사이에 방울양배추를 먹거나 TV 쇼의 파트 사이에 광고를 보는 것은 이 과정을 방해한다. 덜 긍정적인 순간은 뒤에 ⑤ 오는 긍정적인 순간을 다시 새롭게 만들어서 더 즐겁게 만든다.

Why? 왜 정답일까?

긍정적인 경험 사이의 부정적인 경험이 긍정적인 경험의 적응을 막아 긍정적인 경험의 즐거움을 유지시킬 수 있다는 내용이다. 따라서 긍정적인 경험 사이에 덜 긍정적인 경험들을 배치하는 것은 적응을 늦출 수 있다는 것이 맥락상 적절하므로 답은 ④이다.

- adapt ⓥ 적응하다
- commercial ⓝ 광고
- positive ⓐ 긍정적인
- interrupt ⓥ 방해하다
- enjoyable ⓐ 즐거운
- disrupt ⓥ 방해하다

구문 풀이

1행 Because people tend to adapt, interrupting positive things with negative
「tend to 동사원형: ~하는 경향이 있다」 동명사
ones can actually increase enjoyment.
부정대명사(things)

---

31 희소성의 매력   정답률 56% | 정답 ①

다음 빈칸에 들어갈 말로 가장 적절한 것을 고르시오.

- ✔ short supply - 공급 부족
- ② good shape - 좋은 모양새
- ③ current use - 현재 사용
- ④ great excess - 많은 잉여
- ⑤ constant production - 꾸준한 생산

We collect stamps, coins, vintage cars / even when they serve no practical purpose.
우리는 우표, 동전, 빈티지 자동차를 수집한다. / 그것들이 실용적인 목적을 전혀 제공하지 않을 때조차도

The post office doesn't accept the old stamps, / the banks don't take old coins, / and the vintage cars are no longer allowed on the road.
우체국은 오래된 우표를 받지 않고, / 은행은 오래된 동전을 받지 않으며, / 빈티지 자동차는 더 이상 도로에서 허용되지 않는다.

These are all side issues; / the attraction is that they are in short supply.
이것들은 모두 부차적인 문제이다; / 매력은 그것들이 공급이 부족하다는 것이다.

In one study, / students were asked to arrange ten posters in order of attractiveness / — with the agreement / that afterward they could keep one poster / as a reward for their participation.
한 연구에서, / 학생들은 열 개의 포스터를 매력도 순으로 배열하라고 요청받았다. / — 동의와 함께 / 그 후에 하나의 포스터를 가질 수 있다는 / 참여에 대한 보상으로

Five minutes later, / they were told / that the poster with the third highest rating / was no longer available.
5분 후에, / 그들은 들었다. / 세 번째로 높은 평가를 받은 포스터가 / 더 이상 이용할 수 없다는 말을

Then they were asked / to judge all ten from scratch.
그 후 그들은 요청을 받았다. / 모든 열 개를 처음부터 다시 평가하라는

The poster that was no longer available / was suddenly classified as the most beautiful.
더 이상 이용할 수 없게 된 포스터가 / 갑자기 가장 아름다운 것으로 분류되었다.

In psychology, / this phenomenon is called *reactance*: / when we are deprived of an option, / we suddenly deem it more attractive.
심리학에서는, / 이 현상을 *리액턴스*라 부른다: / 우리가 어떤 선택지를 박탈당할 때, / 우리는 갑자기 그것을 더 매력적이라고 여긴다.

우리는 그것들이 실용적인 목적을 수행하지 않더라도 우표, 동전, 빈티지 자동차들을 수집한다. 우체국은 오래된 우표를 받지 않고, 은행은 오래된 동전을 받지 않으며, 그리고 빈티지 자동차는 더 이상 도로에서 허용되지 않는다. 이런 것들은 모두 부수적인 문제이다; 매력은 그들이 부족한 공급에 있다는 것이다. 한 연구에서, 학생들은 포스터 10장을 매력의 순서대로 배열하도록 요청받았다 — 나중에 그들의 참여에 대한 보상으로 포스터 1장을 간직할 수 있다는 합의와 함께. 5분 후, 그들은 세 번째 높은 평가의 포스터가 더 이상 이용 가능하지 않다는 것을 들었다. 그런 다음 그들은 10개의 포스터를 모두 처음부터 평가하라고 요청을 받았다. 더 이상 이용할 수 없는 포스터가 갑자기 가장 아름다운 것으로 분류되었다. 심리학에서, 이러한 현상은 *리액턴스*라고 불린다: 우리가 선택지를 빼앗겼을 때, 우리는 그것을 갑자기 더 매력적으로 여긴다.

Why? 왜 정답일까?

실험 결과에서 더 이상 가질 수 없는 포스터의 인기 순위가 전보다 높아졌으므로, 포스터가 인기 있어진 이유는 공급의 부족이다. 따라서 매력의 이유는 ① 'short supply'이다.

- **stamp** ⓝ 우표
- **vintage** ⓐ 고전적인, 오래된
- **poster** ⓝ 포스터
- **reactance** ⓝ 반발
- **coin** ⓝ 동전
- **attraction** ⓝ 매력
- **psychology** ⓝ 심리학

구문 풀이

11행 The poster that was no longer available was suddenly classified as the most beautiful.
선행사 / 주격 관계대명사 / 수동태

---

32 매몰 비용 오류
정답률 56% | 정답 ③

다음 빈칸에 들어갈 말로 가장 적절한 것을 고르시오.
① reduce profit – 이익을 감소시키다
② offer rewards – 보상을 제공하다
③ cut our losses – 손실을 끊다
④ stick to the plan – 계획을 고수하다
⑤ pay off our debt – 빚을 갚다

If we've invested in something / that hasn't repaid us / — be it money in a failing venture, / or time in an unhappy relationship / — we find it very difficult to walk away.
우리가 어떤 것에 투자했을 때 / 우리에게 보답하지 않은 / — 실패한 사업에 돈을 투자했든, / 불행한 관계에 시간을 투자했든 / — 우리는 그것을 떠나기 매우 어려워한다.

This is the sunk cost fallacy.
이것이 매몰비용 오류이다.

Our instinct is to continue investing money or time / as we hope that our investment will prove to be worthwhile / in the end.
우리의 본능은 돈이나 시간을 계속 투자하는 것이다. / 우리의 투자가 가치가 있음을 증명하기를 바라며 / 결국에

Giving up would mean acknowledging / that we've wasted something we can't get back, / and that thought is so painful / that we prefer to avoid it if we can.
포기하는 것은 인정하는 것을 의미한다. / 우리가 되돌릴 수 없는 것을 낭비했다는 것을, / 그리고 그 생각은 너무나 고통스럽기 때문에 / 가능하다면 그것을 피하는 것을 선호한다.

The problem, of course, / is that if something really is a bad bet, / then staying with it simply increases the amount we lose.
물론 문제는, / 만약 어떤 것이 정말로 나쁜 선택이라면, / 그것을 계속 유지하는 것은 우리가 잃는 양을 단순히 증가시킬 뿐이다.

Rather than walk away from a bad five-year relationship, / for example, / we turn it into a bad 10-year relationship; / rather than accept that we've lost a thousand dollars, / we lay down another thousand and lose that too.
나쁜 5년짜리 관계에서 떠나기보다는, / 예를 들어, / 우리는 그것을 나쁜 10년짜리로 만든다; / 천 달러를 잃었다는 것을 받아들이기보다는, / 우리는 또 다른 천 달러를 걸고 그것도 잃는다.

In the end, / by delaying the pain of admitting our problem, / we only add to it.
결국, / 우리의 문제를 인정하는 고통을 지연시킴으로써, / 우리는 그 고통을 더할 뿐이다.

Sometimes we just have to cut our losses.
때로 우리는 그저 손실을 끊어야 한다.

우리에게 보답해 주지 않는 것에 우리가 투자해 왔다면 — 실패한 사업에 투자한 돈이거나, 불행한 인간관계에 투자한 시간이던 간에 — 우리는 벗어나기가 매우 어렵다는 것을 안다. 이것은 매몰 비용 오류이다. 우리의 본능은 결국에는 우리의 투자가 가치 있는 것으로 입증될 것이라고 희망하면서 돈이나 시간에 투자를 계속 하는 것이다. 포기한다는 것은 우리가 돌이킬 수 없는 무언가를 낭비했다고 인정하는 것을 의미하고, 그런 생각은 너무 고통스러워서 우리가 할 수 있다면 그것을 피하기를 선호한다. 물론, 문제는 어떤 것이 정말 나쁜 투자라면, 그것을 계속하는 것은 우리가 잃는 총액을 증가시킬 뿐이라는 것이다. 예를 들어, 5년의 나쁜 관계에서 벗어나기보다는 우리는 그것을 10년의 나쁜 관계로 바꾸고; 천 달러를 잃었다는 사실을 받아들이기보다는, 또 다른 천 달러를 내놓고 그것도 역시 잃는다. 결국, 우리의 문제를 인정하는 고통을 미룸으로써 우리는 그것에 보탤 뿐이다. 때때로 우리는 손실을 끊어야만 한다.

Why? 왜 정답일까?

매몰 비용 오류에 대해 설명하고 있다. 지금까지 투자한 비용이 아까워서 손실을 인정하지 못하기 때문에 더 큰 손실을 본다고 하였으므로 손실을 끊어야 한다는 ③ 'cut our losses'가 정답이다.

- **invest** ⓥ 투자하다
- **relationship** ⓝ 관계
- **acknowledge** ⓥ 인정하다
- **delay** ⓥ 지연하다
- **fallacy** ⓝ 오류
- **worthwhile** ⓐ 가치 있는
- **instinct** ⓝ 본능

구문 풀이

9행 The problem, of course, is that if something really is a bad bet, then
명사절의 접속사 / 가정법 / 동명사
staying with it simply increases the amount (that) we lose.
목적격 관계대명사 생략

★★★ 등급을 가르는 문제!
33 우주에서의 빛의 이동
정답률 38% | 정답 ①

다음 빈칸에 들어갈 말로 가장 적절한 것을 고르시오. [3점]
☑ see everything in space in the past – 우주의 모든 것을 과거로 본다
② can predict when our sun will go out – 해가 불이 꺼지면 예측할 수 있다
③ lack evidence of life on other planets – 다른 행성에서 생명의 증거가 부족하다
④ rely on the sun as a measure of time – 시간의 측정을 해에 의존하다
⑤ can witness the death of a star as it dies – 별이 죽으면 별의 죽음을 목격할 수 있다

On our little world, / light travels, for all practical purposes, / instantaneously.
우리의 작은 세계에서, / 빛은 이동한다. / 실질적으로, 즉각적으로

If a lightbulb is glowing, / then of course it's physically where we see it, / shining away.
전구가 빛나고 있다면, / 당연히 그것은 우리가 보는 위치에 물리적으로 있다. / 빛나며

We reach out our hand and touch it: / It's there all right, / and unpleasantly hot.
우리가 손을 뻗어 그것을 만지면: / 그것은 분명히 그곳에 있고, / 불쾌할 정도로 뜨겁다.

If the filament fails, / then the light goes out.
필라멘트가 고장 나면, / 빛은 꺼진다.

We don't see it / in the same place, glowing, / illuminating the room / years after the bulb breaks / and it's removed from its socket.
우리는 보지 않는다. / 같은 자리에, 빛나며, 방을 밝히는 것을 / 전구가 깨지고 / 소켓에서 제거된 후 수년이 지나도

The very notion seems nonsensical.
그 개념 자체가 터무니없어 보인다.

But if we're far enough away, / an entire sun can go out / and we'll continue to see it shining brightly; / we won't learn of its death, / it may be, for ages to come / — in fact, for how long it takes light, / which travels fast but not infinitely fast, / to cross the intervening vastness.
하지만 우리가 충분히 멀리 있다면, / 하나의 태양 전체가 꺼져도 / 우리는 그것이 여전히 밝게 빛나는 것을 계속 볼 수 있을 것이다; / 우리는 그것의 죽음을 알지 못할 것이다. / 아마도, 오랜 시간이 지나도록 / — 사실, 빛이 걸리는 시간만큼, / 빠르게 이동하지만 무한히 빠르지는 않은, / 사이의 거대한 공간을 가로지르는 데 걸리는

The immense distances to the stars and the galaxies mean / that we see everything in space in the past.
별과 우주까지의 엄청난 거리는 의미한다. / 우리가 우주의 모든 것을 과거의 것으로 보는 것을

우리의 작은 세상에서, 실제로는 빛은 순간적으로 이동한다. 전구가 켜져 있다면, 당연히 그것은 우리가 보는 그 자리에서 빛을 내고 있다. 우리는 손을 뻗어 그것을 만진다: 그것은 바로 거기에 있고, 불쾌할 정도로 뜨겁다. 필라멘트가 나가면, 그때 빛은 꺼진다. 전구가 망가져서 소켓에서 제거된 몇 년 후, 그 자리에서 빛을 내고 방을 밝히고 있는 그것을 우리는 보지 못한다. 바로 그 개념은 말도 안 되는 것처럼 보인다. 하지만 우리가 충분히 멀리 떨어져 있다면, 항성 전체는 꺼질 수 있지만 우리는 그것이 밝게 빛나는 것을 계속 볼 것이다; 우리는 아마도 오랜 세월동안 — 사실, 빠르지만 무한히 빠르지는 않게, 이동하는 빛이 그 사이에 낀 광대함을 가로지르는데 걸리는 시간 동안 그것의 소멸을 알지 못할 것이다. 별과 은하까지의 엄청난 거리는 우리가 우주 공간의 모든 것을 과거의 모습으로 보고 있다는 것을 의미한다.

Why? 왜 정답일까?

빛의 이동에 대한 이야기이다. 충분히 멀리 떨어져 있다면, 빛이 이동하는 속도 때문에 빛이 도달하기 전까지는 빛을 계속 볼 것이므로, 모든 것을 과거의 모습으로 보고 있다는 ① 'see everything in space in the past'가 정답이다.

- **instantaneously** ⓐⓓ 즉시, 순간적으로
- **intervening** ⓐ 사이에 있는
- **nonsensical** ⓐ 무의미한, 터무니없는
- **evidence** ⓝ 증거
- **filament** ⓝ 필라멘트
- **vastness** ⓝ 광대함
- **witness** ⓥ 목격하다

구문 풀이

8행 But if we're far enough away, an entire sun can go out and we'll continue
가정법 / 조동사+동사원형
to see it shining brightly; we won't learn of its death, it may be, for ages to come
to부정사 명사적 용법 / 조동사+동사원형
— in fact, for how long it takes light, which travels fast but not infinitely fast,
주격 관계대명사
to cross the intervening vastness.
to부정사 부사적 용법

★★ 문제 해결 꿀~팁 ★★

▶ 많이 틀린 이유는?
글은 빛이 이동함을 제시한다. 가까이 있어서 만질 수 있는 전구와 멀리 있어서 만질 수 없는 태양을 비교하며, 태양이 아주 멀리 있기 때문에 태양이 더 이상 빛나지 않아도 우리는 태양의 마지막 빛이 이동하는 동안 태양이 빛나는 걸 볼 수 있다고 설명한다. 빛이 빠르게 이동하지만 거리가 아주 멀다면 빛이 이동하는 것을 볼 수 있기 때문에, 우리는 과거의 태양을 보는 것이다. 따라서 빈칸에 들어갈 알맞은 말은 'see everything in space in the past'이다.

▶ 문제 해결 방법은?
글의 요지를 파악한 후, 어울리는 선지를 고른다. 해당 문제의 경우 글에 제시된 예시를 통해 요지를 파악하여 빛이 이동 속도를 가지며, 빠르지만 완전히 빠르지 않음을 알면 풀 수 있다.

34 금융 시장의 이점
정답률 44% | 정답 ②

다음 빈칸에 들어갈 말로 가장 적절한 것을 고르시오. [3점]

① we can ignore the complexity of financial markets
금융 시장의 복잡함을 우리는 무시할 수 있다
② earning income has been divorced from spending it
소득을 버는 것과 그것을 소비하는 것은 분리되어 있다
③ financial markets can regulate our impulses
금융 시장이 우리의 충동을 조절할 수 있다
④ we sell our crops as soon as we harvest them
우리가 우리의 농작물을 수확하는 즉시 농작물을 판매할 수 있다
⑤ managing working hours has become easier than ever
근무 시간을 조정하는 것이 그 언제보다 쉬워졌다

Financial markets do more / than take capital from the rich / and lend it to everyone else.
금융 시장은 더 한다. / 부자들에게서 자본을 가져와 / 모두에게 빌려주는 일보다

They enable each of us / to smooth consumption over our lifetimes, / which is a fancy way / of saying that we don't have to spend income / at the same time we earn it.
그들은 우리 각자를 할 수 있게 해 준다. / 평생 동안 소비를 원활하게 / 이것은 멋진 표현입니다. / 우리가 수입을 소비할 필요가 없다는 / 돈을 벌 때와 동시에

Shakespeare may have admonished us / to be neither borrowers nor lenders; / the fact / is that most of us will be both at some point.
셰익스피어는 우리에게 충고했을 지도 모른다. / 돈을 빌려주지도, 빌리지도 말라고 / 사실 / 대부분의 우리는 어느 시점에선가 둘 다 될 지도 모른다

If we lived in an agrarian society, / we would have to eat our crops reasonably soon after the harvest / or find some way to store them.
만약 우리가 농업 사회에서 살았다면, / 우리는 수확 후 꽤 빨리 작물을 먹거나 / 아니면 그것들을 저장할 방법을 찾아야 했을 것이다.

Financial markets are a more sophisticated way / of managing the harvest.
금융 시장은 더 정교한 방법이다. / 농작물을 관리하는

We can spend income now / that we have not yet earned / — as by borrowing for college or a home — / or we can earn income now and spend it later, / as by saving for retirement.
우리는 지금 소비할 수 있다. / 아직 벌지 않은 수입을 / 대학이나 주택을 위해 돈을 빌리는 것처럼 / 또는 우리는 지금 수입을 벌고 나중에 소비할 수 있다. / 은퇴를 위해 저축하는 것처럼

The important point / is that earning income has been divorced / from spending it, / allowing us much more flexibility in life.
중요한 점은 / 돈을 버는 것이 갈라진 것이다. / 소비하는 것에서 / 우리에게 삶에서 더 많은 유연성을 허락하며

금융 시장은 부자들로부터 자본을 받아 다른 모든 사람들에게 그것을 빌려주는 것 이상을 한다. 그것들은 우리 각자가 평생에 걸쳐 소비를 원활하게 하도록 해주며, 그리고 이는 우리가 그것(소득)을 얻는 동시에 소득을 소비할 필요가 없다는 것을 말하는 멋진 방식이다. 셰익스피어는 우리가 빌리는 사람도 빌려주는 사람도 되지 말라고 충고했을지도 모른다; 사실 우리 대부분은 어떤 때에는 둘 다 될 것이다. 만약 우리가 농경사회에 산다면, 우리는 우리의 농작물을 수확 직후에 합리적으로 먹거나 또는 그것들을 저장할 어떤 방법을 찾아야 할 것이다. 금융 시장은 수확을 관리하는 더 정교한 방법이다. 우리는 우리가 아직 벌지 않은 소득을 지금 소비할 수도 있고 — 대학이나 주택을 위해 빌리는 것처럼 — 혹은 우리는 은퇴를 위해 저축하는 것처럼, 지금 소득을 벌어서 나중에 그것을 소비할 수도 있다. 중요한 점은 소득을 버는 것이 그것을 소비하는 것과 분리되어 있다는 것이고, 이는 우리에게 삶에서 훨씬 더 많은 유연성을 허용해준다.

Why? 왜 정답일까?
금융 시장이 우리의 소비를 원활하게 해 준다는 이야기이다. 아직 벌지는 않았지만 벌 소득을 미리 사용하게 해주고, 번 소득을 나중에 소비할 수 있게 해준다고 하였으므로 소득을 사용하는 것과 소득을 버는 것이 분리되어 있다는 말이 빈칸에 들어갈 말로 가장 적절하다. 따라서 정답은 ② 'earning income has been divorced from spending it'이다.

- **financial** ⓐ 재정의
- **capital** ⓝ 자본
- **lifetime** ⓝ 평생, 생애
- **reasonably** [ad] 상당히, 꽤
- **sophisticated** ⓐ 정교한, 복잡한
- **market** ⓝ 시장
- **admonish** ⓥ 훈계하다
- **agrarian** ⓐ 농업의
- **retirement** ⓝ 은퇴

구문 풀이

2행 They enable each of us to smooth consumption over our lifetimes, which
　　　　each of + 복수 명사 to 부정사 명사적 용법 / 주격 관계대명사
is a fancy way of saying that we don't have to spend income at the same time we
　　　　　　　　　　명사절의 접속사
earn it.

★★ 문제 해결 꿀~팁 ★★

▶ 많이 틀린 이유는?
금융 시장의 역할에 대한 글이다. 금융 시장은 소득을 버는 것과 소비하는 것의 고정된 순서를 자유롭게 한다고 설명한다. 농경사회의 농작물의 소비와 저장을 예시로 들며 이것이 좀 더 정교해진 것이 금융 시장이라고 비교한다. 아직 벌지 않은 소득을 지금 사용할 수도 있고, 지금 소득을 벌어서 나중에 소비할 수도 있다(We can spend income now that we have not yet earned...or we can earn income now and spend it later, as by saving for retirement.)고 이야기하며 소득을 버는 것과 소비하는 것의 전통적인 순서를 흐리고 있다.

▶ 문제 해결 방법은?
빈칸 문제는 본문의 주제를 파악하고, 선지를 올바르게 해석하는 것이 중요하다. 글의 서두와 말미의 문장에서 주제를 파악한 후, 빈칸에 들어갈 답을 고른다. 해당 문제의 경우 소득을 버는 것과 소비하는 것의 순서를 흐리고 있기 때문에 'earning income has been divorced from spending it'가 정답이다.

35 사용자 매뉴얼의 중요성
정답률 67% | 정답 ③

다음 글에서 전체 흐름과 관계 없는 문장은?

As the old joke goes: / "Software, free. User manual, $10,000."
옛 농담에 이런 말이 있다. / "소프트웨어는 무료. 사용자 설명서는 10,000달러."

But it's no joke.
하지만 이건 농담이 아니다.

A couple of high-profile companies / make their living / selling instruction and paid support for free software.
몇몇 유명한 회사들이 / 수익을 만든다. / 무료 소프트웨어에 대한 설명서와 유료 지원을 판매하여

The copy of code, / being mere bits, / is free.
코드의 복사본은, / 단순한 비트로서, / 무료다.

The lines of free code / become valuable to you / only through support and guidance.
무료 코드의 줄들이 / 당신에게 가치 있게 되는 것은 / 오직 지원과 안내를 통해서이다.

① A lot of medical and genetic information / will go this route / in the coming decades.
많은 의학과 유전 정보가 / 이 경로를 따를 것이다. / 다가오는 몇십 년 동안

② Right now / getting a full copy of all your DNA / is very expensive ($10,000), / but soon it won't be.
지금은 / 모든 DNA의 완전한 복사본을 얻는 것이 / 매우 비싸지만, ($10,000), / 곧 그렇지 않을 것이다.

③ The public exposure of people's personal genetic information / will undoubtedly cause serious legal and ethical problems.
사람들의 개인 유전 정보의 공개는 / 분명히 심각한 법적 및 윤리적 문제를 일으킬 것이다.

④ The price is dropping so fast, / it will be $100 soon, / and then the next year / insurance companies will offer to sequence you for free.
가격이 너무 빨리 떨어져서, / 곧 100달러가 될 것이고, / 그 다음 해에는 / 보험 회사들이 무료로 당신의 유전자 서열을 제공할 것이다.

⑤ When a copy of your sequence costs nothing, / the interpretation of what it means, / what you can do about it, and how to use it / — the manual for your genes — / will be expensive.
당신의 유전자 서열 복사본이 무료가 되면, / 그것이 의미하는 바의 해석, / 그것에 대해 할 수 있는 일, / 그리고 그것을 사용하는 방법 / —당신의 유전자 설명서— / 은 비쌀 것이다.

다음과 같은 옛 농담처럼: "소프트웨어, 무료. 사용자 매뉴얼, 10,000달러." 하지만 그것은 농담이 아니다. 세간의 이목을 끄는 몇몇 기업은 무료 소프트웨어에 대한 지침과 유료 지원을 판매하면서 돈을 번다. 단지 몇 비트일 뿐인 코드 사본은 무료다. 무료 코드의 배열은 지원과 안내를 통해서만 당신에게 가치 있게 된다. ① 다가올 수십 년 안에 많은 의료 및 유전 정보가 이 경로를 따르게 될 것이다. ② 지금은 당신의 모든 DNA의 전체 사본을 얻는 것이 매우 비싸지만 (10,000달러), 곧 그렇지 않게 될 것이다. ③ 사람들의 개인 유전자 정보의 공개는 틀림없이 심각한 법적이고 윤리적인 문제를 야기할 것이다. ④ 가격이 너무 빨리 떨어지고 있어, 곧 100달러가 될 것이고, 그 다음 해에는 보험 회사가 무료로 당신의 유전자 배열 순서를 밝혀줄 것을 제안할 것이다. ⑤ 당신의 배열의 사본에 비용이 들지 않을 때, 그것이 의미하는 것, 당신이 그것에 관해 할 수 있는 것, 그리고 그것을 사용하는 방법에 관한 설명 —당신의 유전자 매뉴얼— 은 비싸질 것이다.

Why? 왜 정답일까?
사용자 매뉴얼 없이 소프트웨어는 무용지물일 것이기 때문에 사용자 매뉴얼이 중요하다고 이야기하며, 유전자 배열 역시 유전자 배열 사용법 없이는 무용지물일 것이라고 이야기하고 있다. 따라서 개인 유전자 정보의 공개가 법적으로 문제가 된다는 ③이 전체 흐름과 관계 없는 문장이다.

- **software** ⓝ 소프트웨어
- **paid** ⓐ 유급의
- **valuable** ⓐ 가치가 큰
- **sequence** ⓝ 서열, 순서
- **ethical** ⓐ 윤리적인
- **instruction** ⓝ 지시, 설명서
- **support** ⓝ 지원, 도움
- **genetic** ⓐ 유전의
- **interpretation** ⓝ 해석

구문 풀이

14행 When a copy of your sequence costs nothing, the interpretation of what
　　　　부사절의 접속사 / 관계대명사
it means, what you can do about it, and how to use it — the manual for your
genes — will be expensive.
조동사 + 동사원형

36 최소한의 양만 처리하는 뇌
정답률 65% | 정답 ②

주어진 글 다음에 이어질 글의 순서로 가장 적절한 것을 고르시오.

① (A) − (C) − (B)　　② (B) − (A) − (C)
③ (B) − (C) − (A)　　④ (C) − (A) − (B)
⑤ (C) − (B) − (A)

Brains are expensive / in terms of energy.
뇌는 비용이 많이 든다. / 에너지 측면에서

Twenty percent of the calories we consume / are used / to power the brain.
우리가 섭취하는 칼로리의 20퍼센트는 / 사용된다. / 뇌를 가동하는 데

(B) So brains try to operate / in the most energy-efficient way possible, / and that means processing only the minimum amount of information / from our senses / that we need to navigate the world.
그래서 뇌는 작동하려고 한다. / 가능한 가장 에너지 효율적인 방법으로, / 그리고 그것은 최소한의 정보를 처리하는 것을 의미한다. / 우리의 감각으로부터 / 우리가 세상을 탐색하는 데 필요한

Neuroscientists weren't the first to discover / that fixing your gaze on something / is no guarantee of seeing it.
신경과학자들이 처음 발견한 것은 아니다. / 무언가에 시선을 고정하는 것이 / 그것을 본다는 보장이 아니라는 것을

Magicians figured this out / long ago.
마술사들은 이 점을 알아냈다. / 오래전에.

(A) By directing your attention, / they perform tricks with their hands / in full view.
당신의 주의를 끌어서, / 그들은 손으로 묘기를 부린다. / 다 보이는 데서

Their actions should give away the game, / but they can rest assured / that your brain processes / only small bits of the visual scene.
그들의 행동은 그 속임수를 드러내겠지만, / 그들은 확신한 채로 있을 수 있다. / 당신의 뇌가 처리한다는 것을 / 시각적 장면의 작은 부분만을

(C) This all helps to explain / the prevalence of traffic accidents / in which drivers hit pedestrians in plain view, / or collide with cars directly in front of them.
이것은 모두 설명하는 데 도움이 된다. / 교통사고의 발생의 빈번함을 / 운전자들이 명백히 보이는 보행자를 치거나, / 또는 그들 앞에 있는 차와 충돌하는

In many of these cases, / the eyes are pointed / in the right direction, / but the brain isn't seeing / what's really out there.
많은 이러한 경우에서, / 눈은 향하고 있지만, / 올바른 방향으로, / 뇌는 보고 있지 않다. / 실제로 거기에 있는 것을

에너지의 측면에서 뇌는 비용이 많이 든다. 우리가 소비하는 칼로리의 20%는 뇌에 동력을 공급하는 데 사용된다.

(B) 따라서 뇌는 가능한 한 가장 에너지 효율적인 방식으로 작동하려고 애쓰며, 그것은 우리가 세상을 항해하는 데 필요로 하는 최소한의 양의 정보만을 우리 감각으로부터 처리하는 것을 의미한다. 신경과학자들은 무언가에 당신의 시선을 고정하는 것이 그것을 본다는 보장이 없다는 사실을 발견한 최초가 아니었다. 마술사들은 오래전에 이것을 알아냈다.

(A) 당신의 주의를 끌어서, 그들은 다 보이는 데서 손으로 속임수를 행한다. 그들의 행동은 그 속임수를 드러내지만, 그들은 당신의 뇌가 시각적 장면의 오직 작은 부분들만을 처리한다는 것을 확신한 채로 있을 수 있다.

(C) 이 모든 것은 운전자가 명백한 시야에 있는 보행자들을 치거나, 바로 앞에 있는 차량들과 충돌하는 교통사고의 빈번함을 설명하는 데 도움이 된다. 많은 이러한 경우에서, 눈은 올바른 방향을 향하고 있지만, 뇌는 실제로 거기에 있는 것을 보고 있지 않다.

Why? 왜 정답일까?

글의 초반에서 우리의 뇌는 에너지를 많이 사용한다고 밝힌다. 따라서 (B)의 뇌는 에너지를 가장 효율적인 방식으로 사용하려고 한다는 문장과 연결된다. 그래서 시선을 고정하는 것이 보는 것이 같은 것이 아니며, 이를 마술사가 밝혀냈다고 문단을 마친다. (A)의 시작 문장인 'By directing your attention, they perform tricks with their hands in full view.'는 마술사의 행동을 묘사하는 문장이므로 이어지는 것이 자연스럽다. (C)의 시작 문장인 운전자 예시는 (A)의 문단에서의 시각적 장면의 일부만 처리한다는 내용과 연결되기 때문에 주어진 글 다음에 이어질 글의 순서로 가장 적절한 것은 ② '(B) - (A) - (C)'이다.

- brain ⓝ 뇌
- calory ⓝ 칼로리
- gaze ⓝ 시선, 응시
- accident ⓝ 사고들
- energy ⓝ 에너지
- neuroscientist ⓝ 신경과학자
- prevalence ⓝ 널리 퍼짐, 유행

구문 풀이

8행 So brains try to operate in the most energy-efficient way possible, and
(to 부정사 명사적 용법 / 최상급)
that means processing only the minimum amount of information from our senses
(지시대명사)
that we need to navigate the world.
(목적격 관계대명사)

★★★ 등급을 가르는 문제!

37 투자와 소비의 차이점   정답률 43% | 정답 ③

주어진 글 다음에 이어질 글의 순서로 가장 적절한 것을 고르시오. [3점]

① (A) - (C) - (B)
②✓ (B) - (C) - (A)
⑤ (C) - (B) - (A)
③ (B) - (A) - (C)
④ (C) - (A) - (B)

Buying a television is current consumption.
텔레비전을 사는 것은 현재 소비다.
It makes us happy today / but does nothing / to make us richer tomorrow.
그것은 오늘 우리를 행복하게 하지만 / 내일 우리를 더 부유하게 만드는 데는 / 아무런 도움이 되지 않는다.
Yes, money spent on a television / keeps workers employed / at the television factory.
물론, 텔레비전에 쓰인 돈은 / 근로자들이 고용된 상태를 유지하게 한다. / 텔레비전 공장에서
(B) But if the same money were invested, / it would create jobs somewhere else, / say for scientists in a laboratory / or workers on a construction site, / while also making us richer in the long run.
하지만 동일한 돈이 투자되었다면, / 그것은 다른 곳에 일자리를 창출할 것이다. / 예를 들어 실험실의 과학자들이나 / 건설 현장의 근로자들에게. / 그러면서도 장기적으로 우리를 더 부유하게 만든다.
(C) Think about college as an example.
대학을 예로 생각해 보자.
Sending students to college / creates jobs for professors.
학생들을 대학에 보내는 것은 / 교수에게 일자리를 창출한다.
Using the same money to buy fancy sports cars / for high school graduates / would create jobs for auto workers.
화려한 스포츠카를 사는 데 동일한 돈을 사용하는 것은 / 고등학교 졸업생들에게 / 자동차 노동자들에게 일자리를 창출할 것이다.
(A) The crucial difference between these scenarios / is that a college education / makes a young person more productive / for the rest of his or her life; / a sports car does not.
이러한 시나리오 간의 중요한 차이는 / 대학 교육이 / 젊은이를 더 생산적으로 만든다는 점이다 / 그의 남은 생 동안; / 스포츠카는 그렇지 않다.
Thus, college tuition is an investment; / buying a sports car is consumption.
따라서, 대학 등록금은 투자다; / 스포츠카를 사는 것은 소비다.

텔레비전을 사는 것은 현재의 소비이다. 그것은 오늘 우리를 행복하게 하지만 내일 우리를 더 부유하게 만드는 데는 아무것도 하지 않는다. 그렇다, 텔레비전에 소비되는 돈은 노동자들이 텔레비전 공장에 계속 고용되게 한다.

(B) 하지만 같은 돈이 투자된다면, 그것은 말하자면 실험실의 과학자들이나 건설 현장의 노동자들을 위한, 어딘가 다른 곳의 일자리를 창출하면서, 또한 장기적으로 우리를 더 부유하게 만들 것이다.

(C) 대학을 예로써 생각해 보자. 학생들을 대학에 보내는 것은 교수들을 위한 일자리를 창출한다. 같은 돈을 고등학교 졸업생에게 멋진 스포츠카를 사주는 데 쓰는 것은 자동차 노동자를 위한 일자리를 창출할 것이다.

(A) 이러한 시나리오들의 중대한 차이점은 대학 교육은 젊은이들이 그 또는 그녀의 남은 삶 동안 더 생산적이게 만들지만; 스포츠카는 그렇지 않다는 것이다. 따라서, 대학 등록금은 투자이다; 스포츠카를 구입하는 것은 소비이다.

Why? 왜 정답일까?

텔레비전 구매, 대학 교육비, 스포츠카 구매를 예로 들며 투자와 소비의 차이점에 대해 이야기하고 있다. 주어진 글은 텔레비전 구매에 대해 이야기하고 있으므로 (B)에서 언급하고 있는 과학자들과 건설 현장 노동자들과는 연관이 없으므로 "But"으로 연결되는 것이 자연스럽다. 'while also making us richer in the long run.'(장기적으로 우리를 더 부유하게 만들 것이다)의 예시로 'Think about college as an example.'(대학을 예로써 생각해 보자.)를 들고 있으므로 (C)가, 대학 교육비와 스포츠카 구매를 비교하는 (A)가 순서대로 오는 것이 가장 적절하다. 따라서 정답은 ③ '(B) - (C) - (A)'이다.

- television ⓝ 텔레비전
- consumption ⓝ 소비

- productive ⓐ 생산적인
- investment ⓝ 투자
- fancy ⓐ 화려한, 값비싼
- sports car ⓝ 스포츠카
- tuition ⓝ 학비

구문 풀이

15행 Using the same money to buy fancy sports cars for high school graduates
(동명사 / to 부정사 부사적 용법)
would create jobs for auto workers.
(조동사 + 동사원형)

★★ 문제 해결 꿀~팁 ★★

▶ 많이 틀린 이유는?
소비와 투자를 비교하는 글이다. 소비의 예시로는 tv와 스포츠카를 사는 것. 투자의 예시로는 대학교 교육비를 들었다. 주어진 글의 마지막 문장에서 tv(소비)를 언급하고 있으니, 'But'으로 투자 이야기를 시작하는 (B)가 오는 것이 자연스럽다. 투자의 예로 대학 교육비에 대해 설명하는 (C)가 연결된다. 마지막으로 (A)에서는 투자(대학 교육비)와 소비(스포츠카)를 비교하며 마무리하고 있기 때문에 (B) - (C) - (A) 순서이다.

▶ 문제 해결 방법은?
주어진 글에 이어질 순서를 맞추는 문제는 해당 글에서 말하고자 하는 주제를 찾은 후 전치사로 힌트를 얻는 것이 좋다. 주의하여 볼 전치사로는 'But', 'However', 'Yet' 등이 있다. 주어진 문단마다의 핵심 단어를 파악하고 이어보자.

38 인터넷의 상호연결적 특징   정답률 48% | 정답 ④

글의 흐름으로 보아, 주어진 문장이 들어가기에 가장 적절한 곳을 고르시오.

The Net differs from most of the mass media it replaces / in an obvious and very important way: / it's bidirectional.
인터넷은 그것이 대체하는 대부분의 대중 매체와 다르다. / 명백하고 매우 중요한 방식에서: / 그것은 양방향이다.
① We can send messages through the network / as well as receive them, / which has made the system all the more useful.
우리는 메시지를 네트워크를 통해 보낼 수 있다. / 메시지를 수신하는 것뿐만 아니라, / 이것이 이 시스템을 더욱 유용하게 만들었다.
② The ability to exchange information online, / to upload as well as download, / has turned the Net into a thoroughfare for business and commerce.
온라인에서 정보를 교환하는 능력, / 다운로드뿐만 아니라 업로드하는 능력은 / 인터넷을 비즈니스와 상업의 대로로 변모시켰다.
③ With a few clicks, / people can search virtual catalogues, / place orders, track shipments, / and update information in corporate databases.
몇 번의 클릭으로, / 사람들은 가상 카탈로그를 검색하고, / 주문을 넣고, 배송을 추적하며, / 기업 데이터베이스에서 정보를 업데이트할 수 있다.
④✓ But the Net doesn't just connect us with businesses; / it connects us with one another.
하지만 인터넷은 우리를 기업과 연결할 뿐만 아니라, / 우리를 서로 연결시킨다.
It's a personal broadcasting medium / as well as a commercial one.
그것은 개인 방송 매체이며 / 상업적인 매체이기도 하다.
⑤ Millions of people use it to distribute their own digital creations, / in the form of blogs, videos, photos, songs, and podcasts, / as well as to critique, edit, or otherwise modify the creations of others.
수백만의 사람들이 그것을 사용하여 자신의 디지털 창작물을 배포한다. / 블로그, 비디오, 사진, 노래, 그리고 팟캐스트의 형태로, / 다른 사람들의 창작물을 비평하거나, 편집하거나, 또는 다른 방식으로 수정하는 것뿐만 아니라

인터넷은 그것이 대체하는 대부분의 대중 매체와 분명하고도 매우 중요한 방식으로 다르다: 그것은 두 방향으로 작용한다. ① 우리는 네트워크를 통해 메시지를 받을 수 있을 뿐만 아니라 그것들을 보낼 수도 있는데, 이것은 그 시스템을 훨씬 더 유용하게 만들었다. ② 온라인에서 정보를 교환하고, 다운로드할 뿐만 아니라 업로드하는 능력은, 인터넷을 비즈니스와 상거래를 위한 통로로 만들었다. ③ 몇 번의 클릭으로, 사람들은 가상 카탈로그를 검색하고, 주문을 하고, 배송을 추적하고, 그리고 기업의 데이터베이스에 정보를 업데이트할 수 있다. ④ 하지만 인터넷은 단지 우리를 기업과 연결하는 것만은 아니다; 그것은 우리를 서로서로 연결한다. 그것은 상업용 매체일 뿐만 아니라 개인 방송 매체이다. ⑤ 수백만 명의 사람들이 다른 사람들의 창작물을 비평하고, 편집하고, 또는 그렇지 않으면 수정하기 위해서 뿐만 아니라, 블로그, 동영상, 사진, 노래, 그리고 팟캐스트의 형태로 자신의 디지털 창작물을 배포하기 위해서 그것을 사용한다.

Why? 왜 정답일까?

인터넷과 대부분의 대중 매체를 비교하며, 인터넷의 가장 큰 특징은 상호 연결성이라는 것이 이 글의 주제이다. 주어진 문장은 인터넷의 상호 연결성에 대하여 직접적으로 언급하고 있다. 'With a few clicks, people can search virtual catalogues, place orders, track shipments, and update information in corporate databases.'(몇 번의 클릭으로, 사람들은 가상 카탈로그를 검색하고, 주문을 하고, 배송을 추적하고, 그리고 기업의 데이터베이스에 정보를 업데이트할 수 있다.)는 인터넷의 상호 작용적 특징이 잘 드러나지 않지만, 다음 문장인 'It's a personal broadcasting medium as well as a commercial one.'(그것은 상업용 매체일뿐만 아니라 개인 방송 매체이다.)에서 인터넷의 상호 연결성에 대하여 직접적으로 언급하고 있어서 ④에 주어진 문장이 들어가는 것이 적절하다.

- differ ⓥ 다르다
- bidirectional ⓐ 양방향의
- catalogue ⓝ 카탈로그
- medium ⓝ 매체
- virtual ⓐ 가상의
- replace ⓥ 대신하다, 대체하다
- receive ⓥ 수신하다
- corporate ⓐ 기업의
- distribute ⓥ 배포하다

구문 풀이

10행 With a few clicks, people can search virtual catalogues, place orders,
(a few + 가산명사 / 동사1 / 동사2)
track shipments, and update information in corporate databases.
(동사3 / 동사4)

★★★ 등급을 가르는 문제!

39 자동화의 일자리 창출   정답률 43% | 정답 ③

글의 흐름으로 보아, 주어진 문장이 들어가기에 가장 적절한 곳을 고르시오.

Imagine that seven out of ten working Americans got fired tomorrow. / What would they all do?
만약 일하는 미국인들 10명 중 7명이 내일 해고된다고 상상해 보라. / 그들이 모두 무엇을 할 것인가?
It's hard to believe / you'd have an economy at all / if you gave pink slips to more than half the labor force.
믿기 어려운 일이다 / 경제가 존재할 것이라는 것은 / 노동력의 절반 이상에게 해고 통지서를 준다면.
But that is what the industrial revolution did / to the workforce of the early 19th century.
그러나 그것이 바로 산업혁명이 했던 일이다 / 19세기 초의 노동력에
Two hundred years ago, / 70 percent of American workers lived on the farm.
200년 전, / 미국 노동자의 70%가 농장에서 살았다.
① Today automation has eliminated / all but 1 percent of their jobs, / replacing them with machines.
오늘날 자동화는 없앴다. / 그들의 일자리 중 1%를 제외한 모든 것을 / 그것들을 기계로 대체하면서
② But the displaced workers did not sit idle.
그러나 일자리를 잃은 노동자들은 가만히 앉아 있지 않았다.
☑ Instead, automation created hundreds of millions of jobs / in entirely new fields.
대신, 자동화는 수억 개의 일자리를 창출했다. / 완전히 새로운 분야에서
Those who once farmed were now manning the factories / that manufactured farm equipment, cars, and other industrial products.
한때 농사를 짓던 사람들은 이제 공장을 운영하고 있었다. / 농기계, 자동차, 그리고 다른 산업 제품을 제조하는
④ Since then, wave upon wave of new occupations have arrived / — appliance repair person, food chemist, photographer, web designer — / each building on previous automation.
그 이후로, 수많은 새로운 직업들이 도래했다. / — 가전제품 수리공, 식품 화학자, 사진작가, 웹 디자이너 — / 각각이 이전의 자동화를 기반으로
⑤ Today, the vast majority of us are doing jobs / that no farmer from the 1800s could have imagined.
오늘날, 우리 대부분은 일을 하고 있다. / 1800년대의 농부들이 상상할 수 없었던

미국인 직장인 10명 중 7명이 내일 해고된다고 상상해 보라. 그들은 모두 무엇을 할까? 노동력의 절반 이상에게 해고 통지서를 보낸다면 경제가 유지될 것이라고 믿기 어려운 일이다. 하지만 그것은 19세기 초 노동력에 산업혁명이 했던 것이다. 200년 전, 미국 노동자의 70%가 농장에서 살았다. ① 오늘날 자동화는 1%를 제외한 모든 일자리를 제거하였고, 그것들을 기계로 대체하였다. ② 하지만 일자리를 잃은 노동자들은 한가롭게 앉아 있지 않았다. ③ 그 대신, 자동화는 완전히 새로운 분야에서 수억 개의 일자리를 창출했다. 한때 농사를 짓던 사람들은 이제 농기구, 자동차, 그리고 기타 산업 제품을 제조하는 공장에서 일하고 있다. ④ 그 이후로, 가전제품 수리공, 식품 화학자, 사진작가, 웹 디자이너 등 이전의 자동화를 기반으로 한 새로운 직업이 계속해서 등장했다. ⑤ 오늘날, 우리 중 대다수는 1800년대의 농부들은 상상도 할 수 없었던 일을 하고 있다.

Why? 왜 정답일까?
자동화의 일자리 창출에 대하여 이야기하고 있다. 글의 초반에는 자동화가 일자리를 없애고 기계로 대체하였다고 언급하고, 글의 후반에서는 자동화가 일자리를 창출했다는 흐름이다. 따라서 글의 흐름이 반전되는 ③에 주어진 문장이 들어가는 것이 가장 적절하다.

- **automation** ⓝ 자동화
- **displaced** ⓐ 대체된, 쫓겨난
- **occupation** ⓝ 직업
- **vast** ⓐ 광대한
- **revolution** ⓝ 혁명
- **wave** ⓝ 물결, 파도
- **appliance** ⓝ 기구, 장치

구문 풀이

9행 Today automation has eliminated all but 1 percent of their jobs, replacing them with machines.
현재완료 ~을 제외하고(= except) 현재분사(~하면서)

★★ 문제 해결 꿀~팁 ★★

▶ 많이 틀린 이유는?
자동화가 많은 일자리를 만들었다고 주장하는 글이다. 글의 윗부분에서는 자동화가 많은 일자리를 없앴다고 하지만 글의 뒷부분에서는 자동화가 많은 일자리를 만들었다고 한다. 따라서 접속사 'Instead'가 어울리고, 자동화가 만든 많은 일자리를 나열한 앞 부분인 ③에 주어진 문장이 들어가는 것이 가장 자연스럽다.

▶ 문제 해결 방법은?
주어진 문장을 글에 넣는 문제는 글의 흐름 파악이 최우선이다. 흐름이 바뀌는 부분과 새로운 개념이 제시되는 부분에 표시를 하여 직관적으로 파악할 수 있게 하자.

40 부러움의 특징 정답률 48% | 정답 ⑤

다음 글의 내용을 한 문장으로 요약하고자 한다. 빈칸 (A), (B)에 들어갈 말로 가장 적절한 것은?

	(A)		(B)		(A)		(B)
①	actions 행동	......	different 다른	②	possessions 소유권	......	unique 고유한
③	goals 목표	......	ordinary 일반적인	④	possessions 소유물	......	favorable 좋아하는
☑⑤	actions 행동	......	alike 비슷한				

Many things spark *envy* : / ownership, status, health, youth, talent, popularity, beauty.
많은 것들이 *부러움*을 유발한다 : / 소유, 지위, 건강, 젊음, 재능, 인기, 아름다움.
It is often confused with jealousy / because the physical reactions are identical.
이는 종종 질투와 혼동된다. / 왜냐하면 신체 반응이 동일하기 때문이다.
The difference: / the subject of *envy* is a thing (status, money, health etc.).
차이점: / *부러움*의 대상은 사물이다 (지위, 돈, 건강 등).
The subject of jealousy / is the behaviour of a third person.
질투의 대상은 / 제3자의 행동이다.
Envy needs two people. / Jealousy, on the other hand, requires three: / Peter is jealous of Sam because the beautiful girl next door rings him instead.
*부러움*은 두 사람을 필요로 한다. / 반면에, 질투는 세 사람이 필요하다: / 피터는 샘을 질투한다, 왜냐하면 옆집의 아름다운 소녀가 그에게 대신 전화를 걸기 때문이다.
Paradoxically, with envy we direct resentments toward those / who are most similar to us in age, career and residence.
역설적으로, 부러움의 경우 우리는 원망을 향하게 한다. / 우리와 나이, 경력, 거주지가 가장 비슷한 사람들에게
We don't envy business people / from the century before last.
우리는 부러워하지 않는다. / 지난 세기의 사업가들을

We don't envy millionaires / on the other side of the globe.
우리는 백만장자를 부러워하지 않는다. / 지구 반대편의
As a writer, I don't envy musicians, managers or dentists, / but other writers.
작가로서 나는 음악가, 관리자, 치과의사들을 부러워하지 않는다. / 하지만 다른 작가들을 부러워한다.
As a CEO / you envy other, / bigger CEOs.
CEO로서 / 당신은 다른, / 더 큰 CEO들을 부러워한다.
As a supermodel / you envy more successful supermodels.
슈퍼모델로서 / 당신은 더 성공한 슈퍼모델들을 부러워한다.
Aristotle knew this: / 'Potters envy potters.'
아리스토텔레스는 이것을 알고 있었다. / '도공들은 도공들을 부러워한다.'
→ Jealousy involves three parties, focusing on the (A) actions of a third person, whereas envy involves two individuals whose personal circumstances are most (B) alike, with one person resenting the other.
질투는 세 당사자를 포함한다. / 제3자의 행동에 집중하며 반면 부러움은 두 개인을 포함한다. / 개인적인 상황이 가장 비슷한 / 한 사람이 다른 사람을 불쾌하게 여기며

많은 것들은 *부러움*을 불러일으킨다: 소유권, 지위, 건강, 젊음, 재능, 인기, 아름다움. 이것은 신체적 반응이 동일하기 때문에 종종 질투와 혼동된다. 차이점: *부러움*의 대상은 사물(지위, 돈, 건강 등)이다. 질투의 대상은 제3자의 행동이다. *부러움*은 두 사람을 필요로 한다. 반면, 질투는 세 사람을 요구한다: Peter는 옆집의 예쁜 여자가 자기가 아니라 Sam에게 전화를 걸기 때문에 그를 질투한다. 역설적이게도, 부러움을 가질 때 우리는 나이, 경력, 거주지에 있어서 우리와 가장 비슷한 사람들에게 불쾌감을 향하게 한다. 우리는 지지난 세기의 사업가들을 부러워하지 않는다. 우리는 지구 반대편의 백만장자를 부러워하지 않는다. 작가로서, 나는 음악가, 매니저 또는 치과 의사가 부럽지 않지만, 다른 작가들을 부러워한다. CEO로서 당신은 다른, 더 큰 CEO들을 부러워한다. 슈퍼 모델로서 당신은 더 성공한 슈퍼 모델들을 부러워한다. 아리스토텔레스는 이를 알고 있었다: '도공은 도공을 부러워한다.'

→ 질투는 세 당사자를 포함하며, 제3자의 (A) 행동에 초점을 맞추는 반면, 부러움은 개인적 상황이 가장 (B) 비슷한 두 사람을 포함하고, 한 사람이 다른 사람을 불쾌하게 여기는 상태이다.

Why? 왜 정답일까?
글은 부러움의 특징에 대하여 설명하며, 부러움은 비슷한 위치에 있는 사람에게 가지는 감정임을 강조한다. 또한 질투와의 차이점을 언급하는데, 'The subject of jealousy is the behaviour of a third person.'(질투의 대상은 제3자의 행동이다.)에서 (A)에 들어갈 적절한 단어가 'actions'임을 알 수 있고, 'Paradoxically, with envy we direct resentments toward those who are most similar to us in age, career and residence.'(역설적이게도, 부러움을 가질 때 우리는 나이, 경력, 거주지에 있어서 우리와 가장 비슷한 사람들에게 불쾌감을 향하게 한다.)에서 (B)에 들어갈 적절한 단어가 'alike'임을 알 수 있다. 따라서 정답은 ⑤ '(A) actions(행동), (B) alike(비슷한)'이다.

- **envy** ⓝ 부러움
- **jealousy** ⓝ 질투
- **resentment** ⓝ 원한, 분노
- **aristotle** ⓝ 아리스토텔레스
- **involve** ⓥ 포함하다
- **circumstance** ⓝ 상황
- **ownership** ⓝ 소유
- **behaviour** ⓝ 처신, 행위, 행동
- **paradoxically** ⓐⓓ 역설적으로
- **potter** ⓝ 도예가
- **party** ⓝ 당사자

구문 풀이

8행 Paradoxically, with envy we direct resentments toward those who are most similar to us in age, career and residence.
주격 관계대명사 「direct A toward B : B에게 A를 곧장 주다, 향하다.」

41·42 면접에서의 확증편향

「We have biases / that support our biases!」 ◀41번의 근거
우리는 편견을 가진다! / 우리의 편견을 뒷받침하는
If we're partial to one option / — perhaps because it's more memorable, / or framed to minimize loss, / or seemingly consistent with a promising pattern — / we tend to search for information / that will (a) justify choosing that option.
만약 우리가 한 옵션에 편향된다면 / — 그것이 아마도 더 잘 기억될만 하거나, / 손실을 최소화하기 위해 짜맞춰졌거나, / 혹은 유망한 패턴과 일치하는 것처럼 보이기 때문에 — / 우리는 정보를 찾는 경향이 있다. / 그 옵션을 선택한 것을 정당화할
On the one hand, / it's sensible to make choices / that we can defend with data and a list of reasons.
한편으로는, / 선택을 하는 것이 현명하다. / 데이터와 이유들의 목록으로 방어할 수 있는
On the other hand, / if we're not careful, / we're (b) likely to conduct an imbalanced analysis, / falling prey to a cluster of errors collectively / known as "confirmation biases."
반면에, / 만약에 우리가 주의를 기울이지 않으면, / 우리는 불균형한 분석을 수행할 가능성이 있어서, / 총체적으로 오류의 덩어리의 희생양이 된다. / '확증 편향'으로 알려져 있는
For example, / nearly all companies include / classic "tell me about yourself" job interviews / as part of the hiring process, / and many rely on these interviews alone / to evaluate applicants.
예를 들어, / 거의 모든 기업들을 포함한다. / 전통적인 "자기소개" 취업면접 / 채용 과정의 일부로 / 그리고 많은 기업이 이러한 면접에만 의존한다. / 지원자를 평가하기 위해서
But it turns out that traditional interviews / are actually one of the (c) least useful tools / for predicting an employee's future success.
하지만 전통적인 면접은 판명된다. / 실제로 가장 유용하지 않은 도구 중 하나라는 것으로 / 직원의 미래 성공을 예측하는 데
This is because interviewers often subconsciously make up their minds about interviewees / based on their first few moments of interaction / and spend the rest of the interview / cherry-picking evidence and phrasing their questions / to (d) confirm that initial impression: / "I see here you left a good position at your previous job. / You must be pretty ambitious, right?" / versus "You must not have been very committed, huh?"
이것은 면접관이 종종 잠재의식적으로 면접 대상자에 대한 결정을 내리고, / 처음 순간의 상호 작용을 바탕으로 / 면접의 나머지 시간을 보내기 때문이다 / 그 첫인상을 확인하기 위해 증거를 고르고 질문을 만드는 데: / "당신은 이전 직장에서 좋은 직책을 두고 나오신 게 보이네요. / 틀림없이 야망이 꽤 크시겠어요, 그렇죠?" / 대 "당신은 그다지 헌신적이지 않았음에 틀림없네요, 그렇죠?"
This means that interviewers can be prone to (e) overlooking significant information / that would clearly indicate / whether this candidate was actually the best person to hire.
이것은 면접관이 중요한 정보를 간과하기 쉽다는 것을 의미한다. / 명확히 보여줄 수 있는 / 이 지원자가 실제로 채용하기에 가장 좋은 사람인지 여부를
'More structured approaches, / like obtaining samples of a candidate's work / or asking how he would respond to difficult hypothetical situations, / are dramatically better at assessing future success, / with a nearly threefold advantage over traditional interviews.' ◀42번의 근거

구조화된 접근 방식은, / 지원자의 업무 샘플을 확보하거나 / 가정된 어려운 상황에 어떻게 그가 대응할지 묻는 것과 같은 보다 / 미래의 성공을 평가하는 데 훨씬 더 낫다. / 전통적인 면접보다, 거의 세 배의 이점으로

우리는 우리의 편견을 뒷받침하는 편견을 가진다! 만약 우리가 한 가지 옵션에 편향된다면 — 그것이 아마도 더 잘 기억할만 하거나, 손실을 최소화하기 위해 짜맞춰 졌거나, 혹은 유망한 패턴과 일치하는 것처럼 보이기 때문에 — 우리는 그 옵션을 선택한 것을 (a) 정당화할 정보를 찾는 경향이 있다. 한편으로는, 데이터와 이유들의 목록으로 방어할 수 있는 선택을 하는 것이 현명하다. 반면에, 만약 우리가 주의를 기울이지 않으면, 우리는 불균형한 분석을 수행할 (b) 가능성이 있어서, 총체적으로 "확증 편향"으로 알려져 있는 오류 덩어리의 희생양이 된다. 예를 들어, 거의 모든 기업이 채용 과정의 일부로 전통적인 "자기소개" 취업 면접을 실시하며, 많은 기업이 지원자를 평가하기 위해서 이러한 면접에만 의존한다. 하지만 전통적인 면접은 실제로 직원의 미래 성공을 예측하는 데 가장 유용하지 (c) 않은 도구 중 하나라는 것으로 판명된다. 이것은 면접관들이 종종 잠재의식적으로 처음 몇 순간의 상호작용을 바탕으로 면접 대상자에 대한 결정을 내리고, 그 첫인상을 (d) 확인하기 위해 증거를 고르고 질문을 만드는 데 면접의 나머지 시간을 보내기 때문이다: "당신은 이전 직장에서 좋은 직책을 두고 나오신 게 보이네요. 틀림없이 야망이 꽤 크시겠어요, 그렇죠?" 대 "당신은 그다지 헌신적이지 않았음에 틀림없네요, 그렇죠?" 이것은 면접관이 이 지원자가 실제로 채용하기에 가장 좋은 사람인지 여부를 명확하게 보여줄 수 있는 중요한 정보를 (e) 알아차리기(→ 간과하기) 쉽다는 것을 의미한다. 지원자의 업무 샘플을 확보하거나 가정된 어려운 상황에 어떻게 그가 대응할지 묻는 것과 같은 보다 구조화된 접근 방식은, 전통적인 면접보다, 거의 세 배의 이점으로 미래의 성공을 평가하는 데 훨씬 더 낫다.

- bias ⓝ 편견
- partial ⓐ 부분의
- confirmation ⓝ 확신
- cherry-picking 원하는 것만 선택하는 것
- impression ⓝ 인상
- support ⓥ 지원하다
- information ⓝ 정보
- include ⓥ 포함하다
- spend ⓥ 소비하다

구문 풀이

25행 More structured approaches, like obtaining samples of a candidate's (동명사1) work or asking how he would respond to difficult hypothetical situations, are (동명사2) dramatically better at assessing future success, with a nearly threefold advantage (비교급)(동명사) over traditional interviews.

41 제목 파악 　　정답률 55% | 정답 ①

윗글의 제목으로 가장 적절한 것은?

☑ Bias Trap: How Our Preconceptions Mislead Us – 편견 함정: 어떻게 선입견이 우리를 잘못 이끄는가
② Utilize the Power of Similar Personality Types! – 비슷한 성격 유형의 힘을 사용해라!
③ More Information Adds Up to Worse Choices – 더 많은 정보는 더 안 좋은 선택으로 이끈다
④ Why Are You Persuaded by Others' Perspectives? – 왜 우리는 타인의 관점에 의해 설득될까?
⑤ Interviews: The Fairest Judgment for All Applicants – 인터뷰: 모든 지원자를 위한 가장 공정한 판단

Why? 왜 정답일까?

확증 편향에 대하여 이야기하는 글이다. 면접에서 자기소개하라는 질문이 면접관의 확증 편향에 영향을 받을 수 있음을 언급하며 확증 편향은 스스로가 갖고 있는 생각에 맞는 상황을 더 크게 인식함을 설명한다. 따라서 윗글의 제목으로 가장 적절한 것은 ① 'Bias Trap: How Our Preconceptions Mislead Us' 이다.

★★★ 등급을 가르는 문제!

42 어휘 추론 　　정답률 40% | 정답 ⑤

밑줄 친 (a) ~ (e) 중에서 문맥상 낱말의 쓰임이 적절하지 않은 것은? [3점]

① (a)　② (b)　③ (c)　④ (d)　☑ (e)

Why? 왜 정답일까?

확증 편향에 대하여 이야기하는 글로, 면접관이 첫인상을 기반으로 지원자에게 갖는 확증 편향이 지원자를 실제로 파악하는 데에 어려움을 준다는 내용이다. 따라서 지원자에 대한 중요한 정보를 간과한다는 것이 문맥상 어울리기 때문에, 알아차린다는 ⑤ 낱말은 문맥상 쓰임이 적절하지 않다.

★★ 문제 해결 꿀~팁 ★★

▶ 많이 틀린 이유는?
확증 편향에 관한 글이다. 면접관이 지원자에게 가진 편견을 바탕으로 확증 편향적 사고를 하기 쉽기 때문에, 면접 질문으로 자기소개는 지원자를 알아가기에 적절한 방법이 아니라고 주장한다.

▶ 문제 해결 방법은?
글에서 면접관이 확증 편향을 갖는 경향이 있고, 자기소개를 하라는 질문은 확증 편향을 강화할 수 있는 질문이기 때문에 좋지 않음을 알 수 있다. 따라서 면접관이 확증 편향 때문에 중요한 정보를 놓칠 수 있다고 하는 것이 글의 맥락상 적절하다.

43-45 진정한 도움

(A)

On Saturday morning, / Todd and his 5-year-old daughter Ava walked out of the store / with the groceries they had just purchased.
토요일 아침에, / Todd와 그의 다섯 살짜리 딸 Ava는 가게에 걸어 나왔다. / 그들이 방금 구입한 식료품을 가지고
As they pushed their grocery cart through the parking lot, / they saw a red car pulling into the space / next to their pick-up truck.
그들이 주차장에서 식료품 카트를 밀면서 갈 때, / 그들은 빨간색 차가 공간에 들어오는 것을 보았다. / 픽업 트럭 옆
A young man named Greg / was driving.
Greg라는 이름의 한 젊은 남자가 / 운전하고 있었다.
「"That's a cool car," Ava said to her dad.」 45번 ①의 근거 일치

"저것은 멋진 차네요."라고 Ava가 그녀의 아빠에게 말했다.
(a) He agreed and looked at Greg, / who finished parking and opened his door.
그는 동의했고 Greg를 보았는데, / 그는 주차를 마치고 그의 문을 열었다.

(C)

As Todd finished loading his groceries, / Greg's door remained open.
Todd가 그의 식료품을 싣는 것을 끝냈을 때, / Greg의 문은 열린 채로 있었다.
「Todd noticed / Greg didn't get out of his car.」 45번 ④의 근거 일치
Todd는 알아차렸다. / Greg가 그의 차에서 내리지 않은 것을
But he was pulling something / from his car.
그러나 그는 무엇인가를 꺼내고 있었다. / 그의 차에서
He put a metal frame / on the ground beside his door.
그는 금속 프레임을 두었다. / 그의 문 옆 바닥에
Remaining in the driver's seat, / he then reached back into (c) his car / to grab something else.
운전석에 머무른 채, / 그는 그의 차 안 뒤쪽으로 손을 뻗었다. / 무엇인가 다른 것을 잡기 위해
Todd realized what he was doing / and considered whether (d) he should try to help him.
Todd는 그가 무엇을 하고 있는지를 깨닫고, / 그가 그를 도와야 할지를 생각했다.
After a moment, / he decided to approach Greg.
잠시 후, / 그는 Greg에게 다가가기로 결심했다.

(B)

「By this time, / Greg had already pulled one thin wheel out of his car / and attached it to the frame.」 45번 ②의 근거 일치
그때쯤, / Greg는 이미 그의 차에서 얇은 바퀴 하나를 꺼냈고 그것을 프레임에 끼웠다.
He was now pulling a second wheel out / when he looked up and saw Todd standing near him.
그는 이제 두 번째 바퀴를 꺼내는 중이었다. / 그가 고개를 들어 그의 근처에 서 있는 Todd를 보았을 때
Todd said, / "Hi there! / Have a great weekend!"
Todd는 말했다. / "안녕하세요! / 주말 잘 보내세요!"라고
Greg seemed a bit surprised, but replied by wishing (b) him a great weekend too.
Greg는 약간 놀란 것처럼 보였지만, / 그에게도 좋은 주말을 보내라고 답했다.
Then Greg added, / "Thanks for letting me have my independence."
그러자 Greg는 덧붙였다. / "내가 독립성을 가질 수 있게 해줘서 고맙습니다."라고
"Of course," / Todd said.
"물론이죠." / 라고 Todd가 말했다.

(D)

「After Todd and Ava climbed into their truck, / Ava became curious.」 45번 ⑤의 근거 일치
Todd와 Ava가 그들의 트럭에 올라탄 후에, / Ava는 호기심이 생겼다.
So she asked / why (e) he didn't offer to help the man / with his wheelchair.
그래서 그녀는 물었다. / 왜 그가 그 남자에게 도움을 제공하지 않았는지를 / 휠체어에 대해
Todd said, / "Why do you insist on brushing your teeth without my help?"
Todd는 말했다. / "왜 너는 내 도움 없이 너의 이를 닦으려고 고집하니?"라고
She answered, / "Because I know how to!
그녀는 대답했다. / "왜냐하면 제가 어떻게 하는지를 알기 때문이죠!"라고
He said, / "And the man knows / how to put together his wheelchair."
그는 말했다. / "그리고 그 남자는 알고 있어. / 어떻게 그의 휠체어를 조립하는지"라고
Ava understood / that sometimes the best way to help someone / is to not help at all.
Ava는 이해했다. / 때때로 누군가를 돕는 가장 좋은 방법은 / 전혀 도와주지 않는 것임을

(A)

토요일 아침에, Todd와 그의 다섯 살짜리 딸 Ava는 그들이 방금 구입한 식료품을 가지고 가게에서 걸어 나왔다. 그들이 주차장에서 식료품 카트를 밀면서 갈 때, 그들은 빨간 차 한 대가 그들의 픽업 트럭 옆 공간으로 들어오는 것을 보았다. Greg라는 이름의 한 젊은 남자가 운전을 하고 있었다. "저것은 멋진 차예요."라고 Ava가 그녀의 아빠에게 말했다. (a) 그는 동의했고 Greg를 보았는데, 그는 주차를 마치고 그의 문을 열었다.

(C)

Todd가 그의 식료품을 싣는 것을 끝냈을 때, Greg의 문은 열린 채로 있었다. Todd는 Greg가 그의 차에서 내리지 않은 것을 알아차렸다. 그러나 그는 그의 차에서 무엇인가를 꺼내고 있었다. 그는 그의 문 옆 바닥에 금속 프레임을 두었다. 운전석에 머무른 채, (c) 그는 무엇인가 다른 것을 잡기 위해 그의 차 안 뒤쪽으로 손을 뻗었다. Todd는 (d) 그가 무엇을 하고 있는지를 깨닫고 그가 그를 도와야 할지를 생각했다. 잠시 후, 그는 Greg에게 다가가기로 결심했다.

(B)

그때쯤, Greg는 이미 그의 차에서 얇은 바퀴 하나를 꺼냈고 그것을 프레임에 끼웠다. 그가 고개를 들어 그의 근처에 서 있는 Todd를 보았을 때 그는 이제 두 번째 바퀴를 꺼내는 중이었다. Todd는 "안녕하세요! 주말 잘 보내세요!"라고 말했다. Greg는 약간 놀란 것처럼 보였지만, (b) 그에게도 좋은 주말을 보내라고 답했다. 그러자 Greg는 "내가 독립성을 가질 수 있게 해줘서 고맙습니다."라고 덧붙였다. "물론이죠."라고 Todd가 말했다.

(D)

Todd와 Ava가 그들의 트럭에 올라탄 후에, Ava는 호기심이 생겼다. 그래서 그녀는 왜 그가 (e) 그 남자에게 휠체어에 대해 도움을 제공하지 않았는지를 물었다. Todd는 "왜 너는 내 도움 없이 너의 이를 닦으려고 고집하니?"라고 말했다. 그녀는 "왜냐하면 제가 어떻게 하는지를 알기 때문이죠!"라고 답했다. 그는 "그리고 그 남자는 그의 휠체어를 어떻게 조립하는지 알고 있어."라고 말했다. Ava는 때때로 누군가를 돕는 가장 좋은 방법은 전혀 도와주지 않는 것임을 이해했다.

- grocery ⓝ 식료품점
- moment ⓝ 순간
- climb ⓥ 오르다
- independence ⓝ 독립
- approach ⓥ 접근하다
- without ~없이
- load ⓥ 짐을 싣다
- walk out 걸어 나가다

구문 풀이

(C) 6행 Todd realized what he was doing and considered whether he should try (관계대명사)(과거진행형)　　(명사절의 접속사)(조동사 + 동사원형) to help him.

43 글의 순서 파악 　　정답률 72% | 정답 ②

주어진 글 (A)에 이어질 내용을 순서에 맞게 배열한 것으로 가장 적절한 것은?

① (B) − (D) − (C)　　　　✓(C) − (B) − (D)
③ (C) − (D) − (B)　　　　④ (D) − (B) − (C)
⑤ (D) − (C) − (B)

Why? 왜 정답일까?

Todd와 Ava가 식료품점에서 장을 보고 나와서부터의 일이다. Ava가 Greg이 주차한 차를 언급했고, Todd가 Greg의 차문이 여전히 열려 있음을 알아차렸다. 따라서 (A) 뒤에 (C)가 오는 것이 자연스럽다. Todd가 Greg이 휠체어를 혼자서 꺼내고 있는 것을 보고 도와주려고 갔지만, Greg이 잘하고 있는 것을 보고 Todd가 인사만 하고 지나갔다. 이 광경을 본 Ava가 왜 Greg을 도와주지 않았냐고 묻자 Greg 혼자서도 할 수 있기 때문이라고 대답하는 순서가 자연스럽다. (B), (D) 순서로 배열하면 ② 'C) − (B) − (D)'가 정답이다.

| **44** | 지칭 추론 | 정답률 68% | 정답 ③ |

밑줄 친 (a) ~ (e) 중에서 가리키는 대상이 나머지 넷과 **다른** 것은?
① (a)　　② (b)　　✓(c)　　④ (d)　　⑤ (e)

Why? 왜 정답일까?

(a), (b), (d), (e)는 모두 Greg을 가리키고 있고, (c)는 Todd를 가리키고 있기 때문에 가리키는 대상이 나머지 넷과 다른 것은 ③ '(c)'이다.

| **45** | 세부 내용 파악 | 정답률 77% | 정답 ③ |

윗글에 관한 내용으로 적절하지 **않은** 것은?
① Ava는 차가 멋지다고 말했다.
② Greg는 얇은 바퀴를 프레임에 끼웠다.
✓Greg는 휠체어를 꺼내준 것에 감사하다고 말했다.
④ Todd는 Greg가 차에서 내리지 않은 것을 알아차렸다.
⑤ Ava는 트럭에 오른 후 호기심이 생겼다.

Why? 왜 정답일까?

Ava는 차가 멋지다고 말했으며("That's a cool car," Ava said to her dad.), Greg는 얇은바퀴를 프레임에 끼웠고(He put a metal frame on the ground beside his door.), Todd는 Greg가 차에서 내리지 않은 것을 알아차렸다(Todd noticed Greg didn't get out of his car.). Ava는 트럭에 오른 후 호기심이 생겼지만(After Todd and Ava climbed into their truck, Ava became curious.), Greg는 휠체어를 꺼내준 것에 감사하다고 말하지 않았기 때문에 윗글에 관한 내용으로 적절하지 않은 것은 ③이다.

어휘 Review Test 06
문제편 060쪽

A	B	C	D
01 죄수, 포로	01 fallacy	01 ⓜ	01 ⓑ
02 요구 사항	02 imminent	02 ⓟ	02 ⓟ
03 자유	03 reinforce	03 ⓖ	03 ⓔ
04 비참한	04 involve	04 ⓞ	04 ⓕ
05 걱정스럽게, 불안하게	05 vintage	05 ⓑ	05 ⓓ
06 원활하게	06 capacity	06 ⓒ	06 ⓒ
07 약점	07 behavior	07 ①	07 ①
08 다양성	08 invest	08 ⓕ	08 ⓐ
09 평가, 추정	09 acknowledge	09 ⓢ	09 ⓡ
10 저항하다, 반대하다	10 envy	10 ①	10 ⓚ
11 수행하다, 공연하다	11 attraction	11 ⓚ	11 ①
12 거래	12 delay	12 ①	12 ⓓ
13 열망하다	13 journal	13 ①	13 ①
14 장식	14 participation	14 ⓐ	14 ①
15 멀리 떨어진, 원격의	15 worthwhile	15 ⓗ	15 ⓗ
16 민족성	16 adapt	16 ⓔ	16 ⓜ
17 개입하다	17 reactance	17 ⓓ	17 ⓖ
18 이점, 혜택	18 disrupt	18 ⓠ	18 ⓢ
19 합의, 의견일치	19 surpass	19 ⓝ	19 ⓗ
20 나누다	20 fancy	20 ①	20 ⓖ

· 정답 ·

18① 19① 20② 21④ 22② ★23④ 24⑤ 25④ 26④ 27⑤ 28③ ★29④ 30③ 31① ★32③
33③ ★34⑤ 35④ 36② 37③ ★38④ ★39③ 40① 41⑤ ★42⑤ 43④ 44② 45③

★ 표기된 문항은 [등급을 가르는 문제]에 해당하는 문항입니다.

| **18** | 자녀의 결석 사유 등록 요청하기 | 정답률 72% | 정답 ① |

다음 글의 목적으로 가장 적절한 것은?
✓자녀의 결석 사유를 등록해 줄 것을 요청하려고
② 학교 홈페이지의 일시적 운영 중단을 공지하려고
③ 자녀가 지각하지 않도록 부모의 지도를 당부하려고
④ 방과 후 프로그램에 대한 부모의 관심을 독려하려고
⑤ 인정 결석은 최대 7일까지 허용된다는 것을 안내하려고

Dear parents,
친애하는 부모님께
Regular attendance at school / is essential in maximizing student potential.
학교에 규칙적으로 출석하는 것은 / 학생의 잠재력을 극대화하는 데 필수적입니다.
Recently, / we've become concerned / about the number of unapproved absences / across all grades.
최근에, / 우리는 우려하고 있습니다. / 승인되지 않은 결석 수에 대해 / 전 학년에 걸쳐
I would like to further clarify / that your role as a parent / is to approve any school absence.
저는 더 명확히 하고 싶습니다. / 부모로서 귀하의 역할이 / 학교 결석을 승인하는 것임을
Parents must provide an explanation for absences / to the school / within 7 days from the first day of any period of absence.
학부모들은 결석에 대한 설명을 제공해야 합니다. / 학교에 / 어떤 기간의 결석이든 첫날로부터 7일 이내에
Where an explanation has not been received / within the 7-day time frame, / the school will record the absence as unjustified / on the student's record.
설명이 주어지지 않을 경우, / 7일의 기간 내에 / 학교는 결석을 정당하지 않은 것으로 기록할 것입니다. / 학생부에
Please ensure / that you go to the parent portal site / and register the reason / any time your child is absent.
반드시 해 주십시오. / 여러분이 학부모 포털 사이트에 들어가서 / 사유를 등록하는 것을 / 자녀가 결석할 때마다
Please approve all absences, / so that your child will not be at a disadvantage.
모든 결석을 승인해 주십시오. / 자녀가 불이익에 처하지 않도록
Many thanks for your cooperation.
협조해 주셔서 대단히 감사합니다.
Sincerely, // Natalie Brown, Vice Principal
교감 Natalie Brown 드림

친애하는 부모님께

학생의 잠재력을 극대화하는 데는 학교에 규칙적으로 출석하는 것이 필수적입니다. 최근에, 우리는 전 학년에 걸쳐 승인되지 않은 결석 수에 대해 우려하고 있습니다. 저는 부모로서 귀하의 역할이 학교 결석을 승인하는 것임을 더 명확히 하고 싶습니다. 학부모들은 결석 기간과 관계없이 첫날로부터 7일 이내에 결석에 대한 설명을 학교에 제공해야 합니다. 7일의 기간 내에 설명이 주어지지 않을 경우, 학교는 결석을 정당하지 않은 것으로 학생부에 기록할 것입니다. 반드시 학부모 포털 사이트에 들어가서 자녀가 결석할 때마다 사유를 등록해 주십시오. 자녀가 불이익에 처하지 않도록 모든 결석을 승인해 주십시오. 협조해 주셔서 대단히 감사합니다.

교감 Natalie Brown 드림

Why? 왜 정답일까?

부모에게 자녀의 결석 사유를 꼭 등록해 달라고 요청하는 글이므로(Please ~ register the reason ~), 글의 목적으로 가장 적절한 것은 ① '자녀의 결석 사유를 등록해 줄 것을 요청하려고'이다.

- attendance ⓝ 출석, 참석
- absence ⓝ 결석
- within prep ~ 이내에
- student's record 학생부
- unapproved ⓐ 승인되지 않은
- clarify ⓥ 밝히다
- unjustified ⓐ 정당하지 않은
- disadvantage ⓝ 불리(한 점)

구문 풀이

8행 Where an explanation has not been received within the 7-day time frame,
　　　부사절 접속사(~할 경우에)　　　　현재완료 수동태
the school will record the absence as unjustified on the student's record.
　　　미래시제

| **19** | 기다리던 인턴십 합격 편지를 받은 Ester | 정답률 84% | 정답 ① |

다음 글에 드러난 Ester의 심경 변화로 가장 적절한 것은?
✓anticipating → excited
　기대하는　　신난
② confident → ashamed
　자신 있는　부끄러운
③ curious → embarrassed
　호기심 어린　당황한
④ surprised → confused
　놀란　　혼란스러운
⑤ indifferent → grateful
　무관심한　　고마운

Ester stood up / as soon as she heard the hum of a hover engine outside.
Ester는 일어섰다. / 그녀가 밖에서 호버 엔진의 윙윙거리는 소리를 듣자마자
"Mail," / she shouted / and ran down the third set of stairs / and swung open the door.
"편지다," / 그녀는 소리치며 / 계단을 세 칸씩 뛰어내려 / 문을 확 열었다.
It was pouring now, / but she ran out into the rain.
비가 쏟아지고 있었지만 / 그녀는 빗속으로 뛰어나갔다.

She was facing the mailbox.
그녀는 우편함을 마주하고 있었다.

There was a single, unopened letter inside.
안에는 뜯지 않은 편지 한 통이 들어 있었다.

She was sure / this must be what she was eagerly waiting for.
그녀는 확신했다. / 이것이 그녀가 간절히 기다리고 있던 게 틀림없다고

Without hesitation, / she tore open the envelope.
망설임 없이 / 그녀는 봉투를 뜯어서 열었다.

She pulled out the paper / and unfolded it.
그녀는 종이를 꺼내 / 그것을 펼쳤다.

The letter said, / 'Thank you for applying to our company. / We would like to invite you to our internship program. / We look forward to seeing you soon.'
편지에는 쓰여 있었다. / '우리 회사에 지원해 주셔서 감사합니다. / 우리는 당신을 인턴십 프로그램에 초대하고 싶습니다. / 우리는 당신을 곧 뵙기를 기대합니다.'라고

She jumped up and down / and looked down at the letter again.
그녀는 펄쩍펄쩍 뛰며 / 다시 편지를 내려다보았다.

She couldn't wait to tell this news to her family.
그녀는 이 소식을 가족들에게 빨리 전하고 싶었다.

밖에서 호버 엔진의 윙윙거리는 소리가 들리자마자 Ester는 일어섰다. "편지다." 소리치며 그녀는 계단을 세 칸씩 뛰어내려 문을 확 열었다. 비가 쏟아지고 있었지만 그녀는 빗속으로 뛰어나갔다. 그녀는 우체통을 마주하고 있었다. 안에는 뜯지 않은 편지 한 통이 들어 있었다. 그녀는 이것이 그녀가 간절히 기다리고 있던 게 틀림없다고 확신했다. 망설임 없이 그녀는 봉투를 뜯어서 열었다. 그녀는 종이를 꺼내 펼쳤다. 편지에는 '우리 회사에 지원해 주셔서 감사합니다. 우리는 당신을 인턴십 프로그램에 초대하고 싶습니다. 우리는 당신을 곧 뵙기를 기대합니다.'라고 쓰여 있었다. 그녀는 펄쩍펄쩍 뛰며 다시 편지를 내려다보았다. 그녀는 이 소식을 가족들에게 빨리 전하고 싶었다.

Why? 왜 정답일까?

어떤 편지를 기다리고 있던(She was sure this must be what she was eagerly waiting for.) Ester가 인턴십 합격 통지를 받고 몹시 기뻐했다(She couldn't wait to tell this news to her family.)는 내용이다. 따라서 Ester의 심경 변화로 가장 적절한 것은 ① '기대하는 → 신난'이다.

- **hum** ⓝ 웅웅거리는 소리
- **pour** ⓥ (비가) 퍼붓다
- **unfold** ⓥ 펼치다
- **swing open** 활짝 열다
- **eagerly** ⓐ 간절히
- **embarrassed** ⓐ 당황한

구문 풀이

5행 She was sure this must be {what she was eagerly waiting for}.
~임에 틀림없다   [ ] : must be의 보어(명사절)

20 신기술의 영향 골고루 평가하기   정답률 85% | 정답 ②

다음 글에서 필자가 주장하는 바로 가장 적절한 것은?
① 기술 혁신을 저해하는 과도한 법률적 규제를 완화해야 한다.
✓ 기술의 도입으로 인한 잠재적인 영향들을 충분히 고려해야 한다.
③ 혁신적 농업 기술을 적용할 때는 환경적인 측면을 검토해야 한다.
④ 기술 진보가 가져온 일자리 위험에 대한 대비책을 마련해야 한다.
⑤ 기술 발전을 위해서는 혁신적 사고와 창의성이 뒷받침되어야 한다.

The introduction of new technologies / clearly has both positive and negative impacts / for sustainable development.
신기술의 도입은 / 긍정적인 영향과 부정적인 영향을 둘 다 분명히 미친다. / 지속 가능한 발전에

Good management of technological resources / needs to take them fully into account.
기술 자원의 좋은 관리는 / 그것들을 충분히 고려해야 한다.

Technological developments in sectors / such as nuclear energy and agriculture / provide examples / of how not only environmental benefits / but also risks to the environment or human health / can accompany technological advances.
분야의 기술 발전은 / 원자력과 농업과 같은 / 예를 제공한다. / 어떻게 환경적 이익뿐만 아니라 / 환경이나 인간의 건강에 대한 위험이 / 기술 발전에 수반될 수 있는지에 대한

New technologies have profound social impacts as well.
새로운 기술은 또한 심오한 사회적 영향을 끼친다.

Since the industrial revolution, / technological advances have changed the nature of skills / needed in workplaces, / creating certain types of jobs / and destroying others, / with impacts on employment patterns.
산업혁명 이후 / 기술의 발전은 기술의 본질을 변화시켜 / 직장에서 요구되는 / 특정 유형의 일자리를 창출하고 / 다른 유형의 일자리는 소멸시켰다 / 고용 패턴에 영향을 미치며

New technologies need to be assessed / for their full potential impacts, / both positive and negative.
신기술은 평가되어야 한다. / 모든 잠재적 영향에 관해 / 즉 긍정적이고 부정적인 영향 둘 다

신기술의 도입은 지속 가능한 발전에 긍정적인 영향과 부정적인 영향을 둘 다 분명히 미친다. 기술 자원을 잘 관리하려면 그것들을 충분히 고려해야 한다. 원자력과 농업과 같은 분야의 기술 발전은 환경적 이익뿐만 아니라 환경이나 인간의 건강에 대한 위험이 어떻게 기술 발전에 수반될 수 있는지에 대한 예를 제공한다. 새로운 기술은 또한 심오한 사회적 영향을 끼친다. 산업혁명 이후 기술의 발전은 직장에서 요구되는 기술의 본질을 변화시켜 고용 패턴에 영향을 미치며 특정 유형의 일자리를 창출하고 다른 유형의 일자리는 소멸시켰다. 신기술은 모든 잠재적 영향, 즉 긍정적이고 부정적인 영향에 관해 다 평가되어야 한다.

Why? 왜 정답일까?

신기술의 잠재적 영향을 좋은 것이든 나쁜 것이든 완전히 평가해야 한다(New technologies need to be assessed for their full potential impacts, both positive and negative.)는 내용이므로, 필자가 주장하는 바로 가장 적절한 것은 ② '기술의 도입으로 인한 잠재적인 영향들을 충분히 고려해야 한다.'이다.

- **sustainable development** (환경적으로) 지속 가능한 개발
- **take into account** ~을 고려하다
- **nuclear** ⓐ 핵의
- **profound** ⓐ 심오한, 깊은
- **sector** ⓝ 부문
- **agriculture** ⓝ 농업
- **assess** ⓥ 평가하다

구문 풀이

4행 Technological developments in sectors such as nuclear energy and
주어   ~와 같은
agriculture provide examples of {how not only environmental benefits but also
동사(복수)   「not only A + but also B : A뿐 아니라 B도」
risks to the environment or human health can accompany technological
advances}. [ ] : of의 목적어(간접의문문)

21 토착 음식 정체성의 약화   정답률 49% | 정답 ④

밑줄 친 have entirely lost our marbles가 다음 글에서 의미하는 바로 가장 적절한 것은? [3점]

① have utterly disrupted our complex food supply chain
우리의 복잡한 식품 공급 사슬을 완전히 파괴했다
② have vividly witnessed the rebirth of our classic recipes
우리의 고전 요리법의 부활을 생생히 목격했다
③ have completely denied ourselves access to healthy food
우리가 건강에 좋은 음식에 접근하지 못하게 완전히 막았다
✓ have become totally confused about our distinctive food identity
우리의 독특한 음식 정체성에 완전히 혼란을 겪고 있다
⑤ have fully recognized the cultural significance of our local foods
우리 지역 음식의 문화적 중요성을 완전히 인식했다

North America's native cuisine / met the same unfortunate fate / as its native people, / save for a few relics / like the Thanksgiving turkey.
북미의 토착 요리는 / 불행한 운명을 맞이했다. / 원주민들과 같은 / 몇 가지 전해 내려오는 풍속을 제외하고 / 추수감사절 칠면조와 같은

Certainly, / we still have regional specialties, / but the Carolina barbecue will almost certainly have California tomatoes in its sauce, / and the Louisiana gumbo is just as likely to contain Indonesian farmed shrimp.
분명 / 우리에게는 여전히 지역 특색 음식이 있지만, / Carolina 바비큐에는 거의 확실히 California 토마토가 그 소스에 들어갈 것이고, / Louisiana 검보에도 인도네시아 양식 새우가 들어있을 것이다.

If either of these shows up on a fast-food menu / with lots of added fats or HFCS, / we seem unable / either to discern or resist the corruption.
만약 이것들 중 하나가 패스트푸드 메뉴에 나타난다면, / 지방이나 액상 과당이 많이 첨가된 형태로 / 우리는 ~할 수 없을 것 같다. / 그 붕괴를 식별하거나 막을 수

We have yet to come up with a strong set of generalized norms, / passed down through families, / for savoring and sensibly consuming / what our land and climate give us.
우리는 아직 강력한 일련의 일반화된 규범을 생각해내지 못했다. / 가계를 통해 전해져 내려오는 / 음미하고 현명하게 소비할 수 있도록 / 우리 땅과 기후가 우리에게 주는 것을

We have, instead, a string of fad diets / convulsing our bookstores and bellies, / one after another, / at the scale of the national best seller.
대신, 우리는 여러 유행하는 식단을 가지고 있다. / 서점과 배에 큰 소동을 일으키는 / 연이어서 / 전국적인 베스트셀러의 규모로

Nine out of ten nutritionists / view this as evidence / that we have entirely lost our marbles.
10명 중 9명의 영양학자들은 / 이것이 증거라고 본다. / 우리가 완전히 우리의 분별력을 잃었다는

추수감사절 칠면조와 같은 몇 가지 전해 내려오는 풍속을 제외하고, 북미의 토착 요리는 원주민들과 같은 불행한 운명을 맞이했다. 분명 우리에게는 여전히 지역 특색 음식이 있지만, Carolina 바비큐 소스에는 거의 확실히 California 토마토가 들어갈 것이고, Louisiana 검보에도 인도네시아 양식 새우가 들어있을 것이다(재료가 옛날과는 많이 다를 것이다). 만약 이것들 중 하나가 지방이나 액상 과당을 많이 첨가한 형태로 패스트푸드 메뉴에 나타난다면, 우리는 그 붕괴를 식별하거나 막을 수 없을 것 같다. 우리는 아직 우리 땅과 기후가 우리에게 주는 것을 음미하고 현명하게 소비할 수 있도록 가계를 통해 전해져 내려오는 강력한 일련의 일반화된 규범을 생각해내지 못했다. 대신, 우리는 전국적인 베스트셀러의 규모로 서점과 배에 연이어 큰 소동을 일으키는 여러 유행하는 식단을 가지고 있다. 10명 중 9명의 영양학자들은 이것이 우리가 완전히 우리의 분별력을 잃었다는 증거라고 본다.

Why? 왜 정답일까?

북미 토착 요리가 붕괴라는 '불행한 운명'을 맞이하고 있다(North America's native cuisine met the same unfortunate fate as its native people. ~)는 내용이 글의 요지이므로, 밑줄 친 부분의 의미로 가장 적절한 것은 ④ '우리의 독특한 음식 정체성에 완전히 혼란을 겪고 있다'이다.

- **save for** ~을 빼고는
- **regional** ⓐ 지역적인
- **HFCS** ⓝ 액상과당
- **corruption** ⓝ 붕괴
- **sensibly** ⓐ 분별력 있게, 현명하게
- **convulse** ⓥ 큰 소동을 일으키다
- **disrupt** ⓥ 파괴하다, 방해하다
- **significance** ⓝ 의미, 중요성
- **relic** ⓝ 전해 내려오는 풍속
- **specialty** ⓝ 특산품, 특색 요리
- **discern** ⓥ 분간하다
- **savor** ⓥ 음미하다
- **fad** ⓝ (일시적) 유행
- **lose one's marble** 분별력을 잃다
- **witness** ⓥ 목격하다

구문 풀이

9행 We have yet to come up with a strong set of generalized norms,
아직 ~하지 못했다(~해야 한다)
passed down through families, for savoring and sensibly consuming what our
과거분사구(norms 보충 설명)   전치사   동명사구
land and climate give us.

22 감정 지능(EI)의 중요성   정답률 62% | 정답 ②

다음 글의 요지로 가장 적절한 것은?
① 감성 지능의 결여는 직장 내 대인 관계 갈등을 심화시킨다.
✓ 미래의 직장에서는 감성 지능의 가치가 더욱 높아질 것이다.
③ 미래 사회에서는 감성 지능을 갖춘 기계가 보편화될 것이다.
④ 미래에는 대부분의 직장 업무를 인공 지능이 대신할 것이다.
⑤ 인간과 인공 지능 간의 상호 작용은 감성 지능의 발달을 저해한다.

Perhaps, / the advent of Artificial Intelligence (AI) in the workplace / may bode well for Emotional Intelligence (EI).
아마도, / 직장에서 인공 지능(AI)의 출현은 / 감정 지능(EI)에 좋은 징조가 될 수 있다.

As AI gains momentum / and replaces people in jobs at every level, / predictions are, / there will be a premium placed on people / who have high ability in EI.

AI가 추진력을 받고 / 모든 수준의 일자리에서 사람들을 대신함에 따라, / 전망이 있다. / 사람들에게 프리미엄이 주어질 것이라는 / 높은 EI 능력을 가진

The emotional messages / people send and respond to while interacting / are, at this point, / far beyond the ability of AI programs to mimic.
감정적인 메시지들은 / 사람들이 상호 작용하는 동안 보내고 반응하는 / 이런 점에서 ~이다. / AI 프로그램의 모방하는 능력을 훨씬 넘어서

As we get further into the age of the smart machine, / it is likely / that sensing and managing emotions / will remain one type of intelligence / that puzzles AI.
우리가 스마트 기기의 시대로 접어들수록, / ~일 것이다. / 감정을 감지하고 관리하는 것은 / 지능의 한 유형으로 남을 것이다. / AI를 당혹스럽게 하는

This means / people and jobs involving EI are safe / from being taken over by machines.
이것은 의미한다. / EI와 관련된 사람들과 직업들이 안전하다는 것을 / 기계에게 점령되는 것으로부터

In a survey, / almost three out of four executives / see EI as a "must-have" skill / for the workplace in the future / as the automatizing of routine tasks / bumps up against the impossibility of creating effective AI for activities / that require emotional skill.
한 설문 조사에서, / 임원 네 명 중 세 명 가량이 / EI를 '필수' 기술로 보고 있다. / 향후 직장을 위한 / 일상적인 업무의 자동화가 / 활동에 효과적인 AI를 만드는 것의 불가능함에 부딪히면서 / 정서적 기술이 필요한

아마도, 직장에서 인공 지능(AI)의 출현은 감성 지능(EI)에 좋은 징조가 될 수 있다. AI가 추진력을 받고 모든 수준의 일자리에서 사람들을 대신함에 따라, 높은 EI 능력을 가진 사람들에게 프리미엄이 주어질 것이라는 전망이 있다. 사람들이 상호 작용하는 동안 보내고 반응하는 감정적인 메시지들은 이런 점에서 AI 프로그램의 모방하는 능력을 훨씬 넘어선다. 우리가 스마트 기기의 시대로 접어들수록, 감정을 감지하고 관리하는 것은 AI를 당혹스럽게 하는 지능의 한 유형으로 남을 것이다. 이것은 EI와 관련된 사람들과 직업들이 기계에게 점령되는 것으로부터 안전하다는 것을 의미한다. 한 설문 조사에서, 일상적인 업무의 자동화가 정서적 기술이 필요한 활동에 효과적인 AI를 만드는 것이 불가능하다는 점에 부딪히면서, 임원 네 명 중 세 명 가량이 EI를 향후 직장의 '필수' 기술로 보고 있다.

Why? 왜 정답일까?

스마트 기기 시대가 발전할수록 감정 지능에 관한 영역은 AI의 손이 닿을 수 없는 영역으로 남아 AI를 당혹스럽게 할 수 있으며, 이에 따라 감정 지능이 향후 더 높은 가치를 지닐 것이라는(~ predictions are, there will be a premium placed on people who have high ability in EI.) 내용이다. 따라서 글의 요지로 가장 적절한 것은 ② '미래의 직장에서는 감성 지능의 가치가 더욱 높아질 것이다.' 이다.

- advent ⓝ 출현
- momentum ⓝ 추진력, 기세
- executive ⓝ 임원
- bump up against ~에 부딪치다, ~와 우연히 만나다
- bode ⓥ ~의 징조가 되다
- take over 장악하다, 탈취하다, 인수하다
- automatize ⓥ 자동화하다

구문 풀이

7행 As we get further into the age of the smart machine, it is likely [that
접속사(~함에 따라)   가주어
sensing and managing emotions will remain one type of intelligence that puzzles
AI]. [ ]: 진주어

★★★ 등급을 가르는 문제!

23 통합 교육을 촉진하는 공통 용어 사용   정답률 35% | 정답 ④

다음 글의 주제로 가장 적절한 것은? [3점]
① difficulties in finding meaningful links between disciplines
   학문 분야 간 유의미한 연결고리를 찾는 것의 어려움
② drawbacks of applying a common language to various fields
   공통 언어를 다양한 분야에 적용하는 것의 단점
③ effects of diversifying the curriculum on students' creativity
   커리큘럼을 다양화하는 것이 학생들의 창의력에 미치는 효과
④ necessity of using a common language to integrate the curriculum
   커리큘럼 통합을 위해 공통된 용어를 사용할 필요성
⑤ usefulness of turning abstract thoughts into concrete expressions
   추상적 사고를 구체적 표현으로 전환하는 것의 유용성

Education must focus on the trunk of the tree of knowledge, / revealing the ways / in which the branches, twigs, and leaves / all emerge from a common core.
교육은 지식의 나무 줄기에 초점을 맞춰야 한다. / 방식을 밝히면서, / 나뭇가지, 잔가지, 잎이 / 모두 공통의 핵심에서 나오는

Tools for thinking stem from this core, / providing a common language / with which practitioners in different fields / may share their experience of the process of innovation / and discover links between their creative activities.
사고를 위한 도구는 이 핵심에서 비롯된다. / 공통 언어를 제공하면서, / 그 언어로 다양한 분야의 실무자들이 / 혁신 과정에 대한 경험을 공유하고 / 그들의 창의적 활동 사이의 연결 고리를 발견할 수 있는

When the same terms are employed across the curriculum, / students begin to link different subjects and classes.
교육과정 전반에 걸쳐 동일한 용어가 사용될 때, / 학생들은 서로 다른 과목들과 수업들을 연결하기 시작한다.

If they practice abstracting in writing class, / if they work on abstracting in painting or drawing class, / and if, in all cases, they call it abstracting, / they begin to understand / how to think beyond disciplinary boundaries.
그들이 글쓰기 수업에서 추상을 연습하고, / 회화나 그림 그리기 수업에서 추상을 연습하고, / 그리고 모든 경우에 그들이 그것을 추상이라고 일컫는다면, / 그들은 이해하기 시작한다. / 학문의 경계를 넘어 사고하는 방법을

They see / how to transform their thoughts / from one mode of conception and expression / to another.
그들은 알게 된다. / 자기 생각을 바꾸는 방법을 / 하나의 개념과 표현 방식에서 / 다른 방식으로

Linking the disciplines comes naturally / when the terms and tools are presented / as part of a universal imagination.
학문들을 연결하는 것은 자연스럽게 이루어진다. / 용어들과 도구들이 제시될 때 / 보편적 상상력의 일부로

교육은 나뭇가지, 잔가지, 잎이 모두 공통의 핵심에서 나오는 방식을 밝히면서, 지식의 나무 줄기에 초점을 맞춰야 한다. 다양한 분야의 실무자들이 혁신 과정에 대한 경험을 공유하고 그들의 창의적 활동 사이의 연결 고리를 발견할 수 있는 공통 언어를 제공하면서, 사고를 위한 도구는 이 핵심에서 비롯된다. 교육과정 전반에 걸쳐 동일한 용어가 사용될 때, 학생들은 서로 다른 과목들과 수업을 연결하기 시작한다. 글쓰기 수업에서 추상을 연습하고, 회화나 그림 그리기 수업에서 추상을 연습하고, 그리고 모든 경우에 그들이 그것을 추상이라고 일컫는다면, 그들은 학문의 경계를 넘어 사고하는 방법을 이해하기 시작한다. 그들은 자기

생각을 하나의 개념과 표현 방식에서 다른 방식으로 바꾸는 방법을 알게 된다. 용어들과 도구들이 보편적 상상력의 일부로 제시될 때 학문들을 연결하는 것은 자연스럽게 이루어진다.

Why? 왜 정답일까?

공통 용어 사용이 다양한 학문을 자연스럽게 연결할 수 있다는(When the same terms are employed across the curriculum, students begin to link different subjects and classes.)는 내용이므로, 글의 주제로 가장 적절한 것은 ④ '커리큘럼 통합을 위해 공통된 용어를 사용할 필요성'이다.

- trunk ⓝ (나무) 줄기
- stem from ~에서 유래하다
- abstract ⓥ 추상하다, (글쓰기) 요약하다
- drawback ⓝ 문제
- emerge from ~에서 생겨나다
- practitioner ⓝ 실무자
- disciplinary ⓐ (학문) 분야의
- necessity ⓝ 필요성

구문 풀이

3행 Tools for thinking stem from this core, providing a common language
        주어   동사구(복수)   분사구문   선행사
[with which practitioners (in different fields) may share their experience of the
「전치사＋관·대」   주어   동사1   목적어1
process of innovation and discover links (between their creative activities)].
                          동사2   목적어2

★★ 문제 해결 꿀~팁 ★★

▶ 많이 틀린 이유는?
글 중반과 후반부에 다양한 학문 별로 공통된 용어를 사용해야 한다는 핵심 내용이 제시된다. ②는 주제와 정면으로 상충하며, ③은 '커리큘럼의 다양화', '창의력' 등 주제와 무관한 소재를 언급하므로 답으로 적절하지 않다.

▶ 문제 해결 방법은?
must가 포함된 첫 문장이 '지식의 나무 줄기'라는 비유로 주제를 제시하기 때문에 추상적으로 느껴진다. 하지만 주제는 반복 제시되기 마련이므로, 처음이 어렵다면 결론에 집중하면 된다.

24 언어의 변화   정답률 53% | 정답 ⑤

다음 글의 제목으로 가장 적절한 것은?
① Original Meanings of Words Fade with Time
   단어의 원래 의미는 시간이 가며 퇴색된다
② Dictionary: A Gradual Continuation of the Past
   사전: 과거의 점진적 지속
③ Literature: The Driving Force Behind New Words
   문학: 새로운 단어 이면의 원동력
④ How Can We Bridge the Ever-Widening Language Gap?
   계속해서 넓어지는 언어 격차를 어떻게 줄일 수 있을까?
✓⑤ Language Evolution Makes Even Shakespeare Semi-literate!
   언어 변화는 심지어 셰익스피어도 글을 반만 이해하게 한다!

New words and expressions emerge continually / in response to new situations, ideas and feelings.
새로운 단어들과 표현들이 계속해서 생겨난다. / 새로운 상황, 생각, 감정에 반응하여

The Oxford English Dictionary / publishes supplements of new words and expressions / that have entered the language.
Oxford 영어 사전은 / 새로운 단어들과 표현들의 추가분을 출판한다. / 그 언어에 등장한

Some people deplore this kind of thing / and see it as a drift from correct English.
어떤 사람들은 이런 일을 한탄하고 / 그것을 올바른 영어에서 벗어났다고 본다.

But it was only in the eighteenth century / that any attempt was made / to formalize spelling and punctuation of English at all.
그러나 18세기에 이르러서야 / 시도가 이루어진 것은 / 영어의 철자와 구두법을 공식화하려는

The language we speak in the twenty-first century / would be virtually unintelligible to Shakespeare, / and so would his way of speaking to us.
21세기에 우리가 사용하는 언어는 / 셰익스피어에게는 사실상 이해되기 어려울 것이며, / 우리에게도 그의 말하기 방식이 그럴 것이다.

Alvin Toffler estimated / that Shakespeare would probably only understand / about 250,000 of the 450,000 words / in general use in the English language now.
Alvin Toffler는 추정했다. / 셰익스피어가 아마도 이해할 것이라고 / 450,000개의 단어 중 약 250,000개만을 / 현재 영어에서 일반적으로 사용되는

In other words, / so to speak, / if Shakespeare were to materialize in London today / he would understand, / on average, / only five out of every nine words in our vocabulary.
다시 말해서, / 가령 / 만약 셰익스피어가 오늘날 런던에 나타난다면, / 그는 이해할 것이다. / 평균적으로 / 우리의 어휘에 있는 9개의 단어당 5개만

새로운 상황, 생각, 감정에 반응하여 새로운 단어들과 표현들이 계속해서 생겨난다. *Oxford 영어 사전*은 그 언어에 등장한 새로운 단어들과 표현들의 추가분을 출판한다. 어떤 사람들은 이런 일을 한탄하고 그것을 올바른 영어에서 벗어났다고 본다. 그러나 영어의 철자와 구두법을 공식화하려는 시도는 18세기에 이르러서야 이루어졌다. 21세기에 우리가 사용하는 언어는 셰익스피어에게는 사실상 이해되기 어려울 것이며, 우리에게도 그의 말하기 방식이 그럴 것이다. Alvin Toffler는 셰익스피어가 현재 영어에서 일반적으로 사용되는 450,000개의 단어 중 약 250,000개만을 이해할 것이라고 추정했다. 다시 말해서, 가령 만약 셰익스피어가 오늘날 런던에 나타난다면, 그는 평균적으로 우리의 어휘에 있는 9개의 단어당 5개만 이해할 것이다.

Why? 왜 정답일까?

언어는 계속해서 변하고, 그에 따라 심지어 언어 사용의 대가라고 여겨지는 셰익스피어조차 오늘날의 언어를 절반 정도밖에 이해하지 못할 것이라는(The language we speak in the twenty-first century would be virtually unintelligible to Shakespeare, and so would his way of speaking to us. / ~ if Shakespeare were to materialize in London today he would understand, on average, only five out of every nine words in our vocabulary.) 비유가 제시되고 있다. 따라서 글의 제목으로 가장 적절한 것은 이 비유를 그대로 차용한 ⑤ '언어 변화는 심지어 셰익스피어도 글을 반만 이해하게 한다!'이다.

- deplore ⓥ 한탄하다
- formalize ⓥ 공식화하다
- virtually ⓐ 거의, 사실상
- materialize ⓥ (갑자기) 나타나다
- ever-widening ⓐ 점점 커지는, 계속 벌어지는
- drift ⓝ 표류, 부유
- punctuation ⓝ 구두법
- unintelligible to ~가 이해할 수 없는
- literature ⓝ 문학

구문 풀이

6행 But **it was** only in the eighteenth century **that** any attempt was made
「it was ~ that ···」 ···한 것은 바로 ~였다(강조 구문)
to formalize spelling and punctuation of English at all.
부사적 용법(목적)

---

25 국가별 공립 초중등 교사 1인당 평균 학생 수 비교 | 정답률 84% | 정답 ④

다음 도표의 내용과 일치하지 <u>않는</u> 것은?

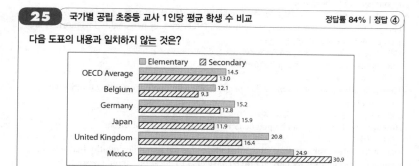

The graph above shows / the average number of students per teacher / in public elementary and secondary schools / across selected countries / in 2019.
위 그래프는 보여준다. / 교사 1인당 평균 학생 수를 / 공립 초·중등학교의 / 선정된 국가들의 / 2019년

① Belgium was the only country / with a smaller number of students per teacher / than the OECD average / in both public elementary and secondary schools.
벨기에는 유일한 / 교사 1인당 학생 수가 더 적은 / OECD 평균보다 / 공립 초등학교와 중등학교 모두에서

② In both public elementary and secondary schools, / the average number of students per teacher / was the largest in Mexico.
공립 초등학교와 중등학교 모두에서, / 교사 1인당 평균 학생 수는 / 멕시코에서 가장 많았다.

③ In public elementary schools, / there was a smaller number of students per teacher on average in Germany / than in Japan, / whereas the reverse was true in public secondary schools.
공립 초등학교에서는 / 교사 1인당 평균 학생 수가 독일에서 더 적은 반면, / 일본보다 / 공립 중등학교에서는 그 반대였다.

☑ The average number of students per teacher / in public secondary schools in Germany / was less than half that in the United Kingdom.
교사 1인당 평균 학생 수는 / 독일 공립 중등학교의 / 영국의 절반보다 적었다.

⑤ Of the five countries, / Mexico was the only country / with more students per teacher in public secondary schools / than in public elementary schools.
5국가 중 / 멕시코는 유일한 나라였다. / 공립 중등학교의 교사 1인당 학생 수가 더 많은 / 공립 초등학교보다

위 그래프는 선정된 국가들의 2019년 공립 초·중등학교 교사 1인당 평균 학생 수를 보여준다. ① 벨기에는 공립 초등학교와 중등학교 모두에서 교사 1인당 학생 수가 OECD 평균보다 더 적은 유일한 나라였다. ② 공립 초등학교와 중등학교 모두에서, 교사 1인당 평균 학생 수는 멕시코에서 가장 많았다. ③ 공립 초등학교에서는 교사 1인당 평균 학생 수가 일본보다 독일에서 더 적은 반면, 공립 중등학교에서는 그 반대였다. ④ 독일 공립 중등학교의 교사 1인당 평균 학생 수는 영국의 절반보다 적었다. ⑤ 5국가 중 멕시코는 공립 중등학교의 교사 1인당 학생 수가 공립 초등학교보다 더 많은 유일한 나라였다.

Why? 왜 정답일까?

도표에 따르면 독일 중등학교의 교사 1인당 평균 학생 수는 12.8명으로, 영국 중등학교의 교사 1인당 평균 학생 수(16.4명)의 절반을 넘는다. 따라서 도표와 일치하지 않는 것은 ④이다.

● secondary ⓐ 중등의   ● reverse ⓝ 역, 반대

---

26 John Ray의 생애 | 정답률 72% | 정답 ④

John Ray에 관한 다음 글의 내용과 일치하지 <u>않는</u> 것은?
① 마을 대장장이의 아들이었다.
② 성직자의 길로 들어서기 전 Cambridge 대학에 다녔다.
③ 병에서 회복하기 위해 자연을 산책하기 시작했다.
☑ Francis Willughby에게 후원받아 홀로 유럽을 여행하였다.
⑤ 동식물의 목록을 만들기 위해 표본을 연구하며 말년을 보냈다.

「Born in 1627 in Black Notley, Essex, England, / John Ray was the son of the village blacksmith.」 ①의근거 일치
1627년 잉글랜드 Essex주 Black Notley에서 태어난 / John Ray는 마을 대장장이의 아들이었다.

「At 16, / he went to Cambridge University, / where he studied widely / and lectured on topics from Greek to mathematics, / before joining the priesthood in 1660.」 ②의근거 일치
16세에 / 그는 Cambridge 대학교에 들어갔다 / 거기서 그는 폭넓게 공부하고 / 그리스어부터 수학까지 강의를 하다가 / 1660년에 성직자의 길로 들어섰다.

「To recover from an illness in 1650, / he had taken to nature walks / and developed an interest in botany.」 ③의근거 일치
1650년 병에서 회복하기 위해, / 그는 자연을 산책하기 시작했고 / 식물학에 대한 관심을 키웠다.

「Accompanied by his wealthy student and supporter Francis Willughby, / Ray toured Britain and Europe in the 1660s, / studying and collecting plants and animals.」 ④의근거 불일치
부유한 학생이자 후원자인 Francis Willughby를 동반해 / Ray는 1660년대에 영국과 유럽을 여행했고 / 식물과 동물을 연구하고 수집했다.

He married Margaret Oakley in 1673 / and, after leaving Willughby's household, / lived quietly in Black Notley to the age of 77.
그는 1673년 Margaret Oakley와 결혼했고, / Willughby 집안을 떠난 후에는 / Black Notley에서 77세까지 조용히 살았다.

「He spent his later years studying samples / in order to assemble plant and animal catalogues.」 ⑤의근거 일치
그는 표본을 연구하면서 말년을 보냈다. / 동식물 목록을 만들기 위해

He wrote more than twenty works / on theology and his travels, / as well as on plants and their form and function.
그는 20편 이상의 저서를 썼다. / 신학과 그의 여행에 관해 / 식물과 그 형태, 기능뿐만 아니라

1627년 잉글랜드 Essex주 Black Notley에서 태어난 John Ray는 마을 대장장이의 아들이었다. 16세에 그는 Cambridge 대학교에 들어가서 폭넓게 공부하고 그리스어부터 수학까지 강의를

하다가 1660년에 성직자의 길로 들어섰다. 1650년 병에서 회복하기 위해, 그는 자연을 산책하기 시작했고 식물학에 대한 관심을 키웠다. 부유한 학생이자 후원자인 Francis Willughby와 함께 Ray는 1660년대에 영국과 유럽을 여행했고 식물과 동물을 연구하고 수집했다. 그는 1673년 Margaret Oakley와 결혼했고, Willughby 집안을 떠난 후에는 Black Notley에서 77세까지 조용히 살았다. 그는 동식물 목록을 만들기 위해 표본을 연구하면서 말년을 보냈다. 그는 식물과 그 형태, 기능뿐만 아니라 신학과 그의 여행에 관해 20편 이상의 저서를 썼다.

Why? 왜 정답일까?

'Accompanied by his wealthy student and supporter Francis Willughby, Ray toured Britain and Europe ~'에서 Ray는 영국 및 유럽 여행에 Francis Willughby의 후원을 받은 동시에 그와 동행도 했다고 하므로, 내용과 일치하지 않는 것은 ④ 'Francis Willughby에게 후원받아 홀로 유럽을 여행하였다.'이다.

Why? 왜 오답일까?

① '~ John Ray was the son of the village blacksmith.'의 내용과 일치한다.
② 'At 16, he went to Cambridge University, ~ before joining the priesthood in 1660.'의 내용과 일치한다.
③ 'To recover from an illness in 1650, he had taken to nature walks ~'의 내용과 일치한다.
⑤ 'He spent his later years studying samples in order to assemble plant and animal catalogues.'의 내용과 일치한다.

● blacksmith ⓝ 대장장이   ● priesthood ⓝ 성직, 사제직
● botany ⓝ 식물학   ● accompany ⓥ ~을 동반하다
● wealthy ⓐ 부유한   ● theology ⓝ 신학

구문 풀이

2행 At 16, he went to Cambridge University, where he studied widely and
장소 선행사   관계부사
lectured on topics from Greek to mathematics, before joining the priesthood in 1660.
~하기 전에

---

27 평화 마라톤 축제 | 정답률 94% | 정답 ⑤

Peace Marathon Festival에 관한 다음 안내문의 내용과 일치하지 <u>않는</u> 것은?
① 출발 시각은 오전 10시이다.
② 5 킬로미터 코스는 참가에 나이 제한이 없다.
③ 참가자는 선착순 1,000명으로 제한된다.
④ 모든 참가자들에게 기념품과 메달이 주어진다.
☑ 물은 결승선에서만 제공된다.

Peace Marathon Festival
평화 마라톤 축제
The Peace Marathon Festival / will be held / to promote world peace / and share compassion for people in need.
평화 마라톤 축제는 / 개최됩니다. / 세계 평화를 장려하고 / 도움이 필요한 사람들을 위한 온정을 나누기 위해
Join us to enjoy running / and make a better world.
달리기를 즐기는 데 동참하고 / 더 나은 세상을 만들어 주세요.

When & Where
일시 & 장소
Sunday, September 3, 2023 「(Start time: 10 a.m.)」 ①의근거 일치
2023년 9월 3일, 일요일 (출발 시각: 오전 10시)
Civic Stadium
시민 스타디움

Participation Fee & Qualification
참가비 & 자격
Full & Half: $30 (20 years or older)
풀 & 하프: $30 (20세 이상)
「10 km & 5 km: $15 (No age limit)」 ②의근거 일치
10km & 5km: $15 (나이 제한 없음)

Registration
등록
「The number of participants is limited to 1,000. (First come, first served.)」 ③의근거 일치
참가자는 1,000명으로 제한됩니다. (선착순입니다.)
Online only at ipmarathon.com
ipmarathon.com에서 온라인으로만 가능

Notes
참고
「Souvenirs and medals will be given to all participants.」 ④의근거 일치
모든 참가자들에게 기념품과 메달이 주어집니다.
Changing rooms will be available at no charge.
탈의실은 무료로 이용 가능합니다.
「Water will be provided every 2.5 km and at the finish line.」 ⑤의근거 불일치
물은 2.5km마다, 그리고 결승선에서 제공됩니다.

Peace Marathon Festival(평화 마라톤 축제)

평화 마라톤 축제는 세계 평화를 장려하고 도움이 필요한 사람들을 위한 온정을 나누기 위해 개최됩니다. 달리기를 즐기는 데 동참하고 더 나은 세상을 만들어 주세요.

일시 & 장소
• 2023년 9월 3일, 일요일 (출발 시각: 오전 10시)
• 시민 스타디움

참가비 & 자격
• 풀 & 하프: $30 (20세 이상)
• 10km & 5km: $15 (나이 제한 없음)

등록
• 참가자는 1,000명으로 제한됩니다. (선착순입니다.)

- ipmarathon.com에서 온라인으로만 가능

참고
• 모든 참가자들에게 기념품과 메달이 주어집니다.
• 탈의실은 무료로 이용 가능합니다.
• 물은 2.5km마다, 그리고 결승선에서 제공됩니다.

Why? 왜 정답일까?

'Water will be provided every 2.5 km and at the finish line.'에서 물은 결승선뿐 아니라 2.5km 단위로 제공된다는 것을 알 수 있다. 따라서 안내문의 내용과 일치하지 않는 것은 ⑤ '물은 결승선에서만 제공된다.'이다.

Why? 왜 오답일까?

① '(Start time: 10 a.m.)'의 내용과 일치한다.
② '10 km & 5 km: $15 (No age limit)'의 내용과 일치한다.
③ 'The number of participants is limited to 1,000. (First come, first served.)'의 내용과 일치한다.
④ 'Souvenirs and medals will be given to all participants.'의 내용과 일치한다.

● compassion ⓝ 연민, 동정
● qualification ⓝ 자격 (사항)

---

28 공원 점심 행사   정답률 91% | 정답 ③

Out to Lunch에 관한 다음 안내문의 내용과 일치하는 것은?
① 일 년 내내 수요일마다 열리는 행사이다.
② 푸드 트럭에서는 가격을 20% 할인해 준다.
✓ ③ 라이브 음악 공연이 마련되어 있다.
④ 개인 의자와 담요를 가지고 올 수 없다.
⑤ 주류를 포함한 음료를 마실 수 있다.

Out to Lunch
점심을 위한 외출
Do you want to enjoy an afternoon / with tasty food and great music?
오후를 즐기고 싶으세요? / 맛있는 음식, 좋은 음악과 함께
'Out to Lunch' is the perfect event / to meet your needs!
'Out to Lunch'는 더할 나위 없는 행사입니다! / 당신의 요구를 충족시켜 주는
Come and enjoy this event / held in Caras Park in downtown Missoula!
오셔서 이 행사를 즐기세요! / Missoula 시내의 Caras 공원에서 열리는
Dates & Times
날짜 & 시간
『Every Wednesday in June, 12 p.m. – 3 p.m.』 ①의 근거 불일치
6월 매주 수요일, 오후 12시 – 오후 3시
Highlights
주요 특징
『10% discount at all food trucks / including Diamond Ice Cream』 ②의 근거 불일치
모든 푸드 트럭에서 10% 할인 / Diamond 아이스크림을 포함한
『Live music performance of the new group Cello Brigade』 ③의 근거 일치
신인 그룹 Cello Brigade의 라이브 음악 공연
Face-painting and water balloon fight for kids
아이들을 위한 페이스 페인팅과 물풍선 놀이
Notices
공지
『Bring your own lawn chairs and blankets.』 ④의 근거 불일치
개인 접이식 의자와 담요를 가져오세요.
Dispose of your waste properly.
개인 쓰레기를 올바르게 처리해 주세요.
『Drinking alcoholic beverages / is strictly banned.』 ⑤의 근거 불일치
주류를 마시는 것은 / 엄격하게 금지됩니다.

Out to Lunch(점심을 위한 외출)

맛있는 음식, 좋은 음악과 함께 오후를 즐기고 싶으세요? 'Out to Lunch'는 당신의 요구를 충족시켜 주는 더할 나위 없는 행사입니다! 오셔서 Missoula 시내의 Caras 공원에서 열리는 이 행사를 즐기세요!

날짜 & 시간
• 6월 매주 수요일, 오후 12시 – 오후 3시

주요 특징
• Diamond 아이스크림을 포함한 모든 푸드 트럭에서 10% 할인
• 신인 그룹 Cello Brigade의 라이브 음악 공연
• 아이들을 위한 페이스 페인팅과 물풍선 놀이

공지
• 개인 접이식 의자와 담요를 가져오세요.
• 개인 쓰레기를 올바르게 처리해 주세요.
• 주류를 마시는 것은 엄격하게 금지됩니다.

Why? 왜 정답일까?

'Live music performance of the new group Cello Brigade'에서 신인 그룹의 라이브 공연이 있을 것이라고 하므로, 안내문의 내용과 일치하는 것은 ③ '라이브 음악 공연이 마련되어 있다.'이다.

Why? 왜 오답일까?

① 'Every Wednesday in June, 12 p.m. – 3 p.m.'에서 6월 한 달간 열리는 행사라고 하였다.
② '10% discount at all food trucks including Diamond Ice Cream'에서 할인율은 10%라고 하였다.
④ 'Bring your own lawn chairs and blankets.'에서 개인 의자와 담요를 가지고 오라고 하였다.
⑤ 'Drinking alcoholic beverages is strictly banned.'에서 주류는 엄격히 금지된다고 하였다.

● dispose of ~을 처리하다, ~을 버리다
● strictly ㉙ 엄히
● ban ⓥ 금지하다

---

29 자기 보고 데이터의 한계   정답률 40% | 정답 ④

다음 글의 밑줄 친 부분 중, 어법상 틀린 것은? [3점]

Research psychologists often work with *self-report data*, / made up of participants' verbal accounts of their behavior.
연구 심리학자들은 종종 *자기 보고 데이터*로 작업하는데, / 이는 자신의 행동에 대한 참가자들의 구두 설명으로 구성되어 있다.
This is the case / ① whenever questionnaires, interviews, or personality inventories / are used to measure variables.
이것은 그러하다. / 설문지, 면접 또는 성격 특성 목록이 / 변인을 측정하기 위해 사용될 때마다
Self-report methods can be quite useful.
자기 보고 방법은 꽤 유용할 수 있다.
They take advantage of the fact / that people have a unique opportunity / to observe ② themselves full-time.
그것들은 사실을 이용한다. / 사람들이 유일한 기회를 갖는다는 / 자신을 풀타임으로 관찰할 수 있는
However, / self-reports can be plagued / by several kinds of distortion.
그러나, / 자기 보고는 오염될 수 있다. / 몇 가지 종류의 왜곡으로
One of the most problematic of these distortions / is the social desirability bias, / which is a tendency / to give ③ socially approved answers / to questions about oneself.
이러한 왜곡 중 가장 문제가 되는 하나는 / 사회적 바람직성 편향인데, / 이것은 경향이다. / 사회적으로 승인된 답을 제공하는 / 자신에 관한 질문에
Subjects who are influenced by this bias / work overtime / trying to create a favorable impression, / especially when subjects ✓ are asked about sensitive issues.
이러한 편향에 영향을 받은 피실험자들은 / 더 노력한다. / 호의적인 인상을 만들기 위해 / 특히 피실험자들이 민감한 문제에 대해 질문받을 때
For example, / many survey respondents will report / that they voted in an election or ⑤ gave to a charity / when in fact it is possible / to determine that they did not.
예를 들어, / 많은 설문 조사 응답자들은 보고할 것이다. / 그들이 선거에서 투표했다거나 자선 단체에 기부했다고 / 사실은 가능할 때도 / 그들이 안 했다고 밝히는 것이

연구 심리학자들은 종종 *자기 보고 데이터*로 작업하는데, 이는 자신들의 행동에 대한 참가자들의 구두 설명으로 구성되어 있다. 변인을 측정하기 위해 설문지, 면접 또는 성격 특성 목록이 사용될 때마다 여기 해당한다. 자기 보고 방법은 꽤 유용할 수 있다. 그것들은 사람들이 자신을 풀타임으로 관찰할 수 있는 유일한 기회를 갖는다는 사실을 이용한다. 그러나, 자기 보고는 몇 가지 종류의 왜곡으로 오염될 수 있다. 이러한 왜곡 중 가장 문제가 되는 하나는 사회적 바람직성 편향인데, 이것은 자신에 관한 질문에 사회적으로 승인된 답을 제공하는 경향이다. 이러한 편향에 영향을 받은 피실험자들은 특히 민감한 문제에 대해 질문받을 때 호의적인 인상을 만들기 위해 더 노력한다. 예를 들어, 많은 설문 조사 응답자들은 사실은 안 했다고 밝히는 것이 가능할 때도 선거에서 투표했다거나 자선 단체에 기부했다고 보고할 것이다.

Why? 왜 정답일까?

문맥상 실험 대상자(subjects)가 질문을 '받는' 상황이므로 ask 대신 are asked를 써야 한다. 타동사 뒤에 목적어도 없다는 점에서 수동태가 필요하다는 힌트를 추가로 얻을 수 있다. 따라서 어법상 틀린 것은 ④이다.

Why? 왜 오답일까?

① '~할 때마다'라는 의미의 복합관계부사 whenever이다.
② to observe의 목적어 themselves는 to observe의 의미상 주어인 people과 동일한 대상이다. 이렇게 같은 행위에 걸리는 주어와 목적어가 같으면 목적어 자리에 재귀대명사를 쓴다.
③ 과거분사 approved를 꾸미는 부사 socially이다.
⑤ voted와 병렬 연결되는 과거시제 동사 gave이다.

● verbal ⓐ 구두의
● questionnaire ⓝ 설문지
● plague ⓥ 괴롭히다, 감염시키다
● subject ⓝ 실험 대상자
● sensitive ⓐ 민감한
● account ⓝ 설명
● variable ⓝ 변수, 변인
● distortion ⓝ 왜곡
● bias ⓝ 편향
● vote ⓥ 투표하다

구문 풀이

5행 They take advantage of the fact [that people have a unique opportunity to observe themselves full-time]. [ ] : 동격절(= the fact)

★★ 문제 해결 꿀~팁 ★★

▶ 많이 틀린 이유는?
⑤의 병렬구조는 전체적인 문맥을 살펴봐야 하기 때문에 까다로웠을 수 있다. 최근의 출제 트렌드 상 병렬구조는 형태만 기계적으로 맞추기보다 의미를 고려해야 하는 유형으로 나오기 때문에 주의가 필요하다.

▶ 문제 해결 방법은?
④의 '능동태 vs. 수동태'는 최다 출제 포인트 중 하나이다. '태'란 주어–동사의 관계를 나타내므로, 동사에 밑줄이 있으면 주어와의 관계를 1순위로 살피도록 한다.

---

30 부유국의 보호 무역 조치   정답률 41% | 정답 ③

다음 글의 밑줄 친 부분 중, 문맥상 낱말의 쓰임이 적절하지 않은 것은? [3점]

Over the past several decades, / there have been some agreements / to reduce the debt of poor nations, / but other economic challenges (like trade barriers) / ① remain.
지난 수십 년 동안, / 몇 가지 합의가 있었지만, / 가난한 나라들의 부채를 줄이려는 / (무역 장벽 등) 다른 경제적 과제는 / 남아 있다.
Nontariff trade measures, / such as quotas, subsidies, and restrictions on exports, / are increasingly prevalent / and may be enacted for policy reasons / having nothing to do with trade.
비관세 무역 조치가 / 할당제, 보조금, 수출 제한과 같은 / 점점 더 널리 퍼지고 있으며, / 정책적 이유로 제정될 수 있다. / 무역과 무관한
However, / they have a ② discriminatory effect / on exports from countries / that lack the resources / to comply with requirements of nontariff measures / imposed by rich nations.
그러나 / 그것들은 차별적인 영향을 끼친다. / 국가들의 수출에 / 자원이 부족한 / 비관세 조치의 요건을 준수할 / 부유한 국가들이 부과한

For example, / the huge subsidies / that ☑ wealthy nations give to their farmers / make it very difficult / for farmers in the rest of the world / to compete with them.
예를 들어, / 막대한 보조금은 / 부유한 국가들이 자국 농부들에게 주는 / 매우 힘들게 만든다. / 전 세계 나머지 국가들의 농부들이 / 그들과 경쟁하기

Another example / would be domestic health or safety regulations, / which, though not specifically targeting imports, / could ④ impose significant costs on foreign manufacturers / seeking to conform to the importer's market.
또 다른 예는 / 국내 보건 또는 안전 규제인데, / 이것은 구체적으로 수입을 타겟으로 하진 않지만, / 외국 제조업체에 상당한 비용을 부과할 수 있다. / 수입자 시장에 맞추려는

Industries in developing markets / may have more ⑤ difficulty / absorbing these additional costs.
개발도상국 시장의 산업은 / 더 많은 어려움을 겪을 수 있다. / 이러한 추가 비용을 부담하는 데

지난 수십 년 동안, 가난한 나라들의 부채를 줄이려는 몇 가지 합의가 있었지만, (무역 장벽 등) 다른 경제적 과제는 ① 남아 있다. 할당제, 보조금, 수출 제한과 같은 비관세 무역 조치가 점점 더 널리 퍼지고 있으며, 무역과 무관한 정책적 이유로 제정될 수 있다. 그러나 그것들은 부유한 국가들이 부과한 비관세 조치의 요건을 준수할 자원이 부족한 국가들의 수출에 ② 차별적인 영향을 끼친다. 예를 들어, ③ 가난한(→ 부유한) 국가들이 자국 농부들에게 주는 막대한 보조금은 전 세계 나머지 국가들의 농부들이 그들과 경쟁하기 매우 힘들게 만든다. 또 다른 예는 국내 보건 또는 안전 규제인데, 이것은 구체적으로 수입을 타겟으로 하진 않지만, 수입자 시장에 맞추려는 외국 제조업체에 상당한 비용을 ④ 부과할 수 있다. 개발도상국 시장의 산업은 이러한 추가 비용을 부담하는 데 더 많은 ⑤ 어려움을 겪을 수 있다.

Why? 왜 정답일까?

가난한 국가들의 국가 부채를 줄이려는 노력이 많이 있었지만 이를 가로막는 부유국의 경제 조치가 여전히 있다는 내용이다. 그런데 ③은 '가난한' 국가가 자국 농부들을 타국 농부들과의 경쟁으로부터 보호하려 한다는 의미이므로 흐름상 어색하다. 따라서 문맥상 낱말의 쓰임이 적절하지 않은 것은 ③이고, 이를 **wealthy**로 고쳐야 한다.

- trade barrier 무역 장벽
- quota ⓝ 할당(제)
- restriction ⓝ 제한, 규제
- enact ⓥ 제정하다
- comply with ~을 준수하다
- domestic ⓐ 국내의, 가정의
- conform to ~에 맞추다, 순응하다
- nontariff ⓐ 비관세의
- subsidy ⓝ 보조금
- prevalent ⓐ 만연한, 널리 퍼진
- discriminatory ⓐ 차별적인
- impose ⓥ 부과하다
- significant ⓐ 상당한

구문 풀이

10행 For example, the huge subsidies [that wealthy nations give to their farmers] make it very difficult for farmers (in the rest of the world) to compete with them.

---

31 규제에서 꽃피는 기업의 혁신 · 정답률 58% | 정답 ①

다음 빈칸에 들어갈 말로 가장 적절한 것을 고르시오.

☑ innovation – 혁신 ② resistance – 저항 ③ fairness – 공정함
④ neglect – 방치 ⑤ unity – 통합

In the course of his research / on business strategy and the environment, / Michael Porter noticed a peculiar pattern: / Businesses seemed to be profiting from regulation.
연구하는 과정에서, / 비즈니스 전략과 환경에 관해 / Michael Porter는 독특한 패턴을 발견했다. / 기업이 규제로부터 이익을 얻는 것처럼 보인다는

He also discovered / that the stricter regulations were prompting more innovation / than the weaker ones.
그는 또한 발견했다. / 더 엄격한 규제가 더 많은 혁신을 유발하고 있다는 것을 / 느슨한 규제보다

The Dutch flower industry provides an illustration.
네덜란드의 꽃 산업은 하나의 예시다.

For many years, / the companies / producing Holland's world-renowned tulips and other cut flowers / were also contaminating the country's water and soil / with fertilizers and pesticides.
수년 동안, / 회사들은 / 네덜란드의 세계적으로 유명한 튤립과 다른 꽃들을 생산하는 / 또한 그 나라의 물과 토양을 오염시키고 있었다. / 비료와 농약으로

In 1991, / the Dutch government adopted a policy / designed to cut pesticide use in half by 2000 — a goal they ultimately achieved.
1991년, / 네덜란드 정부는 정책을 채택했다. / 2000년까지 농약 사용을 절반으로 줄이도록 고안된 / 그들이 궁극적으로 달성한 목표인

Facing increasingly strict regulation, / greenhouse growers realized / they had to develop new methods / if they were going to maintain product quality / with fewer pesticides.
점점 더 엄격한 규제에 직면하면서, / 온실 재배자들은 깨달았다. / 그들이 새로운 방법을 개발해야 한다는 것을 / 그들이 상품의 품질을 유지하려면 / 더 적은 양의 농약으로

In response, / they shifted to a cultivation method / that circulates water in closed-loop systems / and grows flowers in a rock wool substrate.
이에 / 그들은 재배 방식으로 전환했다. / 폐쇄 루프 방식으로 물을 순환시키고 / 암모 배양판에서 꽃을 키우는

The new system not only reduced the pollution / released into the environment; / it also increased profits / by giving companies greater control over growing conditions.
새로운 시스템은 오염을 감소시켰을 뿐만 아니라, / 환경에 배출되는 / 이것은 이익을 증가시켰다. / 회사들이 재배 조건을 더 잘 통제할 수 있게 해서

비즈니스 전략과 환경을 연구하는 과정에서, Michael Porter는 기업이 규제로부터 이익을 얻는 것처럼 보인다는 독특한 패턴을 발견했다. 그는 또한 더 엄격한 규제가 느슨한 규제보다 더 많은 혁신을 유발하고 있다는 것을 발견했다. 네덜란드의 꽃 산업은 하나의 예시다. 수년 동안, 네덜란드의 세계적으로 유명한 튤립과 다른 꽃들을 생산하는 회사들은 또한 비료와 농약으로 그 나라의 물과 토양을 오염시키고 있었다. 1991년, 네덜란드 정부는 2000년까지 농약 사용을 절반으로 줄이도록 고안된 정책을 채택했는데, 이것은 그들이 궁극적으로 달성한 목표였다. 점점 더 엄격한 규제에 직면하면서, 온실 재배자들은 더 적은 양의 농약으로 상품의 품질을 유지하려면 새로운 방법을 개발해야만 한다는 것을 깨달았다. 이에 그들은 폐쇄 루프 방식으로 물을 순환시키고 암모 배양판에서 꽃을 키우는 재배 방식으로 전환했다. 새로운 시스템은 환경에 배출되는 오염을 감소시켰을 뿐만 아니라, 회사들이 재배 조건을 더 잘 통제할 수 있게 해 이익을 증가시켰다.

Why? 왜 정답일까?

네덜란드의 꽃 산업을 예로 들어, 국가적인 엄격한 규제가 생산 주체들로 하여금 새로운 방법과 혁신을 시도하도록 격려한다(Businesses seemed to be profiting from regulation.)는 것을 보여주는 글이다. 따라서 빈칸에 들어갈 말로 가장 적절한 것은 ① '혁신'이다.

- peculiar ⓐ 특이한
- illustration ⓝ (잘 보여주는) 예
- contaminate ⓥ 오염시키다
- pesticide ⓝ 살충제
- substrate ⓝ 배양판
- neglect ⓝ 방치, 태만, 소홀
- prompt ⓥ 유발하다
- world-renowned ⓐ 세계적으로 유명한
- fertilizer ⓝ 비료
- cultivation ⓝ 경작, 재배
- resistance ⓝ 저항

구문 풀이

12행 Facing increasingly strict regulation, greenhouse growers realized (that) they had to develop new methods if they were going to maintain product quality with fewer pesticides.

★★★ 등급을 가르는 문제!

32 능력보다도 시간이나 노력에 돈을 치르려는 경향 · 정답률 39% | 정답 ③

다음 빈칸에 들어갈 말로 가장 적절한 것을 고르시오. [3점]

① prefer money to time – 시간보다 돈을 선호할
② ignore the hours put in – 들인 시간을 무시할
☑ value effort over outcome – 결과보다 노력을 중시할
④ can't stand any malfunction – 어떤 불량도 참지 못할
⑤ are biased toward the quality – 질 쪽으로 편향될

It's hard to pay more / for the speedy but highly skilled person, / simply because there's less effort being observed.
더 많은 돈을 지불하기는 어려운데, / 빠르지만 고도로 숙련된 사람에게 / 그 이유는 단순히 관찰되고 있는 노력이 적기 때문이다.

Two researchers once did a study / in which they asked people / how much they would pay for data recovery.
두 명의 연구원이 연구를 한 적이 있다. / 그들이 사람들에게 묻는 / 그들이 데이터 복구에 얼마를 지불할 것인지를

They found / that people would pay a little more / for a greater quantity of rescued data, / but what they were most sensitive to / was the number of hours / the technician worked.
그들은 발견했다. / 사람들이 조금 더 많은 돈을 지불할 것이지만 / 더 많은 양의 복구된 데이터에 / 사람들이 가장 민감하게 여기는 것은 / 시간이었다는 것을 / 기술자가 일한

When the data recovery took only a few minutes, / willingness to pay was low, / but when it took more than a week / to recover the same amount of data, / people were willing to pay much more.
데이터 복구에 몇 분밖에 걸리지 않았을 때, / 지불 의사는 낮았지만, / 일주일 이상이 걸렸을 때, / 같은 양의 데이터를 복구하는 데 / 사람들은 훨씬 더 많은 비용을 지불할 의사가 있었다.

Think about it: / They were willing to pay more / for the slower service / with the same outcome.
생각해 봐라. / 그들은 더 많은 비용을 기꺼이 지불하고자 했다. / 더 느린 서비스에 / 같은 결과를 내는

Fundamentally, / when we value effort over outcome, / we're paying for incompetence.
근본적으로, / 우리가 결과보다 노력을 중시할 때, / 우리는 무능함에 비용을 지불하는 것이다.

Although it is actually irrational, / we feel more rational, / and more comfortable, / paying for incompetence.
비록 그것이 실제로는 비합리적이지만, / 우리는 더 합리적이라고 느낀다. / 그리고 더 편하다 / 무능함에 지불하면서

빠르지만 고도로 숙련된 사람에게 더 많은 돈을 지불하기는 어려운데, 그 이유는 단순히 관찰되고 있는 노력이 적기 때문이다. 두 명의 연구원이 사람들에게 데이터 복구에 얼마를 지불할 것인지를 묻는 연구를 한 적이 있다. 그들은 사람들이 복구된 데이터가 더 많으면 조금 더 많은 돈을 지불할 것이지만, 사람들이 가장 민감하게 여기는 것은 기술자가 일한 시간이었다는 것을 발견했다. 데이터 복구에 몇 분밖에 걸리지 않았을 때 지불 의사는 낮았지만, 같은 양의 데이터를 복구하는 데 일주일 이상이 걸렸을 때, 사람들은 훨씬 더 많은 비용을 지불할 의사가 있었다. 생각해 보라. 그들은 같은 결과에 대해 더 느린 서비스에 더 많은 비용을 기꺼이 지불하고자 했다. 근본적으로, 우리가 결과보다 노력을 중시할 때, 우리는 무능함에 비용을 지불하는 것이다. 비록 그것이 실제로는 비합리적이지만, 우리는 무능함에 지불하면서 더 합리적이고 더 편하다고 느낀다.

Why? 왜 정답일까?

유능해도 보이는 노력이 적으면 우리는 비용을 덜 치르고 싶어 한다(It's hard to pay more for the speedy but highly skilled person, simply because there's less effort being observed.)는 내용이다. 예시로 언급된 실험에 관해 주제와 같은 결론이 내려져야 하므로, 빈칸에 들어갈 말로 가장 적절한 것은 ③ '결과보다 노력을 중시할'이다.

- rescue ⓥ 복구하다, 구조하다
- incompetence ⓝ 무능
- fundamentally ⓐⓓ 근본적으로
- malfunction ⓝ 불량

구문 풀이

1행 It's hard to pay more for the speedy but highly skilled person, simply because there's less effort being observed.

★★ 문제 해결 꿀~팁 ★★

▶ 많이 틀린 이유는?
①에 '시간'과 '돈'이라는 핵심어가 다 포함되어 있지만, 이 글은 '시간보다 돈이 선호된다'는 내용이 아니다. 똑같은 일에 더 오랜 시간이 소요되었을 때 오히려 돈을 더 기꺼이 내려는 경향을 소개하는 것이 글의 중심 내용이다.

▶ 문제 해결 방법은?
빈칸 문제에서는 핵심어의 반복보다는 주제의 '적절한 재진술'을 찾는 것이 중요하다. 실제로 정답인 ③은 '일에 들인 시간'을 effort로, '복구된 데이터 양'을 outcome으로 재진술하였다.

33 나이가 들수록 닫히는 마음　　　　　정답률 43% | 정답 ③

다음 빈칸에 들어갈 말로 가장 적절한 것을 고르시오. [3점]

① the high dependence on others – 타인에 대한 높은 의존
② the obsession with our inferiority – 우리의 열등함에 대한 강박
✔③ the increasing closing of the mind – 점차적인 마음의 폐쇄
④ the misconception about our psychology – 우리 심리에 대한 오해
⑤ the self-destructive pattern of behavior – 자기 파괴적 행동 패턴

In adolescence / many of us had the experience / of falling under the sway of a great book or writer.
청소년기에 / 우리 중 다수는 경험이 있다 / 위대한 책이나 작가의 영향을 받은
We became entranced / by the novel ideas in the book, / and because we were so open to influence, / these early encounters with exciting ideas / sank deeply into our minds / and became part of our own thought processes, / affecting us decades after we absorbed them.
우리는 매료되었고, / 책 속의 참신한 아이디어에 / 그리고 우리가 영향에 매우 열려 있었기 때문에, / 흥미로운 아이디어와의 이러한 초기 만남은 / 우리의 마음속 깊이 가라앉아 / 우리 사고 과정의 일부가 되었고, / 그것들을 흡수한 지 수십 년이 지난 후에 우리에게 영향을 미쳤다.
Such influences enriched our mental landscape, / and in fact our intelligence depends on the ability / to absorb the lessons and ideas of those / who are older and wiser.
그러한 영향들은 우리의 정신적 풍경을 풍부하게 했고, / 사실 우리의 지성은 능력에 달려 있다 / 사람들의 교훈과 생각을 흡수하는 / 더 나이가 많고 더 현명한
Just as the body tightens with age, / however, / so does the mind.
나이가 들면서 몸이 경직되는 것처럼 / 그러나, / 마음도 그러하다.
And just as our sense of weakness and vulnerability / motivated the desire to learn, / so does our creeping sense of superiority / slowly close us off to new ideas and influences.
그리고 마치 약점과 취약성에 대한 우리의 깨달음이 / 학습 욕구를 자극했듯이, / 슬며시 다가오는 우월감도 / 새로운 생각과 영향력에 대해 서서히 우리를 닫는다.
Some may advocate / that we all become more skeptical in the modern world, / but in fact a far greater danger comes / from the increasing closing of the mind / that burdens us as individuals / as we get older, / and seems to be burdening our culture in general.
어떤 사람들은 주장할지도 모르지만, / 현대 세계에서 우리가 모두 더 회의적이 된다고 / 사실 훨씬 더 큰 위험은 온다 / 점차적인 마음의 폐쇄에서 / 우리에게 개인으로서 부담을 주는 / 우리가 나이 들수록 / 그리고 전반적인 우리 문화에 부담을 주는 듯 보이는

청소년기에 우리 중 다수는 위대한 책이나 작가의 영향을 받은 경험이 있다. 우리는 책 속의 참신한 아이디어에 매료되었고, 영향에 매우 열려 있었기 때문에, 흥미로운 아이디어와의 이러한 초기 만남은 우리의 마음속 깊이 가라앉아 우리 사고 과정의 일부가 되었고, 그것들을 흡수한 지 수십 년이 지난 후에 우리에게 영향을 미쳤다. 그러한 영향들은 우리의 정신적 풍경을 풍부하게 했고, 사실 우리의 지성은 더 나이가 많고 더 현명한 사람들의 교훈과 생각을 흡수하는 능력에 달려 있다. 그러나, 나이가 들면서 몸이 경직되는 것처럼 마음도 그러하다. 그리고 약점과 취약성에 대한 우리의 깨달음이 학습 욕구를 자극했듯이, 슬며시 다가오는 우월감도 새로운 생각과 영향력에 대해 서서히 우리를 닫는다. 어떤 사람들은 현대 세계에서 우리가 모두 더 회의적이 된다고 주장할지도 모르지만, 사실 훨씬 더 큰 위험은 우리가 나이 들수록 우리에게 개인으로서 부담을 주고, 전반적인 우리 문화에 부담을 주는 듯 보이는 점차적인 마음의 폐쇄에서 온다.

Why? 왜 정답일까?

어렸을 때는 위대한 책과 작가의 영향력에 마음이 열려 있지만 나이가 들수록 우리 마음이 닫혀 흡수가 잘 일어나지 않는다(**Just as the body tightens with age, however, so does the mind. And just as our sense of weakness and vulnerability motivated the desire to learn, so does our creeping sense of superiority slowly close us off to new ideas and influences.**)는 내용이다. 따라서 빈칸에 들어갈 말로 가장 적절한 것은 ③ '점차적인 마음의 폐쇄'이다.

- adolescence ⑩ 청소년기, 사춘기
- entrance ⓥ 매료시키다
- encounter ⑩ 만남, 조우
- enrich ⓥ 풍부하게 하다
- vulnerability ⑩ 취약함, 상처받기 쉬움
- superiority ⑩ 우월함
- skeptical ⓐ 회의적인
- inferiority ⑩ 열등함
- sway ⑩ 영향, 지배, 장악
- novel ⓐ 새로운, 신기한
- sink into ~로 가라앉다
- landscape ⑩ 정경, 풍경
- creeping ⓐ 서서히 진행되는
- advocate ⓥ 주장하다, 변호하다, 옹호하다
- obsession ⑩ 강박, 집착

구문 풀이

11행 And just as our sense of weakness and vulnerability motivated the desire
　　　　　　　　　　　　　　　　「just as + A +
to learn, so does our creeping sense of superiority slowly close us off to new
so + B」: 마치 A하듯이 B하다(B는 동의 구문 : so + 대동사 + 주어)
ideas and influences.

★★★ 등급을 가르는 문제!

34 다수가 항상 옳지는 않음을 이해하기　　　　　정답률 28% | 정답 ⑤

다음 빈칸에 들어갈 말로 가장 적절한 것을 고르시오. [3점]

① majority rule should be founded on fairness
　다수결의 법칙은 공정성에 바탕을 둬야 한다
② the crowd is generally going in the right direction
　군중은 일반적으로 맞는 쪽으로 향한다
③ the roles of leaders and followers can change at any time
　리더와 팔로워의 역할은 어느 때든 바뀔 수 있다
④ people behave in a different fashion to others around them
　사람들은 자기 주변의 다른 사람들과 다른 방식으로 행동한다
✔⑤ there is a huge difference between acceptance and intelligence
　수용과 지성 사이에 큰 차이가 있다

Many people look for safety and security / in popular thinking.
많은 사람이 안전과 안심을 찾는다. / 대중적인 사고에서
They figure / that if a lot of people are doing something, / then it must be right.
그들은 생각한다. / 만약 많은 사람이 뭔가 하고 있다면 / 그것은 틀림없이 옳을 것이라고
It must be a good idea.
그것은 좋은 생각임이 틀림없다.
If most people accept it, / then it probably represents fairness, equality, compassion, and sensitivity, / right?
만약 대부분의 사람들이 그것을 받아들인다면, / 그것은 아마도 공정함, 평등함, 동정심, 그리고 민감성을 상징할 것이다. / 그렇지 않은가?

Not necessarily.
꼭 그렇지는 않다.
Popular thinking said / the earth was the center of the universe, / yet Copernicus studied the stars and planets / and proved mathematically / that the earth and the other planets in our solar system / revolved around the sun.
대중적인 사고는 말했지만, / 지구가 우주의 중심이라고 / Copernicus는 별과 행성을 연구했고 / 수학적으로 증명했다. / 지구와 태양계의 다른 행성들이 / 태양 주위를 돈다는 것을
Popular thinking said / surgery didn't require clean instruments, / yet Joseph Lister studied the high death rates in hospitals / and introduced antiseptic practices / that immediately saved lives.
대중적인 사고는 말했지만, / 수술에 깨끗한 도구가 필요하지 않다고 / Joseph Lister는 병원에서의 높은 사망률을 연구했고 / 균균법을 소개했다. / 즉시 생명을 구한
Popular thinking said / that women shouldn't have the right to vote, / yet people like Emmeline Pankhurst and Susan B. Anthony / fought for and won that right.
대중적인 사고는 말했지만 / 여성들이 투표권을 가져선 안 된다고 / Emmeline Pankhurst와 Susan B. Anthony 같은 사람들은 / 그 권리를 위해 싸웠고 쟁취했다.
We must always remember / there is a huge difference / between acceptance and intelligence.
우리는 항상 기억해야 한다. / 큰 차이가 있다는 것을 / 수용과 지성 사이에
People may say / that there's safety in numbers, / but that's not always true.
사람들은 말할지도 모르지만, / 수가 많은 편이 더 안전하다고 / 그것이 항상 사실이진 않다.

많은 사람이 대중적인 사고에서 안전과 안심을 찾는다. 그들은 만약 많은 사람이 뭔가 하고 있다면 그것은 틀림없이 옳을 것이라 생각한다. 그것은 좋은 생각임이 틀림없다. 만약 대부분의 사람들이 그것을 받아들인다면, 그것은 아마도 공정함, 평등함, 동정심, 그리고 민감성을 상징할 것이다. 그렇지 않은가? 꼭 그렇지는 않다. 대중적인 사고는 지구가 우주의 중심이라고 했지만, Copernicus는 별과 행성을 연구했고 지구와 태양계의 다른 행성들이 태양 주위를 돈다는 것을 수학적으로 증명했다. 대중적인 사고는 수술에 깨끗한 도구가 필요하지 않다고 말했지만, Joseph Lister는 병원에서의 높은 사망률을 연구했고 즉시 생명을 구한 균균법을 소개했다. 대중적인 사고는 여성들이 투표권을 가져선 안 된다고 했지만, Emmeline Pankhurst와 Susan B. Anthony 같은 사람들은 그 권리를 위해 싸웠고 쟁취했다. 우리는 항상 수용과 지성 사이에 큰 차이가 있다는 것을 기억해야 한다. 사람들은 수가 많은 편이 더 안전하다고 말할지도 모르지만, 그것이 항상 사실이진 않다.

Why? 왜 정답일까?

많은 사람들이 '받아들이고' 있다고 해서 '합당하고, 공정하고, 맞는' 사실은 아닐 수도 있다(**If most people accept it, then it probably represents fairness, equality, compassion, and sensitivity, right? Not necessarily.**)는 내용이다. 따라서 빈칸에 들어갈 말로 가장 적절한 것은 ⑤ '수용과 지성 사이에 큰 차이가 있다'이다.

- fairness ⑩ 공정
- antiseptic ⓐ 멸균의
- surgery ⑩ 수술
- be founded on ~에 근거를 두다

구문 풀이

9행 Popular thinking said (that) surgery didn't require clean instruments, yet
　　　　　　　　　　　　　　　생략(접속사)
Joseph Lister studied the high death rates in hospitals and introduced antiseptic
　　　　　　　동사1　　　　　　　　　　　　　　동사2　　　　선행사
practices [that immediately saved lives].
　　　　　　 주격 관・대

★★ 문제 해결 꿀~팁 ★★

▶ 많이 틀린 이유는?
글의 핵심은 사람들이 보통 주변 사람들의 사고와 행동을 따르지만, 지식의 발견은 이를 거스를 때 이뤄질 수도 있다는 것이다. 즉 대중적 사고와 진짜 지식이 다를 수 있음을 이해하는 게 중요하다는 것이다. ④를 빈칸에 넣어보면, '사람들이 주변 사람들과 다르게 행동한다'는 것을 기억하라는 의미인데, 이것은 앞서 소개한 사람들의 행동 경향과 반대되며, 지식 발견에 관한 내용과도 무관하다.

▶ 문제 해결 방법은?
정답인 ⑤는 '대중적 사고'를 acceptance로 재진술했고, 예시로 든 '과학적 발견과 투표권 쟁취'를 intelligence로 일반화했다. 이렇듯 지문 표현을 그대로 반복하는 선택지보다 적절히 재진술하고 일반화한 표현이 답일 확률이 높다.

---

35 런던 택시 운전사들의 두뇌 특징　　　　　정답률 58% | 정답 ④

다음 글에서 전체 흐름과 관계 없는 문장은?

Before getting licensed to drive a cab in London, / a person has to pass an incredibly difficult test / with an intimidating name / — "The Knowledge."
런던에서 택시 운전면허를 받기 전에, / 사람은 매우 어려운 시험을 통과해야 한다. / 위협적인 이름을 가진 / 'The Knowledge'라는
① The test involves / memorizing the layout of more than 20,000 streets / in the Greater London area / — a feat that involves an incredible amount of memory resources.
이 시험은 포함하는데, / 2만 개 이상 거리의 구획을 암기하는 것을 / Greater London 지역의 / 이는 엄청난 양의 기억 자원을 포함하는 기술이다.
② In fact, / fewer than 50 percent of the people / who sign up for taxi driver training / pass the test, / even after spending two or three years / studying for it!
사실, / 사람 중 50% 미만이 / 택시 운전사 훈련에 등록한 / 시험을 통과하는데, / 심지어 2～3년을 보낸 후에도 그러하다! / 그것을 공부하며
③ And as it turns out, / the brains of London cabbies / are different from non-cab-driving humans / in ways that reflect their herculean memory efforts.
그리고 밝혀진 바에 따르면, / 런던 택시 운전사들의 두뇌는 / 택시 운전을 하지 않는 사람들과 다르다. / 초인적인 기억 노력을 반영하는 방식 면에서
✔④ In other words, / they must hold a full driving license, / issued by the Driver and Vehicle Licensing Authority, / for at least a year.
즉, / 그들은 정식 운전면허증을 소지해야 한다. / 운전 면허청에서 발급된 / 최소 1년 동안
⑤ In fact, / the part of the brain / that has been most frequently associated with spatial memory, / the tail of the sea horse-shaped brain region / called the hippocampus, / is *bigger* than average / in these taxi drivers.

사실, / 뇌 부위, / 공간 기억과 가장 자주 연관된 / 즉 해마 모양을 한 뇌 영역의 꼬리 부분은 / 해마라 불리는 / 평균보다 *더 크다*. / 이들 택시 운전사들에게서

런던에서 택시 운전면허를 받기 전에, 사람은 'The Knowledge'라는 위협적인 이름의 매우 어려운 시험을 통과해야 한다. ① 이 시험은 Greater London 지역의 2만 개 이상 거리의 구획을 암기하는 것을 포함하는데, 이는 엄청난 양의 기억 자원을 포함하는 기술이다. ② 사실, 택시 운전사 훈련에 등록한 사람 중 50% 미만이 시험을 통과하는데, 심지어 그것을 2~3을 공부한 후에도 그러하다! ③ 그리고 밝혀진 바에 따르면, 런던 택시 운전사들의 두뇌는 초인적인 기억 노력을 반영하는 방식 면에서 택시 운전을 하지 않는 사람들과 다르다. ④ 즉, 그들은 운전 면허청에서 발급된 정식 운전면허증을 최소 1년 동안 소지해야 한다. ⑤ 사실, 공간 기억과 가장 자주 연관된 뇌 부위, 즉 해마라 불리는 해마 모양을 한 뇌 영역의 꼬리 부분은 이들 택시 운전사들에게서 평균보다 *더 크다*.

Why? 왜 정답일까?

런던의 택시 운전 면허 시험은 대단히 방대한 기억 자원을 요하고, 이에 따라 공간 기억을 다루는 해마 부위가 택시 운전사들의 뇌에서 평균보다 더 크다. 하지만 ④는 운전사들의 면허 소지 기간에 관한 내용이므로 흐름상 어색하다. 따라서 전체 흐름과 관계 없는 문장은 ④이다.

- license ⓥ 면허를 주다 ⓝ 면허
- intimidating ⓐ 위협적인
- cabbie(cabby) ⓝ 택시 기사
- hippocampus ⓝ (대뇌의) 해마
- cab ⓝ 택시
- feat ⓝ 능력, 기술
- herculean ⓐ 초인적인

구문 풀이

13행 In fact, the part of the brain [that has been most frequently associated with spatial memory], the tail of the sea horse-shaped brain region called the hippocampus, is *bigger* than average in these taxi drivers.

주어 / 주어 동격 / 분사구 / 동사(단수)

---

36 의도하지 않은 결과의 법칙 정답률 69% | 정답 ②

주어진 글 다음에 이어질 글의 순서로 가장 적절한 것을 고르시오.

① (A) – (C) – (B)　　　✔ (B) – (A) – (C)
③ (B) – (C) – (A)　　　④ (C) – (A) – (B)
⑤ (C) – (B) – (A)

When evaluating a policy, / people tend to concentrate / on how the policy will fix some particular problem / while ignoring or downplaying other effects it may have.
정책을 평가할 때, / 사람들은 집중하는 경향이 있다 / 그것이 어떤 특정한 문제를 어떻게 해결할 것인가에 / 그 정책이 가질 수 있는 다른 효과는 무시하거나 경시하는 한편
Economists often refer to this situation / as *The Law of Unintended Consequences*.
경제학자들은 종종 이 상황을 부른다. / *의도하지 않은 결과의 법칙*이라고
(B) For instance, / suppose / that you impose a tariff on imported steel / in order to protect the jobs of domestic steelworkers.
예를 들어, / 가정해 보자. / 당신이 수입된 철강에 관세를 부과한다고 / 국내 철강 노동자들의 일자리를 보호하기 위해
If you impose a high enough tariff, / their jobs will indeed be protected / from competition by foreign steel companies.
만약 당신이 충분히 높은 관세를 부과한다면, / 그들의 일자리는 실제로 보호될 것이다 / 외국 철강 회사들과의 경쟁으로부터
(A) But / an unintended consequence is / that the jobs of some autoworkers will be lost to foreign competition.
그러나 / 한 가지 의도하지 않은 결과는 ~이다. / 일부 자동차 노동자들의 일자리를 외국 경쟁사에 빼앗기게 된다는 것
Why?
왜일까?
The tariff that protects steelworkers / raises the price of the steel / that domestic automobile makers need / to build their cars.
철강 노동자들을 보호하는 관세는 / 철강의 가격을 높인다. / 국내 자동차 제조업체들이 필요로 하는 / 자동차를 만들기 위해
(C) As a result, / domestic automobile manufacturers / have to raise the prices of their cars, / making them relatively less attractive / than foreign cars.
그 결과, / 국내 자동차 제조업체들은 / 자동차 가격을 인상해야 하고, / 국산 차를 상대적으로 덜 매력적이게 만든다. / 외제 차에 비해
Raising prices tends to reduce domestic car sales, / so some domestic autoworkers lose their jobs.
가격을 올리는 것은 국산 차 판매를 줄이는 경향이 있어서, / 일부 국내 자동차 노동자들은 일자리를 잃는다.

정책을 평가할 때, 사람들은 그것이 어떤 특정한 문제를 어떻게 해결할 것인가에 집중하는 경향이 있으며, 그 정책이 가질 수 있는 다른 효과는 무시하거나 경시한다. 경제학자들은 종종 이 상황을 의도하지 않은 결과의 법칙이라고 부른다. (B) 예를 들어, 국내 철강 노동자들의 일자리를 보호하기 위해 수입된 철강에 관세를 부과한다고 가정해 보자. 만약 당신이 충분히 높은 관세를 부과한다면, 그들의 일자리는 실제로 외국 철강 회사들과의 경쟁으로부터 보호될 것이다. (A) 그러나 한 가지 의도하지 않은 결과는 일부 자동차 노동자들의 일자리를 외국 경쟁사에 빼앗기게 된다는 것이다. 왜일까? 철강 노동자들을 보호하는 관세는 국내 자동차 제조업체들이 자동차를 만드는 데 필요한 철강의 가격을 높인다. (C) 그 결과, 국내 자동차 제조업체들은 자동차 가격을 인상해야 하고, 국산 차를 외제 차에 비해 상대적으로 덜 매력적이게 만든다. 가격을 올리는 것은 국산 차 판매를 줄이는 경향이 있어서, 일부 국내 자동차 노동자들은 일자리를 잃는다.

Why? 왜 정답일까?

'의도하지 않은 결과의 법칙'을 소개하는 주어진 글 뒤로, 국내 철강 회사를 보호하기 위한 무역 조치를 예로 드는 (B), 이 조치의 '의도하지 않은 결과'에 관해 언급하는 (A), 그 최종 영향을 설명하는 (C)가 차례로 연결되어야 한다. 따라서 글의 순서로 가장 적절한 것은 ② '(B) – (A) – (C)'이다.

- downplay ⓥ 경시하다
- unintended ⓐ 의도되지 않은
- import ⓥ 수입하다
- economist ⓝ 경제학자
- consequence ⓝ 결과

구문 풀이

1행 When evaluating a policy, people tend to concentrate on {how the policy
분사구문(= When they evaluate ~) / 전치사 { } : 간접의문문
will fix some particular problem} while ignoring or downplaying other effects [it
분사구문(= while they ignore or downplay ~)
may have.]

---

37 멸종에 취약한 단일 지역 토착종 정답률 58% | 정답 ③

주어진 글 다음에 이어질 글의 순서로 가장 적절한 것을 고르시오.

① (A) – (C) – (B)　　　② (B) – (A) – (C)
✔ (B) – (C) – (A)　　　④ (C) – (A) – (B)
⑤ (C) – (B) – (A)

Species that are found in only one area / are called endemic species / and are especially vulnerable to extinction.
오직 한 지역에서만 발견되는 종들은 / 토착종이라고 불리고 / 특히 멸종에 취약하다.
(B) They exist on islands and in other unique small areas, / especially in tropical rain forests / where most species are highly specialized.
그들은 섬들과 다른 독특한 작은 지역에 있다. / 특히 열대 우림인 / 대부분의 종이 매우 특화된
One example is the brilliantly colored golden toad / once found only in a small area of lush rain forests / in Costa Rica's mountainous region.
한 가지 예는 번쩍이는 색깔의 황금 두꺼비이다. / 무성한 열대 우림의 작은 지역에서만 한때 발견되었던, / 코스타리카의 산악 지역에 있는
(C) Despite living in the country's well-protected Monteverde Cloud Forest Reserve, / by 1989, / the golden toad had apparently become extinct.
그 나라의 잘 보존된 Monteverde Cloud Forest Reserve에서 살았음에도 불구하고, / 1989년 즈음에 / 황금 두꺼비는 멸종된 것으로 보였다.
Much of the moisture / that supported its rain forest habitat / came in the form of moisture-laden clouds / blowing in from the Caribbean Sea.
습기의 많은 부분은 / 그것의 열대 우림 서식지를 지탱해 준 / 습기를 실은 구름의 형태에서 왔다. / 카리브해에서 불어 들어오는
(A) But warmer air from global climate change / caused these clouds to rise, / depriving the forests of moisture, and the habitat for the golden toad and many other species / dried up.
하지만 세계적 기후 변화로 인한 더 따뜻한 공기가 / 이러한 구름들을 상승하게 했고, / 숲에서 습기를 제거하였으며, / 황금 두꺼비와 많은 다른 종들의 서식지가 / 완전히 말라 버렸다.
The golden toad / appears to be one of the first victims of climate change / caused largely by global warming.
황금 두꺼비는 / 기후 변화의 첫 희생양들 중 하나인 것 같다. / 대체로 지구 온난화로 인한

오직 한 지역에서만 발견되는 종들은 토착종이라고 불리고 특히 멸종에 취약하다. (B) 그들은 섬들과 특히 대부분의 종이 매우 특화된 열대 우림인 다른 독특한 작은 지역에 있다. 한 가지 예는 코스타리카의 산악 지역에 있는 무성한 열대 우림의 작은 지역에서만 한때 발견되었던, 번쩍이는 색깔의 황금 두꺼비이다. (C) 그 나라의 잘 보존된 Monteverde Cloud Forest Reserve에서 살았음에도 불구하고, 1989년 즈음에 황금 두꺼비는 멸종된 것으로 보였다. 그것의 열대 우림 서식지를 지탱해 준 습기의 많은 부분은 카리브해에서 불어 들어오는 습기를 실은 구름의 형태에서 왔다. (A) 하지만 세계적 기후 변화로 인한 더 따뜻한 공기가 이러한 구름들을 상승하게 했고, 숲에서 습기를 제거하였으며, 황금 두꺼비와 많은 다른 종들의 서식지가 완전히 말라 버렸다. 황금 두꺼비는 주로 지구 온난화로 인한 기후 변화의 첫 희생양들 중 하나인 것 같다.

Why? 왜 정답일까?

한 가지 서식지에만 있는 생물 종은 멸종에 취약하다는 일반적인 내용의 주어진 글 뒤로, 황금 두꺼비라는 구체적 예를 언급하는 (B)가 먼저 연결된다. 이어서 (C)는 이들이 1989년 무렵 멸종되었다는 내용과 함께 서식지 환경에 관해 설명하고, (A)는 이 환경이 지구 온난화 때문에 '변하면서' 결국 두꺼비가 멸종되었다고 언급한다. 따라서 글의 순서로 가장 적절한 것은 ③ '(B) – (C) – (A)'이다.

- endemic ⓐ 토착의, 풍토의, 고유의
- extinction ⓝ 멸종
- habitat ⓝ 서식지
- brilliantly ⓐⓓ 눈부시게
- mountainous ⓐ 산악의
- apparently ⓐⓓ 겉보기에, 분명히
- vulnerable to ~에 취약한
- deprive A of B A에게서 B를 빼앗다
- victim ⓝ 희생자
- lush ⓐ 무성한, 우거진
- reserve ⓝ 보호 구역
- moisture-laden ⓐ 습기 찬

구문 풀이

15행 Despite living in the country's well-protected Monteverde Cloud Forest
전치사 / 동명사
Reserve, by 1989, the golden toad had apparently become extinct.
동사(과거완료) / 주격 보어

---

38 과학 실험의 조작과 통제 정답률 49% | 정답 ④

글의 흐름으로 보아, 주어진 문장이 들어가기에 가장 적절한 곳을 고르시오.

The fundamental nature of the experimental method / is manipulation and control.
실험 방법의 근본적인 본질은 / 조작과 통제이다.
Scientists manipulate a variable of interest, / and see if there's a difference.
과학자들은 관심 변인을 조작하고, / 차이가 있는지 확인한다.
At the same time, / they attempt to control / for the potential effects of all other variables.
동시에, / 그들은 통제하려고 시도한다. / 다른 모든 변인의 잠재적 영향에 대해
The importance of controlled experiments / in identifying the underlying causes of events / cannot be overstated.
통제된 실험의 중요성은 / 사건의 근본적인 원인을 식별하는 데 있어 / 아무리 강조해도 지나치지 않다.
① In the real-uncontrolled-world, / variables are often correlated.
현실의 통제되지 않은 세계에서, / 변인들은 종종 상관관계가 있다.
② For example, / people who take vitamin supplements / may have different eating and exercise habits / than people who don't take vitamins.
예를 들어, / 비타민 보충제를 섭취하는 사람들은 / 다른 식습관과 운동 습관을 지닐 수 있다. / 비타민을 섭취하지 않는 사람들과는

③ As a result, / if we want to study the health effects of vitamins, / we can't merely observe the real world, / since any of these factors (the vitamins, diet, or exercise) / may affect health.
그 결과, / 만약 우리가 비타민의 건강에 미치는 효과를 연구하고 싶다면, / 우리는 단지 현실 세계만 관찰할 수 없는데, / 왜냐하면 이러한 요소 (비타민, 식단, 운동) 중 어느 것이든 / 건강에 영향을 미칠 수 있기 때문이다.

☑ Rather, / we have to create a situation / that doesn't actually occur in the real world.
오히려, / 우리는 상황을 만들어야 한다. / 현실 세계에서 실제로 일어나지 않는

That's just what scientific experiments do.
그것이 바로 과학 실험이 하는 일이다.

⑤ They try to separate the naturally occurring relationship in the world / by manipulating one specific variable at a time, / while holding everything else constant.
그것들은 세상에서 자연적으로 발생하는 관계를 분리하려고 애쓴다. / 한 번에 하나의 특정 변인을 조작해서 / 그 밖의 다른 모든 것을 일정하게 유지하면서

실험 방법의 근본적인 본질은 조작과 통제이다. 과학자들은 관심 변인을 조작하고, 차이가 있는지 확인한다. 동시에, 다른 모든 변인의 잠재적 영향을 통제하려고 시도한다. 사건의 근본적인 원인을 식별하는 데 있어 통제된 실험의 중요성은 아무리 강조해도 지나치지 않다. ① 현실의 통제되지 않은 세계에서, 변인들은 종종 상관관계가 있다. ② 예를 들어, 비타민 보충제를 섭취하는 사람들은 비타민을 섭취하지 않는 사람들과는 다른 식습관과 운동 습관을 지닐 수 있다. ③ 그 결과, 만약 우리가 비타민의 건강에 미치는 효과를 연구하고 싶다면, 우리는 단지 현실 세계만 관찰할 수 없는데, 왜냐하면 이러한 요소(비타민, 식단, 운동) 중 어느 것이든 건강에 영향을 미칠 수 있기 때문이다. ④ 오히려, 우리는 현실 세계에서 실제로 일어나지 않는 상황을 만들어야 한다. 그것이 바로 과학 실험이 하는 일이다. ⑤ 그것들은 그 밖의 다른 모든 것을 일정하게 유지하면서, 한 번에 하나의 특정 변인을 조작해 세상에서 자연적으로 발생하는 관계를 분리하려고 애쓴다.

Why? 왜 정답일까?

과학 실험의 조작과 통제를 설명하는 글이다. ④ 앞에서 현실 세계만 관찰해서는 여러 변인의 상호작용으로 인해 연구가 잘 이뤄지지 않는다고 하고, 주어진 문장에서는 '그래서 오히려' 현실에 없는 상황을 만들어야 한다고 설명하고 있다. ④ 뒤는 바로 '그 일'이 과학 실험에서 일어나는 일이라는 내용으로 주어진 문장과 자연스럽게 연결된다. 따라서 주어진 문장이 들어가기에 가장 적절한 곳은 ④이다.

- fundamental ⓐ 근본적인
- underlying ⓐ 근본적인, 기저에 있는
- cannot be overstated 아무리 과장해도 지나치지 않다
- correlate ⓥ 상호 관련시키다
- manipulation ⓝ 조작
- constant ⓐ 일정한

구문 풀이

1행 Rather, we have to create a situation [that doesn't actually occur in the real world].
<small>선행사 / 주격 관·대 / 동사(단수)</small>

★★★ 등급을 가르는 문제!

39 지중해 사람들이 더 건강한 이유   정답률 39% | 정답 ③

글의 흐름으로 보아, 주어진 문장이 들어가기에 가장 적절한 곳을 고르시오.

Why do people in the Mediterranean live longer / and have a lower incidence of disease?
왜 지중해 지역의 사람들은 더 오래 살고 / 질병 발생률이 더 낮을까?

Some people say / it's because of what they eat.
몇몇의 사람들은 말한다. / 그것이 그들이 먹는 것 때문이라고

Their diet is full of fresh fruits, fish, vegetables, whole grains, and nuts.
그들의 식단은 신선한 과일, 생선, 채소, 통곡물, 견과류로 가득하다.

Individuals in these cultures / drink red wine / and use great amounts of olive oil.
이러한 문화권의 사람들은 / 적포도주를 마시고 / 많은 양의 올리브유를 사용한다.

Why is that food pattern healthy?
왜 그러한 음식 패턴이 건강에 좋을까?

① One reason is / that they are eating a palette of colors.
한 가지 이유는 ~이다. / 그들이 다양한 색깔을 먹고 있다는 것

② More and more research is surfacing / that shows us the benefits / of the thousands of colorful "phytochemicals" (phyto=plant) / that exist in foods.
점점 더 많은 연구가 부상하고 있다. / 우리에게 이점을 보여주는 / 수천 가지의 다채로운 '생화학 물질'(phyto=식물)의 / 식품에 존재하는

☑ These healthful, non-nutritive compounds in plants / provide color and function to the plant / and add to the health of the human body.
식물에 있는 이 건강에 좋은 비영양성 이 화합물은 / 식물에 색과 기능을 제공하고 / 인체의 건강에 보탬이 된다.

Each color connects to a particular compound / that serves a specific function in the body.
각각의 색깔은 특정 화합물과 연결된다. / 몸에서 특정 기능을 하는

④ For example, / if you don't eat purple foods, / you are probably missing out on anthocyanins, / important brain protection compounds.
예를 들어, / 만약 당신이 보라색 음식을 먹지 않는다면, / 당신은 안토시아닌을 아마도 놓치고 있는 것이다. / 중요한 뇌 보호 화합물인

⑤ Similarly, / if you avoid green-colored foods, / you may be lacking chlorophyll, / a plant antioxidant / that guards your cells from damage.
마찬가지로, / 만약 당신이 녹색 음식을 피한다면, / 당신에게는 엽록소가 부족할 수도 있다. / 식물 산화 방지제인 / 세포가 손상되는 것을 막아주는

왜 지중해 지역의 사람들은 더 오래 살고 질병 발생률이 더 낮을까? 몇몇의 사람들은 그것이 그들이 먹는 것 때문이라고 말한다. 그들의 식단은 신선한 과일, 생선, 채소, 통곡물, 견과류로 가득하다. 이러한 문화권의 사람들은 적포도주를 마시고 많은 양의 올리브유를 사용한다. 왜 그러한 음식 패턴이 건강에 좋을까? ① 한 가지 이유는 그들이 다양한 색깔을 먹고 있기 때문이다. ② 식품에 존재하는 수천 가지의 다채로운 '생화학 물질'(phyto=식물)의 이점을 보여주는 점점 더 많은 연구가 부상하고 있다. ③ 식물에 있는 이 건강에 좋은 비영양성 화합물들은 식물에 색과 기능을 제공하고 인체의 건강에 보탬이 된다. 각각의 색깔은 몸에서 특정 기능을 하는 특정 화합물과 연결된다. ④ 예를 들어, 만약 당신이 보라색 음식을 먹지 않는다면, 당신은 중요한 뇌 보호 화합물인 안토시아닌을 아마도 놓치고 있는 것이다. ⑤ 마찬가지로, 만약 당신이 녹색 음식을 피한다면, 세포가 손상되는 것을 막아주는 식물 산화 방지제인 엽록소가 부족할 수도 있다.

Why? 왜 정답일까?

③ 앞에서 다채로운 생화학 물질이 연구되고 있다고 하는데, 주어진 문장에서는 이 생화학 물질을 These healthful, non-nutritive compounds로 지칭하며 보충 설명한다. ③ 뒤로는 색깔마다

어떤 기능의 화합물과 연관되는지 구체적으로 열거하는 내용이 일관성 있게 제시된다. 따라서 주어진 문장이 들어가기에 가장 적절한 곳은 ③이다.

- Mediterranean ⓝ 지중해 (지역) ⓐ 지중해의
- miss out on ~을 놓치다
- incidence ⓝ (사건의) 발생
- antioxidant ⓝ 산화 방지제

구문 풀이

17행 Similarly, if you avoid green-colored foods, you may be lacking chlorophyll, a plant antioxidant [that guards your cells from damage].
<small>동격(= chlorophyll) / 주격 관·대</small>

★★ 문제 해결 꿀~팁 ★★

▶ 많이 틀린 이유는?
④ 앞에 a particular compound가 나오고, 주어진 문장에도 compounds가 나오기 때문에 얼핏 보면 연결되는 것처럼 보인다. 하지만 'these ~ compounds'는 엄밀히 따지면 복수의 지시어이므로, 앞에 '복수 명사'가 나와야 사용 가능하다.

▶ 문제 해결 방법은?
주어진 문장의 These healthful, non-nutritive compounds가 가리킬 만한 말이 ③ 앞의 복수 명사 phytochemicals 뿐이다. 따라서 아무리 ③ 앞뒤가 내용상 자연스러워 보여도, 지시어로 인해 발생하는 논리적 공백을 메꾸기 위해 ③에 주어진 문장을 넣어야 한다.

40 행동이 결정이나 생각에 무의식적으로 미치는 영향   정답률 57% | 정답 ①

다음 글의 내용을 한 문장으로 요약하고자 한다. 빈칸 (A), (B)에 들어갈 말로 가장 적절한 것은?

	(A)		(B)
☑	favorably <small>호의적으로</small>	……	behavior <small>행동</small>
②	favorably <small>호의적으로</small>	……	instinct <small>본능</small>
③	unfavorably <small>호의적이지 않게</small>	……	feeling <small>감정</small>
④	unfavorably <small>호의적이지 않게</small>	……	gesture <small>몸짓</small>
⑤	irrationally <small>불합리하게</small>	……	prejudice <small>편견</small>

People behave in highly predictable ways / when they experience certain thoughts.
사람들은 매우 예측 가능하게 행동한다. / 그들이 특정한 생각을 할 때

When they agree, / they nod their heads.
그들이 동의할 때 / 그들은 고개를 끄덕인다.

So far, no surprise, / but according to an area of research / known as "proprioceptive psychology," / the process also works in reverse.
여기까지는 놀랍지만 / 하지만 한 연구 분야에 따르면, / '고유 수용 심리학'이라고 알려진 / 그 과정은 거꾸로도 작용한다.

Get people to behave in a certain way / and you cause them to have certain thoughts.
사람들을 특정한 방식으로 행동하게 하라 / 그러면 당신은 그들이 특정한 생각을 갖게 하는 것이다.

The idea was initially controversial, / but fortunately it was supported by a compelling experiment.
이 관념은 처음에는 논란의 여지가 있었지만, / 다행히도 그것은 설득력 있는 실험으로 뒷받침되었다.

Participants in a study / were asked to fixate on various products / moving across a large computer screen / and then indicate / whether the items appealed to them.
한 연구의 참가자들은 / 다양한 제품에 시선을 고정하도록 요청받았다 / 큰 컴퓨터 화면을 가로질러 움직이는 / 그리고 나타내도록 / 그 제품들이 자신한테 매력적인지 아닌지를

Some of the items moved vertically / (causing the participants to nod their heads / while watching), / and others moved horizontally / (resulting in a side-to-side head movement).
일부 제품은 수직으로 움직였고 / (참가자들이 고개를 끄덕이게 하면서 / 보는 동안), / 다른 제품은 수평으로 움직였다 / (그리하여 좌우로 머리를 움직이게 하면서).

Participants preferred vertically moving products / without being aware / that their "yes" and "no" head movements / had played a key role in their decisions.
참가자들은 수직으로 움직이는 제품을 선호했다. / 인지하지 못한 채 / '예'와 '아니오'라는 그들의 머리 움직임이 / 결정에 핵심적인 역할을 했다는 사실을

➡ In one study, / participants responded (A) favorably / to products on a computer screen / when they moved their heads up and down, / which showed / that their decisions were unconsciously influenced / by their (B) behavior.
한 연구에서, / 참가자들은 (A) 호의적으로 반응했는데, / 컴퓨터 화면에 나오는 제품들에 / 그들이 고개를 위아래로 움직일 때 / 이는 보여주었다 / 이들의 결정이 무의식적으로 영향을 받는다는 것을 / 그들의 (B) 행동에 의해서

사람들은 특정한 생각을 할 때 매우 예측 가능하게 행동한다. 그들은 동의할 때 고개를 끄덕인다. 여기까지는 놀랍지 않지만, '고유 수용 심리학'이라고 알려진 한 연구 분야에 따르면, 그 과정은 거꾸로도 작용한다. 사람들을 특정한 방식으로 행동하게 하면, 당신은 그들이 특정한 생각을 갖게 하는 것이다. 이 관념은 처음에는 논란의 여지가 있었지만, 다행히도 설득력 있는 실험으로 뒷받침되었다. 한 연구에서, 참가자들이 큰 컴퓨터 화면을 가로질러 움직이는 다양한 제품에 시선을 고정하고, 그 제품들이 자신한테 매력적인지 아닌지를 나타내도록 요청받았다. 일부 제품은 수직으로 움직였고(참가자들이 보는 동안 고개를 끄덕이게 하면서), 다른 제품은 수평으로 움직였다(좌우로 머리를 움직이게 하면서). 참가자들은 '예'와 '아니오'라는 머리 움직임이 결정에 핵심적인 역할을 했다는 사실을 인지하지 못한 채 수직으로 움직이는 제품을 선호했다.

➡ 한 연구에서, 참가자들은 고개를 위아래로 움직일 때 컴퓨터 화면에 나오는 제품들에 (A) 호의적으로 반응했는데, 이는 이들의 결정이 (B) 행동에 의해서 무의식적으로 영향을 받는다는 것을 보여주었다.

Why? 왜 정답일까?

사람들이 특정한 행동을 하면 특정한 생각을 품게 될 수 있다(Get people to behave in a certain way and you cause them to have certain thoughts.)는 내용이다. 이에 대한 근거로 사람들로 하여금 고개를 끄덕이거나 가로젓으며 제품 만족도를 평가하게 했을 때 고개를 끄덕였던 제품에 대한 선호가 실제로 더 높게 나타났다(Participants preferred vertically moving products without being aware that their "yes" and "no" head movements had played a key role in their decisions.)는 실험이 언급되고 있다. 따라서 요약문의 빈칸 (A), (B)에 들어갈 말로 가장 적절한 것은 ① 'A) favorably(호의적으로), (B) behavior(행동)'이다.

- **controversial** ⓐ 논쟁의 여지가 있는
- **vertically** [ad] 수직으로, 세로로
- **unconsciously** [ad] 무의식적으로
- **prejudice** ⓝ 편견
- **fixate on** ~에 고정시키다
- **horizontally** [ad] 수평으로, 가로로
- **instinct** ⓝ 본능

5행 Get people to behave in a certain way and you cause them to have certain thoughts.
명령문(~하라)↵ 목적어 목적격 보어 접속사(그러면)

41-42 평범하지 않은 것이 더 잘 기억나는 이유

『Events or experiences / that are out of ordinary / tend to be remembered better / because there is nothing competing with them / when your brain tries to access them / from its storehouse of remembered events.』 41번의 근거
사건들이나 경험들은 / 평범하지 않은 / 더 잘 기억되는 경향이 있는데, / 그것들과 경쟁하는 것이 없기 때문이다. / 당신의 뇌가 그것들에 접근하려고 할 때 / 기억된 사건들의 창고에서

In other words, / the reason it can be (a) difficult / to remember what you ate for breakfast two Thursdays ago / is / that there was probably nothing special / about that Thursday or that particular breakfast — consequently, / all your breakfast memories combine together / into a sort of generic impression of a breakfast.
다시 말해, / 어려울 수 있는 이유는 / 2주 전 목요일에 아침 식사로 무엇을 먹었는지 기억하기가 / ~이다. / 아마도 특별한 게 없었다는 것 / 그 목요일이나 그 특정 아침 식사에 대해 / 그 결과, / 당신의 모든 아침 식사 기억은 합쳐진다. / 일종의 일반적인 아침 식사에 대한 인상으로

Your memory (b) merges similar events / not only because it's more efficient to do so, / but also because this is fundamental / to how we learn things / — our brains extract abstract rules / that tie experiences together.
여러분의 기억력은 유사한 사건들을 병합하는데, / 그것은 그렇게 하는 것이 더 효율적일 뿐만 아니라, / 이것이 기본이기 때문이다. / 우리가 어떤 것들을 배우는 방법의/ 우리의 뇌는 추상적인 규칙들을 추출한다. / 경험을 함께 묶는

This is especially true for things / that are (c) routine.
이것은 대상들에 특히 해당된다. / 일상적인

If your breakfast is always the same / — cereal with milk, a glass of orange juice, and a cup of coffee for instance — / there is no easy way / for your brain / to extract the details from one particular breakfast.
만약 당신의 아침 식사가 항상 같다면 / 예를 들어, 우유를 곁들인 시리얼, 오렌지 주스 한 잔, 커피 한 잔 / 쉬운 방법은 없다. / 당신의 뇌가 / 특정한 한 아침 식사에서 그 세부 사항을 추출하기 위한

Ironically, then, / for behaviors that are routinized, / you can remember the generic content of the behavior / (such as the things you ate, / since you always eat the same thing), / but (d) 『particulars to that one instance / can be very difficult to call up / (such as the sound of a garbage truck going by / or a bird that passed by your window) / unless they were especially distinctive.』 42번의 근거
그래서 아이러니하게도, / 일상화된 행동의 경우, / 당신은 그 행동의 일반적인 내용을 기억할 수 있지만, / (가령 당신이 먹었던 것, / 당신은 항상 같은 것을 먹기 때문에) / 그 한 가지 예의 세부 사항들은 / 상기하기가 매우 어려울 수 있다. / (쓰레기 트럭이 지나가는 소리나 / 창문을 지나치는 새소리 같은) / 그것들이 특히 독특하지 않다면

On the other hand, / if you did something unique / that broke your routine — perhaps you had leftover pizza for breakfast / and spilled tomato sauce on your dress shirt — / you are (e) more likely to remember it.
반면에, / 만약 당신이 특이한 일을 했다면 / 일상을 깨뜨리는 / 어쩌면 당신은 아침 식사로 남은 피자를 먹고 / 와이셔츠에 토마토 소스를 쏟았을 수도 있다 / 당신은 그것을 기억하기 더 쉽다.

평범하지 않은 사건들이나 경험들은 당신의 뇌가 기억된 사건들의 창고에서 그것들에 접근하려고 할 때 더 잘 기억되는 경향이 있는데, 그것들과 경쟁하는 것이 없기 때문이다. 다시 말해, 2주 전 목요일에 아침 식사로 무엇을 먹었는지 기억하기가 (a) 어려울 수 있는 이유는 아마도 그 목요일이나 그 특정 아침 식사에 대해 특별한 게 없었기 때문이다. 그 결과, 당신의 모든 아침 식사 기억은 일종의 일반적인 아침 식사에 대한 인상으로 (b) 합쳐진다. 여러분의 기억력은 유사한 사건들을 병합하는데, 그것은 그렇게 하는 것이 더 효율적일 뿐만 아니라, 이것이 우리가 어떤 것들을 배우는 방법의 기본이기 때문이다. 우리의 뇌는 경험을 함께 묶는 추상적인 규칙들을 추출한다. 이것은 (c) 일상적인 것들에 특히 해당된다. 만약 당신의 아침 식사가 항상 같다면 — 예를 들어, 우유를 곁들인 시리얼, 오렌지 주스 한 잔, 커피 한 잔 — 당신의 뇌가 특정한 한 아침 식사에서 그 세부 사항을 추출하기는 쉽지 않다. 그래서 아이러니하게도, 일상화된 행동의 경우, 당신은 그 행동의 일반적인 내용(가령 당신이 먹었던 것, 당신은 항상 같은 것을 먹기 때문에)은 기억할 수 있지만, 그 한 가지 예의 (d) 세부 사항들(쓰레기 트럭이 지나가는 소리나 창문을 지나치는 새소리 같은)은 매우 특이하지 않다면 상기하기가 매우 어려울 수 있다. 반면에, 만약 당신이 일상을 깨뜨리는 특이한 일을 했다면 — 어쩌면 아침 식사로 남은 피자를 먹고 와이셔츠에 토마토 소스를 쏟았을 수도 있다 — 당신은 그것을 기억하기 (e) 덜(→더) 쉽다.

- **out of (the) ordinary** 평범하지 않은
- **merge** ⓥ 병합하다
- **routinize** ⓥ 일상화하다, 습관화하다
- **distinctive** ⓐ 독특한
- **spill** ⓥ 쏟다
- **generic** ⓐ 일반적인
- **extract** ⓥ 추출하다
- **garbage** ⓝ 쓰레기
- **leftover** ⓝ 남긴 ⓝ 남은 음식

1행 Events or experiences [that are out of ordinary] tie to be remembered
주어 동사구
better because there is nothing competing with them when your brain tries to
현재분사구
access them from its storehouse of remembered events.
= events or experiences

41 제목 파악 정답률 46% | 정답 ⑤

윗글의 제목으로 가장 적절한 것은?
① Repetition Makes Your Memory Sharp!
반복은 여러분의 기억이 예리해지게 한다!
② How Does Your Memory Get Distorted?
기억은 어떻게 왜곡되는가?
③ What to Consider in Routinizing Your Work
작업을 일상화할 때 고려할 것

---

④ Merging Experiences: Key to Remembering Details
기억의 통합: 세부 사항을 기억하는 데 있어 핵심
✓ The More Unique Events, the More Vivid Recollection
사건이 더 특이할수록, 기억은 더 생생해진다

특이한 사건이 보통 사건보다 기억이 잘 나는(Events or experiences that are out of ordinary tend to be remembered better ~) 이유에 관한 글이므로, 글의 제목으로 가장 적절한 것은 ⑤ '사건이 더 특이할수록, 기억은 더 생생해진다'이다.

42 어휘 추론 정답률 69% | 정답 ⑤

밑줄 친 (a) ~ (e) 중에서 문맥상 낱말의 쓰임이 적절하지 않은 것은?
① (a) ② (b) ③ (c) ④ (d) ✓ (e)

(e)가 포함된 문장 바로 앞에서, 어떤 사건의 세부 사항은 '특이하지 않은 이상' 일반적인 기억 속에 통합되어 버려 구체적으로 상기되기 어렵다고 한다(particulars to that one instance can be very difficult to call up (such as the sound of a garbage truck going by or a bird that passed by your window) unless they were especially distinctive). 이러한 흐름으로 보아, (e)의 less를 more로 고쳐야 흐름에 적합하다. 따라서 낱말의 쓰임이 문맥상 적절하지 않은 것은 ⑤ '(e)'이다.

43-45 Henrietta의 마음 따뜻한 일화

(A)
Henrietta is one of the greatest "queens of song."
Henrietta는 가장 위대한 '노래의 여왕' 중 한 명이다.
She had to go through a severe struggle / before (a) she attained the enviable position / as the greatest singer Germany had produced.
그녀는 혹독한 시련을 겪어야 했다. / 그녀가 남들의 부러움을 살 위치에 도달하기 전 / 독일이 배출한 가장 위대한 가수라는
『At the beginning of her career / she was hissed off a Vienna stage / by the friends of her rival, Amelia.』 45번 ①의 근거 일치
경력 초기에, / 그녀는 비엔나 무대에서 야유를 받고 쫓겨났다. / 라이벌이었던 Amelia의 친구들에 의해
But in spite of this defeat, / Henrietta endured / until all Europe was at her feet.
그러나 이 좌절에도 불구하고, / Henrietta는 견뎠다. / 모든 유럽이 그녀의 발아래에 있을 때까지

(D)
Many years later, / when Henrietta was at the height of her fame, / one day she was riding through the streets of Berlin.
수년 후, / Henrietta의 명성이 절정에 달했을 때, / 그녀는 어느 날 베를린의 거리를 차를 타고 지나가고 있었다.
『Soon she came across a little girl / leading a blind woman.』 45번 ⑤의 근거 일치
곧 그녀는 여자 아이와 마주쳤다. / 눈먼 여성을 데리고 가는
She was touched by the woman's helplessness, / and she impulsively beckoned the child to (e) her, / saying / "Come here, my child. / Who is that you are leading by the hand?"
그녀는 여성의 무력함에 마음이 움직였고, / 그녀는 충동적으로 아이를 자기 쪽으로 오라고 손짓하며, / 말했다. / "이리 와, 얘야. / 네가 손을 잡고 데리고 가는 사람은 누구니?"라고

(B)
The answer was, / "That's my mother, Amelia Steininger. / She used to be a great singer, / but she lost her voice, / and she cried so much about it / that now (b) she can't see anymore."
대답은 이랬다. / "저분은 제 어머니, Amelia Steininger예요. / 그녀는 훌륭한 가수였지만 / 그녀는 목소리를 잃었고, / 그녀는 이 일로 너무 많이 울어서 / 그녀는 이제 더 이상 앞을 볼 수 없게 됐어요."
Henrietta inquired their address / and then told the child, / "Tell your mother / an old acquaintance will call on her this afternoon."
Henrietta는 그들의 주소를 묻고 나서 / 아이에게 말했다. / "어머니께 말하렴. / 오래된 지인이 오늘 오후에 방문할 것이라고"
『She searched out their place / and undertook the care of both mother and daughter.』
그녀는 그들의 거처를 찾아내서 / 모녀를 돌봤다. 45번 ②의 근거 일치
『At her request, / a skilled doctor tried to restore Amelia's sight, / but it was in vain.』
그녀의 요청에 따라 / 숙련된 의사가 Amelia의 시력을 회복시키려 했지만, / 그것은 허사였다. 45번 ③의 근거 불일치

(C)
But / Henrietta's kindness to (c) her former rival / did not stop here.
그러나 / Henrietta가 자기 예전 경쟁자에게 베푼 친절은 / 여기서 그치지 않았다. 45번 ④의 근거 일치
『The next week / she gave a benefit concert for the poor woman,』 / and it was said / that on that occasion Henrietta sang / as (d) she had never sung before.
그다음 주에 / 그 불쌍한 여성을 위한 자선 콘서트를 열었고, / ~라고 이야기되었다. / 그 자리에서 Henrietta는 노래했다고 / 그녀가 한 번도 불러본 적이 없는 방식으로
And who can doubt / that with the applause of that vast audience / there was mingled the applause of the angels in heaven / who rejoice over the good deeds of those below?
그리고 누가 의심할 수 있겠는가? / 많은 청중의 박수와 함께 / 천국에 있는 천사들의 박수가 섞여 있었다는 것을 / 지상 사람들의 선행에 기뻐하는

(A)
Henrietta는 가장 위대한 '노래의 여왕' 중 한 명이다. (a) 그녀가 독일이 배출한 가장 위대한 가수라는 남들의 부러움을 살 위치에 도달하기 전 그녀는 혹독한 시련을 겪어야 했다. 경력 초기에 그녀는 라이벌이었던 Amelia의 친구들에 의해 비엔나 무대에서 야유를 받고 쫓겨났다. 그러나 이 좌절에도 불구하고, Henrietta는 모든 유럽이 그녀의 발아래에 있을 때까지 견뎠다.

(D)
수년 후, Henrietta의 명성이 절정에 달했을 때, 그녀는 어느 날 베를린의 거리를 차를 타고 지나가고 있었다. 곧 그녀는 눈먼 여성을 데리고 가는 여자 아이와 마주쳤다. 그녀는 여성의 무력함에 마음이 움직였고, 충동적으로 아이를 (e) 자기 쪽으로 오라고 손짓하며, "이리 와, 얘야. 네가 손을 잡고 데리고 가는 사람은 누구니?"라고 말했다.

(B)
대답은 이랬다. "저분은 제 어머니, Amelia Steininger예요. 그녀는 훌륭한 가수였지만 목소리를 잃었고, 그 일로 너무 많이 울어서 (b) 그녀는 이제 더 이상 앞을 볼 수 없게 됐어요." Henrietta는 그들의 주소를 묻고 나서 아이에게 "어머니께 오래된 지인이 오늘 오후에 방문할 것이라고 말하렴."이라고 말했다. 그녀는 그들의 거처를 찾아내서 모녀를 돌봤다. 그녀의 요청에 따라 숙련된 의사가 Amelia의 시력을 회복시키려 했지만 허사였다.

그러나 Henrietta가 (c) 자기 예전 경쟁자에게 베푼 친절은 여기서 그치지 않았다. 그다음 주에 그녀는 그 불쌍한 여성을 위한 자선 콘서트를 열었고, (사람들은) Henrietta가 그 자리에서 (d) 그녀가 전에 한 번도 불러본 적 없는 방식으로 불렀다고 했다. 그리고 많은 청중의 박수와 함께 지상 사람들의 선행에 기뻐하는 천국에 있는 천사들의 박수가 섞여 있었다는 것을 누가 의심할 수 있겠는가?

- **severe** ⓐ 혹독한
- **hiss off** 야유하여 쫓아내다
- **acquaintance** ⓝ 아는 사람, 지인
- **undertake** ⓥ 맡다, 착수하다, 약속하다
- **applause** ⓝ 박수갈채
- **come across** 우연히 마주치다
- **impulsively** ⓐⓓ 충동적으로
- **enviable** ⓐ 부러운, 선망의 대상인
- **endure** ⓥ 견디다
- **call on** 방문하다
- **in vain** 허사가 되어
- **rejoice over** ~에 기뻐하다
- **helplessness** ⓝ 무력함
- **beckon** ⓥ 손짓하다

구문 풀이

[C] 2행 The next week she gave a benefit concert for the poor woman, and it was said that on that occasion Henrietta sang as she had never sung before.
= Henrietta was said to sing on that occasion ~

---

43 글의 순서 파악 　　　정답률 71% | 정답 ④

주어진 글 (A)에 이어질 내용을 순서에 맞게 배열한 것으로 가장 적절한 것은?
① (B) – (D) – (C)
② (C) – (B) – (D)
③ (C) – (D) – (B)
④ (D) – (B) – (C) ✓
⑤ (D) – (C) – (B)

Why? 왜 정답일까?

Henrietta가 '노래의 여왕'이 되기 전 경쟁자 Amelia의 친구들 때문에 좌절을 겪었다는 내용의 (A) 뒤로, (D)에서는 '수년이 지나 그녀가 명성을 얻은 후' 길을 가다가 어느 모녀를 마주쳤다고 한다. 이어서 (B)에서는 그 모녀가 Amelia 모녀였다는 내용과 함께 Henrietta가 이들을 챙겼다는 내용이, (C)에서는 Henrietta가 추가로 베푼 선행에 관한 내용이 전개된다. 따라서 글의 순서로 가장 적절한 것은 ④ '(D) – (B) – (C)'이다.

---

44 지칭 추론 　　　정답률 60% | 정답 ②

밑줄 친 (a)~(e) 중에서 가리키는 대상이 나머지 넷과 다른 것은?
① (a)　　② (b) ✓　　③ (c)　　④ (d)　　⑤ (e)

Why? 왜 정답일까?

(a), (c), (d), (e)는 Henrietta, (b)는 Amelia를 가리키므로, (a)~(e) 중에서 가리키는 대상이 다른 하나는 ② '(b)'이다.

---

45 세부 내용 파악 　　　정답률 77% | 정답 ③

윗글에 관한 내용으로 적절하지 **않은** 것은?
① Amelia와 Henrietta는 라이벌 관계였다.
② Henrietta는 모녀의 거처를 찾아내서 그들을 돌보았다.
③ 숙련된 의사가 Amelia의 시력을 회복시켰다. ✓
④ 불쌍한 여성을 위해 Henrietta는 자선 콘서트를 열었다.
⑤ Henrietta는 눈먼 여성을 데리고 가는 여자 아이와 마주쳤다.

Why? 왜 정답일까?

(B) '~ a skilled doctor tried to restore Amelia's sight, but it was in vain.'에 따르면 숙련된 의사가 Amelia의 시력을 회복시키고자 했지만 허사로 돌아갔다고 하므로, 내용과 일치하지 않는 것은 ③ '숙련된 의사가 Amelia의 시력을 회복시켰다.'이다.

Why? 왜 오답일까?

① (A) '~ she was hissed off a Vienna stage by the friends of her rival, Amelia.'의 내용과 일치한다.
② (B) 'She searched out their place and undertook the care of both mother and daughter.'의 내용과 일치한다.
④ (C) 'The next week she gave a benefit concert for the poor woman, ~'의 내용과 일치한다.
⑤ (D) 'Soon she came across a little girl leading a blind woman.'의 내용과 일치한다.

A	B	C	D
01 출석, 참석	01 disapproved	01 ⓚ	01 ⓒ
02 심오한	02 discern	02 ⓕ	02 ⓕ
03 (일시적) 유행	03 advent	03 ⓜ	03 ⓝ
04 ~에서 유래하다	04 reverse	04 ⓝ	04 ⓐ
05 추상적이다, 요약하다	05 ban	05 ⓛ	05 ⓙ
06 ~을 동반하다	06 strictly	06 ⓑ	06 ⓑ
07 할당(제)	07 subject	07 ⓒ	07 ⓞ
08 설문지	08 domestic	08 ⓞ	08 ⓓ
09 차별적인	09 pesticide	09 ⓟ	09 ⓢ
10 오염시키다	10 malfunction	10 ⓓ	10 ⓔ
11 복구하다, 구조하다	11 advocate	11 ⓠ	11 ⓗ
12 새로운, 신기한	12 feat	12 ⓢ	12 ⓕ
13 위협적인	13 import	13 ⓔ	13 ⓟ
14 ~에 근거를 두다	14 manipulation	14 ⓘ	14 ⓖ
15 근본적인, 기저에 있는	15 prejudice	15 ⓗ	15 ⓚ
16 수직으로, 세로로	16 routinize	16 ⓘ	16 ⓘ
17 독특한	17 cannot be overstated	17 ⓙ	17 ⓜ
18 손짓하다	18 qualification	18 ⓖ	18 ⓘ
19 추출하다	19 embarrassed	19 ⓐ	19 ⓘ
20 (환경적으로) 지속 가능한 개발	20 take into account	20 ⓛ	20 ⓠ

• 정답 •

18 ⑤ 19 ① 20 ② 21 ① 22 ① 23 ② 24 ① 25 ③ 26 ④ 27 ③ 28 ④ 29 ⑤ 30 ⑤ 31 ④ 32 ⑤
33 ① 34 ① 35 ④ 36 ⑤ 37 ③ 38 ④ 39 ② 40 ② 41 ⑤ 42 ④ 43 ④ 44 ⑤ 45 ③

★ 표기된 문항은 [등급을 가르는 문제]에 해당하는 문항입니다.

---

18 책 읽어 주기 자원봉사 참여 요청 | 정답률 93% | 정답 ⑤

다음 글의 목적으로 가장 적절한 것은?

① 도서관의 운영 시간 연장을 제안하려고
② 봉사 활동 시간이 변경된 것을 안내하려고
③ 독서 토론 수업에 참여할 아동을 모집하려고
④ 봉사 활동에 참여하지 못하게 된 것을 사과하려고
☑ 책 읽어 주기 자원봉사에 참여해 줄 것을 요청하려고

Dear Ms. Stevens,
Stevens씨께,
My name is Peter Watson, / and I'm the manager of the Springton Library.
제 이름은 Peter Watson이고, / 저는 Springton 도서관의 관리자입니다.
Our storytelling program has been so well-attended / that we are planning to expand the program / to 6 days each week.
우리 도서관의 스토리텔링 프로그램에 많은 분들이 참석해주셔서 / 프로그램을 확대하는 것을 계획 중입니다. / 주 6일로
This means / that we need to recruit more volunteers / to read to the children.
이것은 의미합니다. / 우리가 자원봉사자를 더 많이 모집해야 한다는 것을 / 아이들에게 책을 읽어 줄
People still talk about the week / you filled in for us / when one of our volunteers couldn't come.
사람들은 그 일주일에 대해서 아직도 이야기합니다. / 당신이 대신 채워준 / 자원봉사자 중 한 명이 올 수 없었을 때
You really brought those stories to life!
당신은 정말 그 이야기들에 생동감을 불어넣었죠!
So, / would you be willing to read to the preschoolers for an hour, / from 10 to 11 a.m. every Friday?
그러니, / 한 시간 동안 미취학 아동들에게 책을 읽어 줄 의향이 있으십니까? / 매주 금요일 오전 10시부터 11시까지
I hope you will take this opportunity / to let more children hear your voice.
저는 당신이 이 기회를 받아들이길 바랍니다. / 더 많은 아이들이 당신의 목소리를 듣게 되도록
We are looking forward to your positive reply.
당신의 긍정적인 답변을 기다리겠습니다.
Best regards, / Peter Watson
Peter Watson 드림

Stevens씨께,

제 이름은 Peter Watson이고, 저는 Springton 도서관의 관리자입니다. 우리 도서관의 스토리텔링 프로그램에 많은 분들이 참석해주셔서 프로그램을 주 6일로 확대하는 것을 계획 중입니다. 이것은 아이들에게 책을 읽어 줄 자원봉사자를 더 많이 모집해야 한다는 것을 의미합니다. 사람들은 우리 자원봉사자 중 한 명이 올 수 없었을 때 당신이 대신 채워준 일주일에 대해서 아직도 이야기합니다. 당신은 정말 그 이야기들에 생동감을 불어넣었죠! 그래서, 매주 금요일 오전 10시부터 11시까지 한 시간 동안 미취학 아동들에게 책을 읽어 줄 의향이 있으십니까? 당신이 이 기회를 받아들여서 더 많은 아이들이 당신의 목소리를 듣게 되길 바랍니다. 당신의 긍정적인 답변을 기다리겠습니다.

Peter Watson 드림

Why? 왜 정답일까?

미취학 아동들에게 책을 읽어주는 자원봉사에 참여할 의향이 있는지(So, would you be willing to read to the preschoolers for an hour, from 10 to 11 a.m. every Friday?) 묻는 내용의 글이므로, 글의 목적으로 가장 적절한 것은 ⑤ '책 읽어 주기 자원봉사에 참여해 줄 것을 요청하려고'이다.

● well-attended ⓐ 많은 사람들이 참석하는
● recruit ⓥ 모집하다
● bring to life (이야기를) 활기 넘치게 하다, 생동감 있게 하다
● expand ⓥ 확대하다
● fill in ~을 대신하다, 채워넣다

구문 풀이

3행 Our storytelling program has been so well-attended that we are planning to expand the program to 6 days each week.
「so ~ that … : 너무 ~해서 …하다」

---

19 오래된 문 뒤에서 거울을 발견한 필자 | 정답률 91% | 정답 ①

다음 글에 드러난 'I'의 심경 변화로 가장 적절한 것은?

☑ terrified → relieved
겁에 질린 → 안도한
② hopeful → nervous
희망찬 → 긴장한
③ confident → anxious
자신 있는 → 불안한
④ annoyed → grateful
짜증이 난 → 고마워하는
⑤ disappointed → thrilled
실망한 → 황홀한

I walked up to the little dark brown door / and knocked.
나는 작고 짙은 갈색 문으로 걸어가서 / 문을 두드렸다.
Nobody answered.
아무도 대답이 없었다.
I pushed on the door carefully.
나는 조심스럽게 그 문을 밀었다.
When the door swung open with a rusty creak, / a man was standing in a back corner of the room.
그 문이 녹슬어서 삐걱거리는 소리와 함께 홱 열렸을 때, / 한 남자가 그 방의 뒤쪽 구석에 서 있었다.
My hands flew over my mouth / as I started to scream.
내 손이 입 위로 향했다 / 내가 소리를 지르기 시작할 때
He was just standing there, watching me!

그는 나를 지켜보면서, 그저 거기 서 있었다!
As my heart continued to race, / I saw that he had also put his hands over his mouth.
내 심장이 계속 요동칠 때, / 나는 그 역시 두 손을 그의 입 위로 올린 것을 보았다.
Wait a minute... // It was a mirror!
잠깐... // 그것은 거울이었다!
I took a deep breath / and walked past a table to the old mirror / that stood in the back of the room.
나는 심호흡을 하고 / 테이블을 지나 오래된 거울로 걸어갔다. / 방 뒤쪽에 세워져 있는
I felt my heartbeat returning to normal, / and calmly looked at my reflection in the mirror.
나는 심장 박동이 정상으로 돌아오는 것을 느꼈고, / 차분하게 거울 속 내 모습을 바라보았다.

나는 짙은 갈색의 작은 문으로 걸어가서 문을 두드렸다. 아무도 대답이 없었다. 나는 조심스럽게 그 문을 밀었다. 녹슬어서 삐걱거리는 소리와 함께 그 문이 홱 열렸을 때, 한 남자가 그 방의 뒤쪽 구석에 서 있었다. 나는 소리를 지르기 시작하며 두 손으로 황급히 입을 가렸다. 그는 나를 지켜보면서, 그저 서 있었다! 내 심장이 계속 요동칠 때, 나는 그 역시 두 손으로 입을 가린 것을 보았다. 잠깐… 그것은 거울이었다! 나는 심호흡을 하고 테이블을 지나 방 뒤쪽에 세워져 있는 오래된 거울로 걸어갔다. 나는 심장 박동이 정상으로 돌아오는 것을 느꼈고, 차분하게 거울 속 내 모습을 바라보았다.

Why? 왜 정답일까?

오래된 문을 열고 들어간 필자가 방에서 사람을 발견하고 깜짝 놀랐다가(My hands flew over my mouth as I started to scream.), 그것이 거울에 비친 자신임을 알고 안도했다(I felt my heartbeat returning to normal, and calmly looked ~)는 내용의 글이다. 따라서 'I'의 심경 변화로 가장 적절한 것은 ① '겁에 질린 → 안도한'이다.

● swing open (문이) 활짝 열리다
● scream ⓥ 비명지르다
● rusty ⓐ 녹슨
● reflection ⓝ (거울이나 물에 비친) 그림자

구문 풀이

5행 As my heart continued to race, I saw {that he had also put his hands over his mouth}.
접속사(~할 때) | 동사(과거완료) | { } : 명사절(목적어)

---

20 성공하게 도와준 사람들에게 감사하는 마음 갖기 | 정답률 91% | 정답 ②

다음 글에서 필자가 주장하는 바로 가장 적절한 것은?

① 원만한 인간관계를 위하여 사고의 유연성을 길러야 한다.
☑ 성공에 도움을 준 사람들에게 감사하는 마음을 가져야 한다.
③ 자신의 분야에서 성공하기 위해서는 경험의 폭을 넓혀야 한다.
④ 원하는 직업을 갖기 위해서는 다른 사람의 조언을 경청해야 한다.
⑤ 타인의 시선을 의식하지 않고 부단히 새로운 일에 도전해야 한다.

In the rush towards individual achievement and recognition, / the majority of those who make it / forget their humble beginnings.
개인의 성취와 인정을 향한 질주 속에서, / 성공한 대다수의 사람들은 / 자신의 작은 시작을 잊는다.
They often forget those / who helped them on their way up.
그들은 종종 사람들을 잊는다. / 성공으로 가는 과정에서 자신을 도와준
If you forget where you came from, / if you neglect those / who were there for you when things were tough and slow, / then your success is valueless.
당신이 어디서 왔는지 잊어버리고, / 당신이 사람들을 소홀히 한다면, / 상황이 힘들고 진척이 없을 때 당신 곁에 있어 준 / 당신의 성공은 가치가 없다.
No one can make it up there / without the help of others.
아무도 성공할 수 없다. / 다른 사람의 도움 없이는
There are parents, friends, advisers, and coaches that help.
도움을 주는 부모님, 친구, 조언자, 코치들이 있다.
You need to be grateful / to all of those who helped you.
당신은 감사할 필요가 있다. / 당신을 도와준 사람들 모두에게
Gratitude is the glue / that keeps you connected to others.
감사는 접착제이다. / 당신과 다른 사람들을 연결해 주는
It is the bridge that keeps you connected with those / who were there for you in the past / and who are likely to be there in the end.
그것은 당신을 사람들과 계속해서 연결해 주는 다리이다. / 당신을 위해 과거에 그곳에 있었고 / 마지막에도 그곳에 있을 것 같은
Relationships and the way you treat others / determine your real success.
관계, 그리고 당신이 다른 사람들을 대하는 방식이 / 당신의 진정한 성공을 결정한다.

개인의 성취와 인정을 향한 질주 속에서, 성공한 대다수의 사람들은 자신의 작은 시작을 잊는다. 그들은 종종 성공으로 가는 과정에서 자신을 도와준 사람들을 잊는다. 당신이 어디서 왔는지 잊어버리고, 상황이 힘들고 진척이 없을 때 곁에 있어 준 사람들을 소홀히 한다면, 당신의 성공은 가치가 없다. 누구도 다른 사람의 도움 없이는 성공할 수 없다. 도움을 주는 부모님, 친구, 조언자, 코치들이 있다. 당신은 당신을 도와준 사람들 모두에게 감사할 필요가 있다. 감사는 당신과 다른 사람들을 연결해 주는 접착제이다. 그것은 당신을 위해 과거에 있었고 마지막에도 있을 것 같은 사람들과 당신을 계속해서 연결해 주는 다리이다. 관계, 그리고 당신이 다른 사람들을 대하는 방식이 당신의 진정한 성공을 결정한다.

Why? 왜 정답일까?

'You need to be grateful to all of those who helped you.'에서 성공에 도움을 주었던 사람들에게 고마워하는 마음을 지니라고 하므로, 필자가 주장하는 바로 가장 적절한 것은 ② '성공에 도움을 준 사람들에게 감사하는 마음을 가져야 한다.'이다.

● achievement ⓝ 성취
● make it 성공하다
● neglect ⓥ 소홀히 하다
● gratitude ⓝ 감사
● recognition ⓝ 인정, 표창
● humble ⓐ 작은, 변변찮은, 겸손한
● valueless ⓐ 가치 없는
● determine ⓥ 결정하다

구문 풀이

1행 In the rush towards individual achievement and recognition, the majority of those [who make it] forget their humble beginnings.
주어(부분 of 전체) | 동사(복수)

21 마케팅에서 중요한 균형　　정답률 58% | 정답 ①

밑줄 친 'give away the house'가 다음 글에서 의미하는 바로 가장 적절한 것은? [3점]

☑ risk the company's profitability – 회사의 수익성을 위태롭게 해서는
② overlook a competitor's strengths – 경쟁자의 강점을 간과해서는
③ hurt the reputation of the company – 회사의 명성에 해를 끼쳐서는
④ generate more customer complaints – 고객 불만을 더 창출해서는
⑤ abandon customer-oriented marketing – 고객 중심 마케팅을 버려서는

For companies interested in delighting customers, / exceptional value and service / become part of the overall company culture.
고객들을 즐겁게 하는 데 관심이 있는 기업들에게, / 뛰어난 가치와 서비스는 / 기업 문화 전반의 일부가 된다.

For example, year after year, / Pazano ranks at or near the top of the hospitality industry / in terms of customer satisfaction.
예를 들어, 해마다, / Pazano는 서비스업 중 최상위 또는 상위권을 차지한다. / 고객 만족이라는 측면에서

The company's passion for satisfying customers / is summed up in its credo, / which promises / that its luxury hotels will deliver a truly memorable experience.
고객을 만족시키려는 그 기업의 열정은 / 그것의 신조에 요약되어 있고, / 이는 약속한다. / 그 기업의 고급 호텔이 진정으로 기억될 만한 경험을 제공할 것을

Although a customer-centered firm / seeks to deliver high customer satisfaction / relative to competitors, / it does not attempt to maximize customer satisfaction.
비록 고객 중심 기업은 / 고객 만족을 제공하고자 하지만, / 경쟁사 대비 높은 / 그것은 고객 만족을 최대화하려고 하지는 않는다.

A company can always increase customer satisfaction / by lowering its price or increasing its services.
기업은 고객 만족을 항상 높일 수 있다. / 가격을 낮추거나 서비스를 증진시켜

But this may result in lower profits.
하지만 이것은 더 낮은 이윤으로 이어질지도 모른다.

Thus, / the purpose of marketing is / to generate customer value profitably.
따라서, / 마케팅의 목적은 ~이다. / 수익을 내면서 고객 가치를 창출하는 것

This requires a very delicate balance: / the marketer must continue / to generate more customer value and satisfaction / but not 'give away the house'.
이것은 매우 섬세한 균형을 필요로 하는데, / 즉 마케팅 담당자는 계속해야 하지만 / 더 많은 고객 가치와 만족을 창출하는 것을 / 하지만, '집을 거저나 다름없이 팔아서는' 안 된다.

─────

고객들을 즐겁게 하는 데 관심이 있는 기업들에게, 뛰어난 가치와 서비스는 기업 문화 전반의 일부가 된다. 예를 들어, 고객 만족이라는 측면에서 Pazano는 해마다 서비스업 중 최상위 또는 상위권을 차지한다. 고객을 만족시키려는 그 기업의 열정은 그것의 신조에 요약되어 있는데, 그 기업의 고급 호텔이 진정으로 기억될 만한 경험을 제공할 것을 약속한다. 고객 중심 기업은 경쟁사 대비 높은 고객 만족을 제공하고자 하지만, 그것은 고객 만족을 *최대화하려고* 하지는 않는다. 기업은 가격을 낮추거나 서비스를 증진시켜 고객 만족을 항상 높일 수 있다. 하지만 이것은 더 낮은 이윤으로 이어질지도 모른다. 따라서, 마케팅의 목적은 수익을 내면서 고객 가치를 창출하는 것이다. 이것은 매우 섬세한 균형을 필요로 하는데, 즉 마케팅 담당자는 더 많은 고객 가치와 만족을 계속해서 창출해야 하지만, '집을 거저나 다름없이 팔아서는' 안 된다.

Why? 왜 정답일까?

마케팅은 고객을 만족시키는 한편으로 수익 창출도 노려야 한다(Thus, the purpose of marketing is to generate customer value profitably.)는 내용으로 보아, 밑줄 친 부분은 고객 만족만을 신경 쓰다가 '수익을 놓쳐서는 안 된다'는 의미일 것이다. 따라서 밑줄 친 부분의 의미로 가장 적절한 것은 ① '회사의 수익성을 위태롭게 해서는'이다.

- **delight** ⓥ (~을) 즐겁게 하다, 기쁘게 하다
- **hospitality industry** 서비스업(호텔 산업, 식당업 등)
- **sum up** 요약하다, 압축해서 보여주다
- **delicate** ⓐ 섬세한, 미묘한
- **overlook** ⓥ 간과하다
- **exceptional** ⓐ 뛰어난, 예외적인
- **relative to** ~에 비해
- **profitably** ⓐⓓ 수익을 내며, 수익성 있게
- **give away** 거저 주다
- **reputation** ⓝ 명성

구문 풀이

4행 The company's passion for satisfying customers is summed up in its credo, [선행사] which promises {that its luxury hotels will deliver a truly memorable experience}.
[계속적 용법] [동사(미래)] { } : 명사절(promises의 목적어)

22 아이에 따라 양육 방식을 맞춤 설계하기　　정답률 86% | 정답 ①

다음 글의 요지로 가장 적절한 것은?

☑ 자녀의 특성에 맞는 개별화된 양육이 필요하다.
② 식물을 키우는 것이 자녀의 창의성 발달에 도움이 된다.
③ 정서적 교감은 자녀의 바람직한 인격 형성에 필수적이다.
④ 자녀에게 타인을 존중하는 태도를 가르치는 것이 중요하다.
⑤ 전문가에 의해 검증된 양육 방식을 따르는 것이 바람직하다.

The problem / with simply adopting any popular method of parenting / is that it ignores the most important variable in the equation: / the uniqueness of your child.
문제는 / 대중적인 양육법을 단순히 채택하는 것의 / 그것이 방정식의 가장 중요한 변수를 무시한다는 것이다. / 즉 자녀의 독특함

So, / rather than insist / that one style of parenting will work with every child, / we might take a page from the gardener's handbook.
그래서, / 주장하기보다는, / 한 가지 양육 방식이 모든 아이들에게 효과가 있을 것이라고 / 우리는 정원사 안내서의 일부를 참고할 수도 있다.

Just as the gardener accepts, / without question or resistance, / the plant's requirements / and provides the right conditions / each plant needs to grow and flourish, / so, too, do we parents need to custom-design our parenting / to fit the natural needs of each individual child.
정원사가 받아들이고, / 의문이나 거부감 없이 / 식물의 요구 사항을 / 적절한 조건을 제공하는 것처럼, / 각각의 식물이 자라고 번성하는 데 필요한 / 우리 부모도 역시 양육을 맞춤 설계할 필요가 있다. / 아이들 각각의 타고난 욕구에 맞게

Although that may seem difficult, / it is possible.
그것이 어려워 보일지 모르지만, / 가능하다.

Once we understand who our children really are, / we can begin to figure out / how to make changes in our parenting style / to be more positive and accepting of each child / we've been blessed to parent.
일단 우리가 우리 아이들이 진정 어떤 아이인지를 알게 되면, / 우리는 알아내기 시작할 수 있다. / 양육 방식에 변화를 줄 방법을 / 각각의 아이에게 보다 긍정적이고 수용적이도록 / 우리가 양육하도록 축복 받은

─────

대중적인 양육법을 단순히 채택하는 것의 문제는 그것이 방정식의 가장 중요한 변수, 즉 자녀의 독특함을 무시한다는 것이다. 그래서, 한 가지 양육 방식이 모든 아이들에게 효과가 있을 것이라고 주장하기보다는, 정원사 안내서의 일부를 참고할 수도 있다. 정원사가 의문이나 거부감 없이 식물의 요구 사항을 받아들이고 각각의 식물이 자라고 번성하는 데 필요한 적절한 조건을 제공하는 것처럼, 우리 부모도 역시 아이들 각각의 타고난 욕구에 맞는 양육을 맞춤 설계할 필요가 있다. 그것이 어려워 보일지 모르지만, 가능하다. 일단 우리가 우리 아이들이 진정 어떤 아이인지를 알게 되면, 우리가 양육하도록 축복 받은 각각의 아이에게 보다 긍정적이고 수용적이도록 양육 방식에 변화를 줄 방법을 알아내기 시작할 수 있다.

Why? 왜 정답일까?

'~ so, too, do we parents need to custom-design our parenting to fit the natural needs of each individual child.'에서 부모는 아이들 각각의 필요에 맞는 양육 방식을 맞춤 설계할 필요성이 있다고 하므로, 글의 요지로 가장 적절한 것은 ① '자녀의 특성에 맞는 개별화된 양육이 필요하다.'이다.

- **adopt** ⓥ 채택하다
- **parenting** ⓝ 양육
- **uniqueness** ⓝ 독특함, 고유함
- **resistance** ⓝ 저항
- **blessed** ⓐ 축복 받은
- **method** ⓝ 방법
- **variable** ⓝ 변수 ⓐ 가변적인
- **insist** ⓥ 주장하다
- **flourish** ⓥ 번성하다

구문 풀이

5행 Just as the gardener accepts, (without question or resistance), the plant's
[접속사(~와 마찬가지로)] [동사1] [삽입구] [목적어1]
requirements and provides the right conditions [each plant needs to grow and
[동사2] [목적어2(선행사)]
flourish], so, too, do we parents need to custom-design our parenting to fit the
「so + 조동사 + 주어 + 동사원형: 긍정 동의(~도 그렇다)」
natural needs of each individual child.

23 예측 불가능성을 향하는 인간의 성향　　정답률 63% | 정답 ②

다음 글의 주제로 가장 적절한 것은?

① considerations in learning foreign languages
외국어 학습에서의 고려 사항
☑ people's inclination towards unpredictability
예측 불가능성을 향하는 인간의 성향
③ hidden devices to make a movie plot unexpected
영화 줄거리를 예측 불가하게 만들기 위한 숨겨진 장치들
④ positive effects of routine on human brain function
일상이 인간의 뇌 기능에 미치는 긍정적 영향
⑤ danger of predicting the future based on the present
현재에 근거해 미래를 예측하는 것의 위험성

In the movie *Groundhog Day*, / a weatherman played by Bill Murray / is forced to relive a single day over and over again.
영화 *Groundhog Day*에서, / Bill Murray가 연기한 기상캐스터는 / 하루를 반복해서 다시 살아야 한다.

Confronted with this seemingly endless loop, / he eventually rebels against living through the same day / the same way twice.
끝이 없어 보이는 이 고리에 직면하여, / 그는 결국 같은 날을 사는 것에 저항한다. / 같은 방식으로 두 번

He learns French, / becomes a great pianist, / befriends his neighbors, / helps the poor.
그는 프랑스어를 배우고, / 위대한 피아노 연주자가 되고, / 이웃들과 친구가 되고, / 가난한 사람들을 도와준다.

Why do we cheer him on?
우리는 왜 그를 응원하는가?

Because we don't want perfect predictability, / even if what's on repeat is appealing.
왜냐하면 우리가 완벽한 예측 가능성은 원하지 않기 때문이다. / 반복되는 것이 매력적일지라도

Surprise engages us.
놀라움은 우리를 끌어들인다.

It allows us to escape autopilot.
그것은 우리를 자동 조종 장치에서 벗어나게 한다.

It keeps us awake to our experience.
그것은 우리가 경험을 계속 인식하게 한다.

In fact, / the neurotransmitter systems involved in reward / are tied to the level of surprise: / rewards delivered at regular, predictable times / yield a lot less activity in the brain / than the same rewards delivered at random unpredictable times.
실제로, / 보상과 관련된 신경 전달 물질 체계는 / 놀라움의 수준과 관련이 있다. / 규칙적이고, 예측 가능한 때에 전달되는 보상은 / 뇌에서 훨씬 적은 활동을 산출한다. / 임의적으로 예측 불가능한 때에 전달되는 동일한 보상보다

Surprise gratifies.
놀라움은 만족감을 준다.

─────

영화 *Groundhog Day*에서, Bill Murray가 연기한 기상캐스터는 하루를 반복해서 다시 살아야 한다. 끝이 없어 보이는 이 고리에 직면하여, 그는 결국 같은 날을 같은 방식으로 두 번 사는 것에 저항한다. 그는 프랑스어를 배우고, 위대한 피아노 연주자가 되고, 이웃들과 친구가 되고, 가난한 사람들을 도와준다. 우리는 왜 그를 응원하는가? 왜냐하면 반복되는 것이 매력적일지라도, 우리는 완벽한 예측 가능성을 원하지 않기 때문이다. 놀라움은 우리를 끌어들인다. 그것은 우리를 자동 조종 장치에서 벗어나게 한다. 그것은 우리가 경험을 계속 인식하게 한다. 실제로, 보상과 관련된 신경 전달 물질 체계는 놀라움의 수준과 관련이 있다. 규칙적이고, 예측 가능한 때에 전달되는 보상은 임의적으로 예측 불가능한 때에 전달되는 동일한 보상보다 뇌에서 훨씬 적은 활동을 산출한다. 놀라움은 만족감을 준다.

Why? 왜 정답일까?

글 중간의 질문에 답을 제시하는 문장에서 주제가 드러나는데, 우리는 완전한 예측 가능성을 원하지 않는다(Because we don't want perfect predictability, ~)는 것이다. 이어서 'Surprise engages us.'와 'Surprise gratifies.'에서 놀라움, 즉 예측 불가한 요소는 우리를 끌어들이는 속성이 있으며, 우리에게 만족감을 준다고 한다. 따라서 글의 주제로 가장 적절한 것은 ② '예측 불가능성을 향하는 인간의 성향'이다.

- **confront** ⓥ 직면하다
- **rebel against** ~에 저항하다
- **cheer on** ~을 응원하다
- **seemingly** ⓐⓓ 겉보기에
- **befriend** ⓥ ~와 친구가 되다
- **predictability** ⓝ 예측 가능성

- appealing ⓐ 매력적인
- yield ⓥ 산출하다
- inclination ⓝ 성향, 경향
- engage ⓥ 사로잡다
- gratify ⓥ 기쁘게 하다, 충족시키다

구문 풀이

3행 Confronted with this seemingly endless loop, he eventually rebels against
수동분사구문(= As he is confronted ~)
living through the same day the same way twice.

---

24 메시지를 표현하는 빌딩
정답률 72% | 정답 ①

다음 글의 제목으로 가장 적절한 것은?

✓① Buildings Do Talk in Their Own Ways! - 빌딩은 자기 식대로 분명 말한다!
② Design of Buildings Starts from Nature - 건물 설계는 자연에서 시작된다
③ Language of Buildings: Too Vague to Grasp - 건물의 언어: 너무 모호해서 이해할 수 없다
④ Which Is More Important, Safety or Beauty? - 안전과 아름다움, 무엇이 더 중요한가?
⑤ How Do Architects Attach Emotions to Buildings? - 건축가들은 건물에 어떻게 감정을 부여하는가?

A building is an inanimate object, / but it is not an inarticulate one.
빌딩은 무생물이지만, / 표현을 제대로 하지 못하는 사물은 아니다.

Even the simplest house always makes a statement, / one expressed in brick and stone, in wood and glass, / rather than in words / — but no less loud and obvious.
아무리 단순한 집이라도 항상 진술을 하는데, / 그것은 벽돌과 돌, 나무와 유리로 표현되지만 / 말보다는 / 꽤 크고 명확하다.

When we see a rusting trailer / surrounded by weeds and abandoned cars, / or a brand-new minimansion with a high wall, / we instantly get a message.
우리가 녹슨 트레일러를 보거나 / 잡초와 버려진 자동차로 둘러싸인 / 높은 벽을 가진 아주 새로운 소형 저택을 볼 때, / 우리는 즉시 메시지를 받는다.

In both of these cases, / though in different accents, / it is "Stay Out of Here."
이 두 경우 모두, / 비록 다른 억양이지만, / 그것은 "여기에 들어오지 마시오"이다.

It is not only houses, of course, / that communicate with us.
물론 집뿐만이 아니다. / 우리와 소통하는 것은

All kinds of buildings / — churches, museums, schools, hospitals, restaurants, and offices — / speak to us silently.
모든 종류의 건물들이 / 교회, 박물관, 학교, 병원, 식당, 사무실 등 / 우리에게 조용히 말한다.

Sometimes the statement is deliberate.
때때로 그 진술은 의도적이다.

A store or restaurant can be designed / so that it welcomes mostly low-income or high-income customers.
가게나 레스토랑은 설계될 수 있다. / 주로 저소득층 또는 고소득층 고객을 맞이하기 위해서

Buildings tell us what to think and how to act, / though we may not register their messages consciously.
건물들은 우리에게 무엇을 생각하고 어떻게 행동해야 하는지를 알려준다. / 우리가 그들의 메시지를 의식적으로 명심하지는 않더라도

빌딩은 무생물이지만, 표현을 제대로 하지 못하는 사물은 아니다. 아무리 단순한 집이라도 항상 진술을 하는데, 그것은 말보다 벽돌과 돌, 나무와 유리로 표현되지만 꽤 크고 명확하다. 잡초와 버려진 자동차로 둘러싸인 녹슨 트레일러나 높은 벽을 가진 아주 새로운 소형 저택을 볼 때, 우리는 즉시 메시지를 받는다. 이 두 경우 모두, 비록 다른 억양이지만, "여기에 들어오지 말라"는 것이다. 물론 우리와 소통하는 것은 집뿐만이 아니다. 교회, 박물관, 학교, 병원, 식당, 사무실 등 모든 종류의 건물들이 우리에게 소리 없이 말한다. 때때로 그 진술은 의도적이다. 가게나 레스토랑은 주로 저소득층 또는 고소득층 고객을 맞이하기 위해서 설계될 수 있다. 건물들은 우리가 그들의 메시지를 의식적으로 명심하지는 않더라도 우리에게 무엇을 생각하고 어떻게 행동해야 하는지를 알려준다.

Why? 왜 정답일까?

첫 문장과 마지막 문장을 통해, 건물은 아무 표현을 하지 하는 무생물이 아니므로 우리에게 메시지를 전달한다(Buildings tell us what to think and how to act, ~)는 주제를 파악할 수 있다. 따라서 글의 주제로 가장 적절한 것은 ① '빌딩은 자기 식대로 분명 말한다'이다.

- inanimate ⓐ 무생물의
- brick ⓝ 벽돌
- abandon ⓥ 버리다
- deliberate ⓐ 의도적인, 고의의
- consciously ⓐ 의식적으로
- make a statement 말하다, 진술하다
- weed ⓝ 잡초
- instantly ⓐ 즉시
- register ⓥ 알아채다, 기억하다
- grasp ⓥ 이해하다

구문 풀이

2행 Even the simplest house always makes a statement, one (expressed in brick and stone, in wood and glass, rather than in words — but no less loud and obvious). ( ): 과거분사구(one 수식)
부정대명사(= a statement)

---

25 5개국 GDP에서 여행 및 관광의 비중
정답률 75% | 정답 ③

다음 도표의 내용과 일치하지 않는 것은?

Travel and Tourism's Contribution to GDP

(unit: billions of US dollars)

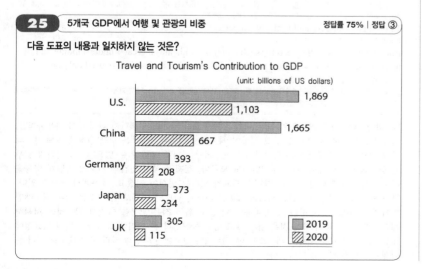

U.S. 1,869 / 1,103
China 1,665 / 667
Germany 393 / 208
Japan 373 / 234
UK 305 / 115
■ 2019 ▨ 2020

The above graph shows travel and tourism's contribution to GDP / for each of the five countries / in 2019 and in 2020.
그래프는 GDP에 대한 여행 및 관광의 기여를 보여 준다. / 5개국 각각에 있어 / 2019년과 2020년

① In all five countries, / travel and tourism's contribution to GDP in 2020 / decreased compared to the previous year.
5개국 모두에서, / 2020년에 GDP에 대한 여행 및 관광의 기여는 / 전년에 비해 감소하였다.

② Both in 2019 and in 2020, / the U.S. showed the largest contribution of travel and tourism to GDP / among the five countries, / followed by China.
2019년과 2020년 모두에서, / 미국이 GDP에 대한 여행 및 관광의 가장 큰 기여를 나타냈고, / 5개국 중 / 중국이 그 뒤를 이었다.

✓③ In China, / travel and tourism's contribution to GDP in 2020 / was less than a third that in 2019.
중국에서, / 2020년에 GDP에 대한 여행 및 관광의 기여는 / 2019년 기여분의 3분의 1 미만이었다.

④ In 2019, / Germany showed a larger contribution of travel and tourism to GDP / than Japan, / whereas the reverse was true in 2020.
2019년에, / 독일은 GDP에 대한 여행 및 관광의 기여가 더 큰 것으로 나타난 반면, / 일본보다 / 2020년에는 그 반대였다.

⑤ In 2020, / the UK was the only country / where the contribution of travel and tourism to GDP / was less than $200 billion.
2020년에는, / 영국이 유일한 국가였다. / GDP에 대한 여행 및 관광의 기여가 / 2,000억 달러 미만인

그래프는 2019년과 2020년 5개국 각각의 GDP에 대한 여행 및 관광의 기여를 보여 준다. ① 5개국 모두에서, 2020년에 GDP에 대한 여행 및 관광의 기여는 전년에 비해 감소하였다. ② 2019년과 2020년 모두에서, 5개국 중 미국이 GDP에 대한 여행 및 관광의 가장 큰 기여를 나타냈고, 중국이 그 뒤를 이었다. ③ 중국에서, 2020년에 GDP에 대한 여행 및 관광의 기여는 2019년 기여분의 3분의 1 미만이었다. ④ 2019년에, 독일은 GDP에 대한 여행 및 관광의 기여가 일본보다 더 큰 것으로 나타난 반면, 2020년에는 그 반대였다. ⑤ 2020년에는, 영국이 GDP에 대한 여행 및 관광의 기여가 2,000억 달러 미만인 유일한 국가였다.

Why? 왜 정답일까?

도표에 따르면 2020년 중국 GDP에서 여행 및 관광이 차지한 액수(6,670억)는 2019년 액수(1조 6,650억)의 3분의 1을 넘으므로, 도표와 일치하지 않는 것은 ③이다.

- contribution ⓝ 기여
- previous ⓐ 이전의
- billion ⓝ 10억
- reverse ⓝ 반대, 역

---

26 제왕나비의 특징
정답률 91% | 정답 ④

monarch butterfly에 관한 다음 글의 내용과 일치하지 않는 것은?

① 날개의 바깥 가장자리에 흰 점이 있다.
② 뒷날개는 앞날개보다 색이 더 밝다.
③ 알은 약 3일에서 5일 후에 부화한다.
✓④ 북부 주의 추운 겨울 기온에 잘 버틴다.
⑤ 4천 킬로미터 넘게 날 수 있다.

The monarch butterfly has lovely bright colors / splashed on its wings.
제왕나비는 예쁜 밝은색이 / 자기 날개 위에 얼룩진

「The wings have white spots on the outer margins.」 ①의 근거 일치
날개 바깥쪽 가장자리에 흰 점들이 있다.

「The hind wings are rounded, / and they are lighter in color than the front wings.」 ②의 근거 일치
뒷날개는 둥글고, / 그것들은 앞날개보다 더 밝은색을 띤다.

The body is black with white spots.
몸통은 검은 바탕에 흰 점이 있다.

「The mother butterfly lays only one egg / on the underside of milkweed leaves, / which hatches about three to five days later.」 ③의 근거 일치
어미 나비는 오직 한 개의 알만 낳고, / 밀크위드 잎 밑면에 / 그것은 약 3일에서 5일 후에 부화한다.

The monarch loves to fly around in the warm sunshine, / from March through October, / all across the United States.
제왕나비는 따뜻한 햇살을 받으며 날아다니는 것을 좋아한다. / 3월부터 10월까지 / 미국 전역에서

「The monarch cannot survive the cold winter temperatures of the northern states.」 ④의 근거 불일치
제왕나비는 북부 주의 추운 겨울 기온에 살아남을 수 없다.

So, / it very wisely migrates / from the northern states to the south, / and hibernates.
그래서, / 그것은 매우 현명하게 이주하여 / 북부 주에서 남부로 / 동면한다.

「The monarch is the only insect / that can fly more than four thousand kilometers / to a warmer climate.」 ⑤의 근거 일치
제왕나비는 유일한 곤충이다. / 4천 킬로미터 넘게 날 수 있는 / 더 따뜻한 지방으로

제왕나비는 날개에 밝은색의 예쁜 얼룩무늬가 있다. 날개 바깥쪽 가장자리에 흰 점들이 있다. 뒷날개는 둥글고, 앞날개보다 더 밝은색을 띤다. 몸통은 검은 바탕에 흰 점이 있다. 어미 나비는 밀크위드 잎 밑면에 오직 한 개의 알만 낳고, 그것은 약 3일에서 5일 후에 부화한다. 제왕나비는 3월부터 10월까지 미국 전역에서 따뜻한 햇살을 받으며 날아다니는 것을 좋아한다. 제왕나비는 북부 주의 추운 겨울 기온에 살아남을 수 없다. 그래서, 그것은 매우 현명하게 북부 주에서 남부로 이주하여 동면한다. 제왕나비는 더 따뜻한 지방으로 4천 킬로미터 넘게 날 수 있는 유일한 곤충이다.

Why? 왜 정답일까?

'The monarch cannot survive the cold winter temperatures of the northern states.'에서 제왕나비는(미국) 북부 주의 겨울 온도에서 생존할 수 없다고 하므로, 내용과 일치하지 않는 것은 ④ '북부 주의 추운 겨울 기온에 잘 버틴다.'이다.

Why? 왜 오답일까?

① 'The wings have white spots on the outer margins.'의 내용과 일치한다.
② 'The hind wings are ~ lighter in color than the front wings.'의 내용과 일치한다.
③ '~ which hatches about three to five days later.'의 내용과 일치한다.
⑤ 'The monarch is the only insect that can fly more than four thousand kilometers to a warmer climate.'의 내용과 일치한다.

- monarch ⓝ 제왕, 군주
- spot ⓝ 점
- rounded ⓐ 둥근
- underside ⓝ 아랫면, 밑면
- migrate ⓥ 이주하다
- splash ⓥ (선명한 색으로) 알록달록하게 장식하다
- margin ⓝ 가장자리
- lay ⓥ (알을) 낳다
- hatch ⓥ 부화하다

4행 The mother butterfly lays <u>only one egg</u> on the underside of milkweed
<u>선행사</u>
leaves, which hatches about three to five days later.
주격 관·대 동사(단수)

---

27 외외인 학생 대상 한국어 말하기 대회 　정답률 95% | 정답 ③

2022 Korean Speech Contest에 관한 다음 안내문의 내용과 일치하지 <u>않는</u> 것은?
① 한국에서 지내는 동안의 경험을 주제로 한다.
② 영상 제출 마감일은 9월 5일이다.
☑ 1등에게는 상금과 한국 전통 인형이 주어진다.
④ 영상 도입부에 이름이 언급되어야 한다.
⑤ 이메일로 영상 파일을 보내야 한다.

2022 Korean Speech Contest
2022 한국어 말하기 대회
Are you a foreign student / who wants to show off your Korean?
당신은 외국인 학생인가요? / 한국어를 뽐내고 싶은
Make your own video / sharing your experiences in Korea.
자신만의 영상을 만들어 보세요. / 한국에서의 경험을 공유하는
『Theme: "My Experiences While Staying in Korea"』 ①의근거 일치
주제: "한국에서 지내는 동안의 경험"
『Video Submission Deadline: September 5th』 ②의근거 일치
영상 제출 마감일: 9월 5일
Prizes
상품
『1st place: $100 and traditional Korean tea』 ③의근거 불일치
1등: $100 및 한국 전통차
2nd place: $50 and a traditional Korean doll
2등: $50 및 한국 전통 인형
Details
세부 사항
『Your name must be mentioned at the beginning of the video.』 ④의근거 일치
당신의 이름이 영상의 도입부에 언급되어야 합니다.
Your video must be between 3 to 5 minutes.
영상은 3분에서 5분 길이여야 합니다.
『Please email your video file to k-speech@kcontest.com.』 ⑤의근거 일치
영상 파일을 k-speech@kcontest.com에 이메일로 보내주십시오.

2022 한국어 말하기 대회

당신은 한국어를 뽐내고 싶은 외국인 학생인가요? 한국에서의 경험을 공유하는 자신만의 영상을 만들어 보세요.

• 주제: "한국에서 지내는 동안의 경험"
• 영상 제출 마감일: 9월 5일
• 상품
  − 1등: $100 및 한국 전통차
  − 2등: $50 및 한국 전통 인형
• 세부 사항
  − 영상의 도입부에 이름이 언급되어야 합니다.
  − 영상은 3분에서 5분 길이여야 합니다.
  − 영상 파일을 k-speech@kcontest.com에 이메일로 보내주십시오.

Why? 왜 정답일까?

'1st place: $100 and traditional Korean tea'에서 1등 수상자에게는 상금 100달러와 한국 전통차가 부상으로 주어진다고 하므로, 안내문의 내용과 일치하지 않는 것은 ③ '1등에게는 상금과 한국 전통 인형이 주어진다.'이다.

Why? 왜 오답일까?

① 'Theme: "My Experiences While Staying in Korea"'의 내용과 일치한다.
② 'Video Submission Deadline: September 5th'의 내용과 일치한다.
④ 'Your name must be mentioned at the beginning of the video.'의 내용과 일치한다.
⑤ 'Please email your video file to k-speech@kcontest.com.'의 내용과 일치한다.

● show off ～을 과시하다　　● mention ⓥ 언급하다

---

28 휴대용 사진 프린터 설명서 　정답률 90% | 정답 ④

EZ Portable Photo Printer 사용에 관한 다음 안내문의 내용과 일치하는 것은?
① LED 표시기의 흰색은 충전 중임을 나타낸다.
② 전원을 한 번 누르면 전원이 꺼진다.
③ 배터리가 완전히 충전되는 데 2시간 이상 걸린다.
☑ 무선 연결을 위해 앱을 다운로드해야 한다.
⑤ 인화지를 로고가 위로 향하도록 넣어야 한다.

EZ Portable Photo Printer / User Manual
EZ 휴대용 사진 프린터 / 사용자 설명서
Note on LED Indicator
LED 표시기에 대한 유의 사항
『White: Power on』 ①의근거 불일치
흰색: 전원 켜짐
Red: Battery charging
빨간색: 배터리 충전 중
How to Operate
작동 방법
Press the power button to turn the printer on.
프린터를 켜려면 전원 버튼을 누르세요.

『Press the power button twice to turn the printer off.』 ②의근거 불일치
프린터를 끄려면 전원 버튼을 두 번 누르세요.
To charge the battery, / connect the cable to the USB port.
배터리를 충전하려면, / 케이블을 USB 포트에 연결하세요.
『It takes 60 – 90 minutes for a full charge.』 ③의근거 불일치
완전 충전은 60～90분이 소요됩니다.
『To connect to the printer wirelessly, / download the 'EZ Printer App' on your mobile device.』 ④의근거 일치
프린터에 무선으로 연결하려면, / 모바일 장치에 'EZ Printer App'을 다운 받으세요.
How to Load Photo Paper
인화지 장착 방법
Lift the printer's top cover.
프린터의 상단 덮개를 들어 올리세요.
『Insert the photo paper with any logos facing downward.』 ⑤의근거 불일치
인화지를 로고가 아래로 향하도록 넣으세요.

EZ 휴대용 사진 프린터
사용자 설명서

LED 표시기에 대한 유의 사항
• 흰색: 전원 켜짐
• 빨간색: 배터리 충전 중
작동 방법
• 프린터를 켜려면 전원 버튼을 누르세요.
• 프린터를 끄려면 전원 버튼을 두 번 누르세요.
• 배터리를 충전하려면, 케이블을 USB 포트에 연결하세요. 완전 충전은 60～90분이 소요됩니다.
• 프린터에 무선으로 연결하려면, 모바일 기기에 'EZ Printer App'을 다운받으세요.
인화지 장착 방법
• 프린터의 상단 덮개를 들어 올리세요.
• 인화지를 로고가 아래로 향하도록 넣으세요.

Why? 왜 정답일까?

'To connect to the printer wirelessly, download the 'EZ Printer App' on your mobile device.'에서 프린터를 무선 연결하려면 앱을 다운로드해야 한다고 하므로, 안내문의 내용과 일치하는 것은 ④ '무선 연결을 위해 앱을 다운로드해야 한다.'이다.

Why? 왜 오답일까?

① 'White: Power on'에서 LED 표시기의 흰색은 전원이 켜져 있다는 의미라고 하였다. 충전 중을 표시하는 색은 빨간색이다.
② 'Press the power button twice to turn the printer off.'에서 전원을 끄려면 버튼을 두 번 누르라고 하였다.
③ 'It takes 60 – 90 minutes for a full charge.'에서 완전 충전까지는 60분에서 90분이 걸린다고 하였다.
⑤ 'Insert the photo paper with any logos facing downward.'에서 인화지는 로고가 아래로 향하도록 넣어야 한다고 하였다.

● portable ⓐ 휴대 가능한　　　● indicator ⓝ 표시(기), 장치, 지표
● wirelessly ⓐⓓ 무선으로　　　● load ⓥ 장착하다, 싣다

---

29 경제 성장의 영향에 대처하기 　정답률 48% | 정답 ⑤

다음 글의 밑줄 친 부분 중, 어법상 틀린 것은? [3점]

Even though institutions like the World Bank / use wealth / ① to differentiate between "developed" and "developing" countries, / they also agree / that development is more than economic growth.
World Bank와 같은 기관들은 / 부를 이용하지만, / '선진' 국가와 '개발도상' 국가를 구별하기 위해 / 그들은 또한 동의한다. / 발전이 경제 성장 그 이상이라는 데
"Development" can also include the social and environmental changes / that are caused by or accompany economic growth, / some of ② which are positive and thus may be negative.
'발전'은 사회적이고 환경적인 변화도 포함할 수 있으며, / 경제 성장에 의해 야기되거나 경제 성장을 수반하는 / 그 변화의 일부는 긍정적이고 그래서 부정적일지도 모른다.
Awareness has grown — and continues to grow — / that the question of how economic growth is affecting people and the planet / ③ needs to be addressed.
인식이 커졌고, 계속해서 커지고 있다. / 경제 성장이 인간과 지구에 어떻게 영향을 미치고 있는지에 대한 문제가 / 다뤄질 필요가 있다는
Countries are slowly learning / that it is cheaper and causes ④ much less suffering / to try to reduce the harmful effects of an economic activity or project at the beginning, / when it is planned, / than after the damage appears.
국가들은 서서히 깨닫고 있다. / 비용이 덜 들고 훨씬 적은 고통을 야기한다는 것을 / 경제 활동이나 프로젝트의 폐해를 초기에 줄이려고 노력하는 것이 / 그것이 계획되는 때인 / 피해가 나타난 이후보다
To do this is not easy and is always imperfect.
이렇게 하는 것은 쉽지 않고 항상 불완전하다.
But an awareness of the need for such an effort / indicates a greater understanding and moral concern / than ☑ did the previous widespread attitude / that focused only on creating new products and services.
그러나 그러한 노력의 필요성에 대한 인식은 / 더 큰 이해와 도덕적 관심을 나타낸다. / 이전의 널리 퍼진 태도가 그랬던 것보다 / 새로운 제품과 서비스를 만드는 데만 집중했던

World Bank와 같은 기관들은 '선진' 국가와 '개발도상' 국가를 구별하기 위해 부를 이용하지만, 그들은 또한 발전이 경제 성장 그 이상이라는 데 동의한다. '발전'은 경제 성장에 의해 야기되거나 경제 성장을 수반하는 사회적이고 환경적인 변화도 포함할 수 있으며, 그 변화의 일부는 긍정적이기에 (일부는) 부정적일지도 모른다. 경제 성장이 인간과 지구에 어떻게 영향을 미치고 있는지에 대한 문제가 다뤄질 필요가 있다는 인식이 커졌고, 계속해서 커지고 있다. 국가들은 경제 활동이나 프로젝트의 폐해를 피해가 나타난 이후보다, 그것이 계획되는 때인 초기에 줄이려고 노력하는 것이 비용이 덜 들고 훨씬 적은 고통을 야기한다는 것을 서서히 깨닫고 있다. 이렇게 하는 것은 쉽지 않고 항상 불완전하다. 그러나 그러한 노력의 필요성에 대한 인식은 새로운 제품과 서비스를 만드는 데만 집중했던 이전의 널리 퍼진 태도보다 더 큰 이해와 도덕적 관심을 나타낸다.

than 앞에 일반동사 indicates가 나오므로, than 뒤의 대동사는 do 동사 형태여야 한다. 이때 문맥상 시제가 과거이므로 was를 did로 고쳐야 한다. 따라서 어법상 틀린 것은 ⑤이다.

Why? 왜 오답일까?

① use가 포함된 3형식의 완전한 구조 뒤에 '~하기 위해'라는 목적의 의미로 주절을 보충하는 to부정사가 바르게 쓰였다.
② 콤마 앞뒤로 접속사 없이 문장이 연결되므로, some of 뒤에 관계대명사가 필요하다. 따라서 앞에 나온 복수 명사 changes를 대신하면서 두 문장을 연결하는 접속사 역할을 하는 which가 알맞게 쓰였다.
③ 주어인 the question이 단수 명사이므로, 동사 또한 단수형인 needs로 바르게 쓰였다.
④ 비교급 less를 강조하는 부사로 much가 바르게 쓰였다.

- **institution** ⓝ 기관
- **differentiate** ⓥ 구별하다
- **environmental** ⓐ 환경적인
- **awareness** ⓝ 인식
- **suffering** ⓝ 고통
- **wealth** ⓝ 부
- **economic growth** 경제 성장
- **accompany** ⓥ 동반하다
- **address** ⓥ 다루다, 처리하다
- **imperfect** ⓐ 불완전한

구문 풀이

4행 "Development" can also include the social and environmental changes [that are caused by or accompany economic growth], some of which are positive and thus may be negative.
(선행사 / 주격 관·대 / = the changes)

---

30 비행 조종에서 기술에 대한 의존이 낳는 역설 | 정답률 48% | 정답 ⑤

다음 글의 밑줄 친 부분 중, 문맥상 낱말의 쓰임이 적절하지 않은 것은?

The most advanced military jets are fly-by-wire:
가장 진보된 군사용 제트기는 전자식 비행 조종 장치이다.
They are so unstable / that they require an automated system / that can sense and act more quickly than a human operator / to maintain control.
그것들은 매우 불안정해서 / 자동화된 시스템을 필요로 한다. / 인간 조작자보다 더 빠르게 감지하고 행동할 수 있는 / 계속 제어하려면
Our dependence on smart technology / has led to a ① paradox.
스마트 기술에 대한 우리의 의존은 / 역설로 이어졌다.
As technology improves, / it becomes more reliable and more efficient, / and human operators depend on it even more.
기술이 향상될수록 / 그 기술은 신뢰성과 효율성이 더 높아지고, / 인간 조작자들은 훨씬 더 그것에 의존한다.
Eventually they lose focus, / become ② distracted, / and check out, / leaving the system to run on its own.
결국 그들은 집중력을 잃고, / 산만해지며, / 떠난다. / 시스템이 스스로 작동하도록 내버려 둔 채로
In the most extreme case, / piloting a massive airliner / could become a ③ passive occupation, / like watching TV.
가장 극단적인 경우, / 대형 여객기를 조종하는 것은 / 수동적인 직업이 될 수 있다. / TV를 보는 것과 같은
This is fine until something unexpected happens.
이것은 예상치 못한 일이 일어나기 전까지는 괜찮다.
The unexpected reveals the value of humans; / what we bring to the table / is the ④ flexibility to handle new situations.
예상치 못한 일은 인간의 가치를 드러낸다. / 우리가 제시하는 것은 / 새로운 상황에 대처할 수 있는 유연성이다.
Machines aren't collaborating in pursuit of a joint goal; / they are merely serving as tools.
기계는 공동의 목표를 추구하기 위해 협력하는 것이 아니라 / 그것들은 단지 도구의 역할을 할 뿐이다.
So when the human operator gives up oversight, / the system is ⑤ more likely to have a serious accident.
따라서 인간 조작자가 관리를 포기하면 / 그 시스템이 심각한 사고를 겪을 가능성이 더 많을 것이다.

가장 진보된 군사용 제트기는 전자식 비행 조종 장치이다. 그것들은 매우 불안정해서 계속 제어하려면 인간 조작자보다 더 빠르게 감지하고 행동할 수 있는 자동화된 시스템이 필요하다. 스마트 기술에 대한 우리의 의존은 ① 역설로 이어졌다. 기술이 향상될수록 그 기술은 신뢰성과 효율성이 더 높아지고, 인간 조작자들은 훨씬 더 그것에 의존한다. 결국, 그들은 집중력을 잃고, ② 산만해지며, 시스템이 스스로 작동하도록 내버려 둔 채로 떠난다. 가장 극단적인 경우, 대형 여객기를 조종하는 것은 TV를 보는 것과 같은 ③ 수동적인 직업이 될 수 있다. 이것은 예상치 못한 일이 일어나기 전까지는 괜찮다. 예상치 못한 일은 인간의 가치를 드러낸다. 우리가 제시하는 것은 새로운 상황에 대처할 수 있는 ④ 유연성이다. 기계는 공동의 목표를 추구하기 위해 협력하는 것이 아니라 단지 도구의 역할을 할 뿐이다. 따라서 인간 조작자가 관리를 포기하면 그 시스템이 심각한 사고를 겪을 가능성이 ⑤ 더 적을(→ 더 많을) 것이다.

Why? 왜 정답일까?

전자식 비행 조종 장치에 다양한 스마트 기술이 도입되면서 인간 조작자는 기술에 더 많이 의지하게 되었지만, 예기치 못한 상황이나 사고 속에서는 인간 조작자의 역할이 여전히 필요하고 중요하다는 내용의 글이다. ⑤가 포함된 문장 앞에서 기술 또는 기계는 인간의 협력자라기보다는 도구에 불과하다고 하므로, 인간 조작자가 관리 의무를 포기한 상황을 설명하는 ⑤는 심각한 사고가 일어날 가능성이 '더 커진다'는 의미여야 한다. 즉 less를 more로 고쳐야 문맥이 자연스럽다. 따라서 문맥상 낱말의 쓰임이 적절하지 않은 것은 ⑤이다.

- **advanced** ⓐ 진보된, 고급의
- **automate** ⓥ 자동화하다
- **dependence** ⓝ 의존
- **lose focus** 집중력을 잃다
- **occupation** ⓝ 직업, 일
- **bring to the table** 제시하다, 화두를 꺼내다
- **in pursuit of** ~을 추구하여
- **unstable** ⓐ 불안정한
- **operator** ⓝ 조작자
- **reliable** ⓐ 믿을 만한
- **distracted** ⓐ 산만한, 주의가 분산된
- **unexpected** ⓐ 예상치 못한
- **flexibility** ⓝ 유연성
- **oversight** ⓝ 관리, 감독

구문 풀이

10행 The unexpected reveals the value of humans; {what we bring to the table} is the flexibility to handle new situations.
(주어1(the + 형용사 : ~한 것) / 동사1 / { } : 주어2(명사절) / 동사2(단수))

---

31 리더 및 추종자 역할의 유동성 | 정답률 45% | 정답 ③

다음 빈칸에 들어갈 말로 가장 적절한 것을 고르시오.
① rigid – 엄격할
② unfair – 불공평할
③ fluid – 유동적일 ✔
④ stable – 안정적일
⑤ apparent – 분명할

Followers can be defined by their position as subordinates / or by their behavior of going along with leaders' wishes.
추종자는 부하라는 직책에 의해 정의될 수 있다. / 또는 리더의 바람에 따르는 행동에 의해
But followers also have power to lead.
그러나 추종자도 이끌 힘이 있다.
Followers empower leaders as well as vice versa.
추종자는 리더에게 힘을 주기도 하고, 그 반대도 마찬가지이다.
This has led some leadership analysts like Ronald Heifetz / to avoid using the word *followers* / and refer to the others in a power relationship / as "citizens" or "constituents."
이로 인해 Ronald Heifetz와 같은 일부 리더십 분석가들은 / 추종자라는 단어를 사용하는 것을 피하고 / 권력 관계에 있는 다른 사람들을 지칭하게 되었다. / '시민' 또는 '구성원'으로
Heifetz is correct / that too simple a view of followers / can produce misunderstanding.
Heifetz의 말은 옳다. / 추종자에 대한 너무 단순한 관점이 / 오해를 불러일으킬 수 있다는
In modern life, / most people wind up being both leaders and followers, / and the categories can become quite fluid.
현대의 삶에서, / 대부분의 사람들은 결국 리더와 추종자 둘 다가 되고, / 그 범주는 꽤 유동적일 수 있다.
Our behavior as followers changes / as our objectives change.
추종자로서의 우리의 행동도 바뀐다. / 우리의 목표가 변함에 따라
If I trust your judgment in music more than my own, / I may follow your lead / on which concert we attend / (even though you may be formally my subordinate in position).
만약 내가 음악에 대한 나의 판단보다 당신의 판단을 더 신뢰한다면, / 나는 당신의 주도를 따를 수 있다. / 우리가 어떤 콘서트에 참석할지에 대해서는 / (당신이 비록 공식적으로 지위상 나의 부하일지라도)
But if I am an expert on fishing, / you may follow my lead on where we fish, / regardless of our formal positions / or the fact that I followed your lead on concerts yesterday.
하지만 내가 낚시 전문가라면, / 당신은 낚시 장소에 대해서는 나를 따를 수 있다. / 공식적인 지위와는 관계없이 / 혹은 내가 어제 콘서트에 대해 당신을 따랐다는 사실과

추종자는 부하라는 직책이나 리더의 바람에 따르는 행동에 의해 정의될 수 있다. 그러나 추종자도 이끌 힘이 있다. 추종자는 리더에게 힘을 주기도 하고, 그 반대도 마찬가지이다. 이로 인해 Ronald Heifetz와 같은 일부 리더십 분석가들은 추종자라는 단어를 사용하는 것을 피하고, 권력 관계에 있는 다른 사람들을 '시민' 또는 '구성원'으로 지칭하게 되었다. 추종자에 대한 너무 단순한 관점이 오해를 불러일으킬 수 있다는 Heifetz의 말은 옳다. 현대의 삶에서, 대부분의 사람들은 결국 리더와 추종자 둘 다가 되고, 그 범주는 꽤 유동적일 수 있다. 우리의 목표가 변함에 따라 추종자로서의 우리의 행동도 바뀐다. 만약 내가 음악에 대한 나의 판단보다 당신의 판단을 더 신뢰한다면, (당신이 비록 공식적으로 지위상 나의 부하일지라도) 우리가 어떤 콘서트에 참석할지에 대해서는 당신의 주도를 따를 수 있다. 하지만 내가 낚시 전문가라면, 우리의 공식적인 지위나 내가 어제 콘서트에 대해 당신을 따랐다는 사실과는 관계없이, 낚시할 장소에 대해서는 당신이 나를 따를 수 있다.

Why? 왜 정답일까?

'Our behavior as followers changes as our objectives change.'에서 목표가 변함에 따라 추종자로서의 행동이 바뀐다고 언급한 후, 상황에 따라 리더와 추종자의 역할이 달라지는 경우를 예로 들고 있다. 따라서 빈칸에 들어갈 말로 가장 적절한 것은 리더와 추종자의 범주가 '변할 수 있다'는 의미의 ③ '유동적일'이다.

- **subordinate** ⓝ 부하, 추종자
- **analyst** ⓝ 분석가
- **constituent** ⓝ 구성원, 구성 요소
- **formally** ⓐⓓ 공식적으로
- **rigid** ⓐ 엄격한
- **empower** ⓥ 권한을 주다
- **refer to A as B** A를 B라고 지칭하다
- **objective** ⓝ 목표
- **regardless of** ~에 관계없이
- **fluid** ⓐ 유동적인

구문 풀이

6행 Heifetz is correct {that too simple a view of followers can produce misunderstanding}.
(주어(too + 형 + a(n) + 명 : 너무 ~한 …) / 동사구)

▶ 많이 틀린 이유는?
④가 나타내듯이 추종자와 리더의 분류가 '안정적'이라면, 빈칸 뒤와 마찬가지로 '목적에 따라 추종자로서의 행동이 바뀌는' 상황이 발생하기 어렵다. 리더의 역할, 추종자의 역할이 안정적인 분류 체계에 따라 굳어질 것이기 때문이다.

▶ 문제 해결 방법은?
빈칸 바로 뒤가 빈칸을 뒷받침하는 내용이다. 즉 '목적이 변하면 행동도 변한다'는 내용을 요약할 수 있는 말을 찾아 빈칸에 넣는다.

---

32 생물학적 작용의 한계에서 비롯되는 인식의 한계 | 정답률 49% | 정답 ⑤

다음 빈칸에 들어갈 말로 가장 적절한 것을 고르시오.
① hindered by other wavelengths – 다른 파장에 의해 방해받는다
② derived from our imagination – 우리의 상상에서 나온다
③ perceived through all senses – 모든 감각을 통해 인식된다
④ filtered by our stereotypes – 우리의 고정관념에 의해 걸러진다
⑤ limited by our biology – 우리의 생물학적 작용에 의해 제한된다 ✔

Color is an interpretation of wavelengths, / one that only exists internally.
색은 파장에 대한 해석으로, / 내부에서만 존재하는 것이다.
And it gets stranger, / because the wavelengths we're talking about / involve only what we call "visible light", / a spectrum of wavelengths / that runs from red to violet.
그리고 그것은 더 생소하게 느껴진다. / 왜냐하면 우리가 말하고 있는 파장은 / '가시광선'이라고 부르는 것만을 포함하기 때문에, / 파장의 스펙트럼인 / 빨간색에서 보라색까지 이어지는

But visible light constitutes / only a tiny fraction of the electromagnetic spectrum / — less than one ten-trillionth of it.
그러나 가시광선은 구성해서 / 전자기 스펙트럼의 극히 일부만을 / 그중 10조 분의 1도 되지 않는다.

All the rest of the spectrum / — including radio waves, microwaves, Xrays, gamma rays, cell phone conversations, wifi, and so on — / all of this is flowing through us right now, / and we're completely unaware of it.
나머지 모든 스펙트럼이 / 전파, 마이크로파, X선, 감마선, 휴대폰 통화, 와이파이 등 / 이 모든 것이 지금 우리를 통해 흐르고 있으며, / 우리는 그것을 완전히 알지 못한다.

This is because we don't have any specialized biological receptors / to pick up on these signals from other parts of the spectrum.
이것은 우리가 어떤 특별한 생물학적 수용체도 가지고 있지 않기 때문이다. / 스펙트럼의 다른 부분으로부터 이러한 신호를 포착할 수 있는

The slice of reality that we can see / is limited by our biology.
우리가 볼 수 있는 현실의 단면은 / 우리의 생물학적 작용에 의해 제한된다.

색은 파장에 대한 해석으로, 내부에서만 존재하는 것이다. 그리고 이것은 더 생소해지는데, 우리가 말하고 있는 파장은 빨간색에서 보라색까지 이어지는 파장의 스펙트럼인 '가시광선'이라고 부르는 것만을 포함하기 때문이다. 그러나 가시광선은 전자기 스펙트럼의 극히 일부만을 구성해서 그중 10조 분의 1도 되지 않는다. 전파, 마이크로파, X선, 감마선, 휴대폰 통화, 와이파이 등 나머지 모든 스펙트럼이 지금 우리를 통해 흐르고 있으며, 우리는 이 모든 것을 완전히 알지 못한다. 이것은 우리가 스펙트럼의 다른 부분으로부터 이러한 신호를 포착할 수 있는 어떤 특별한 생물학적 수용체를 가지고 있지 않기 때문이다. 우리가 볼 수 있는 현실의 단면은 우리의 생물학적 작용에 의해 제한된다.

Why? 왜 정답일까?
우리 주변에는 온갖 종류의 스펙트럼이 흐르고 있지만 우리는 생물학적 수용체의 한계상 극히 일부만 인식할 수 있다(~ we don't have any specialized biological receptors to pick up on these signals from other parts of the spectrum.)는 설명으로 보아, 빈칸에 들어갈 말로 가장 적절한 것은 ⑤ '우리의 생물학적 작용에 의해 제한된다'이다.

- interpretation ⓝ 해석
- internally ⓐⓓ 내부적으로
- fraction ⓝ 부분, 파편
- specialized ⓐ 전문화된, 분화된
- hinder ⓥ 방해하다
- wavelength ⓝ 파장, 주파수
- visible light 가시광선
- unaware ⓐ 알지 못하는
- pick up on ~을 알아차리다

구문 풀이
2행 And it gets stranger, because the wavelengths we're talking about involve only {what we call "visible light"}, a spectrum of wavelengths [that runs from red to violet].
{ }: 선행사   선행사 동격   주격 관·대

★★★ 등급을 가르는 문제!
33 일반 전문직과 저널리즘의 차이점   정답률 32% | 정답 ①

다음 빈칸에 들어갈 말로 가장 적절한 것을 고르시오. [3점]
✓ its lack of independence – 그것의 독립성의 부족
② the constant search for truth – 지속적인 진리 추구
③ the disregard of public opinion – 여론의 무시
④ its balance of income and faith – 수입과 신념의 균형
⑤ its overconfidence in its social influence – 사회적 영향에 대한 과신

What is unusual about journalism as a profession / is its lack of independence.
직업으로서의 저널리즘에서 특이한 점은 / 그것의 독립성의 부족이다.

In theory, / practitioners in the classic professions, / like medicine or the clergy, / contain the means of production in their heads and hands, / and therefore do not have to work / for a company or an employer.
이론적으로, / 고전적 전문직에 종사하는 사람들은 / 의학이나 성직자처럼 / 머리와 손 안에 생산 수단을 지니고 있으므로, / 일할 필요가 없다. / 회사나 고용주를 위해

They can draw their income / directly from their clients or patients.
그들은 수입을 끌어낼 수 있다. / 고객이나 환자로부터 직접

Because the professionals hold knowledge, moreover, / their clients are dependent on them.
게다가, 전문직 종사자들은 지식을 보유하고 있기 때문에, / 그들의 고객은 이들에게 의존한다.

Journalists hold knowledge, / but it is not theoretical in nature; / one might argue / that the public depends on journalists / in the same way that patients depend on doctors, / but in practice a journalist can serve the public / usually only by working for a news organization, / which can fire her or him at will.
언론인들은 지식을 보유하고 있지만, / 그것은 본질적으로 이론적이지 않다. / 어떤 사람들은 주장할지도 모르지만, / 대중이 언론인들에게 의존한다고 / 환자가 의사들에게 의존하는 것과 같은 방식으로 / 실제로 언론인은 대중들에게 봉사할 수 있으며, / 일반적으로 뉴스 기관을 위해 일해야만 / 그 기관은 그 사람을 마음대로 해고할 수 있다.

Journalists' income depends not on the public, / but on the employing news organization, / which often derives the large majority of its revenue from advertisers.
언론인들의 수입은 대중에 의존하지 않고 / 고용한 뉴스 기관에 의존하는데, / 이는 종종 광고주들로부터 수익의 대부분을 얻는다.

직업으로서의 저널리즘에서 특이한 점은 그것의 독립성의 부족이다. 이론적으로, 의학이나 성직자처럼 고전적인 전문직에 종사하는 사람들은 머리와 손 안에 생산 수단을 지니고 있으므로, 회사나 고용주를 위해 일할 필요가 없다. 그들은 고객이나 환자로부터 직접 수입을 끌어낼 수 있다. 게다가, 전문직 종사자들은 지식을 보유하고 있기 때문에, 고객은 이들에게 의존한다. 언론인들은 지식을 보유하고 있지만, 그것은 본질적으로 이론적이지 않다. 어떤 사람들은 환자들이 의사들에게 의존하는 것과 같은 방식으로 대중이 언론인들에게 의존한다고 주장할지도 모르지만, 실제로 언론인은 일반적으로 뉴스 기관을 위해 일해야 대중들에게 봉사할 수 있으며, 그 기관은 그 사람을 마음대로 해고할 수 있다. 언론인들의 수입은 대중이 아닌, 고용한 뉴스 기관에 의존하는데, 이 기관들은 종종 광고주들로부터 수익의 대부분을 얻는다.

Why? 왜 정답일까?
마지막 두 문장(~ but in practice a journalist can serve the public usually only by

---

working for a news organization, which can fire her or him at will. Journalists' income depends not on the public, but on the employing news organization, ~)에서, 언론인은 고전적인 전문직과는 달리 지식을 보유하고 있어도 독립적이지 못한 채 자신을 고용한 뉴스 기관을 위해 일해야 한다고 설명한다. 따라서 빈칸에 들어갈 말로 가장 적절한 것은 ① '그것의 독립성의 부족'이다.

- practitioner ⓝ 전문직 종사자, 현역
- means of production 생산 수단
- theoretical ⓐ 이론적인
- at will 마음대로
- disregard ⓥ 무시
- overconfidence ⓝ 과신
- clergy ⓝ 성직자
- draw A from B A를 B로부터 끌어내다
- in nature 본질적으로
- derive A from B A를 B로부터 얻다
- faith ⓝ 믿음

구문 풀이
1행 {What is unusual about journalism as a profession} is its lack of independence.
{ }: 주어(명사절)   전치사(~로서)   동사(단수)

★★ 문제 해결 꿀~팁 ★★
▶ 많이 틀린 이유는?
저널리스트를 설명하는 글 중후반부에 the public이 많이 등장하므로, 얼핏 보면 public이 포함된 ③이 정답처럼 보인다. 하지만 저널리스트들이 '대중의 의견을 무시'한다는 내용은 글 어디에도 없다.
▶ 문제 해결 방법은?
전문직과 저널리스트를 구별하는 부분을 잘 봐야 한다. 전문직은 자기 분야에 대한 전문성과 지식을 인정받기 때문에, 회사를 위해서 일할 필요가 없으며 의뢰인도 이들의 지식을 신뢰한다는 내용이 글 중반까지 나온다. 하지만 'Journalists hold knowledge, ~' 이후로는 저널리스트들의 상황이 '다르다'는 내용이 주를 이룬다. 이들은 회사에 '종속되어' 일하므로 '업무 독립성에 제약이 있다'는 것이다.

★★★ 등급을 가르는 문제!
34 어느 정도의 정부 개입이 불가피한 자유 시장 경제   정답률 33% | 정답 ①

다음 빈칸에 들어갈 말로 가장 적절한 것을 고르시오. [3점]
✓ markets are rarely left entirely free – 시장이 완전히 자유로운 상태로 맡겨지는 경우는 드물다
② governments are reluctant to intervene – 정부는 개입하기를 꺼린다
③ supply and demand are not always balanced – 수요와 공급은 항상 균형이 맞는 것은 아니다
④ economic inequality continues to get worse – 경제적 불평등은 계속해서 심해지고 있다
⑤ competition does not guarantee the maximum profit – 경쟁은 최대 이익을 보장해주지 못한다

In most of the world, / capitalism and free markets are accepted today / as constituting the best system / for allocating economic resources and encouraging economic output.
세계 대부분에서 / 오늘날 자본주의와 자유 시장은 받아들여지고 있다. / 최고의 시스템을 구성하는 것으로 / 경제적 자원을 분배하고 경제적 생산을 장려하기 위한

Nations have tried other systems, / such as socialism and communism, / but in many cases / they have either switched wholesale / or adopted aspects of free markets.
국가들은 다른 시스템들을 시도했지만, / 사회주의나 공산주의와 같은 / 많은 경우 / 그들은 (자유 시장으로) 완전히 전환하거나 / 자유 시장의 측면들을 받아들였다.

Despite the widespread acceptance of the freemarket system, / markets are rarely left entirely free.
자유 시장 시스템의 광범위한 수용에도 불구하고, / 시장이 완전히 자유로운 상태로 맡겨지는 경우는 드물다.

Government involvement takes many forms, / ranging from the enactment and enforcement of laws and regulations / to direct participation in the economy / through entities like the U.S.'s mortgage agencies.
정부의 개입은 다양한 형태를 취한다. / 법과 규정의 제정과 집행에서부터 / 직접적인 경제 참여에 이르기까지 / 미국의 담보 기관과 같은 실체를 통한

Perhaps the most important form of government involvement, / however, / comes in the attempts of central banks and national treasuries / to control and affect the ups and downs of economic cycles.
아마도 가장 중요한 형태의 정부 개입은 / 그러나 / 중앙은행과 국가 재무기관의 시도로 나타날 것이다. / 경기 주기의 흥망성쇠를 통제하고 영향을 미치려는

오늘날 세계 대부분에서 자본주의와 자유 시장은 경제적 자원을 분배하고 경제적 생산을 장려하기 위한 최고의 시스템을 구성하는 것으로 받아들여지고 있다. 국가들은 사회주의나 공산주의와 같은 다른 시스템들을 시도했지만, 많은 경우 그들은 자유 시장으로 완전히 전환하거나 자유 시장의 측면들을 받아들였다. 자유 시장 시스템의 광범위한 수용에도 불구하고, 시장이 완전히 자유로운 상태로 맡겨지는 경우는 드물다. 정부의 개입은 법과 규정의 제정과 집행에서부터 미국의 담보 기관과 같은 실체를 통한 직접적인 경제 참여에 이르기까지 다양한 형태를 취한다. 그러나 아마도 가장 중요한 형태의 정부 개입은 중앙은행과 국가 재무기관이 경기 주기의 흥망성쇠를 통제하고 영향을 미치려는 시도로 나타날 것이다.

Why? 왜 정답일까?
빈칸 앞에서 오늘날 세계 대부분의 국가가 자유 시장 경제를 받아들였다고 이야기하는데, 빈칸 뒤에서는 자유 시장 경제 체제 안에서도 이루어질 수밖에 없는 정부 개입(Government involvement)에 관해 설명하고 있다. 따라서 빈칸에 들어갈 말로 가장 적절한 것은 ① '시장이 완전히 자유로운 상태로 맡겨지는 경우는 드물다'이다.

- capitalism ⓝ 자본주의
- allocate ⓥ 배분하다, 할당하다
- communism ⓝ 공산주의
- enforcement ⓝ 시행, 집행
- mortgage ⓝ (담보) 대출
- ups and downs 흥망성쇠
- intervene ⓥ 개입하다
- constitute ⓥ 구성하다
- socialism ⓝ 사회주의
- wholesale ⓐⓓ 완전히, 모조리
- regulation ⓝ 규정, 규제
- treasury ⓝ 재무부, 금고
- reluctant ⓐ 꺼리는, 마지못해 하는

구문 풀이
6행 Despite the widespread acceptance of the freemarket system, markets are rarely left entirely free.
전치사(~에도 불구하고)   5형식 수동태   보어(형용사구)

▶ 많이 틀린 이유는?
②는 '정부가 개입을 꺼린다'는 의미인데, 빈칸 뒤를 보면 실제 자본주의 체계에서 일어나는 다양한 정부 개입의 형태를 언급하고 있다. 이는 정부가 시장 개입을 자제한다기보다 오히려 단행한다는 뜻이다.

▶ 문제 해결 방법은?
글 중간에 나온 빈칸에 대한 힌트는 빈칸 뒤에 있음을 명심하자. 여기서도 빈칸 뒤를 보면, 정부 개입은 실제로 다양한 형태로 발생하고, 그중에서도 가장 중요한 개입은 중앙 은행이나 국가 재무기관의 조치로 나타난다는 내용이 제시된다. 이를 토대로 볼 때, '정부 개입이 이뤄진다 = 시장을 가만히 내버려두는 경우는 잘 없다'는 내용이 빈칸에 들어가야 한다.

35 인플레이션에 따르는 위험
정답률 62% | 정답 ④

다음 글에서 전체 흐름과 관계 없는 문장은?

Inflationary risk refers to uncertainty / regarding the future real value of one's investments.
인플레이션에 의한 위험성은 불확실성과 관련되어 있다 / 개인 투자의 미래 실질 가치에 대한

Say, for instance, / that you hold $100 in a bank account / that has no fees and accrues no interest.
예를 들어, 말해보자. / 당신이 은행 계좌에 100달러를 가지고 있다고 / 수수료가 없고 이자가 생기지 않는

If left untouched / there will always be $100 in that bank account.
그대로 내버려 두면, / 그 은행 계좌에는 항상 100달러가 있을 것이다.

① If you keep that money in the bank for a year, / during which inflation is 100 percent, / you've still got $100.
만약 당신이 1년 동안 은행에 그 돈을 보관하고 / 그 기간에 인플레이션이 100퍼센트라면, / 당신은 여전히 100달러만 가지고 있는 것이다.

② Only now, / if you take it out and put it in your wallet, / you'll only be able to purchase half the goods / you could have bought a year ago.
이제, / 만약 당신이 그 돈을 인출해서 지갑에 넣어둔다면, / 당신은 물건들의 반만 구매할 수 있게 될 것이다. / 1년 전에 당신이 살 수도 있었던

③ In other words, / if inflation increases faster / than the amount of interest you are earning, / this will decrease the purchasing power of your investments over time.
다시 말하자면, / 만약 인플레이션이 더 빨리 증가한다면, / 당신이 받고 있는 이자의 양보다 / 이것은 시간이 지남에 따라 당신 투자의 구매력을 감소시킬 것이다.

④ It would be very useful to know in advance / what would happen to your firm's total revenue / if you increased your product's price.
미리 아는 것은 매우 유용할 것이다. / 회사 총수입에 어떤 일이 일어날지를 / 만약 당신이 상품의 가격을 올린다면

⑤ That's why we differentiate / between nominal value and real value.
그것이 우리가 구별하는 이유이다. / 명목 가치와 실질 가치를

인플레이션에 의한 위험성은 개인 투자의 미래 실질 가치에 대한 불확실성과 관련되어 있다. 예를 들어, 당신이 수수료가 없고 이자가 생기지 않는 은행 계좌에 100달러를 가지고 있다고 하자. 그대로 내버려 두면, 그 은행 계좌에는 항상 100달러가 있을 것이다. ① 만약 당신이 1년 동안 은행에 그 돈을 보관하고 그 기간에 인플레이션이 100퍼센트라면, 당신은 여전히 100달러만 가지고 있는 것이다. ② 이제, 만약 당신이 그 돈을 인출해서 지갑에 넣어둔다면, 당신은 1년 전에 당신이 살 수도 있었던 물건들의 반만 구매할 수 있게 될 것이다. ③ 다시 말하자면, 만약 인플레이션이 당신이 받고 있는 이자의 양보다 더 빨리 증가한다면, 이것은 시간이 지남에 따라 당신 투자의 구매력을 감소시킬 것이다. ④ 만약 당신이 상품의 가격을 올린다면 회사 총수입에 어떤 일이 일어날지를 미리 아는 것은 매우 유용할 것이다. ⑤ 그것이 우리가 명목 가치와 실질 가치를 구별하는 이유이다.

Why? 왜 정답일까?

인플레이션에 수반되는 위험에 관해 설명하는 글로, ①부터 예시를 소개한 뒤 마지막 문장에서 이러한 위험 때문에 명목 가치와 실질 가치가 구분되어야 한다는 결론을 도출하고 있다. 하지만 ④는 상품 가격을 올렸을 때 총수입에 어떤 영향이 있을 것인지 알면 좋다는 내용이므로 흐름상 어색하다. 따라서 전체 흐름과 관계 없는 문장은 ④이다.

- uncertainty ⓝ 불확실성
- account ⓝ 계좌, 계정
- differentiate ⓥ 구분하다, 구별하다
- investment ⓝ 투자
- total revenue 총수입

구문 풀이

3행 If (it is) left untouched there will always be $100 in that bank account.
접속사 / 생략 / 과거분사구 / 동사 / 주어

36 촉감 수용체의 분포
정답률 47% | 정답 ⑤

주어진 글 다음에 이어질 글의 순서로 가장 적절한 것을 고르시오.

① (A) - (C) - (B)
② (B) - (A) - (C)
③ (B) - (C) - (A)
④ (C) - (A) - (B)
⑤ (C) - (B) - (A) ✓

Touch receptors are spread over all parts of the body, / but they are not spread evenly.
촉감 수용체는 신체 곳곳에 퍼져 있지만 / 그것들은 골고루 퍼져 있지는 않다.

Most of the touch receptors / are found in your fingertips, tongue, and lips.
대부분의 촉감 수용체는 / 손가락 끝, 혀, 그리고 입술에서 발견된다.

(C) On the tip of each of your fingers, for example, / there are about five thousand separate touch receptors.
예를 들어, 각각의 손가락 끝에는 / 약 5천 개의 서로 떨어져 있는 촉감 수용체가 있다.

In other parts of the body / there are far fewer.
몸의 다른 부분에서는 / 훨씬 더 적다.

In the skin of your back, / the touch receptors may be as much as 2 inches apart.
당신의 등 피부에는 / 촉감 수용체가 2인치만큼 떨어져 있을 수도 있다.

(B) You can test this for yourself.
당신은 스스로 이것을 테스트해 볼 수 있다.

Have someone poke you in the back with one, two, or three fingers / and try to guess how many fingers the person used.
누군가에게 당신의 등을 한 손가락, 두 손가락, 또는 세 손가락으로 찌르게 하고 / 그 사람이 얼마나 많은 손가락을 사용했는지 추측해 보라.

If the fingers are close together, / you will probably think it was only one.
만약 손가락이 서로 가까이 붙어 있다면, / 당신은 아마 그것이 한 개라고 생각할 것이다.

(A) But if the fingers are spread far apart, / you can feel them individually.
하지만 만약 손가락끼리 멀리 떨어져 있다면, / 당신은 그것들을 각각 느낄 수 있다.

Yet if the person does the same thing on the back of your hand / (with your eyes closed, / so that you don't see how many fingers are being used), / you probably will be able to tell easily, / even when the fingers are close together.
하지만 만약 그 사람이 당신의 손등에 똑같이 해보면(당신의 눈을 감은 채로 / 몇 개의 손가락이 사용되고 있는지 당신이 모르도록) / 당신은 아마 쉽게 구별할 수 있을 것이다. / 손가락이 서로 가까이 있을 때조차도

촉감 수용체는 신체 곳곳에 퍼져 있지만 골고루 퍼져 있지는 않다. 대부분의 촉감 수용체는 손가락 끝, 혀, 그리고 입술에서 발견된다.

(C) 예를 들어, 각각의 손가락 끝에는 별개의 촉감 수용체가 약 5천 개있다. 몸의 다른 부분에는 훨씬 더 적다. 당신의 등 피부에는 촉감 수용체가 2인치만큼 떨어져 있을 수도 있다.

(B) 당신은 스스로 이것을 테스트해 볼 수 있다. 누군가에게 당신의 등을 한 손가락, 두 손가락, 또는 세 손가락으로 찌르게 하고 그 사람이 손가락을 몇 개 사용했는지 추측해 보라. 만약 손가락이 서로 가까이 붙어 있다면, 당신은 아마 그것이 한 개라고 생각할 것이다.

(A) 하지만 만약 손가락끼리 멀리 떨어져 있다면, 당신은 그것들을 각각 느낄 수 있다. 하지만 만약 그 사람이 당신의 손등에 똑같이 해보면(몇 개의 손가락이 사용되고 있는지 모르도록 눈을 감은 채로), 당신은 아마 손가락이 서로 가까이 있을 때조차도 쉽게 구별할 수 있을 것이다.

Why? 왜 정답일까?

촉감 수용체의 분포에 관해 언급하는 주어진 글 뒤로, 손가락 끝과 다른 부분을 예를 들어 비교하는 (C), 촉감 수용체를 테스트하는 과정에 대한 설명으로 넘어가는 (B), 설명을 이어 가는 (A)가 차례로 이어져야 자연스럽다. 따라서 글의 순서로 가장 적절한 것은 ⑤ '(C) - (B) - (A)'이다.

- receptor ⓝ 수용체
- individually ⓐⓓ 개별적으로
- poke ⓥ 쿡 찌르다
- fingertip ⓝ 손가락 끝
- for oneself 스스로, 혼자 힘으로
- separate ⓐ 각각의, 별개의 ⓥ 분리하다

구문 풀이

5행 Yet if the person does the same thing on the back of your hand (with your eyes closed, so that you don't see how many fingers are being used), you probably will be able to tell easily, even when the fingers are close together.

37 네크워크 시장에서 역사의 중요성
정답률 64% | 정답 ③

주어진 글 다음에 이어질 글의 순서로 가장 적절한 것을 고르시오. [3점]

① (A) - (C) - (B)
② (B) - (A) - (C)
③ (B) - (C) - (A) ✓
④ (C) - (A) - (B)
⑤ (C) - (B) - (A)

One interesting feature of network markets / is that "history matters."
네트워크 시장의 한 가지 흥미로운 특징은 / '역사가 중요하다'라는 것이다.

A famous example is the QWERTY keyboard / used with your computer.
한 가지 유명한 예는 QWERTY 키보드이다. / 컴퓨터와 함께 사용되는

(B) You might wonder / why this particular configuration of keys, / with its awkward placement of the letters, / became the standard.
당신은 의아해할지도 모른다. / 이 독특한 키의 배열이 왜 / 어색한 문자 배치를 가진, / 표준이 되었는지

The QWERTY keyboard in the 19th century was developed / in the era of manual typewriters with physical keys.
19세기 QWERTY 키보드는 개발되었다. / 물리적 키가 있는 수동 타자기 시대에

(C) The keyboard was designed / to keep frequently used keys (like E and O) physically separated / in order to prevent them from jamming.
그 키보드는 설계되었다. / 자주 사용되는 (E와 O 같은) 키가 물리적으로 떨어져 있도록 / 그것들이 걸리는 것을 막기 위해

By the time the technology for electronic typing evolved, / millions of people had already learned / to type on millions of QWERTY typewriters.
전자 타이핑 기술이 발전했을 무렵, / 수백만 명의 사람들이 이미 배운 상태였다. / 수백만 개의 QWERTY 타자기에서 타자 치는 법을

(A) Replacing the QWERTY keyboard with a more efficient design / would have been both expensive and difficult to coordinate.
QWERTY 키보드를 더 효율적인 디자인으로 교체하는 것은 / 비용이 많이 들고 조정하기 어려웠을 것이다.

Thus, / the placement of the letters / stays with the obsolete QWERTY / on today's English-language keyboards.
따라서, / 문자의 배치는 / 구식 QWERTY로 남아 있다. / 오늘날의 영어 키보드에서

네트워크 시장의 한 가지 흥미로운 특징은 '역사가 중요하다'라는 것이다. 한 가지 유명한 예는 컴퓨터와 함께 사용되는 QWERTY 키보드이다.

(B) 당신은 문자 배치가 어색한 이 독특한 키의 배열이 왜 표준이 되었는지 의아해할지도 모른다. 19세기 QWERTY 키보드는 물리적 키가 있는 수동 타자기 시대에 개발되었다.

(C) 그 키보드는 자주 사용되는 (E와 O 같은) 키가 걸리는 것을 막기 위해 물리적으로 떨어져 있도록 설계되었다. 전자 타이핑 기술이 발전했을 무렵, 수백만 명의 사람들이 이미 수백만 개의 QWERTY 타자기에서 타자 치는 법을 배운 상태였다.

(A) QWERTY 키보드를 더 효율적인 디자인으로 교체하는 것은 비용이 많이 들고 조정하기 어려웠을 것이다. 따라서, 오늘날의 영어 키보드에서 문자의 배치는 구식 QWERTY로 남아 있다.

Why? 왜 정답일까?

네트워크 시장에서 역사가 중요하다는 일반적인 내용과 함께 QWERTY 키보드의 사례를 언급하는 주어진 글 뒤로, 이 독특한 키보드가 수동 타자기 시대에 개발되었다는 배경을 설명하는 (B)가 먼저 연결된다. 이어서 (C)는 QWERTY 배열이 왜 특이하게 설계되었는지를 설명한 후, 전자 타이핑 기술이 발전했을

무렵에는 이미 QWERTY 키보드가 너무 많이 쓰이고 있었음을 언급하고, (A)는 그래서 QWERTY가 계속 그대로 쓰이게 되었다는 결론을 제시한다. 따라서 글의 순서로 가장 적절한 것은 ③ '(B) – (C) – (A)'이다.

- coordinate ⓥ 조정하다
- awkward ⓐ 어색한
- prevent A from B A가 B하지 못하게 하다
- placement ⓝ 배열
- typewriter ⓝ 타자기
- jam ⓥ 걸리다, 움직이지 않게 하다

구문 풀이

4행 Replacing the QWERTY keyboard with a more efficient design
　　　　　동명사구 주어
would have been both expensive and difficult to coordinate.
「would have + 과거분사」: ~했을 것이다(과거 추측)

---

38 온도와 색의 연관성　　　정답률 48% | 정답 ④

글의 흐름으로 보아, 주어진 문장이 들어가기에 가장 적절한 곳을 고르시오. [3점]

One way of measuring temperature occurs / if an object is hot enough to visibly glow, / such as a metal poker / that has been left in a fire.
온도를 측정하는 한 가지 방법은 생긴다. / 물체가 눈에 띄게 빛이 날 정도로 뜨거울 때 / 금속 부지깽이처럼 / 불 속에 놓아둔
① The color of a glowing object / is related to its temperature: / as the temperature rises, / the object is first red and then orange, / and finally it gets white, the "hottest" color.
빛나는 물체의 색은 / 온도와 관련 있는데, / 온도가 상승함에 따라 / 물체는 먼저 빨간색, 이후 주황색으로 변하고, / 마지막으로 '가장 뜨거운' 색인 흰색이 된다.
② The relation / between temperature and the color of a glowing object / is useful to astronomers.
관련성은 / 온도와 빛나는 물체의 색 사이의 / 천문학자들에게 유용하다.
③ The color of stars is related to their temperature, / and since people cannot as yet travel the great distances to the stars / and measure their temperature in a more precise way, / astronomers rely on their color.
별의 색은 별의 온도와 관련이 있고, / 사람들이 아직 별까지 먼 거리를 이동할 수 없기 때문에 / 그리고 더 정확한 방법으로 별의 온도를 측정할 수 없기에, / 천문학자들은 별의 색에 의존한다.
✔ This temperature is of the surface of the star, / the part of the star / which is emitting the light that can be seen.
이 온도는 별 표면의 온도이다. / 별의 부분인, / 보일 수 있는 빛을 방출하는
The interior of the star / is at a much higher temperature, / though it is concealed.
별의 내부는 / 온도가 훨씬 더 높다. / 비록 그것이 숨겨져 있지만
⑤ But / the information obtained from the color of the star / is still useful.
하지만 / 별의 색깔에서 얻은 정보는 / 여전히 유용하다.

온도를 측정하는 한 가지 방법은 불 속에 놓아둔 금속 부지깽이처럼 물체가 눈에 띄게 빛이 날 정도로 뜨거울 때 생긴다. ① 빛나는 물체의 색은 온도와 관련 있는데, 온도가 상승함에 따라 물체는 먼저 빨간색, 이후 주황색으로 변하고, 마지막으로 '가장 뜨거운' 색인 흰색이 된다. ② 온도와 빛나는 물체의 색 사이의 관련성은 천문학자들에게 유용하다. ③ 별의 색은 별의 온도와 관련이 있고, 사람들이 아직 별까지 먼 거리를 이동하고 더 정확한 방법으로 별의 온도를 측정할 수 없기에, 천문학자들은 별의 색에 의존한다. ④ 이 온도는 보일 수 있는 빛을 방출하는 별의 부분인 별 표면의 온도이다. 별의 내부는 비록 숨겨져 있지만, 온도가 훨씬 더 높다. ⑤ 하지만 별의 색깔에서 얻은 정보는 여전히 유용하다.

Why? 왜 정답일까?

④ 앞에서 별의 색은 별의 온도와 관련된다고 하는데, 주어진 문장은 '이 온도'가 별 표면의 온도임을 보충 설명하고, ④ 뒤에서는 표면이 아닌 내부의 온도가 훨씬 더 높음을 자연스럽게 부연한다. 따라서 주어진 문장이 들어가기에 가장 적절한 곳은 ④이다.

- surface ⓝ 표면
- measure ⓥ 측정하다
- glow ⓥ 빛나다
- astronomer ⓝ 천문학자
- rely on ~에 의존하다
- emit ⓥ (빛이나 열을) 뿜다
- visibly ⓐⓓ 눈에 보이게
- poker ⓝ 부지깽이
- precise ⓐ 정확한
- interior ⓝ 내부 ⓐ 내부의

구문 풀이

3행 One way of measuring temperature occurs if an object is hot enough to
　　　　　주어　　　　　　　　　　　　　동사(단수)　　　　「형/부 + enough + to부정사」
visibly glow, such as a metal poker [that has been left in a fire].
~할 만큼 충분히　한/하게)　　선행사　주격 관·대

---

39 창의력 지수　　　정답률 52% | 정답 ②

글의 흐름으로 보아, 주어진 문장이 들어가기에 가장 적절한 곳을 고르시오.

The holy grail of the first wave of creativity research / was a personality test / to measure general creativity ability, / in the same way that IQ measured general intelligence.
창의성 연구의 첫 번째 물결의 성배는 / 성격 검사였다. / 전반적인 창의력을 측정하기 위한 / IQ가 전반적인 지능을 측정했던 것과 같은 방식으로
① A person's creativity score should tell us / his or her creative potential in any field of endeavor, / just like an IQ score is not limited to physics, math, or literature.
한 사람의 창의성 점수는 우리에게 알려줄 것이었다. / 노력하는 어떤 분야에서든 그 사람의 창의적 잠재력을 / IQ 점수가 물리학, 수학 또는 문학에 국한되지 않는 것과 마찬가지로
✔ But by the 1970s, / psychologists realized / there was no such thing as a general "creativity quotient."
그러나 1970년대에, / 심리학자들은 깨달았다. / 전반적인 '창의성 지수' 같은 것은 없음을
Creative people aren't creative in a general, universal way; / they're creative in a specific sphere of activity, / a particular domain.
창의적인 사람들은 전반적이고 보편적으로 창의적인 것은 아니어서, / 이들은 활동의 특정 범위에서 창의적이다. / 즉 특정 영역
③ We don't expect a creative scientist / to also be a gifted painter.
우리는 창의적인 과학자에게 기대하지 않는다. / 재능 있는 화가도 될 것이라고
④ A creative violinist may not be a creative conductor, / and a creative conductor may not be very good / at composing new works.
창의적인 바이올린 연주자는 창의적인 지휘자가 아닐 수도 있고, / 창의적인 지휘자는 매우 뛰어나지 않을 수도 있다. / 새로운 곡을 작곡하는 데

---

⑤ Psychologists now know / that creativity is domain specific.
심리학자들은 이제 안다. / 창의성이 특정 영역에만 한정된 것이라는 것을

창의성 연구의 첫 번째 급증의 궁극적 목표는 IQ가 전반적인 지능을 측정했던 것과 같은 방식으로 전반적인 창의력을 측정하기 위한 성격 검사였다. ① 한 사람의 창의성 점수는 IQ 점수가 물리학, 수학 또는 문학에 국한되지 않는 것과 마찬가지로, 그 사람이 노력하는 어떤 분야에서든 그 사람의 창의적 잠재력을 우리에게 알려줄 것이었다. ② 그러나 1970년대에, 심리학자들은 전반적인 '창의성 지수' 같은 것은 없음을 깨달았다. 창의적인 사람들은 전반적이고 보편적으로 창의적인 것은 아니어서, 이들은 활동의 특정 범위, 즉 특정 영역에서 창의적이다. ③ 우리는 창의적인 과학자가 재능 있는 화가도 되리라고 기대하지 않는다. ④ 창의적인 바이올린 연주자는 창의적인 지휘자가 아닐 수도 있고, 창의적인 지휘자는 새로운 곡을 작곡하는 데 매우 뛰어나지 않을 수도 있다. ⑤ 심리학자들은 이제 창의성이 특정 영역에만 한정된 것이라는 것을 안다.

Why? 왜 정답일까?

창의적 연구 초창기에는 전반적인 창의력을 측정하고자 했다는 내용이 ② 앞에 나오는데, 주어진 문장은 But으로 흐름을 전환시키며 1970년대부터 전반적인 창의력 지수라는 것은 없다는 인식이 생겨났다고 설명한다. ② 뒤에서는 창의적인 사람들이 전반적 또는 보편적으로 창의적인 것은 아니라는 보충 설명으로 주어진 문장 내용을 뒷받침한다. 따라서 주어진 문장이 들어가기에 가장 적절한 곳은 ②이다.

- endeavor ⓝ 노력
- literature ⓝ 문학
- sphere ⓝ 범위, 영역
- conductor ⓝ 지휘자
- physics ⓝ 물리학
- universal ⓐ 보편적인
- domain ⓝ 영역

구문 풀이

1행 The holy grail of the first wave of creativity research was a personality test
　　　　　주어　　　　　　　　　　　　　　　　　　　　　동사(단수)　　　주격 보어
to measure general creativity ability, in the same way that IQ measured general
형용사적 용법　　　　　　　　　　　　　　~와 같은 방법으로
intelligence.

---

40 과학자와 운동선수의 차이점　　　정답률 53% | 정답 ②

다음 글의 내용을 한 문장으로 요약하고자 한다. 빈칸 (A), (B)에 들어갈 말로 가장 적절한 것은?

	(A)		(B)		(A)		(B)
①	confident 자신 있는	······	keep 유지해야	✔②	skeptical 회의적인	······	eliminate 없애야
③	arrogant 거만한	······	express 표현해야	④	critical 비판적인	······	keep 유지해야
⑤	stubborn 고집 센	······	eliminate 제거하다				

The great irony of performance psychology / is that it teaches each sportsman to believe, / as far as he is able, / that he will win.
퍼포먼스 심리학의 큰 아이러니는 / 개개의 운동선수들이 믿도록 가르친다는 것이다. / 그가 능력이 되는 한 / 그가 이길 것이라고
No man doubts.
어느 누구도 의심하지 않는다.
No man indulges his inner skepticism.
어느 누구도 내면의 회의에 빠지지 않는다.
That is the logic of sports psychology.
그것이 스포츠 심리학의 논리이다.
But only one man can win.
하지만 오직 한 사람만이 이길 수 있다.
That is the logic of sport.
그것이 스포츠의 논리이다.
Note the difference between a scientist and an athlete.
과학자와 운동선수의 차이점을 주목하라.
Doubt is a scientist's stock in trade.
의심은 과학자의 일상적인 업무이다.
Progress is made by focusing on the evidence / that refutes a theory / and by improving the theory accordingly.
진보는 증거에 집중함으로 이루어진다. / 이론을 반박하는 / 그리고 그에 따라 이론을 개선하여
Skepticism is the rocket fuel of scientific advance.
회의론은 과학적 진보의 추진 연료이다.
But doubt, to an athlete, is poison.
하지만 운동선수에게 의심은 독이다.
Progress is made by ignoring the evidence; / it is about creating a mindset / that is immune to doubt and uncertainty.
진보는 증거를 무시함으로 만들어지고, / 그것은 사고방식을 만드는 것이다. / 의심과 불확실성에 영향을 받지 않는
Just to reiterate:
다시 한 번 말하자면 이렇다.
From a rational perspective, / this is nothing less than crazy.
이성적인 시각에서 보면 / 이는 미친 짓이나 다름없다.
Why should an athlete convince himself he will win / when he knows / that there is every possibility he will lose?
왜 운동선수는 이길 것이라고 확신해야 하는가? / 그가 알 때 / 자신이 질 거라는 모든 가능성이 있다는 것을
Because, to win, / one must proportion one's belief, / not to the evidence, / but to whatever the mind can usefully get away with.
왜냐하면 이기려면 / 선수는 자기 신념을 할당해야 하기 때문이다. / 증거가 아니라 / 마음이 유용하게 해낼 수 있는 무엇이든지 간에
➡ Unlike scientists / whose (A) skeptical attitude is needed / to make scientific progress, / sports psychology says / that to succeed, / athletes must (B) eliminate feelings of uncertainty / about whether they can win.
과학자들과는 달리, / 회의적인 태도가 요구되는 / 과학적 진보를 이루기 위해 / 스포츠 심리학은 말한다. / 성공하려면 / 운동선수들이 불확실한 감정을 없애야 한다고 / 그들이 이길 수 있는지에 대한

퍼포먼스 심리학의 큰 아이러니는 개개의 운동선수들이 능력이 되는 한 이길 것이라고 믿도록 가르친다는 것이다. 어느 누구도 의심하지 않는다. 어느 누구도 내면의 회의에 빠지지 않는다. 그것이 스포츠 심리학의 논리이다. 하지만 오직 한 사람만이 이길 수 있다. 그것이 스포츠의 논리이다. 과학자와 운동선수의 차이점을 주목하라. 의심은 과학자의 일상적인 업무이다. 진보는 이론을 반박하는 증거에 집중하고 그에 따라 이론을 개선하여 이루어진다. 회의론은 과학적 진보의 추진 연료이다. 하지만 운동선수에게 의심은 독이다. 진보는 증거를 무시함으로써

만들어지고, 그것은 의심과 불확실성에 영향을 받지 않는 사고방식을 만드는 것이다. 다시 말하지만, 이성적인 시각에서 보면 이는 미친 짓이나 다름없다. 왜 운동선수는 자신이 질 거라는 모든 가능성이 있다는 것을 알면서도 이길 것이라고 확신해야 하는가? 선수는 이기려면 증거가 아니라 마음이 유용하게 해낼 수 있는 것이 무엇이든 그것에 자기 신념을 할당해야 하기 때문이다.

➡ 과학적 진보를 이루기 위해 (A) 회의적인 태도가 요구되는 과학자들과는 달리, 스포츠 심리학은 운동선수들이 성공하려면 이길 수 있는지에 대한 불확실한 감정을 (B) 없애야 한다고 한다.

Why? 왜 정답일까?

과학자들과 운동선수 간에 차이가 있다(the difference between a scientist and an athlete)는 내용 뒤로, 과학자는 의심을 추진력으로 삼는 반면에 운동선수는 의심 대신 확신을 지녀야 한다(Skepticism is the rocket fuel of scientific advance. But doubt, to an athlete, is poison.)는 설명이 이어진다. 따라서 요약문의 빈칸 (A), (B)에 들어갈 말로 가장 적절한 것은 ② '(A) skeptical (회의적인), (B) eliminate(없애야)'이다.

- **doubt** ⓥ 의심하다 ⓝ 의심
- **skepticism** ⓝ 회의론
- **stock in trade** 상투적 요소, 장사 도구
- **accordingly** ⓐⓓ 그에 따라
- **proportion** ⓥ 적절한 비율로 조화시키다
- **eliminate** ⓥ 없애다, 제거하다
- **stubborn** ⓐ 고집 센, 완고한
- **indulge** ⓥ (~에) 빠지다, 탐닉하다
- **athlete** ⓝ 운동선수
- **refute** ⓥ 반박하다
- **nothing less than** 다름 아닌
- **get away with** ~을 잘 해내다
- **arrogant** ⓐ 거만한

구문 풀이

[1행] The great irony of performance psychology is {that it teaches each sportsman
　　 주어　　　　　　　　　　　　　　　　　　　 동사(단수)
to believe, (as far as he is able), that he will win}.　{ }: 주격 보어(명사절)
목적격 보어　 ( ): 삽입절

41-42 토론에서의 집단 양극화 현상

Common sense suggests / that discussion with others / who express different opinions / should produce more moderate attitudes / for everyone in the group.
상식은 시사한다. / 사람들과의 토론은 / 다른 의견을 내는 / 좀 온건한 태도를 만들어 낼 것이라고 / 그 집단 내의 모든 사람들에게

Surprisingly, this is not always the case.
놀랍게도, 이것이 항상 사실은 아니다.

In group polarization, / a period of discussion pushes group members / to take more extreme positions / in the direction that they were already inclined to prefer.
집단 양극화에서, / 일정 기간의 토론은 집단 구성원들을 압박한다. / 더 극단적인 입장을 취하도록 / 그들이 이미 선호하는 경향이 있던 방향으로

『Group polarization does not (a) reverse the direction of attitudes, / but rather accentuates the attitudes held at the beginning.』 41번의 근거
집단 양극화는 태도의 방향을 뒤집는 것이 아니라, / 오히려 처음에 가졌던 태도를 강화한다.

『Two pressures appear to push individuals / to take more extreme positions following a group discussion.』 42번의 근거
두 가지 압력이 개인들을 압박하는 것으로 보인다. / 집단 토론 후에 더 극단적인 입장을 취하도록

First, / conformity and desire for affiliation / contribute to group polarization.
첫째, / 순응과 소속 욕구는 / 집단 양극화에 기여한다.

If the majority of a group is leaning in a particular direction, / what could be a better way of fitting in / than (b) agreeing with that majority, / and maybe even taking its argument one step farther?
만약 어떤 집단의 다수가 특정한 방향으로 기울어 있다면, / 더 나은 소속 방법이 무엇이겠는가? / 그 다수에 동의하고, / 어쩌면 심지어 그 주장에서 한 걸음 더 나아가는 것보다

There is also a tendency / for like-minded people to affiliate with one another, / which can provide (c) reinforcement for existing opinions, / increase people's confidence in those opinions, / lead to the discovery of new reasons for those opinions / and counterarguments to opposing views, / and reduce exposure to conflicting ideas.
또한 경향이 있는데, / 생각이 비슷한 사람들이 서로 뭉치는 / 이는 기존 의견에 대한 강화를 제공하고, / 그러한 의견에 대한 사람들의 확신을 높이고, / 그러한 의견에 대한 새로운 근거의 발견을 야기하며 / 그리고 상반되는 관점에 대한 반론(의 발견) / 상충되는 생각에의 노출을 줄일 수 있다.

Second, / exposure to discussion on a topic / introduces new reasons for (d) holding an attitude.
둘째, / 주제에 대한 토론에의 노출은 / 태도를 유지하는 데 대한 새로운 이유를 도입한다.

If you are already opposed to gun control / and you listen to additional arguments supporting your position, / you might end up more (e) opposed / than you were originally.
만약 당신이 이미 총기 규제에 반대하고 있으며 / 그리고 당신이 당신의 입장을 지지하는 추가적인 주장을 듣는다면, / 당신은 결국 반대하게 될지도 모른다. / 당신이 원래 그랬던 것보다

상식에 따르면 다른 의견을 내는 사람들과의 토론은 그 집단 내의 모든 사람들에게 좀 더 온건한 태도를 만들어 낼 것이라고 한다. 놀랍게도, 이것이 항상 사실은 아니다. 집단 양극화에서, 일정 기간의 토론은 집단 구성원들이 이미 선호하는 경향이 있던 방향으로 더 극단적인 입장을 취하도록 압박한다. 집단 양극화는 태도의 방향을 (a) 뒤집는 것이 아니라, 오히려 처음에 가졌던 태도를 강화한다. 두 가지 압력이 집단 토론 후에 개인들이 더 극단적인 입장을 취하도록 압박하는 것으로 보인다. 첫째, 순응과 소속 욕구는 집단 양극화에 기여한다. 만약 어떤 집단의 다수가 특정한 방향으로 기울어 있다면, 그 다수에게 (b) 동의하고, 어쩌면 심지어 그 주장에서 한 걸음 더 나아가는 것보다 더 나은 소속 방법이 무엇이겠는가? 또한 생각이 비슷한 사람들은 서로 뭉치는 경향이 있는데, 이는 기존 의견에 대한 (c) 강화를 제공하고, 그러한 의견에 대한 사람들의 확신을 높이고, 그러한 의견에 대한 새로운 근거 및 상반되는 관점에 대한 반론의 발견을 야기하며, 상충되는 생각에의 노출을 줄일 수 있다. 둘째, 주제에 대한 토론에의 노출은 태도를 (d) 바꿀(→ 유지할) 새로운 이유를 도입한다. 만약 당신이 이미 총기 규제에 반대하고 있으며 당신의 입장을 지지하는 추가적인 주장을 듣는다면, 당신은 결국 원래보다 더 (e) 반대하게 될지도 모른다.

- **common sense** 상식
- **be not the case** 사실이 아니다
- **polarization** ⓝ 양극화
- **like-minded** ⓐ 생각이 비슷한
- **counterargument** ⓝ 반론
- **moderate** ⓐ 온건한, 중간의
- **inclined to** ~하는 경향이 있는
- **lean** ⓥ 기울다, 기대다
- **reinforcement** ⓝ 강화
- **opposing** ⓐ 상반되는, 대립되는

- **gun control** 총기 규제
- **companion** ⓝ 동반자
- **end up** 결국 ~이 되다
- **foster** ⓥ 기르다, 육성하다

구문 풀이

[13행] There is also a tendency for like-minded people to affiliate with one
　　　　　　　　　　　　 주어(선행사)　　　　　 의미상 주어　　 형용사적 용법
another, which can provide reinforcement for existing opinions, increase people's
　　　　 계속적 용법　　　　　 동사1
confidence in those opinions, lead to the discovery (of new reasons for those
　　　　　　　　　　　　　 동사2
opinions and counterarguments to opposing views), and reduce exposure to
　　　　　　　　　　　　　　　　　　　　　　　　　　　　 동사4
conflicting ideas.

★★★ 등급을 가르는 문제!

41 제목 파악　　　　　　　　　　　　　　 정답률 41% | 정답 ⑤

윗글의 제목으로 가장 적절한 것은?
① Have More Companions and Perform Better!
　동반자를 더 많이 두어 성과를 높이라!
② Group Competition: Not Necessarily Harmful
　집단 경쟁: 반드시 해롭지는 않다
③ Exposure to New Ideas Weakens Group Identity
　새로운 아이디어에 대한 노출은 집단 정체성을 약화시킨다
④ Sharing Ideas: The Surest Way to Foster Creativity
　아이디어 공유: 창의력을 키우는 가장 확실한 방법
✓⑤ Black Gets Darker, White Gets Brighter in Group Discussion
　집단 토론에서 검은색은 더 검어지고, 흰색은 더 희어진다

Why? 왜 정답일까?

토론 중 집단 양극화 현상으로 원래 갖고 있던 견해가 강화된다(Group polarization ~ accentuates the attitudes held at the beginning.)는 내용을 설명한 글이므로, 글의 제목으로 가장 적절한 것은 ⑤ '집단 토론에서 검은색은 더 검어지고, 흰색은 더 희어진다'이다.

★★ 문제 해결 꿀~팁 ★★

▶ 많이 틀린 이유는?
이 글의 주제는 다른 의견을 가진 사람들끼리 토론한 뒤 서로 견해가 중화되지 않고 도리어 강화될 수 있다는 것이다. 그러나 최다 오답인 ③은 새로운 아이디어를 접하는 것이 집단 정체성을 '약하게 만든다'는 의미로, 주제를 거꾸로 진술하고 있다.

▶ 문제 해결 방법은?
제목 문제에 비유적 표현이 나오면 한 번 더 주의 깊게 살펴봐야 한다. 'Black Gets Darker, White Gets Brighter'는 '검은 것이 더 검어지고, 흰 것은 더 희어진다'는 의미인데, 이는 토론을 통해 각자의 견해가 중립적이 되기는커녕 서로 더 극단으로 향하는 상황을 올바르게 묘사한다.

★★★ 등급을 가르는 문제!

42 어휘 추론　　　　　　　　　　　　　 정답률 36% | 정답 ④

밑줄 친 (a) ~ (e) 중에서 문맥상 낱말의 쓰임이 적절하지 않은 것은? [3점]
① (a)　　② (b)　　③ (c)　　✓④ (d)　　⑤ (e)

Why? 왜 정답일까?

'Two pressures appear to push individuals to take more extreme positions following a group discussion.' 이후로 집단 양극화로 개인이 원래 갖고 있던 견해를 강화해 나가게 되는 이유를 제시한다. (d)가 포함된 문장은 사람들이 견해를 '바꾸지' 않고 '고수하는' 두 번째 이유에 관한 설명이므로, changing을 holding으로 고쳐야 한다. 따라서 문맥상 낱말의 쓰임이 적절하지 않은 것은 ④ '(d)'이다.

★★ 문제 해결 꿀~팁 ★★

▶ 많이 틀린 이유는?
최다 오답인 ③은 서로 생각이 비슷한 사람끼리 뭉치면 나타나는 결과를 설명하며, 비슷한 사람끼리 있으면 원래 가졌던 견해를 '강화'하게 된다는 의미로 reinforcement를 적절히 썼다. 한편, ⑤를 고른 학생들도 많은데, 원래 총기 난사에 '반대하던' 상황에서 추가적인 반대 근거를 들면 '더 반대하게' 될 수 있다는 의미로 opposed를 쓴 것은 적절하다.

▶ 문제 해결 방법은?
④와 ⑤는 사실상 함께 판단해야 하는 선택지이다. ④가 포함된 문장에 대해 예를 드는 문장이 마지막 문장, 즉 ⑤가 포함된 문장이기 때문이다. 마지막 문장의 핵심 내용은 원래 반대하던 사람이 추가로 반대할 이유를 접하면 '더 심하게' 반대하게 된다는 것이다. 이는 기존의 견해를 '바꾸는' 상황이 아니라 '유지하는' 상황에 해당한다.

43-45 소년이 홀로 차분할 수 있었던 이유

(A)
A businessman boarded a flight.
한 사업가가 비행기에 탑승했다.

『Arriving at his seat, / he greeted his travel companions: / a middle-aged woman sitting at the window, / and a little boy sitting in the aisle seat.
자리에 도착한 후, / 그는 여행 동반자들과 인사를 나눴다. / 즉 창가에 앉아 있는 중년 여성과 / 통로 쪽 좌석에 앉아 있는 어린 소년

After putting his bag in the overhead bin, / he took his place between them.』 45번 ①의 근거 일치
가방을 머리 위 짐칸에 넣은 후, / 그는 그들 사이에 앉았다.

After the flight took off, / he began a conversation with the little boy.
비행기가 이륙한 후, / 그는 어린 소년과 대화를 시작했다.

He appeared to be about the same age as (a) his son / and was busy with a coloring book.
그는 그의 아들과 나이가 비슷해 보였고 / 색칠 공부 책을 칠하느라 바빴다.

(D)
He asked the boy a few usual questions, / such as his age, his hobbies, as well as his favorite animal.

He found it strange / that such a young boy would be traveling alone, / so he decided to keep an eye on (e) him / to make sure he was okay.
그는 이상하다고 생각했다 / 그런 어린 소년이 혼자 여행하는 것을 / 그래서 그는 그를 지켜보기로 했다. / 그가 괜찮은지 확인하기 위해

About an hour into the flight, / the plane suddenly began experiencing turbulence.
비행 시작 1시간여 만에 / 비행기가 갑자기 난기류를 타기 시작했다.

『The pilot told everyone / to fasten their seat belts and remain calm, / as they had encountered rough weather.』 45번 ⑤의 근거 일치
조종사는 모든 사람들에게 말했다. / 안전벨트를 매고 침착하라고 / 그들이 악천후를 만났기 때문에

(B)

『As the plane rose and fell several times, / people got nervous and sat up in their seats.』
비행기가 여러 차례 오르락내리락하자 / 사람들은 긴장해 자리에 똑바로 앉았다. 45번 ②의 근거 일치

The man was also nervous / and grabbing (b) his seat as tightly as he could.
그 남자도 긴장해서 / 자기 좌석을 최대한 꽉 잡고 있었다.

Meanwhile, the little boy was sitting quietly beside (c) him.
그러는 동안에도, 어린 소년은 조용히 그의 옆에 앉아 있었다.

『His coloring book and crayons / were put away neatly in the seat pocket in front of him』, / and his hands were calmly resting on his legs.
그의 색칠 공부 책과 크레용은 / 앞 좌석 주머니에 가지런히 치워져 있었고 / 그의 손은 차분히 다리에 놓여 있었다. 45번 ③의 근거 불일치

Incredibly, he didn't seem worried at all.
놀랍게도, 그는 전혀 걱정하지 않는 것처럼 보였다.

(C)

Then, suddenly, the turbulence ended.
그러다가 문득 난기류가 끝났다.

The pilot apologized for the bumpy ride / and announced that they would be landing soon.
조종사는 험난한 비행에 대해 사과하고 / 그들이 곧 착륙할 것이라고 알렸다.

As the plane began its descent, / the man said to the little boy, / "You are just a little boy, / but (d) I have never met a braver person in all my life!
비행기가 하강하기 시작했을 때, / 그 남자는 어린 소년에게 말했다. / "너는 어린 아이에 불과하지만, / 나는 평생 (너보다) 더 용감한 사람을 만난 적이 없어!

Tell me, / how is it that you remained so calm / while all of us adults were so afraid?"
말해주렴, / 네가 어떻게 그렇게 침착하게 있었는지? / 어른들은 모두가 두려워하는데" 45번 ④의 근거 일치

Looking him in the eyes, he said, / "My father is the pilot, and he's taking me home."』
그의 눈을 바라보며 소년은 말했다. / "저희 아빠가 이 비행기 조종사인데, 아빠가 저를 집으로 데려가고 있어요."

(A)

한 사업가가 비행기에 탑승했다. 자리에 도착한 후, 그는 여행 동반자들, 즉 창가에 앉아 있는 중년 여성과 통로 쪽 좌석에 앉아 있는 어린 소년과 인사를 나눴다. 가방을 머리 위 짐칸에 넣은 후, 그는 그들 사이에 앉았다. 비행기가 이륙한 후, 그는 어린 소년과 대화를 시작했다. 그는 (a) 그의 아들과 나이가 비슷해 보였고 색칠 공부 책을 칠하느라 바빴다.

(D)

그는 소년에게 그의 나이, 취미, 좋아하는 동물과 같은 몇 가지 일상적인 질문을 했다. 그는 그런 어린 소년이 혼자 여행하는 것이 이상하다고 생각해서 그가 괜찮은지 확인하기 위해 (e) 그를 지켜보기로 했다. 비행 시작 1시간여 만에 비행기가 갑자기 난기류를 타기 시작했다. 조종사는 악천후를 만났기 때문에 안전벨트를 매고 침착하라고 모든 사람들에게 말했다.

(B)

비행기가 여러 차례 오르락내리락하자 사람들은 긴장해 자리에 똑바로 앉았다. 그 남자도 긴장해서 (b) 자기 좌석을 최대한 꽉 잡고 있었다. 그러는 동안에도, 어린 소년은 조용히 (c) 그의 옆에 앉아 있었다. 그의 색칠 공부 책과 크레용은 앞 좌석 주머니에 가지런히 치워져 있었고, 그의 손은 차분히 다리 위에 놓여 있었다. 놀랍게도, 그는 전혀 걱정하지 않는 것처럼 보였다.

(C)

그러다가 갑자기 난기류가 끝났다. 조종사는 험난한 비행에 대해 사과하고 곧 착륙할 것이라고 알렸다. 비행기가 하강하기 시작했을 때, 그 남자는 어린 소년에게 말했다. "너는 어린 아이에 불과하지만, (d) 나는 평생 (너보다) 더 용감한 사람을 만난 적이 없어! 어른들 모두가 두려워하는데 어떻게 그렇게 침착하게 있었는지 말해 주겠니?" 그의 눈을 바라보며 소년은 말했다. "저희 아빠가 이 비행기 조종사인데, 아빠가 저를 집으로 데려가고 있어요."

- board ⓥ 탑승하다
- middle-aged ⓐ 중년의
- take off 이륙하다
- neatly ⓐⓓ 가지런히, 깔끔하게
- bumpy ride 험난한 주행, 곤란, 우여곡절
- keep an eye on ~을 주시하다
- greet ⓥ 인사하다
- overhead bin (여객기 객석 위에 있는) 짐 넣는 곳
- grab ⓥ 쥐다, 잡다
- rest on ~ 위에 놓여 있다
- descent ⓝ 하강
- rough weather 악천후

구문 풀이

(A) 1행 Arriving at his seat, he greeted his travel companions: a middle-aged
분사구문(~하자)   동격(~자)
woman sitting at the window, and a little boy sitting in the aisle seat.

(B) 2행 The man was also nervous and grabbing his seat as tightly as he could.
「as + 원급 + as ~ can[could] : 최대한 ~하게」

(D) 2행 He found it strange {that such a young boy would be traveling alone}, ~
5형식 동사 목적격 보어 { }: 진목적어(명사절)

43 글의 순서 파악 정답률 78% | 정답 ④

주어진 글 (A)에 이어질 내용을 순서에 맞게 배열한 것으로 가장 적절한 것은?

① (B) – (D) – (C)
② (C) – (B) – (D)
③ (C) – (D) – (B)
④ (D) – (B) – (C) ✓
⑤ (D) – (C) – (B)

Why? 왜 정답일까?

비행기에 탄 사업가가 옆자리의 한 소년을 만났다는 내용의 (A) 뒤로, 두 사람이 탄 비행기가 난기류를 만났다는 내용의 (D), 모두가 두려워하는 와중에 소년이 혼자 걱정하지 않는 듯 보였다는 내용의 (B), 남자가 소년에게 그 이유를 묻자 소년이 아버지가 조종사라고 답했다는 내용의 (C)가 차례로 이어져야 한다. 따라서 글의 순서로 가장 적절한 것은 ④ '(D) – (B) – (C)'이다.

44 지칭 추론 정답률 76% | 정답 ⑤

밑줄 친 (a) ~ (e) 중에서 가리키는 대상이 나머지 넷과 다른 것은?

① (a) ② (b) ③ (c) ④ (d) ✓ (e)

Why? 왜 정답일까?

(a), (b), (c), (d)는 the businessman, (e)는 the young boy를 가리키므로, (a) ~ (e) 중에서 가리키는 대상이 다른 하나는 ⑤ '(e)'이다.

45 세부 내용 파악 정답률 82% | 정답 ③

윗글에 관한 내용으로 적절하지 않은 것은?

① 사업가는 중년 여성과 소년 사이에 앉았다.
② 비행기가 오르락내리락하자 사람들은 긴장했다.
✓ 소년은 색칠 공부 책과 크레용을 가방에 넣었다.
④ 소년은 자신의 아버지가 조종사라고 말했다.
⑤ 조종사는 사람들에게 안전벨트를 매고 침착하라고 말했다.

Why? 왜 정답일까?

(B) 'His coloring book and crayons were put away neatly in the seat pocket in front of him, ~'에서 소년은 색칠 공부 책과 크레용을 앞 좌석 주머니에 치워놓고 차분히 있었다고 하므로, 내용과 일치하지 않는 것은 ③ '소년은 색칠 공부 책과 크레용을 가방에 넣었다.'이다.

Why? 왜 오답일까?

① (A) 'After putting his bag in the overhead bin, he took his place between them.'의 내용과 일치한다.
② (B) 'As the plane rose and fell several times, people got nervous and sat up in their seats.'의 내용과 일치한다.
④ (C) '~ he said, "My father is the pilot, ~'의 내용과 일치한다.
⑤ (D) 'The pilot told everyone to fasten their seat belts and remain calm, ~'의 내용과 일치한다.

어휘 Review Test 08 문제편 080쪽

A		B		C	D
01 그림자		01 adopt		01 ⓟ	01 ⓝ
02 이론적인		02 parenting		02 ⓝ	02 ①
03 성취		03 register		03 ⓗ	03 ⓕ
04 사고		04 mention		04 ⓚ	04 ⓖ
05 반론		05 reverse		05 ⓞ	05 ⓑ
06 간과하다		06 polarization		06 ①	06 ⓜ
07 기여		07 unexpected		07 ⓢ	07 ①
08 불완전한		08 accompany		08 ①	08 ①
09 방해하다		09 subordinate		09 ⓥ	09 ①
10 직업, 일		10 fraction		10 ①	10 ⓒ
11 제왕, 군주		11 investment		11 ⓖ	11 ⓓ
12 다루다, 처리하다		12 awkward		12 ⓓ	12 ⓐ
13 관리, 감독		13 separate		13 ⓑ	13 ⓢ
14 번성하다		14 refute		14 ①	14 ①
15 과신		15 exceptional		15 ①	15 ⓔ
16 분석가		16 placement		16 ⓡ	16 ⓗ
17 가치 없는		17 interior		17 ⓐ	17 ①
18 이해하다		18 coordinate		18 ⓜ	18 ⓚ
19 영역		19 account		19 ⓔ	19 ⓠ
20 통로		20 blessed		20 ⓒ	20 ⓟ

09 회 | 2021학년도 6월 학력평가 [고2]

| 정답과 해설 |

• 정답 •

18 ⑤ 19 ① 20 ② 21 ① 22 ⑤ 23 ② 24 ③ 25 ④ 26 ③ 27 ⑤ 28 ④ 29 ⑤ 30 ④ 31 ① 32 ②
33 ③ 34 ① 35 ③ 36 ⑤ 37 ③ 38 ④ 39 ② 40 ① 41 ④ 42 ⑤ 43 ② 44 ⑤ 45 ⑤

★ 표기된 문항은 [등급을 가르는 문제]에 해당하는 문항입니다.

18　새 동물 보호소를 짓는 데 필요한 기부금 요청　정답률 93% | 정답 ⑤

다음 글의 목적으로 가장 적절한 것은?

① 사무실을 빌려준 것에 대해 감사하려고
② 동물 병원 설립의 필요성을 주장하려고
③ 새롭게 시행되는 동물 보호법에 대해 설명하려고
④ 동물 보호 단체의 봉사 활동 프로그램을 안내하려고
☑ 새로운 동물 보호소를 짓기 위한 기부를 요청하려고

Dear animal lovers,
동물 애호가들께,
I am writing on behalf of the Protect Animal Organization.
저는 Protect Animal Organization을 대표해서 이 글을 씁니다.
Our organization was founded on the belief / that all animals should be respected and treated with kindness, / and must be protected by law.
우리 단체는 믿음으로 설립되었습니다. / 모든 동물들이 존중받고 애정으로 대우받아야 하며, / 법에 의해 보호되어야 한다는
Over the past 20 years, / we have provided lost animals / with protection, new homes, and sometimes health care.
지난 20년 동안, / 우리는 길 잃은 동물들에게 제공해 왔습니다. / 보호, 새로운 집, 그리고 때로는 의료를
Currently, our animal shelter is full, / and we need your help to build a new shelter.
현재, 우리의 동물 보호소는 가득 찼고, / 그래서 우리는 새로운 보호소를 짓기 위해 당신의 도움이 필요합니다.
We are seeking donations in any amount.
우리는 어떤 금액이든 기부금을 받고 있습니다.
Every dollar raised / goes to building homes for animals in need.
모금된 모든 돈은 / 도움이 필요한 동물들을 위한 집을 짓는 데 사용됩니다.
You can donate to us online at www.protectanimal.org.
당신은 www.protectanimal.org에서 온라인으로 저희에게 기부하실 수 있습니다.
Thank you for considering supporting us.
저희에 대한 지원을 고려해 주셔서 감사합니다.
Sincerely, // Stella Anderson
Stella Anderson 드림

동물 애호가들께,

저는 Protect Animal Organization을 대표해서 이 글을 씁니다. 우리 단체는 모든 동물들이 존중받고 애정으로 대우받아야 하며, 법에 의해 보호되어야 한다는 믿음으로 설립되었습니다. 지난 20년 동안, 우리는 길 잃은 동물들에게 보호, 새로운 집, 그리고 때로는 의료를 제공해 왔습니다. 현재, 우리의 동물 보호소는 가득 찼고, 그래서 우리는 새로운 보호소를 짓기 위해 당신의 도움이 필요합니다. 우리는 액수에 관계없이 기부금을 받고 있습니다. 모금된 모든 돈은 도움이 필요한 동물들을 위한 집을 짓는 데 사용됩니다. www.protectanimal.org에서 온라인으로 저희에게 기부하실 수 있습니다. 저희에 대한 지원을 고려해 주셔서 고맙습니다.

Stella Anderson 드림

Why? 왜 정답일까?

'We are seeking donations in any amount. Every dollar raised goes to building homes for animals in need.'에서 새로운 동물 보호소를 짓기 위해 어떤 액수든 기부를 해 달라고 요청하고 있으므로, 글의 목적으로 가장 적절한 것은 ⑤ '새로운 동물 보호소를 짓기 위한 기부를 요청하려고'이다.

● on behalf of ~을 대표하여
● found(-founded-founded) ⓥ 설립하다
● in need 도움이 필요한

구문 풀이

9행　Every dollar raised goes to building homes for animals in need.
　　 주어　　　과거분사　동사(단수)

19　서핑 도중 상어를 맞닥뜨렸다가 무사히 피한 Dave　정답률 93% | 정답 ①

다음 글에 드러난 Dave의 심경 변화로 가장 적절한 것은?

☑ scared → relieved
　 겁먹은　　안도한
② indifferent → proud
　 무관심한　　자랑스러운
③ amazed → horrified
　 놀란　　　겁에 질린
④ hopeful → worried
　 희망에 찬　걱정스러운
⑤ ashamed → grateful
　 부끄러운　고마워하는

Dave sat up on his surfboard and looked around.
Dave는 그의 서핑보드 위에 앉아 주변을 둘러보았다.
He was the last person in the water that afternoon.
그는 그날 오후 물에 있는 마지막 사람이었다.
Suddenly something out toward the horizon / caught his eye / and his heart froze.
갑자기 수평선 위로 무언가가 / 그의 눈을 사로잡았고 / 그의 심장은 얼어붙었다.
It was every surfer's worst nightmare / — the fin of a shark.
그것은 모든 서퍼들의 최악의 악몽, / 바로 상어 지느러미였다.
And it was no more than 20 meters away!
그리고 그것은 단지 20미터 떨어져 있었다!
He turned his board toward the beach / and started kicking his way to the shore.
그는 그의 보드를 해변 쪽으로 돌렸고 / 해안가 쪽으로 발차기를 시작했다.
Shivering, / he gripped his board tighter and kicked harder.
떨면서, / 그는 그의 보드를 더 꽉 붙잡고 더 열심히 발차기를 했다.

'I'm going to be okay,' he thought to himself.
'나는 괜찮을 거야,' 그는 마음속으로 생각했다.
'I need to let go of the fear.'
'나는 공포를 떨쳐낼 필요가 있어.'
Five minutes of terror that felt like a lifetime passed / before he was on dry land again.
한평생처럼 느껴졌던 공포의 5분이 지나갔다. / 그가 육지에 다시 도착하기 전에
Dave sat on the beach and caught his breath.
Dave는 해변에 앉아 한숨 돌렸다.
His mind was at ease.
그의 마음은 이제 편안해졌다.
He was safe.
그는 안전했다.
He let out a contented sigh / as the sun started setting behind the waves.
그는 만족스러운 한숨을 내쉬었다. / 태양이 파도 뒤로 지기 시작할 때

Dave는 그의 서핑보드 위에 앉아 주변을 둘러보았다. 그는 그날 오후 물에 있는 마지막 사람이었다. 갑자기 수평선 위로 무언가가 그의 눈을 사로잡았고 그의 심장은 얼어붙었다. 그것은 모든 서퍼들의 최악의 악몽, 바로 상어 지느러미였다. 그리고 그것은 단지 20미터 떨어져 있었다! 그는 보드를 해변 쪽으로 돌렸고 해안가 쪽으로 발차기를 시작했다. 떨면서, 그는 보드를 더 꽉 붙잡고 더 열심히 발차기를 했다. '나는 괜찮을 거야,' 그는 마음속으로 생각했다. '나는 공포를 떨쳐낼 필요가 있어.' 한평생처럼 느껴졌던 공포의 5분이 지난 후 그는 육지에 다시 도착했다. Dave는 해변에 앉아 한숨 돌렸다. 그의 마음은 이제 편안해졌다. 그는 안전했다. 그는 태양이 파도 뒤로 지기 시작할 때 만족스러운 한숨을 내쉬었다.

Why? 왜 정답일까?

'Suddenly something out toward the horizon caught his eye and his heart froze.'에서 서핑 도중 상어 지느러미를 발견한 Dave가 두려움으로 몸이 얼어붙었다고 묘사한 데 이어, 'His mind was at ease. He was safe. He let out a contented sigh as the sun started setting behind the waves.'에서는 상어를 무사히 피한 Dave가 안도의 한숨을 내쉬었다고 묘사하고 있다. 따라서 Dave의 심경 변화로 가장 적절한 것은 ① '겁먹은 → 안도한'이다.

● nightmare ⓝ 악몽
● shiver ⓥ (몸을) 떨다
● let go of ~을 놓다
● at ease 편안한
● indifferent ⓐ 무관심한
● no more than 단지 ~일 뿐인
● grip ⓥ 잡다
● catch one's breath 한숨 돌리다, 숨을 고르다
● contented ⓐ 만족한
● horrified ⓐ 겁에 질린

구문 풀이

8행　Five minutes of terror [that felt like a lifetime] passed before he was on dry land again.
　　 주어　　　주격 관계대명사　　　　　동사　접속사(~하기 전에)

20　자녀를 비판적으로 비교하는 말 하지 않기　정답률 79% | 정답 ②

다음 글에서 필자가 주장하는 바로 가장 적절한 것은?

① 아이를 칭찬할 때는 일관성 있게 하라.
☑ 자녀를 서로 비교하는 발언을 자제하라.
③ 아이의 발전을 위하여 경쟁을 활용하라.
④ 아이에게 실패를 두려워하지 말라고 가르쳐라.
⑤ 자녀가 구체적인 목표를 설정하도록 조언하라.

Sibling rivalry is natural, / especially between strong-willed kids.
형제간의 경쟁은 자연스러운 것이다. / 특히 의지가 강한 아이들 사이에서
As parents, / one of the dangers / is comparing children unfavorably with each other, / since they are always looking for a competitive advantage.
부모로서, / 위험들 중 하나는 / 아이들을 서로 호의적이지 않게 비교하는 것인데, / 왜냐하면 그들은 항상 경쟁 우위를 찾기 때문이다.
The issue is not how fast a child can run, / but who crosses the finish line first.
문제는 아이가 얼마나 빨리 달릴 수 있느냐가 아니라, / 누가 먼저 결승선을 통과하느냐다.
A boy does not care how tall he is; / he is vitally interested in who is tallest.
아이는 자신이 얼마나 키가 큰지 신경 쓰지 않으며, / 누가 가장 큰지에 매우 관심이 있다.
Children systematically measure themselves against their peers on everything / from skateboarding ability to who has the most friends.
아이들은 모든 것에 대해 자신을 동료들과 비교해서 체계적으로 평가한다. / 스케이트보드 타는 능력에서부터 누가 가장 많은 친구를 가지고 있는지에 이르기까지
They are especially sensitive to any failure / that is talked about openly within their own family.
그들은 어떠한 실패에든 특히 민감하다. / 자기 가족 내에서 공개적으로 이야기되는
Accordingly, / parents who want a little peace at home / should guard against comparative comments / that routinely favor one child over another.
따라서, / 가정의 소소한 평화를 원하는 부모들은 / 비교의 발언에 대해 경계해야 한다. / 일상적으로 한 아이를 다른 아이보다 편애하는
To violate this principle / is to set up even greater rivalry between them.
이 원칙을 위반하는 것은 / 그들 사이에 훨씬 더 큰 경쟁을 만드는 것이다.

형제간의 경쟁은 특히 의지가 강한 아이들 사이에서 자연스러운 것이다. 부모로서, 위험들 중 하나는 아이들을 서로 호의적이지 않게 비교하는 것인데, 왜냐하면 그들은 항상 경쟁 우위를 찾기 때문이다. 문제는 아이가 얼마나 빨리 달릴 수 있느냐가 아니라, 누가 먼저 결승선을 통과하느냐다. 아이는 자신이 얼마나 키가 큰지 신경 쓰지 않으며, 누가 가장 큰지에 매우 관심이 있다. 아이들은 스케이트보드 타는 능력에서부터 누가 가장 많은 친구를 가지고 있는지에 이르기까지 모든 것에 대해 자신을 동료들과 비교해서 체계적으로 평가한다. 그들은 자기 가족 내에서 공개적으로 이야기되는 어떠한 실패에든 특히 민감하다. 따라서, 가정의 소소한 평화를 원하는 부모들은 일상적으로 한 아이를 다른 아이보다 편애하는 비교의 발언에 대해 경계해야 한다. 이 원칙을 위반하는 것은 그들 사이에 훨씬 더 큰 경쟁을 만드는 것이다.

Why? 왜 정답일까?

'Accordingly, parents who want a little peace at home should guard against comparative comments that routinely favor one child over another.'에서 가정의 평화를 유지하고 싶은 부모라면 자녀들끼리 비교하는 발언을 하지 말아야 한다고 언급하는 것으로 볼 때, 필자가 주장하는 바로 가장 적절한 것은 ② '자녀를 서로 비교하는 발언을 자제하라.'이다.

- **strong-willed** ⓐ 의지가 강한
- **competitive advantage** 경쟁 우위
- **systematically** ⓐⓓ 체계적으로
- **guard against** (~이 생기지 않도록) 경계하다, 조심하다
- **violate** ⓥ 위반하다

- **unfavorably** ⓐⓓ 비판적으로, 호의적이지 않게
- **vitally** ⓐⓓ 극도로, 지극히
- **sensitive** ⓐ 민감한, 예민한

구문 풀이

2행 As parents, one of the dangers is comparing children unfavorably with
전치사(~로서)   주어   →동사(단수)   동사(동명사)
each other, since they are always looking for a competitive advantage.
접속사(~이기 때문에)

★★★ 등급을 가르는 문제! ★★★

21 명문화되지 않은 규칙의 완고함   정답률 48% | 정답 ①

밑줄 친 the silent killers가 다음 글에서 의미하는 바로 가장 적절한 것은?

✓① hidden rules that govern our actions unconsciously
우리의 행동을 무의식적으로 통제하는 숨겨진 규칙
② noises that restrict one's level of concentration
사람들의 집중력을 제한하는 소음
③ surroundings that lead to the death of a cat
고양이의 죽음을 초래하는 환경
④ internal forces that slowly lower our self-esteem
우리의 자존감을 서서히 낮추는 내부적인 힘
⑤ experiences that discourage us from following rules
우리가 규칙을 준수하지 않게 만드는 경험

Author Elizabeth Gilbert / tells the fable of a great saint / who would lead his followers in meditation.
작가 Elizabeth Gilbert는 / 위대한 성자의 우화에 대해 이야기한다. / 명상할 때 그의 신도들을 이끌었던
Just as the followers were dropping into their zen moment, / they would be disrupted by a cat / that would walk through the temple / meowing and bothering everyone.
신도들이 선의 순간에 막 빠질 때, / 그들은 고양이에 의해 방해를 받곤 했다. / 사원을 돌아다니는 / 야옹 하고 울고 모든 사람들을 귀찮게 하며
The saint came up with a simple solution:
성자는 간단한 해결책을 생각해 냈다.
He began to tie the cat to a pole during meditation sessions.
그는 명상 시간 동안 고양이를 기둥에 묶기 시작했다.
This solution quickly developed into a ritual:
이 해결책은 빠르게 하나의 의식으로 발전했다.
Tie the cat to the pole first, meditate second.
즉 먼저 고양이를 기둥에 묶고, 그다음에 명상하다.
When the cat eventually died of natural causes, / a religious crisis followed.
고양이가 결국 자연사했을 때, / 종교적 위기가 뒤따랐다.
What were the followers supposed to do?
신도들이 어떻게 해야 하는 것인가?
How could they possibly meditate / without tying the cat to the pole?
어떻게 그들이 명상을 할 수 있을 것인가? / 고양이를 기둥에 묶지 않고
This story illustrates / what I call invisible rules.
이 이야기는 보여 준다 / 내가 보이지 않는 규칙이라고 부르는 것을
These are habits and behaviors / that have unnecessarily rigidified into rules.
이것들은 습관과 행동들이다. / 불필요하게 규칙으로 굳어진
Although written rules can be resistant to change, / invisible ones are more stubborn.
비록 쓰여진 규칙들은 변화에 저항할 수 있지만, / 보이지 않는 규칙들은 더 완고하다.
They're the silent killers.
그것들은 침묵의 살인자이다.

작가 Elizabeth Gilbert는 명상할 때 신도들을 이끌었던 위대한 성자의 우화에 대해 이야기한다. 신도들이 선의 순간에 막 빠질 때, 야옹 하고 울고 모든 사람들을 귀찮게 하며 사원을 돌아다니는 고양이에 의해 방해를 받곤 했다. 성자는 간단한 해결책을 생각해 냈다. 그는 명상 시간 동안 고양이를 기둥에 묶기 시작했다. 이 해결책, 즉 먼저 고양이를 기둥에 묶고, 그다음에 명상하는 것은 빠르게 하나의 의식으로 발전했다. 고양이가 결국 자연사했을 때, 종교적 위기가 뒤따랐다. 신도들이 어떻게 해야 하는 것인가? 어떻게 고양이를 기둥에 묶지 않고 그들이 명상을 할 수 있을 것인가? 이 이야기는 내가 보이지 않는 규칙이라고 부르는 것을 보여 준다. 이것들은 불필요하게 규칙으로 굳어진 습관과 행동들이다. 비록 쓰여진 규칙들은 변화에 저항할 수 있지만, 보이지 않는 규칙들은 더 완고하다. 그것들은 침묵의 살인자이다.

Why? 왜 정답일까?

명상에 앞서 명상을 방해하는 고양이를 매번 기둥에 묶어두는 일부터 하는 것이 규칙처럼 자리잡자, 막상 고양이가 죽었을 때 사람들이 어찌할 바를 몰랐다는 일화가 제시되고 있다. 즉 이는 '불필요한' 규칙 또는 습관에 불과하지만 명문화되어 있지 않아 도리어 사람들의 의식 속에 더 완고하게 자리잡게 되었다는 것(These are habits and behaviors that have unnecessarily rigidified into rules. Although written rules can be resistant to change, invisible ones are more stubborn.)이 글의 논지이다. 밑줄 친 부분에서 이러한 규칙이 '침묵의 살인자'와 같다고 언급한 것은 이 규칙이 우리의 행동을 얼마나 강하게 통제하고 있는지를 비유적으로 나타낸 것이다. 따라서 밑줄 친 부분이 의미하는 바로 가장 적절한 것은 ① '우리의 행동을 무의식적으로 통제하는 숨겨진 규칙'이다.

- **fable** ⓝ 우화
- **disrupt** ⓥ 방해하다, 지장을 주다
- **ritual** ⓝ 의식
- **crisis** ⓝ 위기
- **invisible** ⓐ 보이지 않는
- **resistant** ⓐ (~에) 저항하는, 내성이 있는
- **restrict** ⓥ 제한하다

- **meditation** ⓝ 명상
- **come up with** ~을 떠올리다
- **religious** ⓐ 종교적인
- **illustrate** ⓥ (예를 들어 분명히) 보여주다
- **unnecessarily** ⓐⓓ 불필요하게
- **stubborn** ⓐ 완고한

구문 풀이

2행 Just as the followers were dropping into their zen moment, they would
접속사(바로 ~할 때) 주어   조동사(과거의 습관)←
be disrupted by a cat [that would walk through the temple meowing and bothering
수동태   선행사↑   분사구문1   분사구문2
everyone].

★★ 문제 해결 꿀~팁 ★★

▶ 많이 틀린 이유는?
글로 쓰이지 않은 규칙은 우리 일상에 완고하게 자리잡았을 때 대단한 영향력을 행사한다는 내용의 글이다. 명상을 방해하는 고양이에 관한 이야기는 예시일 뿐이므로 '침묵의 살인자'라는 표현 자체가 고양이를 죽게 하는 환경과 관련되어 있다는 의미의 ③은 답으로 부적절하다.
▶ 문제 해결 방법은?
밑줄 친 부분의 silent는 규칙이 우리 일상을 '우리도 모르게' 통제하고 있다는 의미를, killer는 그 통제가 매우 완고하고 강력하다는 의미를 나타낸다. ①의 hidden, govern, unconsciously를 주의 깊게 보도록 한다.

22 운동 계획을 작게 세워 시작하기   정답률 93% | 정답 ⑤

다음 글의 요지로 가장 적절한 것은?

① 상황에 따른 유연한 태도가 목표 달성에 효과적이다.
② 올바른 식습관과 규칙적인 운동이 건강 유지에 도움이 된다.
③ 나쁜 습관을 고치기 위해서는 장기적인 계획이 필수적이다.
④ 꿈을 이루기 위해서는 원대한 목표를 세우는 것이 중요하다.
✓⑤ 장기적인 성공을 위해 작은 습관부터 시작하는 것이 필요하다.

When it comes to the decision to get more exercise, / you are setting goals / that are similar to running a half marathon / with very little training!
더 많이 운동을 하려는 결정에 관해 말하자면, / 당신은 목표들을 세우고 있다! / 하프 마라톤을 하는 것과 비슷한 / 거의 훈련을 하지 않고
You make a decision to buy a gym membership / and decide to spend an hour at the gym every day.
당신은 헬스장 회원권을 사기로 결정하고 / 매일 헬스장에서 한 시간을 보내기로 결정한다.
Well, you might stick to that for a day or two, / but chances are / you won't be able to continue to meet that commitment / in the long term.
글쎄, 당신은 하루나 이틀은 그것을 지킬 수도 있겠지만, / 그러나 가능성이 있다. / 당신은 그 다짐을 계속 이행할 수 없을 / 장기적으로
If, however, you make a commitment to go jogging for a few minutes a day / or add a few sit-ups to your daily routine before bed, / then you are far more likely to stick to your decision / and to create a habit / that offers you long-term results.
하지만, 만약 당신이 하루에 몇 분씩 조깅을 하기로 다짐한다면 / 또는 잠자리에 들기 전에 매일 루틴에 몇 번의 윗몸 일으키기를 더하기로 / 당신은 당신의 결정을 지킬 가능성이 훨씬 더 높다. / 그리고 습관을 만들 / 당신에게 장기적인 결과를 제공하는
The key is to start small.
핵심은 작게 시작하는 것이다.
Small habits lead to long-term success.
작은 습관들은 장기적인 성공으로 이어진다.

더 많이 운동을 하려는 결정에 관해 말하자면, 당신은 거의 훈련을 하지 않고 하프 마라톤을 하는 것과 비슷한 목표들을 세우고 있다! 당신은 헬스장 회원권을 사기로 결정하고 매일 헬스장에서 한 시간을 보내기로 결정한다. 글쎄, 당신은 하루나 이틀은 그것을 지킬 수도 있겠지만, 장기적으로 그 다짐을 계속 이행할 수 없을 가능성이 있다. 하지만, 만약 당신이 하루에 몇 분씩 조깅을 하거나 잠자리에 들기 전에 매일 루틴에 몇 번의 윗몸 일으키기를 더하기로 다짐한다면, 당신은 당신의 결정을 지키고 당신에게 장기적인 결과를 제공하는 습관을 만들 가능성이 훨씬 더 높다. 핵심은 작게 시작하는 것이다. 작은 습관들은 장기적인 성공으로 이어진다.

Why? 왜 정답일까?

운동의 목표를 거창하게 설정하기보다 하루 조깅 몇 분, 윗몸 일으키기 몇 번과 같은 식으로 작게 잡아 시작하는 것이 좋다(The key is to start small.)는 내용의 글로, 마지막 두 문장에서 핵심 내용을 잘 제시하고 있다. 따라서 글의 요지로 가장 적절한 것은 ⑤ '장기적인 성공을 위해 작은 습관부터 시작하는 것이 필요하다.'이다.

- **when it comes to** ~에 관하여
- **commitment** ⓝ 약속, 다짐, 헌신

- **stick to** ~을 지키다, 고수하다

구문 풀이

1행 When it comes to the decision to get more exercise, you are setting goals
'when it comes to + 명사': ~에 관하여   선행사
[that are similar to running a half marathon with very little training]!
주격 관계대명사 전치사 동명사

23 상상력을 실현하는 창의성   정답률 82% | 정답 ②

다음 글의 주제로 가장 적절한 것은?

① the various meanings of imagination – 상상력의 다양한 의미
✓② creativity as the realization of imagination – 상상력의 실현인 창의성
③ factors which make imaginative people attractive – 상상력이 풍부한 사람들을 매력적으로 만드는 요인
④ the necessity of art education to enhance creativity – 창의성을 증진시키기 위한 예술 교육의 필요성
⑤ effects of a creative attitude on academic achievement – 창의적인 태도가 학업적 성취에 미치는 영향

Creativity is a step further on from imagination.
창의성은 상상력으로부터 한 단계 더 나아간 것이다.
Imagination can be / an entirely private process of internal consciousness.
상상력은 ~일 수 있다. / 내적 의식의 오로지 사적인 과정일
You might be lying motionless on your bed / in a fever of imagination / and no one would ever know.
당신은 침대 위에 움직임 없이 누워있을지도 모르고 / 상상력의 흥분 속에서 / 어느 누구도 그런 사실을 알지 못할 것이다.
Private imaginings / may have no outcomes in the world at all.
사적인 상상력들은 / 이 세상에서 아무 결과도 가지고 있지 않을지도 모른다.
Creativity does.
창의성은 그렇다.
Being creative involves doing something.
창의적인 것은 무언가 하는 것을 수반한다.
It would be odd / to describe as creative / someone who never did anything.
이상할 것이다. / 창의적이라고 묘사하는 것은 / 어떤 것도 절대로 하지 않았던 사람을
To call somebody creative suggests / they are actively producing something in a deliberate way.

086 고2·5개년 영어 독해 [리얼 오리지널]

[문제편 p.082]

누군가를 창의적이라고 부르는 것은 암시한다. / 그들이 의도적인 방식으로 어떤 것을 적극적으로 만들어 내고 있다는 것을

People are not creative in the abstract; / they are creative in something: / in mathematics, in engineering, in writing, in music, in business, in whatever.
사람들은 추상적인 것에서는 창의적이지 않으며, / 어떤 것에서 창의적이다. / 수학, 공학, 글쓰기, 음악, 사업 등등

Creativity involves putting your imagination to work.
창의성은 당신의 상상력을 작동시키는 것을 수반한다.

In a sense, creativity is applied imagination.
어떤 면에서, 창의성은 적용된 상상력이다.

창의성은 상상력으로부터 한 단계 더 나아간 것이다. 상상력은 내적 의식의 오로지 사적인 과정일 수 있다. 당신은 상상력의 흥분 속에서 침대 위에 움직임 없이 누워있을지도 모르고 어느 누구도 그런 사실을 알지 못할 것이다. 사적인 상상력들은 이 세상에서 아무 결과도 가지고 있지 않을지도 모른다. 창의성은 그렇다(결과를 가진다). 창의적인 것은 무언가 하는 것을 수반한다. 어떤 것도 절대로 하지 않았던 사람을 창의적이라고 묘사하는 것은 이상할 것이다. 누군가를 창의적이라고 부르는 것은 그들이 의도적인 방식으로 어떤 것을 적극적으로 만들어 내고 있다는 것을 암시한다. 사람들은 추상적인 것에서는 창의적이지 않으며, 수학, 공학, 글쓰기, 음악, 사업 등등 (구체적인) 어떤 것에서 창의적이다. 창의성은 당신의 상상력을 작동시키는 것을 수반한다. 어떤 면에서, 창의성은 적용된 상상력이다.

Why? 왜 정답일까?

글 전체에 걸쳐 상상력은 결과를 수반하지 않는 데 반해 창의성은 무언가 해내는 것과 결과를 수반한다고 설명하고 있다. 특히 마지막 문장인 'In a sense, creativity is applied imagination.'에서 창의성은 어떤 면에서 적용된 상상력으로 볼 수 있다는 결론을 제시하는 것으로 보아, 글의 주제로 가장 적절한 것은 ② '상상력의 실현인 창의성'이다.

- entirely [ad] 전적으로
- outcome [n] 결과
- deliberate [a] 의도적인
- realization [n] 실현
- necessity [n] 필요성
- internal [a] 내적인
- odd [a] 이상한
- abstract [n] 추상적인 것 [a] 추상적인
- imaginative [a] 상상력이 풍부한

구문 풀이

6행 It would be odd to describe as creative someone [who never did anything].
가주어 / 진주어 / 선행사 / 주격 관계대명사

---

24 뉴스 정보가 제시되는 방식 정답률 60% | 정답 ③

다음 글의 제목으로 가장 적절한 것은?

① Inverted Pyramid: Logically Impossible Structure – 역 피라미드: 논리적으로 불가능한 구조
② Curiosity Is What Makes Readers Keep Reading – 호기심은 독자가 읽기를 계속하게 만드는 것이다
③ Where to Put Key Points in News Writing – 뉴스 작성 시 요점을 어디에 둘 것인가
④ The More Information, the Less Attention – 정보가 더 많을수록 관심이 더 적어진다
⑤ Readers, Tell the Facts from the Fakes! – 독자들이여, 사실과 거짓을 구별하라!

News reporters are taught / to start their stories with the most important information.
뉴스 리포터들은 배운다. / 가장 중요한 정보로 이야기를 시작하도록

The first sentence, called the lead, / contains the most essential elements of the story.
리드라고 불리는 첫 번째 문장은 / 이야기의 가장 본질적인 요소들을 담는다.

A good lead can convey a lot of information.
좋은 리드는 많은 정보를 전달할 수 있다.

After the lead, / information is presented in decreasing order of importance.
리드 후에, / 정보는 중요도가 감소하는 순서로 제시된다.

Journalists call this the "inverted pyramid" structure / — the most important information (the widest part of the pyramid) / is at the top.
언론인들은 이것을 '역 피라미드' 구조라고 부르는데, / 가장 중요한 정보(피라미드의 가장 넓은 부분)가 / 맨 위에 있는 것이다.

The inverted pyramid is great for readers.
역 피라미드는 독자들에게 아주 좋다.

No matter what the reader's attention span / — whether she reads only the lead or the entire story — / the inverted pyramid maximizes the information she gets.
독자의 주의 지속 시간이 어떻든 간에 / 독자가 리드만 읽든 전체 이야기를 읽든 / 역 피라미드는 독자가 얻는 정보를 극대화한다.

Think of the alternative:
다른 방법을 생각해 보라.

If news stories were written like mysteries / with a dramatic payoff at the end, / then readers who broke off in mid-story / would miss the point.
만약 뉴스 이야기들이 미스터리처럼 쓰여진다면, / 마지막에 극적인 결말이 있는 / 이야기 중반부에서 중단한 독자들은 / 요점을 놓칠 것이다.

Imagine waiting until the last sentence of a story / to find out who won the presidential election or the Super Bowl.
이야기의 마지막 문장까지 기다린다고 상상해 보라. / 누가 대통령 선거 혹은 슈퍼볼에서 이겼는지 알아내기 위해

뉴스 리포터들은 가장 중요한 정보로 이야기를 시작하도록 배운다. 리드라고 불리는 첫 번째 문장은 이야기의 가장 본질적인 요소들을 담는다. 좋은 리드는 많은 정보를 전달할 수 있다. 리드 후에, 정보는 중요도가 감소하는 순서로 제시된다. 언론인들은 이것을 '역 피라미드' 구조라고 부르는데, 가장 중요한 정보(피라미드의 가장 넓은 부분)가 맨 위에 있는 것이다. 역 피라미드는 독자들에게 아주 좋다. 독자의 주의 지속 시간이 어떻든 간에 — 독자가 리드만 읽든 전체 이야기를 읽든 — 역 피라미드는 독자가 얻는 정보를 극대화한다. 다른 방법을 생각해 보라. 만약 뉴스 이야기들이 마지막에 극적인 결말이 있는 미스터리처럼 쓰여진다면, 이야기 중반부에서 중단한 독자들은 요점을 놓칠 것이다. 누가 대통령 선거 혹은 슈퍼볼(매년 미국 프로 미식축구의 우승팀을 결정하는 경기)에서 이겼는지 알아내기 위해 이야기의 마지막 문장까지 기다린다고 상상해 보라.

Why? 왜 정답일까?

첫 두 문장에 따르면 뉴스에서 가장 중요한 정보는 리드라고 불리는 첫 번째 문장에 제시된다(News reporters are taught to start their stories with the most important information. The first sentence, called the lead, contains the most essential elements of the story.)고 한다. 이어서 중요도가 덜할수록 정보가 나중에 제시된다는 설명이 뒤따르고 있다. 따라서 글의 제목으로 가장 적절한 것은 ③ '뉴스 작성 시 요점을 어디에 둘 것인가'이다.

- essential [a] 필수적인, 본질적인
- convey [v] 전달하다

- attention span 주의 지속 시간
- payoff [n] (뜻밖의) 결말
- presidential [a] 대통령 (선거)의
- tell A from B A와 B를 구별하다
- alternative [n] 대안
- break off (갑자기) 중단하다
- logically [ad] 논리적으로

구문 풀이

7행 No matter what the reader's attention span — whether she reads only the
= whatever(무엇이 / ~이든 간에) / 부사절 접속사(~이든 아니든)
lead or the entire story — the inverted pyramid maximizes the information [she gets].
주어 / 동사 / 목적어(선행사)

---

25 국가별 천연가스 생산량 비교 정답률 87% | 정답 ④

다음 표의 내용과 일치하지 않는 것은?

Top Seven Natural Gas Producing Countries Worldwide
(unit: billion cubic meters)

Rank	2014 Country	Amount	Rank	2018 Country	Amount
1	The United States	729	1	The United States	863
2	Russia	610	2	Russia	725
3	Iran	172	3	Iran	248
4	Canada	161	4	Qatar	181
5	Qatar	160	5	China	176
6	China	132	6	Canada	172
7	Norway	108	7	Australia	131

The table above shows / the top seven natural gas producing countries worldwide / in 2014 and 2018.
위 표는 보여준다. / 전 세계의 천연가스 생산 상위 7개 국가들을 / 2014년과 2018년

① The United States, Russia, and Iran / were the top three natural gas producing countries / in both 2014 and 2018.
미국, 러시아, 이란은 / 상위 3개 천연가스 생산 국가였다. / 2014년과 2018년 모두

② In 2014 and 2018 respectively, / the gap of the amount of natural gas production / between Russia and Iran / was larger than 400 billion cubic meters.
2014년과 2018년 각각, / 천연가스 생산량 차이는 / 러시아와 이란 간의 / 4,000억 세제곱미터보다 더 컸다.

③ Canada ranked lower in 2018 than in 2014 / even though the amount of natural gas produced in Canada increased.
캐나다는 2014년보다 2018년에 낮은 순위를 기록했다. / 비록 캐나다의 천연가스 생산량은 증가했지만

④ Between 2014 and 2018, / the increase in natural gas production in China / was more than three times that in Qatar.
2014년과 2018년 사이, / 중국의 천연가스 생산 증가량은 / 카타르의 증가량의 3배 이상이었다.

⑤ Australia, / which was not included among the top seven natural gas producing countries in 2014, / ranked seventh in 2018.
호주는 / 2014년 상위 7개 천연가스 생산 국가에 포함되지 않았던 / 2018년에 7위에 올랐다.

위 표는 2014년과 2018년, 전 세계의 천연가스 생산 상위 7개 국가를 보여준다. ① 미국, 러시아, 이란은 2014년과 2018년 모두 상위 3개 천연가스 생산 국가였다. ② 2014년과 2018년 각각, 러시아와 이란 간의 천연가스 생산량 차이는 4,000억 세제곱미터보다 더 컸다. ③ 비록 캐나다의 천연가스 생산량은 증가했지만 캐나다는 2014년보다 2018년에 낮은 순위를 기록했다. ④ 2014년과 2018년 사이, 중국의 천연가스 생산 증가량은 카타르의 증가량의 3배 이상이었다. ⑤ 2014년 상위 7개 천연가스 생산 국가에 포함되지 않았던 호주는 2018년에 7위에 올랐다.

Why? 왜 정답일까?

도표에 따르면 중국의 천연가스 생산량은 2014년 1,320억 세제곱미터에서 2018년 1,760억 세제곱미터로 증가해 그 차이가 440억 세제곱미터였고, 카타르의 천연가스 생산량은 2014년 1,600억 세제곱미터에서 2018년 1,810억 세제곱미터로 증가해 그 차이는 210억 세제곱미터였다. 즉 중국의 천연가스 생산 증가량은 카타르의 생산 증가량의 2배 정도 되므로, 도표와 일치하지 않는 것은 ④이다.

- respectively [ad] 각각
- cubic [a] 세제곱의, 입체의

---

26 Carol Ryrie Brink의 생애 정답률 93% | 정답 ③

Carol Ryrie Brink에 관한 다음 글의 내용과 일치하지 않는 것은?

① 할머니에 의해 길러졌다.
② Moscow에서 만났던 수학 교수와 결혼했다.
③ 자녀가 태어나기 전에 어린이 이야기를 쓰기 시작했다.
④ 1934년에 그녀의 첫 번째 소설이 출간되었다.
⑤ Caddie Woodlawn으로 Newbery 상을 받았다.

「Born in 1895, / Carol Ryrie Brink was orphaned by age 8 / and raised by her grandmother.」
1895년에 태어난 / Carol Ryrie Brink는 8살 때 고아가 되었고 / 할머니에 의해 길러졌다. ①의 근거 일치

Her grandmother's life and storytelling abilities / inspired her writing.
그녀의 할머니의 삶과 스토리텔링 능력은 / 그녀의 글쓰기에 영감을 주었다.

「She married Raymond Woodard Brink, / a young mathematics professor / she had met in Moscow, Idaho many years before.」 ②의 근거 일치
그녀는 Raymond Woodard Brink와 결혼했다. / 젊은 수학 교수인 / 그녀가 수년 전 Idaho주 Moscow에서 만났던

After their son and daughter were born, / early in her career, / she started to write children's stories / and edited a yearly collection of short stories. ③의 근거 불일치
그들의 아들과 딸이 태어난 후 / 그녀의 경력 초기에 / 그녀는 어린이 이야기를 쓰기 시작했고, / 연간 단편 소설집을 편집했다.

「She and her husband spent several years living in France, / and her first novel Anything Can Happen on the River / was published in 1934.」 ④의 근거 일치
그녀와 그녀의 남편은 프랑스에서 수년간 살았고, / 그녀의 첫 번째 소설인 Anything Can Happen on the River가 / 1934년에 출판되었다.

After that, / she wrote more than thirty fiction and nonfiction books / for children and adults.
그 후, / 그녀는 30권 이상의 소설과 논픽션을 썼다. / 어린이들과 어른들을 위해

「She received the Newbery Award in 1936 for Caddie Woodlawn.」 ⑤의 근거 일치
그녀는 Caddie Woodlawn으로 1936년에 Newbery 상을 받았다.

1895년에 태어난 Carol Ryrie Brink는 8살 때 고아가 되었고 할머니에 의해 길러졌다. 그녀의 할머니의 삶과 스토리텔링 능력은 그녀의 글쓰기에 영감을 주었다. 그녀는 수년 전 Idaho주 Moscow에서 만났던 젊은 수학 교수인 Raymond Woodard Brink와 결혼했다. 그들의 아들과 딸이 태어난 후 경력 초기에 그녀는 어린이 이야기를 쓰기 시작했고, 연간 단편 소설집을 편집했다. 그녀와 그녀의 남편은 프랑스에서 수년간 살았고, 그녀의 첫 번째 소설인 *Anything Can Happen on the River*가 1934년에 출판되었다. 그 후, 그녀는 어린이들과 어른들을 위해 30권 이상의 소설과 논픽션을 썼다. 그녀는 *Caddie Woodlawn*으로 1936년에 Newbery 상을 받았다.

Why? 왜 정답일까?

'After their son and daughter were born, early in her career, she started to write children's stories ~'에서 Carol Ryrie Brink는 아들과 딸이 태어난 이후 어린이 이야기를 쓰기 시작했다고 하므로, 내용과 일치하지 않는 것은 ③ '자녀가 태어나기 전에 어린이 이야기를 쓰기 시작했다.'이다.

Why? 왜 오답일까?

① '~ raised by her grandmother.'의 내용과 일치한다.
② 'She married Raymond Woodard Brink, a young mathematics professor she had met in Moscow, ~'의 내용과 일치한다.
④ '~ her first novel *Anything Can Happen on the River* was published in 1934.'의 내용과 일치한다.
⑤ 'She received the Newbery Award in 1936 for *Caddie Woodlawn*.'의 내용과 일치한다.

- orphan ⓥ 고아로 만들다 ⓝ 고아
- spend A ~ing ~하는 데 A를 쓰다
- inspire ⓥ 영감을 주다
- publish ⓥ 출판하다

구문 풀이

3행 She married Raymond Woodard Brink, a young mathematics professor
동격(= Raymond Woodard Brink)
[(whom) she had met in Moscow, Idaho many years before].
생략(목적격 관·대)

27 박물관 일일 캠프　　정답률 95% | 정답 ⑤

One Day Camp at Seattle Children's Museum에 관한 다음 안내문의 내용과 일치하지 않는 것은?
① 7월 8일 목요일에 진행된다.
② 음악과 춤 활동이 있다.
③ 아이의 참가비는 30달러이다.
④ 모든 아이들은 어른과 동행해야 한다.
☑ 점심 식사는 참가비에 포함되지 않는다.

One Day Camp at Seattle Children's Museum
Seattle 어린이 박물관에서의 일일 캠프
One Day Camp at Seattle Children's Museum / is an experience / that promises to inspire creativity in children.
Seattle 어린이 박물관에서의 일일 캠프는 / 체험입니다. / 아이들에게 창의력을 불어넣을 것을 약속하는
Join us on an amazing journey of discovery!
발견의 놀라운 여행에 함께 하세요!
『Date: Thursday, July 8, 2021』 ①의근거 일치
날짜: 2021년 7월 8일 목요일
Ages: 5 – 10
연령: 5 ~ 10세
Schedule
일정

Time 시간	Activity 활동
10:30 – 12:30	Arts & Crafts 미술 & 공예
12:30 – 13:30	Lunch 점심 식사
13:30 – 15:30	『Music & Dance』②의근거 일치 음악 & 춤

Participation Fees
참가비
『Child: $30』 ③의근거 일치
아이: 30달러
Adult: $10
어른: 10달러
Notes
알림
『All children must be accompanied by an adult.』 ④의근거 일치
모든 아이들은 반드시 어른과 동행해야 합니다.
『The participation fee / includes lunch and materials for the program.』 ⑤의근거 불일치
참가비에는 / 점심 식사와 프로그램 재료비가 포함됩니다.

Seattle 어린이 박물관에서의 일일 캠프

Seattle 어린이 박물관에서의 일일 캠프는 아이들에게 창의력을 불어넣을 것을 약속하는 체험입니다. 발견의 놀라운 여행에 함께 하세요!
- **날짜**: 2021년 7월 8일 목요일
- **연령**: 5 ~ 10세
- **일정**

시간	활동
10:30 – 12:30	미술 & 공예
12:30 – 13:30	점심 식사
13:30 – 15:30	음악 & 춤

- **참가비**
　– 아이: 30달러
　– 어른: 10달러
- **알림**
　– 모든 아이들은 반드시 어른과 동행해야 합니다.
　– 참가비에는 점심 식사와 프로그램 재료비가 포함됩니다.

Why? 왜 정답일까?

'The participation fee includes lunch and materials for the program.'에서 참가비에는 점심 식사와 재료비가 포함된다고 하므로, 안내문의 내용과 일치하지 않는 것은 ⑤ '점심 식사는 참가비에 포함되지 않는다.'이다.

Why? 왜 오답일까?

① 'Date: Thursday, July 8, 2021'의 내용과 일치한다.
② 'Activity / Music & Dance'의 내용과 일치한다.
③ 'Child: $30'의 내용과 일치한다.
④ 'All children must be accompanied by an adult.'의 내용과 일치한다.

- discovery ⓝ 발견
- accompany ⓥ 동반하다, 동행하다

28 록 밴드 콘서트　　정답률 90% | 정답 ④

Summer Rock Concert에 관한 다음 안내문의 내용과 일치하는 것은?
① 이틀간 진행된다.
② 티켓은 현장에서만 구매할 수 있다.
③ 콘서트 관람에 나이 제한은 없다.
☑ 음식은 콘서트 홀에서 허용되지 않는다.
⑤ 공연 중 사진 촬영이 가능하다.

Summer Rock Concert
여름 록 콘서트
Five rock bands will provide / great entertainment, joy, and music / to all visitors.
5개 록 밴드들이 제공할 것입니다. / 훌륭한 오락거리, 즐거움, 그리고 음악을 / 모든 방문객들에게
『Date: Saturday, August 14, 2021』 ①의근거 불일치
날짜: 2021년 8월 14일 토요일
Time: 7 p.m.
시간: 오후 7시
Place: Citizens Hall in the Blue Creek Building
장소: Blue Creek 건물의 시민회관
Details
세부 사항
All seats are $30.
모든 좌석은 30달러입니다.
『Tickets must be purchased online by Saturday, August 7.』 ②의근거 불일치
티켓은 8월 7일 토요일까지 온라인으로 구매되어야 합니다.
『Only 13-year-olds and older can attend the concert.』 ③의근거 불일치
13세 이상만이 콘서트를 관람할 수 있습니다.
Notice
공지
『Food is not allowed in the concert hall.』 ④의근거 일치
음식은 콘서트 홀에서 허용되지 않습니다.
『All forms of photography and video recording / are prohibited / during the performance.』
모든 형태의 사진 촬영과 동영상 녹화는 / 금지됩니다. / 공연 중에는　　⑤의근거 불일치
If you have any questions, please visit www.rock5.info
문의 사항이 있으시면, www.rock5.info로 방문해 주십시오.

여름 록 콘서트

5개 록 밴드들이 모든 방문객들에게 훌륭한 오락거리, 즐거움, 그리고 음악을 제공할 것입니다.
- **날짜**: 2021년 8월 14일 토요일
- **시간**: 오후 7시
- **장소**: Blue Creek 건물의 시민회관
- **세부 사항**
　– 모든 좌석은 30달러입니다.
　– 티켓은 8월 7일 토요일까지 온라인으로 구매되어야 합니다.
　– 13세 이상만이 콘서트를 관람할 수 있습니다.
- **공지**
　– 음식은 콘서트 홀에서 허용되지 않습니다.
　– 공연 중에는 모든 형태의 사진 촬영과 동영상 녹화는 금지됩니다.
　– 문의 사항이 있으시면, www.rock5.info로 방문해 주십시오.

Why? 왜 정답일까?

'Food is not allowed in the concert hall.'에서 콘서트 홀 내에서 음식은 허용되지 않는다고 하였다. 따라서 안내문의 내용과 일치하는 것은 ④ '음식은 콘서트 홀에서 허용되지 않는다.'이다.

Why? 왜 오답일까?

① 'Saturday, August 14, 2021'에서 공연은 8월 14일 하루 열린다는 것을 알 수 있다.
② 'Tickets must be purchased online by Saturday, August 7.'에서 티켓은 현장이 아닌 온라인에서 구매할 수 있다고 하였다.
③ 'Only 13-year-olds and older can attend the concert.'에서 13세 이상만 콘서트에 올 수 있다고 하였다.
⑤ 'All forms of photography and video recording are prohibited during the performance.'에서 공연 중 사진 및 동영상 촬영은 모두 금지된다고 하였다.

- **entertainment** ⓝ 오락
- **prohibit** ⓥ 금지하다
- **purchase** ⓥ 구매하다

★★★ 등급을 가르는 뚫제!

29 긍정적 강화에 대한 실험
정답률 34% | 정답 ⑤

다음 글의 밑줄 친 부분 중, 어법상 틀린 것은? [3점]

While working as a research fellow at Harvard, / B. F. Skinner carried out a series of experiments on rats, / using an invention / that later became known as a "Skinner box."
> Harvard에서 연구원으로 일하는 동안, / B. F. Skinner는 쥐를 대상으로 일련의 실험을 수행했다. / 발명품을 사용하여, / 후에 'Skinner box'로 알려지게 된

A rat was placed in one of these boxes, / ① which had a special bar fitted on the inside.
> 이 상자들 중 하나에 쥐 한 마리를 넣었는데, / 이 상자에는 내부에 끼워져 있는 특별한 막대가 있었다.

Every time the rat pressed this bar, / it was presented with food.
> 쥐가 이 막대를 누를 때마다 / 쥐는 음식을 받았다.

The rate of bar-pressing / was ② automatically recorded.
> 막대를 누르는 비율이 / 자동으로 기록되었다.

Initially, the rat might press the bar accidentally, / or simply out of curiosity, / and as a consequence ③ receive some food.
> 처음에 쥐는 우연히 막대를 눌렀을 것이고, / 또는 단순히 호기심으로 / 그리고 그 결과로 약간의 음식을 받았을 것이다.

Over time, / the rat learned / that food appeared whenever the bar was pressed, / and began to press ④ it purposefully / in order to be fed.
> 시간이 지나면서, / 쥐는 학습했고 / 막대가 눌러질 때마다 음식이 나타난다는 것을 / 일부러 그것을 누르기 시작했다. / 먹이를 받기 위해

Comparing results from rats / ✔ given the "positive reinforcement" of food for their bar-pressing behavior / with those that were not, / or were presented with food at different rates, / it became clear / that when food appeared as a consequence of the rat's actions, / this influenced its future behavior.
> 쥐들에게서 나온 결과를 비교해보니, / 막대 누르는 행동에 대해 음식이라는 '긍정적인 강화'가 주어진 / 그렇지 않았던 쥐들과 / 혹은 음식을 다른 비율로 받은 / 분명해졌다. / 쥐의 행동의 결과로 음식이 나타났을 때, / 이것이 쥐의 향후 행동에 영향을 미쳤다는 것이

Harvard에서 연구원으로 일하는 동안, B. F. Skinner는 후에 'Skinner box'로 알려지게 된 발명품을 사용하여, 쥐를 대상으로 일련의 실험을 수행했다. 이 상자들 중 하나에 쥐 한 마리를 넣었는데, 이 상자에는 내부에 끼워져 있는 특별한 막대가 있었다. 쥐는 이 막대를 누를 때마다 음식을 받았다. 막대를 누르는 비율이 자동으로 기록되었다. 처음에 쥐는 우연히, 또는 단순히 호기심으로 막대를 눌렀을 것이고, 그리고 그 결과로 약간의 음식을 받았을 것이다. 시간이 지나면서, 쥐는 막대가 눌러질 때마다 음식이 나타난다는 것을 학습했고, 먹이를 받기 위해 일부러 그것을 누르기 시작했다. 막대 누르는 행동에 대해 음식이라는 '긍정적인 강화'가 주어진 쥐들과 그렇지 않거나(강화가 없었거나) 음식을 다른 비율로 받은 쥐들과 비교해보니, 쥐의 행동의 결과로 음식이 나타났을 때, 이것이 쥐의 향후 행동에 영향을 미쳤다는 것이 분명해졌다.

Why? 왜 정답일까?
마지막 문장에서 주절이 'it became clear ~'이고 Comparing이 접속사 없이 분사구문으로 쓰인 것으로 볼 때, 문장에 또 다른 동사가 나올 수 없다. 즉 gives는 동사가 아닌 준동사로 바뀌어야 하는데, 여기서는 앞에 나오는 명사 rats를 꾸밀 수 있도록 gives를 과거분사인 given으로 바꾸는 것이 적절하다. 따라서 어법상 틀린 것은 ⑤이다. rats가 '주는' 주체가 아니라 '받는' 대상이기 때문에 giving이 아닌 given을 쓴다는 점에 주의한다.

Why? 왜 오답일까?
① 사물 선행사 one of these boxes를 보충 설명하기 위해 주어가 없는 불완전한 문장을 연결하는 which가 바르게 쓰였다.
② 수동태 동사 was recorded를 꾸미기 위해 부사 automatically가 적절하게 쓰였다.
③ 등위접속사 and 앞뒤로 동사구 might press와 병렬을 이루는 또 다른 동사가 필요하므로 receive가 바르게 쓰였다.
④ 단수 명사 the bar를 받는 단수 대명사 it이 바르게 쓰였다.

- **carry out** ~을 수행하다
- **automatically** ⓐ 자동적으로
- **accidentally** ⓐ 우연히
- **purposefully** ⓐ 일부러, 목적을 갖고
- **present A with B** A에게 B를 주다, 제시하다
- **initially** ⓐ 처음에
- **as a consequence** 그 결과
- **reinforcement** ⓝ 강화

구문 풀이

10행 Comparing results from rats [(that were) given the "positive reinforcement"
(compare + A + 선행사 / 생략)
of food for their bar-pressing behavior] with those [that were not, or were presented
(with + B : A와 B를 비교하다)
with food at different rates], it became clear {that when food appeared as a
(가주어)
consequence of the rat's actions, this influenced its future behavior}. [ ]: 진주어
(진주어)

★★ 문제 해결 꿀~팁 ★★
▶ 많이 틀린 이유는?
③은 and 앞뒤의 병렬구조를 묻는 선택지이다. 'or simply out of curiosity', 'as a consequence' 등 불필요한 부사구를 지워보면 'might press ~'와 'receive ~'가 병렬구조임을 알 수 있다.
▶ 문제 해결 방법은?
정답인 ⑤가 포함된 문장은 분사구문, 관계절, 가주어-진주어 구문 등이 함께 쓰여 그 구조가 복잡하다. 수식어구를 전부 괄호로 묶으면, 주절인 'it became clear ~' 앞의 분사구문은 Comparing A (~) with B (~)의 구조를 띠고, ⑤는 이중 A의 일부인 rats를 꾸미는 수식어구 자리임을 파악할 수 있다.

30 용어를 통한 문제 인식
정답률 53% | 정답 ④

다음 글의 밑줄 친 부분 중, 문맥상 낱말의 쓰임이 적절하지 않은 것은? [3점]

Let's return to a time / in which photographs were not in living color.
> 시기로 돌아가 보자. / 사진이 생생한 색으로 되어 있지 않았던

During that period, / people referred to pictures as "photographs" / rather than "black-and-white photographs" / as we do today.
> 그 기간 동안, / 사람들은 사진을 '사진'이라고 불렀다. / '흑백 사진'이 아닌 / 오늘날 우리가 부르듯이

The possibility of color did not exist, / so it was ① unnecessary / to insert the adjective "black-and-white."
> 색의 가능성은 존재하지 않았고, / 따라서 불필요했다. / '흑백'이라는 형용사를 삽입하는 것은

However, / suppose we did include the phrase "black-and-white" / before the existence of color photography.
> 하지만, / 우리가 흑백이라는 어구를 정말로 포함시켰다고 가정해 보자. / 컬러 사진의 존재 전에

By ② highlighting that reality, / we become conscious of current limitations / and thus open our minds to new possibilities and potential opportunities.
> 그 현실을 강조함으로써, / 우리는 현재의 한계를 의식하게 되고, / 따라서 새로운 가능성과 잠재적 기회에 마음을 연다.

World War I was given that name / only ③ after we were deeply embattled in World War II.
> 제1차 세계대전은 우리가 제2차 세계대전에 깊이 휘말린 후에야 비로소 그 이름이 붙여졌다.

Before that horrific period of the 1940s, / World War I was simply called "The Great War" / or, even worse, "The War to End All Wars."
> 1940년대의 끔찍한 시기 이전에, / 제1차 세계대전은 단순히 '대전쟁'이라고 불렸다. / 또는 더 심하게는 '모든 전쟁을 끝내는 전쟁'이라고

What if we had called it "World War I" back in 1918?
> 만약 우리가 1918년으로 돌아가 그것을 '제1차 세계대전'이라고 불렀더라면 어땠을까?

Such a label might have made / the possibility of a second worldwide conflict / a ✔ greater reality / for governments and individuals.
> 그러한 명칭은 만들었을지도 모른다. / 두 번째 세계적 충돌의 가능성을 / 더 큰 현실로 / 정부와 개인에게

We become conscious of issues / when we explicitly ⑤ identify them.
> 우리는 문제를 의식하게 된다. / 우리가 그것을 명시적으로 확인했을 때

사진이 생생한 색으로 되어 있지 않았던 시기로 돌아가 보자. 그 기간 동안, 사람들은 오늘날 우리가 부르듯이 사진을 '흑백 사진'이 아닌 '사진'이라고 불렀다. 색의 가능성은 존재하지 않았고, 따라서 '흑백'이라는 형용사를 삽입하는 것은 ① 불필요했다. 하지만, 우리가 컬러 사진의 존재 전에 '흑백'이라는 어구를 정말로 포함시켰다고 가정해 보자. 그 현실을 ② 강조함으로써, 우리는 현재의 한계를 의식하게 되고, 따라서 새로운 가능성과 잠재적 기회에 마음을 연다. 제1차 세계대전은 우리가 제2차 세계대전에 깊이 휘말린 ③ 후에야 비로소 그 이름이 붙여졌다. 1940년대의 끔찍한 시기 이전에, 제1차 세계대전은 단순히 '대전쟁', 또는 더 심하게는 '모든 전쟁을 끝내는 전쟁'이라고 불렀다. 만약 우리가 1918년으로 돌아가 그것을 '제1차 세계대전'이라고 불렀더라면 어땠을까? 그러한 명칭은 두 번째 세계적 충돌의 가능성을 정부와 개인에게 ④ 예측할 수 없는(→ 더 큰) 현실로 만들었을지도 모른다. 우리가 문제를 명시적으로 ⑤ 확인했을 때, 우리는 그것을 의식하게 된다.

Why? 왜 정답일까?
글 전반부에서 흑백 사진이 표준이어서 사람들이 흑백 사진을 그냥 '사진'이라고 부르던 시절에 만일 '흑백 사진'이라는 용어를 썼다면 '컬러 사진'이라는 새로운 기회에 대한 인식이 깨어났을지도 모른다고 설명한다. 이어서 제1차 세계대전이 비슷한 예로 언급되는데, 만일 제2차 세계대전이 일어날 줄 모르는 상황 속에서 이미 '제1차 세계대전'이라는 용어를 썼다면 사람들이 '제2차' 세계대전의 가능성을 '더' 현실적으로 인지했을 것이라는 내용이 서술되고 있다. 이러한 흐름으로 보아, ④의 unpredictable을 greater로 고쳐야 한다. 따라서 문맥상 낱말의 쓰임이 적절하지 않은 것은 ④이다.

- **unnecessary** ⓐ 불필요한
- **existence** ⓝ 존재
- **limitation** ⓝ 한계
- **conflict** ⓝ 충돌, 갈등
- **explicitly** ⓐ 명시적으로
- **insert** ⓥ 삽입하다
- **highlight** ⓥ 강조하다
- **embattle** ⓥ 전쟁 준비를 갖추다
- **unpredictable** ⓐ 예측 불가능한
- **identify** ⓥ 확인하다, 알아보다

구문 풀이

9행 World War I was given that name only after we were deeply embattled in
(주어)(4형식 수동태)(목적어)(접속사(~하고 나서야 비로소))
World War II.

31 행동의 연쇄 반응
정답률 61% | 정답 ①

다음 빈칸에 들어갈 말로 가장 적절한 것을 고르시오.

✔ isolation - 고립
② comfort - 위안
③ observation - 관찰
④ fairness - 공정함
⑤ harmony - 조화

The tendency / for one purchase to lead to another one / has a name: / the Diderot Effect.
> 경향에는 / 한 구매가 또 다른 구매로 이어지는 / 이름이 있는데, / 바로 Diderot 효과이다.

The Diderot Effect states / that obtaining a new possession / often creates a spiral of consumption / that leads to additional purchases.
> Diderot 효과는 말한다. / 새로운 소유물을 얻는 것이 / 종종 소비의 소용돌이를 만든다고 / 추가적인 구매로 이어지는

You can spot this pattern everywhere.
> 당신은 이러한 경향을 어디서든지 발견할 수 있다.

You buy a dress / and have to get new shoes and earrings to match.
> 당신은 드레스를 사고 / 어울리는 새 신발과 귀걸이를 사야 한다.

You buy a toy for your child / and soon find yourself purchasing all of the accessories / that go with it.
> 당신은 아이를 위해 장난감을 사고 / 곧 모든 액세서리를 구매하는 자신을 발견한다. / 그것과 어울리는

It's a chain reaction of purchases.
> 이것은 구매의 연쇄 반응이다.

Many human behaviors follow this cycle.
> 많은 인간의 행동들은 이 순환을 따른다.

You often decide what to do next / based on what you have just finished doing.
> 당신은 종종 다음에 무엇을 할지 결정한다. / 당신이 방금 끝낸 것에 근거하여

Going to the bathroom / leads to washing and drying your hands, / which reminds you / that you need to put the dirty towels in the laundry, / so you add laundry detergent to the shopping list, and so on.
> 화장실에 가는 것은 / 손을 씻고 말리는 것으로 이어지고, / 이는 당신으로 하여금 생각이 들게 하고, / 당신이 더러운 수건을 세탁실에 넣을 필요가 있다는 / 그래서 당신은 쇼핑 목록에 세탁 세제를 더하고, 기타 등등을 한다.

No behavior happens in isolation.
> 고립되어 일어나는 행동은 없다.

Each action becomes a cue / that triggers the next behavior.
> 각 행동은 신호가 된다. / 다음 행동을 유발하는

한 구매가 또 다른 구매로 이어지는 경향에는 이름이 있는데, 바로 Diderot 효과이다. Diderot 효과는 새로운 소유물을 얻는 것이 종종 추가적인 구매들로 이어지는 소비의 소용돌이를 만든다고 말한다. 당신은 이러한 경향을 어디서든지 발견할 수 있다. 당신은 드레스를 사고 어울리는 새 신발과 귀걸이를 사야 한다. 당신은 아이를 위해 장난감을 사고 곧 그것과 어울리는 모든 액세서리들을 구매하는 자신을 발견한다. 이것은 구매의 연쇄 반응이다. 많은 인간의 행동들은 이 순환을 따른다. 당신은 종종 당신이 방금 끝낸 것에 근거하여 다음에 무엇을 할지 결정한다. 화장실에 가는 것은 손을 씻고 말리는 것으로 이어지고, 이로 인해 당신은 더러운 수건을 세탁실에 넣을 필요가 있다는 생각이 들고, 그래서 당신은 쇼핑 목록에 세탁 세제를 더하고, 기타 등등을 한다. 고립되어 일어나는 행동은 없다. 각 행동은 다음 행동을 유발하는 신호가 된다.

Why? 왜 정답일까?

마지막 문장인 'Each action becomes a cue that triggers the next behavior.'에서 한 행동은 다음 행동을 유발하는 신호가 된다고 언급하는 것으로 보아, 빈칸이 포함된 문장은 그 어떤 행동도 '따로' 일어나지 않는다는 의미를 나타내야 한다. 따라서 빈칸에 들어갈 말로 가장 적절한 것은 ① '고립'이다.

- possession ⓝ 소유물
- consumption ⓝ 소비
- chain reaction 연쇄 반응
- trigger ⓥ 유발하다
- fairness ⓝ 공정함, 공평함
- spiral ⓝ 소용돌이
- go with ~와 어울리다
- detergent ⓝ 세제
- isolation ⓝ 고립

구문 풀이

1행 The tendency for one purchase to lead to another one has a name: the Diderot Effect.
주어 / 의미상 주어 / 형용사적 용법 / 동사(단수) / 동격(= a name)

★★★ 등급을 가르는 문제!

32 섣부른 결정으로 인한 실패를 피하는 방법
정답률 26% | 정답 ②

다음 빈칸에 들어갈 말로 가장 적절한 것을 고르시오. [3점]
① justifying layoffs – 해고를 정당화하는
② exercising patience – 인내심을 발휘하는
③ increasing employment – 고용을 늘리는
④ sticking to his opinions – 자기 의견을 고수하는
⑤ training unskilled members – 미숙한 구성원들을 훈련시키는

While leaders often face enormous pressures / to make decisions quickly, / premature decisions / are the leading cause of decision failure.
리더들은 종종 큰 압박에 직면하지만, / 빨리 결정들을 내려야 하는 / 섣부른 결정들은 / 결정 실패의 주된 원인이다.

This is primarily / because leaders respond / to the superficial issue of a decision / rather than taking the time / to explore the underlying issues.
이것은 주로 / 리더들이 반응하기 때문이다. / 결정의 피상적인 문제에 / 시간을 보내기보다는 / 근원적인 문제들을 탐색하는 데

Bob Carlson is a good example of a leader / exercising patience in the face of diverse issues.
Bob Carlson은 리더의 좋은 예이다. / 다양한 문제에 직면했을 때 인내심을 발휘하는

In the economic downturn of early 2001, / Reell Precision Manufacturing / faced a 30 percent drop in revenues.
2001년 초의 경기 침체기에, / Reell Precision Manufacturing은 / 총수입의 30퍼센트 하락에 직면했다.

Some members of the senior leadership team favored layoffs / and some favored salary reductions.
몇몇의 고위 지도자 팀의 구성원들은 해고에 찬성했고 / 몇몇은 임금 삭감에 찬성했다.

While it would have been easy / to push for a decision or call for a vote / in order to ease the tension of the economic pressures, / as co-CEO, / Bob Carlson helped the team work together / and examine all of the issues.
쉬웠을 테지만, / 결정을 밀어붙이거나 투표를 요청하는 것이 / 경제적 압박의 긴장 상태를 완화하기 위해서 / 공동 최고 경영자로서, / Bob Carlson은 그 팀이 함께 노력하도록 도왔다. / 그리고 모든 문제들을 검토하도록

The team finally agreed on salary reductions, / knowing that, / to the best of their ability, / they had thoroughly examined the implications of both possible decisions.
그 팀은 마침내 임금 삭감에 동의했다. / 아는 상태로 / 자신들의 최선의 능력으로 / 자신이 두 가지 가능한 결정 모두의 영향을 철저하게 검토했다는 것을

리더들이 종종 빨리 결정들을 내려야 하는 큰 압박에 직면하지만, 섣부른 결정들은 결정 실패의 주된 원인이다. 이것은 주로 리더들이 근원적인 문제들을 탐색하는 데 시간을 보내기보다는 결정의 피상적인 문제에 반응하기 때문이다. Bob Carlson은 다양한 문제들에 직면했을 때 인내심을 발휘하는 리더의 좋은 예이다. 2001년 초의 경기 침체기에, Reell Precision Manufacturing은 총수입의 30퍼센트 하락에 직면했다. 몇몇의 고위 지도자 팀의 구성원들은 해고에 찬성했고 몇몇은 임금 삭감에 찬성했다. 경제적 압박의 긴장 상태를 완화하기 위해서 결정을 밀어붙이거나 투표를 요청하는 것이 쉬웠을 테지만, 공동 최고 경영자로서, Bob Carlson은 그 팀이 함께 노력하고 모든 문제를 검토하도록 도왔다. 그 팀은 마침내 자신들이 최선의 능력으로 두 가지 가능한 결정 모두의 영향을 철저하게 검토했다는 것을 아는 상태로 임금 삭감에 동의했다.

Why? 왜 정답일까?

빈칸 뒤에 제시된 예에 따르면 경기 침체기를 맞아 해고 또는 임금 삭감이라는 두 가지 안 중 하나를 선택해야 하는 상황에서, 회사의 공동 경영자였던 Bob Carlson은 팀원들 모두가 함께 노력하고 모든 문제를 검토하도록 도와주었다(~ as co-CEO, Bob Carlson helped the team work together and examine all of the issues.)고 한다. 이는 리더가 섣불리 결정하지 않고 팀원들의 논의와 검토 과정을 '인내심 있게 기다리는' 행위로 볼 수 있으므로, 빈칸에 들어갈 말로 가장 적절한 것은 ② '인내심을 발휘하는'이다.

- enormous ⓐ 거대한
- primarily ⓐ 주로
- underlying ⓐ 근본적인
- layoff ⓝ 해고
- examine ⓥ 검토하다
- justify ⓥ 정당화하다
- premature ⓐ 너무 이른, 시기상조의
- superficial ⓐ 피상적인
- in the face of ~에 직면하여, ~에도 불구하고
- reduction ⓝ 삭감, 감소
- thoroughly ⓐ 철저하게
- stick to ~을 고수하다

구문 풀이

13행 The team finally agreed on salary reductions, knowing that, (to the best of their ability), they had thoroughly examined the implications of both possible decisions.
분사구문 / 접속사(~것) / ( ): 삽입구 / 주어 / 동사(과거완료)

★★ 문제 해결 꿀~팁 ★★

▶ 많이 틀린 이유는?
리더들이 섣부른 결정을 내리는 이유를 진단하고 이를 해결할 방법을 제시하는 글이다. '해고'는 예시의 일부로 언급될 뿐 글의 핵심 소재가 아니므로 ①은 답으로 부적절하다. ④는 리더가 '자기 의견만 고수한다'라는 의미인데, 이는 글의 주제와 정반대된다.

▶ 문제 해결 방법은?
글에 'patience(인내심)'이라는 단어가 직접 등장하지는 않지만, 예시에서 리더가 팀원들로 하여금 모든 해결책을 꼼꼼히 검토해볼 수 있도록 도와주었다는 내용을 통해, 섣불리 혼자 결정하지 않고 '시간을 들여 기다리는 것'이 필요하다는 결론을 내릴 수 있다.

33 자기불구화 전략
정답률 60% | 정답 ③

다음 빈칸에 들어갈 말로 가장 적절한 것을 고르시오. [3점]
① getting some rest from studying is necessary – 공부하다가 약간 쉬는 것은 필요하기
② failure serves as the foundation for success – 실패는 성공의 기초 역할을 하기
③ you're creating a reason for your failure – 실패에 대한 이유를 만들기
④ studying is not about winning or losing – 공부는 이기고 지는 것의 문제가 아니기
⑤ you have already achieved a lot – 당신은 이미 많은 것을 성취했기

When self-handicapping, / you're engaging in behaviour / that you know will harm your chances of succeeding: / you know / that you won't do as well on the test / if you go out the night before, / but you do it anyway.
자기불구화를 할 때, / 당신은 행동에 관여하고 있는 것인데, / 당신이 알기로 당신의 성공 가능성을 해칠 / 당신은 알고 있지만, / 당신이 시험을 그만큼 잘 치지 못할 것임을 / 당신이 전날 밤 놀러 나가면 / 당신은 어찌되었든 그렇게 한다.

Why would anyone intentionally harm their chances of success?
어떤 사람이 왜 의도적으로 자신의 성공 가능성을 해치겠는가?

Well, here's a possible answer.
여기에 가능한 답이 있다.

Say that you do study hard.
당신이 공부를 정말로 열심히 한다고 해 보자.

You go to bed at a decent time / and get eight hours of sleep.
당신은 적당한 시간에 잠자리에 들고 / 8시간 동안 잠을 잔다.

Then you take the maths test, / but don't do well: / you only get a C.
그러고 나서 당신은 수학 시험에 응시하지만, / 잘 치지 못해서 / 당신은 겨우 C를 받는다.

What can you conclude about yourself?
당신은 당신 자신에 대해 어떤 결론을 내릴 수 있는가?

Probably that you're just not good at maths, / which is a pretty hard blow to your self-esteem.
아마도 당신은 그저 수학을 잘 못한다는 것일 텐데, / 이것은 당신의 자존감에 꽤 타격이다.

But if you self-handicap, / you'll never be in this position / because you're creating a reason for your failure.
하지만 만약 당신이 자기불구화를 한다면, / 당신은 결코 이런 상황에 처하지 않을 것이다. / 당신이 실패에 대한 이유를 만들기 때문이다.

You were bound to get a C, / you can tell yourself, / because you went out till 1 a.m.
당신이 C를 받을 수밖에 없었다고 / 당신은 스스로에게 말할 수 있는 것이다. / 당신이 새벽 1시까지 밖에 있었기 때문에

That C doesn't mean that you're bad at maths; / it just means that you like to party.
그 C는 당신이 수학을 못한다는 것을 뜻하지는 않으며, / 그것은 단지 당신이 파티하는 것을 좋아하는 것을 의미한다.

Self-handicapping seems like a paradox, / because people are deliberately harming their chances of success.
자기불구화 현상은 역설처럼 보이는데, / 사람들이 의도적으로 자신의 성공 가능성을 해치고 있는 것이기 때문이다.

자기불구화를 할 때, 당신은 당신이 알기로 당신의 성공 가능성을 해칠 행동에 관여하고 있는 것인데, 당신은 (시험) 전날 밤 놀러 나가면 시험을 그만큼 잘 치지 못할 것임을 알고 있지만, 어찌되었든 그렇게 한다. 어떤 사람이 왜 의도적으로 성공 가능성을 해치겠는가? 여기에 가능한 답이 있다. 당신이 공부를 정말히 열심히 한다고 해 보자. 당신은 적당한 시간에 잠자리에 들고 8시간 동안 잠을 잔다. 그러고 나서 당신은 수학 시험에 응시하지만, 잘 치지 못해서 겨우 C를 받는다. 당신은 당신 자신에 대해 어떤 결론을 내릴 수 있는가? 아마도 당신은 그저 수학을 잘 못한다는 결론일 텐데, 이것은 당신의 자존감에 꽤 타격이다. 하지만 만약 당신이 자기불구화를 한다면, 당신은 실패에 대한 이유를 만들기 때문에 결코 이런 상황에 처하지 않을 것이다. 당신은 새벽 1시까지 밖에 있었기 때문에 C를 받을 수밖에 없었다고 스스로에게 말할 수 있는 것이다. 그 C는 당신이 수학을 못한다는 것을 뜻하지는 않으며, 단지 당신이 파티하는 것을 좋아한다는 것을 의미한다. 자기불구화 현상은 역설처럼 보이는데, 사람들이 의도적으로 자신의 성공 가능성을 해치고 있는 것이기 때문이다.

Why? 왜 정답일까?

빈칸 앞에서 수학 시험 공부를 열심히 하고 나서 시험을 쳤지만 결과가 좋지 않았을 때에는 능력을 탓할 수 밖에 없을 것이라고 설명하고 있다. 한편 빈칸이 포함된 문장부터는 우리가 자기불구화 전략을 택하는 경우, 즉 시험 전날 늦게까지 나가 놀아서 C를 받을 수밖에 없는 상황을 만드는 경우에는 우리가 능력이 아닌 다른 이유를 탓할 수 있다는 내용이 이어지고 있다. 이로 인해 마지막 문장에서는 자기불구화 전략을 채택하는 경우 사람들은 의도적으로 자신이 성공할 가능성을 망치고 있는 것(~ people are deliberately harming their chances of success.)이라는 결론을 내린다. 따라서 빈칸에 들어갈 말로 가장 적절한 것은 사람들이 스스로 '실패의 핑계를 만들기 위해' 자기불구화 전략을 채택한다는 의미를 완성하는 ③ '실패에 대한 이유를 만들기'이다.

- engage in ~에 관여하다
- intentionally ⓐ 의도적으로
- deliberately ⓐ 의도적으로, 고의로
- foundation ⓝ 기반, 기초
- harm ⓥ 해를 입히다
- paradox ⓝ 역설
- serve as ~의 역할을 하다

구문 풀이

1행 When self-handicapping, you're engaging in behaviour [that (you know)
접속사 / 분사구문 / 선행사 / ( ): 삽입절

will harm your chances of succeeding]: you know that you won't do as well on the test if you go out the night before, but you do it anyway.

★★★ 등급을 가르는 문제!

34 실제 보이는 것을 인식하기   정답률 49% | 정답 ①

다음 빈칸에 들어갈 말로 가장 적절한 것을 고르시오. [3점]

☑ consciously acknowledge what you actually see – 여러분이 실제로 보는 것을 의식적으로 인정하라
② accept different opinions with a broad mind – 넓은 마음으로 다양한 의견을 받아들여라
③ reflect on what you've already learned – 이미 배운 것을 반추해보라
④ personally experience even a small thing – 작은 것이라도 직접 경험하라
⑤ analyze the answers from various perspectives – 다양한 시각에서 답을 분석하라

Early in the term, / our art professor projected an image of a monk, / his back to the viewer, / standing on the shore, / looking off into a blue sea and an enormous sky.
학기 초, / 우리 미술 교수는 수도승의 이미지를 제시했다. / 보는 이를 등지고 / 바닷가에 서서 / 푸른 바다와 거대한 하늘을 바라보고 있는
The professor asked the class, "What do you see?"
교수는 반 학생들에게 물었다, "무엇이 보이나요?"
The darkened auditorium was silent.
어두컴컴한 강당은 조용했다.
We looked and looked and thought and thought / as hard as possible / to unearth the hidden meaning, / but came up with nothing / — we must have missed it.
우리는 보고 또 보고 생각하고 또 생각했지만, / 가능한 한 열심히 / 그 숨겨진 의미를 파헤치기 위해 / 아무것도 생각해 내지 못했다 / 우리는 그것을 놓쳤음에 틀림없다
With dramatic exasperation / she answered her own question, / "It's a painting of a monk! His back is to us! / He is standing near the shore! / There's a blue sea and enormous sky!"
극도로 분노하며 / 그녀는 자신의 질문에 대답했다. / "이것은 수도승의 그림이에요! / 그는 우리를 등지고 있어요! / 그는 해안 근처에 서 있죠! / 푸른 바다와 거대한 하늘이 있네요!"
Hmm... why didn't we see it?
흠... 왜 우리는 그것을 보지 못했을까?
So as not to bias us, / she'd posed the question / without revealing the artist or title of the work.
우리에게 편견을 주지 않기 위해, / 그녀는 질문을 제시했다. / 그 작품의 작가나 제목을 밝히지 않고
In fact, / it was Caspar David Friedrich's *The Monk by the Sea.*
사실, / 그것은 Caspar David Friedrich의 *The Monk by the Sea*였다.
To better understand your world, / consciously acknowledge what you actually see / rather than guess at / what you think you are supposed to see.
여러분의 세상을 더 잘 이해하려면, / 여러분이 실제로 보는 것을 의식적으로 인정하라. / 추측하기보다는 / 여러분이 생각하기에 봐야 한다고 기대되는 것을

학기 초, 우리 미술 교수는 보는 이를 등지고 바닷가에 서서 푸른 바다와 거대한 하늘을 바라보고 있는 수도승의 이미지를 제시했다. 교수는 반 학생들에게 물었다. "무엇이 보이나요?" 어두컴컴한 강당은 조용했다. 우리는 그 숨겨진 의미를 파헤치기 위해 가능한 한 열심히 보고 또 보고 생각하고 또 생각했지만, 아무것도 생각해 내지 못했다 — 우리는 그것을 놓쳤음에 틀림없다. 극도로 분노하며 그녀는 자신의 질문에 대답했다. "이것은 수도승의 그림이에요! 그는 우리를 등지고 있어요! 그는 해안 근처에 서 있죠! 푸른 바다와 거대한 하늘이 있네요!" 흠... 왜 우리는 그것을 보지 못했을까? 우리에게 편견을 주지 않기 위해, 그녀는 그 작품의 작가나 제목을 밝히지 않고 질문을 제시했다. 사실, 그것은 Caspar David Friedrich의 *The Monk by the Sea*였다. 여러분의 세상을 더 잘 이해하려면, 여러분이 생각하기에 봐야 한다고 기대되는 것을 추측하기보다는 여러분이 실제로 보는 것을 의식적으로 인정하라.

Why? 왜 정답일까?

제시된 예에 따르면 교수가 바닷가에 등을 보이고 서 있는 수도승의 이미지를 주었을 때, 학생들은 교수가 기대하는 답 또는 그림의 의미를 찾는 데 골몰하다가 그 이미지를 있는 그대로 감상하지 못했다. 이는 애초에 작가와 작품명도 주지 않고 이미지를 최대한 편견 없이 보기를 바랐던 교수의 기대와는 상반된 결과였다. 이 예시를 토대로 빈칸이 포함된 문장은 이미지를 볼 때 이미지 너머의 것을 추론하기보다는 '보이는 것을 보라'는 결론을 도출하고 있다. 따라서 빈칸에 들어갈 말로 가장 적절한 것은 ① '여러분이 실제로 보는 것을 의식적으로 인정하라'이다.

- project ⓥ 제시하다, 투사하다
- auditorium ⓝ 강당
- come up with ~을 떠올리다
- acknowledge ⓥ 인정하다
- analyze ⓥ 분석하다
- enormous ⓐ 거대한
- unearth ⓥ 파헤치다, 밝혀내다
- bias ⓥ 편견을 갖게 하다 ⓝ 편견
- reflect on ~을 반추하다, 되돌아 보다
- perspective ⓝ 시각, 관점

구문 풀이

1행 Early in the term, our art professor projected an image of a monk,
  주어 동사 목적어
his back to the viewer, standing on the shore, looking off into a blue sea and an
= the monk's   현재분사1   현재분사2(a monk 보충 설명)
enormous us sky.

★★ 문제 해결 꿀~팁 ★★

▶ 많이 틀린 이유는?
세상을 어떤 기대에 맞추어 바라보려고 하기보다 있는 그대로 이해하는 것이 중요하다는 글로, 일화가 생소하여 내용이 쉽게 와닿지 않을 수 있다. 오답인 ②와 ⑤는 모두 의견의 '다양성'을 언급하고 있는데, 이는 글에서 언급되지 않은 소재이므로 답으로 적절하지 않다.

▶ 문제 해결 방법은?
교수의 말을 주의 깊게 읽도록 한다. 수도승 그림에 관해 교수가 언급한 내용은 필자가 첫 문장에서 그림 속 수도승을 '보이는 대로' 묘사한 내용과 일치한다.

35 사회적 증거   정답률 69% | 정답 ③

다음 글에서 전체 흐름과 관계 <u>없는</u> 문장은?

An interesting phenomenon / that arose from social media / is the concept of *social proof.*
흥미로운 현상은 / 소셜 미디어에서 생겨난 / *사회적 증거*라는 개념이다.
It's easier for a person / to accept new values or ideas / when they see that others have already done so.
사람에 있어 더 쉽다. / 새로운 가치나 아이디어를 받아들이기가 / 다른 사람들이 이미 그렇게 하고 있다는 것을 알 때
① If the person / they see accepting the new idea / happens to be a friend, / then social proof has even more power / by exerting peer pressure / as well as relying on the trust / that people put in the judgments of their close friends.
만약 그 사람이 / 새로운 아이디어를 받아들이고 있다고 보는 / 우연히도 친구라면, / 그때 사회적 증거는 훨씬 더 큰 힘을 갖게 된다. / 또래 압력을 발휘함으로써 / 신뢰에 의존할 뿐만 아니라 / 사람들이 자신의 친한 친구들의 판단에 두는
② For example, / a video about some issue / may be controversial on its own / but more credible / if it got thousands of likes.
예를 들어, / 어떤 문제에 대한 영상은 / 그 자체로 논란이 될 수 있지만 / 더 신뢰할 수 있다. / 그것이 수천 개의 좋아요를 얻으면
☑ When expressing feelings of liking to friends, / you can express them / using nonverbal cues such as facial expressions.
친구에게 좋아함의 감정을 표현할 때 / 당신은 그것들을 표현할 수 있다. / 표정과 같은 비언어적 신호를 이용해
④ If a friend recommends the video to you, / in many cases, / the credibility of the idea it presents / will rise / in direct proportion to the trust / you place in the friend recommending the video.
만약에 한 친구가 당신에게 영상을 추천한다면, / 많은 경우 / 영상이 제시하는 아이디어의 신뢰도는 / 상승할 것이다. / 신뢰도와 정비례하여 / 당신이 영상을 추천하는 친구에게 부여하는
⑤ This is the power of social media / and part of the reason / why videos or "posts" can become "viral."
이것이 소셜 미디어의 힘이고 / 이유의 일부다. / 영상이나 '게시물'이 '입소문이 날' 수 있는

소셜 미디어에서 생겨난 흥미로운 현상은 *사회적 증거*라는 개념이다. 사람은 다른 사람들이 이미 새로운 가치나 아이디어를 받아들였다는 것을 알 때 그렇게 하기가 더 쉽다. ① 만약 그들이 새로운 아이디어를 받아들이고 있다고 보는 그 사람이 우연히도 친구라면, 그때 사회적 증거는 사람들이 자신의 친한 친구들의 판단에 두는 신뢰에 의존할 뿐만 아니라 또래 압력을 발휘함으로써 훨씬 더 큰 힘을 갖게 된다. ② 예를 들어, 어떤 문제에 대한 영상은 그 자체로 논란이 될 수 있지만 그것이 수천 개의 좋아요를 얻으면 더 신뢰할 수 있다. ③ 친구에게 좋아함의 감정을 표현할 때 표정과 같은 비언어적 신호를 이용해 그것들을 표현할 수 있다. ④ 만약에 한 친구가 당신에게 영상을 추천한다면, 많은 경우 영상이 제시하는 아이디어의 신뢰도는 당신이 영상을 추천하는 친구에게 부여하는 신뢰도와 정비례하여 상승할 것이다. ⑤ 이것이 소셜 미디어의 힘이고 영상이나 '게시물'이 '입소문이 날' 수 있는 이유의 일부다.

Why? 왜 정답일까?

소셜 미디어의 발전과 함께 등장한 사회적 증거 개념을 설명한 글로, ①, ②, ④, ⑤는 주제에 부합한다. 하지만 ③은 비언어적 신호를 통해 친구에게 호의를 표시하는 경우에 관해 언급하고 있어 흐름에서 벗어난다. 따라서 전체 흐름과 관계 없는 문장은 ③이다.

- phenomenon ⓝ 현상
- controversial ⓐ 논란의 여지가 있는
- nonverbal ⓐ 비언어적인
- rely on ~에 의존하다
- credible ⓐ 신뢰할 만한
- in proportion to ~에 비례하여

구문 풀이

3행 If the person [(whom) they see accepting the new idea] happens to be a
  접속사   주어   생략   주어 지각동사 목적격 보어   동사(단수)
friend, then social proof has even more power by exerting peer pressure as well
  전치사 동명사1
as relying on the trust [that people put in the judgments of their close friends].
  동명사2   선행사   목적격 관계대명사

★★★ 등급을 가르는 문제!

36 협상에서 근원적인 이해관계 살피기   정답률 29% | 정답 ⑤

주어진 글 다음에 이어질 글의 순서로 가장 적절한 것을 고르시오.

① (A) – (C) – (B)   ② (B) – (A) – (C)   ③ (B) – (C) – (A)
④ (C) – (A) – (B)   ☑ (C) – (B) – (A)

Consider the story of two men / quarreling in a library.
두 사람의 이야기를 생각해 보자. / 도서관에서 싸우는
One wants the window open / and the other wants it closed.
한 사람은 창문을 열고 싶어 하고 / 다른 사람은 그것을 닫고 싶어 한다.
They argue back and forth / about how much to leave it open: / a crack, halfway, or three-quarters of the way.
그들은 옥신각신한다. / 그것을 얼마나 많이 열어 둘지에 대해 / 즉 조금, 절반, 혹은 4분의 3 정도 중
(C) No solution satisfies them both.
어떤 해결책도 둘 다를 만족시키지 못한다.
Enter the librarian.
사서로 투입하라.
She asks one why he wants the window open:
사서는 한 명에게 왜 그가 창문을 열고 싶어 하는지 묻는다.
"To get some fresh air."
"신선한 공기를 쐬기 위해서."
She asks the other why he wants it closed:
사서는 다른 사람에게도 왜 창문을 닫고 싶어 하는지 묻는다.
"To avoid a draft."
"외풍을 피하기 위해서."
(B) After thinking a minute, / she opens wide a window in the next room, / bringing in fresh air without a draft.
잠시 생각한 후, / 그녀는 옆방의 창문을 활짝 열고, / 외풍 없이 신선한 공기를 들여온다.
This story is typical of many negotiations.
이 이야기는 많은 협상의 전형이다.
Since the parties' problem / appears to be a conflict of positions, / they naturally tend to talk about positions / — and often reach an impasse.
당사자들의 문제가 / 입장 충돌로 보이기 때문에, / 그들은 자연스레 입장을 말하는 경향이 있고, / 흔히 막다른 상황에 이른다.
(A) The librarian could not have invented the solution she did / if she had focused only on the two men's stated positions / of wanting the window open or closed.
사서는 자신이 생각해 낸 해결책을 생각해 낼 수 없었을 것이다. / 만약 그녀가 말로 언급된 두 사람의 입장에만 집중했다면 / 창문을 열거나 닫기를 원하는

Instead, / she looked to their underlying interests / of fresh air and no draft.
대신에, / 그녀는 그들의 근본적인 이해관계를 살펴보았다. / 신선한 공기가 있고 외풍이 없어야 한다는

두 사람이 도서관에서 싸우는 이야기를 생각해 보자. 한 사람은 창문을 열고 싶어 하고 다른 사람은 그것을 닫고 싶어 한다. 그들은 얼마나 많이, 즉 조금, 절반, 혹은 4분의 3 정도 중 얼마나 열어 둘지에 대해 옥신각신한다.

(C) 어떤 해결책도 둘 다를 만족시키지 못한다. 사서를 투입하라. 사서는 한 명에게 왜 창문을 열고 싶어 하는지 묻는다. "신선한 공기를 쐬기 위해서."(라는 답이 돌아온다.) 사서는 다른 사람에게도 왜 창문을 닫고 싶어 하는지 묻는다. "외풍을 피하기 위해서."(라는 답이 돌아온다.)

(B) 잠시 생각한 후, 사서는 옆방의 창문을 활짝 열고, 외풍 없이 신선한 공기를 들여온다. 이 이야기는 많은 협상의 전형이다. 당사자들의 문제가 입장 충돌로 보이기 때문에, 그들은 자연스레 (자신의) 입장을 말하는 경향이 있고, 흔히 막다른 상황에 이른다.

(A) 만약 창문을 열거나 닫기를 원하는, 말로 언급된 두 사람의 입장에만 집중했다면 사서는 자신이 생각해 낸 해결책을 생각해 낼 수 없었을 것이다. 대신에, 사서는 신선한 공기가 있고 외풍이 없어야 한다는 그들의 근본적인 이해관계를 살펴보았다.

Why? 왜 정답일까?

주어진 글은 도서관에 있는 두 사람 중 한 사람은 창문을 열고 싶어 하고 다른 사람은 창문을 닫고 싶어 하여 충돌이 일어나는 상황을 소개한다. 이어서 (C)는 주어진 글에서 언급되듯이 창문을 약간만 열든, 절반만 열든, 4분의 3을 열든 두 사람 모두를 만족시키기는 어렵기 때문에, 사서를 투입해서 이유를 들어본다고 언급한다. (B)에서는 두 사람의 이야기를 모두 들어본 사서가 잠시 생각한 뒤 옆방 창문을 열어 문제를 해결한다고 설명하고, (A)에서는 이것이 양쪽 입장의 근원적인 욕구에 집중하여 문제를 해결한 사례임을 정리한다. 따라서 글의 순서로 가장 적절한 것은 ⑤ '(C) – (B) – (A)'이다.

- **quarrel** 싸우다
- **crack** ⓝ (좁은) 틈, (갈라진) 금
- **underlying** ⓐ 근본적인, 기저에 있는
- **negotiation** ⓝ 협상
- **argue back and forth** 옥신각신하다, 설왕설래하다
- **state** ⓥ 언급하다, 말하다
- **typical** ⓐ 전형의, 전형적인
- **conflict** ⓝ 충돌, 갈등

구문 풀이

5행 The librarian could not have invented the solution she did if she had
「주어 + 조동사 과거형 + have p.p. ~」
focused only on the two men's stated positions of wanting the window open or
「if + 주어 + had p.p. ~ : 가정법 과거완료(과거 사실의 반대 가정)」
closed.

★★ 문제 해결 꿀~팁 ★★

▶ 많이 틀린 이유는?
도서관에서 싸우는 두 사람을 중재시킨 사서의 예를 통해 협상의 기본 원칙을 보여주는 글로, (C) 이후 나머지 두 단락의 순서를 파악하는 것이 관건이다. (A)의 첫 문장을 살펴보면, 사서가 만일 두 사람이 말로 표현한 입장에만 치중한다면 '그 해결책(the solution)'을 고안할 수 없었을 것이라는 의미이다. 하지만 (C)에서는 아직 해결책이 언급되지 않으므로, (C) 뒤에 (A)를 연결하면 the solution으로 가리킬 내용이 앞에 없어 흐름이 어색해진다.

▶ 문제 해결 방법은?
(B)에서 사서가 옆방 창문을 열어 외풍 없이 신선한 공기를 들여왔다고 하는데, 바로 이 내용을 (A)에서 the solution으로 받았다.

---

37 질문의 프레이밍이 답변에 미치는 영향   정답률 64% | 정답 ③

주어진 글 다음에 이어질 글의 순서로 가장 적절한 것을 고르시오.

① (A) – (C) – (B)   ② (B) – (A) – (C)
✔③ (B) – (C) – (A)   ④ (C) – (A) – (B)
⑤ (C) – (B) – (A)

In one survey, / 61 percent of Americans said / that they supported the government / spending more on 'assistance to the poor'.
한 조사에서, / 61%의 미국인들이 말했다. / 그들이 정부를 지지한다고 / '빈곤층 지원'에 더 많은 돈을 쓰는

(B) But when the same population was asked / whether they supported spending more government money on 'welfare', / only 21 percent were in favour.
그러나 같은 모집단이 질문을 받았을 때, / 그들이 '복지'에 더 많은 정부 예산을 쓰는 것을 지지하느냐는 / 단지 21%만이 찬성했다.

In other words, / if you ask people about individual welfare programmes / — such as giving financial help to people / who have long-term illnesses / and paying for school meals / for families with low income / — people are broadly in favour of them.
다시 말해, / 만약 당신이 개별 복지 프로그램에 관해 사람들에게 질문한다면, / 즉 사람들에게 재정적 도움을 주고 / 오랫동안 병을 앓은 / 학교 급식비를 내주는 것 같은 / 저소득층 가정을 위해 / 사람들은 대체로 그것들에 찬성한다.

(C) But if you ask about 'welfare' / — which refers to those exact same programmes / that you've just listed — / they're against it.
그러나 만약 당신이 '복지'에 관해서 질문한다면 / 정확히 똑같은 프로그램을 가리키는, / 당신이 방금 열거한 것과 / 사람들은 그것에 반대한다.

The word 'welfare' has negative connotations, / perhaps because of the way / many politicians and newspapers portray it.
'복지'라는 단어는 부정적인 함축을 가지고 있다. / 방식 때문일지 몰라도 / 많은 정치인들과 신문들이 그것을 묘사하는

(A) Therefore, / the framing of a question / can heavily influence the answer in many ways, / which matters / if your aim is to obtain / a 'true measure' of what people think.
따라서, / 질문의 프레이밍은 / 여러 가지 방식으로 답변에 큰 영향을 미칠 수 있으며, / 이는 중요하다. / 당신의 목표가 얻는 것이라면 / 사람들이 생각하는 것에 대한 '진정한 척도'를

And next time you hear a politician say / 'surveys prove that the majority of the people agree with me', / be very wary.
그리고 다음번에 어느 정치인이 말하는 것을 듣게 되면, / '설문조사를 통해 대다수 국민들이 제게 동의한다는 점이 입증됩니다'라고 / 아주 조심하라.

한 조사에서, 61%의 미국인들이 '빈곤층 지원'에 더 많은 돈을 쓰는 정부를 지지한다고 말했다.
(B) 같은 모집단이 '복지'에 더 많은 정부 예산을 쓰는 것을 지지하느냐는 질문을 받았을 때, 단지 21%만이 찬성했다. 다시 말해, 만약 당신이 개별 복지 프로그램, 즉 오랫동안 병을

앓은 사람들에게 재정적 도움을 주고 저소득층 가정을 위해 학교 급식비를 내주는 것 같은 프로그램에 관해 사람들에게 질문한다면, 사람들은 대체로 그것들에 찬성한다.

(C) 그러나 만약 당신이 방금 열거한 것과 정확히 똑같은 프로그램을 가리키는, '복지'에 관해서 질문한다면 사람들은 그것에 반대한다. '복지'라는 단어는 많은 정치인들과 신문들이 그것을 묘사하는 방식 때문일지 몰라도 부정적인 함축을 가지고 있다.

(A) 따라서, 질문의 프레이밍은 여러 가지 방식으로 답변에 큰 영향을 미칠 수 있으며, 이는 당신의 목표가 사람들이 생각하는 것에 대한 '진정한 척도'를 얻는 것이라면 중요하다. 그리고 다음번에 어느 정치인이 '설문조사를 통해 대다수 국민들이 제게 동의한다는 점이 입증됩니다'라고 말하는 것을 듣게 되면, 아주 조심하라.

Why? 왜 정답일까?

현안이나 문제를 어떤 말로 묘사하는지가 사람들의 응답에 영향을 미칠 수 있다는 내용의 글이다. 주어진 글에서 미국인들의 61%가 '빈곤층 지원'에 정부 예산을 사용하는 데 호의적이라는 예를 제시한 데 이어, (B)는 만일 빈곤층 지원이라는 단어를 '복지'라는 말로 바꾸면 21%만이 호의적인 태도를 보인다는 내용을 대비하여 제시한다. 이어서 (B)의 마지막 문장과 (C)의 첫 번째 문장은 앞서 언급된 내용을 더 자세한 예로 풀어서, 사람들이 '병원비 또는 저소득층 급식비 지원'에는 찬성하면서도 '복지'라는 단어에는 반대할 수 있다고 설명한다. (A)는 예시를 토대로 질문의 프레이밍, 즉 질문의 언어 표현 방식이 여러모로 답변에 영향을 미친다는 결론을 내린다. 따라서 글의 순서로 가장 적절한 것은 ③ '(B) – (C) – (A)'이다.

- **assistance** ⓝ 도움, 원조
- **influence** ⓥ 영향을 미치다 ⓝ 영향
- **welfare** ⓝ 복지
- **framing** ⓝ 프레이밍, (특정한 방식의) 표현
- **politician** ⓝ 정치인
- **portray** ⓥ 묘사하다

구문 풀이

4행 Therefore, the framing of a question can heavily influence the answer in
계속적 용법(앞 문장)
many ways, which matters if your aim is to obtain a 'true measure' of what people
접속사만약 ~라면   관계대명사(~것)
think.

---

38 위험 관리 방법   정답률 65% | 정답 ④

글의 흐름으로 보아, 주어진 문장이 들어가기에 가장 적절한 곳을 고르시오. [3점]

Risk often arises from uncertainty / about how to approach a problem or situation.
위험은 종종 불확실성으로부터 발생한다. / 문제나 상황에 접근하는 방법에 대한

① One way to avoid such risk / is to contract with a party / who is experienced and knows how to do it.
이 위험을 피할 수 있는 한 가지 방식은 / 당사자와 계약하는 것이다. / 경험이 많고 그렇게 하는 방법을 알고 있는

② For example, / to minimize the financial risk / associated with the capital cost of tooling and equipment / for production of a large, complex system, / a manufacturer might subcontract the production of the system's major components / to suppliers familiar with those components.
예를 들어, / 재정적 위험을 최소화하기 위해, / 도구 및 장비의 자본 비용과 관련된 / 크고 복잡한 시스템의 생산을 위한 / 제조업자는 공급업자들에게 시스템 주요 부품 생산의 하청을 줄지도 모른다. / 그러한 부품에 정통한

③ This relieves the manufacturer of the financial risk / associated with the tooling and equipment / to produce these components.
이것은 제조업자에게 재정적 위험을 덜어 준다. / 도구 및 장비와 관련된 / 이러한 부품을 생산하기 위한

✔ However, / transfer of one kind of risk / often means inheriting another kind.
그러나, / 한 종류의 위험의 이전은 / 종종 다른 종류를 이어받는 것을 의미한다.

For example, / subcontracting work for the components / puts the manufacturer / in the position of relying on outsiders, / which increases the risks / associated with quality control, scheduling, and the performance of the end-item system.
예를 들어, / 부품에 대한 작업을 하청 주는 것은 / 제조업자를 처하게 하고, / 외부 업자들에 의존하는 위치에 / 이것은 위험들을 증가시킨다. / 품질 관리, 일정 관리, 완제품 시스템의 성능과 관련된

⑤ But these risks often can be reduced / through careful management of the suppliers.
그러나 이러한 위험들은 종종 감소될 수 있다. / 공급업자들의 신중한 관리를 통해

위험은 종종 문제나 상황에 접근하는 방법에 대한 불확실성으로부터 발생한다. ① 이 위험을 피할 수 있는 한 가지 방식은 경험이 많고 그렇게 하는 방법을 알고 있는 당사자와 계약하는 것이다. ② 예를 들어, 크고 복잡한 시스템의 생산을 위한 도구 및 장비의 자본 비용과 관련된 재정적 위험을 최소화하기 위해, 제조업자는 시스템의 주요 부품에 정통한 공급업자들에게 그러한 부품 생산의 하청을 줄지도 모른다. ③ 이것은 제조업자에게 이러한 부품을 생산하기 위한 도구 및 장비와 관련된 재정적 위험을 덜어 준다. ④ 그러나, 한 종류의 위험의 이전은 종종 다른 종류(위험)를 이어받는 것을 의미한다. 예를 들어, 부품에 대한 작업을 하청 주는 것은 제조업자를 외부 업자들에 의존하게 만들고, 이로 인해 품질 관리, 일정 관리, 완제품 시스템의 성능과 관련된 위험들을 증가시킨다. ⑤ 그러나 이러한 위험들은 공급업자들의 신중한 관리를 통해 종종 감소될 수 있다.

Why? 왜 정답일까?

위험은 방법의 불확실성으로 발생하기 때문에 잘 아는 사람에게 일을 맡기면 위험을 줄일 수 있고, 이로 인해 제조업자들은 부품을 잘 아는 공급업자들에게 하청을 맡기게 된다는 내용이 ④ 앞까지 전개된다. 이어서 주어진 문장은 However로 흐름을 반전시키며, 한 위험이 감소하면 다른 위험이 높아질 수 있다는 사실을 환기시킨다. ④ 뒤의 문장은 높아지는 '다른' 위험에 대한 예로, 제조업자가 부품 생산 하청을 맡기다 보면 외부 업체 의존도가 커지게 될 것이라는 내용을 언급하고 있다. 따라서 주어진 문장이 들어가기에 가장 적절한 곳은 ④이다.

- **inherit** ⓥ 물려받다
- **uncertainty** ⓝ 불확실성
- **minimize** ⓥ 최소화하다
- **component** ⓝ 부품
- **rely on** ~에 의존하다
- **arise** ⓥ 발생하다
- **experienced** ⓐ 경험이 풍부한
- **manufacturer** ⓝ 제조업체
- **familiar with** ~에 익숙한, 정통한

구문 풀이

4행 One way to avoid such risk is to contract with a party [who is experienced
주어   형용사적 용법   동사(단수) 주격 보어   선행사   동사1
and knows how to do it].
동사2

39 꼬리에 꼬리를 무는 위대한 진보
정답률 50% | 정답 ②

글의 흐름으로 보아, 주어진 문장이 들어가기에 가장 적절한 곳을 고르시오.

Ransom Olds, the father of the Oldsmobile, / could not produce his "horseless carriages" fast enough.
Oldsmobile의 창립자인 Ransom Olds는 / '말 없는 마차'를 충분히 빨리 생산할 수 없었다.

In 1901 he had an idea / to speed up the manufacturing process / — instead of building one car at a time, / he created the assembly line.
1901년에, 그는 아이디어를 내서, / 생산 과정의 속도를 높일 / 한 번에 한 대의 자동차를 만드는 대신에, / 그는 조립 라인을 고안했다.

① The acceleration in production was unheard-of / — from an output of 425 automobiles in 1901 / to an impressive 2,500 cars the following year.
생산의 가속은 전례가 없던 것으로, / 1901년 425대의 자동차 생산량에서 / 이듬해 인상적이게도 2,500대의 자동차로

☑ While other competitors were in awe of this incredible volume, / Henry Ford dared to ask, / "Can we do even better?"
다른 경쟁자들이 이 놀라운 분량에 깊은 감명을 받는 동안, / Henry Ford는 감히 질문했다. / "우리가 훨씬 더 잘할 수 있을까?"라고

He was, in fact, able to improve upon Olds's clever idea / by introducing conveyor belts to the assembly line.
실제로 그는 Olds의 훌륭한 아이디어를 개선할 수 있었다. / 컨베이어 벨트를 조립 라인에 도입함으로써

③ As a result, / Ford's production went through the roof.
그 결과, / Ford사의 생산은 최고조에 달했다.

④ Instead of taking a day and a half to manufacture a Model T, / as in the past, / he was now able to spit them out / at a rate of one car every ninety minutes.
Model T를 제작하는 데 1.5일이 걸리는 대신에, / 과거처럼, / 그는 차를 뽑아낼 수 있게 되었다. / 90분마다 한 대씩의 속도로

⑤ The moral of the story is / that good progress is often the herald of great progress.
이 이야기의 교훈은 / 좋은 진보는 종종 위대한 진보의 선구자라는 것이다.

Oldsmobile의 창립자인 Ransom Olds는 '말 없는 마차(자동차의 초창기 호칭)'를 충분히 빨리 생산할 수 없었다. 1901년에, 그는 생산 과정의 속도를 높일 아이디어를 내서, 한 번에 한 대의 자동차를 만드는 대신에, 조립 라인을 고안했다. ① 생산의 가속은 전례가 없던 것으로, 1901년 425대의 자동차 생산량에서 이듬해 인상적이게도 2,500대의 자동차가 생산되었다. ② 다른 경쟁자들이 이 놀라운 분량에 깊은 감명을 받는 동안, Henry Ford는 감히 "우리가 훨씬 더 잘할 수 있을까?"라고 질문했다. 실제로 그는 컨베이어 벨트를 조립 라인에 도입함으로써 Olds의 훌륭한 아이디어를 개선할 수 있었다. ③ 그 결과, Ford사의 생산은 최고조에 달했다. ④ 과거처럼, Model T를 제작하는 데 1.5일이 걸리는 대신에, 그는 90분마다 한 대씩의 속도로 차를 뽑아낼 수 있게 되었다. ⑤ 이 이야기의 교훈은 좋은 진보는 종종 위대한 진보의 선구자라는 것이다.

Why? 왜 정답일까?

② 앞에서 Oldsmobile의 창립자인 Ransom Olds가 조립 라인을 만들어 자동차 생산 속도를 높였다는 내용이 소개된 후, 주어진 문장은 Henry Ford가 이에 감탄하는 데 그치지 않고 '더 잘할' 방법을 모색하기 시작했다는 내용을 이어 간다. ② 뒤의 문장에서는 Henry Ford를 He로 가리키며, 실제로 Ford가 조립 라인에 컨베이어 벨트를 도입하여 시스템을 한층 더 개선했다는 내용을 제시한다. 따라서 주어진 문장이 들어가기에 가장 적절한 곳은 ②이다.

- **incredible** ⓐ 놀라운, 믿기지 않는
- **manufacturing process** 제조 과정
- **acceleration** ⓝ 가속화
- **impressive** ⓐ 인상적인
- **go through the roof** 치솟다, 급등하다
- **moral** ⓝ (이야기나 경험의) 교훈, 도덕률
- **dare** ⓥ 감히 ~하다
- **assembly** ⓝ 조립
- **unheard-of** ⓐ 전례 없는
- **improve** ⓥ 향상되다
- **spit out** 내뱉다

구문 풀이

11행 Instead of taking a day and a half to manufacture a Model T, as (he did)
전치사(~ 대신에) 동명사 / 접속사(~듯이) / 생략

in the past, he was now able to spit them out at a rate of one car every ninety minutes.
~할 수 있었다

40 선택 구조의 변화로 시작된 식습관의 변화
정답률 64% | 정답 ①

다음 글의 내용을 한 문장으로 요약하고자 한다. 빈칸 (A), (B)에 들어갈 말로 가장 적절한 것은?

	(A)	(B)		(A)	(B)
☑	placement 배치	lowered 줄인다	②	placement 배치	boosted 증가시킨다
③	price 가격	lowered 줄인다	④	price 가격	boosted 증가시킨다
⑤	flavor 맛	maintained 유지시킨다			

Anne Thorndike, a primary care physician in Boston, / had a crazy idea.
Boston의 1차 진료 의사인 Anne Thorndike는 / 아주 좋은 생각을 했다.

She believed / she could improve the eating habits / of thousands of hospital staff and visitors / without changing their willpower or motivation / in the slightest way.
그녀는 믿었다. / 자신이 식습관을 개선할 수 있다고 / 수천 명의 병원 직원들과 방문객들의 / 그들의 의지력이나 동기를 바꾸지 않고 / 가벼운 방식으로

In fact, / she didn't plan on talking to them at all.
사실, / 그녀는 그들에게 말해 줄 계획을 세우지 않았다.

Thorndike designed a study / to alter the "choice architecture" of the hospital cafeteria.
Thorndike는 연구를 설계했다. / 병원 구내식당의 '선택 구조'를 바꾸기 위해서

She started / by changing how drinks were arranged in the room.
그녀는 시작했다. / 공간 안에 음료가 놓여 있는 방식을 바꾸는 것으로

Originally, / the refrigerators / located next to the cash registers in the cafeteria / were filled with only soda.
원래, / 냉장고들은 / 구내식당 내의 금전등록기 옆에 위치했고 / 탄산음료로만 채워져 있었다.

She added water as an option to each one.
그녀는 각각의 냉장고에 선택 사항으로 물을 추가했다.

Additionally, / she placed baskets of bottled water / next to the food stations throughout the room.
게다가, / 그녀는 물병이 담긴 바구니를 놓았다. / 공간 전체에 있는 음식을 두는 장소 옆에

Soda was still in the primary refrigerators, / but water was now available at all drink locations.
탄산음료는 여전히 기본 냉장고에 있었지만, / 물은 이제 음료를 둔 모든 곳에서 이용 가능하게 되었다.

Over the next three months, / the number of soda sales at the hospital / dropped by 11.4 percent.
다음 3개월 동안, / 병원의 탄산음료 판매 숫자는 / 11.4퍼센트만큼 떨어졌다.

Meanwhile, / sales of bottled water increased by 25.8 percent.
반면에, / 물병 판매는 25.8퍼센트만큼 증가했다.

➡ The study performed by Thorndike / showed / that the (A) placement of drinks at the hospital cafeteria / influenced the choices people made, / which (B) lowered the consumption of soda.
Thorndike에 의해 수행된 연구는 / 보여주었다. / 병원 구내식당에 음료를 배치하는 것이 / 사람들이 하는 선택에 영향을 주어, / 탄산음료의 소비를 줄인다는 것을

Boston의 1차 진료 의사인 Anne Thorndike는 아주 좋은 생각을 했다. 그녀는 의지력이나 동기를 바꾸지 않고 가벼운 방식으로 수천 명의 병원 직원들과 방문객들의 식습관을 개선할 수 있다고 믿었다. 사실, 그녀는 그들에게 말해 줄 계획을 세우지 않았다. Thorndike는 병원 구내식당의 '선택 구조'를 바꾸기 위해서 연구를 설계했다. 그녀는 공간 안에 음료가 놓여 있는 방식을 바꾸는 것으로 시작했다. 원래, 구내식당 내의 금전등록기 옆에 있는 냉장고들은 탄산음료로만 채워져 있었다. 그녀는 각각의 냉장고에 선택 사항으로 물을 추가했다. 게다가, 그녀는 공간 전체에 있는 음식을 두는 장소 옆에 물병이 담긴 바구니들을 놓았다. 탄산음료는 여전히 기본 냉장고에 있었지만, 물은 이제 음료를 둔 모든 곳에서 이용 가능하게 되었다. 다음 3개월 동안, 병원의 탄산음료 판매 숫자는 11.4퍼센트만큼 떨어졌다. 반면에, 물병의 판매는 25.8퍼센트만큼 증가했다.

➡ Thorndike에 의해 수행된 연구는 병원 구내식당에 음료를 (A) 배치하는 것이 사람들이 하는 선택에 영향을 주어, 탄산음료의 소비를 (B) 줄인다는 것을 보여주었다.

Why? 왜 정답일까?

개인의 의지력 또는 동기를 자극하지 않고 단지 개인이 선택할 수 있는 구조만 바꾸어도 개인의 식습관 변화가 일어날 수 있다는 내용의 글이다. 글의 마지막 세 문장에 따르면, 구내식당에 음료 비치 코너에 물을 추가하여 어디서든 물을 이용할 수 있게 하자, 탄산음료가 선택 사항에서 빠지지 않았음에도 불구하고 물 소비가 증가하고 탄산음료 소비가 떨어졌다고 한다. 이를 근거로 볼 때, 요약문은 구내식당의 음료 '배치'가 사람들의 선택에 영향을 미칠 수 있으며, 이를 잘 활용하면 사람들의 탄산음료 소비를 '줄일' 수 있다는 의미를 나타내야 한다. 따라서 요약문의 빈칸 (A), (B)에 들어갈 말로 가장 적절한 것은 ① '(A) placement(배치) – (B) lowered(줄인다)'이다.

- **physician** ⓝ (내과) 의사
- **willpower** ⓝ 의지력
- **alter** ⓥ 바꾸다
- **be filled with** ~로 채워지다
- **consumption** ⓝ 소비
- **improve** ⓥ 향상시키다
- **slight** ⓐ 약간의, 조금의, 경미한
- **architecture** ⓝ 구성, 건축
- **additionally** ⓐⓓ 추가적으로, 게다가

구문 풀이

7행 Originally, the refrigerators located next to the cash registers in the cafeteria were filled with only soda.
주어 / 과거분사 / 동사구(~로 채워지다)

41-42 분석에 의한 마비 현상

『Paralysis by analysis / is a state of overthinking and analyzing a particular problem, / but you still end up not making a decision.』 41번의 근거
분석에 의한 마비는 / 특정 문제를 지나치게 생각하고 분석하는 상태이지만 / 당신은 여전히 결정을 내리지 못한다.

One famous ancient fable of the fox and the cat / explains this situation of paralysis by analysis / in the simplest way.
여우와 고양이의 한 유명한 고대 우화는 / 이 분석에 의한 마비 상황을 설명한다. / 가장 간단한 방법으로

In the story, / the fox and the cat discuss / how many ways they have / to escape their hunters.
이야기에서, / 여우와 고양이는 논의한다. / 그들에게 얼마나 많은 방법이 있는지 / 사냥꾼으로부터 탈출할 수 있는

Cat quickly climbs a tree.
고양이는 재빨리 나무에 오른다.

Fox, on the other hand, / begins to analyze all the ways to escape / that he knows.
반면에 여우는 / 모든 탈출 방법을 분석하기 시작한다. / 그가 알고 있는

But unable to decide / which one would be the best, / he (a) fails to act / and gets caught by the dogs.
하지만 결정하지 못한 채, / 어떤 것이 가장 좋을지 / 그는 행동하지 못하고 / 개들에게 잡힌다.

This story perfectly illustrates the analysis paralysis phenomenon: / the (b) inability to act or decide / due to overthinking about available alternatives.
이 이야기는 분석 마비 현상을 완벽하게 설명하는데, / 행동하거나 결정하지 못하는 것이다. / 이용 가능한 대안들에 대한 지나친 생각 때문에

People experience / that although they start with a good intention / to find a solution to a problem, / they often analyze indefinitely about various factors / that might lead to wrong decisions.
사람들은 경험한다. / 비록 그들이 좋은 의도로 시작하지만, / 문제의 해결책을 찾으려는 / 그들은 종종 다양한 요인에 대해 무한히 분석하는 것을 / 잘못된 결정을 초래할지 모를

They don't feel satisfied with the available information / and think they still need (c) more data / to perfect their decision.
그들은 이용 가능한 정보에 만족하지 못하고 / 여전히 더 많은 데이터가 필요하다고 생각한다. / 그들의 결정을 완벽하게 하기 위해

『Most often / this situation of paralysis by analysis / (d) arises / when somebody is afraid of making an erroneous decision / that can lead to potential catastrophic consequences: / it might impact their careers or their organizations' productivity.』 42번의 근거
대부분 / 이러한 분석에 의한 마비 상황은 / 발생하는데 / 누군가가 잘못된 결정을 할까 봐 두려워할 때 / 처참한 잠재적 결과를 초래할 수 있는 / 그것은 그들의 경력이나 조직의 생산성에 영향을 미칠 수 있다.

So that's why people are generally (e) overcautious / in making decisions that involve huge stakes.
그래서 그것이 사람들이 일반적으로 지나치게 조심하는 이유이다. / 막대한 이해관계가 수반되는 결정을 내릴 때

분석에 의한 마비는 특정 문제를 지나치게 생각하고 분석하지만 여전히 결정을 내리지 못하는 상태이다. 여우와 고양이의 한 유명한 고대 우화는 이 분석에 의한 마비 상황을 가장 간단한 방법으로 설명한다. 이야기에서, 여우와 고양이는 그들이 사냥꾼으로부터 탈출할 수 있는 얼마나 많은 방법이 있는지 논의한다. 고양이는 재빨리 나무에 오른다. 반면에 여우는 그가

알고 있는 모든 탈출 방법을 분석하기 시작한다. 하지만 어떤 것이 가장 좋을지 결정하지 못한 채, 그는 행동하지 (a) 못하고 개들에게 잡힌다. 이 이야기는 분석 마비 현상을 완벽하게 설명하는데, 이용 가능한 대안들에 대한 지나친 생각 때문에 행동하거나 결정하지 (b) 못하는 것이다. 사람들은 비록 문제의 해결책을 찾으려는 좋은 의도로 시작하지만, 그들은 종종 잘못된 결정을 초래할지 모를 다양한 요인에 대해 무한히 분석하는 것을 경험한다. 그들은 이용 가능한 정보에 만족하지 못하고 그들의 결정을 완벽하게 하기 위해 여전히 (c) 더 많은 데이터가 필요하다고 생각한다. 대부분 이러한 분석에 의한 마비 상황은 누군가가 처참한 잠재적 결과를 초래할 수 있는 잘못된 결정을 할까 봐 두려워할 때 (d) 발생하고, 그들의 경력이나 조직의 생산성에 영향을 미칠 수 있다. 그래서 그것이 사람들이 일반적으로 막대한 이해관계가 수반되는 결정을 내릴 때 (e) 자신이 있는(→ 지나치게 조심하는) 이유이다.

- **analysis** ⓝ 분석
- **end up ~ing** 결국 ~하게 되다
- **illustrate** ⓥ (예를 들어 분명하게) 보여주다
- **inability** ⓝ ~할 수 없음, 무능력
- **intention** ⓝ 의도
- **arise** ⓥ 발생하다
- **catastrophic** ⓐ 처참한, 재앙 같은
- **impact** ⓥ 영향을 미치다
- **keep A from B** A가 B하지 못하게 하다
- **state** ⓝ 상태
- **fable** ⓝ 우화
- **phenomenon** ⓝ 현상
- **alternative** ⓝ 대안 ⓐ 대체의
- **indefinitely** ⓐⓓ 무한히
- **erroneous** ⓐ 잘못된
- **consequence** ⓝ 결과, 영향
- **productivity** ⓝ 생산성

구문 풀이

7행 But (being) unable to decide which one would be the best, he fails to act
생략(분사구문) 형용사 보어　　의문형용사(어떤)　　동사구1(~하지 못하다)
and gets caught by the dogs.
동사구2

---

41 제목 파악　　　정답률 71% | 정답 ④

윗글의 제목으로 가장 적절한 것은?

① Best Ways to Keep You from Overthinking - 당신이 너무 많은 생각을 하지 않게 할 최선의 방법
② Overthinking or Overdoing: Which Is Worse? - 과한 생각 또는 과한 행동: 어느 것이 더 나쁠까?
③ Costs and Benefits of Having Various Alternatives - 다양한 대안을 갖고 있는 것의 비용과 이점
✔ Overthinking: A Barrier to Effective Decision-making - 과한 생각: 효과적인 의사결정의 장애물
⑤ Trapped in Moral Dilemma: Harmful for Your Survival - 도덕적 딜레마에 갇히는 것: 생존에 해롭다

Why? 왜 정답일까?

첫 문장에서 핵심 소재인 '분석에 의한 마비 현상'을 정의 내린 후 예시를 통해 개념을 쉽게 설명해주는 글이다. 'Paralysis by analysis is a state of overthinking and analyzing a particular problem, but you still end up not making a decision.'에서 분석에 의한 마비 상황이란 어떤 문제에 대해 생각이 너무 많아서 쉽게 결정을 내리지 못하는 상태라고 언급하는 것으로 볼 때, 글의 제목으로 가장 적절한 것은 ④ '과한 생각: 효과적인 의사결정의 장애물'이다.

---

42 어휘 추론　　　정답률 55% | 정답 ⑤

밑줄 친 (a) ~ (e) 중에서 문맥상 낱말의 쓰임이 적절하지 않은 것은? [3점]

① (a)　② (b)　③ (c)　④ (d)　✔ (e)

Why? 왜 정답일까?

'Most often this situation of paralysis by analysis arises when somebody is afraid of making an erroneous decision that can lead to potential catastrophic consequences: ~'에서 분석에 의한 마비 현상은 잘못된 결정으로 처참한 결과가 발생할까봐 우려되는 상황에서 발생한다고 언급한다. 이를 근거로 보면, (e)가 포함된 문장은 사람들이 막대한 이해관계가 수반되는 결정을 해야 할 때 '망설이는' 이유가 바로 분석에 의한 마비 현상 때문이라는 의미여야 하므로, (e)의 confident를 overcautious로 고쳐야 한다. 따라서 문맥상 낱말의 쓰임이 적절하지 않은 것은 ⑤ '(e)'이다.

43-45 위기를 기회로 바꾼 Victor

(A)

『Victor applied for the position of office cleaner / at a very big company.』 45번 ①의 근거 일치
Victor는 사무실 청소부 자리에 지원했다. / 아주 큰 회사의
The manager interviewed him, / then gave him a test: / cleaning, stocking, and supplying designated facility areas.
매니저는 그를 인터뷰한 뒤, / 그를 테스트해 보았다. / 청소하기, 비품 정리하기, 지정된 부서에 비품 보급하기 등
After observing what (a) he was doing, / the manager said, / "You are hired.
그가 하는 일을 지켜본 후, / 매니저는 말했다. / "당신은 채용되었습니다.
Give me your email address, / and I'll send you some documents to fill out."
이메일 주소를 알려 주세요, / 그럼 작성하실 몇 가지 서류들을 보내드리겠습니다."

(C)

Victor replied, / "I don't have a computer, nor an email."
Victor는 대답했다. / "저는 컴퓨터도 없고 이메일도 없습니다."
"I'm sorry," said the manager.
"유감이네요."라고 매니저가 말했다.
And he added, / "If you don't have an email, / how do you intend to do this job?
그리고 그는 덧붙였다. / "만약 당신이 이메일이 없다면 / 이 일을 어떻게 하려고 합니까?
This job requires you to have an email address.
이 작업을 하려면 당신은 이메일 주소를 가지고 있어야 합니다.
I can't hire you."
당신을 채용할 수 없습니다."
Victor left with no hope at all.
Victor는 아무 희망도 없이 떠났다.
(d) He didn't know what to do, / with only 10 dollars in his pocket.
그는 어떻게 해야 할지 몰랐다. / 자기 주머니에 10달러만 가진 채
『He then decided to go to the supermarket / and bought a 10kg box of tomatoes.』
그러고 나서 그는 슈퍼마켓에 가기로 결심하고 / 10kg짜리 토마토 한 상자를 샀다. 45번 ③의 근거 일치

(B)

(b) He then sold the tomatoes / in a door to door round.
그 뒤 그는 토마토를 팔았다. / 집집마다 돌아다니며
『In two hours, / he succeeded to double his capital.』 45번 ②의 근거 일치
2시간 만에, / 그는 자본금을 두 배로 늘리는 데 성공했다.
He repeated the operation three times / and returned home with 60 dollars.
그는 이 작업을 세 번 반복했고 / 60달러를 가지고 집으로 돌아왔다.
Victor realized / that he could survive by this way, / and started to go every day earlier, / and returned late.
Victor는 깨닫고, / 그가 이런 방법으로 살아남을 수 있다는 것을 / 매일 더 일찍 나가기 시작했고, / 늦게 돌아왔다.
Thus, (c) his money doubled or tripled each day.
이런 식으로, 그의 돈은 매일 두 배 또는 세 배로 불었다.
Shortly later, / he bought a cart, then a truck, / and then he had his own fleet of delivery vehicles.
얼마 지나지 않아, / 그는 카트를 사고, 트럭을 사고, 이후 자기 배달 차량을 여러 대 갖게 되었다.

(D)

『Several years later, / Victor's company became the biggest food company in his city.』 45번 ④의 근거 일치
몇 년 후, / Victor의 회사는 그의 시에서 가장 큰 식품 회사가 되었다.
He started to plan his family's future, / and decided to get a life insurance.
그는 가족의 미래를 계획하기 시작했고, / 생명 보험에 가입하기로 결심했다.
He called an insurance broker.
그는 보험 중개인을 불렀다.
When the conversation was concluded, / (e) he asked him his email.
대화가 끝나자, / 그는 그에게 이메일을 물었다.
『Victor replied: / "I don't have an email."』 45번 ⑤의 근거 불일치
Victor는 대답했다. / "저는 이메일이 없어요."
The broker replied curiously, / "You don't have an email, / and yet have succeeded to build an empire.
중개인은 의아해하며 대답했다. / "당신은 이메일이 없는데도 / 성공적으로 제국을 건설했군요.
Do you imagine what you could have been / if you had an email?"
어땠을지 상상되나요? / 이메일이 있었다면"
He thought for a while, / and replied, "An office cleaner!"
그는 잠시 생각한 뒤 / "사무실 청소부가 됐을 겁니다!"라고 대답했다.

(A)

Victor는 아주 큰 회사의 사무실 청소부 자리에 지원했다. 매니저는 그를 인터뷰한 뒤, 청소하기, 비품 정리하기, 지정된 부서에 비품 보급하기 등 그를 테스트해 보았다. (a) 그가 하는 일을 지켜본 후, 매니저는 말했다. "당신은 채용되었습니다. 이메일 주소를 알려 주세요, 그럼 작성하실 몇 가지 서류들을 보내드리겠습니다."

Victor는 대답했다. "저는 컴퓨터도 없고 이메일도 없습니다." "유감이네요."라고 매니저가 말했다. 그리고 그는 덧붙였다. "만약 당신이 이메일이 없다면 이 일을 어떻게 하려고 합니까? 이 작업을 하려면 당신은 이메일 주소를 가지고 있어야 합니다. 당신을 채용할 수 없습니다." Victor는 아무 희망도 없이 떠났다. 주머니에 10달러만 가진 채, (d) 그는 어떻게 해야 할지 몰랐다. 그러고 나서 그는 슈퍼마켓에 가기로 결심하고 10kg짜리 토마토 한 상자를 샀다.

그 뒤 (b) 그는 집집마다 돌아다니며 토마토를 팔았다. 2시간 만에, 그는 자본금을 두 배로 늘리는 데 성공했다. 그는 이 작업을 세 번 반복했고 60달러를 가지고 집으로 돌아왔다. Victor는 이런 방법으로 살아남을 수 있다는 것을 깨닫고, 매일 더 일찍 나가기 시작했고, 늦게 돌아왔다. 이런 식으로, (c) 그의 돈은 매일 두 배 또는 세 배로 불었다. 얼마 지나지 않아, 그는 카트를 사고, 트럭을 사고, 이후 자기 배달 차량을 여러 대 갖게 되었다.

(D)

몇 년 후, Victor의 회사는 시에서 가장 큰 식품 회사가 되었다. 그는 가족의 미래를 계획하기 시작했고, 생명 보험에 가입하기로 결심했다. 그는 보험 중개인을 불렀다. 대화가 끝나자, (e) 그는 그에게 이메일을 물었다. Victor가 대답했다. "저는 이메일이 없어요." 중개인은 의아해하며 대답했다, "당신은 이메일이 없는데도 성공적으로 제국을 건설했군요. 이메일이 있었다면 어땠을지 상상되나요?" 그는 잠시 생각한 뒤 대답했다. "사무실 청소부가 됐을 겁니다!"

- **designate** ⓥ 지정하다
- **fill out** (서류 등을) 작성하다
- **triple** ⓥ 3배가 되다
- **fleet** ⓝ (한 기관이 소유한 전체 비행기·버스·택시 등의) 무리
- **life insurance** 생명 보험
- **curiously** ⓐⓓ 의아해하며, 신기한 듯이
- **facility** ⓝ 시설
- **capital** ⓝ 자본
- **broker** ⓝ 중개인

구문 풀이

(A) 2행 The manager interviewed him, then gave him a test: cleaning, stocking, and supplying designated facility areas.
동격(= a test)

(B) 3행 Victor realized that he could survive by this way, and started to go every
동사1　접속사(~것)　　　　　　동사2
day earlier, and returned late.
동사3

---

43 글의 순서 파악　　　정답률 84% | 정답 ②

주어진 글 (A)에 이어질 내용을 순서에 맞게 배열한 것으로 가장 적절한 것은?

① (B) - (D) - (C)　✔ (C) - (B) - (D)　③ (C) - (D) - (B)
④ (D) - (B) - (C)　⑤ (D) - (C) - (B)

Why? 왜 정답일까?

Victor가 사무실 청소부 자리에 지원하여 합격 통보와 함께 이메일 주소를 요청받았다는 내용의 (A) 뒤로, Victor가 이메일이 없다고 답하여 입사를 취소당한 뒤 주머니에 있던 10달러로 토마토를 한 상자 샀다는 내용의 (C)가 연결된다. 이어서 (B)에서는 Victor가 이 토마토를 팔아 2시간 만에 자본금을 두 배로 늘렸고, 같은 식으로 장사를 계속하여 배달 차량을 여러 개 사들일 정도로 돈을 벌었다는 내용을 전개한다. 마지막으로 (D)는 Victor가 몇 년 뒤 시에서 가장 큰 식품 회사를 갖게 되어 미래 대비 차원으로 보험을 알아보다가 이메일 주소를 다시금 요청받고는 자신의 인생을 되돌아보았다는 내용으로 마무리된다. 따라서 글의 순서로 가장 적절한 것은 ② '(C) - (B) - (D)'이다.

44 지칭 추론
정답률 83% | 정답 ⑤

밑줄 친 (a) ~ (e) 중에서 가리키는 대상이 나머지 넷과 다른 것은?
① (a) ② (b) ③ (c) ④ (d) ☑ (e)

Why? 왜 정답일까?
(a), (b), (c), (d)는 Victor, (e)는 앞 문장의 an insurance broker를 가리키므로, (a) ~ (e) 중에서 가리키는 대상이 다른 하나는 ⑤ '(e)'이다.

45 세부 내용 파악
정답률 87% | 정답 ⑤

윗글의 Victor에 관한 내용으로 적절하지 않은 것은?
① 사무실 청소부 자리에 지원하였다.
② 2시간 만에 자본금을 두 배로 만들었다.
③ 슈퍼마켓에 가서 토마토를 샀다.
④ 그의 회사는 도시에서 가장 큰 식품 회사가 되었다.
☑ 이메일이 있다고 보험 중개인에게 답했다.

Why? 왜 정답일까?
(D) 'Victor replied: "I don't have an email."'에서 알 수 있듯이 Victor는 이메일이 있느냐는 보험 중개인의 질문에 '이메일이 없다'고 답하였다. 따라서 내용과 일치하지 않는 것은 ⑤ '이메일이 있다고 보험 중개인에게 답했다.'이다.

Why? 왜 오답일까?
① (A) 'Victor applied for the position of office cleaner at a very big company.'의 내용과 일치한다.
② (B) 'In two hours, he succeeded to double his capital.'의 내용과 일치한다.
③ (C) 'He then decided to go to the supermarket and bought a 10kg box of tomatoes.'의 내용과 일치한다.
④ (D) 'Several years later, Victor's company became the biggest food company in his city.'의 내용과 일치한다.

어휘 Review Test 09
문제편 090쪽

A	B	C	D
01 대안	01 rely on	01 ①	01 ①
02 (몸을)떨다	02 underlying	02 ①	02 ①
03 분석	03 inspire	03 ⓞ	03 ⓔ
04 호기심	04 intentionally	04 ⓚ	04 ⓐ
05 제한하다	05 dare	05 ⓔ	05 ①
06 향상하다	06 logically	06 ①	06 ⓗ
07 기반, 기초	07 donate	07 ⓐ	07 ⓑ
08 잘못된	08 systematically	08 ⓢ	08 ①
09 충돌, 갈등	09 carry out	09 ①	09 ①
10 묘사하다	10 prohibit	10 ⓖ	10 ⓚ
11 시각, 관점	11 credibility	11 ⓠ	11 ⓟ
12 전적으로	12 quarrel	12 ⓝ	12 ⓜ
13 유발하다	13 religious	13 ⓑ	13 ⓔ
14 ~을 떠올리다	14 invisible	14 ⓡ	14 ⓝ
15 위반하다	15 deliberate	15 ①	15 ⓢ
16 인정하다	16 designate	16 ⓓ	16 ⓒ
17 발견	17 capital	17 ⓗ	17 ①
18 각각	18 assistance	18 ⓒ	18 ⓖ
19 검토하다	19 nonverbal	19 ⓟ	19 ⓗ
20 ~을 대표하여	20 existence	20 ⓜ	20 ⓓ

• 정답 •
18 ① 19 ① 20 ③ 21 ⑤ 22 ⑤ 23 ② 24 ⑤ 25 ⑤ 26 ④ 27 ⑤ 28 ③ 29 ⑤ 30 ③ 31 ① 32 ③ 33 ④ 34 ④ 35 ③ 36 ② 37 ⑤ 38 ④ 39 ① 40 ① 41 ② 42 ⑤ 43 ③ 44 ⑤ 45 ④

★ 표기된 문항은 [등급을 가르는 문제]에 해당하는 문항입니다.

18 축제 개막식 공연 부탁하기
정답률 93% | 정답 ①

다음 글의 목적으로 가장 적절한 것은?
☑ 개막 행사에서 연주를 요청하려고
② 공연 스케줄 변경을 공지하려고
③ 학교 행사 취소를 통보하려고
④ 모금 행사 참여를 독려하려고
⑤ 올해의 음악가 상 수상을 축하하려고

Dear Mr. Stanton:
Stanton 씨에게.
We at the Future Music School / have been providing music education to talented children / for 10 years.
저희 Future Music School에서는 / 재능 있는 아이들에게 음악 교육을 제공해 오고 있습니다. / 십 년 동안
We hold an annual festival / to give our students a chance / to share their music with the community / and we always invite a famous musician / to perform in the opening event.
저희는 매년 축제를 개최하며, / 학생들에게 기회를 주기 위해 / 그들의 음악을 지역 사회와 나눌 / 항상 유명한 음악가를 초청합니다. / 개막 행사에서 연주할
Your reputation as a world-class violinist precedes you / and the students consider you the musician / who has influenced them the most.
세계적인 바이올린 연주자로서의 당신의 명성이 자자하고 / 학생들은 당신을 음악가로 생각합니다. / 그들에게 가장 큰 영향을 준
That's why we want to ask you / to perform at the opening event of the festival.
그래서 저희는 당신에게 요청합니다. / 축제 개막 행사에서 공연해 주시기를
It would be an honor for them / to watch one of the most famous violinists of all time play at the show.
그들에게 큰 영광이 될 것입니다. / 공연에서 역대 가장 유명한 바이올린 연주자 중 한 분의 연주를 본다는 것은
It would make the festival more colorful and splendid.
당신의 연주는 축제를 더 다채롭고 훌륭하게 만들어 줄 것입니다.
We look forward to receiving a positive reply.
긍정적인 답변을 받을 수 있기를 기대하겠습니다.
Sincerely, // Steven Forman
Steven Forman 드림

Stanton 씨에게.

저희 Future Music School에서는 십 년 동안 재능 있는 아이들에게 음악 교육을 제공해 오고 있습니다. 저희는 학생들에게 그들의 음악을 지역 사회와 나눌 기회를 주기 위해 매년 축제를 개최하며, 항상 개막 행사에서 연주할 유명한 음악가를 초청합니다. 세계적인 바이올린 연주자로서의 당신의 명성이 자자하고 학생들은 당신을 그들에게 가장 큰 영향을 준 음악가로 생각합니다. 그래서 저희는 당신이 축제 개막 행사에서 공연해 주시기를 요청합니다. 그들이 공연에서 역대 가장 유명한 바이올린 연주자 중 한 분의 연주를 본다는 것은 큰 영광일 것입니다. 당신의 연주는 축제를 더 다채롭고 훌륭하게 만들어 줄 것입니다. 긍정적인 답변을 받을 수 있기를 기대하겠습니다.

Steven Forman 드림

Why? 왜 정답일까?
'That's why we want to ask you to perform at the opening event of the festival.'에서 개막 행사에서 연주를 해주기를 요청한다는 내용이 언급되므로, 글의 목적으로 가장 적절한 것은 ① '개막 행사에서 연주를 요청하려고'이다.

- talented ⓐ 재능 있는
- reputation ⓝ 명성
- influence ⓥ 영향을 끼치다
- look forward to ~을 고대하다
- annual ⓐ 매년의
- precede ⓥ 앞서다, 선행하다
- splendid ⓐ 훌륭한

구문 풀이
6행 Your reputation as a world-class violinist precedes you and the students
주어1 전치사(~로서) 동사1 주어2
consider you the musician [who has influenced them the most].
동사2 목적어 목적격 보어 부사 최상급

19 말하기 대회 우승자 발표
정답률 92% | 정답 ①

다음 글에 드러난 'I'의 심경 변화로 가장 적절한 것은?
☑ nervous → excited
긴장한   신난
② delighted → jealous
기쁜   질투하는
③ indifferent → thrilled
무관심한   황홀한
④ confident → disappointed
자신감 있는   실망한
⑤ furious → relieved
분노한   안도한

It was time for the results of the speech contest.
말하기 대회의 결과 발표 시간이었다.
I was still skeptical / whether I would win a prize or not.
나는 여전히 회의적이었다. / 내가 상을 탈 수 있을지 없을지에 대해
My hands were trembling due to the anxiety.
내 손은 불안감 때문에 떨리고 있었다.
I thought to myself, / 'Did I work hard enough / to outperform the other participants?'
나는 마음속으로 생각했다. / '내가 충분히 열심히 했는가? / 다른 참가자들보다 우수하다고 할 만큼'

After a long wait, / an envelope was handed to the announcer.
오랜 기다림 끝에, / 봉투가 사회자에게 전달되었다.
She tore open the envelope / to pull out the winner's name.
그녀는 봉투를 찢어 열고 / 우승자의 이름을 꺼냈다.
My hands were now sweating / and my heart started pounding really hard and fast.
내 손은 이제 땀이 나고 있었고, / 심장은 정말 격렬하고 빠르게 뛰기 시작했다.
"The winner of the speech contest is Josh Brown!" / the announcer declared.
"말하기 대회의 우승자는 Josh Brown입니다!"라고 / 사회자가 선언했다.
As I realized my name had been called, / I jumped with joy.
내가 내 이름이 불렸다는 것을 깨달았을 때, / 나는 기쁨에 펄쩍 뛰었다.
"I can't believe it. I did it!" I exclaimed.
"믿을 수 없어. 내가 해냈어!"라고 소리쳤다.
I felt like I was in heaven.
나는 마치 천국에 있는 것처럼 느꼈다.
Almost everybody gathered around me / and started congratulating me for my victory.
거의 모든 사람들이 내 주위에 모여 / 내 우승을 축하해 주기 시작했다.

말하기 대회의 결과 발표 시간이었다. 나는 내가 상을 탈 수 있을지 없을지에 대해 여전히 회의적이었다. 내 손은 불안감 때문에 떨리고 있었다. '내가 다른 참가자들보다 우수하다고 할 만큼 충분히 열심히 했는가?'라고 마음속으로 생각했다. 오랜 기다림 끝에, 봉투가 사회자에게 전달되었다. 그녀는 봉투를 찢어 열고 우승자의 이름을 꺼냈다. 내 손은 이제 땀이 나고 있었고, 심장은 정말 격렬하고 빠르게 뛰기 시작했다. "말하기 대회의 우승자는 Josh Brown입니다!"라고 사회자가 선언했다. 내 이름이 불렸다는 것을 깨달았을 때, 나는 기쁨에 펄쩍 뛰었다. "믿을 수 없어. 내가 해냈어!"라고 소리쳤다. 나는 마치 천국에 있는 것처럼 느꼈다. 거의 모든 사람들이 내 주위에 모여 내 우승을 축하해 주기 시작했다.

Why? 왜 정답일까?

'I was still skeptical whether I would win a prize or not. My hands were trembling due to the anxiety.'에서 말하기 대회 우승자 발표를 기다리며 필자가 몹시 긴장했음을 알 수 있고, 'As I realized my name had been called, I jumped with joy.', 'I felt like I was in heaven.'에서 우승자로 지목된 필자가 몹시 기뻐하며 마치 천국에라도 있는 듯한 기분을 느꼈다는 것을 알 수 있다. 따라서 'I'의 심경 변화로 가장 적절한 것은 ① '긴장한 → 신난'이다.

- **skeptical** ⓐ 회의적인
- **anxiety** ⓝ 불안
- **outperform** ⓥ ~을 능가하다, ~보다 더 나은 결과를 내다
- **tear open** ~을 찢어 열다
- **declare** ⓥ 선언하다, 분명히 말하다
- **gather** ⓥ 모이다
- **indifferent** ⓐ 무관심한
- **tremble** ⓥ 떨다
- **pound** ⓥ (심장이) 세차게 뛰다
- **exclaim** ⓥ 소리치다
- **delighted** ⓐ 기쁜
- **furious** ⓐ 분노한

구문 풀이

9행 As I realized (that) my name had been called, I jumped with joy.
접속사(~할 때) 동사(과거) 접속사(~것) 과거완료 수동태

20 삶을 모험으로 인식하기   정답률 85% | 정답 ③

다음 글에서 필자가 주장하는 바로 가장 적절한 것은?
① 반복되는 경험 속에서 인생의 의미를 발견하라.
② 도전하기 전에 실패의 가능성을 신중하게 생각하라.
✓③ 정해진 일상에 안주하기보다 삶에서 모험을 시도하라.
④ 타인의 삶의 방식을 수용하고 인정하는 자세를 지녀라.
⑤ 결단을 실천으로 옮기는 삶 속에서 즐거움을 발견하라.

We all have set patterns in life.
우리는 모두 삶에 정해진 패턴을 가지고 있다.
We like to label ourselves as this or that / and are quite proud of our opinions and beliefs.
우리는 우리 자신을 이것 또는 저것으로 이름 짓기 좋아하고 / 우리의 의견이나 믿음에 대해 꽤 자랑스러워한다.
We all like to read a particular newspaper, / watch the same sorts of TV programs or movies, / go to the same sort of shops every time, / eat the sort of food that suits us, / and wear the same type of clothes.
우리는 모두 특정한 신문을 읽고, / 똑같은 종류의 TV 프로그램이나 영화를 보고, / 매번 똑같은 종류의 가게에 가고, / 우리에게 맞는 종류의 음식을 먹고, / 똑같은 종류의 옷을 입기를 좋아한다.
And all this is fine.
그리고 이 모든 것은 괜찮다.
But if we cut ourselves off from all other possibilities, / we become boring, rigid, hardened / — and thus likely to get knocked about a bit.
그러나 우리가 우리 자신을 모든 다른 가능성으로부터 차단시킨다면, / 우리는 지루하며 완고하고 경직된 상태가 되어서, / 약간은 지치게 될 가능성이 있다.
You have to see life as a series of adventures.
당신은 삶을 일련의 모험으로 보아야 한다.
Each adventure is a chance / to have fun, / learn something, / explore the world, / expand your circle of friends and experience, / and broaden your horizons.
각각의 모험은 기회이다. / 재미를 느끼고 / 무언가를 배우고 / 세상을 탐험하고 / 교우관계와 경험을 확장시키며 / 당신의 지평을 넓힐
Shutting down to adventure means / exactly that — you are shut down.
모험을 멈추는 것은 의미한다. / 바로 당신이 멈추는 것을

우리는 모두 삶에서 정해진 패턴을 가지고 있다. 우리는 우리 자신을 이것 또는 저것으로 이름 짓기 좋아하고 우리의 의견이나 믿음에 대해 꽤 자랑스러워한다. 우리는 모두 특정한 신문을 읽고, 똑같은 종류의 TV 프로그램이나 영화를 보고, 매번 똑같은 종류의 가게에 가고, 우리에게 맞는 종류의 음식을 먹고, 똑같은 종류의 옷을 입기를 좋아한다. 그리고 이 모든 것은 괜찮다. 그러나 우리가 우리 자신을 모든 다른 가능성으로부터 차단시킨다면, 우리는 지루하며 완고하고 경직된 상태가 되어서, 약간은 지치게 될 가능성이 있다. 당신은 삶을 일련의 모험으로 보아야 한다. 각각의 모험은 재미를 느끼고 무언가를 배우고 세상을 탐험하고 교우관계와 경험을 확장시키며 당신의 지평을 넓힐 기회이다. 모험을 멈추는 것은 바로 당신이 멈추는 것을 의미한다.

Why? 왜 정답일까?

'You have to see life as a series of adventures.'에서 삶의 정해진 패턴을 따르며 살기보다 삶

을 모험으로 바라보는 시각이 필요하다고 말하는 것으로 볼 때, 필자가 주장하는 바로 가장 적절한 것은
③ '정해진 일상에 안주하기보다 삶에서 모험을 시도하라.'이다.

- **label A as B** A를 B라고 이름 짓다
- **hardened** ⓐ 굳어진
- **explore** ⓥ 탐험하다
- **cut off from** ~에서 단절시키다
- **knock about** ~을 혹사시키다
- **broaden** ⓥ 확장하다

구문 풀이

9행 Each adventure is a chance to have fun, learn something, explore the
주어 동사 보어 형용사적 용법1 형용사적 용법2 형용사적 용법3
world, expand your circle of friends and experience, and broaden your horizons.
형용사적 용법4   형용사적 용법5(a chance 꾸밈)

★★★ 등급을 가르는 문제!
21 사회적 삶의 연극적 속성   정답률 38% | 정답 ⑤

밑줄 친 constantly wearing masks가 다음 글에서 의미하는 바로 가장 적절한 것은? [3점]
① protecting our faces from harmful external forces
위험한 외부적 힘으로부터 우리 얼굴을 보호하고 있는
② performing on stage to show off our acting skills
우리의 연기력을 뽐내기 위해 무대에서 공연하고 있는
③ feeling confident by beating others in competition
경쟁에서 남을 이겨서 자신감을 느끼고 있는
④ doing completely the opposite of what others expect
다른 사람들이 기대하는 것과 완전히 반대로 행동하고 있는
✓⑤ adjusting our behavior based on the social context given
주어진 사회적 상황에 기초하여 우리의 행동을 적용하는

Over the centuries / various writers and thinkers, / looking at humans from an outside perspective, / have been struck by the theatrical quality of social life.
수 세기에 걸쳐 / 다양한 작가와 사상가들은 / 외부의 관점에서 인간들을 바라보며 / 사회적 삶의 연극적 속성과 마주해왔다.
The most famous quote expressing this comes from Shakespeare: / "All the world's a stage, / And all the men and women merely players; / They have their exits and their entrances, / And one man in his time plays many parts."
이것을 표현하는 가장 유명한 명언은 셰익스피어에게서 비롯되는데, / "모든 세상은 연극 무대이고, / 모든 인간은 단지 배우일 뿐이다. / 그들은 퇴장하고 입장한다. / 그리고 일생 동안 한 인간은 다양한 역할을 연기한다."
If the theater and actors were traditionally represented / by the image of masks, / writers such as Shakespeare are implying / that all of us are constantly wearing masks.
만약 연극과 배우들이 전통적으로 가면의 이미지로 표현된다면, / 가면의 이미지로 / 셰익스피어와 같은 작가들은 암시하고 있는 것이다. / 우리 모두는 끊임없이 가면을 쓰고 있다는 것을
Some people are better actors than others.
어떤 사람들은 다른 사람보다 더 나은 배우이다.
Evil types such as Iago in the play Othello / are able to conceal their hostile intentions / behind a friendly smile.
연극 Othello 속 Iago와 같은 악역들은 / 그들의 적대적 의도를 숨길 수 있다. / 친근한 미소 뒤에
Others are able to act with more confidence and bravado / — they often become leaders.
다른 사람들은 더 큰 자신감과 허세를 가지고 연기를 할 수 있고, / 그들은 주로 리더가 된다.
People with excellent acting skills / can better navigate our complex social environments / and get ahead.
훌륭한 연기력을 가지고 있는 사람들은 / 우리의 복잡한 사회적 환경을 더 잘 헤쳐 나갈 수 있고 / 앞서갈 수 있다.

수 세기에 걸쳐 다양한 작가와 사상가들은 외부의 관점에서 인간들을 바라보며 사회적 삶의 연극적 속성과 마주해왔다. 이것을 표현하는 가장 유명한 명언은 셰익스피어에게서 비롯되는데, "모든 세상은 연극 무대이고, 모든 인간은 단지 배우일 뿐이다. 그들은 퇴장하고 입장한다. 그리고 일생 동안 한 인간은 다양한 역할을 연기한다." 만약 연극과 배우들이 전통적으로 가면의 이미지로 표현된다면, 셰익스피어와 같은 작가들은 우리 모두는 끊임없이 가면을 쓰고 있다는 것을 암시하고 있다. 어떤 사람들은 다른 사람보다 더 나은 배우이다. 연극 Othello 속 Iago와 같은 악역들은 그들의 적대적 의도를 친근한 미소 뒤에 숨길 수 있다. 다른 사람들은 더 큰 자신감과 허세를 가지고 연기를 할 수 있고, 그들은 주로 리더가 된다. 훌륭한 연기력을 가지고 있는 사람들은 우리의 복잡한 사회적 환경을 더 잘 헤쳐 나갈 수 있고 앞서갈 수 있다.

Why? 왜 정답일까?

삶을 연극 무대에 비유하고 있는 글로, 인간은 배우와 같아서 살면서 다양한 역할을 맡게 된다("All the world's a stage, / And all the men and women merely players; / ~ one man in his time plays many parts.")는 셰익스피어의 인용구가 주제를 잘 제시하고 있다. 특히 밑줄 뒤의 두 문장에서 적의를 친근한 미소 뒤에 숨긴 채 행동하거나, 자신감과 허세를 잘 가장하여 리더가 되는 경우를 언급하고 있다. 이는 사람들이 상황에 따라 자신이 필요한 대로 처세하기 위해 일정한 역할이나 특성을 꾸며낼 수 있음을 뜻하는 것이다. 따라서 밑줄 친 부분이 의미하는 바로 가장 적절한 것은 ⑤ '주어진 사회적 상황에 기초하여 우리의 행동을 적응시키는'이다.

- **perspective** ⓝ 관점
- **merely** ⓐⓓ 단지
- **constantly** ⓐⓓ 끊임없이
- **navigate** ⓥ (상황을) 다루다, (길을 가며) 방향을 찾다
- **harmful** ⓐ 해로운, 위험한
- **theatrical** ⓐ 연극적인
- **represent** ⓥ 표현하다, 나타내다, 대표하다
- **confidence** ⓝ 자신감
- **show off** 뽐내다

구문 풀이

1행 Over the centuries various writers and thinkers, looking at humans from
기간 부사구 주어 분사구문
an outside perspective, have been struck by the theatrical quality of social life.
현재완료 수동태

★★ 문제 해결 꿀~팁 ★★

▶ 많이 틀린 이유는?
이 글은 삶이 연극과 같다는 내용을 제시하고 있으며, 밑줄 친 부분의 masks는 우리가 사회적 상황에서 연기를 하듯 어떤 모습을 꾸며내어 대처하거나 특정한 역할을 담당한다는 것을 비유한 표현이다. ②는 이 masks를 삶에서의 연기가 아닌 무대에서의 연기와 연관짓고 있어 답으로 적절하지 않다.
▶ 문제 해결 방법은?
글에 인용구가 나오면 주제와 직결된다. 여기서도 삶이 연기와 다를 바 없다는 셰익스피어의 인용구를 토대로 '연기, 연극'이 비유적인 표현임을 이해해야 한다.

22 맹점에 관해 조언해줄 수 있는 사람을 곁에 두기
정답률 71% | 정답 ⑤

다음 글의 요지로 가장 적절한 것은?

① 모르는 부분을 인정하고 질문하는 것이 중요하다.
② 폭넓은 인간관계는 성공에 결정적인 영향을 미친다.
③ 자기발전은 실수를 기회로 만드는 능력에서 비롯된다.
④ 주변에 관심을 가지고 타인을 도와주는 것이 바람직하다.
☑ 자신의 맹점을 인지하도록 도와줄 수 있는 사람이 필요하다.

Personal blind spots are areas / that are visible to others but not to you.
개인의 맹점은 부분이다. / 다른 사람들에게는 보이지만 당신에게는 보이지 않는

The developmental challenge of blind spots / is that you don't know what you don't know.
맹점의 발달상의 어려움은 / 당신이 무엇을 모르는지 모른다는 것이다.

Like that area in the side mirror of your car / where you can't see that truck in the lane next to you, / personal blind spots can easily be overlooked / because you are completely unaware of their presence.
당신 차의 사이드미러 속 부분과 같이, / 당신이 옆 차선에 있는 트럭을 볼 수 없는 / 개인의 맹점은 쉽게 간과될 수 있다. / 당신이 그것의 존재를 전혀 인지하지 못하기 때문에

They can be equally dangerous as well.
그것들은 마찬가지로 똑같이 위험할 수 있다.

That truck you don't see? It's really there!
당신이 보지 못하는 그 트럭? 그것은 정말 거기에 있다!

So are your blind spots.
당신의 맹점도 그러하다.

Just because you don't see them, / doesn't mean they can't run you over.
당신이 그것을 볼 수 없다고 해서 / 그것이 당신을 칠 수 없음을 의미하는 것은 아니다.

This is where you need to enlist the help of others.
이 부분이 당신이 다른 사람의 도움을 구해야 할 부분이다.

You have to develop a crew of special people, / people who are willing to hold up that mirror, / who not only know you well enough to see that truck, / but who also care enough about you / to let you know that it's there.
당신은 특별한 동료들을 만들어야 한다. / 기꺼이 그 거울을 들고, / 그 트럭을 볼 수 있을 정도로 충분히 당신을 잘 알 뿐만 아니라 / 또한 충분히 당신을 아끼는 / 트럭이 존재한다는 것을 당신에게 알려 줄 만큼

개인의 맹점은 다른 사람들에게는 보이지만 당신에게는 보이지 않는 부분이다. 맹점이 지닌 발달상의 어려움은 당신이 무엇을 모르는지 모른다는 것이다. 옆 차선의 트럭을 볼 수 없는 당신 차의 사이드미러 속 부분과 같이, 개인의 맹점은 당신이 그것의 존재를 완전히 인지하지 못하기 때문에 쉽게 간과될 수 있다. 그것들은 마찬가지로 똑같이 위험할 수 있다. 당신이 보지 못하는 그 트럭? 그것은 정말 존재한다! 당신의 맹점도 그러하다. 당신이 그것을 볼 수 없다고 해서 그것이 당신을 칠 수 없음을 의미하는 것은 아니다. 여기서 당신이 다른 사람의 도움을 구해야 한다. 당신은 기꺼이 그 거울을 들고, 그 트럭을 볼 수 있을 정도로 충분히 당신을 잘 알 뿐만 아니라 또한 트럭이 존재한다는 것을 당신에게 알려 줄 만큼 충분히 당신을 아끼는 이런 특별한 동료들을 만들어야 한다.

Why? 왜 정답일까?

마지막 두 문장인 'This is where you need to enlist the help of others. You have to develop a crew of special people, people who are willing to hold up that mirror, who not only know you well enough to see that truck, but who also care enough about you to let you know that it's there.'에서 개인의 맹점은 타인에게는 보이지만 자신에게는 보이지 않는 부분이므로 자신에게 맹점에 관해 조언을 해줄 수 있는 특별한 동료를 곁에 두어야 한다는 조언을 제시하고 있다. 따라서 글의 요지로 가장 적절한 것은 ⑤ '자신의 맹점을 인지하도록 도와줄 수 있는 사람이 필요하다.'이다.

- **blind spot** 맹점
- **overlook** ⓥ 간과하다
- **equally** ⓐⓓ 똑같이
- **enlist** ⓥ (협조나 도움을) 구하다, 요청하다
- **developmental** ⓐ 발달상의
- **unaware** ⓐ 인지하지 못하는
- **run over** (차 등이) ~을 치다

구문 풀이

10행 You have to develop a crew of special people, people [who are willing to hold up that mirror], [who not only know you well enough to see that truck, but who also care enough about you to let you know that it's there].
기꺼이 ~하다 / 동격 / not only + A + but also + B : A뿐만 아니라 B도 / 「형/부 + enough + to부정사」: ~할 만큼 충분히 / 「한/하게」

---

23 아이의 행동 제한을 설정할 때 고려할 사항
정답률 74% | 정답 ②

다음 글의 주제로 가장 적절한 것은?

① ways of giving reward and punishment fairly
보상과 처벌을 공정하게 주는 방법
☑ considerations when placing limits on children's behavior
아이들의 행동에 제한을 설정할 때의 고려사항들
③ increasing necessity of parents' participation in discipline
훈육에 있어 부모 참여의 필요성 증가
④ impact of caregivers' personality on children's development
아동 발달에 양육자의 성격이 미치는 영향
⑤ reasons for encouraging children to do socially right things
아이들에게 사회적으로 옳은 일을 하도록 격려해야 하는 이유

A child whose behavior is out of control / improves / when clear limits on their behavior are set and enforced.
행동이 통제되지 않는 아이는 / 개선된다. / 그의 행동에 대한 분명한 제한이 설정되고 시행될 때

However, parents must agree on / where a limit will be set / and how it will be enforced.
그러나 부모들은 반드시 합의를 해야 한다. / 어디에 제한을 두고 / 어떻게 그것이 시행될지에 대해

The limit and the consequence of breaking the limit / must be clearly presented to the child.
제한과 그 제한을 깨뜨리는 것의 결과는 / 반드시 아이에게 분명하게 제시되어야 한다.

Enforcement of the limit should be consistent and firm.
제한의 시행은 일관성 있고 단호해야 한다.

Too many limits are difficult to learn / and may spoil the normal development of autonomy.
너무 많은 제한은 배우기 어렵고 / 자율성의 정상적 발달을 저해할지도 모른다.

The limit must be reasonable / in terms of the child's age, temperament, and developmental level.
제한은 합당해야 한다. / 아이의 나이, 기질, 발달 수준의 측면에서

To be effective, / both parents (and other adults in the home) / must enforce limits.
효과적이려면 / 부모 모두가 (그리고 가정의 다른 어른들도) / 제한을 시행해야 한다.

Otherwise, children may effectively split the parents / and seek to test the limits with the more indulgent parent.
그렇지 않으면, 아이들은 효과적으로 부모들을 따로 떼어서 / 좀 더 멋대로 하게 하는 부모에게 제한을 시험해 보려 한다.

In all situations, to be effective, / punishment must be brief and linked directly to a behavior.
모든 상황에서 효과적이기 위해서는 / 처벌은 간결하고 행동과 직접적으로 관련 있어야 한다.

행동이 통제되지 않는 아이는 행동에 대한 분명한 제한이 설정되고 시행될 때 개선된다. 그러나 부모들은 어디에 제한을 두고 어떻게 그것이 시행될지에 대해 반드시 합의를 해야 한다. 제한과 그 제한을 깨뜨리는 것의 결과는 반드시 아이에게 분명하게 제시되어야 한다. 제한의 시행은 일관성 있고 단호해야 한다. 너무 많은 제한은 배우기 어렵고 자율성의 정상적 발달을 저해할지도 모른다. 제한은 아이의 나이, 기질, 발달 수준의 측면에서 합당해야 한다. 효과적이려면 부모 모두가 (그리고 가정의 다른 어른들도) 제한을 시행해야 한다. 그렇지 않으면, 아이들은 효과적으로 부모들을 따로 떼어서 좀 더 멋대로 하게 하는 부모에게 제한을 시험해 보려 한다. 모든 상황에서 효과적이기 위해서는 처벌은 간결하고 행동과 직접적으로 관련 있어야 한다.

Why? 왜 정답일까?

첫 두 문장인 'A child whose behavior is out of control improves when clear limits on their behavior are set and enforced. However, parents must agree on where a limit will be set and how it will be enforced.'에서 아이의 행동을 개선하기 위한 제한은 어디에 설정되고 어떻게 시행될지에 대한 부모간의 합의를 바탕으로 만들어져야 한다는 핵심 내용을 제시하고 있다. 따라서 글의 주제로 가장 적절한 것은 ② '아이들의 행동에 제한을 설정할 때의 고려사항들'이다.

- **enforce** ⓥ 시행하다
- **present** ⓥ 제시하다
- **spoil** ⓥ 망치다
- **temperament** ⓝ 기질
- **split** ⓥ 갈라놓다, 분리시키다
- **fairly** ⓐⓓ 공정하게, 꽤
- **consequence** ⓝ 결과
- **consistent** ⓐ 일관성 있는
- **autonomy** ⓝ 자율성
- **effectively** ⓐⓓ 효과적으로
- **punishment** ⓝ 처벌
- **discipline** ⓝ 훈육, 규율

구문 풀이

1행 A child [whose behavior is out of control] improves when clear limits on their behavior are set and enforced.
주어 / 소유격 관계대명사 / 자동사 / 주어 / 접속사(~할 때) / 동사구(수동태)

---

24 항상 다시 쓰일 여지가 있는 발명품 기원의 역사
정답률 74% | 정답 ③

다음 글의 제목으로 가장 적절한 것은?

① How Can You Tell Original from Fake? – 모조품과 진품을 어떻게 구별하는가?
② Exploring the Materials of Ancient Pottery – 고대 자기의 재료 탐구하기
☑ Origin of Inventions: Never-Ending Journey – 발명품의 기원: 끝나지 않는 여정
④ Learn from the Past, Change for the Better – 과거로부터 배우고, 더 나은 쪽으로 바뀌어라
⑤ Science as a Driving Force for Human Civilization – 인간 문명의 동인력인 과학

Many inventions were invented thousands of years ago / so it can be difficult to know their exact origins.
많은 발명들은 수천 년 전에 발명이 되어서 / 그것들의 정확한 기원을 아는 것은 어려울 수 있다.

Sometimes scientists discover a model of an early invention / and from this model / they can accurately tell us / how old it is and where it came from.
때때로 과학자들은 초기 발명품의 모형을 발견하고 / 이 모형으로부터 / 정확하게 우리에게 말해 줄 수 있다. / 그것이 얼마나 오래 되었고 어디에서 왔는지를

However, there is always the possibility / that in the future / other scientists will discover an even older model of the same invention / in a different part of the world.
그러나 가능성이 항상 존재한다. / 미래에 / 다른 과학자들이 똑같은 발명품의 훨씬 더 오래된 모형을 발견할 / 세계의 다른 곳에서

In fact, / we are forever discovering the history of ancient inventions.
사실 / 우리는 고대 발명품들의 역사를 계속해서 발견하고 있다.

An example of this is the invention of pottery.
이것의 한 예는 도자기라는 발명품이다.

For many years / archaeologists believed that pottery was first invented / in the Near East (around modern Iran) / where they had found pots dating back to 9,000 B.C.
수년 동안 / 고고학자들은 도자기가 처음 발명되었다고 믿었다. / 근동지역(현대의 이란 근처)에서 / 그들이 기원전 9,000년으로 거슬러 올라가는 도자기를 발견

In the 1960s, however, / older pots from 10,000 B.C. / were found on Honshu Island, Japan.
그러나, 1960년대에 / 기원전 10,000년의 더 오래된 도자기가 / 일본의 혼슈섬에서 발견되었다.

There is always a possibility / that in the future / archaeologists will find even older pots somewhere else.
가능성은 언제나 존재한다. / 미래에 / 고고학자들이 어딘가에서 훨씬 더 오래된 도자기를 발견

많은 발명들은 수천 년 전에 발명이 되어서 그것들의 정확한 기원을 아는 것은 어려울 수 있다. 때때로 과학자들은 초기 발명품의 모형을 발견하고 이 모형으로부터 그것이 얼마나 오래되었고 어디에서 왔는지를 정확하게 우리에게 말해 줄 수 있다. 그러나 미래에 다른 과학자들이 세계의 다른 곳에서 똑같은 발명품의 훨씬 더 오래된 모형을 발견할 가능성이 항상 존재한다. 사실 우리는 고대 발명품들의 역사를 계속해서 발견하고 있다. 이것의 한 예는 도자기라는 발명품이다. 수년 동안 고고학자들은 그들이 기원전 9,000년으로 거슬러 올라가는 도자기를 발견한 근동지역(현대의 이란 근처)에서 도자기가 처음 발명되었다고 믿었다. 그러나, 1960년대에 기원전 10,000년의 더 오래된 도자기가 일본의 혼슈섬에서 발견되었다. 미래에 고고학자들이 어딘가에서 훨씬 더 오래된 도자기를 발견할 가능성은 언제나 존재한다.

Why? 왜 정답일까?

글 중간의 'However, there is always the possibility that in the future other scientists will discover an even older model of the same invention in a different part of the world. In fact, we are forever discovering the history of ancient inventions.'에서 이미 원형이 발견되었다고 여겨진 발명품이라 할지라도 항상 더 오래된 모형이 발견될 여지는 있으며 실제로

그러한 사례가 계속 나오고 있다는 내용이 제시되므로, 글의 제목으로 가장 적절한 것은 이를 적절히 요약한 ③ '발명품의 기원: 끝나지 않는 여정'이다.

- **accurately** @d 정확하게
- **pottery** ⑪ 도자기
- **date back to** ~로 거슬러 올라가다
- **driving force** 동인(動因), 추동하는 힘
- **ancient** @ 고대의
- **archaeologist** ⑪ 고고학자
- **tell A from B** A와 B를 구별하다

구문 풀이

5행 However, there is always the possibility that in the future other scientists
동사(단수)   주어   동격 접속사   주어
will discover an even older model of the same invention in a different part of the
동사   비교급 강조 부사   비교급 형용사
world.

---

25 5개 국의 전기차 재고량   정답률 77% | 정답 ⑤

다음 도표의 내용과 일치하지 않는 것은?

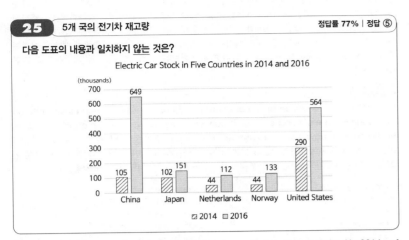

Electric Car Stock in Five Countries in 2014 and 2016

The graph above / shows the amount of the electric car stock in five countries / in 2014 and 2016.
위 그래프는 / 5개국의 전기차 재고량을 보여준다. / 2014년과 2016년에

① All five countries had / more electric car stock in 2016 than in 2014.
5개국 모두 / 2014년보다 2016년에 더 많은 전기차 재고량을 보유했다.

② In 2014, the electric car stock of the United States / ranked first among the five countries, / followed by that of China.
2014년 미국의 전기차 재고량은 / 5개의 국가들 중에서 1위를 차지했고, / 중국이 뒤를 이었다.

③ However, / China showed the biggest increase of electric car stock / from 2014 to 2016, / surpassing the United States in electric car stock in 2016.
그러나 / 중국은 전기차 재고량의 가장 큰 증가를 보였고, / 2014년에서부터 2016년까지 / 2016년에 전기차 재고량에서 미국을 넘어섰다.

④ Between 2014 and 2016, / the increase in electric car stock in Japan / was less than that in Norway.
2014년과 2016년 사이에 / 일본의 전기차 재고량의 증가는 / 노르웨이보다 적었다.

☑ In the Netherlands, / the electric car stock / was more than three times larger in 2016 than in 2014.
네덜란드에서, / 전기차 재고량은 / 2014년보다 2016년에 3배 이상 더 많았다.

위 그래프는 5개국의 2014년과 2016년 전기차 재고량을 보여준다. ① 5개국 모두 2014년보다 2016년에 더 많은 전기차 재고량을 보유했다. ② 2014년 미국의 전기차 재고량은 5개의 국가들 중에서 1위를 차지했고, 중국이 뒤를 이었다. ③ 그러나 중국은 2014년에서부터 2016년까지 전기차 재고량의 가장 큰 증가를 보였고, 2016년에 전기차 재고량에서 미국을 넘어섰다. ④ 2014년과 2016년 사이에 일본의 전기차 재고량의 증가는 노르웨이보다 적었다. ⑤ 네덜란드에서, 전기차 재고량은 2014년보다 2016년에 3배 이상 더 많았다.

Why? 왜 정답일까?

도표에 따르면 2014년 네덜란드의 전기차 재고량은 4만 4천대이고, 2016년의 재고량은 11만 2천 대로, 후자는 전자의 세 배에 미치지 못한다. 따라서 도표와 일치하지 않는 것은 ⑤이다.

- **electric car** 전기 차
- **surpass** ⓥ 넘어서다, 능가하다

---

26 임팔라의 특징   정답률 85% | 정답 ④

impala에 관한 다음 글의 내용과 일치하지 않는 것은?

① 암컷과 수컷 모두 배가 하얗다.
② 수컷은 길고 뾰족한 뿔이 있다.
③ 풀, 과일, 나뭇잎을 먹고 산다.
☑ 우기가 시작될 무렵 번식기를 가진다.
⑤ 평균 수명은 야생에서 13년에서 15년이다.

The impala is one of the most graceful four-legged animals.
임팔라는 가장 우아한 네발 동물 중의 하나이다.

Impalas have the ability / to adapt to different environments of the savannas.
임팔라는 능력이 있다. / 대초원의 여러 환경에 적응하는

『Both male and female impalas / are similar in color, / with white bellies and black-tipped ears.』 ①의근거 일치
수컷과 암컷 임팔라 모두 / 색깔이 비슷한데 / 배가 하얗고 귀 끝부분이 검다.

『Male impalas have long and pointed horns / which can measure 90 centimeters in length.』 ②의근거 일치
수컷 임팔라는 길고 뾰족한 뿔이 있다. / 길이가 90센티미터에 이를 수 있는

Female impalas have no horns.
암컷 임팔라는 뿔이 없다.

『Impalas feed upon grass, fruits, and leaves from trees.』 ③의근거 일치
임팔라들은 풀, 과일, 나뭇잎을 먹고 산다.

When conditions are harsh in the dry season, / they come together to search for food in mixed herds / which can number as many as 100-200 individuals.
건기에 상황이 열악할 때, / 그것들은 먹이를 찾기 위해 뒤섞인 무리로 모인다. / 그 수가 100에서 200마리에 달할 수 있는

『The breeding season occurs / at the end of the wet season around May.』 ④의근거 불일치
번식기는 일어난다. / 5월 무렵 우기의 끝에

Females give birth in an isolated spot away from the herd.
암컷은 무리에서 떨어져 고립된 장소에서 출산한다.

『The average life span of an impala / is between 13 and 15 years in the wild.』 ⑤의근거 일치
임팔라의 평균 수명은 / 야생에서 13년에서 15년 사이이다.

임팔라는 가장 우아한 네발 동물 중의 하나이다. 임팔라는 대초원의 여러 환경에 적응하는 능력이 있다. 수컷과 암컷 임팔라 모두 색깔이 비슷한데 배가 하얗고 귀 끝부분이 검다. 수컷 임팔라는 길이가 90센티미터에 이를 수 있는 길고 뾰족한 뿔이 있다. 암컷 임팔라는 뿔이 없다. 임팔라들은 풀, 과일, 나뭇잎을 먹고 산다. 건기에 상황이 열악할 때, 그것들은 먹이를 찾기 위해 그 수가 100에서 200마리에 달할 수 있는 뒤섞인 무리로 모인다. 번식기는 5월 무렵 우기의 끝에 일어난다. 암컷은 무리에서 떨어져 고립된 장소에서 출산한다. 임팔라의 평균 수명은 야생에서 13년에서 15년 사이이다.

Why? 왜 정답일까?

'The breeding season occurs at the end of the wet season around May.'에서 임팔라의 번식기는 우기가 끝나는 5월 무렵 시작된다고 하므로, 내용과 일치하지 않는 것은 ④ '우기가 시작될 무렵 번식기를 가진다.'이다.

Why? 왜 오답일까?

① 'Both male and female impalas are similar in color, with white bellies ~'의 내용과 일치한다.
② 'Male impalas have long and pointed horns which can measure 90 centimeters in length.'의 내용과 일치한다.
③ 'Impalas feed upon grass, fruits, and leaves from trees.'의 내용과 일치한다.
⑤ 'The average life span of an impala is between 13 and 15 years in the wild.'의 내용과 일치한다.

- **graceful** @ 우아한
- **pointed** @ 뾰족한
- **harsh** @ 혹독한, 가혹한
- **give birth** 출산하다
- **belly** ⑪ 배
- **feed upon** ~을 먹고 살다
- **breeding season** 번식기
- **isolated** @ 고립된

구문 풀이

7행 When conditions are harsh in the dry season, they come together to search
접속사(~할 때)   주어   동사   부사적 용법(~하기 위해)
for food in mixed herds [which can number as many as 100-200 individuals].
선행사   주격 관·대   동사   「as + 원급 + as : ~만큼 …한/하게」

---

27 노인 수영 수업 안내   정답률 89% | 정답 ⑤

Silver Aqua Classes에 관한 다음 안내문의 내용과 일치하지 않는 것은?

① 노인 고객들을 위한 일일 강좌이다.
② 6월 9일 화요일에 진행된다.
③ 오후에 수중 에어로빅 수업이 있다.
④ 1인당 입장료는 5달러이다.
☑ 사전 참가 등록이 필요하다.

Silver Aqua Classes
Silver Aqua 수업

Are you bored with your current exercise routine?
지금의 운동 일과에 지루함을 느끼시나요?

『Parkside Pool will host special one-day water exercise classes / for senior customers.』 ①의근거 일치
Parkside Pool에서 특별한 일일 수중 운동 강좌를 엽니다. / 노인 고객들을 위한

Please come and enjoy our senior-friendly pool.
오셔서 노인 친화적 수영장을 즐겨보세요.

Program
프로그램

『Date: Tuesday, June 9』 ②의근거 일치
날짜: 6월 9일 화요일

Special Classes
특별 수업

9:00 a.m. − 10:00 a.m.: water walking
오전 9:00 − 오전 10:00 : 수중 걷기

10:30 a.m. − 11:30 a.m.: recreational swimming
오전 10:30 − 오전 11:30 : 오락 수영

『2:00 p.m. − 3:00 p.m.: water aerobics』 ③의근거 일치
오후 2:00 − 오후 3:00 : 수중 에어로빅

Admission Fee
입장료

『$5 per person / (This includes all classes.)』 ④의근거 일치
1인당 5달러 / (이것은 모든 수업을 포함합니다.)

Notes
참고사항

『No pre-registration necessary, / just show up and have fun!』 ⑤의근거 불일치
사전 등록은 필요 없으니 / 그냥 오셔서 즐기세요!

For more information, / please visit our website at www.parksidepool.org.
더 많은 정보가 필요하시면, / 저희 웹 사이트 www.parsidepool.org를 방문하세요.

Silver Aqua 수업

지금의 운동 일과에 지루함을 느끼시나요? Parkside Pool에서 노인 고객들을 위한 특별한 일일 수중 운동 강좌를 엽니다. 오셔서 노인 친화적 수영장을 즐겨보세요.

프로그램
- 날짜: 화요일, 6월 9일
- 특별 수업
  오전 9:00 − 오전 10:00 : 수중 걷기
  오전 10:30 − 오전 11:30 : 오락 수영
  오후 2:00 − 오후 3:00 : 수중 에어로빅

입장료

– 1인당 5달러(이것은 모든 수업을 포함합니다.)

참고사항
– 사전 등록은 필요 없으니 그냥 오셔서 즐기세요!
– 더 많은 정보가 필요하시면, 저희 웹 사이트 www.parsidepool.org를 방문하세요.

Why? 왜 정답일까?

'No pre-registration necessary, just show up and have fun!'에서 사전 등록은 필요 없다고 하므로, 안내문의 내용과 일치하지 않는 것은 ⑤ '사전 참가 등록이 필요하다.'이다.

Why? 왜 오답일까?

① 'Parkside Pool will host special one-day water exercise classes for senior customers.'의 내용과 일치한다.
② 'Date: Tuesday, June 9'의 내용과 일치한다.
③ '2:00 p.m. – 3:00 p.m.: water aerobics'의 내용과 일치한다.
④ '$5 per person (This includes all classes.)'의 내용과 일치한다.

- current ⓐ 지금의
- recreational ⓐ 오락의
- pre-registration 사전 등록
- senior-friendly 노인 친화적인
- admission fee 입장료, 참가비

---

28 마술 축제 안내 　　　정답률 87% | 정답 ③

Fanstaville Magic Festival에 관한 다음 안내문의 내용과 일치하는 것은?
① 8시간 동안 진행된다.
② 우천 시 취소된다.
✓ 간단한 마술을 배울 수 있다.
④ 참가자에게 기념품은 제공되지 않는다.
⑤ 입장권은 온라인으로만 구매할 수 있다.

Fanstaville Magic Festival
Fanstaville 마술 축제
Welcome to the Fanstaville Magic Festival!
Fanstaville 마술 축제에 오신 걸 환영합니다!
Enjoy a magical experience with your family / and make special memories!
가족과 함께 마법 같은 경험을 즐기고 / 특별한 추억을 만드세요!
『When: July 4th (Saturday), 12:00 – 18:00』 ①의근거 불일치
언제: 7월 4일(토요일), 12:00 – 18:00
Where: Fanstaville Center playground
어디서: Fanstaville Center 운동장
『(If it rains, the event will be held in the gym.)』 ②의근거 불일치
(우천 시, 행사는 체육관에서 열릴 것입니다.)
What:
무엇:
『Learn simple magic tricks.』 ③의근거 일치
간단한 마술 묘기를 배우세요.
Take pictures at the trick art photo zone.
트릭 아트 포토존에서 사진을 찍으세요.
Watch a magic stage show.
마술 쇼를 관람하세요.
Tickets:
티켓:
$20 per person
1인당 20달러
『All participants will receive a free T-shirt as a gift.』 ④의근거 불일치
모든 참가자들은 기념품으로 무료 티셔츠를 받습니다.
『Purchase tickets online at www.fanstaville.com / or at the entrance on the day of the festival.』 ⑤의근거 불일치
티켓은 www.fanstaville.com에서 온라인으로 구매하시거나 / 축제 당일 입구에서 구매하세요.

Fanstaville 마술 축제

Fanstaville 마술 축제에 오신 걸 환영합니다! 가족과 함께 마법 같은 경험을 즐기고 특별한 추억을 만드세요!
• 일시: 7월 4일(토요일), 12:00 – 18:00
• 장소: Fanstaville Center 운동장
  (우천 시, 행사는 체육관에서 열릴 것입니다.)
• 내용:
  – 간단한 마술 묘기를 배우세요.
  – 트릭 아트 포토존에서 사진을 찍으세요.
  – 마술 쇼를 관람하세요.
• 티켓:
  – 1인당 20달러
  – 모든 참가자들은 기념품으로 무료 티셔츠를 받습니다.
  – 티켓은 www.fanstaville.com에서 온라인으로 구매하시거나 축제 당일 입구에서 구매하세요.

Why? 왜 정답일까?

'Learn simple magic tricks.'에서 축제에서 간단한 마술을 배우라고 하므로, 안내문의 내용과 일치하는 것은 ③ '간단한 마술을 배울 수 있다.'이다.

Why? 왜 오답일까?

① 'When: July 4th (Saturday), 12:00 – 18:00'에서 축제는 6시간 동안 열린다고 하였다.
② '(If it rains, the event will be held in the gym.)'에서 우천 시에는 축제가 체육관에서 열린다고 하였다.
④ 'All participants will receive a free T-shirt as a gift.'에서 모든 참가자에게는 무료 티셔츠가 기념품으로 증정된다고 하였다.
⑤ 'Purchase tickets online at www.fanstaville.com or at the entrance on the day of the festival.'에서 입장권은 온라인 사이트뿐 아니라 축제 당일 입구에서도 구매할 수 있다고 하였다.

- magic trick 마술 묘기
- entrance ⓝ 입구
- participant ⓝ 참가자

---

29 공동체에 더 많은 공로를 돌릴 필요성 　　정답률 37% | 정답 ⑤

다음 글의 밑줄 친 부분 중, 어법상 틀린 것은?

Every farmer knows / that the hard part is getting the field ① prepared.
모든 농부들은 안다. / 밭을 준비하는 것이 어려운 부분임을
Inserting seeds and watching ② them grow / is easy.
씨앗을 심고 그것들이 자라는 것을 보는 것은 / 쉽다.
In the case of science and industry, / the community prepares the field, / yet society tends to give all the credit to the individual / who happens to plant a successful seed.
과학과 산업의 경우, / 공동체가 밭을 준비하지만, / 사회는 우연히 성공적인 씨앗을 심은 / 개인에게 모든 공로를 돌리는 경향이 있다.
Planting a seed / does not necessarily require overwhelming intelligence; / creating an environment / that allows seeds to prosper / ③ does.
씨를 심는 것은 / 반드시 엄청난 지능을 필요로 하지는 않지만, / 환경을 만드는 것은 / 씨앗이 번성하게 해 주는 / 그러하다.
We need to give more credit to the community / in science, politics, business, and daily life.
우리는 공동체에 좀 더 많은 공로를 인정해 줄 필요가 있다. / 과학, 정치, 사업 그리고 일상에서
Martin Luther King Jr. was a great man.
Martin Luther King Jr.는 위대한 사람이었다.
Perhaps his greatest strength was his ability / ④ to inspire people to work together / to achieve, against all odds, revolutionary changes / in society's perception of race and in the fairness of the law.
아마도 그의 가장 큰 강점은 그의 능력이었다. / 사람들이 함께 일하도록 고무시키는 / 모든 역경에 맞서 혁명적인 변화를 성취하기 위해서 / 사회의 인종에 대한 인식과 법의 공정성에서의
But to really understand ✓ what he accomplished / requires looking beyond the man.
그러나 그가 성취한 것을 진정으로 이해하는 것은 / 이 사람 너머를 보는 것을 요구한다.
Instead of treating him as the manifestation of everything great, / we should appreciate his role / in allowing America to show that it can be great.
그를 모든 위대한 것들의 표명으로 여기는 대신에 / 우리는 그의 역할을 인정해야 한다. / 미국이 위대해질 수 있음을 보여주게 한 데 있어

모든 농부들은 밭을 준비하는 것이 어려운 부분임을 안다. 씨앗을 심고 그것들이 자라는 것을 보는 것은 쉽다. 과학과 산업의 경우, 공동체가 밭을 준비하지만, 사회는 우연히 성공적인 씨앗을 심은 개인에게 모든 공로를 돌리는 경향이 있다. 씨를 심는 것은 반드시 엄청난 지능을 필요로 하지는 않지만, 씨앗이 번성하게 해 주는 환경을 만드는 것은 필요로 한다. 우리는 과학, 정치, 사업 그리고 일상에서 공동체에 좀 더 많은 공로를 인정해 줄 필요가 있다. Martin Luther King Jr.는 위대한 사람이었다. 아마도 그의 가장 큰 강점은 모든 역경에 맞서 사회의 인종에 대한 인식과 법의 공정성에서의 혁명적인 변화들을 성취하기 위해서 사람들이 함께 일하도록 고무시키는 능력이었다. 그러나 그가 성취한 것을 진정으로 이해하려면 이 사람 너머를 보는 것이 요구된다. 그를 모든 위대한 것들의 표명으로 여기는 대신에 우리는 미국이 위대해질 수 있음을 보여주게 한 데 있어 그의 역할을 인정해야 한다.

Why? 왜 정답일까?

앞에 선행사가 없고 뒤에 'he accomplished'라는 목적어가 없는 절이 뒤따르는 것으로 보아 that 대신 선행사를 포함하는 관계대명사 what을 써야 한다. 따라서 어법상 틀린 것은 ⑤이다.

Why? 왜 오답일까?

① getting의 목적어인 the field가 '준비된 상태로 만들어지는' 대상이므로 과거분사 목적격 보어인 prepared가 적절하게 쓰였다.
② 앞에 나온 복수 명사 seeds를 받기 위해 복수 대명사 them이 바르게 쓰였다.
③ 주어가 동명사인 creating이고 앞에 일반동사 require가 나오므로 단수 대동사 does가 바르게 쓰였다.
④ his ability를 꾸미는 말로 to inspire가 바르게 쓰였다. attempt, ability, chance, opportunity, effort 등은 to부정사의 꾸밈을 받는 명사임을 기억해 둔다.

- industry ⓝ 산업
- overwhelming 엄청난, 압도적인
- against all odds 모든 역경을 딛고
- perception ⓝ 인식
- accomplish ⓥ 성취하다, 달성하다
- give credit to ~에게 공로를 주다, ~을 믿다
- prosper ⓥ 번성하다
- revolutionary ⓐ 혁명적인
- fairness ⓝ 공정함
- appreciate ⓥ (진가를) 인정하다

구문 풀이

9행 Perhaps his greatest strength was his ability to inspire people to work together to achieve, (against all odds), revolutionary changes in society's perception of race and in the fairness of the law.
(inspire + 목적어 + to부정사: ~이 …하도록 고무시키다)
주어 / 동사 / 보어 / 목적(~하기 위해) / ( ): 삽입구 / to achieve의 목적어

★★ 문제 해결 꿀~팁 ★★

▶ 많이 틀린 이유는?
③의 대동사는 앞에 나오는 동사와 대동사의 주어를 보아 결정한다. 세미콜론(;) 앞에 require라는 일반동사가 나오고, 주어가 단수 취급되는 동명사구 'creating ~'이므로 do/does/did 중 does가 바르게 쓰였다.

▶ 문제 해결 방법은?
정답인 ⑤의 'that vs. what'은 어법 문항에서 가장 많이 출제되는 포인트이므로 경우를 나누어 잘 기억해 둔다. 앞에 선행사가 있으면 관계대명사 that, 앞에 선행사가 없고 뒤에 완전한 문장이 나오면 접속사 that, 앞에 선행사가 없고 뒤에도 불완전한 문장이 나오면 관계대명사 what을 쓴다.

30 갑작스러운 성공 또는 부의 위험성 　　정답률 47% | 정답 ③

다음 글의 밑줄 친 부분 중, 문맥상 낱말의 쓰임이 적절하지 않은 것은? [3점]

Sudden success or winnings can be very dangerous.
갑작스러운 성공이나 상금은 아주 위험할 수 있다.
Neurologically, chemicals are released in the brain / that give a powerful burst of excitement and energy, / leading to the desire to ① repeat this experience.
신경학적으로 화학물질들이 뇌에서 분비되고, / 흥분과 에너지의 강력한 분출을 유발하는 / 이 경험을 반복하고자 하는 욕구로 이어진다.

It can be the start of any kind of addiction or manic behavior.
그것이 어떤 종류의 중독 또는 광적 행동의 출발점일 수 있다.
Also, when gains come quickly / we tend to ② lose sight of the basic wisdom / that true success, to really last, / must come through hard work.
또한, 이익이 빨리 얻어질 때, / 우리는 기본적인 지혜를 보지 못하고 놓치는 경향이 있다. / 진정한 성공이 정말 지속되기 위해서는 / 노력을 통해야 한다는
We do not take into account the role / that luck plays in such ✔ sudden gains.
우리는 역할을 고려하지 않는다. / 그처럼 갑작스러운 이익에 있어 운이 하는
We try again and again to recapture that high / from winning so much money or attention.
우리는 그 황홀감을 되찾기 위해 계속해서 시도한다. / 그만큼의 돈이나 관심을 얻는 것으로부터의
We acquire feelings of superiority.
우리는 우월감을 느낀다.
We become especially ④ resistant to anyone / who tries to warn us — they don't understand, we tell ourselves.
우리는 특히 누구에게든 저항하게 된다 / 우리에게 경고를 하려고 하는 / 그들은 이해하지 못한다고 우리는 스스로에게 말한다.
Because this cannot be sustained, / we experience an inevitable ⑤ fall, / which is all the more painful, / leading to the depression part of the cycle.
이것은 지속될 수 없기 때문에 / 우리는 필연적인 추락을 경험하고, / 몹시 고통스러운 / 이는 그 사이클의 우울기로 이어진다.
Although gamblers are the most prone to this, / it equally applies to businesspeople during bubbles / and to people who gain sudden attention from the public.
도박꾼들이 가장 이러기 쉽지만, / 이것은 거품 경제일 때의 사업가들에게 똑같이 적용된다. / 그리고 대중으로부터 갑작스러운 관심을 얻은 사람들에게도

갑작스러운 성공이나 상금은 아주 위험할 수 있다. 신경학적으로 흥분과 에너지의 강력한 분출을 유발하는 화학물질들이 뇌에서 분비되고, 이 경험을 ① 반복하고자 하는 욕구로 이어진다. 그것이 어떤 종류의 중독 또는 광적 행동의 출발점일 수 있다. 또한, 이익이 빨리 얻어질 때, 우리는 진정한 성공이 정말 지속되기 위해서는 노력을 통해야 한다는 기본적인 지혜를 보지 못하고 놓치는 경향이 있다. 우리는 그처럼 ③ 어렵게 얻은(→ 갑작스러운) 이익에 있어 운이 하는 역할을 고려하지 않는다. 우리는 그만큼의 돈이나 관심을 얻는 것으로부터의 그 황홀감을 되찾기 위해 계속해서 시도한다. 우리는 우월감을 느낀다. 우리는 특히 우리에게 경고를 하려고 하는 누구에게든 ④ 저항하게 된다 — 그들은 이해하지 못한다고 우리는 스스로에게 말한다. 이것은 지속될 수 없기 때문에 우리는 필연적이고도 몹시 고통스러운 ⑤ 추락을 경험하고, 이는 그 사이클의 우울기로 이어진다. 도박꾼들이 가장 이러기 쉽지만, 이것은 거품 경제일 때의 사업가들과 대중으로부터 갑작스러운 관심을 얻은 사람들에게도 똑같이 적용된다.

Why? 왜 정답일까?
③ 앞의 문장에서 우리는 갑작스럽게 성공을 거머쥐다 보면 진정한 성공을 지속시키기 위해 노력이 필요하다는 기본적인 지혜를 놓칠 수 있다고 언급한다. 이 뒤에는 우리가 '갑자기 쉽게 얻은' 성공에 운이 개입하였음을 고려하지 않는다는 내용이 연결되어야 하므로, ③의 hard-earned는 sudden으로 고쳐야 한다. 따라서 문맥상 낱말의 쓰임이 적절하지 않은 것은 ③이다.

- neurologically [ad] 신경학적으로
- addiction [n] 중독
- last [v] 지속되다
- hard-earned 어렵게 얻은
- superiority [n] 우월함
- sustain [v] 지속시키다, 지탱하다
- depression [n] 우울, 낮게 패인 곳
- burst [n] 분출
- manic [a] 광적인
- take into account ~을 고려하다
- recapture [v] 되찾다
- resistant [a] 저항하는
- inevitable [a] 필연적인, 불가피한
- prone to ~하기 쉬운

구문 풀이

11행 We become especially resistant to anyone who tries to warn us — they
　　　　　　　2형식 동사　　　형용사 보어　= whoever
don't understand, we tell ourselves.
직접 목적어　주어 동사　간접 목적어

---

31 과일이 당분으로 과당을 선택한 이유　　정답률 48% | 정답 ①

다음 빈칸에 들어갈 말로 가장 적절한 것을 고르시오. [3점]
✔ full - 배가 부르다　② strong - 튼튼하다　③ tired - 피곤하다
④ dangerous - 위험하다　⑤ hungry - 배가 고프다

When is the right time / for the predator to consume the fruit?
적절한 시기는 언제인가? / 포식자가 과일을 섭취하기에
The plant uses the color of the fruit / to signal to predators that it is ripe, / which means that the seed's hull has hardened / — and therefore the sugar content is at its height.
식물은 과일의 색깔을 이용하며, / 포식자에게 과일이 익었음을 알려주기 위해 / 이는 씨의 껍질이 딱딱해졌음을, / 그리하여 당도가 최고에 이르렀음을 의미한다.
Incredibly, the plant has chosen / to manufacture fructose, instead of glucose, / as the sugar in the fruit.
놀랍게도, 식물은 선택해왔다. / 포도당 대신 과당을 만들기로 / 과일의 당분으로서
Glucose raises insulin levels in primates and humans, / which initially raises levels of leptin, a hunger-blocking hormone / — but fructose does not.
포도당은 영장류와 인간의 인슐린 수치를 높여서, / 처음에는 배고픔을 막는 호르몬인 렙틴의 수치를 높이지만, / 과당은 그렇지 않다.
As a result, / the predator never receives the normal message / that it is full.
그 결과 / 포식자는 결국 일반적인 메시지를 받지 못한다. / 배가 부르다는
That makes for a win-win for predator and prey.
그것이 포식자와 먹이에게 상호 이익이 된다.
The animal obtains more calories, / and because it keeps eating more and more fruit / and therefore more seeds, / the plant has a better chance of distributing more of its babies.
동물은 더 많은 열량을 얻고, / 그것이 계속해서 더 많은 과일을 먹기 때문에, / 따라서 더 많은 씨를 / 식물은 더 많은 후손을 퍼뜨릴 더 높은 가능성을 얻는다.

포식자가 과일을 섭취하기에 적절한 시기는 언제인가? 식물은 포식자에게 과일이 익었음을 알려주기 위해 과일의 색깔을 이용하며, 이는 씨의 껍질이 딱딱해졌음을, 그리하여 당도가 최고에 이르렀음을 의미한다. 놀랍게도, 식물은 과일의 당분으로서 포도당 대신 과당을 만들기로 선택해왔다. 포도당은 영장류와 인간의 인슐린 수치를 높여서, 처음에는 배고픔을 막는 호르몬인 렙틴의 수치를 높이지만, 과당은 그렇지 않다. 그 결과 포식자는 결국 배가 부르다는 일반적인 메시지를 받지 못한다. 그것이 포식자와 먹이에게 상호 이익이 된다. 동물은 더

많은 열량을 얻고, 그것이 계속해서 더 많은 과일을, 따라서 더 많은 씨를 먹기 때문에 식물은 더 많은 후손을 퍼뜨릴 더 높은 가능성을 얻는다.

Why? 왜 정답일까?
'Glucose raises insulin levels in primates and humans, which initially raises levels of leptin, a hunger—blocking hormone—but fructose does not.'에서 포도당과는 달리 과당은 배고픔을 막는 호르몬 분비 증가를 유도하지 않는다고 설명하는 것으로 보아, 빈칸에는 동물이 이로 인해 '배부름'을 느끼지 못한다는 의미를 완성하는 ① '배가 부르다'가 들어가야 적절하다. 마지막 두 문장은 이로 인해 동물이 계속해서 과일을 먹고 결과적으로 과일의 씨도 더 많이 먹게 되므로 과일이 번식할 가능성을 높여준다는 결론을 제시하고 있다.

- predator [n] 포식자
- harden [v] 딱딱해지다
- at one's height 최고조에 이른
- manufacture [v] 생산하다
- glucose [n] 포도당
- distribute [v] 퍼뜨리다, 분포시키다
- ripe [a] (과일 등이) 다 익은
- content [n] 함량
- incredibly [ad] 놀랍게도, 믿기 힘들게도
- fructose [n] 과당
- initially [ad] 처음에는

구문 풀이

2행 The plant uses the color of the fruit to signal to predators that it is ripe,
　　　　　　　　　　　　　목적(~하기 위해)　　to signal의 목적어(선행사)
which means that the seed's hull has hardened — and therefore the sugar content
계속적 용법　접속사(~것)　　주어1　동사1(현재완료)　　　　주어2
is at its height.
동사2

---

32 어떤 것을 선택하기 전에 먼저 작게 시도해보기　　정답률 67% | 정답 ③

다음 빈칸에 들어갈 말로 가장 적절한 것을 고르시오.
① trying out what other people do - 다른 사람들이 하는 것을 시험 삼아 해보는
② erasing the least preferred options - 가장 선호하지 않는 선택권을 지우는
✔ testing the option on a smaller scale - 선택을 좀 더 작은 규모로 시험해보는
④ sharing your plans with professionals - 전문가와 계획을 상의하는
⑤ collecting as many examples as possible - 가능한 많은 사례를 모으는

We are often faced with high-level decisions, / where we are unable to predict the results of those decisions.
우리는 종종 높은 수준의 결정에 직면하는데, / 거기에서 우리는 그 결정의 결과를 예측할 수 없다.
In such situations, / most people end up quitting the option altogether, / because the stakes are high / and results are very unpredictable.
그런 경우에, / 대부분의 사람들은 결국 선택권을 전적으로 포기하는데, / 왜냐하면 위험성이 높고 / 결과가 매우 예측 불가능하기 때문이다.
But there is a solution for this.
그러나 여기에는 해결책이 있다.
You should use the process / of testing the option on a smaller scale.
당신은 과정을 활용해야 한다. / 선택을 좀 더 작은 규모로 시험해보는
In many situations, it's wise / to dip your toe in the water / rather than dive in headfirst.
많은 경우에, 현명하다. / 발끝을 담그는 것이 / 물속에 머리부터 뛰어들기보다는
Recently, I was about to enroll / in an expensive coaching program.
최근에, 나는 등록을 하려고 했었다. / 비싼 코칭 프로그램에
But I was not fully convinced / of how the outcome would be.
그러나 나는 완전히 확신하지 못했다. / 그 결과가 어떠할지
Therefore, I used this process / by enrolling in a low-cost mini course with the same instructor.
그러므로 나는 이러한 과정을 활용했다. / 똑같은 강사의 저렴한 미니 코스에 등록함으로써
This helped me understand his methodology, style, and content; / and I was able to test it / with a lower investment, and less time and effort / before committing fully to the expensive program.
이것은 내가 그의 방법론, 스타일, 그리고 교육 내용을 이해하도록 도왔고, / 나는 그것을 시험해 볼 수 있었다. / 더 적은 투자, 그리고 더 적은 시간과 노력으로 / 비싼 프로그램에 완전히 전념하기 전에

우리는 종종 높은 수준의 결정에 직면하는데, 거기에서 우리는 그 결정의 결과를 예측할 수 없다. 그런 경우에, 대부분의 사람들은 결국 선택권을 전적으로 포기하는데, 왜냐하면 위험성이 높고 결과가 매우 예측 불가능하기 때문이다. 그러나 여기에는 해결책이 있다. 당신은 선택을 좀 더 작은 규모로 시험해보는 과정을 활용해야 한다. 많은 경우에, 물속에 머리부터 뛰어들기보다는 발끝을 담그는 것이 현명하다. 최근에, 나는 비싼 코칭 프로그램에 등록을 하려고 했었다. 그러나 나는 그 결과가 어떠할지 완전히 확신하지 못했다. 그러므로 나는 똑같은 강사의 저렴한 미니 코스에 등록함으로써 이러한 과정을 활용했다. 이것은 내가 그의 방법론, 스타일, 그리고 교육 내용을 이해하도록 도왔고, 비싼 프로그램에 완전히 전념하기 전에 나는 그것을 더 적은 투자, 그리고 더 적은 시간과 노력으로 시험해 볼 수 있었다.

Why? 왜 정답일까?
빈칸 뒤의 'In many situations, it's wise to dip your toe in the water rather than dive in headfirst.'에서 물속에 머리부터 다 뛰어들기보다는 발끝을 담가보는게 현명하다는 비유적인 표현을 통해 어떤 것을 선택하기 앞서 작게 시도해보라는 조언을 제시하고 있다. 이어서 마지막 두 문장 또한 필자가 비싼 코칭 프로그램을 듣기로 결정하기 전에 먼저 미니 코스부터 들어 보아서 비교적 저렴한 비용과 노력으로 의사 결정에 참고할 만한 정보를 얻었다고 언급하고 있다. 따라서 빈칸에 들어갈 말로 가장 적절한 것은 ③ '선택을 좀 더 작은 규모로 시험해보는'이다.

- predict [v] 예측하다
- altogether [ad] 전적으로, 완전히
- enroll in ~에 등록하다
- outcome [n] 결과
- content [n] 내용
- end up 결국 ~하게 되다
- dip [v] 담그다, 적시다
- convinced [a] 확신하는
- methodology [n] 방법론
- investment [n] 투자

구문 풀이

1행 We are often faced with high-level decisions, where we are unable to
　　　　　　　　　　　　　　　　　선행사(추상적 공간)　관계부사　~할 수 없다
predict the results of those decisions.

33 문화적 산물이 사람들에게 미치는 영향   정답률 40% | 정답 ④

다음 빈칸에 들어갈 말로 가장 적절한 것을 고르시오. [3점]

① can provide many valuable views – 여러 가치 있는 시각을 제공해줄 수 있다
② reflects the idea of the sociologists – 사회학자들의 생각을 반영한다
③ forms prejudices to certain characters – 특정 캐릭터에 대한 편견을 형성한다
☑ will have the same effect on everyone – 모든 사람에게 똑같은 영향을 줄 것이라
⑤ might resolve social conflicts among people – 사람들 사이의 사회적 갈등을 해결해줄지 모른다

Sociologists have proven / that people bring their own views and values / to the culture they encounter; / books, TV programs, movies, and music / may affect everyone, / but they affect different people in different ways.
사회학자들은 입증해 왔는데, / 사람들이 자신만의 관점이나 가치를 가져온다는 것을 / 그들이 직면하는 문화로 / 책, TV 프로그램, 영화, 음악은 / 모두에게 영향을 줄지도 모르지만 / 그것들은 다양한 사람들에게 다양한 방식으로 영향을 준다.

In a study, / Neil Vidmar and Milton Rokeach / showed episodes of the sitcom *All in the Family* / to viewers with a range of different views on race.
한 연구에서, / Neil Vidmar와 Milton Rokeach는 / 시트콤 *All in the Family*의 에피소드들을 보여주었다. / 인종에 관한 다양한 관점을 가진 시청자들에게

The show centers on a character named Archie Bunker, / an intolerant bigot / who often gets into fights with his more progressive family members.
이 쇼는 Archie Bunker라는 인물에 초점을 맞춘다. / 편협한 고집쟁이인 / 보다 진보적인 가족 구성원들과 자주 싸움에 휘말리는

Vidmar and Rokeach found / that viewers who didn't share Archie Bunker's views / thought the show was very funny / in the way it made fun of Archie's absurd racism / — in fact, this was the producers' intention.
Vidmar와 Rokeach는 발견했는데 / Archie Bunker의 관점을 공유하지 않는 시청자들이 / 그 쇼가 아주 재미있다고 생각했다는 것을 / Archie의 어처구니없는 인종 차별주의를 비웃는 방식에 있어 / 실은 이것이 제작자의 의도였다.

On the other hand, though, / viewers who were themselves bigots / thought Archie Bunker was the hero of the show / and that the producers meant to make fun of his foolish family!
그러나 반면에, / 스스로가 고집쟁이인 시청자들은 / Archie Bunker가 그 쇼의 영웅이라고 생각했고, / 제작자가 Bunker의 어리석은 가족들을 비웃으려 한다고 생각했다!

This demonstrates / why it's a mistake to assume / that a certain cultural product will have the same effect on everyone.
이것은 보여준다. / 왜 가정하는 것이 잘못인지를 / 특정 문화적 산물이 모든 사람에게 똑같은 영향을 줄 것이라고

사회학자들은 사람들이 그들 자신의 관점이나 가치를 그들이 직면하는 문화로 가져온다는 것을 입증해 왔는데, 책, TV 프로그램, 영화, 음악은 모두에게 영향을 줄지도 모르지만 다양한 사람들에게 다양한 방식으로 영향을 준다. 한 연구에서, Neil Vidmar와 Milton Rokeach는 인종에 관한 다양한 관점을 가진 시청자들에게 시트콤 *All in the Family*의 에피소드들을 보여주었다. 이 쇼는 보다 진보적인 가족 구성원들과 자주 싸움에 휘말리는 편협한 고집쟁이 Archie Bunker라는 인물에 초점을 맞춘다. Vidmar와 Rokeach는 Archie Bunker의 관점을 공유하지 않는 시청자들이 Archie의 어처구니없는 인종 차별주의를 비웃는 방식에 있어 그 쇼가 아주 재미있다고 생각했다는 것을 발견했는데, 실은 이것이 제작자의 의도였다. 그러나 반면에, 스스로가 고집쟁이인 시청자들은 Archie Bunker가 그 쇼의 영웅이라고 생각했고, 제작자가 Bunker의 어리석은 가족들을 비웃으려 한다고 생각했다! 이것은 왜 특정 문화적 산물이 모든 사람에게 똑같은 영향을 줄 것이라고 가정하는 것이 잘못인지를 보여준다.

Why? 왜 정답일까?

첫 문장인 '~ books, TV programs, movies, and music may affect everyone, but they affect different people in different ways.'에서 책, TV 프로, 영화, 음악 등은 모두에게 영향을 주기는 하지만 그 영향의 대상과 양상은 다양하다는 주제를 제시하고 있다. 이를 근거로 할 때, 어느 시각이 '잘못된' 것인지를 지적하는 빈칸에는 주제와는 반대로 모두에게 같은 영향이 갈 것으로 생각한다는 내용이 들어가야 하므로, 답으로 가장 적절한 것은 ④ '모든 사람에게 똑같은 영향을 줄 것이라'이다.

- encounter ⓥ 직면하다, 마주치다
- progressive ⓐ 진보적인
- racism ⓝ 인종 차별주의
- assume ⓥ 가정하다
- have an effect on ~에게 영향을 주다
- intolerant ⓐ 편협한
- absurd ⓐ 어처구니없는, 불합리한
- demonstrate ⓥ 분명히 보여주다
- prejudice ⓝ 편견
- resolve ⓥ 해결하다

구문 풀이

14행 This demonstrates why it's a mistake to assume that a certain cultural
       의문부사 └→가주어   진주어   접속사(~것)
product will have the same effect on everyone.

★★ 문제 해결 꿀~팁 ★★

▶ 많이 틀린 이유는?
첫 문장에 따르면 각종 문화적 산물이 사람마다 미치는 영향이 다른데, 이는 사람들이 문화적 산물을 접할 때 각기 자기만의 견해와 가치관을 투영하기 때문이다. 이를 근거로 할 때, 문화적 산물이 사람들에게 가치로운 견해를 '주는' 입장이라고 서술한 ①은 글의 내용과 맞지 않다. ③ 또한 문화적 산물을 특정 캐릭터들에 대한 편견을 형성시키는 주체로 보고 있어 답으로 부적절하다.

▶ 문제 해결 방법은?
첫 문장에서 주제를 제시한 후 이를 뒷받침하는 연구의 내용을 후술한 글이다. 따라서 연구의 결론을 나타내는 빈칸 문장은 첫 문장과 동일한 내용일 것임을 예측할 수 있다.

34 가용성 휴리스틱   정답률 54% | 정답 ④

다음 빈칸에 들어갈 말로 가장 적절한 것을 고르시오. [3점]

① there is little reliable data about workers – 직원에 대한 신뢰성 있는 데이터가 거의 없기
② the frequent contacts help the relationship – 잦은 접촉이 관계에 도움이 되기
③ they want to evaluate employees objectively – 그들은 직원들을 객관적으로 평가하고 싶어 하기
☑ the recent instances dominate their memories – 최근의 사례들이 그들의 기억을 지배하기
⑤ distorted data have no impact on the evaluation – 왜곡된 데이터는 평가에 전혀 영향을 미치지 않기

The availability heuristic refers to a common mistake / that our brains make / by assuming

[문제편 p.095]

/ that the instances or examples / that come to mind easily / are also the most important or prevalent.
가용성 휴리스틱은 일반적인 오류를 가리킨다. / 우리의 뇌가 저지르는 / 가정함으로써 / 사례들이나 예시들이 / 머릿속에 쉽게 떠오르는 / 역시 가장 중요하거나 널리 퍼져 있다고

It shows that we make our decisions / based on the recency of events.
그것은 우리가 의사 결정을 한다는 것을 보여준다. / 사건들의 최신성에 기반하여

We often misjudge the frequency and magnitude of the events / that have happened recently / because of the limitations of our memories.
우리는 종종 사건들의 빈도와 규모를 잘못 판단한다. / 최근에 발생한 / 우리 기억의 한계 때문에

According to Harvard professor, Max Bazerman, / managers conducting performance appraisals / often fall victim to the availability heuristic.
Harvard 대학교의 교수인 Max Bazerman에 따르면, / 직무 수행 평가를 수행하는 관리자들은 / 종종 이 가용성 휴리스틱의 희생양이 된다.

The recency of events / highly influences a supervisor's opinion / during performance appraisals.
사건의 최신성은 / 관리자의 의견에 크게 영향을 미친다. / 직무 수행 평가 기간 중

Managers give more weight to performance / during the three months prior to the evaluation / than to the previous nine months of the evaluation period / because the recent instances dominate their memories.
관리자들은 수행에 더 무게를 둔다. / 평가 직전 3개월 동안의 / 평가 기간 앞의 9개월보다 / 최근의 사례들이 그들의 기억을 지배하기 때문에

The availability heuristic is influenced / by the ease of recall or retrievability / of information of some event.
가용성 휴리스틱은 영향을 받는다. / 회상의 용이함 또는 복구 가능성에 의해서 / 어떤 사건에 대한 정보의

Ease of recall suggests / that if something is more easily recalled in your memory, / you think that it will occur with a high probability.
회상의 용이함은 시사한다. / 만약 어떤 것이 당신의 기억 속에서 더 쉽게 회상된다면, / 당신은 그것이 높은 가능성으로 일어날 것이라고 생각한다는 것을

가용성 휴리스틱은 우리의 뇌가 머릿속에 쉽게 떠오르는 사례들이 역시 가장 중요하거나 널리 퍼져 있다고 가정함으로써 저지르는 일반적인 오류를 가리킨다. 그것은 우리가 사건들의 최신성에 기반하여 의사 결정을 한다는 것을 보여준다. 우리 기억의 한계 때문에 우리는 종종 최근에 발생한 사건들의 빈도와 규모를 잘못 판단한다. Harvard 대학교의 교수인 Max Bazerman에 따르면, 직무 수행 평가를 수행하는 관리자들은 종종 이 가용성 휴리스틱의 희생양이 된다. 사건의 최신성은 직무 수행 평가 기간 중 관리자의 의견에 크게 영향을 미친다. 최근의 사례들이 그들의 기억을 지배하기 때문에 관리자들은 평가 기간 앞의 9개월보다 평가 직전 3개월 동안의 수행에 더 무게를 둔다. 가용성 휴리스틱은 어떤 사건에 대한 정보의 회상 또는 복구 가능성의 용이함에 의해서 영향을 받는다. 회상의 용이함은 만약 어떤 것이 기억 속에서 더 쉽게 회상된다면 당신은 그것이 높은 가능성으로 일어날 것이라고 생각한다는 것을 시사한다.

Why? 왜 정답일까?

가용성 휴리스틱의 특성을 설명하는 'It shows that we make our decisions based on the recency of events.'에서 우리의 의사 결정은 사건의 최신성에 영향을 받을 수 있다는 내용을 제시하고 있다. 이를 근거로 볼 때, 직무 수행을 평가하고 있는 관리자들은 평가 시점 기준으로 최근에 일어난 사건들에 영향을 받아 의견을 형성하게 될 것임을 유추할 수 있다. 따라서 빈칸에 들어갈 말로 가장 적절한 것은 ④ '최근의 사례들이 그들의 기억을 지배하기'이다.

- availability ⓝ 가용성, 이용 가능성
- heuristic ⓐ (교수법·교육이) 체험적인, 스스로 발견하게 하는
- come to mind 떠오르다
- recency ⓝ 최신성
- magnitude ⓝ 규모
- fall victim to ~의 희생양이 되다
- evaluation ⓝ 평가
- objectively ⓐⓓ 객관적으로
- prevalent ⓐ 널리 퍼진, 만연한
- misjudge ⓥ 잘못 판단하다
- limitation ⓝ 한계
- supervisor ⓝ 관리자, 상사
- probability ⓝ 가능성
- distorted ⓐ 왜곡된

구문 풀이

1행 The availability heuristic refers to a common mistake [that our brains
                                                           └→접속사(~것)   선행사   목적격 관·대
make by assuming that the instances or examples {that come to mind easily} are
       ~함으로써   주어   동사(복수)
also the most important or prevalent].
       보어(최상급 형용사)

35 목표에 따라 수요에 다양한 영향을 가하는 마케팅   정답률 65% | 정답 ③

다음 글에서 전체 흐름과 관계 없는 문장은?

Marketing management is concerned / not only with finding and increasing demand / but also with changing or even reducing it.
마케팅 경영은 관련이 있다. / 수요를 찾고 증가시키는 것뿐만 아니라 / 그것을 바꾸거나 심지어 줄이는 것과도

For example, / Uluru (Ayers Rock) might have too many tourists / wanting to climb it, / and Daintree National Park in North Queensland / can become overcrowded in the tourist season.
예를 들어, / Uluru (Ayers Rock)에는 너무 많은 관광객이 있을지도 모르고, / 그것을 등반하기를 원하는 / 그리고 North Queensland의 Daintree 국립공원은 / 관광 시즌에 과도하게 붐비게 될 수 있다.

① Power companies sometimes have trouble meeting demand / during peak usage periods.
전력 회사들은 때때로 수요를 충족시키는 데 어려움이 있다. / 최고 사용 기간 중

② In these and other cases of excess demand, / the needed marketing task, called demarketing, / is to reduce demand temporarily or permanently.
과도한 수요의 이런저런 경우들에서, / 요구되는 마케팅 과업, 즉 역 마케팅은 / 일시적 혹은 영구적으로 수요를 줄이는 것이다.

☑ Efforts should be made / to compensate for the losses / caused by the increase in supply.
노력이 이루어져야 한다. / 손실들을 보상하기 위해서 / 공급 증가에 의해 유발된

④ The aim of demarketing / is not to completely destroy demand, / but only to reduce / or shift it to another time, or even another product.
역 마케팅의 목적은 / 수요를 완전히 없애는 것이 아니라, / 단지 그것을 줄이거나 / 또는 다른 시기 또는 심지어 다른 제품으로 이동시키는 것이다.

⑤ Thus, marketing management / seeks to affect the level, timing, and nature of demand / in a way that helps the organisation achieve its objectives.
따라서, 마케팅 경영은 / 수요의 수준, 시기, 그리고 특성에 영향을 주는 것을 추구한다. / 조직이 그것의 목표를 달성하는 것을 돕는 방식으로

마케팅 경영은 수요를 찾고 증가시키는 것뿐만 아니라 그것을 바꾸거나 심지어 줄이는 것과도 관련이 있다. 예를 들어, Uluru (Ayers Rock)에는 그것을 등반하기를 원하는 너무 많은 관광객이 있을지도 모르고, 그리고 North Queensland의 Daintree 국립공원은 관광 시즌에 과도하게 붐비게 될 수 있다. ① 전력 회사들은 때때로 최고 사용 기간 중 수요를 충족시키는 데 어려움이 있을지 모른다. ② 과도한 이런저런 경우들에서, 요구되는 마케팅 과업, 즉 역 마케팅은 일시적 혹은 영구적으로 수요를 줄이는 것이다. ③ 공급 증가에 의해 유발된 손실들을 보상하기 위해서 노력해야 한다. ④ 역 마케팅의 목적은 수요를 완전히 없애는 것이 아니라, 단지 그것을 줄이거나 또는 다른 시기 또는 심지어 다른 제품으로 이동시키는 것이다. ⑤ 따라서, 마케팅 경영은 조직이 그것의 목표들을 달성하는 것을 돕는 방식으로 수요의 수준, 시기, 그리고 특성에 영향을 주는 것을 추구한다.

Why? 왜 정답일까?

마케팅은 수요를 창출하는 과정뿐 아니라 바꾸거나 줄이는 과정과도 연관되어 있다는 내용을 다룬 글로, 첫 문장과 마지막 문장에 주제가 일관되게 제시된다. 한편 ③은 공급의 증가로 나타난 손실을 보상하고자 노력해야 한다는 내용으로 글의 주제와 무관하다. 따라서 전체 흐름과 관계없는 문장은 ③이다.

- overcrowded ⓐ 과하게 붐비는
- demarketing ⓝ 역 마케팅(수요 억제를 위한 선전 활동)
- temporarily ⓐⓓ 일시적으로　　　● permanently ⓐⓓ 영구적으로
- compensate for ~을 보상하다, 상쇄하다　　● objective ⓝ 목표

구문 풀이

12행 Thus, marketing management seeks to affect the level, timing, and nature of demand in a way [that helps the organisation achieve its objectives].

---

36 기계식 시계의 발명과 그 영향　　정답률 52% | 정답 ②

주어진 글 다음에 이어질 글의 순서로 가장 적절한 것을 고르시오.
① (A) − (C) − (B)　　✓ (B) − (A) − (C)
③ (B) − (C) − (A)　　④ (C) − (A) − (B)
⑤ (C) − (B) − (A)

The invention of the mechanical clock / was influenced by monks / who lived in monasteries / that were the examples of order and routine.
기계식 시계의 발명은 / 수도사들에 의해 영향을 받았다. / 수도원에 살았던 / 질서와 규칙적인 일상의 예시인

(B) They had to keep accurate time / so that monastery bells could be rung at regular intervals / to announce the seven hours of the day / reserved for prayer.
그들은 정확한 시간을 지켜야 했다. / 수도원의 종이 규칙적인 간격으로 울릴 수 있도록 / 하루의 일곱 시간을 알리기 위해 / 기도를 위해 지정된

Early clocks were nothing more than a weight / tied to a rope wrapped around a revolving drum.
초기의 시계들은 무게추에 불과했다. / 회전하는 드럼통 주위에 감긴 줄에 묶인

(A) Time was determined / by watching the length of the weighted rope.
시간은 정해졌다. / 무게를 단 줄의 길이를 관찰하여

The discovery of the pendulum in the seventeenth century / led to the widespread use of clocks and enormous public clocks.
17세기의 흔들리는 추의 발견은 / 시계와 큰 대중 시계의 광범위한 사용으로 이어졌다.

Eventually, / keeping time turned into serving time.
마침내, / 시간을 지키는 것은 시간에 복종하는 것이 되었다.

(C) People started to follow the mechanical time of clocks / rather than their natural body time.
사람들은 기계식 시계의 시간을 따르기 시작했다. / 그들의 자연적 생체 시간보다는

They ate at meal time, / rather than when they were hungry, / and went to bed when it was time, / rather than when they were sleepy.
그들은 식사 시간에 먹었고, / 그들이 배고플 때보다는 / 시간이 되었을 때 자러 갔다. / 그들이 졸릴 때보다는

Even periodicals and fashions became "yearly."
심지어 정기 간행물들과 패션들도 '연간으로' 되었다.

The world had become orderly.
세상은 질서 정연해졌다.

기계식 시계의 발명은 질서와 규칙적인 일상의 예시인 수도원에 살았던 수도사들에 의해 영향을 받았다.

(B) 그들은 기도를 위해 지정된 하루의 일곱 시간을 알리기 위해 수도원의 종이 규칙적인 간격으로 울릴 수 있도록 정확한 시간을 지켜야 했다. 초기의 시계들은 회전하는 드럼통 주위에 감긴 줄에 묶인 무게추에 불과했다.

(A) 시간은 무게를 단 줄의 길이를 관찰하여 정해졌다. 17세기의 흔들리는 추의 발견은 시계와 큰 대중 시계의 광범위한 사용으로 이어졌다. 마침내, 시간을 지키는 것은 시간에 복종하는 것이 되었다.

(C) 사람들은 그들의 자연적 생체 시간보다는 기계식 시계의 시간을 따르기 시작했다. 그들은, 그들이 배고플 때보다는 식사 시간에 먹었고, 졸릴 때보다는 시간이 되었을 때 자러 갔다. 심지어 정기 간행물들과 패션들도 '연간으로' 되었다. 세상은 질서 정연해졌다.

Why? 왜 정답일까?

기계식 시계의 발명이 수도원의 수도사들로 인해 영향을 받았다는 내용의 주어진 글 뒤에는 수도사들을 They로 받아 이들이 기도하기 위해 시간을 잘 지켜 종을 울려야 했다는 설명을 제시하는 (B)가 연결된다. 이어서 (A)는 (B) 후반부에 이어 초기 시계의 특징을 설명하고, (C)는 시계추의 발견 이후 시계가 보다 자리잡고 그 사용이 널리 이루어지면서 사람들이 생체 시간보다는 기계식 시간을 따르게 되었다는 결과를 언급한다. 따라서 글의 순서로 가장 적절한 것은 ② '(B) − (A) − (C)'이다.

- invention ⓝ 발명　　　　　● mechanical ⓐ 기계의
- monk ⓝ 수도사, 승려　　　● widespread ⓐ 널리 퍼진
- enormous ⓐ 거대한, 엄청난　● accurate ⓐ 정확한
- interval ⓝ 간격　　　　　　● periodical ⓝ 정기 간행물
- orderly ⓐ 질서 정연한

구문 풀이

8행 They had to keep accurate time so that monastery bells could be rung at
목적(~하도록)　　　　　　　　조동사 수동태
regular intervals to announce the seven hours of the day reserved for prayer.
목적(~하기 위해)　　　　　명사구　　　　　과거분사구

★★★ 등급을 가르는 문제!
37 편향의 영향력을 제한하기 위한 노력　　정답률 39% | 정답 ⑤

주어진 글 다음에 이어질 글의 순서로 가장 적절한 것을 고르시오. [3점]
① (A) − (C) − (B)　　② (B) − (A) − (C)　　③ (B) − (C) − (A)
④ (C) − (A) − (B)　　✓ (C) − (B) − (A)

Since we know we can't completely eliminate our biases, / we need to try to limit the harmful impacts / they can have on the objectivity and rationality / of our decisions and judgments.
우리는 우리의 편향을 완전히 없앨 수 없다는 것을 알고 있기 때문에, / 우리는 해로운 영향들을 제한하도록 노력할 필요가 있다. / 편향이 객관성과 합리성에 끼칠 수 있는 / 우리의 결정과 판단의

(C) It is important / that we are aware / when one of our cognitive biases is activated / and make a conscious choice to overcome that bias.
중요하다. / 우리가 인지하고, / 언제 우리의 인지적 편향 중 하나가 활성화되는지를 / 그 편향을 극복하기 위한 의식적 결정을 내리는 것이

We need to be aware of the impact / the bias has on our decision making process and our life.
우리는 영향력을 인지할 필요가 있다. / 편향이 우리의 의사 결정 과정과 삶에 끼치는

(B) Then we can choose an appropriate de-biasing strategy / to combat it.
그때 우리 적절한 반(反) 편향 전략을 선택할 수 있다. / 편향과 싸우기 위해

After we have implemented a strategy, / we should check in again / to see if it worked in the way we had hoped.
우리가 전략을 실행해 본 이후에, / 우리는 한 번 더 확인해야 한다. / 그것이 우리가 희망했던 방식대로 작동했는지를 보기 위해

(A) If it did, / we can move on / and make an objective and informed decision.
만약 그랬다면, / 우리는 넘어가서 / 객관적이고 정보에 근거한 결정을 내릴 수 있다.

If it didn't, / we can try the same strategy again / or implement a new one / until we are ready to make a rational judgment.
만약 그러지 않았다면, / 우리는 똑같은 전략을 다시 시도하거나 / 새로운 것을 실행할 수 있다. / 우리가 이성적 판단을 내릴 준비가 될 때까지

우리는 우리의 편향을 완전히 없앨 수 없다는 것을 알고 있기 때문에, 우리는 편향이 우리의 결정과 판단의 객관성과 합리성에 끼칠 수 있는 해로운 영향들을 제한하도록 노력할 필요가 있다.

(C) 우리가 언제 우리의 인지적 편향 중 하나가 활성화되는지를 인지하고, 그 편향을 극복하기 위한 의식적 결정을 내리는 것이 중요하다. 우리는 편향이 우리의 의사 결정 과정과 삶에 끼치는 영향력을 인지할 필요가 있다.

(B) 그때 우리는 편향과 싸우기 위해 적절한 반(反) 편향 전략을 선택할 수 있다. 우리가 전략을 실행해 본 이후에, 우리는 그것이 우리가 희망했던 방식대로 작동했는지를 보기 위해 한 번 더 확인해야 한다.

(A) 만약 그러했다면, 우리는 넘어가서 객관적이고 정보에 근거한 결정을 내릴 수 있다. 만약 그러지 않았다면, 우리는 우리가 이성적 판단을 내릴 준비가 될 때까지 똑같은 전략을 다시 시도하거나 새로운 것을 실행할 수 있다.

Why? 왜 정답일까?

편향의 영향력을 제한하기 위해 노력할 필요가 있다는 내용의 주어진 글 뒤에는, 우리가 편향이 언제 작동하는지를 이해하고 이를 극복하기 위한 의식적인 결정을 내릴 수 있어야 한다는 설명으로 주어진 글의 내용을 뒷받침하는 (C)가 먼저 연결된다. 이어서 (B)는 (C)의 후반부 내용을 받아 '편향이 삶에 미치는 영향력을 우리가 인지할 때' 바로 반 편향 전략 사용으로 나아갈 수 있다는 내용을 제시한다. 마지막으로 (A)는 (B)의 후반부 내용을 받아 전략이 우리가 기대한 대로 작용했는지 그렇지 못했는지에 따라 이어지는 결과를 소개하고 있다. 따라서 글의 순서로 가장 적절한 것은 ⑤ '(C) − (B) − (A)'이다.

- eliminate ⓥ 없애다, 제거하다　● bias ⓝ 편향, 편견
- harmful ⓐ 해로운　　　　　　● objectivity ⓝ 객관성
- rationality ⓝ 합리성　　　　● informed ⓐ 정보에 근거한
- implement ⓥ 실행하다　　　● appropriate ⓐ 적절한
- combat ⓥ 싸우다　　　　　　● cognitive ⓐ 인지적인
- overcome ⓥ 극복하다

구문 풀이

9행 After we have implemented a strategy, we should check in again to see if
접속사(~인지 아닌지)　접속사(~한 이후에)　현재완료　　　　　　　　　목적(~하기 위해)
it worked in the way [we had hoped].
과거완료(worked보다 먼저 일어남)

★★ 문제 해결 꿀~팁 ★★

▶ **많이 틀린 이유는?**
(C)에 이어 (A)와 (B) 중 어느 단락이 이어질지 파악하는 것이 풀이의 관건이다. (C) 뒤에 (A)가 바로 이어질 경우, '편견이 우리의 의사 결정에 영향을 미친다면 우리가 객관적이고 정보에 근거한 판단을 내릴 수 있다'는 의미가 완성되어 맥락에 부합하지 않는다.

▶ **문제 해결 방법은?**
(B) 후반부의 'if it worked in the way we had hoped'를 (A)에서 'if it did ~'와 'if it didn't ~'로 나누어 설명하고 있음을 파악하면 쉽게 답을 고를 수 있다.

---

38 인간과 컴퓨터의 결합　　정답률 56% | 정답 ④

글의 흐름으로 보아, 주어진 문장이 들어가기에 가장 적절한 곳을 고르시오.

It is important to remember / that computers can only carry out instructions / that humans give them.

기억하는 것이 중요하다. / 컴퓨터들은 지시 사항들을 단지 수행만 할 수 있다는 것을 / 인간이 그들에게 부여한

Computers can process data accurately at far greater speeds / than people can, / yet they are limited in many respects — most importantly, they lack common sense.
컴퓨터들은 훨씬 더 빠른 속도로 정확하게 데이터를 처리할 수 있지만, / 사람들이 할 수 있는 것보다 / 그것들은 많은 측면에서 제한되어 있는데, / 가장 중요하게도 이것들은 상식이 부족하다.

① However, / combining the strengths of these machines with human strengths / creates synergy.
그러나, / 이러한 기계들의 강점과 인간의 강점을 결합하는 것은 / 시너지를 생성한다.

② Synergy occurs / when combined resources produce output / that exceeds the sum of the outputs of the same resources / employed separately.
시너지는 일어난다. / 결합된 자원이 산출을 생성할 때 / 바로 그 자원들의 산출의 합을 초과하는 / 각각 사용된

③ A computer works quickly and accurately; / humans work relatively slowly and make mistakes.
컴퓨터는 빠르고 정확하게 작동하지만, / 인간은 상대적으로 느리게 일하고 실수를 한다.

☑A computer cannot make independent decisions, however, / or formulate steps for solving problems, / unless programmed to do so by humans.
그러나, 컴퓨터는 독립적인 결정을 하거나 / 문제를 해결하기 위한 단계를 만들어낼 수 없다. / 인간에 의해서 그렇게 하도록 프로그램되지 않는 한

Even with sophisticated artificial intelligence, / which enables the computer / to learn and then implement what it learns, / the initial programming must be done by humans.
정교한 인공지능조차, / 컴퓨터가 ~할 수 있게 하는 / 학습을 하고 학습한 것을 실행하도록 / 최초의 프로그래밍은 인간에 의해 수행되어야 한다.

⑤ Thus, a human-computer combination / allows the results of human thought / to be translated into efficient processing of large amounts of data.
따라서, 인간-컴퓨터 결합은 / 인간 사고의 결과들이 ~하게 한다. / 많은 데이터의 효율적 처리로 변환되도록

컴퓨터들은 인간이 그들에게 부여한 지시 사항들을 단지 수행만 할 수 있다는 것을 기억하는 것이 중요하다. 컴퓨터들은 사람들이 할 수 있는 것보다 훨씬 더 빠른 속도로 정확하게 데이터를 처리할 수 있지만, 그것들은 많은 측면에서 제한되어 있는데, 가장 중요하게도 이것들은 상식이 부족하다. ① 그러나, 이러한 기계들의 강점과 인간의 강점을 결합하는 것은 시너지를 생성한다. ② 시너지는 결합된 자원들이 바로 그 자원들을 각각 사용한 산출의 합을 초과하는 산출을 생성할 때 일어난다. ③ 컴퓨터는 빠르고 정확하게 작동하지만, 인간은 상대적으로 느리게 일하고 실수를 한다. ④ 그러나, 컴퓨터는 인간에 의해서 그렇게 하도록 프로그램되지 않는 한, 독립적인 결정을 하거나 문제를 해결하기 위한 단계들을 만들어낼 수 없다. 컴퓨터가 학습을 하고 학습한 것을 실행할 수 있게 하는 정교한 인공지능조차, 최초의 프로그래밍은 인간에 의해 수행되어야 한다. ⑤ 따라서, 인간-컴퓨터 결합은 인간 사고의 결과들이 많은 데이터의 효율적 처리로 변환되도록 한다.

Why? 왜 정답일까?

컴퓨터는 결국 인간의 개입을 필요로 한다는 내용을 다룬 글로, ④ 앞뒤의 논리적 공백을 잘 살펴야 한다. ④ 앞에서는 인간이 느리고 실수도 하는 반면 컴퓨터는 빠르고 정확하게 작동한다고 언급한다. 한편 ④ 뒤의 문장은 제 아무리 정교한 인공지능도 초기 프로그래밍은 결국 인간에 의해 이루어져야 한다는 내용을 제시한다. 즉 ④ 앞뒤로 컴퓨터의 능력에 대한 시각이 상반되는 것으로 볼 때, 흐름을 반전시키는 however가 포함된 주어진 문장이 들어가기에 가장 적절한 곳은 ④이다.

- formulate ⓥ 만들어 내다, 공식화하다
- lack ⓥ ~이 부족하다
- separately ⓐⓓ 각각, 별개로
- relatively ⓐⓓ 상대적으로, 비교적
- initial ⓐ 최초의, 초기의
- instruction ⓝ 지시
- employ ⓥ 사용하다
- accurately ⓐⓓ 정확하게
- sophisticated ⓐ 정교한, 세련된
- efficient ⓐ 효율적인

구문 풀이

1행 A computer cannot make independent decisions, however, or formulate steps for solving problems, unless programmed to do so by humans.

★★★ 등급을 가르는 문제!

| 39 | 인간의 비언어적 의사소통 | 정답률 31% | 정답 ① |

글의 흐름으로 보아, 주어진 문장이 들어가기에 가장 적절한 곳을 고르시오. [3점]

For hundreds of thousands of years / our hunter-gatherer ancestors could survive / only by constantly communicating with one another / through nonverbal cues.
수십만 년 동안 / 우리의 수렵-채집인 조상들은 생존할 수 있었다 / 서로 끊임없이 의사소통해야만 / 비언어적 신호를 통해서

Developed over so much time, / before the invention of language, / that is how the human face became so expressive, / and gestures so elaborate.
오랜 시간에 걸쳐 발달되어, / 언어의 발명 이전에 / 그렇게 인간의 얼굴은 매우 표현적이고 / 몸짓은 매우 정교해지게 되었다.

☑We have a continual desire to communicate our feelings / and yet at the same time / the need to conceal them for proper social functioning.
우리는 우리의 감정을 전달하고자 하는 끊임없는 욕망을 지니고 있다. / 하지만 동시에 / 적절한 사회적 기능을 위해 그것들을 감추고자 하는 욕구도

With these counterforces battling inside us, / we cannot completely control what we communicate.
이 반대 세력이 우리 내면에서 다투면서, / 우리는 우리가 전달하는 것을 완전히 통제할 수 없다.

② Our real feelings continually leak out / in the form of gestures, tones of voice, facial expressions, and posture.
우리의 진짜 감정은 끊임없이 새어 나온다. / 몸짓, 목소리의 톤, 얼굴 표정, 그리고 자세의 형태로

③ We are not trained, however, / to pay attention to people's nonverbal cues.
그러나 우리는 훈련받지 않는다. / 사람들의 비언어적 신호에 주의를 기울이도록

④ By sheer habit, we fixate on the words people say, / while also thinking about what we'll say next.
순전한 습관으로 우리는 사람들이 하는 말에 집착하며 / 동시에 또한 우리가 다음번에 말할 것을 생각한다.

⑤ What this means is / that we are using only a small percentage of the potential social skills / we all possess.
이것이 의미하는 것은 / 우리가 잠재적인 사회적 기술들 중 오직 작은 부분만 사용하고 있다는 것이다. / 우리 모두 소유한

수십만 년 동안 우리의 수렵-채집인 조상들은 비언어적 신호들을 통해서 서로 끊임없이 의사소통해야만 생존할 수 있었다. 언어의 발명 이전에 오랜 시간에 걸쳐 발달되어, 그렇게 인간의 얼굴은 매우 표현적이고 몸짓은 매우 정교해지게 되었다. ① 우리는 우리의 감정을 전달

하고자 하는 끊임없는 욕망을 지니고 있지만 동시에 적절한 사회적 기능을 위해 그것들을 감추고자 하는 욕구를 지니고 있다. 이 반대 세력이 우리 내면에서 다투면서, 우리는 우리가 전달하는 것을 완전히 통제할 수 없다. ② 우리의 진짜 감정은 몸짓, 목소리의 톤, 얼굴 표정, 그리고 자세의 형태로 끊임없이 새어 나온다. ③ 그러나 우리는 사람들의 비언어적 신호에 주의를 기울이도록 훈련받지 않는다. ④ 순전한 습관으로 우리는 사람들이 하는 말에 집착하며 동시에 또한 우리가 다음번에 말할 것을 생각한다. ⑤ 이것이 의미하는 것은 우리 모두가 소유한 잠재적인 사회적 기술들 중 오직 작은 부분만을 우리가 사용하고 있다는 것이다.

Why? 왜 정답일까?

인간의 비언어적 의사소통에 관해 설명한 글로, ① 뒤의 지시어에 주목한다. ① 뒤의 문장에서 these counterforces를 언급하는데 앞에는 '상충되는 힘'으로 나타낼 만한 것이 없다. 이때 주어진 문장은 인간이 감정을 나타내고 싶어 하지만 동시에 감정을 감추고 싶어 한다는 내용이므로, 이 'desire to communicate ~'와 'need to conceal ~'을 ① 뒤의 문장에서 these counterforces로 가리키고 있음을 알 수 있다. 따라서 주어진 문장이 들어가기에 가장 적절한 곳은 ①이다.

- continual ⓐ 끊임없는
- constantly ⓐⓓ 끊임없이, 지속적으로
- invention ⓝ 발명
- elaborate ⓐ 정교한
- in the form of ~의 형태로
- possess ⓥ 소유하다
- functioning ⓝ 기능
- nonverbal ⓐ 비언어적인
- expressive ⓐ (감정을) 나타내는, 표현력이 있는
- leak out 새어 나오다
- fixate on ~에 집착하다, ~을 고수하다

구문 풀이

6행 Developed over so much time, before the invention of language, that is how the human face became so expressive, and gestures (became) so elaborate.

★★ 문제 해결 꿀~팁 ★★

▶ 많이 틀린 이유는?
'With these counterforces ~' 이후로 네 문장에 걸쳐 우리가 우리의 의사소통 내용을 완벽히 통제하지 못하기에 비언어적 단서의 형태로 자꾸 진정한 감정을 내비치게 되지만, 우리는 비언어적 단서에 주목하도록 훈련받지 않아서 주로 언어적 단서에 집착한다는 내용이 논리적 공백 없이 기술되어 있다. 따라서 ②, ③, ④는 모두 오답이다.

▶ 문제 해결 방법은?
① 뒤의 these counterforces가 가리키는 바에 주목한다. 만일 주어진 문장이 ①에 들어가지 않으면, these counterforces로 받을 만한 명사는 human face와 gestures 뿐인데, '얼굴과 몸짓'을 '상충하는 힘'으로 일반화하기에는 근거가 부족하다.

| 40 | 인간이 서로 돕고 사는 이유 | 정답률 61% | 정답 ① |

다음 글의 내용을 한 문장으로 요약하고자 한다. 빈칸 (A), (B)에 들어갈 말로 가장 적절한 것은?

	(A)		(B)
☑	advantages 이익	......	repay 되갚다
②	patience 인내	......	evaluate 평가하다
③	wisdom 지혜	......	forget 잊다
④	advantages 이익	......	accept 받아들이다
⑤	patience 인내	......	appreciate 감사하다

Why do we help?
우리는 왜 돕는가?

One widely held view is / that self-interest underlies all human interactions, / that our constant goal is to maximize rewards and minimize costs.
널리 받아들여지는 한 가지 관점은 / 자기 이익이 인간의 모든 상호 작용의 기초가 되고, / 우리의 지속적인 목표가 보상을 극대화하고 비용을 최소화하는 것이라는 것이다.

Accountants call it *cost-benefit analysis*.
회계사들은 그것을 *비용-수익 분석*이라고 부른다.

Philosophers call it *utilitarianism*.
철학자들은 그것을 *공리주의*라고 부른다.

Social psychologists call it social exchange theory.
사회 심리학자들은 그것을 사회적 교환 이론이라고 부른다.

If you are considering whether to donate blood, / you may weigh the costs of doing so (time, discomfort, and anxiety) / against the benefits (reduced guilt, social approval, and good feelings).
만약 당신이 헌혈할지를 생각한다면, / 당신은 그렇게 하는 것의 비용(시간, 불편함, 그리고 걱정)을 따져 볼지도 모른다. / 이익들(죄책감 감소, 사회적 인정, 그리고 좋은 감정)에 대비해서

If the rewards exceed the costs, / you will help.
만약 보상이 비용을 초과한다면 / 당신은 도울 것이다.

Others believe / that we help because we have been socialized to do so, / through norms that prescribe how we ought to behave.
다른 사람들은 믿는다. / 우리가 그렇게 하도록 사회화되어 왔기 때문에 돕는다고 / 우리가 어떻게 행동해야 하는지를 규정하는 규범들을 통해

Through socialization, / we learn the reciprocity norm: / the expectation that we should return help, not harm, / to those who have helped us.
사회화를 통해서 / 우리는 상호성 규범을 배운다. / 즉 우리는 해가 아닌 도움을 돌려주어야 한다는 기대 / 우리를 도와주었던 사람들에게

In our relations with others of similar status, / the reciprocity norm compels us / to give (in favors, gifts, or social invitations) / about as much as we receive.
유사한 지위의 타인과의 관계에서, / 상호성 규범은 우리로 하여금 강요한다. / (호의, 선물, 혹은 사회적 초대를) 주도록 / 대략 우리가 받은 만큼

➡ People help / because helping gives them (A) advantages, / but also because they are socially learned to (B) repay / what others have done for them.
사람들은 돕는다. / 돕는 것이 그들에게 이익을 주기 때문만이 아니라, / 그들이 되갚아야 한다고 사회적으로 학습되기 때문에 / 타인이 그들에게 한 것을

우리는 왜 돕는가? 널리 받아들여지는 한 가지 관점은 자기 이익이 인간의 모든 상호 작용의

기초가 되고, 우리의 지속적인 목표는 보상을 극대화하고 비용을 최소화하는 것이라는 것이다. 회계사들은 그것을 *비용-수익 분석*이라고 부른다. 철학자들은 그것을 *공리주의*라고 부른다. 사회 심리학자들은 그것을 사회적 교환 이론이라고 부른다. 만약 당신이 헌혈할지를 생각한다면, 당신은 그렇게 하는 것의 이익들(죄책감 감소, 사회적 인정, 그리고 좋은 감정) 대비 비용들(시간, 불편함, 그리고 걱정)을 따져 볼지도 모른다. 만약 그 보상들이 비용들을 초과한다면 당신은 도울 것이다. 다른 사람들은 우리가 어떻게 행동해야 하는지를 규정하는 규범들을 통해서, 우리가 그렇게 하도록 사회화되어 왔기 때문에 돕는다고 믿는다. 사회화를 통해서 우리는 상호성 규범, 즉 우리는 우리를 도와주었던 사람에게 해가 아닌 도움을 돌려주어야 한다는 기대를 배운다. 유사한 지위의 타인들과의 관계에서, 상호성 규범은 우리로 하여금 대략 우리가 받은 만큼 (호의, 선물들, 혹은 사회적 초대를) 주도록 강요한다.

➡ 사람들은 돕는 것이 그들에게 (A) 이익을 주기 때문만이 아니라, 타인이 그들에게 한 것을 (B) 되갚아야 한다고 사회적으로 학습되기 때문에 돕는다.

Why? 왜 정답일까?

인간이 서로 돕고 사는 이유에 관해 설명한 글로, 'One widely held view is that self-interest underlies all human interactions, that our constant goal is to maximize rewards and minimize costs.'에서는 인간이 자기 이익을 추구하는 존재이기 때문에 비용을 초과하는 이득이 있을 때 남을 돕는다고 설명한다. 이어서 'Others believe that ~ we learn the reciprocity norm: ~'에서는 우리가 상호성의 규범, 즉 자신에게 도움을 제공했던 사람에게 보답을 해야 한다는 점을 학습하기 때문에 도움을 베풀게 되는 것임을 추가적으로 설명한다. 따라서 요약문의 빈칸에 들어갈 말로 가장 적절한 것은 ① '(A) advantages(이익), (B) repay(되갚다)'이다.

- **underlie** ⓥ ~의 기초를 이루다
- **analysis** ⓝ 분석
- **utilitarianism** ⓝ 공리주의
- **approval** ⓝ 인정, 승인
- **prescribe** ⓥ 규정하다, 처방하다
- **compel** ⓥ 강요하다
- **accountant** ⓝ 회계사
- **philosopher** ⓝ 철학자
- **weigh** ⓥ (결정을 내리기 전에) 따져 보다
- **discomfort** ⓝ 불편함
- **reciprocity** ⓝ 상호성

구문 풀이

12행 Through socialization, we learn the reciprocity norm: the expectation that we should return help, not harm, to those [who have helped us].
주어 / 동사 / 목적어(B + (but) not + A : A가 아니라 B인) / 동격 / 동격 접속사 / 선행사

41-42 적절한 휴지기와 유지 보수의 중요성

An organization imported new machinery / with the capacity to produce quality products at a lesser price.
한 조직이 새로운 기계를 수입했다. / 질 좋은 제품을 더 낮은 가격으로 생산할 능력이 있는

A manager was responsible for large quantities / in a relatively short span of time.
한 관리자는 많은 양을 책임지고 있었다. / 상대적으로 짧은 시간에

He started with the (a) full utilization of the new machinery.
그는 새로운 기계를 꽉 채워 사용하는 것으로 시작했다.

He operated it 24/7 at maximum capacity.
그는 그것을 최대 성능으로 24시간 7일 내내 작동시켰다.

He paid the least attention / to downtime, recovery breaks or the general maintenance of the machinery.
그는 최소의 주의를 기울였다. / 비가동 시간, 회복을 위한 휴지기, 또는 기계의 일반적인 유지 보수에는

As the machinery was new, / it continued to produce results / and, therefore, the organization's profitability (b) soared / and the manager was appreciated for his performance.
그 기계가 새것이었으므로 / 그것은 계속해서 결과물을 만들어 냈고, / 그리하여 그 조직의 수익성은 치솟았으며 / 그 관리자는 성과를 인정받았다.

Now after some time, / this manager was promoted / and transferred to a different location.
이제 얼마의 시간이 흘러, / 이 관리자는 승진하였고 / 다른 지점으로 옮겼다.

A new manager came in his place / to be in charge of running the manufacturing location.
새로운 관리자가 그의 자리를 채우러 왔다. / 제조 지점 운영을 담당하기 위해

But this manager realized / that with heavy utilization and without any downtime for maintenance, / a lot of the parts of the machinery / were significantly (c) worn / and needed to be replaced or repaired.
그러나 이 관리자는 / 과도한 사용과 유지 보수를 위한 비가동 시간의 부재로 인해 / 기계의 많은 부품들이 / 상당히 닳았고 / 대체되거나 수리될 필요가 있다는 것을 깨달았다.

41, 42번의 근거
「The new manager had to put significant time and effort / into repair and maintenance of the machines, / which resulted in lower production / and thus a loss of profits.」
새 관리자는 상당한 시간과 노력을 들여야만 했고, / 그 기계의 수리와 유지 보수에 / 더 낮은 생산을 초래했다. / 그에 따른 이익의 손실과

The earlier manager / had only taken care of the goal of production / and (d) ignored the machinery / although he had short-term good results.
이전의 관리자는 / 생산 목표만을 신경 썼고 / 기계를 무시했다. / 비록 그가 단기간에 좋은 결과를 얻었을지라도

But ultimately not giving attention to recovery and maintenance / resulted in long-term (e) negative consequences.
그러나 궁극적으로 회복과 유지 보수에 주의를 기울이지 않은 것은 / 장기간의 부정적인 결과들을 초래했다.

한 조직이 질 좋은 제품을 더 낮은 가격으로 생산할 수 있는 새로운 기계를 수입했다. 한 관리자는 상대적으로 짧은 시간에 많은 양을 책임지고 있었다. 그는 새로운 기계를 (a) 꽉 채워 사용하는 것으로 시작했다. 그는 그것을 최대 성능으로 24시간 7일 내내 작동시켰다. 그는 비가동 시간, 회복을 위한 휴지기, 또는 기계의 일반적인 유지 보수에는 최소의 주의를 기울였다. 그 기계가 새것이었으므로 그것은 계속해서 결과물을 만들어 냈고, 그리하여 그 조직의 수익성은 (b) 치솟았으며 그 관리자는 성과를 인정받았다. 이제 얼마의 시간이 흘러, 이 관리자는 승진하였고 다른 지점으로 옮겼다. 새로운 관리자가 제조 지점 운영을 담당하기 위해 그의 자리를 채우러 왔다. 그러나 이 관리자는 과도한 사용과 유지 보수를 위한 비가동 시간의 부재로 인해 기계의 많은 부품들이 상당히 (c) 닳았고 대체되거나 수리될 필요가 있다는 것을 깨달았다. 새 관리자는 상당한 시간과 노력을 그 기계의 수리와 유지 보수에 들여야만 했고, 그것은 생산 감소와 그에 따른 이익의 손실을 초래했다. 이전의 관리자는 비록 단기간에 좋은 결과를 얻었을지라도 생산 목표만을 신경 썼고 기계를 (d) 무시했다. 그러나 궁극적으로 회복과 유지 보수에 주의를 기울이지 않은 것은 장기간의 (e) 긍정적인(→ 부정적인) 결과들을 초래했다.

구문 풀이

13행 But this manager realized that with heavy utilization and without any
접속사(~것)
downtime for maintenance, a lot of the parts of the machinery were significantly
주어(복수) 동사구1
worn and needed to be replaced or repaired.
동사구2

41 제목 파악 정답률 45% | 정답 ②

윗글의 제목으로 가장 적절한 것은?
① Why Are Quality Products Important?
왜 양질의 제품이 중요한가?
✓② Give Machines a Break to Avoid Overuse
과도한 사용을 막기 위해 기계에게 휴식을 주라
③ Providing Incentives to Maximize Workers' Abilities
근로자의 능력을 최대화하기 위해 인센티브를 제공하는 것
④ Tip for Managers: The Right Man in the Right Place
관리자들을 위한 조언: 적재적소(적당한 사람을 적합한 곳에)
⑤ Wars for High Productivity in a World of Competition
경쟁의 세계에서 높은 생산성을 위한 전쟁

Why? 왜 정답일까?

생산성이 좋은 기계를 쉴 틈 없이 최대 능력치로 가동했다가 결국에는 많은 부품이 빨리 닳게 되어 유지 보수 비용과 생산성 면에서 손해가 야기되었다는 내용을 다룬 글이다. 특히 'The new manager had to put significant time and effort into repair and maintenance of the machines, which resulted in lower production and thus a loss of profits.'에서 기계의 과도한 사용으로 인한 부정적 결과가 잘 나타나므로, 이를 반영한 글의 제목으로 가장 적절한 것은 ② '과도한 사용을 막기 위해 기계에게 휴식을 주라'이다.

42 어휘 추론 정답률 41% | 정답 ⑤

밑줄 친 (a) ~ (e) 중에서 문맥상 낱말의 쓰임이 적절하지 않은 것은?
① (a) ② (b) ③ (c) ④ (d) ✓⑤ (e)

Why? 왜 정답일까?

'The new manager had to put significant time and effort into repair and maintenance of the machines, which resulted in lower production and thus a loss of profits.'에서 내내 돌아가던 기계가 부품이 많이 닳고 상하는 바람에 기존의 관리자 이후에 부임해 온 사람은 기계를 유지 보수하는 데 많은 시간과 비용을 써야만 했다고 설명하고 있다. 이를 근거로 볼 때, 마지막 문장은 제때 유지 보수에 관심을 기울이지 않았던 것이 장기적으로는 '부정적인' 결과를 초래했다는 결론으로 끝나야 하므로, (e)의 positive는 negative로 고쳐야 한다. 따라서 문맥상 낱말의 쓰임이 적절하지 않은 것은 ⑤ '(e)'이다.

43-45 딸과 함께 Karen 가족을 위한 크리스마스 선물을 마련한 Maria

(A)
「Maria Sutton was a social worker in a place / where the average income was very low.」 **45번 ①의 근거** 일치
Maria Sutton은 지역의 사회복지사였다. / 평균 소득이 매우 낮은

Many of Maria's clients had lost their jobs / when the coal industry in a nearby town collapsed.
Maria의 많은 고객들은 일자리를 잃었다. / 근처 마을의 석탄 산업이 붕괴되었을 때

Every Christmas season, / knowing how much children loved presents at Christmas, / Maria tried to arrange a special visit from Santa Claus for one family.
크리스마스 시즌마다 / 아이들이 크리스마스에 얼마나 선물을 좋아하는지 알았기 때문에, / Maria는 한 가족을 위해 산타클로스의 특별 방문을 계획하려 했다.

Alice, the seven-year-old daughter of Maria, / was very enthusiastic / about helping with (a) her mother's Christmas event.
Maria의 7살 된 딸 Alice는 / 매우 열성적이었다. / 자기 엄마의 크리스마스 이벤트를 돕는 것에

(C)
「This year's lucky family was / a 25-year-old mother named Karen and her 3-year-old son, / who she was raising by herself.」 **45번 ③의 근거** 일치
올해 행운의 가족은 / Karen이라는 이름의 25살 된 엄마와 그녀의 3살 된 아들이었고, / 그를 그녀는 혼자서 키우고 있었다.

However, things went wrong.
그러나, 상황이 나빠졌다.

「Two weeks before Christmas Day, / a representative from a local organization / called Maria to say / that the aid she had requested for Karen had fallen through.」 **45번 ④의 근거** 불일치
크리스마스 2주 전, / 지역 단체의 대표가 / Maria에게 전화해서 말했다. / 그녀가 Karen을 위해 요청했던 지원이 성사되지 않았다고

No Santa Claus.
산타클로스는 없었다.

No presents.
선물도 없었다.

Maria saw the cheer disappear from Alice's face at the news.
Maria는 그 소식에 Alice의 얼굴에서 생기가 사라지는 것을 보았다.

After hearing this, (c) she ran to her room.
이 말을 듣고 난 뒤, 그녀는 자기 방으로 달려갔다.

(D)
When Alice returned, / her face was set with determination.
Alice가 돌아왔을 때, / 그녀의 얼굴은 결의에 차 있었다.

She counted out the coins from her piggy bank: $4.30.
그녀는 그녀의 돼지 저금통에서 동전들을 세면서 꺼냈다, $4.30

"Mom," she told Maria, / "(d) I know it's not much. / But maybe this will buy a present for the kid."
"엄마," 그녀는 Maria에게 말했다. / "전 이것이 얼마 되지 않는다는 것을 알아요. / 그러나 아마도 이것으로 그 아이를 위한 선물을 살 수 있을 거예요."라고

Maria gave her daughter a lovely hug.
Maria는 그녀의 딸을 사랑스럽게 안아주었다.

The next day, / Maria told her coworkers about her daughter's latest project.
그다음 날, / Maria는 그녀의 동료들에게 딸의 최근 프로젝트에 대해 말했다.

To (e) her surprise, / staff members began to open their purses.
그녀로서는 놀랍게도, / 직원들이 그들의 지갑을 열기 시작했다.

The story of Alice's gift / had spread beyond Maria's office, / and 「Maria was able to raise $300」 / — plenty for a Christmas gift for Karen and her son. 〔45번 ⑤의 근거 일치〕
Alice의 선물 이야기는 / Maria의 사무실을 넘어 퍼졌고, / Maria는 300달러를 모금할 수 있었는데, / 이것은 Karen과 아들의 크리스마스 선물을 위해 충분했다.

(B)

On Christmas Eve, / Maria and Alice visited Karen's house with Christmas gifts.
크리스마스 전날, / Maria와 Alice는 크리스마스 선물들을 가지고 Karen의 집을 방문했다.

When Karen opened the door, / Maria and Alice wished the astonished woman a merry Christmas.
Karen이 문을 열었을 때, / Maria와 Alice는 그 깜짝 놀란 여성에게 즐거운 크리스마스를 빌어주었다.

「Then Alice began to unload the gifts from the car, / handing them to Karen one by one.」 〔45번 ②의 근거 일치〕
그런 다음 Alice는 차에서 선물들을 내리기 시작했고, / 그것들을 하나씩 Karen에게 건넸다.

Karen laughed in disbelief, / and said she hoped / she would one day be able to do something similar / for someone else in need.
Karen은 믿기지 않는다는 듯 웃었고, / 자신이 바란다고 말했다. / 자신이 언젠가 비슷한 어떤 일을 할 수 있기를 / 어려운 다른 사람을 위해

On her way home, Maria said to Alice, / "God multiplied (b) your gift."
집으로 돌아가는 길에, Maria는 Alice에게 말했다. / "신이 네 선물을 늘렸구나."라고

(A)

Maria Sutton은 평균 소득이 매우 낮은 지역의 사회복지사였다. Maria의 많은 고객들은 근처 마을의 석탄 산업이 붕괴되었을 때 일자리를 잃었다. 아이들이 크리스마스에 얼마나 선물을 좋아하는지 알았기 때문에, 크리스마스 시즌마다 Maria는 한 가족을 위해 산타클로스의 특별 방문을 계획하려 했다. Maria의 7살 된 딸 Alice는 (a) 자기 엄마의 크리스마스 이벤트를 돕는 것에 매우 열성적이었다.

(C)

올해 행운의 가족은 Karen이라는 이름의 25살 된 엄마와 그녀의 3살 된 아들이었고, 그를 그녀는 혼자서 키우고 있었다. 그러나, 상황이 나빠졌다. 크리스마스 2주 전, 지역 단체의 대표가 Maria에게 전화해서 그녀가 Karen을 위해 요청했던 지원이 성사되지 않았다고 말했다. 산타클로스는 없었다. 선물도 없었다. Maria는 그 소식에 Alice의 얼굴에서 생기가 사라지는 것을 보았다. 이 말을 듣고 난 뒤, (c) 그녀는 자기 방으로 달려갔다.

(D)

Alice가 돌아왔을 때, 그녀의 얼굴은 결의에 차 있었다. 그녀는 그녀의 돼지 저금통에서 동전들을 세면서 꺼냈고, $4.30였다. "엄마," 그녀는 Maria에게 "(d) 전 이것이 얼마 되지 않는다는 것을 알아요. 그러나 아마도 이것으로 그 아이를 위한 선물은 살 수 있을 거예요."라고 말했다. Maria는 그녀의 딸을 사랑스럽게 안아주었다. 그다음 날, Maria는 그녀의 동료들에게 딸의 최근 프로젝트에 대해 말했다. (e) 그녀로서는 놀랍게도, 직원들이 그들의 지갑을 열기 시작했다. Alice의 선물 이야기는 Maria의 사무실을 넘어 퍼졌고, Maria는 300달러를 모금할 수 있었는데, 이것은 Karen과 아들의 크리스마스 선물을 위해 충분했다.

(B)

크리스마스 전날, Maria와 Alice는 크리스마스 선물들을 가지고 Karen의 집을 방문했다. Karen이 문을 열었을 때, Maria와 Alice는 그 깜짝 놀란 여성에게 즐거운 크리스마스를 빌어주었다. 그런 다음 Alice는 차에서 선물들을 내리기 시작했고, 그것들을 하나씩 Karen에게 건넸다. Karen은 믿기지 않는다는 듯 웃었고, 자신이 언젠가 어려운 다른 사람을 위해 비슷한 어떤 일을 할 수 있기를 바란다고 말했다. 집으로 돌아가는 길에, Maria는 Alice에게, "신이 (b) 네 선물을 늘렸구나."라고 말했다.

- social worker 사회 복지사
- enthusiastic ⓐ 열성적인
- unload ⓥ (짐을) 내리다
- in need 어려운, 도움이 필요한
- representative ⓝ 대표 ⓐ 대표하는, 나타내는
- determination ⓝ 결의
- collapse ⓥ 붕괴하다
- astonished ⓐ 깜짝 놀란
- disbelief ⓝ 믿기지 않음, 불신
- multiply ⓥ 배가시키다
- fall through 성사되지 않다, 실현되지 못하다

구문 풀이

[A] 3행 Every Christmas season, knowing how much children loved presents at (분사구문(~하면서) 의문부사(얼마나))
Christmas, Maria tried to arrange a special visit from Santa Claus for one family. (~하려고 노력하다)

[B] 5행 Karen laughed in disbelief, and said (that) she hoped (that) she would one (동사1) (동사2) (접속사(~것)) (주어) (동사구)
day be able to do something similar for someone else in need. (~할 수 있다)

[C] 3행 Two weeks before Christmas Day, a representative from a local organization (주어)
called Maria to say that the aid [she had requested for Karen] had fallen through. (동사) (부사적 용법(~하기 위해)) (주어) (동사(과거완료))

---

43 글의 순서 파악　　　　정답률 68% | 정답 ③

주어진 글 (A)에 이어질 내용을 순서에 맞게 배열한 것으로 가장 적절한 것은?

① (B) - (D) - (C)
② (C) - (B) - (D)
③ (C) - (D) - (B) ✓
④ (D) - (B) - (C)
⑤ (D) - (C) - (B)

Why? 왜 정답일까?

가난한 지역에서 사회복지사로 일하는 Maria가 매년 크리스마스 시즌에 한 가정을 상대로 특별 방문

행사를 준비하곤 했다는 배경을 설명하는 (A) 뒤에는, 올해에는 Karen과 그 아들이 선정되었지만 이들을 위한 지원 준비가 원활히 이루어지지 않았다는 내용의 (C), Maria의 딸 Alice가 자신의 저금통을 깨 Karen의 아들에게 선물을 사주겠다는 결의를 보였고 이 이야기를 알리자 Maria의 동료들이 모금에 참여했다는 내용의 (D), Maria와 Alice가 마침내 크리스마스 선물을 잘 전달했다는 내용의 (B)가 차례로 이어져야 한다. 따라서 글의 순서로 가장 적절한 것은 ③ '(C) - (D) - (B)'이다.

44 지칭 추론　　　　정답률 55% | 정답 ⑤

밑줄 친 (a)~(e) 중에서 가리키는 대상이 나머지 넷과 다른 것은?

① (a)　② (b)　③ (c)　④ (d)　✓(e)

Why? 왜 정답일까?

(a), (b), (c), (d)는 Alice를, (e)는 앞 문장의 Maria를 가리키므로, (a)~(e) 중에서 가리키는 대상이 다른 하나는 ⑤ '(e)'이다.

45 세부 내용 파악　　　　정답률 78% | 정답 ④

윗글에 관한 내용으로 적절하지 않은 것은?

① Maria는 평균 소득이 매우 낮은 지역의 사회복지사였다.
② 크리스마스 전날 Karen은 선물을 받았다.
③ Karen은 세 살 된 아들을 키우고 있었다.
✓ Maria는 지역 단체 대표의 연락을 받지 못했다.
⑤ Maria는 300달러를 모금할 수 있었다.

Why? 왜 정답일까?

(C) 'Two weeks before Christmas Day, a representative from a local organization called Maria to say that the aid she had requested for Karen had fallen through.'에서 크리스마스 2주 전 지역 단체 대표가 Maria에게 연락하여 Karen을 위해 요청한 지원이 성사되지 않았음을 알려주었다고 하므로, 내용과 일치하지 않는 것은 ④ 'Maria는 지역 단체 대표의 연락을 받지 못했다.'이다.

Why? 왜 오답일까?

① (A) 'Maria Sutton was a social worker in a place where the average income was very low.'의 내용과 일치한다.
② (B) 'On Christmas Eve, ~ Alice began to unload the gifts from the car, handing them to Karen one by one.'의 내용과 일치한다.
③ (C) 'This year's lucky family was a 25-year-old mother named Karen and her 3-year-old son, who she was raising by herself.'의 내용과 일치한다.
⑤ (D) '~ Maria was able to raise $300 ~'의 내용과 일치한다.

어휘 Review Test 10

문제편 100쪽

A	B	C	D
01 번성하다	01 distorted	01 ①	01 ⓓ
02 훈육, 규율	02 progressive	02 ⓑ	02 ⓝ
03 깜짝 놀란	03 addiction	03 ①	03 ①
04 망치다	04 rationality	04 ⓓ	04 ①
05 광적인	05 autonomy	05 ⓗ	05 ⓗ
06 시행하다	06 permanently	06 ⓞ	06 ⓐ
07 상호성	07 show off	07 ⓔ	07 ①
08 선언하다, 분명히 말하다	08 racism	08 ⓐ	08 ①
09 ~의 희생양이 되다	09 indifferent	09 ①	09 ⓚ
10 훌륭한	10 furious	10 ⓖ	10 ⓔ
11 편협한	11 anxiety	11 ⓗ	11 ⓜ
12 붕괴하다	12 surpass	12 ①	12 ⓑ
13 ~을 찢어서 열다	13 reputation	13 ⓜ	13 ①
14 새어 나오다	14 run over	14 ⓚ	14 ⓞ
15 ~을 혹사시키다	15 interval	15 ⓒ	15 ⓒ
16 A와 B를 구별하다	16 nonverbal	16 ⓢ	16 ⓟ
17 해로운, 위험한	17 label A as B	17 ①	17 ①
18 강요하다	18 graceful	18 ⓠ	18 ⓠ
19 인정, 승인	19 prejudice	19 ⓟ	19 ①
20 확장하다	20 investment	20 ①	20 ⓢ

정답

18 ① 19 ② 20 ⑤ 21 ① 22 ⑤ 23 ② 24 ④ 25 ④ 26 ④ 27 ⑤ 28 ★ 29 ④ 30 ★ 31 ③ 32 ★
33 ① 34 ⑤ 35 ③ 36 ⑤ 37 ③ 38 ② 39 ④ 40 ① 41 ① 42 ④ 43 ② 44 ③ 45 ③

★ 표기된 문항은 [등급을 가르는 문제]에 해당하는 문항입니다.

---

18 마감 기한 연장 요청   정답률 92% | 정답 ①

다음 글의 목적으로 가장 적절한 것은?
☑ 상담 경력 증명서의 제출 기한 연장을 요청하려고
② 서류 심사 결과 발표의 지연에 대해 항의하려고
③ 전문 상담 강좌의 추가 개설을 제안하려고
④ 대학의 편의 시설 확충을 건의하려고
⑤ 대학 진학 상담 예약을 취소하려고

To whom it may concern,
관계자분께,
My name is Peter Jackson / and I am thinking of applying for the Advanced Licensed Counselor Program / that the university provides.
저의 이름은 Peter Jackson입니다. / 그리고 Advanced Licensed Counselor Program에 지원하려고 합니다. / 대학교에서 제공하는
I found / that the certification for 100 hours of counseling experience is required / for the application.
저는 알았습니다. / 100시간의 상담 경력 증명서가 필요하다는 것을 / 지원을 위해
However, / I do not think / I could possibly complete the required counseling experience / by the current deadline.
그러나 / 저는 생각하지 않습니다. / 아마도 필요한 상담 경험을 완료할 수 있다고 / 현재 마감 기한까지
So, / if possible, / I kindly request an extension of the deadline / until the end of this summer vacation.
그래서 / 가능하시다면 / 저는 마감 기한의 연장을 정중하게 요청합니다. / 이번 여름 방학 말까지
I am actively working / on obtaining the certification, / and I am sure / I will be able to submit it / by then.
저는 열심히 노력하고 있습니다. / 증명서를 얻으려고 / 그리고 확신합니다. / 그것을 제출할 수 있을 것이라고 / 그때까지
I understand the importance / of following the application process, / and would greatly appreciate your consideration / of this request.
저는 중요성을 이해합니다. / 지원 과정을 따르는 것의 / 그리고 귀하의 고려에 대단히 감사하겠습니다. / 이 요청에 대한
I look forward to your response.
저는 귀하의 회신을 기다리겠습니다.
Sincerely, Peter Jackson
진심을 담아, Peter Jackson

관계자분께,

저의 이름은 Peter Jackson이고, 대학교에서 제공하는 Advanced Licensed Counselor Program에 지원하려고 합니다. 저는 지원을 위해 100시간의 상담 경력 증명서가 필요하다는 것을 알았습니다. 그러나 저는 아마도 현재 마감 기한까지 필요한 상담 경험을 완료할 수 없다고 생각합니다. 그래서 가능하시다면 저는 이번 여름 방학 말까지 마감 기한의 연장을 정중하게 요청합니다. 저는 증명서를 얻으려고 열심히 노력하고 있고, 저는 제가 그때까지 그것을 제출할 수 있을 것이라고 확신합니다. 저는 지원 과정을 따르는 것의 중요성을 이해하며, 이 요청에 대한 귀하의 고려에 대단히 감사하겠습니다. 저는 귀하의 회신을 기다리겠습니다.

진심을 담아,
Peter Jackson 드림

Why? 왜 정답일까?

지원에 필요한 조건을 채우기 위해 마감 기한을 늘려달라는 글(So, if possible, I kindly request an extension of the deadline until the end of this summer vacation.)이므로, 글의 목적으로 가장 적절한 것은 ① '상담 경력 증명서의 제출 기한 연장을 요청하려고'이다.

● certification ⓝ증명서
● application ⓝ지원
● consideration ⓝ고려
● counseling ⓝ상담
● submit ⓥ제출하다

구문 풀이

4행 I found that the certification for 100 hours of counseling experience
　　　　　　　　　　　　접속사
is required for the application.
수동태

---

19 입국 심사 통과하기   정답률 89% | 정답 ②

다음 글에 드러난 'I'의 심경 변화로 가장 적절한 것은?
① angry → ashamed
　화난　　부끄러운
③ bored → grateful
　지루한　감사한
⑤ hopeful → disappointed
　희망찬　　실망한
☑ nervous → relieved
　긴장한　　안도한
④ curious → frightened
　궁금한　　놀란

The passport control line was short / and the inspectors looked relaxed; / except the inspector at my window.
입국 심사 줄은 짧았다. / 그리고 심사관들은 편안해 보였다. / 그런데 내 창구의 심사관은 예외였다.
He seemed to want to model / the seriousness of the task at hand / for the other inspectors.
그는 모범을 보여주고 싶어 하는 것 같았다. / 당면한 업무의 심각성에 대해 / 다른 심사관들에게
Maybe that's why / I felt uneasy / when he studied my passport more carefully / than I expected.
아마도 그것이 이유였다. / 내가 불안감을 느꼈던 / 그가 내 여권을 더 꼼꼼히 살펴볼 때 / 내가 예상했던 것보다
"You were here in September," / he said.
"9월에 여기 계셨네요." / 라고 그가 말했다.
"Why are you back so soon?" / "I came in September to prepare to return this month," / I replied with a trembling voice, / considering if I missed any Italian regulations.
"왜 이렇게 빨리 돌아오셨어요?" / "이번 달에 돌아올 것을 준비하기 위해 9월에 왔어요." / 나는 떨리는 목소리로 대답했다. / 내가 이탈리아의 규정을 놓친 것이 아닌지 생각하면서
"For how long?" / he asked.
"얼마나 오래요?" / 라고 그가 물었다.
"One month, this time," / I answered truthfully.
"이번에는 한 달 동안입니다." / 나는 정직하게 대답했다.
I knew / it was not against the rules to stay / in Italy for three months.
나는 알고 있었다. / 체류하는 것이 규정에 어긋나지 않는다는 것을 / 이탈리아에 세 달 동안
"Enjoy your stay," / he finally said, / as he stamped my passport.
"즐거운 여행 되세요." / 그가 마침내 말했다. / 내 여권에 도장을 찍으면서
Whew! / As I walked away, / the burden I had carried, / even though I did nothing wrong, / vanished into the air.
휴! / 내가 걸어 나갈 때 / 내가 짊어지고 있던 짐이 / 나는 아무 잘못도 하지 않았는데도 / 허공으로 사라졌다.
My shoulders, / once weighed down, / now stretched out with comfort.
내 어깨가 / 한때 눌렸던 / 이제 편한 마음과 함께 쭉 펴졌다.

입국 심사 줄은 짧았고 심사관들은 편안해 보였는데, 내 창구의 심사관은 예외였다. 그는 다른 심사관들에게 당면한 업무의 심각성에 대해 모범을 보여 주고 싶어 하는 것 같았다. 아마 그것이 내가 예상했던 것보다 그가 내 여권을 더 꼼꼼히 살펴볼 때 불안감을 느꼈던 이유였다. "9월에 여기 계셨네요."라고 그가 말했다. "왜 이렇게 빨리 돌아오셨어요?" 나는 내가 이탈리아의 규정을 놓친 것이 아닌지 생각하면서 "이번 달에 돌아올 것을 준비하기 위해 9월에 왔어요."라고 떨리는 목소리로 대답했다. "얼마나 오래요?"라고 그가 물었다. 나는 "이번에는 한 달 동안입니다."라고 정직하게 대답했다. 나는 이탈리아에 세 달 동안 체류하는 것이 규정에 어긋나지 않는다는 것을 알고 있었다. "즐거운 여행 되세요." 그가 마침내 내 여권에 도장을 찍으며 말했다. 휴! 내가 걸어 나갈 때, 나는 아무 잘못도 하지 않았는데도, 내가 짊어지고 있던 짐이 허공으로 사라졌다. 한때 눌렸던 내 어깨가 이제 편한 마음과 함께 쭉 펴졌다.

Why? 왜 정답일까?

입국 심사를 기다리면서부터 혹시 통과하지 못할까봐 불안했다(Maybe that's why I felt uneasy when he studied my passport more carefully than I expected.)가 무사히 심사를 끝내고 안도했다(Maybe that's why I felt uneasy when he studied my passport more carefully than I expected.)는 글이다. 따라서 'I'의 심경 변화로 가장 적절한 것은 ② '긴장한 → 안도한'이다.

● passport control 입국 심사, 출국 수속
● inspector ⓝ 심사관
● studied ⓥ 살펴보다
● prepare ⓥ 준비하다
● regulation ⓥ 규정
● weigh down ~을 짓누르다
● relaxed ⓐ 편안한
● seriousness ⓝ 심각함, 진지함
● expected ⓐ 예상되는
● trembling ⓐ 떨리는
● truthfully ⓐ 정직하게

구문 풀이

7행 "I came in September to prepare to return this month," I replied with a
　　　　　　　　　　　　to부정사(부사적용법)
trembling voice, considering if I missed any Italian regulations.
　　　　　　　분사구문

---

20 스스로 멈출 수 있는 걱정   정답률 91% | 정답 ⑤

다음 글에서 필자가 주장하는 바로 가장 적절한 것은?
① 아이가 죄책감과 책임감을 구분하도록 가르쳐야 한다.
② 아이가 스스로 불안의 원인을 찾도록 도와주어야 한다.
③ 아이의 감정에 공감하고 있음을 구체적으로 표현해야 한다.
④ 부모로서 느끼는 감정에 관해 아이와 솔직하게 대화해야 한다.
☑ 아이에게 자기 의지로 걱정을 멈출 수 있음을 알려주어야 한다.

Merely convincing your children / that worry is senseless / and that they would be more content / if they didn't worry / isn't going to stop / them from worrying.
여러분의 아이들을 설득하는 것만으로는 / 걱정은 의미 없을 것이라고 / 그리고 그들이 더 만족할 것이라고 / 그들이 걱정하지 않는다면 / 멈추게 하지 않을 것이다. / 그들이 걱정하는 것을
For some reason, / young people seem to believe / that worry is a fact of life over / which they have little or no control.
어떤 이유로 / 아이들은 믿는 것 같다. / 걱정이 삶의 사실이라고 / 자신이 거의 통제할 수 없거나 아예 통제할 수 없는
Consequently, / they don't even try to stop.
결과적으로 / 그들은 멈추려고 노력하지도 않는다.
Therefore, / you need to convince them / that worry, / like guilt and fear, / is nothing more than an emotion, / and like all emotions, / is subject to the power of the will.
따라서 / 여러분은 그들을 설득할 필요가 있다. / 걱정이 / 죄책감과 두려움처럼 / 감정에 지나지 않는다고 / 그리고 모든 감정과 같이 / 의지의 힘에 의해 영향을 받기 쉽다고
Tell them / that they can eliminate worry / from their lives / by simply refusing to attend to it.
아이들에게 알려주어라. / 그들이 걱정을 없앨 수 있다는 것을 / 자신의 삶으로부터 / 단순히 걱정에 주의를 기울이려 하지 않음으로써
Explain to them / that if they refuse to act worried / regardless of how they feel, / they will eventually stop feeling worried / and will begin to experience the contentment / that accompanies a worry-free life.
아이들에게 설명하라. / 그들이 걱정하며 행동하는 것을 거부한다면 / 어떻게 느끼는지와 상관없이 / 그들은 결국 걱정하는 것을 멈출 것이라고 / 그리고 만족감을 경험하기 시작할 것이라고 / 걱정 없는 삶을 수반하는

걱정은 의미 없고 그들이 걱정하지 않는다면 더 만족할 것이라고 여러분의 아이들을 설득하는 것만으로는 그들이 걱정하는 것을 멈추게 하지 않을 것이다. 어떤 이유로, 아이들은 걱정이 자신이 거의 통제할 수 없거나 아예 통제할 수 없는 삶의 사실이라고 믿는 것 같다. 결과적으로, 그들은 멈추려고 노력하지도 않는다. 따라서, 여러분은 걱정이 죄책감과 두려움처럼 감정에 지나지 않고, 모든 감정과 같이 의지의 힘에 영향을 받기 쉽다고 그들을 설득할 필요가 있다. 아이들에게 단순히 걱정에 주의를 기울이려 하지 않음으로써 그들이 자신의 삶으로부터 걱정을 없앨 수 있다는 것을 알려주어라. 아이들에게 그들이 어떻게 느끼는지와 상관없이 걱정하며 행동하는 것을 거부한다면, 그들은 결국 걱정하는 것을 멈추고 걱정 없는 삶을 수반하는 만족감을 경험하기 시작할 것이라고 설명하라.

Why? 왜 정답일까?

걱정은 죄책감과 두려움처럼 감정에 불과하며 걱정에 주의를 기울이지 않음으로써 없앨 수 있다는 것을 아이들에게 알려주라(Tell them that they can eliminate worry from their lives by simply refusing to attend to it.)고 조언하는 글이므로, 필자가 주장하는 바로 가장 적절한 것은 ⑤ '아이에게 자기 의지로 걱정을 멈출 수 있음을 알려주어야 한다.'이다.

- convince ⓥ 설득하다
- eliminate ⓥ 없애다
- content ⓝ 내용
- regardless of ~와 상관없이

구문 풀이

1행 Merely convincing your children that worry is senseless and that they
（주어(동명사)）　　　　　　　（접속사(병렬1)）　　　　　　（접속사(병렬2)）
would be more content if they didn't worry isn't going to stop them from
　　　　　　　　　　　　　　　　　（단수동사）
worrying.

21　오늘날 기업의 추구성　　정답률 56% | 정답 ①

밑줄 친 Build a jazz band가 다음 글에서 의미하는 바로 가장 적절한 것은?

☑ Foster variation within an organization. – 조직 내 다양성을 길러라
② Limit the scope of variability in businesses. – 사업 변동성의 범위를 제한하라
③ Invent a new way of minimizing risk-taking. – 위험 감수를 최소화하는 새로운 길을 찾아라
④ Promote teamwork to forecast upcoming changes. – 팀워크를 촉진하여 향후 변경 사항을 예측하라
⑤ Share innovations over a sufficient period of time. – 충분한 기간 동안 혁신을 공유하라

In today's information age, / in many companies and on many teams, / the objective is no longer error prevention and replicability.
오늘날 정보화 시대에는 / 많은 기업과 팀에서 / 목표는 더 이상 오류 방지와 반복 가능성이 아니다.
On the contrary, / it's creativity, speed, and keenness.
반대로 / 그것은 창의성, 속도, 그리고 명민함이다.
In the industrial era, / the goal was to minimize variation.
산업화 시대에는 / 목표는 변화를 최소화하는 것이었다.
But in creative companies today, / maximizing variation is more essential.
그런데 오늘날의 창의적 기업에서는 / 변화를 극대화하는 것이 더 필수적이다.
In these situations, / the biggest risk isn't / making a mistake or losing consistency; / it's failing to attract top talent, / to invent new products, / or to change direction quickly / when the environment shifts.
이러한 상황에서 / 가장 큰 위험은 ~것이 아니다. / 실수를 하거나 일관성을 잃는 / 반면에 가장 재능 있는 사람을 끌어들이는 것에 실패하는 것이다. / 새로운 제품을 만드는 것 / 혹은 방향을 빠르게 바꾸는 것 / 상황이 변할 때
Consistency and repeatability are more likely / to suppress fresh thinking / than to bring your company profit.
일관성과 반복 가능성이 더 높다. / 새로운 생각을 짓누를 / 여러분의 회사에 이익을 가져오기보다
A lot of little mistakes, / while sometimes painful, / help the organization learn quickly / and are a critical part / of the innovation cycle.
많은 작은 실수는 / 때때로 고통스럽지만 / 조직이 빠르게 배우는 것을 돕는다. / 그리고 중요한 부분이다. / 혁신 주기의
In these situations, / rules and process are no longer the best answer.
이러한 상황에서 / 규칙과 과정은 더 이상 최선의 답이 아니다.
A symphony isn't / what you're going for.
교향악단은 아니다. / 여러분이 추구하는 것이
Leave the conductor and the sheet music behind.
지휘자와 악보는 내버려두어라.
Build a jazz band instead.
대신 재즈 밴드를 구성하라.

오늘날 정보화 시대에는, 많은 기업과 팀에서 목표는 더 이상 오류 방지와 반복 가능성이 아니다. 반대로, 그것은 창의성, 속도 그리고 명민함이다. 산업화 시대에서, 목표는 변화를 최소화하는 것이었다. 그런데 오늘날의 창의적 기업에서는 변화를 극대화하는 것이 더 필수적이다. 이러한 상황에서, 가장 큰 위험은 실수를 하거나 일관성을 잃는 것이 아니라, 가장 재능 있는 사람을 끌어들이는 것, 새로운 제품을 만드는 것, 혹은 상황이 변할 때 방향을 빠르게 바꾸는 것에 실패하는 것이다. 일관성과 반복 가능성은 여러분의 회사에 이익을 가져오기보다 새로운 생각을 짓누를 가능성이 더 높다. 많은 작은 실수는 때때로 고통스럽지만, 조직이 빠르게 배우는 것을 돕고 혁신 주기의 중요한 부분이다. 이러한 상황에서, 규칙과 과정은 더 이상 최선의 답이 아니다. 교향악단은 여러분이 추구하는 것이 아니다. 지휘자와 악보는 내버려두어라. 대신 재즈 밴드를 구성하라.

Why? 왜 정답일까?

산업화 시대와 달리, 정보화 시대에는 변화를 추구하며 규칙과 과정을 지양한다(In these situations, rules and process are no longer the best answer.)는 내용으로 보아, 밑줄 친 부분의 의미로 가장 적절한 것은 ① 'Foster variation within an organization.(조직 내 다양성을 길러라)'이다.

- replicability ⓝ 반복 가능성
- variation ⓝ 변화
- repeatability ⓝ 반복성
- innovation ⓝ 혁신
- foster ⓥ 기르다
- keenness ⓝ 명민함
- consistency ⓝ 일관성
- suppress ⓥ 짓누르다
- conductor ⓝ 지휘자

구문 풀이

11행 A lot of little mistakes, while (they are) sometimes painful, help the
　　　　　　　　　　　　　　　　（생략）　　　　　　　　　　（동사병렬1）
organization learn quickly and are a critical part of the innovation cycle.
（목적보어(= to learn)）　　（동사(병렬2)）

22　긴박한 상황에서의 소문　　정답률 84% | 정답 ⑤

다음 글의 요지로 가장 적절한 것은?

① 소수에 의한 정보 독점은 합리적 의사 결정을 방해한다.
② 대중의 지속적 관심이 뉴스의 공정성을 향상시킬 수 있다.
③ 위기에 처한 사람은 권위 있는 전문가의 의견을 구하려고 한다.

Any new or threatening situation may require / us to make decisions / and this requires information.
어떤 새롭거나 긴박한 상황은 요한다. / 우리가 결정을 내리도록 / 그리고 이것은 정보를 요한다.
So important is communication / during a disaster / that normal social barriers are often lowered.
소통이 매우 중요해서 / 재난 상황 중에는 / 보통의 사회적 장벽이 자주 낮아진다.
We will talk to strangers / in a way / we would never consider normally.
우리는 낯선 사람에게 말을 걸 것이다. / 방식으로 / 평상시에는 전혀 고려하지 않을
Even relatively low grade disruption of our life / such as a fire drill or a very late train / seems to give us the permission / to break normal etiquette / and talk to strangers.
우리 삶에서의 비교적 낮은 수준의 혼란조차도 / 소방 훈련이나 매우 연착된 기차와 같은 / 허용해 주는 것처럼 보인다. / 보통의 에티켓을 어기는 것 / 그리고 낯선 사람에게 말을 거는 것
The more important an event to a particular public, / the more detailed and urgent the requirement / for news becomes.
어떠한 사건이 특정 사람들에게 중요할수록 / 요구가 더 상세하고 긴박해진다. / 소식에 대한
Without an authoritative source of facts, / whether that is a newspaper or trusted broadcast station, / rumours often run riot.
사실에 대한 공신력 있는 출처 없이 / 그것이 신문이든 신뢰할 만한 방송국이든 / 소문은 자주 제멋대로 뻗어나간다.
Rumours start / because people believe their group to be in danger / and so, although the rumour is unproven, / feel they should pass it on.
소문은 시작된다. / 사람들이 자신이 속한 집단이 위험에 처해 있다고 믿기 때문에 / 입증되지 않은 소문임에도 불구하고 / 이를 전달해야 한다고 생각하기
For example, / if a worker heard / that their employer's business was doing badly / and people were going to be made redundant, / they would pass that information / on to colleagues.
예를 들어 / 한 근로자가 들으면 / 그의 고용주의 사업이 잘 안되어서 / 사람들이 해고될 것이라고 / 그들은 그 정보를 전달할 것이다. / 동료들에게

어떤 새롭거나 긴박한 상황은 우리가 결정을 내리도록 하고 이것은 정보를 요한다. 재난 상황 중에는 소통이 매우 중요해서 보통의 사회적 장벽이 자주 낮아진다. 우리는 평상시에는 전혀 고려하지 않을 방식으로 낯선 사람에게 말을 걸 것이다. 소방 훈련이나 매우 연착된 기차와 같은 우리 삶에서의 비교적 낮은 수준의 혼란조차도 보통의 에티켓을 어기고 낯선 사람에게 말을 거는 것을 허용해 주는 것처럼 보인다. 어떠한 사건이 특정 사람들에게 중요할수록, 소식에 대한 요구가 더 상세하고 긴박해진다. 그것이 신문이든 신뢰할 만한 방송국이든, 사실에 대한 공신력 있는 출처 없이, 소문은 자주 제멋대로 뻗어나간다. 소문은 사람들이 자신이 속한 집단이 위험에 처해 있다고 믿어서, 입증되지 않은 소문임에도 불구하고, 이를 전달해야 한다고 생각하기 때문에 시작된다. 예를 들어, 한 근로자가 그의 고용주의 사업이 잘 안되어서 사람들이 해고될 것이라고 들으면, 그들은 그 정보를 동료들에게 전달할 것이다.

Why? 왜 정답일까?

재난처럼 긴박한 상황이나 해고와 같은 위험에 처한 상황에서는 소문이 사실과 상관없을지라도 퍼져나가기 쉽다(Rumours start because people believe their group to be in danger and so, although the rumour is unproven, feel they should pass it on.)는 내용이다. 따라서 글의 요지로 가장 적절한 것은 ⑤ '위기 상황에서는 확인되지 않은 정보라도 전달하려는 경향이 크다.'이다.

- permission ⓝ 허용
- authoritative ⓐ 권위 있는
- unproven ⓐ 입증되지 않은
- redundant ⓐ (일시)해고된
- urgent ⓐ 긴급한
- run riot 제멋대로 뻗어나가다
- badly [ad] 안 좋게

구문 풀이

8행 The more important an event to a particular public, the more detailed and
『the 비교급 ~, the 비교급 ~ : ~하면 할수록 ~하다』
urgent the requirement for news becomes.

23　예술과 다른 과학의 특징　　정답률 71% | 정답 ②

다음 글의 주제로 가장 적절한 것은?

① misconceptions on how experimental data should be measured
실험 데이터를 측정하는 방법에 관한 오해
☑ views on whether science is free from cultural context or not
과학이 문화적 맥락에서 자유로운지 아닌지에 관한 견해
③ ways for minimizing cultural bias in scientific pursuits
과학적 추구에서 문화적 편견을 최소화하는 법
④ challenges in achieving objectivity in scientific studies
과학적 연구에서 객관성을 달성하기 위한 과제
⑤ functions of science in analyzing cultural phenomena
문화 현상을 분석하는 과학의 기능

People seem to recognize / that the arts are cultural activities / that draw on (or react against) certain cultural traditions, / certain shared understanding, / and certain values and ideas / that are characteristic of the time and place / in which the art is created.
사람들은 인식하는 것 같다. / 예술을 문화적 활동이라고 / 특정 문화적 전통에 기반한(또는 이에 반하는) / 특정 공유 지식 / 그리고 특정 가치와 아이디어에 / 시기와 장소에 특유한 / 예술이 만들어진
In the case of science, / however, / opinions differ.
과학의 경우에는 / 하지만 / 의견이 갈린다.
Some scientists, / like the great biologist J. B. S. Haldane, / see science in a similar light / — as a historical activity / that occurs in a particular time and place, / and that needs to be understood / within that context.
일부 과학자들은 / 위대한 생물학자 J. B. S. Haldane과 같은 / 유사한 관점에서 과학을 본다. / 역사적 활동으로써 / 특정한 시기와 장소에서 발생하는 / 그리고 이해될 필요가 있는 / 그 맥락에서
Others, / however, / see science as a purely "objective" pursuit, / uninfluenced by the cultural viewpoint and values / of those who create it.
다른 사람들은 / 하지만 / 과학을 순전히 '객관적인' 일로 본다. / 문화적 관점과 가치에 영향을 받지 않는 / 그것을 만들어내는 사람들의
In describing this view of science, / philosopher Hugh Lacey speaks of the belief / that there is an underlying order of the world / which is simply there to be discovered / — the world of pure "fact" / stripped of any link with value.
과학에 대한 이러한 관점을 묘사할 때 / 철학자 Hugh Lacey는 믿음에 대해 말한다. / 세계의 근원적인 질서가 있다는 / 단순히 거기에 있어서 발견되는 / 이것은 순전한 '사실'의 세계이다. / 가치와 어떠한 연관도 없는
The aim of science / according to this view / is to represent this world of pure "fact", /

independently of any relationship / it might bear contingently / to human practices and experiences.
과학의 목적은 / 이러한 관점에 따라 / 이러한 순전한 '사실'의 세계를 나타내는 것이다. / 어떠한 관계와 무관하게 / 그것이 혹여라도 맺을 수 있는 / 인간의 관습 및 경험과

사람들은 예술을 예술이 만들어진 시기와 장소에 특유한 특정 문화적 전통, 특정 공유 지식, 그리고 특정 가치와 아이디어에 기반한(또는 이에 반하는) 문화적 활동이라고 인식하는 것 같다. 하지만 과학의 경우에는 의견이 갈린다. 위대한 생물학자 J. B. S. Haldane과 같은 일부 과학자들은 유사한 관점에서 과학을 보는데, 특정한 시기와 장소에서 발생하고 그 맥락 안에서 이해될 필요가 있는 역사적 활동으로 보는 것이다. 하지만 다른 사람들은 과학을 그것을 만들어 내는 사람들의 문화적 관점과 가치에 의해 영향을 받지 않는 순전히 '객관적인' 일로 본다. 과학에 대한 이러한 관점을 묘사할 때, 철학자 Hugh Lacey는 단순히 거기에 있어서 발견되는 세계의 근원적인 질서가 있다는 믿음에 대해 말하는데, 이것은 가치와 어떠한 연관도 없는 순전한 '사실'의 세계이다. 이러한 관점에 따라 과학의 목적은 이러한 순전한 '사실'의 세계를 나타내는 것인데, 그것이 인간의 관습 및 경험과 혹여라도 맺을 수 있는 어떠한 관계와도 무관하게 말이다.

Why? 왜 정답일까?

과학은 예술과 달리 문화적 관점과 가치에 영향을 받지 않는 순전한 사실의 세계(The aim of science according to this view is to represent this world of pure "fact", independently of any relationship it might bear contingently to human practices and experiences.)라고 주장하는 글이다. 따라서 글의 주제로 가장 적절한 것은 ② 'views on whether science is free from cultural context or not(과학이 문화적 맥락에서 자유로운지 아닌지에 관한 견해)'이다.

- differ ⓥ 다르다
- pursuit ⓥ 추구하다
- strip of ~을 빼앗다
- misconception ⓝ 오해
- purely [ad] 순전히
- underlying @ 근본적인
- contingently [ad] 혹여라도

24 나이로 규정할 수 없는 정신적 발달의 정도
정답률 69% | 정답 ④

다음 글의 제목으로 가장 적절한 것은?

① Adult Influence Is Key to Child Development
성인의 영향력은 아동 발달의 핵심이다
② How Can Social Codes Limit People's Cognition?
어떻게 소셜 코드가 사람들의 인식을 제한할 수 있을까?
③ Democracy Grows Only with Responsible Youth
오직 책임감 있는 젊은이들과 함께 성장하는 민주주의
✓④ Setting Responsibilities Based on Age: Is It Appropriate?
연령에 기반한 책임 설정: 적절한가?
⑤ Aging: A Possible Obstacle to Consistent Personal Growth
노화: 지속적인 개인 성장의 장애물이 될 가능성

Mental development / consists of individuals increasingly mastering social codes and signals themselves, / which they can master only in social situations / with the support of more competent individuals, / typically adults.
정신적 발달은 / 개인이 점점 더 사회적 규범과 신호를 스스로 습득하는 것으로 이루어지는데 / 그들은 사회적 상황에서만 이를 습득할 수 있다 / 더 유능한 개인들의 도움을 받는 / 일반적으로 성인들의

In this sense, / mental development consists of / internalizing social patterns and gradually becoming a responsible actor / among other responsible actors.
이러한 의미에서 / 정신적 발달은 이루어진다. / 사회적 양식을 내면화하는 것으로 / 그리고 점차 책임 있는 행위자가 되는 것으로 / 다른 책임 있는 행위자들 사이에서

In Denmark, / the age of criminal responsibility is 15 years, / which means / that we then say / that people have developed sufficient mental maturity / to be accountable for their actions / at this point.
덴마크에서 / 형사 책임 연령은 15세이다. / 이는 의미한다. / 그러면 우리가 말할 수 있음을 / 사람들이 충분한 정신적 성숙을 발현했다고 / 자신의 행위에 책임을 지기에 / 이 시점에서

And / at the age of 18 / people are given the right to vote / and are thereby formally included / in the basic democratic process.
그리고 / 18세에 / 사람들은 투표권을 받는다. / 그리고 그것에 의해 공식적으로 포함된다. / 기본적인 민주적 과정에

I do not know / whether these age boundaries are optimal, / but it is clear / that mental development takes place / at different rates for different individuals, / and depends especially on the social and family environment / they have been given.
나는 모르겠다. / 이러한 연령 경계가 최적인지 / 하지만 이것은 분명하다. / 정신적 발달이 일어난다는 것은 / 다른 개인에게 다른 속도로 / 그리고 사회적 환경과 가정환경에 따라 특히 달라진다는 것은 / 그들에게 주어져 있는

Therefore, / having formal limits for responsibility / from a specific age / that apply to everyone / is a somewhat questionable practice.
따라서 / 책임에 대한 공식적인 제한을 두는 것은 / 특정 연령부터 / 모든 사람에게 적용되는 / 다소 의심스러운 관행이다.

But the question, / of course, / is whether it can be done any differently.
그러나 문제는 / 물론 / 그것이 조금이나마 다르게 행해질 수 있는지이다.

정신적 발달은 개인들이 점점 더 사회적 규범과 신호를 스스로 습득하는 것으로 이루어지는데, 그들은 더 유능한 개인들, 일반적으로 성인들의 도움을 받는 사회적 상황에서만 이를 습득할 수 있다. 이러한 의미에서 정신적 발달은 사회적 양식을 내면화하고 다른 책임 있는 행위자들 사이에서 점차 책임 있는 행위자가 되는 것으로 이루어진다. 덴마크에서 형사 책임 연령은 15세인데, 이는 그러면 우리가 사람들이 이 시점에서 자신의 행위에 책임을 지기에 충분한 정신적 성숙을 발현했다고 말할 수 있음을 의미한다. 그리고 18세에 사람들은 투표권을 받고, 그것에 의해 기본적인 민주적 과정에 공식적으로 포함된다. 나는 이러한 연령 경계가 최적인지는 모르겠지만, 정신적 발달이 다른 개인에게 다른 속도로 일어나고, 특히 그들에게 주어져 있는 사회적 환경과 가정환경에 따라 달라진다는 것은 분명하다. 따라서 특정 연령부터 모든 사람에게 적용되는 책임에 대한 공식적인 제한을 두는 것은 다소 의심스러운 관행이다. 그러나 물론 문제는 그것이 조금이나마 다르게 행해질 수 있는지이다.

Why? 왜 정답일까?

정신적 발달은 주변과의 사회화를 통해 이루어지므로(I do not know whether these age

---

boundaries are optimal, but it is clear that mental development takes place at different rates for different individuals, and depends especially on the social and family environment they have been given.) 특정 연령에 기반하여 일률적으로 적용하는 것은 적절하지 않아 보인다고 주장하는 내용이므로, 글의 제목으로 가장 적절한 것은 ④ 'Setting Responsibilities Based on Age: Is It Appropriate?(연령에 기반한 책임 설정: 적절한가?)'이다.

- consist of ~로 구성되다
- gradually [ad] 점차
- maturity ⓝ 성숙함
- thereby [ad] 그렇게 함으로써
- competent @ 유능한
- sufficient @ 충분한
- be accountable for ~에 대해 책임이 있다
- somewhat [ad] 다소

25 캐나다의 무급 돌봄 제공 비율
정답률 86% | 정답 ④

다음 도표의 내용과 일치하지 않는 것은?

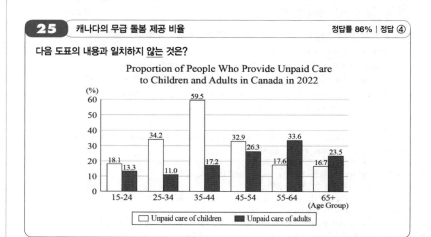

Proportion of People Who Provide Unpaid Care
to Children and Adults in Canada in 2022

The graph above shows / the percentage of people / who provided unpaid care to children and adults / by age group in Canada/ in 2022.
위 그래프는 보여 준다. / 사람의 비율을 / 아동과 성인에게 무급 돌봄을 제공한 / 캐나다의 연령 집단별 / 2022년

① Notably, / the 35 – 44 group had the highest percentage of individuals / providing unpaid care to children, / reaching 59.5%.
특히 / 35 ~ 44세 집단은 사람의 비율이 가장 높았다. / 아동에게 무급 돌봄을 제공하는 / 이는 59.5%에 달했다.

② However, / the highest percentage of individuals / providing unpaid care to adults / was found in the 55 – 64 group.
하지만 / 사람의 가장 높은 비율은 / 성인에게 무급 돌봄을 제공하는 / 55 ~ 64세 집단에서 발견되었다.

③ Compared to the 25 – 34 group, / the 15 – 24 group had a lower percentage of individuals / providing unpaid care to children / and a higher percentage of individuals / providing unpaid care to adults.
25 ~ 34세 집단에 비해 / 15 ~ 24세 집단은 사람의 비율이 더 낮았다. / 아동에게 무급 돌봄을 제공하는 / 그리고 사람의 비율이 더 높았다. / 성인에게 무급 돌봄을 제공하는

✓④ The percentage of people / providing unpaid care to adults / in the 45 – 54 group / was more than twice as high as / that in the 35 – 44 group.
사람의 비율은 / 성인에게 무급 돌봄을 제공하는 / 45 ~ 54세 집단에서 / ~보다 두 배 넘게 높았다. / 35 ~ 44세 집단의 비율

⑤ The 55 – 64 group and the 65 and older group showed / a similar percentage of individuals / providing unpaid care to children, / with a difference of less than 1 percentage point.
55 ~ 64세 집단과 65세 이상 집단은 보였다. / 사람의 비슷한 비율을 / 아동에게 무급 돌봄을 제공하는 / 1퍼센트 포인트 미만의 차이로

위 그래프는 2022년 캐나다의 연령 집단별 아동과 성인에게 무급 돌봄을 제공한 사람의 비율을 보여 준다. ① 특히 35~44세 집단은 아동에게 무급 돌봄을 제공하는 사람의 비율이 가장 높았는데, 이는 59.5%에 달했다. ② 하지만 성인에게 무급 돌봄을 제공하는 사람의 가장 높은 비율은 55~64세 집단에서 발견되었다. ③ 25~34세 집단에 비해, 15~24세 집단은 아동에게 무급 돌봄을 제공하는 사람의 비율이 더 낮았고, 성인에게 무급 돌봄을 제공하는 사람의 비율이 더 높았다. ④ 45~54세 집단에서 성인에게 무급 돌봄을 제공하는 사람의 비율은 35~44세 집단의 비율보다 두 배 넘게 높았다. ⑤ 55~64세 집단과 65세 이상 집단은 아동에게 무급 돌봄을 제공하는 사람의 비율이 1퍼센트 포인트 미만의 차이로 비슷한 비율을 보였다.

Why? 왜 정답일까?

도표에 따르면 45~54세 집단에서 성인에게 무급 돌봄을 제공하는 사람의 비율은 26.3%이고, 35~44세 집단의 비율은 17.2%이므로 두 배 넘게 차이나지 않는다는 것을 알 수 있다. 따라서 도표와 일치하지 않는 것은 ④이다.

- unpaid @ 무급의
- reach ⓥ 도달하다
- care ⓝ 돌봄, 치료

26 Charles Elton의 생애
정답률 95% | 정답 ④

Charles Elton에 관한 다음 글의 내용과 일치하지 않는 것은?

① 대학에서 동물학을 공부했다.
② 대학 졸업 후 가르치는 일을 시작했다.
③ 생물학 컨설턴트로서 한 회사와 함께 일했다.
✓④ 마지막으로 쓴 저서는 Animal Ecology였다.
⑤ 1932년에 Journal of Animal Ecology의 편집자가 되었다.

『Born in the English city of Liverpool, / Charles Elton studied zoology / under Julian Huxley at Oxford University / from 1918 to 1922.』 ①의근거 일치

영국의 도시 Liverpool에서 태어난 / Charles Elton은 동물학을 공부했다. / Oxford 대학에서 Julian Huxley 아래에서 / 1918년부터 1922년까지

『After graduating, / he began teaching as a part-time instructor / and had a long and distinguished teaching career / at Oxford / from 1922 to 1967.』 ②의근거 일치

졸업 후 / 그는 시간제 강사로 가르치는 일을 시작했다. / 그리고 장기간의 훌륭한 교수 경력을 가졌다. / Oxford 대학에서 / 1922년부터 1967년까지

『After a series of arctic expeditions with Huxley, / he worked with a fur-collecting and trading company / as a biological consultant, / and examined the company's records / to study animal populations.』 ③의근거 일치

Huxley와 함께한 일련의 북극 탐험 후 / 그는 한 모피 수집 및 무역 회사와 함께 일했고, / 생물학 컨설턴트로서 / 그리고 그 회사의 기록을 검토했다. / 동물 개체군을 연구하기 위해

『In 1927, / he wrote his first and most important book, *Animal Ecology*, / in which he demonstrated the nature / of food chains and cycles.』 ④의근거 불일치

1927년 / 그의 처음이자 가장 중요한 저서인 *Animal Ecology*를 썼다. / 그리고 그 저서에서 그는 본질을 설명했다. / 먹이 사슬과 순환의 본질을

In 1932, / he helped establish / the Bureau of Animal Population at Oxford.

1932년에 / 그는 설립하는 것을 도왔다. / Oxford 대학에서 Bureau of Animal Population을

『In the same year / he became the editor / of the new *Journal of Animal Ecology*.』 ⑤의근거 일치

같은 해에 / 그는 편집자가 되었다. / 새로운 *Journal of Animal Ecology*의

Throughout his career, / Elton wrote six books / and played a major role / in shaping the modern science of ecology.

그의 경력을 통틀어서 / Elton은 여섯 권의 저서를 썼다. / 그리고 주요한 역할을 했다. / 현대 생태학을 형성하는 데

영국의 도시 Liverpool에서 태어난 Charles Elton은 1918년부터 1922년까지 Oxford 대학에서 Julian Huxley 아래에서 동물학을 공부했다. 졸업 후 그는 시간제 강사로 가르치는 일을 시작했고 1922년부터 1967년까지 Oxford 대학에서 장기간의 훌륭한 교수 경력을 가졌다. Huxley와 함께한 일련의 북극 탐험 후, 그는 생물학 컨설턴트로서 한 모피 수집 및 무역 회사와 함께 일했고, 동물 개체군을 연구하기 위해 그 회사의 기록을 검토했다. 1927년 그의 처음이자 가장 중요한 저서인 *Animal Ecology*를 썼고, 그 저서에서 그는 먹이 사슬과 순환의 본질을 설명했다. 1932년에 그는 Oxford 대학에서 Bureau of Animal Population을 설립하는 것을 도왔다. 같은 해에 그는 새로운 *Journal of Animal Ecology*의 편집자가 되었다. 그의 경력을 통틀어서 Elton은 여섯 권의 저서를 썼고, 현대 생태학을 형성하는 데 주요한 역할을 했다.

Why? 왜 정답일까?

'He was dissatisfied with his economic education at Princeton University ∼'에서 Charles는 처음이자 가장 중요한 저서인 Animal Ecology를 썼다고 하므로, 내용과 일치하지 않는 것은 ④ '마지막으로 쓴 저서는 Animal Ecology였다.'이다.

Why? 왜 오답일까?

① 'Born in the English city of Liverpool, Charles Elton studied zoology under Julian Huxley at Oxford University from 1918 to 1922.'의 내용과 일치한다.

② 'After graduating, he began teaching as a part-time instructor and had a long and distinguished teaching career at Oxford from 1922 to 1967.'의 내용과 일치한다.

③ 'After a series of arctic expeditions with Huxley, he worked with a fur-collecting and trading company as a biological consultant, and examined the company's records to study animal populations.'의 내용과 일치한다.

⑤ 'In the same year he became the editor of the new Journal of Animal Ecology'의 내용과 일치한다.

- zoology ⓝ 동물학
- distinguished ⓐ 유명한
- expedition ⓝ 탐험
- population ⓝ 개체
- establish ⓥ 설립하다
- instructor ⓝ 강사
- arctic ⓝ 북극
- biological ⓐ 생물학의
- demonstrate ⓥ 입증하다
- ecology ⓝ 생태학

구문 풀이

1행 (Being) Born in the English city of Liverpool, Charles Elton studied
생략 분사구문
zoology under Julian Huxley at Oxford University from 1918 to 1922.

---

27 2024 Clifton Fall 청소의 날 정답률 88% | 정답 ⑤

Clifton Fall Clean-up Day 2024에 관한 다음 안내문의 내용과 일치하지 <u>않는</u> 것은?

① 매년 열리는 행사이다.
② 10명씩 조를 이루어 청소할 것이다.
③ 푸드 트럭이 설치될 것이다.
④ 행사 로고가 있는 티셔츠가 제공될 것이다.
✔ 청소 도구를 가져와야 한다.

Clifton Fall Clean-up Day 2024
2024 Clifton Fall 청소의 날

『Join us for this annual event / to clean up the fallen leaves / in Central Park, / and enjoy meeting your neighbors!』 ①의근거 일치

매년 열리는 이 행사에 참여하세요. / 낙엽을 청소하는 / Central Park에서 / 그리고 이웃과의 만남을 즐기세요.

When: Sunday, October 20th, 1 p.m. – 3 p.m.

일시: 10월 20일 일요일 오후 1시부터 3시까지

Details
세부사항

『Clean-up will be done / in groups of 10 people / based on age.』 ②의근거 일치

청소할 것입니다. / 10명씩 조를 이루어 / 연령에 따라

After the clean-up, / you can enjoy a casual gathering / with neighbors.

청소 후 / 가벼운 모임을 즐길 수 있습니다. / 이웃과

『Food trucks will be set up / for your gathering.』 ③의근거 일치

푸드 트럭이 설치될 것입니다. / 모임을 위해

Notes
유의사항

『A T-shirt with the event's logo / will be provided / as a gift.』 ④의근거 일치

행사 로고가 있는 티셔츠가 / 제공될 것입니다. / 선물로

『You'll be supplied with cleaning materials, / such as bags and gloves, / so you don't have to bring them.』 ⑤의근거 불일치

청소 도구가 제공될 것입니다. / 봉지와 장갑 같은 / 그러니 여러분은 그것들을 가져올 필요가 없습니다.

We're looking forward / to seeing you there!
우리는 고대합니다. / 그곳에서 여러분을 만나기를

2024 Clifton Fall 청소의 날

Central Park에서 낙엽을 청소하는 매년 열리는 이 행사에 참여하여 이웃과의 만남을 즐기세요!

일시: 10월 20일 일요일 오후 1시부터 3시까지

세부사항
- 연령에 따라 10명씩 조를 이루어 청소할 것입니다.
- 청소 후 이웃과 가벼운 모임을 즐길 수 있습니다.
- 푸드 트럭이 모임을 위해 설치될 것입니다.

유의사항
- 행사 로고가 있는 티셔츠가 선물로 제공될 것 입니다.
- 봉지와 장갑 같은 청소 도구가 제공될 것이니 여러분은 그것들을 가져올 필요가 없습니다.

우리는 그곳에서 여러분을 만나기를 고대합니다!

Why? 왜 정답일까?

'You'll be supplied with cleaning materials, such as bags and gloves, so you don't have to bring them.'에서 청소 도구가 제공된다고 하므로, 안내문의 내용과 일치하지 않는 것은 ⑤ '청소 도구를 가져와야 한다.'이다.

Why? 왜 오답일까?

① 'Join us for this annual event to clean up the fallen leaves in Central Park, and enjoy meeting your neighbors!'의 내용과 일치한다.

② 'Clean-up will be done in groups of 10 people based on age.'의 내용과 일치한다.

③ 'Food trucks will be set up for your gathering.'의 내용과 일치한다.

④ 'A T-shirt with the event's logo will be provided as a gift.'의 내용과 일치한다.

- leaf ⓝ 잎사귀 (복수형: leaves)
- casual ⓐ 가벼운
- material ⓝ 도구, 재료
- based on ∼에 기초하여
- gathering ⓝ 모임, 수집
- bring ⓥ 가져오다, 데려오다

---

28 2024 지속 가능한 패션 축제 정답률 91% | 정답 ④

Sustainable Fashion Festival 2024에 관한 다음 안내문의 내용과 일치하는 것은?

① 금요일 오전에 진행된다.
② 티켓 조기 구매 할인은 행사 사흘 전 종료된다.
③ 장터에서 새 의류를 구입할 수 없다.
✔ 5개 이하의 의류 물품을 교환할 수 있다.
⑤ 사전 등록 없이도 지속 가능 제품을 판매할 수 있다.

Sustainable Fashion Festival 2024
2024 지속 가능한 패션 축제

Sustainable Fashion Festival 2024 is coming!
2024 지속 가능한 패션 축제가 다가오고 있습니다!

Be inspired / and learn / how to live sustainably / while looking fabulous.
영감을 받으세요. / 그리고 배우세요. / 지속 가능하게 사는 방법을 / 멋지게 보이면서

When & Where
일시와 장소

『Friday, September 13th, 5 p.m.5 – 9 p.m.』 ①의근거 불일치

9월 13일 금요일 오후 5시부터 9시까지

Aimes Community Center
Aimes 시민 회관

Tickets: $20 for early birds / $25 at the door
티켓: 조기 구매 20달러 / 현장 구매 25달러

『(Early purchase discount ends / two days before the event.)』 ②의근거 불일치

(조기 구매 할인은 종료됩니다. / 행사 이틀 전에)

Programs
프로그램

『Marketplace for sustainable products: / You can sell or buy / new, vintage, or upcycled clothing.』 ③의근거 불일치

지속 가능 제품을 위한 장터 / 사고팔 수 있습니다. / 새 의류, 빈티지 의류, 또는 업사이클 의류를

Talks from eco-fashion experts / on fashion's sustainable future
친환경 패션 전문가들의 강연 / 패션의 지속 가능한 미래에 대한

『Clothing exchange: / You can exchange 5 or fewer items.』 ④의근거 일치

의류 교환 / 여러분은 5개 이하의 의류 물품을 교환할 수 있습니다.

Runway showcase / of sustainable designs
패션쇼 / 지속가능한 디자인의

『To sell your sustainable products / at our marketplace, / registration is required / in advance.』

지속 가능 제품을 판매하려면 / 장터에서 / 등록을 하셔야 합니다. / 사전에 ⑤의근거 불일치

Contact us on social media / for more information.
소셜 미디어로 우리에게 연락해주세요. / 더 많은 정보를 원하시면

2024 지속 가능한 패션 축제

2024 지속 가능한 패션 축제가 다가오고 있습니다! 멋지게 보이면서 영감을 받고 지속 가능하게 사는 방법을 배워 보세요.

일시와 장소
- 9월 13일 금요일 오후 5시부터 9시까지
- Aimes 시민 회관

티켓: 조기 구매 20달러 / 현장 구매 25달러 (조기 구매 할인은 행사 이틀 전에 종료됩니다.)

프로그램
- 지속 가능 제품을 위한 장터: 새 의류, 빈티지 의류 또는 업사이클 의류를 사고팔 수 있습니다.
- 패션의 지속 가능한 미래에 대한 친환경 패션 전문가들의 강연

- 의류 교환: 여러분은 5개 이하의 의류 물품을 교환할 수 있습니다.
- 지속 가능한 디자인의 패션쇼

※ 장터에서 지속 가능 제품을 판매하려면 사전에 등록을 하셔야 합니다.

더 많은 정보를 원하시면 소셜 미디어로 우리에게 연락해 주세요.

Why? 왜 정답일까?

'Clothing exchange: You can exchange 5 or fewer items.'에서 5개 이하의 의류 물품을 교환할 수 있다고 하므로, 안내문의 내용과 일치하는 것은 ④ '5개 이하의 의류 물품을 교환할 수 있다.'이다.

Why? 왜 오답일까?

① 'Friday, September 13th, 5 p.m. – 9 p.m.'에서 금요일 오후에 진행된다고 말하고 있다.
② 'Early purchase discount ends two days before the event.'에서 조기 구매 할인은 이틀 전에 종료된다고 말하고 있다.
③ 'Marketplace for sustainable products: You can sell or buy new, vintage, or upcycled clothing.'에서 새 의류를 구입할 수 있다고 말하고 있다.
⑤ 'To sell your sustainable products at our marketplace, registration is required in advance.'에서 사전에 등록해야 물건을 판매할 수 있다고 말하고 있다.

- sustainable ⓐ 지속 가능한
- fabulous ⓐ 굉장한
- clothing ⓝ 의류, 옷
- few ⓐ 적은
- inspire ⓥ 영감을 주다
- sell ⓥ 팔다
- expert ⓝ 전문가
- in advance 사전에

★★★ 등급을 가르는 문제!

29 관점의 변화를 통한 발전 정답률 52% | 정답 ④

다음 글의 밑줄 친 부분 중, 어법상 틀린 것은? [3점]

One well-known shift took place / when the accepted view / — that the Earth was the center of the universe / — changed to one / where we understood / that we are only inhabitants / on one planet ① orbiting the Sun.
잘 알려진 한 가지 변화가 일어났다. / 용인된 관점이 ~했을 때 / 지구가 우주의 중심이라는 / 관점으로 바뀌었을 때 / 우리가 이해하는 / 우리가 거주자일 뿐이라고 / 태양을 공전하는 하나의 행성에 사는

With each person / who grasped the solar system view, / ② it became easier / for the next person / to do so.
각각의 사람이 있어서 / 태양계의 관점을 이해하는 / 이것은 더 쉬워졌다 / 그 다음 사람이 / 그렇게 하는 것이

So / it is with the notion / that the world revolves / around the human economy.
그래서 / 이 개념도 마찬가지이다. / 세계가 돌아간다는 / 인간의 경제를 중심으로

This is slowly being replaced / by the view / that the economy is a part of the larger system / of material flows / that connect all living things.
이것은 서서히 대체되고 있다. / 관점으로 / 경제가 더 거대한 시스템의 일부라는 / 물질 흐름의 / 모든 생명체를 연결하는

When this perspective shifts into place, / it will be obvious / that our economic well-being requires / that we account for, and ③ respond to, factors of ecological health.
이러한 관점이 바뀌어 자리를 잡으면 / ~는 것이 분명해질 것이다. / 우리의 경제적 안녕이 필요로 한다 / 우리가 책임지고 대응하는 / 것을 / 생태학적 건강의 요인에

Unfortunately / we do not have a century or two / ✔ to make the change.
불행하게도 / 우리는 한두 세기의 시간이 없다. / 변화를 만들어 낼

By clarifying the nature / of the old and new perspectives, / and by identifying actions / ⑤ on which we might cooperate / to move the process along, / we can help / accelerate the shift.
본질을 명확히 함으로써 / 오래된 관점과 새로운 관점의 / 그리고 행동을 밝힘으로써 / 협력할지도 모를 / 그 과정을 진전시키기 위해 / 우리는 도움을 줄 수 있다. / 그 변화를 가속화 하는데

지구가 우주의 중심이라는 용인된 관점이 우리가 태양을 공전하는 하나의 행성에 사는 거주자일 뿐이라고 이해하는 관점으로 바뀌었을 때 잘 알려진 한 가지 변화가 일어났다. 태양계의 관점을 이해하는 각각의 사람이 있어서, 그 다음 사람이 그렇게 하는 것이 더 쉬워졌다. 그래서 세계가 인간의 경제를 중심으로 돌아간다는 이 개념도 마찬가지이다. 이것은 경제가 모든 생명체를 연결하는 물질 흐름의 더 거대한 시스템의 일부라는 관점으로 서서히 대체되고 있다. 이러한 관점이 바뀌어 자리를 잡으면, 우리의 경제적 안녕이 우리가 생태학적 건강의 요인에 책임지고, 대응하는 것을 필요로 한다는 것이 분명해질 것이다. 불행하게도 우리는 변화를 만들어 낼 한두 세기의 시간이 없다. 오래된 관점과 새로운 관점의 본질을 명확히 하고, 그 과정을 진전시키기 위해 협력할지도 모를 행동을 밝힘으로써 우리는 그 변화를 가속화하는데 도움을 줄 수 있다.

Why? 왜 정답일까?

문장 안에 이미 본동사(do not have)가 존재하므로 make를 to 부정사의 형용사적 용법인 to make로 고쳐야 한다. 따라서 어법상 틀린 것은 ④이다.

Why? 왜 오답일까?

① planet을 수식하며 능동적 관계이므로 현재분사 orbiting이 오는 것이 맞다.
② 진주어 to do를 대신하는 가주어 it이 오는 것이 맞다.
③ account와 병렬구조이므로 respond가 오는 것이 맞다.
⑤ actions를 수식하고 있으며, 뒤에 주어 we와 동사 might cooperate가 있는 것으로 보아 완전한 절을 이끌고 있으므로 전치사＋관계대명사 형태인 on which가 오는 것이 맞다.

- inhabitant ⓝ 주민
- grasp ⓥ 잡다, 이해하다
- notion ⓝ 개념
- flow ⓝ 흐름
- shift ⓝ 변화
- accelerate ⓥ 가속화하다
- orbit ⓥ 궤도를 돌다
- solar system 태양계
- economy ⓝ 경제학
- perspective ⓝ 관점
- account for 설명하다

구문 풀이

1행 One well-known shift took place when the accepted view — that the
                                                              동격
Earth was the center of the universe — changed to one where we understood
                                                    관계부사
that we are only inhabitants on one planet (which was) orbiting the Sun.
접속사   생략

★★ 문제 해결 꿀~팁 ★★

▶ 많이 틀린 이유는?
문법 문제의 경우 자주 등장하는 유형들이 있는데 '전치사＋관계 대명사'의 유형이 낯설어 해당 답지를 선택하면서 오답률이 높았던 문제이다. 문법 문제의 경우 밑줄 친 부분이 포함된 문장 내에서만 옳고 그른지를 따져보면 되므로 차분히 살펴보자.

▶ 문제 해결 방법은?
문법 문제의 대부분은 주어와 동사를 찾는 것만으로도 많은 선택지를 지울 수 있다. 한 문장에 동사가 두 번 등장하지 않는지, 주어와 동사의 수가 일치하는 지, 분사의 경우 능동과 수동의 형태가 제대로 쓰였는지 등을 확인하면 된다. 관계대명사는 자주 등장하는 문제로 그 뒤의 문장이 완전한 문장인지 아닌지 살펴보는 것이 중요한데, '전치사＋관계대명사'의 경우에는 그 뒤에 완전한 문장이 온다. 'on which'뒤로 주어와 동사 목적어가 포함된 완전한 문장이 왔으므로 올바르게 쓰인 것을 알 수 있다.

30 신체의 변화에 따른 영역 확장 정답률 75% | 정답 ⑤

다음 글의 밑줄 친 부분 중, 문맥상 낱말의 쓰임이 적절하지 않은 것은?

The first human beings probably evolved / in tropical regions / where survival was possible / without clothing.
최초의 인간은 아마도 진화했다. / 열대 지역에서 / 생존이 가능한 / 의복 없이

It is likely / that they had very dark skin / because light skin would have given ① little protection / against the burning rays of the sun.
가능성이 있다. / 그들은 매우 어두운 피부를 가졌다 / 밝은 피부는 보호를 거의 제공하지 못했을 것이기 때문에 / 강렬한 태양 광선에 대한

There is a debate / about whether these people spread / into other parts of the world / or, instead, / whether people developed independently / in various parts of the world.
논쟁이 있다. / 이 사람들이 퍼져 나갔는지에 대해서는 / 세계의 다른 지역으로 / 아니면 대신에 / 사람들이 독립적으로 발생했는지 / 세계의 다른 지역에서

Whichever the case, / it is believed / that in time they became ② capable of spreading out / from Africa, / eventually to most of the world.
어느 경우이든 / 믿어진다. / 언젠가 그들은 퍼져 나갈 수 있게 되었다고 / 아프리카에서부터 / 결국 세계 대부분의 지역으로

This was probably / because their ③ physical characteristics changed.
이것은 아마도 ~ 것이다. / 그들의 신체적 특성이 바뀌기 때문일

For instance, / early hominids probably did not walk upright, / but when they developed that ability, / they could travel more efficiently.
예를 들어 / 초기 인류는 아마도 직립 보행을 하지 않았을 것이다. / 하지만 그들이 그 능력을 발달시켰을 때 / 그들은 더 효율적으로 이동할 수 있었다.

More important, / perhaps, / was their ④ development of tool making.
더 중요한 것은 / 아마도 / 그들의 도구 제작의 발달이었다.

With tools, / they could hunt other animals, / so they could consume more protein and fat / than their low-energy vegetarian diet would have provided.
도구를 이용하여 / 그들은 다른 동물을 사냥할 수 있었다. / 그래서 그들은 더 많은 단백질과 지방을 섭취할 수 있었다. / 그들의 저에너지 채식 식단이 제공했을 것보다

Not only their bodies but also their brains / would have been changed / with more energy.
그들의 신체뿐만 아니라 뇌도 / 변화되었을 것이다. / 더 많은 에너지와 함께

The brain needs / lots of energy / to grow.
뇌는 필요하다. / 더 많은 에너지가 / 성장하기 위해

As their diet ✔ expanded, / hominids could physically and intellectually expand their territory.
그들의 식단이 확장되면서 / 초기 인류는 신체적으로 그리고 지적으로 그들의 영역을 확장할 수 있었다.

최초의 인간은 아마도 의복 없이 생존이 가능한 열대 지역에서 진화했다. 밝은 피부는 강렬한 태양 광선에 대한 보호를 거의 제공하지 못했을 것이기 때문에 그들은 매우 어두운 피부를 가졌을 가능성이 있다. 이 사람들이 세계의 다른 지역으로 퍼져나갔는지, 아니면 대신에 사람들이 세계의 다른 지역에서 독립적으로 발생했는지에 대해서는 논쟁이 있다. 어느 경우이든, 언젠가 그들은 아프리카에서부터, 결국 세계 대부분의 지역으로 퍼져 나갈 수 있게 되었다고 믿어진다. 이것은 아마도 그들의 신체적 특성이 바뀌었기 때문일 것이다. 예를 들어, 초기 인류는 아마도 직립 보행을 하지 않았을 것이지만, 그들이 그 능력을 발달시켰을 때, 그들은 더 효율적으로 이동할 수 있었다. 더 중요한 것은 아마도 그들의 도구 제작의 발달이었다. 도구를 이용하여, 그들은 다른 동물을 사냥할 수 있어서, 그들의 저에너지 채식 식단이 제공했을 것보다 더 많은 단백질과 지방을 섭취할 수 있었다. 그들의 신체뿐만 아니라 뇌도 더 많은 에너지와 함께 변화되었을 것이다. 뇌는 성장하기 위해 많은 에너지가 필요하다. 초기 인류의 식단이 축소되면서(→ 확장되면서) 그들은 신체적으로 그리고 지적으로 그들의 영역을 확장할 수 있었다.

Why? 왜 정답일까?

신체적 특성이 변화함에 따라 이동을 할 수 있게 되었고(This was probably because their physical characteristics changed.), 이후 도구의 발달로 채식뿐만 아니라 단백질과 지방을 섭취하게 되었다고 이야기하고 있으므로(With tools, they could hunt other animals, so they could consume more protein and fat than their low-energy vegetarian diet would have provided.) 식단이 '확장되었다'는 설명이 알맞다. 따라서 reduced를 expanded로 고쳐야 한다.

- probably ⓐⓓ 아마도
- debate ⓝ 논쟁
- became capable of ~할 수 있다
- efficiently ⓐⓓ 효율적으로
- hunt ⓥ 사냥하다
- intellectually ⓐⓓ 지적으로
- territory ⓝ 지역
- protection ⓝ 보호
- independently ⓐⓓ 독립적으로
- hominid ⓝ 인류
- perhaps ⓐⓓ 아마도
- diet ⓝ 식단
- expand ⓥ 확장하다

구문 풀이

13행 More important, perhaps, was their development of tool making.
         보어(도치)   동사   주어

★★★ 등급을 가르는 문제!

31 불리한 결과에 관한 믿음 정답률 34% | 정답 ③

다음 빈칸에 들어갈 말로 가장 적절한 것을 고르시오. [3점]

① expect – 기대할　　② diversify – 다양화할　　✓ externalize – 외부화할
④ generate – 발생할　　⑤ overestimate – 과대평가할

When we get an unfavorable outcome, / in some ways / the *last* thing we want to hear is / that the process was fair.
우리가 불리한 결과를 얻을 때 / 어떤 면에서 / 우리가 '가장' 듣고 싶지 않은 말은 / 그 과정이 공정했다는 말이다.

As outraging / as the combination of an unfavorable outcome and an unfair process is, / this combination also brings / with it a consolation prize: / the possibility of attributing / the bad outcome to something other than ourselves.
분노를 불러일으키지만 / 불리한 결과와 불공정한 과정의 결합이 / 이 결합은 또한 가져다준다. / 그것과 더불어 / 위로의 상 / 즉 탓으로 돌릴 가능성을 / 나쁜 결과를 우리 자신 이외의 다른 무언가의

We may reassure ourselves / by believing / that our bad outcome had little to do / with us / and everything to do / with the unfair process.
우리는 우리 자신을 안심시킬지도 모른다. / 믿음으로써 / 우리의 나쁜 결과가 거의 관련이 없었고 / 우리와는 / 그리고 전적으로 관련이 있었다고 / 불공정한 과정과

If the process is fair, / however, / we cannot nearly as easily externalize the outcome; / we got / what we got "fair and square."
그 과정이 공정하다면 / 하지만 / 우리는 결과를 거의 마찬가지로 쉽게 외부화할 수 없다. / 우리는 얻은 것이다. / 우리가 '정정당당하게' 얻은 것을

When the process is fair / we believe / that our outcome is deserved, / which is another way of saying / that there must have been something about ourselves / (what we did or who we are) / that caused the outcome.
그 과정이 공정할 때 / 우리는 믿게 된다. / 우리의 결과가 마땅하다고 / 이는 말하는 또 다른 방식이다. / 우리 자신에 관한 무언가가 틀림없이 있었을 것이라고 / 우리가 무엇을 했는지 또는 우리가 누구인지 / 그 결과를 초래한

우리가 불리한 결과를 얻을 때, 어떤 면에서 우리가 '가장 듣고 싶지 않은' 말은 그 과정이 공정했다는 말이다. 불리한 결과와 불공정한 과정의 결합이 분노를 불러일으키지만, 이 결합은 또한 위로의 상, 즉 나쁜 결과를 우리 자신 이외의 다른 무언가의 탓으로 돌릴 가능성을 더불어 가져다준다. 우리는 우리의 나쁜 결과가 우리와는 거의 관련이 없었고 불공정한 과정과 전적으로 관련이 있었다고 믿음으로써 우리 자신을 안심시킬지도 모른다. 하지만 그 과정이 공정하다면, 우리는 결과를 거의 마찬가지로 쉽게 외부화할 수 없으며, 우리는 우리가 '정정당당하게' 얻은 것을 얻은 것이다. 그 과정이 공정할 때 우리는 우리의 결과가 마땅하다고 믿게 되는데, 이는 그 결과를 초래한 우리 자신(우리가 무엇을 했는지 또는 우리가 누구인지)에 관한 무언가가 틀림없이 있었을 것이라고 말하는 또 다른 방식이다.

Why? 왜 정답일까?
불리한 결과를 얻었을 때 과정이 불공정하다면 그 결과의 원인이 자신 이외의 것에 있다고 믿을 수 있으므로 위로가 될 수 있다(As outraging as the combination of an unfavorable outcome and an unfair process is, this combination also brings with it a consolation prize: the possibility of attributing the bad outcome to something other than ourselves.)는 이야기를 하고 있다. 과정이 공정하다면 원인이 자신 즉 내부에 있다는 것을 뜻하므로 빈칸에 들어갈 말로 가장 적절한 것은 ③ '외부화할'이다.

- unfavorable ⓐ 불리한
- fair ⓐ 공정한, 공평한
- combination ⓝ 결합
- attribute ⓥ ~의 탓으로 돌리다
- unfair ⓐ 불공정한
- outcome ⓝ 결과, 성과
- outrage ⓝ 분노
- consolation ⓝ 위로
- reassure ⓥ 안심시키다
- deserved ⓐ 마땅한

구문 풀이
2행 As outraging as the combination of an unfavorable outcome and an
「As ~ as+주어+동사 : 비록 ~일지라도」
unfair process is, this combination also brings with it a consolation prize: the possibility of attributing the bad outcome to something other than ourselves.
「other than : 제외하고」

★★ 문제 해결 꿀~팁 ★★
▶ 많이 틀린 이유는?
단어가 빈칸 처리된 경우 오답으로 반의어가 등장하는 경우도 있지만, 어떤 단어를 넣었을 때 논리적으로 그럴 듯한 문장이 되는 경우도 있다. 따라서 반드시 글의 주제와 일치하는지 글에 언급되지 않은 것과 연결되어 있는지 따져보아야 한다.

▶ 문제 해결 방법은?
이 글은 불리한 결과를 얻을 때 과정이 공정하지 않았다는 얘기를 들으면 화가 나지만 그 결과가 나로 인한 것이 아니라 외부적인 요인에 인한 것이라는 생각에 안심이 될 수 있다고 말하고 있다. 빈칸이 포함된 문장은 'However'라는 접속사를 포함하고 있는데 반대로 과정이 공정하다면 결과를 ~할 수 없다고 이야기하고 있다. 앞 주장과 반대되는 개념에 대해 이야기 하고 있기 때문에 '외부화할' 수 없다고 이야기 하는 것이 옳다. 빈칸에 '기대할'이라는 단어가 들어가는 것도 문장만 봐서는 논리적으로 보이지만 글 전체 내용과는 상관없으므로 답이 될 수 없다.

★★★ 등급을 가르는 문제! ★★★
32 여성 이브닝드레스에 관한 연구　　정답률 40% | 정답 ①

다음 빈칸에 들어갈 말로 가장 적절한 것을 고르시오. [3점]
✓ a profoundly regular phenomenon – 매우 규칙적인 현상
② a practical and progressive trend – 실용적이고 진보적인 추세
③ an intentionally created art form – 의도적으로 만들어진 예술 형식
④ a socially influenced tradition – 사회적으로 영향을 받은 전통
⑤ a swiftly occurring event – 빠르게 발생하는 사건

The well-known American ethnologist / Alfred Louis Kroeber made a rich and in-depth study / of women's evening dress in the West, / stretching back about three centuries / and using reproductions of engravings.
미국의 잘 알려진 민속학자인 / Alfred Louis Kroeber는 풍부하고 심도 있는 연구를 수행했다. / 서양의 여성 이브닝드레스에 대한 / 약 3세기 전으로 거슬러 올라가 / 판화 복제품을 사용하여

Having adjusted the dimensions of these plates / due to their diverse origins, / he was able to analyse / the constant elements in fashion features / and to come up with a study / that was neither intuitive nor approximate, / but precise, mathematical and statistical.

이 판들의 크기를 조정하여 / 다양한 기원 때문에 / 그는 분석할 수 있었다. / 패션 특징에서의 일정한 요소를 / 그리고 연구를 구상할 수 있었다. / 직관적이지도 대략적이지도 않은 / 정확하고 수학적이며 통계적인

He reduced women's clothing to a certain number of features: / length and size of the skirt, / size and depth of the neckline, / height of the waistline.
그는 여성 의류를 몇 가지 특징들로 정리했다. / 스커트의 길이와 크기 / 목선의 크기와 깊이 / 허리선의 높이와 같은

He demonstrated unambiguously / that fashion is a profoundly regular phenomenon / which is not located at the level of annual variations / but on the scale of history.
그는 분명하게 보여주었다. / 패션이 매우 규칙적인 현상이라는 것을 / 매년 일어나는 변화의 수준이 아니라 / 역사의 척도에 위치하는

For practically 300 years, / women's dress was subject / to a very precise periodic cycle: / forms reach the furthest point in their variations / every fifty years.
거의 300년 동안 / 여성 드레스는 영향을 받았다. / 매우 정확한 주기적인 순환의 / 형식은 변화의 정점에 도달했다. / 50년마다

If, / at any one moment, / skirts are at their longest, / fifty years later / they will be at their shortest; / thus skirts become long again fifty years / after being short/ and a hundred years / after being long.
만약 / 어느 한 시기에 / 스커트가 가장 길었다면 / 50년 후에 / 가장 짧아질 것이다. / 따라서 스커트는 50년 후에 다시 길어진다. / 짧아진 데서 / 그리고 100년 후에 / 길어진 데서

미국의 잘 알려진 민속학자인 Alfred Louis Kroeber는 약 3세기 전으로 거슬러 올라가 판화 복제품을 사용하여 서양의 여성 이브닝드레스에 대한 풍부하고 심도 있는 연구를 수행했다. 다양한 기원 때문에 이 판들의 크기를 조정하여, 그는 패션 특징에서의 일정한 요소를 분석해서 직관적이지도 대략적이지도 않은, 정확하고 수학적이며 통계적인 연구를 구상할 수 있었다. 그는 여성 의류를 스커트의 길이와 크기, 목선의 크기와 깊이, 허리선의 높이와 같은 몇 가지 특징들로 정리했다. 그는 패션이 매년 일어나는 변화의 수준이 아니라 역사의 척도에 위치하는 매우 규칙적인 현상이라는 것을 분명하게 보여주었다. 거의 300년 동안 여성 드레스는 매우 정확한 주기적인 순환의 영향을 받았는데, 형식은 50년마다 변화의 정점에 도달했다. 만약 어느 한 시기에 스커트가 가장 길었다면 50년 후에 가장 짧아질 것이고, 따라서 스커트는 짧아진 데서 50년 후에 다시 길어지고, 길어진 데서 100년 후에 길어진다.

Why? 왜 정답일까?
여성 이브닝드레스에 대한 연구를 통해 스커트의 특징이 일정 주기에 따라 특징이 변화했다는 것을 발견했다(For practically 300 years, women's dress was subject to a very precise periodic cycle: forms reach the furthest point in their variations every fifty years.)는 내용이므로, 빈칸에 들어갈 말로 가장 적절한 것은 ① 'a profoundly regular phenomenon(매우 규칙적인 현상)'이다.

- ethnologist ⓝ 민족학자
- engraving ⓝ 판화
- diverse ⓐ 다양한
- constant ⓐ 끊임없는
- intuitive ⓐ 직관적인
- precise ⓐ 정확한
- variation ⓝ 변화
- periodic ⓐ 주기적인
- reproduction ⓝ 복제품
- dimension ⓝ 크기
- origin ⓝ 기원
- feature ⓝ 특징
- approximate ⓐ 대략적이지 않은
- unambiguously [ad] 분명하게
- practically [ad] 사실상

구문 풀이
11행 He demonstrated unambiguously that fashion is a profoundly regular
접속사
phenomenon which is not located at the level of annual variations but on the
관계대명사(주격)　「not A but B : A가 아니라 B이다」
scale of history.

★★ 문제 해결 꿀~팁 ★★
▶ 많이 틀린 이유는?
글에서 등장하는 단어가 뜻이 같은 다른 단어로 다시 등장하는 경우가 많다. 따라서 앞 뒤 내용을 살펴보고 글의 주제와 논리적으로 흐름을 같이 하고 있는 답지를 고르면 된다. 이 때, 본인의 어떤 편견에 의해 넘겨짚지 않도록 주의해야 한다.

▶ 문제 해결 방법은?
이 글은 여성 이브닝 드레스의 변화에 대한 연구를 주제로 하고 있다. 빈칸이 포함된 문장 뒤로 어떻게 변화하는지 자세하게 설명해주고 있는데, '순환의 영향'을 받았다고 뒷받침하고 있다. 순환은 50년마다 변화의 흐름을 ерш 이루어지고 있는 것을 알 수 있다. 따라서 빈칸에 들어갈 답으로 알맞은 것은 '매우 규칙적인 현상'이다. '실용적이고 진보적인 추세'는 이 글에서 드레스의 특징들이 실용적이거나 진보적이라고 언급되지 않았으므로 답이 될 수 없다.

★★★ 등급을 가르는 문제! ★★★
33 시장 메커니즘에서 발생할 수 있는 문제점　　정답률 51% | 정답 ①

다음 빈칸에 들어갈 말로 가장 적절한 것을 고르시오. [3점]
✓ not receiving a share of society's prosperity at all – 사회의 부의 몫을 전혀 받지 않음
② making too large of an investment in new areas – 새로운 영역에 너무 많은 투자를 할
③ not fully comprehending technological terms – 기술 용어를 완전히 이해하지 못할
④ unconsciously wasting the rewards from their work – 무의식적으로 업무로부터 얻은 보상을 낭비할
⑤ not realizing the reason to raise their cost of living – 생활비를 인상해야 하는 이유를 깨닫지 못할

Over the last few centuries, / humanity's collective prosperity has skyrocketed, / as technological progress has made us far wealthier / than ever before.
지난 몇 세기 동안 / 인류의 집합적 부가 급증했다. / 기술 발전이 우리를 훨씬 더 부유하게 만듦에 따라 / 그 어느 때보다

To share out those riches, / almost all societies have settled upon the market mechanism, / rewarding people in various ways for the work / that they do / and the things / that they own.
이러한 부를 나누기 위해 / 거의 모든 사회는 시장 메커니즘을 채택했다. / 사람들에게 일에 대해 다양한 방식으로 보상하는 / 그들이 하는 / 그리고 ~것에 대해 / 그들이 소유한

But rising inequality, / itself often driven by technology, / has started to put that mechanism under strain.
그러나 증가하는 불평등은 / 그 자체가 기술로 인해 자주 생기는데 / 그 메커니즘에 부담을 주기 시작했다.

Today, / markets already provide immense rewards / to some people / but leave many others with very little.
오늘날 / 시장은 이미 막대한 보상을 제공한다. / 일부 사람들에게는 / 하지만 많은 다른 사람들에게는 거의 아무것도 남기지 않는다.

And now, / technological unemployment threatens / to become a more radical version / of the same story, / taking place in the particular market / we rely upon the most: / the labor market.
그리고 이제 / 기술 혁신에 의한 실업은 우려가 있다. / 좀 더 급진적인 형태가 될 / 같은 이야기의 / 특정 시장에서 발생하여 / 우리가 가장 의존하는 / 즉 노동 시장

As that market begins to break down, / more and more people will be in danger of / not receiving a share of society's prosperity at all.
그 시장이 무너짐에 따라 / 점점 더 많은 사람들이 위험에 처하게 될 것이다. / 사회의 부의 몫을 전혀 받지 않을

지난 몇 세기 동안 기술 발전이 우리를 그 어느 때보다 훨씬 더 부유하게 만듦에 따라, 인류의 집합적 부가 급증했다. 이러한 부를 나누기 위해 거의 모든 사회는 사람들에게 그들이 하는 일과 그들이 소유한 것에 대해 다양한 방식으로 보상하는 시장 메커니즘을 채택했다. 그러나 증가하는 불평등은, 그 자체가 기술로 인해 자주 생기는 데, 그 메커니즘에 부담을 주기 시작했다. 오늘날 시장은 이미 일부 사람들에게는 막대한 보상을 제공하지만 많은 다른 사람들에게는 거의 아무것도 남기지 않는다. 그리고 이제, 기술 혁신에 의한 실업은 우리가 가장 의존하는 특정 시장, 즉 노동 시장에서 발생하여, 같은 이야기의 좀 더 급진적인 형태가 될 우려가 있다. 그 시장이 무너짐에 따라 점점 더 많은 사람들이 사회의 부의 몫을 전혀 받지 않을 위험에 처하게 될 것이다.

Why? 왜 정답일까?

시장은 기술이 발전함에 따라 일과 소유한 것에 따라 차별적으로 보상을 해왔는데, 점점 불평등이 증가하면서 격차가 벌어졌다고 이야기하고 있다(Today, markets already provide immense rewards to some people but leave many others with very little.). 기술 혁신에 의한 실업으로 인해 시장이 무너지고 있다고 이야기하고 있으므로 빈칸에 들어갈 말로 가장 적절한 것은 ① 'not receiving a share of society's prosperity at all(사회의 부의 몫을 전혀 받지 않을)'이다.

- prosperity ⓝ 번영
- share ⓥ 공유하다, 나누다
- inequality ⓝ 불평등
- immense ⓐ 엄청난
- unemployment ⓝ 실업
- radical ⓐ 급진적인
- break down ⓥ 무너지다
- skyrocket ⓥ 급증하다
- settle ⓥ 정착하다, 해결하다
- strain ⓝ 부담, 압박
- leave ⓥ 떠나다, 남기다
- threaten ⓥ 위협하다
- rely ⓥ 의지하다, 믿다
- comprehend ⓥ 이해하다

구문 풀이

3행 To share out those riches, almost all societies have settled upon the
to부정사(부사적용법) / 현재완료
market mechanism, rewarding people in various ways for the work that they do
분사구문 / 관계대명사(목적격)
and the things that they own.

★★ 문제 해결 꿀~팁 ★★

▶ 많이 틀린 이유는?
조금 추상적이게 느껴질 수 있는 경제 관련 지문이지만 사전 지식이 없더라도 차분히 읽으면 충분히 답을 찾을 수 있다.

▶ 문제 해결 방법은?
빈칸이 포함된 문장을 먼저 해석해보고 이후 처음부터 읽으며 답을 찾아보는 것이 좋다. 빈칸이 포함된 문장에서는 '시장이 무너짐에 따라 어떤 위험에 처하게 될 것'이라고 이야기하고 있다. 다시 글의 처음으로 돌아가 살펴보면, 시장 메커니즘은 일과 소유에 따라 다양한 방식으로 보상하는 것을 따르는데 증가하는 불평등으로 인해 부담이 생겼다고 이야기 하고 있다. 오늘 날의 시장에 대해 이야기하는 부분을 살펴보면 어떤 사람에게는 막대한 보상을 제공하는 한편, 다른 사람들에게는 아무것도 제공하지 않는다고 이야기하고 있다. 따라서 이 뒤에는 '사회의 부의 몫을 전혀 받지 않을'위험에 처해있다는 내용이 오는 것이 논리적으로 알맞다.

★★★ 등급을 가르는 문제!

34 전문가의 암시성 | 정답률 36% | 정답 ⑤

다음 빈칸에 들어갈 말로 가장 적절한 것을 고르시오. [3점]

① the greater efforts you have to put into your work
업무에 더 많은 노력을 쏟는다
② the smaller number of strategies you use to solve problems
문제 해결에 사용하는 전략의 수가 적다
③ the less you tend to show off your excellent skills to others
다른 사람들에게 뛰어난 기술을 뽐내는 경향이 적다
④ the more detail-oriented you are likely to be for task completion
작업 완료를 위해 더 자세한 것을 지향할 가능성이 높다
✓⑤ the less conscious awareness you often have of the fundamentals
여러분은 흔히 기본에 대해 덜 의식적인 인식을 지닌다

It's often said / that those who can't do, teach.
흔히 말이 있다. / 할 줄 모르는 사람이 가르친다는

It would be more accurate to say / that those who can do, / can't teach the basics.
말하는 것이 더 정확할 것이다. / 할 수 있는 사람은 / 기본을 가르칠 수 없다고

A great deal of expert knowledge is implicit, / not explicit.
많은 전문 지식은 암시적이다. / 명시적이지 않고

The further you progress toward mastery, / the less conscious awareness / you often have of the fundamentals.
숙달을 향해 더 나아갈수록 / 덜 의식적인 인식을 지닌다. / 여러분은 흔히 기본에 대해

Experiments show / that skilled golfers and wine aficionados have a hard time / describing their putting and tasting techniques / — even asking them to explain their approaches / is enough to interfere with their performance, / so they often stay on autopilot.
실험에 따르면 / 숙련된 골퍼와 와인 애호가들은 어려움을 겪는다. / 자신의 퍼팅과 시음 기술을 설명하는데 / 심지어 설명해 달라고 요청하는 것은 / 그들의 접근 방식을 / 그들의 수행에 방해가 되기에 충분하기 때문에 / 그렇기 때문에 그들은 자주 자동 조종 상태에 있다.

When I first saw / an elite diver do four and a half somersaults, / I asked / how he managed to spin so fast.
내가 처음 봤을 때 / 한 엘리트 다이버가 공중제비를 4회 반 도는 것을 / 나는 물었다. / 어떻게 그렇게 빨리 회전할 수 있었는지

His answer: / "Just go up in a ball."
그의 대답은 ~였다. / "그냥 공 모양으로 올라가기만 해면 돼요"

Experts often have an intuitive understanding / of a route, / but they struggle / to clearly express / all the steps to take.

전문가들은 자주 직관적인 지식을 가지고 있다. / 방법에 대해 / 하지만 그들은 고전한다. / 분명하게 표현하는 데 / 취해야 할 모든 단계를

Their brain dump / is partially filled with garbage.
그들이 이것저것 표현하는 것은 / 부분적으로는 쓰레기로 차 있다

흔히 할 줄 모르는 사람이 가르친다는 말이 있다. 할 수 있는 사람은 기본을 가르칠 수 없다고 말하는 것이 더 정확할 것이다. 많은 전문 지식은 명시적이지 않고 암시적이다. 숙달을 향해 더 나아갈수록 여러분은 흔히 기본에 대해 덜 의식적인 인식을 지닌다. 실험들에 따르면 숙련된 골퍼와 와인 애호가들은 자신의 퍼팅과 시음 기술을 설명하는데 어려움을 겪으며, 심지어 그들의 접근 방식을 설명해 달라고 요청하는 것은 그들의 수행에 방해가 되기에 충분하기 때문에 그들은 자주 자동 조종 상태에 있다. 내가 한 엘리트 다이버가 공중제비를 4회 반 도는 것을 처음 봤을 때, 나는 어떻게 그렇게 빨리 회전할 수 있었는지 물었다. 그의 대답은 "그냥 공 모양으로 올라가기만 하면 돼요"였다. 전문가들은 자주 방법에 대해 직관적인 지식을 가지고 있지만, 취해야 할 모든 단계를 분명하게 표현하는 데 고전한다. 그들이 이것저것 표현하는 것은 부분적으로는 쓰레기로 차 있다.

Why? 왜 정답일까?

실험에 의하면, 숙련된 전문가들은 자신의 전문 분야에서 직관적인 지식을 갖고 있을 뿐 세세하게 설명할 수 있다고(Experts often have an intuitive understanding of a route, but they struggle to clearly express all the steps to take.) 이야기하고 있다. 따라서 빈칸에 들어갈 말로 가장 적절한 것은 ⑤ 'the less conscious awareness you often have of the fundamentals(여러분은 흔히 기본에 대해 덜 의식적인 인식을 지닌다)'이다.

- accurate ⓐ 정확한
- explicit ⓐ 명시적
- aficionado ⓝ 애호가
- somersault ⓝ 공중제비
- garbage ⓝ 쓰레기
- completion ⓝ 완료
- implicit ⓐ 암시적
- mastery ⓝ 숙달
- interfere with ~을 방해하다
- partially ⓐⓓ 부분적으로
- detail-oriented 자세한 것을 지향하는

구문 풀이

1행 It's often said that those who can't do, teach.
가주어 / 진주어 / 관계대명사(주격)

★★ 문제 해결 꿀~팁 ★★

▶ 많이 틀린 이유는?
시험에 등장하는 모든 지문이 그렇지만, 특히 빈칸 문제는 문장을 정확하게 해석하는 연습을 하는 것이 중요하다.

▶ 문제 해결 방법은?
실험이나 연구가 등장하면 그 결과가 주제가 될 확률이 높다. 이 실험에 의하면 숙련된 전문가들은 뛰어난 기술을 행할 수 있지만 그 원리에 대해 자세하게 설명할 수 없다고 이야기하고 있다. ①, ②, ④번은 언급되지 않은 내용이므로 이 글을 통해 알 수 없고, ③번의 경우는 기술을 행하는 데는 문제가 없어 뽐내는 것과는 관련이 없기 때문에 정답이 될 수 없다.

35 가공을 최소화하는 것의 장점 | 정답률 68% | 정답 ③

다음 글에서 전체 흐름과 관계 없는 문장은?

Minimal processing can be one of the best ways / to keep original flavors and taste, / without any need to add artificial flavoring / or additives, / or too much salt.
최소한의 가공은 가장 좋은 방법 중 하나일 수 있다. / 본연의 풍미와 맛을 유지하는 / 인공 향료를 넣을 필요 없이 / 첨가물이나 / 또는 과도한 소금을

This would also be the efficient way / to keep most nutrients, / especially the most sensitive ones / such as many vitamins and anti-oxidants.
이것은 또한 효율적인 방법일 수 있다. / 대부분의 영양소를 유지하는 / 특히 가장 민감한 영양소를 / 많은 비타민과 항산화물질과 같은

① Milling of cereals / is one of the most harsh processes / which dramatically affect nutrient content.
곡물을 제분하는 것은 / 가장 가혹한 과정 중 하나이다. / 영양소 함량에 크게 영향을 미치는

② While grains are naturally very rich / in micronutrients, anti-oxidants and fiber / (i.e. in wholemeal flour or flakes), / milling usually removes / the vast majority of minerals, vitamins and fibers / to raise white flour.
곡물에는 자연적으로 매우 풍부하지만 / 미량 영양소, 항산화물질, 그리고 섬유질에 / 즉 통밀가루 또는 플레이크에는 / 제분이 일반적으로 제거한다. / 대부분의 미네랄, 비타민, 그리고 섬유질을 / 흰 밀가루를 만들기 위해

✓③ To increase grain production, / the use of chemical fertilizers should be minimized, / and insect-resistant grain varieties should be developed.
곡물 생산을 늘리려면 / 화학비료 사용이 최소화되어야 한다. / 그리고 해충에 강한 곡물 품종이 개발되어야 한다.

④ Such a spoilage of key nutrients and fiber / is no longer acceptable / in the context of a sustainable diet / aiming at an optimal nutrient density and health protection.
주요 영양소와 섬유질의 그러한 손상은 / 더 이상 받아들여질 수 없다. / 지속 가능한 식단의 맥락에서 / 최적의 영양소 밀도와 건강 보호를 목표로 하는

⑤ In contrast, / fermentation of various foodstuffs or germination of grains / are traditional, / locally accessible, low-energy and highly nutritious processes / of sounded interest.
대조적으로, / 다양한 식품의 발효나 곡물의 발아는 / 전통적이다. / 현지에서 접근 가능하며 / 에너지가 적게 들고 매우 영양가 있는 과정이다. / 알려진 관심을 받는

최소한의 가공은 인공 향료나 첨가물, 또는 과도한 소금을 넣을 필요 없이 본연의 풍미와 맛을 유지하는 가장 좋은 방법 중 하나일 수 있다. 이것은 또한 대부분의 영양소, 특히 많은 비타민과 항산화물질과 같은 가장 민감한 영양소를 유지하는 효율적인 방법일 수 있다. ① 곡물을 제분하는 것은 영양소 함량에 크게 영향을 미치는 가장 가혹한 과정 중 하나이다. ② 곡물에는 (즉 통밀가루 또는 플레이크에는) 미량 영양소, 항산화물질, 그리고 섬유질이 자연적으로 매우 풍부하지만, 제분이 일반적으로 흰 밀가루를 만들기 위해 대부분의 미네랄, 비타민 그리고 섬유질을 제거한다. ③ 곡물 생산을 늘리려면 화학비료 사용이 최소화되어야 하고 해충에 강한 곡물 품종이 개발되어야 한다. ④ 주요 영양소와 섬유질의 그러한 손상은 최적의 영양소 밀도와 건강 보호를 목표로 하는 지속 가능한 식단의 맥락에서 더 이상 받아들여질 수 없다. ⑤ 대조적으로, 다양한 식품의 발효나 곡물의 발아는 알려진 관심을 받는 전통적이고, 현지에서 접근 가능하며, 에너지가 적게 들고, 매우 영양가 있는 과정이다.

Why? 왜 정답일까?

최소한의 가공은 본연의 풍미와 맛을 유지할 수 있으며 또한 본래 가지고 있는 영양소를 유지할 수 있다고 이야기하고 있는데, ③은 곡물 생산을 늘리는 방법에 대해 이야기하고 있다. 따라서 전체 흐름과 관계없는 문장은 ③이다.

- flavor ⓝ 맛
- additive ⓝ 첨가물
- sensitive ⓐ 민감한
- mill ⓥ 제분하다
- micronutrient ⓝ 미량영양소
- fertilizer ⓝ 비료
- density ⓝ 밀도
- germination ⓝ 발아
- nutritious ⓐ 영양가가 높은
- artificial ⓐ 인공적인
- nutrient ⓝ 영양소
- anti-oxidants 항산화물질
- harsh ⓐ 가혹한
- fiber ⓝ 섬유질
- spoilage ⓝ 부패
- fermentation ⓝ 발효
- accessible ⓐ 접근 가능한

구문 풀이

1행 Minimal processing can be one of the best ways to keep original flavors
『one + of + the + 최상급 + 복수명사 : 가장 ~한 것들 중 하나』 to부정사(형용사적용법)
and taste, without any need to add artificial flavoring or additives, or too much salt.
to부정사(형용사적용법)

36 능력에 관한 역설적 사실   정답률 58% | 정답 ⑤

주어진 글 다음에 이어질 글의 순서로 가장 적절한 것을 고르시오.
① (A) – (C) – (B)
② (B) – (A) – (C)
③ (B) – (C) – (A)
④ (C) – (A) – (B)
✓⑤ (C) – (B) – (A)

It would seem obvious / that the more competent someone is, / the more we will like that person.
명확해 보일 것이다. / 누군가가 더 능력이 있을수록, / 우리가 그 사람을 더 많이 좋아할 것이라는 점은

By "competence," / I mean a cluster of qualities: / smartness, the ability to get things done, wise decisions, etc.
'능력'이라는 것을 / 나는 총체적인 특징을 뜻하는 것으로 말한다. / 똑똑함, 일을 수행하는 능력, 지혜로운 결정 등과 같은

(C) We stand a better chance of doing well / at our life tasks / if we surround ourselves with people / who know what they're doing / and have a lot to teach us.
우리는 잘될 더 나은 가능성이 있다. / 우리의 인생 과업에서 / 우리가 사람 주변에 있을 때 / 자신이 무엇을 하고 있는지를 아는 / 그리고 우리를 가르칠 많은 것들을 갖고 있는

But the research evidence is paradoxical: / In problem-solving groups, / the participants / who are considered the most competent / and have the best ideas tend not to be the ones / who are best liked.
그러나 연구 증거는 역설적이다. / 문제 해결 집단에서 / 참여자들은 / 가장 능력이 있다고 여겨지는 / 그리고 가장 좋은 생각을 갖고 있는 / 사람이 아닌 경향이 있다. / 가장 선호되는 사람들이

Why?
왜 그럴까?

(B) One possibility is that, / although we like to be / around competent people, / those who are *too* / competent make us uncomfortable.
하나의 가능성은 ~이다. / 비록 우리는 있고 싶어 하지만 / 능력 있는 사람들 주위에 / '너무' 능력 있는 사람들은 / 우리를 불편하게 만든다는 것

They may seem unapproachable, distant, superhuman / — and make us look bad / (and feel worse) / by comparison.
그들은 접근할 수 없고, 멀고, 초인간적으로 보일 수가 있다. / 그리고 우리가 형편없어 보이게 만든다. / 그리고 기분이 더 나쁘게 / 비교해 보면

(A) If this were true, / we might like people more / if they reveal some evidence of fallibility.
만약에 이것이 사실이라면 / 우리는 사람들을 더 좋아할지도 모른다. / 그들이 실수를 저지를 수 있다는 어떤 증거를 드러낼 때

For example, / if your friend is a brilliant mathematician, superb athlete, and gourmet cook, / you might like him or her better / if, every once in a while, they screwed up.
예를 들면 / 여러분의 친구가 훌륭한 수학자, 뛰어난 운동선수, 그리고 미식 요리사라면 / 여러분은 더 좋아할지도 모른다. / 그들이 가끔 일을 망친다면

누군가가 더 능력이 있을수록, 우리가 그 사람을 더 많이 좋아할 것이라는 점은 명확해 보일 것이다. 나는, '능력'이라는 것을, 똑똑함, 일을 수행하는 능력, 지혜로운 결정 등과 같은 총체적인 특징을 뜻하는 것으로 말한다.

(C) 우리는 자신이 무엇을 하고 있는지를 알고 우리를 가르칠 많은 것들을 갖고 있는 사람 주변에 있을 때, 우리의 인생 과업에서 잘될 더 나은 가능성이 있다. 그러나 연구 증거는 역설적이다. 문제 해결 집단에서, 가장 능력이 있다고 여겨지고 가장 좋은 생각을 갖고 있는 참여자들은 가장 선호되는 사람들이 아닌 경향이 있다. 왜 그럴까?

(B) 하나의 가능성은, 비록 우리는 능력 있는 사람들 주위에 있고 싶어 하지만, '너무' 능력 있는 사람들은 우리를 불편하게 만든다는 것이다. 그들은 접근할 수 없고, 멀고, 초인간적으로 보일 수가 있어서, 비교해 보면 우리가 형편없어 보이게(그리고 기분이 더 나쁘게) 만든다.

(A) 만약에 이것이 사실이라면, 사람들이 실수를 저지를 수 있다는 어떤 증거를 드러낼 때 그들을 더 좋아할지도 모른다. 예를 들면, 여러분의 친구가 훌륭한 수학자, 뛰어난 운동선수, 그리고 미식 요리사라면, 여러분은 가끔 그들이 일을 망친다면 그들을 더 좋아할지도 모른다.

Why? 왜 정답일까?

주어진 글에서 능력에 대해 정의하면서 이후 (C)에서 능력이 있는 사람이 선호되는 사람들이 아닐 수 있다는 의문을 제기하고 있다. 그 다음은 능력이 있는 사람이 왜 선호되지 않는지에 대해 이야기하고 있는 (B)가 오는 것이 자연스럽다. 이후 (A)에서는 앞서 제기된 의문이 사실이라면 어떨지에 대해 이야기하고 있다. 따라서 글의 순서로 가장 적절한 것은 ⑤ '(C) – (B) – (A)'이다.

- obvious ⓐ 분명한
- fallibility ⓝ 실수
- superb ⓐ 뛰어난
- screw up 망치다
- unapproachable ⓐ 접근할 수 없는
- paradoxical ⓐ 역설적인
- cluster ⓝ 집단
- brilliant ⓐ 훌륭한
- gourmet ⓝ 미식가
- possibility ⓝ 가능성
- comparison ⓝ 비교
- participant ⓝ 참가자

구문 풀이

10행 One possibility is that, although we like to be around competent people,
접속사
those who are too competent make us uncomfortable.
관계대명사(주격)   동사   목적격보어(형용사)

37 컴퓨터 알고리즘과 벌의 차이   정답률 59% | 정답 ③

주어진 글 다음에 이어질 글의 순서로 가장 적절한 것을 고르시오. [3점]
① (A) – (C) – (B)
② (B) – (A) – (C)
✓③ (B) – (C) – (A)
④ (C) – (A) – (B)
⑤ (C) – (B) – (A)

A computational algorithm / that takes input data / and generates some output from it / doesn't really embody any notion of meaning.
컴퓨터를 사용하는 알고리즘은 / 입력 데이터를 받아 / 그것으로부터 어떤 출력을 생성하는 / 실제로 의미라는 그 어떤 개념도 구현하지 않는다.

Certainly, / such a computation / does not generally have as its purpose / its own survival and well-being.
분명히 / 그러한 컴퓨터 계산은 / 일반적으로 목적으로 하지 않는다. / 그 자체의 생존과 안녕을

(B) It does not, in general, assign / value to the inputs.
이것은 일반적으로 부여하지 않는다. / 입력에 가치를

Compare, / for example, / a computer algorithm / with the waggle dance of the honeybee, / by which means a foraging bee conveys to others in the hive / information about the source of food / (such as nectar) / it has located.
비교해 보라. / 예를 들어 / 컴퓨터 알고리즘을 / 꿀벌의 8자 춤과 / 먹이를 찾아다니는 벌이 벌집 안의 다른 벌들에게 알려주는 수단인 / 먹이의 출처에 대한 정보를 / 꿀과 같은 / 그것이 위치를 찾아낸

(C) The "dance" / — a series of stylized movements on the comb / — shows / the bees how far away the food is / and in which direction.
그 '춤' / 즉 벌집에서의 일련의 양식화된 움직임은 / 보여 준다. / 벌들에게 먹이가 얼마나 멀리 있는지 / 그리고 어느 방향으로 있는지

But / this input does not simply program / other bees to go out and look for it.
그러나 / 이 입력은 단순히 프로그래밍 하는 것이 아니다. / 다른 벌들이 나가서 먹이를 찾도록

Rather, / they evaluate this information, / comparing it with their own knowledge / of the surroundings.
오히려 / 그것들은 이 정보를 평가한다. / 그들 자신의 지식과 비교하면서 / 주변 환경에 대한

(A) Some bees might not bother to make the journey, / considering it not worthwhile.
일부 벌들은 굳이 그 이동을 하지 않을 수도 있다. / 그 이동이 가치가 없다고 생각해서

The input, / such as it is, / is processed in the light of the organism's own internal states and history; / there is nothing prescriptive about its effects.
그 입력은 / 대단한 것은 아니지만 / 유기체 자체의 내부 상태와 역사에 비추어 처리된다 / 그 결과에 대해 규정하는 것은 없다.

입력 데이터를 받아 그것으로부터 어떤 출력을 생성하는 컴퓨터를 사용하는 알고리즘은 실제로 의미라는 그 어떤 개념도 구현하지 않는다. 분명히, 그러한 컴퓨터 계산은 일반적으로 그 자체의 생존과 안녕을 목적으로 하지 않는다.

(B) 이것은 일반적으로 입력에 가치를 부여하지 않는다. 예를 들어, 컴퓨터 알고리즘을, 먹이를 찾아다니는 벌이 벌집 안의 다른 벌들에게 그것이 위치를 찾아낸 (꿀과 같은) 먹이의 출처에 대한 정보를 알려주는 수단인 꿀벌의 8자 춤과 비교해 보라.

(C) 그 '춤', 즉 벌집에서의 일련의 양식화된 움직임은 벌들에게 먹이가 얼마나 멀리 있고 어느 방향으로 있는지 보여준다. 그러나 이 입력은 다른 벌들이 나가서 먹이를 찾도록 단순히 프로그래밍하는 것이 아니다. 오히려 그것들은 이 정보를 주변 환경에 대한 그들 자신의 지식과 비교하면서 정보를 평가한다.

(A) 일부 벌들은 그 이동이 가치가 없다고 생각해서 굳이 그 이동을 하지 않을 수도 있다. 그 입력은, 대단한 것은 아니지만, 유기체 자체의 내부 상태와 역사에 비추어 처리되며, 그 결과에 대해 규정하는 것은 없다.

Why? 왜 정답일까?

주어진 글에서 컴퓨터를 사용하는 알고리즘에 대해 이야기하고 있다. 이후 (B)에서 '이것'은 일반적으로 입력에 가치를 부여하지 않는다며 주어진 글에 나온 내용을 언급하고 있다. (B)의 마지막 부분에 나온 벌의 춤에 대해서 (C)에서 이어서 등장하고 있으며 (A)에서 일부 벌들의 행동을 통해 주어진 글에서의 주장을 강화하고 있다. 따라서 글의 순서로 가장 적절한 것은 ③ '(B) – (C) – (A)'이다.

- computational ⓐ 컴퓨터의
- input ⓝ 입력
- embody ⓥ 구현하다
- purpose ⓝ 목적
- prescriptive ⓐ 규정하는
- foraging ⓝ 수렵, 채집
- stylize ⓥ 양식화하다
- evaluate ⓥ 평가하다
- algorithm ⓝ 알고리즘
- generate ⓥ 발생하다
- notion ⓝ 개념
- worthwhile ⓐ 가치 있는
- assign ⓥ 부여하다
- convey ⓥ 전달하다
- comb ⓝ 벌집

구문 풀이

1행 A computational algorithm that takes input data and generates some
주어   관계대명사(주격)
output from it doesn't really embody any notion of meaning.
단수동사

38 바이러스 전염과 행동의 전염   정답률 59% | 정답 ②

글의 흐름으로 보아, 주어진 문장이 들어가기에 가장 적절한 곳을 고르시오.

There are deep similarities / between viral contagion and behavioral contagion.
깊은 유사성이 있다. / 바이러스성의 전염과 행동의 전염 사이에

① For example, / people in close or extended proximity / to others infected by a virus / are themselves more likely to become infected, / just as people are more likely to drink excessively / when they spend more time / in the company of heavy drinkers.
예를 들어 / 아주 근접해 있거나 어느 정도 근접해 있는 사람들은 / 바이러스에 감염된 다른 사람들과 / 그들도 감염될 가능성이 더 높다. / 사람들이 술을 과도하게 마실 가능성이 더 높은 것과 마찬가지로 / 사람들이 시간을 많이 보낼 때 / 술을 많이 마시는 사람들과 함께

✔ But / there are also important differences / between the two types of contagion.
하지만 / 중요한 차이점들도 있다. / 두 종류의 전염 사이에

One is / that visibility promotes behavioral contagion / but inhibits the spread of infectious diseases.
한 가지는 ~는 것이다. / 가시성이 행동의 전염을 촉진한다는 것 / 하지만 감염성 질병의 확산은 억제한다

③ Solar panels / that are visible from the street, / for instance, / are more likely to stimulate neighboring installations.
태양 전지판은 / 거리에서 볼 수 있는 / 예를 들어 / 이웃의 설치를 북돋을 가능성이 더 높다.

④ In contrast, / we try to avoid others / who are visibly ill.
대조적으로 / 우리는 다른 사람들을 피하려고 노력한다. / 눈에 띄게 몸이 아픈

⑤ Another important difference is / that whereas viral contagion is almost always a bad thing, / behavioral contagion is sometimes negative / — as in the case of smoking / — but sometimes positive, / as in the case of solar installations.
또 다른 중요한 차이는 ~ 것이다. / 바이러스성의 전염은 거의 항상 나쁜 것인 반면 / 행동의 전염은 때로는 부정적이다. / 흡연의 경우와 같이 / 하지만 때때로 긍정적이라는 / 태양 전지판 설치의 경우와 같이

바이러스성의 전염과 행동의 전염 사이에 깊은 유사성이 있다. 예를 들어, 바이러스에 감염된 다른 사람들과 아주 근접해 있거나 어느 정도 근접해 있는 사람들은 그들도 감염될 가능성이 더 높은데, 이는 사람들이 술을 많이 마시는 사람들과 함께 시간을 많이 보낼 때 술을 과도하게 마실 가능성이 더 높은 것과 마찬가지이다. 하지만 두 종류의 전염 사이에 중요한 차이점들도 있다. 한 가지는 가시성이 행동의 전염을 촉진하지만, 감염성 질병의 확산은 억제한다는 것이다. 예를 들어, 거리에서 볼 수 있는 태양 전지판은 이웃의 설치를 북돋을 가능성이 더 높다. 대조적으로, 우리는 눈에 띄게 몸이 아픈 다른 사람들을 피하려고 노력한다. 또 다른 중요한 차이는 바이러스성의 전염은 거의 항상 나쁜 것인 반면, 행동의 전염은 흡연의 경우와 같이, 때로는 부정적이지만, 태양 전지판 설치의 경우와 같이, 때때로 긍정적이라는 것이다.

Why? 왜 정답일까?

② 앞은 바이러스성 전염과 행동의 전염 사이에 유사성이 있다고 주장하고 있는데, ② 뒤에서는 차이점에 대해서 이야기하고 있다. 주어진 문장은 차이점들도 있다고 이야기하고 있으므로 주어진 문장이 들어가기에 가장 적절한 곳은 ②이다.

- contagion ⓝ 전염
- proximity ⓝ 가까움
- visibility ⓝ 가시성
- infectious ⓐ 전염되는
- viral ⓐ 바이러스의
- excessively ⓐⓓ 과도하게
- inhibit ⓥ 억제하다
- stimulate ⓥ 촉진하다

구문 풀이

10행 Solar panels <u>that are visible from the street</u>, for instance, <u>are</u> more likely
주어 　　관계대명사(주격)　　　　　　　　　　복수동사
to stimulate neighboring installations.

---

39 동면과 수면의 차이 　　　　　정답률 62% | 정답 ④

글의 흐름으로 보아, 주어진 문장이 들어가기에 가장 적절한 곳을 고르시오. [3점]

Sleep is clearly about more / than just resting.
잠은 분명 이상이다. / 단지 휴식하는 것

One curious fact is / that animals that are hibernating also / have periods of sleep.
한 가지 호기심을 끄는 것은 ~는 점이다. / 동면하고 있는 동물들 또한 / 잠자는 기간을 가진다

It comes as a surprise to most of us, / but hibernation and sleep are not the same thing at all, / at least not from a neurological and metabolic perspective.
그것은 우리 대부분에게 놀라움으로 다가온다. / 하지만 동면과 수면은 전혀 같은 것이 아니다. / 적어도 신경학적이고 신진대사적인 관점에서 볼 때

① Hibernating is more like being anesthetized: / the subject is unconscious / but not actually asleep.
동면은 마취되는 것과 더욱 비슷하다. / 그 대상은 의식이 없다. / 그러나 실제로 잠들어 있지는 않다.

② So / a hibernating animal needs / to get a few hours of conventional sleep each day / within the larger unconsciousness.
그래서 / 동면하고 있는 동물은 필요가 있다. / 매일 몇 시간의 전형적인 잠을 잘 / 더 큰 무의식 속에서

③ A further surprise to most of us is / that bears, the most famous of wintry sleepers, / don't actually hibernate.
우리 대부분에게 더욱 놀라운 점은 ~이다. / 겨울에 잠을 자는 동물 중 가장 유명한 곰도 / 실제로는 동면하지 않는다는 것

✔ Real hibernation involves profound unconsciousness and a dramatic fall in body temperature / — often to around 32 degrees Fahrenheit.
실제 동면은 포함한다. / 깊은 무의식과 체온의 급격한 하락을 / 자주 대략 화씨 32도로 떨어진다.

By this definition, / bears don't hibernate, / because their body temperature stays near normal / and they are easily awakened.
이러한 정의에 따르면 / 곰은 동면하지 않는다. / 그것들의 체온은 정상 근처를 유지하기 때문에 / 그리고 쉽게 잠에서 깨어나기 때문에

⑤ Their winter sleeps are more accurately called / a state of torpor.
그것들의 겨울잠은 더 정확하게는 불린다. / 휴면 상태라고

잠은 분명 단지 휴식하는 것 이상이다. 한 가지 호기심을 끄는 사실은 동면하고 있는 동물들 또한 잠자는 기간을 가진다는 점이다. 그것은 우리 대부분에게 놀라움으로 다가오지만, 동면과 수면은 적어도 신경학적이고 신진대사적인 관점에서 볼 때 전혀 같은 것이 아니다. 동면은 마취되는 것과 더욱 비슷한데, 그 대상은 의식이 없지만 실제로 잠들어 있지는 않다. 그래서 동면하고 있는 동물은 더 큰 무의식 속에서 매일 몇 시간의 전형적인 잠을 잘 필요가 있다. 우리 대부분에게 더욱 놀라운 점은 겨울에 잠을 자는 동물 중 가장 유명한 곰도 실제로는 동면하지 않는다는 것이다. 실제 동면은 깊은 무의식과 체온의 급격한 하락을 포함하는데, 자주 대략 화씨 32도로 떨어진다. 이러한 정의에 따르면, 곰의 체온은 정상 근처를 유지하기 때문에 그것들은 동면하지 않고 쉽게 잠에서 깨어나기 때문에 그것들은 동면하지 않는다. 그것들의 겨울잠은 더 정확하게는 휴면 상태라고 불린다.

Why? 왜 정답일까?

동면과 수면은 다르다고 이야기하고 있는데, 동면하는 동물로 알려진 곰을 예시로 들고 있다. 곰은 실제로 동면하지 않는다고 하는데 주어진 문장은 그에 대한 이유이므로 들어가기에 가장 적절한 곳은 ④이다.

- hibernation ⓝ 동면
- unconsciousness ⓝ 무의식
- neurological ⓐ 신경의
- profound ⓐ 깊은
- Fahrenheit ⓝ 화씨의
- metabolic ⓐ 신진대사적인

- anesthetize ⓥ 마취시키다
- awakened ⓥ 깨다
- wintry ⓐ 겨울의
- torpor ⓝ 휴면

구문 풀이

12행 A further surprise to most of us is that bears, {the most famous of wintry
　　　　　　주어　　　　　　　　단수동사　　　주어
sleepers,} don't actually hibernate.　{ }: 수식
　　　　　　복수동사

---

40 Ervin Staub의 연구 　　　　　정답률 54% | 정답 ①

다음 글의 내용을 한 문장으로 요약하고자 한다. 빈칸 (A), (B)에 들어갈 말로 가장 적절한 것은?

	(A)		(B)		(A)		(B)
✔	presence 있음	……	evaluated 평가받는	②	presence 있음	……	motivated 동기를 부여 받는
③	absence 없음	……	viewed 보는	④	absence 없음	……	assisted 도움 받는
⑤	audience 청중인	……	trained 훈련 받는				

The concern about how we appear to others / can be seen in children, / though work by the psychologist Ervin Staub suggests / that the effect may vary with age.
걱정은 / 우리가 다른 사람들에게 어떻게 보이는지에 대한 / 아이들에게서 보일 수 있다. / 하지만 심리학자 Ervin Staub의 연구는 시사한다. / 그 영향이 나이에 따라 달라질 수 있다고

In a study / where children heard another child in distress, / young children (kindergarten through second grade) / were more likely to help the child in distress / when with another child / than alone.
한 연구에서 / 아이들이 곤경에 처한 다른 아이의 소리를 들었던 / 어린 아이들(유치원에서 2학년까지)은 / 곤경에 처한 아이를 도울 가능성이 더 높았다. / 다른 아이와 함께 있을 때 / 혼자 있을 때 보다

But for older children — in fourth and sixth grade / — the effect reversed: / they were less likely to help a child in distress / when they were with a peer / than when they were alone.
하지만 4학년과 6학년과 같이 나이가 더 많은 아이들의 경우에는 / 그 결과가 뒤바뀌었는데 / 그들은 곤경에 처한 아이를 도울 가능성이 더 낮았다. / 또래와 함께 있을 때 / 혼자 있을 때 보다

Staub suggested / that younger children might feel more comfortable acting / when they have the company of a peer, / whereas older children might feel more concern / about being judged by their peers / and fear feeling embarrassed by overreacting.
Staub는 말했다. / 더 어린 아이들은 행동하는데 더 편안함을 느낄지도 모른다고 / 또래와 함께 있을 때 / 반면에 나이가 더 많은 아이들은 더욱 걱정할 것이다. / 자기 또래들에게 판단 받는 것을 / 그리고 창피함을 느끼는 것을 두려워할 지도 모른다고 / 과잉 반응에 의해

Staub noted / that "older children seemed to discuss the distress sounds less / and to react to them less openly / than younger children."
Staub는 언급했다. / 나이가 더 많은 아이들은 곤경(에 처한 아이들)의 소리에 대해 덜 이야기 하는 것처럼 보였다고 / 그리고 덜 공공연하게 반응하는 것처럼 보였다고 / 더 어린 아이들에 비해

In other words, / the older children were deliberately putting on a poker face / in front of their peers.
다시 말해서 / 더 나이가 많은 아이들은 의도적으로 무표정한 얼굴을 하고 있었다. / 자기 또래들 앞에서

➡ The study suggests / that, contrary to younger children, / older children are less likely to help / those in distress / in the (A) presence of others / because they care more / about how they are (B) evaluated.
연구는 시사한다. / 더 어린 아이들과는 반대로 / 나이가 더 많은 아이들은 도울 가능성이 더 낮다. / 곤경에 처한 아이들을 / 다른 사람들이 있을 때 / 그 이유는 그들이 더 많이 신경 쓰기 때문이라고 / 자신이 어떻게 평가 받는지에 대해

우리가 다른 사람들에게 어떻게 보이는지에 대한 걱정은 아이들에게서 보일 수 있지만, 심리학자 Ervin Staub의 연구는 그 영향이 나이에 따라 달라질 수도 있다고 시사한다. 아이들이 곤경에 처한 다른 아이의 소리를 들었던 연구에서, 어린 아이들(유치원에서 2학년까지)은 혼자 있을 때보다 다른 아이와 함께 있을 때 곤경에 처한 아이를 도울 가능성이 더 높았다. 하지만 4학년과 6학년과 같이 나이가 더 많은 아이들의 경우에는, 그 결과가 뒤바뀌었는데, 그들은 혼자 있을 때보다 또래와 함께 있을 때 곤경에 처한 아이를 도울 가능성이 더 낮았다. Staub은 더 어린 아이들은 또래와 함께 있을 때 행동하는데 편안함을 느낄지도 모르는 데 반해, 나이가 더 많은 아이들은 자기 또래들에게 판단 받는 것을 두려워하며 과잉 반응에 의해 창피함을 느끼는 것을 두려워할지도 모른다고 말했다. Staub은 '나이가 더 많은 아이들은 더 어린 아이들에 비해 곤경(에 처한 아이들)의 소리에 대해 덜 이야기하고, 덜 공공연하게 반응하는 것처럼 보였다.'라고 언급했다. 다시 말해서, 더 나이가 많은 아이들은 의도적으로 자기 또래들 앞에서 무표정한 얼굴을 하고 있었다.

➡ 연구는 더 어린 아이들과는 반대로, 나이가 더 많은 아이들은 다른 사람들이 (A) 있을 때 곤경에 처한 아이들을 도울 가능성이 더 낮으며, 그 이유는 그들은 자신이 어떻게 (B) 평가받는지에 대해 더 많이 신경 쓰기 때문이라고 시사한다.

Why? 왜 정답일까?

Ervin Staub의 연구에 의하면 나이가 더 많은 아이들의 경우 또래와 함께 있을 때 곤경에 처한 아이들을 도울 가능성이 낮고(But for older children — in fourth and sixth grade — the effect reversed: they were less likely to help a child in distress when they were with a peer than when they were alone.)말하며, 그 이유는 또래에게 판단 받는 것을 걱정하여 과잉 반응에 의해 창피함을 느끼고 이를 두려워할지도 모르기 때문이라고(Staub suggested that younger children might feel more comfortable acting when they have the company of a peer, whereas older children might feel more concern about being judged by their peers and fear feeling embarrassed by overreacting.) 말한다. 따라서 요약문의 빈칸 (A), (B)에 들어갈 말로 가장 적절한 것은 ① 'A) presence(있을), (B) evaluated(평가받는)'이다.

- psychologist ⓝ 심리학자
- reverse ⓥ 뒤집다
- overreact ⓥ 과잉 반응을 보이다
- deliberately ⓐⓓ 의도적으로
- distress ⓝ 곤경
- vary ⓥ 다르다
- peer ⓝ 또래
- note ⓥ 주목하다
- contrary to ~와 반대로

구문 풀이

1행 The concern about how we appear to others can be seen in children,
　　　　　　　　　　　관계부사　　　　　　　　　동사
though work by the psychologist Ervin Staub suggests that the effect may vary
　　　　　　　　　　　　　　　　　　　　　　　　접속사
with age.

What makes / questioning authority so hard?
무엇이 만들까? / 권위에 의문을 제기하는 것을 그토록 어렵게

The (a) difficulties start in childhood, / when parents — the first and most powerful authority figures / — show children "the way things are."
그 어려움은 유년 시절에 시작한다. / 최초이자 가장 영향력 있는 권위자인 부모가 ~ 할 때 / 아이들에게 '사물이 존재하는 방식'을 제시하는

This is a necessary element of learning language and socialization, / and certainly most things learned in early childhood / are (b) noncontroversial: / the English alphabet starts with A and ends with Z, / the numbers 1 through 10 come before the numbers 11 through 20, / and so on.
이것은 언어 학습과 사회화의 필수적인 요소이다. / 그리고 확실히 초기 유년기에 학습되는 것 대부분은 / 논쟁의 여지가 없다. / 영어 알파벳은 A에서 시작해서 Z로 끝난다는 것 / 숫자 1부터 10은 숫자 11부터 20보다 이전에 나온다는 것 / 등등처럼

Children, / however, / will spontaneously question / things that are quite obvious / to adults and even to older kids.
아이들은 / 하지만 / 즉흥적으로 의문을 제기할 것이다. / 꽤 명백한 것들에 / 어른들과 심지어 더 나이 많은 아이들에게도

The word "why?" / becomes a challenge, / as in, "Why is the sky blue?"
"왜요?"라는 말은 / 도전이 된다. / "왜 하늘이 파랄까요?"에서처럼

Answers such as "because it just is" or "because I say so" / tell children / that they must unquestioningly (c) accept / what authorities say "just because," / and children who persist in their questioning / are likely to find / themselves dismissed or yelled / at for "bothering" adults / with "meaningless" or "unimportant" questions.
"그냥 그러니까" 혹은 "내가 그렇다고 하니까"와 같은 대답은 / 아이들에게 말한다. / 아이들이 의심 없이 받아들여야 한다고 / 권위자들이 "단지 그러니까"라고 말하는 것을 / 그리고 의문을 제기하는 것을 지속하는 아이들은 / 알게 될 가능성이 높다. / 그들 자신이 쫓겨나거나 고함을 듣는다는 것을 / 어른들을 '성가시게 하는' 것 때문에 / '무의미한' 혹은 '중요하지 않은' 질문으로

But these questions are in fact perfectly (d) reasonable.
하지만 이러한 질문들은 / 실제로 완벽하게 합리적이다.

Why is the sky blue?
왜 하늘은 파랄까?

「Many adults do not themselves know / the answer.」 [42번의 근거]
많은 어른들은 자신도 알지 못한다. / 그 대답

And who says the sky's color needs to be called "blue," / anyway?
그리고 누가 말하는가? / 하늘의 색깔이 '파란색'으로 불려야 한다고 / 어쨌든

How do we know / that what one person calls "blue" is the same color / that another calls "blue"?
어떻게 우리가 아는가? / 한 사람이 '파란색'이라고 부르는 것이 같은 색깔인지 / 또 다른 사람이 '파란색'이라고 부르는 것과

The scientific answers come from physics, / but those are not the answers / that children are seeking.
과학적인 답은 물리학에서 나온다. / 하지만 그것들은 답은 아니다. / 아이들이 찾고 있는

「They are trying to understand the world, / and no matter how (e) irritating the repeated questions may become / to stressed and time-pressed parents, / it is important to take them seriously / to encourage kids to question authority / to think for themselves.」 [41번의 근거]
그들은 세계를 이해하려고 노력하고 있다. / 그리고 반복되는 질문들이 아무리 짜증스러울지라도 / 스트레스가 쌓이고 시간에 쫓기는 부모들에게 / 아이들이 그것들을 진지하게 받아들이는 것이 중요하다. / 아이들이 권위에 의문을 제기하도록 독려하여 / 스스로 생각하도록

무엇이 권위에 의문을 제기하는 것을 그토록 어렵게 만들까? 그 (a) 어려움은 유년 시절에 시작하는데, 이는 최초이자 가장 영향력 있는 권위자인 부모가 아이들에게 '사물이 존재하는 방식'을 제시하는 때이다. 이것은 언어 학습과 회화의 필수적인 요소이고, 확실히 초기 유년기에 학습되는 것 대부분은 (b) 논쟁의 여지가 없는데, 영어 알파벳은 A에서 시작해서 Z로 끝난다는 것, 숫자 1부터 10은 숫자 11부터 20보다 이전에 나온다는 것 등등처럼 말이다. 하지만 아이들은 어른들과 심지어 더 나이 많은 아이들에게도 꽤 명백한 것들에 즉흥적으로 의문을 제기할 것이다. "왜요?"라는 말은 "왜 하늘은 파랄까요?"에서처럼 도전이 된다. "그냥 그러니까" 혹은 "내가 그렇다고 하니까"와 같은 대답들은 권위자들이 "단지 그러니까"라고 말하는 것을 아이들이 의심 없이 (c) 받아들여야 한다고 아이들에게 말해주며, 의문을 제기하는 것을 지속하는 아이들은 '무의미한' 혹은 '중 하지 않은' 질문으로 어른들을 '성가시게 하는' 것 때문에 그들 자신이 쫓겨나거나 고함을 듣는다는 것을 알게 될 가능성이 높다. 하지만 이러한 질문들은 실제로 완벽하게 (d) 비합리적(→ 합리적)이다. 왜 하늘은 파랄까? 많은 어른들은 자신도 그 대답을 알지 못한다. 그리고 어쨌든 누가 하늘의 색깔이 '파란색'으로 불려야 한다고 말하는가? 한 사람이 '파란색'이라고 부르는 것이 또 다른 사람이 '파란색'이라고 부르는 것과 같은 색깔인지 어떻게 우리가 아는가? 과학적인 답은 물리학에서 나오지만, 그것들은 아이들이 찾고 있는 답은 아니다. 그들은 세계를 이해하려고 노력하고 있고, 반복되는 질문들이 스트레스가 쌓이고 시간에 쫓기는 부모들에게 아무리 (e) 짜증스러울지라도, 아이들이 권위에 의문을 제기하도록 독려하여 스스로 생각하도록 그것들을 진지하게 받아들이는 것이 중요하다.

- figure ⓝ 인물
- socialization ⓝ 사회화
- spontaneously ⓐⓓ 자발적으로
- persist ⓥ 계속하다
- yell ⓥ 소리치다
- unreasonable ⓐ 비합리적인
- encourage ⓥ 독려하다
- necessary ⓐ 필요한
- noncontroversial ⓐ 논란의 여지가 없는
- unquestioningly ⓐⓓ 의문을 품지 않고
- dismiss ⓥ 묵살하다
- bother ⓥ 성가시게 하다
- irritate ⓥ 짜증나게 하다

구문 풀이

[21행] How do we know that what one person calls "blue" is the same color
접속사 ↳ 관계대명사(선행사포함)
that another calls "blue"?
관계대명사(목적격)

41 제목 파악 　　　정답률 58% | 정답 ①

윗글의 제목으로 가장 적절한 것은?
✓① Things Plain to You Aren't to Children: Let Them Question
아이들에게는 평범한 일이 아니다 : 질문하게 하라
② Children's Complaints: Should Parents Accept All of Them?
아이들의 불만 : 부모는 모든 것을 받아들여야 할까?
③ Want More Challenges? They'll Make Your Energy Dry Up!
더 많은 도전을 원하는가? 에너지가 고갈될 것이다!
④ Authority Has Hidden Power to Nurture Children's Morality
당국은 아이들의 도덕성을 기를 숨겨진 힘을 갖고 있다

---

⑤ Answering Is More Crucial than Questioning for Quick Learning
빠른 학습을 위해서는 질문 보다 답변이 더 중요하다

Why? 왜 정답일까?

아이들이 발달 과정에서 논쟁의 여지가 없는 당연한 질문들을 하는 것은 성가실 수 있지만, 권위에 의문을 제기하도록 독려하여 스스로 생각하도록 도와줄 수 있으므로 진지하게 받아들여야 한다(**They are trying to understand the world, and no matter how irritating the repeated questions may become to stressed and time-pressed parents, it is important to take them seriously to encourage kids to question authority to think for themselves.**)는 내용이다. 따라서 글의 제목으로 가장 적절한 것은 ① 'Things Plain to You Aren't to Children: Let Them Question(아이들에게는 평범한 일이 아니다 : 질문하게 하라)'이다.

42 어휘 추론 　　　정답률 62% | 정답 ④

밑줄 친 (a) ~ (e) 중에서 문맥상 낱말의 쓰임이 적절하지 않은 것은?
① (a)　② (b)　③ (c)　✓④ (d)　⑤ (e)

Why? 왜 정답일까?

유년 시절 발달 과정 중 하나인 질문하기는 논쟁의 여지가 없고 당연한 것처럼 보여서 무의미하고 성가신 것으로 느껴질 수 있는데 사실 이는 어른도 답을 알 수 없는 질문(**Many adults do not themselves know the answer.**)으로 unreasonable 대신 reasonable을 써야 자연스럽다. 따라서 낱말의 쓰임이 문맥상 적절하지 않은 것은 ④ '(d)'이다.

43-45 　남들보다 조금 느리게 성장한 Benjamin

(A)
My two girls grew up without challenges / with respect to development and social interaction.
나의 두 딸은 어려움 없이 성장했다. / 발달과 사회적 상호 작용에 있어서

My son Benjamin, / however, / was quite delayed.
나의 아들 Benjamin은 / 하지만 / 꽤 더뎠다.

「He struggled through his childhood, / not fitting in with the other children and wondering / what he was doing wrong / at every turn.」 [45번 ①의 근거] 일치
그는 어린 시절 동안 고생했다. / 다른 아이들과 잘 어울리지 않으면서 / 그리고 궁금해 하며 / 그가 무엇을 잘못했는지 / 언제나

He was teased by the other children / and frowned upon / by a number of unsympathetic adults.
그는 다른 아이들에게 괴롭힘을 받았다. / 그리고 눈살을 찌푸리게 했다. / 인정 없는 많은 어른들의

But his Grade 1 teacher was a wonderful, caring person / who took the time to ask / why Benjamin behaved the way (a) he did.
하지만 그의 1학년 선생님은 훌륭하고 친절한 사람이었다. / 물어보는 시간을 갖는 / 왜 Benjamin이 그가 했던 방식으로 행동했는지

(C)
The teacher was determined to understand Benjamin / and to accept him / as he was.
그 선생님은 결심했다. / Benjamin을 이해하겠다고 / 그리고 받아들이겠다고 / 있는 그대로

One day / he came home / with a note from his teacher.
어느 날 / 그는 집으로 왔다. / 그의 선생님으로부터 받은 한 쪽지를 가지고

「He suggested / I go to the school library.」 [45번 ④의 근거] 일치
그는 제안했다. / 내가 학교 도서관에 방문할 것을

They were having a sale, / and (c) he thought / my son would like one of the books.
그들은 판매를 하고 있었다. / 그리고 그는 생각했다. / 나의 아들이 책 중 하나를 좋아할 거라고

I couldn't go for a couple of days / and was concerned / I'd missed the opportunity.
나는 며칠 동안 갈 수 없었다. / 그리고 걱정했다. / 내가 기회를 놓쳤을까 봐

When I finally went to the school, / his teacher told me that / the sale had ended / but that the library had saved the book / for my little boy.
내가 마침내 학교에 갔을 때 / 그의 선생님은 나에게 말했다. / 판매는 끝났다고 / 하지만 도서관이 책을 남겨두었다고 / 내 아이를 위해

(B)
「I suspected / the teacher had paid for it / out of his own pocket.」 [45번 ②의 근거] 일치
나는 짐작했다. / 선생님이 그것을 지불한 것이 아닌가 / 자비로

It was a story-board book / with a place for a photo.
그것은 스토리보드 책이었다. / 사진을 위한 공간이 있는

On each page / there was an outline of an animal and a hole / so that the face in the photo appeared / to be the face of the animal.
쪽마다 / 동물의 윤곽과 구멍이 있었다. / 그래서 사진 속의 얼굴이 보였다. / 그 동물의 얼굴인 것처럼

Wondering if Benjamin would really be interested / in the book, / I brought it home.
Benjamin이 정말로 흥미가 있을지 궁금해 하며 / 그 책에 / 나는 그것을 집으로 가져왔다.

「He loved it!」 [45번 ③의 근거] 불일치
그는 그것을 좋아했다!

Through that book, / he saw that (b) he could be anything he wanted to be: / a cat, an octopus, a dinosaur — even a frog!
그 책을 통해 / 그는 알았다. / 그가 자신이 되길 원하는 어떠한 것도 될 수 있음을 / 고양이, 문어, 공룡, 그리고 심지어 개구리까지 말이다.

(D)
Benjamin joyfully embarked / on an imaginative journey / through the book, / and little did we know, / it laid the groundwork for his future successes.
Benjamin은 즐겁게 시작했다. / 상상의 여행을 / 그 책을 통해 / 그리고 우리가 거의 알지는 못했다. / 그것은 토대를 마련했다 / 그의 미래 성공을 위한

And thankfully, / his teacher had taken the time / to observe and understand (d) him / and had discovered a way to help / him reach out of his own world and join ours / through a story-board book.
그리고 감사하게도 / 그의 선생님은 시간을 가졌다. / 그를 관찰하고 이해하기 위한 / 그리고 돕는 방법을 발견했다. / 그가 자신만의 세상을 벗어나 우리의 세상에 참여하도록 / 스토리 보드책을 통해

「My son later became a child actor / and performed for seven years / with a Toronto casting agency.」 [45번 ⑤의 근거] 일치
내 아들은 나중에 아역 배우가 됐다. / 그리고 7년 동안 공연을 했다. / Toronto에 있는 캐스팅 회사와 함께

(e) He is now a published author / who writes fantasy and science-fiction!
그는 이제 출판 작가이다! / 판타지와 공상과학 소설을 쓰는

Who would have guessed?
누가 짐작이나 했을까?

(A)

나의 두 딸은 발달과 사회적 상호 작용에 있어서 어려움 없이 성장했다. 하지만, 나의 아들 Benjamin은 꽤 더뎠다. 그는 다른 아이들과 잘 어울리지 않고 언제나 그가 무엇을 잘못했는지 궁금해 하며, 어린 시절 동안 고생했다. 그는 다른 아이들에게 괴롭힘을 받았고 인정 없는 많은 어른들의 눈살을 찌푸리게 했다. 하지만 그의 1학년 선생님은 왜 Benjamin이 (a) 그가 했던 방식으로 행동했는지 물어보는 시간을 갖는, 훌륭하고 친절한 사람이었다.

(C)

그 선생님은 Benjamin을 이해하고 그를 있는 그대로 받아들이겠다고 결심했다. 어느 날 그는 그의 선생님으로부터 받은 한 쪽지를 가지고 집으로 왔다. 그는 내가 학교 도서관에 방문할 것을 제안했다. 그들은 판매를 하고 있었고, (c) 그는 나의 아들이 책 중 하나를 좋아할 거라고 생각했다. 나는 며칠 동안 갈 수 없었고, 기회를 놓쳤을까 봐 걱정했다. 내가 마침내 학교에 갔을 때, 그의 선생님은 나에게 판매는 끝났지만 도서관이 내 아이를 위해 책을 남겨 두었다고 말했다.

(B)

나는 선생님이 그것을 자비로 지불한 것이 아닌가 짐작했다. 그것은 사진을 위한 공간이 있는 스토리보드 책이었다. 쪽마다 동물의 윤곽과 구멍이 있어서 사진 속의 얼굴이 그 동물의 얼굴인 것처럼 보였다. Benjamin이 그 책에 정말로 흥미가 있을지 궁금해 하며 나는 그것을 집으로 가져왔다. 그는 그것을 좋아했다! 이 책을 통해 그는 (b) 그가 자신이 되길 원하는 어떠한 것도 될 수 있음을 알았는데, 고양이, 문어, 공룡 그리고 심지어 개구리까지 말이다!

(D)

Benjamin은 그 책을 통해 상상의 여행을 즐겁게 시작했고, 우리가 거의 알지는 못하지만, 그것은 그의 미래 성공을 위한 토대를 마련했다. 그리고 감사하게도, 그의 선생님은 (d) 그를 관찰하고 이해하기 위한 시간을 가졌고, 스토리 보드책을 통해 그가 자신만의 세상을 벗어나 우리의 세상에 참여하도록 돕는 방법을 발견했다. 내 아들은 나중에 아역 배우가 되었고 Toronto에 있는 캐스팅 회사와 함께 7년 동안 공연을 했다. (e) 그는 이제 판타지와 공상과학 소설을 쓰는 출판 작가이다! 누가 짐작이나 했을까?

- interaction ⓝ 상호 작용
- unsympathetic ⓐ 인정 없는
- suspect ⓥ 의심하다
- accept ⓥ 받아들이다
- embark ⓥ 시작하다
- journey ⓝ 여정
- observe ⓥ 관찰하다
- author ⓝ 작가
- struggle ⓥ 고군분투하다
- behave ⓥ 행동하다
- determine ⓥ 결심하다
- concern ⓝ 걱정
- imaginative ⓐ 상상력이 풍부한
- groundwork ⓝ 준비작업
- publish ⓥ 출판하다
- guess ⓥ 짐작하다

구문 풀이

[C] 7행 When I finally went to the school, his teacher told me that the sale had
접속사(부사절)　　　　　　　　　　　　　접속사(병렬1)
ended but that the library had saved the book for my little boy.
접속사(병렬2)

---

43 글의 순서 파악　　　　　　　　　정답률 85% | 정답 ②

주어진 글 (A)에 이어질 내용을 순서에 맞게 배열한 것으로 가장 적절한 것은?

① (B) − (D) − (C)　　　　　　✔②(C) − (B) − (D)
③ (C) − (D) − (B)　　　　　　④ (D) − (B) − (C)
⑤ (D) − (C) − (B)

Why? 왜 정답일까?

두 딸과 달리 아들은 발달이 더뎠다는 (A) 뒤로, 1학년 선생님이 Benjamin을 있는 그대로 받아들이고 책을 준비했다는 내용의 (C), Benjamin이 그 책을 통해 자신이 무엇이든 될 수 있다고 알게 되며 좋아했다는 내용의 (B), 이를 토대로 후에 아역배우가 되었다는 내용의 (D)가 순서대로 이어져야 자연스럽다. 따라서 글의 순서로 가장 적절한 것은 ② '(C) − (B) − (D)'이다.

44 지칭 추론　　　　　　　　　정답률 84% | 정답 ③

밑줄 친 (a)∼(e) 중에서 가리키는 대상이 나머지 넷과 다른 것은?

① (a)　　② (b)　　✔③ (c)　　④ (d)　　⑤ (e)

Why? 왜 정답일까?

(a), (b), (d), (e)는 Benjamin을, (c)는 선생님을 가리키므로, (a)∼(e) 중에서 가리키는 대상이 다른 하나는 ③ '(c)'이다.

45 세부 내용 파악　　　　　　　　　정답률 82% | 정답 ③

윗글에 관한 내용으로 적절하지 않은 것은?

① Benjamin은 어린 시절 다른 아이들과 잘 어울리지 않았다.
② 'I'는 선생님이 책값을 지불했다고 짐작했다.
✔③ Benjamin은 'I'가 가져온 책을 좋아하지 않았다.
④ 선생님은 'I'에게 학교 도서관에 방문할 것을 제안했다.
⑤ Benjamin은 아역 배우가 되었다.

Why? 왜 정답일까?

(B) 'He loved it!'에서 Benjamin은 그 책을 좋아했다고 말하므로, 내용과 일치하지 않는 것은 ③ 'Benjamin은 'I'가 가져온 책을 좋아하지 않았다.'이다.

Why? 왜 오답일까?

① (A) 'He struggled through his childhood, not fitting in with the other children and wondering what he was doing wrong at every turn.'의 내용과 일치한다.
② (B) 'I suspected the teacher had paid for it out of his own pocket.'의 내용과 일치한다.

④ (C) 'He suggested I go to the school library.'의 내용과 일치한다.
⑤ (D) 'My son later became a child actor and performed for seven years with a Toronto casting agency.'의 내용과 일치한다.

어휘 Review Test 11　　　　　　　　　문제편 110쪽

A	B	C	D
01 상담	01 instructor	01 ⓞ	01 ⓠ
02 증명서	02 demonstrate	02 ⓔ	02 ⓒ
03 고려	03 expedition	03 ⓛ	03 ⓓ
04 준비하다	04 casual	04 ⓣ	04 ⓗ
05 심각함, 진지함	05 material	05 ⓐ	05 ⓚ
06 정직하게	06 sustainable	06 ⓙ	06 ⓞ
07 변화	07 fabulous	07 ⓕ	07 ⓛ
08 짓누르다	08 expert	08 ⓑ	08 ⓝ
09 혁신	09 inhabitant	09 ⓢ	09 ⓕ
10 권위 있는	10 accelerate	10 ⓜ	10 ⓜ
11 입증되지 않은	11 flow	11 ⓗ	11 ⓒ
12 긴급한	12 debate	12 ⓠ	12 ⓔ
13 순전히	13 perhaps	13 ⓖ	13 ⓢ
14 오해	14 intellectually	14 ⓟ	14 ⓣ
15 점차	15 territory	15 ⓘ	15 ⓟ
16 다소	16 unfavorable	16 ⓒ	16 ⓐ
17 그렇게 함으로써	17 consolation	17 ⓚ	17 ⓖ
18 도달하다	18 reassure	18 ⓓ	18 ⓑ
19 돌봄, 치료	19 unfair	19 ⓡ	19 ⓡ
20 유명한	20 reproduction	20 ⓝ	20 ⓘ

• 정답 •

18 ⑤ 19 ① 20 ⑤ 21 ③ 22 ④ 23 ⑤ 24 ③ 25 ⑤ 26 ③ 27 ④ 28 ④ 29 ② 30 ④* 31 ① 32 ④
33 ② 34 ② 35 ③* 36 ⑤ 37 ③ 38 ⑤ 39 ④ 40 ① 41 ① 42 ⑤ 43 ③ 44 ② 45 ②

★ 표시된 문항은 [등급을 가르는 문제]에 해당하는 문항입니다.

---

18 | 버스 무정차 시정 요청 | 정답률 90% | 정답 ⑤

다음 글의 목적으로 가장 적절한 것은?

① 버스 운전기사 채용 계획을 문의하려고
② 버스 정류장의 위치 변경을 요청하려고
③ 도로 공사로 인한 소음에 대해 항의하려고
④ 출퇴근 시간의 버스 배차 간격 단축을 제안하려고
☑ 버스 정류장 무정차 통과에 대한 시정을 요구하려고

To whom it may concern,
담당자 귀하
I would like to draw your attention to a problem / that frequently occurs with the No. 35 buses.
저는 문제에 대해 귀하의 주의를 환기하고 싶습니다. / 35번 버스에서 자주 발생하는
There is a bus stop about halfway along Fenny Road, / at which the No. 35 buses are supposed to stop.
Fenny Road를 따라 중간쯤 버스 정류장이 있고, / 그곳에 35번 버스가 정차하게 되어 있습니다.
It would appear, however, / that some of your drivers / are either unaware of this bus stop / or for some reason choose to ignore it, / driving past even though the buses are not full.
그러나 ~한 것으로 보입니다. / 귀사의 버스 기사들 중 일부는 / 이 버스 정류장을 인식하지 못하거나 / 무슨 이유인지 그것을 무시하기로 해서 / 버스가 꽉 차지 않았는데도 지나쳐가는
I would be grateful / if you could remind your drivers / that this bus stop exists / and that they should be prepared to stop at it.
고맙겠습니다. / 귀하가 기사들에게 상기시켜 주시면 / 이 버스 정류장이 존재하고, / 그곳에 정차할 준비를 해야 한다는 것을
I look forward to seeing an improvement in this service soon.
곧 이 서비스가 개선되기를 기대합니다.
Yours faithfully, // John Williams
John Williams 드림

담당자 귀하

35번 버스에서 자주 발생하는 문제에 대해 귀하의 주의를 환기하고 싶습니다. Fenny Road를 따라 중간쯤 버스 정류장이 있고, 그곳에 35번 버스가 정차하게 되어 있습니다. 그러나 귀사의 버스 기사들 중 일부는 이 버스 정류장을 인식하지 못하거나 무슨 이유인지 그것을 무시하기로 해서 버스가 꽉 차지 않았는데도 지나쳐가는 것으로 보입니다. 기사들에게 이 버스 정류장이 존재하고, 그곳에 정차할 준비를 해야 한다는 것을 상기시켜 주시면 고맙겠습니다. 곧 이 서비스가 개선되기를 기대합니다.

John Williams 드림

Why? 왜 정답일까?

버스가 종종 정차하지 않고 지나는 정류장에 대해 기사들의 주의를 환기시켜 달라고 요구하는 글이다(I would be grateful if you could remind your drivers that this bus stop exists and that they should be prepared to stop at it.). 따라서 글의 목적으로 가장 적절한 것은 ⑤ '버스 정류장 무정차 통과에 대한 시정을 요구하려고'이다.

- to whom it may concern 담당자 귀하
- unaware ⓐ 모르는
- be supposed to ~하기로 되어 있다
- grateful ⓐ 고마워하는

구문 풀이

3행 There is a bus stop about <u>halfway</u> along Fenny Road, <u>at which</u> the No. 35 buses <u>are supposed to</u> stop.
약, 대략 / 계속적 용법(= where) / ~하기로 되어 있다

---

19 | 아이의 사랑 가득한 선물에 기뻐진 필자 | 정답률 84% | 정답 ①

다음 글에 드러난 'I'의 심경 변화로 가장 적절한 것은?

☑ annoyed → delighted
   짜증 난 / 기쁜
② ashamed → relieved
   수치스러운 / 안도한
③ excited → confused
   신난 / 혼란스러운
④ scared → confident
   겁에 질린 / 자신 있는
⑤ indifferent → jealous
   무관심한 / 질투하는

My 10-year-old appeared, / in desperate need of a quarter.
내 열 살짜리 아이가 와서 / 25센트 동전을 간절히 원했다.
"A quarter? / What on earth do you need a quarter for?"
"25센트 동전? / 도대체 25센트 동전이 왜 필요하지?"
My tone bordered on irritation.
나의 말투는 거의 짜증에 가까웠다.
I didn't want to be bothered / with such a trivial demand.
나는 방해받고 싶지 않았다. / 그런 사소한 요구에
"There's a garage sale up the street, / and there's something I just gotta have! / It only costs a quarter. Please?"
"거리 위쪽에서 중고 물품 판매 행사를 하는데, / 꼭 사야 할 게 있어요! / 25센트밖에 안 해요. 네?"
I placed a quarter in my son's hand.
나는 아들의 손에 25센트 동전을 쥐어 주었다.

[문제편 p.111]

Moments later, / a little voice said, / "Here, Mommy, this is for you."
잠시 후 / 작은 목소리가 말했다. / "여기요, 엄마, 엄마 주려고 산 거예요."라고
I glanced down at the hands of my little son / and saw a four-inch cream-colored statue / of two small children hugging one another.
나는 내 어린 아들의 손을 힐끗 내려다보았고, / 4인치짜리 크림색의 조각상을 보았다. / 두 어린아이가 서로 껴안고 있는
Inscribed at their feet / were words / that read *It starts with 'L' ends with 'E' / and in between are 'O' and 'V.'*
그들의 발밑에는 / 말이 있었다. / ~라고 읽히는 / 'L'로 시작하여 'E'로 끝나고, / 사이에 'O'와 'V'가 있다
As I watched him race back to the garage sale, / I smiled with a heart full of happiness.
아이가 중고 물품 판매 행사로 서둘러 돌아가는 모습을 바라보며 / 나는 행복이 가득한 마음으로 미소를 지었다.
That 25-cent garage sale purchase / brought me a lot of joy.
그 25센트짜리 중고 물품 판매 행사 구입품은 / 내게 큰 기쁨을 가져다 주었다.

내 열 살짜리 아이가 와서 25센트 동전을 간절히 원했다. "25센트 동전? 도대체 25센트 동전이 왜 필요하지?" 나의 말투는 거의 짜증에 가까웠다. 나는 그런 사소한 요구에 방해받고 싶지 않았다. "거리 위쪽에서 중고 물품 판매 행사를 하는데, 꼭 사야 할 게 있어요! 25센트밖에 안 해요. 네?" 나는 아들의 손에 25센트 동전을 쥐어 주었다. 잠시 후 작은 목소리가 "여기요, 엄마, 엄마 주려고 산 거예요."라고 말했다. 나는 내 어린 아들의 손을 힐끗 내려다보았고, 두 어린아이가 서로 껴안고 있는 4인치짜리 크림색 조각상을 보았다. 그들의 발밑에는 'L'로 시작하여 'E'로 끝나고, 사이에 'O'와 'V'가 있다는 말이 새겨져 있었다. 아이가 중고 물품 판매 행사로 서둘러 돌아가는 모습을 바라보며 나는 행복이 가득한 마음으로 미소를 지었다. 그 25센트짜리 중고 물품 판매 행사 구입품은 내게 큰 기쁨을 가져다 주었다.

Why? 왜 정답일까?

어린 아들이 느닷없이 동전을 달라고 하자 짜증이 났던(My tone bordered on irritation.) 필자가 아들의 사랑이 담긴 선물을 받고 행복해했다는(~ I smiled with a heart full of happiness.) 내용이다. 따라서 'I'의 심경 변화로 가장 적절한 것은 ① '짜증 난 → 기쁜'이다.

- in need of ~이 필요한, ~이 없는
- quarter ⓝ 25센트 동전
- irritation ⓝ 짜증
- trivial ⓐ 사소한
- inscribe ⓥ 새기다
- delighted ⓐ 기쁜
- jealous ⓐ 질투하는
- desperate ⓐ 간절한
- border on 거의 ~에 달하다
- be bothered with ~로 귀찮다
- glance ⓥ 흘깃 보다
- annoyed ⓐ 짜증 난
- confused ⓐ 혼란스러운

구문 풀이

10행 <u>Inscribed at their feet were words</u> [that read *It starts with 'L' ends with 'E' and in between are 'O' and 'V.'*]
「도치 구문: p.p. + be + 주어」 / 주격 관·대

---

20 | 직원의 '행동'에 관해 피드백하기 | 정답률 80% | 정답 ⑤

다음 글에서 필자가 주장하는 바로 가장 적절한 것은?

① 직원의 개인적 성향을 고려하여 업무를 배정하라.
② 업무 효율성 향상을 위해 직원의 자율성을 존중하라.
③ 조직의 안정을 위해 직원의 심리 상태를 수시로 확인하라.
④ 직원의 업무상 고충을 이해하기 위해 직원과 적극적으로 소통하라.
☑ 문제를 보이는 직원에게 인격적 특성보다는 행동 방식에 대해 제안하라.

Managers frequently try to play psychologist, / to "figure out" why an employee has acted in a certain way.
관리자들은 자주 심리학자 역할을 하려 한다. / 직원이 왜 특정한 방식으로 행동했는지를 '알아내려고'
Empathizing with employees / in order to understand their point of view / can be very helpful.
직원들과 공감하는 것은 / 그들의 관점을 이해하려고 / 매우 도움이 될 수 있다.
However, / when dealing with a problem area, in particular, / remember / that it is not the person who is bad, / but the actions exhibited on the job.
하지만, / 특히 문제 영역을 다룰 때, / 기억하라. / 나쁜 것은 사람이 아니라 / 근무 중에 나타나는 행동임을
Avoid making suggestions to employees / about personal traits / they should change; / instead suggest more acceptable ways of performing.
직원들에게 제안하기를 피하라 / 인격적 특성에 대해 / 그들이 바뀌어야 할 / 대신 더 용인되는 수행 방법을 제안하라.
For example, / instead of focusing on a person's "unreliability," / a manager might focus on the fact / that the employee "has been late to work seven times this month."
예를 들어, / 어떤 사람의 '미덥지 못함'에 집중하는 대신, / 관리자는 사실에 초점을 맞출 수도 있을 것이다. / 그 직원이 '이번 달에 회사에 일곱 번 지각했다'는
It is difficult / for employees to change who they are; / it is usually much easier / for them to change how they act.
어렵다. / 직원들이 자신이 어떤 사람인지를 바꾸기는 / 일반적으로 훨씬 더 쉽다. / 자신이 행동하는 방식을 바꾸는 것은

관리자들은 직원이 왜 특정한 방식으로 행동했는지를 '알아낼' 목적으로 자주 심리학자 역할을 하려 한다. 직원들의 관점을 이해하려고 그들과 공감하는 것은 매우 도움이 될 수 있다. 하지만, 특히 문제 영역을 다룰 때, 나쁜 것은 사람이 아니라 근무 중에 나타나는 행동임을 기억하라. 직원들에게 그들이 바꿔야 할 인격적 특성에 대해 제안하기를 피하고, 대신 더 용인되는 수행 방법을 제안하라. 예를 들어, 관리자는 어떤 사람의 '미덥지 못함'에 집중하는 대신, 그 직원이 '이번 달에 회사에 일곱 번 지각했다'는 사실에 초점을 맞출 수도 있을 것이다. 직원들은 자신이 어떤 사람인지를 바꾸기는 어렵다. 일반적으로 자신이 행동하는 방식을 바꾸기가 훨씬 더 쉽다.

Why? 왜 정답일까?

직원이 문제를 보일 때 나쁜 것은 사람이 아니라 행동임을 명심하고, 인격적 특성보다는 수행 방법에 대해 피드백하라는(~ instead suggest more acceptable ways of performing.) 내용이다. 따라서 필자가 주장하는 바로 가장 적절한 것은 ⑤ '문제를 보이는 직원에게 인격적 특성보다는 행동 방식에 대해 제안하라.'이다.

- certain ⓐ 특정한, 어떤
- point of view 관점, 견해
- make a suggestion 제안하다
- trait ⓝ 특성
- unreliability ⓝ 미덥지 못함
- empathize with ~에 공감하다
- deal with ~을 다루다, ~에 대처하다
- personal ⓐ 개인적인, 인격의
- acceptable ⓐ 수용 가능한

4행 However, when dealing with a problem area, in particular, remember that
분사구문(= when you deal ~) 명령문(~하라)
it is not the person who is bad, but the actions exhibited on the job.
「not+A+but+B : A가 아니라 B인」 과거분사

---

21 출판을 넘어 이해되어야 비로소 완성되는 과학 연구   정답률 62% | 정답 ③

밑줄 친 forward "thinking"이 다음 글에서 의미하는 바로 가장 적절한 것은?

① responsible for the invasion of foreign species
외래종 침입에 책임이 있는
② eager to support the dominance of one species
어느 한 종의 우세를 열렬히 지지하는
✓③ aware that diversity leads to the stability of forests
다양성이 숲의 안정성으로 이어진다는 것을 알고 있는
④ indifferent to helping forests regenerate after collapse
숲이 붕괴 후 재생하는 것을 돕는 데 관심이 없는
⑤ careful that their territories are not occupied by other species
그들의 영역이 다른 종에 의해 지배되지 않도록 주의를 기울이는

I suspect / fungi are a little more forward "thinking" / than their larger partners.
나는 짐작한다 / 균류가 좀 더 앞서 '생각한다'고 / 더 큰 상대보다

Among trees, / each species fights other species.
나무들 사이에서 / 각 종은 다른 종들과 싸운다.

Let's assume / the beeches native to Central Europe / could emerge victorious in most forests there.
가정해 보자 / 중부 유럽 태생의 너도밤나무가 / 그쪽 숲 대부분에서 우세하게 나타날 수 있다고

Would this really be an advantage?
이건 정말 이점일까?

What would happen / if a new pathogen came along / that infected most of the beeches and killed them?
어떻게 될까? / 만약 새로운 병원균이 출현한다면 / 대부분의 너도밤나무를 감염시켜 죽게 만드는

In that case, / wouldn't it be more advantageous / if there were a certain number of other species around / — oaks, maples, or firs — / that would continue to grow / and provide the shade needed / for a new generation of young beeches / to sprout and grow up?
이 경우, / 더 유리하지 않을까? / 주변에 일정한 수의 다른 종이 있다면 / 참나무, 단풍나무 또는 전나무와 같은 / 계속 자라서 / 필요한 그늘을 제공할 / 새로운 세대의 어린 너도밤나무가 / 싹을 틔우고 자라는 데

Diversity provides security for ancient forests.
다양성은 오래된 숲에 안전을 제공한다.

Because fungi are also very dependent on stable conditions, / they support other species underground / and protect them from complete collapse / to ensure that one species of tree doesn't manage to dominate.
균류도 또한 안정적인 조건에 매우 의존하기 때문에, / 그들은 땅속에서 다른 종을 지원하고, / 그것들이 완전히 붕괴되지 못하게 한다. / 한 종의 나무가 우세해지지 않도록 확실히 하고자

나는 균류가 더 큰 상대보다 좀 더 앞서 '생각한다'고 짐작한다. 나무들 사이에서 각 종은 다른 종들과 싸운다. 중부 유럽 태생의 너도밤나무가 그쪽 숲 대부분에서 우세하게 나타날 수 있다고 가정해 보자. 이건 정말 이점일까? 만약 대부분의 너도밤나무를 감염시켜 죽게 만드는 새로운 병원균이 출현한다면 어떻게 될까? 이 경우, 주변에 참나무, 단풍나무 또는 전나무와 같은 일정한 수의 다른 종이 계속 자라서 새로운 세대의 어린 너도밤나무가 싹을 틔우고 자라는 데 필요한 그늘을 제공한다면 더 유리하지 않을까? 다양성은 오래된 숲에 안전을 제공한다. 균류도 또한 안정적인 조건에 매우 의존하기 때문에, 그들은 한 종의 나무가 우세해지지 않도록 확실히 하고자 땅속에서 다른 종을 지원하고, 그것들이 완전히 붕괴되지 못하게 한다.

Why? 왜 정답일까?

마지막 두 문장의 핵심 내용은 균류가 숲속에서 어느 한 종의 나무가 우세해지지 않도록 다른 종의 나무를 도와준다는 것이다. 이는 생태 다양성을 지켜 환경의 안정성을 확보하려는 균류의 노력이다. 이를 근거로 할 때, 밑줄 친 부분의 의미로 가장 적절한 것은 ③ '다양성이 숲의 안정성으로 이어진다는 것을 알고 있는'이다.

- fungus (pl. fungi) ⓝ 균류
- native to ~의 원산지인
- victorious ⓐ 승리한, 우세한
- infect ⓥ 감염시키다
- maple ⓝ 단풍나무
- sprout ⓥ 싹을 틔우다
- security ⓝ 안정(성)
- collapse ⓝ 붕괴 ⓥ 붕괴되다, 무너지다, 쓰러지다
- dominate ⓥ 우세하다, 지배하다
- foreign species 외래종
- regenerate ⓥ 재생되다
- occupy ⓥ 점유하다, 차지하다
- beech ⓝ 너도밤나무
- emerge ⓥ 부상하다, 출현하다
- pathogen ⓝ 병원균
- oak ⓝ 떡갈나무, 오크
- fir ⓝ 전나무
- diversity ⓝ 다양성
- stable ⓐ 안정된
- ensure ⓥ 확실히 하다
- invasion ⓝ 침입
- stability ⓝ 안정성
- territory ⓝ 영역, 영토

구문 풀이

7행 In that case, wouldn't it be more advantageous if there were a certain
가정법 과거(if + 주어 + 과거 동사 ~, 주어 + would + 동사원형)
number of other species around — oaks, maples, or firs — [that would continue
선행사
to grow and provide the shade needed for a new generation of young beeches
과거분사   의미상의 주어
to sprout and grow up]?
to부정사구

---

22 낙관적인 상상의 부작용   정답률 47% | 정답 ④

다음 글의 요지로 가장 적절한 것은?

① 과도한 목표 지향적 태도는 삶의 만족감을 떨어뜨린다.
② 긍정적 자세로 역경을 극복할 때 잠재 능력이 발휘된다.
③ 편안함을 느끼는 상황에서 자기 개선에 대한 동기가 생긴다.
✓④ 낙관적인 상상은 소망을 실현하는 데 필요한 동력을 약화시킨다.
⑤ 막연한 목표보다는 명확하고 구체적인 목표가 실현 가능성이 크다.

It's remarkable / that positive fantasies help us relax / to such an extent that it shows up in physiological tests.
주목할 만하다. / 낙관적인 상상이 우리가 긴장을 푸는 데 도움이 된다는 것 / 그것이 생물학적 검사로 나타날 정도로

If you want to unwind, / you can take some deep breaths, / get a massage, / or go for a walk / — but you can also try simply closing your eyes / and fantasizing about some future outcome / that you might enjoy.
만약 여러분이 긴장을 풀고 싶다면 / 여러분은 심호흡하거나 / 마사지를 받거나 / 산책을 할 수도 있지만, / 여러분은 단순히 눈을 감고 / 미래의 결과에 대해 상상해 볼 수도 있다. / 여러분이 누릴지도 모를

But what about / when your objective is to make your wish a reality?
하지만 ~라면 어떨까? / 여러분의 목표가 소망을 실현하는 것인 경우

The *last* thing you want to be / is relaxed.
여러분이 가장 피해야 할 상태는 / 긴장이 풀려 있는 것이다.

You want to be energized enough / to get off the couch and lose those pounds / or find that job or study for that test, / and you want to be motivated enough / to stay engaged / even when the inevitable obstacles or challenges arise.
여러분은 충분히 활력을 얻어야 한다 / 소파에서 일어나 살을 빼거나 / 직업을 찾거나 시험공부를 할 수 있을 만큼 / 그리고 여러분은 충분히 동기 부여되어야 한다. / 계속 전념할 수 있도록 / 피할 수 없는 장애물이나 문제가 발생할 때도

The principle of "Dream it. Wish it. Do it." / does not hold true, / and now we know why: / in dreaming it, / you undercut the energy / you need to do it.
'꿈꾸라. 소망하라. 실현하라.'라는 원칙은 / 사실이 아니며, / 우리는 이제 그 이유를 안다. / 꿈꾸고 있을 때, / 여러분은 에너지를 약화시킨다. / 여러분이 그걸 하는 데 필요한

You put yourself / in a temporary state of complete happiness, calmness / — and inactivity.
여러분은 빠지게 된다. / 완전한 행복과 고요의 일시적인 상태에 / 그리고 비활동

낙관적인 상상이 우리가 긴장을 푸는 데 도움이 되어서 그것이 생물학적 검사로 나타날 정도라는 것은 주목할 만하다. 만약 여러분이 긴장을 풀고 싶다면 심호흡하거나 마사지를 받거나 산책을 할 수도 있지만, 단순히 눈을 감고 여러분이 누릴지도 모를 미래의 결과에 대해 상상해 볼 수도 있다. 하지만 여러분의 목표가 소망을 실현하는 것인 경우라면 어떨까? 여러분이 *가장 피해야* 할 상태는 긴장이 풀려 있는 것이다. 여러분은 소파에서 일어나 (지금 쪄 있는) 살을 빼거나, (원하는) 직업을 찾거나 (붙고 싶은) 시험공부를 할 수 있을 만큼 충분히 활력을 얻어야 하고, 피할 수 없는 장애물이나 문제가 발생할 때도 계속 전념할 수 있도록 충분히 동기 부여되어야 한다. '꿈꾸라. 소망하라. 실현하라.'라는 원칙은 사실이 아니며, 우리는 이제 그 이유를 안다. 꿈꾸고 있을 때, 여러분은 그걸 하는 데 필요한 에너지를 약화시킨다. 여러분은 완전한 행복, 고요, 그리고 비활동의 일시적인 상태에 빠지게 된다.

Why? 왜 정답일까?

'But what about ~' 문장 이후로 주제가 제시되는데, 낙관적 상상이 긴장을 푸는 데는 도움이 되지만 목표 실현에는 도움이 안 된다(~ in dreaming it, you undercut the energy you need to do it.)는 것이다. 따라서 글의 요지로 가장 적절한 것은 ④ '낙관적인 상상은 소망을 실현하는 데 필요한 동력을 약화시킨다.'이다.

- remarkable ⓐ 두드러지는
- unwind ⓥ 긴장을 풀다. (감긴 것을) 풀다
- objective ⓝ 목표
- inevitable ⓐ 피할 수 없는, 필연적인
- arise ⓥ 발생하다
- undercut ⓥ 약화하다
- inactivity ⓝ 무활동
- physiological ⓐ 생리학적인
- outcome ⓝ 결과
- be motivated to ~하도록 동기 부여받다
- obstacle ⓝ 장애물
- hold true 사실이다
- temporary ⓐ 일시적인

구문 풀이

1행 It's remarkable {that positive fantasies help us relax to such an extent that
동사 목·보
it shows up in physiological tests}.   [{ } : 진주어]
목적어   ~할 정도로(원형부정사)

---

23 집에서 요리하는 일이 줄어들면서 생긴 변화   정답률 63% | 정답 ⑤

다음 글의 주제로 가장 적절한 것은?

① current trends in commercial cooking equipment
상업용 조리 장치의 최근 동향
② environmental impacts of shifts in dietary patterns
식생활 패턴의 변화가 환경에 미치는 영향
③ cost-effective ways to cook healthy meals at home
집에서 건강한 음식을 요리하는 가성비 좋은 방법
④ reasons behind the decline of the food service industry
외식업 쇠퇴의 이면에 있는 이유들
✓⑤ benefits of reduced domestic cooking duties through outsourcing
(기업에의) 외부 위탁을 통한, 집에서 요리하는 일이 감소한 것의 이득

If cooking is as central / to human identity, biology, and culture / as the biological anthropologist Richard Wrangham suggests, / it stands to reason / that the decline of cooking in our time / would have serious consequences for modern life, / and so it has.
요리가 그렇게 중요하다면, / 인간의 정체성, 생물학 및 문화에 / 생물 인류학자인 Richard Wrangham이 말하는 것만큼 / 당연하다 / 우리 시대의 요리 감소가 / 현대 생활에 심각한 결과로 이어진다는 것은 / 그리고 실제로 그랬다.

Are they all bad?
그게 다 나쁜 걸까?

Not at all.
전혀 그렇지 않다.

The outsourcing of much of the work of cooking to corporations / has relieved women / of what has traditionally been their exclusive responsibility / for feeding the family, / making it easier for them / to work outside the home and have careers.
요리의 많은 부분을 기업에 위탁한 것은 / 여성들에게서 덜어주었고, / 전통적으로 그들의 전적인 책임이었던 것을 / 가족을 먹이는 것에 관한 / 그들이 ~하기 더 쉽게 만들었다. / 집 밖에서 일하고 직업을 갖는 것을

It has headed off many of the domestic conflicts / that such a large shift in gender roles and family dynamics / was bound to spark.
그것은 가정 내 갈등을 많이 막아냈다. / 그토록 큰 성 역할 및 가정 역학의 큰 변화가 / 촉발할

It has relieved other pressures in the household, / including longer workdays and overscheduled children, / and saved us time / that we can now invest in other pursuits.
그것은 집안의 다른 곤란을 덜어주었고, / 더 많은 근무일과 일정이 지나치게 바쁜 아이들을 포함한 / 우리에게 시간을 아껴주었다 / 이제 우리가 다른 일에 시간을 들일 수 있는

It has also allowed us / to diversify our diets substantially, / making it possible / even for people with no cooking skills and little money / to enjoy a whole different cuisine.
그것은 또한 우리가 ~하게 해주었고 / 우리의 식단을 상당히 다양화할 수 있게 / 가능하게 해주었다 / 요리 기술이 없고 돈이 거의 없는 사람들까지도 / 완전히 색다른 요리를 즐기는 것

All that's required / is a microwave.
필요한 것은 / 전자레인지뿐이다.

생물 인류학자인 Richard Wrangham이 말하는 것만큼 요리가 인간의 정체성, 생물학 및 문화에 중요하다면, 우리 시대의 요리 감소가 현대 생활에 심각한 결과로 이어진다는 것은 당연하고, 실제로 그랬다. 그게 다 나쁜 걸까? 전혀 그렇지 않다. 요리의 많은 부분을 기업에 위탁한 것은 전통적으로 그들의 전적인 책임이라 여겨진 가족을 먹이는 일을 여성들에게서 덜어주었고, 그들이 집 밖에서 일하고 직업을 갖기 더 쉽게 했다. 그것은 그토록 큰 성 역할 및 가정 역학의 큰 변화가 촉발한 많은 가정 내 갈등을 막아냈다. 그것은 더 많은 근무일과 일정이 지나치게 바쁜 아이들을 포함한 집안의 다른 곤란을 덜어주었고, 이제 우리가 시간을 아껴 다른 일에 시간을 들이게 했다. 그것은 또한 우리의 식단을 상당히 다양하게 해주었고, 요리 기술이 없고 돈이 거의 없는 사람까지도 완전히 색다른 요리를 즐길 수 있게 해 주었다. 필요한 것은 전자레인지뿐이다.

Why? 왜 정답일까?
요리를 기업들에 맡기면서 여성들이 밖에서 일하기 더 쉬워지고 가정 내 곤란이나 갈등은 줄어들었으며 식단은 다양해졌다는 내용이다. 따라서 글의 주제로 가장 적절한 것은 ⑤ '(기업에의) 외부 위탁을 통한, 집에서 요리하는 일이 감소한 것의 이득'이다.

- **anthropologist** ⓝ 인류학자
- **decline** ⓝ 감소, 쇠퇴 ⓥ 줄어들다
- **outsource** ⓥ (외부에) 위탁하다
- **exclusive** ⓐ 전적인, 배타적인
- **domestic** ⓐ 가정의
- **be bound to** ~하게 마련이다
- **pursuit** ⓝ (시간과 에너지를 들여 하는) 활동, 취미
- **cuisine** ⓝ 요리
- **dietary** ⓐ 식단의
- **stand to reason** 당연하다, 이치에 맞다
- **consequence** ⓝ 결과, 영향
- **corporation** ⓝ 회사, 기업
- **head off** ~을 막다, 차단하다
- **gender role** 성 역할
- **spark** ⓥ 촉발하다
- **substantially** ⓐ 상당히
- **microwave** ⓝ 전자레인지
- **cost-effective** ⓐ 가성비 좋은

구문 풀이

1행 If cooking is as central to human identity, biology, and culture as the
「as + 원급 +
biological anthropologist Richard Wrangham suggests, it stands to reason {that
as : ~만큼 …한,
가주어
the decline of cooking in our time would have serious consequences for modern
{ } : 진주어
life}, and so it has.
대동사(= has had serious consequences)

---

24 사려 깊은 소비로 기업에 영향을 주기   정답률 67% | 정답 ③

다음 글의 제목으로 가장 적절한 것은?
① Green Businesses: Are They Really Green?
친환경 기업: 그들은 정말이 친환경적일까?
② Fair Trade Does Not Always Appeal to Consumers
공정 무역이 항상 소비자에게 어필하는 것은 아니다
✓③ Buy Consciously, Make Companies Do the Right Things
양심 있게 구매하고, 회사들이 옳은 일을 하게 하라
④ Do Voters Have a Powerful Impact on Economic Policy?
유권자들은 경제 정책에 강력한 영향을 끼칠까?
⑤ The Secret to Saving Your Money: Record Your Spending
돈을 아끼는 비결: 소비를 기록하라

As you may already know, / what and how you buy can be political.
당신이 이미 알고 있겠지만, / 당신이 무엇을 어떻게 구매하는지는 정치적일 수 있다.
To whom do you want to give your money?
당신의 돈을 누구에게 주고 싶은가?
Which companies and corporations do you value and respect?
어떤 회사와 기업을 가치 있게 여기고 존중하는가?
Be mindful about every purchase / by carefully researching the corporations / that are taking our money / to decide if they deserve our support.
모든 구매에 주의를 기울이라. / 기업을 면밀히 조사해서 / 우리 돈을 가져가는 / 우리의 지원을 받을 자격이 있는지를 결정하기 위해
Do they have a record of polluting the environment, / or do they have fair-trade practices and an end-of-life plan / for the products they make?
그들은 환경을 오염시킨 기록이 있는가, / 아니면 그들은 공정 거래 관행과 제품 수명 종료 계획을 갖췄는가? / 그들이 만드는 제품에 대한
Are they committed to bringing about good in the world?
그들은 헌신하고 있는가? / 세상에 득이 되는 것에
For instance, / my family has found a company / producing recycled, plastic-packaging-free toilet paper / with a social conscience.
예를 들어, / 우리 가족은 회사를 발견했다. / 재활용되고 플라스틱 포장이 없는 화장지를 생산하는 / 사회적 양심을 가지고
They contribute 50 percent of their profits / to the construction of toilets around the world, / and we're genuinely happy / to spend our money on this special toilet paper each month.
그들은 수익의 50%를 기부하고, / 전 세계 화장실 건설에 / 우리는 정말 기쁘다. / 이 특별한 화장지에 매달 돈을 쓸 수 있어서
Remember / that the corporate world is built on consumers, / so as a consumer you have the power / to vote with your wallet / and encourage companies to embrace healthier and more sustainable practices / with every purchase you choose to make.
기억하라. / 기업의 세계는 소비자를 기반으로 구축되므로, / 소비자로서 당신은 힘이 있다는 것을 / 당신의 지갑으로 투표하고 / 회사들이 더 건강하고 더 지속 가능한 관행을 받아들이도록 권할 / 당신이 선택한 모든 구매를 통해

이미 알고 있겠지만, 당신이 무엇을 어떻게 구매하는지는 정치적일 수 있다. 당신의 돈을 누구에게 주고 싶은가? 어떤 회사와 기업을 가치 있게 여기고 존중하는가? 우리의 지원을 받을 자격이 있는지를 결정하기 위해 우리 돈을 가져가는 기업을 면밀히 조사해 모든 구매에 주의를 기울이라. 그들은 환경을 오염시킨 기록이 있는가, 아니면 그들이 만드는 제품에 대한 공정 거래 관행과 제품 수명 종료 계획이 있는가? 그들은 세상에 득이 되는 것에 헌신하고 있는가? 예를 들어, 우리 가족은 사회적 양심을 가지고 재활용되고 플라스틱 포장이 없는 화장지를 생산하는 회사를 발견했다. 그들은 수익의 50%를 전 세계 화장실 건설에 기부하고, 우리는 이 특별한 화장지에 매달 돈을 쓸 수 있어서 정말 기쁘다. 기업의 세계는 소비자를 기반으로 구축되므로, 소비자로서 당신은 지갑으로 투표하고 당신이 선택한 모든 구매를 통해 회사들이 더 건강하고 더 지속 가능한 관행을 받아들이도록 권할 힘이 있다는 것을 기억하라.

Why? 왜 정답일까?
회사들을 많이 알아보고 책임감 있게 물건을 구매하여, 회사들로 하여금 정말로 옳은 일을 할 수 있도록

영향력을 행사하라(~ vote with your wallet and encourage companies to embrace healthier and more sustainable practices with every purchase you choose to make.)는 내용의 글이다. 따라서 글의 제목으로 가장 적절한 것은 ③ '양심 있게 구매하고, 회사들이 옳은 일을 하게 하라'이다.

- **deserve** ⓥ ~을 받을 만하다
- **fair-trade** ⓐ 공정 무역의
- **end-of-life plan** 수명 종료 계획(제품, 폐기, 교체, 중단 등에 관한 계획)
- **be committed to** ~에 헌신하다, 전념하다
- **conscience** ⓝ 양심
- **genuinely** ⓐ 진짜로
- **embrace** ⓥ 받아들이다, 수용하다
- **pollute** ⓥ 오염시키다
- **practice** ⓝ 관행
- **bring about** ~을 초래하다
- **contribute** ⓥ 기부하다
- **vote** ⓥ 투표하다

구문 풀이

15행 Remember {that the corporate world is built on consumers, so as a
동사(명령문)   주어1   동사1   ~로서
consumer you have the power to vote with your wallet and encourage companies
주어2   동사2   목적어   형용사적 용법1   형용사적 용법2(encourage + 목적어 + to부정사)
to embrace healthier and more sustainable practices with every purchase [you
선행사
choose to make]}.

---

25 영국 남녀별 스마트 TV 사용 비교   정답률 83% | 정답 ⑤

다음 도표의 내용과 일치하지 않는 것은?

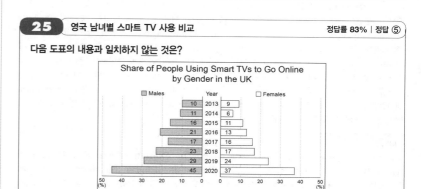

Share of People Using Smart TVs to Go Online by Gender in the UK

Males	Year	Females
10	2013	9
11	2014	6
16	2015	11
21	2016	13
17	2017	16
23	2018	17
29	2019	24
45	2020	37

The graph above shows the findings of a survey / on the use of smart TVs to go online / in the UK / from 2013 to 2020, / by gender.
위 그래프는 설문 조사 결과를 보여준다. / 온라인 접속을 위한 스마트 TV 사용에 대한 / 영국에서 / 2013년부터 2020년까지 / 성별에 따라
① In each year from 2013 to 2020, / the percentage of male respondents / who used smart TVs to access the Internet / was higher than that of female respondents.
2013년부터 2020년까지 매년, / 남성 응답자의 비율은 / 인터넷 접속을 위해 스마트 TV를 사용한 / 여성 응답자의 비율보다 더 높았다.
② The percentage gap between the two genders / was the largest in 2016 and in 2020, / which both had an 8 percentage point difference.
두 성별 간 비율의 차이는 / 2016년과 2020년에 가장 컸고, / 두 해 모두 8퍼센트포인트 차이가 있었다.
③ In 2020, / the percentage of respondents / who reported using smart TVs to go online / was higher than 30% for both males and females.
2020년에 / 응답자의 비율은 / 온라인 접속을 위해 스마트 TV를 사용했다고 말한 / 남성과 여성 둘 다에서 30%를 넘겼다.
④ For male respondents, / 2017 was the only year / that saw a decrease in the percentage / of those accessing the Internet via smart TVs / compared to the previous year, / during the given period.
남성 응답자의 경우, / 2017년은 유일한 해였다. / 비율에서 감소를 보인 / 스마트 TV를 통하여 인터넷에 접속한 사람의 / 전년도에 비해 / 해당 기간 중
✓⑤ In 2014, / the percentage of females / using smart TVs to access the Internet / was the lowest during the given period at 6%, / and it was still below 10% in 2015.
2014년에 / 여성의 비율은 / 인터넷 접속을 위해 스마트 TV를 사용한 / 6%로 주어진 기간 중 가장 낮았고, / 2015년에 여전히 10% 미만이었다.

위 그래프는 2013년부터 2020년까지 영국에서 온라인 접속을 위한 스마트 TV 사용에 대한 설문 조사 결과를 성별에 따라 보여준다. ① 2013년부터 2020년까지 매년, 인터넷 접속을 위해 스마트 TV를 사용한 남성 응답자의 비율은 여성 응답자의 비율보다 더 높았다. ② 두 성별 간 비율의 차이는 2016년과 2020년에 가장 컸고, 두 해 모두 8퍼센트포인트 차이가 있었다. ③ 2020년에 온라인 접속을 위해 스마트 TV를 사용했다고 말한 응답자의 비율은 남성과 여성 둘 다 30%를 넘겼다. ④ 남성 응답자의 경우, 해당 기간 중 2017년은 전년도에 비해 스마트 TV를 통하여 인터넷에 접속한 사람의 비율이 감소한 유일한 해였다. ⑤ 2014년에 인터넷 접속을 위해 스마트 TV를 사용한 여성의 비율은 6%로 주어진 기간 중 가장 낮았고, 2015년에 여전히 10% 미만이었다.

Why? 왜 정답일까?
도표에 따르면 온라인에 접속하려고 스마트 TV를 사용한 영국 여성의 비율은 2015년에 10%를 넘겼다(11%). 따라서 도표와 일치하지 않는 것은 ⑤이다.

- **survey** ⓝ 설문 조사
- **respondent** ⓝ 응답자
- **go online** 온라인에 접속하다
- **access** ⓥ 접속하다

---

26 Camille Flammarion의 생애   정답률 90% | 정답 ③

Camille Flammarion에 관한 다음 글의 내용과 일치하지 않는 것은?
① 어린 나이에 천문학에 흥미가 생겼다.
② 1858년에 Le Verrier의 조수가 되었다.
✓③ 19세에 쓴 책에서 외계 생명체의 존재를 부인했다.
④ 자신의 자금으로 Juvisy에 천문대를 세웠다.
⑤ French Astronomical Society를 설립했다.

Camille Flammarion was born / at Montigny-le-Roi, France.
Camille Flammarion은 태어났다. / 프랑스 Montigny-le-Roi에서
⌜He became interested in astronomy at an early age, / and when he was only sixteen / he

wrote a book on the origin of the world. **①의 근거** 일치
그는 어린 나이에 천문학에 흥미가 생겼고, 그가 불과 16세였을 때 / 그는 세상의 기원에 관한 책을 썼다.

The manuscript was not published at the time, / but it came to the attention of Urbain Le Verrier, / the director of the Paris Observatory.
그 원고는 그 당시 출판되지 않았지만, / 그것은 Urbain Le Verrier의 관심을 끌게 되었다. / Paris Observatory 소장이었던

『He became an assistant to Le Verrier in 1858 / and worked as a calculator.』 **②의 근거** 일치
그는 1858년에 Le Verrier의 조수가 되었고 / 계산원으로 일했다.

『At nineteen, / he wrote another book called *The Plurality of Inhabited Worlds*, / in which he passionately claimed / that life exists outside the planet Earth.』 **③의 근거** 불일치
19세에 / 그는 *The Plurality of Inhabited Worlds*라는 또 다른 책을 썼는데, / 이 책에서 그는 열정적으로 주장했다. / 외계에 생명체가 존재한다고

His most successful work, *Popular Astronomy*, / was published in 1880, / and eventually sold 130,000 copies.
그의 가장 성공적인 저서인 *Popular Astronomy*는 / 1880년에 출판되었고, / 결국 130,000부가 판매되었다.

『With his own funds, / he built an observatory at Juvisy / and spent May to November of each year there.』 **④의 근거** 일치
자신의 자금으로 / 그는 Juvisy에 천문대를 세웠고, / 매년 5월에서 11월까지 거기서 지냈다.

『In 1887, / he founded the French Astronomical Society / and served as editor of its monthly publication.』 **⑤의 근거** 일치
1887년에 / 그는 French Astronomical Society를 설립했고 / 거기서 월간 간행물의 편집자로 일했다.

Camille Flammarion은 프랑스 Montigny-le-Roi에서 태어났다. 그는 어린 나이에 천문학에 흥미가 생겼고, 불과 16세에 그는 세상의 기원에 관한 책을 썼다. 그 원고는 그 당시 출판되지 않았지만, Paris Observatory의 소장이었던 Urbain Le Verrier의 관심을 끌게 되었다. 그는 1858년에 Le Verrier의 조수가 되었고 계산원으로 일했다. 19세에 그는 *The Plurality of Inhabited Worlds*라는 또 다른 책을 썼는데, 이 책에서 그는 외계에 생명체가 존재한다고 열정적으로 주장했다. 그의 가장 성공적인 저서인 *Popular Astronomy*는 1880년에 출판되었고, 결국 130,000부가 판매되었다. 그는 자신의 자금으로 Juvisy에 천문대를 세웠고, 매년 5월에서 11월까지 거기서 지냈다. 1887년에 그는 French Astronomical Society를 설립했고 거기서 월간 간행물의 편집자로 일했다.

Why? 왜 정답일까?
'At nineteen, he wrote another book called *The Plurality of Inhabited Worlds*, in which he passionately claimed that life exists outside the planet Earth.'에서 Camille Flammarion은 외계 생명체의 존재 가능성을 열정적으로 주장했다고 하므로, 내용과 일치하지 않는 것은 ③ '19세에 쓴 책에서 외계 생명체의 존재를 부인했다.'이다.

Why? 왜 오답일까?
① 'He became interested in astronomy at an early age, ~'의 내용과 일치한다.
② 'He became an assistant to Le Verrier in 1858 and worked as a calculator.'의 내용과 일치한다.
④ 'With his own funds, he built an observatory at Juvisy ~'의 내용과 일치한다.
⑤ 'In 1887, he founded the French Astronomical Society ~'의 내용과 일치한다.

- **astronomy** ⓝ 천문학
- **publish** ⓥ 출판하다, 게재하다
- **calculator** ⓝ 계산원, 계산기
- **inhabit** ⓥ 거주하다
- **serve as** ~로 일하다, ~의 역할을 하다
- **manuscript** ⓝ 원고
- **observatory** ⓝ 천문대
- **plurality** ⓝ 다원성, 많은 수
- **passionately** ⓐⓓ 열정적으로
- **publication** ⓝ 간행물, 발행

구문 풀이

7행 At nineteen, he wrote another book called *The Plurality of Inhabited Worlds*,
선행사
in which he passionately claimed {that life exists outside the planet Earth}.
『전치사 + 관계대명사』 명사절(claimed의 목적어)

---

27 가상 운동회 | 정답률 95% | 정답 ④

Roselands Virtual Sports Day에 관한 다음 안내문의 내용과 일치하지 <u>않는</u> 것은?
① 10월 16일부터 22일까지 열린다.
② 총 10개의 도전 과제가 있다.
③ 학교 웹사이트에서 도전 과제를 설명하는 영상을 볼 수 있다.
✔ 학부모와 교사는 참여할 수 없다.
⑤ 제출할 영상파일 용량이 500MB를 초과하면 안 된다.

Roselands Virtual Sports Day
Roselands Virtual Sports Day(Roselands 가상 운동회)
Roselands Virtual Sports Day is an athletic competition / that you can participate in from anywhere.
Roselands Virtual Sports Day는 운동 시합입니다. / 여러분이 어디에서나 참여할 수 있는

『When: October 16th – 22nd, 2023』 **①의 근거** 일치
시기: 2023년 10월 16일~22일

How the event works
행사 진행 방식

『There are 10 challenges in total.』 **②의 근거** 일치
총 10개의 도전 과제가 있습니다.

『You can see videos / explaining each challenge / on our school website.』 **③의 근거** 일치
여러분은 영상을 볼 수 있습니다. / 각 도전 과제를 설명하는 / 우리 학교 웹사이트에서

The more challenges you complete, / the more points you will gain for your class.
여러분이 더 많은 도전 과제를 완수할수록, / 학급을 위한 더 많은 점수를 얻을 수 있습니다.

The class with the most points / will get a prize.
가장 많은 점수를 얻은 학급은 / 상을 받을 것입니다.

『Parents and teachers can also participate.』 **④의 근거** 불일치
학부모와 교사도 참여할 수 있습니다.

How to submit your entry
출품작 제출 방법

Email us videos / of you completing the challenges / at virtualsportsday@roselands.com.
이메일로 영상을 보내주세요. / 여러분이 도전 과제를 완수하는 / virtualsportsday@roselands.com으로

『The size of the video file / must not exceed 500MB.』 **⑤의 근거** 일치
제출할 영상파일 용량은 / 500MB를 초과하면 안 됩니다.

Roselands Virtual Sports Day
(Roselands 가상 운동회)

Roselands Virtual Sports Day는 여러분이 어디에서나 참여할 수 있는 운동 시합입니다.

시기: 2023년 10월 16일~22일

행사 진행 방식
- 총 10개의 도전 과제가 있습니다.
- 여러분은 우리 학교 웹사이트에서 각 도전 과제를 설명하는 영상을 볼 수 있습니다.
- 여러분이 더 많은 도전 과제를 완수할수록, 학급을 위한 더 많은 점수를 얻을 수 있습니다.
- 가장 많은 점수를 얻은 학급은 상을 받을 것입니다.
- 학부모와 교사도 참여할 수 있습니다.

출품작 제출 방법
- 여러분이 도전 과제를 완수하는 영상을 virtualsportsday@roselands.com으로 이메일로 보내주세요.
- 제출할 영상파일 용량이 500MB를 초과하면 안 됩니다.

Why? 왜 정답일까?
'Parents and teachers can also participate.'에서 학부모와 교사도 참가할 수 있다고 하므로, 안내문의 내용과 일치하지 않는 것은 ④ '학부모와 교사는 참여할 수 없다.'이다.

Why? 왜 오답일까?
① 'When: October 16th – 22nd, 2023'의 내용과 일치한다.
② 'There are 10 challenges in total.'의 내용과 일치한다.
③ 'You can see videos explaining each challenge on our school website.'의 내용과 일치한다.
⑤ 'The size of the video file must not exceed 500MB.'의 내용과 일치한다.

- **virtual** ⓐ 가상의
- **exceed** ⓥ 초과하다, 능가하다
- **athletic** ⓐ 운동의, 육상의

---

28 신학기 물품 나눔 행사 | 정답률 88% | 정답 ④

Back-to-school Giveaway Event에 관한 다음 안내문의 내용과 일치하는 것은?
① 토요일 오후에 진행된다.
② 우천 시에는 취소된다.
③ Easton시 주민이 아니어도 참여할 수 있다.
✔ 가방 500개가 선착순으로 배부될 것이다.
⑤ 부모 또는 보호자만 와도 가방을 받을 수 있다.

Back-to-school Giveaway Event
Back-to-school Giveaway Event(개학 무료 나눔 행사)
The City of Easton will host a free back-to-school giveaway event.
Easton시는 신학기 무료 나눔 행사를 주최합니다.

Join us for this fun event / to help children of all ages / prepare to go back to school after summer vacation.
이 즐거운 행사에 함께하세요. / 모든 연령의 아이들이 ~하게 돕는 / 여름 방학 후 학교로 돌아가는 것을 준비할 수 있게

『When: Saturday, September 2nd, 9 a.m. – 11 a.m.』 **①의 근거** 불일치
일시: 9월 2일 토요일 오전 9시~11시

Location: City of Easton Central Park
장소: Easton시 중앙 공원

『(This event will be held rain or shine.)』 **②의 근거** 불일치
(이 행사는 날씨와 관계없이 열릴 예정입니다.)

Participation requirements
참여요건

『Open to City of Easton residents only』 **③의 근거** 불일치
Easton시 주민만 참여할 수 있음

Must bring a valid ID
유효한 신분증을 꼭 가져올 것

Note
유의사항

『500 backpacks will be given out / on a first-come, first-served basis.』 **④의 근거** 일치
가방 500개가 배부될 것입니다. / 선착순으로

『A parent or a guardian must come with their child / to receive the backpack.』 **⑤의 근거** 불일치
부모 또는 보호자께서 아이와 함께 오셔야 합니다. / 가방을 받으시려면

For more information, / call the City Council at 612-248-6633.
더 많은 정보를 알고 싶으시면, / 612-248-6633으로 시의회에 전화 주세요.

Back-to-school Giveaway Event
(개학 무료 나눔 행사)

Easton시는 신학기 무료 나눔 행사를 주최합니다. 모든 연령의 아이들이 여름 방학 후 학교로 돌아가는 것을 준비할 수 있게 돕는 이 즐거운 행사에 함께하세요.

일시: 9월 2일 토요일 오전 9시~11시

장소: Easton시 중앙 공원
(이 행사는 날씨와 관계없이 열릴 예정입니다.)

참여요건
- Easton시 주민만 참여할 수 있음
- 유효한 신분증을 꼭 가져올 것

유의사항
- 가방 500개가 선착순으로 배부될 것입니다.
- 가방을 받으시려면, 부모 또는 보호자께서 아이와 함께 오셔야 합니다.

더 많은 정보를 알고 싶으시면, 612-248-6633으로 시의회에 전화 주세요.

Why? 왜 정답일까?
'500 backpacks will be given out on a first-come, first-served basis.'에서 가방 500개

가 선착순으로 배부될 예정이라고 공지하므로, 안내문의 내용과 일치하는 것은 ④ '가방 500개가 선착순으로 배부될 것이다.'이다.

Why? 왜 오답일까?

① 'When: Saturday, September 2nd, 9 a.m.–11 a.m.'에서 행사는 토요일 오전이라고 하였다.
② 'This event will be held rain or shine.'에서 날씨에 관계없이 진행된다고 하였다.
③ 'Open to City of Easton residents only'에서 Easton시에 거주하는 사람만 참여 가능하다고 하였다.
⑤ 'A parent or a guardian must come with their child to receive the backpack.'에서 가방을 받으려면 부모나 보호자가 반드시 아이와 함께 와야 한다고 하였다.

- giveaway ⓝ 무료 나눔, 증정
- give out 나눠주다
- valid ⓐ 유효한, 타당한
- on a first-come, first-served basis 선착순으로

---

29 | 생산자 – 소비자의 행동에 영향을 미치는 판매 유효 기간 | 정답률 50% | 정답 ②

다음 글의 밑줄 친 부분 중, 어법상 틀린 것은?

There is little doubt / that we are driven by the sell-by date.
의심할 여지가 거의 없다. / 우리가 판매 유효 기한에 따라 움직인다는 것은
Once an item is past that date / it goes into the waste stream, / further ① increasing its carbon footprint.
일단 어떤 품목이 그 기한을 지나면 / 그것은 폐기물 흐름으로 들어가고, / 이는 물품의 탄소 발자국을 더욱더 증가시킨다.
Remember / those items have already travelled hundreds of miles / ✓to reach the shelves / and once they go into waste / they start a new carbon mile journey.
기억하라. / 그러한 품목들이 이미 수백 마일을 이동해서, / 선반에 도달되고 / 일단 그것들이 버려지면 / 그것들은 새로운 탄소 마일 여정을 시작한다는 것을
But we all make our own judgement about sell-by dates; / those brought up during the Second World War / ③ are often scornful of the terrible waste / they believe such caution encourages.
그러나 우리 모두는 판매 유효 기한에 대해 알아서 판단을 내린다. / 제2차 세계 대전 중에 자란 사람들은 / 끔찍한 낭비를 흔히 경멸한다. / 그들이 생각하기로 그런 경고가 조장하는
The manufacturer of the food has a view / when making or growing something / ④ that by the time the product reaches the shelves / it has already been travelling / for so many days and possibly many miles.
식품 제조업자는 관점을 지닌다. / 뭔가 만들거나 재배할 때 / 제품이 선반에 도달할 무렵에는 / 그것이 이미 이동해 왔다는 / 매우 오랫동안, 그리고 아마 상당한 거리를
The manufacturer then decides / that a product can reasonably be consumed within say 90 days / and 90 days minus so many days for travelling / gives the sell-by date.
그래서 제조업자는 판단한다. / 제품이 이를테면 90일 이내에는 무리 없이 소비될 수 있고, / 90일에서 이동에 필요한 여러 날을 빼면 / 판매 유효 기한이 나온다고
But / ⑤ whether it becomes toxic / is something / each individual can decide.
그러나 / 그것이 유독해지는지는 / 뭔가이다. / 개인이 각자 결정할 수 있는
It would seem to make sense / not to buy large packs of perishable goods / but non-perishable items may become cost-effective.
이치에 맞아 보이겠지만, / 상하기 쉬운 제품을 대량으로 사지 않는 것이 / 상하지 않는 품목들의 경우에는 비용 효율이 높아질 수도 있다.

우리가 판매 유효 기한에 따라 움직인다는 것은 의심할 여지가 거의 없다. 일단 어떤 품목이 그 기한을 지나면 폐기물 흐름으로 들어가고, 이는 물품의 탄소 발자국을 더욱더 증가시킨다. 그러한 품목들이 이미 수백 마일을 이동해 선반에 도달했고, 일단 버려지면 그것들은 새로운 탄소 마일 여정을 시작한다는 것을 기억하라. 그러나 우리 모두는 판매 유효 기한에 대해 알아서 판단을 내린다. 가령, 제2차 세계 대전 중에 자란 사람들은 그런 경고가 조장한다고 생각하는 끔찍한 낭비를 흔히 경멸한다. 식품 제조업자는 뭔가 만들거나 재배할 때, 제품이 선반에 도달할 무렵에는 그것이 이미 매우 오랫동안, 그리고 아마 상당한 거리를 이동해 왔다는 관점을 지닌다. 그래서 제조업자는 제품이 이를테면 90일 이내에는 무리 없이 소비될 수 있고, 90일에서 이동에 필요한 여러 날을 빼면 판매 유효 기한이 나온다고 판단한다. 그러나 그것이 유독해지는지는 개인이 각자 결정할 수 있는 것이다. 상하기 쉬운 제품을 대량으로 사지 않는 것이 이치에 맞아 보이겠지만, 상하지 않는 품목들의 경우에는 비용 효율이 높아질 수도 있다.

Why? 왜 정답일까?

Remember의 목적절에서 접속사 that은 생략되고 주어 those items와 동사 have already travelled가 나왔으므로, ②는 주절을 보충 설명하는 부사구 자리이다. 즉 동사 reach 대신 to부정사 to reach의 형태로 써야 적합하다. 따라서 어법상 틀린 것은 ②이다.

Why? 왜 오답일까?

① 콤마 뒤로 주절을 보충하는 분사구문이다.
③ 주어가 those이므로 동사의 복수형을 적절히 썼다.
④ a view를 설명하는 동격 명사절을 이끄는 접속사이다.
⑤ '~인지 아닌지'라는 의미의 명사절 접속사 whether이다.

- sell-by date 판매 유효 기한
- carbon footprint 탄소 발자국
- scornful ⓐ 경멸하는
- manufacturer ⓝ 제조업체
- toxic ⓐ 유독한
- perishable ⓐ 상하기 쉬운
- stream ⓝ 흐름
- bring up 양육하다
- terrible ⓐ 끔찍한
- consume ⓥ 소비하다
- make sense 이치에 맞다

구문 풀이

6행 But we all make our own judgement about sell-by dates; those (brought up during the Second World War) are often scornful of the terrible waste [(that) (they believe) such caution encourages].
(주어 / 과거분사 / 동사복수 / 선행사 / 생략 (목적격 관·대) / 삽입절)

---

30 | 카페인을 분해하는 속도 | 정답률 63% | 정답 ④

다음 글의 밑줄 친 부분 중, 문맥상 낱말의 쓰임이 적절하지 않은 것은?

The "jolt" of caffeine does wear off.
카페인의 '충격'은 확실히 점차 사라진다.
Caffeine is ① removed from your system / by an enzyme within your liver, / which gradually degrades it over time.
카페인은 신체로부터 제거되는데, / 여러분 간 속의 효소에 의해 / 이 효소는 시간이 지남에 따라 그것을 점진적으로 분해한다.
Based in large part on genetics, / some people have a more efficient version of the enzyme / that degrades caffeine, / ② allowing the liver / to rapidly clear it from the bloodstream.
대체로 유전적 특징 때문에, / 어떤 사람들은 더 효율적인 형태의 효소를 갖고 있는데, / 카페인을 분해하는 / 이는 간이 ~하도록 허용한다. / 그것을 혈류로부터 더 빠르게 제거하도록
These rare individuals can drink an espresso with dinner / and fall fast asleep at midnight without a problem.
이 몇 안 되는 사람들은 저녁과 함께 에스프레소를 마실 수 있다 / 그리고 아무 문제 없이 한밤중에 깊이 잠든다.
Others, however, / have a slower-acting version of the enzyme.
그러나 다른 사람들은 / 더 느리게 작용하는 형태의 효소를 가지고 있다.
It takes far ③ longer / for their system to eliminate the same amount of caffeine.
훨씬 더 오래 걸린다. / 이들의 신체가 같은 양의 카페인을 제거하는 데
As a result, / they are very ✓sensitive to caffeine's effects.
결과적으로, / 그들은 카페인의 효과에 매우 민감하다.
One cup of tea or coffee in the morning / will last much of the day, / and should they have a second cup, / even early in the afternoon, / they will find it difficult / to fall asleep in the evening.
아침에 마시는 차 또는 커피 한 잔은 / 그날 대부분 동안 지속될 것이고, / 그들이 혹시 또 한 잔을 마신다면 / 심지어 이른 오후라도 / 이들은 어렵다는 것을 깨닫는다. / 저녁에 잠들기가
Aging also ⑤ alters the speed of caffeine clearance: / the older we are, / the longer it takes / our brain and body to remove caffeine, / and thus the more sensitive we become in later life / to caffeine's sleep-disrupting influence.
또한, 노화는 카페인 제거 속도를 변화시킨다. / 즉, 우리가 나이 들수록 / 더 오래 걸리고, / 우리 뇌와 신체가 카페인을 제거하는 데 / 따라서 우리는 노후에 더 민감해진다. / 카페인의 수면을 방해하는 효과에

카페인의 '충격'은 확실히 점차 사라진다. 카페인은 여러분 간 속의 효소에 의해 신체로부터 ① 제거되는데, 이 효소는 시간이 지남에 따라 그것을 점진적으로 분해한다. 대체로 유전적 특징 때문에, 어떤 사람들은 카페인을 분해하는 더 효율적인 형태의 효소를 갖고 있는데, 이는 간이 그것을 혈류로부터 더 빠르게 제거하도록 ② 허용한다. 이 몇 안 되는 사람들은 저녁과 함께 에스프레소를 마시고도 아무 문제 없이 한밤중에 깊이 잠들 수 있다. 그러나 다른 사람들은 더 느리게 작용하는 형태의 효소를 가지고 있다. 이들의 신체는 같은 양의 카페인을 제거하는 데 훨씬 ③ 더 오래 걸린다. 결과적으로, 그들은 카페인의 효과에 매우 ④ 둔감하다(→ 민감하다). 아침에 마시는 차 또는 커피 한 잔은 그날 대부분 동안 지속될 것이고, 심지어 이른 오후라도 혹시 또 한 잔을 마신다면 이들은 저녁에 잠들기가 어렵다는 것을 깨닫는다. 또한, 노화는 카페인 제거 속도를 ⑤ 변화시킨다. 즉, 우리가 나이 들수록 우리 뇌와 신체가 카페인을 제거하는 데 더 오래 걸리고, 따라서 우리는 노후에 카페인의 수면을 방해하는 효과에 더 민감해진다.

Why? 왜 정답일까?

'Others, however, ~' 이후로 카페인 분해 속도가 느린 사람들을 언급한다. 이들은 카페인을 몸 밖으로 배출하는 시간이 '더 오래' 걸리기 때문에, 한 잔만 먹어도 효과가 오래 가서 카페인의 영향에 '더 취약하다'는 설명이 적합하다. 즉 ④에는 insensitive 대신 sensitive가 적합하므로, 문맥상 낱말의 쓰임이 적절하지 않은 것은 ④이다.

- jolt ⓝ 충격
- enzyme ⓝ 효소
- gradually ⓐ 점점
- genetics ⓝ 유전적 특징
- bloodstream ⓝ 혈류
- fast asleep 깊이 잠든
- insensitive ⓐ 둔감한
- clearance ⓝ 없애기, 정리
- disrupt ⓥ 지장을 주다
- wear off 차츰 사라지다, 없어지다
- liver ⓝ 간
- degrade ⓥ 분해하다, 저하시키다
- efficient ⓐ 효율적인
- rare ⓐ 몇 안 되는, 드문
- eliminate ⓥ 제거하다
- alter ⓥ 변화시키다
- sensitive ⓐ 민감한

구문 풀이

10행 One cup of tea or coffee in the morning will last much of the day, and should they have a second cup, even early in the afternoon, they will find it difficult to fall asleep in the evening.
(가정법 미래(= if they should have ~) / 가목적어 / 동사 / 목적격 보어 / 진목적어(~것))

★★★ 등급을 가르는 문제!

31 | 반항 경향을 이용한 마케팅 | 정답률 45% | 정답 ①

다음 빈칸에 들어갈 말로 가장 적절한 것을 고르시오. [3점]

✓ reversal – 반전
② imitation – 모방
③ repetition – 반복
④ conformity – 순응
⑤ collaboration – 협력

Rebels may think they're rebels, / but clever marketers influence them / just like the rest of us.
반항자들은 자기가 반항자라고 생각할지도 모르지만, / 영리한 마케터들은 그들에게 영향을 준다. / 나머지 우리에게 그러듯이
Saying, "Everyone is doing it" / may turn some people off from an idea.
"모두가 그렇게 하고 있다."라고 말하는 것은 / 일부 사람들이 어떤 생각에 흥미를 잃게 할지도 모른다.
These people will look for alternatives, / which (if cleverly planned) can be / exactly what a marketer or persuader wants you to believe.
이 사람들은 대안을 찾을 것이고, / 그것은 (만약 영리하게 계획된다면) ~일 수 있다. / 정확히 마케터나 설득자가 여러분이 믿기를 원하는 것
If I want you to consider an idea, / and know you strongly reject popular opinion / in favor of maintaining your independence and uniqueness, / I would present the majority option first, / which you would reject in favor of my actual preference.
만약 내가 여러분이 어떤 아이디어를 고려하길 바라는데, / 여러분이 대중적인 의견을 강하게 거부한다는 것을 안다면, / 독립성과 고유성을 유지하기 위해서 / 나는 대다수가 선택하는 것을 먼저 제시할 것이고, / 여러분은 내 실제 선호에 따라 그것을 거부할 것이다.
We are often tricked / when we try to maintain a position of defiance.
우리는 종종 속는다. / 우리가 반항의 입장을 유지하려 할 때
People use this reversal / to make us independently" choose an option / which suits their purposes.
사람들은 이러한 반전을 사용한다. / 우리가 선택지를 '독자적으로' 택하도록 만들기 위해 / 그들의 목적에 맞는

Some brands have taken full effect of our defiance towards the mainstream / and positioned themselves as rebels; / which has created even stronger brand loyalty.
일부 브랜드들은 주류에 대한 우리의 반항을 온전히 활용 / 반항자로 자리 잡았으며, / 이는 훨씬 더 강력한 브랜드 충성도를 만들어 왔다.

반항자들은 자기가 반항자라고 생각할지도 모르지만, 영리한 마케터들은 나머지 우리에게 그러듯이 그들에게 영향을 준다. "모두가 그렇게 하고 있다."라고 말하는 것은 일부 사람들이 어떤 생각에 흥미를 잃게 할지도 모른다. 이 사람들은 대안을 찾을 것이고, 그것은 (만약 영리하게 계획된다면) 정확히 마케터나 설득자가 여러분이 믿기를 원하는 것일 수 있다. 만약 내가 여러분이 어떤 아이디어를 고려하길 바라는데, 여러분이 독립성과 고유성을 유지하기 위해서 대중적인 의견을 강하게 거부한다는 것을 안다면, 나는 대다수가 선택하는 것을 먼저 제시할 것이고, 여러분은 내 실제 선호에 따라 그것을 거부할 것이다. 우리는 반항의 입장을 유지하려 할 때 종종 속는다. 사람들은 우리가 그들의 목적에 맞는 선택지를 '독자적으로' 택하도록 만들기 위해 이러한 반전을 사용한다. 일부 브랜드들은 주류에 대한 우리의 반항을 온전히 활용해 반항자로 자리 잡았으며, 이는 훨씬 더 강력한 브랜드 충성도를 만들어 왔다.

Why? 왜 정답일까?
반항자들을 대상으로 한 마케팅 기법을 소개하고 있다. 반항자들은 스스로의 독립성과 고유성을 중시하기 때문에, 대중의 생각을 제시하면 그에 반감을 보이고, 실은 그 '반감 형성'이 마케터들의 의도라는 것이다. (Some brands have taken full effect of our defiance towards the mainstream and positioned themselves as rebels; which has created even stronger brand loyalty.)따라서 반항적인 행동 경향을 '역이용'하여 본래의 마케팅 목적을 달성한다는 의미로, 빈칸에 들어갈 말로 가장 적절한 것은 ① '반전'이다.

- rebel ⓝ 반항아
- turn off ~을 지루하게 만들다
- reject ⓥ 거부하다
- independence ⓝ 독립
- majority ⓝ 대다수
- defiance ⓝ 반항
- mainstream ⓝ 주류
- repetition ⓝ 반복
- clever ⓐ 영리한
- alternative ⓐ 대안
- in favor of ~을 위해
- uniqueness ⓝ 고유성
- trick ⓥ 속이다
- suit ⓥ ~에 맞추다
- loyalty ⓝ 충성도
- conformity ⓝ 순응

구문 풀이

6행 If I want you to consider an idea, and know {(that) you strongly reject 접속사(~라면) 동사1 동사2 접속사
popular opinion in favor of maintaining your independence and uniqueness}, I
would present the majority option first, which you would reject in favor of my 선행사 계속적 용법
actual preference.

★★ 문제 해결 꿀~팁 ★★

▶ 많이 틀린 이유는?
'누구나 다 하고 있다'는 인용구만 보면 남들을 '따라 한다'는 의미의 ②를 고르기 쉽다. 하지만 글에서 언급된 반항자들은 대중의 의견을 따르기보다는 '반대하는' 사람들이므로 '모방'이라는 단어는 적절하지 않다.

▶ 문제 해결 방법은?
대중적인 의견에 반대하려는 성향을 '오히려 이용해서' 브랜드에 대한 강한 충성도를 형성한다는 내용을 요약하는 단어가 필요하다.

32 드라마 속 추상적인 세계 정답률 47% | 정답 ④
다음 빈칸에 들어갈 말로 가장 적절한 것을 고르시오. [3점]
① is separated from the dramatic contents – 극적인 내용과 분리되어 있기
② is a reflection of our unrealistic desires – 비현실적인 욕망의 반영이기
③ demonstrates our poor taste in TV shows – TV 쇼에 대한 우리의 형편없는 취향을 보여주기
④ is built on an extremely familiar framework – 매우 친숙한 틀 위에서 만들어졌기
⑤ indicates that unnecessary details are hidden – 불필요한 세부사항이 숨겨져 있다는 의미이기

A typical soap opera creates an abstract world, / in which a highly complex web of relationships connects fictional characters / that exist first only in the minds of the program's creators / and are then recreated in the minds of the viewer.
전형적인 드라마는 추상적인 세계를 만들어내는데, / 그 세계에는 매우 복잡한 관계망이 허구의 캐릭터를 연결한다 / 프로그램 제작자들의 마음속에만 먼저 존재하다가 / 이후에 시청자의 마음속에 재현되는

If you were to think about / how much human psychology, law, and even everyday physics the viewer must know / in order to follow and speculate about the plot, / you would discover it is considerable / — at least as much as the knowledge / required to follow and speculate about a piece of modern mathematics, / and in most cases, much more.
만약 여러분이 생각해보면, / 시청자가 얼마나 많은 인간 심리학, 법, 그리고 심지어 일상에서의 물리학을 알아야 하는지 / 줄거리를 따라가고 그것에 대해 추측하려면 / 여러분은 그 양이 상당하다는 것을 알게 된다. / 적어도 지식만큼, / 현대 수학의 한 부분을 따라가고 거기에 대해 추측하는 데 필요한 / 나아가 대부분의 경우 훨씬 더 많다는 것을 알게 된다.

Yet viewers follow soap operas with ease.
하지만 시청자들은 드라마를 쉽게 따라간다.

How are they able to cope with such abstraction?
그들은 어떻게 그런 추상에 대처할 수 있을까?

Because, of course, / the abstraction is built on an extremely familiar framework.
왜냐하면 당연하게도, / 그 추상은 매우 친숙한 틀 위에서 만들어졌기 때문이다.

The characters in a soap opera / and the relationships between them / are very much like the real people and relationships / we experience every day.
드라마 속 인물들과 / 그들 사이의 관계는 / 실제 사람들 및 관계와 매우 흡사하다. / 우리가 매일 경험하는

The abstraction of a soap opera / is only a step / removed from the real world.
드라마의 추상은 / 불과 한 걸음이다. / 현실 세계에서 떨어져 있는

The mental "training" required to follow a soap opera / is provided by our everyday lives.
드라마를 따라가는 데 필요한 정신적 '훈련'은 / 우리의 일상생활에 의해 제공된다.

전형적인 드라마는 추상적인 세계를 만들어내는데, 그 세계에서는 매우 복잡한 관계망이

프로그램 제작자들의 마음속에만 먼저 존재하다가 이후에 시청자의 마음속에 재현되는 허구의 캐릭터들을 연결한다. 만약 줄거리를 따라가고 그것에 대해 추측하려면 시청자가 얼마나 많은 인간 심리학, 법, 그리고 심지어 일상에서의 물리학을 알아야 하는지 생각해보면, 여러분은 그 양이 상당하다는 것을 알게 된다. 적어도 현대 수학의 한 부분을 따라가기에 거기에 대해 추측하는 데 필요한 지식만큼, 나아가 대부분의 경우 훨씬 더 많다는 것을 알게 된다. 하지만 시청자들은 드라마를 쉽게 따라간다. 그들은 어떻게 그런 추상에 대처할 수 있을까? 왜냐면 당연하게도, 그 추상은 매우 친숙한 틀 위에서 만들어졌기 때문이다. 드라마 속 인물들과 그들 사이의 관계는 우리가 매일 경험하는 실제 사람들 및 관계와 매우 흡사하다. 드라마의 추상은 현실 세계에서 불과 한 걸음 떨어져 있다. 드라마를 따라가는 데 필요한 정신적 '훈련'은 우리의 일상생활에 의해 제공된다.

Why? 왜 정답일까?
빈칸 뒤 내용의 핵심은 드라마 속 추상이 우리 일상과 가깝다는 것이다(The mental "training" required to follow a soap opera is provided by our everyday lives.). 따라서 빈칸에 들어갈 말로 가장 적절한 것은 ④ '매우 친숙한 틀 위에서 만들어졌기'이다.

- soap opera 드라마, 연속극
- complex ⓐ 복잡한
- fictional ⓐ 허구의
- psychology ⓝ 심리
- speculate ⓥ 추측하다
- cope with ~에 대처하다
- reflection ⓝ 반영
- framework ⓝ 틀, 뼈대
- abstract ⓐ 추상적인
- web ⓝ 망
- recreate ⓥ 되살리다
- physics ⓝ 물리학
- considerable ⓐ 상당한
- abstraction ⓝ 추상
- demonstrate ⓥ 입증하다, 보여주다

구문 풀이

5행 If you were to think about {how much human psychology, law, and even
가정법 미래 종속절(if + 주어 + were to + 동사원형 ~) { } : 명사절
everyday physics the viewer must know in order to follow and speculate about
the plot}, you would discover it is considerable — at least as much as the
가정법 미래 주절(주어 + 조동사 과거형 + 동사원형 ~)
knowledge required to follow and speculate about a piece of modern mathematics,
└ 과거분사
and in most cases, much more.

★★★ 등급을 가르는 문제!
33 진화적 군비 경쟁 정답률 32% | 정답 ②
다음 빈칸에 들어갈 말로 가장 적절한 것을 고르시오. [3점]
① been in a fierce war over scarce food sources
희소한 식량 자원을 두고 맹렬한 전쟁을 치러
② been engaged in a life-or-death sensory arms race
수백만 년 동안 생사를 가르는 감각 군비 경쟁에 참여해
③ invented weapons that are not part of their bodies
그들의 신체 일부가 아닌 무기를 발명해
④ evolved to cope with other noise-producing wildlife
소음을 만들어내는 다른 야생 생물에 대처하도록 진화해
⑤ adapted to flying in night skies absent of any lights
아무 빛도 없는 밤하늘을 나는 데 적응해

As always happens with natural selection, / bats and their prey / have been engaged in a life-or-death sensory arms race / for millions of years.
자연 선택에서 항상 그렇듯이, / 박쥐와 그 먹잇감은 / 생사를 가르는 감각 군비 경쟁에 참여해 왔다. / 수백만 년 동안

It's believed / that hearing in moths arose / specifically in response to the threat of being eaten by bats.
여겨진다. / 나방의 청력은 생겨났다고 / 특히 박쥐에 잡아먹히는 위험에 대한 반응으로

(Not all insects can hear.)
(모든 곤충이 들을 수 있는 것은 아니다.)

Over millions of years, / moths have evolved the ability / to detect sounds at ever higher frequencies, / and, as they have, / the frequencies of bats' vocalizations have risen, too.
수백만 년 동안, / 나방은 능력을 발달시켰고, / 계속 더 높아진 주파수의 소리를 감지하는 / 그것들이 그렇게 하면서 / 박쥐의 발성 주파수도 높아졌다.

Some moth species have also evolved / scales on their wings / and a fur-like coat on their bodies; / both act as "acoustic camouflage," / by absorbing sound waves in the frequencies / emitted by bats, / thereby preventing those sound waves from bouncing back.
또한 일부 나방 종은 진화시켰다. / 날개의 비늘과 / 몸에 모피와 같은 외피를 / 둘 다 '음향 위장'의 역할을 한다. / 주파수의 음파를 흡수함으로써 / 박쥐에 의해 방출되는 / 그렇게 하여 음파가 박쥐에게로 되돌아가는 것을 방지함으로써

The B-2 bomber and other "stealth" aircraft / have fuselages / made of materials / that do something similar with radar beams.
B-2 폭격기와 그 밖의 '스텔스' 항공기는 / 재료로 만들어진 기체를 가지고 있다. / 레이더 전파에 유사하게 반응하는

자연 선택에서 항상 그렇듯이, 박쥐와 그 먹잇감은 수백만 년 동안 생사를 가르는 감각 군비 경쟁에 참여해 왔다. 나방의 청력은 특히 박쥐에게 잡아먹히는 위험에 대한 반응으로 생겨났다고 여겨진다. (모든 곤충이 들을 수 있는 것은 아니다.) 수백만 년 동안, 나방은 계속 더 높아진 주파수의 소리를 감지하는 능력을 발달시켰고, 그것들이 그렇게 하면서 박쥐의 발성 주파수도 높아졌다. 또한 일부 나방 종은 날개의 비늘과 몸에 모피와 같은 외피를 진화시켰다. 둘 다 '음향 위장'의 역할을 해서, 박쥐에 의해 방출되는 주파수의 음파를 흡수하여 음파가 박쥐에게로 되돌아가는 것을 방지한다. B-2 폭격기와 그 밖의 '스텔스' 항공기는 레이더 전파에 유사하게 반응하는 재료로 만들어진 기체를 가지고 있다.

Why? 왜 정답일까?
박쥐의 먹잇감인 나방은 잡아먹히지 않기 위해 박쥐가 내는 고주파음을 듣도록 진화해왔고, 그에 따라 박쥐는 더 높은 주파수를 낼 수 있도록 같이 진화해왔다는 내용이다. 이렇듯 두 종이 더 잡아먹고 덜 잡아 먹히기 위해 경쟁적으로 진화하는 과정을 '군비 경쟁'으로 볼 수 있으므로, 빈칸에 들어갈 말로 가장 적절한 것은 ② '수백만 년 동안 생사를 가르는 감각 군비 경쟁에 참여해'이다.

- natural selection 자연 선택
- moth ⓝ 나방
- detect ⓥ 감지하다
- vocalization ⓝ 발성
- acoustic ⓐ 청각적인
- absorb ⓥ 흡수하다
- prey ⓝ 먹이 동물
- threat ⓝ 위협
- frequency ⓝ 주파수
- scale ⓝ 비늘
- camouflage ⓝ 위장
- emit ⓥ 방출하다

[문제편 p.114]

- **bounce back** 반항하다, (튕겨서) 되돌아가다
- **stealth** ⓐ (레이더가 탐지하기 힘든) 스텔스기의, 숨어서 하는
- **fuselage** ⓝ (비행기의) 기체
- **arms race** 군비 경쟁(군사적 우위를 차지하기 위한 소모적 경쟁)
- **wildlife** ⓝ 야생 생물
- **bomber** ⓝ 폭격기
- **fierce** ⓐ 맹렬한
- **absent of** ~이 없는

구문 풀이

3행 It's believed that hearing in moths arose specifically in response to the
= Hearing in moths is believed to have arisen ~
threat of being eaten by bats.
동명사의 수동태(being p.p.)

★★ 문제 해결 꿀~팁 ★★

▶ 많이 틀린 이유는?
예시의 지엽적 내용에만 집중하면 '소음을 만들어낸다'는 표현이 들어간 ④를 고르기 쉽다. 하지만 빈칸 뒤에 예시가 나오면 이를 적절히 일반화해야 정답을 도출할 수 있다.

▶ 문제 해결 방법은?
박쥐가 더 높은 주파수의 소리를 내고, 나방이 소리를 더 잘 듣게 계속 진화하는 이유는 각자 더 '생존'에 유리해지기 위함이다. 이 진화가 '경쟁적으로' 일어난다는 점도 포인트이다.

★★★ 등급을 가르는 문제!

34 인간의 인지 작용 　　　　정답률 33% | 정답 ②

다음 빈칸에 들어갈 말로 가장 적절한 것을 고르시오. [3점]

① tend to favor learners with great social skills
사교성이 뛰어난 학습자를 선호하는 경향이 있다
✓② are marked by a steady elimination of information
정보의 지속적인 제거로 특징지어진다
③ require an external aid to support our memory capacity
우리 기억력을 보조하고자 외부의 도움을 필요로 한다
④ are determined by the accuracy of incoming information
유입되는 정보의 정확성에 의해 결정된다
⑤ are facilitated by embracing chaotic situations as they are
혼돈의 상황을 있는 그대로 받아들이는 것으로부터 촉진된다

Much of human thought / is designed to screen out information / and to sort the rest into a manageable condition.
인간 사고의 많은 부분은 / 정보를 걸러내도록 설계된다. / 그리고 나머지는 처리하기 쉬운 상태로 분류하도록

The inflow of data from our senses / could create an overwhelming chaos, / especially given the enormous amount of information / available in culture and society.
우리 감각에서 오는 데이터의 유입은 / 압도적인 혼란을 낳을 수 있다. / 특히 엄청난 양의 정보를 고려할 때, / 문화와 사회에서 이용할 수 있는

Out of all the sensory impressions and possible information, / it is vital / to find a small amount / that is most relevant to our individual needs / and to organize that into a usable stock of knowledge.
모든 감각적 인상과 가능한 정보 중에서, / 중요하다. / 적은 양을 찾는 것이 / 우리의 개인적인 필요와 가장 관련이 있는 / 그리고 그것을 사용 가능한 지식체로 구성하는 것이

Expectancies accomplish some of this work, / helping to screen out information / that is irrelevant to what is expected, / and focusing our attention on clear contradictions.
예상들은 이 작업의 일부를 수행하여 / 정보를 걸러내는 데 도움이 되고, / 예상되는 것과 무관한 / 명확한 모순에 우리의 주의를 집중시킨다.

The processes of learning and memory / are marked by a steady elimination of information.
학습과 기억의 과정은 / 정보의 지속적인 제거로 특징지어진다.

People notice only a part of the world around them.
사람들은 그들 주변 세계의 일부분만을 인지한다.

Then, / only a fraction of what they notice / gets processed and stored into memory.
그런 다음, / 그들이 알아차린 것의 일부만 / 처리되어 기억에 저장된다.

And / only part of what gets committed to memory / can be retrieved.
그리고 / 기억에 넘겨진 것의 일부만 / 생각해 낼 수 있다.

인간 사고의 많은 부분은 정보를 걸러내고 나머지는 처리하기 쉬운 상태로 분류하도록 설계된다. 특히 문화와 사회에서 이용할 수 있는 엄청난 양의 정보를 고려할 때, 우리 감각에서 오는 데이터의 유입은 압도적인 혼란을 낳을 수 있다. 모든 감각적 인상과 가능한 정보 중에서, 우리의 개인적인 필요와 가장 관련된 적은 양을 찾아서 그것을 사용 가능한 지식체로 구성하는 게 중요하다. 예상들은 이 작업의 일부를 수행하여 예상되는 것과 무관한 정보를 걸러내는 데 도움이 되고, 명확한 모순에 우리의 주의를 집중시킨다. 학습과 기억의 과정은 정보의 지속적인 제거로 특징지어진다. 사람들은 그들 주변 세계의 일부분만을 인지한다. 그런 다음, 그들이 알아차린 것의 일부만 처리되어 기억에 저장된다. 그리고 기억에 넘겨진 것의 일부만 생각해 낼 수 있다.

Why? 왜 정답일까?

빈칸 뒤에서 우리는 세계의 일부만 인지하고, 인지한 것 중 일부만 저장하고, 저장된 것의 일부만 회상할 수 있다고 한다. 말인즉 정보를 점점 줄여가는 것이 우리의 인지 과정이라는 것이므로, 빈칸에 들어갈 말로 가장 적절한 것은 ② '정보의 지속적인 제거로 특징지어진다'이다.

- **screen out** 차단하다
- **inflow** ⓝ 유입
- **chaos** ⓝ 혼돈
- **vital** ⓐ 매우 중요한
- **accomplish** ⓥ 해내다, 성취하다
- **contradiction** ⓝ 모순
- **commit A to memory** A를 기억하다
- **accuracy** ⓝ 정확성
- **manageable** ⓐ 처리하기 쉬운, 감당할 만한
- **overwhelming** ⓐ 압도적인
- **enormous** ⓐ 막대한
- **stock** ⓝ 저장, 축적 ⓥ 저장하다, 보관하다
- **irrelevant** ⓐ 무관한
- **fraction** ⓝ 부분
- **retrieve** ⓥ 생각해 내다
- **facilitate** ⓥ 촉진하다

구문 풀이

5행 Out of all the sensory impressions and possible information, it is vital
가주어
to find a small amount [that is most relevant to our individual needs] and to organize
진주어1　　　선행사　　　주격 관·대　　　　　　　　　　　　　진주어2
that into a usable stock of knowledge.
대명사(= the small amount)

★★ 문제 해결 꿀~팁 ★★

▶ 많이 틀린 이유는?
외부에서 들어오는 데이터나 정보를 차단하고 줄여야 한다는 내용 때문에 '기억력을 외부에서 보조해 줘야 한다'는 의미의 ③을 고르게 될 수도 있다. 하지만 '외부의 보조'에 관해서는 전혀 언급되지 않았다.

▶ 문제 해결 방법은?
빈칸 뒤가 인간의 인지적 과정을 잘 요약하고 있다. 주변 정보를 선별적으로 받아들이고, 받아들인 정보 중 일부만을 저장하고, 저장된 정보 중 일부만을 기억하게 된다는 것은 결국 '계속 정보를 지워간다'는 의미와 같다. 본문의 **screen out**이 ②의 **elimination**과 연결된다.

★★★ 등급을 가르는 문제!

35 과거 유럽의 통치 권력 　　　정답률 35% | 정답 ③

다음 글에서 전체 흐름과 관계 없는 문장은?

The irony of early democracy in Europe / is that it thrived and prospered precisely / because European rulers for a very long time were remarkably weak.
유럽 초기 민주주의의 아이러니는 / 바로 그것이 번성하고 번영했다는 것이다. / 유럽의 통치자들이 매우 오랫동안 현저하게 약했기 때문에

① For more than a millennium after the fall of Rome, / European rulers lacked the ability / to assess what their people were producing / and to levy substantial taxes based on this.
로마의 멸망 후 천 년 넘게, / 유럽의 통치자들은 능력이 부족했다. / 백성들이 생산하고 있었던 것을 평가해 / 이를 바탕으로 상당한 세금을 부과할

② The most striking way to illustrate European weakness / is to show / how little revenue they collected.
유럽의 연약함을 설명하는 가장 눈에 띄는 방법은 / 보여주는 것이다. / 그들이 거둔 세입이 얼마나 적은지를

✓③ For this reason, / tax collectors in Europe / were able to collect a huge amount of revenue / and therefore had a great influence / on how society should function.
이러한 이유로, / 유럽의 세금 징수원은 / 막대한 액수의 세입을 거둘 수 있었고, / 그리하여 큰 영향을 미쳤다. / 사회가 어떻게 기능해야 하는지에

④ Europeans would eventually develop strong systems of revenue collection, / but it took them an awfully long time to do so.
유럽인들은 결국 강력한 세입 징수 시스템을 개발했지만, / 그렇게 하는 데 엄청나게 오랜 시간이 걸렸다.

⑤ In medieval times, / and for part of the early modern era, / Chinese emperors and Muslim caliphs / were able to extract much more of economic production / than any European ruler / with the exception of small city-states.
중세 시대와 / 초기 근대의 일부 동안, / 중국의 황제들과 이슬람 문명의 칼리프들은 / 경제적 생산물 중 훨씬 많은 양을 뜯어낼 수 있었다. / 그 어느 유럽 통치자들보다 / 작은 도시 국가를 제외하고

유럽 초기 민주주의의 아이러니는 바로 유럽의 통치자들이 매우 오랫동안 현저하게 약했기 때문에 그것이 번성하고 번영했다는 것이다. 로마의 멸망 후 천 년 넘게, 유럽의 통치자들은 백성들이 생산하고 있었던 것을 평가해 이를 바탕으로 상당한 세금을 부과할 능력이 부족했다. 유럽의 연약함을 설명하는 가장 눈에 띄는 방법은 그들이 거둔 세입이 얼마나 적은지를 보여주는 것이다. ③ 이러한 이유로, 유럽의 세금 징수원은 막대한 액수의 세입을 거둘 수 있었고, 그리하여 사회가 어떻게 기능해야 하는지에 큰 영향을 미쳤다. ④ 유럽인들은 결국 강력한 세입 징수 시스템을 개발했지만, 그렇게 하는 데 엄청나게 오랜 시간이 걸렸다. ⑤ 중세 시대와 초기 근대의 일부 동안, 중국의 황제들과 이슬람 문명의 칼리프들은 작은 도시 국가를 제외한 그 어느 유럽 통치자들보다 경제적 생산물 중 훨씬 많은 양을 뜯어낼 수 있었다.

Why? 왜 정답일까?

유럽의 적은 세금 수입을 보면 유럽의 통치 권력이 강하지 않았다는 것을 알 수 있다는 내용인데, ③은 유럽의 징수원이 막대한 세금을 거둬들일 수 있었다는 모순되는 내용이다. 따라서 전체 흐름과 관계 없는 문장은 ③이다.

- **democracy** ⓝ 민주주의
- **prosper** ⓥ 번영하다
- **assess** ⓥ 평가하다
- **substantial** ⓐ 상당한
- **illustrate** ⓥ 분명히 보여주다
- **huge** ⓐ 거대한, 막대한
- **medieval** ⓐ 중세의
- **emperor** ⓝ 황제
- **extract** ⓥ 뜯어내다, 얻어내다
- **thrive** ⓥ 번성하다
- **remarkably** ⓐⓓ 현저하게
- **levy** ⓥ 부과하다
- **striking** ⓐ 눈에 띄는
- **revenue** ⓝ 세입, 수입
- **awfully** ⓐⓓ 몹시, 지독히
- **era** ⓝ 시대
- **caliph** ⓝ 칼리프(과거 이슬람 국가의 통치자)
- **with the exception of** ~을 제외하고

구문 풀이

11행 Europeans would eventually develop strong systems of revenue collection, but it took them an awfully long time to do so.
= it took an awfully long time for them to do so(의미상 주어 활용)

★★ 문제 해결 꿀~팁 ★★

▶ 많이 틀린 이유는?
유럽의 통치 권력이 약했다는 것을 적은 세금 수입으로 알 수 있다는 내용인데, ④에서 갑자기 '세금 징수 체계'를 언급하므로 흐름상 부자연스러워 보일 수 있다. 하지만 이 문장의 진짜 의미는 유럽에서 (세금을 더 잘 거두기 위해) 세입 체계를 만들기는 했지만 그렇게 하는 데도 시간이 오래 걸렸을 정도로 '통치 권력이 약했다'는 것이다.

▶ 문제 해결 방법은?
모든 문장에서 '세금 징수'가 언급되고 있으므로, 소재가 어긋나는 문장은 없다. 이럴 때는 주제와 반대되는 문장이 없는지 살펴보면 된다.

★★★ 등급을 가르는 문제!

36 광고를 하는 이유 　　　　정답률 33% | 정답 ⑤

주어진 글 다음에 이어질 글의 순서로 가장 적절한 것을 고르시오.

① (A) – (C) – (B)　　② (B) – (A) – (C)　　③ (B) – (C) – (A)
④ (C) – (A) – (B)　　✓⑤ (C) – (B) – (A)

If you drive down a busy street, / you will find many competing businesses, / often right next to one another.
만약 여러분이 번화한 거리를 운전한다면, / 여러분은 경쟁하는 많은 업체들을 발견할 것이다. / 흔히 바로 서로 옆에서

For example, / in most places / a consumer in search of a quick meal / has many choices, / and more fast-food restaurants appear all the time.
예를 들어, / 대부분의 장소에서 / 간단한 식사를 찾는 소비자에게는 / 선택권이 많고, / 항상 여러 패스트푸드 식당들이 눈에 띈다.

(C) These competing firms advertise heavily.
이 경쟁 업체들은 광고를 많이 한다.

The temptation is / to see advertising as driving up the price of a product / without any benefit to the consumer.
유혹은 ~이다. / 광고가 제품의 가격을 올린다고 본다는 것 / 소비자에게 어떤 혜택도 없이

(B) However, / this misconception doesn't account for / why firms advertise.
그러나 / 이러한 오해는 설명해주지 않는다. / 회사들이 광고하는 이유를

In markets / where competitors sell slightly differentiated products, / advertising enables firms / to inform their customers about new products and services.
시장에서, / 경쟁사들이 약간씩 차별화된 제품들을 판매하는 / 광고는 회사들이 ~할 수 있게 해 준다. / 소비자들에게 새로운 제품과 서비스를 알릴

(A) Yes, costs rise, / but consumers also gain information / to help make purchasing decisions.
물론 가격이 상승하기는 하지만, / 소비자들은 도움이 되는 정보도 얻는다. / 구매 결정을 내리는 데

Consumers also benefit from added variety, / and we all get a product / that's pretty close to our vision of a perfect good / — and no other market structure delivers that outcome.
또한 소비자들은 추가된 다양성으로부터 혜택을 얻고, / 우리 모두는 제품을 얻는데, / 완벽한 제품에 대한 우리의 상상에 매우 근접한 / 다른 어떤 시장 구조도 그러한 결과를 제공하지 않는다.

만약 여러분이 번화한 거리를 운전한다면, 여러분은 바로 서로 옆에서 경쟁하는 많은 업체들을 흔히 발견할 것이다. 예를 들어, 대부분의 장소에서 간단한 식사를 찾는 소비자에게는 선택권이 많고, 항상 여러 패스트푸드 식당들이 눈에 띈다.
(C) 이 경쟁 업체들은 광고를 많이 한다. 광고라고 하면 소비자에게 어떤 혜택도 없이 제품의 가격을 올린다고 보기 쉽다.
(B) 그러나 이러한 오해는 회사들이 광고하는 이유를 설명해주지 않는다. 경쟁사들이 약간씩 차별화된 제품들을 판매하는 시장에서, 광고는 회사들이 소비자들에게 새로운 제품과 서비스를 알릴 수 있게 해 준다.
(A) 물론 가격이 상승하기는 하지만, 소비자들은 구매 결정을 내리는 데 도움이 되는 정보도 얻는다. 또한 소비자들은 추가된 다양성으로 혜택을 얻고, 우리 모두는 완벽한 제품에 대한 우리의 상상에 매우 근접한 제품을 얻는데, 다른 어떤 시장 구조도 그러한 결과를 제공하지 않는다.

Why? 왜 정답일까?

주어진 글은 우리가 일상에서 경쟁 관계에 있는 업체들을 많이 볼 수 있다는 내용이고, (C)는 '이 업체들'이 살아남기 위해 많은 광고를 한다는 내용이다. 특히 (C)의 후반부는 우리가 광고 때문에 제품 가격이 올라간다고 여기기 쉽다고 하는데, (B)는 이런 '오해'가 광고의 이유를 설명해주지 못한다면서 광고의 효과를 설명하기 시작한다. (A) 또한 (B)에 이어 광고의 이득과 효과를 언급하므로, 글의 순서로 가장 적절한 것은 ⑤ '(C) – (B) – (A)'이다.

- **misconception** ⓝ 오해
- **slightly** [ad] 약간
- **temptation** ⓝ 유혹
- **account for** ~을 설명하다
- **differentiate** ⓥ 차별(화)하다, 구별하다

구문 풀이

12행 In markets [where competitors sell slightly differentiated products],
장소 선행사 관계부사절
advertising enables firms to inform their customers about new products and
『enable + 목적어 + to부정사: ~이 …할 수 있게 해주다』
services.

★★ 문제 해결 꿀~팁 ★★

▶ 많이 틀린 이유는?
(C)의 driving up the price of a product 다음에 (A)의 Yes, costs rise가 와도 자연스러워 보이지만, (A) 다음 (B)가 자연스럽지 않다. (A)에서 '오해'로 볼 만한 내용이 언급되지 않기 때문이다.

▶ 문제 해결 방법은?
(C)의 see advertising as driving up the price of a product without any benefit to the consumer가 (B)의 this misconception으로 연결되고, also가 포함된 (A)에서 광고의 이점에 대한 내용을 추가하는 흐름이다.

---

37 기계와 알고리즘을 이용한 '창의적' 작업 정답률 43% | 정답 ③

주어진 글 다음에 이어질 글의 순서로 가장 적절한 것을 고르시오. [3점]

① (A) – (C) – (B) ② (B) – (A) – (C)
③ (B) – (C) – (A) ④ (C) – (A) – (B)
⑤ (C) – (B) – (A)

Architects might say / a machine can never design an innovative or impressive building / because a computer cannot be "creative."
건축가들은 말할지도 모른다. / 기계는 결코 혁신적이거나 인상적인 건물을 디자인하지 못한다고 / 컴퓨터는 '창의적일' 수 없기 때문에

Yet consider the Elbphilharmonie, / a new concert hall in Hamburg, / which contains a remarkably beautiful auditorium / composed of ten thousand interlocking acoustic panels.
그러나 Elbphilharmonie를 생각해보라, / Hamburg에 있는 새로운 콘서트 홀인 / 이곳에는 놀랍도록 아름다운 강당이 있다. / 1만 개의 서로 맞물리는 음향 패널로 구성된

(B) It is the sort of space / that makes one instinctively think / that only a human being / — and a human with a remarkably refined creative sensibility, at that — / could design something so aesthetically impressive.
그것은 부류의 공간이다. / 우리를 본능적으로 생각하게 만드는 / 인간만이, / 그것도 놀랍도록 세련된 창의적 감수성을 가진 인간만이 / 그토록 미적으로 인상적인 것을 디자인할 수 있을 거라고

Yet the auditorium was, / in fact, / designed algorithmically, / using a technique known as "parametric design."
하지만 그 강당은 / 사실 / 알고리즘 방식으로 설계되었다. / '파라메트릭 디자인'이라고 알려진 기술을 사용해

(C) The architects gave the system a set of criteria, / and it generated a set of possible designs / for the architects to choose from.
건축가들은 그 시스템에 일련의 기준을 부여했고, / 그것은 일련의 가능한 디자인을 만들어냈다. / 건축가들이 선택할 수 있는

Similar software has been used / to design lightweight bicycle frames and sturdier chairs, / among much else.
비슷한 소프트웨어가 이용돼 왔다. / 경량 자전거 프레임과 더 튼튼한 의자를 디자인할 목적으로 / 다른 많은 것들보다도

(A) Are these systems behaving "creatively"?
이러한 시스템들은 '창의적으로' 작동하고 있는가?

No, / they are using lots of processing power / to blindly generate varied possible designs, / working in a very different way from a human being.
아니다, / 그것들은 많은 처리 능력을 사용해 / 여러 가능한 디자인을 닥치는 대로 만들면서, / 인간과는 매우 다른 방식으로 일하고

건축가들은 컴퓨터는 '창의적일' 수 없기 때문에 기계는 결코 혁신적이거나 인상적인 건물을 디자인하지 못한다고 말할지도 모른다. 그러나 Hamburg에 있는 새로운 콘서트 홀인 Elbphilharmonie를 생각해보라, 이곳에는 1만 개의 서로 맞물리는 음향 패널로 구성된 놀랍도록 아름다운 강당이 있다.
(B) 그것은 인간만이, 그것도 놀랍도록 세련된 창의적 감수성을 가진 인간만이 그토록 미적으로 인상적인 것을 디자인할 수 있을 거라고 본능적으로 생각하게 만드는 부류의 공간이다. 하지만 사실 그 강당은 '파라메트릭 디자인'이라고 알려진 기술을 사용해 알고리즘 방식으로 설계되었다.
(C) 건축가들은 그 시스템에 일련의 기준을 부여했고, 그것은 건축가들이 선택할 수 있는 일련의 가능한 디자인을 만들어냈다. 다른 많은 것들보다도 경량 자전거 프레임과 더 튼튼한 의자를 디자인할 목적으로 비슷한 소프트웨어가 이용돼 왔다.
(A) 이러한 시스템들은 '창의적으로' 작동하고 있는가? 아니다, 그것들은 많은 처리 능력을 사용해 여러 가능한 디자인을 닥치는 대로 만들면서, 인간과는 매우 다른 방식으로 일하고 있다.

Why? 왜 정답일까?

주어진 글에서 언급된 콘서트 홀(Elbphilharmonie)을 (B)에서는 It으로 가리키며 이것이 알고리즘에 의해 디자인됐다고 설명한다. 이어서 (C)는 건축가들이 이 콘서트홀을 만들었던 과정을 설명한 뒤, 경량 자전거 프레임 등 다른 분야에도 이런 식의 소프트웨어가 이용되고 있다고 한다. (A)는 '이런 시스템들'이 진정한 의미로 '창의적'이지는 않지만, 인간과는 매우 다른 방식으로 작업을 이어간다는 내용이다. 따라서 글의 순서로 가장 적절한 것은 ③ '(B) – (C) – (A)'이다.

- **interlock** ⓥ 서로 맞물리다
- **instinctively** [ad] 본능적으로
- **sensibility** ⓝ 감수성
- **architect** ⓝ 건축가
- **sturdy** @ 튼튼한, 견고한
- **generate** ⓥ 만들어내다, 생성하다
- **refine** ⓥ 개선하다
- **aesthetically** [ad] 미적으로
- **criterion** (pl. criteria) ⓝ 기준

구문 풀이

3행 Yet consider the Elbphilharmonie, a new concert hall in Hamburg, which
동격(선행사) 계속적 용법
contains a remarkably beautiful auditorium (composed of ten thousand interlocking
과거분사구
acoustic panels).

---

38 뇌의 연료 자원 사용 정답률 54% | 정답 ④

글의 흐름으로 보아, 주어진 문장이 들어가기에 가장 적절한 곳을 고르시오.

The brain is a high-energy consumer of glucose, / which is its fuel.
뇌는 포도당의 고에너지 소비자이다. / 자기 연료인

Although the brain accounts for merely 3 percent of a person's body weight, / it consumes 20 percent of the available fuel.
비록 뇌는 사람 체중의 단지 3퍼센트를 차지하지만, / 그것은 사용 가능한 연료의 20퍼센트를 소비한다.

① Your brain can't store fuel, however, / so it has to "pay as it goes."
하지만 여러분의 뇌는 연료를 저장할 수 없고, / 따라서 '활동하는 대로 대가를 지불'해야 한다.

② Since your brain is incredibly adaptive, / it economizes its fuel resources.
여러분의 뇌는 놀라울 정도로 적응력이 뛰어나기 때문에, / 그것의 연료 자원을 경제적으로 사용한다.

③ Thus, / during a period of high stress, / it shifts away from the analysis of the nuances of a situation / to a singular and fixed focus on the stressful situation at hand.
따라서, / 극심한 스트레스를 받는 중이라면, / 뇌는 상황의 미묘한 차이를 분석하는 것으로부터 옮겨 간다. / 눈에 닥친 스트레스 상황에 대한 단일하고 고정된 집중으로

✔ You don't sit back / and speculate about the meaning of life / when you are stressed.
여러분은 앉아서 / 삶의 의미에 대해 사색하지 않는다. / 여러분이 스트레스를 받을 때

Instead, / you devote all your energy / to trying to figure out what action to take.
대신에, / 여러분은 모든 에너지를 쏟는다. / 어떤 행동을 취해야 할지 알아내려고 노력하는 데

⑤ Sometimes, however, / this shift from the higher-thinking parts of the brain / to the automatic and reflexive parts of the brain / can lead you / to do something too quickly, without thinking.
그러나 때때로 / 이런 식으로 뇌의 고차원적 사고 영역에서 이동하는 것은 / 뇌의 자동적이고 반사적인 영역으로 / 여러분이 ~하도록 이끌 수 있다. / 무언가를 생각 없이 너무 빨리 하도록

뇌는 자기 연료인 포도당의 고에너지 소비자이다. 비록 뇌는 사람 체중의 단지 3퍼센트를 차지하지만, 사용 가능한 연료의 20퍼센트를 소비한다. ① 하지만 여러분의 뇌는 연료를 저장할 수 없고, 따라서 '활동하는 대로 대가를 지불'해야 한다. ② 여러분의 뇌는 놀라울 정도로 적응력이 뛰어나기 때문에, 그것의 연료 자원을 경제적으로 사용한다. ③ 따라서, 극심한 스트레스를 받는 중이라면, 뇌는 상황의 미묘한 차이를 분석하는 것으로부터 눈에 닥친 스트레스 상황에 대한 단일하고 고정된 집중으로 옮겨 간다. ④ 여러분은 스트레스를 받을 때 앉아서 삶의 의미에 대해 사색하지 않는다. 대신에, 여러분은 어떤 행동을 취해야 할지 알아내려고 노력하는 데 모든 에너지를 쏟는다. ⑤ 그러나 때때로 이런 식으로 뇌의 고차원적 사고 영역에서 자동적이고 반사적인 영역으로 이동하는 것은 여러분이 무언가를 생각 없이 너무 빨리 하도록 이끌 수 있다.

Why? 왜 정답일까?

④ 앞에서 극도로 스트레스를 받는 상황을 제시하며, 이때 우리 뇌는 상황의 미묘한 차이까지 관심을

기울이기보다는 눈에 닥친 것들에 주목하게 된다고 한다. 이어서 주어진 문장은 우리가 스트레스 상황일 때 삶의 의미를 생각하지는 않는다고 하고, ④ 뒤의 문장은 '그 대신(Instead)' 우리가 '(이 상황에서 지금) 뭘 할지'에 초점을 맞추게 된다고 설명한다. 따라서 주어진 문장이 들어가기에 가장 적절한 곳은 ④이다.

- **glucose** ⓝ 포도당
- **merely** 團 단지, 그저
- **economize** ⓥ 절약하다, 아끼다
- **nuance** ⓝ 미묘한 차이
- **at hand** 당면한, 눈앞에 있는
- **fuel** ⓝ 연료 ⓥ 부추기다
- **adaptive** ⓐ 적응하는
- **analysis** ⓝ 분석
- **fixed** ⓐ 고정된
- **reflexive** ⓐ 반사적인

구문 풀이

11행 Instead, you devote all your energy to trying to figure out {what action to take}.
「devote + A + to ~ing : A를 ~하는 데 바치다」 「what + 명사 + to부정사 : 어떤 ~할지」

---

39 몰입의 원인
정답률 47% | 정답 ④

글의 흐름으로 보아, 주어진 문장이 들어가기에 가장 적절한 곳을 고르시오. [3점]

Much research has been carried out on the causes of engagement, / an issue that is important / from both a theoretical and practical standpoint: / identifying the drivers of work engagement / may enable us / to manipulate or influence it.
몰입의 원인에 대한 많은 연구가 수행되었는데, / 이는 중요한 문제이다. / 이론적 및 실제적 둘 다의 관점에서 / 업무 몰입의 동기를 알아내는 것은 / 우리가 ~할 수 있게 할 것이다. / 우리가 그것을 조작하거나 그것에 영향을 줄

① The causes of engagement fall into two major camps: / situational and personal.
몰입의 원인은 두 가지 주요한 분야로 나뉜다. / 상황적인 것과 개인적인 것이라는

② The most influential situational causes / are job resources, feedback and leadership, / the latter, of course, / being responsible for job resources and feedback.
가장 영향력 있는 상황적 원인은 / 직무 자원, 피드백, 그리고 리더십이며, / 후자는 당연하게도 / 직무 자원과 피드백에 대한 책임이다.

③ Indeed, / leaders influence engagement / by giving their employees / honest and constructive feedback on their performance, / and by providing them with the necessary resources / that enable them to perform their job well.
실제로 / 리더들은 몰입에 영향을 미친다. / 직원들에게 제공해서 / 수행에 대한 솔직하고 건설적인 피드백 / 그리고 직원들에게 필요한 자원을 제공해서 / 그들이 자기 직무를 잘 수행할 수 있도록

☑ It is, however, noteworthy / that although engagement drives job performance, / job performance also drives engagement.
그러나 주목할 점은 / 몰입이 직무 수행의 동기가 되지만, / 직무 수행도 몰입의 동기가 된다는 것이다.

In other words, / when employees are able to do their jobs well / — to the point that they match or exceed their own expectations and ambitions — / they will engage more, / be proud of their achievements, / and find work more meaningful.
즉, / 직원들이 직무를 잘 수행할 수 있을 때 / 자기 기대와 포부에 부합하거나 그것을 능가할 정도로 / 직원들은 더 많이 몰입하고, / 자기 성과를 자랑스러워하며, / 업무를 더 의미 있게 생각할 것이다.

⑤ This is especially evident / when people are employed in jobs / that align with their values.
이것은 특히 분명하다. / 사람들이 직무에 종사했을 때 / 자기 가치와 일치하는

몰입의 원인에 대한 많은 연구가 수행되었는데, 이는 이론적 및 실제적 둘 다의 관점에서 중요한 문제이다. 업무 몰입의 동기를 알아내는 것은 우리가 그것을 조작하거나 그것에 영향을 줄 수 있게 할 것이다. ① 몰입의 원인은 상황적인 것과 개인적인 것이라는 두 가지 주요한 분야로 나뉜다. ② 가장 영향력 있는 상황적 원인은 직무 자원, 피드백, 그리고 리더십이며, 후자는 당연하게도 직무 자원과 피드백에 대한 책임이다. ③ 실제로 리더들은 직원들에게 수행에 대한 솔직하고 건설적인 피드백을 제공하고 직원들이 자기 직무를 잘 수행할 수 있도록 필요한 자원을 제공하여 몰입에 영향을 미친다. ④ 그러나 주목할 점은 몰입이 직무 수행의 동기가 되지만, 직무 수행도 몰입의 동기가 된다는 것이다. 즉, 직원들이 자기 기대와 포부에 부합하거나 그것을 능가할 정도로 직무를 잘 수행할 수 있을 때 직원들은 더 많이 몰입하고, 자기 성과를 자랑스러워하며, 업무를 더 의미 있게 생각할 것이다. ⑤ 이것은 사람들이 자기 가치와 일치하는 직무에 종사했을 때 특히 분명하다.

Why? 왜 정답일까?
④ 앞에서 리더들이 직원의 수행에 대해 주는 피드백이 업무에 대한 몰입을 촉진할 수 있다고 한다. 이에 대해 주어진 문장은 거꾸로 '수행' 역시 몰입의 원인이 될 수 있다고 설명하고, ④ 뒤의 문장은 직무 수행력이 좋아졌을 때 직원의 업무 몰입이 상승할 수도 있다는 말로 주어진 문장 내용을 다시 풀어(**In other words**) 설명한다. 따라서 주어진 문장이 들어가기에 가장 적절한 곳은 ④이다.

- **noteworthy** ⓐ 주목할 만한
- **carry out** 수행하다
- **standpoint** ⓝ 관점, 견지
- **manipulate** ⓥ 조작하다
- **be employed in** ~에 종사하다
- **engagement** ⓝ 몰입, 참여
- **theoretical** ⓐ 이론적인
- **identify** ⓥ 식별하다, 알아내다
- **evident** ⓐ 분명한
- **align with** ~과 일치하다

구문 풀이

9행 The most influential situational causes are job resources, feedback and leadership, the latter, of course, being responsible for job resources and feedback.
의미상 주어 / 분사구문

---

40 도움을 주려는 동기에 대한 연구
정답률 45% | 정답 ①

다음 글의 내용을 한 문장으로 요약하고자 한다. 빈칸 (A), (B)에 들어갈 말로 가장 적절한 것은?

	(A)		(B)
☑	sustained 지속될	……	decline 감소
②	sustained 지속될	……	maximization 극대화
③	indirect 간접적일	……	variation 변화
④	discouraged 좌절될	……	reduction 감소
⑤	discouraged 좌절될	……	increase 증가

In 2006, / researchers conducted a study / on the motivations for helping / after the

---

September 11th terrorist attacks / against the United States.
2006년에 / 연구자들은 연구를 수행했다. / 도움을 주려는 동기에 대한 / 9.11 테러 공격 이후에 / 미국을 향한

In the study, / they found / that individuals who gave money, blood, goods, or other forms of assistance / because of other-focused motives / (giving to reduce another's discomfort) / were almost four times more likely / to still be giving support one year later / than those whose original motivation was to reduce personal distress.
이 연구에서, / 그들은 발견했다. / 돈, 혈액, 물품 또는 다른 형태의 도움을 주었던 사람들이 / 타인에게 초점을 맞춘 동기 때문에 / (다른 사람의 곤란을 줄이기 위해 베푸는 것) / 가능성이 거의 네 배 더 높다는 것을 / 일 년 후에도 여전히 지원을 제공할 / 원래 동기가 자신의 고통을 줄이는 것이었던 사람들에 비해

This effect likely stems from differences in emotional arousal.
이 결과는 감정적 자극의 차이에서 비롯된 것 같다.

The events of September 11th / emotionally affected people throughout the United States.
9.11의 사건들은 / 미국 전역의 사람들에게 감정적으로 영향을 미쳤다.

Those who gave to reduce their own distress / reduced their emotional arousal with their initial gift, / discharging that emotional distress.
자기 고통을 줄이기 위해 베푼 사람들은 / 초기의 베풂을 통해 그 감정적 고통을 해소하면서 / 감정적 자극을 줄였다.

However, / those who gave to reduce others' distress / did not stop empathizing with victims / who continued to struggle long after the attacks.
하지만, / 다른 사람들의 고통을 줄이기 위해 베푼 사람들은 / 피해자들에게 공감하기를 멈추지 않았다. / 공격 이후 오랫동안 계속 고생하는

➡ A study found / that the act of giving / was less likely to be (A) sustained / when driven by self-centered motives / rather than by other-focused motives, / possibly because of the (B) decline in emotional arousal.
한 연구는 발견했다. / 베푸는 행위가 / 지속될 가능성이 더 낮았는데, / 자기 중심적 동기에 의해 유도될 때 / 타인에 초점을 맞춘 동기보다는 / 아마도 감정적 자극의 감소 때문이라는 것을

2006년에 연구자들은 미국을 향한 9.11 테러 공격 이후에 도움을 주려는 동기에 대한 연구를 수행했다. 이 연구에서, 그들은 타인에게 초점을 맞춘 동기(다른 사람의 곤란을 줄이기 위해 베푸는 것) 때문에 돈, 혈액, 물품, 또는 다른 형태의 도움을 주었던 사람들이 원래 동기가 자신의 고통을 줄이는 것이었던 사람들에 비해 일 년 후에도 여전히 지원을 제공할 가능성이 거의 네 배 더 높다는 것을 발견했다. 이 결과는 감정적 자극의 차이에서 비롯된 것 같다. 9.11의 사건들은 미국 전역의 사람들에게 감정적으로 영향을 미쳤다. 자기 고통을 줄이기 위해 베푼 사람들은 초기의 베풂을 통해 그 감정적 고통을 해소하면서 감정적 자극을 줄였다. 하지만, 다른 사람들의 고통을 줄이기 위해 베푼 사람들은 공격 이후 오랫동안 계속 고생하는 피해자들에게 계속해서 공감했다.

➡ 한 연구는 베푸는 행위가 타인에 초점을 맞춘 동기보다는 자기 중심적 동기에 의해 유도될 때 (A) 지속될 가능성이 더 낮았는데, 아마도 감정적 자극의 (B) 감소 때문이라는 것을 발견했다.

Why? 왜 정답일까?
베푸는 행위가 자기 중심적 동기에 바탕을 둘 때에는 도움의 행위가 덜 지속되는 경향이 있었는데, 아마도 감정적 자극이 줄어들면서 그런 것 같다(Those who gave to reduce their own distress reduced their emotional arousal with their initial gift, discharging that emotional distress.)는 연구 내용을 소개하는 글이다. 따라서 요약문의 빈칸 (A), (B)에 들어갈 말로 가장 적절한 것은 ① '(A) sustained(지속될), (B) decline(감소)'이다.

- **motivation** ⓝ 동기
- **distress** ⓝ (정신적) 고통
- **arousal** ⓝ 자극
- **indirect** ⓐ 간접적인
- **discomfort** ⓝ 불편
- **stem from** ~에서 기인하다
- **discharge** ⓥ 해소하다, 내보내다
- **discourage** ⓥ 낙담시키다, 좌절시키다

구문 풀이

18행 A study found that the act of giving was less likely to be sustained when
접속사(~것) / ~할 가능성이 적다
(it was) driven by self-centered motives rather than by other-focused motives,
생략
possibly because of the decline in emotional arousal.
전치사(~ 때문에)

41-42 나이에 대한 사회적 규범과 인식

In England in the 1680s, / it was unusual / to live to the age of fifty.
1680년대 영국에서 / 이례적인 일이었다. / 50세까지 사는 것은

This was a period / when knowledge was not spread (a) widely, / there were few books / and most people could not read.
이때는 시절였다. / 지식이 널리 보급되지 않았고, / 책이 거의 없었으며, / 대부분의 사람들이 읽을 수 없던

As a consequence, / knowledge passed down / through the oral traditions of stories and shared experiences.
결과적으로, / 지식은 전수되었다. / 이야기와 공유된 경험이라는 구전 전통으로

And since older people had accumulated more knowledge, / the social norm was / that to be over fifty was to be wise.
그리고 더 나이 든 사람들이 더 많은 지식을 축적했기 때문에, / 사회적 규범은 ~이었다. / 50세가 넘으면 지혜롭다는 것

「This social perception of age / began to shift with the advent of new technologies / such as the printing press.」 **41번의 근거**
나이에 대한 이런 사회적 인식은 / 새로운 기술의 출현으로 변화하기 시작했다. / 인쇄기와 같은

Over time, / as more books were printed, / literacy (b) increased, / and the oral traditions of knowledge transfer / began to fade.
시간이 지나면서 / 더 많은 책이 인쇄됨에 따라 / 문해력이 증가했고, / 지식 전달의 구전 전통이 / 사라지기 시작했다.

With the fading of oral traditions, / the wisdom of the old became less important / and as a consequence / being over fifty was no longer seen / as (c) signifying wisdom.
구전 전통이 사라지면서 / 노인들의 지혜는 덜 중요해졌고, / 결과적으로 / 50세가 넘은 것은 더 이상 여겨지지 않았다. / 지혜로움을 의미하는 것으로

「We are living in a period / when the gap between chronological and biological age / is changing fast / and where social norms are struggling to (d) adapt.」 **42번의 근거**
우리는 시기에 살고 있다. / 생활 연령과 생물학적 연령 사이의 격차가 / 빠르게 변하고, / 사회적 규범이 적응하기 위해 분투하는

In a video / produced by the AARP (formerly the American Association of Retired Persons), / young people were asked / to do various activities 'just like an old person'.
영상에서 / AARP(이전의 American Association of Retired Persons)에 의해 제작된 / 젊은이들은 요청받았다. / 다양한 활동을 '마치 꼭 노인처럼' 하도록

When older people joined them in the video, / the gap between the stereotype and the older people's actual behaviour / was (e) striking.

영상에서 노인들이 그들에 합류했을 때, / 고정관념과 노인들의 실제 행동 사이의 격차는 / 두드러졌다.

「It is clear / that in today's world / our social norms need to be updated quickly.」 **41번의 근거**

분명하다. / 오늘날의 세상에서 / 우리의 사회적 규범은 신속하게 갱신되어야 한다는 것이

1680년대 영국에서 50세까지 사는 것은 이례적인 일이었다. 이 시기는 지식이 (a) 널리 보급되지 않았고, 책이 거의 없었으며, 대부분의 사람들이 (글자를) 읽을 수 없었던 때였다. 결과적으로, 지식은 이야기와 공유된 경험이라는 구전 전통으로 전수되었다. 그리고 더 나이 든 사람들이 더 많은 지식을 축적했기 때문에, 사회적 규범은 50세가 넘으면 지혜롭다는 것이었다. 나이에 대한 이런 사회적 인식은 인쇄기와 같은 새로운 기술의 출현으로 변화하기 시작했다. 시간이 지나면서 더 많은 책이 인쇄됨에 따라 문해력이 (b) 증가했고, 지식 전달의 구전 전통이 사라지기 시작했다. 구전 전통이 사라지면서 노인들의 지혜는 덜 중요해졌고, 결과적으로 50세가 넘은 것은 더 이상 지혜로움을 (c) 의미하는 것으로 여겨지지 않았다. 우리는 생활 연령과 생물학적 연령 사이의 격차가 빠르게 변화하고, 사회적 규범이 (d) 적응하기 위해 분투하는 시기에 살고 있다. AARP(이전의 American Association of Retired Persons)에 의해 제작된 영상에서 젊은이들은 다양한 활동을 '마치 꼭 노인처럼' 하도록 요청받았다. 영상에서 노인들이 그들에 합류했을 때, 고정관념과 노인들의 실제 행동 사이의 격차는 (e) 눈에 띄지 않았다(→ 두드러졌다). 오늘날의 세상에서 우리의 사회적 규범은 신속하게 갱신되어야 한다는 것이 분명하다.

- **spread** ⓥ 퍼뜨리다
- **pass down** 전해지다
- **perception** ⓝ 인식
- **literacy** ⓝ 문해력, 읽고 쓰는 능력
- **fade** ⓥ 사라지다, 엷어지다
- **chronological age** (신체적·정신적 수준을 비추어볼 때 실제로 산) 생활 연령
- **biological age** 생물학적 연령
- **stereotype** ⓝ 고정관념
- **as a consequence** 결과적으로
- **accumulate** ⓥ 축적하다
- **advent** ⓝ 출현, 도래
- **transfer** ⓝ 이동, 전파
- **signify** ⓥ 의미하다
- **formerly** ⓐⓓ 이전에
- **unnoticeable** ⓐ 눈에 띄지 않는

구문 풀이

6행 And since older people had accumulated more knowledge, the social
~ 때문에 / 과거완료(was보다 이전 시점)
norm was {that to be over fifty was to be wise}. [ ]: 명사절
주어 / 주격 보어

---

41 제목 파악 정답률 53% | 정답 ①

윗글의 제목으로 가장 적절한 것은?

✓① Our Social Norms on Aging: An Ongoing Evolution
노화에 대한 우리의 사회적 규범: 지속적 변화
② The Power of Oral Tradition in the Modern World
현대 세계에서의 구전의 힘
③ Generational Differences: Not As Big As You Think
세대별 차이: 생각보다 크지 않다
④ There's More to Aging than What the Media Shows
노화에는 미디어가 보여주는 것보다 더 많은 것이 있다
⑤ How Well You Age Depends on Your Views of Aging
나이를 얼마나 잘 먹는가는 나이를 보는 시각에 달려 있다

Why? 왜 정답일까?

과거에는 50세를 넘겨 살기도 힘들었고, 사람들의 문해력도 충분히 발달하지 못한 시기였기에 나이가 든다는 것이 지혜의 상징처럼 여겨졌지만, 오늘날에는 기술적 변화와 함께 노화에 대한 이러한 사회적 규범이 변하게 되었다(This social perception of age began to shift ~)는 내용이다. 따라서 글의 제목으로 가장 적절한 것은 ① '노화에 대한 우리의 사회적 규범: 지속적 변화'이다.

---

42 어휘 추론 정답률 55% | 정답 ⑤

밑줄 친 (a) ~ (e) 중에서 문맥상 낱말의 쓰임이 적절하지 않은 것은? [3점]

① (a) ② (b) ③ (c) ④ (d) ✓⑤ (e)

Why? 왜 정답일까?

두 번째 단락의 핵심 내용은 실제 살아가는 나이와 먹은 나이 사이의 격차가 점점 벌어지고 있고 사회적 규범이 이 격차를 부지런히 따라가야 한다는 것이다. 즉 고정관념 속 노인과 실제 노인의 모습이 '다르고', 이에 맞춰 사회적 규범을 빨리 변화시켜야 한다는 결론이 되도록 (e)의 unnoticeable을 striking으로 고쳐야 한다. 따라서 낱말의 쓰임이 가장 적절하지 않은 것은 ⑤ '(e)'이다.

43-45 내면의 용기로 풍요로움을 쌓아온 Jack

(A)

When Jack was a young man in his early twenties / during the 1960s, / he had tried to work in his father's insurance business, / as was expected of him.
Jack이 20대 초반의 청년이었을 때, / 1960년대에 / 그는 아버지의 보험 회사에서 일하려고 했다. / 자기가 기대받았던 대로

「His two older brothers fit in easily / and seemed to enjoy their work.」 **45번 ①의 근거** 일치
그의 두 형은 쉽게 적응했고 / 자기 일을 즐기는 것처럼 보였다.

But Jack was bored with the insurance industry.
그러나 Jack은 보험 업계에 실증이 났다.

"It was worse than being bored," / he said. / "I felt like I was dying inside."
"그것은 지루함 그 이상으로 나빴다."라고 그는 말했다. / "나는 내면이 죽어가는 것 같았다."

Jack felt drawn to hair styling / and dreamed of owning a hair shop with a lively environment.
Jack은 미용에 매력을 느꼈고, / 활기찬 분위기의 미용실을 갖는 것을 꿈꿨다.

He was sure / that (a) he would enjoy the creative and social aspects of it / and that he'd be successful.
그는 믿었다. / 자신이 미용의 창의적이고 사회적인 면을 즐길 것이고, / 자기가 성공할 것이라고

(C)

「When he was twenty-six, / Jack approached his father / and expressed his intentions of leaving the business / to become a hairstylist.」 **45번 ①의 근거** 일치
그가 26세였을 때 / Jack은 아버지에게 가서 / 회사를 떠나겠다는 의사를 밝혔다. / 미용사가 되기 위해

As Jack anticipated, / his father raged / and accused Jack of being selfish, ungrateful, and unmanly.

Jack이 예상했던 대로, / 그의 아버지는 화를 내며 / Jack이 이기적이고 배은망덕하며 남자답지 못하다고 비난했다.

In the face of his father's fury, / Jack felt confusion and fear.
아버지의 분노 앞에서, / Jack은 혼란과 두려움을 느꼈다.

His resolve became weak.
그의 결심은 약해졌다.

But then a force filled (d) his chest / and he stood firm in his decision.
그러나 그때 어떤 힘이 (d) 그의 가슴을 채웠고 / 그는 자기 결정에 확고해졌다.

「In following his path, / Jack not only ran three flourishing hair shops, / but also helped his clients experience their inner beauty / by listening and encouraging them / when they faced dark times.」 **45번 ⑤의 근거** 일치
자신의 길을 가면서, / Jack은 번창하는 미용실 세 군데를 운영했을 뿐 아니라, / 또한 고객들이 내면의 아름다움을 경험하도록 도왔다. / 그들의 말을 들어주고 격려해주어 / 그들이 힘든 시기에 직면했을 때

(D)

「His love for his work / led to donating time and talent at nursing homes, / which in turn led to becoming a hospice volunteer, / and eventually to starting fundraising efforts / for the hospice program in his community.」 **45번 ⑤의 근거** 일치
자기 일에 대한 그의 사랑은 / 요양원에 시간과 재능을 기부하는 것으로 이어졌고 / 이것은 결과적으로 호스피스 자원봉사가 되고, / 마침내 기금 모금 운동을 시작하는 것으로 이어졌다. / 자기 지역사회에서 호스피스 프로그램을 위한

And / all this laid a strong stepping stone / for another courageous move in his life.
그리고 / 이 모든 것은 견고한 디딤돌을 놓았다. / 그의 삶에서 또 다른 용기 있는 움직임을 위한

When, after having two healthy children of their own, / Jack and his wife, Michele, / decided to bring an orphaned child into their family, / (e) his father threatened to disown them.
건강한 아이들 둘을 낳고 나서 / Jack과 그의 아내 Michele이 / 고아가 된 아이를 가정에 데려오기로 결정했을 때, / 그의 아버지는 그들과 의절하겠다고 위협했다.

(B)

Jack understood that his father feared adoption, / in this case especially / because the child was of a different racial background / than their family.
Jack은 아버지가 입양을 두려워하고 있는 것을 이해했다. / 특히 이 경우에는 / 아이가 다른 인종적 배경 출신이었기 때문임을 / 그들 가족과는

「Jack and Michele risked rejection / and went ahead with the adoption.」 **45번 ②의 근거** 불일치
Jack과 Michele은 거부의 위험을 무릅쓰고 / 입양을 진행했다.

It took years / but eventually Jack's father loved the little girl / and accepted (b) his son's independent choices.
몇 년이 걸렸지만, / 결국 Jack의 아버지는 어린 손녀를 사랑했고 / 자기 아들의 독립적인 선택을 받아들였다.

Jack realized / that, although he often felt fear and still does, / he has always had courage.
Jack은 깨달았다. / 그가 비록 자주 두려움을 느꼈고 여전히 그렇지만, / 항상 그에게는 용기가 있다는 것을

In fact, / courage was the scaffolding / around which (c) he had built richness into his life.
사실, / 용기는 발판이었다. / 그가 삶에 풍요로움을 쌓아온

(A)

1960년대에 Jack이 20대 초반의 청년이었을 때, 그는 자기가 기대받았던 대로 아버지의 보험 회사에서 일하려고 했다. 그의 두 형은 쉽게 적응했고 자기 일을 즐기는 것처럼 보였다. 그러나 Jack은 보험 업계에 실증이 났다. "그것은 지루함 그 이상으로 나빴다."라고 그는 말했다. "나는 내면이 죽어가는 것 같았다." Jack은 미용에 매력을 느꼈고, 활기찬 분위기의 미용실을 갖는 것을 꿈꿨다. 그는 (a) 자신이 미용의 창의적이고 사회적인 면을 즐길 것이고, 성공할 것이라고 믿었다.

(C)

26세에 Jack은 아버지에게 가서 회사를 떠나 미용사가 되겠다는 의사를 밝혔다. Jack이 예상했던 대로, 그의 아버지는 화를 내며 Jack이 이기적이고 배은망덕하며 남자답지 못하다고 비난했다. 아버지의 분노 앞에서, Jack은 혼란과 두려움을 느꼈다. 그의 결심은 약해졌다. 그러나 그때 어떤 힘이 (d) 그의 가슴을 채웠고 그는 자기 결정에 확고해졌다. 자신의 길을 가면서, Jack은 번창하는 미용실 세 군데를 운영했을 뿐만 아니라, 또한 고객들이 힘든 시기에 직면했을 때 그들의 말을 들어주고 격려해주어 그들이 내면의 아름다움을 경험하도록 도왔다.

(D)

자기 일에 대한 그의 사랑으로 인해 그는 요양원에서 시간과 재능을 기부하게 되었고, 이는 결과적으로 그가 호스피스 자원봉사가 되고, 마침내 자기 지역사회에서 호스피스 프로그램을 위한 기금 모금 운동을 시작하는 결과로 이어졌다. 그리고 이 모든 것은 그의 삶에서 또 다른 용기 있는 움직임을 위한 견고한 디딤돌을 놓았다. Jack과 그의 아내 Michele이 건강한 아이들 둘을 낳고 나서 고아가 된 아이를 가정에 데려오기로 결정했을 때, (e) 그의 아버지는 그들과 의절하겠다고 위협했다.

(B)

Jack은 아버지가 입양을 두려워하고 있으며, 특히 이 경우에는 아이가 그들 가족과 다른 인종적 배경 출신이었기 때문임을 이해했다. Jack과 Michele은 거부의 위험을 무릅쓰고 입양을 진행했다. 몇 년이 걸렸지만, 결국 Jack의 아버지는 어린 손녀를 사랑했고 (b) 자기 아들의 독립적인 선택을 받아들였다. Jack은 비록 자주 두려움을 느꼈고 여전히 그렇지만, 항상 자신에게 용기가 있다는 것을 깨달았다. 사실, 용기는 (c) 그가 삶에 풍요로움을 쌓아온 발판이었다.

- **insurance** ⓝ 보험
- **rejection** ⓝ 거부
- **scaffolding** ⓝ 발판
- **rage** ⓥ 분노하다
- **selfish** ⓐ 이기적인
- **unmanly** ⓐ 남자답지 못한
- **fury** ⓝ 분노
- **flourishing** ⓐ 무성한, 번영하는
- **hospice** ⓝ 호스피스(말기 환자용 병원)
- **orphaned** ⓐ 고아인
- **adoption** ⓝ 입양
- **courage** ⓝ 용기
- **anticipate** ⓥ 예상하다
- **accuse A of B** A를 B에 대해 비난하다
- **ungrateful** ⓐ 배은망덕한
- **in the face of** ~에도 불구하고
- **resolve** ⓝ 결심 ⓥ 결심하다
- **in turn** 결과적으로
- **fundraising** ⓝ 모금
- **disown** ⓥ 의절하다

구문 풀이

(B) 8행 In fact, courage was the scaffolding around which he had built richness into his life.
= where

(D) 6행 When, (after having two healthy children of their own), Jack and his wife,
= after they had / 주어
Michele, decided to bring an orphaned child into their family, his father
동사 / 주어
threatened to disown them.
동사구(~하겠다고 협박하다)

주어진 글 (A)에 이어질 내용을 순서에 맞게 배열한 것으로 가장 적절한 것은?

① (B) – (D) – (C)　　　　② (C) – (B) – (D)
✓③ (C) – (D) – (B)　　　　④ (D) – (B) – (C)
⑤ (D) – (C) – (B)

Why? 왜 정답일까?

Jack이 아버지의 보험 회사에서 일하다가 미용에 관심을 갖게 되었다는 (A) 뒤로, Jack이 비난을 무릅쓰고 회사를 나와 미용실을 성공적으로 운영하기 시작했다는 (C), Jack이 각종 봉사를 이어가다가 아이 입양 문제로 다시금 아버지와 대립했다는 (D), 입양을 감행한 Jack이 결국 손녀와 잘 지내기 시작한 아버지를 보며 자기 안의 용기를 깨달았다는 (B)가 차례로 연결되어야 자연스럽다. 따라서 글의 순서로 가장 적절한 것은 ③ '(C) – (D) – (B)'이다.

---

44 지칭 추론　　　　　　정답률 70% | 정답 ②

밑줄 친 (a)~(e) 중에서 가리키는 대상이 나머지 넷과 다른 것은?

① (a)　　✓② (b)　　③ (c)　　④ (d)　　⑤ (e)

Why? 왜 정답일까?

(a), (c), (d), (e)는 Jack을, (b)는 his father를 가리키므로, (a)~(e) 중에서 가리키는 대상이 다른 하나는 ② '(b)'이다.

---

45 세부 내용 파악　　　　　　정답률 77% | 정답 ②

윗글의 Jack에 관한 내용으로 적절하지 않은 것은?

① 두 형은 자신들의 일을 즐기는 것으로 보였다.
✓② 아버지의 반대로 입양을 포기했다.
③ 아버지에게 회사를 떠나겠다는 의사를 밝혔다.
④ 세 개의 번창하는 미용실을 운영했다.
⑤ 지역사회에서 모금 운동을 시작했다.

Why? 왜 정답일까?

(B) 'Jack and Michele risked rejection and went ahead with the adoption.'에서 아버지의 반대를 감수하고 Jack은 아내와 함께 아이를 입양했다고 하므로, 내용과 일치하지 않는 것은 ② '아버지의 반대로 입양을 포기했다.'이다.

Why? 왜 오답일까?

① (A) 'His two older brothers fit in easily and seemed to enjoy their work.'의 내용과 일치한다.
③ (C) 'When he was twenty-six, Jack approached his father and expressed his intentions of leaving the business to become a hairstylist.'의 내용과 일치한다.
④ (C) 'In following his path, Jack not only ran three flourishing hair shops ~'의 내용과 일치한다.
⑤ (D) '~ eventually to starting fundraising efforts for the hospice program in his community.'의 내용과 일치한다.

어휘 Review Test 12

문제편 120쪽

A		B		C		D	
01	~이 필요한	01	grateful	01	ⓠ	01	ⓟ
02	~에 공감하다	02	remarkable	02	ⓜ	02	①
03	싹을 틔우다	03	infect	03	ⓚ	03	①
04	장애물	04	security	04	ⓞ	04	ⓐ
05	응답자	05	corporation	05	ⓐ	05	ⓝ
06	경멸하는	06	inhabit	06	ⓟ	06	ⓝ
07	차츰 사라지다, 없어지다	07	make sense	07	ⓡ	07	ⓑ
08	반항	08	degrade	08	①	08	ⓔ
09	추상적인	09	conformity	09	①	09	ⓗ
10	방출하다	10	cope with	10	ⓔ	10	ⓒ
11	압도적인	11	considerable	11	①	11	①
12	~을 설명하다	12	fierce	12	ⓒ	12	ⓚ
13	(정신적) 고통	13	democracy	13	ⓗ	13	ⓢ
14	자극	14	architect	14	ⓑ	14	ⓓ
15	고정관념	15	reflexive	15	ⓢ	15	①
16	사라지다, 옅어지다	16	literacy	16	ⓓ	16	①
17	관점, 견지	17	insurance	17	ⓖ	17	①
18	분명한	18	perception	18	①	18	ⓖ
19	유혹	19	align with	19	①	19	ⓜ
20	~하도록 동기 부여받다	20	trivial	20	①	20	ⓓ

[문제편 p.117]

• 정답 •

18 ④　19 ②　20 ①　21 ⑤　22 ②　23 ②　24 ①　25 ③　26 ⑤　27 ④　28 ②　29 ④　30 ③　31 ③　32 ①　33 ①　34 ③　35 ④　36 ④　37 ②　38 ③　39 ③　40 ②　41 ①　42 ⑤　43 ④　44 ④　45 ③

★ 표시된 문항은 [등급을 가르는 문제]에 해당하는 문항입니다.

---

18 큰 글자판 잡지가 있는지 문의하기　　　　　　정답률 94% | 정답 ④

다음 글의 목적으로 가장 적절한 것은?

① 잡지 기삿거리를 제보하려고
② 구독 기간 변경을 신청하려고
③ 구독료 인상에 대해 항의하려고
✓④ 잡지의 큰 글자판이 있는지 문의하려고
⑤ 잡지 기사 내용에 대한 정정을 요구하려고

Dear Customer Service,
고객 서비스팀께,
I am writing in regard to my magazine subscription.
저는 잡지 구독과 관련하여 글을 씁니다.
Currently, / I have just over a year / to go on my subscription to *Economy Tomorrow* / and would like to continue my subscription / as I have enjoyed the magazine for many years.
현재, / 저는 일 년 조금 넘게 남았는데 / 저의 *Economy Tomorrow* 구독을 계속하는 데 / 저는 구독을 계속하고 싶습니다. / 제가 수년간 귀사의 잡지를 즐겨왔기 때문에
Unfortunately, / due to my bad eyesight, / I have trouble reading your magazine.
안타깝게도, / 제 시력이 나빠서 / 저는 귀사의 잡지를 읽는 데 어려움이 있습니다.
My doctor has told me / that I need to look for large print magazines and books.
의사 선생님은 제게 말씀하셨습니다. / 제가 큰 글자판의 책과 잡지를 찾아봐야 할 필요가 있다고
I'd like to know / whether there's a large print version of your magazine.
저는 알고 싶습니다. / 귀사 잡지의 큰 글자판이 있는지
Please contact me / if this is something you offer.
저에게 연락 부탁드립니다. / 귀사에서 이를 제공한다면
Thank you for your time.
시간 내주셔서 감사합니다.
I look forward to hearing from you soon.
조만간 소식을 들을 수 있기를 기대합니다.
Sincerely, // Martin Gray
Martin Gray 드림

고객 서비스팀께,

저는 잡지 구독과 관련하여 글을 씁니다. 현재 저의 *Economy Tomorrow* 구독이 일 년 조금 넘게 남았는데, 저는 수년간 귀사의 잡지를 즐겨왔기 때문에 구독을 계속하고 싶습니다. 안타깝게도, 제 시력이 나빠서 귀사의 잡지를 읽는 데 어려움이 있습니다. 의사 선생님 말씀이 큰 글자판의 책과 잡지를 찾아봐야 할 필요가 있다고 합니다. 저는 귀사 잡지의 큰 글자판이 있는지 알고 싶습니다. 이를 제공한다면 저에게 연락 부탁드립니다. 시간 내주셔서 감사합니다. 조만간 소식을 들을 수 있기를 기대합니다.

Martin Gray 드림

Why? 왜 정답일까?

'I'd like to know whether there's a large print version of your magazine. Please contact me if this is something you offer.'에서 현재 구독하고 있는 잡지의 큰 글자판이 있는지 알고 싶다고 하므로, 글의 목적으로 가장 적절한 것은 ④ '잡지의 큰 글자판이 있는지 문의하려고'이다.

● in regard to ~에 관해서
● subscription ⓝ 구독
● have trouble ~ing ~하는 데 어려움이 있다
● look forward to ~하기를 고대하다
● currently ⓐ 현재
● eyesight ⓝ 시력
● print ⓝ 활자

구문 풀이

5행 Unfortunately, due to my bad eyesight, I have trouble reading your magazine.
~ 때문에　　「have trouble+동명사: ~하는 데 어려움이 있다」

---

19 글쓰기 과제로 칭찬을 받아 기뻐한 필자　　　　　　정답률 83% | 정답 ②

다음 글에 나타난 'I'의 심경 변화로 가장 적절한 것은?

① relieved → scared
　안도한　　겁에 질린
✓② nervous → delighted
　긴장한　　기쁜
③ bored → confident
　지루한　　자신 있는
④ satisfied → depressed
　만족한　　우울한
⑤ confused → ashamed
　혼란스러운　　수치스러운

There was no choice next morning / but to turn in my private reminiscence of Belleville.
다음 날 아침 ~할 수밖에 없었다. / Belleville에 대한 나의 개인적인 회상을 제출할
Two days passed / before Mr. Fleagle returned the graded papers, / and he returned everyone's but mine.
이틀이 흘렀고, / Fleagle 선생님이 채점된 과제들을 돌려주기까지 / 그는 내 것을 제외하고 모든 사람들의 과제를 돌려주었다.
I was anxiously expecting for a command / to report to Mr. Fleagle immediately after school for discipline / when I saw him lift my paper from his desk / and rap for the class's attention.
나는 지시를 초조하게 기다리고 있었다. / 학교 끝나고 즉시 벌을 받으러 Fleagle 선생님에게 오라는 / 그가 책상에서 내 과제를 집어드는 것을 보았을 때 / 그리고 책상을 두드려 학생들의 주의를 끄는 것을

"Now, boys," / he said, / "I want to read you an essay. / This is titled 'The Art of Eating Spaghetti.'"
"자, 여러분," / 그가 말했다. / "나는 여러분에게 글 한 편을 읽어주고 싶습니다. / 이 글의 제목은 '스파게티를 먹는 기술'입니다."
And he started to read.
그리고 그는 읽기 시작했다.
My words!
내 글!
He was reading *my words* out loud / to the entire class.
그는 *내* 글을 소리 내어 읽어주고 있었다. / 우리 반 모두에게
What's more, / the entire class was listening attentively.
더욱이, / 온 학급이 주의 깊게 듣고 있었다.
Then somebody laughed, / then the entire class was laughing, / and not in contempt and ridicule, / but with openhearted enjoyment.
그 후 누군가가 웃었고, / 그러자 온 학급이 웃고 있었다. / 경멸이나 조소가 아니고 / 숨김없는 즐거움으로
I did my best to avoid showing pleasure, / but what I was feeling / was pure ecstasy at this startling demonstration / that my words had the power to make people laugh.
나는 기쁨을 드러내지 않으려고 애를 썼지만, / 내가 느낀 것은 / 이 놀라운 시연에 대한 순수한 환희였다. / 내 글이 사람들을 웃게 만드는 힘을 가졌다는

다음 날 아침 Belleville에 대한 나의 개인적인 회상을 제출할 수밖에 없었다. Fleagle 선생님이 채점된 과제들을 돌려주기까지 이틀이 흘렀고, 그는 내 것을 제외하고 모든 사람들의 과제를 돌려주었다. 그가 책상에서 내 과제를 집어들고 책상을 두드려 학생들의 주의를 끄는 것을 보았을 때, 나는 학교 끝나고 즉시 벌을 받으러 Fleagle 선생님에게 오라는 지시를 초조하게 기다리고 있었다. 그가 말했다. "자, 여러분, 나는 여러분에게 글 한 편을 읽어주고 싶습니다. 이 글의 제목은 '스파게티를 먹는 기술'입니다." 그리고 그는 읽기 시작했다. 내 글! 그는 *내* 글을 우리 반 모두에게 소리 내어 읽어주고 있었다. 더욱이, 온 학급이 주의 깊게 듣고 있었다. 그 후 누군가가 웃었고, 그러자 온 학급이 경멸이나 조소가 아니고, 숨김없는 즐거움으로 웃고 있었다. 나는 기쁨을 드러내지 않으려고 애를 썼지만, 내가 느낀 것은 내 글이 사람들을 웃게 만드는 힘을 가졌다는 이 놀라운 시연에 대한 순수한 환희였다.

Why? 왜 정답일까?

글쓰기 과제를 혼자 돌려받지 못해 초조해하던 필자가(I was anxiously expecting for ~) 선생님이 읽어 주시는 자신의 글을 듣고 모두가 순수하게 웃자 기뻐했다(I did my best to avoid showing pleasure, but what I was feeling was pure ecstasy ~)는 내용의 글이다. 따라서 'I'의 심경 변화로 가장 적절한 것은 ② '긴장한 → 기쁜'이다.

- **there is no choice but** ~할 수밖에 없다
- **command** ⓝ 지시, 명령
- **rap** ⓥ (빠르게) 톡톡 두드리다
- **attentively** ⓐⓓ 주의 깊게
- **ridicule** ⓝ 조롱, 조소
- **anxiously** ⓐⓓ 걱정스럽게, 불안하게
- **discipline** ⓝ 훈육, 징계
- **read out loud** 소리 내어 읽다
- **contempt** ⓝ 경멸
- **openhearted** ⓐ 솔직한, 숨김없는

구문 풀이

4행 I was anxiously expecting for a command to report to Mr. Fleagle immediately after school for discipline when I saw him lift my paper from his desk and rap for the class's attention.
지각동사 ← 목적어 → 원형부정사1
원형부정사2

20 자신을 위한 시간이 필요함을 느끼기 정답률 90% | 정답 ①

다음 글에서 필자가 주장하는 바로 가장 적절한 것은?
✓① 나를 위한 시간의 중요성을 인식해야 한다.
② 자신의 잘못을 성찰하는 자세를 가져야 한다.
③ 어려운 일이라고 해서 처음부터 회피해서는 안 된다.
④ 사회의 건강과 행복을 위하여 타인과 연대해야 한다.
⑤ 급변하는 사회에서 가치 판단을 신속하게 할 수 있어야 한다.

We usually take time out / only when we really need to switch off, / and when this happens / we are often overtired, sick, and in need of recuperation.
우리는 보통 휴식을 취하고, / 우리가 정말로 신경을 꺼야 할 때만 / 이러한 상황이 발생할 때 / 우리는 종종 지나치게 피곤하거나 아프거나 회복해야 한다.
Me time is complicated by negative associations / with escapism, guilt, and regret / as well as overwhelm, stress, and fatigue.
나를 위한 시간은 부정적인 연상에 의해 복잡해진다. / '현실 도피, 죄책감, 후회'와의 / '압도감, 스트레스, 피로감' 뿐만 아니라
All these negative connotations mean / we tend to steer clear of it.
이러한 모든 부정적인 함축은 의미한다. / 우리가 그것을 피하려는 경향이 있음을
Well, / I am about to change your perception of the importance of me time, / to persuade you / that you should view it as vital / for your health and wellbeing.
자 / 나는 이제 나를 위한 시간의 중요성에 관한 당신의 인식을 바꾸고, / 설득하고자 한다. / 당신이 이것을 필수적인 것으로 간주해야 한다고 / 당신의 건강과 행복에
Take this as permission / to set aside some time for yourself!
이것을 허락으로 받아 들여라! / 당신 자신을 위해 일부 시간을 할애하는 것에 대한
Our need for time / in which to do what we choose / is increasingly urgent / in an overconnected, overwhelmed, and overstimulated world.
시간이 필요하다는 것은 / 우리가 선택하는 일을 할 / 점점 절박해지고 있다. / 지나치게 연결되고 압도적이며 지나치게 자극적인 세상에서

우리는 보통 정말로 신경을 꺼야 할 때만 휴식을 취하고, 이러한 상황이 발생할 때 우리는 종종 지나치게 피곤하거나 아프거나 회복해야 한다. 나를 위한 시간은 '압도감, 스트레스, 피로감' 뿐만 아니라 '현실 도피, 죄책감, 후회'와의 부정적인 연상에 의해 복잡해진다. 이러한 모든 부정적인 함축은 우리가 그것을 피하려는 경향이 있음을 의미한다. 나는 이제 나를 위한 시간의 중요성에 관한 당신의 인식을 바꾸고, 당신이 이것을 건강과 행복에 필수적인 것으로 간주해야 한다고 설득하고자 한다. 이것을 당신 자신을 위해 일부 시간을 할애하는 것에 대한 허락으로 받아 들여라! 우리가 선택하는 일을 할 시간이 필요하다는 것은 지나치게 연결되고 압도적이며 지나치게 자극적인 세상에서 점점 절박해지고 있다.

Why? 왜 정답일까?

'Well, I am about to change your perception of the importance of me time, to

---

persuade you that you should view it as vital for your health and wellbeing.' 이후로 자신을 위한 시간이 부정적인 것이 아니라 건강과 행복에 실로 중요한 요소임을 깨달아야 한다는 내용이 이어지고 있다. 따라서 필자가 주장하는 바로 가장 적절한 것은 ① '나를 위한 시간의 중요성을 인식해야 한다.'이다.

- **time out** (경기의) 타임 아웃, 휴식
- **overtired** ⓐ 지나치게 피곤한
- **escapism** ⓝ 현실 도피
- **regret** ⓝ 후회, 유감
- **set aside** ~을 따로 두다, 마련하다
- **switch off** (신경을) 끄다
- **complicated** ⓐ 복잡한
- **guilt** ⓝ 죄책감
- **steer clear of** ~을 피하다, 가까이 가지 않다
- **overstimulate** ⓥ 과도하게 자극하다

구문 풀이

9행 Our need for time in which to do what we choose is increasingly urgent
주어 = when 동사(단수)
in an overconnected, overwhelmed, and overstimulated world.

21 침묵 효과가 발생하는 이유 정답률 69% | 정답 ⑤

밑줄 친 the innocent messenger who falls before a firing line이 다음 글에서 의미하는 바로 가장 적절한 것은? [3점]
① the employee being criticized for being silent
침묵해서 비난당하는 직원
② the peacemaker who pursues non-violent solutions
비폭력적 해결책을 추구하는 중재자
③ the negotiator who looks for a mutual understanding
상호 이해를 탐색하는 협상가
④ the subordinate who wants to get attention from the boss
상사에게 관심을 얻으려는 부하직원
✓⑤ the person who gets the blame for reporting unpleasant news
불쾌한 소식을 전했다고 비난받는 사람

Perhaps worse / than attempting to get the bad news out of the way / is / attempting to soften it or simply not address it at all.
아마도 더 나쁜 것은 / 나쁜 소식부터 처리하고 넘어가려고 하는 것보다 / ~이다. / 그것을 부드럽게 말하거나 전혀 다루지 않으려고 하는 것
This "Mum Effect" / — a term coined by psychologists Sidney Rosen and Abraham Tesser in the early 1970s — / happens / because people want to avoid / becoming the target of others' negative emotions.
이 '침묵 효과'는 / 1970년대 초반에 심리학자인 Sidney Rosen과 Abraham Tesser가 만든 용어인 / 발생한다. / 사람들이 피하고 싶기 때문에 / 다른 사람들의 부정적인 감정의 표적이 되는 것
We all have the opportunity to lead change, / yet it often requires of us the courage / to deliver bad news to our superiors.
우리 모두는 변화를 이끌 기회를 가지고 있으나, / 그것은 종종 우리에게서 용기를 필요로 한다. / 우리의 상사에게 나쁜 소식을 전달하기 위한
We don't want to be the innocent messenger / who falls before a firing line.
우리는 무고한 전령이 되고 싶어 하지는 않는다. / 사선 앞에서 쓰러지는
When our survival instincts kick in, / they can override our courage / until the truth of a situation gets watered down.
우리의 생존 본능이 발동하면, / 이것은 우리의 용기를 무효화시킬 수 있다. / 어떤 상황의 진상이 희석될 때까지
"The Mum Effect and the resulting filtering / can have devastating effects in a steep hierarchy," / writes Robert Sutton, / an organizational psychologist.
"침묵 효과와 그로 인해 발생하는 필터링은 / 가파른 위계 관계에서 파괴적인 결과를 가져올 수 있다"라고 / Robert Sutton은 말한다. / 조직 심리학자인
"What starts out as bad news / becomes happier and happier / as it travels up the ranks / — because after each boss hears the news from his or her subordinates, / he or she makes it sound a bit less bad / before passing it up the chain."
"나쁜 소식으로 시작한 것이 / 점점 좋아진다. / 그것이 단계를 올라갈수록 / 그 이유는 각 단계의 상사가 자기 부하 직원으로부터 그 소식을 듣고 나서 / 그 사람은 그것이 다소 덜 나쁘게 들리도록 만들기 때문이다. / 그것을 다음 단계로 올려 보내기 전에"

나쁜 소식부터 처리하고 넘어가려고 하는 것보다 아마도 더 나쁜 것은 그것을 부드럽게 말하거나 전혀 다루지 않으려고 하는 것이다. 1970년대 초반에 심리학자인 Sidney Rosen과 Abraham Tesser가 만든 용어인 이 '침묵 효과'는 사람들이 다른 사람들의 부정적인 감정의 표적이 되는 것을 피하고 싶기 때문에 발생한다. 우리 모두는 변화를 이끌 기회를 가지고 있으나, 그것은 종종 우리의 상사에게 나쁜 소식을 전달하기 위한 용기를 필요로 한다. 우리는 사선 앞에서 쓰러지는 무고한 전령이 되고 싶어 하지는 않는다. 우리의 생존 본능이 발동하면, 이것은 어떤 상황의 진상이 희석될 때까지 우리의 용기를 무효화시킬 수 있다. "침묵 효과와 그로 인해 발생하는 (언어) 필터링은 가파른 위계 관계에서 파괴적인 결과를 가져올 수 있다"라고 조직 심리학자 Robert Sutton은 말한다. "나쁜 소식으로 시작한 것이 단계를 올라갈수록 점점 좋아진다. 그 이유는 각 단계의 상사가 자기 부하직원으로부터 그 소식을 듣고 나서 다음 단계로 올려 보내기 전에 그것을 다소 덜 나쁘게 들리도록 만들기 때문이다."

Why? 왜 정답일까?

사람들은 타인의 부정적 감정에 희생되고 싶어 하지 않으며(people want to avoid becoming the target of others' negative emotions), 생존하겠다는 본능 때문에 나쁜 소식을 전해야만 하는 상황에서 용기가 수그러든다(our survival instincts ~ can override our courage until the truth of a situation gets watered down.)는 내용으로 보아, 우리가 되고 싶지 않은 모습을 묘사하는 밑줄 친 부분의 의미로 가장 적절한 것은 ⑤ '불쾌한 소식을 전했다고 비난받는 사람'이다.

- **out of the way** 처리된, 끝난
- **superior** ⓝ 상사, 윗사람 ⓐ 상위의, 우등한
- **kick in** 효과가 나타나다
- **water down** (물로) 희석하다
- **hierarchy** ⓝ 위계질서
- **mutual** ⓐ 서로의, 상호의
- **mum** ⓝ 침묵 ⓐ 잠자코 있는
- **firing line** (화기가 발사되는) 사선, 방화선
- **override** ⓥ 중단시키다
- **devastating** ⓐ 파괴적인
- **subordinate** ⓝ 부하직원

구문 풀이

1행 Perhaps worse than attempting to get the bad news out of the way
보어(비교급 형용사)+
is attempting to soften it or simply not address it at all.
동사+주어 : 도치 구문

22 부모 본인의 평정심 유지하기
정답률 77% | 정답 ②

다음 글의 요지로 가장 적절한 것은?
① 자녀의 행동 변화를 위해 부모의 즉각적인 반응이 필요하다.
② 부모의 내적 성장을 통한 평정심 유지가 양육에 중요하다.
③ 부모는 자녀가 감정을 다스릴 수 있게 도와주어야 한다.
④ 부모와 자녀는 건설적인 의견을 나눌 수 있어야 한다.
⑤ 바람직한 양육은 자녀에게 모범을 보이는 것이다.

Most parents think / that if our child would just "behave," / we could stay calm as parents.
대부분의 부모은 생각한다. / 자녀가 그저 '잘 행동하면' / 우리가 부모로서 침착함을 유지할 수 있다고

The truth is / that managing our own emotions and actions / is what allows us to feel peaceful as parents.
진실은 ~이다. / 감정과 행동을 관리하는 것이 / 우리가 부모로서 평안함을 느끼도록 해준다는 것

Ultimately / we can't control our children or the obstacles they will face / — but we can always control our own actions.
궁극적으로 / 우리는 우리의 자녀나 그들이 마주할 장애물을 통제할 수는 없다 / 하지만 우리는 항상 우리 자신의 행동을 통제할 수 있다.

Parenting isn't about what our child does, / but about how we respond.
양육은 우리 자녀가 무엇을 하는지에 대한 것이 아니라 / 우리가 어떻게 반응하는지에 대한 것이다.

In fact, / most of what we call parenting / doesn't take place between a parent and child / but within the parent.
사실, / 우리가 양육이라고 부르는 것의 대부분은 / 부모와 자녀 사이에서 발생하는 것이 아니라 / 부모 안에서 발생하는 것이다.

When a storm brews, / a parent's response will either calm it / or trigger a full-scale tsunami.
폭풍이 일어나려고 할 때, / 부모의 반응은 그것을 잠재우거나 / 아니면 최대치의 해일을 유발할 것이다.

Staying calm enough / to respond constructively to all that childish behavior / — and the stormy emotions behind it — / requires that we grow, too.
충분히 침착함을 유지하는 것은 / 그 모든 아이 같은 행동에 건설적으로 반응할 수 있을 만큼 / 그리고 그 이면의 폭풍 같은 감정 / 우리에게도 성장을 요구한다.

If we can use those times when our buttons get pushed to reflect, / not just react, / we can notice when we lose equilibrium / and steer ourselves back on track.
만약 우리가 우리 버튼이 눌리는 그런 순간을 성찰하기 위해 이용할 수 있다면, / 그저 반응하는 목적이 아니라 / 우리는 우리가 언제 평정심을 잃는지 알아차릴 수 있고 / 다시 제자리로 돌아갈 수 있다.

This inner growth is the hardest work there is, / but it's what enables you to become a more peaceful parent, / one day at a time.
이러한 내면의 성장이 세상에서 가장 힘든 일이지만, / 그것은 당신이 더욱 평안한 부모가 될 수 있도록 해주는 것이다. / 하루하루

대부분의 부모들은 자녀가 그저 '잘 행동하면' 부모로서 침착함을 유지할 수 있다고 생각한다. 진실은 우리가 감정과 행동을 관리하는 것이 부모로서 평안함을 느끼도록 해준다는 것이다. 궁극적으로 우리는 우리의 자녀나 그들이 마주할 장애물을 통제할 수는 없지만, 항상 우리 자신의 행동을 통제할 수 있다. 양육은 우리 자녀가 무엇을 하는지에 대한 것이 아니라 우리가 어떻게 반응하는지에 대한 것이다. 사실, 우리가 양육이라고 부르는 것의 대부분은 부모와 자녀 사이가 아니라 부모 안에서 발생한다. 폭풍이 일어나려고 할 때, 부모의 반응은 그것을 잠재우거나, 아니면 최대치의 해일을 유발할 것이다. 그 모든 아이 같은 행동—그리고 그 이면의 폭풍 같은 감정—에 건설적으로 반응할 수 있을 만큼 침착함을 유지하는 것은 우리에게도 성장을 요구한다. 만약 우리 버튼이 눌리는 그런 순간을 그저 반응하는 목적이 아니라 성찰하는 데 이용할 수 있다면, 우리는 우리가 언제 평정심을 잃는지 알아차릴 수 있고 다시 제자리로 돌아갈 수 있다. 이러한 내면의 성장이 세상에서 가장 힘든 일이지만, 그것은 당신이 하루하루 더욱 평안한 부모가 될 수 있도록 해주는 것이다.

Why? 왜 정답일까?
부모가 평정심을 유지하려면 자녀의 행동이나 반응보다는, 자기 자신의 감정과 행동을 관리하는 데 노력을 들일 필요가 있으며(The truth is that managing our own emotions and actions is what allows us to feel peaceful as parents.), 이러한 내적 성장이 더 좋은 부모가 되도록 이끌어준다(This inner growth is ~ what enables you to become a more peaceful parent, one day at a time.)는 내용의 글이다. 따라서 글의 요지로 가장 적절한 것은 ② '부모의 내적 성장을 통한 평정심 유지가 양육에 중요하다.'이다.

- **obstacle** ⓝ 장애물
- **brew** ⓥ (불쾌한 일이 일어나려고) 태동하다. (차가) 끓다
- **constructively** ⓐⓓ 건설적으로
- **equilibrium** ⓝ 평정, 균형
- **back on track** 정상 궤도로 돌아온
- **parenting** ⓝ 양육
- **childish** ⓐ 유치한
- **steer** ⓥ 조종하다

구문 풀이
9행 Staying calm enough to respond constructively to all that childish behavior — (and the stormy emotions behind it) — requires that we (should) grow, too.
(동명사 주어 / 삽입구 / 동사(단수) / 생략)

23 학습에 도움을 주는 잠
정답률 78% | 정답 ②

다음 글의 주제로 가장 적절한 것은?
① how to get an adequate amount of sleep
적절한 양의 수면을 취하는 방법
② the role that sleep plays in the learning process
잠이 학습 과정에 수행하는 역할
③ a new method of stimulating engagement in learning
학습 참여를 촉진하는 새로운 방법
④ an effective way to keep your mind alert and active
정신을 초롱초롱하고 활동적으로 유지하는 효과적인 방법
⑤ the side effects of certain medications on brain function
특정 약물이 뇌 기능에 끼치는 부작용

We have already seen / that learning is much more efficient / when done at regular intervals: / rather than cramming an entire lesson into one day, / we are better off spreading out the learning.
우리는 이미 보았다. / 학습이 훨씬 더 효율적이라는 것을 / 규칙적인 간격으로 이뤄질 때 / 즉, 모든 과업을 하루에 밀어 넣기보다 / 우리는 그 과업을 분산하는 것이 더 좋다.

The reason is simple: / every night, / our brain consolidates / what it has learned during the day.
그 이유는 간단한데. / 매일 밤 / 우리의 뇌는 통합 정리하기 때문이다. / 뇌가 그날 학습한 것을

This is / one of the most important neuroscience discoveries of the last thirty years: / sleep is not just a period of inactivity / or a garbage collection of the waste products / that the brain accumulated while we were awake.
이것은 ~이다. / 지난 30년 동안 이뤄진 가장 중요한 신경과학 발견들 중 하나 / 잠은 단순한 비활동이 아니라는 것 / 혹은 쓸모없는 생산물들의 쓰레기 수집 기간이 / 우리가 깨어있는 동안 뇌가 축적한

Quite the contrary: / while we sleep, our brain remains active; / it runs a specific algorithm / that replays the important events / it recorded during the previous day / and gradually transfers them into a more efficient compartment of our memory.
정반대로, / 우리가 자는 동안 우리의 뇌는 활동적인 상태를 유지하며, / 그것은 특별한 알고리듬을 가동한다. / 중요한 사건들을 재상영하고 / 그것이 전날 하루 동안 기록한 / 그것을 우리 기억의 더 효율적인 구획으로 점진적으로 이동시키는

우리는 학습이 규칙적인 간격으로 이뤄질 때 훨씬 더 효율적이라는 것을 이미 보았다. 즉, 모든 과업을 하루에 밀어 넣기보다 그 과업을 분산하는 것이 더 좋다. 그 이유는 간단한데, 매일 밤 우리의 뇌는 그날 학습한 것을 통합 정리하기 때문이다. 이것은 지난 30년 동안 이뤄진 가장 중요한 신경과학 발견들 중 하나로, 잠은 단순한 비활동이나 우리가 깨어있는 동안 뇌가 축적하는 쓸모없는 생산물들의 쓰레기 수집 기간이 아니라는 것이다. 정반대로, 우리가 자는 동안 우리의 뇌는 활동적인 상태를 유지하며, 전날 하루 동안 기록한 중요한 사건들을 재상영하고 그것을 우리 기억의 더 효율적인 구획으로 점진적으로 이동시키는 특별한 알고리듬을 가동한다.

Why? 왜 정답일까?
우리가 자는 동안 뇌가 오히려 활성화 상태를 유지하여 그날 배운 것을 정리하고 조직화하는 과정이 이뤄진다(Quite the contrary: while we sleep, our brain remains active; it runs a specific algorithm ~)는 마지막 문장 내용으로 보아, 글의 주제로 가장 적절한 것은 ② '잠이 학습 과정에 수행하는 역할'이다.

- **interval** ⓝ 간격
- **well off** 잘 사는, 사정이 좋은
- **inactivity** ⓝ 비활동
- **quite the contrary** 그와는 정반대이다
- **compartment** ⓝ 구획
- **cram** ⓥ 밀어 넣다, 벼락치기하다
- **spread out** 펼쳐놓다
- **accumulate** ⓥ 축적하다, 모으다
- **gradually** ⓐⓓ 점진적으로, 점차
- **side effect** 부작용

구문 풀이
1행 We have already seen that learning is much more efficient when (it is) done at regular intervals: ~
(비교급 강조(훨씬) / 접속사 / 생략 / 과거분사)

24 병원 치료만큼이나 중요한 예방적 공공 보건 서비스
정답률 50% | 정답 ①

다음 글의 제목으로 가장 적절한 것은? [3점]
① Public Healthcare: A Co-Star, Not a Supporting Actor
공공 보건 서비스: 조연이 아닌 공동 주연
② The Historical Development of Medicine and Surgery
의학과 수술의 역사적 발달
③ Clinical Care Controversies: What You Don't Know
병원 치료의 논란: 여러분이 모르는 것
④ The Massive Similarities Between Different Mythologies
다양한 신화 간의 엄청나게 큰 유사성
⑤ Initiatives Opening up Health Innovation Around the World
전 세계 보건 혁신을 가능케 하는 계획

From the earliest times, / healthcare services have been recognized to have two equal aspects, / namely clinical care and public healthcare.
가장 초기의 시대부터. / 의료 서비스는 두 가지의 동등한 영역을 포함하는 것으로 인식되어 왔다. / 즉 병원 치료와 공공 보건

In classical Greek mythology, / the god of medicine, Asklepios, / had two daughters, / Hygiea and Panacea.
고대 그리스 신화에서 / 의료의 신 아스클레피오스는 / 두 딸을 두었다. / 하이지아와 파나시아라는

The former was the goddess of preventive health and wellness, or hygiene, / and the latter the goddess of treatment and curing.
전자는 예방적 건강과 건강 관리, 즉 위생의 여신이었고, / 후자는 치료와 치유의 여신이었다.

In modern times, / the societal ascendancy of medical professionalism / has caused treatment of sick patients / to overshadow those preventive healthcare services / provided by the less heroic figures of sanitary engineers, biologists, and governmental public health officers.
현대 시대에. / 의료 전문성에 대한 사회적 우세는 / 아픈 환자들의 치료를 ~하게 만들었다. / 그러한 예방적 보건 서비스가 빛을 잃게 / 위생 공학자, 생물학자, 정부 공공 건강 관료와 같은 덜 영웅적인 인물들에 의해서 제공되는

Nevertheless, / the quality of health / that human populations enjoy / is attributable / less to surgical dexterity, innovative pharmaceutical products, and bioengineered devices / than to the availability of public sanitation, sewage management, and services / which control the pollution of the air, drinking water, urban noise, and food for human consumption.
그럼에도 불구하고, / 건강의 질은 / 인류가 향유하는 / 바탕을 둔다. / 수술적 기민함, 혁신적 제약 제품, 그리고 생물 공학적 장비에 덜 / 공공 위생, 하수 관리, 그리고 서비스들의 이용 가능성에 비해 / 대기 오염, 식수, 도시 소음, 인간이 소비하는 음식을 관리하는

The human right to the highest attainable standard of health / depends on public healthcare services / no less than on the skills and equipment of doctors and hospitals.
달성 가능한 최고 수준의 건강에 대한 인간의 권리는 / 공공 보건 서비스에 달려 있다. / 의사와 병원의 기술과 장비 못지않게

가장 초기의 시대부터, 의료 서비스는 두 가지의 동등한 영역, 즉 병원 치료와 공공 보건을 포함하는 것으로 인식되어 왔다. 고대 그리스 신화에서 의료의 신 아스클레피오스에게는 하이지아와 파나시아라는 두 딸이 있었다. 전자는 예방적 건강과 건강 관리, 즉 위생의 여신이었고, 후자는 치료와 치유의 여신이었다. 현대 시대에, 의료 전문성에 대한 사회적 우세는 아픈 환자들의 치료로 인해 위생 공학자, 생물학자, 정부 공공 건강 관료와 같은 덜 영웅적인 인물들에 의해서 제공되는 그러한 예방적 보건 서비스가 빛을 잃게 만들었다. 그럼에도 불구하고, 인류가 향유하는 건강의 질은 공공 위생, 하수 관리, 그리고 대기 오염, 식수, 도시 소음, 인간이 소비하는 음식을 관리하는 서비스들의 이용 가능성에 비해 수술적 기민함, 혁신적 제약 제품, 그리고 생물 공학적 장비에 덜 바탕을 둔다. 달성 가능한 최고 수준의 건강에 대한 인간의 권리는 의사와 병원의 기술과 장비 못지않게 공공 보건 서비스에 달려 있다.

건강 수준을 높이기 위해서는 병원 치료뿐 아니라 위생과 관련된 예방적 공공 보건 서비스도 중요한 역할을 한다(The human right to the highest attainable standard of health depends on public healthcare services no less than on the skills and equipment of doctors and hospitals.)고 하므로, 글의 제목으로 가장 적절한 것은 ① '공공 보건 서비스: 조연이 아니라 공동 주연'이다.

- healthcare service 공공 보건 서비스
- mythology ⓝ 신화
- wellness ⓝ 건강
- overshadow ⓥ 빛을 잃게 하다, 가리다
- be attributable to ~에 기인하다
- pharmaceutical ⓐ 약학의
- attainable ⓐ 달성 가능한
- co-star ⓝ 공동 주연 ⓥ 공동 주연을 맡다

- clinical care 임상 진료
- preventive ⓐ 예방적인
- hygiene ⓝ 위생
- heroic ⓐ 영웅적인
- surgical ⓐ 수술적인
- sewage ⓝ 오물
- no less than ~에 못지 않게

구문 풀이

1행 From the earliest times, healthcare services have been recognized to
기간 부사구 / 현재완료 수동태
have two equal aspects, namely clinical care and public healthcare.

---

25 OECD 회원국들의 부문별 원유 수요 정답률 87% | 정답 ③

다음 도표의 내용과 일치하지 <u>않는</u> 것은?

Distribution of oil demand in the OECD in 2020, by sector

- Electricity generation 3%
- Rail & domestic waterways 1.8%
- Marine bunkers 3.6%
- Aviation 4.4%
- Residential / commercial / agricultural 9.8%
- Other industry 12.6%
- Petrochemicals 16.2%
- Road transportation 48.6%

The above graph shows / the distribution of oil demand by sector / in the OECD in 2020.
위 그래프는 보여준다. / 원유 수요에 따른 부문별 분포를 / 2020년 OECD에서의

① The Road transportation sector, / which took up 48.6%, / was the greatest oil demanding sector / in the OECD member states.
도로 교통 부문은 / 48.6%를 차지한 / 가장 큰 원유 수요 부문이었다. / OECD 회원국들에서

② The percentage of oil demand in the Petrochemicals sector / was one-third that of the Road transportation sector.
석유화학 부문의 원유 수요 비율은 / 도로 교통 부문의 원유 수요 비율의 3분의 1이었다.

✔ The difference in oil demand / between the Other industry sector and the Petrochemicals sector / was smaller / than the difference in oil demand / between the Aviation sector and the Electricity generation sector.
원유 수요 차이는 / 기타 산업 부문과 석유화학 부문 사이의 / 더 작았다. / 원유 수요 차이보다 / 항공 부문과 전기 생성 부문 사이의

④ The oil demand in the Residential, commercial and agricultural sector / took up 9.8% of all oil demand in the OECD, / which was the fourth largest among all the sectors.
주거, 상업, 그리고 농업 부문의 원유 수요는 / OECD의 총 원유 수요의 9.8%를 차지했는데, / 이는 전체 부문 중 네 번째로 컸다.

⑤ The percentage of oil demand in the Marine bunkers sector / was twice that of the oil demand in the Rail & domestic waterways sector.
해상 벙커 부문의 원유 수요 비율은 / 철도와 국내 수로 부문의 원유 수요 비율의 두 배였다.

위 그래프는 2020년 OECD에서의 원유 수요에 따른 부문별 분포를 보여준다. ① 48.6%를 차지한 도로 교통 부문은 OECD 회원국들에서 가장 큰 원유 수요 부문이었다. ② 석유화학 부문의 원유 수요 비율은 도로 교통 부문의 원유 수요 비율의 3분의 1이었다. ③ 기타 산업 부문과 석유화학 부문 사이의 원유 수요 차이는 항공 부문과 전기 생성 부문 사이의 원유 수요 차이보다 작았다. ④ 주거, 상업, 그리고 농업 부문의 원유 수요는 OECD의 총 원유 수요의 9.8%를 차지했는데, 이는 전체 부문 중 네 번째로 컸다. ⑤ 해상 벙커 부문의 원유 수요 비율은 철도와 국내 수로 부문의 원유 수요 비율의 두 배였다.

Why? 왜 정답일까?

도표에 따르면 기타 산업과 석유화학 부문은 3.6%만큼, 항공 부문과 전기 생성 부문은 1.4%만큼 차이가 난다. 즉 기타 산업 부문과 석유화학 부문 사이의 차이가 더 크므로, 도표의 내용과 일치하지 않는 것은 ③이다.

- distribution ⓝ 분배, 분포
- take up ~을 차지하다
- aviation ⓝ 항공
- domestic ⓐ 국내의, 가정의
- sector ⓝ 부문, 분야
- petrochemical ⓐ 석유화학의
- residential ⓐ 거주의, 주거의

구문 풀이

5행 The difference (in oil demand) (between the Other industry sector and the
주어
Petrochemicals sector) was smaller than the difference (in oil demand) (between
동사(단수) '비교급 + than ~보다 더 …한'
the Aviation sector and the Electricity generation sector).

---

26 Carl-Gustaf Rossby의 생애 정답률 90% | 정답 ⑤

Carl-Gustaf Rossby에 관한 다음 글의 내용과 일치하지 <u>않는</u> 것은?
① Stockholm에서 성장하면서 전통적인 교육을 받았다.
② University of Stockholm에서 수리 물리학 학위를 받았다.

③ 1925년에 장학금을 받았다.
④ polar front theory를 지지했다.
✔ University of Stockholm에 마련된 직책을 거절했다.

Carl-Gustaf Rossby was one of a group of notable Scandinavian researchers / who worked with the Norwegian meteorologist Vilhelm Bjerknes / at the University of Bergen.
Carl-Gustaf Rossby는 저명한 스칸디나비아 연구자들 중 한 명이었다. / 노르웨이 기상학자인 Vilhelm Bjerknes와 함께 일했던 / Bergen 대학에서

「While growing up in Stockholm, / Rossby received a traditional education.」 ①의 근거 일치
Stockholm에서 성장하면서, / Rossby는 전통적인 교육을 받았다.

「He earned a degree in mathematical physics / at the University of Stockholm in 1918,」 / ②의 근거 일치
but after hearing a lecture by Bjerknes, / and apparently bored with Stockholm, / he moved to the newly established Geophysical Institute in Bergen.
그는 수리 물리학 학위를 받았지만, / 1918년에 University of Stockholm에서 / Bjerknes의 강의를 듣고 나서 / 그리고 아마도 Stockholm에 대한 지루함 때문에 / 그는 Bergen에 새로 설립된 지구 물리학 연구소로 옮겼다.

「In 1925, / Rossby received a scholarship from the Sweden-America Foundation / to go to the United States, / where he joined the United States Weather Bureau.」 ③의 근거 일치
1925년에 / Rossby는 스웨덴-미국 재단으로부터 장학금을 받아 / 미국으로 갔고, / 그곳에서 그는 미국 기상국에 입사했다.

Based in part on his practical experience in weather forecasting, / 「Rossby had become a supporter of the "polar front theory," / which explains the cyclonic circulation / that develops at the boundary between warm and cold air masses.」 ④의 근거 일치
일기 예보에 대한 그의 실질적인 경험을 일부 바탕으로 하여, / Rossby는 'polar front theory'의 지지자가 되었다. / 사이클론 순환을 설명하는 / 고온 기단과 저온 기단 사이의 경계에서 발생하는

「In 1947, / Rossby accepted the chair of the Institute of Meteorology, / which had been set up for him at the University of Stockholm, / where he remained until his death ten years later.」 ⑤의 근거 불일치
1947년에 / Rossby는 기상 연구소장 직책을 받아들였고, / University of Stockholm에 자신을 위해 마련된 / 그곳에서 그는 10년 후 생을 마감할 때까지 재직했다.

Carl-Gustaf Rossby는 Bergen 대학에서 노르웨이 기상학자인 Vilhelm Bjerknes와 함께 일했던 저명한 스칸디나비아 연구자들 중 한 명이었다. Stockholm에서 성장하면서, Rossby는 전통적인 교육을 받았다. 그는 1918년에 University of Stockholm에서 수리 물리학 학위를 받았지만, Bjerknes의 강의를 듣고 나서 아마도 Stockholm에 대한 지루함 때문에 Bergen에 새로 설립된 지구 물리학 연구소로 옮겼다. 1925년에 Rossby는 스웨덴-미국 재단으로부터 장학금을 받아 미국으로 갔고, 그곳에서 미국 기상국에 입사했다. 일기 예보에 대한 그의 실질적인 경험을 일부 바탕으로 하여, Rossby는 고온 기단과 저온 기단 사이의 경계에서 발생하는 사이클론 순환을 설명하는 'polar front theory'의 지지자가 되었다. 1947년에 Rossby는 University of Stockholm에 자신을 위해 마련된 기상 연구소장 직책을 받아들였고, 그곳에서 10년 후 생을 마감할 때까지 재직했다.

Why? 왜 정답일까?

'In 1947, Rossby accepted the chair of the Institute of Meteorology, which had been set up for him at the University of Stockholm, ~'에 따르면 Carl-Gustaf Rossby는 University of Stockholm에 마련된 기상 연구소장 직책을 수락했고, 여기서 사망할 때까지 재직했다고 한다. 따라서 내용과 일치하지 않는 것은 ⑤ 'University of Stockholm에 마련된 직책을 거절했다.'이다.

Why? 왜 오답일까?

① 'While growing up in Stockholm, Rossby received a traditional education.'의 내용과 일치한다.
② 'He earned a degree in mathematical physics at the University of Stockholm in 1918, ~'의 내용과 일치한다.
③ 'In 1925, Rossby received a scholarship ~'의 내용과 일치한다.
④ '~ Rossby had become a supporter of the "polar front theory," ~'의 내용과 일치한다.

- notable ⓐ 저명한
- earn a degree 학위를 받다
- in part 부분적으로
- weather forecasting 기상 예보
- circulation ⓝ 순환
- meteorologist ⓝ 기상학자
- receive a scholarship 장학금을 받다
- practical ⓐ 실질적인, 현실적인
- cyclonic ⓐ 사이클론의, 격렬한

구문 풀이

10행 Based in part on his practical experience in weather forecasting, Rossby
분사구문 주어
had become a supporter of the "polar front theory," which explains the cyclonic
선행사 계속적 용법
circulation [that develops at the boundary between warm and cold air masses].

---

27 멸종 위기 동물을 돕기 위한 자선 경주 행사 정답률 96% | 정답 ④

The Colchester Zoo Charity Race에 관한 다음 안내문의 내용과 일치하지 <u>않는</u> 것은?

① 2시간 동안 진행된다.
② 등록비에는 음식과 음료가 포함된다.
③ 코스 길이는 10km이다.
✔ 모든 참가자는 메달을 받는다.
⑤ 행사 티셔츠는 동물원에서 구입할 수 있다.

The Colchester Zoo Charity Race
The Colchester Zoo Charity Race(Colchester 동물원 자선 경주)

Join us for a charity event to help endangered species.
멸종 위기종을 돕기 위한 자선 행사에 참여하세요.

You will be running through Colchester Zoo, / home to over 260 species!
당신은 Colchester 동물원을 통과하여 달릴 것입니다! / 260종 이상의 서식지인

Date: Sunday, Sep. 25th, 2022
날짜: 2022년 9월 25일 일요일

「Time: 9:00 a.m. – 11:00 a.m.」 ①의 근거 일치
시간: 오전 9시 – 오전 11시

Registration Fee: $50
등록비: 50달러

『Registration fee includes / a free pass to the zoo, / food and drinks, / and official photos.』②의 근거 일치
등록비는 포함합니다. / 동물원 무료 입장권, / 음식과 음료, / 그리고 공식 사진을
Register at www.info.colchesters.com.
www.info.colchesters.com에서 등록하세요.
『Course Length: 10km』③의 근거 일치
코스 길이: 10km
Every runner will run 1km of the race through the zoo / before going out to the main road.
모든 주자는 동물원을 통과하여 1km를 달립니다. / 주 도로로 나가기 전에
Other Information
기타 정보
『Only the runners who complete the race / will receive a medal at the finish line.』④의 근거 불일치
오직 경주를 완주한 주자만 / 결승선에서 메달을 받을 것입니다.
『Event T-shirts can be purchased at the zoo.』⑤의 근거 일치
행사 티셔츠는 동물원에서 구입할 수 있습니다.

The Colchester Zoo Charity Race
(Colchester 동물원 자선 경주)

멸종 위기종을 돕기 위한 자선 행사에 참여하세요. 당신은 260종 이상의 서식지인 Colchester 동물원을 통과하여 달릴 것입니다.

날짜: 2022년 9월 25일 일요일

시간: 오전 9시 – 오전 11시

등록비: 50달러
• 등록비에는 동물원 무료 입장권, 음식과 음료, 그리고 공식 사진이 포함되어 있습니다.
• www.info.colchesters.com에서 등록하세요.

코스 길이: 10km
• 모든 주자는 동물원을 통과하여 1km를 달린 후 주 도로로 나갑니다.

기타 정보
• 오직 경주를 완주한 주자만 결승선에서 메달을 받을 것입니다.
• 행사 티셔츠는 동물원에서 구입할 수 있습니다.

Why? 왜 정답일까?

'Only the runners who complete the race will receive a medal at the finish line.'에서 경주를 완주한 참가자만 메달을 받는다고 하므로, 안내문의 내용과 일치하지 않는 것은 ④ '모든 참가자는 메달을 받는다.'이다.

Why? 왜 오답일까?

① 'Time: 9:00 a.m. – 11:00 a.m.'의 내용과 일치한다.
② 'Registration fee includes a free pass to the zoo, food and drinks, and official photos.'의 내용과 일치한다.
③ 'Course Length: 10km'의 내용과 일치한다.
⑤ 'Event T-shirts can be purchased at the zoo.'의 내용과 일치한다.

● charity event 자선 행사
● species ⓝ (생물) 종
● finish line 결승선
● endangered ⓐ 멸종 위기에 처한
● official ⓐ 공식적인

28 문학적 글쓰기 대회 　　　　　정답률 86% | 정답 ②

7-Day Story Writing Competition에 관한 다음 안내문의 내용과 일치하는 것은?

① 17세 미만 누구나 참여할 수 있다.
☑ 참가자들은 동일한 주제에 대하여 글을 쓴다.
③ 참가자들은 12가지 문학 장르 중 하나를 선택할 수 있다.
④ 1인당 출품작을 최대 3편까지 제출할 수 있다.
⑤ 결승 진출자 전원에게 상금이 수여된다.

7-Day Story Writing Competition
7-Day Story Writing Competition(7일 이야기 글짓기 대회)
Is writing your talent?
글쓰기가 당신의 재능인가요?
This is the stage for you.
여기 당신을 위한 무대가 있습니다.
When: From Monday, Dec. 5th to Sunday, Dec. 11th, 2022
날짜: 2022년 12월 5일 월요일부터 12월 11일 일요일까지
『Age: 17 and over』①의 근거 불일치
연령: 17세 이상
Content
내용
『All participants will write about the same topic.』②의 근거 일치
모든 참가자들은 동일한 주제에 대하여 글을 씁니다.
『You will be randomly assigned / one of 12 literary genres for your story.』③의 근거 불일치
당신은 무작위로 12가지 문학 장르 중 하나를
You'll have exactly 7 days / to write and submit your story.
여러분에게는 정확히 7일이 있습니다. / 이야기를 작성하고 제출하기 위한
Submission
제출
『Only one entry per person』④의 근거 불일치
1인당 한 출품작만 가능
You can revise and resubmit your entry / until the deadline.
당신은 출품작을 수정하여 다시 제출할 수 있습니다. / 마감 기한까지
Prize
시상
We will choose 12 finalists, one from each genre, / and the 12 entries will be published online and shared via social media.
각 장르에서 한 명씩 12명의 결승 진출자를 선발할 것이고, / 12편의 작품들은 온라인으로 출판되며 소셜 미디어를 통해 공유됩니다.
『From the 12 finalists, / one overall winner will be chosen and awarded $500.』⑤의 근거 불일치
12명의 결승 진출자 중에서 / 한 명의 전체 우승자가 선발되어, 500달러를 받을 것입니다.

To register and for more information, / visit our website at www.7challenge_globestory.com.
등록하거나 더 많은 정보를 보시려면, / www.7challenge_globestory.com에 방문하세요.

7-Day Story Writing Competition
(7일 이야기 글짓기 대회)

글쓰기가 당신의 재능인가요? 여기 당신을 위한 무대가 있습니다.

날짜: 2022년 12월 5일 월요일부터 12월 11일 일요일까지

연령: 17세 이상

내용
• 모든 참가자들은 동일한 주제에 대하여 글을 씁니다.
• 당신은 12가지 문학 장르 중 하나를 무작위로 배정받습니다.
• 이야기를 작성하고 제출하는 데 정확히 7일이 주어집니다.

제출
• 1인당 한 출품작만 가능
• 당신은 마감 기한까지 출품작을 수정하여 다시 제출할 수 있습니다.

시상
• 각 장르에서 한 명씩 12명의 결승 진출자를 선발할 것이고, 12편의 작품들은 온라인으로 출판되며 소셜 미디어를 통해 공유됩니다.
• 12명의 결승 진출자들 중에서 한 명의 전체 우승자가 선발되어, 500달러를 받을 것입니다.

※ 등록하거나 더 많은 정보를 보시려면, www.7challenge_globestory.com에 방문하세요.

Why? 왜 정답일까?

'All participants will write about the same topic.'에서 글쓰기 대회 참가자들이 모두 같은 주제로 글을 쓴다고 하므로, 안내문의 내용과 일치하는 것은 ② '참가자들은 동일한 주제에 대하여 글을 쓴다.'이다.

Why? 왜 오답일까?

① 'Age: 17 and over'에서 17세 미만이 아닌 17세 이상이 참가 대상이라고 하였다.
③ 'You will be randomly assigned one of 12 literary genres for your story.'에서 참가자들은 자신이 장르를 선택하지 못하고, 무작위로 배정된다고 하였다.
④ 'Only one entry per person'에서 1인당 출품작은 하나만 낼 수 있다고 하였다.
⑤ 'From the 12 finalists, one overall winner will be chosen and awarded $500.'에서 12인의 결승 진출자 중 선출된 종합 우승자 1인에게만 상금이 지급된다고 하였다.

● talent ⓝ 재능
● literary ⓐ 문학의
● revise ⓥ 수정하다
● randomly ⓐⓓ 무작위로
● genre ⓝ 장르

29 자기 행동의 영향력을 금방 인식하는 유아 　　정답률 54% | 정답 ④

다음 글의 밑줄 친 부분 중, 어법상 틀린 것은? [3점]

By noticing the relation / between their own actions and resultant external changes, / infants develop self-efficacy, / a sense ① that they are agents of the perceived changes.
관계를 알아차림으로써, / 자신의 행동과 그에 따른 외부 변화 사이에서의 / 유아들은 자아 효능감을 발전시킨다. / 즉 그들이 인지된 변화의 주체라는 인식
Although infants can notice the effect of their behavior / on the physical environment, / it is in early social interactions / that infants most ② readily perceive the consequence of their actions.
유아들은 자신의 행동의 영향을 알아차릴 수 있지만, / 물리적 환경에 미치는 / 바로 초기 사회적 상호작용이다. / 유아가 가장 쉽게 자기 행동의 결과를 인지하는 상황은
People have perceptual characteristics / that virtually ③ assure that infants will orient toward them.
사람들은 지각적 특성을 가지고 있다. / 유아들이 확실히 그들 쪽으로 향하게 할
They have visually contrasting and moving faces.
사람들은 시각적으로 구별되고 달라지는 얼굴 표정을 지닌다.
They produce sound, / provide touch, / and have interesting smells.
사람들은 소리를 만들고, / 촉각을 제공하고, / 흥미로운 냄새를 가지고 있다.
In addition, / people engage with infants / by exaggerating their facial expressions and inflecting their voices / in ways that infants find ☑ fascinating.
또한, / 사람들은 유아들과 관계를 맺는다. / 얼굴 표정을 과장하고 목소리를 조절하며 / 유아들이 매력적이라고 느끼는 방식으로
But most importantly, / these antics are responsive / to infants' vocalizations, facial expressions, and gestures; / people vary the pace and level of their behavior / in response to infant actions.
그러나 다른 무엇보다 중요한 것은, / 이러한 익살스러운 행동이 호응해준다는 것인데, / 유아들의 발성, 얼굴 표정, 몸짓에 / 사람들은 자기 행동의 속도와 수준을 다양하게 한다. / 유아들의 행동에 맞춰
Consequentially, / early social interactions provide a context / ⑤ where infants can easily notice the effect of their behavior.
결과적으로, / 초기 사회적 상호 작용은 맥락을 제공한다. / 유아들이 자기 행동의 영향을 쉽게 알아차릴 수 있는

유아들은 자신의 행동과 그에 따른 외부 변화 사이에서의 관계를 알아차림으로써, 그들이 인지된 변화의 주체라는 인식, 즉 자아 효능감을 발전시킨다. 유아들은 자신의 행동이 물리적 환경에 미치는 영향을 알아차릴 수 있지만, 유아들이 가장 쉽게 자기 행동의 결과를 인지하는 상황은 바로 초기 사회적 상호작용이다. 사람들은 유아들이 확실히 그들 쪽으로 향하게 할 지각적 특성을 가지고 있다. 사람들은 얼굴 표정이 시각적으로 구별되고 달라진다. 사람들은 소리를 만들고, 촉각을 제공하고, 흥미로운 냄새를 가지고 있다. 또한, 사람들은 유아들이 매력적이라고 느끼는 방식으로 얼굴 표정을 과장하고 목소리를 조절하며 유아들과 관계를 맺는다. 그러나 다른 무엇보다 중요한 것은, 이러한 익살스러운 행동이 유아들의 발성, 얼굴 표정, 몸짓에 호응해준다는 것인데, 사람들은 유아들의 행동에 맞춰 자기 행동의 속도와 수준을 다양하게 한다. 결과적으로 초기 사회적 상호 작용은 유아들이 자기 행동의 영향을 쉽게 알아차릴 수 있는 맥락을 제공한다.

Why? 왜 정답일까?

④가 포함된 주격 관계대명사 that절의 선행사는 ways인데, 이는 '매혹시키는' 주체이므로 fascinated 대신 fascinating을 써야 한다. 따라서 어법상 틀린 것은 ④이다.

① a sense를 보충 설명하는 동격 명사절의 접속사 that이 바르게 쓰였다. that 뒤에 완전한 2형식 구조가 나왔음을 참고한다.
② 동사 perceive를 꾸미기 위해 부사 readily가 바르게 쓰였다.
③ 선행사 perceptual characteristics가 복수 명사이므로, 주격 관계대명사 that 뒤의 동사 또한 복수 동사여야 한다. 따라서 assure가 바르게 쓰였다.
⑤ 관계부사 where가 장소의 선행사 a context를 어법상 적절하게 꾸미고 있다.

- resultant ⓐ 그로 인한
- self-efficacy ⓝ 자기 효능감
- perceptual ⓐ 지각과 관련된
- virtually ⓐⓓ 실제로
- exaggerate ⓥ 과장하다
- consequentially ⓐⓓ 결과적으로
- external ⓐ 외부적인
- readily ⓐⓓ 쉽게, 순조롭게
- characteristic ⓝ 특성
- engage with ~와 관계를 맺다, ~을 상대하다
- fascinated ⓐ 매혹된

구문 풀이

9행 In addition, people engage with infants by exaggerating their facial expressions and inflecting their voices in ways [that infants find fascinating].
선행사 | 목적격 관·대 | 동사 | 목적격 보어

★★★ 등급을 가르는 문제!

30 Adam Smith의 전문화 개념　　　　정답률 45% | 정답 ③

다음 글의 밑줄 친 부분 중, 문맥상 낱말의 쓰임이 적절하지 않은 것은?

Adam Smith pointed out / that specialization, / where each of us focuses on one specific skill, / leads to a general improvement of everybody's well-being.
Adam Smith는 지적했다. / 전문화, 즉 우리 각자가 하나의 특정한 기술에 집중하는 것이 / 모든 사람의 복지의 전반적인 향상으로 이어진다고

The idea is simple and powerful.
그 개념은 간단하고 강력하다.

By specializing in just one activity / — such as food raising, clothing production, or home construction — / each worker gains ① mastery over the particular activity.
단 하나의 분야에만 전문화함으로써, / 예컨대 식량 재배, 의류 생산, 혹은 주택 건설과 같은 / 각각의 노동자는 특정한 활동에 숙달하게 된다.

Specialization makes sense, however, / only if the specialist can subsequently ② trade his or her output / with the output of specialists in other lines of activity.
하지만 전문화는 성립한다. / 전문가가 그 이후 자신의 생산물을 거래할 수 있을 때만 / 다른 활동 라인 전문가들의 생산물과

It would make no sense / to produce more food than a household needs / unless there is a market outlet / to exchange that ✔ excess food for clothing, shelter, and so forth.
의미가 없을 것이다. / 한 가구가 필요로 하는 양보다 더 많이 식량을 생산하는 것은 / 만약 시장 판매처가 없다면 / 그 넘치는 식량을 의류, 주거지 등등으로 교환할

At the same time, / without the ability to buy food on the market, / it would not be possible / to be a specialist home builder or clothing maker, / since it would be ④ necessary / to farm for one's own survival.
동시에, / 시장에서 식량을 구매할 능력이 없다면, / 불가능할 텐데, / 전문 주택 건축가나 전문 의류 제작자가 되는 것은 / 필요성이 있기 때문이다. / 스스로의 생존을 위해 농사를 지어야 할

Thus Smith realized / that the division of labor is ⑤ limited / by the extent of the market, / whereas the extent of the market is determined / by the degree of specialization.
따라서 Smith는 알았다. / 노동의 분업은 제한된다는 것을 / 시장의 규모에 의해 / 시장의 규모는 결정되는 반면에, / 전문화의 정도에 따라

Adam Smith는 전문화, 즉 우리 각자가 하나의 특정한 기술에 집중하는 것이 모든 사람의 복지의 전반적인 향상으로 이어진다고 지적했다. 그 개념은 간단하고 강력하다. 예컨대 식량 재배, 의류 생산, 혹은 주택 건설과 같은 단 하나의 분야에만 전문화함으로써, 각각의 노동자는 특정한 활동에 ① 숙달하게 된다. 하지만 전문화는 전문가가 그 이후 자신의 생산물을 다른 활동 라인 전문가들의 생산물과 ② 거래할 수 있을 때만 성립한다. 만약 그 ③ 부족한(→ 넘치는) 식량을 의류, 주거지 등등으로 교환할 시장 판매처가 없다면 한 가구가 필요로 하는 양보다 더 많이 식량을 생산하는 것은 의미가 없을 것이다. 동시에, 시장에서 식량을 구매할 능력이 없다면, 전문 주택 건축가나 전문 의류 제작자가 되는 것은 불가능할 텐데, 스스로의 생존을 위해 농사를 지어야 할 ④ 필요성이 있기 때문이다. 따라서 Smith는 시장의 규모는 전문화의 정도에 따라 결정되는 반면에, 노동의 분업은 시장의 규모에 의해 ⑤ 제한된다는 것을 알았다.

Why? 왜 정답일까?

②가 포함된 문장에서 전문화는 시장 거래가 가능할 때만 의의가 있다고 하는데, 이러한 거래는 한 가정에서 필요한 양 '이상의', 즉 '남는' 생산물을 대상으로 할 것이기에, ③의 scarce를 excess로 고쳐야 한다. 따라서 문맥상 낱말의 쓰임이 적절하지 않은 것은 ③이다.

- specialization ⓝ 전문화
- improvement ⓝ 향상, 개선
- make sense 말이 되다, 의의가 있다
- trade ⓥ 교역하다, 거래하다
- division of labor 분업
- specific ⓐ 특정한
- raise ⓥ 기르다, 키우다
- subsequently ⓐⓓ 차후에
- and so forth 기타 등등

구문 풀이

11행 At the same time, without the ability to buy food on the market, it
= if it were not for(~이 없다면)
would not be possible to be a specialist home builder or clothing maker, ~
가정법 과거 주절

★★ 문제 해결 꿀~팁 ★★

▶ 많이 틀린 이유는?
전문화의 이점을 언급하는 글로, 특히 글 중간의 however 뒤에서는 이 전문화가 시장의 존재를 전제로 한다는 내용을 다루고 있다. 시장이 있어야 많이 생산된 식량을 교환할 수도 있고, 식량이 아닌 '다른' 재화를 생산해 식량과 바꿀 수도 있게 되므로 결국 시장의 규모가 분업이나 전문화의 정도까지도 '결정한다'는 것이다. ⑤는 시장의 규모에 따라 분업, 즉 전문화의 정도에 영향이 간다는 의미로 limited를 적절하게 썼다.

▶ 문제 해결 방법은?
③이 포함된 문장은 문맥상 시장이 있어서 '남는' 음식을 처분할 수 없다면 음식을 더 많이 생산할 필요가 없을 것이라는 의미이다.

31 농지 분산의 이점　　　　정답률 57% | 정답 ③

다음 빈칸에 들어갈 말로 가장 적절한 것을 고르시오. [3점]

① land leveling – 땅 평평하게 고르기
② weed trimming – 잡초 손질
✔ ③ field scattering – 농지 흩어놓기
④ organic farming – 유기농법
⑤ soil fertilization – 토지 비옥하게 만들기

It is not the peasant's goal / to produce the highest possible time-averaged crop yield, / averaged over many years.
농부의 목표가 아니다. / 최고로 가능한 시간 평균적인 농작물 생산량을 만드는 것은 / 여러 해에 걸쳐서 평균을 내는

If your time-averaged yield is marvelously high / as a result of the combination of nine great years and one year of crop failure, / you will still starve to death in that one year of crop failure / before you can look back / to congratulate yourself on your great time-averaged yield.
당신의 시간 평균적인 생산량이 엄청나게 높더라도, / 좋았던 9년과 농사에 실패한 1년을 합친 결과로 / 당신은 농사에 실패한 바로 그 한 해에 굶어 죽을 것이다. / 당신이 돌아보기도 전에 / 훌륭한 시간 평균적인 생산량에 있어서 스스로를 축하하려고

Instead, / the peasant's aim is / to make sure to produce a yield above the starvation level in every single year, / even though the time-averaged yield may not be highest.
대신에, / 농부의 목표는 ~이다. / 굶어 죽지 않을 수준 이상의 생산량을 매년 확실히 만들어내는 것이다. / 시간 평균적인 생산량이 가장 높지 않을지라도

That's why field scattering may make sense.
그것이 바로 농지 흩어놓기가 합리적인 이유이다.

If you have just one big field, / no matter how good it is on the average, / you will starve / when the inevitable occasional year arrives / in which your one field has a low yield.
만일 당신이 그냥 하나의 큰 농지를 가지고 있다면, / 그것이 평균적으로 아무리 좋다고 할지라도, / 당신은 굶주리게 될 것이다. / 그 가끔 오는 불가피한 때가 오면 / 당신의 유일한 농지가 낮은 생산량을 내는

But if you have many different fields, / varying independently of each other, / then in any given year / some of your fields will produce well / even when your other fields are producing poorly.
그러나 만일 당신이 농지들을 가지고 있다면, / 서로 상관없는 다른 / 어느 해에 / 당신의 농지 중 일부는 잘 생산할 것이다. / 당신의 다른 농지들이 빈약하게 생산하고 있을 때조차도

여러 해에 걸쳐서 평균을 내는, 최고로 가능한 시간 평균적인 농작물 생산량을 만드는 것은 농부의 목표가 아니다. 당신의 시간 평균적인 생산량이 (농사 결과가) 좋았던 9년과 농사에 실패한 1년을 합친 결과로 엄청나게 높더라도, 당신은 훌륭한 시간 평균적인 생산량에 있어서 스스로를 축하하려고 돌아보기도 전에 농사에 실패한 바로 그 한 해에 굶어 죽을 것이다. 대신에, 농부의 목표는 시간 평균적인 생산량이 가장 높지 않을지라도, 굶어 죽지 않을 수준 이상의 생산량을 매년 확실히 만들어내는 것이다. 그것이 바로 농지 흩어놓기가 합리적인 이유이다. 만일 당신이 그냥 하나의 큰 농지를 가지고 있다면, 그것이 평균적으로 아무리 좋다고 할지라도, 당신은 유일한 농지가 낮은 생산량을 내는 그 가끔 오는 불가피한 때가 오면 굶주리게 될 것이다. 그러나 만일 당신이 서로 상관없는 다른 농지들을 가지고 있다면, 어느 해에 당신의 다른 농지들이 빈약하게 생산하고 있을 때조차도 당신의 농지 중 일부는 잘 생산할 것이다.

Why? 왜 정답일까?

빈칸 뒤에서 큰 농지를 하나 가지고 있을 때와 여러 개의 분산된 농지를 갖고 있을 때를 대조하며, 전자의 경우 그 농지 수확이 낮으면 꼼짝없이 위기를 맞지만 후자의 경우 어느 한 땅이 안 좋아도 다른 땅이 벌충해 줄 수 있어 좋다(But if you have many different fields, varying independently of each other, then in any given year some of your fields will produce well ~)고 설명하고 있다. 따라서 빈칸에 들어갈 말로 가장 적절한 것은 ③ '농지 흩어놓기'이다.

- peasant ⓝ 농부, 소작농
- marvelously ⓐⓓ 놀랍도록
- make sure to 확실히 ~하다
- occasional ⓐ 이따금의
- leveling (땅을) 고름, 평평하게 함
- fertilization ⓝ (땅을) 비옥하게 하기
- yield ⓝ 수확량, 산출량
- starve to death 굶어 죽다
- inevitable ⓐ 불가피한
- independently of ~와 상관없이
- scatter ⓥ 흩어놓다

구문 풀이

2행 If your time-averaged yield is marvelously high as a result of the
접속사(조건) | 현재시제 | ~의 결과로
combination of nine great years and one year of crop failure, you will still starve
미래시제
to death in that one year of crop failure before you can look back to congratulate
부사적 용법(목적)
yourself on your great time-averaged yield.

★★★ 등급을 가르는 문제!

32 다른 사람의 도움이 자존감에 해가 되는 순간　　　　정답률 44% | 정답 ①

다음 빈칸에 들어갈 말로 가장 적절한 것을 고르시오.

✔ ① make you feel bad about yourself
당신이 스스로를 안 좋게 느끼도록 만들
② improve your ability to deal with challenges
어려움에 대처하는 능력을 높여줄
③ be seen as a way of asking for another favor
또 다른 부탁을 하는 방법으로 여겨질
④ trick you into thinking that you were successful
스스로 성공했다고 착각하게 할
⑤ discourage the person trying to model your behavior
당신의 행동을 본보기로 삼으려는 사람을 낙담시킬

There are several reasons / why support may not be effective.
몇몇 이유들이 있다. / 도움이 효과적이지 않을 수 있는

One possible reason is / that receiving help could be a blow to self-esteem.
한 가지 가능한 이유는 / 도움을 받는 것이 자존감에 타격이 될 수 있다는 것이다.

A recent study by Christopher Burke and Jessica Goren at Lehigh University / examined this possibility.
Lehigh 대학의 Christopher Burke와 Jessica Goren에 의한 최근 한 연구는 / 이 가능성을 조사했다.

According to the threat to self-esteem model, / help can be perceived as supportive and loving, / or it can be seen as threatening / if that help is interpreted as implying incompetence.
자존감 위협 모델 이론에 따르면, / 도움은 협력적이고 애정 있는 것으로 여겨질 수도 있고, / 혹은 그것은 위협적으로 보여질 수도 있다. / 만약 그 도움이 무능함을 암시하는 것으로 해석된다면

According to Burke and Goren, / support is especially likely to be seen as threatening / if it is in an area that is self-relevant or self-defining / — that is, in an area / where your own success and achievement are especially important.
Burke와 Goren에 따르면 / 도움은 특히 위협으로 보여질 가능성이 있다. / 그것이 자기 연관적이거나 자기 정의적인 영역 안에 있는 경우 / 다시 말해, 영역에서 / 자신의 성공과 성취가 특히 중요한

Receiving help with a self-relevant task / can make you feel bad about yourself, / and this can undermine the potential positive effects of the help.
자기 연관적인 일로 도움을 받는 것은 / 당신이 스스로를 안 좋게 느끼도록 만들 수 있고, / 이것은 도움의 잠재적인 긍정적 영향에 해를 줄 수 있다.

For example, / if your self-concept rests, in part, on your great cooking ability, / it may be a blow to your ego / when a friend helps you prepare a meal for guests / because it suggests / that you're not the master chef you thought you were.
예를 들어, / 만약 당신의 자아 개념이 훌륭한 요리 실력에 일부 기초한다면, / 이는 당신의 자아에 타격이 될 수 있는데 / 친구가 당신이 손님들을 위해 식사를 준비하는 것을 도울 때 / 이는 암시하기 때문이다. / 당신이 생각했던 만큼 유능한 요리사가 아니라는 것을

도움이 효과적이지 않을 수 있는 몇몇 이유들이 있다. 한 가지 가능한 이유는 도움을 받는 것이 자존감에 타격이 될 수 있다는 것이다. Lehigh 대학의 Christopher Burke와 Jessica Goren에 의한 최근 한 연구는 이 가능성을 조사했다. 자존감 위험 모델 이론에 따르면, 도움은 협력적이고 애정 있는 것으로 여겨질 수도 있고, 혹은 만약 그 도움이 무능함을 암시하는 것으로 해석된다면 위협적으로 보여질 수 있다. Burke와 Goren에 따르면 도움이 자기 연관적이거나 자기 정의적인 영역 — 다시 말해, 자신의 성공과 성취가 특히 중요한 영역 — 안에 있는 경우, 그것은 특히 위협으로 보여질 가능성이 있다. 자기 연관적인 일로 도움을 받는 것은 당신이 스스로를 안 좋게 느끼도록 만들 수 있고, 이것은 도움의 잠재적인 긍정적 영향에 해를 줄 수 있다. 예를 들어, 만약 당신의 자아 개념이 훌륭한 요리 실력에 일부 기초한다면, 친구가 당신이 손님들을 위해 식사를 준비하는 것을 도울 때 이는 당신의 자아에 타격이 될 수 있는데 이는 당신이 생각했던 만큼 유능한 요리사가 아니라는 뜻이기 때문이다.

Why? 왜 정답일까?

도움이 효과적이지 않은 순간 중 하나는 도움이 자존감에 타격을 줄 때(One possible reason is that receiving help could be a blow to self-esteem.)임을 설명하는 글이므로, 빈칸에 들어갈 말로 가장 적절한 것은 ① '당신이 스스로를 안 좋게 느끼도록 만들'이다.

- blow ⓝ 타격, 충격
- threat ⓝ 위협
- self-relevant ⓐ 자아 관련의
- self-concept ⓝ 자아 개념
- trick A into B A를 속여 B하게 하다
- self-esteem ⓝ 자아 존중감
- incompetence ⓝ 무능
- undermine ⓥ 손상시키다
- rest on ~에 놓여 있다
- discourage ⓥ 낙담시키다

구문 풀이

14행 ~ it may be a blow to your ego when a friend helps you prepare a meal for guests because it suggests that you're not the master chef [(you thought) you were].
선행사 / 삽입절 / [ ] : 형용사절(were의 보어가 없는 불완전한 절)

★★ 문제 해결 꿀~팁 ★★

▶ 많이 틀린 이유는?
'~ support is especially likely to be seen as threatening ~' 문장에서 과업의 자기 관련성이 높은(self-relevant or self-defining) 경우 타인의 도움이 오히려 위험으로 여겨질 수 있다고 했다. ②의 경우, 이런 과업에서 타인의 도움을 받으면 위기 대처 능력이 '향상된다'는 의미이므로 주제와 정반대된다. ④는 자기 관련성이 높은 과업에서 타인의 도움을 받을 때 '우리가 성공했다는 착각에 빠질 수 있다'는 의미인데, 성공에 대한 착각은 글에서 언급되지 않았다.

▶ 문제 해결 방법은?
마지막 문장의 a blow to your ego를 ①에서 feel bad about yourself로 바꾸었다.

---

33 도덕적 성찰을 돕기 위한 역사 연구 정답률 47% | 정답 ①

다음 빈칸에 들어갈 말로 가장 적절한 것을 고르시오.
✓ source of moral lessons and reflections – 도덕적 교훈과 성찰의 근원
② record of the rise and fall of empires – 제국의 흥망성쇠에 관한 기록
③ war against violence and oppression – 폭력과 억압에 대항하는 전쟁
④ means of mediating conflict – 갈등 중재의 수단
⑤ integral part of innovation – 혁신의 필수 요소

As well as making sense of events through narratives, / historians in the ancient world established the tradition of history / as a source of moral lessons and reflections.
이야기를 통해서 사건을 이해했을 뿐 아니라 / 고대 사회의 역사가들은 역사의 전통을 확립했다. / 도덕적 교훈과 성찰의 근원으로서

The history writing of Livy or Tacitus, / for instance, / was in part designed / to examine the behavior of heroes and villains, / meditating on the strengths and weaknesses / in the characters of emperors and generals, / providing exemplars for the virtuous to imitate or avoid.
Livy나 Tacitus의 역사적인 기술은 / 예를 들면, / 부분적으로는 만들어져, / 영웅과 악당의 행동을 살펴보도록 / 장점과 단점을 숙고해 / 황제와 장군들의 성격에서의 / 도덕적인 사람들이 모방하거나 피해야 할 표본을 제공한다.

This continues to be one of the functions of history.
이것이 계속되어 역사의 기능 중 하나가 된다.

French chronicler Jean Froissart said / he had written his accounts of chivalrous knights / fighting in the Hundred Years' War / "so that brave men should be inspired thereby to follow such examples."
프랑스의 연대기 학자인 Jean Froissart는 말했다. / 그가 기사도적인 기사들의 이야기를 썼다고 / 백년전쟁에서 싸운 / '용맹스러운 자들이 영감을 받아 이러한 본보기를 따르도록'

Today, / historical studies of Lincoln, Churchill, Gandhi, or Martin Luther King, Jr. / perform the same function.
오늘날 / Lincoln, Churchill, Gandhi 또는 Martin Luther King, Jr.에 대한 역사적 연구는 / 같은 기능을 수행한다.

고대 사회의 역사가들은 이야기를 통해서 사건을 이해했을 뿐 아니라 도덕적 교훈과 성찰의 근원으로서 역사의 전통을 확립했다. 예를 들면, Livy나 Tacitus의 역사적인 기술은 부분적으로 만들어져, 황제와 장군들의 성격적 장점과 단점을 숙고해 영웅과 악당의 행동을 살펴보도록 만들어져, 도덕적인 사람들이 모방하거나 피해야 할 표본을 제공한다. 프랑스의 연대기 학자인 Jean Froissart는 백년전쟁에서 싸운 기사도적인 기사들의 이야기를 '용맹스러운 자들이 영감을 받아 이러한 본보기를 따르도록' 썼다고 말했다. 오늘날 Lincoln, Churchill, Gandhi 또는 Martin Luther King, Jr.에 대한 역사적 연구는 같은 기능을 수행한다.

Why? 왜 정답일까?

빈칸 뒤의 예시에서 역사적 인물의 장단점을 연구해 사람들이 보고 따를 만한 도덕적 인간의 표본을 만들어낸다(~ providing exemplars for the virtuous to imitate or avoid.)고 하므로, 빈칸에 들어갈 말로 가장 적절한 것은 ① '도덕적 교훈과 성찰의 근원'이다.

- villain ⓝ 악당
- emperor ⓝ 황제
- virtuous ⓐ 도덕적인
- account ⓝ 설명
- empire ⓝ 제국
- meditate on ~에 관해 곰곰이 생각해보다
- exemplar ⓝ 본보기
- chronicler ⓝ 연대기 작가, 기록가
- rise and fall 흥망성쇠
- oppression ⓝ 억압

구문 풀이

8행 French chronicler Jean Froissart said he had written his accounts of
과거완료
chivalrous knights fighting in the Hundred Years' War "so that brave men should
접속사(~하도록)
be inspired thereby to follow such examples."
be inspired + to부정사 : ~하도록 영감을 받다

---

34 어떤 행동을 막을 수 있는 효과적인 기법 정답률 57% | 정답 ③

다음 빈칸에 들어갈 말로 가장 적절한 것을 고르시오.
① ignore what experts say – 전문가들의 말을 무시할
② keep a close eye on the situation – 상황을 면밀히 관찰할
✓ shift our emphasis from behavior to character – 행동에서 품성으로 강조점을 옮길
④ focus on appealing to emotion rather than reason – 이성보다 감정에 호소하는 데 초점을 둘
⑤ place more importance on the individual instead of the group – 집단 대신 개인에 더 중점을 둘 때

Psychologist Christopher Bryan finds / that when we shift our emphasis from behavior to character, / people evaluate choices differently.
심리학자인 Christopher Bryan은 밝힌다. / 우리가 행동에서 품성으로 강조점을 옮길 때, / 사람들은 선택을 다르게 평가하는 것

His team was able to cut cheating in half: / instead of "Please don't cheat," / they changed the appeal / to "Please don't be a cheater."
그의 팀은 속이는 행위를 반으로 줄일 수 있었는데, / '속이지 마세요'라는 문구 대신에, / 그들은 호소를 전환했다. / '속이는 사람이 되지 마세요'라는 문구로

When you're urged not to cheat, / you can do it / and still see an ethical person in the mirror.
당신이 속이지 말라고 강요받을 때, / 당신은 그렇게 하고도 / 여전히 거울 속에서 도덕적인 사람을 마주할 수 있다.

But when you're told not to be a cheater, / the act casts a shadow; / immorality is tied to your identity, / making the behavior much less attractive.
하지만 당신이 속이는 사람이 되지 말라고 들을 때는 / 그 행동이 그림자를 드리우는데, / 비도덕성이 당신의 정체성과 결부되어 / 그 행동을 훨씬 덜 매력적으로 만든다.

Cheating is an isolated action / that gets evaluated with the logic of consequence: / Can I get away with it?
속이는 행동은 독립적인 행위이다. / 결과의 논리에 따라 평가되는 / 내가 들키지 않을 수 있을까?

Being a cheater evokes a sense of self, / triggering the logic of appropriateness: / What kind of person am I, / and who do I want to be?
속이는 사람이 되는 것은 자의식을 환기시키며 / 적절함에 대한 논리를 촉발한다. / 나는 어떤 종류의 사람인가, / 그리고 나는 어떤 사람이 되고 싶은가?

In light of this evidence, / Bryan suggests / that we should embrace nouns more thoughtfully.
이러한 증거에 비추어 볼 때, / Bryan은 제안한다. / 우리가 명사를 더욱 사려 깊게 받아들여야 한다고

"Don't Drink and Drive" could be rephrased as: / "Don't Be a Drunk Driver."
'음주운전 하지 마세요'는 ~라고 바꿔 말할 수 있다. / '음주 운전자가 되지 마세요'

The same thinking can be applied to originality.
같은 논리가 독창성에도 적용될 수 있다.

When a child draws a picture, / instead of calling the artwork creative, / we can say "You are creative."
아이가 그림을 그릴 때, / 작품이 창의적이라고 말하는 대신에 / 우리는 '너는 창의적이구나'라고 말해줄 수 있다.

심리학자인 Christopher Bryan은 우리가 행동에서 품성으로 강조점을 옮길 때, 사람들은 선택을 다르게 평가한다는 것을 밝힌다. 그의 팀은 속이는 행위를 반으로 줄일 수 있었는데, '속이지 마세요'라는 문구 대신에, 그들은 '속이는 사람이 되지 마세요'라는 문구로 호소를 전환했다. 당신이 속이지 말라고 강요받을 때, 당신은 속이고 나서도 여전히 거울 속에서 도덕적인 사람을 마주할 수 있다. 하지만 당신이 속이는 사람이 되지 말라고 들을 때는 그 행동이 그림자를 드리우는데, 비도덕성이 당신의 정체성과 결부되어 그 행동을 훨씬 덜 매력적으로 만든다. 속이는 행동은 결과의 논리에 따라 평가되는 독립적인 행위이다. 내가 들키지 않을 수 있을까? 속이는 사람이 되는 것은 자의식을 환기시키며 적절함에 대한 논리를 촉발한다. 나는 어떤 종류의 사람인가, 그리고 나는 어떤 사람이 되고 싶은가? 이러한 증거에 비추어 볼 때, Bryan은 우리가 명사를 더욱 사려 깊게 받아들여야 한다고 제안한다. '음주운전 하지 마세요'는 '음주 운전자가 되지 마세요'로 바꿔 말할 수 있다. 같은 논리가 독창성에도 적용될 수 있다. 아이가 그림을 그릴 때, 작품이 창의적이라고 말하는 대신에 우리는 '너는 창의적이구나'라고 말해줄 수 있다.

Why? 왜 정답일까?

빈칸 뒤의 예시에 따르면, 어떤 행동을 막고 싶을 때 단지 그 행동을 하지 말라는 메시지보다는, 그 행동

과 정체성을 연결시킨 메시지를 이용할 때 더 효과적일 수 있다고 한다. 즉, 단지 '～하지 말라'는 메시지보다는 '～하는 사람이 되지 말라'는 식으로 자의식이나 품성을 건드릴 수 있는 진술이 행동 방지 효과를 더 크게 나타낸다는 것이다. 따라서 빈칸에 들어갈 말로 가장 적절한 것은 ③ '행동에서 품성으로 강조점을 옮길이다.

- cut in half 절반으로 줄이다
- urge ⓥ 촉구하다
- cast a shadow 그림자를 드리우다
- be tied to ～와 결부되다
- get away with ～에서 벗어나다
- appropriateness ⓝ 적절성
- emphasis ⓝ 강조, 역점
- cheat ⓥ 속이다
- ethical ⓐ 도덕적인, 윤리적인
- immorality ⓝ 부도덕함
- isolated ⓐ 고립된, 동떨어진
- evoke ⓥ (감정 등을) 불러일으키다
- in light of ～에 비추어볼 때
- place importance on ～에 중점을 두다

6행 But when you're told not to be a cheater, the act casts a shadow;
be told not + to부정사: ～하지 말라고 듣다
immorality is tied to your identity, making the behavior much less attractive.
분사구문

---

35 마케팅에서 입장을 취하는 것의 중요성 　　정답률 60% | 정답 ④

다음 글에서 전체 흐름과 관계 없는 문장은?

Taking a stand is important / because you become a beacon for those individuals / who are your people, your tribe, and your audience.
입장을 취하는 것은 중요하다. / 당신이 그 개개인들에게 횃불이 되기 때문에 / 당신의 사람, 부족, 청중인

① When you raise your viewpoint up like a flag, / people know where to find you; / it becomes a rallying point.
당신이 당신의 견해를 깃발처럼 들 때, / 사람들은 당신을 어디서 찾아야 할지를 안다. / 그것은 집합 지점이 된다.

② Displaying your perspective / lets prospective (and current) customers know / that you don't just sell your products or services.
당신의 관점을 보여주는 것은 / 장래 (및 현재) 고객들이 깨닫게 한다. / 당신이 그저 물건과 서비스만 파는 것이 아님을

③ The best marketing is never just about selling a product or service, / but about taking a stand / — showing an audience / why they should believe in what you're marketing enough / to want it at any cost, / simply because they agree with what you're doing.
최고의 마케팅은 결코 제품이나 서비스를 판매하는 것에 대한 것이 아니라 / 입장을 취하는 데 관한 것으로, / 청중에게 보여주는 것이다. / 그들이 당신이 마케팅하고 있는 것을 충분히 믿어야 하는 이유를 / 반드시 원하게 될 만큼 / 그들은 그저 당신의 행동에 동의하기 때문에

✔ If you want to retain your existing customers, / you need to create ways / that a customer can feel like another member of the team, / participating in the process of product development.
만약 당신이 기존의 고객을 유지하고 싶다면, / 당신은 방법을 만들어낼 필요가 있다. / 고객이 팀의 또 다른 구성원이 된 기분을 느낄 수 있게 할 / 상품 개발 과정에 참여하면서

⑤ Products can be changed or adjusted / if they aren't functioning, / but rallying points align with the values and meaning / behind what you do.
상품은 바꾸거나 고칠 수 있지만, / 그것이 기능하지 않으면 / 집합 지점은 가치 및 의미와 같은 선상에 있다. / 당신의 행위 이면에 있는

입장을 취하는 것은 당신의 사람, 부족, 청중인 그 개개인들에게 당신이 횃불이 되기 때문에 중요하다. ① 당신이 당신의 견해를 깃발처럼 들 때, 사람들은 당신을 어디서 찾아야 할지를 안다. 그것은 집합 지점이 된다. ② 당신의 관점을 보여주는 것은 당신이 그저 물건과 서비스만 파는 것이 아님을 장래 (및 현재) 고객들이 깨닫게 한다. ③ 최고의 마케팅은 결코 제품이나 서비스를 판매하는 것에 대한 것이 아니라 입장을 취하는 데 관한 것으로, 청중들은 그저 당신의 행동에 동의하기 때문에 그들이 당신이 마케팅하고 있는 것을 반드시 원하게 될 만큼 충분히 믿어야 하는 이유를 그들에게 보여주는 것이다. ④ 만약 당신이 기존의 고객을 유지하고 싶다면, 당신은 고객이 상품 개발 과정에 참여하면서 팀의 또 다른 구성원이 된 기분을 느낄 수 있게 할 방법을 만들어낼 필요가 있다. ⑤ 상품은 기능하지 않으면 바꾸거나 고칠 수 있지만, 집합 지점은 당신의 행위 이면에 있는 가치 및 의미와 같은 선상에 있다.

마케팅에서 특정 입장을 취하는 것이 중요하다는 내용으로, 첫 문장과 문장 ③이 핵심 내용을 잘 제시한다. 반면 ④는 고객을 상품 개발 과정에 참여시켜 기존 고객을 유지할 방법에 관해 논하므로 글의 흐름에서 벗어난다. 따라서 전체 흐름과 관계 없는 문장은 ④이다.

- take a stand 입장을 취하다
- viewpoint ⓝ 견해, 시각
- at any cost 반드시, 기필코
- product development 상품 개발
- tribe ⓝ 부족
- prospective ⓐ 장래의
- existing ⓐ 기존의
- align with ～와 나란히 있다

4행 Displaying your perspective lets prospective (and current) customers
　　　　　　　　　　　사역동사　　　　　　　　　목적어
know that you don't just sell your products or services.
원형부정사

---

36 환경과 경험의 중요성 　　정답률 58% | 정답 ④

주어진 글 다음에 이어질 글의 순서로 가장 적절한 것을 고르시오.

① (A) - (C) - (B)　　② (B) - (A) - (C)　　③ (B) - (C) - (A)
✔ (C) - (A) - (B)　　⑤ (C) - (B) - (A)

If DNA were the only thing that mattered, / there would be no particular reason / to build meaningful social programs / to pour good experiences into children / and protect them from bad experiences.
만약 DNA가 유일하게 중요한 것이라면, / 특별한 이유가 없을 것이다. / 의미 있는 사회 프로그램을 만들 / 아이들에게 좋은 경험을 제공하고 / 그들을 해로운 경험으로부터 보호하는

(C) But brains require the right kind of environment / if they are to correctly develop.
하지만 뇌는 적절한 종류의 환경을 필요로 한다. / 그것이 제대로 발달하려면

When the first draft of the Human Genome Project / came to completion / at the turn of the

---

millennium, / one of the great surprises was / that humans have only about twenty thousand genes.
Human Genome Project의 첫 번째 초안이 / 완성되었을 때, / 새천년에 들어 / 큰 놀라움 중 하나는 ～이었다. / 인간이 대략 2만 개의 유전자만 갖고 있다는 것

(A) This number came as a surprise to biologists: / given the complexity of the brain and the body, / it had been assumed / that hundreds of thousands of genes would be required.
이 숫자는 생물학자들에게 놀라움으로 다가왔는데, / 뇌와 신체의 복잡성을 고려했을 때 / 추정되어 왔기 때문이다 / 수십만 개의 유전자가 필요할 것이라고

(B) So how does the massively complicated brain, / with its eighty-six billion neurons, / get built / from such a small recipe book?
그러면 극도로 복잡한 뇌가 어떻게, / 860억 개의 뉴런을 갖고 있는 / 만들어질 수 있었을까? / 그렇게 작은 요리책으로부터

The answer relies on a clever strategy / implemented by the genome: / build incompletely and let world experience refine.
그 해답은 한 영리한 전략에 있다. / 게놈에 의해 실행된 / 즉 불완전하게 만들고 세상 경험으로 정교하게 다듬는다는 것

만약 DNA가 유일하게 중요한 것이라면, 아이들에게 좋은 경험을 제공하고 해로운 경험으로부터 보호하는 의미 있는 사회 프로그램을 만들 특별한 이유가 없을 것이다.

(C) 하지만 뇌는 제대로 발달하려면 적절한 종류의 환경을 필요로 한다. Human Genome Project의 첫 번째 초안이 새천년에 들어 완성되었을 때, 큰 놀라움 중 하나는 인간이 대략 2만 개의 유전자만 갖고 있다는 것이었다.

(A) 이 숫자는 생물학자들에게 놀라움으로 다가왔는데, 뇌와 신체의 복잡성을 고려했을 때 수십만 개의 유전자가 필요할 것이라고 추정되어 왔기 때문이다.

(B) 그러면 860억 개의 뉴런을 갖고 있는 극도로 복잡한 뇌가 어떻게 그렇게 작은 요리책으로부터 만들어질 수 있었을까? 그 해답은 게놈에 의해 실행된 한 영리한 전략, 즉 불완전하게 만들고 세상 경험으로 정교하게 다듬는다는 데 있다.

만일 DNA만 중요하다면 경험과 환경의 의미가 약해질 것이라는 주어진 글 뒤로, '하지만' 뇌 발달에는 적절한 환경이 중요하다는 내용의 (C)가 먼저 연결된다. 한편 (C)의 후반부에서 인간의 유전자는 대략 2만 개에 불과하다고 하는데, (A)는 '이 숫자'가 생각보다 너무 적어서 과학자들이 놀랐다는 설명을 이어 간다. 마지막으로 (B)는 이렇게 턱없이 부족한 유전자만 갖고도 뇌가 그토록 복잡해질 수 있는 까닭은 '경험' 때문이라는 결론을 적절히 제시한다. 따라서 글의 순서로 가장 적절한 것은 ④ '(C) - (A) - (B)'이다.

- pour ⓥ 쏟아 붓다
- come as a surprise 놀라움으로 다가오다
- massively ⓐⓓ 엄청나게
- refine ⓥ 다듬다, 정제하다
- come to completion 완수되다
- protect A from B A를 B로부터 보호하다
- hundreds of thousands of 수십만의, 다수의
- implement ⓥ 실행하다
- first draft 초안
- at the turn of ～의 전환기에

5행 ~ given the complexity of the brain and the body, it had been assumed
　　　　분사구문(～을 고려하면)　　　　　　　　　　　　　　　　과거완료 수동태
that hundreds of thousands of genes would be required.
접속사(～것)

★★★ 등급을 가르는 문제!
37 겸손을 길러주는 근거와 주장 　　정답률 46% | 정답 ②

주어진 글 다음에 이어질 글의 순서로 가장 적절한 것을 고르시오. [3점]

① (A) - (C) - (B)　　✔ (B) - (A) - (C)
③ (B) - (C) - (A)　　④ (C) - (A) - (B)
⑤ (C) - (B) - (A)

One benefit of reasons and arguments is / that they can foster humility.
근거와 주장의 한 가지 이점은 ～이다. / 겸손을 기를 수 있다는 점

If two people disagree without arguing, / all they do is yell at each other.
만약에 두 사람이 논쟁 없이 의견만 다르다면, / 그들이 하는 것은 서로에게 고함을 지르는 것뿐이다.

No progress is made.
어떠한 발전도 없다.

(B) Both still think that they are right.
양측은 여전히 자신이 옳다고 생각한다.

In contrast, / if both sides give arguments / that articulate reasons for their positions, / then new possibilities open up.
대조적으로, / 양측이 주장을 제시한다면, / 자신의 입장에 대한 이유를 분명하게 말하는 / 새로운 가능성이 열린다.

One of the arguments gets refuted / — that is, it is shown to fail.
이러한 주장 중 한쪽이 반박된다. / 즉, 틀렸다는 것이 드러난다.

In that case, / the person who depended on the refuted argument / learns that he needs to change his view.
이런 경우에 / 반박된 주장에 의지했던 사람은 / 자신의 관점을 바꿀 필요가 있다는 것을 배운다.

(A) That is one way to achieve humility / — on one side at least.
이것은 겸손을 얻는 한 가지 방식이다. / 적어도 한쪽에서는

Another possibility is / that neither argument is refuted.
또 다른 가능성은 ～이다. / 어떤 주장도 반박되지 않는 것

Both have a degree of reason on their side.
둘 다 자기 입장에 대해 어느 정도 근거가 있다.

Even if neither person involved is convinced by the other's argument, / both can still come to appreciate the opposing view.
두 대화자 모두 상대의 주장에 설득되지 않더라도, / 양측은 그럼에도 불구하고 반대 견해를 이해하게 된다.

(C) They also realize / that, even if they have some truth, / they do not have the whole truth.
또한 그들은 인식하게 된다. / 자신이 약간의 진실을 갖고 있더라도 / 그들이 완전한 진실은 가지고 있지 않다는 점을

They can gain humility / when they recognize and appreciate the reasons / against their own view.
그들은 겸손을 얻을 수 있다. / 그들이 근거를 인식하고 이해할 때 / 자신의 견해에 반대되는

근거와 주장의 한 가지 이점은 겸손을 기를 수 있다는 점이다. 만약에 두 사람이 논쟁 없이 의견만 다르다면, 그들이 하는 것은 서로에게 고함을 지르는 것뿐이다. 어떠한 발전도 없다.

(B) 양측은 여전히 자신이 옳다고 생각한다. 대조적으로, 양측이 자신의 입장에 대한 이유를 분명하게 말하는 주장을 제시한다면, 새로운 가능성이 열린다. 이러한 주장 중 한쪽이

반박된다. 즉, 틀렸다는 것이 드러난다. 이런 경우에 반박된 주장에 의지했던 사람은 자신의 관점을 바꿀 필요가 있다는 것을 배운다.

(A) 이것은 적어도 한쪽에서는 겸손을 얻는 한 가지 방식이다. 또 다른 가능성은 어떤 주장도 반박되지 않는 것이다. 둘 다 자기 입장에 대해 어느 정도 근거가 있다. 두 대화자 모두 상대의 주장에 설득되지 않더라도, 양측은 그럼에도 불구하고 반대 견해를 이해하게 된다.

(C) 또한 그들은 자신이 약간의 진실은 몰라도 완전한 진실은 가지고 있지 않다는 점을 인식하게 된다. 그들은 자신의 견해에 반대되는 근거를 인식하고 이해할 때 겸손을 얻을 수 있다.

Why? 왜 정답일까?

근거와 주장은 겸손에 도움이 될 수 있다는 내용과 함께 서로 의견 차이를 좁히지 못하는 두 사람의 예를 드는 주어진 글 뒤에는, 양쪽이 적절한 근거를 들어 말하다가 한쪽의 결함이 드러나는 경우를 설명하는 (B)가 먼저 연결된다. 이어서 (A)는 두 주장에 모두 합당한 근거가 있는 '또 다른' 경우를 언급하고, (C)는 이들 또한 각자 주장이 '온전히' 맞지 않음을 수긍하며 겸손을 배울 수 있게 된다고 설명한다. 따라서 글의 순서로 가장 적절한 것은 ② '(B) − (A) − (C)'이다.

- **yell at** ~에게 소리 지르다
- **refute** ⓥ 반박하다
- **appreciate** ⓥ 제대로 이해하다
- **whole** ⓐ 온전한, 전체의
- **progress** ⓝ 진전, 진행
- **a degree of** 어느 정도의
- **opposing** ⓐ 반대되는, 상충하는

구문 풀이

11행 One of the arguments gets refuted — that is, it is shown to fail.
「be shown+to부정사: ~함이 드러나다」

★★ 문제 해결 꿀~팁 ★★

▶ 많이 틀린 이유는?
(B)를 자세히 읽어보면, 견해가 다른 두 사람 중 한쪽의 주장이 반박당하는 경우를 설명하고 있다. 하지만 (C)는 '둘 중 아무도 온전한 진실을 갖고 있지 않은 경우'를 다루므로 (B)와 연결되지 않는다. 이때 (A)가 '둘 중 어느 주장도 반박되지 않는 경우'를 말하고 있으므로, 이 상황에 대한 보충 설명이 (C)임을 알 수 있다.

▶ 문제 해결 방법은?
단순히 지시어나 연결어 등 형태적인 힌트에만 의존하면 답을 찾기 어렵다. 다른 쉬운 문제(심경, 도표, 안내문 등)를 빨리 풀고 남은 시간을 투자해 단락별 내용을 깊이 파악해야 한다.

38 순응과 구별되는 적응의 특성
정답률 53% | 정답 ③

글의 흐름으로 보아, 주어진 문장이 들어가기에 가장 적절한 곳을 고르시오. [3점]

Adaptation involves changes in a population, / with characteristics / that are passed from one generation to the next.
적응은 개체군의 변화를 수반한다. / 특성과 함께 / 한 세대로부터 다음 세대로 전해지는
This is different from acclimation / — an individual organism's changes / in response to an altered environment.
이것은 순응과는 다르다. / 개별 유기체의 변화인 / 변화된 환경에 반응한
① For example, / if you spend the summer outside, / you may acclimate to the sunlight: / your skin will increase its concentration of dark pigments / that protect you from the sun.
예를 들어, / 당신이 여름을 야외에서 보낸다면, / 당신은 햇빛에 순응하게 되어, / 당신의 피부는 어두운 색소의 농도를 증가시킬 것이다. / 당신을 태양으로부터 보호하는
② This is a temporary change, / and you won't pass the temporary change on / to future generations.
이것은 일시적인 변화이고, / 당신은 그 일시적인 변화를 물려주지 않을 것이다. / 미래 세대에
☑ However, / the capacity to produce skin pigments / is inherited.
하지만, / 피부 색소를 생산하는 능력은 / 유전된다.
For populations living in intensely sunny environments, / individuals with a good ability to produce skin pigments / are more likely to thrive, or to survive, / than people with a poor ability to produce pigments, / and that trait becomes increasingly common in subsequent generations.
햇빛이 강렬한 환경에 사는 사람들의 경우, / 피부 색소를 생산하는 능력이 좋은 사람들이 / 더 번영하거나 생존하기 쉽고, / 색소 생산 능력이 좋지 않은 사람들보다 / 그 특징은 다음 세대에서 더욱 흔해진다.
④ If you look around, / you can find countless examples of adaptation.
당신이 주변을 둘러보면, / 당신은 적응의 수많은 사례를 찾을 수 있다.
⑤ The distinctive long neck of a giraffe, / for example, / developed / as individuals that happened to have longer necks / had an advantage / in feeding on the leaves of tall trees.
기린의 특징인 긴 목은 / 예를 들어, / 발달했다. / 우연히 더 긴 목을 갖게 된 개체들이 / 이점을 가짐에 따라 / 키 큰 나무의 잎을 먹는 데

적응은 한 세대로부터 다음 세대로 전해지는 특성과 함께 개체군의 변화를 수반한다. 이것은 변화된 환경에 반응한 개별 유기체의 변화인 순응과는 다르다. ① 예를 들어, 당신이 여름을 야외에서 보낸다면, 당신은 햇빛에 순응하게 되어, 당신의 피부는 당신을 태양으로부터 보호하는 어두운 색소의 농도를 증가시킬 것이다. ② 이것은 일시적인 변화이고, 당신은 그 일시적인 변화를 미래 세대에 물려주지 않을 것이다. ③ 하지만, 피부 색소를 생산하는 능력은 유전된다. 햇빛이 강렬한 환경에 사는 사람들의 경우, 피부 색소를 생산하는 능력이 좋은 사람들이 색소 생산 능력이 좋지 않은 사람들보다 더 번영하거나 생존하기 쉽고, 그 특징은 다음 세대에서 더욱 흔해진다. ④ 주변을 둘러보면, 당신은 적응의 수많은 사례를 찾을 수 있다. ⑤ 예를 들어, 기린의 특징인 긴 목은 우연히 더 긴 목을 갖게 된 개체들이 키 큰 나무의 잎을 먹는 데 유리해짐에 따라 발달했다.

Why? 왜 정답일까?

③ 앞에서 여름 햇빛에 반응해 생기는 일시적 변화를 순응의 예로 언급하는데, 주어진 문장은 이와는 달리 피부 색소를 생산하는 능력의 경우 유전적으로 전해질 수 있는 '적응'의 예시임을 설명한다. ③ 뒤의 문장은 주어진 문장에 이어 피부 색소를 생산해내는 능력에 관해 부연 설명한다. 따라서 주어진 문장이 들어가기에 가장 적절한 곳은 ③이다.

- **inherit** ⓥ 물려주다, 상속하다
- **adaptation** ⓝ 적응

- **acclimation** ⓝ (새 환경에 대한) 순응
- **concentration** ⓝ 농도
- **thrive** ⓥ 번성하다
- **distinctive** ⓐ 독특한
- **alter** ⓥ 바꾸다, 변경하다
- **intensely** ⓐⓓ 강렬하게
- **trait** ⓝ 특성

구문 풀이

14행 The distinctive long neck of a giraffe, for example, developed as individuals [that happened to have longer necks] had an advantage in feeding on the leaves of tall trees.
주어 / 자동사(~함에 따라) / 접속사 / 우연히 ~하다

39 지구의 대기 대순환
정답률 49% | 정답 ③

글의 흐름으로 보아, 주어진 문장이 들어가기에 가장 적절한 곳을 고르시오.

On any day of the year, / the tropics / and the hemisphere that is experiencing its warm season / receive much more solar radiation / than do the polar regions and the colder hemisphere.
연중 어느 날이든, / 열대 지방과 / 따뜻한 계절을 보내고 있는 반구는 / 훨씬 더 많은 태양 복사열을 받는다. / 극지방과 더 추운 반구가 받는 것보다
① Averaged over the course of the year, / the tropics and latitudes up to about 40° / receive more total heat / than they lose by radiation.
일 년 중 평균적으로, / 열대 지역과 위도 약 40도까지의 지역은 / 더 많은 전체 열을 받는다. / 복사에 의해 잃는 열보다
② Latitudes above 40° receive less total heat / than they lose by radiation.
위도 40도 이상의 지역은 더 적은 전체 열을 받는다. / 복사열에 의해 잃는 것보다
☑ This inequality produces the necessary conditions / for the operation of a huge, global-scale engine / that takes on heat in the tropics / and gives it off in the polar regions.
이러한 불균형은 필요조건을 만들어 낸다. / 거대한 전 지구 규모의 엔진 작동을 위한 / 열대 지방에서 열을 받아서 / 극지방에서 그 열을 방출하는
Its working fluid is the atmosphere, / especially the moisture it contains.
그것의 작동유는 대기인데, / 특히 그것이 품고 있는 수분이다.
④ Air is heated over the warm earth of the tropics, / expands, rises, and flows away both northward and southward at high altitudes, / cooling as it goes.
공기는 열대 지방의 따뜻한 땅 위에서 데워지고, / 확장되고, 상승해서 높은 고도에서 북쪽과 남쪽 두 방향으로 흐르게 되고, / 이동하면서 식는다.
⑤ It descends and flows toward the equator again / from more northerly and southerly latitudes.
그것은 하강하여 다시 적도를 향해 흘러간다. / 더 북쪽과 남쪽의 위도로부터

연중 어느 날이든, 열대 지방과 따뜻한 계절을 보내고 있는 반구는 극지방과 더 추운 반구가 받는 것보다 훨씬 더 많은 태양 복사열을 받는다. ① 일 년 중 평균적으로, 열대 지역과 위도 약 40도까지의 지역은 복사에 의해 잃는 열보다 더 많은 전체 열을 받는다. ② 위도 40도 이상의 지역은 복사열에 의해 잃는 것보다 더 적은 전체 열을 받는다. ③ 이러한 불균형은 열대 지방에서 열을 받아서 극지방에서 그 열을 방출하는 거대한 전 지구 규모의 엔진 작동을 위한 필요조건을 만들어 낸다. 그것의 작동유는 대기인데, 특히 그것이 품고 있는 수분이다. ④ 공기는 열대 지방의 따뜻한 땅 위에서 데워지고, 확장되고, 상승해서 높은 고도에서 북쪽과 남쪽 두 방향으로 흐르게 되고, 이동하면서 식는다. ⑤ 그것은 하강하여 더 북쪽과 남쪽의 위도에서 다시 적도를 향해 흘러간다.

Why? 왜 정답일까?

③ 앞에서 열대 지방과 위도 40도까지의 지역은 위도 40도를 넘는 지역보다 전체적으로 더 많은 열을 받는다고 하는데, 주어진 문장은 바로 이런 '불균형' 때문에 열대에서 쌓인 열이 극지방에서 방출되는 과정이 일어날 수밖에 없다고 설명한다. ③ 뒤의 문장은 이 과정에서 열을 전달해주는 매체(Its working fluid)가 바로 공기, 특히 그 안의 수분임을 부연 설명한다. 따라서 주어진 문장이 들어가기에 가장 적절한 곳은 ③이다.

- **necessary condition** 필요조건
- **tropics** ⓝ 열대
- **polar** ⓐ 극지방의
- **radiation** ⓝ (열, 에너지 등의) 복사
- **equator** ⓝ 적도
- **take on** ~을 떠맡다
- **give off** 방출하다, 내뿜다
- **hemisphere** ⓝ 반구
- **working fluid** 작동유(동력을 전달해주는 매체)

구문 풀이

11행 Air is heated over the warm earth of the tropics, expands, rises, and flows away both northward and southward at high altitudes, cooling as it goes.
동사1 / 동사2 / 동사3 / 동사4 / 대명사(= air)

40 그린워싱의 교묘한 수법
정답률 59% | 정답 ②

다음 글의 내용을 한 문장으로 요약하고자 한다. 빈칸 (A), (B)에 들어갈 말로 가장 적절한 것은? [3점]

(A)	(B)
① permanently 영구적으로	manipulated 조종당한
② temporarily 일시적으로 ☑	misinformed 잘못된 정보를 받은
③ momentarily 잠시	advocated 옹호된
④ ultimately 궁극적으로	underestimated 과소평가된
⑤ consistently 지속적으로	analyzed 분석된

Greenwashing involves misleading a consumer into thinking / that a good or service is more environmentally friendly / than it really is.
그린워싱은 소비자가 생각하도록 현혹시키는 것을 포함한다. / 재화나 서비스가 더 친환경적이라고 / 실제 그것이 그런 것보다
Greenwashing ranges / from making environmental claims required by law, / and therefore irrelevant (CFC-free for example), / to puffery (exaggerating environmental claims) / to fraud.
그린워싱은 ~에 이른다. / 법에 의해 요구되는 환경적 주장을 하는 것부터 / 그래서 무의미한 것(예를 들어 '염화불화탄소 없음')에서부터 / 과대 광고(환경적 주장을 과장하는 것)와 / 사기까지
Researchers have shown / that claims on products are often too vague or misleading.
연구자들은 보여준다. / 제품에 관한 주장은 종종 지나치게 모호하거나 현혹적이라는 것을

Some products are labeled "chemical-free," / when the fact is everything contains chemicals, / including plants and animals.
몇몇 제품에는 '화학물질 없음'이라고 표기되어 있다. / 사실은 모든 것에 화학물질이 들어있는데 / 식물과 동물 포함해서
Products with the highest number of misleading or unverifiable claims / were laundry detergents, household cleaners, and paints.
현혹적이고 확인할 수 없는 주장이 가장 많이 포함된 제품은 / 세탁 세제, 가정용 세제, 그리고 페인트였다.
Environmental advocates agree / there is still a long way to go / to ensure shoppers are adequately informed / about the environmental impact of the products they buy.
환경 옹호자들이 동의하기로, / 여전히 갈 길이 멀다. / 소비자들이 확실히 정보를 적절하게 제공받으려면 / 그들이 구매하는 제품의 환경적 영향력에 대하여
The most common reason for greenwashing / is to attract environmentally conscious consumers.
그린워싱의 가장 흔한 이유는 / 환경적으로 의식 있는 소비자들을 유인하기 위해서이다.
Many consumers do not find out about the false claims / until after the purchase.
많은 소비자들은 거짓 주장을 발견하지 못한다. / 구매를 끝내기 전까지
Therefore, / greenwashing may increase sales in the short term.
그러므로 / 그린워싱은 단기적으로는 판매량을 증가시킬 수도 있다.
However, / this strategy can seriously backfire / when consumers find out they are being deceived.
하지만, / 이 전략은 심각하게 역효과를 낼 수 있다. / 자신들이 기만당하고 있다는 것을 소비자들이 알게 될 때
➡ While greenwashing might bring a company profits (A) temporarily / by deceiving environmentally conscious consumers, / the company will face serious trouble / when the consumers figure out they were (B) misinformed.
그린워싱이 일시적으로 회사에 이익을 가져다줄 수 있지만, / 환경적인 의식이 있는 소비자들을 속여 / 회사는 심각한 문제에 직면할 것이다. / 소비자들이 자신들이 잘못된 정보를 받은 것을 알게 됐을 때

그린워싱은 소비자가 재화나 서비스를 실제보다 더 친환경적이라고 생각하도록 현혹시키는 것을 포함한다. 그린워싱은 법에 의해 요구되는 환경적 주장을 하는 것, 그래서 무의미한 것(예를 들어 '염화불화탄소 없음')에서부터 과대 광고(환경적 주장을 과장하는 것), 사기에까지 이르는 것을 포함한다. 연구자들에 따르면, 제품에 관한 주장은 종종 지나치게 모호하거나 현혹적이다. 몇몇 제품들에는 실제로 식물과 동물을 포함해서 모든 것에 화학물질이 들어있음에도 '화학물질 없음'이라고 표기되어 있다. 현혹적이고 확인할 수 없는 주장이 가장 많이 포함된 제품은 세탁 세제, 가정용 세제, 그리고 페인트였다. 환경 옹호자들이 동의하기로, 소비자들이 구매하는 제품의 환경적 영향력에 대하여 확실히 정보를 적절하게 제공받으려면 여전히 갈 길이 멀다. 그린워싱의 가장 흔한 이유는 환경적으로 의식 있는 소비자들을 유인하기 위해서이다. 많은 소비자들은 구매를 끝내기 전까지 거짓 주장을 발견하지 못한다. 그러므로 그린워싱은 단기적으로는 판매량을 증가시킬 수도 있다. 하지만, 이 전략은 자신들이 기만당하고 있다는 것을 소비자들이 알게 될 때 심각하게 역효과를 낼 수 있다.

➡ 그린워싱이 환경적인 의식이 있는 소비자들을 속여 (A) 일시적으로 회사에 이익을 가져다 줄 수 있지만, 소비자들이 (B) 잘못된 정보를 받은 것을 알게 됐을 때 회사는 심각한 문제에 직면할 것이다.

Why? 왜 정답일까?

마지막 네 문장에 핵심 내용이 제시된다. 그린워싱은 흔히 환경에 신경을 쓰는 소비자들을 유인하기 위해 이용되고, 실제로 단기적으로는 회사에 이득을 가져다주지만, 결과적으로 소비자들이 속았다는 것을 깨달으면 심각한 역효과를 초래할 수 있다는(~ greenwashing may increase sales in the short term. However, this strategy can seriously backfire when consumers find out they are being deceived.)는 것이다. 따라서 요약문의 빈칸 (A), (B)에 들어갈 말로 가장 적절한 것은 ② '(A) temporarily(일시적으로), (B) misinformed(잘못된 정보를 받은)'이다.

- greenwashing ⓝ 그린워싱, 위장 환경주의
- range from A to B A부터 B에 이르다
- exaggerate ⓥ 과장하다
- unverifiable ⓐ 증명할 수 없는
- in the short term 단기적으로
- permanently ⓐⓓ 영구적으로
- mislead ⓥ 현혹하다, 오도하다
- puffery ⓝ 과대 선전
- vague ⓐ 애매모호한
- detergent ⓝ 세제
- backfire ⓥ 역효과를 낳다

구문 풀이

1행 Greenwashing involves misleading a consumer into thinking a good or
                                   목적어(동명사)
service is more environmentally friendly than it really is.
                                              대동사(= is environmentally friendly)

41-42 소외된다는 두려움을 즐거움으로 바꾸기

The driver of FOMO (the fear of missing out) / is the social pressure / to be at the right place with the right people, / whether it's from a sense of duty / or just trying to get ahead, / we feel (a) obligated to attend certain events / for work, for family and for friends.
FOMO(소외되는 것에 대한 두려움)의 동기는 / 사회적 압박인데, / 적재적소에 있어야 한다 / 그것이 의무감으로부터 오든, / 또는 앞서 나가려는 데서 오든 간에, / 우리는 어떤 행사에 참석해야만 한다는 의무감을 느낀다. / 직장, 가족, 친구를 위해서
This pressure from society combined with FOMO / can wear us down.
FOMO와 결합된 사회로부터의 이러한 압박은 / 우리를 지치게 할 수 있다.
According to a recent survey, / 70 percent of employees admit / that when they take a vacation, / they still don't (b) disconnect from work.
최근 연구에 따르면 / 직원들 중 70%는 인정했다 / 그들이 휴가를 가서도 / 그들은 여전히 직장에서 단절되지 않는다고
Our digital habits, / which include constantly checking emails, and social media timelines, / have become so firmly established, / it is nearly impossible to simply enjoy the moment, / along with the people / with whom we are sharing these moments.
디지털 습관은 / 끊임없이 이메일, 소셜미디어 타임라인을 확인하는 것을 포함한 / 너무 굳어지게 되어서 / 거의 불가능하다. / 그저 즐기는 것이 / 사람들과 / 우리가 그 순간을 나누고 있는 《41번의 근거》
『JOMO (the joy of missing out) / is the emotionally intelligent antidote to FOMO / and is essentially about being present / and being (c) content with where you are at in life.』
JOMO(소외되는 것에 대한 즐거움)는 / FOMO에 대한 정서적으로 현명한 해독제이고, / 본질적으로 현재에 있으면서 / 현재의 삶에 만족하는 데 관한 것이다.
You do not need to compare your life to others / but instead, practice tuning out the background noise of the "shoulds" and "wants" / and learn to let go of worrying / whether you are doing something wrong.
당신은 다른 사람들과 자신의 삶을 비교할 필요가 없다. / 대신에, '해야 하는 것'과 '원하는 것'의 배경 소음을 듣지 않는 연습을 하라 / 그리고 걱정을 버리는 법을 배워라. / 당신이 뭔가 잘못된 일을 하고 있는 것인지 아닌지를
JOMO allows us / to live life in the slow lane, / to appreciate human connections, / to be

(d) intentional with our time, / to practice saying "no," / to give ourselves "tech-free breaks," / and to give ourselves permission / to acknowledge where we are and to feel emotions.
JOMO는 여러분이 ~하게 해준다. / 느리게 사는 삶을 살고, / 인간관계의 연결을 이해하며, / 자기 시간에 의도를 갖고, / 거절하는 법을 연습하고, / 스스로에게 '기기에서 벗어나는 휴식 시간'을 주며, / 우리 자신에게 허락하게 / 현재 있는 곳을 인식하고 감정을 느끼도록
『Instead of constantly trying to keep up with the rest of society, / JOMO allows us / to be who we are in the present moment.』 《42번의 근거》
사회의 나머지 사람들을 따라 잡으려고 끊임없이 애쓰는 대신, / JOMO는 우리가 ~할 수 있게 해준다. / 현재 이 순간에 우리 자신이 될
When you (e) free up that competitive and anxious space in your brain, / you have so much more time, energy, and emotion / to conquer your true priorities.
당신이 뇌 속 경쟁적이고 걱정스러운 공간을 벗어날 때, / 당신은 더욱 많은 시간과 에너지를 가질 수 있다. / 당신의 진정한 우선순위를 정복해나가게 해주는

FOMO(소외되는 것에 대한 두려움)의 동기는 적재적소에 있어야 한다는 사회적 압박인데, 그것이 의무감으로부터 오든, 또는 앞서 나가려는 데서 오든 간에, 우리는 직장, 가족, 친구를 위해서 어떤 행사에 참석해야만 한다는 (a) 의무감을 느낀다. FOMO와 결합된 사회로부터의 이러한 압박은 우리를 지치게 할 수 있다. 최근 연구에 따르면 직원들 중 70%는 휴가를 가서도 여전히 직장에서 (b) 단절되지 않는다고 인정했다. 끊임없이 이메일, 소셜 미디어 타임라인을 확인하는 것을 포함한 디지털 습관은 너무 굳어져서, 그 순간을 나누고 있는 사람들과 그저 즐기는 것이 거의 불가능하다.
JOMO(소외되는 것에 대한 즐거움)는 FOMO에 대한 정서적으로 현명한 해독제이고, 본질적으로 현재에 있으면서 현재의 삶에 (c) 만족하는 데 관한 것이다. 당신은 다른 사람들과 자신의 삶을 비교할 필요가 없다. 대신에, '해야 하는 것'과 '원하는 것'의 배경 소음을 듣지 않는 연습을 하고, 당신 행동의 옳고 그름에 대한 걱정을 버리는 법을 배워라. JOMO는 여러분이 느리게 사는 삶을 살고, 인간관계의 연결을 이해하며, 자기 시간에 (d) 의도를 갖고, 거절하는 법을 연습하고, 스스로에게 '기기에서 벗어나는 휴식 시간'을 주며, 현재 있는 곳을 인식하고 감정을 느끼도록 허락할 수 있게 해준다. 사회의 나머지 사람들을 따라잡으려고 끊임없이 애쓰는 대신, JOMO는 현재 이 순간에 우리 자신이 될 수 있게 해준다. 당신이 뇌 속 경쟁적이고 걱정스러운 공간을 (e) 활성화할(→ 벗어날) 때, 당신은 진정한 우선순위를 정복해나가게 해주는 더욱 많은 시간과 에너지를 가질 수 있다.

- miss out 놓치다, 소외되다
- wear down ~을 지치게 하다
- along with ~와 함께
- let go of ~을 버리다, 놓아주다
- conquer ⓥ 정복하다, 이기다
- feel obligated to ~해야 한다는 의무감이 들다
- established ⓐ 확립된, 자리 잡은
- tune out ~을 듣지 않다, 무시하다
- keep up with ~을 따라잡다
- catch up with ~을 따라잡다, ~에 발맞추다

구문 풀이

8행 Our digital habits, which include constantly checking emails, and social media timelines, have become so firmly established, it is nearly impossible to
「so ~ that : 너무 ~해서 …하다(that 대신 콤마)」
simply enjoy the moment, along with the people [with whom we are sharing
「전치사 + 목적격 관·대」
these moments].

★★★ 등급을 가르는 문제!

41 제목 파악 정답률 40% | 정답 ①

윗글의 제목으로 가장 적절한 것은?

✓① Missing Out Has Its Benefits
소외는 나름의 이점이 있다
② JOMO: Another Form of Self-Deception
JOMO: 또 다른 형태의 자기 기만
③ How to Catch up with Digital Technology
디지털 기술을 따라잡는 방법
④ Being Isolated from Others Makes You Lonely
다른 사람들로부터 고립되면 외로워진다
⑤ Using Social Media Wisely: The Dos and Don'ts
소셜 미디어 현명하게 쓰기: 해야 할 일과 하지 말아야 할 일

Why? 왜 정답일까?

첫 문단에서 소외되는 것을 두려워하는 현상인 FOMO를 소개한 뒤, 이것을 극복하기 위해서는 JOMO, 즉 소외 상태를 즐기고 현재에 집중하기를 선택해야 한다고 설명하고 있다. 따라서 글의 제목으로 가장 적절한 것은 ① '소외는 나름의 이점이 있다'이다.

★★ 문제 해결 꿀~팁 ★★

▶ 많이 틀린 이유는?
이 글은 FOMO와 반대되는 개념인 JOMO를 소개하고, 이를 채택하기를 권하고 있다. 즉 타인과 내내 연결되어 막연한 의무감이나 사회적 비교로 고통받으며 살아가기보다는, 잠시 연결을 내려놓고 자기 삶에 만족하라는 것이다. 최다 오답인 ②는 이 JOMO가 '자기 기만적인' 측면을 지닌다는 부정적인 내용이므로 답으로 적절하지 않다.

▶ 문제 해결 방법은?
정답인 ①은 JOMO라는 키워드를 그대로 옮기는 대신 'missing out에 장점이 있다'는 표현을 썼다. 이렇듯 제목 문제의 정답에는 키워드가 그대로 나오기보다는 키워드를 암시하는 간접적 표현이나 비유가 흔히 등장한다.

★★★ 등급을 가르는 문제!

42 어휘 추론 정답률 39% | 정답 ⑤

밑줄 친 (a) ~ (e) 중에서 문맥상 낱말의 쓰임이 적절하지 않은 것은?

① (a) ② (b) ③ (c) ④ (d) ✓⑤ (e)

Why? 왜 정답일까?

'Instead of constantly trying to keep up with the rest of society, ~' 문장에서 다른 사람들을 자꾸 따라잡으려고 애쓰는 대신 지금 이 순간 자기 자신이 되는 것이 곧 JOMO임을 설명하고 있다. 즉, 우리 마음속 걱정과 불안의 영역을 '활성화하기'보다는, 그러한 영역에서 '해방되어' 자기 자신을 되찾는

 [문제편 p.127]

것이 JOMO의 핵심이므로, (e)의 **activate**는 **free up**으로 고쳐야 한다. 따라서 문맥상 낱말의 쓰임이 적절하지 않은 것은 ⑤ '(e)'이다.

43-45 온 세상을 녹색으로 칠하려 했던 남자

(A)

『There was a very wealthy man / who was bothered by severe eye pain.
아주 부유한 남자가 있었다. / 심한 눈 통증으로 괴로워하는
He consulted many doctors / and was treated by several of them.』 45번 ①의 근거 일치
그는 많은 의사와 상담했고, / 이들 중 여러 명에게 치료받았다.
He did not stop consulting a galaxy of medical experts; / he was heavily medicated / and underwent hundreds of injections.
그는 멈추지 않고 수많은 의료 전문가들과 상담했다 / 그는 많은 약을 복용했고 / 주사를 수백 번 맞았다.
However, / the pain persisted / and was worse than before.
하지만 / 통증이 지속되었고, / 전보다 심해졌다.
At last, / (a) he heard about a monk / who was famous for treating patients with his condition.
결국 / 그는 한 수도사에 대해 듣게 되었다. / 자신 같은 질환의 환자들을 치료하는 것으로 유명한
Within a few days, / the monk was called for by the suffering man.
며칠 후, / 그 수도사는 고통받는 그 남자에게 불려갔다.

(D)

The monk understood the wealthy man's problem / and said / that for some time (e) he should concentrate only on green colours / and not let his eyes see any other colours.
수도사는 그 부자의 문제를 이해했고 / 말했다. / 일정 시간 동안 그가 녹색에만 집중하고 눈으로 / 다른 색을 봐서는 안 된다고
『The wealthy man thought / it was a strange prescription, / but he was desperate and decided to try it.』 45번 ④의 근거 일치
부자는 생각했다 / 그것이 이상한 처방이라고 하지만 그는 절박해서 그것을 시도하기로 하였다.
『He got together a group of painters / and purchased barrels of green paint / and ordered / that every object he was likely to see / be painted green / just as the monk had suggested.』
그는 페인트공들을 불러 모았고 / 녹색 페인트를 많이 구매하여 / 지시했다. / 그가 볼 가능성이 있는 모든 물체가 / 녹색으로 칠해져야 한다고 수도사가 제안한 대로

(B)

In a few days / everything around (b) that man was green.
며칠 후 / 그 남자 주변의 모든 것은 녹색이 되었다.
The wealthy man made sure / that nothing around him could be any other colour.
부자는 확실히 하였다. / 자기 주변의 어떤 것도 다른 아무 색이 되지 않도록
『When the monk came to visit him after a few days, / the wealthy man's servants ran with buckets of green paint / and poured them all over him / because he was wearing red clothes.』 45번 ②의 근거 일치
며칠 후 수도사가 그를 찾아왔을 때, / 부자의 하인들은 녹색 페인트통을 들고 달려와서 / 그의 몸 전체에 부었다. / 그가 붉은 옷을 입고 있었기 때문에
(c) He asked the servants / why they did that.
그는 하인들에게 물었다. / 왜 그들이 그렇게 했는지

(C)

They replied, / "We can't let our master see any other colour."
그들은 대답했다. / "우리는 주인님이 다른 어떤 색도 보게 할 수 없어요." 45번 ③의 근거 불일치
Hearing this, / the monk laughed and said / "If only you had purchased a pair of green glasses for just a few dollars, / you could have saved these walls, trees, pots, and everything else / and you could have saved a large share of (d) his fortune.』 / You cannot paint the whole world green."
이것을 듣고 / 수도사는 웃으며 말했다. / "만약에 당신들이 단돈 몇 달러밖에 하지 않는 녹색 안경 하나만 구매했다면, / 당신들은 이러한 벽, 나무, 항아리, 그리고 다른 모든 것을 지킬 수 있었을 것이고 / 또한 당신은 그의 재산의 많은 부분을 아낄 수 있었을 것입니다. / 당신들은 온 세상을 녹색으로 칠할 수는 없어요."

(A)

심한 눈 통증으로 괴로워하는 아주 부유한 남자가 있었다. 그는 많은 의사와 상담했고, 이들 중 여러 명에게 치료받았다. 그는 멈추지 않고 수많은 의료 전문가들과 상담했으며, 많은 약물을 복용했고 주사를 수백 번 맞았다. 하지만 통증은 지속되었고, 전보다 심해졌다. 결국 (a) 그는 자신 같은 질환의 환자들을 치료하는 것으로 유명한 한 수도사에 대해 듣게 되었다. 며칠 후, 그 수도사는 고통받는 그 남자에게 불려갔다.

(D)

수도사는 그 부자의 문제를 이해했고 일정 시간 동안 (e) 그가 녹색에만 집중하고 눈으로 다른 색을 봐서는 안 된다고 말했다. 부자는 그것이 이상한 처방이라고 생각했지만, 절박해서 그것을 시도하기로 하였다. 그는 페인트공들을 불러 모았고 녹색 페인트를 많이 구매하여 수도사가 제안한 대로 그가 볼 가능성이 있는 모든 물체를 녹색으로 칠하라고 지시했다.

(B)

며칠 후 (b) 그 남자 주변의 모든 것은 녹색이 되었다. 부자는 주변의 어떤 것도 다른 색이 되지 않도록 확실히 하였다. 며칠 후 수도사가 그를 찾아왔을 때, 그는 붉은 옷을 입고 있었기 때문에 부자의 하인들은 녹색 페인트통을 들고 달려와서 그의 몸 전체에 부었다. (c) 그는 하인들에게 왜 그들이 그렇게 했는지 물었다.

(C)

그들은 대답했다. "우리는 주인님이 다른 어떤 색도 보게 할 수 없어요." 이것을 듣고 수도사는 웃으며 말했다. "만약에 당신들이 단돈 몇 달러밖에 하지 않는 녹색 안경 하나만 구매했다면, 이러한 벽, 나무, 항아리, 그리고 다른 모든 것을 지킬 수 있었을 것이고 또한 (d) 그의 재산의 많은 부분을 아낄 수 있었을 것입니다. 당신들은 온 세상을 녹색으로 칠할 수는 없어요."

- **wealthy** ⓐ 부유한
- **medical expert** 의료 전문가
- **undergo** ⓥ 겪다, 경험하다
- **call for** ~을 필요로 하다, 데리러 가다, 부르다
- **severe** ⓐ 심각한
- **medicate** ⓥ 약을 투여하다
- **persist** ⓥ 지속되다
- **desperate** ⓐ 절박한

구문 풀이

(C) 2행 Hearing this, the monk laughed and said "If only you had purchased a [if (only) + 주어 + had p.p. ~] pair of green glasses for just a few dollars, you could have saved these walls, [주어 + 조동사 과거형 + have p.p.: 가정법 과거완료] trees, pots, and everything else ~"

(D) 5행 He ~ ordered that every object [he was likely to see] (should) be painted [동사(명령) 접속사 주어 동사구] green just as the monk had suggested.

---

43 글의 순서 파악 정답률 83% | 정답 ④

주어진 글 (A)에 이어질 내용을 순서에 맞게 배열한 것으로 가장 적절한 것은?
① (B) – (D) – (C)　　② (C) – (B) – (D)
③ (C) – (D) – (B)　　✔ (D) – (B) – (C)
⑤ (D) – (C) – (B)

Why? 왜 정답일까?

한 부자가 눈 통증이 너무 심해 여러 의사를 전전하다 수도사를 불러들였다는 내용의 (A) 뒤에는, 초록색만 봐야 한다는 수도사의 처방에 따라 부자가 하인들을 시켜 모든 사물을 녹색으로 칠하게 했다는 내용의 (D)가 이어진다. 한편, (B)에서는 며칠 후 수도사가 붉은 옷을 입고 부자의 집을 방문하자 하인들이 수도사의 몸에 초록색 페인트를 부었다는 내용이 전개되고, (C)에서는 그 이유를 들은 수도사가 그저 초록색 안경 하나만 샀으면 됐을 것이라고 알려주었다는 내용이 이어진다. 따라서 글의 순서로 가장 적절한 것은 ④ '(D) – (B) – (C)'이다.

44 지칭 추론 정답률 70% | 정답 ③

밑줄 친 (a) ~ (e) 중에서 가리키는 대상이 나머지 넷과 다른 것은?
① (a)　　② (b)　　✔ (c)　　④ (d)　　⑤ (e)

Why? 왜 정답일까?

(a), (b), (d), (e)는 the wealthy man, (c)는 the monk를 가리키므로, (a) ~ (e) 중에서 가리키는 대상이 다른 하나는 ③ '(c)'이다.

45 세부 내용 파악 정답률 78% | 정답 ③

윗글에 관한 내용으로 적절하지 않은 것은?
① 부자는 눈 통증으로 여러 명의 의사에게 치료받았다.
② 수도사는 붉은 옷을 입고 부자를 다시 찾아갔다.
✔ 하인들은 녹색 안경을 구입했다.
④ 부자는 수도사의 처방이 이상하다고 생각했다.
⑤ 부자는 주변을 모두 녹색으로 칠하게 했다.

Why? 왜 정답일까?

(C) 'If only you had purchased a pair of green glasses for just a few dollars, you could have saved ~'에서 수도사는 만일 부자가 주변을 온통 초록색으로 칠하는 대신 그저 녹색 안경 하나만 샀다면 많은 자원을 아꼈을 것이라고 말해주고 있다. 즉, 녹색 안경을 산 것은 실제 일어난 일이 아니므로, 내용과 일치하지 않는 것은 ③ '하인들은 녹색 안경을 구입했다.'이다.

Why? 왜 오답일까?

① (A) 'There was a very wealthy man who was bothered by severe eye pain. He consulted many doctors and was treated by several of them.'의 내용과 일치한다.
② (B) '~ because he was wearing red clothes.'의 내용과 일치한다.
④ (D) 'The wealthy man thought it was a strange prescription, ~'의 내용과 일치한다.
⑤ (D) '~ ordered that every object he was likely to see be painted green just as the monk had suggested.'의 내용과 일치한다.

A	B	C	D
01 오물	01 steer	01 ①	01 ⓚ
02 간격	02 eyesight	02 ①	02 ⑨
03 예방적인	03 thrive	03 ⑨	03 ⓡ
04 구독	04 readily	04 ⓜ	04 ①
05 신화	05 command	05 ⓒ	05 ⓝ
06 파괴적인	06 undermine	06 ①	06 ①
07 악당	07 ethical	07 ⓑ	07 ①
08 축적하다, 모으다	08 pour	08 ⓐ	08 ⓜ
09 분배, 분포	09 wellness	09 ⓢ	09 ⓑ
10 위계질서	10 override	10 ⓔ	10 ⓔ
11 항공	11 progress	11 ①	11 ⓐ
12 본보기	12 anxiously	12 ①	12 ①
13 실질적인, 현실적인	13 circulation	13 ⓓ	13 ①
14 서로의, 상호의	14 scatter	14 ①	14 ①
15 후회, 유감	15 residential	15 ①	15 ⓓ
16 특성	16 specialization	16 ⓞ	16 ⓠ
17 무작위로	17 official	17 ⓝ	17 ⓒ
18 제대로 이해하다	18 revise	18 ⓠ	18 ⓗ
19 놀랍도록	19 desperate	19 ⓚ	19 ①
20 타격, 충격	20 account	20 ⓗ	20 ⓢ

14회 | 2021학년도 9월 학력평가   고2

• 정답 •

18 ① 19 ① 20 ② 21 ④ 22 ①   23 ⑤ 24 ① 25 ⑤ 26 ④ 27 ⑤   28 ③ 29 ⑤ 30 ③ ★ 31 ② 32 ① ★
33 ① 34 ① ★ 35 ③ 36 ② 37 ③   38 ③ ★ 39 ⑤ ★ 40 ② 41 ④ 42 ③   43 ④ 44 ④ 45 ⑤

★ 표기된 문항은 [등급을 가르는 문제]에 해당하는 문항입니다.

18   강당 수리 예정 안내   정답률 84% | 정답 ①

다음 글의 목적으로 가장 적절한 것은?

✔ ① 수리로 인한 강당 폐쇄를 안내하려고
② 캠퍼스 투어 프로그램 일정을 조정하려고
③ 강당 사용을 위한 신청 방법을 공지하려고
④ 강당 신축을 위한 기금 모금 행사를 홍보하려고
⑤ 집짓기 행사에 참여할 자원 봉사자를 모집하려고

Dear parents and students of Douglas School,
Douglas school의 학부모님과 학생 여러분에게,
As you know, / our school was built over 150 years ago.
여러분들도 아시다시피, / 우리 학교는 150년도 더 전에 지어졌습니다.
While we are proud of our school's history, / the facilities are not exactly what they should be / for modern schooling.
우리는 학교의 역사가 자랑스럽지만, / 학교의 시설들이 정확히 마땅한 모습이지는 않습니다. / 현대 교육을 위해
Thanks to a generous donation to the school foundation, / we will be able to start renovating those parts of our campus / that have become outdated.
학교 재단에 아낌없이 기부해 주신 덕분에, / 우리는 캠퍼스의 그러한 요소들에 대한 보수를 시작할 수 있을 것입니다. / 구식이 되어버린
We hope / this will help provide our students / with the best education possible.
우리는 바랍니다. / 이 보수작업이 우리 학생들에게 제공하는 데 도움이 되기를 / 가능한 최고의 교육을
I'm writing to inform you / that the auditorium will be the first building / closed for repairs.
이 편지로 여러분께 알려드립니다. / 강당이 첫 번째 건물이 될 것이라는 점을 / 수리로 인해 폐쇄되는
Students will not be able to use the auditorium / for about one month / while the repairs are taking place.
학생들은 강당을 이용할 수 없게 됩니다. / 약 한 달 동안 / 수리가 진행되는 동안
We hope / that you will understand / how this brief inconvenience will encourage community-wide benefits / for years to come.
우리는 바랍니다. / 여러분이 이해해 주시기를 / 이 짧은 불편함이 지역사회 전체의 혜택을 어떻게 장려할 것인지 / 향후 몇 년 동안
Sincerely, // Vice Principal Kyla Andrews
교감 Kyla Andrews 드림

Douglas school의 학부모님과 학생 여러분에게,

여러분들도 아시다시피, 우리 학교는 150년도 더 전에 지어졌습니다. 우리는 학교의 역사가 자랑스럽지만, 학교의 시설들이 현대 교육을 위해 정확히 맞지는 않습니다. 학교 재단에 아낌없이 기부해 주신 덕분에, 우리는 구식이 되어버린 캠퍼스의 그러한 요소들에 대한 보수를 시작할 수 있을 것입니다. 우리는 이 보수작업으로 우리 학생들에게 가능한 최고의 교육을 제공하는 데 도움이 되기를 바랍니다. 강당이 수리로 인해 폐쇄되는 첫 번째 건물이 될 것이라는 점을 이 편지로 알려드립니다. 학생들은 수리가 진행되는 동안 약 한 달 동안 강당을 이용할 수 없게 됩니다. 이 짧은 불편함이 향후 몇 년 동안 지역사회 전체의 혜택을 어떻게 장려할 것인지 이해해 주시기를 바랍니다.

교감 Kyla Andrews 드림

Why? 왜 정답일까?

글 후반부에서 캠퍼스 내 보수작업이 강당에서 처음 진행됨에 따라 앞으로 한 달간 강당을 이용할 수 없게 된다고 하므로(I'm writing to inform you that the auditorium will be the first building closed for repairs.), 글의 목적으로 가장 적절한 것은 ① '수리로 인한 강당 폐쇄를 안내하려고'이다.

- **facility** ⓝ 시설
- **foundation** ⓝ 재단
- **outdated** ⓐ 구식인, 시대에 뒤처진
- **inconvenience** ⓝ 불편, 폐
- **generous** ⓐ 관대한, 너그러운
- **renovate** ⓥ 수리하다, 보수하다
- **auditorium** ⓝ 강당

구문 풀이

8행 I'm writing to inform you that the auditorium will be the first building
    부사적 용법(목적)   접속사(~것)
closed for repairs.
    과거분사구

19   시드니를 떠나게 되어 충격받고 당황한 Evan   정답률 89% | 정답 ①

다음 글에 드러난 Evan의 심경으로 가장 적절한 것은?

✔ ① shocked and worried – 충격받고 걱정하는
② excited and pleased – 신나고 기쁜
③ grateful and relieved – 감사하고 안도한
④ bored and indifferent – 지루하고 무관심한
⑤ jealous and envious – 질투 나고 부러운

Evan's eyes opened wide / and his mouth made the shape of an O, / which happened whenever something surprised him.
Evan은 눈이 휘둥그레지고 / 입은 O자 모양이 되었는데, / 이는 그가 무언가로 놀랄 때마다 일어나는 일이었다.
"You don't mean we're leaving Sydney?" / he asked.
"우리가 시드니를 떠난다는 말은 아니죠?" / 그가 물었다.

His mother had just told him / they were leaving Sydney for his father's work.
그의 어머니는 막 그에게 이야기한 참이었다. / 그들이 아버지의 일을 위해 시드니를 떠난다고

"But what about school?" said Evan, / interrupting her, / a thing he knew he was not supposed to do / but which he felt he would be forgiven for on this occasion.
"그런데 학교는 어쩌고요?"라고 Evan은 말했다. / 어머니의 말을 가로막고는 / 평소에는 하지 않았을 행동이라는 걸 알지만 / 이번 만큼은 용서를 받을 수 있을 것이라 느끼며

"And what about Carl and Daniel and Martin?
"Carl과 Daniel과 Martin은요?

How will they know where I am / when we want to do things together?"
얘네는 내가 있는 곳을 어떻게 알죠? / 우리가 뭔가 함께 하고 싶을 때"

His mother told him / that he would have to say goodbye to his friends for the time being / but that she was sure / Evan would see them again.
그의 어머니는 그에게 말했다. / 그가 지금 당장은 친구들과 작별인사를 해야 하지만 / 그녀는 확신한다고 / Evan이 그들을 다시 보게 될 것이라고

"Say goodbye to them? Say goodbye to them?"
"작별인사를 하라고요? 작별인사요?"

He kept repeating himself, / sounding more and more anxious with every repetition.
그는 반복해서 혼잣말을 했고, / 반복할 때마다 목소리에는 더욱 근심이 어렸다.

Evan은 눈이 휘둥그레지고 입은 O자 모양이 되었는데, 이는 그가 무언가로 놀랄 때마다 일어나는 일이었다. "우리가 시드니를 떠난다는 말은 아니시죠?" 그가 물었다. 그의 어머니는 막 그에게 아버지의 일을 위해 시드니를 떠난다고 이야기한 참이었다. Evan은 평소에는 하지 않았을 행동이라는 걸 알지만 이번만큼은 용서를 받을 수 있을 것이라 느끼며 어머니의 말을 가로막고는 "그런데 학교는 어쩌고요?"라고 말했다. "Carl과 Daniel과 Martin은요? 뭔가 함께 하고 싶을 때 얘네는 내가 있는 곳을 어떻게 알죠?" 그의 어머니는 그에게 지금 당장은 친구들과 작별인사를 해야 하지만 Evan이 그들을 다시 보게 될 것이라고 확신한다고 말했다. "작별인사를 하라고요? 작별인사요?" 그는 반복해서 혼잣말을 했고, 반복할 때마다 목소리에는 더욱 근심이 어렸다.

Why? 왜 정답일까?

첫 문장(~ which happened whenever something surprised him.)과 마지막 문장(~ sounding more and more anxious with every repetition.)을 통해, 아버지의 일 때문에 시드니를 떠나야 한다는 말을 들은 Evan이 충격과 근심을 동시에 느꼈음을 알 수 있다. 따라서 Evan의 심경으로 가장 적절한 것은 ① '충격받고 걱정하는'이다.

- interrupt ⓥ 끼어들다, 간섭하다
- anxious ⓐ 걱정하는
- indifferent ⓐ 무관심한
- envious ⓐ 부러워하는
- occasion ⓝ 경우, 때
- grateful ⓐ 고마워하는
- jealous ⓐ 질투하는

구문 풀이

1행 Evan's eyes opened wide and his mouth made the shape of an O, which
선행사 / 계속적 용법
happened whenever something surprised him.
복합관계부사(~할 때마다)

---

20 협력의 기술을 지도하기 　　　　정답률 91% | 정답 ②

다음 글에서 필자가 주장하는 바로 가장 적절한 것은?
① 학생의 참여가 활발한 수업 방법을 개발해야 한다.
✓ ② 학생에게 성공적인 협동을 위한 기술을 가르쳐야 한다.
③ 학생의 의견을 존중하는 학교 분위기를 조성해야 한다.
④ 학생의 전인적 발달을 위해 체육활동을 강화해야 한다.
⑤ 정보를 올바르게 선별하도록 미디어 교육을 실시해야 한다.

Without guidance from their teacher, / students will not embark on a journey of personal development / that recognizes the value of cooperation.
선생님의 지도 없이는 / 학생들은 개인적 발달의 여정에 나서지 않을 것이다. / 협력의 가치를 인정하는

Left to their own devices, / they will instinctively become increasingly competitive with each other.
하고 싶은 대로 내버려 두면, / 그들은 본능적으로 서로 점점 더 경쟁적이 될 것이다.

They will compare scores, reports, and feedback / within the classroom environment / — just as they do in the sporting arena.
그들은 점수, 성적표, 피드백을 비교할 것이다. / 교실 환경 내의 / 그들이 스포츠 경기장에서 하는 것과 마찬가지로

We don't need to teach our students / about winners and losers.
우리는 학생들에게 가르칠 필요가 없다. / 승자와 패자에 대해

The playground and the media do that for them.
운동장과 미디어가 그들을 위해 그렇게 하는 것이다.

However, / we do need to teach them / that there is more to life than winning / and about the skills they need for successful cooperation.
하지만, / 우리는 정말로 가르쳐 줄 필요가 있다. / 그들에게 삶에 승리보다 더 많은 것이 있다는 것과 / 성공적인 협력을 위해 그들이 필요로 하는 기술에 대해

A group working together successfully / requires individuals / with a multitude of social skills, / as well as a high level of interpersonal awareness.
성공적으로 함께 일하는 그룹은 / 개인들을 필요로 한다. / 다양한 사회적 기술을 가진 / 고도의 대인 의식뿐만 아니라

While some students inherently bring a natural understanding of these skills with them, / they are always in the minority.
일부 학생들은 본래 이러한 기술에 대한 타고난 이해를 가지고 있지만, / 그들은 항상 소수이다.

To bring cooperation between peers into your classroom, / you need to teach these skills consciously and carefully, / and nurture them continuously throughout the school years.
당신의 교실 안에 또래들 사이의 협력을 불러일으키기 위해서, / 당신은 의식적이고 주의 깊게 이러한 기술들을 가르쳐야 하고, / 학창시절 내내 계속해서 그것들을 육성해야 한다.

선생님의 지도 없이는 학생들은 협력의 가치를 인정하는 개인적 발달의 여정에 나서지 않을 것이다. 하고 싶은 대로 내버려 두면, 그들은 본능적으로 서로 점점 더 경쟁적이 될 것이다. 그들은 스포츠 경기장에서와 마찬가지로 교실 환경 내의 점수, 성적표, 피드백을 비교할 것이다. 우리는 학생들에게 승자와 패자에 대해 가르칠 필요가 없다. 운동장과 미디어가 그들을 위해 그렇게 하는 것이다. 하지만, 우리는 그들에게 삶에 승리보다 더 많은 것이 있다는 것과 성공적인 협력을 위해 필요한 기술에 대해 정말로 가르쳐 줄 필요가 있다. 성공적으로 함께 일하는 그룹은 고도의 대인 의식뿐만 아니라 다양한 사회적 기술을 가진 개인들을 필요

로 한다. 일부 학생들은 본래 이러한 기술에 대한 타고난 이해를 가지고 있지만, 그들은 항상 소수이다. 당신의 교실에 또래들 사이의 협력을 불러일으키기 위해서, 당신은 의식적이고 주의 깊게 이러한 기술들을 가르쳐야 하고, 학창시절 내내 계속해서 그것들을 육성해야 한다.

Why? 왜 정답일까?

'However, we do need to teach them that there is more to life than winning and about the skills they need for successful cooperation.'에서 선생님은 학생들에게 성공적인 협력을 위해 필요한 기술을 지도해야 한다고 하므로, 필자가 주장하는 바로 가장 적절한 것은 ② '학생에게 성공적인 협동을 위한 기술을 가르쳐야 한다.'이다.

- embark on ~에 착수하다
- leave ~ to one's devices ~을 자기 뜻대로 하게 내버려두다
- instinctively ⓐⓓ 본능적으로
- a multitude of 다수의, 아주 많은
- inherently ⓐⓓ 본래, 선천적으로
- continuously ⓐⓓ 계속해서
- arena ⓝ 경기장, 무대
- interpersonal ⓐ 대인 관계에 관련된
- nurture ⓥ 육성하다

구문 풀이

3행 Left to their own devices, they will instinctively become increasingly
수동분사구문(= If they are left ~) / 주어 / 동사구 / 주격 보어(형용사구)
competitive with each other.

---

21 팀이 최고의 수행을 하기 위한 조건 　　　정답률 63% | 정답 ④

밑줄 친 bringing together contradictory characteristics가 다음 글에서 의미하는 바로 가장 적절한 것은?
① establishing short-term and long-term goals – 단기적 및 장기적 목표를 수립하는 것
② performing both challenging and easy tasks – 어려운 과업과 쉬운 과업을 둘 다 수행하는 것
③ adopting temporary and permanent solutions – 일시적 해결책과 영구적 해결책을 채택하는 것
✓ ④ utilizing aspects of both experts and rookies – 전문가와 신참의 면을 둘 다 활용하는 것
⑤ considering processes and results simultaneously – 과정과 결과를 동시에 고려하는 것

The creative team exhibits paradoxical characteristics.
창의적인 팀은 역설적인 특징을 보인다.

It shows tendencies of thought and action / that we'd assume to be mutually exclusive or contradictory.
그것은 생각과 행동의 경향을 보여준다. / 우리가 상호 배타적이거나 모순된다고 여기는

For example, / to do its best work, / a team needs deep knowledge of subjects / relevant to the problem / it's trying to solve, / and a mastery of the processes involved.
예를 들어, / 최고의 작업을 수행하기 위해서는 / 팀에는 주제에 대한 깊은 지식이 필요하다. / 문제와 관련된 / 팀이 해결하려는 / 그리고 수반되는 과정의 숙달이

But at the same time, / the team needs fresh perspectives / that are unencumbered / by the prevailing wisdom or established ways of doing things.
그러나 동시에, / 팀에는 신선한 관점이 필요하다. / 방해받지 않는 / 널리 퍼져 있는 지혜나 자리 잡힌 일 처리 방식에

Often called a "beginner's mind," / this is the newcomers' perspective: / people who are curious, even playful, / and willing to ask anything / — no matter how naive the question may seem — / because they don't know what they don't know.
종종 '초심자의 마음'이라고 불리는 / 이것은 신참의 관점이다. / 호기심 많고, 심지어 장난기 넘치는 사람들, / 그리고 무엇이든 기꺼이 물어보는 / 질문이 아무리 모자라 보일지라도 / 자신이 모르는 것이 무엇인지도 모르기 때문에

Thus, / bringing together contradictory characteristics / can accelerate the process of new ideas.
따라서 / 모순되는 특징들을 한데 모으는 것이 / 새로운 아이디어의 과정을 가속화할 수 있다.

창의적인 팀은 역설적인 특징을 보인다. 그것은 우리가 상호 배타적이거나 모순된다고 여기는 생각과 행동의 경향을 보여준다. 예를 들어, 최고의 작업을 수행하기 위해서는 팀이 해결하려는 문제와 관련된 주제에 대한 깊은 지식과 수반되는 과정의 숙달이 필요하다. 그러나 동시에, 널리 퍼져 있는 지혜나 (이미) 자리 잡힌 일 처리 방식에 방해받지 않는 신선한 관점이 필요하다. 종종 '초심자의 마음'이라고 불리는 이것은 신참의 관점이다. 즉, 이런 사람들은 호기심 많고, 심지어 장난기 넘치고, 질문이 아무리 모자라 보일지라도 무엇이든 기꺼이 물어보는데, 이것은 자신이 모르는 것이 무엇인지도 모르기 때문이다. 따라서 모순되는 특징들을 한데 모으는 것이 새로운 아이디어의 과정을 가속화할 수 있다.

Why? 왜 정답일까?

For example 이하로 팀이 최고의 작업을 수행하려면 관련 주제에 대한 방대한 지식을 갖추고 일 처리 과정도 숙달할 필요가 있지만 동시에 신참내기의 관점, 즉 기존의 방법에 구애받지 않는 신선한 관점을 지녀야 한다는 내용이 제시된다. 이를 근거로 보아, 밑줄 친 부분이 의미하는 바로 가장 적절한 것은 ④ '전문가와 신참의 면을 둘 다 활용하는 것'이다.

- paradoxical ⓐ 역설적인
- contradictory ⓐ 모순적인
- prevailing ⓐ 만연한, 널리 퍼진
- naive ⓐ (경험이 못하여) 모자란, 순진한
- challenging ⓐ 힘드는, 까다로운
- rookie ⓝ 초보자
- mutually exclusive 상호 배타적인
- relevant to ~에 관련 있는
- established ⓐ 확립된, 자리를 잡은
- accelerate ⓥ 가속화하다
- permanent ⓐ 영구적인
- simultaneously ⓐⓓ 동시에

구문 풀이

8행 Often called a "beginner's mind," this is the newcomers' perspective:
수동분사구문 / 보어
people [who are curious, even playful, and willing to ask anything] — (no matter
선행사
how naive the question may seem) — because they don't know what they don't
삽입절(아무리 ~하더라도) / 의문사(무엇)
know.

---

22 도시 재생에서 가장 중요하게 고려되어야 하는 요소 　　정답률 83% | 정답 ①

다음 글의 요지로 가장 적절한 것은?
✓ ① 도시 재생을 위한 공공정책은 건설보다 사람에 중점을 두어야 한다.
② 대중 교통 이용이 편리하도록 도시 교통 체계를 구축해야 한다.

③ 사회기반시설 확충을 통해 지역 경제를 활성화해야 한다.
④ 에너지를 절감할 수 있는 친환경 건물을 설계해야 한다.
⑤ 문화유산 보존을 우선하는 도시 계획을 수립해야 한다.

Too many officials in troubled cities / wrongly imagine / that they can lead their city back to its former glories / with some massive construction project / — a new stadium or light rail system, / a convention center, / or a housing project.
문제가 있는 도시의 너무 많은 공무원들은 / 잘못 상상하고 있다. / 그들이 그들의 도시를 이전의 영광으로 되돌릴 수 있다고 / 대규모 건설 프로젝트를 통해 / 새로운 경기장 또는 경전철 시스템, / 컨벤션 센터, / 또는 주택 프로젝트와 같은

With very few exceptions, / no public policy can slow the tidal forces of urban change.
거의 예외 없이 / 어떤 공공 정책도 도시 변화의 조석력을 늦출 수는 없다.

We mustn't ignore the needs of the poor people / who live in the Rust Belt / but public policy should help poor *people*, / not poor places.
우리는 가난한 사람들의 요구를 무시해서는 안 되고 / Rust Belt에 사는 / 공공 정책이 가난한 *사람들*을 돕도록 해야 한다. / 가난한 지역을 돕는 것이 아닌

Shiny new real estate may dress up a declining city, / but it doesn't solve its underlying problems.
반짝이는 새로운 부동산은 쇠퇴하는 도시를 꾸밀 수는 있지만, / 이것은 기저에 있는 문제를 해결하지는 못한다.

The hallmark of declining cities is / that they have *too much* housing and infrastructure / relative to the strength of their economies.
쇠퇴하는 도시의 특징은 / 이들이 *너무 많은* 주택과 기반시설을 가지고 있다는 것이다. / 그들의 경제력에 비해서

With all that supply of structure and so little demand, / it makes no sense / to use public money to build more supply.
그 모든 건축물의 공급과 너무 적은 수요로 인해 / 의미가 없다. / 더 많은 공급을 만들어 내기 위해 공공 자금을 사용하는 것은

The folly of building-centric urban renewal reminds us / that cities aren't structures; / cities are people.
건물 중심의 도시 재생의 어리석음은 우리에게 상기시킨다. / 도시는 구조물이 아니라 / 사람이라는 것을

문제가 있는 도시의 너무 많은 공무원들은 새로운 경기장 또는 경전철 시스템, 컨벤션 센터, 주택 프로젝트와 같은 대규모 건설 프로젝트를 통해 그들의 도시를 이전의 영광으로 되돌릴 수 있다고 잘못 상상하고 있다. 거의 예외 없이 어떤 공공 정책도 도시 변화의 흐름을 늦출 수는 없다. 우리는 Rust Belt에 사는 가난한 사람들의 요구를 무시해서는 안 되고 공공 정책이 가난한 지역을 돕는 것이 아닌 가난한 *사람들*을 돕도록 해야 한다. 반짝이는 새로운 부동산은 쇠퇴하는 도시를 꾸밀 수는 있지만, 이것은 기저에 있는 문제를 해결하지는 못한다. 쇠퇴하는 도시의 특징은 이들이 경제력에 비해서 *너무 많은* 주택과 기반시설을 가지고 있다는 것이다. 그 모든 건축물의 공급과 너무 적은 수요로 인해 더 많은 공급을 만들어 내기 위해 공공 자금을 사용하는 것은 의미가 없다. 건물 중심의 도시 재생의 어리석음은 우리에게 도시는 구조물이 아니라 사람이라는 것을 상기시킨다.

Why? 왜 정답일까?
'~ public policy should help poor *people*, not poor places.'와 'The folly of building-centric urban renewal reminds us that cities aren't structures; cities are people.'에서 도시 재생을 위한 공공 정책은 장소나 건설이 아닌 사람에 집중해야 한다는 논지를 일관되게 제시하는 것으로 볼 때, 글의 요지로 가장 적절한 것은 ① '도시 재생을 위한 공공정책은 건설보다 사람에 중점을 두어야 한다.'이다.

- massive ⓐ 거대한
- exception ⓝ 예외
- ignore ⓥ 무시하다
- underlying ⓐ 기저에 있는, 근본적인
- infrastructure ⓝ 기반 시설
- construction ⓝ 건설
- tidal ⓐ (바다) 조수의
- decline ⓥ 쇠퇴하다
- hallmark ⓝ 특징
- folly ⓝ 어리석음, 판단력 부족

구문 풀이

1행 Too many officials in troubled cities wrongly imagine that they can lead
　　　 주어　　　　　　　　　　　　　　　　　　동사　　 접속사(~것)
their city back to its former glories with some massive construction project —
(a new stadium or light rail system, a convention center, or a housing project).
( ): 동격(= some massive construction project)

---

23 인간이 바다의 침입종 확산에 미친 영향　　정답률 52% | 정답 ⑤

다음 글의 주제로 가장 적절한 것은?
① benefits of recreational ocean fishing – 취미로 하는 바다 낚시의 이점
② ways to maintain marine biodiversity – 해양 생물 다양성을 유지하는 방법
③ potential value of the ocean for ecotourism – 생태 관광에 있어 해양의 잠재적 가치
④ contribution of ocean farming to food supply – 바다 양식의 식량 공급에 대한 기여
✔ human influence on the spread of invasive species – 침입종의 확산에 대한 인간의 영향

Many marine species / including oysters, marsh grasses, and fish / were deliberately introduced / for food or for erosion control, / with little knowledge of the impacts they could have.
많은 해양 종들은 / 굴, 습지 풀, 그리고 물고기를 포함한 / 의도적으로 도입되었다. / 식량이나 침식 방제를 위해 / 그것들이 미칠 수 있는 영향에 대한 정보가 거의 없는 상태에서

Fish and shellfish / have been intentionally introduced / all over the world / for aquaculture, / providing food and jobs, / but they can escape / and become a threat / to native species, ecosystem function, or livelihoods.
어패류는 / 의도적으로 도입되어 / 전 세계에 / 양식을 위해 / 음식과 일자리를 제공하지만, / 그것들은 탈출해서 / 위협이 될 수 있다. / 토착종, 생태계 기능, 또는 생계에

Atlantic salmon are reared in ocean net-pens / in Washington State and British Columbia.
대서양 연어는 해양 그물 어장에서 길러진다. / Washington State와 British Columbia에 있는

Many escape each year, / and they have been recovered / in both saltwater and freshwater / in Washington State, British Columbia, Alaska.
매년 많은 연어가 탈출해, / 그들은 발견된다. / 해수와 담수 모두 / Washington State, British Columbia, Alaska의

Recreational fishing can also spread invasive species.
취미로 하는 낚시 또한 침입종을 전파시킬 수 있다.

Bait worms from Maine / are popular throughout the country.
Maine의 미끼용 벌레들은 / 전국적으로 인기가 있다.

They are commonly packed in seaweed / which contains many organisms.
그것들은 보통 해초에 싸여 있다 / 많은 다른 유기체들을 포함하는

If the seaweed is discarded, / it or the organisms on it / can colonize new areas.
만약 해초가 버려지면, / 해초나 해초 위에 있는 유기체들은 / 새로운 영역에 군락을 이룰 수 있다.

Fishing boots, recreational boats, and trailers / can pick up organisms at one location / and move them elsewhere.
낚시용 장화, 여가용 보트와 트레일러는 / 유기체들을 한 장소에서 집어 올려 / 다른 곳으로 옮길 수 있다.

굴, 습지 풀, 그리고 물고기를 포함한 많은 해양 종들은 그것들이 미칠 수 있는 영향에 대한 정보가 거의 없는 상태에서 의도적으로 식량이나 침식 방제를 위해 도입되었다. 어패류는 양식을 위해 전 세계에 의도적으로 도입되어 음식과 일자리를 제공하지만, 탈출해 토착종, 생태계 기능, 또는 생계에 위협이 될 수 있다. 대서양 연어는 Washington State와 British Columbia의 해양 그물 어장에서 길러진다. 매년 많은 연어가 탈출해, 그들은 Washington State, British Columbia, Alaska의 해수와 담수에서 모두 발견된다. 취미로 하는 낚시 또한 침입종을 전파시킬 수 있다. Maine의 미끼용 벌레들은 전국적으로 인기가 있다. 그것들은 보통 많은 다른 유기체들을 포함하는 해초에 싸여 있다. 만약 해초가 버려지면, 해초나 해초 위에 있는 유기체들은 새로운 영역에서 군락을 이룰 수 있다. 낚시용 장화, 여가용 보트와 트레일러는 유기체를 한 장소에서 집어 올려 다른 곳으로 옮길 수 있다.

Why? 왜 정답일까?
첫 두 문장에서 많은 해양종이 사전 정보 없이 식량이나 침식 방제를 위해 인간에 의해 의도적으로 도입되어 이득이 주지만 생태계에 대한 악영향도 준다(Fish and shellfish have been intentionally introduced all over the world ~, but they can ~ become a threat to native species, ecosystem function, or livelihoods.)고 언급하고 있다. 따라서 글의 주제로 가장 적절한 것은 ⑤ '침입종의 확산에 대한 인간의 영향'이다.

- oyster ⓝ (바다) 굴
- deliberately ⓐⓓ 의도적으로
- intentionally ⓐⓓ 의도적으로
- rear ⓥ 기르다, 재배하다
- invasive ⓐ 침입의
- marsh ⓝ 습지
- erosion ⓝ 침식
- threat ⓝ 위협
- spread ⓥ 퍼뜨리다
- discard ⓥ 버리다

구문 풀이

1행 Many marine species (including oysters, marsh grasses, and fish)
　　　 주어
were deliberately introduced for food or for erosion control, with little knowledge
동사　　　　　　　　　　　　　　　 부사구1　　　　　　 부사구2
of the impacts [they could have].
　　　　　 선행사

---

24 쓰레기 매립지에 심어진 밀밭　　정답률 69% | 정답 ①

다음 글의 제목으로 가장 적절한 것은?
✔ Living Public Art Grows from a Landfill
　 살아있는 대중 예술이 쓰레기 매립지로부터 자라다
② Why Does Art Fade Away in Urban Areas?
　 왜 미술은 도시 지역에서 사라져 가는가?
③ New York: Skyscraper Capital of the World
　 뉴욕: 세계 고층 건물의 수도
④ Art Narrows the Gap Between the Old and Young
　 예술은 노년층과 청년층의 격차를 좁힌다
⑤ How City Expansion Could Affect Food Production
　 도시 확장은 식량 생산에 어떻게 영향을 미칠 수 있는가

Before the fancy high-rises, financial headquarters, tourist centers, and souvenir peddlers / made their way to Battery Park City, / the area behind the World Trade Center / was a giant, gross landfill.
화려한 고층 건물, 금융 본부, 관광 센터, 기념품 행상인들이 ~하기 이전에, / Battery Park City로 나아가기 / 세계 무역 센터 뒤편의 지역은 / 거대하고 혐오스러운 쓰레기 매립지였다.

In 1982, / artist Agnes Denes decided to return that landfill / back to its roots, / although temporarily.
1982년, / 예술가 Agnes Denes는 그 매립지를 되돌리기로 결정했다. / 다시 원래의 뿌리로 / 비록 일시적이긴 하지만

Denes was commissioned by the Public Art Fund / to create one of the most significant and fantastical pieces of public work / Manhattan has ever seen.
Denes는 Public Art Fund로부터 의뢰를 받았다. / 가장 의미심장하며 환상적인 공공 사업 작품 중 하나를 만들어 달라는 / Manhattan에서 지금까지 본

Her concept was not a traditional sculpture, / but a living installation / that changed the way the public looked at art.
그녀의 콘셉트는 전통적인 조형물이 아니라 / 살아있는 설치 조형물이었다. / 대중이 미술을 보는 방식을 바꾼

In the name of art, / Denes put a beautiful golden wheat field / right in the shadow of the gleaming Twin Towers.
예술의 이름으로, / Denes는 아름다운 황금 밀밭을 만들었다. / 반짝이는 쌍둥이 빌딩의 그림자에

For *Wheatfield — A Confrontation,* / Denes and volunteers removed trash from four acres of land, / then planted amber waves of grain atop the area.
작품 *Wheatfield — A Confrontation*을 위해, / Denes와 자원 봉사자들은 4에이커의 땅에서 쓰레기를 치운 다음 / 그 지역 위에 황색 빛깔의 너울거리는 곡물을 심었다.

After months of farming and irrigation, / the wheat field was thriving and ready.
수개월의 농사와 관개 후에 / 밀밭은 무성해지고 준비가 되었다.

The artist and her volunteers / harvested thousands of pounds of wheat / to give to food banks in the city, / nourishing both the minds and bodies of New Yorkers.
그 예술가와 자원 봉사자들은 / 수천 파운드의 밀을 수확하여 / 뉴욕의 푸드 뱅크에 기부하였고, / 뉴욕 사람들의 마음과 몸을 모두 풍요롭게 해주었다.

화려한 고층 건물, 금융 본부, 관광 센터, 기념품 행상인들이 Battery Park City로 나아가기 전에, 세계 무역 센터 뒤편의 지역은 거대하고 혐오스러운 쓰레기 매립지였다. 1982년, 예술가 Agnes Denes는 비록 일시적이긴 하지만 그 매립지를 다시 원래의 뿌리로 되돌리기로 결정했다. Denes는 Public Art Fund로부터 Manhattan에서 지금까지 본 가장 의미심장하며 환상적인 공공 사업 작품 중 하나를 만들어 달라는 의뢰를 받았다. 그녀의 콘셉트는 전통적인 조형물이 아니라 대중이 미술을 보는 방식을 바꾼 살아있는 설치 조형물이었다. 예술의 이름으로, Denes는 반짝이는 쌍둥이 빌딩의 그림자에 아름다운 황금 밀밭을 만들었다. 작품 *Wheatfield — A Confrontation*을 위해, Denes와 자원 봉사자들은 4에이커의 땅에서 쓰레기를 치운 다음 그 지역 위에 황색 빛깔의 너울거리는 곡물을 심었다. 수개월의 농사와 관개 후에 밀밭은 무성해지고 준비가 되었다. 그 예술가와 자원 봉사자들은 수천 파운드의 밀을 수확하여 뉴욕의 푸드 뱅크에 기부하여 뉴욕 사람들의 마음과 몸을 모두 풍요롭게 해주었다.

She decided to concentrate on ophthalmology, / which is the branch of medicine / that works with eye diseases and disorders.

Why? 왜 정답일까?

글 전체에 걸쳐 예술가 Agnes Denes가 쓰레기 매립지였던 땅에 예술의 명목으로 아름다운 황금 밀밭을 만들어 대중이 예술을 바라보는 관점을 바꾸는 데 기여했다(a living installation that changed the way the public looked at art)는 내용이 제시되고 있다. 따라서 글의 제목으로 가장 적절한 것은 ① '살아있는 대중 예술이 쓰레기 매립지로부터 자라다'이다.

- high-rise ⑩ 고층 건물
- souvenir ⑩ 기념품
- gross ⓐ 혐오스러운, 징그러운
- temporarily ⓓ 일시적으로
- significant ⓐ 중대한
- confrontation ⑩ 대립
- nourish ⓥ 풍요롭게 하다, 영양분을 공급하다
- narrow the gap 격차를 좁히다
- headquarter ⑩ 본부
- peddler ⑩ 행상인, 판매원
- landfill ⑩ 쓰레기 매립지
- commission ⑩ 의뢰하다
- gleaming ⓐ 반짝이는, 빛나는
- irrigation ⑩ 관개, 물 대기
- fade away 사라지다, (생명, 불꽃 등이) 꺼지다

구문 풀이

16행 The artist and her volunteers harvested thousands of pounds of wheat
to give to food banks in the city, nourishing both the minds and bodies of New
부사적 용법(목적) · · · · · · · · · · · · · · · · · 분사구문(그리고 ~하다)
Yorkers.

---

25 한국 고궁 방문객 수 비교
정답률 83% | 정답 ⑤

다음 도표의 내용과 일치하지 <u>않는</u> 것은?

The Number of Korean and Foreign Visitors to Korean Palaces

Changgyeonggung Palace (in thousands)

	Korean	Foreign	Total
2018	1,716	345	2,061
2019	874	94	968
Overall Total			3,029

Deoksugung Palace (in thousands)

	Korean	Foreign	Total
2018	767	77	844
2019	2,414	369	2,783
Overall Total			3,627

※ Note: Details may not add to totals due to rounding.

The tables above show / the number of Korean and foreign visitors / to Korean palaces / in 2018 and 2019.
위 도표는 보여준다. / 한국인 방문객과 외국인 방문객의 수를 / 한국의 궁을 방문한 / 2018년과 2019년에
① For the two-year period of 2018 to 2019, / the overall total number of visitors to Deoksugung Palace / was larger than that to Changgyeonggung Palace.
2018년부터 2019년까지 2년의 기간 동안 / 덕수궁의 총 방문객 수는 / 창경궁의 총 방문객의 수보다 컸다.
② While the total number of visitors to Changgyeonggung Palace / decreased from 2018 to 2019, / the total number of visitors to Deoksugung Palace / increased during the same period.
창경궁의 총 방문객 수는 / 2018년부터 2019년까지 감소했으나, / 덕수궁의 방문객 수는 / 같은 기간 동안 증가했다.
③ During both 2018 and 2019, / the two palaces had more Korean visitors than foreign visitors.
2018년과 2019년 두 해 모두, / 그 두 궁은 한국인 방문객이 외국 방문객보다 많았다.
④ In 2018, / the number of Korean visitors to Deoksugung Palace / was less than half the number of Korean visitors to Changgyeonggung Palace.
2018년에 / 덕수궁의 한국인 방문객 수는 / 창경궁의 한국인 방문객 수의 절반보다 적었다.
☑ In 2019, / the number of Korean visitors to Changgyeonggung Palace / was more than 10 times the number of foreign visitors.
2019년에 / 창경궁의 한국인 방문객 수는 / 외국인 방문객 수의 10배보다 많았다.

위 도표는 2018년과 2019년에 한국의 궁을 방문한 한국인 방문객과 외국인 방문객의 수를 보여준다. ① 2018년부터 2019년까지 2년의 기간 동안 덕수궁의 총 방문객 수는 창경궁의 총 방문객의 수보다 컸다. ② 2018년부터 2019년까지 창경궁의 총 방문객 수는 감소했으나, 같은 기간 동안 덕수궁의 방문객 수는 증가했다. ③ 2018년과 2019년 두 해 모두, 그 두 궁은 한국인 방문객이 외국 방문객보다 많았다. ④ 2018년에 덕수궁의 한국인 방문객 수는 창경궁의 한국인 방문객 수의 절반보다 적었다. ⑤ 2019년에 창경궁의 한국인 방문객 수는 외국인 방문객 수의 10배보다 많았다.

Why? 왜 정답일까?

2019년 창경궁의 한국인 방문객 수는 874명, 외국인 방문객은 94명으로, 전자는 후자의 10배에 미치지 못한다. 따라서 도표와 일치하지 않는 것은 ⑤이다.

- palace ⑩ 궁, 궁전
- overall ⓐ 전반적인

---

26 Patricia Bath의 생애
정답률 76% | 정답 ④

Patricia Bath에 관한 다음 글의 내용과 일치하지 <u>않는</u> 것은?
① 뉴욕 시의 Harlem 지역에서 성장했다.
② 1968년에 의과 대학을 졸업했다.
③ 의과 대학에서 학생을 가르쳤다.
☑ 1976년에 AiPB를 단독으로 설립했다.
⑤ 의료 장비 특허를 받았다.

Patricia Bath spent her life advocating for eye health.
Patricia Bath는 눈 건강을 옹호하며 일생을 보냈다.
「Born in 1942, / she was raised in the Harlem area of New York City.」 ①의근거 일치
1942년에 태어난 / 그녀는 New York City의 Harlem 지역에서 성장했다.
「She graduated from Howard University's College of Medicine in 1968.」 ②의근거 일치
그녀는 1968년에 Howard 의과 대학을 졸업했다.
It was during her time as a medical intern / that she saw / that many poor people and Black people were becoming blind / because of the lack of eye care.
수련의로서 시간을 보내는 동안이었다 / 그녀는 알게된 것은 / 많은 가난한 사람과 흑인이 눈이 멀게 되고 있음을 / 눈 관리 부족으로

She decided to concentrate on ophthalmology, / which is the branch of medicine / that works with eye diseases and disorders.
그녀는 안과학에 몰두하기로 결심했다. / 의학 분야인 / 눈 질병과 장애를 연구하는
「As her career progressed, / Bath taught students in medical schools / and trained other doctors.」 ③의근거 일치
그녀의 경력이 쌓이면서 / 그녀는 의과 대학에서 학생을 가르쳤고 / 다른 의사들을 훈련시켰다.
「In 1976, / she co-founded the American Institute for the Prevention of Blindness (AiPB) / with the basic principle / that "eyesight is a basic human right."」 ④의근거 불일치
1976년에 / 그녀는 미국시각장애예방협회(AiPB)를 공동 설립했다. / 기본 원칙으로 / "시력은 기본적인 인권이다"라는
In the 1980s, / Bath began researching the use of lasers in eye treatments.
1980년대에 / Bath는 눈 치료에서 레저저 사용을 연구하기 시작했다.
「Her research led to her / becoming the first African-American female doctor / to receive a patent for a medical device.」 ⑤의근거 일치
그녀의 연구는 그녀를 ~하게 했다. / 최초의 아프리카계 미국 흑인 여성 의사가 되게 / 의료 장비 특허를 받은

Patricia Bath는 눈 건강을 옹호하며 일생을 보냈다. 1942년에 태어난 그녀는 New York City의 Harlem 지역에서 성장했다. 그녀는 1968년에 Howard 의과 대학을 졸업했다. 수련의로서 시간을 보내는 동안 그녀는 눈 관리 부족으로 많은 가난한 사람과 흑인이 눈이 멀게 되고 있음을 알게 되었다. 그녀는 눈 질병과 장애를 연구하는 의학 분야인 안과학에 몰두하기로 결심했다. 경력이 쌓이면서 그녀는 의과 대학에서 학생을 가르쳤고 다른 의사들을 훈련시켰다. 1976년에 그녀는 "시력은 기본적인 인권이다"라는 기본 원칙으로 미국시각장애예방협회(AiPB)를 공동 설립했다. 1980년대에 Bath는 눈 치료에서 레이저 사용을 연구하기 시작했다. 그녀의 연구로 인해 그녀는 의료 장비 특허를 받은 최초의 아프리카계 미국 흑인 여성 의사가 되었다.

Why? 왜 정답일까?

'In 1976, she co-founded the American Institute for the Prevention of Blindness (AiPB) ~'에서 Patricia Bath는 AiPB를 공동 설립했다고 하므로, 내용과 일치하지 않는 것은 ④ '1976년에 AiPB를 단독으로 설립했다.'이다.

Why? 왜 오답일까?

① '~ she was raised in the Harlem area of New York City.'의 내용과 일치한다.
② 'She graduated from Howard University's College of Medicine in 1968.'의 내용과 일치한다.
③ 'As her career progressed, Bath taught students in medical schools ~'의 내용과 일치한다.
⑤ 'Her research led to her becoming the first African-American female doctor to receive a patent for a medical device.'의 내용과 일치한다.

- advocate for ~을 옹호하다
- concentrate on ~에 집중하다
- disorder ⑩ 장애, 이상
- prevention ⑩ 예방
- medical device 의료 기기
- lack ⑩ 부족, 결여
- ophthalmology ⑩ 안과학
- progress ⓥ 진척하다, 진행하다
- patent ⑩ 특허

구문 풀이

4행 It was during her time as a medical intern that she saw that many poor
「it is[was] ~ that : 강조구문 : · · 한 것은 바로 ~이다(이었다)」
people and Black people were becoming blind because of the lack of eye care.

---

27 불우이웃을 위한 걷기 대회
정답률 94% | 정답 ⑤

Bright Future Walkathon에 관한 다음 안내문의 내용과 일치 하지 <u>않는</u> 것은?
① 오전 9시에 시작한다.
② 모든 등록비는 기부될 것이다.
③ B 코스는 15세 이상 참가자가 선택할 수 있다.
④ 코스를 완주한 참가자는 티셔츠를 받는다.
☑ 취소 시 환불이 가능하다.

Bright Future Walkathon
Bright Future Walkathon
Sunny Side Foundation is hosting the annual Bright Future Walkathon / in support of people in need.
Sunny Side 재단은 연례 Bright Future Walkathon을 개최합니다. / 어려운 사람들을 돕고자
Date & Place
날짜 & 장소
Date: Saturday, September 25th 「(Start Time: 9:00 a.m.)」 ①의근거 일치
날짜: 9월 25일, 토요일 (시작 시간: 오전 9시)
Place: Green Brook Park
장소: Green Brook 공원
Registration
등록
Fee: $10
등록비: $10
「All registration fees will be donated to local charities.」 ②의근거 일치
모든 등록비는 지역 자선 단체에 기부될 것입니다.
Register online at www.ssfwalkathon.com.
www.ssfwalkathon.com에서 온라인으로 등록하세요.
Course (Choose one)
코스 (하나를 선택)
Course A: 3 km (all ages welcome)
A 코스: 3km (전 연령 환영)
「Course B: 5 km (for ages 15 and older)」 ③의근거 일치
B 코스: 5km (15세 이상)
Details
세부 사항
「Each participant who completes the course / will receive a T-shirt.」 ④의근거 일치
코스를 완주한 참가자는 / 티셔츠를 받을 것입니다.
「No refund will be made for cancellations.」 ⑤의근거 불일치
취소 시 환불이 되지 않습니다.

Bright Future Walkathon

Sunny Side 재단은 어려운 사람들을 돕고자 연례 Bright Future Walkathon을 개최합니다.

날짜 & 장소
- 날짜: 9월 25일, 토요일 (시작 시간: 오전 9시)
- 장소: Green Brook 공원

등록
- 등록비: $10
- 모든 등록비는 지역 자선 단체에 기부될 것입니다.
- www.sfwalkathon.com에서 온라인으로 등록하세요.

코스 (하나를 선택)
- A 코스: 3km (전 연령 환영)
- B 코스: 5km (15세 이상)

세부 사항
- 코스를 완주한 참가자는 티셔츠를 받을 것입니다.
- 취소 시 환불이 되지 않습니다.

Why? 왜 정답일까?

'No refund will be made for cancellations.'에서 취소 시 환불은 불가하다고 하므로, 안내문의 내용과 일치하지 않는 것은 ⑤ '취소 시 환불이 가능하다.'이다.

Why? 왜 오답일까?

① '(Start Time: 9:00 a.m.)'의 내용과 일치한다.
② 'All registration fees will be donated to local charities.'의 내용과 일치한다.
③ 'Course B: 5 km (for ages 15 and older)'의 내용과 일치한다.
④ 'Each participant who completes the course will receive a T-shirt.'의 내용과 일치한다.

- **walkathon** ⓝ 걷기 대회, 장거리 경보
- **in need** 도움이 필요한, 불우한
- **in support of** ~을 후원하여
- **cancellation** ⓝ 취소

---

28 · 고등학교 동창회
정답률 92% | 정답 ③

South High School Reunion에 관한 다음 안내문의 내용과 일치하는 것은?

① 오후 7시부터 오후 11시까지 진행된다.
② 11월 1일 이후에 티켓 환불이 가능하다.
☑ 퀴즈 쇼 챔피언은 영화 티켓 두 장을 받는다.
④ 정해진 복장 규정은 없다.
⑤ 친구는 네 명까지 초대할 수 있다.

South High School Reunion
South High School 동창회
Class of 2011
2011년 졸업
Don't you miss your old friends from high school?
여러분은 고등학교의 오랜 친구들이 그립지 않습니까?
Come meet them / and remember your high school days!
그들을 만나러 와서 / 여러분의 고등학교 시절을 추억하세요!
When & Where
일시 & 장소
『Saturday, November 6th, 2021 7:00 p.m. − 10:00 p.m.』 ①의 근거 불일치
2021년 11월 6일 토요일 오후 7시 ~ 오후 10시
Bay Street Park
Bay Street 공원
Ticket Reservation (per person)
티켓 예약 (1인당)
Ticket price: $40
티켓 가격: $40
If you reserve by October 15th, / the price will be $30.
10월 15일까지 예약하면 / 티켓 가격은 30달러입니다.
『Refunds will only be available until October 31st.』 ②의 근거 불일치
환불은 10월 31일까지만 가능합니다.
Main Events
주요 행사
Quiz Show: / Answer 50 questions / about our old buddies, teachers, and memories.
퀴즈 쇼: / 50개의 문제에 답하세요. / 우리의 오랜 친구들, 선생님들, 추억에 관한
『The champion will receive two movie tickets.』 ③의 근거 일치
챔피언은 영화 티켓 두 장을 받게 될 것입니다.
The barbecue party will start at 8:00 p.m.
바비큐 파티는 오후 8시에 시작될 것입니다.
Notes
주의 사항
『Dress Code: / Wear a red jacket / to show your South High School spirit.』 ④의 근거 불일치
복장 규정: / 빨간색 재킷을 입어야 합니다. / South 고등학교의 정신을 보여주는
『Feel free to invite up to three friends.』 ⑤의 근거 불일치
친구는 세 명까지 초대할 수 있습니다.

South High School 동창회
2011년 졸업

여러분은 고등학교의 오랜 친구들이 그립지 않습니까? 그들을 만나러 와서 여러분의 고등학교 시절을 추억하세요!

◎ **일시 & 장소**
- 2021년 11월 6일 토요일 오후 7시 ~ 오후 10시
- Bay Street 공원

◎ **티켓 예약 (1인당)**
- 티켓 가격: $40
- 10월 15일까지 예약하면 티켓 가격은 30달러입니다.

- 환불은 10월 31일까지만 가능합니다.

◎ **주요 행사**
- 퀴즈 쇼: 우리의 오랜 친구들, 선생님들, 추억에 관한 50개의 문제에 답하세요. 챔피언은 영화 티켓 두 장을 받게 될 것입니다.
- 바비큐 파티는 오후 8시에 시작될 것입니다.

◎ **주의 사항**
- 복장 규정: South 고등학교의 정신을 보여주는 빨간색 재킷을 입어야 합니다.
- 친구는 세 명까지 초대할 수 있습니다.

Why? 왜 정답일까?

'The champion will receive two movie tickets.'에서 퀴즈 쇼 챔피언은 영화 티켓 두 장을 받게 된다고 하므로, 안내문의 내용과 일치하는 것은 ③ '퀴즈 쇼 챔피언은 영화 티켓 두 장을 받는다.'이다.

Why? 왜 오답일까?

① 'Saturday, November 6th, 2021 7:00 p.m.−10:00 p.m.'에서 오후 7시부터 10시까지 진행된다고 하였다.
② 'Refunds will only be available until October 31st.'에서 환불은 10월 31일까지만 가능하다고 하였다.
④ 'Dress Code: Wear a red jacket to show your South High School spirit.'에서 빨간색 재킷을 입어야 한다는 복장 규정이 제시되었다.
⑤ 'Feel free to invite up to three friends.'에서 친구는 세 명까지 초대할 수 있다고 하였다.

- **reunion** ⓝ (오랫동안 만나지 못한 사람들의) 모임, 재결합
- **refund** ⓝ 환불
- **dress code** 복장 규정
- **feel free to** 자유롭게 ~하다

---

29 · 심해 유기체들의 특성
정답률 64% | 정답 ⑤

다음 글의 밑줄 친 부분 중, 어법상 틀린 것은? [3점]

Organisms living in the deep sea / have adapted to the high pressure / by storing water in their bodies, / some ① consisting almost entirely of water.
심해에 사는 유기체들은 / 고압에 적응해 왔고, / 몸에 물을 저장하여 / 일부는 거의 물로만 구성되어 있다.
Most deep-sea organisms lack gas bladders.
대부분의 심해 유기체들은 부레가 없다.
They are cold-blooded organisms / that adjust their body temperature to their environment, / allowing them ② to survive in the cold water / while maintaining a low metabolism.
그들은 냉혈 유기체들로, / 주변 환경에 체온을 맞추는 / 이는 그들이 차가운 물에서 생존하게 한다. / 낮은 신진대사를 유지하고 있는 동안
Many species lower their metabolism so much / that they are able to survive without food / for long periods of time, / as finding the sparse food ③ that is available / expends a lot of energy.
많은 종들은 신진대사를 아주 많이 낮추어 / 그들은 먹이 없이 생존이 가능하다. / 오랜 기간 / 구할 수 있는 드문 먹이를 찾는 것이 / 많은 에너지를 소비하기 때문에
Many predatory fish of the deep sea / are equipped with enormous mouths and sharp teeth, / enabling them to hold on to prey and overpower ④ it.
심해의 많은 포식성 물고기는 / 거대한 입과 날카로운 이빨을 가지고 있고, / 이는 물고기들이 먹이를 붙잡고 제압하게 한다.
Some predators / hunting in the residual light zone of the ocean / ☑ have excellent visual capabilities, / while others are able to create their own light / to attract prey or a mating partner.
일부 포식자들은 / 해양의 잔광 구역에서 먹이를 잡는 / 뛰어난 시력을 가지고 있다. / 다른 포식자들은 자신의 빛을 만들어 낼 수 있는 반면 / 먹이나 짝을 끌어들이기 위해

심해에 사는 유기체들은 몸에 물을 저장하여 고압에 적응해 왔고, 일부는 거의 물로만 구성되어 있다. 대부분의 심해 유기체들은 부레가 없다. 그들은 주변 환경에 체온을 맞추는 냉혈 유기체로, 이는 그들이 낮은 신진대사를 유지하고 있는 동안 차가운 물에서 생존하게 한다. 구할 수 있는 드문 먹이를 찾는 것이 많은 에너지를 소비하기 때문에, 많은 종들은 신진대사를 아주 많이 낮추어 오랜 기간 먹이 없이 생존이 가능하다. 심해의 많은 포식성 물고기는 거대한 입과 날카로운 이빨을 가지고 있고, 이는 물고기들이 먹이를 붙잡고 제압하게 한다. 해양의 잔광 구역에서 먹이를 잡는 일부 포식자들은 뛰어난 시력을 가지고 있는 반면, 다른 포식자들은 먹이나 짝을 끌어들이기 위해 빛을 만들어 낼 수 있다.

Why? 왜 정답일까?

주어가 복수 명사인 Some predators이므로, 동사 또한 단수형인 has가 아닌 have로 써 주어야 적절하다. 주어와 동사 사이의 'hunting ~'은 주어를 꾸민다. 따라서 어법상 틀린 것은 ⑤이다.

Why? 왜 오답일까?

① 앞에 완전한 주절이 나온 뒤 의미상 주어 some 뒤로 분사구문이 이어지는 것이다. 따라서 현재분사 consisting은 알맞게 쓰였다.
② allow는 목적격 보어 자리에 to부정사를 쓰는 동사이므로, allowing them 뒤로 to survive가 알맞게 쓰였다.
③ 뒤에 주어가 없는 관계절이 나와 the sparse food를 꾸미고 있으므로, 주격 관계대명사 that은 알맞게 쓰였다.
④ 앞에 나온 불가산명사 prey를 가리키기 위해 단수 대명사 it을 쓴 것은 적절하다.

- **entirely** ⓐⓓ 전적으로
- **sparse** ⓐ 드문, (밀도가) 희박한
- **predatory** ⓐ 포식성의
- **enormous** ⓐ 거대한
- **residual** ⓐ 잔여의
- **metabolism** ⓝ 신진대사
- **expend** ⓥ 소비하다
- **be equipped with** ~을 갖추다
- **overpower** ⓥ 제압하다, 압도하다

구문 풀이

7행 Many species lower their metabolism so much that they are able to survive without food for long periods of time, as finding the sparse food [that is available] expends a lot of energy.
so ~ that : 너무 ~해서 …하다 / 접속사(이유) / 주어(동명사구)
[ ] : the sparse food 수식 / 동사(단수)

30 생물 다양성을 고려한 경작의 필요성 정답률 39% | 정답 ③

다음 글의 밑줄 친 부분 중, 문맥상 낱말의 쓰임이 적절하지 않은 것은? [3점]

Human innovation in agriculture / has unlocked modifications in apples, tulips, and potatoes / that never would have been realized / through a plant's natural reproductive cycles.
농업에서 인류의 혁신은 / 사과, 튤립, 감자의 개량을 가능하게 했다. / 결코 실현할 수 없었던 / 식물의 자연적 번식 주기를 통해서는

This cultivation process / has created some of the recognizable vegetables and fruits / consumers look for in their grocery stores.
이러한 경작 과정은 / 알아볼 수 있는 몇몇 채소나 과일을 만들어냈다. / 소비자들이 식료품 가게에서 찾는

However, / relying on only a few varieties of cultivated crops / can leave humankind ① vulnerable / to starvation and agricultural loss / if a harvest is destroyed.
그러나 / 소수의 재배된 작물에만 의존하는 것은 / 인류를 취약한 상태에 둘 수도 있다. / 기아나 농업의 손실에 / 만약 추수가 망쳐지면

For example, / a million people died / over the course of three years / during the Irish potato famine / because the Irish relied ② primarily on potatoes and milk / to create a nutritionally balanced meal.
예를 들어, / 1백만 명의 사람들이 사망했는데, / 3년이라는 기간에 걸쳐 / 아일랜드 감자 기근 동안 / 아일랜드 사람들이 주로 감자와 우유에 의존했기 때문이다. / 영양학적으로 균형 있는 식사를 마련하기 위해

In order to continue its symbiotic relationship with cultivated plants, / humanity must allow for biodiversity / and recognize the potential ☑ drawbacks / that monocultures of plants can introduce.
재배 식물과 공생 관계를 유지하려면, / 인류는 생물의 다양성을 고려해야만 하고 / 잠재적 결점에 대해서도 인식해야만 한다. / 식물의 단일 경작이 가져올 수 있는

Planting seeds of all kinds, / even if they don't seem immediately useful or profitable, / can ④ ensure the longevity of those plants / for generations to come.
모든 종류의 씨앗을 심는 것은 / 설령 그것들이 당장은 유용하고 이득이 되어 보이지는 않아도, / 그러한 식물들이 오래 지속되는 것을 보장해 줄 수 있다. / 다가올 세대들을 위해

A ⑤ balance must be struck / between nature's capacity for wildness / and humanity's desire for control.
균형이 유지되어야 한다. / 야생에 대한 자연의 능력과 / 통제에 대한 인간의 욕망 사이에서

농업에서 인류의 혁신은 식물의 자연적 번식 주기를 통해서는 결코 실현할 수 없었던 사과, 튤립, 감자의 개량을 가능케 했다. 이러한 경작 과정은 소비자들이 식료품 가게에서 찾는 (여러분이) 알아볼 수 있는 몇몇 채소나 과일을 만들어냈다. 그러나 만약 추수가 망쳐지면 소수의 재배된 작물에만 의존하는 것은 인류를 기아나 농업의 손실에 ① 취약한 상태에 둘 수도 있다. 예를 들어, 아일랜드 감자 기근 동안 1백만 명의 사람들이 3년이라는 기간에 걸쳐 사망했는데, 아일랜드 사람들이 영양학적으로 균형 있는 식사를 마련하기 위해 ② 주로 감자와 우유에 의존했기 때문이다. 재배 식물과 공생 관계를 유지하려면, 인류는 생물의 다양성을 고려해야만 하고 식물의 단일 경작이 가져올 수 있는 잠재적 ③ 이점(→ 결점)에 대해서도 인식해야만 한다. 설령 그것들이 당장은 유용하고 이득이 되어 보이지는 않아도, 모든 종류의 씨앗을 심는 것은 다가올 세대들을 위해 그러한 식물들이 오래 지속되는 것을 ④ 보장해 줄 수 있다. 야생에 대한 자연의 능력과 통제에 대한 인간의 욕망 사이에서 ⑤ 균형이 유지되어야 한다.

Why? 왜 정답일까?

'However, relying on only a few varieties of cultivated crops ~'에서 몇 가지 작물에만 의존하는 것은 인류를 기아나 농업적 손실에게 취약하게 만들 수 있다고 언급하고, 이어서 아일랜드 감자 기근이 예로 제시된다. 이러한 맥락으로 볼 때, ③이 포함된 문장은 식물의 단일 경작이 낳을 수 있는 '결점'을 인지하고 식물의 다양성을 지킬 방법을 고민해야 한다는 의미여야 한다. 즉 ③의 benefits를 drawbacks로 바꾸어야 맥락이 자연스러워진다. 따라서 문맥상 낱말의 쓰임이 적절하지 않은 것은 ③이다.

- agriculture ⓝ 농업
- reproductive ⓐ 번식의, 재생의
- recognizable ⓐ 알아보기 쉬운
- starvation ⓝ 기아, 굶주림
- nutritionally 쪤 영양학적으로
- monoculture ⓝ 단일 경작
- longevity ⓝ 오래 감, 장수
- strike a balance 균형을 유지하다
- modification ⓝ 개량, 수정
- cultivation ⓝ 재배, 경작
- vulnerable ⓐ 취약한
- famine ⓝ 기근
- biodiversity ⓝ 생물 다양성
- profitable ⓐ 수익성 있는
- generations to come 후대, 후세

구문 풀이

9행 For example, a million people died over the course of three years during
<small>주어 ___ 동사 ___ ~라는 기간에 걸쳐 ___ 전치사(~ 동안)</small>
the Irish potato famine because the Irish relied primarily on potatoes and milk
<small>접속사(이유) 「the + 형용사 : ~한 사람들」</small>
to create a nutritionally balanced meal.
<small>부사적 용법(목적)</small>

★★ 문제 해결 꿀~팁 ★★

▶ 많이 틀린 이유는?
② 앞에서 소수 재배 작물에만 의지하면 인간이 기근 등의 위기에 '취약해진다'고 했다. 이에 대한 예시로 감자 기근 당시 아일랜드 사람들에 관한 내용이 제시되는 것이므로, 아일랜드 사람들이 '주로' 감자에만 의존했기에 감자 기근에 그토록 취약했다는 의미를 나타내는 ② primarily는 바르게 쓰였다.
또한 ④가 포함된 문장은 앞 내용과 마찬가지로 다양한 작물 재배를 옹호하기 위해, 여러 작물을 재배하는 것이 당장은 이득이 안 되어 보여도 결국 식물 다양성 유지를 '보장해준다'라고 설명하고 있다. 따라서 ④의 ensure 또한 맥락에 맞는 어휘이다.

▶ 문제 해결 방법은?
However 이후로 단일 경작보다는 식물의 다양성을 존중한 경작이 인류에 이롭다는 내용이 일관되게 제시된다. 주제에 비추어 각 어휘 선택을 판단하도록 한다.

31 상대적 비교에 따라 결정되는 음식 양 정답률 54% | 정답 ②

다음 빈칸에 들어갈 말로 가장 적절한 것을 고르시오.
① Originality – 독창성   ☑ Relativity – 상대성
③ Visualization – 시각화   ④ Imitation – 모방
⑤ Forgetfulness – 건망증

Relativity works as a general mechanism for the mind, / in many ways and across many different areas of life.
상대성은 정신을 위한 일반적인 메커니즘으로 작용한다. / 여러 면에서 그리고 삶의 많은 다른 영역에 걸쳐

For example, / Brian Wansink, author of *Mindless Eating*, / showed / that it can also affect our waistlines.
예를 들어, / *Mindless Eating*의 저자 Brian Wansink는 / 보여주었다. / 이것이 우리의 허리 둘레에도 영향을 미칠 수 있다는 것을

We decide how much to eat / not simply as a function of how much food we actually consume, / but by a comparison to its alternatives.
우리는 우리가 먹을 양을 결정한다. / 단순히 우리가 실제로 먹는 음식 양의 함수로서가 아니라 / 그것의 대안과의 비교를 통해서

Say we have to choose / between three burgers on a menu, / at 8, 10, and 12 ounces.
우리가 선택해야 한다고 하자. / 메뉴에 있는 버거 세 개 사이에서 / 8온스, 10온스, 12온스의

We are likely to pick the 10-ounce burger / and be perfectly satisfied at the end of the meal.
우리는 10온스 버거를 고르고 / 식사가 끝날 때쯤이면 완벽하게 만족할 수 있을 것이다.

But if our options are instead 10, 12, and 14 ounces, / we are likely again to choose the middle one, / and again feel equally happy and satisfied / with the 12-ounce burger / at the end of the meal, / even though we ate more, / which we did not need / in order to get our daily nourishment / or in order to feel full.
하지만 만약 대신에 우리의 선택권이 10온스, 12온스, 14온스라면, / 우리는 다시 중간의 것을 선택할 것이고, / 똑같이 행복감과 만족감을 다시 느낄 수 있을 것이다. / 12온스의 햄버거로 / 식사가 끝날 때 / 비록 우리가 더 많이 먹었더라도, / 우리가 필요하지 않았던 / 매일 영양분을 섭취하기 위해 / 혹은 포만감을 느끼기 위해

상대성은 여러 면에서 그리고 삶의 많은 다른 영역에 걸쳐 정신을 위한 일반적인 메커니즘으로 작용한다. 예를 들어, *Mindless Eating*의 저자 Brian Wansink는 이것이 우리의 허리 둘레에도 영향을 미칠 수 있다는 것을 보여주었다. 우리는 단순히 우리가 실제로 먹는 음식 양의 함수로서가 아니라 대안과의 비교를 통해서 우리가 먹을 양을 결정한다. 우리가 메뉴에 있는 8온스, 10온스, 12온스의 버거 세 개 중 하나를 선택해야 한다고 하자. 우리는 10온스 버거를 고르고 식사가 끝날 때쯤이면 완벽하게 만족할 수 있을 것이다. 하지만 만약 대신에 우리의 선택권이 10온스, 12온스, 14온스라면, 우리는 다시 중간의 것을 선택할 것이고, 비록 우리가 더 많이 먹었더라도, 식사가 끝날 때 매일 영양분을 섭취하거나 포만감을 느끼기 위해 필요하지 않았던 12온스의 햄버거에 똑같이 행복감과 만족감을 다시 느낄 수 있을 것이다.

Why? 왜 정답일까?

예시 앞의 'We decide how much to eat not simply as a function of how much food we actually consume, but by a comparison to its alternatives.'에서 우리는 대안 간의 비교를 통해 얼마나 먹을지를 결정하게 된다고 하므로, 빈칸에 들어갈 말로 가장 적절한 것은 '비교'를 다른 말로 재진술한 ② '상대성'이다.

- function ⓝ (수학) 함수
- alternative ⓝ 대안
- originality ⓝ 독창성
- forgetfulness ⓝ 건망증, 잘 잊어버림
- consume ⓥ 먹다, 마시다
- nourishment ⓝ 영양분
- relativity ⓝ 상대성

구문 풀이

4행 We decide how much to eat not simply as a function (of how much food
<small>「not simply[only] + ___ A +</small>
we actually consume), but by a comparison (to its alternatives).
<small>but (also) + B : A뿐 아니라 B도」</small>

32 철학적 대화에서 이루어지는 무지의 인식 정답률 36% | 정답 ①

다음 빈칸에 들어갈 말로 가장 적절한 것을 고르시오.
☑ recognition of ignorance – 무지의 인식
② emphasis on self-assurance – 자기 확신에 대한 강조
③ conformity to established values – 확립된 가치관에 대한 순응
④ achievements of ancient thinkers – 고대 사상가들의 업적
⑤ comprehension of natural phenomena – 자연 현상에 대한 이해

Philosophical activity is based on the recognition of ignorance.
철학적 활동은 무지의 인식에 기초를 둔다.

The philosopher's thirst for knowledge / is shown through attempts / to find better answers to questions / even if those answers are never found.
지식에 대한 철학자의 갈망은 / 시도를 통해 나타나게 된다. / 질문에 대한 더 나은 답을 찾으려는 / 그 답이 결코 발견되지 않는다 하더라도

At the same time, / a philosopher also knows / that being too sure / can hinder the discovery of other and better possibilities.
동시에, / 철학자는 또한 알고 있다. / 지나치게 확신하는 것이 / 다른 가능성들과 더 나은 가능성들의 발견을 방해할 수 있다는 것을

In a philosophical dialogue, / the participants are aware / that there are things / they do not know or understand.
철학적 대화에서, / 참여자들은 인식한다. / 일들이 있다는 것을 / 자신이 알지 못하거나 이해하지 못하는

The goal of the dialogue is / to arrive at a conception / that one did not know or understand beforehand.
그 대화의 목표는 / 생각에 도달하는 것이다. / 아무도 전부터 알지 못했거나 이해하지 못했던

In traditional schools, / where philosophy is not present, / students often work with factual questions, / they learn specific content listed in the curriculum, / and they are not required to solve philosophical problems.
전통적인 학교에서, / 철학이 존재하지 않는 / 학생들은 흔히 사실적 질문에 대해 공부하고, / 그들은 교육과정에 실린 특정한 내용을 배우며, / 그들은 철학적인 문제를 해결하도록 요구받지 않는다.

However, / we know / that awareness of what one does not know / can be a good way to acquire knowledge.
하지만 / 우리는 안다. / 누구도 알지 못하는 것에 대한 인식이 / 지식을 습득하는 좋은 방법이 될 수 있다는 것을

Knowledge and understanding are developed / through thinking and talking.
지식과 이해는 발달한다. / 사색과 토론을 통해

Putting things into words makes things clearer.
생각을 말로 표현하는 것은 생각을 더 분명하게 만든다.

Therefore, / students must not be afraid of / saying something wrong / or talking without first being sure that they are right.
따라서 / 학생들은 두려워해서는 안 된다. / 틀린 것을 말하거나 / 처음에 그들이 옳다는 것을 확신하지 못하는 상태로 이야기하는 것을

철학적 활동은 무지의 인식에 기초를 둔다. 지식에 대한 철학자의 갈망은 그 답이 결코 발견

되지 않는다 하더라도 질문에 대한 더 나은 답을 찾으려는 시도를 통해 나타나게 된다. 동시에, 철학자는 또한 지나치게 확신하는 것이 다른 가능성들과 더 나은 가능성들의 발견을 방해할 수 있다는 것을 알고 있다. 철학적 대화에서 참여자들은 자신이 알지 못하거나 이해하지 못하는 것이 있다는 것을 인식한다. 그 대화의 목표는 아무도 전부터 알지 못했거나 이해하지 못했다는 생각에 도달하는 것이다. 철학이 존재하지 않는 전통적 학교에서, 학생들은 흔히 사실적 질문에 대해 공부하고, 교육과정에 실린 특정한 내용을 배우며, 철학적인 문제를 해결하도록 요구받지 않는다. 하지만 우리는 누구도 알지 못하는 것에 대한 인식이 지식을 습득하는 좋은 방법이 될 수 있다는 것을 안다. 생각을 말로 표현하는 것은 생각을 더 분명하게 만든다. 따라서 학생들은 틀린 것을 말하거나 처음에 그들이 옳다는 것을 확신하지 못하는 상태로 이야기하는 것을 두려워해서는 안 된다.

Why? 왜 정답일까?

'In a philosophical dialogue, the participants are aware that there are things they do not know or understand.'에서 철학적 대화를 하다 보면 사람들은 자신이 모르고 있거나 이해하지 못하고 있는 것이 있음을 알게 된다고 언급한 후, 'However, we know that awareness of what one does not know can be a good way to acquire knowledge.'에서는 이러한 무지에 대한 인식이 우리가 지식을 습득하는 좋은 방법이 될 수 있다고 설명한다. 따라서 빈칸에 들어갈 말로 가장 적절한 것은 ① '무지의 인식'이다.

- philosophical ⓐ 철학적인
- discovery ⓝ 발견
- specific ⓐ 특정한
- acquire ⓥ 습득하다
- ignorance ⓝ 무지
- self-assurance ⓝ 자기 확신
- phenomenon ⓝ 현상
- hinder ⓥ 방해하다
- factual ⓐ 사실적인
- awareness ⓝ 인식
- put into words 말로 옮기다
- emphasis ⓝ 강조
- conformity ⓝ 순응

구문 풀이

10행 In traditional schools, where philosophy is not present, students often work with factual questions, they learn specific content listed in the curriculum, and they are not required to solve philosophical problems.

★★ 문제 해결 꿀~팁 ★★

▶ 많이 틀린 이유는?
'In a philosophical dialogue, ~'와 'The goal of the dialogue ~'에서 철학적 대화를 통해 인간은 스스로 알지 못하거나 모르고 있다는 사실을 인지하게 된다고 했다. 따라서 철학적 대화나 활동을 통해 인간이 자기 확신에 이른다는 내용인, self-assurance를 포함한 ②는 답으로 적절하지 않다.

▶ 문제 해결 방법은?
주제를 제시하는 However가 포함된 문장의 'awareness of what one does not know'를 재진술한 표현이 바로 ①의 'recognition of ignorance'임을 파악하면 쉽게 답을 고를 수 있다.

33 기쁨의 경험   정답률 62% | 정답 ①

다음 빈칸에 들어갈 말로 가장 적절한 것을 고르시오. [3점]

✓① your biological treasure map to joy – 기쁨으로 가는 생물학적 보물지도
② your hidden key to lasting friendships – 오래 지속되는 우정에 이르는 숨겨진 열쇠
③ a mirror showing your unique personality – 독특한 성격을 보여주는 거울
④ a facilitator for communication with others – 다른 사람들과의 의사소통에 대한 촉진제
⑤ a barrier to looking back to your joyful childhood – 즐거운 어린 시절을 돌아보는 데 있어서의 장애물

The most powerful emotional experiences / are those / that bring joy, inspiration, / and the kind of love / that makes suffering bearable.
가장 강력한 감정적 경험은 / 경험이다. / 기쁨, 영감을 가져다주는 / 그리고 일종의 사랑을 / 고통을 견딜 수 있게 만들어주는
These emotional experiences / are the result of choices and behaviors / that result in our feeling happy.
이러한 감정적 경험은 / 선택과 행동의 결과이다. / 우리가 행복하다고 느끼게 만드는
When we look at happiness through a spiritual filter, / we realize / that it does not mean the absence of pain or heartache.
우리가 정신적 필터를 통해 행복을 바라볼 때, / 우리는 깨닫는다. / 그것이 고통이나 마음의 아픔이 없다는 것을 뜻하는 것이 아님을
Sitting with a sick or injured child, / every parent gets to know the profound joy / that bubbles over / when a son or daughter begins to heal.
아프거나 다친 아이와 함께 앉아 있으면, / 모든 부모는 깊은 기쁨을 알게 된다. / 벅차오르는 / 아들 혹은 딸이 치유되기 시작할 때
This is a simple example / of how we can be flooded with happiness / that becomes more intense / as we contrast it with previous suffering.
이것은 간단한 예이다. / 어떻게 우리가 행복으로 넘쳐날 수 있는지의 / 더욱 강렬해진 / 우리가 그것을 이전의 고통과 대조함에 따라
Experiences such as this / go into the chemical archives of the limbic system.
이와 같은 경험은 / 변연계의 화학적 기록 보관소에 들어간다.
Each time you experience true happiness, / the stored emotions are activated / as you are flooded with even deeper joy / than you remembered.
여러분이 진정한 행복을 경험할 때마다, / 저장된 감정이 활성화된다. / 여러분이 훨씬 더 깊은 기쁨으로 벅차오르면서 / 여러분이 기억했던 것보다
Your spiritual genes are, / in a sense, / your biological treasure map to joy.
당신의 정신적 유전자는 / 어떤 의미에서, / 기쁨으로 가는 생물학적 보물지도이다.

가장 강력한 감정적 경험은 기쁨, 영감, 고통을 견딜 수 있게 만들어주는 일종의 사랑을 가져다주는 경험이다. 이러한 감정적 경험은 우리가 행복하다고 느끼게 만드는 선택과 행동의 결과이다. 우리가 정신적 필터를 통해 행복을 바라볼 때, 우리는 그것이 고통이나 마음의 아픔이 없다는 것을 뜻하는 것이 아님을 깨닫는다. 아프거나 다친 아이와 함께 앉아 있으면, 모든 부모는 아들 혹은 딸이 치유되기 시작할 때 벅차오르는 깊은 기쁨을 알게 된다. 이것은 이전의 고통과 대조함에 따라 어떻게 우리가 더욱 강렬해진 행복으로 넘쳐날 수 있는지의 간단한 예이다. 이와 같은 경험은 변연계의 화학적 기록 보관소에 들어간다. 진정한 행복을 경험할 때마다, 기억했던 것보다 훨씬 더 깊은 기쁨이 벅차오르면서 저장된 감정이 활성화된다. 어떤 의미에서, 당신의 정신적 유전자는 기쁨으로 가는 생물학적 보물지도이다.

Why? 왜 정답일까?

'Each time you experience true happiness, the stored emotions are activated as you are flooded with even deeper joy than you remembered.'에서 우리가 행복을 경험할 때마다 우리의 기억 속에 저장되어 있던 기쁨이 한층 증폭되어 활성화된다고 언급하는 것으로 보아, 감정과 관련된 우리의 정신 기제를 설명하는 빈칸에 들어갈 말로 가장 적절한 것은 ① '기쁨으로 가는 생물학적 보물지도'이다.

- inspiration ⓝ 영감
- spiritual ⓐ 정신적인
- profound ⓐ 깊은
- intense ⓐ 강렬한
- archive ⓝ 기록 보관소
- facilitator ⓝ 촉진제
- bearable ⓐ 견딜 수 있는
- absence ⓝ 부재
- be flooded with ~로 넘쳐나다
- contrast A with B A와 B를 대조하다
- lasting ⓐ 지속되는
- look back to ~을 돌아보다

구문 풀이

1행 The most powerful emotional experiences are those [that bring joy, inspiration, and the kind of love [that makes suffering bearable]].

★★★ 등급을 가르는 문제!
34 우리가 고지방 음식을 찾는 이유   정답률 35% | 정답 ①

다음 빈칸에 들어갈 말로 가장 적절한 것을 고르시오. [3점]

✓① actually be our body's attempt to stay healthy – 실제로 건강을 유지하려는 우리 몸의 시도일
② ultimately lead to harm to the ecosystem – 궁극적으로 생태계에 대한 피해를 낳을
③ dramatically reduce our overall appetite – 우리의 전반적 식욕을 극적으로 줄일
④ simply be the result of a modern lifestyle – 단지 현대 생활 방식의 결과일
⑤ partly strengthen our preference for fresh food – 신선 식품에 대한 우리의 선호를 부분적으로 강화할

Deep-fried foods are tastier than bland foods, / and children and adults develop a taste for such foods.
기름에 튀긴 음식은 싱거운 음식보다 더 맛있고, / 어린이와 어른들은 그런 음식에 대한 취향을 발달시킨다.
Fatty foods cause the brain to release oxytocin, / a powerful hormone with a calming, antistress, and relaxing influence, / said to be the opposite of adrenaline, / into the blood stream; / hence the term "comfort foods."
지방이 많은 음식은 뇌로 하여금 옥시토신을 분비하게 하고 / 진정, 항스트레스와 진정 효과를 가진 강한 호르몬인, / 아드레날린의 반대로 알려진 / 혈류에 / 그로 인해 '위안을 주는 음식'이란 용어가 있다.
We may even be genetically programmed / to eat too much.
심지어 우리는 유전적으로 프로그램되어 있을지도 모른다. / 너무 많이 먹도록
For thousands of years, / food was very scarce.
수천 년 동안, / 음식은 매우 부족했다.
Food, along with salt, carbs, and fat, / was hard to get, / and the more you got, the better.
소금, 탄수화물, 지방이 있는 음식은 / 구하기 어려웠고, / 더 많이 구할수록 더 좋았다.
All of these things are necessary nutrients in the human diet, / and when their availability was limited, / you could never get too much.
이러한 모든 것은 인간의 식단에 필수적 영양소이고, / 그것들의 이용 가능성이 제한되었을 때, / 여러분은 아무리 많이 먹어도 지나침은 없었다.
People also had to hunt down animals or gather plants / for their food, / and that took a lot of calories.
사람들은 또한 동물을 사냥하거나 식물을 채집해야 했고, / 음식을 위해 / 그것은 많은 칼로리를 필요로 했다.
It's different these days.
오늘날은 이와 다르다.
We have food at every turn / — lots of those fast-food places / and grocery stores with carry-out food.
우리에게는 도처에 음식이 있다. / 많은 패스트푸드점과 / 포장음식이 있는 식료품점과 같이
But that ingrained "caveman mentality" says / that we can't ever get too much to eat.
하지만 그 뿌리 깊은 '원시인 사고방식'은 말한다. / 우리가 너무 많아 못 먹는 만큼을 구할 수는 없다고
So / craving for "unhealthy" food / may actually be our body's attempt to stay healthy.
그래서 / '건강하지 않은' 음식에 대한 갈망은 / 실제로 건강을 유지하려는 우리 몸의 시도일 수 있다.

기름에 튀긴 음식은 싱거운 음식보다 더 맛있고, 어린이와 어른들은 그런 음식에 대한 취향을 발달시킨다. 지방이 많은 음식은 뇌로 하여금 진정, 항스트레스와 진정 효과를 가진 강한 호르몬인, 아드레날린의 반대로 알려진 옥시토신을 혈류에 분비하게 하고 그로 인해 '위안을 주는 음식'이란 용어가 있다. 심지어 우리는 너무 많이 먹도록 유전적으로 프로그램되어 있을지도 모른다. 수천 년 동안, 음식은 매우 부족했다. 소금, 탄수화물, 지방이 있는 음식은 구하기 어려웠고, 더 많이 구할수록 더 좋았다. 이러한 모든 것은 인간의 식단에 필수적 영양소이고, 이용 가능성이 제한되었을 때, 아무리 많이 먹어도 지나침은 없었다. 사람들은 또한 음식을 위해 동물을 사냥하거나 식물을 채집해야 했고, 그것은 많은 칼로리를 필요로 했다. 오늘날은 이와 다르다. 많은 패스트푸드점의 음식과 식료품점의 포장음식과 같이 도처에 음식이 있다. 하지만 그 뿌리 깊은 '원시인 사고방식'은 우리가 너무 많아 못 먹는 만큼을 구할 수는 없다고 말한다. 그래서 '건강하지 않은' 음식에 대한 갈망은 실제로 건강을 유지하려는 우리 몸의 시도일 수 있다.

Why? 왜 정답일까?

'It's different these days.' 앞에서 아주 오랫동안 음식은 매우 부족했고, 어떤 영양소든 먹어두는 것이 다 필요하고 좋았기에 지나친 섭취라는 개념이 없었다고 언급한다. 오늘날에는 상황이 비록 달라졌지만, 'But that ingrained "caveman mentality" says that we can't ever get too much to eat.'에 따르면 우리의 사고방식은 여전히 음식이 부족하던 시대에 머물러 있다고 한다. 즉 우리가 고지방 음식을 찾는 것은 옛날 관점에서 생각하면 '필요하게' 여겨지는 행위일 수 있다는 것이다. 따라서 빈칸에 들어갈 말로 가장 적절한 것은 ① '실제로 건강을 유지하려는 우리 몸의 시도일'이다.

- bland ⓐ 싱거운, 담백한, 특징 없는
- calming ⓐ 진정시키는
- comfort food 위안을 주는 음식(힘들거나 아플 때 먹고 기운을 차리는 음식), 기분 좋게 해주는 음식
- genetically ⓐⓓ 유전적으로
- carry-out food 포장음식
- ultimately ⓐⓓ 궁극적으로
- strengthen ⓥ 강화하다
- release ⓥ 분비하다
- scarce ⓐ 드문
- mentality ⓝ 사고방식
- dramatically ⓐⓓ 극적으로

구문 풀이

8행 Food, (along with salt, carbs, and fat), was hard to get, and the more you
주어　　( ): 삽입구　　　　　　동사　　　　　　「the + 비교급 ~,
got, the better.
「the + 비교급 … : ~할수록 더 …하다」

★★ 문제 해결 꿀~팁 ★★

▶ 많이 틀린 이유는?

우리가 기름진 음식을 선호하는 이유로 우리 뇌가 아직 과거에 머물러 있기 때문(caveman mentality) 이라는 내용을 다룬 글이다. 글에 따르면 과거에는 식량이 부족해서 음식을 구하는 대로 다 먹어두면 좋았지만, 오늘날에는 식량이 풍부해졌고, 따라서 기름진 음식이 '건강하지 않게' 여겨지게 되었음에도 우리의 몸은 계속해서 기름진 음식을 찾는다고 하였다. 최다 오답인 ④에서는 우리가 기름진 음식을 찾는 까닭이 현대적 생활 방식(a modern lifestyle)에 있다고 하는데, 이는 정답의 주요 근거인 'caveman mentality'라는 표현과 정반대된다.

▶ 문제 해결 방법은?

더 이상 건강하게 여겨지지 않는 기름진 음식이 과거에는 사람이 살아남고 건강을 유지하는 데 도움이 되는 것이었기에, 그 시절 사고방식이 아직 박혀 있는 인간으로서는 '건강을 유지하기 위해' 기름진 음식을 찾는 것이라는 내용을 완성시키는 말이 빈칸에 들어가야 한다.

---

35 간호사들의 중간자적 역할　　정답률 54% | 정답 ③

다음 글에서 전체 흐름과 관계 <u>없는</u> 문장은?

Nurses hold a pivotal position in the mental health care structure / and are placed at the centre of the communication network, / partly because of their high degree of contact with patients, / but also because they have well-developed relationships with other professionals.
간호사들은 정신 건강 관리 체계에서 중추적인 역할을 맡고 있으며 / 의사소통망의 중심에 위치해 있는데, / 부분적으로는 그들의 환자들과의 높은 접촉 정도 때문이다 / 뿐만 아니라 그들이 다른 전문직 종사자들과 잘 발달된 관계를 유지하기 때문이다.

① Because of this, / nurses play a crucial role in interdisciplinary communication.
이런 이유로 / 간호사들은 여러 학문 분야가 관련된 의사소통에서 중요한 역할을 한다.

② They have a mediating role / between the various groups of professionals / and the patient and carer.
그들은 중개 역할을 한다. / 다양한 전문직 종사자들 집단과 / 환자와 보호자 집단 사이에서

✓ Mental healthcare professionals / are legally bound to protect the privacy of their patients, / so they may be, / rather than unwilling, / unable to talk about care needs.
정신건강 관리 전문직 종사자들은 / 법적으로 자신의 환자의 사생활을 보호하기로 되어 있어, / 그들은 ~일지도 모른다. / 꺼린다기보다도, / 치료에 필요한 것에 관해 말할 수 없는 것일

④ This involves / translating communication between groups into language / that is acceptable and comprehensible to people / who have different ways of understanding mental health problems.
이것은 포함한다. / 언어로 집단 간 의사소통을 번역하는 것을 / 사람들에게 납득 가능하고 이해 가능한 / 정신 건강 상의 문제를 이해하는 다양한 방식을 가진

⑤ This is a highly sensitive and skilled task, / requiring a high level of attention to alternative views / and a high level of understanding of communication.
이것은 고도로 민감하고 숙련된 작업이며 / 대안적 시각에 대한 높은 수준의 관심을 요구한다. / 그리고 높은 수준의 의사소통 이해를

간호사들은 정신 건강 관리 체계에서 중추적인 역할을 맡고 있으며 의사소통망의 중심에 위치해 있는데, 부분적으로는 그들의 환자들과의 높은 접촉 정도 뿐만 아니라 다른 전문직 종사자들과 잘 발달된 관계를 유지하기 때문이다. ① 이런 이유로 간호사들은 여러 학문 분야가 관련된 의사소통에서 중요한 역할을 한다. ② 그들은 다양한 전문직 종사자들 집단과 환자와 보호자 집단 사이에서 중개 역할을 한다. ③ 정신건강 관리 전문직 종사자들은 법적으로 자신의 환자의 사생활을 보호하기로 되어 있어, 그들은 치료에 필요한 것에 관해 말하기를 꺼린다기보다도, 말할 수 없는 것일지도 모른다. ④ 이것은 정신 건강 상의 문제를 이해하는 다양한 방식을 가진 사람들에게 납득 가능하고 이해 가능한 언어로 집단 간 의사소통을 번역하는 것을 포함한다. ⑤ 이것은 고도로 민감하고 숙련된 작업이며 대안적 시각에 대한 높은 수준의 관심과 높은 수준의 의사소통 이해를 요구한다.

Why? 왜 정답일까?

간호사들은 여러 분과 간의 소통, 의료인과 환자 간의 소통 등에서 중요한 역할을 한다는 내용의 글이다. ①, ②는 간호사들이 주로 중간자적 역할을 담당한다는 내용을, ④, ⑤는 그 역할의 구체적 내용을 제시하지만, ③은 환자의 사생활 보호에 관해 언급하며 주제에서 벗어난다. 따라서 전체 흐름과 관계 없는 문장은 ③이다.

- **pivotal** ⓐ 핵심적인
- **structure** ⓝ 구조, 체계
- **communication** ⓝ 의사소통
- **well-developed** 잘 발달된[다듬어진]
- **crucial** ⓐ 중요한
- **mediate** ⓥ 중재하다
- **be bound to** ~하게 되어 있다
- **translate** ⓥ 번역하다
- **comprehensible** ⓐ 이해 가능한
- **skilled** ⓐ 숙련된, 노련한
- **care** ⓝ 돌봄, 관리
- **centre** ⓝ 중심, 가운데
- **contact** ⓝ 접촉, 연락
- **professional** ⓝ 전문직 종사자
- **interdisciplinary** ⓐ 여러 학문 분야가 관련된
- **legally** ⓐⓓ 법적으로
- **unwilling** ⓐ ~하려 하지 않는, 내키지 않는
- **acceptable** ⓐ 용인되는
- **sensitive** ⓐ 민감한, 예민한
- **alternative** ⓐ 대안이 되는

구문 풀이

11행 This involves translating communication between groups into language
동사　　목적어(동명사)　　　　　　　　　　　선행사
[that is acceptable and comprehensible to people [who have different ways of
주격 관·대　　　　　　　　　　　　　선행사　주격 관·대
understanding mental health problems]].

---

36 캐나다 이누이트족의 민족 정신 유지　　정답률 43% | 정답 ②

주어진 글 다음에 이어질 글의 순서로 가장 적절한 것을 고르시오. [3점]

① (A) − (C) − (B)　　✓ (B) − (A) − (C)　　③ (B) − (C) − (A)
④ (C) − (A) − (B)　　⑤ (C) − (B) − (A)

When trying to sustain an independent ethos, / cultures face a problem of critical mass.
독립적인 민족(사회) 정신을 유지하려고 할 때, / 문화는 임계 질량의 문제에 직면한다.

No single individual, / acting on his or her own, / can produce an ethos.
어떤 한 개인도 / 자신 혼자서 행동하는 / 민족 정신을 만들어 낼 수 없다.

(B) Rather, / an ethos results from the interdependent acts of many individuals.
오히려 / 민족 정신은 많은 개인의 상호의존적인 행위에서 비롯된다.

This cluster of produced meaning / may require some degree of insulation / from larger and wealthier outside forces.
생성된 의미의 이러한 군집은 / 어느 정도의 단절을 필요로 할 수 있다. / 더 크고 더 부유한 외부 세력으로부터

The Canadian Inuit maintain their own ethos, / even though they number no more than twenty-four thousand.
캐나다 이누이트족은 그들만의 민족 정신을 유지하고 있다. / 그들이 수는 비록 2만 4천 명에 불과하지만

(A) They manage this feat / through a combination of trade, / to support their way of life, / and geographic isolation.
그들은 이러한 업적을 해낸다. / 무역의 조합을 통해 / 그들의 삶을 유지하기 위해 / 지리적 고립과

The Inuit occupy remote territory, / removed from major population centers of Canada.
이누이트족은 멀리 떨어진 영토를 차지하고 있다. / 캐나다의 주요 인구 중심지에서 따로 떨어진

If cross-cultural contact were to become sufficiently close, / the Inuit ethos would disappear.
만약 문화 간 접촉이 충분히 긴밀해진다면, / 이누이트인들의 민족 정신이 사라지게 될 것이다.

(C) Distinct cultural groups of similar size do not, / in the long run, / persist in downtown Toronto, Canada, / where they come in contact with many outside influences / and pursue essentially Western paths for their lives.
비슷한 규모의 다른 문화 집단은 ~하진 않는다 / 결국 / 캐나다 토론토 도심에서는 지속되지 / 여기서 그들은 많은 외부 영향과 접촉하고 / 살아가기 위해 본질적으로 서구적 방식을 추구한다.

독립적인 민족(사회) 정신을 유지하려고 할 때, 문화는 임계 질량(바람직한 결과를 얻기 위해 필요한 양)의 문제에 직면한다. 자신 혼자서 행동하는 어떤 한 개인도 민족 정신을 만들어 낼 수 없다.

(B) 오히려 민족 정신은 많은 개인의 상호의존적인 행위에서 비롯된다. 생성된 의미의 이러한 군집은 더 크고 더 부유한 외부 세력으로부터 어느 정도의 단절을 필요로 할 수 있다. 캐나다 이누이트족은 비록 2만 4천 명에 불과하지만 그들만의 민족 정신을 유지하고 있다.

(A) 그들은 삶을 유지하기 위해 무역과 지리적 고립의 조합을 통해 이러한 업적을 해낸다. 이누이트족은 캐나다의 주요 인구 중심지에서 따로 멀리 떨어진 영토를 차지하고 있다. 만약 문화 간 접촉이 충분히 긴밀해진다면, 이누이트인들의 민족 정신이 사라지게 될 것이다.

(C) 비슷한 규모의 다른 문화 집단은 캐나다 토론토 도심에서는 결국 지속되지 않는데, 여기서 그들은 많은 외부 영향과 접촉하고 본질적으로 서구적 생활 방식을 추구한다.

Why? 왜 정답일까?

주어진 글에서는 독립적인 민족 정신을 유지하는 데 있어 임계 질량의 문제가 있다고 언급하며, 한 명의 구성원만 가지고는 민족 정신이 유지되지 않는다고 설명한다. 여기에 **Rather**로 연결되는 **(B)**는 한 명이 아닌 많은 개인의 상호의존적 행위가 필요하다고 언급하며 2만 4천 명 규모의 캐나다 이누이트족을 예로 든다. **(A)**는 이누이트족들이 어떻게 민족 정신을 유지하는지 설명한다. 마지막으로 **(C)**는 비슷한 규모의 다른 문화 집단은 이누이트족과는 달리 민족 정신을 유지하지 못하고 있음을 대비시켜 언급한다. 따라서 글의 순서로 가장 적절한 것은 ② '**(B) − (A) − (C)**'이다.

- **sustain** ⓥ 지속하다
- **critical mass** 임계 질량
- **combination** ⓝ 조합
- **geographic** ⓐ 지리적인
- **occupy** ⓥ 차지하다, 점유하다
- **territory** ⓝ 지역, 영토
- **sufficiently** ⓐⓓ 충분히
- **cluster** ⓝ 군집, 무리
- **insulation** ⓝ 단절, 절연
- **persist** ⓥ 지속하다
- **pursue** ⓥ 추구하다
- **path** ⓝ (행동) 계획[방식]
- **independent** ⓐ 독립된
- **feat** ⓝ 위업, 공적
- **trade** ⓝ 거래, 무역
- **isolation** ⓝ 고립
- **remote** ⓐ 외진, 외딴
- **cross-cultural** 여러 문화가 섞인
- **disappear** ⓥ (눈앞에서) 사라지다, 보이지 않게 되다
- **require** ⓥ 필요[요구]하다, 필요로 하다
- **distinct** ⓐ 구별되는, 다른
- **come in contact with** ~와 접촉하다
- **essentially** ⓐⓓ 본질적으로

구문 풀이

7행 If cross-cultural contact were to become sufficiently close,
「if + 주어 + were to + 동사원형 ~
the Inuit ethos would disappear.
주어 + 조동사 과거형 + 동사원형 : 가정법 미래(가능성이 없거나 희박한 일 가정)」

---

37 동물과 인간의 차이　　정답률 51% | 정답 ③

주어진 글 다음에 이어질 글의 순서로 가장 적절한 것을 고르시오. [3점]

① (A) − (C) − (B)　　② (B) − (A) − (C)　　✓ (B) − (C) − (A)
④ (C) − (A) − (B)　　⑤ (C) − (B) − (A)

Heat is lost at the surface, / so the more surface area you have relative to volume, / the harder you must work to stay warm.
열은 표면에서 손실되므로, / 당신이 체적에 대비하여 더 많은 표면적을 가질수록 / 당신은 따뜻함을 유지하기 위해 더 열심히 움직여야 한다.

That means / that little creatures have to produce heat / more rapidly than large creatures.
그것은 의미한다. / 작은 생물이 열을 생산해야 함을 / 큰 생물보다 더 빠르게

(B) They must therefore lead completely different lifestyles.
그러므로 그들은 완전히 다른 생활방식으로 살아가야 한다.

An elephant's heart beats just thirty times a minute, / a human's sixty, / a cow's between fifty and eighty, / but a mouse's beats six hundred times a minute — ten times a second.
코끼리의 심장은 1분에 단 30회를 뛰고 / 인간은 60회, / 소는 50회에서 80회를 뛰지만, / 생쥐는 1분에 600회를 뛴다. / 즉 1초에 10회

Every day, just to survive, / the mouse must eat about 50 percent of its own body weight.
매일 단지 살아남기 위해, / 생쥐는 자신의 몸무게의 약 50퍼센트를 먹어야 한다.

(C) We humans, / by contrast, / need to consume only about 2 percent of our body weight / to supply our energy requirements.
우리 인간은 / 대조적으로 / 우리 체중의 단지 약 2퍼센트만 먹으면 된다. / 에너지 요구량을 공급하기 위해

One area where animals are curiously uniform / is with the number of heartbeats / they have in a lifetime.
동물이 기묘하게도 동일한 하나의 영역은 / 심박수라는 부분이다. / 동물이 평생 동안 갖는
(A) Despite the vast differences in heart rates, / nearly all mammals have about 800 million heartbeats in them / if they live an average life.
심박수의 엄청난 차이에도 불구하고 / 거의 모든 포유동물은 약 8억 회의 심장 박동 수를 갖는다. / 만약 그들이 평균수명을 산다면
The exception is humans.
예외는 인간이다.
We pass 800 million heartbeats after twenty-five years, / and just keep on going for another fifty years / and 1.6 billion heartbeats or so.
우리는 25년 이후 8억 회를 넘어서고 / 또 다른 50년 동안 계속해서 심장이 뛰어 / 약 16억 회 정도의 심박수를 갖는다.

열은 표면에서 손실되므로, 당신이 체적에 대비하여 더 많은 표면적을 가질수록 당신은 따뜻함을 유지하기 위해 더 열심히 움직여야 한다. 그것은 작은 생물이 큰 생물보다 더 빠르게 열을 생산해야 함을 의미한다.

(B) 그러므로 그들은 완전히 다른 생활방식으로 살아야만 한다. 코끼리의 심장은 1분에 단 30회를 뛰고 인간은 60회, 소는 50회에서 80회를 뛰지만, 생쥐는 1분에 600회, 즉 1초에 10회를 뛴다. 매일 단지 살아남기 위해 생쥐는 자신의 몸무게의 약 50퍼센트를 먹어야 한다.

(C) 대조적으로 우리 인간은 에너지 요구량을 공급하기 위해 우리 체중의 단지 약 2퍼센트만 먹으면 된다. 동물이 기묘하게도 동일한 하나의 영역은 동물이 평생 동안 뛰는 심박수라는 부분이다.

(A) 심박수의 엄청난 차이에도 불구하고 거의 모든 포유동물은 만약 그들이 평균수명을 산다면 약 8억 회의 심장 박동 수를 갖는다. 예외는 인간이다. 우리는(태어나고) 25년 이후 8억 회를 넘어서고 또 다른 50년 동안 계속해서 심장이 뛰어 약 16억 회 정도의 심박수를 갖는다.

Why? 왜 정답일까?

작은 생물이 큰 생물에 비해 열을 더 많이 생산해내야 체온을 유지한다는 내용의 주어진 글 뒤로, (B)는 그리하여 작은 생물과 큰 생물의 삶의 방식이 아예 다르다고 설명한다. (C)는 (B)에서 언급된 동물들과 대비되는 예로 인간을 언급한 후, 서로 다른 동물들끼리 비슷한 점이 하나 있다고 말하며 심박수를 언급한다. (A)는 심박수에 대한 내용을 이어 간다. 따라서 글의 순서로 가장 적절한 것은 ③ '(B) − (C) − (A)' 이다.

- surface ⓝ 표면, 지면
- volume ⓝ 부피, 체적
- rapidly ⓐⓓ 빠르게
- vast ⓐ 큰, 방대한
- heartbeat ⓝ 심장 박동
- requirement ⓝ 필요, 요구
- curiously ⓐⓓ 기묘하게도
- lifetime ⓝ 일생, 평생
- relative to ~에 비해
- creature ⓝ 생명이 있는 존재, 생물
- despite ⓟⓡⓔⓟ …에도 불구하고
- nearly ⓐⓓ 거의
- completely ⓐⓓ 완전히
- supply ⓥ 공급[제공]하다
- uniform ⓐ 동일한

구문 풀이

> 1행 Heat is lost at the surface, so the more surface area you have relative to
> 「the+비교급 ~,
> volume, the harder you must work to stay warm.
> the+비교급 … : ~할수록 더 …하다」

★★★ 등급을 가르는 문제!
38 아동 문학 텍스트의 입지 　　　　　정답률 38% | 정답 ③

글의 흐름으로 보아, 주어진 문장이 들어가기에 가장 적절한 곳을 고르시오.

Interest in ideology in children's literature / arises from a belief / that children's literary texts are culturally formative, / and of massive importance / educationally, intellectually, and socially.
아동 문학에서의 이데올로기에 대한 관심은 / 믿음에서 비롯된다. / 아동문학의 텍스트가 문화적으로 형성되고, / 매우 중요하다는 / 교육적, 지적, 사회적으로
① Perhaps more than any other texts, / they reflect society / as it wishes to be, / as it wishes to be seen, / and as it unconsciously reveals itself to be, / at least to writers.
아마 다른 어떤 텍스트보다도 / 그것들은 사회를 반영한다. / 그것이 바라는 대로, / 그것이 보이게 하고 싶은 대로, / 그리고 그것이 무의식적으로 드러나 있는 그대로를 / 적어도 작가에게는
② Clearly, / literature is not the only socialising agent / in the life of children, / even among the media.
분명히, / 문학만이 유일한 사회화 동인은 아니다. / 아이들의 삶에서, / 또 심지어 매체들 가운데에서도
✔ It is possible to argue, / for example, / that, today, / the influence of books is vastly overshadowed / by that of television.
주장할 수 있다. / 예를 들어, / 오늘날 책의 영향은 크게 가려진다고 / 텔레비전의 영향력에 의해
There is, therefore, / a considerable degree of interaction / between the two media.
그러나 ~이 있다. / 상당한 수준의 상호작용이 / 두 매체 사이에
④ Many so-called children's literary classics are televised, / and the resultant new book editions strongly suggest / that viewing can encourage subsequent reading.
소위 아동문학 고전이라고 불리는 많은 책이 TV로 방영되고 있으며, / 그 결과 나온 새로운 판본의 책은 강력하게 시사한다. / TV를 시청하는 것이 추가적으로 이어지는 독서를 장려할 수 있다는 것을
⑤ Similarly, / some television series for children / are published in book form.
마찬가지로, / 아동을 위한 몇몇 텔레비전 시리즈는 / 책 형태로 출판되기도 한다.

아동 문학에서의 이데올로기에 대한 관심은 아동문학의 텍스트가 문화적으로 형성되고, 교육적, 지적, 사회적으로 매우 중요하다는 믿음에서 비롯된다. ① 적어도 작가에게는 아동 문학의 텍스트는 아마 다른 어떤 텍스트보다도 사회를 그 사회가 바라는 대로, 보이게 하고 싶은 대로, 그리고 그것이 무의식적으로 드러나 있는 그대로를 반영한다. ② 분명히, 문학만이 아이들의 삶 속에서, 또 심지어 매체들 가운데에서도 유일한 사회화 동인은 아니다. ③ 예를 들어, 오늘날 책의 영향은 텔레비전의 영향력에 의해 크게 가려진다고 주장할 수 있다. 그러나 두 매체 사이에는 상당한 수준의 상호작용이 있다. ④ 소위 아동문학 고전이라고 불리는 많은 책이 TV로 방영되고 있으며, 그 결과 나온 새로운 판본의 책은 TV를 시청하는 것이 추가적으로 이어지는 독서를 장려할 수 있다는 것을 강력하게 시사한다. ⑤ 마찬가지로, 아동을 위한 몇몇 텔레비전 시리즈는 책 형태로 출판되기도 한다.

Why? 왜 정답일까?

③ 앞의 문장에서 오늘날 아동문학은 아이들에게 영향력을 발휘하는 유일한 매체는 아니라고 언급한 뒤, 주어진 문장에서는 예컨대 텔레비전의 영향력과 비교하면 책의 영향력이 많이 가려진다고 설명한다. 이어서 ③ 뒤의 문장은 however로 흐름을 반전시키며 두 매체, 즉 주어진 문장에서 언급된 텔레비전과 문학 사이에 많은 상호작용이 이루어지고 있다는 내용을 제시한다. 따라서 주어진 문장이 들어가기에 가장 적절한 곳은 ③이다.

- vastly ⓐⓓ 크게
- ideology ⓝ 이데올로기, 이념
- arise from ~에서 발생하다
- formative ⓐ 모양을 만드는, 형성하는
- reflect ⓥ 반영하다
- reveal ⓥ 드러내다
- agent ⓝ 중요한 작용을 하는 사람[것], 동인
- so-called ⓐ 소위 말하는
- resultant ⓐ 그 결과로 생긴, 그에 따른
- overshadow ⓥ 그늘을 드리우다, 가리다.
- literature ⓝ 문학
- literary ⓐ 문학의
- intellectually ⓐⓓ 지적으로
- unconsciously ⓐⓓ 무의식적으로
- socialise ⓥ 사회화시키다
- considerable ⓐ 상당한
- televise ⓥ 텔레비전으로 방송하다
- subsequent ⓐ 뒤이은

구문 풀이

> 3행 Interest in ideology in children's literature arises from a belief {that
> 　　　　　　　주어　　　　　　　　　　　동사　　　　　　보어
> children's literary texts are culturally formative, and of massive importance
> educationally, intellectually, and socially}. ( ): 동격절(=a belief) (massively important)
>
> 5행 Perhaps more than any other texts, they reflect society {as it wishes to be}, {as it wishes to be seen}, and {as it unconsciously reveals itself to be}, at least to writers.
> {A}, {B}, and {C}: 병렬 구조

★★ 문제 해결 꿀~팁 ★★

▶ 많이 틀린 이유는?
④ 앞뒤에 논리적 공백이 있는지 확인해 보면, 먼저 ④ 앞에서 두 미디어 간의 상호작용(a considerable degree of interaction between the two media)을 언급한 후, ④ 뒤에서 아동 문학 고전이 텔레비전으로 방송되는 경우를 예로 들고 있다. 즉 ④ 앞뒤로 일반론과 예시가 자연스럽게 연결되므로, ④에 주어진 문장이 들어갈 만한 논리적 공백이 존재하지 않는다.

▶ 문제 해결 방법은?
정관사 힌트에 주목해야 한다.
③ 앞에서 '두 미디어'로 지칭할 만한 대상이 언급되지 않았는데, ③ 뒤에서는 'the two media'라는 표현을 사용하고 있다. 이로 미루어 보아, books와 television이라는 두 가지 대상을 언급하는 주어진 문장이 ③에 반드시 들어가야 함을 알 수 있다.

★★★ 등급을 가르는 문제!
39 임무가 종료된 인공 위성의 처리 문제 　　　　　정답률 41% | 정답 ⑤

글의 흐름으로 보아, 주어진 문장이 들어가기에 가장 적절한 곳을 고르시오. [3점]

The United Nations asks / that all companies remove their satellites from orbit / within 25 years / after the end of their mission.
국제연합은 요청하고 있다. / 모든 기업들이 위성을 궤도에서 제거해 줄 것을 / 25년 이내에 / 인공위성의 임무 종료 후
This is tricky to enforce, though, / because satellites can (and often do) fail.
하지만 이것은 시행하기에 까다롭다. / 인공위성이 작동하지 않을 수 있기(그리고 종종 정말로 작동하지 않기) 때문에
① To tackle this problem, / several companies around the world / have come up with novel solutions.
이 문제를 해결하기 위해 / 전세계의 몇몇 회사들이 / 새로운 해결책을 내놓았다.
② These include / removing dead satellites from orbit / and dragging them back into the atmosphere, / where they will burn up.
이것은 포함하는데, / 수명이 다한 인공위성을 궤도에서 제거하고, / 대기권으로 다시 끌어들이는 것을 / 여기서 그것은 다 타 버리게 될 것이다.
③ Ways we could do this / include / using a harpoon to grab a satellite, / catching it in a huge net, / using magnets to grab it, / or even firing lasers to heat up the satellite, / increasing its atmospheric drag / so that it falls out of orbit.
우리가 이렇게 할 수 있는 방법은 / 포함한다. / 작살을 이용해서 위성을 잡거나, / 거대한 그물로 그것을 잡거나, / 자석을 이용하여 위성을 잡거나, / 혹은 레이저를 발사하여 위성을 가열하는 것을 / 그것의 대기 항력을 증가시키면서 / 그것이 궤도에서 떨어져 나오도록
④ However, / these methods are only useful / for large satellites orbiting Earth.
하지만, / 이러한 방법은 오직 유용하다. / 지구 궤도를 도는 큰 위성들에게만
✔ There isn't really a way for us / to pick up smaller pieces of debris / such as bits of paint and metal.
우리로서는 방법이 정말로 없다. / 작은 잔해물을 치울 수 있는 / 페인트 조각이나 금속 같은
We just have to wait for them / to naturally re-enter Earth's atmosphere.
우리는 그것들을 기다려야 할 뿐이다. / 자연적으로 지구의 대기로 다시 들어오기를

국제연합은 모든 기업들이 인공위성의 임무 종료 후 25년 이내에 위성을 궤도에서 제거해 줄 것을 요청하고 있다. 하지만 인공위성이 작동하지 않을 수 있기(그리고 종종 정말로 작동하지 않기) 때문에 이것은 시행하기에 까다롭다. ① 이 문제를 해결하기 위해 전세계의 몇몇 회사들이 새로운 해결책을 내놓았다. ② 이것은 수명이 다한 인공위성을 궤도에서 제거하고, 대기권으로 다시 끌어들이는 것을 포함하는데, 여기서 그것은 다 타 버리게 될 것이다. ③ 우리가 이렇게 할(인공위성을 대기권으로 끌고 들어가) 수 있는 방법은 위성이 궤도에서 떨어져 나오도록 대기 항력을 증가시키면서 위성을 작살을 이용해서 잡거나, 거대한 그물로 잡거나, 자석을 이용하여 잡거나, 레이저를 발사하여 가열하는 것을 포함한다. ④ 하지만, 이러한 방법은 오직 지구 궤도를 도는 큰 위성들에게만 유용하다. ⑤ 우리가 페인트 조각이나 금속 같은 작은 잔해물을 치울 수 있는 방법은 정말로 없다. 우리는 그것들이 자연적으로 지구의 대기로 다시 들어오기를 기다려야 할 뿐이다.

Why? 왜 정답일까?

⑤ 앞의 문장에서 임무가 종료된 인공위성을 대기권으로 끌어들여 태우는 방법은 지구 궤도를 도는 큰 위성들에게만 유용하다고 언급한다. 주어진 문장은 우리가 '작은' 잔해물을 처리할 방법이 없다고 언급하며 ⑤ 앞의 문장 내용을 보충 설명한다. ⑤ 뒤의 문장은 주어진 문장에서 언급된 smaller pieces of debris를 them으로 받으며, 작은 잔해물은 알아서 대기로 들어오기를 바랄 수밖에 없다고 언급한다. 따라서 주어진 문장이 들어가기에 가장 적절한 곳은 ⑤이다.

- **debris** ⓝ 잔해
- **orbit** ⓝ 궤도
- **tricky** ⓐ 까다로운
- **tackle** ⓥ 다루다, 해결하다
- **novel** ⓐ 새로운, 신기한
- **atmosphere** ⓝ (지구의) 대기
- **magnet** ⓝ 자석, 자철
- **fall out of** ~을 빠져나오다, 떨어져 나오다
- **satellite** ⓝ 인공위성
- **mission** ⓝ 임무
- **enforce** ⓥ 시행하다
- **come up with** ~을 떠올리다
- **drag** ⓝ 항력, 끌림
- **burn up** 타 버리다
- **heat up** 데우다, 열을 가하다
- **method** ⓝ 방법

구문 풀이

10행 Ways [we could do this] include using a harpoon to grab a satellite, 〔주어(복수)〕 〔동사〕 〔목적어1〕 catching it in a huge net, using magnets to grab it, or even firing lasers to heat up 〔목적어2〕 〔목적어3〕 〔목적어4〕 the satellite, increasing its atmospheric drag so that it falls out of orbit. 〔분사구문(~하면서)〕 〔접속사(~하도록, ~하기 위해)〕

★★ 문제 해결 꿀~팁 ★★

▶ **많이 틀린 이유는?**
수명이 다한 인공위성의 사후 처리에 관한 글로, 대명사 힌트를 잘 활용하면 오답을 쉽게 소거할 수 있다. ③ 앞에서 인공위성을 다시 대기로 끌어들여 없애는 방법을 언급한 데 이어, ③ 뒤이자 ④ 앞의 문장에서는 이를 do this로 가리킨다. 또한 이 문장의 'using ~, catching ~, using ~, or even firing ~'을 ④ 뒤에서 these methods로 가리킨다. 즉 ③, ④ 앞뒤에서 대명사 사용이 모두 적절하기 때문에 주어진 문장은 이 두 곳에 들어갈 수 없다.

▶ **문제 해결 방법은?**
정답을 골라내는 데에도 대명사 힌트가 큰 역할을 한다. ⑤ 앞의 문장에서는 대기로 끌어당기는 갖가지 방법이 큰 인공위성(large satellites)에만 적용될 수 있다고 하는데, ⑤ 뒤의 문장은 '이 방법을 사용하지 못하고 그저 자연스럽게 지구로 다시 오기를 기다려야 하는' 대상을 them으로 가리키고 있다. 즉 them이 large satellites와 일치하지 않으므로, 주어진 문장이 ⑤에 들어가야 함을 알 수 있다.

---

40 음악에 영향을 받을 수 있는 협력성 〔정답률 76%〕 〔정답 ②〕

다음 글의 내용을 한 문장으로 요약하고자 한다. 빈칸 (A), (B)에 들어갈 말로 가장 적절한 것은?

	(A)		(B)
①	uncomfortable 불편하게	……	competitive mood 경쟁적 분위기
✓②	cooperative 협동적이게	……	shared rhythm 공유된 리듬
③	distracted 산만해지게	……	shared rhythm 공유된 리듬
④	attentive 주의 집중하게	……	competitive mood 경쟁적 분위기
⑤	indifferent 무관심하게	……	disturbing pattern 골치 아픈 패턴

Music is used / to mold customer experience and behavior.
음악은 사용된다. / 고객의 경험과 행동을 형성하기 위해
A study was conducted / that explored / what impact it has on employees.
연구가 수행되었다 / 탐구하는 / 그것이 직원에게 어떤 영향을 끼치는지를
Results from the study indicate / that participants who listen to rhythmic music / were inclined to cooperate more / irrespective of factors / like age, gender, and academic background, / compared to those who listened to less rhythmic music.
연구 결과는 보여준다 / 리듬감 있는 음악을 듣는 참가자가 / 더 협력하는 경향이 있다는 것을 / 요인에 관계없이 / 나이, 성별, 학력과 같은 / 리듬감이 덜 있는 음악을 듣는 참가자에 비해
This positive boost / in the participants' willingness to cooperate / was induced / regardless of whether they liked the music or not.
이러한 긍정적인 촉진제는 / 참가자의 협력하려는 자발성의 / 야기되었다 / 그들이 음악을 좋아하는지 혹은 그렇지 않은지와 상관없이
When people are in a more positive state of mind, / they tend to become more agreeable and creative, / while those on the opposite spectrum / tend to focus on their individual problems / rather than giving attention to solving group problems.
사람들이 좀 더 긍정적인 심리 상태에 있을 때, / 그들이 더 기분이 좋고 창의적이 되는 경향이 있다. / 반면 반대 스펙트럼에 있는 사람은 / 자신의 개별 문제에 초점을 두는 경향이 있다 / 집단 문제 해결에 주의를 기울이기보다는
The rhythm of music has a strong pull / on people's behavior.
음악의 리듬은 강하게 끌어당긴다 / 사람들의 행동을
This is because / when people listen to music with a steady pulse, / they tend to match their actions to the beat.
이것은 ~이기 때문이다. / 사람이 일정한 박자로 음악을 들을 때, / 자신의 행동을 박자에 맞추는 경향이 있기
This translates to better teamwork / when making decisions / because everyone is following one tempo.
이것은 더 좋아지는 팀워크로 이해된다. / 결정을 내릴 때 / 모두가 한 박자를 따르고 있어
➡ According to the study, / the music played in workplaces / can lead employees to be (A) cooperative / because the beat of the music / creates a (B) shared rhythm for working.
연구에 따르면 / 직장에서 연주되는 음악은 / 직원이 협동적이게 이끌 수 있다. / 음악의 박자가 ~하기 때문에 / 작업 동안 공유된 리듬을 만들기

음악은 고객의 경험과 행동을 형성하는 데 사용된다. 그것이 직원에게 어떤 영향을 끼치는지를 탐구하는 연구가 수행되었다. 연구 결과는 리듬감 있는 음악을 듣는 참가자가 리듬감이 덜 있는 음악을 듣는 참가자에 비해 나이, 성별, 학력과 같은 요인에 관계없이 더 협력하는 경향이 있다는 것을 보여준다. 이러한 참가자의 협력하려는 자발성의 긍정적인 촉진제는 그들이 음악을 좋아하는지 혹은 그렇지 않은지와 상관없이 야기되었다. 사람들이 좀 더 긍정적인 심리 상태에 있을 때, 그들이 더 기분이 좋고 창의적이 되는 경향이 있는 반면, 반대 스펙트럼에 있는 사람은 집단 문제 해결에 주의를 기울이기보다는 자신의 개별 문제에 초점을 두는 경향이 있다. 음악의 리듬은 사람들의 행동을 강하게 끌어당긴다. 이것은 사람이 일정한 박자로 음악을 들을 때, 자신의 행동을 박자에 맞추는 경향이 있기 때문이다. 이것은 모두가 한 박자를 따르고 있어 결정을 내릴 때 더 좋아지는 팀워크로 이해된다.
➡ 연구에 따르면 작업 동안 음악의 박자가 (B) 공유된 리듬을 만들기 때문에 직장에서 연주되는 음악은 직원이 (A) 협동적이게 이끌 수 있다.

Why? 왜 정답일까?

'Results from the study indicate that participants who listen to rhythmic music were inclined to cooperate more ~'에서 리듬이 있는 음악을 듣는 사람들은 리듬이 덜한 음악을 듣는 이들에 비해 더 협력적이라고 하는데, 마지막 두 문장에 따르면 이는 사람들이 듣고 있는 음악의 박자에 행동을 맞추는 경향이 있어 모두가 같은 박자를 따를 때 팀워크가 증진되는 현상과 관련이 있다. 따라서 요약문의 빈칸 (A), (B)에 들어갈 말로 적절한 것은 ② '(A) cooperative(협동적이게), (B) shared rhythm(공유된 리듬)'이다.

- **mold** ⓥ 형성하다, 빚다
- **indicate** ⓥ 보여주다
- **be inclined to** ~하는 경향이 있다
- **academic background** 학력
- **willingness** ⓝ (기꺼이) ~하려는 마음
- **regardless of** ~와 상관없이
- **spectrum** ⓝ 스펙트럼, 빛 띠
- **steady** ⓐ 고정적인, 한결같은
- **beat** ⓝ 박자, 운율
- **tempo** ⓝ 박자, 속도
- **distracted** ⓐ 산만해진
- **employee** ⓝ 직원
- **rhythmic** ⓐ 리드미컬한, 리듬감이 있는
- **irrespective of** ~와 관계없이
- **boost** ⓝ 증진
- **induce** ⓥ 유발하다
- **agreeable** ⓐ 기분 좋은, 선뜻 동의하는
- **rhythm** ⓝ 리듬
- **pulse** ⓝ 리듬, 맥박
- **translate to** ~로 이해되다, 해석되다
- **workplace** ⓝ 직장, 업무 현장
- **disturbing** ⓐ 골치 아픈, 불안감을 주는

구문 풀이

3행 Results from the study indicate that participants [who listen to rhythmic 〔접속사(~것)〕 〔주어〕 music] were inclined to cooperate more irrespective of factors (like age, gender, 〔동사〕 〔~와 관계없이〕 and academic background), compared to those [who listened to less rhythmic 〔분사구문(~와 비교해서)〕 →선행사 music].

14회

41-42 이메일을 더 친환경적으로 사용하기 위해 노력할 필요성

In this day and age, / it is difficult / to imagine our lives without email.
요즘 같은 시대에 / 어렵다. / 이메일이 없는 우리의 삶을 상상하기
But how often do we consider / the environmental impact of these virtual messages?
그러나 얼마나 자주 우리는 고려하는가? / 이러한 가상 메시지의 환경적 영향을
At first glance, / digital messages appear to (a) save resources.
얼핏 보면 / 디지털 메시지가 자원을 절약하는 것처럼 보인다.
Unlike traditional letters, / no paper or stamps are needed; / nothing has to be packaged or transported.
전통적인 편지와는 달리, / 종이나 우표가 필요하지 않다. / 즉, 어떤 것도 포장되거나 운송될 필요가 없다.
Many of us tend to assume / that using email requires little more than the electricity / used to power our computers.
우리 중 많은 사람은 추정하는 경향이 있다. / 이메일을 사용하는 것이 전기 정도만 필요로 한다고 / 컴퓨터 전원을 켜는 데 사용되는 것
It's easy / to (b) overlook the invisible energy usage / involved in running the network / — particularly when it comes to sending and storing data.
쉽다. / 보이지 않는 에너지 사용을 간과하기 / 네트워크 실행에 수반되는 / 특히 데이터 전송과 저장에 관해
Every single email in every single inbox in the world / is stored on a server.
세계의 모든 받은편지함에 있는 모든 이메일은 / 서버에 저장된다.
The incredible quantity of data / requires huge server farms — gigantic centres with millions of computers / which store and transmit information.
엄청난 양의 데이터는 / 엄청난 양의 서버 팜을 필요로 한다. / 수백만 대의 컴퓨터가 있는 거대한 센터인 / 정보를 저장하고 전송하는
These servers consume (c) massive amounts of energy, 24 hours a day, / and require countless litres of water, or air conditioning systems, / for cooling.
이러한 서버는 하루 24시간 엄청나게 많은 양의 에너지를 소비하며 / 수많은 리터의 물 또는 에어컨 시스템이 필요하다. / 냉각을 위해
『The more messages we send, receive and store, / the (d) more servers are needed / — which means more energy consumed, / and more carbon emissions.』 42번의 근거
우리가 더 많은 메시지를 보내고, 받고, 저장할수록 / 더 많은 서버가 필요한데, / 이는 더 많은 에너지 소비를 의미한다. / 그리고 더 많은 탄소 배출
『Clearly, / sending and receiving electronic messages / in an environmentally conscious manner / is by no means enough to stop climate change.
분명히, / 전자 메시지를 보내고 받는 것은 / 환경 의식이 있는 방식으로 / 결코 기후 변화를 멈추기에 충분하지 않다.
But with a few careful, mindful changes, / (e) unnecessary CO₂ emissions can easily be avoided.』 41번의 근거
그러나 몇몇 주의 깊고 신중한 변화로 / 불필요한 CO_2 배출은 쉽게 회피될 수 있다.

요즘 같은 시대에 이메일이 없는 우리의 삶을 상상하기 어렵다. 그러나 얼마나 자주 우리는 이러한 가상 메시지의 환경적 영향을 고려하는가? 얼핏 보면 디지털 메시지가 자원을 (a) 절약하는 것처럼 보인다. 전통적인 편지와는 달리, 종이나 우표가 필요하지 않다. 즉, 어떤 것도 포장되거나 운송될 필요가 없다. 우리 중 많은 사람은 이메일을 사용하는 것이 컴퓨터 전원을 켜는 데 사용되는 전기 정도만 필요로 한다고 추정하는 경향이 있다. 특히 데이터 전송과 저장에 관해, 네트워크 실행에 수반되는 보이지 않는 에너지 사용을 (b) 간과하기 쉽다. 세계의 모든 받은편지함에 있는 모든 이메일은 서버에 저장된다. 엄청난 양의 데이터는 엄청난 양의 서버 팜을 필요로 하는데, 이것은 정보를 저장하고 전송하는 수백만 대의 컴퓨터가 있는 거대한 센터이다. 이러한 서버는 하루 24시간 (c) 최소한의(→ 엄청나게 많은) 양의 에너지를 소비하며 냉각을 위해 수많은 리터의 물 또는 에어컨 시스템이 필요하다. 더 많은 메시지를 보내고, 받고, 저장할수록 (d) 더 많은 서버가 필요한데, 이는 더 많은 에너지 소비와 더 많은 탄소 배출을 의미한다. 분명히, 환경 의식이 있는 방식으로 전자 메시지를 보내고 받는 것은 결코 기후 변화를 멈추기에 충분하지 않다. 그러나 몇몇 주의 깊고 신중한 변화로 (e) 불필요한 CO_2 배출은 쉽게 회피될 수 있다.

- **impact** ⓝ 영향
- **at first glance** 언뜻 보기에는
- **package** ⓥ 포장하다
- **overlook** ⓥ 간과하다
- **particularly** ⓐⓓ 특히
- **incredible** ⓐ 믿어지지 않을 정도인
- **huge** ⓐ 거대한
- **transmit** ⓥ 전송하다
- **minimum** ⓐ 최소한의, 최저의
- **virtual** ⓐ 가상의
- **resource** ⓝ 자원, 재원(財源)
- **transport** ⓥ 운송하다, 수송하다
- **invisible** ⓐ 눈에 보이지 않는
- **when it comes to** ~에 관해서
- **quantity** ⓝ 양
- **gigantic** ⓐ 거대한
- **consume** ⓥ 소비하다, 소모하다
- **countless** ⓐ 무수히 많은

- **air conditioning** 에어컨
- **carbon** ⑪ 탄소
- **environmentally conscious** 환경 의식이 있는
- **unnecessary** ⓐ 불필요한
- **cooling** ⑪ 냉각
- **emission** ⑪ (빛·열·가스 등의) 배출
- **mindful** ⓐ 의식하는, 유념하는
- **record** ⑪ 기록

구문 풀이

13행 The incredible quantity of data requires huge server farms — (gigantic centres with millions of computers [which store and transmit information]).

선행사 / 주격 관·대 / ( ): 동격(= server farms)

---

41 제목 파악 | 정답률 75% | 정답 ②

윗글의 제목으로 가장 적절한 것은?

① Recycling Makes Your Life Even Better – 재활용은 여러분의 삶을 훨씬 더 좋게 만든다
✓② Eco-friendly Use of Email Saves the Earth – 이메일의 친환경적 사용이 지구를 지킨다
③ Traditional Letters: The Bridge Between Us – 전통적 편지: 우리를 연결해주는 다리
④ Email Servers: Records of Past and Present – 이메일 서버: 과거와 현재의 기록
⑤ Technicians Looking for Alternative Energy – 대체 에너지를 찾고 있는 기술자들

Why? 왜 정답일까?

통념과는 달리 이메일을 사용하는 데에는 많은 에너지와 자원이 들어가므로, 보다 환경을 생각하는 방식으로 이메일을 이용하기 위해 노력해야 한다는 내용의 글이다. 특히 마지막 두 문장에서, 환경 의식이 있는 방식으로 이메일을 사용하고자 노력한다고 해서 바로 기후 변화가 멈춰지는 것은 아니지만, 적어도 불필요한 탄소 배출을 줄일 수는 있게 될 것이라고 언급하며 변화를 촉구하고 있다. 따라서 글의 제목으로 가장 적절한 것은 ② '이메일의 친환경적 사용이 지구를 지킨다'이다.

---

42 어휘 추론 | 정답률 74% | 정답 ③

밑줄 친 (a)~(e) 중에서 문맥상 낱말의 쓰임이 적절하지 않은 것은?

① (a)　② (b)　✓③ (c)　④ (d)　⑤ (e)

Why? 왜 정답일까?

이메일을 더 많이 보낼수록 서버가 더 많이 필요하고, 에너지 소비량과 탄소 배출량이 증가한다(The more messages we send, receive and store, the more servers are needed — which means more energy consumed, and more carbon emissions.)는 내용으로 보아, (c)가 포함된 문장 또한 이메일 서버 팜의 '많은' 에너지 소비에 관해 언급해야 한다. 따라서 (c)의 minimum을 massive로 고쳐야 한다.

43-45 발레에 재능을 갖고 태어난 Melanie

(A)

There once lived a girl named Melanie.
옛날에 Melanie라는 소녀가 살았다.
She wanted to be a ballet dancer.
그녀는 발레 댄서가 되고 싶었다.
『One day, / Melanie's mother saw her dancing / with the flawless steps and enthusiasm of a ballerina.』 45번 ①의 근거 일치
어느 날, / Melanie의 엄마는 Melanie가 춤추는 것을 보았다. / 발레리나의 흠 없는 스텝과 열정을 갖고
"Isn't it strange?
"놀랍지 않아요?
Melanie is dancing so well without any formal training!" / her mother said.
Melanie는 정규 교육을 받지 않고도 춤을 너무 잘 춰요!"라고 / 그녀의 엄마가 말했다.
"I must get (a) her professional lessons / to help her polish her skill."
"나는 아이가 전문적인 수업을 받도록 해야겠어요. / 아이가 기술을 연마하는 것을 돕기 위해"

(D)

『The following day, / Melanie accompanied her mother to a local dance institute』 45번 ④의 근거 일치
다음날, / Melanie는 지역 댄스 학원에 엄마와 동행했다.
Upon meeting the dance teacher, Mr. Edler, / her mother requested to admit Melanie to his institute.
댄스 교사인 Mr. Edler를 만나자마자 / 엄마는 Melanie를 학원에 받아달라고 요청했다.
The teacher asked Melanie to audition.
교사는 Melanie에게 오디션을 보라고 했다.
(e) She was happy / and showed him some of her favorite dance steps.
그녀는 기뻐하며 / 그에게 자신이 가장 좋아하는 댄스 스텝을 보여 주었다.
『However, he wasn't interested in her dance.』 45번 ⑤의 근거 불일치
하지만, 그는 그녀의 춤에 관심이 없었다.
He was busy with other tasks in the dance room.
그는 댄스실에서 다른 일들로 바빴다.
"You can leave now! / The girl is just average.
"이제 가셔도 됩니다! / 이 소녀는 평범합니다.
Don't let her waste her time aspiring to be a dancer," / he said.
그녀가 댄서가 되기를 꿈꾸며 시간을 낭비하게 하지 마세요."라고 / 그가 말했다.
Melanie and her mother were shocked to hear this.
Melanie와 엄마는 이 말을 듣고 충격을 받았다.

(B)

Disappointed, they returned home, / tears rolling down Melanie's cheeks.
실망하여 그들은 집으로 돌아왔고, / Melanie의 뺨에 눈물이 흘러내렸다.
With her confidence and ego hurt, / Melanie never danced again.
자신감과 자아가 상처받은 채, / Melanie는 결코 다시는 춤을 추지 않았다.
(b) She completed her studies / and became a schoolteacher.
그녀는 학업을 마치고 / 학교 교사가 되었다.
One day, / the ballet instructor at her school was running late, / and Melanie was asked to keep an eye on the class / so that they wouldn't roam around the school.
어느 날, / 그녀가 학교의 발레 강사가 늦게 오는 중이었고, / Melanie는 학생들을 지켜봐 달라는 요청을 받았다. / 그들이 학교를 배회하지 않도록
Once inside the ballet room, / she couldn't control herself.

발레실 안으로 들어가자, / Melanie는 자신을 통제할 수 없었다.
『She taught the students some steps / and kept on dancing for some time.』 45번 ②의 근거 일치
그녀는 소녀들에게 몇 가지 스텝을 가르쳤고 / 얼마 동안 계속해서 춤을 추었다.
Unaware of time or the people around her, / (c) she was lost in her own little world of dancing.
시간과 그녀를 둘러싼 사람들도 인식하지도 못한 채, / 그녀는 자신만의 작은 춤의 세계에 빠져 있었다.

(C)

Just then, / the ballet instructor entered the classroom / and was surprised to see Melanie's incredible skill.
바로 그때, / 발레 강사가 교실로 들어와 / Melanie의 훌륭한 기술을 보고 놀랐다.
"What a performance!" / the instructor said with a sparkle in her eyes.
"대단한 공연이에요!"라고 / 강사는 눈을 반짝이며 말했다.
Melanie was embarrassed / to see the instructor in front of her.
Melanie는 당황했다. / 자신 앞에 서 있는 강사를 보고
"Sorry, Ma'am!" she said.
"죄송해요, 강사님!"이라고 그녀는 말했다.
"For what?" the instructor asked.
"뭐가요?"라고 강사가 물었다.
"You are a true ballerina!"
"당신은 진정한 발레리나예요!"
The instructor invited Melanie / to accompany (d) her to a ballet training center, / and Melanie has never stopped dancing since.
강사는 Melanie에게 요청했고, / 발레 교습소로 자신과 함께 가자고 / 이후 Melanie는 결코 무용을 그만두지 않았다.
『Today, she is a world-renowned ballet dancer.』 45번 ③의 근거 일치
오늘날, 그녀는 세계적으로 유명한 발레 무용수이다.

(A)

옛날에 Melanie라는 소녀가 살았다. 그녀는 발레 댄서가 되고 싶었다. 어느 날, Melanie의 엄마는 Melanie가 발레리나의 흠 없는 스텝과 열정을 갖고 춤추는 것을 보았다. "놀랍지 않아요? Melanie는 정규 교육을 받지 않고도 춤을 너무 잘 춰요!"라고 그녀의 엄마가 말했다. "아이가 기술을 연마하는 것을 돕기 위해 (a) 아이가 전문적인 수업을 받도록 해야겠어요.

(D)

다음날, Melanie는 지역 댄스 학원에 엄마와 동행했다. 댄스 교사인 Mr. Edler를 만나자마자 엄마는 Melanie를 학원에 받아달라고 요청했다. 교사는 Melanie에게 오디션을 보라고 했다. (e) 그녀는 기뻐하며 그에게 자신이 가장 좋아하는 댄스 스텝을 보여 주었다. 하지만, 그는 그녀의 춤에 관심이 없었다. 그는 댄스실에서 다른 일들로 바빴다. "이제 가셔도 됩니다! 이 소녀는 평범합니다. 댄서가 되길 꿈꾸며 시간을 낭비하게 하지 마세요."라고 그가 말했다. Melanie와 엄마는 이 말을 듣고 충격을 받았다.

(B)

실망하여 그들은 집으로 돌아왔고, Melanie의 뺨에 눈물이 흘러내렸다. 자신감과 자아가 상처받은 채, Melanie는 결코 다시는 춤을 추지 않았다. (b) 그녀는 학업을 마치고 학교 교사가 되었다. 어느 날, 그녀가 근무하는 학교의 발레 강사가 늦게 (학교에) 오는 중이었고, Melanie는 학생들이 학교를 배회하지 않도록 지켜봐 달라는 요청을 받았다. 발레실 안으로 들어가자, Melanie는 자신을 통제할 수 없었다. 그녀는 소녀들에게 몇 가지 스텝을 가르쳤고 얼마 동안 계속해서 춤을 추었다. 시간과 그녀를 둘러싼 사람들도 인식하지도 못한 채, (c) 그녀는 자신만의 작은 춤의 세계에 빠져 있었다.

(C)

바로 그때, 발레 강사가 교실로 들어와 Melanie의 훌륭한 기술을 보고 놀랐다. "대단한 공연이에요!"라고 강사는 눈을 반짝이며 말했다. Melanie는 자신 앞에 서 있는 강사를 보고 당황했다. "죄송해요, 강사님!"이라고 그녀는 말했다. "뭐가요?"라고 강사가 물었다. "당신은 진정한 발레리나예요!" 강사는 Melanie에게 발레 교습소로 (d) 자신과 함께 가자고 요청했고, 이후 Melanie는 결코 무용을 그만두지 않았다. 오늘날, 그녀는 세계적으로 유명한 발레 무용수이다.

- **flawless** ⓐ 흠 없는
- **formal** ⓐ 공식적인, 형식적인
- **cheek** ⑪ 볼, 뺨
- **ego** ⑪ 자아, 에고
- **run late** 늦다
- **control oneself** 자제하다, 통제하다
- **sparkle** ⑩ 반짝거림
- **accompany** ⑩ 동반하다, 데리고 가다
- **request** ⑩ 요청하다
- **average** ⓐ 평균의
- **aspire** ⑩ 열망하다, 바라다
- **enthusiasm** ⑪ 열정
- **polish** ⑩ 연마하다, 다듬다
- **confidence** ⑪ 자신감
- **instructor** ⑪ 강사
- **roam** ⑩ 이리저리 돌아다니다, 배회하다
- **unaware** ⓐ 알지 못하는
- **embarrassed** ⓐ 당황한
- **world-renowned** ⓐ 세계적으로 유명한
- **admit** ⑩ (입학 등을) 받아주다
- **waste** ⑩ 낭비하다

구문 풀이

(A) 2행 One day, Melanie's mother saw her dancing with the flawless steps and enthusiasm of a ballerina.
지각동사 목적어 → 목적격 보어(현재분사)

(B) 4행 One day, the ballet instructor at her school was running late, and Melanie was asked to keep an eye on the class so that they wouldn't roam around the school.
「be asked + to부정사」: ~하도록 요청받다 / 접속사(~하도록)

(C) 4행 Melanie was embarrassed to see the instructor in front of her.
감정 형용사 / 부사적 용법(감정의 원인)

(D) 2행 Upon meeting the dance teacher, Mr. Edler, her mother requested to admit Melanie to his institute.
~하자마자 / 동격 / 동사 / 목적어

---

43 글의 순서 파악 | 정답률 85% | 정답 ④

주어진 글 (A)에 이어질 내용을 순서에 맞게 배열한 것으로 가장 적절한 것은?

① (D) – (B) – (C)　② (C) – (B) – (D)
③ (C) – (D) – (B)　✓④ (D) – (B) – (C)
⑤ (D) – (C) – (B)

[문제편 p.137]

배운 적이 없어도 춤을 잘 추었던 Melanie를 보고 엄마가 감탄했다는 내용의 (A) 뒤에, 다음날 Melanie와 엄마가 학원에 찾아가서 춤을 선보였지만 평균에 불과하다는 말을 듣고 낙심했다는 내용의 (D)가 먼저 이어진다. 이어서 (B)에서는 이후 커서 교사가 된 Melanie가 어느 날 우연히 늦게 온 발레 강사를 대신해 아이들에게 스텝을 가르쳐주다가 혼자만의 춤에 빠져들었다는 내용이 전개된다. 마지막으로 (C)에서는 Melanie의 실력에 감탄한 발레 강사가 Melanie에게 발레 수업을 권했고, 마침내 Melanie가 유명한 발레리나가 되었다는 결말이 제시된다. 따라서 글의 순서로 가장 적절한 것은 ④ '(D) – (B) – (C)'이다.

44 지칭 추론 정답률 70% | 정답 ④

밑줄 친 (a) ~ (e) 중에서 가리키는 대상이 나머지 넷과 다른 것은?

① (a) ② (b) ③ (c) ✔ (d) ⑤ (e)

Why? 왜 정답일까?

(a), (b), (c), (e)는 Melanie, (d)는 the ballet instructor at her school을 가리키므로, (a) ~ (e) 중에서 가리키는 대상이 다른 하나는 ④ '(d)'이다.

45 세부 내용 파악 정답률 80% | 정답 ⑤

윗글에 관한 내용으로 적절하지 않은 것은?

① 엄마는 Melanie가 발레리나의 열정을 가지고 춤추는 것을 보았다.
② Melanie는 학생들에게 스텝을 가르쳤다.
③ Melanie는 세계적으로 유명한 발레 댄서이다.
④ Melanie는 지역 댄스 학원에 엄마와 동행했다.
✔ Mr. Edler는 Melanie의 춤에 관심을 보였다.

Why? 왜 정답일까?

(D) 'However, he wasn't interested in her dance.'에서 Melanie가 찾아갔던 댄스 학원의 Mr. Edler는 Melanie의 춤에 관심을 보이지 않았다고 하므로, 내용과 일치하지 않는 것은 ⑤ 'Mr. Edler는 Melanie의 춤에 관심을 보였다.'이다.

Why? 왜 오답일까?

① (A) 'One day, Melanie's mother saw her dancing with ~ enthusiasm of a ballerina.'의 내용과 일치한다.
② (B) 'She taught the students some steps ~'의 내용과 일치한다.
③ (C) 'Today, she is a world-renowned ballet dancer.'의 내용과 일치한다.
④ (D) 'The following day, Melanie accompanied her mother to a local dance institute.'의 내용과 일치한다.

어휘 Review Test 14
문제편 140쪽

	A		B		C		D
01	끼어들다, 간섭하다	01	cancellation	01	ⓘ	01	ⓘ
02	반영하다	02	drag	02	ⓣ	02	ⓒ
03	분비하다	03	continuously	03	ⓠ	03	ⓠ
04	강화하다	04	regardless of	04	ⓕ	04	ⓕ
05	지속하다	05	countless	05	ⓓ	05	ⓓ
06	의도적으로	06	longevity	06	ⓛ	06	ⓘ
07	유발하다	07	occupy	07	ⓝ	07	ⓗ
08	잔여의	08	pivotal	08	ⓐ	08	ⓢ
09	힘드는, 까다로운	09	threat	09	ⓞ	09	ⓝ
10	기근	10	hallmark	10	ⓑ	10	ⓘ
11	대안	11	ignorance	11	ⓜ	11	ⓔ
12	상대성	12	formal	12	ⓔ	12	ⓐ
13	기묘하게도	13	relative to	13	ⓟ	13	ⓚ
14	당황한	14	aspire	14	ⓘ	14	ⓖ
15	궤도	15	souvenir	15	ⓒ	15	ⓘ
16	강렬한	16	gigantic	16	ⓢ	16	ⓕ
17	예방	17	entirely	17	ⓗ	17	ⓜ
18	순응	18	commission	18	ⓚ	18	ⓟ
19	대립	19	enforce	19	ⓖ	19	ⓑ
20	크게	20	absence	20	ⓕ	20	ⓓ

15 회 | 2020학년도 9월 학력평가 [고2]

• 정답 •

18 ①	19 ②	20 ⑤	21 ①	22 ③	23 ⑤★	24 ①	25 ⑤	26 ⑤	27 ④	28 ⑤	29 ③	30 ②★	31 ②	32 ③★
33 ①	34 ①	35 ③	36 ②	37 ⑤	38 ④★	39 ③	40 ①	41 ①	42 ④★	43 ②	44 ④	45 ②

★ 표기된 문항은 [등급을 가르는 문제]에 해당하는 문항입니다.

18 반려견 소음 관리에 신경 써줄 것을 요청하기 정답률 94% | 정답 ①

다음 글의 목적으로 가장 적절한 것은?

✔ 반려견이 짖는 소리를 최소화 해줄 것을 요청하려고
② 아파트 내 반려동물 출입 가능 구역을 안내하려고
③ 아파트 공사로 인한 소음 발생에 대해 사과하려고
④ 반려견 대소변 관련 민원처리 결과를 공지하려고
⑤ 반려동물과 외출 시 목줄 사용을 당부하려고

Dear Residents,
주민께,
We truly value / and appreciate all of our residents, / including those with pets.
우리는 (모든 주민들을) 진심으로 소중하게 생각하고 / 모든 주민들께 감사하고 있습니다. / 반려동물이 있는 분들을 포함하여
We believe / that allowing people to live with their pets / enriches their lives.
우리는 생각합니다. / 사람들이 반려동물과 함께 살게 하는 것은 / 그들의 삶을 풍요롭게 한다고
While we encourage you to enjoy your pets, / we also want to ensure / that you do not do so / at the expense of your neighbors or your community.
우리는 여러분이 반려동물과 즐겁게 지내기를 장려하지만, / 우리는 또한 확실히 하고자 합니다. / 여러분이 그렇게 하지는 않을 것을 / 여러분의 이웃이나 지역사회에 폐를 끼치면서까지
We have received reports / that some residents have been disturbed / by noise from dogs barking.
우리는 신고를 접수했습니다. / 일부 주민들이 방해받고 있다는 / 반려견이 짖는 소리로 인한 소음으로
Excessive barking by dogs / disrupts everyone within hearing, / particularly those who are elderly or sick / or who have small children.
개가 과도하게 짖는 것은 / 그 소리를 들을 수 있는 모든 분에게 피해를 줍니다. / 특히 나이가 많거나 아픈 분, / 혹은 어린 자녀가 있는 분들
We kindly ask / that you keep your dogs' noise levels / to a minimum.
우리는 정중히 요청합니다. / 여러분이 반려견 소음을 유지해 주시기를 / 최소한으로
Thank you for your assistance with this.
이 일에 협조해주셔서 감사합니다.
Regards, Conway Forest Apartments Management Office
Conway Forest 아파트 관리소

주민들께,

우리는 반려동물이 있는 분들을 포함하여 모든 주민들을 진심으로 소중하게 생각하고 주민들께 감사합니다. 우리는 사람들이 반려동물과 함께 살게 하는 것은 그들의 삶을 풍요롭게 한다고 생각합니다. 우리는 여러분이 반려동물과 잘 지내기를 장려하지만, 또한 여러분의 이웃이나 지역사회에 폐를 끼치면서까지 여러분이 그렇게 하지는 않을 것을 확실히 하고자 합니다. 우리는 일부 주민들이 반려견이 짖는 소리로 인한 소음으로 방해받고 있다는 신고를 접수했습니다. 개가 과도하게 짖는 것은 그 소리를 들을 수 있는 모든 분, 특히 나이가 많거나 아픈 분, 혹은 어린 자녀가 있는 분들에게 피해를 줍니다. 우리는 여러분이 반려견 소음을 최소한으로 유지해 주시기를 정중히 요청합니다. 이 일에 협조해주셔서 감사합니다.

Conway Forest 아파트 관리소

Why? 왜 정답일까?

'We kindly ask that you keep your dogs' noise levels to a minimum.'에서 반려견의 소음을 될 수 있는 대로 작게 유지해주기를 아파트 주민들에게 요청한다고 하므로, 글의 목적으로 가장 적절한 것은 ① '반려견이 짖는 소리를 최소화 해줄 것을 요청하려고'이다.

● enrich ⓥ 풍요롭게 하다 ● ensure ⓥ 확실히 하다
● at the expense of ~을 희생하여 ● disturb ⓥ 방해하다, 어지럽히다
● excessive ⓐ 과도한 ● disrupt ⓥ 방해하다, 지장을 주다

구문 풀이
접속새(~하는 반면)
4행 While we encourage you to enjoy your pets, we also want to ensure that
「encourage + 목적어 + to부정사 : ~이 …하기를 장려하다」 접속새(~것)
you do not do so at the expense of your neighbors or your community.
= enjoy your pets ↳~을 희생하여

19 물에 빠진 개를 구하기 위해 빗속에서 수영한 Meghan 정답률 81% | 정답 ②

다음 글의 상황에 나타난 분위기로 가장 적절한 것은?

① grave and solemn – 심각하고 엄숙한 ✔ tense and urgent – 긴박하고 다급한
③ calm and peaceful – 고요하고 평화로운 ④ festive and lively – 축제 같고 활기찬
⑤ monotonous and boring – 단조롭고 지루한

Meghan looked up / and saw angry gray clouds / rolling across the water.
Meghan은 고개를 들어 / 성난 회색 구름을 보았다. / 물 위로 밀려오는 것을
The storm had turned / and was coming her way.
폭풍이 방향을 바꿔서 / 그녀 쪽으로 다가오고 있었다.
She stood up / and reached for her sandals.
그녀는 일어나서 / 그녀의 샌들을 향해 손을 뻗었다.
That's when she spotted the dog splashing / around in the middle of the lake.
그때 그녀는 첨벙거리고 있는 개를 발견했다. / 호수 한 가운데서
At first / she thought he was playing.
처음에 / 그녀는 그 개가 놀고 있다고 생각했다.
She watched for a second or two, / then realized the dog wasn't playing.

그녀는 1, 2초 정도 지켜봤고, / 그리고 나서 그 개가 놀고 있는 것이 아니라는 것을 깨달았다.

He was trying / to keep from going under.
그는 애쓰고 있었다. / 가라앉지 않으려고

With her heart pounding like a trip-hammer, / she ran into the water / and started swimming / toward the dog.
심장이 스프링 해머처럼 쿵쾅거리며 / 그녀는 물속으로 뛰어 들어가 / 헤엄치기 시작했다. / 그 개를 향해

Before she got to the dog, / the rain started.
그녀가 그 개에 닿기 전에 / 비가 내리기 시작했다.

She saw the dog, / and seconds later / he was gone.
그녀는 개를 보았고, / 그리고 몇 초 후에 / 그 개는 사라졌다.

She pushed forward frantically, / her arms reaching out in long strokes, / her legs kicking harder and faster.
그녀는 미친 듯이 앞으로 나아갔다. / 팔을 길게 뻗어 저으며, / 다리를 더욱 힘차고 빠르게 차면서

Meghan은 고개를 들어 성난 회색 구름이 물 위로 밀려오는 것을 보았다. 폭풍이 방향을 바꿔서 그녀 쪽으로 다가오고 있었다. 그녀는 일어나서 그녀의 샌들을 향해 손을 뻗었다. 그때 그녀는 호수 한가운데에서 첨벙거리고 있는 개를 발견했다. 처음에 그녀는 그 개가 놀고 있다고 생각했다. 그녀는 1, 2초 정도 지켜봤고, 그러고 나서 그 개가 놀고 있는 것이 아님을 깨달았다. 그는 가라앉지 않으려고 애쓰고 있었다. 심장이 스프링 해머처럼 쿵쾅거리며 그녀는 물속으로 뛰어 들어가 그 개를 향해 헤엄치기 시작했다. 그녀가 그 개에 닿기 전에 비가 내리기 시작했다. 그녀는 개를 보았고, 몇 초 후에 그 개는 사라졌다. 그녀는 팔을 길게 뻗어 저으며, 다리를 더욱 힘차고 빠르게 차면서 미친 듯이 앞으로 나아갔다.

Why? 왜 정답일까?

'With her heart pounding like a trip-hammer, she ran into the water and started swimming toward the dog.', 'She pushed forward frantically, her arms reaching out in long strokes, her legs kicking harder and faster.'에서 물에 빠진 개가 절박하게 첨벙거리는 것을 발견한 Meghan이 개를 구조하기 위해 필사적으로 헤엄치는 장면을 묘사하고 있다. 따라서 글의 분위기로 가장 적절한 것은 ② '긴박하고 다급한'이다.

- splash ⓥ 첨벙거리다
- stroke ⓝ (수영에서 팔을) 젓기
- solemn ⓐ 엄숙한
- frantically ⓐ 미친 듯이
- grave ⓐ (문제 등이) 심각한
- monotonous ⓐ 단조로운

구문 풀이

7행 With her heart pounding like a trip-hammer, she ran into the water and
「with + 명사 + 분사 : ~한 채로, ~하면서」 동사1
started swimming toward the dog.
동사2

---

20 자녀가 만들어낸 가상의 친구를 존중해주기   정답률 91% | 정답 ⑤

다음 글에서 필자가 주장하는 바로 가장 적절한 것은?

① 아이들의 상상력을 자극하는 질문을 해야 한다.
② 식사 시간을 자녀와 대화하는 기회로 삼아야 한다.
③ 사회성 발달을 위해 단체 활동에 적극 참여해야 한다.
④ 자녀의 노력을 구체적으로 칭찬하는 부모가 되어야 한다.
☑ 부모는 자녀의 가상의 친구를 존중하고 받아들여야 한다.

Children may develop imaginary friends / around three or four years of age.
아이들은 가상의 친구를 만들어 낼 수도 있다. / 서너 살 즈음에

Imaginary friends are only a concern / if children replace all social interactions / with pretend friends.
가상의 친구는 오로지 걱정거리이다. / 아이들이 모든 사회적 상호작용을 대체할 때에 / 가상의 친구로

As long as children are developing socially / with other children, / then imaginary friends are beneficial.
아이들이 사회적으로 성장하는 한, / 다른 아이들과 함께 / 가상의 친구는 유익하다.

Parents often will need reassurance / about imaginary friends; / they should be respectful of the pretend friends, / as well as of their child.
부모는 종종 안심할 필요가 있을 것이며, / 가상의 친구에 대해 / 그들은 가상의 친구도 존중해야 한다. / 자신의 자녀 뿐 아니라

Children who create imaginary friends / should never be teased, humiliated, or ridiculed / in any way.
가상의 친구를 만들어 낸 아이들이 / 절대 놀림 받거나 창피당하거나 조롱당해서는 안 된다. / 어떤 식으로든

Parents may tire of including the friends / in daily activities, / such as setting an extra plate at dinner, / but they should be reassured / that the imaginary friends stage will pass.
부모는 그 친구를 포함시키는 일에 지칠 수 있지만, / 일상생활에 / 저녁식사 시간에 여분의 접시를 놓는 일과 같은 / 그들은 안심해야 한다. / 가상의 친구 시기는 지나갈 것이라고

Until then, / imaginary friends should be respected and welcomed by parents / because they signify a child's developing imagination.
그때까지는 / 가상의 친구는 부모에 의해서 존중되어야 하고 받아들여져야 한다. / 가상의 친구가 자녀의 자라나는 상상력을 의미하는 것이므로

아이들은 서너 살 즈음에 가상의 친구를 만들어 낼 수도 있다. 가상의 친구는 아이들이 모든 사회적 상호작용을 가상의 친구로 대체할 때에만 걱정거리이다. 아이들이 다른 아이들과 함께 사회적으로 성장하는 한, 가상의 친구는 유익하다. 부모는 종종 가상의 친구에 대해 안심할 필요가 있을 것이며, 그들은 자신의 자녀뿐 아니라 가상의 친구도 존중해야 한다. 가상의 친구를 만들어 낸 아이들이 절대 어떤 식으로든 놀림 받거나 창피당하거나 조롱당해서는 안 된다. 부모는 저녁 식사 시간에 여분의 접시를 놓는 일과 같은 일상생활에 그 친구를 포함시키는 일에 지칠 수 있지만, 가상의 친구 시기가 지나갈 것이라고 안심해야 한다. 그때까지는 부모는 가상의 친구가 자녀의 자라나는 상상력을 의미하는 것이므로 가상의 친구를 존중하고 받아들여야 한다.

Why? 왜 정답일까?

'~ imaginary friends should be respected and welcomed by parents because they signify a child's developing imagination.'에서 부모는 자녀가 만들어낸 가상의 친구를 받아들이고 존중해줄 필요가 있다고 언급하는 것으로 볼 때, 필자가 주장하는 바로 가장 적절한 것은 ⑤ '부모는 자녀의 가상의 친구를 존중하고 받아들여야 한다.'이다.

- replace A with B A를 B로 대체하다
- pretend ⓐ 가상의 ⓥ ~인 체하다

- reassurance ⓝ 안심
- humiliate ⓥ 창피를 주다
- tire of ~에 지치다, 싫증 내다
- tease ⓥ 놀리다
- ridicule ⓥ 조롱하다

구문 풀이

4행 As long as children are developing socially with other children, then
조건 접속사(~하는 한) 현재진행(~하고 있다)
imaginary friends are beneficial.

★★★ 등급을 가르는 문제!

21 이전에 버렸던 방식을 되짚어가며 창작을 이어가는 예술가들   정답률 35% | 정답 ①

밑줄 친 got "colder"가 다음 글에서 의미하는 바로 가장 적절한 것은? [3점]

☑ moved away from the desired outcome
바라던 결과에서 멀어졌다
② lost his reputation due to public criticism
대중의 비판으로 인해 명성을 잃었다
③ became unwilling to follow new art trends
새로운 예술 사조를 따르기를 꺼렸다
④ appreciated others' artwork with less enthusiasm
남들의 예술작품을 덜 열정적으로 감상했다
⑤ imitated masters' styles rather than creating his own
자신의 스타일을 만들기보다 거장들의 스타일을 모방했다

If creators knew / when they were on their way to fashioning a masterpiece, / their work would progress only forward: / they would halt their idea-generation efforts / as they struck gold.
만약 창작자들이 안다면, / 그들이 언제 걸작을 만들어 가고 있는지를 / 그들의 작품은 오직 앞으로만 나아갈 것이다. / 그들은 아이디어를 만들어내는 노력을 멈출 것이다. / 그들이 금광을 발견했을 때

But in fact, / they backtrack, / returning to versions / that they had earlier discarded / as inadequate.
그러나 사실 / 그들은 역추적하여 / 버전으로 되돌아간다. / 이전에 그들이 폐기했던 / 부적절하다고

In Beethoven's most celebrated work, the Fifth Symphony, / he scrapped the conclusion of the first movement / because it felt too short, / only to come back to it later.
베토벤의 가장 유명한 작품인 제5번 교향곡에서, / 그는 제1악장의 결말 부분을 폐기했고, / 그것이 너무 짧다고 느껴져 / 결국 나중에 되돌아왔다.

Had Beethoven been able / to distinguish an extraordinary from an ordinary work, / he would have accepted his composition immediately as a hit.
베토벤이 ~할 수 있었다면 / 비범한 작품과 평범한 작품을 구분할 / 그는 자기 작곡을 성공으로 바로 받아들였을 것이다.

When Picasso was painting his famous *Guernica* / in protest of fascism, / he produced 79 different drawings.
피카소가 그의 유명한 *Guernica*를 그릴 때, / 파시즘에 저항하여 / 그는 79점의 다른 스케치들을 그렸다.

Many of the images in the painting / were based on his early sketches, / not the later variations.
이 그림의 많은 이미지들은 / 그의 초기 스케치에 바탕을 두었다. / 이후의 변형물이 아니라

If Picasso could judge his creations / as he produced them, / he would get consistently "warmer" / and use the later drawings.
만약 피카소가 자신의 작품을 판단할 수 있었다면, / 그가 작품을 만들면서 / 그는 일관되게 '더 뜨겁게' 되고 / 나중에 그린 스케치를 사용했을 것이다.

But in reality, / it was just as common / that he got "colder."
하지만 실제로는 / 그만큼 흔한 일이었다. / 그가 '더 차갑게' 된 것은

만약 창작자들이 그들이 언제 걸작을 만들어가고 있는지를 안다면, 그들의 작품은 오직 앞으로만 나아갈 것이다. 그들은 금광을 발견했을 때 아이디어를 만들어내는 노력을 멈출 것이다. 하지만 사실 그들은 (창작 과정을) 되짚어가서 이전에 부적당하다고 폐기했던 버전으로 되돌아간다. 베토벤의 가장 유명한 작품인 제5번 교향곡에서 그는 제1악장의 결말 부분이 너무 짧다고 느껴져 폐기했고, 결국 나중에야 그것에 복귀했다. 베토벤이 비범한 작품과 평범한 작품을 구분할 수 있었다면 그는 자기 작곡을 바로 성공으로 받아들였을 것이다. 피카소가 파시즘에 저항하여 유명한 *Guernica*를 그릴 때, 그는 79점의 다른 스케치들을 그렸다. 이 그림의 많은 이미지들은 이후의 변형물이 아니라, 그의 초기 스케치에 바탕을 두었다. 만약 피카소가 작품을 만들면서 자신의 작품을 판단할 수 있었다면, 그는 일관되게 '더 뜨거워지고' 나중에 그린 스케치를 사용했을 것이다. 하지만 실제로는 그가 '더 차가워진' 것은 그만큼 흔한 일이었다.

Why? 왜 정답일까?

첫 두 문장에서 예술가들은 창작 도중에는 어떤 것이 걸작인지 바로 파악할 수 없기에 작품을 만들어가는 과정을 때때로 되짚어가며 버렸던 것을 다시 가져와 작품을 완성한다고 설명한 후, 베토벤과 피카소의 예를 들고 있다. 특히 피카소의 예에서, 피카소가 만일 작품을 그리던 도중에 어느 스케치가 괜찮은지를 알아볼 수 있었다면 피카소는 초기 스케치를 되살릴 필요 없이 꾸준히 '더 뜨거워졌을' 것이라고 언급하고 있다. 여기서 '뜨거워지다'는 피카소가 걸작에 일관되게 가까워지는 과정을 비유한 표현으로 볼 수 있다. 이에 근거할 때, 피카소가 실제로는 '더 차가워졌다'는 말은 피카소가 걸작에 꾸준히 가까워지지 못하고 초기 스케치에 미치지 못하는 중간 스케치들을 생산해내는 과정을 묘사한 말로 볼 수 있다. 따라서 밑줄 친 부분이 의미하는 바로 가장 적절한 것은 ① '바라던 결과에서 멀어졌다'이다.

- fashion ⓥ (특히 손으로) 만들다, 빚다
- strike gold 노다지를 캐다, 큰 성공을 거두다
- discard A as B A를 B로 간주해서 폐기하다
- scrap ⓥ 폐기하다, 버리다
- composition ⓝ 작곡, 구성
- variation ⓝ 변형, 변주
- generation ⓝ 발생, 유발, 생성
- backtrack ⓥ (왔던 길을) 되짚어가다
- inadequate ⓐ 부적당한, 불충분한
- distinguish A from B A와 B를 구별하다
- in protest of ~에 저항하는
- consistently ⓐ 일관되게

구문 풀이

8행 Had Beethoven been able to distinguish an extraordinary from an ordinary
「had + 주어 + p.p. : 가정법 과거완료 종속절(if 생략 후 도치)」
work, he would have accepted his composition immediately as a hit.
「주어 + 조동사 과거형 + have p.p. : 가정법 과거완료 주절」

★★ 문제 해결 꿀~팁 ★★

▶ 많이 틀린 이유는?
예술가들의 창작 과정이 항상 앞으로만 향하지는 않는다는 내용의 글로, '예술 사조'나 '거장의 스타일을 모방하는' 행위 등은 언급되지 않기 때문에 ③, ⑤는 모두 오답이다.

▶ 문제 해결 방법은?
앞에 나온 get "warmer"의 의미를 잘 이해해야 한다. 이는 피카소가 *Guernica*를 작업하는 도중 어느 스케치가 더 나은지를 바로 판단할 수 있었다면 제작 과정에서 계속 더 발전된 쪽으로 나아가는 요소들만 선택했을 것이기 때문에 그가 추구하는 좋은 작품에 '꾸준히 더 가까워졌을' 것이라는 의미를 나타내는 표현이다. 밑줄 친 got "colder"는 이와 반대되는 의미로 이해해야 한다.

---

22 손으로 하는 활동이 정신 건강에 미치는 긍정적 영향   정답률 83% | 정답 ③

다음 글의 요지로 가장 적절한 것은?
① 긍정적인 감정은 타인에게 쉽게 전이된다.
② 감정 조절은 대인 관계 능력의 핵심 요소이다.
☑ 수작업 활동은 정신 건강에 도움을 줄 수 있다.
④ 과도한 신체활동은 호르몬 분비의 불균형을 초래한다.
⑤ 취미 활동을 통해 여러 분야의 사람들을 만날 수 있다.

The psychology professor Dr. Kelly Lambert's research explains / that keeping what she calls the "effort-driven rewards circuit" well engaged / helps you deal with challenges / in the environment around you / or in your emotional life / more effectively and efficiently.
심리학 교수인 Kelly Lambert 박사의 연구는 설명한다. / 그녀가 '노력 주도 보상 회로'라고 부르는 것을 잘 작동되는 상태로 유지하는 것이 / 당신이 도전들을 처리하는 데 도움이 된다고 / 당신 주변의 환경에서나 / 당신의 정서 생활에서 / 더 효과적이고 효율적으로

Doing hands-on activities / that produce results you can see and touch / — such as knitting a scarf, / cooking from scratch, / or tending a garden — / fuels the reward circuit / so that it functions optimally.
수작업 활동을 하는 것은 / 여러분이 보고 만질 수 있는 결과를 만들어내는 / 목도리를 뜨거나 / 처음부터 직접 요리하거나 / 정원을 손질하는 것과 같이 / 보상 회로를 활성화시킨다. / 그것이 최적으로 작동하도록

She argues / that the documented increase in depression among Americans / may be directly correlated / with the decline of purposeful physical activity.
그녀는 주장한다. / 문서로 기록된 미국인들의 우울증 증가는 / 직접적으로 관련이 있을 수도 있다고 / 목적이 있는 신체 활동의 감소와

When we work with our hands, / it increases the release / of the neurochemicals dopamine and serotonin, / both responsible for generating positive emotions.
우리가 손으로 일을 할 때, / 그것은 분비를 증가시키는데, / 신경 화학 물질인 도파민과 세로토닌의 / 둘 다 긍정적인 감정을 발생시키는 것을 담당한다.

She also explains / that working with our hands / gives us / a greater sense of control over our environment / and more connection to the world around us.
그녀는 또한 설명한다. / 우리의 손으로 작업하는 것은 / 우리에게 준다고 / 환경에 대한 더 큰 통제감과 / 우리 주변 세계와의 더 많은 연결을

All of which contributes / to a reduction in stress and anxiety / and builds resilience / against the onset of depression.
이 모든 것이 기여하고 / 스트레스와 불안의 감소에 / 회복력을 키워준다. / 우울증 발생에 대한

심리학 교수인 Kelly Lambert 박사의 연구는 그녀가 '노력 주도 보상 회로'라고 부르는 것을 잘 작동되는 상태로 유지하는 것이, 당신이 당신 주변의 환경에서나 당신의 정서 생활에서의 도전들을 더 효과적이고 효율적으로 처리하는 데 도움이 된다고 설명한다. 목도리를 뜨거나 처음부터 직접 요리하거나 정원을 손질하는 것과 같이 여러분이 보고 만질 수 있는 결과를 만들어내는 수작업 활동을 하는 것은 보상 회로가 최적으로 작동하도록 활성화시킨다. 그녀는 문서로 기록된 미국인들의 우울증 증가는 목적이 있는 신체 활동의 감소와 직접적으로 관련이 있을 수도 있다고 주장한다. 우리가 손으로 일을 할 때, 신경 화학 물질인 도파민과 세로토닌의 분비를 증가시키는데, 둘 다 긍정적인 감정을 발생시키는 것을 담당한다. 그녀는 또한 우리의 손으로 작업하는 것은 우리에게 환경에 대한 더 큰 통제감과 우리 주변 세계와의 더 많은 연결을 준다고 설명한다. 이 모든 것이 스트레스와 불안의 감소에 기여하고 우울증 발생에 대한 회복력을 키워준다.

Why? 왜 정답일까?
마지막 세 문장에서 손으로 하는 활동은 긍정적인 감정을 발생시키는 화학 물질의 분비를 촉진하고, 환경에 대한 통제감과 주변 세계에 대한 연결감을 주어서 불안을 감소시키고 우울증 발생을 막는 데 도움을 준다고 설명하고 있다. 따라서 글의 요지로 가장 적절한 것은 이러한 수작업 활동의 효과를 일반화해 서술한 ③ '수작업 활동은 정신 건강에 도움을 줄 수 있다.'이다.

- hands-on 손으로 하는, 직접 해보는
- tend ⓥ 돌보다, 보살피다
- depression ⓝ 우울(증), 침체
- neurochemical ⓝ 신경 화학 물질
- resilience ⓝ 회복력, 탄력성
- from scratch 처음부터
- optimally ⓐⓓ 최적으로
- correlate ⓥ 연관성이 있다
- anxiety ⓝ 불안
- onset ⓝ (특히 불쾌한 일의) 시작

구문 풀이
5행 Doing hands-on activities [that produce results {you can see and touch}]
　　　　　동명사구 주어　　선행사　　　주격 관·대　　동사(복수)　　　목적격
— such as knitting a scarf, cooking from scratch, or tending a garden — fuels the
　　　　　동명사1　　　　　동명사2　　　　　　동명사3　　　　　동사(단수)
reward circuit so that it functions optimally.
　　　　　접속사(~하도록)

---

23 문화 연구와 이해에 도움을 주는 유머   정답률 71% | 정답 ⑤

다음 글의 주제로 가장 적절한 것은?
① typical process of cultural assimilation – 문화적 동화의 전형적 과정
② function of laughter in building friendship – 우정 형성에 있어 웃음의 역할
③ educational need for intercultural competence – 문화 간 역량에 대한 교육적 필요
④ roles of humor in criticizing social problems – 사회 문제를 비판하는 데 있어 유머의 역할
☑ humor as a tool for understanding a culture – 문화를 이해하기 위한 도구로서의 유머

It has long been held / that the capacity for laughter / is a peculiarly human characteristic.
오랫동안 여겨져 왔다. / 웃음의 능력은 / 인간의 독특한 특징이라고

The witty Lucian of Samosata (2nd century A.D.) noted / that the way to distinguish a man from a donkey / is that one laughs and the other does not.

(기원후 2세기) Samosata의 재치 있는 Lucian이 지적했다. / 인간을 당나귀와 구별하는 방법으로 / 한쪽은 웃고 다른 한쪽은 그렇지 않다는 것을

In all societies / humor is important / not only in individual communication / but also as a molding force of social groups, / reinforcing their norms and regulating behavior.
모든 사회에서 / 유머는 중요하다. / 개인적인 의사소통에서뿐 아니라 / 사회 집단들을 형성하는 힘으로서도 / 규범을 강화하고 행동을 규제하면서

"Each particular time, each era, in fact each moment, / has its own condition and themes for laughter . . . / because of the major preoccupations, concerns, interests, activities, relations, and mode / prevailing at the time."
"각각 특정한 시간, 각각의 시대, 사실상 각각의 순간은 / 웃음에 대한 그 자체의 조건과 주제를 가지고 있다… / 주된 사고, 관심사, 흥미, 활동, 관계, 그리고 방식 때문에 / 그 당시에 널리 퍼져있는."

The ultimate goal of anyone / who studies another culture, / such as ancient Greece, / is to understand the people themselves / who were more than the sum total / of monuments, historical incidents, or social groupings.
누군가의 궁극적인 목표는 / 다른 문화를 연구하는 / 고대 그리스와 같은 / 사람들 그 자체를 이해하는 것이다. / 총합계 이상이었던 / 유물들, 역사적 사건들, 혹은 사회적 집단화의

One way to approach this goal directly / is to study the culture's humor.
이 목표에 바로 접근하는 한 가지 방법은 / 그 문화의 유머를 연구하는 것이다.

As Goethe aptly observed: / "Men show their characters in nothing more clearly / than in what they think laughable."
괴테가 적절하게 언급한대로 / "사람의 특성을 명확히 보여주는 것도 없다. / 그들이 무엇을 웃기다고 여기는지만큼"

웃음의 능력은 인간의 독특한 특징이라고 오랫동안 여겨져 왔다. (기원후 2세기) Samosata의 재치 있는 Lucian이 인간을 당나귀와 구별하는 방법으로 한쪽은 웃고 다른 한쪽은 그렇지 않다는 것을 지적했다. 모든 사회에서 유머는 규범을 강화하고 행동을 규제하면서, 개인적인 의사소통에서뿐 아니라 사회 집단들을 형성하는 힘으로서도 중요하다. "각각 특정한 시간, 각각의 시대, 사실상 각각의 순간은 웃음에 대한 그 자체의 조건과 주제를 가지고 있다… 그 당시에 널리 퍼져있는 주된 사고, 관심사, 흥미, 활동, 관계, 그리고 방식 때문에." 고대 그리스와 같은 다른 문화를 연구하는 누군가의 궁극적인 목표는 기념물들, 역사적 사건들, 혹은 사회적 집단화의 총합계 이상이었던 사람들 그 자체를 이해하는 것이다. 이 목표에 바로 접근하는 한 가지 방법은 그 문화의 유머를 연구하는 것이다. 괴테가 적절하게 언급한 대로, "사람이 무엇을 웃기다고 여기는지만큼 사람의 특성을 명확히 보여주는 것도 없다."

Why? 왜 정답일까?
마지막 두 문장에서 어떤 문화의 유머를 연구하면 그 문화와 그에 속한 구성원들의 특성을 이해할 수 있다 (One way to approach this goal directly is to study the culture's humor. ~ "Men show their characters in nothing more clearly than in what they think laughable.")고 하므로, 글의 주제로 가장 적절한 것은 ⑤ '문화를 이해하기 위한 도구로서의 유머'이다.

- peculiarly ⓐⓓ 독특하게
- reinforce ⓥ 강화하다
- prevail ⓥ 만연하다, 팽배하다
- aptly ⓐⓓ 적절하게
- assimilation ⓝ 동화
- mold ⓥ 만들다, 주조하다
- preoccupation ⓝ 생각, 집착
- monument ⓝ 기념물
- observe ⓥ (의견을) 말하다
- intercultural ⓐ 문화 간의

구문 풀이
11행 The ultimate goal of anyone [who studies another culture, such as
　　　　　　주어　　　　　　　　선행사　　주격 관계대명사
ancient Greece], is to understand the people themselves [who were more than
　　　　　　　동사(단수)　　주격 보어(~것)　　선행사　　선행사 강조　주격 관계대명사
the sum total of monuments, historical incidents, or social groupings].

---

24 그린 프라이데이   정답률 86% | 정답 ②

다음 글의 제목으로 가장 적절한 것은?
① Compare Deals, Save Money
　구매를 비교해서 돈을 아껴라
☑ Turning Black Friday Green
　블랙 프라이데이를 친환경적으로 바꾸기
③ Online Shops for Green Consumers
　친환경 소비자들을 위한 온라인 매장
④ Marketing Tricks Used on Black Friday
　블랙 프라이데이에 이용되는 마케팅 기술
⑤ What Makes You Spend Beyond Your Budget?
　무엇이 당신으로 하여금 예산을 초과해 소비하게 하는가?

Since the early 1980s, / Black Friday has been a kind of unofficial U.S. holiday / marking the beginning of the holiday season / and, consequently, the most profitable time / for retailers / in the year.
1980년대 초반부터, / 블랙 프라이데이는 일종의 비공식적인 미국 휴일이었고, / 휴가 시즌의 시작을 나타내는 / 그 결과 수익이 가장 높은 시기였다. / 소매상들에게 있어 / 일 년 중

But in recent years, / a new movement has come to light, / adding a more ecological philosophy.
그러나 최근 몇 년 동안 / 새로운 움직임이 나타났다. / 좀 더 생태학적인 철학이 더해져서

The movement is called Green Friday, / and it seeks to raise awareness / about the damage / that Black Friday brings to the environment.
이 운동은 그린 프라이데이라고 불리며, / 그것은 의식을 높이는 것을 추구한다. / 피해에 대한 / 블랙 프라이데이가 환경에 가져오는

Think of / the carbon emissions caused by driving to the mall, / the shipping of millions of items around the world, / the plastic waste produced by packaging, / and even the long-term waste / produced by mindlessly buying things / we don't need.
생각해 보라. / 쇼핑몰까지 운전하면서 발생되는 탄소 배출, / 수백만 개의 물건의 전 세계 배송, / 포장에 의해 발생되는 플라스틱 폐기물, / 그리고 심지어 오랫동안 남게 될 쓰레기까지 / 물건을 생각 없이 구매함으로써 생긴 / 우리가 필요하지도 않은

Green Friday is about changing the way / we see this day / and switching our mindset / from "buy, buy, buy" / to finding alternative ways / to give gifts during the holiday season / so we don't cause further damage to the Earth.
그린 프라이데이는 방식을 바꾸는 것에 관한 것이며, / 우리가 그날(블랙 프라이데이)을 보는 / 우리의 사고방식을 바꾸는 것이다. / "사고, 사고, 사는 것"에서 / 대안적인 방법을 찾는 것으로 / 그 휴가 시즌에 선물을 하는 / 그래서 우리가 지구에 더 많은 피해를 주지 않도록 한다.

Even if only a small percentage of the population makes the switch, / it'll mean great things for the environment.
비록 인구의 단지 일부만이 변화한다 하더라도, / 그것은 환경에 큰 의미가 있을 것이다.

1980년대 초반부터, 블랙 프라이데이는 휴가 시즌의 시작을 나타내는 일종의 비공식적인 미국 휴일이었고, 그 결과 소매상들에게 있어 일 년 중 수익이 가장 높은 시기였다. 그러나 최근 몇 년 동안 좀 더 생태학적인 철학이 더해져서 새로운 움직임이 나타났다. 이 운동은 그린

15회

프라이데이라고 불리며, 블랙 프라이데이가 환경에 가져오는 피해에 대한 의식을 높이는 것을 추구한다. 쇼핑몰까지 운전하면서 발생하는 탄소 배출, 수백만 개의 물건의 전 세계 배송, 포장 때문에 발생하는 플라스틱 폐기물, 그리고 심지어 우리가 필요하지도 않은 물건을 생각 없이 구매함으로써 오랫동안 남게 될 쓰레기까지 생각해보라. 그린 프라이데이는 우리가 그날(블랙 프라이데이)을 보는 방식을 "사고, 사고, 사는 것"에서 그 휴가 시즌에 선물하는 것에 대한 대안적인 방법을 찾는 것으로 우리의 사고방식을 바꾸는 것에 관한 것이며, 그래서 우리가 지구에 더 큰 피해를 주지 않도록 한다. 비록 인구의 단지 일부만이 변화한다고 하더라도, 그것은 환경에 큰 의미가 있을 것이다.

Why? 왜 정답일까?

'But in recent years, ~' 이후로 블랙 프라이데이 행사로 초래되는 환경적 피해에 대한 인식이 높아지면서 블랙 프라이데이를 보다 친환경적으로 바꾸기 위한 노력이 이루어지고 있다는 내용이 서술된다. 따라서 글의 제목으로 가장 적절한 것은 ② '블랙 프라이데이를 친환경적으로 바꾸기'이다.

- unofficial ⓐ 비공식적인
- come to light 나타나다, 드러나다, 밝혀지다
- emission ⓝ 배출
- consequently ⓐⓓ 결과적으로
- ecological ⓐ 생태학적인
- mindlessly ⓐⓓ 생각 없이, 무분별하게, 어리석게

구문 풀이

1행 Since the early 1980s, Black Friday has been a kind of unofficial U.S.
기간 부사구(since + 과거) / 현재완료(~해 왔다) / 주격 보어1
holiday marking the beginning of the holiday season and, consequently, the most
현재분사 / 주격 보어2
profitable time for retailers in the year.

---

25 미국의 도시 매립 쓰레기 물질 　　　　　　　정답률 84% | 정답 ⑤

다음 도표의 내용과 일치하지 않는 것은?

Materials Landfilled as Municipal Waste in the U.S.

(unit: thousand of tons)

2000		2017	
Material	Amount	Material	Amount
Paper	40,450	Plastics	26,820
Plastics	19,950	Paper	18,350
Metals	10,290	Metals	13,800
Wood	9,910	Wood	12,140
Glass	8,100	Textiles	11,150
Textiles	6,280	Glass	6,870
Other Materials	6,360	Other Materials	7,930
Total	101,340	Total	97,060

※ Note: Details may not add to totals due to rounding.

The tables above show the materials / landfilled as municipal waste / in the U.S. in 2000 and 2017.
위 표는 물질들을 보여준다. / 도시 쓰레기로 매립된 / 2000년과 2017년 미국에서
① The total amount of materials landfilled in 2017 / was smaller than in 2000.
2017년에 매립된 물질들의 합계는 / 2000년보다 적었다.
② While paper was the material / most landfilled as municipal waste in 2000, / plastics were the most landfilled material in 2017.
종이는 물질이었지만, / 2000년에 도시 쓰레기로 가장 많이 매립된 / 2017년에는 플라스틱이 가장 많이 매립된 물질이었다.
③ In 2000, / metals and wood were the third and fourth most landfilled materials, respectively, / and this remained the same in 2017.
2000년에 / 금속과 나무는 세 번째와 네 번째로 각각 가장 많이 매립된 물질이었고, / 이것은 2017년에도 동일하게 유지되었다.
④ More glass was landfilled than textiles in 2000, / but more textiles were landfilled than glass in 2017.
2000년에 유리가 직물보다 더 많이 매립되었지만 / 2017년에는 직물이 유리보다 더 많이 매립되었다.
✓ The amount of textiles landfilled in 2017 / was more than twice that in 2000.
2017년에 매립된 직물의 양은 / 2000년의 그것의 두 배 이상이었다.

위 표는 2000년과 2017년 미국에서 도시 쓰레기로 매립된 물질들을 보여준다. ① 2017년에 매립된 물질들의 합계는 2000년보다 적었다. ② 종이는 2000년에 도시 쓰레기로 가장 많이 매립된 물질이었지만, 2017년에는 플라스틱이 가장 많이 매립된 물질이었다. ③ 2000년에 금속과 나무는 각각 세 번째와 네 번째로 가장 많이 매립된 물질이었고, 이것은 2017년에도 동일하게 유지되었다. ④ 2000년에 유리가 직물보다 더 많이 매립되었지만 2017년에는 직물이 유리보다 더 많이 매립되었다. ⑤ 2017년에 매립된 직물의 양은 2000년의 두 배 이상이었다.

Why? 왜 정답일까?

도표에 따르면 2017년에 미국에서 도시 쓰레기로 매립된 직물의 양(11,150,000톤)은 2000년에 매립된 직물 양(6,280,000톤)의 2배에 미치지 못한다. 따라서 도표와 일치하지 않는 것은 ⑤이다.

- landfill ⓥ 매립하다 ⓝ 매립 쓰레기
- respectively ⓐⓓ 각각
- municipal ⓐ 도시의
- textile ⓝ 직물

---

26 Vera Rubin의 생애 　　　　　　　정답률 91% | 정답 ⑤

Vera Rubin에 관한 다음 글의 내용과 일치하지 않는 것은?
① Washington, D.C.에서 천문학에 대한 관심을 키우기 시작했다.
② 1954년에 Georgetown 대학교에서 박사 학위를 받았다.
③ 은하의 움직임에 관한 이론으로 과학자들을 놀라게 했다.
④ Hale 망원경을 사용하도록 허가받은 최초의 여성이었다.
✓ 노벨상을 포함하여 많은 상을 받았다.

Vera Rubin was born in 1928 in Philadelphia / and grew up in Washington, D.C.
Vera Rubin은 1928년에 Philadelphia에서 태어났고, / Washington, D.C.에서 자랐다.
『It was in Washington, D.C. / that she started to develop an interest in astronomy.』 ①의근거 일치
바로 Washington, D.C.였다. / 그녀가 천문학에 대한 관심을 키우기 시작했던 곳은
『She earned a master's degree / from Cornell University in 1951 / and a doctor's degree / from Georgetown University in 1954.』 ②의근거 일치
그녀는 석사 학위를 받았고, / 1951년에 Cornell 대학교에서 / 박사 학위를 받았다. / 1954년에 Georgetown 대학교에서

『At the age of 22, / she made headlines and shocked scientists / with her theory about the motion of galaxies.』 ③의근거 일치
22살의 나이에 / 그녀는 대서특필되었고 과학자들을 놀라게 했다. / 은하의 움직임에 관한 그녀의 이론으로
『In 1965, / Rubin started as a researcher / at the Carnegie Institution / and became the first woman / permitted to use the Hale Telescope.』 ④의근거 일치
1965년에 / Rubin은 연구자로서 일을 시작했고, / Carnegie Institution에서 / 최초의 여성이었다. / Hale 망원경을 사용하도록 허가받은
She made groundbreaking observations / that provided evidence / for the existence of a vast amount of dark matter / in the universe.
그녀는 혁신적인 관측을 했다. / 증거를 제공하는 / 막대한 양의 암흑물질의 존재에 대한 / 우주에 있는
『She won many prizes for her work, / but never the Nobel Prize.』 ⑤의근거 불일치
그녀는 많은 상을 받았지만, / 그녀의 연구로 / 결코 노벨상을 받지 못했다.
She died in 2016 / and is celebrated as someone / who worked to lead the way for women / in astronomy and physics.
그녀는 2016년에 죽었고, / 인물로 칭송받는다. / 여성들에 있어 선도적 역할을 한 / 천문학과 물리학 분야에서

Vera Rubin은 1928년에 Philadelphia에서 태어났고, Washington, D.C.에서 자랐다. Washington, D.C.는 바로 그녀가 천문학에 대한 관심을 키우기 시작했던 곳이었다. 1951년에 Cornell 대학교에서 석사 학위를 받았고, 1954년에 Georgetown 대학교에서 박사 학위를 받았다. 22살의 나이에 그녀는 은하의 움직임에 관한 이론으로 대서특필되었고 과학자들을 놀라게 했다. 1965년에 Rubin은 Carnegie Institution에서 연구자로서 일을 시작했고, Hale 망원경을 사용하도록 허가받은 최초의 여성이었다. 그녀는 우주의 막대한 양의 암흑물질의 존재에 대한 증거를 제공하는 혁신적인 관측을 했다. 그녀는 연구로 많은 상을 받았지만, 결코 노벨상을 받지 못했다. 그녀는 2016년에 죽었고, 천문학과 물리학 분야에서 여성들에 있어 선도적 역할을 한 인물로 칭송받는다.

Why? 왜 정답일까?

'She won many prizes for her work, but never the Nobel Prize.'에서 Vera Rubin은 연구를 통해 많은 상을 받았지만 노벨상은 받지 못했다고 하므로, 내용과 일치하지 않는 것은 ⑤ '노벨상을 포함하여 많은 상을 받았다.'이다.

Why? 왜 오답일까?

① 'It was in Washington, D.C. that she started to develop an interest in astronomy.'의 내용과 일치한다.
② 'She earned ~ a doctor's degree from Georgetown University in 1954.'의 내용과 일치한다.
③ '~ shocked scientists with her theory about the motion of galaxies.'의 내용과 일치한다.
④ '~ and became the first woman permitted to use the Hale Telescope.'의 내용과 일치한다.

- astronomy ⓝ 천문학
- groundbreaking ⓐ 혁신적인, 획기적인
- vast ⓐ 막대한, 광대한
- make headlines 대서특필되다, 화제가 되다
- existence ⓝ 존재
- celebrate ⓥ 칭송하다, 기념하다

구문 풀이

2행 It was in Washington, D.C. that she started to develop an interest in astronomy.
「it is[was] + 강조 어구 + that ~」: ~한 것은 바로 …이다[였다]

---

27 어린이 대상 게임 코딩 워크숍 　　　　　　　정답률 93% | 정답 ④

2020 Game-Coding Workshop에 관한 다음 안내문의 내용과 일치하지 않는 것은?
① 토요일 오후에 진행된다.
② Lansing 키즈 클럽 회원은 참가비가 무료이다.
③ 온라인 등록이 가능하다.
✓ 참가자들에게 노트북 컴퓨터가 제공된다.
⑤ 코딩에 대한 사전 지식이 필요 없다.

2020 Game-Coding Workshop
2020 게임 코딩 워크숍
Turn your children's love for computer games / into a skill.
자녀의 컴퓨터 게임에 대한 애정을 바꾸세요. / 기술로
This game-coding workshop will teach them / to use block-based coding software / to create their own games!
이 게임 코딩 워크숍은 아이들에게 가르칠 것입니다! / 블록기반 코딩 소프트웨어를 사용하도록 / 자신만의 게임을 만들기 위해
Date & Time
날짜와 시간
『Saturday, December 12th, 1:00 pm to 3:00 pm』 ①의근거 일치
12월 12일 토요일, 오후 1시에서 오후 3시까지
Registration
등록
Closes Friday, November 27th
11월 27일 금요일에 마감
Participation fee is $30 / 『(free for Lansing Kids Club members)』 ②의근거 일치
참가비는 30달러입니다. / (Lansing 키즈 클럽 회원은 무료)
『Sign up in person at Kid's Coding Center / or online at www.lanskidscoding.com.』 ③의근거 일치
Kid's Coding Center에서 직접 등록하거나 / www.lanskidscoding.com에서 온라인으로 등록하십시오
Requirements
요구 사항
Open only to children 9 to 12 years old
9세에서 12세까지의 어린이만을 대상으로 함
『Laptops will not be provided.』 ④의근거 불일치
노트북 컴퓨터는 제공되지 않습니다.
Participants must bring their own.
참가자들은 자신의 노트북 컴퓨터를 가져와야 합니다.
『No prior coding knowledge is required.』 ⑤의근거 일치
코딩에 대한 사전 지식이 필요하지 않습니다.
Please visit our website / for more information.
우리 웹사이트를 방문하십시오. / 더 많은 정보를 위해서는

2020 Game-Coding Workshop
(2020 게임 코딩 워크숍)

자녀의 컴퓨터 게임에 대한 애정을 기술로 바꾸세요. 이 게임 코딩 워크숍은 아이들에게 자신만의 게임을 만들기 위해 블록 기반 코딩 소프트웨어를 사용하도록 가르쳐줄 것입니다!

□ 날짜와 시간
• 12월 12일 토요일, 오후 1시 ~ 오후 3시

□ 등록
• 11월 27일 금요일에 마감
• 참가비는 30달러입니다(Lansing 키즈 클럽 회원은 무료.
• Kid's Coding Center에서 직접 등록하거나 www.lanskidscoding.com에서 온라인으로 등록하십시오.

□ 요구 사항
• 9세에서 12세까지의 어린이만을 대상으로 함
• 노트북 컴퓨터는 제공되지 않습니다. 참가자들은 자신의 노트북 컴퓨터를 가져와야 합니다.
• 코딩에 대한 사전 지식이 필요하지 않습니다.

더 많은 정보를 위해서는 우리 웹 사이트를 방문하십시오.

Why? 왜 정답일까?

'Laptops will not be provided.'에서 참가자들에게 노트북 컴퓨터가 제공되지 않는다고 하므로, 안내문의 내용과 일치하지 않는 것은 ④ '참가자들에게 노트북 컴퓨터가 제공된다.'이다.

Why? 왜 오답일까?

① 'Saturday, December 12th, 1:00 pm to 3:00 pm'의 내용과 일치한다.
② '(free for Lansing Kids Club members)'의 내용과 일치한다.
③ 'Sign up ~ online at www.lanskidscoding.com.'의 내용과 일치한다.
⑤ 'No prior coding knowledge is required.'의 내용과 일치한다.

● sign up 등록하다
● prior ⓐ 사전의
● in person 직접

---

28 영화 제작 대회 　　　　정답률 89% | 정답 ⑤

Young Filmmakers Contest에 관한 다음 안내문의 내용과 일치하는 것은?

① 중학생을 대상으로 한다.
② 각 출품작의 전체 길이는 15분 이상이어야 한다.
③ 참가자는 세 개의 주제 중 하나를 선택해야 한다.
④ 출품작은 우편으로 제출할 수 있다.
✓ 모든 수상작은 공식 웹사이트에 게시될 것이다.

Young Filmmakers Contest
Young Filmmakers Contest(젊은 영화 제작자 대회)
Join our annual Young Filmmakers Contest, / and demonstrate your filmmaking skills!
매년 열리는 Young Filmmakers Contest에 참여하여 / 당신의 영화 제작 기술들을 보여주세요!
Contest Rules
대회 규칙
「Contest is open only to high school students.」 ①의 근거 불일치
대회는 오직 고등학생만 대상으로 합니다.
「Total running time of each entry / must be less than fifteen minutes.」 ②의 근거 불일치
각 출품작의 전체 길이는 / 15분 미만이어야 합니다.
「Participants must choose one of the following two topics: / Family | Friendship」 ③의 근거 불일치
참가자는 다음 두 가지 주제 중 하나를 선택해야 합니다: / 가족 | 우정
Submission
제출
Submit by Wednesday, September 16th.
9월 16일 수요일까지 제출하세요.
「Do not mail entries to our offices.」 ④의 근거 불일치
출품작을 저희 사무실에 우편으로 보내지 마세요.
Only submissions / uploaded to our official Young Filmmakers Contest website / will be accepted.
오로지 제출만 / 저희 공식 Young Filmmakers Contest 웹사이트에 업로드된 / 허용됩니다.
Prizes
상금
1st place: $300 | 2nd place: $200 | 3rd place: $100
1등: 300달러 | 2등: 200달러 | 3등: 100달러
「All winning entries will be posted / on the official website.」 ⑤의 근거 일치
모든 수상작은 게시될 것입니다. / 공식 웹사이트에
If you have any questions, / please visit www.2020yfc.org.
문의 사항이 있다면, / www.2020yfc.org에 방문하시오.

Young Filmmakers Contest
(젊은 영화 제작자 대회)

매년 열리는 Young Filmmakers Contest에 참여하여 당신의 영화 제작 기술들을 보여주세요!

◇ 대회 규칙
• 대회는 오직 고등학생만 대상으로 합니다.
• 각 출품작의 전체 길이는 15분 미만이어야 합니다.
• 참가자는 다음 두 가지 주제 중 하나를 선택해야 합니다:
가족 | 우정

◇ 제출
• 9월 16일 수요일까지 제출하세요.
• 출품작을 저희 사무실에 우편으로 보내지 마세요. 저희 공식 Young Filmmakers Contest 웹사이트에 업로드된 제출만 허용됩니다.

◇ 상금
• 1등: 300달러 | 2등: 200달러 | 3등: 100달러
• 모든 수상작은 공식 웹사이트에 게시될 것입니다.

문의 사항이 있다면, www.2020yfc.org에 방문하시오.

Why? 왜 정답일까?

'All winning entries will be posted on the official website.'에서 모든 수상작은 웹사이트에 게시될 예정이라고 하므로, 안내문의 내용과 일치하는 것은 ⑤ '모든 수상작은 공식 웹사이트에 게시될 것이다.'이다.

Why? 왜 오답일까?

① 'Contest is open only to high school students.'에서 대회는 고등학생을 대상으로 열린다고 하였다.
② 'Total running time of each entry must be less than fifteen minutes.'에서 각 출품작은 15분을 넘기지 않도록 제작되어야 한다고 하였다.
③ 'Participants must choose one of the following two topics: Family | Friendship'에서 가족과 우정이라는 두 가지 주제 중 하나를 선택할 수 있다고 하였다.
④ 'Do not mail entries to our offices.'에서 출품작은 우편으로 제출하지 말라고 하였다.

● demonstrate ⓥ 보여주다, 입증하다
● submission ⓝ 제출
● entry ⓝ 출품(작)

---

29 사회적 관계의 필수적 기반 역할을 하는 도덕성 　　정답률 53% | 정답 ③

다음 글의 밑줄 친 부분 중, 어법상 틀린 것은? [3점]

All social interactions / require some common ground / upon which the involved parties can coordinate their behavior.
모든 사회적 상호 작용은 / 어떤 공통의 기반을 요구한다. / 관련된 당사자들이 그들의 행동을 조정할 수 있는
In the interdependent groups / ① in which humans and other primates live, / individuals must have even greater common ground / to establish and maintain social relationships.
상호 의존적인 집단에서, / 인간과 그 외의 영장류들이 사는 / 개인들은 훨씬 더 큰 공통의 기반을 가져야 한다. / 사회적 관계를 확립하고 유지하기 위해
This common ground is morality.
이러한 공통의 기반은 도덕성이다.
This is why / morality often is defined / as a shared set of standards / for ② judging right and wrong / in the conduct of social relationships.
이는 이유이다. / 도덕성이 자주 정의되는 / 공유된 일련의 기준으로 / 옳고 그름을 판단하기 위한 / 사회적 관계의 행위에서
No matter how it is conceptualized — whether as trustworthiness, cooperation, justice, or caring — / morality ✓ is always about the treatment of people / in social relationships.
그것이 어떻게 개념화되더라도 / 신뢰성, 협력, 정의 혹은 복지든 간에 / 도덕성은 항상 사람을 대하는 것에 관한 것이다. / 사회적 관계에서
This is likely why / there is surprising agreement / across a wide range of perspectives / ④ that a shared sense of morality is necessary to social relations.
이것은 아마 이유일 것이다. / 놀라운 일치가 있는 / 광범위한 관점에 걸쳐 / 공유된 도덕 관념이 사회적 관계에 필수적이라는
Evolutionary biologists, sociologists, and philosophers all / seem to agree with social psychologists / that the interdependent relationships within groups / that humans depend on / ⑤ are not possible without a shared morality.
진화 생물학자와 사회학자와 철학자 모두 / 사회 심리학자의 의견에 동의하는 듯하다. / 집단 내에서의 상호 의존적 관계가 / 인간이 의존하는 / 공유된 도덕성 없이는 가능하지 않다

모든 사회적 상호 작용은 관련된 당사자들이 그들의 행동을 조정할 수 있는 어떤 공통의 기반을 요구한다. 인간과 그 외의 영장류들이 사는 상호 의존적인 집단에서, 개인들은 사회적 관계를 확립하고 유지하기 위해 훨씬 더 큰 공통의 기반을 가져야 한다. 이러한 공통의 기반은 도덕성이다. 이는 도덕성이 사회적 관계의 행위에서 옳고 그름을 판단하기 위한 공유된 일련의 기준으로 자주 정의되는 이유이다. 도덕성은 어떻게 개념화되더라도 (신뢰성, 협력, 정의 혹은 배려든 간에) 항상 사회적 관계에서 사람을 대하는 것에 관한 것이다. 이것이 아마 공유된 도덕 관념이 사회적 관계에 필수적이라는 광범위한 관점에 걸쳐 놀라운 일치가 있는 이유이다. 진화 생물학자와 사회학자와 철학자 모두 인간이 의존하는 집단 내에서의 상호 의존적 관계가 공유된 도덕성 없이는 가능하지 않다는 사회 심리학자의 의견에 동의하는 듯하다.

Why? 왜 정답일까?

No matter how(어떻게 ~하더라도)와 whether(~이든 아니든)가 이끄는 부사절에 이어 주어 morality가 나오므로, 주어와 호응하는 동사가 뒤따라야 한다. 따라서 준동사 to be를 동사 is로 고쳐야 한다. 어법상 틀린 것은 ③이다.

Why? 왜 오답일까?

① 선행사 the interdependent groups 뒤로 1형식의 완전한 관계절이 연결되는 것으로 보아 '전치사 + 관계대명사' 형태의 in which를 쓴 것은 적절하다. 이는 여기서 where와 같다.
② 전치사 for 뒤로 동명사 judging을 쓴 것은 적절하다.
④ agreement의 내용을 보충 설명하는 완전한 동격절을 연결하기 위해 접속사 that을 쓴 것은 적절하다.
⑤ 주어인 the interdependent relationships가 복수 명사이므로 복수 동사 are가 적절하게 쓰였다.

● coordinate ⓥ 조정하다
● primate ⓝ 영장류
● morality ⓝ 도덕성
● trustworthiness ⓝ 신뢰성
● evolutionary ⓐ 진화의
● interdependent ⓐ 상호 의존적인
● establish ⓥ 확립하다
● conceptualize ⓥ 개념화하다
● perspective ⓝ 관점

구문 풀이

8행 No matter how it is conceptualized — whether as trustworthiness,
=however(어떻게 ~하더라도) 　　　　　~이든 아니든
cooperation, justice, or caring — morality is always about the treatment of people
　　　　　　　　　　　　　주어　　동사
in social relationships.

★★★ 등급을 가르는 문제!
30 오래된 이야기를 더 잘 믿는 사람들 　　정답률 38% | 정답 ②

다음 글의 밑줄 친 부분 중, 문맥상 낱말의 쓰임이 적절하지 않은 것은?

Spine-tingling ghost stories are fun to tell / if they are really scary, / and even more so / if you claim that they are true.

등골이 오싹한 유령 이야기는 들려주기에 재밌고, / 그것들이 정말 무섭다면 / 훨씬 더 그렇다. / 만약 당신이 그 이야기가 사실이라고 주장하면

People get a ① thrill / from passing on those stories.
사람들은 스릴을 느낀다. / 그런 이야기를 전달하는 것으로부터

The same applies to miracle stories.
같은 것이 기적 이야기에도 적용된다.

If a rumor of a miracle gets written down in a book, / the rumor becomes hard to ☑ challenge, / especially if the book is ancient.
만약 기적에 대한 소문이 어떤 책에 쓰이면, / 의문을 제기하기 힘들어진다. / 특히 그 책이 아주 오래되었을 경우

If a rumor is ③ old enough, / it starts to be called a "tradition" instead, / and then people believe it all the more.
만약 소문이 충분히 오래된 것이라면, / 그것은 대신 '전통'으로 불리기 시작하고, / 그러면 사람들은 그것을 한결 더 믿는다.

This is rather odd / because you might think / they would realize / that older rumors have had more time to get ④ distorted / than younger rumors / that are close in time / to the alleged events themselves.
이것은 다소 이상한데, / 그 이유는 당신이 생각할 수 있기 때문이다. / 그들이 깨달을 것이라고 / 오래된 소문이 왜곡될 시간이 더 많다는 점을 / 최근의 소문보다 / 시간상 가까운 / (근거 없이) 주장된 사건 그 자체에

Elvis Presley and Michael Jackson lived too ⑤ recently / for traditions to have grown up, / so not many people believe stories / like "Elvis seen on Mars."
Elvis Presley와 Michael Jackson은 너무 최근에 살아서 / 전통이 생겨나기에는 / 이야기를 믿는 사람이 많지 않다. / "Elvis가 화성에서 목격되었다"와 같은

등골이 오싹한 유령 이야기는 정말 무섭다면 들려주기에 재밌고, 만약 당신이 그 이야기가 사실이라고 주장하면 훨씬 더 그렇다. 사람들은 그런 이야기를 전달하는 것으로부터 ① 스릴을 느낀다. 같은 것이 기적 이야기에도 적용된다. 만약 기적에 대한 소문이 어떤 책에 쓰이면, 특히 그 책이 아주 오래되었을 경우 그 소문은 ② 믿기(→ 의문을 제기하기) 힘들어진다. 만약 소문이 충분히 ③ 오래된 것이라면, 그것은 대신 '전통'으로 불리기 시작하고, 그러면 사람들은 그것을 한결 더 믿는다. 이것은 다소 이상한데, 그 이유는 그들이 (근거 없이) 주장된 사건 그 자체에 시간상 가까운 최근의 소문보다 오래된 소문이 ④ 왜곡될 시간이 더 많다는 점을 깨달을 것이라고 당신이 생각할 수 있기 때문이다. Elvis Presley와 Michael Jackson은 전통이 생겨나기에는 너무 ⑤ 최근에 살아서 "Elvis가 화성에서 목격되었다"와 같은 이야기를 믿는 사람은 많지 않다.

Why? 왜 정답일까?

'If a rumor is old enough, ~' 이후로 오래된 소문일수록 '전통'처럼 취급되어 사람들이 더 잘 믿는다는 내용이 언급되고 있다. 이에 근거할 때, 아주 오래된 책에 적힌 이야기는 사람들의 믿음을 더 많이 사게 되어 이 이야기에 대한 '의문을 제기하기'가 어려워질 것을 유추할 수 있다. 따라서 ②의 believe는 challenge로 고쳐야 한다. 문맥상 낱말의 쓰임이 적절하지 않은 것은 ②이다.

- spine-tingling 등골이 오싹한, 스릴 넘치는
- ancient ⓐ 아주 오래된, 고대의
- alleged ⓐ (증거 없이) 주장된, ~이라고는 말하는
- pass on ~을 전해주다
- distort ⓥ 왜곡하다

구문 풀이

8행 This is rather odd because you might think (that) they would realize that
접속사(~ 때문에) / 생략(접속사) / 접속사(~것)
older rumors **have had** more time to get distorted than younger rumors [that are
현재완료 / 선행사 / 주격 관계대명사
close in time to the alleged events **themselves**].
재귀대명사(events 강조)

★★ 문제 해결 꿀~팁 ★★

▶ 많이 틀린 이유는?
④가 포함된 문장은 오래된 루머가 왜 신뢰를 얻는지에 대한 의문을 제기하고 있다. 즉 더 오래된 루머는 생겨난 지 오래라 그만큼 '왜곡될' 기회도 더 많았을 텐데 왜 더 믿을 만하다고 여겨지는지 궁금해 한다는 의미를 나타내기 위해 ④의 distorted가 바르게 쓰였다. 또한 ⑤가 포함된 문장의 so 뒤에서 사람들이 Elvis에 관한 루머를 잘 믿지 않는다고 언급하는데, 이는 글의 논리에 따르면 그가 비교적 '최근에' 살았던 사람이기 때문일 것임을 유추할 수 있다. 따라서 recently도 맞게 쓰였다.
▶ 문제 해결 방법은?
'소문이 오래될수록 더 잘 믿어진다'는 주제문과 'especially if the book ~'를 힌트로 삼도록 한다.

---

31 산업의 집중화 경향   정답률 43% | 정답 ②

다음 빈칸에 들어갈 말로 가장 적절한 것을 고르시오.
① Automation – 자동화
☑ Concentration – 집중
③ Transportation – 교통
④ Globalization – 세계화
⑤ Liberalization – 자유화

Firms in almost every industry / tend to be clustered.
거의 모든 산업의 회사들은 / 밀집되는 경향이 있다.

Suppose / you threw darts at random / on a map of the United States.
가정해보라. / 당신이 무작위로 다트를 던진다고 / 미국 지도에

You'd find the holes / left by the darts / to be more or less evenly distributed / across the map.
당신은 구멍들을 보게 될 것이다 / 다트에 의해 남겨진 / 다소 고르게 분포된 것을 / 지도 전체에

But the real map of any given industry / looks nothing like that; / it looks / more as if someone had thrown all the darts in the same place.
하지만 어떤 특정 산업의 실제 지도는 / 전혀 그렇게 보이지 않는다. / 그것은 보인다. / 마치 어떤 사람이 던진 것처럼 모든 다트를 같은 지역에

This is probably in part because of reputation; / buyers may be suspicious of a software firm / in the middle of the cornfields.
이것은 아마 부분적으로는 평판 때문일 것이다. / 구매자들은 소프트웨어 회사를 수상쩍게 여길 것이다. / 옥수수 밭 한가운데 있는

It would also be hard / to recruit workers / if every time you needed a new employee / you had to persuade someone / to move across the country, / rather than just poach one from your neighbor.
또한 어려울 것이다. / 직원을 채용하는 것이 / 만약 당신이 새로운 직원을 필요로 할 때마다 / 당신이 누군가를 설득해야 한다면 / 나라를 가로질러 이주하도록 / 근처에서 인력을 빼내기보다는 오히려

There are also regulatory reasons: / zoning laws often try to concentrate / dirty industries in one place / and restaurants and bars in another.

또한 규제상의 이유도 있다. / 토지 사용 제한법들은 종종 집중시키려 노력한다. / 공해 유발 산업들을 한 지역에, / 그리고 식당들과 술집들을 다른 지역에

Finally, / people in the same industry / often have similar preferences / (computer engineers like coffee, / financiers show off with expensive bottles of wine).
마지막으로, / 같은 산업에 종사하는 사람들은 / 종종 유사한 선호도를 가진다. / 컴퓨터 엔지니어들은 커피를 좋아하고, / 금융업 종사자들은 비싼 와인을 가지고 뽐낸다.

Concentration makes it easier / to provide the amenities they like.
집중이 더 쉽게 해준다. / 그들이 좋아하는 생활 편의시설을 제공하는 것을

거의 모든 산업의 회사들은 밀집되는 경향이 있다. 당신이 미국 지도에 무작위로 다트를 던진다고 가정해보라. 당신은 다트에 의해 남겨진 구멍들이 지도 전체에 다소 고르게 분포된 것을 보게 될 것이다. 하지만 어떤 특정 산업의 실제 지도는 전혀 그렇게 보이지 않고, 마치 어떤 사람이 모든 다트를 같은 지역에 던진 것처럼 보인다. 이것은 아마 부분적으로는 평판 때문일 것이다. 구매자들은 옥수수밭 한가운데 있는 소프트웨어 회사를 수상쩍게 여길 것이다. 당신이 새로운 직원을 필요로 할 때마다 근처에서 인력을 빼내기보다는 오히려 누군가로 하여금 나라를 가로질러 이주하도록 설득해야 한다면 직원을 채용하는 것이 또한 어려울 것이다. 또한 규제상의 이유도 있다. 토지 사용 제한법들은 종종 공해 유발 산업들을 한 지역에, 식당들과 술집들을 다른 지역에 집중시키려 노력한다. 마지막으로, 같은 산업에 종사하는 사람들은 종종 유사한 선호도를 보인다. (컴퓨터 엔지니어들은 커피를 좋아하고 금융업 종사자들은 비싼 와인을 가지고 뽐낸다.) 집중이 그들이 좋아하는 생활 편의시설을 제공하는 것을 더 쉽게 해준다.

Why? 왜 정답일까?

첫 문장인 'Firms in almost every industry tend to be clustered.'에서 어느 산업 부문에서건 회사들은 밀집하는 경향이 있다고 언급하는 것으로 볼 때, 빈칸에 들어갈 말로 가장 적절한 것은 '밀집'을 다른 말로 나타낸 ② '집중'이다.

- cluster ⓥ 밀집하다, 모이다
- distribute ⓥ 분포하다
- suspicious ⓐ 수상쩍어하는, 의심스러운
- regulatory ⓐ 규제의, 단속력을 지닌
- financier ⓝ 금융업자, 자본가
- automation ⓝ 자동화
- evenly ⓐⓓ 고르게
- reputation ⓝ 평판, 명성
- recruit ⓥ 채용하다, 모집하다
- concentrate ⓥ 집중시키다
- amenity ⓝ 편의시설
- liberalization ⓝ 자유화

구문 풀이

4행 But the real map of any given industry looks nothing like that; it looks more as if someone had thrown all the darts in the same place.
「as if + 주어 + had p.p. : 가정법 과거완료(마치 ~했던 것처럼)」

★★★ 등급을 가르는 문제!

32 격앙된 감정을 다스리는 데 도움이 되는 타임아웃   정답률 27% | 정답 ③

다음 빈칸에 들어갈 말로 가장 적절한 것을 고르시오. [3점]
① restrain your curiosity – 호기심을 억누르는
② mask your true emotions – 진실된 감정을 가리는
☑ spare innocent bystanders – 무고한 구경꾼들을 구하는
④ provoke emotional behavior – 감정적 행동을 촉발시키는
⑤ establish unhealthy relationships – 건강하지 않은 관계를 만드는

When we are emotionally charged, / we often use anger / to hide our more primary and deeper emotions, / such as sadness and fear, / which doesn't allow / for true resolution to occur.
우리가 감정적으로 격앙되어 있을 때, / 우리는 자주 분노를 사용하는데, / 우리의 더 원초적이고 더 깊은 감정을 숨기기 위해 / 슬픔과 공포와 같은 / 그것은 허용하지 않는다. / 진정한 해결책이 생기는 것을

Separating yourself / from an emotionally upsetting situation / gives you the space you need / to better understand what you are truly feeling / so you can more clearly articulate your emotions / in a logical and less emotional way.
자신을 분리하는 것은 / 감정적으로 화가 나는 상황으로부터 / 당신에게 필요한 공간을 제공하기에 / 당신이 진정으로 느끼고 있는 것을 더 잘 이해하기 위해 / 당신은 감정을 더 명확하게 표현할 수 있다. / 논리적이고 덜 감정적인 방법으로

A time-out also helps spare innocent bystanders.
타임아웃은 또한 무고한 구경꾼들을 구하는 데 도움이 된다.

When confronted with situations / that don't allow us to deal with our emotions / or that cause us to suppress them, / we may transfer those feelings / to other people or situations / at a later point.
우리가 상황에 직면했을 때, / 우리가 우리의 감정을 다스리도록 허용하지 않는 / 혹은 우리가 그 감정들을 억누르게 만드는 / 우리는 그러한 감정을 전이할 수도 있다. / 다른 사람들이나 상황에 / 나중에

For instance, / if you had a bad day at work, / you may suppress your feelings at the office, / only to find / that you release them / by getting into a fight with your kids or spouse / when you get home / later that evening.
예를 들어, / 만약 당신이 직장에서 기분이 나쁜 하루를 보냈다면, / 당신은 사무실에서 당신의 감정을 억누를 수 있지만, / 결과적으로 발견하게 된다. / 당신이 그것들을 표출하는 것을 / 당신의 아이들이나 배우자와 다툼으로써 / 당신이 집에 도착했을 때 / 그 후 저녁에

Clearly, / your anger didn't originate at home, / but you released it there.
분명히, / 당신의 분노는 집에서 비롯된 것이 아니었지만, / 당신은 거기서 그것을 표출했다.

When you take the appropriate time / to digest and analyze your feelings, / you can mitigate hurting or upsetting other people / who have nothing to do with the situation.
당신이 적절한 시간을 가질 때, / 당신의 감정을 소화하고 분석하는 데 / 당신은 다른 사람들을 상처주거나 화나게 하는 것을 완화시킬 수 있다. / 그 상황과 무관한

우리가 감정적으로 격앙되어 있을 때, 우리는 자주 슬픔과 공포와 같은 우리의 더 원초적이고 더 깊은 감정을 숨기기 위해 분노를 사용하는데, 이것은 진정한 해결책이 생기는 것을 허용하지 않는다. 감정적으로 화가 나는 상황으로부터 자신을 분리하는 것은 진정으로 느끼고 있는 것을 더 잘 이해하는 데 필요한 공간을 제공하기에 당신은 논리적이고 덜 감정적인 방법으로 감정을 더 명확하게 표현할 수 있다. 타임아웃은 또한 무고한 구경꾼들을 구하는 데 도움이 된다. 우리가 우리의 감정을 다스리도록 허용되지 않는 상황 혹은 그 감정을 억누르게 만드는 상황에 직면했을 때, 우리는 그러한 감정을 나중에 다른 사람들이나 상황에 전이할 수도 있다. 예를 들어, 만약 당신이 직장에서 기분이 나쁜 하루를 보냈다면, 당신은 사무실에서 당신의 감정을 억누를 수 있지만, 결과적으로 그 후 저녁에 당신이 집에 도착했을 때 당신의 아이들이나 배우자와 다툼으로써 그것들을 표출하는 것을 발견하게 된다. 분명히, 당신의 분노는 집에서 비롯된 것이 아니었지만, 당신은 거기서 그것을 표출했다. 당신의 감정을

을 소화하고 분석하는 데 적절한 시간을 가질 때, 당신은 그 상황과 무관한 다른 사람들을 상처 주거나 화나게 하는 것을 완화시킬 수 있다.

Why? 왜 정답일까?

마지막 문장인 'When you take the appropriate time to digest and analyze your feelings, you can mitigate hurting or upsetting other people who have nothing to do with the situation.'에서 감정을 소화하고 분석할 시간을 갖고 나면 무관한 사람들에게 상처를 주고 화나게 할 일이 적어진다고 서술하고 있다. 따라서 빈칸에 들어갈 말로 가장 적절한 것은 ③ '무고한 구경꾼들을 구하는'이다.

- primary ⓐ 원초적인, 기본적인
- articulate ⓥ 명확하게 표현하다
- suppress ⓥ 억누르다
- spouse ⓝ 배우자
- appropriate ⓐ 적절한
- analyze ⓥ 분석하다
- restrain ⓥ 억누르다, 제한하다
- provoke ⓥ 촉발시키다, 자극하다
- resolution ⓝ 해결책, 결심
- confront ⓥ 직면하게 하다
- transfer ⓥ 전이하다, 옮기다
- originate ⓥ 비롯되다, 기원하다
- digest ⓥ 소화하다
- have nothing to do with ~와 무관하다
- innocent ⓐ 무고한, 순진한

구문 풀이

4행 Separating yourself from an emotionally upsetting situation gives you the space [you need to better understand what you are truly feeling] so (that) you can more clearly articulate your emotions in a logical and less emotional way.

★★ 문제 해결 꿀~팁 ★★

▶ 많이 틀린 이유는?
글에서 감정을 '식히기' 위한 시간을 가질 것을 조언하고 있지만, 이는 감정을 '숨기라'는 의미는 아니므로 ②는 답으로 부적절하다. 또한 감정을 식히는 시간을 갖는데 '감정적인 행위가 촉발되지'는 않을 것이므로 ④도 답으로 부적합하다.
▶ 문제 해결 방법은?
빈칸 문장에 also가 있는 것으로 보아, 앞에 이어 새로이 추가되는 내용이 중요함을 알 수 있다. 즉 빈칸 앞보다는 뒤를 중점적으로 읽고 핵심을 요약하여 빈칸에 들어갈 말을 찾아야 한다.

33 사람들의 얼굴을 머릿속에 그릴 수 있는 개들 정답률 59% | 정답 ①

다음 빈칸에 들어갈 말로 가장 적절한 것을 고르시오.
☑ form mental images of people's faces – 사람들의 얼굴에 대한 심상을 형성하는
② sense people's moods from their voices – 사람들의 목소리로부터 그들의 기분을 파악하는
③ detect possible danger and prepare for it – 가능한 위험을 감지하고 그것에 대비하는
④ imitate their guardians' habitual behaviors – 그들의 보호자의 습관적 행동을 따라 하는
⑤ selectively obey commands from strangers – 낯선 사람들의 명령에 선택적으로 복종하는

A recent study shows / that dogs appear to form mental images of people's faces.
최근의 한 연구는 보여준다. / 개들이 사람들의 얼굴에 대한 심상을 형성하는 것처럼 보인다는 것을
Scientists placed 28 dogs / in front of a computer monitor / blocked by an opaque screen, / then played a recording / of the dog's human guardian or a stranger / saying the dog's name five times / through speakers in the monitor.
과학자들은 28마리의 개들을 놓고, / 컴퓨터 모니터 앞에 / 불투명한 스크린으로 가려진 / 그리고 나서 녹음을 틀어주었다. / 개의 보호자나 낯선 사람이 / 개의 이름을 5번 부르는 / 모니터의 스피커를 통해
Finally, / the screen was removed / to reveal / either the face of the dog's human companion / or a stranger's face.
마지막으로, / 스크린을 제거했다. / 드러내기 위해 / 개의 인간 동반자의 얼굴이나 / 낯선 사람의 얼굴을
The dogs' reactions were videotaped.
개들의 반응이 비디오로 녹화되었다.
Naturally, / the dogs were attentive to the sound of their name, / and they typically stared about six seconds at the face / after the screen was removed.
당연히, / 개들은 자신의 이름을 부르는 소리에 주의를 기울였고, / 그들은 일반적으로 약 6초 동안 얼굴을 응시했다. / 스크린이 제거된 후
But they spent significantly more time / gazing at a strange face / after they had heard the familiar voice of their guardian.
그러나 그들은 훨씬 더 많은 시간을 보냈다. / 낯선 사람의 얼굴을 응시하는 것에 / 그들이 보호자의 친숙한 목소리를 들은 후
That they paused for an extra second or two / suggests / that they realized something was wrong.
그들이 1~2초 동안 더 멈췄다는 것은 / 보여준다. / 그들이 뭔가 잘못된 것을 파악했음을
The conclusion drawn is / that dogs form a picture in their mind, / and that they can think about it / and make predictions / based on that picture.
도출된 결론은 ~이다. / 개들이 머릿속에 그림을 형성하고 / 그들이 그것에 대해서 생각할 수 있고 / 예측할 수 있다는 것 / 그 그림을 바탕으로
And, like us, / they are puzzled / when what they see or hear doesn't match / what they were expecting.
그리고 우리와 마찬가지로, / 개들은 당황한다. / 그들이 보거나 듣는 것이 일치하지 않을 때 / 그들이 기대했던 것과

최근의 한 연구는 개들이 사람들의 얼굴에 대한 심상을 형성하는 것처럼 보인다는 것을 보여준다. 과학자들은 28마리의 개들을 불투명한 스크린으로 가려진 컴퓨터 모니터 앞에 놓고, 그리고 나서 모니터의 스피커를 통해 개의 보호자나 낯선 사람이 개의 이름을 5번 부르는 녹음을 틀어주었다. 마지막으로 스크린을 제거해 개의 인간 동반자의 얼굴이나 낯선 사람의 얼굴을 드러냈다. 개들의 반응이 비디오로 녹화되었다. 당연히, 개들은 자신의 이름을 부르는 소리에 주의를 기울였고, 스크린이 제거된 후 그들은 일반적으로 약 6초 동안 얼굴을 응시했다. 그러나 그들은 보호자의 친숙한 목소리를 들은 후 낯선 사람의 얼굴을 응시하는 데 훨씬 더 많은 시간을 보냈다. 그들이 1~2초 동안 더 멈췄다는 것은 그들이 뭔가 잘못된 것을 파악했음을 보여준다. 도출된 결론은 개들이 머릿속에 그림을 형성하고 그것에 대해서 생각할 수 있고 그림을 바탕으로 예측할 수 있다는 것이다. 그리고 우리와 마찬가지로, 개들은 그들이 보거나 듣는 것이 기대했던 것과 일치하지 않을 때 당황한다.

Why? 왜 정답일까?

연구의 결론을 제시하는 'The conclusion drawn is that dogs form a picture in their mind, and that they can think about it and make predictions based on that picture.'에서 개들은 목소리 녹음을 듣고 목소리 주인의 얼굴에 대한 머릿속 이미지를 만들어냈으며 그 이미지를 바탕으로 예측도 할 수 있었던 것으로 보인다고 언급하므로, 빈칸에 들어갈 말로 가장 적절한 것은 ① '사람들의 얼굴에 대한 심상을 형성하는'이다.

- companion ⓝ 동반자
- typically ⓐⓓ 일반적으로, 전형적으로
- significantly ⓐⓓ 상당히, 현저히, 유의미하게
- make a prediction 예측하다
- detect ⓥ 감지하다
- selectively ⓐⓓ 선택적으로
- attentive ⓐ 주의를 기울이는
- stare ⓥ 응시하다
- gaze at ⓥ ~을 응시하다
- puzzled ⓐ 당황한
- habitual ⓐ 습관적인

구문 풀이

15행 The conclusion drawn is that dogs form a picture in their mind, and that they can think about it and make predictions based on that picture.

34 사회적 기업을 위한 새로운 자금 조달 방법의 필요성 정답률 50% | 정답 ①

다음 빈칸에 들어갈 말로 가장 적절한 것을 고르시오. [3점]
☑ alternatives to the traditional forms of financing – 금융의 전통적 형태들의 대안
② guidelines for promoting employee welfare – 직원 복지를 증진시키기 위한 지침
③ measures to protect employees' privacy – 직원들의 사생활 보호를 위한 조치
④ departments for better customer service – 더 나은 고객 서비스를 위한 부서
⑤ incentives to significantly increase productivity – 생산성을 현저히 증가시키는 장려금

In the current landscape, / social enterprises tend to rely / either on grant capital (e.g., grants, donations, or project funding) / or commercial financing products (e.g., bank loans).
현재 상황에서 / 사회적 기업들은 의존하는 경향이 있다. / 보조금 자본(예를 들어, 보조금, 기부금, 혹은 프로젝트 기금) / 또는 상업 금융 상품(예를 들어, 은행 대출)에
Ironically, / many social enterprises / at the same time / report of significant drawbacks / related to each of these two forms of financing.
아이러니하게도, / 많은 사회적 기업들은 / 동시에 / 중대한 결점을 보고한다. / 이러한 자금 조달의 두 가지 형태 각각에 관련된
Many social enterprises are for instance reluctant / to make use of traditional commercial finance products, / fearing / that they might not be able to pay back the loans.
예를 들어, 많은 사회적 기업들은 꺼린다. / 전통적인 상업 금융 상품들을 이용하는 것을 / 두려워하여 / 그들이 대출금을 상환하지 못할 수 있다는 것을
In addition, / a significant number of social enterprise leaders report / that relying too much on grant funding / can be a risky strategy / since individual grants are time limited / and are not reliable in the long term.
게다가 / 상당히 많은 사회적 기업 리더들은 말한다. / 보조금 조달에 너무 많이 의존하는 것은 / 위험한 전략일 수 있다고 / 개별적 보조금은 시간 제한적이고 / 장기적으로 신뢰할 수 없으므로
Grant funding can also lower the incentive / for leaders and employees / to professionalize the business aspects, / thus leading to unhealthy business behavior.
보조금 조달은 또한 동기를 낮출 수 있고, / 리더들과 직원들이 / 사업적인 면들을 전문화하려는 / 그로 인해 건강하지 않은 사업 행위를 초래한다.
In other words, / there seems to be a substantial need / among social enterprises / for alternatives to the traditional forms of financing.
다시 말해서, / 상당한 필요가 있는 것처럼 보인다. / 사회적 기업들 사이에서 / 금융의 전통적 형태들의 대안에 대한

현재 상황에서 사회적 기업들은 보조금 자본(예를 들어, 보조금, 기부금, 혹은 프로젝트 기금) 또는 상업 금융 상품(예를 들어, 은행 대출)에 의존하는 경향이 있다. 아이러니하게도, 많은 사회적 기업들은 동시에 이러한 자금 조달의 두 가지 형태 각각에 관련된 중대한 결점을 보고한다. 예를 들어, 많은 사회적 기업들은 대출금을 상환하지 못할 수 있다는 것을 두려워하여 전통적인 상업 금융 상품들을 이용하는 것을 꺼린다. 게다가 개별적 보조금들은 시간 제한적이고 장기적으로는 신뢰할 수 없으므로 상당히 많은 사회적 기업 리더들은 보조금 조달에 너무 많이 의존하는 것은 위험한 전략일 수 있다고 말한다. 보조금 조달은 또한 리더들과 직원들이 사업적인 면들을 전문화하려는 동기를 낮출 수 있고, 그로 인해 건강하지 않은 사업 행위를 초래한다. 다시 말해서, 사회적 기업들 사이에서 금융의 전통적 형태들의 대안에 대한 상당한 필요가 있는 것처럼 보인다.

Why? 왜 정답일까?

'Ironically, many social enterprises at the same time report of significant drawbacks related to each of these two forms of financing.'에 따르면 사회적 기업들은 두 가지 전통적인 자금 조달 형태에 중대한 결점이 있음을 지적한다고 한다. 이를 근거로 할 때, 빈칸에 들어갈 말로 가장 적절한 것은 새로운 자금 조달 형태가 필요할 것이라는 의미를 완성하는 ① '금융의 전통적 형태들의 대안'이다.

- enterprise ⓝ 기업
- significant ⓐ 중대한, 중요한, 상당한
- reluctant ⓐ 꺼리는, 마지못해 하는
- rely on ~에 의존하다
- professionalize ⓥ 전문화하다
- alternative ⓝ 대안
- productivity ⓝ 생산성
- ironically ⓐⓓ 반어적으로
- drawback ⓝ 결점
- make use of ~을 이용하다
- reliable ⓐ 신뢰할 수 있는
- substantial ⓐ 상당한
- welfare ⓝ 복지

구문 풀이

8행 In addition, a significant number of social enterprise leaders report relying too much on grant funding can be a risky strategy since individual grants are time limited and are not reliable in the long term.

35 대양의 연결성과 유동성 정답률 56% | 정답 ③

다음 글에서 전체 흐름과 관계 없는 문장은?

The major oceans are all interconnected, / so that their geographical boundaries are less clear / than those of the continents.

주요 대양은 모두 서로 연결되어 있어, / 그것들의 지리적 경계가 덜 명확하다. / 대륙의 경계보다

As a result, / their biotas show fewer clear differences / than those on land.
결과적으로 / 그들의 생물 군집은 명확한 차이를 덜 보여준다. / 육지에서의 생물 군집보다

① The oceans themselves / are continually moving / because the water within each ocean basin / slowly rotates.
대양 자체가 / 끊임없이 움직인다. / 왜냐하면 각 해저분지 안의 물이 / 천천히 회전하기에

② These moving waters / carry marine organisms from place to place, / and also help the dispersal of their young or larvae.
이 이동하는 물은 / 해양 생물을 여기저기로 운반하며, / 또한 그들의 새끼나 유충의 분산을 돕는다.

☑ In other words, / coastal ocean currents / not only move animals / much less often than expected, / but they also trap animals / within near-shore regions.
즉, / 연안 해류는 / 동물들을 이동시킬 뿐 아니라 / 예상보다 훨씬 덜 / 동물을 가두기도 한다. / 근해 지역 내로

④ Furthermore, / the gradients / between the environments of different areas of ocean water mass / are very gradual / and often extend over wide areas / that are inhabited by a great variety of organisms / of differing ecological tolerances.
더욱이 / 변화도는 / 다양한 지역의 대양 해수 덩어리 환경 사이의 / 매우 점진적이며, / 종종 넓은 지역으로 확장된다. / 매우 다양한 유기체가 서식하는 / 생태학적 내성이 다른

⑤ There are no firm boundaries / within the open oceans / although there may be barriers / to the movement of organisms.
확실한 경계는 없다. / 넓은 대양 / 방해물이 있을 수 있지만, / 유기체의 이동에

주요 대양은 모두 서로 연결되어 있어, 그것들의 지리적 경계가 대륙의 경계보다 덜 명확하다. 결과적으로 그들의 생물 군집은 육지에서의 생물 군집보다 명확한 차이를 덜 보여준다. ① 각 해저분지 안의 물이 천천히 회전하기 때문에 대양 자체가 끊임없이 움직인다. ② 이 이동하는 물은 해양 생물을 여기저기로 운반하며, 또한 그들의 새끼나 유충의 분산을 돕는다. ③ 즉 연안 해류는 예상보다 훨씬 덜 동물들을 이동시킬 뿐 아니라 근해 지역 내로 동물을 가두기도 한다. ④ 더욱이 다양한 지역의 대양 해수 덩어리 환경 사이의 변화도는 매우 점진적이며, 종종 생태학적 내성이 다른 매우 다양한 유기체가 서식하는 넓은 지역으로 확장된다. ⑤ 유기체의 이동에 방해물이 있을 수 있지만, 넓은 대양에 확실한 경계는 없다.

Why? 왜 정답일까?

주요 대양은 서로 연결되어 있으며 그 경계가 대륙보다 불명확하므로 대양 안의 생물은 아주 넓은 지역까지 이동하고 퍼져나갈 수 있다는 내용의 글이다. ①, ②, ④, ⑤는 주제를 적절히 뒷받침하지만, ③은 연안 해류가 동물을 예상보다 덜 이동시키고 동물을 가두기도 한다는 내용을 다루며 흐름에서 벗어난다. 따라서 전체 흐름과 관계없는 문장은 ③이다.

- interconnected ⓐ 상호 연결된
- continually ⓐⓓ 계속해서
- rotate ⓥ 회전하다
- larva ⓝ 유충, 애벌레
- inhabit ⓥ ~에 거주하다
- geographical ⓐ 지리적인
- basin ⓝ 분지, (큰 강의) 유역
- dispersal ⓝ 분산
- gradual ⓐ 점진적인
- tolerance ⓝ 내성, 관용

구문 풀이

1행 The major oceans are all interconnected, so that their geographical
　　　　　　　　　　　　　　　　　　　　　┌ *less + 원급 + than : ~보다 덜 …이다*
boundaries are less clear than those of the continents.
　　　　　　　　　　　　　　　　　　= boundaries

---

36 환경 변화에 따른 순응 작용　　　　　정답률 74% | 정답 ②

주어진 글 다음에 이어질 글의 순서로 가장 적절한 것을 고르시오.
① (A) - (C) - (B)　　☑ (B) - (A) - (C)　　③ (B) - (C) - (A)
④ (C) - (A) - (B)　　⑤ (C) - (B) - (A)

When a change in the environment occurs, / there is a relative increase or decrease in the rate / at which the neurons fire, / which is how intensity is coded.
환경에서 변화가 일어날 때, / 속도에서의 상대적인 증가나 감소가 있는데, / 뉴런이 발화하는 / 이것이 강도가 암호화되는 방법이다.
Furthermore, / relativity operates / to calibrate our sensations.
게다가 / 상대성은 작용한다. / 우리의 감각을 조정하기 위해
(B) For example, / if you place one hand in hot water / and the other in iced water / for some time / before immersing them both / into lukewarm water, / you will experience conflicting sensations of temperature / because of the relative change in the receptors / registering hot and cold.
예를 들어, / 만약 당신이 한 손을 뜨거운 물에 넣고, / 다른 한 손을 얼음물에 담가두면, / 얼마간 / 두 손을 담가 두기 전 / 미지근한 물에 / 당신은 온도 감각이 상충하는 것을 경험할 것이다. / 수용체들의 상대적인 변화 때문에 / 뜨거운 것과 차가운 것을 인식하는
(A) Although both hands are now in the same water, / one feels / that it is colder / and the other feels warmer / because of the relative change / from prior experience.
비록 지금은 두 손이 같은 물속에 있지만, / 한 손은 느낀다 / 더 차갑게 / 그리고 다른 손은 더 따뜻하게 느낀다. / 상대적인 변화 때문에 / 이전 경험으로부터의
This process, called *adaptation*, / is one of the organizing principles / operating throughout the central nervous system.
순응이라고 불리는 이 과정은 / 작동 원리 중 하나이다. / 중추신경계 전반에 걸쳐 작용하는
(C) It explains / why you can't see well inside a dark room / if you have come in from a sunny day.
그것은 설명한다. / 당신이 왜 어두운 방 안에서 잘 볼 수 없는지를 / 당신이 햇볕이 쨍쨍한 날에 실내로 들어온다면
Your eyes have to become accustomed / to the new level of luminance.
당신의 눈은 익숙해져야 한다. / 새로운 수준의 밝기에
Adaptation explains / why apples taste sour / after eating sweet chocolate / and why traffic seems louder in the city / if you normally live in the country.
순응은 설명한다. / 왜 사과가 신맛이 나는지 / 달콤한 초콜릿을 먹은 후 / 그리고 왜 도시에서 교통이 더 시끄러운 것 같은지를 / 만약 당신이 보통 때는 시골에 산다면

환경에서 변화가 일어날 때, 뉴런이 발화하는 속도에서의 상대적인 증가나 감소가 있는데, 이것이 강도가 암호화되는 방법이다. 게다가 상대성은 우리의 감각을 조정하기 위해 작용한다. (B) 예를 들어, 당신이 두 손을 미지근한 물에 담그기 전 얼마간 한 손을 뜨거운 물에, 다른 한 손을 얼음물에 담가두면, 뜨거운 것과 차가운 것을 인식하는 수용체들의 상대적인 변화 때문에 온도 감각이 상충하는 것을 경험할 것이다. (A) 비록 지금은 두 손이 같은 물속에 있지만, 이전 경험으로부터의 상대적인 변화 때문에 한 손은 더 차갑게 느끼고 다른 손은 더 따뜻하게 느낀다. 순응이라고 불리는 이 과정은 중추신경계 전반에 걸쳐 작용하는 작동 원리 중 하나이다.

(C) 그것은 당신이 햇볕이 쨍쨍한 날에 실내로 들어온다면, 왜 어두운 방 안에서 잘 볼 수 없는지를 설명한다. 당신의 눈은 새로운 수준의 밝기에 익숙해져야 한다. 순응은 달콤한 초콜릿을 먹은 후 왜 사과가 신맛이 나는지와 만약 당신이 보통 때는 시골에 산다면 왜 도시에서 교통이 더 시끄러운 것 같은지를 설명한다.

Why? 왜 정답일까?

환경에 변화가 일어날 때 우리의 감각을 조정하고자 상대성이 작용하기 시작한다는 내용을 언급한 주어진 글 뒤에는, 두 손을 똑같이 미지근한 물에 넣기 전 한 손은 차가운 물에, 다른 손은 뜨거운 물에 담가두었다면 서로 다른 감각을 느낄 것이라는 내용의 (B)가 연결된다. 이어서 (A)는 이전 경험의 차이로 인해 같은 대상을 다르게 경험하게 되는 이러한 현상을 '순응'이라는 용어로 정리하며 설명한다. 마지막으로 (C)에서는 순응의 다양한 예를 추가로 들고 있다. 따라서 글의 순서로 가장 적절한 것은 ② '(B) - (A) - (C)'이다.

- intensity ⓝ 강도
- sensation ⓝ (자극을 받아서 느끼는) 감각
- immerse ⓥ (액체 속에) 담그다, 몰두하게 만들다
- conflicting ⓐ 상충하는, 모순되는
- register ⓥ 인식하다, 알아채다, 등록하다
- normally ⓐⓓ 보통
- relativity ⓝ 상대성
- adaptation ⓝ 순응, 적응
- lukewarm ⓐ 미지근한
- receptor ⓝ 수용체
- accustomed to ~에 익숙한

구문 풀이

1행 When a change in the environment occurs, there is a relative increase or
　　　접속사(~할 때)　　주어　　　　　자동사　　　　　　　주어
decrease in the rate [at which the neurons fire], which is how intensity is coded.
선행사　　「전치사 + 관·대」　　　계속적 용법(주절 보충)

---

37 변화를 받아들이고 놓아주는 법을 배우기　　정답률 60% | 정답 ⑤

주어진 글 다음에 이어질 글의 순서로 가장 적절한 것을 고르시오.
① (A) - (C) - (B)　　② (B) - (A) - (C)　　③ (B) - (C) - (A)
④ (C) - (A) - (B)　　☑ (C) - (B) - (A)

When an important change takes place in your life, / observe your response.
중요한 변화가 당신의 삶에서 일어났을 때, / 당신의 반응을 관찰하라.
If you resist accepting the change / it is because you are afraid; / afraid of losing something.
만약 당신이 이 변화를 받아들이는 것을 저항한다면 / 그것은 당신이 두려워하기 때문인데, / 즉 무언가를 잃을까 두려워하기 때문이다.
(C) Perhaps you might lose / your position, property, possession, or money.
아마도 당신은 잃을지도 모른다. / 당신의 지위, 재산, 소유물, 혹은 돈을
The change might mean / that you lose privileges or prestige.
이 변화는 의미할지도 모른다. / 당신이 특권이나 명성을 잃는 것을
Perhaps with the change / you lose the closeness of a person or a place.
아마도 이 변화로 / 당신은 어떤 사람이나 장소의 친밀함을 잃게 된다.
(B) In like manner, / all these things come and go / and then others appear, / which will also go.
인생에서 / 이러한 모든 것들은 있다가 없어지고 / 그러고 나서 다른 것들이 나타나며 / 그것 또한 사라진다.
It is like a river in constant movement.
그것은 끊임없이 움직이는 강과 같다.
If we try to stop the flow, / we create a dam; / the water stagnates / and causes a pressure / which accumulates inside us.
만약 우리가 그 흐름을 멈추려고 노력한다면, / 우리는 댐을 만들고, / 물은 고여서 / 압박을 유발한다. / 우리 안에 축적되는
(A) To learn to let go, / to not cling / and allow the flow of the river, / is to live without resistances; / being the creators of constructive changes / that bring about improvements / and widen our horizons.
놓아주는 법을 배우는 것, / 즉 집착하지 않고 / 강물의 흐름을 허용하는 것은 / 저항 없이 살아가는 것이며, / 건설적인 변화의 창조자가 되는 것이다. / 개선을 가져오고 / 우리의 시야를 넓히는

당신의 삶에서 중요한 변화가 일어났을 때, 당신의 반응을 관찰해라. 당신이 이 변화를 받아들이는 것을 저항한다면 그것은 당신이 두려워하기 때문인데, 즉 무언가를 잃을까 두려워하기 때문이다.

(C) 아마도 당신은 당신의 지위, 재산, 소유물, 혹은 돈을 잃을지도 모른다. 이 변화는 당신이 특권이나 명성을 잃는 것을 의미할지도 모른다. 아마도 이 변화로 당신은 어떤 사람이나 장소의 친밀함을 잃게 된다.

(B) 인생에서 이러한 모든 것들은 있다가 없어지고 그러고 나서 다른 것들이 나타났다가 또한 사라진다. 그것은 끊임없이 움직이는 강과 같다. 만약 우리가 그 흐름을 멈추려고 노력한다면, 우리는 댐을 만들고, 물은 고여서 우리 안에 축적되는 압박을 유발한다.

(A) 놓아주는 법을 배우는 것, 즉 집착하지 않고 강물의 흐름을 허용하는 것은 저항 없이 살아가는 것이며, 개선을 가져오고 우리의 시야를 넓히는 건설적인 변화의 창조자가 되는 것이다.

Why? 왜 정답일까?

우리가 어떤 중요한 변화를 받아들이기 어려운 까닭은 손실에 대한 두려움 때문임을 언급한 주어진 글 뒤에는, 이 손실이 지위, 재산, 소유물, 돈, 혹은 특권이나 명성과 관련되어 있을지도 모른다는 설명으로 주어진 글을 뒷받침하는 (C)가 먼저 연결된다. 이어서 (B)는 (C)에서 열거된 대상을 all these things로 가리키며 인생은 끊임없이 흐르는 강물과 같아서 모든 것이 왔다 사라진다는 내용을 덧붙인다. 마지막으로 (A)는 놓아주는 법을 배우고 생의 '흐름'을 받아들이라는 결론을 제시한다. 따라서 글의 순서로 가장 적절한 것은 ⑤ '(C) - (B) - (A)'이다.

- cling ⓥ 집착하다, 고수하다
- constructive ⓐ 건설적인
- improvement ⓝ 개선, 향상
- accumulate ⓥ 축적되다
- possession ⓝ 소유물
- prestige ⓝ 명성, 위신
- resistance ⓝ 저항
- bring about ~을 가져오다
- constant ⓐ 끊임없는
- property ⓝ 재산, 특성
- privilege ⓝ 특권

구문 풀이

4행 To learn to let go, to not cling and allow the flow of the river, is to live
　　　부정사구 주어　　　　　　　주어 동격　　　　　동사+보어
without resistances; being the creators of constructive changes [that bring about
　　　　　　　　　　　　　　　　　　　　　　　선행사(복수)　　주격 관·대　동사1
improvements and widen our horizons].
　　　　　　　　　동사2

38 중요한 요소와 중추적 요소의 차이   정답률 39% | 정답 ④

글의 흐름으로 보아, 주어진 문장이 들어가기에 가장 적절한 곳을 고르시오. [3점]

Some resources, decisions, or activities / are *important* / (highly valuable on average) / while others are *pivotal* / (small changes make a big difference).
어떤 자원들, 결정들 또는 활동들은 / *중요하다.* / (평균적으로 매우 가치 있는) / 다른 것들은 중추적인 반면 / (작은 변화가 큰 차이를 만든다)

Consider / how two components of a car / relate to a consumer's purchase decision: / tires and interior design.
생각해보자. / 어떻게 자동차의 두 구성요소가 / 소비자의 구매결정과 관련이 있는지 / 즉 타이어와 내부 디자인

Which adds more value on average?
어떤 것이 평균적으로 더 큰 가치를 부가시키는가?

The tires.
타이어이다.

① They are essential / to the car's ability to move, / and they impact both safety and performance.
타이어는 필수적이고 / 차의 운행 능력에 / 그것은 안전과 성능 모두에 영향을 준다.

② Yet tires generally do not influence purchase decisions / because safety standards guarantee / that all tires will be very safe and reliable.
하지만 타이어는 일반적으로 구매 결정에 영향을 미치지 않는데, / 그 이유는 안전기준들이 보장해주기 때문이다. / 모든 타이어가 매우 안전하고 믿을 만하다고

③ Differences in interior features / — optimal sound system, / portable technology docks, / number and location of cup holders — / likely have far more effect / on the consumer's buying decision.
내부 디자인 사양 차이가 / 최적의 음향 시스템, / 스마트기기 거치대, / 컵홀더의 개수와 위치와 같은 / 아마도 훨씬 더 큰 영향을 미친다. / 소비자의 구매 결정에

✔ In terms of the overall value of an automobile, / you can't drive without tires, / but you can drive / without cup holders and a portable technology dock.
자동차의 전반적인 가치 측면에서, / 당신은 타이어 없이는 운전할 수 없지만 / 운전할 수 있다. / 컵홀더나 스마트기기 거치대가 없어도

Interior features, however, / clearly have a greater impact / on the purchase decision.
하지만 내부 디자인 사양들은 / 확실히 더 큰 영향을 미친다. / 구매 결정에

⑤ In our language, / the tires are important, / but the interior design is pivotal.
우리 표현으로 하자면, / 타이어는 중요하지만 / 내부 디자인은 중추적이다.

어떤 자원들, 결정들 또는 활동들은 *중요한*(평균적으로 매우 가치 있는) 반면 다른 것들은 중추적(작은 변화가 큰 차이를 만든다)이다. 자동차의 두 구성요소인 타이어와 내부 디자인이 어떻게 소비자의 구매 결정과 관련이 있는지 생각해보자. 어떤 것이 평균적으로 더 큰 가치를 부가시키는가? 타이어이다. ① 타이어는 차의 운행 능력에 필수적이고 안전과 성능 모두에 영향을 준다. ② 하지만 타이어는 일반적으로 구매 결정에 영향을 미치지 않는데, 그 이유는 안전기준들이 모든 타이어가 매우 안전하고 믿을 만하다고 보장해주기 때문이다. ③ 최적의 음향 시스템, 스마트기기 거치대, 컵홀더의 개수와 위치와 같은 내부 디자인 사양 차이가 아마도 소비자의 구매 결정에 훨씬 더 큰 영향을 미친다. ④ 자동차의 전반적인 가치 측면에서, 당신은 타이어 없이는 운전할 수 없지만 컵홀더나 스마트기기 거치대가 없어도 운전할 수 있다. 하지만 내부 디자인 사양들은 확실히 구매 결정에 더 큰 영향을 미친다. ⑤ 우리 표현으로 하자면, 타이어는 중요하지만 내부 디자인은 중추적이다.

Why? 왜 정답일까?

자동차 구매 결정에 영향을 미치는 두 가지 요소로서 타이어와 내부 디자인을 예로 들어 비교한 글이다. ④ 앞의 두 문장에서 타이어는 보통 안전기준상 안전함을 보장받기 때문에 구매 결정에 큰 영향을 미치지 않지만, 내부 디자인은 구매 결정에 큰 영향을 미친다고 설명한다. 이어서 주어진 문장은 전반적인 가치 측면으로 보자면 타이어가 훨씬 중요하다는 점을 서술한다. 여기에 however로 연결되는 ④ 뒤의 문장은 그럼에도 불구하고 내부 디자인 사양이 구매 결정에 큰 영향을 끼친다는 점을 다시 기술한다. 따라서 주어진 문장이 들어가기에 가장 적절한 곳은 ④이다.

- in terms of ~의 면에서
- dock ⓝ 거치대
- essential ⓐ 필수적인
- reliable ⓐ 믿을 만한
- optimal ⓐ 최적의
- portable ⓐ 휴대용의
- pivotal ⓐ 중추적인
- impact ⓥ 영향을 미치다 ⓝ 영향
- feature ⓝ 기능, 특징
- have (an) effect on ~에 영향을 미치다

구문 풀이

4행 Some resources, decisions, or activities are *important* (highly valuable on average) while others are *pivotal* (small changes make a big difference).
접속사(~한 반면) = other resources

★★ 문제 해결 꿀~팁 ★★

▶ 많이 틀린 이유는?
③ 앞에서 타이어는 구매 결정에 큰 영향을 끼치지 않는다고 서술한 데 이어, ③ 뒤에는 '타이어보다 더 큰' 영향을 끼칠 수 있는 요소로 내부 디자인 사양을 언급하고 있다. 즉 ③ 앞뒤는 타이어와 내부 디자인이 소비자의 구매 결정에 미치는 영향력의 크기를 비교하며 서로 자연스럽게 연결된다.

▶ 문제 해결 방법은?
④ 앞뒤는 똑같이 '내부 디자인 사양'에 관해 언급하는데, ④ 뒤의 문장에는 however가 있다. 즉 ④ 앞에서 내부 디자인을 언급했다가, 잠시 주어진 문장을 통해 타이어에 관해 언급한 후, ④ 뒤에서 다시 내부 디자인에 관해 설명하는 흐름임을 알 수 있다.

39 일부 아프리카 부족의 음악의 즉흥성   정답률 33% | 정답 ③

글의 흐름으로 보아, 주어진 문장이 들어가기에 가장 적절한 곳을 고르시오. [3점]

In the West, / an individual composer writes the music / long before it is performed.
서양에서, / 개인 작곡가는 음악을 작곡한다. / 음악이 연주되기 오래 전에

The patterns and melodies we hear / are pre-planned and intended.
우리가 듣는 패턴과 멜로디들은 / 사전에 계획되고 의도된다.

① Some African tribal music, however, / results from collaboration by the players / on the spur of the moment.
그러나 일부 아프리카 부족의 음악은 / 연주자들의 협연의 결과로 생겨난다. / 즉석에서

② The patterns heard, / whether they are the silences / when all players rest on a beat / or the accented beats / when all play together, / are not planned but serendipitous.
들리는 패턴은 / 휴지(休止)이든, / 모든 연주자가 어느 한 박자에서 쉴 때의 / 강박(強拍)이든 간에 / 모든 연주자가 함께 연주할 때의 / 계획된 것이 아니라 우연히 얻은 것이다.

✔ When an overall silence appears / on beats 4 and 13, / it is not because each musician is thinking, / "On beats 4 and 13, I will rest."
전반적인 휴지가 나타날 때, / 4박자와 13박자에 / 그것은 각각의 음악가가 생각하고 있기 때문이 아니다. / "4박자와 13박자에 나는 쉴 거야."라고

Rather, / it occurs randomly / as the patterns of all the players converge / upon a simultaneous rest.
오히려, / 그것은 무작위로 일어난다. / 모든 연주자의 패턴이 한데 모아질 때 / 동시에 쉬는 것으로

④ The musicians are probably as surprised as their listeners / to hear the silences at beats 4 and 13.
그 음악가들도 아마 청중만큼 놀란다. / 4박자와 13박자에 휴지를 듣고서

⑤ Surely that surprise is one of the joys / tribal musicians experience / in making their music.
확실히 그 놀라움은 기쁨 중 하나이다. / 부족의 음악가들이 경험하는 / 음악을 연주할 때

서양에서 개인 작곡가는 음악이 연주되기 오래 전에 음악을 작곡한다. 우리가 듣는 패턴들과 멜로디들은 사전에 계획되고 의도된다. ① 그러나 일부 아프리카 부족의 음악은 연주자들의 협연의 결과로 즉석에서 생겨난다. ② 모든 연주자가 어느 한 박자에서 쉴 때의 휴지(休止)이든, 모든 연주자가 함께 연주할 때의 강박(強拍)이든 간에 들리는 패턴은 계획된 것이 아니라 우연히 얻은 것이다. ③ 전반적인 휴지가 4박자와 13박자에 나타날 때, 그것은 각각의 음악가가 "4박자와 13박자에 나는 쉴 거야."라고 생각하고 있기 때문이 아니다. 오히려, 이것은 모든 연주자의 패턴이 동시에 쉬는 것으로 한데 모아질 때 무작위로 일어난다. ④ 그 음악가들도 아마 4박자와 13박자에 휴지를 듣고서 청중만큼 놀란다. ⑤ 확실히 그 놀라움은 부족의 음악가들이 음악을 연주할 때 경험하는 기쁨 중 하나이다.

Why? 왜 정답일까?

일부 아프리카 부족의 음악 연주에서 관찰되는 우연성과 즉흥성을 설명한 글이다. ③ 앞에서 모든 연주자가 연주 도중 함께 쉬든 혹은 함께 특정 박자를 세게 치든 모든 것은 계획에 따른 것이 아니라 우연히 이루어진다고 서술한다. 주어진 문장은 이에 대한 예로 4박과 13박에서 휴지가 일어났을 때를 언급하며 이것이 모든 연주자가 생각하고 있던 것이 아니라고 설명한다. ③ 뒤의 문장은 주어진 문장에 Rather로 연결되어 '그렇다기보다는' 각 연주자의 연주 패턴이 동시에 쉬는 것으로 우연히 한데 모일 때 전체 휴지가 무작위로 발생하는 것임을 설명한다. 따라서 주어진 문장이 들어가기에 가장 적절한 곳은 ③이다.

- composer ⓝ 작곡가
- on the spur of the moment 즉석에서, 순간적인 충동으로
- accent ⓥ 강조하다
- tribal ⓐ 부족의
- randomly ⓐ 무작위로
- simultaneous ⓐ 동시의

구문 풀이

5행 The patterns heard, (whether they are the silences when all players rest on a beat or the accented beats when all play together), are not planned but serendipitous.
주어 / 과거분사 / 「whether+A+or+B : A이든 B이든」 / ( ) : 부사절 / 동사 「not+A+but+B : A가 아니라 B인」

★★ 문제 해결 꿀~팁 ★★

▶ 많이 틀린 이유는?
④ 앞에서 모두가 4박과 13박에서 멈추는 현상이 '계획되지 않고 무작위로' 일어난다고 말한 데 이어, ④ 뒤에서는 그래서 아마 음악가들도 청중만큼 '놀랄' 수도 있다고 설명하고 있다. 즉 놀람의 이유가 무작위로 일어난 휴지(休止) 때문이므로 ④ 앞뒤는 논리적으로 자연스럽게 연결된다.

▶ 문제 해결 방법은?
앞에서 not A가 나오면 but B를 떠올려야 한다. 여기서도 주어진 문장이 not(it is not because ~)이 나오므로 뒤에 but B가 이어져야 하는데, ③ 뒤의 문장이 but을 대신할 수 있는 Rather(오히려, 대신에)로 시작하며 자연스럽게 이어진다.

40 취미에 들인 시간과 일에 대한 자기 효능감의 관계   정답률 52% | 정답 ①

다음 글의 내용을 한 문장으로 요약하고자 한다. 빈칸 (A), (B)에 들어갈 말로 가장 적절한 것은?

	(A)		(B)
✔	confidence 자신감	……	different 다른
②	productivity 생산성	……	connected 연결된
③	relationships 관계	……	balanced 균형 잡힌
④	creativity 창의성	……	separate 분리된
⑤	dedication 헌신	……	similar 비슷한

Some researchers at Sheffield University / recruited 129 hobbyists / to look at / how the time spent on their hobbies / shaped their work life.
Sheffield 대학교 몇몇 연구자들은 / 취미에 열정적인 사람들 129명을 모집했다. / 보기 위해 / 어떻게 취미에 쓴 시간이 / 그들의 직장 생활에 영향을 미치는지를

To begin with, / the team measured the seriousness of each participant's hobby, / asking them to rate their agreement / with statements like "I regularly train for this activity," / and also assessed / how similar the demands of their job and hobby were.
먼저, / 연구팀은 각 참가자의 취미가 있는 취미의 진지함을 측정하며, / 그들에게 동의하는 정도를 평가하도록 요청하며, / "나는 이 (취미)활동을 위해 정기적으로 연습을 한다."와 같은 / 또한 평가했다. / 그들의 일과 취미에 대한 필요한 것들이 얼마나 비슷한지를

Then, each month for seven months, / participants recorded / how many hours they had dedicated to their activity, / and completed a scale / measuring their belief / in their ability to effectively do their job, / or their "self-efficacy."
그 뒤, 7개월 동안 매달, / 참가자들은 기록하고 / 그들의 취미활동에 몇 시간을 투자했는지를 / 평가표를 작성했다. / 그들의 믿음을 측정하는 / 그들의 직업을 효과적으로 수행하는 능력에 대한 / 즉, '자기 효능감'을

The researchers found / that when participants spent longer than normal / doing their leisure activity, / their belief in their ability to perform their job / increased.

연구자들은 발견했다. / 참가자들이 보통 수준보다 더 긴 시간을 썼을 때 / 취미활동을 하면서 / 그들의 직업 수행능력에 대한 믿음이 / 증가하였다는 것을

But this was only the case / when they had a serious hobby / that was dissimilar to their job.
하지만 이는 오직 그러했다. / 그들이 진지한 취미를 가지고 있을 때에만 / 그들의 직업과 다른

When their hobby was both serious and similar to their job, / then spending more time on it / actually decreased their self-efficacy.
그들의 취미가 진지하면서 직업과 유사할 때, / 그러면 취미에 시간을 많이 보내는 것이 / 실제로 그들의 자기 효능감을 낮추었다.

Research suggests / that spending more time on serious hobbies / can boost (A) confidence at work / if the hobbies and the job are sufficiently (B) different.
연구는 시사한다. / 진지한 취미에 더 많은 시간을 보내는 것이 / 일에서의 자신감을 높여줄 수 있다고 / 취미와 직업이 충분히 다른 경우

Sheffield 대학교 몇몇 연구자들은 취미에 쓴 시간이 어떻게 직장 생활에 영향을 미치는지를 보기 위해 취미에 열정적인 사람들 129명을 모집했다. 먼저 연구팀은 '나는 이 (취미)활동을 위해 정기적으로 연습을 한다.'와 같은 진술에 동의하는 정도를 평가하도록 요청하며, 각 참가자가 가지고 있는 취미의 진지함을 측정하고, 또한 그들의 일과 취미를 하는 데 필요한 것들이 얼마나 비슷한지도 평가했다. 그 뒤, 7개월 동안 매월, 참가자들은 취미활동에 몇 시간을 투자했는지를 기록하고 그들의 직업을 효과적으로 수행하는 능력에 대한 믿음, 즉 '자기 효능감'을 측정하는 평가표를 작성했다. 연구자들은 참가자들이 보통 수준보다 취미활동에 더 긴 시간을 썼을 때 그들의 직업 수행능력에 대한 믿음이 증가하였다는 것을 발견했다. 하지만 이는 오로지 그들이 직업과 다른 진지한 취미를 가지고 있을 때만 그러했다. 그들의 취미가 진지하면서 직업과 유사할 때, 취미에 시간을 많이 보내는 것이 실제로 그들의 자기 효능감을 낮추었다.

➡ 연구에 따르면 취미와 직업이 충분히 (B) 다른 경우 진지한 취미에 더 많은 시간을 보내는 것이 일에서의 (A) 자신감을 높여줄 수 있다.

Why? 왜 정답일까?

마지막 세 문장에서 연구 참가자들은 직업과 다른 진지한 취미에 더 많은 시간을 들일 때 일에 대한 자기 효능감이 상승했으며, 직업과 취미가 비슷할 때에는 오히려 자기 효능감이 떨어지는 결과가 나타났다고 설명하고 있다. 따라서 요약문의 빈칸 (A), (B)에 들어갈 말로 가장 적절한 것은 일에 대한 자신감이 일과 충분히 다른 취미에 종사할 때 높아질 수 있다는 의미를 완성하는 ① '(A) confidence(자신감), (B) different (다른)'이다.

- **seriousness** ⓝ 진지함
- **dedicate** ⓥ 바치다, 전념하다
- **self-efficacy** 자기 효능감
- **boost** ⓥ 높이다, 신장시키다
- **confidence** ⓝ 자신감
- **assess** ⓥ 평가하다
- **effectively** ⓐⓓ 효과적으로
- **dissimilar** ⓐ 다른, 같지 않은
- **sufficiently** ⓐⓓ 충분히

구문 풀이

1행 Some researchers at Sheffield University recruited 129 hobbyists to look at how the time spent on their hobbies shaped their work life.
~하기 위해
의문사 / 주어 / 과거분사 / 동사

41-42 미국 민간 항공사의 오류 보고 시스템

U.S. commercial aviation / has long had an extremely effective system / for encouraging pilots / to submit reports of errors.
미국 민항 사업에는 / 매우 효과적인 시스템이 오랫동안 있어 왔다. / 조종사들을 장려하는 / 오류 보고서를 제출하도록

The program has resulted in numerous improvements / to aviation safety.
이 프로그램은 많은 개선점들을 만들어 왔다. / 항공 안전에

It wasn't easy to establish: / pilots had severe self-induced social pressures / against (a) admitting to errors.
그것을 정착시키기가 쉽지는 않았다. / 조종사들은 스스로 만들어낸 심한 사회적 압박감을 느꼈다. / 오류를 인정하는 것에 대해

Moreover, / to whom would they report them?
더구나, / 누구에게 그 오류들을 보고한단 말인가?

Certainly not to their employers.
분명 그들의 고용주에게는 아닐 것이다.

Not even to the Federal Aviation Authority (FAA), / for then they would probably be punished.
심지어 미국연방항공청(FAA)에게는 더욱 아닐 것이다. / 그러면 그들이 처벌을 받을 수도 있기에

「**The solution / was to let the National Aeronautics and Space Administration (NASA) / set up a (b) voluntary accident reporting system / whereby pilots could submit semi-anonymous reports of errors / they had made or observed in others.**」 **41번의 근거**
해결책은 / 항공우주국(NASA)으로 하여금 ~하게 하는 것이었다. / 자발적인 사고 보고 체계를 만들도록 / 조종사들이 오류에 대해 반(半)익명의 오류 보고서를 제출할 수 있는 / 그들이 저질렀거나 다른 조종사에게서 목격한

Once NASA personnel had acquired the necessary information, / they would (c) detach the contact information from the report / and mail it back to the pilot.
일단 NASA 인사부가 필요한 정보를 얻어내면, / 그들은 보고서에 있던 연락처 정보를 떼어내어 / 조종사에게 돌려보냈다.

「**This meant / that NASA no longer knew / who had reported the error,**」 / **which made it impossible / for the airline companies or the FAA / (which enforced penalties against errors) / to find out who had (d) submitted the report.** **42번의 근거**
이것은 의미했고, / NASA가 더 이상 알지 못한다는 것을 / 오류를 누가 보고했는지를 / 이는 불가능하게 만들었다. / 항공사나 FAA가 / (오류에 대해 제재를 가할 수 있는) / 누가 보고서를 제출했는지 알아내는 것을

If the FAA had independently noticed the error / and tried to invoke a civil penalty or certificate suspension, / the receipt of self-report / automatically exempted the pilot from punishment.
만일 FAA가 독립적으로 오류를 발견하고 / 민사상 처벌 또는 면허정지를 실시하려고 하면, / 자기 보고서의 접수가 / 자동으로 해당 조종사가 처벌을 면하게 해주었다.

When a sufficient number of similar errors / had been collected, / NASA would analyze them / and issue reports and recommendations / to the airlines and to the FAA.
충분한 수의 유사한 오류가 / 수집되면, / NASA는 그것들을 분석하여 / 보고서와 권고안을 발송하곤 했다. / 항공사들과 FAA에

These reports also helped the pilots realize / that their error reports were (e) valuable tools / for increasing safety.
이러한 보고서는 또한 조종사들로 하여금 깨닫는 데 도움을 주었다. / 그들의 오류 보고서가 가치 있는 도구였다는 것을 / 안전을 높이는 데

미국 민항 사업에는 조종사들이 오류 보고서를 제출하도록 장려하는 매우 효과적인 시스템이 오랫동안 있어 왔다. 이 프로그램은 항공 안전에 있어 많은 개선점을 만들어 왔다. 그것을

정착시키기가 쉽지는 않았다. 조종사들은 오류를 (a) 인정하는 것에 대해 스스로 만들어낸 심한 사회적 압박감을 느꼈다. 더구나, 누구에게 그 오류들을 보고한단 말인가? 분명 그들의 고용주에게는 아닐 것이다. 처벌을 받을 수도 있기에 심지어 미국 연방 항공청(FAA)에게는 더욱 아닐 것이다. 해결책은 항공 우주국(NASA)으로 하여금 조종사들이 그들이 저질렀거나 다른 조종사에게서 목격한 오류에 대해 반(半)익명의 오류 보고서를 제출할 수 있는 (b) 자발적인 사고 보고 체계를 만들도록 하는 것이었다. 일단 NASA 인사부가 필요한 정보를 얻어 내면, 보고서에 있던 연락처 정보를 (c) 떼어내어 조종사에게 돌려보냈다. 이것은 NASA가 오류를 누가 보고했는지를 더 이상 알지 못한다는 것을 의미했고, 이는 (오류에 대해 제재를 가할 수 있는) 항공사나 FAA가 누가 보고서를 (d) 거절했는지(→ 제출했는지) 알아내는 것을 불가능하게 만들었다. 만일 FAA가 독립적으로 오류를 발견하고 민사상 처벌 또는 면허정지를 실시하려고 하면, 자기 보고서의 접수가 자동으로 해당 조종사가 처벌을 면하게 해주었다. 유사한 오류가 충분히 수집되면, NASA는 그것들을 분석하여 보고서와 권고안을 항공사들과 FAA에 발송하곤 했다. 이러한 보고서는 또한 조종사들로 하여금 그들의 오류 보고서가 안전을 높이는 데 (e) 가치 있는 도구였다는 것을 깨닫게 하는 데 도움을 주었다.

- **aviation** ⓝ 항공
- **numerous** ⓐ 수많은
- **self-induced** 자기 유도의, 저절로 생긴
- **punish** ⓥ 처벌하다
- **acquire** ⓥ 얻다, 습득하다
- **enforce** ⓥ 집행하다, 실시하다
- **civil penalty** 민사상 처벌(주로 벌금형)
- **suspension** ⓝ 정지, 연기, 보류
- **exempt A from B** A로 하여금 B를 면하게 하다
- **controversy** ⓝ 논란
- **extremely** ⓐⓓ 매우, 극도로
- **improvement** ⓝ 개선, 향상
- **admit to** ~을 인정하다
- **anonymous** ⓐ 익명의
- **detach** ⓥ 떼어내다, 분리시키다
- **invoke** ⓥ 적용하다, 들먹이다
- **certificate** ⓝ 자격(증)
- **automatically** ⓐⓓ 자동으로, 저절로
- **sufficient** ⓐ 충분한

구문 풀이

16행 This meant that NASA no longer knew {who had reported the error},
→ 계속적 용법(앞 문장 보충)
which made it impossible for the airline companies or the FAA (which enforced
가목적어 / 목적격 보어 / 의미상 주어
penalties against errors) to find out {who had submitted the report}.
진목적어 / { } : 간접의문문(누가 ~했는지)

41 제목 파악 정답률 63% | 정답 ①

윗글의 제목으로 가장 적절한 것은?

☑ ① Aviation Safety Built on Anonymous Reports - 익명 보고서로 구축된 항공 안전
② More Flexible Manuals Mean Ignored Safety - 더 융통성 있는 매뉴얼은 안전 무시를 의미한다
③ Great Inventions from Unexpected Mistakes - 예기치 못한 실수로부터 나온 위대한 발명품
④ Controversies over New Safety Regulations - 새 안전 규정에 대한 논란
⑤ Who Is Innovating Technology in the Air? - 누가 공중에서 기술을 혁신하고 있는가?

Why? 왜 정답일까?

첫 두 문장에서 미국 민간 항공사에 오류를 보고하는 효과적인 체계가 있음을 언급한 뒤, 'The solution was ~'에서는 이 체계가 반익명의 오류 보고서를 특징으로 한다는 점을 제시한다. 따라서 글의 제목으로 가장 적절한 것은 ① '익명 보고서로 구축된 항공 안전'이다.

42 어휘 추론 정답률 48% | 정답 ④

밑줄 친 (a) ~ (e) 중에서 문맥상 낱말의 쓰임이 적절하지 않은 것은? [3점]

① (a)   ② (b)   ③ (c)   ☑ ④ (d)   ⑤ (e)

Why? 왜 정답일까?

(c)가 포함된 문장과 'This meant that NASA no longer knew who had reported the error, ~'에 따르면 NASA에서는 오류 보고를 수렴한 후 보고자의 연락처를 지워서 다시 조종사들에게 돌려보냈고 누가 오류를 보고했는지에 대한 정보를 더 이상 보관하지 않았다고 한다. 이에 근거할 때, (d)가 포함된 문장은 추후 항공사나 FAA에서 누가 오류 보고서를 '제출했는지' 알려 해도 알 수 없었다는 의미를 나타내야 한다. 따라서 (d)의 rejected를 submitted로 고쳐야 한다. 문맥상 낱말의 쓰임이 적절하지 않은 것은 ④ '(d)'이다.

43-45 스위스 기차 여행 중 경험한 친절

(A)

I was on a train in Switzerland.
나는 스위스에서 기차를 타고 있었다.

The train came to a stop, / and the conductor's voice over the loudspeaker delivered a message / in German, then Italian, then French.
기차가 멈췄고 / 차장의 목소리가 스피커를 통해 메시지를 전했다. / 독일어, 이탈리아어, 그다음 프랑스어로

I had made the mistake / of not learning any of those languages / before my vacation.
나는 실수를 했다. / 그 언어 중에 어떠한 것도 배우지 않는 / 휴가를 떠나기 전에

「**After the announcement, / everyone started getting off the train,**」 **45번 ①의 근거** 일치 / **and an old woman saw / I was confused and stressed.**
안내방송 후, / 모두가 기차에서 내리기 시작했고, / 한 노부인이 보았다. / 내가 혼란스러워하고 스트레스를 받는 것을

(a) She came up to me.
그녀가 나에게 다가왔다.

(C)

「**She spoke some English, / and she told me / that an accident had happened on the tracks.**」 **45번 ③의 근거** 일치
그녀는 영어를 조금 할 수 있었고 / 나에게 말했다. / 선로에서 사고가 발생했다고

「**She asked me / where I was trying to get to, / then she got off the train / and went to a woman in the ticket booth.**」 **45번 ④의 근거** 일치
그녀는 나에게 물었으며, / 내가 어디로 가려고 하는지 / 그 뒤 그녀는 기차에서 내려 / 티켓 부스에 있는 여자에게 갔다.

The old woman got a rail map and timetable from (c) her / and came back to tell me / that we'd have to hop trains three or four times / to get there.
노부인은 그녀에게서 기차 노선표와 기차 시간표를 얻었고, / 나에게 돌아와서 말했다. / 우리는 서너 번 기차를 갈아타야 한다고 / 거기 가려면

I was really glad / (d) she was headed the same way / because it would have been hopeless / for me to figure it out on my own.
나는 정말로 기뻤다. / 그녀가 나와 같은 방향으로 간다는 것이 / 가망이 없었을 것이기 때문에. / 나 혼자서는 그 사실을 알아내는 것은

So we went from one train station to the next, / getting to know each other along the way.
그래서 우리는 여러 기차역을 이동했고, / 그동안 서로에 대해 알아갔다.

It was a 2.5-hour journey in total, / and when we finally made it to the destination, / we got off and said our goodbyes.
총 2.5시간의 여행이었으며 / 마침내 우리가 목적지에 도착했을 때 / 우리는 기차에서 내렸고 작별의 인사를 했다.

「I had made it just in time / to catch my train to Rome, / and she told me / she had a train to catch too.」 **45번 ②의 근거** 불일치
나는 딱 제때 도착했고, / 로마로 가는 기차를 타기 위해 / 그녀는 나에게 말했다. / 그녀 역시 기차를 타야 한다고

I asked (b) her / how much farther she had to go, / and it turned out / her home was two hours back the other way.
나는 그녀에게 물었고, / 얼마나 더 가야 하는지 / 그리고 밝혀졌다. / 그녀의 집은 반대 방향으로 두 시간 거리에 있다는 것이

(D)

She had jumped from train to train / and traveled the whole way / just to make sure I made it.
그녀는 기차를 갈아타면서 / 끝까지 계속 이동했다. / 단지 내가 잘 도착하는지를 확인하기 위해

"You are the nicest person / I've ever met," / I said.
"당신은 가장 친절한 사람이에요. / 내가 만난 사람 중에서."라고 / 나는 말했다.

She smiled gently / and hugged me / and told me / I'd better hurry off / so I wouldn't miss my train.
그녀는 부드럽게 미소 지었고 / 나를 안아주며 / 내게 말했다. / 내가 서두르는 게 좋겠다고 / 그러면 기차를 놓치지 않을 것이라고

This woman spent her entire day / sitting on trains / taking (e) her hours away from her home / just to help out a confused tourist / visiting her country.
이 여성은 하루 종일 보냈다. / 기차에 앉아 / 그녀의 집에서 몇 시간이나 떨어진 곳으로 그녀를 실어가는 / 단지 혼란스러워하는 여행객을 돕기 위해 / 그녀의 나라를 방문한

「No matter how many countries I visit or sites I see, / I always say / the most beautiful country in the world / is Switzerland.」 **45번 ⑤의 근거** 일치
아무리 많은 나라를 방문하거나 장소를 보더라도, / 나는 항상 말한다. / 세계에서 가장 아름다운 나라는 / 스위스라고

(A)
나는 스위스에서 기차를 타고 있었다. 기차가 멈췄고 스피커를 통해 차장의 목소리가 독일어로, 이탈리아어로, 그다음 프랑스어로 메시지를 전했다. 나는 휴가를 떠나기 전에 이 언어 중에 어떠한 것도 배우지 않는 실수를 했다. 안내방송 후, 모두가 기차에서 내리기 시작했고, 한 노부인이 내가 혼란스러워하고 스트레스를 받는 것을 보았다. (a) 그녀가 나에게 다가왔다.

(C)
그녀는 영어를 조금 할 수 있었고, 나에게 선로에서 사고가 발생했다고 말했다. 그녀는 나에게 어디로 가려고 하는지 물었으며, 그 후 기차에서 내려 티켓 부스에 있는 여자에게 갔다. 노부인은 (c) 그녀에게서 기차 노선표와 기차 시간표를 얻었고, 나에게 돌아와서 우리가 거기 가려면 서너 번 기차를 갈아타야 한다고 말했다. 나 혼자서는 그 사실을 알아낼 가망이 없었을 것이기 때문에, 나는 (d) 그녀가 나와 같은 방향으로 간다는 것이 정말로 기뻤다.

(B)
그래서 우리는 여러 기차역을 이동했고, 그동안 서로에 대해 알아갔다. 총 2.5시간의 여행이었으며 마침내 목적지에 도착했을 때 우리는 기차에서 내렸고 작별의 인사를 했다. 나는 로마로 가는 기차 시간에 딱 맞추어 도착했고, 그녀는 나에게 그녀 역시 기차를 타야 한다고 말했다. 나는 (b) 그녀에게 얼마나 더 가야 하는지 물었고, 알고 보니 그녀의 집은 반대 방향으로 두 시간 거리에 있었다.

(D)
그녀는 단지 내가 잘 도착하는지를 확인하기 위해 기차를 갈아타면서 끝까지 계속 이동했다. "당신은 내가 만난 사람 중에서 가장 친절한 사람이에요."라고 나는 말했다. 그녀는 부드럽게 미소 지었고 나를 안아주며 내가 서두르지 않으면 기차를 놓칠 것이라고 내게 말했다. 이 여성은 단지 자신의 나라를 방문한 혼란스러워하는 여행객을 돕기 위해 자신의 집에서 몇 시간이나 떨어진 곳으로 (e) 자신을 실어가는 기차에 앉아 하루 종일 보냈다. 아무리 많은 나라를 방문하거나 장소를 보더라도, 나는 세계에서 가장 아름다운 나라는 스위스라고 항상 말한다.

- come to a stop 멈추다, 서다
- destination ⓝ 목적지
- hopeless ⓐ 가망 없는, 절망적인
- conductor ⓝ 차장, 안내원, 지휘자
- in time 때맞춰, 제시간에
- gently ⓐⓓ 부드럽게

구문 풀이

(A) 3행 I had made the mistake of not learning any of those languages before my vacation.
과거완료 / 전치사 / 'not+동명사 : 동명사 부정 표현'

(B) 6행 I asked her {how much farther she had to go}, and it turned out (that) her home was two hours back the other way.
4형식 동사 / 간접 목적어 { } : 직접 목적어(간접의문문) / ~임이 판명되다

(C) 7행 I was really glad (that) she was headed the same way because it would have been hopeless for me to figure it out on my own.
생략(접속사) / 접속사(~ 때문에) / 가주어 / ~했을 것 주어 / 의미상 주어 / 진주어(~것)

(D) 5행 This woman spent her entire day sitting on trains taking her hours away from her home just to help out a confused tourist visiting her country.
'spend+시간+동명사 : ~하는 데 …을 들이다, 쓰다' / 목적(단지 ~하기 위해)

---

43 글의 순서 파악 　　　　　 정답률 81% | 정답 ②

주어진 글 (A)에 이어질 내용을 순서에 맞게 배열한 것으로 가장 적절한 것은?
① (B) - (D) - (C)　　　☑ (C) - (B) - (D)
③ (C) - (D) - (B)　　　④ (D) - (B) - (C)
⑤ (D) - (C) - (B)

Why? 왜 정답일까?
스위스에서 기차 여행을 하던 도중 갑자기 방송이 나와 모두가 기차에서 내리는 모습을 보고 필자가 당황했다는 내용의 주어진 글 (A) 뒤에는, 필자에게 한 노부인이 다가와 상황을 설명해주고 기차 노선표와 시간표

를 구해다 주었다는 내용의 (C), 약 2.5시간을 함께 간 끝에 필자가 로마로 가는 기차를 타기 위해 도착했을 때 사실은 노부인의 집이 반대 방향에 있었다는 사실을 알게 되었다는 내용의 (B), 필자가 노부인의 친절에 감동과 감사를 느꼈음을 서술하는 (D)가 차례로 이어져야 한다. 따라서 글의 순서로 가장 적절한 것은 ② '(C) - (B) - (D)'이다.

44 지칭 추론 　　　　　 정답률 72% | 정답 ③

밑줄 친 (a) ~ (e) 중에서 가리키는 대상이 나머지 넷과 다른 것은?
① (a)　　② (b)　　☑ (c)　　④ (d)　　⑤ (e)

Why? 왜 정답일까?
(a), (b), (d), (e)는 모두 필자를 도와준 the old woman을 가리키지만, (c)는 앞 문장의 a woman in the ticket booth를 가리키므로, (a) ~ (e) 중에서 가리키는 대상이 다른 하나는 ③ '(c)'이다.

45 세부 내용 파악 　　　　　 정답률 82% | 정답 ②

윗글에 관한 내용으로 적절하지 <u>않은</u> 것은?
① 안내 방송 후 모두가 기차에서 내리기 시작했다.
☑ 'I'는 로마로 가는 기차 시간에 맞춰 도착하지 못했다.
③ 노부인은 선로에서 사고가 발생했다고 말했다.
④ 노부인은 기차에서 내려 티켓 부스로 갔다.
⑤ 'I'는 세계에서 가장 아름다운 나라가 스위스라고 항상 말한다.

Why? 왜 정답일까?
(B) 'I had made it just in time to catch my train to Rome, ~'에서 나는 로마로 가는 기차 시간에 딱 맞추어 도착했다고 하므로, 내용과 일치하지 않는 것은 ② "I는 로마로 가는 기차 시간에 맞춰 도착하지 못했다."이다.

Why? 왜 오답일까?
① (A) 'After the announcement, everyone started getting off the train. ~'의 내용과 일치한다.
③ (C) '~ she told me that an accident had happened on the tracks.'의 내용과 일치한다.
④ (C) '~ then she got off the train and went to a woman in the ticket booth.'의 내용과 일치한다.
⑤ (D) '~ I always say the most beautiful country in the world is Switzerland.'의 내용과 일치한다.

어휘 Review Test 15 　　　　　 문제편 150쪽

A	B	C	D
01 다른, 같지 않은	01 assimilation	01 ⓘ	01 ⓐ
02 떼어내다, 분리시키다	02 enforce	02 ⓑ	02 ⓚ
03 ~에 거주하다	03 distort	03 ⓛ	03 ⓞ
04 정지, 연기, 보류	04 punish	04 ⓐ	04 ⓕ
05 촉발시키다, 자극하다	05 mold	05 ⓓ	05 ⓓ
06 논란	06 privilege	06 ⓝ	06 ⓗ
07 배우자	07 tease	07 ⓒ	07 ⓙ
08 명성, 위신	08 possession	08 ⓗ	08 ⓝ
09 집중시키다	09 vast	09 ⓔ	09 ⓙ
10 미지근한	10 adaptation	10 ⓘ	10 ⓖ
11 고르게	11 ridicule	11 ⓞ	11 ⓒ
12 내성, 관용	12 reluctant	12 ⓖ	12 ⓘ
13 등골이 오싹한, 스릴 넘치는	13 municipal	13 ⓚ	13 ⓔ
14 복지	14 anxiety	14 ⓕ	14 ⓛ
15 배출	15 digest	15 ⓜ	15 ⓘ
16 자유화	16 morality	16 ⓠ	16 ⓠ
17 처음부터	17 coordinate	17 ⓘ	17 ⓢ
18 강화하다	18 scrap	18 ⓡ	18 ⓘ
19 영장류	19 splash	19 ⓟ	19 ⓡ
20 유충, 애벌레	20 drawback	20 ⓢ	20 ⓟ

정답 •

18② 19② 20⑤ 21④ 22① 23① 24③ 25④ 26③ 27④ 28④ 29⑤ 30⑤ 31① 32①
33⑤ 34② 35③ 36② 37③ 38③ 39④ 40① 41① 42⑤ 43③ 44⑤ 45⑤

★ 표기된 문항은 [등급을 가르는 문제]에 해당하는 문항입니다.

---

18 농구장 개장 시간 조절 부탁　정답률 96% | 정답 ②

다음 글의 목적으로 가장 적절한 것은?

① 체육관의 바닥 교체 공사를 요구하려고
✔ 농구 코트의 운영 시간 제한을 요청하려고
③ 문화 센터 시설의 대관 날짜를 변경하려고
④ 건강 증진 프로그램 신청 방법을 문의하려고
⑤ 지역 내 체육 시설의 증설 가능 여부를 확인하려고

To whom it may concern,
관계자 귀하,
I am writing / to inform you / of an ongoing noise issue / that I am experiencing.
저는 글을 쓰고 있습니다. / 알려 드리기 위해 / 지속되는 소음 문제에 대해 / 제가 겪고 있는
My apartment / faces / the basketball courts / of the community center.
저의 아파트는 / 향하고 있습니다. / 농구 코트를 / 문화 센터의
While I fully support / the community center's services, / I am constantly / being disrupted / by individuals / playing basketball / late at night.
저는 전적으로 지지하고 있지만 / 문화 센터의 서비스를, / 저는 끊임없이 / 방해받고 있습니다. / 개인들에 의해 / 농구를 하는 / 밤늦게
Many nights, / I struggle / to fall asleep / because I can hear / people / bouncing balls / and shouting / on the basketball courts / well after 11 p.m.
많은 밤마다 / 저는 애를 먹습니다. / 잠을 자는 데 / 왜냐하면 들을 수 있기 때문입니다. / 사람들이 / 공을 튀기는 것을 / 그리고 소리 치는 것을 / 농구 코트에서 / 오후 11시가 한참 넘어서도
Could you restrict / the time / the basketball court is open / to before 9 p.m.?
제한해 주실 수 있으십니까? / 시간을 / 농구 코트가 열려 있는 / 밤 9시 이전으로
I'm sure / I'm not the only person / in the neighborhood / that is affected / by this noise issue.
저는 확신합니다. / 제가 유일한 사람이 아님을 / 이 근처에서 / 영향을 받는 / 이 소음 문제에 의해
I appreciate / your assistance.
저는 감사드립니다. / 당신의 협조에
Sincerely,
진심을 담아,
Ian Baldwin
Ian Baldwin이

관계자 귀하,
저는 제가 겪고 있는 지속되는 소음 문제에 대해 알려 드리기 위해 이 편지를 씁니다. 저의 아파트는 문화 센터의 농구 코트를 향하고 있습니다. 저는 문화 센터의 서비스를 전적으로 지지하고 있지만, 밤늦게 농구를 하는 사람들에 의해 끊임없이 방해받고 있습니다. 많은 밤마다, 밤 11시가 한참 넘어서도 저는 사람들이 농구 코트에서 공을 튀기고 소리치는 것을 들어야 해서 잠을 자는 데 애를 먹습니다. 당신은 농구 코트를 여는 시간을 밤 9시 이전으로 제한해 주실 수 있으십니까? 저는 이 근처에서 이 소음 문제에 의해 영향 받는 유일한 사람이 아님을 확신합니다. 당신의 협조에 감사드립니다.

진심을 담아,
Ian Baldwin

Why? 왜 정답일까?
문화 센터의 농구 코트를 향하고 있는 아파트에서 소음 문제에 힘들어 하고 있으므로, 농구 코트 개장 시간을 조정해 달라고 한다('Could you restrict the time the basketball court is open to before 9 p.m.?'). 따라서 글의 목적으로 가장 적절한 것은 ② '농구 코트의 운영 시간제한을 요청하려고'이다.

● inform ⓥ 알리다　　● ongoing ⓐ 진행 중인
● experience ⓥ 경험하다　　● bounce ⓥ 튀기다
● neighborhood ⓝ 이웃

구문 풀이
4행 While I fully support the community center's services, I am constantly
반면에
being disrupted by individuals (who are) playing basketball late at night.
수동태　by + 행위자　→ 주격관계대명사 + be동사 생략

---

19 부족 청년들의 통과 의례　정답률 84% | 정답 ②

다음 글에 드러난 Chaske의 심경 변화로 가장 적절한 것은?

① nervous → doubtful　　✔ horrified → relieved
　긴장한　의심스러운　　　무서운　안심한
③ disappointed → curious　④ ashamed → frightened
　실망한　궁금한　　　　　부끄러운　놀란
⑤ bored → delighted
　지루한　기쁜

Chaske, / a Cherokee boy, / was sitting / on a tree stump.
Chaske는 / 체로키 소년인 / 앉아 있었다. / 나무 그루터기에
As a rite of passage / for youths / in his tribe, / Chaske had to survive / one night / in the forest / wearing a blindfold, / not knowing / he was observed / by his father.
통과 의례로 / 청년들을 위한 / 그의 부족의 / Chaske는 살아남아야 했다. / 하룻밤을 / 숲속에서 / 눈가리개를 쓰고, / 모른 채로 / 그가 관찰되고 있다는 것을 / 그의 아버지에 의해
After the sunset, / Chaske could hear / all kinds of noises.
해가 지고 난 후에, / Chaske는 들을 수 있었다. / 모든 종류의 소리를

The wind / blew the grass / and shook / his stump.
바람이 / 풀을 휘저었다. / 그리고 흔들었다. / 그의 그루터기를
A sense of dread / swept through / his body.
두려움이 / 휩쓸었다. / 그의 몸을
What if / wild beasts / are looking at me?
만약 / 야생 짐승들이 / 나를 보고 있다면?
I / can't stand this!
나는 / 견딜 수가 없어 / 이것을!
Just as he was about to take off / the blindfold, / to run away, / a voice / came in / from somewhere.
그가 막 벗으려고 했을 때 / 눈가리개를 / 도망가기 위해, / 한 음성이 / 들려왔다. / 어디선가
"I'm here / around you. / Don't give up, / and complete your mission."
"나는 여기 있어. / 네 주변에 있어. / 포기하지 마, / 그리고 너의 임무를 완수해."
It was / his father's voice.
그것은 / 그의 아버지의 목소리였다.
He has been / watching me / from nearby!
그는 계속해서 / 나를 지켜보고 있었구나! / 근처에서
With just / the presence of his father, / the boy / regained stability.
단지 / 그의 아버지의 존재만으로도, / 소년은 / 안정을 되찾았다.
What panicked him awfully / a moment ago / vanished / into thin air.
그를 끔찍하게 겁에 질리게 한 것들이 / 조금 전까지 / 사라졌다. / 온데간데없이

체로키족 소년인 Chaske는 나무 그루터기에 앉아 있었다. 그의 부족 청년들에 대한 통과 의례로, Chaske는 그의 아버지가 지켜보는 것을 모른 채로 눈가리개를 쓰고 숲속에서 하룻밤을 살아남아야 했다. 해가 지고 난 후에, Chaske는 모든 종류의 소리를 들을 수 있었다. 바람이 풀을 휘저으며 그의 그루터기를 흔들었다. 두려움이 그의 몸을 휩쓸었다. '만약 야생 짐승들이 나를 바라보고 있다면 어떡하지? 나는 이것을 견딜 수가 없어!' 그가 도망가기 위해 눈가리개를 막 벗으려고 했을 때 어디선가 한 음성이 들려왔다. "나는 여기 네 주변에 있어. 포기하지 말고 너의 임무를 완수해." 그것은 그의 아버지의 목소리였다. '그가 근처에서 나를 지켜보고 있었구나!' 그의 아버지의 존재만으로도 소년은 안정을 되찾았다. 조금 전까지 그를 끔찍하게 겁에 질리게 한 것들이 온데간데없이 사라졌다.

Why? 왜 정답일까?
눈가리개를 쓰고 숲속에서 모든 종류의 소리를 들으며 두려워했지만('A sense of dread swept through his body.'), 아버지의 목소리를 듣고는 안정을 되찾았다('With just the presence of his father, the boy regained stability.'). 따라서 감정 변화로 알맞은 것은 ② 'horrified → relieved'이다.

● stump ⓝ 그루터기　　● rite ⓝ 의례
● survive ⓥ 살아남다　　● observe ⓥ 관찰하다

구문 풀이
12행 What panicked him awfully a moment ago vanished into thin air.
관계대명사(= the thing that)　　동사

---

20 농업의 의미　정답률 87% | 정답 ⑤

다음 글에서 필자가 주장하는 바로 가장 적절한 것은?

① 토양의 질을 개선하기 위해 친환경 농법의 연구와 개발이 필요하다.
② 세계 인구의 증가에 대응하기 위해 농산물 품종의 다양화가 필요하다.
③ 기후 변화에 대한 지속 가능한 대책은 경제적 관점에서 고려되어야 한다.
④ 다른 산업 분야와의 공동 연구를 통해 상품성을 가진 농작물을 개발해야 한다.
✔ 농업이 직면한 문제 해결 및 식량과 농산물의 지속적 생산을 위한 방안이 필요하다.

Agriculture / includes / a range of activities / such as planting, / harvesting, / fertilizing, / pest management, / raising animals, / and distributing food and agricultural products.
농업은 포함한다. / 다양한 활동들을 / 파종, / 수확, / 비료 주기, / 해충 관리, / 동물 사육, / 그리고 식량 및 농산물 분배와 같은
It is / one of the oldest and most essential / human activities, / dating back thousands of years, / and has played / a critical role / in the development of human civilizations, / allowing people / to create stable food supplies / and settle / in one place.
그것은 / 가장 오래되고 필수적인 것 중 하나이다. / 인간 활동 중에서 / 수천 년으로 거슬러 올라가는, / 그리고 해왔다. / 중요한 역할을 / 인류 문명의 발전에 있어서 / 사람들을 허락해 주며, / 안정적인 식량 공급을 생산하게 / 그리고 한 곳에 정착할 수 있게
Today, / agriculture / remains / a vital industry / that feeds the world's population, / supports rural communities, / and provides raw materials / for other industries.
오늘날, / 농업은 / 남아있다. / 중요한 산업으로 / 전 세계 인구를 먹여 살리고, / 농업 공동체를 지원하며 / 원료를 공급하는 / 다른 산업에
However, / agriculture / faces / numerous challenges / such as climate change, / water scarcity, / soil degradation, / and biodiversity loss.
그러나, / 농업은 / 직면하고 있다. / 수많은 문제에 / 기후 변화와 같은, / 물 부족, / 토질 저하, / 그리고 생물 다양성 손실
As the world's population / continues to grow, / it is essential / to find sustainable solutions / to address the challenges / facing agriculture / and ensure / the continued production / of food and other agricultural products.
세계 인구가 / 계속해서 증가함에 따라, / 필수적이다. / 지속 가능한 해결책을 찾는 것이 / 문제를 다루기 위해 / 농업이 직면한 / 그리고 보장하기 위해 / 지속적인 생산을 / 식량과 다른 농산물의

농업은 파종, 수확, 비료 주기, 해충 관리, 동물 사육, 그리고 식량 및 농산물 분배와 같은 다양한 활동들을 포함한다. 그것은 수천 년 전으로 거슬러 올라가는 가장 오래되고 필수적인 인간 활동 중 하나이고, 인류 문명의 발전에 중요한 역할을 해 왔으며, 사람들이 안정적인 식량을 생산하고 한곳에 정착할 수 있게 허락해 주었다. 오늘날, 농업은 전 세계 인구를 먹여 살리고 농업 공동체를 지원하며 다른 산업에 원료를 공급하는 중요한 산업으로 남아 있다. 그러나, 농업은 기후 변화, 물 부족, 토질 저하, 생물 다양성 손실과 같은 수많은 문제에 직면하고 있다. 세계 인구가 계속해서 증가함에 따라, 농업이 직면한 문제를 다루고 식량과 다른 농산물의 지속적인 생산을 보장하기 위한 지속 가능한 해결책을 찾는 것이 필수적이다.

Why? 왜 정답일까?
농업이 중요함에도 불구하고, 수많은 문제에 직면하였으므로(However, agriculture faces numerous challenges such as climate change, water scarcity, soil degradation, and biodiversity loss.) 지속 가능한 해결책을 찾아야 한다고 하였다. 따라서 글에서 필자가 주장하는 바로 가장 적절한 것은 ⑤ '농업이 직면한 문제 해결 및 식량과 농산물의 지속적 생산을 위한 방안이 필요하다.'이다.

- agriculture ⓝ 농업
- fertilize ⓥ 비료를 주다
- agricultural ⓐ 농업의
- critical ⓐ 대단히 중요한
- remain ⓥ 남아 있다
- material ⓝ 원료, 재료
- include ⓥ 포함하다
- degradation ⓝ 저하
- essential ⓐ 필수적인
- civilization ⓝ 문명
- vital ⓐ 극히 중대한, 필수적인
- challenge ⓝ 도전

구문 풀이

3행 It is one of the oldest and most essential human activities, dating back
동사1　　　　　　　　　　　　　　　　　　　　　현재분사
thousands of years, and has played a critical role in the development of human
　　　　　　　　　　　현재분사
civilizations, allowing people to create stable food supplies and settle in one place.
현재분사　　　　　to부정사1　　　　　　　　　　to부정사2

---

21 예술의 정서적 연결　　정답률 48% | 정답 ④

밑줄 친 be more than just sugar on the tongue이 다음 글에서 의미하는 바로 가장 적절한 것은? [3점]

① play a role in relieving psychological anxiety – 심리학적 불안을 푸는 역할을 하다
② enlighten us about the absoluteness of beauty – 아름다움의 완벽함에 대해 우리에게 깨우쳐 주다
③ conceal the artist's cultural and ethnic traditions – 예술가의 문화적 그리고 민족적 전통을 숨기다
✔④ embrace a variety of experiences beyond pleasure – 쾌락 너머 경험의 다양성을 포용하다
⑤ distort the viewers' accurate understanding of history – 역사의 시청자들의 정확한 이해를 왜곡하다

The arts and aesthetics / offer / emotional connection / to the full range of human experience.
예술과 미학은 / 제공한다. / 정서적인 연결을 / 다양한 인간 경험에 대한

"The arts / can be / more than just sugar on the tongue," / Anjan Chatterjee, / a professor at the University of Pennsylvania, / says.
"예술은 / 될 수 있다. / 단순히 혀 위의 설탕 이상의 것" / Anjan Chatterjee는, / Pennsylvania 대학교의 교수인 / 말한다.

"In art, / when there's something challenging, / which can also be uncomfortable, / this discomfort, / if we're willing to engage / with it, / offers / the possibility / of some change, / some transformation.
"예술에서, / 무언가 도전적인 것이 있을 때 / 또한 불편할 수도 있는, / 이 불편은, / 우리가 기꺼이 참여하려 한다면 / 그것에, / 제공한다. / 가능성을 / 어떤 변화의, 어떤 변형의

That / can also be / a powerful / aesthetic experience."
그것은 / 또한 될 수 있다. / 강력한 / 미적 경험이"

The arts, / in this way, / become / vehicles / to contend / with ideas and concepts / that are difficult and uncomfortable otherwise.
예술은, / 이런 방식으로, / 된다. / 매개체가 / 싸우기 위한 / 아이디어 및 개념들과 / 그렇지 않았더라면 어렵고 불편한

When Picasso / painted / his masterpiece *Guernica* / in 1937, / he / captured / the heartbreaking and cruel nature / of war, / and offered / the world / a way to consider / the universal suffering / caused by the Spanish Civil War.
피카소가 / 그렸을 때 / 그의 걸작 *Guernica*를 / 1937년에, / 그는 / 포착했다. / 가슴 아프고 잔인한 본질을 / 전쟁의, / 그리고 제공했다. / 세상에 / 숙고할 방법을 / 보편적 고통을 / 스페인 내전으로 인한

When Lorraine Hansberry wrote / her play *A Raisin in the Sun*, / she gave us / a powerful story / of people struggling with / racism, / discrimination, / and the pursuit of the American dream / while also offering / a touching portrait / of family life.
Lorraine Hansberry가 썼을 때 / 그녀의 희곡 *A Raisin in the Sun*을 / 그녀는 우리에게 주었다. / 강력한 이야기를 / 맞서 싸우는 사람들의 / 인종차별, / 차별, / 그리고 아메리칸드림의 추구를 위해 / 또한 제공하면서 / 감동적인 초상화를 / 가족생활에 대한

예술과 미학은 다양한 인간 경험에 대한 정서적인 연결을 제공한다. "예술은 단순히 혀 위의 설탕 이상의 것이 될 수 있다."라고 Pennsylvania 대학교의 교수인 Anjan Chatterjee는 말한다. "예술에서, 무언가 도전적인 것이 있고 그것이 또한 불편할 수 있을 때, 이 불편은, 만약 우리가 기꺼이 그것에 참여하려 한다면, 어떤 변화, 어떤 변형의 가능성을 제공한다. 그것은 또한 강력한 미적 경험이 될 수 있다." 예술은, 이런 방식으로, 그렇지 않았더라면 어렵고 불편한 아이디어 및 개념들과 싸우는 매개체가 된다. Picasso가 그의 걸작 *Guernica*를 1937년에 그렸을 때, 그는 가슴 아프고 잔인한 전쟁의 본질을 포착했고, 스페인 내전으로 인한 보편적인 고통을 숙고할 방법을 세상에 제공했다. Lorraine Hansberry가 그녀의 희곡 *A Raisin in the Sun*을 썼을 때, 그녀는 또한 가족생활에 대한 감동적인 초상화를 제공하면서 인종 차별, 차별, 아메리칸드림의 추구를 위해 고군분투하는 사람들의 강력한 이야기를 우리에게 주었다.

Why? 왜 정답일까?

피카소의 작품 Guernica와 로랜 한즈베리의 A Raisin in the Sun을 예로 들며 예술이 그저 아름답기만 한 것이 아니며, 그 이상의 의미를 가질 수 있다고 주장한다. 따라서 밑줄 친 글이 의미하는 바로 가장 적절한 것은 ④ 'embrace a variety of experiences beyond pleasure'이다.

- aesthetics ⓝ 미학
- connection ⓝ 연결
- possibility ⓝ 가능성
- vehicle ⓝ 매개체, 수단
- discrimination ⓝ 차별
- emotional ⓐ 감정적인
- uncomfortable ⓐ 불편한
- transformation ⓝ 변형, 변모
- masterpiece ⓝ 걸작, 명작
- portrait ⓝ 초상화

구문 풀이

4행 In art, when there's something challenging, which can also be
　　　　　　~때　　　　　　　　　　주격관계대명사
uncomfortable, this discomfort, if we're willing to engage with it, offers the
　　　　　　　　　　주어　　　　　　　　　　to부정사　　　　　　동사
possibility of some change, some transformation.
→ this discomfort

---

22 시간 측정의 유용성　　정답률 79% | 정답 ①

다음 글의 요지로 가장 적절한 것은?

✔① 공공 시계는 서양 사회의 경제적 진보에 영향을 미쳤다.
② 서양에서 생산된 시계는 세계적으로 정교함을 인정받았다.
③ 서양의 시계는 교역을 통해 전파되어 세계적으로 대중화되었다.
④ 기계 시계의 발명은 다른 측량 장비들의 개발에 도움을 주었다.
⑤ 중세 시대의 시계 발명은 자연법칙을 이해하는 데 큰 전환점이 되었다.

Many historians / have pointed / to the significance / of accurate time measurement / to Western economic progress.
많은 역사가들은 / 시사해 왔다. / 중요성을 / 정확한 시간 측정의 / 서양의 경제적 진보에 있어서

The French historian / Jacques Le Goff / called / the birth of the public mechanical clock / a turning point / in Western society.
프랑스 역사가 / Jacques Le Goff는 / 불렀다. / 공공 기계 시계의 탄생을 / 전환점으로 / 서구 사회에서의

Until the late Middle Ages, / people had / sun or water clocks, / which did not play / any meaningful role / in business activities.
중세 말기까지, / 사람들은 가지고 있었다. / 해시계나 물시계를, / 그것들은 하지 못했다. / 아무런 의미 있는 역할을 / 경제 활동에 있어

Market openings / and activities / started / with the sunrise / and typically ended / at noon / when the sun was / at its peak.
시장 개장 / 그리고 활동들은 / 시작되었다. / 일출과 함께 / 그리고 일반적으로 끝났다. / 정오에 / 태양이 있을 때 / 그것의 최고점에

But / when the first public mechanical clocks / were introduced / and spread / across European cities, / market times / were set / by the stroke of the hour.
그러나 / 최초의 공공 기계 시계들이 / 도입됐을 때 / 그리고 확산되었을 때, / 유럽 도시들 전역으로 / 시장 시간은 / 정해졌다. / 시간을 알리는 소리에 의해

Public clocks / thus greatly contributed / to public life and work / by providing / a new concept of time / that was easy for everyone / to understand.
공공 시계들은 / 따라서 크게 기여했다. / 공공의 생활과 일에 / 제공함으로써 / 새로운 시간 개념을 / 모든 사람에게 쉬운 / 이해하기에

This, / in turn, / helped / facilitate trade and commerce.
이것은, / 결과적으로, / 도움을 주었다. / 무역과 상업을 촉진하는 데

Interactions and transactions / between consumers, retailers, and wholesalers / became less irregular.
상호작용과 거래는 / 소비자, 소매업자, 그리고 도매업자 간의 / 덜 불규칙해졌다.

Important town meetings / began to follow / the pace of the clock, / allowing people / to better plan their time / and allocate resources / in a more efficient manner.
중요한 마을 회의들은 / 따르기 시작했다. / 시계의 페이스를, / 사람들을 허락해 주면서 / 더 그들의 시간을 더 잘 계획하도록 / 그리고 자원들을 분배하도록 / 더 효율적인 방식으로

많은 역사가들은 서양의 경제적 진보에 있어서 정확한 시간 측정의 중요성을 시사해 왔다. 프랑스 역사가 Jacques Le Goff는 공공 기계 시계의 탄생을 서구 사회에서의 전환점이라고 불렀다. 중세 말기까지, 사람들은 해시계와 물시계를 가지고 있었는데, 그것들은 경제 활동에 있어서 아무런 의미 있는 역할을 하지 못했다. 시장 개장과 활동들은 일출과 함께 시작했고 태양이 최고점에 이르는 정오에 일반적으로 끝났다. 그러나 최초의 공공 기계 시계들이 도입되고 유럽 도시들 전역으로 확산되었을 때, 시장 시간은 시간을 알리는 소리에 의해 정해졌다. 따라서 공공 시계들은 모든 사람이 이해하기 쉬운 시간의 새로운 개념을 제공함으로써 공공의 생활과 일에 크게 기여했다. 그 결과, 이것은 무역과 상업을 촉진하는 데 도움을 주었다. 소비자, 소매업자, 그리고 도매업자 간의 상호 작용과 거래는 덜 불규칙해졌다. 중요한 마을 회의는 시계의 페이스를 따르기 시작했고, 이것은 사람들이 그들의 시간을 더 잘 계획하고 더 효율적인 방식으로 자원들을 분배하는 것을 허락해 주었다.

Why? 왜 정답일까?

서양의 경제적 진보에 있어서 시간 측정이 중요했다는 글이다. 특히 공공으로의 시계의 보급은 무역과 상업의 촉진에 도움이 되었다(This, in turn, helped facilitate trade and commerce.)고 하며 시계의 대중 보급이 큰 역할을 했다고 시사한다. 따라서 글의 요지로 가장 적절한 것은 ① '공공 시계는 서양 사회의 경제적 진보에 영향을 미쳤다.'이다.

- historian ⓝ 역사학자
- accurate ⓐ 정확한
- mechanical ⓐ 기계의
- meaningful ⓐ 의미 있는
- stroke ⓝ (시계·종 등의) 치는 소리, 울림
- commerce ⓝ 상업
- transaction ⓝ 거래, 매매
- significance ⓝ 중요성, 중대성
- measurement ⓝ 측량, 측정
- turning point 전환점, 전기
- typically ⓐⓓ 일반적으로, 보통
- contribute ⓥ 기여하다
- interaction ⓝ 상호 작용
- allocate ⓥ 배분하다, 할당하다

구문 풀이

4행 Until the late Middle Ages, people had sun or water clocks, which did not
　　　　~까지　　　　　　　　　　　　　　　　　　　　　주격관계대명사
play any meaningful role in business activities.
　　　　　　　　　　　　　　　　　　　(sun or water clocks)

---

23 쇼핑 카트 사용하기　　정답률 62% | 정답 ①

다음 글의 주제로 가장 적절한 것은?

✔① persuasive power of peer behavior – 군중 행동의 설득적인 힘
② methods to help consumers shop less – 소비자들이 덜 쇼핑하게 돕는 방법
③ innovative ways to reduce waste in retail – 소매에서 쓰레기를 감소시키는 혁신적인 방법
④ hidden nature of human beings to support materialism – 물질주의를 지지하는 인간의 숨은 본성
⑤ importance of a store layout based on customer needs – 소비자들의 필요에 따른 가게 구성의 중요성

Sylvan Goldman / invented / the shopping cart / and introduced it / in his stores / in 1937.
Sylvan Goldman은 / 발명했다. / 쇼핑 카트를 / 그리고 그것을 도입했다. / 그의 가게에 / 1937년에

It was / an excellent device / that would make it easy / for shoppers to buy / as much as they wanted / without getting tired / or seeking others' help.
그것은 / 훌륭한 장치였다. / 쉽게 만들어 준 / 쇼핑객들이 구매하는 것을 / 그들이 원했던 만큼 / 지치거나 / 다른 사람들의 도움을 구하지 않고

But Goldman / discovered / that in spite of his repeated advertisements and explanations, / he could not persuade / his shoppers / to use / the wheeled carts.
그러나 Goldman은 / 알게 됐다. / 그의 반복적인 광고와 설명에도 불구하고, / 그는 설득할 수 없다는 것을 / 그의 쇼핑객들을 / 사용하도록 / 바퀴 달린 카트를.

Men / were reluctant / because they thought / they would appear weak / if they pushed / such carts / instead of carrying / their shopping.
남자들은 / 꺼렸다. / 왜냐하면 그들은 생각했다. / 나약해 보일 것이라고 / 만약 그들이 민다면 / 그런 카트를 / 들고 다니는 대신 / 그들의 쇼핑 물건을

Women / wouldn't touch / them / because the carts / reminded them / of baby carriages.
여성들은 / 손대지 하지 않았다. / 그것들에 / 왜냐하면 그 카트들이 / 그들에게 연상시키기 때문에 / 유모차를

It was only a few elderly shoppers / who used them.
오직 몇 명의 노인 쇼핑객들뿐이었다. / 그것들을 사용하는 사람들은

That / made the carts / even less attractive / to the majority of the shoppers.
그것은 / 카트를 만들었다. / 훨씬 덜 매력적이도록 / 대다수의 쇼핑객들에게

Then Goldman / hit upon / an idea.
그때 Goldman이 / 떠올렸다. / 한 아이디어를
He / hired / several models, / men and women, / of different ages / and asked / them / to wheel the carts / in the store / and shop.
그는 / 고용했다 / 여러 모델들을 / 남자와 여자, / 다른 연령대의 / 그리고 요청했다. / 그들에게 / 카트를 밀도록 / 가게 안에서 / 그리고 쇼핑하도록
A young woman employee / standing near the entrance / told / the regular shoppers, / 'Look, / everyone is using the carts. / Why don't you?'
한 젊은 여성 직원이 / 입구 근처에 서 있던 / 말했다. / 일반 쇼핑객들에게 / '보세요, / 모든 사람이 카트를 사용하고 있습니다. / 해 보는 게 어때세요?'
That was / the turning point.
그것이 / 전환점이었다.
A few shills / disguised as regular shoppers / easily accomplished / what logic, explanations, and advertisements / failed to do.
몇몇 바람잡이들이 / 일반 쇼핑객들로 위장한 / 쉽게 달성했다. / 논리, 설명, 그리고 광고가 / 하지 못한 것을
Within a few weeks / shoppers / readily accepted / those carts.
몇 주 만에 / 쇼핑객들은 / 기꺼이 받아들였다. / 그 카트들을

Sylvan Goldman은 쇼핑 카트를 발명하고 1937년에 그의 가게들에 그것을 도입했다. 그것은 쇼핑객들이 지치거나 다른 사람들의 도움을 구하지 않고 그들이 원했던 만큼 구매하는 것을 쉽게 만들어 준 훌륭한 장치였다. 하지만 Goldman은 그의 반복적인 광고와 설명에도 불구하고, 그의 쇼핑객들에게 바퀴 달린 카트들을 사용하도록 설득할 수 없다는 것을 알게 됐다. 남성들은 그들의 쇼핑한 물건을 들고 다니는 대신 만약 그들이 그런 카트들을 민다면 그들이 나약해 보일 것으로 생각했기 때문에 꺼렸다. 여성들은 카트들이 그들에게 유모차를 연상시키기 때문에 그것들에 손대려 하지 않았다. 그것들을 사용하는 사람들은 오직 몇 명의 노인 쇼핑객들뿐이었다. 그것은 카트들을 대다수 쇼핑객들에게 훨씬 덜 매력적이도록 만들었다. 그때 Goldman이 한 아이디어를 떠올렸다. 그는 다른 연령대의 남자와 여자 모델들을 고용했고, 그들에게 상점에서 카트를 밀고 쇼핑하도록 요청했다. 입구 근처에 서 있던 한 젊은 여성 직원이 일반 쇼핑객들에게 '보세요, 모든 사람이 카트를 사용하고 있습니다. 해 보는 게 어때세요?'라고 말했다. 그것이 전환점이었다. 일반 쇼핑객들로 위장한 바람잡이들이 논리, 설명, 그리고 광고가 하지 못한 것을 쉽게 달성했다. 몇 주 만에 쇼핑객들은 그 카트들을 기꺼이 받아들였다.

Why? 왜 정답일까?
쇼핑 카트가 나약해 보이거나 유모차를 연상시킨다고 생각하여 쇼핑 카트를 사용하지 않았지만, Goldman의 군중 심리를 파악한 아이디어로 모두가 쇼핑 카트를 사용하게 되었다는 글이다. 따라서 제목으로 적절한 것은 ① 'persuasive power of peer behavior'이다.

- introduce ⓥ 도입하다
- discover ⓥ 알아내다
- persuade ⓥ 설득하다
- elderly ⓐ 연세가 드신, 나이가 지긋한
- employee ⓝ 종업원
- shill ⓝ 바람잡이
- accomplish ⓥ 달성하다
- device ⓝ 장치, 기구
- advertisement ⓝ 광고
- reluctant ⓐ 꺼리는
- attractive ⓐ 매력적인
- regular ⓐ 보통의
- disguise ⓥ 변장하다

구문 풀이
17행 A few shills disguised as regular shoppers easily accomplished what
a few + 가산명사　　～로써
logic, explanations, and advertisements failed to do.
　　　　to부정사 명사적 용법

24 로봇 친구에 대한 도덕적 관점　　정답률 49% | 정답 ③

다음 글의 제목으로 가장 적절한 것은?
① The Importance of Protecting Human Dignity
　인간 존엄성을 지키는 것의 중요성
② Robots Can't Surpass Human Beings in Nursing Jobs
　로봇은 요양 직업에서 인간을 능가할 수 없다
③ Why Robots for Vulnerable People Should Look Like Robots
　취약한 사람들에게 로봇이 로봇처럼 보여야 하는 이유
④ Can Robots Learn Ethical Behavior Through Human Interaction?
　로봇이 인간과의 상호 작용을 통해 도덕적인 행동을 배울 수 있는가
⑤ Healthcare Robots: Opening the Era of Online Medical Checkups
　헬스 케어 로봇: 온라인 의료 진료의 시대를 열다

In response to human-like care robots, / critics might charge / that human-robot interactions / create moral hazards / for dementia patients.
인간을 닮은 돌봄 로봇들에 대한 반응으로, / 비평가들은 주장할지도 모른다 / 인간－로봇의 상호작용이 / 도덕적 위험을 만들어 낸다고 / 치매 환자들에게
Even if / deception / is sometimes allowed / when it serves / worthy goals, / should it be allowed / for vulnerable users?
설령 / 속임수가 / 때때로 허용된다고 하더라도 / 그것이 달성할 때 / 가치 있는 목표를, / 그것이 허용되어야 할까? / 취약한 사용자들에게
Just as / children on the autism spectrum / with robot companions / might be easily fooled / into thinking of robots as friends, / older adults / with cognitive deficits / might be.
마치 / 자폐성 스펙트럼을 가진 아이들이 / 로봇 친구가 있는 / 쉽게 속을 수 있는 것처럼 / 로봇을 친구로 생각하도록, / 노인들도 / 인지 결함을 가진 / 그럴 수 있다.
According to Alexis Elder, / a professor at UMD, / robots are / *false* friends, / inferior to true friendship.
Alexis Elder에 따르면, / UMD의 교수인, / 로봇은 / '가짜' 친구이다. / 진정한 우정보다 열등한
Reasoning along similar lines, / John Sullins, / a professor at Sonoma State University, / holds that / robots should "remain iconic / or cartoonish / so that they are / easily distinguished / as synthetic / even by unsophisticated users."
비슷한 방향에서 생각하자면, / John Sullins는 / Sonoma 주립 대학교 교수인 / 주장한다. / 로봇은 "상징적이거나 / 만화같이 / 남아 있어야 한다 / 그래서 그들이 / 쉽게 구별될 수 있도록 / 진짜가 아닌 것으로 / 심지어 순수한 사용자들에 의해서도."
At least then / no one is fooled.
적어도 그러면 / 아무도 속지 않는다.
Making robots / clearly fake / also avoids / the so-called "uncanny valley," / where robots are perceived / as scary / because they / so closely resemble us, / but not quite.
로봇을 만드는 것은 / 명백히 가짜로 / 또한 피하게 한다. / 소위 '불쾌한 골짜기'라고 불리는 것을 / 그곳에서 로봇이 인지된다 / 무섭다고 / 왜냐하면 그것이 / 우리를 아주 가깝게 닮았기 때문에 / 완전히는 아니지만
Other critics / of robot deception / argue that / when care recipients / are deceived into thinking / that robots care, / this crosses a line / and violates / human *dignity*.

다른 비평가들은 / 로봇 속임수에 대한 / 주장한다. / 돌봄을 받는 사람들이 / 생각하도록 속임을 당할 때 / 로봇이 돌봐 준다고 / 이것은 선을 넘는다. / 그리고 침해한다. / 인간의 '존엄성'을

인간을 닮은 돌봄 로봇들에 대한 반응으로, 비평가들은 인간－로봇의 상호 작용이 치매 환자들에게 도덕적 위험을 만들어 낸다고 비난할지도 모른다. 속임수가 그것이 가치 있는 목표를 달성할 때 때때로 허용된다고 하더라도, 취약한 사용자들에게 그것이 허용되어야 할까? 로봇 친구가 있는 자폐성 스펙트럼을 가진 아이들이 로봇을 친구로 생각하도록 쉽게 속을 수 있는 것처럼, 인지 결함을 가진 노인들도 그럴 수 있다. UMD의 교수인 Alexis Elder에 따르면, 로봇은 진정한 우정보다, 열등한 '가짜' 친구이다. 비슷한 방향에서 생각하자면, Sonoma 주립 대학교 교수인 John Sullins는 로봇이 '심지어 순수한 사용자들에 의해서도 그것들이 진짜가 아닌 것으로 쉽게 구별될 수 있도록 상징적이거나 만화같이 남아 있어야 한다.'라고 주장한다. 적어도 그러면 아무도 속지 않는다. 로봇을 명백히 가짜로 만드는 것은 또한 로봇이 우리를 완전히는 아니지만, 아주 가깝게 닮았기 때문에 무섭다고 인지되는 소위 '불쾌한 골짜기'라고 불리는 것을 피하게 한다. 로봇 속임수에 대한 다른 비평가들은 돌봄을 받는 사람들이 로봇이 돌봐 준다고 생각하도록 속임을 당할 때, 이것은 선을 넘고 인간의 '존엄성'을 침해한다고 주장한다.

Why? 왜 정답일까?
취약한 사용자들에게 사람과 똑같이 생긴 로봇 친구는 인간의 '존엄성'을 침해하는 도덕적 위험을 만들어 낸다(Other critics of robot deception argue that when care recipients are deceived into thinking that robots care, this crosses a line and violates human dignity.)고 주장한다. 따라서 글의 제목으로 가장 적절한 것은 ③ 'Why Robots for Vulnerable People Should Look Like Robots'이다.

- response ⓝ 답변
- charge ⓥ 고소하다
- dementia ⓝ 치매
- vulnerable ⓐ 취약한, 연약한
- cognitive ⓐ 인지의, 인식의
- critic ⓝ 비평가
- moral hazard 도덕적 위험
- deception ⓝ 속임수
- autism ⓝ 자폐성
- inferior ⓐ 열등한

구문 풀이
15행 Other critics of robot deception argue that when care recipients
　　　　　　　　　　　　　　　　　　　접속사　　～때
are deceived into thinking that robots care, this crosses a line and violates human
　수동태　　　　　　　접속사　　　　　　　　　동사1　　　　　　　　　동사2
dignity.

25 2019년 표적 온라인 광고에 대한 미국인의 견해　　정답률 89% | 정답 ④

다음 도표의 내용과 일치하지 않는 것은?

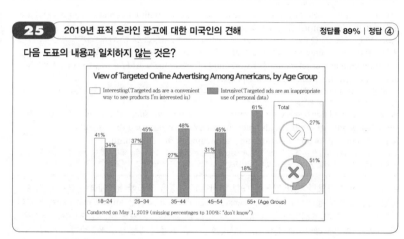

View of Targeted Online Advertising Among Americans, by Age Group
□ Interesting(Targeted ads are a convenient way to see products I'm interested in.)　■ Intrusive(Targeted ads are an inappropriate use of personal data)

Age Group	Interesting	Intrusive
18–24	41%	34%
25–34	37%	45%
35–44	48%	27%
45–54	31%	45%
55+	18%	61%
Total	27%	51%

Conducted on May 1, 2019. (missing percentages to 100%: "don't know")

The graph above / shows / the results of a 2019 survey on / the views of American age groups / on targeted online advertising.
위의 그래프는 / 보여 준다. / 2019년 설문 조사의 결과를 / 미국 연령층의 견해에 관한 / 표적 온라인 광고에 대한
① In total, / while 51% of the respondents said / targeted ads were intrusive, / 27% said / they were interesting.
전체적으로, / 응답자의 51%는 말한 반면, / 표적 광고들이 침해적이라고, / 27%는 대답하였다. / 그것들이 흥미롭다고
② The percentage of respondents / who believed that targeted ads were interesting / was the highest / in the age group of 18 to 24.
응답자의 비율은 / 표적 광고들이 흥미롭다고 믿는 / 가장 높았다. / 18세에서 24세 연령층에서
③ The percentage of respondents aged 25 to 34 / who said that targeted ads were intrusive / was the same as that / of respondents aged 45 to 54 / who said the same.
25세에서 34세 응답자들의 비율은 / 표적 광고들이 침해적이라고 응답한 / 그것과 똑같았다. / 45세에서 54세의 응답자들 / 똑같이 응답한
④ Among all age groups, / the gap between respondents / who said targeted ads were interesting / and those who believed them to be intrusive / was the largest / in the 35-to-44 age group.
모든 연령층에서, / 응답자들 간의 차이는 / 표적 광고들이 흥미롭다 말한 응답자들과 / 그것들이 침해적이라고 믿는 응답자들 / 가장 컸다. / 35세에서 44세의 연령층에서
⑤ The age group of 55 and above / was the only group / where the percentage of respondents / who believed targeted ads were intrusive / was more than 50%.
55세 이상의 연령층은 / 유일한 집단이었다. / 응답자들의 비율이 / 표적 광고들이 침해적이라고 믿는 / 50%가 넘는

위의 그래프는 표적 온라인 광고에 대한 미국 연령층들의 견해에 관한 2019년 설문 조사의 결과를 보여 준다. ① 전체적으로, 응답자의 51%는 표적 광고들이 침해적이라고 말한 반면, 27%는 그것들이 흥미롭다고 대답하였다. ② 표적 광고들이 흥미롭다고 믿는 응답자들의 비율은 18세와 24세 연령층에서 가장 높았다. ③ 표적 광고들이 침해적이라고 응답한 25세에서 34세 응답자들의 비율은 똑같이 응답한 45세에서 54세 응답자들의 그것과 똑같았다. ④ 모든 연령층에서, 표적 광고들이 흥미롭다고 말한 응답자들과 그것들이 침해적이라고 믿는 응답자들 간의 차이는 35세에서 44세 연령층에서 가장 컸다. ⑤ 55세 이상의 연령층은 표적 광고들이 침해적이라고 믿는 응답자들의 비율이 50%가 넘는 유일한 집단이었다.

Why? 왜 정답일까?
광고가 흥미롭다고 한 응답자와 침해적이라고 믿는 응답자 간의 차이는 55세 이상의 연령층에서 가장 컸기 때문에, 도표의 내용과 일치하지 않는 것은 ④ 'Among all age groups, the gap between respondents who said targeted ads were interesting and those who believed them

to be intrusive was the largest in the 35-to-44 age group.'이다.

- **survey** ⓝ 조사
- **advertisement** ⓝ 광고
- **intrusive** ⓐ 침해적
- **targeted** ⓐ 표적이 된
- **respondent** ⓝ 응답자

구문 풀이

8행 Among all age groups, the gap between respondents who said targeted
〜중에 　　　　　　주어　　　　　　　　주격관계대명사
ads were interesting and those who believed them to be intrusive was the largest
　　　　　　　　　　　　　　　 주격관계대명사　 targeted ads　 동사↵　 최상급
in the 35-to-44 age group.

---

26 Maggie L. Walker의 일생　　　　　정답률 80% | 정답 ③

Maggie L. Walker에 관한 다음 글의 내용과 일치하지 않는 것은?
① 아프리카계 미국인을 위해 설립된 학교에 다녔다.
② 졸업 후 자신이 공부했던 학교에서 교사로 일했다.
☑ 인종 차별로 인해 은행 금융법 공부를 시작할 수 없었다.
④ 자선 단체와 대중 간의 소통을 장려하고자 신문을 설립했다.
⑤ 그녀가 설립한 은행은 대공황에서 살아남아 다른 은행들과 합병했다.

Maggie L. Walker / achieved national prominence / as a businesswoman and community leader.
Maggie L. Walker는 / 전국적 명성을 얻었다. / 여성 사업가와 커뮤니티 리더로서
『She / was among the earliest Black students / to attend newly-established public schools / for African Americans.』①의근거 일치
그녀는 / 초기 흑인 학생들 중 하나였다. / 새롭게 설립된 공립 학교에 다닌 / 아프리카계 미국인들을 위해
『After graduating, / she worked as a teacher / for three years / at the Valley School, / where she had studied.』②의근거 일치
졸업 이후, / 그녀는 교사로 근무했다. / 3년 동안 / Valley School에서, / 그녀가 공부했던
In the early 1900s, / Virginia banks owned by white bankers / were unwilling to do business / with African American organizations or individuals.
1900년대 초반에, / 백인 은행가들에 의해 소유된 Virginia의 은행들은 / 거래하기를 꺼렸다. / 아프리카계 미국인의 단체나 개인들과
『The racial discrimination by white bankers / drove her / to study banking and financial laws.』③의근거 불일치
백인 은행가들에 의한 인종 차별은 / 그녀로 하여금 만들었다. / 은행 금융법을 공부하도록
『She / established / a newspaper / to promote closer communication / between the charitable organization she belonged to / and the public.』④의근거 일치
그녀는 / 설립했다. / 신문사를 / 더 긴밀한 소통을 장려하고자 / 그녀가 속한 자선 단체와 / 대중 간의
『Soon after, / she / founded the St. Luke Penny Savings Bank, / which survived the Great Depression / and merged with two other banks.』⑤의근거 일치
곧이어, / 그녀는 / 설립했다. / St. Luke Penny Savings Bank를, / 이 은행은 대공황에서 살아남아 / 두 개의 다른 은행들과 합병했다.
It / thrived / as the oldest continually African American-operated bank / until 2009.
그것은 / 번창했다. / 가장 오래된 지속적인 아프리카계 미국인 운영 은행으로서 / 2009년까지.
Walker / achieved successes / with the vision to make improvements / in the way of life for African Americans.
Walker는 / 성공을 거두었다. / 개선을 이루고자 하는 비전으로 / 아프리카계 미국인들을 위한 삶의 방식에서

Maggie L. Walker는 여성 사업가와 커뮤니티 리더로서 전국적 명성을 얻었다. 그녀는 아프리카계 미국인들을 위해 새롭게 설립된 공립 학교에 다닌 초기 흑인 학생들 중 하나였다. 졸업 이후, 그녀는 그녀가 공부했던 Valley School에서 교사로서 3년 동안 근무했다. 1900년대 초반에, 백인 은행가들에 의해 소유된 Virginia의 은행들은 아프리카계 미국인의 단체나 개인들과 거래하기를 꺼렸다. 백인 은행가들에 의한 인종 차별은 그녀로 하여금 은행 금융법을 공부하게 만들었다. 그녀는 그녀가 속한 자선 단체와 대중 간의 더 긴밀한 소통을 장려하고자 신문사를 설립했다. 곧이어, 그녀는 St. Luke Penny Savings Bank를 설립했는데, 그것은 대공황에서 살아남아 두 개의 다른 은행들과 합병했다. 그것은 2009년까지 지속적으로 아프리카계 미국인에 의해 운영되는 가장 오래된 은행으로서 번창했다. Walker는 아프리카계 미국인들을 위한 삶의 방식에서 개선을 이루고자 하는 비전으로 성공을 거두었다.

Why? 왜 정답일까?
인종 차별로 인해 은행 금융법 공부를 시작했다(The racial discrimination by white bankers drove her to study banking and financial laws.)고 했으므로 글의 내용과 일치하지 않는 것은 ③ '인종 차별로 인해 은행 금융법 공부를 시작할 수 없었다.'이다.

Why? 왜 오답일까?
① 'She was among the earliest Black students to attend newly-established public schools for African Americans.'의 내용과 일치한다.
② 'After graduating, she worked as a teacher for three years at the Valley School, where she had studied.'의 내용과 일치한다.
④ 'She established a newspaper to promote closer communication between the charitable organization she belonged to and the public.'의 내용과 일치한다.
⑤ 'Soon after, she founded the St. Luke Penny Savings Bank, which survived the Great Depression and merged with two other banks.'의 내용과 일치한다.

- **prominence** ⓝ 명성
- **individual** ⓝ 개인
- **merge** ⓥ 합병하다
- **organization** ⓝ 조직
- **promote** ⓥ 홍보하다

구문 풀이

4행 After graduating, she worked as a teacher for three years at the Valley
　　　　　　동명사
School, where she had studied.
관계부사 　　　　～로써

---

27 2024 Youth Tennis Camp　　　정답률 94% | 정답 ④

2024 Youth Tennis Camp에 관한 다음 안내문의 내용과 일치하지 않는 것은?

① 자격을 가진 테니스 선수가 지도한다.
② 금요일에는 강습이 없다.
③ 등록비에는 점심 식사가 포함된다.
☑ 강습 당일 취소 시 환불받을 수 있다.
⑤ 참가자들은 테니스 장비를 가져와야 한다.

2024 Youth Tennis Camp
2024 청소년 테니스 캠프
『2024 Youth Tennis Camp / is where your child can get instruction / from qualified tennis players / at indoor tennis courts.』①의근거 일치
2024 청소년 테니스 캠프는 / 여러분의 자녀가 지도를 받을 수 있는 곳입니다. / 자격을 가진 테니스 선수들로부터 / 실내 테니스 코트에서
It / will provide / fundamental tennis skills / to your children!
그것은 / 제공할 것입니다! / 기본적인 테니스 기술을 / 여러분의 자녀들에게
Who: Ages 13 to 18
누가: 13세부터 18세까지
When: January 15 – 18, 2024
언제: 2024년 1월 15일부터 18일까지
『Monday to Thursday, 9:00 a.m. – 12:00 p.m.』②의근거 일치
월요일부터 목요일까지, 오전 9시 – 오후 12시
『Registration Fee: $100 (lunch included)』③의근거 일치
등록비: $100 (점심 식사 포함)
Cancellation Policy
취소 방침
5 days before the class: 100% refund
강습 5일 전까지: 100% 환불
1 – 4 days before the class: 50% refund
강습 1 – 4일 전까지: 50% 환불
『On the day of the class and afterwards: No refund』④의근거 불일치
강습 당일 이후: 환불 불가
Notes
참고
No outside food / is allowed.
외부 음식은 / 허용되지 않습니다.
『Participants / must bring / their own tennis equipment.』⑤의근거 일치
참가자들은 / 가져와야 합니다. / 자신들의 테니스 장비를
Registration / is ONLY available online / and will start / on December 16.
등록은 / 온라인으로만 가능하며, / 시작할 것입니다. / 12월 16일에
Visit our website at / www.ytc2024.com / to register.
우리의 웹사이트를 방문해 주세요. / www.ytc2024.com / 등록을 위해

2024 청소년 테니스 캠프

2024 청소년 테니스 캠프는 여러분의 자녀가 실내 테니스 코트에서 자격을 가진 테니스 선수들로부터 지도를 받을 수 있는 곳입니다. 그것은 기본적인 테니스 기술들을 여러분의 자녀들에게 제공할 것입니다!

누가: 13세부터 18세까지
언제: 2024년 1월 15일부터 18일까지
　　　월요일부터 목요일까지, 오전 9시 – 오후 12시
등록비: $100(점심 식사 포함)

취소 방침
• 강습 5일 전까지: 100% 환불
• 강습 1-4일 전까지: 50% 환불
• 강습 당일 이후: 환불 불가

참고
• 외부 음식은 허용되지 않습니다.
• 참가자들은 자신들의 테니스 장비를 가져와야 합니다.

등록은 온라인으로만 가능하며, 12월 16일에 시작할 것입니다. 등록을 위해 우리의 웹사이트인 www.ytc2024.com을 방문해 주세요.

Why? 왜 정답일까?
'Cancellation Policy'의 'On the day of the class and afterwards: No refund'에 따르면 강습 당일 취소 시 환불을 받을 수 없다고 했으므로 안내문의 내용과 일치하지 않는 것은 ④ '강습 당일 취소 시 환불 받을 수 있다.'이다.

Why? 왜 오답일까?
① '2024 Youth Tennis Camp is where your child can get instruction from qualified tennis players at indoor tennis courts.'의 내용과 일치한다.
② 'Monday to Thursday, 9:00 a.m. – 12:00 p.m.'의 내용과 일치한다.
③ 'Registration Fee: $100(lunch included)'의 내용과 일치한다.
⑤ 'Participants must bring their own tennis equipment.'의 내용과 일치한다.

- **instruction** ⓝ 지도
- **indoor** ⓐ 실내의
- **refund** ⓝ 환불
- **qualified** ⓐ 자격이 있는
- **fundamental** ⓐ 기초의

---

28 Cherrywood 고등학교 티셔츠 디자인 대회　　정답률 92% | 정답 ④

Cherrywood High School's T-shirt Design Contest에 관한 다음 안내문의 내용과 일치하는 것은?
① 교사들이 수상 디자인을 선정할 예정이다.
② 수상자 발표일은 제출 마감일 다음 날이다.
③ 출품작은 학생회실에 제출해야 한다.
☑ 종이에 자신의 학번과 이름을 써야 한다.
⑤ 사용 가능한 색상 수에 제한이 없다.

Cherrywood High School's T-shirt Design Contest

체리우드 고등학교의 티셔츠 디자인 대회
Help us / to design / our new school shirts!
우리를 도와주세요! / 디자인하는 것을 / 우리의 새로운 학교 셔츠를
『A panel of student council members / will select / the winning design.』 ①의 근거 불일치
학생회 위원들의 패널이 / 선정할 것입니다. / 수상 디자인을
Take this chance / at being the designer / for the new school T-shirt.
기회를 잡으세요. / 디자이너가 될 / 새 학교 티셔츠의
This contest / is open / to all students!
이 대회는 / 열려 있습니다! / 모든 학생에게
Submission Deadline: 16:00 on December 22, 2023
제출 마감 기한: / 2023년 12월 22일 16:00
『Winner Announcement Date: December 29, 2023』 ②의 근거 불일치
수상자 발표일: 2023년 12월 29일
『Location for Submissions: Art Teacher's Office』 ③의 근거 불일치
제출 장소: 미술 교사의 사무실
Contest Rules
대회 규칙
Sketch your design / on a piece of plain paper.
여러분의 디자인을 스케치하세요. / 백지 한 장에
『Write your student number and name / on your paper.』 ④의 근거 일치
여러분의 학생 번호와 이름을 쓰세요. / 종이에
Include the school name and logo / in your design.
학교 이름과 로고를 포함하세요. / 여러분의 디자인에
『Max of 4 colors / can be used.』 ⑤의 근거 불일치
최대 4개의 색상이 / 사용될 수 있습니다.
Good luck / and thanks / for your participation!
행운을 빕니다. / 그리고 감사합니다. / 참여해 주셔서!

Cherrywood 고등학교 티셔츠 디자인 대회

우리가 우리의 새로운 학교 티셔츠를 디자인하는 것을 도와주세요! 학생회 위원단이 수상 디자인을 선정할 것입니다. 새로운 학교 티셔츠의 디자이너가 되는 이 기회를 잡으세요. 이 대회는 모든 학생에게 열려 있습니다!

제출 마감 기한: 2023년 12월 22일 16시
수상자 발표일: 2023년 12월 29일
제출 장소: 미술 교사 사무실

대회 규칙
• 백지 한 장에 여러분의 디자인을 스케치하세요.
• 여러분의 종이에 여러분의 학번과 이름을 쓰세요.
• 학교 이름과 로고를 여러분의 디자인에 포함하세요.
• 최대 4개의 색상이 사용될 수 있습니다.

행운을 빌며 참여해 주셔서 감사합니다!

Why? 왜 정답일까?
'Write your student number and name on your paper.'에서 얘기하듯, 종이에 자신의 학번과 이름을 써야 한다고 했으므로 안내문의 내용과 일치하는 것은 ④ '종이에 자신의 학번과 이름을 써야 한다.'이다.

Why? 왜 오답일까?
① 'A panel of student council members will select the winning design.'라고 하였기 때문에 학생 패널이 수상 디자인을 선정할 예정이다.
② 'Submission Deadline'이 22일이고, 'Winner Announcement Date'가 29일이므로 수상자 발표일은 제출 마감일 일주일 후이다.
③ 'Location for Submissions: Art Teacher's Office'에서 출품작을 미술 선생님의 사무실에 제출해야 함을 알 수 있다.
⑤ 'Max of 4 colors can be used'에서 사용 가능한 색상 수가 4가지임을 알 수 있다.

● contest ⓝ 대회
● council ⓝ 의회
● announcement ⓝ 발표
● design ⓥ 디자인하다
● submission ⓝ 제출

---

29 렉틴의 역할 정답률 55% | 정답 ⑤

다음 글의 밑줄 친 부분 중, 어법상 틀린 것은?

Lectins / are large proteins / that serve as a crucial weapon / that plants use to defend / ① themselves.
렉틴은 / 큰 단백질이다. / 중요한 무기로서 역할을 하는 / 식물이 방어하기 위해 사용하는 / 그들 스스로를
The lectins in most plants / bind to carbohydrates / as we consume the plant.
대부분의 식물에서의 렉틴은 / 탄수화물에 결합한다. / 우리가 식물을 섭취할 때.
They / also / bind to sugar molecules / ② found in the gut, / in the brain, / between nerve endings, / in joints and in all bodily fluids.
그들은 / 또한 / 당 분자에 결합한다. / 장에서 발견되는, / 뇌에서, / 신경 말단 사이에서, / 관절과 모든 체액에서
According to Dr. Steven Gundry, / these sticky proteins / can interrupt messaging / between cells and / ③ cause toxic and inflammatory reactions.
Steven Gundry 박사에 따르면, / 이러한 끈적한 단백질은 / 메시지 전달을 방해할 수 있으며 / 세포 간의 / 독성 및 염증 반응을 유발한다.
Brain fog / is just one result / of lectins interrupting communication / between nerves.
두뇌 흐림증은 / 단지 한 가지 결과일 뿐이다. / 렉틴이 소통을 방해할 때. / 신경 간의
An upset stomach / is another common symptom / of lectin overload.
속이 불편한 것은 / 또 다른 일반적인 증상이다. / 렉틴 과다 섭취로 인한.
Dr. Gundry / lists / a wide range of other health problems / including aching joints, / dementia, / headaches and infertility / ④ that have been resolved in his patients / once they eliminated lectins from their diets.
Gundry 박사는 / 나열한다. / 광범위한 다양한 건강문제들을 / 아픈 관절, / 치매, / 두통 및 불임을 포함한 / 그의 환자들에게서 해결되어 왔던 / 그들의 식단에서 렉틴을 제거했을 때.
Dr. Paul Saladino / writes / that the hypothesis / that lectins are involved in Parkinson's disease / is also gaining support, / with animal studies / ✓ showing that / 'lectins, once eaten, / may be damaging the gut / and travelling to the brain, / where they appear to be toxic / to dopaminergic neurons'.

Paul Saladino 박사는 / 기록한다. / 그 가설이 / 렉틴이 파킨슨병에 관련되어 있다는 / 지지를 얻고 있다고, / 동물 연구들과 함께 / 그것을 보여주는 / '렉틴이 한 번 섭취되면 / 장을 손상시킬 수 있으며 / 뇌로 이동하여, / 독성을 일으키는 것처럼 보이는 / 도파민 작동성 신경 세포'

렉틴은 식물들이 그들 스스로를 방어하기 위해 사용하는 중요한 무기로서 역할을 하는 커다란 단백질이다. 대부분의 식물에 있는 렉틴은 우리가 식물을 섭취할 때 탄수화물과 결합한다. 그것들은 또한 장, 뇌, 신경 말단 사이, 관절 및 모든 체액에서 발견되는 당 분자들과 결합한다. Dr. Steven Gundry에 따르면, 이러한 끈적끈적한 단백질은 세포들 간의 메시지 전달을 방해하고 독성 및 염증성의 반응을 일으킬 수 있다. 뇌 피로 현상은 렉틴이 신경들 간의 소통을 방해하는 단지 하나의 결과에 지나지 않는다. 위장 장애는 렉틴 과다의 또 다른 흔한 증상이다. Dr. Gundry는 그의 환자들이 자신의 식단에서 렉틴을 제거하였을 때 해결되어 왔던 관절통, 치매, 두통, 그리고 불임을 포함한 광범위한 다양한 건강 문제들을 나열한다. Dr. Paul Saladino는 렉틴이 파킨슨병과 관련이 있다는 가설이 '렉틴이 일단 섭취되면, 장에 손상을 입히고 뇌로 이동해 그곳에서 그것들이 도파민 작동성 신경 세포에 독성을 일으키는 것처럼 보인다.'는 것을 보여 주는 동물 연구들과 함께 또한 지지를 얻고 있다고 기록한다.

Why? 왜 정답일까?
that절의 study를 꾸며줘야 하므로 'showed' 대신 'showing'이 오는 것이 알맞다.

Why? 왜 오답일까?
① 주어와 같은 'they'가 목적어로 왔으므로 재귀대명사 'themselves'가 오는 것이 알맞다.
② 'molcules (that are) found'이므로, 'found'가 오는 것이 알맞다.
③ 'these sticky proteins'를 주어로 하고, 'interrupt'와 병렬이므로 'cause'가 오는 것이 적절하다.
④ 뒤 문장에 주어가 없으므로 주격관계대명사 'that'이 오는 것이 알맞다.

● protein ⓝ 단백질
● weapon ⓝ 무기
● inflammatory ⓐ 염증성의
● crucial ⓐ 중요한
● eliminate ⓥ 제거하다

구문 풀이

13행 Dr. Paul Saladino writes that the hypothesis that lectins are involved in [접속사] [접속사] Parkinson's disease is also gaining support, with animal studies showing that [현재분사] [접속사] 'lectins, once eaten, may be damaging the gut and travelling to the brain, where [현재분사1] [현재분사2] [관계부사] they appear to be toxic to dopaminergic neurons'.

---

30 감시 카메라 확산에 대한 입장 정답률 55% | 정답 ⑤

다음 글의 밑줄 친 부분 중, 문맥상 낱말의 쓰임이 적절하지 않은 것은? [3점]

Technology / changes / how individuals and societies understand / the concept of privacy.
기술은 / 변화시킨다. / 개인과 사회가 이해하는 방식을 / 사생활의 개념에 대해
The fact / that someone has a new ability / to access information or watch the actions of another / does not ① justify / doing so.
그 사실은 / 누군가가 새로운 능력을 갖고 있다는 / 다른 사람의 정보에 접근하거나 행동을 관찰하는 / 정당화하지 않는다. / 그렇게 하는 것을
Rather, / advances in technology / require / citizens and policy makers to consider / how privacy protections should be expanded.
오히려, / 기술의 발전은 / 요구한다. / 시민들과 정책 입안자들이 고려할 것을 / 어떻게 사생활 보호가 확장되어야 하는지
For example, / when cameras first became available / for commercial and private use, / nations and citizens / struggled / over whether new laws should be enacted / to ② protect individuals / from being photographed / without their permission.
예를 들어, / 카메라가 처음으로 사용될 수 있게 되었을 때 / 상업적 및 개인적 용도로 / 국가와 시민들은 / 투쟁했다. / 새로운 법이 제정되어야 하는지에 대해 / 개인을 보호하기 위해 / 사진에 찍히는 것으로부터 / 그들의 허가 없이
The ③ reconsideration of privacy / brought about by this new technology / re-affirmed a distinction / between private and public spaces.
사생활에 대한 재고는 / 이 새로운 기술이 가져온 / 구별을 재확인했다. / 사적 및 공적 공간의
It was determined by most cultures / that people automatically gave ④ consent / to being seen — and thus recorded — / once they voluntarily stepped / into a public space.
대부분의 문화에서 결정되었다. / 사람들이 자발적으로 동의하는 것으로 / 보여지고, 따라서 녹화되는 것에 / 일단 사람들이 자발적으로 발을 들여놓으면 / 공공장소에
Although some people / might be uncomfortable / with the spread of surveillance cameras, / citizens in most cultures / have adjusted to the fact / that giving up the right not to be observed / in these circumstances / causes ✓ less harm to the community / than failing to have surveillance.
일부 사람들은 / 불편하게 여겨질지도 모르지만 / 감시 카메라들의 확산을, / 대부분의 문화권에 있는 시민들은 / 사실에 순응해 왔다. / 관찰되지 않을 권리를 포기하는 것이 / 이러한 상황에서 / 더 적은 해를 끼친다는 / 감시받지 못하는 것보다.

기술은 개인들과 사회가 사생활의 개념을 이해하는 방식을 변화시킨다. 누군가가 정보에 접근하거나 다른 사람의 행동을 관찰하는 새로운 능력을 갖추고 있다는 사실은 그렇게 하는 것을 ① 정당화하지 않는다. 오히려, 기술의 발전은 시민들과 정책 입안자들이 어떻게 사생활 보호가 확장되어야 하는지 고려할 것을 요구한다. 예를 들어, 카메라들이 상업적이고 사적인 용도로 처음 사용될 수 있게 되었을 때, 국가들과 시민들은 그들의 허가 없이 개인이 사진에 찍히는 것으로부터 ② 보호하기 위해 새로운 법들이 제정되어야 하는지에 대해 투쟁했다. 이 새로운 기술이 가져온 사생활에 대한 ③ 재고는 사적 및 공적 공간의 구별을 재확인했다. 일단 사람들이 자발적으로 공공장소에 발을 들여놓으면, 보여지고, 따라서 녹화되는 것에 자동적으로 ④ 동의하는 것으로 대부분의 문화에서 결정되었다. 일부 사람들은 감시 카메라들의 확산을 불편하게 여길지도 모르지만, 대부분의 문화권에 있는 시민들은 이러한 상황에서 관찰되지 않을 권리를 포기하는 것이 감시받지 못하는 것보다 지역 사회에 ⑤ 더 많은(→ 더 적은) 해를 끼친다는 사실에 순응해 왔다.

Why? 왜 정답일까?
감시 카메라의 확장에 대한 찬성과 반대의 입장을 설명하는 글이다. 감시 카메라의 확산을 불편해 할지도 모르지만, 대부분의 사람들은 감시 카메라가 지역 사회에 기여하는 바가 크다고 동의한다고 하였으므로, 더 많은 해가 아닌 더 적은 해를 끼친다는 문장이 알맞다. 따라서 ⑤ 'more'를 'less'로 바꾸는 것이 적절하다.

● technology ⓝ 기술
● access ⓥ 접근하다

- **citizen** ⓝ 시민
- **commercial** ⓐ 상업의, 상업적인
- **privacy** ⓝ 사생활
- **consent** ⓥ 동의하다
- **surveillance** ⓝ 감시
- **protection** ⓝ 보호
- **permission** ⓝ 허락, 허가
- **distinction** ⓝ 구별, 차이
- **voluntarily** ⓐ 자발적으로, 자진해서

구문 풀이

4행 Rather, advances in technology require citizens and policy makers
주어 / 동사
to consider how privacy protections should be expanded.
to부정사 / 관계부사(= the way)

---

31 기적이 아닌 기적
정답률 46% | 정답 ①

다음 빈칸에 들어갈 말로 가장 적절한 것을 고르시오. [3점]

✓① ignorance – 무지
② flexibility – 유연성
③ excellence – 멋짐
④ satisfaction – 만족
⑤ exaggeration – 과장

Coincidence / that is statistically impossible / seems / to us / like an irrational event, / and some / define / it / as a miracle.
우연은 / 통계적으로 불가능한 / 보인다. / 우리에게 / 비이성적인 사건처럼 / 그리고 어떤 이들은 / 정의한다. / 그것을 / 기적이라고

But, / as Montaigne has said, / "the origin of a miracle / is in our ignorance, / at the level of our knowledge of nature, / and not in nature itself."
하지만, / 몽테뉴가 말했듯이, / "기적의 기원은 / 우리의 무지에 있다. / 자연에 대한 우리의 지식수준에서, / 자연 그 자체가 아니라."

Glorious miracles / have been later on discovered / to be obedience / to the laws of nature / or a technological development / that was not widely known / at the time.
영광스러운 기적들은 / 나중에 발견되어 왔다. / 순응으로서 / 자연의 법칙에 대한 / 혹은 기술적 발전으로서 / 널리 알려지지 않았던 / 당시에는

As the German poet, / Goethe, / phrased it: / "Things that are *mysterious* / are *not* yet / *miracles.*"
독일 시인인 / Goethe가 / 말하길: / "*신비한* 것들은 / 아직 *아니다.* / *기적이*"

The miracle / assumes the intervention of a "higher power" / in its occurrence / that is beyond / human capability to grasp.
기적은 / 가정한다. / '더 높은 힘'의 개입을 / 그것의 발생에 있어서 / 그 너머에 있는 / 인간이 이해할 수 있는 능력

Yet / there are methodical and simple ways / to "cause a miracle" / without divine revelation and inspiration.
그러나 / 체계적이고 간단한 방법들이 있다. / '기적을 일으키는' / 신적인 계시와 영감 없이

Instead of checking it out, / investigating and finding / the source of the event, / we / define / it / as a miracle.
그것을 확인하는 것 대신에 / 조사하고 찾는 것 / 그 사건의 근원 / 우리는 / 정의한다. / 그것을 / 기적으로

The miracle, / then, / is the excuse / of those who are too lazy / to think.
기적은 / 그렇다면 / 핑계이다. / 너무 게으른 사람들의 / 생각하는 데

통계적으로 불가능한 우연은 우리에게 비이성적인 사건처럼 보이고, 어떤 이들은 그것을 기적으로 정의한다. 그러나, Montaigne가 말했듯이, "기적의 기원은 자연 그 자체가 아니라 자연에 대한 우리의 지식수준에서, 우리의 무지에 있다." 영광스러운 기적들은 자연의 법칙에 대한 순응으로서, 혹은 당시에는 널리 알려지지 않았던 기술적 발전으로서 나중에 발견되어 왔다. 독일 시인 Goethe가 그것을 표현했듯이, "'*신비한*' 것들은 아직 '*기적*'이 '*아니다*'." 기적은 그것의 발생에 있어서 인간이 이해할 수 있는 능력 너머의 '더 높은 힘'의 개입을 가정한다. 하지만, 신적인 계시와 영감 없이 '기적을 일으키는' 체계적이고 간단한 방법들이 있다. 그것을 확인하는 것, 즉, 그 사건의 근원을 조사하고 찾는 것 대신에, 우리는 그것을 기적으로 정의한다. 그렇다면, 기적은 생각하는 데 너무 게으른 사람들의 핑계이다.

Why? 왜 정답일까?

기적이 사실은 기적이 아니라는 글이다. 기적은 자연의 법칙에 대한 순응이며, 기술적 발전으로 설명이 된다(Glorious miracles have been later on discovered to be obedience to the laws of nature or a technological development that was not widely known at the time.)고 하기 때문에 빈칸에 들어갈 알맞은 말은 ① 'ignorance'이다.

- **statistically** ⓐ 통계적으로
- **define** ⓥ 정의하다, 규정하다
- **ignorance** ⓝ 무지, 무식
- **phrase** ⓥ 표현하다, 말로 나타내다
- **intervention** ⓝ 개입
- **divine** ⓐ 신의, 신성한
- **excuse** ⓝ 변명
- **irrational** ⓐ 비합리적인
- **miracle** ⓝ 기적
- **obedience** ⓝ 순응, 복종
- **assume** ⓥ 가정하다, 추정하다
- **methodical** ⓐ 체계적인
- **revelation** ⓝ 계시

구문 풀이

5행 Glorious miracles have been later on discovered to be obedience to the
수동태 현재완료
laws of nature or a technological development that was not widely known at the
주격관계대명사 / 수동태
time.

★★★ 등급을 가르는 문제!

32 불완전한 진술
정답률 29% | 정답 ①

다음 빈칸에 들어갈 말로 가장 적절한 것을 고르시오. [3점]

✓① this new information will be rejected
새로운 정보가 거부될 것이다
② people will deny the experience of forgetting
사람들은 잊어버리는 경험을 거부할 것이다
③ interference between conflicting data will occur
충돌하는 정보끼리의 방해가 일어날 것이다
④ the unconscious will be involved in the recall process
다시 떠올리는 과정에서 무의식이 관여할 것이다
⑤ a recent event will last longer in memory than a distant one
최근의 사건이 과거의 더 먼 기억보다 오래 기억에 남을 것이다

Information / encountered after an event / can influence / subsequent remembering.
정보는 / 사건 이후에 접한 / 영향을 줄 수 있다. / 이후의 기억하는 것에

External information / can easily integrate / into a witness's memory, / especially / if the

---

event / was poorly encoded / or the memory / is from a distant event, / in which case time and forgetting / have degraded / the original memory.
외부 정보는 / 쉽게 통합될 수 있다. / 목격자의 기억 / 특히 / 사건이 / 불충분하게 부호화되었거나 / 기억이 / 먼 사건으로부터 온 것이라면, / 시간과 망각이 / 저하시켜 온 / 원래의 기억

With reduced information / available in memory / with which to confirm / the validity of post-event misinformation, / it is less likely / that this new information will be rejected.
줄어든 정보를 가지면 / 기억에서 사용할 수 있는 / 확인하기 위해 / 유효성 / 사건 후의 잘못된 정보의 / 덜 그럴 듯하다. / 이 새로운 정보가 / 거부될 것

Instead, / especially when it fits / the witness's current thinking / and can be used / to create a story / that makes sense / to him or her, / it / may be integrated / as part of / the original experience.
대신, / 특히 그것이 맞을 때 / 목격자의 현재 생각과 / 그리고 사용될 수 있을 때 / 하나의 이야기를 / 이해가 되는 / 그 또는 그녀에게 / 그것은 / 통합될 수 있다. / 일부로서 / 원래 경험의

This process / can be explicit / (i.e., the witness / knows / it is happening), / but it is / often unconscious.
이 과정은 / 명시적일 수 있다. / (즉, 목격자는 / 알고 있다. / 그것이 일어나고 있다는 것을) / 하지만 / 그것은 / 종종 무의식적이다.

That is, / the witness / might find / himself or herself / thinking about the event / differently / without awareness.
즉, 목격자는 / 발견할지도 모른다. / 그 자신 또는 그녀 자신을 / 사건에 대해 생각하는 / 다르게 / 의식하지 못한 채

Over time, / the witness / may not even know / the source of information / that led to the (new) memory.
시간이 지남에 따라, / 목격자는 / 모를지도 모른다. / 정보의 출처조차 / (새로운) 기억으로 이끄는

Sources of misinformation / in forensic contexts / can be encountered anywhere, / from discussions / with other witnesses / to social media searches / to multiple interviews / with investigators or other legal professionals, / and even in court.
잘못된 정보의 출처는 / 법정의 상황에서 / 마주쳐질 수 있다. / 어디에서나 / 토론에서부터 / 다른 목격자들과의 / 소셜 미디어 조사들 / 다중 인터뷰들 / 수사관 또는 기타 법률 전문가들과의 / 그리고 심지어 법정에서까지

사건 후에 마주친 정보는 이후의 기억하는 것에 영향을 미칠 수 있다. 특히 사건이 불충분하게 부호화되었거나, 그 기억이 시간과 망각이 원래의 기억을 저하시켜 온 먼 사건으로부터 온 것이라면, 외부 정보는 목격자의 기억에 쉽게 통합될 수 있다. 사건 후의 잘못된 정보의 유효성을 확인하기 위해 기억에서 사용할 수 있는 줄어든 정보를 가지면, 이 새로운 정보가 덜 거부될 듯하다. 대신, 특히 그것이 목격자의 현재 생각과 맞고 그 또는 그녀에게 이해되는 하나의 이야기를 만드는 데 사용될 수 있을 때, 그것은 원래 경험의 일부로서 통합될 수 있다. 이 과정은 명시적일 수 있지만(즉, 목격자는 그것이 일어나고 있다는 것을 알고 있다), 흔히 무의식적이다. 즉, 목격자는 의식하지 못한 채 그 사건에 대해 다르게 생각하는 그 자신 또는 그녀 자신을 발견할지도 모른다. 시간이 지남에 따라, 목격자는 (새로운) 기억으로 이끄는 정보의 출처조차 모를지도 모른다. 법정의 상황에서의 잘못된 정보의 출처는 다른 목격자들과의 토론에서부터 소셜 미디어 조사들, 수사관 또는 기타 법률 전문가들과의 다중 인터뷰들, 심지어 법정에서까지 어디에서나 마주쳐질 수 있다.

Why? 왜 정답일까?

사건이 일어난 후 접한 정보가 기억에 끼치는 영향에 대해 얘기하고 있다. 따라서 사건 후의 잘못된 정보를 접했을 때 사건에 대한 기억에 영향을 끼쳐 거부되지 않는다는 문장이 알맞다. 빈칸에 들어갈 말로 적절한 것은 ① 'this new information will be rejected'이다.

- **encounter** ⓥ 마주치다
- **confirm** ⓥ 확인하다
- **legal** ⓐ 법적의
- **influence** ⓝ 영향
- **investigator** ⓝ 조사관

구문 풀이

9행 Instead, especially when it fits the witness's current thinking and can be
관계부사 / 동사1 / 동명사 / 동사2
used to create a story that makes sense to him or her, it may be integrated as
수동태 / 주격관계대명사 / 수동태 / ~로써
part of the original experience.

★★ 문제 해결 꿀~팁 ★★

▶ 많이 틀린 이유는?

글의 내용은 사건 이후에 접한 정보가 목격자의 기억에 어떻게 영향을 미칠 수 있는지를 설명하고 있다. 특히, 사건이 잘 입력 않았거나 오래된 사건일 경우, 기억이 퇴화되면서 새로운 정보가 기존의 기억에 통합될 가능성이 크다는 것을 예를 들며 언급하고 있다. 즉, 사실이 아닌 정보가 사실인 것처럼 여겨질 수 있다고 한다. 기억의 유효성을 확인할 근거 정보가 적을수록 사건 이후의 정보가 기억에 통합될 가능성을 제시한다.

▶ 문제 해결 방법은?

기억의 형성 및 변형을 파악해야한다. 특히, 외부 정보가 기존 기억과 통합되는 과정을 강조하고 있으므로, 빈칸에 들어갈 내용은 새로운 정보가 거부되지 않는다는 것이 가장 알맞다.

★★★ 등급을 가르는 문제!

33 상관관계와 인과관계
정답률 28% | 정답 ⑤

다음 빈칸에 들어갈 말로 가장 적절한 것을 고르시오. [3점]

① stay away from simply accepting the data as they are
정보를 있는 그대로 단순히 받아들이는 것에서부터 멀어지기
② point out every phenomenon in light of cause and effect
모든 인과관계의 및 현상을 짚어내기
③ apply a psychological approach to color preferences
색깔 선호에 심리적인 접근 적용하기
④ admit that correlations are within the framework of causality
상관관계가 인과관계 틀 안에 있음을 인정하기
✓⑤ hold off from trying to explain the reason behind the correlations
상관관계 배후에 있는 이유를 설명하려 하지 않기

Correlations / are powerful / because the insights they offer / are relatively clear.
상관관계는 / 강력하다. / 왜냐하면 그들이 제공하는 통찰은 / 비교적 명확하기 때문에

These insights / are often covered up / when we bring / causality back / into the picture.
이러한 통찰은 / 종종 가려진다. / 우리가 가져올 때 / 인과관계를 다시 / 그 상황으로

For instance, / a used-car dealer / supplied data / to statisticians / to predict / which of the vehicles / available for purchase / at an auction / were likely to have problems.
예를 들어, / 중고차 딜러가 / 데이터를 제공했다. / 통계학자들에게 / 예측하기 위해 / 어떤 차량이 / 구매 가능한 / 경매에서 / 문제가 있을 가능성이 높은지를

A correlation analysis / showed / that orange-colored cars / were far less likely / to have defects.
상관관계 분석은 / 보여 주었다. / 오렌지색 차량이 / 가능성이 훨씬 낮다는 것을 / 결함을 가질

Even as we read this, / we / already think / about why it might be so:
우리가 이것을 읽을 때도, / 우리는 / 이미 생각한다. / 왜 그럴지에 대해

Are orange-colored car owners / likely to be car enthusiasts / and take better care / of their vehicles?
오렌지색 차량 소유자들이 / 자동차 애호가이고 / 더 잘 돌볼 가능성이 있을까? / 그들의 차량을

Or, / is it because orange-colored cars / are more noticeable / on the road / and therefore / less likely / to be in accidents, / so they're / in better condition / when resold?
아니면, / 오렌지색 차들이 / 더 눈에 띈다. / 도로에서 / 그러므로 / 가능성이 낮다 / 사고에 연루될 / 그래서 그들이 / 더 좋은 상태에 있을까? / 재판매 될 때

Quickly / we / are caught / in a web / of competing causal hypotheses.
곧 / 우리는 / 갇힌다. / 함정에 / 경쟁적인 인과 가설의

But / our attempts / to illuminate things / this way / only make / them / cloudier.
그러나 / 우리의 시도는 / 무언가를 설명하려는 / 이러한 방식으로 / 만들 뿐이다. / 그것들을 / 더 흐리게

Correlations / exist; / we / can show / them / mathematically.
상관관계는 / 존재한다.; / 우리는 / 보여줄 수 있다. / 그것을 / 수학적으로

We / can't easily do the same / for causal links.
우리는 / 쉽게 똑같이 할 수 없다. / 인과 관계에 대해서는

So / we / would do well / to hold off / from trying / to explain the reason / behind the correlations.
그러므로 / 우리는 / 하는 것이 좋다. / 시작하지 않는 것 / 시도하기 / 이유를 설명하려고 / 상관관계의 배후에 있는

상관관계는 그것들이 제공하는 통찰력이 비교적 명확하기 때문에 강력하다. 이러한 통찰력은 종종 우리가 인과 관계를 그 상황으로 다시 가져올 때 가려진다. 예를 들어, 한 중고차 딜러가 경매에서 구입할 수 있는 차량들 중 어떤 차량에 문제가 발생할 가능성이 있는지를 예측하기 위한 데이터를 통계학자들에게 제공했다. 한 상관관계 분석은 주황색 차들이 결함이 있을 가능성이 훨씬 적다는 것을 보여 줬다. 심지어 우리가 이것을 읽으면서도, 우리는 이미 왜 그럴지에 대해 생각한다. 주황색 차를 소유한 사람들이 자동차 애호가여서 그들의 차량을 더 잘 관리할 가능성이 있는가? 아니면, 주황색 차들이 도로에서 더 눈에 띄고, 그래서 사고가 날 가능성이 적어 재판매될 때 그것들이 상태가 더 좋은 것이기 때문인가? 곧 우리는 경쟁적인 인과 가설의 함정에 빠진다. 하지만 이런 식으로 무언가를 설명하려는 우리의 시도는 그것들을 더 흐리게 만들 뿐이다. 상관관계는 존재하며 우리는 그것들을 수학적으로 보여 줄 수 있다. 우리는 인과 관계에 대해서는 쉽게 똑같이 할 수 없다. 따라서 우리는 상관관계의 배후에 있는 이유를 설명하려 하지 않는 것이 좋다.

Why? 왜 정답일까?

상관관계가 명확한 통찰력을 제공하고, 우리는 상관관계의 인과 관계를 떠올리려고 하지만 상관관계만큼 수학적으로 계산할 수 없기 때문에 더욱 혼란스러워진다(But our attempts to illuminate things this way only make them cloudier.)고 설명한다. 따라서 명확한 상관관계에서 이점을 보려면 인과관계를 떠올리면 안 된다고 주장하므로 빈칸에 들어갈 알맞은 말은 ⑤ 'hold off from trying to explain the reason behind the correlations'이다.

- correlation ⓝ 상관관계
- statistician ⓝ 통계학자
- mathematically ⓪ 수학적으로
- compete ⓥ 경쟁하다
- cover up 숨기다, 가리다
- hypothesis ⓝ 가설
- causal ⓐ 원인의

구문 풀이

13행 But our attempts to illuminate things this way only make them cloudier.
　　　　　　　　　　　　to부정사　　　　　　　　　　동사　　things

★★ 문제 해결 꿀~팁 ★★

▶ 많이 틀린 이유는?
글은 상관관계가 제공하는 통찰력이 명확하지만, 인과관계를 고려할 때 이러한 통찰력이 가려지는 과정을 설명하고 있다. 특히, 'But our attempts to illuminate things this way only make them cloudier.'에서 알 수 있듯이, 주어진 예시에서 오렌지색 자동차가 결함이 적다는 사실을 통해 우리는 다양한 원인에 대한 가설을 세우게 되지만, 이러한 시도가 오히려 상황을 복잡하게 만든다고 말하고 있다. 따라서 "우리는 상관관계 뒤에 있는 이유를 설명하려는 시도를 삼가는 것이 좋다"는 내용이 자연스럽게 이어진다.

▶ 문제 해결 방법은?
글의 흐름을 이해하고, 상관관계와 인과관계의 복잡성을 인식하는 것이 중요하다. 인과관계로 돌아가는 것이 오히려 혼란을 초래한다고 강조하고 있으므로, 원인을 설명하려는 시도를 보류하는 것이 최선이라는 점을 파악해야 한다.

---

34 쥐의 수명　　　　　　　　　　　　정답률 49% | 정답 ②

다음 빈칸에 들어갈 말로 가장 적절한 것을 고르시오.

① the distance that migrating species can travel for their survival
이동하는 종들이 생존을 위해 이동할 수 있는 거리
② the average time that this animal species can survive in the wild
이 동물 종이 야생에서 생존할 수 있는 평균 시간
③ the amount of energy that members of the species expend in a day
종의 구성원이 하루에 소비하는 에너지의 양
④ the extent to which this species is able to protect its source of food
이 종이 식량 공급원을 보호할 수 있는 정도
⑤ the maximum size of the habitat in which it and its neighbors coexist
이 동물과 이웃 동물이 공존하는 서식지의 최대 크기

Most mice in the wild / are eaten or die / before their life span of two years is over.
대부분의 쥐들은 / 먹히거나 죽는다 / 그들의 2년 수명이 끝나기 전에

They die / from *external causes*, / such as disease, starvation, or predators, / not due to *internal causes*, / such as aging.
그들은 죽는다. / *외부 원인* 때문에 / 예를 들어 질병, 기아, 또는 포식자 / *내부 원인* 때문이 아니라, / 예를 들어 노화

That is why nature has made mice / to live, / on average, / for no longer than two years.
그것이 자연이 쥐를 만들었던 이유다. / 살도록 / 평균적으로 / 2년을 넘지 않도록

Now they / we have arrived at an important point: / The average life span of an animal species, / or the rate at which it ages, / is determined by / the average time / that this animal species can survive in the wild.

이제 우리는 중요한 지점에 도착했다.: / 한 동물 종의 평균 수명, / 또는 그것이 나이 드는 속도는, / 결정된다. / 평균 시간에 의해 / 그 동물 종이 야생에서 생존할 수 있는

That explains / why a bat can live / to be 30 years old.
그것은 설명한다. / 왜 박쥐가 살 수 있는지 / 30세까지

In contrast to mice, / bats can fly, / which is why they can escape from danger / much faster.
쥐와 대조적으로, / 박쥐는 날 수 있다. / 그것이 그들이 위험에서 탈출할 수 있는 이유이다. / 훨씬 더 빨리

Thanks to their wings, / bats can also cover longer distances / and are better able to find food.
그들의 날개 덕분에, / 박쥐는 또한 더 긴 거리를 이동할 수 있고 / 더 잘 음식을 찾을 수 있다.

Every genetic change in the past / that made it possible for a bat to live longer / was useful, / because bats are much better able than mice / to flee from danger, / find food, / and survive.
과거의 모든 유전적 변화는 / 박쥐가 더 오래 살 수 있게 만든 / 유용했다. / 왜냐하면 박쥐는 쥐보다 훨씬 더 잘 할 수 있기 때문이다 / 위험에서 도망치고, / 음식을 찾고, / 생존하는 것을

야생에 있는 대부분의 쥐들은 2년의 수명이 끝나기 전에 잡아먹히거나 죽는다. 그들은 노화와 같은 '내부적인 원인들' 때문이 아니라 질병, 굶주림 또는 포식자와 같은 '외부적인 원인들'로 죽는다. 그것이 자연이 쥐를 평균적으로 2년 이상 살지 못하게 만든 이유이다. 이제 우리는 중요한 지점에 도달했다. 동물 종의 평균 수명, 또는 그것이 노화하는 속도는 이 동물 종이 야생에서 생존할 수 있는 평균 시간에 의해 결정된다. 그것은 왜 박쥐가 30세까지 살 수 있는지를 설명해 준다. 쥐와 대조적으로 박쥐는 날 수 있고, 이것은 그들이 위험에서 훨씬 더 빨리 도망칠 수 있는 이유이다. 그들의 날개 덕분에, 박쥐들은 또한 더 긴 거리를 이동할 수 있고 먹이를 더 잘 찾을 수 있다. 박쥐가 더 오래 사는 것을 가능하게 해 준 과거의 모든 유전적 변화는 박쥐가 쥐보다 위험으로부터 도망치고, 먹이를 찾고, 생존하는 것을 훨씬 더 잘 할 수 있기 때문에 유용했다.

Why? 왜 정답일까?

야생 쥐가 내부적인 원인이 아니라 외부적인 원인으로 죽기 때문에 쥐의 수명이 2년이라고 한다. 이를 박쥐의 수명과 비교하며 쥐와 박쥐의 유전적 변화의 차이라고 설명한다. 즉, 박쥐가 쥐보다 야생에서 살아남기 유리하기 때문에 더 오래 산다고 얘기한다. 따라서 빈칸에 들어갈 알맞은 말은 ② 'the average time that this animal species can survive in the wild'이다.

- mouse ⓝ 쥐(*pl.* mice)
- external ⓐ 외부의
- predator ⓝ 포식자
- span ⓝ 기간
- starvation ⓝ 기아
- escape ⓥ 탈출하다

구문 풀이

4행 That is why nature has made mice to live, on average, for no longer than two years.
　　　　　　　　관계부사　　　　　현재완료　　　　　　　　　　　　　비교급

---

35 도덕적 우수성 획득　　　　　　　　정답률 63% | 정답 ③

다음 글에서 전체 흐름과 관계 없는 문장은? [3점]

Moral excellence, / according to Aristotle, / is the result of habit / and repetition, / though modern science would also suggest / that it may have an innate, genetic component.
도덕적 탁월함은, / 아리스토텔레스에 따르면, / 습관의 결과이다. / 그리고 반복의, / 하지만 현대 과학은 또한 제안할 것이다. / 그것이 타고난, 유전적 요소를 가질 수 있다고

① This means that / moral excellence will be broadly set / early in our lives, / which is why the question of how early to teach it / is so important.
이것은 의미한다. / 도덕적 탁월함이 대체로 설정될 것이라는 것을 / 우리의 삶 초기에, / 그것이 왜 그것을 얼마나 일찍 가르칠 것인지에 대한 질문이 / 그렇게 중요한 이유인

② Freud suggested / that we don't change our personality much / after age five or thereabouts, / but as in many other things, / Freud was wrong.
프로이트는 제안했다. / 우리가 성격을 많이 바꾸지 않는다고 / 5살 이후나 그쯤에, / 하지만 많은 다른 것들에서처럼, / 프로이트는 틀렸다.

✓③ A person of moral excellence / cannot help doing good / — it is as natural / as the change of seasons or the rotation of the planets.
도덕적 탁월함을 지닌 사람은 / 선행을 하지 않을 수 없다. / —그것은 자연스럽다 / 계절의 변화나 행성의 회전만큼

④ Recent psychological research shows / that personality traits stabilize / around age thirty / in both men and women / and regardless of ethnicity / as the human brain continues to develop, / both neuroanatomically / and in terms of cognitive skills, / until the mid-twenties.
최근의 심리학 연구는 보여 준다. / 성격 특성이 안정화된다는 것을 / 30세쯤에 / 남녀 모두에서 / 인종에 관계없이 / 인간의 뇌가 계속 발달함에 따라, / 신경 해부학적으로나 / 인지 능력 면에서, / 20대 중반까지

⑤ The advantage of this new understanding / is that we can be a bit more optimistic / than Aristotle and Freud / about being able to teach moral excellence.
이 새로운 이해의 장점은 / 우리가 좀 더 낙관적일 수 있다는 것이다. / 아리스토텔레스와 프로이트보다 / 도덕적 탁월함을 가르칠 수 있는 것에 대해

비록 현대 과학은 그것이 선천적, 즉, 유전적인 요소를 가지고 있다고 또한 주장하지만, Aristotle에 따르면 도덕적 우수성은 습관과 반복의 결과물이다. ① 이것은 도덕적 우수성이 우리 삶에 있어서 이른 시기에 광범위하게 설정될 것임을 의미하며, 이것이 얼마나 일찍 그것을 가르쳐야 할지에 대한 질문이 매우 중요한 이유이다. ② Freud는 우리가 5세 혹은 그 무렵 이후에는 우리의 성격을 많이 바꾸지 않는다고 제시했지만, 다른 많은 것들에서처럼 Freud는 틀렸다. ③ 도덕적으로 우수한 사람은 좋은 일을 하지 않을 수 없으며, 그것은 계절의 변화나 행성의 자전만큼이나 자연스럽다. ④ 최근의 심리 연구는 20대 중반까지 신경 해부학적으로 그리고 인지 기능 면에서 인간의 뇌가 계속해서 발달함에 따라 남성과 여성 모두에게 있어서 그리고 민족에 상관없이 성격 특성이 30세 무렵에 안정된다는 것을 보여 준다. ⑤ 이 새로운 이해의 이점은 우리가 Aristotle이나 Freud보다 도덕적 우수성을 가르칠 수 있다는 점에서 조금 더 낙관적일 수 있다는 것이다.

Why? 왜 정답일까?

Aristotle과 Freud, 그리고 과학적인 관점에서 도덕적 우수성의 획득에 대해 쓴 글이다. Aristotle은 습관과 반복의 결과라고 하였고, Freud는 5세 즈음에 성격이 고정된다고 하였지만 최근 과학의 연구는 이후에도 성격의 발달이 이루어짐을 제시한다. 따라서 도덕적으로 우수한 사람의 행동 변화는 글의 전체 흐름과 관계가 없다. 따라서 정답은 ③이다.

- neuroanatomically ⓪ 신경 해부학적으로
- suggest ⓥ 제안하다
- develop ⓥ 발달하다
- excellence ⓝ 우수성
- personality ⓝ 성격

[문제편 p.155]

1행 Moral excellence, according to Aristotle, is the result of habit and

삽입구문

repetition, though modern science would also suggest that it may have an innate,

비록(= even though)　　　　　　　　　　　접속사→ moral excellence

genetic component.

---

36 종의 크기의 원인　　　　　　　　　　정답률 61% | 정답 ②

주어진 글 다음에 이어질 글의 순서로 가장 적절한 것을 고르시오.

① (A) – (C) – (B)　　　　　✔ (B) – (A) – (C)
③ (B) – (C) – (A)　　　　　④ (C) – (A) – (B)
⑤ (C) – (B) – (A)

The size of a species / is not accidental.
종의 크기는 / 우연이 아니다.

It's a fine-tuned interaction / between a species / and the world it inhabits.
그것은 정교하게 조정된 상호작용이다. / 한 종과 / 그 종이 서식하는 세계 사이의

Over large periods of time, / size fluctuations / have often signalled / significant changes in the environment.
오랜 시간에 걸쳐, / 크기 변동은 / 종종 신호를 보냈다. / 환경에서의 중요한 변화를

(B) Generally speaking, / over the last five hundred million years, / the trend has been / towards animals getting larger.
(일반적으로 말하자면, / 지난 5억 년 동안, / 경향은 ~였다. / 동물이 더 커지는 쪽으로

It's particularly notable / in marine animals, / whose average body size / has increased 150-fold / in this time.
그것은 특히 두드러진다. / 해양 동물에서, / 그들의 평균 체격이 / 150배 증가했다. / 이 기간 동안

(A) But we are beginning to see / changes in this trend.
하지만 우리는 보기 시작하고 있다. / 이 경향에서의 변화를

Scientists have discovered / that many animals are shrinking.
과학자들은 발견했다. / 많은 동물이 줄어들고 있다는 것을

Around the world, / species in every category / have been found / to be getting smaller, / and one major cause / appears to be the heat.
전 세계적으로, / 모든 범주의 종들이 / 발견되었다. / 더 작아지고 있다는 것이, / 그리고 하나의 주요 원인은 / 열인 것 같다.

(C) Animals living in the Italian Alps, / for example, / have seen temperatures rise / by three to four degrees Celsius / since the 1980s.
이탈리아 알프스에 사는 동물들은, / 예를 들어, / 기온이 상승하는 것을 목격해 왔다. / 섭씨 3도에서 4도 정도 / 1980년대 이후로

To avoid overheating, / chamois goats now spend / more of their days resting / rather than searching for food, / and as a result, / in just a few decades, / the new generations of chamois / are 25 percent smaller.
과열을 피하기 위해, / 샤무아 염소들은 이제 보낸다. / 그들의 하루 대부분을 휴식하며 / 음식을 찾는 대신에. / 그 결과, / 단 몇 십 년 만에, / 새로운 세대의 샤무아 염소들은 / 25퍼센트 더 작아졌다.

종의 크기는 우연인 것이 아니다. 그것은 한 종과 그것이 서식하는 세계 사이의 미세 조정된 상호 작용이다. 오랜 시간에 걸쳐, 크기의 변동은 종종 환경에서의 상당한 변화를 나타내 왔다.

(B) 일반적으로 말해서, 지난 5억 년 동안, 그 경향은 동물들이 점점 커지는 쪽으로 되어 왔다. 그것은 특히 해양 동물들에게서 두드러지는데, 그들의 평균 몸 크기는 이 시기에 150배로 증가해 왔다.

(A) 하지만 우리는 이 경향에서 변화를 관찰하기 시작하고 있다. 과학자들은 많은 동물이 작아지고 있다는 것을 발견해 왔다. 전 세계적으로, 모든 범주의 종들이 점점 작아지고 있는 것으로 발견되어 왔고, 한 가지 주요 원인은 열인 것으로 보인다.

(C) 예를 들어, 이탈리아 알프스에 살고 있는 동물들은 1980년대 이후로 기온이 섭씨 3에서 4도까지 상승하는 것을 보아 왔다. 과열을 피하기 위해서, 샤무아 염소들은 이제 먹이를 찾는 것보다 휴식을 취하는 데 더 많은 그들의 날들을 보내고, 결과적으로, 단지 몇 십 년 만에, 새로운 세대들의 샤무아는 25% 더 작아져 있다.

Why? 왜 정답일까?

주어진 글은 종의 크기에는 환경적 영향이 크다고 얘기한다. (B)에서는 환경적 영향이 해양 동물에서 두드러짐을 언급하고, (A)는 이와 반대로 동물들이 작아진다는 것을 제시한다. 따라서 내용이 전환되는 (B)와 (A)가 이어져야 하고, 그 이후에 동물들이 작아지는 것의 세부적인 예시를 든 (C)가 오는 것이 가장 자연스럽다. 따라서 정답은 ② '(B) – (A) – (C)'이다.

- species ⑪ 종
- increase ⑫ 증가하다
- generation ⑪ 세대
- accidental ⓐ 우연한
- temperature ⑪ 온도

구문 풀이

15행　→to부정사 부사적 용법
To avoid overheating, chamois goats now spend more of their days
　　　　　　　　　　　　　동명사

resting rather than searching for food, and as a result, in just a few decades,
현재분사　　　　　　　　　　　　　　　　　　a few + 가산명사

the new generations of chamois are 25 percent smaller.
주어

★★★ 등급을 가르는 문제!

37 디지털 시대의 데이터 분석　　　　　정답률 38% | 정답 ③

주어진 글 다음에 이어질 글의 순서로 가장 적절한 것을 고르시오. [3점]

① (A) – (C) – (B)　　　　② (B) – (A) – (C)
✔ (B) – (C) – (A)　　　　④ (C) – (A) – (B)
⑤ (C) – (B) – (A)

For a long time, / random sampling / was a good shortcut.
오랫동안, / 무작위 표본 추출은 / 좋은 지름길이었다.

It made analysis / of large data problems / possible / in the pre-digital era.
그것은 분석을 가능하게 만들었다. / 대규모 데이터 문제의 / 디지털 시대 이전에

(B) But much as converting a digital image or song / into a smaller file / results in loss of

---

data, / information is lost / when sampling.
하지만 디지털 이미지나 노래를 변환하는 것처럼 / 더 작은 파일로 / 데이터 손실을 초래하는 것처럼, / 정보는 손실된다. / 표본 추출을 할 때

Having the full (or close to the full) dataset / provides a lot more freedom / to explore, / to look at the data from different angles / or to look closer at certain aspects of it.
전체 데이터 세트 (또는 거의 전체)에 접근하는 것은 / 훨씬 더 많은 자유를 제공한다. / 탐구할 / 데이터를 다른 각도에서 바라보거나 / 특정 측면을 더 자세히 보는

(C) A fitting example / may be the light-field camera, / which captures / not just a single plane of light, / as with conventional cameras, / but rays from the entire light field, / some 11 million of them.
적절한 예시는 / 라이트 필드 카메라일 수 있다. / 그것은 포착한다. / 단순히 한 평면의 빛을 포착하는 것이 아니라, / 일반 카메라처럼, / 전체 빛 필드에서 나오는 광선을, / 약 1,100만 개의

The photographers / can decide later / which element of an image / to focus on / in the digital file.
사진작가들은 / 나중에 결정할 수 있다. / 이미지의 어느 요소를 / 초점을 맞출지 / 디지털 파일에서

(A) There is no need / to focus at the beginning, / since collecting all the information / makes it possible / to do that afterwards.
필요가 없다. / 처음에 초점을 맞출 필요가, / 왜냐하면 모든 정보를 수집하는 것이 / 가능하게 하기 때문에. / 나중에 그것을 할 수 있도록

Because rays from the entire light field / are included, / it is closer / to all the data.
전체 빛 필드의 광선이 / 포함되기 때문에, / 그것은 더 가깝다. / 모든 데이터에

As a result, / the information is more "reuseable" / than ordinary pictures, / where the photographer has to decide / what to focus on / before she presses the shutter.
결과적으로, / 그 정보는 더 "재사용 가능하다." / 일반 사진보다. / 그곳에서는 사진작가가 결정해야 한다. / 무엇에 초점을 맞출지 / 셔터를 누르기 전에

오랫동안, 무작위 추출법은 좋은 지름길이었다. 그것은 디지털 시대 이전에 상당한 데이터 문제 분석을 가능하게 했다.

(B) 그러나 디지털 이미지나 노래를 더 작은 파일로 변환하는 것이 데이터 손실을 유발하는 것과 마찬가지로, 추출을 할 때 정보가 손실된다. 전체(또는 전체에 가까운) 데이터 세트를 가지는 것은 탐색하거나 다른 각도에서 데이터를 살펴보거나 그것의 특정 측면들을 더 자세히 보게 하는 자유를 훨씬 더 많이 제공한다.

(C) 라이트 필드 카메라가 적절한 비유가 될 수 있는데, 그것은 기존 카메라처럼 한 평면의 빛만 포착할 뿐만 아니라 약 1,100만 개에 달하는 전체 라이트 필드로부터의 광선들도 포착한다. 사진사들은 디지털 파일에서 이미지의 어느 요소에 초점을 맞출지를 나중에 결정할 수 있다.

(A) 모든 정보를 수집하는 것은 그것을 나중에 하는 것을 가능하게 만들기 때문에, 처음에 초점을 맞출 필요는 없다. 전체 라이트 필드의 빛이 포함되기 때문에, 그것은 모든 데이터에 더 가깝다. 결과적으로 사진사가 셔터를 누르기 전에 그녀가 무엇에 초점을 맞출지를 결정해야 하는 일반 사진들보다 그 정보는 더 '재사용 가능'하다.

Why? 왜 정답일까?

디지털 시대의 데이터 분석에 대해 얘기하고 있다. 주어진 글에서는 디지털 시대 이전에는 무작위 추출법이 좋다고 하였으나 이제는 그렇지 않다는 (B)가 이어지는 것이 자연스럽다. 무작위 추출법이 좋지 않은 이유를 (C)에서 라이트 필드 카메라를 통해 설명하고 있으므로 (C)가 다음, (A)에서 라이트 필드 카메라의 세부 작동 방식에 대해 언급하므로 (A)가 마지막에 와야 내용이 이어진다. 따라서 답은 ③ '(B) – (C) – (A)'이다.

- shortcut ⑪ 지름길
- reusable ⓐ 재사용이 가능한
- element ⑪ 요소
- analysis ⑪ 분석
- freedom ⑪ 자유

구문 풀이

7행 As a result, the information is more "reuseable" than ordinary pictures,
　　　　　　　　　　　　　　　　　　　　　　　　　　~로써
where the photographer has to decide what to focus on before she presses the
관계부사　　　　　　　　　　　　　　　관계대명사(= the thing that)
shutter.

★★ 문제 해결 꿀~팁 ★★

▶ 많이 틀린 이유는?
문단 마다 전달하고자 하는 메시지와 그 연관성을 명확히 인지하지 못하면 답을 찾기 어렵다. 이 문제에서는 샘플링과 전체 데이터셋의 관계, 그리고 라이트 필드 카메라의 기능과 글에서 갖는 의미를 파악해야한다. (B)는 데이터 손실을 언급하고 (C)는 이를 보완하는 방법으로 라이트 필드 카메라를 소개하는 방식으로 이어진다.

▶ 문제 해결 방법은?
다른 문제와 마찬가지로 문맥을 파악하는 것이 우선시 된다. (B)에서 샘플링의 한계를 인식하고, (C)에서 그 한계를 보완하는 예시를 제시한 후, (A)에서 "there is no need to focus at the beginning"이라고 하여 전체 데이터를 수집하는 것의 중요성을 강조하는 흐름을 이해하며 읽는 것이 직관적인 문제 풀이에 도움이 될 수 있다.

---

38 내향적인 리더들의 장점　　　　　　정답률 46% | 정답 ③

글의 흐름으로 보아, 주어진 문장이 들어가기에 가장 적절한 곳을 고르시오.

Introverted leaders / do have to overcome / the strong cultural presumption / that extroverts are more effective leaders.
내성적인 리더들은 / 극복해야 한다. / 강한 문화적 추정을 / 외향적인 사람들이 더 효과적인 리더라는

① Although the population / splits into almost equal parts / between introverts and extroverts, / more than 96 percent / of managers and executives / are extroverted.
비록 인구가 / 거의 같은 비율로 나뉘지만, / 내성적인 사람들과 외향적인 사람들 사이에서, / 96퍼센트 이상이 / 관리자들과 임원들 중 / 외향적이다.

② In a study done in 2006, / 65 percent of senior corporate executives / viewed introversion / as a barrier to leadership.
2006년에 수행된 연구에서, / 65퍼센트의 고위 기업 임원들이 / 내성적 성향을 보았다. / 리더십에 대한 장벽으로

✔ We must / reexamine this stereotype, / however, / as it doesn't always hold true.
우리는 / 이 고정관념을 재검토해야 한다. / 그러나, / 항상 사실은 아니기 때문에.

Regent University / found that / a desire to be of service to others / and to empower them to grow, / which is / more common among introverts than extroverts, / is a key factor / in becoming a leader / and retaining leadership.
리젠트 대학교는 / 발견했다. / 다른 사람들을 돕고자 하는 열망과 / 그들이 성장할 수 있도록 함을 실어주는 것이, / 그것은 / 외향적인 사람들보다 내성적인 사람들 사이에서 더 흔한데, / 중요한 요소이다. / 리더가 되는 데 있어서 / 그리고 리더십을 유지하는 데
④ So-called servant leadership, / dating back to ancient philosophical literature, / adheres to the belief / that a company's goals / are best achieved / by helping workers or customers / achieve their goals.
이른바 서번트 리더십은 / 고대 철학 문헌까지 거슬러 올라가는, / 그 믿음을 따른다. / 회사의 목표가 / 가장 잘 달성된다는 / 직원들이나 고객들이 / 그들의 목표를 달성하게 도와줌으로써
⑤ Such leaders / do not seek attention / but rather want / to shine a light / on others' wins and achievements; / servant leadership / requires humility, / but that humility / ultimately pays off.
그런 리더들은 / 주목받기를 원하지 않으며 / 오히려 원한다. / 빛을 비추는 것을 / 다른 사람들의 성공과 성과에; / 서번트 리더십은 / 겸손을 요구한다. / 그러나 그 겸손은 / 결국 보상을 준다.

내향적인 리더들은 외향적인 사람들이 더 유능한 리더라는 강력한 문화적 억측을 극복해야 한다. ① 비록 인구는 내향적인 사람과 외향적인 사람 사이에서 거의 동등한 비율로 나뉘지만, 관리자와 임원의 96% 이상이 외향적이다. ② 2006년에 실시된 한 연구에서, 기업 고위 임원의 65%가 내향성을 리더십의 장애물로 간주했다. ③ 하지만 그것이 항상 맞는 것은 아니기 때문에 우리는 이 고정 관념을 재검토해야 한다. Regent 대학교는 다른 사람들에게 도움이 되고 그들이 성장할 수 있도록 힘을 주고자 하는 열망이 리더가 되고 리더십을 유지하는 데 핵심적인 요소이고, 그것이 외향적인 사람들보다 내향적인 사람들 사이에서 더 일반적이라는 것을 발견했다. ④ 고대 철학 문헌으로 거슬러 올라가는 소위 서번트 리더십은 한 회사의 목표가 근로자나 고객이 그들의 목표를 달성하도록 도움으로써 가장 잘 달성된다는 믿음을 고수한다. ⑤ 그런 리더들은 관심을 추구하는 것이 아니라 오히려 다른 사람들의 승리와 업적에 빛을 비추고 싶어 하고, 서번트 리더십은 겸손을 필요로 하지만, 그 겸손은 궁극적으로 결실을 맺는다.

Why? 왜 정답일까?
글에서는 내향적인 리더와 외향적인 리더를 비교하며 외향적인 리더가 더욱 이상적인 리더라고 여겨지지만 내향적인 리더 역시 장점이 있음을 언급한다. 주어진 문장은 내향적인 리더의 장점을 소개하는 문장 앞인 ③에 오는 것이 가장 적절하다.

- reexamine ⓥ 재검토하다
- introverted ⓐ 내성적인
- split ⓥ 나누다
- retain ⓥ 유지하다
- literature ⓝ 문헌
- stereotype ⓝ 고정관념
- population ⓝ 인구
- executive ⓝ 임원
- philosophical ⓐ 철학적인

구문 풀이

9행 Regent University found that a desire to be of service to others and
to empower them to grow, which is more common among introverts than extroverts,
is a key factor in becoming a leader and retaining leadership.

★★★ 등급을 가르는 문제!
39 완벽한 단위를 만들기 위한 노력 정답률 43% | 정답 ④
글의 흐름으로 보아, 주어진 문장이 들어가기에 가장 적절한 곳을 고르시오.

By the nineteenth century, / France had developed / a system of precisely defined units of measurement / to capture space, time, and more, / and had begun / to get other nations / to adopt the same standards.
19세기까지, / 프랑스는 개발했다. / 정확하게 정의된 측정 단위를 / 공간, 시간 등을 포착하기 위해, / 그리고 시작했다. / 다른 국가들이 / 같은 기준을 채택하게
① Just half a century later, / in the 1920s, / the discoveries of quantum mechanics / forever destroyed / the dream of comprehensive and perfect measurement.
불과 반세기 후, / 1920년대에, / 양자역학의 발견은 / 영원히 파괴했다. / 포괄적이고 완벽한 측정의 꿈을
② And yet, / outside a relatively small circle of physicists, / the mindset of humankind's drive / to flawlessly measure / continued among engineers and scientists.
그러나, / 비교적 작은 물리학자 집단을 제외하고, / 인류의 노력에 대한 사고방식은 / 완벽하게 측정하려는 / 엔지니어들과 과학자들 사이에서 계속되었다.
③ In the world of business / it even expanded, / as the precision-oriented sciences / of mathematics and statistics / began to influence / all areas of commerce.
비즈니스 세계에서는 / 그것이 심지어 확장되었으며, / 정확성을 지향하는 과학들이 / 수학과 통계학의 / 영향을 미치기 시작했다. / 모든 상업 분야에
☑However, / contrary to the trend of the past several decades, / in many new situations / that are occurring today, / allowing for imprecision / — for messiness — / may be a positive feature, / not a shortcoming.
그러나, / 지난 수십 년간의 추세와 반대로, / 오늘날 발생하는 / 많은 새로운 상황에서, / 부정확성을 허용하는 것이 — 혼란을 허용하는 것 — / 긍정적인 특징일 수 있으며, / 결함이 아니다.
As a tradeoff / for relaxing the standards of allowable errors, / one can get a hold of / much more data.
허용 가능한 오류의 기준을 완화하는 대가로, / 더 많은 데이터를 / 얻을 수 있다.
⑤ It isn't just that / "more is better than some," / but that, in fact, / sometimes "more is greater than better."
단순히 / "많은 것이 적은 것보다 낫다."는 것이 아니라, / 실제로는 / 때때로 "많음이 더 나음보다 더 크다."는 것이다.

19세기까지, 프랑스는 공간, 시간, 그리고 더 많은 것을 포착하기 위해 정밀하게 규정된 측정 단위의 체계를 개발했고, 다른 국가들이 동일한 기준을 채택하도록 만들기 시작했다. ① 불과 반세기 후, 1920년대에, 양자 역학의 발견은 포괄적이고 완벽한 측정에 대한 꿈을 영원히 깨 버렸다. ② 그러나 비교적 소수 집단의 물리학자를 제외하고 공학자와 과학자 사이에서 완벽하게 측정하려고 하는 인류의 추진 정신은 계속되었다. ③ 정확성을 지향하는 수학과 통계학이라는 과학이 상업의 모든 영역에 영향을 미치기 시작하면서 비즈니스의 세계에서 그것은 심지어 확장하였다. ④ 그러나, 지난 수십 년간의 경향과 반대로, 오늘날 발생하는 많은 새로운 상황에서 부정확성, 즉, 번잡함을 허용하는 것은 단점이 아니라 긍정적인 특성이 될 수 있다. 허용할 오류의 기준을 완화하기 위한 거래로서 사람은 훨씬 더 많은 데이

터를 얻을 수 있다. ⑤ 그것은 단순히 '더 많은 것이 조금보다 더 나을' 뿐만 아니라, 사실은 때때로 '더 많은 것이 더 좋은 것보다 더 훌륭하기'도 하다

Why? 왜 정답일까?
완벽한 단위를 만들기 위한 인간의 노력에 대한 얘기다. 주어진 문장은 'allowing for imprecision'의 긍정적 효과를 설명하는 내용으로, ④번에서 'relaxing the standards of allowable errors'라는 문장이 이어진다.

- contrary ⓐ 반대의, 상반되는
- messiness ⓝ 어지러움, 지저분함
- quantum mechanics ⓝ 양자 역학
- comprehensive ⓐ 포괄적인, 종합적인
- continue ⓥ 계속하다
- commerce ⓝ 상업
- occur ⓥ 발생하다
- shortcoming ⓝ 결점, 단점
- destroy ⓥ 파괴하다
- mindset ⓝ 사고방식, 태도
- oriented ⓐ 유래된

구문 풀이

4행 By the nineteenth century, France had developed a system of precisely
과거완료1
defined units of measurement to capture space, time, and more, and had begun
to부정사 부사적 용법   과거완료2
to get other nations to adopt the same standards.
to부정사 명사적 용법   to부정사 부사적 용법

★★ 문제 해결 꿀~팁 ★★

▶ 많이 틀린 이유는?
주어진 문장인 "However, contrary to ~ not a shortcoming."은 ④의 이전 문장에서 이야기하는 정밀도와 측정의 변화에 대한 논의와 잘 연결된다. 많은 사람들이 이러한 논리적 흐름을 이해하지 못하면 정답을 찾기가 어렵다.
▶ 문제 해결 방법은?
글의 초반에서 글의 주제를 파악하고, 흐름이 어색한 부분을 찾으면 된다. 본문에서는 'precisely defined units of measurement'와 'quantum mechanics'의 발견이 정밀 측정의 꿈을 깨뜨렸다고 언급한 후, 그 이후에도 "the mindset of humankind's drive to flawlessly measure"가 여전히 존재한다고 설명하고 있다. 주어진 문장이 허용 가능한 오차의 기준을 완화하는 대가로 더 많은 데이터를 얻을 수 있다는 내용을 언급하므로, 이전 문장에서 정밀도를 추구하는 경향이 여전히 존재함을 언급한 후, 새로운 접근 방식의 필요성을 자연스럽게 연결하는 역할을 한다.

40 협력의 힘 정답률 58% | 정답 ①
다음 글의 내용을 한 문장으로 요약하고자 한다. 빈칸 (A), (B)에 들어갈 말로 가장 적절한 것은?

(A)	(B)		(A)	(B)
✔generosity	benefit		② hostility	support
관대함	혜택		적대감	지지
③ generosity	humiliation		④ hostility	hospitality
관대함	수치심		적대감	환대
⑤ tolerance	dishonor			
인내	불명예			

Multiple laboratory studies show / that cooperative people / tend to receive social advantages / from others.
여러 실험실 연구들이 / 협력적인 사람들이 / 사회적 이점을 받는 경향이 있다는 것을 / 다른 사람들로부터
One way / to demonstrate this / is to give people the opportunity / to act positively or negatively / toward contributors.
하나의 방법은 / 이것을 입증하기 위한 / 사람들에게 기회를 주는 것이다. / 긍정적 또는 부정적으로 행동할 / 기여자들에 대해
For example, / Pat Barclay, a professor at the University of Guelph, / had participants play / a cooperative game / where people could contribute money / toward a group fund / which helped all group members,
예를 들어, / Pat Barclay, 구엘프 대학교의 교수는, / 참가자에게 하게 했다. / 협력 게임을 / 사람들이 돈을 기여할 수 있는 / 그룹 기금에 / 그 기금이 모든 그룹 구성원을 돕는
and then / allowed participants / to give money / to other participants / based on their reputations.
그런 다음 / 참가자들에게 허락했다. / 돈을 주는 것을 / 다른 참가자들에게 / 그들의 평판에 기반하여
People who / contributed more to the group fund / were given responsibility for more money / than people who contributed less.
더 많이 기여한 사람들은 / 그룹 기금에 / 더 많은 돈에 대한 책임을 부여받았다. / 덜 기여한 사람들보다
Similar results / have been found by other researchers.
비슷한 결과들이 / 다른 연구자들에 의해 발견되었다.
People who / contribute toward their groups / are also chosen more often / as interaction partners, / preferred as leaders, / rated as more desirable partners / for long-term relationships, / and are perceived / to be trustworthy / and have high social status.
자신의 그룹에 기여하는 사람들은 / 또한 더 자주 선택된다. / 상호작용 파트너로서, / 리더로서 선호되고, / 더 바람직한 파트너로 평가되며 / 장기적인 관계에서, / 그리고 인식된다. / 신뢰할 수 있다고 / 그리고 높은 사회적 지위를 가지고 있다고
Uncooperative people / tend to receive verbal criticism / or even more severe punishment.
비협동적인 사람들은 / 언어적 비판을 받는 경향이 있다. / 혹은 더 심각한 처벌을 받기도 한다.
➡ Studies suggest that individuals / who act with (A) generosity / toward their communities / are more likely / to be viewed as deserving of (B) benefit / by members of that community / than those who don't.
연구들은 제안한다. / 개인들이 / 관대하게 행동하는 / 그들의 공동체를 향해 / 더 가능성이 크다고 / 혜택을 받을 자격이 있다고 / 여겨질 / 그 공동체의 구성원들에 의해 / 그렇게 하지 않는 사람들보다

여러 실험실 연구들은 협력적인 사람들이 다른 사람들로부터 사회적인 혜택들을 받는 경향이 있다는 것을 보여 준다. 이것을 증명하는 한 가지 방법은 사람들에게 기여자들을 향해 긍정적이거나 부정적으로 행동할 기회를 주는 것이다. 예를 들어, Guelph 대학교의 교수인, Pat Barclay는 참가자들로 하여금 모든 집단 구성원들을 도와주는 집단 기금에 사람들이 돈을 기부할 수 있는 협동 게임을 하도록 한 다음, 참가자들이 그들의 평판을 바탕으로 다른 참가자들에게 돈을 줄 수 있도록 허락했다. 집단 기금에 더 많이 기부한 사람들은 덜 기부한 사람들보다 더 많은 돈에 대한 책임이 주어졌다. 유사한 결과들이 다른 연구자들에 의해 발견되었다. 또한 그들의 집단에 기여하는 사람들은 상호 작용 파트너로서 더 자주 선택되고, 리더로서 선호되며, 장기적인 관계를 위한 더 바람직한 파트너로서 평가되고, 신뢰할 수 있고 사회적 지위가 높은 것으로 인식된다. 비협조적인 사람들은 언어적인 비판이나 심지어 더 심한 벌을 받는 경향이 있다.

[문제편 p.156]

➡ 연구들은 그들의 공동체에 (A) <u>관대함</u>을 가지고 행동하는 사람들이 그렇게 하지 않은 사람들보다 그 공동체의 구성원들에 의해 (B) <u>혜택</u>을 누릴 만하다고 보여질 가능성이 더 크다고 이야기한다.

Why? 왜 정답일까?

실험 결과를 통해 협력적인 사람과 비협력적인 사람을 비교하며, 협력적인 사람이 사회적으로 이득을 본다는 글이다. 'People who contribute toward their groups are also chosen more often as interaction partners, preferred as leaders, rated as more desirable partners for long-term relationships, and are perceived to be trustworthy and have high social status.'와 'Uncooperative people tend to receive verbal criticism or even more severe punishment.'를 미루어 보았을 때, 빈칸에 들어갈 알맞은 말은 ① '(A) generosity(관대함), (B) benefit(혜택)'이다.

- **laboratory** ⓝ 연구실
- **receive** ⓥ 받다
- **reputation** ⓝ 명성
- **contribute** ⓥ 기여하다
- **cooperative** ⓐ 협력적인
- **advantage** ⓝ 이점, 유리한 점
- **trustworthy** ⓐ 신뢰할 수 있는, 믿을 만한

구문 풀이

9행 People who contributed more to the group fund were given responsibility
주어 / 주격관계대명사 / 동사
for more money than people who contributed less.
주격관계대명사

41-42 연주자와 청중의 소통

In Western society, / many music performance settings / make a clear distinction / between performers and audience members: / the performers are / the "doers" / and those in the audience / take a decidedly passive role.
서구 사회에서, / 많은 음악 공연 환경은 / 명확한 구분을 한다. / 연주자들과 관객들 사이에: / 연주자들은 / "행동하는 자"이고 / 그리고 관객들은 / 단호하게 수동적인 역할을 맡는다.

The performance space / itself may further / (a) <u>reinforce</u> the distinction / with a physical separation / between the stage and audience seating.
공연 공간 자체가 / 더 강화할 수 있다. / 그 구분을 / 물리적 분리로 / 무대와 관객석 사이의

Perhaps because / this distinction is so common, / audiences seem to / greatly value opportunities / to have special "access" / to performers / that affords understanding / about performers' style of music.
아마도 / 이 구분이 매우 흔하기 때문에, / 관객들은 / 크게 가치를 두는 것 같다. / 특별한 "접근"의 기회를 / 연주자들에게 / 그것은 이해를 제공한다. / 연주자들의 음악 스타일에 대한

Some performing musicians / have won great approval / by regularly / (b) <u>incorporating</u> "audience participation" / into their concerts.
일부 연주하는 음악가들은 / 큰 찬사를 받았다. / 정기적으로 / "관객 참여"를 포함함으로써 / 그들의 콘서트에

Whether by leading / a sing-along activity / or teaching a rhythm / to be clapped at certain points, / including audience members / in the music making / can (c) <u>boost</u> the level of engagement / and enjoyment / for all involved. 41번의 근거
노래를 함께 부르는 활동을 이끌거나 / 또는 리듬을 가르침으로써 / 특정 지점에서 박수를 치도록, / 관객을 포함하는 것은 / 음악 만들기에 / 몰입도와 즐거움을 높일 수 있다 / 모든 참여자들에게

Performers / who are uncomfortable / leading audience participation / can still connect / with the audience / simply by giving / a special glimpse / of the performer (d) <u>perspective</u>.
연주자들은 / 불편함을 느끼는 / 관객 참여를 이끄는 데에 / 여전히 소통할 수 있다. / 관객들과 / 단순히 제공함으로써 / 특별한 엿봄을 / 연주자 관점의

It is quite common / in classical music / to provide audiences / with program notes.
꽤 흔하다. / 클래식 음악에서 / 관객들에게 제공하는 것이 / 프로그램 노트를

Typically, / this text in a program / gives background information / about pieces of music / being performed / and perhaps / biographical information / about historically significant composers.
일반적으로, / 프로그램의 이 글은 / 배경 정보를 제공한다. / 음악 작품들에 대한 / 연주되고 있는 / 그리고 아마도 / 전기적 정보도 / 역사적으로 중요한 작곡가들에 대한

What may be / of more interest / to audience members / is background information / about the very performers / who are onstage, / including an explanation / of why / they have chosen / the music they are presenting.
더 흥미로울 수 있는 것은 / 관객들에게 / 배경 정보이다. / 바로 그 연주자들에 대한 / 무대 위에 있는, / 포함하여 설명을 / 왜 / 그들이 선택했는지에 대한 / 그들이 연주하는 음악을

Such insight / can make audience members / feel (e) <u>close</u> to the musicians / onstage, / both metaphorically and emotionally.
그러한 통찰은 / 관객들과 가까움을 / 무대 위의, / 은유적으로도 감정적으로도

『This connection / will likely enhance / the expressive and communicative experience.』
이 연결은 / 아마도 향상시킬 것이다. / 표현적이고 소통적인 경험을 42번의 근거

서양 사회에서, 많은 음악 공연 상황은 공연자와 청중 사이에 명확한 구분을 만든다. 공연자들은 '행위자들'이고, 청중 속 사람들은 분명히 수동적인 역할을 맡는다. 공연 공간 그 자체가 무대와 청중석 사이의 물리적 분리로 구분을 더 (a) 강화할 수 있다. 아마도 이러한 구분이 너무 흔하기 때문에, 청중들은 공연자의 음악 스타일에 대한 이해를 제공하는 공연자에 대한 특별한 '접근'을 할 기회들에 크게 가치를 부여하는 것처럼 보인다. 일부 공연 음악가는 정기적으로 그들의 콘서트에 '청중 참여'를 (b) 포함함으로써 큰 호응을 받아 왔다. 함께 노래 부르기 활동을 하든지 지정된 지점에서 박수를 치도록 리듬을 가르치든지, 음악을 만드는 데 있어서 청중 구성원을 포함하는 것은 모든 참여자의 참여와 즐거움의 수준을 (c) 높일 수 있다. 청중 참여를 이끄는 것에 불편함을 느끼는 공연자들은 단순히 그 공연자 (d) 관점을 특별히 흘깃 보여줌으로써 청중과 여전히 이어질 수 있다. 클래식 음악에서는 청중에게 프로그램 해설을 제공하는 것이 상당히 흔하다. 전형적으로, 이러한 프로그램의 텍스트는 연주되는 음악 작품에 대한 배경 정보와 아마도 역사적으로 중요한 작곡가들에 대한 전기(傳記) 정보를 제공한다. 청중들에게 더 흥미로울 수도 있는 것은 공연자들이 그들이 선보이고 있는 음악을 왜 선택했는지에 대한 설명을 포함한, 무대 위에 있는 바로 그 연주가에 관한 배경 정보이다. 그러한 통찰력은 청중들이 무대 위에 있는 음악가들에게 비유적이고 감정적으로 (e) 멀게(→ 더 가까이) 느끼게 만들 수 있다. 이러한 연결은 표현적이고 소통적인 경험을 아마 향상시킬 것이다.

- **performance** ⓝ 수행
- **passive** ⓐ 수동적인
- **separation** ⓝ 분리, 구분
- **audience** ⓝ 청중
- **reinforce** ⓥ 강화하다
- **access** ⓝ 접근 ⓥ 접근하다

- **regularly** ⓐⓓ 규칙적으로
- **perspective** ⓝ 관점
- **clap** ⓥ 박수를 치다
- **biographical** ⓐ 전기체의

구문 풀이

4행 The performance space itself may further reinforce the distinction with a
재귀대명사 / 조동사 + 동사원형
physical separation between the stage and audience seating.
between A and B : A와 B 사이

★★★ 등급을 가르는 문제!

41 제목 파악
정답률 45% | 정답 ①

윗글의 제목으로 가장 적절한 것은?

☑① Bridge the Divide and Get the Audience Involved
분열을 해소하고 청중 참여 유도
② Musical Composition Reflects the Musician's Experience
뮤지션의 경험을 반영한 음악 작곡
③ Why a Performer's Style Changes with Each Performance
공연마다 공연자의 스타일이 바뀌는 이유
④ Understanding Performers on Stage: An Audience's Responsibility
무대 위 공연자 이해: 관객의 책임
⑤ The Effect of Theater Facilities on the Success of a Performance
극장 시설이 공연 성공에 미치는 영향

Why? 왜 정답일까?

연주자와 청중 간의 참여와 이해의 중요성에 대해 얘기하고 있다. 따라서 윗글의 제목으로 가장 적절한 것은 ① 'Bridge the Divide and Get the Audience Involved'이다.

★★ 문제 해결 꿀~팁 ★★

▶ 많이 틀린 이유는?
주어진 글에서는 "performers and audience members" 간의 구별과 연결, 그리고 "audience participation"의 중요성을 강조하고 있다. 특히, "audiences seem to greatly value opportunities to have special 'access' to performers"라는 문장에서 관객이 공연자와의 연결을 중요하게 여김을 알 수 있다. 지나치게 글의 세부사항에 집중하거나, 공연자의 스타일 변화나 공연 시설의 효과와 같은 주제로 제목을 선택하면 다른 주제로 이해할 수 있다.

▶ 문제 해결 방법은?
글의 제목을 찾는 문제는 무엇보다 글의 주제를 파악하는 것이 중요하다. 해당 글에서는 공연자와 관객 간의 관계와 공연에서의 관객 참여의 중요성을 다루고 있으므로 제목에 들어가는 것이 좋다고 생각할 수 있다.

42 어휘 추론
정답률 59% | 정답 ⑤

밑줄 친 (a) ~ (e) 중에서 문맥상 낱말의 쓰임이 적절하지 <u>않은</u> 것은?

① (a) ② (b) ③ (c) ④ (d) ☑⑤ (e)

Why? 왜 정답일까?

'distant'는 문맥상 청중과 연주자 사이의 거리를 느끼게 하는 부정적인 뉘앙스가 있다. 하지만 이 문맥에서는 연주자와 청중이 가까워지는 것을 강조하고 있기 때문에, 'close'와 같은 긍정적인 단어가 더 적절하다.

43-45 울타리 대신 다리

(A)
Once upon a time, / two brothers, Robert and James, / who lived on neighboring farms / fell into conflict.
옛날에, / 두 형제, 로버트와 제임스가, / 이웃하는 농장에서 살았는데 / 갈등에 빠졌다.

『It was / the first serious fight / in 40 years of farming side by side.』 45번 ①의 근거 일치
그것은 / 첫 번째 심각한 싸움이었다. / 40년 동안 나란히 농사를 지어온 동안

It began / with a small misunderstanding / and it grew / into a major argument, / and finally it exploded / into an exchange of bitter words / followed by weeks of silence.
그것은 시작되었다. / 작은 오해로 / 그리고 커졌다. / 큰 논쟁으로, / 결국 폭발했다. / 심한 말다툼으로 / 그 후 몇 주 동안 침묵으로 이어진

One morning / there was a knock / on Robert's door.
어느 날 아침 / 문을 두드리는 소리가 들렸다. / 로버트의 문에서

(a) He opened it / to find a carpenter / with a toolbox.
그가 그것을 열었을 때 / 목수를 발견했다. / 공구함을 들고 있는

(C)
Looking at Robert, / the carpenter said, / "I'm looking for a few days' work. / Do (c) <u>you</u> have anything to repair?"
로버트를 보며, / 목수가 말했다, / "며칠 동안 일할 곳을 찾고 있습니다. / 고칠 것이 있나요?"

"I have nothing to be repaired, / but I have a job for you. / Look across the creek / at that farm.
"수리할 것은 없지만, / 할 일이 있어요. / 개울 건너편을 보세요. / 저 농장을

『Last week, / my younger brother James / took his bulldozer / and put that creek / in the meadow between us.』 45번 ③의 근거 일치
지난주에, / 내 동생 제임스가 / 불도저를 가져와서 / 그 개울을 만들었어요. / 우리 사이의 초원에

Well, / (d) <u>I will do even worse</u>. / I want you to build me / an 8-foot tall fence / which will block him / from seeing my place," / said Robert.
그래요, / 더 심하게 할 거예요. / 당신에게 8피트짜리 울타리를 / 지어 달라고 부탁하고 싶어요. / 그가 내 집을 / 보지 못하게," / 로버트가 말했다.

The carpenter / seemed to understand the situation.
목수는 / 상황을 이해한 것 같았다.

(D)
『Robert / prepared all the materials / the carpenter needed.』 45번 ④의 근거 일치
로버트는 / 모든 재료를 준비했다. / 목수가 필요로 하는

The next day, / Robert left / to work on another farm, / so he couldn't watch / the carpenter for some days.
다음날, / 로버트는 떠났다. / 다른 농장에서 일하러, / 그래서 그는 지켜볼 수 없었다. / 며칠 동안 목수를

When Robert returned / and saw the carpenter's work, / his jaw dropped.

로버트가 돌아와서 / 목수의 일을 보았을 때, / 그의 턱이 떨어졌다.
『Instead of a fence, / the carpenter had built a bridge / that stretched / from one side of the creek / to the other.』 45번 ⑤의 근거 불일치
울타리 대신에, / 목수는 다리를 지었다. / 뻗어나간 / 개울 한쪽에서 / 다른 쪽까지
His brother / was walking over, / waving (e) his hand in the air.
그의 형제는 / 다리를 건너오고 있었다. / 공중에서 손을 흔들며
Robert laughed / and said to the carpenter, / "You really can fix anything."
로버트는 웃으며 / 목수에게 말했다. / "당신은 정말 뭐든지 고칠 수 있군요."

(B)
The two brothers / stood awkwardly for a moment, / but soon / met on the bridge / and shook hands.
두 형제는 / 어색하게 잠시 서 있었지만, / 곧 / 다리 위에서 만났고 / 악수했다.
They saw / the carpenter leaving / with his toolbox.
그들은 보았다. / 목수가 떠나는 것을 / 그의 공구함을 들고
『"No, wait! / Stay a few more days." / Robert told him.』 45번 ②의 근거 일치
"아니, 잠깐만요! / 며칠 더 머물러 주세요." / 로버트가 그에게 말했다.
"Thank you / for (b) your invitation. / But I need to go / build more bridges.
"감사합니다. / 당신의 초대에 / 하지만 저는 가야 해요. / 더 많은 다리를 지으러
Don't forget. / The fence leads to isolation / and the bridge to openness," / said the carpenter.
잊지 마세요. / 울타리는 고립으로 이어지고 / 다리는 개방으로 이어집니다." / 목수가 말했다.
The two brothers / nodded / at the carpenter's words.
두 형제는 / 고개를 끄덕였다. / 목수의 말에

(A)
옛날 옛적에, 가까운 농장에 사는 두 형제인 Robert와 James가 갈등에 빠졌다. 그것은 함께 나란히 농사를 지은 지 40년 만에 최초의 심각한 싸움이었다. 그것은 작은 오해로 시작하여 보다 중대한 논쟁이 되었고, 마침내 그것은 독설을 주고받는 것으로 폭발했고 몇 주간의 침묵이 뒤따랐다. 어느 날 아침 Robert의 문에 노크가 있었다. (a) 그(Robert)는 그것을 열고 공구 상자를 가진 목수를 발견했다.

(C)
Robert를 바라보며 그 목수는 말했다. "저는 며칠 동안 할 일을 찾고 있어요. (c) 당신(Robert)은 수리할 것이 있나요?" "수리될 것은 없지만 당신이 해 줄 일이 있어요. 샛강 저편에 저 농장을 보세요. 지난주에, 제 동생 James가 그의 불도저를 가지고 우리 사이의 초원에 샛강을 만들었어요. 음, 제(Robert)의 불도저가 훨씬 더 나쁘게 할 거예요. 저는 당신이 그가 제 장소를 보지 못하게 막는 8피트 높이의 울타리를 지어 주기를 원해요." Robert가 말했다. 목수는 그 상황을 이해한 것처럼 보였다.

(D)
Robert는 그 목수가 필요로 하는 모든 재료를 준비해 주었다. 다음 날, Robert는 또 다른 농장으로 일하러 떠났고, 그래서 그는 며칠 동안 그 목수를 볼 수 없었다. Robert가 돌아와서 그 목수의 작업을 보았을 때, 그의 입이 쩍 벌어졌다. 울타리 대신에, 그 목수는 샛강의 한쪽에서 다른 쪽까지 펼쳐진 다리 하나를 만들었다. 그의 동생은 (e) 그(James)의 손을 공중에 흔들며 걸어오고 있었다. Robert는 웃었고 그 목수에게 말했다. "당신은 정말 어떤 것이든 고칠 수 있군요."

(B)
그 두 형제는 잠시 동안 어색하게 서 있었지만, 곧 다리 위에서 만나 악수를 했다. 그들은 그 목수가 그의 공구 상자를 가지고 떠나는 것을 보았다. "안 돼요, 기다려 주세요! 며칠 더 머물러 주세요." Robert가 그에게 말했다. "(b) 당신의(Robert) 초대에 감사드립니다. 하지만 저는 더 많은 다리들을 만들러 가야 해요. 잊지 마세요. 울타리는 고립으로 이끌고 다리는 관대함으로 이끕니다." 목수가 말했다. 그 두 형제는 목수의 말에 끄덕여 동의를 표시했다.

- once upon a time 옛날에
- carpenter ⓝ 목수
- shake hand 악수하다
- isolation ⓝ 고립
- nod ⓥ 고개를 끄덕이다
- creek ⓝ 개울
- walk over 건너오다
- side by side 나란히
- awkwardly [ad] 어색하게
- invitation ⓝ 초대
- openness ⓝ 개방
- repair ⓥ 수리하다
- block ⓥ 막다

구문 풀이

[B] 1행 The two brothers stood awkwardly for a moment, but (they) soon met on
  〔잠시 동안〕 〔주어 생략〕 〔동사1〕
the bridge and shook hands.
  〔동사2〕

43 글의 순서 파악
정답률 72% | 정답 ③

주어진 글 (A)에 이어질 내용을 순서에 맞게 배열한 것으로 가장 적절한 것은?
① (B) – (C) – (D)　　② (C) – (B) – (D)
✓③ (C) – (D) – (B)　　④ (D) – (B) – (C)
⑤ (D) – (C) – (B)

Why? 왜 정답일까?
주어진 글은 Robert와 James의 싸움으로 시작한다. 목수가 Robert에게 할 일을 찾는 (C), Robert가 시킨 일 대신 다리를 만든 목수 (D), 그리고 목수의 재치로 화해하는 (B)의 순서가 가장 알맞다. 따라서 답은 ③ '(C) – (D) – (B)'이다.

44 지칭 추론
정답률 64% | 정답 ⑤

밑줄 친 (a) ~ (e) 중에서 가리키는 대상이 나머지 넷과 다른 것은?
① (a)　　② (b)　　③ (c)　　④ (d)　　✓⑤ (e)

Why? 왜 정답일까?
(a), (b), (c), (d) 모두 Robert를 가리키기 때문에, James를 뜻하는 (e)는 가리키는 대상이 나머지 넷과 다르다. 따라서 답은 ⑤ '(e)'이다.

45 세부 내용 파악
정답률 77% | 정답 ⑤

윗글에 관한 내용으로 적절하지 않은 것은?
① Robert와 James는 40년간 나란히 농사를 지었다.
② Robert는 떠나려는 목수에게 더 머무르라고 말했다.
③ James는 불도저로 초원에 샛강을 만들었다.
④ Robert는 목수가 필요로 하는 재료를 준비해 주었다.
✓⑤ 목수는 샛강에 다리 대신 울타리를 설치했다.

Why? 왜 정답일까?
(D)의 'Instead of a fence, the carpenter had built a bridge that stretched from one side of the creek to the other.'에서 알 수 있듯이, 목수는 샛강에 울타리 대신 다리를 설치했다. 따라서 적절하지 않은 것은 ⑤ '목수는 샛강에 다리 대신 울타리를 설치했다.'이다.

Why? 왜 오답일까?
① (A) 'It was the first serious fight in 40 years of farming side by side.'의 내용과 일치한다.
② (B) '"No, wait! Stay a few more days." Robert told him.'의 내용과 일치한다.
③ (C) 'Last week, my younger brother James took his bulldozer and put that creek in the meadow between us.'의 내용과 일치한다.
④ (D) 'Robert prepared all the materials the carpenter needed.'의 내용과 일치한다.

어휘 Review Test 16
문제편 160쪽

A	B	C	D
01 알리다	01 accomplish	01 ⓕ	01 ⓞ
02 진행 중인	02 persuade	02 ⓐ	02 ⓙ
03 이웃	03 response	03 ⓙ	03 ⓒ
04 청년	04 inferior	04 ⓗ	04 ⓠ
05 관찰하다	05 cognitive	05 ⓢ	05 ⓛ
06 농업	06 survey	06 ⓠ	06 ⓝ
07 저하	07 intrusive	07 ⓑ	07 ⓜ
08 대단히 중요한	08 individual	08 ⓡ	08 ⓐ
09 도전	09 instruction	09 ⓖ	09 ⓔ
10 가능성	10 fundamental	10 ⓛ	10 ⓕ
11 초상화	11 submission	11 ⓘ	11 ⓢ
12 매개체, 수단	12 announcement	12 ⓟ	12 ⓗ
13 역사학자	13 weapon	13 ⓓ	13 ⓙ
14 일반적으로, 보통	14 crucial	14 ⓣ	14 ⓑ
15 기여하다	15 eliminate	15 ⓒ	15 ⓡ
16 상업	16 privacy	16 ⓚ	16 ⓟ
17 기계의	17 voluntarily	17 ⓜ	17 ⓓ
18 도입하다	18 surveillance	18 ⓝ	18 ⓖ
19 장치, 기구	19 statistically	19 ⓞ	19 ⓘ
20 꺼리는	20 methodical	20 ⓔ	20 ⓚ

· 정답 ·

18 ③ 19 ① 20 ④ 21 ③ 22 ④　23 ② 24 ② 25 ③ 26 ⑤ 27 ④　28 ⑤ 29 ④ 30 ⑤ 31 ② 32 ①
33 ① 34 ② 35 ④ 36 ② 37 ③　38 ⑤ 39 ④ 40 ① 41 ③ 42 ②　43 ⑤ 44 ⑤ 45 ④

★ 표기된 문항은 [등급을 가르는 문제]에 해당하는 문항입니다.

---

18 상품권 기부 요청　　정답률 92% | 정답 ③

다음 글의 목적으로 가장 적절한 것은?

① 행사 홍보물 게시가 가능한지를 문의하려고
② 학교 퀴즈 행사에 사용할 물품 제작을 의뢰하려고
☑ 우승 상품으로 사용할 상품권을 기부해 줄 것을 요청하려고
④ 학교 행사로 예상되는 소음 발생에 대해 양해를 구하려고
⑤ 퀴즈 행사 개최를 위한 장소 사용 허가를 받으려고

Dear local business owners,
지역 상점 주인분들께
My name is Carol Williams, / president of the student council at Yellowstone High School.
제 이름은 Carol Williams이고 / Yellowstone 고등학교의 학생회장입니다.
We are hosting our annual quiz night on March 30 / and plan to give prizes to the winning team.
저희는 3월 30일에 연례 퀴즈의 밤을 개최할 것이고, / 우승팀에게 상품을 제공할 계획입니다.
However, / this event won't be possible / without the support of local businesses / who provide valuable products and services.
그러나 / 이 행사는 불가능할 것입니다. / 지역 상점의 후원 없이는 / 유용한 상품과 서비스를 제공해 주는
Would you be willing to donate a gift certificate / that we can use as a prize?
상품권을 흔쾌히 기부해 주실 수 있으신가요? / 저희가 상품으로 사용할
We would be grateful / for any amount on the certificate.
감사히 여길 것입니다. / 어떤 액수의 상품권 기부든
In exchange for your generosity, / we would place an advertisement for your business / on our answer sheets.
귀하의 관대함에 대한 대가로 / 저희는 귀하의 사업 광고를 싣겠습니다. / 저희 답안지에
Thank you for taking time / to read this letter and consider our request.
시간 내주셔서 감사합니다. / 이 편지를 읽고 저희 요청을 고려해주셔서
If you'd like to donate or need more information, / please call or email me.
만약 여러분이 기부를 원하시거나 더 많은 정보가 필요하시면 / 제게 전화나 이메일을 주십시오.
I look forward to hearing from you soon.
귀하로부터 곧 소식 듣기를 기대하겠습니다.
Carol Williams
Carol Williams 드림

지역 상점 주인분들께

제 이름은 Carol Williams이고 Yellowstone 고등학교의 학생회장입니다. 저희는 3월 30일에 연례 퀴즈의 밤을 개최할 것이고, 우승팀에게 상품을 제공할 계획입니다. 그러나 이 행사는 유용한 상품과 서비스를 제공해 주는 지역 상점의 후원 없이는 불가능할 것입니다. 저희가 상품으로 사용할 상품권을 흔쾌히 기부해 주실 수 있으신가요? 어떤 액수의 상품권 기부든 감사히 여길 것입니다. 귀하의 관대함에 대한 대가로 저희 답안지에 귀하의 사업 광고를 싣겠습니다. 시간 내주셔서 이 편지를 읽고 저희 요청을 고려해주셔서 감사합니다. 만약 기부를 원하시거나 더 많은 정보가 필요하시면 제게 전화나 이메일을 주십시오. 귀하로부터 곧 소식 듣기를 기대하겠습니다. Carol Williams 드림

Why? 왜 정답일까?

편지 중반에 퀴즈의 밤 행사의 우승 상품으로 사용할 상품권을 기부해줄 수 없는지(**Would you be willing to donate a gift certificate that we can use as a prize?**) 묻는 말이 나오므로, 글의 목적으로 가장 적절한 것은 ③ '우승 상품으로 사용할 상품권을 기부해 줄 것을 요청하려고'이다.

- student council 학생회
- support ⓝ 후원, 지지
- be willing to 기꺼이 ~하다
- grateful for ~에 감사하는
- generosity ⓝ 관대함
- host ⓥ 주최하다
- valuable ⓐ 가치 있는
- gift certificate 상품권
- in exchange for ~에 대한 대가로

구문 풀이

7행 Would you be willing to donate a gift certificate [that we can use as a prize]?
「be willing to + 동사원형 : 기꺼이 ~하다」　[ ] : 목적격 관계대명사절

---

19 파트너 대신 발표를 무사히 마치고 안도한 필자　　정답률 84% | 정답 ①

다음 글에 드러난 'I'의 심경 변화로 가장 적절한 것은?

☑ ① panicked → relieved
　　당황한　　안도한
② sorrowful → indifferent
　　슬픈　　무관심한
③ sympathetic → content
　　연민 어린　　만족한
④ jealous → delighted
　　질투하는　　기쁜
⑤ confused → humiliated
　　혼란스러운　　굴욕스러운

Dan and I were supposed to make a presentation that day.
그날, Dan과 나는 발표를 하기로 돼 있었다.
Right after the class started, / my phone buzzed.
수업이 시작된 직후에 / 내 전화가 진동했다.
It was a text from Dan saying, / "I can't make it on time. / There's been a car accident on the road!"
그것은 ~라고 Dan이 보낸 문자 메시지였다. / "나 제때 도착할 수 없어. / 도로에서 교통사고가 났어!"
I almost fainted. / 'What should I do?'
나는 거의 쓰러질 뻔했다. / '어떻게 하지?'
Dan didn't show up before our turn, / and soon I was standing in front of the whole class.
Dan은 우리 차례 전에 나타나지 않았고 / 곧 나는 반 전체 학생 앞에 서 있었다.
I managed to finish my portion, / and my mind went blank for a few seconds, / wondering what to do.
나는 겨우 내 부분을 다 끝냈고 / 내 정신은 몇 초간 멍해졌다. / 어떻게 할지 생각하면서
'Hold yourself together!' / I quickly came to my senses / and worked through Dan's part of the presentation / as best as I could.
'정신 차려!' / 나는 재빨리 정신을 가다듬고 / Dan의 발표 부분을 해 나갔다. / 내가 할 수 있는 한 최선을 다해
After a few moments, / I finished the entire presentation on my own.
잠시 후, / 나는 혼자서 전체 발표를 끝냈다.
Only then did the tension vanish.
그제서야 긴장감이 사라졌다.
I could see our professor's beaming face.
나는 우리 교수님의 웃음 띤 얼굴을 볼 수 있었다.

그날, Dan과 나는 발표를 하기로 돼 있었다. 수업이 시작된 직후에 내 전화가 진동했다. "나 제때 도착할 수 없어. 도로에서 교통사고가 났어!"라고 Dan이 보낸 문자 메시지였다. 나는 거의 쓰러질 뻔했다. '어떻게 하지?' Dan은 우리 차례 전에 나타나지 않았고 곧 나는 반 전체 학생 앞에 서 있었다. 나는 겨우 내 부분을 다 끝냈고 어떻게 할지 생각하면서 정신이 몇 초간 멍해졌다. '정신 차려!' 나는 재빨리 정신을 가다듬고 내가 할 수 있는 한 최선을 다해 Dan의 발표 부분을 해 나갔다. 잠시 후, 나는 혼자서 전체 발표를 끝냈다. 그제서야 긴장감이 사라졌다. 나는 우리 교수님의 웃음 띤 얼굴을 볼 수 있었다.

Why? 왜 정답일까?

발표를 함께 하기로 한 친구가 제때 도착하지 못해 기절할 정도로 아찔해했던(**I almost fainted.** 'What should I do?') 필자가 무사히 발표를 마치고 긴장이 풀렸다(**Only then did the tension vanish.**)는 내용의 글이다. 따라서 'I'의 심경 변화로 가장 적절한 것은 ① '당황한 → 안도한'이다.

- buzz ⓥ (윙윙) 울리다
- go blank (마음 따위가) 텅 비다
- come to one's senses 의식을 되찾다, 정신을 차리다
- tension ⓝ 긴장
- beaming ⓐ 미소 띤, 기쁨에 넘치는
- sympathetic ⓐ 연민 어린
- humiliated ⓐ 굴욕을 느끼는, 수치스러운
- faint ⓥ 기절하다
- hold oneself together 정신을 차리다
- vanish ⓥ 사라지다
- panicked ⓐ 당황한, 공포에 질린
- content ⓐ 만족한

구문 풀이

10행 Only then did the tension vanish.
「준부정어 + 조동사 + 주어 + 동사원형 : 도치 구문」

---

20 조직원에 대한 평가의 명확성　　정답률 42% | 정답 ④

다음 글에서 필자가 주장하는 바로 가장 적절한 것은?

① 조직이 구성원에게 제공하는 보상은 즉각적이어야 한다.
② 조직의 발전을 위해 구성원은 동료의 능력을 신뢰해야 한다.
③ 조직 내 구성원의 능력에 맞는 명확한 목표를 설정해야 한다.
☑ 조직의 신뢰 형성을 위해 구성원에 대한 평가 요소가 명확해야 한다.
⑤ 구성원의 의견 수용을 위해 신뢰에 기반한 조직 문화가 구축되어야 한다.

Clarity in an organization / keeps everyone working in one accord / and energizes key leadership components / like trust and transparency.
조직에서의 명확성은 / 모두가 계속 조화롭게 일하게 하고, / 핵심적인 리더십 요소에 활력을 준다. / 신뢰와 투명성 같은
No matter who or what is being assessed in your organization, / what they are being assessed on must be clear / and the people must be aware of it.
조직에서 누가 또는 무엇이 평가되고 있든 간에 / 그들이 무엇을 평가받는지는 분명해야 하고 / 사람들은 그것을 알고 있어야 한다.
If individuals in your organization are assessed / without knowing what they are being assessed on, / it can cause mistrust and move your organization away from clarity.
만약 여러분 조직에 있는 개개인들이 평가받는다면, / 그들이 무엇에 대해 평가받고 있는지를 알지 못한 채로 / 이것은 불신을 초래하고 / 여러분의 조직이 명확성으로부터 멀어지게 할 수 있다.
For your organization to be productive, cohesive, and successful, / trust is essential.
여러분의 조직이 생산적이고 응집력이 높고 성공적이게 하려면 / 신뢰가 필수적이다.
Failure to have trust in your organization / will have a negative effect / on the results of any assessment.
조직에 대한 신뢰를 갖지 못하는 것은 / 부정적인 영향을 끼칠 것이다. / 어떤 평가 결과에든
It will also significantly hinder the growth of your organization.
그것은 또한 여러분의 조직의 성장을 상당히 방해할 것이다.
To conduct accurate assessments, / trust is a must — which comes through clarity.
정확한 평가를 수행하려면 / 신뢰는 필수적이며, / 이는 명확성으로부터 온다.
In turn, / assessments help you see clearer, / which then empowers your organization / to reach optimal success.
결국 / 평가는 여러분이 더 분명하게 볼 수 있도록 도와주는데, / 이는 이후 여러분의 조직이 ~할 힘을 준다. / 최적의 성공에 도달할

조직에서의 명확성은 모두가 계속 조화롭게 일하게 하고, 신뢰와 투명성 같은 핵심적인 리더십 요소에 활력을 준다. 조직에서 누가 또는 무엇이 평가되고 있든 간에 그들이 무엇을 평가받는지는 분명해야 하고, 사람들은 그것을 알고 있어야 한다. 만약 여러분 조직에 있는 개개인들이 무엇에 대해 평가되고 있는지를 알지 못한 채로 평가받는다면, 이것은 불신을 초래하고 여러분의 조직이 명확성으로부터 멀어지게 할 수 있다. 여러분의 조직이 생산적이고 응집력이 높고 성공적이게 하려면 신뢰가 필수적이다. 조직에 대한 신뢰를 갖지 못하는 것은 어떤 평가 결과에든 부정적인 영향을 끼칠 것이다. 그것은 또한 조직의 성장을 상당히 방해할 것이다. 정확한 평가를 수행하려면 신뢰는 필수적이며, 이는 명확성으로부터 온다. 결국 평가는 여러분이 더 분명하게 볼 수 있도록 도와주는데, 이는 이후 여러분의 조직이 최적의 성공에 도달할 힘을 준다.

Why? 왜 정답일까?

'**To conduct accurate assessments, trust is a must — which comes through clarity.**'에서 정확한 평가를 하려면 신뢰가 갖춰져야 하고, 신뢰는 명확성에서 나온다는 핵심 내용을 제시한다.

따라서 필자가 주장하는 바로 가장 적절한 것은 ④ '조직의 신뢰 형성을 위해 구성원에 대한 평가 요소가 명확해야 한다.'이다.

- **clarity** ⓝ 명확성
- **component** ⓝ 구성 요소
- **assess** ⓥ 평가하다
- **productive** ⓐ 생산적인
- **significantly** 젣 현저히, 상당히
- **accurate** ⓐ 정확한
- **optimal** ⓐ 최적의
- **in one accord** 합심하여, 이구동성으로
- **transparency** ⓝ 투명성
- **mistrust** ⓝ 불신
- **cohesive** ⓐ 응집력 있는
- **hinder** ⓥ 막다, 방해하다
- **empower** ⓥ 권한을 부여하다

구문 풀이

3행 No matter who or what is being assessed in your organization, what they
누가 혹은 무엇이 ~하든 간에(= whoever or whatever)　주어1(명사절)
are being assessed on must be clear and the people must be aware of it.
동사1　주어2　동사2

21　하루 에너지 수준에 맞춰 일과 세우기　정답률 55% | 정답 ③

밑줄 친 "eating my problems for breakfast"가 다음 글에서 의미하는 바로 가장 적절한 것은?

① thinking of breakfast as fuel for the day
아침을 하루의 연료로 생각하는 것
② trying to reflect on pleasant events from yesterday
어제 있었던 즐거운 일을 반추해보려고 하는 것
③ handling the most demanding tasks while full of energy
가장 활기 넘칠 때 가장 까다로운 일을 처리하는 것
④ spending the morning time improving my physical health
아침 시간을 신체 건강 증진에 쓰는 것
⑤ preparing at night to avoid decision making in the morning
아침에 의사 결정하는 것을 피하기 위해 밤에 준비하는 것

Research in the science of peak performance and motivation / points to the fact / that different tasks should ideally be matched / to our energy level.
최상의 수행과 동기 부여에 관한 과학 연구는 / 사실을 지적한다. / 각기 다른 일이 이상적으로 맞춰져야 한다는 / 우리 에너지 수준에
For example, / analytical tasks are best accomplished / when our energy is high / and we are free from distractions and able to focus.
예를 들어 / 분석적인 일은 가장 잘 수행된다. / 우리 에너지가 높고 / 우리가 방해물이 없으며 집중할 수 있을 때
I generally wake up energized.
나는 보통 활기찬 상태로 일어난다.
Over the years, / I have consistently stuck to the habit / of "eating my problems for breakfast."
몇 년 동안 / 나는 습관을 꾸준히 고수해 왔다. / '내 문제를 아침 식사로 먹는'
I'm someone / who tends to overthink different scenarios and conversations / that haven't happened yet.
나는 사람이다. / 다양한 시나리오와 대화를 과하게 생각하는 경향이 있는 / 아직 일어나지 않은
When I procrastinate on / talking with an unhappy client / or dealing with an unpleasant email, / I find / I waste too much emotional energy during the day.
내가 미룰 때, / 불만족한 고객과 이야기하거나 / 불쾌한 이메일을 처리하는 것을 / 나는 깨닫는다. / 내가 낮 동안 감정적 에너지를 너무 많이 낭비하고 있음을
It's as if the task hangs over my head, / and I'll spend more time worrying about it, / talking about it, / and avoiding it, / than it would actually take to just take care of it.
마치 그 일이 뇌리에서 떠나지 않는 것 같고, / 나는 더 많은 시간 동안 그 일에 관해 걱정하고 / 이야기하고 / 피할 것이다. / 그냥 그 일을 처리하는 데 실제로 드는 것보다
So for me, / it'll always be the first thing / I get done.
그래서 나로 말하자면, / 그 일은 항상 첫 번째가 될 것이다. / 내가 끝내버리는
If you know you are not a morning person, / be strategic / about scheduling your difficult work later in the day.
만약 여러분 자신이 아침형 인간이 아니란 것을 알고 있다면, / 전략적으로 되라. / 어려운 일을 오후 늦은 시간에 하는 것에 관해

최상의 수행과 동기 부여에 관한 과학 연구는 각기 다른 일이 우리 에너지 수준에 이상적으로 맞춰져야 한다는 사실을 지적한다. 예를 들어 분석적인 일은 우리 에너지가 높고 방해물이 없으며 집중할 수 있을 때 가장 잘 수행된다. 나는 보통 활기찬 상태로 일어난다. 몇 년 동안 나는 '내 문제를 아침 식사로 먹는' 습관을 꾸준히 고수해 왔다. 나는 아직 일어나지 않은 다양한 시나리오와 대화를 과하게 생각하는 경향이 있는 사람이다. 불만족한 고객과 이야기하거나 불쾌한 이메일을 처리하는 것을 미룰 때, 나는 내가 낮 동안 감정적 에너지를 너무 많이 낭비하고 있음을 깨닫는다. 마치 그 일이 뇌리에서 떠나지 않는 것 같고, 나는 그냥 그 일을 처리하는 데 실제로 드는 것보다 더 많은 시간 동안 그 일에 관해 걱정하고 이야기하고 피할 것이다. 그래서 나로 말하자면, 늘 그 일부터 가장 먼저 끝내버릴 것이다. 만약 여러분 자신이 아침형 인간이 아니란 것을 알고 있다면, 전략적으로 어려운 일을 오후 늦은 시간에 하도록 일정을 짜라.

Why? 왜 정답일까?

첫 문장에 따르면 최적의 수행과 동기 부여는 우리 에너지 수준에 맞춰 과업을 배치할 때 가능해진다(~ different tasks should ideally be matched to our energy level.)고 한다. 이어서 필자는 자신이 아침에 활기가 넘치기 때문에, 활기가 덜한 낮 시간보다는 아침에 문제가 되는 일부터 처리해 버린다고 설명한다. 이를 근거로 볼 때, '문제를 아침 식사로 먹는다'는 밑줄 친 부분의 의미로 가장 적절한 것은 ③ '가장 활기 넘칠 때 가장 까다로운 일을 처리하는 것'이다.

- **peak** ⓝ 최상, 정점
- **point to** ~을 지적하다
- **accomplish** ⓥ 성취하다
- **consistently** 젣 꾸준하게, 일관성 있게
- **overthink** ⓥ 과도하게 생각하다
- **unpleasant** ⓐ 불쾌한
- **strategic** ⓐ 전략적인
- **performance** ⓝ 수행, 성과
- **ideally** 젣 이상적으로
- **distraction** ⓝ 방해물, 정신을 산만하게 하는 것
- **stick to** ~을 고수하다
- **procrastinate** ⓥ 미루다
- **take care of** 처리하다, 다루다
- **demanding** ⓐ 까다로운

구문 풀이

1행 Research in the science of peak performance and motivation points to
주어(불가산) 동사
the fact [that different tasks should ideally be matched to our energy level].
[ ] : the fact 동격

22　새로운 시작과 연관된 날짜와 목표 추진의 동기　정답률 80% | 정답 ④

다음 글의 요지로 가장 적절한 것은?

① 새로운 시작을 하기 전에 장기적인 계획을 세우는 것이 바람직하다.
② 자신이 해야 할 일을 일정표에 표시하는 것이 목표 달성에 효과적이다.
③ 문제 행동을 개선하기 위해 원인이 되는 요소를 파악할 필요가 있다.
④ 날짜가 시작이라는 의미와 관련지어질 때 목표 추구에 강한 동기가 부여된다.
⑤ 상세한 일정표를 작성하는 것은 여러 목표를 동시에 달성하는 데 도움이 된다.

In one study, / when researchers suggested / that a date was associated with a new beginning / (such as "the first day of spring"), / students viewed it / as a more attractive time to kick-start goal pursuit / than when researchers presented it / as an unremarkable day / (such as "the third Thursday in March").
한 연구에서 / 연구자들이 제시했을 때, / 어떤 날짜가 새로운 시작과 관련이 있다고 / (예컨대 '봄의 첫날') / 학생들은 그 날짜를 간주했다. / 목표 추구를 시작할 더 매력적인 시기로 / 연구자들이 그날을 제시했을 때에 비해 / 평범한 날로 / (예컨대 '3월의 세 번째 목요일')
Whether it was starting a new gym habit / or spending less time on social media, / when the date that researchers suggested / was associated with a new beginning, / more students wanted to begin changes right then.
새로운 운동 습관을 시작하는 것이든, / 혹은 소셜 미디어에 시간을 덜 쓰는 것이든, / 연구자들이 제시하는 날짜가 / 새로운 시작과 관련될 때 / 더 많은 학생들이 바로 그때 변화를 시작하려 했다.
And more recent research by a different team found / that similar benefits were achieved / by showing goal seekers modified weekly calendars.
그리고 다른 팀에 의한 더 최근의 연구는 알아냈다. / 비슷한 이점이 얻어졌다는 것을 / 목표를 추구하는 사람들에게 수정된 주간 일정표를 보여줘서
When calendars depicted the current day / (either Monday or Sunday) / as the first day of the week, / people reported feeling more motivated / to make immediate progress on their goals.
달력이 오늘을 표현했을 때, / (월요일이든 일요일이든) / 한 주의 첫날로 / 사람들은 더 의욕적인 기분을 느낀다고 보고했다. / 자기 목표에 대한 즉각적인 진전을 이루는 데

한 연구에서 연구자들이 어떤 날짜가 새로운 시작(예컨대 '봄의 첫날')과 관련이 있다고 제시했을 때, 학생들은 연구자들이 그 날짜를 평범한 날(예컨대 '3월의 세 번째 목요일')로 제시했을 때에 비해 그날을 목표 추구를 시작할 더 매력적인 시기로 간주했다. 새로운 운동 습관을 시작하는 것이든, 혹은 소셜 미디어에 시간을 덜 쓰는 것이든, 연구자들이 제시하는 날짜가 새로운 시작과 관련될 때 더 많은 학생들이 바로 그때 변화를 시작하려고 했다. 그리고 다른 팀에 의한 더 최근의 연구는 목표를 추구하는 사람들에게 수정된 주간 일정표를 보여줘서 비슷한 이점을 얻었다는 것을 알아냈다. 달력이 오늘을 (월요일이든 일요일이든) 한 주의 첫날로 표현했을 때, 사람들은 자기 목표에 대한 즉각적인 진전을 이루는 데 더 의욕적인 기분을 느낀다고 보고했다.

Why? 왜 정답일까?

두 연구를 예로 들어 날짜가 달이든 주이든 시작과 관련되어 있을 때 목표 추구에 더 강한 동기가 부여된다는 결론을 이끌어내는 글이다. 따라서 글의 요지로 가장 적절한 것은 ④ '날짜가 시작이라는 의미와 관련지어질 때 목표 추구에 강한 동기가 부여된다.'이다.

- **kick-start** ⓥ 시동을 걸다
- **present A as B** A를 B라고 제시하다
- **modify** ⓥ 수정하다
- **progress** ⓝ 진전
- **pursuit** ⓝ 추구
- **unremarkable** ⓐ 특별할 것 없는, 평범한
- **depict** ⓥ 묘사하다, 설명하다

구문 풀이

1행 ~ when researchers suggested that a date was associated with a new
접속사(~것)
beginning (such as "the first day of spring"), students viewed it as a more
「view +A＋ as + B : A를 B라고 여기다」
attractive time to kick-start goal pursuit than when researchers presented it as
「비교급 + than : ~보다 더 …한」 (= the date)
an unremarkable day (such as "the third Thursday in March").

23　전쟁에서 노래와 춤을 이용하는 것의 이점　정답률 52% | 정답 ②

다음 글의 주제로 가장 적절한 것은?

① cultural differences in honoring war victims
전쟁 희생자를 기념하는 데 있어 문화적 차이
② benefits of utilizing sound and motion in warfare
전쟁에서 소리와 움직임을 이용하는 것의 이점
③ functions of music in preventing or resolving conflicts
갈등을 방지하거나 해결하는 데 있어서의 음악의 기능
④ strategies of analyzing an enemy's vulnerable points in war
전쟁에서 적의 취약점을 분석하는 전략
⑤ effects of religious dances on lowering anxiety on the battlefield
종교적인 춤이 전쟁터에서 불안을 낮추는 데 끼치는 영향

Native Americans often sang and danced / in preparation for launching an attack.
북미 원주민들은 종종 노래를 부르고 춤을 췄다. / 공격을 개시하기 위한 준비로
The emotional and neurochemical excitement / that resulted from this preparatory singing / gave them stamina / to carry out their attacks.
감정적이고 신경 화학적인 흥분 상태가 / 이러한 준비의 노래에서 비롯된 / 그들에게 힘을 제공해주었다. / 공격을 수행할
What may have begun as an unconscious, uncontrolled act / — rushing their victims with singing and beating drums in a frenzy — / could have become a strategy / as the victors saw firsthand the effect / their actions had on those they were attacking.
무의식적이고 억제되지 않는 행동으로 시작했을지도 모르는 것, / 즉 격분하여 노래를 부르고 북을 치며 희생자를 공격하는 것은 / 전략이 되었을 수도 있다. / 승리자들이 영향을 직접 목격하면서 / 자신들이 공격 중인 사람들에게 자신들의 행동이 미치는
Although war dances risk warning an enemy of an upcoming attack, / the arousal and synchronizing benefits for the attackers / may compensate for the loss of surprise.
비록 전쟁의 춤이 적에게 곧 있을 공격을 경고해 주는 위험을 감수하는 것임에도 불구하고, / 공격자들에게 주는 정서적 자극과 동시에 하는 이점이 / 기습의 상실을 보상해 줄 수 있다.
Humans who sang, danced, and marched / may have enjoyed a strong advantage on the battlefield / as well as intimidated enemies / who witnessed such a spectacle.
노래하고, 춤추고, 행진했던 사람들은 / 전쟁터에서 강한 우세를 누렸을지도 모른다. / 적들을 겁먹게 했을 뿐 아니라 / 그러한 장관을 목격한

Nineteenth-and twentieth-century Germans / feared no one more than the Scots — / the bagpipes and drums were disturbing / in their sheer loudness and visual spectacle.
19세기와 20세기의 독일인들은 / 스코틀랜드인들을 가장 무서워했는데, / 백파이프와 북은 교란시켰다 / 그것의 순전한 시끄러움과 시각적인 장관으로

북미 원주민들은 공격을 개시하기 위한 준비로 종종 노래를 불렀고 춤을 췄다. 이러한 준비의 노래에서 비롯된 감정적이고 신경 화학적인 흥분 상태가 공격을 수행할 힘을 제공해주었다. 무의식적이고 억제되지 않는 행동으로 시작됐을지도 모르는 것, 즉 격분하여 노래를 부르고 북을 치며 희생자를 공격하는 것은 승리자들이 자신들이 공격 중인 사람들에게 자신들의 행동이 미치는 영향을 직접 목격하면서 전략이 되었을 수도 있다. 비록 전쟁의 춤이 적에게 곧 있을 공격을 경고해 주는 위험을 감수하는 것임에도 불구하고, 공격자들에게 주는 정서적 자극과 동시에 움직이게 하는 이점이 기습의 상실을 보상해 줄 수 있다. 노래하고, 춤추고, 행진했던 사람들은 그러한 장관을 목격한 적들을 겁먹게 했을 뿐만 아니라 전쟁터에서 강한 우세를 누렸을지도 모른다. 19세기와 20세기의 독일인들은 스코틀랜드인들을 가장 무서워했는데, (이들의) 백파이프와 북은 순전한 시끄러움과 시각적인 장관으로 (적을) 교란시켰다.

Why? 왜 정답일까?

전쟁에서 노래와 춤을 이용하는 쪽이 우세를 누렸다(Humans who sang, danced, and marched may have enjoyed a strong advantage on the battlefield as well as intimidated enemies who witnessed such a spectacle.)는 점을 언급하며 그 이유를 추측하는 글이므로, 글의 주제로 가장 적절한 것은 ② '전쟁에서 소리와 움직임을 이용하는 것의 이점'이다.

- **launch** ⓥ 개시하다, 시작하다
- **arousal** ⓝ 자극, 흥분
- **compensate for** ~을 보충하다, 보상하다
- **witness** ⓥ 목격하다
- **disturb** ⓥ 교란시키다
- **utilize** ⓥ 이용하다
- **vulnerable** ⓐ 취약한
- **anxiety** ⓝ 불안, 걱정
- **carry out** ~을 수행하다
- **synchronize** ⓥ 동시에 움직이게 하다
- **intimidate** ⓥ 위협하다
- **spectacle** ⓝ 장관
- **sheer** ⓐ 순전한, 큰
- **warfare** ⓝ 전쟁, 싸움
- **religious** ⓐ 종교적인

구문 풀이

4행 What may have begun as an unconscious, uncontrolled act — (rushing
명사절 주어
their victims with singing and beating drums in a frenzy) — could have become
동사구(과거에 대한 추측: ~했을 수도 있다)
a strategy as the victors saw firsthand the effect [their actions had on those they were attacking.]

24 자전거 타기의 의미 변화 정답률 50% | 정답 ②

다음 글의 제목으로 가장 적절한 것은?

① Cycling Contributes to a City's Atmosphere and Identity
자전거 타기는 도시 분위기와 정체성에 이바지한다
✓ The Rise of Cycling: A New Status Symbol of City Dwellers
자전거 타기의 증가: 도시 거주자들에게 있어 지위의 새로운 상징물
③ Cycling Is Wealth-Building but Worsens Social Inequality
자전거 타기는 부를 축적하지만 사회적 불평등을 악화시킨다
④ How to Encourage and Sustain the Bicycle Craze in Urban Areas
도시 지역의 자전거 열풍을 촉진하고 유지시킬 방법
⑤ Expanding Bike Lane Networks Can Lead to More Inclusive Cities
자전거 도로망 확장이 더 폭넓은 도시를 만든다

The recent "cycling as a lifestyle" craze / has expressed itself / in an increase in the number of active cyclists / and in growth of cycling club membership / in several European, American, Australian and Asian urban areas.
최근 '라이프스타일로서의 자전거' 열풍은 / 나타났다 / 적극적으로 자전거를 타는 사람들 수의 증가와 / 자전거 타기 클럽 회원의 성장으로 / 유럽, 미국, 호주, 그리고 아시아의 몇몇 도시 지역에서
It has also been accompanied / by a symbolic reinterpretation of the bicycle.
그것은 또한 동반되었다 / 자전거의 상징적인 재해석과
After the bicycle had been associated with poverty for many years, / expensive recreational bicycles or recreationally-inspired commuting bicycles / have suddenly become aspirational products / in urban environments.
자전거가 수년 간 가난과 연관지어진 이후로, / 비싼 여가용 자전거나 여가에서 영감을 얻은 통근용 자전거가 / 갑자기 열망의 상품이 되었다 / 도시 환경에서
In present times, / cycling has become an activity / which is also performed for its demonstrative value, / its role in identity construction / and its effectiveness in impressing others and signaling social status.
오늘날 / 자전거 타기는 활동이 되었다 / 그것의 표현적 가치 때문에 수행되기도 하는 / 그것이 정체성 형성에서 수행하는 역할, / 그리고 타인에게 깊은 인상을 주고 사회적 지위를 나타내는 데 있어서의 효과성
To a certain extent, / cycling has turned into a symbolic marker of the well-off.
어느 정도는 / 자전거 타기가 부유한 사람들의 상징적 표시로 바뀌었다.
Obviously, / value-laden consumption behavior / is by no means limited to cycling.
분명히, / 가치를 지닌 소비 행위는 / 결코 자전거 타기에 한정되지 않는다.
However, / the link with identity construction and conspicuous consumption / has become particularly manifest / in the case of cycling.
그러나 / 정체성 형성과 과시적 소비와의 연관성은 / 특히 분명해졌다 / 자전거 타기에 있어

최근 '라이프스타일로서의 자전거' 열풍은 유럽, 미국, 호주, 그리고 아시아의 몇몇 도시 지역에서 적극적으로 자전거를 타는 사람들 수의 증가와 자전거 타기 클럽 회원의 성장으로 나타났다. 그것은 또한 자전거의 상징적인 재해석과 동반되었다. 자전거가 수년 간 가난과 연관지어진 이후로, 비싼 여가용 자전거나 여가에서 영감을 얻은 통근용 자전거가 도시 환경에서 갑자기 열망의 상품이 되었다. 오늘날 자전거 타기는 그것의 표현적 가치, 그것이 정체성 형성에서 수행하는 역할, 그리고 그것이 타인에게 깊은 인상을 주고 사회적 지위를 나타내는 데 있어서의 효과성 때문에 수행되기도 하는 활동이 되었다. 어느 정도는 자전거 타기가 부유한 사람들의 상징적 표시로 바뀌었다. 분명히, 가치를 지닌 소비 행위는 결코 자전거 타기에 한정되지 않는다. 그러나 정체성 형성과 과시적 소비와의 연관성은 자전거 타기에 있어 특히 분명해졌다.

Why? 왜 정답일까?

자전거의 의미가 과거와 달라졌음을 설명하는 글이다. 과거에는 자전거가 가난과 주로 연관되었지만, 오늘날에는 비싼 여가용 자전거 등이 개발되면서 자전거가 도시 사람들의 정체성 형성과 과시적 소비와 관련

성을 띠게 되었다(cycling has become an activity which is also performed for its demonstrative value, its role in identity construction and its effectiveness in impressing others and signaling social status)는 내용이다. 따라서 글의 제목으로 가장 적절한 것은 ② '자전거 타기의 증가: 도시 거주자들에게 있어 지위의 새로운 상징물'이다.

- **accompany** ⓥ 동반하다, 수반하다
- **poverty** ⓝ 가난
- **demonstrative** ⓐ 표현적인, 분명히 나타내는
- **effectiveness** ⓝ 유효성
- **well-off** ⓐ 부유한
- **value-laden** 가치 판단적인, 개인의 의견에 영향을 받는
- **by no means** 결코 ~않다
- **manifest** ⓥ 나타내는, 분명한
- **inequality** ⓝ 불평등
- **reinterpretation** ⓝ 재해석
- **inspire** ⓥ 영감을 주다
- **construction** ⓝ 구축, 건설
- **social status** 사회적 지위
- **conspicuous** ⓐ 눈에 잘 띄는
- **dweller** ⓝ 거주자

구문 풀이

1행 The recent "cycling as a lifestyle" craze has expressed itself in an
재귀대명사(= The recent ~ craze)
increase in the number of active cyclists ~

25 지역별 아동의 2차 홍역 백신 접종 비율 정답률 69% | 정답 ③

다음 도표의 내용과 일치하지 않는 것은?

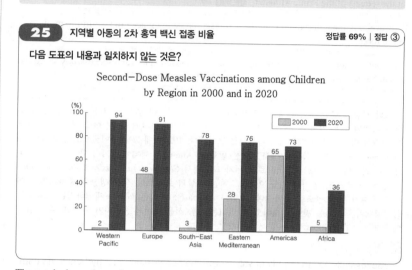

Second-Dose Measles Vaccinations among Children by Region in 2000 and in 2020

The graph above shows the percentage of children / who received second-dose measles vaccinations in six regions / in 2000 and in 2020.
위 그래프는 아이들의 비율을 보여 준다. / 6개 지역에서 2차 홍역 백신을 접종한 / 2000년과 2020년에
① The percentage of vaccinated children in the Western Pacific / was lower than that of Europe in 2000, / but the vaccination percentage in 2020 of the Western Pacific / exceeded that of Europe by 3 percentage points.
서태평양에서 백신을 접종한 아이들의 비율은 / 2000년에는 유럽에 비해 낮았지만 / 2020년 서태평양의 백신 접종율은 / 유럽을 3퍼센트포인트 앞질렀다.
② Among all regions, / South-East Asia achieved the second biggest increase / in its percentage of vaccinated children / over the two decades, / and it ranked third / in the percentage of vaccinated children / among the six regions in 2020.
모든 지역들 중에서, / 동남아시아는 두 번째로 큰 증가를 이뤘고, / 백신 접종이 완료된 아이들의 비율에 있어 / 지난 20년간 / 이 지역은 3위를 차지했다. / 백신 접종된 아이들의 비율에서 / 2020년 6개 지역 중
✓ In the Eastern Mediterranean, / the percentage of vaccinated children / more than doubled from 2000 to 2020, / but did not exceed that of the Americas in either year.
동 지중해에서 / 백신을 접종한 아이들의 비율은 / 2000년에서 2020년까지 2배 이상 증가했지만, / 두 해 모두 아메리카의 비율을 뛰어넘지는 못했다.
④ The percentage of vaccinated children in the Americas / was the highest among the six regions in 2000, / but it increased the least of all regions / over the two decades.
아메리카에서 백신을 접종한 아이들의 비율은 / 2000년에 여섯 지역 중 가장 높았지만, / 이는 모든 지역 중 가장 적게 증가했다. / 지난 20년간
⑤ In Africa, / the percentage of children / who received the vaccine in 2020 / was more than seven times higher than in 2000, / but was still the lowest among the six regions in 2020.
아프리카에서 / 아이들의 비율은 / 2020년에 백신을 접종한 / 2000년보다 7배 이상 높았지만, / 2020년에도 여전히 여섯 지역 중 최하였다.

위 그래프는 2000년과 2020년에 6개 지역에서 2차 홍역 백신을 접종한 아이들의 비율을 보여 준다. ① 서태평양에서 백신을 접종한 아이들의 비율은 2000년에는 유럽에 비해 낮았지만 2020년 서태평양의 백신 접종율은 유럽을 3퍼센트포인트 앞질렀다. ② 모든 지역들 중에서, 동남아시아는 백신 접종이 완료된 아이들의 비율에 있어 지난 20년간 두 번째 증가를 이뤘고, 이 지역은 2020년 백신 접종된 아이들의 비율에서 6개 지역 중 3위를 차지했다. ③ 동 지중해에서 백신을 접종한 아이들의 비율은 2000년에서 2020년까지 2배 이상 증가했지만, 두 해 모두 아메리카를 뛰어넘지는 못했다. ④ 아메리카에서 백신을 접종한 아이들의 비율은 2000년에 여섯 지역 중 가장 높았지만, 이는 지난 20년간 모든 지역 중 가장 적게 증가했다. ⑤ 아프리카에서 2020년에 백신을 접종한 아이들의 비율은 2000년보다 7배 이상 높았지만, 2020년에도 여전히 여섯 지역 중 최하였다.

Why? 왜 정답일까?

도표에 따르면 동 지중해 지역에서 2차 홍역 백신 접종을 완료한 아동의 비율은 2000 ~ 2020년 사이 28%에서 76%로 증가했고, 2020년의 경우 아메리카(73%)보다도 그 수치가 높았다. 따라서 도표와 일치하지 않는 것은 두 해 모두 아메리카보다 낮다고 잘못 기술한 ③이다.

- **dose** ⓝ (약의) 투여량, 복용량
- **vaccination** ⓝ 백신 접종
- **measles** ⓝ 홍역
- **Mediterranean** ⓐ 지중해의

26 Janaki Ammal의 생애 정답률 89% | 정답 ⑤

Janaki Ammal에 관한 다음 글의 내용과 일치하지 않는 것은?

① 관습을 따르지 않고 대학에 입학하기로 결심했다.
② 세계에서 가장 단 사탕수수 품종 개발에 기여했다.
③ Chromosome Atlas of Cultivated Plants를 공동 집필했다.

④ 식량 생산을 증가시키는 데 도움을 주기 위해 인도로 돌아갔다.
☑ 수력 발전 댐의 건설로부터 Silent Valley를 지키는 데 실패했다.

Janaki Ammal, one of India's most notable scientists, / was born in 1897, / and was expected / to wed through an arranged marriage.
인도의 가장 유명한 과학자 중 한 명인 Janaki Ammal은 / 1897년에 태어나 / 기대되었다. / 중매결혼을 할 것으로
『Despite living at a time / when literacy among women in India was less than one percent, / she decided to reject tradition and attend college.』 ①의근거 일치
시기에 살았음에도 불구하고, / 인도 여성들의 식자율이 1%보다 낮았던 / 그녀는 관습을 따르지 않고 대학에 입학하기로 결심했다.
In 1924, / she went to the U.S. / and eventually received a doctorate in botany / from the University of Michigan.
1924년에 / 그녀는 미국으로 갔고, / 마침내 식물학 박사 학위를 받았다. / Michigan 대학교에서
『Ammal contributed to the development / of the sweetest sugarcane variety in the world.』 ②의근거 일치
Ammal은 개발에 기여했다. / 세계에서 가장 단 사탕수수 품종
『She moved to England / where she co-authored the *Chromosome Atlas of Cultivated Plants*.』 ③의근거 일치
그녀는 영국으로 건너갔다. / 그녀가 *Chromosome Atlas of Cultivated Plants*를 공동 집필한 곳인
『Following a series of famines, / she returned to India / to help increase food production / at the request of the Prime Minister.』 ④의근거 일치
연이은 기근 이후, / 그녀는 인도로 돌아갔다. / 식량 생산을 증가시키는 데 도움을 주기 위해 / 수상의 요청으로
However, / Ammal disagreed with the deforestation taking place / in an effort to grow more food.
그러나 / Ammal은 삼림벌채가 일어나는 것에 반대하였다. / 더 많은 식량을 재배하려는 노력으로
『She became an advocate / for the preservation of native plants / and successfully saved the Silent Valley / from the construction of a hydroelectric dam.』 ⑤의근거 불일치
그녀는 옹호자가 되었고, / 토종 식물 보존의 / Silent Valley를 성공적으로 지켰다. / 수력 발전 댐의 건설로부터

인도의 가장 유명한 과학자 중 한 명인 Janaki Ammal은 1897년에 태어나 중매결혼을 할 것으로 기대되었다. 인도 여성들의 식자율이 1%보다 낮았던 시기에 살았음에도 불구하고, 그녀는 관습을 따르지 않고 대학에 입학하기로 결심했다. 1924년에 그녀는 미국으로 갔고, 마침내 Michigan 대학교에서 식물학 박사 학위를 받았다. Ammal은 세계에서 가장 단 사탕수수 품종 개발에 기여했다. 그녀는 영국으로 건너가 그곳에서 *Chromosome Atlas of Cultivated Plants*를 공동 집필했다. 연이은 기근 이후, 그녀는 수상의 요청으로 식량 생산을 증가시키는 데 도움을 주기 위해 인도로 돌아갔다. 그러나 Ammal은 더 많은 식량을 재배하려는 노력으로 삼림벌채가 일어나는 것에 반대하였다. 그녀는 토종 식물 보존의 옹호자가 되었고, 수력 발전 댐의 건설로부터 Silent Valley를 성공적으로 지켰다.

Why? 왜 정답일까?
'~ successfully saved the Silent Valley from the construction of a hydroelectric dam.'에 따르면 Janaki Ammal은 수력 발전 댐의 건설로부터 Silent Valley를 성공적으로 지켜냈다고 하므로, 내용과 일치하지 않는 것은 ⑤ '수력 발전 댐의 건설로부터 Silent Valley를 지키는 데 실패했다.'이다.

Why? 왜 오답일까?
① '~ she decided to reject tradition and attend college.'의 내용과 일치한다.
② 'Ammal contributed to the development of the sweetest sugarcane variety in the world.'의 내용과 일치한다.
③ 'She moved to England where she co-authored the *Chromosome Atlas of Cultivated Plants*.'의 내용과 일치한다.
④ '~ she returned to India to help increase food production ~'의 내용과 일치한다.

- notable ⓐ 유명한, 저명한
- arranged marriage 중매결혼
- doctorate ⓝ 박사 학위
- co-author ⓥ 공동 저술하다
- deforestation ⓝ 삼림벌채
- preservation ⓝ 보존
- be expected to ~할 것으로 예상되다
- literacy ⓝ 문해력, 식자율
- botany ⓝ 식물학
- famine ⓝ 기근
- advocate ⓝ 지지자, 옹호자
- hydroelectric ⓐ 수력 전기의

구문 풀이

3행 Despite living at a time [when literacy among women in India was less than one percent], she decided to reject tradition and attend college.

Note
참고
『The parking fee is $5 / and includes tram service to the ticket booth.』 ④의근거 불일치
주차비는 5달러이며, / 매표소로 가는 트램 서비스가 포함됩니다.
『If you are interested in volunteering, / complete an application form / and email it to manager@strawberryfestival.org.』 ⑤의근거 일치
여러분이 자원봉사에 관심이 있으시다면, / 신청서를 작성하여 / 그것을 manager@strawberryfestival.org로 이메일로 보내 주십시오.

2022 딸기 축제

즐거운 가족 축제에 함께하세요. 올해에는 Berry Square에서 대면 행사를 다시 개최하게 되었습니다!

□ 날짜: 2022년 11월 26일(오전 11시-오후 5시)
□ 티켓: 1인당 20달러 (6세 이하의 아이들은 무료입니다.)

□ 특별행사
• 오전 11시 : 아이들을 위한 베이킹 수업
• 오후 1시 : 딸기파이 먹기 대회
• 오후 3시 : 딸기 의상 대회

□ 참고
• 주차비는 5달러이며, 매표소로 가는 트램 서비스가 포함됩니다.
• 자원봉사에 관심이 있으시다면, 신청서를 작성하여 manager@strawberryfestival.org로 이메일을 보내 주십시오.

Why? 왜 정답일까?
'The parking fee is $5 and includes tram service to the ticket booth.'에서 주차비 5달러에는 매표소까지 가는 트램 서비스가 포함되어 있다고 하므로, 안내문의 내용과 일치하지 않는 것은 ④ '매표소로 가는 트램 서비스는 주차비에 포함되지 않는다.'이다.

Why? 왜 오답일까?
① 'This year, we are back to hosting an in-person event in Berry Square!'의 내용과 일치한다.
② '(Children 6 and under are FREE.)'의 내용과 일치한다.
③ '1:00 p.m. : Strawberry Pie-Eating Contest'의 내용과 일치한다.
⑤ 'If you are interested in volunteering, complete an application form and email it to manager@strawberryfestival.org.'의 내용과 일치한다.

- in-person ⓐ 직접 하는, 대면의
- square ⓝ 광장

---

28 조명 예술 전시회 안내   정답률 91% | 정답 ⑤

Maple Spring Light Art Exhibition에 관한 다음 안내문의 내용과 일치하는 것은?
① 매주 월요일은 운영하지 않는다.
② 밤 11시 이후에도 입장이 가능하다.
③ 관람 경로가 담긴 지도는 종이로만 제공한다.
④ 기념품은 현장에서만 구매 가능하다.
☑ 지역 주민은 입장료의 10% 할인을 받을 수 있다.

Maple Spring Light Art Exhibition
Maple Spring 조명 예술 전시회
The Maple Spring Light Art Exhibition will illuminate you, / with a route surrounded by light artwork.
Maple Spring 조명 예술 전시회는 여러분을 비춰줄 것입니다. / 조명 예술품으로 둘러싸인 경로를 따라
Admire the beautiful light artwork / as you walk through Maple Spring.
아름다운 조명 예술품들을 감상하세요. / 여러분이 Maple Spring을 걸으면서
Date: December 1 – 31, 2022 / 『(closed on the 2nd and 4th Monday of the month)』 ①의근거 불일치
날짜: 2022년 12월 1일부터 12월 31일까지 / (둘째 주와 넷째 주 월요일은 운영하지 않음.)
『Time: 7 p.m. – 11 p.m.』 ②의근거 불일치
시간: 오후 7시부터 오후 11시까지
Entrance Fee: $5 per person
입장료: 1인당 5달러
Exhibition Route: alongside the Bow River in central Maple Spring / 『(Only digital maps of the route are available.)』 ③의근거 불일치
전시 경로: Maple Spring 중심부의 Bow 강을 따라 / (관람 경로의 디지털 지도만 제공합니다.)
『Souvenirs will be available on site and online.』 ④의근거 불일치
기념품은 현장과 온라인에서 구매 가능합니다.
『Local residents can get a 10% discount off the entrance fee.』 ⑤의근거 일치
지역 주민은 입장료의 10% 할인을 받을 수 있습니다.
Please visit www.maplespringlight.com for more information.
더 많은 정보를 위해 www.maplespringlight.com을 방문하십시오.

Maple Spring 조명 예술 전시회

Maple Spring 조명 예술 전시회는 조명 예술품으로 둘러싸인 경로를 따라 여러분을 비춰줄 것입니다. Maple Spring을 걸으면서 아름다운 조명 예술품들을 감상하세요.

□ **날짜**: 2022년 12월 1일부터 12월 31일까지
  (둘째 주와 넷째 주 월요일은 운영하지 않음.)
□ **시간**: 오후 7시부터 오후 11시까지
□ **입장료**: 1인당 5달러
□ **전시 경로**: Maple Spring 중심부의 Bow 강을 따라(관람 경로의 디지털 지도만 제공합니다.)

• 기념품은 현장과 온라인에서 구매 가능합니다.
• 지역 주민은 입장료의 10% 할인을 받을 수 있습니다.

더 많은 정보를 위해 www.maplespringlight.com을 방문하십시오.

---

27 딸기 축제 공지   정답률 87% | 정답 ④

2022 Strawberry Festival에 관한 다음 안내문의 내용과 일치하지 <u>않는</u> 것은?
① 올해는 대면 행사로 개최된다.
② 6세 이하의 어린이에게는 입장료를 받지 않는다.
③ 딸기파이 먹기 대회가 오후에 열린다.
☑ 매표소로 가는 트램 서비스는 주차비에 포함되지 않는다.
⑤ 자원봉사에 관심이 있다면 신청서를 이메일로 보내야 한다.

2022 Strawberry Festival
2022 딸기 축제
Join us for a fun family festival.
즐거운 가족 축제에 함께하세요.
『This year, / we are back to hosting an in-person event in Berry Square!』 ①의근거 일치
올해에는 / Berry Square에서 대면 행사를 다시 개최하게 되었습니다!
Date: November 26, 2022 (11:00 a.m. – 5:00 p.m.)
날짜: 2022년 11월 26일(오전 11시-오후 5시)
Tickets: $20 per person / 『(Children 6 and under are FREE.)』 ②의근거 일치
티켓: 1인당 20달러 / (6세 이하의 아이들은 무료입니다.)
Special Events
특별행사
11:00 a.m. : Baking Class for Kids
오전 11시 : 아이들을 위한 베이킹 수업
『1:00 p.m. : Strawberry Pie-Eating Contest』 ③의근거 일치
오후 1시 : 딸기파이 먹기 대회

Why? 왜 정답일까?

'Local residents can get a 10% discount off the entrance fee.'에서 지역 주민은 입장료를 10퍼센트 할인받을 수 있다고 하므로, 안내문의 내용과 일치하는 것은 ⑤ '지역 주민은 입장료의 10% 할인을 받을 수 있다.'이다.

Why? 왜 오답일까?

① '(closed on the 2nd and 4th Monday of the month)'에서 둘째 주와 넷째 주 월요일에만 운영되지 않는다고 하였다.
② 'Time: 7 p.m. – 11 p.m.'에서 마감 시간이 밤 11시라고 하였다.
③ 'Only digital maps of the route are available.'에서 관람 경로 지도는 디지털 형태로만 제공된다고 하였다.
④ 'Souvenirs will be available on site and online.'에서 기념품은 현장뿐 아니라 온라인에서도 구매 가능하다고 하였다.

- **exhibition** ⓝ 전시
- **artwork** ⓝ 예술 작품
- **on site** 현장에서
- **illuminate** ⓥ 비추다
- **souvenir** ⓝ 기념품

---

29 선매 행위의 개념과 종류 · 정답률 67% | 정답 ④

다음 글의 밑줄 친 부분 중, 어법상 틀린 것은? [3점]

Pre-emption means / that a strategy is designed / to prevent a rival from starting some particular activity.
선매 행위는 의미한다. / 어떤 전략이 만들어진다는 것을 / 경쟁자가 어떤 특정한 활동을 시작하는 것을 막고자
In some case / a pre-emptive move / may simply be an announcement of some intent / ① that might discourage rivals from doing the same.
어떤 경우 / 선제적 조치는 / 단순히 어떤 의도의 공표일 수도 있다. / 경쟁자들이 똑같이 하지 못하게 할 수 있는
The idea of pre-emption implies / that timing is sometimes very important / — a decision or an action at one point in time / might be much more rewarding / than ② doing it at a different time point.
선매 행위 개념은 암시하는데, / 때로 타이밍이 매우 중요하다는 것을 / 즉 어떤 시점의 결정이나 조치는 / 훨씬 더 득이 될 수 있다. / 그것을 다른 시점에 행하는 것보다
Pre-emption may involve up-weighting advertising / for a period / before and during ③ when a new entrant launches into a market.
선매 행위에는 광고의 가중치를 높이는 것이 포함될 수 있다. / 기간에 / 새로운 진입자가 시장에 진출하기 이전과 진출 도중에
The intent is / to make it more difficult / for the new entrant's advertising / to make an impression on potential buyers.
그 취지는 ~이다. / 더 어렵게 만드는 것 / 신규 진입자의 광고가 / 잠재적 구매자들에게 인상을 남기는 것을
Product proliferation is another potential pre-emption strategy.
제품 확산은 또 다른 잠재적인 선매 행위 전략이다.
The general idea is / to launch a large variety of product variants / so that there is very little in the way of market demand / that ✓ is not accommodated.
그 개념은 ~이다. / 다양한 제품 변형을 출시하는 것 / 시장 수요 방식이 거의 없도록 / 수용되지 않는
Arguably, / if a market is already filled with product variants / it is more difficult / for competitors to find ⑤ untapped pockets of market demand.
거의 틀림없이, / 만약 시장이 제품 변형으로 이미 채워져 있다면 / 더 어렵다. / 경쟁자들이 / 아직 점유되지 않은 시장 수요 주머니를 찾기가

선매 행위는 경쟁자가 어떤 특정한 활동을 시작하는 것을 막고자 어떤 전략이 만들어진다는 것을 의미한다. 어떤 경우 선제적 조치는 단순히 경쟁자들이 똑같이 하지 못하게 할 수 있는 어떤 의도의 공표일 수도 있다. 선매 행위 개념은 때로 타이밍이 매우 중요하다는 것을, 즉 어떤 시점의 결정이나 조치는 다른 시점에 행하는 것보다 훨씬 더 득이 될 수 있다는 것을 암시하는데, 즉 어떤 시점의 결정이나 조치는 다른 시점에 행하는 것보다 훨씬 더 득이 될 수 있다. 선매 행위에는 새로운 진입자가 시장에 진출하기 이전과 진출 도중에 광고의 가중치를 높이는 것이 포함될 수 있다. 그 취지는 신규 진입자의 광고가 잠재적 구매자들에게 인상을 남기는 것을 더 어렵게 만드는 것이다. 제품 확산은 또 다른 잠재적인 선매 행위 전략이다. 그 개념은 수용되지 않는 시장 수요 방식이 거의 없도록 다양한 제품 변형을 출시하는 것이다. 거의 틀림없이, 만약 시장이 제품 변형으로 이미 채워져 있다면 경쟁자들은 아직 점유되지 않은 시장 수요 주머니를 찾기가 더 어렵다.

Why? 왜 정답일까?

주격 관계대명사절의 동사는 선행사와 수 일치되는데, **market demand**가 불가산명사임에도 불구하고 **that** 뒤에 복수 동사 **are**가 나왔다. 이는 어법상 옳지 않으므로, **are**를 **is**로 고쳐야 한다. 따라서 어법상 틀린 것은 ④이다.

Why? 왜 오답일까?

① **some intent**를 꾸미면서 뒤에 주어가 없는 불완전한 구조를 연결하고자 주격 관계대명사 **that**을 썼다.
② 비교의 **than** 뒤에 '~하는 것'이라는 의미의 동명사 **doing**을 썼다.
③ 일반적인 시간 선행사 **the time**이 생략된 자리에 관계부사 **when**이 알맞게 쓰였다.
⑤ '**pockets of market demand**'가 '손이 안 닿은' 대상이므로 과거분사 **untapped**가 알맞게 쓰였다.

- **pre-emption** ⓝ 선매 행위
- **rewarding** ⓐ 보람된
- **entrant** ⓝ 갓 들어온 사람, 진입자, 출전자
- **variant** ⓝ 변형
- **arguably** ⓐ 거의 틀림없이
- **discourage A from B** A가 B하지 못하게 단념시키다
- **weight** ⓥ 가중치를 두다 ⓝ 가중치, 무게
- **proliferation** ⓝ 확산
- **accommodate** ⓥ (수요나 필요를) 맞추다, 수용하다
- **untapped** ⓐ 아직 손대지 않은

구문 풀이

2행 In some case a pre-emptive move may simply be an announcement of some intent [that might discourage rivals from doing the same]. [ ]: 주격 관계대명사절
선행사 · 'discourage + A + from + B : A가 B하지 못하게 막다'

★★★ 등급을 가르는 문제!

30 카운터쉐이딩의 개념 · 정답률 29% | 정답 ⑤

다음 글의 밑줄 친 부분 중, 문맥상 낱말의 쓰임이 적절하지 않은 것은? [3점]

Countershading is the process of optical flattening / that provides camouflage to animals.
카운터쉐이딩은 시각적으로 평평하게 하는 과정이다. / 동물에게 위장을 제공하는
When sunlight illuminates an object from above, / the object will be brightest on top.
햇빛이 물체를 위에서 비출 때, / 그 물체는 맨 위가 가장 밝을 것이다.
The color of the object / will gradually shade darker / toward the ① bottom.
물체의 색깔은 / 점차 더 어두운색으로 음영이 생길 것이다. / 맨 아래로 향할수록
This shading gives the object ② depth / and allows the viewer to distinguish its shape.
이러한 음영은 물체에 농도를 주고, / 보는 사람이 그것의 모양을 식별하게 해 준다.
Thus even if an animal is exactly, but uniformly, the same color as the substrate, / it will be easily ③ visible when illuminated.
따라서 비록 동물이 정확하게, 하지만 균일하게 밑바탕과 같은 색일지라도 / 그것은 빛을 받을 때 쉽게 눈에 띌 것이다.
Most animals, however, / are darker above / than they are below.
그러나 동물 대부분은 / 윗부분이 더 어둡다. / 아랫부분보다
When they are illuminated from above, / the darker back is lightened / and the lighter belly is shaded.
그들이 위에서 빛을 받을 때, / 더 어두운 등은 밝아지고 / 더 밝은 복부에 음영이 진다.
The animal thus appears to be a ④ single color / and easily blends in with the substrate.
따라서 동물은 하나의 색처럼 보이고 / 밑바탕과 쉽게 섞인다.
This pattern of coloration, or countershading, / ✓ destroys the visual impression of shape in the organism.
이런 형태의 배색, 즉 카운터쉐이딩은 / 생물체의 모양의 시각적 인상을 파괴한다.
It allows the animal / to blend in with its background.
그것은 동물이 ~하게 해 준다. / 자신의 배경에 섞여들게

카운터쉐이딩(명암 역위형 보호색)은 시각적으로 평평하게 하는 과정으로 동물에게 위장을 제공한다. 햇빛이 물체를 위에서 비출 때, 그 물체는 맨 위가 가장 밝을 것이다. 물체의 색깔은 ① 맨 아래로 향할수록 점차 더 어두운색으로 음영이 생길 것이다. 이러한 음영은 물체에 ② 농도를 주고, 보는 사람이 그것의 모양을 식별하게 해 준다. 따라서 비록 동물이 밑바탕과 정확하게, 하지만 균일하게 같은 색일지라도 빛을 받을 때 쉽게 ③ 눈에 띌 것이다. 그러나 동물 대부분은 아랫부분보다 윗부분이 더 어둡다. 그들이 위에서 빛을 받을 때, 더 어두운 등은 밝아지고 더 밝은 복부에 음영이 진다. 따라서 동물은 ④ 하나의 색처럼 보이고 밑바탕과 쉽게 섞인다. 이런 형태의 배색, 즉 카운터쉐이딩은 생물체의 모양의 시각적 인상을 ⑤ 강화한다(→ 파괴한다). 그것은 동물이 자신의 배경에 섞여들게 해 준다.

Why? 왜 정답일까?

동물이 주변 색에 섞여들게 하는 장치인 카운터쉐이딩에 관해 설명한 글이다. 전반적으로 색이 균일한 물체를 향해 위에서 빛을 주면 아래로 갈수록 음영이 지면서 형태감이 생기는데, 동물 대부분은 몸 위쪽 색이 더 어둡기에 위에서 빛을 비추더라도 아래로 갈수록 색이 비슷해지게 되고 만다. 따라서 동물은 '하나의' 색깔처럼 보이고, 형태감이 오히려 '무너져' 배경에 섞여버리게 된다는 것이다. 이를 근거로 할 때, 시각적 인상은 '파괴된다'는 설명이 적절하므로 ⑤의 **reinforces를 destroys**로 고쳐야 한다. 따라서 문맥상 낱말의 쓰임이 적절하지 않은 것은 ⑤이다.

- **optical** ⓐ 시각적인
- **gradually** ⓐ 점점
- **uniformly** ⓐ 균일하게
- **visible** ⓐ 눈에 띄는
- **reinforce** ⓥ 강화하다
- **camouflage** ⓝ 위장
- **distinguish** ⓥ 구별하다
- **substrate** ⓝ 밑바탕, 기질(基質)
- **blend in with** ~에 섞여들다

구문 풀이

6행 Thus even if an animal is exactly, but uniformly, the same color as the substrate, it will be easily visible when (it is) illuminated.
설령 ~하더라도 / 생략

★★ 문제 해결 꿀~팁 ★★

▶ 많이 틀린 이유는?
몸이 햇빛을 받으면 대체로 위가 밝고 아래가 어두워지므로, 아예 위쪽 몸을 더 어둡게 해서 형태가 분간되지 않도록 보호하는 **countershading**에 관해 설명하는 글이다. ③의 전후 문맥을 보면, 몸 색깔이 전체적으로 균일하면 빛을 받을 때 형태가 더 '잘 보일' 것이라고 한다. 이는 실제로 동물들이 **countershading** 전략을 취하는 이유를 적절히 설명한 것이다. 이어서 ④를 보면, 위쪽 몸의 색깔이 더 어두울 때 빛을 받으면 아래쪽 몸의 색상 톤과 비슷해지면서 '한 가지' 색깔로 보이게 된다고 설명한다. 색상이 '하나로' 보인다는 것은 입체 형태가 잘 분간되지 않는다는 의미이고, 그렇기에 **countershading** 전략과 잘 맞는 설명이다.
▶ 문제 해결 방법은?
어휘 문제는 항상 전후 문맥을 잘 봐야 한다. 특히 ⑤가 포함된 문장을 보충 설명하는 마지막 문장에 밑줄이 없으므로, 이 문장은 '맞는' 진술이다. 따라서 이를 근거로 ⑤를 판단한다.

---

31 예측 불가능한 자극이 있을 때 일어나는 학습 · 정답률 57% | 정답 ②

다음 빈칸에 들어갈 말로 가장 적절한 것을 고르시오.

① audible - 잘 들리는지
② ✓ predictable - 예측 가능한지
③ objective - 객관적인지
④ countable - 셀 수 있는지
⑤ recorded - 녹음된 것인지

No learning is possible / without an error signal.
어떤 학습도 가능하지 않다. / 오류 신호 없이는
Organisms only learn / when events violate their expectations.
유기체는 오로지 학습한다. / 사건이 기대에 어긋날 때
In other words, / surprise is one of the fundamental drivers of learning.
다시 말해 / 놀람은 학습의 근본적인 동력 중 하나이다.
Imagine hearing a series of identical notes, AAAAA.
일련의 똑같은 음인 AAAAA를 듣는 것을 상상해 보라.
Each note draws out a response / in the auditory areas of your brain / — but as the notes repeat, / those responses progressively decrease.
각각의 음은 반응을 끌어내지만, / 여러분의 뇌의 청각 영역에서 / 그 음이 반복되면서 / 그 반응은 점진적으로 감소한다.
This is called "adaptation," / a deceptively simple phenomenon / that shows / that your brain is learning to anticipate the next event.
이것은 '적응'이라 불리며, / 현혹될 정도로 단순해 보이는 현상으로 / 알려주는 / 뇌가 다음 사건을 예상하는 법을 배울 것임을

17회

Suddenly, the note changes: AAAAA#.
문득, 그 음이 AAAAA#로 바뀐다.
Your primary auditory cortex / immediately shows a strong surprise reaction: / not only
does the adaptation fade away, / but additional neurons begin to vigorously fire / in
response to the unexpected sound.
당신의 일차 청각 피질은 / 즉시 강한 놀람의 반응을 보이는데, / 즉 적응이 점차 사라질 뿐만 아니라 / 추가적인 뉴런이 힘차게 활성
화되기 시작한다. / 예상치 못한 소리에 대한 반응으로
And it is not just repetition / that leads to adaptation: / what matters is / whether the notes
are predictable.
그리고 단순한 반복이 아니라, / 적응을 유발하는 것은 / 중요한 것은 ~이다. / 그 음이 예측 가능한지이다.
For instance, / if you hear an alternating set of notes, / such as ABABA, / your brain gets
used to this alternation, / and the activity in your auditory areas / again decreases.
예를 들어 / 만약 당신이 일련의 교차하는 음을 듣는다면, / ABABA와 같이 / 당신의 뇌는 이 교차에 익숙해지고, / 당신의 청각 영역
내 활동은 / 다시 감소한다.
This time, however, / it is an unexpected repetition, / such as ABABB, / that triggers a
surprise response.
그러나 이번에는 / 바로 예상치 못한 반복이다. / ABABB와 같은 / 놀람의 반응을 일으키는 것은

어떤 학습도 오류 신호 없이는 가능하지 않다. 유기체는 사건이 기대에 어긋날 때에만 학습
한다. 다시 말해 놀람은 학습의 근본적인 동력 중 하나이다. 일련의 똑같은 음인 AAAAA를
듣는다는 것을 상상해 보라. 각각의 음은 여러분의 뇌의 청각 영역에서 반응을 끌어내지만, 음이
반복되면서 그 반응은 점진적으로 감소한다. 이것은 '적응'이라 불리며, 뇌가 다음 사건을
예상하는 법을 배울 것임을 알려주는 현혹될 정도로 단순해 보이는 현상이다. 문득, 그 음이
AAAAA#으로 바뀐다. 당신의 일차 청각 피질은 즉시 강한 놀람의 반응을 보이는데, 즉 적
응이 점차 사라질 뿐만 아니라 예상치 못한 소리에 대한 반응으로 추가적인 뉴런이 힘차게
활성화되기 시작한다. 그리고 적응을 유발하는 것은 단순한 반복이 아니며, 중요한 것은 그
음이 예측 가능한지이다. 예를 들어 만약 당신이 ABABA와 같이 일련의 교차하는 음을 듣는
다면, 당신의 뇌는 이 교차에 익숙해지고, 당신의 청각 영역 내 활동은 다시 감소한다. 그러나
이번에는 놀람의 반응을 일으키는 것은 바로 ABABB와 같은 예상치 못한 반복이다.

Why? 왜 정답일까?

첫 세 문장에서 학습이 가능한 것은 오류 신호, 즉 '예측을 벗어나는 놀람'이 있을 때라고 한다(Organisms
only learn when events violate their expectations. In other words, surprise is one
of the fundamental drivers of learning.). 이어서 우리 뇌는 자극에 '적응하는' 능력을 지니고 있
기에 반복되는 패턴에 주의를 덜 기울이고, 예측에 벗어나는 변칙이 주어질 때 '놀라면서' 비로소 학습하려
한다는 설명이 제시된다. 따라서 빈칸에 들어갈 말로 가장 적절한 것은 ② '예측 가능한지'이다.

- violate ⓥ 위반하다
- identical @ 동일한
- draw out ~을 끌어내다
- progressively [ad] 점진적으로
- phenomenon ⓝ 현상
- primary @ 1차의, 주요한, 기본적인
- fade away 흐려지다, 옅어지다
- alternate ⓥ 번갈아 나오다, 교대로 나오다
- predictable @ 예측 가능한
- fundamental @ 근본적인
- note ⓝ 음
- auditory @ 청각의
- deceptively [ad] 현혹될 정도로
- anticipate ⓥ 기대하다, 예상하다
- cortex ⓝ (대뇌의) 피질
- vigorously [ad] 힘차게
- audible @ 잘 들리는, 들을 수 있는

구문 풀이

9행 Your primary auditory cortex immediately shows a strong surprise
reaction: not only does the adaptation fade away, but additional neurons begin
「부정어구＋조동사＋주어＋동사원형」: 도치 구문
to vigorously fire in response to the unexpected sound.

32 두려움과 불확실성으로 인해 위태로워질 수 있는 금융 시장   정답률 53% | 정답 ①

다음 빈칸에 들어갈 말로 가장 적절한 것을 고르시오.

✓① Fear and uncertainty can be damaging
  두려움과 불확실성은 해가 될 수 있다
② Unaffordable personal loans may pose a risk
  감당 못할 개인 부채가 위험을 끼칠 수도 있다
③ Ignorance about legal restrictions may matter
  법적 제재에 대한 무지가 문제가 될 수 있다
④ Accurate knowledge of investors can be poisonous
  투자자에 대한 정확한 정보가 유해할 수 있다
⑤ Strong connections between banks can create a scare
  은행 간의 강한 유대가 두려움을 낳을 수 있다

The connectedness of the global economic market / makes it vulnerable to potential
"infection."
전 세계 경제 시장의 연결성은 / 시장이 잠재적 '감염'에 취약하게 만든다.
A financial failure can make its way / from borrowers to banks to insurers, / spreading like
a flu.
금융상의 실패는 나아갈 수 있다. / 채무자에서부터 은행, 보증인까지 / 독감처럼 퍼지면서
However, / there are unexpected characteristics / when it comes to such infection in the
market.
그러나 / 예상치 못한 특징들이 있다. / 시장 내 그러한 감염에 관한
Infection can occur / even without any contact.
감염은 일어날 수 있다. / 심지어 아무런 접촉 없이도
A bank might become insolvent / even without having any of its investments fail.
은행은 지급 불능이 될 수 있다. / 어떠한 투자에 실패하지 않고도
Fear and uncertainty / can be damaging to financial markets, / just as cascading failures
due to bad investments.
두려움과 불확실성은 / 금융 시장에 해가 될 수 있다. / 어떤 나쁜 투자 때문에 일어나는 연속된 실패처럼
If we all woke up tomorrow / and believed that Bank X would be insolvent, / then it would
become insolvent.
만약 우리 모두가 내일 일어나서 / X은행이 지급 불능이 될 것이라고 믿는다면, / 그러면 그것은 지급 불능이 될 것이다.
In fact, / it would be enough for us to fear / that others believed that Bank X was going to
fail, / or just to fear our collective fear!
사실 / 우리가 두려워하는 것으로 충분할 것이다. / 다른 사람들이 X은행이 망할 거라고 믿고 있다는 것을 / 혹은 단지 우리의 집단적
인 두려움을 겁내는 것으로
We might all even know / that Bank X was well-managed with healthy investments, / but if
we expected others to pull their money out, / then we would fear being the last / to pull our
money out.

우리 모두 심지어 알 것이다 / X은행이 건전한 투자로 잘 운영된다는 것을 / 하지만 만약 우리가 다른 사람들이 자기 돈을 인출해 갈
것이라고 예상한다면 / 우리는 마지막 사람이 되는 것을 겁낼 것이다. / 자기 돈을 인출하는
Financial distress can be self-fulfilling / and is a particularly troublesome aspect of
financial markets.
재정적인 고통은 자기 충족적일 수 있으며, / 금융 시장에서 각별히 골치 아픈 측면이다.

전 세계 경제 시장의 연결성은 시장이 잠재적 '감염'에 취약하게 만든다. 금융상의 실패는
독감처럼 퍼지면서 채무자에서부터 은행, 보증인까지 나아갈 수 있다. 그러나 시장 내 그러한
감염에 관한 예상치 못한 특징들이 있다. 감염은 심지어 아무런 접촉 없이도 일어날 수 있다.
은행은 어떠한 투자에 실패하지 않고도 지급 불능이 될 수 있다. 어떤 나쁜 투자들 때문에
일어나는 연속된 실패처럼, 두려움과 불확실성은 금융 시장에 해가 될 수 있다. 만약 우리
모두가 내일 일어나서 X은행이 지급 불능이 될 것이라고 믿는다면, 그것은 지급 불능이 될
것이다. 사실 우리가 다른 사람들이 X은행이 망할 거라고 믿고 있다는 것을 두려워하거나,
단지 우리의 집단적인 두려움을 겁내는 것으로 충분할 것이다. 우리 모두 심지어 X은행이
건전한 투자로 잘 운영된다는 것을 알지라도 만약 우리가 다른 사람들이 (거기서) 자기 돈을
인출해 갈 것이라고 예상한다면, 우리는 자기 돈을 인출하는 마지막 사람이 되는 것을 겁낼 것
이다(남들보다 돈을 먼저 인출하려 할 것이다). 재정적인 고통은 자기 충족적일 수 있으며,
금융 시장에서 각별히 골치 아픈 측면이다.

Why? 왜 정답일까?

빈칸 뒤 예시에 따르면 X은행이 실제로 잘 운영되고 있음에도 불구하고, 사람들이 X은행이 망할까봐
'두려워하는' 마음만으로 X은행에 위기가 닥칠 수 있다고 한다. 즉 재정적 고통이 닥칠지도 모른다는
두려움과 불확실성 자체가 금융 시장에 생각지 못한 위기를 가져올 수 있다는 것이므로, 빈칸에 들어갈
말로 가장 적절한 것은 ① '두려움과 불확실성은 해가 될 수 있다'이다.

- infection ⓝ 감염
- insolvent @ 지급 불능의, 파산한
- cascading @ 연속된
- well-managed @ 잘 경영되는
- pull out 꺼내다, 인출하다
- self-fulfilling @ 자기 충족적인, 예고대로 성취되는
- troublesome @ 골치 아픈
- damaging @ 해로운
- restriction ⓝ 제재, 제한
- scare ⓝ 놀람, 공포 ⓥ 겁먹게 하다
- insurer ⓝ 보증인, 보험업자
- investment ⓝ 투자
- collective @ 집단적인
- healthy @ 건전한
- distress ⓝ 고통
- uncertainty ⓝ 불확실성
- unaffordable @ 감당할 수 없는
- poisonous @ 유독한, 유해한

구문 풀이

1행 The connectedness of the global economic market makes it vulnerable
대명사(= the global economic market)
to potential "infection."

33 음수 기호 사용을 꺼리는 경향   정답률 37% | 정답 ①

다음 빈칸에 들어갈 말로 가장 적절한 것을 고르시오.

✓① sidestep the dreaded negative sign
  그 두려운 음수의 기호를 피하기
② resolve stock market uncertainties
  주식 시장의 불확실성을 해결하기
③ compensate for complicated calculating processes
  복잡한 계산 과정을 보완하기
④ unify the systems of expressing numbers below zero
  영 이하의 수를 표현하는 체계를 통합하기
⑤ face the truth that subtraction can create negative numbers
  뺄셈으로 음수가 생길 수 있다는 진리를 직시하기

Negative numbers are a lot more abstract than positive numbers / — you can't see negative
4 cookies / and you certainly can't eat them — / but you can think about them, / and you
have to, / in all aspects of daily life, / from debts to contending with freezing temperatures
and parking garages.
음수는 양수에 비해 훨씬 더 추상적이다 / 여러분이 –4개의 쿠키를 볼 수 없고 / 여러분이 분명 이를 먹지 못한다는 점에서 / 그러나
여러분은 음수에 관해 생각할 수 있으며, / 여러분은 생각해야만 한다. / 일상의 모든 측면에서 / 빚부터 시작해서 몹시 추운 기온과
주차장에서 씨름하는 것에 이르기까지
Still, / many of us haven't quite made peace with negative numbers.
그럼에도 불구하고, / 우리 중 많은 사람들은 음수와 잘 지내지 못했다.
People have invented all sorts of funny little mental strategies / to sidestep the dreaded
negative sign.
사람들은 온갖 우스꽝스럽고 사소한 정신적 전략들을 만들어 냈다. / 그 두려운 음수의 기호를 피하기 위해
On mutual fund statements, / losses (negative numbers) are printed in red / or stuck in
parentheses / with no negative sign to be found.
뮤추얼 펀드 설명서에서 / 손실(음수)은 빨갛게 인쇄되거나 / 괄호 안에 갇혀 있다. / 음수 기호를 찾아볼 수 없는 채로
The history books tell us / that Julius Caesar was born in 100 B.C., / not -100.
역사책은 우리에게 알려준다. / Julius Caesar는 기원전 100년에 태어났다고 / –100year이 아닌
The underground levels in a parking garage / often have designations / like B1 and B2.
주차장의 지하층은 / 종종 명칭을 가지고 있다. / B1과 B2와 같은
Temperatures are one of the few exceptions: / folks do say, / especially here in Ithaca, New
York, / that it's -5 degrees outside, / though even then, / many prefer to say 5 below zero.
기온은 몇 안 되는 예외 중 하나인데, / 사람들은 정말로 말한다. / 특히 이곳 New York의 Ithaca에서 / 바깥의 기온이 –5도라고 /
하지만 심지어 이때도 / 많은 이들이 영하 5도라고 말하길 선호한다.
There's something about that negative sign / that just looks so unpleasant.
그 음수의 기호에 관해서는 무언가 있다. / 정말 불쾌하게만 보이는

음수는 여러분이 –4개의 쿠키를 볼 수 없고 분명 이를 먹지 못한다는 점에서 양수에 비해
훨씬 더 추상적이지만, 여러분은 음수에 관해 생각할 수 있으며, 빚부터 시작해서 몹시 추운
기온과 주차장에서 씨름하는 것에 이르기까지 일상의 모든 측면에서 생각해야만 한다. 그럼
에도 불구하고, 우리 중 많은 사람들은 음수와 잘 지내지 못했다. 사람들은 그 두려운 음수
의 기호를 피하기 위해 온갖 우스꽝스럽고 사소한 정신적 전략들을 만들어 냈다. 뮤추얼 펀드
(계약형 투자 신탁) 설명서에서 손실(음수)은 빨갛게 인쇄되거나 음수 기호를 찾아볼 수 없는
채로 괄호 안에 갇혀 있다. 역사책에서 우리에게 알려주기로 Julius Caesar는 –100년이 아닌
기원전 100년에 태어났다고 한다. 주차장의 지하층은 종종 B1과 B2와 같은 명칭을 가지고
있다. 기온은 몇 안 되는 예외 중 하나인데, 특히 이곳 New York의 Ithaca에서 사람들은 바깥
의 기온이 –5도라고 하지만 심지어 이때도 많은 이들이 영하 5도라고 말하길 선호한다. 그
음수의 기호에 관해서는 정말 불쾌하게만 보이는 무언가가 있다.

구문 풀이

6행 Confounding factors are variables (known or unknown) [that make it difficult for epidemiologists to isolate the effects of the specific variable being studied].
분사구(진행수동태)

---

35 질투가 까다로운 이유
정답률 52% | 정답 ④

다음 글에서 전체 흐름과 관계 없는 문장은?

Of all the human emotions, / none is trickier or more elusive than envy.
인간의 모든 감정 중, / 질투보다 더 까다롭거나 더 이해하기 어려운 것은 없다.
It is very difficult / to actually discern the envy / that motivates people's actions.
매우 어렵다. / 질투를 실제로 알아차리기는 / 사람들의 행동을 자극하는
① The reason for this elusiveness / is simple: / we almost never directly express the envy / we are feeling.
이러한 모호함의 이유는 / 간단한데, / 우리는 질투를 대부분 절대 직접적으로 표현하지 않는다. / 우리가 느끼고 있는
② Envy entails the admission to ourselves / that we are inferior to another person / in something we value.
질투는 자기 자신에 대한 인정을 수반한다. / 우리가 또 다른 사람보다 열등하다는 / 우리가 가치 있게 여기는 어떤 것에서
③ Not only is it painful / to admit this inferiority, / but it is even worse for others to see / that we are feeling this.
고통스러울 뿐 아니라, / 이 열등감을 인정하기가 / 다른 사람들이 알게 되는 것은 훨씬 더 나쁘다. / 우리가 이것을 느끼고 있는 것을
✔④ Envy can cause illness / because people with envy can cast the "evil eye" / on someone they envy, / even unwittingly, / or the envious person can become ill / from the emotion.
질투는 질병을 유발할 수도 있는데, / 질투하는 사람이 '증오에 찬 눈초리'를 보낼 수도 있고, / 자신이 부러워하는 사람에게 / 무의식적으로라도 / 질투심이 강한 사람이 몸이 아플 수 있기 때문이다. / 그 감정으로 인해
⑤ And so almost as soon as we experience the initial feelings of envy, / we are motivated to disguise it to ourselves / — it is not envy we feel / but unfairness at the distribution of goods or attention, / resentment at this unfairness, / even anger.
그래서 우리는 최초의 질투를 느끼는 거의 바로 그 순간 / 우리는 그것을 자신에게서 감추려고 한다. / 즉, 우리는 질투를 느끼는 것이 아니라, / 재산의 분배나 관심에 대한 불공평함, / 이 불공평함에 대한 분개, / 심지어 분노를 느끼는 것이다.

인간의 모든 감정 중, 질투보다 더 까다롭거나 더 이해하기 어려운 것은 없다. 사람들의 행동을 자극하는 질투를 실제로 알아차리기는 매우 어렵다. ① 이러한 모호함의 이유는 간단한데, 우리는 우리가 느끼고 있는 질투를 대부분 절대 직접적으로 표현하지 않는다. ② 질투는 우리가 가치 있게 여기는 어떤 것에서 또 다른 사람보다 열등하다는, 자기 자신에 대한 인정을 수반한다. ③ 이 열등감을 인정하기가 고통스러울 뿐 아니라, 우리가 이것을 느끼고 있는 것을 다른 사람들이 알게 되는 것은 훨씬 더 나쁘다. ④ 질투는 질병을 유발할 수도 있는데, 질투하는 사람이 무의식적으로라도 자신이 부러워하는 사람에게 '증오에 찬 눈초리'를 보낼 수도 있고, 질투심이 강한 사람이 그 감정으로 인해 몸이 아플 수 있기 때문이다. ⑤ 그래서 우리는 최초의 질투를 느끼는 거의 바로 그 순간 그것을 자신에게서 감추려고 한다. 즉, 우리는 질투를 느끼는 것이 아니라, 재산의 분배나 관심에 대한 불공평함, 이 불공평함에 대한 분개, 심지어 분노를 느끼는 것이다.

Why? 왜 정답일까?

질투의 모호함을 설명하는 글인데, ④는 질투가 신체적 질병을 야기할 수 있다는 내용이므로 흐름상 어색하다. 따라서 전체 흐름과 관계 없는 문장은 ④이다.

● elusive ⓐ 이해하기 어려운 ● envy ⓝ 부러움, 질투
● discern ⓥ 분간하다, 알아차리다 ● elusiveness ⓝ 모호함, 이해하기 어려움
● entail ⓥ 수반하다 ● inferior to ~보다 열등한
● inferiority ⓝ 열등함 ● cast ⓥ 던지다
● unwittingly 고ⓓ 자기도 모르게 ● unfairness ⓝ 불공평함
● resentment ⓝ 분개

구문 풀이

1행 Of all the human emotions, none is trickier or more elusive than envy.
모든 ~ 중에서 「부정 주어+비교급+than : ~보다 더 …한 것은 없다(최상급 의미)」

★★★ 등급을 가르는 문제!

36 잊힐 권리
정답률 30% | 정답 ②

주어진 글 다음에 이어질 글의 순서로 가장 적절한 것을 고르시오.

① (A) – (C) – (B)   ✔② (B) – (A) – (C)
③ (B) – (C) – (A)   ④ (C) – (A) – (B)
⑤ (C) – (B) – (A)

The right to be forgotten / is a right / distinct from but related to a right to privacy.
잊힐 권리는 / 권리이다. / 사생활 권리와 구별되지만 연관성이 있는
The right to privacy is, / among other things, / the right for information / traditionally regarded as protected or personal / not to be revealed.
사생활 권리는 ~이다. / 무엇보다도 / 정보에 대한 권리이다. / 전통적으로 보호되거나 개인적인 것으로 여겨지는 / 공개되지 않아야 할
(B) The right to be forgotten, / in contrast, / can be applied to information / that has been in the public domain.
잊힐 권리는 / 반면에 / 정보에 적용될 수 있다. / 공공의 영역에 있었던
The right to be forgotten / broadly includes the right of an individual / not to be forever defined by information / from a specific point in time.
잊힐 권리는 / 폭넓게 개인의 권리를 포함한다. / 정보에 의해 영원히 규정되지 않을 / 특정 시점의
(A) One motivation for such a right / is to allow individuals / to move on with their lives / and not be defined by a specific event or period in their lives.
그러한 권리의 한 가지 이유는 / 개인이 ~하도록 해 주는 것이다. / 자기 삶을 영위하고 / 삶의 특정 사건이나 기간에 의해 한정되지 않도록
For example, / it has long been recognized in some countries, / such as the UK and France,

---

Why? 왜 정답일까?

빈칸 뒤에서 음수를 괄호 처리하거나, -100년 대신 '기원전' 100년이라는 호칭을 쓰거나, 지하 1층, 2층을 'B1, B2'와 같이 표시함으로써 음수 기호 사용을 최대한 피하는 경우를 예로 들고 있다. 따라서 이러한 예시를 아우르는 빈칸에 들어갈 말로 가장 적절한 것은 ① '그 두려운 음수의 기호를 피하기'이다. 마지막 문장에서 음수 기호가 '불쾌하다(unpleasant)'고 언급한 것을 통해서도 결론에 대한 힌트를 얻을 수 있다.

● negative ⓐ (수가) 음수인 ● abstract ⓐ 추상적인
● positive ⓐ (수가) 양수인 ● contend with ~와 씨름하다
● make peace with ~와 잘 지내다 ● statement ⓝ 설명(서)
● parentheses ⓝ 괄호 ● designation ⓝ 명칭, 직함
● unpleasant ⓐ 불쾌한 ● sidestep ⓥ 회피하다
● dread ⓥ 두려워하다, 겁내다 ● resolve ⓥ 해결하다
● subtraction ⓝ 빼기, 뺄셈

구문 풀이

1행 Negative numbers are a lot more abstract than positive numbers — (you
비교급 수식(훨씬)
can't see negative 4 cookies and you certainly can't eat them) — but you can
( ) : 삽입절
think about them, and you *have to*, in all aspects of daily life, from debts to
대명사(= negative numbers) 대동사(= have to think about them)
contending with freezing temperatures and parking garages.

---

34 인간에 대한 연구를 어렵게 하는 교란 변수
정답률 34% | 정답 ②

다음 빈칸에 들어갈 말로 가장 적절한 것을 고르시오. [3점]

① distort the interpretation of the medical research results
의학 연구 결과의 해석을 왜곡하기
✔② isolate the effects of the specific variable being studied
연구되고 있는 특정한 변수의 영향을 분리하기
③ conceal the purpose of their research from subjects
자신의 연구 목적을 실험 참가자로부터 숨기기
④ conduct observational studies in an ethical way
관찰 연구를 윤리적 방식으로 수행하기
⑤ refrain from intervening in their experiments
자신의 실험에 개입하기를 자제하기

Observational studies of humans / cannot be properly controlled.
인간에 대한 관찰 연구는 / 적절하게 통제될 수 없다.
Humans live different lifestyles and in different environments.
인간은 다양한 생활 방식으로 다양한 환경에서 산다.
Thus, / they are insufficiently homogeneous / to be suitable experimental subjects.
따라서 / 그들은 충분히 동질적이지 않다. / 적절한 실험 대상이 되기에
These *confounding factors* undermine our ability / to draw sound causal conclusions / from human epidemiological surveys.
이러한 *교란 변수*는 우리의 능력을 약화시킨다. / 타당한 인과적 결론을 도출하는 / 인간 역학 조사로부터
Confounding factors are variables (known or unknown) / that make it difficult / for epidemiologists / to isolate the effects of the specific variable being studied.
교란 변수는 (알려지거나 알려지지 않은) 변수이다. / 어렵게 하는 / 역학자가 / 연구되고 있는 특정한 변수의 영향을 분리하기
For example, / Taubes argued / that since many people who drink also smoke, / researchers have difficulty determining the link / between alcohol consumption and cancer.
예를 들어, / Taubes는 주장했다. / 술을 마시는 많은 사람들이 흡연도 하기 때문에 / 연구자들이 연관성을 파악하는 데 어려움을 겪는다고 / 알코올 섭취와 암 사이의
Similarly, / researchers in the famous Framingham study / identified a significant correlation / between coffee drinking and coronary heart disease.
마찬가지로 / 유명한 Framingham 연구의 연구자들은 / 상당한 상관관계를 확인했다. / 커피를 마시는 것과 관상 동맥성 심장 질환 사이에
However, / most of this correlation disappeared / once researchers corrected for the fact / that many coffee drinkers also smoke.
그러나 / 이러한 상관관계의 대부분은 사라졌다. / 연구자들이 사실에 대해 수정하자 / 커피를 마시는 많은 사람들이 흡연도 한다는
If the confounding factors are known, / it is often possible / to correct for them.
교란 변수들이 알려져 있다면 / 종종 가능하다. / 그것들을 수정하는 것이
However, if they are unknown, / they will undermine the reliability of the causal conclusions / we draw from epidemiological surveys.
그러나 그것들이 알려져 있지 않다면, / 그것들은 인과적 결론의 신뢰성을 손상시킬 것이다. / 우리가 역학 조사로부터 도출하는

인간에 대한 관찰 연구는 적절하게 통제될 수 없다. 인간은 다양한 생활 방식으로 다양한 환경에서 산다. 따라서 그들은 적절한 실험 대상이 되기에 충분히 동질적이지 않다. 이러한 교란 변수는 인간 역학 조사로부터 타당한 인과적 결론을 도출하는 우리의 능력을 약화시킨다. 교란 변수는 역학자가 연구되고 있는 특정한 변수의 영향을 분리하기 어렵게 하는 (알려지거나 알려지지 않은) 변수이다. 예를 들어, Taubes는 술을 마시는 많은 사람들이 흡연도 하기 때문에 연구자들이 알코올 섭취와 암 사이의 연관성을 파악하는 데 어려움을 겪는다고 주장했다. 마찬가지로 유명한 Framingham 연구의 연구자들은 커피를 마시는 것과 관상 동맥성 심장 질환 사이에 상당한 상관관계를 확인했다. 그러나 연구자들이 커피를 마시는 많은 사람들이 흡연도 한다는 사실에 대해 수정하자 이러한 상관관계의 대부분은 사라졌다. 교란 변수들이 알려져 있다면 그것들을 수정하는 것이 종종 가능하다. 그러나 그것들이 알려져 있지 않다면, 그것들은 우리가 역학 조사로부터 도출하는 인과적 결론의 신뢰성을 손상시킬 것이다.

Why? 왜 정답일까?

첫 문장과 마지막 두 문장의 내용을 종합하면, 교란 변수가 알려진 경우에는 이를 수정할 수 있지만 알려지지 않은 경우 수정되기 어렵기 때문에, 인간을 대상으로 한 연구는 적절히 통제되기 어렵다는 것이 글의 결론이다. 여기서 '통제되기 어렵다'는 말은 결국 실험 결과에 영향을 미치는 다른 변수, 즉 교란 변수를 연구 대상인 변수로부터 '분리해내' 수정하기가 어렵다는 의미로 이해할 수 있다. 따라서 빈칸에 들어갈 말로 가장 적절한 것은 ② '연구되고 있는 특정 변수의 영향을 분리하기'이다.

● observational ⓐ 관찰의 ● insufficiently 고ⓓ 불충분하게
● homogeneous ⓐ 동질적인 ● suitable ⓐ 적절한
● confounding factor (결과에 간섭하는) 교란 변수 ● undermine ⓥ 약화시키다
● draw a conclusion 결론을 내리다 ● epidemiological ⓐ 역학의
● epidemiologist ⓝ 전염병학자, 역학자 ● correlation ⓝ 상관관계
● coronary ⓐ 관상 동맥의 ● reliability ⓝ 신뢰도
● distort ⓥ 왜곡하다 ● isolate ⓥ 분리하다

/ that even past criminal convictions should eventually be "spent" / and not continue to affect a person's life.
예를 들어, / 일부 국가에서는 오랫동안 인식되어 왔다. / 영국과 프랑스와 같은 / 과거의 범죄 유죄 판결조차도 결국 '다 소모되어야' 한다고 / 그리고 한 사람의 삶에 계속 영향을 미치지 않아야 한다고

(C) Despite the reason / for supporting the right to be forgotten, / the right to be forgotten / can sometimes come into conflict with other rights.
이유에도 불구하고, / 잊힐 권리를 지지하는 / 잊힐 권리는 / 다른 권리와 때때로 충돌할 수 있다.

For example, / formal exceptions are sometimes made / for security or public health reasons.
예를 들어, / 공식적인 예외가 때때로 생겨난다. / 안보와 공공 보건의 이유로 인해

잊힐 권리는 사생활 권리와 구별되지만 연관성이 있는 권리이다. 사생활 권리는 무엇보다도 전통적으로 보호되거나 공개되지 않아야 할 개인적인 것으로 여겨지는 정보에 대한 권리이다.
(B) 반면에 잊힐 권리는 공공의 영역에 있었던 정보에 적용될 수 있다. 잊힐 권리는 개인이 특정 시점의 정보에 의해 영원히 규정되지 않을 권리를 폭넓게 포함한다.
(A) 그러한 권리의 한 가지 이유는 개인이 자기 삶을 영위하고 삶의 특정한 사건이나 기간에 의해 한정되지 않도록 해 주는 것이다. 예를 들어, 영국과 프랑스와 같은 일부 국가에서는 과거의 범죄 유죄 판결조차도 결국 '다 소모되고' 한 사람의 삶에 계속 영향을 미치지 않아야 한다고 오랫동안 인식되어 왔다.
(C) 잊힐 권리를 지지하는 이유에도 불구하고, 잊힐 권리는 다른 권리와 때때로 충돌할 수 있다. 예를 들어, 공식적인 예외가 안보와 공공 보건의 이유로 인해 때때로 생겨난다.

Why? 왜 정답일까?
잊힐 권리의 개념과 필요성을 설명하는 글이다. 주어진 글에서 '사생활 권리'를 잊힐 권리와 대비되는 개념으로 언급한 후, in contrast로 시작하는 (B)는 잊힐 권리로 다시 돌아와 예시와 함께 의미를 설명한다. (A)에서는 잊힐 권리가 왜 필요한지 이유를 설명하고, (C)에서는 그런 이유에도 불구하고 가끔 예외 상황은 생길 수 있음을 덧붙인다. 따라서 글의 순서로 가장 적절한 것은 ② '(B) – (A) – (C)'이다.

- right to be forgotten 잊힐 권리
- reveal ⓥ 드러내다, 폭로하다
- criminal ⓐ 형사상의, 범죄의
- spent ⓐ 소모된, 영향력이 없어진
- formal ⓐ 공식적인
- right to privacy 사생활 권리
- define ⓥ 규정하다, 한정짓다
- conviction ⓝ 유죄 판결
- domain ⓝ 영역
- security ⓝ 안보

구문 풀이

2행 The right to privacy is, (among other things), the right for information
동사 ( ): 삽입구 주격 보어
traditionally regarded as protected or personal not to be revealed.
~라고 여겨지는

★★ 문제 해결 꿀~팁 ★★

▶ 많이 틀린 이유는?
주어진 글과 (B)를 연결하고 난 다음이 문제이다. (B)의 마지막은 '잊힐 권리'의 범위(includes ~)를 언급하며 끝나는데, (A)는 이 권리가 필요한 이유를, (C)는 이 권리가 다른 권리와 충돌을 일으킨다는 내용을 각각 다룬다. 즉 (C)에서 글의 흐름이 전환되고 있으므로 (B)-(C)를 바로 연결하는 ③은 답으로 적절치 않다.
▶ 문제 해결 방법은?
(A)의 motivation이 바로 '이유'를 말하는 표현이다. (B)에서 잊힐 권리의 개념과 범위를 소개한 뒤, 이런 권리를 지지하는 '한 가지 이유'를 말하는 (A)가 먼저 나오고, '그런 이유에도 불구하고' 권리 충돌이 발생한다는 내용의 (C)가 마지막에 나와야 적절하다.

★★★ 등급을 가르는 문제!

37 행동에 관한 경제학적 관점 정답률 31% | 정답 ③

주어진 글 다음에 이어질 글의 순서로 가장 적절한 것을 고르시오. [3점]
① (A) – (C) – (B)
② (B) – (A) – (C)
✓③ (B) – (C) – (A)
④ (C) – (A) – (B)
⑤ (C) – (B) – (A)

To an economist / who succeeds in figuring out a person's preference structure / — understanding whether the satisfaction gained from consuming one good / is greater than that of another — / explaining behavior / in terms of changes in underlying likes and dislikes / is usually highly problematic.
경제학자에게 있어, / 한 사람의 선호 구조를 알아내는 것에 성공한 / 즉 한 상품을 소비하여 얻는 만족이 ~한지 아닌지를 이해하는 데 성공한 / 또 다른 상품을 소비하여 얻는 만족보다 더 큰지 / 행동을 설명하는 것은 / 기저에 있는 호불호의 변화 측면에서 / 대체로 아주 문제가 많다.

(B) To argue, / for instance, / that the baby boom and then the baby bust / resulted in an increase and then a decrease / in the public's inherent taste for children / rather than a change in relative prices / against a background of stable preferences, / places a social scientist in an unsound position.
주장하는 것은 / 예를 들어 / 베이비 붐과 그 이후의 출생률 급락이 / 증가 후 감소에서 비롯되었다고 / 아기에 대한 대중의 내재적 선호의 / 상대적 비용의 변화보다는 / 변동 없는 선호도를 배경으로 한 / 사회과학자를 불안정한 입지에 둔다.

(C) In economics, / such an argument about birth rates / would be equivalent to saying / that a rise and fall in mortality / could be attributed to an increase / in the inherent desire change for death.
경제학에서 / 출생률에 대한 그러한 주장은 / 말하는 것과 같다. / 사망률의 상승과 하락이 / 증가에서 비롯된다고 / 죽음에 대한 내재적 욕구 변화의

For an economist, / changes in income and prices, / rather than changes in tastes, / affect birth rates.
경제학자에게는 / 소득과 물가의 변화가 / 기호의 변화보다는 / 출생률에 영향을 미친다.

(A) When income rises, / for example, / people want more children / (or, as you will see later, / more satisfaction derived from children), / even if their inherent desire for children / stays the same.
소득이 증가할 때 / 예를 들어 / 사람들은 더 많은 자녀를 원한다. / (또는 여러분이 나중에 알게 되겠지만, / 아이로부터 오는 더 큰 만족감) / 자녀에 대한 내재적 욕구가 / 그대로 유지되더라도

(우측 단)

있는 호불호의 변화 측면에서 설명하는 것은 대체로 아주 문제가 많다.

(B) 예를 들어 베이비 붐과 그 이후의 출생률 급락이 변동 없는 선호도를 배경으로 한 상대적 비용의 변화보다는, 아기에 대한 대중의 내재적 선호가 이후 떨어진 것에서 비롯되었다고 주장하는 것은 사회과학자를 불안정한 입지에 둔다.

(C) 경제학에서 출생률에 대한 그러한 주장은 사망률의 상승과 하락이 죽음에 대한 내재적 욕구 변화의 증가에서 비롯된다고 말하는 것과 같다. 경제학자에게는 기호의 변화보다는 소득과 물가의 변화가 출생률에 영향을 미친다.

(A) 예를 들어 소득이 증가할 때 사람들은 자녀에 대한 내재적 욕구가 그대로 유지되더라도 더 많은 자녀(또는 여러분이 나중에 알게 되겠지만, 아이로부터 오는 더 큰 만족감)를 원한다.

Why? 왜 정답일까?
경제학적으로 볼 때 선호도 변화로 행동을 설명하는 것은 문제가 있다는 주어진 글에 이어, (B)는 베이비 붐 시대의 인구 증가와 그 이후 세대의 인구 감소를 설명할 때를 예로 든다. (C)는 (B)에서 소개되었듯이 아기에 대한 대중의 선호 변화라는 관점에서 인구 증가를 설명하는 '그러한 주장'이 경제학적으로 타당하지 않다는 내용을 제시한다. 마지막으로 (A)는 (C)의 마지막 부분에서 언급되었듯이, 선호도보다는 '소득'의 변화가 출산율에 영향을 미칠 수 있음을 구체적 사례로 설명한다. 따라서 글의 순서로 가장 적절한 것은 ③ '(B) – (C) – (A)'이다.

- underlying ⓐ 기저에 있는
- income ⓝ 소득, 수입
- baby boom 베이비 붐
- stable ⓐ 안정된
- mortality ⓝ 사망률
- like and dislikes 호불호
- inherent ⓐ 내재된
- baby bust 출생률 급감
- unsound ⓐ 불안정한, 불건전한
- rise and fall 증감, 흥망성쇠
- be attributed to ~에서 비롯되다, 기인하다

구문 풀이

1행 To an economist [who succeeds in figuring out a person's preference
주격 관계대명사
structure] — understanding {whether the satisfaction gained from consuming one
동명사 주어1 : 명사절(~인지 아닌지)
good} is greater than that of another — explaining behavior in terms of changes
동사1 동명사 주어2
in underlying likes and dislikes is usually highly problematic.
동사2

★★ 문제 해결 꿀~팁 ★★

▶ 많이 틀린 이유는?
④는 정답과 마찬가지로 (C)-(A)를 잘 연결했지만 (B)를 맨 뒤에 배치했는데, 이는 적절한 선택이 아니다. 주어진 글에서 '출생률에 관한 주장'을 다루지 않았는데, (C)에서는 '그러한 주장'을 언급하기 때문이다. 이 주장을 언급한 단락은 (B)이다. 따라서 (B)가 먼저 배치된 후 '그러한 주장'에 관해 평가하는 (C)를 배치하는 것이 옳다.
▶ 문제 해결 방법은?
어떤 두 단락이 인접한다면, 앞 단락의 마지막 부분에서 언급된 내용이 뒷 단락의 처음 부분에서 다시 언급되는 식이다. 가령 (C)의 첫 문장에서 '출생률에 관한 그러한 주장'을 언급하려면 앞에 '베이비 붐, 출산율'과 관련된 '주장'을 제시하는 (B)가 나와야 하는 식이다.

★★★ 등급을 가르는 문제!

38 아이들이 채소를 싫어하는 까닭 정답률 32% | 정답 ⑤

글의 흐름으로 보아, 주어진 문장이 들어가기에 가장 적절한 곳을 고르시오.

In the natural world, / if an animal consumes a plant / with enough antinutrients / to make it feel unwell, / it won't eat that plant again.
자연계에서 / 만약 어떤 동물이 어떤 식물을 섭취한다면, / 충분한 항영양소가 들어 있는 / 몸이 안 좋아질 만큼 / 그 동물은 그 식물을 다시는 먹지 않을 것이다.
Intuitively, / animals also know / to stay away from these plants.
직관적으로 / 동물은 또한 안다. / 이러한 식물을 멀리하는 법을
Years of evolution and information being passed down / created this innate intelligence.
오랜 시간의 진화와 전해 내려오는 정보는 / 이 타고난 지능을 만들어 냈다.
① This "intuition," / though, / is not just seen in animals.
이 '직관'은 / 그러나 / 동물에게서만 보이는 것은 아니다.
② Have you ever wondered / why most children hate vegetables?
여러분은 궁금해한 적이 있는가? / 왜 아이들 대부분이 채소를 싫어하는지
③ Dr. Steven Gundry justifies this / as part of our genetic programming, / our inner intelligence.
Dr. Steven Gundry는 이것을 정당화한다. / 우리의 유전적 프로그래밍, / 즉 우리의 내적 지능의 일부라고
④ Since many vegetables are full of antinutrients, / your body tries to keep you away from them / while you are still fragile and in development.
많은 야채들은 항영양소로 가득 차 있어서, / 여러분의 몸은 여러분이 그것을 멀리하게 하려고 노력한다. / 여러분이 아직 연약하고 성장기일 때
✓ It does this / by making your taste buds perceive these flavors / as bad and even disgusting.
그것은 이렇게 한다. / 여러분의 미뢰(味蕾)가 이러한 맛을 인식하게 만들어 / 나쁘고 심지어 역겹다고
As you grow / and your body becomes stronger enough / to tolerate these antinutrients, / suddenly they no longer taste as bad as before.
여러분이 성장하고 / 여러분의 신체가 충분히 더 강해지면, / 이러한 항영양소를 견딜 만큼 / 갑자기 그것들은 더 이상 전처럼 맛이 안 좋다고 느껴지지 않는다.

자연계에서 만약 항영양소가 몸이 안 좋아질 만큼 들어 있는 식물을 어떤 동물이 섭취한다면, 그 동물은 그 식물을 다시는 먹지 않을 것이다. 직관적으로 동물은 또한 이러한 식물을 멀리할 줄 안다. 오랜 시간의 진화와 전해 내려오는 정보는 이 타고난 지능을 만들어 냈다. ① 그러나 이 '직관'은 동물에게서만 보이는 것은 아니다. ② 여러분은 왜 아이들 대부분이 채소를 싫어하는지 궁금해한 적이 있는가? ③ Dr. Steven Gundry는 이것을 우리의 유전적 프로그래밍, 즉 우리의 내적 지능의 일부라고 정당화한다. ④ 많은 야채들은 항영양소로 가득 차 있어서, 여러분이 아직 연약하고 성장기일 때 여러분의 몸은 여러분이 그것을 멀리하게 하려고 노력한다. ⑤ 그것은 여러분의 미뢰(味蕾)가 이러한 맛을 나쁘고 심지어 역겹다고 인식하게 만들어 그렇게 한다. 여러분이 성장하고 여러분의 신체가 이러한 항영양소를 견딜 만큼 충분히 더 강해지면, 갑자기 그것들은 더 이상 전처럼 맛이 안 좋다고 느껴지지 않는다.

한 사람의 선호도 구조를 알아내는 것, 즉 한 상품을 소비하여 얻는 만족도가 또 다른 상품을 소비하여 얻는 만족도보다 더 큰지를 이해하는 데 성공한 경제학자에게 있어, 행동을 기저에

왼쪽 단

Why? 왜 정답일까?

어린 시절에는 식물에 든 항영양소로 인해 몸이 나빠질 수 있어 직관적으로 채소를 꺼리게 된다는 내용의 글이다. ⑤ 앞에서 이 이야기가 본격적으로 언급되어서, 우리가 아직 어리고 자라는 중일 때는 우리 몸에서 채소를 멀리하게 만들려고 한다는 내용이 제시된다. 주어진 문장은 '채소를 멀리하게 하려고 한다'는 내용을 does this로 가리키며, 어떤 식으로 이런 노력이 이뤄지는지를 보충 설명한다. ⑤ 뒤로는 우리가 다 자라고 나면 상황이 달라진다는 결론이 연결된다. 따라서 주어진 문장이 들어가기에 가장 적절한 곳은 ⑤이다.

- **taste bud** 맛봉오리, 미뢰(味蕾)
- **disgusting** ⓐ 역겨운
- **intuitively** [ad] 직관적으로
- **intuition** ⓝ 직관
- **genetic** ⓐ 유전적인
- **tolerate** ⓥ 견디다
- **flavor** ⓝ 맛, 풍미
- **antinutrient** ⓝ 항영양소
- **innate** ⓐ 타고난
- **justify** ⓥ 정당화하다, 옳음을 보여주다
- **fragile** ⓐ 연약한

구문 풀이

5행 Years of evolution and information being passed down created this innate intelligence.
(주어1 / 주어2 / 수식어구 / 동사)

★★ 문제 해결 꿀~팁 ★★

▶ 많이 틀린 이유는?
가장 헷갈리는 ④ 앞의 두 문장을 보면, 아이들이 채소를 싫어하는 이유를 '우리의 내적 지능'으로 설명할 수 있다고 한다. 그리고 ④ 뒤는 채소가 우리 몸이 연약할 때는 멀리해야 하는 항영양소로 가득 차 있다고 설명한다. 즉, 앞에서 언급된 '내적 지능'을 부연 설명하기 위한 예시가 뒤에 등장하는 문맥이므로 ④ 앞뒤는 논리적 공백 없이 자연스럽다.

▶ 문제 해결 방법은?
주어진 문장의 It은 ⑤ 앞의 your body이고, does this는 keep you away from them을 가리킨다.

---

39 조수간만의 차
정답률 35% | 정답 ③

글의 흐름으로 보아, 주어진 문장이 들어가기에 가장 적절한 곳을 고르시오. [3점]

The difference in the Moon's gravitational pull / on different parts of our planet / effectively creates a "stretching force."
달 중력의 차이는 / 우리 행성의 여러 부분에 대한 / 효과적으로 '잡아 늘리는 힘'을 만든다.

① It makes our planet / slightly stretched out along the line of sight to the Moon / and slightly compressed along a line perpendicular to that.
그것은 우리 행성을 ~하게 만든다. / 달이 보이는 쪽으로 약간 늘어나고, / 그것에 직각을 이루는 선을 따라 약간 눌리게

② The tidal stretching / caused by the Moon's gravity / affects our entire planet, / including both land and water, inside and out.
조수의 팽창은 / 달의 중력으로 발생하는 / 우리 행성 전체에 영향을 미친다. / 땅과 물을 포함한 안팎으로

✔ However, the rigidity of rock means / that land rises and falls with the tides / by a much smaller amount than water, / which is why we notice only the ocean tides.
하지만 / 암석의 단단함은 의미한다 / 땅이 조수와 함께 오르락내리락한다는 것을 / 물보다는 훨씬 적은 양만큼 / 이 이유로 우리는 오로지 바다의 조수만을 알아차리게 된다.

The stretching also explains / why there are generally *two* high tides / (and two low tides) / in the ocean each day.
또한, 그 팽창은 설명한다. / 왜 일반적으로 두 번의 만조가 발생하는지 / (그리고 두 번의 간조) / 매일 바다에서

④ Because Earth is stretched / much like a rubber band, / the oceans bulge out / both on the side facing toward the Moon / and on the side facing away from the Moon.
지구가 늘어나기 때문에, / 고무줄처럼 / 바다는 팽창해 나간다. / 달을 향하는 쪽에서도, / 달에서 멀어지는 쪽에서도

⑤ As Earth rotates, / we are carried through both of these tidal bulges each day, / so we have high tide / when we are in each of the two bulges / and low tide / at the midpoints in between.
지구가 자전함에 따라 / 우리는 매일 이 두 개의 조수 팽창부를 통과하게 된다 / 그래서 우리는 만조를 겪는다 / 우리가 각각 두 개의 팽창부에 있을 때 / 그리고 간조를 / 그 사이 중간 지점에서

우리 행성의 여러 부분에 대한 달 중력의 차이는 효과적으로 '잡아 늘리는 힘'을 만든다. ① 그것은 우리 행성이 달이 보이는 쪽으로 약간 늘어나고, 그것에 직각을 이루는 선을 따라 약간 눌리게 만든다. ② 달의 중력으로 발생하는 조수의 팽창은 땅과 물을 포함한 우리 행성 전체에 안팎으로 영향을 미친다. ③ 하지만 암석의 단단함은 땅이 물보다는 훨씬 적은 양만큼 조수와 함께 오르락내리락한다는 것을 의미하며, 이 이유로 우리는 오로지 바다의 조수만을 알아차리게 된다. 또한, 그 팽창은 왜 일반적으로 매일 바다에서 두 번의 만조(그리고 두 번의 간조)가 발생하는지 설명한다. ④ 지구가 고무줄처럼 늘어나기 때문에, 바다는 달을 향하는 쪽에서도, 달에서 멀어지는 쪽에서도 팽창해 나간다. ⑤ 지구가 자전함에 따라 우리는 매일 이 두 개의 조수 팽창부를 통과하게 되어서, 우리가 각각 두 개의 팽창부에 있을 때 만조를 겪고 그 사이 중간 지점에 있을 때 간조를 겪는다.

Why? 왜 정답일까?

조수간만의 차가 발생하는 이유를 설명하는 글이다. 달의 중력은 지구의 영역마다 다르게 작용하기 때문에 지구가 달을 보는 쪽을 따라 늘어나고, 이와 직각을 이루는 지점에서는 줄어든다는 배경 설명이 ③ 앞까지 이어진다. 이때 주어진 문장은 암석으로 이뤄진 지구의 땅은 팽창과 수축이 덜 드러나는 반면, 바다의 물은 보다 크게 차이를 보인다고 설명한다. also로 시작하는 ③ 뒤의 문장부터는 조수간만의 차가 일어나는 횟수에 관해 언급하며 앞과 내용상 달라진다. 따라서 주어진 문장이 들어가기에 가장 적절한 곳은 ③이다.

- **rigidity** ⓝ 단단함
- **gravitational** ⓐ 중력의
- **perpendicular** ⓐ 직각을 이루는
- **tide** ⓝ 조수, 밀물과 썰물
- **compress** ⓥ 압축하다, 수축하다
- **bulge** ⓥ 팽창하다 ⓝ 튀어나온 것

구문 풀이

1행 However, the rigidity of rock means that land rises and falls with the tides by a much smaller amount than water, which is why we notice only the ocean tides.
(선행사[문장] / 계속적 용법)

★★★ 등급을 가르는 문제!

40 유사한 배경 출신의 동료와 일하고자 하는 경향
정답률 33% | 정답 ①

다음 글의 내용을 한 문장으로 요약하고자 한다. 빈칸 (A), (B)에 들어갈 말로 가장 적절한 것은? [3점]

	(A)	(B)
✔①	preference 선호	outweigh ~보다 중요하다
②	hesitation 망설임	reinforce 강화하다
③	preference 선호	strengthen 강화하다
④	hesitation 망설임	overwhelm 압도하다
⑤	inability ~할 수 없음	underlie ~의 근간이 되다

A study investigated the economic cost of prejudice / based on blind assumptions.
한 연구는 선입견의 경제적인 비용을 연구했다. / 맹목적인 가정에 근거한

Researchers gave a group of Danish teenagers / the choice of working with one of two people.
연구자들은 한 무리의 덴마크 십 대들에게 주었다. / 두 사람 중 한 명과 함께 일하는 선택권을

The teenager had never met either of them.
십 대는 둘 중 어느 한 명과도 만난 적이 없었다.

One of the people had a name / that suggested / they were from a similar ethnic or religious background to the teenager.
둘 중 한 명은 이름을 지니고 있었다. / 암시하는 / 그들이 그 십 대와 유사한 인종 또는 종교적 배경의 출신임을

The other had a name / that suggested / they were from a different ethnic or religious background.
다른 한 사람은 이름을 지니고 있었다. / 암시하는 / 그들이 다른 인종 또는 종교적 배경의 출신임을

The study showed / that the teenagers were prepared / to earn an average of 8% less / if they could work with someone / they thought came from the same ethnic or religious background.
그 연구는 보여 주었다. / 만약 십 대들이 준비가 되어 있다는 것을 / 평균 8% 더 적게 벌 / 그들이 사람과 함께 일할 수 있다면 / 같은 인적적 또는 종교적 배경 출신이라고 생각하는

And this prejudice was evident / among teenagers with ethnic majority names / as well as those with ethnic minority names.
그리고 이러한 선입견은 분명했다. / 다수 인종의 이름을 가진 십 대들 사이에서도 / 소수 인종의 이름을 가진 십 대들뿐만 아니라

The teenagers were blindly making assumptions / about the race of their potential colleagues.
십 대들은 맹목적으로 추정했다. / 잠재적인 동료의 인종에 대해

They then applied prejudice to those assumptions, / to the point / where they actually allowed that prejudice to reduce *their own* potential income.
그리고 나서 그들은 선입견을 가정에 적용했다. / 정도까지 / 그 선입견이 실제로 하게 할 / *자기 자신의* 잠재적인 소득을 줄이게

The job required the two teenagers / to work together for just *90 minutes*.
그 일은 두 명의 십 대들에게 요구했다. / *90분*간만 함께 일할 것을

➡ A study / in which teenagers expressed a(n) (A) preference / to work with someone of a similar background, / even at a financial cost to themselves, / suggests / that an assumption-based prejudice can (B) outweigh rational economic behavior.
한 연구는 / 십 대들이 선호를 표현했던 / 비슷한 배경의 사람과 함께 일하는 것에 / 심지어 자신에게 경제적 손실이 따르는데도 / 시사한다. / 가정에 근거한 선입견이 합리적인 경제 행위보다 중요할 수 있다는 것을

한 연구는 맹목적인 가정에 근거한 선입견의 경제적인 비용을 연구했다. 연구자들은 한 무리의 덴마크 십 대들에게 두 사람 중 한 명과 함께 일하는 선택권을 주었다. 십 대는 둘 중 어느 한 명과도 만난 적이 없었다. 둘 중 한 명은 그 십 대와 유사한 인종 또는 종교적 배경의 출신임을 암시하는 이름을 지니고 있었다. 다른 한 사람은 다른 인종 또는 종교적 배경의 출신임을 암시하는 이름을 지니고 있었다. 그 연구는 만약 십 대들이 같은 인종적 또는 종교적 배경 출신이라고 생각되는 사람과 함께 일할 수 있다면 평균 8% 더 적게 벌 준비가 되어 있다는 것을 보여 주었다. 그리고 이러한 선입견은 소수 인종의 이름을 가진 십 대들뿐만 아니라 다수 인종의 이름을 가진 십 대들 사이에서도 분명했다. 십 대들은 맹목적으로 잠재적인 동료의 인종에 대해 추정했다. 그러고 나서 그들은 그 선입견이 *자기 자신의* 잠재적인 소득을 줄이는 것을 실제로 허용할 정도까지 선입견을 가정에 적용하였다. 그 일은 두 명의 십 대들에게 90분간만 함께 일할 것을 요구했다(그렇게 짧게 같이 일하는 것인데도 불구하고 이런 선입견이 작용했다).

➡ 십 대들이 심지어 자신에게 경제적 손실이 따르는데도 비슷한 배경의 사람과 함께 일하는 것에 (A) 선호를 표현했던 한 연구는 가정에 근거한 선입견이 합리적인 경제 행위보다 (B) 중요할 수 있다는 것을 시사한다.

Why? 왜 정답일까?

실험의 결론을 제시하는 'They then applied prejudice to those assumptions, to the point where they actually allowed that prejudice to reduce *their own* potential income.'에서, 참가자들은 금전적 손해를 감수하면서까지 유사한 인종 및 종교적 배경 출신이라고 여겨지는 동료와 일하려는 경향을 보였다고 한다. 따라서 요약문의 빈칸 (A), (B)에 들어갈 말로 가장 적절한 것은 ① '(A) preference(선호), (B) outweigh(~보다 중요하다)'이다.

- **investigate** ⓥ 조사하다, 연구하다
- **assumption** ⓝ 가정, 추정
- **evident** ⓐ 명백한
- **reduce** ⓥ 줄이다, 감소시키다
- **outweigh** ⓥ ~보다 중요하다
- **strengthen** ⓥ 강화하다
- **inability** ⓝ ~하지 못함, 무능
- **prejudice** ⓝ 편견
- **ethnic** ⓐ 민족적인
- **race** ⓝ 인종
- **financial** ⓐ 재정적인
- **hesitation** ⓝ 망설임
- **overwhelm** ⓥ 압도하다
- **underlie** ⓥ ~의 근간이 되다

구문 풀이

10행 And this prejudice was evident among teenagers with ethnic majority names as well as those with ethnic minority names.
(A+ / as well as + B : B뿐만 아니라 A도)

★★ 문제 해결 꿀~팁 ★★

▶ 많이 틀린 이유는?
실험의 결과(The study showed ~)를 보면, 배경이 다른 사람과 일할 때가 더 많은 돈을 벌 수 있

는데도 십 대들은 비슷한 배경을 가진 파트너와 일하기를 선호했다고 한다. 이 경우 경제적으로 생각하면 '배경이 다른' 사람과 일하기를 선택하는 것이 '합리적'인데, 이 행동은 비슷한 배경에 대한 선호가 '더 중요하게' 작용하는 바람에 약해졌다. 따라서 ②나 ③처럼 (B)에 reinforce나 strengthen을 쓰면 어색하다.

▶ 문제 해결 방법은?
결론인 'The teenagers were blindly making assumptions ~. They then applied prejudice ~.'와 요약문은 서로 같은 말이다.

41-42 정보를 얻지 못할 때 세부 사항을 꾸며내 우리를 '속이는' 뇌

A neuropsychologist, Michael Gazzaniga / conducted a study / that shows that our brains (a) excel / at creating coherent (but not necessarily true) stories / that deceive us.
신경 심리학자 Michael Gazzaniga는 / 연구를 수행했다 / 우리 뇌가 탁월하다는 것을 보여 주는 / 일관성 있는 (하지만 꼭 사실은 아닌) 이야기를 만들어 내는 데 / 우리를 속이는

In the study, / split-brain patients were shown an image / such that it was visible to only their left eye / and asked to select a related card with their left hand.
이 연구에서는 / 분리 뇌 환자들에게 이미지를 보여 주고 / 왼쪽 눈에만 보이도록 / 왼손으로 관련 있는 카드를 선택하도록 요청했다.

Left-eye vision and left-side body movement / are controlled by the right hemisphere.
왼쪽 눈의 시력과 왼쪽 몸의 움직임은 / 우뇌에 의해 제어된다.

『In a split-brain patient, / the connection between the right and left hemispheres / has been broken, / meaning no information can cross / from one hemisphere to the other.』 42번의 근거
분리 뇌 환자에 있어 / 우뇌와 좌뇌 사이의 연결은 / 끊어져 있는데 / 이는 정보가 건너갈 수 없다는 것을 의미한다 / 한쪽 뇌에서 다른 쪽 뇌로

Therefore, / in this experiment, / the right hemisphere was doing all of the work, / and the left hemisphere was (b) unaware of what was happening.
따라서 / 이 실험에서 / 우뇌가 모든 작업을 수행하고 있었고 / 좌뇌는 무슨 일이 일어나고 있는지 모르고 있었다.

Gazzaniga then asked participants / why they chose the card / that they did.
그 뒤 Gazzaniga는 참가자들에게 물었다 / 그들이 그 카드를 왜 선택했는지 / 그들이 고른

Because language is processed and generated in the left hemisphere, / the left hemisphere is required to respond.
언어는 좌뇌에서 처리되고 생성되기 때문에 / 좌뇌가 응답하도록 요구된다.

However, / because of the experiment's design, / only the right hemisphere knew / why the participant selected the card.
그러나 / 그 실험의 설계 때문에 / 오직 우뇌만이 알고 있었다 / 왜 그 참가자가 그 카드를 선택했는지

As a result, / Gazzaniga expected the participants to be (c) silent / when asked to answer the question.
결과적으로 / Gazzaniga는 참가자들이 침묵할 것이라고 예상했다 / 질문에 답할 것을 요청받았을 때

But instead, / every subject fabricated a response.
하지만 그 대신 / 모든 피실험자는 응답을 꾸며 냈다.

The left hemisphere was being asked / to provide a (d) rationalization / for a behavior done by the right hemisphere.
좌뇌는 요청을 받고 있었다 / 설명을 제공하라고 / 우뇌에 의해 행해진 행동에 대한

The left hemisphere didn't know the answer.
좌뇌는 답을 알지 못했다.

But that didn't keep it from fabricating an answer.
그러나 그것이 좌뇌가 답을 꾸며 내는 것을 막지는 못했다.

That answer, however, / had no basis in reality.
하지만 그 대답은 / 사실 근거를 가지고 있지 않았다.

Now if this study had been limited to split-brain patients, / it would be interesting / but not very (e) relevant to us.
자, 만약 이 연구가 분리 뇌 환자에게 제한됐다면 / 그것은 흥미롭지만 / 우리와 매우 관련 있는 일은 아닐 것이다.

It turns out / split-brain patients aren't the only ones / who fabricate reasons.
~라고 밝혀진다 / 분리 뇌 환자들이 유일한 사람은 아니라고 / 이유를 꾸며 내는

We all do it.
우리 모두 그렇게 한다.

『We all need a coherent story about ourselves, / and when information in that story is missing, / our brains simply fill in the details.』 41번의 근거
우리 모두는 자신에 대한 일관성 있는 이야기를 필요로 하고 / 그 이야기에서 정보가 빠져 있을 때 / 우리의 뇌는 그저 세부 사항을 채워넣는다.

신경 심리학자 Michael Gazzaniga는 우리 뇌가 우리를 속이는 일관성 있는 (하지만 꼭 사실은 아닌) 이야기를 만들어 내는 데 (a) 탁월함을 보여 주는 연구를 수행했다. 이 연구에서는 분리 뇌 환자들에게 왼쪽 눈에만 보이도록 이미지를 보여 주고 왼손으로 관련 있는 카드를 선택하도록 요청했다. 왼쪽 눈의 시력과 왼쪽 몸의 움직임은 우뇌에 의해 제어된다. 분리 뇌 환자에게 있어 우뇌와 좌뇌 사이의 연결은 끊어져 있는데, 이는 한쪽 뇌에서 다른 쪽 뇌로 정보가 건너갈 수 없다는 것을 의미한다. 따라서 이 실험에서 우뇌가 모든 작업을 수행하고 있었고, 좌뇌는 무슨 일이 일어나고 있는지 (b) 알고(→ 모르고) 있었다. 그 뒤 Gazzaniga는 참가자들에게 그들이 고른 그 카드를 왜 선택했는지 물었다. 언어는 좌뇌에서 처리되고 생성되기 때문에 좌뇌가 응답하도록 요구된다. 그러나 그 실험의 설계 때문에 오직 우뇌만이 왜 그 참가자가 그 카드를 선택했는지 알고 있었다. 결과적으로 Gazzaniga는 참가자들이 질문에 답할 것을 요청받았을 때 (c) 침묵할 것이라고 예상했다. 하지만 그 대신, 모든 피실험자는 응답을 꾸며 냈다. 좌뇌는 우뇌에 의해 행해진 행동에 대한 (d) 설명을 제공하라는 요청을 받고 있었다. 좌뇌는 답을 알지 못했다. 그러나 그것이 좌뇌가 답을 꾸며 내는 것을 막지는 못했다. 하지만 그 대답은 사실 근거를 가지고 있지 않았다. 자, 만약 이 연구가 분리 뇌 환자에게만 제한됐다면, 그것은 흥미롭지만 우리와 매우 (e) 관련 있는 일은 아닐 것이다. 밝혀지기로, 분리 뇌 환자들이 이유를 꾸며 내는 유일한 사람은 아니다. 우리 모두 그렇게 한다. 우리 모두는 자신에 대한 일관성 있는 이야기를 필요로 하고, 그 이야기에서 정보가 빠져 있을 때, 우리의 뇌는 그저 세부 사항을 채워넣는다.

- **neuropsychologist** ⓝ 신경 심리학자
- **deceive** ⓥ 속이다
- **hemisphere** ⓝ 반구, (뇌의 한쪽) 뇌
- **generate** ⓥ 만들어내다, 생성하다
- **fabricate** ⓥ 꾸며내다, 날조하다
- **behavior** ⓝ 행동
- **basis** ⓝ 근거, 기반
- **deceptive** ⓐ 속이는, 교묘한
- **activate** ⓥ 활성화하다

- **coherent** ⓐ 일관성 있는
- **split** ⓐ 분리된, 쪼개진
- **process** ⓥ 처리하다
- **respond** ⓥ 반응하다, 응수하다
- **rationalization** ⓝ 합리적 설명, 합리화
- **keep A from B** A가 B하지 못하게 하다
- **relevant** ⓐ 관련 있는, 적절한
- **insight** ⓝ 통찰력
- **dominance** ⓝ 우세

12행 Gazzaniga then asked participants [why they chose the card that they did].
4형식 동사   간접목적어
[ ]: 직접목적어(간접의문문)
대동사(=chose)

41 제목 파악   정답률 41% | 정답 ③

윗글의 제목으로 가장 적절한 것은?
① Which Side of the Brain Do We Tend to Use More?
우리는 어느 쪽 뇌를 더 사용하는 경향이 있을까?
② How Our Brain's Hemispheres Interact in Storytelling
이야기할 때 우리 뇌의 두 반구가 상호작용하는 방식
✓③ The Deceptive Brain: Insights from a Split-Brain Patient Study
속이는 뇌: 분리 뇌 환자 연구에서 나온 통찰
④ To Be Creative, Activate Both Hemispheres of Your Brain!
창의적이 되려면, 여러분 뇌 양쪽을 모두 활성화하라!
⑤ The Dominance of the Left Brain in Image Processing
이미지 처리에 있어 좌뇌의 우세

Why? 왜 정답일까?

분리 뇌 환자들의 연구 사례를 통해, 우리 뇌는 정보가 없을 때 세부 사항을 '그저 채워넣기' 위해 꼭 사실은 아닐 수도 있는 정보를 만들어 낸다(We all need a coherent story about ourselves, and when information in that story is missing, our brains simply fill in the details.)는 결론을 이끌어내는 글이다. 따라서 글의 제목으로 가장 적절한 것은 ③ '속이는 뇌: 분리 뇌 환자 연구에서 나온 통찰'이다.

42 어휘 추론   정답률 39% | 정답 ②

밑줄 친 (a) ~ (e) 중에서 문맥상 낱말의 쓰임이 적절하지 않은 것은? [3점]
① (a)   ✓② (b)   ③ (c)   ④ (d)   ⑤ (e)

Why? 왜 정답일까?

분리 뇌 환자들의 상태를 설명하는 'In a split-brain patient, the connection between the right and left hemispheres has been broken, meaning no information can cross from one hemisphere to the other.'에서, 이런 환자들의 두 뇌 사이에는 연결이 끊어져 있어 어느 한쪽 뇌에서 받아들인 정보가 다른 쪽 뇌에 전달되지 않는다고 설명한다. 이를 근거로 볼 때, 우뇌가 하는 일을 좌뇌는 '모른다'는 의미가 되도록 (b)의 aware를 unaware로 고쳐야 한다. 따라서 문맥상 낱말의 쓰임이 적절하지 않은 것은 ② '(b)'이다.

43-45 쌍둥이 자매와의 연습으로 숫 감각을 향상시킨 Chanel

(A)

The basketball felt like it belonged in Chanel's hands / even though it was only a practice game.
농구공은 마치 Chanel의 것인 듯했다. / 그것이 단지 연습 경기이기는 했지만

She decided not to pass the ball / to her twin sister, Vasha.
그녀는 공을 패스하지 않기로 결심했다. / 자기 쌍둥이 자매인 Vasha에게

Instead, / (a) she stopped, jumped, and shot the ball toward the basket, / but it bounced off the backboard.
대신 / 그녀는 멈춰서서 점프해 공을 골대 쪽으로 던졌지만, / 그것은 백보드를 맞고 튕겨 나갔다.

『Chanel could see / that her teammates were disappointed.』 45번①의 근거 일치
Chanel은 볼 수 있었다 / 자신의 팀원들이 실망하는 것을

The other team got the ball and soon scored, / ending the game.
상대 팀이 공을 가져가 이내 득점했고 / 경기는 끝났다.

(D)

When the practice game ended, / Chanel felt her eyes sting with tears.
연습 경기가 끝났을 때, / Chanel은 눈이 눈물로 따끔거리는 것을 느꼈다.

"It's okay," / Vasha said in a comforting voice.
"괜찮아," / Vasha가 위로하는 목소리로 말했다.

Chanel appreciated her, / but Vasha wasn't making her feel any better.
Chanel은 그녀에게 고마웠지만, / Vasha 덕에 기분이 더 나아지지는 않았다.

Vasha wanted to help her twin improve.
Vasha는 그녀의 쌍둥이가 나아지도록 돕고 싶었다.

She invited her twin to practice with (e) her.
그녀는 자기 쌍둥이에게 자신과 함께 연습하자고 권유했다.

『After school, / they got their basketball / and started practicing their basketball shots.』 45번⑤의 근거 일치
방과 후에 / 그들은 농구공을 가지고 / 농구 숫을 연습하기 시작했다.

(C)

At first, / Chanel did not like practicing with Vasha / because every time Vasha shot the ball, / it went in.
처음에 / Chanel은 Vasha와 연습하는 것이 좋지 않았는데, / Vasha가 숫을 할 때마다 / 숫이 들어가기 때문이었다.

But whenever it was Chanel's turn, / she missed.
하지만 Chanel의 차례마다 / 그녀는 숫을 넣지 못했다.

(c) She got frustrated / at not making a shot.
그녀는 좌절했다. / 숫을 넣지 못해

"Don't give up!" / Vasha shouted after each missed shot.
"포기하지 마!" / 숫이 실패할 때마다 Vasha가 외쳤다.

After twelve misses in a row, / her thirteenth shot went in / and she screamed, / "I finally did it!" 45번④의 근거 불일치
12번의 연이은 실패 후에 / 13번째 숫이 들어갔고, / 그녀가 외쳤다. / "마침내 내가 해냈어!"라고

Her twin said, / "I knew (d) you could! / Now let's keep practicing!"
그녀의 쌍둥이는 말했다. / "네가 해낼 줄 알았어! / 자, 계속 연습하자!"

(B)

『The next day, / Chanel played in the championship game / against a rival school.』 45번②의 근거 일치
다음 날, / Chanel은 챔피언십 경기에 출전했다. / 라이벌 학교에 대항하여

It was an intense game / and the score was tied / when Chanel was passed the ball by Vasha, / with ten seconds left in the game.
팽팽한 경기였고, / 점수는 동점이었다. / Chanel이 Vasha에게 공을 패스받았을 때 / 경기가 10초 남은 상황에서

(b) She leaped into the air / and shot the ball.
그녀는 공중으로 뛰어올라 / 공을 던졌다.
『It went straight into the basket!
그것은 곧바로 골대 안으로 들어갔다!
Chanel's last shot / had made her team the champions.』 45번 ③의 근거 일치
Chanel의 마지막 슛은 / 그녀의 팀을 우승팀으로 만들었다.
Vasha and all her other teammates / cheered for her.
Vasha와 모든 다른 팀원들은 / 그녀에게 환호를 보냈다.

(A)
단지 연습 경기이기는 했지만 농구공은 마치 Chanel의 것인 듯했다. 그녀는 자기 쌍둥이 자매인 Vasha에게 공을 패스하지 않기로 결심했다. 대신 (a) 그녀는 멈춰서서 점프해 공을 골대 쪽으로 던졌지만, 그것은 백보드를 맞고 튕겨 나갔다. Chanel은 팀원들이 실망하는 것을 볼 수 있었다. 상대 팀이 공을 가져가서 이내 득점했고 경기는 끝났다.

(D)
연습 경기가 끝났을 때, Chanel은 눈이 눈물로 따끔거리는 것을 느꼈다. "괜찮아," Vasha가 위로하는 목소리로 말했다. Chanel은 그녀에게 고마웠지만, Vasha 덕분에 기분이 더 나아지지는 않았다. Vasha는 그녀의 쌍둥이가 나아지도록 돕고 싶었다. 그녀는 자기 쌍둥이에게 (e) 자신과 함께 연습하자고 권유했다. 방과 후에 그들은 농구공을 가지고 농구 슛을 연습하기 시작했다.

(C)
처음에 Chanel은 Vasha와 연습하는 것이 좋지 않았는데, Vasha가 슛을 할 때마다 슛이 들어갔기 때문이었다. 하지만 Chanel은 자기 차례마다 슛을 넣지 못했다. (c) 그녀는 슛을 넣지 못해 좌절했다. "포기하지 마!" 슛이 실패할 때마다 Vasha가 외쳤다. 12번의 연이은 실패 후에 13번째 슛이 들어갔고, 그녀가 "마침내 내가 해냈어!"라고 외쳤다. 그녀의 쌍둥이는 말했다. "(d) 네가 해낼 줄 알았어! 자, 계속 연습하자!"

(B)
다음날 Chanel은 라이벌 학교와의 챔피언십 경기에 출전했다. 팽팽한 경기였고, 경기가 10초 남은 상황에서 Chanel이 Vasha에게 공을 패스받았을 때 점수는 동점이었다. (b) 그녀는 공중으로 뛰어올라 공을 던졌다. 그것은 곧바로 골대 안으로 들어갔다! Chanel의 마지막 슛으로 인해 그녀의 팀은 우승팀이 되었다. Vasha와 모든 다른 팀원들은 그녀에게 환호를 보냈다.

- bounce off 튕겨져 나오다
- intense ⓐ 격렬한
- leap ⓥ 뛰어오르다
- give up 포기하다
- scream ⓥ (무서움이나 흥분으로) 비명을 지르다
- comfort ⓥ 위로하다
- disappointed ⓐ 실망한
- tie ⓥ 동점을 이루다
- cheer for ~을 응원하다
- in a row 연속으로
- sting ⓥ 따끔거리다, 쓰라리다
- appreciate ⓥ 고마워하다

구문 풀이

[C] 3행 She got frustrated at not making a shot.
전치사 ↵ 동명사(부정 표현)

43 글의 순서 파악   정답률 75% | 정답 ⑤

주어진 글 (A)에 이어질 내용을 순서에 맞게 배열한 것으로 가장 적절한 것은?
① (B) − (D) − (C)   ② (C) − (B) − (D)
③ (C) − (D) − (B)   ④ (D) − (B) − (C)
☑ (D) − (C) − (B)

Why? 왜 정답일까?

연습 게임에서 Chanel이 결정적인 슛을 실패해 팀에 패배를 안겼다는 내용의 (A) 뒤에는, 경기 후 쌍둥이 자매 Vasha가 함께 연습하자고 제안했다는 내용의 (D), Vasha와 계속 연습하며 Chanel이 다시 슛을 성공하게 되었다는 내용의 (C), 슛 감각을 완전히 찾은 Chanel이 본 게임에서는 멋지게 결정 골을 넣었다는 내용의 (B)가 차례로 연결되어야 한다. 따라서 글의 순서로 가장 적절한 것은 ⑤ '(D) − (C) − (B)' 이다.

44 지칭 추론   정답률 64% | 정답 ⑤

밑줄 친 (a) ~ (e) 중에서 가리키는 대상이 나머지 넷과 다른 것은?
① (a)   ② (b)   ③ (c)   ④ (d)   ☑ (e)

Why? 왜 정답일까?

(a), (b), (c), (d)는 Chanel, (e)는 Vasha를 가리키므로, (a) ~ (e) 중에서 가리키는 대상이 다른 하나는 ⑤ '(e)'이다.

45 세부 내용 파악   정답률 84% | 정답 ④

윗글의 Chanel에 관한 내용으로 적절하지 않은 것은?
① 연습 경기 중에 팀원들의 실망한 모습을 보았다.
② 라이벌 학교와의 챔피언십 경기에 출전했다.
③ 팀을 우승시키는 마지막 슛을 성공했다.
☑ 슛 연습에서 연이은 실패 후에 12번째 슛이 들어갔다.
⑤ 방과 후에 농구 슛을 연습하기 시작했다.

Why? 왜 정답일까?

(C) 'After twelve misses in a row, her thirteenth shot went in ~'에서 Chanel은 슛을 12번 실패한 후 13번째 슛을 성공시켰음을 알 수 있다. 따라서 내용과 일치하지 않는 것은 ④ '슛 연습에서 연이은 실패 후에 12번째 슛이 들어갔다.'이다.

Why? 왜 오답일까?

① (A) 'Chanel could see that her teammates were disappointed.'의 내용과 일치한다.

② (B) 'Chanel played in the championship game against a rival school.'의 내용과 일치한다.
③ (B) 'Chanel's last shot had made her team the champions.'의 내용과 일치한다.
⑤ (D) 'After school, they ~ started practicing their basketball shots.'의 내용과 일치한다.

어휘 Review Test 17   문제편 170쪽

A	B	C	D
01 관대함	01 productive	01 ⓜ	01 ⓞ
02 평가하다	02 support	02 ⓐ	02 ⓝ
03 ~을 고수하다	03 accurate	03 ⓣ	03 ⓐ
04 까다로운	04 ideally	04 ⓘ	04 ⓜ
05 개시하다, 시작하다	05 progress	05 ⓝ	05 ⓛ
06 종교적인	06 inspire	06 ⓒ	06 ⓟ
07 걱정	07 vaccination	07 ⓑ	07 ⓒ
08 동반하다, 수반하다	08 exhibition	08 ⓓ	08 ⓓ
09 유명한, 저명한	09 discourage A from B	09 ⓔ	09 ⓘ
10 직접 하는, 대면의	10 optical	10 ⓕ	10 ⓢ
11 (수요나 필요를) 맞추다, 수용하다	11 fundamental	11 ⓕ	11 ⓔ
12 위반하다	12 anticipate	12 ⓠ	12 ⓚ
13 고통	13 identical	13 ⓢ	13 ⓕ
14 명칭, 직함	14 resolve	14 ⓖ	14 ⓖ
15 유죄 판결	15 envy	15 ⓚ	15 ⓗ
16 직관적으로	16 flavor	16 ⓘ	16 ⓘ
17 민족적인	17 process	17 ⓗ	17 ⓙ
18 격렬한	18 famine	18 ⓙ	18 ⓠ
19 가중치를 두다, 가중치, 무게	19 poverty	19 ⓞ	19 ⓑ
20 굴욕을 느끼는, 수치스러운	20 valuable	20 ⓟ	20 ⓘ

17회

---

18 버스 운행 중단 계획 반대   정답률 80% | 정답 ②

다음 글의 목적으로 가장 적절한 것은?

① 버스 노선 변경에 항의하려고
✔ 버스 운행 중단 계획에 반대하려고
③ 버스 배차 간격 조정을 요청하려고
④ 자전거 전용 도로 설치를 건의하려고
⑤ 통학로 안전 관리 강화를 촉구하려고

직독 직해

To whom it may concern,
관계자 분께

I am a parent of a high school student / who takes the 145 bus to commute to Clarkson High School.
저는 고등학생의 부모입니다. / Clarkson 고등학교로 통학하기 위해 145번 버스를 타는

This is the only public transport available from our area / and is used by many students.
이것은 우리 지역에서 이용할 수 있는 유일한 대중교통이며 / 많은 학생들에 의해 이용됩니다.

Recently, / I heard / that the city council is planning to discontinue this service.
최근 / 저는 들었습니다. / 시 의회가 이 노선을 중단하는 것을 계획하고 있다고

My husband and I start work early in the morning / and this makes it impossible / for us to drop our son off at school.
제 남편과 저는 아침 일찍 일을 시작하며 / 이 점이 불가능하게 만듭니다. / 저희가 아들을 학교에 태워다주는 것을

It would take him nearly an hour to walk to school / and there is a lot of traffic in the morning, / so I do not consider it safe to bike.
제 아들이 학교에 걸어가는 데는 거의 한 시간이 걸릴 것이며 / 아침에는 교통량이 많아서 / 저는 자전거를 타는 것이 안전하다고 생각하지 않습니다.

This matter will place many families, / including ours, / under a lot of stress.
이런 문제점은 많은 가족들을 처하게 할 것입니다. / 저희를 포함한 / 엄청난 곤경에

As a resident of Sunnyville, / I think such a plan is unacceptable.
Sunnyville의 거주자로서 / 저는 그러한 계획을 받아들이기 어렵다고 생각합니다.

I urge the council to listen to the concerns of the community.
저는 의회가 지역 사회의 우려를 경청할 것을 촉구하는 바입니다.

Sincerely, // Lucy Jackson
Lucy Jackson 드림

관계자 분께

저는 Clarkson 고등학교로 통학하기 위해 145번 버스를 타는 고등학생의 부모입니다. 이것은 우리 지역에서 이용할 수 있는 유일한 대중교통이며 많은 학생들이 이용합니다. 최근 저는 시 의회가 노선을 중단하는 것을 계획하고 있다고 들었습니다. 제 남편과 저는 아침 일찍 일을 시작하며 이 점 때문에 저희가 아들을 학교에 태워다주는 것이 불가능합니다. 제 아들이 학교에 걸어가는 데는 거의 한 시간이 걸릴 것이며, 아침에는 교통량이 많아서 저는 자전거를 타는 것이 안전하다고 생각하지 않습니다. 이런 문제점은 저희를 포함한 많은 가족들을 엄청난 곤경에 처하게 할 것입니다. Sunnyville의 거주자로서 저는 그러한 계획을 받아들이기 어렵다고 생각합니다. 저는 의회가 지역 사회의 우려를 경청할 것을 촉구하는 바입니다.

Lucy Jackson 드림

Why? 왜 정답일까?

최근 의회에서 계획한 버스 운행 중단에 대해 주민으로서 반대 의견을 표명한(As a resident of Sunnyville, I think such a plan is unacceptable.)는 내용의 글이다. 따라서 글의 목적으로 가장 적절한 것은 ② '버스 운행 중단 계획에 반대하려고'이다.

- commute ⓥ 통근하다, 통학하다
- city council 시 의회
- drop off (차로) 내려주다
- urge ⓥ 촉구하다, 권고하다
- public transport 대중 교통
- discontinue ⓥ 중단하다
- unacceptable ⓐ 받아들일 수 없는

구문 풀이

6행 My husband and I start work early in the morning and this makes it impossible for us to drop our son off at school.
목적격 보어 / 의미상 주어 / 진목적어 / 5형식 동사 / 가목적어

---

19 기대했던 승진 통보를 받지 못한 Ted   정답률 87% | 정답 ①

다음 글에 드러난 Ted의 심경 변화로 가장 적절한 것은?

✔ hopeful → shocked
기대하는 / 충격받은
② relaxed → lonely
여유로운 / 외로운
③ ashamed → relieved
부끄러운 / 안도한
④ indifferent → upset
무관심한 / 언짢은
⑤ embarrassed → pleased
당황한 / 기쁜

One Friday afternoon, / Ted was called to the vice president of human resources.
어느 금요일 오후 / Ted는 인사과의 부사장에게 호출되었다.

Ted sat down, beaming in anticipation.
Ted는 기대감에 차 밝게 웃으며 앉았다.

Today was the big day / and this meeting would mark a turning point in his career!
오늘은 중요한 날이었으며 / 이 만남은 그의 경력에 있어 전환점을 찍게 될 것이었다!

Ted felt sure / that it was for his promotion / and that the vice president would make him the marketing manager.
Ted는 확신했다. / 이것이 자신의 승진을 위한 자리이며 / 부사장이 자신을 마케팅 매니저로 만들어줄 것이라고

"Ted, there is no easy way to say this."
"Ted, 이런 말을 하기가 쉽지는 않네요."

Ted suddenly realized / this meeting wasn't going to be as he expected.
Ted는 돌연 깨달았다. / 이 만남이 자신이 예상했던 대로 되지는 않을 것임을

Ted's mind went blank.
Ted의 머릿속이 하얘졌다.

The vice president continued, / "Ted, I know you've desperately wanted this promotion, / but we decided Mike is more suitable."
부사장은 계속해서 말을 이어 나갔다. / "Ted, 당신이 이번 승진을 간절히 원해 왔다는 것을 알고 있지만, / 우리는 Mike가 더 적합하다고 결정했습니다."

Ted just sat there, frozen.
Ted는 얼어붙은 채 그저 그곳에 앉아 있었다.

He felt as if he had been hit by a truck.
그는 마치 트럭에 치인 것 같은 기분이었다.

Don't panic.
당황하지 말자.

All he was able to do was / repeat that sentence over and over to himself.
그가 할 수 있었던 전부라고는 ~였다. / 그 문장을 계속해서 자신에게 되풀이하는 것

어느 금요일 오후 Ted는 인사과의 부사장에게 호출되었다. Ted는 기대감에 차 밝게 웃으며 앉았다. 오늘은 중요한 날이었으며 이 만남은 그의 경력에 있어 전환점을 찍게 될 것이었다! Ted는 이것이 자신의 승진을 위한 자리이며 부사장이 자신을 마케팅 매니저로 만들어줄 것이라고 확신했다. "Ted, 이런 말을 하기가 쉽지는 않네요." Ted는 돌연 이 만남이 자신이 예상했던 대로 되지는 않을 것임을 깨달았다. Ted의 머릿속이 하얘졌다. 부사장은 계속해서 말을 이어 나갔다. "Ted, 당신이 이번 승진을 간절히 원해 왔다는 것을 알고 있지만, 우리는 Mike가 더 적합하다고 결정했습니다." Ted는 얼어붙은 채 그저 그곳에 앉아 있었다. 그는 마치 트럭에 치인 것 같은 기분이었다. 당황하지 말자. 그가 할 수 있었던 전부라고는 그 문장을 계속해서 자신에게 되풀이하는 것뿐이었다.

Why? 왜 정답일까?

승진을 기대하던(beaming in anticipation) Ted가 기대했던 바와 다른 결과를 듣고 충격받았다(Ted just sat there, frozen. He felt as if he had been hit by a truck.)는 내용의 글이다. 따라서 Ted의 심경 변화로 가장 적절한 것은 ① '기대하는 → 충격받음'이다.

- vice president 부사장
- beam ⓥ 활짝 웃다
- desperately ⓐ 간절히
- suitable ⓐ 적합한
- human resources (회사) 인사과
- anticipation ⓝ 기대
- promotion ⓝ 승진

구문 풀이

9행 He felt as if he had been hit by a truck.
「as if 가정법 과거완료 : (실제로 ~하지 않았지만) 마치 ~했던 것처럼」

---

20 판매 시 희소성의 원칙 이용하기   정답률 80% | 정답 ③

다음 글에서 필자가 주장하는 바로 가장 적절한 것은?

① 상품 판매 시 실현 가능한 판매 목표를 설정해야 한다.
② 판매를 촉진하기 위해서는 가격 경쟁력을 갖추어야 한다.
✔ 효과적인 판매를 위해서는 상품의 희소성을 강조해야 한다.
④ 고객의 신뢰를 얻기 위해서는 일관된 태도를 유지해야 한다.
⑤ 고객의 특성에 맞춰 다양한 판매 전략을 수립하고 적용해야 한다.

In 2003, / British Airways made an announcement / that they would no longer be able / to operate the London to New York Concorde flight twice a day / because it was starting to prove uneconomical.
2003년에 / 영국 항공은 발표했는데 / 자신들이 더 이상 ~할 수 없을 것이라고 / 런던에서 뉴욕까지 가는 콩코드 항공편을 하루에 두 번 운항할 / 왜냐하면 그것이 경제성이 없다고 판명되기 시작하고 있었기 때문이었다.

Well, / the sales for the flight on this route / increased the very next day.
그런데 / 이 노선의 항공편 판매가 / 바로 다음날 증가했다.

There was nothing / that changed about the route / or the service offered by the airlines.
아무것도 없었다. / 노선에 있어서 달라진 것은 / 또는 항공사에 의해 제공되는 서비스(에 있어서)

Merely because it became a scarce resource, / the demand for it increased.
단지 그것이 부족한 자원이 되었기 때문에 / 그것에 대한 수요가 증가했다.

If you are interested in persuading people, / then the principle of scarcity can be effectively used.
만약에 여러분이 사람들을 설득하는 데에 관심이 있다면, / 희소성의 원리가 효과적으로 사용될 수 있다.

If you are a salesperson / trying to increase the sales of a certain product, / then you must not merely point out the benefits / the customer can derive from the said product, / but also point out its uniqueness / and what they will miss out on / if they don't purchase the product soon.
만약 여러분이 판매원이라면, / 특정 상품의 판매를 증가시키려 노력하는 / 여러분은 단지 혜택을 강조할 뿐만이 아니라, / 고객이 언급된 상품으로부터 얻을 수 있는 / 그것의 유일함을 또한 강조해야만 한다. / 그리고 그들이 무엇을 놓치게 될 것인지를 / 만약에 그들이 그것을 빨리 구매하지 않는다면

In selling, / you should keep in mind / that the more limited something is, / the more desirable it becomes.
판매에 있어 / 여러분은 명심해야 한다. / 무언가가 더 한정적일수록 / 그것이 더 가치 있게 된다는 것을

2003년에 영국 항공은 더 이상 런던에서 뉴욕까지 가는 콩코드 항공편을 하루에 두 번 운항할 수 없을 것이라고 발표했는데 왜냐하면 그것이 경제성이 없다고 판명되기 시작하고 있었기 때문이었다. 그런데 바로 다음날 이 노선의 항공편 판매가 증가했다. 노선이나 항공사에 의해 제공되는 서비스에 있어서 달라진 것은 아무것도 없었다. 단지 그것이 부족한 자원이 되었기 때문에 그것에 대한 수요가 증가했다. 만약에 여러분이 사람들을 설득하는 데에 관심이 있다면, 희소성의 원리가 효과적으로 사용될 수 있다. 만약 여러분이 특정 상품의 판매를 증가시키려 노력하는 판매원이라면, 여러분은 단지 고객이 언급된 상품으로부터 얻을 수 있는 혜택

을 강조할 뿐만이 아니라 그것의 유일함과 만약에 그들이 그 상품을 빨리 구매하지 않는다면 무엇을 놓치게 될 것인지를 또한 강조해야만 한다. 판매에 있어 여러분은 무언가가 더 한정적일수록 더 가치 있게 된다는 것을 명심해야 한다.

'~ then the principle of scarcity can be effectively used.'에서 판매를 위해 설득할 때 희소성의 원리를 효과적으로 이용할 수 있다고 하므로, 필자가 주장하는 바로 가장 적절한 것은 ③ '효과적인 판매를 위해서는 상품의 희소성을 강조해야 한다.'이다.

- make an announcement 발표하다
- scarce ⓐ 부족한, 희소한
- derive A from B B로부터 A를 얻어내다
- miss out on ~을 놓치다
- uneconomical ⓐ 비경제적인, 수익이 안 나는
- effectively [ad] 효과적으로
- uniqueness ⓝ 유일함, 고유함
- desirable ⓐ 바람직한, 가치 있는

구문 풀이

12행 In selling, you should keep in mind that the more limited something is,
「the + 비교급 ~, the + 비교급 … : ~할수록 더 …하다」
the more desirable it becomes.

---

21 미디어 다이어트의 필요성   정답률 79% | 정답 ②

밑줄 친 a "media diet"가 다음 글에서 의미하는 바로 가장 적절한 것은?

① balancing the consumption of traditional and online media
기존 미디어 소비와 온라인 미디어 소비의 균형을 유지하는 것
✔② regulating the use of media devices with a set schedule
정해진 시간 계획으로 미디어 기기 사용을 통제하는 것
③ avoiding false nutritional information from the media
미디어 출처의 잘못된 영양 정보를 피하는 것
④ stimulating your brain with various media sources
다양한 언론매체로 뇌를 자극하는 것
⑤ separating yourself from toxic media contents
유독한 매체 콘텐츠로부터 자신을 분리하는 것

The most dangerous threat / to our ability to concentrate / is not that we use our smartphone during working hours, / but that we use it too irregularly.
가장 위험한 위협은 / 우리의 집중력에 / 우리가 근무 시간 동안 스마트폰을 사용한다는 것이 아니라 / 그것을 지나치게 불규칙적으로 사용한다는 것이다.

By checking our emails every now and then on the computer / and our text messages here and there on our phone / with no particular schedule or rhythm in mind, / our brain loses its ability to effectively filter.
이따금 컴퓨터로 이메일을 확인하고 / 전화로 문자 메시지를 어디서든 확인함으로써 / 특별한 일정이나 규칙성을 염두에 두지 않은 채 / 우리의 뇌는 효과적으로 여과하는 능력을 잃는다.

The solution is to regulate your devices / as if you were on a strict diet.
해결책은 기기를 조절하는 것이다. / 마치 여러분이 엄격한 다이어트 중인 것처럼

When it comes to nutrition, / sticking to a fixed time plan for breakfast, lunch, and dinner / allows your metabolism to adjust, / thereby causing less hunger during the in-between phases.
영양에 관해서라면 / 아침, 점심 그리고 저녁 식사를 위한 정해진 시간 계획을 고수하는 것이 / 여러분의 신진대사를 적응시키고, / 그렇게 함으로써 중간 단계 동안 허기를 덜 유발한다.

Your belly will start to rumble around 12:30 p.m. each day, / but that's okay / because that's a good time to eat lunch.
여러분의 배는 매일 오후 12시 반쯤 우르르 울리기 시작할 것이지만 / 그것은 괜찮다. / 그때는 점심을 먹기에 좋은 시간이기 때문에

If something unexpected happens, / you can add a snack every now and then / to get fresh energy, / but your metabolism will remain under control.
만약 예기치 않은 무언가가 일어난다면 / 여러분은 이따금 간식을 추가할 수 있지만 / 활기를 얻기 위해 / 여러분의 신진대사는 계속 통제된 상태에 있을 것이다.

It's the same with our brain / when you put it on a "media diet."
우리의 뇌 또한 그렇다. / 여러분이 뇌를 '미디어 다이어트' 상태로 두었을 때

우리의 집중력에 가장 위험한 위협은 우리가 근무 시간 동안 스마트폰을 사용한다는 것이 아니라 그것을 지나치게 불규칙적으로 사용한다는 것이다. 특별한 일정이나 규칙성을 염두에 두지 않은 채 이따금 컴퓨터로 이메일을 확인하고 전화로 문자 메시지를 어디서든 확인함으로써 우리의 뇌는 효과적으로 여과하는 능력을 잃는다. 해결책은 마치 여러분이 엄격한 다이어트 중인 것처럼 기기 (사용)를 조절하는 것이다. 영양에 관해서라면 아침, 점심 그리고 저녁 식사를 위한 정해진 시간 계획을 고수하는 것이 여러분의 신진대사를 적응시키고, 그렇게 함으로써 식사와 식사 사이 시간 동안 허기를 덜 유발한다. 여러분의 배는 매일 오후 12시 반쯤 우르르 울리기 시작할 것이지만 그때는 점심을 먹기에 좋은 시간이기 때문에 괜찮다. 만약 예기치 않은 무언가가 일어난다면 여러분은 활기를 얻기 위해 이따금 간식을 추가할 수 있지만, 여러분의 신진대사는 계속 통제된 상태에 있을 것이다. 여러분이 뇌를 '미디어 다이어트' 상태로 두었을 때 뇌 또한 그렇다.

집중력에 가장 중대한 위험은 스마트폰을 아무 때나 사용하는 것이므로, 마치 다이어트 중 식이를 조절할 때처럼 엄격하게 기기 사용을 '조절해야'(The solution is to regulate your devices as if you were on a strict diet.) 한다는 내용의 글이다. 따라서 밑줄 친 부분이 의미하는 바로 가장 적절한 것은 ② '정해진 시간 계획으로 미디어 기기 사용을 통제하는 것'이다.

- concentrate ⓥ 집중하다
- every now and then 이따금, 가끔
- strict ⓐ 엄격한
- stick to ~을 고수하다
- metabolism ⓝ 신진대사
- irregularly [ad] 불규칙적으로
- regulate ⓥ 조절하다, 통제하다
- nutrition ⓝ 영양
- fixed ⓐ 고정된
- adjust ⓥ 적응하다

구문 풀이

1행 The most dangerous threat to our ability to concentrate is not {that we
주어   전명구   형용사적 용법   동사
use our smartphone during working hours}, but {that we use it too irregularly}.
「not + (A) + but + (B) : (A)가 아니라 (B)인」

---

22 스토리텔링에서 독자 또는 시청자를 몰입하게 하는 요소   정답률 87% | 정답 ⑤

다음 글의 요지로 가장 적절한 것은?

① 독자의 공감을 얻기 위해 구체적인 인물 묘사가 중요하다.
② 이야기의 줄거리를 단순화시키는 것이 독자의 이해를 높인다.
③ 거리를 두고 주인공의 상황을 객관적으로 바라볼 필요가 있다.
④ 주인공의 역경과 행복이 적절히 섞여야 이야기가 흥미로워진다.
✔⑤ 주인공에 대한 지속적인 궁금증 유발이 독자의 몰입을 도와준다.

Who is this person?
이 사람은 누구지?
This is the question all stories ask.
이것은 모든 이야기가 물어보는 질문이다.
It emerges first at the ignition point.
그것은 발화 지점에서 가장 먼저 나타난다.
When the initial change strikes, / the protagonist overreacts / or behaves in an otherwise unexpected way.
처음 변화가 발생할 때 / 주인공은 과민 반응하거나 / 혹은 다른 예상치 못한 방식으로 행동한다.
We sit up, suddenly attentive.
우리는 일어나 앉아 갑자기 주의를 기울인다.
Who is this person who behaves like this?
이렇게 행동하는 이 사람은 누구야?
The question then re-emerges / every time the protagonist is challenged by the plot / and compelled to make a choice.
그러고 나서 그 질문은 / 주인공이 줄거리에 도전받을 때마다 / 그리고 선택을 하도록 강요받을
Everywhere in the narrative / that the question is present, / the reader or viewer will likely be engaged.
이야기의 모든 곳에서 / 그 질문이 존재하는 / 독자 또는 시청자는 몰입하게 될 것이다.
Where the question is absent, / and the events of drama move out of its narrative beam, / they are at risk of becoming detached / — perhaps even bored.
그 질문이 부재하는 곳에서 / 그리고 드라마의 사건들이 이야기의 빛줄기에서 벗어나는 / 그들은 무심해질 위험에 놓인다. / 심지어는 지루해할
If there's a single secret to storytelling / then I believe it's this.
만약 스토리텔링에 한 가지 비밀이 있다면 / 나는 이것이 비밀이라 믿는다.
Who is this person?
이 사람은 누구지?
Or, from the perspective of the character, / *Who am I?*
또는 등장인물의 관점에서 / 나는 누구지?
It's the definition of drama.
그것이 드라마의 정의이다.
It is its electricity, its heartbeat, its fire.
그것이 드라마의 전기이고 심장 박동이자 불이다.

이 사람은 누구지? 이것은 모든 이야기가 물어보는 질문이다. 그것은 발화 지점에서 가장 먼저 나타난다. 처음 변화가 발생할 때 주인공은 과민 반응하거나 다른 예상치 못한 방식으로 행동한다. 우리는 일어나 앉아 갑자기 주의를 기울인다. 이렇게 행동하는 이 사람은 누구야? 그러고 나서 그 질문은 주인공이 줄거리에 도전받고 선택을 하도록 강요받을 때마다 다시 나타난다. 그 질문이 존재하는 이야기의 모든 곳에서 독자 또는 시청자는 몰입하게 될 것이다. 그 질문이 부재하고 드라마의 사건들이 이야기의 빛줄기에서 벗어나는 곳에서 그들은 무심해지거나, 심지어는 지루해질 위험에 처할 수도 있다. 만약 스토리텔링에 한 가지 비밀이 있다면 나는 이것이 비밀이라 믿는다. 이 사람은 누구지? 또는 등장인물의 관점에서 나는 누구지? 라는 질문 말이다. 그것이 드라마의 정의이다. 그것이 드라마의 전기이고 심장 박동이자 불이다.

주인공이 누구인가에 대한 물음은 드라마 전체에 걸쳐 지속되며, 독자 또는 시청자를 몰입하게 만드는 원천(Everywhere in the narrative that the question is present, the reader or viewer will likely be engaged.)이라는 내용의 글이다. 따라서 글의 요지로 가장 적절한 것은 ⑤ '주인공에 대한 지속적인 궁금증 유발이 독자의 몰입을 도와준다.'이다.

- emerge ⓥ 나타나다, 출현하다
- attentive ⓐ 주의를 기울이는
- engaged ⓐ 몰입한
- at risk of ~할 위험에 처한
- overreact ⓥ 과민 반응하다
- compel ⓥ 강요하다
- absent ⓐ 부재한
- definition ⓝ 정의

구문 풀이

8행 Where the question is absent, and the events of drama move out of its
접속사(~한 곳에서, ~한 경우에)
narrative beam, they are at risk of becoming detached — perhaps even bored.
주어   동사   보어

---

23 눈이 깜박이는 속도로 나타나는 두려움   정답률 80% | 정답 ③

다음 글의 주제로 가장 적절한 것은?

① eye contact as a way to frighten others – 다른 사람들을 겁주기 위한 방법인 눈 맞춤
② fast blinking as a symptom of eye fatigue – 눈 피로의 증상인 빠른 눈 깜박임
✔③ blink speed as a significant indicator of fear – 두려움의 중요한 척도인 눈 깜박임 속도
④ fast eye movement as proof of predatory instinct – 포식자 본능의 증거인 빠른 눈 움직임
⑤ blink rate as a difference between humans and animals – 인간과 동물의 차이점인 눈 깜박임 속도

Shutter speed refers to the speed of a camera shutter.
셔터 속도는 카메라 셔터의 속도를 지칭한다.
In behavior profiling, / it refers to the speed of the eyelid.
행동 프로파일링에서는 / 그것은 눈꺼풀의 속도를 지칭한다.
When we blink, / we reveal more than just blink rate.
우리가 눈을 깜박일 때 / 우리는 단지 눈을 깜박이는 속도보다 더 많은 것을 드러낸다.
Changes in the speed of the eyelid / can indicate important information; / shutter speed is a measurement of fear.
눈꺼풀 속도의 변화는 / 중요한 정보를 나타내는데, / 즉 셔터 속도가 두려움의 척도라는 것이다.
Think of an animal / that has a reputation for being fearful.
동물을 생각해 보라. / 겁이 많다는 평판이 있는
A Chihuahua might come to mind.
치와와가 생각날지도 모른다.

In mammals, / because of evolution, / our eyelids will speed up / to minimize the amount of time / that we can't see an approaching predator.
포유동물의 경우 / 진화 때문에, / 우리의 눈꺼풀은 속도를 높일 것이다. / 시간의 양을 최소로 하기 위하여 / 우리가 다가오는 포식자를 볼 수 없는
The greater the degree of fear an animal is experiencing, / the more the animal is concerned with an approaching predator.
동물이 경험하고 있는 두려움의 정도가 더 클수록 / 그 동물은 다가오는 포식자에 대해 더 걱정한다.
In an attempt to keep the eyes open as much as possible, / the eyelids involuntarily speed up.
가능한 한 많이 눈을 뜨고 있으려는 시도로 / 눈꺼풀은 무의식적으로 속도를 높인다.
Speed, / when it comes to behavior, / almost always equals fear.
속도는 / 행동에 관한 한 / 거의 항상 두려움과 같다.
In humans, / if we experience fear about something, / our eyelids will do the same thing as the Chihuahua; they will close and open more quickly.
인간의 경우 / 만약 우리가 무언가에 대한 두려움을 경험한다면, / 우리의 눈꺼풀은 치와와와 똑같아질 것이어서, / 그것은 더 빠르게 닫히고 열릴 것이다.

셔터 속도는 카메라 셔터의 속도를 지칭한다. 행동 프로파일링에서는 그것은 눈꺼풀의 속도를 지칭한다. 우리가 눈을 깜박일 때 우리는 단지 눈을 깜박이는 속도보다 더 많은 것을 드러낸다. 눈꺼풀 속도의 변화는 중요한 정보를 나타내는데, 즉 셔터 속도가 두려움의 척도라는 것이다. 겁이 많다는 평판이 있는 동물을 생각해 보라. 치와와가 생각날지도 모른다. 포유동물의 경우 진화 때문에, 우리가 다가오는 포식자를 볼 수 없는 시간의 양을 최소로 하기 위하여 우리의 눈꺼풀은 속도를 높일 것이다. 동물이 경험하고 있는 두려움의 정도가 더 클수록 그 동물은 다가오는 포식자에 대해 더 걱정한다. 가능한 한 많이 눈을 뜨고 있으려는 시도로 눈꺼풀은 무의식적으로 속도를 높인다. 행동에 관한 한 속도는 거의 항상 두려움과 같다. 인간의 경우 만약 우리가 무언가에 대한 두려움을 경험한다면, 우리의 눈꺼풀은 치와와와 똑같아질 것이어서, 즉 더 빠르게 닫히고 열릴 것이다.

Why? 왜 정답일까?

'~ shutter speed is a measurement of fear.'에서 눈을 깜빡이는 속도는 두려움의 척도라는 핵심 내용이 제시되므로, 글의 주제로 가장 적절한 것은 ③ '두려움의 중요한 척도인 눈 깜박임 속도'이다.

- profiling ⓝ 프로파일링, (개요 작성을 위한) 자료 수집
- blink ⓝ 눈을 깜박거림 ⓥ 눈을 깜박이다
- measurement ⓝ 척도
- minimize ⓥ 최소화하다
- involuntarily [ad] 모르는 사이에, 본의 아니게
- fatigue ⓝ 피로
- indicator ⓝ 지표, 표시
- rate ⓝ 속도, 비율
- reputation ⓝ 평판, 명성
- predator ⓝ 포식자
- frighten ⓥ 겁을 주다
- significant ⓐ 중요한, 유의미한
- instinct ⓝ 본능

구문 풀이

> **12행** In humans, if we experience fear about something, our eyelids will do the
> 접속사(조건)   동사(현재)   동사1(미래)
> same thing as the Chihuahua; they will close and open more quickly.
>   동사2(미래)

24 자유 시장의 순기능　정답률 57% | 정답 ②

다음 글의 제목으로 가장 적절한 것은?
① Trade War: A Reflection of Human's Innate Violence
무역 전쟁: 인간의 타고난 폭력의 반영
✓ Free Market: Winning Together over Losing Together
자유 시장: 함께 지키보다 함께 이기기
③ New Economic Framework Stabilizes the Free Market
새로운 경제 체제는 자유 시장을 안정시킨다
④ Violence Is the Invisible Hand That Disrupts Capitalism!
폭력은 자본주의를 교란하는 보이지 않는 손이다!
⑤ How Are Governments Involved in Controlling the Market?
정부는 시장 통제에 어떻게 관여하는가?

The free market has liberated people / in a way that Marxism never could.
자유 시장은 사람들을 자유롭게 해 왔다. / 마르크스주의가 결코 할 수 없었던 방식으로
What is more, / as A. O. Hirschman, the Harvard economic historian, / showed in his classic study *The Passions and the Interests*, / the market was seen / by Enlightenment thinkers Adam Smith, David Hume, and Montesquieu / as a powerful solution / to one of humanity's greatest traditional weaknesses: / violence.
게다가 / 하버드 대학 경제 역사학자인 A. O. Hirschman이 / 자신의 대표적 연구인 *The Passions and the Interests*에서 / 보여주었듯이, / 시장은 여겨졌다. / 계몽주의 사상가들인 Adam Smith, David Hume 그리고 Montesquieu에 의해 / 강력한 해결책으로 / 인류의 가장 큰 전통적 약점들 중 하나에 대한 / 즉 폭력
When two nations meet, / said Montesquieu, / they can do one of two things: / they can wage war or they can trade.
두 국가가 만날 때 / Montesquieu가 말했던 바로, / 그들은 두 가지 중 하나를 할 수 있는데, / 즉 전쟁을 벌이거나 거래를 할 수 있다.
If they wage war, / both are likely to lose in the long run.
만약 그들이 전쟁을 벌인다면, / 둘 다 장기적으로 손해를 볼 가능성이 있다.
If they trade, / both will gain.
만약 그들이 거래를 한다면, / 둘 다 이득을 얻을 것이다.
That, of course, was the logic / behind the establishment of the European Union: / to lock together the destinies of its nations, / especially France and Germany, / in such a way that they would have an overwhelming interest / not to wage war again / as they had done to such devastating cost / in the first half of the twentieth century.
그것이 물론 논리였다. / 유럽 연합의 설립 이면에 있는 / 연합의 국가들의 운명을 한데 묶는 것 / 특히 프랑스와 독일 / 그들이 저항할 수 없는 이해관계를 가질 그런 방식으로 / 전쟁을 다시는 벌이지 않는다는 / 그들이 너무나도 파괴적인 대가를 치르며 벌였던 것처럼 / 20세기 전반에

자유 시장은 마르크스주의가 결코 할 수 없었던 방식으로 사람들을 자유롭게 해 왔다. 게다가 하버드 대학 경제 역사학자인 A. O. Hirschman이 대표적 연구인 *The Passions and the Interests*에서 보여주었듯이, 시장은 계몽주의 사상가들인 Adam Smith, David Hume 그리고 Montesquieu에 의해 인류의 가장 큰 전통적 약점들 중 하나인 폭력에 대한 강력한 해결책으로 여겨졌다. Montesquieu가 말했던 바로, 두 국가는 만나서 두 가지 중 하나를 할 수 있는데, 즉 전쟁을 벌이거나 거래를 할 수 있다. 만약 그들이 전쟁을 벌인다면, 둘 다 장기적으로 손해를 볼 가능성이 있다. 만약 그들이 거래를 한다면, 둘 다 이득을 얻을 것이다. 물론 그것이 유럽 연합의 설립 이면에 있는 논리였다. 즉 연합의 국가들, 특히 프랑스와 독일의 운명을 한데 묶었는데, 그렇게 함으로써 그들은 20세기 전반에 너무나도 파괴적인 대가를 치르며 벌였던 전쟁을 다시는 벌이지 않는다는 저항할 수 없는 이해관계를 가졌을 것이다.

Why? 왜 정답일까?

'~ the market was seen ~ as a powerful solution to ~ violence.'에서 자유 시장은 국가 간 폭력에 대한 강력한 해결책으로 여겨졌다는 핵심 내용을 제시한다. 이어서 예시에 따르면 어떤 두 국가가 만났을 때 전쟁 또는 거래라는 선택지가 주어지는데, 전쟁은 둘 다에 실이 되는 한편 거래는 둘 다에 득이 되기에 유럽 연합 등의 기구가 출현하여 자유 시장을 촉진하고 전쟁을 억제하는 기능을 수행하게 되었다고 한다. 따라서 글의 제목으로 가장 적절한 것은 자유 시장의 순기능을 적절히 요약한 ② '자유 시장: 함께 지기보다 함께 이기기'이다.

- classic ⓐ 전형적인, 고전적인
- Enlightenment ⓝ (18세기) 계몽주의
- establishment ⓝ 설립
- devastating ⓐ 참담한
- disrupt ⓥ 교란시키다
- passion ⓝ 열정
- wage war 전쟁을 벌이다
- overwhelming ⓐ 저항할 수 없는, 압도적인
- reflection ⓝ 반영, 성찰

구문 풀이

> **9행** That, of course, was the logic behind the establishment of the European
> 주어   동사   보어
> Union: {to lock together the destinies of its nations, (especially France and
>   ( ): 보어 동격   ( ): 삽입구
> Germany), in such a way [that they would have an overwhelming interest not to
> wage war again as they had done to such devastating cost in the first half of the
>   접속사(~듯이)
> twentieth century]}.

25 e-스포츠 참여 비율　정답률 84% | 정답 ③

다음 표의 내용과 일치하지 않는 것은?

Share of Respondents Familiar with/Engaged in E-Sports in 2020

Country	Familiarity (%)	Engagement (%)
China	72	47
Denmark	67	10
Indonesia	57	40
U.S.	34	8
Spain	33	17
UAE	26	19
Iraq	26	16

The above table shows the share of respondents / familiar with or engaged in e-sports / in selected countries / in 2020.
위 표는 응답자들의 비율을 보여 준다. / e-스포츠에 친숙하거나 참여하는 / 선택된 나라들에서 / 2020년에
① Among the countries in the table, / China was the country with the highest percentage / both in e-sports familiarity and in e-sports engagement.
표 안의 나라들 중, / 중국은 가장 높은 비율을 가진 나라였다. / e-스포츠 친숙도와 e-스포츠 참여도 모두에서
② When it comes to e-sports familiarity, / Denmark showed a higher percentage than Indonesia, / but the percentage of e-sports engagement in Denmark / was lower than Indonesia's.
e-스포츠 친숙도에 있어서, / 덴마크가 인도네시아보다 더 높은 비율을 보였으나, / 덴마크의 e-스포츠 참여도 비율은 인도네시아보다 더 낮았다.
✓ The percentage of U.S. respondents familiar with e-sports / was higher than that of Spanish respondents, / and with e-sports engagement, / the percentage in the U.S. was more than twice that of Spain.
e-스포츠에 친숙한 미국 응답자들의 비율은 / 스페인 응답자들보다 더 높았고, / e-스포츠 참여도에 있어서 / 미국의 비율은 / 스페인의 두 배 이상이었다.
④ While the percentage of e-sports familiarity in Spain / was higher than that in the UAE, / the percentage of e-sports engagement in Spain / was two percentage points lower than that in the UAE.
스페인의 e-스포츠 친숙도 비율은 / 아랍 에미리트 연방보다 더 높았지만, / 스페인의 e-스포츠 참여도 비율은 / 아랍 에미리트 연방보다 2퍼센트포인트 더 낮았다.
⑤ As for e-sports familiarity, / among the selected countries, / the UAE and Iraq showed the lowest percentage, / where fewer than a third of respondents in each country / were familiar with e-sports.
e-스포츠 친숙도에 있어서, / 선택된 나라들 중, / 아랍 에미리트 연방과 이라크는 가장 낮은 비율을 보였는데, / 각 나라의 3분의 1보다 적은 응답자들이 / e-스포츠에 친숙했다.

위 표는 2020년에 선택된 나라들에서 e-스포츠에 친숙하거나 참여하는 응답자들의 비율을 보여 준다. ① 표 안의 나라들 중, 중국은 e-스포츠 친숙도와 e-스포츠 참여도 모두에서 비율이 가장 높은 나라였다. ② e-스포츠 친숙도에 있어서, 덴마크가 인도네시아보다 더 높은 비율을 보였으나, 덴마크의 e-스포츠 참여도 비율은 인도네시아보다 더 낮았다. ③ e-스포츠에 친숙한 미국 응답자들의 비율은 스페인 응답자들보다 더 높았고, e-스포츠 참여도에 있어서 미국의 비율은 스페인의 두 배 이상이었다. ④ 스페인의 e-스포츠 친숙도 비율은 아랍 에미리트 연방보다 더 높았지만, 스페인의 e-스포츠 참여도 비율은 아랍 에미리트 연방보다 2퍼센트포인트 더 낮았다. ⑤ e-스포츠 친숙도에 있어서, 선택된 나라들 중, 아랍 에미리트 연방과 이라크는 가장 낮은 비율을 보였는데, 각 나라의 3분의 1보다 적은 응답자들이 e-스포츠에 친숙했다.

Why? 왜 정답일까?

도표에 따르면 2020년 e-스포츠 참여도에 있어 미국의 비율(8%)은 스페인(17%)과 비교했을 때 절반에도 미치지 못했다. 따라서 도표와 일치하지 않는 것은 ③이다.

- familiar with ~에 친숙한
- engagement ⓝ 참여, 몰입

26 John Bowlby의 생애　정답률 91% | 정답 ④

John Bowlby에 관한 다음 글의 내용과 일치하지 않는 것은?
① 아버지는 왕의 의료진의 일원이었다.
② 어머니와 많은 시간을 보내지 못했다.
③ 기숙 학교로 보내진 것이 성장에 있어 충격적인 일이었다.

✔ Trinity 대학에 심리학을 공부하기 위해 입학했다.
⑤ 세계 보건 기구에서 정신 건강 자문 위원으로 일했다.

John Bowlby, British developmental psychologist and psychiatrist, / was born in 1907, / to an upper-middle-class family.
영국 발달 심리학자이자 정신과 의사인 John Bowlby는 / 1907년에 태어났다. / 상위 중산 계급 가정에서
「His father, / who was a member of the King's medical staff, / was often absent.」 ①의근거 일치
그의 아버지는 / 왕의 의료진의 일원이었던 / 자주 집을 비웠다.
「Bowlby was cared for primarily by a nanny / and did not spend much time with his mother, / as was customary at that time for his class.」 ②의근거 일치
Bowlby는 주로 유모에게 보살핌을 받았고 / 어머니와 많은 시간을 보내지 못했는데, / 이는 당시 그의 계급에서 관례적이었다.
「Bowlby was sent to a boarding school at the age of seven.
Bowlby는 7살에 기숙 학교로 보내졌다.
He later recalled this / as being traumatic to his development.」 ③의근거 일치
그는 나중에 이것을 회상했다. / 자신의 성장에 있어 충격적인 일이었다고
This experience, / however, / proved to have a large impact on Bowlby, / whose work focused on children's development.
이 경험은 / 그러나 / Bowlby에게 큰 영향을 미쳤던 것으로 판명되었고 / 그의 연구는 아동의 발달에 중점을 두었다.
「Following his father's suggestion, / Bowlby enrolled at Trinity College, Cambridge / to study medicine, / but by his third year, / he changed his focus to psychology.」 ④의근거 불일치
아버지의 제안을 따라, / Bowlby는 Cambridge의 Trinity 대학에 입학했으나 / 의학을 공부하기 위해 / 3년째 되던 해에 그는 관심 분야를 심리학으로 바꿨다.
「During the 1950s, / Bowlby briefly worked as a mental health consultant / for the World Health Organization.」 ⑤의근거 일치
1950년대에 / Bowlby는 잠시 정신 건강 자문 위원으로 활동했다. / 세계 보건 기구에서
His attachment theory has been described / as the dominant approach / to understanding early social development.
그의 애착 이론은 평가되어 오고 있다. / 주요한 접근법으로 / 어린 시절의 사회적 발달을 이해하는 데 있어

영국 발달 심리학자이자 정신과 의사인 John Bowlby는 1907년에 상위 중산 계급 가정에서 태어났다. 왕의 의료진의 일원이었던 그의 아버지는 자주 집을 비웠다. Bowlby는 주로 유모에게 보살핌을 받았고 어머니와 많은 시간을 보내지 못했는데, 이는 당시 그의 계급에서 관례적이었다. Bowlby는 7살에 기숙 학교로 보내졌다. 그는 나중에 이것을 자신의 성장에 있어 충격적인 일이었다고 회상했다. 그러나 이 경험은 Bowlby에게 큰 영향을 미쳤던 것으로 판명되었고 그의 연구는 아동의 발달에 중점을 두었다. 아버지의 제안을 따라, Bowlby는 Cambridge의 Trinity 대학에 의학을 공부하기 위해 입학했으나 3년째 되던 해에 관심 분야를 심리학으로 바꿨다. 1950년대에 Bowlby는 잠시 세계 보건 기구에서 정신 건강 자문 위원으로 활동했다. 그의 애착 이론은 어린 시절의 사회적 발달을 이해하는 데 있어 주요한 접근법으로 평가되어 오고 있다.

Why? 왜 정답일까?
'Following his father's suggestion, Bowlby enrolled at Trinity College, Cambridge to study medicine, but by his third year, he changed his focus to psychology.'에 따르면 Bowlby는 의학을 공부하러 Trinity 대학에 입학했지만 3년째 되던 해에 심리학으로 관심을 틀었다고 한다. 따라서 내용과 일치하지 않는 것은 ④ 'Trinity 대학에 심리학을 공부하기 위해 입학했다.'이다.

Why? 왜 오답일까?
① 'His father, who was a member of the King's medical staff, ~'의 내용과 일치한다.
② 'Bowlby ~ did not spend much time with his mother, ~'의 내용과 일치한다.
③ 'Bowlby was sent to a boarding school at the age of seven. He later recalled this as being traumatic to his development.'의 내용과 일치한다.
⑤ '~ Bowlby briefly worked as a mental health consultant for the World Health Organization.'의 내용과 일치한다.

- **psychiatrist** ⓝ 정신과 의사
- **nanny** ⓝ 유모
- **boarding school** 기숙 학교
- **enroll at** ~에 등록하다
- **dominant** ⓐ 지배적인
- **primarily** ⓐⓓ 주로
- **customary** ⓐ 관습적인
- **have an impact on** ~에 영향을 미치다
- **attachment** ⓝ (유아와 부모의) 애착

---

27 호박 굴리기 경주 소개   정답률 94% | 정답 ④

The Great Pumpkin Roll에 관한 다음 안내문의 내용과 일치하지 <u>않는</u> 것은?
① 2021년 5월의 마지막 일요일에 열린다.
② 경기에 사용하는 호박의 최소 너비에 제한이 있다.
③ 참가자는 팔을 아래로 내려 호박을 굴려야 한다.
✔ 참가자에게 호박을 굴릴 수 있는 기회를 여러 번 준다.
⑤ Lucky Spot에 호박을 넣은 모두가 상금을 균등하게 나눠 갖는다.

The Great Pumpkin Roll
성대한 호박 굴리기
Let's race pumpkins by rolling them down a hill!
호박들을 언덕 아래로 굴리면서 경주하게 합시다!
How far will they go across the road?
그것들은 길을 건너 얼마나 멀리까지 갈까요?
「Date: The last Sunday of May, 2021」 ①의근거 일치
날짜: 2021년 5월의 마지막 일요일
Location: Branford Hill in the town of Goomeri
장소: Goomeri 마을의 Branford Hill
Registration Fee: $10 for adults, $2 for teens
등록비: 성인 10달러, 십 대 2달러
Rules
규칙
The participant / who rolls their pumpkin farthest / wins.
참가자가 / 자신의 호박을 가장 멀리 굴린 / 우승합니다.
「Pumpkins must be at least 15 cm in width.」 ②의근거 일치
호박은 너비가 최소 15센티미터여야 합니다.
「Participants must roll pumpkins / only using an underarm action.」 ③의근거 일치
참가자들은 호박을 굴려야 합니다. / 팔을 아래로 내리는 동작만을 사용하여
「Each participant has only one opportunity / to roll a pumpkin.」 ④의근거 불일치

각 참가자는 기회를 단 한 번만 갖습니다. / 호박을 굴릴 수 있는
Prizes
상금
$1,000 for the person / whose pumpkin lands in the Lucky Spot
사람에게 1,000달러 / 자신의 호박이 Lucky Spot에 안착한
(「If more than one participant lands their pumpkin in the Lucky Spot, / the money will be divided equally.」) ⑤의근거 일치
(한 명 이상의 참가자가 Lucky Spot에 자신의 호박을 안착시키면, / 그 상금은 균등하게 분배될 것입니다.)
$500 for the adult champion / and $200 for the teen champion
성인 우승자에게 500달러, / 십 대 우승자에게 200달러
Please visit www.goomeripumpkinfestival.com.
www.goomeripumpkinfestival.com을 방문해 주십시오.

성대한 호박 굴리기

호박들을 언덕 아래로 굴리면서 경주하게 합시다! 그것들은 길을 건너 얼마나 멀리까지 갈까요?
☐ **날짜:** 2021년 5월의 마지막 일요일
☐ **장소:** Goomeri 마을의 Branford Hill
☐ **등록비:** 성인 10달러, 십 대 2달러
☐ **규칙**
• 호박을 가장 멀리 굴린 참가자가 우승합니다.
• 호박은 너비가 최소 15센티미터여야 합니다.
• 참가자들은 팔을 아래로 내리는 동작만을 사용하여 호박을 굴려야 합니다.
• 각 참가자는 호박을 굴릴 수 있는 기회를 단 한 번만 갖습니다.
☐ **상금**
• 호박이 Lucky Spot에 안착한 사람에게 1,000달러(한 명 이상의 참가자가 Lucky Spot에 호박을 안착시키면, 상금은 균등하게 분배될 것입니다.)
• 성인 우승자에게 500달러, 십 대 우승자에게 200달러

www.goomeripumpkinfestival.com을 방문해 주십시오.

Why? 왜 정답일까?
'Each participant has only one opportunity to roll a pumpkin.'에서 각 참가자에게 호박을 굴릴 기회는 단 한 번만 주어진다고 하므로, 안내문의 내용과 일치하지 않는 것은 ④ '참가자에게 호박을 굴릴 수 있는 기회를 여러 번 준다.'이다.

Why? 왜 오답일까?
① 'Date: The last Sunday of May, 2021'의 내용과 일치한다.
② 'Pumpkins must be at least 15 cm in width.'의 내용과 일치한다.
③ 'Participants must roll pumpkins only using an underarm action.'의 내용과 일치한다.
⑤ 'If more than one participant lands their pumpkin in the Lucky Spot, the money will be divided equally.'의 내용과 일치한다.

- **width** ⓝ 너비
- **land** ⓥ 착륙하다
- **underarm** ⓐ (투구 시) 팔을 내려서 하는
- **equally** ⓐⓓ 균등하게

---

28 달리기와 쓰레기 줍기를 동시에 할 수 있는 행사 소개   정답률 84% | 정답 ④

Plogging Event에 관한 다음 안내문의 내용과 일치하는 것은?
① 2016년에 영국에서 시작되었다.
② 매달 첫 번째 일요일 오전 9시에 열린다.
③ 운동화를 포함한 장비들이 지급된다.
✔ 참가비는 무료이다.
⑤ 참가하려면 예약이 필요하다.

Plogging Event
플로깅 행사
Have you heard of Plogging?
플로깅에 대해 들어본 적 있으신가요?
It comes from the Swedish word for pick up, "plocka upp" / and is a combination of jogging and picking up litter.
그것은 줍는다는 의미의 스웨덴어 단어인 'plocka upp'에서 왔으며 / 조깅과 쓰레기 줍기가 결합된 말입니다.
「In 2016, / it started in Sweden / and has recently come to the UK, / becoming a new movement for saving nature.」 ①의근거 불일치
2016년에, / 그것은 스웨덴에서 시작되었고 / 최근 영국으로 건너와 / 자연을 보호하기 위한 새로운 운동이 되었습니다.
When & Where
일시 및 장소
「9 a.m. on the first Monday of each month」 ②의근거 불일치
매달 첫 번째 월요일 오전 9시
Outside the ETNA Centre, East Twickenham
East Twickenham에 있는 ETNA 센터 밖
What to Prepare
준비물
「Just bring your running shoes, / and we will provide all the other equipment.」 ③의근거 불일치
운동화만 가져오세요 / 그러면 우리가 다른 모든 장비를 지급합니다.
「There is no fee to participate」, / but you are welcome to donate toward our conservation work. ④의근거 일치
참가비는 무료이나 / 우리의 자연보호 활동을 위한 기부는 기꺼이 받습니다.
「No reservations are necessary to participate.」 ⑤의근거 불일치
참가하기 위해 예약은 필요하지 않습니다.
For more information, visit www.environmenttrust.org.
더 많은 정보를 원하시면 www.environmenttrust.org를 방문하십시오.

플로깅 행사

플로깅에 대해 들어본 적 있으신가요? 줍는다는 의미의 스웨덴어 단어인 'plocka upp'에서 왔으며 조깅과 쓰레기 줍기가 결합된 말입니다. 2016년에 스웨덴에서 시작되었고 최근 영국으로 건너와 자연을 보호하기 위한 새로운 운동이 되었습니다.

일시 및 장소
• 매달 첫 번째 월요일 오전 9시
• East Twickenham에 있는 ETNA 센터 밖

준비물
• 운동화만 가져오시면 다른 모든 장비를 지급합니다.
• 참가비는 무료이나 우리의 자연보호 활동을 위한 기부는 기꺼이 받습니다.

※ 참가하기 위해 예약은 필요하지 않습니다.

더 많은 정보를 원하시면 www.environmenttrust.org를 방문하십시오.

Why? 왜 정답일까?

'There is no fee to participate, ~'에서 참가비는 없다고 하므로, 안내문의 내용과 일치하는 것은 ④ '참가비는 무료이다.'이다.

Why? 왜 오답일까?

① 'In 2016, it started in Sweden and has recently come to the UK, ~'에서 플로깅 행사가 시작된 곳은 스웨덴이고 영국에는 최근 건너온 것임을 알 수 있다.
② '9 a.m. on the first Monday of each month'에서 매달 첫 월요일에 행사가 열린다고 하였다.
③ 'Just bring your running shoes, and we will provide all the other equipment.'에서 운동화는 참가자가 준비해야 한다고 하였다.
⑤ 'No reservations are necessary to participate.'에서 참가를 위해 예약할 필요는 없다고 하였다.

• litter ⓝ 쓰레기
• conservation ⓝ (환경) 보호
• equipment ⓝ 장비

★★★ 등급을 가르는 문제!

29 기준점 편향 정답률 37% | 정답 ⑤

다음 글의 밑줄 친 부분 중, 어법상 틀린 것은? [3점]

Anchoring bias describes the cognitive error you make / when you tend to give more weight / to information arriving early in a situation / ① compared to information arriving later / — regardless of the relative quality or relevance of that initial information.
기준점 편향은 여러분이 저지르는 인지 오류를 말한다. / 여러분이 더 비중을 두는 경향이 있을 때 / 어떠한 상황에서 일찍 도착하는 정보에 / 나중에 도착하는 정보에 비해 / 그 초기 정보의 상대적인 질이나 적절성과 상관없이
Whatever data is presented to you first / when you start to look at a situation / can form an "anchor" / and it becomes significantly more challenging / ② to alter your mental course away from this anchor / than it logically should be.
여러분에게 처음으로 제시되는 어떤 정보든 / 여러분이 어떠한 상황을 보기 시작할 때 / '기준점'을 형성할 수 있고, / 상당히 더 어려워진다. / 생각의 방향을 이 기준점에서 벗어나도록 바꾸는 것은 / 논리적으로 그래야 하는 것보다도
A classic example of anchoring bias in emergency medicine / is "triage bias," / ③ where whatever the first impression you develop, or are given, about a patient / tends to influence all subsequent providers / seeing that patient.
응급 진료에서 기준점 편향의 고전적인 예는 / '부상자 분류 편향'인데, / 이는 여러분이 환자에 대해 갖거나 받는 어떤 첫인상이든 / 다음의 모든 의료 종사자들에게 영향을 미치는 경향이 있다는 것이다. / 그 환자를 보는
For example, / imagine two patients / presenting for emergency care with aching jaw pain / that occasionally ④ extends down to their chest.
예를 들어, / 두 명의 환자들을 상상해 보라. / 쑤시는 턱 통증으로 응급 치료를 받으러 온 / 이따금 가슴까지 아래로 퍼지는
Differences in how the intake providers label the chart / — "jaw pain" vs. "chest pain," for example — / ⑤ create anchors / that might result in significant differences / in how the patients are treated.
환자를 예진하는 의료 종사자들이 어떻게 차트로 분류하는가의 차이, / 예를 들어 '턱 통증' 대 '가슴 통증' / 기준점을 만든다. / 중대한 차이를 초래할 수도 있는 / 그 환자들이 어떻게 치료하는가에 있어

기준점 편향은 초기 정보의 상대적인 질이나 적절성과 상관없이, 여러분이 어떠한 상황에서 나중에 도착하는 정보에 비해 일찍 도착하는 정보에 더 비중을 두는 경향이 있을 때 저지르는 인지 오류를 말한다. 여러분이 어떠한 상황을 보기 시작할 때 처음으로 제시되는 어떤 정보든 '기준점'을 형성할 수 있고, 생각의 방향을 이 기준점에서 벗어나도록 바꾸는 것은 논리적으로 그래야 하는 것보다도 상당히 더 어려워진다. 응급 진료에서 기준점 편향의 고전적인 예는 '부상자 분류 편향'인데, 이는 여러분이 환자에 대해 어떠한 첫인상을 갖거나 받은 그것이 그 환자를 보는 다음의 모든 의료 종사자들에게 영향을 미치는 경향이 있다는 것이다. 예를 들어 이따금 가슴까지 아래로 퍼지는 쑤시는 턱 통증으로 응급 치료를 받으러 온 두 명의 환자들을 상상해 보라. 환자를 예진하는 의료 종사자들이 어떻게 차트로 분류하는가의 차이, 예를 들어 '턱 통증' 대 '가슴 통증' 중 무엇으로 분류하는지는 그 환자들이 어떻게 치료받는가에 있어 중대한 차이를 초래할 수도 있는 기준점을 만든다.

Why? 왜 정답일까?

복수 명사 주어 Differences 뒤로 동사가 필요하므로 creating을 create로 고쳐야 한다. 따라서 어법상 틀린 것은 ⑤이다.

Why? 왜 오답일까?

① '~에 비해'라는 뜻의 분사구문 관용표현인 compared to[with]가 어법상 알맞다.
② 가주어 it에 대응하는 진주어 to alter가 어법상 알맞다.
③ 뒤에 주어인 명사절 'whatever the first impression you develop, or are given, ~', 동사 'tends to ~'로 구성된 완전한 문장이 나오므로 관계부사 where가 어법상 알맞다. triage bias는 공간 선행사로 취급되었다.
④ 선행사 aching jaw pain이 불가산 명사이므로, 이를 꾸미는 주격 관계대명사절의 동사 또한 단수형으로 써야 한다. 따라서 extends가 어법상 알맞다.

• anchor ⓥ 닻을 내리다, 정박하다, 기준점을 잡다 ⓝ 기준점
• cognitive ⓐ 인지적인
• regardless of ~와 관계없이
• significantly ⓐⓓ 상당히
• present ⓥ (환자가) 진찰을 받으러 가다, (증상이) 나타나다
• occasionally ⓐⓓ 때때로
• give weight to ~을 중요시하다
• relevance ⓝ 적절성
• subsequent ⓐ 다음의, 이후의

구문 풀이

4행 {Whatever data is presented to you first when you start to look at a situation}
복합관계형용사(어떤 ~이든지)   [ ]: 주어1
can form an "anchor" and it becomes significantly more challenging to alter your
동사1   주어2(가주어)   동사2   보어   진주어
mental course away from this anchor than it logically should be.

★★ 문제 해결 꿀~팁 ★★

▶ 많이 틀린 이유는?
③은 관계부사의 쓰임을 묻고 있다. where가 나오면 흔히 which와 비교해야 하는데, 뒤에 완전한 문장이 나오면 관계부사 where를, 뒤에 불완전한 문장이 나오면 관계대명사 which를 쓴다. 이 문제에서 where 뒤의 구조를 분석하면 'whatever ~ about a patient'가 '~하는 어떤 것이든'이라는 의미의 명사절 주어이고, tends to influence가 동사구, 'all subsequent providers ~'가 목적어이다. 따라서 which가 아닌 where를 쓴 것이 알맞다.

▶ 문제 해결 방법은?
복합관계사 whatever가 주어, 목적어, 보어 역할을 하는 명사절을 이끈다는 사실을 기억해 둔다. 또한, 어법 문제에서 수식어구를 동반한 긴 주어가 나오면 동사가 어디에 있는지 체크하고, 동사의 수 일치 또한 확인하도록 한다.

30 세부 사항의 망각 정답률 52% | 정답 ④

다음 글의 밑줄 친 부분 중, 문맥상 낱말의 쓰임이 적절하지 않은 것은?

In order for us to be able / to retain valuable pieces of information, / our brain has to ① forget in a manner / that is both targeted and controlled.
우리가 ~할 수 있기 위해서 / 가치 있는 정보의 조각들을 기억할 / 우리의 뇌는 ~한 방식으로 잊어야만 한다. / 조준되면서도 통제된
Can you recall, for example, your very first day of school?
예를 들어 여러분은 학교에서의 맨 첫날을 기억할 수 있는가?
You most likely have one or two noteworthy images in your head, / such as putting your crayons and pencils into your pencil case.
여러분은 아마도 주목할 만한 심상 한두 개를 머릿속에 가지고 있을 것이다. / 크레용과 연필을 필통에 넣는 것 같은
But that's probably the extent of the ② specifics.
하지만 그것은 아마도 세부 사항의 범위일 것이다.
Those additional details / that are apparently unimportant / are actively deleted from your brain / the more you go about remembering the situation.
그러한 추가적인 세부 사항들은 / 명백히 중요하지 않은 / 여러분의 뇌에서 적극적으로 삭제된다. / 여러분이 그 상황을 계속 기억하려고 할수록
The reason for this is / that the brain does not consider it ③ valuable / to remember all of the details / as long as it is able to convey the main message / (i.e., your first day of school was great).
이것의 이유는 ~이다. / 뇌가 가치 있다고 여기지 않는 것 / 모든 세부 사항을 기억하는 것을 / 주요 메시지를 전달할 수 있는 한 / (즉, 여러분의 학교 첫날이 좋았다)
In fact, / studies have shown / that the brain actively ✔ controls regions / responsible for insignificant or minor memory content / that tends to disturb the main memory.
사실 / 연구에서 보여준다 / 뇌가 영역을 적극적으로 억제한다고 한다. / 중요하지 않거나 사소한 기억 내용을 담당하는 / 주기억을 저해하는 경향이 있는
Over time, / the minor details vanish more and more, / though this in turn serves / to ⑤ sharpen the most important messages of the past.
시간이 지나면서 / 그 사소한 세부 사항들은 점점 더 사라지지만, / 그래도 이것은 결국 도움이 된다. / 과거의 가장 중요한 메시지들을 선명하게 하는 데

우리가 가치 있는 정보의 조각들을 기억할 수 있기 위해서 우리의 뇌는 조준되면서도 통제된 방식으로 ① 잊어야만 한다. 예를 들어 여러분은 학교에서의 맨 첫날을 기억할 수 있는가? 여러분은 아마도 크레용과 연필을 필통에 넣는 것 같은 주목할 만한 심상 한두 개를 머릿속에 가지고 있을 것이다. 하지만 그것은 아마도 ② 세부 사항의 범위일 것이다. 명백히 중요하지 않은 그러한 추가적인 세부 사항들은 여러분이 그 상황을 계속 기억하려고 할수록 뇌에서 적극적으로 삭제된다. 이것의 이유는 뇌가 주요 메시지(가령, 학교 첫날이 좋았다)를 전달할 수 있는 한 모든 세부 사항을 기억하는 것을 ③ 가치 있다고 여기지 않기 때문이다. 사실 연구에 따르면 주기억을 저해하는 경향이 있는 중요하지 않거나 사소한 기억 내용을 담당하는 영역을 뇌가 적극적으로 ④ 강화한다(→ 억제한다)고 한다. 시간이 지나면서 그 사소한 세부 사항들은 점점 더 사라지지만, 그래도 이것은 결국 과거의 가장 중요한 메시지들을 ⑤ 선명하게 하는 데 도움이 된다.

Why? 왜 정답일까?

주기억에 도움이 되지 않는 세부 사항은 점점 적극적으로 잊혀 간다는 핵심 내용으로 보아, ④가 포함된 문장은 세부 사항에 대한 기억을 담당하는 뇌 영역이 '강화되기'보다는 더 '약해진다'는 의미를 나타내야 한다. 따라서 strengthens를 controls로 고쳐야 한다. 문맥상 낱말의 쓰임이 적절하지 않은 것은 ④이다.

• retain ⓥ 지니다, 보유하다
• noteworthy ⓐ 주목할 만한
• specific ⓝ 세부 사항, 구체적인 것
• convey ⓥ 전달하다
• insignificant ⓐ 중요하지 않은
• sharpen ⓥ 선명하게 하다, 연마하다
• recall ⓥ 기억하다, 회상하다
• extent ⓝ 정도, 범위
• apparently ⓐⓓ 명백히
• responsible for ~을 담당하는, 책임지는
• disturb ⓥ 저해하다, 방해하다

구문 풀이

9행 The reason for this is that the brain does not consider it valuable
가목적어 ── it valuable ── 5형식 동사 / 목적격 보어
to remember all of the details as long as it is able to convey the main message
진목적어 / 접속사(~하는 한)
(i.e., your first day of school was great).

31 맛 선호도의 발달 정답률 54% | 정답 ①

다음 빈칸에 들어갈 말로 가장 적절한 것을 고르시오.

✔ Taste preferences – 맛 선호도
③ Migration patterns – 이주 패턴
⑤ Periodic starvations – 주기적 굶주림
② Hunting strategies – 사냥 전략
④ Protective instincts – 보호 본능

The elements any particular animal needs / are relatively predictable.
어떤 특정한 동물이 필요로 하는 요소들은 / 상대적으로 예측 가능하다.
They are predictable based on the past: / what an animal's ancestors needed / is likely to be what that animal also needs.

[문제편 p.174]

그것들은 과거에 기반하여 예측 가능한데, / 즉 어떤 동물의 조상들이 필요로 했던 것은 / 그 동물이 현재에도 필요로 하는 것일 가능성이 있다.

Taste preferences, therefore, can be hardwired.
그러므로 맛 선호도는 타고나는 것일 수 있다.

Consider sodium (Na).
나트륨(Na)을 생각해 보라.

The bodies of terrestrial vertebrates, / including those of mammals, / tend to have a concentration of sodium / nearly fifty times that of the primary producers on land, / plants.
육생 척추동물의 몸은 / 포유동물의 몸을 포함하여 / 나트륨 농도를 지니고 있는 경향이 있다. / 육지의 주된 생산자의 농도의 50배인 / 즉, 식물

This is, in part, because vertebrates evolved in the sea / and so evolved cells / dependent upon the ingredients / that were common in the sea, / including sodium.
이는 부분적으로는 척추동물이 바다에서 진화했고 / 따라서 세포를 진화시켰기 때문이다. / 성분에 의존한 / 바다에서 흔했던 / 나트륨을 포함하여

To remedy the difference / between their needs for sodium and that available in plants, / herbivores can eat fifty times more plant material / than they otherwise need / (and eliminate the excess).
격차를 해결하기 위해 / 나트륨에 대한 욕구와 식물에서 얻을 수 있는 나트륨 사이의 / 초식 동물은 50배 더 많은 식물을 섭취할 수 있다. / 그들이 그렇지 않은 경우 필요로 하는 것보다 / (그리고 초과분을 배설한다)

Or they can seek out other sources of sodium.
또는 나트륨의 다른 공급원을 찾아다닐 수 있다.

The salt taste receptor rewards animals for doing the latter, / seeking out salt / in order to satisfy their great need.
짠맛 수용기는 후자의 행위에 대해 동물에게 보상을 한다. / 즉 소금을 찾아다니는 것 / 그들의 엄청난 욕구를 충족시키기 위해

어떤 특정한 동물이 필요로 하는 요소들은 상대적으로 예측 가능하다. 그것들은 과거에 기반하여 예측 가능한데, 즉 어떤 동물의 조상들이 필요로 했던 것은 그 동물이 현재에도 필요로 하는 것일 가능성이 있다. 그러므로 맛 선호도는 타고나는 것일 수 있다. 나트륨(Na)을 생각해 보라. 포유동물의 몸을 포함하여 육생 척추동물의 몸은 육지의 주된 생산자인 식물보다 나트륨 농도가 거의 50배인 경향이 있다. 이는 부분적으로는 척추동물이 바다에서 진화했고, 따라서 나트륨을 포함하여 바다에서 흔했던 성분들에 의존한 세포를 진화시켰기 때문이다. 나트륨에 대한 욕구와 식물에서 얻을 수 있는 나트륨 사이의 격차를 해결하기 위해 초식 동물은 그렇지 않은 경우 필요로 하는 것보다 50배 더 많은 식물을 섭취할 수 있다(그리고 초과분을 배설한다). 또는 나트륨의 다른 공급원을 찾아다닐 수 있다. 짠맛 수용기는 후자의 행위, 즉 엄청난 욕구를 충족시키기 위해 소금을 찾아다니는 것에 대해 동물에게 보상을 한다.

Why? 왜 정답일까?

예시에 따르면 본래 바다에서 진화한 육생 동물들은 식물에 비해 체내 나트륨 비율이 훨씬 높아서, 필요한 만큼 나트륨을 먹으려면 식물을 아주 많이 먹어야 하거나 다른 나트륨 공급원을 찾아야 하는 상황이라고 한다. 그리고 마지막 문장에서는 이들의 짠맛 수용기가 나트륨을 더 찾아나서는 행위에 '보상'을 해준다고 한다. 이는 짠맛에 대한 선호로 이어지게 될 것이므로, 빈칸에 들어갈 말로 가장 적절한 것은 ① '맛 선호도'이다.

- **predictable** ⓐ 예측 가능한
- **concentration** ⓝ 농도
- **remedy** ⓥ 해결하다, 바로잡다
- **receptor** ⓝ (신체의) 수용기, 감각기
- **periodic** ⓐ 주기적인
- **hardwired** ⓐ 타고난, 내장된
- **dependent upon** ~에 의존하는
- **eliminate** ⓥ 배설하다, 제거하다
- **reward** ⓥ 보상하다

구문 풀이

10행 To remedy the difference between their needs for sodium and that
부사적 용법(~하기 위해) 「between + A + and + B : A와 B 사이에」
available in plants, herbivores can eat fifty times more plant material than they
「배수표현 + 비교급 + than : ~보다 …배 더 한」
otherwise need (and eliminate the excess).

★★★ 등급을 가르는 문제!

32 찰나의 인식에 의해 형성되는 직감   정답률 46% | 정답 ①

다음 빈칸에 들어갈 말로 가장 적절한 것을 고르시오. [3점]
☑ result of our cognitive processing system – 우리의 인지 처리 체계의 결과
② instance of discarding negative memories – 부정적 기억을 버리는 것의 예시
③ mechanism of overcoming our internal conflicts – 우리의 내적 갈등을 극복하는 기제
④ visual representation of our emotional vulnerability – 우리의 정서적 취약성의 시각적 표현
⑤ concrete signal of miscommunication within the brain – 뇌 속의 의사소통 오류에 대한 구체적 신호

We might think / that our gut instinct is just an inner feeling / — a secret interior voice — / but in fact it is shaped / by a perception of something visible around us, / such as a facial expression or a visual inconsistency / so fleeting that often we're not even aware we've noticed it.
우리는 생각할지도 모르지만, / 우리의 직감이 단지 내면의 느낌이라고 / 즉 비밀스러운 내적 목소리 / 사실 그것은 형성된다 / 우리 주변의 가시적인 무언가에 대한 인식에 의해 / 얼굴 표정 또는 시각적 불일치와 같이 / 너무 빨리 지나가서 보통 우리가 그것을 알아차렸음을 의식하지도 못하는

Psychologists now think of this moment / as a 'visual matching game'.
오늘날 심리학자들은 이러한 순간을 생각한다. / '시각적 연결시키기 게임'으로

So / a stressed, rushed or tired person / is more likely to resort to this visual matching.
그렇다면 / 스트레스를 받거나, 서두르고 있거나 피곤한 사람이 / 이 시각적 연결시키기에 의존할 가능성이 더 높다.

When they see a situation in front of them, / they quickly match it to a sea of past experiences / stored in a mental knowledge bank / and then, based on a match, / they assign meaning to the information in front of them.
그들이 눈앞의 상황을 볼 때 / 그들은 그것을 과거 경험의 바다와 그것을 재빨리 연결해 보고, / 정신의 지식 저장고 안에 보관된 / 그다음 연결에 기초하여 / 그들은 앞에 있는 정보에 의미를 부여한다.

The brain then sends a signal to the gut, / which has many hundreds of nerve cells.
그리고 나서 뇌가 창자로 신호를 보내는데 / 이것은 수백 개의 신경세포를 가지고 있다.

So / the visceral feeling we get in the pit of our stomach / and the butterflies we feel / are a result of our cognitive processing system.
따라서 / 우리가 우리의 뱃속에서 받는 본능적인 느낌과 / 우리가 느끼는 긴장감은 / 우리의 인지 처리 체계의 결과이다.

우리는 우리의 직감이 단지 내면의 느낌, 즉 비밀스러운 내적 목소리라고 생각할지도 모르지만, 사실 그것은 얼굴 표정 또는 시각적 불일치와 같이 너무 빨리 지나가서 보통 우리가 그것을 알아차렸음을 의식하지도 못하는, 우리 주변의 가시적인 무언가에 대한 인식에 의해 형성

된다. 오늘날 심리학자들은 이러한 순간을 '시각적 연결시키기 게임'으로 생각한다. 그렇다면 스트레스를 받거나, 서두르고 있거나 피곤한 사람이 이 시각적 연결시키기에 의존할 가능성이 더 높다. 그들이 눈앞의 상황을 볼 때 정신의 지식 저장고 안에 보관된 과거 경험의 바다와 그것을 재빨리 연결해 보고, 그다음 연결에 기초하여 앞에 있는 정보에 의미를 부여한다. 그러고 나서 뇌가 창자로 신호를 보내는데 이것은 수백 개의 신경세포를 가지고 있다. 따라서 우리가 뱃속에서 받는 본능적인 느낌과 우리가 느끼는 긴장감은 우리의 인지 처리 체계의 결과이다.

Why? 왜 정답일까?

첫 문장에서 우리의 직감은 단지 내면의 느낌에 불과한 것이 아니라 아주 찰나에 이루어지는, 주변 정보에 대한 처리에 기반하여 형성된다(~ shaped by a perception ~ so fleeting that often we're not even aware we're notice it)고 한다. 이를 가리켜 '시각적 연결시키기 게임'이라고 정리한 후 예시가 이어지고, 빈칸은 예시의 결론 부분에 있으므로 첫 문장의 주제와 동일한 내용일 것이다. 따라서 빈칸에 들어갈 말로 가장 적절한 것은 ① '우리의 인지 처리 체계의 결과'이다.

- **instinct** ⓝ 본능, 직감
- **inconsistency** ⓝ 불일치, 모순
- **assign A to B** A를 B에 부여하다, 할당하다
- **vulnerability** ⓝ 취약성, 연약함
- **interior** ⓐ 내부의
- **fleeting** ⓐ 순식간의, 잠깐 동안의
- **discard** ⓥ 버리다
- **concrete** ⓐ 구체적인

구문 풀이

1행 We might think that our gut instinct is just an inner feeling — a secret
동격
interior voice — but in fact it is shaped by a perception of something visible
-thing + 형용사
around us, such as a facial expression or a visual inconsistency [(which is)
선행사   생략
so fleeting that often we're not even aware we've noticed it].
「so ~ that … : 너무 ~해서 …하다」

★★ 문제 해결 꿀~팁 ★★

▶ 많이 틀린 이유는?
글에 따르면 직감은 그저 느낌이 아니라, 우리도 모르는 새에 스쳐간 정보를 재빨리 분석한 결과이다. 이 일련의 과정은 '시각적 연결시키기 게임'과 비슷하다고 하는데, 이는 정보 분석의 과정을 비유하는 설명일 뿐 직감 자체가 시각적 표현이라는 의미는 아니다. 따라서 ④는 빈칸에 적합하지 않다.
▶ 문제 해결 방법은?
빈칸이 마지막 문장에 있으면 앞에 제시된 요지를 반복하거나 예시를 일반화하는 말을 답으로 골라야 한다. 이 문제에서도 예시 앞의 주제인 첫 문장이 가장 큰 힌트이다.

33 내륙 지역의 기후를 건조하게 만드는 산   정답률 52% | 정답 ③

다음 빈칸에 들어갈 말로 가장 적절한 것을 고르시오. [3점]
① increase annual rainfall in dry regions – 건조한 지역에서 연간 강우량을 늘리다
② prevent drastic changes in air temperature – 급격한 기온 변화를 방지하다
☑ play a huge role in stopping the flow of moisture – 수분의 흐름을 막는 데 큰 역할을 한다
④ change wind speed as air ascends and descends them – 공기가 오르내림에 따라 풍속을 바꾸다
⑤ equalize the amount of moisture of surrounding land areas – 주변 토지의 습도를 균등하게 하다

When it comes to climates / in the interior areas of continents, / mountains play a huge role / in stopping the flow of moisture.
기후에 있어서 / 대륙의 내륙 지역 / 산은 큰 역할을 한다. / 수분의 흐름을 막는 데

A great example of this / can be seen along the West Coast of the United States.
이것의 좋은 예를 / 미국의 서해안을 따라 확인할 수 있다.

Air moving from the Pacific Ocean toward the land / usually has a great deal of moisture in it.
태평양에서 육지로 이동하는 공기는 / 보통 많은 수분을 함유한다.

When this humid air moves across the land, / it encounters the Coast Range Mountains.
이 습한 공기가 육지를 가로질러 이동할 때, / 그것은 코스트산맥 산들과 마주친다.

As the air moves up and over the mountains, / it begins to cool, / which causes precipitation on the windward side of the mountains.
공기가 상승하여 산맥 위로 이동하면서 / 그것은 식기 시작하고, / 이는 산의 풍상측(風上側)에 강수를 발생시킨다.

Once the air moves down the opposite side of the mountains / (called the leeward side) / it has lost a great deal of moisture.
공기가 산의 반대편으로 내려갈 때쯤이면 / (풍하측(風下側)이라고 불리는) / 그것은 많은 수분을 잃어버린다.

The air continues to move / and then hits the even higher Sierra Nevada mountain range.
공기는 계속 움직이고 / 그러고 나서 훨씬 더 높은 시에라네바다 산맥과 부딪힌다.

This second uplift causes most of the remaining moisture / to fall out of the air, / so by the time it reaches the leeward side of the Sierras, / the air is extremely dry.
이 두 번째 상승은 남아 있는 수분 대부분이 ~하게 하며 / 공기로부터 빠져나오게 / 그래서 그것이 시에라 산맥의 풍하측에 도달할 때쯤이면 / 공기는 극도로 건조하다.

The result is / that much of the state of Nevada is a desert.
그 결과는 ~이다 / 네바다주 대부분이 사막이라는 것

대륙의 내륙 지역의 기후에 있어서 산은 수분의 흐름을 막는 데 큰 역할을 한다. 이것의 좋은 예를 미국의 서해안을 따라 확인할 수 있다. 태평양에서 육지로 이동하는 공기는 보통 많은 수분을 함유한다. 이 습한 공기가 육지를 가로질러 이동할 때, 그것은 코스트산맥 산들과 마주친다. 공기는 상승하여 산맥 위로 이동하면서 식기 시작하고, 이는 산의 풍상측(風上側)에 강수를 발생시킨다. 공기가 (풍하측(風下側)이라고 불리는) 산의 반대편으로 내려갈 때쯤이면 그것은 많은 수분을 잃어버린다. 공기는 계속 움직이고 그러고 나서 훨씬 더 높은 시에라네바다 산맥과 부딪힌다. 이 두 번째 상승은 남아 있는 수분 대부분을 공기로부터 빠져나오게 하며, 그래서 공기는 시에라 산맥의 풍하측에 도달할 때쯤이면 극도로 건조하다. 그 결과 네바다주 대부분이 사막이 된다.

Why? 왜 정답일까?

태평양에서 육지로 이동하는 공기는 본래 많은 수분을 포함하고 있지만 산 위로 상승해 온도가 떨어져 비로 내리는 과정 속에서 그 수분을 거의 잃고 건조해진다(~ most of the remaining moisture to fall out of the air, so ~ the air is extremely dry.)고 한다. 따라서 빈칸에 들어갈 말로 가장 적절한 것은 ③ '수분의 흐름을 막는 데 큰 역할을 한다'이다.

- continent ⓝ 대륙
- precipitation ⓝ 강수
- leeward ⓐ 바람이 가려지는 쪽의
- uplift ⓝ 상승
- extremely ⓐⓓ 매우, 극도로
- ascend ⓥ 올라가다
- encounter ⓥ 마주치다, 접하다
- windward ⓐ 바람이 불어오는 쪽의
- a great deal of 많은 양의
- fall out of ~에서 빠져나오다
- drastic ⓐ 급격한, 과감한
- equalize ⓥ 균등하게 하다

구문 풀이

11행 This second uplift <u>causes</u> most of the remaining moisture <u>to fall out of</u>
「cause + 목적어 + to부정사」: ~이 …하게 야기하다

the air, <u>so</u> <u>by the time</u> it reaches the leeward side of the Sierras, the air is
접속사(~할 무렵)

extremely dry.

★★★ 등급을 가르는 문제!

34 시장 사고방식에 의한 관습의 변질   정답률 20% | 정답 ⑤

다음 빈칸에 들어갈 말로 가장 적절한 것을 고르시오. [3점]

① people can put aside their interests for the common good
사람들이 공익을 위해 그들의 이익을 제쳐둘 수 있는지
② changing an existing agreement can cause a sense of guilt
기존의 합의를 바꾸는 것은 죄책감을 유발할 수 있는지
③ imposing a fine can compensate for broken social contracts
벌금 부과가 사회 계약 위반을 보상할 수 있는지
④ social bonds can be insufficient to change people's behavior
사회적 유대감이 사람들의 행동을 바꾸기에 불충분할 수 있는지
✓⑤ a market mindset can transform and undermine an institution
시장 사고방식이 관습을 변질시키고 훼손시킬 수 있는지

One vivid example / of how a market mindset can transform and undermine an institution / is given by Dan Ariely in his book *Predictably Irrational*.
한 생생한 예가 / 어떻게 시장 사고방식이 관습을 변질시키고 훼손시킬 수 있는지에 대한 / Dan Ariely의 저서 *Predictably Irrational*에서 주어진다.

He tells the story of a day care center in Israel / that decided to fine parents / who arrived late to pick up their children, / in the hope that this would discourage them from doing so.
그는 이스라엘의 한 어린이집에 관한 이야기를 들려준다. / 부모들에게 벌금을 부과하기로 결정했던 / 아이를 데리러 늦게 도착한 / 이것이 그들이 그렇게 행동하는 것을 막을 수 있기를 바라면서

In fact, the exact opposite happened.
실제로는 정반대의 일이 일어났다.

Before the imposition of fines, / parents felt guilty about arriving late, / and guilt was effective / in ensuring that only a few did so.
벌금 부과 전에 / 부모들은 늦게 도착한 것에 대해 죄책감을 느꼈고 / 죄책감은 효과적이었다 / 몇 안 되는 사람들만이 그렇게 하도록 하는 데

Once a fine was introduced, / it seems / that in the minds of the parents / the entire scenario was changed / from a social contract to a market one.
일단 벌금이 도입되자 / ~처럼 보인다 / 부모들의 마음속에서 / 전체 시나리오가 바뀌었던 / 사회 계약에서 시장 계약으로

Essentially, / they were paying for the center / to look after their children after hours.
근본적으로 / 그들은 어린이집에 비용을 지불하고 있었다 / 방과 후에 아이를 봐주도록

Some parents thought the price, / and the rate of late arrivals increased.
일부 부모들은 그것이 값어치를 한다고 생각했고 / 늦은 도착의 비율이 증가했다.

Significantly, / once the center abandoned the fines / and went back to the previous arrangement, / late arrivals remained at the high level / they had reached during the period of the fines.
중요하게는, / 어린이집이 벌금을 포기하고 / 이전 방식으로 돌아갔을 때, / 늦은 도착은 그 높은 수준으로 유지되었다. / 그들이 벌금 기간 중 달했던

어떻게 시장 사고방식이 관습을 변질시키고 훼손시킬 수 있는지에 대한 한 생생한 예가 Dan Ariely의 저서 *Predictably Irrational*에서 주어진다. 그는 아이를 데리러 늦게 도착한 부모들에게 벌금을 부과하기로 결정했던 이스라엘의 한 어린이집에 관한 이야기를 들려주는데, 이는 벌금이 그들의 그런 행동을 막을 수 있기를 바라서였다. 실제로는 정반대의 일이 일어났다. 벌금 부과 전에 부모들은 늦게 도착한 것에 대해 죄책감을 느꼈고, 죄책감은 늦는 사람이 얼마 없도록 하는 데 효과적이었다. 일단 벌금이 도입되자 부모들의 마음속에서 전체 시나리오가 사회 계약에서 시장 계약으로 바뀌었던 것으로 보인다. 근본적으로 그들은 방과 후에 아이를 돌봐주는 데 대해 어린이집에 비용을 지불하고 있었다. 일부 부모들은 그것이 값어치를 한다고 생각했고 늦은 도착의 비율이 증가했다. 중요하게는, 어린이집이 벌금을 포기하고 이전 방식으로 돌아갔을 때, 늦은 도착은 벌금 기간 중 달했던 그 높은 수준으로 유지되었다.

Why? 왜 정답일까?

예시에 따르면 어린이집이 아이를 늦게 데리러 온 부모에게 벌금을 물리기 시작하자 부모들이 점차 어린이집에 지불하는 '비용'을 의식하게 되면서 오히려 더 많이 늦게 왔다고 한다. 이어서 마지막 문장에서는 이후 결국 어린이집이 벌금을 없앴음에도 이 늦는 비율이 줄어들지 않았다고 한다. 즉 이 예시는 사회 계약으로 인식되던 관계가 '시장 계약'으로 변화했을 때 기존의 관습이 어떻게 무너지는지를 보여준다고 정리할 수 있다. 따라서 빈칸에 들어갈 말로 가장 적절한 것은 ⑤ '시장 사고방식이 관습을 변질시키고 훼손시킬 수 있는지'이다.

- vivid ⓐ 생생한
- discourage A from B A를 B하지 못하게 하다
- guilty ⓐ 죄책감이 드는
- abandon ⓥ (하다가) 포기하다, 그만두다
- compensate for ~을 보상하다
- undermine ⓥ 훼손하다, (기반을) 약화시키다
- irrational ⓐ 불합리한
- imposition ⓝ 부과
- contract ⓝ 계약
- put aside ~을 무시하다, 제쳐두다, 따로 떼어놓다
- insufficient ⓐ 불충분한
- institution ⓝ 제도, 관습

구문 풀이

11행 Some parents thought <u>it worth the price</u>, and the rate of late arrivals
5형식 동사   목적어 목적격 보어(worth + 명사: ~할 가치가 있는)

increased.

★★ 문제 해결 꿀~팁 ★★

▶ 많이 틀린 이유는?
글에 따르면 부모들과 어린이집은 본래 '사회 계약' 관계에 있었지만, 어린이집이 지각하는 부모들에게 벌금을 물리기 시작하며 '돈'이 매개가 되는 '시장 계약'으로 관계가 변화한다고 한다. 오답 중 ③은

벌금이 사회 계약을 복구시키는 수단이 될 수 있다는 의미이므로 답으로 적절하지 않다. 또한, 이 글이 사회적 유대 관계가 행동을 바꾼다는 내용도 아니므로 ④도 답으로 부적절하다.

▶ 문제 해결 방법은?
⑤의 an institution은 본문의 a social contract과 문맥적 의미가 같다. 즉 부모들에게 벌금을 물리기 이전에 '부모가 어린이집에 제때 와서 아이를 데려가기로 하는' 암묵적 합의가 있었던 상황을 요약하는 말이다.

---

35 인간의 사고력에 대한 믿음   정답률 49% | 정답 ④

다음 글에서 전체 흐름과 관계 없는 문장은?

There is a pervasive idea in Western culture / that humans are essentially rational, / skillfully sorting fact from fiction, / and, ultimately, arriving at timeless truths about the world.
서구권 문화에는 널리 스며 있는 관념이 있다. / 인간이 본질적으로 이성적이며, / 사실과 허구를 능숙하게 가려내고, / 최종적으로 세상에 대한 영원한 진리에 도달한다는

① This line of thinking holds / that humans follow the rules of logic, / calculate probabilities accurately, / and make decisions about the world / that are perfectly informed by all available information.
이러한 사고방식은 주장한다 / 인간은 논리의 규칙을 따르고, / 가능성을 정확히 계산하며, / 판단을 세상에 대해 내린다고 / 모든 이용 가능한 정보에 의해 완벽히 정보를 갖춘

② Conversely, / failures to make effective and well-informed decisions / are often attributed to failures of human reasoning / — resulting, say, from psychological disorders or cognitive biases.
반대로 / 효과적이고 정보를 잘 갖춘 판단을 내리지 못하는 것은 / 흔히 인간 사고의 실패 탓으로 여겨지는데, / 예를 들면 심리적 장애나 인지적 편견에서 비롯된다고 여겨진다.

③ In this picture, / whether we succeed or fail / turns out to be a matter / of whether individual humans are rational and intelligent.
이러한 상황에서 / 우리가 성공할 것인가 실패할 것인가는 / 문제인 것으로 판명된다. / 개개인이 이성적이고 지적인지 아닌지의

✓④ Our ability to make a reasonable decision / has more to do with our social interactions / than our individual psychology.
이성적인 판단을 내리는 우리의 능력은 / 우리의 사회적 상호작용과 더욱 관련이 있다. / 우리의 개인적 심리보다

⑤ And so, / if we want to achieve better outcomes / — truer beliefs, better decisions — / we need to focus on improving individual human reasoning.
그러므로, / 우리가 더 나은 결과를 성취하기를 원한다면, / 더 참된 신념과 더 나은 판단과 같은 / 우리는 개개인의 사고를 향상하는 것에 집중할 필요가 있다.

서구권 문화에는 인간이 본질적으로 이성적이며, 사실과 허구를 능숙하게 가려내고, 최종적으로 세상에 대한 영원한 진리에 도달한다는 널리 스며 있는 관념이 있다. ① 이러한 사고방식은 인간은 논리의 규칙을 따르고, 가능성을 정확히 계산하며, 모든 이용 가능한 정보에 의해 완벽히 정보를 갖춘 판단을 세상에 대해 내린다고 주장한다. ② 반대로 효과적이고 정보를 잘 갖춘 판단을 내리지 못하는 것은 흔히 인간 사고의 실패 탓으로 여겨지는데, 예를 들어 심리적 장애나 인지적 편견에서 비롯된다고 여겨진다. ③ 이러한 상황에서 우리가 성공할 것인가 실패할 것인가는 개개인이 이성적이고 지적인지 아닌지의 문제인 것으로 판명된다. ④ 이성적인 판단을 내리는 우리의 능력은 우리의 개인적 심리보다 우리의 사회적 상호작용과 더욱 관련이 있다. ⑤ 그러므로 우리가 더 참된 신념과 더 나은 판단과 같은 더 나은 결과를 성취하기를 원한다면, 우리는 개개인의 사고를 향상하는 것에 집중할 필요가 있다.

Why? 왜 정답일까?

서구권에서 인간은 이성적 존재로 여겨지기에 판단의 실패는 개인의 능력 부족 탓으로 여겨지며, 문제 해결의 실마리 또한 개인의 능력 향상에 있다고 간주된다는 내용의 글이다. 하지만 ④는 인간의 이성적 사고 능력이 개인의 심리보다는 사회적 상호작용과 더 관련이 있다는 내용이므로 흐름에서 벗어난다. 따라서 전체 흐름과 관계 없는 문장은 ④이다.

- sort A from B A와 B를 가려내다
- timeless ⓐ 영원한
- probability ⓝ 확률, 가능성
- be attributed to ~의 탓이다
- outcome ⓝ 결과
- ultimately ⓐⓓ 궁극적으로
- calculate ⓥ 계산하다
- accurately ⓐⓓ 정확하게
- have to do with ~와 관련이 있다

구문 풀이

1행 There is a pervasive idea in Western culture {that humans are essentially
동사   주어

rational, skillfully sorting fact from fiction, and, ultimately, arriving at timeless

truths about the world}.   [ ]: 주어 동격

---

36 식품 생산의 책임에 관한 개념의 차이   정답률 64% | 정답 ②

주어진 글 다음에 이어질 글의 순서로 가장 적절한 것을 고르시오.

① (A) − (C) − (B)   ✓② (B) − (A) − (C)
③ (B) − (C) − (A)   ④ (C) − (A) − (B)
⑤ (C) − (B) − (A)

Regarding food production, / under the British government, / there was a different conception of responsibility / from that of French government.
식품 생산과 관련하여 / 영국 정부에서는 / 다른 책임 개념이 있었다. / 프랑스 정부의 그것과는

In France, / the responsibility for producing good food / lay with the producers.
프랑스에서 / 좋은 식품을 생산하는 것에 대한 책임은 / 생산자들에게 있었다.

(B) The state would police their activities / and, if they should fail, / would punish them / for neglecting the interests of its citizens.
정부가 그들의 활동을 감시하곤 했고, / 만약 그들이 실패했다면, / 그들을 처벌했을 것이다. / 시민들의 이익을 등한시한 이유로

By contrast, / the British government / — except in extreme cases — / placed most of the responsibility with the individual consumers.
대조적으로 / 영국 정부는 / 극단적인 경우를 제외하고 / 그 책임의 대부분을 개인 소비자들에게 두었다.

(A) It would be unfair / to interfere with the shopkeeper's right / to make money.
부당했을 것이다. / 가게 주인의 권리를 침해하는 것은 / 돈을 벌기 위한

In the 1840s, / a patent was granted for a machine / designed for making fake coffee beans out of chicory, / using the same technology / that went into manufacturing bullets.

1840년대에 / 기계에 특허권이 승인되었다. / 치커리로부터 가짜 커피콩을 만들어 내기 위해 고안된 / 똑같은 기술을 이용해서 / 총알을 제조하는 데 들어갔던

(C) This machine was clearly designed / for the purposes of swindling, / and yet the government allowed it.
이 기계는 분명히 고안되었지만 / 사기의 목적으로 / 그런데도 정부는 그것을 허가했다.

A machine for forging money / would never have been licensed, / so why this?
돈을 위조하기 위한 기계였다면 / 결코 허가를 받을 수 없었을 텐데 / 그렇다면 이것은 왜 허가됐을까?

As one consumer complained, / the British system of government / was weighted against the consumer / in favour of the swindler.
한 소비자가 불평했던 것처럼 / 영국의 정부 체제는 / 소비자에게는 불리하도록 치우쳐 있었다. / 사기꾼의 편을 들고

식품 생산과 관련하여 영국 정부하에서는 프랑스 정부의 책임의 개념과는 다른 개념이 있었다. 프랑스에서 좋은 식품을 생산하는 것에 대한 책임은 생산자들에게 있었다.

(B) 정부가 그들의 활동들을 감시하곤 했고, 만약 그들이 실패했다면, 시민들의 이익을 등한시한 이유로 그들을 처벌했을 것이다. 대조적으로 영국 정부는 극단적인 경우들을 제외하고 그 책임의 대부분을 개인 소비자들에게 두었다.

(A) 돈을 벌기 위한 가게 주인의 권리를 침해하는 것은 부당했을 것이다. 1840년대에, 총알을 제조하는 데 들어갔던 똑같은 기술을 이용해서 치커리로부터 가짜 커피콩을 만들어 내기 위해 고안된 기계에 특허권이 승인되었다.

(C) 이 기계는 분명히 사기의 목적으로 고안되었지만 정부는 그것을 허가했다. 돈을 위조하기 위한 기계였다면 결코 허가를 받을 수 없었을 텐데, 그렇다면 이것은 왜 허가됐을까? 한 소비자가 불평했던 것처럼 영국의 정부 체제는 사기꾼의 편을 들고 소비자에게는 불리하도록 치우쳐 있었다.

Why? 왜 정답일까?

프랑스에서 좋은 식품 생산에 대한 책임은 생산자에 있었다는 내용의 주어진 글 뒤로, **(B)**에서는 정부가 이들을 감독하는 설명을 덧붙인 뒤 영국 정부를 대조적 사례로 언급한다. 이어서 **(A)**는 총알 제조 기술을 이용해 치커리로 가짜 커피콩을 만드는 기계를 영국 정부가 승인했다는 예를 들고, **(C)**는 이 허가 행위를 통해 영국 정부가 생산자보다는 소비자에 책임론을 돌리는 입장이었음을 알 수 있다고 한다. 따라서 글의 순서로 가장 적절한 것은 ② '**(B) – (A) – (C)**'이다.

- **unfair** ⓐ 부당한
- **grant** ⓥ (공식적으로) 주다
- **neglect** ⓥ 등한시하다
- **patent** ⓝ 특허
- **manufacture** ⓥ 생산하다, 제조하다
- **weigh against** ~에 불리하다

구문 풀이

15행 A machine for forging money would never have been licensed, so why this?
「would have p.p. : ~했을 것이다(과거에 대한 추측)」

---

37 생태계의 회복력　　　　정답률 51% | 정답 ⑤

주어진 글 다음에 이어질 글의 순서로 가장 적절한 것을 고르시오. [3점]

① (A) – (C) – (B)　　② (B) – (A) – (C)
③ (B) – (C) – (A)　　④ (C) – (A) – (B)
☑ (C) – (B) – (A)

Because we are told that the planet is doomed, / we do not register the growing number of scientific studies / demonstrating the resilience of other species.
우리는 지구가 운이 다한 것이라고 듣기 때문에 / 우리는 증가하는 수의 과학적 연구를 기억하지 않는 / 다른 종의 회복력을 증명하는

For instance, / climate-driven disturbances / are affecting the world's coastal marine ecosystems / more frequently and with greater intensity.
예를 들어 / 기후로 인한 교란이 / 세계 해안의 해양 생태계에 영향을 미치고 있다. / 더 자주, 더 큰 강도로

(C) This is a global problem / that demands urgent action.
이것은 세계적인 문제이다. / 긴급한 조치를 요구하는

Yet, as detailed in a 2017 paper in *BioScience*, / there are also instances / where marine ecosystems show remarkable resilience / to acute climatic events.
하지만 *BioScience*의 2017년 논문에서 자세히 설명된 것처럼, / 경우들이 또한 있다. / 해양 생태계가 놀라운 회복력을 보여주는 / 극심한 기후의 사건들에

(B) In a region in Western Australia, for instance, / up to 90 percent of live coral was lost / when ocean water temperatures rose, / causing what scientists call coral bleaching.
예를 들어 Western Australia의 한 지역에서 / 살아 있는 산호의 90퍼센트까지 소실되어 / 바닷물 온도가 상승했을 때, / 과학자들이 산호 백화라 부르는 것을 야기했다.

Yet in some sections of the reef surface, / 44 percent of the corals recovered within twelve years.
하지만 암초 표면의 몇몇 부분에서 / 산호의 44퍼센트가 12년 이내에 회복했다.

(A) Similarly, / kelp forests hammered by intense El Niño water-temperature / increases recovered within five years.
마찬가지로 / 극심한 엘니뇨 수온 상승에 의해 강타당한 켈프 숲이 / 5년 이내에 회복했다.

By studying these "bright spots," / situations where ecosystems persist / even in the face of major climatic impacts, / we can learn what management strategies help / to minimize destructive forces and nurture resilience.
이러한 '밝은 지점들'을 연구함으로써, / 즉 생태계가 지속되는 상황들을 / 중대한 기후의 영향에 직면한 순간에도 / 우리는 어떠한 관리 전략들이 도움이 되는지를 배울 수 있다. / 파괴적인 힘을 최소화하고 회복력을 키우는 데

우리는 지구가 운이 다한 것이라고 듣기 때문에 다른 종의 회복력을 증명하는 과학적 연구의 증가를 기억하지 않는다. 예를 들어 기후로 인한 교란이 세계 해안의 해양 생태계에 더 자주, 더 큰 강도로 영향을 미치고 있다.

(C) 이것은 긴급한 조치를 요구하는 세계적인 문제이다. 하지만 *BioScience*의 2017년 논문에서 자세히 설명된 것처럼, 해양 생태계가 극심한 기후의 사건들에 놀라운 회복력을 보여주는 경우들이 또한 있다.

(B) 예를 들어 Western Australia의 한 지역에서 바닷물 온도가 상승했을 때, 살아 있는 산호의 90퍼센트까지 소실되어 과학자들이 산호 백화라 부르는 것을 야기했다. 하지만 암초 표면의 몇몇 부분에서 산호의 44퍼센트가 12년 이내에 회복했다.

(A) 마찬가지로 극심한 엘니뇨 수온 상승에 의해 강타당한 켈프 숲이 5년 이내에 회복했다.

이러한 '밝은 지점들', 즉 중대한 기후의 영향에 직면한 순간에도 생태계가 지속되는 상황들을 연구함으로써, 우리는 어떠한 관리 전략들이 파괴적인 힘을 최소화하고 회복력을 키우는 데 도움이 되는지를 배울 수 있다.

Why? 왜 정답일까?

해양 생태계가 기후 교란에 큰 영향을 받고 있음을 언급하는 주어진 글 뒤로 **(C)**는 '이것'이 세계적 문제임을 언급한 후, 희망적이게도 해양 생태계의 회복력에 관한 사례들이 존재함을 상기시킨다. **for instance**로 연결되는 **(B)**는 산호의 회복 사례를 언급하고, **Similarly**로 시작되는 **(A)**는 켈프 숲 회복 사례를 추가로 열거한다. 따라서 글의 순서로 가장 적절한 것은 ⑤ '**(C) – (B) – (A)**'이다.

- **register** ⓥ (흔히 부정문에서) 알아채다, 기억하다
- **disturbance** ⓝ 교란
- **persist** ⓥ 지속되다
- **destructive** ⓐ 파괴적인
- **bleaching** ⓝ 표백
- **remarkable** ⓐ 놀라운, 주목할 만한
- **demonstrate** ⓥ 입증하다
- **intensity** ⓝ 강도
- **in the face of** ~에 직면하여, ~에도 불구하고
- **nurture** ⓥ 양성하다, 키우다
- **reef** ⓝ 암초

구문 풀이

1행 Because we are told {that the planet is doomed}, we do not register the
동사(4형식 수동태)　　　{ } : 목적어
growing number of scientific studies demonstrating the resilience of other species.
↖ 현재분사

★★★ 등급을 가르는 문제!

38 소리의 밝기　　　　정답률 41% | 정답 ⑤

글의 흐름으로 보아, 주어진 문장이 들어가기에 가장 적절한 곳을 고르시오. [3점]

Brightness of sounds means much energy in higher frequencies, / which can be calculated from the sounds easily.
소리의 밝기는 더 높은 주파수에서의 많은 에너지를 의미하며, / 이는 소리로부터 쉽게 계산될 수 있다.

A violin has many more overtones compared to a flute / and sounds brighter.
바이올린은 플루트에 비해 더 많은 상음(上音)을 가지고 있고 / 더 밝게 들린다.

① An oboe is brighter than a classical guitar, / and a crash cymbal brighter than a double bass.
오보에가 클래식 기타보다 더 밝고, / 크래시 심벌이 더블 베이스보다 더 밝다.

② This is obvious, / and indeed people like brightness.
이것은 명백하고 / 실제로 사람들은 밝음을 좋아한다.

③ One reason is / that it makes sound subjectively louder, / which is part of the loudness war / in modern electronic music, / and in the classical music of the 19th century.
한 가지 이유는 ~이며, / 그것이 소리를 주관적으로 더 크게 들리도록 만든다는 것 / 이는 소리의 세기 전쟁의 일환이다. / 현대 전자 음악과 / 19세기 클래식 음악에서

④ All sound engineers know / that if they play back a track to a musician / that just has recorded this track / and add some higher frequencies, / the musician will immediately like the track much better.
모든 음향 기사들은 안다. / 만약 그들이 음악가에게 곡을 틀어 주고 / 방금 이 곡을 녹음한 / 약간의 더 높은 주파수를 더하면, / 그 음악가는 곧바로 그 곡을 훨씬 더 좋아하게 되리라는 것

☑ But this is a short-lived effect, / and in the long run, / people find such sounds too bright.
하지만 이것은 일시적인 효과이고 / 장기적으로 / 사람들은 그러한 소리가 너무 밝다는 것을 알게 된다.

So it is wise / not to play back such a track with too much brightness, / as it normally takes quite some time / to convince the musician / that less brightness serves his music better in the end.
따라서 현명한데 / 그러한 곡을 너무 밝게 틀어 주지 않는 것이 / 왜냐하면 보통 시간이 꽤 걸리기 때문에 / 그 음악가에게 납득시키는 데 / 더 적은 밝기가 결국 음악에 더 도움이 된다는 것

소리의 밝기는 더 높은 주파수에서의 많은 에너지를 의미하며, 이는 소리로부터 쉽게 계산될 수 있다. 바이올린은 플루트에 비해 더 많은 상음(上音)을 가지고 있고 더 밝게 들린다. ① 오보에가 클래식 기타보다 더 밝고, 크래시 심벌이 더블 베이스보다 더 밝다. ② 이것은 명백하고 실제로 사람들은 밝음을 좋아한다. ③ 한 가지 이유는 그것이 소리를 주관적으로 더 크게 들리도록 만든다는 것이며, 이는 현대 전자 음악과 19세기 클래식 음악에서 소리의 세기 전쟁의 일환이다. ④ 모든 음향 기사들은 만약 방금 이 곡을 녹음한 음악가에게 곡을 틀어 주고 약간의 더 높은 주파수를 더하면, 그 음악가는 곧바로 그 곡을 훨씬 더 좋아하게 되리라는 것을 안다. ⑤ 하지만 이것은 일시적인 효과이고, 장기적으로 사람들은 그러한 소리가 너무 밝다는 것을 알게 된다. 따라서 그러한 곡을 너무 밝게 틀어 주지 않는 것이 현명한데 왜냐하면, 그 음악가에게 더 적은 밝기가 결국 음악에 더 도움이 된다는 것을 납득시키는 데 보통 시간이 꽤 걸리기 때문이다.

Why? 왜 정답일까?

소리는 밝을수록 더 크게 느껴진다는 설명 뒤로, ⑤ 앞의 문장은 만일 음악을 녹음해서 조금 더 높은 주파수를 첨가해 틀어주면 음악가가 그 소리를 더 좋아하게 될 것이라는 예를 든다. 하지만 ⑤ 뒤의 문장은 곡을 너무 밝게 틀어주지 않는 것이 현명하다는 내용이므로, 밝은 소리가 선호될 것이라는 ⑤ 앞의 내용과 상충한다. 따라서 But으로 시작하며 밝아진 소리에 대한 선호가 일시적임을 지적하는 주어진 문장이 들어가기에 가장 적절한 곳은 ⑤이다.

- **short-lived** ⓐ 단기적인
- **subjectively** ⓐⓓ 주관적으로
- **convince** ⓥ 납득시키다
- **frequency** ⓝ 주파수
- **normally** ⓐⓓ 보통
- **serve** ⓥ 도움이 되다

구문 풀이

13행 So it is wise not to play back such a track with too much brightness, as
가주어　　　　　　　　　　　　　　　　진주어
it normally takes quite some time to convince the musician that less brightness
「it takes + 시간 + to부정사 : ~이 …하는 데 ~의 시간이 걸리다」
serves his music better in the end.

★★ 문제 해결 꿀~팁 ★★

▶ 많이 틀린 이유는?
③에 주어진 문장을 넣으면 '밝은 소리는 주관적으로 크게 들린다 → 그런데 이 효과는 일시적이다 →

그 이유는 소리가 크게 들리기 때문이다'라는 흐름이 얼핏 자연스러워 보인다. 하지만 ③을 답으로 고르면, ⑤ 앞뒤의 흐름 단절이 해소되지 않은 상태로 남기 때문에 전체적인 논리 전개가 부자연스럽다.

▶ 문제 해결 방법은?

⑤ 뒤의 문장에 So가 있고, So 뒤로 곡을 너무 밝게 틀어주면 안 된다는 결론이 나오므로, ⑤ 앞에는 '밝게 틀어주는 것의 한계'를 언급하는 말이 나와야 한다. 본문에서 이 한계는 ⑤ 앞 문장이 아닌, 주어진 문장에서 언급된다(find such sounds too bright).

---

39   어둠 속에서의 식물 생장   정답률 57% | 정답 ③

글의 흐름으로 보아, 주어진 문장이 들어가기에 가장 적절한 곳을 고르시오. [3점]

Scientists who have observed plants growing in the dark / have found / that they are vastly different in appearance, form, and function / from those grown in the light.
어둠 속에서 식물이 자라는 것을 관찰해 온 과학자들은 / 발견해 왔다. / 그것들이 생김새, 형태, 기능 면에서 상당히 다르다는 것을 / 빛 속에서 길러진 것들과

① This is true / even when the plants in the different light conditions / are genetically identical / and are grown under identical conditions of temperature, water, and nutrient level.
이것은 적용된다. / 다른 빛 조건에 있는 식물들이 ~할 때에도 / 유전적으로 같고, / 동일한 온도, 물, 영양소 수준의 조건에서 길러질

② Seedlings grown in the dark / limit the amount of energy going to organs / that do not function at full capacity in the dark, / like cotyledons and roots, / and instead initiate elongation of the seedling stem / to propel the plant out of darkness.
어둠 속에서 길러진 묘목은 / 기관으로 가는 에너지의 양을 제한하고, / 어둠 속에서 완전히 기능하지 않는 / 떡잎이나 뿌리처럼, / 대신 묘목 줄기의 연장을 시작한다. / 그 식물을 어둠 바깥으로 나아가게 하기 위하여

☑ In full light, / seedlings reduce the amount of energy / they allocate to stem elongation.
충분한 빛 속에서 / 묘목은 에너지의 양을 줄인다. / 그것들이 줄기 연장에 배분하는

The energy is directed / to expanding their leaves / and developing extensive root systems.
그 에너지는 향한다. / 그것들의 잎을 확장하고 / 광범위한 근계(根系)를 발달시키는 데로

④ This is a good example of phenotypic plasticity.
이것이 표현형 적응성의 좋은 예이다.

⑤ The seedling adapts to distinct environmental conditions / by modifying its form / and the underlying metabolic and biochemical processes.
묘목은 별개의 환경 조건에 적응한다. / 그것의 형태를 바꿈으로써 / 그리고 근원적인 신진대사 및 생화학적 과정을

어둠 속에서 식물이 자라는 것을 관찰해 온 과학자들은 그것들이 빛 속에서 길러진 것들과 생김새, 형태, 기능 면에서 상당히 다르다는 것을 발견해 왔다. ① 이것은 다른 빛 조건에 있는 식물들이 유전적으로 같고, 동일한 온도, 물, 영양소 수준의 조건에서 길러질 때에도 적용된다. ② 어둠 속에서 길러진 묘목은 떡잎이나 뿌리처럼, 어둠 속에서 완전히 기능하지 않는 기관으로 가는 에너지의 양을 제한하고, 대신 그 식물을 어둠 바깥으로 나아가게 하기 위하여 묘목 줄기를 연장하기 시작한다. ③ 충분한 빛 속에서 묘목은 줄기 연장에 배분하는 에너지의 양을 줄인다. 그 에너지는 잎을 확장하고 광범위한 근계(根系)를 발달시키는 데로 향한다. ④ 이것이 표현형 적응성의 좋은 예이다. ⑤ 묘목은 형태와 근원적인 신진대사 및 생화학적 과정을 바꿈으로써 별개의 환경 조건에 적응한다.

Why? 왜 정답일까?

어둠 속에서 길러진 묘목이 떡잎이나 뿌리로 가는 에너지 양을 줄이고 줄기를 연장시킨다는 ③ 앞의 내용에 이어, 주어진 문장은 빛이 충분해지면 줄기 연장에 할당되는 에너지 양이 다시 줄어듦을 설명한다. 이어서 ③ 뒤의 문장은 대신에 에너지가 묘목의 잎을 확장하고 뿌리를 확장시키는 쪽으로 이용됨을 설명한다. 따라서 주어진 문장이 들어가기에 가장 적절한 곳은 ③이다.

- seedling ⓝ 묘목
- stem ⓝ 줄기
- genetically ⓐⓓ 유전적으로
- nutrient ⓝ 영양소
- propel ⓥ 나아가게 하다, 추진시키다
- distinct ⓐ 별개의, 다른
- allocate ⓥ 할당하다
- vastly ⓐⓓ 상당히, 대단히, 엄청나게
- identical ⓐ 동일한
- initiate ⓥ 시작하다
- extensive ⓐ 광범위한
- underlying ⓐ 기저의, 근본적인

구문 풀이

8행 Seedlings grown in the dark limit the amount of energy going to organs
    주어   과거분사   동사1   선행사
[that do not function at full capacity in the dark, like cotyledons and roots], and
  주격 관·대
instead initiate elongation of the seedling stem to propel the plant out of darkness.
       동사2   부사적 용법(~하기 위해서)

---

40   기대에 좌우되는 예측   정답률 63% | 정답 ①

다음 글의 내용을 한 문장으로 요약하고자 한다. 빈칸 (A), (B)에 들어갈 말로 가장 적절한 것은?

	(A)	(B)
☑	wish 희망	affected 영향을 미쳤다
②	wish 희망	contradicted 모순되었다
③	disregard 무시	restricted 제한했다
④	disregard 무시	changed 바꾸었다
⑤	assurance 확신	realized 실현시켰다

In a study, / Guy Mayraz, a behavioral economist, / showed his experimental subjects / graphs of a price rising and falling over time.
한 연구에서 / 행동 경제학자인 Guy Mayraz는 / 실험 대상자들에게 보여주었다. / 시간이 지나면서 오르내린 가격에 대한 도표들을

The graphs were actually of past changes in the stock market, / but Mayraz told people / that the graphs showed recent changes in the price of wheat.
그 도표들은 사실 주식 시장에서의 과거 변동에 관한 것이었으나 / Mayraz는 사람들에게 말했다. / 그 도표들이 밀 가격의 최근 변동을 보여준다고

He asked each person to predict / where the price would move next / — and offered them a reward / if their forecasts came true.
그는 각각의 사람에게 예측하도록 요청했으며, / 가격이 다음에 어디로 움직일지를 / 그들에게 보상을 제공했다. / 그들의 예측이 실현되면

But Mayraz had also divided his participants into two categories, / "farmers" and "bakers".
그러나 Mayraz는 또한 자신의 참가자들을 두 개의 범주로 나누었다. / '농부'와 '제빵사'라는

Farmers would be paid extra / if wheat prices were high.
농부들은 추가 보상을 받을 것이었다. / 밀 가격이 높으면

Bakers would earn a bonus / if wheat was cheap.
제빵사들은 보너스를 받을 것이었다. / 밀이 저렴하면

So the subjects might earn two separate payments: / one for an accurate forecast, / and a bonus if the price of wheat moved in their direction.
따라서 실험 대상자들은 두 가지 별개의 보상을 받았을지도 모르는데, / 즉 정확한 예측에 대한 보상과 / 밀의 가격이 자기 쪽으로 움직이게 될 경우의 보너스였다.

Mayraz found / that the prospect of the bonus influenced the forecast itself.
Mayraz는 발견했다. / 보너스에 대한 기대가 예측 자체에 영향을 미쳤음을

The farmers hoped and *predicted* / that the price of wheat would rise.
농부들은 희망하고 *예측했다*. / 밀의 가격이 올라갈 것이라고

The bakers hoped for — and predicted — the opposite.
제빵사들은 그 반대를 희망하고 예측했다.

They let their hopes influence their reasoning.
그들은 자신들의 희망이 추론에 영향을 미치게 했다.

➡ When participants were asked / to predict the price change of wheat, / their (A) wish for where the price would go, / which was determined by the group they belonged to, / (B) affected their predictions.
참가자들이 요청받았을 때, / 밀의 가격 변동을 예측하도록 / 가격이 어디로 이동할 것인가에 대한 그들의 희망은 / 자신들이 속했던 집단에 의해 정해졌고 / 그들의 예측에 영향을 미쳤다.

한 연구에서 행동 경제학자인 Guy Mayraz는 시간이 지나면서 오르내린 가격을 보여주는 도표들을 실험 대상자들에게 보여주었다. 그 도표들은 사실 주식 시장에서의 과거 변동에 관한 것이었으나 Mayraz는 사람들에게 그 도표들이 밀 가격의 최근 변동을 보여준다고 말했다. 그는 각각의 사람에게 가격이 다음에 어디로 움직일지를 예측하도록 요청했으며, 예측이 실현되면 그들에게 보상을 제공했다. 그러나 Mayraz는 참가자들을 '농부'와 '제빵사'라는 두 개의 범주로 나누었다. 농부들은 밀 가격이 높으면 추가 보상을 받을 것이었다. 제빵사들은 밀이 저렴하면 보너스를 받을 것이었다. 따라서 실험 대상자들은 두 가지 별개의 보상을 받았을지도 모르는데, 즉 정확한 예측에 대한 보상과 밀의 가격이 자기 (집단에 유리한) 쪽으로 움직이게 될 경우의 보너스였다. Mayraz는 보너스에 대한 기대가 예측 자체에 영향을 미쳤음을 발견했다. 농부들은 밀의 가격이 올라갈 것이라고 희망하고 *예측했다*. 제빵사들은 그 반대를 희망하고 예측했다. 그들은 자신들의 희망이 추론에 영향을 미치게 했다.

➡ 참가자들이 밀의 가격 변동을 예측하도록 요청받았을 때, 가격이 어디로 이동할 것인가에 대한 그들의 (A) 희망은 자신들이 속했던 집단에 의해 정해졌고 그들의 예측에 (B) 영향을 미쳤다.

Why? 왜 정답일까?

실험에 따르면 밀 가격이 높을 때 보상을 받기로 한 '농부' 집단은 밀 가격의 상승을 바라고 예측했으며, 반대로 가격이 낮을 때 보상을 받기로 한 '제빵사' 집단은 밀 가격의 하락을 바라고 예측했다. 이를 마지막 문장에서는 희망에 따라 추론에 영향을 받았다(They let their hopes influence their reasoning.)고 정리하므로, 요약문의 빈칸 (A), (B)에 들어갈 말로 가장 적절한 것은 ① '(A) wish(희망), (B) affected (영향을 미쳤다)'이다.

- stock market 주식 시장
- forecast ⓝ 예측, 예보
- accurate ⓐ 정확한
- reasoning ⓝ 추론
- disregard ⓝ 무시 ⓥ 무시하다
- wheat ⓝ 밀
- separate ⓐ 별개의
- prospect ⓝ 예상, 전망
- contradict ⓥ ~와 모순되다
- assurance ⓝ 확언, 장담, 자신감

구문 풀이

5행 He asked each person to predict {where the price would move next} —
       동사1   목적어   목적격 보어   { } : 간접의문문
and offered them a reward if their forecasts came true.
      동사2   직접목적어   └ 접속사(만일 ~라면)
   간접목적어

41~42   신호와 이야기에 주의를 기울이도록 이루어진 진화

Stories populate our lives.
이야기는 우리 삶에 거주한다.

If you are not a fan of stories, / you might imagine / that the best world is a world without them, / where we can only see the facts in front of us.
만약 여러분이 이야기를 좋아하지 않는다면, / 여러분은 생각할지도 모른다. / 가장 좋은 세상이란 이야기가 없는 세상이라고 / 우리가 우리 앞에 있는 사실들만 볼 수 있는

But to do this is / to (a) deny how our brains work, / how they are *designed* to work.
그러나 이렇게 하는 것은 / 우리의 뇌가 어떻게 작동하는지를 부인하는 것이다. / 즉 어떻게 그것들이 작동하도록 *설계되어* 있는지를

Evolution has given us minds / that are alert to stories and suggestion / because, through many hundreds of thousands of years of natural selection, / minds that can attend to stories / have been more (b) successful / at passing on their owners' genes.
진화는 우리에게 사고방식을 주었다. / 이야기와 암시에 주의를 기울이는 / 왜냐하면 수십만 년의 자연 선택을 거쳐, / 이야기에 주의를 기울일 수 있는 사고방식이 / 더 성공해 왔기 때문에, / 그들 주인의 유전자를 물려주는 데에

Think about what happens, / for example, / when animals face one another in conflict.
무슨 일이 일어나는지 생각해 보라. / 예를 들어 / 동물들이 싸움에서 서로 직면할 때

They rarely plunge into battle right away.
그것들은 좀처럼 즉시 전투에 뛰어들지 않는다.

No, they first try to (c) signal in all kinds of ways / what the *outcome* of the battle is going to be.
아니, 그것들은 온갖 종류의 방법으로 신호를 보내려 애를 쓴다. / 먼저 전투의 *결과*가 무엇이 될지

They puff up their chests, / they roar, / and they bare their fangs.
그것들은 가슴을 잔뜩 부풀리고, / 그것들은 포효하며, / 그것들은 송곳니를 드러낸다.

「Animals evolved to attend to stories and signals / because these turn out to be an efficient way / to navigate the world. 」41번의 근거
동물들은 이야기와 신호에 주의를 기울이도록 진화했다. / 그것들이 효율적인 방법이 되기 때문에, / 세상을 항해하는

If you and I were a pair of lions on the Serengeti, / and we were trying to decide the strongest lion, / it would be most (d) unwise — for both of us — / to plunge straight into a conflict.
만약 여러분과 내가 세렝게티의 한 쌍의 사자이고 / 우리가 가장 강한 사자를 결정하려 한다면, / 가장 어리석은 일은 / 우리 둘 다에게 / 싸움에 곧바로 뛰어드는 것이

『It is far better for each of us / to make a show of strength, / to tell the *story* of how our victory is inevitable. 42번의 근거

우리 각자에게 있어 훨씬 낫다. / 힘을 과시하는 것, 즉 어떻게 자신의 승리가 불가피한지에 대한 *이야기*를 하는 것이

If one of those stories is much more (e) convincing than the other, / we might be able to agree on the outcome / without actually having the fight.

그 이야기들 중 하나가 다른 쪽보다 훨씬 더 설득력이 있다면, / 우리는 그 결과에 동의할 수 있을지도 모른다. / 실제로 싸우지 않고도

이야기는 우리 삶에 거주한다. 만약 여러분이 이야기를 좋아하지 않는다면, 여러분은 가장 좋은 세상이란 이야기 없이 우리가 우리 앞에 있는 사실들만 볼 수 있는 세상이라고 생각할지도 모른다. 그러나 이렇게 하는 것은 우리의 뇌가 어떻게 작동하는지, 즉 어떻게 그것들이 작동하도록 (a) 설계되어 있는지를 (a) 부인하는 것이다. 수십만 년의 자연 선택을 거쳐, 이야기에 주의를 기울일 수 있는 사고방식이 그들 주인의 유전자를 물려주는 것에 더 (b) 성공해 왔기 때문에, 진화는 우리에게 이야기와 암시에 주의를 기울이는 사고방식을 주었다. 예를 들어 동물들이 싸움에서 서로를 직면할 때 무슨 일이 일어나는지 생각해 보라. 그것들은 좀처럼 즉시 전투에 뛰어들지 않는다. 오히려, 그것들은 먼저 전투의 결과가 무엇이 될지 온갖 종류의 방법으로 (c) 신호를 보내려 애쓴다. 그것들은 가슴을 잔뜩 부풀리고, 포효하며, 송곳니를 드러낸다. 이야기와 신호가 세상을 항해하는 효율적인 방법이 되기 때문에, 동물들은 이것들에 주의를 기울이도록 진화했다. 만약 여러분과 내가 세렝게티의 한 쌍의 사자이고 우리가 가장 강한 사자를 결정하려 한다고 할 때, 우리 둘 다 싸움에 곧바로 뛰어드는 것이 가장 (d) 분별 있는(→ 어리석은) 일일 것이다. 우리 각자가 힘을 과시하는 것, 즉 어떻게 자신의 승리가 불가피한지에 대한 *이야기*를 하는 것이 훨씬 낫다. 그 이야기들 중 하나가 다른 쪽보다 훨씬 더 (e) 설득력이 있다면, 우리는 실제로 싸우지 않고도 그 결과에 동의할 수 있을지도 모른다.

- **populate** ⓥ 거주하다
- **natural selection** 자연 선택
- **conflict** ⓝ 갈등
- **puff up** 부풀리다
- **bare** ⓥ (신체의 일부를) 드러내다
- **make a show of** ~을 과시하다, 자랑하다
- **convincing** ⓐ 설득력 있는
- **deny** ⓥ 부인하다
- **pass on** ~을 전해주다
- **plunge into** ~에 뛰어들다
- **roar** ⓥ 으르렁거리다
- **sensible** ⓐ 분별 있는
- **inevitable** ⓐ 불가피한

구문 풀이

15행 If you and I were a pair of lions on the Serengeti, and we were trying to
「if + 주어1 + 과거동사1 ~   주어2 + 과거동사2 ~
decide the strongest lion, it would be most sensible — for both of us — to plunge
(가주어 + 조동사 과거형 + 동사원형 : 가정법 과거)   진주어
straight into a conflict.

41 제목 파악
정답률 48% | 정답 ③

윗글의 제목으로 가장 적절한 것은?

① The Light and Dark Sides of Storytelling
스토리텔링의 명암
② How to Interpret Various Signals of Animals
동물의 다양한 신호를 해석하는 방법
✔ Why Are We Built to Pay Attention to Stories?
왜 우리는 이야기에 집중하도록 만들어졌을까?
④ Story: A Game Changer for Overturning a Losing Battle
이야기: 지는 전투를 뒤집기 위한 게임 체인저
⑤ Evolution: A History of Human's Coexistence with Animals
진화: 인간과 동물의 공존의 역사

Why? 왜 정답일까?

'Animals evolved to attend to stories and signals because these turn out to be an efficient way to navigate the world.'에서 이야기와 신호가 세상을 살아가는 데 도움이 되기 때문에 동물은 이것들에 주의를 기울이도록 진화해왔다고 한다. 따라서 글의 제목으로 가장 적절한 것은 이러한 요지를 정답으로 유도할 수 있는 질문 형태인 ③ '왜 우리는 이야기에 집중하도록 만들어졌을까?'이다.

★★★ 등급을 가르는 문제!

42 어휘 추론
정답률 45% | 정답 ④

밑줄 친 (a) ~ (e) 중에서 문맥상 낱말의 쓰임이 적절하지 않은 것은? [3점]

① (a)   ② (b)   ③ (c)   ✔ (d)   ⑤ (e)

Why? 왜 정답일까?

'It is far better for each of us ~'에서 누가 강한지를 결정할 때 곧바로 싸우는 것보다 서로의 힘에 관해 '이야기'하는 것이 더 효과적이라고 하므로, 바로 싸움에 뛰어드는 것이 '어리석다'는 지적의 의미를 나타낼 수 있도록 (d)의 sensible을 unwise로 고쳐야 한다. 따라서 문맥상 낱말의 쓰임이 적절하지 않은 것은 ④ '(d)'이다.

★★ 문제 해결 꿀~팁 ★★

▶ 많이 틀린 이유는?
가장 헷갈리는 ⑤ (e)가 포함된 문장은 싸움을 앞두고 신호로 이야기를 전달하고 있는 두 사자에 관한 내용이다. 두 사자의 이야기 중 어느 한쪽의 이야기가 '설득력이 있다면' 실제로 싸워보지 않고도 서열을 결정할 수 있게 되고, 이 점이 신호 또는 이야기를 통한 이득이라는 것이 글의 결론이다. 따라서 convincing은 앞뒤 문맥상 적절하다.

▶ 문제 해결 방법은?
정답인 ④ (d)는 이야기의 이득을 설명하기 위한 예시인데, 여기서 '이야기를 전달하기도 전에 싸움에 뛰어드는' 상황을 지지하면 부자연스럽다. 따라서 sensible은 문맥상 어색하다.

43-45 노숙자 여자의 따뜻한 마음에 감동한 Jennifer

(A)

Jennifer was on her way home.
Jennifer는 집으로 가던 중이었다.
『She decided to stop at a gas station to get coffee. 45번 ①의 근거 일치

그녀는 커피를 사기 위해 주유소에 들르기로 결정했다.
After she paid for her coffee, / she got back into her car, / but before she started it, / she noticed a woman / standing outside in front of the building.
그녀가 커피값을 지불한 후에 / 그녀는 자신의 차로 돌아왔는데, / 그녀가 차의 시동을 걸기 전에 / 그녀는 한 여자를 알아챘다. / 건물 앞 바깥에서 서 있는
(a) She could tell / that the woman was homeless / by her appearance.
그녀는 알 수 있었다. / 그녀가 노숙자임을 / 그 여자의 겉모습을 보고
Her clothes were worn / and she was nothing but skin and bones.
그녀의 옷은 닳았고 / 그녀는 거죽과 뼈만 남아 있었다.
She must have not had enough money / to get something to eat.
이 사람은 충분한 돈을 가지고 있지 않았음이 틀림없어. / 먹을 것을 사기 위한
Jennifer thought to herself, / feeling pity for her.
Jennifer는 혼자 생각했다. / 그녀에게 동정심을 느끼며

(D)

Suddenly, / a dog walked up to the front of the building.
갑자기, / 개 한 마리가 건물 앞으로 걸어갔다.
Being a dog lover, / Jennifer noticed that the dog was a German Shepherd.
개를 사랑하는 사람이어서 / Jennifer는 그 개가 저먼 셰퍼드라는 것을 알아챘다.
『She could also tell that the dog was a mother, / because anyone could notice / that she had been feeding puppies. 45번 ⑤의 근거 일치

그녀는 또한 그 개가 어미라는 것을 알 수 있었는데, / 왜냐하면 누군가 알아차릴 수 있었기 때문이었다. / 그 개가 강아지들에게 젖을 먹여 왔음을
The dog was terribly in need of something to eat / and (e) she felt so bad for her.
그 개는 먹을 것을 너무나 필요로 하고 있었고 / 그녀는 개에게 너무나 안쓰러움을 느꼈다.
She knew / if the dog didn't eat soon, / she and her puppies would not make it.
그녀는 알았다. / 만약 그 개가 곧 먹지 않는다면, / 그 개와 강아지들이 살아남을 수 없을지도 모른다는 것을

(C)

Jennifer sat in her car, / looking at the dog.
Jennifer는 자신의 차에 앉아 있었다. / 개를 쳐다보면서
『She noticed that people were walking by / without paying attention to the dog. 45번 ③의 근거 일치

그녀는 사람들이 지나가는 것을 알아챘다. / 개에게 관심을 보이지 않고
But (c) she still did not do anything.
그러나 그럼에도 그녀는 어떤 것도 하지 않았다.
However, someone did.
하지만 누군가는 했다.
The homeless woman, / who Jennifer thought did not have money / to buy herself anything to eat, / went into the store.
노숙자 여자가, / Jennifer가 생각하기에 돈이 없었던 / 스스로에게 어떤 먹을 것도 사줄 / 가게에 들어갔다.
And what she did brought tears to Jennifer's eyes.
그리고 그녀가 한 일로 Jennifer는 눈물을 흘렸다.
『She had gone into the store, / bought a can of dog food, / and fed that dog. 45번 ④의 근거 불일치

그녀는 가게에 들어가서 / 개의 먹이 한 캔을 샀고 / 그 개에게 먹였다.
(d) She looked so happy to do it as well.
그녀는 또한 그 일을 하면서 매우 행복해 보였다.

(B)

Watching the scene changed Jennifer's life entirely.
그 장면을 본 것이 Jennifer의 삶을 완전히 바꾸었다.
『You see, that day was Mother's Day. 45번 ②의 근거 일치

실은 그날은 어머니날이었다.
It took a homeless woman / to show (b) her what selfless giving and love is.
한 명의 노숙자 여자가 필요했다. / 그녀에게 이타적인 베풂과 사랑이 무엇인지를 보여 주는 데
From that day on, / Jennifer has helped people in trouble, / especially mothers struggling to raise children.
그날 이후로, / Jennifer는 곤경에 처한 사람들을 돕고 있다. / 특히 아이들을 키우기 위해 애쓰는 엄마들을
The homeless woman made Jennifer a better person.
노숙자 여자가 Jennifer를 더 나은 사람으로 만들었다.

(A)

Jennifer는 집으로 가던 중이었다. 그녀는 커피를 사기 위해 주유소에 들르기로 결정했다. 커피값을 지불한 후에 그녀는 자신의 차로 돌아왔는데, 차의 시동을 걸기 전에 그녀는 건물 앞 바깥에 서 있는 한 여자에게 주목했다. (a) 그녀는 여자의 겉모습을 보고 노숙자임을 알 수 있었다. 그녀의 옷은 닳았고 그녀는 거죽과 뼈만 남아 있었다. *이 사람은 먹을 것을 사기 위한 충분한 돈을 가지고 있지 않았음이 틀림없어.* Jennifer는 그녀에게 동정심을 느끼며 혼자 생각했다.

(D)

갑자기 개 한 마리가 건물 앞으로 걸어갔다. 개를 사랑하는 사람인 Jennifer는 그 개가 저먼 셰퍼드라는 것을 알아챘다. 그녀는 또한 그 개가 어미라는 것을 알 수 있었는데, 왜냐하면 누군든 그 개가 강아지들에게 젖을 먹여 왔음을 알아차릴 수 있었기 때문이었다. 그 개는 먹을 것을 너무나 필요로 하고 있었고 (e) 그녀는 개에게 너무나 안쓰러움을 느꼈다. 그녀는 만약 그 개가 곧 먹지 않는다면, 그 개와 강아지들이 살아남을 수 없을지도 모른다는 것을 알았다.

(C)

Jennifer는 자신의 차에 앉아서 개를 쳐다보았다. 그녀는 사람들이 개에게 관심을 보이지 않고 지나가는 것을 알아챘다. 그러나 그럼에도 (c) 그녀는 어떤 것도 하지 않았다. 하지만 누군가는 했다. Jennifer가 생각하기에 자신이 먹을 것을 살 돈이 전혀 없었던 노숙자 여자가 가게에 들어갔다. 그리고 그녀가 한 일로 Jennifer는 눈물을 흘렸다. 그녀는 가게에 들어가서 개의 먹이 한 캔을 샀고 그 개에게 먹였다. (d) 그녀는 또한 그 일을 하면서 매우 행복해 보였다.

(B)

그 장면을 본 것이 Jennifer의 삶을 완전히 바꾸었다. 실은 그날은 어머니날이었다. (b) 그녀에게 이타적인 베풂과 사랑이 무엇인지를 보여 주는 데 한 명의 노숙자 여자가 필요했다. 그날 이후로 Jennifer는 곤경에 처한 사람들, 특히 아이들을 키우기 위해 애쓰는 엄마들을 돕고 있다. 노숙자 여자가 Jennifer를 더 나은 사람으로 만들었다.

- **appearance** ⓝ 겉모습
- **entirely** ⓐⓓ 완전히
- **bring tears to one's eyes** ~의 눈물을 짓게 하다
- **pity** ⓝ 유감, 연민
- **selfless** ⓐ 이타적인
- **in need of** ~이 필요한

구문 풀이

(A) 6행 *She must have not had enough money to get something to eat.*
「must have p.p. : ~했음에 틀림없다」

(C) 3행 The homeless woman, {who (Jennifer thought) did not have money to
주어(선행사)　　　　주격 관·대　　　( ): 삽입절
buy herself anything to eat}, went into the store.
{ }: 주어 보충　　　　　　　동사
(D) 1행 Being a dog lover, Jennifer noticed that the dog was a German Shepherd.
분사구문(=As she was ~)　　　　　　접속사(~것)

43 글의 순서 파악　　　　　정답률 66% | 정답 ⑤

주어진 글 (A)에 이어질 내용을 순서에 맞게 배열한 것으로 가장 적절한 것은?

① (B) – (D) – (C)　　　　② (C) – (B) – (D)
③ (C) – (D) – (B)　　　　④ (D) – (B) – (C)
✓⑤ (D) – (C) – (B)

Why? 왜 정답일까?

커피를 사러 주유소에 들렀던 Jennifer가 남루한 차림의 노숙자 여자를 우연히 보았다는 내용의 (A) 뒤로, 이어서 Jennifer가 굶주린 어미 개를 보았다는 내용의 (D), 모두가 외면하고 있던 개에게 노숙자 여자가 먹을 것을 사 먹이는 것을 보고 Jennifer가 감동을 받았다는 내용의 (C), 이후로 Jennifer가 어려운 사람들을 돕기 시작했다는 내용의 (B)가 차례로 연결된다. 따라서 글의 순서로 가장 적절한 것은 ⑤ '(D) – (C) – (B)'이다.

44 지칭 추론　　　　　정답률 66% | 정답 ④

밑줄 친 (a) ~ (e) 중에서 가리키는 대상이 나머지 넷과 다른 것은?

① (a)　　② (b)　　③ (c)　　✓④ (d)　　⑤ (e)

Why? 왜 정답일까?

(a), (b), (c), (e)는 Jennifer, (d)는 the homeless woman을 가리키므로, (a) ~ (e) 중에서 가리키는 대상이 다른 하나는 ④ '(d)'이다.

45 세부 내용 파악　　　　　정답률 68% | 정답 ④

윗글에 관한 내용으로 적절하지 않은 것은?

① Jennifer는 커피를 사기 위해 주유소에 들렀다.
② 사건이 일어난 날은 어머니날이었다.
③ 지나가던 사람들은 개에게 관심을 보이지 않았다.
✓④ Jennifer는 가게에 들어가서 개의 먹이를 샀다.
⑤ Jennifer는 개가 어미 개라는 것을 알았다.

Why? 왜 정답일까?

(C) 'She had gone into the store, bought a can of dog food, and fed that dog.'에서 상점으로 들어가 개 먹이를 사서 나온 사람은 Jennifer가 아닌 노숙자 여자이다. 따라서 내용과 일치하지 않는 것은 ④ 'Jennifer는 가게에 들어가서 개의 먹이를 샀다.'이다.

Why? 왜 오답일까?

① (A) 'She decided to stop at a gas station to get coffee.'의 내용과 일치한다.
② (B) '~ that day was Mother's Day.'의 내용과 일치한다.
③ (C) 'She noticed that people were walking by without paying attention to the dog.'의 내용과 일치한다.
⑤ (D) 'She could also tell that the dog was a mother, ~'의 내용과 일치한다.

어휘 Review Test 18　　　　　문제편 180쪽

A	B	C	D
01 받아들일 수 없는	01 discontinue	01 ①	01 ⑨
02 기대	02 desirable	02 ⓗ	02 ①
03 균등하게	03 specific	03 ⓐ	03 ⓟ
04 주의를 기울이는	04 abandon	04 ①	04 ①
05 동일한	05 unfair	05 ⓝ	05 ①
06 중요한, 유의미한	06 reward	06 ①	06 ⓠ
07 확률, 가능성	07 selfless	07 ⓑ	07 ⓔ
08 생산하다, 제조하다	08 retain	08 ⓠ	08 ⓑ
09 속도, 비율	09 reputation	09 ⓓ	09 ①
10 중요하지 않은	10 irrational	10 ⓖ	10 ⓢ
11 조절하다, 통제하다	11 outcome	11 ⓢ	11 ①
12 포식자	12 primarily	12 ⓡ	12 ①
13 저항할 수 없는, 압도적인	13 prospect	13 ⓒ	13 ⓐ
14 주식 시장	14 emerge	14 ⓔ	14 ⓡ
15 완전히	15 occasionally	15 ①	15 ⓜ
16 입증하다	16 reflection	16 ⓞ	16 ⓗ
17 죄책감이 드는	17 concentrate	17 ⓜ	17 ⓚ
18 기억하다, 회상하다	18 customary	18 ⓚ	18 ⓗ
19 겉모습	19 continent	19 ⓟ	19 ⓒ
20 장비	20 normally	20 ①	20 ⓓ

・정답・

18④ 19① 20⑤ 21⑤ 22③ 23② 24② 25③ 26② 27⑤ 28③ 29③ 30⑤ 31② 32③
33① 34⑤ 35③ 36④ 37⑤ 38④ 39③ 40① 41① 42⑤ 43② 44② 45③

★ 표기된 문항은 [등급을 가르는 문제]에 해당하는 문항입니다.

18 학교 운동장 사용 허가 요청　　　　　정답률 95% | 정답 ④

다음 글의 목적으로 가장 적절한 것은?

① 학생 동아리 운영 성과를 보고하려고
② 댄스 동아리 특별 공연을 홍보하려고
③ 댄스 동아리실 시설 보수를 건의하려고
✓④ 댄스 동아리의 운동장 사용 허락을 요청하려고
⑤ 학생 동아리 부원 모집 기간의 연장을 부탁하려고

To the Principal of Gullard High School,
Gullard 고등학교 교장 선생님 귀하,
My name is Nancy Watson, / and I am the captain of the student dance club at Gullard
High School.
제 이름은 Nancy Watson이고 / 저는 Gullard 고등학교 학생 댄스 동아리 회장입니다.
We are one of the biggest faces of the school, / winning a lot of awards and trophies.
우리는 학교의 가장 중요한 얼굴 중 하나입니다. / 많은 상과 트로피를 받는
However, / the school isn't allowing our club to practice on the school field / because a lot
of teachers worry / that we are going to mess up the field.
그러나 / 학교는 우리 동아리가 운동장에서 연습하는 것을 허락하지 않고 있습니다. / 많은 선생님들께서 염려하시기 때문에 / 우리가
학교 운동장을 엉망으로 만들 것을
This is causing us to lose practice time / and ultimately results in creating a bad high
school experience for us.
이것은 우리가 연습 시간을 잃게 만들고 / 결국 우리에게 안 좋은 고등학교 경험을 만들어 주게 됩니다.
We promise to use the space respectfully.
우리는 그 공간을 소중히 사용할 것을 약속드립니다.
Therefore, / I'm asking you / to allow us to use the school field for our dance practice.
그러므로, / 저는 교장 선생님께 요청드립니다. / 우리가 댄스 연습을 위해 학교 운동장을 사용하도록 허락해 주시기를
I would be grateful / if you reconsider your decision.
저는 고맙겠습니다. / 교장 선생님께서 그 결정을 재고해 주신다면
Thank you very much.
대단히 감사합니다.
Sincerely, // Nancy Watson
Nancy Watson 올림

Gullard 고등학교 교장 선생님 귀하,

제 이름은 Nancy Watson이고 Gullard 고등학교 학생 댄스 동아리 회장입니다. 우리는 학교의 가장 중요한 얼굴 중 하나로 많은 상과 트로피를 받고 있습니다. 그러나 많은 선생님들께서 우리가 학교 운동장을 엉망으로 만들 것을 염려하시기 때문에 학교는 우리 동아리가 운동장에서 연습하는 것을 허락하지 않고 있습니다. 이로 인해 우리는 연습 시간을 잃고, 결국 안 좋은 고등학교 경험이 생기게 됩니다. 우리는 그 공간을 소중히 사용할 것을 약속드립니다. 그러므로, 저는 교장 선생님께 우리가 댄스 연습을 위해 학교 운동장을 사용하도록 허락해 주시기를 요청드립니다. 교장 선생님께서 그 결정을 재고해 주신다면 고맙겠습니다. 대단히 감사합니다.

Nancy Watson 올림

Why? 왜 정답일까?

'Therefore, I'm asking you to allow us to use the school field for our dance practice.'에서 댄스 동아리가 연습 때 운동장을 사용할 수 있도록 허가해 줄 것을 요청하고 있으므로, 글의 목적으로 가장 적절한 것은 ④ '댄스 동아리의 운동장 사용 허락을 요청하려고'이다.

● mess up 엉망으로 만들다, 어지럽히다　　　● ultimately ⓐⓓ 결국, 궁극적으로
● respectfully ⓐⓓ 공손히, 정중하게　　　● grateful ⓐ 감사하는
● reconsider ⓥ 재고하다

구문 풀이

4행 However, the school isn't allowing our club to practice on the school field
이유 접속사　　　　　　5형식 동사　　목적어　　　목적격 보어
because a lot of teachers worry that we are going to mess up the field.
　　　　　　　　　타동사　접속사(~것)

19 여름 방학을 삼촌과 숙모의 농장에서 보내게 되어 실망한 Ryan　　정답률 91% | 정답 ①

다음 글에 드러난 Ryan의 심경 변화로 가장 적절한 것은?

✓① excited → disappointed　　② furious → regretful
　신이 난　　실망한　　　　　　분노한　　후회하는
③ irritated → satisfied　　④ nervous → relaxed
　짜증 난　　만족한　　　　　　긴장한　　여유로운
⑤ pleased → jealous
　기쁜　　질투하는

Ryan, an eleven-year-old boy, / ran home as fast as he could.
11살 소년 Ryan은 / 가능한 한 빨리 집으로 달려갔다.
Finally, summer break had started!
마침내, 여름 방학이 시작되었다!
When he entered the house, / his mom was standing in front of the refrigerator, / waiting
for him.
그가 집으로 들어갔을 때 / 그의 엄마는 냉장고 앞에 서서 / 그를 기다리고 있었다.
She told him to pack his bags.
그녀는 그에게 가방을 싸라고 말했다.

Ryan's heart soared like a balloon.
Ryan의 심장이 풍선처럼 날아올랐다.
Pack for what?
왜 가방을 싸지?
Are we going to Disneyland?
우리가 디즈니랜드에라도 가나?
He couldn't remember the last time / his parents had taken him on a vacation.
그는 마지막으로 ~했던 때가 기억나지 않았다. / 부모님이 자신을 데리고 휴가를 갔던
His eyes beamed.
그의 두 눈이 반짝거렸다.
"You're spending the summer with uncle Tim and aunt Gina."
"너는 Tim 삼촌과 Gina 숙모와 함께 여름을 보내게 될 거야."
Ryan groaned.
Ryan은 불만의 신음소리를 냈다.
"The whole summer?"
"여름 내내요?"
"Yes, the whole summer."
"그렇단다. 여름 내내."
The anticipation he had felt / disappeared in a flash.
그가 느꼈던 기대감이 / 순식간에 사라졌다.
For three whole miserable weeks, / he would be on his aunt and uncle's farm.
끔찍한 3주 내내, / 그는 자신의 삼촌과 숙모의 농장에서 지내게 될 것이었다.
He sighed.
그는 한숨을 쉬었다.

11살 소년 Ryan은 가능한 한 빨리 집으로 달려갔다. 마침내, 여름 방학이 시작되었다! 그가 집으로 들어갔을 때 그의 엄마는 냉장고 앞에 서서 그를 기다리고 있었다. 그녀는 그에게 가방을 싸라고 말했다. Ryan의 심장은 풍선처럼 날아올랐다. *왜 가방을 싸지? 우리가 디즈니랜드에라도 가나?* 그는 마지막으로 부모님이 자신을 데리고 휴가를 갔던 때가 기억나지 않았다. 그의 두 눈이 반짝거렸다. "너는 Tim 삼촌과 Gina 숙모와 함께 여름을 보내게 될 거야." Ryan은 불만의 신음소리를 냈다. "여름 내내요?" "그렇단다. 여름 내내." 그가 느꼈던 기대감이 순식간에 사라졌다. 끔찍한 3주 내내, 그는 삼촌과 숙모의 농장에서 지내게 될 것이었다. 그는 한숨을 쉬었다.

Why? 왜 정답일까?

'Ryan's heart soared like a balloon.'와 'His eyes beamed.'에 따르면 방학이 시작된 날 어머니로부터 짐을 싸라는 이야기를 들은 Ryan은 기대감에 부풀었지만, 'The anticipation he had felt disappeared in a flash.' 이후에 따르면 방학 내내 삼촌과 숙모의 농장에서 지낼 것이라는 사실을 알고는 불만을 느꼈다. 따라서 Ryan의 심경 변화로 가장 적절한 것은 ① '신이 난 → 실망한'이다.

- **pack** ⓥ (가방이나 짐을) 싸다
- **beam** ⓥ 빛나다, 활짝 웃다
- **anticipation** ⓝ 기대감
- **in a flash** 순식간에
- **regretful** ⓐ 후회하는, 유감스러운
- **soar** ⓥ 날아오르다, 솟구치다
- **groan** ⓥ 신음소리를 내다
- **disappear** ⓥ 사라지다
- **miserable** ⓐ 끔찍한, 비참한
- **irritated** ⓐ 짜증 난

구문 풀이

8행 The anticipation [he had felt] disappeared in a flash.
　　　　주어　　　　　　　　　자동사

---

20 타인을 설득하는 방법에 관한 조언　　정답률 84% | 정답 ⑤

다음 글에서 필자가 주장하는 바로 가장 적절한 것은?
① 타인의 신뢰를 얻기 위해서는 일관된 행동을 보여 주어라.
② 협상을 잘하기 위해 질문에 담긴 상대방의 의도를 파악하라.
③ 논쟁을 잘하려면 자신의 가치관에서 벗어나려는 시도를 하라.
④ 원만한 대인 관계를 유지하려면 상대를 배려하는 태도를 갖춰라.
✓⑤ 설득하고자 할 때 상대방이 스스로 관점을 돌아보게 하는 질문을 하라.

When trying to convince someone to change their mind, / most people try to lay out a logical argument, / or make a passionate plea / as to why their view is right / and the other person's opinion is wrong.
누군가 마음을 바꾸도록 설득하고자 할 때 / 대부분의 사람들이 논리적 주장을 펼치거나 / 열정적으로 항변한다. / 또는 왜 자신의 관점이 옳고 / 다른 사람의 의견이 틀린지에 대해
But when you think about it, / you'll realize that this doesn't often work.
하지만 여러분이 그것에 대해 생각해 보면 / 여러분은 이것이 종종 효과가 없다는 것을 깨달을 것이다.
As soon as someone figures out / that you are on a mission to change their mind, / the metaphorical shutters go down.
누군가 알아차리자마자 / 여러분이 자신의 마음을 바꾸려는 임무를 띠고 있다는 것을 / 은유적인 셔터는 내려간다.
You'll have better luck / if you ask well-chosen, open-ended questions / that let someone challenge their own assumptions.
여러분은 더 좋은 운이 따를 것이다. / 만약 여러분이 잘 선택된, 다양한 대답이 가능한 질문을 한다면 / 누군가에게 본인의 가정을 의심하도록 하는
We tend to approve of an idea / if we thought of it first / — or at least, if we *think* we thought of it first.
우리는 어떤 견해를 인정하려는 경향이 있다. / 만약 우리가 그 견해를 먼저 생각해 냈다면 / 혹은 최소한 우리가 그것을 먼저 생각해 냈다고 *생각한다면*
Therefore, / encouraging someone to question their own worldview / will often yield better results / than trying to force them into accepting your opinion as fact.
그러므로, / 누군가에게 자기 자신의 세계관에 의문을 갖도록 장려하는 것은 / 종종 더 나은 결과를 가져올 것이다. / 그들에게 여러분의 의견을 사실로 받아들이도록 강요하려고 하는 것보다
Ask someone well-chosen questions / to look at their own views from another angle, / and this might trigger fresh insights.
누군가에게 잘 선택된 질문을 하라. / 그들 자신의 관점을 다른 각도에서 바라보도록 / 그러면 이것은 새로운 통찰력을 유발할 것이다.

누군가를 그 마음을 바꾸도록 설득하고자 할 때 대부분의 사람들이 논리적 주장을 펼치거나 또는 왜 자신의 관점이 옳고 다른 사람의 의견이 틀린지에 대해 열정적으로 항변한다. 하지만 여러분이 그것에 대해 생각해 보면 여러분은 이것이 종종 효과가 없다는 것을 깨달을 것이다. 누군가가 여러분이 자신의 마음을 바꾸려는 임무를 띠고 있다는 것을 알아차리자마자 은유적인 (마음의) 셔터는 내려간다. 만약 여러분이 누군가에게 자기 자신의 가정을 의심하도록

하는 잘 선택된, 다양한 대답이 가능한 질문을 한다면 여러분은 더 좋은 운이 따를 것이다. 만약 우리가 어떤 견해를 먼저 생각해 냈거나 최소한 우리가 그것을 먼저 생각해 냈다고 *생각한다면*, 우리는 그 견해를 인정하려는 경향이 있다. 그러므로 누군가에게 자기 자신의 세계관에 의문을 갖도록 장려하는 것은 그들에게 여러분의 의견을 사실로 받아들이도록 강요하려고 하는 것보다 종종 더 나은 결과를 가져올 것이다. 누군가에게 그들 자신의 관점을 다른 각도에서 바라보도록 잘 선택된 질문을 하면, 이것은 새로운 통찰력을 유발할 것이다.

Why? 왜 정답일까?

'Therefore, encouraging someone to question their own worldview will often yield better results than trying to force them into accepting your opinion as fact. Ask someone well-chosen questions to look at their own views from another angle, ~'에서 상대방을 설득하려고 할 때 의견을 관철하기보다는 상대방이 스스로 자기 자신의 견해를 돌아보게 할 수 있는 잘 선택된 질문을 던지는 것이 좋다고 하므로, 필자가 주장하는 바로 가장 적절한 것은 ⑤ '설득하고자 할 때 상대방이 스스로 관점을 돌아보게 하는 질문을 하라.'이다.

- **convince** ⓥ 설득하다
- **make a plea** 항변하다, 간청하다
- **metaphorical** ⓐ 비유의, 은유의
- **assumption** ⓝ 가정
- **yield** ⓥ (결과를) 내다, 산출하다
- **lay out** 펼치다
- **passionate** ⓐ 열정적인
- **open-ended** ⓐ 정해진 답이 없는, 주관식의
- **approve of** ~을 인정하다
- **trigger** ⓥ 유발하다

구문 풀이

9행 Therefore, encouraging someone to question their own worldview
동명사구 주어 「encourage + 목적어 + to부정사 : ~이 …하게 장려하다」
will often yield better results than trying to force them into accepting your opinion
동사구　　　　　목적어　　　　　동명사구(주어와 병렬)
as fact.

---

21 현대의 과학 교과서가 법칙을 기술하는 방법에 있어 범하는 오류　　정답률 51% | 정답 ⑤

밑줄 친 turns the life stories of these scientists from lead to gold가 다음 글에서 의미하는 바로 가장 적절한 것은? [3점]
① discovers the valuable relationships between scientists
과학자들 간의 소중한 관계를 발견해낸다
② emphasizes difficulties in establishing new scientific theories
새로운 과학 이론을 세우는 것의 어려움을 강조한다
③ mixes the various stories of great scientists across the world
전 세계 위대한 과학자들의 다양한 이야기들을 섞는다
④ focuses more on the scientists' work than their personal lives
과학자들의 사생활보다 그들의 공적에 집중한다
✓⑤ reveals only the scientists' success ignoring their processes and errors
과학자들의 과정과 오류는 무시한 채 오로지 그들의 성공만을 드러내 보인다

In school, / there's one curriculum, / one right way to study science, / and one right formula / that spits out the correct answer on a standardized test.
학교에는 / 하나의 교육과정이 있다. / 과학을 공부하는 하나의 올바른 방식, / 그리고 하나의 올바른 공식 / 표준화된 시험의 정답을 내어놓는
Textbooks with grand titles / like *The Principles of Physics* / magically reveal "the principles" in three hundred pages.
대단한 제목을 가진 교과서들은 / *물리학의 원리*와 같은 / 300페이지에 걸쳐 '그 원리들'을 마법처럼 보여 준다.
An authority figure then steps up to the lectern / to feed us "the truth."
그러고 나서 권위자가 강의대로 다가간다. / 우리에게 '진실'을 알려 주기 위해서
As theoretical physicist David Gross explained in his Nobel lecture, / textbooks often ignore the many alternate paths / that people wandered down, / the many false clues they followed, / the many misconceptions they had.
이론 물리학자 David Gross가 자신의 노벨상 수상자 강연에서 설명했듯이, / 교과서들은 종종 그 많은 다른 경로들을 묵살한다. / 사람들이 헤매고 다닌 / 그들이 따랐던 그 많은 잘못된 단서들을 / 그들이 가졌던 그 많은 오해들을
We learn about Newton's "laws" / — as if they arrived / by a grand divine visitation or a stroke of genius / — but not the years / he spent exploring, revising, and changing them.
우리는 뉴턴의 '법칙들'에 대해 배우지만, / 마치 그것들이 도래하는 것처럼 / 대단한 신의 방문이나 한 번의 천재성에 의해 / 여러 해에 대해서는 배우지 않는다. / 그가 그것들을 탐구하고 수정하고 변경하는 데 들인
The laws that Newton failed to establish / — most notably his experiments in alchemy, / which attempted, and spectacularly failed, / to turn lead into gold — / don't make the cut / as part of the one-dimensional story / told in physics classrooms.
뉴턴이 확립하는 데 실패한 법칙들, / 즉 가장 공공연하게는 그의 연금술 실험은 / 시도했으나 엄청나게 실패했던 / 납을 금으로 바꾸기 위해 / 선택되지 못한다. / 일차원적인 이야기의 일부로 / 물리학 수업에서 언급되는
Instead, / our education system / turns the life stories of these scientists / from lead to gold.
대신에, / 우리의 교육 시스템은 / 이런 과학자들의 인생 이야기들을 바꿔 버린다. / 납에서 금으로

학교에는 하나의 교육과정, 과학을 공부하는 하나의 올바른 방식, 표준화된 시험의 정답을 내어놓는 하나의 올바른 공식이 있다. *물리학의 원리*와 같은 대단한 제목을 가진 교과서들은 300페이지에 걸쳐 '그 원리들'을 마법처럼 보여 준다. 그러고 나서 권위자가 우리에게 '진실'을 알려 주기 위해서 강의대로 다가간다. 이론 물리학자 David Gross가 자신의 노벨상 수상자 강연에서 설명했듯이, 교과서들은 종종 사람들이 헤매고 다닌 그 많은 다른 경로들과 그들이 따랐던 그 많은 잘못된 단서들과 그들이 가졌던 그 많은 오해들을 묵살한다. 우리는 뉴턴의 '법칙들'에 대해 마치 그것들이 대단한 신의 방문이나 한 번의 천재성에 의해 도래하는 것처럼 배우지만, 그가 그것들을 탐구하고 수정하고 변경하는 데 들인 여러 해에 대해서는 배우지 않는다. 뉴턴이 확립하는 데 실패한 법칙들, 즉 가장 공공연하게는 납을 금으로 바꾸기 위해 시도했으나 엄청나게 실패했던 그의 연금술 실험은 물리학 수업에서 언급되는 일차원적인 이야기의 일부로 선택되지 못한다. 대신에, 우리의 교육 시스템은 이런 과학자들의 인생 이야기들을 납에서 금으로 바꿔 버린다.

Why? 왜 정답일까?

'~ textbooks often ignore the many alternate paths that people wandered down, the many false clues they followed, the many misconceptions they had.' 이후로 오늘날 과학 교과서는 과학적 법칙 이면에 있는 과학자들의 무수한 실패나 오류를 묵살한 채 과학자들이 마치 '납을 금으로 바꾸기라도 한 듯이' 천재적으로 그 법칙을 발견해 낸 것처럼 묘사한다는 내용이 이어진다. 이를 근거로 볼 때, 과학자들의 인생 이야기가 '납에서 금으로 바뀌어 버렸다'고 언급한 밑줄 친 부분이 의미하는 바로 가장 적절한 것은 ⑤ '과학자들의 과정과 오류는 무시한 채 오로지 그들의 성공만을 드러내 보인다'이다.

- **formula** ⓝ 공식, 제조법
- **standardize** ⓥ 표준화하다, 규격화하다

- reveal ⓥ 드러내다
- alternate ⓐ 대안의
- visitation ⓝ (격식) 방문, 시찰
- establish ⓥ 확립하다
- spectacularly ⓐ 구경거리로, 볼 만하게
- make the cut 목표를 달성하다, 최종 명단에 들다, 성공하다
- emphasize ⓥ 강조하다
- authority figure 권위자
- misconception ⓝ 오해
- stroke of genius 천재성, 신의 한 수
- notably ⓐ 특히, 현저히

구문 풀이

6행 As theoretical physicist David Gross explained in his Nobel lecture,
접속사(~대로, ~듯이)
textbooks often ignore the many alternate paths [that people wandered down],
주어   동사   목적어1
the many false clues [they followed], the many misconceptions [they had].
목적어2   목적어3

---

22 적자생존의 법칙보다는 관계 능력에 좌우되는 성공   정답률 85% | 정답 ③

다음 글의 요지로 가장 적절한 것은?
① 효율적인 업무 배분은 조직의 생산성을 향상시킨다.
② 유연한 사고방식은 원활한 의사소통에 도움이 된다.
✓ 사람들과 잘 어울려 일하는 능력이 성공을 가능하게 한다.
④ 비판적 사고 능력은 정확성을 추구하는 태도에서 출발한다.
⑤ 치열한 경쟁 사회에서 최고의 실력을 갖추는 것이 필수적이다.

The vast majority of companies, schools, and organizations / measure and reward "high performance" / in terms of individual metrics / such as sales numbers, resume accolades, and test scores.
대부분의 회사, 학교, 조직이 / '높은 성과'를 측정하고 보상한다. / 개인의 수치적 관점에서 / 매출, 수상 이력, 시험 성적과 같은
The problem with this approach is / that it is based on a belief / we thought science had fully confirmed: / that we live in a world of "survival of the fittest."
이러한 접근법의 문제는 / 그것이 믿음에 바탕을 두고 있다는 점이다. / 우리가 과학이 완전히 확인해 주었다고 생각하는 / 즉 우리가 '적자생존'의 세상에서 살고 있다는
It teaches us / that those with the best grades, / or the *most* impressive resume, / or the *highest* point score, / will be the ONLY ones to succeed.
그것은 우리에게 가르친다. / 최고의 성적을 가진 사람들이 / 혹은 *가장* 인상적인 이력서, / 혹은 *최상의* 점수를 / 성공할 '유일한' 사람들일 것이라고
The formula is simple: / be better and smarter and more creative than everyone else, / and you will be successful.
이 공식은 간단하다. / 즉, 다른 누구보다 더 잘하고 더 똑똑하고 더 창의적이 되어라 / 그러면 여러분은 성공할 것이다.
But this formula is inaccurate.
그러나 이 공식은 정확하지 않다.
Thanks to new research, / we now know / that achieving our highest potential / is not about survival of the fittest / but survival of the best fit.
새로운 연구 덕분에 / 우리는 이제 안다. / 우리의 최상의 가능성을 성취하는 것이 / 가장 적응하는 사람의 생존이 아니라 / 가장 잘 어울리는 사람의 생존에 관한 것임을
In other words, / success is not just about how creative or smart or driven you are, / but how well you are able to connect with, / contribute to, / and benefit from the ecosystem of people around you.
다시 말해서, / 성공은 단지 여러분이 얼마나 창의적이고, 똑똑하고, 열의가 있는가에 관한 것이 아니라, / 여러분이 얼마나 ~와 잘 관계를 맺고, / ~에 기여하고, / 여러분의 주변에 있는 사람들의 생태계로부터 이익을 얻는지에 관한 것이다.

대부분의 회사, 학교, 조직이 매출, 수상 이력, 시험 성적과 같은 개인의 수치적 관점에서 '높은 성과'를 측정하고 보상한다. 이러한 접근법의 문제는 그것이 우리가 과학이 완전히 확인해 주었다고 생각하는 믿음, 즉 우리가 '적자생존'의 세상에서 살고 있다는 믿음에 바탕을 두고 있다는 점이다. 그것은 우리에게 최고의 성적, *가장* 인상적인 이력서, 혹은 *최상의* 점수를 가진 사람들이 성공할 '유일한' 사람들일 것이라고 가르친다. 이 공식은 간단하다. 즉, 다른 누구보다 더 잘하고 더 똑똑하고 더 창의적이 되면 여러분은 성공할 것이다. 그러나 이 공식은 정확하지 않다. 새로운 연구 덕분에 우리는 이제 최상의 가능성을 성취하는 것이, 가장 잘 적응하는 사람의 생존이 아니라 가장 잘 맞는 사람의 생존에 관한 것임을 안다. 다시 말해서, 성공은 단지 여러분이 얼마나 창의적이고, 똑똑하고, 열의가 있는가에 관한 것이 아니라, 여러분의 주변에 있는 사람들의 생태계와 얼마나 잘 관계를 맺고, 그것에 기여하고, 그로부터 이익을 얻는지에 관한 것이다.

Why? 왜 정답일까?
글 전반부에 걸쳐 적자생존의 법칙과 그에 따른 성과 중심 주의, 경쟁 중심 풍토 등이 언급된 후, 'But this formula is inaccurate.'부터 글의 흐름이 반전된다. 특히 마지막 문장에서 단지 창의적이고 똑똑하고 열의가 있으면 성공하는 것이 아니라, 주변 사람들과 관계를 잘 맺을 수 있어야 성공한다(In other words, success is ~ about ~ how well you are able to connect with, contribute to, and benefit from the ecosystem of people around you.)고 언급하는 것으로 보아, 글의 요지로 가장 적절한 것은 ③ '사람들과 잘 어울려 일하는 능력이 성공을 가능하게 한다.'이다.

- metrics ⓝ 수량적 분석
- survival of the fittest 적자생존
- inaccurate ⓐ 부정확한
- ecosystem ⓝ 생태계
- confirm ⓥ (맞다고) 확인하다
- impressive ⓐ 인상적인
- driven ⓐ 투지가 넘치는, 주도적인

구문 풀이

12행 In other words, success is not just about {how creative or smart or driven you are}, but {how well you are able to connect with, contribute to, and benefit
not just + A
from the ecosystem of people around you}.
but + B : A뿐 아니라 B도(A, B 자리에 간접의문문)

---

23 사람들이 원을 그리며 걷는 이유   정답률 70% | 정답 ②

다음 글의 주제로 가장 적절한 것은?

---

① abilities to construct a mental map for walking – 걷기에 대한 정신적 지도를 구성하는 능력
✓ factors that result in people walking in a circle – 사람이 원을 그리며 걷게 되는 원인
③ reasons why dominance exists in nature – 자연에 우성이 존재하는 이유
④ instincts that help people return home – 사람들이 집으로 돌아갈 수 있도록 도와주는 본능
⑤ solutions to finding the right direction – 올바른 방향을 찾는 데 관한 해법

I was brought up to believe / that if I get lost in a large forest, / I will sooner or later end up where I started.
나는 믿도록 길러졌다. / 만약 내가 넓은 숲에서 길을 잃었다면, / 머지않아 내가 출발했던 곳으로 결국 올 것을
Without knowing it, / people who are lost / will always walk in a circle.
그것을 알지 못한 채, / 길을 잃은 사람들은 / 항상 원을 그리며 걸을 것이다.
In the book *Finding Your Way Without Map or Compass*, / author Harold Gatty confirms / that this is true.
지도나 나침반 없이 길 찾기라는 책에서 / 저자인 Harold Gatty는 확인해 준다 / 이것이 사실임을
We tend to walk in circles for several reasons.
우리는 몇 가지 이유로 원을 그리며 걷는 경향이 있다.
The most important is / that virtually no human has two legs of the exact same length.
가장 중요한 것은 / 실제로 어떤 사람도 정확히 똑같은 길이의 두 다리를 가지지 않는다는 점이다.
One leg is always slightly longer than the other, / and this causes us to turn without even noticing it.
한쪽 다리는 항상 다른 쪽보다 조금 더 길고 / 이는 우리가 심지어 그것을 알아채지 못한 채 돌도록 한다.
In addition, if you are hiking with a backpack on, / the weight of that backpack / will inevitably throw you off balance.
게다가 만약 여러분이 배낭을 메고 도보 여행을 하는 중이라면, / 그 배낭의 무게가 / 여러분을 불가피하게 균형을 잃게 할 것이다.
Our dominant hand factors into the mix too.
우리의 주로 쓰는 손도 이 조합의 한 요소가 된다.
If you are right-handed, / you will have a tendency to turn toward the right.
만약 여러분이 오른손잡이라면 / 여러분은 오른쪽으로 돌려는 경향을 갖고 있을 것이다.
And when you meet an obstacle, / you will subconsciously decide to pass it on the right side.
그리고 여러분이 장애물을 만났을 때 / 여러분은 무의식적으로 그것을 오른쪽으로 지나가겠다고 결정할 것이다.

나는 만약 내가 넓은 숲에서 길을 잃었다면, 머지않아 내가 출발했던 곳으로 결국 올 것을 믿도록 길러졌다. 길을 잃은 사람들은 항상 원을 그리며 걷는데, 이를 알지 못한 채 그렇게 한다. 지도나 나침반 없이 길 찾기라는 책에서 저자인 Harold Gatty는 이것이 사실임을 확인해 준다. 우리는 몇 가지 이유로 원을 그리며 걷는 경향이 있다. 가장 중요한 것은 실제로 어떤 사람도 두 다리 길이가 정확히 똑같지 않다는 점이다. 한쪽 다리는 항상 다른 쪽보다 조금 더 길고 이는 우리가 심지어 그것을 알아채지 못한 채 돌도록 한다. 게다가 만약 여러분이 배낭을 메고 도보 여행을 하는 중이라면, 그 배낭의 무게로 인해 여러분은 불가피하게 균형을 잃게 될 것이다. 우리가 주로 쓰는 손도 이 조합의 한 요소가 된다. 만약 여러분이 오른손잡이라면 여러분은 오른쪽으로 돌려는 경향을 갖고 있을 것이다. 그리고 여러분이 장애물을 만났을 때 여러분은 무의식적으로 그것을 오른쪽으로 지나가겠다고 결정할 것이다.

Why? 왜 정답일까?
'We tend to walk in circles for several reasons.' 이후로 사람은 두 다리의 길이가 같지 않고 주로 쓰는 손 쪽으로 움직여가는 경향을 갖고 있어 원을 그리며 걷게 된다는 내용이 제시되고 있다. 따라서 글의 주제로 가장 적절한 것은 ② '사람이 원을 그리며 걷게 되는 원인'이다.

- end up 결국 ~이다
- virtually ⓐ 거의, 사실상
- weight ⓝ 무게 ⓥ 무게가 ~이다
- factor into ~을 요인으로 포함하다
- subconsciously ⓐ 무의식적으로
- instinct ⓝ 본능
- compass ⓝ 나침반
- slightly ⓐ 약간
- inevitably ⓐ 불가피하게
- obstacle ⓝ 장애물
- dominance ⓝ (유전적) 우성, 우세함, 지배

구문 풀이

8행 In addition, if you are hiking with a backpack on, the weight of that
조건 접속사   현재시제(진행)
backpack will inevitably throw you off balance.
미래시제

---

24 분명한 언어 사용의 중요성   정답률 64% | 정답 ②

다음 글의 제목으로 가장 적절한 것은?
① Earn Trust with Reliable Goods Rather Than with Words!
말보다는 믿을 수 있는 상품으로 신뢰를 얻으라!
✓ Linguistic Precision: A Key to Successful Economic Transactions
언어적 정확성: 성공적인 경제 거래의 열쇠
③ Difficulties in Overcoming Language Barriers and Distrust in Trade
무역에서 언어 장벽과 불신을 극복하는 데 있어서의 어려움
④ The More the Economy Grows, the More Complex the World Gets
경제가 성장할수록 세계는 더 복잡해진다
⑤ Excessive Confidence: The Biggest Reason for Miscommunication
지나친 신뢰: 잘못된 의사소통의 가장 큰 이유

In government, / in law, / in culture, / and in routine everyday interaction beyond family and immediate neighbours, / a widely understood and clearly formulated language / is a great aid to mutual confidence.
정치 체제에서, / 법에서, / 문화에서, / 그리고 가족 및 가까운 이웃을 넘어서는 일상적인 매일의 상호작용에서, / 폭넓게 이해되고 확실하게 표현된 언어가 / 상호 신뢰에 굉장한 도움이 된다.
When dealing with property, / with contracts, / or even just with the routine exchange of goods and services, / concepts and descriptions need to be as precise and unambiguous as possible, / otherwise misunderstandings will arise.
재산을 다룰 때, / 계약서를 / 혹은 심지어 단순히 상품과 서비스의 일상적인 교환을 / 개념과 설명은 가능한 한 정확하고 모호하지 않아야 하며, / 그렇지 않으면 오해가 생길 것이다.
If full communication with a potential counterparty in a deal / is not possible, / then uncertainty and probably a measure of distrust / will remain.
만약 거래에서 잠재적 상대방과의 완전한 의사소통이 / 가능하지 않다면 / 불확실성과 아마 어느 정도의 불신이 / 남아있을 것이다.
As economic life became more complex in the later Middle Ages, / the need for fuller and more precise communication / was accentuated.
경제 생활이 중세 시대 후반에 더 복잡해지면서 / 더욱 완전하고 더욱 정확한 의사소통에 대한 필요가 / 강조되었다.
A shared language / facilitated clarification and possibly settlement of any disputes.
공유된 언어는 / 해명과 아마도 어떤 분쟁의 해결을 용이하게 했다.

[문제편 p.182]

In international trade also / the use of a precise and well-formulated language / aided the process of translation.
국제무역에서도 또한 / 정확하고 잘 표현된 언어의 사용은 / 통역의 과정을 도왔다.
The Silk Road could only function at all / because translators were always available at interchange points.
실크로드는 그나마 기능할 수 있었다. / 교환 지점에서 통역가들이 항상 이용 가능했기 때문에

정치 체제, 법, 문화, 그리고 가족 및 가까운 이웃을 넘어서는 일상적인 매일의 상호작용에서, 폭넓게 이해되고 확실하게 표현된 언어가 상호 신뢰에 굉장한 도움이 된다. 재산이나 계약서, 심지어 단순히 상품과 서비스의 일상적인 교환을 다룰 때 개념과 설명은 가능한 한 정확하고 모호하지 않아야 하며, 그렇지 않으면 오해가 생길 것이다. 만약 거래에서 잠재적 상대방과의 완전한 의사소통이 가능하지 않다면 불확실성과 아마도 어느 정도의 불신이 남아있을 것이다. 경제 생활이 중세 시대 후반에 더 복잡해지면서 더욱 완전하고 더욱 정확한 의사소통에 대한 필요가 강조되었다. 공유된 언어는 해명과 아마도 어떤 분쟁의 해결을 용이하게 했다. 국제무역에서도 또한 정확하고 잘 표현된 언어의 사용은 통역의 과정을 도왔다. 실크로드는 교환 지점에서 통역가들이 항상 이용 가능했기 때문에 그나마 기능할 수 있었다.

Why? 왜 정답일까?
첫 문장에서 명확한 언어 사용이 상호 신뢰를 구축하는 데 도움이 된다고 언급된 데 이어, 중반 이후에 특히 거래 등 경제 상황에서 명확하고 완전한 의사소통이 중요하게 여겨진다는 내용이 나온다. 따라서 글의 제목으로 가장 적절한 것은 ② '언어적 정확성: 성공적인 경제 거래의 열쇠'이다.

- **immediate** ⓐ 가까운, 당면한, 즉각적인
- **mutual** ⓐ 상호의
- **contract** ⓝ 계약서
- **unambiguous** ⓐ 모호하지 않은
- **counterparty** ⓝ 한쪽 당사자
- **facilitate** ⓥ 용이하게 하다
- **dispute** ⓝ 논쟁
- **excessive** ⓐ 지나친, 과도한
- **formulate** ⓥ 만들어내다, 표현하다
- **confidence** ⓝ 신뢰, 자신감
- **precise** ⓐ 정확한
- **arise** ⓥ 발생하다
- **uncertainty** ⓝ 불확실성
- **clarification** ⓝ 해명, 설명
- **transaction** ⓝ 거래, 매매

구문 풀이

4행 When dealing with property, with contracts, or even just with the routine
접속사 / 분사구문 / 전명구1 / 전명구2 / 전명구3
exchange of goods and services, concepts and descriptions need to be
주어1 / 동사구1
as precise and unambiguous as possible, otherwise misunderstandings
「as + 원급 + as possible : 가능한 한 ~한/하게」 / 그렇지 않으면 / 주어2
will arise.
동사구2(자동사)

---

25 친환경 통근 수단별 사용자 비율 정답률 76% | 정답 ③

다음 도표의 내용과 일치하지 <u>않는</u> 것은?

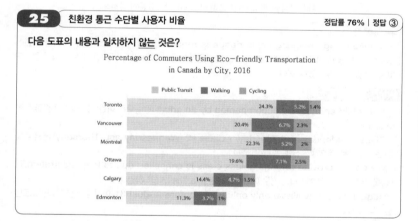

Percentage of Commuters Using Eco-friendly Transportation in Canada by City, 2016

City	Public Transit	Walking	Cycling
Toronto	24.3%	5.2%	1.4%
Vancouver	20.4%	6.7%	2.3%
Montréal	22.3%	5.2%	2%
Ottawa	19.6%	7.1%	2.5%
Calgary	14.4%	4.7%	1.5%
Edmonton	11.3%	3.7%	1%

The above graph shows the percentage of commuters / using eco-friendly transportation to get to work / in six large cities in Canada in 2016.
위 도표는 통근자의 비율을 보여 준다. / 출근 시 친환경 교통수단을 사용한 / 2016년에 캐나다의 6개 대도시에서
① For all six given cities, / the percentage of people / who commuted by public transit / was the highest, / while the percentage of people / who commuted by cycling / was the lowest.
주어진 6개의 도시 모두에서 / 사람들의 비율이 / 대중교통으로 통근한 / 가장 높았다. / 사람들의 비율이 / 자전거를 타고 통근한 / 가장 낮았던 반면에
② The percentages of people / who commuted by walking / were the same in both Toronto and Montreal / even though the percentages of people / who commuted by public transit / in those two cities / were different.
사람들의 비율은 / 걸어서 통근한 / 토론토와 몬트리올에서 서로 같았다. / 비록 사람들의 비율이 / 대중교통으로 통근한 / 그 두 도시의 / 달랐지만
③ In Vancouver, / the percentage of people / who commuted by public transit / was over ten times higher / than that of people who commuted by cycling.
밴쿠버에서 / 사람들의 비율이 / 대중교통으로 통근한 / 10배 이상 더 높았다. / 자전거를 타고 통근한 사람들의 비율보다
④ Even though Ottawa ranked fourth / in the percentage of people / who commuted by public transit, / this city was in first place / in the percentage of people / who commuted by walking or cycling.
비록 오타와는 4위를 차지했으나 / 사람들의 비율에서 / 대중교통으로 통근한 / 이 도시는 1위를 했다. / 사람들의 비율에서는 / 걷거나 자전거를 타고 통근한
⑤ Compared with Calgary, / Edmonton recorded lower percentages / for all three given types of eco-friendly transportation.
캘거리와 비교하면, / 에드먼턴이 더 낮은 비율을 기록했다. / 주어진 세 가지 유형의 친환경 교통수단 모두에서

위 도표는 2016년에 캐나다의 6개 대도시에서 출근시 친환경 교통수단을 사용한 통근자의 비율을 보여 준다. ① 주어진 6개의 도시 모두에서 대중교통으로 통근한 사람들의 비율이 가장 높았던 반면 자전거를 타고 통근한 사람들의 비율이 가장 낮았다. ② 토론토와 몬트리올에서, 비록 대중교통으로 통근한 사람들의 비율은 달랐지만 걸어서 통근한 사람들의 비율은 서로 같았다. ③ 밴쿠버에서 대중교통으로 통근한 사람들의 비율이 자전거를 타고 통근한 사람들의 비율보다 10배 이상 더 높았다. ④ 비록 오타와는 대중교통으로 통근한 사람들의 비율에서 4위를 차지했으나 걷거나 자전거를 타고 통근한 사람들의 비율에서는 1위를 했다.

---

⑤ 캘거리와 비교하면, 에드먼턴이 주어진 세 가지 유형의 친환경 교통수단 모두에서 더 낮은 비율을 기록했다.

Why? 왜 정답일까?
도표에 따르면 밴쿠버의 대중교통 통근자 비율(20.4%)은 자전거 통근자 비율(2.3%)의 10배에 미치지 못한다. 따라서 도표와 일치하지 않는 것은 ③이다.

- **transportation** ⓝ 교통수단
- **public transit** 대중교통

---

26 Alice Coachman의 생애 정답률 92% | 정답 ②

Alice Coachman에 관한 다음 글의 내용과 일치하지 <u>않는</u> 것은?
① 집 근처에서 맨발로 달리며 훈련했다.
☑ 육상 경기에서의 재능을 고등학교 때부터 보였다.
③ 런던 올림픽에서 높이뛰기 올림픽 기록과 미국 기록을 세웠다.
④ 흑인 여성 최초로 올림픽 금메달리스트가 되었다.
⑤ 9개의 명예의 전당에 올랐다.

Alice Coachman was born in 1923, / in Albany, Georgia, U.S.A.
Alice Coachman은 1923년 태어났다. / 미국 Georgia의 Albany에서
Since she was unable to access athletic training facilities / because of the racism of the time, / she trained / using what was available to her, / 「running barefoot along the dirt roads near her home」 / and using homemade equipment to practice her jumping. ①의근거 일치
그녀는 운동 훈련 시설을 이용할 수 없었기 때문에 / 당시의 인종 차별 때문에 / 그녀는 훈련했다. / 자신에게 이용 가능한 것을 사용하여 / 자신의 집 근처 비포장도로를 따라 맨발로 달리고, / 점프를 연습하기 위해 집에서 만든 장비를 사용하면서
「Her talent in track and field / was noticeable as early as elementary school.」 ②의근거 불일치
육상 경기에서의 그녀의 재능은 / 일찍이 초등학교 때 눈에 띄었다.
Coachman kept practicing hard / and gained attention with her achievements in several competitions / during her time in high school and college.
Coachman은 계속 열심히 연습하여 / 여러 대회에서의 자신의 성취로 주목을 받았다. / 고등학교와 대학교 시절 동안
「In the 1948 London Olympics, / Coachman competed in the high jump, / reaching 5 feet, 6.5 inches, / setting both an Olympic and an American record.」 ③의근거 일치
1948년 런던 올림픽에서 / Coachman은 높이뛰기에 출전해 / 5피트 6.5인치에 도달하여 / 올림픽과 미국 기록을 둘 다 세웠다.
「This accomplishment made her the first black woman / to win an Olympic gold medal.」 ④의근거 일치
이 성과는 그녀를 최초의 흑인 여성으로 만들었다. / 올림픽 금메달을 딴
「She is in nine different Halls of Fame, / including the U.S. Olympic Hall of Fame.」 ⑤의근거 일치
그녀는 9개의 각기 다른 명예의 전당에 올랐다. / 미국 올림픽 명예의 전당을 포함하여
Coachman died in 2014, at the age of 90 in Georgia / after she had dedicated her life to education.
Coachman은 2014년에 Georgia에서 90세의 나이에 사망했다. / 그녀의 일생을 교육에 바친 후

Alice Coachman은 1923년 미국 Georgia의 Albany에서 태어났다. 당시의 인종 차별 때문에 운동 훈련 시설을 이용할 수 없었기 때문에, 그녀는 자신에게 이용 가능한 것을 사용하여, 자신의 집 근처 비포장도로를 따라 맨발로 달리고, 점프를 연습하기 위해 집에서 만든 장비를 사용하면서 훈련했다. 육상 경기에서의 그녀의 재능은 일찍이 초등학교 때 눈에 띄었다. Coachman은 계속 열심히 연습하여 고등학교와 대학교 시절 동안 여러 대회에서의 자신의 성취로 주목을 받았다. 1948년 런던 올림픽에서 Coachman은 높이뛰기에 출전해 5피트 6.5인치에 도달하여 올림픽과 미국 기록을 둘 다 세웠다. 이 성과로 그녀는 올림픽 금메달을 딴 최초의 흑인 여성이 되었다. 그녀는 미국 올림픽 명예의 전당을 포함하여, 9개의 각기 다른 명예의 전당에 올랐다. Coachman은 일생을 교육에 바친 후 2014년에 Georgia에서 90세의 나이에 사망했다.

Why? 왜 정답일까?
'Her talent in track and field was noticeable as early as elementary school.'에서 Alice Coachman은 초등학교 시절부터 육상 경기에 대한 재능을 보였다고 하므로, 내용과 일치하지 않는 것은 ② '육상 경기에서의 재능을 고등학교 때부터 보였다.'이다.

Why? 왜 오답일까?
① '~ she trained ~ running barefoot along the dirt roads near her home ~'의 내용과 일치한다.
③ 'In the 1948 London Olympics, Coachman competed in the high jump, reaching 5 feet, 6.5 inches, setting both an Olympic and an American record.'의 내용과 일치한다.
④ 'This accomplishment made her the first black woman to win an Olympic gold medal.'의 내용과 일치한다.
⑤ 'She is in nine different Halls of Fame, ~'의 내용과 일치한다.

- **athletic** ⓐ 운동의, 육상의
- **racism** ⓝ 인종 차별주의
- **noticeable** ⓐ 눈에 띄는, 두드러지는
- **dedicate A to B** A를 B에 바치다
- **facility** ⓝ 시설
- **barefoot** ⓐⓓ 맨발로
- **accomplishment** ⓝ 성취

구문 풀이

2행 Since she was unable to access athletic training facilities because of the
접속사(~ 때문에) / 전치사(~ 때문에)
racism of the time, she trained using what was available to her, running barefoot
분사구문1 ┗관계대명사(~것)
along the dirt roads near her home and using homemade equipment to practice
분사구문3 / 목적(~하기 위해)
her jumping.

---

27 쓰레기 없는 날 행사 안내 정답률 92% | 정답 ⑤

Zero Waste Day 2020에 관한 다음 안내문의 내용과 일치하지 <u>않는</u> 것은?
① 우천 시에도 행사가 예정대로 진행된다.
② 의류와 신발은 건조된 상태의 것만 받는다.
③ 해지거나 찢어진 침구류도 기부가 가능하다.
④ 전자 기기에 저장된 모든 정보는 삭제되어야 한다.
☑ 기부 물품 접수가 거절되면 현장에서 버릴 수 있다.

19회

Zero Waste Day 2020
2020 쓰레기 없는 날
Zero Waste Day (ZWD) 2020 is an opportunity for you / to clean out your attic and donate items for reuse.
2020 쓰레기 없는 날(ZWD)은 여러분에 있어 기회입니다. / 다락방을 치워 재사용을 위한 물품을 기부할
When & Where: / First Saturday in November (November 7, 2020), / 9:00 a.m. – 12:00 p.m. 「(rain or shine)」 ①의근거 일치
언제 그리고 어디서: / 11월 첫 번째 토요일 (2020년 11월 7일), / 오전 9시부터 오후 12시까지 (날씨와 상관없이)
At 400 Union Square
400 Union Square에서
Accepted Items: / Wearable clothes / shoes
접수 물품: / 입을 수 있는 의류 / 신발
「All sizes of clothes and shoes MUST BE DRY.」 ②의근거 일치
모든 치수의 의류와 신발은 '건조된 상태여야만 합니다.'
Bedding (pillows, blankets, or mattress covers)
침구류(베개, 담요, 또는 매트리스 커버)
「Worn or torn is fine, / but no oil stains are allowed.」 ③의근거 일치
헤지거나 찢어져도 괜찮지만 / 기름 얼룩은 절대 허용되지 않습니다.
Electronics (computers, laptops, or cell phones)
전자 기기(컴퓨터, 노트북, 또는 휴대폰)
「All data on the device must be deleted.」 ④의근거 일치
기기에 저장된 모든 정보는 삭제되어야 합니다.
Note: / 「If an item isn't accepted, / please be prepared to take it home.
주의 사항: / 만약 물품이 접수되지 않으면 / 그것을 집으로 가져갈 준비를 해 오십시오.
There is no place / for you to drop off garbage.」 ⑤의근거 불일치
장소가 없습니다. / 여러분이 쓰레기를 버릴
ZWD is open to ALL!
ZWD는 '모두'에게 열려 있습니다!
For more information, please visit www.zwd.org.
더 많은 정보를 원하시면, www.zwd.org를 방문해 주십시오.

2020 쓰레기 없는 날

2020 쓰레기 없는 날(ZWD)은 여러분이 다락방을 치워 재사용을 위한 물품을 기부할 기회입니다.

시간 & 장소:
11월 첫 번째 토요일 (2020년 11월 7일),
오전 9시부터 오후 12시까지 (날씨와 상관없이)
400 Union Square에서

접수 물품:
• 입을 수 있는 의류 / 신발
  모든 치수의 의류와 신발은 '건조된 상태여야만 합니다.'
• 침구류(베개, 담요, 매트리스 커버)
  헤지거나 찢어져도 괜찮지만 기름 얼룩은 절대 허용되지 않습니다.
• 전자 기기(컴퓨터, 노트북, 휴대폰)
  기기에 저장된 모든 정보는 삭제되어야 합니다.

주의 사항: 만약 물품이 접수되지 않으면 그것을 집으로 가져갈 준비를 해 오십시오. 쓰레기를 버릴 장소가 없습니다.

ZWD는 '모두'에게 열려 있습니다!
더 많은 정보를 원하시면, www.zwd.org를 방문해 주십시오.

Why? 왜 정답일까?
'If an item isn't accepted, please be prepared to take it home. There is no place for you to drop off garbage.'에서 현장에 쓰레기를 버릴 공간이 없으므로 접수가 거절되었을 경우 물품을 도로 가져갈 수 있도록 준비해 달라고 했다. 따라서 안내문의 내용과 일치하지 않는 것은 ⑤ '기부 물품 접수가 거절되면 현장에서 버릴 수 있다.'이다.

Why? 왜 오답일까?
① '(rain or shine)'의 내용과 일치한다.
② 'All sizes of clothes and shoes MUST BE DRY.'의 내용과 일치한다.
③ 'Worn or torn is fine, but no oil stains are allowed.'의 내용과 일치한다.
④ 'All data on the device must be deleted.'의 내용과 일치한다.

• attic ⑪ 다락방
• rain or shine 날씨에 상관없이
• wear(-wore-worn) ⓥ 닳다, 마모되다

---

28 수화 수업 안내 정답률 87% | 정답 ③

Sign Language Class에 관한 다음 안내문의 내용과 일치하는 것은?
① 어린이들도 어른 동반 없이 참여할 수 있다.
② 수업은 주 3일 진행된다.
③ 수화 경험이 없어도 참여할 수 있는 수업이 있다. ✔
④ 환불은 예외 없이 불가능하다.
⑤ 현장 등록이 가능하다.

Sign Language Class
수화 수업
If you've ever considered studying sign language, / our class is one of the best ways to do it!
만약 여러분이 수화를 배우는 것을 고려한 적이 있다면, / 우리 수업이 그것을 할 가장 좋은 방법 중 하나입니다!
「The class is open to people of all ages, / but all children must be accompanied by an adult.」 ①의근거 불일치
수업은 모든 연령대의 사람들에게 열려 있으나 / 모든 어린이들은 어른의 동반이 필요합니다.
Class Schedule
수업 일정
Where: / Coorparoo Community Center
어디: / Coorparoo 주민센터
When: / September – October, 2020 / (7:00 p.m. – 9:00 p.m.)

언제: / 2020년 9월에서 10월까지 / (오후 7시부터 오후 9시까지)
Levels
수준
Class #1 (Monday and Tuesday), ②의근거 불일치
수업 #1 (월요일, 화요일)
「No previous sign language experience is required.」 ③의근거 일치
이전의 수화 경험이 필요 없습니다.
Class #2 (Wednesday and Thursday),
수업 #2 (수요일, 목요일)
Knowledge of at least 1,000 signs / is required.
최소 1,000개의 수화 동작 지식이 / 필요합니다.
Note
주의 사항
Tuition is $100.
수업료는 $100입니다.
「We do not provide refunds / unless class is cancelled due to low registration.」 ④의근거 불일치
우리는 환불을 제공하지 않습니다. / 저조한 등록으로 수업이 취소되지 않는 한
「Registration is available only online and before August 31.」 ⑤의근거 불일치
등록은 온라인으로만 8월 31일 전에 가능합니다.
Visit our website at www.CRsignlgs.com.
우리 웹사이트 www.CRsignlgs.com을 방문하십시오.

수화 수업

만약 여러분이 수화를 배우는 것을 고려한 적이 있다면, 우리 수업이 그것을 할 가장 좋은 방법 중 하나입니다! 수업은 모든 연령대의 사람들에게 열려 있으나 모든 어린이들은 어른의 동반이 필요합니다.

수업 일정
• 어디: Coorparoo 주민센터
• 언제: 2020년 9월에서 10월까지
  (오후 7시부터 오후 9시까지)

수준
• 수업 #1 (월요일, 화요일)
  – 이전의 수화 경험이 필요 없습니다.
• 수업 #2 (수요일, 목요일)
  – 최소 1,000개의 수화 동작 지식이 필요합니다.

주의 사항
• 수업료는 $100입니다.
• 우리는 저조한 등록으로 수업이 취소되지 않는 한 환불을 제공하지 않습니다.
• 등록은 온라인으로만 8월 31일 전에 가능합니다.
  우리 웹사이트 www.CRsignlgs.com을 방문하십시오.

Why? 왜 정답일까?
'No previous sign language experience is required.'에서 수업 #1의 경우 수화를 이전에 경험해보지 않았어도 참여할 수 있다고 하므로, 안내문의 내용과 일치하는 것은 ③ '수화 경험이 없어도 참여할 수 있는 수업이 있다.'이다.

Why? 왜 오답일까?
① '~ all children must be accompanied by an adult.'에서 모든 어린이는 필히 어른과 동반 참여해야 한다고 하였다.
② 'Class #1 (Monday and Tuesday) / Class #2 (Wednesday and Thursday)'에서 수화 수업은 수준별로 주 2일씩 진행된다고 하였다.
④ 'We do not provide refunds unless class is cancelled due to low registration.'에서 등록 저조로 수업이 취소되는 경우 예외적으로 환불이 가능하다고 하였다.
⑤ 'Registration is available only online and before August 31.'에서 등록은 온라인으로만 가능하다고 하였다.

• sign language 수화, 수어
• previous ⓐ 이전의
• accompany ⓥ 동반하다
• registration ⑪ 등록

★★★ 등급을 가르는 문제!
29 곤충의 몸 구성 정답률 46% | 정답 ③

다음 글의 밑줄 친 부분 중, 어법상 틀린 것은? [3점]

One of the keys to insects' successful survival in the open air / ① lies in their outer covering / — a hard waxy layer / that helps prevent their tiny bodies from dehydrating.
야외에서 곤충의 성공적인 생존의 비결 중 하나는 / 그들의 외피에 있다. / 단단한 밀랍 같은 층인 / 그들의 작은 몸이 탈수되지 않도록
To take oxygen from the air, / they use narrow breathing holes in the body-segments, / which take in air ② passively / and can be opened and closed as needed.
공기로부터 산소를 흡수하기 위해 / 그들은 몸의 마디에 있는 좁은 호흡구들을 사용하는데, / 이들은 공기를 수동적으로 흡입하고 / 필요할 때 열리고 닫힐 수 있다.
Instead of blood ③ contained in vessels, / they have free-flowing hemolymph, / which helps keep their bodies rigid, / aids movement, / and assists the transportation of nutrients and waste materials / to the appropriate parts of the body.
혈관에 담긴 피 대신 / 그들은 자유롭게 흐르는 혈림프를 갖고 있는데, / 이는 그들의 몸이 단단하게 유지되도록 돕고 / 움직임을 거들고 / 영양분과 노폐물이 이동하는 것을 도와준다. / 몸의 적절한 부위로
The nervous system is modular — / in a sense, / each of the body segments / has ④ its own individual and autonomous brain / — and some other body systems show a similar modularization.
신경 체계가 모듈식으로 되어 있는데, / 어떤 의미에서는 / 몸의 각 마디가 / 그 자체의 개별적이고 자율적인 뇌를 갖고 있으며, / 몇몇 다른 몸의 체계가 유사한 모듈화를 보여 준다.
These are just a few of the many ways / ⑤ in which insect bodies are structured and function / completely differently from our own.
이것들은 많은 방식들 중 몇 가지일 뿐이다. / 곤충의 몸이 구조화되어 있고 기능하는 / 우리의 것과는 완전히 다르게

야외에서 곤충의 성공적인 생존의 비결 중 하나는 그들의 작은 몸이 탈수되지 않도록 돕는 단단한 밀랍 같은 층인 외피에 있다. 그들은 공기로부터 산소를 흡수하기 위해 몸의 마디에 있는 좁은 호흡구들을 사용하는데, 이들은 공기를 수동적으로 흡입하고 필요할 때 열리고 닫힐 수 있고

닫힐 수 있다. 혈관에 담긴 피 대신 그들은 자유롭게 흐르는 혈림프를 갖고 있는데, 이는 그들의 몸이 단단하게 유지되도록 돕고 움직임을 거들고 영양분과 노폐물이 몸의 적절한 부위로 이동하는 것을 도와준다. 신경 체계가 모듈식으로 되어 있는데, 어떤 의미에서는 몸의 각 마디가 그 자체의 개별적이고 자율적인 뇌를 갖고 있으며, 몇몇 다른 몸의 체계가 유사한 모듈화를 보여 준다. 이것들은 곤충의 몸이 우리의 것과는 완전히 다르게 구조화되어 있고 기능하는 많은 방식들 중 몇 가지일 뿐이다.

Why? 왜 정답일까?

분사의 꾸밈을 받는 명사 blood가 혈관 속에 '포함되는' 대상이므로, 현재분사 containing 대신 과거분사 contained를 사용해야 한다. 어법상 틀린 것은 ③이다.

Why? 왜 오답일까?

① 'one of the + 복수 명사'가 주어이므로 단수 동사인 lies가 바르게 쓰였다.
② 관계절의 동사인 take in을 꾸미기 위해 부사인 passively가 바르게 쓰였다.
④ 단수 취급하는 'each of the + 복수 명사'의 소유격을 나타내기 위해 단수 대명사 its가 바르게 쓰였다.
⑤ 관계절에 are structured라는 수동태 동사와 자동사 function을 포함한 완전한 구조가 나온다. 따라서 관계부사와 마찬가지로 뒤에 완전한 절을 수반하는 '전치사 + 관계대명사' 형태의 in which가 바르게 쓰였다.

- **covering** ⓝ 외피, 피복
- **segment** ⓝ (동물의) 몸의 마디
- **rigid** ⓐ 단단한, 엄격한
- **appropriate** ⓐ 적절한
- **dehydrate** ⓥ 탈수 상태가 되다, 건조시키다
- **passively** ⓐd 수동적으로
- **vessel** ⓝ 혈관
- **nutrient** ⓝ 영양분
- **autonomous** ⓐ 자율적인

구문 풀이

1행 One of the keys to insects' successful survival in the open air lies in their
「one of the + 복수 명사」: ~ 중 하나 / 동사(단수)
outer covering — a hard waxy layer [that helps prevent their tiny bodies from
동격(= their ~ covering) / 주격 관·대 / 「help + 원형부정사」: ~하는 것을 돕다
dehydrating].

★★ 문제 해결 꿀~팁 ★★

▶ 많이 틀린 이유는?
② '형용사 vs. 부사', ④ '대명사의 수 일치', ⑤ '전치사 + 관계대명사' 등 빈출 포인트로 구성된 어법 문제이다. 특히 ⑤의 경우 뒤에 나오는 문장 구조를 잘 파악해야 한다. '전치사 + 관계대명사'는 관계부사와 기능상 같아서 뒤에 완전한 절이 연결되어야 한다.

▶ 문제 해결 방법은?
③ '현재분사 vs. 과거분사'는 분사가 꾸미거나 보충 설명하는 명사가 분사의 행위 주체인지 아니면 행위 대상인지를 구별해야 한다. 여기서는 분사의 수식을 받는 blood가 혈관에 무엇인가를 '포함시키는' 주체가 아니라 혈관에 '담기는' 대상이므로 과거분사를 써야 한다.

30 | 건축에서의 디자인과 실용성 | 정답률 53% | 정답 ⑤

(A), (B), (C)의 각 네모 안에서 문맥에 맞는 낱말로 가장 적절한 것은?

	(A)		(B)		(C)
①	relevant 관련 있다		distinction 구분		shape 형성한다
②	relevant 관련 있다		connection 연결		overlook 간과한다
③	irrelevant 무관하다		distinction 구분		overlook 간과한다
④	irrelevant 무관하다		connection 연결		overlook 간과한다
✓⑤	irrelevant 무관하다		distinction 구분		shape 형성한다

On projects in the built environment, / people consider safety and functionality nonnegotiable.
건축 환경에서의 설계에 대해 / 사람들은 안전성과 기능성은 협상의 여지가 없다고 여긴다.

But the aesthetics of a new project / — how it is *designed* — / is too often considered (A) irrelevant.
하지만 새로운 설계의 미학은 / 어떻게 그것이 *디자인*되어 있는지와 같은 / 너무 종종 무관하다고 여겨진다.

The question of how its design *affects* human beings / is rarely asked.
어떻게 그것의 디자인이 인간에게 *영향을 미치는지*에 대한 질문은 / 거의 하지 않는다.

People think / that design makes something highfalutin, called architecture, / and that architecture differs from building, / just as surely as the Washington National Cathedral differs from the local community church.
사람들은 생각한다 / 디자인이 (미학적) 건축물이라고 불리는, 허세를 부리는 것을 만들어 낸다고 / 그리고 그 건축물은 (일반적) 건축물과 다르다고 생각한다. / 워싱턴 국립 대성당이 지역 사회 교회와는 다른 것과 마찬가지로 분명하게

This (B) distinction between architecture and building / — or more generally, between design and utility — / couldn't be more wrong.
(미학적) 건축물과 (일반적) 건축물 사이의 구분은 / 더 일반적으로는 디자인과 실용성 사이의 / 더할 나위 없이 잘못된 것이다.

More and more we are learning / that the design of all our built environments / matters so profoundly / that safety and functionality must not be our only urgent priorities.
우리는 더욱더 알아가고 있다. / 우리의 모든 건축 환경의 디자인이 / 너무나도 대단히 중요해서 / 안전성과 기능성이 우리의 유일한 시급한 우선순위여서는 안 된다는 것을

All kinds of design elements influence people's experiences, / not only of the environment but also of themselves.
모든 종류의 디자인 요소는 사람들의 경험에 영향을 미친다. / 환경뿐 아니라 자신에 대한

They (C) shape our cognitions, emotions, and actions, / and even our well-being.
그것들은 우리의 인지, 감정, 그리고 행동을 형성한다. / 그리고 심지어 우리의 행복까지

They actually help constitute our very sense of identity.
그것들은 실제로 우리의 정체성까지 만들어 내도록 돕는다.

건축 환경에서의 설계에 대해 사람들은 안전성과 기능성은 협상의 여지가 없다고 여긴다. 하지만 어떻게 그것이 *디자인*되어 있는지와 같은 새로운 설계의 미학은 너무 종종 (A) 무관하다고 여겨진다. 어떻게 그것의 디자인이 인간에게 *영향을 미치는지*에 대한 질문은 거의 하지 않는다. 사람들은 디자인이 (미학적) 건축물이라고 불리는, 허세를 부리는 것을 만들어 낸다고 생각하며, 워싱턴 국립 대성당이 지역 사회 교회와는 다른 것과 마찬가지로 분명하게 (미학적) 건축물은 (일반적) 건축물과 다르다고 생각한다. (미학적) 건축물과 (일반적) 건축물,

---

더 일반적으로는 디자인과 실용성 사이의 이러한 (B) 구분은 더할 나위 없이 잘못된 것이다. 우리의 모든 건축 환경의 디자인이 너무나도 대단히 중요해서 안전성과 기능성만이 우리의 시급한 우선순위여서는 안 된다는 것을 우리는 더욱더 알아가고 있다. 모든 종류의 디자인 요소들은 환경뿐 아니라 자신에 대한 사람들의 경험에도 영향을 미친다. 그것들은 우리의 인지, 감정, 행동, 심지어 행복까지 (C) 형성한다. 그것들은 실제로 우리의 정체성까지 만들어 내도록 돕는다.

Why? 왜 정답일까?

(A) 'The question of how its design *affects* human beings is rarely asked.'에서 건물의 미학적 디자인이 어떻게 인간에게 영향을 미치는지에 관해서는 거의 질문이 제기되지 않는다고 언급하고 있다. 이를 토대로, 사람들은 건물의 안전성과 기능성에 대해서는 중요하게 생각하면서도 디자인은 '별 상관이 없다'고 여기고 있다는 내용을 추론할 수 있다. 따라서 (A)에는 irrelevant가 적절하다.
(B) 'People think ~ that architecture differs from building, ~'에서 사람들은 보통 디자인적 고려가 들어간 '건축물'이 일반 '빌딩'과는 다르다고 생각하는 경향이 있다고 언급한다. 이를 토대로, 건물의 디자인과 실용성에 대해서 일반적으로 '구분'이 이루어지고 있다는 내용을 유추할 수 있다. 따라서 (B)에는 distinction이 적절하다.
(C) 'All kinds of design elements influence people's experiences, not only of the environment but also of themselves.'에서 모든 디자인적 요소는 환경뿐 아니라 자신에 대한 사람들의 경험에도 영향을 미친다고 언급한다. 이를 근거로 할 때, 디자인적 요소는 사람들의 인지, 감정, 행동, 심지어 행동에도 두루 영향을 미친다는 의미가 되도록 (C)에는 shape이 들어가야 한다. 따라서 (A), (B), (C)의 각 네모 안에서 문맥에 맞는 낱말로 가장 적절한 것은 ⑤ 'A) 무관하다 – (B) 구분 – (C) 형성한다'이다.

- **functionality** ⓝ 기능성
- **irrelevant** ⓐ 무관한
- **architecture** ⓝ 건축(물)
- **profoundly** ⓐd 완전히, 깊이
- **shape** ⓥ 형성하다, 영향을 미치다
- **constitute** ⓥ 구성하다
- **nonnegotiable** ⓐ 협상의 여지가 없는
- **aesthetics** ⓝ 미학
- **distinction** ⓝ 구분
- **overlook** ⓥ 간과하다
- **cognition** ⓝ 인지

구문 풀이

10행 More and more we are learning that the design of all our built environments
「비교급 + and + 비교급: 점점 더 ~한/하게」 / 접속사(~것) / 주어 / 동사 / 주어
matters so profoundly that safety and functionality must not be our only urgent
동사 / 「so ~ that …: 너무 ~해서 …하다」
priorities.

★★★ 등급을 가르는 문제!

31 | 생명체의 출현으로 인한 지구의 대기 변화 | 정답률 29% | 정답 ②

다음 빈칸에 들어갈 말로 가장 적절한 것을 고르시오.

① a barrier to evolution – 진화에 있어 장벽
✓② a consequence of life – 생명체의 결과
③ a record of primitive culture – 원시 문화의 기록
④ a sign of the constancy of nature – 자연의 불변성에 대한 신호
⑤ a reason for cooperation among species – 종들 간 협력의 이유

Over 4.5 billion years ago, / the Earth's primordial atmosphere / was probably largely water vapour, carbon dioxide, sulfur dioxide and nitrogen.
45억 년도 더 전에 / 지구의 원시 대기는 / 아마도 대부분 수증기, 이산화탄소, 이산화황과 질소였을 것이다.

The appearance and subsequent evolution of exceedingly primitive living organisms / (bacteria-like microbes and simple single-celled plants) / began to change the atmosphere, / liberating oxygen and breaking down carbon dioxide and sulfur dioxide.
극히 원시적인 생물체의 출현과 연이은 진화는 / (박테리아 같은 미생물과 단순한 단세포 식물) / 대기를 변화시키기 시작했다. / 산소를 유리(遊離)시키고 이산화탄소와 이산화황을 분해하면서

This made it possible / for higher organisms to develop.
이것은 가능하게 했다. / 더 상위 유기체가 발달하는 것을

When the earliest known plant cells with nuclei / evolved about 2 billion years ago, / the atmosphere seems to have had / only about 1 percent of its present content of oxygen.
가장 최초라고 알려진 핵이 있는 식물 세포가 / 약 20억 년 전 진화했을 때, / 대기에 있었던 것 같다. / 현재 산소 함량의 고작 약 1%만이

With the emergence of the first land plants, / about 500 million years ago, / oxygen reached about one-third of its present concentration.
최초의 육지 식물이 출현하면서 / 약 5억 년 전에 / 산소는 현재 농도의 약 3분의 1에 달했다.

It had risen to almost its present level / by about 370 million years ago, / when animals first spread on to land.
그것은 거의 현재 수준으로 증가했고, / 약 3억 7천만 년 전까지 / 그때 동물들이 처음 육지에 퍼졌다.

Today's atmosphere is thus / not just a requirement to sustain life / as we know it — / it is also a consequence of life.
그러므로 오늘날의 대기는 / 생명체를 유지하기 위한 필요조건인 것만이 아니라, / 우리가 알고 있듯이 / 생명체의 결과이기도 하다.

45억 년도 더 전에 지구의 원시 대기는 아마도 대부분 수증기, 이산화탄소, 이산화황과 질소였을 것이다. 극히 원시적인 생물체(박테리아 같은 미생물과 단순한 단세포 식물)의 출현과 연이은 진화는 산소를 유리(遊離)시키고 이산화탄소와 이산화황을 분해하면서 대기를 변화시키기 시작했다. 이것은 더 상위 유기체가 발달하는 것을 가능하게 했다. 가장 최초라고 알려진 핵이 있는 식물 세포가 약 20억 년 전 진화했을 때, 대기에 현재 산소 함량의 고작 1%만이 있었던 것 같다. 약 5억 년 전에 최초의 육지 식물이 출현하면서 산소는 현재 농도의 약 3분의 1에 달했다. 그것은 약 3억 7천만 년 전까지 거의 현재 수준으로 증가했고, 그때 동물들이 처음 육지에 퍼졌다. 그러므로 오늘날의 대기는 우리가 알고 있듯이 생명체를 유지하기 위한 필요조건인 것만이 아니라, 생명체의 결과이기도 하다.

Why? 왜 정답일까?

첫 두 문장에서 지구의 원시 대기는 수증기, 이산화탄소, 이산화황, 질소 등으로 이루어져 있었을 것이나 생명체의 탄생 이후 산소가 유리되고 이산화탄소와 이산화황이 분해되는 등 변화를 맞이하게 되었다고 한다. 이어서 핵이 있는 최초의 식물 세포, 최초의 육지 식물 등이 출현하며 산소 농도 또한 점점 더 많은 생명체가 살기 적합하도록 높아졌다는 내용이 전개된다. 이러한 흐름으로 보아, 빈칸 문장은 대기가 생명체의 탄생으로 말미암아 '결과적으로' 변화해온 것이라는 결론을 적합하게 제시해야 한다. 따라서 빈칸에 들어갈 말로 가장 적절한 것은 ② '생명체의 결과'이다.

- billion ⓝ 10억
- subsequent ⓐ 연이은, 그다음의
- liberate ⓥ (화학) 유리시키다
- emergence ⓝ 출현
- requirement ⓝ 필요조건
- consequence ⓝ 결과
- nitrogen ⓝ 질소
- exceedingly ⓐⓓ 극히, 대단히
- nucleus ⓝ (생물) 핵, 세포핵 (pl. nuclei)
- concentration ⓝ 농도
- sustain ⓥ 유지하다, 지탱하다
- constancy ⓝ 불변성

구문 풀이

12행 It had risen to almost its present level by about 370 million years ago,
(과거완료) (시간 선행사)
when animals first spread on to land.
(관계부사(계속적 용법))

★★ 문제 해결 꿀~팁 ★★

▶ 많이 틀린 이유는?
지구의 대기가 생물체 출현에 따라 '변화해' 왔다는 것이 글의 주제이므로, ④의 constancy(불변성, 항구성)는 주제와 정반대되는 단어이다. 또한 글에서 '원시 문화'에 관해 언급하지 않으므로 ③도 답으로 부적절하다.

▶ 문제 해결 방법은?
첫 두 문장에서 초창기 대기는 오늘날과 많이 달랐으나 생물체의 진화에 따라 대기가 변화되기 시작했다는 내용을 파악하면 답이 ②임을 알 수 있다.

32 음악이 기억 회상에 미치는 영향   정답률 56% | 정답 ③

다음 빈칸에 들어갈 말로 가장 적절한 것을 고르시오.

① analyzing memories of the event thoroughly
   사건에 대한 기억을 면밀히 분석하는 것
② increasing storage space for recalling the event
   사건을 기억하기 위한 저장 공간을 늘리는 것
③ re-hearing the same music associated with the event ✓
   그 사건과 연관된 바로 그 음악을 다시 듣는 것
④ reconstructing the event in the absence of background music
   배경 음악 없이 사건을 재구성하는 것
⑤ enhancing musical competence to deliver emotional messages
   감정적인 메시지를 전달하는 음악적 능력을 향상시키는 것

One of the primary ways / by which music is able to take on significance in our inner world / is by the way it interacts with memory.
주요한 방법 중 하나는 / 음악이 우리의 내면세계에서 중요성을 가질 수 있는 / 그것이 기억과 상호작용하는 방식에 의해서이다.
Memories associated with important emotions / tend to be more deeply embedded in our memory / than other events.
중요한 감정과 연관된 기억들은 / 우리 기억 속에 더욱 깊이 박혀 있는 경향이 있다. / 다른 사건들보다
Emotional memories / are more likely to be vividly remembered / and are more likely to be recalled with the passing of time / than neutral memories.
감정적인 기억들은 / 생생히 기억될 가능성이 더 크고 / 시간이 지나도 기억될 가능성이 더 크다. / 중립적인 기억들보다
Since music can be extremely emotionally evocative, / key life events can be emotionally heightened by the presence of music, / ensuring that memories of the event become deeply encoded.
음악이 감정을 엄청나게 불러일으킬 수 있기 때문에 / 삶의 중요한 사건들은 음악의 존재에 의해 감정적으로 고조될 수 있고, / 이는 그 사건에 대한 기억이 확실히 깊이 부호화되도록 해 준다.
Retrieval of those memories / is then enhanced by contextual effects, / in which a recreation of a similar context / to that in which the memories were encoded / can facilitate their retrieval.
그러한 기억들의 회복은 / 그러고 나서 맥락 효과에 의해 강화되는데, / 이 맥락 효과에서는 비슷한 맥락의 재창조가 / 그 기억들이 부호화되었던 것과 / 그것들의 회복을 촉진시킬 수 있다.
Thus, / re-hearing the same music associated with the event / can activate intensely vivid memories of the event.
따라서 / 그 사건과 연관된 바로 그 음악을 다시 듣는 것이 / 그 사건에 대한 강렬하게 생생한 기억들을 활성화할 수 있다.

음악이 우리의 내면세계에서 중요성을 가질 수 있는 주요한 방법 중 하나는 그것이 기억과 상호작용하는 방식에 의해서이다. 중요한 감정과 연관된 기억들은 다른 사건들보다 우리 기억 속에 더욱 깊이 박혀 있는 경향이 있다. 감정적인 기억들은 생생히 기억될 가능성이 더 크고 중립적인 기억들보다 시간이 지나도 기억될 가능성이 더 크다. 음악이 감정을 엄청나게 불러일으킬 수 있기 때문에 삶의 중요한 사건들은 음악의 존재에 의해 감정적으로 고조될 수 있고, 이는 그 사건에 대한 기억들이 확실히 깊이 부호화되도록 해 준다. 그러고 나서 그러한 기억들의 회복은 맥락 효과에 의해 강화되는데, 그 기억이 부호화되었던 맥락과 비슷한 맥락의 재창조가 기억의 회복을 촉진시킬 수 있다. 따라서 그 사건과 연관된 바로 그 음악을 다시 듣는 것이 그 사건에 대한 강렬하게 생생한 기억들을 활성화할 수 있다.

Why? 왜 정답일까?
음악은 듣는 이의 감정을 고조시키고, 감정적인 기억은 더 생생히 저장되게 하는 경향이 있기 때문에, 어떤 사건이 일어날 때 특정한 음악을 듣고 있었다면 나중에 그 음악을 다시 듣는 '맥락'이 조성될 때 관련된 사건을 기억해내기가 훨씬 쉬워진다(~ a recreation of a similar context to that in which the memories were encoded can facilitate their retrieval.)는 내용의 글이다. 따라서 빈칸에 들어갈 말로 가장 적절한 것은 ③ '그 사건과 연관된 바로 그 음악을 다시 듣는 것'이다.

- take on (특징 등을) 띠다, (일을) 맡다
- vividly ⓐⓓ 생생하게
- neutral ⓐ 중립적인
- heighten ⓥ 고조시키다
- encode ⓥ 부호화하다
- facilitate ⓥ 용이하게 하다
- intensely ⓐⓓ 강렬하게, 매우
- in the absence of ~이 없을 때, ~의 부재 시에
- significance ⓝ 중요성
- with the passing of time 시간이 지남에 따라
- extremely ⓐⓓ 극도로
- presence ⓝ 존재
- enhance ⓥ 강화하다
- activate ⓥ 활성화하다
- thoroughly ⓐⓓ 면밀하게, 철저하게
- competence ⓝ 능력, 능숙함

구문 풀이

10행 Retrieval of those memories is then enhanced by contextual effects,
        (동사구(수동태))   (선행사)
in which a recreation of a similar context to that [in which the memories were
=where   (주어)   (지시대명사(=context))   =where
encoded] can facilitate their retrieval.
                (동사)

★★★ 등급을 가르는 문제! ★★★

33 환경에 대한 인간의 영향력   정답률 45% | 정답 ①

다음 빈칸에 들어갈 말로 가장 적절한 것을 고르시오. [3점]

① imposing ourselves on nature ✓ – 우리 자신을 자연에게 강요하고 있으며
② limiting our ecological impact – 우리의 생물학적 영향력을 제한하고 있으며
③ yielding our land to mammals – 우리의 땅을 포유류에게 내주고 있으며
④ encouraging biological diversity – 생물학적 다양성을 장려하고 있으며
⑤ doing useful work for the environment – 환경에 유용한 일을 하고 있으며

We are now imposing ourselves on nature, / instead of the other way around.
우리는 지금 우리 자신을 자연에게 강요하고 있다. / 그 반대의 경우는 대신
Perhaps the clearest way to see this / is to look at changes / in the biomass — the total worldwide weight — of mammals.
아마도 이것을 알 수 있는 가장 분명한 방법은 / 변화를 보는 것이다. / 전 세계 포유류 무게의 총합, 즉 생물량의
A long time ago, / all of us humans together / probably weighed only about two-thirds as much / as all the bison in North America, / and less than one-eighth as much / as all the elephants in Africa.
오래전에 / 우리 인간은 모두 합쳐도 / 아마 대략 3분의 2 정도의 무게였고, / 북미에 있는 모든 들소 무게의 / 8분의 1 무게보다 적었다. / 아프리카의 모든 코끼리의
But in the Industrial Era / our population exploded / and we killed bison and elephants / at industrial scale and in terrible numbers.
하지만 산업 시대에 / 우리의 인구는 폭발적으로 증가했고 / 우리는 들소와 코끼리를 죽였다. / 엄청난 규모와 끔찍한 숫자로
The balance shifted greatly as a result.
그 결과 균형이 엄청나게 바뀌었다.
At present, / we humans weigh more than 350 times as much / as all bison and elephants put together.
현재는 / 우리 인간이 350배가 넘는 무게가 나간다. / 모든 들소와 코끼리를 합친 무게의
We weigh over ten times more / than all the earth's wild mammals combined.
우리는 10배 이상 무게가 나간다. / 지구상의 모든 야생 포유류를 합친 것보다
And if we add in all the mammals we've domesticated / — cattle, sheep, pigs, horses, and so on — / the comparison becomes truly ridiculous: / we and our tamed animals / now represent 97 percent of the earth's mammalian biomass.
그리고 만약 우리가 사육해 온 모든 포유류를 포함한다면 / 소, 양, 돼지, 말 등 / 그 비교는 정말로 터무니없어지는데, / 우리와 우리가 길들인 동물은 / 현재 지구 포유류 생물량의 97%에 해당한다.
This comparison illustrates a fundamental point: / instead of being limited by the environment, / we learned to shape it to our own ends.
이러한 비교는 기본적인 핵심을 보여주고 있는데, / 환경에 의해 제약을 받는 것이 아니라, / 우리는 우리 자신의 목적에 맞게 그것을 만들도록 배웠다.

우리는 지금 우리 자신을 자연에게 강요하고 있으며, 그 반대의 경우는 아니다. 아마도 이것을 알 수 있는 가장 분명한 방법은 전 세계 포유류 무게의 총합, 즉 생물량의 변화를 보는 것이다. 오래전에 우리 인간은 모두 합쳐도 아마 북미에 있는 모든 들소 무게의 대략 3분의 2 정도의 무게였고, 아프리카의 모든 코끼리의 8분의 1 무게보다 적었다. 하지만 산업 시대에 우리의 인구는 폭발적으로 증가했고 우리는 엄청난 규모와 끔찍한 숫자의 들소와 코끼리를 죽였다. 그 결과 균형이 엄청나게 바뀌었다. 현재는 우리 인간이 모든 들소와 코끼리를 합친 무게의 350배가 넘는 무게가 나간다. 우리는 지구상의 모든 야생 포유류를 합친 것보다 10배 이상 무게가 나간다. 그리고 만약 우리가 사육해 온 소, 양, 돼지, 말 등 모든 포유류를 포함한다면 그 비교는 정말로 터무니없어지는데, 우리와 우리가 길들인 동물은 현재 지구 포유류 생물량의 97%에 해당한다. 이러한 비교는 기본적인 핵심을 보여주고 있는데, 우리는 환경에 의해 제약을 받는 것이 아니라, 우리 자신의 목적에 맞게 그것을 만들도록 배웠다.

Why? 왜 정답일까?
마지막 문장에서 생물량을 비교해보면 우리 인간은 환경에 제약을 받는 대신 오히려 우리 자신의 목적에 맞게 환경을 만들어나가는 법을 배웠다(~ instead of being limited by the environment, we learned to shape it to our own ends.)는 점을 알 수 있다고 했다. 따라서 빈칸에 들어갈 말로 가장 적절한 것은 인간이 환경에 영향을 받는 대상이라기보다는 영향력을 직접 행사하는 주체라는 뜻의 ① '우리 자신을 자연에게 강요하고 있으며'이다.

- the other way around 반대로, 거꾸로
- mammal ⓝ 포유류
- at industrial scale 대규모로
- domesticate ⓥ 가축화하다, 길들이다
- tame ⓥ 길들이다
- illustrate ⓥ (예를 들어) 보여주다
- to one's end ~의 목적을 위해서
- yield ⓥ (~에게) 양도하다
- biomass ⓝ (특정 지역 내의) 생물량
- explode ⓥ 폭발적으로 증가하다
- shift ⓥ 변화하다, 바뀌다
- ridiculous ⓐ 터무니없는, 우스꽝스러운
- represent ⓥ 나타내다
- fundamental ⓐ 기본적인
- impose ⓥ 강요하다, (의무나 책임을) 부과하다

구문 풀이

11행 We weigh over ten times more than all the earth's wild mammals combined.
「배수사+비교급+than : ~보다 … 배 더 ~한/하게」   (과거분사)

★★ 문제 해결 꿀~팁 ★★

▶ 많이 틀린 이유는?
본래 인간은 북미 모든 들소 무게의 약 2/3, 아프리카 모든 코끼리 무게의 1/8 미만 정도를 차지했으나, 산업화 이후 인구는 폭발적으로 늘고 들소와 코끼리는 죽어 나가면서 비중이 완전히 역전되었다는 것이 글의 주된 내용이다. ②, ③은 모두 인간이 자연에서 차지하는 비중이 '늘었다'는 내용과 정반대되는 선택지이다.

▶ 문제 해결 방법은?
마지막 문장 이전까지 부연과 예시가 주를 이루다가 마지막 문장에서 결론을 제시하고 있다. 앞의 숫자 위주로 비교적 가볍게 읽고 마지막 문장의 의미를 정확히 파악한 뒤, 오답 선택지를 소거하며 풀도록 한다.

★★★ 등급을 가르는 문제! ★★★

34 확실성을 추구하는 인간   정답률 43% | 정답 ⑤

다음 빈칸에 들어갈 말로 가장 적절한 것을 고르시오. [3점]

① weigh the pros and cons of our actions – 우리 행동의 장단점을 따져 본다
② develop the patience to bear ambiguity – 모호함을 참을 수 있는 인내심을 기른다
③ enjoy adventure rather than settle down – 안주하기보다 모험을 즐긴다
④ gain insight from solving complex problems – 복잡한 문제를 해결하여 통찰력을 얻는다
✔ lose our ability to interact with the unknown – 미지의 것과 상호 작용하는 우리의 능력을 잃어버린다

In the modern world, / we look for certainty in uncertain places.
현대 세계에서 / 우리는 불확실한 곳에서 확실성을 찾는다.
We search for order in chaos, / the right answer in ambiguity, / and conviction in complexity.
우리는 혼란 속에서 질서를 찾는다. / 애매모호함에서 정답을, / 복잡함에서 확신을
"We spend far more time and effort / on trying to control the world," / best-selling writer Yuval Noah Harari says, / "than on trying to understand it."
"우리는 훨씬 더 많은 시간과 노력을 쏟는다. / 세상을 통제하려고 하는 것에" / 베스트셀러 작가인 Yuval Noah Harari가 말하기를, / "세상을 이해하려고 하는 것보다"
We look for the easy-to-follow formula.
우리는 쉽게 따라할 수 있는 공식을 찾는다.
Over time, / we lose our ability to interact with the unknown.
시간이 지나면서 / 우리는 미지의 것과 상호 작용하는 우리의 능력을 잃어버린다.
Our approach reminds me / of the classic story of the drunk man / searching for his keys under a street lamp at night.
우리의 접근법은 나에게 떠올리게 한다. / 술 취한 남자에 대한 전형적인 이야기를 / 밤에 가로등 아래에서 자신의 열쇠를 찾는
He knows / he lost his keys somewhere on the dark side of the street / but looks for them underneath the lamp, / because that's where the light is.
그는 안다 / 자신이 열쇠를 어두운 길가 어딘가에 잃어버렸다는 것을 / 가로등 밑에서 그것을 찾는데, / 왜냐하면 그곳에 빛이 있는 곳이기 때문이다.
Our yearning for certainty / leads us to pursue seemingly safe solutions / — by looking for our keys under street lamps.
확실성에 대한 우리의 열망은 / 우리가 겉으로 보기에 안전한 해결책을 추구하도록 이끈다. / 가로등 아래에서 우리의 열쇠를 찾음으로써
Instead of taking the risky walk into the dark, / we stay within our current state, / however inferior it may be.
어둠 속으로 위험한 걸음을 내딛는 대신, / 우리는 우리의 현재 상태 안에 머문다. / 그것이 아무리 열등할지 몰라도

현대 세계에서 우리는 불확실한 곳에서 확실성을 찾는다. 우리는 혼란 속에서 질서를, 애매모호함에서 정답을, 복잡함에서 확신을 찾는다. 베스트셀러 작가인 Yuval Noah Harari가 말하기를, "우리는 쉽게 따라할 수 있는 것보다 세상을 통제하려고 하는 것에 훨씬 더 많은 시간과 노력을 쏟는다." 우리는 쉽게 따라할 수 있는 공식을 찾는다. 시간이 지나면서 우리는 미지의 것과 상호 작용하는 우리의 능력을 잃어버린다. 우리의 접근법은 내게 밤에 가로등 아래에서 자신의 열쇠를 찾는 술 취한 남자에 대한 전형적인 이야기를 떠올리게 한다. 그는 자신이 열쇠를 어두운 길가 어딘가에 잃어버렸다는 것을 알지만 가로등 밑에서 그것을 찾는데, 왜냐하면 그곳에 빛이 있기 때문이다. 확실성에 대한 우리의 열망은 우리가 가로등 아래에서 열쇠를 찾음으로써 겉으로 보기에 안전한 해결책을 추구하도록 이끈다. 어둠 속으로 위험한 걸음을 내딛는 대신, 우리는 우리의 현재 상태가 아무리 열등할지 몰라도 그 안에 머문다.

Why? 왜 정답일까?

마지막 두 문장에서 우리는 확실성을 추구하기 때문에 겉보기에 안전해 보이는 선택지를 취하려 하며, 미지의 어둠 속을 탐색하는 대신 부족하고 열등한 현재 상태일지라도 그대로 유지하려는 경향이 있다(Our yearning for certainty leads us to pursue seemingly safe solutions ~. Instead of taking the risky walk into the dark, we stay within our current state, however inferior it may be.)고 언급한다. 따라서 빈칸에 들어갈 말로 가장 적절한 것은 새롭고 불확실한 것을 점점 덜 알아보려 한다는 의미의 ⑤ '미지의 것과 상호 작용하는 우리의 능력을 잃어버린다'이다.

- certainty ⓝ 확실성
- ambiguity ⓝ 애매모호함
- complexity ⓝ 복잡성
- formula ⓝ 공식, 제조법
- pursue ⓥ 추구하다
- inferior ⓐ 열등한
- patience ⓝ 인내심
- insight ⓝ 통찰력
- uncertain ⓐ 불확실한
- conviction ⓝ 확신
- easy-to-follow ⓐ 따르기 쉬운
- yearning ⓝ 갈망, 열망
- seemingly ⓐd 겉보기에
- pros and cons 장단점
- bear ⓥ 참다, (아이를) 낳다
- unknown ⓝ 미지의, 알려지지 않은

구문 풀이

3행 "We spend far more time and effort on trying to control the world,"
「spend + 시간/노력 + on + 동명사: ~하는 데 시간/노력을 들이다」
(best-selling writer Yuval Noah Harari says), "than on trying to understand it."
( ): 삽입절   병렬구조(than 앞의 on trying과 연결됨)

★★ 문제 해결 꿀~팁 ★★

▶ 많이 틀린 이유는?
빈칸이 있는 문장 바로 앞의 'We look for ~'에서 우리는 쉽게 따라할 수 있는 것을 좇는 경향이 있다고 하므로, '어려운 문제를 풀며 영감을 얻는다'는 의미의 ④는 맥락상 상충한다.

▶ 문제 해결 방법은?
어두운 길가에서 열쇠를 잃어버렸음에도 빛이 있는 가로등 밑에서 열쇠를 찾아 헤매는 남자의 예는 '새롭고 위험할지라도 시도해봐야 하지만 안전한 현재 상태만 고수하고 있는' 우리의 모습을 비유한 것이다. 빈칸 문장은 이 상태가 지속되면 결국 우리가 '미지의 것을 살펴보는 능력 자체를 잃게 된다'는 전망을 제시하는 것이다.

---

35 머리카락의 영적 중요성   정답률 66% | 정답 ③

다음 글에서 전체 흐름과 관계 없는 문장은?

As far back as the seventeenth century, / hair had a special spiritual significance in Africa.
과거 17세기 정도에 / 머리카락은 아프리카에서 특별한 영적 중요성을 가졌다.
Many African cultures saw the head / as the center of control, communication, and identity in the body.

많은 아프리카의 문화들은 머리를 여겼다. / 신체에서 지배, 소통, 그리고 정체성의 중심이라고
① Hair was regarded as a source of power / that personified the individual / and could be used for spiritual purposes / or even to cast a spell.
머리카락은 힘의 원천으로 여겨졌다. / 개인을 인격화하는 / 영적인 목적을 위해서 사용될 수 있었다. / 또는 심지어 주문을 걸기 위해서
② Since it rests on the highest point on the body, / hair itself was a means to communicate with divine spirits / and it was treated in ways / that were thought to bring good luck or protect against evil.
그것이 신체의 가장 높은 지점에 있기 때문에, / 머리카락은 그 자체로 신성한 영혼들과 소통할 수 있는 수단이었고 / 그것은 방식으로 다루어졌다. / 행운을 가져오거나 악으로부터 지켜준다고 생각되는
✔ People had the opportunity to socialize / while styling each other's hair, / and the shared tradition of hair was passed down.
사람들은 사귀는 기회를 가졌고 / 서로의 머리카락을 스타일링해 주면서 / 머리카락에 대한 공유된 전통이 대대로 전해졌다.
④ According to authors Ayana Byrd and Lori Tharps, / "communication from the gods and spirits / was thought to pass through the hair to get to the soul."
작가 Ayana Byrd와 Lori Tharps에 따르면, / "신과 영혼들로부터의 의사소통이 / 머리카락을 통과하여 영혼에 다다른다고 여겨졌다."
⑤ In Cameroon, for example, / medicine men attached hair to containers / that held their healing potions / in order to protect the potions and enhance their effectiveness.
예를 들어 Cameroon에서는 / 치료 주술사들이 머리카락을 용기에 붙였다. / 자신의 치료 물약을 담은 / 물약을 보호하고 그 효과성을 높이기 위해

과거 17세기 정도에 머리카락은 아프리카에서 특별한 영적 중요성을 가졌다. 많은 아프리카의 문화들은 신체에서 머리를 지배, 소통, 그리고 정체성의 중심이라고 여겼다. ① 머리카락은 개인을 인격화하는 힘의 원천으로 여겨졌고 영적인 목적을 위해서나 심지어 주문을 걸기 위해서 사용될 수 있었다. ② 머리카락은 신체의 가장 높은 지점에 있기 때문에, 그 자체로 신성한 영혼들과 소통할 수 있는 수단이었고 행운을 가져오거나 악으로부터 지켜준다고 생각되는 방식으로 다루어졌다. ③ 사람들은 서로의 머리카락을 스타일링해 주면서 사귀는 기회를 가졌고 머리카락에 대한 공유된 전통이 대대로 전해졌다. ④ 작가 Ayana Byrd와 Lori Tharps에 따르면, "신과 영혼들로부터의 의사소통이 머리카락을 통과하여 영혼에 다다른다고 여겨졌다." ⑤ 예를 들어 Cameroon에서는 치료 주술사들이 치료 물약을 보호하고 그 효과성을 높이기 위해 머리카락을 자신의 물약을 담은 용기에 붙였다.

Why? 왜 정답일까?

아프리카 문화권에서 머리카락은 영적 의미를 가진 대상으로 이해되었다는 내용의 글로, ①, ②, ④, ⑤는 모두 주제를 뒷받침한다. 하지만 ③은 사람들이 머리 스타일을 만져주며 서로를 사귀었고 머리카락에 관한 공유된 전통이 대대로 전해졌다는 무관한 내용을 다룬다. 따라서 전체 흐름과 관계없는 문장은 ③이다.

- spiritual ⓐ 영적인
- identity ⓝ 정체성
- cast a spell 주문을 걸다
- socialize ⓥ (사람을) 사귀다, 어울리다
- enhance ⓥ 강화하다, 향상시키다
- significance ⓝ 중요성
- personify ⓥ 인격화하다
- divine ⓐ 성스러운, 신성한
- pass down 전해주다

구문 풀이

4행 Hair was regarded as a source of power [that personified the individual ┌주격 관계대명사
「A + be regarded as + B : A가 B로 간주되다」   동사1
and could be used for spiritual purposes or even to cast a spell].
동사2   부사구1   부사구2(목적)

---

36 더 새로운 정보의 원천이 될 수 있는 약한 유대관계   정답률 61% | 정답 ④

주어진 글 다음에 이어질 글의 순서로 가장 적절한 것을 고르시오.

① (A) – (C) – (B)   ② (B) – (A) – (C)
③ (B) – (C) – (A)   ✔ (C) – (A) – (B)
⑤ (C) – (B) – (A)

Mark Granovetter examined the extent / to which information about jobs / flowed through weak versus strong ties / among a group of people.
Mark Granovetter는 정도를 조사했다. / 직업에 대한 정보가 / 약한 유대관계 대비 강한 유대관계를 통해 유입되는 / 한 무리의 사람들 사이에서
(C) He found / that only a sixth of jobs that came via the network / were from strong ties, / with the rest coming via medium or weak ties; / and with more than a quarter coming via weak ties.
그는 발견했다. / 관계망을 통해 오는 직업의 6분의 1만이 / 강한 유대관계로부터 오며 / 나머지는 중간이나 약한 유대관계를 통해 오고 / 4분의 1 이상이 약한 유대관계로부터 온다는 것을
Strong ties can be more homophilistic.
강한 유대관계는 더 동족친화적일 수 있다.
Our closest friends are often those / who are most like us.
우리의 가장 친한 친구들은 종종 사람들이다. / 우리와 가장 비슷한
(A) This means / that they might have information / that is most relevant to us, / but it also means / that it is information / to which we may already be exposed.
이것은 의미하지만 / 그들이 정보를 가지고 있을지도 모른다는 것을 / 우리와 가장 관련 있는 / 또한 이는 의미한다. / 그것이 정보라는 것을 / 우리가 이미 접하고 있을지도 모르는
In contrast, / our weaker relationships are often with people / who are more distant both geographically and demographically.
대조적으로, / 우리의 더 약한 인간 관계는 종종 사람들을 상대로 한다. / 지리적으로나 인구통계학적으로 더 먼
(B) Their information is more novel.
그들의 정보는 더 새롭다.
Even though we talk to these people less frequently, / we have so many weak ties / that they end up being a sizable source of information, / especially of information to which we don't otherwise have access.
우리는 이러한 사람들과 덜 빈번하게 이야기를 하지만, / 우리는 매우 많은 약한 유대관계를 가지고 있어서 / 결국 그것이 정보의 엄청난 원천이 된다. / 특히 우리가 그렇지 않다면 접근하지 못하는 정보의

Mark Granovetter는 한 무리의 사람들 사이에서 직업에 대한 정보가 약한 유대관계 대비 강한 유대관계를 통해 유입되는 정도를 조사했다.
(C) 그는 관계망을 통해 오는 직업의 6분의 1만이 강한 유대관계로부터 오며 나머지는 중간이나 약한 유대관계를 통해 오고 4분의 1 이상이 약한 유대관계로부터 온다는 것을 발견했다. 강한 유대관계는 더 동족친화적일 수 있다. 우리의 가장 친한 친구들은 종종 우리와 가장 비슷한 사람들이다.

(A) 이것은 그들이 우리와 가장 관련 있는 정보를 가지고 있을지 모른다는 것을 의미하지만 또한 이는 그것이 우리가 이미 접하고 있을지도 모르는 정보라는 것을 의미한다. 대조적으로, 우리의 더 약한 인간관계는 종종 지리적으로나 인구통계학적으로나 더 먼 사람들을 상대로 한다.

(B) 그들의 정보는 더 새롭다. 우리는 이러한 사람들과 덜 빈번하게 이야기를 하지만, 우리는 매우 많은 약한 유대관계를 가지고 있어서 결국 그것이 정보, 특히 우리가 그렇지 않다면 접근하지 못하는 정보의 엄청난 원천이 된다.

Why? 왜 정답일까?

주어진 글에서 한 연구자가 약한 유대관계와 강한 유대관계에서 각각 직업에 관한 정보가 유입되는 정도를 조사했다고 언급한 데 이어, (C)는 연구자를 He로 받으며 그가 밝힌 결과를 제시한다. 특히 (C)의 후반부에서는 결과의 이유를 밝히기 위해 강한 유대관계의 특성부터 설명하며, 흔히 가장 친한 친구들은 자신과 가장 비슷하기 마련이라고 언급하는데, (A)에서는 바로 그렇기 때문에 이들(they)로부터 오는 정보를 우리가 이미 알고 있는 정보일 수 있음을 지적한다. 이어서 (A)의 후반부에서는 약한 인간관계의 특성을 언급하고, (B)에서는 이들을 Their로 받으며 이들이 우리와 더 '멀기' 때문에 이들이 가진 정보가 오히려 더 새롭다는 점을 상기시킨다. 따라서 글의 순서로 가장 적절한 것은 ④ '(C) – (A) – (B)'이다.

- examine ⓥ 조사하다
- geographically [ad] 지리적으로
- frequently [ad] 자주
- otherwise [ad] 그렇지 않으면
- relevant ⓐ 관련 있는
- novel ⓐ 새로운, 신기한
- sizable ⓐ (크기 등이) 상당한
- have access to ~을 이용하다, ~에 접근하다

구문 풀이

9행 Even though we talk to these people less frequently, we have so many
접속사(~에도 불구하고)
「so ~ that …: 너무 ~해서 …하다」
weak ties that they end up being a sizable source of information, especially of
결국 ~하게 되다
information [to which we don't otherwise have access].
선행사 「전치사 + 관계대명사」

---

37 문화에 대한 인간의 인식 정답률 58% | 정답 ⑤

주어진 글 다음에 이어질 글의 순서로 가장 적절한 것을 고르시오. [3점]

① (A) – (C) – (B) ② (B) – (A) – (C)
③ (B) – (C) – (A) ④ (C) – (A) – (B)
☑ (C) – (B) – (A)

When we think of culture, / we first think of human cultures, / of *our* culture.
우리가 문화에 대해 생각할 때, / 우리는 먼저 인간의 문화를 생각한다. / 즉 우리의 문화를

We think of computers, airplanes, fashions, teams, and pop stars.
우리는 컴퓨터, 비행기, 패션, 팀, 그리고 팝 스타를 생각한다.

For most of human cultural history, / none of those things existed.
대부분의 인간 문화의 역사에서 / 그러한 것들 중 어느 것도 존재하지 않았다.

(C) For hundreds of thousands of years, / no human culture had a tool with moving parts.
수십만 년 동안, / 어떤 인간의 문화도 움직이는 부품이 있는 도구를 가지지 않았다.

Well into the twentieth century, / various human foraging cultures / retained tools of stone, wood, and bone.
20세기까지도 / 다양한 인간의 수렵 채집 문화는 / 돌, 나무, 그리고 뼈로 된 도구를 보유했다.

We might pity human hunter-gatherers for their stuck simplicity, / but we would be making a mistake.
우리는 수렵 채집인들을 그들의 꽉 막힌 단순함 때문에 동정할지도 모르지만, / 우리는 실수를 범하고 있는 것일 수 있다.

(B) They held extensive knowledge, / knew deep secrets of their lands and creatures.
그들은 광범위한 지식을 가졌고 / 그들의 땅과 생명체의 깊은 비밀을 알았다.

And they experienced rich and rewarding lives; / we know so / because when their ways were threatened, / they fought to hold on to them, to the death.
그리고 그들은 풍요롭고 가치 있는 삶을 경험했는데, / 우리는 그것을 알고 있다. / 그들의 (삶의) 방식이 위협받았을 때 ~했기 때문에 / 그것을 고수하기 위해 죽을 때까지 그들이 싸웠기

(A) Sadly, this remains true / as the final tribal peoples get overwhelmed / by those who value money above humanity.
슬프게도 이것은 여전히 사실이다. / 마지막 부족민들이 제압당할 때도 / 인간성보다 돈을 가치 있게 여기는 사람들에 의해

We are living in their end times / and, to varying extents, / we're all contributing to those endings.
우리는 그들의 종말의 시대에 살고 있고, / 다양한 정도로 / 우리는 모두 그러한 종말에 원인이 되고 있다.

Ultimately our values may even prove self-defeating.
결국 우리의 가치들이 스스로를 파괴하고 있다는 것을 증명하는 것일 수도 있다.

우리가 문화에 대해 생각할 때, 우리는 먼저 인간의 문화, 우리의 문화를 생각한다. 우리는 컴퓨터, 비행기, 패션, 팀, 그리고 팝 스타를 생각한다. 그러한 것들 중 어느 것도 대부분의 인간 문화의 역사에서 존재하지 않았다.

(C) 수십만 년 동안, 어떤 인간의 문화도 움직이는 부품이 있는 도구를 가지지 않았다. 20세기까지도 다양한 인간의 수렵 채집 문화는 돌, 나무, 그리고 뼈로 된 도구를 보유했다. 우리는 수렵 채집인들을 그들의 꽉 막힌 단순함 때문에 동정할지도 모르지만, 우리는 실수를 범하고 있는 것일 수 있다.

(B) 그들은 광범위한 지식을 가졌고 그들의 땅과 생명체의 깊은 비밀을 알았다. 그리고 그들은 풍요롭고 가치 있는 삶을 경험했는데, 그들의 (삶의) 방식이 위협받았을 때 그것을 고수하기 위해 죽을 때까지 그들이 싸웠기 때문에 우리는 그것을 알고 있다.

(A) 슬프게도 인간성보다 돈을 가치 있게 여기는 사람들에 의해 마지막 부족민들이 제압당할 때도 이것은 여전히 사실이다. 우리는 그들의 종말의 시대에 살고 있고, 다양한 정도로 우리는 모두 그러한 종말에 원인이 되고 있다. 결국 우리의 가치들이 스스로를 파괴하고 있다는 것을 증명하는 것일 수도 있다.

Why? 왜 정답일까?

주어진 글에서 인간은 '문화'라는 말을 들으면 '현대 우리의' 문화를 떠올리는 경향이 있지만 사실 현대 문화의 역사는 매우 짧다고 언급한 데 이어, (C)는 수십만 년 동안 현대의 '움직이는 부품'은 존재하지 않았으며 20세기까지만 해도 수렵 채집 문화에서는 돌, 나무, 뼈 등을 사용했다는 부연 설명을 이어간다. 특히 (C)의 후반부에서는 현대의 우리가 수렵채집 문화권의 사람들을 단순하다고 동정하는 것이 실수일 수 있다고 지적하는데, (B)에서는 '수렵채집인'들을 They로 받으며 이들이 광범위한 지식을 지니고 있었

다는 점과 풍요롭고 가치로운 삶 또한 누렸다는 점을 보충 설명한다. (A)는 '슬프게도' 우리가 이들이 종말을 맞는 시대에 살고 있으며, 이로 인해 우리 자신의 가치를 파괴하는 과정에 있는 것인지도 모른다는 결론을 제시한다. 따라서 글의 순서로 가장 적절한 것은 ⑤ '(C) – (B) – (A)'이다.

- tribal ⓐ 부족의
- varying ⓐ 다양한, 바뀌는
- self-defeating ⓐ 스스로를 파괴하는, 자멸적인
- rewarding ⓐ 가치 있는, 보람 있는
- retain ⓥ 보유하다
- overwhelm ⓥ 압도하다, 제압하다
- ultimately [ad] 결국, 궁극적으로
- extensive ⓐ 광범위한
- hold on to ~을 고수하다
- simplicity ⓝ 단순함

구문 풀이

5행 Sadly, this remains →형용사 보어 true as the final tribal peoples get overwhelmed by
2형식 동사   접속사(~할 때)
those [who value money above humanity].
선행사   주격 관계대명사

---

38 액체의 파괴력 정답률 60% | 정답 ④

글의 흐름으로 보아, 주어진 문장이 들어가기에 가장 적절한 곳을 고르시오.

Liquids are destructive.
액체는 파괴적이다.

Foams feel soft / because they are easily compressed; / if you jump on to a foam mattress, / you'll feel it give beneath you.
발포 고무는 부드럽게 느껴지는데, / 그것이 쉽게 압축되기 때문에 / 만약 여러분이 발포 고무 매트리스 위로 점프를 한다면 / 여러분은 그것이 여러분의 밑에서 휘어지는 것을 느끼게 될 것이다.

① Liquids don't do this; / instead they flow.
액체는 이렇게 하지 않고, / 대신에 액체는 흐른다.

② You see this in a river, / or when you turn on a tap, / or if you use a spoon to stir your coffee.
여러분은 강에서 이것을 보게 된다. / 혹은 여러분이 수도꼭지를 틀 때나, / 혹은 여러분이 스푼을 사용하여 자신의 커피를 젓는다면

③ When you jump off a diving board / and hit a body of water, / the water has to flow away from you.
여러분이 다이빙 도약대에서 뛰어내려 / 많은 양의 물을 치게 될 때 / 그 물은 여러분에게서 비켜나 흘러나가야만 한다.

☑ But the flowing takes time, / and if your speed of impact is too great, / the water won't be able to flow away fast enough, / and so it pushes back at you.
그러나 흘러나가는 것은 시간이 걸리며, / 만약 여러분의 충돌 속도가 너무나도 엄청나다면 / 그 물이 충분히 빠르게 흘러나가지 못할 것이며 / 따라서 그것은 여러분을 밀어낸다.

It's that force / that stings your skin / as you belly-flop into a pool, / and makes falling into water from a great height / like landing on concrete.
바로 그 힘이다. / 여러분의 피부를 쓰리게 하며, / 여러분이 배로 수면을 치며 수영장 물속으로 떨어질 때 / 굉장한 높이에서 물속으로 떨어지는 것을 만드는 것이 / 콘크리트 위에 떨어지는 것처럼

⑤ The incompressibility of water is also / why waves can have such deadly power, / and in the case of tsunamis, / why they can destroy buildings and cities, / tossing cars around easily.
물의 비압축성은 또한 / 파도가 그러한 치명적인 힘을 가질 수 있는 이유이고, / 해일의 경우, / 그것이 건물과 도시를 부수는 이유인 것이다. / 자동차를 쉽게 던져버리며

액체는 파괴적이다. 발포 고무는 쉽게 압축되기 때문에 부드럽게 느껴지는데, 만약 여러분이 발포 고무 매트리스 위로 점프를 한다면 여러분은 그것이 밑에서 휘어지는 것을 느끼게 될 것이다. ① 액체는 이렇게 하지 않고 대신에 흐른다. ② 강에서나, 여러분이 수도꼭지를 틀 때나, 혹은 여러분이 스푼을 사용하여 자신의 커피를 젓는다면 여러분은 이것을 보게 된다. ③ 여러분이 다이빙 도약대에서 뛰어내려 많은 양의 물을 치게 될 때 그 물은 여러분에게서 비켜나 흘러나가야만 한다. ④ 그러나 흘러나가는 것은 시간이 걸리며, 만약 여러분의 충돌 속도가 너무나도 엄청나다면 그 물은 충분히 빠르게 흘러나가지 못할 것이며 따라서 여러분을 밀어낸다. 여러분이 배로 수면을 치며 수영장 물속으로 떨어질 때 여러분의 피부를 쓰리게 하며, 굉장한 높이에서 물속으로 떨어지는 것을 콘크리트 위에 떨어지는 것처럼 만드는 것이 바로 그 힘이다. ⑤ 물의 비압축성은 또한 파도가 그러한 치명적인 힘을 가질 수 있는 이유이고, 해일의 경우 그것이 건물과 도시를 부수며 자동차를 쉽게 던져버릴 수 있는 이유인 것이다.

Why? 왜 정답일까?

물은 흐르는 속성 때문에 파괴적인 힘을 가질 수 있음을 설명한 글로, ④ 앞의 문장은 다이빙대에서 뛰어내리는 경우를 예로 들고 있다. 이에 이어 주어진 문장은 다이빙처럼 급격히 떨어지는 경우 물이 흘러나가기까지 시간이 걸리기 때문에 만일 물 표면에 충돌하는 속도가 엄청나다면 물이 충분히 빨리 흘러나가지 못하여 우리를 '밀어내게' 된다고 설명한다. ④ 뒤의 문장은 바로 그러한 이유로 너무 빨리 물로 뛰어들었을 때 피부에 쓰림이 발생하고 수면이 아닌 콘크리트에라도 부딪친 것 같은 강력한 충격을 경험하게 된다고 설명한다. 따라서 주어진 문장이 들어가기에 가장 적절한 곳은 ④이다.

- impact ⓝ 충격, 충돌
- foam ⓝ (매트리스에 주로 쓰이는) 발포 고무
- stir ⓥ 젓다
- sting ⓥ 쓰리게 하다, 쏘다, 찌르다
- belly-flop ⓥ 배로 수면을 치며 뛰어들다, 엎드린 자세로 활강하다
- height ⓝ 높이, 고도
- incompressibility ⓝ 비압축성
- in the case of ~의 경우에
- destructive ⓐ 파괴적인
- tap ⓝ 수도꼭지
- a body of (양이) 많은
- land on ~에 착륙하다
- deadly ⓐ 치명적인
- toss ⓥ 던지다

구문 풀이

10행 「it is ~ that 강조구문: ~한 것은 바로 ~이다」 It's that force that stings your skin as you belly-flop into a pool, and
동사1   접속사(~할 때)
makes falling into water from a great height like landing on concrete.
동사2   목적어(동명사구)   목적격 보어(전명구)

★★★ 등급을 가르는 문제!
39 생각과 행동의 전파 정답률 50% | 정답 ③

글의 흐름으로 보아, 주어진 문장이 들어가기에 가장 적절한 곳을 고르시오. [3점]

In the late twentieth century, / researchers sought to measure / how fast and how far news, rumours or innovations moved.

20세기 후반 / 연구자들은 측정하고자 했다. / 뉴스, 소문, 혁신이 얼마나 빨리 그리고 얼마나 멀리 이동하는지를
① More recent research has shown / that ideas — even emotional states and conditions — / can be transmitted through a social network.
더 최근의 연구는 보여주었다. / 생각, 즉 감정 상태와 상황까지도 / 사회 관계망을 통해 전파될 수 있다는 것을
② The evidence of this kind of contagion / is clear:
이러한 종류의 전염의 증거는 / 분명하다.
'Students with studious roommates / become more studious.
즉 '학구적인 룸메이트와 함께 하는 학생들은 / 더욱 학구적이 된다.
Diners sitting next to heavy eaters / eat more food.'
폭식하는 사람 옆에 앉아 식사하는 사람은 / 더 많은 음식을 먹는다.'
☑ However, according to Christakis and Fowler, / we cannot transmit ideas and behaviours / much beyond our friends' friends' friends / (in other words, across just three degrees of separation).
그러나 Christakis와 Fowler에 따르면, / 우리는 생각과 행동을 전파할 수 없다. / 우리의 친구의 친구의 친구를 훨씬 넘어서, / (다시 말해 고작 세 단계의 분절을 건너서는)
This is because the transmission and reception of an idea or behaviour / requires a stronger connection / than the relaying of a letter / or the communication that a certain employment opportunity exists.
이것은 생각이나 행동의 전파와 수용이 / 더 강한 연결을 요구하기 때문이다. / 편지를 전달하는 것보다 / 혹은 어떤 고용 기회가 있다는 말의 전달이나
④ Merely knowing people is not the same / as being able to influence them to study more or over-eat.
단지 사람을 아는 것은 같지 않다. / 그들이 더 공부하거나 과식하도록 영향을 미칠 수 있는 것과는
⑤ Imitation is indeed the sincerest form of flattery, / even when it is unconscious.
모방은 실로 가장 순수한 형태의 아첨이다. / 그것이 무의식적일 때조차도

20세기 후반 연구자들은 뉴스, 소문, 혁신이 얼마나 빨리 그리고 얼마나 멀리 이동하는지를 측정하고자 했다. ① 더 최근의 연구는 생각, 즉 감정 상태와 상황까지도 사회 관계망을 통해 전파될 수 있다는 것을 보여주었다. ② 이러한 종류의 전염의 증거는 분명한데, '학구적인 룸메이트와 함께 하는 학생들은 더욱 학구적이 되고, 폭식하는 사람 옆에 앉아 식사하는 사람은 더 많은 음식을 먹는다.' ③ 그러나 Christakis와 Fowler에 따르면 우리는 우리의 친구의 친구의 친구를 훨씬 넘어서(다시 말해 고작 세 단계의 분절을 건너서는) 생각과 행동을 전파할 수 없다. 이것은 생각이나 행동의 전파와 수용이 편지나 어떤 고용 기회가 있다는 말을 전달하는 것보다 더 강한 연결을 요구하기 때문이다. ④ 단지 사람을 아는 것은 그들이 더 공부하거나 과식하도록 영향을 미칠 수 있는 것과는 같지 않다. ⑤ 모방은 그것이 무의식적일 때조차도 실로 가장 순수한 형태의 아첨이다.

Why? 왜 정답일까?
③ 앞에서 뉴스, 소문, 혁신뿐 아니라 감정 상태나 상황 또한 흔히 사람들 간에 전염처럼 번질 수 있다고 언급한 데 이어, 주어진 문장은 친구의 친구의 친구, 즉 세 단계를 걸쳐 아는 사람들을 넘어서면 그 전파력이 잘 발휘되지 않는다는 상반된 내용을 제시한다. ③ 뒤의 문장은 주어진 문장 내용을 This로 받으며, 생각이나 행동의 전파 또는 수용이 편지나 정보를 단순히 전달하는 경우보다 더 강한 유대나 연결을 요구하기 때문이라는 이유를 제시한다. 따라서 주어진 문장이 들어가기에 가장 적절한 곳은 ③이다.

- transmit Ⓥ 전달하다
- innovation Ⓝ 혁신
- studious Ⓐ 학구적인
- relaying Ⓝ (정보나 뉴스 등의) 전달
- unconscious Ⓐ 무의식적인
- separation Ⓝ 단절, 분리
- contagion Ⓝ 전염
- reception Ⓝ 수용
- merely ⓐd 단지, 그저

구문 풀이
6행 More recent research has shown that ideas — (even emotional states and conditions) — can be transmitted through a social network.
접속사(~것), 주어, ( ): 삽입구, 조동사 수동태

★★ 문제 해결 꿀~팁 ★★
▶ 많이 틀린 이유는?
④ 앞에서 생각이나 행동을 전파할 때는 단순히 소식이나 정보를 전달할 때보다 더 강한 연결이 필요하다고 설명한다. 이어서 ④ 뒤의 문장에서는 단지 사람을 안다고 해서 그 사람의 행동에 영향을 미칠 수 있다고 볼 수는 없다고 언급한다. 즉 ④ 앞뒤로 생각이나 행동에 영향을 미치려면 '알고 있는 것 이상'의 강한 연결고리가 필요하다는 내용이 일관성 있게 제시되므로, 주어진 문장은 ④에 들어갈 수 없다.
▶ 문제 해결 방법은?
③ 앞뒤로 '생각·행동이 사회 관계망을 통해 전파되는 경우 vs. 그 전파가 어려운 경우'가 대비되고 있음을 파악하도록 한다.

40 기억의 왜곡을 유발하는 외부적 요인 정답률 53% | 정답 ①

다음 글의 내용을 한 문장으로 요약하고자 한다. 빈칸 (A), (B)에 들어갈 말로 가장 적절한 것은?

(A)	(B)
☑ stable 안정된	······ falsified 왜곡된
② fragile 허술한	······ modified 수정된
③ stable 안정된	······ intensified 강화된
④ fragile 허술한	······ solidified 공고히 된
⑤ concrete 수동적인	······ maintained 유지하는

In 2011, / Micah Edelson and his colleagues / conducted an interesting experiment / about external factors of memory manipulation.
2011년 / Micah Edelson과 그의 동료들이 / 흥미로운 실험을 했다. / 기억 조작의 외부 요인들에 대한
In their experiment, / participants were shown a two minute documentary film / and then asked a series of questions about the video.
그들의 실험에서 / 참가자들은 2분짜리 다큐멘터리 영상을 보고 나서 / 그 영상에 대한 일련의 질문을 받았다.
Directly after viewing the videos, / participants made few errors in their responses / and were correctly able to recall the details.
그 영상을 본 직후 / 참가자들은 응답에서 거의 실수를 하지 않았고 / 세부 사항을 정확하게 기억해 낼 수 있었다.

Four days later, / they could still remember the details / and didn't allow their memories to be swayed / when they were presented with any false information about the film.
4일 후에 / 그들은 여전히 세부 사항을 기억할 수 있었고 / 자신의 기억이 흔들리게 두지 않았다. / 그들이 영상에 관한 어떤 잘못된 정보를 제시받았을 때에도
This changed, however, / when participants were shown fake responses about the film / made by other participants.
그러나 이것이 바뀌었다. / 참가자들이 그 영상에 관한 거짓 응답을 봤을 때 / 다른 참가자들이 한
Upon seeing the incorrect answers of others, / participants were also drawn toward the wrong answers themselves.
다른 사람들의 올바르지 않은 응답을 보자마자 / 참가자들 자신 또한 잘못된 응답 쪽으로 이끌려 갔다.
Even after they found out / that the other answers had been fabricated / and didn't have anything to do with the documentary, / it was too late.
심지어 그들이 알아낸 뒤에도 / 다른 응답들은 조작되었으며 / 그 다큐멘터리와 아무 상관이 없다는 것을 / 이는 너무 늦어버린 후였다.
The participants were no longer able / to distinguish between truth and fiction.
참가자들은 더 이상 ~할 수 없었다. / 진실과 허구를 구분하는
They had already modified their memories / to fit the group.
그들은 이미 자신의 기억을 수정했다. / 집단에 맞게끔
➡ According to the experiment, / when participants were given false information itself, / their memories remained (A) stable, / but their memories were (B) falsified / when they were exposed to other participants' fake responses.
실험에 따르면, / 참가자들이 거짓된 정보 자체를 제공받았을 때 / 그들의 기억은 안정된 상태로 남아있었으나 / 그들의 기억이 왜곡되었다. / 그들이 다른 참가자들의 거짓 응답에 노출되었을 때

2011년 Micah Edelson과 그의 동료들이 기억 조작의 외부 요인들에 대한 흥미로운 실험을 했다. 그들의 실험에서 참가자들은 2분짜리 다큐멘터리 영상을 보고 나서 그 영상에 관한 일련의 질문을 받았다. 그 영상을 본 직후 참가자들은 응답에서 거의 실수를 하지 않았고 세부 사항들을 정확하게 기억해 낼 수 있었다. 4일 후에 그들은 여전히 세부 사항을 기억할 수 있었고 영상에 관한 어떤 잘못된 정보가 제시되었을 때에도 자신의 기억이 흔들리게 두지 않았다. 그러나 참가자들이 그 영상에 관한 다른 참가자들이 한 거짓 응답을 봤을 때 이것이 바뀌었다. 다른 사람들의 올바르지 않은 응답을 보자마자 참가자들 자신 또한 잘못된 응답 쪽으로 이끌려 갔다. 심지어 그들이 다른 응답들은 조작되었으며 그 다큐멘터리와 아무 상관이 없다는 것을 알아낸 뒤에도, 이는 너무 늦어버린 후였다. 참가자들은 더 이상 진실과 허구를 구분할 수 없었다. 그들은 이미 자신의 기억을 집단에 맞게끔 수정했다.

➡ 실험에 따르면 참가자들이 거짓된 정보 자체를 제공받았을 때 그들의 기억은 (A) 안정된 상태로 남아있었으나 다른 참가자들의 거짓 응답에 노출되었을 때 그들의 기억이 (B) 왜곡되었다.

Why? 왜 정답일까?
'This changed, however, when participants were shown fake responses about the film made by other participants.' 이후로, 사람들은 본래 혼자서는 정확히 기억하고 있던 것도 다른 사람들이 제공했다는 '잘못된' 정보에 노출되면 혼동하기 시작한다는 내용이 이어지고 있다. 이는 마지막 문장에서 말하듯이 사람들이 집단 기억에 맞추어 자신의 기억을 수정하는 경향이 있기(They had already modified their memories to fit the group.) 때문임을 알 수 있다. 따라서 요약문의 빈칸에 들어갈 말로 가장 적절한 것은 ① '(A) stable(안정된), (B) falsified(왜곡된)'이다.

- external Ⓐ 외부의
- a series of 일련의
- sway Ⓥ 흔들다, 동요시키다
- fabricate Ⓥ (거짓 정보를) 날조하다, 조작하다
- distinguish between A and B A와 B를 구별하다
- modify Ⓥ 수정하다
- solidify Ⓥ 공고히 하다
- manipulation Ⓝ 조작
- recall Ⓥ 회상하다, 기억하다
- present A with B A에게 B를 제시하다
- intensify Ⓥ 강화하다

구문 풀이
11행 Upon seeing the incorrect answers of others, participants were also drawn toward the wrong answers themselves.
「upon + 동명사」: ~하자마자, 주어, 동사(수동태), 재귀대명사(주어 강조)

41-42 사회성으로 인한 인간의 뇌 발달

「Evolutionary biologists believe / sociability drove the evolution of our complex brains.」
진화생물학자들은 믿는다. / 사회성이 우리의 복잡한 뇌의 진화를 이끌었다고 (41번의 근거)
Fossil evidence shows / that as far back as 130,000 years ago, / it was not (a) unusual for Homo sapiens / to travel more than a hundred and fifty miles / to trade, share food and, no doubt, gossip.
화석 증거는 보여준다. / 13만 년 전이라는 먼 옛날에 / 호모사피엔스로서는 이상한 일이 아니었다는 것을 / 150마일 이상을 이동하는 것이 / 거래하러, 음식을 공유하러, 그리고 의심의 여지없이 잡담을 하러
Unlike the Neanderthals, / their social groups extended far beyond their own families.
네안데르탈인과는 다르게 / 그들의 사회 집단은 그들 자신의 가족을 훨씬 넘어서서 뻗어 있었다.
Remembering all those (b) connections, / who was related to whom, and where they lived / required considerable processing power.
모든 그런 연결을 기억하는 것은 / 누가 누구와 관련이 있는지 그리고 그들이 어디에 사는지 / 상당한 처리 능력을 요구했다.
It also required wayfinding savvy.
그것은 또한 길 찾기 요령을 요구했다.
Imagine trying to (c) maintain a social network / across tens or hundreds of square miles of Palaeolithic wilderness.
사회 관계망을 유지하려고 한다고 상상해 보라. / 구석기 시대 황야의 수십 혹은 수백 제곱 마일을 가로지르는
You couldn't send a text message to your friends / to find out where they were / — you had to go out and visit them, / remember where you last saw them / or imagine where they might have gone.
여러분은 친구들에게 문자 메시지를 보낼 수도 없다. / 그들이 어디에 있는지 알아내기 위해 / 여러분은 나가서 그들을 방문하거나, / 마지막으로 그들을 어디에서 보았는지 기억해 내거나 / 혹은 그들이 어디로 갔을지 상상해야만 했다.
To do this, / you needed navigation skills, spatial awareness, a sense of direction, / the ability to store maps of the landscape in your mind / and the motivation to travel around.
이것을 하기 위해, / 여러분은 길 찾기 능력, 공간 인식, 방향 감각을 필요로 했다. / 풍경의 지도를 머릿속에 저장하는 능력, / 그리고 여기저기를 이동할 동기
「Canadian anthropologist Ariane Burke believes / that our ancestors (d) developed all these attributes / while trying to keep in touch with their neighbours.」
캐나다 인류학자 Ariane Burke는 믿는다. / 우리 조상들이 이 모든 속성을 발전시켰다고 / 그들의 이웃들과 연락하려고 애쓰는 동안

캐나다 인류학자인 Ariane Burke는 믿는다. / 우리의 조상이 이러한 모든 특징들을 발달시켰다고 / 자신의 이웃과 연락하고 지내려고 하는 동안

Eventually, our brains became primed for wayfinding. 42번의 근거

마침내 우리의 두뇌가 길 찾기를 위한 준비를 하게 된 것이다.

Meanwhile / the Neanderthals, / who didn't travel as far, / never fostered a spatial skill set; / despite being sophisticated hunters, / well adapted to the cold / and able to see in the dark, / they went extinct.

한편, / 네안데르탈인은 / 그만큼 멀리 이동하지 않았고 / 다양한 공간 능력을 전혀 발전시키지 못했다. / 수준 높은 사냥꾼이었음에도 불구하고, / 추위에 잘 적응했으며 / 어둠 속에서도 볼 수 있었지만 / 그들은 멸종하게 되었다.

In the prehistoric badlands, / nothing was more (e) useful than a circle of friends.

선사 시대의 불모지에서는 / 그 어떤 것도 친구 집단보다 도움이 되는 것은 없었다.

진화생물학자들은 사회성이 우리의 복잡한 뇌의 진화를 이끌었다고 믿는다. 화석 증거는 13만 년 전이라는 먼 옛날에 호모사피엔스가 거래하러, 음식을 공유하러, 의심의 여지없이 잡담을 하러 150마일 이상을 이동하는 것이 (a) 이상한 일이 아니었다는 것을 보여준다. 네안데르탈인과는 다르게 그들의 사회 집단은 그들 자신의 가족을 훨씬 넘어서서 뻗어 있었다. 누가 누구와 관련이 있는지 그리고 그들이 어디에 사는지 모든 그런 (b) 연결을 기억하는 것은 상당한 처리 능력을 요구했다. 그것은 또한 길 찾기 요령을 요구했다. 구석기 시대 황야의 수십 혹은 수백 제곱 마일을 가로지르는 사회 관계망을 (c) 유지하려고 한다고 상상해 보라. 여러분은 친구들이 어디에 있는지 알아내기 위해 그들에게 문자 메시지를 보낼 수도 없다. 여러분은 나가서 그들을 방문하거나, 마지막으로 그들을 어디에서 보았는지 기억해 내거나 혹은 그들이 어디로 갔을지 상상해야만 했다. 이것을 하기 위해, 여러분은 길 찾기 능력, 공간 인식, 방향 감각, 풍경의 지도를 머릿속에 저장하는 능력, 그리고 여기저기를 이동할 동기를 필요로 했다. 캐나다 인류학자인 Ariane Burke는 우리의 조상이 자신의 이웃과 연락하고 지내려고 하는 동안 이러한 모든 특징들을 (d) 발달시켰다고 믿는다. 마침내 우리의 두뇌가 길 찾기를 위한 준비를 하게 된 것이다. 한편, 네안데르탈인은 그만큼 멀리 이동하지 않았고 다양한 공간 능력을 전혀 발전시키지 못했다. 수준 높은 사냥꾼이었으며 추위에 잘 적응했으며 어둠 속에서도 볼 수 있었음에도 불구하고, 그들은 멸종하게 되었다. 선사 시대의 불모지에서는 그 어떤 것도 친구 집단보다 (e) 쓸모없는 (→ 도움이 되는) 것은 없었다.

- sociability ⓝ 사교성, 사회성
- considerable ⓐ 상당한
- spatial ⓐ 공간의
- anthropologist ⓝ 인류학자
- keep in touch with ~와 연락하다
- sophisticated ⓐ 수준 높은, 정교한
- prehistoric ⓐ 선사 시대의
- extend ⓥ 뻗다, 확장하다
- wilderness ⓝ 황무지
- landscape ⓝ 풍경
- attribute ⓝ 특성
- primed for ~의 준비가 된
- extinct ⓐ 멸종된
- badland ⓝ 악지, 불모지

구문 풀이

2행 Fossil evidence shows that as far back as 130,000 years ago, it was not
접속사(~것) 가주어
unusual for Homo sapiens to travel more than a hundred and fifty miles to trade,
의미상 주어 진주어 to부정사구 부정사구1
share food and, no doubt, gossip.
부정사구2 부정사구3(~하기 위해)

---

41 제목 파악 정답률 58% | 정답 ①

윗글의 제목으로 가장 적절한 것은?

✓① Social Networks: An Evolutionary Advantage
사회적 연결망: 진화적 이점
② Our Brain Forced Us to Stay Close to Our Family!
우리 뇌는 우리가 가족의 근처에 있도록 강요했다!
③ How We Split from Our Way and Kept Going on My Way
우리는 어떻게 우리의 길에서 벗어나와 나의 길을 가는가
④ Why Do Some People Have Difficulty in Social Relationships?
왜 어떤 사람들은 사회적 관계에 어려움을 겪는가?
⑤ Being Connected to Each Other Leads to Communicative Skills
서로 연결되는 것이 의사소통 능력으로 이어진다

Why? 왜 정답일까?

첫 문장인 '~ sociability drove the evolution of our complex brains.'에서 인간의 사회성은 인간의 뇌 발달을 이끌어낸 요소라는 주제를 제시하므로, 글의 제목으로 가장 적절한 것은 ① '사회적 연결망: 진화적 이점'이다.

---

42 어휘 추론 정답률 61% | 정답 ⑤

밑줄 친 (a)~(e) 중에서 문맥상 낱말의 쓰임이 적절하지 않은 것은? [3점]

① (a)   ② (b)   ③ (c)   ④ (d)   ✓⑤ (e)

Why? 왜 정답일까?

'~ our ancestors developed all these attributes while trying to keep in touch with their neighbours. Eventually, our brains became primed for wayfinding.'에서 인간은 이웃과 계속 연락하고 지내려고 노력하는 동안 길 찾기에 필요한 능력을 갖추게 되었다고 언급한다. 즉 '친구 집단'이 우리의 뇌 발달에 도움이 되었다는 것이다. 이를 근거로 할 때, (e)의 useless는 반의어인 useful로 고쳐야 한다. 문맥상 낱말의 쓰임이 적절하지 않은 것은 ⑤ '(e)'이다.

43-45 크리스마스에 Martha 가족에게 생긴 일

(A)

"You've been a very good girl this year, Emma.

"Emma, 올해 너는 참 착한 아이였어.

Tonight, / Santa will drop by our house / to leave you some presents."

오늘밤, / 산타 할아버지가 우리 집에 들러서 / 너에게 선물을 몇 개 두고 가실 거야."

Martha told (a) her little girl, smiling.

Martha가 자신의 귀여운 딸에게 웃으며 말했다.

"And for you too, Fred," she added.

"Fred 너에게도." 그녀가 덧붙였다.

"Fred 너에게도." 그녀가 덧붙였다.

She wanted to give her two children so much more, / but this year had been especially hard for Martha. 45번 ①의 근거 일치

그녀는 자신의 두 아이들에게 훨씬 많은 것을 주길 원했지만 / 올해는 Martha에게 특히 힘들었다.

She had worked day and night / to buy some Christmas gifts for her children.

그녀는 밤낮으로 일했다. / 자신의 두 아이들에게 크리스마스 선물을 사 주기 위해

(C)

That night, after everyone had gone to bed, / Emma slowly climbed out of bed.

그날 밤, 모두가 잠들고 난 후 / Emma는 천천히 침대 밖으로 기어 나왔다.

She took out a page from a notebook / to write a letter to Santa. 45번 ④의 근거 일치

그녀는 공책 한 장을 찢어 냈다. / 산타 할아버지에게 편지를 쓰기 위해

She whispered to herself as she wrote.

그녀는 쓰면서 혼자 작은 소리로 속삭였다.

"Dear Santa, / will you send a few smiles and laughs for my mother?

"산타 할아버지께, / 저희 엄마에게 미소와 웃음을 조금 보내주실 수 있나요?

(c) She doesn't laugh much.

엄마는 별로 웃지 않아요.

And will you send a few toys for Fred as well? / Thank you."

그리고 Fred를 위한 장난감도 몇 개 보내주실 수 있나요? / 고맙습니다."

Emma folded the letter twice / and sealed it within an envelope.

Emma는 그 편지를 두 번 접어 / 그것을 봉투에 넣고 붙였다.

She left the envelope outside the front door / and went back to sleep.

그녀는 현관 밖에 그 봉투를 두고 나서 / 다시 잠자리에 들었다.

(B)

Emma came running up to her mother the next morning.

다음 날 아침 Emma가 엄마에게 뛰어왔다.

"Mommy, Santa really did come last night!"

"엄마, 어젯밤 정말로 산타 할아버지가 오셨어요!"

Martha smiled, / thinking of the candies and cookies / (b) she must have found in her socks.

Martha가 미소 지었다. / 사탕과 쿠키를 떠올리며 / 양말 속에서 딸이 틀림없이 발견했을

"Did you like his gifts?"

"산타 할아버지가 주신 선물들이 마음에 들었니?"

"Yes, they are wonderful.

"네, 멋져요.

Fred loves his toys, too." 45번 ②의 근거 일치

Fred도 그분이 주신 장난감들이 마음에 든대요."

Martha was confused.

Martha는 혼란스러웠다.

She wondered / how the candies and cookies had become toys overnight.

그녀는 궁금했다. / 사탕과 쿠키가 하룻밤 사이에 어떻게 장난감이 되었는지

Martha ran into Emma's room / and saw a small red box that was half open. 45번 ③의 근거 불일치

Martha는 Emma의 방으로 뛰어 들어가서 / 반쯤 열려 있는 작은 빨간 상자를 보았다.

She knelt down and glanced inside to see its contents.

그녀는 무릎을 꿇고 그 내용물을 보기 위해 안을 들여다보았다.

(D)

The box contained some toys, countless little candies and cookies.

그 상자는 장난감 몇 개, 그리고 셀 수 없이 많은 작은 사탕과 쿠키를 담고 있었다.

"Mommy, this is for you from Santa."

"엄마, 이건 산타 할아버지가 엄마에게 주신 거예요."

Emma said / holding out a card towards Martha. 45번 ⑤의 근거 일치

Emma가 말했다. / Martha를 향해 카드 하나를 내밀며

Puzzled, (d) she opened it.

당황한 채로, 그녀는 그것을 열었다.

It said, / "Dear Emma's mother.

거기에는 쓰여 있었다. / "Emma 어머님께.

A very merry Christmas!

정말 메리 크리스마스입니다!

Hi, I am Amelia.

안녕하세요, 저는 Amelia입니다.

I found your child's letter blowing across the street last night.

어젯밤 길 건너편에서 자녀분이 쓴 편지가 바람에 날아다니고 있는 걸 보았어요.

I was touched and couldn't help but respond.

제가 감동 받아 답장을 하지 않을 수 없었습니다.

Please accept the gift as a Christmas greeting."

부디 이 선물을 크리스마스 인사로 받아주세요."

Martha felt tears falling down (e) her cheeks.

Martha는 눈물이 자신의 볼을 타고 흘러내리는 것을 느꼈다.

She slowly wiped them off and hugged her daughter.

그녀는 천천히 눈물을 닦고 딸을 껴안았다.

"Merry Christmas, Emma.

"Emma, 메리 크리스마스.

Didn't I tell you Santa would come?"

엄마가 너에게 산타 할아버지가 오실 거라고 말했었지?"

(A)

"Emma, 올해 너는 참 착한 아이였어. 오늘밤, 산타 할아버지가 우리 집에 들러서 너에게 선물을 몇 개 두고 가실 거야." Martha가 (a) 자신의 귀여운 딸에게 웃으며 말했다. "Fred 너에게도." 그녀가 덧붙였다. 그녀는 두 아이들에게 훨씬 더 많은 것을 주길 원했지만 올해는 Martha에게 특히 힘들었다. 그녀는 두 아이들에게 크리스마스 선물을 사 주기 위해 밤낮으로 일했다.

(C)

그날 밤, 모두가 잠들고 난 후 Emma는 천천히 침대 밖으로 기어 나왔다. 그녀는 산타 할아버지에게 편지를 쓰기 위해 공책 한 장을 찢어 냈다. 그녀는 쓰면서 혼자 작은 소리로 속삭였다. "산타 할아버지께, 저희 엄마에게 미소와 웃음을 조금 보내주실 수 있나요? (c) 엄마는 별로 웃지 않아요. 그리고 Fred를 위한 장난감도 몇 개 보내주실 수 있나요? 고맙습니다." Emma는 그 편지를 두 번 접어 봉투에 넣고 붙였다. 그녀는 현관 밖에 그 봉투를 두고 나서 다시 잠자리에 들었다.

(B)

다음 날 아침 Emma가 엄마에게 뛰어왔다. "엄마, 어젯밤 정말로 산타 할아버지가 오셨어요!" 양말 속에서 (b) 딸이 틀림없이 발견했을 사탕과 쿠키를 떠올리며 Martha가 미소 지었다. "산타 할아버지가 주신 선물들이 마음에 들었니?" "네, 멋져요. Fred도 그분이 주신 장난감들이 마음에 든대요." Martha는 혼란스러웠다. 그녀는 사탕과 쿠키가 하룻밤 사이에 어떻게

장난감이 되었는지 궁금했다. Martha는 Emma의 방으로 뛰어 들어가서 반쯤 열려 있는 작은 빨간 상자를 보았다. 그녀는 무릎을 꿇고 그 내용물을 보기 위해 안을 들여다보았다.

(D)

그 상자는 장난감 몇 개, 그리고 셀 수 없이 많은 작은 사탕과 쿠키를 담고 있었다. "엄마, 이건 산타 할아버지가 엄마에게 주신 거예요." Emma가 Martha를 향해 카드 하나를 내밀며 말했다. 당황한 채로, (d) 그녀는 그것을 열었다. 거기에는 이렇게 쓰여 있었다. "Emma 어머님께. 정말 메리 크리스마스입니다! 안녕하세요, 저는 Amelia입니다. 어젯밤 길 건너편에서 자녀분이 쓴 편지가 바람에 날아다니고 있는 걸 보았습니다. 제가 감동 받아 답장을 하지 않을 수 없었습니다. 부디 이 선물을 크리스마스 인사로 받아주세요." Martha는 눈물이 (e) 자신의 볼을 타고 흘러내리는 것을 느꼈다. 그녀는 천천히 눈물을 닦고 딸을 껴안았다. "Emma, 메리 크리스마스. 엄마가 너에게 산타 할아버지가 오실 거라고 말했었지?"

- drop by ~에 들르다
- kneel down 꿇어 앉다
- whisper ⓥ 속삭이다
- seal ⓥ 봉인하다
- countless ⓐ 무수히 많은
- overnight [ad] 하룻밤 사이에
- glance 홀긋 보다
- fold ⓥ 접다
- envelope ⓝ 봉투

구문 풀이

(A) 3행 She wanted to give her two children so much more, but this year
주어1 동사1 주어2
had been especially hard for Martha.
동사2(과거완료 : wanted보다 이전)

(B) 2행 Martha smiled, thinking of the candies and cookies [(that) she must have
분사구문(~하면서) 선행사 생략 「must have
found in her socks].
p.p. : ~했음에 틀림없다」

(D) 5행 I was touched and couldn't help but respond.
「cannot help but + 동사원형 : ~하지 않을 수 없다」

---

43 글의 순서 파악　　　　　　　　정답률 82% | 정답 ②

주어진 글 (A)에 이어질 내용을 순서에 맞게 배열한 것으로 가장 적절한 것은?
① (B) − (D) − (C)
② (C) − (B) − (D) ✓
③ (C) − (D) − (B)
④ (D) − (B) − (C)
⑤ (D) − (C) − (B)

Why? 왜 정답일까?

시간적 단서를 잘 활용해야 하는 순서 문제이다. (A)에서 Martha가 크리스마스를 맞이해 아이들에게 선물을 사주기 위해 밤낮으로 일하고 있었다는 상황을 묘사한 데 이어, (C)에서는 산타클로스를 기다리던 '그날 밤(That night)' 딸인 Emma가 어머니에게 미소와 웃음을 달라는 편지를 쓰고 잠들었다는 내용을 제시한다. 이어서 (B)는 '다음 날 아침(the next morning)' 딸과 아들에게 자신이 준비한 쿠키 대신 장난감 선물이 주어졌다는 것을 안 Martha가 딸의 방에 들어가 상자를 확인해 보았다는 내용을 제시한다. 마지막으로 (D)는 Martha가 편지를 통해 Amelia라는 이웃이 Emma의 편지를 우연히 발견하고는 선물을 대신 준비해주었음을 알게 되었다는 결말을 제시한다. 따라서 글의 순서로 가장 적절한 것은 ② '(C) − (B) − (D)'이다.

---

44 지칭 추론　　　　　　　　정답률 66% | 정답 ②

밑줄 친 (a) ~ (e) 중에서 가리키는 대상이 나머지 넷과 다른 것은?
① (a)
② (b) ✓
③ (c)
④ (d)
⑤ (e)

Why? 왜 정답일까?

(a), (c), (d), (e)는 Martha를, (b)는 Emma를 가리키므로, (a) ~ (e) 중에서 가리키는 대상이 다른 하나는 ② '(b)'이다.

---

45 세부 내용 파악　　　　　　　　정답률 77% | 정답 ③

윗글에 관한 내용으로 적절하지 <u>않은</u> 것은?
① 올해는 Martha에게 힘든 한 해였다.
② Fred가 선물받은 장난감을 마음에 들어 했다.
③ Martha가 자신의 방에서 작은 빨간 상자를 보았다. ✓
④ Emma가 산타에게 편지를 썼다.
⑤ Emma가 Martha에게 산타가 보냈다고 말하며 카드를 내밀었다.

Why? 왜 정답일까?

(B) 'Martha ran into Emma's room and saw a small red box that was half open.'에 따르면 Martha가 빨간 상자를 발견한 곳은 자신의 방이 아닌 딸 Emma의 방이다. 따라서 내용과 일치하지 않는 것은 ③ 'Martha가 자신의 방에서 작은 빨간 상자를 보았다.'이다.

Why? 왜 오답일까?

① (A) '~ but this year had been especially hard for Martha.'의 내용과 일치한다.
② (B) 'Fred loves his toys, too.'의 내용과 일치한다.
④ (C) 'She took out a page from a notebook to write a letter to Santa.'의 내용과 일치한다.
⑤ (D) '"Mommy, this is for you from Santa." Emma said holding out a card towards Martha.'의 내용과 일치한다.

• 정답 •

18 ① 19 ⑤ 20 ② ★21 ① 22 ⑤ 23 ③ 24 ② 25 ④ 26 ④ 27 ④ 28 ③ 29 ④ 30 ② 31 ① ★32 ②
33 ⑤ 34 ② 35 ④ 36 ③ ★37 ④ 38 ③ 39 ④ 40 ① 41 ③ ★42 ④ 43 ② 44 ⑤ 45 ④

★ 표기된 문항은 [등급을 가르는 문제]에 해당하는 문항입니다.

---

18 초청 연사 강연 요청
정답률 93% | 정답 ①

다음 글의 목적으로 가장 적절한 것은?

☑ 회사 행사에 초청 연사로 와 줄 것을 요청하려고
② 회사의 행사 일정이 변경된 이유를 설명하려고
③ 체계적인 시간 관리 방법을 제안하려고
④ 기업의 효율적 경영에 대한 조언을 부탁하려고
⑤ 의사 결정 과정에서 토의의 중요성을 강조하려고

Dear Mr. Coleman,
Coleman 씨 귀하.

I'm Aaron Brown, the director of TAC company.
저는 TAC 회사의 이사 Aaron Brown입니다.

To celebrate our company's 10th anniversary / and to boost further growth, / we have arranged a small event.
저희 회사의 10주년을 기념하고 / 추가적인 성장을 촉진시키기 위해, / 저희는 작은 행사를 마련했습니다.

It will be an informative afternoon / with enlightening discussions on business trends.
그 행사는 유익한 오후가 될 것입니다. / 사업 동향에 대해 깨우침을 주는 토론이 있는

I recently attended your lecture / about recent issues in business / and it was really impressive.
최근에 저는 당신의 강연에 참석하였고 / 사업의 새로운 논쟁점에 대한 / 그것은 매우 인상적이었습니다.

I am writing this letter to request / that you be our guest speaker for the afternoon.
저는 요청하기 위해 이 편지를 쓰고 있습니다. / 귀하가 오후 행사에 초청 연사가 되어줄 것을

Your experience and knowledge / will benefit our businesses in many ways.
귀하의 경험과 지식이 / 저희 사업에 다방면으로 도움이 될 것입니다.

It would be a pleasure to have you with us.
귀하께서 저희와 함께 해주신다면 기쁠 것입니다.

The planned schedule includes a guest speaker's speech / and a question and answer session / on Thursday, the 21st of November, 2019 at 3:00 p.m.
계획된 일정은 초청 연사 강연을 포함합니다. / 그리고 질의응답 시간을 / 2019년 11월 21일 목요일 오후 3시에

We would sincerely appreciate it / if you could make some time for us.
저희는 진심으로 감사하겠습니다. / 귀하께서 저희를 위해 시간을 내주신다면

We will be looking forward to hearing from you soon.
저희는 귀하의 빠른 답변을 기대하고 있겠습니다.

Yours Sincerely, // Aaron Brown
Aaron Brown 드림

Coleman 씨 귀하,

저는 TAC 회사의 이사 Aaron Brown입니다. 저희 회사의 10주년을 기념하고 추가적인 성장을 촉진시키기 위해, 저희는 작은 행사를 마련했습니다. 그 행사는 사업 동향에 대해 깨우침을 주는 토론이 있는 유익한 오후가 될 것입니다. 최근에 저는 사업의 새로운 논쟁점에 대한 당신의 강연에 참석하였고 그것은 매우 인상적이었습니다. 저는 귀하가 오후 행사에 초청 연사가 되어줄 것을 요청하기 위해 이 편지를 쓰고 있습니다. 귀하의 경험과 지식이 저희 사업에 다방면으로 도움이 될 것입니다. 귀하께서 저희와 함께 해주신다면 기쁠 것입니다. 계획된 일정은 2019년 11월 21일 목요일 오후 3시에 초청 연사 강연과 질의응답 시간을 포함합니다. 귀하께서 저희를 위해 시간을 내주신다면 저희는 진심으로 감사하겠습니다. 귀하의 빠른 답변을 기대하고 있겠습니다.

Aaron Brown 드림

Why? 왜 정답일까?

'I am writing this letter to request that you be our guest speaker for the afternoon.'에서 초청 연사로 와 주기를 부탁하기 위해 편지를 쓴다는 내용이 나오므로, 글의 목적으로 가장 적절한 것은 ① '회사 행사에 초청 연사로 와 줄 것을 요청하려고'이다.

● informative ⓐ 유익한
● impressive ⓐ 인상적인
● enlightening ⓐ 깨우침을 주는
● appreciate ⓥ 감사하다

구문 풀이

6행 I am writing this letter to request that you (should) be our guest speaker for the afternoon.
「request + that + 주어 + (should) 동사원형 : ～이 ～하기를 요청하다」

---

19 파티 도중 공습이 시작되어 겁에 질린 필자 일행
정답률 86% | 정답 ⑤

다음 글에 드러난 'I'의 심경 변화로 가장 적절한 것은?

① indifferent → satisfied
  무관심한   만족한
② relaxed → envious
  여유로운 부러워하는
③ frustrated → relieved
  좌절한   안도한
④ excited → bored
  신난   지루한
☑ pleased → terrified
  유쾌한   공포에 질린

One night, my family was having a party / with a couple from another city / who had two daughters.
어느 날 밤 우리 가족은 파티를 하고 있었다. / 다른 도시에서 온 부부와 / 두 딸이 있는

The girls were just a few years older than I, / and I played lots of fun games together with them.
그 소녀들은 나보다 단지 몇 살 많았고, / 나는 그들과 함께 많은 재미있는 게임을 했다.

The father of the family had an amusing, jolly, witty character, / and I had a memorable night / full of laughter and joy.
그 가족의 아버지는 재미있고 쾌활하며 재치 있는 성격이셨고, / 나는 잊지 못할 밤을 보냈다. / 웃음과 기쁨으로 가득한

While we laughed, joked, and had our dinner, / the TV suddenly broadcast an air attack, / and a screeching siren started to scream, / announcing the "red" situation.
우리가 웃고 농담하며 저녁을 먹는 동안, / TV에서 갑자기 공습을 알렸고, / 날카로운 사이렌이 울리기 시작했다. / '긴급' 상황을 알리며

We all stopped dinner, / and we squeezed into the basement.
우리는 모두 저녁 식사를 멈추고, / 지하실로 비집고 들어갔다.

The siren kept screaming / and the roar of planes was heard in the sky.
사이렌은 계속 울렸고 / 비행기의 굉음이 하늘에서 들렸다.

The terror of war was overwhelming.
전쟁의 공포는 압도적이었다.

Shivering with fear, / I murmured a panicked prayer / that this desperate situation would end quickly.
두려움에 떨며, / 나는 겁에 질린 기도를 중얼거렸다. / 이 절망적인 상황이 빨리 끝나게 해달라는

어느 날 밤 우리 가족은 다른 도시에서 온 두 딸이 있는 부부와 파티를 하고 있었다. 그 소녀들은 나보다 단지 몇 살 많았고, 나는 그들과 함께 많은 재미있는 게임을 했다. 그 가족의 아버지는 재미있고 쾌활하며 재치 있는 성격이셨고, 나는 웃음과 기쁨으로 가득한 잊지 못할 밤을 보냈다. 우리가 웃고 농담하며 저녁을 먹는 동안, TV에서 갑자기 공습을 알렸고, 날카로운 사이렌이 '긴급' 상황을 알리며 울리기 시작했다. 우리는 모두 저녁 식사를 멈추고 지하실로 비집고 들어갔다. 사이렌은 계속 울렸고 비행기의 굉음이 하늘에서 들렸다. 전쟁의 공포는 압도적이었다. 두려움에 떨며, 나는 이 절망적인 상황이 빨리 끝나게 해달라는 겁에 질린 기도를 중얼거렸다.

Why? 왜 정답일까?

'～ the TV suddenly broadcast an air attack, ～' 앞뒤로 글의 흐름이 반전된다. 앞에서는 필자가 다른 가족과의 파티를 즐기며 웃음과 기쁨으로 가득한 밤을 보내고 있었다는(～ I had a memorable night full of laughter and joy.) 내용이 주를 이루는 반면, 뒤에서는 사이렌이 울리고 전쟁의 공포가 상황을 압도하는 가운데 필자 일행이 두려움에 떨었다는(The terror of war was overwhelming. Shivering with fear, I murmured a panicked prayer that this desperate situation would end quickly.) 내용이 주로 묘사되고 있다. 따라서 'I'의 심경 변화로 가장 적절한 것은 ⑤ '유쾌한 → 공포에 질린'이다.

● amusing ⓐ 재미있는
● witty ⓐ 재치 있는
● squeeze into ～로 비집고 들어가다
● overwhelming ⓐ 압도적인
● murmur ⓥ 중얼거리다
● indifferent ⓐ 무관심한
● terrified ⓐ 공포에 질린
● jolly ⓐ 쾌활한
● screeching ⓐ 날카로운 소리를 내는
● roar ⓝ 굉음, 함성
● shiver ⓥ 떨다
● desperate ⓐ 절망적인
● frustrated ⓐ 좌절한

구문 풀이

11행 Shivering with fear, I murmured a panicked prayer [that this desperate situation would end quickly].
분사구문(～하면서)   동격 접속사(= a panicked prayer)

---

20 기억의 중요성
정답률 88% | 정답 ②

다음 글에서 필자가 주장하는 바로 가장 적절한 것은?

① 창의력 신장을 학습 활동의 목표로 삼아야 한다.
☑ 배운 것을 활용하기 위해서는 내용을 기억해야 한다.
③ 기억력 저하를 예방하기 위해 자신의 일상을 기록해야 한다.
④ 자연스러운 분위기를 만들 수 있는 농담을 알고 있어야 한다.
⑤ 학습 의욕을 유지하기 위해서는 실천 가능한 계획을 세워야 한다.

Over the years, / memory has been given a bad name.
수년간 / 기억은 오명을 받아 왔다.

It has been associated with rote learning / and cramming information into your brain.
그것은 암기 학습과 연관되어 왔다. / 그리고 정보를 뇌 속으로 주입하는 것과

Educators have said / that understanding is the key to learning, / but how can you understand something / if you can't remember it?
교육자들이 말해 왔지만 / 이해가 학습의 핵심이라고 / 여러분은 어떻게 어떤 것을 이해할 수 있겠는가? / 만약 여러분이 그것을 기억해내지 못한다면

We have all had this experience: / we recognize and understand information / but can't recall it when we need it.
우리는 모두 이러한 경험을 해본 적이 있다. / 우리가 정보를 인식하고 이해하지만, / 우리가 그것을 필요로 할 때 그것을 기억해 내지 못하는

For example, how many jokes do you know?
예를 들어, 여러분은 몇 개의 농담을 알고 있는가?

You've probably heard thousands, / but you can only recall about four or five right now.
여러분은 아마도 수천 개를 들었겠지만 / 지금 당장은 대략 네 다섯 개만 겨우 기억해 낼 수 있다.

There is a big difference / between remembering your four jokes / and recognizing or understanding thousands.
큰 차이가 있다. / 네 개의 농담을 기억해 내는 것과 / 수천 개를 인식하거나 이해하는 것 사이에는

Understanding doesn't create use: / only when you can instantly recall what you understand, / and practice using your remembered understanding, / do you achieve mastery.
이해는 사용을 만들어 내지 않으며, / 오직 여러분이 이해한 것을 즉각적으로 기억해 내고 / 여러분의 기억된 이해를 사용하는 것을 시행할 수 있을 때 / 여러분은 숙달에 이른다.

Memory means storing what you have learned; / otherwise, why would we bother learning in the first place?
기억은 여러분이 배운 것을 저장하는 것을 의미하는데, / 그렇지 않다면 애초에 우리는 왜 굳이 배우는가?

수년간 기억은 오명을 받아 왔다. 그것은 (기계적인) 암기 학습과 정보를 뇌 속으로 주입하는 것과 연관되어 왔다. 교육자들이 이해가 학습의 핵심이라고 말해 왔지만, 만약 여러분이 어떤 것을 기억해내지 못한다면 어떻게 그것을 이해할 수 있겠는가? 우리는 모두 우리가 정보를 인식하고 이해하지만, 우리가 그것을 필요로 할 때 그것을 기억해 내지 못하는 이러한 경험을 해본 적이 있다. 예를 들어, 여러분은 몇 개의 농담을 알고 있는가? 여러분은 아마도 수천 개

를 들었겠지만 지금 당장은 대략 네 다섯 개만 겨우 기억해 낼 수 있다. 네 개의 농담을 기억해 내는 것과 수천 개를 인식하거나 이해하는 것 사이에는 큰 차이가 있다. 이해는 사용을 만들어 내지 않으며, 오직 여러분이 이해한 것을 즉각적으로 기억해 내고 여러분의 기억된 이해를 사용하는 것을 시행할 수 있을 때 여러분은 숙달에 이른다. 기억은 여러분이 배운 것을 저장하는 것을 의미하는데, 그렇지 않다면 애초에 우리는 왜 굳이 배우는가?

'~ only when you can instantly recall what you understand, and practice using your remembered understanding, do you achieve mastery. Memory means storing what you have learned; otherwise, why would we bother learning in the first place?'에서 배운 것을 이해하더라도 우선 기억하고 사용해야 숙달의 경지에 이를 수 있다고 하므로, 필자의 주장으로 가장 적절한 것은 ② '배운 것을 활용하기 위해서는 내용을 기억해야 한다.'이다.

- be associated with ~와 연관되다
- cram into ~에 쑤셔 넣다
- mastery ⑩ 숙달
- bother ⓥ 굳이 ~하다
- rote learning (기계적인) 암기 학습
- instantly [ad] 즉각적으로
- otherwise [ad] 그렇지 않으면
- in the first place 애초에

구문 풀이

10행 Understanding doesn't create use: only when you can instantly recall what you understand, and practice using your remembered understanding, do you achieve mastery.
「only + 부사절 +」
「조동사 + 주어 + 동사원형 : 도치 구문」

★★★ 등급을 가르는 문제!

21 크라우드 펀딩과 기업 자금 조달   정답률 36% | 정답 ①

밑줄 친 the democratization of business financing이 다음 글에서 의미하는 바로 가장 적절한 것은?

☑ More people can be involved in funding a business.
더 많은 사람들이 사업 자금 조달에 관여할 수 있다.
② More people will participate in developing new products.
더 많은 사람들이 신제품 개발에 참여하게 된다.
③ Crowdfunding can reinforce the conventional way of financing.
크라우드 펀딩은 전통적 자금 조달 방식을 강화할 수 있다.
④ Crowdfunding keeps social networking from facilitating funding.
크라우드 펀딩은 소셜 네트워크가 펀딩을 용이하게 하지 못하게 만든다.
⑤ The Internet helps employees of a company interact with each other.
인터넷은 한 회사의 직원들이 서로 상호작용하는 것을 돕는다.

Crowdfunding is a new and more collaborative way / to secure funding for projects.
크라우드 펀딩은 새롭고 더 협력적인 방법이다. / 프로젝트를 위한 자금을 확보하는
It can be used in different ways / such as requesting donations / for a worthy cause anywhere in the world / and generating funding for a project with the contributors / then becoming partners in the project.
그것은 다양한 방식들로 사용될 수 있다. / 기부를 요청하는 것 같은 / 세계 어느 곳에서나 가치 있는 명분을 위한 / 그리고 기부자들과 함께 프로젝트를 위한 자금을 조성하는 것 / 이후에 프로젝트의 파트너가 되는
In essence, / crowdfunding is the fusion / of social networking and venture capitalism.
본질적으로, / 크라우드 펀딩은 융합이다. / 소셜 네트워킹과 벤처 자본주의의
In just the same way / as social networks have rewritten the conventional rules / about how people communicate and interact with each other, / crowdfunding in all its variations / has the potential to rewrite the rules / on how businesses and other projects get funded in the future.
동일한 방식으로 / 소셜 네트워킹이 전통적인 규칙을 다시 쓴 것과 / 사람들이 서로 의사소통하고 상호작용하는 방법에 대한 / 온갖 다양한 방식의 크라우드 펀딩은 / 규칙을 다시 쓸 잠재력을 가진다. / 미래에 기업과 다른 프로젝트가 자금을 얻는 방법에 대한
Crowdfunding can be viewed / as the democratization of business financing.
크라우드 펀딩은 여겨질 수 있다. / 기업 자금 조달의 민주화로
Instead of restricting capital sourcing and allocation / to a relatively small and fixed minority, / crowdfunding empowers everyone / connected to the Internet / to access both the collective wisdom and the pocket money of everyone else / who connects to the Internet.
자본 조달과 할당을 한정하는 대신에 / 비교적 소규모의 고정된 소수에 / 크라우드 펀딩은 모든 사람에게 권한을 준다. / 인터넷에 연결된 / 다른 모든 사람의 집단 지혜와 쌈짓돈 둘 다에 다가갈 / 인터넷에 접속하는

크라우드 펀딩은 프로젝트를 위한 자금을 확보하는 새롭고 더 협력적인 방법이다. 그것은 세계 어느 곳에서나 가치 있는 명분을 위한 기부를 요청하고, 이후에 프로젝트의 파트너가 되는 기부자들과 함께 프로젝트를 위한 자금을 조성하는 등 다양한 방식들로 사용될 수 있다. 본질적으로, 크라우드 펀딩은 소셜 네트워킹과 벤처 자본주의의 융합이다. 소셜 네트워킹이 사람들이 서로 의사소통하고 상호작용하는 방법에 대한 전통적인 규칙을 다시 쓴 것과 동일한 방식으로, 온갖 다양한 방식의 크라우드 펀딩은 미래에 기업과 다른 프로젝트가 자금을 얻는 방법에 대한 규칙을 다시 쓸 잠재력을 가진다. 크라우드 펀딩은 기업 자금 조달의 민주화로 여겨질 수 있다. 자본 조달과 할당을 비교적 소규모의 고정된 소수에 한정하는 대신에 크라우드 펀딩은 인터넷에 연결된 모든 사람이 인터넷에 접속하는 다른 모든 사람의 집단 지혜와 쌈짓돈 둘 다에 다가갈 수 있게 해준다.

Why? 왜 정답일까?

마지막 문장에서 크라우드 펀딩을 통해 기업들은 고정된 소수에서 자본 조달과 할당을 받는 대신에 인터넷에 연결된 모든 사람들의 지혜와 돈에 접근할 수 있게 된다(~ crowdfunding empowers everyone connected to the Internet to access both the collective wisdom and the pocket money of everyone else ~.)고 설명한다. 따라서 밑줄 친 부분이 의미하는 바로 가장 적절한 것은 ① '더 많은 사람들이 사업 자금 조달에 관여할 수 있다.'이다.

- collaborative ⓐ 협력적인
- worthy ⓐ 가치 있는
- contributor ⑩ 기부자
- fusion ⑩ 융합, 혼합
- conventional ⓐ 전통적인
- democratization ⑩ 민주화
- collective wisdom 집단 지혜
- reinforce ⓥ 강화하다
- facilitate ⓥ 용이하게 하다
- secure ⓥ 확보하다
- cause ⑩ 대의명분
- in essence 본질적으로
- capitalism ⑩ 자본주의
- variation ⑩ 변주, 변형
- restrict ⓥ 한정시키다, 제한하다
- pocket money 쌈짓돈, 용돈
- keep A from B A가 B하지 못하게 하다

구문 풀이

6행 In just the same way as social networks have rewritten the conventional
딱 ~한 방식과 마찬가지로
rules about [how people communicate and interact with each other], crowdfunding
전치사 관계부사(~하는 방법)   주어
in all its variations has the potential to rewrite the rules on [how businesses and
동사   형용사적 용법   전치사 └관계부사(~하는 방법)┘
other projects get funded in the future].

★★ 문제 해결 꿀~팁 ★★

▶ 많이 틀린 이유는?
밑줄 친 부분의 의미를 마지막 문장에서 풀어서 서술하고 있다. 즉 기존에는 기업 자금이 주로 소수의 정해진 이들에 의해 조달되었지만 이제는 '인터넷에 연결된 모든 이들로부터' 조달될 수 있게 되었다는 것이다. ④의 경우 크라우드 펀딩이 소셜 네트워크를 통한 자금 조달을 도리어 '막는다'는 의미를 나타내므로 주제와 상충한다.

▶ 문제 해결 방법은?
글에 따르면 기업 자금 조달에 더 많은 사람들, 나아가 인터넷에 연결된 모든 사람들을 관여시킬 수 있는 수단이 바로 크라우드 펀딩이다. 이를 비유적으로 나타낸 표현이 바로 '민주화'임을 파악하도록 한다.

22 긍정적인 태도의 중요성   정답률 83% | 정답 ⑤

다음 글의 요지로 가장 적절한 것은?
① 근거 없는 낙관주의는 문제 해결을 어렵게 한다.
② 차이에 대한 관용은 조화로운 공동체 생활에 필요하다.
③ 인식과 행동의 일관성은 정신적 스트레스를 감소시킨다.
④ 적극적인 의사 표현이 효율적 의사소통에 도움이 된다.
☑ 긍정적인 태도를 갖는 것이 삶의 변화를 가져온다.

You meet many different kinds of people in your life.
여러분은 인생에서 많은 다양한 부류의 사람을 만난다.
Sometimes you run into those / who are full of energy, / and you wonder / if they are from the same planet as you.
때때로 여러분은 사람을 마주치고, / 활기로 가득한 / 여러분은 궁금해한다. / 그들이 여러분과 같은 행성에서 왔는지
After a closer look, / you realize / that they too face challenges and problems.
면밀한 관찰 후에 / 여러분은 알아차린다. / 그들 또한 힘든 일과 문제에 직면한다는 것을
They are under the same amount of pressure and stress as you.
그들은 여러분과 같은 양의 압박과 스트레스를 받는다.
One word makes a world of difference: / attitude!
하나의 단어가 엄청난 변화를 가져온다. / 태도!
Attitude is your psychological disposition, / a proactive way to approach life.
태도는 여러분의 심리적 기질로, / 삶에 접근하는 주도적인 방식이다.
It is a personal predetermination / not to let anything or anyone / take control of your life or manipulate your mood.
그것은 개인의 사전 결정이다. / 어떤 것이나 어떤 사람에게 내버려두지 않는 / 여러분의 삶을 통제하거나 여러분의 기분을 조종하도록
Attitude allows you / to anticipate, excuse, forgive and forget, / without being naive or stupid.
태도는 여러분에게 허용해준다. / 기대하고, 너그러이 봐주고, 용서하고, 잊어버리도록 / 고지식하거나 어리석지 않으면서
It is a personal decision / to stay in control and not to lose your temper.
그것은 개인의 결심이다. / 평정심을 유지하고 화내지 않겠다는
Attitude provides safe conduct / through all kinds of storms.
태도는 안전 통행권을 제공한다. / 온갖 폭풍우를 헤쳐 나갈
It helps you to get up every morning / happy and determined to get the most out of a brand new day.
그것은 여러분이 매일 아침 일어나게 도와준다. / 행복하게 그리고 새로운 하루를 최대한 활용하겠다는 결의에 찬 채
Whatever happens — good or bad — / the proper attitude makes the difference.
좋든 나쁘든 어떤 일이 일어나더라도 / 적절한 태도는 변화를 가져온다.
It may not always be easy to have a positive attitude; nevertheless, you need to remember / you can face a kind or cruel world / based on your perception and your actions.
긍정적인 태도를 가지기가 언제나 쉽지는 않을 수 있지만, / 그럼에도 여러분은 기억할 필요가 있다. / 여러분이 친절하거나 잔인한 세상에 직면할 수 있다는 것을 / 여러분의 인식과 행동에 기초하여

여러분은 인생에서 많은 다양한 부류의 사람을 만난다. 때때로 여러분은 활기로 가득한 사람을 마주치고, 그들이 여러분과 같은 행성에서 왔는지 궁금해 한다. 면밀한 관찰 후에 여러분은 그들 또한 힘든 일과 문제에 직면한다는 것을 알아차린다. 그들은 여러분과 같은 양의 압박과 스트레스를 받는다. 하나의 단어가 엄청난 변화를 가져온다. 태도! 태도는 여러분의 심리적 기질로, 삶에 접근하는 주도적인 방식이다. 그것은 어떤 것이나 어떤 사람이 여러분의 삶을 통제하거나 기분을 조종하도록 두지 않는 개인의 사전 결정이다. 태도는 여러분이 고지식하거나 어리석지 않으면서, 기대하고, 너그러이 봐주고, 용서하고, 잊어버리도록 해준다. 그것은 평정심을 유지하고 화내지 않겠다는 개인의 결심이다. 태도는 온갖 폭풍우를 헤쳐 나갈 안전 통행권을 제공한다. 그것은 여러분이 매일 아침 행복하게 그리고 새로운 하루를 최대한 활용하겠다는 결의에 찬 채 일어나게 도와준다. 좋든 나쁘든 어떤 일이 일어나더라도 적절한 태도는 변화를 가져온다. 긍정적인 태도를 가지기가 언제나 쉽지는 않을 수 있지만, 그럼에도 여러분은 여러분의 인식과 행동에 기초하여 친절하거나 잔인한 세상에 직면할 수 있다는 것을 기억할 필요가 있다.

Why? 왜 정답일까?

마지막 두 문장에서 어떤 일이 일어나더라도 긍정적인 태도를 지니고 있으면 변화를 맞이할 수 있다(Whatever happens — good or bad — the proper attitude makes the difference. It may not always be easy to have a positive attitude; nevertheless, you need to remember you can face a kind or cruel world based on your perception and your actions.)는 결론을 제시하므로, 글의 요지로 가장 적절한 것은 ⑤ '긍정적인 태도를 갖는 것이 삶의 변화를 가져온다.'이다.

- run into ~을 마주치다
- proactive ⓐ 상황을 앞서서 주도하는
- manipulate ⓥ 조종하다, 조작하다
- naive ⓐ 고지식한, 순진한
- get the most out of ~을 최대한 활용하다
- disposition ⑩ 기질
- predetermination ⑩ 사전 결정, 선결
- anticipate ⓥ 기대하다
- lose temper 화가 나 이성을 잃다

[20회] 2019학년도 11월 205

14행 Whatever happens — (good or bad) — the proper attitude makes the difference.
복합관계대명사(부사절: 무엇이 ~하든 간에) ( ): 삽입구   주어   동사구

---

23 무해한 자극을 유해하다고 지각하는 인간의 뇌   정답률 71% | 정답 ③

다음 글의 주제로 가장 적절한 것은?

① the role of instinct in deciding to flee or fight
도피 또는 투쟁하기로 결정하는 데 있어 본능의 역할
② benefits of danger perception for humans' survival
인간 생존을 위한 위험 인식의 이점
✓③ our perception of harmless situations as threatening
무해한 상황을 위협적으로 보는 우리의 인식
④ the human brain's evolution for telling friend from foe
친구와 적을 구별하기 위한 인간 뇌의 진화
⑤ primitive people's ways of quickly dealing with dangers
위험을 빨리 처리하는 원시시대 사람들의 방식

Our world today is comparatively harmless.
오늘날 우리의 세계는 비교적 무해하다.
We don't have to be careful every moment / that a tiger is behind us.
우리는 매 순간 주의해야 할 필요가 없다. / 우리 뒤에 호랑이가 있는지
We do not have to worry about starving.
우리는 굶주림에 대해 걱정할 필요가 없다.
Our dangers today are, for example, / high blood pressure or diabetes.
예를 들어, 오늘날 우리의 위험은 / 고혈압이나 당뇨병이다.
To be clear, we have a Stone Age brain / that lives in a modern world.
정확히 하자면, 우리는 석기 시대의 뇌를 가지고 있다. / 현대 세계에 사는
Because of this, / many situations are considered a threat by our brains, / although they are harmless to our survival.
이 때문에 / 많은 상황이 우리의 뇌에 의해 위협으로 간주된다. / 그것이 우리의 생존에 무해할지라도
In the past, danger meant / we either had to flee or fight.
과거에는 위험은 의미했다. / 우리가 도망치거나 싸워야만 한다는 것을
If we have an appointment but are stuck in a traffic jam, / that does not really threaten our lives.
만약 우리가 약속이 있지만 교통 체증에 갇혀 있다면, / 그것이 우리의 생명을 실제로 위협하지는 않는다.
However, our brain considers this a danger.
하지만 우리의 뇌는 이것을 위험으로 간주한다.
That is the point.
그것이 핵심이다.
There is no danger, / but our brain rates it as such.
위험은 없지만, / 우리의 뇌는 그것을 그렇게 여긴다.
If we have an unpleasant conversation with our partner, / it does not threaten our lives, / and we do not have to flee or fight.
만약 우리가 파트너와 불쾌한 대화를 나눈다면, / 그것은 우리의 생명을 위협하지 않으며, / 우리는 도망치거나 싸울 필요가 없다.
The danger is an illusion.
그 위험은 착각이다.
Our Stone Age brain sees a mortal danger / that is not there.
우리의 석기 시대적 뇌는 치명적인 위험을 본다. / 거기에 존재하지 않는

오늘날 우리의 세계는 비교적 무해하다. 우리는 우리 뒤에 호랑이가 있는지 매 순간 주의해야 할 필요가 없다. 우리는 굶주림에 대해 걱정할 필요가 없다. 예를 들어, 오늘날 우리의 위험은 고혈압이나 당뇨병이다. 정확히 하자면, 우리는 석기 시대의 뇌를 가지고 현대 세계에 살고 있다. 이 때문에 많은 상황이 우리의 생존에 무해할지라도 우리의 뇌에 의해 위험으로 간주된다. 과거에는 위험이 우리가 도망치거나 싸워야만 한다는 것을 의미했다. 만약 우리가 약속이 있지만 교통 체증에 갇혀 있다면, 그것이 우리의 생명을 실제로 위협하지는 않는다. 하지만 우리의 뇌는 이것을 위험으로 간주한다. 그것이 핵심이다. 위험은 없지만, 우리의 뇌는 그것을 그렇게 여긴다. 만약 우리가 파트너와 불쾌한 대화를 나눈다면, 그것은 우리의 생명을 위협하지 않으며, 우리는 도망치거나 싸울 필요가 없다. 그 위험은 착각이다. 우리의 석기 시대적 뇌는 거기에 존재하지 않는 치명적인 위험을 본다.

Why? 왜 정답일까?

'~ many situations are considered a threat by our brains, although they are harmless to our survival.'에서 생존에 무해한 상황일지라도 석기 시대에 머물러 있는 우리의 뇌는 이를 위험으로 간주한다는 핵심 내용을 언급하는 것으로 볼 때, 글의 주제로 가장 적절한 것은 ③ '무해한 상황을 위험하다고 보는 우리의 인식'이다.

● comparatively @ 비교적
● threat ⓝ 위협
● flee ⓥ 도피하다, 도망하다
● illusion ⓝ 환상
● instinct ⓝ 본능
● foe ⓝ 적, 원수
● starve ⓥ 굶어죽다
● harmless @ 무해한
● rate A as B A를 B로 여기다, 평가하다
● mortal @ 치명적인
● tell A from B A와 B를 구별하다

구문 풀이

5행 Because of this, many situations are considered a threat by our brains,
이유 전치사(~ 때문에)   「A + be considered + B : A가 B라고 간주되다」
although they are harmless to our survival.
~에 무해한

---

24 우리의 공격성을 반영하는 전투적 스포츠   정답률 71% | 정답 ②

다음 글의 제목으로 가장 적절한 것은?

① Is There a Distinction among Combative Sports?
전투적 스포츠를 사이에 구별이 있는가?
✓② Combative Sports Mirror Human Aggressiveness
전투적 스포츠는 인간의 공격성을 반영한다
③ Never Let Your Aggressive Impulses Consume You!
절대 당신의 공격적인 충동이 당신을 사로잡게 하지 마라!
④ International Conflicts: Creating New Military Alliances
국가 간 충돌: 새로운 군사동맹을 만들어내다
⑤ Combative Sports Are More Common among the Oppressed
전투적 스포츠는 억압받는 사람들 사이에서 더 흔하다

There has been a general belief / that sport is a way of reducing violence.
일반적인 믿음이 있다. / 스포츠가 폭력을 감소시키는 방법이라는
Anthropologist Richard Sipes tests this notion / in a classic study of the relationship between sport and violence.
인류학자인 Richard Sipes는 이 개념을 검증한다. / 스포츠와 폭력의 관계에 대한 고전적인 연구에서
Focusing on what he calls "combative sports," / those sports including actual body contact between opponents or simulated warfare, / he hypothesizes / that if sport is an alternative to violence, / then one would expect to find an inverse correlation / between the popularity of combative sports / and the frequency and intensity of warfare.
그가 '전투적인 스포츠'라고 부르는 것에 초점을 맞추며, / 상대 간의 실제 신체 접촉과 모의 전투를 포함하는 그러한 스포츠와 같이 / 그는 가설을 세운다. / 만약 스포츠가 폭력에 대한 대체물이라면, / 어떤 사람은 역 상관관계를 찾을 것을 기대할 것이라고 / 전투적인 스포츠의 인기 / 전투의 빈도 및 강도 사이에
In other words, / the more combative sports (e.g., football, boxing) / the less likely warfare.
다시 말해서, / 전투적인 스포츠(예를 들면, 축구, 권투)가 더 많을수록, / 전투는 덜 일어난다.
Using the Human Relations Area Files and a sample of 20 societies, / Sipes tests the hypothesis / and discovers a significant relationship between combative sports and violence, / but a direct one, not the inverse correlation of his hypothesis.
Human Relations Area Files와 20개 사회의 샘플을 사용하여 / Sipes는 그 가설을 검증하고 / 전투적인 스포츠와 폭력 사이의 중요한 관련성을 발견한다. / 그가 가정한 역 상관관계가 아닌 직접적인 상관관계를
According to Sipes' analysis, / the more pervasive and popular / combative sports are in a society, / the more likely that society is to engage in war.
Sipes의 분석에 따르면, / 더 만연하고 더 인기가 많을수록, / 전투적인 스포츠가 한 사회에서 / 그 사회는 전쟁에 더 참여할 것이다.
So, Sipes draws the obvious conclusion / that combative sports are not alternatives to war / but rather are reflections / of the same aggressive impulses in human society.
그러므로 Sipes는 분명한 결론을 도출해낸다. / 전투적인 스포츠가 전쟁에 대한 대체물이 아니라 / 오히려 반영이라는 / 인간 사회의 바로 그 공격적인 충동의

스포츠가 폭력을 감소시키는 방법이라는 일반적인 믿음이 있다. 인류학자인 Richard Sipes는 스포츠와 폭력의 관계에 대한 고전적인 연구에서 이 개념을 검증한다. 상대 간의 실제 신체 접촉과 모의 전투를 포함하는 그러한 스포츠와 같이 그가 '전투적인 스포츠'라고 부르는 것에 초점을 맞추며, 그는 만약 스포츠가 폭력에 대한 대체물이라면, 어떤 사람은 전투적인 스포츠의 인기와 전투의 빈도 및 강도 사이에 역 상관관계를 찾을 것을 기대할 것이라고 가설을 세운다. 다시 말해서, 전투적인 스포츠(예를 들면, 축구, 권투)가 더 많을수록 전투는 덜 일어난다는 것이다. Human Relations Area Files와 20개 사회의 샘플을 사용하여 Sipes는 그 가설을 검증하고 전투적인 스포츠와 폭력 사이의 중요한 관련성, 그가 가정한 역 상관관계가 아닌 직접적인 상관관계를 발견한다. Sipes의 분석에 따르면, 전투적인 스포츠가 한 사회에서 더 만연하고 더 인기가 많을수록, 그 사회는 전쟁에 더 참여할 것이다. 그러므로 Sipes는 전투적인 스포츠가 전쟁에 대한 대체물이 아니라 오히려 인간 사회의 바로 그 공격적인 충동의 반영이라는 분명한 결론을 도출해낸다.

Why? 왜 정답일까?

'~ combative sports are not alternatives to war but rather are reflections of the same aggressive impulses in human society.'에서 전투적 스포츠는 전쟁이나 폭력의 대체로 기능하기보다 우리의 공격성을 반영하는 것이라는 결론을 제시하고 있다. 따라서 글의 제목으로 가장 적절한 것은 ② '전투적 스포츠는 인간의 공격성을 반영한다'이다.

● combative @ 전투적인
● simulated @ 모의의, 모조의
● hypothesize ⓥ 가설을 세우다
● correlation ⓝ 상관관계
● significant @ 중요한
● aggressive @ 공격적인
● consume ⓥ 사로잡다
● opponent ⓝ 상대방
● warfare ⓝ 전투, 전쟁
● inverse @ 역의, 정반대의
● intensity ⓝ 강도
● reflection ⓝ 반영(물)
● impulse ⓝ 충동
● alliance ⓝ 동맹

구문 풀이

3행 Focusing on what he calls "combative sports," those sports including (~을 포함해서)
분사구문(~하면서, ~한 채로)   동격(= combative sports)
actual body contact between opponents or simulated warfare, he hypothesizes
주어   동사
that (if sport is an alternative to violence), then one would expect to find an
접속사(~것)   ( ): 부사절   주어   동사   목적어
inverse correlation between the popularity of combative sports and the frequency and intensity of warfare.

---

25 전 세계 재생 가능 에너지 기술 분야 일자리 수   정답률 77% | 정답 ④

다음 표의 내용과 일치하지 않는 것은?

Jobs in Renewable Energy Technology in 2014 and 2015

Year of 2014		Year of 2015	
Renewable Energy Technology	Jobs (thousands)	Renewable Energy Technology	Jobs (thousands)
Solar Photovoltaic	2,495	Solar Photovoltaic	2,772
Liquid Biofuels	1,788	Liquid Biofuels	1,678
Wind Power	1,027	Wind Power	1,081
Biomass	822	Solar Heating/Cooling	939
Solar Heating/Cooling	764	Biomass	822
Biogas	381	Biogas	382
Small Hydropower	209	Small Hydropower	204
Geothermal Energy	154	Geothermal Energy	160
Total	**7,600**	**Total**	**8,000**

* Note: Figures may not add to total shown because of rounding.

The tables above show the number of jobs / in renewable energy technology around the world / in 2014 and 2015.
위 표들은 일자리 수를 보여준다. / 전 세계 재생 가능 에너지 기술 분야에서의 / 2014년과 2015년의
① The total number of jobs / was larger in 2015 than in 2014.
일자리의 총계는 / 2014년보다 2015년에 더 많았다.

② In both years, / solar photovoltaic had the largest number of jobs, / and the number of jobs increased in 2015.
두 해 모두 / 태양광 발전이 가장 많은 일자리 수를 보였고, / 그 일자리의 수는 2015년에 증가했다.

③ The rank of liquid biofuels / remained the same in both years / though the number of jobs decreased in 2015.
액체 바이오 연료의 순위는 / 두 해 모두 동일했다. / 일자리 수는 2015년에 감소했지만

☑ Solar heating/cooling ranked higher in 2015 / than in 2014, / but still had fewer than 900 thousand jobs.
태양열 냉난방은 2015년에 더 높은 순위에 올랐으나 / 2014년보다 / 여전히 90만 개보다 적은 일자리를 보였다.

⑤ Among the lowest three ranks in 2014, / only small hydropower showed a decrease / in the number of jobs in 2015.
2014년의 최하위 세 개의 순위 중에서 / 단지 소규모 수력 발전만 감소를 보였다. / 2015년에 일자리 수에서

위 표들은 2014년과 2015년의 전 세계 재생 가능 에너지 기술 분야에서의 일자리 수를 보여 준다. ① 일자리의 총계는 2014년보다 2015년에 더 많았다. ② 두 해 모두 태양광 발전이 가장 많은 일자리 수를 보였고, 그 일자리의 수는 2015년에 증가했다. ③ 액체 바이오 연료의 일자리 수는 2015년에 감소했지만, 순위는 두 해 모두 동일했다. ④ 태양열 냉난방은 2014년보다 2015년에 더 높은 순위에 올랐으나 여전히 90만 개보다 적은 일자리를 보였다. ⑤ 2014년의 최하위 세 개의 순위 중에서 단지 소규모 수력 발전만 2015년에 일자리 수에서 감소를 보였다.

Why? 왜 정답일까?

도표에 따르면 2015년에 태양열 냉난방 분야의 일자리 수는 약 93만 9천 개에 이르러 90만 개를 넘었다. 따라서 도표와 일치하지 않는 것은 ④이다.

- renewable ⓐ 재생 가능한
- biofuel ⓝ 바이오 연료
- photovoltaic ⓐ 광발전의
- hydropower ⓝ 수력 발전

---

26 Lotte Laserstein의 생애
정답률 86% | 정답 ④

Lotte Laserstein에 관한 다음 글의 내용과 일치하지 <u>않는</u> 것은?
① 어린 나이에 회화와 소묘를 배웠다.
② Berlin Academy of Arts에 입학 허가를 받았다.
③ 나치당의 권력 장악 이후 독일에서 작품 전시를 금지 당했다.
☑ 이전에 누렸던 명성을 스웨덴에서 되찾았다.
⑤ 가장 가까운 친구인 Gertrud Rose를 그렸다.

Lotte Laserstein was born into a Jewish family in East Prussia.
Lotte Laserstein은 동프로이센의 유대인 가정에서 태어났다.

『One of her relatives ran a private painting school, / which allowed Lotte / to learn painting and drawing at a young age.』 ①의 근거 일치
그녀의 친척 중 한 명은 사립 미술 학교를 운영했는데, / 이것은 Lotte에게 허용해주었다 / 어린 나이에 회화와 소묘를 배우도록

『Later, she earned admission to the Berlin Academy of Arts / and completed her master studies / as one of the first women in the school.』 ②의 근거 일치
나중에, 그녀는 Berlin Academy of Arts에 입학 허가를 받았고 / 석사 과정을 마쳤다. / 그 학교에서 최초의 여성 중 한 명으로

In 1928 her career skyrocketed / as she gained widespread recognition, / 『but after the seizure of power by the Nazi Party, / she was forbidden to exhibit her artwork in Germany.』 ③의 근거 일치
1928년에 그녀의 경력은 급부상했지만, / 그녀가 폭넓은 인정을 받으며 / 나치당의 권력 장악 이후, / 그녀는 독일에서 자신의 작품 전시를 금지 당했다.

In 1937 she emigrated to Sweden.
1937년에 그녀는 스웨덴으로 이주했다.

『She continued to work in Sweden / but never recaptured the fame / she had enjoyed before.』 ④의 근거 불일치
그녀는 스웨덴에서 계속 활동했지만 / 결코 명성을 되찾지 못했다. / 그녀가 이전에 누렸던

『In her work, Lotte repeatedly portrayed Gertrud Rose, / her closest friend.』 ⑤의 근거 일치
자신의 작품에서 Lotte는 Gertrud Rose를 반복해서 그렸다. / 자신의 가장 가까운 친구인

To Lotte, / she embodied the type of the "New Woman" / and was so represented.
Lotte에게 있어, / 그녀는 '신여성'의 전형을 상징했고 / 그렇게 표현되었다.

Lotte Laserstein은 동프로이센의 유대인 가정에서 태어났다. 그녀의 친척 중 한 명은 사립 미술 학교를 운영했는데, 이것은 Lotte가 어린 나이에 회화와 소묘를 배우도록 해주었다. 나중에, 그녀는 Berlin Academy of Arts에 입학 허가를 받았고 그 학교에서 최초의 여성 중 한 명으로 석사 과정을 마쳤다. 그녀는 폭넓은 인정을 받으며 1928년에 경력이 급부상했지만, 나치당의 권력 장악 이후, 그녀는 독일에서 자신의 작품 전시를 금지 당했다. 1937년에 그녀는 스웨덴으로 이주했다. 그녀는 스웨덴에서 계속 활동했지만 그녀가 이전에 누렸던 명성을 결코 되찾지 못했다. 자신의 작품에서 Lotte는 자신의 가장 가까운 친구인 Gertrud Rose를 반복해서 그렸다. Lotte에게 있어, 그녀는 '신여성'의 전형을 상징했고 그렇게 표현되었다.

Why? 왜 정답일까?

'She continued to work in Sweden but never recaptured the fame she had enjoyed before.'에서 Laserstein은 스웨덴으로 가서 활동했지만 이전의 명성을 결코 회복하지 못했다고 하므로, 내용과 일치하지 않는 것은 ④ '이전에 누렸던 명성을 스웨덴에서 되찾았다.'이다.

Why? 왜 오답일까?

① '~ allowed Lotte to learn painting and drawing at a young age.'의 내용과 일치한다.
② 'Later, she earned admission to the Berlin Academy of Arts ~'의 내용과 일치한다.
③ '~ after the seizure of power by the Nazi Party, she was forbidden to exhibit her artwork in Germany.'의 내용과 일치한다.
⑤ 'In her work, Lotte repeatedly portrayed Gertrud Rose, her closest friend.'의 내용과 일치한다.

- Jewish ⓐ 유대인의 ⓝ 유대인
- skyrocket ⓥ 급부상하다, 급증하다
- exhibit ⓥ 전시하다
- recapture ⓥ 되찾다, 다시 붙잡다
- master ⓝ 석사 학위
- widespread ⓐ 폭넓은, 널리 퍼진
- emigrate to ⓥ ~로 이주하다
- repeatedly ⓐd 반복해서

구문 풀이

5행 In 1928 her career skyrocketed as she gained widespread recognition,
                      └자동사   └~하면서 / ~함에 따라

but after the seizure of power by the Nazi Party, she was forbidden to exhibit her
    └전치사(~ 후에)   └'be forbidden + to부정사': ~하는 것을 금지 당하다

artwork in Germany.

---

27 마을 사진 대회 안내
정답률 94% | 정답 ④

Springfield Photo Contest에 관한 다음 안내문의 내용과 일치하지 <u>않는</u> 것은?
① 모든 수상작은 공식 여행 안내 책자에 수록될 것이다.
② 1등 상금은 2등 상금의 두 배이다.
③ Springfield에서 촬영한 사진이어야 한다.
☑ 컬러 사진 및 흑백 사진이 허용된다.
⑤ 12월 27일까지 웹 사이트로 제출이 완료되어야 한다.

Springfield Photo Contest
Springfield 사진 대회

Show off your pictures / taken in this beautiful town.
여러분의 사진을 뽐내 보세요. / 이 아름다운 마을에서 촬영한

『All the winning entries will be included / in the official Springfield tour guide book!』 ①의 근거 일치
모든 수상작은 수록될 것입니다! / Springfield 공식 여행 안내 책자에

Prizes
상금

『1st Place: $500
1등: 500달러
2nd Place: $250』 ②의 근거 일치
2등: 250달러
3rd Place: $150
3등: 150달러

Contest Rules
대회 규칙

Limit of 5 photos per entrant
참가자당 5개의 사진으로 제한합니다.

『Photos must be taken in Springfield.』 ③의 근거 일치
사진은 Springfield에서 촬영한 것이어야 합니다.

Photos must be submitted digitally as JPEG files.
사진은 JPEG 디지털 파일로 제출되어야 합니다.

『Photos should be in color / (black-and-white photos are not accepted).』 ④의 근거 불일치
사진은 컬러여야 합니다 / (흑백 사진은 허용되지 않습니다).

『The submission must be completed / on our website (www.visitspringfield.org) / by December 27, 2019.』 ⑤의 근거 일치
제출은 완료되어야 합니다. / 우리 웹 사이트(www.visitspringfield.org)로 / 2019년 12월 27일까지

Please email us at info@visitspringfield.org / for further information.
info@visitspringfield.org로 우리에게 이메일을 보내주세요. / 더 많은 정보를 원하시면

Springfield 사진 대회

이 아름다운 마을에서 촬영한 여러분의 사진을 뽐내 보세요. 모든 수상작은 Springfield 공식 여행 안내 책자에 수록될 것입니다!

상금
• 1등: 500달러
• 2등: 250달러
• 3등: 150달러

대회 규칙
• 참가자당 5개의 사진으로 제한합니다.
• 사진은 Springfield에서 촬영한 것이어야 합니다.
• 사진은 JPEG 디지털 파일로 제출되어야 합니다.
• 사진은 컬러여야 합니다(흑백 사진은 허용되지 않습니다).

제출은 2019년 12월 27일까지 우리 웹 사이트(www.visitspringfield.org)로 완료되어야 합니다.

더 많은 정보를 원하시면 info@visitspringfield.org로 우리에게 이메일을 보내주세요.

Why? 왜 정답일까?

'Photos should be in color (black-and-white photos are not accepted).'에서 사진은 컬러만이 가능하고 흑백은 허용되지 않는다고 하므로, 안내문의 내용과 일치하지 않는 것은 ④ '컬러 사진 및 흑백 사진이 허용된다.'이다.

Why? 왜 오답일까?

① 'All the winning entries will be included in the official Springfield tour guide book!'의 내용과 일치한다.
② '1st Place: $500 / 2nd Place: $250'의 내용과 일치한다.
③ 'Photos must be taken in Springfield.'의 내용과 일치한다.
⑤ 'The submission must be completed on our website (www.visitspringfield.org) by December 27, 2019.'의 내용과 일치한다.

- show off ~을 뽐내다
- accept ⓥ 수용하다
- complete ⓥ 완료하다
- entrant ⓝ 참가자, 출전자
- submission ⓝ 제출

---

28 업사이클링 축제 안내
정답률 91% | 정답 ③

2019 Upcycling Festival에 관한 다음 안내문의 내용과 일치하는 것은?
① 입장료가 있고 예약이 필요하다.
② 토요일 오전부터 시작된다.
☑ 어린이를 위한 체험 활동이 있다.
④ 예술 작품이 회의실에 전시된다.
⑤ 주차 요금은 무료이다.

2019 Upcycling Festival
2019 업사이클링 축제

The Riverside Art Center is proud / to announce the 2019 Upcycling Festival, / a festival for the whole family / to create, see and learn about the art of upcycling.
Riverside 아트 센터는 자랑스럽습니다. / 2019 업사이클링 축제를 알리게 되어 / 온 가족을 위한 축제인 / 업사이클링 예술을 만들고, 보고, 배울 수 있는

『There is no admission fee / and booking is not needed.』 ①의근거 불일치
입장료가 없고 / 예약은 필요 없습니다.
Date & Time
날짜와 시간
『Saturday, November 23, 2:00 pm − 5:00 pm』 ②의근거 불일치
11월 23일 토요일 오후 2시부터 5시까지
Location
장소
The Riverside Art Center
Riverside 아트 센터
Programs
프로그램
『Hands-on activities for children: / making art pieces / utilizing used or waste materials at the center's garden』 ③의근거 일치
어린이를 위한 직접 체험 활동: / 예술 작품 만들기 / 센터 정원의 낡거나 쓸모없는 재료를 이용하여
『Exhibition: famous upcycled artwork in the lobby』 ④의근거 불일치
전시: 로비에 유명 업사이클 예술 작품 전시
Movie: documentaries on environmental topics in the meeting room
영화: 회의실에서 환경 주제에 관한 다큐멘터리 상영
Parking
주차
The parking lot is open from 1:00 pm to 6:00 pm.
주차장은 오후 1시부터 6시까지 개방됩니다.
『The parking fee is $5.』 ⑤의근거 불일치
주차 요금은 5달러입니다.
For more information, please call 123-456-0987.
더 많은 정보를 원하시면, 123-456-0987로 전화하세요.

2019 업사이클링 축제

Riverside 아트센터는 온 가족이 업사이클링 예술을 만들고, 보고, 배울 수 있는 축제인 2019 업사이클링 축제를 알리게 되어 자랑스럽습니다. 입장료가 없고 예약은 필요 없습니다.

날짜와 시간
11월 23일 토요일 오후 2시부터 5시까지

장소
Riverside 아트 센터

프로그램
• 어린이를 위한 직접 체험 활동: 센터 정원의 낡거나 쓸모없는 재료를 이용하여 예술 작품 만들기
• 전시: 로비에 유명 업사이클 예술 작품 전시
• 영화: 회의실에서 환경 주제에 관한 다큐멘터리 상영

주차
• 주차장은 오후 1시부터 6시까지 개방됩니다.
• 주차 요금은 5달러입니다.

더 많은 정보를 원하시면, 123-456-0987로 전화하세요.

Why? 왜 정답일까?
'Hands-on activities for children: ~'에서 어린이들이 직접 해볼 수 있는 체험 활동으로 예술품 만들기를 언급하므로, 안내문의 내용과 일치하는 것은 ③ '어린이를 위한 체험 활동이 있다.'이다.

Why? 왜 오답일까?
① 'There is no admission fee and booking is not needed.'에서 입장료가 없고 예약이 필요하지 않다고 하였다.
② 'Saturday, November 23, 2:00 pm − 5:00 pm'에서 축제는 토요일 오후에 개최된다고 하였다.
④ 'Exhibition: famous upcycled artwork in the lobby'에서 작품 전시는 로비에서 이루어진다고 하였다.
⑤ 'The parking fee is $5.'에서 주차 요금은 5달러라고 하였다.

• upcycling ⓝ 업사이클링(재활용품으로 더 품질이 좋거나 가치가 높은 새 제품을 만드는 과정)
• hands-on 직접 해보는   • utilize ⓥ 이용하다

29 사람들이 녹음된 음악에 끌리는 이유   정답률 55% | 정답 ④
다음 글의 밑줄 친 부분 중, 어법상 틀린 것은? [3점]

There is a reason / why so many of us are attracted to recorded music these days, / especially considering / personal music players are common / and people are listening to music through headphones a lot.
이유가 있다. / 요즘 우리 중 그렇게나 많은 사람이 녹음된 음악에 끌리는 / 특히 고려할 때, / 개인용 음악 플레이어가 흔하고 / 사람들이 헤드폰으로 음악을 많이 듣는 것을
Recording engineers and musicians / have learned to create special effects / that tickle our brains by exploiting neural circuits / that evolved ① to discern important features of our auditory environment.
녹음 엔지니어와 음악가는 / 특수 효과를 만들어 내는 것을 배웠다. / 신경회로를 이용함으로써 우리의 뇌를 자극하는 / 우리 청각 환경의 중요한 특징들을 분간하도록 진화한
These special effects are similar in principle / to 3-D art, motion pictures, or visual illusions, / none of ② which have been around long enough / for our brains to have evolved special mechanisms to perceive them.
이러한 특수 효과들은 원리상 비슷하지만, / 3-D 아트, 모션 픽처, 또는 착시와 / 그것들 중에 어느 것도 충분히 오랫동안 주변에 존재하지 않았다 / 우리의 뇌가 그것들을 인식하기 위한 특수한 방법을 진화시킬 만큼
Rather, 3-D art, motion pictures, and visual illusions / leverage perceptual systems / that ③ are in place to accomplish other things.
오히려 3-D 아트, 모션 픽처, 그리고 착시는 / 인식 체계를 이용한다. / 다른 것들을 성취하기 위해 자리 잡고 있는
Because they use these neural circuits in novel ways, / we find them especially ✔ interesting.
그것들이 이러한 신경회로를 새로운 방식으로 이용하기 때문에, / 우리는 그것들이 특히 흥미롭다고 여긴다.
The same is true of the way / ⑤ that modern recordings are made.
동일한 것이 방법에도 적용된다. / 현대의 녹음된 음악이 만들어지는

개인용 음악 플레이어가 흔하고 사람들이 헤드폰으로 음악을 많이 듣는 것을 특히 고려할 때, 요즘 우리 중 그렇게나 많은 사람이 녹음된 음악에 끌리는 이유가 있다. 녹음 엔지니어와 음악가는 우리 청각 환경의 중요한 특징들을 분간하도록 진화한 신경회로를 이용함으로써 우리의 뇌를 자극하는 특수 효과를 만들어 내는 것을 배웠다. 이러한 특수 효과들은 원리상 3-D 아트, 모션 픽처, 또는 착시와 비슷하지만, 그것들 중에 어느 것도 우리의 뇌가 그것들을 인식하기 위한 특수한 방법을 진화시킬 만큼 충분히 오랫동안 주변에 존재하지는 않았다. 오히려 3-D 아트, 모션 픽처, 그리고 착시는 다른 것들을 성취하기 위해 자리 잡고 있는 인식 체계를 이용한다. 그것들(특수 효과)이 이러한 신경회로를 새로운 방식으로 사용하기 때문에, 우리는 그것들이 특히 흥미롭다고 여긴다. 동일한 것이 현대의 녹음된 음악이 만들어지는 방법에도 적용된다.

Why? 왜 정답일까?
find의 목적어인 them은 앞 문장에 나오는 3-D art, motion pictures, and visual illusions를 받는데, 이들은 '흥미롭게 하는' 주체이다. 따라서 interested를 interesting으로 고쳐야 한다. 어법상 틀린 것은 ④이다.

Why? 왜 오답일까?
① '~하도록'의 의미를 나타내는 to부정사가 바르게 쓰였다.
② 앞에 나오는 명사 3-D art, motion pictures, or visual illusions를 대신하면서 앞뒤로 절을 연결하는 계속적 용법의 관계대명사 which가 바르게 쓰였다.
③ 선행사 systems가 복수 명사이므로 관계절의 동사 자리에 are라는 복수 동사가 바르게 쓰였다.
⑤ 방법의 way, 이유의 reason이 선행사일 때 that은 흔히 관계부사를 대체한다. 여기서도 관계부사 역할의 that이 바르게 쓰였고, 이어서 완전한 구조가 뒤따랐다.

• attracted to ~에 끌리는, 매혹되는   • considering prep ~을 고려할 때
• tickle ⓥ 자극하다, 간질이다   • exploit ⓥ 이용하다
• circuit ⓝ 회로   • discern ⓥ 분간하다, 식별하다
• feature ⓝ 특징   • in principle 원리적으로
• visual illusion 착시   • mechanism ⓝ 기제
• perceive ⓥ 인식하다   • accomplish ⓥ 성취하다
• novel ⓐ 새로운   • true of ~에 해당하는, 적용되는

구문 풀이
4행 Recording engineers and musicians have learned to create special effects [that tickle our brains by exploiting neural circuits {that evolved to discern important features of our auditory environment}].

30 이야기와 신뢰   정답률 63% | 정답 ②
(A), (B), (C)의 각 네모 안에서 문맥에 맞는 낱말로 가장 적절한 것은? [3점]

	(A)	(B)	(C)
①	exists 존재한다	deceptive 기만적인	Respecting 존중하는 것
✔②	exists 존재한다	sacrificial 희생적인	Respecting 존중하는 것
③	exists 존재한다	sacrificial 희생적인	Wasting 낭비하는 것
④	vanishes 사라진다	sacrificial 희생적인	Respecting 존중하는 것
⑤	vanishes 사라진다	deceptive 기만적인	Wasting 낭비하는 것

A story is only as believable as the storyteller.
이야기는 오직 이야기하는 사람만큼만 믿을 만하다.
For story to be effective, / trust must be established.
이야기가 효과적이려면 / 신뢰가 확립되어야 한다.
Yes, trust.
그렇다, 신뢰다.
Whenever someone stops to listen to you, / an element of unspoken trust (A) exists.
누군가가 여러분의 말을 듣기 위해 멈출 때마다, / 무언의 신뢰라는 요소가 존재한다.
Your listener unconsciously trusts you / to say something worthwhile to him, / something that will not waste his time.
여러분의 이야기를 듣는 사람은 무의식적으로 신뢰한다 / 여러분이 가치 있는 어떤 것을 그에게 말할 것이라고 / 즉 그의 시간을 낭비하지 않을 어떤 것
The few minutes of attention / he is giving you / is (B) sacrificial.
몇 분간의 관심은 / 그가 여러분에게 주는 / 희생적이다.
He could choose to spend his time elsewhere, / yet he has stopped to respect your part in a conversation.
그는 다른 어딘가에 자신의 시간을 보내는 걸 선택할 수 있었지만, / 그는 대화에서 여러분의 말을 존중하기 위해 멈추었다.
This is where story comes in.
여기가 이야기가 들어오는 곳이다.
Because a story illustrates points clearly / and often bridges topics easily, / trust can be established *quickly*, / and recognizing this time element to story / is essential to trust.
이야기는 요점을 분명하게 설명하고, / 종종 주제들을 쉽게 연결하기 때문에 / 신뢰가 빨리 확립될 수 있으며, / 이러한 이야기의 시간적 요소를 인지하는 것이 / 신뢰에 필수적이다.
(C) Respecting your listener's time / is the capital letter / at the beginning of your sentence / — it leads the conversation into a sentence / worth listening to / if trust is earned and not taken for granted.
여러분의 이야기를 듣는 사람의 시간을 존중하는 것이 / 대문자(시작점)이다. / 여러분의 문장 맨 앞의 / 그것은 대화를 문장으로 이끈다. / 들을 만한 가치가 있는 / 만약 신뢰가 얻어지고 당연하게 여겨지지 않는다면

이야기는 오직 이야기하는 사람만큼만 믿을 만하다. 이야기가 효과적이려면 신뢰가 확립되어야 한다. 그렇다, 신뢰다. 누군가가 여러분의 말을 듣기 위해 멈출 때마다, 무언의 신뢰라는 요소가 (A) 존재한다. 여러분의 이야기를 듣는 사람은 여러분이 가치 있는 어떤 것, 즉 그의 시간을 낭비하지 않을 어떤 것을 그에게 말할 것이라고 무의식적으로 신뢰한다. 그가 여러분에게 주는 몇 분간의 관심은 (B) 희생적이다. 그는 다른 어딘가에 자신의 시간을 보내는 걸 선택할 수 있었지만 대화에서 여러분의 말을 존중하기 위해 멈추었다. 여기가 이야기가 들어오는 곳이다. 이야기는 요점을 분명하게 설명하고, 종종 주제들을 쉽게 연결하기 때문에 신뢰가 빨리 확립될 수 있으며, 이러한 이야기의 시간적 요소를 인지하는 것이 신뢰에 필수적이다. 여러분의 이야기를 듣는 사람의 시간을 (C) 존중하는 것이 여러분의 문장 맨 앞의 대문자(시작점)

이다. 만약 신뢰가 얻어지고 당연하게 여겨지지 않는다면 그것은 대화를 들을 만한 가치가 있는 문장으로 이끈다.

Why? 왜 정답일까?

(A) 뒤에서 청자는 화자가 가치 있는 어떤 것을 이야기하리라고 무의식적으로 '신뢰한다'고 언급하는 것으로 보아, (A)에는 신뢰가 '있다'는 의미를 완성하는 **exists**가 들어가야 적절하다.
(B) 뒤에서 대화 상대방은 다른 일을 할 수도 있는 시간에 우리 이야기를 듣기로 선택했다는 이야기가 나오는데, 이는 상대가 우리를 위해 '희생하고' 있다는 사실을 상기시키는 진술이다. 따라서 (B)에는 **sacrificial**이 들어가야 적절하다.
(C) 앞에서 대화의 시간적 요소를 '인지하라'고 언급하므로, (C)에는 이를 달리 표현한 **Respecting**이 들어가야 적절하다. 따라서 각 네모 안에서 문맥에 맞는 낱말로 가장 적절한 것은 ② '(A) 존재한다 – (B) 희생인 – (C) 존중하는 것'이다.

- **establish** ⓥ 확립하다
- **vanish** ⓥ 사라지다
- **worthwhile** ⓐ 가치 있는
- **sacrificial** ⓐ 희생적인
- **illustrate** ⓥ 분명하게 보였다
- **essential** ⓐ 필수적인, 본질적인
- **unspoken** ⓐ 무언의, 이야기되지 않은
- **unconsciously** ⓐⓓ 무의식적으로
- **deceptive** ⓐ 기만적인
- **part** ⓝ (배역의) 말, 대사
- **bridge** ⓥ 연결하다

구문 풀이

11행 Respecting your listener's time is the capital letter at the beginning of
동명사구 주어 / 동사(단수)
your sentence — it leads the conversation into a sentence worth listening to if
~의 시작점에 / 「lead + A + into + B : A를 B로 이끌다」 / 「worth + 동명사 : ~할 가치가 있는」
trust is earned and not taken for granted.

---

31 자기 소유의 물건의 가치를 과대평가하는 경향 정답률 71% | 정답 ①

다음 빈칸에 들어갈 말로 가장 적절한 것을 고르시오.

✓ ① overvalue – 과대평가할 ② exchange – 교환할 ③ disregard – 무시할
④ conceal – 숨길 ⑤ share – 공유할

Once we own something, / we're far more likely to overvalue it.
일단 우리가 어떤 것을 소유하면, / 우리는 그것을 과대평가할 가능성이 훨씬 더 높다.
In a study conducted at Duke University, / students who won basketball tickets / in an extremely onerous lottery / (one that they had to wait in line to enter for more than a day) / said they wouldn't sell their tickets / for less than, on average, $2,400.
Duke 대학교에서 실시된 한 연구에서, / 농구 티켓을 얻은 학생들은 / 극도로 성가신 추첨에서 / (그들이 참여하기 위해 하루 이상 줄을 서서 기다려야 하는 것) / 자신의 티켓을 팔지 않을 것이라고 말했다. / 평균적으로 2,400달러 아래로는
But students who had waited and hadn't won / said they would only pay, on average, $170 per ticket.
그러나 기다렸지만 티켓을 얻지 못한 학생들은 / 단지 평균적으로 티켓당 170달러를 지불할 것이라고 말했다.
Once a student owned the tickets, / he or she saw them / as being worth much more in the market / than they were.
일단 학생이 티켓을 소유하면 / 그 또는 그녀는 그것을 여겼다. / 시장에서 훨씬 더 많은 가치가 있다고 / 실제로 그러한 것보다
In another example, / during the housing market crash of 2008, / a real estate website conducted a survey / to see / how homeowners felt the crash affected the price of their homes.
또 다른 사례에서 / 2008년의 주택시장 붕괴 동안에 / 부동산 웹 사이트가 설문조사를 실시했다. / 알아보기 위해 / 주택 소유자들이 느끼기에 이 붕괴가 자신들의 주택의 가격에 어떻게 영향을 미쳤는지를
92% of respondents, aware of nearby foreclosures, asserted / these had hurt the price of homes in their neighborhood.
인근의 압류를 인식하고 있는 응답자 중 92%가 단언했다. / 이것이 자신의 지역에 있는 주택의 가격을 손상시켰다고
However, when asked about the price of their *own* home, / 62% believed it had increased.
하지만 그들 소유의 주택 가격에 대해 질문을 받았을 때, / 62%는 그것이 상승했다고 믿었다.

일단 우리가 어떤 것을 소유하면, 우리는 그것을 과대평가할 가능성이 훨씬 더 높다. Duke 대학에서 실시된 한 연구에서, 극도로 성가신 추첨(참여하기 위해 하루 이상 줄을 서서 기다려야 하는 것)에서 농구 티켓을 얻은 학생들은 평균적으로 2,400달러 아래로는 자신의 티켓을 팔지 않을 것이라고 말했다. 그러나 기다렸지만 티켓을 얻지 못한 학생들은 단지 평균적으로 티켓당 170달러를 지불할 것이라고 말했다. 일단 학생이 티켓을 소유하면 그 또는 그녀는 실제로 그러한 것보다 그것이 시장에서 훨씬 더 많은 가치가 있다고 여겼다. 또 다른 사례에서 2008년의 주택시장 붕괴 동안에 부동산 웹 사이트가 주택 소유자들이 느끼기에 그 붕괴가 자신들의 주택의 가격에 어떻게 영향을 미쳤는지를 알아보기 위해 설문조사를 실시했다. 인근의 압류를 인식하고 있는 응답자 중 92%가 이것이 자신의 지역에 있는 주택의 가격을 손상시켰다고 단언했다. 하지만 그들 소유의 주택 가격에 대해 질문을 받았을 때, 62%는 그것이 상승했다고 믿었다.

Why? 왜 정답일까?

첫 문장인 주제문을 완성하는 빈칸 문제로, 빈칸 이후의 두 예시를 적절히 일반화하여 빈칸에 들어갈 말을 추론해야 한다. 예시의 결론 문장에서 각각 티켓을 소유한 학생은 실제보다 티켓의 가치를 높게 보았고, 자기 소유의 주택가에 대해 질문을 받은 사람들은 가격이 상승했다고 믿었다는 내용이 나온다. 이를 일반화하면, 사람들은 자신이 소유하게 된 것의 가치를 실제보다 크게 추산하는 경향이 있다는 결론을 도출할 수 있다. 따라서 빈칸에 들어갈 말로 가장 적절한 것은 ① '과대평가할'이다.

- **extremely** ⓐⓓ 극도로
- **wait in line** 줄을 서서 기다리다
- **real estate** 부동산
- **overvalue** ⓥ 과대평가하다, 지나치게 가치를 두다
- **lottery** ⓝ 추첨, 도박, 복권
- **crash** ⓝ 붕괴, 도산
- **assert** ⓥ 단언하다, 확고히 하다
- **disregard** ⓥ 무시하다

구문 풀이

2행 In a study conducted at Duke University, / students [who won basketball tickets in an extremely onerous lottery] / (one [that they had to wait in line
과거분사 / 주어(선행사) / 주격 관계대명사 / = a lottery / 목적격 관계대명사
to enter for more than a day]) / said (that) they wouldn't sell their tickets for less
부사적 용법(~하기 위해) / 동사 / 생략(접속사)
than, on average, $2,400.

★★★ 등급을 가르는 문제!

32 소비자의 행동에 따라 좌우되는 재화 간 관계 정답률 52% | 정답 ②

다음 빈칸에 들어갈 말로 가장 적절한 것을 고르시오.

① interaction with other people – 다른 사람들과의 상호 작용
✓ ② individual consumer's behavior – 개별 소비자의 행동
③ obvious change in social status – 사회적 지위의 명백한 변화
④ innovative technological advancement – 혁신적인 기술 진보
⑤ objective assessment of current conditions – 현재 상황에 대한 객관적 평가

Are the different types of mobile device, / smartphones and tablets, / substitutes or complements?
다른 유형의 모바일 기기인 / 스마트폰과 태블릿은 / 대체재인가 또는 보완재인가?
Let's explore this question / by considering the case of Madeleine and Alexandra, / two users of these devices.
이 질문을 탐구해보자. / Madeleine과 Alexandra의 사례를 생각하면서 / 이 기기들의 두 사용자인
Madeleine uses her tablet / to take notes in class.
Madeleine은 자신의 태블릿을 사용한다. / 수업 중에 필기하기 위해
These notes are synced to her smartphone wirelessly, / via a cloud computing service, / allowing Madeleine to review her notes on her phone / during the bus trip home.
이 필기는 무선으로 스마트폰에 동기화되어 / 클라우드 컴퓨팅 서비스를 통해 / Madeleine이 전화기로 자신의 필기를 복습하도록 해준다. / 집으로 버스를 타고 가는 동안
Alexandra uses both her phone and tablet / to surf the Internet, write emails and check social media.
Alexandra는 자신의 전화기와 태블릿을 둘 다 사용한다. / 인터넷을 검색하고, 이메일을 쓰고, 소셜 미디어를 확인하기 위해
Both of these devices / allow Alexandra to access online services / when she is away from her desktop computer.
이러한 두 기기 모두 / Alexandra가 온라인 서비스에 접근하도록 해준다. / 그녀가 데스크톱 컴퓨터로부터 떨어져 있을 때
For Madeleine, smartphones and tablets are *complements*.
Madeleine에게 스마트폰과 태블릿은 *보완재*이다.
She gets greater functionality out of her two devices / when they are used together.
그녀는 그녀의 두 기기로부터 더 큰 기능성을 얻는다. / 그것들이 함께 사용될 때
For Alexandra, they are *substitutes*.
Alexandra에게 그것들은 *대체재*이다.
Both smartphones and tablets / fulfill more or less the same function in Alexandra's life.
스마트폰과 태블릿 둘 다 / Alexandra의 생활에서 거의 같은 기능을 수행한다.
This case illustrates the role / that an individual consumer's behavior plays / in determining the nature of the relationship / between two goods or services.
이 사례는 역할을 보여준다. / 개별 소비자의 행동이 행하는 / 관계의 속성을 결정하는 데 있어 / 두 개의 상품 또는 서비스 사이의

다른 유형의 모바일 기기인 스마트폰과 태블릿은 대체재인가, 보완재인가? 이 기기들의 두 사용자인 Madeleine과 Alexandra의 사례를 생각하면서 이 질문을 탐구해보자. Madeleine은 수업 중에 필기하기 위해 자신의 태블릿을 사용한다. 이 필기는 클라우드 컴퓨팅 서비스를 통해 무선으로 스마트폰에 동기화되어 Madeleine이 집으로 버스를 타고 가는 동안 전화기로 자신의 필기를 복습하도록 해준다. Alexandra는 인터넷을 검색하고, 이메일을 쓰고, 소셜 미디어를 확인하기 위해 자신의 전화기와 태블릿을 둘 다 사용한다. 이러한 두 기기 모두 Alexandra가 데스크톱 컴퓨터로부터 떨어져 있을 때 그녀가 온라인 서비스에 접근하도록 해준다. Madeleine에게 스마트폰과 태블릿은 *보완재*이다. 두 기기가 함께 사용될 때, 그녀는 그것들로부터 더 큰 기능성을 얻는다. Alexandra에게 그것들은 *대체재*이다. 스마트폰과 태블릿 둘 다 Alexandra의 생활에서 거의 같은 기능을 수행한다. 이 사례는 개별 소비자의 행동이 두 개의 상품 또는 서비스 사이의 관계의 속성을 결정하는 데 있어 행하는 역할을 보여준다.

Why? 왜 정답일까?

첫 문장인 주제문을 완성하는 빈칸 문제로, 빈칸 앞의 예시를 적절히 일반화하여 빈칸에 들어갈 말을 추론해야 한다. 두 번째 문장 이후로 Madeleine와 Alexandra의 예를 통해, 스마트폰과 태블릿이 사용자에 따라 보완재 또는 대체재로 모두 이용될 수 있음을 보여주고 있다. 따라서 빈칸에 들어갈 말로 가장 적절한 것은 똑같은 두 상품이 각 사용자의 사용 행위 패턴에 따라 서로 다른 관계에 놓일 수 있다는 뜻을 완성하는 ② '개별 소비자의 행동'이다.

- **substitute** ⓝ 대체재, 대체물
- **be synced to** ~에 동기화되다
- **via** ⓟⓡⓔⓟ ~을 통해
- **functionality** ⓝ 기능성
- **more or less** 거의, 대략
- **nature** ⓝ 속성, 본질
- **complement** ⓝ 보완재, 보충물
- **wirelessly** ⓐⓓ 무선으로
- **access** ⓥ 접속하다
- **fulfill** ⓥ 수행하다, 달성하다
- **illustrate** ⓥ 분명히 보여주다
- **assessment** ⓝ 평가

구문 풀이

14행 This case illustrates the role [that an individual consumer's behavior
선행사 / 목적격 관계대명사
plays in determining the nature of the relationship between two goods or
~함에 있어
services].

★★ 문제 해결 꿀~팁 ★★

▶ 많이 틀린 이유는?
글에서 태블릿과 스마트폰이 언급되기는 하지만, 이는 같은 두 재화 사이의 관계가 사용자의 행위 유형에 따라 달라질 수 있음을 보여주기 위한 예시이다. 두 단어만 보고 ④의 '기술적 진보'에 관한 글이라고 오해하지 않도록 한다.
▶ 문제 해결 방법은?
앞에 나오는 예시를 읽고 직접 요약된 결론을 도출해야 하는 빈칸 문제이므로, Madeleine과 Alexandra의 '차이'에 집중하여 글 전체를 주의 깊게 읽어야 한다.

33 고객의 요구를 고려하여 제품을 발명할 필요가 있음을 깨달은 에디슨 정답률 63% | 정답 ⑤

다음 빈칸에 들어갈 말로 가장 적절한 것을 고르시오. [3점]

① consider the likelihood of mass production – 대량 생산의 가능성을 고려하고
② simplify the design of his inventions – 그의 발명품의 디자인을 단순화하고

[20회] 2019학년도 11월 **209**

③ work with other inventors regularly – 다른 발명가들과 정기적으로 작업하고
④ have knowledge of law in advance – 법을 미리 알고
✓ put the customers' needs first – 고객의 요구를 우선시하고

Thomas Edison was indeed a creative genius, / but it was not until he discovered / some of the principles of marketing / that he found increased success.
토마스 에디슨은 정말 창의적인 천재였지만 / 그가 발견한 후에야 / 어떠한 마케팅 원칙을 / 그는 비로소 큰 성공에 도달했다.
One of his first inventions was, / although much needed, a failure.
그의 최초 발명품 중 하나는 / 매우 필요함에도 불구하고, 실패였다.
In 1869, he created and patented an electronic vote recorder, / which recorded and totalled the votes / in the Massachusetts state legislature / faster than the chamber's old manual system.
1869년에 그는 전자식 투표 기록 장치를 만들어 특허를 얻었는데, / 이것은 투표를 더 빠르게 기록하고 합계를 냈다. / Massachusetts 주 의회에서의 / 의회의 오래된 수기 시스템보다
To Edison's astonishment, it failed.
에디슨으로서는 놀랍게도 그것은 실패했다.
Edison had not taken into account legislators' habits.
에디슨은 의원들의 습관을 고려하지 않았다.
They didn't like to vote quickly and efficiently.
그들은 빠르고 효율적으로 투표하는 것을 원하지 않았다.
They liked to lobby their fellow legislators / as voting took place.
그들은 자신의 동료 의원에게 로비하는 것을 원했다. / 투표가 진행될 때
Edison had a great idea, / but he completely misunderstood the needs of his customers.
에디슨은 훌륭한 아이디어를 가졌으나 / 그는 자신의 고객의 요구를 완전히 잘못 이해했다.
He learned from his failure / the relationship between invention and marketing.
그는 자신의 실패로부터 배웠다. / 발명과 마케팅의 관계를
Edison learned / that marketing and invention must be integrated.
에디슨은 알게 되었다. / 마케팅과 발명이 통합되어야 함을
"Anything that won't sell, / I don't want to invent," / he said.
"팔리지 않을 어떤 것도 / 나는 발명하고 싶지 않다."라고 / 그가 말했다.
"Its sale is proof of utility, / and utility is success."
"그것의 판매량이 유용성의 증거이며, / 유용성이 성공이다."
He realized / he needed to put the customers' needs first / and tailor his thinking accordingly.
그는 깨달았다. / 자신이 고객의 요구를 우선시하고 / 자신의 생각을 그에 따라 맞출 필요가 있다는 것을

토마스 에디슨은 정말 창의적인 천재였지만 어떠한 마케팅 원칙을 발견한 후에야 그는 비로소 큰 성공에 도달했다. 매우 필요함에도 불구하고, 그의 최초 발명품 중 하나는 실패였다. 1869년에 그는 전자식 투표 기록 장치를 만들어 특허를 얻었는데, 이것은 Massachusetts 주 의회에서의 투표를 의회의 오래된 수기 시스템보다 더 빠르게 기록하고 합계를 냈다. 에디슨으로서는 놀랍게도 그것은 실패했다. 에디슨은 의원들의 습관을 고려하지 않았다. 그들은 빠르고 효율적으로 투표하는 것을 원하지 않았다. 투표가 진행될 때 그들은 자신의 동료 의원에게 로비하는 것을 원했다. 에디슨은 훌륭한 아이디어를 가졌으나 자신의 고객의 요구를 완전히 잘못 이해했다. 그는 자신의 실패로부터 발명과 마케팅의 관계를 배웠다. 에디슨은 마케팅과 발명이 통합되어야 함을 알게 되었다. "팔리지 않을 어떤 것도 나는 발명하고 싶지 않다."라고 그가 말했다. "그것의 판매량이 유용성의 증거이며, 유용성이 성공이다." 그는 자신이 고객의 요구를 우선시하고 자신의 생각을 그에 따라 맞출 필요가 있다는 것을 깨달았다.

Why? 왜 정답일까?
'He learned from his failure ~ that marketing and invention must be integrated.'에서 에디슨은 고객의 요구를 잘못 파악하여 발명품 판매에 실패했으며, 그 실패로부터 마케팅과 발명이 통합되어야 한다는 사실을 배웠다고 진술한다. 이에 비추어 볼 때, 빈칸에 들어갈 말로 가장 적절한 것은 고객의 요구를 고려하여 발명품을 만들어야 한다는 뜻을 완성하는 ⑤ '고객의 요구를 우선시하고'이다.

- genius ⓝ 천재
- manual ⓐ 손으로 하는, 수기의
- take into account ~을 고려하다
- integrate ⓥ 통합시키다
- tailor ⓥ ~에 맞추다
- mass production 대량 생산
- legislature ⓝ 의회
- astonishment ⓝ 놀람
- efficiently ⓐ𝖽 효율적으로
- utility ⓝ 유용성
- accordingly ⓐ𝖽 그에 따라

구문 풀이

1행 Thomas Edison was indeed a creative genius, but it was not until he
「it is not until ~」
discovered some of the principles of marketing that he found increased success.
「that+주어+동사 : ~한 후에야 비로소 …하다」

★★★ 등급을 가르는 문제!
34 야생 동물 (관리)에 대한 태도 형성에 영향을 미치는 요소   정답률 32% | 정답 ②

다음 빈칸에 들어갈 말로 가장 적절한 것을 고르시오. [3점]
① attitude drives the various forms of belief
태도가 다양한 형태의 믿음을 이끌어내어
✓ all aspects of attitude are consistent with each other
태도의 모든 측면이 서로 일치하여
③ cognitive components of attitude outweigh affective ones
태도의 인지적 요소가 감정적 요소보다 중요하여
④ the components of attitude are not simultaneously evaluated
태도의 요소들이 동시에 평가되지 않아
⑤ our biased attitudes get in the way of preserving biodiversity
우리의 편향된 태도가 생물 다양성 보존을 방해하여

Attitude has been conceptualized into four main components: / affective (feelings of liking or disliking), / cognitive (beliefs and evaluation of those beliefs), / behavioral intention / (a statement of how one would behave / in a certain situation), / and behavior.
태도는 네 가지 주요한 요소로 개념화되어 왔다. / 감정적 요소(좋아하거나 싫어한다는 느낌), / 인지적 요소(신념 및 그러한 신념에 대한 평가), / 행동적 의도 요소 / (누군가 어떤 상황에서 / 어떻게 행동할 것인가에 대한 진술), / 행동 요소로
Public attitudes toward a wildlife species and its management / are generated / based on the interaction of those components.
야생 동물종과 그 관리에 대한 대중의 태도는 / 생성된다. / 그러한 요소들의 상호작용에 기초하여
In forming our attitudes toward wolves, / people strive to keep their affective components of attitude / consistent with their cognitive component.
늑대에 대한 우리의 태도를 형성할 때, / 사람들은 태도의 감정적 요소를 유지하려고 노력한다. / 그들의 인지적 요소에 일치되게

For example, I could dislike wolves; / I believe they have killed people / (cognitive belief), / and having people killed is of course bad / (evaluation of belief).
예를 들어, 나는 늑대를 싫어할 수 있다. / 나는 그것들이 사람들을 죽였다고 믿는다 / (인지적 신념). / 그리고 사람을 죽게 하는 것은 당연히 나쁘다 / (신념에 대한 평가).
The behavioral intention that could result from this / is to support a wolf control program / and actual behavior may be a history of shooting wolves.
이것으로부터 생길 수 있는 행동적 의도는 / 늑대 통제 프로그램을 지지하는 것이고, / 실제 행동은 늑대 사냥의 역사일 것이다.
In this example, / all aspects of attitude are consistent with each other, / producing a negative overall attitude toward wolves.
이 예에서는, / 태도의 모든 측면이 서로 일치하여 / 늑대에 대해 부정적인 전체 태도를 만들어 낸다.

태도는 네 가지 주요한 요소로 개념화되어 왔는데, 바로 감정적 요소(좋아하거나 싫어한다는 느낌), 인지적 요소(신념 및 그러한 신념에 대한 평가), 행동적 의도 요소(누군가 어떤 상황에서 어떻게 행동할 것인가에 대한 진술), 행동 요소이다. 야생 동물종과 그 관리에 대한 대중의 태도는 그러한 요소들의 상호작용에 기초하여 생성된다. 늑대들에 대한 우리의 태도를 형성할 때, 사람들은 태도의 감정적 요소를 그들의 인지적 요소에 일치되게 유지하려고 노력한다. 예를 들어, 나는 늑대를 싫어할 수 있다. 나는 그것들이 사람들을 죽였다고 믿는다(인지적 신념). 그리고 사람을 죽게 하는 것은 당연히 나쁘다(신념에 대한 평가). 이것으로부터 생길 수 있는 행동적 의도는 늑대 통제 프로그램을 지지하는 것이고, 실제 행동은 늑대 사냥의 역사일 것이다. 이 예에서는, 태도의 모든 측면이 서로 일치하여 늑대에 대해 부정적인 전체 태도를 만들어 낸다.

Why? 왜 정답일까?
글의 서두에서 태도에 4가지 주요 요소가 있다고 언급하고, 이 요소들의 상호작용에 의해 대중의 태도가 형성된다고 했다. 또한 For example 앞에서 사람들은 감정적 요소를 인지적 요소에 '일치되게' 유지하려고 노력한다(~, people strive to keep their affective components of attitude consistent with their cognitive component.)고 설명한다. 마지막 문장은 예시의 결론을 다시 한번 정리하는 문장이므로, 빈칸에 들어갈 말로 가장 적절한 것은 예시 앞 문장과 같은 의미를 지닌 ② '태도의 모든 측면이 서로 일치하여'이다.

- conceptualize ⓥ 개념화하다
- affective ⓐ 감정적인
- behavioral ⓐ 행동의
- consistent with ~와 일관되는, 일치하는
- simultaneously ⓐ𝖽 동시에
- biodiversity ⓝ 생물 다양성
- component ⓝ 구성 요소
- evaluation ⓝ 평가
- generate ⓥ 생성하다, 만들어 내다
- outweigh ⓥ ~보다 중요하다
- get in the way of ~을 방해하다

구문 풀이

6행 In forming our attitudes toward wolves, people strive to keep
~함에 있어, ~할 때   동사구(~하기 위해 노력하다)
their affective components of attitude consistent with their cognitive component.
목적어   목적격 보어

★★ 문제 해결 꿀~팁 ★★

▶ 많이 틀린 이유는?
글에 따르면 태도에는 네 가지 요소가 있고, 우리는 이 요소 각각에 부합하는 방향으로 어떤 대상에 대한 태도를 형성하는 경향이 있다. 글에서 태도의 인지적 요소와 정의적 요소의 영향력을 비교하고 있지는 않으므로 ③은 정답이 아니다. 또한 ①에서 언급하는 '믿음'은 태도의 결과물이 아닌 태도의 구성 요소이다. 따라서 태도가 다양한 믿음을 파생시킨다는 진술은 글의 내용과 다르다.
▶ 문제 해결 방법은?
'주제 – 예시 – 결론(= 주제)' 구조의 글에서 마지막에 빈칸이 나온 문제이므로, 예시 앞 부분을 집중적으로 읽어 답을 도출하도록 한다.

35 문화적 세계화의 중심지를 다수 지니고 있는 아시아   정답률 66% | 정답 ④

다음 글에서 전체 흐름과 관계 없는 문장은?

Cultural globalization has multiple centers in Asia / like Bollywood movies made in India / and Kung Fu movies made in Hong Kong.
문화적 세계는 아시아에 다수의 중심지가 있다. / 인도에서 제작된 Bollywood 영화와 / 홍콩에서 제작된 Kung Fu 영화와 같이
① They are subtitled in as many as 17 languages / and distributed to specific diasporas.
그것들은 무려 17개 언어로 자막 처리가 되며 / 특정 디아스포라에 배급된다.
② These cultural spaces, / which are dominated by languages like Hindi and Mandarin, / ignore and challenge the spread of English.
이러한 문화적 장소들은 / 힌디 어, 만다린 어와 같은 언어들에 지배되는 / 영어의 확산을 무시하고 이에 저항한다.
③ Professor Vaish has shown / how Chinese and Indian children in Singapore / are networked into the pan-Chinese and pan-Indian culture / through their engagement / with Chinese pop music and Indian movies respectively.
Vaish 교수는 보여주었다. / 싱가포르의 중국인 아이들과 인도인 아이들이 어떻게 / 범중국 문화와 범인도 문화로 연결되는지를 / 그들의 참여를 통해 / 각각 중국 대중음악과 인도 영화에 대한
✓ As the world's two most populous nations, / China is India's largest trading partner, / with the size of trade between them valuing $71.5 billion.
전 세계에서 가장 인구가 많은 두 나라로서, / 중국은 인도의 가장 큰 무역 파트너이며, / 그들 사이의 무역 규모가 715억 달러의 가치에 이른다.
⑤ She thus empirically challenges the idea / that Asian youth are passive victims of cultural globalization, / or "world culture" that comes out of the West.
그래서 그녀는 생각에 실증적으로 이의를 제기한다. / 아시아 젊은이들이 문화적 세계의 수동적 희생자라는 / 즉 서구로부터 퍼져 나온 세계 문화'의

문화적 세계화는 인도에서 제작된 Bollywood 영화와 홍콩에서 제작된 Kung Fu 영화와 같이 아시아에 다수의 중심지가 있다. ① 그것들은 무려 17개 언어로 자막 처리가 되며 특정 디아스포라에 배급된다. ② 힌디 어, 만다린 어와 같은 언어들에 지배되는 이러한 문화적 장소들은 영어의 확산을 무시하고 이에 저항한다. ③ Vaish 교수는 싱가포르의 중국인 아이들과 인도인 아이들이 각각 중국 대중음악과 인도 영화에 대한 참여를 통해 범중국 문화와 범인도 문화로 어떻게 연결되는지를 보여주었다. ④ 전 세계에서 가장 인구가 많은 두 나라로서, 중국은 인도의 가장 큰 무역 파트너이며, 두 국가 사이의 무역 규모는 715억 달러의 가치에 이른다. ⑤ 그래서 그녀는 아시아 젊은이들이 문화적 세계화, 즉 서구로부터 퍼져 나온 '세계 문화'의 수동적 희생자라는 생각에 실증적으로 이의를 제기한다.

Why? 왜 정답일까?

아시아는 문화적 세계화에 수동적으로 희생되는 지역이 아니라 오히려 다수의 중심지를 두고 문화적 세계화에 참여하고 있는 곳이라는 내용의 글로, 인도 및 홍콩의 영화 또는 중국 대중음악의 예가 주제를 뒷받침하고 있다. 하지만 ④는 중국과 인도의 무역 규모 및 관계에 관해 언급하여 흐름에서 벗어난다. 따라서 전체 흐름과 관계없는 문장은 ④이다.

- **subtitle** ⓥ 자막 처리를 하다, 자막을 달다
- **specific** ⓐ 특정한
- **challenge** ⓥ 저항하다, 반박하다, 도전하다
- **engagement** ⓝ 참여, 관여
- **empirically** ⓐⅾ 실증적으로
- **distribute** ⓥ 배급하다, 분포시키다
- **dominate** ⓥ 지배하다
- **spread** ⓝ 확산 ⓥ 퍼뜨리다
- **respectively** ⓐⅾ 각각
- **victim** ⓝ 희생자

구문 풀이

`12행` She thus empirically challenges the idea [that Asian youth are passive victims of cultural globalization, or "world culture" {that comes out of the West}].

---

36 연꽃 식물의 잎 정화 원리를 이용한 페인트 개발 　정답률 71% | 정답 ③

주어진 글 다음에 이어질 글의 순서로 가장 적절한 것을 고르시오.

① (A) – (C) – (B)　　　② (B) – (A) – (C)
✓③ (B) – (C) – (A)　　　④ (C) – (A) – (B)
⑤ (C) – (B) – (A)

The lotus plant (a white water lily) / grows in the dirty, muddy bottom of lakes and ponds, / yet despite this, / its leaves are always clean.
연꽃 식물(흰 수련)은 / 호수와 연못의 더럽고 진흙투성이인 바닥에서 성장하지만, / 그럼에도 불구하고 / 그것의 잎은 항상 깨끗하다.

(B) That is because / whenever the smallest particle of dust lands on the plant, / it immediately waves the leaf, / directing the dust particles to one particular spot.
그것은 ~ 때문이다. / 먼지 같은 가장 작은 입자가 그 식물에 떨어질 때마다, / 그것이 즉시 잎을 흔들어서 / 먼지 입자들을 어떤 특정 장소로 향하도록 하기 때문이다.

Raindrops falling on the leaves / are sent to that same place, / to thus wash the dirt away.
잎에 떨어지는 빗방울들이 / 그 동일한 장소로 보내져 / 먼지를 씻어낸다.

(C) This property of the lotus / led researchers to design a new house paint.
연꽃의 이러한 특성은 / 연구자들이 새로운 주택용 페인트를 고안하도록 이끌었다.

Researchers began working on how to develop paints / that wash clean in the rain, / in much the same way as lotus leaves do.
연구자들은 페인트를 어떻게 개발할지에 대한 연구를 시작했다. / 비가 올 때 깨끗하게 씻기는 / 연꽃잎이 하는 것과 대체로 똑같이

(A) As a result of this investigation, / a German company produced a house paint.
이 연구의 결과로 / 한 독일 회사가 주택용 페인트를 생산했다.

On the market in Europe and Asia, / the product even came with a guarantee / that it would stay clean for five years without detergents or sandblasting.
유럽과 아시아의 시장에서 / 이 제품은 심지어 보증됐다 / 그것이 세제나 모래 분사 세척 없이 5년 동안 깨끗한 상태로 유지된다고

연꽃 식물(흰 수련)은 호수와 연못의 더럽고 진흙투성이인 바닥에서 성장하지만, 그러함에도 불구하고 그것의 잎은 항상 깨끗하다.

(B) 그것은 먼지 같은 가장 작은 입자가 그 식물에 떨어질 때마다, 즉시 잎을 흔들어서 먼지 입자들을 어떠한 특정 장소로 향하도록 하기 때문이다. 잎에 떨어지는 빗방울들이 그 동일한 장소로 보내져 먼지를 씻어낸다.

(C) 연꽃의 이러한 특성은 연구자들이 새로운 주택용 페인트를 고안하도록 이끌었다. 연구자들은 연꽃잎이 하는 것과 대체로 똑같이 비가 올 때 깨끗하게 씻기는 페인트를 어떻게 개발할지에 대한 연구를 시작했다.

(A) 이 연구의 결과로 한 독일 회사가 주택용 페인트를 생산했다. 유럽과 아시아의 시장에서 이 제품은 심지어 세제나 모래 분사 세척 없이 5년 동안 깨끗한 상태로 유지된다고 보증했다.

Why? 왜 정답일까?

연꽃 식물이 더러운 환경에서 자람에도 잎은 늘 깨끗하다고 설명한 주어진 글 뒤에는, 주어진 글의 내용을 That으로 받아 그 이유를 설명하는 (B)가 먼저 이어져야 한다. (B)에서는 먼지 같은 입자가 떨어질 때마다 연꽃이 잎을 즉시 흔들어서 입자들을 다른 곳으로 보낸다는 점을 언급하는데, (C)는 이를 This property of the lotus로 가리키며, 이 특성을 접목하여 탄생한 것이 새로운 주택용 페인트임을 설명한다. (A)에서는 (C)의 후반부에 이어 페인트 개발에 관한 연구와 그 결과를 언급하고 있다. 따라서 글의 순서로 가장 적절한 것은 ③ '(B) – (C) – (A)'이다.

- **lotus** ⓝ 연꽃, 수련
- **guarantee** ⓥ 보증하다
- **sandblasting** ⓝ 모래 분사
- **property** ⓝ 특성
- **investigation** ⓝ 연구, 조사
- **detergent** ⓝ 세제
- **particle** ⓝ 입자

구문 풀이

`13행` Researchers began working on how to develop paints [that wash clean in the rain], in much the same way as lotus leaves do.

★★★ 등급을 가르는 문제! ★★★

37 과학에서의 획기적 발견 　정답률 53% | 정답 ④

주어진 글 다음에 이어질 글의 순서로 가장 적절한 것을 고르시오. [3점]

① (A) – (C) – (B)　　　② (B) – (A) – (C)
③ (B) – (C) – (A)　　　✓④ (C) – (A) – (B)
⑤ (C) – (B) – (A)

Like the physiological discoveries of the late nineteenth century, / today's biological

breakthrough / has fundamentally altered our understanding / of how the human organism works / and will change medical practice fundamentally and thoroughly.
19세기 후반 생리학의 발견처럼, / 오늘날 생물학의 획기적인 발견은 / 우리의 이해를 근본적으로 바꿔놓았고, / 인간 유기체가 작동하는 방식에 대한 / 의료 행위를 본질적이면서도 철저하게 변화시킬 것이다.

(C) The word "breakthrough," however, / seems to imply in many people's minds / an amazing, unprecedented revelation / that, in an instant, makes everything clear.
그러나 '획기적인 발견'이라는 말은 / 많은 사람들의 마음속에서는 의미하는 것처럼 보인다. / 놀랍고 전례 없는 발견을 / 순식간에 모든 것을 명확하게 만드는

Science doesn't actually work that way.
사실 과학은 그런 방식으로 작동하지 않는다.

(A) Remember the scientific method, / which you probably first learned / about back in elementary school?
과학적 방법을 기억하는가? / 여러분이 아마 처음 배웠을 / 대략 초등학교 때

It has a long and difficult process / of observation, hypothesis, experiment, testing, modifying, retesting, / and retesting again and again and again.
그것은 길고 어려운 과정을 지닌다. / 관찰, 가설, 실험, 검증, 수정, 재검증 / 그리고 재차 반복되는 재검증이라는

(B) That's how science works, / and the breakthrough understanding of the relationship / between our genes and chronic disease / happened in just that way, / building on the work of scientists / from decades — even centuries — ago.
그것이 과학이 작동하는 방식이고, / 관계에 대한 획기적 이해도 / 우리 유전자와 만성 질환 사이의 / 바로 그러한 방식으로 일어났다. / 과학자들의 연구를 기반으로 하여 / 수십 년, 심지어 수백 년 전으로부터의

In fact, it is still happening; / the story continues to unfold / as the research presses on.
사실, 그 이야기는 여전히 일어나고 있으며 / 그것은 계속 펼쳐진다. / 연구가 계속되는 한

19세기 후반 생리학의 발견처럼, 오늘날 생물학의 획기적인 발견은 인간 유기체가 작동하는 방식에 대한 우리의 이해를 근본적으로 바꿔놓았고, 의료 행위를 본질적이면서도 철저하게 변화시킬 것이다.

(C) 그러나 '획기적인 발견'이라는 말은 많은 사람들의 마음속에서는 순식간에 모든 것을 명확하게 만드는 놀랍고 전례 없는 발견을 의미하는 것처럼 보인다. 사실 과학은 그런 방식으로 작동하지 않는다.

(A) 여러분이 대략 초등학교 때 아마 처음 배웠을 과학적 방법을 기억하는가? 그것은 관찰, 가설, 실험, 검증, 수정, 재검증, 그리고 재차 반복되는 재검증이라는 길고 어려운 과정을 지닌다.

(B) 그것이 과학이 작동하는 방식이고, 우리 유전자와 만성 질환 사이의 관계에 대한 획기적 이해도 수십 년, 심지어 수백 년 전으로부터의 과학자들의 연구를 기반으로 하여 바로 그러한 방식으로 일어났다. 사실, 그것은 여전히 일어나고 있으며 연구가 계속되는 한 그 이야기는 계속 펼쳐진다.

Why? 왜 정답일까?

오늘날 생물학의 획기적 발견을 화두로 제시하는 주어진 글 뒤에는, however로 흐름을 반전시키며 사실 과학에는 순식간에 모든 것을 정리해주는 '획기적 발견'이라는 것이 존재하지 않는다고 언급하는 (C)가 먼저 이어진다. 이어서 (A)는 과학이 관찰, 가설, 실험, 검증, 수정, 재검증 등의 길고 복잡한 과정을 통해 이루어진다는 점을 상기시키고, (B)는 그러한 긴 과정이 곧 과학의 진정한 작동 방식이라는 결론을 제시한다. 따라서 글의 순서로 가장 적절한 것은 ④ '(C) – (A) – (B)'이다.

- **physiological** ⓐ 생리학적인
- **fundamentally** ⓐⅾ 근본적으로, 본질적으로
- **hypothesis** ⓝ 가설
- **chronic** ⓐ 만성의
- **unprecedented** ⓐ 전례 없는
- **breakthrough** ⓝ 획기적 발견
- **thoroughly** ⓐⅾ 철저히
- **modify** ⓥ 수정하다
- **unfold** ⓥ 펼쳐지다, 펴다
- **revelation** ⓝ 발견

구문 풀이

`10행` That's how science works, and the breakthrough understanding of the relationship between our genes and chronic disease happened in just that way, building on the work of scientists from decades — even centuries — ago.

★★ 문제 해결 꿀~팁 ★★

▶ 많이 틀린 이유는?
(C)와 (B)에 나오는 breakthrough만 보고 (C) – (B)를 곧장 연결시켜서는 안 된다. (C)는 'Science doesn't actually work that way.'로 끝나는데, 이 뒤에 (B)의 'That's how science works, ~'가 이어지면 '과학은 그런 식으로 작동하지 않는다. vs. 바로 그렇게 과학이 작동한다.'와 같이 상충되는 의미의 두 문장이 역접의 연결어 없이 이어져 버린다.

▶ 문제 해결 방법은?
맥락상 (C) 뒤에 관찰, 가설, 실험, 검증, 수정, 재검증 등을 언급하며 과학의 작동 원리를 설명하는 (A)가 먼저 나오고, 이것이 바로 과학의 작동 원리가 맞다고 확인해주는 (B)가 연결되어야 적절한 흐름이 완성된다.

---

38 소유권/이용권 공유 서비스 　정답률 58% | 정답 ③

글의 흐름으로 보아, 주어진 문장이 들어가기에 가장 적절한 곳을 고르시오.

Car-sharing is now a familiar concept, / but creative companies are making it possible / for their clients to share / ownership and access to just about everything, / such as villas, handbags and even diamond necklaces.
자동차 공유는 지금 익숙한 개념이지만 / 창의적인 회사들은 가능하게 하고 있다. / 그들의 고객들이 공유하는 것을 / 거의 모든 것에 대한 소유권과 이용권을 / 별장, 핸드백, 그리고 심지어 다이아몬드 목걸이와 같은

① According to a Portuguese saying, / "You should never have a yacht; / you should have a friend with a yacht."
포르투갈의 한 속담에 따르면, / '여러분은 절대 요트를 가져서는 안 되고 / 요트가 있는 친구를 가져야 한다.'

② By joining a yacht sharing service, / members can live the Portuguese dream / by sharing a yacht with up to seven other people.
요트 공유 서비스에 가입함으로써, / 회원들은 포르투갈인들의 꿈을 성취할 수 있다. / 최대 7명의 다른 사람들과 한 대의 요트를 공유함으로써

✓ In describing the service, / a recent newspaper article warned consumers / that sharing the yacht means / "there is no guarantee / you will always be able to use it when you want."

그 서비스를 설명하면서, / 최근 한 신문 기사는 소비자에게 경고했다. / 요트를 공유하는 것은 의미한다고 / '보장은 없다'는 것을 / '여러분이 원할 때 그것을 항상 이용할 수 있을 것이라는'

This apparent limitation is / precisely what helps consumers make it a treat.
이 외견상의 제한이 / 바로 소비자들이 그것을 큰 기쁨으로 만들도록 돕는 것이다.

④ Limiting your access to everything / from sandwiches to luxury cars / helps to reset your cheerometer.
모든 것에 여러분의 이용권을 제한하는 것이 / 샌드위치부터 고급 자동차까지 / 여러분의 활기 온도계를 재설정하도록 돕는다.

⑤ That is, / knowing you can't have access to something all the time / may help you appreciate it more / when you do.
즉, / 어떤 것에 여러분이 항상 이용권을 가질 수는 없다는 것을 아는 것이 / 그것에 대해 더 감사하도록 도울 것이다. / 여러분이 이용권을 가질 때

자동차 공유는 지금 익숙한 개념이지만 창의적인 회사들은 그들의 고객들이 별장, 핸드백, 그리고 심지어 다이아몬드 목걸이와 같은 거의 모든 것에 대한 소유권과 이용권을 공유하는 것을 가능하게 하고 있다. ① 포르투갈의 한 속담에 따르면, '여러분은 절대 요트를 가져서는 안 되고 요트가 있는 친구를 가져야 한다.' ② 요트 공유 서비스에 가입함으로써, 회원들은 최대 7명의 다른 사람들과 한 대의 요트를 공유함으로써 포르투갈인들의 꿈을 성취할 수 있다. ③ 그 서비스를 설명하면서, 최근 한 신문 기사는 요트를 공유하는 것은 '여러분이 원할 때 여러분이 그것을 항상 이용할 수 있을 것이라는' 보장은 없다'는 것을 의미한다고 소비자에게 경고했다. 이 외견상의 제한이 바로 소비자들이 그것을 큰 기쁨으로 만들도록 돕는 것이다. ④ 샌드위치부터 고급 자동차까지 모든 것에 여러분의 이용권을 제한하는 것이 여러분의 활기 온도계를 재설정하도록 돕는다. ⑤ 즉, 어떤 것에 여러분이 항상 이용권을 가질 수는 없다는 것을 아는 것이 여러분이 이용권을 가질 때 그것에 대해 더 감사하도록 도울 것이다.

Why? 왜 정답일까?

③ 앞에서 요트 공유 서비스를 예로 들어 거의 모든 재화에 대한 소유권 및 이용권 공유가 활발히 이루어지고 있는 상황을 제시하는데, ③ 뒤에서는 공유 서비스의 '외견상 제한'을 언급하고 있다. 즉 ③ 앞뒤로 공유 서비스에 대한 논조가 상반되어 논리적 공백이 생겨나므로, 주어진 문장이 들어가기에 가장 적절한 곳은 ③이다.

- guarantee ⓝ 보장 ⓥ 보장하다
- apparent ⓐ 외관상의, 겉보기의
- precisely ⓐ 정확히, 꼭
- cheerometer ⓝ 활기 온도계(사람의 활기를 측정하는 장치라는 뜻의 비유적 표현)
- appreciate ⓥ 감사하다
- ownership ⓝ 소유권
- limitation ⓝ 제한

구문 풀이

4행 Car-sharing is now a familiar concept, but creative companies are making **it** possible for their clients **to share** ownership and access to just about everything, such as villas, handbags and even diamond necklaces.
「make+가목적어+목적격 보어+의미상 주어+진목적어: ~이 …하는 것을 ~하게 만들다」

---

39 건물 스타일의 지역적 제한   정답률 57% | 정답 ④

글의 흐름으로 보아, 주어진 문장이 들어가기에 가장 적절한 곳을 고르시오. [3점]

In the US, / regional styles of speech have always been associated / with regional styles of building: / the Midwestern farmhouse, the Southern plantation mansion, and the Cape Cod cottage / all have their equivalent in spoken dialect.
미국에서는, / 말투의 지역적 스타일이 항상 연결되어 왔다. / 건물의 지역적 스타일과 함께 / 중서부의 농장 주택, 남부의 대농장 저택, 그리고 Cape Cod 지역의 오두막 / 모두가 구어 방언에서 그에 상응하는 것을 가진다.

① These buildings may be old and genuine, / or they may be recent reproductions, / the equivalent of an assumed rather than a native accent.
이 건물들은 오래되고 진품일 수도 있고 / 또는 최근의 복제품일 수도 있다. / 그 지방 고유의 방언이라기보다는 꾸며진 방언에 상응하는 것인

② As James Kunstler says, / "half-baked versions of Scarlett O'Hara's Tara / now stand replicated in countless suburban subdivisions / around the United States."
James Kunstler가 말한 것처럼, / "Scarlett O'Hara의 Tara의 어설픈 변형들이 / 요즘 수없이 많은 교외 지역에 복제되어 세워져 있다. / 미국 전역의"

③ In some cities and towns, / especially where tourism is an important part of the economy, / zoning codes may make a sort of artificial authenticity compulsory.
몇몇 도시와 마을에서는 / 특히 관광 사업이 경제의 중요한 일부분일 때 / 지역제(地域制) 규칙이 일종의 인위적인 진정성을 의무로 정할 수 있다.

✔Houses in the historic district of Key West, Florida, for example, / whether new or remodeled, / must be built of wood in a traditional style, / and there are only a few permissible colors of paint, / white being preferred.
예를 들어, 플로리다 주 Key West의 역사적으로 유명한 지역에 있는 주택들은 / 신축이거나 리모델링이거나 / 전통적 양식에 따라 목재로 지어져야만 하고, / 허용되는 페인트의 색깔이 몇 가지 뿐이며, / 흰색이 선호되고 있다.

From the street / these houses may look / like the simple sea captains' mansions they imitate.
거리에서 보면 / 이 주택들은 보일 수도 있다. / 그것들이 모방하고 있는 단순한 선장의 저택처럼

⑤ Inside, however, / where zoning does not reach, / they often contain modern lighting and state-of-the-art kitchens and bathrooms.
그러나, 내부에는 / 지역제가 미치지 않는 / 그것들은 흔히 현대적인 조명과 최신식 부엌과 욕실을 포함하고 있다.

미국에서는 말투의 지역적 스타일이 건물의 지역적 스타일과 함께 항상 연결되어 왔다. 중서부의 농장 주택, 남부의 대농장 저택, 그리고 Cape Cod 지역의 오두막 모두가 구어 방언에서 그에 상응하는 것을 가진다. ① 이 건물들은 오래되고 진품일 수도 있고 또는 그 지방 고유의 방언이라기보다는 꾸며진 방언에 상응하는 것인 최근의 복제품일 수도 있다. ② James Kunstler가 말한 것처럼, "Scarlett O'Hara의 Tara의 어설픈 변형들이 요즘 미국 전역의 수없이 많은 교외 지역에 복제되어 세워져 있다." ③ 특히 관광 사업이 경제의 중요한 일부분인 몇몇 도시와 마을에서는 지역제(地域制) 규칙이 일종의 인위적인 진정성을 의무로 정할 수 있다. ④ 예를 들어, 플로리다 주 Key West의 역사적으로 유명한 지역에 있는 주택들은 신축이거나 리모델링이거나 전통적 양식에 따라 목재로 지어져야만 하고, 허용될 수 있는 페인트의 색깔이 몇 가지 뿐이며, 흰색이 선호되고 있다. 거리에서 보면 이 주택들은 그것들이 모방하고 있는 단순한 선장의 저택처럼 보일 수도 있다. ⑤ 그러나, 지역제가 미치지 않는 내부에는, 그것은 흔히 현대적인 조명과 최신식 부엌과 욕실을 포함하고 있다.

Why? 왜 정답일까?

④ 앞에서 건물 스타일의 지역적 규칙이 특정 지역 내의 주택 건축 양식을 의무로 정할 수 있다고 언급한 데 이어, **for example**이 포함된 주어진 문장은 Key West 지역의 주택을 예로 제시한다. ④ 뒤의

문장은 주어진 문장에 언급된 주택들을 **these houses**로 언급한다. 따라서 주어진 문장이 들어가기에 가장 적절한 곳은 ④이다.

- district ⓝ 지역
- plantation ⓝ 대농장
- cottage ⓝ 오두막
- dialect ⓝ 방언
- replicate ⓥ 복제하다
- authenticity ⓝ 진정성
- state-of-the-art 최신식의
- permissible ⓐ 허용 가능한
- mansion ⓝ 저택
- equivalent ⓝ 상응하는 것, 등가물 ⓐ 상응하는
- genuine ⓐ 진품의, 진짜인
- artificial ⓐ 인공의
- compulsory ⓐ 의무적인, 필수의

구문 풀이

1행 Houses in the historic district of Key West, Florida, for example,
주어1
whether new or remodeled, **must be built** of wood in a traditional style, and there
「whether+A or+B : A이든 B이든」 동사1(조동사 수동태)
are only a few permissible colors of paint, white being preferred.
동사2   주어2   의미상 주어   └ 분사구문(그리고 ~되고 있다)

---

40 외부 요인에 영향을 받는 인간의 인식과 행동   정답률 59% | 정답 ①

다음 글의 내용을 한 문장으로 요약하고자 한다. 빈칸 (A), (B)에 들어갈 말로 가장 적절한 것은?

	(A)		(B)			(A)		(B)
✔①	exposure 노출	⋯⋯	corresponding 일치하는		②	resistance 저항	⋯⋯	irrelevant 무관한
③	exposure 노출	⋯⋯	contrary 대조적인		④	resistance 저항	⋯⋯	similar 비슷한
⑤	preference 선호	⋯⋯	comparable 맞먹는					

Psychologist John Bargh did an experiment / showing human perception and behavior can be influenced / by external factors.
심리학자 John Bargh는 실험을 했다. / 인간의 인식과 행동이 영향을 받을 수 있다는 것을 보여주는 / 외부 요인에 의해

He told a bunch of healthy undergraduates / that he was testing their language abilities.
그는 한 무리의 건강한 대학생들에게 말했는데, / 그가 그들의 언어 능력을 검사하고 있다고

He presented them with a list of words / and asked them to create a coherent sentence from it.
그는 그들에게 단어 목록 한 개를 보여주고 / 그것으로부터 의미 통하는 한 개의 문장을 만들어 보라고 요구했다.

One of the lists was / "DOWN SAT LONELY THE MAN WRINKLED BITTERLY THE WITH FACE OLD".
목록 중 하나는 / 'DOWN SAT LONELY THE MAN WRINKLED BITTERLY THE WITH FACE OLD'이었다.

"Bitterly, the lonely old man with the wrinkled face sat down" / is one possible solution.
'Bitterly, the lonely old man with the wrinkled face sat down(씁쓸하게도, 얼굴에 주름이 가득한 외롭고 나이 든 남자가 앉았다)'은 / 한 가지 가능한 해답이다.

But this was no linguistics test.
그러나 이것은 어학 시험이 아니었다.

Bargh was interested / in how long it took the students / to leave the lab and walk down the hall / after they were exposed to the words.
Bargh는 관심이 있었다. / 학생들이 얼마나 오래 걸리는지에 / 연구실을 나와 복도를 걷는 데 / 그들이 그 단어들에 노출이 되고 나서

What he found was extraordinary.
그가 발견한 것은 놀라웠다.

Those students who had been exposed / to an "elderly" mix of words / took almost 40 percent longer / to walk down the hall / than those who had been exposed to "random" words.
노출되었던 학생들은 / '늙은'과 관련된 단어들의 조합에 / 거의 40%나 더 오래 걸렸다. / 복도를 걸어가는 데 / '무작위의' 단어들에 노출되었던 학생들보다

Some students even walked / with their shoulders bent forwards, / dragging their feet as they left, / as if they were 50 years older than they actually were.
어떤 학생들은 심지어 걷기도 했다. / 떠날 때 어깨를 앞으로 구부리고 / 자신의 발을 끌면서 / 그들이 실제보다 마치 50살이 더 많은 것처럼

➡ In an experiment about human perception and behavior, / participants who experienced (A) exposure / to words related to "elderly" / showed pace, / and some of them even showed posture, / (B) corresponding to what the words suggested.
인간의 인식과 행동에 대한 실험에서, / 노출을 경험한 참가자들은 / '늙은'과 관련된 단어들에 대한 / 속도를 보였고, / 심지어 몇몇 참가자들은 자세까지 보이기도 했다. / 그 단어들이 암시하는 것과 일치하는

심리학자 John Bargh는 인간의 인식과 행동이 외부 요인에 의해 영향을 받을 수 있다는 것을 보여주는 실험을 했다. 그는 한 무리의 건강한 대학생들에게 그가 그들의 언어 능력을 검사하고 있다고 말했다. 그는 그들에게 단어 목록 한 개를 보여주고 그것으로부터 의미가 통하는 한 개의 문장을 만들어 보라고 요구했다. 목록 중 하나는 'DOWN SAT LONELY THE MAN WRINKLED BITTERLY THE WITH FACE OLD'이었다. 'Bitterly, the lonely old man with the wrinkled face sat down(씁쓸하게도, 얼굴에 주름이 가득한 외롭고 나이 든 남자가 앉았다)'은 한 가지 가능한 해답이다. 그러나 이것은 어학 시험이 아니었다. Bargh는 학생들이 그 단어들에 노출이 되고 나서 연구실을 나와 복도를 걸어가는 데 얼마나 오래 걸리는지에 관심이 있었다. 그가 발견한 것은 놀라웠다. '늙은'과 관련된 단어들의 조합에 노출되었던 학생들은 '무작위의' 단어들에 노출되었던 학생들보다 복도를 걸어가는 데 거의 40%나 더 오래 걸렸다. 어떤 학생들은 실제보다 마치 50살이 더 많은 것처럼, 떠날 때 심지어 어깨를 앞으로 구부리고 자신의 발을 끌면서 걷기도 했다.

➡ 인간의 인식과 행동에 대한 실험에서, '늙은'과 관련된 단어들에 대한 (A) 노출을 경험한 참가자들은 그 단어들이 암시하는 것과 (B) 일치하는 속도를 보였고, 심지어 몇몇 참가자들은 자세까지 보이기도 했다.

Why? 왜 정답일까?

첫 문장에서 인간의 인식과 행동은 외부 요인에 영향을 받는다(~ human perception and behavior can be influenced by external factors.)는 핵심 내용을 제시한 뒤 실험의 예가 이어지고 있다. 실험의 결론을 제시하는 마지막 두 문장에서, '늙은'과 관련된 단어를 접했던 학생들은 복도를 걸어가는 속도도 느렸고, 자세 또한 노인과 더 닮아 있었다고 하는 것으로 보아, 특정한 단어에의 노출이 그 의미와 일치하는 학생들의 행동을 이끌어냈다는 내용을 유추할 수 있다. 따라서 요약문의 빈칸 (A)와 (B)에 들어갈 말로 가장 적절한 것은 ① '(A) exposure(노출), (B) corresponding(일치하는)'이다.

- perception ⓝ 인식
- undergraduate ⓝ 대학생, 학부생
- external ⓐ 외부의
- present A with B A에게 B를 제시하다

- **coherent** @ 일관되는, 조리 있는
- **bitterly** [ad] 쓰쓸하게도
- **extraordinary** @ 놀라운, 대단한
- **comparable** @ 맞먹는, 필적할 만한
- **wrinkled** @ 주름이 진
- **linguistics** ⓝ 언어학
- **corresponding** @ (~와) 일치하는, 부합하는

41-42 예측 가능성과 새로움의 균형을 필요로 하는 우리 뇌

We're creatures who live and die / by the energy stores we've built up in our bodies.
우리는 살고 죽는 생명체이다. / 우리가 몸 안에 쌓아온 에너지 저장량에 의해

Navigating the world is a difficult job / that requires moving around and using a lot of brainpower / — an energy-expensive endeavor.
세상을 향해하는 것은 어려운 일이다 / 여기저기로 이동하는 것과 많은 지력을 사용하는 것을 필요로 하는 / 즉 에너지가 많이 드는 수고로움이다.

When we make correct (a) predictions, / that saves energy.
우리가 정확한 예측을 할 때, / 그것은 에너지를 아껴준다.

When you know / that edible bugs can be found beneath certain types of rocks, / it saves turning over *all* the rocks.
여러분이 알 때, / 먹을 수 있는 곤충이 특정한 종류의 바위 아래에서 발견될 수 있다는 것을 / 그것은 모든 바위를 뒤집어야 하는 일을 덜어준다.

The better we predict, / the less energy it costs us.
우리가 더 잘 예측할수록, / 그것은 우리에게 더 적은 에너지를 들게 한다.

Repetition makes us more confident in our forecasts / and more efficient in our actions.
반복은 우리의 예측에 있어서 우리를 더 자신 있게 만든다. / 그리고 우리의 행동에 있어서 더 효율적으로

So there's something (b) appealing about predictability.
그래서 예측 가능성에 관해서는 매력적인 무언가가 있다.

But if our brains are going to all this effort / to make the world predictable, / that begs the question: / if we love predictability so much, / why don't we, for example, just replace our televisions / with machines that emit a rhythmic beep / twenty-four hours a day, / predictably?
하지만 만약 우리의 뇌가 이 모든 노력을 하고 있다면, / 세상을 예측 가능한 것으로 만들기 위해 / 그것은 이 질문을 하게 만든다. / 만약 우리가 예측 가능성을 이토록 좋아한다면, / 예를 들어, 왜 우리는 우리의 텔레비전을 교체하지 않을까? / 규칙적인 소리를 내보내는 기계 / 하루 24시간 / 예측 가능하도록

The answer is / that there's a problem with a (c) lack of surprise.
그 대답은 / 놀라움의 결핍에는 문제가 있다는 것이다.

「The better we understand something, / the less effort we put into thinking about it.」 42번의 근거
우리가 어떤 것을 더 잘 이해할수록, / 우리는 그것에 대해 생각하는 데 노력을 덜 기울인다.

Familiarity (d) breeds indifference.
친숙함은 무관심을 키운다.

Repetition suppression sets in / and our attention diminishes.
반복 억제가 생겨나고 / 우리의 주의가 감소한다.

This is why / — no matter how much you enjoyed watching the World Series — / you aren't going to be satisfied / watching that same game over and over.
이것은 이유이다. / 여러분이 월드 시리즈 시청을 아무리 즐길 수 할지라도 / 여러분이 만족하지 않을 / 같은 경기를 반복해서 시청하며

「Although predictability is reassuring, / the brain strives to (e) incorporate new facts / into its model of the world.」
비록 예측 가능성이 안도감을 주지만, / 뇌는 새로운 사실을 포함시키려 노력한다. / 세상에 대한 그것의 모형에

It always seeks novelty. 41번의 근거
그것은 항상 새로움을 추구한다.

우리는 우리의 몸 안에 쌓아온 에너지 저장량에 의해 살고 죽는 생명체이다. 세상을 향해하는 것은 여기저기로 이동하는 것과 많은 지력을 사용하는 것을 필요로 하는 어려운 일, 즉 에너지가 많이 드는 수고로움이다. 우리가 정확한 (a) 예측을 할 때, 그것은 에너지를 아껴준다. 여러분이 먹을 수 있는 곤충이 특정한 종류의 바위 아래에서 발견될 수 있다는 것을 알 때, 그것은 모든 바위를 뒤집어야 하는 일을 덜어준다. 우리가 더 잘 예측할수록, 그것은 우리에게 더 적은 에너지를 들게 한다. 반복은 우리의 예측에 있어서 우리를 더 자신 있게 만들고 우리의 행동에 있어서 더 효율적으로 만든다. 그래서 예측 가능성에 관해서는 (b) 매력적인 무언가가 있다. 하지만 만약 우리의 뇌가 세상을 예측 가능한 것으로 만들기 위해 이 모든 노력을 하고 있다면, 그것은 이 질문을 하게 만든다. 만약 우리가 예측 가능성을 이토록 좋아한다면, 예를 들어, 왜 우리는 예측 가능하도록 우리의 텔레비전을 하루 24시간 규칙적인 소리를 내보내는 기계로 교체하지 않을까? 그 대답은 놀라움의 (c) 결핍에는 문제가 있다는 것이다. 우리가 어떤 것을 더 잘 이해할수록, 우리는 그것에 대해 생각하는 데 노력을 덜 기울인다. 친숙함은 무관심을 (d) 줄인다(→ 키운다). 반복 억제(반복이 주는 억제)가 생겨나고 우리의 주의가 감소한다. 이것 때문에 여러분은 월드 시리즈 시청을 아무리 즐길 수 있다 할지라도 같은 경기를 반복해서 시청하며 만족하지 않을 것이다. 비록 예측 가능성이 안도감을 주지만, 뇌는 세상에 대한 그것의 모형에 새로운 사실을 (e) 포함시키려 노력한다. 그것은 항상 새로움을 추구한다.

- **endeavor** ⓝ 수고, 노력
- **appealing** @ 매력적인
- **beg the question** 질문을 하게 만든다
- **put effort into** ~에 노력을 들이다
- **indifference** ⓝ 무관심
- **reassuring** @ 안심시키는
- **novelty** ⓝ 새로움
- **expertise** ⓝ 전문성, 전문기술
- **edible** @ 먹을 수 있는
- **predictability** ⓝ 예측 가능성
- **emit** ⓥ 내보내다, 방출하다
- **familiarity** ⓝ 익숙함
- **suppression** ⓝ 억제
- **incorporate** ⓥ 포함시키다, 통합시키다
- **rerun** ⓝ 재방송
- **at the expense of** ~을 희생하여

---

41 제목 파악　　　　정답률 58% | 정답 ③

윗글의 제목으로 가장 적절한 것은?

① Why Are Television Reruns Still Popular?
　무엇이 TV 재방송을 여전히 인기 있게 만드는가?
② Predictability Is Something Not to Be Feared!
　예측 가능성은 두려워할 대상이 아니다!
✓③ What Really Satisfies Our Brain: Familiarity or Novelty
　무엇이 우리 뇌를 정말로 만족시키는가: 익숙함이 새로움인가
④ Repetition Gives Us Expertise at the Expense of Creativity
　반복은 창의성을 희생하여 우리에게 전문성을 준다
⑤ Our Hunter-Gatherer Ancestors Were Smart in Saving Energy
　우리의 수렵채집인 조상들은 에너지를 똑똑하게 아꼈다

Why? 왜 정답일까?

글의 결론을 제시하는 마지막 두 문장에서 비록 예측 가능성이 우리를 안심시켜 주지만, 우리 뇌는 계속해서 새로움을 추구한다(Although predictability is reassuring, the brain strives to incorporate new facts into its model of the world. It always seeks novelty.)고 언급하고 있다. 따라서 글의 제목으로 가장 적절한 것은 이와 같은 핵심 내용을 답으로 유도할 수 있는 질문인 ③ '무엇이 우리 뇌를 정말로 만족시키는가: 익숙함이 새로움인가'이다.

★★★ 등급을 가르는 문제!

42 어휘 추론　　　　정답률 46% | 정답 ④

밑줄 친 (a) ~ (e) 중에서 문맥상 낱말의 쓰임이 적절하지 않은 것은? [3점]

① (a)　② (b)　③ (c)　✓④ (d)　⑤ (e)

Why? 왜 정답일까?

'The better we understand something, the less effort we put into thinking about it.' 에서 우리는 어떤 대상을 더 잘 이해할수록 그 대상에 관해 덜 생각하게 된다고 하는 것으로 보아, (d)가 포함된 문장은 익숙함이 무관심을 '키운다'는 의미를 나타내야 한다. 따라서 (d)의 reduces를 반의어인 breeds로 고쳐야 한다. 문맥상 낱말의 쓰임이 적절하지 않은 것은 ④ '(d)'이다.

★★ 문제 해결 꿀~팁 ★★

▶ 많이 틀린 이유는?
맨 마지막 문장에서 우리 뇌는 새로움을 항상 추구한다고 언급하는 것으로 보아, 우리 뇌가 예측 가능성과 더불어 새로운 사실도 '통합시키기' 위해 애쓴다는 뜻의 (e)는 바르게 쓰였다.

▶ 문제 해결 방법은?
(d) 바로 뒤의 문장에서 어떤 것이 반복되어 익숙해지면 '주의력이 감소한다'고 언급하고 있다. 이는 다른 말로 바꾸면 익숙함이 무관심을 '키운다'는 것이다.

43-45 선행을 돌려받은 Bahati

(A)

Bahati lived in a small village, / where baking bread for a hungry passerby is a custom / when one misses someone.
Bahati는 작은 마을에 살았는데, / 그곳에서는 배고픈 행인을 위해 빵을 굽는 것이 관습이다. / 어떤 사람이 누군가를 그리워할 때

「She had an only son living far away / and missed him a lot, 45번 ①의 근거 일치
/ so (a) she baked an extra loaf of bread / and put it on the window sill every day, / for anyone to take away.
그녀는 멀리 살고 있는 외아들이 있었고, / 그를 몹시 그리워했기에 / 그녀는 여분의 빵을 구워 / 매일 창틀에 그것을 두었다. / 누구든 가져갈 수 있도록

Every day, a poor old woman took away the bread, / just muttering "The good you do, comes back to you!" / instead of expressing gratitude.
매일 한 가난한 노파가 그 빵을 가져가면서 / "당신이 행하는 선한 일은 당신에게로 돌아옵니다!"라고 중얼거리기만 했다. / 고마움을 표현하는 대신에

(C)

"Not a word of gratitude," / Bahati said to herself.
"감사의 말도 한마디 없어."라고 / Bahati는 혼잣말을 했다.

「One day, irritated, / she was tempted to stop baking extra bread, / but soon changed her mind.
어느 날, 짜증이 나서 / 그녀는 여분의 빵 굽기를 그만두고 싶은 마음이 들었지만 / 곧 그녀의 마음을 바꾸었다.

She baked an extra loaf and kept doing good / because the words of the poor old woman / kept coming back to her.」 45번 ④의 근거 불일치
그녀는 여분의 빵을 구웠고 선행을 계속했다. / 가난한 노파의 말이 / 그녀에게 계속 생각났기 때문에

(d) She placed the bread on the window sill.
그녀는 그 빵을 창틀에 두었다.

The poor old woman took away the loaf as usual, / muttering the same words.
가난한 노파는 평소처럼 빵 덩어리를 가져갔다. / 같은 말을 중얼거리며

(B)

This time, instead of being irritated, / Bahati decided to offer a prayer. 「For years, she had got no news of her son. 45번 ②의 근거 일치
이번에는 짜증을 내는 대신에, / Bahati는 기도하기로 결심했다. / 몇 년 동안, 그녀는 아들의 소식을 듣지 못했다.

(b) She prayed for his safety.
그녀는 그의 안전을 위해 기도했다.

That night, there was a knock on the door.
그날 밤, 문을 두드리는 소리가 났다.

As she opened it, / (c) she was surprised / to find her son standing in the doorway.
그녀가 문을 열었을 때, / 그녀는 놀랐다. / 문간에 서 있는 아들을 발견하고

He had grown thin and lean.
그는 말랐고 야위어 있었다.

His clothes were torn.
그의 옷은 찢겨 있었다.

「Crying and hugging her son, / she gave him clothes to change into and some food.」
울며 아들을 껴안은 후에 / 그녀는 갈아입을 옷과 약간의 음식을 그에게 가져다주었다. 45번 ③의 근거 일치

(D)

After taking some rest, Bahati's son said, / "On my way home, / I was so starved that I collapsed.
잠시 쉰 후에, Bahati의 아들은 말했다. / "집으로 오는 길에, / 저는 너무 굶주려서 쓰러졌어요.

약간의 휴식을 취한 후에 Bahati의 아들은 말했다. / "집에 오는 길에 / 저는 너무 배가 고파서 쓰러졌어요.
I saw an old woman with a loaf of bread.
저는 빵 한 덩어리를 가진 노파를 봤어요.
I begged her for a small piece of bread.
저는 그녀에게 작은 빵 한 조각을 구걸했어요.
But (e) she gave me the whole loaf / saying my need was greater than hers."
그런데 그녀는 그 빵 덩어리 전부를 저에게 주었어요. / 제 어려움이 자신의 어려움보다 더 크다고 말하며"
「It was then that Bahati finally realized / the meaning of the words of the poor old woman:」   45번 ⑤의 근거 일치
/ "The good you do, comes back to you!"」
바로 그때 Bahati는 마침내 깨달았다. / 그 가난한 노파의 말의 의미를 / "당신이 행하는 선한 일은 당신에게로 돌아옵니다!"

(A)
Bahati는 작은 마을에 살았는데, 그곳에서는 어떤 사람이 누군가를 그리워할 때 배고픈 행인을 위해 빵을 굽는 것이 관습이다. 그녀는 멀리 살고 있는 외아들이 있었고, 그를 몹시 그리워했기에 (a) 그녀는 매일 여분의 빵을 구워 누구든 가져갈 수 있도록 창틀에 그것을 두었다. 매일 한 가난한 노파가 그 빵을 가져가면서 고마움을 표현하는 대신에 "당신이 행하는 선한 일은 당신에게로 돌아옵니다!"라고 중얼거리기만 했다.

(C)
"감사의 말도 한마디 없어."라고 Bahati는 혼잣말을 했다. 어느 날, 짜증이 나서 그녀는 여분의 빵 굽기를 그만두고 싶은 마음이 들었지만 곧 마음을 고쳐먹었다. 가난한 노파의 말이 계속 생각났기 때문에 그녀는 여분의 빵을 구웠고 선행을 계속했다. (d) 그녀는 그 빵을 창틀에 두었다. 가난한 노파는 같은 말을 중얼거리며 평소처럼 빵 덩어리를 가져갔다.

(B)
이번에는 짜증을 내는 대신에, Bahati는 기도하기로 결심했다. 몇 년 동안, 그녀는 아들의 소식을 듣지 못했다. (b) 그녀는 그의 안전을 위해 기도했다. 그날 밤, 문을 두드리는 소리가 났다. 문을 열었을 때, (c) 그녀는 문간에 서 있는 아들을 발견하고 놀랐다. 그는 말랐고 야위어 있었다. 그의 옷은 찢겨 있었다. 그녀는 울며 아들을 껴안은 후에 갈아입을 옷과 약간의 음식을 그에게 가져다주었다.

(D)
약간의 휴식을 취한 후에 Bahati의 아들은 말했다. "집에 오는 길에 저는 너무 배가 고파서 쓰러졌어요. 저는 빵 한 덩어리를 가진 한 노파를 봤어요. 저는 그녀에게 작은 빵 한 조각을 구걸했어요. 그런데 (e) 그녀(an old woman)는 제 어려움이 자신의 어려움보다 더 크다고 말하며 그 빵 덩어리 전부를 저에게 주었어요." 바로 그때 Bahati는 마침내 그 가난한 노파의 말의 의미를 깨달았다. "당신이 행하는 선한 일은 당신에게로 돌아옵니다!"

- passerby ⑩ 행인
- loaf ⑩ (빵) 덩어리
- mutter ⓥ 중얼거리다
- irritated ⓐ 짜증 난
- starved ⓐ 굶주린
- custom ⑩ 관습
- sill ⑩ (문이나 창문의) 틀
- gratitude ⑩ 감사
- lean ⓐ 야윈
- collapse ⓥ 쓰러지다, 붕괴하다

구문 풀이

[A] 1행 Bahati lived in a small village, where baking bread for a hungry passerby
          장소 선행사   관계부사   동명사구 주어
is a custom when one misses someone.
동사(단수)   ~할 때
[A] 2행 She had an only son living far away and missed him a lot, so she baked
          동사1   현재분사구   동사2   동사3
an extra loaf of bread and put it on the window sill every day, for anyone to take
          동사4   의미상 주어
away.   부사적 용법(~하도록)
[C] 1행 One day, irritated, she was tempted to stop baking extra bread, but soon
          수동분사구문(~된 채로)   동사1   ~하기를 멈추다
changed her mind.
동사2
[D] 4행 It was then that Bahati finally realized the meaning of the words of the
          「it is ~ that : 강조구문 ~한 것은 바로 ~이다」
poor old woman: "The good you do, comes back to you!"
          동격(윗줄의 the words ~)

---

43 글의 순서 파악   정답률 79% | 정답 ②

주어진 글 (A)에 이어질 내용을 순서에 맞게 배열한 것으로 가장 적절한 것은?
① (B) - (D) - (C)
☑ ② (C) - (B) - (D)
③ (C) - (D) - (B)
④ (D) - (B) - (C)
⑤ (D) - (C) - (B)

Why? 왜 정답일까?

아들이 그리워 여분의 빵을 구워 창틀에 놓아두던 Bahati와 그 빵을 가져가는 노파를 소개한 (A) 뒤에는, 노파가 감사의 말 한마디 하지 않는 데 불만이었던 Bahati가 빵 굽기를 그만두려다가 계속해서 빵을 구웠다는 내용의 (C)가 먼저 연결된다. 이어서 Bahati가 몇 년간 소식도 없었던 아들과 재회하게 되었다는 내용의 (B), 집에 오던 중 배가 고파 쓰러졌던 아들이 노파에게서 빵 덩이를 얻었음이 밝혀지는 (D)가 차례로 뒤따른다. 따라서 글의 순서로 가장 적절한 것은 ② '(C) - (B) - (D)'이다.

---

44 지칭 추론   정답률 81% | 정답 ⑤

밑줄 친 (a) ~ (e) 중에서 가리키는 대상이 나머지 넷과 다른 것은?
① (a)   ② (b)   ③ (c)   ④ (d)   ☑ ⑤ (e)

Why? 왜 정답일까?

(a), (b), (c), (d)는 Bahati를, (e)는 두 문장 앞의 an old woman을 가리키므로, (a) ~ (e) 중에서 가리키는 대상이 다른 하나는 ⑤ '(e)'이다.

---

45 세부 내용 파악   정답률 80% | 정답 ④

윗글의 Bahati에 관한 내용으로 적절하지 <u>않은</u> 것은?

① 멀리 살고 있는 아들을 몹시 그리워했다.
② 수년간 아들의 소식을 듣지 못했다.
③ 아들에게 갈아입을 옷과 음식을 주었다.
☑ ④ 여분의 빵을 굽는 일을 그만두었다.
⑤ 결국은 노파의 말의 의미를 깨달았다.

Why? 왜 정답일까?

(C) 'One day, irritated, she was tempted to stop baking extra bread, but soon changed her mind. She baked an extra loaf ~'에서 Bahati는 여분의 빵 굽기를 그만두려다가 곧 마음을 고쳐먹고 빵을 구웠다고 하므로, 내용과 일치하지 않는 것은 ④ '여분의 빵을 굽는 일을 그만두었다.'이다.

Why? 왜 오답일까?

① (A) 'She had an only son living far away and missed him a lot, ~'의 내용과 일치한다.
② (B) 'For years, she had got no news of her son.'의 내용과 일치한다.
③ (B) 'Crying and hugging her son, she gave him clothes to change into and some food.'의 내용과 일치한다.
⑤ (D) 'It was then that Bahati finally realized the meaning of the words of the poor old woman: ~'의 내용과 일치한다.

어휘 Review Test 20   문제편 200쪽

A	B	C	D
01 놀람	01 novelty	01 ⓗ	01 ⓐ
02 지배하다	02 expertise	02 ⓓ	02 ①
03 ~에 해당되는, 적용되는	03 coherent	03 ①	03 ⓝ
04 특성	04 modify	04 ①	04 ⓓ
05 ~을 고려할 때	05 chronic	05 ①	05 ⓔ
06 실증적으로	06 real estate	06 ⓖ	06 ⓒ
07 동맹	07 behavioral	07 ⓐ	07 ⑩
08 진정성	08 perception	08 ①	08 ⓗ
09 전투적인	09 integrate	09 ⓑ	09 ①
10 내보내다, 방출하다	10 discern	10 ⑩	10 ⓑ
11 화가 나 이성을 잃다	11 naive	11 ⓔ	11 ⓖ
12 야윈	12 show off	12 ⑩	12 ⓚ
13 기질	13 fusion	13 ⓚ	13 ①
14 ~보다 중요하다	14 opponent	14 ⓒ	14 ⑩
15 굶어죽다	15 murmur	15 ⓞ	15 ①
16 익숙함	16 collapse	16 ⓢ	16 ①
17 언어학	17 mutter	17 ⓟ	17 ⓠ
18 ~에 맞추다	18 deceptive	18 ①	18 ⓢ
19 사라지다	19 threat	19 ①	19 ⓟ
20 쌈짓돈, 용돈	20 aggressive	20 ⓠ	20 ①

MEMO

MEMO